THE OXFORD COMPANION TO THE

SECOND WORLD WAR

THE OXFORD COMPANION TO THE SECOND WORLD WAR

General Editor

I. C. B. DEAR

Consultant Editor

M. R. D. FOOT

Oxford New York

OXFORD UNIVERSITY PRESS

1995

Oxford University Press, Walton Street, Oxford OX2 6DP
Oxford New York
Athens Auckland Bangkok Bombay
Calcutta Cape Town Dar es Salaam Delhi
Florence Hong Kong Istanbul Karachi
Kuala Lumpur Madras Madrid Melbourne
Mexico City Nairobi Paris Singapore
Taipei Tokyo Toronto
and associated companies in
Berlin Ibadan

Oxford is a trade mark of Oxford University Press

First published 1995 as The Oxford Companion to the Second World War
and The Oxford Companion to World War II (USA and Canada only)

British Library Cataloguing in Publication Data
Data available

Library of Congress Cataloging in Publication Data
Data available
ISBN 0-19-214168-6 (The Oxford Companion to the Second World War)

ISBN 0-19-866225-4 (The Oxford Companion to World War II)

1 3 5 7 9 10 8 6 4 2

Typeset by Selwood Systems
Printed in the United States of America
on acid-free paper

Table of Contents

List of Maps

List of Maps

Colour maps

Advisory Editors

Professor Norman Davies, *School of Slavonic and East European Studies, University of London*
USSR, Eastern and Central Europe, the Balkans, and Persia

Professor Wilhelm Deist, *University of Freiburg*
Germany and Austria

Professor John Gooch, *University of Leeds*
Western Europe, the Mediterranean, the Middle East, and Africa

Professor David M. Kennedy, *Stanford University*
The Americas and the Pacific

Professor Robert O'Neill, *Chichele Professor of the History of War, University of Oxford*
South East Asia, India, Japan, China, and Australasia

Contributors

Unsigned entries are written by the General Editor.

Professor Akashi Yogi, Nanzan University, Japan

Professor Louis Allen, late Durham University

Professor Martin S. Alexander, Department of History, University of Southampton

Mark Almond, Oriel College, Oxford

Professor Stephen E. Ambrose, formerly Department of History, University of New Orleans

Lord Amery

Dr Christopher Andrew, Corpus Christi College, Cambridge

Dr C. Andreyev, Christ Church, Oxford

Dr Ian D. Armour

P. M. H. Bell, formerly Department of History, Liverpool University

Dr Ralph Bennett, formerly Master of Magdalene College, Cambridge

Dr Richard Bessel, Department of History, Open University

Professor Michael Biddiss, Department of History, University of Reading

Claus Bjørn, Centre for the Research in Humanities, University of Copenhagen

Professor Martin Blumenson

Revd Canon Michael Bourdeaux, Keston College, Kent

Alexander Boyd

Professor H. W. Brands, Department of History, Texas A & M University

Stephanie Brookins

Professor Judith Brown, Beit Professor of Commonwealth History, University of Oxford

Dr Angus Calder, The Open University in Scotland

Peter Calvocoressi

Professor A. E. Campbell, Department of History, Birmingham University

Professor D'Ann Campbell, Dean of Arts &

Sciences, Austin Peay State University, Clarksville, Tennessee

Professor Clayborne Carson, Department of History, Stanford University

Dr Martin Ceadel, New College, Oxford

Robert Cecil, late Reader in Contemporary German History, Reading University

Professor Lucio Ceva, Milan

Professor John Chapman, University of Sussex

Professor R. N. Chapman, Department of History, Francis Marion College, South Carolina

Professor Richard Clogg, King's College London

Commander Richard Compton-Hall, formerly Director Royal Navy Submarine Museum, Gosport

Dr Martin Conway, Balliol College, Oxford

Nicholas Coote, Assistant General Secretary, Catholic Bishops of England and Wales

Sebastian Cox, Air Historical Branch, MoD

Professor Richard Crampton, St Edmund Hall, Oxford

Professor Robert Dallek, Department of History, University of Texas at Austin

Dr Gordon Daniels, Department of History, University of Sheffield

Professor Norman Davies, Area Advisory Editor

Professor Peter Davies, Department of Economic and Social History, University of Liverpool

I. C. B. Dear, General Editor

Dr Dennis Deletant, Department of East European Language and Literature, School of Slavonic and East European Studies, University of London

David Dorrell

Stanley L. Falk, US Army Center of Military History, Washington, DC

General Sir Anthony Farrar-Hockley

M. R. D. Foot, Consultant Editor

Dr Jürgen Förster, Military Historical Research Office, Potsdam, Germany

Dr A. N. Frankland, former Director Imperial War Museum

Professor Martin Fritz, Department of Economic History, Göteborg University

Ali Gheissari, Department of Sociology, University of California, San Diego

Martin Gilbert, Merton College, Oxford

Professor John Gooch, Area Advisory Editor

Professor Ian Gow, Scottish Centre for Japanese Studies, University of Stirling

Professor Dominick Graham, formerly Department of History, University of Fredericton, Canada

Professor J. L. Granatstein, Department of History, York University, Ontario

Eric Grove, Deputy Director, Centre for Security Studies, University of Hull

Dr William Hale, School of Oriental and African Studies, University of London

H. Hanak, School of Slavonic and East European Studies, University of London

Dr Joanna Hanson

Dr Mark Harrison, Wellcome Institute for the History of Medicine

Professor Hatano Sumio, Institute of Social Sciences, University of Tsukuba, Japan

Captain Winfried Heinemann, Military Historical Research Office, Potsdam, Germany

Professor Waldo Heinrichs, Department of History, College of Arts and Letters, San Diego State University

Dr Ulrich Herbert, Director, Forschungsstelle für die Geschichte des Nationalsozialismus, Hamburg, Germany

Sir F. H. Hinsley, St John's College, Cambridge

Dr Gerhard Hirschfeld, Director, Bibliothek für Zeitgeschichte, Stuttgart, Germany

Ian Hogg, full-time writer specializing in defence journalism

Dr Brian Holden Reid, Resident Historian, The Staff College, Camberley

Dr Robert Holland, Institute of Commonwealth Studies, University of London

Dr Tom Hone

Alistair Horne

Richard Hough

Professor Sir Michael Howard, formerly Regius Professor of History, Oxford

Janet Howarth, St Hilda's College, Oxford

Contributors

General Sir William Jackson

Dr Keith Jeffery, Department of History, University of Ulster at Jordanstown, Northern Ireland

Richard Jensen, University of Illinois at Chicago

Air Vice-Marshal Johnnie Johnson

Professor R. V. Jones, Emeritus Professor of Natural Philosophy, University of Aberdeen

Barry M. Katz, Department of Mechanical Engineering, Stanford University

Professor Roderick Kedward, School of European Studies, University of Sussex

Lt-Commander Peter Kemp, late Head of Naval Historical Branch, MoD

Professor David M. Kennedy, Area Advisory Editor

Professor Warren Kimball, Department of History, Rutgers, State University of New Jersey

Professor Clayton R. Koppes, Department of History, Oberlin College, Ohio

Tony Lane, Department of Sociology, Social Policy and Social Work Studies, University of Liverpool

Dr Stephen Large, Japanese Research Centre and Wolfson College, Cambridge

Dr Paul Latawski, School of Slavonic and East European Studies, London

Professor J. M. Lee, formerly Department of Politics, University of Bristol

Professor Heinz-Dietrich Löwe, Faculty of History, University of Heidelberg, Germany

Professor L. Y. Luciuk, Department of Politics and Economics, Royal Military College of Canada, Ontario

Dr Martin McCauley, School of Slavonic Studies, London

Professor W. David McIntyre, Department of History, University of Canterbury, Christchurch, New Zealand

Kenneth Macksey, formerly Royal Tank Regiment

Dr Klaus A. Maier, Military Historical Research Office, Potsdam, Germany

Lt-Colonel Charles Messenger

Professor T. B. Millar, late Head, Sir Robert Menzies Centre for Australian Studies, University of London

Professor Marc Milner, Department of History, University of New Brunswick, Canada

Dr Rolf-Dieter Müller, Military Historical Research Office, Potsdam, Germany

Dr Thomas Munch-Peterson, Department of Scandinavian Studies, University College London

E. A. Munday, formerly Air Historical Branch, MoD

Dr Richard Nile, Australian Studies Centre, University of Queensland, Australia

Professor Ian Nish, Emeritus Professor of International History, London School of Economics

Dr Vincent Orange, Department of History, University of Canterbury, Christchurch, New Zealand

Dr Rüdiger Overmans, Military Historical Research Office, Potsdam, Germany

Professor Richard Overy, Department of History, King's College, London

Professor Larry Owens, Department of History, University of Massachusetts at Amherst

Stevan Pavlowitch, Department of History, University of Southampton

Dr Wolfgang Petter, Military Historical Research Office, Potsdam, Germany

Professor I. R. Phimister, Department of History, University of Cape Town, South Africa

Professor Antony Polonsky, Brandeis University, Massachusetts

Dr Alfred Price

Denis Richards

Dr Richard Rigby, Department of Foreign Affairs, Canberra, Australia

Professor Olav Riste, Director Norwegian Institute for Defence Studies, Tollbugt

Professor Keith Robbins, Principal, Saint David's University College, Lampeter, Wales

Professor Adam Roberts, Montague Burton Professor of International Relations, University of Oxford

Professor Giorgio Rochat, Milan

Professor Jeffrey J. Safford, Professor of History, Department of History and Philosophy, College of Letters and Science, Montana State University

Dr J. E. O. Screen, School of Slavonic and East European Studies, University of London

Professor Robert Service, School of Slavonic and East European Studies, University of London

Professor Martin J. Sherwin, Nuclear Age History and Humanities Center, Tufts University Massachusetts

Dr Ben-Ami Shillony, Institute of Asian and African Studies, Hebrew University of Jerusalem

Dr Malcolm Smith, St David's University College, Lampeter, Wales

Professor Ronald Spector, Elliot School of International Affairs, George Washington University

Professor Peter Stansky, Department of History, Stanford University

Shelby Stanton, Distinguished Adjunct Fellow, Center of Strategic & International Studies, USA

Dr A. Streim, Zentrale Stelle der Landesjustizverwaltungen Ludwigsburg, Germany

Dr Brian R. Sullivan, Institute for National Strategic Studies, National Defense University, Fort McNair, Washington, DC

Dr Keith Sword, School of Slavonic and East European Studies, London

Dr Sean Swords, Department of Microelectronics and Electrical Engineering, Trinity College, Dublin

Dr Elsie K. Tipton, School of Asian Studies, University of Sydney

Dr Johannes Tuchel, Leiter Gedenkstätte Deutscher Widerstand, Berlin, Germany

Dr Gerd R. Ueberschär, Military Historical Research Office, Potsdam, Germany

Dr Hans Umbreit, Military Historical Research Office, Potsdam, Germany

Professor Anthony Upton, Department of Modern History, University of St Andrews, Fife

Professor Lyman P. Van Slyke, Department of History, Stanford

Dr Bernd Wegner, Military Historical Research Office, Potsdam, Germany

Professor G. L. Weinberg, Department of History, University of North Carolina, Chapel Hill

Dr Mark Wheeler, School of Slavonic and East European Studies, University of London

Dr J. M. Winter, Pembroke College, Cambridge

Professor John D. Wirth, Department of History, Stanford University

Professor Z. A. B. Zeman, St Edmund Hall, Oxford

Professor Earl Ziemke, Department of History, Franklin College of Arts and Sciences, University of Georgia

Note to the Reader

Entries are arranged in alphabetical order up to the first punctuation in the headword. Cross-references are indicated by an asterisk or by the use in brackets of 'See' followed by the entry title, or part of it, in small capitals. Occasionally, 'See also' is used to inform the reader of related subjects which may be of interest. Normally, a cross reference only appears once in an entry.

All battles and biographical entries (except Churchill, Hitler, Mussolini, Roosevelt, and Stalin) are cross-referenced. Otherwise cross-references appear only where reference is likely to increase understanding of the entry being read. Countries are not normally cross-referenced. This is to avoid confusion with the battles named after some of them, though the entries for colonies and smaller countries involved in the war often contain details of that involvement and are cross-referenced where appropriate. Longer country entries have been divided into sections and have a mini index.

Unless stated otherwise, all times are local, tonnage of merchant shipping is gross registered tonnage (see the table on p. 1203 for the definition of different types of tonnage), and tonnage of warships is displacement tonnage. The Wade–Giles system has been used to romanize the Chinese language in the text.

Wherever possible, place-names in the text and on the maps have been given their English names. Where no English version exists the name as current in the country the place belonged to on 1 September 1939 is used. However, as clarification, an alternative name has sometimes been given in brackets. If a place-name has changed since 1945, its modern equivalent will be found in the place-name appendix on p. 1339.

Hereditary titles, and knighthoods conferred on British and Commonwealth citizens, are given where known if they were held prior to or during the war. Ranks in biographical headwords are the highest reached during the war by the individual concerned. British equivalents of foreign ranks have normally been used, but see the entry on ranks for a full explanation.

Readers who know nothing of military matters might find it useful to read the entries on ranks and formations before proceeding further, and for those who know nothing of the Second World War the Introduction and the entry on the origins of the war are good starting points. The entries on demography and statistics give some basic facts and figures in tabular form. The Chronology lists the dates of some of the war's more important and interesting events, including declarations of war.

The reader must not be surprised if the statistics, and indeed the text in this book sometimes conflict. Historians, and sources for statistics, don't always agree with each other. I have made no attempt to make them do so.

Acknowledgement

I am deeply grateful for the help and advice given by the advisory board and by the consultant editor. They have been unstinting with the time they have given to the project and unfailingly generous in coming to my aid when needed. I would also like to thank Peter Masters for his help in collecting many of the photographs which appear in this book.

I. C. B. Dear

Introduction

Comradeship in war is vital, for it is the glue that holds fighting sub-units together: without it, navies, armies, air forces dissolve into mobs. Yet war is not a companionable business—taken literally, the title of this volume inevitably sits ill with its subject.

Moreover purists, especially Chinese purists, might hold that the Second World War was fought centuries before ever the Christian era began. However, these pages follow current popular Anglo-American usage; their subject is the war that raged from 1 September 1939 to 2 September 1945.

Fighting is as natural as breathing. Wars are only too common; world wars are not uncommon—Sir George Clark counted four between 1689 and 1763.[1] One world war above all others, this century's first, dominated commanders' and statesmen's minds during the second: the Great War that was fought from 1914 to 1918, cost more than 12 million dead in battle, brought down four great empires, and ended with an influenza epidemic which killed even more millions than battle did. From the awkwardness of the *Versailles settlement that ended it, from the consequences of a major world depression, from a single man's mesmeric will to evil, and from the sluggishness of early opposition to him, the next world war arose. Fortunately, it is not the task of this book to explore its *origins in detail. Behind the diplomatic reasons for and against it lay, for several of the countries involved, a sound and ancient reason for fighting: to stop foreigners coming to tell them how to behave. Better the devil you know.

This 'second' world war shaped the world of yesterday and of today; even those born after it ended have had their fates moulded by it. Hence its interest and relevance for current study. Social and domestic history, all but bloodless, are currently much taught and much researched; warfare, a bloody business, sets all the stages on which social and domestic history are enacted. Military historians remain aware that not much even of domestic life is quite unaffected by war; in this volume they reach out to a more general readership.

The study of war, like the practice of it, is not for the squeamish. The glamour that attached to it as recently as 1914, when Rupert Brooke could write 'Now, God be thanked Who has matched us with His hour', has entirely faded. It is a dreary, dull, protracted process of terror and counter-terror; yet sometimes it has to be undertaken, lest still worse befall: 1939 was one of those times. 'War is horrible, but slavery is worse', as Churchill put it even before the fighting started.[2]

War's dullness, one of its outstanding features for those who take part in it, is hardly ever reflected in articles or books about it; but it is inescapable. Soldiers have a sound saying: 'War is ninety-nine per cent boredom and one per cent fright.' Even in the forefront of battle—on watch in a warship, on sentry in a weapon pit, in the tail turret of a bomber—a fighting man might be bored, lonely, and sleepy almost beyond bearing, kept alert only by knowing that his comrades' lives as well as his own depended entirely on himself. Modern battlefields are empty

[1] *English History: a survey* (1971), pp. 336–7.

[2] On 7 January 1939; epigraph to Martin Gilbert, *Winston Churchill: the Wilderness Years* (1991).

by comparison with the crowds who thronged Cannae, Bouvines, Pavia, Borodino, Gettysburg, Mukden, even Verdun; emptiness does not enhance liveliness or excitement.

Besides the dullness was the dreariness: war is drab. *Blackout, unavoidable in most of wartime Europe, was tiresome and dangerous; food in towns was usually short, sometimes not to be had; decent clothes, shoes, furnishings vanished; entertainments were scarce. This was before the age of mass television; sound broadcasting was heavily laced with propaganda; actors were called up; cinemas had trouble with heating; cafés ran out of coffee, pubs ran out of beer.

Total War, the best single-volume account,[3] is well named: this was a war that reached all over the world, and penetrated every aspect of existence for almost all the people then alive in it. In the remotest parts even of the New World the war brought dislocations galore, of society, trade, methods of work and play; and from the New World fighting men travelled by millions to the Old, where it had begun, to share in the dangers and the dreariness.

Yet although the war was total, it was not simply two-sided, Us against Them, goodies against baddies. Some experts maintain that the war in East Asia and the Pacific was a separate war from the war in Europe and North Africa, though fought at the same time and by some of the same combatant states. Within Europe there were many-sided campaigns. The Poles, whose land was first divided between, and then fought over by, Germany and the Soviet Union detested both. War in Yugoslavia was even more complicated by race, religion, and politics, as the troubles that erupted there half a century later show. Even in France, a prefect (nominally a creature of *Vichy, but in secret touch with *resistance) was once, when travelling by motor car in his own *département*, held up in a single day by five bodies of armed men, each of which at a pinch might have opened fire on any of the other four.[4] As the planet gets more overloaded with humankind, polygonal wars are likely to become more common.

Wide diversity of views about the war will be reflected in the pages that follow: historians are no more likely to take a single view now than combatants were then. Whether *BARBAROSSA, the German invasion of the USSR in June 1941, was delayed by the *Balkan campaign is, for instance, still a matter that divides them. Conflicts of opinion are unavoidable, given the various national origins and the diverse training of the contributors, and no attempt has been made to eradicate them. The editor has done his best not to be biased; but admits an Anglo-American orientation to the text, mitigated by contributors from Germany, Italy, and Japan. German readers, for example, will find that *Rommel and *Manstein are treated in terms that may appear to them over-generous: reflecting an Anglo-American wartime view of them which still largely prevails.

This was an especially nasty war, marked not merely by danger, if fighting happened to come close, but by *atrocities. Tales of torture abound from it, as from many other wars; this time there was an added frightfulness, the attempt by one nation to eradicate another race entirely—genocide. Before we all throw up our hands in horror, and cry shame at the very thought, we need to remember that even genocide was not without precedent. The Old Testament seems to glance at it,[5] and, long before biblical times, what happened to Neanderthal man? If he was stamped out by *Homo habilis*, there are not many Europeans or 'white' north Americans who do not have genocidal ancestors. The fate of the Carthaginians and of the aboriginal Tasmanians is clear and comparatively recent.

[3] By Peter Calvocoressi, Guy Wint and John Pritchard (2nd edn., New York, 1989).

[4] P. Trouillé, *Journal d'un Préfet pendant l'Occupation* (Paris, 1964). pp. 202–3.

[5] See, for instance, Deuteronomy, ch. 29.

Not too much notice needs to be taken of the extremists who pretend the Holocaust never happened; but, as usual, faults are not only to be found on one side, the Germans'. Here was mid-century Europe, in Edmund Wilson's memorable words,

> not as she appeared
> To the bland eye of Henry James,
> But agonized and mad with war,
> With her barbarity lying bare.[6]

Quite how bare, American soldiers discovered with a rude shock when they entered *Dora, *Buchenwald, *Flossenbürg; and British soldiers, when they entered *Bergen-Belsen. When *Hoess, the commandant of *Auschwitz, was found in the summer of 1945 hiding in the British zone of occupied Germany, his first interrogator accused him of having killed some hundreds of thousands of Jews; to which Hoess replied, in pride and precision, with an exact figure of over two million dead—he did not bother to distinguish Jews from Aryans—during his spell of command.[7]

Auschwitz had been taken by the Red Army, like the other large killing camps, *Chelmno, *Sobibor, *Treblinka, and Auschwitz's own sub-camp of Birkenau. But the Soviets had a reason for not trumpeting too loud what they had found there: they had too many camps of their own, the *GUlag, in which there were deaths past numbering. Only since the collapse of the USSR has it been admitted in Moscow that almost all the captured officers of the Polish Army were massacred by the Soviet police forces in *Katyń and elsewhere in 1940; Katyń was only a pinnacle on an iceberg of inhumanity, in which millions of souls were done to death. History, like the life it reflects, is full of paradoxes. One of the oddest to crop up this century was that the free world's chance to remain free was preserved against the Nazi menace by those two monsters of tyranny, Stalin and *Beria.

Moreover the British and American air forces returned upon Germany in 1943–5, many times over, the severity of bombing attack on civilian populations that Germany had applied to Poland, the Netherlands, England, and Yugoslavia in 1939–41. In revenge for the ruins of Warsaw, *Rotterdam, London, and Belgrade, the RAF and USAAF laid waste Cologne, *Hamburg, *Dresden, *Berlin, and many cities more. (Bonn was subsequently chosen to be capital of western Germany only because it was the one place of its size in which as many as half the buildings were left standing.) To days—day after day, regularly as clockwork—on which *Himmler killed ten thousand Jews, nights followed, night after night, on which *Harris killed a thousand Germans; both of them killing indirectly, as is the fashion with modern commanders. (Contrast Homer's *Iliad* with Warlimont's *Inside Hitler's Headquarters*.) Sometimes Harris's body-count outreached Himmler's. What differences Saint Michael will see on the day of judgement between burning a baby to death in Dresden, and gassing a baby to death in Birkenau, is a question rather for the theologian than for the historian; but one difference at least is obvious: Germany's cities were heavily defended, so that the aircrew who attacked them put their own lives at risk; very few such resources were available to the victims of concentration camps.

A change of key and tempo—no, the musical metaphors are too mild: an abrupt, revolutionary

[6] Leon Edel (ed.), Edmund Wilson, *The Twenties* (1975), pp. 70–1.

[7] Private information from an eyewitness. Hoess was hanged, after trial; the gallows on which he died still stands at Auschwitz.

shift in methods of warfare followed, on 6 and 9 August 1945, with the only uses ever yet made in combat of nuclear weapons. Within ten days, Japan agreed to surrender; within a month, the fighting stopped.

No subject in modern military history is as important; none has been so ineptly handled by journalists, propagandists, and troublemakers. Those who deck their vehicles with the slogan 'No more Hiroshimas' are unaware or choose to ignore or to dispute that the use of these two *atomic bombs saved hundreds of thousands of lives, Japanese as well as Allied, at the time; nor have they paused to think how many millions of lives the existence of nuclear bombs has saved since. There has never yet been a war between states, both of which own nuclear weapons; statesmen have not, so far, been that foolhardy.

The use of the bombs gave a fillip to pacifist feeling, which for the previous six years had been only a feeble force. Television broadcasts of scenes of warfare have had plenty of political influence, since the fighting in Vietnam invaded American homes in the 1960s; and from them a good deal of the nastiness of war can be inferred, though neither the vast size of a world war, nor the predominant role of luck in battle, can be projected through the screen. Moreover war shown on television, however actual it seems to be, is to this extent cleansed before display: the fragments of dismembered bodies which are a commonplace of battlefields are not as a rule laid out before a viewing public.

Telecasting warfare has begun to develop powerful popular revulsion against war, to fit in with the belief of the world's intelligentsia that future world wars are unthinkable. No such feelings were prevalent in mid-century, once it had become clear that the Allied Great War slogan 'the War to end War' had been a hollow sham. That it was a sham was evident, if not from 1931 then from 1935, or at least from 1936. Indeed from the moment of Hitler's arrival in power on 30 January 1933 it became axiomatic, on the political left, that there would be another major war.[8] From 1939 to 1945 there was not much anti-war protest, on any side: nothing to parallel liberal opposition in England to the South African war of 1899–1902, or the opposition by intellectuals in France to the Algerian war of independence, or in the USA to the war in Vietnam.[9] Under secret police regimes—Germany, Italy, the USSR—such protests never had any chance at all. It was official state doctrine in Italy that *fascism 'believes neither in the possibility nor the utility of perpetual peace'.[10] In Japan, almost everyone who thought about politics at all favoured expansion, by force of arms—the simplest, most familiar way. In France, before the catastrophe of 1940, the nation was divided between those determined to settle the German question this time (*faut en finir* was their motto) and those who held, with the French Communist Party, that imperialist wars were all evil and should be attacked, in Marx's phrase of 1848, by 'the forcible overthrow of all existing social conditions'.[11] In England, as in the USA, opinion hardened in favour of war. English opinion hardened much faster than American, under the blows of the Luftwaffe in the battle of *Britain and the Blitz. A handful of pacifists in both countries held out against compulsory armed service, usually on religious grounds; and were accommodated.

Warfare in the present century has become much more destructive, as weapons technology has advanced; but war has never been a kindly business. Hamburg and *Hiroshima were both

[8] Cp. Stephen Spender, *Life and the Poet* (1942), p. 9.

[9] See David L. Schalk, *War and the Ivory Tower* (New York, 1991).

[10] Mussolini in *Enciclopedia Italiana* (Treviso 1932), xiv.849a, tr. Jane Soames as a pamphlet, *The Political and Social Doctrine of Fascism* (1933), p. 11.

[11] K. Marx and F. Engels, *The Communist Manifesto, ad fin.*

burned out by air attack (of the two, more people were killed in Hamburg). They join a long list of burned-out cities, that goes back through Washington, Magdeburg, and Rome to Troy. So destructive did explosives become, even before the atomic bomb, that over half the war's battle casualties were due to *artillery fire. A great many Christian soldiers, especially in the United States army, remained so impressed with the commandment 'Thou shalt not kill',[12] which they had learned in boyhood, that they were unable ever to point a rifle at anybody else, even when they could bring themselves to fire it in action at all.[13] Saint Augustine's and Aquinas's doctrines about just wars left them unmoved.

Explosives provided by no means the only field for technological improvement during the six years of war. One of the war's decisive actions, at *Taranto, fatal to the prospects of battleships, was won in 1940 by single-engined biplanes with a top speed of less than 250 kph; by the end of the war, jet aircraft with top speeds touching 800 kph were in action, and supersonic rockets were already in the air, foreshadowing the intercontinental ballistic missiles of the present day. Besides, there were almost magical improvements in means of communication, which came with the development of *radar and the start of *electronic warfare. These improvements were of special importance in the world of *intelligence.

Care has been taken to include in this book what two leading experts in the field, Andrew and Dilks, have called the missing dimension of studies of diplomacy and war:[14] the field of intelligence, broadly considered, to include deception, sabotage, and escape as well as the more conventional subject of information about the enemy. Beside general articles on sea, land, and air warfare, we have placed a general article on subversion, quite as important as the three more usual aspects in which wafare is regarded.

Intelligence certainly played a larger part than usual in the conduct of the Second World War, but was not (it never is) all-sufficient or all-embracing. The skills of secret analysts—some of them very skilful indeed—needed to be sustained by fighting men in the field. Every intelligence staff officer dreams of securing the enemy's full order of battle. The French got it, from *ULTRA secret sources, in May 1940; whereupon they underwent a catastrophic defeat, in which their British allies were lucky not to become engulfed as well.

This book glances at the once intensely secret business of decipher; a business as much subject to myth as any other. We have, we hope, punctured some mythical balloons; a few are worth special mention.

By now it has become a commonplace to talk of Great Britain's stand alone against Germany after the fall of *France in the summer of 1940. The UK did indeed stand alone among the world's great powers: Italy and Japan were formally and the USSR informally allied to the enemy, France was prostrate, the USA firmly neutral. But with Great Britain there stood all four of the old dominions, as indispensable and voluntary allies, as well as the vast Indian and colonial territories, whose share in the war was taken for granted. Moreover, *governments-in-exile were beginning to assemble in London—the president of Poland, the queen of the Netherlands and the king of Norway were already there—and the first glimmerings were to be seen of the flame of *resistance that was eventually to blaze up among the peoples of occupied Europe, who were almost universally unhappy with their conquered state.

[12] Exodus, 20: 13.

[13] S. L. A. Marshall, *Men Against Fire* (Washington, 1947). pp. 50–61, 72–8.

[14] Christopher Andrew and David Dilks (eds.), *The Missing Dimension: Governments and Intelligence Communities in the Twentieth Century* (1984).

Introduction

Resistance has been the source of far too many tales, including the tale that resisters were only bandits pretending to be respectable. We have done our best to re-examine the myths; while recognizing that some resistance was indeed sublime, as—we hope—a few entries on such exceptional characters as Pearl *Witherington show.

The cost in lives and in disruption remains appalling. Wars are always horrible; sometimes, like this one, they are necessary, and even at their dreadful cost, are worth it.

As usual, war acted as an accelerator, politically and socially as well as technically. Of technique enough has already been said in outline; politics and society also each deserve attention, for war, politics, and society are tied tightly together.

The First World War had disposed of the personal empires of the Habsburg, Hohenzollern, Ottoman, and Romanov families; it had also fatally weakened the will to imperial power of both the British and the French electorates. The world war that followed marked the beginning of the end of both the British and the French empires. The British withdrew from India in 1947, and had left almost all their colonies by 1970; French North and West Africa and Indo-China became independent as well; and the Dutch, Belgian, and Portuguese colonial empires foundered also. The Russian empire lasted a few years longer.

The Soviets provided extra stability through their system of political commissars. In Macaulay's day, every schoolboy knew that William the Conqueror's half-brother Odo, bishop of Bayeux, rode into battle with him at Hastings, armed with a mace—to kill by stunning, for the Church was not supposed to shed blood. It is not quite fanciful to compare Odo's presence beside William with Khrushchev's beside *Timoshenko, to ensure doctrinal purity on the battlefield.

For the time being, the war favoured the development of communist regimes; a great propaganda effort supported the view that the communists had everywhere been the dominant element in resistance to nazism and fascism, a doctrine rather short of historical truth to back it. War experience also seemed to show that there was much to be said for state direction of industry and of other parts of the national effort.

In the longer run, such views have not stood the test of time, as the collapse of communist power in eastern Europe in 1989–91 showed. Indeed, looking back on the war (as historians do: we disapprove hindsight, but cannot avoid using it) it is clear that what scuppered Hitler's bid for world power was his challenge in December 1941 to the industrial might of the USA, quite as much as his overreaching onslaught on the USSR six months earlier. Even the U-boat menace, that had terrified Churchill (lightly though it weighs on Professor Milner as he reveals in his article on the battle of the *Atlantic), shrank to manageable proportions when confronted by a nation that could build a 10,000-ton *Liberty ship in a single week, so that by 1944 Allied shipbuilding was keeping comfortably ahead of submarine losses.

Only in Japan did the armed forces drive wartime policy direct: Emperor *Hirohito gave his formal assent, but, like Wilhelm II in the previous world war, left all the decisions to the experts in uniform. (It is another paradox that the Japanese have come much farther towards creating their *Greater East Asia Co-Prosperity Sphere by peaceful commerce than they ever did by force of arms.) In Germany, Italy, and the USSR a single dictator, each with a dictatorial party to back him, was in charge. In the USA, the United Kingdom, and the British dominions, elected leaders responsible to debating assemblies ran the war. France started with the same system, but after defeat fell back on a dictator, *Pétain. India came remotely under Westminster's control, through a small, strong civil service and a powerful viceroy. One of the reasons why *Mountbatten set up his headquarters as supreme commander in south-east Asia in Ceylon rather than in India was to get out of the shadow of the viceroy, *Wavell.

Other political aspects of this world war await proper study. Not enough is known about how people reacted to the shock and disgrace of national defeat, or how ready they were to adopt a new set of attitudes towards their conquerors; some of whom expected them to be welcoming and subservient—as some, but by no means all, of them were. There is also more work to be done on the impact of war as a socially cohesive force, and a solvent of class divisions. Bombs fall, like God's rain, on the just and on the unjust, on the poor and the rich alike (though the rich may have afforded deeper shelters); bombardment can sometimes enhance a spirit of 'we're all in this together'.

At some times, and in some countries, a sense of communal effort transcending political differences did develop: whether in unoccupied states, that still had something to fight for, such as the United Kingdom, or in occupied ones, that had only too much to fight against, such as Poland or the Netherlands. In all occupied countries, the resistance effort split, to reflect the split that ran through the *Grand Alliance: the communists and their friends were never able to agree entirely with the anti-communists, differences that degenerated into the *Cold War of 1944 to 1989.

The First World War had done much to free women from the shackles of 19th-century domesticity; the next world war did even more. Few women took a combatant part in battle, but millions of them could not help finding themselves in the front line of civilians subjected to air attack where they showed strength and courage equal to any fighting soldier's. Many more women made invaluable contributions to warfare as makers of armaments; others played crucial roles in resistance, as well as in the armed services.

Many marriages did not stand the strain of separation, even if the husbands returned alive and whole. Sex outside marriage, usually thought shocking in the 1930s, had become commonplace by the 1960s; partly because the war had helped to make it so, partly because the war had stimulated research into birth control, which had become much more readily available. *Patria potestas*, the father's power over his wife and children and children's children, a concept familiar from Roman law, has now all but vanished from Europe and north America, replaced by doctrines of equality between the sexes which seem set to spread elsewhere.

No history can ever be quite definitive, and some historical surprises may yet be waiting to be sprung. Many points once utterly secret (see *secrecy) are at last seeping out into view. Soviet archives, long closed, are now starting to become available; 3,000 cubic feet of American secret archives went public in the early 1990s; those of SOE's papers that survive—an eighth of its original paperasserie—are in process of being released to the Public Record Office. There will not yet be adjustments and revisions to be made to the tale set out below. A few points of importance will never surface: points so secret that they were never written down at the time, covered in private talks between those who are all now dead. Historical insight can sometimes infer what they may have been; and historians' ranges of interest change with fashion, thus constantly revising the perspective in which the present views the past.

The articles that follow are all written by historians, who have done their best to write history, rather than to pursue sensation. Recent events in eastern Europe have opened up wide fields for revisionists, in which we try to operate. Far too much sensation-mongering about the war has gone on already; and many 'revisionist' volumes appear based purely on speculation. We do our best to avoid either sensation or speculation, and can echo Lord Palmerston's words to the House of Commons, that what would have happened if that which did happen had not happened, we cannot undertake to say. There are lessons worth learning, all the same, from this as from any other honest history; about how humankind has behaved, might behave, even ought to behave, under pressure. Before all the survivors of the great war against Adolf Hitler's Germany are dead, one at least of them must go on record here to remind the present age that that evil man, and the evil system he created, came close to conquering Europe, as they meant one day to conquer the world.

M. R. D. Foot
February 1993

All books cited are published in London, unless another place of origin is given.
* Asterisks preface the titles of entries in this volume, and refer the reader to them for further details.

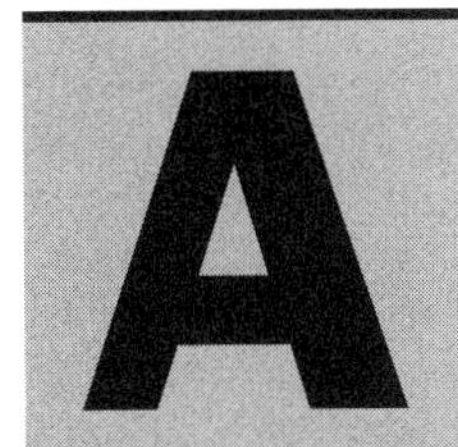

Aachen, German city situated close to the Dutch and Belgian borders, the scene of the first major battle fought by *Eisenhower's forces on German soil during the fighting which began the battle for *Germany. The *West Wall ran close to here and from 12 to 15 September 1944 *Hodges's First US Army attempted to penetrate it south of the city, but without success. Renewing his attacks on 2 October, this time in the north as well, Hodges eventually overcame the German defences, surrounded Aachen on 16 October, and after several days of bitter street fighting forced its surrender on 21 October. Colonel Gerhard Wilck's stubborn defence of Aachen delayed Hodges's advance for more than five weeks and cost him about 8,000 casualties. See also WEREWOLVES.

CHARLES MESSENGER

AB AKTION (Ausserordentliche BefriedungsAKTION, or Extraordinary Pacification Action). Nazi codename for the liquidation of Polish intellectuals and other leaders which took place during and after the *Polish campaign. It has been estimated that about 3,500 were killed from September 1939 to June 1940. See also EINSATZGRUPPEN.

ABC-1 Plan, the outcome of secret American–British–Canadian military discussions in Washington which took place from January to March 1941. The plan, which had already been recommended to Roosevelt as part of the *Rainbow plans, envisaged that if the USA entered the war a joint strategy would be pursued in which Germany would be the prime target. A war of attrition would be waged against Japan until Germany had been defeated. The primary measures to be taken against Germany were blockade, aerial attack, and subversion. The plan bound no one at the time, but it was confirmed at the first Washington conference in December 1941 (see ARCADIA) and resulted in the US Navy reinforcing the Atlantic at the expense of the Pacific, while British units were sent to reinforce Singapore (see PRINCE OF WALES).

ABDA Command, first attempt at a combined Allied command, which was agreed at the first Washington conference in December 1941 (see ARCADIA). ABDA (American–British–Dutch–Australian) was activated on 15 January 1942 to defend Singapore and the *Netherlands East Indies (NEI). ABDA's area of operations covered Burma, the Malayan peninsula, the NEI, Thailand, South China Sea, and the northern and north-western coasts of Australia (see Map F). It was commanded by General *Wavell, who had his HQ at Lembang on Java. Lt-General G. Brett of the USAAF was his deputy, Lt-General Henry Pownall, whose post as C-in-C Far East now lapsed, acted as his Chief of Staff, and the C-in-C of the US Asiatic Fleet, Admiral *Hart (Vice-Admiral C. Helfrich from 14 February) was his naval commander (ABDAFLOAT).

But ABDA 'was too complicated for truly effective co-operation and rapid communication ... Moreover ... the naval and air forces at Wavell's command were negligible, and he had no troops as a strategic reserve ... National animosities and the basic differences between American and British interests were other weaknesses' (A. Marder *et al.*, *Old Friends, New Enemies*, Vol. 2, Oxford, 1992, pp. 31–2). On 25 February it was disbanded when Wavell had to flee from his HQ ahead of a Japanese invasion of Java on 1 March.

Abwehr ('defence'), German military intelligence and counter-intelligence organization formed after the *First World War. Although the *Versailles settlement of 1919 had prohibited Germany from establishing an intelligence organization, a counter-espionage group was set up within the defence ministry in 1920. It was called the 'Abwehr' as it was the nation's defence against foreign espionage, and it retained this name throughout its existence, although its role was to evolve. It was not until after 1933 that the Abwehr went beyond merely defensive assignments and became involved in espionage. However, since its espionage networks abroad only then began to be set up, the task of establishing them proved extremely difficult and was by no means completed by the outbreak of the Second World War.

In January 1935, Captain (later Admiral) *Canaris was put in charge of the Abwehr. He proved an appropriate choice for the job. During the First World War he had been involved in clandestine supply operations for the Imperial Navy in South America, he had travelled widely, and he had a good command of foreign languages, especially Spanish. Canaris set to work to convert the Abwehr from a gentlemanly but largely inefficient club into a modern intelligence organization. Although he had had no formal training on the job, he was quick to grasp the essential elements of espionage and counter-espionage. When the war ministry was finally merged into the Oberkommando der Wehrmacht (OKW, or Armed Forces Supreme Command) in February 1938, Canaris was appointed one of its departmental commanders. Late in 1939 his organization, now called Amt Ausland/Abwehr (*Amt*, office; *Ausland*, abroad), acquired the structure it was to retain for most of the war as a branch of OKW (see Table).

It consisted of one *Amtsgruppe* (*Ausland*) and four *Abteilungen* (departments). Amtsgruppe Ausland was responsible for attaché work and other forms of non-covert intelligence. A Central Department (Abteilung Z) carried out administrative duties. It was headed by Maj.-General *Oster, who was to become one of the Abwehr's most influential officers.

Departments I, II, and III were entrusted with the classical elements of any secret service. The espionage department (Abteilung I) was under the command of Colonel Hans Piekenbrock; sabotage and subversion, Abteilung II, at first headed by Major (later Colonel)

Abwehr: Organization of Amt Ausland/Abwehr

		Admiral Wilhelm Canaris		
Amtsgruppe Ausland	*Abteilung Z*	*Abteilung I*	*Abteilung II*	*Abteilung III*
Vice Admiral Bürkner	1938–43 Maj-General Oster	1937–43 Colonel Piekenbrock	1938–9 Major Groscurth	1933–9 Major Bamler
	1943–4 Colonel Jakobsen	1943–4 Colonel Hansen	1939–43 Colonel Lahousen 1943–4 Colonel von Freytag-Loringhoven	1939–44 Colonel von Bentivegni
Non-covert Intelligence; Military Attachés	Organization Personnel Archives	Espionage	Sabotage Subversion Regiment, later Division, Brandenburg	Counter-Intelligence

Source: Contributor.

Helmuth Groscurth, was run by the enigmatic and resourceful Colonel Erwin Lahousen from 1939 to 1943; counter-espionage, Abteilung III, enjoyed its greatest successes under Colonel Egbert von Bentivegni who ran it from 1939 to 1944. Unlike the British system (see UK, 8) all the branches functioned within the same organizational structure, and there was very little rivalry between them. The Abwehr was not predominant in the field of technical intelligence. In particular, signals interception was largely left to the intelligence branches of the army, navy, and air force respectively (see GERMANY, 7).

Throughout the period from 1935 to 1944 the Abwehr was in constant rivalry with the Sicherheitsdienst (SD) (see RSHA), the *SS security service headed initially by Reinhard *Heydrich, and later by Walter *Schellenberg. The SD regarded the Abwehr as politically unreliable; the Abwehr in turn resented party encroachment upon what it felt was purely military territory. Basically, this conflict was merely a watered-down version of the major power struggle between army and party organizations, notably the SS. Canaris achieved a reasonably good working relationship with Heydrich, who had once been a naval officer. In March 1942, they reached an agreement which permitted the SD to conduct its own counter-espionage operations alongside those of the Abwehr, which, in turn, was no longer supposed to report on internal affairs such as the mood of the German people. Shortly afterwards, Heydrich was killed in Czechoslovakia. Between Canaris and Heydrich's successors there was fierce rivalry. Schellenberg, head of the SD foreign service, and Walter Huppenkothen, head of the *Gestapo's counter-intelligence section (E), were to become Canaris' chief enemies; Huppenkothen eventually saw him hanged.

The Abwehr's foreign espionage networks in the Balkans, Portugal and, above all, Spain, were well informed. The Spanish secret service facilitated German surveillance of Allied shipping in the Mediterranean, and negotiations between Hitler and *Franco about Spain's entry into the war were conducted by Canaris, who was a personal friend of Franco's. Similarly, the Abwehr conducted secret talks with the Greek dictator, General Ioannis Metaxas (1871–1941), just before his death early in 1941, aimed at avoiding German intervention in the Balkans. In France, penetration had been achieved only to a minor degree, and most networks were blown soon after war broke out. However, the attempt to set up an espionage network in the UK and the USA had failed completely. By the end of 1939, no German agents were operating in the UK. All attempts to smuggle new agents into the country, usually by parachute or submarine, ended in failure; some agents were hanged, most were turned round (see XX-COMMITTEE). The Abwehr only once got anywhere near the best-guarded British military secret, *ULTRA (see SIGNALS INTELLIGENCE WARFARE, 7 for details). An attempt to co-operate with the *Irish Republican Army in order to subvert British fighting strength operating from Northern Ireland failed, as did all attempts to lure Eire into the Axis fold. But although the espionage service never lived up to expectations, the other two branches of the Abwehr were quite successful.

Abwehr II fulfilled its first major tasks even before the outbreak of the Second World War. It was instrumental in organizing pro-German uprisings (see VOLKSDEUTSCHE) which formed the pretext for the annexation of Czechoslovakia; it was also involved in a rather unsuccessful disinformation campaign before and during the Anschluss of Austria in 1938. When, in August 1939, Hitler postponed the attack on Poland at the very last minute, the Abwehr II group which had been charged with securing the strategically important Yablunka Pass across the Beskides mountains, could not be recalled in time. They successfully attacked the Polish platoon guarding the tunnel, only to give it up again when they learned that the invasion had not started after all. Raids like this were the essence of Abwehr II. They secured bridges in the opponent's rear, operated behind the other side's lines, and were largely involved in attempts to stir up nationalist trouble in areas under attack, mostly on the Eastern Front. For administrative reasons, these subversive units were classed together as *Brandenburgers. Towards the end of the war, these reached the strength of a full infantry division. However, this also led to an increasing use of élite Brandenburg units as mere infantry, squandering valuable resources when manpower was beginning to be critically short. Abwehr II also took part in raising nationalist troops from among former *prisoners-of-war (see SOVIET EXILES AT WAR).

Counter-intelligence (Abwehr III) had its most spectacular success when, with the Gestapo (see RHSA), it broke into and then destroyed the large Soviet espionage and resistance network known as the *Rote Kapelle (Red Orchestra) and the head of the Abwehr in the Netherlands, Lt-Colonel Hermann Giskes, was instrumental in running the war's best-known *Funkspiel* ('radio game') when British *SOE and *MI6 agents were captured and turned (see ENGLANDSPIEL).

The Abwehr played a major role in the German resistance against Hitler (see SCHWARZE KAPELLE). The direct, unfiltered, information about Nazi war crimes available to the Abwehr was enough to convince anybody of the evil nature of the regime. Its secret channels of communication and its ability to employ 'shadowy' (that is, politically unreliable) elements made it the ideal vehicle for clandestine opposition. Most conspiratorial activities, if discovered, could be explained away as being part of normal duties. The attempt to overthrow Hitler in 1938 was mostly engineered by Abwehr personnel, among them Oster, Groscurth, and Canaris himself. Later on, the Abwehr was actively engaged in providing means of communicating unobtrusively with the enemy. Through Abwehr channels, the resistance tried to obtain assurances of lenient treatment for Germany in the event of an attempted *coup d'état*. However the British, in particular, realizing that the Abwehr was involved in these approaches, tended to mistrust them. Finally, it was through Abwehr channels that the resistance obtained the explosives, captured from SOE agents, used in several attempts on Hitler's life.

The Abwehr's involvement in the conspiracy against the regime was to contribute to its eventual downfall. The SD had always had misgivings about the precarious agreement reached between Canaris and Heydrich in March 1942, and they continued to search for mistakes on the part of the Abwehr which would eventually bring about its ruin. Canaris had bluntly expressed his pessimism about the likely outcome of the war, thereby losing most of the support he still enjoyed at OKW and estranging himself from Hitler as well.

In the autumn of 1942, German police began to investigate major foreign currency deals operated through Abwehr channels. The affair ended up with the RSHA (Reichssicherheitshauptamt), which was all too eager to find an excuse to investigate the SD's rival organization. One of the suspects had been party to General Oster's 1938–40 conspiracies, and when hard pressed and seemingly deserted by his Abwehr colleagues, he began to tell his torturers what he knew. This led to large-scale arrests within the Abwehr and Oster's dismissal. Not only was the resistance against Hitler decisively weakened (it would not find a similar power base until Colonel Claus von Stauffenberg made his resources as Chief of Staff of the C-in-C, Replacement Army, available), but the position of Canaris and his organization was also seriously undermined. The defection to the British of a minor agent in Istanbul and the continuation of underground attacks against British targets in Spain, against the obvious wishes of the Spaniards, dealt a final blow to the Abwehr. On 12 February 1944, Hitler ordered Canaris to stay out of Berlin and German intelligence was put under *Himmler's command. Colonel Hansen, who had taken over Abteilung I in 1943, was given the department for military affairs within the new service, which effectively operated under the Abwehr's former adversaries. Both Hansen and Canaris himself eventually fell victim to the fury of the Gestapo in the wake of the attempt on Hitler's life on 20 July 1944.

The Abwehr's espionage achievements were sometimes overrated. On the other hand, it has not always been given full credit for its notable successes in counter-espionage and, above all, sabotage and subversion.

WINFRIED HEINEMANN

There is a paucity of recent English-language publications on the Abwehr. The best are probably:
Höhne, H., *Canaris* (London, 1976).
Kahn, D., *Hitler's Spies. German Military Intelligence in World War II* (London, 1978).
See also, although it contains some factual errors: Paine, L., *German Military Intelligence in World War II. The Abwehr* (New York, 1984), who maintains that Abwehr espionage was in fact a success.
For the view of a participant see: Leverkuehn, P., *Der geheime Nachrichtendienst der deutschen Wehrmacht im Kriege* (2nd edn., Frankfurt, 1957).

Abyssinia (Ethiopia), an ancient East African kingdom of some ten million people ruled by an emperor, *Haile Selassie. In October 1935 Abyssinia was invaded by Italian forces from the neighbouring Italian territories of Italian Somaliland and Eritrea, and in March 1936 Haile Selassie's forces were decisively defeated by *Badoglio; the emperor was forced into exile in the UK.

The country became part of Italian East Africa, with *Graziani as its governor-general and viceroy, and the population was ruthlessly repressed. When Italy entered the war in June 1940 it became a springboard from which the Italians attacked frontier posts in the Sudan and Kenya, and for the capture of British Somaliland. But with internal rebellion threatening them the Italians failed to capitalize on these successes and were eventually defeated in the *East African campaign by British and Commonwealth forces. Haile Selassie was returned to his throne by *Wingate and his *Gideon Force in May 1941 and later managed to wrest control of his country from his British allies. See also MUSSOLINI, 3.

ack-ack was an Allied term for anti-aircraft fire or guns. For anti-aircraft guns, see ARTILLERY.

acoustic weapons, see MINE WARFARE, 2 and GUIDED WEAPONS.

Aden was a British protectorate and port in the Arabian peninsula. The protectorate which covered 112,000 sq. mi. stretched from the port to the border of Oman. The port was acquired by the British as a coaling station in 1839. It became a crown colony in 1937, having been previously administered from India, and Indian troops recaptured British Somaliland from it in March 1941. In 1967 longstanding territorial claims by Yemen on it were successful.

Adlertag (Eagle Day) was the 13 August 1940, the day *Göring started operation ADLERANGRIFF (Eagle Attack), a two-week assault on RAF Fighter Command's aircraft, airfields, and installations as a preliminary to the invasion of the UK (see SEALION). Poor weather and muddled orders made *Adlertag* itself less than a resounding success, but ADLERANGRIFF nearly brought the Luftwaffe the supremacy in the air it was seeking. For German historians it is also the day that marks the beginning of the battle of *Britain. For the British it started on 10 July.

Admin Box battle, fought in February 1944, the first major British success against the Japanese during the *Burma campaign.

On 4 February 1944 the 55th Japanese Division, commanded by Lt-General Hanaya Tadashi, launched an operation designed to defeat Lt-General *Christison's British 15th Corps which had advanced from India into the Arakan as far as Maungdaw, and to pin down any British reinforcements which could be used against the Japanese *Imphal offensive due to start that March.

To support Christison's own offensive—its objective was to capture the Akyab airfields, a vital requisite for retaking Rangoon—an administrative and supply base had been constructed near Sinzweya. It was this box, just 1,000 m. (1,100 yd.) square, that gave the battle its name, for it was here that a regiment from Hanaya's division attacked. Although the British were aware of his plan, Hanaya achieved total tactical surprise. The HQ of the 7th Indian Division under Maj-General *Messervy was overrun and the Box was soon surrounded. But the British stood their ground and were soon reinforced. Tanks, which Hanaya did not have, regular airborne supplies, superior air power, and better artillery kept the Japanese at bay.

What won the day for the British, against the swift encircling tactics that had always previously defeated them, was the three-dimensional nature of their defences. The Box, defended and supplied as it was from the air, was really a cube, while the Japanese, short of fire-power and aircraft, had to rely on a two-dimensional attack. It failed, and once additional Indian Army forces had closed in from the north and west, the Japanese were themselves encircled and then destroyed. Hanaya's failure at Sinzweya enabled *Slim to fly in reinforcements to defend Imphal at a crucial moment in the Japanese offensive against it. British casualties amounted to 3,506; the Japanese, according to their own sources, had 5,335 including 3,106 killed.

Turnbull, P., *The Battle of the Box* (Shepperton, 1979).

Admiral Graf Spee, see RIVER PLATE.

Admiralty Islands, Pacific group which lies 320 km. (200 mi.) north-east of what was then the Australian mandate of New Guinea of which they formed a part. The Japanese developed air bases there after occupying the islands in April 1942 and Seeadler harbour provided an ideal fleet anchorage. Their capture was therefore an essential requisite for General *MacArthur's plan to isolate and reduce *Rabaul, and he gave the task of seizing the islands to Lt-General Walter Krueger's *Alamo Force. On 29 February 1944 the 1st Cavalry Division, supported by 73rd Wing of the Royal Australian Air Force, landed on one of the principal islands, Los Negros, before moving to the other, Manus, the following week. The Japanese garrison, which included two infantry battalions and naval detachments, resisted tenaciously and the islands were not declared secure until 18 May. The 1st Cavalry Division lost 326 men killed and 1,189 wounded.

Aegean Islands, overall name for numerous islands and island groups in the Aegean Sea including the Cyclades, Dodecanese, and Sporades groups. The larger islands were occupied by Axis forces after the *Balkan campaign and the fall of *Crete in June 1941. When the Italians surrendered in September 1943 the Germans and the British fought the *Dodecanese campaign for the possession of some of them.

Afghanistan, a neutral oligarchy ruled by Mohammed Zahir Shah. It joined the *League of Nations in 1934 and in 1937 signed a non-aggression pact with Turkey and Persia. From 1935 until the outbreak of the Second World War, German influence increased markedly, but though the sympathies of the ruling élite were mainly with the Axis they kept the country strictly neutral. Economic and political ties were maintained with Germany, a position the USSR at first chose not to, and the UK was unable to, alter. However, once Hitler invaded the USSR in June 1941 (see BARBAROSSA) the Afghan government was successfully pressed into severing all ties with the Axis powers and expelled their citizens.

A Force, see DECEPTION.

African Americans at war. As was the case during the previous wars of the USA, African Americans responded to the nation's involvement in the Second World War with a mixture of patriotic sacrifice and racial militancy. Wartime mobilization offered many opportunities for African Americans to demonstrate, through military service and employment in war industries, that they were loyal to the nation and crucial to its defence. The vulnerability of the USA to external threats from Nazi Germany also provided leverage for blacks seeking to challenge racially discriminatory practices that undermined the nation's unity and democratic self-image. The 'Double-V' campaign, initiated by the *Pittsburgh Courier* in 1942, symbolized the widely held desire of African Americans for victory over fascism abroad and over racism at home. Although some of the racial gains of the Second World War period did not endure after the war, changes in prevailing patterns of racial attitudes and black–white relations caused by wartime exigencies provided a foundation for many of the civil rights advances of the post-war era. In particular, the increasing black militancy of the period provided models for the more extensive racial protests of the 1950s and 1960s.

Even before American entry into the war, some African Americans became actively concerned with international issues. The Italian invasion of Abyssinia in 1935 became a particularly important cause for blacks because of that nation's symbolic importance as a source of African culture. An International Council of Friends lobbied on behalf of Abyssinia at the *League of Nations, and black Americans raised funds to aid the beleaguered African kingdom. As fascism spread in Europe, some black leftists joined the Abraham Lincoln Brigade and fought on behalf of the Republican cause in the *Spanish Civil War.

In 1941, while the nation debated its role in the expanding European war, the March on Washington Movement (MOWM), under the leadership of the black labour leader A. Philip Randolph, made visible the widespread discontent of blacks facing racial discrimination in employment. Resentment was most acute in union-controlled fields, where some affiliates in the American Federation of Labour maintained rules against black membership. After mobilizing support for the march in black communities throughout the nation, Randolph called off the threatened march shortly before its scheduled start in June 1941, when Roosevelt issued Executive Order No. 8802 establishing a Fair Employment Practice Committee (FEPC) within the Office of Production Management. The new committee, the result of the first presidential executive order on behalf of blacks since the Civil War, was mandated to ensure 'full and equitable participation of all workers in the defense industries, without discrimination because of race, creed, color, or national origin.' Although the FEPC did not become permanent until after the war, and had little power to enforce its rulings or to combat segregation in the military, the planned march demonstrated the potential impact of mass activism as a means of achieving racial gains. For several years thereafter the MOWM remained in existence and continued to pressure government officials.

After the Japanese attack on *Pearl Harbor in December 1941, black leaders generally supported the war effort even while continuing to speak out against racial discrimination. Although the Selective Service Act of 1940 prohibited discrimination in the administration of the draft and in the training of soldiers (see SELECTIVE SERVICE SYSTEM), the War Department refused to allow integrated military units on the grounds that it would undermine the morale of white soldiers. In September 1940 Randolph and other black leaders spoke out against these discriminatory policies, but they had little success. When the USA entered the war, there were only about 5,000 black enlisted men and only a few dozen black officers.

Despite wartime manpower shortages, military leaders remained reluctant to use blacks as officers or in combat roles, relenting somewhat only towards the end of the war. Because military leaders resisted the idea of an integrated military, black recruits were less likely to be accepted in military service, and when accepted they were assigned to segregated units that were represented in disproportionately large numbers in particular branches and arms, such as the army's Quartermaster Corps and Engineer Corps. The 92nd and 93rd Infantry Divisions and the 2nd Cavalry Division became the largest concentrations of black soldiers. The US Navy had traditionally employed blacks only in servile roles, and did not accept black volunteers or conscripts until Roosevelt's Executive Order No. 9279, issued in December 1942, forced all services to end such restrictions. Even after this presidential order, more than 95% of the blacks in the navy served as messmen, and the *WAVES refused to accept black women until forced to do so at the end of 1944. In July 1945 a small group of black WAVES was accepted for training at Hunter College Naval Training School. The Army Air Corps (Army Air Forces from June 1941) resisted accepting blacks until it was compelled to include a few black squadrons; even then most of these squadrons were assigned to airfield maintenance. The 99th Fighter Squadron, a black unit trained at a segregated facility at Tuskegee, Alabama, and deployed in the Mediterranean in April 1943, was the first group of black pilots to see action during the war, and only three other such squadrons would see action before it ended. Such racial restrictions led to the resignation in January 1943 of former federal judge William H. Hastie, the black civilian aide to the secretary of war. In his resignation statement, Hastie condemned the military's 'reactionary' policies that continued to view integrated forces as an experiment likely to fail and that restricted black service in the air command to a few segregated units.

Secretary of War Henry L. *Stimson defended military policies regarding the deployment of black soldiers. He asserted that they were less capable of handling modern weapons, a claim that was hotly disputed by the black press and by Hastie's successor as civilian aide, Truman K. Gibson.

Only as the war continued and casualties mounted did military leaders gradually accept the idea of using black units in combat. Black soldiers who served overseas discovered that their roles were limited to support activities, usually under the command of white officers. Thus, when the 2nd Cavalry arrived in North Africa in March 1944, it was deactivated as a combat unit and black soldiers in it were assigned to service roles. In the *Pacific war black marines assigned to work at ammunition depots in the South Pacific came under fire and found themselves pressed into the battle for *Iwo Jima.

Despite such racial barriers, blacks made limited advances towards equality in the military. They were admitted to officer training schools in all the armed services, studying with white officer candidates in a few instances. By the end of 1944, increasing opportunities for promotion had led to the commissioning of more than 5,000 black soldiers, including the promotion of one, Benjamin O. Davis of the Inspector General's Department to brig-general. By this time there were more than 700,000 blacks serving in the US Army (see Table) with more than half overseas. An additional 165,000 were in the navy, 5,000 in the coast guard, and 17,000 in the marine corps.

The 99th Fighter Squadron performed well in the *Italian campaign, and 761st Tank Battalion was commended for its service in the *Ardennes campaign. In the 614th Tank Destroyer Battalion, which fought in north-west Europe, 8 soldiers won the Silver Star for distinguished service, 28 won the Bronze Star, and 79 won the Purple Heart (see DECORATIONS). Yet, the burden of fighting racism in the military at the same time as the nation's foreign enemies often hampered the effectiveness of black units. African American soldiers often gave expression to their resentment of racial discrimination in the services. When white soldiers in the UK tried to impose segregation at recreational facilities, black soldiers responded with angry clashes that sometimes grew into riots. Black soldiers in Salina, Kansas, were angered when they were barred from eating at a restaurant that served German prisoners-of-war. In July 1944 at Port Chicago, California, several hundred black seamen loaders refused to return to the docks after an ammunition explosion killed more than 300 people. Despite criticism from the black press and civil rights leaders, 44 soldiers were tried and convicted of *mutiny and given sentences ranging from eight to fifteen years' hard labour. Mutinies and racial conflicts also occurred at numerous other military bases, including major clashes at Mabry Field, Florida, and Brookley Field, Alabama, in May 1944, at Camp Claiborn, Louisiana, in August 1944, and in Hawaii early in 1945.

In January 1945, encouraged by reports that black soldiers had performed well, the War Department initiated a plan to recruit black volunteers who would be assigned to platoons that would fight alongside white combat units in north-west Europe. In order to be eligible for the experiment, blacks had to gain high scores on the Army General Classification Test, and black non-commissioned officers were allowed to participate only if they accepted demotion. More than 5,000 black soldiers volunteered for such assignments, and 2,500 were trained in platoons led by white officers. A military study of the effectiveness of the black platoons later concluded that they performed very well in the opinion of most white officers, a finding that was disparaged by many military leaders. Segregation would remain the basic policy of the military until 1948, when President *Truman issued an executive order calling for equal treatment and opportunity for black servicemen.

Race relations on the home front during the war followed patterns similar to those in the military—the gradual overcoming of pervasive discriminatory policies in the utilization of black skills combined with numerous instances of racial militancy and violent black–white conflicts. The Communist Party of the United States, once in the vanguard of racial advancement efforts in the 1930s, was displaced by other organizations such as the anti-communist and all-black MOWM that were less willing to compromise civil rights concerns in order to support the war effort. In addition to the MOWM, groups such as the National Association for the Advancement of Colored People (NAACP) and the National Urban League attempted to eliminate discriminatory practices through lobbying and litigation. The Supreme Court's decision in Smith V. Allwright (1944) invalidating white primary elections that excluded blacks was the most significant NAACP victory during the war years. A series of meetings involving black and white southerners culminated in 1944 with the establishment of the Southern Regional Council, a group dedicated to racial reform. While most leaders of mainstream racial advancement organizations abjured mass protest during the war, black and white advocates of direct action protest, including a few veterans of MOWM, banded together in 1943 to form the Congress of Racial Equality (CORE). CORE activists in several northern cities staged small-scale sit-ins protesting against segregation in restaurants and other public facilities. While CORE was active mainly in the North, the Southern Negro Youth Congress, founded in 1937, kept alive a tradition of anti-segregation agitation in the South. Among the few black organizations that actively opposed the war effort was the Nation of Islam, a small Islamic group advocating racial separatism. The group's leader, Elijah Muhammad, went to prison rather than serve in the military.

White resentment of the modest black employment gains of the war years led to several major outbreaks of violence. In 1943, after large numbers of blacks had

African Americans at War: Quarterly strength of African Americans, by category, in US Army and percentage of total strength of the Army, December 1941–December 1945

Quarter of month	Male Officers	Enlisted Men	Nurses	Dietitians	Physical Therapists	Warrant Officers	Flight Officers	WAAC and WAC Officers	WAAC and WAC Enlisted	Total African Americans	Total Strength of the Army	Per cent of African Americans	African American Enlisted Personnel	Total Enlisted Personnel	Per cent of African Americans Enlisted to Total Enlisted
1941															
December	462	98,686	45	0	0	13	0	0	0	99,206	1,685,403	5.88	98,686	1,562,256	6.32
1942															
March	534	142,967	45	0	0	10	0	0	0	143,556	2,387,746	6.01	142,967	2,236,547	6.39
June	594	178,032	76	0	0	6	0	0	0	178,708	3,074,184	5.81	178,032	2,867,762	6.21
September	1,525	253,952	44	0	0	24	0	0	0	255,545	3,971,016	6.44	253,952	3,673,876	6.91
December	1,921	397,246	81	0	0	26	0	19	161	399,454	5,397,674	7.40	397,407	5,000,275	7.95
1943															
March	2,687	498,956	165	0	0	90	0	65	2,467	504,430	6,508,854	7.75	501,423	6,010,032	8.34
June	3,358	548,319	158	4	1	166	9	105	3,056	555,176	6,993,102	7.94	551,375	6,413,526	8.60
September	3,859	589,253	195	8	1	336	0	105	2,907	596,664	7,273,784	8.20	592,160	6,622,951	8.94
December	4,475	625,449	198	9	1	507	4	103	2,702	633,448	7,482,434	8.47	628,151	6,790,754	9.25
1944															
March	4,690	663,164	219	10	2	603	14	115	3,060	671,877	7,757,629	8.66	666,224	7,021,758	9.49
June	4,949	689,565	213	8	2	636	32	117	3,389	698,911	7,992,868	8.74	692,954	7,215,888	9.60
September	4,728	692,229	247	9	2	613	84	121	3,645	701,678	8,108,129	8.65	695,874	7,293,480	9.54
December	5,027	681,376	256	9	6	656	151	120	3,920	691,521	8,052,693	8.59	685,296	7,212,210	9.50
1945															
March	5,073	684,097	336	7	9	685	234	115	3,787	694,343	8,157,386	8.51	687,884	7,288,292	9.44
June	5,411	684,091	464	9	11	682	301	117	3,732	694,818	8,266,373	8.41	687,823	7,374,710	9.33
September	5,718	642,719	466	8	10	592	312	105	3,633	653,563	7,564,514	8.64	646,352	6,679,773	9.68
December	3,799	366,016	318	8	7	306	225	80	1,610	372,369	4,228,936	8.81	367,626	3,572,577	10.29

Source: Lee, V., *US Army in World War Two: The Employment of Negro Troops* (Washington, 1966).

migrated to Detroit to fill industrial jobs, white workers staged a strike to protest against the promotion of some blacks to more skilled jobs at the Packard Motor Plant. On 20 June a small fight escalated into a major race riot involving white mobs attacking blacks. Roosevelt declared a state of emergency and sent federal troops to the city. Twenty-five blacks and nine whites were killed. A less serious race riot occurred at the Mobile, Alabama, shipyard after black workers were upgraded. Later in the summer, disaffected blacks in Harlem, New York City, attacked police and white businesses before the uprising was suppressed by police and State Guard troops. In other communities, whites attacked uniformed black soldiers.

After the Second World War, as with previous wars, many black soldiers returning home with a new sense of militancy encountered resistance from whites determined to return race relations to earlier patterns. In the South, there were many instances of violence directed against returning black soldiers, attacks intended to keep the race 'in its place'. Some of the wartime employment gains were also reversed as white soldiers returned expecting to resume civilian jobs. Nevertheless, the war led to enduring changes in American race relations. The idealism associated with the fight against fascism led many white Americans to oppose racial practices that contradicted the nation's professed political ideals.

In addition, the wartime experiences of Americans established a foundation for future changes in race relations by prompting massive migrations of blacks to urban areas. In the West and Midwest, large numbers of blacks assumed new employment roles. Although the *First World War era is often described as a period of massive black migration from the South, net migration of non-whites out of the South during the 1940s was far larger than during the 1910s, totaling more than 1.5 million. During and immediately after the Second World War, housing shortages and competition for jobs led to greater racial conflicts in some cities, but increasing urbanization and upward mobility fostered the emergence of a new generation of black activists who would play leading roles in stimulating the civil rights upsurge of the 1950s and 1960s. The publication of Gunnar Myrdal's *An American Dilemma* in 1944 reflected the widespread realization that overt racial barriers were not only contrary to the 'American Creed' but also inconsistent with the increasing geographic mobility of blacks and their increasing participation in the US economy.

CLAYBORNE CARSON

Buchanan, A. R., *Black Americans in World War II* (Santa Barbara, Cal., 1977).
James, C. L. R. *et al., Fighting Racism in World War II* (New York, 1980).
MacGregor, M. J. Jr., *Integration of the Armed Forces, 1940–1965* (Washington, DC, 1981).
Motley, M. P. (ed.), *The Invisible Soldier: The Experience of the Black Soldier, World War II* (Detroit, 1975).

Afrika Korps, or Deutsches Afrika Korps (DAK), was the formation *Rommel, then a maj-general, commanded tactically from February to August 1941 in the *Western Desert campaigns. From August 1941 to March 1943 it was always the spearhead of his several larger commands (Panzer Group Africa, Panzer Army Africa, and German–Italian Panzer Army), and when he was appointed C-in-C of Army Group Africa in March 1943 it became part of the Italian First Army under General *Messe.

The dispatch of a German force to the Western Desert was first discussed in December 1940. Italian defeats prompted Hitler to issue his directive No. 22 on 11 January 1941 ordering the formation of a *Sperrverband* (special blocking detachment) to bolster the Italian defence of western Libya. To carry out this operation (SONNENBLUME), the 5th Light Division was formed and was soon joined by the 15th Panzer Division, and on 3 February Rommel was appointed 'Commander of German Army troops in Africa'. The new formation was officially named the Deutsches Afrika Korps on 19 February 1941, by which time part of the 5th Light Division (renamed 21st Panzer Division, 1 October 1941) had already arrived at Tripoli. Later, various Italian formations were attached to it and it was supported from the air by units detached from 10th Fliegerkorps based in Italy under the command of a Fliegerführer Afrika.

It says much for Rommel's powers of leadership that the two German divisions initially under his command, which were both hastily formed from an assortment of units, none of them with any desert experience, were welded so soon into a formation with so strong an identity, which quickly became legendary. 'Between Rommel and his troops there was that mutual understanding which cannot be explained and analysed,' wrote one of his staff officers, 'but which is the gift of the gods. The Afrika Korps followed Rommel wherever he led, however hard he drove them.'

Rommel was technically subordinate to the Italian C-in-C in North Africa, and through him to the Italian High Command (see COMANDO SUPREMO), but as he had the right to appeal to Berlin his independent command was unfettered by Italian wishes or orders. However, he was hamstrung by several limiting factors: *ULTRA intelligence often revealed his plans, though he did not always follow them; his supply line during the battle for supremacy in the *Mediterranean was always threatened and frequently disrupted; his main port, Tripoli, was inadequate; and Hitler and his subordinates, absorbed in greater events elsewhere, viewed the Western Desert as no more than a holding campaign.

The tactics of the DAK reversed the generally accepted contemporary theory that tanks were best employed to destroy other tanks before penetrating the infantry's lines to attack the rear areas. Rommel stood this principle on its head by using an anti-tank gun line to destroy the oncoming armour, enabling his tanks to deal with the opposing infantry. These tactics were employed during the British offensive (BATTLEAXE) of June 1941. They resulted in a victory for the DAK which did much to create the pride and self-confidence that marked its later battles and it remained a formidable force throughout Rommel's time in the western desert and in the *North African campaign. It was a DAK Assault Group which was largely responsible for his victory at the *Kasserine Pass in February 1943 and it was one of the last units to surrender in Tunisia, when, just before midnight on 12 May 1943, its commander signalled: 'Ammunition shot off. Arms and equipment destroyed. In accordance with order received Afrika Korps has fought itself to the condition where it can fight no more. The German Afrika Korps must rise again. *Heia Safari!*'

Heia Safari was the DAK's Swahili warcry. Meaning 'Let's go get 'em', or 'Tallyho!', it proved entirely appropriate.

Lewin, R., *The Life and Death of the Afrika Korps* (London, 1977).

AFS, Auxiliary Fire Services; see also Civil Defence and Defence Forces sections of major powers.

Agency Africa, Franco-Polish intelligence network which was also known as Agency Rygor after its leader, Major (later Maj-General) Rygor Slowikowski, who escaped to France after the end of the *Polish campaign in October 1939. He formed an intelligence network in France and in July 1941 was ordered by the Polish government-in-exile to start one in French North Africa. Unknown to him initially, his orders were in fact coming from, and his intelligence going to, *MI6 (though it was later channelled through the *Office of Strategic Services). His territory was vast, from the Libyan–Tunisian border to French West Africa, but, posing as a wealthy porridge-making businessman and using Algiers as a base, he organized nine outposts in Algeria, Tunisia, French Morocco, and Dakar in French West Africa. His intelligence officers were Polish but his agents were all French. By the time of the *North African campaign landings (TORCH) in November 1942, for which Agency Africa provided valuable intelligence on ports and airfields and the location of *Vichy French military units and installations, it had two radio stations, a counter-intelligence on port, and no fewer than 92 principal agents. After TORCH the network was mainly concerned with interrogating Polish *prisoners-of-war who had fought for the Germans. Slowikowski was awarded the British OBE and the American Legion of Merit (see DECORATIONS). See also SPIES.

Slowikowski, M. R., *In the Secret Service: The Lighting of the Torch* (London, 1988).

A-GŌ, codename for the Japanese operation during the *Pacific war to deny the Mariana Islands to US forces. It was originally Vice-Admiral *Koga's Operation 'Z' which detailed the destruction by Japanese air and sea forces of the US Pacific Fleet as it approached the Marianas, but in May 1944 the plan was revamped by Koga's successor, Admiral *Toyoda, as A-GŌ leading to the battle of the *Philippine Sea. Details of the operation were captured and passed to the Americans well before the battle by Allied guerrillas in the Philippines after Koga's Chief of Staff, who carried details of it, crashed in his aircraft near the Filipino island of Cebu.

airborne warfare. In 1922, Soviet soldiers were dropped successfully by parachute from aircraft. This experiment aroused the interest of German officers attached to the Red Army as technical advisers. When Hitler rearmed in the mid-1930s, however, the army lacked enthusiasm for the airborne concept. It was adopted by the Luftwaffe with the intention of sending parachutists to attack targets inaccessible to aerial bombs. After a period of uncertainty, an air force officer, Maj-General *Student, was ordered in 1938 to command and expand an airborne striking arm.

The pioneers had already developed equipment and training, including use of a 'static line' instead of a ripcord for parachute opening. The line attached to the aircraft pulled the parachute out automatically as the user fell away, finally releasing the canopy, which reduced individual misjudgements in falling and permitted the dropping of men much closer to the ground. The trainee was taught to pack his own parachute and was exercised vigorously in exit and landing techniques. Those recruited were volunteers who made six descents to qualify. About three-quarters of each course passed.

The Germans had a suitable transport aircraft in service, the Ju52. With seventeen parachutists its range was 1,370 km. (850 mi.). However, until these troops had landed and assembled, they were vulnerable to ground forces; and even when gathered, they lacked vehicles or heavy weapons, so Student decided to carry these in *gliders. The DFS230, specially designed, lifted troops or freight up to 1,135 kg. (2,500 lb.) when towed by an empty Ju52. Men and aircraft were incorporated into the 7th Fliegerdivision and an army division was made available to form an airborne corps.

German airborne operations were planned but not executed against Czechoslovakia and Austria in 1938–9, and for the *Polish campaign. The world's first airborne operation was mounted on 9 April 1940 when divisional elements were used in the *Norwegian campaign, with smaller numbers in the invasion of Denmark. One month later, in a variety of aircraft, Junkers, Heinkel 59 *float planes and DFS 230 gliders, the corps joined the assault into the Low Countries that led to the fall of *France. Combined airlanding and parachute operations at The Hague were unsuccessful, but glider and parachute troops captured two important bridges over the Meuse and the massive Belgian fortress at *Eben Emael.

These operations alarmed the Allies. During the remainder of the fighting there were frequent reports of parachutists landing which, though false, contributed to the crises preceding the Allied defeat and evacuation (see DUNKIRK).

On 6 June 1940 Churchill gave instructions for the

In one of the best known examples of **airborne warfare**, British paratroops land on the outskirts of Arnhem during Operation MARKET-GARDEN, 17 September 1944.

'Deployment of parachute troops on a scale equal to five thousand'. These were to complement sea raiders (later called commandos) to harry German garrisons in continental Europe, the policy of what Churchill called 'butcher and bolt'.

The Central Landing Establishment and School was formed at RAF Ringway, Manchester, to gather suitable parachutes and gliders, and to train volunteers for airborne operations. A few Whitley bombers were provided, converted to drop parachutists from a hole in the fuselage floor, and to tow gliders. The American 'statichute' was purchased but was prone to malfunction. It was successfully modified by Raymond Quilter of the GQ Parachute Company, and further developed as the Type X with Leslie Irvin. Webbing was adopted for the static line. The General Aircraft and Airspeed Companies quickly produced a range of gliders including the light Hotspur, which was relegated to training, the 32-seat Horsa, and the Hamilcar, a large 40-seater which could also carry several light vehicles or guns. A Glider Training Squadron opened at Ringway.

Training began, but progress was slow. Bomber Command was opposed to surrendering its aircraft. The air staff suggested that, despite German success in the Low Countries, 'it was at least possible that this was the last time that parachute troops are used in major operations'; gliders might be better employed for aerial refuelling or bomb carrying, but training of pilots would slow the expansion of RAF aircrew. Many army commanders resented the loss of the thousands of high-calibre officers and men volunteering for parachuting. Of these, training facilities could cope with only 500 for several months. Churchill's persistence overcame these objections. The first unit, No. 2 Commando, became the 11th Special Air Service Battalion, and finally the 1st Parachute Battalion. Plans were made to form a parachute brigade of three battalions with detachments from all arms.

On the night of 10/11 February 1941, Major T. A. G. Prichard with 35 members of the commando landed by parachute in southern Italy and demolished an aqueduct at *Tragino to deprive local military ports of water. This operation (COLOSSUS) was a pinprick in the war effort, but the raid alarmed the Italian government, causing the diversion of considerable forces to guard duties. A year later, a company from the 2nd Battalion carried off German *radar equipment from *Bruneval, near Le Havre.

In the meantime the Germans had again demonstrated the strategic potential of airborne forces. Beginning on 20 May 1941, Student launched an operation (MERKUR) against *Crete. Against all expectations, it was successful, although a quarter of the parachutists were killed. This triumph influenced the formation of the 1st British Airborne Division with one 'airlanding' (gliderborne) and two parachute brigades, supporting Arms and Services under Maj-General *Browning. The object was no longer simply raiding but to provide a force for strategic intervention. A wing, later Thirty-eighth Group, Royal Air Force, was formed to complement the division. The USA also began to develop parachute and glider units during 1941, including the CG4A WACO glider. When they joined the war, two items of American equipment were welcomed by British airborne forces, the C47 Dakota aircraft with its door exit, and the *jeep.

British and American parachute detachments took part in the invasion of French North Africa in November 1942 (see NORTH AFRICAN CAMPAIGN), and in greater numbers at the start of the *Sicilian campaign in July 1943. Many lessons were learned in these operations. The British 1st Parachute Brigade also earned a high reputation in ground operations in Tunisia; the Germans called them 'Red Devils', partly because of the distinctive maroon berets worn by British airborne forces. A fourth parachute brigade was raised in the Middle East, principally from British units in the Indian Army; another body, the 6th Airborne Division, included a Canadian battalion, formed in the UK. The 1st Airborne returned home to join them in 1943, leaving one reinforced formation—2nd Independent Parachute Brigade—for operations in Italy, Greece, and Southern France. The two British divisions with the American 82nd and 101st formed a part of General *Eisenhower's command for the reoccupation of north-west Europe (see OVERLORD).

Allied delivery techniques, training, and special operational equipment had advanced considerably by 1944. The number of fatalities in early parachute training had been greatly reduced. In the UK, Stirling, Albemarle, and, most importantly, Halifax bombers had been brought into service for parachute and equipment dropping, and as glider tugs. Numbers of gliders and pilots had been organized to provide carriage for essential light vehicles and heavy weapons for the parachute units, men and freight for those airlanding. Dakota aircraft also dropped cylindrical containers for the troops aboard, and each parachutist carried on his person light equipment and a Sten machine carbine (see SMALL ARMS) for immediate action on landing. Dropping and landing patterns and rallying drills had been perfected.

Maj-General James Gavin's 82nd, Maj-General Maxwell D. Taylor's 101st, and Maj-General R. N. Gale's 6th Airborne Divisions took part in the assault phase of OVERLORD when they landed ahead of the seaborne forces in Normandy on 6 June 1944. Their objective was to secure both flanks which they did successfully, having been preceded by pathfinder companies whose task was to mark the dropping and landing zones (DZs and LZs). Though some units were scattered, the majority of the airborne tasks were accomplished, and the divisions remained in action on the ground for some weeks.

In August 1944 all Allied airborne formations became part of Lt-General *Brereton's Allied Airborne Army which comprised 1st British Airborne Corps and the 18th US Airborne Corps. As the Allies advanced, Browning, who commanded the 1st Airborne Corps, co-ordinated planning of sixteen operations between August and September. None was executed. The seventeenth, *MARKET-GARDEN, involved the two American divisions, 1st Airborne Division, and the Polish Parachute Brigade whose task was to capture bridgeheads across the Dutch Maas, Waal, and Lower Rhine rivers, and their associated canals to facilitate the advance of *Horrocks's 30th Corps on the ground. There were insufficient aircraft to lift the corps simultaneously, which contributed to the prolonged isolation of 1st Airborne under German armoured pressure at Arnhem. A Rhine bridgehead was thereby denied. However, the 6th British and 17th US Airborne Divisions of Lt-General Matthew B. Ridgway's 18th Airborne Corps dropped successfully beyond the Rhine in one lift in the following March, the final such operation of the war.

In some of these operations, Allied troops fought German parachutists because, after Crete, the latter were used as ground forces, Hitler having decided that large-scale airborne operations were too expensive. The Axis thus missed an opportunity to capture Malta in 1942 using Student's veterans and the high-quality Italian Folgore Airborne Division which was, instead, used—and destroyed—at *El Alamein. Still, Student used a small detachment to free Mussolini from his captors.

Soviet airborne warfare was largely confined to minor deployments, several of which were in conjunction with defensive *amphibious warfare operations on the *Black Sea coast. Airborne warfare had been under the patronage of Marshal Mikhail Tukhachevsky (1893–1937) up to his tenure as chief of armaments in 1931 and he had encouraged the early development of assault gliders and parachutes; it had been neglected after he was murdered in Stalin's pre-war purges.

Adverse terrain mostly prevented large-scale employment of airborne forces in the Far East, but the Japanese, with the aid of German instructors, began the training of paratroops in 1940, and they were as well advanced in this type of warfare as they were in amphibious operations. The Japanese Navy was quick to grasp the potential of airborne forces—which could capture vital airfields before they could be destroyed—and 1,800 Japanese marines received paratroop training in which they were taught to jump from low altitudes at the very short interval of one second, reducing their dispersion on the ground. They were formed into two battalions, the 1st and 3rd Yokosuka Special Naval Landing Forces. Each battalion, comprising 844 officers and men, included three infantry companies, an HQ company, and an anti-tank unit. In January 1942 they mounted their first operation when, during the Japanese invasion of the *Netherlands East Indies, they captured the airfield at Menado on Celebes. This was successful, as was a remarkable assault by a small team of paratroops to capture the oil fields at Palembang in Sumatra, though neither of these operations was properly co-ordinated with amphibious forces. But on 20 February 1942 this co-ordination was achieved when 308 men of the 3rd Yokosuka Special Naval Landing Force took part in the first vertical envelopment of an enemy force in history when they dropped behind Allied lines in *Timor and held up their retreat until the landing forces had advanced and started to encircle them. Apart from these early offensive operations, Japanese paratroops were mostly used as raiding forces.

The Allies also employed airborne forces during the *Pacific war, most notably the 11th US Airborne Division which landed on Luzon by sea and from the air in January 1945 during the recapture of the Philippines. Also, during the *Burma campaign, the 50th Indian Parachute Brigade played an important part in the ground fighting around *Imphal, and a composite Gurkha Parachute Battalion captured Elephant Point at Rangoon by airborne assault in May 1945.

ANTHONY FARRAR-HOCKLEY

Farrar-Hockley, A., *Student* (New York, 1973).
MacDonald, C., *By Air to Battle* (New York, 1969).
Otway, T., *Airborne Forces* (London, 1951).

Air Commando, officially called No. 5318 Air Force Unit of the US Army Air Forces, which was commanded by Colonel Philip Cochran. Formed to support and supply the second operation of the *Chindits during the *Burma campaign in March 1944, it transported two Chindit brigades behind Japanese lines in gliders. Its strength included 30 fighters, 12 bombers, 225 gliders, 100 light aircraft, and 6 helicopters. Withdrawn in May 1944, it was later used to transport supplies and troops over the *Hump from India to China.

aircraft, see BOMBERS, FIGHTERS, FLOAT PLANES, FLYING BOATS, GLIDERS, and HELICOPTERS. For carrier aircraft see CARRIERS. See also AIR POWER

aircraft carriers, see CARRIERS.

Air Defence of Great Britain (ADGB), pre-war command abolished in 1936 when it was replaced by various Commands named by function. However it continued to be used occasionally in connection with the relations between C-in-C Fighter Command and those air defences—such as anti-aircraft guns—which were provided by the army but controlled by Fighter Command. The title was resurrected in November 1943 when Allied fighter forces were reorganized for the Normandy landings in June 1944 (see OVERLORD). As part of the Allied Expeditionary Air Force the ADGB comprised five fighter groups which were commanded by Air Marshal Roderic Hill who also controlled all anti-aircraft guns, *barrage balloons, and *searchlights. These groups were responsible for the defence not only of the UK but of the English Channel while the invasion was taking place, and of the initial lodgement area in Normandy.

air gap, mid-Atlantic, area south of Greenland in which Allied *convoys could not be given air cover against U-boat attacks during much of the battle of the *Atlantic (see Map 1). It was therefore ideal for the operation of Admiral *Dönitz's wolf-packs, though aircraft launched from merchant ships (see CAM SHIPS, FIGHTER CATAPULT SHIPS, and MAC SHIPS), and later escort carriers, were used to try to cover it. Until May 1941 air cover was very limited but from that month land-based aircraft began operating 965 km. (600 mi.) eastwards from New-foundland, 645 km. (400 mi.) southwards from Iceland, and 1,125 km. (700 mi.) westwards from Northern Ireland. However, this still left a 480 km. (300 mi.) gap south of Greenland where merchant shipping losses continued to be high. A decision at the Casablanca conference in January 1943 (see SYMBOL) to cover this with additional very long range Liberator bombers was not implemented as they were badly needed for use in the *Pacific war and the *strategic air offensive against Germany. However, a recommendation by the *Washington Convoy conference, held in March 1943, that 20 be supplied to the Royal Canadian Air Force to cover the gap, was heeded, and by the end of May sufficient were operating to close it.

Until January 1943, there was also a gap east of the *Azores, which affected the Gibraltar and West African convoys, another west of the Azores, and another in the South Atlantic. The one west of the Azores was called the 'Black Pit' by the Germans because they sank so many ships there, but it was eventually closed when air bases in the Azores were opened in October 1943.

air power. Before the Second World War, there was no general agreement about the importance or capabilities of air power. In the UK, for instance, while the government was worrying about a possible 'knock-out blow' from the Luftwaffe, the Admiralty was cheerfully asserting that its warships at sea had little to fear from the air. This was not surprising. A mere infant in 1914, military aviation had become a vigorous young adult by 1918, but the achievements of the air forces during those years, though important, had been far from decisive. Since 1919, and particularly in the later 1930s, there had been abundant technical development but very little—except in the *China Incident and the *Spanish Civil War—in the way of actual combat experience. As service attitudes were firmly entrenched, soldiers and sailors tended to play down the potential of air power, airmen to exaggerate it.

To some extent these differences of view arose from a very simple fact, so obvious as to be rarely stated, and for that reason often overlooked. A single bomber, unopposed, may do enormous damage: a dozen bombers, opposed, may do no damage at all. Those who entertained the most horrific visions of devastation tended to ignore,

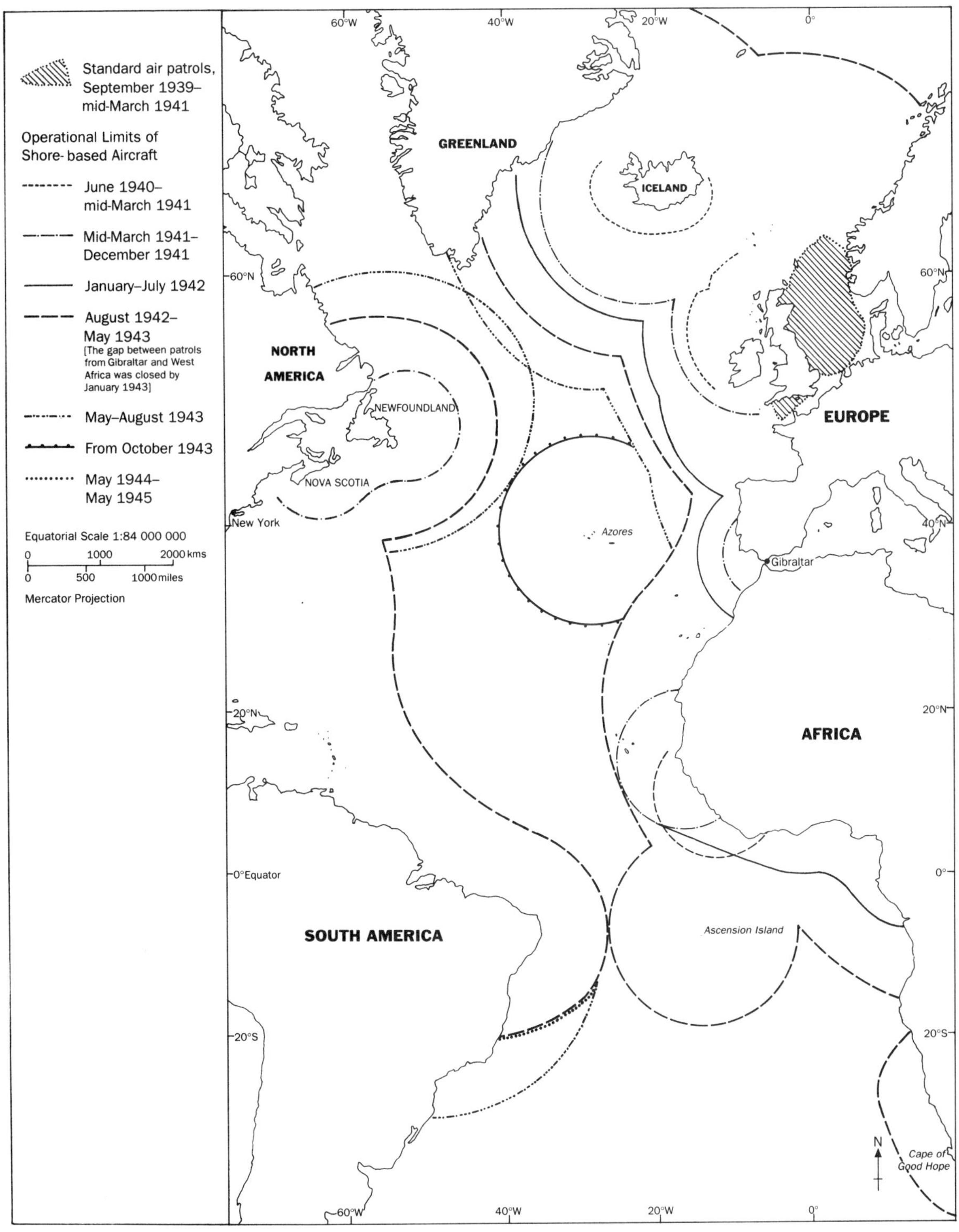

1. **Air gap**: Atlantic air cover by Allied land-based aircraft, 1940–5

or disbelieve in, the possibilities of effective air defence.

During the *First World War most of the main tasks of air power had become established: reconnaissance, artillery observation, bombing (tactical and strategic), strafing, and air fighting. For these, specialized aircraft had quickly developed. So, too, had aircraft for maritime work such as *air-sea rescue—aircraft with floats (*float planes) or hulls (*flying boats) for operating from water, and aircraft which could take off from, and return to, a ship adapted as a carrier (see CAM SHIPS, FIGHTER CATAPULT SHIPS, and MAC SHIPS). Airships, too, had done valuable work in the maritime sphere, although their vulnerability to bad weather and enemy opposition, as seen during the Zeppelin raids, was to deny them a significant military future (but see BLIMPS).

In the years after 1919 a further task had emerged: mass transportation (see AIR TRANSPORT COMMAND, for example). Few countries could maintain a sizeable force of transport aircraft for purely military purposes, but many could use their developing civil aviation in emergency for wartime needs as the USA did when it formed the *Civil Air Patrol.

As a development or refinement of the transport function was later to come the dropping of parachutists or the landing of troops from aircraft or gliders to seize an objective behind enemy lines (see AIRBORNE WARFARE).

A country's capacity for developing air power inevitably depends on its industrial, economic, and technical resources. The availability of a large industrial base, scientific knowledge, skilled manpower, facilities for training, and supplies of fuel (whether home-produced or imported under the shield of a strong navy) are some of the most obvious requirements. Accordingly in 1939 only the more developed industrial nations could hope to exercise any significant degree of air power.

In Europe, the USSR's air force came first in terms of numbers, Germany's second and Britain's third. France and Italy—the latter with hundreds of obsolescent machines—also maintained sizeable air establishments. Figures of first-line strength in 1939 can be quoted (e.g. Luftwaffe 3,609, RAF 1,911, Armée de l'Air 1,792), but they mean very little without reference to reserves or quality, about which generalization is difficult. In terms of aircraft production in 1939, the picture was much the same: the USSR produced more than 10,000 aircraft during the year, Germany more than 8,000, the UK—catching up fast—just under 8,000.

Outside Europe by far the strongest air force, excluding the Soviet Union's, was that of Japan, with the USA well behind. In both countries the naval and military elements were rigidly separated from each other, being component parts of the navy or army. In 1939 Japan produced nearly 4,500 aircraft of all types, the USA around 5,800. But the USA had enormous industrial potential which, when the need came, would transform this narrow margin into a huge superiority. By 1942 American aircraft production was more than five times that of Japan.

Among nearly all nations the primary task envisaged for air power was direct assistance to troops on the ground. Maritime duties were also considered important, but only the American, Japanese, and British navies operated a large number of carriers. Japanese aviation, especially had some bold ideas, and was well equipped to carry them out. It had, for instance, developed plans for an 'all carrier' naval task force, and its equipment, besides exceptionally efficient torpedoes, included the first monoplane carrier-borne fighters. Only two countries, the UK and the USA, had by 1939 pursued their ideas of 'strategic' bombing not immediately linked with military operations, and had in production suitable bombers for the task. Italy had warmed to the theory of strategic bombardment, but possessed nothing effective with which to put it into practice.

The first emphatic demonstration of air power in the war was provided by the Luftwaffe. Following the death of General Walther Wever, its principal proponent of strategic bombing, in an air accident in 1936, and the cancellation the following year of his four-engined 'Ural' bomber project, the Luftwaffe, though an independent service, had become largely committed to working directly with the German Army. The 'volunteers' of its Kondor Legion, supporting Nationalist troops in the Spanish Civil War, had gained valuable experience in this kind of work, and Hitler duly entrusted the opening of the *Polish campaign to his air force. Contrary to popular belief, *Göring had every intention of building a strategic bombing force (including long-range bombers capable of reaching the USA), but the four-engined He177 was plagued with development problems and very few were built.

With more than 1,500 aircraft allotted to the campaign, the Luftwaffe had no difficulty in demolishing the Polish air force, only some 400 combat aircraft strong, and thereafter could bomb more or less at will. Close support Junkers 87 dive-bombers—'Stukas'—screamed down with pinpoint accuracy on any opposition to the advancing German tanks, while medium-range bombers attacked military depots and factories and wrecked the Polish lines of communication. Transport aircraft carrying supplies kept the German columns moving swiftly, and finally relentless bombing helped to force Warsaw into submission. Thus was revealed to the world a new kind of war, the *Blitzkrieg ('lightning war'), the pattern of much to follow: a war of aircraft in association with fast-moving armoured and motorized columns on the ground.

During the *phoney war which followed the defeat of Poland the Luftwaffe and the RAF largely confined their attacks to shipping. An innovation in long-range reconnaissance was the RAF's introduction of the 'stripped' unarmed Spitfire flying at 12,000 m. (40,000 ft.) and almost immune to interception. A whole new sphere of high-level *photographic reconnaissance and its interpretation was to spring from this advance. In addition to its other tasks, the RAF also dropped leaflets over Germany (see POLITICAL WARFARE EXECUTIVE). There is no evidence that this last use of air power had any significant effect: propaganda delivered from the skies had hastened Austro-Hungarian disintegration in 1918, but propaganda against victorious and well-fed opponents was notably less effective. A further use of air power by both sides during this period was the laying of sea mines from the air.

For the *Norwegian campaign and their occupation of Denmark in April 1940 the Germans employed some 500 transport planes, some to carry parachutists, most to ferry supplies and reinforcements across the Baltic once Norwegian airfields had been captured. Except in the Narvik area, where two RAF Hurricane squadrons opposed them vigorously, the Luftwaffe soon had virtually free range. Using some 800 aircraft from captured airfields against negligible opposition, it was able to harry at will the Norwegian troops and the Anglo-French forces which came to their aid in central Norway. Only because German bombers were not yet efficient at night were these forces able to make good their escape.

In France, as in Belgium, the main pattern of air operations followed that set in Poland. For their campaign in the west the Germans held a considerable numerical superiority, having amassed some 3,500 aircraft, excluding transports and gliders, while the Allies deployed only around 2,000. Their initial onslaught destroyed scores of aircraft on the ground, and dive-bombers and fighters then attacked front-line troops and strong-points while the longer-range bombers hit depots, railways, and road junctions. Both in Belgium and the Netherlands parachutists captured key points (see EBEN EMAEL, for example) and the Luftwaffe's raid on *Rotterdam was the principal factor in bringing about the surrender of the latter. Particular care was taken to sever the communications between the main French armies and the Allied forces soon cut off in the north. German fighters for the most part effectively protected their bombers from Anglo-French fighter opposition, and German mobile anti-aircraft guns massed at key points like the Albert Canal and Meuse crossings did enormous execution among the attacking Allied bombers. In the Sedan sector, the Ju87s wrought appalling havoc among the French Ninth Army's horses, so that much of its artillery became immobilized.

*Dunkirk was to reveal that German air power, thus far all-conquering, had its limits. Göring had boasted that he would prevent the evacuation, but in the event the spoiling operations of RAF fighters from British bases, the hours of darkness and daytime mist, stout resistance at the perimeter by the trapped forces, and the heroic efforts of the French and British navies, the merchantmen, and the 'little ships' combined to foil the Luftwaffe and bring about 'the miracle of deliverance'.

In the first days of June, as the evacuation proceeded, the Luftwaffe for the first time attacked strategic targets remote from the battlefield, including aircraft plants in Marseilles and Paris. The moral effect was at least as great as the physical, and soon the French, in retreat, were deciding not to defend their capital. It became apparent that, as in September 1938 and March 1939, air power could achieve results by its mere existence. The threat it posed could be sufficient in itself.

For all its successes, during the fall of *France the Luftwaffe lost nearly 1,400 aircraft. Its consequent need to recuperate, as well as its need to regroup, gave Hitler's remaining opponent an invaluable few weeks in which to prepare for the inevitable onslaught.

The battle of *Britain which followed the collapse of France was the first major campaign to be contested between air forces without fighting taking place on the ground below. It was also the first sustained refutation of prime minister, Stanley Baldwin's 1928 pronouncement, 'the bomber will always get through'. *Dowding, the C-in-C of Fighter Command, showed that the system of scientific air defence he had built up in RAF Fighter Command during the later 1930s could cope, in daylight at least, with attacking forces far more numerous than those at his own disposal. It was a system dependent on fast, modern, well-armed fighters—mainly Hurricanes and Spitfires—directed from the ground into visual contact with raiding aircraft on information of the attackers' approach derived from *radar and the Observer Corps (see UK, 6), and on information of the defending fighters' own movements derived from their *pip-squeak signal emissions picked up by direction-finding stations. Buttressing this fighter system were the ground defences of anti-aircraft guns, *searchlights, and *barrage balloons. It was a triumph, for the first time in the war, of defensive air power.

It also showed how far air power could be blunted by misdirection. While the Germans were attacking the southern airfields, they were doing relatively well. The key indicator was that, in the fortnight before 7 September, Fighter Command lost more aircraft than it could replace from repair and manufacture. It also suffered great damage to its ground installations. But on 7 September the Luftwaffe transferred its attack from the airfields to London, and thereafter Hurricane and Spitfire replacements well exceeded losses. The switch to London had strong reasons behind it: not merely Hitler's desire to avenge attacks on Berlin, but also the imperatives of his late September invasion timetable: the German need to create administrative chaos in the British capital and to bring to battle what were thought to be the last resources of Fighter Command before deteriorating weather conditions made Operation *SEALION impossible. It was a decision flawed not only by faulty intelligence but by neglect of an obvious technical factor: the very short range of the otherwise excellent German escort fighter, the Me109. From their cross-Channel bases the 109s could fly and fight over London for only ten minutes. Lacking sustained escort the German bombers suffered unacceptable losses, and the whole tide of the battle turned against Germany.

German air power thus demonstrated an inbuilt

weakness. The Luftwaffe lacked the aircraft—heavier, faster, better protected bombers carrying a bigger bomb load, and better long-range escort fighters—to wage a strategic campaign effectively by day against a strong defence. It accordingly turned to night operations against the UK, partly for intimidation, partly to strike at British industry and commerce and, in conjunction with the U-boats, to set up a blockade.

The Luftwaffe conducted these night operations economically enough: in eight months' bombing of London and other cities and ports it lost about 600 aircraft, or only 1.5% of the sorties flown. But without the pressure of German armies, these nightly attacks by 100–200 bombers could achieve nothing decisive against a resolute people. Unlike the British bombers of the time they had the benefit of radio beams for navigation (see ELECTRONIC NAVIGATION SYSTEMS) which usually brought them into the vicinity of their objectives, but they were normally unable to hit precise key targets. The *Blitz (in the Londoners' term) caused misery and loss of production, but left Hitler as far as ever from subduing the UK. It ceased not because it was becoming more expensive—though it was, as better British night-fighters, directed from the ground into airborne radar range of German aircraft, gained in effectiveness—but because Hitler needed most of his aircraft for his forthcoming attack on the USSR (see BARBAROSSA).

Between the battle of Britain and the invasion of the USSR in June 1941 the RAF tried to exert air power in Europe in three main ways: by offensive sweeps (see CIRCUSES and RHUBARBS) over France and the Low Countries; by the night bombing of Germany, two attempts at daylight bombing in 1939 having proved disastrous; and by incessant activity at sea, including reconnaissance, the protection of *convoys, and anti-shipping and anti-U-boat operations. For the offensive sweeps and the night bombing the resources available were inadequate, both technically and numerically, to achieve significant results, but the maritime work helped to surmount the first great crisis in the battle of the *Atlantic.

With Italy a belligerent and Germany in control of the entire north-west European coastline, the losses of Allied and neutral shipping increased dramatically. For April 1941 they reached the massive figure of 644,000 tons, far beyond replacement capacity. U-boats and *auxiliary cruisers accounted for the greater part of this total, but nearly half was sunk by aircraft, especially the long-range converted airliners, the Focke-Wolf Condors, operating mainly from France. But just as German air power helped to bring about this crisis, so British air power helped to overcome it. Increases in the strength of RAF Coastal Command, including the introduction of Beaufighters; the provision of small escort carriers; the development of much improved ASV (air to surface vessel) radar and more effective depth-charges (see ANTI-SUBMARINE WEAPONS); the establishment of new air bases in Iceland, Northern Ireland, the Hebrides, and West Africa; the pinning down of the **Scharnhorst* and *Gneisenau* in Brest by bombing; the spotting of the **Bismarck* by an RAF Catalina and its crippling by Fleet Air Arm Swordfish—all these, like the much more systematic use of convoys, contributed greatly to the resolution of the crisis. By July–August 1941 the monthly average of merchant shipping losses had fallen to a very sustainable 125,000 tons.

Meanwhile in the Mediterranean and Middle East some 200–300 not very modern RAF aircraft had proved fully capable of overwhelming Italian opponents twice as numerous but flying for the most part outdated machines. This greatly helped in the spectacular British advance from Egypt across Cyrenaica in December 1940, and later in the *East African campaign. So too did the remarkable feat of the Fleet Air Arm crippling the Italian fleet at *Taranto in November 1940, an exploit which had repercussions for years to come. Even the detachment of squadrons from Egypt to sustain Greek resistance to Mussolini's invasion (see BALKAN CAMPAIGN) did not at first end the RAF's run of success; but the arrival of Luftwaffe units in Sicily in January 1941 and in Libya the following month, together with the formation of *Rommel's *Afrika Korps and the German incursion into the Balkans, swiftly changed the picture. The loss of Cyrenaica (apart from Tobruk), the collapse of Yugoslavia after the savage bombing of Belgrade (which killed thousands of civilians), and the expulsion of the British from Greece were among the results. But once more the ineffectiveness of the Luftwaffe at night helped the Royal Navy to save most of the *British Expeditionary Force from capture or destruction.

In Cyrenaica and Greece the Luftwaffe had followed its normal pattern of neutralizing the opposing air force, giving close support on the battlefield, and attacking more distant communications. In the airborne invasion of *Crete, however, it brought off one of the most unorthodox operations of the whole war.

Most of the hastily concocted plan was known to the British through *ULTRA intelligence (see also FLIVOS), and the Royal Navy was able to defeat the sea-borne element of the invasion. But the capture of just one airfield, Maleme, decided the issue. It was an issue which seemed for a while to hang by a thread, but in fact it might have been read in advance in the air power available to the opposing sides. To defend Crete there were initially about 24 fighters, including obsolescent Gladiators and Fulmars; to attack it the Germans could bring to bear from their new Aegean bases about 430 bombers and 180 fighters, in addition to 80 gliders and more than 500 transport aircraft. Including long-range bomber support from Egypt, the RAF managed to fly only about 20 sorties a day. The Luftwaffe flew many hundreds.

The sharpest lesson of Crete was that learned by the Royal Navy about air power. With great devotion and skill it had held the Cretan seas while there was any point in doing so, but in the course of this it had lost nine warships from air attack and suffered damage to another seven-

Allied **air power**: US B29 bombers return to North Field, Guam, after a bombing mission over Japan.

teen. However much warships might still be able to look after themselves in mid-ocean, it was now clear, that they ventured within range of a strong hostile shore-based air force only at their mortal peril. The capture of an island defended by an overwhelmingly strong navy was, for all to see, a portent: air power victorious over traditional sea power.

Shortly before Crete, a minor lesson in air power had been given in Iraq. When the usurper *Rashid Ali besieged the RAF base at Habbaniya, the home of No. 4 Flying Training School, his forces were driven off by combined ground and air action, the latter supplied in the main by training aircraft flown by the instructors and senior pupils. The lesson was that against little opposition in the air, even out-of-date aircraft, if flown by resolute crews, can enormously influence the military situation.

In the titanic struggle between Germany and the Soviet Union (see GERMAN–SOVIET WAR), air power was in the main employed tactically. For BARBAROSSA the Luftwaffe deployed about 2,800 aircraft—60% of its strength—against opponents with about 10,000 first-line aircraft west of the Urals. The Luftwaffe, however, by its initial surprise attacks on airfields, at once greatly reduced this disparity. On 27 June 1941, after only a week, the German High Command claimed the destruction of over 4,000 Soviet planes as against a loss of 150 by the Luftwaffe. Whatever the degree of exaggeration, Soviet losses were still stupendous. On both sides the fight against the opposing air force, and direct support of the armies by reconnaissance and by attacks on tanks, columns, points of resistance, and communications, became the staple pattern of operations. On the German side the medium-range bombers (Ju88s and He111s), as well as the Stukas, the fighter bombers, and the fighters, were expected to make low-flying attacks on troop positions in daylight. Anti-shipping attacks and mining also formed part of the Luftwaffe's programme, but on both sides long-range strategical operations were uncommon. There were notable exceptions, as when just before the German offensive against *Kursk in July 1943 Luftwaffe bombers ranged far afield to attack a tank factory, rubber works, and oil targets, but such ventures were too infrequent to have much effect. Without definite air superiority, and in the face of the Soviets' very strong anti-aircraft artillery, they also tended to be expensive.

Other important features in the four years' fighting included the Soviets' ability to maintain a higher rate of serviceability in the winter than the Luftwaffe, the remarkable mobility of the Luftwaffe (thanks to transport aircraft and an effective ground organization), and the degree to which German operations suffered from the lack of a good long-range bomber. The increasing use by the Germans of air supply, too, was very notable. It peaked catastrophically when Hitler gave the Luftwaffe the impossible task of supplying the 500,000 troops locked up in *Stalingrad. The effort cost the Germans almost half of their by then 1,000-strong transport fleet.

But perhaps the most surprising feature of all—certainly to Hitler, who had expected complete victory within six weeks—was the ability of the Soviets to move equipment east from their overrun territories and to develop in the Moscow area and behind the Urals an extremely strong aircraft and armaments industry (see USSR, 2). The massive *Lend-Lease supplies which came in from the British and Americans, together with the effects of the Allied bombing of Germany, enabled the USSR to outperform the Germans in manufacture and to build up a huge air force which finally outnumbered the Luftwaffe on the Eastern Front by as much as 20:1. By 1944, the Soviets were producing more than 3,000 aircraft a month; in the whole war they produced about 40,000 more aircraft than Germany.

At an early stage, too, Luftwaffe units had to be withdrawn from the Eastern Front to bolster up the Axis forces in the Mediterranean, and later to strengthen the air defences of the Reich against the Allied bombing. Until 1942 the Luftwaffe more than held its own on the Eastern Front, but the force of 3,000 aircraft it managed to build up there was by 1944 whittled down to about 1,700—an impossibly small number to give all the support needed over a 1,600 km. (1,000 mi.) front. In the end, German air power there simply wore out from the incessant demands made upon it.

In the Mediterranean and Middle East from 1941 to 1943 air power was in the main employed tactically, but there was a big exception in the *logistics battle. Attacks from Egypt on such Axis ports as Benghazi and Tripoli were a constant and productive feature of RAF operations throughout the *Western Desert campaigns. Most important in this connection was lifting the siege of *Malta: keeping Malta going as a staging-post for the delivery of aircraft to the Middle East and as a base from which to attack Italian ports and the shipping supplying the Axis forces in Africa, became a key element in British strategy, just as eliminating it became important for the Germans. Unquestionably the interruption of supplies—including, critically, fuel—to the German and Italian forces in Libya and later Tunisia played a major part in their defeat; and in this work aircraft based on Malta shared the main honours with submarines. The fact that the Axis did not attempt to invade this vital 'unsinkable aircraft carrier', as at one time planned, stands out as a glaring failure in German policy a failure which was at least partly due to *Kesselring's conviction that the island had been neutralized by his aircraft.

On the tactical side, it was in the desert campaigns that the RAF really learned how to give the army effective close support. Apart from increased forces, many of them obtained by opening up an air route to Egypt from West Africa (see TAKORADI AIR ROUTE), and aircraft of higher performance, two key elements were a new degree of mobility, and new high levels of maintenance in mobile conditions. Essential to the whole close support technique was to have *fighters, fighter-bombers, and *bombers with excellent air-to-ground *radio communications, and forward joint RAF–army posts which could issue calls for action in the light of exact up-to-date information. Features such as the *cab rank waiting in the sky to respond instantly to calls from below first proved their worth in North Africa and then helped the Allied armies to liberate Europe; but such refinements were possible only when superiority over the opposing air force had first been established.

For the air power to be applied effectively, the British Army had to make its own improvements in communications. In Norway, in France, and in Greece, the army had ascribed most of its problems to German air power. But in Libya in May–June 1942 it was still compelled to retreat, by forces under *Rommel numerically inferior to its own, despite the fact that the RAF by then held a clear air superiority—indeed it was only this superiority which enabled the British troops to withdraw into Egypt relatively unscathed. The lesson emerged, and was applied by *Montgomery, that the army itself must develop better communications with and between its tanks, so that they could be properly controlled and their whereabouts exactly known. Without this, air support could not be applied with full effectiveness.

Before the British and Americans could build up forces powerful enough to liberate Europe, they had first to win the battle of the Atlantic. Here again, air power was finally a deciding factor. After the U-boats' early run of success had been ended in the summer of 1941, they soon found it profitable to concentrate on the areas not covered, or only poorly covered, by Allied aircraft (see AIR GAP). This tactic caused heavy shipping losses, but the introduction of auxiliary carriers (see CAM SHIPS, FIGHTER CATAPULT SHIPS, and MAC SHIPS) and of very long-range aircraft (mainly US Liberators) first of all narrowed and then closed the gaps. With new short-wave (10 cm.) ASV radar, undetectable for some time to the Germans, to locate the U-boat, with Leigh lights (see SEARCHLIGHTS) to illuminate them at night, and with more powerful depth charges filled with Torpex (see EXPLOSIVES) and fitted with better pistols, aircraft became not only U-boat spotters but also U-boats killers. By the end of the war the number of U-boats destroyed by the RAF, including those by bombing and aerial mine-laying, exceeded the number sunk by the Royal Navy.

When the Allies at length gathered their forces for the return to the Continent (see OVERLORD), air power exercised in a wide variety of ways was fundamental to the success of the invasion. By landing or parachuting agents and supplies from the UK it first helped to build up the Resistance and acquired essential intelligence. Then, in the weeks before OVERLORD, the RAF and the USAAF wrought havoc with the railway system in northern France, effectively sealing off the projected lodgement areas (and others, for the sake of *deception) from any possibility of rapid reinforcement by the Germans. At the same time the strength of the British air defences denied the Luftwaffe the possibility of assessing the invasion preparations by reconnaissance. Next, during the invasion itself, air patrols protected the Allied vessels, 'spoof' air patrols falsely indicated a landing in the Pas de Calais, and air attacks, almost unopposed, on batteries, radar stations, troops, and airfields put the defenders at an impossible disadvantage. Airborne landings, too, played their part, and subsequently the whole panoply of air support techniques which had been developed in North Africa speeded the progress of the Allied ground forces (see CARPET BOMBING).

Not merely was this air support superb in quality, it was completely overwhelming in quantity. For OVERLORD the Allied Expeditionary Air Force numbered no fewer than 9,000 aircraft, supported by another 3,000 from other Commands. Against this vast array the Luftwaffe locally could initially pit only some 300 machines, later to be increased to upwards of 1,000. On D-Day itself, Allied aircraft flew nearly 15,000 sorties in support of the invading forces, the Luftwaffe barely 100 against them.

The achievements of tactical and maritime air power, of reconnaissance, and of military air transport were soon universally acknowledged. About the Anglo-American *strategic air offensive against Germany, however, there was and still is controversy. The main points of contention have concerned the morality of attacks on civilian centres, the wisdom of devoting such large resources to a virtually unproved form of warfare, and the actual results of the offensive.

With regard to the moral issue, both sides at the outset declared their intention of restricting bombing to strictly 'military' targets. Later, the British felt themselves freed from this inhibition by the German bombing of Warsaw, Rotterdam, London itself, and Belgrade. But a shift in bombing policy came not so much from changed moral attitudes as from the discovery that long-range strategic missions could not be flown in daylight against a good defence without heavy losses. The Germans found this out in the battle of Britain, and in the autumn of 1940 went over to night bombing, which with its greater inaccuracy inevitably killed many civilians. They also began attacking non-industrial targets (see BAEDEKER RAIDS). On the British side, RAF Bomber Command, having discovered as early as 1940 that it could not bomb Germany in daylight, later discovered that it had seriously misjudged its attempts to bomb precise targets by night. In December 1940 it first introduced *area bombing, which meant deliberately bombing whole industrial and administrative areas, which were easier to find and hit. Inevitably, attacks of this kind, which became regular from mid-1941 onwards, especially after the *Butt Report of August 1941, caused much loss of life among civilians.

When the Eighth US Army Air Force arrived in the UK in 1942 its intentions were those originally cherished by the British—to attack only precise targets. Its leaders contended that the defensive power of their multi-gunned B17 Flying Fortresses, operating in formation, taken in conjunction with the bombing accuracy from great heights conferred by the new Norden bomb-sight, would permit *precision bombing in daylight without unacceptable losses. The course of the Americans' operations over Germany was to show that, after many difficulties, they were in fact able to make good their claim. They did so finally, however, only after the development of good long-distance escort fighters, notably the P51 Mustang with drop tanks, possessing a combination of range, speed, and fighting power no one had thought possible at the outset of hostilities. For its part, RAF Bomber Command became progressively more effective in its night bombing. Successive radio or radar aids (see ELECTRONIC NAVIGATION SYSTEMS) in combination with the new Mark XIV bomb-sight and more sophisticated *pathfinder and marker techniques (see SHAKER TECHNIQUE) brought greater accuracy to navigation and bomb-aiming. Heavier concentration of attack to saturate the defences, tactical routeing (occasionally in the light of ULTRA intelligence), and the dropping of metallic foil (see ELECTRONIC WARFARE) to disrupt the German radar, all helped to keep losses within acceptable limits. More specialized and much more powerful *bombs and a more intensive use of incendiaries inflicted ever greater damage. Better aircraft, notably the four-engined Lancaster and the fast twin-engined wooden Mosquito (used over Germany largely for *'intruder', reconnaissance, and pathfinding purposes) reached the targets and brought the crews, except the unlucky four or five in every hundred, safely back again. Finally the point was reached, in the last months of the war, when the RAF's night bombing, reverting increasingly to precise targets like oil installations, was actually more accurate than the USAAF's daylight bombing, which was often done at excessive heights on account of the strength of the ground defences.

To the criticism that the strategic offensive involved a vast misuse of resources there is a simple answer. After the fall of France bombing was the only form of attack by which the UK could directly damage Germany, not only in 1940 but for years to come. Equally, when the USA became involved in the war, bombers could be flown to Europe and be in action long before American ground forces could be brought across in sufficient numbers to attempt an invasion.

After January 1943, however, the air offensive against Germany was essentially geared to the strategy decided upon at the Casablanca conference (see SYMBOL). It was to be waged with the object of weakening Germany to the point where it could not effectively repel an invasion. So in the end the foremost proponents of the strategic offensive—*Portal and *Harris on the British side, *Arnold, *Spaatz, and *Eaker on the American—were never given the resources, around 6,000 heavy bombers, which they had considered necessary to weaken Germany fatally without major fighting on land. Though Harris relinquished that dream only with the greatest reluctance, their task became, essentially, to reduce Germany's industrial capacity, to weaken or destroy the Luftwaffe, and then to assist, by both tactical and strategic operations, the progress of the Allied ground forces.

The results of the offensive, which at its height occupied some 3,000 British and American bombers, have in recent years been seriously undervalued. Much has been made of the fact that during the peak period of Allied bombing German aircraft production actually increased; but a high proportion of these aircraft were fighters for Reich defence, much more easily manufactured than bombers, the production of which declined sharply. In 1939, 31% of German aircraft production consisted of fighters, 26% of bombers. In 1944 the proportions were 75% fighters, 11% bombers. This in itself was a victory for Allied air power.

The strategic air offensive in fact had profoundly important results. Though it failed to destroy German morale it greatly reduced German war production. Among other effects it finally brought about a shortage of oil (see RAW MATERIALS) so acute that fuel could not even be found to give proper training to the Luftwaffe's new pilots. After the introduction of the long-range fighter it also, through the efforts of the Americans, fatally weakened the Luftwaffe by attacks on aircraft factories (see SCHWEINFURT, for example) and by combat in the skies.

This was far from being all. In the final stages, the offensive destroyed communications in Western Germany and utterly disrupted German troop movements. It caused Luftwaffe units to be withdrawn from the Eastern Front, so that only 32% of its forces were engaged there in 1944 as compared with 65% in 1941. In its last year it kept 2,000 or more German fighters, and nearly 20,000 anti-aircraft guns, many of which could have been used as anti-tank guns, pinned down to the defence of the Reich. As intended, it threw Germany on the defensive, and the combination of daylight attacks by the USAAF and night attacks by the RAF finally proved irresistible. The mature judgement of Albert *Speer, Hitler's armaments minister, ran thus: 'The real importance of the air war was that it opened a second front long before the invasion of Europe. That front was the skies of Germany ... This was the greatest lost battle on the German side.'

In the final stages of the air war in Europe the Germans displayed great technological inventiveness. In addition to the flying-bomb and the long-range rocket (see V-WEAPONS) they produced a bewildering variety of rocket and turbo-jet aircraft—22 types in all. The Me262, a heavily armed (4x30 mm. cannon) twin turbo-jet capable of around 870 kph (540 mph), was produced in the greatest quantity. First operational in the spring of 1944, it had an enormous advantage in speed over any Allied fighter and could have taken a deadly toll of the American daylight bombers. But Hitler foolishly demanded a modification for bomb-carrying, which delayed production, and it was not until March 1945, far too late to have much effect, that all Me262 resources were devoted to the fighter defence of the Reich.

Despite their ingenuity the German jets, were unreliable compared with the only British turbo-jet to go into service during the war, the Gloster Meteor, operational from August 1944. Some 80–95 kph (50–60 mph) slower than the Me262, it had the advantage of Rolls-Royce engines soundly derived from the designs of the inventor of the British jet engine, Air Commodore Frank Whittle. Used at first against the flying bomb, and then for ground attack, it never encountered the Me262. Its importance, like that of the German jets, was less for its achievements in the war than for beginning the 'jet revolution' that was soon to transform both military and civil aviation.

It was in the Far East that some of the most dramatic achievements of air power occurred. To begin with there were the devastating attacks by Japanese carrier aircraft against the US Pacific Fleet at *Pearl Harbor in December 1941—an operation influenced by the events at Taranto the previous November—and by land-based machines from Formosa against *MacArthur's aircraft in the Philippines (see CLARK FIELD). It was largely thanks to these initial blows, and the superiority of the Japanese Navy's Zero fighter to anything it was to meet for two years to come, that the Japanese were able to sweep through the ill-defended British and Dutch possessions in South-East Asia without the Allies being able to interrupt their communications. At the outset, too, the sinking of the **Prince of Wales* and the *Repulse* by Japanese aircraft ruined the British chances of interfering with the invasion of Malaya and confirmed, as had the Royal Navy's losses off Crete, that sea power could no longer be exercised without air power.

When the Americans had recovered and in 1942 were

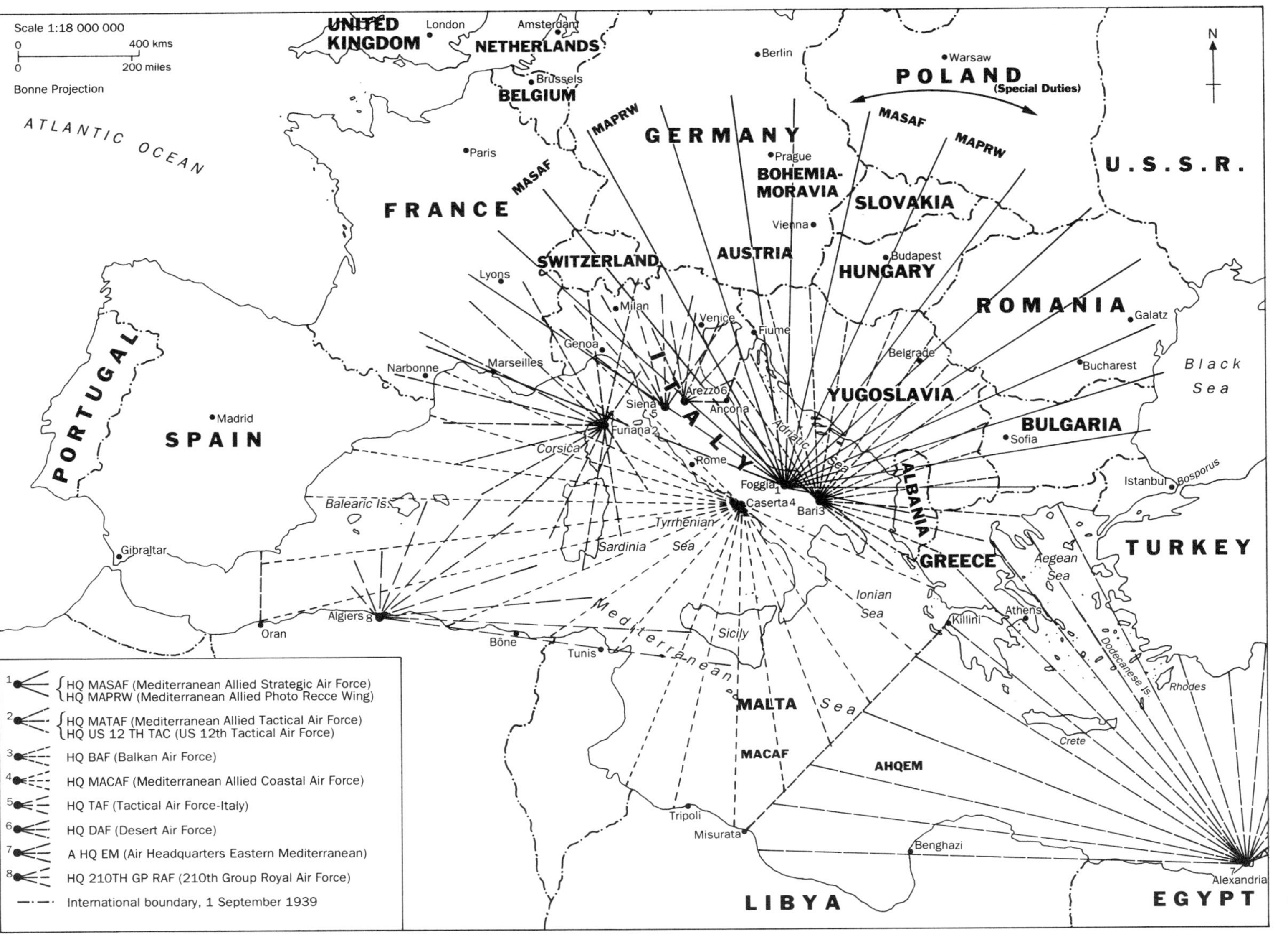

2. An example of range and flexibility of Allied **air power**: the Mediterranean, July–August 1944

contesting the further Japanese incursions into New Guinea and the Philippines, two great sea battles marked a new epoch in naval history and in the history of air power. In the *Coral Sea and off *Midway Island the Japanese and American fleets fought by means of their aircraft. These two engagements, which turned the tide in the *Pacific war, were the first occasions on which surface fleets fought an action without ever coming within sight or gunfire range of each other. Sea power, basic and essential, had come to depend on aircraft as well as surface vessels and submarines, and the hegemony of the battleship was over (for example, see MUSASHI AND YAMATO). Outside the range of shore-based aircraft, the carrier now ruled the surface of the seas.

There were other unprecedented achievements of air power during the prolonged struggle which turned the Japanese back from the gates of India and recovered Burma. In addition to all their normal reconnaissance and combat roles, Allied aircraft played a major part in transport and supply. They made possible *Wingate's *Chindit expeditions and the *Hump supply and transport service from Assam to China; kept a force of 150,000 supplied during the siege of *Imphal (and evacuated 35,000 wounded and non-combatants); maintained supply to large formations of the British Fourteenth Army behind the Japanese lines, formations which had been landed not simply for raiding purposes but as outposts for a subsequent advance.

All this could not have been done without mastery in the air, but as time went on and the Allies were reinforced, Japanese air superiority evaporated. The figures of British air strength tell the story. In 1941 the RAF had five squadrons in northern India, mostly on out-of-date aircraft; by 1944 it had more than 60 squadrons, on modern aircraft, allocated to the *Burma campaign. Against more than 1,000 Allied aircraft in Burma, the Japanese could finally pit only 200.

But it was in the final attacks on the Japanese homeland that air power achieved its most rapid, complete, and terrifying results. First there was the struggle to obtain air bases, which in the Far East meant capturing islands sufficiently close to Japan. In the course of these advances the Americans gained such complete air superiority over the Japanese that the latter's raw new pilots were forced to resort to *Kamikaze or suicide missions. The capture of the Mariana Islands in November 1944 provided an invaluable return landing point for the new B29 Superfortresses which had been operating against Japan from China. US landings on *Iwo Jima in January 1945 and on *Okinawa in April then made fighter escort possible; and everywhere the American's ability to construct bases and landing grounds rapidly was a key factor in their success (see ENGINEERS and SEABEES). However, it was not, until they went over to the decried RAF tactics of area bombing by night, using incendiaries filled with napalm, that the Americans achieved big results (see STRATEGIC AIR OFFENSIVES, 3). Finally, the dropping of *atomic bombs on *Hiroshima and *Nagasaki was decisive. Strategic bombing, though far from being the only cause of Japan's defeat, had unquestionably delivered the *coup de grâce*.

Air power: Numbers of military aircraft produced by four of the major air powers, 1938–44 (000s)

Year	*Germany*	*Japan*	*UK*	*USA*
1938	5.6	3.2	2.8	1.8
1939	8.3	4.5	7.9	2.1
1940	10.8	4.8	15.0	6.1
1941	11.8	5.1	20.1	29.4
1942	15.6	8.9	23.7	47.8
1943	25.5	16.7	26.3	85.9
1944	39.8	28.2	26.5	96.3

The substantial increases by Germany and Japan in 1943–4 reflect their growing concentration on defence and the manufacture of relatively easily produced single-engined fighters. These types accounted for 24% of Germany's aircraft production in 1941, 65% in 1944.

There are no regular figures of comparable reliability for the USSR, but it is estimated that production there rose from approximately 10,000 in 1940 to approximately 40,000 in 1944.

Source: Contributor.

Many factors lay behind the massive air power finally wielded by the Allies. The British and Americans harnessed their scientific resources to the war effort more systematically, and to more immediately practicable purposes, than did the Axis powers. The Allies gained, and held, a general advantage in the vital work of code-breaking (see SIGNALS INTELLIGENCE WARFARE); their structure for the higher direction of the war was superior (see GRAND ALLIANCE); and the ready availability of fuel, and the huge open spaces of the USA and the British Empire, safe from hostile interference, gave the Allies inestimable benefits when it came to training (see BRITISH EMPIRE AIR TRAINING SCHEME). But it was above all the Allies' enormous industrial capacity which was the foundation of their air power (see Table). By the beginning of 1945, Allied aircraft outnumbered their opponents on all fronts by at least five to one. 'God is on the side of the big battalions' especially, when, as in this case, they are well-equipped, well-trained, well-informed, and well-led.

Curiously enough, the final consummation in the Far East may have marked the apogee of air power. Air forces would certainly remain key, even decisive, elements in warfare; but within a few years rockets would replace manned aircraft as the major delivery system for the most powerful weapons of mass destruction. In the new era, there would be a new fear: 'the missile will always get through'.

DENIS RICHARDS

Higham, R., *Air Power: a Concise History* (London, 1972).
Overy, R. J., *The Air War 1939–45* (London, 1980).
Stokesbury, J. L., *A Short History of Air Power* (New York, 1984).

air-sea rescue, the equipment and organization used to pick up air crew forced to 'ditch' in the sea. The efficiency of this service, for Allied airmen at least, increased as the war progressed, which was not only good for morale but a sensible measure as aircrew were always in short supply.

Germany was far in advance of other combatants in providing an air-sea rescue service for its air crews, having created the Seenotdienst within the Luftwaffe as early as 1936. From September 1939 *float plane and *flying boat patrols, marked with the Red Cross emblem, covered the North Sea and these were extended to the English Channel when the battle of *Britain started. In case they were unable to land to pick up a ditched crew immediately these aircraft carried collapsible rubber dinghies equipped with radio transmitters, which transmitted on the international distress frequency, and by October 1940 there were 150 aircraft divided into five Seenotflugkommandos. Additionally, sea rescue floats equipped with bunks, food, and water for four men were positioned in the middle of the English Channel.

In March 1940 the British established a unified system of communications which enabled fast RAF launches, or Army Lysander light aircraft with survival equipment, to reach a downed crew quickly, but liaison between the services was initially poor. During the battle of Britain RAF pilots had only inflatable jackets (nicknamed Mae Wests after the busty *Hollywood actress) to keep them afloat; but the German rubber dinghy was soon copied, as was the marker dye, which allowed the dinghy to be spotted from the air, and the radio transmitter. In January 1941 a Directorate of Air-Sea Rescue was established in the air ministry which improved co-ordination. From that time the chances of a pilot surviving improved considerably and from February to August 1941 444 crewmen were rescued out of the 1,200 who ditched.

In August 1941 the UK's Coastal Command took over operational responsibility for 'deep search' air-sea rescue at sea, though Fighter Command remained in charge around the coastline, and the following month four special air-sea rescue squadrons (275–278) were formed within Fighter Command. By the end of 1942 another three (279–281) were formed, two of which joined Coastal Command for deep search operations.

During the course of the war the US Army Air Forces formed seven air-sea rescue squadrons and by September 1944 about 90% of US aircrews forced down at sea in the European Theatre of Operations (see ETOUSA) were being rescued. The record in the *Pacific war was equally impressive with 1,841 lives being saved from July 1943 to April 1945. But the survival of crews depended largely on luck, weather conditions, and the type of aircraft being flown. Bombers were mostly ditched—the B17 Flying Fortress would often float for up to half an hour—but fighter pilots preferred to bail out as their aircraft (especially the Mustang, whose radiator scoop dragged it under immediately), were notoriously hard to ditch.

What improved the chances of all Allied crews immeasurably was the introduction in 1942 of the *Gibson Girl radio transmitter, a development of the German air-sea rescue transmitter first captured by the British in 1941. This was a more reliable form of establishing a downed crew's position than the navigator's estimate dispatched by *carrier pigeons which had originally been part of a British aircraft's air-sea rescue equipment. A further aid came in 1943 when Allied crews were equipped with an automatic oscillator ('Walter') which registered on the searching aircraft's *radar. Emergency survival packs such as the Thornaby Bag, which could be dropped to help crews once they had been found, became increasingly sophisticated and by 1944 a powered lifeboat was available which could be dropped by parachute.

The aircraft most widely used for Allied air-sea rescue was the ubiquitous, amphibious Catalina, but in the Pacific the B29 Superfortress, heavily armed and of great endurance, soon proved itself ideal for delivering survival equipment when it began operating in 1944. *Helicopters were also used from 1944 onwards by the US Coast Guard and by June 1945 they were in regular use in emergency rescue squadrons. Vital though aircraft were in dropping lifeboats and rescue equipment, most downed Allied crews were rescued by ships.

Air Transport Auxiliary, British civilian organization which flew aircraft from the factories to their air bases. Of 1,152 male and 166 female pilots, some of them American, many of whom were trained at its flying schools, 98 men and 15 women lost their lives. Altogether it delivered 308,567 aircraft at an annual loss rate that never exceeded 0.39%.

Air Transport Command (ATC) controlled the US Army Air Forces' world-wide system of air transport. Originally known as the US Air Corps Ferrying Command, established in May 1941 to deliver *Lend-Lease aircraft to the UK, it was renamed Air Transport Command in June 1942. Its aircraft (which could become troop carriers or air ambulances when not flying freight, passengers, or mail) and its organization were based on, and developed from, US civil airlines such as Pan American. Its principal aircraft were the twin-engined Douglas DC3, the Dakota, called the C47 in military parlance (C53 when a passenger plane), the four-engined DC4 (C54), and the twin-engined Curtiss C46 (Commando). Converted bombers were also used, the B24 Liberator, designated C87 (C109 when a tanker), being the most important.

Through its wing organizations overseas ATC retained control over local base troops and installations (though not over crews and their aircraft passing through). This ran counter to the principle of unified command but the theatre commander could, and sometimes did, draw on ATC transport in an emergency when his own troop carrier forces became overloaded (see MOUNTBATTEN). The basis of ATC's operations was running what amounted to a number of major airlines which spanned the world and linked the US with every theatre of war. For example, the South Atlantic route, which linked the USA with Liberia and British West Africa via the Caribbean, Brazil, and Ascension Island, fed Lend-Lease aircraft to the British (see TAKORADI AIR ROUTE) and to the USSR via Persia. The 3,555 km. (2,210 mi.) north-west air route, was inaugurated to ensure reinforcement of Alaska when it appeared the Japanese might invade (see ALEUTIAN ISLANDS) and it later delivered Lend-Lease aircraft to the USSR.

ATC's maximum strength was 200,000 men and 3,700 aircraft. Its achievements included such vital supply operations as those which sustained the Chinese war effort over the *Hump and British resistance to the Japanese *Imphal offensive in March 1944. In one month alone (July 1945) it flew 275,000 passengers and 100,000 tons of cargo, and it ferried more than a quarter of a million aircraft and evacuated more than 300,000 sick and wounded personnel. ATC was a crucial part of Allied *logistics which contributed a new dimension to 20th-century warfare. See also ATLANTIC FERRY ORGANIZATION.

Alam Halfa, battle of, fought from 30 August to 7 September 1942 when *Rommel made his last attempt to break through the British line defending Egypt. It was, from the British point of view, one of the best examples of army–air co-operation in the *Western Desert campaigns. See ULTRA, 1 for the important role intelligence played in this battle; see also WESTERN DESERT CAMPAIGNS.

Alamo Force was the task force *MacArthur created for CARTWHEEL, the operation launched in June 1943 to reduce *Rabaul. Its forces comprised Lt-General Walter Krueger's Sixth US Army whose HQ and commanding general it shared. Alamo Force came directly under MacArthur's command, thus effectively removing all US troops from the operational control of MacArthur's *South-West Pacific Area Allied Land Forces commander, General *Blamey. Forces controlled by, or assigned to, Alamo Force landed on the Trobriand Islands, *New Britain, the *Admiralty Islands, and at Saidor and *Hollandia in Dutch New Guinea, and they also took part in liberating the *Philippines.

Alaska, the most north-western part of North America, which includes the Aleutian Islands. It was purchased by the USA from Russia in 1867, but did not become the 49th state until 1959. It had a governor and the laws of Oregon were applied to its 72,000 population, half of whom were indigenous Inuit. From these, and from Aleuts and Indians, were drawn the men who composed the 2,700-strong Alaskan Territorial Guard, known as the Tundra Army, formed in 1941 to defend the territory against a Japanese attack. In fact, Alaska, with two Aleutian islands being occupied by the Japanese during the *Aleutian Islands campaigns as well as Japanese attacks on Dutch Harbor, saw more of the war than the rest of the USA, though the Tundra Army's only chance for action was when its members shot down Japanese *balloon bombs. A number of air and military bases were rapidly built there to counter the Japanese threat and the Alaska Highway was started. When this was completed in 1943 it ran for 2,450 km. (1,523 mi.) from Dawson Creek in British Columbia to Fairbanks. Officially called the Alcan Military Highway, it was a joint Canadian–US defence project which involved 11,000 US and 16,000 Canadian troops, as well as civilians.

Albania, tribal monarchy of just over a million inhabitants, the governments of which after the *First World War tended to look to the UK for guidance and protection. Between the wars Italy and Yugoslavia contended for influence in Albania and although King *Zog had come to power with Yugoslav aid, he had little alternative to accepting increasing Italian influence in economic, cultural, and political matters. He was persuaded to dispense with his British advisers, but the Italians aspired to take control of the country, Mussolini seeing it as a useful bridgehead to extent Italian power in the Balkans to Greece and beyond.

Italy invaded Albania on 7 April—Good Friday—1939. The only resistance was conducted by Colonel Abas Kupi who, with two battalions and some tribal levies, held up the Italian advance from Durazzo for 36 hours, enabling King Zog, with his queen and their new-born son, to escape. The king eventually settled in the UK for the duration of the war. Although treated as a distinguished guest there, he was not recognized by the foreign office as an Allied head of state because the UK had recognized the annexation of Albania in a final attempt to prevent Italy from joining Germany in the approaching war. The Italian King, *Victor Emmanuel III, was declared king of Albania and a fascist-type administration was installed in Tirana; anti-Italian elements were imprisoned or went into exile.

By the spring of 1940, the D organization (later part of *SOE) had persuaded the British government to prepare a revolt in Albania against the Italians. Geography as well as history suggested that the launching pad for this revolt should be the Yugoslav province of Kosovo, which was largely populated by ethnic Albanians. A prominent clan there, the Kryezius, were invited to form an Albanian United Front, to be led by Abas Kupi—already something of a legend because of his resistance to the Italian invasion. Mustafa Jinishi, a young communist, was also co-opted. The United Front was at first well received, but with the collapse of Yugoslav resistance in the face of the German invasion of April 1941 (see BALKAN CAMPAIGN), which resulted in Kosova being transferred to Albania, the revolt melted away.

However, after the Axis defeats at *El Alamein and *Stalingrad the political climate began to change once more. A few young men, mostly communists, took to the mountains in the south. Mustafa Jinishi was among them and Enver Hoxha (1908–83) emerged as their leader. They were encouraged by emissaries from *Tito to form a Partisan movement. Also in the south, some of the more liberal landowners and intellectuals began to form a more traditionalist resistance movement, the Balli Kombetar, while in central and northern Albania, Abas Kupi and other tribal leaders began mobilizing their clans. As reports came in of growing resistance, SOE sent in two agents, Colonel Neil McLean and Major David Smiley, to reconnoitre. They made contact with Hoxha Partisans and urged that support should be sent to both the communist Partisans and the Balli Kombetar, also that additional SOE missions should be sent to the areas where the tribal leaders held sway.

At this point (July 1943) Mussolini was overthrown and the different Albanian resistance groups came together in a United Front which rose in a general insurrection. Two of the Italian divisions occupying the country obeyed the orders of the new Italian prime minister Marshal *Badoglio to join the Partisans, and were soon disarmed and dispersed. Of the remaining three divisions, some units went over to the Germans, others simply disintegrated. By the end of September the guerrillas and miscellaneous citizens had captured the equipment of much of the Italian garrison. For a few days much of Albania was liberated, the Italians only holding out in Valona, Durazzo, Scutari, and Tirana, and even there they were negotiating with members of the British military missions. The Germans, however, reacted promptly. A strong force was flown in to Tirana, which quickly cleared the insurgents out of the towns in the centre and north of the country, while another division brought in from Macedonia cleared the south. A short phase of savage reprisals against the civilian population deprived the guerrilla forces of much local support.

Having instilled fear into the population, the Germans released most of the Albanian leaders imprisoned by the Italians and offered the country neutral status. They repealed the fascist constitution and persuaded Mehdi Frasheri, a former governor of Jerusalem under the Ottomans, to form a Council of Regency and a government together with other respected men. They allowed a measure of freedom of association and of the press. The new government, however, had no power beyond the main towns and the coastal plain, and the rest of Albania relapsed into anarchy, under rival chiefs and guerrilla leaders.

Calculating that the Germans had lost the war and would soon withdraw their forces, Hoxha decided to break up the United Front and direct his energies to suppressing the Balli Kombetar. The Germans, quick to encourage internecine conflict, helped the Tirana government to re-equip Ballist groups and send them back into the mountains as counter-guerrillas, enabling the Partisans to accuse the Ballists of *collaboration. Civil war developed in southern Albania on much the same lines that had already divided the Greek and Yugoslav resistance movements.

By the beginning of 1944 the Germans had regained control of the coast and the principal Albanian cities and it seemed likely that they would retreat from Greece through Albania. The problem was how to bring the Albanians to harrass their withdrawal most effectively. The key seemed to lie in persuading the Albanian leaders to abandon their civil war and comply with British military directives in harassing the retreating Germans. The strategy to be pursued was determined by *Balkan Air Force headquarters in Bari. The task of trying to co-ordinate the activities of the British missions in northern and central Albania, and of reconciling the tribal leaders with the Partisans in the south, was given to McLean and Lt-Colonel Anthony Palmer, the principal British liaison officer with the Partisans. McLean was authorized to promise arms to any group once it had begun to fight the Germans.

Abas Kupi and his fellow tribal leaders, having begun operations against the Germans, received a few drops of arms from Bari. But the communists, also re-equipped from British sources, moved into central Albania and began to attack Abas Kupi's forces and those of his allies. The British mission with the Partisans proved powerless to restrain them and a British officer sent in to mediate was killed in an air raid. The civil war spread in due course to the north, where pro-Tito forces from Kosovo began to operate against the Kryezius. No further supplies were sent to Abas Kupi and the other non-communist forces. There is little doubt that the headquarters of the Balkan Air Force had become strongly pro-Partisan, and parts of it had certainly been infiltrated by communist sympathizers.

The Germans began to retreat in earnest in September 1944 and were attacked by Abas Kupi whose forces had been swelled by the Balli Kombetar, retreating before pressure from the communists, and by some Tirana government troops who had defected. It might still have been possible to raise the whole of northern Albania against them, but by this time it had been decided that all British support was to be concentrated on the communist Partisans who controlled south Albania, though they were still weak elsewhere. The McLean mission was evacuated to Italy, to be followed successively by Abas Kupi with four of his principal officers and the Ballist leaders. The communists took over the government of Albania, initially under Yugoslavian supervision, and were recognized by the UK and the USA. However, in October 1946 two British warships were damaged, with serious loss of life, by mines in the Corfu channel. When the Albanians rejected the Hague Court's finding that they were responsible and must pay compensation, the UK and USA broke off relations with Tirana.

Albania moved into a phase of open hostility to the West, but over the years fell out with all the powers of the communist bloc in succession. Enver Hoxha retreated into isolation, relying on the mutual jealousies of Yugoslavia, Greece, and Italy to protect the country from

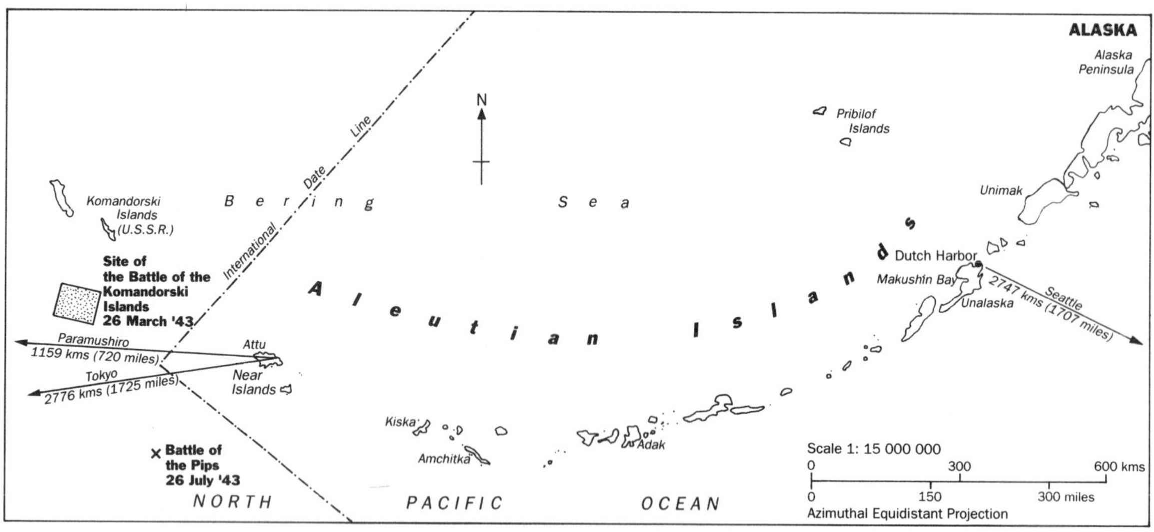

3. **Aleutian Islands**

attack. He himself eliminated most of his wartime colleagues and survived to die in bed. JULIAN AMERY

Aleutian Islands campaigns. Kiska and Attu, two of the most westerly of these US-owned islands, which stretch across the north Pacific between Alaska and Japan, were occupied by Japanese forces in June 1942 (see Map 3). Though the Japanese feared the islands might be used as American bases to bomb, or even invade, Japan, they were principally occupied to help draw part of the US Pacific Fleet north before it was brought to battle off *Midway in the central Pacific by Admiral *Yamamoto's Combined Fleet. But Admiral *Nimitz, C-in-C US Pacific Fleet, forewarned of Japanese intentions by *ULTRA intelligence, sent his most powerful units to ambush Yamamoto off Midway and formed Task Force 8 (later known as North Pacific Force) to defend the Aleutians. Commanded by Rear-Admiral Robert Theobald, the force included 5 cruisers, 14 destroyers, 6 submarines, and 85 Army Air Forces aircraft.

From the start neither, side knew much about the other's dispositions or intentions and both forces were frequently shrouded in the fog and rain squalls that often prevailed. The Americans also feared the islands could be used as an invasion route and Theobald decided, quite contrary to the intelligence estimates that had been given him, that the Japanese invasion transports were heading for Alaska, an error which placed his forces in the wrong area.

Opposing Theobald's force were the offensive components of the Japanese Fifth Fleet, commanded by Vice-Admiral Hosogaya Boshiro, which was divided into four groups. Rear-Admiral Kakuta Kakuji's Mobile Force, built around two light carriers and a seaplane carrier; the Kiska Occupation Force; the Adak-Attu Occupation Force; and the supply ships which were escorted by Hosogaya's flagship, the heavy cruiser *Nachi*, and two destroyers. Yamamoto's Midway Force had also detached a powerful Aleutian Screening Force to act as distant cover for Kakuta but this was withdrawn when the battle off Midway failed to go Yamamoto's way. As part of the plan to induce Nimitz to divide his fleet, Kakuta twice raided a new US base at Dutch Harbor on Unalaska in the eastern Aleutians. This caused considerable damage, but a second raid, on US destroyers in Makushin Bay, failed.

Theobald's error in supposing Alaska was Hosogaya's objective meant that the Japanese landings on Attu on 5 June 1942, and on Kiska two days later, were unopposed, and they remained unknown to the Americans until 10 June. Kiska was then raided by American bombers—Attu was beyond their range—but they did little damage, and a naval bombardment was hardly more effective. On 27 August the Japanese began transferring the Attu garrison to Kiska, but in October Attu was reoccupied and then reinforced.

For the next nine months the Japanese were harassed from the sea, and from the air by USAAF bombers operating from air strips specially built on two other islands, Adak and Amchitka, just 145 km. (90 mi.) and 95 km. (60 mi.) respectively from Kiska. But adverse weather conditions hindered any real attrition of the occupying Japanese and it was not until March 1943 that sufficient Allied forces became available to drive them from American soil.

The weather also made American air support unreliable as Rear-Admiral Charles McMorris discovered when it failed to arrive after he encountered Hosogaya's more powerful force on 26 March 1943. However, the battle of the *Komandorski Islands which followed prevented the 2,630-strong Japanese garrison on Attu from receiving any further infantry reinforcements before

11,000 men of the 7th US Infantry Division landed there on 11 May 1943 with the support of a battleship bombardment and, for the first time in the *Pacific war, with air support supplied by an escort carrier. The Japanese, commanded by Colonel Yamazaki Yasuyo, resisted stubbornly and on 16 May the commanding US general was dismissed when he remarked that it would need six months to conquer the island. But Yamazaki and his men, outnumbered and poorly supported from the air and sea, were gradually pushed into the last high ground. Then, before dawn on 29 May, they launched one of the biggest *banzai* charges of the war which overran two command posts and a medical station before being halted. The battle went on all day and the next morning the surviving Japanese made a final attack before most of the survivors committed suicide. Only 28 prisoners were taken and 2,351 bodies were counted. The Americans lost 600 killed and 1,200 wounded.

Vice-Admiral Thomas Kinkaid, who had succeeded Theobald in January 1943, now turned his attention to Kiska. He imposed a destroyer blockade and ordered intensified air and sea attacks on the garrison. However, by then the Japanese had decided to evacuate the island and on the night of 28/29 July, while US naval patrol ships were refuelling after the *'Battle of the Pips', the Japanese Navy expertly evacuated 5,183 troops and civilians under cover of fog. Air reconnaissance failed to establish that Kiska was no longer occupied and as ground fire was reported on several occasions it was suspected that the Japanese might be hiding. So on 15 August 1943 a force of 34,000 US and Canadian troops landed, but it took them some days to discover the Japanese had departed. In doing so 56 men were killed or wounded when friendly patrols fired on one another.

If nothing else, the campaign taught the Americans some useful lessons in *amphibious warfare which were soon put to good use elsewhere in the Pacific war. For the Japanese the whole diversionary effort was a disaster and a waste of valuable men and *matériel*.

Alexander, Albert V. (1885–1965), British Labour Party politician who succeeded Churchill as First Lord of the Admiralty in May 1940, a post he held throughout the war. In June 1940 he flew to Bordeaux with the First Sea Lord, Admiral *Pound, to persuade the *Vichy French government to put the French navy beyond Hitler's grasp. The failure of this mission led directly to the bombardment of the French fleet at *Mers-el-Kébir.

Alexander, Field Marshal Sir Harold (1891–1961), British Army officer who, from commanding the 1st British Division during the fall of *France rose to become Allied Supreme Commander in the *Mediterranean.

Alexander, who was the fourth son of the Earl of Caledon, served with great distinction in the *First World War, and by 1937 was the youngest general in the British Army. He took command of the *British Expeditionary Force during the *Dunkirk evacuation of May–June 1940, was promoted lt-general that December, and succeeded *Auchinleck at Southern Command. In March 1942 he was sent to reverse British defeats in the *Burma campaign but could only organize the retreat of his forces into India, which he did very ably. Promoted to general in April 1942, he was appointed C-in-C First Army for the *North African campaign which started that November. However, in August, Churchill appointed him C-in-C *Middle East Command with *Montgomery under him. It was a formidable team which turned the tide of war in the *Western Desert campaigns. Alexander, with typical generosity, but also as a deliberate policy, always insisted that the victories were Montgomery's; but it was Alexander's tactful handling of his brilliant but difficult subordinate which gave Montgomery the scope and the resources he needed.

In January 1943 Alexander was summoned to the Casablanca conference (see SYMBOL) where he was appointed *Eisenhower's deputy and ground commander of the Allied armies then fighting the North African campaign. As C-in-C of the newly formed Eighteenth Army Group, he took command on 20 February 1943, reorganized the confused Allied front and, in a campaign of great panache, forced the surrender of all Axis forces in North Africa that May. He was then appointed C-in-C Fifteenth Army Group, which launched the *Sicilian campaign in July 1943. He was later criticized for his handling of the campaign as he appeared rather too ready to accept what Montgomery told him and not ready enough to employ the mobility and striking power of *Patton's raw but aggressive Seventh US Army. In the *Italian campaign which followed, Alexander served as C-in-C of all Allied forces and then, from 27 November 1944, as Allied Supreme Commander in the Mediterranean. On the same day he was promoted field marshal, back-dated to 4 June 1944, the day his troops had entered Rome. With the main Allied effort taking place in north-west Europe, Italy became a backwater. But instead of allowing the campaign to fade into stalemate, Alexander planned the destruction of the German forces facing him, and on 29 April 1945 he personally accepted their *unconditional surrender.

Alexander was no original thinker but he had many virtues, not the least of which were his personal courage, his imperturbability in battle, and his ability to make friends among whom Churchill counted himself one. He was a charming, affable man who, it was said, defeated his enemies without making any. Having been knighted in 1942, he was created a viscount in 1946, and became governor-general of Canada, a post he held until 1952 when he was created Earl Alexander of Tunis. See also LAND POWER.

Keegan, J. (ed.), *Churchill's Generals* (London, 1991).
Nicolson, N., *Alex: The Life of Field Marshal Earl Alexander of Tunis* (London, 1973).
North, J. (ed.), *The Alexander Memoirs 1940–45* (London, 1962).

Algeria, French North African colony divided into three provinces. Each was administered by a governor-general who was responsible to the French ministry of the interior. In 1939 the colony had 6.6 million inhabitants, including nearly a million Europeans.

In September 1940 General *Weygand was appointed the *Vichy government's delegate-general in North Africa and his presence in Algeria encouraged the French settlers (*colons*) to accept the regime he represented. Repressive measures were taken against the local Jews, whose French citizenship was withdrawn, and against nationalist Muslims. This pushed the more moderate Muslims such as Ferhat Abbas into the radicals' camp, and the radicals such as Messali Hadj into prison. In December 1941 General *Juin replaced Weygand who sided with the Allies when they occupied Algeria at the start of the *North African campaign in November 1942.

The presence of the Allies in Algeria, and General *Giraud's decision to re-form Algerian army units, gave Ferhat Abbas the opportunity he sought. He presented an independence manifesto to the governor-general, Marcel Peyrouton, who accepted it and the need for change. However, in June 1943 the *French Committee for National Liberation, which had its HQ in Algiers, replaced Peyrouton with General *Catroux. He introduced more liberal policies, but opposed the immediate unconditional independence the followers of Messali Hadj demanded, as did the *Brazzaville conference in January 1944. On V-E Day in May 1945 civil disturbances erupted which were repressed with great severity, and independence was not finally achieved, after much bloodshed, until 1962.

A number of Algerian *Tirailleur regiments took part in the fighting which preceded the fall of *France in June 1940 and two fought with the Allies during the North African campaign. See also FRANCE, 4.

Allied Control Commissions were formed to oversee the implementation of the terms of the various *armistices the Allies imposed on some of the Axis powers. They were controlled by the Allied power which had borne the burden of the fighting against the country surrendering. In the case of Italy the terms of the armistice, and the running of the Commission, were organized by the Americans and the British; with the Finnish armistice in September 1944 it was the USSR, though there were British observers on the Commission.

With Austria and Germany the Commissions were the organizations formed by the Allied occupying powers along the lines drawn up by the *European Advisory Commission and confirmed at the Yalta conference in February 1945 (see ARGONAUT). Both countries and their capitals were divided into American, British, French, and Soviet zones of occupation, and military governments established in each (see Map I). To co-ordinate the administration of the occupied countries, which included the right for each occupying power to hold *war crimes trials within its zone (see also NUREMBERG TRIALS), the Cs-in-C of the occupying armies formed an Allied Control Council, or Commission, with a committee to implement its decisions, and both capitals also had an inter-Allied Governing Authority (Kommandatura). Besides having zones of occupation, Vienna also had a central district controlled jointly by all four powers. Military government, as defined by *Montgomery, was rule by the 'issue of orders, obedience to which will be exacted ... Military government is the instrument, so far as the civil population is concerned, by which these orders will be conveyed and enforced.' The Americans established it first near Aachen in September 1944, but the areas captured were so small that the German civil administration was retained (see also WEREWOLVES). The British first occupied German territory near Geilenkirchen, north of Aachen, in November 1944 but the civil population was evacuated. Military government in the western Allied zones differed from earlier organizations, such as the *Allied Military government of Occupied Territories, in that it was an integral part of the occupying forces' command system.

Allied Forces Headquarters (AFHQ). Formed in August 1942 as *Eisenhower's HQ for the *North African campaign, it then became the HQ for the supreme commander in the *Mediterranean theatre. It was based in Algiers from November 1942 until it moved to Caserta in Italy in July 1944. As the forerunner of *SHAEF, it was the first Allied inter-service HQ to be created equally from British and US personnel.

Allied Intelligence Bureau (AIB). Established at Brisbane, Australia, in July 1942 this co-ordinated all Allied intelligence services in *MacArthur's *South-West Pacific Area. Its controller was an Australian officer, Col. C. Roberts, who had a US deputy. Initially, it had four sections: A, was *Special Operations Australia (SOA), which collected information and mounted sabotage behind enemy lines. B, a part of *MI6 known as Secret Intelligence Australia, was funded and controlled from London and was responsible for espionage and *subversive warfare in Japanese-held territories. C, called a field intelligence unit, was the Australian *Coast Watchers Service. When this became part of the AIB it was divided into three regional sub-sections which covered the north-east area, the Philippines, and the Netherlands East Indies (NEI). The head of the last was a Dutch naval officer who, for sabotage and intelligence-gathering operations in the NEI, was responsible to the head of SOA. D, was responsible for propaganda, but in September 1942, as the Far Eastern Liaison Office, it was put under the Australian Chiefs of Staff and the Australian Department of External Affairs.

In April 1943 the AIB was reorganized on a regional, not a functional, basis and Section C's sub-sections became independent field intelligence sections answerable directly to the controller. Consequently, the NEI section (later, Division III of the Netherlands Forces

Intelligence Service) no longer came under SOA for clandestine operations in the NEI.

Allied Military Government of Occupied Territories (AMGOT). The rules annexed to the *Hague Convention state that an occupying army must ensure public order and safety. To comply, the Allies formed AMGOT for the military government of Sicily before the *Sicilian campaign began in July 1943 (and soon became known to the rest of the British Army as Ancient Military Gentlemen on Tour). It was based on British experience in Libya where their Enemy Occupied Territory Administration (EOTA) was operating. The C-in-C, General *Alexander, acted as military governor in Sicily and he was advised by a Chief Civil Affairs officer who had a deputy and six divisions under him: legal, financial, civilian supply, public health, public safety, and enemy property. Civil affairs officers naturally came under the control of local military commanders in combat zones. But once an area had become non-operational it was administered quite separately from the occupying forces and was responsible only to the supreme commander, *Eisenhower.

AMGOT, having unwittingly helped to revive the *Mafia in Sicily, was later extended to Italy, though Marshal *Badoglio's government administered the four southern provinces in the name of the king, *Victor Emmanuel III, and once Italy became a co-belligerent in October 1943 it operated only in combat zones. AMGOT had some difficulties in north-west Italy at the end of the war when the First French Army refused to withdraw and frustrated AMGOT's establishment there. Roosevelt resolved the situation by refusing the French any more military supplies until they withdrew, which they did on 10 June 1945. There were also some difficulties in *Trieste, which *Tito's forces had occupied, but this was also solved eventually.

Having a separate chain of command from the army made AMGOT unsatisfactory, and it was not used in Germany or Austria, where the *Allied Control Commissions ran the civil administration, or in France, where de *Gaulle took over at once.

Allied powers, those countries which actively opposed the *Axis powers. The principal ones were China, France, the UK and its empire, the USA, and the USSR. From January 1942 all countries, including the *governments-in-exile of those countries occupied by the Germans, which became a party to the *United Nations Declaration were also regarded as Allied powers. See also GRAND ALLIANCE.

Alsace-Lorraine, disputed German-speaking provinces (Elsass-Lothringen), on France's eastern borders, which became French territory in the late 17th and early 18th centuries. In 1871, as a result of the Franco-Prussian war, Alsace (the departments of Haut-Rhin and Bas-Rhin) and northern Lorraine (mainly the department of Moselle), were annexed to the new German Empire, the Second Reich. They were called the Reichsland, and governed from Berlin by a viceroy (*Statthalter*) in Strasbourg. The coking coal of Lorraine was welcome to the steelworks of Krupp and others in the Ruhr, and assisted the Second Reich's armaments programme. The inhabitants were given the option of staying or leaving for France; 45,000 left.

French politicians of the Third Republic dreamed of recapturing Alsace-Lorraine; it was a *terra irredenta*, a sore spot for decades in Franco-German relations. 'Think of it always; never speak of it' was their motto; a few who did speak of it before the *First World War got sympathy, but no government backing. During that war it became an acknowledged French grievance.

By the *Versailles settlement of 1919, the provinces again became French, again subject to French law and apparently happy at the change. In the summer of 1940, after the fall of *France (though the point was not covered in the *armistice terms), they were reannexed to Germany, and became part of two *Gaue* (see GAULEITER) in the Third Reich (see Map 43). At a few hours' notice 200,000 French-speaking inhabitants were evicted westwards.

The coking coal was again useful to the German armaments industry. The provinces were subjected to the full rigours of Nazi law—directed labour, directed education, elimination of Jews (see FINAL SOLUTION), restrictions on religious meetings, and conscription. *Prisoners-of-war born in them, captured in the French Army, were most of them simply put into German uniforms and became part of the German Army. Some of the more ardently pro-German were accepted as volunteers for the Waffen-*SS.

The remaining inhabitants, German-speakers but few of them pro-Nazi in sentiment, were given no opportunity to express any feelings of resentment they might have had. In 1945, as automatically as in 1919, they reverted to French control, where they remain.

M. R. D. FOOT

Alsos missions, US intelligence teams dispatched to Europe in 1943–4 to track down Axis scientific research teams. They were particularly interested in the advances made by German scientists, led by Werner *Heisenberg, towards producing an *atomic bomb, but initially a small team was dispatched to Italy by Brig-General Leslie Groves (*alsos* is Greek for 'grove'), the military commander of the American development of the bomb. Nothing of great significance was found there but the fact that such a mission proved feasible led to a much larger team, which included *Counter Intelligence Corps agents and scientists from the *Office of Scientific Research and Development, being sent to north-west Europe after the Normandy landings in June 1944 (see OVERLORD). This team methodically tracked down all suspect scientists, and eventually Heisenberg himself, and established that although German scientists had begun their research into an atomic bomb two years before the Allies they had made little headway.

Goudsmit, S., *Alsos: The Failure of German Science* (London, 1947).

Altmark, a 14,367-ton German tanker employed as the supply ship (see also LOGISTICS) for the pocket battleship *Admiral Graf Spee* when it operated in the South Atlantic and Indian Oceans in 1939. It also acted as a prison ship for the crews of ships which the German warship had sunk. Following the scuttling of the *Admiral Graf Spee*, after the battle of the *River Plate in December 1939, *Altmark* sailed for Germany and on 14 February 1940 her presence off Norway was reported. Captain Philip Vian, commanding a British destroyer flotilla, was ordered to intercept her, but neutral Norwegian destroyers prevented this and *Altmark* escaped into Jössenfjord. On Admiralty instructions Vian entered the fjord in his destroyer *Cossack* and, in a skilled operation which immediately caught the imagination of the British public, boarded *Altmark* and rescued 303 Allied merchant seaman.

Ambrosio, General Vittorio (1879–1958), commander of Italian occupation forces in Yugoslavia before becoming Army Chief of Staff in January 1942. In February 1943 he replaced *Cavallero as Chief of the Italian High Command (see COMANDO SUPREMO), a post in which he intrigued against Mussolini, whose fall he helped to bring about. On 9 September 1943, after the announcement of the Italian *armistice with the Allies, he fled from Rome before the Germans occupied it, and was subsequently appointed minister of war in *Badoglio's government while remaining head of Comando Supremo. In November 1943 he relinquished both posts and was appointed Inspector-General of Italian forces.

America, see USA and LATIN AMERICA AT WAR.

America First Committee, the principal national American organization which sought to mobilize public opinion in the USA against intervention in the European War. Formed in September 1940 in the wake of the fall of *France as questions of aid to the UK arose, America First fought to preserve traditional American non-entanglement in Europe's quarrels. Arrayed against it in the so-called Great Debate of 1940–1 was the *Committee to Defend America by Aiding the Allies and later the even more interventionist *Fight For Freedom Committee.

The instigator of America First was a 24-year-old Princeton graduate at Yale Law School, R. Douglas Stuart Jr. By consulting leading isolationists in Congress and using family connections with prominent businessmen in Chicago, Stuart drew together the diverse voices of non-intervention. He prevailed on General Robert E. Wood, the innovative and reformist head of Sears Roebuck, to become national chairman. Wood had served as quartermaster general of the army in the *First World War and had initially been a supporter of the New Deal. Also active at the national level were the businessmen Hanford MacNider, William H. Regnery, and Jay C. Hormel, former diplomat William R. Castle, William Benton of the University of Chicago, Chester Bowles, advertising executive, Philip LaFollette, former governor of Wisconsin, and the author John T. Flynn. At its peak, membership of America First exceeded 800,000.

America Firsters were strong American nationalists. Like most Americans they were suspicious of Europe, horrified by the bloodshed of the First World War, and disillusioned at the failure of the peace. They had no objection to selling arms to the UK on a cash and carry basis (see NEUTRALITY ACTS), but they did not see Britain or the Soviet Union as an asset to American security, nor Nazi Germany as a threat to it. They argued that the USA should build up its own military forces, defend the *Western Hemisphere, and rely on the broad Atlantic as protection. Involvement in Europe's wars, they believed, would only weaken American democracy.

America First fought an uphill battle. In a time of world peril, its message was essentially negative. It was hard to argue that the USA would be safer in the long run by defending its own side of the Atlantic than by seizing the moment to keep the war on the other side by sustaining the UK, and later the Soviet Union, especially when *German surface raiders, U-boats, and *auxiliary cruisers were already sinking ships off American shores. More than most such national pressure groups, it suffered from the disparate and often contradictory viewpoints of its members. Its core was anti-New Deal Republican, business-oriented, and Midwestern (especially Chicago). This bedrock conservatism sat poorly with liberals, who joined America First in fear that foreign involvement would wreck their domestic reform agenda. Meanwhile the leadership's support of military preparedness discomfited pacifists.

Unwelcome as they were to the national leadership, members of pro-Nazi and fascist organizations strayed into local chapters. One prominent America First speaker proved to be a German agent. The anglophobia of many America Firsters was also a handicap at a time of prevailing sympathy for the UK's plight.

Most damaging to the committee, however, was the reputation it earned for *anti-Semitism as a result of Charles *Lindbergh's speech under its auspices at Des Moines on 11 September 1941. The Lone Eagle, as the famous transatlantic solo pilot was nicknamed, expressed sympathy for Jewish hatred of Nazi Germany but warned against their 'agitating for war.' Tolerance, he said, could not survive war, and the Jewish people would be the first to suffer its loss. Jews carried great weight on the question of intervention, he pointed out, on account of 'their large ownership and influence in our motion pictures, our press, our radio, and our government'.

In spite of its weaknesses and embarrassments,

Fighters belonging to the **American Volunteer Group** known as the 'Flying Tigers'.

America First fought on. Most prominent were its mass rallies with a clutch of admired speakers such as Senator Burton K. Wheeler and Lindbergh. It also organized repeated letter-writing campaigns to Congress, provided speakers for local meetings, sent transcriptions of speeches to radio stations, sponsored polls, and distributed pamphlets, auto stickers, newsletters, and posters.

By the time of *Pearl Harbor in December 1941, the Great Debate had reached a bitter impasse while neither side emerged a clear winner, America First was, in the last analysis, the loser. At no point in the successive battles over intervention—*Lend-Lease, escort of *convoys during the battle of the *Atlantic, repeal of the remaining neutrality acts—did it score a victory. The Roosevelt administration moved warily against the isolationist bloc but never ceased its progressive intervention in the war and the public, by and large, went along with it. America First's fight represented the last stand of American detachment from world politics. It was disbanded after Pearl Harbor. WALDO HEINRICHS

Cole, W. C., *America First: The Battle Against Intervention, 1940–1941* (Madison, Wis., 1953).

Schneider, J. C., *Should America Go to War? The Debate Over Foreign Policy in Chicago, 1939–1941* (Chapel Hill, NC, 1989).

Americal Division, US Army division formed in May 1942 from Task Force 6184 which garrisoned New Caledonia in the *Pacific war. After the destruction of the Philippine division in the *Philippines campaign early in 1942, it was the only division in the US Army to have a name not a number. Its 164th Regiment was one of the first army units into combat when it reinforced US Marines in October 1942 during the *Guadalcanal campaign. The remainder of the division then moved there and its commander, Maj-General *Patch, assumed operational control of the campaign in December 1942. It later fought in the *Bougainville campaign and took part in the second *Philippines campaign.

American Military Mission to China, see CHINA-BURMA-INDIA THEATRE.

American Volunteer Group (AVG). Known as the 'Flying Tigers', because of the bared fangs painted on the noses of their fighters, this formation was the brainchild of Captain *Chennault, a retired US Army Air Corps officer who was an adviser to the Chinese government and a colonel in its air force.

In April 1941 the Chinese agreed to Chennault's scheme that a number of American squadrons, manned by volunteer pilots from the US Army and Navy on one-year contracts, could operate in China against the invading Japanese (see CHINA INCIDENT). About 100 pilots and 200 ground staff were recruited and the British made an air base at Toungoo in Burma available for training, which began in September 1941. By November three squadrons, equipped with Tomahawk (P40) fighters, had been formed there, and Chennault was busy teaching them the tactics he had evolved from years of studying Japanese methods: stay in pairs; don't *dogfight; use the Tomahawk's superior diving speed to make one pass, shoot, and break away (see also FIGHTERS, 2).

Once Japan was at war with the Allies, *Chiang Kai-shek kept a previous promise that the AVG could be employed in Burma if that country were attacked, and one squadron was used to defend Rangoon at the start of the *Burma campaign while the other two were stationed in the Chinese city of Kunming from where they patrolled the *Burma Road. All three squadrons were soon in action when Japanese bombers attempted to raid Kunming on 20 December 1941, and three days later 60 Japanese bombers attacked Rangoon's docks and the AVG's airfield at Mingaladon. Two AVG aircraft were shot down during these encounters, and two more were lost during a raid on Christmas Day, but the AVG and RAF squadrons accounted for 30 Japanese aircraft between them despite being heavily outnumbered.

On 4 January 1942 about 30 Japanese fighters tried to break through Rangoon's air defences but were driven off by the AVG, and on 23 January they launched their main effort to overwhelm the aircraft defending the city. Between that date and 29 January there was continuous fighting above Rangoon in which about 50 Japanese aircraft were probably destroyed while the RAF lost ten and the AVG two. Another, and final, attempt to overwhelm the defences was made on 25 and 26 February, but out of a force of 170 bombers and fighters about 34 were destroyed, most of them by the AVG. This victory enabled ships carrying reinforcements to arrive safely and for the evacuation of Rangoon to proceed without interference. But by 27 February Allied operational air strength had been reduced to only ten fighters, many of which had been damaged or lacked spares, and after the Japanese entered Rangoon on 8 March the surviving AVG aircraft were withdrawn to Magwe. Eventually they joined the other two squadrons in Kunming and were later deployed against Japanese bombers attacking Chinese cities.

It had been hoped that the induction of the AVG into Chennault's new command, the China Air Task Force, which was to be part of Tenth USAAF, would proceed smoothly. But when their contracts ran out in July 1942 only five pilots stayed on though another 20 agreed to remain until replacements could be found.

Total AVG losses amounted to 50 aircraft and 9 pilots for 286 Japanese aircraft destroyed. See also AIR POWER.

Chennault, A., *Chennault and the Flying Tigers* (New York, 1963).

Amiens prison raid. A daylight *precision bombing operation (JERICHO) was mounted against the prison on 18 February 1944 by British aircraft. Its objective was to release important French resistance workers needed to implement sabotage plans once the Normandy landings had taken place in June (see OVERLORD). Out of 1,000 inmates, about 180 of whom were prisoners of the Germans, 87 prisoners were killed but more than 250 escaped. They included Raymond Vivant, a key resistance leader, and twelve other resistance workers who were about to be executed.

amphibians, vehicles for *amphibious warfare, produced mostly by the USA. The most successful were the Alligator, an amphibious tractor officially designated a Land Vehicle, Tracked (LVT); and a six-wheeled, boat-shaped truck called from its factory serial numbers the DUKW (D=model year, U=amphibian, K=all-wheel drive, W=dual rear axles). The LVT developed from vehicles used for rescue purposes in the Florida swamp, was used in the *Pacific war to lift personnel across coral, mud, or swamp, while armoured, gun-carrying LVTs gave covering fire. The British, who called them 'buffaloes', used them during the *Scheldt Estuary battle. DUKWs, of which more than 20,000 were built, were used first in the *Sicilian campaign. The British, who had their own, unsuccessful, amphibious truck called the 'terrapin', acquired 2,000 of them through *Lend-Lease. The Germans manufactured an amphibious Volkswagen car and an amphibious tractor, but the former was used only for reconnoitring Soviet lakes and rivers during the *German–Soviet war, and few of the latter were constructed.

Japan, the UK, the US, and the USSR also converted tanks for amphibious use. British and American ones with propellers and detachable flotation screens were known as DD (duplex drive) tanks, and were widely employed during, and after, the Normandy landings in June 1944 (see OVERLORD).

amphibious warfare is the invasion of enemy-held territory from the sea. In the west it is at least as old as the battle of Marathon (490 BC) while in the Far East Japan had practised it beyond its borders even before then. During the Second World War it meant transporting specially trained troops to a designated landing beach in enemy-held territory; putting them, their tanks, artillery, and stores ashore from *landing craft under an umbrella of supporting fire from the air and sea; and ensuring that the build-up in men and *matériel* was sufficient to overwhelm any opposition and to secure a beachhead from which an advance inland could be made.

Undertaking such an operation implied the full integration of all air, land, and sea forces, from the planning stage onwards, a new concept. Churchill called it triphibious warfare and it was, according to both Admiral *King and *Eisenhower, the most difficult to mount as it required careful planning, special training, and a high degree of technical competence on the part of the participants.

Between 1939 and 1942 methods were crude and techniques often faulty but by 1945 the US Marine Corps in the *Pacific war had brought amphibious warfare near to perfection. Terminology varied, but by 1945 a landing force was normally divided into assault formations, which invariably included a floating reserve; follow-up formations; and build-up formations. Assault formations were 'combat' stowed—that is, supplies and equipment were loaded so that they could be unloaded in the order they were needed ashore—but build-up formations were stowed to make the most economical use of space, while the follow-up formations were a mixture of the other two, which was known as 'tactical' stowing. Assault forces were landed from landing craft or *amphibians formed into 'flights'. A flight usually carried a complete military unit and each was broken down into 'waves'. Each wave was timed to touch down together and they were arranged so that a military unit was landed in the correct tactical order. They were formed up out of gunfire range on a line-of-departure which ran parallel to the landing beaches and was normally marked by control boats. Equipped with special navigational aids, including *radar, the control boats also guided the assault waves in and then shepherded the subsequent traffic to and from the beach, always a major problem in any amphibious operation.

Early amphibious operations did not have this degree of sophistication, but their most important, and most vulnerable, moment was always when the first wave of troops hit the beach, and all calculations, including the complicated timetable for air and sea support, were tied to it. Amphibious doctrine recognized that this moment, generally known as 'H-Hour', could be altered by circumstances beyond the control of the planners after the operation had been launched. If this happened all other activities relating to the landing had to be altered, too, which brought about the terminology, 'H-Hour minus 32 minutes' or 'H-Hour plus 12 minutes'.

The first practitioners of modern amphibious methods were the Japanese, who landed troops from a specially constructed landing ship at Tientsin in 1937 at the start of the *China Incident. But unlike the Allies, whose navies predominated, it was the Japanese Army which developed the necessary expertise in amphibious warfare and developed and constructed the specialized landing craft, and all large amphibious operations were reserved for it. The Japanese Navy, though in theory responsible for the assault phase of any landing, in practice took on a supporting role, its capture of *Wake Island and *Guam being notable exceptions. The necessity for local air and naval supremacy, for careful planning, intelligence, and surprise, were well understood. Night landings were preferred to gain surprise, and to avoid air attacks, but also because the Japanese were adept at night infiltration of their opponents' defences. The principal drawback to landing at night, confusion, they overcame by sound doctrine, rigorous training, the formation of élite troops for arranging the disembarkation, and the liberal use of luminous paint. Japanese amphibious doctrine, though sound, tended to be over-rigid. This gave the participants little flexibility to cope with the unexpected, but the numerous amphibious operations Japan mounted in 1941–2 met with little opposition. It was only the Americans at the battle of *Midway and during the *Guadalcanal campaign—both amphibious operations nipped in the bud—that stopped Japan expanding further.

The Germans mounted the first amphibious operation of the war in Europe, and a brilliantly successful one, when they invaded Norway in April 1940 (see NORWEGIAN CAMPAIGN). Uniquely for them they formed a special temporary joint staff to do so. However, the Wehrmacht was really only geared for land warfare. It jibbed at invading England in 1940 (see SEALION), though it did undertake a number of amphibious operations in the *Baltic Sea in June 1941, and later in the *Black Sea. These were both areas where the Soviet Navy also launched large numbers of landings. Early German pressure during the *German–Soviet war meant that many were undertaken as defensive measures to aid the Red Army on shore and they were often inadequately planned and hastily improvised—according to one Soviet source 61 of the 113 Soviet amphibious operations mounted during the war were prepared in less than 24 hours (see Bartlett below). Proper co-ordination between the services was often lacking. Also, the Soviet Navy had no specialized landing craft, so that the different speeds, general unseaworthiness, and low carrying capacity of the boats used often resulted in troops being landed at different times in insufficient quantity and in the wrong places. Under these circumstances it is laudable that, according to another Soviet statistic, surprise was achieved in 76 of the operations (ibid.).

The Soviets learned quickly from these early mistakes. They continued to lack specialized landing craft (though some were acquired under *Lend-Lease very late in the war), but their later amphibious operations, such as those in Korea, were carefully planned and properly co-ordinated, and had the proper level of air and sea support. By 1945, 40 naval infantry brigades had been formed for amphibious operations, and it has been estimated that 340,000 men took part in them.

Though supporting the Red Army with amphibious operations was one of the Soviet Navy's principal functions, amphibious warfare remained peripheral to Soviet strategy as a whole. To the British and Americans, however, it was central to their conduct of the war. In June 1940, the British, who had practised amphibious warfare for centuries, formed a new headquarters, *Combined Operations, their term for amphibious warfare, to take the war to the Germans. The first permanent, fully integrated, inter-service organization, its major contributions to the Allied war effort were the development of larger landing craft and proper methods of training, and the mounting of a series of raids where many practical lessons were learned. After the *Dieppe raid of August 1942 it was recognized that a heavy preliminary air and sea bombardment was essential. Equally important were surprise, proper intelligence on such matters as beach gradients and heavily defended beaches, and the necessity for close support landing craft which could continue firing until the troops were almost ashore. Inadequate communications also highlighted the necessity for a specialized HQ ship to control the operation, a lack some American operations continued to suffer until January 1944.

The *North African campaign landings of November 1942 were mounted too soon after Dieppe for some of these lessons to have been absorbed, while others were ignored. Lack of training and inadequate surveys of the beaches beforehand caused the loss of 94% of the first wave of landing craft at Algiers and 35% at Casablanca. But there were no specialized beach recovery and repair teams to salvage damaged craft and vehicles; no equipment to bridge the water-gap between landing craft and shore; and no properly trained beach parties for unloading and handling supplies. Men drowned because they were overburdened and the US ship-to-shore technique, where infantry, armour, and artillery all had to be laboriously transferred from large ships to small landing craft, proved unsatisfactory. It was just as well that the maintenance of total secrecy was the one unqualified success of the landings, as this resulted in their being largely unopposed.

By the start of the *Sicilian campaign the following July many of these faults had been corrected. The beaches were properly surveyed by *Combined Operations Pilotage Parties; larger landing craft enabled a shore-to-shore technique to be employed by some of the assault force; specially converted landing craft delivered a last-minute bombardment; and the new amphibian DUKW, pontoon causeways which bridged the water gap, and specially trained beach parties speeded the handling of supplies, armour, and artillery ashore. However, the British did not develop really successful beach organizations—they called them 'bricks'—until the *Salerno landings in September 1943.

The ability of the Americans to match British experience at this time was undoubtedly due to the US Marine Corps who were early experimenters in amphibious techniques and doctrine. Between the wars they had begun to tailor their weapons and tactical units to fit the ships transporting them; experimented with the *Higgins boat and with amphibians; introduced the technique of combat loading; helped evolve the Attack Destroyer Transport designed to carry a marine raiding force; and developed the use of close air support with the navy which had been first practised in Nicaragua in the 1920s.

Their exemplary record in the Pacific notwithstanding, the greatest contribution the marines made to Allied victory was doctrinal. Apart from the six marine divisions which fought in the Pacific war, they trained the 1st and 9th US Infantry Divisions which landed in North Africa, Sicily, and Normandy (see OVERLORD); the 3rd US Infantry Division which landed in North Africa, Sicily, and *Anzio; and the 7th US Infantry Division which recaptured Attu and Kiska during the *Aleutian Islands campaign, seized Kwajalein during the *Marshall Islands campaign, and landed on Leyte (see PHILIPPINES CAMPAIGNS) and on *Okinawa.

Though the marines were brought to the brink of disaster at the start of their first amphibious operation, *Guadalcanal, their doctrine soon proved itself viable, and in *MacArthur's *South-West Pacific Area US forces soon became experts at this kind of operation. Their first real test was a series of operations (CARTWHEEL) designed to isolate and reduce *Rabaul began in June 1943 with the *New Georgia campaign landings. These were accomplished at a speed the Japanese regarded as miraculous and by the time the campaign had been completed, and the *New Guinea and Philippines campaigns also won, MacArthur had become an expert at, to use his own terminology, 'hitting 'em where they ain't'. He was often able to leapfrog heavily defended areas and then isolate them, and could also frequently maintain surprise before landing on comparatively lightly defended beaches. He was also sometimes able to employ the 'amphibious end run' where secondary landings were made to the rear of the main ones. This 'hammer and anvil' effect of crushing the defenders between two blows was used most successfully during the Leyte landings in October 1944. Between Leyte and the end of the Pacific war, MacArthur's Eighth Army made 52 amphibious landings; in one 44-day period there was a landing every day and a half.

The marines who took part in the spectacular drive across the central Pacific, which started in November 1943, fought under different conditions, for their objectives were often too small and too obvious a target to avoid the Japanese defences. Instead, techniques were devised for landing on fortified beaches where surprise or light opposition could be discounted. Known as amphibious assaults, they required the use of armoured amphibians, total isolation of the objective, and heavy, sustained bombardments. To implement them the US Pacific Fleet, supported by a *logistics system astonishing in its scale and efficiency (see also FLEET TRAIN), was divided into three parts: the amphibious force, a vast array of landing ships, transports, and close support craft for landing the marines; the bombardment fleet, which comprised the older battleships supplemented by cruisers and destroyers, and later by escort carriers; and the fleet carriers and their escorts which sealed the objective from any reinforcement and protected the landings from air attack. With surprise of no consequence, bombardments often lasted days, and sometimes weeks, and the landings took place in daylight to maximize the accuracy of the preliminary bombardment.

These techniques only evolved as the Pacific war progressed. Those used at *Tarawa, the first central Pacific objective, failed to work as the bombardment saturated the island without destroying its fortified positions. Because of poor communications (a specialized HQ ship was not used) the bombardment was also lifted too early and there were too few amphibians (LVTs) to cross the coral reefs that, because the tide had been incorrectly assessed, barred the way for landing craft. The result was heavy marine losses with the Japanese very nearly inflicting a crushing defeat on the shoreline.

Improvements followed quickly for the seizure of the Marshall Islands beginning in January 1944. A specialized HQ ship controlled the operation; the preparatory bombardment used interdicting fire from much closer inshore, and was supplemented by artillery positioned on unoccupied islets; star shell was used to illuminate ground liable to night infiltration by the Japanese defenders; and a last-minute bombardment was delivered by specially converted landing craft of which the rocket-firing variety (see ROCKET WEAPONS) were the most deadly. LVTs, which took the entire assault force ashore, were taken as close to the beaches as possible by LSTs, underwater demolition teams were used for the first time to clear natural and man-made obstacles (see FROGMEN), and the US fleet, aided by ground fire control parties, remained to support the advance inland.

These techniques were so successful that they became standard procedure in the Pacific landings which followed. Though these did not always proceed smoothly—the Japanese displayed great courage and ingenuity in countering American tactics on islands such as *Saipan and *Peleliu—the Marshalls was a watershed in amphibious warfare in the Pacific. *Tinian was called 'the perfect amphibious operation of the Pacific war', but the Marshall Islands showed how it should be done and by April 1945, when Okinawa was invaded, the US Navy and Marines had stood on its head the pre-war theory that the best way to defeat an amphibious operation was while it was taking place. At Tarawa the Japanese almost managed to do this, but at Okinawa they did not even attempt to defend the beaches. 'The power of the American warships and aircraft,' commented the Japanese commander on *Iwo Jima which fell in March 1945, 'makes every landing operation possible to whatever beachhead they like.'

In Europe amphibious warfare was shown at its most complex and ingenious during the Normandy landings in June 1944, the largest operation of its kind in the history of warfare. It was mounted in daylight and relied to a large degree on *deception for its ultimate success. Within a month a million men were ashore, an astonishing feat to which every previous Allied amphibious operation of the war had in some way contributed.

The last amphibious operation of the war (ZIPPER) took place after the Japanese had surrendered as it seemed the most practicable way for the British to regain control of Malaya; and on 9 September 1945 their forces landed unopposed near Port Swettenham and north of Port Dickson.

Bartlett, M. (ed.), *Assault from the Sea: Essays on the History of Amphibious Warfare* (Annapolis, MD, 1983).
Clifford, K., *Amphibious Warfare Development in Britain and America from 1920–1940* (NY, 1983; despite its title this covers the whole war).
Fergusson, B., *The Watery Maze* (London, 1961).

Anami Korechika, General (1887–1945), Japanese vice-minister of war in Prince *Konoe's cabinet in 1940 and the leader of the faction which brought General *Tōjō to power in October 1941. He subsequently commanded the Eleventh Army in China (see CHINA INCIDENT) and the Second Area Army in Manchukuo. In November 1943 parts of the Second Area Army were transferred to strengthen Japanese forces fighting in the *New Guinea campaign and Anami took control of operations there. In December 1944 he was made inspector-general of army aviation and chief of the army's aeronautical department before being appointed minister of war in *Suzuki Kantarō's cabinet in April 1945.

In the months that followed he agonized between wanting peace and preventing dishonourable surrender. He was not for peace at any price and was sympathetic towards those who wanted to make a last glorious stand. However, when his support was canvassed by those junior army officers determined to defy the government's decision to surrender, he offered no encouragement. On the evening of 14 August these officers committed the impiety of invading the royal palace to remove the recording of the Emperor *Hirohito's surrender announcement, which was to be broadcast at noon the next day. Anami waited to ensure that this insurrection had failed and then committed *seppaku* (see BUSHIDŌ) in expiation of the army's sins. His suicide ended any confusion and any further possibility of revolt by the army against the surrender decision.

Andaman and Nicobar Islands, adjacent groups in the Bay of Bengal (Indian Ocean) which were administered by India. In March 1942, after Rangoon had fallen to the Japanese at the start of the *Burma campaign, the British garrison was withdrawn. The same month the islands were occupied by the Japanese who, at the end of 1943, handed over their administration, but not their defence, to Subhas Chandra *Bose's Provisional government of Free India. The islands were strategically placed but in December 1943 it was decided at the Cairo conference (see SEXTANT) to postpone a plan (BUCCANEER) to capture them—all available landing craft were needed for the Normandy landings in Europe (see OVERLORD)—and the Japanese garrison, harassed by Allied air raids, remained there until the war ended.

Anders' Army. Popular name given to the 2nd Polish Corps which fought in the *Italian campaign under the command of General Władysław Anders (1892–1970).

After the German attack on the Soviet Union in June 1941 (see BARBAROSSA), the signing of the Polish–Soviet Treaty (see POLAND, 2) provided for the release of all Polish citizens (an estimated 1.5 million) held captive by the Soviet authorities and for the formation of Polish military units on Soviet soil. To command the new force the Polish C-in-C, General *Sikorski, chose Anders, a cavalry officer, who had been wounded and captured during the *Polish campaign and later held in Moscow's Lubianka prison. Only army units were to be organized on Soviet soil (navy and air force personnel were to be sent to the UK). It was agreed that these would owe allegiance to the Polish government-in-exile in London (see POLAND, 2(e)) but would be under Soviet operational control. They were to be armed and supplied by the Soviets, partly using *Lend-Lease supplies. A full military agreement was signed in Moscow on 14 August and a Polish headquarters established at Buzuluk on 18 August.

Once news spread that the army was forming, Poles began to flood from all parts of the Soviet Union to join up. Most were in the last stages of hunger and exhaustion, and many did not survive the long journeys. By mid-October 1941 some 25,000 officers and men had enlisted. Recruits were directed to the 5th Infantry Division forming at Tatishchevo on the River Volga, and the 6th Division at Totsk. In the early part of 1942 the Polish forces moved to locations near the Chinese and Afghan borders. Most of the camps they occupied were in the Uzbek Republic, with headquarters at Jangi-Jul, situated between Samarkand and Tashkent.

Towards the end of 1941 Polish–Soviet relations began to sour. Anders insisted that he would not send any of his units to the Russian front unless they were fully armed and supplied. The Soviet government for its part refused to allow recruitment to the Polish units of Ukrainians, Belorussians, and Jews from the Polish eastern provinces occupied by the Red Army in 1939. Evidence reached the Polish authorities of Soviet reluctance to release Poles in some areas. Moreover, there was great concern about the non-appearance of several thousand Polish officers known to have been captured by the Red Army in 1939 (see KATYŃ).

In December 1941 Sikorski, as head of the Polish government-in-exile, visited Moscow to discuss these and other difficulties with Stalin. It was agreed that the Poles could form six divisions of some 11,000 men each, with a reserve of 30,000 (i.e. some 96,000 men in all). Subsequently, however, Soviet attitudes hardened. On 18 March 1942 when the strength of the army had reached 72,000, Stalin told Anders that owing to supply difficulties the Polish force would have to be cut to 44,000 men. As a result of this decision, a partial evacuation of some 33,000 troops was made to British control in Persia, transports crossing the Caspian Sea from Krasnovodsk to Pahlevi. When it became clear that the Soviets were not going to arm more than one division, Anders, who had never trusted Stalin's good intentions, evacuated the remaining 44,000 troops, plus large numbers of civilian dependants, in August. This exodus brought further evidence of the *GUlag and the system of *forced labour it employed.

Once they had crossed the border into Persia, Anders' units were merged with Polish units in the Middle East and came under the command of the British Persia and Iraq Force (see PAIFORCE). A corps was formed which incorporated General Kopański's *Carpathian Brigade. The 2nd Polish Corps was structured along British lines and during 1942–3, as part of Paiforce, took on the role of defending the Iraqi oilfields, whilst engaging in intensive training and manoeuvres. In August 1943 the corps was transferred to Palestine where more than 3,000 out of the 4,000 soldiers of Jewish origin became *deserters. Many of them, including Menachem *Begin, joined underground terrorist organizations. In November it moved to Egypt, where it made final preparations for taking part in the Italian campaign. At this point the corps included the 3rd Carpathian Rifle Division, the 5th Border Infantry Division, two armoured brigades, an artillery group, and a reconnaissance regiment, with communications, sapper battalions, and so on. It numbered some 52,000 men.

During the first weeks of 1944, the 2nd Polish Corps became involved in the *Italian campaign, where it came under the operational command of the British Eighth Army. It was based initially in the River Sangro area and in May, along with the British 10th and 13th Corps, took part in the final, successful *Monte Cassino battle. After a week of fighting, Polish troops eventually stormed the monastery, moving on to dislodge a further German stronghold at Piedimonte. The defeat of the German stronghold at Cassino opened the road north to Rome, but in June the Poles were directed east to the Adriatic coast. They took a leading part in the battles for Ancona (July 1944), against the *Gothic Line, and for Pescara and Faenza, and in April 1945 they took Bologna, in the last major battle of the Italian campaign (see ARGENTA GAP). In a tribute to the Poles, Lt-General *McCreery pointed out that the corps had faced three of the Germans' best divisions and had pushed them back. In the process, though, they suffered more than 11,000 casualties.

At the end of the war General Anders' troops were engaged in occupation duties in Italy. Their presence proved something of a magnet for the many displaced Poles and released Polish *prisoners-of-war who found themselves in Austria or southern Germany. Anders and the majority of his men were bitterly opposed to the Teheran–Yalta accords, under which Poland was apportioned to the Soviet sphere of influence (see GRAND ALLIANCE). They refused to return to Poland under communist rule, and in late 1946 were transported to the UK where they were demobilized (see POLISH RESETTLEMENT CORPS). In September 1946 the provisional government in Warsaw stripped Anders and

US Marine Raider patrol on Bougainville, December 1943. Dogs were one of the most useful **animals** in the Pacific war, where thick jungle made them invaluable scouts.

75 other officers of their Polish citizenship—in Anders' case, for 'conducting abroad activities detrimental to the Polish State'. KEITH SWORD

Anders, W., *An Army in Exile* (London, 1981).
General Sikorski Institute, London, *Polskie Siły Zbrojne w II Wojnie Swiatowej, Vol. II, part 2 (London, 1975).*

Anderson shelter, standard British garden bomb shelter erected by bolting together two curved walls of corrugated galvanized steel in a 3 ft. (.91 m.) pit and then covering them with earth. Designed by William Paterson it was named after the Lord Privy Seal, John Anderson, who was given special responsibility for British civil defence (see UK, 6) in 1938. Two million were issued free during the early months of the war until a shortage of steel led to their being discontinued.

Anglo-Soviet Treaty, signed by the British foreign secretary, Anthony *Eden, and his Soviet counterpart, Vyacheslav *Molotov, in London on 26 May 1942. It was preceded by tough negotiations in which the British refused to acknowledge Stalin's demands for recognition of the USSR's boundaries prior to the start of the *German–Soviet war in June 1941 which encompassed eastern Poland and the Baltic states. However, it decreased both parties' fears by stipulating that no armistice or peace with Germany or its Axis allies would be negotiated or concluded by one party without the consent of the other. Other clauses expressed the willingness of both parties to help each other in the war against Germany and that both parties were bound by the 'two principles of not seeking territorial aggrandisement for themselves and of non-interference in the internal affairs of other states'. Other clauses detailed joint actions to be taken after the war.

animals were employed by every combatant country for a variety of tasks, including transporting supplies (see LOGISTICS), hauling artillery, finding mines, and as mascots.

General *Slim listed *carrier pigeons, dogs, ponies, mules, horses, bullocks, buffaloes, and elephants as all being used by his Fourteenth Army in the *Burma campaign. His elephant companies helped build hundreds of bridges as well as laying log causeways, launching ships, and transporting supplies. The Japanese used elephants to transport mortars and ammunition during their advance into Burma from Thailand in 1941 and they used a column of 350 of them during their *Imphal offensive in March 1944. The British prized them highly and managed to capture more than 1,600 from the Japanese.

During the *North African campaign the British Royal Army Service Corps formed animal transport companies which each contained 308 load-carrying mules. As every mule could carry 72 kg. (160 lb.) this gave each company the ability to 'lift' about 22 tons. Mules were also used extensively during the *Sicilian and *Italian campaigns with the Fifth US Army employing fifteen Italian pack trains totalling nearly 4,000 mules in the Apennines during the last winter of the war. In Italy the *French Expeditionary Corps, whose North African *Goums were skilled in mountain warfare, were almost entirely reliant on them for their logistics.

But, as in the *First World War, the horse was the most commonly used animal in combat. Cavalry was more widely employed than might be supposed and two American generals, *Patton and *Truscott, were convinced that if they had had a cavalry division during the Sicilian campaign they could have prevented Axis forces from escaping across the Straits of Messina. The French and the Poles used cavalry units during the first months of the war, as did the British. The last cavalry charge of the war probably took place in November 1941, when the Red Army's 44th Mongolian Cavalry Division was wiped out near the village of Musino by a German infantry division during the *German–Soviet War, but the Red Army, as well as the Germans (see SOVIET EXILES AT WAR) and Japanese, continued to use cavalry divisions throughout the war for patrolling and mopping-up operations.

Horses were most commonly used for hauling guns and transport wagons, with the German Army relying on them the most. In 1939 a German infantry division required between 4,077 and 6,033 horses to move, and even panzer divisions used them. The Germans assembled 625,000 horses for the invasion of the USSR in June 1941 (see BARBAROSSA). Of these 180,000 were lost during the first winter. The casualty rates for horses on the Eastern Front were staggeringly high, with the USSR, which also used horses extensively until *Lend-Lease trucks became available, losing two-thirds of its 21 million horses.

Dogs were used for patrol and guard duties—one was reportedly parachuted on operations mounted by the *Special Air Service—and in the *Pacific war scout dogs were trained to detect Japanese troops at 27 m. (30 yd.) in all conditions and sometimes as far away as 275 m. (300 yd.). The UK and USSR also trained dogs to detect mines, engineers using them throughout the *Normandy campaign of June–August 1944, and later in the Netherlands. One Soviet mine dog, called Zucha, apparently found 2,000 mines in 18 days. The Red Army also used dogs to destroy German tanks by training them to crawl under them. An explosive charge with a trigger device was strapped to the animal's back and when the trigger device touched the tank's underside it detonated the 11.8 kg. (26 lb.) charge. During the *Stalingrad and *Kursk battles 25 tanks were destroyed by dogs, but the method proved a double-edged weapon as the animals, having been trained with Soviet tanks, were more inclined to crawl under them than under German ones. An astonishing variety of animals was kept by many members of the armed forces of the combatant nations as pets and mascots, but perhaps the most unusual was Wojtek, a brown bear cub acquired by soldiers of *Anders' Army in Persia. Wojtek saw action during the battle for *Monte Cassino with the 22nd Transport Company of the Polish Army Service Corps when he helped move ammunition boxes. After the war he was given to Edinburgh zoo and lived to the age of 22.

Cooper, J., *Animals in War* (London, 1983).
Williams, J. H., *Elephant Bill* (London, 1950).

Anschluss (joining together), Germany's annexation of Austria in March 1938.

anti-aircraft guns, see ARTILLERY.

Anti-Comintern pact, an agreement between Germany and Japan, signed in November 1936, to exchange information on the activities of Soviet-backed international communist parties (see COMINTERN). Hitler wanted a stronger anti-Soviet commitment from Japan, which was traditionally opposed to Russian expansion in Asia. But Japan had no desire to be drawn into a European war and was only encouraged to sign after the USSR had made a treaty of mutual assistance with Outer Mongolia the previous April which Japan saw as threatening its interests. A secret protocol pledged the signatories to neutrality if one of them was at war with the USSR, but the pact was not a military alliance and the protocol did not apply to Italy when it joined in November 1937—by which time the pact appeared more anti-British than anti-Soviet. Two years later Hungary, Manchukuo, and Spain joined, and in November 1941 Bulgaria, Croatia, Denmark, Finland, Romania, *Wang Ching-wei's government in Nanking (see CHINA, 3(b)), and Slovakia also signed. See also DIPLOMACY.

anti-imperialism. The Second World War is widely believed to have encouraged the forces of anti-imperialism within the international system at large and undermined the viability of the various European colonial empires. John Darwin, for example, has argued (in his book *Britain and Decolonization, Retreat from Empire in the Post-War World*, Basingstoke, 1989) that it was this experience and its effects which functioned as the 'trigger' for the long fuse of British decolonizations which exploded at intervals in subsequent decades, while one of the few major texts focusing on colonial aspects of the 1939–45 struggle, by Wm. Roger Louis, is tellingly entitled *Imperialism at Bay* (Oxford, 1977). Paradoxically, other historians have been impressed by the fact that the same years witnessed a remarkable *revival* of imperial confidence and virility, not least in the case of the UK (for example, see J. Gallagher, *The Decline, Revival and Fall of the British Empire*, Cambridge, 1982).

The colonized areas most dramatically affected were those in South-East Asia following the outbreak of the *Pacific war. There the assault on the status quo, with its medley of British, French, Dutch, and American administrations, lent itself easily to Japanese propaganda as 'a sacred war for the liberation of Asia', and the fall of *Singapore—the greatest *imperial* military defeat suffered by the British since Yorktown in 1781—was a massive blow to European (i.e. white) mystique throughout the region. Nor, for all the lasting resentments that they were undoubtedly to bring upon themselves, did Japanese invocations to their *Greater East Asia Co-Prosperity Sphere as an authentic Asian nationalism fall upon deaf ears. As one Indian administrator employed in the

Malayan Civil Service later recalled his volatile emotions, 'though his reason utterly rebelled against it, his sympathies had instinctively ranged themselves in their Japanese fight against the Anglo-Saxons'; one may guess that at the time reason was even more pliable than such recollections allow. The persecution disproportionately suffered by Chinese individuals and communities at the hands of the *Kempei (the Japanese secret police) naturally made them less susceptible to the siren calls of Tokyo, many fleeing into the Malayan countryside to escape; ironically, the guns which the British filtered through to the Chinese resistance groups which then established themselves were later (in the post-1948 'Emergency') to be turned against themselves. In China proper, however, the legacy of *Chiang Kai-shek's misrule and corruption meant that the Japanese were not without their supporters even there. Racial exclusivity, in short, was the Achilles' heel of the Western, self-proclaimedly 'democratic', powers in the Orient, and it was one that they were never entirely able to recover from.

The effects of Japanese rule on conquered territories were more profound than the implications flowing from the humiliating sight of Europeans boxed into their prison-cages. In identifying local politicians with whom they could work, the Japanese authorities provided openings for such figures as 'Engineer' *Sukarno in Java, *Ba Maw in Burma, and Subhas Chandra *Bose as 'Great Leader and Hero' of the *Indian National Army, to sharpen their own brand of often charismatic anti-imperial leadership, and more widely nurtured the development of a secular politics which the Europeans had long sought to repress. One historian has, indeed, emphasized a qualitative difference in the methods employed by Europeans and Japanese in ruling subordinate populations in this part of the world. Where the former before 1942 had blocked off avenues by which local people might project themselves into the public arena, promoting instead the virtues of family life in the villages, the Japanese actually encouraged group endeavours in sports associations, religious organizations and even, in the Putera movement in Java, embracing displays of martial arts. Of course, all this hectic activity was intended to be firmly at Tokyo's behest, but there was implicit in it a measure of mobilization, of refreshing innovation, which was not easily compatible with any future restoration of European hegemony. The parting gesture by which the Japanese, with defeat looming in 1945, allowed power to be usurped by those indigenous elements least likely to welcome the Europeans back into their traditional haunts—such as the communists under *Ho Chi Minh in French Indo-China—only capped this situation. 'The Japanese', remarked one French observer who had spent most of the war imprisoned in Batavia, 'though defeated in a general sense, have "won the war" in this corner of Asia.'

The Middle East, including North Africa, was the other major region outside Europe whose internal politics and society were most directly affected by the war. The fall of *France in June 1940 excited hopes of a rapid advance to freedom among Syrian and Lebanese nationalists; at the same time it heightened French determination to keep a grip on those overseas possessions which were now virtually that country's sole claim to Great Power status. This was a recipe for confusion and bloodshed; it culminated in the disastrous French cannonade on Damascus in November 1944. The unseemly mess in the Levant in which *Vichy Frenchmen fought with their Gaullist compatriots, and where British and French 'allies' were constantly at verbal and sometimes even physical odds with each other, sapped collective European prestige among the indigenous inhabitants much as in the Far East. Furthermore, if the British hoped to gain some scarce credit with Arab opinion by distancing themselves from French reaction in the region, they were soon disappointed. The emergence of a pro-German element in Iraq, and the investment of the RAF garrisons in that country during April 1941, were important in highlighting just how fragile the British imperium was in much of the Middle East. The revolt in Iraq was put down, and pro-British politicians propped up anew, but the episode left a strain of bitterness which continued into the post-war world and came to a climax with the revolution in Baghdad in 1958.

It was Egypt, the 'main base' of the UK's 'Mediterranean Strategy', where the political and social consequences of the war in the Middle East were, however, to be most pronounced. With so many expatriate personnel crammed into strange and often congested conditions, it was predictable that relations with the local population should prove unstable. Thus the 'tarbush game'—revolving around the purloining of headgear from innocent passers-by—became a favourite competitive pastime for off-duty English squaddies roaming the streets of the Egyptian capital. Anglo-Egyptian dealings at a personal level had never been easy; under the pressure of war they were to become more brittle than ever, until by 1945 the ill-feeling which contributed to the Suez débâcle just over a decade later was plainly to be seen. But social matters, with their racial connotations, apart, the very salience of Egypt for the British war effort gave rise to political misunderstandings which military success, initially against the Italians, and later (after many setbacks) against *Rommel's *Afrika Korps, only served to accentuate. Local newspapers and other organs of opinion held that the British could never have succeeded in holding on to their position in North Africa without the help and co-operation of Egypt, so that the latter should be rewarded immediately with *Istiqual-el-tam*, or complete independence (as opposed to the quasi-independence which had prevailed since 1922); the English, on the other hand, thought that the Egyptians should be grateful for having been saved from German and Italian clutches, and never ceased impressing the fact upon them. This missing of minds and sympathies was perhaps most starkly illustrated by the incident in 1942 when the

British High Commissioner, Sir Miles Lampson, furious at the appointment of an anti-British premier by King Farouk (1920–65), surrounded the Abdin Palace with troops and browbeat the monarch into changing his nominee. In London this was regarded as an impressive display of strength, Lampson himself being elevated to the peerage, but the underlying effect was to humiliate the royal house on which the British connection had long depended for some of its access to political decision-making in Cairo. Decolonization, it has been alleged, is at bottom the result of imperial systems running out of the collaborators on which their local foundations rest; in Egypt the British had virtually exhausted its always scarce reserves of this commodity by the end of the Second World War.

Although India did not become an 'active' theatre, except very marginally, after 1939, the fortunes of imperialism and anti-imperialism were deeply affected by events. By declaring war against Germany on India's behalf as well as its own, without any attempt to sound indigenous opinion, the British government allowed the initiative within the Indian National Congress (see INDIA, 3) to swing back towards the 'extremists'—including *Gandhi and *Nehru—who had opposed any participation in the British reforms under the 1935 government of India Act. All provincial Congress governments immediately resigned from office. Afterwards the crucial issue was whether the imperial administration would 'go the whole hog' and impose a war economy without negotiation with popular politicians, or strike a bargain in which concessions regarding a move to self-government were traded against Congress's assistance in mobilizing military resources. Since bargaining with Indians was one of Churchill's pet aversions, it was probably inevitable that the talks between the mission led by Stafford *Cripps and leading Indian nationalists in March 1942 should break down over what appeared to be points of detail. The 'Quit India' rebellion which followed in August of that year was the biggest such protest since the Mutiny of 1857–8; it ended with the incarceration of almost the entire echelon of senior Congress leaders. Having Gandhi, the 'seditious fakir' of old, behind bars again was one of Churchill's 'finest hours' during the course of the Second World War; whilst the manner in which Congress nationalism was swept off the streets of the cities, and the sub-continent applied anew to great imperial purposes, was an achievement which few Englishmen a few years before would have believed possible.

In India, however, as in Egypt, there was a high political and psychological price to pay for this vicarious triumph. The Raj had always been based on a complex system of compromises and accommodations with local society; in squeezing recruits and commodities out of this greatest of dependencies the bureaucracy proceeded to break many of the unwritten rules on which its acceptability had been based. To give just one instance: in fending off the famine in Bengal during 1942–3 threatening the entire war effort in the region, the surplus grain of the Punjab became liable to official sequestration, causing intense alienation among the rich peasant classes on whose co-operation the status quo depended. British rule in that strategic province was never to be the same again. More widely than this, industrialization and urbanization arising from the economic growth which war has always brought in its wake altered Indian society to a degree that made the 'thin white line' of alien rule suddenly appear unsustainable in the longer, or even medium, term; when General *Auchinleck returned in 1943 as C-in-C he found that he scarcely recognized the country in which many years of his professional life had been passed. These new, and inevitably unruly, conditions meant that by the end of the war British guarantees of 'law and order' in India, the basic test of any presiding power, had ceased to be credible. Overall, in India the hopes of the anti-imperialists after September 1939, that their foreign masters would quickly be forced into a political capitulation, were frustrated, but they had the more leisurely consolation (often in captivity) of watching the British sink deeper and deeper into a political quagmire largely of their own making. When Churchill told R. A. Butler in 1945 that all that remained for the UK in its once so lustrous 'jewel' was to get her army and administrators out in one piece, and leave the locals to a 'good civil war' of their own, he was only evoking with a typically savage twist what everyone knew to be the case.

Compared to the Middle East and Asia, sub-Saharan Africa was a backwater in the military history of the era. In the *First World War there had been large-scale campaigning between British and German forces in East Africa, with much disruption to native life; during the Second the fighting was on a much smaller scale (see DAKAR EXPEDITION and the FEZZAN and GABON CAMPAIGNS). The impact on social and economic structures, though less than in India, was none the less of great importance for the future. In the words of the British Colonial Secretary, Lord Cranborne, after early 1942 colonial Africa became 'a vast armoury for the war effort', and in tracing what this meant in practice one scholar has remarked that Tanganyika came to experience 'colonialism with the gloves off'; much the same could be said for other territories. Yet if some Africans lost out materially during the conflict, others indubitably gained on the inflationary roller-coaster that was set in motion, so that in general the result was a more stratified and combustible society. 'The war had brought more division because it had brought more money,' John Lonsdale has commented in his article 'The Depression and the Second World War in the Transformation of Kenya' (D. Killingray and R. Rathbone (eds), *Africa and the Second World War*, London, 1986, p. 125). 'Money brought more politics.' This expanded politics set black increasingly against black in the struggle for the post-colonial succession whose outlines now became discernible, and the climax of which in

Kenya was to be the Mau Mau 'emergency' in the 1950s. Most importantly, or at least more vividly, it set white settlers against the African majority, since the former were able to exploit the administrative machinery of war in those colonies where they were concentrated to regain a primacy which had slipped away from them during the preceding depression. In this sense the war established the terms on which black nationalism and white privilege were to vie after 1945, though the structural shift which also took shape at this time, from an 'old' Africa, with its close European supervision and collaborationist tribal chiefs, to the 'new' Africa with mushrooming cities and a recognizably modern proletariat, may be said to have made the final outcome inevitable.

Finally, what of the argument that the war gave an immense boost to anti-imperialism in general within the world political system? In this regard emphasis is usually given to the *Atlantic Charter of August 1941, in which Roosevelt manoeuvred a reluctant Churchill into issuing a joint statement, Article III of which asserted 'the right of all peoples to choose the form of government under which they will live'. Scarcely was this declaration made before the British leader began to backtrack by pointing out that the principle only applied in Europe, while simultaneously promoting an alternative ethic of 'What We Have We Hold'. Yet the Charter did give an ideological and, as it were, moral respectability to anti-imperialism which it had previously lacked; certainly the self-confidence and maturity evident in the Pan-African Congress held in Manchester in July 1945 would have been inconceivable six years earlier. By much the same token, imperial agencies were forced (if only to deflect American criticisms) to adopt more respectable rationales and methods than hitherto; the British colonial office, for example, spent much of its war evolving a fresh credo for empire summed up in the phrase 'Development and Welfare'. Under the exigencies of the moment this may not have meant a great deal, but before long such liberal presuppositions were to limit critically the options open to imperial rulers when faced with recurrent challenges after 1945. The world did not as a consequence become the oyster for the enemies of territorial empire, but it did become a safer place in which to conduct their activities than it had been before the conflagration began (though even here there were bloody exceptions to prove the rule, as the massacre of Muslim protesters at Sétif in French Algeria during May 1945 illustrated). Perhaps even more telling in the end was the fact that the two main 'victor' powers of the Second World War—the USA and the USSR—were both, in their different guises, ill-disposed to European colonialism, so that as time went by the British, French, Dutch, Belgian, and Portuguese empires were to be deprived of the oxygen they needed to survive.

Any discussion of imperialism and its antithesis, however, must always end in caveats and ambiguities, and this one is no exception. 'It is our turn to bat in Asia,' an American official encapsulated what was, for him, the real benefit of the sacrifices that had been made in the Second World War, while the Yalta agreements of February 1945 (see GRAND ALLIANCE) meant that it was the Soviet Union's turn to bat in Eastern Europe. The upheavals between 1939 and 1945 did not, therefore, so much resolve the issue between imperialism and anti-imperialism, as shake up the *dramatis personae* in the perennial contest for mastery between nations, peoples, and élites. See also COLLABORATION and Map H.

ROBERT HOLLAND

Benda, H., *The Crescent and the Rising Sun: Indonesian Islam and the Japanese Occupation, 1942–45* (The Hague, 1958).
Killingray, D., and Rathbone, R. (eds.), *Africa and the Second World War* (London, 1986).
Thorne, C., *Allies of a Kind: The United States, Britain and the War against Japan, 1941–5* (London, 1978).
—— *The Issue of War: States, Societies and the Far Eastern Conflict of 1941–45* (London, 1985).

anti-Semitism is not a concept on which there can be any general consensus. Its dictionary meaning, 'hatred of Jews', gives only limited guidance, since the term is used to refer to a very wide range of attitudes, from petty prejudice to genocide. Many Jewish authors maintain that anti-Semitism is a unique phenomenon, that the *Final Solution during the Second World War was the culmination of 2,000 years of Christian anti-Semitism. Religious, political, economic, social, and racial categories of anti-Semitism are often distinguished. Other commentators, in contrast, would argue that anti-Semitism is just one variant of the racism and xenophobia that can be found among members of any community, including Jews. The racist anti-Semitism which was propagated in Nazi Germany is often set apart from the kind of recriminations against Jews which flourished alongside other similar intercommunal antagonisms, especially in the multi-ethnic societies of eastern Europe. More recently, anti-Semitism has been used to describe widespread prejudice in the western world against Arabs (who, like the Jews, are Semites).

Anti-Semitism of the most virulent racist type formed a central theme of *Nazi ideology. In **Mein Kampf*, Hitler made numerous ugly references to the Jews as 'parasites' and 'degenerates' whose presence was supposedly poisoning the purity of German blood. He also identified Communism as a Jewish movement, giving the struggle against 'Jewish Bolshevism' the highest priority in his programme. Once in power the Nazis gave legal expression to their views. According to the Nuremberg Laws of 1935, it was a criminal offence for Jews and non-Jews to marry or to have sexual intercourse. Jewishness was defined by kinship criteria within three generations, and was used to withdraw civil rights from all people coming within its purview. Jews were not the only group to be classed as *Untermenschen* or 'sub-humans', nor were they the only people to be murdered en masse, simply for what they were. But the so-called Final Solution of

1941–5 was certainly the largest single campaign of genocide which the Nazis put into execution.

It is relevant to note that Nazi anti-Semitism flourished in a country where the Jews represented less than 1% of the population and where they were highly assimilated into German culture. It would seem that the more extreme anti-Semitic fantasies thrived on the fact that the scapegoats were scarce. It is difficult to say how many Germans shared the Nazis' views and how many rejected them in private, but there were few public protests.

In Poland, where the Jewish community was ten times larger than in Germany and much less assimilated, racist anti-Semitism of the Nazi type was rare. Tensions between Jews and non-Jews had certainly been rising in the last years before the war, and they were to rise still further in 1939 when the Jews of eastern Poland were widely suspected of welcoming the Soviet invasion. The nationalist wing of public opinion had always been notoriously xenophobic, and the various religious and ethnic minorities had to suffer a tide of threats, jibes, and petty discrimination. Religious anti-Semitism involving the ancient 'blood-libel' was not uncommon. At the same time, pre-war Poland had granted far-reaching political and cultural autonomy to the Jewish *kahals*, or communes. Since the Middle Ages legal *ghettos had disappeared, until their formation by the Nazis in 1939–40, and organized violence was at most sporadic. The *SS located their death camps (see OPERATION REINHARD) in occupied Poland for the simple reason that the majority of the intended victims lived there: they could *not* count on any significant measure of support from a Polish population which was itself terrorized. In the period of segregation, a class of *szmalcowniks* or 'greasers' was used by the *Gestapo to betray fugitive Jews for money. (The Gestapo had a similar practice of keeping Jewish informers alive on licence in order to report on the Polish underground.) Despite widespread apathy and complacency in Poland about the fate of the Jews, many individuals risked their lives in order to render assistance (see ZEGOTA). The most eloquent commentary on Polish anti-Semitism is to be found at the Yad-Vashem Holocaust Memorial Centre in Jerusalem, where Polish names form the largest single group in the avenue of 'the Righteous among Nations'.

Elsewhere in Europe the patterns of anti-Semitism were extremely varied. There was a strong dislike of Jews in many English upper-class and academic circles, and British attitudes were also coloured by the activities of Zionist terrorists in Palestine (see IRGUN and STERN GANG). France received a large influx of Jewish refugees in the period preceding the German occupation, and popular reactions were not always generous. French police in the occupied zone, like the *Vichy authorities in the south, followed Nazi demands to round up Jews for deportation. Hitler's fascist allies in Italy were less enthusiastic, and Italy's Jewish community was largely left intact, though similar laws to the Nuremberg ones were passed in November 1938 (in the provisions for the Defence of the Italian Race). The Dutch also gained a good reputation, although only 20% of the Jews in the Netherlands survived. Hungary's Jews stayed in place as long as the *Horthy regime was in power. In the brief German occupation of 1944–5, the Hungarian Arrow Cross (see HUNGARY, 3) collaborated willingly. But others, such as *Wallenberg, made elaborate attempts to limit the deportations. Romania witnessed a wave of native pogroms in 1939–41, long before the Nazis arrived to finish the job more systematically. In the Baltic States, the Nazis recruited auxiliary units to assist in their work. In Ukraine, it was reported that civilians spontaneously joined in the murderous work of the **Einsatzgruppen*. In the Soviet Union, anti-Semitism was officially regarded as a vice exclusive to the fascist enemy, but in practice it was alive and growing. The Stalinist purges against the old Bolsheviks, many of whom were Jewish, had heightened the climate of suspicion; and no arrangements were made to evacuate Jews from areas threatened in 1941–2 by the Nazi advance. It is often said that a full-scale anti-Semitic purge was only prevented by Stalin's death in 1953.

In any fair analysis, however, collective guilt and stereotypes are to be avoided. Anti-Semitism could be found in most countries, while no nation could be collectively characterized as anti-Semitic. The climate of public opinion was usually set by political regimes, but individual reactions to that climate were often unpredictable.

NORMAN DAVIES

anti-submarine weapons. The object of an anti-submarine (A/S) weapon was (and is) to pierce or rupture a submarine's pressure hull and let the submariner's worst enemy—the sea itself—make the kill. Although only tactical A/S weapons are reviewed here, ground and moored mines (see MINE WARFARE, 2) were responsible for numerous submarine losses during the Second World War—probably one-third of those suffered by the Royal Navy.

A submarine on the surface, or to a lesser extent at periscope/**Schnorchel* depth, was vulnerable to *torpedoes fired by other submarines as well as to guns, air-dropped weapons, or ramming; but, except when torpedoed by a submerged submarine, a boat could often dive deep quickly enough to avoid being hit provided that a sharp visual or electronic lookout was being kept. It was therefore imperative for A/S units, aircraft in particular, to attack without delay, which led to more than a few 'own goals' due to wrong identification. The most effective aerial means of detecting a submarine on the surface was centimetric *radar; at night this could be used in conjunction with a powerful *searchlight. The Americans also developed the Magnetic Anomaly Device (MAD) to detect submarines from the air, even when submerged, and a Catalina *flying boat had the first success with this when it sank a U-boat in the Straits of Gibraltar in 1944.

If a submarine was fully submerged the hunters had to explode a weapon in the right position at the right depth

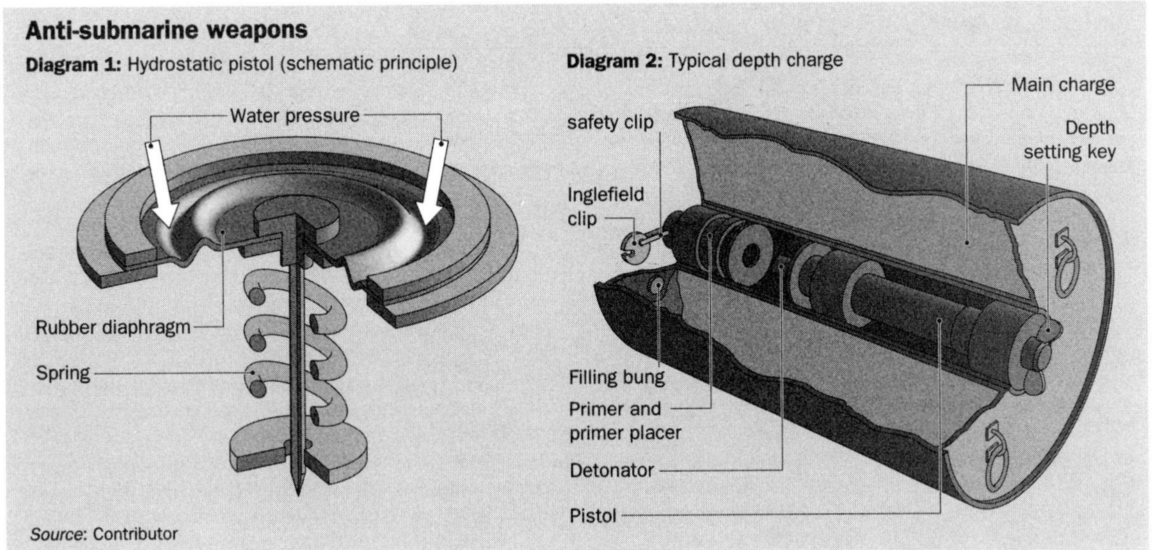

Source: Contributor

which might be anything down to 300 m. (985 ft.). The exact depth was always hard to estimate. Moreover, an attack could often be predicted by a submarine commander who was able to alter course, speed, and depth drastically, and/or release a bubble-making decoy (the Germans called the device a *Pillenwerfer*) at the critical time.

A single A/S weapon stood little chance of success unless it had a homing capability: the US Navy therefore produced the Fido air-dropped, acoustic-homing torpedo in 1943 (see also GUIDED WEAPONS). The Japanese developed a non-homing torpedo that spiralled down to 200 m. (656 ft.) in the (mostly vain) hope of hitting its target at some point.

The most common weapon was the depth charge (D/C). Similar in all navies, it was simply a strong canister of high explosive—90–136 kg. (198–300 lb.) in weight but less for small patrol craft—actuated by a hydrostatic device at a pre-set depth. The British 'Mark VII Heavy' had the deepest maximum setting at 259 m. (850 ft.): lethal range was 9 m. (29.5 ft.). D/Cs dropped from aircraft had fins like the A/S bombs aircraft also carried. Typically, surface warships dropped D/Cs in patterns, like the Five of Clubs, with a spacing of 37–55 m. (120–180 ft.), three being rolled over rails at the stern and one being discharged on each quarter by throwers. A depth bracket could be achieved by alternating heavy charges (quicker sinking) with lighter ones. Of all German U-boats destroyed 43% were sunk with D/Cs.

The attacker's *ASDIC lost contact in the final 180 m. (590 ft.) of a D/C run over the target: that 'deaf-time' as it was called, together with the D/Cs' sinking time, afforded the submarine precious moments to take vigorous evasive action. However, even if the explosions were not close they could cause extensive damage, shake a crew's morale, and, most important, keep the submarine deep and impotent. The answer to 'deaf-time' was ahead-throwing weapons which only the Allies developed satisfactorily. A widely fitted type was the British Hedgehog (adopted by the US Navy in parallel with, and preferred to, the smaller Mousetrap) comprising 24 light projectiles mounted on six rows of spigots. Each row tilted to compensate the ship's rolling; and each spigot was slightly angled to spread the weapons over a circular area, some 40 m. (130 ft.) in diameter, well ahead of the firing ship so that it could maintain contact with the target. The disadvantage of Hedgehog was that it only exploded on contact: it did not have a depth charge's deterrent value.

Squid, its uniquely British successor in late 1943, was a large three-barrelled mortar, eventually mounted in pairs, which fired projectiles carrying 91 kg. (200 lb.) of powerful Minol II (see EXPLOSIVES). These sank rapidly at 13.4 m. (44 ft.) per second (nearly three times as fast as a D/C) and exploded at an automatically set depth in triangular patterns with 37 m. (120 ft.) sides. A double mounting produced two depth layers 18 m. (59 ft.) apart. Double Squid, besides reintroducing the deterrent effect, theoretically raised the kill probability to 50% from 6% with depth charges and 20% with Hedgehog.

RICHARD COMPTON-HALL

Compton-Hall, R., Chapter 9, 'The Enemy Above', in *The Underwater War 1939–1945* (Poole, Dorset, 1982).
Hackmann, W., *Asdics in World War II: measures and countermeasures* (London, 1984), ch. 12.

anti-tank weapons. The first anti-tank weapons in 1916 were armour-piercing bullets fired by machine-guns, low velocity (LV) HE shells from 77 mm. (3 in.) artillery pieces, with a 1:25 chance of a hit at ranges beyond 300 m. (1,000

Anti-tank weapons: Anti-tank guns

	Weight in action kg. 1 Kg = 2.2 lb	*Weight of shell kg*	*Maximum range m 1 metre = 1.09 yards*	*Muzzle velocity m./sec.*
Germany				
28 cm PzB41[a]	229	0.13	500	1,400
37 mm PAK36	432	0.68	500	762
42 mm PJK41[a]	642	0.34	1,000	1,265
50 mm PAK38	986	2.25	1,000	823
75 mm PAK40	1,425	6.80	1,800	792
75 mm PAK41[a]	1,356	2.59	2,000	1,125
76 mm PAK36 (r)[b]	1,730	7.54	2,000	740
88 mm PAK43	3,700	10.4	2,000	1,000
128 mm PAK44	10,160	28.3	3,000	1,000
Italy				
47 mm Mod 35	265	1.5	8,200	630
Japan				
37 mm Mod 94	370	0.7	4,600	700
47 mm Mod 01	755	1.1	7,675	830
UK				
2 pdr Mk 9	800	0.9	7,300	853
6 pdr Mk 2	1,144	2.7	5,030	820
17 pdr Mk 1	2,100	7.7	9,150	884
USA				
37 mm M3	414	0.9	11,750	884
57 mm M1	1,275	2.8	9,380	854
3 in M5	2,662	7.0	14,720	792
USSR				
45 mm M1942	570	2.1	8,900	820
57 mm M1943	1,150	3.8	8,400	990
100 mm M1944	3,455	15.8	20,000	900

[a] taper bore
[b] captured and converted Soviet field gun
Ranges given are maximum effective engagement ranges.

Source: Ian Hogg.

ft.), and the 57 mm. (2.2 in.) LV guns mounted in some British and German tanks. Also a few mines were laid, predecessors of millions laid in the Second World War (see MINE WARFARE, 1).

Between the World Wars, however, development focused on much more accurate, high velocity (HV) guns firing solid shot to penetrate armour by kinetic energy (KE). Pieces with calibres ranging from 13 mm. (.5 in.) to 50 mm. (2 in.) with muzzle velocities (MV) up to 850 m./sec. (2,800 ft./sec.) were in general use in tanks by 1939 and with the infantry on towed field carriages. Also, very significantly, German doctrine (not initiated, as sometimes stated, by Hitler himself), stipulated the use of their 88 mm. (3.4 in.) anti-aircraft gun with an MV of 811 m./sec. (2,660 ft./sec.) in the dual anti-tank role, when possible.

The gun versus armour contest which began in the 1920s (see TANKS) made inevitable increases in weapon size and weight to defeat the thicker, higher quality, and sloped armour being fitted to tanks and assault guns. The appearance in 1941 of the Soviet KV1 tank, with frontal armour which at medium ranges defeated even the dual-purpose German 88 mm. gun, not only necessitated the use of the 105 mm. (4 in.) field gun which had an MV of 835 m./sec. (2,740 ft./sec.) with a 14.5 kg. (32 lb.) shot to score a kill, but also made essential the fitting of the 88 mm. to the heavy German Tiger tank to cope with T34/76s. And as a stopgap, improved 50 mm. and 75 mm. (2.9 in.) guns with longer barrels and more sophisticated ammunition, to increase MV, had to be mounted in the standard Mark III and IV tanks. For example, the mounting of a 48 calibres long 75 mm. gun in the up armoured Mark IV in 1942 enabled it to defeat T34/76 out to 2,000 m. (2,190 yd.) whereas the T34's 76 mm. (2.9 in.) gun failed against the up armoured Mark IV at 1000 m. (1,095 yd.).

Improved projectiles were as important as larger calibres and longer barrels. At an early stage the Germans recognized that solid armour piercing (AP) shot broke up against face-hardened armour. To prevent this they added a soft metal cap to AP shot (making APC) and later increased MV by adding a streamlined ballistic cap, making APCBC. They also increased MV by fitting a rigid metal carrier round a lightweight shot (APCR) to raise (for example) the 88's MV from 811 m./sec. with APCBC to 936 m./sec. (3,070 ft./sec.), but with the penalty of impaired accuracy beyond 600 m. (2,000 ft.). The British sub-calibre shot in a plastic sabot (or carrier), which was discarded after firing (APDS) was far superior to APCR as reduced air resistance increased MV and there was no loss in accuracy. But accuracy also depended on good optical instruments (the Germans' were best) and range estimation by eye, the latter being difficult beyond 400 m. (1,300 ft.). This was a contest in which neither the Japanese nor the Italians seriously engaged. The former used no gun larger than 57 mm., field or vehicle mounted, while the latter's largest tank-mounted gun was 47 mm. (1.8 in.), though they did have a 75 mm. self-propelled gun (see ARTILLERY). However, the larger field pieces in their service were mainly of German or Allied manufacture.

By the middle of the war the vastly increased size of KE anti-tank guns had become an embarrassment. They were difficult to conceal, clumsy, expensive to manufacture, and required bulky ammunition which created stowage and *logistics problems. The invention of the hollow charge (see EXPLOSIVES) chemical energy (CE) projectile seemed to offer a solution. On the principle that a shaped charge of high explosive directs a very high velocity jet of molten gas and debris through armour with pressures as much as 200 tonnes/per square inch, High Explosive Anti-Tank (HEAT) warheads were developed by both sides for both conventional artillery pieces and small hand-held projectors (see PIAT and ROCKET WEAPONS). Since a HEAT warhead's effect is degraded when spun—that is, fired from a rifled barrel—they were of more use in unrifled projectors for the infantry. It was not economically viable to produce armour which defeated these weapons, but as their maximum range was about 100 m. (330 ft.) the most effective counter was closer infantry escort and fire support for tanks.

Aircraft mounting HV guns up to 57 mm. (2.2 in.), or rockets, were also a threat to tanks. Of the two the gun was the more deadly since ballistically unstable rockets had only a 0.5% chance of a hit/kill—they were credited with grossly inflated destruction of tanks during the *Normandy campaign and elsewhere.

In the final analysis the tank was the best anti-tank weapon system, followed by the tracked assault gun; the small field anti-tank gun, though cost effective in 1940, had become too cumbersome and vulnerable towards the war's end. For anti-tank rifles see SMALL ARMS.

KENNETH MACKSEY

Macksey, K., *Tank versus Tank* (London, 1991).
Ogorkiewicz, R., *Armour* (London, 1960).

Antonescu, Marshal Ion (1886–1946), Romanian Army officer, minister of war since 1932, was appointed prime minister by King Carol (1893–1953) in September 1940. Carol then abdicated and Antonescu, modelling himself on Mussolini, established a Fascist-style dictatorship in conjunction with the Fascist Iron Guard organization, which he later used the army to suppress. He fought alongside the Germans when they invaded the USSR in June 1941 (see BARBAROSSA). He recaptured Bessarabia and northern Bucovina, promoted himself marshal, and when Odessa was captured in October 1941 the port was renamed after him. But as the war progressed the Romanian Army suffered terrible casualties and Antonescu's popularity waned. He started to negotiate for peace after the Axis defeat at *Stalingrad in January 1943, but the negotiations foundered as he could not accept the Allied terms of *unconditional surrender. He continued to prevaricate until, in August 1944, King Michael (b.1921) had him arrested and an *armistice was signed. Eventually he was tried and executed for *collaboration. See also ROMANIA, 3.

ANVIL, see FRENCH RIVIERA LANDINGS.

Anzac area, Pacific command formed in January 1942 (see Map F). It was a sea command only and came under a US naval officer, Vice-Admiral H. F. Leary. Its naval squadron, Anzac force, comprised a number of Australian, New Zealand, and US warships and was commanded by Rear-Admiral J. G. Crace. The Command was dissolved on 22 April 1942 and both area and force were then absorbed into *South-West Pacific Area or *South Pacific Area commands.

Anzio. After the *Salerno landings had been mounted in September 1943, the Allies planned a second landing on the west coast of Italy during the battle for the *Mediterranean to try to break the deadlock in the *Italian campaign, by breaching the *Winter Line and hastening the capture of Rome. One plan was cancelled but the second (SHINGLE), decided upon at the *Marrakesh conference with Churchill in the chair, was mounted on 22 January 1944 by Maj-General John Lucas's 6th US Corps of Mark *Clark's Fifth US Army. Churchill later wrote he had hoped that the Allies were hurling a wild cat on to the shore but all they got was a stranded whale. The reality did, indeed, turn out to be very different from Churchill's hopes and it was the opinion of the US Navy's official historian that putting such a modest force ashore was akin to sending a boy on a man's errand.

Lucas's corps comprised the 1st British Infantry Division and a British Commando Brigade, which landed north of Anzio; and 3rd US Infantry Division, reinforced with tanks and Ranger battalions (see USA, 5(f)), which landed in or south of the port. In all, 378 ships took part and air support was drawn from Maj-General John Cannon's immensely strong Mediterranean Allied Tactical Air Force. By contrast, German naval and air forces were weak. Their *explosive motor boats and *human torpedoes did attack Allied shipping off the beachhead but they were largely ineffectual.

The landings, as indicated by *ULTRA intelligence, achieved total tactical surprise and were virtually unopposed. However, the operation had been hastily mounted and Lucas's orders made its immediate objectives far from clear. Moreover, contrary to the expectations of the Marrakesh Conference, Lucas decided against exploiting the surprise he had achieved. Instead, he consolidated his position.

In the days that followed German bombers caused some damage to the naval forces and bad weather hindered the Allied build-up, and it was not until he knew reinforcements were arriving that Lucas agreed to advance. But by then it was too late, for the German commander in Italy, Field Marshal *Kesselring, reacted with brilliant improvisation, and by 26 January he had the core of no less than six divisions of a hastily improvised Fourteenth Army, commanded by General Eberhard von Mackensen, surrounding the Allied perimeter. This cordon proved highly effective: when Lucas advanced, two battalions of Rangers near Cisterna were wiped out in an ambush; by 30 January the 3rd US Division had 3,000 casualties; the British who, with American armoured help, had created a salient towards Osteriaccia, had 2,100. These losses forced Lucas on to the defensive again.

However, during the last days of January ULTRA intelligence provided details of German plans and tank strengths—a senior intelligence officer on General Alexander's staff considered it 'one of Ultra's most important triumphs' (quoted in R. Bennett, *Ultra and Mediterranean Strategy*, London, 1989, p. 269)—and it enabled the Allied commanders to defend the perimeter with maximum effectiveness. The elimination of the Osteriaccia salient could not be prevented, but heavy losses were inflicted on the Germans; and when a few days later German forces began moving into the area around Aprilia it was known that it was a build-up to a counter-offensive. This was launched on 16 February but, aided by foreknowledge, powerful air support, heavy artillery concentrations, and sturdy defence, the Allies halted it after four days with little territorial loss and 5,389 German casualties. On 22 February Lucas was replaced by his deputy, Maj-General *Truscott, who drove off a second German attack on 29 February. When the attack failed, Kesselring abandoned any hope of eliminating the landings, although he continued to attack the perimeter to keep the Allied landing beaches under fire. It was not until the spring that 6th Corps, now heavily reinforced, broke out and linked up with Fifth Army's 2nd Corps on 25 May and began the triumphant advance on Rome.

The cost of Anzio was heavy for the Allies: some 7,000 killed and 36,000 wounded or missing in action; 44,000 were disabled with injuries or sickness. German losses were estimated by Kesselring to have been 40,000 including 5,000 killed and 4,500 captured.

D'Este, C., *Fatal Decision* (London, 1991).

Arab League, collective security pact signed in Cairo in March 1945 between Egypt, which proposed it, Iraq, Transjordan, Saudi Arabia, Syria, Lebanon, and Yemen. The League, based on the Alexandria Protocol issued in Alexandria in September 1944, was prompted by Zionist demands in Palestine and by French intervention in Lebanon the previous year, and it gave full status to an Arab Palestinian state. It is still functioning and now has 22 members.

Arakan campaign, see BURMA CAMPAIGN.

ARCADIA, codename for the first Washington conference (22 December 1941 to 14 January 1942) at which Churchill, Roosevelt, and their military advisers hammered out future strategy and the mechanisms to be used to co-ordinate their war effort (see GRAND ALLIANCE). At the suggestion of the Americans, General *Wavell was appointed to command *ABDA. Other discussion included the possibility of invading North Africa, *MacArthur's urgent requests for action to stop the Japanese in the *Philippines, and the crucial issue of *Lend-Lease for the USSR (see THREE-POWER CONFERENCE). The dispatch of US troops to Northern Ireland and Iceland was agreed upon, as was the wording of the *United Nations Declaration issued on New Year's Day 1942. *Beaverbrook, who flew to join Churchill in Washington, urged Roosevelt and Donald Nelson, the executive director of the newly-established *War Production Board, to set US production targets higher. This was achieved with such alacrity that apart from aircraft (the deliveries of which had to be cut by half because of USAAF expansion) the UK, during the first six months of 1942, suffered no shortages through a shortfall of Lend-Lease. See also DIPLOMACY.

Arctic convoys transported *matériel* from UK and Icelandic ports for the Soviet war effort via the Norwegian and Barents seas. A total of 4.43 million tons was shipped by this route, 22.7% of the total Soviet *Lend-Lease supplies. The loss rate of *matériel* was 7%, while the loss rate of eastbound merchant ships was 7.8% and 3.8% for empty westbound ones, far higher than any other route for Allied *convoys. The first convoy, which sailed from Scapa Flow in Scotland on 21 August 1941, carried Hurricane fighters and essential *raw materials. It was not allotted a lettered codename, but the next one, which sailed in September from Iceland, was codenamed PQ1—the letters apparently originating from the initials of an officer working in the British Admiralty.

Early shipments proved of little use, but the supplies of US trucks, boots, and telephone equipment shipped up to the beginning of 1942 were, almost certainly, of critical importance to the USSR during the fighting that summer in the *German–Soviet war though Soviet historians were only just beginning to acknowledge the part played by Lend-Lease before the USSR was dissolved in December 1991. Although the tonnage delivered was small at first, the convoys were—apart from the *strategic air offensive against Germany—the only weapon Churchill possessed with which to counter Stalin's demands for a Second Front (see GRAND ALLIANCE).

The available routes were severely restricted by climatic and geographical factors, and their crews had to face heavy weather conditions and extreme cold. Though the long (or total) winter nights gave them some chance of escaping undetected, ice forced them closer to the Norwegian coastline and so within easier operational range of German forces based there.

Eastbound convoys normally kept as far from Norway as the prevailing ice conditions allowed and made either for the ice-free port of Murmansk or the White Sea ports of Archangel and Molotovsk. Each had a close escort of destroyers and smaller warships, and a distant escort of cruisers which were later replaced by a larger number of destroyers. Escorts were drawn predominantly from the Royal Navy, but also included US and Soviet ships, the latter not being as much in evidence as the Admiralty would have liked. Allied air patrols were also an essential element in protecting the convoys, though their range was limited, as were British and Soviet submarine patrols, part of whose task it was to watch the entrances of the Norwegian fjords containing, at different times, major German surface units. After PQ12 escaped an attack by the German battleship **Tirpitz* in March 1942, distant cover by main units of the Home Fleet was also available to counter any threat that might develop from them. Later, when the convoys increased to 30 or more merchant ships, air cover was provided by aircraft from *CAM ships and escort carriers, and anti-aircraft (A-A) ships were also deployed.

The Germans, confident of an early victory after launching their invasion of the USSR in June 1941 (see BARBAROSSA), took no interest in the early convoys and up to mid-March 1942 only two ships were lost. However, when they realized BARBAROSSA was not going to bring them a quick victory, they began, from December 1941, to increase their air and sea strength in northern Norway. This quickly became known to the Admiralty through *ULTRA intelligence, and eastbound and westbound convoys were ordered to sail simultaneously so that both could be given adequate cover.

PQ13 was the first convoy to have appreciable losses. After sailing on 20 March 1942 it was attacked not only by aircraft and U-boats but by destroyers from Kirkenes in northern Norway. ULTRA intelligence gave due warning of this and one destroyer was sunk and two damaged by the cruiser *Trinidad*, but the convoy still lost five ships. Air attack now became increasingly lethal. On one day alone, 27 May 1942, no fewer than 108 aircraft attacked PQ16 from which seven ships were eventually lost. It was such heavy losses, and the sinking of two escorting cruisers and a number of other escorts, that led the First Sea Lord, Admiral *Pound, to comment that the convoys were 'a most unsound operation with the dice loaded against us in every direction'. But he failed to persuade Churchill, who was under immense political pressure, to discontinue them.

By far the most disastrous convoy was the controversial PQ17 which sailed from Iceland on 27 June 1942. The Admiralty, aware of an impending attack, laid elaborate plans to safeguard it, and it was given a strong close escort of destroyers, A-A ships, and smaller vessels, and a distant escort of cruisers. But on the evening of 4 July ULTRA intelligence revealed that *Tirpitz*, the cruiser *Hipper*, and possibly the pocket battleship *Lützow*, with a force of destroyers, had joined another cruiser, *Admiral Scheer*, at Altenfjord, and that this powerful force was poised to overwhelm PQ17's cruiser escort before destroying the convoy itself. Pound consulted the *Naval Intelligence Division's Operational Intelligence Centre, but this could only offer evidence that suggested *Tirpitz* had not put to sea. After deliberating with his staff Pound ordered the convoy to scatter and its escort to return. The individual ships were immediately pounced on by U-boats and bombers, and only 11 out of the original 37 reached their destination. After air reconnaissance had corrected an earlier error that PQ17's cruiser escort included a battleship, and had established that the British Home Fleet was too distant to interfere, the *Tirpitz* force sailed the next afternoon (5 July), but it was soon recalled when it was realized that the convoy was already being eliminated. About 3,850 trucks and vehicles, 430 tanks, and 2,500 aircraft were lost, and 153 seamen died.

With hindsight, PQ17 might have been saved if it had been ordered to reverse course when the movements of *Tirpitz* and *Admiral Hipper* were first detected by ULTRA intelligence on 3 July. It could then have remained under the cover of the Home Fleet's major units until the situation had become clearer. But what seems virtually certain is that, if the order to scatter had not been given, neither escort nor convoy could have escaped almost total destruction once the *Tirpitz* force had intercepted them, which it would have done on 6 July.

This catastrophe, and a dearth of escorts (which were being employed to help break the siege of *Malta), forced Churchill to suspend the convoys, much to Stalin's annoyance, and PQ18 did not sail until nine weeks later. By that time the C-in-C of the Home Fleet, Admiral *Tovey, had planned new tactics. Instead of eastbound and westbound convoys sailing together a Fighting Destroyer Escort (FDE) of 12 to 16 destroyers was formed which would transfer from the eastbound to the westbound convoy in the Barents Sea. Tovey also added an escort carrier to the defending force, and transferred to Soviet soil some search and strike aircraft. Although these tactics did not

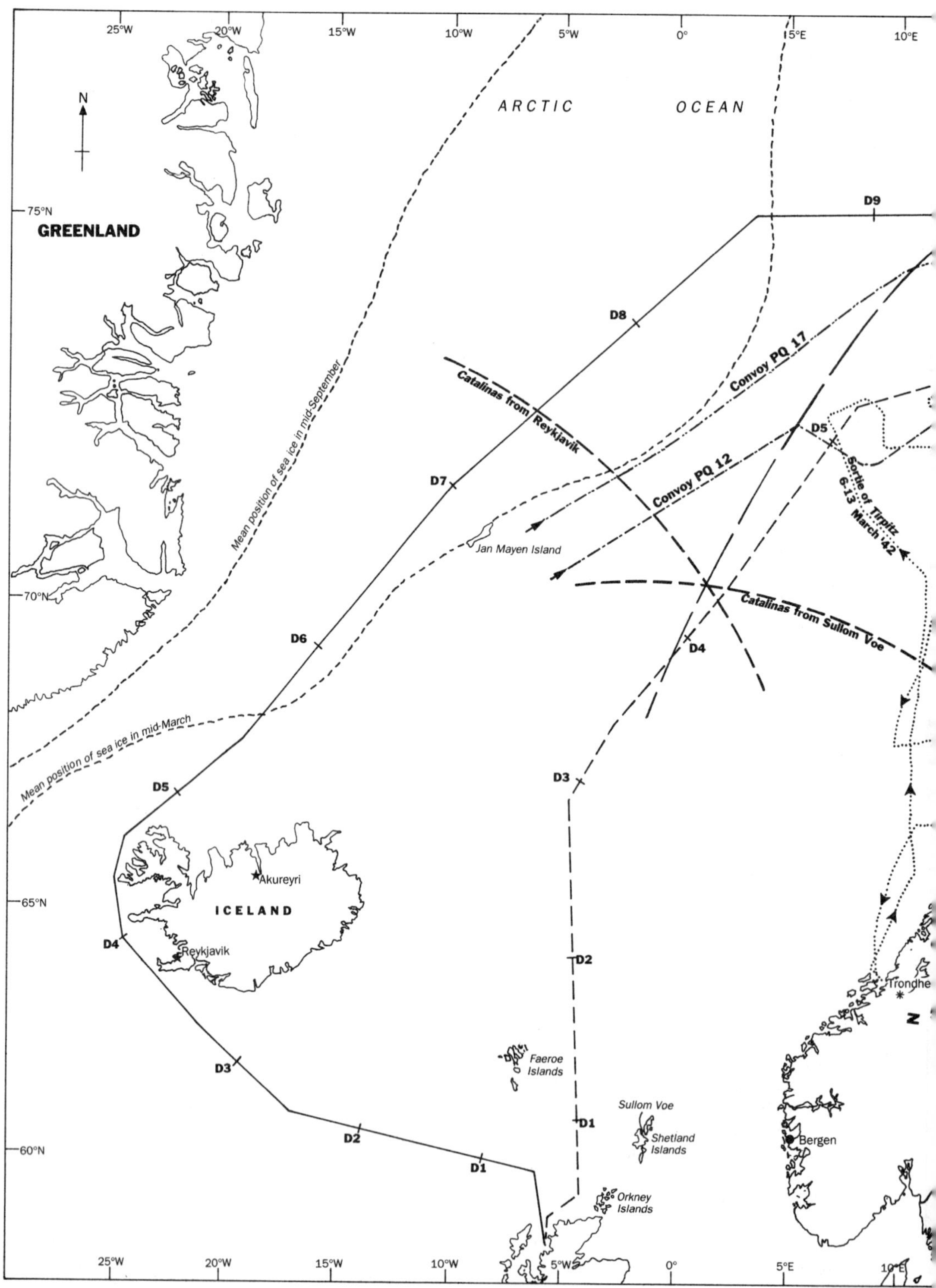

4. **Arctic convoys**, 1941–2

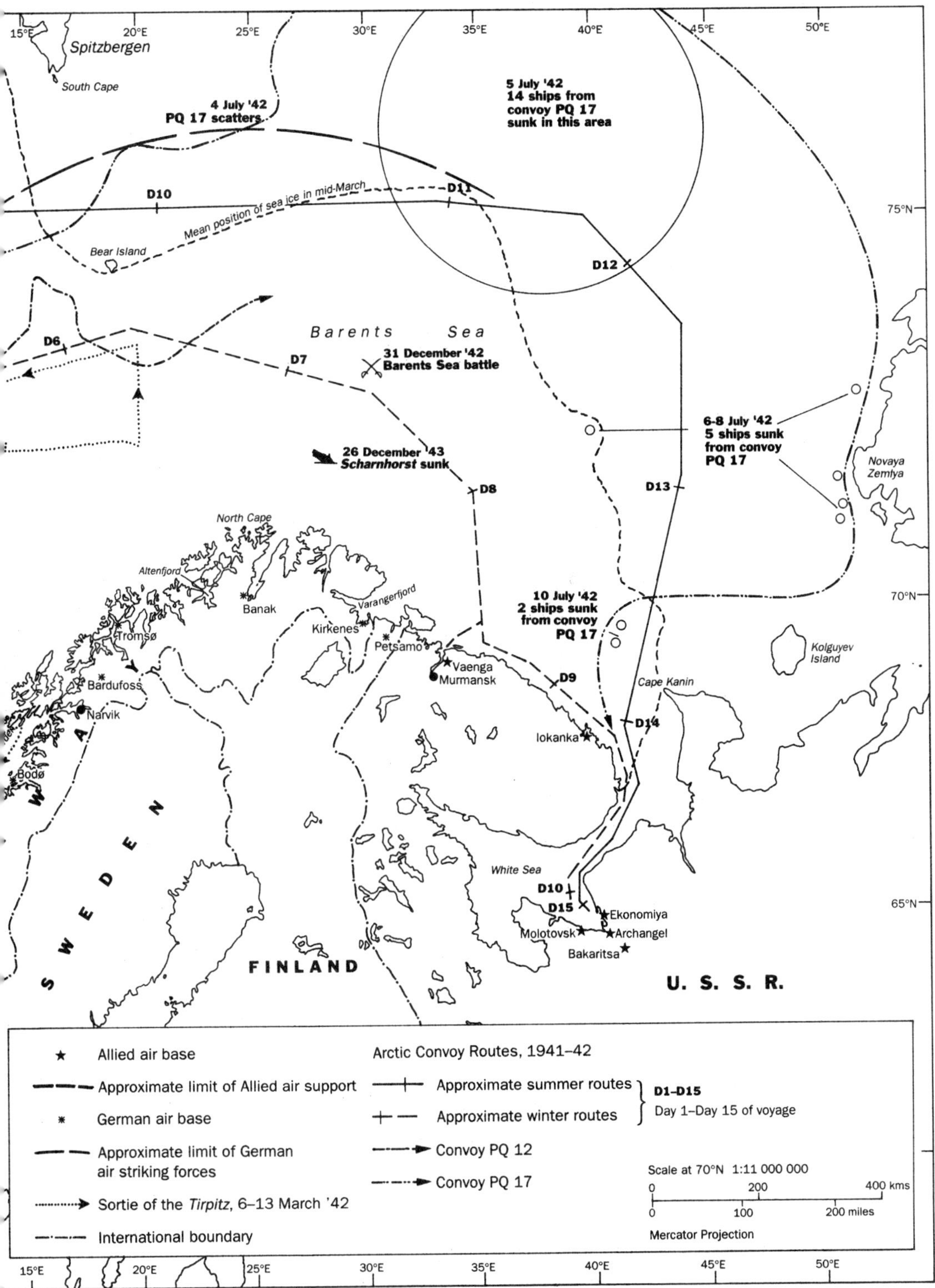

Spitzbergen
South Cape
4 July '42
PQ 17 scatters
5 July '42
14 ships from
convoy PQ 17
sunk in this area
Mean position of sea ice in mid-March
Bear Island
Barents Sea
31 December '42
Barents Sea battle
26 December '43
Scharnhorst sunk
6-8 July '42
5 ships sunk
from convoy
PQ 17
Novaya
Zemlya
North Cape
Altenfjord
Banak
Varangerfjord
Kirkenes
Petsamo
Tromsø
Bardufoss
Narvik
Bodø
Vaenga
Murmansk
10 July '42
2 ships sunk
from convoy
PQ 17
Kolguyev
Island
Cape Kanin
Iokanka
White Sea
Ekonomiya
Molotovsk
Archangel
Bakaritsa
NORWAY
SWEDEN
FINLAND
U. S. S. R.
D1–D15
Day 1–Day 15 of voyage
Allied air base
Approximate limit of Allied air support
German air base
Approximate limit of German air striking forces
Sortie of the Tirpitz, 6–13 March '42
International boundary
Arctic Convoy Routes, 1941–42
Approximate summer routes
Approximate winter routes
Convoy PQ 12
Convoy PQ 17
Scale at 70°N 1:11 000 000
0 200 400 kms
0 100 200 miles
Mercator Projection

prevent the loss of 16 ships from the next two convoys, the Germans lost 4 U-boats and 41 aircraft.

After PQ18, the Arctic convoys were once more suspended as all available shipping was needed for the Allied *North African campaign landings in November 1942. By the time the convoys were restarted in December much of the German air strength in northern Norway had been transferred to the *Mediterranean, thus substantially reducing the threat. Each convoy was now given a new lettered code, JW for the outward convoy and RA for the homeward one, both starting with the number 51. Their size was such that it was decided to run them in two sections a fortnight apart so that they could be adequately escorted.

The first JW convoy was not detected and arrived intact, but JW51B was attacked on 31 December 1942 by *Lützow*, *Admiral Hipper*, and six destroyers. In the running battle which followed, known as the battle of the Barents Sea, the convoy was skilfully defended by its destroyer escort under Captain Robert Sherbrooke which, helped by the distant escort of cruisers, drove the German force off. The British lost two destroyers, including Sherbrooke's flagship, and a minesweeper, and had one merchantman damaged. However, the failure of the force, which lost one destroyer, to eradicate the convoy so infuriated Hitler that he ordered the decommissioning of all heavy ships. This was not carried out, but the German Navy's C-in-C, Admiral *Raeder, resigned and *Admiral Hipper* and another cruiser, *Köln*, were recalled to the Baltic.

The next two eastbound convoys were smaller and were therefore not divided. Both reached their destination unharmed, but the two westbound convoys lost five ships. In March 1943 the battle-cruiser **Scharnhorst*, having escaped from Brest the previous February (see CERBERUS), joined *Tirpitz* and *Lützow* in Norway. This added threat coincided with the climax of the battle of the *Atlantic, so once again the Arctic convoys were suspended while their escorts were transferred to the Atlantic, and they were not resumed until November 1943. By then *Tirpitz* had been crippled by British *midget submarines and *Lützow* had returned to Germany, and the one remaining threat, *Scharnhorst*, was sunk in December when she tried to attack JW55B. The convoys were suspended once again between May and July 1944 because of the Normandy landings in June (see OVERLORD). From February 1944 to 16 April 1945, when the last one sailed, the convoys were no longer divided. But they were so heavily defended that U-boats, even those equipped with homing torpedoes and *Schnorchels, were rarely able to penetrate the defensive screen, and only eight ships were lost. See also GERMAN SURFACE RAIDERS.

Schofield, B., *The Arctic Convoys* (London, 1977).

Ardeatine Caves massacre. German massacre of 335 political and Jewish prisoners which was carried out in the caves of Via Ardeatina, near Rome, in March 1944. It was in retaliation for the ambush of German troops by Italian partisans. See also ATROCITIES.

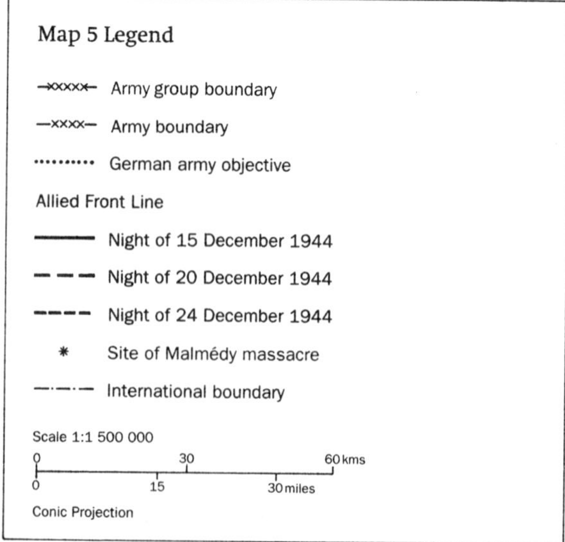

Ardennes campaign, Hitler's final counter-offensive in north-west Europe launched in December 1944 and also known as the battle of the Bulge. Aimed at splitting the Allied armies in half and recapturing Antwerp, the Allies' most vital supply port (see also SCHELDT), it achieved total strategic and tactical surprise and was launched in poor weather (see METEOROLOGICAL INTELLIGENCE) which, as Hitler had calculated, neutralized Allied *air power.

To make the quick breakthrough essential to the success of the offensive, Hitler created the Sixth *SS Panzer Army of four SS Panzer Divisions and gave command of it to 'Sepp' *Dietrich, one of his most trusted SS officers. Dietrich's army represented the *Schwerpunkt* (main thrust) which was launched from the northern Ardennes around Monschau. Simultaneously, another new panzer army, *Manteuffel's Fifth, would attack in the centre and Lt-General Erich Brandenberger's Seventh Army in the south. These armies, totalling 30 divisions and supported by more than 1,000 aircraft of Brigadier Dietrich Peltz's 2nd Fighter Corps, were assembled in the greatest secrecy and screened by the most sophisticated deception plans. Even the codename Hitler initially gave to the offensive, WACHT AM RHEIN ('watch on the Rhine'), was intended by its defensive connotations to mislead. To start with he also deliberately misled *Rundstedt, his C-in-C West, about his intentions. When Rundstedt eventually heard about them he was appalled. He thought the choice of the almost impenetrable Ardennes 'a stroke of genius' but that the offensive lacked 'all, absolutely all' the right conditions for success. Rundstedt was merely a figurehead. The tactical commander was one of Hitler's favourites, *Model, C-in-C Army Group B, but he, too, considered the plan unrealistic. Both suggested a less ambitious one which Hitler contemptuously dismissed.

To speed the advance towards Antwerp two special

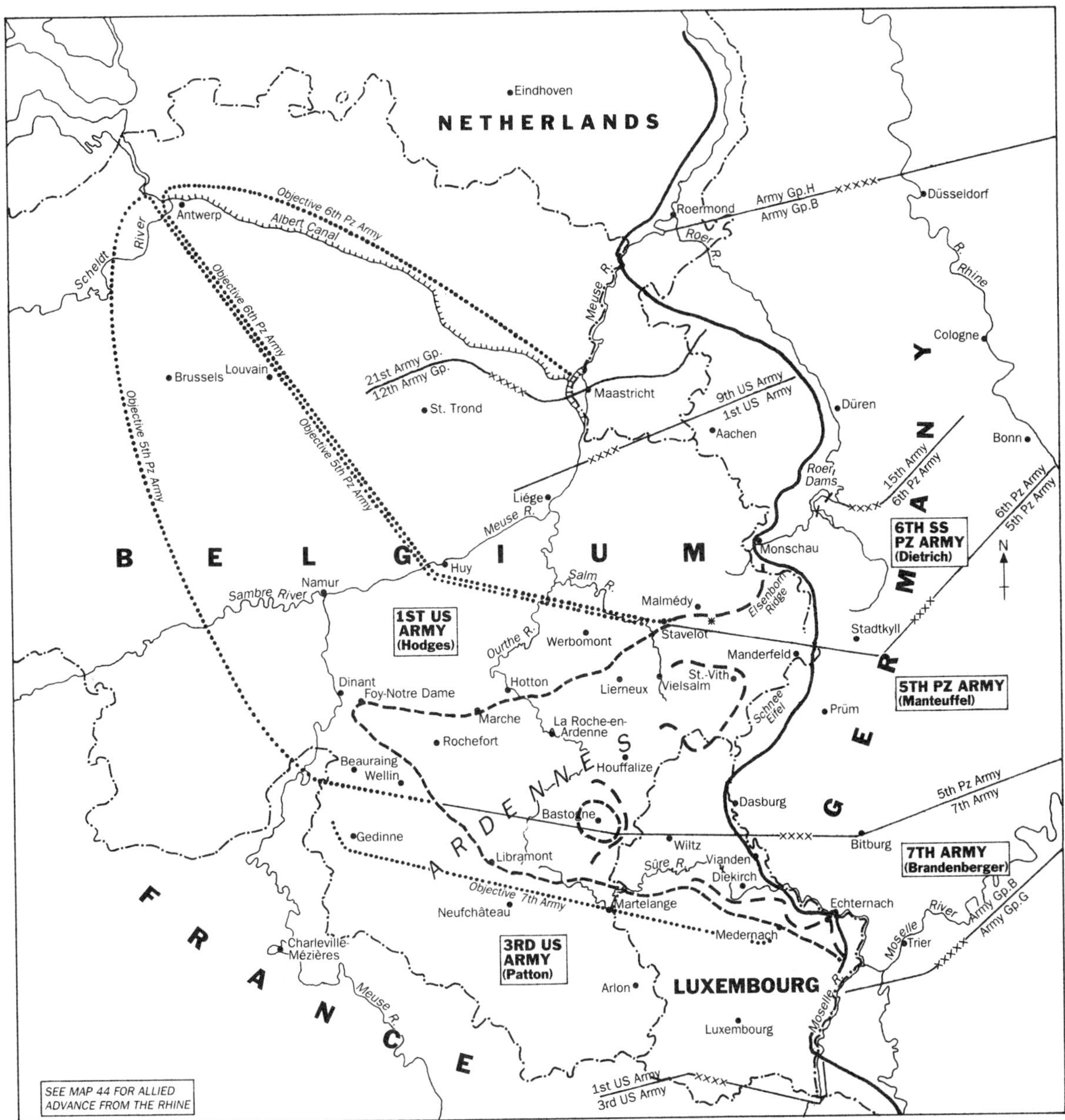

5. **Ardennes campaign**, December 1944–January 1945

units were ordered to break through early to capture bridges across the River Meuse, and a small force of paratroops was to be employed to block US reinforcements moving south. Neither the paratroopers, who were widely scattered when they were dropped, nor *Skorzeny's 150th SS Brigade, which included a handful of English-speaking troops dressed in American uniform and driving US vehicles, achieved any significant military advantage, but they did create a lot of confusion and apprehension. On the other hand, SS Standartenführer (Colonel) Joachim Peiper's Kampfgruppe (battle group), formed from Dietrich's powerful 1st SS Panzer Division, proved a serious threat and was past *Malmédy before it was trapped and destroyed.

Lt-General *Hodges's First US Army, part of *Bradley's Twelfth Army Group, was responsible for the Ardennes, but most of his strength was in the Aachen area where he was pushing to capture the Roer dams. The Ardennes was the chosen area for new or recuperating divisions and only five defended the 130 km. (80 mi.) front: 99th and 106th from Hodges's 5th Corps, 28th and 4th from his 8th Corps, with 9th Armoured in reserve.

This lack of strength—a calculated risk the Allies had taken in order to pursue their objectives north and south of the Ardennes—could have been counter-balanced by good intelligence. But at a tactical level the Germans had imposed strict radio silence; Allied *photographic reconnaissance flights were grounded by the weather; and though *ULTRA intelligence had revealed that German forces were being massed, it was wrongly judged, in the atmosphere of optimism that prevailed, that they were being accumulated to counter-attack the next Allied offensive building either side of the Ardennes. Bradley saw an attack in the Ardennes as 'only a remote possibility' and *Montgomery, 24 hours before it occurred, said the Germans were incapable of staging 'any major offensive operations'. So surprise was complete when German infantry, visually aided by the beams of searchlights reflected from the lowering clouds, attacked at 0530.

News from the front was slow to arrive at Bradley's HQ as a heavy German artillery preparation had knocked out many telephone lines. When information did arrive, it was initially thought to be a local attack. But *Eisenhower, the supreme Allied commander, ordered 10th Armoured Division of *Patton's Third US Army, fighting south of the Ardennes, and 7th Armoured Division of Lt-General W. H. *Simpson's Ninth US Army to the north of Hodges, to reinforce the frontline infantry divisions. It was as well he did so immediately for the first few days were critical, with Hodges's frontline divisions in the north and south hanging on by a thread. In the north 99th Division was soon reinforced by two others, 1st and 2nd, and later by 9th. These held out against Dietrich around Elsenborn ridge, east of Malmédy, while in the south the 4th US Division also managed to contain the advance of Brandenberger's **Volksgrenadier*. But though both shoulders held, 28th and 106th Divisions in the centre collapsed as Manteuffel's panzers headed for two important centres of the local road network, St Vith and *Bastogne. Two regiments of 106th Division on the Schnee Eifel were cut off and forced to surrender, but its third helped put up a stout defence before St Vith. The 7th Armoured also performed prodigies of valour at St Vith, but by 22 December the defensive horseshoe had become a vulnerable salient and the defending forces were ordered to retire behind the River Salm. At Bastogne 101st Airborne Division and part of 10th Armoured were rushed into the area and threw a defensive ring around the town just before Manteuffel attacked and surrounded it.

On 19 December, Eisenhower, now alerted by ULTRA intelligence that the Germans were heading for the Meuse, stopped all Allied offensive action along his front. He ordered Patton, under whose command Hodges's most southerly corps now came, to change the axis of his advance and attack northwards, an order Patton executed with astonishing swiftness. By launching such an attack it was also hoped to relieve some of the pressure on Hodges. Montgomery, who now took command of Bradley's two northern armies, concentrated his reserve, the British 30th Corps, between Liège and Louvain. Though very few of 30th Corps saw action, this commitment enabled Hodges, who had realigned his army in as remarkable a manner as Patton, to poise his 7th Corps ready to counter-attack when the moment was ripe. But the fighting was so fierce that part of 7th Corps, although it later attacked as planned, had to be committed to blunt Manteuffel's 2nd Panzer Division which had managed, by 24 December, to reach Foy-Notre Dame, just 5 km. (3 mi.) from the Meuse.

With Dietrich thwarted in the north, Hitler, too late, gave permission for the weight of the attack to be switched behind Manteuffel. Dietrich's reserve panzer divisions were committed to the Fifth Panzer Army on 20 December, but Bastogne, where resistance sucked in as many as nine German divisions, remained a severe hindrance to Manteuffel's advance. With American forces restricting the width and speed of his offensive, Rundstedt, on 22 December, requested permission to withdraw. Hitler refused. The same day the skies began to clear, allowing Allied fighter-bombers to take off in large numbers for the first time. Ninth US Army Force flew nearly 1,300 sorties on 23 December and on Christmas Eve 2,000 Allied aircraft attacked 31 separate targets. This intervention was of critical importance, for it shattered the already inadequate German supply organization and further decreased the mobility of the panzers which were already badly hampered by fuel shortages, poor roads, dogged defence, and the narrowness of their front. In a last desperate bid for air superiority, every available German fighter took to the air on New Year's Day to attack 27 Allied airfields. They destroyed 156 aircraft, but lost more than 300 themselves, a blow from which the Luftwaffe never recovered.

With the 2nd Panzer Division's thrust to Foy-Notre Dame, the Bulge—65 km. (40 mi.) wide at its base, 95 km. (60 mi.) deep—reached its furthest limit. Weakened by Bastogne's refusal to capitulate, and by heavy losses and acute supply problems, Manteuffel could advance no further, and on 3 January Hodges's 7th Corps began its attack southwards, aiming to meet Patton's northward thrust at Houffalize. Deep snow delayed the two pincers closing on Houffalize until 16 January, and by then the German armies, more used to dealing with the winter conditions, had escaped. But they had suffered 100,000 casualties out of the 500,000 men committed and the loss of nearly all their tanks and aircraft. The Allies had suffered almost as many losses, but they could replace them while the Germans could not.

The Ardennes campaign caused the Anglo-American command crisis Hitler had hoped for; but it was overcome, and did not prevent the Allies acting with swift accord. The US Army's astonishing mobility was the key to success: in four days its infantry numbers in the Ardennes doubled and its armour tripled. Churchill

The German **Ardennes offensive** was launched on 16 December 1944 in winter conditions which initially neutralized Allied air power. Here, men of Third US Army trudge northwards through the snow to relieve Bastogne.

called it the greatest American battle of the war which would 'be regarded as an ever famous American victory'. Certainly Hitler's determination to maintain the offensive long after there was any chance of its objective being achieved, dissipated Germany's last reserves and hastened her end.

Macdonald, C., *The Battle of the Bulge* (London, 1984).

area bombing was the technique whereby whole cities and not just specified targets were bombed. Its aim was not only destruction but the shattering of civilian morale. RAF Bomber Command exploited its full potential against Germany (see STRATEGIC AIR OFFENSIVES, 1) after *photographic reconnaissance had revealed in 1941 the failure of its attempts at *precision bombing (see BUTT REPORT). It was also used by Twentieth US Army Air Force against Japan (see STRATEGIC AIR OFFENSIVES, 3), and the most extreme examples of it were the destruction of *Hiroshima and *Nagasaki by *atomic bombs. See also BOMBERS, 2.

Argenta Gap, battle of, generic term for the final Allied offensive in the *Italian campaign, launched in April 1945 under the codename GRAPESHOT. The plan had been drawn up by General Mark *Clark during the winter and was designed to trap General Heinrich von Vietinghoff's Army Group C between the Fifth US and Eighth British Armies. Vietinghoff expected an attack, once the ground dried out, and wanted to conduct a delaying operation based on the numerous river lines, but Hitler ordered him to stand and fight in place. However, shortage of fuel and the prolonged Allied air interdiction campaign had, drastically reduced his mobility. After a preliminary operation by British Special Forces on Lake Comacchio, which was designed to tie down the German Adriatic flank, the Eighth Army struck first, on 9 April. Further operations on Lake Comacchio helped to turn the German flank, enabling the British to force the vital Argenta Gap, just west of the lake which was then twice its modern size. The Fifth US Army, with the whole weight of Allied air power switched to its support, attacked on 15 April. Eight days later the two armies linked up north of Bologna and the back of the German resistance was broken. Thereafter the Allies advanced rapidly northwards and westwards, with the Americans entering Genoa on 27 April, and Milan two days later, while the British also reached Venice on 29 April. On this same day the Germans signed an *unconditional surrender at Caserta. This came into effect on 2 May and marked the end of the war in Italy, although the Fifth US Army continued to advance into Austria, linking up with the Seventh US Army in the Brenner Pass on 6 May. CHARLES MESSENGER

Graham, D., and Bidwell, S., *Tug of War: The Battle for Italy, 1943–45* (London, 1986).

Argentina pursued a neutral policy after the USA entered the war in December 1941, but failed to induce Chile, Paraguay, and Peru to form a neutral bloc. It managed to water down the motions of the *Rio conference, held in January 1942, and continued to defy US pressures to align itself with the Allies, and was therefore not invited to the *Hot Springs conference in May 1943. The UK, 40% of whose meat was imported from Argentina, did not press it with the same urgency. A military *coup d'état* in June 1943, and the uncovering of a Nazi espionage network, led to Argentina severing diplomatic relations with Germany and Japan on 26 January 1944. This prompted Colonel Juan Perón (1895–1974) to lead a 'palace revolution' and a new president was installed. These events convinced Cordell *Hull, the US secretary of state, that the fascists had finally got the upper hand, and in July the US ambassador was withdrawn. The UK reluctantly withdrew its ambassador, too, and, under pressure from the USA, did not renew the meat contract, but continued to purchase on a month-by-month basis. After illness forced Hull's resignation in October 1944, the USA took a more conciliatory line, and as a result of the Mexico City conference (see CHAPULTEPEC) Argentina declared war on the Axis powers on 27 March 1945—the last American power to do so—and on 9 April 1945 its government was recognized by the UK and USA. But Argentina did not sign the *United Nations Declaration and was not invited to the *San Francisco conference, to which it was only admitted after other American states refused to co-operate in allowing Belorussia and the Ukraine to participate until Argentina was allowed to do so. After the war, when escape lines were set up for war criminals (see ODESSA ORGANIZATION and VATICAN), Argentina became a refuge for Nazis and for those, such as Ante *Pavelić, who had collaborated with them. It has been estimated that perhaps as many as 40 high-ranking Nazis were given sanctuary there, including *Eichmann who was found there in 1962. See also LATIN AMERICA.

ARGONAUT, codename for the Allied conference at Yalta in the Crimea which was held from 4 to 11 February 1945 to discuss future strategy (see GRAND ALLIANCE) and the division of post-war Germany. Present were Churchill, Roosevelt, and Stalin, and their diplomatic and military advisers, totalling 700 people. ARGONAUT was also the codename for preliminary meetings held by Edward *Stettinius, Anthony *Eden, and the *Combined Chiefs of Staff in Malta from 30 January to 3 February, and where Churchill and Roosevelt also met twice.

The military topics discussed included the strategy of the western allies in the final phase of the battle for *Germany; their liaison with Soviet forces during the course of this campaign; and how the occupation of Germany and Austria would be arranged (see ALLIED CONTROL COMMISSIONS). The first topic was covered at the Malta meetings; the other two were discussed at Yalta. But apart from agreeing to an Allied Control Commission for Germany, and that France should be one of the occupying powers, little was achieved.

Unlike earlier summit conferences, where military strategy predominated, the three leaders were primarily involved in diplomatic negotiations on the shape of the post-war world (see CONSEQUENCES OF THE WAR). A secret agreement was reached, without Churchill's knowledge, that covered Soviet demands in return for entering the war against Japan. Although Chinese interests were affected by this agreement, *Chiang Kai-shek was not informed of them. They included the preservation of the status quo of Mongolia, the return of the southern part of Sakhalin Island to the USSR, and the acquisition by the USSR of the Kurile Islands.

The most difficult discussions centred on the Polish government (see LUBLIN COMMITTEE) and Poland's frontiers (see ODER–NEISSE LINE). However an agreement, if only temporary, was reached; voting rights in the United Nations (see SAN FRANCISCO CONFERENCE), which the *Dumbarton Oaks conference had failed to resolve, were settled; affirmation was given to an agreement that all nationals accused of being *deserters or traitors should be returned to their countries of origin (see SOVIET EXILES); and the *Declaration on Liberated Europe was issued. See also DIPLOMACY.

armed forces, see under armed forces sections of major powers. Otherwise see under country.

armed merchant cruisers, British and Dominion liners, varying in size from 6,267 tons to 22,575 tons, which were requisitioned and armed by the Admiralty for blockade purposes, or as escorts for *convoys during the battle of the *Atlantic. In these operations 56 were used, and they soon proved no match for the German surface raiders they encountered: *Rawalpindi* was sunk by *Scharnhorst* and *Gneisenau* in November 1939; *Jervis Bay* fell victim to *Admiral Scheer* in November 1940; and of the ships which engaged the German *auxiliary cruiser *Thor* at different times during her first cruise, two were outfought and the third was sunk. Altogether fifteen were lost, ten to U-boats. Churchill thought them 'an immense expense and also a care and anxiety', and by October 1941 most had been withdrawn for use as troop transports.

armistice, mutual agreement whereby the fighting stops so that permanent peace terms can be agreed upon later. Several were agreed during the course of the War, some of them on more lenient terms than the *unconditional surrender mostly demanded by the Allies. Those dictated by the Allies were controlled by *Allied Control Commissions.

The first armistice to be signed was between France and Germany in June 1940. Marshal *Pétain, using the Spanish government as an intermediary, requested one immediately he was appointed French prime minister on 17 June 1940. Hitler, who desired it as much as the French, did not demand total surrender as he did not want to risk the French government carrying on the war from North Africa, where it could have escaped with the French fleet and at least some aircraft. He therefore decreed that France should survive as a sovereign power, and that there should be no demands concerning her empire, in case this forced the colonies to side with the UK. He decided, too, that only part of France would be occupied. The French Army would be demobilized in the unoccupied zone, but some units could be retained to maintain law and order. The French fleet was to be neutralized under German or Italian control, but no demands were to be made for it to be handed over and the French government was to be assured that once peace terms had been agreed the fleet would be returned to it. Any territorial demands on France would be a matter for a peace settlement.

On 21 June the French delegation, headed by General *Huntziger, met Hitler and other Nazi leaders in the same railway coach in the forest of Compiègne where the armistice had been signed in 1918. Peace terms were not discussed as Hitler wanted to see first what the British would do. Instead, Huntziger was simply handed an armistice convention of 24 articles which he was told were immutable. It was signed the next day but only came into force after there had been an armistice with Italy, which, after declaring war on the Allies on 10 June, had launched an attack on France on 21 June. Mussolini, who had been vainly hoping for some success against the French before agreeing to an armistice—the only town of any size the Italians had taken was Menton—realized he was in no position to delay. The French delegation signed the armistice in Rome on the evening of 24 June, hostilities ceased at 0135 the next morning, and an Italian zone of occupation was established (see Map 34). Negotiations were continued between the Germans and the French to establish peace terms. But none were ever signed and in November 1942 the Germans, and the Italians, violated the terms of the armistice by occupying the whole of France.

Once Sicily was invaded by the Allies in July 1943 it became obvious that Italy could not remain in the war. Mussolini's advisers attempted to make him seek an agreement from Hitler that Italy should seek an armistice with the Allies, but this came to nothing. Mussolini fell from power on 25 July, but Italy, with German troops pouring into the country, remained in the war on the Axis side, though the new prime minister, Marshal *Badoglio, began secret, if ambivalent, negotiations with the Allies who insisted on Italy's unconditional surrender. With the king, *Victor Emmanuel III, constantly assuring the Germans that Italy would not desert them, and Badoglio still ambivalent as to whether he would honour its terms, the armistice was signed secretly by General Giuseppe Castellano on 3 September, the day of the Allied landings at *Reggio di Calabria, near Syracuse in Sicily, and was announced just before the Allies landed at *Salerno at 0330 hours on 9 September. Known as the 'short' armistice, this covered the military surrender only, and included the repatriation of prisoners-of-war and the use of Italy as an Allied base. Its final clause provided that Italy would observe additional political, economic, and financial terms to be imposed at a later date. Known as the 'long' armistice, these were signed by Badoglio and *Eisenhower on 29 September at Malta. They gave the Allies complete control over every aspect of the Italian state and the *Allied Military government of Occupied Territories which had been formed to administer Sicily was extended to Italy, though the Italian government soon controlled some parts of the country. The Italian fleet escaped to Malta as ordered (one battleship was lost to German air attack), but on land the Germans forced the surrender of all Italian forces in Italy and the Balkans, the principal Italian cities were occupied, and the German occupation of Italy was announced.

Other armistices included those between *Vichy French forces and the Allies at Acre in July 1941 after the *Syrian campaign; between Finland and the Allies; and between Romania and the Allies, in which, among other matters, the territorial realignment of parts of Bessarabia were formalized; and between Bulgaria and the Allies. All these armistices took place in September–October 1944, with the USSR dictating the terms and running the Allied Control Commission. Preliminary terms for an armistice with the USSR were also agreed by Hungary's Admiral *Horthy in October 1944 but the Nazis organized a coup and he was forced to denounce it after broadcasting its terms on 15 October 1944.

armoured warfare, see TANKS, 2.

Arnhem, battle of, see MARKET-GARDEN.

Arnold, General of the Army Henry ('Hap') (1886–1950), US Army officer who commanded the Army Air Forces and was a member of the US *Joint Chiefs of Staff, and the *Combined Chiefs of Staff, committees.

Though only an average student at West Point Military Academy, by 1918 Arnold, who had been taught to fly by the Wright brothers in 1911, was the assistant chief of the US Air Service (US Army Air Corps from 1926) and the youngest colonel in the army. He arrived in Europe too late to fight in the *First World War but by September 1938 he was a major-general and chief of the Army Air Corps. In October 1940 he also became a deputy chief of staff under *Marshall, the Army Chief of Staff, and in June 1941 the corps became the US Army Air Forces (USAAF), an independent organization within the US Army with its own air staff and with Arnold at its head. In December 1941 he was promoted to lt-general and in March 1942 became Commanding General of the USAAF. He received his fourth star a year later and his fifth in December 1944, and after the war he was the US Air Force's first five-star general.

Arnold was the father of the US Army Air Forces. From a strength of 20,000 men and a few hundred old aircraft he built it into the most powerful air force in the world with 2.4 million men and 80,000 modern aircraft. He was a likeable, good-natured man, hence his nickname 'Hap' which was short for happy. 'His leadership, drive, experience and imagination,' said another USAAF general, *Eaker, 'were the primary factors in the accomplishments of the USAAF during the war, especially in the field of *logistics and training.' He worked a twelve hour day and eventually wore himself out. During the war he had four heart attacks, and the last of several more killed him. See also GRAND ALLIANCE.

Arnold, H., *Global Mission* (New York, 1949).

ARP (Air Raid Precautions), see Civil Defence sections of major powers.

Arrow Cross, the Hungarian fascist party. See HUNGARY, 3.

art, see culture section of major powers; see also WAR ARTISTS.

artillery. (See separate entries for ANTI-TANK WEAPONS and MORTARS.)

1. Design and development

Artillery equipments are categorized in many different ways; the most common terms in use include *field guns*—those guns forming part of the infantry or armoured division; *heavy artillery*—the major-calibre weapons acting as support and generally controlled at corps or army level; *self-propelled artillery*—guns and howitzers mounted on wheeled or tracked motor carriages; and *assault guns*—tracked artillery resembling tanks but used for close support of assaulting infantry. The weapons are classed according to their function as *guns*—firing at high velocity and with a relatively flat trajectory; *howitzers*—firing at low velocity with a high trajectory to pass over intervening obstacles; and **mortars*—firing only at angles over 45° so as to drop their projectile steeply behind cover.

The artillery weapons in use in 1939 were principally those which had been developed since 1930, and were based upon technological lessons learned in the *First World War. The British Army was exceptional in that all its artillery was mechanized; the German and Soviet, and to a lesser extent the American and Japanese, armies still used a large proportion of horse-drawn artillery (see ANIMALS). The design of shells and fuzes, the chemistry of propellants, the manufacture of the actual weapons, had all benefited from developments introduced in 1914–18 and perfected in the subsequent years.

Development of artillery from 1939 onwards can be divided into two spheres; the first was that continual improvement which can be expected in any technology—the adaptation of new methods of manufacture, of new materials, and of the results of theoretical research. The second was the production of new weapons in response to particular tactical developments. The two spheres obviously acted together, so that, for example, advances in metallurgy allowed the development of lighter guns, while research into the physical performances of gases was reflected in the development of recoilless weapons.

The UK and USA began their war with good new designs (though inadequate in quantity) which were capable of improvement and which were thus able to last throughout the war. Their principal task, therefore, was to produce these weapons in the necessary numbers, making refinements and improvements to meet particular demands. Thus the standard British field gun, the 25-pounder (see table, below, for an explanation of pounder) was improved by the addition of a muzzle brake to allow the firing of an armour-piercing projectile at high velocity, and was developed into a lighter version with a narrower wheel track to permit loading into the Dakota transport aircraft; other than that the 1945 gun was little different from that of 1939. In each country the design and development of guns was firmly in the hands of one official ordnance body which ruled upon the suitability of designs and authorized production.

In Germany, on the other hand, the development of weapons of any sort was open to a number of competing authorities, further complicated by political influence. As a result, much effort and time went into the development of weapons which were, tactically and strategically, useless but which bestowed prestige upon those connected with the project. The two gigantic railway guns 'Gustav' and 'Dora', of 800 mm. (31 in.) calibre firing a 7-ton shell, which were deployed during the siege of *Sevastopol took several years to design and build; it is doubtful if, between them, they fired 100 effective shots and they did nothing to influence the outcome of the war. The 15 cm. (5.9 in.) 'High Pressure Pump' gun (see V-WEAPONS) was even more ineffective.

For the most part German development paralleled that of the UK and USA, which meant the constant improvement of existing designs to meet changing tactical requirements. An early example of this, supposedly Hitler's own idea, was the adaptation of the standard 88 mm. (3.4 in.) air defence gun so that it became a highly effective anti-tank weapon. Similarly, the standard 105 mm. (4 in.) divisional howitzer, after experience in the *German–Soviet war, was redeveloped to become a weapon capable of a 360° traverse and higher elevation so that it could be emplaced in forests and fired in any direction, a reflection of the frequent instances where German artillery had been surrounded by Soviet troops. Unfortunately, and largely due to political decisions, much of this type of development began too late and was not ready for full production when the war ended.

Soviet development of artillery was influenced by the enormous losses (more than 20,000 guns) after the German invasion of June 1941 (see BARBAROSSA). Their first priority was, therefore, to mass-produce artillery to make good these losses, and the opportunity was taken to redesign so as to simplify manufacture. There was no innovation; but gun carriages were designed to mount different barrels, allowing anti-tank and field guns to use the same carriage and thus rationalize manufacture, and advantage was taken of the massive tank and tractor manufacturing base to develop a series of self-propelled (SP) assault guns using existing field gun barrels.

German SP artillery design was similar to Russian—tank chassis carrying field artillery pieces, used as a direct support weapon for the infantry. Britain and the USA, on the other hand, regarded SP artillery as normal field artillery with the ability to move more easily across country, and it was handled exactly like any other field artillery, organized in batteries and firing in the indirect role. The prime mover in this field was the USA and, except for one or two designs produced in small numbers by the British, the majority of Allied SP guns were of US origin. Even the British 'Sexton' was a British 25-pounder gun on a Canadian-built version of the American Sherman tank chassis.

Mountain artillery consisted of light guns and howitzers capable of being dismantled and carried piecemeal on mules, or even by men, into positions inaccessible to ordinary artillery. Mountain weapons were extensively used by the German and Soviet armies in the Caucasus during the German–Soviet war, by the German and British armies in the *Italian campaign and by the British in the *Burma campaign. In the latter case the terrain was not always mountainous but the ability to dismantle and mule-pack guns was of great value in the jungle.

Anti-aircraft artillery was of conventional form and relied simply upon better ammunition design and, from time to time, the enlargement of the weapon so as to be able to reach higher and fire at faster aircraft. This class divided into two: the light weapons of 37–40 mm. (1.4–1.6 in.) calibre, intended to defend against low-flying aircraft and dive-bombers, and the medium and heavy weapons of 76–150 mm. (3–5.8 in.) calibre to deal with heavy bombers at greater altitudes. The former included the 40 mm. Bofors automatic gun, of Swedish origin, and the 20 mm. Oerlikon and Hispano automatic cannons, used by virtually all combatants. The latter included the UK's 3.7 in. and 4.5 in., the German 88 mm. and 105 mm., and the USA's 90 mm. guns, However, experience showed that there was also a 'middle zone' where an aircraft was too low and moving too quickly to allow a heavy gun to engage it but too high for small-calibre weapons. This led to an attempt to produce 'intermediate A-A guns' of about 50 mm. (1.9 in.) calibre, but although the UK and Germany tried, neither produced a successful design before the war ended.

Recoilless (RCL) guns were introduced by Germany in the battle for *Crete in May 1941, since the lightness of these weapons was attractive to the airborne forces used in the assault. In brief, the RCL gun relies upon burning a very large propelling charge and allowing four-fifths of the explosion gas to be directed through a nozzle at the rear of the gun. The mass × velocity of this gas is equal to the mass × velocity of the projectile being launched up the barrel, and the gun remains stationary. Thus there is no need for a heavy carriage to withstand the firing shock, nor for a heavy and complex recoil braking system. The UK and the USA took up development of these weapons after 1941, and the USA managed to produce two shortly before the fighting ended, a 57 mm. and a 75 mm., for use in the *Pacific war. The British designs were ready for production in 1945 but were cancelled at the end of the war to allow further research and did not appear until the 1950s.

Little need be said about coast defence artillery; most countries used the same weapons they had emplaced in the 1900–18 period, and the subsequent improvements were either better mountings to permit longer range, or better fire control systems to permit more accurate long-range fire. The only modern designs were small-calibre quick-firing guns to protect harbours against raids by fast motor craft. Even the defences of Singapore, perhaps the most modern coast fortress, relied upon 9.2 in. (23 cm.) and 15 in. (38 cm.) guns of 1914–18 vintage, albeit controlled by a much improved fire control system.

IAN HOGG

2. Warfare

The Second World War was an artillery war; over half the battle casualties were caused by artillery fire, in spite of the commonly held view that tanks and *air power were the dominant weapons. The Red Army had enormous quantities of guns and howitzers, but the other combatants employed fewer pieces of artillery than they had in the First World War. This was largely because the trench warfare of 1914–18 had called for different tactics, but also because improvements in command and control meant that fewer needed to be deployed.

Nevertheless, to preserve scarce infantry, the western Allies used immense concentrations of fire and barrages (see below) to support their assaults, methods familiar in the final stages of the First World War. With the help of *radio communications, longer-ranged guns—field gun ranges had doubled to about 11,000 m. (12,000 yd.)—and excellent survey and *meteorological intelligence, they were able to concentrate the shells of many hundreds of guns in a matter of minutes. The Soviets, who enjoyed air superiority from 1943, concentrated their artillery in almost wheel-to-wheel style close to the front. This obviated their weakness in survey, their poor maps, dearth of radios, unreliable meteorological information, and irregular calibrations. But the open spaces of the Eastern Front offered more opportunity for surprise and made it less necessary to use sophisticated techniques for which they were ill-equipped.

Artillery, 2: Weapons used by chief combatants. (See also ANTI-TANK WEAPONS.)

Weapon	Weight in action kg 1kg = 2.2 lb	Weight of shell kg	Maximum range m 1 metre = 1.09 yards	Muzzle velocity m/sec
1. Germany				
Field				
75 mm LeIG 18	400	6.0	3,375	210
75 mm Geb G 36	750	5.7	9,150	475
75 mm LeFK 18	1,120	5.83	9,425	485
105 mm Geb H 40	1,660	14.5	16,740	565
105 mm LeFH 18	1,985	14.8	10,675	470
105 mm K 17	3,300	18.5	16,500	650
10 cm K18	5,642	15.1	19,075	835
15 cm SIG 33	1,700	38.0	4,700	240
15 cm sFH 18	5,512	43.5	13,250	495
15 cm K 18	12,760	43.0	24,500	890
17 cm K 18	17,520	62.8	29,600	925
21 cm Mrs 18	16,700	113.0	16,700	565
21 cm K 38	25,300	120.0	33,900	905
24 cm K 3	54,866	151.4	37,500	970
Railway				
15 cm K(E)	74,000	43.0	22,500	805
21 cm K12 (E)	302,000	107.5	115,000	1,500
24 cm k Bruno (E)	129,000	240	29,500	820
28 cm n Bruno (e)	150,000	265	36,600	995
28 cm K 5 (E)	218,000	248	86,500[a]	1,130
38 cm Siegfried	294,000	495	55,700	1,050
80 cm Gustav	1,350,000	4,800	47,000	820
[a]rocket-assisted shell				
Coast defence				
105 mm SK L/60	11,750	15.1	17,500	900
15 cm Tbts c/36		45.5	19,525	835
17 cm SK L/40		62.8	27,200	875
28 cm SK L/50		284	39,100	905
38 cm Siegfried		475	55,700	1,050
40.6 cm Adolf		610	56,000	1,050
Weights depended upon type of mounting and emplacement, but were always in the 100+ ton category.				
Anti-aircraft				
37 mm Flak 18	1,748	0.6	4,800[b]	820
50 mm Flak 41	3,100	2.2	5,600[b]	840
88 mm Flak 18–37	4,985	9.4	8,000[b]	820
88 mm Flak 41	7,800	9.4	10,675[b]	1,000
105 mm Flak 39	10,224	14.8	9,450[b]	881
128 mm Flak 40	13,000	26.0	10,675[b]	880
[b]effective ceiling				
for anti-tank role of 88 mm, see ANTI-TANK WEAPONS.				
Recoilless				
75 mm LG40	145	5.83	6,800	350
105 mm LG40	388	14.8	7,950	335
105 mm LG42	552	14.8	7,950	335
2. Italy				
Field				
75 mm Mod 37	1,185	6.3	12,500	600
105 mm Mod 42	3,860	17.5	17,600	710
149 mm How Mod 20	5,690	40.8	16,000	375
149 mm Mod 35	11,480	50.8	22,000	800
210 mm Mod 35	15,800	102	16,000	570

Artillery, 2: (*cont.*)

Weapon	Weight in action kg 1kg = 2.2 lb	Weight of shell kg	Maximum range m 1 metre = 1.09 yards	Muzzle velocity m/sec
Anti-aircraft				
75 mm Mod 35	3,350	6.5	9,300[b]	715
75 mm Mod 38	5,200	6.5	8,400[b]	975
90 mm Mod 38	5,180	10.0	12,000[b]	840
102 mm Mod 38		13.2	9,500[b]	755

[b] effective ceiling

3. Japan

Weapon	Weight in action kg	Weight of shell kg	Maximum range m	Muzzle velocity m/sec
Field				
70 mm Inf H M92	212	3.8	2,800	200
75 mm Mtn M94	535	6.5	8,300	385
75 mm Mod 38	945	5.9	8,250	510
75 mm Mod 95	1,105	6.5	14,950	700
105 mm Mod 14	3,110	15.8	15,000	620
105 mm Mod 92	3,720	15.8	18,250	760
105 mm H Mod 91	1,495	15.8	10,765	545
150 mm Mod 89	10,400	45.8	19,900	685
150 mm H Mod 96	4,135	31.2	11,850	805
240 mm Mod 45		181	10,335	365
410 mm How	81,280	997	19,380	535
Anti-aircraft				
40 mm Mod 91	890	0.8	3,950[b]	610
75 mm Mod 88	2,440	6.5	8,850[b]	720
75 mm Type 4	3,400	6.5	10,050[b]	860
80 mm Mod 99	6,575	9.0	9,750[b]	800
105 mm Mod 14	4,480	15.8	10,950[b]	700
120 mm Type 3	22,000	26.0	14,650[b]	855

[b] effective ceiling

4. UK

Weapon	Weight in action kg	Weight of shell kg	Maximum range m	Muzzle velocity m/sec
Field				
25 pdr Mk 2[c]	1,800	11.3	12,250	518
3.7 in How	842	9.1	5,485	244
4.5 in How	1,493	15.9	6,400	308
4.5 in Gun	5,842	24.9	18,745	686
5.5 in Gun	6,190	45.4	14,815	510
7.2 in How Mk 6	14,763	90.7	17,925	587
Anti-aircraft				
40 mm Mk 1	1,981	0.9	1,525[b]	823
3 in 20 cwt[c]	2,722	7.5	4,785[b]	610
3.7 in Mk 1	9,317	12.7	9,755[b]	792
3.7 in Mk 6	17,400	12.7	13,715[b]	1,044
4.5 in Mk 2	14,990	24.5	10,515[b]	732
5.25 in Mk 2	30,785	36.3	13,105[b]	853

[b] effective ceiling

Weapon	Weight in action kg	Weight of shell kg	Maximum range m	Muzzle velocity m/sec
Coast defence				
6 pdr Twin[c]	10,040	2.7	4,710	720
6 in Mk 24	16,285	45.4	22,400	861
9.2 in Mk 10	127,000	172.4	33,560	823
15 in Mk 2	378,990	879	38,405	817

Artillery, 2: *(cont.)*

Weapon	*Weight in action kg 1kg = 2.2lb*	*Weight of shell kg*	*Maximum range m 1 metre = 1.09 yards*	*Muzzle velocity m/sec*
Recoilless				
3.45 in Mk 1	34.02	4.99	914	183
3.7 in Mk 1	170.1	10.21	1,825	305
95 mm Mk 1	1,066	11.34	9,875	488
7.2 in P 1	1,626	54.43	6,400	275

[c] The notation 'pdr' indicating 'pounder', was a traditional British method of classifying guns which lingered into this period; it was occasionally useful to distinguish a particular gun from others of the same calibre. The notation 'cwt' for 'hundredweight' (112 lbs) was of similar value, being the nominal weight of the gun barrel and distinguishing a particular gun from others of the same calibre. The 2 pdr gun had a calibre of 1.575 in (40 mm); the 6 pdr gun of 2.244 in (57 mm), the 17 pdr gun of 3 in (76 mm), and the 25 pdr gun of 3.45 in (87 mm).

5. USA

Weapon	Weight in action kg	Weight of shell kg	Maximum range m	Muzzle velocity m/sec
Field				
75 mm How M1	607	6.4	8,787	381
75 mm Gun M2	1,564	6.7	11,686	596
105 mm How M2	2,260	15.0	11,160	472
155 mm How M1	5,428	43.1	14,955	564
155 mm Gun M1	13,880	43.1	23,220	853
8 in How M1	14,380	90.7	16,925	594
8 in Gun M1	31,435	109	32,585	866
240 mm How M1	18,734	156.5	14,996	518
Anti-aircraft				
37 mm M1	2,777	0.6	3,200[b]	792
40 mm M1	2,517	0.9	3,355[b]	875
3 in M3	5,534	5.8	8,504[b]	853
90 mm M2	14,650	10.6	10,300[b]	823
105 mm M3	15,212	14.8	11,275[b]	853
120 mm M1	22,135	22.7	14,445[b]	945

[b] effective ceiling

Weapon	Weight in action kg	Weight of shell kg	Maximum range m	Muzzle velocity m/sec
Coast defence				
6 in M1	71,465	47.6	24,825	853
8 in Mk VI	71,670	118.8	30,160	838
12 in Gun M1917	189,015	408.2	26,700	710
12 in Mor M1912	74,980	474.5	10,748	365
14 in M1910	309,355	753	20,850	716
16 in M1919	492,156	1,061	38,040	838
Recoilless				
57 mm T15	22.11	1.22	4,510	371
75 mm M20	75.07	6.53	6,360	302

6. USSR

Weapon	Weight in action kg	Weight of shell kg	Maximum range m	Muzzle velocity m/sec
Field				
76 mm Gun M1939	1,484	6.1	12,185	670
76 mm Gun M1942	1,116	6.2	13,000	680
122 mm How M1938	2,250	21.7	11,795	500
122 mm Gun M1937	7,120	24.9	20,800	800
152 mm How M1938	4,165	40	12,400	508
152 mm Gun M1935	18,350	48.9	26,975	880
203 mm How M1931	17,700	98.5	18,000	606
210 mm Gun M1939	43,180	135	30,430	800
Anti-aircraft				
37 mm M39	2,000	0.7	6,000[b]	960
76.2 mm M1938	4,300	6.6	9,500[b]	815
85 mm M1939	4,300	9.2	8,280[b]	800
85 mm M1944	4,890	9.2	10,200[b]	900

[b] effective ceiling

Artillery fire fell into two groups: targets of opportunity, in which a forward observer saw a target and called for fire; and fire plans, employed to accompany an attack, or form part of a defensive plan, in which specific targets were selected and the necessary data prepared—predicted fire, as it was called—before battle was joined. For offensive actions fire plans used barrages in which a line of bursting shells was placed to act as a barrier or protective screen. These could be 'standing', where the position of the bursts remained the same; 'creeping', in which the line of fire moved in steps towards the objective, the infantry keeping behind its protection; or 'rolling', in which two lines of fire were laid down, the rearmost leapfrogging the other so that the advancing belt of bursting shells was thicker and more destructive. For defensive purposes fire plans used concentrations of fire, where the guns all aimed at the same spot. When the Americans concentrated the artillery of an entire corps, some 200 guns, on a target they called it a 'serenade'. When this was fired by what was known as TOT (time on target), that is each shell's trajectory was calculated so that they all arrived simultaneously, the effect was devastating. These techniques were used by all combatants, but the British also had an additional 'quick fire plan' known as a stonk (standard regimental concentration). This was based upon the frontage of two of a regiment's field batteries with the third superimposed and produced a 440 m. (525 yd.) block of fire, though it came to mean any brief and sudden bombardment. It could be rapidly prepared to support a small infantry action using a graphical template. This was simply a piece of celluloid with the spacing of the guns marked on it in black ink at the correct scale (1/25000) of the artillery plotting map. It was laid over the target and the ranges and bearings to the various points for each gun could then be calculated using a scale and a protractor.

Apart from having a greater range, the guns of 1939 were little different, ballistically, from those of 1918. The ammunition was improved, the shells being more efficient, with more reliable fuzes, and, as the war progressed, many different types of shell were developed. The US 105 mm. (4 in.) howitzer, for example, fired no fewer than thirteen different kinds, from high explosive to propaganda leaflets. During the inter-war years much work had gone into the improvement of predicted fire. However, predicted fire demanded precise meteorological information, and this depended upon the method of determination; it was not until late in the war that radar-tracking of balloons carrying radio-sounding apparatus measuring air density and temperature produced really reliable data from which the necessary corrections could be made.

Of equal importance was the ability to communicate. During 1914–18 the artillery received target information from forward observers; as soon as the infantry advanced and the observer was removed from his telephone, target information ceased to flow and subsequent firing was usually done on a timed basis, hoping that the advance had reached its scheduled point in synchrony with the artillery. In 1939–45 the ability of observers to carry radio equipment and speak directly to the guns was of vital importance. Furthermore, the ability to link an observer by radio to higher formations gave him the ability to call for fire from formations larger than his own. The forward observer for an artillery battery was not confined to firing his own battery; he could call for the guns of the regiment, division, army corps, or even army, according to the importance of the target. In the British Army a regiment could answer a call for fire in less than three minutes, and an army corps could be made available in less than half an hour. It was this flexibility and rapid response which made artillery fire much more effective and formidable than previously.

Tactical flexibility was also enhanced by mechanization and the self-propelled gun. In 1914–18 the infantry frequently advanced beyond the support of their own artillery because horse-drawn guns could not cross the shell-torn country fast enough. In 1939–45, although the German and Soviet armies still used many horses, as a general rule mobile operations were supported by mechanized or self-propelled weapons which had a far better cross-country performance and could thus keep up with the advance.

The spotting of targets also benefited from technological advances. The air direction of artillery fire had been pioneered by the Germans as early as 1914 and, using the manoeuvrable Storch light aircraft, they were again in the forefront in 1940. The British Army, and later the American, also adopted light aircraft such as the Auster which were operated by artillery officers as flying observation posts. These proved to be highly effective for the detection and engagement of targets out of sight of the forward observers on the ground. Moreover it was found that the presence of an artillery spotter aircraft frequently caused the opposing side's artillery to cease firing for fear of retaliation.

Sound ranging, originally developed in 1917, was improved by the availability of better electrical devices. This system relied upon a chain of buried microphones to detect the noise of an enemy gun firing and, by measuring the time taken for the sound to cross the microphone array, could provide a series of bearings which crossed at the gun's location. This system could detect guns to an accuracy of 50 m. (160 ft.) and it could be used 'in reverse' to detect the sound of shells falling and derive corrections to bring gunfire to bear against the enemy gun.

Flash spotting was a technique involving observation of the front by skilled observers to detect the flash of artillery firing from otherwise concealed positions. This, too, depended upon good communication between observers and plotting stations but was capable of producing accurate locations. However, the gradual adoption of flashless propellant powders, particularly by the German Army, led to this system becoming less reliable towards the end of the war. It was, however, used in 1944–5 to detect the launch of V-2 rockets.

Artillery employment was broadly the same in all armies except the Red Army; the basic tactical formation was the division, and this was the lowest level which carried its own organic artillery with its own artillery commander. The division would contain one field artillery regiment/battalion per brigade, plus air defence and anti-tank units and might have a medium regiment attached. In the case of a British infantry division, this would mean 72 25-pounder guns, perhaps 12 5.5 in. guns, about 24 17-pounder anti-tank guns, manned by specialist infantrymen as well as those belonging to the artillery arm, and 24 40 mm. (1.5 in.) air defence guns. The corps would have a number of divisions, each with its own artillery, and in addition would have extra, usually heavy-calibre, artillery at the disposition of the corps commander. Generally speaking the divisional artillery was primarily concerned with the support of the division's operations; the corps artillery was available for 'counter-bombardment'—the shelling of enemy artillery so as to neutralize it—or for heavy support to those divisional operations which required it; and at army level there was an army artillery commander disposing of artillery units attached to the army for support of the various corps in their operations. Heavy air defence guns were generally a separate organization which could be distributed in accordance with the air threat; in the German organization, they were controlled by the Luftwaffe.

The Red Army lacked the sophisticated techniques at the disposal of the Germans or the western Allies. For easier control of its artillery it was therefore normal to find divisions, corps, and even armies made up entirely of artillery. These were superimposed upon the infantry organization so as to provide the support they required but remained totally independent formations.

Anti-aircraft guns are also artillery. In 1939, they were directed by predictors on which operators followed the flight of aircraft mechanically. This could not be done at night or in poor visibility. *Radar, on the other hand, determined the course, height, and speed of hostile aircraft and the future positions of shell and aircraft could be calculated electronically, a process which could also be done at night when radar-directed *searchlights caught a plane in their beams. An alternative, throwing up barrages of shells through which aircraft would have to fly was, at first, only marginally more effective than that used in 1917. It was a different matter when the height and speed of a bomber stream was determined by radar, for even if radar did not lock on to individual planes, it could place the barrage in the centre of the stream. The increased lethality of shells, more powerful guns and, in the *Air Defence of Great Britain (ADGB), the introduction of the *proximity fuze in June 1944 made barrages fearsome particularly at an altitude below 6,000 m. (20,000 ft.). In the campaign against the V-1 flying bomb, ADGB anti-aircraft guns, particularly 40 mm. light anti-aircraft Bofors, destroyed more of them than fighter planes.

DOMINICK GRAHAM/IAN HOGG

Bailey, J. B. A., *Field Artillery and Firepower* (Oxford, 1989).
Bidwell, S., *Gunners at War* (London, 1970).
—and Graham, D., *Firepower; British Army Weapons and Theories of War 1904–1945* (London, 1982).
Hogg, I. V., *British & American Artillery of World War Two* (London, 1978).
—*German Artillery of World War Two* (London, 1975).
—*The Guns of World War Two* (London, 1976).

art treasures, see LOOT.

Ascension Island, British south Atlantic colony which, from mid-1942, was the base of the 1st Composite Squadron of the US Army Air Forces employed on anti-submarine patrols (see LACONIA). The airfield, Wideawake, was also an important staging post for ferrying aircraft from the USA to Africa (see also TAKORADI AIR ROUTE).

ASDIC, acronym of Allied Submarine Detection Investigation Committee, an Anglo-French organization which in 1917 began evolving a system of detecting submerged submarines by sound: it emitted a pulse which was then picked up when it rebounded from a submarine's hull. By 1938 it had been fully developed by the British who, for a time, regarded it as the answer to *submarine warfare. But though it was, within limits, effective, it could only gauge the distance and direction of the target which was why a pattern of depth charges had to be set to explode at different depths (see ANTI-SUBMARINE WEAPONS). The US Navy developed a similar system which it called Sonar and in 1943 the Royal Navy adopted the same name.

Athenia, 13,500-ton liner, the first British ship of the war to be sunk when it was torpedoed on 3 September 1939 near the Hebrides off Scotland's west coast. The ship was attacked without warning despite Hitler's orders that U-boats were to obey the *Hague Conventions. Out of the 128 who lost their lives, 28 were Americans, which greatly exacerbated anti-Nazi feeling in the USA. German newspapers accused Churchill of deliberately arranging the incident to create bad German–US relations, but it later transpired that the U-boat had mistaken the liner for a *Q-ship or *auxiliary cruiser.

Atlantic, battle of the, popular name for the six-year struggle from 1939 to 1945 to secure the Atlantic routes vital to Allied victory. It was not, therefore, a battle in the traditional sense like Trafalgar, Jutland, or *Midway, but rather a long fight to organize, protect, and manage the movement of war materials and shipping efficiently in response to the conflicting pressures of global war. To win in the Atlantic the Allies had to overcome more than the Germans. The Germans, in turn, never possessed the forces to achieve victory.

RAF Liberator bomber attacks a U-boat during the **battle of the Atlantic**.

The shooting war in the Atlantic was actually a series of campaigns, in which the immediate and long-term objectives of German strategy varied while those of the Allies remained essentially constant. For the Allies the Atlantic war had three objectives: blockade of Axis Europe, security of Allied sea movements, and the freedom to project military power overseas as required. The preponderance of Allied naval power meant that the blockade was never seriously challenged (but see BLOCKADE RUNNERS). Allied *amphibious warfare potential took time to develop, but that was due to the limits of air and land forces and depended on the availability of suitable *landing craft. Security of trade movements at sea posed the greatest problem for Allied navies due to the small, but powerful and modern, German surface fleet and more importantly the Germans' innovative use of submarines.

The battle of the Atlantic was therefore a response to German initiatives, since most objectives of Allied strategy could be met without direct attack on Germany's maritime interests. The initiative in the Atlantic fell on the Kriegsmarine (German Navy), a service woefully unprepared for a major naval war. The massive expansion of *Raeder's 'Z' Plan of 1939 would have provided the required forces, but not before 1944 (see GERMANY, Table 11). When the Kriegsmarine found itself at war with the UK in September 1939 naval planners were left to wonder 'What now?'

German naval strategy during the *phoney war was thus an adjunct to the main thrust in the west by the army and air forces. The Kriegsmarine harassed and contained Allied naval forces through a war on shipping conducted largely by surface ships. These included the heavy units of the main fleet (see GERMAN SURFACE RAIDERS), as well as *auxiliary cruisers, but although dramatic, these operations were never more than a qualified success. The fleet made a major contribution to the invasion of Norway in April 1940, but suffered crippling losses. The importance of U-boats remained to be demonstrated during the phoney war, and torpedo failures marred their contribution to the *Norwegian campaign.

The battle began in earnest after the fall of *France in June 1940. That collapse gave impetus to the naval war in two ways. First, French and Norwegian bases partially allowed the Germans to overcome the Allied blockade, permitting breakout through the Greenland–UK gap and giving them advanced bases on the Atlantic. Second, the collapse of western Europe provided the Kriegsmarine with a clear and simple strategic objective with potential war-winning results: defeat of the UK by severing her maritime communications. It was this battle, begun in earnest in the late summer of 1940, that Churchill dubbed the battle of the Atlantic. It was, in fact, the only time in the war when the Germans were within a measurable distance of victory at sea (see Graph for comparison of losses, September 1939–May 1945).

Unfortunately the Germans had no way to measure the distance accurately and lacked the means to execute the strategy. Karl *Dönitz, commander of the U-boat fleet, estimated that if Germany destroyed 600,000 to 750,000 tons of British shipping per month for a year the UK would sue for peace. German 'certainty' of the scale of the task contrasts sharply with British knowledge about their shipping and import situation. Attempts in 1938 by the British to estimate their requirements and shipping resources failed to produce uniformly agreed results. It seemed that the UK needed 47 million tons of imports per year, and that British shipping alone could handle the requirement. The availability of neutral shipping for some carriage would easily fill the gap to achieve the UK's estimated peacetime import total of 50–60 million tons.

To attack this amorphous target the Kriegsmarine applied all its resources over the winter of 1940–1, but they were unequal to the task. Large raiders ended up either blockaded in French ports or destroyed, and the loss of the **Bismarck* in May 1941 effectively ended attempts to use heavy ships in the Atlantic. German surface raiders caused the Allies anxiety, but their destruction of Allied shipping was negligible: only 6.1% of shipping destroyed by Germany during the war. By comparison, 6.5% was accounted for by mines, 13.4% by aircraft, 4.8% by unknown causes, and some 70% by U-boats. As the last figure indicates, Germany came to rely on its U-boat fleet. Dönitz had long argued that only a submarine campaign would defeat the UK and that this required 300 ocean-going U-boats. In August 1940 he had only 27 for operations and over the winter of 1940–1 the number available declined, to a low of 21 in February. Moreover, only about a third were on station at a time: 13 in August 1940 and only 8 in January 1941. The number of U-boats increased dramatically in the spring of 1941, but by then Dönitz's chance had passed.

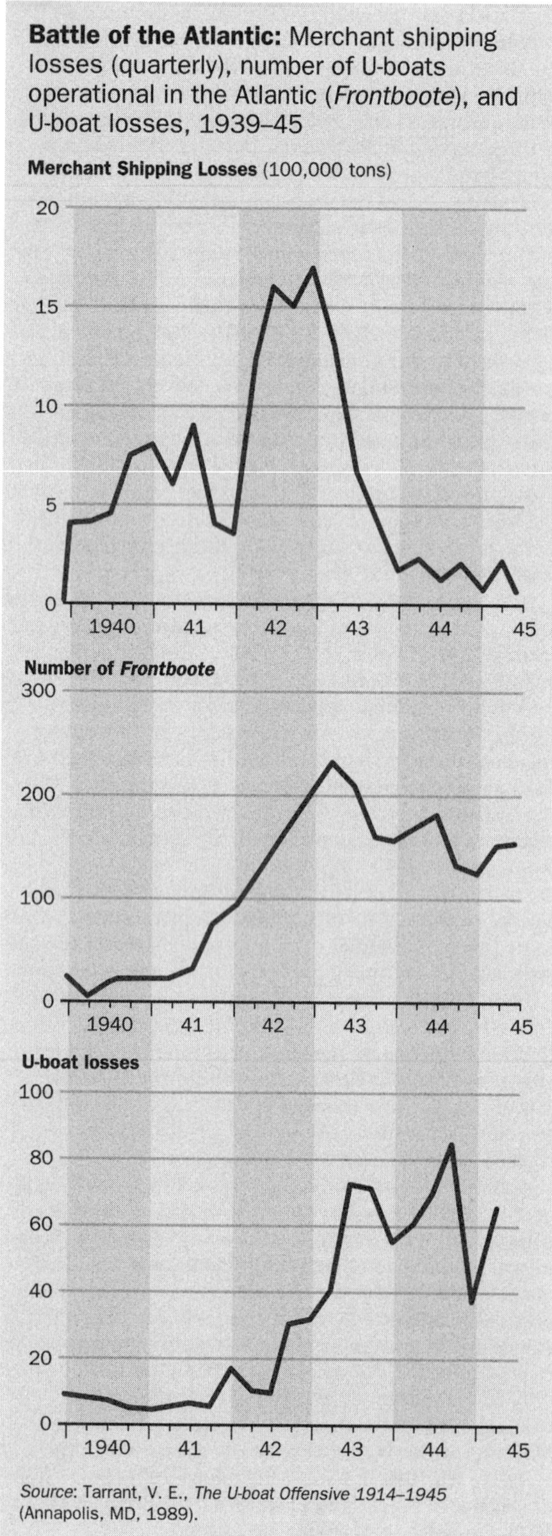

German U-boat operations in the second winter of the war were none the less highly successful; their innovative tactics caught the RN by surprise and produced the first 'Happy Time' for German submariners. Through the first year of the war the Allies defended shipping by routeing it away from danger, sweeping inshore waters with aircraft to keep U-boats down and immobilized, aggressive patrolling, and escorting ocean *convoys with a mixture of forces appropriate to the threat. Since it was believed that air power and convoys forced submarines to operate inshore and submerged, anti-submarine (A/S) escort extended initially only to 12° West. Beyond that convoys were protected by cruisers, battleships, and even Allied submarines. Submariners could move further seaward in search of easy targets, but once away from the channelling effect of coasts, where shipping routes converged, targets and good firing positions were difficult for individual submariners to obtain.

Dönitz developed a system to solve both the search and the attack problems on the high seas. The search problem was resolved by establishing patrol lines of U-boats perpendicular to the convoy route, controlled by a shore-based plot through high-frequency *radio communications. Acting like a huge drift net and manoeuvred on the basis of intelligence, these 'wolf-packs' covered a wide area of open ocean. Once in contact with a convoy, shadowers from the pack transmitted position reports to the shore staff, who then directed the pack on to the target, and sent a medium-frequency homing signal to draw in the pack. Attack on the convoy followed once a number of U-boats were assembled, and it was left to the individual submariners to conduct it. Typically attacking at night, the U-boats slipped inside the escort screen and often inside the convoy itself on highspeed surface runs. Initially defence against such attacks was so feeble that U-boat captains could pick the biggest targets and fire all their loaded torpedo tubes before retiring. Escape was simply a fast run astern of the convoy or, if pressed by an escort, a quick dive.

The RN was unprepared for this type of warfare and losses to some convoys were alarming. At the end of October 1940 SC7, a slow east-bound convoy of 30 ships, lost 21 of its number and HX79, a fast convoy following close behind, lost 12 of its 49 ships. The British responded in several ways, but the main thrust was the progressive denial of both tactical and strategic surface manoeuvrability to the U-boats. Over the winter of 1940–1 steps were taken to extend the range of naval and air anti-submarine escort, culminating in the establishment of bases in Iceland in April 1941. In the same month a distinct Western Approaches Command was established in Liverpool to co-ordinate and oversee defence of trade convoys from submarine attack.

Icelandic bases permitted defence of convoys by small ships to about 35° West, but a gap remained in A/S escort between Iceland-based forces and those from the convoy terminals in Canada. In May 1941 the Royal Canadian Navy (RCN) moved to Newfoundland to fill that gap and in June began escorting convoys between the Grand Banks and Iceland (see NEWFOUNDLAND ESCORT FORCE). The *air gap between the limits of Iceland and Newfoundland-based aircraft remained for another two years and profoundly affected the development of the battle (see Map 1).

Providing ocean A/S escort for convoys did not defeat the German attack: Dönitz's tactics were designed to cope with escorted convoys. Although some notable U-boat 'aces' were killed or captured early in the year, the Germans had little trouble from escorts during 1941. The Allies lacked an effective, modern *radar to detect U-boats on the surface at night, tactical responses to successful penetrations of the escort screen were still primitive, and the teamwork required for escort group cohesion was still developing. What 'saved' the UK in the spring of 1941 was a generally improving situation. Imports had declined sharply over the winter of 1940–1 as the UK adjusted to closed east coast ports, as weather-damaged shipping lay idle, and as demoralized European merchant seamen obstructed sailings. These problems eased as winter gave way to spring, the UK adjusted to new shipping patterns, requirements were sweated down to essentials, the USA moved alongside, and war with the USSR drew German attention. Moreover, German success in the war against tonnage fell far short of expectations—and of the typically inflated claims by U-boat captains. Merchant shipping losses over 1941 amounted to 3.6 million tons—an average of above 250,000 tons per month—of which 2.1 million fell to U-boats. The savings in British tonnage from rationalizing imports and reducing port congestion during 1941 amounted to about 3 million tons, while some 1.2 million tons of new merchant shipping were launched. The UK actually ended 1941 with a surplus in tonnage. Over the same year it imported only about half of its estimated pre-war rate and much less than the amount thought necessary for waging war. In 1942 the UK would manage to live and fight—just—on approximately 23 million tons of imports. Moreover, in 1941 the prospect in the short term looked good as over 7 million tons of new shipping was on order in US yards. Only for brief periods in 1942 and 1944 did the UK draw on its reserves of key commodities; in all other years imports outpaced consumption.

The U-boat war in 1941 was therefore dramatic but not decisive. Despite some dips and alarms the tonnage available to carry the UK's imports remained remarkably constant (see table, UK, 9). The official British history of wartime shipping concludes that there was little wastage in the management of British shipping during the war, although port delays reduced efficiency and diversion to other tasks, such as the build-up of forces for the Normandy landing in June 1944 (see OVERLORD), cut sharply into import programmes. In contrast, it is estimated that American wastage of carrying capacity was prodigious, reaching perhaps 9 million tons a year by 1945—three times the total American tonnage lost to enemy action in the war.

The winter of 1940–1 was the only time the Germans could have achieved a decisive victory in the Atlantic, and they failed. From the summer of 1941 until the spring of 1943, then, German strategy aimed to embarrass Allied plans and forestall the development of the Second Front. In this they enjoyed a modicum of success. But several new elements weighed heavily against Germany in the Atlantic by mid-1941. The invasion of the USSR in June 1941 (see BARBAROSSA) drew German air strength east, and drew U-boats into a defensive posture off Norway by November in response to Hitler's fears for his northern flank. British persistence in the battle for the *Mediterranean also drew U-boats there by the autumn. By the early summer of 1941 the British had achieved a major breakthrough in the German U-boat cipher system (see ULTRA, 1), and by August they were reading Atlantic U-boat signal traffic with some regularity and rapidity. This, along with the general intelligence picture derived from conventional means, allowed convoys to be routed well clear of danger for much of the period. It was not a perfect system, and some rather dramatic battles around slow convoys developed in September and October. One historian has argued that ULTRA saved 300 ships for the Allies in the last half of 1941, a figure that is impossible to refute—or to verify conclusively.

The other major change in the Atlantic war during 1941 was the increasingly active involvement of the USA. The US Navy's participation in defence of shipping followed Roosevelt's and Churchill's historic meeting in August at *Placentia Bay, when they divided the world into spheres of strategic control. The USA took control of the western Atlantic, including Iceland and in mid-September the USN began to escort fast convoys between the Grand Banks and Iceland, working alongside the Royal Canadian Navy (RCN) which took responsibility for slow convoys. The USN was therefore involved in the battles around Canadian-escorted slow convoys in September and October 1941. The Canadians performed so poorly and slow convoys were so vulnerable that one was sent back to Canada when confronted by a U-boat concentration. German withdrawals to the Mediterranean and Norway eased the crisis around the slow convoys by November, while moves were afoot to reinforce the beleaguered Canadians.

The Atlantic war entered a new phase after the Japanese attack on *Pearl Harbor in December 1941. American industry and manpower gave the Allies promise of victory, but in the meantime vast new theatres for Axis attack were opened up. For the Germans the most important of these was the eastern seaboard of the USA, where a rich harvest of Allied shipping sailed virtually unprotected. The first victim fell on 12 January 1942 and by the spring individual U-boats were enjoying their second 'Happy Time'. In May and June alone U-boats sank over a million tons in US waters—half their total score for 1941 in two months. Allied merchant shipping losses peaked in 1942: according to the USN's official history, some 8.3 million tons were lost to enemy action. By British estimates, 6.1

million tons of this fell to U-boats, which averaged over half a million tons per month. It was the closest Dönitz got to his earlier objective, but it could not be sustained. The curve of new shipping construction surged past losses in the autumn of 1942, as American industry gained momentum. Moreover, the U-boats' success in the western Atlantic was the result of a monumental American strategic blunder.

Like the British in 1939–40, the Americans in 1942 trusted in offensive patrols by surface and air forces, protected lanes, and independently routed coastal shipping to defeat the U-boat menace. The result was one of the real disasters of the war. U-boats enjoyed freedom of movement inshore as patrols and merchant ships proceeded independent of one another along predictable routes. Routine patrols made operating areas more secure for U-boats, while individual ships made easy victims. Only the progressive extension of a convoy system within a wide and effectively patrolled air corridor reduced the threat from lone submariners. The quality of the naval escort, the basis for much American concern since they preferred destroyers and there were too few of these, was less important than the system. Air patrols made wolf-pack operations impossible, while convoys eliminated easy victims and threatened U-boats with counter-attack. Even if a lone U-boat could find a convoy it could anticipate only one good shot before the escort reacted and the convoy evaded the attacker. As this system was extended, the ratio of Dönitz's basic formula for success—the amount of tonnage sunk per U-boat day at sea—was reduced, and forced U-boats to move on. Much of 1942, then, saw the progressive denial of operating areas for U-boats dependent upon surface manoeuvrability for both tactical and strategic success.

American failure to institute a coastal convoy system immediately has mystified historians, but recent Canadian scholarship sheds light on this issue in two ways. First, the infrastructure needed to establish a convoy system was in place by the end of 1941. The Canadians ran, on behalf of the British, a naval network which controlled shipping in major American ports, and in early 1941 the USN was brought into it. Ottawa was privy to intelligence as it affected merchant shipping, and controlled shipping movements in the western Atlantic until the Americans took over in July 1942. The Anglo-Canadian system, with local help, could have organized a convoy system from American ports at the end of 1941. Secondly, American delay in establishing convoys probably owed more to doctrinal issues, and was no doubt the result of experience alongside the struggling Canadians in late 1941. The USN's predilection for offensive measures and belief that poorly escorted slow convoys were dangerous, as was demonstrated in September and October 1941, clearly carried more weight than advice from the British.

By September 1942, New York had become the western terminus for transatlantic convoys, and a complete interlocking convoy system extended into the southern hemisphere. In the process the Allies abandoned Iceland as a relay point for transatlantic escorts, and convoys sailed between the Grand Banks and Ireland with a single Mid-Ocean Escort Force group, which could make the passage provided the convoy stayed close to the great circle route. With the Germans busy elsewhere restricted routeing was not a problem, but it made the main routes more vulnerable when wolf-packs returned to the air gap in the autumn. By September 1942 the soft theatres were gone, and the Atlantic war reached its moment of decision.

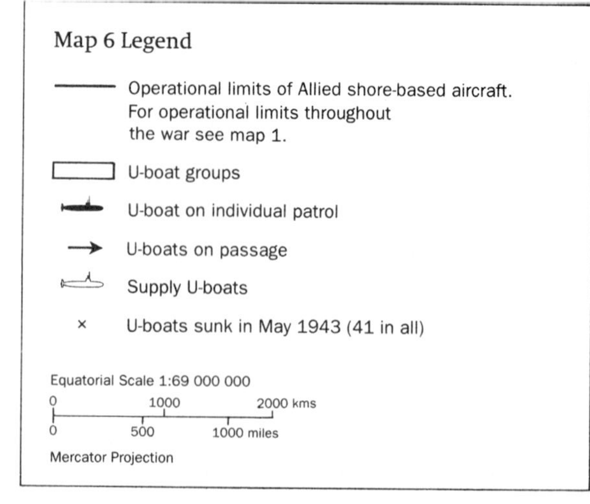

The winter of 1942–3 is the most complex period of the Atlantic war. Allied fortunes changed dramatically, with victories at *Stalingrad, *Guadalcanal, and in the *North African campaign. Offensives put more demands on shipping, while North African operations drew more heavily on British war reserves than planners had anticipated. The situation was further complicated by drawing the escorts needed for the North African landings from the direct UK–West Africa convoy route. Thereafter all south Atlantic shipping was routed through the western Atlantic convoy system and to the UK along the main routes. This extended sailing times and reduced carrying capacity. The UK therefore became utterly dependent on the main convoy routes just as the Germans were driven to attack them in force. As a final point, the situation was further aggravated by the fact that the bulk of new merchant shipping was American (see USA, 7) while the vast majority of losses were British. These broad strategic developments therefore pushed the UK into its gravest import crisis of the war just as the battle in mid-ocean built to a climax. The Germans returned to the air gap in increasing numbers in August 1942, with enough U-boats to operate two large packs. Over the next eight months the number of packs and their size increased dramatically.

The naval and air tactics, doctrine, and equipment necessary to deal with wolf-packs had improved markedly by 1942. Air patrols previously hovered directly over

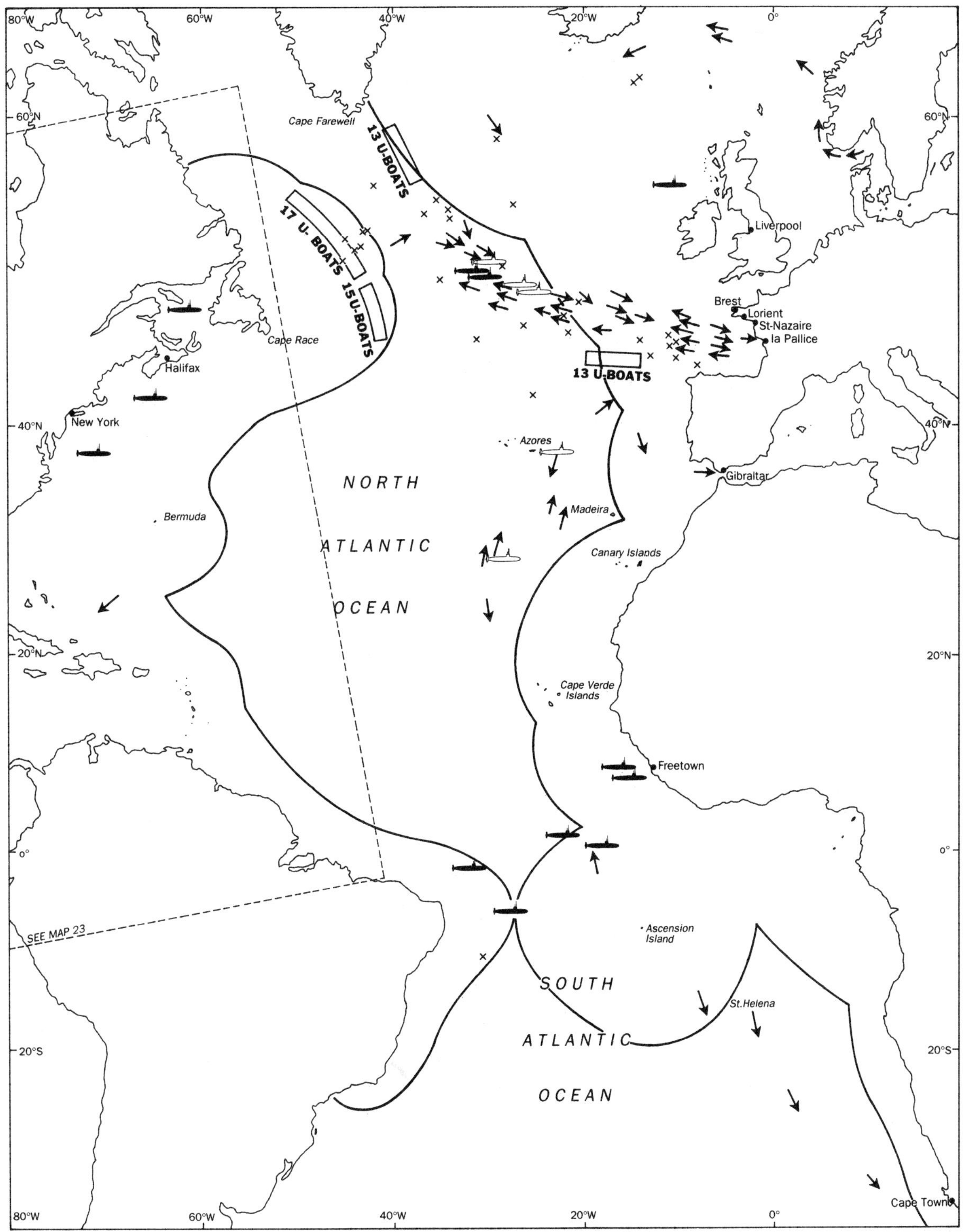

6. **Battle of the Atlantic**: U-boat dispositions, 1 May 1943

convoys, or patrolled over vast areas in support of several convoys. By 1942 air patrols were synchronizing their efforts more effectively with convoy movements by flying slightly ahead and on either side of a convoy's line of advance to forestall the assembling of a pack: these tactics also produced more sightings. The introduction of white paint schemes, which made aircraft harder to spot, higher patrol altitudes, and more effective fuzes for depth charges (see ANTI-SUBMARINE WEAPONS) contributed to more and more successful air support. In August a few specially equipped very long range (VLR) Liberator aircraft penetrated to the depths of the air-gap, a development noted with concern by the Germans. Naval escorts now enjoyed the benefits of 18 months of steady operational and tactical leadership, the development of sound and workable tactics and doctrine, and new equipment. The latter included 10 cm. radar with an automated 360° sweep, which made it possible to establish an effective barrier around the convoy at night in good weather. The assembly of the pack around the convoy could now be forestalled by ship-borne High Frequency Direction Finding sets (see HUFF-DUFF), which revealed the position of U-boats sending contact and shadowing reports. Destroyers of the escort screen raced out and drove the U-boats off. Shipborne HF/DF was not completely successful (destroyers had to conserve fuel), but it usually reduced the number of attackers that the radar barrier had to handle. The only element missing from the naval escort in 1942 were small escort carriers which, like so many other resources, had been drawn off for the North African landings and the *Arctic convoys.

These developments affected the dynamic of convoy battles. Good leadership, group familiarity, and the tactical intelligence provided by modern sensors allowed the six RN mid-ocean groups to win their battles in late 1942. It helped that the RN escorted the bulk of the fast convoys. The other five groups, four of them Canadian and one nominally American, lacked modern equipment and enough destroyers, and their convoys—the bulk of them slow—were easy marks for German submariners. The results were hardly surprising: Canadian escorted convoys accounted for 80% of mid-Atlantic losses from July to December. It was, in fact a repeat of autumn 1941. The British were so alarmed that they removed Canadian groups from the mid-ocean for several months in early 1943.

The only bright spot for the mid-Atlantic at the very end of the year was the re-penetration of the Atlantic U-boat cipher. The gap in this part of the ULTRA picture had endured since February, but with individual U-boats roving inshore enough intelligence was available from conventional sources and other decrypts to keep track of them. However, as the mid-ocean filled with U-boats precise intelligence became increasingly crucial. Through the winter of 1943 the number of operational U-boats ranged from 403 to 435, with an average of more than 100 at sea each month, most in the Atlantic. Dönitz, who became head of the Kriegsmarine in January 1943, had his magic number and a free hand.

The battle of the Atlantic reached a climax in early 1943, building to a crisis for the Allies very quickly, spurred by bad winter weather, the rising numbers of U-boats, and another gap in ULTRA intelligence in the first three weeks of March. The situation was so bad in early March that all North Atlantic convoys were located by the Germans, half were attacked, and some 22% of shipping in those convoys sunk. The grim news brought alarm to the Allied camp, but the seeds of the German defeat were already sown. In January 1943 Churchill, Roosevelt, and their senior advisers met in Casablanca (see SYMBOL) to plot Allied strategy. Pressured by the need to get on with the build-up for the Normandy landings and the mounting UK import crisis, the Allies finally gave the Atlantic first priority. With that decision the longstanding pleas by naval authorities for more VLR aircraft, more destroyers, and escort carriers to eliminate the air gap found fertile ground. By late March support groups, one of them with a carrier, were established to reinforce convoy escorts during their transit of the air gap. In March, as well, the allocation of VLR Liberator aircraft was finally agreed at the *Washington Convoy conference and by May they were making their presence felt in the mid-Atlantic. The Allied offensive in the air gap was aided immeasurably by moderating weather in April, which gave freer rein to the escorts' radars and 'Huff-Duff' directed destroyer sweeps.

ULTRA's re-penetration of the main U-boat cipher in the third week of March allowed these resources to be applied with devastating results. Since not all convoys could now be routed clear of U-boats, routeing and reinforcement were used to draw U-boats into a battle of attrition they could not win. The RN was prepared to trade the loss of two merchant ships for the certain destruction of a U-boat in the spring of 1943, as confrontations were sought and U-boats punished heavily. VLR Liberators closed the air gap in May, and more escort carriers arrived to join the battle. Nearly 100 U-boats were sunk in the Atlantic during the first five months of 1943: 47 in May alone (see Map 6). At the end of May, Dönitz withdrew his battered packs: as far as the course of the war was concerned, the battle of the Atlantic was decided by the spring of 1943.

Historians point to the decisive role of ULTRA in the Atlantic war, particularly in early 1943 when the German defeat followed quickly after the breakthrough in late March. However, the elimination of the air gap would have defeated the wolf-packs without ULTRA, although special intelligence allowed it to happen faster and with more telling effect. It was air power that forced submarines to operate fully submerged as a normal mode. Maritime air power, directed by ULTRA, also devastated the U-boat fleet when it attempted to renew the offensive with acoustic homing torpedoes in late summer. Air power held the U-boat in check for the balance of the war.

The decisiveness of the Allied victory over Germany's submariners in 1943 was a highlight in the naval war, and most histories of the Atlantic end there. As far as the war itself is concerned, the scale and drama of the victory over the U-boats were of less importance than the check in shipping losses it represented. These were already a localized and declining proportion of Allied tonnage by late 1942. Allied shipping losses from January to May 1943 averaged 450,000 tons per month, most of this to U-boats. In the last seven months losses averaged approximately 200,000 with only about 40–60,000 tons accounted for by submarines. To the victory of 1943 can be added the opening of the Mediterranean in the summer and the enormous volume of new construction from American yards over the year. An open Mediterranean improved the usefulness of available shipping, while Allied shipyards launched 14 million tons of new shipping in 1943, outstripping losses by about 11.5 million tons. Unfortunately for the UK, the new shipping was almost entirely American and only Roosevelt's intervention gave the British access to it. Shortages of shipping and strict regulation by the UK's ministry of war transport plagued British action for the balance of the war, while the percentage of British controlled shipping under bareboat charter (that is, without crews) increased substantially. These factors contributed to the UK's post-war economic crisis. It remains to be demonstrated, however, whether war losses of shipping materially affected the course of the war. MARC MILNER

Behrens, C. B. A., *Merchant Shipping and the Demands of War* (London, 1955).
Ministry of Defence (Navy), *The U-Boat War in the Atlantic 1939–1945* (London, 1989).
Milner, M., *North Atlantic Run: The Royal Canadian Navy and the Battle for the Convoys* (Toronto, 1985).
Morison, S. E., *History of the United States Navy in World War II*, Vols. I and X (Boston, 1947, 1956).
Roskill, S. W., *The War at Sea*, 3 vols. (London, 1954–61).

Atlantic Charter, document agreed by Churchill and Roosevelt during the *Placentia Bay conference of August 1941. It comprised eight points: (1) neither country sought any kind of aggrandisement, nor (2) desired territorial changes without the freely expressed agreement of the peoples concerned. (3) The right of all peoples to choose their governments was respected and it was desired that self-government be returned to all who had been forcibly deprived of it. (4) The two powers would endeavour, with due respect to their existing obligations, to give to all states, 'victor or vanquished', equality of access to the world's trade and raw materials which were needed for their economic prosperity. (5) Both powers supported the collaboration of all nations in the economic field, with the object of securing for all peoples improved labour standards, economic advancement, and social security. (6) After the destruction of Nazi tyranny they hoped to establish a lasting peace which would give all nations 'the means of dwelling safely within their own boundaries, and would allow all peoples to 'live out their lives in freedom from fear and want'. (7) Such a peace should enable all men to sail the high seas unhindered, and (8) all nations must abandon force. The USSR adhered to the Charter which was subsequently the basis of the *United Nations Declaration.

Atlantic Ferry Organization (ATFERO). Allied transatlantic air ferry service which, from November 1940 to August 1941, flew US-built combat aircraft to the UK, after which delivery became the responsibility of RAF Ferry Command. It was initiated by *Beaverbrook and organized by the Canadian Pacific Railway. Because of the *Neutrality Acts the first two aircraft were delivered close to the Canadian border, and a team of horses then hauled them into Canada, but the Acts' stringent regulations were soon relaxed. The aircraft were flown by British, Canadian, and US pilots, mostly civilians, and from May to August 1941 US service pilots delivered them to Montreal, the US government having created the Air Corps Ferrying Command (see AIR TRANSPORT COMMAND) for this purpose. During the war about 10,000 US aircraft were delivered to the UK. See also TAKORADI AIR ROUTE.

Atlantic Wall, Hitler's name for the line of fortifications which stretched, though not continuously, for 2,685 km. (1,670 mi.) along the coastline from the Netherlands to Spain to prevent an Allied landing. The *Todt Organization, which built it, began work in the summer of 1942. It became a cornerstone of Hitler's **Festung Europa* (Fortress Europe). But though the early fortifications proved their worth during the *Dieppe raid of August 1942—and its gun batteries, bunkers, observation towers, and *radar posts eventually absorbed 17.3 million cubic tons of concrete—it failed to prevent the Normandy landings of June 1944 (see OVERLORD). Much of it still stands.

Partridge, C., *Hitler's Atlantic Wall* (Guernsey, CI, 1976).

atomic bomb.

1. Development

Following the discovery of radioactivity by the French scientist Henri Becquerel in 1896, measurements of the kinetic energies of alpha-particles emitted by radioactive atoms led the British scientists Ernest Rutherford and Frederick Soddy to conclude in 1903 that atoms contained immense stores of energy; and in 1904 Soddy was speculating to the British Corps of Royal Engineers that this energy might ultimately form the basis of a devastating weapon based on atomic fission. In 1911 Rutherford found that the mass of an atom, and therefore its energy, was almost entirely concentrated in its nucleus; and in 1920 Arthur Eddington concluded, from Einstein's equivalence of mass and energy and from Francis Aston's measurements of the masses of hydrogen and helium nuclei, that enormous amounts of energy would be released if hydrogen nuclei could be fused together to make helium nuclei, and that this process was a main source of energy in stars. Thus by 1920 it was realized that weapons might be based on the fission of heavy nuclei or the fusion of light ones.

In 1932, at Cambridge, James Chadwick discovered the neutron, and this proved easily capable of penetrating atomic nuclei because, unlike protons and electrons, it was neither repelled nor attracted by the inherent nuclear charge. Some nuclei, when they absorbed a neutron, became radioactive and then might emit charged particles or even further neutrons. If these in turn could penetrate the nuclei of nearby atoms, a chain reaction might be started, as Leo *Szilard patented in 1934. Two German scientists working in Berlin, Otto Hahn and Fritz Strassmann, investigating the effects of bombarding uranium with neutrons, found in 1938 that this created new elements, and their careful work forced them to the surprising conclusion that one of these elements was barium and not, as they had expected, an element heavier than uranium. Over Christmas 1938 the Austrian scientists Otto Frisch and Lise Meitner, then working in Denmark and Sweden respectively, successfully explained the results as indicating that neutrons were penetrating uranium nuclei, each of which then split into two smaller nuclei, sometimes with some smaller fragments. Since the total mass of the fission products was less than that of a uranium nucleus, much energy must have been emitted in the process. The global physics community then realized that if there were neutrons among the minor fragments in the fission process, a chain reaction might be possible; and so thoughts were now seriously directed towards atomic weapons.

To appreciate the subsequent turn of events, a survey of the relevant knowledge in early 1940 may help. In 1939, Niels *Bohr and John Wheeler, building on George Gamow's model of a nucleus as a minute drop of liquid, developed a model of the fission process; and Bohr concluded from this model that it was the lighter uranium isotope U235 that was being split. The drop was held together by attractive forces between the protons and neutrons of which it was composed, against the electric forces of repulsion between its protons. In the common isotope of uranium, U238, there were 92 protons and 146 neutrons. This nucleus was hard to split by bombarding it with a further neutron; but the rarer isotope, U235, with 92 protons and 143 neutrons was less stable, particularly to 'slow' neutrons. One possible route to a bomb might therefore depend on the fission of U235 by slow neutrons, but these would take so long (a millisecond or so) to diffuse through a block of uranium that the bomb would blow itself apart long before its full explosive power could be realized. This difficulty, and others, inevitably appealed to many physicists who tended to hope that nature had subtly set insuperable obstacles in the way of humanity's achieving command of such devastating power; and, anyway, most British physicists were already completely absorbed in the effort to develop *radar and *electronic warfare, both of which were much more urgent in 1940.

Maj-General Leslie R. Groves (right), head of the Manhattan Project, inspects the remains of the steel tower on which the first **atomic bomb** was placed when it was tested near Alamogordo, New Mexico in July 1945. With him is the physicist Dr Robert J. Oppenheimer, who was director of the atomic bomb project at Los Alamos. The intense heat of the bomb melted the tower, and seared the surrounding sands into jade green glasslike cinders.

There was, though, a group of physicists so far excluded from the war effort: the Jewish physicists from Germany and Austria to whom the British had given shelter. Two of these, Otto Frisch and Rudolph Peierls, working in the University of Birmingham, concluded that a bomb might be made if the U235 isotope could be isolated from its less reactive and preponderating counterpart, U238, and Peierls's calculation suggested that, against the opinion of most other workers in Europe and the US, the amount required for a bomb might be no more than a few kilograms (there was a critical size, which had to be great enough for neutrons from one fission to have sufficient chance of striking a second nucleus before escaping outside). It might be small enough to be within the potential of existing methods for separating isotopes, if vigorously developed. For a bomb with 5 kg. (11 lbs.) of U235, Peierls and Frisch estimated an explosive power equivalent to 'several thousand tons of dynamite': these figures proved impressively close to those which were realized in the atomic bombs of 1945.

The consequent memorandum by Peierls and Frisch led to the formation in the UK of the *M.A.U.D. committee under George Thomson in April 1940 to investigate the bomb's potential. A second route towards a bomb had been suggested by Hans von Halban and Lew Kowarski, who had escaped from France and joined the British effort. This route, which had also been identified in the USA, started with the 140:1 mixture of U238 and U235 in natural uranium, where bombardment of the U235 nuclei could result in surplus neutrons which might then penetrate U238 nuclei, converting them into a new element, neptunium, of atomic weight 239, which by radioactive decay could produce nuclei of a new element of atomic weight 239 and atomic number 94 (uranium's atomic number was 92). The attractive possibility of this hitherto unknown element, for which the name 'plutonium' was suggested, was that from the Bohr–Wheeler model it was expected to resemble U235 as a bomb material, while being capable of separation by simple chemistry from its uranium parent, whereas U235 separation involved very difficult physical techniques. Moreover, the 'useless' and much commoner U238 isotope could now itself be transformed into a bomb material.

One snag in this route was that the neutrons emitted by U235 on fission had too high a speed for them to be captured most efficiently by other U235 nuclei, and so the chances were that any such neutrons would be captured by the much more numerous U238 nuclei. While this capture would ultimately result in plutonium nuclei, if it occurred too frequently there would not be enough neutrons left over to maintain the fission chain in the U235 nuclei. The solution was therefore to form the natural uranium into small blocks from which the fission neutrons could temporarily escape and encounter a surrounding 'moderator' made up of light nuclei such as deuterium (heavy water) or carbon (graphite) from which they would rebound back into a uranium block with a speed reduced sufficiently to favour their preferential capture by U235 nuclei, and so maintain the fission chain in these nuclei while the surplus neutrons were used to convert U238 into plutonium. The best source of deuterium was heavy water produced at the Norske Hydro Works at Rjukan in Norway (see VEMORK); and this, or its less effective counterpart, pure carbon (graphite), was therefore vital to the production of plutonium.

Such was the state of knowledge in the UK in 1940 where work started the following year on the large-scale separation of uranium isotopes; and in October 1941 a new body, a division of the Department of Scientific and Industrial Research, codenamed TUBE ALLOYS, was formed to supervise all British nuclear energy research. At that time scientists in other countries had failed to spur their respective governments into urgent action. In Japan K. Hagiwara foresaw the possibility of a bomb with U235, but no serious effort ensued. In Germany, the possibility of a fast-neutron bomb based on U235 was largely overlooked; it was thought that some tons of separated uranium would be necessary for a bomb, and this would not be feasible before the end of the war, although a 'boiler'—that is, a controlled reaction releasing a new kind of energy—might be achieved. In the USA scientists who had fled the Nazi threat became deeply concerned that a nuclear bomb might be under development in Germany. Three of them, Szilard, Eugene Wigner, and Edward Teller, went in August 1939 to see the doyen of the scientific community, Albert Einstein (1879–1955), and persuaded him to write to President Roosevelt to warn him of this danger. However, the American research that resulted was based on fission by slow neutrons and, with the USA still at peace, lacked the necessary urgency, though by April 1941 enough plutonium (one four-millionth of a gram) had been made to suggest that it was indeed fissionable by slow neutrons.

In the USSR Igor Kurchatov had also alerted his government to the possibility of a weapon based on nuclear fission. The idea was not pursued, but after the Soviet physicist Georgi Flerov stated in May 1942 that his country 'must build a uranium bomb without delay' an intense espionage effort against the US programme began, and the knowledge thereby gained was of much help to Kurchatov's post-war programme.

During 1941 American scientists visited the UK to see the progress being made there, and were so impressed by the British conviction, based on the analysis of Frisch and Peierls, that in December 1941 they recommended a full-scale American effort. Up to that time, according to the American physicist Arthur Compton, not a single member of the American committee 'really believed that uranium fission would become of critical importance in the Second World War'. A further agent in convincing the Americans was Mark Oliphant, an Australian pupil of Rutherford, who pressed on Ernest Lawrence (the inventor of the cyclotron) and Vannevar Bush, who headed the *Office of Scientific Research and Development, the British conviction that a bomb could be made. The result was a huge effort in the USA, codenamed MANHATTAN PROJECT, to which workers from the existing British effort were transferred (see Map 7). An establishment for basic bomb development was formed at Los Alamos, New Mexico, under *Oppenheimer; another, at Oak Ridge in Tennessee, worked on the separation of U235 from U238 by gaseous diffusion and electromagnetic techniques; and a third, at Hanford on the Columbia river, produced plutonium in graphite piles.

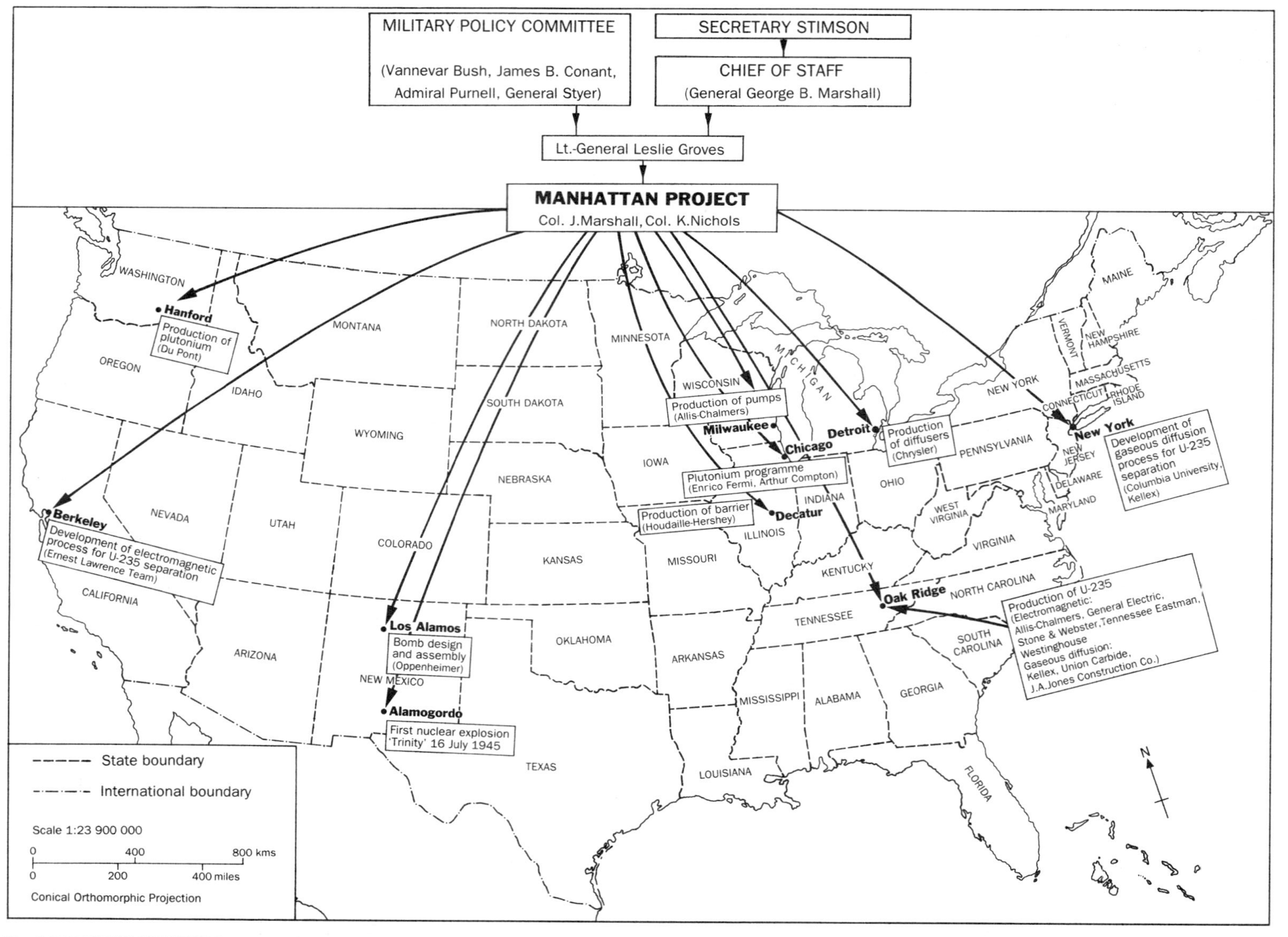

7. MANHATTAN PROJECT for development of the **atomic bomb**

As head of the entire project in Washington a military engineer, Colonel (later Lt-General) Leslie R. Groves was appointed in September 1942; previously he had built the *Pentagon. In addition, in 1944 J. D. Cockcroft headed an Anglo-Canadian-French establishment at Chalk River, west of Ottawa, where ample hydroelectric power was available to produce heavy water for plutonium production.

In 1942 Enrico *Fermi, working in Chicago with Compton, built a 'pile' of suitably disposed 'bricks' of graphite interspersed with sealed 'cans' each containing about 27 kg. (60 lb.) of uranium oxide powder and also some blocks of natural uranium metal. As with a bomb, there was a critical size for a pile: if it was too small too many neutrons would escape outside before they were absorbed by uranium nuclei; and Fermi gradually built up his pile until on 2 December 1942 it 'went critical' and showed that it could produce both energy and plutonium.

By early 1945 bomb-grade U235 was being produced at Oak Ridge and plutonium at Hanford. A key question then was how to keep the explosive in a bomb inert until the instant of detonation. The obvious solution, once the critical mass had been determined from previous measurements, was to keep such a mass in two separate halves, each of which would be safe by itself; if these were then brought rapidly together to form a mass of critical size an explosion would result. With uranium, this solution proved practicable: one half was made into a 'slug' for a 'gun' which fired the slug at the other half as a target. This was the device used in the trial bomb 'Little Boy' dropped on *Hiroshima on 6 August 1945. With Plutonium, however, even a velocity of approach of the masses at 915 m./sec. (3,000 ft./sec.) was too slow—the spontaneous radioactivity in the plutonium halves would cause them to heat up too quickly as they approached, and the 'bomb' would fizzle rather than explode.

An alternative approach was to use the fact that plutonium will suddenly collapse to a more compact form at high pressure which forces its atoms together, almost doubling its density; neutrons generated in one nuclear fission will then have a greater chance of encountering other nuclei before they can escape outside. A suitably chosen mass of plutonium of normal density can then be placed between suitably disposed and shaped masses of conventional explosives, which on detonation produce shock waves which will compress the plutonium to below its critical volume; it will then explode. This is a much faster process than impact from a gun, and it was tried out at the first nuclear explosion, 'Trinity', at Alamogordo on 16 July 1945; it was then used in the bomb 'Fat Man' dropped on *Nagasaki on 9 August 1945.

By then the war with Germany had already ended, and it was clear that German atomic work had been far behind. Although a bomb had been contemplated, the project had been given up in 1942, partly because the amount of U235 required for a bomb had not been nearly so carefully estimated as in Britain, resulting in over-estimates running up to tons, and these would have required an effort far beyond German resources. And although the plutonium route had been conceived by individuals, it was not seriously pursued. The German effort, led by Werner *Heisenberg, from 1942 onwards therefore concentrated on developing a 'boiler' with natural uranium and heavy water; but this work, which might incidentally have opened up the plutonium route, was seriously handicapped because insufficient heavy water was available for a pile, thanks to the sabotage by Norwegian patriots at the plant at Vemork.

The making of the atomic bomb had been a prodigious enterprise, by far the most sophisticated large-scale effort ever made by man. According to Groves (see below) the cost was $2,000,000,000, and the workforce was more than 600,000. For comparison, the Great Pyramid, Herodotus relates, required a continuous force of 100,000 men working for twenty years; and the Great Wall of China may have involved 1,000,000 men.

The atomic bomb effort, particularly in engineering and construction was, of course, predominantly American, while much of the earlier stimulus came from émigré scientists, where the memorandum by Frisch and Peierls was crucial. It was that memorandum, and the subsequent report of the M.A.U.D. committee under G.P. Thomson, which was responsible for 'the encouragement and support at the highest level' acknowledged by General Groves, who also wrote that: 'Prime Minister Churchill was probably the best friend that the Manhattan Project ever had.'

It was natural that thoughts among the outstanding body of scientific talent at Los Alamos should turn to the possible release of energy by the fusion of hydrogen into helium. For this it was necessary that the nuclei of hydrogen (or better, deuterium, because of its greater mass) should be forced together at speeds sufficient to overcome the repulsion between the nuclear charges. This entailed heating to very high temperatures, some hundreds of millions of degrees centigrade, which might be generated in a priming explosion by a uranium or plutonium bomb, giving an explosion equivalent to millions rather than thousands of tons of TNT. The development of such bombs in the USA, the USSR, and the UK belongs to post-war history. R. V. JONES

2. Politics

The two most revolutionary events of the 20th century, the discovery of nuclear fission and the Second World War, marked the year 1939. In February, the news of fission was published in the British science journal *Nature*, and on the first day of September German forces invaded Poland. In the six years that followed, as the international order was destroyed on the battlefields of Europe and Asia, the nuclear age was created, in fear and in secrecy, by American, British, and Canadian scientists in laboratories located throughout North America. This marriage of Mars and Minerva, of cataclysmic war and revolutionary science, altered the course of history.

The birth of the nuclear age marked both an end and a beginning. The war that launched the atomic bomb project destroyed the rising German and Japanese empires, crippled the global influence of the UK and France, and set the ambitions of the most powerful members of the *Grand Alliance, the USA and the USSR, on a collision course. As these expanding great powers amassed their strength during the last year of the war, scientists at the secret and isolated Los Alamos laboratory, on a mesa high above the desert in New Mexico, were completing the design, assembly, and testing of the weapon that would radically alter the military and diplomatic power of the USA.

The idea that the atomic bomb would play an important role in US-Soviet relations after the war took hold early. 'There was never from about two weeks from the time I took charge of this project,' General Leslie R. Groves reported, 'any illusion on my part but that Russia was our enemy and the project was conducted on that basis'. Groves's boss, Secretary of War Henry L. *Stimson, less harsh in his judgement of America's wartime ally, nevertheless informed Roosevelt in late 1944 that, 'troubles with Russia ... [were connected] to the future of S-1 the [atomic bomb].'

The more awesome implications of the revolution that science was creating were also recognized and brought to the president's attention. 'Modern civilization might be completely destroyed' by a future nuclear war, if some form of post-war international control of atomic energy were not implemented, Stimson told President *Truman in April 1945, less than two weeks after Roosevelt's death. It is one of the many ironies associated with the early history of the atomic bomb that the concern to avoid a post-war nuclear arms race—and a war that was expected to be the inevitable result—contributed to the atomic bombings of Hiroshima and Nagasaki on 6 and 9 August 1945. 'If the bomb were not used in the present war,' Arthur Compton, the director of the Metallurgical (Nuclear Research) Laboratory at the University of Chicago, wrote to Stimson, criticizing opposition to the military use of the atomic bomb, 'the world would have no adequate warning as to what was to be expected if war should break out again.'

The organization of the MANHATTAN PROJECT, the codename for the massive two-billion-dollar industrial, technical, and scientific enterprise responsible for the construction of nuclear weapons, was not an inevitable response to the discovery of fission. On the contrary, it was a tardy (and ultimately miscalculated) response to a terrifying prospect: that scientists in Germany, where fission had been discovered, were racing to develop this new weapon. Why German scientists failed to take this initiative has become an increasingly controversial issue. While most historians have argued that it resulted from scientific miscalculations by Germany's leading physicist, Werner Heisenberg, historian Thomas Powers has asserted (*Heisenberg's War: The Secret History of the German Atomic Bomb*, London, 1993) that Heisenberg's pessimistic estimates were based on his moral opposition to the development of such a weapon. Whichever interpretation one accepts, the scientific and technological uncertainties surrounding the question of whether a German atomic bomb could have been constructed are staggeringly complex.

Scientists in the USA also had the highest regard for German science, but their esteem inspired the opposite reaction, and they managed to bring their fears to Roosevelt's attention. Introduced to the implications of the discovery of fission in 1939, through a letter from Albert Einstein, which concluded, ominously, that 'Germany has actually stopped the sale of uranium from the Czechoslovakian mines', the president's initial response was disappointingly cautious. He authorized the formation of a scientific committee to study whether a nuclear weapon was feasible. The question remained unanswered for two years, when Otto Frisch and Rudolph Peierls, refugee physicists from Germany working in the UK, suggested a method of uranium separation that held out the possibility that a nuclear weapon could be produced within a few years.

In the summer of 1941 the British government forwarded the report of the M.A.U.D. committee, 'we have now reached the conclusion that it will be possible to make an effective uranium bomb ... ' to the American 'uranium committee'. Following the strong recommendation of scientists, who were now convinced that their German rivals had a two-year head start, Roosevelt approved a crash programme to build atomic bombs. Vannevar Bush, head of the Office of Scientific Research and Development (OSRD), organized the project and, in the autumn of 1942, the War Department took over, assigning it the code name MANHATTAN ENGINEER DISTRICT, soon abbreviated to the MANHATTAN PROJECT. Even before the project had been launched, émigré physicists such as the Hungarians Leo Szilard, Edward Teller, and Eugen Wigner, the Italian Enrico Fermi, the German Swiss Albert Einstein, and numerous native American physicists such as Ernest Lawrence, J. Robert Oppenheimer, and Arthur and Karl Compton, among others, warned high officials that the first nation to attain nuclear weapons could not be defeated. The atomic bomb was not merely a better bomb, it was an unprecedented force, 'a winning weapon'.

Although viewed at first as a defensive response to a perceived German threat, the bomb quickly evolved into an instrument for defeating the Japanese and controlling the Soviets. The point of use of the first bomb was discussed, the minutes of the Military Policy Committee meeting of 5 May 1943 report, and the general view appeared to be that its best point of use would be on a Japanese fleet concentration in the Harbor of Truk ... The Japanese were selected, 'the minutes go on to say without any touch of irony, as they would not be so apt to secure knowledge from it as would the Germans'.

Having launched the project believing that atomic bombs were powerful enough to win the war, planners did not require exceptional perspicacity to conclude that a monopoly of such a weapon had significant potential post-war military and diplomatic advantages. Roosevelt shared this conclusion with Churchill; Stimson shared it with Bush and with Lord Cherwell (see LINDEMANN), the prime minister's scientific adviser; and Stalin, informed of the MANHATTAN PROJECT by Soviet agents, shared it with the great Soviet physicist Igor Kurchatov. Ideas that threatened to neutralize the Anglo-American post-war nuclear advantage, such as the great Danish physicist Niels Bohr's proposal to Roosevelt and Churchill that they approach Stalin with a plan for the international control of atomic energy, were rejected, and Bohr became suspect. Enquiries should be made regarding the activities of Professor Bohr, Roosevelt and Churchill agreed in September 1944, and steps taken to ensure that he is responsible for no leakage of information, particularly to the Soviets. Thus, by this date, the Churchill–Roosevelt strategy was set. As the Hyde Park *aide-mémoire* noted: 'Full collaboration between the United States and the British government in developing TUBE ALLOYS atomic weapons for military and commercial purposes should continue after the defeat of Japan unless and until terminated by joint agreement.'

When Roosevelt died on 12 April 1945 he left both a wartime and a post-war legacy. The wartime legacy was that the bomb would be used militarily against Japan as soon as it was ready. The post-war legacy was that in the aftermath of the war it would be used diplomatically, as a bargaining chip against the USSR. During the early months of Truman's administration these legacies merged. The expectation that the military use of the bomb during the war would reinforce its post-war diplomatic value emerged as a central consideration for Stimson, for the new Secretary of State, James F. *Byrnes, and for Truman.

As problems with the Soviets mounted, the hopes invested in the value of the bomb increased. It was viewed as a virtual panacea for confronting impending post-war diplomatic difficulties. Stimson referred to it in his diary as a royal straight flush and a 'mastercard', a potential 'Frankenstein' or the saviour of 'the peace of the world'. But in almost every instance, he noted, through one remark or another, that 'over any such tangled wave of problems between the USA and the USSR the S-1 secret would be dominant.'

At the Potsdam conference in July–August 1945 (see TERMINAL), the news of the successful test of the first atomic bomb, on 16 July at Alamogordo, New Mexico, prompted joy and relief among the Americans. Churchill reported that Truman suddenly 'stood up to the Russians in a most emphatic and decisive manner'. Virtually cooing with relief, Stimson wrote in his diary, 'Now with our new weapon we would not need the assistance of the Russians to conquer Japan.'

Whether the USA needed the 'Russians' or even the atomic bomb to 'conquer Japan' (by which Stimson meant inducing the Japanese to surrender) will for ever remain a source of controversy. But the argument that the decision to use those weapons was taken strictly to save the lives of American soldiers, as Truman and Stimson reported in books, articles, and public statements, has become increasingly unsupportable as documents are prised out of their archival shelters.

In the end, the issue of Japanese surrender turned on modifying the doctrine of *'unconditional surrender'. Introduced by Roosevelt in 1943, and accepted by the American public as the appropriate basis upon which to end the war, the doctrine had become something of a political shibboleth by the time Truman entered office. But it had also become a barrier to surrender. Having broken the Japanese diplomatic code (see MAGIC) early in the war, the Department of State's Far Eastern specialists were united in their belief that Japan would surrender if assured that it could maintain Emperor *Hirohito and the imperial dynasty. In the end, after the two existing atomic bombs had destroyed their targets, and the Soviets had entered the war, the Japanese continued to insist on such guarantees. They would surrender, the Japanese announced on 10 August, on the condition that the Potsdam Declaration 'does not comprise any demand which prejudices the prerogatives of His Majesty as Sovereign Ruler'. In response to subtle assurances from the USA that the emperor would continue to occupy the throne, Japan surrendered on 14 August. 'History might find that the United States,' Stimson wrote in his autobiography, 'in its delay in stating its position on unconditional surrender terms, had *prolonged* the war.'

What Stimson did not say was that the availability of nuclear weapons was the source of that delay. Until they were used, until the power of the atomic bomb had been demonstrated, the nuclear option precluded all other options—modifying unconditional surrender among them—because it promised dividends. The shock of the bombs dropped on Hiroshima and Nagasaki would not only be felt in Tokyo, American leaders calculated, they also would be noted in Moscow. The military use of atomic weapons was expected not only to end the war; it was assumed that it would help to organize an American peace. While these expectations and decisions may be understandable in the context of four years of scientific secrecy and brutal war, they were not inevitable. They were avoidable. In the end, that is the most important lesson of Hiroshima for the nuclear age.

MARTIN J. SHERWIN

Alperovitz, G., *Atomic Diplomacy: Hiroshima and Potsdam* (New York, 1985).

Glasstone, S., *Source Book on Atomic Energy* (2nd edn., Princeton, 1958).

Gowing, M., *Britain and Atomic Energy 1939–1945* (London, 1964).

Groueff, S., *Manhattan Project* (London, 1967).

Groves, L. R., *Now it can be told* (London, 1963).

Rhodes, R., *The Making of the Atomic Bomb* (New York, 1986).

Sherwin, M. J., *A World Destroyed: Hiroshima and the Origin of the Arms Race* (New York, 1986).

atrocities. Accusations of atrocity have long been a norm of warfare. Early in the *First World War the British and American press resounded with tales of barbarities committed by invading Germans on civilians in Belgium; many of which turned out to have been mere fabrications, dreamed up by sensation-mongers. Reaction against these horror stories led to a great deal of scepticism next time round, sometimes with unfortunate results.

War is indeed an atrocious business. Admiral Jackie Fisher preached constantly, early in the century, that 'The essence of war is violence. Moderation in war is imbecility.' By the 1940s this doctrine had been generally enough accepted for the governments of great powers to agree quite readily to the mass extermination of civilians. In spite of the *Hague Convention, both the German Army and RAF Bomber Command consciously made a target of civilian housing, which each repeatedly set on fire; not often making any attempt to make sure the houses were empty of people first (see also SCORCHED EARTH POLICY). The Americans joined the British in bombing civilians; the Germans moved on from bombing civilians to systematically exterminating them in *concentration camps. Such acts became routine measures of policy.

There is no need to linger on the fact that no *written* order by Hitler directing the wholesale massacre of Jews has ever emerged (see FINAL SOLUTION): everybody in the business was aware that *es war des Führers Wunsch*, that was what the Leader wanted (see also SECRECY).

The Germans showed in 1939 with their bombing of Warsaw, and in 1940 with their bombing of *Rotterdam, that a nation's will to fight could soon be broken by air attack on civilians. Even though the rumoured 30,000 dead in Rotterdam turned out, on ultimate investigation, to number fewer than a thousand, the rumour did its work, and brought the Dutch to surrender. When in November 1940 the Luftwaffe attacked *Coventry, doing severe damage to its aircraft factories as well as killing some 550 civilians, *Göring coined a new German verb, *coventrieren*; so that when the Luftwaffe's attacks were revenged in a still more frightful form by the RAF and the USAAF, German protesters at the onslaught on, say, *Dresden could be checked with the remark, *Dresden war coventriert*: though Dresden was very much harder hit, it was hit by Göring's methods.

When in August 1945 the Americans, with unquestioning British support, dropped two small nuclear weapons on Japan, the results were at once atrocious and satisfactory. The horrors of *Hiroshima and *Nagasaki instantly became proverbial, but the Japanese at once surrendered, and it has been claimed that as many as a million lives were saved by these two devastating blows (but see ATOMIC BOMB, 2).

Yet reflection on what the effects of bombing Barcelona had been during the *Spanish Civil War—the attacks only stiffened Catalan resistance—might have led air staffs, and governments, to pause. There was no certainty that atrocity from the air would bring instant surrender: it might only make the opponent more angry. Similarly, the exaction of stiff reprisals for unexpected attacks on troops remote from the fighting front might cow the local population, or might stimulate them to more aggressive *resistance. Reactions varied largely with time, place, and historic background.

In the USSR the historic background favoured strong government action. Concentration camps in northern Russia and Siberia (see GULAG) were already a part of the terror regime that ran that unhappy state, before the Nazis came to power; deaths from forced migration and other police perils in Stalin's USSR were probably as numerous as deaths from terror in Hitler's Germany, though exact figures are lacking. Both regimes depended on delation, or sneaking: a social atrocity that could have ghastly results.

In Asia, and in eastern and south-eastern Europe, war was generally more atrocious than in the comparatively sanitized African desert, or in Italy, or in north-west Europe. France still shudders at the memory of *Oradour; yet in Poland and western Russia there was hardly an unburned village. In Greece, village-burning was a routine reprisal after any act of sabotage; a villager once remarked to an *SOE saboteur that he hoped the damage done to the Germans would this time be serious enough to make the damage done to the village worthwhile.

The Japanese treatment of their *prisoners-of-war is too well documented to need dwelling on (see BURMA–THAILAND RAILWAY, for example); that, according to one recent history of the Japanese Army (M. and S. Harries, *Soldiers of the Sun*, London, 1991, p. 389), a number of Japanese soldiers, who had surrendered to an Australian unit, were marched into the jungle where they were massacred by revengeful Borneo tribesmen while the Australians looked on, is less well known.

Within this avalanche of nastiness, a few additional sharp fragments were to be found, which later ages recall with especial agony. Some individual, or small-group, activities are held to be extra atrocious: refusal to take prisoner men who have cast away their arms and held up their hands, who are shot instead (see, for example, BISCARI and MALMÉDY); killing of women, children, old men in cold blood; killing of hostages. The Germans found precedent for the killing of hostages from their conduct in France during the war of 1870–1, and repeatedly adopted it as a police measure: they shot 41 Frenchmen at Nantes in October 1941 in reprisal for the killing of a German colonel, more than 300 Italians in 1944 in the *Ardeatine caves massacre; as late as March–April 1945, more than 250 Dutchmen for an unsuccessful (indeed accidental) ambush of a senior *SS officer; more than 3,000 Yugoslavs in two days in October 1941 for a run of suburban attacks on their troops.

Sometimes atrocities were forced on the well-meaning: as witness a Yugoslav mother who had to strangle her new-born baby, lest its cries attract some passing Germans into a cave where she and several others were hiding. Much more usually, they derived from original sin. A lively literary sub-industry subsists on recounting atrocity stories, tending to make them more atrocious each time round, and indulging in fanciful explanations. The brute fact is that men tend to be brutes to other men.

M. R. D. Foot

ATS (Auxiliary Territorial Service), see UK, 7(b).

Attlee, Clement R. (1883–1967), British Labour politician who was deputy prime minister in Churchill's coalition government from May 1940 to July 1945, when he became prime minister.

After serving in the *First World War, which he finished as a major, Attlee became Labour MP for Limehouse in 1922 and by 1935 was Labour Party leader. In May 1940, when *Chamberlain could not continue as prime minister of a Conservative administration without Labour support, Attlee asked the Labour National Executive committee two questions: would it serve under Chamberlain and would it serve under someone else? When the answer was 'no' to the first question and 'yes' to the second, Chamberlain resigned.

Though not officially given the title until February 1942, Attlee was, *de facto*, deputy prime minister from the start of the new government. Both he and his deputy, Arthur Greenwood, were members of the war cabinet (Greenwood stepped down in February 1942) and Attlee served as Lord Privy Seal until February 1942, then as secretary for the dominions until September 1943 when he was appointed lord president of the council. His main responsibilities lay with the civil side of government but he also ran the government's day-to-day business in the House of Commons and chaired the war cabinet and the Defence Committee in Churchill's absence.

Given their very different personalities and political beliefs the two men worked together with a remarkable degree of harmony. Attlee's loyalty rarely wavered, nor did he ever push his socialist programme of reform beyond acceptable limits, a stance which proved unpopular with some of his more left-wing colleagues. He was a man of few words but his criticisms could be biting.

Attlee accompanied the foreign secretary, Anthony *Eden, to the founding conference of the United Nations in *San Francisco in May 1945, but returned early for the July general election which gave him a majority of 170 seats. One of his first tasks was to take Churchill's place at the Potsdam conference (see TERMINAL) and he served as prime minister until 1951. See also UK, 3.

Attlee, C., *As It Happened* (London, 1954).
Harris, K., *Attlee* (London, 1982).

Auchinleck, General Sir Claude (1884–1981), British army officer who served for most of his career in the Indian Army and who became C-in-C *Middle East Command at a crucial stage in the *Western Desert campaigns against *Rommel.

Auchinleck's successful career in the Indian Army had, by 1939, raised him to the rank of maj-general. He returned to the UK to command 4th Corps, British troops in the *Norwegian campaign (from 13 May 1940), then 5th Corps and Southern Command in England where one of his tasks was organizing the Home Guard (see UK, 6). He was promoted lt-general in July 1940 and then general that November when he was appointed C-in-C India. In April 1941 he dispatched troops to quell the revolt in Iraq and his swift response to this crisis pleased Churchill who that June appointed him C-in-C Middle East Command in place of *Wavell. But though Auchinleck acted with panache when necessary—as C-in-C, he authorized the formation of the *Special Air Service—differences between the two men then arose. Churchill urged immediate action; Auchinleck refused to budge until he was ready. This was not until November 1941 but the success of his offensive (CRUSADER) was shortlived and the ground gained was lost again the following summer, as was *Tobruk, and twice during this period Auchinleck had to replace his Eighth Army commander. On the second occasion he assumed personal command and in the first *El Alamein battle that July stopped Rommel in his tracks. It was also at least partly his plan that led to Rommel's defeat at *Alam Halfa in September, but by then Churchill had replaced him with *Alexander. He was offered, but refused, the Iran–Iraq theatre (see PAIFORCE) as a separate command and was on leave until June 1943 when he became C-in-C India again. Now an administrative post, it was also one of his most important: he mobilized India's resources, trained troops for the *Burma campaign, and supplied *South-East Asia Command. He remained C-in-C until 1947 having been promoted field marshal in 1946.

Auchinleck was a man of great charm and ability who had scant respect for traditional and orthodox military methods. Though his time as C-in-C Middle East was not very successful, and nor was his selection or handling of subordinate commanders, his defensive victory at El Alamein was crucial to eventual British success in the Western Desert. He was knighted in 1940. See also LAND POWER.

Connell, J., *Auchinleck* (London, 1959).
Keegan, J. (ed.), *Churchill's Generals* (London, 1991).

Aung San (1916–47), Burmese *Thakin leader who fled his country in August 1940. He helped the Japanese form the *Burma Independence Army, a later version of which he led from August 1942 to August 1943 as a Japanese maj-general. When Japan made Burma independent in August 1943 he became *Ba Maw's minister of defence. In August 1944 he secretly formed the Anti-Fascist Organization (later the Anti-Fascist People's Freedom League) which organized resistance against the Japanese, and in March 1945 he and his army openly swapped sides. After the war he was in the forefront of his country's political life. In January 1947 he signed an agreement in London, which led to Burma's independence in 1948, but was assassinated on the orders of a political opponent, U *Saw, that July.

Auschwitz was the German name for Oswiecim, a town in southern Poland which was annexed to the Reich after the *Polish campaign in September–October 1939. The name is now reserved for the complex of three Nazi *concentration camps, and 36 sub-camps, which were built outside the town in 1940–2. Auschwitz I was built in June 1940 for Polish political prisoners; Auschwitz II, or Birkenau, which could accommodate over 100,000 inmates, opened in October 1941; and Auschwitz III grew out of a camp at nearby Monowitz which supplied *forced labour for the nearby I. G. Farben synthetic rubber and oil plant. To help implement the *Final Solution gas chambers and crematoria capable of disposing of 2,000 bodies at a time, and using *Zyklon-B gas, were constructed at Birkenau, making part of it a death-camp similar to those built for *Operation REINHARD. By 1944, according to some sources over 6,000 a day were being murdered and 250,000 Jews from Hungary were exterminated in six weeks. Elsewhere in the complex hundreds were dying daily from maltreatment, from the pseudo-medical experiments of Dr *Mengele, or from execution.

A resistance network operated within Auschwitz from the start, two Polish escapees from Auschwitz I brought the first detailed news of conditions within the camps to the outside world in 1942. The full extent of Birkenau's genocidal operations was not known, however, until two years later when three Jewish escapees reached Slovakia. In October 1944 there was a revolt when one gas chamber was blown up with explosives smuggled in from a nearby armaments factory, and another was set on fire. About 250 then escaped but they were all shot, as were another 200 who were also involved. Some weeks before the camps were liberated by Soviet forces in January 1945, the *SS had begun to demolish the installations, and all the surviving inmates fit to walk had been marched into Germany.

Later, the Soviet government announced that four million people may have died at Auschwitz; and this impossible figure passed unchallenged into conventional wisdom. Only in 1991, after the fall of *communism, did the Auschwitz museum issue a revised estimate of 1.2–1.5 million victims, of whom about 800,000 were Jews.

NORMAN DAVIES

Garlinski, J., *Fighting Auschwitz* (London, 1975).
Gilbert, M., *Auschwitz and the Allies* (London, 1981).

AUSTRALIA

1. Introduction

In September 1939 Australia was an independent democracy within the British Empire. While its people were expecting another major war in Europe, in 1939 they lacked the exuberance of 1914, when the prime minister, Andrew Fisher, pledged the nation to the 'last man and last shilling'. The sacrifices of 1914–18, 60,000 dead and a further 30,000 who died of their wounds over the next decade, had killed any enthusiasm for war in the following generation.

In the 1920s and 1930s Australia had sought security through the imperial connection, and the government of the late 1930s supported *Chamberlain's policy of appeasement. The British declaration of war in September 1939 did not surprise Australians, but it caught them unprepared. Spending on defence had been reduced during the 1930s depression to almost 1% of Gross Domestic Product. Australia could raise armed forces readily enough—over 10% of the workforce was unemployed—but it could neither equip nor supply them fully. The country was also in difficulty in repaying British loans for capital works. The debt burden was substantial and not until 1942 did defence spending approach the levels of other Allied powers. Yet Australians served in almost all theatres of war, from the Atlantic to the Pacific.

2. Domestic life, economy, and war effort

At the outbreak of war, firm price controls and rising employment enabled Australia to avoid restricting the production and consumption of consumer goods. The Communist Party of Australia (CPA) was banned from 1939 to 1942. But communists who headed key unions soon promoted strikes and continued to impede the war effort until the USSR entered the fray in June 1941 (see BARBAROSSA). Then they urged workers to show greater co-operation and productivity in support of the war effort. After the ban was lifted the communist influence increased and by 1944 the CPA had a membership of 20,000, making it one of the largest political organizations in Australia at that time. Real industrial expansion was achieved in arms production (see Tables 1 and 2) and by mid-1941 the labour

Australia, 2, Table 1: Aircraft production, 1941–5

	1941–2	*1942–3*	*1943–4*	*1944–5*	*Total 1939 to 31 Aug 1945*	*Number Ordered*
Aircraft						
Beaufort	76	285	312	27	700	700
Beaufighter			3	281	329	450
Lancaster-Lincoln						61
Lancaster-Tudor						12
Wirraway	320		30	60	717	870
Wackett Trainer	187				200	200
Boomerang		105	102	43	250	250
Mustang				4	18	350
Tiger Moth	508	66		35	1,070	1,070
DH.84 Dragon		87			87	87
Mosquito			6	82	115	370
Engines						
Twin Row Wasp	74	223	343	228	870	870
Single Row Wasp	152	85	32		680	680
Gypsy Major	315	460	230		1,300	1,300
Merlin						100

Excludes 2 C.A.C. Bombers and 8 gliders.

Source: Butlin, S. J. and Schedvin, C. B., *War Economy 1942–45* (Canberra, 1977), in *Australia in the War of 1939–45* series.

force engaged in munitions manufacture numbered some 53,000. In order to obtain accurate statistics for manpower allocation decisions involving reserved occupations, essential services, munitions production, and the armed forces, all persons above the age of 16 were required to register, and to carry an identity card. Enemy aliens were interned. Conscription into the army was introduced but only, as had been the case in the *First World War, for home service, which technically included service in Papua and the mandated territory of New Guinea. Some civilian occupations were 'reserved', i.e. the holders of these positions were exempt from military service, and one of the government's first acts was to obtain the services of the industrialist Essington Lewis, and the newspaper proprietor Keith Murdoch, to co-ordinate, respectively, the production of munitions and of propaganda.

The announcement of war was almost a relief for an expectant but sometimes laconic people who had been deeply affected by the depression. Some felt that only a major war, followed by a proper peace settlement, would set the world to rights and provide decent people with a fresh start, in fairness and dignity. Also released were desires for instant gratification—sport, dancing, sex—and people who had been in low spirits for so long now seemed intent on seizing what pleasure they could and enjoying it for as long as it would last. Moreover, some believed that the state had let the people down badly during the depression and therefore resented any request for a greater effort. Young men and women who had known only piecemeal or seasonal work in between long stretches of unemployment might jump at the offer of a full-time job in the forces, but they were also wary of bureaucracies which grew with war. Some felt ambivalent towards a nation and empire which figured so negatively in their normal lives and which gave every impression of being incompetent in an emergency. Others were strongly moved by ties of sentiment and kinship with the UK, and by the realization that a free way of life was now under threat, to step forward and offer their services to the armed forces.

A survey of public attitudes in 1941 revealed the 'disillusion, disappointment, futility, distrust, disgust, diffidence and indifference which so many possess with regard to politics and society in general and the war in particular.' Perhaps because of this general feeling of disenchantment many turned even more avidly than usual to sport. Cricket attendances swelled in the season 1939–40 before fixtures were suspended for the duration, and the amount spent legally—and probably illegally—on gambling increased each year of the war, as did the numbers attending horse-racing and both codes of football. However, as insurance against the hour, attendance at church and worship generally also increased.

A change in public perception towards the war became apparent only after the Japanese raid on *Pearl Harbor in December 1941, and the sweeping Japanese victories in South-East Asia in the early part of 1942 which brought home a growing realization that Australia might be invaded. The government introduced more and more stringent controls, including civil conscription, so that, technically, men or women could be ordered into any occupation. A Manpower Priorities Board and a Manpower Directorate were created; wages and prices were pegged; food, clothing, tobacco, and petrol were quite severely rationed; and civil defence preparations (see below) were made and coastal defences improved.

The fall of *Singapore in February 1942 had an even greater psychological impact on the country. *Curtin, who had replaced Robert *Menzies as prime minister a few months before, told Australians that its capture 'opens the battle for Australia'. Another blow fell when, a few days later, on 19 February, the Japanese raided *Darwin. For the first time since the coming of the Europeans and the dispossession of the indigenous Aborigines, Australians were killed on Australian soil by enemy action. The raid caused widespread panic: shops were looted, wholesale drunkenness took place, and evacuation plans against an expected invasion deteriorated into farce.

An invasion which did occur—the arrival of many thousands of US servicemen—as well as Australia's own wartime needs, led to the creation of a Civil Construction Corps (CCC) within an Allied Works Council, to build the necessary accommodation and other facilities. Those aged 45–60 were recruited or conscripted into the CCC and by June 1943 numbered 53,500, of whom 16,600 had been conscripted.

A Department of War Organization of Industry was set up, directed initially at distribution, commerce, and finance. It simplified clothing manufacture, restricted retail delivery transport, reduced packaging, and zoned bread and milk deliveries. The use of certain essential materials such as iron, steel, copper, and industrial chemicals was either prohibited or restricted. Tea was rationed to 227 g. (8 oz.) per person per five-week period, sugar to 454 g. (1 lb.) a week. The production of beer and other liquors was reduced by a third, and 'quotas' of cigarettes similarly. Sale of motor car tyres was restricted and petrol rationed: after February 1942 8 hp cars had a two-monthly ration of 13.6 l. (3 gal.), 30 hp cars a two-monthly ration of 36.3 l. (8 gal.). The estimated mileage allowed to private users was 26 km. (16 mi.) per week. Profit margins were pegged by government decree. Black marketeering sprang up, resulting in legislation providing fines or imprisonment for offenders. After the loss of *Nauru and Ocean Islands, the sale of fertilizer had to be restricted.

The build-up of US forces in Australia and, later, the

Australia, 2, Table 2: Munitions production January to September 1943

	Monthly production rate	
	Jan–Jun	*Jul–Sept*
Artillery		
25-pound Howitzer	45	9
24-pound Short	3	21
2-pounder A.T.	19	10
6-pounder A.T.	78	31
40 mm Bofors A-A	10	14
3.7 in A-A	16	4
Guns and mortars		
Owen sub-machine	2,322	1,541
Austen sub-machine	1,633	1,659
Rifles, .303 in	12,717	16,420
3 in mortars	104	11
Ammunition, artillery		
25-pounder H.E.	295,610	273,578
40 mm A-A	13,424	38,408
3.7 in A-A	20,924	18,907
Small arms ammunition		
.303 in ball	27.2 million	20.5 million
9 mm ball–Owen and Austen	7.2 million	5.9 million
Ammunition–mortar and grenades		
3 in mortar H.E.	141,846	68,608
Grenades No. 36–hand, rifle	121,244	71,178
Mines		
Mines A.T.	51,685	48,983

Source: Butlin and Schedvin.

Australia, 2, Table 3: War expenditure on goods and services

	1938–9	*1939–40*	*1940–1*	*1941–2*	*1942–3*	*1943–4*	*1944–5*	*1945–6*
Gross National Product £Am	938	999	1,082	1,255	1,431	1,464	1,409	1,423
War Expenditure on goods and services £Am	9	38	133	293	518	547	452	292
As percentage of GNP	1	4	12	23	36	37	32	21

Source: National Income and Expenditure 1946–7.

Australia, 2, Table 4: Agricultural production and goals, main commodities, 1942–3 to 1944–5

Item	*Unit (see note)*	Production *average 1937–9*	*1942–3*		*1943–4*		*1944–5*	
			Goal	*Production*	*Goal*	*Production*	*Goal*	*Production*
1.1 Total milk	m gals	1,142	1,200	1,129	1,210	1,067	1,210	976
1.2 Butter	tons 000	185	190	171	175	156	—	142
1.3 Cheese	tons 000	24	39	36	45	36	—	35
1.4 Fresh milk	m gals	165	170	180	—	195	200	195
2.1 Total meat	tons 000	985	1,040	1,023	1,180	1,027	1,000	900
2.2 Beef & Veal	tons 000	567	560	517	560	473	485	440
2.3 Mutton & Lamb	tons 000	319	380	415	477	424	380	335
2.4 Pigmeat	tons 000	86	100	91	145	130	135	125
3.1 Fish	lbs m	—	—	—	63	55	61	60
4.1 Vegetables	acres 000	109	—	158	252	192	246	220
5.1 Potatoes	acres 000	114	*500*	*483*	174	182	278	233
6.1 Eggs	doz m	65	75	80	100	89	105	105
7.1 Rice	acres 000	24	*55*	*57*	40	41	40	25
8.1 Sugar	tons 000	817	643	650	600	507	600	646
9.1 Wheat	bushels m	164	110	156	100	110	*9.0*	*8.4*

Notes, general: Figures have been rounded. Figures in italics are expressed in units different from those indicated, as explained below. Rows 1.2 to 1.4 are components of Row 1.1, and Rows 2.2 to 2.4 exponents of Row 2.1.

Notes, by row: 1.2 and 1.3, goals for 1944–5 expressed as a composite, milk for processing; 2.1 to 2.4, meat goals, and production set for calendar years, so that 1942–3 refers to 1943 and so on; 5.1, goal and production in 1942–3 expressed in thousands of tons; 6.1 production in 1937–9 is an estimate; 7.1, goal and production for 1942–3 expressed in thousands of tons; 9.1, goal and production for 1944–5 expressed in millions of acres.

Source: Butlin and Schedvin.

prospective arrival of elements of the British Pacific Fleet (see TASK FORCE 57), required land-based installations, and this posed considerable manpower problems. In August 1944 the government directed that 30,000 men be discharged from the army and 15,000 from the air force within the ensuing ten months. Even so, there was a shortage of labour for essential services, and a shortfall in army requirements for the campaigns in *New Guinea and elsewhere. A partial solution was found in the use of Italian *prisoners-of-war on farms and in other occupations—more than 10,000 were so employed. An Australian Women's Land Army, formed in 1942, added some 2,000 women to the rural workforce.

A side-effect of the presence of US servicemen in Australia was the friendships that developed between many of them and young Australian women. Eventually a total of more than 10,000 Australian wives or fiancées of such servicemen went to the USA.

Industrial disputes were a continuing problem throughout the war, especially in 1940 and in the closing years, when they caused a serious shortage of coal, the main source of energy. Railway services had to be reduced, and other industries were affected.

War expenditure on goods and services rose to over a third of gross national product, being financed by greatly increased taxation and low-interest public loans (see Table 3).

Since the 1920s, Australian governments had followed a deliberate policy of industrialization. By the 1940s manufacturing, the major employer of labour, had displaced agriculture as the largest sector of the economy. But agricultural production also rose, sometimes exceeding the goals set for principal commodities (see Table 4).

3. Government

The conservative United Australia Party (UAP) had been in government for most of the 1930s. But in September 1939 its leader, Robert Menzies, had been prime minister for only a few months, having succeeded Joseph Lyons who had died in office in April 1939. Menzies was his party's first choice. But the UAP's junior coalition partner, the Country Party (CP), was sceptical of his abilities and the coalition was rendered inoperable when the CP leader, Earle Page, accused Menzies in front of his colleagues—and, worse, in front of the opposition—of cowardice and opportunism. Menzies, Page said, had chosen to pursue his legal career instead of enlisting during the First World War; and he even hinted that Menzies had contributed to his predecessor's death by resigning as attorney general and deputy leader of the UAP just as Lyons's health was deteriorating. At the dissolution of the coalition Menzies formed a minority government, but an election had to be held in 1940. The coalition was mended in time and the new UAP–CP government, with the help of two independents, survived the voters, but the Labor Party (ALP) was the largest single party in parliament. In August 1941 Menzies again lost CP support and resigned in favour of the CP leader, Arthur *Fadden. But he, after 40 days, lost the support of the independents, and therefore parliament, and on 7 October 1941 the ALP formed a government with John Curtin as prime minister. Like Fadden, Curtin had a majority of only one but in a subsequent election in August 1943 the ALP won a resounding victory and remained in government for the rest of the war.

In September 1939 Menzies formed a war cabinet which as the war progressed took increasing control of Australia's war policies. The war cabinet was advised by a Chiefs of Staff Committee and an Advisory War Council. The latter, formed in September 1940 and consisting of four war cabinet ministers and four members of the opposition, had been formed as a compromise when the opposition refused to join the Menzies administration in an all-party government. When Curtin became prime minister the war cabinet and the Advisory War Council worked as an integrated team and divided much of the work between them. During the war the war cabinet met 354 times, the Advisory War Council 174 times.

In September 1939 Australia's population amounted to only 7,000,000. The majority lived in the six state capital cities but the national territory spanned 7.7 million sq. km. (3 million sq. mi.). Therefore, there may have seemed at that time little alternative but to seek Australian security through an unqualified declaration of support for the UK and its empire, as Menzies did when he committed his country to war without recourse to parliament. But when Japan assaulted American, British, and Dutch colonial possessions in South-East Asia in December 1941, Curtin insisted that Australia make its own declaration of war. Moreover, once the USA had entered the war and the UK's weakness in South-East Asia had been exposed, the Americans became the Australians' main ally. In his prime-ministerial message to the nation on 27 December 1941, Curtin announced to the world 'I make it quite clear that Australia looks to America, free of any pangs as to our traditional links or kinship with the United Kingdom.' The statement marked a turning-point in Australian history. From this point forth, Australia would put its role in Pacific affairs ahead of its involvement with Europe. Curtin ordered the immediate recall of the three army divisions serving in the Middle East, precipitating a serious argument with Churchill. Eventually, a compromise was reached, in which two of the divisions were to be returned, but a further attempt by Churchill to delay their date of departure, and a later plan hatched to have the divisions diverted to protect British interests in India, incensed the Australians.

Despite an increasing reliance on the USA—first brought home by General *MacArthur setting up his *South-West Pacific Area (SWPA) GHQ in Brisbane in April 1942 and then by the influx of US troops—a new mood of nationalism was reflected by government and people. These changes were facilitated through the new institutional basis of a strong central government. War traditionally gives governments increased powers. For Australia the Second World War shifted the balance of power away from the states and in favour of the federal government, with the permanent move of the powers of taxation to the centre. Moreover, the federal government's increased controls over goods and services, including manufacturing and transport, gave it confidence to experiment with a planned mixed economy.

In February 1943 the Curtin government passed what was commonly known as the Militia Bill to allow the deployment of conscripts overseas, though this was to be limited to the South-West Pacific Area. The act was passed through parliament with some skill by Curtin and his ministers without the attendant resistance—in which Curtin had taken a vociferous part—that similar efforts had met a generation earlier. It has remained something of a historical paradox that Curtin, who initially established his political credentials as a pacifist and anti-conscriptionist, should be, firstly, a wartime leader and, secondly, the man who initiated conscription for war service in Australia. Information released in 1992 points to pressure being brought to bear on the Australian government by the Americans. In particular, MacArthur argued that it was bad for US morale to have battalions of Australian soldiers available who were not legally obliged to take part in the Allied *island-hopping campaign towards the Philippines which MacArthur was to launch later in 1943 (see PACIFIC WAR).

The conscripts, known in Australia as 'chockos' (short for 'chocolate soldiers'), had become an embarrassment to relations between the two allies and resentment grew within the US forces that Australians were not pulling their weight. Curtin was a man of deep emotion and commitment, and to introduce conscription was an especially difficult decision for him to take. In the end, the war effort came first. The compromise he reached was that conscripts would fight only in those theatres which immediately affected the security of Australia. Curtin thus persuaded public opinion to accept a policy more amenable to Australia's allies. Engaging the enemy on the approaches to Australia itself, Australians came to accept, was quite different from sending conscripts to distant wars. It was on this principle that in 1965 Australian conscripts were made liable for war service in Vietnam and this commitment ultimately became a strong reason for the Whitlam government's decision to withdraw from the Vietnam conflict in 1972 and to end conscription once more.

Australia had four wartime prime ministers: Menzies, Fadden, Curtin, and Ben Chifley (1885–1951), who was sworn in just as the war was about to finish. None was ever really fully in control of the war around him. Under Menzies and Fadden, Australia concentrated on supporting the UK against Hitler; under Curtin and Chifley the country was subordinate to the Americans, particularly MacArthur, whose imposing military ego sometimes made the foreign general a more powerful figure in local politics than the national prime minister.

Although the relationship between Curtin and MacArthur was amiable, there were sometimes tensions. Australians generally, and servicemen especially, resented MacArthur's apparent desire to make the Pacific theatre the setting for an American triumph, while much of the fighting was in fact being done by the Australians. For all their gratitude towards him, the Australian public sometimes believed that MacArthur took too much credit for himself instead of sharing the credits of victory and co-operating as a true ally. MacArthur's determined personality and unfamiliar American ways and mannerisms—which were less subtle if more effective than the seemingly unobtrusive British method of command—also ruffled feathers.

The end of empire—along with the fact that Australia had been on the winning side in war—contributed to new Australian confidence in the international arena. In September 1939, Australia had only had a small, inchoate department of external affairs and overseas diplomatic links with the UK, where it had been represented by a high commissioner since Federation. By the end of the war Australia, guided by its minister for external affairs, Herbert *Evatt, had established formal relations with the USA, China, Japan, Canada, the Netherlands, the USSR, New Zealand, India, Brazil, and France. It also had representatives in Indonesia, Thailand, Singapore, and New Caledonia, and a mission in Berlin. Evatt claimed that Australia was 'a principal Pacific power', and set his diplomatic sights accordingly for the post-war period.

4. Civil defence and defence forces

From early 1940 various informal groups of citizens began to be formed, some under the influence of members of the banned Communist Party, with the purpose of defending Australia. These were encouraged to join one of the armed services, or the part-time Volunteer Defence Corps (VDC), of which 5,000 members were called up for aerodrome defence and coast watching. The VDC had been formed originally by the Returned Soldiers' League, and was mainly composed of men who had served in the First World War. It was taken over by the government and expanded to include any man aged 18–60 willing to give up evenings or weekends for training. The VDC was given the tasks of local defence, guarding key points, providing local intelligence, and later of manning anti-aircraft and coastal defences, thus replacing some 4,000 men of the military forces. In February 1942 it was decided to increase the VDC from 50,000 to 80,000, and later to 100,000. In May 1944 when the threat to Australia had substantially reduced, about half of the VDC were freed from attendance at regular parades.

In the major cities lighting was restricted, and Air Raid Precaution (ARP) wardens and fire watchers were organized. Air raid warning sirens were installed, and relevant public buildings camouflaged. The development of civil defence was governed by the scale of bombing anticipated, and the estimated number of casualties. The state governments were made responsible for ARP, with the federal government initially providing advice and pamphlets, co-ordination, and (after a time) limited financial support. There was a minister for home security, and state governments appointed ministers for civil defence. There were differences of opinion between state and central authorities as to which areas were 'vulnerable' or 'vital' and thus demanding special protective measures. Firefighting equipment had to be imported, as did light civilian respirators and even sandbags.

There was considerable debate on the question of evacuating the civil population, and on the provision of public air raid shelters. Federal government policy was that 'the normal dispersion of the civil population in their own homes provides the best means for their protection'; that where industrial enterprises were situated in vital areas and employing large numbers engaged on essential war work, shelters should be provided in basements or trenches; and that in general the provision of splinter- and blast-proof shelters was not warranted. Private persons were to provide their shelters at their own cost. Some coastal towns prepared plans for evacuation of women, children, and invalids, but these were never put into effect except for *Darwin (women and children), although many individuals moved inland, or to the south, of their own accord at the height of the fear of invasion in 1942.

In the event, Japanese air raids were launched only against northern targets—Darwin in the Northern Territory; Wyndham, Derby, and Broome in Western Australia; and Townsville and Thursday Island in Queensland. But *Sydney harbour, in New South Wales, was attacked by *midget submarines and further north Newcastle was shelled by their bigger brethren, although with few casualties. As the war receded from Australia, civil defence measures became less imperative and by late 1944 the organizations had been largely disbanded.

5. Armed forces and special forces

(a) High Command

In the South African and First World Wars, Australia's armed services had been incorporated with their British counterparts. Australians were often commissioned into the British Army, Navy, and Air Force while the highest posts in the Australian services were frequently filled by British officers on secondment. In September 1939 the heads of the three Australian services, who were all British, were formed into a Chiefs of Staff committee. As individuals they also served on the Defence Committee which, *inter alia*, advised the minister of defence and co-ordinated the administrative requirements of the Naval, Military, and Air Boards. As a committee the Chiefs of Staff advised the war cabinet and were, collectively, its executive agent. In theory, the committee was therefore responsible for operations, but in practice—and quite unlike the British *Chiefs of Staff—it was confined to technical matters such as strategic appreciations, while as individuals its members controlled only the administrative functions of their respective services. This was because operational control of the majority of Australian forces was in the hands of the Cs-in-C of the theatres in which those forces were serving. For example, General *Blamey, who commanded Australian Army forces fighting in the *Western Desert and *Balkan campaigns during 1940 and 1941, was under the control of the C-in-C Middle East, not of the Australian Chief of the General Staff. However, he had the right to communicate direct with the Australian government, and to protest if he believed that British orders unduly hazarded his force. In April 1942, when MacArthur's South-West Pacific Area (SWPA) was formed, Australian commanders took their orders directly from MacArthur, although they also had the right of appeal to the Australian government.

(b) Army

On the outbreak of war with Germany, the Australian Army numbered 82,800, of whom 80,000 were partly trained volunteer militia. The regular component consisted mainly of cadres of officers, warrant officers and NCOs, clerks and storemen, and some coastal artillery units.

In 1939 the government was reluctant to repeat the level of sacrifice that had been demanded of its people in the First World War. (For casualties by service and theatre during the Second World War, see Table 5.) It would have liked to delay promising troops to fight in Europe, but New Zealand took the initiative and offered a division, whereupon Australia (on 15 September) did the same. Conscription was introduced for home defence only, and a special force of four divisions (6th, 7th, 8th, and 9th, the Second Australian Imperial Force, or AIF) had to be specially recruited for service abroad. In effect Australia now had two separate armies, one for home defence (including Papua and New Guinea) and one for overseas service.

The first contingent to go overseas was 6th Division. It was intended that it should support the *British Expeditionary Force in France but staged in Palestine to complete its training. Part of the division did go to the UK, and became the nucleus of 9th Division. After the fall of *France in June 1940, 6th, 7th, and 9th Divisions, making up the 1st Australian Corps under Lt-General Blamey, joined British forces in Egypt and took part in the defeat of the Italians in the early Western Desert campaigns. In April 1941 part of 6th Division was sent to join British and New Zealand troops engaged in the Balkan campaign, and was involved in the débâcle on *Crete the following month, and in July 1941, 7th Division fought in the *Syrian campaign. In the Western Desert 9th Division helped defend *Tobruk and later took part in the defence of and breakout from *El Alamein before it was withdrawn in late 1942 to participate in the *Pacific war. By then the other two divisions had already been withdrawn: 6th Division went directly to Australia, but in March 1942, 7th Division was diverted to Colombo when Ceylon was threatened (see INDIAN OCEAN). Part of 7th Division also went to Java when the Japanese invaded the *Netherlands East Indies, and was captured there.

Australia had been apprehensive of Japan for nearly half a century and these fears strengthened as Japanese forces advanced first into China (see CHINA INCIDENT) and later into French Indo-China. Such Australian strategic planning as had taken place had been founded on the assumption that Singapore was the key to the security of the region and by August 1941 two brigades of 8th Division, and two squadrons of Royal Australian Air Force aircraft, were stationed in Malaya. The 8th Division also had a battalion at *Rabaul in New Britain (part of the Australian mandate of New Guinea), and other units were scattered on the island chain north-east of New Guinea. When the Japanese swept southwards to take Malaya and Singapore they captured 8th Division. Pressing on into the Netherlands East Indies in early 1942, they overcame 7th Division's 3,000-strong force on Java, a battalion on Ambon, the light defensive forces in New Britain, New Ireland, and the Solomon Islands, and an Independent Company (see SPECIAL FORCES, below) on *Timor.

At this time the land forces in Australia comprised an armoured division (which had few tanks) and seven militia divisions, incompletely trained and inadequately equipped. h 1942, General MacArthur arrived in Australia and Blamey was made, under him, commander of all ground forces in MacArthur's South-West Pacific Area.These comprised the seven militia divisions, the 6th and 7th Australian Divisions, and the 41st US Division, to hich the 32nd US Division and other combat and base nits were later added. In April 1942 Blamey reorganized he Australian Army for the defence of the mainland, the reatest concentration being between Newcastle and

Australia, 5, Table 5: Australian battle casualties in the Second World War

Particulars	*Royal Australian Navy*	*Australian Army*	*Royal Australian Air Forces*	*All Services*
War against Germany				
Killed—				
Killed in action and missing, presumed dead	900	2,610	5,036	8,546
Died of wounds	3	700	58	761
Died of wounds while prisoner-of-war		56	9	65
Died of sickness, disease, and injury while prisoner-of-war		95	14	200
Presumed died while prisoner-of-war		91		
TOTAL KILLED	903	3,552	5,117	9,572
Prisoners-of-war escaped, recovered, or repatriated	25	6,874	1,020	7,919
Wounded and injured in action (cases)	26	8,925	529	9,480
TOTAL	954	19,351	6,666	26,971
War against Japan				
Killed—				
Killed in action and missing, presumed dead	840	6,294	1,140	8,274
Died of wounds	41	1,090	65	1,196
Died of wounds while prisoner-of-war		50		
Died of sickness, disease, and injury while prisoner-of-war	116	5,336	138	8,031
Presumed died while prisoner-of-war		2,391		
TOTAL KILLED	997	15,161	1,343	17,501
Prisoners-of-war escaped, recovered, or repatriated	238	13,872	235	14,345
Wounded and injured in action (cases)	553	13,191	253	13,997
TOTAL	1,788	42,224	1,831	45,843

These tables do not include deaths and illnesses from natural causes. The army casualties do not include 85 Papuan and New Guinea soldiers or members of the Royal Papuan Constabulary killed in action or wounded.

Casualties other than in battle suffered by the army in operational areas were

Killed, died of injuries, etc.	1,165
Wounded, injured, etc. (cases)	33,396
TOTAL	34,561

Source: Long, G., *The Final Campaigns* (Canberra, 1963), in *Australia in the War of 1939–45.*

risbane. To replace the existing commands and military istricts (see Map 8), the First (Queensland and New South Wales) and Second (Victoria, South Australia, and Tasmania) Armies were created; Western Command became 3rd Corps; 6th Division, soon to become Northern Territory Force, absorbed the 7th Military District; and the 8th Military District became New Guinea Force (for dispositions in April 1943 see Map 9).

By mid-1942, the only Australian ground forces fighting the Japanese were an Australian Independent Company and sub-units of the militia New Guinea Volunteer Rifles, in contact with Japanese units which had landed near Lae and Salamaua on New Guinea's northern coastline in March. But by November 1942 both 6th and 7th Divisions, and two militia brigades defending the Papuan capital, Port Moresby, on the south coast, were engaged in the *New Guinea campaign. In February 1943 the Militia Bill was made law (see GOVERNMENT, above) which stipulated that conscripts could be used in a defined area outside Australian territory (see Map 9). However, by 1944, the main offensive against Japan had passed almost wholly out of Australian hands. From October 1944 onwards, Australian forces replaced American ones—needed for the second *Philippines campaign—in mopping-up operations on *Bougainville (3rd Division), *New Britain (5th Division), and in New Guinea (6th Division). But as a finale 7th and 9th Divisions were used in the assault on Borneo (*Balikpapan, *Tarakan, and Brunei) and by the time the war ended on 15 August 1945 had substantially defeated Japanese forces there.

Total enlistments in the army during the war were 691,400 men and 35,800 women.

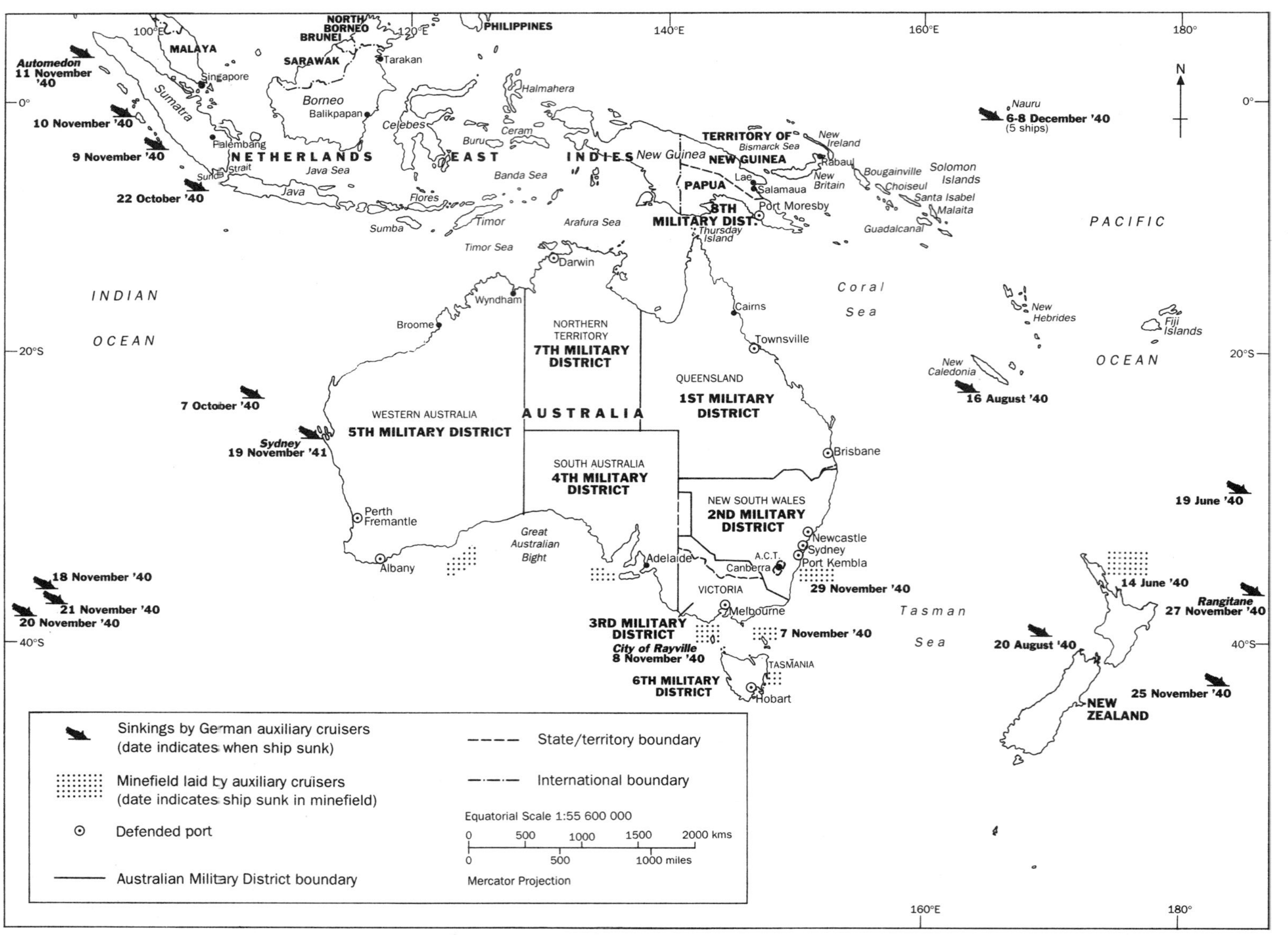

8. **Australian** military districts until April 1942, and activities of German auxiliary cruisers in Australasian waters

(c) Navy

In September 1939, the Royal Australian Navy had two 8 in. (20 cm.) cruisers (*Australia* and *Canberra*), four 6 in. (15 cm.) cruisers (*Adelaide, Hobart, Perth*, and *Sydney*), five old destroyers, and two sloops. All were in the Australian area except HMAS *Perth* which was in the West Indies. Three liners converted into *armed merchant cruisers for the Royal Navy, but manned by Australians, and two others commissioned for the RAN, sailed to join the China station (for British stations and fleets see UK, 7(c)). Several small coastal vessels were converted into minesweepers. The five destroyers were sent to join the British fleet in the battle for the *Mediterranean, and the *Perth* joined the British East Indies station. *Australia* and *Canberra*, plus the British battleship *Ramillies*, escorted the first Australian and New Zealand troop convoys to Egypt, and RAN ships did much of the escorting of the subsequent eight convoys sent there. *Sydney* was sent to the Mediterranean after Italy entered the war in June 1940, and sank the Italian destroyer *Espero*, was largely responsible for the sinking of the cruiser *Bartolomeo Colleoni*, and took part in a raid through the straits of Otranto before returning home in December 1940, being replaced by *Perth*. *Australia* was placed at the disposal of the British Home Fleet, and en route to Europe took part in the *Dakar expedition; *Canberra*, two sloops and an armed merchant cruiser joined the East Indies station; and *Hobart*, also sent to the Middle East, helped in the British withdrawal from British Somaliland, before returning to Australia in December. All the Australian ships in the Mediterranean (now supplemented by additional destroyers) were engaged in operations against the German and Italian fleets, in the supply of *Malta, the escort of convoys, and the bombardment of Italian positions in Libya and the *Dodecanese Islands. They helped land Australian and other troops in Greece and Crete and subsequently to take them off, and the cruiser *Perth* and destroyer *Stuart* took part in the battle of *Cape Matapan.

In fact, Australian warships saw action in all the campaigns in the Middle East during 1940 and 1941 and *Canberra* sank two German *auxiliary cruisers' supply ships in the Indian Ocean in 1941. Though one destroyer was torpedoed and sunk off Tobruk the first really severe blow to the RAN came in November 1941 when **Sydney* was sunk off the coast of Western Australia by a German auxiliary cruiser with the loss of her entire crew. By then nearly all Australian ships in the Middle East had been withdrawn to the Australian or Singapore stations and from the opening of the war against Japan, most Australian naval operations took place in its own region, initially as part of *ABDA command, and then under direct American command (MacArthur and *Nimitz). The destroyer *Vampire* rescued survivors from the **Prince of Wales* and *Repulse*, sunk off Kuantan at the outset of the *Malayan campaign, before being sunk herself by Japanese carrier aircraft during the Japanese raid into the Indian Ocean in April 1942. The cruiser *Perth* was sunk on 28 February 1942 after attacking a Japanese invasion convoy in the Sunda Strait (see JAVA SEA). A few days later the sloop *Yarra* was also sunk and seven other ships were lost during the Japanese air raid on Darwin.

Australian warships later took part in Allied operations in SWPA and the *South Pacific Area. They took a small part in the *Coral Sea battle in May 1942 and three Australian cruisers joined the bombarding and support force for the US assaults on *Guadalcanal and the nearby island of Tulagi. One of them, *Canberra*, was sunk during the *Savo Island battle and in July 1943 another, *Hobart*, was also sunk in the Solomons. Three Australian armed merchant cruisers took part in the US assault on New Britain and Australian warships participated in the recapture of the Philippines where the cruiser *Australia* was hit by what may have been the first Japanese *kamikaze attack. In the last stages of the war Australian warships were used to support Australian operations in Borneo, while three destroyers took part in the *Burma campaign, subsequently serving with the British Pacific Fleet (see TASK FORCE 57) in operations against the Japanese home islands.

Total enlistments during the war were 45,800 men and 3,100 women.

(d) Air Force

Australia had only a small air force when the war began, with 164 combat aircraft, most of them obsolete or obsolescent—Anson bombers, commercial *flying boats, and the Australian-built Wirraway which was essentially a training aircraft but was used, disastrously, as a fighter. There were nominally twelve Royal Australian Air Force (RAAF) squadrons, two being only in nucleus. The government offered the UK an expeditionary force of four bomber and two fighter squadrons, but this was abandoned in favour of training Allied flying personnel by participating in the *British Empire Air Training Scheme. Although there were some 'Australian' units in the RAF, most Australian airmen were dispersed throughout it and saw action in Europe, the Middle East, and in the Burma campaign. In the UK, Australian squadrons formed part of Bomber Command (especially), Fighter Command, and Coastal Command. In the Middle East, Australian squadrons were part of the *Western Desert Air Force and these later participated in the *Italian campaign and about 150 men served with the Balkan Air Force. One squadron moved to Corsica and supported the *French Riviera landings in August 1944.

In the Far East, four RAAF squadrons, two equipped with Hudson bombers and two with obsolescent Brewster Buffalo fighters, operated during the Malayan campaign. When the Japanese swept south the Hudsons were withdrawn to Palembang in Sumatra, then to Java, before finally returning to Australia in March 1942. Two other squadrons of Hudsons based in the Netherlands East Indies, also returned to Australia.

The RAAF in SWPA came under MacArthur's command. With a high proportion of the trained personnel serving

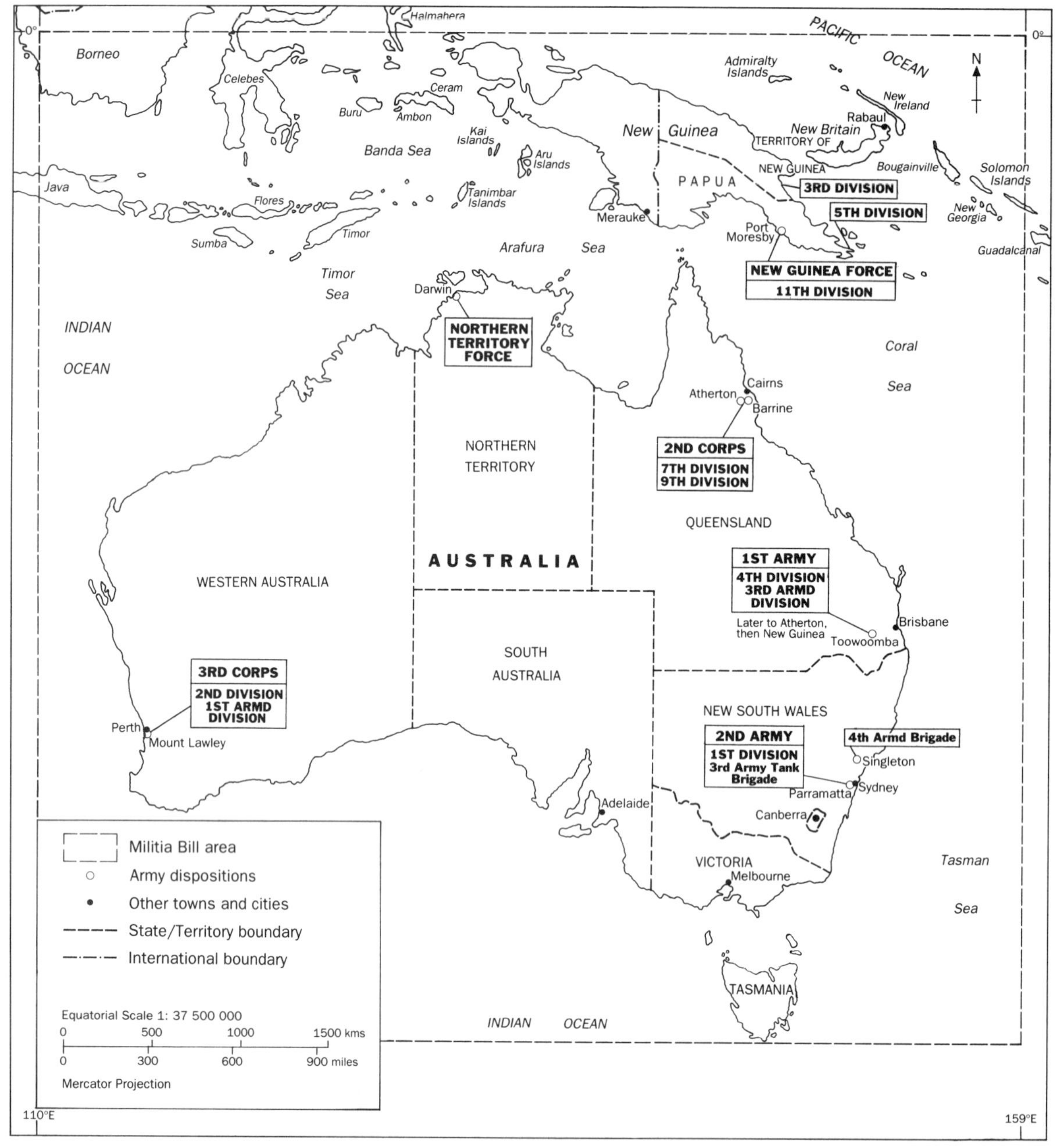

9. **Australian** Army dispositions, April 1943, and area covered by Militia Bill

with British forces, and with the UK making such heavy demands on aircraft for the defence of Britain and the Middle East campaign, the RAAF was weak and ineffective against the much more numerous and better equipped Japanese. It could offer only token resistance to Japanese attacks on Rabaul, Darwin, Broome, Wyndham, and Port Moresby. However, three new squadrons were equipped with US Kittyhawk fighters, and these began to contest the initiative with the Japanese, supporting the ground operations in Papua and New Guinea, and Australian aircraft joined in the successful battle of the *Bismarck Sea in March 1943. By then the RAAF had squadrons of Kittyhawk, Hudson, Boston, Beaufighter, Beaufort, and Wirraway combat aircraft, to which was added an RAF Spitfire wing of one British and two Australian squadrons. The force was active for the rest of the war in supporting

Allied ground and amphibious operations, in attacking Japanese bases and ships, and in minelaying. In the Burma campaign, Australians served in eighteen of the RAF squadrons fighting the Japanese there.

Total enlistments in the RAAF were 189,700 men and 27,200 women.

(e) Special forces

In 1940, acting on British advice, the Australian Army began to train Independent Companies for special activities behind enemy lines. Within a year three such companies, each of 17 officers and 256 men, had been formed, and the number was raised to eleven by 1944. One, 2/1 Independent Company, was deployed in July 1941 to help with the defence of the New Hebrides, New Britain, New Ireland, and the Solomon Islands. 2/2 Independent Company was sent to Portuguese Timor, subsequently reinforced by 2/4 Company, and carried out a remarkably successful guerrilla campaign against the Japanese, until evacuated in late 1942–early 1943. From January to August 1942, 2/3 Independent Company was in New Caledonia to support the Free French administration. These and other companies took part in Australian ground operations in Papua, New Guinea, Bougainville, and Borneo. In mid-1943 the units' designation was changed to Cavalry (Commando) Squadrons, and the following year to Commando Squadrons, which were brought together into three commando regiments.

Some of the men in these units transferred to clandestine activities conducted by the *Allied Intelligence Bureau, whose operations included a successful raid on Japanese shipping in Singapore in 1943, and an unsuccessful one in 1944 (see CANOEISTS).

6. Intelligence

At the outbreak of war, the three armed forces each had a modest directorate of Intelligence, concerned primarily with military information. A Combined Operational Intelligence Centre was set up in 1941 to provide some co-ordinated intelligence to Australian commanders, and a Joint Intelligence Committee was created on the British model, which included the three service intelligence chiefs and a representative of the department of external affairs.

A counter-espionage 'Special Intelligence Bureau', set up in 1916 and reorganized in 1919 as the Investigation Branch (later called the Commonwealth Investigation Branch, CIB), was attached to the attorney-general's department. This was transformed into the Security Service in March 1941, but never functioned to maximum effectiveness.

In March 1942 *SOE sent Major G. Egerton Mott to establish *Special Operations Australia and another British officer, Commander J. C. R. Proud, set up the Far East Liaison Office (FELO) to disseminate covert propaganda. Both these organizations, along with the Royal Australian Navy's intelligence gathering organization, the *Coast Watchers, became part of MacArthur's Allied Intelligence Bureau when this was formed in July 1942.

7. Merchant marine

Australia had never possessed a significant merchant service, although ships had been bought in the First World War to transport Australian grain to Europe, and a small Australian National Line was established. In 1939, the only merchant ships registered in Australia were the 154 engaged in the coastal trade, including several passenger ships which were converted into armed merchant cruisers or troop transports. Because of the distances involved, and the changes in railway guages between the states, some 80–90% of Australian interstate trade was carried by sea. The co-ordination between the state and federal governments of all transport thus became necessary, but it did not really begin until after the fall of *France.

In 1941 the National Security (Shipping Control) Regulations were promulgated, to be administered by a shipping control board, whereby all ships registered in Australia and most ships on the Australian run or under charter to Australian interests were made subject to direction, requisition, or control by the Australian government. Later that year, a Commonwealth Ships Chartering committee was set up to mainly control shipping used for the export of wheat and flour and return imports. This committee's authority was extended to interstate shipping also, and eventually controlled nearly 40 vessels, including 26 under charter, one captured vessel, one requisitioned vessel, and merchant ships built by the federal government. In 1942 the Committee's overall administration was transferred from the Department of Commerce to the Department of Supply. But with nearly 100% of exports and imports carried by sea, Australia was forced to rely on the merchant ships of other nations, especially of the UK and USA.

A Combined Raw Materials Board, a Combined Shipping Adjustment Board, and a Munitions Assignment Board were set up in Washington, with parallel bodies in London. All Australian requests for munitions or *matériel*, and the shipping to transport them, had to be referred to these boards. From early in the war mines laid by German auxiliary cruisers had caused shipping casualties around Australia's coastline (see Map 8). By the end of 1941 nine merchant ships had been lost because of them. From early 1942 Japanese attacks increased shipping losses sharply with twenty being sunk during that year. But by late 1943 Japanese activity near Australia had reduced dramatically, and shipping south of Brisbane was no longer escorted. At the *Commonwealth Prime Ministers' conference in London in May 1944 agreement was reached on planning for the control of all shipping to meet the requirements of the United Nations in an orderly manner. Prime Minister Curtin emphasized Australia's need for an adequate merchant navy and shipbuilding and repair facilities. Even so, Australian forces fighting in the SWPA in 1944–5 suffered from a shortage of adequate shipping.

8. Culture

Australian culture during the war tended to emphasize patriotism, but nationalism in 1939 was still too unformed for Australians to have a clearly separate identity from that of the UK. On 27 December 1941 Prime Minister Curtin, emphasizing Australia's independence of Britain, sought protection and support from the United States. Soon the rapidly growing US involvement in the Pacific theatre brought more than a million foreign servicemen through Australia and the *GIs made an immediate impact. They sounded like the American movie stars Australians had grown up with in the 1920s and 1930s. Although *Hollywood continued to dominate the Australian cinema public, attempts were made to revive the promising Australian film industry which had not survived the 1920s. The war strengthened demand for newsreels but Australia's movie epic was *Forty Thousand Horsemen*, a celebration of the famous Light Horse of the First World War, made by Charles Chauvel in 1944 and starring Chips Rafferty who would become a household name in the 1950s. Australian radio programmes and magazines also gained in popularity—one of the most influential and important cultural journals over the next half century, *Meanjin*, was founded in Brisbane in 1942—as did comic books which, despite paper shortages, rivalled the well established *Boy's Own* and *Girl's Own Annuals*.

Australian literature generally flourished, due not least to the patronage of the Australian government. In September 1939, the Commonwealth Literature Fund (CLF) was reconstituted and its support for writers made more substantial. With general mobilization only a few months away, the new CLF paved the way for writers to work within government agencies. A number of established writers joined the department of information, deploying their literary skills to aid the war effort. Apprentice writers who were to become well known after the war—T. G. Hungerford and Alan Marshall among them—also learned their craft in the service of their country at war. This increase in writing in turn boosted the Australian publishing industry. Before the war the handful of Australian books that had been published had been produced by British publishers in limited 'colonial editions' in expensive hardback format. After 1939 local publishing flourished in the absence of competition from overseas companies, a factor which helped consolidate the novel as the preferred literary genre and social realism as the dominant literary style. In 1944 the CLF underwrote the publication of 25 Australian titles (mostly novels) in print runs of 25,000, all of which were published by Australian publishing companies in cheap paperback editions intended mainly for servicemen. This was the largest government-sponsored Australian literary enterprise up to that time and did much to increase the confidence of Australian writers in the mass market.

With a short-term American boost to the population of almost 10%, British hegemony was successfully challenged and the Australian ethos changed dramatically. The Americans brought more than colourful conversation and nylon stockings; their music dominated radio and public performances. In the two decades leading up to the war Australians had imitated 'blue notes' and jazz rythms but now they had the real thing as dance clubs proliferated to meet the demand for swing and jive. With the music came new fashions which also heralded a new wave of youth culture. Not everyone responded positively to the Yanks. Hysteria broke out in Melbourne when an American serviceman became Australia's first serial killer, and fights between Australians and Americans were commonplace, the most notorious being the 'Battle of Brisbane' in 1942, a riot which resulted in one death and several wounded. Capturing the mood of unease some artists—Albert Tucker was one—depicted the Americans as sexually preoccupied, and painters such as Russell Drysdale, William Dobell, and Sidney Nolan moved the visual arts in the opposite direction to literature, away from realism towards expressionism.

With the passing of the immediate threat of invasion the government re-cast its priorities in favour of post-war reconstruction, or the 'Light on the Hill' as it was called. Culture similarly focused on shaping a new Australia as intellectual élites sought to utilize the experience and consolidate the prestige they had gained as a consequence of their prominence in the nation's time of need. In culture as in politics the Second World War was a major turning point in Australia's history. T. B. Millar

Richard Nile (Culture)

Hasluck, Paul, *Australia in the war of 1939–1945: Civil: The government and the People*, 2 vols. (Canberra, 1952–70).

Horner, D. M., *High Command. Australia and Allied Strategy 1939–1945* (Sydney, 1982).

——*SAS, Phantoms of the Jungle* (Sydney, 1989).

Long, G., *The Six Year War. A Concise History of Australia in the 1939–45 War* (Canberra, 1973).

McKernan, M., *All in! Australia during the Second World War* (Melbourne, 1983).

Millar, T. B., *Australia in Peace and War* (Canberra, 1979).

Robertson, J., *Australia at War 1939–1945* (Melbourne, 1981).

Austria. The Republic of Austria (Republik Österreich) had emerged in 1918 out of the shattered Habsburg Imperial and Royal Monarchy. The name Deutsch-österreich, which it had initially adopted, was disallowed at the *Versailles settlement, as was the original intention of union with the German Republic. After settling the disputed borders with Italy, Yugoslavia, Hungary, and Czechoslovakia, Austria comprised an area of barely 84,000 sq. km. (32,400 sq. mi.) with 6.7 million inhabitants (see Map A for Austrian territorial losses after the First World War).

Austria was the first victim of Nazi aggression and

expansion. Its incorporation into the Third Reich in March 1938 meant an inestimable gain in military personnel, manpower, raw materials, energy, and industrial potential for Germany and at the same time improved Germany's strategic position by allowing for an easier economic penetration of the Balkans and the elimination of Czechoslovakia, which was to be Hitler's next objective.

While a majority of Austrians no doubt initially welcomed the Anschluss, or union with the Reich, dissatisfaction with German tutelage later increased, particularly during the war, which was perceived as being less and less in Austria's own interest. Finally, the reaction of the population to the defeat of the Reich and the recovery of their sovereignty was one of relief.

From the beginning of its existence the internal stability of the Republic suffered from differences between the political parties–Christian Socialists and Social Democrats as well as German Nationalist and German Liberal groups—that were difficult to reconcile. This resulted in short-lived coalition governments and often bloody clashes, triggered off by private political armies, the so-called *Wehrverbände* (defence units), a phenomenon which brought about the assassination of the chancellor, Engelbert Dollfuss (1892–1934), during a National Socialist putsch in July 1934.

After 1933, when the National Socialists came to power under Hitler, Austria came under increasing political pressure from Germany. In an attempt to strengthen its position *vis-à-vis* Germany, the Austrian government founded a rightist, non-party Vaterländische Front which, after the model of Italian and German united parties, was intended to become the basis for an authoritarian, corporative Austrian state. It proved ineffective and even Kurt von Schuschnigg (1897–1977), federal chancellor from July 1934, became less and less able to stand up to German interference. Italian support for Austrian independence grew weaker as Rome and Berlin formed closer political ties. The German–Italian Axis was seen, as the Austrians sarcastically put it, as a roasting spit on which the country was to be browned. An agreement of 11 July 1936 between Germany and Austria, under the terms of which Austria undertook to conduct its foreign policy as a 'German state' and Berlin promised to respect its sovereignty, could not halt the course of events. Berlin used the agreement primarily as a pretext for exacting from Austria the subordination it required.

Schuschnigg, summoned to *Berchtesgaden by Hitler on 12 February 1938, found himself confronted by further German demands, among them the dismissal of the Austrian Chief of General Staff and the inclusion in the government, as minister of the interior, of the National Socialist Artur *Seyss-Inquart, who would become responsible for security. A last-ditch attempt by Schuschnigg to obtain a substantial majority vote for the maintenance of an independent Austrian state through a referendum, planned for 13 March and announced on 9 March, forced Hitler's hand. On 11 March Schuschnigg was replaced by Seyss-Inquart and the next day the Wehrmacht, which had been partially—and not wholly successfully—mobilized, entered the country. It did so unopposed as the Austrian government had already decided that military opposition was pointless, a decision to which the balance of power between Austria and Germany, the lack of any foreign help, and the split in the population, which had led the Austrian National Socialists to prepare themselves for the Anschluss, all contributed.

The German occupying forces, over 100,000 strong, drawn mainly from Wehrkreis (military district) VII [Munich] and XIII [Nuremberg], were combined to form the Eighth Army. For political reasons their C-in-C, General von *Bock, was not given executive powers; however the troops were instructed to be extremely ruthless if necessary in breaking up any opposition. Hitler wanted to give Operation OTTO, as it was called, as unwarlike a character as possible and to allow it to unfold as 'a peaceful incursion welcomed by the population'. This was, indeed, what transpired. However, what was then and still remains controversial was the measure of acceptance given to the Anschluss by the Austrians: many, possibly the majority, greeted it with enthusiasm, though there were also consternation, despair, flight across the frontiers, and some cases of suicide. While Hitler was welcomed with great jubilation during his appearance in Linz and Vienna, the numerous police and *SS who had arrived in the country made their first arrests and were soon sending transports of prisoners to the German *concentration camps. A year later a concentration camp was set up on Austrian soil at *Mauthausen near Linz.

Seyss-Inquart had induced President Wilhelm Miklas (1872–1956) to step down and had taken over the presidential rights. On orders from Berlin he introduced a law on 13 March 1938 which announced the 'reunification' of Austria with the German Reich and provided for a plebiscite to be held on 10 April. It was enacted as a law of the German Reich on the same day and, after the dissolution of the Reichstag (parliament) and according to the wishes of the National Socialist rulers, the German people were also to be given the opportunity to record, in a plebiscite, their assent to the creation of the new 'Greater German Reich'.

On 15 March Hitler appointed Seyss-Inquart as Reich Governor of Vienna and put him in charge of running the Austrian *Landesregierung* (provincial government). Josef Bürckel, **Gauleiter* of the German province of the Saar-Palatinate, was also sent to Vienna to reform the organization of the National Socialist Party and prepare the plebiscite, which produced the customary result in totalitarian states: 99.08% of those entitled to vote agreed to the proposed 'reunification'. Thereafter 73 deputies represented the former Austrian state at the Reichstag in Berlin.

Work on the assimilation of the new territory into the Altreich (Old Reich) started immediately. *Göring secured *raw materials (iron ore, magnesite, wood, and mineral oil), industrial plant, and foreign exchange reserves for his Four Year Plan; and the German police and SS began mass arrests of opponents of the regime and of Jews (see FINAL SOLUTION) even before they had the legal authority to do so. In order to speed up the integration of Austria into the Reich, Bürckel was appointed 'Reich Commissioner for the reunification of Austria and the German Reich'. As Hitler's personal representative, he was given authority to issue directives to all administrative departments of the state and the party, and Seyss-Inquart was pushed aside. Austria, ruled for the moment by a kind of 'authoritarian anarchy', was re-christened Ostmark, its administrative unity was broken up and the name Österreich was formally eradicated from everyday language.

From May 1939, the former republic was divided into seven *Reichsgaue* (party regions), some of them bearing what were at the time novel names: Greater Vienna, Lower Danube, Upper Danube, Styria, Carinthia, Tyrol, and Salzburg. Upper and Lower Danube had been enlarged after the *Munich agreement of September 1938 with the incorporation of Sudeten German territories (see SUDETENLAND) which had been taken from Czechoslovakia. An 'Ostmark Law' of 14 April 1939 brought the state administration into line with the new regional organization. The *Gauleiter*, all of whom were at that time National Socialists from what had been Austria, also acted in most cases as Reich governors of their districts. It was intended that the same system should be adopted in Germany at a later date. In January 1942 the concept of Ostmark was abandoned in an attempt to suppress memories of *Austrian* sovereignty in what were now called the 'Alps and Danube Reich Regions'.

Bürckel, who had been constantly at loggerheads with the highest state and party authorities in the Old Reich and under whom disagreements between the citizens of the Old and New Reichs had been greatly exacerbated, had in August 1940 been replaced as *Gauleiter* in Vienna by Baldur von Schirach (1907–74), a former *Hitler Youth leader. However, his competence for the post was soon called into question, even by fellow party members. Schirach, who considered himself a man of letters, was meant to turn the former capital into the second cultural centre of the Reich. To achieve this he made continuous use of well-known personalities such as Heinz Hilpert, Lothar Müthel, Karl Böhm, and Wilhelm Furtwängler, from the worlds of the theatre and music. When he had become Gauleiter in the summer of 1940, Schirach had also been given by Hitler the task of winning over the Viennese (whom Hitler absolutely distrusted) to the New Order (see GERMANY, 4). However thanks to his knowledge of modern art he not only irritated Hitler but also antagonized *Goebbels, the Reich minister for propaganda. This isolated him from the Nazi leadership while at the same time in Vienna he became less and less able to control a resurgence of Austrian national feeling and an upsurge of determination to revive the country's cultural heritage. The wave of nostalgia, expressed on the stage and in concert halls, was much to Schirach's annoyance flaunted openly and ostentatiously.

In the mid-thirties, during which period the federal chancellor also acted as federal minister for defence, the Austrian government had decided to increase the size of the army by the end of 1939. Conscription was introduced on 1 April 1936. By 1938 the Federal Army, supported by front-line militia, was about 60,000 men strong which included seven infantry divisions, a motorized division, and two air force regiments equipped with 90 obsolescent aircraft. On mobilization these numbers were doubled, but the army possessed neither modern aircraft nor modern tanks. Two days after the German invasion of 12 March 1938 the German Army ordered the Austrian armed forces to take the oath of loyalty to Hitler (125 refused to do so), and three days later the civil service was ordered to do likewise. After excluding those deemed 'unworthy to bear arms' and undesirables, and reinstating previously discharged National Socialist officers, the Federal Army was integrated into the Wehrmacht. This entailed restructuring the units, adapting their equipment and training to those of the Wehrmacht, and the immediate call-up of several age groups for military service. Compulsory retirements and what were felt to be discriminatory procedures, such as the sometimes unfavourable adjustment of Austrian service ranks to those in the German Army, caused resentment; this was exacerbated by a lack of sensitivity on the part of senior officers drafted in from the Altreich and by the distribution of Ostmark soldiers among Wehrmacht units, where the rule that they were not to exceed 25% of the complement of any unit was regarded by them as reflecting German mistrust and arrogance.

The former Austria was divided into Army District XVII (Vienna) and XVIII (Salzburg) and 1,600 Austrian officers, two infantry, two mountain, and one light divisions were immediately added to the strength of the Wehrmacht. These, along with an armoured division drawn from Germany, were merged into three army corps (XVII, XVIII, and XIX) under the command of Fifth Army Group with headquarters in Vienna. Air Force District XVII (Vienna) and an air force command which formed the nucleus of the Fourth Air Fleet were set up in March 1939.

After the war began, the Reich districts in what had been Austria, like the rest of the Reich, had continually to contribute to the formation of a variety of new units. By 1945 at least 220 Ostmark soldiers had reached the rank of general in the Wehrmacht, the Waffen-SS, or the police; and 326 soldiers had been awarded the Knight's Cross (see DECORATIONS). The Austrian share of Wehrmacht losses amounted to approximately 230,000 men; and about 104,000 people lost their lives through the Allied *strategic air offensives on such targets as Vienna (fuel works); Steyn (ball bearing and aircraft industries); Linz (steel and fuel industries); Innsbuck (road/rail communications); and Wiener Neustadt (aircraft and motor vehicle industries).

The German invasion was soon followed by growing disillusionment, frustration, and discontent. Many of the methods of 'assimilation' in the administrative, military, and economic spheres were felt to amount to discrimination and undeserved slights, and aroused increasing dissatisfaction. The rapid fall in unemployment—which was linked to the dispatch of workers to Germany—and a short-lived economic upturn which was checked by the outbreak of war did not make up for the mounting feeling that Austria was being subjected to foreign rule.

The realities of life under a totalitarian regime, and increasing restrictions and impositions imposed after the start of the war, soon restricted cultural activities. The suppression of religious communities and practices, and propaganda hostile to the Church, offended the traditions of the country and were generally rejected.

The repressive measures immediately taken against racial and ethnic minorities, particularly against the Jewish population who were deprived of all their rights, often met with incomprehension and refusal to co-operate. Of barely 200,000 Austrian Jews more than half were forced to emigrate; the others mostly died later in concentration camps. During the second half of the war the general mood of the population changed for the worse as a result of Allied air raids, which by the summer of 1943 had begun to reach as far as the south-eastern part of the Reich.

After the German invasion resistance groups were formed in socialist, monarchist, and nationalist circles, and although they were continually broken up by a strong police force it proved impossible completely to eradicate opposition to a German presence that was regarded as foreign rule. The opposition had links with resistance groups in Germany and from 1943 was encouraged by the fact that the Axis powers were being defeated on all fronts. It was further stimulated by the outcome of the conference of foreign ministers in Moscow in November 1943, at which the Allies—who had more or less acquiesced in the Anschluss in 1938—officially declared that the former republic had been the first victim of German politics of aggression and held out prospects for the liberation of its people. Attempts by the Austrians to shake off German domination were to be given consideration when, in due course, assessments were made about Austrian participation in and responsibility for Hitler's war.

After the bomb plot of 20 July 1944 (see SCHWARZE KAPELLE) in which officers of the Vienna Wehrkreiskommando (regional army command) were involved, a new wave of arrests took place; but in view of the evident decline of the National Socialist regime the Germans became less and less able to suppress the spread of resistance in Austria. This resistance soon established contacts with the Allies and with Austrian émigrés who, being split into a number of factions, had not been able to form a *government-in-exile. Specific acts of resistance—for which, right up to the end, the price had to be paid in loss of lives—prepared the ground for the change of government, separation from the Reich, and the restoration of sovereignty. HANS UMBREIT

Bell, P. M. H., *The Origins of the Second World War* (London, 1986).
Keyserlingk, R. H., *Austria in World War II* (Toronto, 1989).
Williams. M., 'German Imperialism and Austria, 1938', *Journal of Contemporary History*, 14 (1979), 139–54.

Automedon, Singapore-bound British merchant ship seized by the German *auxiliary cruiser *Atlantis* on 11 November 1940. Aboard were British war cabinet minutes of 15 August 1940 which were being taken by hand to the C-in-C Far East, Air Chief Marshal *Brooke-Popham. These recorded British policies towards Japan and a *Chiefs of Staff report on Singapore's defences which concluded that Hong Kong, French Indo-China, Malaya, and the Netherlands East Indies were indefensible. On 12 December the Germans passed the documents on to the Japanese who considered them of such importance that the captain of *Atlantis* was subsequently presented with a samurai sword, an award only granted to two other Germans, *Göring and *Rommel.

The fate of the documents was known in the UK by the end of the year, but neither Brooke-Popham nor the British public, nor any of Britain's allies, were told of their loss. It only became public knowledge when *MAGIC intelligence decrypts, including a signal from the Japanese attaché in Berlin which was not deciphered until after the war, were declassified in the USA in 1980.

auxiliary cruisers were warships disguised as merchantmen which the Axis used to prey on Allied shipping routes (see Maps 8 and 10).

By far the most successful were the ten German ones, modern vessels between 3,860 and 9,400 tons. All carried *float planes and were armed with 15 cm. (5.9 in.) guns, torpedoes, and smaller armaments, which were hidden behind hinged bulwarks, or under false deckhouses and skylights. Five carried mines. They flew the flags of neutral or Allied nations and altered their outlines to appear like the ships under whose names they masqueraded. So cleverly did they disguise themselves, and so adept were they at employing all kinds of ruses that, before the *check-mate system was introduced in October 1942, Allied warships had the greatest difficulty telling friend from foe. Their chief function was to disperse scarce Allied naval resources, and disrupt the flow of trade (see also WORLD TRADE AND WORLD ECONOMY), but between them they sank or captured over 800,000 tons of shipping. They were normally kept fuelled and provisioned by supply ships (see also LOGISTICS), though Japanese island bases were used to refit and refuel some of them while Japan was still officially neutral.

Part of the British Admiralty's problem in hunting

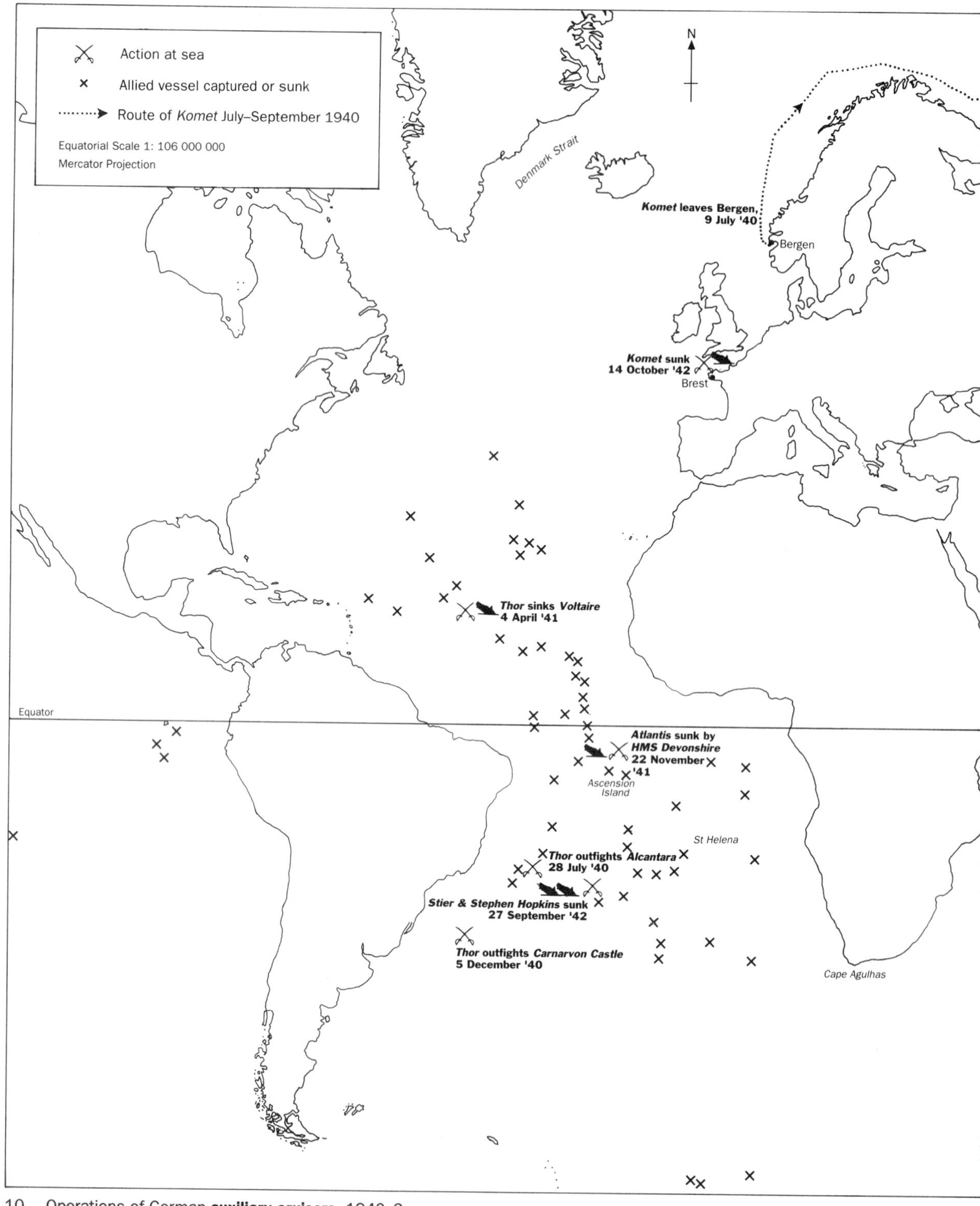

10. Operations of German **auxiliary cruisers**, 1940–3

Passage of *Komet* through ice helped by Soviet icebreakers
JAPAN
Yokohama
Thor blew up 30 November '42
Michel sunk by US submarine 17 October '43
Ramb 1 sunk by *HMNZS Leander*, 27 February '41
Pinguin sunk by *HMS Cornwall* 8 May '41
Equator
INDIAN OCEAN
Thor sinks *Nankin*, 10 May '42
SEE MAP 8 FOR ACTIVITIES OF GERMAN AUXILIARY CRUISERS IN AUSTRALIAN WATERS

these German raiders down was that only the *ENIGMA key they used in home waters had been broken by *Bletchley Park. This restricted any *ULTRA intelligence-based attacks against them to when they were attempting to leave or return by the English Channel.

The first to leave Germany was *Atlantis* (ex-*Goldenfels*) on 31 March 1940. Disguised as a Soviet merchant ship she escaped from Germany into the Atlantic via the Denmark Strait. After laying mines off Cape Agulhas she entered the Indian Ocean where one of her victims yielded current copies of the Merchant Navy Code and secret call-signs which enabled her to intercept other Allied vessels. One of these, **Automedon*, had highly secret mail aboard which gave invaluable intelligence. Eventually, after sinking or capturing 22 ships, *Atlantis* was sunk by the British cruiser *Devonshire* in the central Atlantic.

The next to leave Germany was *Orion* (ex-*Kurmark*) on 6 April 1940. En route for the Pacific she sank several ships and in October 1940 joined another raider, *Komet* (ex-*Ems*). *Komet* had left Bergen the previous July and, with Soviet help, had entered the Pacific by using the Arctic route north of Siberia. Together the two raiders sank the New Zealand liner *Rangitane*, before mounting an attack on phosphate ships off the Pacific island of Nauru, sinking four. *Orion* then returned to Germany having logged the longest voyage of any raider, 233,000 km. (144,700 mi.). She was sunk by a Soviet air attack in May 1945. *Komet* returned to Nauru and shelled its installations, before returning to Germany in November 1941. In October 1942 she left on a second voyage, but ULTRA intelligence revealed her position and she was sunk in the English Channel.

The third raider to leave, *Widder* (ex-*Neumark*), took or sank ten ships in the Atlantic from May to October 1940, before returning to Brest. But she proved mechanically unreliable and was later dismantled to arm another raider, *Michel*.

The fourth to sail, *Thor* (ex-*Santa-Cruz*), showed just how dangerous the German auxiliary cruisers were. After leaving Germany on 6 June 1940 she sank eleven merchant ships, and on the three occasions she was intercepted by British *armed merchant cruisers she outfought them and actually sank one, *Voltaire*. She returned to Germany in April 1941, but left again the following year, and from January to October 1942 took or sank over 29,000 tons of Allied shipping. While operating in the Indian Ocean she captured the Australian steamer **Nankin*, aboard which was top secret correspondence. She then captured or sank four more ships before putting into the Japanese port of Yokohama in October 1942 where she was later accidentally destroyed by fire.

In terms of tonnage, *Pinguin* (ex-*Kandelfels*) was the most successful. She left Germany on 22 June 1940 and after sinking or taking several ships in Australian and Antarctic waters her crew converted two of her prizes into mine layers, and it was her mines which sank *City of Rayville* on 8 November 1940, the first US merchant ship to be lost in the war. *Pinguin* later sank three British ships near the equator, but the distress signal from one of them brought the British cruiser *Cornwall*, which sank her on 8 May 1941. During ten months she had sunk or captured 28 ships totalling 136,551 tons.

These first six raiders constituted what the Germans called the 'first wave'. The first ship of the 'second wave', *Kormoran* (ex-*Steiermark*), at 9,400 tons the largest of the German auxiliary cruisers, sank several ships en route for the Indian Ocean before encountering the Australian cruiser **Sydney* off the West Australian coast on 19 November 1941. At the time *Kormoran* was masquerading as a Dutch ship. It must have been a convincing disguise for the cruiser approached too close for safety and in the ensuing action both ships sank.

The next 'second wave' raider, *Michel* (ex-*Bielsko*), left Kiel on 9 March 1942. To increase her lethal potential, she had aboard a 10-ton motor torpedo boat which her captain employed with good effect. After sinking or taking fourteen ships he took refuge in a Japanese port early in 1943, but during a second sortie, in which he claimed three more victims, he was sunk by a US submarine.

The last German raider to see action was *Stier* (ex-*Cairo*). She left the Gironde estuary in Western France on 20 May 1942 and after sinking several ships in the central Atlantic she encountered the armed US *Liberty ship *Stephen Hopkins*. The American ship put up such resistance that *Stier*, after sinking her, went down too.

In February 1943 one more raider, *Coronel* (ex-*Togo*), attempted to break out into the Atlantic, but ULTRA intelligence revealed her presence in the English Channel. She was bombed and disabled, and was eventually forced to return. By that time German U-boats had a much longer range and promised a much higher return than the auxiliary cruisers for the limited resources available, and no further attempt was made to use them.

Five other auxiliary cruisers, two Japanese and three Italian, were also employed by the Axis powers, but none achieved the success of their German counterparts. One of the Italian ships, *Ramb 1*, was sunk by the New Zealand cruiser *Leander*, in February 1941. See also GERMAN SURFACE RAIDERS.

Muggenthaler, A., *German Raiders of World War II* (London, 1978).

Axiom Mission. This was dispatched to London and Washington in February 1944 by the Supreme Commander of *South-East Asia Command, Admiral *Mountbatten, to present his future operations. Mountbatten wanted an *amphibious warfare operation (CULVERIN) against Sumatra to open a supply route to China by sea; but his deputy, Lt-General *Stilwell, was determined to open one overland by retaking northern Burma and then completing the *Ledo Road. The mission, led by Mountbatten's deputy Chief of Staff, Maj-General *Wedemeyer, was to present both points of view, but Stilwell sent his own mission to Washington without informing Mountbatten. The British *Chiefs of Staff and the US *Joint Chiefs of Staff could not see eye to eye on the subject, but both were opposed to CULVERIN. It was dropped, but by then the Japanese had solved the problem by starting their *Imphal offensive of March 1944 which proved their undoing in Burma.

Axis Powers. A treaty signed in 1936 between Germany and Italy formed what was known as the Rome–Berlin Axis, hence the name. This was reinforced in May 1939 with the *Pact of Steel. Japan became associated with Germany and Italy when it signed the *Anti-Comintern Pact in November 1936, and allied itself to them with the *Tripartite Pact signed in September 1940. Romania, Bulgaria, and Hungary were the other principal Axis powers. See also AXIS STRATEGY AND CO-OPERATION.

Wiskemann, E., *The Rome–Berlin Axis* (London, 1949).

'Axis Sally' was an American called Mildred Gillars (1900–88) who broadcast propaganda (see SUBVERSIVE WARFARE) on German radio. After the war she was convicted of treason and given a twelve-year sentence, but was parolled in 1951.

Axis strategy and co-operation. Although the leaders of the Axis spoke frequently in public of their co-operation, and they were bound by various treaties (see TRIPARTITE PACT, PACT OF STEEL, and ANTI-COMINTERN PACT), in practice there was extraordinarily little co-ordination of military or diplomatic activities during the war. Hitler and Mussolini, the leaders of Germany and Italy, undoubtedly admired each other immensely, but this admiration was not shared by their respective military and naval leaders nor by their respective peoples. Furthermore, each of the two powers conducted its policy without much regard for—and often without giving much notice to—the other. Very much the same thing was true of the relationship of each of them to their third major partner in the conflict: Japan. In that case there was perhaps something of an inversion of the situation between Germany and Italy, in that the military and naval leaders did have a high regard for the abilities of their wartime partners, but there is no evidence that the two European Axis leaders and *Tōjō Hideki, the leader of Japan until the summer of 1944, particularly cared for each other. As for Tōjō's successors *Koiso Kuniaki and *Suzuki Kantarō, neither had a high opinion of the European Axis leaders, who in turn appear to have known next to nothing about either.

The Germans had begun the Second World War at a time when Italy was not ready to join in, having only just been promised several years of peace by the Germans, while the Japanese were affronted by the *Nazi–Soviet Pact of August 1939 which appeared to them to violate their own prior agreements with Germany and which was signed while Japanese and Soviet forces were actually engaged in combat (see JAPANESE–SOVIET CAMPAIGNS). Italy joined Germany in the war in June 1940 on the assumption that the hostilities were amost over, with no real plans for fighting either France or the UK. Furthermore, when the Germans occupied Romania in September 1940, as part of their preparation for the invasion of the Soviet Union (something they had failed to explain to the Italians), Mussolini decided that he would in effect pay them back for their advance in the Balkans by attacking Greece (see BALKAN CAMPAIGN). The defeat suffered by Italian forces in Greece, combined with the failure of Italy's armed forces in the *Western Desert campaigns during the winter of 1940–1 made any future independent conduct of war by Italy impossible.

Because Italy's defeats in Greece and North Africa threatened the very existence of Mussolini's regime, the Germans decided to help Italy out. But that help was to be limited to a rescue operation; Germany did not propose to commit large forces to a part of the world where Italy's living-space, not Germany's, was at stake. As for what in Italian eyes was the critical issue of control of the central Mediterranean, which they believed, probably correctly, could be attained only by taking *Malta, the Germans baulked. The casualties incurred by German airborne units in the seizure of *Crete in May 1941 made Hitler unwilling to try such an operation again, and as the Italians had predicted, the operations of the Axis in North Africa were thereafter too much at the mercy of Allied submarines and aircraft.

Although the Germans contributed only minimal forces to the rescue of Mussolini's regime in the Mediterranean, the Italians reciprocated by sending troops to the Eastern Front to help their allies in the *German–Soviet war. However, that measure by Mussolini to assert his role in the Axis led to disaster for the Italian Army caught up in the aftermath of the great German defeat at *Stalingrad. Mussolini's conclusion from all this, namely that Germany would be well advised to make peace with the Soviet Union and concentrate all efforts on defeating the western Allies, fell on deaf ears in Berlin.

At the start of the *North African campaign in November 1942, both Germany and Italy moved substantial forces into Tunisia, aided at the critical moment by the acquiescence of the *Vichy French resident-general there, Admiral *Estéva. The subsequent campaign for Tunisia served to delay the Allied invasion in the west from 1943 to 1944, but the frictions between German and Italian military leaders which had characterized the earlier fighting in North Africa continued. In May 1943 the troops of both had to surrender. The last joint military effort of the Axis was the attempted defence of Sicily after the Allied landings in July 1943 (see SICILIAN CAMPAIGN). It showed the Italians that they could not resist invasion, and it demonstrated to the Germans that their Italian ally was, in effect, finished with fighting on their side.

In some practical areas Germany and Italy did manage

to co-operate, but always with accompanying friction. Large numbers of Italian workers were sent to Germany, but there were always complaints about their treatment. On the other hand, Germany provided Italy with substantial quantities of coal, needed to keep Italy's industry functioning, but there were always complaints about inadequacies in the supply. One area in which the two proved totally at odds was that of the extermination of Jews. The Italians simply refused to go along with the German programme for the *Final Solution and in fact sabotaged German efforts to implement it in the Axis-occupied parts of Europe, especially Yugoslavia, Greece, and France. Italian unwillingness to share in the mass killing of Jews, which had the highest priority for the Germans, confirmed the latter in their view that the Italians were unreliable and inefficient allies; while the stubborn insistence of the Nazis, which looked like insanity to the Italians, only served to confirm in their eyes that the Germans were still rather like the barbarians who had invaded the Roman Empire centuries before.

The Italian surrender in September 1943 served once again to confirm both Axis partners in their negative views of each other. The Germans believed themselves betrayed and took fearful vengeance on their former ally. Hundreds of Italians were shot; hundreds of thousands were carted off to *forced labour camps in Germany. The shadow government Mussolini was allowed to set up under German auspices in northern Italy (see ITALY, 3(b)) had no means of preventing the exactions and atrocities of the Germans, though one could argue that in the resistance to both the Germans and Mussolini's new regime the Italian people were able to create the founding myth of their post-war republic. The willingness of German military commanders in northern Italy to negotiate a surrender behind Mussolini's back (see WOLFF) illuminates the lack of co-ordination between the Axis partners in defeat—just as their *rivalries in south-east Europe had done when it looked as if they might win.

If the victory of Germany in western Europe in May–June 1940 had led Mussolini to take Italy into the war, it had a similar, if slightly delayed, effect on the Japanese. Those elements in Tokyo looking towards the seizure of a vast empire in South and South-East Asia believed that the time had come to move forward. In this they were constantly encouraged by the Germans who hoped that the USA would be diverted to the Pacific while they were still building up their own navy to fight the Americans; if, on the other hand, the Japanese went to war with the USA, the Germans promised to join them immediately on the basis that then they would have the world's third largest navy on their side right away. When the Japanese did move in December 1941 by attacking *Pearl Harbor, both Germany and Italy immediately declared war against the USA; but no close co-ordination of strategy resulted.

The Japanese had neither told the Germans when they would move nor explained to them their plans, either beforehand or afterwards. There were meetings of military commissions and conferences between Japanese representatives and German naval and military leaders, but it proved impossible to co-ordinate strategy. The obvious way for them to work together was to try to meet in the Indian Ocean and Middle East; the insistence of Admiral *Yamamoto on the *Midway operation in June 1942, followed soon after by the American landing on *Guadalcanal that August, which touched off a six-month struggle for that island, prevented the Japanese from following up on what they, as well as the Germans, recognized as their best chance of turning the whole tide of the war. The failure of the Japanese to make any effective strategic decision about Guadalcanal—to put in overwhelming strength or to cut their losses and advance elsewhere—meant that in the second half of 1942, the time when the powers of the Tripartite Pact had their best opportunity of the war, was consumed by a battle of attrition in the Solomon Islands which the Japanese lost.

By the time Japanese forces were evacuated from Guadalcanal in early 1943, the Axis armies in North Africa were bottled up in Tunisia and had been driven back on the southern portion of the Eastern Front; the Germans and Japanese could talk about meeting thereafter, but they would never again have any prospect of doing so. Furthermore, the Japanese were unwilling to co-operate with the Germans in the effort to paralyse the Allies by attacks on merchant shipping. Having always thought of their submarines as primarily for use against warships, the Japanese failed to grasp Germany's emphasis on the war on Allied convoys. By the time they began to do so, it was too late; not only was the tide of battle turning in the *Atlantic during 1943 but the American strategy of bypassing large Japanese garrisons in the *Pacific war meant that a large proportion of Japan's submarines had to be employed in the task of supplying these isolated forces with ammunition, medicine, and food. The effort to make up for this divergence on the issue of submarine employment, the stationing of a number of German submarines at bases provided by the Japanese in Malaya, so that these submarines could attack shipping in the Indian Ocean and off the coast of Australia, was to prove extremely costly to the Germans and, though certainly adding to the rate of sinkings, was probably not a cost-effective employment.

One field in which the powers of the Tripartite Pact did co-operate fairly effectively in spite of all sorts of attendant frictions was in the use of *blockade runners. Until they attacked the Soviet Union, the Germans had been able to secure important *raw materials from East Asia across the Soviet Union on the Trans-Siberian Railway. Once this ended in June 1941, when the Germans invaded the USSR (see BARBAROSSA), they made arrangements for ships to get through the blockade with key raw materials needed for the German war effort, especially tin and rubber. In exchange the Germans sent patents, blueprints, and some special goods to the Japanese. Although the blockade runners, which came to include both German and Italian submarines, were increasingly intercepted by the Allies, they were able to relieve some of the most critical shortages in Germany's war effort. On the other hand, the endless discussion of air transport between Europe and Japan produced next to nothing practical: one Italian aircraft made the trip east and back, but that was all.

Like the Italians, and it should be added Germany's other satellites and collaborators, the Japanese repeatedly urged Berlin to make peace with the Soviet Union. They began to advocate this line in the latter part of 1941 and came back to it throughout the war, but to no effect. There were repeated signs that the Soviets were interested, but the Germans certainly were not. On the other hand, the Germans were upset, to put it mildly, that vast quantities of American *Lend-Lease supplies—about half the total—were being shipped to Soviet East Asian ports literally under the noses of the Japanese. In exchange for a Soviet refusal to allow American aircraft to bomb the Japanese home islands from Soviet bases, the Japanese refused to interfere with the shipment of US aid to the Soviet Union; the lack of co-ordination between the powers of the Tripartite Pact was particularly obvious in this regard.

There were, it should be noted, some fields in which there was at least a modicum of co-operation. The Japanese and Italians in particular appear to have collaborated in the field of *signals intelligence warfare and the Germans provided the Japanese with a considerable amount of advanced technical information about weapons and industrial processes. There is, however, no evidence that the Japanese were able to make much use of this information in the time available to them, and, ironically, much of what they learned became known to the Allies because of their ability to intercept and decode a high proportion of the messages containing such information sent by Japanese representatives from Europe to Tokyo by wireless (see ULTRA, 2).

Perhaps the relationship between the European Axis and Japan is best symbolized by a portion of the records of the German–Japanese Society, a friendship organization established by the Germans to promote good relations between the two peoples. Included among the records seized at the end of the war was a thick file of agitated correspondence about a most troublesome question: could non-Aryans like Japanese join the German–Japanese Society? G. L. WEINBERG

Chapman, J. W. M., 'Signals Intelligence Collaboration among the Tripartite Pact States on the Eve of Pearl Harbor', *Japan Forum*, 3 (1991), 231–56.
Deakin, F. W., *The Brutal Friendship: Mussolini, Hitler and the Fall of Italian Fascism* (New York, 1962).
Meskill, J. M., *Hitler and Japan: The Hollow Alliance* (New York, 1966).
Sadkovich, J. J., 'Of Myths and Men: Rommel and the Italians in North Africa, 1940–1942', *International History Review*, 13 (1991), 284–313.
Schreiber, G., *Die italienischen Militärinternierten im deutschen Machtbereich 1943 bis 1945*; 'The Italian Military Internees under German Control 1943–1945', the only significant study of this important subject (Munich, 1990).
Steinberg, J., *All or Nothing: The Axis and the Holocaust 1941–43* (London, 1990).
Weinberg, G. L., *The World At Arms: A New History of World War II* (Cambridge, 1993).

Azores, Portuguese Colony, which has nine islands and is situated 800 km. (500 mi.) into the Atlantic Ocean from Portugal. It was to be the Portuguese seat of government if Portugal were overrun by Germany, a not unlikely prospect in 1941. In May 1941 Roosevelt had 25,000 men poised to occupy the islands should the Germans look like doing so. In October 1943, after protracted negotiations with Portugal, its oldest ally, the UK began using air bases there to increase the number of aircraft in the battle of the *Atlantic. US forces were at first excluded, a problem that was only resolved in 1944 by disguising US aircraft as British ones. Aircraft from the bases closed an *air gap, enabling *convoys to be given continuous air cover in that part of the Atlantic.

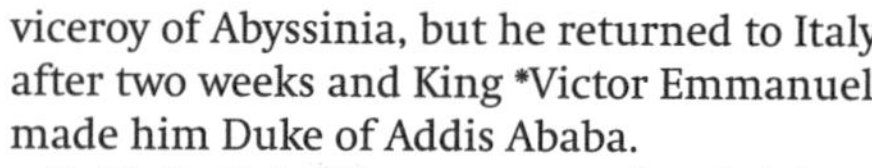

Babi Yar, see FINAL SOLUTION.

Badoglio, Marshal Pietro (1871–1956), Italian Army officer who was chief of the Supreme General Staff (see COMANDO SUPREMO) from June to December 1940, and head of government after Mussolini was deposed in July 1943.

During the *First World War Badoglio rose rapidly from lt-colonel in 1915 to general in 1917 and became army chief of staff in 1919. He resigned in 1921 and, though initially opposed to fascism, became Mussolini's ambassador in Brazil in 1923. In 1925 he was appointed both army chief of staff and chief of the Supreme General Staff and retained the latter post when he was appointed governor of Libya in 1928. When he returned in 1934 he became involved in opposing Mussolini's plans for invading *Abyssinia, but was appointed commander of Italian forces there in November 1935 when they became bogged down in the fighting, and in March 1936 he defeated Emperor *Haile Selassie's forces at Maych'ew. In May he was appointed viceroy of Abyssinia, but he returned to Italy after two weeks and King *Victor Emmanuel made him Duke of Addis Ababa.

Initially Badoglio was opposed to Italy's intervention in the Second World War in June 1940, but he eventually acquiesced in Mussolini's plans and under him enjoyed some control of Italian strategy. However, he openly disapproved of Italy's invasion of Greece in October 1940 (see BALKAN CAMPAIGN) and when it proved disastrous he was quick to blame Mussolini for the fiasco. A newspaper then publicly accused Badoglio of incompetence and when Mussolini did not order a retraction from its editor Badoglio resigned in December 1940 and was replaced by Marshal *Cavallero. For the next two and a half years Badoglio remained in the background, but by the time of Mussolini's arrest in July 1943 he had worked sufficiently hard behind the scenes to emerge as the Duce's most suitable successor. His negotiations with the Allies, while assuring the Germans that the Italians would continue to fight, were inept. When the *armistice

Marshal **Badoglio** aboard HMS *Nelson* off Malta after signing the 'long' armistice terms, 29 September 1943. On his left is General Eisenhower and behind him (left to right) are Air Chief Marshal Tedder, Lt-General Mason-MacFarlane, and General Alexander.

Japanese *Baka* bomb.

was announced on 8 September he fled Rome before it was occupied by the Germans and established his government first at Brindisi and then Salerno, but when the capital was liberated in June 1944 he was forced to resign by the Committee of National Liberation and was replaced by *Bonomi. See also ITALY, 3.

Baedeker raids, tip-and-run Luftwaffe bombing raids which, from April to June 1942, were mounted against the English cities of Bath, Canterbury, Exeter, Norwich, and York. They resulted in 1,637 civilians being killed and 1,760 injured.

The raids, undertaken in retaliation for the RAF's *area bombing of the German civilian populations of Lübeck and Rostock, were so called because a German foreign office official announced the campaign at a press conference by saying that the Luftwaffe would bomb every English building marked with three stars in the Baedeker guidebook.

Rothnie, N., *The Baedeker Blitz* (Shepperton, 1992).

Bailey bridge, see ENGINEERS.

***Baka* bomb,** small rocket-driven plane with a 816 kg. (1,800 lb.) explosive nose, which the Japanese first used in April 1945 at *Okinawa during the *Pacific war. *Baka* means 'idiot' in Japanese, and it was so called by the Allies because it was guided on to its target by its suicide pilot. The Japanese called it *ohka* (cherry blossom) or *jinrai* (thunderbolt). The parent aircraft which delivered it close to its target was so slow that it was never a serious threat. See also KAMIKAZE PILOTS.

Balikpapan, Dutch oil port situated in the south-east corner of Dutch Borneo (see NETHERLANDS EAST INDIES) which was occupied by the Japanese in February 1942. The 7th Australian Division, supported by Australian, Dutch, and US air and naval units, launched an amphibious assault against it on 1 July 1945. By 9 July the division had captured the port and its two airfields, and by the time Japan surrendered in mid-August an area within 24–32 km. (15–20 mi.) of the port had been cleared. Balikpapan's capture, which cost the Australians 229 dead and 634 wounded, was the war's last large-scale operation and the largest amphibious one carried out by Australian troops.

Balkan Air Force (BAF), small Allied inter-service headquarters formed at the Adriatic port of Bari in southern Italy in June 1944. It became the co-ordinating authority for air, land, sea, and special operations in and across the Adriatic, and for those mounted in the Aegean and Ionian seas.

The air component was formed from the eight squadrons and one flight of aircraft which since May 1942 had been dropping supplies to Yugoslav partisans and which, from late 1943, had been giving them direct air support. It was commanded operationally by Air Vice-Marshal W. Elliot, who was the BAF's first commander. The air component was additionally responsible for aircraft supplying Italian partisans and flying missions for *SOE and the *Office of Strategic Services in the Balkans, Poland, and south-east Europe. The BAF also co-ordinated the efforts of the naval forces under the Flag Officer, Taranto; Brigadier *Maclean's mission attached to Tito's HQ; Force 399 which ran special operations in Yugoslavia and Albania; and Land Forces Adriatic.

Men from eight nations—Greece, co-belligerent Italy, Poland, South Africa, the UK, USA, USSR, and Yugoslavia—used as many as fifteen different types of aircraft. Between its inception and May 1945 the BAF flew 38,340 sorties and dropped 6,650 tons of bombs, delivered 16,440 tons of supplies, and flew 2,500 individuals into Yugoslavia and 19,000, mostly wounded, out. On 1 September 1944, a week after the Germans began withdrawing from the Aegean and Ionian islands, BAF mounted 'Rat Week' in which aircraft co-operated with Tito's partisans to stop for one week all German traffic through Yugoslavia and between garrisons within Yugoslavia.

Land Forces Adriatic, helped by Allied *MTBs, operated from the Adriatic island of Vis, raiding German garrisons on other islands and attacking their supply convoys. Some units were part of the *British expedition to Greece, and in the last phases of the war, when Land Forces comprised the *Long Range Desert Group, the Special Boat Squadron (see SPECIAL BOAT SECTION), and the *Raiding Support Regiment. These harassed German garrisons during the Fourth Yugoslav Army's offensive up the coast towards *Trieste, which began on 19 March 1945, and helped locate targets for Allied aircraft and warships. However, on 13 April Yugoslav partisans arrested members of the Special Boat Squadron, an early indication of the *Cold War. Though they were quickly released, all British ground forces were withdrawn, but BAF aircraft, operating from Zadar, continued to support the Partisan offensive. Between 19 March and 3 May 1945 these flew 2,727 sorties, attacking the German withdrawal route from Sarajevo to Zagreb and supporting the Fourth Yugoslav Army advancing from Bihac to Fiume.

Balkan campaign, fought firstly by Greek troops and RAF units against Italian forces which invaded Greece in October 1940; then by Greek, British, and Commonwealth forces which resisted the German invasion of Greece the following April; and finally by the Yugoslavs when their country was invaded by Axis forces at the same time as the Germans entered Greece (see Maps 11 and 12).

After Italy invaded Albania in April 1939 Mussolini gave a formal assurance that he had no designs on Greece. Nevertheless, the British and French governments immediately pledged themselves to maintain the independence of Greece and Romania, and Germany and Italy reacted by signing the *Pact of Steel.

When Italy declared war on 10 June 1940 Mussolini still maintained that he had no interest in Greece, but on 28 October 1940, after accusing Greece of allowing the UK to violate its neutrality, he sent troops across the border from Albania. Though its forces were dangerously stretched at home, and by the battle for the *Mediterranean, the UK immediately dispatched five RAF squadrons to Greece and established an inter-service mission there.

The Italian offensive, which was grossly under strength, collapsed when it met determined Greek resistance, and by 14 November the Greeks had begun a counter-offensive to drive the Italians back into Albania. The Greek C-in-C, General Alexandros Papagos (1883–1955), determined to strike before the Italians could be reinforced, pushed boldly forward. In December he captured Santa Quaranta and by 10 January 1941 had taken Klissoura, while British bombers, despite adverse weather, struck at Italian port facilities and lines of communication and supported the Greek advance on Valona.

In November 1940 the Germans began their own preparations for the invasion of Greece through Romania and Bulgaria, not so much to help the Italians as to protect the Romanian oilfields and secure their southern flank for their planned invasion of the USSR (see BARBAROSSA). The Luftwaffe made its appearance in the area for the first time and in January 1941 a build-up of German troops started in Romania, which after the fall of *France had repudiated the Anglo-French pledge and aligned itself with the Nazis. The presence of Luftwaffe units in Bulgaria, and other indicators of German intentions, were revealed by *ULTRA intelligence, and by other sources, and by the second week in February—diplomatic efforts by the Germans to halt the fighting having so far proved fruitless—it was clear that Greece was to be attacked a second time.

During January 1941, in an atmosphere of mutual suspicion—the Greeks thought the British wanted to commit them to a long conflict against the Germans, while the British suspected the Greeks wanted to make a separate peace with the Italians—a British offer of ground forces and a Greek request for *matériel* were both refused. To ensure the continued commitment of the Greeks Churchill sent a mission under Anthony *Eden. Aiming to get Yugoslavia and Turkey to resist any German invasion of Greece, Eden told the Greeks on 22 February that the British would send troops to help defend their country on condition that the Greeks agreed to abandon Thrace to the Axis forces by withdrawing south to a new defensive position, the Aliakmon Line, which ran from the mouth of the River Aliakmon, through Veroia and Edessa, to the Yugoslav frontier. The British understood the Greeks to have agreed to this plan. But when Eden returned to Athens on 2 March, having failed to embroil Turkey and with Yugoslavia still equivocal, he found that Papagos (whose understanding had been that forming the Aliakmon Line had been conditional on Yugoslavia's reply to Eden's request for support) had done nothing to organize the withdrawal of his troops to it.

On 9 March the Italians launched a second offensive against the Greeks on the Albanian front, but despite now having 28 divisions at their disposal they were unable to break through. During this month Yugoslavia was under constant pressure from Germany to join the *Tripartite Pact and eventually did so on 25 March. This precipitated an anti-Nazi *coup d'état* and, having reluctantly agreed to the withdrawal of his troops from

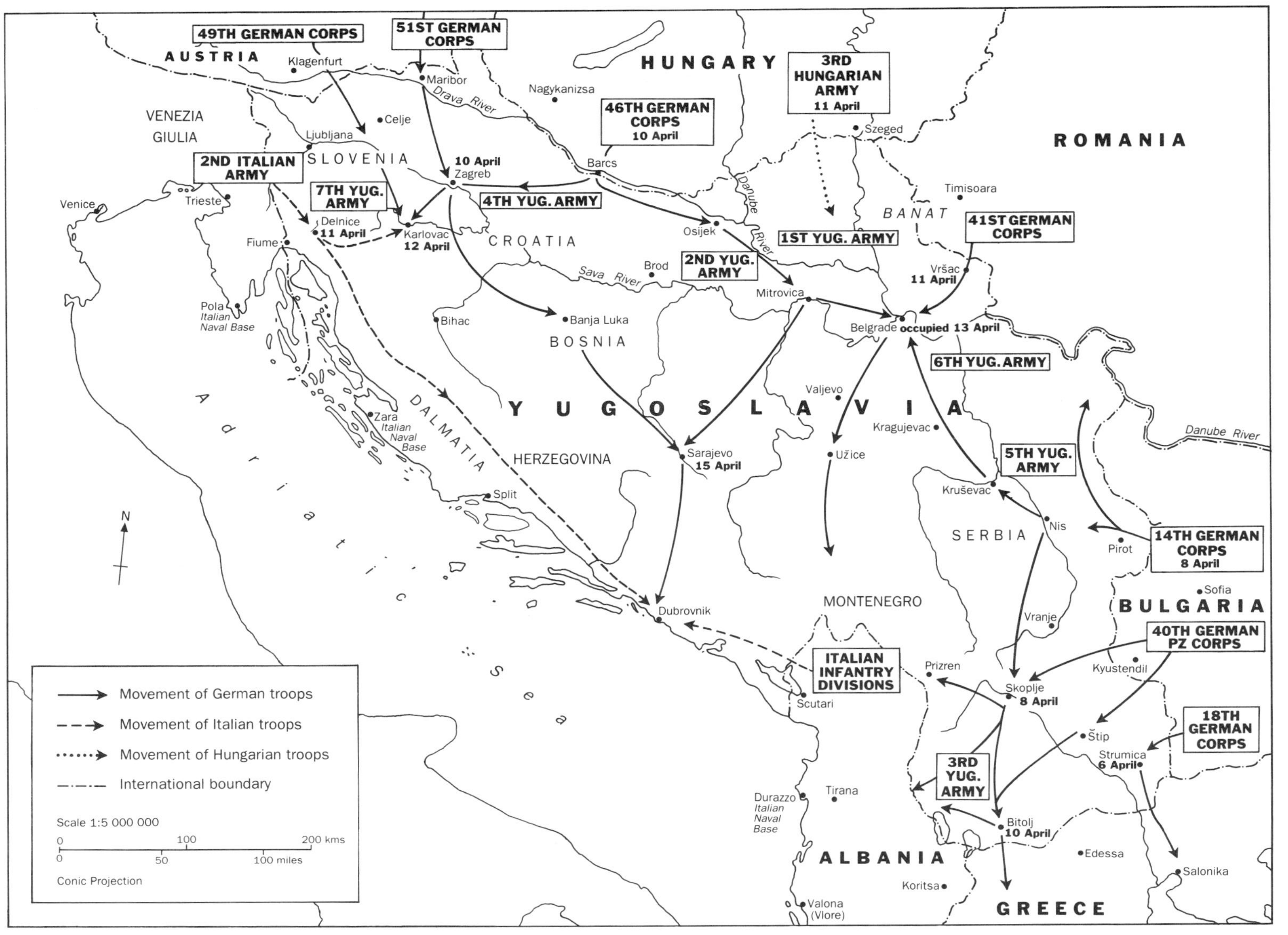

11. **Balkan campaign**: Yugoslavia, April 1941

Thrace, Papagos now reversed his decision. This left three and a half Greek divisions manning the Metaxas Line to protect Salonika while another three formed the Aliakmon Line with a British and Commonwealth force commanded by Lt-General Maitland *Wilson. Rushed from the Middle East, this force comprised the New Zealand Division and 6th and 7th Australian Divisions of the 1st Australian Corps under Lt-General *Blamey with supporting tanks and artillery. The total of RAF squadrons was now seven, and though aided by two squadrons of *Western Desert Air Force bombers for night operations, two of these were operating with the Greeks on the Albanian front, and what remained were no match for the 800 or more operational aircraft the Germans had at their command.

On 6 April the Germans bombed Belgrade, inflicting heavy casualties. The same day *List's Twelfth Army began the simultaneous invasion of southern Yugoslavia and Greece from Bulgaria, and on 8 and 10 April German, Italian, and Hungarian armies attacked from surrounding countries into northern and central Yugoslavia. The Yugoslav Army amounted to a million men, but it was antiquated and riven by dissent, *mutinies, and inefficiency. Only 151 Germans were killed; Belgrade fell on 12 April; and the government capitulated on 17 April.

Lack of Yugoslav resistance allowed List's 40th Corps to move from southern Yugoslavia into Greece, outflanking the Aliakmon Line and isolating the Greek troops that Papagos had refused to withdraw from the Albanian front. At the same time List's 18th Corps broke through the Metaxas Line and captured Salonika on 9 April. Wilson was immediately obliged to adjust his defensive line to meet the threat by 40th Corps, and by 10 April was already beginning to withdraw to another line further back. On 14 April, with the Germans in Belgrade, he was forced to withdraw yet again, this time to Thermopylae. Though under constant pressure, Wilson's moves were well timed, and were in part due to the ULTRA intelligence he received. He was also told its source, the first time a commander in the field had been made privy to the secret. But overall 'it is unlikely that Ultra assisted much in the defence of Greece, and certain that it could not have prevented defeat'. (R. Bennett, *Ultra and Mediterranean Strategy*, London, 1989, p. 50.)

Though it suffered a rebuff at Ptolemais the advance of the 40th Corps into Greece also threatened the Greek Army on the Albanian front which until 9 April had continued to attack the Italians. Papagos, knowing the effect on morale that an unforced withdrawal would cause, hesitated, and did not order his army back to a new defensive line until 12 April, which was too late. On the east coast New Zealand units, while withdrawing through the Olympus Pass on 14 April, mauled forward units of the advancing 18th Corps, but the plight of the Greek Army, now split from the British forces, became increasingly hopeless, and on 21 April the British decided to evacuate Greece. The same day the Greek Army opposing the Italians surrendered to the Germans after officers had deposed its commander.

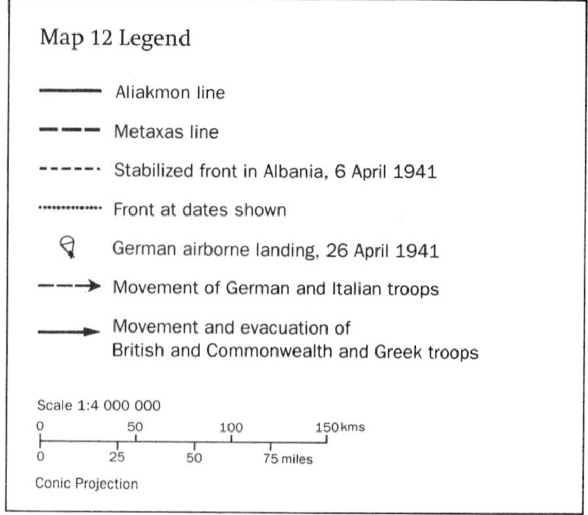

The evacuation posed immense problems for the C-in-C Mediterranean, Admiral *Cunningham, but he eventually mustered an evacuation force which included 7 cruisers, 20 destroyers, 2 infantry assault ships, and 19 medium-sized troopships. Units of New Zealand Division and 6th Australian Division defended the Thermopylae Line as the withdrawal to the beaches began, with 25th New Zealand Battalion fighting a notable defensive action at Molos on 24 April. Embarkation from the Peloponnese beaches, and from those around Athens, began on the night of 24/25 April and lasted seven nights. The acute shortage of shipping meant that most troops were offloaded at Crete though some went direct to Alexandria. The few remaining RAF aircraft had been flown to Crete to avoid certain destruction. Thus the Luftwaffe could attack unhindered, and two destroyers and four transports were sunk with heavy loss of life. Early on 26 April German parachutists captured the bridge across the Corinth Canal. This cut off many units from their beaches, including the rearguard 4th New Zealand Brigade at Erithrae, but they were eventually picked up from Port Raphti.

The evacuation was completed on the night of 30 April/1 May, though for months afterwards small groups of stragglers and individuals continued to escape as best they could. In total 50,732 men of several nationalities were saved from the beaches, while more were rescued by *flying boats operating between the Greek mainland and Crete. German ground forces had little opportunity to attack the evacuation beaches, though at Kalamata on 29 April some 7,000 Allied troops waiting to embark had to be abandoned and were subsequently forced to surrender.

The decision to send British troops to Greece was considered by General *Brooke 'a definite strategic blunder' and in September 1941 Churchill remarked that

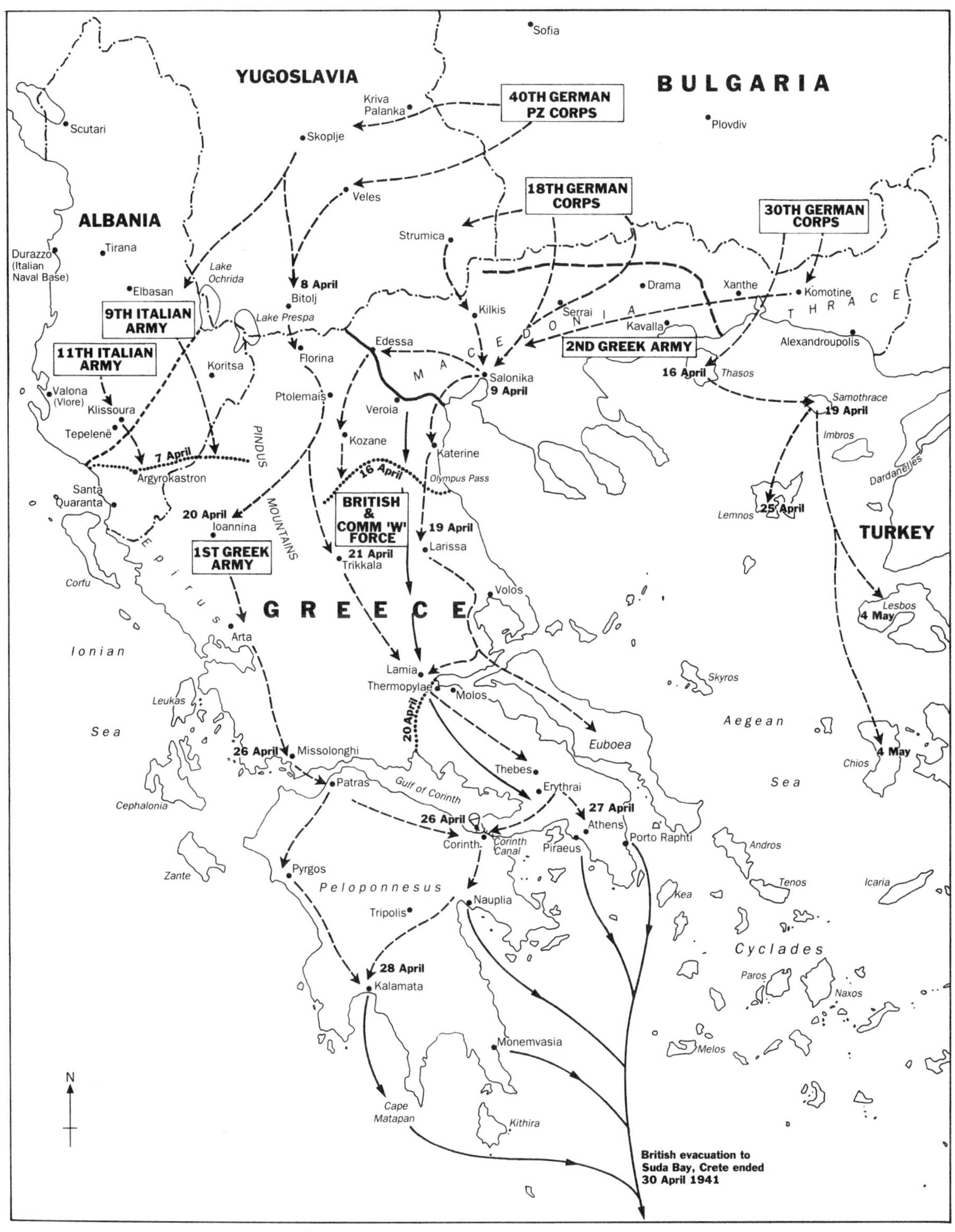

12. **Balkan campaign**: Greece, April 1941

it was the only error his government had so far made. Certainly, by stripping *Wavell of his reserves, it handed the initiative to the Axis in the *Western Desert campaigns. See also LAND POWER.

balloon bombs, balloons with explosive and/or incendiary devices suspended beneath them. The British experimented with them in 1939, but an attempt to dispatch incendiary versions to set the Black Forest alight—the Germans were short of timber—ignited only an East Anglian plantation when the wind changed. Later in the war the Japanese employed them on a fairly large scale with only marginally greater success. The ones they used were nearly 28 m. (91 ft.) round and made of bonded mulberry paper, and thousands of them were released between November 1944 and March 1945 in the hope that the prevailing winds would carry them to the USA. They were kept at the optimum height by a mechanism which, if the balloon went too high or too low, released helium from the sac or jettisoned a sandbag. About 200 landed in Mexico and Canada, as well as in Alaska and other parts of the USA, and it was initially feared they carried deadly bacteria as part of a Japanese *biological warfare campaign. One killed a woman in Helena, Montana; another killed six Oregon fishermen; otherwise they did little material harm. See also BOMBS.

Balloon Command, see UK, 7(d); see also BARRAGE BALLOONS.

Baltic Sea operations. The German bombardment of the Polish naval garrison at *Westerplatte (Danzig) on 1 September 1939 was the first act of war in the Baltic and one of the first of the *Polish campaign. German naval forces quickly overwhelmed the small Polish Baltic Navy of fifteen warships, though some managed to escape to the UK and thereafter fought on the British side under the direction of the Polish *government-in-exile in London.

In November 1939, at the start of the *Finnish–Soviet war, the Soviet Baltic Red Banner fleet blockaded Finnish sea communications with Sweden and bombarded the Finnish coast. But otherwise there were no naval operations in the Baltic until the German Navy, as a preliminary to Germany's invasion of the USSR in June 1941 (see BARBAROSSA), moved 48 small warships into Finnish waters to reinforce its small units already in the Baltic. The German Navy also established a naval base at Helsinki, and laid extensive minefields which caused heavy Soviet losses once the *German–Soviet war had begun. Surface actions during the initial phase of this conflict were confined to skirmishes, but Soviet ships were bombed and their bases seized. *Amphibious warfare was mostly confined to the capture and recapture of islands in the gulfs of Riga and Finland, though some small amphibious raids were mounted by Soviet forces behind German lines on the mainland. In September 1941 Hitler formed a Baltic fleet, which included the battleship **Tirpitz*, to prevent Soviet ships fleeing to Sweden when *Leningrad fell, but the city remained defiant and the fleet proved to be short-lived as its ships were soon needed elsewhere.

On paper the Soviet fleet was much superior to those opposing it. Besides having its own air arm of 656 aircraft, based on coastal airfields, it had 2 old battleships, 2 cruisers, 19 destroyers, 65 submarines, and numerous smaller craft. But its organization was weak, it was operationally inexperienced, and from the start it seemed paralysed by overcaution. When Finland, though still officially neutral, occupied the Åland Islands on the day the German–Soviet war began (22 June 1941), both Soviet battleships were nearby, but neither interfered. Instead, they withdrew to Kronstadt and remained there throughout the war, one being subsequently sunk by air attack.

The Soviet fleet's inactivity can be at least partially explained by its early losses from the minefields the Germans laid before they launched BARBAROSSA. These mounted further when the fleet evacuated Tallinn for Kronstadt and Leningrad in August 1941: 5 destroyers, 3 submarines, 10 smaller warships, and 42 merchant ships were sunk by mines off Cape Juminda, and from that time the Soviet High Command appeared unwilling to risk its larger units.

During 1942 Soviet submarines slipped through the minefields into the Baltic and sank 23 German or Finnish ships, and damaged others. Though ten were lost this was a great improvement on 1941, when they sank only one ship. However, they also sank five Swedish ships, forcing the Swedes to introduce escorted convoys. Because of these operations the Germans laid anti-submarine nets across the Gulf of Finland, and until September 1944 no more Soviet submarines entered the Baltic.

In January 1944 the fleet completed lifting by night 44,000 troops from *Leningrad to a beachhead around Oranienbaum, a considerable feat of *deception as the Germans were led to believe that the troops were being withdrawn not landed. This force then participated in the advance which forced the final withdrawal of the Germans from Leningrad. In March the fleet began clearing the German minefields from the Gulf of Finland. The Germans tried to prevent these operations, but Soviet air superiority caused them heavy losses. In September 1944, the month the Finns changed sides to fight with the USSR (see ARMISTICE), the Germans attempted to sieze the Finnish island of Suursaan (Hogland) in the Gulf of Finland, but were repulsed by Finnish and Soviet forces. The same month Soviet troops began clearing the islands in the Gulf of Riga, the largest *amphibious operations in which the Baltic Red Banner Fleet was involved during the war.

Once the Normandy landings of June 1944 had succeeded (see OVERLORD), the Germans sent all available surface warships, and even some submarines, into the Baltic to delay the advancing Red Army. Mines dropped by the RAF in the western Baltic hampered this

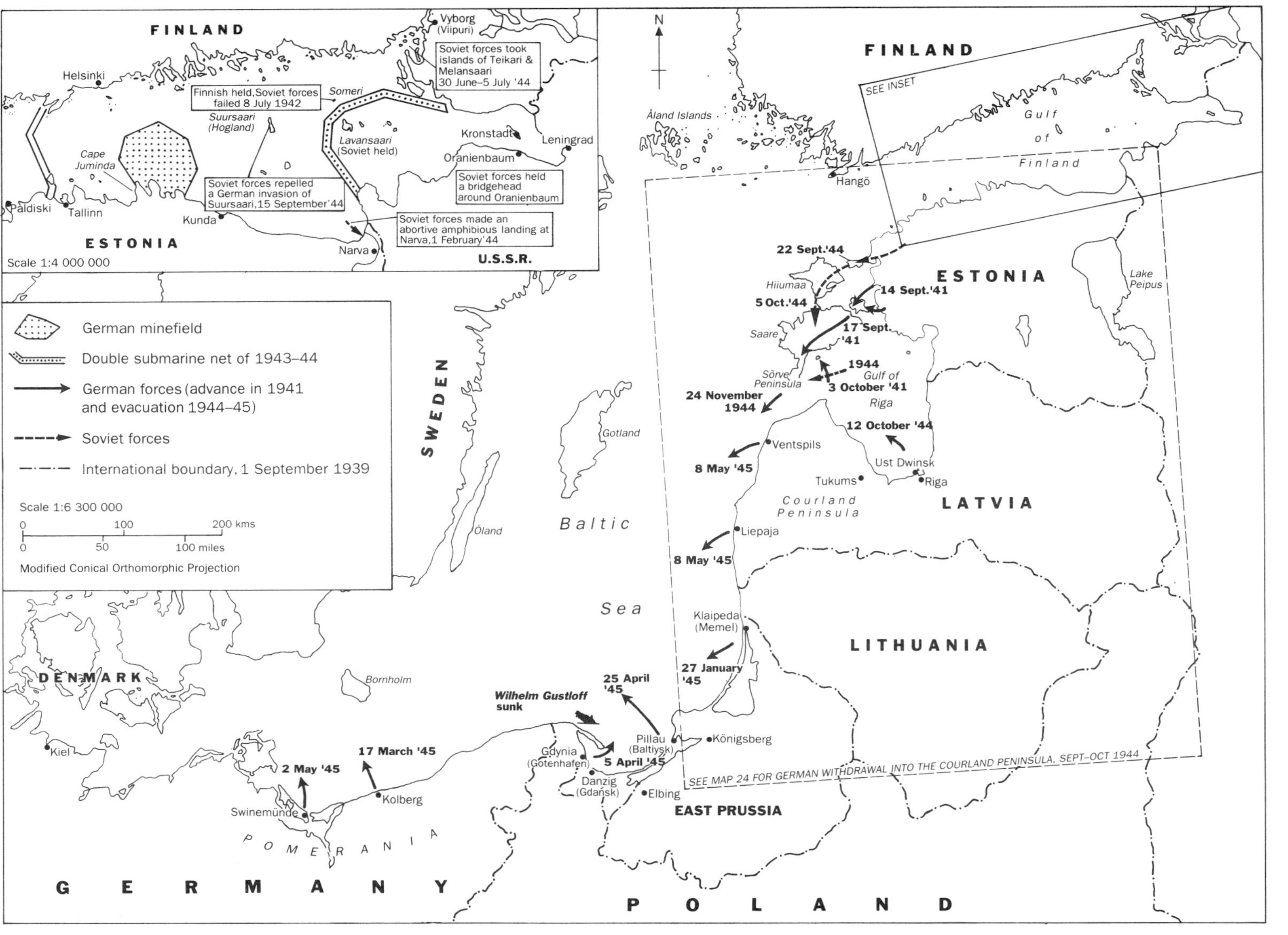

13. **Baltic Sea operations**

move, but the heavy cruiser *Prinz Eugen* and the pocket battleships *Lützow* and *Admiral Scheer* were employed to cover the German Army's retreat, and German troops were evacuated from besieged Baltic ports. By May 1945 about one million Axis servicemen and 1.5 million refugees had been rescued, the largest evacuation in maritime history, during which 15,000 lives were lost. Most of the deaths were caused by the sinking of three rescue ships, including the **Wilhelm Gustloff*, by Soviet submarines. But despite Soviet submarine and air attacks the Germans retained their naval supremacy, and they continued to supply their divisions trapped in the Courland peninsula, enabling them to hold out there until the war ended.

Soviet Second World War naval losses have not so far been published but it has been estimated that its Baltic fleet lost a battleship, 15 destroyers, 39 submarines, 40 minesweepers, and numerous smaller ships. The Finns lost a monitor, 6 minesweepers, 39 merchantmen, and about a dozen smaller ships. Germany lost 12 destroyers, 7 submarines, 67 minesweepers, and 129 smaller warships and landing craft, and 160 merchantmen; their single biggest loss was among their last when the old 13,000-ton battleship *Schlesien* was sunk by a mine on 4 May 1945.

Baltic States. The history of the three Baltic States (See ESTONIA, LATVIA, and LITHUANIA) followed a very similar pattern during the Second World War. They formed an important part of the broad swathe of eastern Europe where Soviet and German interests overlapped, and which suffered the double tyranny of both Soviet and Nazi invasions. There were three successive periods of occupation: the first Soviet occupation, 1940–1; the Nazi occupation from 1941 to 1944–5; and the second Soviet occupation starting in 1944.

In 1939 the independent sovereign status of the Baltic States had been established and confirmed by international recognition, by membership of the *League of Nations, and by treaties signed with the government of the USSR, including a series of bilateral pacts of non-aggression. There was little legal, moral, or political basis for the subsequent Soviet claims which sought to include the Baltic States within a Soviet 'sphere of influence' (as recognized by the *Nazi–Soviet Pact of 23 August 1939), and which, from June 1940, sought to justify their forcible incorporation into the Soviet Union. Although the western powers never formally acquiesced in the fruits of Stalin's aggression against the Baltic States, the politics of the *Grand Alliance barred any effective protest.

The inhabitants of the Baltic States played no part in the political decisions which determined their fate. The national governments which survived until June 1940 had no role in Nazi–Soviet negotiations, and were obliged to accept the resultant ultimatums that were put to them. They had no means to resist the ominous Treaties of Friendship and Co-operation with the USSR, nor the introduction of Soviet garrisons under the terms of those treaties, nor the subsequent political agitation conducted by Soviet agencies. The elections, which accompanied Soviet occupation in July 1940, were stage-managed operations imposed in conditions of nascent mass terror. The demands for annexation to the USSR, consummated in August 1940, were a total sham. The arrival of German forces in June–July 1941 was widely welcomed on the mistaken assumption that the Third Reich might practise policies similar to those of Imperial Germany during the *First World War. In reality, Soviet terror was replaced by a Nazi terror directed largely, though not exclusively, at the Jewish population. The Nazis took no steps to restore Baltic independence, leaving all three states under the military government of the Reich Commissariat *Ostland. The return of Soviet forces in 1944–5 produced a third wave of terror, with the Stalinist security organs conducting vast purges of collaborators, real or imagined.

The multinational population of the Baltic States—Estonian, Latvian, Lithuanian, German, Jewish, Polish, and Russian—was radically altered by the war. In 1939 it was still coloured by 19th-century experiences under tsarist rule, when the German minority had commanded considerable social and political power and an important Jewish community held a strong position in such cities as Riga and *Wilno. The Polish community was still very influential in large parts of Lithuania. Most pre-war social, ethnic, and cultural patterns were destroyed from 1939 onwards. The purges of the first Soviet occupation of 1940–1 were often directed at the Estonian, Latvian, and Lithuanian intelligentsia, who had served or been educated by the national regimes, and who were decimated by methods bordering on genocide. The Baltic Germans were evacuated under the terms of a Nazi–Soviet agreement, and resettled either in Germany or in territory seized by Germany from Poland. The Nazi occupation resulted in the mass murder of virtually all Baltic Jews (see also FINAL SOLUTION), the formation of a number of Waffen-*SS divisions, and the persecution of Poles and Russians. The second Soviet occupation restarted the earlier purges, while supervising the evacuation of most of the remaining Poles. It also saw the beginning of a mass influx of Russians and of other Soviet immigrants, especially to Estonia and Latvia.

Baltic war losses are not easily calculated, since they have been officially subsumed and concealed within statistics pertaining to the Soviet Union as a whole. It is certain, however, that the victims of political terror and genocide far outnumbered military casualties, also that in percentage terms Baltic losses considerably exceeded the Soviet average.

In 1945, the re-incorporation of the Baltic States into the USSR as the 'Soviet Republics' of Estonia, Latvia, and Lithuania clearly breached international law; but it passed without challenge. NORMAN DAVIES

Ba Maw (1893–1977), British-educated lawyer who, as leader of the Sinyetha (People's) Party, served as Burma's first prime minister from April 1937 to March 1939. A fervent nationalist, he was in regular contact with the Japanese and was imprisoned for sedition by the British in August 1940. In August 1942 the Japanese appointed him to head Burma's civil administration. He adopted the title *Ahnashin* ('lord of authority'), and the Sinyetha Party then forged an alliance with the *Thakins to support him. After Japan granted Burma its independence in August 1943, he chose the title *Adipati* ('chief') and led an authoritarian, one-party state. He escaped to Japan in 1945 and was gaoled there briefly by the Allies, but returned to Burma in July 1946. He then formed a new political party but was imprisoned twice more by the Burmese before he died. See also ANTI-IMPERIALISM.

Ba Maw, *Breakthrough in Burma: Memoirs of a Revolutionary 1939–1946* (New Haven, Conn., 1968).

Bandera, Stepan (1909–59), leader of a breakaway faction of the Organization of Ukrainian Nationalists (see UKRAINE). His declaration of an independent Ukrainian state on 30 June 1941, eight days after the start of the *German–Soviet War (see also BARBAROSSA), was ignored by the Germans who imprisoned him and his prime minister, *Stetsko, in *Sachsenhausen. He was released in September 1944 to intensify Ukrainian resistance against the advancing Red Army. His death in Munich from poison was the work of Soviet agents.

BANDIT, Allied codename for an aircraft identified as hostile.

Bangalore torpedo, a light steel tube, 38 mm. (1.5 in.) in diameter, filled with *explosives, which was used for breaching wire obstacles and clearing a path through minefields. It was issued in sections 1.8 m. (6 ft.) long which could be fitted together.

***banzai* charge,** the name given to an all-out attack by Japanese infantry who advanced *en masse* regardless of the strength of their opponents or their own casualties. As on Attu, during the *Aleutian Islands campaigns, and on *Saipan, it was almost always the last action of a defeated force whose members were more concerned to follow the Japanese code of honour, or *Bushidō, than to achieve any tactical advantage. Losses were often catastrophic and survivors frequently committed suicide rather than become *prisoners-of-war. The name derives from the Japanese battle cry '*Tenno heika banzai*' ('Long Live the Emperor').

BARBAROSSA, German codename for the invasion of the USSR which took place on 22 June 1941 (see Map 14). Launched by Hitler in violation of the existing non-aggression treaty with Stalin (see NAZI–SOVIET PACT), it was designed to provide the Reich with 'living space in the East' (see LEBENSRAUM). The German dictator had advocated the conquest of the USSR as early as 1924 in his book, **Mein Kampf*. At the same time, the campaign was to lay the foundations for the expected conflict with the two Anglo-Saxon powers for primacy as a world power and to free Germany of the *economic warfare the Allies were waging against it.

The first operational studies for the invasion of the USSR were started as early as the summer of 1940 and corresponding map exercises took place that autumn. Finally, Hitler was briefed on the results of both on 5 December 1940, and even at this early stage the first serious differences became apparent. It was a question of deciding whether the main thrust was to be directed against *Moscow or the two flanks in the north and south of the field of operations. Hitler wanted the forces to wheel north and south from the centre after piercing the enemy line; the Army High Command (OKH) favoured Moscow as the point of main effort.

As a basis for operations, Directive No. 21, Operation BARBAROSSA, and the Army High Command Deployment Directive were issued on 18 December 1940 and 31 January 1941 respectively. Their objective was 'to crush Soviet Russia in a swift campaign' which involved rapid offensive operations to destroy Soviet troops located in the west of the USSR. The OKH assumed that it would be able to defeat the Red Army west of the Dvina–*Dnieper rivers. Subsequently, both the Donets basin, important to the war economy, in the south and Moscow were to be seized. However, the question of how the war was to be terminated after reaching the 'line Volga (Astrakhan)–Archangel' if the Wehrmacht did not succeed in destroying the Red Army west of the Dvina and Dnieper remained unanswered.

After Hitler had ordered the invasion of the Soviet Union on 20 June 1941 by issuing the codeword DORTMUND, the German *formations launched a surprise attack on a wide front between 0300 and 0330 hours on 22 June 1941. With almost 3.6 million German and other Axis soldiers, around 3,600 tanks and over 2,700 aircraft, the largest force in European military history, crossed the border with the USSR between the Baltic and the Black seas. Under the overall command of Field-Marshal von *Brauchitsch, it was organized into three army groups—North, Centre and South (commanded by Field Marshals von *Leeb, von *Bock, and von *Rundstedt)—and three tactical air forces (commanded by General Alfred Keller, Field Marshal *Kesselring and General *Löhr).

The assault by the 153 divisions succeeded. It had been delayed at least twice and opinions differ among scholars as to whether the postponements were caused by the German intervention in Greece (see BALKAN CAMPAIGN) or for other reasons—a late thaw was probably a prime cause—but Brauchitsch's troops were able to pierce the Soviet frontier positions and conduct their operations according to plan. The Luftwaffe achieved air supremacy over the theatre of operations within the first few days. The Red Army formations in the western military districts, comprising about 140 divisions and 40 brigades, totalling about 2.9 million men, 10–15,000 tanks, some of which were obsolescent, and 8,000 aircraft, suffered heavy defeats. The Soviet High Command was surprised by the force of the German assault. Despite numerous warnings by his agents (see SORGE, for example), Stalin had not reckoned with such an attack by Hitler at this time, expecting instead a new political reconciliation of interests with Berlin.

The German invasion marked the beginning of a rapacious war of annihilation and conquest in which a *scorched earth policy was employed by both sides. Hitler intended a 'ruthless Germanization' of the occupied eastern territories, conducted with great severity. Orders violating international law, such as the *Kommissarbefehl*, the order to execute all Red Army political *commissars, and the 'Barbarossa Jurisdiction Decree', which exempted German soldiers from prosecution if they committed a crime against any Soviet civilian, meant a departure from traditional military conduct for the Wehrmacht. At the same time, **Einsatzgruppen* were to carry out the murder of Jewish and Slav elements of the population.

When Stalin had regained his composure after this embarrassing surprise, he called upon his people to mount a 'relentless struggle' against the German intruders. On 3 July he proclaimed the 'patriotic war' against the Germans, calling for scorched earth actions and partisan warfare behind German lines.

As a result of the military successes of the first few weeks, Hitler and OKH expected a swift campaign with the victory parade taking place in Moscow as early as the end of August. OKH was already occupied with new, large-scale operations against the industrial region in the Urals. Hitler ordered that Moscow and Leningrad were to be razed to the ground; their inhabitants were to be annihilated or driven out by starvation. These intentions were part of the 'General Plan East'. Drafts for a future settlement and regional planning in the East were hastily drawn up. They envisaged gigantic resettlement schemes involving more than 30 million inhabitants who were to be exchanged for 'German and Germanic' peoples.

At a conference on 16 July, Hitler was already distributing the spoils. He said it was obvious that the Third Reich would never again leave the conquered regions of the USSR. He stated that the main objectives of German occupation policy were: 'firstly to rule, secondly to administer, and thirdly to exploit'. In order to implement this policy against all opposition by the inhabitants, 'a simple solution' was recommended: the best way to pacify the conquered territories was 'to shoot dead anyone looking askance'. In addition, Hitler intended to have the Jews in the conquered eastern territories and throughout Europe systematically annihilated. Accordingly, on 31 July, *Göring gave the instruction to make 'all preparations necessary' for a 'total solution to the Jewish question in the German sphere of influence in Europe' (see FINAL SOLUTION).

Despite the initial large-scale battles of encirclement at *Bialystok–Minsk and *Smolensk, it became apparent

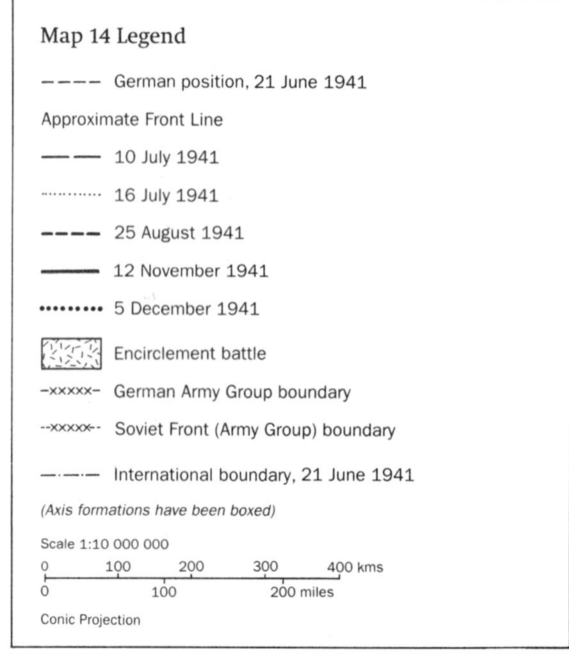

that the Germans were mistaken in their low opinion of the Soviet military potential. The Red Army's will to defend and readiness to perform remained unbroken. With increasing frequency, the Wehrmacht had to ward off vigorous counter-attacks. In August, *Goebbels and Hitler admitted that they had 'obviously underestimated completely Soviet striking power and, above all, the equipment of the Soviet Union'. They were forced to realize that Moscow had succeeded in creating a new industrial base in the far east of the country, which enabled the Soviet leadership to make good very quickly the heavy *matériel* losses in the battles of encirclement. Despite severe losses of personnel, *matériel*, and terrain, the Red Army defended stubbornly and with growing skill. In this way, it was able to prevent the rapid conquest of Leningrad, Moscow, and the industrial region in the Donets basin as planned by the Germans. German *logistics in the hinterland were also hampered by partisan actions following Stalin's appeal (see USSR, 8). Another reason for difficulties in the bringing-up of supplies was that the Germans had failed to provide sufficient *matériel* and transportation for lengthy, force-consuming operations.

After the victory at Smolensk, Hitler reverted to his old concept of concentrating the main effort on the wings. He ordered his forces to wheel south and north in order to capture rapidly the regions in the Ukraine and around Leningrad containing *raw materials and industries vital to the war effort; Army Group Centre was to go on to the defensive for the time being. As a result, the Soviet forces before Moscow gained time for fierce counter-thrusts and for the development of new defensive positions. On the

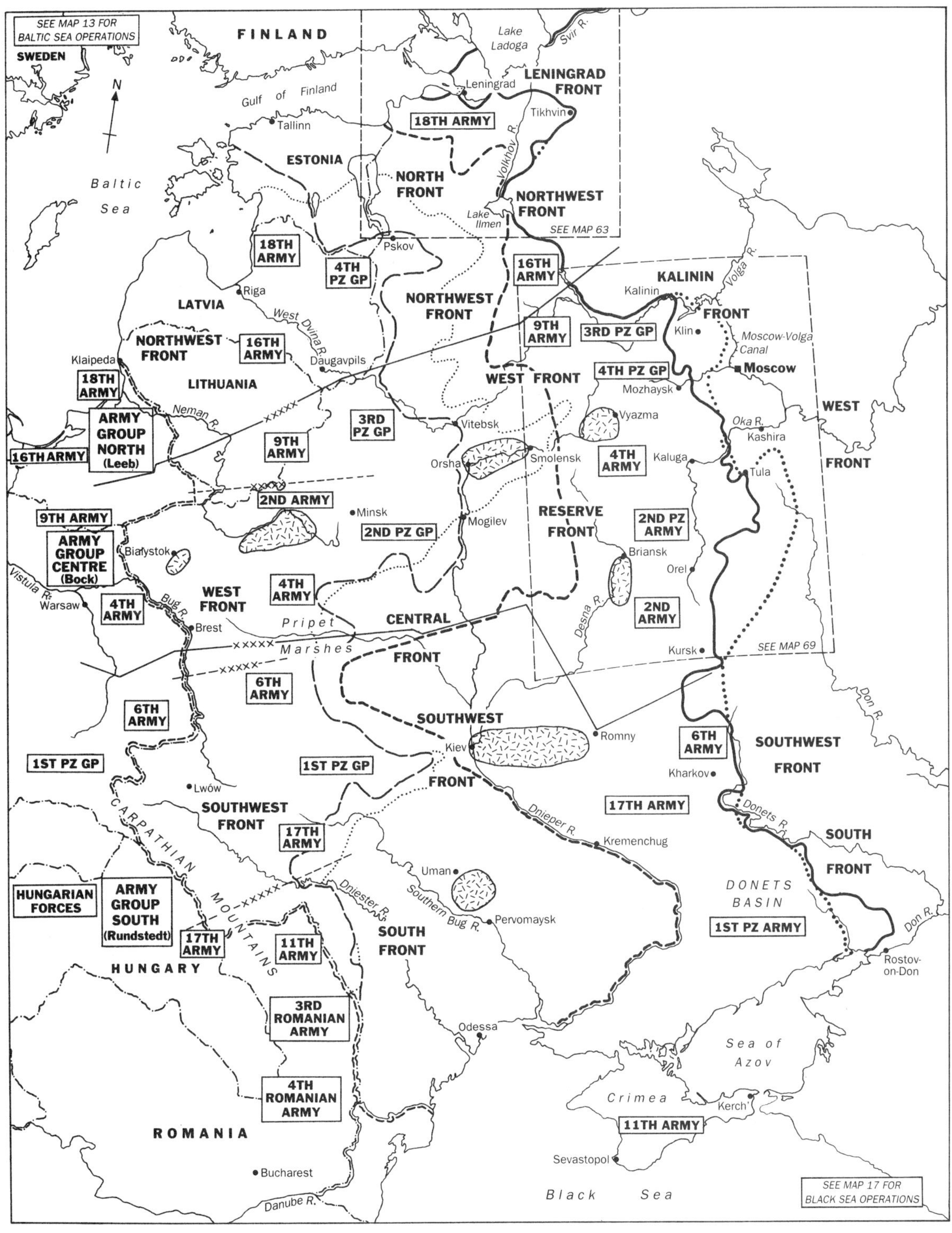

14. **BARBAROSSA:** The German invasion of the USSR, June–December 1941

other hand, the completion of the encirclement of *Kiev on the southern sector of the front at the end of September was an overwhelming success for the Wehrmacht. Hitler was convinced that the military strength of the USSR was now exhausted. For this reason, the advance to Moscow was to take place after all, in order to capture the city, before the onset of winter. However, the Germans had great difficulty in bringing up the most urgently required replacements for this new attack (TYPHOON). With no more strategic reserves, the offensive strength of the German divisions was bound to diminish thenceforth.

Late in September, the attack on Moscow was launched by Army Group Centre with six armies or panzer groups, supported by one tactical air force with three air and anti-aircraft artillery corps. In an address on 2 October, Hitler called this operation 'the last large-scale decisive battle of this year'; he said it would 'shatter the USSR'. He placed particular stress on the idea of a European 'crusade against Bolshevism'; all the nations of Europe, he went on, saw this struggle as a combined action to 'save the most valuable continent of civilization'.

At first it looked as though Hitler's predictions were to come true. In the course of the massive twin battles of *Briansk–Vyazma, Army Group Centre was able to encircle and capture almost eight Soviet armies. Hitler was already busy working out the details of the planned destruction of the Soviet capital. However, the Soviet forces quickly managed to construct new defensive positions and bring up fresh forces. In addition, the onset of muddy weather hampered the mobility of the German troops and favoured the defenders. In the period that followed, both sides suffered from the difficult autumn weather conditions. However, for the German side, the effects of the weather on the supply situation, which was already strained, were devastating.

Nevertheless, in mid-October the Army High Command decided that the attack on Moscow was to be continued towards Vologda in the north and Voronezh in the south. However, after initial penetrations, the Red Army's resistance stiffened noticeably, with the result that the advance by the German formations came to a standstill. By bringing up new formations from Siberia and the Far East (where by now it was apparent that Japan was going to attack southwards and not into the USSR) and by activating militia divisions and battalions of labourers recruited from the population of Moscow, the Moscow leadership was able to reinforce the defensive front. Just how seriously the Soviet leaders took the threat to Moscow is shown by the relocation of most government, party, and military authorities to Kuibyshev, 800 km. (500 mi.) away on the Volga, from mid-October onwards. In addition, about a million inhabitants of Moscow were evacuated, the Kremlin was prepared for demolition and Lenin's coffin was removed from its mausoleum and taken to a safe place; but Stalin remained in Moscow. When German panzer formations conquered Mozhaisk on 18 October, thereby penetrating the Moscow defensive position, Stalin declared the capital a fortress. Moreover, the Kremlin dictator exhorted the units marching to the front straight from the traditional military parade commemorating the 24th anniversary of the October Revolution to withstand the impending threat with all their might.

In the course of the fierce fighting, there was an intensification of the ruthless conduct of war on both sides. Special inflammatory orders and orders of the day issued by German commanders revealed their willingness to play a part in Hitler's war of annihilation, based on racial ideology, against the USSR. This also applies to the assistance they gave to the campaigns of terror and murder conducted by *SS units against the civilian population in the conquered territories. However, not all German officers accepted or morally supported this involvement in the executions of Jews as easily as was expressed, for instance, in the army orders issued by Generals von *Reichenau, Hoth, and von *Manstein. They called upon their soldiers to make 'the merciless extermination of alien insidiousness and brutality' the goal of their struggle.

At a conference chaired by the Chief of the General Staff, *Halder, on 13 November 1941 at Orsha near Smolensk, the differences of opinion of the German staffs concerning the continuation of the operations became apparent. Given the exhausted condition of their units, the field commanders were opposed to further attacks. On the other hand, Hitler and OKH decided to resume the offensive and, by making a supreme effort, risk an attempt to conquer Moscow. This 'final effort of willpower' was regarded as decisive in the effort to vanquish the already teetering Red Army. The Germans staked their all on one throw.

Once again, they were able to drive the Red Army back. The German panzer formations came to within 30 km. (18 mi.) of the city. By the end of the month, however, German offensive strength was exhausted, and the attack came to a standstill. The Quartermaster General, Edward Wagner, stated: 'we are at the end of our personnel and *matériel* strength.'

Early in December, the German panzer armies finally had to discontinue their attack. They hoped that this would be followed by a lengthy breathing-space until the next spring, for the German Army was not adequately equipped to fight a winter war. On 5/6 December 1941, however, the Red Army launched a surprise counter-offensive which broke through the weak German lines, with the result that large gaps appeared in the front and it seemed that several German formations might become encircled. As the Germans were not able to withdraw reserves from any other theatre of war, the Eastern Front threatened to collapse. Only a few days later, on 15 December, the Soviet authorities were able to return from Kuibyshev to Moscow.

Although the German front commanders several times demanded the withdrawal of the troops, Hitler refused and ordered instead that not an inch of ground was to be surrendered. Over the next few days, several Cs-in-C and generals were replaced or dismissed by him or asked to be relieved of their command. On 19 December 1941, Hitler assumed the additional function of C-in-C of the army from Brauchitsch, making an example of those who were to blame for the defeat. But while Hitler was forced to realize that his military concept had failed, the looming disaster before Moscow was overshadowed by the surprise Japanese attack on the US fleet at *Pearl Harbor on 7 December. In keeping with earlier assurances, Hitler entered the war against the USA on Japan's side.

By the end of December, the Red Army had finally eliminated the threat posed to Moscow by the German divisions. The Wehrmacht had been repelled up to 280 km. (175 mi.) from Moscow and had suffered heavy casualties. BARBAROSSA had failed. At the same time, the myth of invincibility of the Wehrmacht, which had grown accustomed to victory, was shattered. By 31 January 1942, it had lost almost 918,000 men, wounded, captured, missing, and dead—28.7% of the 3.2 million soldiers involved. The Wehrmacht never recovered from these heavy personnel and *matériel* losses. The Red Army, too, suffered heavy casualties. By the end of 1941, 3.35 million Soviet soldiers had been taken prisoner by the Germans, but the USSR had not collapsed militarily. The Red Army's victory before Moscow also considerably enhanced the politico-military importance of the USSR. The successful warding off of the German attack—before *Lend-Lease had started on a large scale—strengthened the morale of the Red Army and the Soviet population. It also enhanced the international reputation of the USSR, which on 1 January 1942 was a major co-signatory of the *United Nations Declaration.

For Hitler's political objectives, the defeat before Moscow was a serious setback, an indisputable failure of the *blitzkrieg concept. Hitler's plans and aims for *Lebensraum* and its rapacious exploitation had also failed totally. Subsequently, Berlin had to fight the war against the Soviet Union at the same time as it was fighting the UK and the new enemy, the USA. It was now a question of how long the Third Reich and its Axis partners would be able to withstand the superior resources of the Allied powers. See also GERMAN–SOVIET WAR. For the Soviet point of view of BARBAROSSA, see USSR, 4.

GERD R. UEBERSCHÄR

Bartov, O., *The Eastern Front, 1941–1945: German Troops and the barbarisation of war* (London, 1985).
Boog, H., *et al.*, *Germany and the Second World War*, Vol. 4: *The Attack on the Soviet Union* (Oxford, 1994).
Clark, A., *Barbarossa. The Russian–German Conflict 1941–45* (New York, 1965).
Erickson, J., *The Road to Stalingrad* (London, 1975).

Barbie, Klaus (1913–91), *SS Hauptsturmführer (captain) who as the head of the Gestapo in Lyons from November 1942 to August 1944, tortured and murdered Jews and members of the French Resistance (see MOULIN). Though wanted as a war criminal he was employed by the US *Counter Intelligence Corps in February 1947 which protected him from the French and then helped him reach Bolivia. He was extradited to France in 1983, found guilty of *war crimes, and sentenced to life imprisonment in 1987. At the time of his trial the US government expressed 'its deep regrets' about Barbie's concealment, but it has been denied that the relevant authorities were, at the time, aware of the extent of his crimes.

Bardia, battle of, fought in December 1940–January 1941 between General Annibale Bergonzoli's 23rd Italian Corps, holding the fortified Libyan town of Bardia, and *O'Connor's 13th British Corps. British intelligence had grossly underestimated both Bergonzoli's strength and the determination of his men, but on 4 January 1941 two brigades of 6th Australian Division, in action for the first time, captured the town and took 40,000 *prisoners-of-war. See also WESTERN DESERT CAMPAIGNS.

Barents Sea, battle of, see ARCTIC CONVOYS.

Bari, raid on. Despite Air Marshal *Coningham's remark during the *Italian campaign that he would regard it 'as a personal affront and insult' if the Luftwaffe launched any major raid, German Ju88 bombers successfully used DÜPPEL (see ELECTRONIC WARFARE), to launch a surprise attack on this southern Italian port on the evening of 2 December 1943. They destroyed two Allied ammunition ships and fourteen others, with the loss of 39,000 tons of cargo. More than a thousand people were killed, and among the many casualties 617, of whom 83 later died, occurred when mustard gas, secretly brought to Italy aboard a US merchantman, spread across the harbour when the ship was hit. The gas, which had been deployed as a retaliatory weapon in case the Germans decided to introduce *chemical warfare, covered men in the water from other sunken ships with a solution of mustard gas and oil. The crew of a US destroyer, which had picked up 30 casualties from the water, was contaminated and temporarily incapacitated. Many civilians were also killed by the gas and efforts to keep the incident a secret failed. See also AIR POWER.

Infield, G., *Disaster at Bari* (London, 1974).

barrage balloons. Large balloons whose wire cables, which tethered them to the ground, were an effective defence against low-flying aircraft. They were flown by both sides above likely targets, including ships. In the UK, where thousands were used, they were often handled by WAAF personnel of the RAF's Balloon Command. In February–March 1941 they downed seven German aircraft and those deployed against the V-1 (see V-WEAPONS) destroyed 231. They were introduced into the *Pacific war in November 1943 at *Bougainville, when the Americans flew them from landing craft, but the experiment was not repeated as they revealed a task force's position to Japanese reconnaissance aircraft.

Bastogne, battle for, Belgian town held by the US Army during the German *Ardennes offensive of December 1944. A vital centre of the area's road network, its defence fatally weakened the Fifth Panzer Army's drive to the River Meuse.

Having lost the race to reach the town before the 101st Airborne Division, commanded by Brig-General Anthony McAuliffe, and part of the 10th Armoured Division had thrown a defensive ring around it, the Germans left behind forces to besiege it which they needed for their drive westwards. By 22 December the defenders were low on ammunition and snow started falling. But when McAuliffe heard that 4th Armoured Division of *Patton's Third US Army was racing north to break the encirclement his laconic reply to surrender demands was 'Nuts!'

Ammunition air-dropped on 23 December helped frustrate a German attack on Christmas Day and Patton's armour then broke through. But the Germans were desperate to capture this centre of resistance in their 95 km. (60 mi.) bulge into the Allied front. They attacked twice more, unsuccessfully, with increased forces, but were eventually forced to withdraw.

Bataan peninsula, siege of, a strip of land 40 km. (25 mi.) long and 32 km. (20 mi.) wide at its base, on the Filipino island of Luzon, the last refuge for 67,500 Filipino troops, 12,500 US service personnel, and 26,000 civilians after Lt-General *Homma's Fourteenth Army landed on the island in December 1941 (see also PHILIPPINES CAMPAIGNS).

The US commander, Lt-General *MacArthur, ordered the withdrawal to begin on 24 December. Manila was declared an open city and MacArthur moved with his HQ to *Corregidor, an island at the peninsula's tip. One Japanese general compared the withdrawal to a cat entering a sack, and a quick victory was expected. But the peninsula, though isolated by Japanese air and sea forces, was ideal defensive country, and the withdrawal was a planned one. Supplies had been stockpiled there and hospitals and other key installations constructed. However, insufficient food meant the besieged existed on half rations.

Before he could attack, Homma's best division was withdrawn for the invasion of the *Netherlands East Indies. But, confident of immediate success, he assigned the Kimura Detachment and the inexperienced 65th Brigade to take the peninsula. These broke through MacArthur's defences after they attacked on 9 January, but failed to breach his secondary line to which his two corps withdrew, and attempts to land behind American lines were eradicated. The offensive then stalled, and on 8 February Homma was forced to call a halt. With 2,700 dead, more than 4,000 wounded, and 13,000 sick, his command had all but ceased to exist.

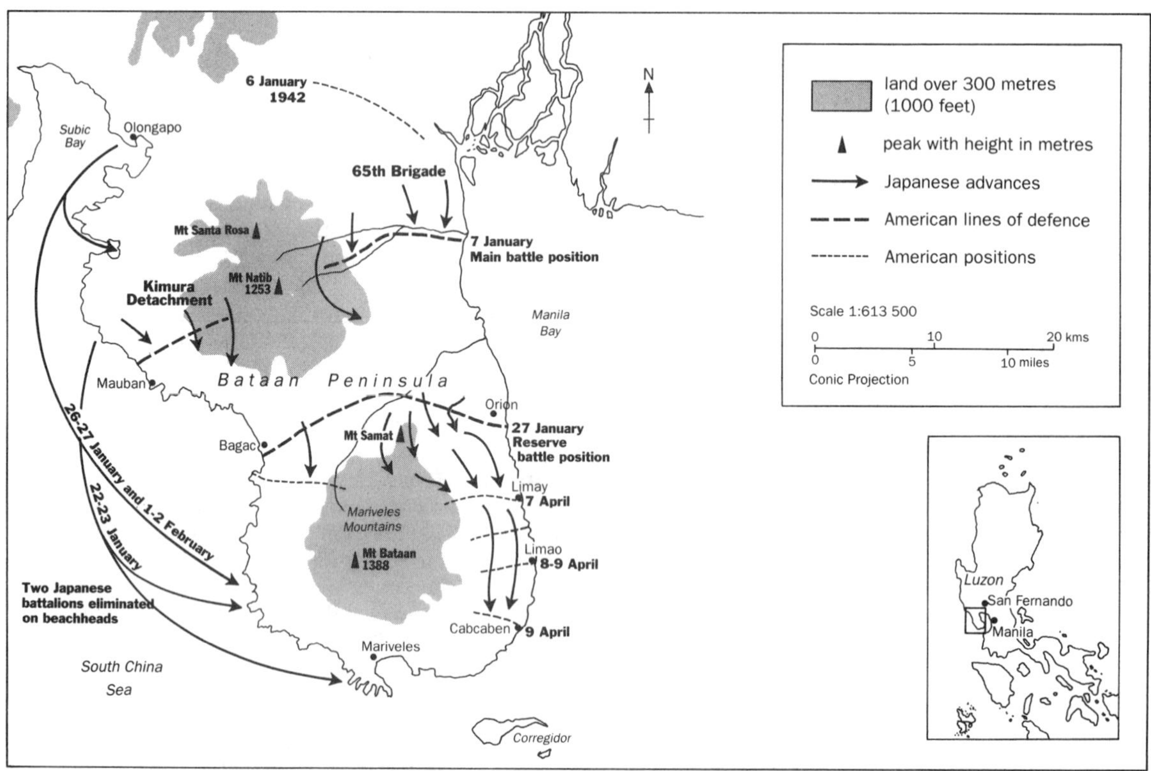

15. **Siege of Bataan peninsula**, January–April 1942

Some of the US troops who were taken prisoner after the end of the siege of the **Bataan peninsula** in April 1942. They were photographed by a Japanese during the Death March which followed the US defeat.

On 11 March MacArthur obeyed Roosevelt's order to go to Australia. His successor, Maj-General *Wainwright, inherited an army debilitated by malnutrition and disease (see also MEDICINE), and its morale had plummeted when it was realized no help would be forthcoming. The end, when it came, was swift. Homma's reinforcements smashed through Wainwright's forces a few days after Homma attacked on 3 April. A counterattack failed. Wainwright, ordered by MacArthur not to surrender, could not authorize his ground commander, Maj-General Edward King, to do so. But King, to prevent unnecessary slaughter, ignored MacArthur's orders and on 9 April he capitulated.

Only about 2,000 of the defenders escaped to Corregidor. The rest, some 78,000, were herded out of the peninsula in what became known as the Bataan Death March on which, beaten, clubbed, and bayoneted, they were forced to walk the 105 km. (65 m.) from Mariveles to San Fernando. Many died before they got there and after the war Homma was arraigned before a regional court (see FAR EAST WAR CRIMES TRIALS) and accused of being responsible for the Death March.

'Battle of the Pips', so-called because of the blips, or pips, that appear on a *radar screen to indicate contact with a ship or aircraft. At 0007 on 26 July 1943, a US flying boat reported radar contact with seven ships 320 km. (200 mi.) south-west of Attu, one of the Aleutian Islands in the North Pacific. American warships patrolling off another Aleutian island, Kiska, which had been occupied by the Japanese during the *Aleutian Islands campaign, went to investigate. They, too, picked up radar contact and, thinking it was a convoy bound for Kiska, they engaged it.

A total of a thousand shells were fired, the wakes of torpedoes were sighted, and flares and lights reported. Below decks men felt the 'shock' of imagined near misses and one had a battle-induced nervous breakdown. While the 'battle' was raging the Japanese evacuated Kiska undisturbed and it was dawn before the radar targets were identified as return echoes from mountains more than 160 km. (100 mi.) away.

battles, except Battle of the Pips, above, see under name.

Bazna, Elyeza (1905–71), agent of the Nazi security service, the Sicherheitsdienst or SD (see RSHA), which gave him the codename CICERO. In July 1943 he was employed as the manservant of the British ambassador in Ankara and in October 1943 he began photographing documents in the ambassador's safe and selling the film to the Germans. In return he received the equivalent of £150,000 in Turkish currency (which the local SD representative obtained by selling forged British currency supplied by Berlin) and in December 1943 Bazna received £50,000 for impressions of the ambassador's keys. The documents were mostly summaries of meetings between the British and Turkish foreign secretaries and between Churchill, Roosevelt, and the Turkish president, *Inönü, but there were also numerous diplomatic telegrams. This material gave the Germans insight into Allied negotiations for Turkey to enter the war on their side, but as Allied policy was well known in this respect little damage was done.

The British first knew there had been a leakage in December 1943 and in January 1944 a German agent working for the *Office of Strategic Services in Switzerland (see DULLES) produced German foreign office telegrams that confirmed it. However, Bazna was cleared in the ensuing investigation (he was thought to be too stupid) and at the end of February 1944 he left his post and did not work for the Germans again, although he continued to receive a monthly salary from them. The full story emerged only after the war when Walther *Schellenberg and others were interrogated. Not all the documents that Bazna photographed have been identified, but none referred to the Normandy landings (see OVERLORD) or to any Allied conference, nor did they enable the Germans to break the foreign office cipher. See also SPIES.

bazooka, see ROCKET WEAPONS.

BBC (British Broadcasting Corporation), an independent organization established in 1922. Its television broadcasts, which had begun in 1936, closed down on 1 September 1939, but through radio the BBC played an important role in *subversive warfare and in boosting the morale of servicemen and the civilian population. Its monitoring service kept track of foreign broadcasts and it had its own *war correspondents. By the time of the Normandy landings in June 1944 (see OVERLORD) a special 'War Reporting Unit' had been formed to supply eye-witness accounts of the fighting in Normandy and later elsewhere in north-west Europe.

Broadcasting propaganda to Allied and neutral countries via the BBC was guided by the Ministry of Information, while broadcasts to enemy and occupied countries were organized by the *Political Warfare Executive (PWE). By the end of 1943 the BBC was broadcasting in 45 languages and the broadcasting services throughout the British Empire retransmitted many of its programmes. It was over the BBC that *Chamberlain announced that war had been declared, that Churchill spoke to the nation, that de *Gaulle made his rallying call to his countrymen on 18 June 1940, and that King *George VI read his annual Christmas message to his people. *SOE also arranged for the broadcasting, on a regular basis, of coded messages to resistance groups in occupied countries.

Initially, domestic broadcasting was restricted to one wavelength (called the Home Service) so that if one transmitter had to be shut down—because it might help guide German bombers to their targets—other transmitters were able to take over. However, the Forces Programme, using two wavelengths, which was started in January 1940 to entertain troops in France, soon attracted larger civilian audiences in the UK than the Home Service. During the course of the war programmes included such diverse favourites as *The Brains Trust*, with Professor C. E. M. Joad on its panel, Tommy Handley's *ITMA* (It's That Man Again), which by 1942 had become 'as much a national institution as the BBC itself' (A. Briggs, *The BBC: The First Fifty Years*, Oxford, 1985, p. 215), and Vera Lynn, 'the sweetheart of the forces' singing in her programme *Sincerely Yours*.

But it was the news bulletins which had the largest audiences and their reliability, both at home and in occupied Europe, became renowned. They were read by broadcasters (such as Alvar Liddell) who always announced their names at the start of each bulletin so that listeners could become familiar with their voices and would know that the source genuinely was the BBC. The commitment of these bulletins to the truth, slanted though it was by the need to sustain morale, probably made them the most effective propaganda the BBC broadcast during the war years.

Briggs, A., *The History of Broadcasting in the United Kingdom*, Vol. 3: *The War of Words* (Oxford, 1970).

BCRA, see BUREAU CENTRAL DE RENSEIGNEMENTS ET D'ACTION.

B-Dienst (Beobachtungs-Dienst, or Observation Service), German naval cryptanalysis service which unbuttoned the Royal Navy's Administrative Code—used by ratings for less secret communications—before the war. This then led to B-Dienst making headway in breaking the Naval Cypher, which was used by officers for more secret communications. 'By April 1940 it was reading without delay 30 to 50% of the traffic intercepted, though it should be added that the evidence suggests that it had no success with traffic enciphered in the tables used by the Commanders-in-Chief and Flag Officers' (F. H. Hinsley, *British Intelligence in the Second World War*, Vol. 2, London, 1981, p. 635). B-Dienst's success adversely affected British naval forces during the *Norwegian campaign; and though both code and cipher were replaced in August 1940—the Administrative Code with Naval Code No. 1 and the Naval Cypher with Naval Cypher No. 2—B-Dienst's ability to decrypt both was closely linked from then on as they had similiar characteristics.

Initially B-Dienst had limited success against Naval Cypher No. 2. But from September 1941 until January 1942, when the cipher was replaced by Naval Cypher No. 4, its ability to read it was extensive, and by October 1942 it was also having some success with decrypting No. 4. More marked, however, was B-Dienst's successes with Naval Cypher No. 3, the British 'Convoy Cypher', the means of communication between the British, Canadian, and US navies during the battle of the *Atlantic. This was introduced in June 1941 and by February 1942 the Germans were reading as much as 80% of the radio traffic sent in it, and though they had minor setbacks they were often able to obtain between 10 and 20 hours' advance warning of the movements of *convoys, with disastrous results for the Allies. This success coincided with the introduction by the Germans of the four-wheel *ENIGMA machine in their U-boats whose signals the British were not immediately able to decrypt, and which, therefore, prevented the British from gleaning from *ULTRA intelligence that their cipher had been compromised. However, other decrypts raised the suspicion that it might have been, and this was finally confirmed when U-boat ENIGMA signals began being read at the end of 1942. It took time to introduce a new system and in the intervening period extra precautions were taken until, in June 1943, both No. 3 and No. 4 were replaced by Naval Cypher No. 5 which B-Dienst was unable to break. From November 1943 onwards Naval Cypher No. 5 was replaced in British–Canadian–US communications in the Atlantic by the Combined Cypher Machine (see TYPEX).

Equally vital to German U-boat successes was B-Dienst's ability to read the British Merchant Navy Code which, in January 1940, replaced the International Code and Naval Appendix used to communicate with merchant ships. By March it was able to read some of the signals and after May 1940, the month when copies of the code were captured at Bergen, it was able to read most with little delay. In April 1942 the Merchant Navy Code was replaced by the Merchant Ships Code, but B-Dienst, aided by the capture of a copy of the new code-book before it was even introduced, was able to read this with equal facility. That helped it to break Naval Cypher No. 3 and gained it important intelligence about convoy movements after Naval Cypher No. 5 was introduced. But the introduction of precautions in December 1943, and of further ones in September 1944, gradually eliminated the Code as an intelligence source for the Germans. See also SIGNALS INTELLIGENCE WARFARE.

Beaverbrook, Lord (1879–1964), British newspaper magnate, born (William) Maxwell Aitken in Canada. He was appointed minister of aircraft production and a member of the war cabinet, in which he served until 1942, immediately his friend Churchill became prime minister on 10 May 1940. His task was to increase aircraft production and, with ruthless efficiency and inspirational leadership, he did just that; although he was later accused of sacrificing long-term advantages for immediate returns, 2,729 aircraft were produced between January and April 1940, 4,576 between May and August. Thus he contributed to a large degree to the RAF's ultimate success in the battle of *Britain. He became minister of state in May 1941, minister of supply the following month, and minister of production in February 1942, but almost immediately fell ill and resigned. From September 1943 he served as Lord Privy Seal. He was, said Churchill, at his best when things were at their worst.

Taylor, A. J. P., *Beaverbrook* (London, 1972).

Beck, Colonel Jósef (1894–1944), anti-communist and anti-fascist Polish foreign minister from 1932 until 1939 who followed a policy of non-alignment between Germany and the USSR. He believed that Nazism and Stalinism were equally hostile to Poland's independence, and placed undue trust in the good intentions of the western powers. Having rejected Hitler's proposals for a settlement of German claims on the so-called *Polish corridor and for an anti-Soviet partnership, he signed the treaty which produced the British guarantee of Poland (see POLAND, GUARANTEE OF). These events led directly to the outbreak of the Second World War. When his country was invaded in the *Polish campaign of September 1939 he joined the Polish government in Romania, where he was interned.

Beck, General Ludwig (1880–1944), anti-Nazi German Army officer who served as a staff officer during the *First World War. From October 1933 he was head of the Truppenamt, the clandestine staff organization set up after the German General Staff had been banned by the *Versailles settlement. When the Truppenamt became the German Army's General Staff again in July 1935 he remained at its head and was promoted lt-general that October. But he was implacably opposed to Hitler's regime and in August 1938 he resigned in protest against Hitler's proposal to invade Czechoslovakia (see ORIGINS OF THE WAR). He was promoted general on retiring and was not employed again. He remained a leading opponent of the Nazis and was designated head of state by those planning to remove Hitler. Arrested when the July 1944 bomb plot failed (see SCHWARZE KAPELLE), he bungled his suicide and had to be finished off by an army sergeant.

Beda Fomm, battle of. In February 1941, early in the *Western Desert campaigns, units of *O'Connor's 13th British Corps cut off the retreat of Marshal *Graziani's Tenth Italian Army to Tripoli by moving inland across the desert and severing the coastal road south of Beda Fomm. It was a high-risk tactic, but the British knew through *signals intelligence that the Italians thought such a move impossible. After fierce fighting the British took 25,000 *prisoners-of-war, and the Italian Air Force and Tenth Army were shattered.

Macksey, K., *Beda Fomm* (London, 1971).

Bedell Smith, see SMITH.

BEF, see BRITISH EXPEDITIONARY FORCE.

Begin, Menachem (1913–92), ultra-nationalist Polish Jew who, in September 1940, was imprisoned in the USSR on charges of espionage, but released after the German invasion of the USSR in June 1941 (see BARBAROSSA). He joined *Anders' Army but deserted in Palestine and joined the *Irgun, which he led from December 1943. He served as Israel's prime minister from 1977 to 1983.

Perlmutter, A., *Life and Times of Menachem Begin* (New York, 1987).

Belgian Congo, Central African colony of 10.4 million inhabitants which included 25,000 whites. With the mandate of Ruanda and Urundi, it covered 3.9 million sq. km. (1.5 million sq. mi.), about 80 times bigger than Belgium.

After some hesitation, and some opposition from Belgian colonists who favoured neutrality, the Congo's immense mineral resources (see RAW AND SYNTHETIC MATERIALS) were put at the UK's disposal by the Belgian *government-in-exile in January 1941 and the British subsequently bought the whole wartime production of Katanga's copper mines, totalling 800,000 tons. The Congo also produced 67% of the world's diamonds, was the world's largest producer of radium and cobalt, and provided the initial supplies of uranium for the *MANHATTAN PROJECT as well as quantities of tungsten and tin.

After the Belgian government-in-exile declared war on Italy in January 1941, the Belgian Congo's Force Publique provided a total of 40,000 men towards the Allied war effort. One contingent took part in the *East African campaign—its commanding officer received the surrender of Italian troops in Gallo Sidano in July 1941—and another served in Nigeria and then the Middle East. During the war years a rural rebellion, urban strikes and riots, and a mutiny, were early indicators of the country's post-war problems which led to its independence in 1960. See also ANTI-IMPERIALISM.

BELGIUM

1. Introduction

Belgium, a constitutional monarchy of 8.2 million people, entered the Second World War, as it had the *First, as a neutral state. After the *Versailles settlement of 1919, the country had concluded a series of diplomatic and military alliances with the western powers but in 1935 and 1936 the tripartite Socialist–Catholic–Liberal government, supported by King *Léopold III, renounced these agreements and declared the goal of Belgium's foreign policy to be the defence of its territory. This 'policy of independence' was both a response to the collapse of the system of collective security and an attempt to rally all sections of the nation behind a policy of enhanced national defence.

The Belgian state dated from a diplomatic settlement of 1830 and, though its rapid economic growth during the 19th century and participation in the First World War had fostered a sense of patriotism and national unity, there remained strong tensions among its socially, ethnically, and ideologically diverse populations. The principal division was linguistic. Belgium was divided between the Dutch-speaking Flemish provinces of the north (Antwerp, Limburg, East and West Flanders) and the French-speaking Walloon area in the south (Liège, Namur, the Hainaut, and the Luxemburg). The latter, together with the francophone populations of the capital city, Brussels, and the largely French-speaking bourgeoisie of Flanders, had long controlled much of the wealth and administration of the country, but during the 1920s and 1930s they had faced mounting pressure for greater rights from a Flemish nationalist movement, the Vlaamsch Nationaal Verbond (VNV), which in 1940 had some 25,000 members and 17 seats in parliament.

2. Government, domestic life, and economy

(a) *Pre-occupation*

The government, headed by Hubert Pierlot (1883–1963), as prime minister, reacted to the outbreak of war in September 1939 by reiterating its resolve to defend the country against attacks from any quarter. The army was initially deployed along both the German and French frontiers but there could be little doubt as to the principal threat to Belgium and, after invasion alerts in November 1939 and January 1940, preparations to repulse a German attack were reinforced. The German invasion on 10 May 1940 (see FALL GELB) did not therefore take the Belgian authorities by surprise. Intelligence from their Berlin embassy had predicted the offensive and the army was in a high state of alert. Nor did the outcome of the campaign at first seem a foregone conclusion. The German airborne attack and motorized offensive, however, rapidly overwhelmed the Belgian defences (see ARMED FORCES, below) and on 25 May the king and his principal ministers, including Pierlot and the foreign minister, Paul-Henri Spaak (1899–1972), met at the château of Wynendaele to assess the critical military situation. The events at this tense meeting were to determine much of the course of Belgian politics both during and after the war and remain a subject of considerable controversy. None of those present doubted the need to end the untenable military situation but, while the ministers advocated that the king and the government should withdraw to France to continue the struggle alongside the Allies, King Léopold argued that the impossibility of continuing the conflict on Belgian soil should mark the end of Belgian involvement in the war and stated his determination to remain in the country and share the fate of his defeated troops.

Léopold negotiated a surrender of the Belgian forces on 28 May and returned to his palace at Laeken outside Brussels where he remained as a self-proclaimed prisoner for the next four years. The ministers travelled to France, where they declared the king to be unable to reign by virtue of his imprisonment and at an improvised session of the Belgian parliament at Limoges on 31 May they echoed Allied criticism of Léopold's actions. Bitterness between the two sides ran deep, not least because the dispute revealed the tensions between the monarch and a political élite whose failure to provide strong government for the country he had long deplored. Thus, when in June the fall of *France led the ministers to abandon their hopes of continuing the war and seek a *rapprochement* with the king, Léopold rebuffed their advances. He, like almost all Belgians at this time, believed the war to be at an end and hoped by negotiations with the Germans to restore a measure of Belgian independence and, if possible, to create a new government within Belgium.

(b) *Government of occupation*

At a meeting with Hitler at *Berchtesgaden on 19 November 1940, Léopold sought guarantees as to the future status of Belgium in the hope that this would open the way to a more general political settlement between the two countries. Hitler, however, was preoccupied by the continued military conflict and refused to be drawn on the future he envisaged for Belgium. The meeting, therefore, ended inconclusively and Léopold returned to Belgium where, until his deportation to the German Reich in June 1944, he remained a mute though not uninfluential political force. He continued to rebuff all approaches from those whom he regarded as the 'traitors' of the Belgian government-in-exile in London (see below) and a number of the members of his entourage appeared to give encouragement to the advocates of a New Order within Belgium. Support for the king had been overwhelming in the summer of 1940 but, as the war continued, it declined rapidly and his stance became ever more clearly at odds with much of the Belgian population.

After the surrender of 28 May 1940, the victorious German authorities rapidly imposed an occupation regime on Belgium. The frontier cantons of Eupen, Malmédy, and St Vith, which had been transferred from Germany to Belgium in 1919, had been reincorporated into the Reich by a special Führer decree on 18 May 1940. The remainder of Belgium, together with the French departments of the Nord and Pas-de-Calais, was ruled by a Wehrmacht military administration or *Militärverwaltung*. Its nominal head was General von *Falkenhausen, but most decisions were the responsibility of the president of the military administration (*Militärverwaltungschef*) Eggert Reeder. The various other German authorities in Belgium including the foreign ministry and the *SS were subordinated to Reeder's military administration and, though *Himmler among others always resented this military supremacy and sought to enact his own policies within the country, Reeder, who proved to be a skilful administrator, was able to repulse most of these challenges to his authority. Only in July 1944, shortly before the German retreat from Belgium, did the military administration finally give way to a civil administration (*Zivilverwaltung*) headed by Reich Commissioner Grohé (see also GERMANY, 4).

Racial and practical concerns determined that Reeder's priorities as the *de facto* ruler of Belgium were threefold. In accordance with an order of Hitler of July 1940 he sought to support the Germanic Flemish population while according no favours to the francophone Walloons. This policy was, however, always mitigated by his two other concerns: to ensure that Belgian industry contributed to the German war effort and to administer Belgium with the minimum deployment of German manpower. These priorities obliged Reeder and his colleagues to work closely with the existing Belgian authorities. A law passed by the Belgian parliament on 10 May 1940 had delegated wide powers to civil servants to administer the country in the absence of their political superiors and, consequently, during the occupation the senior officials of each government department, the *secrétaires-généraux*, became in effect the administrators of much of the life of occupied Belgium. Conflict between these civil servants and the military administration soon developed over a number of contentious issues, but such disputes never destroyed the system of German indirect rule and, as the war progressed, Reeder and the *secrétaires-généraux* became to some extent allies. They agreed on the need to maintain industrial and agricultural output and ensure law and order, and also sought to defend the political status quo against the attacks of the SS and their collaborationist allies and of radical elements within the resistance.

The power exercised during the occupation by the *secrétaires-généraux* mirrored the more general influence exerted by the social and economic élite. Though the national politicians had been excluded, many of the other notables of Belgian life retained or even enhanced their positions. In the economic sphere, a group of leading bankers and industrialists (the Comité Galopin) regulated much of the pattern of economic activity, encouraging the production of essential materials and allowing trade with Germany while seeking to prevent the subordination of Belgium's economy to the German war machine. Similarly, the Catholic Church was treated with considerable respect by the Wehrmacht authorities who allowed the clergy and the Catholic education system to operate largely unhindered (see also RELIGION).

As elsewhere in German-occupied Europe, pro-German collaborationist groups also developed in Belgium (see COLLABORATION). In Flanders, the Flemish nationalists of the VNV, under the direction of Staf De Clercq and subsequently of Hendrik Elias, emerged in 1940 as close allies of the German authorities. Many supporters of the VNV were appointed to positions of responsibility in central and local government and members of the movement served in German military units in Belgium and on the Eastern Front. In francophone Belgium, the small quasi-fascist Rexist movement led by Léon *Degrelle also supported the German cause. It was initially shunned by the Wehrmacht authorities, but, after it established a Légion Wallonie which fought with some distinction on the Eastern Front, it became a close ally of the SS within Belgium.

Though subjected to serious dislocation and German exploitation, the Belgian economy continued to operate during the occupation. Certain industrial sectors, such as the substantial arms industry, were taken under German control but most other enterprises remained in Belgian hands. The Belgian authorities encouraged agricultural and industrial output and the material sufferings of the population were relatively modest compared with those experienced in other parts of Europe. Nevertheless, there was some serious deprivation, notably in the early years of the war when severe food shortages were only very imperfectly compensated for by a substantial black market.

Daily life in occupied Belgium was a mixture of enhanced individualism and a heightened sense of solidarity. The experience of occupation varied greatly between different regions, but for the majority of the population the struggle to find sufficient food, fuel, and clothing acquired a primary role in their lives. The pattern of daily life was disrupted in many ways. Travel was often difficult and Allied bombing of railway junctions in the lead-up to the liberation caused substantial damage as well as costing many civilian lives. Families were frequently split up by the events of the war: in addition to the many thousands of men who were arrested by the

German authorities or were deported (or volunteered) to work in the Reich, some 70,000 largely francophone *prisoners-of-war remained interned in camps in Germany throughout the war as a result of Hitler's decision to liberate only those Belgian soldiers who were of Flemish origin.

For some Belgians, especially the young, the war provided unprecedented opportunities for adventure and freedom from social constraints, but for most life was hard and remorselessly drab. Cultural life was dominated by a desire for escapism and the boom in demand for popular literature, films, spectator sports, and swing dance music all reflected this trend. Some aspects of the occupation, such as the food shortages, heightened divisions between town and country and between a relatively prosperous *haute bourgeoisie* and the majority of the population; but in general the war years eroded the traditional barriers of class, language, and religion. Whether in the resistance (see below) or in more prosaic aspects of daily life, the occupation threw people into contact with each other and enabled them, through a shared antipathy to the Germans and to the sufferings of the war, to work together.

(c) *Government-in-exile*

Prevented by the German authorities from returning to Belgium, Pierlot and his colleagues languished at Vichy throughout the summer of 1940. One minister, Marcel-Henri Jaspar, rebelled in June against the attitude of his colleagues and journeyed to London where, like de *Gaulle, he used the *BBC to declare his determination to continue the military struggle. His unilateral action was promptly disavowed by the Belgian government in France, but Jaspar remained undaunted and, in collaboration with a small group of predominantly socialist refugees in London, he proclaimed the formation of a new pro-British government on 5 July 1940. This alarmed his erstwhile colleagues and Albert De Vleeschauwer, the colonial minister in the Pierlot government, hurried from Lisbon to London to prevent British recognition of the rival administration. Thanks especially to his assurances that the considerable economic resources of the Belgian Congo would be made available to the British cause, London withheld recognition of the Jaspar government; but the rebel minister and his supporters did not abandon their efforts and throughout the summer a complex struggle was pursued between De Vleeschauwer, aided by the finance minister Camille Gutt, and Jaspar and his allies for the backing of the British authorities. After the failure of their attempts to initiate a dialogue with King Léopold and the Germans, Pierlot and Spaak arrived in England where, with De Vleeschauwer and Gutt, they announced on 31 October the reconstitution of the Belgian government. This Pierlot government gradually won official recognition from the Allied authorities as the legal government of Belgium.

Contact between the Pierlot government in London and occupied Belgium developed considerably during the war. While in the summer of 1940 Belgian public opinion had overwhelmingly supported the king, by 1941 the government-in-exile had become for most Belgians the legitimate representative of their nation. This change owed less to the somewhat tarnished reputation of the government's principal figures than to its identification with the Allied cause. The government concluded co-operation agreements with Britain in January 1941 and subsequently became a signatory of the *United Nations Declaration. Pierlot and his colleagues were not without their critics among the Belgian refugee community but the government gradually grew in stature and a steady trickle of escapers from Belgium enabled its bureaucracy in Eaton Square in central London to be expanded. Radio Belgique was established in 1940 to broadcast to occupied Belgium and in the latter years of the war the Pierlot administration participated in discussions on economic and political reconstruction with other exiled governments which contributed significantly to the post-war enthusiasm for European integration.

The development of Belgian armed forces in exile was severely restricted by a shortage of manpower. In October 1940 a number of somewhat heterogenous elements were formed into a battalion based at Tenby in Wales; by 1941 they amounted to some 3,000 men of whom only 1,600 were equipped. At the end of 1942 the Pierlot government decided to form the nucleus of a new Belgian Army under the command of Major Jean Piron. The Piron Brigade was constituted in 1943 and by 1944 it had an effective strength of some 2,000 men. In August 1944 it was transferred to France and subsequently participated in the Allied liberation of Belgium and the battle of Arnhem (see MARKET-GARDEN). Small Belgian commando and *Special Air Service units, numbering fewer than 300 men, were also formed within the British armed forces; a Belgian unit was created in the RAF by 1942 with a total strength of 1,200 men of whom 200 were killed; some 300 men served in the Section Belge of the Royal Navy and two small warships—*Godetia* and *Buttercup*—were manned by Belgian officers and men.

The Belgian Congo remained under Allied control throughout the war and its armed forces (the Force Publique), composed of some 40,000 men, participated in the *East African campaign. After the Allied liberation of 1944, the Belgian and Allied authorities rapidly constituted a new Belgian Army in which approximately 75,000 men served during the remaining months of the war.

(d) *Liberation and the post-occupation government*

Most of Belgium's territory was rapidly liberated in early September 1944. The speed of *liberation precluded any prolonged power vacuum and the excesses experienced in certain other countries were largely avoided. The Pierlot government's prompt return was facilitated by the absence of the king, who had been deported to Germany in June 1944, and his brother, Prince Charles, was installed as regent. The government did not, however, enjoy universal support. Its failure to deal energetically with the purging of collaborators and with the problems of food and coal supplies was widely criticized and, though it was remodelled to include certain new figures drawn from the resistance, it was seen by many as an outmoded relic of the pre-war political order. Its problems came to a head in November 1944 when it sought to force resistance units to surrender their weapons. Pierlot and his colleagues had to rely on Allied assistance and Maj-General Erskine, head of the *SHAEF mission in Belgium, made it clear that he would not tolerate any challenge to the government. Eventually, after a violent demonstration outside parliament, almost all resistance fighters were disarmed.

In February 1945 Pierlot resigned and was replaced by a socialist. Achille Van Acker, who had remained in the country during the war. The major political problem facing the government was now that of the king, who was released from detention at the end of the war. Negotiations were begun between him and Van Acker but they failed to reach an agreement on the conditions for his return to Belgium and Léopold was forced to remain a reluctant exile in Switzerland. This unresolved problem was to cast a long shadow over Belgium's post-war politics and it culminated in the crisis of 1950 when Léopold sought unsuccessfully to regain his throne.

3. Armed forces

Mobilization had begun on 25 August 1939 and by May 1940 Belgium's armed forces amounted to a field army of 18 infantry divisions, 2 divisions of Chasseurs Ardennais (partly motorized), and 2 motorized cavalry divisions, amounting to some 600,000 men in all. It lacked anti-aircraft artillery, its armour amounted to just 10 tanks, and of the 250 aircraft (90 fighters, 12 bombers, 120 reconnaissance planes) at its disposal only 50 were relatively modern types. There was no navy, only a number of small vessels for fishery protection and patrol duties. King Léopold acted as C-in-C of the armed forces and during the winter of 1939–40 limited discussions were initiated with the French and British military commands. After the initial line of defence along the Albert Canal, which centred on the *Eben Emael fortress, had been breached by German airborne attack on 10 May 1940, the king withdrew the bulk of the army to a fortified defensive line east of Brussels (see Map 44). Both British and French troops had entered Belgium on 10 May and they reinforced the new line of defence between Antwerp and Namur (see DYLE LINE). The surprise German attack through the Ardennes, however, rendered this defensive plan useless and within a few days the Belgian forces joined the Allied retreat, abandoning Brussels and other principal centres of population. King Léopold was well aware of the gravity of the situation and as early as 16 May warned the government of the possibility of eventual defeat. Nevertheless, on 24 May the Belgian forces, now grouped in defence of a small area of West Flanders, engaged the Wehrmacht in the only major battle of the campaign. German superiority over the by now demoralized and disorganized Belgian Army was soon apparent and on 28 May the king surrendered. Much blame was wrongly directed at the Belgian authorities for this action at the time, but the Germans considered the Belgian Army tough opponents and the official historian of the 18th German Division spoke of the 'extraordinary bravery' of its soldiers. In 18 days of the most bitter fighting Belgian losses amounted to 6,098 officers and men killed and more than 500 missing, and a further 2,000 prisoners-of-war died in captivity.

4. Resistance

Organized resistance movements appeared gradually. Veterans of anti-German activities during the First World War together with small groups of army officers were active from the outset and a number of intelligence networks as well as a substantial clandestine press had emerged by the end of 1940. It was only, however, during the subsequent years that the realization of a possible Nazi military defeat combined with the oppressive policies of the German authorities gradually led significant numbers of Belgians to engage actively in resistance to the German occupation. Participants were drawn from a wide variety of backgrounds but a prominent contribution was made by the Belgian Communist Party which in May 1941 (before the Nazi attack on the Soviet Union) helped to organize a wave of strikes and subsequently founded the Front de l'Indépendence (FI).

One of the distinctive features of resistance in Belgium was the important role played by intelligence networks and escape lines for Allied airmen (see also MI9). Especially during the latter years of the occupation, much valuable information on German military operations was sent to London and a considerable number of Allied pilots shot down over Belgium were protected and subsequently returned to the UK via escape lines through France and Spain. There were, however, also several substantial armed groupings. The most important of these were the *partisans armés*, who operated within the FI, and the more army-officer-dominated Armée Secrète. Both groups benefited significantly from the introduction by the German authorities of labour conscription measures in 1942 which obliged young Belgian men to work in factories in Germany. Many Belgians chose to evade this legislation and they provided a steady stream of recruits for resistance organizations.

Relations between the Belgian government in London and the resistance groups, though often close, were not without their difficulties. The pretensions of the Pierlot government to dictate internal Belgian developments were not always welcomed by resistance groups while the London authorities distrusted both the potentially pro-Léopold sympathies of the Armée Secrète and the ambitions of radical elements within the FI to prepare a national uprising. In the event, the rapid Allied liberation of Belgium in September 1944 offered the armed resistance groups little opportunity to engage the German forces in direct combat; their greatest military achievement on the eve of *liberation was to seize the port of Antwerp and to prevent its destruction by the departing German armies.

5. Merchant marine

Most of the Belgian merchant fleet of some 100 ships evaded capture by the Germans and, under the terms of an accord signed in July 1940, these ships—together with 3,350 sailors—were placed under British control.

MARTIN CONWAY

Conway, M., *Collaboration in Belgium: Léon Degrelle and the Rexist Movement 1940–1944* (New Haven, 1993).

De Jonghe, A., 'La lutte Himmler-Reeder pour la nomination d'un HSSPF à Bruxelles'. *Cahiers d'histoire de la seconde guerre mondiale*, 3–8 (1974–84).

De Jonghe, E., *L'Occupation en France et en Belgique 1940–1944*, 2 vols. (Lille, 1987–8).

Gérard-Libois, J., and Gotovitch, J., *L'an 40: la Belgique occupée* (Brussels, 1971).

Willequet, J., *La Belgique sous la botte: résistances et collaborations 1940–1945* (Paris, 1986).

Bell, George (1883–1958), British ecumenical churchman; dean of Canterbury, 1924–9; bishop of Chichester, 1929–58. Outstanding for his moral courage and for his concern that all humankind should act as Christ intended, he was a strong supporter of the World Council of Churches and of the Confessional Church in Germany in its struggles against Nazification. Bell visited Stockholm in 1942 and was there approached by Dietrich *Bonhoeffer, an emissary of German resisters (see SCHWARZE KAPELLE), who sent messages through him to *George VI. They did not realize how slight the king's actual power was, nor how unsuitable Bell was as any sort of intermediary to the British government: having already spoken out in the House of Lords against the indiscriminate bombing of civilians (see STRATEGIC AIR OFFENSIVES, 1), he was no longer *persona grata* to Churchill. In the aftermath of war, Bell led the movement to re-establish links between the English and German churches. See also RELIGION.

M. R. D. FOOT

Belorussia (*belo* or *byelo*, white). Having failed to defend the independence which it had briefly achieved at the end of the *First World War, Belorussia found itself divided between a western region that formed part of the Republic of Poland and an eastern region that, as the Belorussian SSR, was part of the USSR. Its ethnically mixed population of eight million consisted of a Belorussian or 'White Ruthenian' majority, interspersed with substantial communities of Poles, Jews, and Russians. There were strong contrasts between the primitive countryside, inhabited by peasantry surrounded by huge areas of forest swamp and wilderness, and the cities, such as Minsk, Grodno, Białystok, or Pinsk, where Jewish influences often predominated.

At the outbreak of war in September 1939, the eastern part of the country was still reeling from a decade of mass killings which accompanied Soviet campaigns to eradicate the national movement, to collectivize the peasantry, and to terrorize the population at large. A complex of mass graves at Kuropaty near Minsk which dates from 1938–9 is thought to contain several hundred thousand victims of Stalin's terror.

In September 1939, when western Belorussia was incorporated into the Soviet Union as a result of the *Nazi–Soviet Pact and the invasion of Poland (see POLISH CAMPAIGN), the Stalinist terror moved westwards into the newly annexed territories. A stage-managed referendum was held to justify the annexation. Delegates supporting the 'reunion' were hand-picked by the Soviet security organs and citizens daring to vote against it were promptly arrested. A police cordon remained in place against movement to the rest of the USSR, whilst mass deportations took place over many months. Anyone connected in any way with Polish state institutions, or with independent Polish, Jewish, and Belorussian organizations, could expect to be eliminated. In addition to land awarded by the Nazi–Soviet Pact, Belorussia was given the district of Białystok bought by the Soviet government for cash (see Map 88).

From June 1941, Belorussia bore the brunt of the German invasion of the USSR (see BARBAROSSA) and the subsequent German occupation, which lasted for three years, and it formed the largest element of the Reich Commissariat *Ostland. Jewish *ghettos were established in all the towns and cities, where many of the worst atrocities of the *Final Solution occurred. Underground resistance movements were particularly strong in Belorussia's forests; and German fears for their lines of communication to the front line provoked repeated reprisals (see KHATIN). Units of the Polish Home Army (see POLAND, 4) mingled uneasily in the woods with Jewish refugees and with increasing bands of Soviet partisans who infiltrated behind the German lines. Huge numbers of civilians were killed by military action or by random brutality, or were removed for *forced labour in the Reich.

The Soviet reoccupation of Belorussia took place between January and July 1944. From the start, the Soviet authorities assumed that the frontiers of September 1939 would be restored; and they made every effort to complete the sovietization begun in 1939–41. Renewed purges and deportations were launched to destroy all forms of opposition. The Belorussian SSR, though admitted to membership of the United Nations (see SAN FRANCISCO CONFERENCE), possessed no independent powers. The ruling Communist Party was run from Moscow, and had been drained of all national sentiment. The Polish community was decimated and the Jewish community had disappeared. Religious and cultural life, including the state-run Russian Orthodox Church (see

RELIGION), was completely subordinated to political control.

Belorussia's war losses were usually concealed within the statistics for the USSR as a whole, which rarely made reference to the separate republics and never differentiated between different nationalities or between the victims of Stalinist and Nazi oppression. In all probability, civilian losses approaching two million were similar in absolute numbers to those of Russia; total losses of perhaps 25% stood well above the Soviet average, being similar in percentage terms to those of neighbouring Ukraine. NORMAN DAVIES

Belsen, see BERGEN-BELSEN.

Belzec was a Nazi death camp on the Lublin-*Lwów railway line 160 km. (100 mi.) south-east of Warsaw. Part of *Operation REINHARD, construction on it began in November 1941 and it opened in March 1942. It had the capacity to kill 1,500 daily. Before it was razed to the ground in the autumn of 1943 an estimated 600,000 died there. It was the most difficult of all the camps to escape from and only two people are known to have succeeded, though Jan *Karski, disguised as a camp guard, managed to get in and out again, and report what he had seen to incredulous politicians and notables in the west. See also CONCENTRATION CAMPS and FINAL SOLUTION.

Beneš, Edvard (1884–1948). President of Czechoslovakia at the time of the *Munich agreement in September 1938, he was forced the next month to resign as Hitler regarded him with suspicion. He took up an academic appointment in the USA where he remained until July 1939 when he settled in London, established a National Council, and became the spokesman for his now dismembered country.

At first he had great difficulty in establishing his credentials, his National Council being recognized as representative only of the Czech and Slovak people. But in July 1941, largely on account of his influence with the Czech resistance, and the intelligence he received from it (see THÜMMEL), both the UK and USSR recognized him as the head of the Czechoslovak *government-in-exile.

Though the British and the French had betrayed him by signing the Munich agreement, Beneš was active in organizing Czech forces to fight with the Allies, and it was he who gave the order for *Heydrich's assassination in Prague, appointed General *Svoboda as C-in-C of the Czech Army, and did what he could to aid the Slovak rising in Slovakia in August 1944. Having signed an agreement with Stalin, he returned to Czechoslovakia in 1945 and was re-elected president, but following the communists's seizure of power, against which he had constantly battled during the war, he resigned in 1948.

Bennett, Lt-General Henry Gordon (1887–1962), youngest maj-general in the Australian Army after returning to the active list in 1939. In February 1941 he was appointed to command the 8th Australian Division which fought in the *Malayan campaign and during the fall of *Singapore. He escaped to Java in a junk and then made his way back to Australia. He was promoted lt-general in April 1942, but never held another operational command. After the war his conduct was investigated by both military and civilian courts of enquiry. The military court found that he had not been justified in abandoning his troops in Singapore, but the civilian one called his decision an error of judgement and found he had not lacked courage or patriotism.

Berchtesgaden was Hitler's retreat in the Bavarian Alps. Apart from his house there, the Berghof, he had high up above it the 'Eagle's Nest', a small house amidst panoramic views. The Berghof and its surrounding buildings were razed to the ground after the war, but the 'Eagle's Nest' can still be visited.

Bergen-Belsen, situated near Hanover, was officially a *Krankenlager* (sick camp). In fact, it was first an *internment camp and then, from July 1943, a *concentration camp. One of its two sections was used for the 'privileged', such as political prisoners and Jews of foreign nationality being held for use in repatriation deals. By March 1945 its numbers had swelled to 60,000, and typhus and other epidemics swept the camps. When the British liberated it the following month they found, according to one source, 10,000 unburied dead and mass graves containing 40,000 bodies. Of the 38,500 who remained alive, perhaps as many as 28,000 died soon afterwards. See also FINAL SOLUTION.

Beria, Lavrenti P. (1899–1953), a Georgian by birth who was, after Stalin, the most feared man in the Soviet Union during the Second World War. He had joined the Bolsheviks in the revolutionary period and became a member of the secret police at the end of the Russian civil war. Having risen through the police ranks, he was transferred to the highest party offices in Georgia in 1931 and in the Transcaucasus as a whole in 1932. Stalin brought him to Moscow to head the People's Commissariat of Internal Affairs (or *NKVD) from 1938; he was consequently in charge of the country's security apparatus. It is true that, under his auspices and at Stalin's command, the Great Terror did not rage in full spate. But Beria was no 'moderate' nor was his tenure of office marked by moderation in the techniques of keeping law and order. The labour camps (see GULAG) retained their millions of starved slave-labourers; and citizens who had their freedom learned to walk in fear of the NKVD.

Beria was responsible for the incursion of security troops into the areas incorporated into the USSR in 1939–40: eastern Poland, Lithuania, Latvia, Estonia, Bessarabia, southern Finland. In all instances there were hundreds of thousands of arrests. Beria's functionaries were instructed to regard the administrative, cultural, and military élites with extreme suspicion. The arrest and summary mass execution of Polish army officers in *Katyń forest was but one among many examples of his grisly handiwork. In his private life, too, he was a moral reprobate. He is said to have married his wife only after forcibly abducting her, and to have ordered his associates to kidnap very young women off the street for his sexual gratification. He also interrogated and beat prominent purge victims in person. Among the generals in the 1940s the shorthand for being arrested and beaten up was 'having coffee with Beria'.

His position as Stalin's confederate was enhanced with the German attack on the Soviet Union in June 1941 (see BARBAROSSA). Beria was appointed to the State Committee of Defence at its formation in June 1941. Oversight of security remained his main function. The *deportations of nationalities thought suspect by Stalin—Chechens, Kalmucks, Crimean Tatars, and Volga Germans—were handled by him. His men also intimidated the High Command with sporadic arrests. It was in the Second World War, moreover, that Beria assumed a role outside the NKVD. In particular, he was charged by Stalin with making the abortive overture via the Bulgarian envoy to Hitler in quest of a separate peace with Germany in July 1941.

As the Red Army's successes mounted in 1943–4, Beria not only tightened the regime's grip on the armed forces but also redeployed the instrumentalities of the purges in the reincorporated regions of the USSR. After the campaign crossed into non-Soviet territory he recruited and trained communist-dominated bodies which, when communist regimes were established, were turned into local security apparatuses subject to his direction in Moscow. He was moved by Stalin at the end of the war from direct control of the secret police, but his influence with it endured since his protégé Viktor Abakumov was appointed in his place. Beria, while ingratiating himself with Stalin, became ever friendlier with Georgy Malenkov (1902–88), who was widely regarded as Stalin's favourite to succeed him; and Stalin showed much hostility to Beria in 1951–2.

Only Stalin's death removed the threat to Beria. But Beria's own lunge at power was thwarted, and he paid for the hatred he had incurred for so keenly purging military commanders in wartime, when his arrest was effected with the help of the high command in June 1953. He was executed in December. ROBERT SERVICE

Knight, A. *Beria: Stalin's First Lieutenant* (Princeton, 1994)

Berlin air offensive, RAF defeat which followed air offensives against the *Ruhr (March–July 1943) and *Hamburg (July–August 1943). After the success of the latter RAF Bomber Command's C-in-C, *Harris, was determined to concentrate maximum effort against Berlin in the belief that if the same destruction could be inflicted on the German capital as on Hamburg then it could bring about the surrender of Germany. The *Combined Chiefs of Staff raised no objection to Harris's proposal, even though the Quebec conference in August 1943 (see QUADRANT), had excluded attacks on morale as a specific means of achieving the aims of the *Combined Bomber Offensive (CBO).

During the period from 23 August to 4 September 1943 the RAF mounted three attacks against Berlin, but they proved costly, with 126 bombers (7.7%) failing to return out of a total of 1,647 dispatched. Harris therefore decided to postpone the start of the offensive until the longer winter nights and also until various new electronic countermeasures (see ELECTRONIC WARFARE) then under development had come into service. He also hoped that the Eighth US Army Air Force, then still smarting from their severe reverse in the Regensburg–*Schweinfurt raid of 17 August, would join the offensive. A second disastrous raid on Schweinfurt in October and diversion of replacement aircraft from the Eighth Army Air Force to the newly formed Fifteenth US Army Air Force in the Mediterranean meant that this was not to be.

Consequently, Harris was forced to proceed alone, before some of his *electronic navigation systems were ready, and on the night of 18/19 November made his first attack. Out of 444 aircraft sent to Berlin, only nine failed to return. Much of the reason for this was a large diversionary raid against Mannheim–Ludwigshafen, which attracted most of the night fighters. Three more raids against the capital were mounted before the month was out and aircraft casualties remained encouragingly low. Thick cloud over the city, however, meant that few crews actually saw their target and post-raid photographs were hard to obtain. The same was true for the four attacks against Berlin in December, but there was an increase in the bomber loss rate from just over 4% to just under 5%. Harris, however, persisted, even though the weather worsened in January, and he was being pressed by the air ministry to concentrate on targets which would wear down the Luftwaffe, a primary objective of the CBO. Five attacks were made in January, but just over 6.1% of the 2,563 sorties dispatched failed to return. The weather during the first half of February was too adverse for major operations, but when the bombers returned to Berlin on the night of 15/16 February 42 out of 891 were posted as missing.

By now it was becoming clear to Harris that the weather and the German defences meant that his bombers were not making the hoped-for impression on Berlin. Indeed, he did not attack it again until the night of 24/25 March, when 9.1% of the aircraft were lost. Even though a rejuvenated Eighth US Army Air Force was now belatedly attacking Berlin by day, it was too late. It had proved too tough a target for the RAF's capabilities. In any event, the end of the time allotted to the CBO was fast approaching and Harris and *Spaatz, in spite of their protests, were about to be placed under *Eisenhower's control in order to help prepare the ground for the long awaited cross-

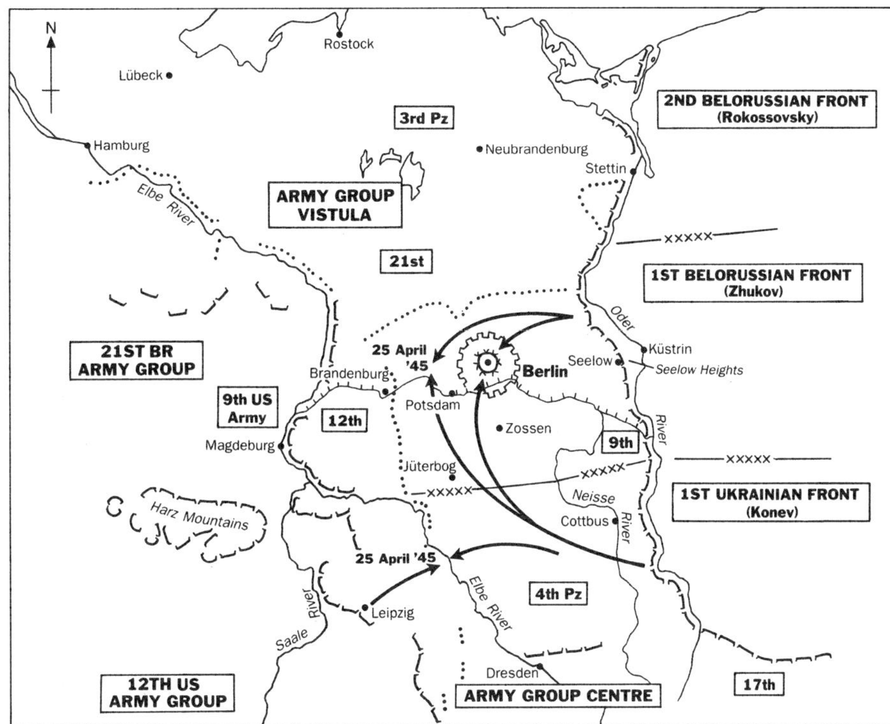

16. **Fall of Berlin**, April 1945

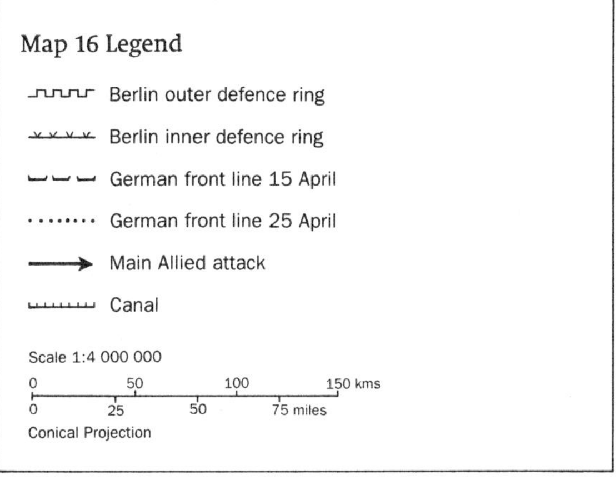

Channel invasion (see OVERLORD). Total Bomber Command losses against Berlin amounted to 492 bombers, and though the city was badly damaged it did not cease to function as the German capital. See also STRATEGIC AIR OFFENSIVES, 1. CHARLES MESSENGER

Messenger, C., *'Bomber' Harris and the Strategic Bombing Offensive, 1939–1945* (London, 1984).
Middlebrook, M., *The Berlin Raids, RAF Bomber Command, Winter 1943–44* (London, 1988).

Berlin, fall of (see Map 16). To Germany's opponents, Berlin was the centre of Prussian, Imperial, and Nazi militarism from which Hitler had directed his drive for European and world hegemony; hence, its capture would deal a decisive blow to the Germans' passion for national aggrandizement. Hitler had proposed some day to make Berlin the architectural symbol of Germany, but preferring his field headquarters and his retreat in *Berchtesgaden, he had spent little time there during the war. On 15 January 1945, he returned from his Western Front headquarters to the Reich Chancellery in Berlin, where bombing soon forced him to move into an underground bunker.

Soviet Marshal *Zhukov's First Belorussian *front* (army group) and Marshal *Konev's First Ukrainian *front*, completing the initial phase of an offensive during the battle for *Germany which had begun three weeks earlier, closed to the River Oder in early February. From his position at Küstrin, on the Oder 57 km. (35 mi.) east of Berlin, Zhukov could in all likelihood have overrun Berlin and gone on to the River Elbe and beyond in another three weeks, but Stalin delayed the second phase. On the city's direct approaches, Hitler had only the shattered remnants of Third Panzer and Ninth Armies under a newly formed headquarters, Army Group Vistula, and he lacked the troops and *matériel* to exploit fully the time Stalin allowed him. An advance across the Oder to the River Neisse which Konev made against the Fourth Panzer Army in February also created a threat to Berlin from the south. In March, Hitler ordered that

regardless of what happened at the front, the city would be defended 'to the last man and the last shot' on concentric rings. The outermost lay about 32 km. (20 mi.) from the city centre, the next 16 km. further in, then one following the S-Bahn, or suburban railway. The innermost, designated 'Z' for *Zitadelle* (citadel), embraced the government district and the Führerbunker.

On 31 March, alarmed at the progress the Americans and British were making east of the Rhine, Stalin ordered Zhukov and Konev to regroup and resume the offensive into Germany. Zhukov would have the honour of taking Berlin, Konev would support him on the left and strike towards Dresden, and Marshal *Rokossovsky's Second Belorussian *front* would deploy on the lower Oder to give support on the right. Together, the three *fronts* had 2.5 million troops, 6,250 armoured vehicles, and 7,500 aircraft.

Zhukov, expecting to make a frontal sweep to and over Berlin, mounted an assault against the Seelow Heights west of the Oder before dawn on 16 April. He had deployed batteries of *searchlights to blind the Germans and illuminate their positions, but in the ensuing smoke and glare, his own attack collapsed. The next day, six armies, two of them tank armies, failed again. On 18 April, after the armies had made two fairly deep dents in the line but no breakthrough, Stalin ordered Zhukov to shift weight to the right and go around Berlin on the north. Konev, who had crossed the Neisse on 16 April, was ordered to aim his two tank armies at and around Berlin from the south; and Rokossovsky would bear south to help Zhukov complete the encirclement. Hitler imagining he might yet win the battle, ordered the Ninth Army to stand fast on the Oder—and thereby eased the way to Berlin for Konev.

On 20 April, Konev's tanks reached Jüterbog, the German Army's largest ammunition depot and were approaching Zossen, its communications centre. Hitler gave those of his entourage who came to congratulate him on his birthday that day permission to leave Berlin before all the roads were closed. He, he said, would see the battle through where he was.

Three of Zhukov's armies reached the Berlin outer defensive ring on 21 April, and his and Konev's armour closed the encirclement on 25 April. Hitler then set about trying to organize a relief, but his largest force, the Ninth Army, was itself encircled and being destroyed and *Wenck's Twelfth Army approaching from the west, in an attempt to break through to the capital, was far too weak to help. Berlin was being defended by regular troops unlucky enough to have been pushed back into the city and by recently enlisted old men and boys (see HITLER YOUTH). On 29 April the city commandant, Lt-General Karl Weidling, reported that ammunition would probably run out the next day. Early on 30 April, the chief of the Armed Forces High Command (OKW), Field Marshal *Keitel, reported from outside the pocket that the relief was not progressing at any point. That afternoon, while Soviet troops were storming the Reichstag building 400 m. (440 yd.) away, Hitler killed himself. During an impromptu cease-fire the next day, the Chief of the General Staff, Lt-General *Krebs, tried unsuccessfully to bargain for less than unconditional surrender. On 2 May, Weidling surrendered the city. EARL ZIEMKE

Chuikov, V. I., *The Fall of Berlin* (New York, 1968).
Zhukov, G. K., *Memoirs of Marshal Zhukov* (London, 1971).
Ziemke, E. F., *Battle for Berlin* (London, 1968).

The Soviet flag is hoisted over the Reichstag after the **fall of Berlin**, 1 May 1945.

Berling's Army. Following the evacuation of *Anders' Army from the Soviet Union during 1942, tens of thousands of Poles remained on Soviet soil. The break in diplomatic relations in April 1943 over the *Katyń massacre provided Stalin with the opportunity to go ahead with the creation of further Polish units without consulting the Polish government in London. The new force was formed at Sielce, between the rivers Don and Oka, and was known as the Kościuszko Division (ironically after the 18th-century Polish hero of an abortive rising against Russian rule). It was formally under the direction of the Union of Polish Patriots, the pro-communist group of Poles in the Soviet Union headed by Wanda *Wasilewska. Command of the division fell to Lt-Colonel Zygmunt Berling (1896–1980). Berling had been Chief of Staff of General Anders' 5th Division and had supervised evacuation arrangements for Anders' forces at the Caspian port of Krasnovodsk. However, at the last moment he refused to leave the Soviet Union, thus effectively deserting from the Polish Army.

Formation of the Kościuszko Division, which began in May 1943, progressed rapidly, and there were soon sufficient recruits to form a reserve Polish unit (the Dąbrowski Division). Further units were foreseen and in August the two divisions were transformed into a corps. However there was a shortage of officers which was made good by drafting in Soviet officers, some of whom were of Polish origin but not all of whom could speak Polish. In October 1943 Berling—promoted to maj-general by a Soviet decree—led his division into battle against the Germans at Lenino, near Mogilev, where they formed part of the Thirty-third Soviet Army. The division was ill-prepared, poorly supplied, and insufficiently trained. It suffered heavy losses, failed in its objective to reach the River Dnieper, and was withdrawn from the front line to undergo further training.

In April 1944 Berling's force was transformed once more, becoming the Polish Army in the USSR (it was eventually to number six divisions) and was transferred to the Ukraine. On 29 April it was placed under the operational command of General *Rokossovsky, commander of the Belorussian *front* (army group). On 21 July, Rokossovsky's *front* crossed the River Bug, the partition line agreed in the *Nazi–Soviet Pact, and within days had reached the outskirts of the Polish capital. When the *Warsaw rising broke out on 1 August, Rokossovsky scrupulously observed Stalin's order that the Red Army was not to intervene. During the seventh week of the rising, however, on 15 September, Berling sent a group of his men across the Vistula to establish contact with the insurgents. When Rokossovsky's Belorussian *front* resumed its advance in January 1945, Berling had been removed from his command of the First Polish Army. The new commander was General S. Popławski.

The First Army, comprising some five infantry divisions and 78,000 men, continued in the direction of Bydgoszcz and the Baltic coast (Kołobrzeg, Stettin), eventually taking part in the fall of *Berlin. In the south, in the closing weeks of the war a Second Polish Army of five infantry divisions (numbering eventually 90,000 men) took part in Ukrainian *front* operations, including the *liberation of Prague.

In the post-war period, the army of the Polish People's Republic was largely created by former 'Berling's Army' officers, several of whom rose to political prominence. Berling himself subsequently studied at the General Staff Academy in Moscow, and in 1948 was appointed commandant of the equivalent Polish institution in Warsaw. He retired in 1953. KEITH SWORD

Biegański, W. (ed.), *Polski Czyn Zbrojny w 11 Wojnie Swiatowej. Ludowe Wojsko Polskie, 1943–45* (Warsaw, 1973).
Muś, W., *W Służbie Boga Wojny (memoir, Warsaw, 1983).*
Sokorski, W., Polacy pod Lenino (Warsaw, 1971).

Bermuda. Self-governing since 1620, this British island colony lies off the US Atlantic coast. After the conclusion of the *destroyers-for-bases agreement a US base was built there. It was also the site of a *British Security Coordination outstation which intercepted mail, and radio and telegraphic traffic, from the *Western Hemisphere to occupied Europe. From its population of 30,000 a contingent of the Bermuda Volunteer Rifle Corps was raised. This served with a British regiment in Europe, while members of the Bermuda Militia Infantry were part of the Caribbean Regiment (see BRITISH WEST INDIES).

Bermuda conference, held behind closed doors between British and US officials in April 1943 to discuss the plight of European Jewry, in particular the fate of 70,000 Romanian Jews who had been deported to Transnistria, and the refugee problem posed by the *Final Solution. It began on the same day as the Germans started their final assault on the Warsaw ghetto (see WARSAW RISINGS) and lasted nine days. Proposals submitted by the *Jewish Agency executive for an approach to Hitler to alleviate the plight of Jews in occupied Europe, and to abandon temporarily British policies limiting Jewish immigration into Palestine, were among the ideas rejected as being impracticable. The only concrete achievement of the conference was the opening of a refugee centre in North Africa. Its final report was not made public at the time 'for fear of aiding the Axis and harming refugees'.

Bernadotte, Count Folke (1895–1948), a nephew of King Gustav of Sweden, whose diplomatic skills the Nazis attempted to use to avoid *unconditional surrender.

As vice-president of the Swedish Red Cross, Bernadotte twice arranged for the exchange of sick and disabled *prisoners-of-war. In February 1945 *Himmler, without Hitler's authority, asked Bernadotte to mediate with the western Allies. Bernadotte, a skilful negotiator, agreed, provided Danish and Norwegian political prisoners were released from *Sachsenhausen. On 24 April Himmler asked him to negotiate the capitulation of German forces to the western Allies, whose forces were to face the Red Army, but three days later Bernadotte informed him this proposal had been rejected. (On hearing about these negotiations Hitler ordered Himmler's arrest and had his adjutant shot.)

Bernadotte became president of the Swedish Red Cross in 1946 and was assassinated by Jewish extremists while acting as a mediator for the United Nations Security Council. See also INTERNATIONAL RED CROSS COMMITTEE.

Bernhard, Prince (b.1911), German-born husband of Princess Juliana, the heir to the Dutch throne, who renounced his German citizenship on his marriage in 1937. When the Germans invaded the Netherlands in May 1940 (see FALL GELB) he escaped to the UK where he trained as a pilot. In November 1940 Juliana's mother, Queen Wilhelmina, appointed him liaison officer between the British and Dutch forces and he also reorganized Dutch intelligence in London. He flew three missions over France and Italy with the US Army Air Forces and also took part in a number of fighter sorties. In September 1944 *Eisenhower appointed him C-in-C of all Dutch forces, including the various resistance factions which he did much to unite and encourage from his Brussels HQ during the last months of the war.

Bernhardt Line, series of German defensive positions, sometimes no more than light field works, held during the *Italian campaign. The line ran from near Minturno, north-west of Naples, along the River Garigliano, through the mountains to Venafro and Castel di Sangro. It then continued across the Maiella range, north of the River Sangro, to the east coast at Fossacesia. It was initially only intended to be lightly defended for delaying tactics. But when, in October 1943, Hitler ordered his C-in-C, *Kesselring, to hold firm on the line Gaeta–Ortona it was strongly fortified. The Bernhardt Line, from which the Germans began withdrawing in December 1943, later became known as the *Gustav Line, the name originally given to the Bernhardt Line's most important fall-back (Switch) position. The whole network of defences, including the *Hitler Line, was called the Winter Line by the Allies.

Bertrand, Gustave (1896–1976), head of the French Army decipher service in the 1930s. He ran a useful spy—Hans-Thilo Schmidt—who provided early details of *ENIGMA prefixes, thus helping Poles and French to break some ENIGMA traffic. Bertrand continued work on ENIGMA in southern France, near Uzès, 1940–2, lived under house arrest in Paris January–August 1944, and survived to become a general and to write *Enigma* (Paris, 1973).

M. R. D. Foot

Bessarabia, region between the rivers Dniester and Prut (see Map 80) with a predominantly Romanian population which, except for a period under Russian rule between 1812 and 1918, formed the eastern half of the Romanian principality of Moldavia. In March 1918 a national assembly of Bessarabian Romanians voted for the union of the province with Romania. The new Soviet government refused to recognize the union and, in order to formalize its opposition to Romania's annexation of the province and to offer a nucleus for a 'liberated' Bessarabia, created in 1924 the Autonomous Moldavian Republic (AMR) in the partly Romanian-inhabited area of south-western Ukraine on the east bank of the Dniester. The Soviet interest in Bessarabia was conceded by Germany in a secret protocol to the *Nazi–Soviet Pact of August 1939.

On 26 June 1940 the Romanian government received a Soviet ultimatum demanding the cession of Bessarabia and Northern Bukovina and, bereft of international support, decided to accede. From the union of most of Bessarabia with the western part of the AMR (the areas around Tiraspol, Dubossary, and Rebnitsa) was created on 2 August 1940 the Moldavian Soviet Socialist Republic. The greater eastern part of the AMR was returned to the Ukrainian Soviet Socialist Republic, thus revealing that its creation in 1924 was merely a political stratagem to give credibility to the Soviet claim to Bessarabia. By restoring most of the AMR's territory to the Ukrainian SSR the Soviet government admitted the fiction of 'Moldavian' in the autonomous republic's official name.

Immediately after the annexation of Bessarabia the Soviet authorities nationalized the land and private enterprises were taken over by the state. The process of sovietization was facilitated by the transfer of 13,000 specialists from Russia, the Ukraine, and Belorussia. *Deportations of Romanians now took place from the new republic to Central Asia in order to work in factories and collective farms as replacements for those drafted into the army. Estimates of the total number of Romanians resettled in this way vary from 100,000 to half a million. The deportations were interrupted by the German attack of 22 June 1941 on the Soviet Union (see BARBAROSSA) in which Romania, under General *Antonescu, participated in order to recover Bessarabia and Northern Bukovina (see also ROMANIA, 4(a)). These lost provinces were regained by 27 July. If deportation had been one of the sinister features of Soviet rule in Bessarabia, it was now the turn of the Romanian authorities to indulge in it. In the winter of 1941–2 there were large deportations of Jews and gypsies from Bessarabia to camps in Transnistria, a region east of Bessarabia which Antonescu had annexed from the Ukraine in August 1941. In December 1941 it was reported to Antonescu that 108,000 persons had been resettled there. Many of the deportees were packed into railway wagons without sufficient food and water and arrived at their destination dead. A large number of those who survived the journey were shot, buried, or starved to death in the Transnistrian camps by German and Romanian units.

The reconquest of Bessarabia was accomplished by the Red Army on 20 August 1944 when the Soviet generals *Malinovsky and *Tolbukhin successfully launched a massive assault of almost one million troops and 1,500 tanks against the combined German and Romanian forces straddling the Prut. Most of Bessarabia was reincorporated into the Moldavian SSR in its August 1940 frontiers, the former southern Bessarabian districts of Ismail and Cetatea Albă being assimilated into the Ukrainian SSR. These territorial realignments were formalized in the Soviet–Romanian Armistice Convention of September 1944 and confirmed by the Peace Treaty of 1947 with Romania.

Dennis Deletant

Dima, N., *Bessarabia and Bukovina: the Soviet–Romanian territorial dispute* (Boulder, Colo., 1982).

Manoliu-Manea, M. (ed.), *The Tragic Plight of a Border Area: Bessarabia and Bucovina* (Los Angeles, 1983).

Betio, see TARAWA.

Bevin, Ernest (1881–1951), leader of Britain's largest trade union, the Transport and General Workers, whom Churchill made minister of labour and national service in his coalition cabinet of May 1940, though he was not an MP at the time. It was an unorthodox appointment, and an inspired one, for the mass of the civil population responded to Bevin's leadership. The Emergency Powers Act passed the same month gave him absolute control over the country's manpower—and womanpower—and by 1943 nearly seven million men and women had been co-opted for the war effort. He joined the war cabinet in September 1940. When *Attlee won the general election in July 1945 Bevin was appointed foreign secretary, and attended the Potsdam conference (see TERMINAL).

Bullock, A., *The Life and Times of Ernest Bevin*, Vol. 2: *Minister of Labour 1940–1945* (London, 1967).

Bevin boys were those chosen by ballot—one in ten of all men aged between 18 and 25—to serve in the British mining industry instead of in the armed forces. They were named after the British wartime minister of labour (above) who introduced the system in December 1943 because the industry was short of manpower. See also UK, 2.

Biak, battle for, fought during the *New Guinea campaign on this island 56 km. (35 mi.) long off the northern coast of Dutch New Guinea when reinforced elements of the 41st US Division landed there on 27 May 1944. A key Japanese air base, its airfields were needed to support *MacArthur's advance on the *Philippines, but it was stubbornly defended by 11,400 Japanese. About 1,200 reinforcements were also landed, though two Japanese destroyers were lost in the process. The Americans' progress was slow and on 14 June MacArthur, who had already announced victory on Biak, approved the replacement of the task force commander by Lt-General *Eichelberger. He quickly turned the battle around but Ibdi Pocket, brilliantly defended, held out until 28 July, and it was not until an amphibious landing was made at Wardo Bay on 17 August that all remaining Japanese resistance was quelled. US battle casualties were 400 killed and 2,000 wounded. Non-battle casualties exceeded 7,000, most of whom suffered from scrub typhus or an undiagnosed fever (see also MEDICINE).

Białystok–Minsk. On 22 June 1941, the day the German invasion of the USSR was launched (see BARBAROSSA) at the start of the *German–Soviet war, German armoured forces began their first true pincers movement (*Zangenangriff*), a double envelopment designed to be executed from an initially relatively straight front. From positions 250 km. (155 mi.) apart on the flanks of the Soviet West *front* (army group) (four armies under General D. G. Pavlov), the Second and Third Panzer groups struck eastwards on at first parallel courses which they would later bend inwards to close an encirclement east of Białystok. The pincers movement could have been quite easily frustrated by a retreat, but Pavlov's orders were to defend the border and they prohibited evasive manoeuvres of any kind; moreover, Soviet doctrine declared the Red Army impervious to *blitzkrieg tactics.

Aware by the fourth day that the Soviet forces between them were in turmoil, the panzer group commanders, Generals Hermann Hoth (Third) and *Guderian (Second), decided to press eastwards and let the infantry armies following behind them close the Białystok pocket. By now Pavlov had lost contact with his own commands and with Moscow, and by 29 June, having gone 325 km. (200 mi.), Hoth's and Guderian's tanks had formed a second pocket around Minsk. The twin pockets yielded 328,000 prisoners and 3,300 tanks and eliminated organized Soviet resistance forward of the western banks of the upper *Dnieper and Dvina rivers, which the panzer groups reached on 6 July. Stalin had Pavlov recalled to Moscow on 30 June, where, after a brief investigation, he, his chief of staff, and his artillery and intelligence chiefs were executed.

EARL ZIEMKE

Bidault, Georges (1899–1975), French politician and resistance worker who, as leader of the French Catholic left during the 1930s, was imprisoned by the Germans in 1940. He was released the following year and worked for the *National Council for Resistance when it was formed in May 1943. Only just keeping one step ahead of the Gestapo, he became its head after *Moulin's death in June 1943. When France was liberated he became foreign minister in de *Gaulle's cabinet and in December 1944 signed the *Franco-Soviet Treaty.

Big Red One, nickname of the battle-hardened 1st US Infantry Division which derived from its large red '1' shoulder-patch. The US Army's oldest active division, it

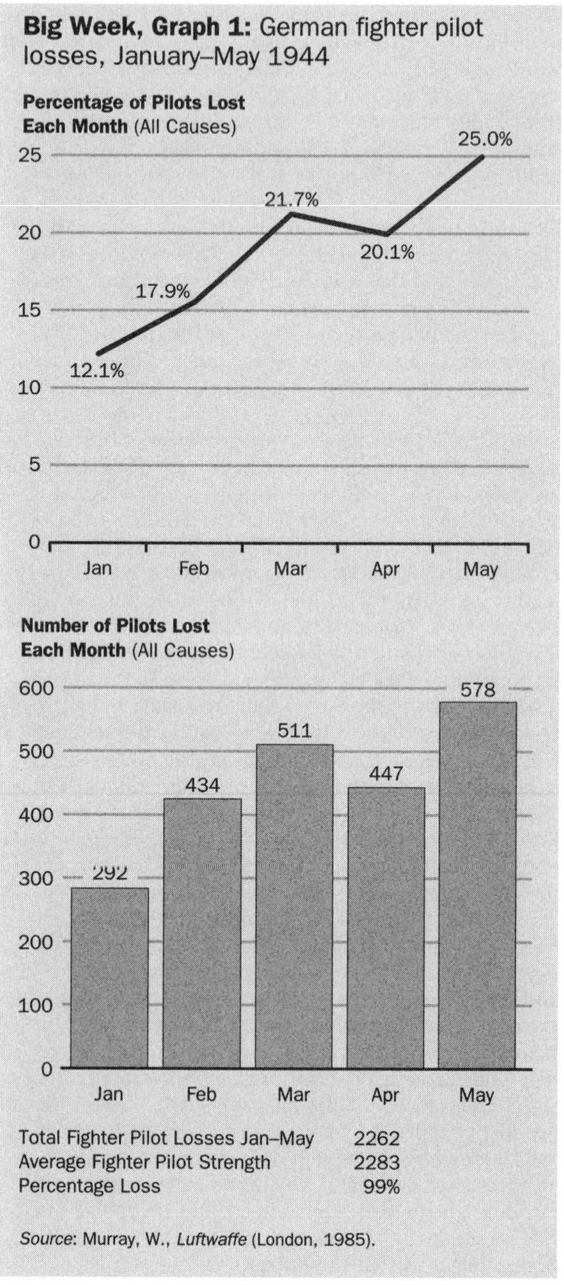

was also known as 'The First Team'. It saw action in the *North African and *Sicilian campaigns, and in north-west Europe after it landed on *OMAHA beach during the Normandy landings (see OVERLORD).

Big Week was the name given later to the co-ordinated six-day air offensive (ARGUMENT) launched in February 1944 by RAF Bomber Command and the US Strategic Air Forces in Europe (USSTAF) as part of the *Combined Bomber Offensive.

USSTAF had been formed under General *Spaatz on 1 January 1944. It comprised the Eighth and Ninth US Army Air Forces, based in the UK, and the Fifteenth USAAF which was based in Italy. The previous year Eighth USAAF had suffered heavy losses during raids on *Schweinfurt and elsewhere. Consequently, US daylight raids deep into Germany had been suspended until long-range fighters to escort the bombers had been delivered, and good weather made the raids viable.

When both these conditions were met, starting on 20 February 1944, more than 3,800 USSTAF bombers and 2,351 from RAF Bomber Command dropped between them nearly 20,000 tons of *bombs on German fighter factories and associated industries, the British at night, the Americans during the day. American losses amounted to 254 aircraft, including 28 fighters, while RAF Bomber Command lost 157. These were heavy losses—Eighth USAAF had a rate of attrition for February which amounted to almost 20%—but Big Week put German fighter production back two months. Its purpose had also been to begin the attrition of German fighter pilots to undermine the Luftwaffe's continuing will to resist. In this Big Week was successful as a precursor to the escorted raids that followed it (see Graphs 1 and 2). From that time the daylight bombing campaign was only partially countered and during the Normandy landings in June 1944 (see OVERLORD) only a handful of German aircraft were immediately available to oppose them.

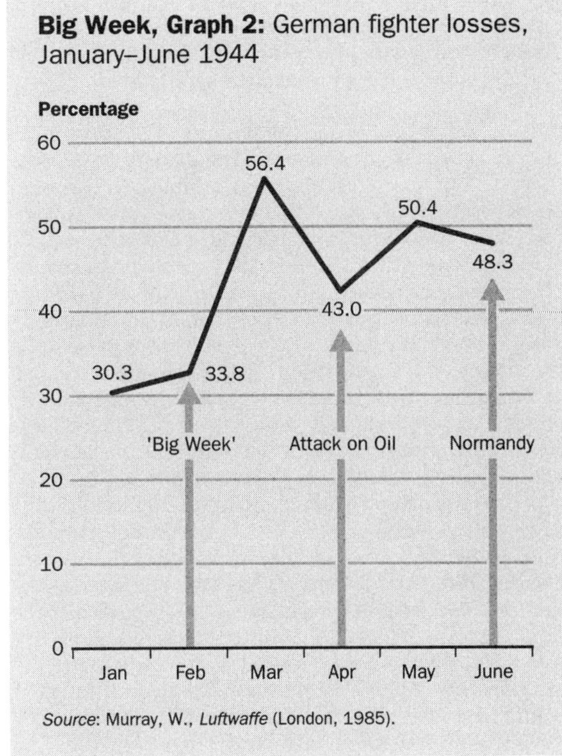

Source: Murray, W., *Luftwaffe* (London, 1985).

biological warfare (BW) was employed only by Japan during the *China Incident and, on a minuscule scale, by the Polish Home Army (see POLAND, 4) which in 1943 killed a few hundred German soldiers and *Gestapo agents with typhoid-fever microbes and lice.

During the 1930s the Japanese formed two BW units, both of which had various branches. Unit 100 was created to develop and employ BW for sabotage purposes while Unit 731, or Ishii Detachment—named after its commanding officer, Lt-Colonel (later lt-general) Ishii Shiro, an army physician—was formed to develop and wage BW on a much larger scale. It was established in Manchukuo in 1936 under the command of the *Kwantung Army, and, using a cover name, the Kwantung Army Epidemic Prevention and Water Supply Unit, it developed such weapons as a porcelain bomb which could deliver plague fleas unharmed to their target; the Ha bomb, to spread anthrax or tetanus on the battlefield, its anti-personnel shrapnel creating wounds infected with these bacteria; and the Uji bomb, for use against civilians and feeding herds. To develop these fearful weapons hundreds, perhaps thousands, of petty criminals and Chinese *prisoners-of-war were used in fatal experiments, but that Allied service personnel were also used as guinea pigs has not so far been substantiated. When the Soviet Army invaded Manchukuo in August 1945 the Japanese destroyed the buildings of Unit 731, obliterated all evidence of BW research, and evacuated the staff.

Though there is no conclusive evidence, a Japanese suicide squad from the unit probably contaminated the River Khalka with typhus, paratyphus, and cholera during the fighting with Soviet troops there in August 1939 (see JAPANESE–SOVIET CAMPAIGNS); and cholera, typhus, and plague were disseminated in and around the Chinese port of Ningpo in October 1940 and plague-infested fleas and grain were dropped on to Changteh city in 1941, causing several epidemics.

A more lethal employment of BW by the Japanese occurred in the China Incident when the germs of cholera, dysentery, typhoid, plague, anthrax, and paratyphoid were used against *Chiang Kai-shek's forces during Japanese advances into Chekiang and Kiangsi provinces in 1942, causing not only 'inestimable' casualties to the Chinese but accidentally infecting 10,000 Japanese troops as well. During the same campaign 3,000 Chinese prisoners-of-war were allegedly given food injected with typhoid and paratyphoid before being returned to their own lines. Plans were also made to attack US forces with plague fleas after they had captured *Saipan, but the ship with the team sent to accomplish this was sunk.

The Allies did not employ BW but they were certainly preparing to do so if they had to. The UK had ratified the *Geneva Convention protocol barring biological weapons, but experiments with anthrax were started in Britain during the 1930s—the Scottish island of Gruinard was not declared decontaminated until 1986—and a programme of producing cattle-feed filled with anthrax, for dropping over Germany, was begun in December 1941. A small anthrax bomb was also developed, which was passed to the Americans for production. They had started research on botulin and anthrax in 1942—the USA had signed the protocol but not ratified it—and by 1944 had reached an advanced stage. By the end of that year the US Chemical Warfare Service had a factory poised to produce 500,000 4 lb. (1.8 kg.) anthrax bombs a month and a method of delivering a botulin solution over a short range had also been devised. Work was in progress, too, on other agents like brucellosis and glanders as well as on chemicals against plants (also developed in the UK), classified at the time as a form of biological, not *chemical, warfare.

In February 1944 Lord Cherwell (see LINDEMANN) recommended that Churchill should request anthrax bombs from the Americans, and later that year, when the V-1 (see V-WEAPONS) caused heavy civilian casualties, the *Chiefs of Staff committee assessed the possibility of employing them in 1945 when it was thought they would be available in sufficient quantities. But though it was agreed to share development, production, and intelligence information, British requests for a joint policy on the use of BW—as had been agreed with chemical warfare—were rejected by the USA which, presumably, wanted a free hand to use BW against Japan if the need arose.

When the V-1 became known to the British it was greatly feared that it might be a BW weapon—the normal detonation of the first one was received with relief—and before the Normandy landings in June 1944 (see OVERLORD) an effort was made to deter the Germans from employing BW. Disinformation was leaked to them that self-inoculating syringes containing botulin antidote were being distributed to 100,000 troops participating in the landings, thereby giving the impression that the Allies not only possessed methods of countering BW but were perhaps capable of employing it offensively. However, unlike the UK and USA, and probably the USSR, Germany did not attempt to develop offensive BW weapons, and such development, despite the threat that the Allies might employ it, was expressly forbidden by Hitler though *Himmler did attempt to circumvent this ban.

In 1949, at Khabarovsk in eastern Siberia, the USSR tried twelve Japanese connected with developing and employing BW for *war crimes. They were all sentenced to various terms of imprisonment, but though the chief medical officer at Mukden prison camp was hanged and its commandant imprisoned, no member of Unit 731 in American hands, including Ishii, was prosecuted. All were given immunity in exchange for the unit's scientific data which were then employed to improve America's own capacity for BW. Details of this deal did not emerge until the 1980s.

Harris, R., and Paxman, J., *A Higher Form of Killing* (London, 1982).
Harris, S. H., *Factories of Death* (London, 1994).

Bir Hakeim, fortress held in May–June 1942 by Maj-General *Koenig's 1st Free French Brigade Group during the *Western Desert campaign. Its pivotal position at the southern end of the British *Gazala Line, which had been established west of *Tobruk in Libya made it of critical importance to *Rommel when he advanced eastwards to take Tobruk. Though heavily attacked, and eventually surrounded, the French, supported by the *Western Desert Air Force, refused to surrender until, on the night of 10/11 June 1942, they were ordered to withdraw. Out of a total of 3,600 who had fought off the first attack 2,700 made their way to safety. Bir Hakeim did much to establish the Free French as a fighting force.

Birkenau, see AUSCHWITZ; see also CONCENTRATION CAMPS.

Biscari massacres. In two separate incidents during the *Sicilian campaign of July–August 1943, 76 German and Italian *prisoners-of-war were shot by US troops of the 45th Division's 180th Regiment near Biscari airfield. The army commander, Lt-General *Patton, directed the men's corps commander, Lt-General *Bradley, to tell 'the officer responsible for the shootings to certify that the dead men were snipers or had attempted to escape or something'. Bradley refused and as a result of the first incident, in which 34 Italians and 2 Germans were shot, Sergeant Horace West was charged with their murder. West admitted he had shot most of the prisoners himself believing, following a pre-invasion speech by Patton, that he was obeying orders. In the second incident, when 40 Italian prisoners were shot, the accused, Captain John Compton, also of the 180th Regiment, quoted Patton's speech, too, and said that he thought he was carrying out the orders of a superior officer. He was acquitted and was killed in action shortly afterwards. West was sentenced to life imprisonment, but a year later, after Compton was acquitted, this was commuted and he returned to the army as a private.

As one account has pointed out (I. Sayer and D. Botting, *Hitler's Last General*, London, 1989, p. 358), if the US officers commanding the men involved in these *atrocities had received the same treatment as those German officers found guilty after the war of the *Malmédy massacre, their sentences would have been as follows: Patton—life imprisonment; Bradley—ten years; the regimental commander, Colonel E. Cookson—death.

The German battleship ***Bismarck*** engaging HMS *Hood* and HMS *Prince of Wales*, 24 May 1941. The photograph was taken from *Prinz Eugen*.

***Bismarck*, sinking of.** The destruction by British naval forces of this powerful 42,000-ton German battleship, armed with eight 38 cm. (15 in.) guns, took place in the Atlantic on 27 May 1941 after she and the heavy cruiser *Prinz Eugen* had left Germany to attack Allied Atlantic *convoys.

Swedish intelligence had forewarned the British that *Bismarck* was to sail and on 20 May the British naval attaché in Stockholm was tipped off by a Norwegian who had been told at a cocktail party that two large German warships had been sighted that day heading north through the Kattegat. This information alerted British patrols and both ships were sighted in the Denmark Strait by the cruiser *Norfolk*. They were initially engaged by the Polish destroyer *Piorun*, and then by the battle-cruiser *Hood* and the battleship *Prince of Wales*. The angle of interception prevented the full armament of the two British warships from being brought to bear; and while the British divided their fire both Germans concentrated all theirs on *Hood*. She was soon hit and blew up with only three survivors, and *Prince of Wales*, new and not fully operational, had to disengage after being hit. However, *Bismarck*, which had been damaged in the encounter and subsequently hit by a torpedo aircraft from the carrier *Victorious*, was leaking fuel, and decided to head for Brest while *Prinz Eugen* slipped away westwards.

British naval forces now converged on the area, but until she blundered by breaking wireless silence *Bismarck*'s whereabouts were unknown. Even so, she nearly escaped for the bearings on her position were incorrectly plotted, which led to the Home Fleet, commanded by Admiral *Tovey, sailing in the wrong direction. But she was eventually sighted at 1030 on 26 May by a Coastal Command Catalina flying boat flown by a US Navy pilot. Torpedo aircraft from the carrier *Ark Royal*, part of the Gibraltar-based *Force H under Admiral *Somerville, then wrecked her steering gear making her an easy target the next morning for the battleships *King George V* and *Rodney*. The cruiser *Dorsetshire* then performed the *coup de grâce* with *torpedoes. Only 115 out of *Bismarck*'s crew of 2,222 were saved. Given the close proximity of German aircraft and submarines operating from France, the margin of victory had been a narrow one. Her remains, found in 1989, lent credence to German claims that she had been scuttled. See also GERMAN SURFACE RAIDERS and SEA POWER.

Bismarck Archipelago, group of about 200 Pacific islands which lie in a crescent shape off the east coast of what was the Australian mandate of New Guinea. They include *New Britain, *New Ireland, and the *Admiralty Islands which all saw fighting during the *Pacific war. See also BISMARCK SEA, below.

Bismarck Sea, battle of. The most devastating air attack on shipping since the Japanese raid on *Pearl Harbor in December 1941 took place in March 1943 in the waters which divide New Guinea from the Bismarck Archipelago. But on this occasion it was Allied aircraft which sank many Japanese vessels.

After suffering a series of reverses in the *New Guinea campaign, the Japanese decided to reinforce the Lae and Salamaua area on New Guinea's north-eastern coast with nearly 7,000 men of 51st Division, part of Lt-General Adachi Hatazo's Eighteenth Army. On the night of 28 February 1943 these men, loaded aboard eight transports and escorted by eight destroyers, sailed from *Rabaul.

The Americans, however, had been alerted to Japanese intentions by naval *ULTRA intelligence and had had time to move their aircraft forward, and even to have a full-scale rehearsal of the tactics to be employed. The convoy was first attacked on the night of 2 March when aircraft of Kenney's Fifth US Army Air Force sank one of the transports and damaged two others. Then at dawn Australian Beaufighters and US bombers attacked again. Some aircraft were equipped for *skip bombing, while others had been specially altered for low-level strafing. Out of 37 500 lb. (227 kg.) *bombs dropped by the first wave, 28 hit their targets leaving the way for later waves to inflict further damage. After *PT boats attacked that night, and bombers finished off two crippled destroyers the following day, only four destroyers escaped destruction. Though 950 survivors reached Lae, and many were rescued by the surviving destroyers, more than 3,660 Japanese troops were killed in the water. See also AIR POWER.

Black Book, the *Sonderfuhndungliste GB* (Special Search List GB) which was prepared by the *SS functionary Walter *Schellenberg in May 1940. It was a list of 2,820 British subjects and European exiles who were to be arrested should *SEALION, the proposed German invasion of the UK be successful. It also included a list of institutions and establishments which were of particular interest to the Nazis. Apart from obvious candidates such as Churchill and Anthony *Eden there were writers, journalists, publishers, and financiers. Noël Coward, H. G. Wells, E. M. Forster, Aldous Huxley, Violet Bonham-Carter, Victor Gollancz, and Bernard Baruch were among those listed. The man chosen to head the operation to arrest them was an SS *Standartenführer* (colonel), Franz Six. He was to be based in London and have six **Einsatzgruppen* working for him in London, Bristol, Birmingham, Liverpool, Manchester, and Edinburgh. After the war Six was sentenced to 20 years' imprisonment at the *Nuremberg trials for war crimes in the USSR.

The British had their own list of people to be arrested if the Germans invaded. Among the 82 names of suspected collaborators was the writer on military strategy Maj-General J. F. C. Fuller, who was *Mosley's military adviser.

A facsimile edition of the Black Book was published by the Imperial War Museum in London in 1989.

Black code, US military attaché cipher used by Colonel Frank Bonner Fellers, the US military attaché in Cairo. See ITALY, 6.

Blackett, Patrick M. S. (1897–1974), British physicist, Nobel Prize winner, and a member of the *Tizard committee from its inception in January 1935. In August 1940 he became scientific adviser to the C-in-C of Anti-Aircraft Command and during the next two years he revolutionized the command's operational techniques and then those of Coastal Command. In January 1942 he transferred to the Admiralty as director of *operational research and his work there exerted a major influence on the anti-submarine techniques employed in the battle of the *Atlantic. He was a member of the *M.A.U.D. committee and dissented from its findings by recommending that the *atomic bomb be constructed in the US, a recommendation the British government followed. See also SCIENTISTS AT WAR.

Black Orchestra, see SCHWARZE KAPELLE.

blackout was imposed in every belligerent country in 1939–40, as a necessary precaution to protect homes and factories from air attack. From a civilian's point of view, it was an infernal nuisance. It meant that several minutes had to be taken up, twice a day, with putting up and taking down screens or blinds on every window in a room where a light would be used after dark; and that anyone who went out at night in a town had to remember to carry a torch to find the way about the darkened streets. Motoring, with headlights blacked out to a single narrow slit a few centimetres long, became nightmarish, except for those with exceptional night vision. Restrictions applied as sharply to the armed forces as they did to civilians. In factories, particularly factories with large glass roofs, blackout made a perceptible hole in the accounts; black paint could be used to cover the roof (as it did, for example, in main-line railway stations), but buying it and applying it cost money and time, and more money had to be spent again on lighting the workfloor by day.

No one seems to have consulted the air authorities about whether blackout was really necessary. Bomber pilots found that they could navigate best at night by looking out for water, which shows up clearly from the air by starlight as well as by moonlight; so that, on clear nights, they should have been able to orient themselves without too much trouble, whether anything on the ground was lit up or not. Next to lakes and rivers, railways also showed up clearly; so did large roads.

Blackout was one of the ways in which the totality of this total war declared itself for it was universally imposed in Germany, France, Italy, the UK, and elsewhere. Switzerland was not blacked out at the start of the war, but provided such excellent navigation beacons for Allied aircraft that German and Italian diplomatic pressure persuaded the Swiss, too, to agree to what was becoming almost a European norm.

Sweden, Spain, and Portugal remained un-blacked-out. The Balkan countries had to do their best to black out, hurriedly, when they were invaded; there was hardly time to assemble the quantities of black cloth or shuttering material that were needed. In the USSR, also, there were difficulties of supply, with which the regime and the citizenry coped as best they could.

A side-effect of blackout, noticed by common people, was the increase it brought in police power: in the UK, for example, the local air raid warden, a neighbour known by sight to all those he (or she) looked after, became a somewhat feared and disliked figure, because wardens had to insist so firmly that no chink of light was shown; while in Germany and France, the already considerable power of the *Blockwart* and the concierge was increased. Blackout also provided a mass of opportunities for the cartoonist and the humorist, as well as a number of tragedies, from individuals killed in the sharply increased number of road accidents.

When the USA entered the war, most of its citizens had heard of blackout because the *BBC news service from Europe was so good; but, knowing themselves to be out of range of the Luftwaffe, they left it to the Europeans. The happiest of the U-boats' 'happy times', in the Caribbean in early 1942, was much assisted by the un-blacked-out towns on the coasts of Florida, Texas, and Louisiana; thereafter federal effort ensured a degree of 'grey-out', at least, in coastal areas (see also CONVOYS).

The Japanese blacked out carefully: they needed to. But it was no protection against the daylight raids that devastated Tokyo, or those that dropped the *atomic bombs which ushered in the ending of the war.

M. R. D. Foot.

black propaganda see SUBVERSIVE WARFARE.

Black Sea operations (see Map 17). Germany did not move any warships to the Black Sea before its invasion of the USSR in June 1941 (see BARBAROSSA) as it did to the *Baltic. However, during the course of the *German–Soviet war, several hundred small ones were subsequently transported there. They included six submarines and Italian *Tenth Light Flotilla units, which mostly had to be shipped by rail or road and reassembled at Romania's principal naval base, Constanţa, or brought down the Danube. They were needed, for Romania possessed only four destroyers, three submarines, three minelayers, and some torpedo and gun boats, and, apart from one Romanian submarine, these were all employed defensively to escort convoys. All Axis ships were commanded by the German Admiral, Black Sea.

Opposing these Axis naval forces was the Soviet Black Sea fleet of one old battleship, 6 cruisers, 21 destroyers, 84 MTBs, 47 submarines, a variety of small craft, and an air arm of 626 aircraft. It was commanded first by Vice-Admiral F. S. Oktyabrsky and from May 1943 to March 1944 by Vice-Admiral Lev Vladimirsky. Their command included flotillas based on the Volga and Don rivers, the Caspian Sea, and the Sea of Azov. Though more powerful than the Axis forces, at no time did the Soviet Black Sea fleet dominate. Its submarines were not very effective, and when German bombers sank three of its destroyers in October 1943 Stalin banned the employment of its larger units altogether. Its smaller ships bombarded German positions, harassed Axis convoys, laid mines, ran in supplies and reinforcements to the beleaguered Red Army ashore, and mounted numerous hit-and-run raids, but the fleet's main offensive role was to support the Red Army with *amphibious warfare.

The Soviet fleet's first *amphibious operation took place on 22 September 1941 when it landed 2,000 naval troops behind the Romanians besieging Odessa. Co-ordinated with a small parachute drop, it forced the Romanians to abandon the positions from which they were bombarding the port. But the city still had to be abandoned and between 1 and 16 October the fleet, in a notable operation, 'itself a small Dunkirk' (J. Erickson, *The Road to Stalingrad*, London, 1975, p. 211), evacuated 86,000 soldiers, 15,000 civilians, and on the final night took off more than 1,000 lorries, 20,000 tons of ammunition, 400 guns, and 32,000 men of General I. Petrov's Independent Maritime Army, all needed to try to prevent the capture of *Sevastopol by General von *Manstein's forces.

Also successful in the short term were Soviet landings on the German-occupied Kerch peninsula in the Crimea to try and relieve Sevastopol. On the night of 25/26 December 1941 there were 25 separate landings in 10 different areas, and though only four succeeded these were soon reinforced. Then on 28 December Feodosiya on the Crimea's southern coast was stormed and by 31 December more than 40,000 troops had been landed, forcing the German evacuation of the peninsula. But the Soviet execution of the land battle was poor and Feodosiya was soon recaptured; by May the peninsula had been cleared of Soviet troops by the Germans.

The Kerch landings probably extended Sevastopol's resistance by as much as six months, but it fell in July 1942, and in early September the Germans crossed the Kerch strait on to the Taman peninsula in small vessels. They surprised the defenders and quickly occupied the peninsula. Novorossisk fell on 7 September, and an amphibious operation two weeks later failed to recapture it, but the German offensive petered out before the fleet's remaining Caucasian bases were reached.

In February 1943 a more powerful Soviet naval force made two landings near Novorossisk. The larger was wiped out but a smaller one succeeded. It was quickly reinforced and all German attempts to dislodge it failed. But the port was held by the Germans until the night of 9/10 September 1943 when 130 small boats of the Soviet fleet entered it and landed troops. This landing, and several others which followed, drove the Germans out. Soon afterwards they began withdrawing from the bridgehead they had formed the previous year and which the defeat at *Stalingrad in January 1943 had made untenable. Several courageous attempts were made by the fleet to establish and maintain bridgeheads to hinder their retreat. Nearly all ultimately failed, though one on the Kerch peninsula at Eltigen held out from October until December 1943. Less impressive were the fleet's efforts to prevent more than 250,000 German troops of *Kleist's Army Group A, their transport and supplies—and 27,000 civilians—being ferried back across the Kerch strait in September–October 1943, an operation completed with few losses.

It was now the turn of the Germans to defend Sevastopol and their ships helped supply and reinforce it. Hitler, after ordering it to be held, approved its evacuation of 6 May 1944, but the reprieve came too late and ships taking off troops from the beaches of Cape Kherson were heavily bombed and attacked by Soviet torpedo boats and submarines. During the last days of the evacuation 27 ships and barges were sunk and 8,000 men drowned, and though 130,000 German and Romanian troops were saved about 78,000 men were killed or made *prisoners-of-war. If Stalin had allowed the Soviet fleet's larger units to operate the casualties would have been far higher; but, apart from two final amphibious landings behind German lines, made in August just days before Bulgaria and Romania capitulated, only Soviet submarines operated offensively in the western Black Sea that summer.

The Germans say they lost 50 vessels, the Soviets claim 191. Soviet Second World War naval losses have not so far been published but German estimates are 103 ships, including a cruiser and 3 destroyers, 191 aircraft, and 86 merchantmen.

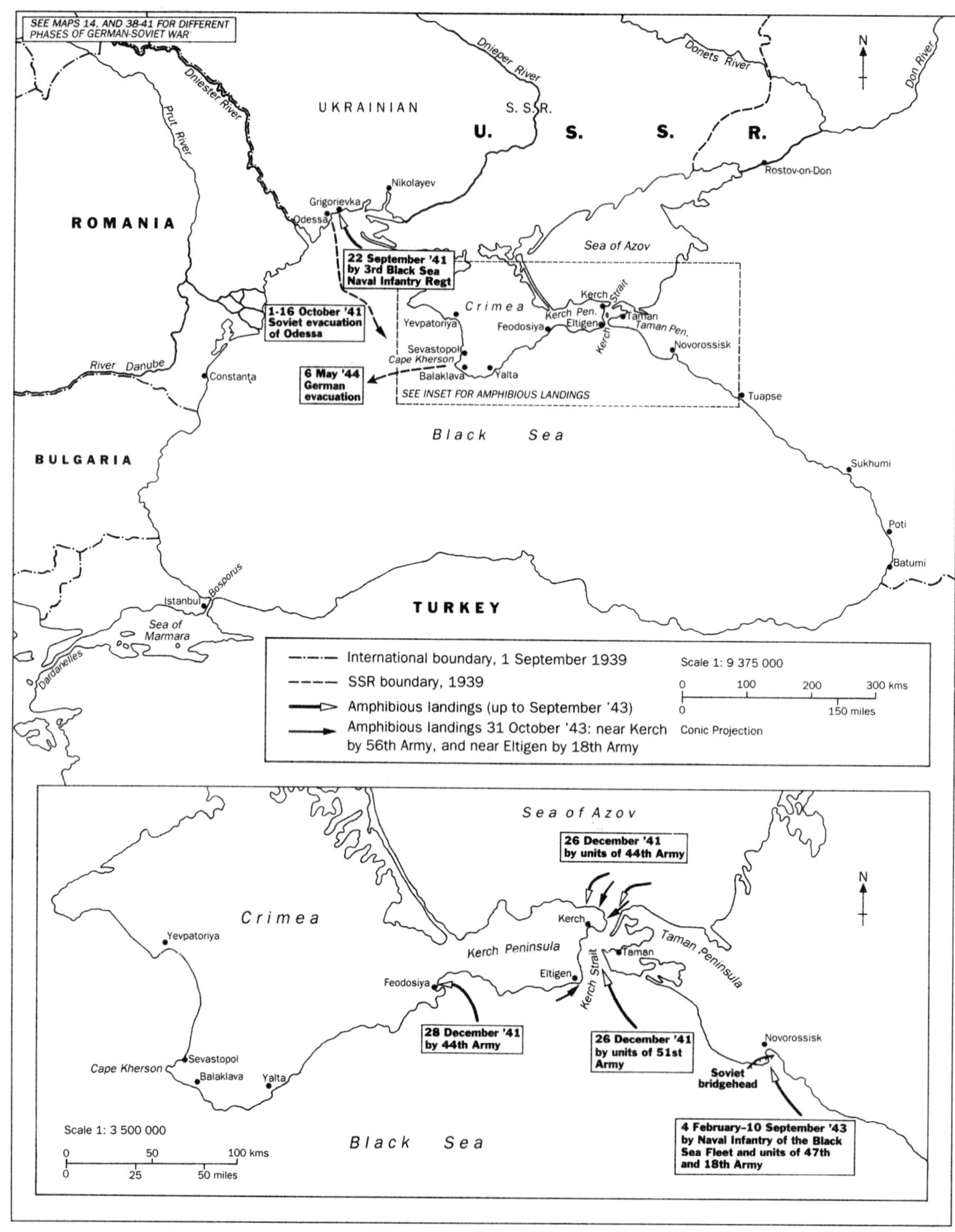

17. **Black Sea operations**

Blackshirts, Italian Fascist militia, who wore black shirts as part of their uniform, later copied by *Mosley's followers in the UK. See FASCISM and ITALY, 5(c).

Blamey, General Sir Thomas (1884–1951), Australian Army officer who served on General John Monash's staff during the *First World War. He subsequently resigned his commission, spent twelve years between the wars as chief of police in the State of Victoria, and was knighted in 1935. As a staff officer he had not seen any action during the First World War and his appointment in 1939 as C-in-C of Australian ground forces was resented by those serving officers who felt that bringing him out of retirement was a vote of no confidence in their abilities. Moreover, Blamey jealously guarded his authority, was loath to delegate, and in consequence spread himself too thin to be an effective strategist or leader.

From February 1940 he commanded the Australian Corps (later Anzac Corps) which took part in the early, and successful, battles of the *Western Desert campaigns, and in the disastrous *Balkan campaign in April–May 1941. He then supervised the evacuation of Allied forces from *Crete and became, briefly, Deputy C-in-C of Middle East Forces under *Auchinleck before he returned to Australia. In March 1942 he was appointed C-in-C Australian Military Forces and Allied land commander in the *South-West Pacific Area (SWPA).

Until Japan entered the war, the Australian armed forces had been substantially under British command, but from April 1942 they came under the operational command of General *MacArthur, SWPA's Supreme Commander. When, during the *New Guinea campaign, it looked as if the Japanese might reach Port Moresby via the *Kokoda trail, MacArthur ordered Blamey to assume personal command of Allied land forces in New Guinea. But MacArthur thought him too slow and after the capture of *Buna in January 1943 Blamey returned to his HQ in Australia; MacArthur then created *Alamo Force to ensure that all US troops in SWPA came under his personal command.

Blamey's appointment as an Allied commander now became a nominal one and when, from October 1944, Australians began replacing US troops in the New Guinea and Solomons combat areas, he was criticized for carrying on what became known as an 'unnecessary war' against entrapped Japanese troops whose lines of communication had been severed by MacArthur's advancing forces (see BOUGAINVILLE and NEW BRITAIN, for example). In these campaigns Blamey acted without the authority of parliament and without the backing of MacArthur, who said the actions were ill-conceived. Blamey came under intense pressure to resign, with criticism of his command being made in parliament, in the papers, in the streets, and even within the ranks of his own forces. Although his actions were 'retrospectively' endorsed by the government they revealed not only Blamey's limited imagination but also Australia's diminished role as an ally of the Americans. Nevertheless, he was promoted field marshal in 1950, the first and only Australian to achieve this rank.

RICHARD NILE

Blaskowitz, General Johannes (1883–1948), commander of the Eighth German Army which suffered the only German reverse during the *Polish campaign, at *Kutno, he subsequently headed the army of occupation in Poland when he succeeded *Rundstedt as C-in-C East and came into immediate conflict both with the governor-general, Hans *Frank, and with the *SS over the atrocities that were being perpetuated by the **Einsatzgruppen* and others. His protests to Hitler, who went into a tirade about his 'childish ideas', were ignored and at Frank's request he was removed from his post in May 1940. In October 1940 he was appointed commander of the First German Army garrisoning France and remained in this post until May 1944 when he was appointed to command Army Group G which opposed the Allied *French Riviera landings that August. He was replaced in September but in January 1945 he took over from General *Student as commander of Army Group H in the Netherlands, his post being renamed C-in-C Festung Holland (Fortress Holland) that April. He committed suicide before appearing at the *Nuremberg trials to face lesser war crimes.

Bleicher, Sergeant Hugo (b.1899), German *Abwehr counter-intelligence agent who recruited Mathilde *Carré, the betrayer of the Franco-Polish **Interallié* intelligence network, as a *double agent. Odette *Sansom was arrested by him. At the end of the war he was caught in Amsterdam and imprisoned.

Bletchley Park, Victorian mansion situated 80 km. (50 mi.) north-west of London. Known as Station X, from 1939 it was the site of the British Government Code and Cypher School (Government Communications HQ from 1942). This had been formed in 1919, from the cryptanalytical sections of the Admiralty (Room 40 O.B.) and the War Office, 'to advise as to the security of codes and cyphers used by all Government departments and to assist in their provision', but it was also secretly ordered to 'study the methods of cypher communications used by foreign powers'. This meant that its staff worked to break those ciphers and it was, in fact, not a school at all but a highly secret organization which came under the aegis of the head of *MI6.

In 1939 the staff, headed by Alistair Denniston, numbered about 150, but it grew so rapidly that wooden huts were erected to accommodate the overflow. By late 1942 the numbers had risen to about 3,500, and to more than 10,000 by 1945. Some were civilians (see TURING); others came from the armed services of several nations, including France, Poland, and the USA. They worked on the decryption of German and Japanese hand codes and ciphers; on the *ENIGMA and *PURPLE machine ciphers, which produced *ULTRA and *MAGIC intelligence; and on the *Geheimschreiber transmissions. Initially, 'bombes'—devices which simulated the workings of an ENIGMA—helped decrypt signals, but by June 1944 the first electronic digital computer, COLOSSUS II, was being used. Staff in Hut 6 deciphered the German Army and Luftwaffe ENIGMA signals, the latter task often being simplified by the signals sent by *Flivos; those in Hut 3 translated and interpreted them, and dispatched the resulting intelligence to *Special Liaison Units and other recipients; and those in Huts 4 and 8 dealt with naval ENIGMA signals which were passed to the *Naval Intelligence Division.

Bletchley had three cryptanalytical outposts overseas: the *Combined Bureau, Middle East, the Wireless Experimental Centre at Delhi, and the *Far East Combined Bureau, all of which had their own outposts.

The Germans never knew the purpose of Bletchley Park, though at least one person mentioned in the *Black Book was listed as having gone 'to Bletchley'.

Calvocoressi, P., *Top Secret Ultra* (London, 1980).
Hinsley, F. H., *British Intelligence in the Second World War*, 5 vols. (London, 1979–90).
—and Stripp, A. (eds), *Codebreakers: The Inside Story of Bletchley Park* (Oxford, 1993)
Lewin, R., *Ultra Goes To War* (London, 1978).
Stripp, A., *Codebreaker in the Far East* (London, 1989).

blimps were 45-knot airships used by the US Navy for anti-submarine patrols off the US eastern seaboard, and later in the Gulf of Mexico, the Caribbean, and off Brazil. Organized as Fleet Airship Wings, they were equipped with *radar and armed with depth charges (see ANTI-SUBMARINE WEAPONS) and machine guns, but they were more effective in raising morale in the *convoys they protected than in sinking U-boats.

Blitz. Taken from the German word **Blitzkrieg* ('lightning war'), this was the British name for the Luftwaffe's sustained night attacks against their cities from August 1940 to mid-May 1941.

The Blitz began as the daylight battle of *Britain was nearing its climax and at a time when the invasion of the UK (see SEALION), for which the battle was a necessary preliminary, was still on the German agenda. For the Germans, who never committed more than a third of their twin-engined bomber force to daylight raids during the battle of Britain, it was first an extension of the battle—in that they wanted to destroy British aircraft factories and thus deny the RAF the reinforcements it required—and then a war of attrition when they failed to achieve the necessary air superiority to launch SEALION. If an invasion was not immediately possible, then surely, German planners surmised, the UK could be bombed into submission by destroying its means of communication and supply as well as its armaments factories and, if necessary, by terrorizing its citizens. However, despite Hitler's directive of 5 September 'for disruptive attacks on the population and air defences of major British cities, including London, by day and night', the primary objective of the Luftwaffe remained to destroy the RAF and the factories that sustained it. But now that London was a legitimate target it was decided that Air Fleet 2, stationed in the Low Countries, would carry out daylight raids on the Capital's infrastructure—in fact, it participated in the night raids as well—while Air Fleet 3, based in France, would attack at night 'until the docks and all supply- and power-sources of the city have been annihilated'. But by October, when it became apparent that the battle of Britain had been lost, the attacks became increasingly a matter of inflicting terror and exhaustion in the ebbing hope that British morale would collapse.

From the British point of view the raids were simply terror tactics and were presented as such by *war correspondents and propaganda (see SUBVERSIVE WARFARE) to an increasingly sympathetic American public. At first there was little the British could do to oppose them. At that time few of the defending anti-aircraft (A-A) batteries were equipped with fire-control *radar; *searchlights were rarely effective at altitudes greater than 3,600 m. (12,000 ft.); few night-fighters were fitted with AI (airborne interception) radar; and ground-controlled interception radar (GCI), which tracked incoming aircraft overland, was still being developed. It was, therefore, unusual for a raider to be seen by the defenders and rare for one to be shot down.

Though counter-measures (see ELECTRONIC WARFARE) were already being taken against the radio beams by which the bombers were directed to their targets (see ELECTRONIC NAVIGATION SYSTEMS), there was initially a lack of coherence in the defences. There were preliminary raids elsewhere—Birmingham was attacked on 25/26 August, Liverpool on the nights of 28–31 August and 4–6 September—before London was attacked on 7 September 1940, the date normally associated with the start of the Blitz. Only 92 guns were available to defend the city. The fire control system for these failed miserably (as did the night-fighter squadrons) and for three nights the city was pounded with hardly a gun being fired in retaliation. However, General Frederick Pile, C-in-C of Anti-Aircraft Command, quickly doubled the number of guns and on the night of 11 September the gunners were allowed to fire at will. The huge barrage of A-A fire that resulted, accompanied by a blaze of searchlights, heartened the civilian population and drove the attackers to a more respectful height, but otherwise had little effect.

In this opening phase of the Blitz, which lasted until mid-November, an average of 200 raiders, including Italian aircraft based in Belgium, bombed London each night except one, and to these attacks were added daylight raids by fighter-bombers, and by single bombers attacking targets of opportunity on cloudy days. The one on 7 September began in the afternoon when 300 bombers, escorted by 600 fighters, attacked in two waves. The docks were the main target, but many of the *bombs

St Paul's cathedral surrounded by burning buildings at the height of the **Blitz**, 29 December 1940.

fell on surrounding residential areas. That night another 180 bombers converged on the capital and altogether 430 Londoners were killed and some 1,600 seriously injured.

An even heavier attack took place on the capital on the night of 15 October while others were mounted against Birmingham and Bristol. It was a bright moonlight night and the 400 bombers began their attack at 2040, continuing through until 0440 the following morning. The railway system was hit particularly hard, with many of the terminals being put out of action; Becton gas works, Battersea Power Station, and the *BBC headquarters at Portland Place were also hit; three large water mains were fractured and there was widespread damage to residential areas. More than 900 fires were reported, six of which were 'major' and nine 'serious'. The RAF sent up 41 fighters but only one Heinkel was shot down.

By mid-November, when the bombers switched temporarily to attack provincial cities such as *Coventry, Southampton, Birmingham, Liverpool, Bristol, and Plymouth, the Germans had dropped over 13,000 tons of high explosive bombs on London and nearly one million incendiaries with the loss rate to themselves of less than 1%. Between mid-November and the end of February 1941, fourteen attacks were mounted on ports, nine on industrial inland targets, and eight on London, while in January Cardiff, Portsmouth, and Avonmouth became targets for the first time. However, although these raids cost the Luftwaffe only 75 aircraft, the German High Command was becoming increasing critical of what was being achieved. Grand Admiral *Raeder persuaded Hitler to issue a directive on 6 February that gave attacks on ports the highest priority, and from 19 February to 12 May 46 raids were mounted against Plymouth, Portsmouth, Bristol and Avonmouth, Swansea, Merseyside, Belfast, Clydeside, Hull, Sunderland, and Newcastle, while only seven were directed against London, Birmingham, Coventry, and Nottingham. Initially, German losses were again minimal, but by May—when the Blitz began to peter out as German bomber squadrons were withdrawn to take part in the German invasion of the USSR (see

BARBAROSSA)—British night defences had been much improved as the highly effective Beaufighter had become operational and more A-A guns and *searchlights were radar controlled. Fitted with the latest version of AI radar, the Beaufighter could now be guided on to targets by GCI sets that worked effectively.

The Blitz caused enormous damage to the country's infrastructure and housing stock, cost the lives of more than 43,000 civilians (a further 139,000 were injured), and tied up precious human and *matériel* resources. All this was achieved by the Luftwaffe for the loss of about 600 bombers, or about 1.5% of the sorties flown; and a sizeable proportion of those had been wrecked in landing accidents caused by bad weather. But it did not seriously impair British aircraft production and notably failed to bring the UK to its knees, just as a second Blitz (see V-WEAPONS) failed to do in 1944. See also BAEDEKER RAIDS and UK, 2(d).

ALFRED PRICE

Calder, A., *The People's War* (London, 1969).
Price, A., *Blitz on Britain* (Shepperton, 1977).

blitzkrieg, ('lightning war') a German word, now Anglicized, which has been attributed to Hitler, and was probably coined for intimidation purposes. First used in the *Polish campaign in September 1939 it combined *air power, tanks, and *subversive warfare actuated by dynamic command and control through *radio and rapidly laid line communications. Simultaneous with air attacks upon enemy airfields and lines of communications, a campaign of lies and half-truths was aimed at the opposing side's morale as concentrated land forces, supported by bombing, either broke through or outflanked their defences. Sometimes, as in the *Norwegian campaign in April and in the Netherlands in May 1940 (see FALL GELB), *airborne warfare was also used when paratroops were landed at vital centres in the rear of the front and held them until relieved by deep penetration thrusts by fast-moving armoured columns (see EBEN EMAEL, for example), so that the opposing forces were outpaced and enveloped. Such disorder was created that, in the fighting which led to the fall of *France in June and in the *Balkan campaign of April 1941, national resistance collapsed. But when the Nazis invaded the USSR in June 1941 (see BARBAROSSA) blitzkrieg failed because, for the first time, German *logistics were unable to maintain their momentum to sufficient depth to achieve ultimate victory. Thereafter German blitzkrieg was countered by similar methods in which surprise, flexibility, and concentration of force were as potent in defence as attack.

KENNETH MACKSEY

blockade runners, part of *economic warfare, were merchant ships, submarines, or motor gun boats (MGBs), employed to carry vital materials through the opposing side's naval blockade.

While still neutral Japan supplied essential *raw materials such as rubber and tin to Germany via the USSR, and received heavy machinery, vehicles, locomotives, armour plate, and aircraft in return. After Germany invaded the USSR in June 1941 (see BARBAROSSA) this trade had to be sent by blockade runners, called Yanagi transports, which had been operating on a small scale since the beginning of the year. As Japan was very short of merchant ships most of the transports were German, though some were Italian.

During the first phase of these operations, from April 1941 to June 1942, twelve out of the sixteen merchantmen which sailed from the Far East to Europe safely delivered 75,000 tons of raw materials, as did all six which sailed with 32,540 tons of engines, commercial goods, and chemical goods in the opposite direction. But at the end of 1942 *ULTRA intelligence revealed to the British that blockade runners were being allocated strips of water, lanes 320 km. (200 mi.) wide, west of the French and African coasts, to ensure their safe passage through U-boat infested waters. This breakthrough pinpointed the positions of blockade runners and an additional bonus occurred in August 1943 when *Bletchley Park broke the *ENIGMA key used for transmissions between the blockade runners themselves.

As a result of these cryptographic successes, and of more efficient air and sea patrols, Axis losses began to mount. Five ships were damaged in the Gironde estuary in western France in December 1942 (see CANOEISTS); of the fifteen ships which sailed from the Far East between August 1942 and May 1943, seven were sunk and four were forced to turn back; and of the seventeen which sailed in the opposite direction four were sunk and three were forced to turn back. These losses discouraged further sailings for some months. Then, between September and December 1943, three blockade runners were bombed and sunk in the Bay of Biscay, and in January 1944 three more were caught by US warships in the South Atlantic. Out of the 33,095 tons of cargo aboard the homeward-bound blockade runners only 6,890 tons were unloaded in France. Hitler then agreed that all further sailings be cancelled and the eight ships which had been waiting to sail to the Far East were eventually scuttled in French ports.

In addition to surface ships, German, Italian, and Japanese submarines were employed carrying cargoes vital to the German armaments industry, and sometimes important personnel, the Indian revolutionary Subhas Chandra *Bose being one. But the amount of cargo that could be carried was negligible compared to that which merchant ships could accommodate, and the submarines, too, suffered heavy losses. Out of the 56 which sailed from 1942 onwards, 29 were sunk and one interned.

Though blockade runners were principally used by the Axis, the Allies also had to use them. In 1942 the Americans used submarines to transport urgent supplies to their besieged troops on *Bataan and *Corregidor (see also PHILIPPINES CAMPAIGNS), but their efforts to use surface ships from Australia failed. The USSR also used submarines to ferry supplies into *Sevastopol and the British used them when *Malta was besieged.

The British also used merchant ships to transport vital steel products from neutral Sweden. These ships, all Norwegian-owned but subsequently chartered to the British ministry of shipping (later ministry of war transport), had been stranded by the war in Swedish ports. In the first operation (RUBBLE) four freighters and an empty tanker, all crewed by British, Norwegian, and Swedish seamen, slipped unseen through the Skagerrak on the night of 23/24 January 1941. They were bombed the next day but reached the UK safely with their 25,000 tons of ball bearings, steel tubing, and other products which had been purchased under an Anglo-Swedish trade agreement of October 1939, and were desperately needed in the UK.

The success of RUBBLE led to a second operation (PERFORMANCE), also organized by *SOE, in which ten Norwegian ships, manned mostly by Norwegians and captained by British volunteers, tried in March 1942 to run the gauntlet of German patrols after being impounded by Sweden. Four were scuttled, two returned to Göteborg, and the rest, after being forced out to sea by Swedish warships, tried to steam through the Skagerrak in daylight. Two were sunk by German aircraft and only two reached Britain.

PERFORMANCE caused a diplomatic furore between Germany and Sweden, another between the UK and Sweden because the ships had been illegally armed, and a third between the UK and the Norwegian *government-in-exile which objected to losing so many ships. A third operation, to allow the escape of the two ships still in Göteborg, had to be cancelled. Instead, SOE was requested to obtain the cargo in them and five MGBs were converted to carry 45 tons of cargo each. The Swedes, who were informed of the operation (BRIDFORD), raised no objections apart from insisting that the cargo was loaded from shore, not direct from the ships, and in a series of six voyages between October 1943 and March 1944 the MGBs brought back 347 tons of ball bearings, machine tools, and other vital equipment with the loss of only one of their number. See also WORLD TRADE and WORLD ECONOMY.

Barker, R., *The Blockade Busters* (London, 1976).

blockbuster bomb, see BOMBS.

Blomberg, Field Marshal Werner von (1878–1946), German Army officer who served as a staff officer during the *First World War. From 1927 to 1929 he was head of the clandestine staff organization (Truppenamt) after the *Versailles settlement of 1919 had banned the German General Staff, and in January 1933 he became defence minister (later war minister) in Hitler's first cabinet and, in April, C-in-C of the Wehrmacht.

Blomberg's agreement that the armed forces should no longer have the right to keep order domestically was an essential precondition to Hitler's plans for turning Germany into a National Socialist state. In return, Hitler confirmed his commitment to rearm and ignored, for the time being, the demands of some of his followers that the armed forces should become part of the Nazi Party apparatus. It was this alliance, based on common interests and goals, which proved to be 'one of the main guarantees of the stability of the regime in the following years' (Deist *et al.*, *Germany and the Second World War*, Vol. 1, Oxford, 1990, p. 401).

In 1936 Blomberg was promoted the regime's first field marshal but the scandalous reputation of his second wife, which *Göring and other Nazi leaders quickly turned to their own advantage, forced his resignation in January 1938. This gave Hitler—who disposed of the army's C-in-C, *Fritsch, at the same time—the opportunity to become war minister himself and gain complete control of the army. Blomberg took no part in the war and died while in internment at Nuremberg.

Barnett, C. (ed.), *Hitler's Generals* (London, 1989).

Blue Division, volunteer Spanish force which fought in the *German–Soviet war on Germany's side.

Formed in 1941, and so called because of the colour of the Falangist Party uniforms its members initially wore, it was commanded first by Maj-General Augustín Muñoz Grandes, from December 1942 by Maj-General Esteban Infantes, and initially numbered 17,692 officers and men. When the division reached Germany in July 1941 it was officially numbered 250 and reorganized along German Army lines so that it comprised the 262nd, 263rd, and 269th Regiments, and 250th Artillery Regiment, plus a reserve battalion and other support units. Its members were given German uniforms and equipment though some continued to wear their blue shirts. All swore allegiance to Hitler, though the wording was modified to specify that this applied only to 'the battle against Bolshevism'. The division first saw action in October 1941 when, under the German 38th Corps of Sixteenth Army, it took over the defence of a 48 km. (30 mi.) front, from Lubkovo on the west bank of the River Volkhov southwards to Kurisko on Lake Ilmen. The following August it was assigned to the German 54th Corps of the Eighteenth Army and was put in the line close to *Leningrad. There the division fought off a Soviet advance at the battle of Krasny Bor in February 1943 and suffered 2,253 casualties.

Allied pressure and a shift in Spanish policy brought about the division's return to Spain—the last volunteers had returned home by the end of 1943—but the much smaller *Spanish Legion, made up of volunteers from the Blue Division, remained until spring 1944.

It has been estimated that of the 47,000 Spaniards who served at different times in the division, 22,000 became casualties, 4,500 were killed or died, and fewer than 300 *prisoners-of-war were repatriated from the USSR in

1954. Many received German and Spanish awards for bravery (see DECORATIONS).

The Spaniards also provided the Germans with sufficient pilots for five squadrons of fighters. Known as the Blue Squadrons these served consecutively on the Eastern Front with Army Group Centre providing fighter support for German bombers. They shot down 156 aircraft and lost only 22 men missing or killed before returning home with the Spanish Legion.

Spaniards also fought on the Allied side. About 70 belonged to that part of *Layforce which failed to be evacuated after the battle for *Crete, and there were many Spaniards active in the French resistance in southern France, and thousands fought in the *Zouave regiments of France's Armée d'Afrique.

Kleinfeld, G., and Tambs, L., *Hitler's Spanish Legion: The Blue Division in Russia* (Carbondale, Ill., 1979).

bocage is the belt of higher ground that runs across the base of the Cherbourg peninsula in western France. During the early phase of the *Normandy campaign its topography of steep valleys and wooded hills, criss-crossed by narrow lanes bordered by high hedges, made it ideal defensive terrain for the Germans which helped them delay the Allies' breakout from their bridgehead.

Bock, Field Marshal Fedor von (1880–1945), German Army officer who, as the son of a Prussian general, was born and bred to his career. He detested National Socialism, but supported Hitler's military aims. 'Tall and thin, he was a humourless, ambitious, arrogant, opinionated, and energetic zealot' (S. W. Mitcham, *Hitler's Field Marshals and their Battles*, London, 1988, p. 145). Unlike many high-ranking German officers during the Second World War, he gained first-hand experience of commanding infantry in battle when he served as a battalion commander in 1917–18, winning what was then Germany's highest decoration, the Pour le Mérite.

Between the wars Bock rose rapidly in rank. He was promoted general on 1 March 1938, commanded the forces which occupied Austria later that month, then Army Group North in the *Polish campaign, and Army Group B during the fighting which led to the fall of *France. Promoted field marshal in July 1940, he was appointed C-in-C Army Group Centre for the invasion of the USSR in June 1941 (see BARBAROSSA) which destroyed Red Army *formations at *Bialystok–Minsk, *Smolensk, and *Briansk–Vyazma, and at the end of November got to within 32 km. (20 mi.) of *Moscow. But Bock's forces suffered heavy casualties when Stalin launched his counter-offensive, and on 19 December, the day Hitler took personal control of the war on the Eastern Front from *Brauchitsch, Bock returned home on sick leave (he had stomach ulcers) and was replaced by *Kluge.

Bock's sick leave did not last long for on 17 January 1942 *Reichenau, the C-in-C Army Group South, died and Bock was ordered to replace him. At the end of May he inflicted a heavy defeat on *Timoshenko's force before launching the second phase of Hitler's offensive (BLUE) towards the Caucasus the following month (see GERMAN–SOVIET WAR, 4). The plan included the division of the Army Group into A and B, with Bock taking command of B. But Bock deviated from Hitler's plan and BLUE was delayed, and in mid-July Hitler gave command of the newly activated Army Group B to General Maximilian von Weichs instead.

Bock's prestige in Germany was so great that the pretence was maintained for some time that he still held his command, but he was never employed again. On 4 May 1945 he was killed when his car was shot up by a British aircraft.

BODYGUARD, codename for *deception operations decided upon at the Allied Cairo conference in December 1943 (see SEXTANT). The object of BODYGUARD was to persuade the Germans that though a large-scale cross-Channel invasion was being planned it was not going to take place until the end of the summer of 1944 and that the Allies had other large-scale operations in mind elsewhere. Although various ploys were implemented, BODYGUARD failed to divert Hitler's immediate attention from the Channel coast. The codename originated from Churchill's remark at the Teheran conference in November 1943 (see EUREKA) that 'in wartime truth is so precious that she should always be attended by a bodyguard of lies'.

BOGEY, Allied codename for an unidentified aircraft.

Bohemia and Moravia, see CZECHOSLOVAKIA.

Bohr, Niels (1885–1962), Danish physicist and 1922 Nobel Prize winner in physics who dominated nuclear research during the first three decades of the 20th century. Many of his fellow scientists rated him second only to Albert Einstein (1879–1955). As a Jew he was in constant danger of being arrested and in September 1943 he escaped to Sweden before a round-up of Danish Jews by the *Gestapo began. His appeal to King Gustav to give sanctuary to all Danish Jews was successful and many reached the safety of Sweden. Bohr subsequently worked in the USA as an adviser on developing the *atomic bomb. In 1944 he sought to persuade Roosevelt and Churchill of the need to avoid a post-war arms race by internationalizing the control of atomic weapons. This could only be achieved, he argued, by inviting the USSR to participate in post-war atomic energy planning before the bomb was an actuality and before the war ended. A modified version of his approach was adopted by Henry *Stimson in 1945, but after Churchill met Bohr he became convinced that he was a security risk and the Dane was put under close surveillance. But Bohr was not advocating that any nuclear secrets be shared with the USSR and when Einstein considered doing just that Bohr 'convinced him of the perils of stepping out of line' (R. Clark, *The Greatest*

Power on Earth, London, 1980, p. 179). See also SCIENTISTS AT WAR.

Moore, R., *Niels Bohr: The man and the Scientist* (London, 1967).

Bolivia broke off diplomatic relations with the Axis powers at the *Rio conference in January 1942, declared war on them on 7 April 1943, and signed the *United Nations Declaration the following month. A further declaration of war was made on 4 December 1943 as the Bolivian Congress had not been consulted the first time. This was followed by a *coup d'état* by a military junta with pro-Nazi members, though its members were soon purged. Bolivia was the Allies' most important producer of tin (see also RAW AND SYNTHETIC MATERIALS). See also LATIN AMERICA.

bomb alley was the Allied nickname given to the area between Crete and Libya. Axis bombers attacked Malta-bound Allied *convoys from Alexandria during the battle for the *Mediterranean.

Bomber Command, see UK, 7(d).

bombers. (For carrier aircraft, see CARRIERS, 2.)

1. Design and development

Most of the bombers in service in 1939 were twin-engined all-metal monoplanes with bomb loads of 454–2,040 kg. (1,000–4,500 lb.) and, for the larger machines, a range of up to 4,025 km. (2,500 mi.).

Germany started with three main types, early versions of which had been tested in the *Spanish Civil war: the Heinkel He111, the smaller and faster Dornier Do17, and the single-engined Junkers Ju87 dive-bomber (or 'Stuka'). All had a weak defensive armament of hand-trained machine-guns and were vulnerable to modern fighters. German aircraft, however, were the first to be fitted with self-sealing fuel tanks.

Purpose designed and stressed, the Ju87 remained stable in a nearly vertical dive and could hit targets with great accuracy. Just entering service, the twin-engined Ju88 was fast and manoeuvrable, had a strong structure, and had been modified during development to undertake dive-bombing; it proved to be the most versatile German aircraft of the war.

Fully comparable with the German bombers was Poland's P.Z.L. P37 Łoś, which could carry a bigger load of *bombs than its own empty weight, but only 36 of these machines were in service. France, caught with a fleet of antiquated bombers, was re-equipping (too late) with new types such as the Lioré et Olivier LeO451, the fastest of all bombers in 1939.

The fighting in May–June 1940 which preceded the fall of *France revealed the inadequacy of Britain's Fairey Battle single-engined day bombers; too slow and without fighter escort, they suffered appalling losses. Smallest and fastest of the British twin-engined bombers was the Bristol Blenheim, past its prime but bearing the brunt of daylight operations. It was backed by three 'heavy' bombers: the Armstrong Whitworth Whitley, Handley Page Hampden, and Vickers-Armstrongs Wellington. The most outstanding of these was the Wellington whose unusual structure—fabric covering over a geodetic light-alloy framework—was immensely strong, could absorb massive battle damage, and was an efficient load-carrier over long distances. Like most British bombers, the Wellington had power-operated gun turrets (pioneered by the UK from 1934 onwards), but even these proved inadequate on unescorted daylight raids, hence RAF Bomber Command's switch to night bombing during the *strategic air offensive against Germany.

Italy's principal bomber, the Savoia-Marchetti SM79, had three engines (offsetting low unit power), was built largely of wood to conserve metals, and on replacement by the larger Cant Z1007—another trimotor of wooden construction—was used very successfully as a torpedo-bomber. In between was the twin-engined Fiat BR20 of metal construction and unimpressive performance. Defensive armament of the Italian machines was weak.

Soviet bombers, apart from the long-range Ilyushin Il4, were used mainly for army support. Twin-engined tactical types included the obsolete Tupolev SB2 (first used in Spain), which was succeeded by the Petlyakov Pe2—a fast machine capable of shallow dive-bombing—and, from 1943, by the larger and more heavily armed Tupolev Tu2. A unique type, built in greater numbers than any other warplane, was the single-engined Ilyushin Il2 'Shturmovik' (assault aircraft), which had an armoured 'bath' to protect engine and crew against ground fire.

In early 1941 the UK introduced two types of four-engined bombers, the Short Stirling and Handley Page Halifax, and in March 1942 the Avro Lancaster, the finest night heavy bomber of the war, became operational. In general, these machines carried double the bomb load of foreign designs—the Lancaster a record 9,979 kg. (22,000 lb.). Also operational in 1942 was the all-wood twin-engined de Havilland Mosquito which was unarmed and relied on its speed—over 645 kmph (400 mph)—to escape interception; its loss rate was the lowest of any bomber.

Germany made less progress. The Dornier Do217 was a new design with four times the Do17's bomb load, the Ju188 was simply a development of the Ju88, and the Heinkel He177—an attempt at a long-range heavy bomber—suffered from over-complication (notably its pairs of coupled engines) and saw little effective use. Few of Germany's many advanced projects came to fruition, an exception being the Arado AR234. This carried a bomb load of 1,500 kg. (3,308 lb.) and was the world's first jet bomber when it was first delivered in June 1944. Powered by two Junkers Jumo jet engines, its speed (730 km/h. or 457 mph) put it almost beyond reach.

Prominent in the *Pacific war was the Japanese Navy's Mitsubishi G4M (Allied codename 'Betty'), a land-based twin-engined bomber which achieved its exceptional range of 6,059 km. (3,765 mi.) at the cost of light

Bombers, 1: Principal bomber aircraft types

Type	Crew	Powerplant	Wing Span	Loaded Weight	Max. Speed	Service Ceiling	Range	Armament	Remarks
1. France									
Lioré et Olivier LeO451	4	2 x 1,060 hp Gnome-Rhone 14N	22.52 m (73 ft 10.1/2 in)	11,400 kg (25,132 lb)	480 km/h (298 mph)	9,000 m (29,530 ft)	2,900 km (1,802 miles)	1,400 kg (3,086 lb); 1 x 20 mm cannon and 5 x 7.5 mm mg	373 delivered by armistice. Continued in production for Vichy French Air Force.
2. Germany									
Heinkel He111H-6	5	2 x 1,340 hp Jumo 211F	22.60 m (74 ft 1 3/4 in)	11,338 kg (25,000 lb)	415 km/h (258 mph)	7,775 m (25,500 ft)	2,820 km (1,740 miles)	2,500 kg (5,510 lb) bombs; 1 x 20 mm cannon and 6 x 7.9 mm machine-guns	Approx. 7,300 built. Served throughout war.
Dornier Do17Z-2	4	2 x 1,000 hp Bramo 323P	18.00 m (59 ft 5/8 in)	8,590 kg (18,937 lb)	410 km/h (255 mph)	8,200 m (26,900 ft)	1,360 km (845 miles)	1,000 kg (2,205 lb) bombs; 4-8 x 7.9 mm mg	Approx. 1,100 built (all versions). Phased out 1942.
Junkers Ju87B-2	2	1 x 1,200 hp Jumo 211 Da	13.80 m (45 ft 3 1/3 in)	4,335 kg (9,560 lb)	383 km/h (238 mph)	8,000 m (26,250 ft)	790 km (490 miles)	500 kg (1,102 lb) bombs; 3 x 7.9 mm mg	5,709 built. The 'Stuka' dive-bomber. Later used as tank-buster. Served throughout war.
Junkers Ju88A-4	4	2 x 1,340 hp Jumo 211J	20.00 m (65 ft 7 1/2 in)	14,000 kg (30,684 lb)	470 km/h (292 mph)	8,200 m (26,900 ft)	1,780 km (1,106 miles)	3,000 kg (6,614 lb) bombs; 6 x 7.9 mm mg	14,676 built, of which approx, 9,000 were bombers. Served throughout war.
Dornier Do217E-2	4	2 x 1,580 hp BMW 801L	19.00 (62 ft 4 in)	14,998 kg (33,070 lb)	515 km/h (320 mph)	7,500 m (24,600 ft)	2,300 km (1,430 miles)	4,000 kg (8,818 lb) bombs; 1 x 15 mm cannon, 2 x 13 mm and 3 x 7.9 mm mg	1,905 built (all versions). Operational March 1941.
Junkers Ju188E-1	5	2 x 1,600 hp BMW 801ML	22.00 m (72 ft 2 in)	14,510 kg (31,989 lb)	500 km/h (311 mph)	9,300 m (31,510 ft)	1,950 km (1,211 miles)	3,000 kg (6,614 lb) bombs; 2 x 20 mm cannon, and 2 x 13 mm mg	1,076 built (all versions). Operational August 1943. Derived from Ju88.
Heinkel He177A-5	6	2 x 3,100 hp Daimler-Benz DB610 coupled engines	31.44 m (103 ft 1 3/4 in)	31,000 kg 68,342 lb	488 km/h (303 mph)	8,000 m (26,245 ft)	4,990 km (3,100 miles)	6,000 kg (13,228 lb) bombs; 2 x 20 mm cannon, 3 x 13 mm and 3 x 7.9 mm mg	1,146 built. Operational late 1942. Long-range strategic bomber.
Arado Ar234B-2	1	2 x 1,764 lb-thrust BMW 003A-1	14.44 m (46 ft 3 1/2 in)	9,800 kg (21,605 lb)	742 km/h (461 mph)	10,000 m (32,810 ft)	1,630 km (1,013 miles)	2,200 kg (4,409 lb) bombs; 2 x 20 mm cannon	Approx. 210 built. World's first jet bomber. Operational November 1944.
3. Italy									
Savoia-Marchetti SM79	4/5	3 x 780 hp Alfa Romeo 126RC34	21.20 m (69 ft 6 1/2 in)	10,725 kg (23,644 lb)	430 km/h (267 mph)	6,500 m (21,325 ft)	3,300 km (2,050 miles)	1,250 kg (2,755 lb) bombs; 3 x 12.7 mm and 1 x 7.7 mm mg	1,330 built. Later used as torpedo-bomber.
Fiat BR20M	5/6	2 x 1,000 hp Fiat A.80 RC41	21.56 m (70 ft 8 3/4 in)	10,448 kg (23,038 lb)	430 km/h (267 mph)	7,600 m (24,935 ft)	2,000 km (1,243 miles)	1,600 kg (3,527 lb) bombs; 1 x 12.7 mm and 2 x 7.7 mm mg	Approx. 600 built. Used for raids on Britain, November 1940.
CRDA (Cant) Z1007bis	5	3 x 1,000 hp Piaggio P.XIbis RC40	24.80 m (81 ft 4 1/2 in)	13,621 kg (30,029 lb)	450 km/h (280 mph)	8,100 m (26,575 ft)	2,657 km (1,650 miles)	3,000 kg (6,615 lb) bombs; 2 x 12.7 mm and 2 x 7.7 mm mg	Approx. 660 built.

Bombers, 1: *(cont.)*

Type	*Crew*	*Powerplant*	*Wing Span*	*Loaded Weight*	*Max. Speed*	*Service Ceiling*	*Range*	*Armament*	*Remarks*
4. Japan									
Mitsubishi Ki21 IIb ('Sally')	5	2 x 1,500 hp Mitsubishi Ha-101	22.50 m (73 ft 9 3/4 in)	10,610 kg (23,391 lb)	486 km/h (302 mph)	10,000 m (32,810 ft)	2,700 km (1,680 miles)	1,000 kg (2,205 lb) bombs; 1 x 12.7 mm and 4 x 7.7 mm mg	Approx. 2,060 built. Army bomber.
Mitsubishi G4M2 ('Betty')	7	2 x 1,800 hp Mitsubishi MK4P Kasei 21	25.00 m (82 ft 1/4 in)	12,500 kg (27,558 lb)	438 km/h (272 mph)	8,950 m (29,365 ft)	6,059 km (3,765 miles)	1,000 kg (2,205 lb) bombs, or torpedo; 2 x 20 mm cannon and 4 x 7.7 mm mg	2,414 built. Land-based navy bomber. Also carried ohka (Baka) suicide bomb.
Mitsubishi Ki67 ('Peggy')	6/8	2 x 1,900 hp Mitsubishi Ha-104	22.50 m (73 ft 9 3/4 in)	13,765 kg (30,347 lb)	537 km/h (334 mph)	9,470 m (31,070 ft)	2,800 km (1,740 miles)	1,070 kg (2,360 lb) bombs; 1 x 20 mm cannon and 4 x 12.7 mm mg	698 built. Army bomber; also used by navy as torpedo-bomber. Entered service October 1944.
5. Poland									
P.Z.L. P.37 Loś B	4	2 x 918 hp Bristol Pegasus XX	17.93 m (58 ft 10 in)	8,560 kg (18,872 lb)	445 km/h (276 mph)	6,000 m (19,680 ft)	2,600 km (1,615 miles)	2,200 kg (4,850 lb) bombs; 3 x 7.7 mm mg	108 built. Max. bomb load 3,020 kg (6,657 lb)
6. UK									
Fairey Battle I	3	1 x 1,030 hp Rolls-Royce Merlin III	16.46 m (54 ft 0 in)	4,895 kg (10,792 lb)	388 km/h (241 mph)	7,165 m (23,500 ft)	1,690 km (1,050 miles)	454 kg (1,000 lb) bombs; 2 x 0.303 in mg	2,203 built. Proved ineffective in France, May 1940; used mainly for training thereafter.
Bristol Blenheim IV	3	2 x 920 hp Bristol Mercury XV	17.17 m (56 ft 4 in)	6,530 kg (14,400 lb)	428 km/h (266 mph)	6,705 m (22,000 ft)	2,350 km (1,460 miles)	454 kg (1,000 lb) bombs; 3-5 x 0.303 in mg	Approx. 6,200 built (all versions). Withdrawn from bomber operations 1943.
Armstrong Whitworth Whitley V	5	2 x 1,145 hp RR Merlin X	25.60 m (84 ft 0 in)	15,196 kg (33,500 lb)	357 km/h (222 mph)	5,365 m (17,600 ft)	2,655 km (1,650 miles)	1,360 kg (3,000 lb) bombs; 5 x 0.303 in mg	1,676 built. Max. bomb load 3,175 kg (7,000 lb). Last bombing raid April 1942.
Handley Page Hampden I	4	2 x 1,000 hp Bristol Pegasus XVIII	21.08 m (69 ft 2 in)	9,526 kg (21,000 lb)	409 km/h (254 mph)	5,790 m (19,000 ft)	1,931 km (1,200 miles)	1,814 kg (4,000 lb) bombs; 6 x 0.303 in m.g.	1,430 built. Last bombing raid September 1942.
Vickers Wellington III	6	2 x 1,500 hp Bristol Hercules XI	26.26 m (86 ft 2 in)	15,422 kg (34,000 lb)	411 km/h (255 mph)	5,790 m (19,000 ft)	2,478 km (1,540 miles)	2,041 kg (4,500 lb) bombs; 8 x 0.303 in mg	11,461 built (all versions). Last bombing raid March 1945.
Short Stirling III	7/8	4 x 1,650 hp Bristol Hercules XVI	30.20m (99 ft 1 in)	31,790 kg (70,000 lb)	435 km/h (270 mph)	5,180 m (17,000 ft)	949 km (590 miles)	6,350 kg (14,000 lb) bombs; 8 x 0.303 in mg	2,374 built. Range 3,237 km (2,010 mi) with reduced bomb load. Operational February 1941.
Handley Page Halifax VI	7	4 x 1,800 hp Bristol Hercules 100	31.75 m (104 ft 2 in)	29,480 kg (65,000 lb)	496 km/h (308 mph)	6,705 m (22,000 ft)	2,028 km (1,260 miles)	5,896 kg (13,000 lb) bombs; 9 x 0.303 in mg	6,176 built. Operational March 1941.
Avro Lancaster I	7	4 x 1,460 hp RR Merlin XX	31.09 m (102 ft 0 in)	30,845 kg (68,000 lb)	462 km/h (287 mph)	7,470 m (24,500 ft)	2,671 km (1,660 miles)	6,350 kg (14,000 lb) bombs; 8 x 0.303 in mg	7,377 built. Max. bomb load 9,979 kg (22,000 lb) Operational March 1942.
De Havilland Mosquito XVI	2	2 x 1,680 hp RR Merlin 72	16.51 m (54 ft 2 in)	10,430 kg (23,000 lb)	668 km/h (415 mph)	11,887 m (39,000 ft)	2,206 km (1,370 miles)	1,814kg (4,000 lb) bombs; no defensive weapons	7,781 built (all versions). Operational May 1942.

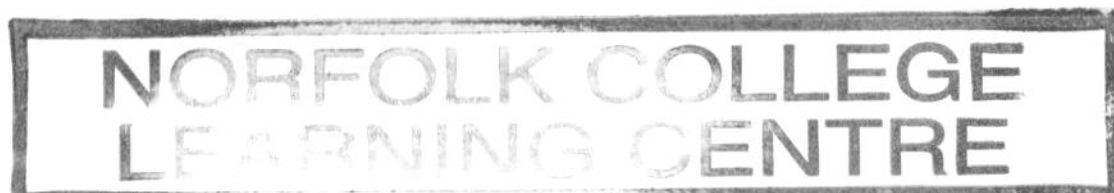

Bombers, 1: *(cont.)*

Type	*Crew*	*Powerplant*	*Wing Span*	*Loaded Weight*	*Max. Speed*	*Service Ceiling*	*Range*	*Armament*	*Remarks*
7. USA									
Boeing B17G Fortress	10	4 x 1,200 hp Wright Cyclone R-1820-97	31.62 m (103 ft 9 in)	29,025 kg (64,000 lb)	462 km/h (287 mph)	10,850 m (35,600 ft)	3,220 km (2,000 miles)	2,722 kg (6,000 lb) bombs; 13 x 0.50 in mg	12,731 built. Max. bomb load 7,983 kg (17,600 lb) for short missions
Douglas A20G Havoc	3	2 x 1,600 hp Wright R-2600-23	18.69 m (61 ft 4 in)	12,338 kg (27,200 lb)	546 km/h (339 mph)	7,865 m (25,800 ft)	1,754 km (1,090 miles)	1,179 kg (2,600 lb) bombs; 8 x 0.50 in mg	7,385 built. A-20G version equivalent to RAF Boston IV.
Consolidated B24J Liberator	8/10	4 x 1,200 hp Pratt & Whitney R-1830-65	33.53 m (110 ft 0 in)	29,484 kg (65,000 lb)	467 km/h (290 mph)	8,535 m (28,000 ft)	3,688 km (2,290 miles)	3,992 kg (8,800 lb) bombs; 10 x 0.50 in mg	18,313 built (most numerous US warplane in history).
North American B25J Mitchell	6	2 x 1,700 hp Wright R-2600-92	20.60 m (67 ft 7 in)	15,876 kg (35,000 lb)	438 km/h (272 mph)	7,375 m (24,200 ft)	2,173 km (1,350 miles)	2,720 kg (6,000 lb) bombs; 12 x 0.50 in mg	Approx. 11,400 built. Operational February 1942.
Martin B26C Marauder	7	2 x 2,000 hp Pratt & Whitney R-2800-43	21.64 m (71 ft 0 in)	15,513 kg (34,200 lb)	454 km/h (282 mph)	6,615 m (21,700 ft)	1,850 km (1,150 miles)	1,361 kg (3,000 lb) bombs; 12 x 0.50 in mg	5,157 built. Operational April 1942.
Douglas A26B invader	3	2 x 2,000 hp Pratt & Whitney R-2800-79	21.35 m (70 ft 0 in)	15,880 kg (35,000 lb)	572 km/h (355 mph)	6,735 m (22,100 ft)	2,253 km (1,400 miles)	1,814 kg (4,000 lb) bombs; 10 x 0.50 in mg	2,446 built during war. Operational November 1944.
Boeing B29A Superfortress	10	4 x 2,200 hp Wright R-3350-57	43.46 m (142 ft 3 in)	64,003 kg (141,000 lb)	550 km/h (342 mph)	9,695 m (31,800 ft)	6,598 km (4,100 miles)	5,442 kg (12,000 lb) bombs; 1 x 20 mm cannon and 12 x 0.50 in mg	3,970 built. Operational June 1944. Served solely in Far East. Max. bomb load 9,072 kg (20,000 lb)
8. USSR									
Tupolev SB2bis	3	2 x 1,100 hp Klimov M-100A	20.33 m (66 ft 8 1/2 in)	7,800 kg (17,196 lb)	450 km/h (280 mph)	10,400 m (34,120 ft)	1,600 km (994 miles)	1,000 kg (2,205 lb) bombs; 4 x 7.62 mm mg	Approx. 6,660 built. Original version first flew 7 October 1934.
Ilyushin Il4	4	2 x 1,100 hp Tumansky M-88B	21.44 m (70 ft 4 1/4 in)	10,000 kg (22,046 lb)	411 km/h (255 mph)	10,000 m (32,810 ft)	3,587 km (2,228 miles)	2,500kg (5,510 lb) bombs; 3 x 12.7 mm mg	Approx. 6,800 built. Wood replaced much of metal structure in late-war production.
Petlyakov Pe2	3	2 x 1,260 hp Klimov M-105PF	17.16 m (56 ft 3 1/2 in)	8,495 kg (18,728 lb)	580 km/h (360 mph)	8,800 m (28,870 ft)	1,200 km (746 miles)	1,000 kg (2,205 lb) bombs; 4 x 12.7 mm and 2 x 7.62 mm mg	11,427 built. Fitted with brakes for shallow dive-bombing.
Tupolev Tu2	4	2 x 1,850 hp Shvetsov ASh-82FN	18.86 m (61 ft 10 1/2 in)	12,800 kg (28,219 lb)	550 km/h (342 mph)	9,500 m (31,170 ft)	2,500 km (1,553 miles)	2,270kg (5,004 lb) bombs; 2 x 20 mm cannon and 3 x 12.7 mm mg	Entered service 1943.
Ilyushin Il2m3	2	1 x 1,770 hp Mikulin AM-38F	14.60 m (48 ft 0 1/2 in)	6,360 kg (14,021 lb)	404 km/h (251 mph)	6,000 km (19,685 ft)	600 km (373 miles)	600 kg (1,321 lb) bombs and/or rockets; 2 x 23 mm cannon, 1 x 12.7 mm and 2 x 7.62 mm mg	36,000-plus built. The 'Shturmovik' ground-attack aircraft. Initial version was a single-seater.

In many cases the bomb load quoted is the maximum that could be accommodated, but this was reduced if the range was increased. Towards the end of the war on raids on Berlin the RAF's Mosquito (2 crew) and the USAAF's B17G Fortress (10 crew) delivered exactly the same bomb load —1,814 kg (4,000 lb).

Source: Contributor.

construction and poor protection for the crew and fuel tanks. Comparable army types were the less impressive Mitsubishi Ki21 ('Sally') and, from October 1944, the fast and manoeuvrable Mitsubishi Ki67 ('Peggy').

In 1935 the USA produced the first truly modern all-metal four-engined monoplane bomber, the Boeing B17 which, because of its five gun positions, was nicknamed "'Flying Fortress'. A robust machine designed to fly at high altitudes, its armament of hand-trained guns was deceptively weak. Between then and mid-1942, when the USAAF embarked on its unescorted daylight raids, the Fortress's armament was progressively increased (thirteen

0.5 in. (12.7 mm.) guns on the B17G), but at the expense of range and/or bomb load.

First used in action by the French in May 1940, the Douglas DB7 (RAF Boston, USAAF A20 Havoc) was a fast, twin-engined attack bomber with a tricycle undercarriage, a feature perpetuated on most subsequent US bomber designs. Later, and larger, twin-engined bombers were the North American B25 Mitchell, Martin B26 Marauder, and Douglas A26 Invader.

The four-engined Consolidated B24 Liberator of 1939 had, thanks to its high aspect ratio Davis wing, a very long range and was first used by the RAF on anti-submarine patrols, helping to close the *air gap in the Atlantic. More Liberators—18,313 of them—were built during the war than any other US type.

Culmination of US bomber design and produced specifically for the Pacific war was the Boeing B29 Superfortress, which could carry a 2,268 kg. (5,000 lb.) load of bombs 5,233 km. (3,250 mi.). Twice as heavy as a Lancaster, the B29 operated at high altitude, had pressurized cabins for its crew, and used remotely controlled gun turrets. This was the aircraft that dropped the *atomic bombs on Japan. DAVID DORRELL

2. Tactics

The 1930s brought a rapid advance not only in the design of bombers but in the theories and tactics of how they were to be used; and for the Germans, in particular, participation in the Spanish Civil War gave the Luftwaffe an early chance to test many of its new ideas in combat.

Broadly speaking, the bomber of the Second World War was employed strategically (attacks on an adversary's communications, factories, sources of supply, civilian population), or tactically (attacks on an adversary's armed forces in support of one's own, and on an adversary's lines of communication and such specific targets as shipping).

The best demonstration of the tactical use of a bomber early in the war was the use of the German Junkers Ju87 dive-bomber. It was the spearhead of the *blitzkrieg which proved so successful during the *Polish campaign of September 1939 and in the fighting which led to the fall of France in June 1940. Its task was to destroy strong-points in the path of the advancing ground forces and it did so with pinpoint accuracy—within 30 m. (100 ft.) of its target—by diving vertically at it. It then released its bomb(s) at low altitude at the bottom of its dive, a method that proved four times more accurate than normal horizontal bombing from altitude.

The RAF had no effective army support bomber during the fighting in France. This lack was rectified in 1941 during the *Western Desert campaigns when Hurricane fighters were equipped to carry bombs. Their success led later to the widescale employment of the RAF Typhoon and the P47 Thunderbolt and P51 Mustang of the US Army Air Forces (USAAF) in the role of fighter-bombers (see Figure 1), and these were often employed in *cab ranks. Each could carry a bomb- or rocket-load of up to 907 kg. (2,000 lb.)—twice that of many 1939 twin-engined bombers—and after the load had been released the aircraft had the performance and manoeuvrability to defend itself.

Another tactic for supporting ground troops was developed by Air Chief Marshal *Tedder in the Middle East, and came to be known as 'Tedder's Carpet'. It was not unlike a rolling barrage (see ARTILLERY, 2), in that bombers saturated the ground ahead of the advancing forces with high-explosive and napalm bombs, and was used to help the Allied break-out (COBRA) from the Normandy beachhead during the *Normandy campaign. After a preliminary bombardment by fighter-bombers, 1,500 US heavy bombers dropped 3,000 tons of bombs on German positions around St Lô. On both occasions some dropped short killing 100 servicemen, including Lt-General Lesley McNair, and wounding 600 others, but it was very effective in clearing the way for the advancing infantry and tanks, and certainly contributed to the success of the operation.

Strategic bombing demanded defensive, not offensive, tactics and the Luftwaffe bombers which raided British cities in daylight in the battle of *Britain flew in formations designed to give the maximum mutual protection; this proved of little avail, however, and the bombers were later provided with fighter escorts where possible. Single bombers were, also used to mount 'tip-and-run' raids on any nearby coastal target and they then escaped across the Channel before British fighters could be vectored on to them. But it was the bombers employed to mount the Allied strategic air offensives that were continually forced to evolve different tactics to counter German air and ground defences. Because RAF Bomber Command mostly mounted unescorted *area bombing night raids the tactics employed were different from those of the Eighth USAAF whose bombers attacked during the day using *precision bombing. Initially the British bombers were widely dispersed when they flew to their targets and this enabled the night fighters of the German *Kammhuber Line to cause casualties among each succeeding flight as they passed through the various 'boxes'. To counter this the bomber-stream, first used for the *thousand-bomber raid on Cologne in May 1942, was introduced. Instead of bombers converging on their target from their airfields separately they were gathered in one stream by giving each bomber a time and height to fly over a predetermined point. This created, by the time the Kammhuber Line was being approached, a mass of aircraft 112 km. (70 mi.) long and some 1,200 m. (4,000 ft.) deep, which, with any luck, completely overwhelmed the Kammhuber defensive box through which it flew. Air gunners had strict orders never to open fire unless attacked as a bomber was more likely to survive by evasion in the dark than by taking the offensive. If attacked, the corkscrew manoeuvre was the best tactic to employ (see Figure 2); Martin Middlebrook relates (see *The Nuremberg Raid*, London, 1973, p. 31) how one German night-fighter ace followed a corkscrewing Lancaster

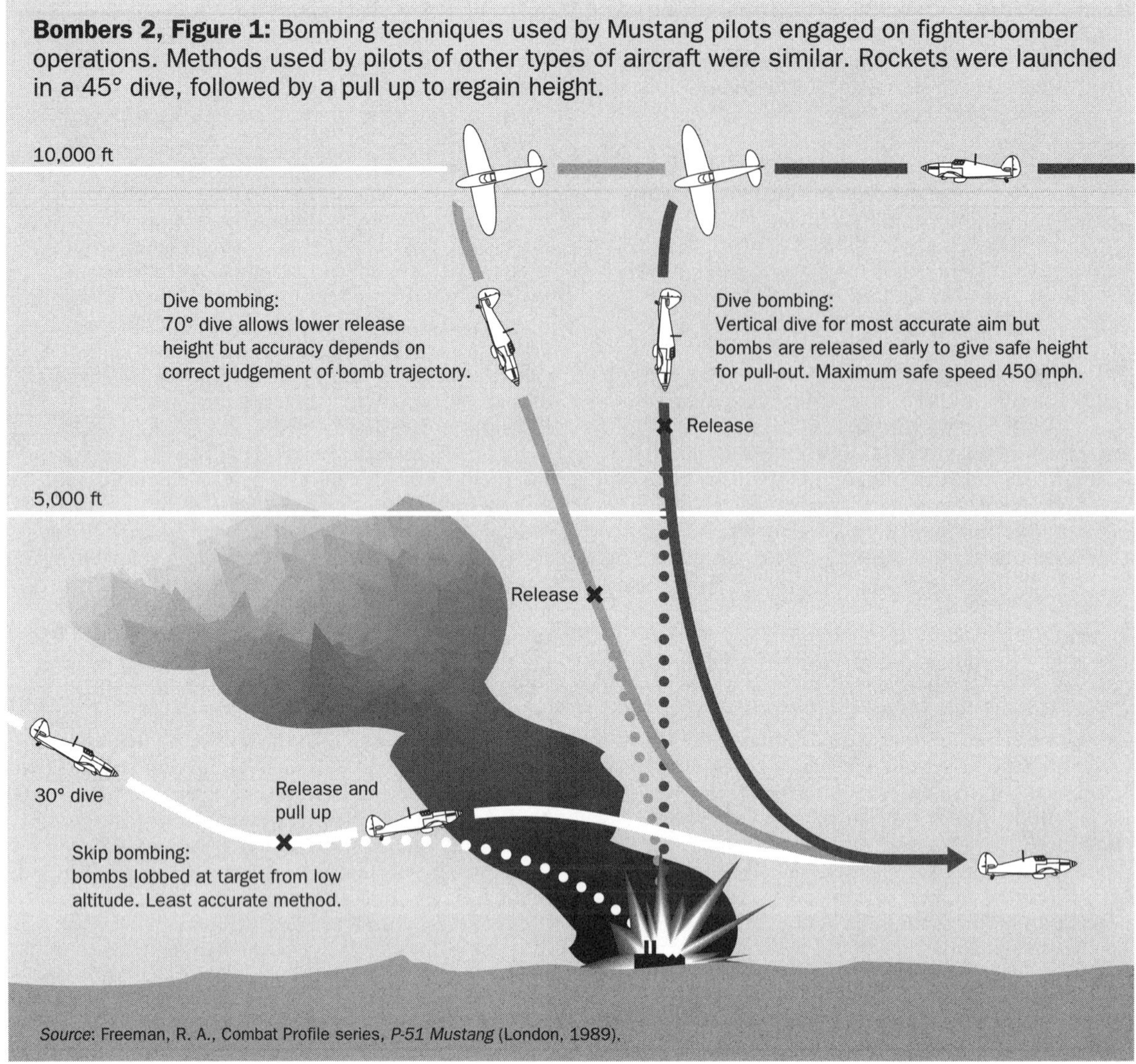

Bombers 2, Figure 1: Bombing techniques used by Mustang pilots engaged on fighter-bomber operations. Methods used by pilots of other types of aircraft were similar. Rockets were launched in a 45° dive, followed by a pull up to regain height.

Source: Freeman, R. A., Combat Profile series, *P-51 Mustang* (London, 1989).

bomber for three-quarters of an hour without once being able to get into a firing position.

As the war progressed all kinds of *electronic warfare devices were brought into play to confuse German *radar and thus misdirect the German night-fighters scrambled to intercept the bomber-stream. 'Spoof' raids were also started to draw them off from the bomber-stream. These were first employed on a large scale during the air offensive against *Berlin, which started in August 1943. Non-operational aircraft were assembled over the UK and flown towards the target area before, or simultaneously with, the bomber-stream. If they timed it right they turned back after the fighter defences had been committed to attacking them but before they could themselves be caught, and the main bomber-stream was able to avoid attack. 'Spoof' raids were also mounted by small numbers of the bomber version of the Mosquito, operational from mid-1942, which was too fast to be caught. When bombing real targets Mosquitoes often attacked in two formations, one at low level co-ordinated with the other making a shallow dive, a tactic which split the defences very effectively.

Because it employed precision bombing during the day against its targets the USAAF faced different problems in devising methods to protect its aircraft. Until long-range fighters became operational in early 1944 the bombers had to rely on their own armament and employ formations which gave maximum mutual defensive firepower. To this end the numbers of aircraft in a formation, and the compactness of the formation, increased as the war progressed. As both the B17 Fortresses and the B24 Liberators were heavily armed it

Bombers 2, Figure 2:
The Corkscrew Manoeuvre

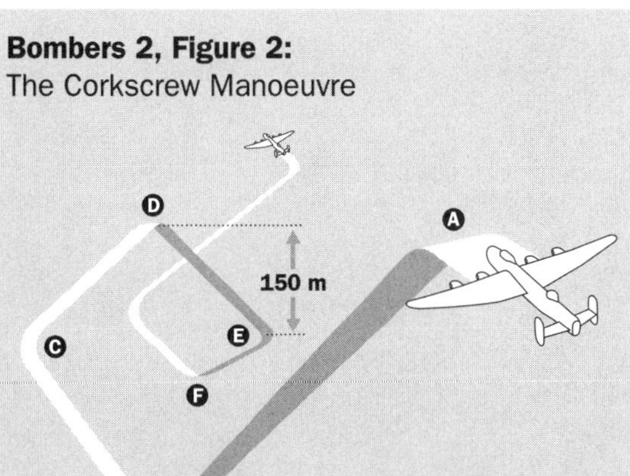

A If the fighter attacks from the port side, the bomber pilot banks at 45° and dives to port at full throttle.

B After descending for about 300m. (1,000ft) the pilot starts climbing. He is still turning to port.

C Halfway through the climb he banks to starboard, but continues to climb. This reduces his speed sharply which sometimes induces the attacking fighter to overshoot.

D After regaining the same altitude, and while still turning to starboard, the pilot starts another dive.

E He descends half the distance of the previous dive, then turns to port.

F If the pilot has not shaken off the fighter, he can repeat the manoeuvre.

Source: Cross, R., *The Bomber* (London, 1987).

was initially believed that they were capable of fighting their way to and from their targets in the Eighth USAAF's basic formation of six aircraft (see Figure 3). Four of these formations flown together, but as much as 6.4 km. (4 m.) apart, allowed plenty of manoeuvrability when bombing but proved quite inadequate for defence. So in September 1942 18-aircraft groups were introduced (see Figure 4) which brought the aircraft closer together and concentrated their firepower. But it was somewhat inflexible and when the formation turned it tended to cause stragglers—the death knell for any bomber. Though this was revised in December 1942 German fighters still caused heavy losses and from March 1943 the 54-aircraft combat wing formation began being used. Three 18-aircraft groups were brought together into a compact unit which was about 2,000 m. (2,200 yd.) wide and 800 m. (880 yd.) deep with 550 m. (600 yd.) between the first and last aircraft. This increased mutual fire support considerably but required new bombing techniques, including *pattern bombing. The 'tucked in' 54-aircraft wing formation followed soon afterwards which squeezed the aircraft even closer together so that they used nearly 75% less air space. This presented a truly formidable concentration of firepower as well as a reduced target for the head-on fighter attacks that the Luftwaffe had developed. This formation continued to be used until the introduction of the long-range fighter in early 1944, and then the appearance of massed anti-aircraft batteries that defended German cities in early 1945, each of which prompted a change of formation. With fighters to accompany bombers throughout a raid, self-protection became a lower priority than maximizing the use of those with the latest *electronic navigation systems which were in short supply. One of these aircraft led a squadron of twelve, with three squadrons flying together in an arrow-shaped group. Finally, in February 1945, four squadrons of nine aircraft each were flown in one group. This made them easy to protect and as each squadron flew at a different height made it difficult for the German gunners to shift fire from one squadron to another.

In the Pacific war, where air-to-air bombing was a frequent Japanese tactic, the bomber tactics of the USAAF attacking Japan with the new B29 also underwent a number of radical changes. At first the air commanders used the tried and tested tactics of day precision bombing from high altitude, but this produced disappointing results, due partly to strong winds at such a height. So, in January 1945, Maj-General *LeMay was brought in with orders to mount area bombing raids with incendiaries. He achieved a startling success which, in the opinion of the US official air historians, marked him 'as one of the very greatest of operational air commanders of the war' (W. Craven and J. Cate, eds., *The Army Air Forces in World War II*, Vol. 5, Chicago, 1958, p. 608). He achieved it by adopting a daring tactic. His bombers, packed with incendiaries, began flying lower altitude sorties at night (around 1,830 m. or 6,000 ft.), and, to increase their speed and bomb load, he had all their armament stripped

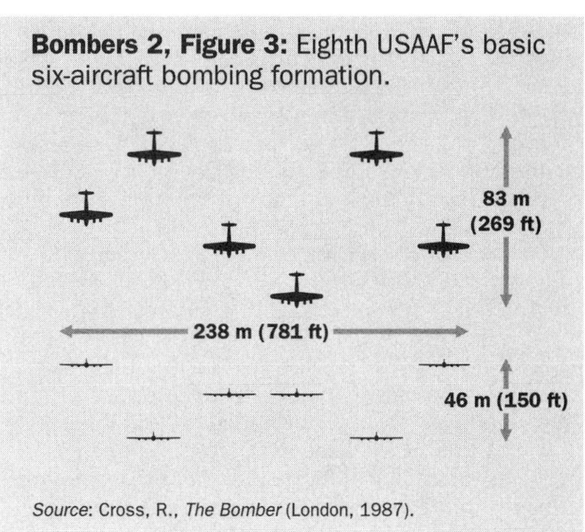

Bombers 2, Figure 3: Eighth USAAF's basic six-aircraft bombing formation.

Source: Cross, R., *The Bomber* (London, 1987).

Bombers 2, Figure 4: Eighteen-aircraft bombing formation introduced in September 1942.

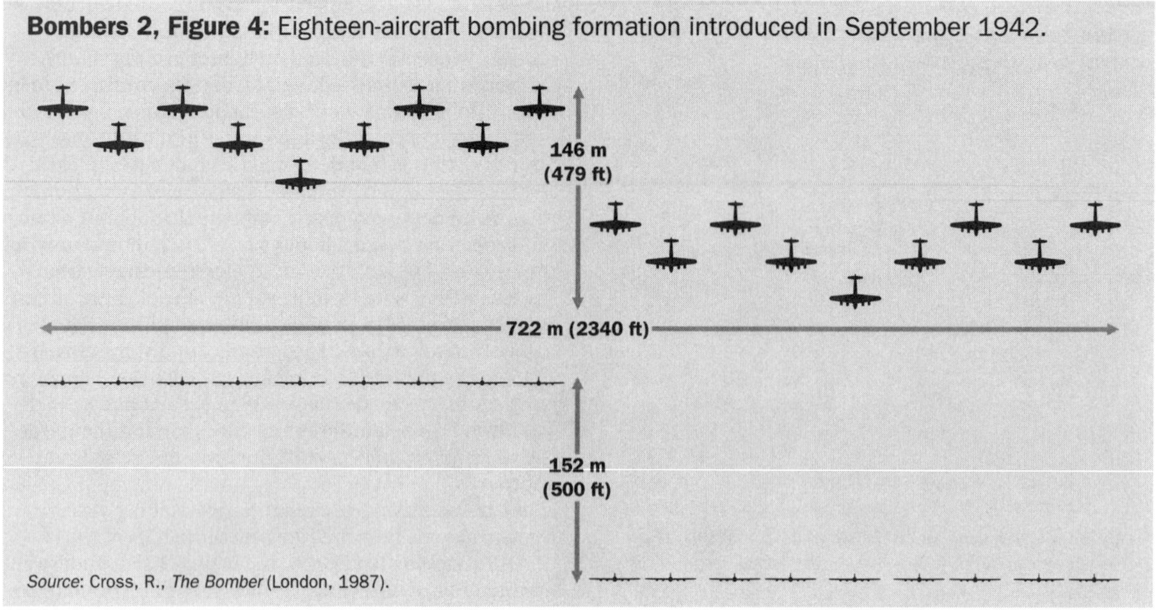

Source: Cross, R., *The Bomber* (London, 1987).

except the tail gun. This tactic was first used to raid Tokyo on the night of 9/10 March. It was a calculated gamble which paid off. These 'Fire Raids' inflicted greater material damage on Japan than the two atomic bombs.

I. C. B. DEAR

Cross, R., *The Bombers—the Illustrated History of Offensive Strategy and Tactics in the Twentieth Century* (London, 1987).
Francillon, R. J., *Japanese Aircraft of the Pacific War* (London, 1987).
Green, W., *Warplanes of the Third Reich* (London, 1970).
Saundby, R., *Air Bombardment* (London, 1961).
Swanborough, G., and Bowers, P. M., *United States Military Aircraft since 1908* (3rd end., London, 1989).
Thetford, O., *Aircraft of the Royal Air Force since 1918* (8th edn., London, 1988).

bombs were used by bombers and fighter-bombers (see FIGHTERS and BOMBERS, 2) of all combatant powers, the principal ones being high explosive (HE), incendiary, anti-personnel, armour-piercing, fragmentation, target indicator, and smoke. There was also the US fire bomb, an aircraft fuel tank filled with napalm (petrol thickened with *na*phthalic and *palm*itic acids), employed from mid-1943.

Fuzes could detonate bombs on impact or delay the explosion for several seconds—or several hours—but the percentage of duds on both sides was astonishingly high, perhaps as much as 20%. *Proximity fuzes, which could explode bombs in the air, had by 1944 proved the best method of maximizing their destructiveness. In certain types of attack parachutes were used to delay the impact, or to ensure an aerial detonation. Most of the aerial mines which the Luftwaffe dropped on British cities were delivered this way, as were the *atomic bombs which destroyed *Hiroshima and *Nagasaki.

The principal German HE bombs were the SC (thin-cased general purpose bomb), SD (thick-cased semi-armoured-piercing fragmentation bomb), and the PC (armour-piercing bomb). Eight out of ten bombs dropped on the UK were SC bombs weighing between 50 kg. and 2,000 kg. (110–4,410 lb.), the 1,000 kg. (2,205 lb.) bomb being known as the 'Hermann' because its bulbous casing was reminiscent of *Göring's girth. The larger 2,500 kg. (5,510 lb.) bomb, nicknamed 'Max', was also used during the *Blitz. The smaller bombs were often fitted with a device, the Gerät Jericho (Jericho apparatus), which emitted a wind-induced shriek similar to that of a German Stuka dive-bomber to intimidate their human targets.

Other bombs developed by Germany included two radio command types (see GUIDED WEAPONS); a concrete-cased bomb containing scrap metal; a rocket-assisted bomb for attacking fortified targets, which the British also developed; and the lethal 2 kg. (4.4 lb.), 9 cm. (3.5 in.) anti-personnel *Splitterbombe* (splinter bomb). Called the butterfly bomb by the Allies, it was copied almost exactly by the Americans. It could not be defused and was delivered one hundred at a time in a container, which was dubbed a 'Molotov bread (or egg) basket' by the Finns who had been on the receiving end of a similar device during the *Finnish–Soviet War.

Only the British, whose three main types of HE bomb were the General Purpose (GP), Medium Capacity (MC), and High Capacity (HC), produced bombs bigger than the 2,500 kg. 'Max'. The higher the capacity the higher the charge-weight ratio, the charge of some HC bombs being as much as 80% of their weight. This gave them very thin casings which resulted in a high blast effect but minimum penetration. Over half a million 500 lb. (225 kg.) GP bombs were dropped by RAF Bomber Command during the *strategic air offensive against Germany (see Table), but they were less efficient than their German counterparts having a lower charge-weight ratio. As a result of the shortcomings of GP bomb, 500 lb., 1,000 lb. (450 kg.), and 4,000 lb. (1,810 kg.) MC bombs were developed but were often in short supply. The biggest breached the dykes on Walcheren Island in October 1944 during the *Scheldt Estuary battle. The 12,000 lb. (5,430 kg.) *'Tallboy' or 'Earthquake', and the 22,000 lb. (10,955 kg.) *'Grand Slam', were also MC bombs. HC bombs came in four sizes—2,000 lb. (905 kg.), 4,000 lb., 8,000 lb. (3,620 kg.), and 12,000 lb.—and were known generically as 'blockbusters'. The British also developed HE bombs for special targets, the most famous being the bouncing 9,250 lb. (4,195 kg.) cylindrical, rotating bomb invented by Barnes *Wallis for the *Dam Busters raid.

By 1945 Allied HE bombs had increased in power five-fold. But by then, on an equal-weight basis, incendiaries such as the US 70 lb. (30 kg.) M47, which used napalm, were far more effective, though the liquid-filled British 30 lb. (13.6 kg.) 'J' bomb, first used by RAF Bomber Command in April 1944, was a failure as it often failed to work. Early British incendiaries filled with thermite—a mixture of iron oxide and powdered aluminium—produced great heat but this dissipated quickly and was confined to a small area. The Germans overcame this with their highly effective 1 kg. (2.2 lb.) bomb by making thermite its primary igniting substance and metallic magnesium the principal incendiary material. This made it burn with great heat for a long time and it could not be doused with water.

Japan produced an incendiary bomb of a radically different design. It contained more than 700 open-end iron cylinders filled with thermite and was fused to burst at about 60 m. (200 ft.) above the ground which scattered the cylinders over a radius of 150 m. (500 ft.).

The 4 lb. (1.8 kg.) incendiary filled with thermate—a mixture of thermite and oxidizing agents—was the one most used by the Allies, almost 30 million being dropped on Europe in special containers called clusters. Almost 10 million were also dropped during the *strategic air offensive against Japan, though the most frequently employed was the 6 lb. (2.7 kg.) M69 oil bomb which had cloth ribbons instead of metal fins. It acted like a small

Incendiary **bombs** caused devastation in Japanese cities. Here Osaka, where 100,000 people were killed and 310,000 houses were damaged or destroyed, is seen ablaze during the night of 15/16 June 1945.

Bombs: Numbers and types of bombs dropped by RAF Bomber Command, 1939–45, during the 389,809 sorties flown. The total came to 955,044 tons.

Type	*Total no.*
Fragmentation (F)	
20 lb	5,000
General purpose (GP)	
40 lb	42,939
250 lb	149,656
500 lb	531,334
1,000 lb	82,164
1,900 lb	2,141
4,000 lb	217
Semi-armour-piercing (SAP)	
500 lb	11,600
Armour-piercing (AP)	
2,000 lb	Exact figure is not known but less than 10,000
High Capacity (HC)	
2,000 lb	28,633
4,000 lb	68,000
8,000 lb	1,088
12,000 lb	193
Medium Capacity (MC)	
500 lb	403,000
1,000 lb	253,800
4,000 lb	21,000
12,000 lb Tallboy	854
22,000 lb Grand Slam	41
Incendiaries	
4 lb	80,000,000
25 lb	20,000
30 lb (Phosphorus)	3,000,000
30 lb 'J'	413,000
250 lb	7,000

Source: Macbean, J. A. and Hogben, A. S., *Bombs Gone*, (Yeovil, 1990).

mortar, ejecting its filling of napalm several yards after being dropped in clusters, and it was these that burnt out 41.5 sq. km. (16 sq. mi.) of Tokyo in March 1945.

Mills bombs, *sticky bombs, and *Gammon bombs were not bombs but hand *grenades.

Bonhoeffer, Dietrich (1906–45), German Protestant theologian and pastor who was one of the first to protest against Nazi domination of the church in his country. For a short time he worked in London as a pastor to the German community, but when Christians who were resisting the Nazis founded their own seminaries he returned to prepare candidates for ordination, and was banned from teaching at the University of Berlin for doing so. In 1939, after coming into conflict with the *Gestapo, he was persuaded to leave for the USA. But he soon returned, convinced that if he were to play a role in the eventual spiritual renewal of his country he could not remain outside it during the time of its greatest crisis.

In May 1942 he met George *Bell, the bishop of Chichester, in Stockholm with proposals from the conspirators against Hitler. They wanted to bring about a negotiated peace once Hitler had been overthrown, but the proposals were rejected by the British Foreign Office. He was imprisoned in Berlin in April 1943 and then moved to *Buchenwald. During this time he wrote his *Letters and Papers from Prison* (published in English in 1953) in which he proposed a 'religionless Christianity'; many of his writings have also been translated into English. He was executed at Flossenbürg on 5 April 1945. See also GERMANY, 9; GERMAN CHRISTIANS; and RELIGION

Bonin Islands, the Japanese Ogasawara Gunto chain of 27 islands lying between Japan and the *Volcano Islands some 965 km. (600 mi.) south of Tokyo. They figured in US strategy as being one way of approaching Japan's home islands and their garrisons were attacked in September 1944 by a US Navy task force and were frequently bombed thereafter. They were administered by the USA from 1945 to 1968.

Bonomi, Ivanoe (1873–1951), veteran anti-fascist Italian politician who, after the Italian *armistice in September 1943 and the German occupation of Rome, went underground and became chairman of the Rome Committee of National Liberation. When the city was liberated in June 1944 the committee forced the removal of King *Victor Emmanuel and his prime minister, *Badoglio, and Bonomi then formed a six-party government. This survived until November 1944 when it was replaced by a new government under Bonomi which lasted until June 1945. In 1949 he was elected president of the Italian Senate. See also ITALY, 3(b).

booty, see LOOT.

Bor-Komorowski, Lt-General, see KOMOROWSKI.

Bormann, Martin (1900–45), Hitler's crude and coarse private secretary who by the end of the war had become one of the most powerful men in the Nazi regime.

Bormann, who was born at Halberstadt, was a drop-out from school. After serving briefly in the *First World War he became a trainee on an estate in Mecklenburg and then a farm manager. He joined the Nazi Party in 1925 after serving a year's imprisonment as an accomplice to murder, and worked for the party's district executive in Weimar. He then rose steadily through the party hierarchy and in November 1933 was elected as a Nazi delegate to the Reichstag. From July 1933 to May 1941 he held the post of *chef de cabinet* in *Hess's office, acting as his right-hand man and personal secretary. It was during these years that he mastered the intricacies of the Nazi bureaucratic machinery, and established Hitler's confidence in his abilities and loyalty by administering the Führer's finances.

After Hess's mysterious flight to England in May 1941 Bormann, to all intents and purposes, took his place. He was made head of the party chancellery, where his apparent self-effacement hid a vicious and remorseless ambition, and in April 1943 took over Hess's old post as Hitler's secretary. The anonymity of his position proved ideal for increasing his influence, fostering intrigue, and pushing for a hard line on the Nazi Party's most cherished policies on racial and domestic matters. He was especially keen to crush once and for all any influence the church might still wield and was as strongly anti-clerical as he was *anti-Semitic.

Bormann's position enabled him to regulate who had access to Hitler, to play on his master's weaknesses and foibles, and to manipulate his rivals. Hitler called him 'my loyal Party comrade' and appointed him the political head of the Volkssturm (see GERMANY, 5) in September 1944. He also made him the witness of his political testament, in which he appointed Bormann the party minister, and of his marriage to Eva *Braun. Bormann left the Führerbunker on the night of 1/2 May to try and join the new German government in Flensburg, but either committed suicide or was killed while still in Berlin. He was sentenced to death *in absentia* at the *Nuremberg trials, and human remains, identified as his, were found in Berlin in December 1972.

Smelser, R., and Zitelmann, R. (eds.), *The Nazi Elite* (London, 1993).

Borneo, see BRITISH BORNEO and NETHERLANDS EAST INDIES.

Bose, Subhas Chandra (1897–1945), Bengali politician and nationalist whose policy of violent revolt against the British, to obtain India's independence, brought him increasing notoriety and several terms of imprisonment.

In September 1939 Bose, whose rallying cry was 'give me blood and I promise you freedom', was president of the *Indian National Congress. By then he had broken with *Gandhi, whose methods were diametrically opposed to his own, and he saw the war in Europe as the opportunity he had been seeking to throw off British rule. He was quickly arrested after war broke out but escaped and fled to Afghanistan, eventually reaching Germany in January 1941. There he found the *Nazi ideology congenial and attractive, and he copied Hitler by adopting the title *Netaji* (leader). But his efforts to arouse German help for his cause only resulted in sporadic propaganda and the formation of the ineffectual *Indian Legion.

Invited by the Japanese to lead the 'Free India' movement, Bose left Germany in February 1943, travelling first in a German, then a Japanese, submarine, not reaching Tokyo until June. He then became the President of the *Indian Independence League and leader of a reconstituted 13,000-strong *Indian National Army (INA), the Azad Hind Fauj. Then, on 23 October 1943, he announced the formation of the Provisional government of Free India (Arzi Hukumat-e-Azad-Hind) which was based in Singapore (Rangoon from January 1944 to April 1945). The next day the Provisional government declared war on the USA and the UK, and at the Greater East Asia Conference (see GREATER EAST ASIA CO-PROSPERITY SPHERE), which Bose attended in November 1943, it was given the civil administration of the Andaman and Nicobar islands. Bose, convinced that rebellion against the British in India would follow any invasion by the INA, broadcast propaganda to the Indian Army and created the slogan *Chalo Delhi* ('on to Delhi'). But the INA shared in the Japanese defeats during the *Imphal offensive into India in March 1944, and in the British advance into Burma that followed. Bose wanted to remain in Rangoon and fight, but in April 1945 the Japanese persuaded him to move to Thailand. However, Bose insisted that INA units remain in the Burmese capital to maintain order until the British arrived. He continued his propaganda broadcasts from Bangkok before moving to Saigon. When he heard of the Japanese surrender in August 1945 he was determined to continue the struggle to free India, but on 18 August his aircraft, which was taking him to Dairen in Manchukuo, crashed on take off from an airfield in Formosa. 'I believe India will soon be free,' were almost his last words before he died. 'Nobody can hold India captive now.' Rumours that he had survived persisted for years and in 1956 the Indian government sent a mission to Japan to enquire into his death.

Fujiwara Awaichi, the Japanese officer who first organized the INA, wrote immediately after the war that Bose 'had a zealous fighting spirit though in outward appearance he was very gentle. His earnest and precise mind, his vigorous actions, and his initiative, together with his love for the masses without any discrimination between classes, won for him respect which later became reverence . . . When contacting the Japanese his motto was "Freedom and Equality".' (Quoted in L. Allen, *The End of the War in Asia*, London, 1976, p. 155.)

Toye, H., *The Springing Tiger* (London, 1959).

Bougainville campaign, fought during the *Pacific war from November 1943 to August 1945 on this Pacific island when US and then Australian troops tried to clear the island of its Japanese garrison. Bougainville, 200 km. (125 mi.) long, was the largest of the *Solomons group (see Map 83) and part of the Australian mandate of North-East New Guinea.

With successes in the *New Guinea and *New Georgia campaigns US Pacific forces began closing in on *Rabaul, the main Japanese base in the area. Bougainville was the last Japanese bastion between it and Admiral *Halsey's land forces advancing up the Solomons, and elements of Lt-General Hyakutake Haruyoshi's Seventeenth Army were therefore rushed to reinforce it. But most of his 37,500 men were sent to Buin at its southern end, or to various offshore islands, so when the 3rd US Marine Division landed at Empress Augusta Bay on 1 November 1943, after the 3rd New Zealand Division had seized the nearby Treasury Islands, it met only light opposition. A defensive perimeter was quickly established and work on airstrips begun, but the initial fighting for the beachhead was in the air and at sea. In the battle of Empress Augusta Bay, fought before dawn on 2 November, the US Navy's Task Force 39 sank a cruiser and a destroyer of Vice-Admiral Omori Sentaro's Eighth Fleet; while Lt-General Kenney's Fifth USAAF bombed Japanese airfields, and fought off Japanese air attacks on TF39 and on the beachhead. However, by far the most dangerous threat to the American campaign was the appearance of Vice-Admiral *Kurita's powerful task force at Rabaul. Halsey's only option to avert disaster was to attack Kurita before he left Rabaul and, in what he later called his 'most desperate emergency', Halsey sent his two-carrier task force within range of Japanese air power. It was a gamble—he expected to lose the carriers—but, protected by land-based aircraft, both remained untouched while their aircraft wrought such damage that Kurita withdrew to *Truk. Then, aided by the completed airstrips on Bougainville, further Allied bombing raids soon forced the complete withdrawal of Japanese air and naval units from Rabaul.

With Rabaul neutralized the Americans quickly built up their forces on Bougainville. By 15 December 1943, when Maj-General Oscar Griswold and his 14th Corps HQ took command, they had defeated several counter-attacks and extended their perimeter, and by 9 March 1944, the day Hyakutake launched a full-scale offensive, Griswold commanded 62,000 men. Though Hyakutake broke through at some points, he lost more than 5,000 men killed and on 27 March he withdrew. After Griswold had further enlarged his perimeter, a virtual truce ensued until 2nd Australian Corps under Lt-General Stanley Savige, which completed relieving the Americans in December 1944, started their own offensive. The wisdom of doing so was later seriously questioned in Australia, but the Allies had mistakenly estimated the strength of the Japanese to be between 12,000 and 25,000, when in fact they then numbered about 40,000. However, Pearl Ridge in the island's centre was captured and one brigade was able to push northwards to contain the Japanese in the Bonis peninsula. But when 3rd Division moved southwards down the west coast towards Buin the Japanese resisted fiercely, and mounted several determined counter-attacks, particularly in the area of Slater's Knoll. But by the time Japan surrendered they had been confined to an area about 48 km. by 24 km. (30 mi. by 15 mi.).

Australian casualties were 516 dead and 1,572 wounded during Savige's offensive. About 8,500 Japanese were killed during the course of it, 9,800 died of disease (see MEDICINE), and 23,571 surrendered.

Bourguiba, Habib (b.1903), Tunisian politician, leader of his country's nationalist party, the Neo-Destour, which fought for independence from France. Arrested by the French in 1938 he was later imprisoned in Marseilles. He apparently remained pro-Allied, but the Germans insisted on his release in April 1943, and the following month he returned to Tunisia via Rome just before the *North African campaign culminated in the Axis surrender there. His negotiations with the Free French over independence failed and in March 1945 he went to Cairo from where he carried on his struggle for independence which was finally achieved in 1956.

Bracero programme. The manpower needs of the military, and the internment of some 110,000 *Japanese-Americans, many of whom were farmers or farm workers, created an acute agricultural labour shortage in the western USA in the early months of American belligerency. A remedy was found in an agreement with the Mexican government in 1942, which brought in some 200,000 Mexican workers—called *braceros*—on temporary work visas. Most helped to harvest the fruit and grain crops of the western states, but many also worked on railway construction and maintenance crews. Texas was at first excluded from eligibility for the Bracero programme because of State Department fears that exploitative labour practices there might precipitate a diplomatic incident with Mexico, menacing the Good Neighbor Policy which was a corner-stone of American hemispheric defence arrangements. The Bracero programme outlived the war by two decades, becoming a fixed feature of the agricultural economy in many western states. DAVID M. KENNEDY

Bracken, Brendan (1901–58), British Conservative member of parliament and friend of Churchill, whose parliamentary private secretary he was from September 1939 until he became minister of information in July 1941. He was one of the three political chiefs of the *Political Warfare Executive.

Bradley, General Omar N. (1893–1981), US Army officer and a West Point classmate of *Eisenhower, whose most trusted field commander he later became.

Born in Clark, Missouri, Bradley did not see active service during the *First World War. But by the time the USA was involved in the Second, he had risen to the rank of brigadier-general and was commanding the Infantry School at Fort Benning. His deep and abiding interest in infantry warfare was soon to pay great dividends. After commanding and training the 82nd and then the 28th Division in Louisiana with the rank of maj-general, Bradley became, in February 1943, Eisenhower's 'eyes and ears' in the *North African campaign, following which he was appointed *Patton's deputy at 2nd US Corps, and in April his successor. He showed his exceptional ability immediately during the last phase of the North African campaign and in June 1943 was promoted three-star general. He then commanded 2nd US Corps in Patton's Seventh Army during the *Sicilian campaign that started the following month, and his success there made him a natural choice for high command in north-west Europe.

Bradley arrived in the UK in September 1943 and in due course was given command of the First US Army, comprising 21 divisions, that landed on *OMAHA and *UTAH beaches during the Normandy landings in June 1944 (see OVERLORD). In early August Bradley assumed command of the newly formed Twelfth US Army Group which performed with such precision during the *Normandy campaign. He contained the German counter-attack at Mortain and then, with the help of the British, virtually destroyed the German Seventh Army at Falaise. This enabled both Army Groups to turn their forces towards Paris, their momentum eventually sweeping them across France before the advance ran out of steam.

The bitter differences that then arose between *Montgomery and Eisenhower over strategy, and over the allocation of supplies, found Bradley firmly on the side of Eisenhower and his policy of fighting on a broad front. But though the Supreme Commander considered him 'the greatest battle-line commander I have met in this war' they did not always agree; and when Eisenhower assigned the First Army, now commanded by *Hodges, to Montgomery during the *Ardennes campaign Bradley reacted furiously. But at the height of the crisis he behaved with great coolness, ordering *Bastogne to be held and launching Patton's Third Army in a brilliant flank attack to relieve it. Once the German advance had been stemmed and then broken the final phase of the war began. One of Hodges's armoured columns seized the bridge at *Remagen and by 23 March Bradley had three corps east of the Rhine; the formal link-up with Soviet troops around *Torgau on 25 April followed.

At the time of the German surrender Bradley's command had grown to four field armies and 1.3 million men. As a field commander he combined an icy calm and plain commonsense with great tactical flair. He was promoted to four-star general in March 1945 and to general of the army in 1950. See also LAND POWER.

Bradley, O., and Blair, C., *A General's Life* (New York, 1983).
Carver, M. (ed.), *The War Lords* (London, 1976).

Brand, Joel (1906–64), Hungarian Jew who was a leading member of the Jewish Aid and Rescue Committee in Hungary. In May 1944 *Eichmann, then inflicting the *Final Solution on Hungarian Jews, ordered him to contact *Jewish Agency emissaries in Turkey. Through Brand, Eichmann proposed exchanging Hungarian Jews for merchandise—10,000 trucks, to be used only in the *German–Soviet war, 80 tons of coffee, 20 tons of cocoa, 20 tons of tea, and 2 million bars of soap. For every truck supplied, or for its equivalent in cash or goods, 100 Jews would be released. The deal was authorized by *Himmler and was almost certainly more a peace feeler than a serious offer. The British opposed it, but went along with the Americans who wished to keep open the negotiations in case they might at least delay the deportation of Hungarian Jews to *Auschwitz. The Soviets, though they knew nothing about the condition attached to the trucks, refused to consider the matter. Brand, who had been arrested by the British in Aleppo in June, was released in October after the negotiations had failed, and went to Palestine.

Brand, J., and Weissberg, A., *Desperate Mission* (New York, 1958).

Brandenburgers, a German commando force used to facilitate the German advance or to hinder the opposing side's movement by employment of special weapons, co-operation with undercover agents and *ruses de guerre* which often violated the rules of war (for example, they wore Red Army uniforms in some operations behind Soviet lines).

During the preparations for the *Polish campaign an organizational framework became necessary for undercover agents and those who had volunteered to execute raids. In October 1939 the Baulehr-Kompanie zbV 800 (Baulehr: construction training; zbV: special duties), the nucleus of all later Brandenburger units, was formed in Brandenburg in Germany under the command of their founder Captain Dr von Hippel. Because of a strong inflow of ethnic German volunteers and soldiers from other units this company soon increased to battalion strength and became the Baulehr-Battalion zbV 800. This and later increases in size were initiated more by military leaders in the field than by central authorities.

Subordinated to the *Abwehr under the command of Admiral *Canaris, the Brandenburgers were the only force at the immediate disposal of the Armed Forces High Command (OKW). For special missions Brandenburger commandos were attached to regular army units. The suggestion that Canaris created the Brandenburgers to assist with a proposed coup against Hitler does not fit in with either the pattern of their development or with their widely scattered deployment. First significant successes were the captures of the Belt bridge in Denmark during the *Norwegian campaign in April 1940 and the bridge over the River Maas near Gennep in the Netherlands after Hitler had launched his campaign in the West in May 1940 (see FALL GELB). These successes and additional personnel led to further expansion to regimental size and it was renamed the Lehr-Regiment Brandenburg zbV 800 which included some other special units such as a *Küstenjägerabteilung* (marine battalion) or a *Fallschirmjägerbataillon* (paratroop battalion).

In the *Balkan campaign the Brandenburgers protected the oil facilities of *Ploesti in Romania and secured the bridge across the River Vardar in Yugoslavia, to the west of Axiopoulos. During the invasion of the USSR in June 1941 (see BARBAROSSA) they assisted the German advance by missions such as capturing the bridge across the River Dvina at Daugavpils in Latvia and the city of *Lwów. In

1942 they were deployed in North Africa and on the Eastern Front.

By the end of 1942 the regiment was first regrouped as the Sonderverband (Special Forces) 800 with five regiments, then as the Brandenburg Division. Unlike regular army forces the divisional staff remained in Berlin while the units were widely scattered over all theatres of war. The spectacular successes during the early years of the war were offset later by heavy losses and failures. Costly and lengthily prepared operations had to be abandoned because of Hitler's changing priorities. This and the morally controversial methods the Brandenburgers used, as well as the precious resources in men, *matériel*, and finances they squandered, made them unpopular with other Wehrmacht units.

With the change of the division's commander in early 1943 and its increasing deployment in anti-partisan operations, and in regular infantry tasks, it lost its character as a commando unit, becoming an OKW reserve. After the removal of the division's commander, Maj-General von Pfuhlstein, because of his connections with the resistance movement against Hitler (see SCHWARZE KAPELLE), and as a consequence of the take-over of the Abwehr by the *SS in February 1944, the division was relieved of its duties, renamed the Panzergrenadier-Division Brandenburg, and integrated into the army. Some of those soldiers who were experienced in commando operations volunteered for the SS-Jagdverbände, and only the Kurfürst Regiment retained the original commando role.

At the end of the war the division was captured by the Red Army near Deutsch-Brod, north-west of Brno.

RÜDIGER OVERMANS

Spaeter, H., *Die Brandenburger* (Munich, 1976).
Kriegsheim, H., *Getarnt, Getäuscht und doch Getreu* (Berlin, 1958).

Brauchitsch, Field Marshal Walter von (1881–1948), German Army officer who served as C-in-C of the German Army from February 1938 to December 1941.

Brauchitsch distinguished himself as a member of the German General Staff during the *First World War and, when the General Staff was forbidden by the *Versailles settlement, in its clandestine substitute, the Truppenamt. A talented artilleryman, he was involved in developing the 88 mm. dual-purpose gun, the Germans' most potent artillery piece of the war. By 1936 he was a lt-general and in January 1938, when *Fritsch was suspended from duty for an alleged homosexual offence, he was nominated to the army's highest post by *Keitel, who wanted an unpolitical C-in-C to please Hitler.

But it was more Brauchitsch's private life than his lack of political acumen which enabled Hitler to obtain the compliance of his new C-in-C and further the process of subordinating the army to the Nazi Party. Brauchitsch wanted a divorce in order to remarry, but he could not meet his wife's demands for a financial settlement. Hitler gave him the money, at least 80,000 Reichsmarks, and Brauchitsch's second wife, a fervent Nazi of dubious reputation, never allowed Brauchitsch to forget the Führer's munificence; the prospect of unsavoury publicity about her was another source of potential blackmail. By taking the money, and by accepting the post of C-in-C before Fritsch had even been tried, Brauchitsch weakened not only his own position but the chance of the army's leaders uniting to depose Hitler.

Throughout his time as C-in-C Brauchitsch was aware of a conspiracy to remove Hitler, but though he sympathized with the conspirators he did nothing to encourage them (see also X-REPORT). He did try to rally his fellow generals against Hitler's designs on Czechoslovakia, but was made to look merely faint-hearted when the *Munich agreement gave the Führer what he wanted. He was in favour of attacking Poland when Hitler assured him it would not lead to a more widespread conflict, and was able to conduct the *Polish campaign without interference. But, fearing the consequences, he did raise objections to a western offensive (see FALL GELB), which Hitler announced without consulting Brauchitsch beforehand. He was ignored, and after it was launched he was ignored again when he urged Hitler that the halt order before the *Dunkirk perimeter be reversed.

Brauchitsch, having been promoted general in February 1938, was given his field marshal's baton in July 1940. Unlike *Raeder, he was optimistic about the prospects of invading the UK (see SEALION) and he showed how far he had been drawn into the Nazi fold when he signed an order for the deportation of all able-bodied British males between 17 and 45 for *forced labour after the UK had been occupied.

As C-in-C of the German Army during its invasion of the USSR in June 1941 (see BARBAROSSA), Brauchitsch and his chief-of-staff, *Halder, were able to take credit for the planning of the operation and the early sweeping victories. But when Brauchitsch urged that *Moscow be captured immediately Hitler ignored his C-in-C yet again, and by the time he had changed his mind it was too late. The failure of the German offensive against the Soviet capital led directly to Brauchitsch's dismissal on 19 December 1941, when he was replaced by Hitler himself.

Brauchitsch spent the rest of the war in retirement. He gave perjured evidence at the *Nuremberg trials concerning, among other matters, his complicity in Hitler's orders to murder Soviet *commissars. He died before he could be tried himself, but historians have not exonerated him. 'Although it was Hitler who wanted to transform BARBAROSSA into a war of extermination against Bolshevism and Jewry, it was the Wehrmacht senior officers and their legal advisers who cast his ideological intentions into legally valid form' (Jürgen Förster, quoted in C. Barnett (ed.), *Hitler's Generals*, London, 1989, p. 89).

Mitcham, S., *Hitler's Field Marshals and their Battles* (London, 1988).

Braun, Eva (1912–45), daughter of a schoolteacher who became Hitler's mistress in 1932. He married her on 29

April 1945 in the Führerbunker where she had voluntarily gone to share his fate. She took poison the next day and her body was burnt.

Braun, Wernher von (1912–77), German engineer, educated at the Berlin Institute of Technology, who developed the A-4 rocket which became the V-2 (see V-WEAPONS).

After astronomy had inspired him to become involved in the theoretical problems of space flight, Braun was appointed to the German Army Ordnance Office in October 1932 to work on its rocket programme (permitted by the *Versailles settlement which did not include rockets in its definition of weapons). He became the Ordnance Office's technical director in 1937 and went with it to *Peenemünde on the Baltic coast. Despite the low priority given to his work on the A-4 rocket, his efforts were eventually rewarded when Hitler ordered the V-2 in 1943. In the face of many difficulties, which included an RAF attack on his installations and arrest by the *SS when *Himmler tried to seize control of the programme, the first V-2 was launched against the UK in September 1944. In March 1945 he and more than 100 of his staff escaped the advancing Soviet Army and were subsequently taken to the USA where they became an essential part of the US space programme and where many of them, including Braun, became naturalized US citizens. See also SCIENTISTS AT WAR.

Brazil. After the US entered the war in December 1941, Brazil declared solidarity with it while still maintaining diplomatic relations with the main Axis powers. However, any hope of preserving neutrality was soon abandoned and the severance of diplomatic relations with the Axis was announced at the *Rio conference in February 1942. Brazil was an important source of *raw materials for the Allied war effort, as well as being a vital link in the *Takoradi air route to the Middle East from Florida.

The sinking of its shipping drove Brazil, on 22 August 1942, to declare war on Germany and Italy—the first South American state to do so. It signed the *United Nations Declaration the following February and declared war on Japan on 5 June 1945. The 25,000-strong Brazilian Expeditionary Force saw action in the *Italian campaign with General *Clark's Fifth US Army; Air Force personnel fought with 350th Squadron USAAF; and Brazilian warships co-operated with the US Navy in patrolling the Brazilian coastline. See also LATIN AMERICA.

Brazzaville conference, convened by de *Gaulle in the capital of the Equatorial Federation (see FRENCH EQUATORIAL AFRICA). It was held from 30 January to 8 February 1944 to discuss the future of French colonies, but it had no powers to implement its conclusions. Most of the governors of French colonies outside Africa were unable, or unwilling, to attend, but those from Africa were present, as were those from Madagascar and Réunion. Félix Eboué, the governor of the Equatorial Federation, was the only black man present. De Gaulle gave the opening speech, but it was his commissioner for the colonies, René Pleven, who presided. The conference started by decreeing that eventual self-government for any of the colonies was unthinkable, but then went on to agree that the colonies must be given greater economic and social freedom, and that the indigenous populations must take a greater part in the running of their countries. This latter consensus started the movement towards independence by nearly all French colonies, a process that was mostly completed by 1962. For the Brazzaville declaration and ordinances of October 1940, see DE GAULLE.

Brereton, Lt-General Lewis H. (1890–1967), US Army officer who commanded US Far East Army Air Forces from October 1941. Most of his bombers were destroyed on the ground when the Japanese attacked *Clark field in the first *Philippines campaign on 7 December 1941. He later commanded the Ninth USAAF in the Middle East, organizing the raids against Romania's *Ploesti oilfields from Libya. In August 1944 he took command of the newly formed First Allied Airborne Army. The army's 1st Airborne Corps failed to gain a bridgehead across the Rhine River at Arnhem the following month (see MARKET-GARDEN), but the 18th Airborne Corps successfully dropped its two divisions beyond the Rhine in March 1945.

Brereton, L., *The Brereton Diaries* (New York, 1946).

Breskens pocket, the area around this Dutch port which was held by the Germans during the 85-day *Scheldt Estuary battle which began in September 1944. Hitler designated it a fortress and, from 5 to 22 September, despite the best efforts of the Allied air power, more than 82,000 men of the Fifteenth German Army, more than 530 artillery pieces, 4,600 vehicles, 4,000 horses (see ANIMALS), and a massive quantity of supplies were ferried across to Walcheren from the pocket. By 20 September the pocket had been much reduced, but the flooded polderland was ideal defensive country and the 3rd Canadian Infantry Division suffered 2,000 casualties before the pocket was eventually eliminated on 2 November.

Breslau Festung. Breslau, the chief city of Silesia, was designated a *Festung*, or fortress, by Hitler as the Red Army advanced on Berlin in early 1945. The bulk of the civilian population was forcibly evacuated by the Nazi authorities. The city was defended by 35,000 troops with no armour, little artillery, and a complement of civilian volunteers. The main Soviet offensive by-passed Breslau, though repeated attempts were made to take it by storm. Supplied by a makeshift airstrip and reinforced by two parachute battalions, the garrison held out until the day before Germany surrendered on 8 May. Large numbers of evacuees from Breslau were killed by the bombing of *Dresden.

Brest-Litovsk, Polish (Bréść nad Bugiem) fortress town on the River Bug, scene of the Russo-German peace treaty of 3 March 1918, which was remarkably favourable to Germany. It was relinquished by Germany to the USSR at the end of the *Polish campaign in October 1939, when the Gestapo and *NKVD exchanged parties of refugees. At the start of the *German–Soviet war in June 1941 (see BARBAROSSA), NKVD frontier troops and elements of two Red Army divisions stubbornly held out in the old fortress until 27 June, causing the 45th German Infantry Division heavy losses. It was reoccupied by the Red Army in July 1944. As Brest, it remained part of the USSR after the war. Post-war Soviet propaganda alleged that the siege had lasted until 20 July, or even later; in 1965 the town received the title of 'hero-fortress'.

Bretton Woods conference, also known as the United Nations Monetary and Financial conference, this meeting was held at Bretton Woods, New Hampshire, from 1 to 22 July 1944. It was largely the inspiration of the British economist Maynard Keynes and the US treasury assistant Harry Dexter White (who was, incidentally, a spy of Stalin's), and was attended by delegates from 44 nations. Its objective was to outline plans for post-war economic co-operation on a world-wide scale parallel to the political co-operation delineated by the *Atlantic Charter and the *Four-Power Declaration. For this purpose it was agreed to form the International Monetary Fund, which began functioning in December 1945 with 22 countries as members, and an International Bank for Reconstruction and Development (now known as the World Bank) with an authorized capital of $10 billion. Four nations—Haiti, Liberia, New Zealand, and the USSR—refused to be party to the conference's decisions.

Briansk–Vyazma encirclements. After having been stopped for a month east of *Smolensk by Hitler's order, Field Marshal Fedor von *Bock's Army Group Centre resumed its advance eastwards on 2 October 1941. Bock's next objective was now *Moscow, 350 km. (217 mi.) away; and he had more armour than in the earlier operations, Third and Fourth Panzer Groups and the Second Panzer Army (formerly also a group). On the Soviet side, three army groups, *Konev's West *front* (seven armies) in the north, *Eremenko's Briansk *front* (three armies in the south and *Budenny's Reserve *front* (five armies) at the rear, covered the approaches to the Soviet capital.

The Fourth Panzer Group drove deep along the West *front*–Briansk *front* boundary, diverting columns to the left and right to meet Third Panzer Group and Second Panzer Army spearheads coming from the north and south. An encirclement closed in the north at Vyazma on 10 October, and another closed in the south around Briansk three days later. Konev's and Eremenko's main forces were engulfed in the pockets, which yielded 663,000 prisoners. *Zhukov took over the remains and Reserve *front* on 10 October, but the panzer formations pressed ahead without a pause, aiming towards and around Moscow. Hitler, like the American and British military attachés in Moscow, believed the war's end was near. On 18 October, panic and looting broke out in the capital. However, rain that had intermittently slowed movement since 10 October was turning the whole landscape into a quagmire impassable to both tanks and infantry. See also BARBAROSSA and GERMAN–SOVIET WAR.

EARL ZIEMKE

Britain, see UK.

Britain, battle of, term coined beforehand by Churchill to describe the attempt by the German High Command (OKW) to gain air superiority over southern England, and to soften British morale, the necessary prerequisites for Operation *SEALION, the proposed invasion of the UK. In Britain the period of the battle is normally defined as being from mid-June to mid-September 1940. In fact, although there was a prolonged period of fencing before the battle proper, the Luftwaffe did not launch its main assault until 13 August, *Adlertag ('Eagle Day'), and British fighters continued to be heavily committed to containing daylight raids well into the autumn.

British preparations had been handicapped in the 1930s by the air ministry's reluctance to accept the possibility of close fighter defence, preferring the doctrine of defence through counter-attack by bombers. The diplomatic requirements of appeasement had also favoured priority for bombers, as a form of deterrent against German aggrandizement. It was not until early 1938 that Fighter Command was given full priority. Air Chief Marshal *Dowding, commander of Fighter Command since its formation in 1936, therefore had very little time to make his force ready. The technological breakthroughs which were to be so important in the battle, moreover, were of only recent origin: the basic principle of *radar was first demonstrated only in 1935; the Spitfire and Hurricane fighters only began to enter service in any numbers in 1939. Dowding had to work rapidly to link these developments together with an efficient communications network based on the group and the sector system, the basic system of fighter control used in the battle (see Figure and Map 18). In the circumstances, it was hardly surprising that some slight flaws were to be detected in Fighter Command's ground organization. In August 1940, however, the virtually untried matrix of technology meshed successfully together.

Fighter Command's problems were compounded by the defeats of the first year of the war. The campaigns on the European mainland reduced Dowding's aircraft and pilot reserves. Though the mobilization of the aircraft industry in the last year of peace was bearing fruit by the summer of 1940, so much so that Fighter Command was never seriously worried by lack of aircraft during that year, the provision of fully-trained pilots to make good losses was to prove more problematical. New dispositions

Fighter pilots 'scramble' from an airfield on the east coast of England during the **battle of Britain**. The scene was recorded by a *Life* magazine photographer on 25 July 1940.

also had to be made hurriedly to cover attacks from the Low Countries (Luftflotte 2) and northern France (Luftflotte 3), as well as long-range attacks from Scandinavia (Luftflotte 5). The weight of the attacks was likely to fall on 11 Group in the South-East, commanded by Air Vice Marshal *Park, and on 12 Group in east Anglia and the Midlands, commanded by Air Vice Marshal *Leigh-Mallory, but Dowding could not expose his flanks by denuding 10 Group in the South-West or 13 Group in the North and Scotland. In the early summer of 1940, Fighter Command hoped to have 60 squadrons ready by September, whereas some in the air ministry calculated that 120 squadrons were needed to achieve security. Dowding would have to rely on economy of effort or mistakes on the part of the Luftwaffe commanders.

On paper the Luftwaffe appeared to have the distinct advantage. In Field Marshals *Kesselring and *Sperrle and General *Stumpff, commanding of Luftflotten 2, 3, and 5 respectively, Dowding was confronted with the most successful commanders the age of *air power had yet seen. He could reckon on a steadily growing front line, but began the battle with approximately 900 fighters, of which he could expect to put at best some 600 in the air simultaneously. Luftflotten 2, 3, and 5, between them, had some 1,260 long-range bombers available, about 320 dive-bombers, 800 single-engined and 280 twin-engined fighters, and a number of reconnaissance aircraft. The distance that Luftflotte 5 would have to fly, however, meant that they would be without single-engined fighter cover, and this left the burden of the task to Luftflotten 2 and 3. In practice, then, with only two-thirds of the front line normally available, the Luftwaffe would rely on a core of some 750 long-range bombers, about 250 dive-bombers, rather more than 600 single-engined, and 150 twin-engined fighters. The Luftwaffe, moreover, suffered from some weaknesses in equipment. Though the Messerschmitt 109s were probably the best interceptors in the air in 1940, their short range was to limit the time they could spend in British air space; the twin-engined Me110 fighters were to prove too sluggish against a sophisticated air force; the dive-bombing Ju87s, spectacular though they appeared in newsreels, had neither the speed nor the payload to make any decisive impression on the RAF; and the longer-ranged Heinkel 111s, Dornier 17s, and Junkers 88s, were medium rather than heavy bombers, and found it difficult to inflict damage of strategic importance. Moreover, even with the experience of the *Polish campaign and the fall of *France behind them, German crews had not worked up the necessary accuracy to make the most of their equipment.

The aim of the German offensive itself was also problematic. The Luftwaffe owed its recent success to the fact that it had been working in close support of the army. This time it was given an independent task: to prepare for SEALION, which would not proceed until this task had been achieved. Any short-term success, therefore, could

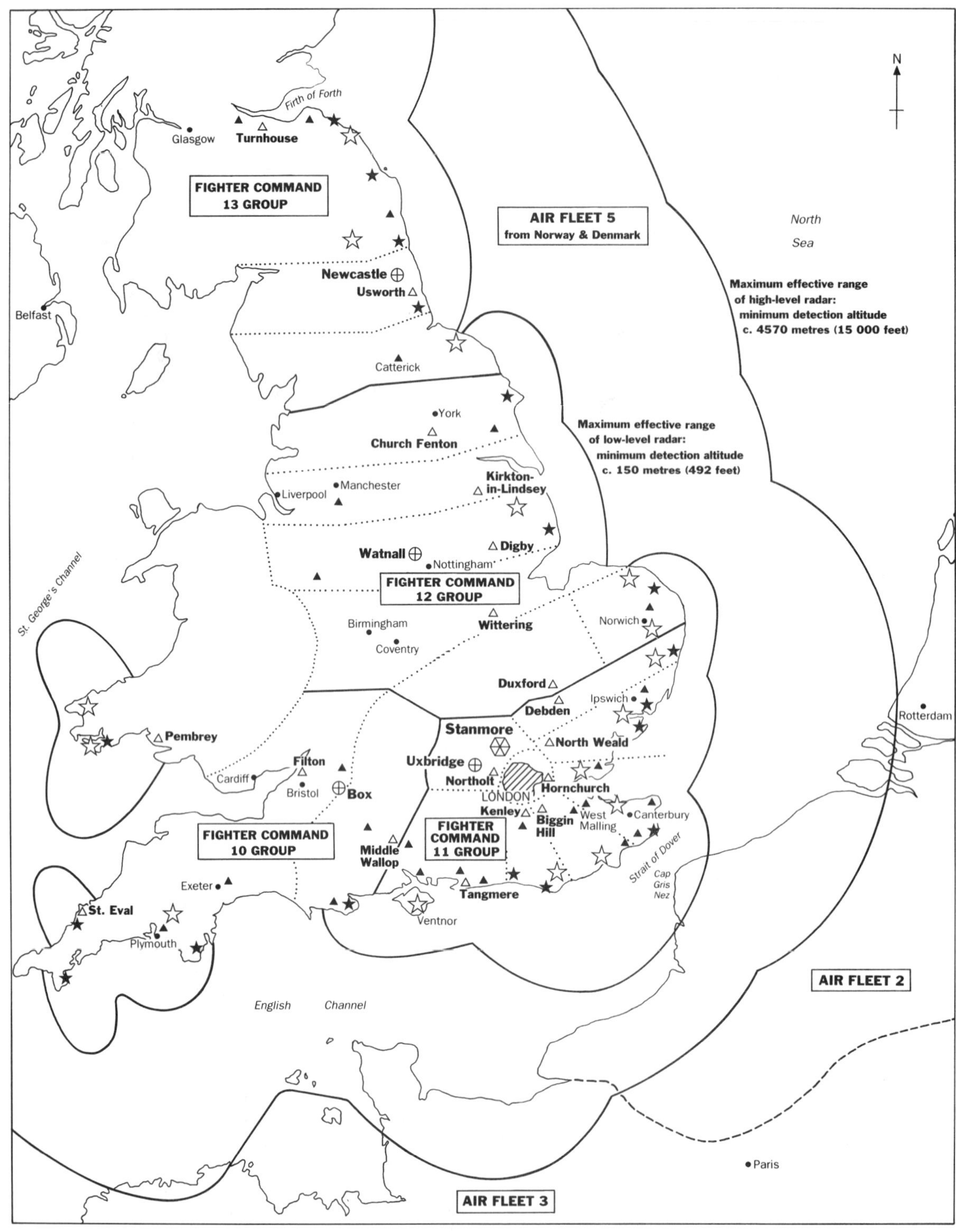

18. British air defences during the **battle of Britain**, 1940

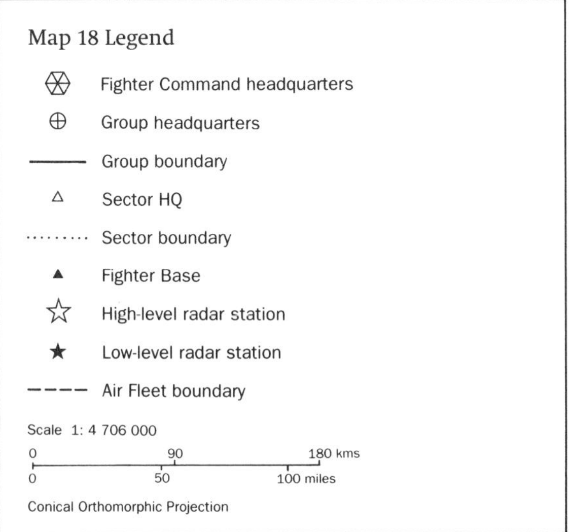

not be immediately followed up on the ground. There was also to be some confusion as to how the aim should be achieved. Target selection moved between coastal convoys, Fighter Command advanced aerodromes, sector stations, the aerodromes of Coastal and Bomber Commands (the utility of which was questionable in a search for command of the air), aircraft and related industries, as well as other industrial targets which were of general military value but not vital to the air war. In particular, the Luftwaffe did not make any concerted attempt to destroy the eyes of Fighter Command, the radar chain.

The weaknesses of the Luftwaffe were not apparent at the time. It took only six minutes to cross the Channel to Dover, and only ten minutes longer for German bombers to be over 11 Group's sector airfields. The bomber waves could be picked up by radar as they massed south of Cap Gris Nez, but it took four minutes for radar information to reach the squadrons and thirteen minutes for a Spitfire to get to 6,100 m. (20,000 ft.), while top-cover Me109 escorts often came in at 7,900 m. (26,000 ft.). Expert though they became, radar operators often found it difficult to predict the size and height of approaching bomber formations. Fighter Command's advanced information was sparse and rarely covered planned raids in the degree of detail Dowding needed for effective preparation. The gravest danger was that diversionary raids would commit 11 Group to attack well away from their airfields while the main attack then fell on their ground organization. To guard against this, 12 Group was often committed to guard 11's airfields. This enforced dispersal meant that Fighter Command was seldom able to achieve the kind of concentration that could wreak havoc among the bombers. Before September, Park's 11 Group was rarely given time to mass an attack on the bombers. The Luftwaffe's basic tactical unit was the *Gruppe* of 30 aircraft, while that of Fighter Command was the squadron of 12. To attack before the bombers reached their targets, Park often had little option but to commit his fighters cumulatively in penny packets of single-squadron strength. Only as experience was gained, and as the bomber attacks became more predictable, was it possible to mount simultaneous multi-squadron attacks as a matter of course. Eventually 12 Group was able to build the Duxford 'Big Wing', five squadrons of Hurricanes and Spitfires working as a single tactical unit of 60 aircraft (see also FIGHTERS, 2).

Through June and July and up to 12 August, the Luftwaffe concentrated its attack on shipping in the Channel, hoping to stretch Fighter Command's resources by forcing the British to adopt close fighter escort for this important coastal traffic. These attacks were supplemented by relatively light raids on south coast ports. In this period 30,000 tons of shipping were lost, but that was out of a total of almost a million tons a week passing through the Channel. By the end of July, meanwhile, German planning for SEALION had reached something of an impasse, with the army and navy commands at odds over the landing zones and the time it would take to transport the initial echelons across the Channel. Hitler accepted that the invasion could not take place before mid-September, and that it could not take place at all in 1940 unless the RAF was defeated. The Luftwaffe was therefore ordered to destroy the British Air Force as soon as possible. On 12 August, which saw the first concerted attacks on British fighter aerodromes, the Ventnor radar station was put out of service. During the next two weeks, however, the Luftwaffe failed to concentrate on these most important targets. 'Eagle Day', 13 August, proved a damp squib when bad weather led to a series of badly co-ordinated Luftwaffe attacks. Two days later, the three Luftflotten attacked in concert, but the weakly defended attack from Scandinavia suffered particularly heavy losses to 12 and 13 Groups, the Luftwaffe losing 75 aircraft in 24 hours to Fighter Command's 34. This was to prove to be Luftflotte 5's first and last major intervention in the battle of Britain.

Both sides were already greatly overestimating the losses they had inflicted on one another, but the German intelligence failures were to prove the more fateful. The Luftwaffe believed that the British were down to a front line strength of only 300. In fact, Dowding had lost only 200 aircraft and the front line remained at about 600. Nevertheless, the next stage in the battle was to prove the most dangerous for the British. In the brief respite afforded by poor weather between 19 and 24 August, Göring decided on a change of tactics, forcing air battles between fighters to break what he believed was the dwindling strength of Fighter Command. This was to be achieved by smaller concentrations of bombers, with relatively larger and closer escort forces, attacking targets the British were bound to defend, airfields in particular. The remaining bombers were to concentrate on unescorted night attacks to stretch the defences and to maintain the strain on British nerves. This was to prove

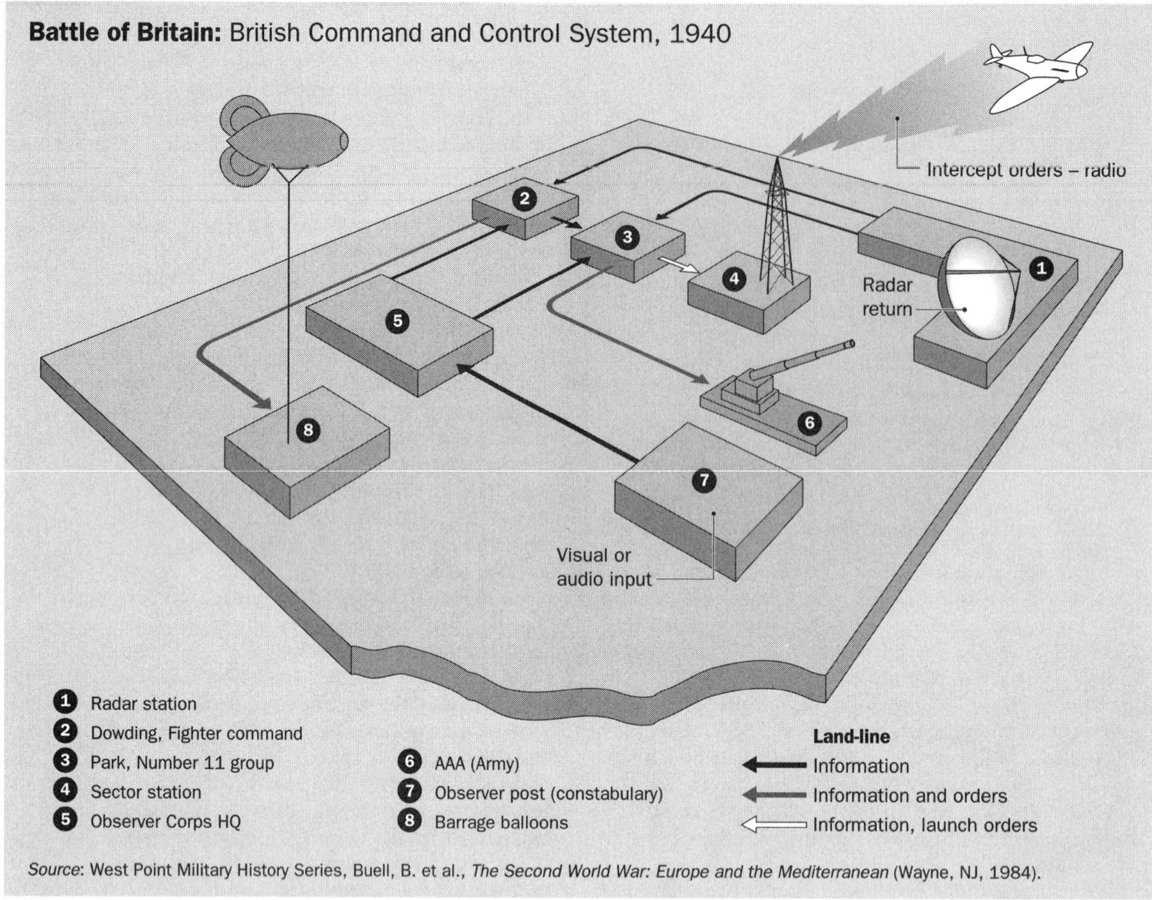

Source: West Point Military History Series, Buell, B. et al., *The Second World War: Europe and the Mediterranean* (Wayne, NJ, 1984).

a much more effective policy but, in that it was based on the assumption that Fighter Command was already close to defeat, its failure to bring early decisive results tested German confidence in the feasibility of launching SEALION in 1940. Fighter Command believed that it had too often allowed itself to get involved in battles with the escorts, and that it should concentrate more closely on the bombers. This approach was to be blocked by the new German tactics, and British losses edged close to those of the Luftwaffe in the next weeks.

Strong and partly successful attacks on Biggin Hill, Hornchurch, North Weald, and West Malling severely tested 11 Group's organization at the end of August and the beginning of September. This led to a dispute between the commanders of 11 and 12 Groups about the defence of 11's airfields while Park's fighters were in the air. It was 12 Group's contention that requests for support from 11 often came too late and that the massing of larger formations of defenders to hit the bombers would have much greater effect, even if this took time. Events were soon to provide an opportunity for the 'Big Wing' tactics to be put to the proof.

There is still much controversy about the origins of the German decision to switch the weight of their bombing from the airfields to London. One view is that an unintentional German attack on London prompted the British air ministry to attack Berlin on 25 August, an attack which so incensed Hitler that he determined to retaliate. The Luftwaffe High Command appears to have believed that such an attack would force Dowding to commit his last reserves, finally break Fighter Command and soften British resistance to the invasion. Whether, at this stage, Hitler still intended to launch SEALION is uncertain. Clearly, the invasion could not be contemplated before the RAF was defeated, but that defeat might itself make SEALION redundant, effectively neutralizing the UK for the time being and leaving the Germans free to concentrate on the long-term aim of achieving *Lebensraum* in the east (see BARBAROSSA). Heavy air attacks on London and other British cities might therefore be a substitute for the dangerous and perhaps unnecessary invasion.

The attacks on London began in earnest in daylight on 7 September. Fighter Command, expecting continued attacks on its airfields, was caught unprepared. Huge fires were left burning in the East End, providing beacons for the follow-up night attack. The next day, however, the Duxford wing abandoned the airfields it was asked to defend north of the Thames and met the bombers as they came over south-west London, an intervention which may have unnerved some in 11 Group but the success of which was to be confirmed a week later. On 15 September the Luftwaffe abandoned its usual practice of sending up feints and diversions, so that the radar network was left in no doubt about the main attack by mid-morning. Park was thus given time to meet the bombers with paired squadrons as far forward as Canterbury, and the 'Big Wing' made contact over East London. A second attack in the afternoon met a similarly prepared defence. On 'Battle of Britain Day', 15 September, the defence claimed to have shot down 185 German aircraft. In fact, the Luftwaffe had lost only 60, but that brought the tally of losses since 7 September to about 175, enough to test severely the confidence of a force which had been engaged virtually continuously for two months, and which had believed it was on the verge of victory. Two days later SEALION was indefinitely postponed. Although daylight raids continued until the weather worsened in October, their strength was gradually reduced as the bombers switched to night attacks. The Luftwaffe priority was no longer only the defeat of the RAF; the battle of Britain had merged imperceptibly into the *Blitz on London and other cities.

The figures of losses remain controversial, but the best estimates suggest that, between 10 July and 31 October, Fighter Command had lost approximately 788 and the Luftwaffe 1,294 aircraft. MALCOLM SMITH

Collier, B., *The Defence of the United Kingdom* (London, 1957).
Hough, R., and Richards, D., *The Battle of Britain: A Jubilee History* (London, 1990).
Murray, W., *Luftwaffe* (London, 1985).

British Army Aid Group (BAAG), escape and evasion organization formed in south China by an Australian doctor, Lt-Colonel Lindsay Ride, after *Hong Kong fell in December 1941. It was part of *MI9. Its medical posts gave succour to escapers while its Hong Kong Chinese agents acted as *Coast Watchers, undertook intelligence-gathering missions, and maintained contact with prisoner-of-war camps in Hong Kong. BAAG also helped acquire smuggled tin, rubber, and wolfram (see also RAW AND SYNTHETIC MATERIALS) from Thailand and French Indo-China; disrupted the Hong Kong shipyards by encouraging key personnel to escape; and formed the China Unit from available Hong Kong service personnel which fought as the Hong Kong Volunteer Company in the *Burma campaign. Having been replaced in early 1945 by the US equivalent of MI9, *MIS-X, by May 1945 it had assisted 1,886 servicemen and civilians—including 40 US airmen—to safety.

British Borneo, British colonies situated within Borneo, the world's third largest island. They comprised North Borneo (and Labuan Island), Brunei, and Sarawak (ruled by the British Brooke family since 1841). The rest of the island was Dutch Borneo, part of the *Netherlands East Indies.

Borneo was situated strategically across the region's main sea routes, but neither the British nor the Dutch were able adequately to defend their possessions on it when the Japanese launched their offensive against them in December 1941. The British opted only to defend Kuching airfield in Sarawak, but they destroyed the oilfields there, and at Seria in Brunei, before the Japanese landed at both places on 16 December 1941. At Kuching a lone regular battalion of Indian troops was soon forced into Dutch Borneo where those remaining eventually surrendered after further fighting.

In October 1943 the Chinese population, which numbered about 50,000, helped by the indigenous Dyaks, rebelled against the Japanese occupation troops. They seized the coastal town of Jesselton, but were later overwhelmed and many were executed. The same month the first of several *Special Operations Australia (SOA) parties was landed for intelligence-gathering purposes and others were dropped into the interior of Sarawak in March and April 1945. These trained and armed local people in advance of landings by the 9th Australian Division at Labuan and Brunei Bay in June which were opposed by elements of the 31,000-strong Japanese garrison in Borneo. The landing forces stayed on the coast and it devolved upon the SOA guerrilla forces to contain Japanese troops inland, some of whom did not surrender until October 1945.

British Cameroons, southern part of the German colony of Cameroon which became a British mandate after the *First World War and was administered by the neighbouring British colony of Nigeria. The other part became French Cameroons. German residents outnumbered the British and nearly all were Nazi Party members. A few escaped to Germany; the rest were interned in June 1940. The German influence resulted in a poor rate of recruitment from the local population of 400,000, only some 3,500 enlisting.

British Central Africa comprised the colonies of Northern Rhodesia (1.5 million blacks, 14,300 whites) and Southern Rhodesia (1.4 million blacks, 65,000 whites), and the Protectorate of Nyasaland (1.8 million blacks, 1,800 whites). About 60,000 blacks, half of them from Nyasaland, and 11,000 whites, including 1,500 women, joined the armed forces and many saw action in African regiments in the *East African, *Western Desert, and *Burma campaigns, and on *Madagascar.

Southern Rhodesia's embryo air force fought in East Africa before becoming part of the RAF (as 237 Squadron). Three other RAF squadrons were also formed from Southern Rhodesian personnel, and ten air schools were constructed in the colony. The Rhodesian Air Askari Corps was formed in 1941 to defend airfields and lines of communication.

Personnel from all three countries served in East Africa Command, and some of Southern Rhodesia's continued to do so after October 1942 when it was grouped with South Africa as part of Southern Command. As a result of this reorganization, General *Smuts became C-in-C of the colony's armed forces and the Southern Rhodesia Armoured Car Regiment served with the 6th SA Armoured Division in the *Italian campaign.

Northern Rhodesia's copper was highly valued early in the war but production peaked at 250,000 tons in 1943, after which demand slackened. Zinc, vanadium (a metal used for manufacturing armour plate), cobalt, mica (employed in the manufacture of valves for oxygen masks), and lead were also produced in the colony, while gold remained Southern Rhodesia's most important source of income, though it also produced high grade asbestos, chrome, and coal. See also RAW AND SYNTHETIC MATERIALS.

Macdonald, J., *The War History of Southern Rhodesia*, 2 vols. (Salisbury, S. Rhodesia, 1947–50).

British Commonwealth Air Training Plan, see BRITISH EMPIRE AIR TRAINING SCHEME.

British East Africa comprised the colonies of Kenya, whose 4.9 million population in 1939 included 22,800 Europeans, Uganda (4.2 million including 2,200 Europeans), and Zanzibar (232,000 including 3,000 Europeans), and the mandate of Tanganyika (6.5 million including 7,900 Europeans). Unlike the *First World War, when there was fighting in German East Africa (Tanganyika), there were no hostilities in British East Africa, but troops were recruited from the population, many of whom fought as two divisions in the *East African campaign and on *Madagascar. These divisions were later disbanded, or their men were absorbed into the 11th (East Africa) Division when it was formed in February 1943 out of brigades from British Central Africa (three battalions), British East Africa (fourteen battalions), and British Somaliland (one battalion), to fight in the *Burma campaign. Probably as many as 100,000 East Africans served in the armed forces in one capacity or another.

After Hitler came to power in January 1933 the German settlers remaining in Tanganyika formed offshoots of the Nazi Party. The number of German settlers increased steadily, so that by 1939 there were more than 3,000. When war was declared they were all interned, as were a number of local activists in Kenya. Tanganyika provided the only *raw materials, rubber and sisal, of any quantity though Uganda did also produce some rubber. After the Japanese Navy's raid into the *Indian Ocean in April 1942, the British Eastern Fleet was based for a time at Mombasa's port, Kilindini.

British Empire, see UK, 5.

British Empire Air Training Scheme. This was Canada's major air contribution to the Allied war effort. On 26 September 1939, the British government asked Canada to establish a British Empire Air Training Scheme (BEATS) after its formation was suggested by the Australian (S. M. Bruce) and Canadian (Vincent Massey) High Commissioners in London. It aimed to produce no fewer than 20,000 pilots and 30,000 personnel. To achieve this, it was estimated that about ninety elementary and advanced flying training schools were needed. Each month the plan was to graduate 520 pilots with elementary training, 544 with service training, 340 observers, and 580 wireless operator/air gunners. It was estimated that the scheme would need 3,540 aircraft—or more than twelve times the pre-war aircraft strength of the Royal Canadian Air Force (RCAF)—33,000 officers and men, and 6,000 civilians.

This was a tall order for the tiny RCAF; it was also an expensive one for the Canadian government to swallow. After long and bitter negotiations that lasted until December 1939, the total cost of the BEATS was set at $607 million of which the UK was to pay $185 million, Australia $39.9 million, and New Zealand $28.6 million. Canada was to find $353.4 million over 42 months. In return for this huge outlay, for so it seemed in 1939, Canada bargained hard, insisting that the RCAF had to administer the scheme, that the UK help the other Dominions to find the dollars necessary to pay their share, and that London state that the BEATS would take priority over all other forms that a Canadian contribution to the war might take. The Canadian prime minister, Mackenzie *King, believed that air casualties could not possibly be as numerous as army ones, and if the British government accorded priority to the BEATS, then Canada would be spared a manpower crisis. These conditions were eventually accepted in London. But the sharpest struggle came over Ottawa's insistence that Canadian aircrew be identified with Canada to the maximum extent possible once their training was complete. The British hoped to merge RCAF aircrew into Royal Air Force units, fearing that other Dominions would inevitably make the same demand if Canada's was conceded. Essentially, the question of 'Canadianization' was left unresolved and later in the war would cause serious ructions.

Despite its rocky beginnings, the BEATS, which was called the British Commonwealth Air Training Plan from June 1942, was a huge success. Extended into 1945, the plan cost $2.2 billion in all, of which, in the end, Canadnada paid $1.6 billion. In all, 168,622 graduated from Canada and other Dominions, more than 75,000 of whom were pilots.

British and Empire aircrew also trained in South Africa, which had its own air training scheme, in Southern Rhodesia, and in Australia and New Zealand (see Table).

J. L. GRANATSTEIN

British Expeditionary Force (BEF), the UK's contribution to the Anglo-French alliance which took part in the fighting which preceded the fall of *France in June 1940. It initially comprised some 152,000 men formed into two corps of two infantry divisions each, plus their sup-

British Empire Air Training Scheme: Aircrew trained under the scheme

Type and year of output	*Canada*	*Australia*	*New Zealand*	*South Africa*	*Southern Rhodesia*	*Total*
1940						
Pilots	240	60	318	—	110	728
Navigators	112	39	—	—	—	151
Others	168	54	—	—	—	222
TOTAL	520	153	318	—	110	1,101
1941						
Pilots	9,637	1,367	1,292	341	1,284	13,921
Navigators	2,884	681	—	629	23	4,217
Others	4,132	1,296	—	—	110	5,538
TOTAL	16,653	3,344	1,292	970	1,417	23,676
1942						
Pilots	14,135	3,033	943	1,529	1,666	21,306
Navigators	7,404	1,375	—	2,541	237	11,557
Air Bombers	1,742	—	—	170	—	1,912
Others	6,896	2,280	—	—	387	9,563
TOTAL	30,177	6,688	943	4,240	2,290	44,338
1943						
Pilots	15,894	3,869	836	2,309	2,083	24,991
Navigators	8,144	1,662	—	3,250	239	13,295
Air Bombers	6,445	—	—	918	—	7,363
Others	8,695	3,838	—	—	419	12,952
TOTAL	39,178	9,369	836	6,477	2,741	58,601
1944 (to 30 September)						
Pilots	8,807	1,684	502	2,025	1,188	14,206
Navigators	7,953	696	—	2,403	180	11,232
Air Bombers	5,131	—	—	742	—	5,873
Others	7,998	1,328	—	—	309	9,635
TOTAL	29,889	3,708	502	5,170	1,677	40,946
TOTAL	116,417	23,262	3,891	16,857	8,235	168,662
Summary						
Pilots	75,152					
Navigators	40,452					
Air Bombers	15,148					
Others	37,910					
GRAND TOTAL	168,662 to 30 September 1944					

Source: Golley J., *Aircrew Unlimited* (Yeovil, 1993).

porting arms, though ultimately it was hoped to field two armies of two corps each. Commanded by *Gort, it began its move to France on 4 September 1939 and was placed in the line on the Belgian border between the French First and Seventh Armies. The 1st Corps, commanded by Lt-General *Dill, then by Lt-General M. Barker, comprised 1st and 2nd Divisions and the 2nd Corps, under *Brooke, 3rd and 4th Divisions, and there was also an air component of 9,392 RAF personnel and 12 squadrons of aircraft.

Though mechanized, or rather motorized, the BEF was a purely defensive force. It had no armoured division, few tanks, inadequate communications, equipment, and training, and insufficient air power for any kind of offensive operation even if the French Army, under whose command it came, had been in any frame of mind to initiate one. It was, as the commander of its 3rd Division, *Montgomery, remarked, 'totally unfit to fight a first class war on the Continent of Europe'. Instead, it prepared defensive positions, did some much-needed training, and waited to see what would happen (see PHONEY WAR).

In December 1939 the BEF was reinforced by the newly formed 5th Division (withdrawn in April 1940) and the following April the 51st (Highland) Division was sent to the *Maginot Line on the Saar Front. Eight territorial divisions were also added between January and April 1940, though half of these had little equipment and less training and were really nothing more than labour battalions (nevertheless, they fought with great tenacity when they found themselves in the path of the German Army Group A). By May the BEF's strength totalled 394,165 men, though more than 150,000 of these were in the rear areas and were mostly without military training.

When the German offensive started on 10 May the BEF advanced to the *Dyle Line in Belgium, but it was soon forced to withdraw and six days later began its evacuation from *Dunkirk. But this still left 140,000 British troops in France. Some, including the remnant of the 1st Armoured Division—which had lost two-thirds of its strength after arriving in France on 21 May—escaped across the River Seine; 2,137 were evacuated from Veules-les-Roses and more than 10,000 from Le Havre; but the 51st (Highland) Division was forced to surrender at St-Valéry-en-Caux on 12 June. The next day Brooke, having replaced Gort, arrived at Cherbourg to command a reconstituted BEF reinforced by the 1st Canadian Division and the 52nd (Highland) Division. But the new French C-in-C, *Weygand, had already advised the French government to seek an armistice and Brooke, with difficulty, persuaded Churchill that a Brittany redoubt was impossible and that all troops must be withdrawn immediately. Some 136,000 men and 310 guns, plus 20,000 Polish troops, were safely evacuated though more than 3,000 perished when the 20,000-ton liner *Lancastria* was bombed at St Nazaire.

Thanks to Dunkirk and other evacuations the BEF's casualties—68,111 killed, wounded, and captured, plus 599 deaths through non-battle causes—were not as disastrous as they would otherwise have been. But its *matériel* losses, which included nearly 64,000 vehicles and 2,472 guns, were little short of catastrophic, while RAF losses amounted to 931 aircraft and 1,526 casualties.

British expedition to Greece, operation (MANNA) mounted in October 1944 after Stalin had agreed that Greece fell within the British sphere of influence (see TOLSTOY). It was sent to prevent the Communist party-controlled EAM taking over the country when the Germans began to withdraw, and to ensure the return of the Greek *government-in-exile.

A powerful force of British warships (Force 120) began operating in the Aegean Sea in September 1944 to intercept any German evacuation by sea, and a military force (Force 140) led by Lt-General Ronald Scobie was assembled at Alexandria. Two reconnaissance forces landed on the Peloponnese and one of them, the Special Boat Squadron (see SPECIAL BOAT SECTION), landed at Patras to capture Araxos airfield and then liberated the rest of the Peloponnese. Both, along with a parachute battalion dropped at Megara on 4 October, then entered Athens on 14 October, and two days later the main British force, supported by the *Balkan Air Force, landed at Piraeus.

The expedition achieved its objective in the short term for, on 18 October, the Greek prime minister, George Papandreou, arrived in Athens on 18 October to form an administration (see GREECE, 3(c)). But in the long run it did not prevent a civil war.

British Free Corps (BFC), unit formed in Germany in 1944 from British and Dominion *prisoners-of war to fight in the *German–Soviet war. It was the idea of a British renegade, John Amery, who called it the Legion of St George, but he only ever found one recruit and never led it. It was subordinated to the *SS, and commanded by an SS officer. The few recruits—there were never more than 57—who saw action during the fall of *Berlin wore ordinary field-grey uniforms with collar patches of three leopards and a 'British Free Corps' cuff band on the left sleeve with a Union Jack above it. Post-war trials condemned Amery to death—he was executed—and some BFC members were given prison sentences.

Weale, A., *Renegades: Hitler's Englishmen* (London, 1994).

British Security Co-ordination, intelligence organization established in New York in August 1940 by the Canadian-born William *Stephenson. In its early days it represented *MI6 and *SOE in the *Western Hemisphere, and, until 1943, *MI5 in Canada and the Caribbean. After the USA entered the war it acted as the liaison office between SOE and MI6 and the *Office of Strategic Services (OSS), and, when the OSS and the US Federal Bureau of Investigation (see USA, 7) took over many of its intelligence gathering and counter-espionage activities, it became the channel for intelligence between these organizations and Whitehall; it also administered *Camp X which trained SOE and OSS personnel.

British Somaliland, British East African colony, part of Somalia which had been divided between France (see FRENCH SOMALILAND), Italy (see ITALIAN SOMALILAND), and the UK at the end of the nineteenth century. In August 1940, during the *East African campaign, it was occupied by Italian troops after its neighbour, French Somaliland, on whose support its defences relied, joined the *Vichy regime. The colony was retaken in March 1941 when the British Navy landed two Indian battalions at Berbera. Its sole indigenous army unit was the 550-strong Somaliland Camel Corps.

British Union, name given to the British Union of Fascists (founded in 1932) in the autumn of 1937. Led by Oswald *Mosley its membership was then in decline from its height of 50,000 in June 1934, and by the summer of 1939 was about 11,000. The Italian government supported it early on, but there is no evidence that Germany did so or was interested in using it for intelligence purposes. In May 1940 Mosley and 33 other BU leaders were arrested under the Defence Regulations (18B) and interned. Altogether 747 BU members were detained, 200 of whom were still in detention in December 1941, 130 in the spring of 1943, and 15 in September 1944. The BU was never actually proscribed, but by September 1940 it was judged to be defunct.

British West Africa, British colonies or protectorates totalling about 41 million inhabitants. They were Nigeria (which administered British Cameroons), Gambia, Sierra Leone, and the Gold Coast, the last administering Togo (later Togo trans-Volta), that part of Togoland mandated to the UK after the *First World War. The colonies proved invaluable to the British war effort, not only for providing troops and labourers for the West African Military Labour Corps, but for *raw materials. Freetown, the capital of Sierra Leone, became an important naval base and staging post for *convoys, and the Gold Coast was the starting point for the *Takoradi air route along which aircraft reinforcements flew to the Middle East.

British West African regiments already existing in 1939 were enlarged to include seven new West African brigades (three from Nigeria, two from the Gold Coast, one each from Sierra Leone and Gambia) which were formed in 1940. These became part of the 1st and 2nd (East Africa) Divisions which fought in the *East African campaign. In 1943, when recruitment had reached 169,000 men, these brigades were formed into the 81st and 82nd (West Africa) Divisions. With one exception all these brigades fought in the *Burma campaign—where they suffered nearly 2,000 casualties, including 494 killed—and one participated in the second *Chindit operation.

British West Indies, British Caribbean colonies of nearly 3 million people comprising the Bahamas (where the Duke of *Windsor was governor), Barbados, British Guiana (which produced bauxite in large quantities), British Honduras, Jamaica, Leeward Islands, Trinidad and Tobago (the UK's largest source of oil in 1938), and the Windward Islands. US air and sea bases were established on several of the islands under the *destroyers-for-bases agreement, which helped bring a degree of prosperity, and skilled West Indian workers went to work in the UK, as did 500 woodsmen from British Honduras who were employed in the Scottish forests. The latter were poorly treated and were returned home in 1943. A number of Jamaicans joined the Royal Engineers in 1941, and in 1944 the 1st Caribbean Regiment was raised from volunteers. After training in the USA and Italy, it went to Egypt, but did not see action. About 300 West Indians also enlisted in the RAF for aircrew duties and subsequently about 5,500 volunteered for ground duties. See also CARIBBEAN AT WAR.

Brooke, Field Marshal Sir Alan (1883–1963), British *Chief of the Imperial General Staff (CIGS) from December 1941 to January 1946 and a member of the *Combined Chiefs of Staff committee who, with Churchill, 'formed an incomparable partnership in the higher direction of the Second World War' (David Fraser in J. Keegan, ed., *Churchill's Generals*, London, 1991, p. 101).

Brooke was the ninth and youngest child of parents who were both of ancient Ulster lineage. However, his mother preferred France to Fermanagh, and it was there that Brooke was born and brought up and went to school. After attending Woolwich Military Academy he joined the Royal Artillery and during the *First World War rose from lieutenant to lt-colonel. At the battle of the Somme he introduced the first 'creeping barrage' with great success and his incisiveness and efficiency marked him out between the wars as an officer of outstanding merit.

He was promoted maj-general in 1935 and in 1937 commanded the first Mobile Division, the prototype of the later armoured divisions. In 1938 he was promoted lt-general and was given command of the newly reshaped Anti-Aircraft Corps which soon expanded into the Anti-Aircraft Command. In August 1939 he became C-in-C Southern Command and from the following month commanded the *British Expeditionary Force's 2nd Corps in France.

During the fighting which led to the fall of *France in June 1940 Brooke showed consummate skill in extracting his corps and organizing its retreat to *Dunkirk, but he was recalled to London before the evacuation and ordered to form an Allied bridgehead in Brittany, which proved impossible. Shortly afterwards he was promoted general and was made C-in-C, Home Forces, in which post he reorganized the remnants of the British Army and prepared for a German invasion.

In December 1941 he replaced *Dill as CIGS and became the chairman of the *Chiefs of Staff committee in March 1942. As principal military adviser to the war cabinet, he was at Churchill's elbow during nearly all the Allied conferences (see GRAND ALLIANCE) and by his side when all the crucial military decisions were made. He saw it as his task to steer Churchill away from some of his more improbable schemes, though he managed to turn others into military realities. That they could disagree—and often did so with some vehemence—yet still work amicably together was of inestimable importance in the running of the war. On one occasion, thwarted by Brooke over some cherished project, Churchill exploded that the CIGS hated him and must go. When told this, Brooke replied: 'I don't hate him, I love him, but when the day comes that I tell him he is right when I believe him to be wrong, it will be time for him to get rid of me.' Later in the war Brooke believed Churchill was losing his grip, and he was perhaps over-hasty in condemning the prime minister's political vision, which was wider than his own.

Brooke communicated his ideas in a way which was at once lucid and compelling, a priceless asset when dealing with Churchill and in negotiating with the Americans.

The US *Joint Chiefs of Staff were wary of the speed and clarity of his thinking—he never did get on with *Marshall—but they soon accepted that they were dealing with someone who was ruthlessly professional, and his advice, especially early on, carried great weight. Brooke's other strength was the great skill with which he chose his generals and the loyalty with which he backed them. *Alexander, *Montgomery, and *Slim were among his protégés and after the war Montgomery wrote to him: 'I can only say again that any success I may have achieved in the field is due basically to you: it is all your doing.'

Brooke had little opportunity for active command. Churchill offered him the post of C-in-C Middle East in succession to *Auchinleck in August 1942, but Brooke had only been CIGS eight months and he decided he would serve his country better by remaining at Churchill's side. However, he was bitterly disappointed when *Eisenhower was offered the post of Supreme Commander for the Normandy landings (see OVERLORD), the more so because Churchill had earlier promised Brooke that he should have it. His passion for ornithology helped him bear the great strain of high command with marvellous equanimity, and he would take time off in the afternoons to feed the birds in St James's Park and so be fresh for Churchill's long, late-night meetings.

Promoted field marshal in 1944, when peace came Brooke received high honours from the Allied nations. He was knighted in 1940, created Baron Alanbrooke of Brookeborough in September 1945, and was later created a viscount.

Bryant, A. (ed.), *The Turn of the Tide, 1939–1943* and *Triumph in the West, 1943–1946*. A History of the War Years based on the diaries of Field Marshal Lord Alanbrooke, Chief of the Imperial General Staff (London, 1957, 1959).

Fraser, D., *Alanbrooke* (London, 1982).

Brooke-Popham, Air Chief Marshal Sir (Henry) Robert (1878–1953), British airman who returned to the RAF in 1939 after serving as governor and C-in-C Kenya. He led the mission to Canada which helped form the *British Empire Air Training Scheme, and then went to South Africa to help that country form its own air training scheme. In October 1940 he was appointed to the newly created post of C-in-C Far East. This made him responsible to the British *Chiefs of Staff for the defences of Singapore, Malaya, Burma, British Borneo, and Hong Kong. His appointment, which 'was designed to solve the problem of co-ordinating the defence of that area, did little more than add another cog to an already somewhat complex machine. Since control of naval forces was excluded, there were two Commanders-in-Chief in Singapore, each responsible to a different authority in London. The Governors of the Straits Settlements (see MALAYA, Hong Kong, and Burma) received their policy directives from the Colonial Office while, for the administration and financing of local defence, the General Officers Commanding, Malaya, Hong Kong, and Burma, continued to be responsible to the War Office, and the Air Officer Commanding, Far East, to the Air Ministry' (S. W. Kirby, *The War Against Japan*, Vol. 1, London, 1957, p. 51).

To add to this recipe for disaster, Brooke-Popham was not an inspiring leader and he was somewhat out of touch with ideas of modern warfare. His recommendations for increased forces, particularly *air power, were largely ignored and he did little to press them. Inevitably, he was blamed for the disasters which followed; he was replaced by Lt-General Henry Pownall on 27 December 1941 and retired in May 1942. He was knighted in 1927. See also AUTOMEDON.

Browning, Lt-General Frederick (1896–1965), British Army officer who pioneered the employment of British airborne forces and oversaw their use in the *Bruneval raid and during the *North African and *Sicilian campaigns. From January 1944 he commanded the 1st Airborne Corps which was subsequently employed during the Normandy landings in June 1944 (see OVERLORD). He then became deputy commander of the First Allied Airborne Army and took a leading part in the planning of *MARKET-GARDEN, the objective of which was to create a bridgehead across several water obstacles, the furthest being the River Rhine at Arnhem. ('I think,' he said to *Montgomery when they discussed the operation prior to its launch on 17 September 1944, 'we might be going a bridge too far.') In November 1944 he was appointed *Mountbatten's Chief of Staff at *South-East Asia Command.

Bruneval raid. British airborne operation mounted on the night of 27/28 February 1942 to obtain details and parts of the German Würzburg *radar set adapted to control night fighters opposing the Allied *strategic air offensive against Germany (see also KAMMHUBER LINE). After *photographic reconnaissance had revealed a set at Bruneval near Le Havre, details of the area and the defences were obtained from further air reconnaissance and from the French resistance. Diversionary bombing raids were then mounted while paratroops and an RAF radar mechanic were dropped close by. After overcoming opposition, the force took parts of the Würzburg back to the UK by sea for examination. Its capture proved a valuable aid in the *electronic warfare both sides were waging and the raid's success ensured the future of British paratroops.

Millar, G., *The Bruneval Raid* (London, 1974).

BRUTUS, see GARBY-CZERNIAWSKI.

Buchenwald, a *concentration camp situated near Weimar in central Germany. It opened in July 1937 and supplied *forced labour to local armament manufacturers. It is estimated that out of the 238,980 imprisoned there over eight years, 56,545 died, yet it contained more long-term survivors than most concentration camps. Its 20,000 inmates rose in revolt on 11 April 1945 so that it was already liberated when the US Army arrived there that afternoon. See also FINAL SOLUTION.

Buckmaster, Colonel Maurice (1902–92), public relations expert, intelligence officer with the *British Expeditionary Force in France, 1939–40, and on the *Dakar expedition, head of *SOE's F (independent French) section, 1941–4. Tall, with a buoyant personality and outgoing manners, he encouraged many successful agents, whose spirits he did much to keep up. About 470 were sent—the exact number has never been settled—and almost one in four of them, instead of the expected one in two, were lost. He was occasionally outwitted by the *Gestapo. Forbidden to go on operations himself, he conducted a triumphal tour of France in the autumn of 1944, rewarding loyal assistants after the liberation, and made sure his section was not forgotten when *decorations were distributed. M. R. D. FOOT

Bucovina, see BUKOVINA.

Budapest, siege of. In December 1944, as the Red Army's Second and Third Ukrainian *fronts*, commanded by Marshal *Malinovsky and General *Tolbukhin respectively, began surrounding the Hungarian capital, Hitler issued a directive that it become a fortress, that is that it must be held to the last man. Making it a fortress did not prove difficult, for Buda on the river Danube's west bank was dominated by the Gelerthey Heights and Palace Hill; while Pest on the east bank had solidly-built government buildings and factories which were easily fortified.

By 26 December the city was surrounded, but it was strongly held by four German divisions (13th Panzer, *SS Feldherrnhalle, and two SS cavalry divisions), and Soviet units could not get beyond the outer suburbs. A German counter-attack, by the 4th Panzer Corps, almost succeeded and on 24 January came within 25 km. (15 mi.) of the city's southern suburbs. The German defenders could now have broken out, but Hitler wanted Budapest defended and was not interested in having its garrison rescued.

Though Tolbukhin was under severe pressure on the Danube's west bank, on the eastern side Malinovsky's troops penetrated the Pest suburbs and his artillery began pounding German defensive positions in Buda. On 12 January, when the specially formed Budapest Group Corps drove for the city centre, the Germans disputed every street and every building. It took six days for Malinovsky to take Pest and the Germans lost 35,000 killed and 62,000 taken prisoner. Then, as Tolbukhin parried further German armoured thrusts, Malinovsky mounted an attack on Buda. But the German garrison, well entrenched in the heights, held out until 13 February before capitulating. Malinovsky took another 30,000 prisoners and three days later the remnants of the garrison, some 16,000 strong, were surrounded and destroyed while attempting to break out to the north-west. See also GERMAN–SOVIET WAR, 10 and 11.

Budenny, Marshal Semyon (1883–1973), a legendary hero of the Russian Civil War, owing to his having commanded Stalin's much-vaunted creation, the First Cavalry Army, Budenny became a marshal in 1935. In 1941, as first deputy defence commissar and a member of the *Stavka, Stalin's general headquarters committee, he co-ordinated the South-West and South *fronts* (army groups) during the encirclement of *Kiev (August–September) and thereafter (until 15 October) took over the Reserve *front* in the *Moscow sector. In the 1942 summer campaign (see GERMAN–SOVIET WAR, 4) he commanded the North Caucasus *front* until September, when it was dissolved after having been practically driven out of the North Caucasus region. In 1943, the title Commander of Red Army Cavalry was created for him, and thereafter he was engaged in trying to devise a place for cavalry in mechanized warfare. EARL ZIEMKE

Bukovina, historically a Romanian territory whose northern part was demanded in an ultimatum presented by the Soviet government to Romania on 26 June 1940 (see Map 80). Despite the fact that northern Bukovina had never formed part of the Russian Empire, the USSR was able to base its claim on the fact that the predominant majority of this part of the province was Ukrainian (300,000 Ukrainians, 50,000 Romanians). This area of roughly 6,000 sq. km. (2,315 sq. mi.) was ceded by Romania and incorporated into the Ukrainian Soviet Socialist Republic. The recovery of Northern Bukovina and Bessarabia was the principal motive for Romania's involvement in the German invasion of the Soviet Union on 22 June 1941 (see BARBAROSSA) and was achieved by 27 July at the cost of 10,486 Romanian dead (see ROMANIA, 4(a)). In the winter of 1941–2 there were massive *deportations of Jews and gypsies from the whole of Bukovina to camps in Transnistria, an area of the Ukraine Romania annexed in August 1941, where many died at the hands of German and Romanian units. Bukovina was overrun by the Red Army in the early autumn of 1944 and its northern part reincorporated into the Ukrainian SSR.

DENNIS DELETANT

Dima, N., *Bessarabia and Bukovina: the Soviet–Romanian territorial dispute* (Boulder, Colo., 1982).

Manoliu-Manea, M. (ed.), *The Tragic Plight of a Border Area: Bessarabia and Bucovina* (Los Angeles, 1983).

Bulgaria, (see Map B). Balkan monarchy with a population of 6,341,000 (1940) which, by September 1939, was the only power defeated in 1918 not to have received some territorial redress. This, plus the predominance of Germany in Bulgaria's external trade and as a supplier of arms, acted as a strong impulse driving Bulgaria towards the Axis. However, King Boris III (1894–1943), who dominated foreign policy-making, was not prepared to make a definite commitment to either side. He wanted to keep Bulgaria neutral and hoped that an Anglo-German settlement might be achieved before the Balkans were affected by the conflict. The *Nazi–Soviet Pact of August 1939 eased his position in that his predominantly Russophile people and his mainly pro-German officer corps were content with this uncommitted policy.

On 7 September 1940 Bulgaria received its first territorial compensation when the Treaty of Craiova (see ROMANIA, 3) returned to it Southern Dobruja. Thereafter the pressures from Germany to join the *Tripartite Pact increased sharply. Bulgarian receptivity to such pressure also increased when it became known that the November talks between *Ribbentrop and *Molotov had raised the prospect that Bulgaria be included in the Soviet sphere of influence. The possibility of British intervention in Greece (see BALKAN CAMPAIGN) and Hitler's preparations for the attack on the Soviet Union (see BARBAROSSA) increased Bulgaria's strategic significance and King Boris's government committed itself to joining the Axis at an unspecified future date. When the Germans became involved in the Balkan campaign by invading Greece (Operation MARITA), they first had to cross Bulgaria and therefore on 1 March 1941 Minister President Bogdan Filov signed an agreement in Vienna whereby Bulgaria entered the Tripartite Pact and the following day German troops crossed the Danube en route to Greece (see also AXIS STRATEGY AND CO-OPERATION.) As a result the UK severed diplomatic relations with Bulgaria on 5 March, but it was not until 13 December that Bulgaria declared war on both the UK and the USA; Sofia hoped, in vain, that this would be a 'platonic war'. Bulgaria never declared war on the USSR, King Boris insisting that his army was not equipped for a modern, mechanized conflict, and that its peasant conscripts would not fight effectively far from their Balkan homes; furthermore, Bulgarian troops would be needed to contain any possible forward move by the Turks, and to counter partisan activity and any projected Allied landing in the Balkans. Boris also feared that the extreme right might use a successful Bulgarian military leader to impose a republican, fascist regime.

Although a member of the Axis, Bulgaria's interests and activities remained purely Balkan. Bulgarian troops took part in the invasion of Yugoslavia, and in the subsequent partition of that country Bulgaria was given the right to administer a large share of Yugoslav Macedonia; full ownership was to await a peace treaty at the end of the war. When Greece was conquered the Bulgarians were given similar rights in eastern Macedonia and most of western Thrace, though much of Macedonia, including Salonika, remained under German control.

The Bulgarians had always regarded Macedonia as theirs by right. Their rule therefore saw the introduction of Bulgarian education, including the establishment of a university in Skoplje, and the incorporation of Macedonia into the Bulgarian Church. However, they overplayed their hand: excessive centralization, graft, and corruption eventually made Sofia's emissaries as unpopular in Macedonia as their Serbian predecessors had been. In Thrace there was not even an initial honeymoon. By September 1941 the harshness of Bulgarian rule enabled local opposition to stage a rising, based on Dráma, which was suppressed with great ferocity.

In military terms Bulgaria's contribution to the German conquest of the Balkans was a minor one. The Bulgarians, with the help of an armoured German division, were to guard the Wehrmacht's left flank during MARITA, and after the defeat of Yugoslavia and Greece three divisions of the Bulgarian Second and Fifth Armies were moved into Macedonia and Thrace to allow the Germans to concentrate their forces elsewhere. German attempts to persuade Boris to commit men, even volunteers, to the *German–Soviet war were resolutely resisted, particularly after *Stalingrad, and in the summer of 1943 the king even refused to extend Bulgaria's commitment against the partisans in Yugoslavia and Albania. In the *Black Sea, Bulgaria's few minor warships were restricted to escorting *convoys.

Just as it refused to make a full commitment to the Nazi war effort, so in its internal affairs Bulgaria rejected some important aspects of Hitler's New Order in Europe (see GERMANY, 4). But compromises were inescapable. In July 1940, partially to parry German pressure to sign the Tripartite Pact, Bulgaria promised to institute measures against its Jews (see also FINAL SOLUTION). The Freemasons were ordered to dissolve their lodges, which occasioned not a little embarrassment as many Bulgarian politicians, including Filov and most of his cabinet, were Masons. The Jewish question did not allow of such an easy solution. There was little *anti-Semitism in Bulgaria, where Jews formed only 1% of the population. German pressure forced the Bulgarian government to promulgate a 'Defence of the Nation Act' in October 1940, the bill being passed by parliament in December. The Bill forbade sexual relations, inside or outside marriage, between Jews and non-Jews, Jews were not to hold land, they were to be banned from the army, and certain industries, including publishing, and were to be subjected to a *numerus clausus* in the free professions. The definition of 'Jewish' was, however, religious rather than racial and rapid conversion offered an escape for many Jews.
The king accepted this distasteful legislation on the assumption that it was better for Bulgaria itself to introduce it rather than have it imposed from without. Further restrictions on the Jews were to follow in January 1941 and in 1942 but Boris, with the demonstrably passionate backing of all but the extreme right-wing, adamantly refused to deport Bulgarian Jews. Those living in areas under Bulgarian occupation could not be saved, but the 55,000 Jews of Bulgaria proper survived, although they had to be sent to provincial labour camps and labouring gangs.

In political terms Bulgaria remained under authoritarian rather than totalitarian rule. Filov and his cabinet were essentially controlled by King Boris and his close circle of advisers and there was little real opposition in parliament. The government acted severely against attempted communist subversion, which flared up briefly after 22 June 1941, while the extreme right suffered the loss of a prominent leader when General Hristo Loukov, a pro-German hero of the *First World War, was murdered in February 1943.

The most important domestic political development came on 28 August 1943 with the death of King Boris. Given his age (he was only 49) and the fact that he had recently had a stormy meeting with Hitler, there were inevitably rumours that he had been poisoned. If that was the case, the instigators of the act have never been revealed. The king's death made great difficulties for Bulgaria. Boris had already begun to seek an escape from the war; the regency which followed moved along the same path but did not have his skill, his experience, or his authority, both at home and abroad.

Filov was replaced as premier on 14 September by Dobri Bozhilov, who intensified negotiations with the western Allies but was at the same time desperate to avoid the fate visited upon Italy and Hungary when they attempted to slip the Nazi noose.

Soon after the death of King Boris the war reached the Bulgarian population. There had been small bombing raids upon Sofia and other centres since 1941 but it was not until 19 November 1943 that the first heavy attack was experienced. More followed and after a huge onslaught on 30 March 1944 on Sofia many of the capital's population fled to the countryside.

By late 1943 the Bulgarian urban population was suffering from increasing food shortages. In May 1940 the government had set up the Directorate of Civilian Mobilization, which had wide powers to conscript economic enterprises in the event of war; in the following month a Directorate for Foreign Trade was established. A centralized grain purchasing agency, Hranoiznos, had been in existence since the early 1930s and had expanded its operations to include other products. After March 1941 central control of these crops meant requisitioning for sale in Germany and, particularly after the severe drought of 1942, for supplying the Bulgarian Army. Too much was taken and to make matters worse peasants switched rapidly to unregulated crops such as potatoes and beans where larger profits were to be made. Bread rationing and meatless days were introduced and by 1944 official food prices in Sofia were 563% of their 1939 levels, while on the black market, frequently the only source of supply, they were 738%. Consumer goods were also less plentiful both because Bulgarian industry had moved towards war production and because armaments made up an ever-increasing proportion of Bulgarian imports.

Although the Bulgarian terrain is well-suited to resistance activity, such activity was not widespread. Some communists were landed in 1941 but they were soon rounded up. Acts of murder and sabotage were isolated and not effective, at least until the spring of 1944. By that time a maximum of 18,000 partisans, organized into eleven brigades, had enlisted with the forces of the Otechestven Front (Fatherland Front), a coalition formed in 1941 of communists, left-wing Agrarians, Zvenari (an authoritarian group responsible for a *coup d'état* in 1934), and Social Democrats.

Support for the Fatherland Front increased as a result of Allied bombing, the advances of the Red Army, and Soviet diplomatic pressure applied in Sofia after April 1944 demanding that Bulgaria leave the Axis. By July Bozhilov had given way to Ivan Bagrianov who was known to have pro-western feelings. His attempts to extricate Bulgaria from the war before the Red Army arrived on the Danube were wrecked by the Romanian coup of 23 August (see ROMANIA, 3). By early September the Soviets were exercising immense pressure for a Bulgarian declaration of war on Germany. This another new prime minister, Konstantin Muraviev, conceded on 8 September. On the same day Soviet forces crossed into Bulgaria. On 9 September the Fatherland Front, aided by a partisan detachment, engineered a bloodless coup in Sofia. The communists secured control of the ministries of the interior and justice whilst in the provinces local Fatherland Front committees instituted savage purges of their former opponents.

After the coup the Bulgarian Army joined the campaign against Germany. Some 339,000 troops of the First, Second, and Fourth Bulgarian Armies were attached to *Tolbukhin's Third Ukrainian *front* (army group) and fought their way through the Balkans and eventually into Hungary and Austria. The cost was 32,000 killed, many of them in the bitter battles for *Budapest and, early in March 1945, in the German counter-attack south of Lake Balaton (See also GERMAN–SOVIET WAR, 11).

The Bulgarian Army was also remodelled on the Soviet pattern. On 20 September 1944 'assistant commanders', i.e. political commissars, were appointed and in the following weeks 800 officers were removed for political reasons. In December 1944 Colonel Ivan Kinov, who had served for many years in the Red Army, was appointed C-in-C.

By the end of the fighting in Europe the communists were entrenching their position inside Bulgaria.

RICHARD CRAMPTON

Groueff, S., *Crown of Thorns* (Lanham, Md., 1987).
Hoppe, H.-J., *Bulgarien—Hitlers eigenwilliger Verbündeter* (Stuttgart, 1979).
Miller, M. L., *Bulgaria During the Second World War* (Stanford, Calif., 1975).

Bulge, battle of the, see ARDENNES CAMPAIGN.

Bullet Decree (*Kugelerlass*), issued by the German High Command (OKW) in March 1944. It ordered that all escaped and recaptured *prisoners-of-war, with the exception of American and British nationals, were to be handed over to the Sicherheitsdienst (see RSHA) and transferred to *Mauthausen to be shot.

Buna, battle for, fought during the *New Guinea campaign when, in November 1942, two Allied divisions assaulted a Japanese beachhead established on Papua's north-eastern coast the previous July. While the 7th Australian Division attacked the 18 km. (11 mi.) well-fortified perimeter at its north-western end (see GONA), the 32nd US Division advanced on Buna village and mission at the south-eastern end, and two airstrips on nearby Cape Endaiadere. The numbers defending the perimeter had been badly underestimated, and the raw 32nd Division was untrained in jungle warfare and inadequately equipped. Casualties mounted and on 30 November *MacArthur ordered *Eichelberger, to the front to take Buna 'or not come back alive'.

Eichelberger found demoralized, half-starved men in rags, many of them riddled with malaria (see also MEDICINE). He relieved most senior officers, improved supplies and brought in armour and reinforcement. Helped by a fresh battalion airlifted to the front, Buna village was taken on 14 December. But the Japanese around the mission held out until 2 January 1943, the same day as Cape Endaiadere was seized, and it took another three weeks of hard fighting to clear the beachhead completely.

MacArthur's reputation hung by a thread at Buna. It was saved by Eichelberger and his 32nd Division whose losses, out of 10,825 frontline troops, amounted to 9,688, including 7,125 sick, a casualty rate of almost 90%. Never again did US troops go into battle with so little preparation and such inadequate *logistics.

Burcorps, contraction of Burma Corps, which was formed on 19 March 1942 by the British C-in-C Burma, *Alexander. It comprised nearly all the British forces fighting the Japanese in the *Burma campaign: the 1st Burma Division, 17th Indian Division, and 7th Armoured Brigade and was commanded by *Slim. After it escaped into India it became part of 4th Corps.

Bureau Central de Rensignements et d'Action (BCRA) (Central Bureau of Information and Action) was the intelligence service of de *Gaulle and the Free French, formed in January 1942 and headed by André *Dewavrin alias Colonel Passy. Its original title was BCRAM, but the 'M' (*militaire*) was dropped in July 1942 when a sixth, non-military, section was added to the other five. The sections were: command, including liaison with Allied commands; intelligence, including liaison with *MI6; recruitment and assignment of agents (see also SPIES), including liaison with *SOE; counter-intelligence, including liaison with *MI5; and a technical section dealing with ciphers, accounts, and similar matters.

Burma. (For the fighting in Burma see BURMA CAMPAIGN, below.) British colony, the largest country on the South-East Asia mainland, with an area of 680,000 sq. km. (262,000 sq. m.). It is a country of contrasts: high mountains, jungle hills, swampy coastal plains, alluvial deltas, with a dry central plain at its core. It is affected by a monsoon biannually and malaria was endemic (see MEDICINE). There are several large rivers running north to south—Chindwin, Irrawaddy, Sittang, Salween—and these were the principal means of communication, the Irrawaddy Flotilla Company (see also FORCE VIPER) running regular services along the 1,300 km. (800 mi.) navigable length of the river, as well as on the Chindwin. Almost all the roads and railways which connected the capital, Rangoon, with inland towns ran north–south, too, though the *Burma Road, opened in 1938, ran eastwards from Lashio into China.

The country's central plain is ringed on all sides by mountains (reaching to 6,000 m./20,000 ft. in the far north), which in 1941 were populated by about a million hill tribesmen (Kachins, Chins, Nagas). The balance of the 17 million population—10 million Burmans, 4 million Karens, and 2 million Shans—inhabited the rest of the country. As the British had made Burma administratively part of India in 1862, there was also an immigrant Indian population of about one million which held great power in the country's bureaucracy and trade. Many of these died when they fled to India in front of the advancing Japanese.

Under the government of Burma Act of 1935, Burma ceased to be governed from India in 1937, and a House of Representatives and a Senate were established. The former had 123 seats and was to be elected every five years; half of the latter was appointed by the governor (Reginald Dorman-Smith from May 1941). About a third of the male population, and about 10% of the women, were enfranchised. The governor retained control of such crucial matters as foreign affairs, the administration of the hill tribes, and the country's defence. The Burmese also had no control over the economy of their country. Their natural resources of timber—they were the world's greatest exporter of teak—oil, rubber, and tungsten (see also RAW AND SYNTHETIC MATERIALS) remained under British control, while the Chinese and Indians, Burma's entrepreneurs, handled the rice trade to which 70% of Burma's agriculture was committed. The main oil wells were at Yenangyaung and the oil was then piped direct to refinery plants around Syriam, south-east of Rangoon. The mines at Mawchi produced 10% of the world's tungsten supplies.

The Burmans and the Shans were Buddhists. The former lived in central Burma; the latter mostly on the country's central and north-eastern borders. The Burmans had ruled Burma until the British, from 1824, progressively took it over, and the educated minority did not want colonial rule. There was a long history of civil disturbances during the 1930s and two premiers, *Ba Maw and U *Saw, negotiated secretly with the Japanese to oust the British, as did the *Thakin student leader *Aung San. But the Karens, who were mostly Christians and lived in the Irrawaddy delta and in the hills between the Sittang and Salween rivers, were pro-British, as colonial rule had suppressed persecution of them by the Burmans. The

Kachins, Chins, and Nagas were pro-British, too, and had long provided men for the local militia and police. After the Japanese occupation of Burma the British raised levies from them and they provided members of *V-Force.

At the time of the Japanese invasion there were 27,000 troops garrisoning Burma: 15,000 were indigenous Burmese, most of whom were serving as infantry in the Burma Frontier Force and the 1st and 2nd Burma Rifles. The Burma Rifles, which normally took recruits only from the Karens, Kachins, and Chins, had formed extra battalions by recruiting Burmans. By December 1941 this had brought the number of native battalions up to fourteen, and these were divided among the brigades of the 1st Burma Division which had been formed in July 1941. The only local artillery belonged to the Burma Auxiliary Force, a territorial unit manned by Europeans, Anglo-Burmans, and Anglo-Indians, and the Burma Royal Naval Volunteer Reserve possessed just five motor launches and a few miscellaneous vessels. All these units fought with the British forces defending Burma, but, like them, they were no match for the Japanese. Many escaped to India with those British forces that had survived, others just melted away, but by the end of the Burma campaign in August 1945 thirteen battalions, all drawn from the Kachins, Karens, and Chins, had been re-formed. In March 1945 Karen levies some 10,000 strong, armed and led by British officers, played an important role in preventing the Japanese from reinforcing Toungoo in southern Burma from the east, and they killed many thousands of them.

Once the British had been ousted from Burma in 1942 the Japanese initially entrusted the civil administration of some occupied areas to the *Burma Independence Army (BIA). However, this was not successful and the BIA was responsible for some unpleasant atrocities against the minority populations. Then, in May 1942, Thakin Tun Oke, a Burmese dissident trained in Japanese administration, was appointed to head a Central Burmese government (Bama Baho) which concluded a treaty with the Japanese, but in August this was replaced by a more extensive civilian administration under Ba Maw. The Burmans, having looked to the Japanese to rid them of the British, now looked to them for their freedom. But though Burma was given independence in August 1943, when Ba Maw formed a one-party state and declared war on the Allies, the country remained subservient to the Japanese occupying forces. It was stripped of two Shan states, Kengtun and Mongpan, which were given to Thailand, and remained firmly part of the Japanese *Greater East Asia Co-Prosperity Sphere. By 1944 many Burmans were working secretly against the Japanese, just as they had earlier worked against the British, and in August 1944 Aung San formed the Anti-Fascist Organization (later the Anti-Fascist People's Freedom League), an underground, communist-inspired movement to fight the Japanese. Aung San, who had served as his country's minister of defence after independence, defected with his army to the British in March 1945. He later formed the first post-war administration and negotiated Burma's independence with the British, but he was assassinated on the orders of U Saw shortly before Burma was declared an independent state on 4 January 1948. LOUIS ALLEN

Ba Maw, *Breakthrough in Burma* (New Haven, Conn., 1968).
Thakin Nu, *Burma under The Japanese* (London, 1954).

Burma campaign (see Map 19). Waged between the Japanese and the Allies, this was the longest campaign in which the British Army participated during the Second World War, lasting from December 1941 to August 1945. However, 'British' is a totally inappropriate description as Indian troops predominated within *Slim's victorious Fourteenth Army and a wide variety of races, including Burmese, Chinese, Chins, Gurkhas, Kachins, Karens, Nagas, and black troops from British East Africa and British West Africa also took part. Ultimate victory was therefore principally won not by the Americans and the British, but by the Indian Army, albeit under British leadership. It was fought over equally diverse terrain which included not only jungle but mountains, open plains, coastal waters, and wide rivers, too. On the plains, during the *Imphal campaign, tanks played an essential role, while air transport and supply gave the campaign a vital additional dimension.

Japan's initial purpose in invading Burma was to protect the flank of its troops fighting in the *Malayan campaign and the capture of *Singapore. Later the occupation of the country, which effectively closed the only remaining supply route to China of any consequence (see BURMA ROAD), provided the westernmost bastion of the newly extended Japanese empire. Even in the days of utter defeat in 1945, the Japanese Army held on to a corner of Tenasserim to block any Allied overland advance on Bangkok. Burma was also a shop-window. The granting of a form of independence to it in August 1943, however inadequate, gave some substance to Japanese claims to be liberators of South-East Asia from the colonial powers (see GREATER EAST ASIAN CO-PROSPERITY SPHERE). Finally, in the view of the Japanese prime minister General *Tōjō, as well as in that of Lt-General *Mutaguchi who launched the Imphal offensive into Manipur State, Burma was the stepping-stone to India.

The British wanted to retake a country lost by military defeat and to avenge that defeat, but the means to that end were not always clear. During most of the campaign, higher command in London and Washington envisaged by-passing the rigours of an overland battle in order to capture Rangoon by sea. The British wanted Rangoon as a staging post to Singapore; the Americans wanted it, at least until the *Ledo Road was completed, in order to clear the road from Rangoon north into China. Churchill also favoured such ventures as a landing on the northern tip of Sumatra (CULVERIN), and the appointment of Admiral *Mountbatten, former Chief of *Combined Operations, to command *South-East Asia Command (SEAC) in September 1943 clearly fore-shadowed

Burma campaign

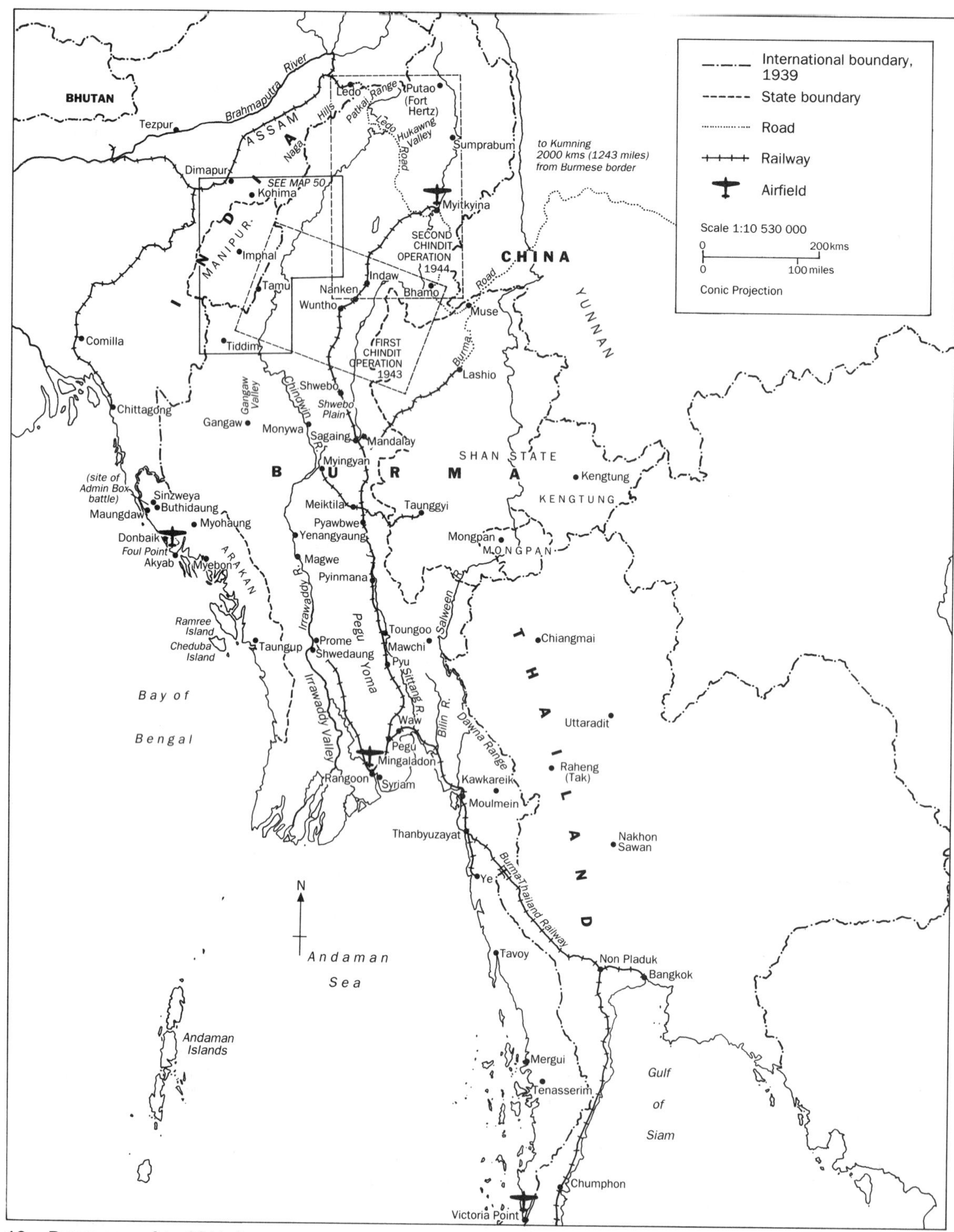

19. **Burma campaign**, 1941–5

The **Burma campaign** was the longest land campaign of the war. This photograph shows British troops in action with a 4.2 in. mortar during the fighting for Meiktila, February–March 1945.

*amphibious warfare playing the main role. This never happened, largely because the necessary *landing craft were not made available from other theatres. In the end, although Rangoon was taken from the sea by an amphibious hook, the fact that the city was deserted when the British entered it was due to their victorious advance overland. And this advance was, in turn, created by Slim's decisive defeat of Mutaguchi's Imphal offensive which was launched in March 1944.

The USA saw in Burma the last means available to feed supplies to *Chiang Kai-shek and thus keep China in the war against Japan (see also CHINA INCIDENT). This in turn would draw off large Japanese forces which might otherwise intervene in the *Pacific war and would also provide air bases in China from which long-range bombers could bomb industrial centres in Japan (see also STRATEGIC AIR OFFENSIVES, 3). The USA was therefore concerned chiefly with the campaign in North Burma to permit a road and an oil pipeline to be opened from Ledo in Assam to Kunming in Yunnan, and soon after this was achieved in January 1945 the American contribution to the Burma campaign effectively ceased (see CHINA–BURMA–INDIA THEATRE). Under Chiang Kai-shek, China saw the training and equipping of its forces in India as a contribution to the solving of post-war internal disputes rather than as a full participation in Allied offensives. The British found US support for Nationalist China misplaced. Neither India, which provided the bulk of the fighting power for the Allied forces, nor Burma, which was their battleground, was consulted by the Americans or the British in the planning of the campaign.

The first Japanese move into Burma was when Victoria Point and its airfield, at the southernmost tip of Burma adjacent to Thailand, were occupied by Uno Force (143rd Infantry Regiment, 55th Division) on 14 December 1941. This prevented air reinforcements reaching Malaya from India. Then, on 19 January 1942, two divisions (33rd and 55th) of Lt-General Iida Shojiro's Fifteenth Army, supported by the 10th Air Brigade and guided by rebels of the *Burma Independence Army, took Tavoy and attacked Kawkareik and Moulmein from Thailand across the Dawna Range. The 17th Indian Division, commanded by Maj-General John Smyth, planned to fight behind a succession of river barriers—the Salween, Bilin, and Sittang—but the blowing of the *Sittang Bridge on 23 February ended in disaster and Smyth's dismissal. Rangoon was taken by the 33rd Japanese Division on 8 March; and the Burma Army under Lt-General *Alexander, who had recently superseded Lt-General Tom Hutton, narrowly evaded capture when a Japanese roadblock on the Prome road prevented their escape northwards. They attacked it several times without success but the local Japanese commander, sticking rigidly to his divisional commander's plan, then withdrew it in order to enter Rangoon, as ordered, from the west.

Chinese reinforcements, reluctantly accepted by the head of *ABDA Command, Lt-General *Wavell, came south as far as Toungoo, but were pushed back by the advance of the 56th Division which, with the 18th Division, had reinforced Iida's Fifteenth Army by advancing through the Shan States from Thailand. The 38th Chinese Division helped extricate the 1st Burma Division from defeat at Yenangyaung before marching out through Imphal to be re-formed in India. In March Slim took command of the newly constituted *Burcorps, which comprised most of what remained of the British Forces in Burma, and led it back to India in a fighting retreat, the longest in the history of the British Army, which was completed by May 1942.

Iida's 18th and 56th Divisions reached the Chinese frontier at the end of April and the northernmost point reached by the Japanese, Sumprabum, was captured on 17 June. Akyab, with its airfields on the Bay of Bengal, was in Japanese hands on 4 May. Taking over as C-in-C, India, after the collapse of his ABDA command, Wavell had already begun to plan the recapture of Burma in April, but the 14th Indian Division's attempt to re-take Akyab in December 1942 ended in failure. There was a brief pause before it tried to take Akyab again, and failed again, and an attempt to reach Donbaik was repulsed in March 1943. After months of fighting, the British in Arakan were back where they had been in October 1942. In the meantime in northern Burma Brigadier *Wingate launched his *Chindits on 13 February 1943 in an operation (LONGCLOTH) which penetrated behind Japanese lines, using air supply. He lost one third of his 3,000 men, but the subsequent publicity boosted British morale and valuable lessons were learned on the use of air supply.

In March 1943 the Japanese reorganized their higher command, creating the Burma Area Army under Lt-General Kawabe Masakazu and placing Mutaguchi, the commander of 18th Division, in command of the Fifteenth Army in succession to Iida. Burma's independence, under Japanese aegis, was proclaimed in August 1943. The Allies also reorganized their higher command by forming SEAC in September and the Fourteenth Army—previously India's Eastern Army—under Slim in October; it came under SEAC's newly formed 11th Army Group, not under C-in-C India. A counter-offensive was now planned, to take three forms. In Arakan, Slim's 15th Corps, commanded by Lt-General *Christison, would advance southwards and take Akyab. Secondly, a combined force of American-trained Chinese and US infantry (see GALAHAD) under Lt-General *Stilwell's Northern Combat Area Command would co-operate with Chiang Kai-shek's forces from Yunnan to take the Hukawng Valley and occupy *Myitkyina. This would permit the completion of the Ledo Road from Assam to take supplies to Kunming in China, thus replacing the old Burma Road, now in Japanese hands. The advance was to be supported by a second Wingate Chindit expedition, six brigades strong, most of which would be air-transported across the Japanese lines of communication facing Stilwell. Thirdly, on the central (Assam) front, the 17th and 20th Indian Divisions of Slim's 4th Corps, commanded by Lt-General Scoones, would push forward stocks and reconnaissance patrols into Burma via Tiddim and Tamu respectively. To oppose this counter-offensive further Japanese armies were created—the Twenty-eighth Army, commanded by Lt-General Sakurai Shōzō, in the Arakan, and Thirty-third Army, commanded by Lt-General Honda Masaki, in North Burma—and two Japanese operations were planned to anticipate it. HA-GŌ was designed to surround, trap, and annihilate two of Christison's divisions (5th and 7th) in the Arakan (see ADMIN BOX). This would prevent reinforcements being sent from there to the Central Front, and would also serve to distract Allied attention from U-GŌ, the Imphal offensive, which was a much more ambitious plan for the invasion of India across the Chindwin into Manipur State. When both these operations failed Kawabe and Mutaguchi were sacked and the entire staff of the Fifteenth Army, save one, were dismissed. The failure of the Imphal offensive was the biggest defeat the Japanese Army had known in its entire history. The Allied divisions pursued the Japanese to the Chindwin, and then began to cross it back into Burma in December 1944.

North of the Central Front, where Stilwell was opposed by Honda, a combined force of two Chinese divisions and GALAHAD had, by March 1944, taken the whole of the Hukawng Valley. After putting pressure on Chiang Kai-shek to produce reinforcements from Yunnan, Stilwell had five Chinese divisions in North Burma, with Wingate's Special Force of Chindits (9,000-strong, flown in on 5 March) operating against Japanese communications to the south of him. By 17 May, GALAHAD and the Chinese had taken the Myitkyina airfield, a valuable prize from which 40,000 tons of supplies were flown into China by October, though the Japanese held on to the town until 3 August.

On the Arakan flank 15th Corps' 82nd West African Division took Buthidaung and then, in conjunction with

Burma campaign: Casualties

Operations, with dates	British and Commonwealth casualties[a]	Japanese casualties[a]
1st Burma (25 December 1941–12 May 1942)	13,463 (1,499)	2,431 (1,999)
1st Arakan (23 October 1942–15 May 1943)	5,057 (916)	1,100 (estimated) (400)
1st Wingate (February–June 1943)	1,138 (28)	205 (68)
2nd Arakan (February–July 1944)	7,951	5,335 (3,106)
2nd Wingate (March–August 1944)	3,786 (1,034)	5,311 (4,716)
Imphal Kohima (March–December 1944)		
Preliminaries (Assam)	920	
Kohima	4,064	5,764
Imphal	12,603	54,879 (13,376)
Irrawaddy Crossings; Mandalay (January–March 1945)	10,096 (1,472)	Combined Japanese losses in these two battles for Fifteenth Army and Thirty-third Army 12,912 (6,513)
Meiktila (February–March 1945)	8,099 (835)	
Pyawbwe to Rangoon	2,166 (446)	7,015 (6,742)
Rangoon to Surrender (Breakout & Sittang Bend) May–August 1945	1,901 (435)	11,192 (9,791)
TOTALS	71,244	106,144

[a] Killed in brackets

Source: Allen, L., *Burma: The Longest War*, (London, 1984).

the 81st West African Division, occupied the Japanese communications centre of Myohaung on 25 January 1945. The 25th Indian Division reached Foul Point on 26 December 1944 and landed on Akyab in January to find it had been abandoned by most of Sakurai's forces, including his 55th Division, which had withdrawn to meet the pressure from the Africans. Its transfer to the Irrawaddy valley left only Sakurai's 54th Division to face the Allied advance in Arakan. A British Royal Marine unit, the 3rd Commando Brigade, took Myebon, and then, with 26th Division took the islands of Ramree and Cheduba at the end of the month. These operations cut off a Japanese escape route to the south and made possible the construction of air strips to support Slim's main axis of advance to Rangoon.

Slim's pursuit of the Japanese into central Burma, and the capture of Rangoon (CAPITAL followed by EXTENDED CAPITAL), involved a *deception plan on the grand scale. The 19th Indian Division, part of Slim's 33rd Corps commanded by Lt-General *Stopford, was across the Irrawaddy by mid-January 1945, making for *Mandalay from the north, while the Corps' 2nd British and 20th Indian Divisions, and 7th Indian Division, now part of 4th Corps, crossed at various points west of Sagaing in February, the longest opposed river crossing of the Second World War (the Irrawaddy in that area was between 900 m. and 4,100 m. wide (1,000–4,500 yd.). The 20th Division pushed south to cut the road and rail communications to Rangoon, while 2nd Division moved east to come upon Mandalay from the south, though, in fact, the 19th Division took it from the north on 20 March. The prestige of its name made Mandalay a symbolic victory, but Lt-General Kimura Hyōtarō, the new Japanese C-in-C of the Burma Area Army, did not intend to fight to the death for it. Slim had at first assumed Kimura would meet him for an encounter battle in the Shwebo plain, with the Irrawaddy at his back, but Kimura had no intention of offering Slim an easy victory in conditions which would have permitted Allied deployment of armour. So Slim devised another strategy. He would fight the decisive battle south of Mandalay, at *Meiktila in Central Burma.

Once this had been won—it was Slim's greatest strategic triumph of the campaign—the way to Rangoon was open, although the Japanese put up a stiff resistance at Pyawbwe. While Stopford's 33rd Corps advanced down the Irrawaddy valley, through the oilfields and Prome towards the capital, the 5th and 17th Divisions of 4th Corps, now commanded by Lt-General *Messervy, leapfrogged through Pyinmana and Toungoo. Messervy covered 400 km. (250 mi.) in nineteen days, his hillward flank protected by *Aung San's Burma Independence Army (now renamed Patriotic Burmese Forces) and by 29 April his 17th Division was on the edge of Pegu, 80 km. (50 mi.) from Rangoon. That day, and the following one, torrential rains swept the town, hampering air support and the movement of trucks and tanks. It would have been poetic justice for Maj-General D. T. Cowan, who had succeeded

Smyth as commander of the 17th Indian Division in the dark days of 1942, to have led 4th Corps back into Rangoon, but Slim could not afford gestures. Rangoon had to be taken before the monsoon set in, and it was finally captured by a sea-borne amphibious landing (DRACULA) by Christison's 26th Indian Division from Akyab and Ramree. The landings were an anticlimax as the Japanese had already fled the city, Kimura and his Burma Area Army HQ having escaped to Moulmein on 23 April. The following month Slim left the Fourteenth Army, whose HQ moved to India, and a new command, Twelfth Army, was formed under Stopford to control British Forces in Burma.

At the end of July, Sakurai's Twenty-eighth Army moved eastwards out of Arakan into the Pegu Yomas range north of Rangoon. Sakurai then tried, with the help of a diversionary attack on Waw by the remains of Honda's shattered Thirty-third Army, which struck from the Sittang estuary, to break through the cordon of British divisions stretched along the Mandalay–Rangoon road. But his battle plan had been captured weeks beforehand, and within ten days he suffered 17,000 casualties. The British lost 95, perhaps the greatest disproportion of casualties during any battle in the war. Sporadic fighting east of the Sittang came to an end with the signing of the preliminary surrender arrangements in Rangoon by Field Marshal *Terauchi's chief of staff on 28 August.

The Japanese took Burma in 1942 at a cost of 2,000 dead (see Table). Added to their 3,500 dead in the Malayan campaign, they destroyed the British Empire in the Far East for roughly 5,000 men. LOUIS ALLEN

Allen, L., *Burma: the Longest War 1941–1945* (London, 1984).
Callahan, R., *Burma 1942–1945* (London, 1978).
Calvert, M., *Prisoners of Hope* (new edn. London, 1971).
Fergusson, B., *The Wild Green Earth* (London, 1946).
Slim, Viscount, *Defeat into Victory* (London, 1956).

Burma Independence Army (BIA). Formed in December 1941, the BIA fought alongside the Japanese at the start of the *Burma campaign, but was more important as a political symbol of Burmese independence which the Japanese claimed to support.

In February 1941 a Japanese officer, Colonel Suzuki Keiji, formed the secret Minami Kikan (Minami Organization, see also JAPAN, 6) to encourage armed insurrection among disaffected Burmese, mostly *Thakins, with the objective of closing the *Burma Road. Suzuki was a fervent and honest believer in Burmese independence and after the Thakin leader *Aung San fled to Japanese-occupied China (see CHINA INCIDENT) in August 1940 he worked with him to form an army. A nucleus of 30 Thakins, later known as the 'Thirty Comrades', were trained on *Hainan Island and BIA columns, totalling about 300 men, led the Japanese invasion into Burma from Thailand in January 1942. Suzuki, to achieve the greatest political impact, then began recruiting as many Burmese as possible for the BIA and 1,300 BIA troops fought the retreating British around Shwedaung in southern Burma. But, ignorant of modern warfare, they suffered heavy casualties and 300 deserted. From then on the BIA followed in the wake of the invading Japanese, setting up civilian administrations to fill the vacuum left by the departing British. Mob rule, and worse, by BIA civil administrations terrorized local minority populations and irritated the Japanese Army of occupation whose *Kempei had to clear many towns of BIA troops. By June 1942 the Japanese Army had had enough of Suzuki, who refused to co-operate with it, and his BIA. Suzuki returned to Tokyo, and in August 1942 the BIA was dissolved and Aung San, now a maj-general in the Japanese Army, headed a newly formed 3,000-strong Burma Defence Army using BIA personnel. Japanese trained and equipped, this became the 10,000-strong Burma National Army (BNA) on Burma's independence in August 1943. Aung San then became the BNA's political supremo as minister of defence and its command was given to Bo Ne Win, one of the 'Thirty Comrades', a colonel in the Japanese Army. Unlike the *Indian National Army, the BNA was not allowed to fight alongside the Japanese in the *Imphal offensive of March 1944 and, when the offensive failed and the Japanese were in full retreat, Aung San and the BNA, encouraged by *SOE, defected to the British in April 1945. It then changed its name yet again, this time to the Patriotic Burmese Forces. This helped cover the flank of *Messervy's 4th Corps as it advanced on Rangoon, but otherwise played little part in the final weeks of the campaign.

Burma Road, supply route 565 km. (350 mi.) long for *Chiang Kai-shek's nationalist forces which connected Burma with China (see Map 19). Built by 200,000 Chinese labourers, it was completed in 1938, and ran from Kunming in Yunnan province to Wanting in China where it joined the road that ran from there, through Lashio, to Mandalay and Rangoon. After Japan had captured most of China's coastline in 1938 (see CHINA INCIDENT), and then closed the Haiphong–Yunnan railway (see FRENCH INDO-CHINA) in 1940—when Stalin also closed the one from the USSR—it was Chiang's principal supply route. Japanese diplomatic pressure on the British stopped it being used from July to October 1940; when it reopened they conspired with nationalist Burmans (see THAKIN) to close it again, and they launched their invasion of Burma in December 1941 partly to ensure its closure. Allied supplies for China then had to be flown from India by an air route known as the *Hump, until the Japanese were cleared from northern Burma and the *Ledo Road was connected to it in January 1945. See also LOGISTICS.

Burma–Thailand railway, (see Map 19) Japanese supply route which linked Nong Pladuk in Thailand to Thanbyuzayat in Burma, where it joined the existing Moulmein–Ye railway. The rapid expansion of Japanese occupied territory in South-East Asia had left Japan with inadequate shipping resources (see JAPAN, 7) and the railway was built to provide a safer supply line for the

Japanese fighting in the *Burma campaign than the exposed sea route to Rangoon. It was a formidable engineering feat, for the line had to be cut through 420 km. (260 mi.) of mountainous jungle which was climatically among the most unhealthy areas in the world. Construction began in July 1942, when 3,000 Allied *prisoners-of-war from *Changi started building base camps, and was completed in October 1943. But the railway failed to carry the tonnage that had been anticipated. In 1944 Allied bombing destroyed parts of it, including the bridge over the River Kwai (in fact, the bridge over the Kwae Yai west of Tamarkan), and it was abandoned in early 1945.

To build the railway the Japanese used 61,000 Australian, British, and Dutch *prisoners-of-war, and impressed or lured upwards of 270,000 native labourers from Burma, Malaya, Thailand, and the Netherlands East Indies. They regarded this labour force as entirely expendable and a starvation diet, combined with the appalling conditions and various epidemics, led to a high death rate. Figures vary but one authority, Louis Allen, has estimated that 12,000 Allied prisoners and 90,000 native labourers perished.

Kinvig, C., *River Kwai Railway* (London, 1992).

Burns, Lt-General Eedson (1897–1985), Canadian Army officer who commanded the 2nd Canadian Division in the UK and the 5th Canadian Armoured Division in the *Italian campaign before taking command of the 1st Canadian Corps in March 1944 which in Italy broke through the *Hitler Line that May and the *Gothic Line in August. However, Burns did not have the confidence of his army commander, *Leese, who in July requested he be replaced, which he was eventually, by *Foulkes, in November 1944.

Busch, Field Marshal Ernst (1885–1945), German Army officer and fervent Nazi Party supporter who served as a German corps commander during the *Polish campaign in September 1939. He then commanded the Sixteenth Army during the fighting which preceded the fall of *France in June 1940, and in the invasion of the USSR in June 1941 (see BARBAROSSA) where the Sixteenth Army was placed on the southern flank of Army Group North. He was promoted field marshal in February 1943 and took command of Army Group Centre that October when *Kluge was injured in a car accident. Although promoted beyond his capacities, Busch did manage to win a few defensive battles, but his blind obedience to Hitler's orders forbidding any retreat resulted in the virtual destruction of the Army Group during the Soviet offensive of June 1944 (See GERMAN–SOVIET WAR, 9). At the end of June he was dismissed and replaced by *Model. For a while he languished in obscurity but in March 1945 he was appointed C-in-C North-West. In this capacity he authorized the initial negotiations which led to the tactical surrender to *Montgomery at *Lüneburg Heath of all German armed forces in Denmark, the Netherlands, and north-west Germany on 4 May 1945. He died a few weeks later in captivity.

Bushidō (the way of the warrior) was the code of the long-abolished Japanese samurai warrior caste kept alive by officers of the Imperial Japanese Army. Its essence was that a soldier should aim to die rather than face capture, and surrender was punishable by death. 'Harshness, endurance, the carrying out ruthlessly of impossible orders, vengeance, and the duty in circumstances of disgrace to commit *seppaku*—more vulgarly known as *hara-kiri* (self-slaughter by a peculiarly courageous and painful method of disembowelment)—were its subjects: it is helpful to appreciate that the Japanese regarded neither the heart nor the intellect but the bowel as the seat of the soul . . . Bushidō was a deeply fatalistic cult' (J. Pritchard, in P. Calvocoressi *et al.*, *Total War*, 2nd edn., London, 1989, pp. 648–9). It bred the *kamikaze pilots, the **banzai* charge, and the atrocious treatment of Allied *prisoners-of-war (see BURMA–THAILAND RAILWAY, for example).

Butt report, analysis of damage done to 28 German targets during 100 night raids mounted by RAF Bomber Command between 2 June and 25 July 1941. It was ordered by Churchill's scientific adviser *Lindemann, and carried out by a member of the war cabinet secretariat, D. M. Butt, who studied 633 photographs of the damage (see PHOTOGRAPHIC RECONNAISSANCE). His conclusions were that of the 6,103 sorties dispatched against the 28 targets only 4,065 actually attacked them. Of this latter figure only one aircraft in three dropped its bombs within 8 km. (5 mi.) of the target. The report caused a furore which led to the introduction of systematic *area bombing, and the intensification of research into *electronic navigation systems. See also STRATEGIC AIR OFFENSIVES and OPERATIONAL RESEARCH.

Byelorussia, see BELORUSSIA.

Byrnes, James F. (1879–1972), US Democrat senator, lawyer, judge, and a close friend of Roosevelt, who directed the newly established Office of Economic Stabilization in October 1942 and then the Office of War Mobilization which Roosevelt formed in May 1943. This made him the chief planner of the American wartime economy, a position so powerful that he became known as the assistant president. He accompanied Roosevelt to the Yalta conference in February 1945 (see ARGONAUT), became *Truman's secretary of state when Roosevelt died, and attended the Potsdam conference in July 1945 (see TERMINAL). See also USA, 3.

cab rank, a small formation of Allied airborne aircraft, usually those armed with *rocket weapons, which were controlled from the ground by VHF radio telephone (see RADIO COMMUNICATIONS) to give support to ground forces at short notice. It was first employed by the *Western Desert Air Force during the *Italian campaign.

Cactus Air Force, mixed force of US aircraft, mostly Marine Corps aviation, which played a critical part in the *Guadalcanal campaign, CACTUS being the codename for the US landings there on 7 August 1942. Its aircraft flew from a captured Japanese airstrip, Henderson field, with 19 fighters and 12 torpedo bombers of 23rd Marine Air Group being the first to arrive. These were later reinforced by other units including aircraft from US carriers sunk or damaged during the six-month campaign.

Cairo Conference, see SEXTANT; see also GRAND ALLIANCE.

camouflage, see DECEPTION.

campaign medals. Besides *decorations and orders awarded to service and civilian personnel for gallantry and outstanding services to their countries, most combatant countries awarded medals to those taking part in certain campaigns or those who served for a certain amount of time in one of the services, perhaps in a particular area. It is only possible to list here some of the campaign medals of the major powers involved in the war.

Belgium. Escaper's Cross, Medal for Volunteers, War Commemorative Medal, African War Medal, Medal for Civil Resistance, Medal for Defaulters (from German *forced labour or military service), Medal for the Military Fighter of the War.

France. Colonial Medal (bars to this medal were awarded for various African battles and campaigns), Medal for Voluntary Service in the Free French Forces, War Commemorative Medal, and two medals for those deported or interned for resistance activities. The *Vichy French government also awarded a Colonial Medal and a Medal of Merit for Black Africa.

Germany. Medal for the Winter Campaign in the east, Medal for the Italo-German *North African campaign (*Afrika Korps Medal), Bravery and Commemorative Medal of the Spanish *Blue Division. Cuff titles—bands worn on the left forearm embroidered with the name of certain campaigns—were also awarded, as were war badges and shields to combatant troops of every category, to civilians, and to Nazi Party members.

Italy. Medal for the campaign against France, 1940; War Commemorative Medal, 1940–3, Medal for the War of Liberation, 1943–5; and Medal for the Italo-German campaign in North Africa.

UK. Eight campaign stars and two medals were issued for the war. The maximum number of stars that could be worn was five. Any additional stars for which an individual qualified were added as bars (represented by a heraldic rose in undress uniform ribbons) to the five already worn, but no star could have more than one bar. The stars were: 1939–45 Star (battle of *Britain air crew were authorized to wear the bar 'Battle of Britain' on it); Atlantic Star; Air Crew Europe; Africa Star (two bars, 'First Army' and 'Eighth Army', represented by the figures 1 and 8 in silver, were authorized for this star, as well as one, 'North Africa 1942–3', for the Royal Navy, Merchant Navy, and RAF); Pacific Star; Burma Star; Italy Star; and France and Germany Star. The two medals were the Defence Medal and 1939–45 War Medal.

British Commonwealth countries and colonies had the same system, but additionally awarded the Australia Service Medal, the Canadian Voluntary Service Medal, the New Zealand War Service Medal, and the (South) Africa Service Medal.

USA. American Defense Service Medal, 1939–41, awarded to US armed forces personnel serving between 8 September 1939 and 7 December 1941; American Campaign Medal; Asiatic-Pacific Campaign Medal; European–African–Middle Eastern Campaign Medal; Women's Army Corps Service Medal; World War II Victory Medal; and Merchant Marine Victory Medal.

The Mariner's Medal, the Combat Bar, the Merchant Marine Defense Bar, Merchant Marine Victory Medal, and Bars for the three war zones, Atlantic, Mediterranean, and Pacific, were all awarded to members of the US Merchant Marine.

USSR. Campaign medals were issued for the defence of *Leningrad, *Moscow, Odessa, *Sevastopol, *Stalingrad, the Caucasus, and the Soviet Arctic. There were also campaign medals for the capture of certain cities—*Budapest, Kaliningrad, Vienna, and *Berlin—and for the *liberation of Belgrade, Warsaw, and Prague. Also issued were the Medal for Victory over Germany in the Great Patriotic War (see GERMAN–SOVIET WAR), the Medal for Victory over Japan, and the Medal for Valiant Labour in the Great Patriotic War.

Like the Germans, the Soviet forces also issued metal badges for certain specialist troops.

Purves, A., *The Medals, Decorations, and Orders of World War Two* (Polstead, Suffolk, 1986).

camp X, preliminary training camp for *SOE personnel which opened on 9 December 1941. Officially designated Special Training School No. 103, it was situated near Oshawa, Ontario, Canada, and was administered by *British Security Co-ordination. Originally, the idea for its

A pilot climbs aboard his Hurricane fighter before it is catapulted from the foredeck of a **CAM ship**.

construction was to help the Americans acquire SOE's methods of clandestine warfare in anticipation of the USA entering the war, and until 1944, when it closed, it gave basic training to some 500 recruits from Canada, the UK, and the USA. It also housed a telecommunications centre, which became the principal channel between London, Ottawa, and Washington for top secret intelligence material.

Stafford, D., *Camp X* (Toronto, 1986).

CAM ships (Catapult Aircraft Merchantmen) were British merchant ships converted to carry catapult equipment for launching a single aircraft. These protected *convoys, primarily in the battle of the *Atlantic, from air attack, but after taking off their pilots had to bail out or ditch as the parent ship had no flight deck. Unlike *fighter catapult ships, which flew the Royal Navy's White Ensign, they continued to fly the Red Ensign of the merchant navy. See also MAC SHIPS.

CANADA

1. Introduction

As a British Dominion, Canada's attitude at the beginning of the Second World War was one of resignation. The memory of the heavy casualties in the *First World War, when 60,000 Canadians died and 172,000 were wounded, naturally weighed heavily on the nation. The Great Depression had devastated the economy for ten years and continued unabated in its severity. And *French Canadians, bitterly resentful of the way in which the anglophone majority had imposed conscription in 1917, had no desire to see Canada enter into another 'British' war in Europe that might lead to heavy casualties and inevitably to renewed demands for compulsory military service. On the other hand, many, perhaps most, English Canadians still assumed that when Britain was at war, so was Canada. The Liberal government of Mackenzie *King managed to bring this reluctant, divided country into the war through King's political skill, a feat that was accomplished by promising that there would be no conscription for overseas service and by pledging a war of 'limited liability'. Those attitudes prevailed for ten months. Not until the fall of *France did most Canadians, including their government, take the war seriously as a struggle for survival; not until the summer of 1940 did war orders from the UK or the Canadian government begin to reach the factories in quantity. From that point until the victory over Japan in August 1945, the Canadian war effort increased exponentially.

2. Domestic life, war effort, and economy

Canada's population in 1939 was only 11.5 million scattered across a vast area reaching from the Atlantic to the Pacific. Just under half the Canadian people were of British origin, with another third being French Canadians. The remainder were of immigrant stock, largely European (with Germans and Ukrainians predominating). A majority of the population lived in cities, though only eight urban populations were bigger than 100,000 and none was greater than a million.

The economy in 1939 was still caught in the toils of the Depression. Official estimates, probably understating the problem, had 400,000 workers unemployed and a million men, women, and children on direct relief. On 1 October 1939, only 3.8 million were gainfully employed, with 2 million men and women in agriculture and the rest in non-agricultural industry or self-employed. The country's Gross National Product was $5.6 billion. The war dramatically altered these numbers. The GNP in 1945 was $11.8 billion, a figure slightly below the 1944 total. Unemployment had disappeared and 5.1 million were gainfully employed, with 3.2 million in non-agricultural industry and 1.9 million working in agriculture. The manufacturing sector of the economy had almost doubled in six years, and war industry at its peak in October 1943 employed 1.2 million men and women, or 13.3% of the total population over 14 years of age.

Production quantities increased dramatically in every sector. In agriculture, good weather helped produce bumper crops of grain—556 million bushels in 1942, for example. The production of pork more than doubled and of beef increased by more than a third, and the country's agricultural exports rose from $332 million in 1939 to $1.12 billion in 1944, $409 million of that total going to the UK.

In the iron and steel sectors, increases were similarly dramatic. Pig iron and steel ingot production more than doubled between 1939 and 1944, and this fuelled astonishing developments in war industry. A country that in 1939 had built no merchant ships had produced 345 by 1944; aircraft production was 14,700 by the end of 1944; while 707,000 military vehicles and 45,710 armoured vehicles were built. Plant expansion was heavily financed by government which established numerous Crown corporations (for example, to produce synthetic rubber) and which financed corporate expansion.

The total of war production in Canada, supervised by C. D. *Howe, was $10.9 billion by 1945, fourth among the Allies. Canada's war production amounted to one-seventh of total British Empire production, but only 30% of this production was used by the Canadian forces. Virtually all the rest was given freely to Canada's allies as gifts or under *Canadian Mutual Aid, with the lion's share going to the UK. Mutual Aid, its financial planning directed by a team headed by the finance minister, J. L. *Ilsley, was a contribution to the Allied war effort, but it was also an investment in full employment in Canada, something of which the government was fully aware. In effect, Ottawa decided it was better to give war production away rather than to see the economy run down in the middle of the war. For the hard-pressed British, the aid was important. As a Dominions Office paper noted in August 1946, 'during the war we were never, from shortage of finance, prevented from securing all Canada could let us have for the war effort'.

Extraordinarily, the economic war effort simultaneously raised living standards at home to peaks never before attained. It was not that wages rose so much as that there was work for everyone. Full employment and all the overtime anyone wanted meant that families, often with every member over the age of 15 gainfully employed, had the money to eat better, even with rationing of meat, butter, sugar, tea, and coffee. Moreover, the fact that consumer goods were unavailable meant that savings rose, a cushion for the expected post-war downturn. The government's tough economic policies controlled inflation well. From the beginning of the war until October 1941, when wage and price controls were imposed, the cost of living rose by 17.8%; but from October 1941 to April 1945, the increase was a mere 2.8%. This was the most successful record of all the belligerents.

3. Government

The federal election of 1935 had replaced the Conservative government of R. B. Bennett with the Liberals under King, previously prime minister 1921–6 and 1926–30. King was cautious and colourless, a fussy bachelor in his sixties, but he was a consummate political tactician with a clear idea of the forces that weighed on his country—the USA, with whom Canada shared the continent, and the UK, the Mother Country across the sea. The struggle between continentalism and imperialism was as old as Canada, as current as today's newspaper, and King had to deal with it. He also had to handle the tensions within the country. French-speaking Canadians, largely but not exclusively concentrated in Quebec, were separated by language and by religion from most of their English-speaking and Protestant countrymen (see also RELIGION). Their political support was traditionally given to the Liberal Party, and King, dependent on it, had to tread carefully on foreign policy questions and on any prospect of Canadian involvement in war.

The Statute of Westminster in 1931 had declared that Canada, like the other Dominions, was independent in foreign policy, just as it had been in domestic matters, but there still remained some doubt that Canada had a right to neutrality, or whether it was bound by a declaration of war issued by its sovereign, *George VI, on behalf of Great Britain. Neutralist sentiment had a powerful voice in King's key foreign policy adviser, Dr Oscar *Skelton, but the Gordian knot was cut by King in September 1939. The UK declared war on 3 September and, the Canadian parliament approving, the government asked King George to declare war on its behalf on 9 September. The next day Canada was at war with Germany. In the week between Britain's and Canada's declarations, the USA had considered Canada to be neutral, sending some war supplies across the border. Canada's independent decision to enter the war, the fulfilment of a much-repeated promise by King, did much to bring a relatively united country into the Second World War.

King then had to withstand a challenge to the war effort in Quebec when, later in September, Premier Maurice Duplessis called a snap election and charged Ottawa with using the conflict as an excuse to pursue centralist policies. Extraordinarily, the federal cabinet ministers from Quebec told the province's voters that they would resign if Duplessis was re-elected. That, they said, would leave Quebec exposed to conscription. The voters listened and elected a Liberal government. In January 1940, by contrast, the Ontario legislature voted to condemn the federal government's lackadaisical war effort. King seized the opportunity to call a snap election of his own for 26 March which he won with 51.5% of the popular vote and a majority of 117 over the combined opposition parties. The Liberal government was in power for the duration.

As important, King had got the election out of the way before the *phoney war turned into an Allied disaster. The defeats in Scandinavia, the Low Countries, and France put enormous pressure on the government to step up the war effort, and King responded by personally drafting the National Resources Mobilization Act (NRMA) which he introduced into the House of Commons on 18 June 1940. This act authorized conscription for home defence and called for a national registration. The prime minister pledged again that his government would not implement conscription for overseas service. While there was some opposition in French Canada to the NRMA, the prompt internment of the mayor of Montreal, Camillien Houde, who had urged his compatriots not to register, ended it quickly.

By late 1941, however, there were pressures for 'total war' everywhere in the country. At a meeting in November the opposition Conservative Party selected Arthur Meighen, the draftsman of the First World War conscription measure and twice prime minister in the 1920s, to be its leader, and the press began calling for full conscription. Within King's cabinet, his minister of national defence, J. Layton *Ralston, and several of his colleagues supported conscription. The attack on *Pearl Harbor, the entry of the USA into the war, and the developing threat to the west coast from Japan increased the pressure. But King felt bound by his repeated pledges to Quebec, and his solution was to stage a plebiscite on 27 April 1942 to ask the electorate to release the government from its past commitments restricting methods of raising men for military service. This plebiscite, asking all Canada to release King from promises made to Quebec, outraged French Canadians. A 'non' campaign was run by La Ligue pour la défense du Canada that effectively out-organized the feeble 'oui' campaign in Quebec. The result saw 72.9% of Quebeckers vote 'non', an overwhelming majority of the French-speaking population. Elsewhere in Canada, though the 'yes' vote won very large majorities, the French-speaking, German, and Ukrainian populations voted 'no' by large margins. King's response, once he had recovered from his shock, was to introduce a bill in parliament to delete the clause in the NRMA restricting the use of conscripts, by now known derogatorily as Zombies, to Canada. But his policy, brilliantly expressed in the phrase, 'Not necessarily conscription but conscription if necessary', remained unchanged. Canada still would not send conscripts overseas unless it was necessary; the definition of necessity was nowhere specified.

Not until the autumn of 1944, by which time the Canadian Army was heavily engaged in the *Italian and *Normandy campaigns, did necessity become an issue. Because of General Staff miscalculations of the numbers of infantry reinforcements, because Canada relied on outdated British 'wastage' rates, by October 1944 there was a projected shortage of some 15,000 infantrymen. Expedients had already been tried and failed, and the only source for trained infantry seemed to be the 60,000 NRMA soldiers in Canada. An enormous political crisis erupted in late October and November, one that saw King sack Ralston in one of the most dramatic cabinet confrontations in Canadian history. His replacement was General *McNaughton, until late 1943 the General Officer Commanding the First Canadian Army. McNaughton failed to find reinforcements, and his army commanders in Canada were increasingly rebellious. King then used the military's unhappiness as the excuse to reverse course on 22 November: the government now would dispatch 16,000 NRMA infantry overseas. The reaction of Quebec MPs was bitter and public opinion angry at what was seen as a betrayal. But clearly King had delayed the inevitable as long as possible, and the anger died away quickly.

What, after all, could Quebec do? The Conservatives were for all-out conscription and had scarcely any French-speaking supporters; the social-democratic Co-operative Commonwealth Federation (CCF) was mistrusted in Quebec; and the francophone Bloc Populaire Canadien, while nationalist in its orientation, was woodenly led. King seemed the only option.

In part that was because the Liberal government had run the war superbly, the question of conscription aside. Quebec received its share of war contracts and prosperity, too. Moreover, the Liberals had announced in September 1943 their intention of creating a social welfare state, largely because the mandarins of the federal financial bureaucracy had concluded that only through government outlays could a post-war return to depression be averted. To some extent, as well, the new government thrust was a response to political pressures. In 1942, the Conservative Party had changed its name to Progressive Conservative, elected a new leader in the Liberal-Progressive Premier of Manitoba, John Bracken, and adopted a programme that included social welfare measures. The CCF, with its firm commitment to welfare policies, was making substantial gains in opinion polls, in federal by-elections, and in provincial elections in Ontario and Saskatchewan. But the Liberals were in power, and beginning in 1944 they moved into action. Family allowances were introduced, offering mothers a cash payment for each child. Through an order in council (PC 1003, 17 February 1944), employees' rights to join and form unions were confirmed and machinery for defining and certifying bargaining units laid out. In effect, Canadian labour had its Magna Carta. At the same time, massive sums were pumped into housing, into the re-establishment of veterans, into export promotion. The government even pledged itself to the goal of full employment early in 1945. Keynesianism had arrived in Canada with a vengeance, and the era of small government was gone. In 1939, the federal budget had been $680 million; by 1945, swollen with war expenditure, it was $5.1 billion, and Ottawa was making clear that it was prepared to spend just as freely in the peace.

At the same time, the country had begun to assert itself in Allied councils. Arguing that Canada had contributed more in certain areas than all but the Great Powers, the department of external affairs, its able staff now headed by Norman *Robertson, insisted on and won a seat on some of the Anglo-American Combined Boards (see COMBINED CHIEFS OF STAFF) and on *UNRRA's supply committee. King also played a prominent role in the formation of the United Nations in 1945 (see SAN FRANCISCO CONFERENCE), and his people, despite themselves and despite their ambivalence toward their prime minister, were impressed.

Thus when the federal election was held on 11 June 1945, fortuitously after the war in Europe had ended and before Canada's promise of a division for the *Pacific war had time to be implemented. King's government was re-elected with 41% of the popular vote and 125 seats, a bare majority. In Quebec, however, King won 53 of 65 seats and, as one academic noted in an election analysis, 'Quebec Saves Our King'. It was precisely true, though the Liberals did win more seats outside Quebec than any other party.

4. Canada–US relations

Before the outbreak of the Second World War, Canada's diplomatic relations with the USA were, while close, largely limited to economic and boundary matters. Prime Minister King and President Roosevelt were friendly enough, something that helped with the crafting of major trade agreements in 1935 and 1938, but Canada remained a British country, more than a little suspicious of the Yankee power to the south. The war changed all this, forcing Canada and the USA closer together economically, militarily, and politically.

The economic pressure produced by wartime expansion led to substantial increases in imports from the USA and the incorporation of American-made components into munitions and *matériel* destined for the UK. But the British could not pay for their needs, and Canada's burgeoning trade deficit with the USA was out of control by 1941. The answer was the *Hyde Park declaration of 1941. This resolved the short-term problem but the resulting integration of the two North American economies would never be undone.

The same thing happened with defence. While there had been secret talks between the two countries' Chiefs of Staff before the war, little had been done to prepare continental defences. But the fall of *France, coupled with the possibility that the UK might be occupied, obliged the two countries to co-ordinate their efforts. In August 1940, King and Roosevelt met and drafted a plan for a *Permanent Joint Board on Defence that began at once to work out plans to defend both the east and west coasts. The two countries worked closely together in fighting the battle of the *Atlantic from 1941 on, and plans were made to move US troops into the maritime provinces to meet any Nazi threat. The Japanese threat similarly sped the process in the Pacific, both countries informally co-ordinating their actions with respect to treatment of their citizens of Japanese origin (see JAPANESE-AMERICANS and JAPANESE-CANADIANS). More directly, American troops moved into Canada to build the Alaska Highway (see ALASKA), a number of weather stations (see also METEOROLOGICAL INTELLIGENCE), and an oil pipeline in the north. The trend was not one-sided, however. When Japan occupied two islands in the Aleutians, Royal Canadian Air Force (RCAF) squadrons were based in Alaska. In 1943 a Canadian infantry brigade, equipped with US weapons, participated in the attack on Kiska during the *Aleutian Islands campaigns. At the same time, Canada provided troops for the First Special Service Force (see USA, 5(f)), which fought in Italy and elsewhere.

There was, however, a certain tension in the military relationship, a fear that the USA had designs on Canada. The Canadian government insisted on paying full value for every American base and fixed installation in Canada at the end of the war, an all-too-obvious effort to eliminate every vestige of an American claim on Canada. None the less, the military links forged during the war remained and they were restored and refurbished when the *Cold War began.

Politically, the relations between the two countries also strengthened during the war. The friendship between King and Roosevelt grew, and the American government, while not according Canada a place at the Allied council tables when high strategy was being discussed, paid more attention to Ottawa than did London. Sometimes this caused difficulties, as in 1941 when Free French forces occupied *St Pierre and Miquelon and Secretary of State Cordell *Hull ordered Canada to evict them, a demand that was ignored. But Churchill and Whitehall all too often still treated Canada like a colony, and the Americans shrewdly used Ottawa's resentment to foster increased links. This was evident in trade matters, for example, where London's parlous financial plight led to restrictions on hard currency imports before the end of the war. Ottawa and Washington reacted similarly to this, and significantly Ottawa imposed the same terms as the USA on the British loan negotiated in 1946.

5. Civil defence and defence forces

At the outbreak of war, the federal government established a civil defence organization in areas it designated as dangerous. Some provincial governments, such as those in Ontario and Saskatchewan, supplemented this service with organizations of their own, and occasionally, as in the latter province, such home guards sniffed out suspect foreigners and verged on vigilantism. By 1943 the federal organization had a strength of some 225,000, including 45,000 women. Nurses, doctors, stretcher-bearers, and rescue squad members formed units in the designated areas and awaited the call which happily never came. In February 1945, except for specified areas in Nova Scotia and, more specifically, British Columbia, where Japanese *balloon bombs were posing a minor threat to the province's forests, the organization disbanded.

6. Armed forces

(a) Introduction

Canada's armed forces at the outbreak of war were organized on a British model, including a Chiefs of Staff Committee composed of the heads of the three services. These services were tiny, ill-trained for the most part, and equipped with obsolescent weapons. The Royal Canadian Navy (RCN) had a regular force strength of 1,990 officers and ratings, ludicrously small but still double its complement three years before. There were in addition 1,700 reservists. Its fleet consisted of four relatively modern destroyers, two older ones, and four minesweepers. The Permanent Force of the Canadian Army had a strength of 4,261 officers and men, along with 4 modern anti-aircraft guns, 5 mortars, 82 Vickers machine guns, 10 Bren guns, and 2 light tanks. Even trucks were in short supply. The militia numbered some 51,000. Nor was the situation any better for the Royal Canadian Air Force (RCAF). Regular force strength was 298 officers and 2,750 airmen and, although it had 270 aircraft of 23 types, only 37 were remotely combat-ready. There were in addition 1,000 reservists organized in seven auxiliary squadrons. It was a slender base on which to build the *British Empire Air Training Scheme, which the British requested Canada to start, but the plan became the country's major air contribution to the Allies' victory.

From under 9,000 regulars, the armed forces expanded more than a hundredfold over the course of the war. The navy enlisted 106,522 men and women, the army 730,159, and the air force 249,662. Officers who had never seen a company in the field, let alone commanded one, led divisions in action. Inevitably, there were serious problems in all three services as demands outpaced resources and training, but on the whole the military effort was more than creditable.

Overall, Canadian military casualties were heavy: 42,042 dead, 54,414 wounded, and 8,995 taken prisoner. The direct cost of the war, in monetary terms, was $21.7 billion, a total that does not include pensions or long-term medical care. Was it worth it? Few Canadians, in 1945 or later, would argue that it was not. And they were very proud of their role in the war, something that the world seemed to notice too. At the *San Francisco conference in the spring of 1945, a Soviet delegate told a Canadian 'that there were only four countries that had really fought this war and they were the USSR, the US, the UK, and Canada.' There was political guile in that Soviet comment, but Canadians wanted to believe it.

(b) Army

The government's policy of 'limited liability' declared in September 1939 meant that Canada would fight the war with volunteers and without exerting itself, in the First World War phrase, 'to the last man and the last dollar'. For a brief period there seemed some doubt that the cabinet would even authorize the dispatch of a division overseas, but on 19 September the people were informed that Canada would raise two divisions, of which one was to be prepared immediately for overseas service. To command this 1st Canadian Division, the government called on McNaughton, a scientific soldier, one who believed in using modern science to keep casualties low. That exactly suited the government which desperately feared high casualties which would inevitably lead to conscription. At the outset there was no shortage of volunteers—54,844 came forward in September, more than enough to get training under way. The first drafts of the 1st Division left Canada for England in December 1939.

The army's expansion proceeded slowly until the fall of France galvanized efforts. Fewer than 35,000 men enlisted between October 1939 and May 1940, but in June and July 60,000 volunteered. In all, 122,000 enlisted in 1940, 94,000 in 1941, 130,000 in 1942, 77,000 in 1943, and 75,000 in 1944. By 1942 the army had defined its overseas plans: a First Canadian Army of two corps incorporating three infantry and two armoured divisions with an additional two armoured brigades. By mid-1943, there were also the equivalent of three divisions defending the Atlantic and Pacific coasts. This was a very substantial force indeed for a small country, and its size greatly troubled the prime minister who continued to fear the effect of casualties on national unity.

But for three years army casualties were light. The 1st Division, training in England, became involved in the débâcle in France only peripherally. After *Dunkirk, elements of the division landed in France as part of an effort to re-establish a defence line, but this was quickly abandoned—along with some of the division's equipment. Thereafter the Canadians, soon joined by the 2nd Division and now organized into a corps, shared in the defence of the UK. For a time, the 1st Division was the only well-equipped and trained formation available for this task. But after the likelihood of invasion receded, the Canadians, their numbers always expanding, continued to train.

The hunger for action of the Canadian people was substantial, and that pressure undoubtedly led to the army's two major disasters. In September 1941, Ottawa accepted a request to send troops to *Hong Kong, and in late November two infantry battalions and a brigade headquarters arrived there. The Japanese attack on 8 December involved the Winnipeg Grenadiers and the Royal Rifles of Canada in a desperate struggle that ended with surrender on Christmas Day 1941. Of the 1,975 Canadians, 40% were killed or wounded in the fighting; 268 subsequently died after brutal treatment in *prisoner-of-war cages in Hong Kong and Japan. The swift Japanese victory—and the stunning speed of Japan's victories throughout the Pacific—caused near panic in British Columbia, led to the enforced evacuation of 23,000 *Japanese-Canadians (see also JAPANESE-AMERICANS) from the coast, and obliged the government to increase substantially its military presence on the Pacific coast.

Even more costly than the Hong Kong débâcle was the Canadian raid on *Dieppe on 19 August 1942 which involved 4,963 men of the 2nd Canadian Division. Only 2,211 returned to England, almost half of whom had never been sent ashore, 656 died in the raid, and 1,946 became *prisoners-of-war, more than in the whole campaign in north-west Europe after D-Day. But the lessons of Dieppe were said to have played their part in the success of the *Sicilian campaign (HUSKY) and *OVERLORD, and Canadians were heavily involved in both operations, though General McNaughton, from 6 April 1942 in command of the First Canadian Army, had resisted efforts to divide his force. The Canadians were to be the spearhead pointing at Berlin in his view. But public pressure for action more successful than that at Hong Kong and Dieppe, as well as the obvious necessity to get some officers and men experienced in combat, led the government to overrule McNaughton and to agree to participate in HUSKY.

The 1st Canadian Division, led by Maj-General *Simonds, and the 1st Canadian Armoured Brigade landed near Pachino on 10 July 1943, and quickly moved inland. The Wehrmacht was not encountered for five days, but then the unblooded troops quickly learned what it meant to face a skilful defence. Operating in difficult terrain, the Canadian advance through the centre of the island was repeatedly slowed by well-planned delaying actions. The most notable of these occurred at Valguarnero (after which Field Marshal *Kesselring reported that his troops had encountered 'Mountain Boys' trained for Alpine fighting), Leonforte, and Assoro before the division was pulled from the line on 2 August. Casualties in Sicily numbered 2,310, including 562 dead.

Although Ottawa's intention had been that the Canadians would return to the UK once Sicily was taken, the division then participated in the Italian campaign, going ashore at Reggio Calabria on 3 September. It was soon joined by the 5th Canadian Armoured Division and the 1st Canadian Corps HQ under General *Crerar. As part of the Eighth Army, the corps participated in the advance up the Italian boot, most notably in the cracking of the German *Bernhardt Line which was anchored at the River Moro on the Adriatic, two miles south of Ortona. The 1st Division had the task of taking Ortona, defended by the 90th Light Panzer Grenadiers and the 1st Parachute Division. It took nearly all of December 1943 and some of the most savage fighting of the war, but Ortona fell on 27 December at a cost of 2,339 Canadian officers and men.

Crerar returned to the UK in March 1944 to take over the First Canadian Army and was succeeded by Lt-General *Burns. The 1st Division played a major part in the attack on the *Gustav Line on 16 May, and the Canadians, fighting for the first time as a corps, cracked the *Hitler Line a week later. The Germans' brilliant defence dissolved into a rout that did not stop until well north of Rome. Then the *Gothic Line was breached in late August as the 1st Canadian Corps aimed for Rimini. By September 1944 the Canadians had broken through the Apennine barrier, and by December they stood at the River Senio. Now led by Lt-General *Foulkes, the corps waited out an appalling winter—and an eventual transfer to join up with the First Canadian Army in the Netherlands. Almost 93,000 Canadians served in Italy and more than a quarter of them became casualties: 5,399 killed, 19,486 wounded, and 1,004 captured.

In north-west Europe the Canadians played a major part in OVERLORD. The 3rd Canadian Division and the 2nd Canadian Armoured Brigade landed on *JUNO Beach, overcoming stiff defences, and some units actually surpassed their D-Day objectives. The first German counter-attacks, launched by the 25th SS Panzer-Grenadier Regiment, then fell heavily on units of the 9th Canadian Infantry Brigade on 7 June, and the result was a bloody nose. The untried teenage Germans were better trained than the equally raw Canadians; and German equipment, especially tanks, was better, too. A series of brutal struggles occurred over the next few days, and the Canadians learned everything their training had not taught them: the 3rd Division lost 2,831 casualties in six days. Later during the Normandy campaign the Canadians closed the Falaise pocket and then took the Channel flank of the advance and moved through Dieppe, Boulogne, Calais, and into Belgium. There followed the long and wearing battle of the *Scheldt Estuary, the Canadians fighting in the mud on both banks of the estuary. Fierce fighting took place on Walcheren Island, where Simonds demonstrated a high degree of tactical innovation, and in the *Breskens pocket. The Scheldt was cleared by 3 November, but 6,367 casualties had been the price.

Not until February 1945 did the First Canadian Army go back into action, a respite that greatly eased the pressures in Canada after the conscription crisis of November 1944. With Crerar now commanding thirteen divisions (including British, American, Dutch, and Polish), it was the largest force ever led by a Canadian; its task was to clear the German forces west of the Rhine. Again the fighting took place in dreadful conditions, the Canadian divisions having to clear the *Reichswald and Hochwald forests. By the beginning of March the task was complete, and the First Canadian Army, now including the 1st Corps from Italy, crossed the Rhine on 23 March. The final tasks assigned to the Canadians were to liberate the north-eastern and western parts of the Netherlands and occupy the German coast east to the Elbe, and these were accomplished before the German capitulation. Fatal casualties in north-west Europe in eleven months of operations were 11,336.

(c) Navy

The Royal Canadian Navy's major contribution to the war, and arguably the major Canadian contribution to victory, came in the battle of the Atlantic. The war for the *convoys pitted the navy's corvettes, manned by prairie farm boys and Toronto clerks and captained by weekend yachtsmen, against Hitler's U-boats. In February 1940, Ottawa placed contracts for 64 corvettes, the first of 122 to be built in Canada. As soon as the little escorts, initially with a 47-man crew, came off the ways they were crewed, worked up, and thrown into the unequal struggle. Initially, training was below standard, and convoy escorts had to learn their trade on the job. Moreover, few Canadian ships had *radar, and when they got Canadian-designed and -built sets, they were inadequate. Naval Service Headquarters in Ottawa always seemed to be slow to get new equipment and armament fitted on RCN vessels.

Still, as resources improved, the quality of the naval escort began to rise. By mid-1941, the RCN had assumed responsibility for all convoy escort in the area of Newfoundland. Thus convoys leaving Halifax were escorted by the RCN to a rendezvous point at which the *Newfoundland Escort Force took over. At 35° West, ships of the Iceland Escort Force joined, and at 18° West, British-based ships took responsibility. Air cover, provided by RAF Coastal Command and the RCAF was also complete, except for the *air gap in the RCN's North Atlantic sector. Advantage still lay with the U-boats, however, as the fate of Convoy SC-42 in September 1941 demonstrated. The convoy's 64 ships were initially protected by one RCN destroyer and three corvettes; two additional corvettes joined while the convoy was under attack by at least eight submarines. Sixteen merchantmen were sunk while the RCN claimed one U-boat. After-action evaluation concluded that the escort had been too small, that group training was inadequate, and that the fundamentals of anti-submarine warfare had yet to be learned.

It took time for those lessons to be mastered. In 1942 the U-boats moved right into the Gulf of St Lawrence, sinking two escorts and fourteen cargo ships in Canadian waters. Ottawa's panicky response was to close the Gulf to shipping for most of the rest of the war, a measure that enormously increased the strain on Canada's rail network and the port of Halifax. The strain was heaviest, of course, on the navy which seemed to be falling further behind in the struggle. After RN assessments showed in November and December 1942 that four-fifths of merchantmen recently sunk had been lost under RCN escort, the hard decision was taken to pull RCN escort groups out of the North Atlantic for re-training on the easier UK–Gibraltar convoy route.

But now the tide turned, as new technology, improved air cover, and better *anti-submarine weapons arrived at last. In March 1943, the RCN took over responsibility in a newly created North–West Atlantic Command, west of the meridian 47° West and south to 29° North and quickly established command of the sea in the area. Of the 33 submarines sunk by the RCN, 22 were destroyed after March 1943.

The navy was also doing more than fighting U-boats. RCN destroyers played a major role in the English Channel before and after the Normandy landings. *Armed merchant cruisers served in the Mediterranean, the Pacific, and the Normandy invasion. In 1944, the RCN operated two aircraft carriers, except for their air crews, and that year and the next it acquired two heavy cruisers. The idea that the RCN, which had begun the war with under 2,000 men, would man 365 ships by 1945, and be the third largest Allied navy, would have been thought simply incredible a few years before. The navy's fatal casualties numbered 2,024 and 24 ships were lost.

(d) Air Force

The Royal Canadian Air Force sent 48 squadrons and 94,000 officers and men overseas. Tens of thousands served in RAF squadrons, most quite happily, but it took enormous pressure on London from the air minister, C. G. *Power, to get substantial Canadian formations created. Power's policy of Canadianization succeeded none the less, and there were soon RCAF fighter wings and a bomber group. Fighter pilots fought in the battle of *Britain, in *Malta, in the *Western Desert campaigns, and in north-west Europe; two transport squadrons flew out of Burma; and a Catalina squadron served notably on Ceylon. The RCAF also had responsibility for home defence, notably on the east and west coasts. It also provided fighter squadrons in support of US forces in Alaska.

But it was in the bomber war that Canada made its greatest operational contribution. The RCAF formed its first bomber squadron in June 1941, entirely from Canadians serving with the RAF. The next year, seven more squadrons took to the air, and on 1 January 1943, No. 6 Group of eight squadrons came into being. Based in Yorkshire, a long distance from their targets, the RCAF Group suffered serious teething problems. It flew older Wellington bombers; it had bad luck, and it lost more than a hundred aircraft and crews between March and June 1943; it suffered in consequence from morale problems. Not until the disciplinarian Air Vice-Marshal 'Black Mike' *McEwen took over command in January 1944, and not until Lancasters and Halifaxes had replaced the Group's Wellingtons, did matters improve. Thereafter the Canadians played their part well. In all, the group's aircraft flew 41,000 operations and dropped 126,000 tons of bombs, one-eighth of Bomber Command's total. The cost was 3,500 dead; another 4,700 RCAF officers and men died in other Bomber Command squadrons. In all, 17,101 members of the RCAF were killed during the war, a number almost exactly equal to the army's combat losses in the European theatre.

7. Intelligence

Canada's overall share in the secret war was small. In 1939 the Royal Canadian Mounted Police provided the country's intelligence and security service, and not very effectively. Its Intelligence Branch consisted of some 20 men across the country and two at HQ; all were obsessed with the communist threat and neglected the dangers posed by Nazi and fascist groups, and supporters of Japan. However, in a clumsy fashion happily mitigated by an appeals procedure that allowed for the correction of mistakes, suspects were swept up and interned in September 1939, June 1940, and December 1941.

The armed forces, tiny and undermanned as they were at the beginning of the war, operated a few listening stations in Ottawa to pick up German communications between South America and Hamburg. Military intelligence officers also kept watch, as in British Columbia where 23,000 Japanese-Canadians lived, on 'suspect' elements in the population. As the war progressed, the RCN's signals interception work (see SIGNALS INTELLIGENCE WARFARE) made a substantial contribution to monitoring U-boat communications, and by 1942 its Operational Intelligence Centre in Ottawa had earned sole charge of the Western Atlantic area.

The key player, however, soon became the Department of External Affairs. In 1940, after the military rejected the idea of establishing a cryptographic bureau on grounds of cost, the department, in co-operation with the National Research Council, established the Examination Unit, so-called because it suggested little to the curious, and hid its modest costs under the NRC's budget. The amateurishness of the operation, which never grew very large, instantly became apparent when Ottawa recruited as the Unit's first head Herbert Yardley, the US cryptographer who in 1931 had published a book that compromised American efforts against Japan. Yardley was *persona non grata* in Washington and London, and the Examination Unit effectively received nothing from Canada's allies until he was dismissed. His successors came from the British deciphering centre, *Bletchley Park, and the unit then did useful work in monitoring *Vichy French communications from the legation in Ottawa, the embassy in Washington, and French Indo-China, in deciphering *Abwehr traffic from South America, and in reading Japanese wireless communications intercepted by a station at Victoria, BC, including messages that implicated Spanish diplomats in Tokyo's spying. In September 1942, the unit created a Special Intelligence Section to analyse the last product; the section did especially well because its head was E. Herbert Norman, a Canadian diplomat who was one of the leading academic experts on Japan. As the unpublished history of the unit noted, 'Ottawa grew in three years to the stature of London and Washington in those two fields (French and Japanese) on which we have worked'. That was perhaps a pardonable exaggeration.

The Examination Unit put Canada in close contact with US intelligence agencies, *British Security Co-ordination in New York, and Bletchley Park. In effect, the war led Canada into the Allied signals intelligence network, and made it a *de facto* member of its intelligence community from the beginning of formalized Anglo-American co-operation.

8. Merchant marine

In 1939, Canada had a tiny ocean-going merchant fleet: 37 ships averaging under 6,000 tons and manned by 1,450 seamen. There had been no merchant ship construction during the inter-war years, and there were only a handful of yards capable of building a ship of 10,000-ton capacity. All this changed during the course of the war as shipbuilding accelerated dramatically under the control of a crown corporation, Wartime Shipbuilding Ltd. By July 1943, ships delivered and on order numbered 366 of 10,000 tons and 36 of 4,700 tons. By the end of the war, 410 ships had been delivered, their cost being $692 million. Shipbuilding employed 126,000 men and women.

At sea, the government moved to control the use of this new construction. Another crown corporation, Park Steamship Co. Ltd., was formed in April 1942 to supervise and control the shipment of munitions and supplies; its ships were leased to private companies. At its peak, Park received from the yards and operated 176 vessels, six of which were lost. All the remainder were sold or chartered at the end of the war.

During the war 68 Canadian flag carriers were lost, taking 1,148 seamen to their deaths.

9. Culture

Canada produced no great cultural achievements during the war. Canadian literature in French and English was in its infancy, the native theatre scarcely existed, and little music of note was being written. Aside from some armed forces shows, such as the immensely popular *Meet the Navy*, what stood out were two areas: war art and documentary films.

Canadian *war artists, commissioned and attached to units of all three services, produced a splendid array of oils, water-colours, and sketches. Artists such as Bruno and Molly Lamb Bobak, Charles Comfort, and Alex Colville produced some of their most powerful work, portraits that convey the shock of war on the human spirit, and battlefield studies that capture the impact of modern technology on human flesh. It was all too true to be propaganda.

The National Film Board of Canada, created on 2 May 1939 just before the outbreak of war, and led by its commissioner, the Scottish filmmaker John Grierson, presented open propaganda with brilliant effect. Its astonishing output, efficiently distributed to every corner of the land, glorified Canadians to themselves at the same time as it tried to explain the causes and purposes of the war in which they were involved. Nor were Canada's allies ignored—for example, films on the Soviets' struggle against Hitler were immensely popular. Fulfilling its commissioner's ideas, the NFB also used its short features with didactic intent to crusade for a new, more progressive world in peacetime. If the ideas were sometimes simplistic, the NFB's films undoubtedly had a major impact on Canadians. J. L. GRANATSTEIN

Granatstein, J. L., *Canada's War: The Politics of the Mackenzie King Government, 1939–1945* (2nd edn., Toronto, 1990).
Stacey, C. P., *Arms, Men and Governments: The War Policies of Canada 1939–1945* (Ottawa, 1970).

Canadian Mutual Aid, the Canadian equivalent of American *Lend-Lease, though the proportion of Canada's budget that was allotted to it was very much larger than that allotted by the USA to Lend-Lease. It was the main economic means by which Canada assisted the UK and other Allied countries with foodstuffs, raw materials, and armaments, and followed on its gift of $1 billion to the UK in 1942 to buy supplies from Canada. Started in 1943, the Mutual Aid programme was run by a board which supervised all Allied purchases in Canada bought with Canadian funds. It helped the UK at a time when its gold and dollar reserves were badly depleted. It also sustained Canada's production, which was the basis of the country's wartime prosperity. In 1943 the bulk of $722.8 million went to the UK but the USSR, Australia, China, India, and the British West Indies also benefited. Altogether, the UK received $4 billion from Canada, and a debt of $425 million for the cost of *British Empire Air Training Scheme was written off. See also CANADA, 2.

Canaris, Admiral Wilhelm (1887–1945), head of the *Abwehr, the German military intelligence and counter-intelligence organization, who was an early conspirator against Hitler (see SCHWARZE KAPELLE).

The son of a wealthy industrialist, Canaris joined the German Navy in 1905. During and after the *First World War he showed a penchant for clandestine operations and secret negotiations which earned him a reputation as being something of a super-spy. In January 1935 he became head of the Abwehr, and was promoted rear admiral shortly afterwards. He soon became one of Hitler's confidants and his standing in the military hierarchy rose steadily. Between 1938 and 1940 he was promoted vice-admiral, then admiral, and the Foreign Intelligence Office (Amt Ausland/Abwehr) of the German High Command (OKW), which controlled the attachés in friendly and neutral countries as well as the Abwehr, was formed under him.

In July 1938 Canaris learned of the Führer's plans to annex the Sudetenland, and like a number of army officers he was appalled. He dabbled with the idea of joining a *coup d' état* that was being planned, but it was not until he witnessed Hitler in a rage that he fully comprehended the kind of person he was serving. 'I've just seen a madman,' he said to his deputy, Hans *Oster. Though Canaris must have known that he was himself in indirect contact with the Allies via his mistress Halina Szymanski, an *MI6 agent who lived in Switzerland, he recoiled from the outright treachery Oster practised. Instead, he engaged in duplicity and ambivalence, his apparently genuine friendship with his arch-rival Reinhard *Heydrich being a typical example. He did what he could for the Jews, saving hundreds from extermination (see also FINAL SOLUTION)—and in February 1942 was temporarily suspended for doing so—yet he failed to curb the activities of his Secret Field Police who behaved with the same ruthlessness in Eastern Europe as the **Einsatzgruppen* and *Gestapo.

He still retained some admirers in the Nazi hierarchy, but in March 1942—the same month as the Abwehr traitor Paul *Thümmel was rearrested, and shortly after the *Bruneval raid which had prompted a furious Hitler to ask how much the Abwehr knew about British *radar—he was forced to allow Heydrich's Nazi security service, the Sicherheitsdienst (see RSHA), to appropriate some Abwehr functions. By then his influence had long been on the wane and, suffering from fits of apathy and despair, he began to make peace overtures to Allied representatives in neutral countries which served only to alert further an already suspicious Gestapo. But it was the defection of an Abwehr officer stationed in Istanbul, and an act of sabotage by the Abwehr which alienated the Spaniards, which finally led to his downfall in February 1944 and to the subordination of the Abwehr to the Sicherheitsdienst. However, he was not dismissed and in June 1944 was appointed chief of the department for economic warfare, a sinecure. After the July 1944 Bomb Plot to assassinate Hitler (see SCHWARZE KAPELLE), in which he was not involved, a confession by a conspirator led to his arrest. The hidden records of the 1938 coup came to light, as did his diaries, and he was arrested, imprisoned, and eventually hanged at *Flossenbürg in April 1945.

Höhne, H., *Canaris* (London, 1976).

canoeists were employed, primarily by the British and Australians, to sabotage shipping and other targets, and for reconnaissance. They were also often used for clandestine purposes such as landing agents from submarines. For example, Maj-General Mark *Clark was taken ashore in a canoe from a submarine to negotiate with the French before the *North African campaign landings in November 1942. The British formed a number of special units which employed either folding canoes, called folboats, or the more robust 4.8 m. (16 ft.) Cockle Mk II. These units included *Combined Operations Pilotage Parties, the *Special Boat Section, and the Royal Marine Boom Patrol Detachment, which damaged German *blockade runners in the Gironde Estuary in western France (FRANKTON) with *limpet mines in December 1942 and which later, as part of *Raiding Forces, attacked German warships in the *Dodecanese. *Special Operations Australia mounted a successful operation with canoes (JAYWICK) in September 1943, when British and Australian personnel, using a captured Japanese motor vessel, *Krait*, as their base, employed three folboats to destroy 50,000 tons of Japanese shipping in Singapore harbour. But a repeat operation (RIMAU), mounted in September 1944, was a disaster and all 23 participants were either killed or executed. Those engaged in RIMAU were equipped with, but did not use, the 3.6 m. (12 ft.), electrically driven 'sleeping beauty', a one-man Motor Submersible Canoe the driver of which wore oxygen breathing apparatus. These were only used operationally once, when two released from a British submarine sank two Japanese ships in Thailand's Phuket harbour.

Cape Esperance, battle of, one of the many naval night actions fought off *Guadalcanal during the *Pacific war. It took place on the night of 11/12 October 1942 when a US Navy Task Force under Rear-Admiral Norman Scott engaged a Japanese bombardment force commanded by Rear-Admiral Gotō Aritomo which was to shell US marines ashore while two seaplane carriers put ashore reinforcements for Japanese troops fighting on the island. The Americans, who had a new type of surface *radar, caught the Japanese unawares; and though the Japanese troop reinforcements, which included heavy artillery, got ashore, one Japanese heavy cruiser and a destroyer were sunk, another heavy cruiser was damaged, and Gotō was killed. The next day two more Japanese destroyers were sunk by US aircraft. Three US ships were damaged and one destroyer was lost, but it was the US Navy's first successful night action and greatly heartened the marines who were fighting ashore.

Cape Matapan, battle of, naval night action off southern Greece which took place on 28 March 1941 between units of the British and Italian navies during the battle for the *Mediterranean.

In September 1940 *Bletchley Park broke the Italian Navy's C38M machine cipher enciphered on a machine which was a derivative of the German *ENIGMA. The cipher was withdrawn the following summer, but before that, on 25 March 1941, *ULTRA intelligence derived from it made it evident that the Italian fleet, urged by the Germans, were planning to attack British *convoys ferrying troops and *matériel* from Egypt to Greece for the *Balkan campaign. The C-in-C Mediterranean, Admiral *Cunningham, promptly diverted two convoys from the area, ordered four cruisers and nine destroyers to lie in wait south-west of Gavdo Island, and on the night of 27 March sailed from Alexandria with his battle squadron and the British carrier *Formidable*.

Air reconnaissance revealed three groups of Italian warships, one of which included the battleship *Vittorio Veneto* with a strong escort. She was pursued by the British cruisers and by aircraft from *Formidable*, but though torpedoes slowed her and stopped the cruiser *Pola*, the results were inconclusive. Knowing that some of the faster Italian ships might have been damaged, Cunningham decided to risk a night action with his slower battle squadron. However, alerted by *radar—which the Italian ships did not have—that *Pola* was damaged, he diverted to try and find her. In doing so he ran across two cruisers, *Zara* and *Fiume*, escorted by two destroyers, which the Italian C-in-C, Admiral Angelo Iachino, who supposed the main British force was still in Alexandria, had sent back to aid *Pola*. It was a disastrous mistake, for Cunningham sank them all, including *Pola*, though *Vittorio Veneto* and her escorts eluded the pursuing cruisers. See also SEA POWER.

Cape Spartivento, naval actions off, early encounters during the battle for the *Mediterranean between British warships and those of Admiral Inigo Campioni's Italian fleet which took place on 9 July 1940 (off Calabria's Cape Spartivento) and 27 November 1940 (off Sardinia's Cape Spartivento). In the first action Campioni had the advantage of knowing *Cunningham's operational orders, which Italian naval intelligence had intercepted and decrypted, but he had been ordered not to risk his fleet and failed to press home an attack with his superior forces. One Italian battleship was hit. In the second, where only cruisers and light forces were engaged, Campioni again failed to make use of his superior forces. One British cruiser of *Somerville's Force H and one Italian destroyer were damaged.

Caribbean at war. The battle for the Caribbean began on the night of 16 February 1942 with the torpedoing of five shallow draught tankers (see also LANDING CRAFT) bringing oil from Lake Maracaibo in Venezuela to the large Royal Dutch refinery on Aruba Island. The refinery itself was also shelled in a most visible challenge to American and British control of the Caribbean basin. By the time the *North African campaign landings relieved the pressure on the area in November 1942, 270 ships had been lost and for several months supplies of vital *raw materials such as bauxite from Dutch Guiana and oil from Venezuela were disrupted. Yet, as the submarines pulled back to North Atlantic waters, effective counter-measures were at last in place, including *convoys and co-ordinated air-sea operations. The development of US air bases in Puerto Rico, Cuba, Haiti, and the Dominican Republic in 1941, and especially of the UK's base sites in Jamaica, Antigua, St Lucia, Trinidad, and British Guiana (resulting from the September, 1940 *destroyers-for-bases agreement), provided an effective shield and the Caribbean became unsafe for U-boats.

It was the building of these bases, and the large labour force of locals that was needed, that involved the USA even more intimately than before in the daily life of the basin as a whole. For example, strikes in the British West Indies were tied in to pressures to achieve home rule, although US Army officers were quick to blame German agitators as the cause. The circulation of labour among the islands and outside was also highlighted by the war. Both Cuba and the Dominican Republic resented the presence of Haitian cane cutters, while Panama refused to accept more black Jamaicans for work on the canal and new air bases, settling for Salvadorans and Colombians, instead—both would become large senders of labour in the future—and Puerto Rico's mainland links were reinforced. The Caribbean was coming into its own as a labour-exporting region.

Wartime stability and prosperity, under strong men like Cuba's Fulgencio Batista and the Dominican Republic's Raphael Trujillo Molina and Haiti's mulatto oligarchy, were bolstered by commodity purchasing agreements. With the fall of *France, the UK and USA were their only export markets. Starting in 1942, for example, Cuba's entire sugar crop was purchased by the USA. In Puerto Rico, the rise of Luis Marín and his Partido Popular Democrático, in tandem with Governor Rexford Tugwell, the New Dealer, marked a shift from colonial rule towards commonwealth status which was achieved in 1948, and an emphasis on economic development.

For their part, both powers depended heavily on oil and bauxite shipments from the region and were careful not to arouse the long-standing territorial interests of other nations. Thus British troops guarding Dutch Aruba and Curaçao, and parts of Dutch Guiana, were replaced by US forces in February 1942 though Venezuela had offered to send its forces. Brazil's offer to garrison Dutch Guiana resulted in the sending of a military mission, which the USA encouraged, though it decided to send its own troops there instead. The *Vichy regime in the French West Indies (Martinique, Guadeloupe, and French Guiana) was replaced in mid-1943 but without the aid of Latin American troops. The potential espionage threat of private German airlines, which had networks of local businessmen and landing rights close to the Panama Canal, was neutralized when the companies were, by 1940, broken up in Colombia at the request of Washington. This was well before the USA established its Caribbean Defense Command in May 1941 (see also USA, 5(a)) and put in place a force that eventually reached 119,000 men, over half of whom were assigned to defending the Panama Canal. JOHN D. WIRTH

Stetson C., Engleman, R. C., and Fairchild, B., *Guarding the United States and Its Outposts. The U.S. Army in World War II, The Western Hemisphere*, Vol. 2 (Washington, 1964).

Carlson's Raiders was the name given to 2nd Raider Battalion (see USA, 5(f)). It was commanded by Lt-Colonel Evans Carlson of the US Marine Corps who had first suggested that the marines should have commando-type units such as the Raiders. Having observed Chinese guerrillas in action against the Japanese during the *China Incident, Carlson adopted the Chinese communist phrase *gung-ho* ('work together') as his unit's motto. During the *Pacific war he led it on the *Makin Island raid and then on a 30-day patrol during the *Guadalcanal campaign which became a legend in US Marine Corps history.

Caroline Islands, a group of 680 Japanese Pacific islands, islets, and atolls situated between the Mariana Islands and New Guinea. In September 1944, during the *Pacific war, US forces occupied Ulithi Atoll, which proved to be a valuable anchorage for the US Pacific Fleet, and two islands in the Palaus. But Ponape and Yap—and *Truk, an important Japanese sea and air base—were bypassed by the Americans.

Carpathian Brigade, Polish unit, some 5,800 strong, full title the 1st Independent Carpathian Fusilier Brigade. It was formed in Syria in May 1940 within General *Weygand's French forces there. Its personnel, all high-quality volunteers, came from Polish troops who had escaped through the Balkans after the *Polish campaign. After the fall of *France in June 1940, the brigade moved to Palestine to avoid falling under *Vichy control, and then to *Tobruk where its commander, Maj-General Stanisław Kopański, commanded the Allied garrison after the Australian garrison had been replaced. In November 1941 it took part in the CRUSADER offensive in the *Western Desert campaigns before being withdrawn to Palestine in March 1942 having suffered 200 killed and 424 wounded. It was then reorganized as the 3rd Carpathian Division which subsequently took part in the *Italian campaign as part of the 2nd Polish Corps (see ANDERS' ARMY). The brigade's name reflected the soldiers' hopes that they would be able to liberate their homeland by crossing Southern Europe and traversing the Carpathian mountains.

carpet bombing was the US Army Air Forces' equivalent of the RAF's *area bombing, except that aircraft dropped their bombs in a uniform pattern over the target area. For the technique known as 'Tedder's Carpet' see BOMBERS, 2.

Carré, Mathilde (b.1910), French nurse recruited into the Franco-Polish **Interallié* intelligence network which she helped betray to the *Abwehr. She became a double agent (see BLEICHER) but confessed to this to a member of *SOE's F section. She was then taken to the UK, a move approved by the Germans who wanted her to penetrate SOE, but an attempt to make her a triple agent failed and she was imprisoned. In 1945 she was deported to France. She was sentenced to death but was reprieved and was freed from prison in 1954. Nicknamed 'The Cat' she always began her messages, 'The Cat reports ...'

Carré, M., *I Was The Cat* (London, 1960).

carrier pigeons, like other *animals, were employed—by both sides—more frequently than might be supposed. British birds were conscripted into the National Pigeon Service and were used most often by the RAF whose aircraft carried them for *air-sea rescue purposes. A Falcon Control Unit was formed to protect them, as was a Falcon (Interceptor) Unit whose members were trained to bring down suspect pigeons. British intelligence dropped them in containers over occupied France and British police, *war correspondents, *spies, *war photographers, and even businesses all used them to send messages. Their military application was limited, but by December 1944 US carrier pigeons operating out of 28 lofts in 15 locations during the *Italian campaign—where the mountainous terrain inhibited *radio communications—carried more than 10,000 messages. They were especially useful in this theatre to Italian partisans who used them extensively to dispatch information about German defences. Five hundred pigeons were sent on the Normandy landings (see OVERLORD); both the Australians and the Japanese employed them in the *New Guinea campaign; as did the US Navy at *Okinawa.

carriers.

1. Design and development

Before the Second World War, aircraft carrier design was driven by naval aircraft characteristics and by the constraints of the 1922 Treaty for the Limitation of Armament (known as the Washington Treaty). In the 1920s and 1930s, aircraft became faster, larger, and heavier, and their combat ranges and weapon loads increased. The treaty, however, set an upper limit of 121,500 metric displacement tons on the carrier tonnage allowed the US Navy (USN) and the Royal Navy (RN). The Imperial Japanese Navy (IJN) was allowed 72,900 metric tons. These three were the only combatant powers to build and operate fleet carriers during the war, though the Canadian Navy provided the crew for two escort carriers. The French did have one under construction (*Béarn*) while Germany's 'Z' Plan of 1938 included the construction of four by 1948, and ultimately eight (see GERMANY, Table 11). But only one, *Graf Zeppelin*, was launched, in December 1938, but work on completing her stopped in 1943. A second, unnamed, was started, but was broken up in 1940. Inter-service rivalry was the principal reason for the demise of the German carriers for *Göring never allowed the German Navy to have a separate air arm, nor did he encourage naval-air co-operation, and the Luftwaffe therefore never developed a suitable aircraft for carrier warfare. Italy's lack of carriers was also caused by inter-service rivalry; Mussolini's veto on his navy's having a separate air arm was only lifted after its defeat at the battle of *Cape Matapan in March 1941. The transatlantic liner *Roma* was then converted into a carrier but she had only just been completed at the time of Italy's surrender in September 1943. Work on converting another liner, *Augustus*, remained unfinished.

The Washington Treaty limited any individual carrier to 24,300 metric tons, but allowed the USA and Japan to

Japanese aircraft being cheered as it takes off from a **carrier** to raid Pearl Harbor, 7 December 1941.

convert two uncompleted battle-cruisers or battleships each to large carriers displacing no more than 29,700 metric tons. Improvements in aircraft, based on more powerful engines, made larger carriers more attractive. But the limits on overall carrier tonnage kept the three major navies from having many carriers at all, which increased the risk that, in wartime, the few available carriers would quickly be put out of action. There was a conflict between size and numbers. Advancing technology pushed up size, which reduced the numbers of carriers built. The desire to put more carriers to sea pushed the other way.

In 1939 the RN, USN, and IJN had several basic kinds of carriers afloat or building (see Table 1). There were small, slow experimental types, such as HMS *Argus*, USS *Langley*, and the IJN's *Hōshō*; there were converted cruisers and battle-cruisers such as HMS *Courageous*, USS *Lexington*, and the IJN's *Akagi*; and there were also some effective carriers designed on the basis of experience with the older ships: HMS *Ark Royal*, USS *Enterprise*, and the IJN's *Hiryu*. All three navies also studied variations of the flying-deck cruiser (half-cruiser, half-carrier) and of merchant ship conversions (see CAM, FIGHTER CATAPULT, and MAC SHIPS) as ways of increasing the numbers of aircraft which their fleets could take to sea. For the Allies there was also the need to give some kind of air cover to *convoys during the battle of the *Atlantic.

In 1940 the RN completed the first of a series of heavily armoured carriers (*Illustrious* class), with reduced aircraft complements. The US and Japanese navies, on the other hand, continued to build lightly armoured vessels (*Essex*, *Shokaku*) with more than double the number of planes carried by ships such as *Illustrious*. War experience suggested to the British that they needed more aircraft, but the armoured decks of the British Pacific Fleet (see TASK FORCE 57) did give some protection against Japanese *kamikaze attacks. The Americans and Japanese, now freed from treaty restrictions, opted for more armour *and* size, producing *Midway* (1945: 42,650 metric tons) and *Taiho* (1944: 30,300 metric tons).

All three navies also built many war emergency types: converted liners, light carriers based on cruiser hulls, and escort carriers based on merchant ship designs. The Imperial Navy converted three submarine tenders to produce *Zuiho* and *Shoho* (10,170 metric tons each) and *Ryuho* (12,060 metric tons). Two seaplane carriers (*Chitose* and *Chiyoda*, 10,080 metric tons each) and seven liners were also converted. The largest liner conversions were *Junyō* and *Hiyo*, each of 21,720 metric tons. In the mid-1930s, the USA had also planned passenger liner

Carriers, Table 1: Royal Navy, US Navy, Imperial Japanese Navy

Class/Type	*Number*	*Commissioned*	*Tonnage*	*No. of A/C*	*Overall Length (in metres/feet)*
Royal Navy					
Argus (experimental)	1	1918	13,000	20	172.2 (565)
Eagle "	1	1924	20,340	23	203.3 (667)
Hermes "	1	1924	9,765	25	181.8 (600)
Furious (converted)	1	1925	20,205	36	239.5 (786)
Courageous "	2	1928–30	20,250	48	239.5 (786)
Ark Royal (fleet)	1	1938	19,800	60	243.8 (800)
Illustrious "	3	1940–1	20,700	33	225.5 (740)
Indomitable "	1	1941	20,700	45	229.5 (763)
Implacable "	2	1944	21,105	60	233.4 (766)
Unicorn (light)	1	1943	13,275	35	195.0 (640)
Colossus (light)	7	1944–6	11,871	37	211.2 (693)
Escort Carriers (9 classes)	44	1941–4	9,180–17,685	6–24	
US Navy					
Langley (experimental)	1	1922	11,430	24	165.2 (542)
Lexington (converted)	2	1927	33,840	63	270.6 (888)
Ranger (fleet)	1	1934	13,120	76	234.4 (769)
Yorktown "	3	1937–41	17,900	96	246.6 (809)
Wasp "	1	1940	13,230	76	219.4 (720)
Essex "	24	1942–50	24,480	91	265.8 (872)
Independence (light)	9	1943	9,600	30	189.5 (622)
Midway (fleet)	3	1945–7	42,660	137	295.0 (968)
Saipan (light)	2	1946–7	13,050	48	208.2 (683)
Escort Carriers (5 classes)	86	1941–6	7,380–17,000	16–36	
Imperial Japanese Navy					
Hosho (experimenatal)	1	1922	6,730	26	167.9 (551)
Akagi (converted)	1	1927	32,850	91	260.6 (855)
Kaga "	1	1928	34,380	90	238.3 (782)
Ryujo (light)	1	1933	9,000	37	179.8 (590)
Soryu (fleet)	1	1937	14,400	63	227.4 (746)
Hiryu "	1	1939	15,600	64	227.1 (745)
Shokaku "	2	1941	23,130	72	257.5 (844)
Zuiho (converted)	2	1940–2	10,170	30	204.5 (671)
Ryuho "	1	1942	12,060	31	215.4 (707)
Junyo "	2	1942	21,720	53	219.1 (719)
Taiho (fleet)	1	1944	26,370	53	260.6 (855)
Chitose (converted)	2	1943–4	10,080	30	192.3 (631)
Shinano "	1	1944	55,800	70	265.8 (872)
Unryu (fleet)	3	1944	15,435	65	227.4 (746)
Escort carriers (3 classes)	5	1941–3	12,240–16,050	24–33	

All displacements are standard (that is, with 2/3 stores, no ammunition, and no aviation fuel or lubricating oil, aircraft were included) and in metric tons (.99 cu m=one imperial displacement ton). All USN, RN, and IJN carriers at sea on 3 Sept. 1939, used as carriers during the war, or meant to be used during the war are included. *Langley* had been converted to a seaplane carrier before the war. Her figures are included so that she can be compared with *Argus* and *Hosho*.

Source: Contributor.

conversions, but these were never pursued because of their cost and the time it would have taken to make the conversions. Instead, the USN co-operated with the RN to produce 'auxiliary aircraft carriers,' or merchant ship conversions. Basic types were *Casablanca* (8,400 metric tons; 50 built) and *Commencement Bay* (17,000 metric tons; 19 built). Most RN escort carriers were obtained through *Lend-Lease, such as the eleven *Attacker* type (10,360 metric tons), but there were also very austere additions of flight decks and three or four aircraft to each of nineteen grain and oil bulk carriers.

2. Warfare

Carrier forces revolutionized war at sea. In the *Pacific war they were the principal maritime offensive weapon; in the battle of the Atlantic, where escort carriers eventually helped tip the scales against the U-boat, and in the battle for the *Mediterranean, where they fought Axis *air power to break the siege of *Malta, their presence was vital. Before the war, the three major navies (the Royal Navy (RN), the United States Navy (USN), and the Imperial Japanese Navy (IJN)) foresaw the carrier's major roles: (1) strikes against other carriers to gain air superiority over the battle area, (2) reconnaissance, (3) attacks against warships and shipping, (4) fixing the enemy's battle line so that friendly battleships could engage it, (5) attacking targets ashore, and (6) convoy escort. It was not clear, however, just which role or roles would matter the most. British pre-war experiments and exercises suggested to the RN that carrier bombers and torpedo planes could not by themselves eliminate battleships. American and Japanese trials, on the other hand, indicated that, suitably armed, carrier aircraft could be the decisive weapon. Those uncertainties, and the fact that the Washington Treaty of 1922 restricted the number of carriers (and hence also the number of carrier aircraft) which navies could field, made war experience the final arbiter of the carrier's status.

The three major navies designed and built carrier forces to deal with what they thought would be their primary tactical problems. For Japan and the USA, the challenge was to mass as many strike aircraft as possible so as to overwhelm the opposing side's defensive fighters and wipe out their aircraft carriers early in an engagement. Consequently, their carriers sacrificed armour protection for large, strike-heavy air groups. The British worried about endurance in the face of damage. The RN wanted damage-resistant carriers that could stay with its battle line and aircraft that could scout, attack, and spot shellfire for its surface formations. As a result, British carriers designed immediately after *Ark Royal*, completed in 1938, had armoured flight decks and reduced air complements (33 planes for *Illustrious*, 60 for *Ark Royal*, and 96 for the USN's contemporary, *Hornet*).

Different fleet doctrines led to different types of aircraft as well as different carrier designs. As Table 2 shows, the RN, constrained by limited hangar capacities and committed to the role of supporting its battle line, procured multi-purpose aircraft. The USN and IJN, on the other hand, developed highly specialized fighters, scout bombers, and torpedo planes. Japanese carrier aircraft, such as the Zero, were designed with very great ranges, and this gave the IJN not only a tactical advantage in carrier-versus-carrier clashes, but also a strategic edge as Japanese naval formations accompanied by carriers had the advantage of finding Allied ships before they themselves were found. Zeros could also keep Allied reconnaissance planes at a distance, so that Japanese commanders usually knew more about Allied movements than the Allies knew about theirs. This strategic advantage was the key to the great success of Japanese naval forces in the first six months of the Pacific war. Even in 1944, most Japanese carrier aircraft outranged their US opponents. The pre-war plan of the IJN was to combine carrier strikes with attacks by long-range, land-based bombers. The carrier planes would strike by day, the bombers by night. Japanese tactics were foiled through the USN's effective application of *radar to tactical fighter control and by the growing power of its fighters. Just before the war, the USN sponsored the development of large, powerful radial aircraft engines. The fighters built with these engines, such as the famous F4U Corsair, outmatched their Japanese contemporaries and gave the USN the ability to eliminate Japan's naval pilots even if its bombers and torpedo planes could not find and sink all Japan's carriers.

War experience demonstrated how important and how vulnerable carriers were. Of the seven carriers which the RN had on hand in September 1939, two (*Courageous* and *Glorious*) were lost in less than a year, *Ark Royal* was sunk in 1941, and two more of the remaining five (*Eagle* and *Hermes*) were sunk in 1942. The USN also started its war with seven carriers. After one year of operations, only three of the seven (*Enterprise*, *Saratoga*, and *Ranger*) were still afloat. The IJN suffered even more. Four of its six large carriers were lost at the battle of *Midway in June 1942.

Carrier warfare varied with the theatre. In the Atlantic and Mediterranean, RN carriers fought submarines and land-based aircraft. In the Pacific, US and Japanese carriers first fought each other; then, when US carriers had virtually wiped out Japan's carrier pilots (at the battle of the *Philippine Sea), US carrier forces went after Japanese naval and merchant ships and also fought successfully against Japanese land-based air forces. In the *Okinawa campaign (April–June 1945), USN carriers (supported by an RN carrier task force) were primarily fighting land-based Japanese kamikaze aircraft. By the end of the war, US carrier aircraft were ranging over Japan's home islands.

In the summer of 1940, with France in German hands and Italy a declared enemy, the RN's fleet carriers acted with other ships to protect the UK from surface blockade and to contest control of the Mediterranean with Italian forces (see TARANTO, and CAPE MATAPAN). In such actions, British carrier aircraft, acting in support of RN forces, successfully attacked ships which lacked effective air cover at sea. Around Malta, however, in support of the struggle to resupply British forces there, in which the US carrier *Hornet* also took part on two occasions, RN carriers fought sustained battles against land-based air units. The cost was high. Apart from the loss of *Ark Royal*, *Illustrious* was severely battered by German dive-bombers in January 1941; *Formidable* was similarly damaged in May 1941; and *Victorious* and *Indomitable* were also hit during a resupply effort in August 1942. The fact that their armoured deck carriers could not carry many aircraft at all, let alone many high performance fighters, placed British carriers at a grave disadvantage when assaulted by repeated waves of experienced German land-based dive-bomber squadrons. There were just not enough effective fighters to defend against German attacks or to

Carriers, Table 2: Carrier aircraft (fighters, unless indicated otherwise in left-hand column)

Type	Span	Length	All-up Weight	Power Plant	Armament (Cannon/ Machine guns)	Weapons (Max) Bomrbs or rockets (or torpedoes)	Optimum Performance	Radius	Crew	Year of entry into service
UK										
Fulmer 1	14.1 m (46 ft 4 in)	12.3 m (40 ft 2 in)	4,636 kg (10,200 lb)	1 x Merlin 1,300 hp	8 x .303 in mg	—	438 kph @ 2,133 m (272 mph/7,000 ft)	644 km (400 mi)	2	1940
Firefly 1	13.7 m (44 ft 6 in)	11.6 m (37 ft 7 in)	6,364 kg (14,000 lb)	1 x Griffon 2,245 hp	4 x 20 mm	909 kg (2,000 lbs) or 8 rockets	508 kph @ 4,267 m (316 mph/14,000 ft)	805 km (500 mi)	2	1943
Swordfish Torpedo/ strike A/c	14 m (45 ft 6 in)	11.1 m (36 ft 4 in)	4,205 kg (9,250 lb)	1 x Bristol Pegasus 750 hp	1 mg (forward) 1 mg (rear)	1 x torpedo (18 in) 736 kg (1,620 lb), or equivalent in bombs, mines, depth charges	222 kph @ 1448 m (138 mph/4750 ft)	1,280 km (795 mi) (in recce role)	2/3	1936
Baracuda II Torpedo/ strike A/c	15.1 m (49 ft 2 in)	12.2 m (39 ft 9 in)	6,410 kg (14,100 lb)	1 x Merlin 1640 hp	2 mg (rear)	1 x torpedo (18 in) 736 kg or equivalent in bombs or depth charges	365 kph @ 534 m (227 mph/1,750 ft)	805 km (500 m)	3	1944
Skua Dive bomber	14.1 m (45 ft 11 in)	10.9 m (35 ft 7 in)	3,740 kg (8,228 lb)	1 x Perseus 905 hp	4 mg (forward) 1 mg (rear)	1 x 227 kg (500 lb) bomb	362 kph @1,982 m (225 mph/6,502 ft)	805 km	2	1938
Japan										
Mitsubishi A6M2 Zero-Sen ('Zeke' 22)	12.1 m (39 ft 4 in)	9.1 m (29 ft 9 in)	2,414 kg (5,313 lb)	1 x Sakae 12 925 hp	2 x 20 mm 2 mg	114 kg (250 lb)	540 kph @ 5,791 m (336 mph/19,000 ft)	965 km (600 m)	1	1940
Mitsubishi A6M5 Zero-Sen ('Zeke' 52)	11 m (35 ft 10 in)	9.1 m	2,749 kg (6,047 lb)	1 x Sakae 31 1,130 hp	2 x 20 mm cannons 2 x 13.2 mn mg	114 kg	554 kph @ 6,000 m (344 mph/19,685 ft)	1,126 km (700 mi)	1	1944
Aicni D3A2 ('Val') Dive bomber	14,5 m (47 ft 2 in)	10.2 m (33 ft 5 in)	3,658 kg (8,047 lb)	1 x Mitsubishi kinsei 1,300 hp	2 x mg (forward) 1 mg (rear)	363 kg (800 lb)	397 kph @ 2,317 m (247 mph/7,600 ft)	1,126 km	2	1940
Nakajima B5N2 ('Kate') Torpedo/ strike A/c	15.6 m (50 ft 11 in)	10.3 m (33 ft 9 in)	4,109 kg (9,039 lb)	1 x Sakae 21 1,115 hp	2 mg (forward) 1 mg (rear)	1 x torpedo 18 in 802 kg (1,765 lb) or equivalent in bombs	378 kph @ 3600 m (235 mph/11,810 ft)	980 km (609 mi)	3	1938
Nakajima B6N2 ('Jill') Torpedo/ strike A/c	15 m (48 ft 10 in)	10.9 m	5,662 kg (12,456 lb)	1 x Mitsubishi Kasei 25	1 mg (forward) 1 mg (rear)	1 x torpedo (18 in) 802 kg (1,765 lb) or equivalent in bombs	480 kph @ 4,877 m (299 mph/16,000 ft)	1,126 km	2	1944
USA										
Brewster F2A-3 Buffalo	10.7 m (35 ft)	8.1 m (26 ft 4 in)	3,254 kg (7,159 lb)	1 x Wright R-1820 1,200 hp	4 mg	91 kg (200 lb)	516 mph @ 5,029 m (321 mph/16,500 ft)	724 km	1	1939
Grumman F4F-3 Wildcat	11.7 m (38 ft)	8.8 m (28 ft 9 in)	3,705 kg (8,152 lb)	1 x Pratt & Whitney R-1830 1,200 hp	4 mg	91 kg (200 lb)	528 kph @ 6,400 m (328 mph/21,000 ft)	676 km (420 mi)	1	1941

Carriers, Table 2: *(cont.)*

Type	*Span*	*Length*	*All-up Weight*	*Power Plant*	*Armament (Cannon / Machine guns)*	*Weapons (Max) Bomrbs or rockets (or torpedoes)*	*Optimum Performance*	*Radius*	*Crew*	*Year of entry into service*
Grumman F6F–5 Hellcat	13.2 m (42 ft 10 in)	10.3 m (33 ft 7 in)	5,682 kg (12,500 lb)	1 x Pratt & Whitney R–2800 2,000 hp	6 mg	909 kg or 6 rockets	621 kph @ 5,273 m (386 mph/17, 300 ft)	322 km	1	1943
Grumman F7F–3 Tigercat	15.8 m (51 ft 6 in)	13.1 m (45 ft 4 in)	11,691 kg (25,720 lb)	2 x Pratt & Whitney R–2800 2,100 hp	4 x 20 mm 4 mg	—	700 kph @ 6,767 m (435 mph/22,200 ft)	1,207 km (750 mi)	1	1945
Grumman F8F–1 Bearcat	11 m (35 ft 10 in)	8.7 m (28ft 3 in)	5,885 kg (12,9471 lb)	1 x Pratt & Whitney R–2800 2,100 hp	4 mg	909 kg or 4 rockets	677 kph @ 6,005 m (421 mph/19,700 ft)	1,529 km (750 mi.)	1	1945
Vought F4U–1D Corsair	12.6 m (40 ft 11 in)	10.3 m	5,964 kg (13,120 lb)	1 x Pratt & Whitney R–2800 2,250 hp	6 mg	909 kg or 8 rockets	684 kph @ 6,096 m (425 mph/20,000 ft)	1,207 km (750 mi)	1	1942
Vought F4U–4 Corsair	12.6 m	10.4 m	6,668 kg (14,670 lb)	1 x Pratt & Whitney R–2800 2,450 hp	6 mg	909 kg or 8 rockets	718 kph @ 7,986 m (446 mph/26,200 ft)	1,207 km	1	1945
Goodyear F2G–1 Corsair (development of F4U–4)	12.6 m	10.3 m	7,010 kg (15,422 lb)	1 x Pratt & Whitney R–4360 3,000 hp	4 x mg All US mg .5 in (12.7 mm) except where shown	909 kg or 8 rockets	693 kph @ 4,998 m (431 mph/16,400 ft)	1,529 km	1	—
Douglas SBD Dauntless dive/scout bomber	12.7 m (41 ft 6 in)	10.1 m (33 ft)	4,934 kg (10,855 lb)	1 x Wright R–1820 1,000 hp	2 x 0.50 mg (forward) 1 x 0.30 mg (rear)	1,023 kg (max) (2,250 lb)	394 kph @ 4,815 m 245 mph @ 15,800 ft	965 km (600 mi)	2	1941
Grumman TBF–1/TBM–3 Avenger Torpedo/ strike A/c	16.6 m (54 ft 2 in)	12.3 m	8295 kg (18,250 lb)	1 x Wright R 2600 1,700 hp	1 mg (forward) 2 mg rear	1 x torpedo or 909 kg in bombs	429 kph @ 4,572 m 267 mph @ 15,000 ft	1,448 km (900 mi)	3	1942
Curtiss SB2C–4 Helldiver dive-bomber	15.3 m (49 ft 9 in)	11.3 m (36 ft 8 in)	7,553 kg (16,616 lb)	1 x Wright R–2600 1900 hp	2 x 20 mg Cannon (forward) 2 x 0.30 mg (rear)	909 kg max	475 kph @ 5,090 m 295 mph @ 16,700 ft	1,440 km	2	1943

NB All the above aircraft, while designed to operate from carriers, could also operate from land.

Source: E. A. Munday.

escort British strike aircraft on raids against Axis airfields.

Escort carriers, designed to provide air cover for convoys and for amphibious landings, lacked the speed to stay with the larger fleet carriers, but they performed invaluable service for the Allies in both the Atlantic and the Pacific. Poorly protected internally, they were suited to combat in areas where the enemy air threat was weak or non-existent. In the Atlantic their aircraft hounded German submarines in areas beyond the reach of land-based patrol bombers, and one was instrumental in the capture of U-505 in June 1944. In October of that year, sixteen escort carriers (designated CVEs in the US Navy) and their destroyer guard were caught in a surprise daylight surface engagement with a force of four Japanese battleships, six cruisers, and many destroyers in the battle of *Leyte Gulf. One CVE was lost, and others were damaged (several by kamikaze aircraft), but the Japanese force was driven off with the loss of three cruisers. Such ship-to-ship combat was the exception for escort carriers. Most provided air cover for units fighting ashore or defending themselves against submarines.

In the Pacific war, carrier warfare began with a massed carrier raid by Japan on *Pearl Harbor (which caught none of the US carriers in port) and the retaliatory *Doolittle raid, then progressed to violent carrier-against-carrier duels—one of them, the battle of the *Coral Sea, was the first-ever naval encounter in which neither side's warships were visible to the other's—and finally circled back to massed raids by US carriers against Japan. When the Pacific war began, both USN and IJN carrier aircraft complements were heavily weighted towards bombers and torpedo planes. Both sides understood the need to attack first, with overwhelming power, and at the longest possible range. In pursuing this doctrine, the IJN went so far as to deprive its pilots of adequately armoured planes. In addition, US carriers faced a special dilemma once US forces began to invade Japanese-held islands: whether to establish and maintain air supremacy during an amphibious assault (see AMPHIBIOUS WARFARE) or to hunt Japanese carriers, and by failing to solve it Vice-Admiral *Fletcher very nearly turned initial success into disaster, at *Guadalcanal.

The 1942 carrier battles were decided by which side found the other first, and by the striking power each side could deliver before suffering its own losses. By 1944, however, things had changed. Radar-directed air patrols and radar-directed ships' anti-aircraft guns downed Japanese pilots faster than the IJN could train them, allowing the USN simultaneously to cover amphibious landings and defeat Japanese carrier attacks.

US carriers survived massed kamikaze attacks at Okinawa because, unlike the RN at Malta, their fighter complements were large and their fighter-control system based on improved radars. Despite these advances, however, eight large, one light, and three escort carriers were seriously damaged by suicide aircraft. Massed kamikaze raids were such a threat to the carriers and the amphibious forces that B29 bombers were ordered to crater the airfields where the Japanese aircraft were organized for their assaults. However, despite the damage they sustained at Okinawa, US carriers demonstrated that carrier aviation could wage sustained campaigns against land targets. That understanding formed the basis for the development of modern carrier battle groups armed with nuclear weapons. See also SEA POWER.

TOM HONE

Friedman, N., *British Carrier Aviation* (London, 1988).
——*Carrier Air Power* (London, 1981).
——*U.S. Aircraft Carriers* (Annapolis, Md., 1983).
Hughes, W. P., *Fleet Tactics: Theory and Practice* (Annapolis, Md., 1986), ch. 4.

Casablanca conference, see SYMBOL; see also GRAND ALLIANCE.

cash and carry act, see NEUTRALITY ACTS.

Cassino, see MONTE CASSINO.

Castelrosso (Greek: Kastellorizo), small (23 sq. km./9 sq. mi.) Italian-owned island which lies off the southern Turkish coast 130 km. (80 mi.) east of Rhodes and 240 km. (150 mi.) west of Cyprus. It was briefly occupied in February 1941 by the British No. 50 Middle East Commando (see LAYFORCE), which withdrew after the Royal Navy failed to prevent an Italian counter-attack. When the Italians surrendered in September 1943 the British occupied the island. They remained there after the *Dodecanese campaign of October–November 1943 and used it as a base for raiding operations into the Aegean. In 1947 it was ceded to Greece and is now usually recognized as being part of the Dodecanese Islands.

Catroux, General Georges (1877–1969), French army officer who was governor-general of French Indo-China from August 1939 until he was replaced in June 1940 by a *Vichy government nominee. He was the only army general to join de *Gaulle and the Free French in 1940, and was condemned to death by Marshal *Pétain for doing so. De Gaulle gave him command of the Free French forces for the *Syrian campaign and he then became 'Delegate-General and Plenipotentiary' for the Levant. One of the original members of the *French Committee for National Liberation, formed in June 1943, he was appointed governor-general of his birthplace, Algeria, the same month before being appointed the minister for French North Africa that September. In February 1945 he became French ambassador to Moscow, remaining there until 1948.

Caucasus. The Soviet republics of Georgia, Armenia, and Azerbaijan, jointly known as 'Transcaucasus', are separated from Russia by the peaks of the Caucasus range. The region attracted attention during the war both through the strategic value of its oilfields at Baku,

Grozny, and Maikop, and through the allegedly separatist tendencies of its population.

In the spring of 1940, when the USSR was making massive deliveries of oil to Germany, a British plan to bomb Baku was only called off at the last minute.

In the summer of 1942, the Wehrmacht's southern offensive was aimed at the oilfields (see GERMAN–SOVIET WAR, 4). German troops occupied Maikop in the northern Caucasus, scaled Mount Elbruz (5,630 m./18,470 ft.), Europe's highest peak, and entered the valley of the Terek (August 1942). But growing complications on their northern flank at *Stalingrad forced a halt. They neither crossed the mountains nor reached the Caspian shore. In 1944 Stalin ordered that many of the mountain peoples of the northern Caucasus—Chechens, Ingushi, and others who were suspected of *collaboration—be forcibly deported to central Asia (see DEPORTATIONS). Though remnants were allowed to return 20 years later, the ethnic composition of the population was permanently changed.

The whole of the region was re-occupied by Soviet forces in the course of 1943. NORMAN DAVIES

Cavallero, Marshal Count Ugo (1880–1943), Mussolini's most outstanding military commander who served as chief of the Italian High Command from December 1940 to February 1943 (see COMANDO SUPREMO).

Cavallero served with great distinction during the *First World War, rising to the rank of brigadier-general. He left the army in 1920 and later served for three years as under-secretary of war. In November 1937 he was appointed commander of Italian forces in East Africa but resigned in May 1939 after which Mussolini made him president of the *Pact of Steel co-ordinating committee. He succeeded his rival *Badoglio as head of the Comando Supremo and then, in early December 1940, also took personal command of the Albanian Front where the Greeks were counter-attacking Italian forces in the *Balkan campaign. There, his efforts to save Klissoura failed, but he stopped the Greeks from taking Valona.

He returned to Rome in May 1941, demanded, and received, greater control of the army, and began to create a proper High Command staff which had at least some authority over all three services. For nearly two years he tried to deal with Mussolini's demands for victories which were beyond the capabilities of his forces; with German insistence that Italy conform to German strategic policies; and with the large, ill-equipped, poorly trained Italian armed forces which were widely dispersed on a number of fronts. But in January 1943, after the Axis had been driven out of Libya by the second *El Alamein battle, he was dismissed. When Mussolini fell from power in July 1943 Cavallero was arrested by Badoglio, but was released by the Germans after Italy's *armistice with the Allies that September. The same month he apparently committed suicide while a guest of *Kesselring after refusing to fight on the side of the Germans.

cavalry, see ANIMALS and armed forces section of major powers.

cavity magnetron, an electronic vacuum valve which originated in the UK in 1940 as a generator of microwaves suitable for high-power pulse (10 kW) airborne *radar. With the aid of American resources and development skills, it brought about centimetric radar which was used with decisive effect during the battle of the *Atlantic and the *strategic air offensives from 1943 onwards.

The operational deficiencies of the existing 1.5 m (200 MHz) airborne radar systems were the driving force behind the British development of the cavity magnetron. With AI (Aircraft Interception) radars, unwanted ground return from a broad antenna pattern prevented any target being detected which was beyond the intercepting aircraft's height. Small wavelengths (10 cm) obviated this problem and allowed the use of compact antennas of high gain and narrow beam-width. What was then needed was a valve that would deliver workable power at 10 cm.

Devised by J. T. Randall and H. A. Boot at the Nuffield Laboratory of the University of Birmingham, the cavity magnetron had a six-segment copper anode. It first operated on 21 February 1940; was redesigned by E. C. S. Megaw at the General Electric Company, Wembley; and eventually emerged in its final form suitable for airborne use in June 1940. One was taken by the *Tizard mission to the USA in August 1940 (see Figures 1 and 2) and one American scientific writer, with understandable hyperbole, later stated that it was 'the most valuable cargo ever brought to our shores' (J. Baxter, *Scientists Against Time*, Boston, 1946, p. 142). It was the heart of the new radar's transmitter while another microwave valve, the klystron, was the equivalent vital organ in the receiver.

The basic magnetron diode valve can trace its origins to A. W. Hull of the USA, who in 1921 produced a cylindrical thermionic diode in which the behaviour of the electrons flowing from cathode to anode was controlled by an axial magnetic field. Pre-war studies on magnetrons were carried out in many countries. During 1936–7, in the Soviet Union, N. F. Alekseev and D. E. Malyarov produced demountable water-cooled cavity magnetrons, while, in Japan S. Nakajima and Y. Ito experimented successfully with cavity magnetrons from 1933 onwards. These achievements, however, were not translated into successful microwave programmes and were unknown to Randall and Boot, whose discovery in 1940 became the starting-point for the world-wide development of microwave radars.

On 2 February 1943, a Stirling bomber with an *H2S ground mapping radar crashed near Rotterdam and its self-destruct mechanism failed to work. The Germans set up a special 'Rotterdam' Commission and by 22 June 1943 had constructed a prototype of the captured equipment which delivered some 40 kW peak power at 9.1 cm. Thereafter German cavity magnetron development was undertaken and well-engineered centimetric

Cavity magnetron

Figure 1 shows the internal construction of an early GEC, Wembley, (E1189) eight-segment magnetron which was taken to the USA by the *Tizzard Mission in 1940 and copied by the Bell Laboratories. The Allies used magnetrons operating at 25 cm, 10 cm, 3 cm and 1.5 cm and the peak power achieved for a 10 cm magnetron by the end of the war was 1MW.

Figure 2 shows a cross-section of the cavity resonators. The operation of the magnetron has been quite accurately likened to the manner in which a sound wave builds up in a bottle when you blow air across its mouth. An oscillating electromagnetic field (radio wave) builds up as a result of electrons from the cathode sweeping past the cavity openings and, as in the sound wave analogy, the frequency of the waves is the resonant frequency of the cavities.

Figure 2

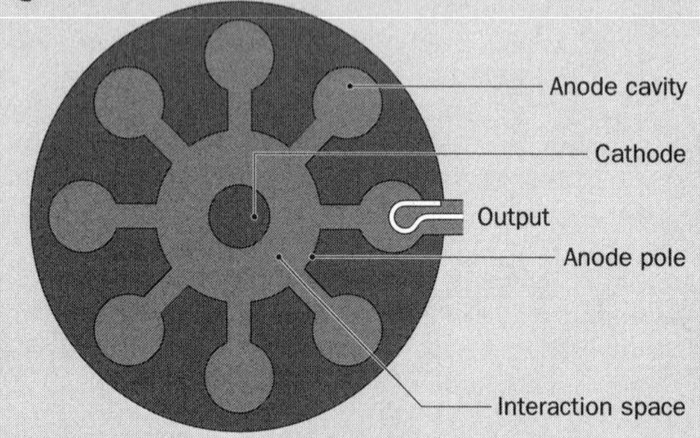

Figure 1

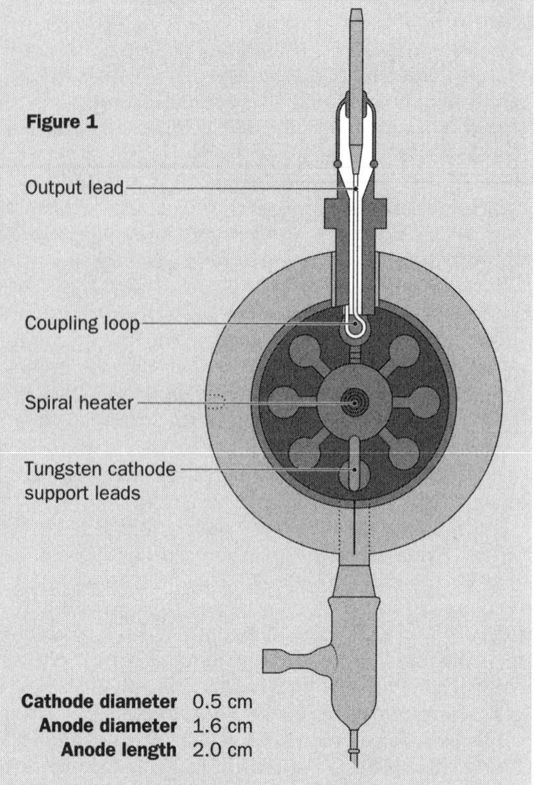

Sources: Figure 1: Megaw, E.C.S., 'The High-Power Pulsed Magnetron: A Review of Early Developments', *J. Instn. Elect. Engrs.*, 1946, *93*, Part III A, pp. 977–84. Figure 2: Terman, S. E., *Electronic and Radio Engineering* (NY, 1955).

radars were produced, but, broadly speaking, Germany lagged behind the Allies in their microwave programme by almost two years. SEAN SWORDS

Bowen, E., *Radar Days* (Bristol, 1987).
Collins, G., *Microwave Magnetrons* (New York, 1948).

CBI, see CHINA–BURMA–INDIA THEATRE.

Celebes Islands, see NETHERLANDS EAST INDIES.

censorship, both of the *press and of post, telephone, and telegraph, is automatic in police states. It was applied with rigour in all the Axis powers throughout the war, and was regarded in all of them as a necessary measure of state security. In the USSR it was applied with equal severity. The newspapers in all these countries printed only what government wanted, when government wanted each item to appear; no one who opposed the regime could safely say so, in print, in manuscript, or by telephone. Radio broadcasts were just as firmly under control.

The UK and its empire also imposed censorship, though more mildly. Movements of warships, troops, and military aircraft were no longer reported in the press—in peacetime they had been, regularly. Newspapers sent *war correspondents to report on each campaign; they were given plenty of facilities, but not shown secret equipment, and they sent their dispatches through service censors, who might delete anything they thought helpful to the other side. Government did not take over the *BBC, but had a comfortable understanding with it. The French made similar arrangements until the fall of *France; *Pétain's regime was more stringent.

The letters home of British servicemen were censored by their junior officers, whose own letters were liable to chance censorship at base. Letters, from civilians and serving men alike, going overseas were channelled through a central censorship bureau in Liverpool, where random inspection produced a certain amount of useful intelligence, most of it on the state of home morale. Here, and in many other censors' offices, letters were often as

Each combatant power had its own methods of **censorship**. Here, an Australian censor is at work in Melbourne in July 1943, snipping out indiscreet passages from letters.

a matter of routine criss-crossed with an X of brush-strokes intended to develop any secret ink; if hidden messages did appear, the letter was at once whisked off to the security authorities, as evidence that *spies might be at work.

No one with any sense ever supposed that telephone calls or telegrams or cables were private. The near-monopoly of Cable & Wireless over the world cable system provided the British Admiralty with much valuable intelligence.

In the USA, censorship was regarded as unconstitutional, in principle; informal arrangements were satisfactorily made for war correspondents at the fighting fronts, and Congress approved some degree of censorship of serving men's letters. M. R. D. FOOT

CERBERUS, German codename for naval operation mounted on 11 February 1942 to dispatch the two battle-cruisers **Scharnhorst* and *Gneisenau* and the heavy cruiser *Prinz Eugen* to Norway from Brest, via the English Channel. It was ordered by Hitler, who feared an imminent Allied invasion of Norway. Grand Admiral *Raeder, the German Navy's C-in-C, was so appalled at the risks it entailed that he refused to take any responsibility for the operation.

The British had calculated that the Germans might take this gamble and had long-laid plans to counter it, principally with attacks by aircraft of Bomber Command. *ULTRA intelligence, which revealed the areas being cleared of mines for the passage of the warships and the gathering of additional German air and sea forces to protect the squadron, gave clear warning that the break-out was imminent. But through a series of mischances, the clever jamming (see ELECTRONIC WARFARE)—and breakdown—of British *radar, and the mistaken assumption that the German squadron would steam through the Channel at night, the Admiralty was not alerted when it sailed at 2245 on 11 February 1942, and remained in ignorance of its presence until the three ships had passed Boulogne in broad daylight. By then it was much too late to mount a co-ordinated attack. Only *MTBs, some torpedo bombers, and six destroyers were available (the Home Fleet could not be risked), for C-in-C Bomber Command had, without telling the Admiralty, stood down over half the bombers allotted to the operation and the remainder were on four hours' notice instead of the required two. Piecemeal attacks were mounted—a complete flight of six torpedo bombers was destroyed—but all three ships eventually reached Germany, an achievement that was rightly seen by the Germans as a triumph, and by the British as a blow to their prestige which caused a public outcry.

In fact the operation was assessed by the German Naval High Command as a tactical success but a strategic failure as the ships presented a much greater threat when based at Brest. It also transpired that both battle-cruisers had been damaged by mines which British aircraft had laid in the areas already swept by the Germans; and though both *Scharnhorst* and *Prinz Eugen* eventually reached Norway, *Gneisenau* was so badly damaged by RAF *bombs while in dry-dock that her refit was abandoned. See also SEA POWER.

Polter, J., *Fiasco* (London, 1970).

Četniks, see MIHAILOVIĆ AND THE ČETNIKS.

Ceylon, Indian Ocean island 435 km. (270 mi.) long inhabited by some six million Sinhalese and Tamils which had been a British colony since 1818. By March 1942 it was one of the few remaining sources of natural rubber for the Allies. More important, it was strategically crucial if British contact with India was to be maintained. Soon after Japan entered the war in December 1941 Australian troops were temporarily garrisoned there until British forces arrived, and the British Eastern Fleet was initially based there. To avoid the failures that had occurred in *Singapore as a result of divided control (see BROOKE-POPHAM), Churchill, when he appointed Vice-Admiral Geoffrey Layton C-in-C Ceylon in March 1942, gave him unparalleled powers over civilians and military alike to make the island ready to defend itself. Layton was given little time to prepare, for the following month a powerful Japanese naval task force launched a raid into the *Indian Ocean (see Map 51) and attacked the capital, Colombo, and the port of Trincomalee, but it eventually withdrew and the island saw no more fighting. In June 1944 Kandy became the HQ of *South-East Asia Command and that December a British committee of enquiry arrived to investigate the island's desire for independence which was granted in 1948.

chaff, see ELECTRONIC WARFARE.

Chamberlain, (Arthur) Neville (1869–1940), British Conservative prime minister from May 1937 to May 1940. His policy of appeasement when dealing with Hitler—it was his signature on the *Munich agreement—earned him a post-war reputation for weakness, though it has been cogently argued that appeasement was essential to gain time for rearmament. In fact he was a determined and principled politician, who strove to maintain peace by pursuing what was at the time an almost universally accepted policy. His real, and fatal, weakness lay in his inability to comprehend the type of man with whom he was dealing, and continuing to strive for compromise for far longer than was prudent. He also had an unfortunate habit of mistiming his public announcements, saying for example that Hitler had 'missed the bus' just before the Germans invaded Norway in April 1940 (see NORWEGIAN CAMPAIGN). The debate on Norway in the House of Commons turned into a personal attack on Chamberlain, and though the government retained a comfortable majority (81) when the vote was taken on 8 May, he had obviously lost the confidence of his supporters. On 9 May he summoned his two most likely successors, *Halifax and Churchill, to a meeting with the chief whip, David Margesson. He said that he doubted if he could continue and offered the premiership to Halifax, who refused it, and it then became evident that the mantle would fall on Churchill. That same evening Chamberlain asked the Labour Party if it would serve in a national government under him. It refused and though Chamberlain hesitated to resign when Hitler's attack was launched the next morning (see FALL GELB), he was soon left in no doubt by his erstwhile supporters that he had little choice but to do so. However, he remained the leader of the Conservative Party, and retained powerful backing amongst Conservative backbenchers. He served in Churchill's cabinet as Lord President of the Council, his last political act being to draw up the charter for *SOE, in mid-July 1940. Illness forced him to resign in October 1940, and he died of cancer the following month. See also ORIGINS OF THE WAR and UK, 3.

Changi was a prison camp for Allied servicemen and civilians situated on a promontory at the eastern end of *Singapore. It was set up by the Japanese after the British colony fell to them in February 1942 in barracks belonging to the British garrison. Initially it contained 50,000 British and Commonwealth troops, but many were soon sent to work in Japan and Japanese-occupied countries, and some to the *Burma–Thailand railway. In May 1943 the 6,000 prisoners remaining in the camp were moved to another barracks and in May 1944, when the 2,800 civilians were interned elsewhere, to Changi gaol.

Because of the large numbers involved the Japanese made those in Changi camp responsible for their own administration, organization, and discipline, and it was guarded by members of the *Indian National Army not by the Japanese. See also PRISONERS-OF-WAR.

Channel Islands. Situated about 32 km. (20 mi.) west of the Cherbourg peninsula, they were the only part of the UK to be occupied. On 28 June 1940 the Germans bombed the two principal islands, Guernsey and Jersey, causing 44 deaths, and two days later they began occupying them. About 30,000 civilians had already been evacuated, but about twice that number remained. The British authorities instructed the islanders not to resist occupation, but some hid Soviet *prisoners-of-war who were being used by the *Todt Organization to build fortifications for the *Atlantic Wall—they were deported to Germany for doing so—and there were a few other acts of isolated resistance.

Life for the ordinary islander was harsh. In September 1942, 2,000 British-born civilians were sent to *internment camps in Germany. Another 200 were deported in January 1943 as a reprisal for a British commando raid, one of several mounted against the German garrison during the war. Starvation, imprisonment, and harsh fines were commonplace. *Collaboration—working voluntarily for the Germans, black marketeering, or being an informer—was not unusual, and quite a number of women consorted with the garrison (they were called 'Jerry bags'). Post-war claims that the occupation had been moderate reflected the experience of the islands' administrators who had been well treated. This was not the experience of the ordinary islander, and the post-war 'determination by the islands' rulers and the British government to hide collaboration in high places (was) shaming indeed' (P. King, *The Channel Islands War: 1940–1945*, London, 1991, p. 172). Documentation released into the public domain in 1992 confirmed that some of the islands' administrators collaborated with the Germans and helped in the round-up and deportation of a number of Jews to *concentration camps.

Chapultepec, Act of, signed at the pan-American conference in Mexico City held 21 February–8 March 1945. The conference was held in a museum on Chapultepec Hill, hence the Act's name, and was first proposed by Argentina the government of which was not recognized by the Allied powers. The US secretary of state, Edward *Stettinius, regarded Argentina's request to have the conference to discuss its relations with other

American powers as a 'brazen and insincere move', but Mexico pressed for the conference to be held in order to discuss existing problems as the war approached its end. But Argentina was not invited and discussion about it was relegated to the penultimate item on the agenda.

'The problems at the heart of the conference were those of world organization, the future of the inter-American system, and the social and economic difficulties of Latin America both during and after the transition from war to peace' (R. Humphreys, *Latin America and the Second World War*, Vol. 2, London, 1982, p. 213). The first matter to be agreed, concerned the harbouring of war criminals, was never held to. 'Under the resolutions adopted here,' Stettinius stated, 'no Axis leader, official, or agent who is guilty of crimes against law and civilization in this war will be able to escape punishment by finding refuge in this hemisphere.' (see BARBIE, EICHMANN, MENGELE).

The Act, which was signed at the end of the conference, stated that any act of aggression on any American state, from without or within, would be considered an act of aggression on all. The conference also recommended an Inter-American Defence Treaty and one was eventually signed at Rio de Janeiro in 1947. As a result of a motion passed at the conference, Argentina declared war on the Axis powers and signed the Act, and on 9 April its government was recognized by the UK and USA. See also LATIN AMERICA.

chariots, see HUMAN TORPEDOES.

check-mate system, a means by which British warships patrolling for German *auxiliary cruisers and other disguised Axis vessels would obtain by radio verification of a ship's identity from the Admiralty. It was introduced in October 1942 after a British ship in German hands had twice passed herself off as a sister ship when challenged. It did not become fully operational until May 1943.

Chelmno (also known as Kulmhof), the first, and highly secret, Nazi death camp which killed gypsies and Jews from the Łódź *ghetto. It was situated 65 km. (40 mi.) north-west of Łódź, Poland, and was opened in December 1941. Figures vary, but probably about 152,000 Jews were killed there, being gassed as soon as they arrived. Only ten people are known to have escaped from it. See also FINAL SOLUTION and OPERATION REINHARD.

chemical warfare (CW) is usually understood to mean the employment of toxic materials such as mustard gas, nerve gas, and phosgene. The Italians used mustard gas in Abyssinia, but chemical weapons were not used during the Second World War, though the Japanese may have used them during the *China Incident. But smokescreens and *flamethrowers, also technically part of CW, were widely employed by both sides.

Morality played little part in the reluctance of either side to use CW. As with *biological warfare, fear of retaliation was a major factor, and the speed of modern warfare also militated against its use. Although CW was never used, chemical weapons were deployed (see BARI), and with the experience of the *First World War behind them the European combatants of the Second were, by September 1939, well advanced in their defensive preparations against it. British gas protection, detection, and decontamination equipment were considered the best in the world, while anti-gas installations were part of the *Maginot Line and of communal shelters in Paris. Germany and the USSR, too, were well prepared to take defensive measures, though in Germany there was a shortage of gas masks.

In September 1939 the only power in the northern hemisphere to have developed an offensive capability with the various gases they possessed was the USSR. The Germans had about 2,900 tons of CW gases, but no adequate means of delivering them as Hitler banned their offensive use. Nevertheless, the Germans did use toxic smoke during the siege of *Sevastopol; and they were the first to begin the production of a nerve gas, Tabun, in 1942. Another, Sarin, was ready for production by the end of the war, by which time the still more lethal Soman was also under development.

At the height of the invasion scare in July 1940 the British had a mere 410 tons of gas. This was rapidly increased until by December 1941 they had stockpiled 15,262 tons of mustard, phosgene, and other gases which could be delivered by artillery shells or bombs, and this quantity had more than doubled by the end of the war. Apart from possibly using it against a German invasion in 1940 (see SEALION), the only other time Churchill seriously considered employing this stockpile, against German cities, was when the V-1 attacks on London started in June 1944 (see V-WEAPONS). But the idea was vetoed by the *Chiefs of Staff as impracticable.

The USA called its mortar units chemical warfare companies, a hangover from the First World War when mortars were used to lay down smoke or gas; but like the UK it was lacking in CW weapons when it entered the war. A joint agreement on their use was soon worked out with the UK, whereby their first use had to be agreed between the two powers, but either could retaliate without the other's permission. The Eighth US Army Air Force based in the UK was supplied by the British with 10,000 phosgene-filled bombs. But American production of CW weapons was quickly started and thirteen new plants were built for this purpose during the war. By 1945 the USA had stockpiled 87,000 tons of toxic chemicals, but a plan to use some of it against the Japanese on *Iwo Jima was vetoed by Roosevelt who had twice publicly declared he would only use CW in retaliation.

Japan was the only combatant nation which may have employed CW, though *Tōjō and other Japanese officials insisted that they had only used tear and sneezing gases. Documentary evidence to the contrary is lacking, but one report states that the Japanese had employed gas in the China Incident 876 times up to the end of June 1941. It was also alleged that in October 1941 Japanese aircraft dropped gas bombs on the suburbs of Ichang, the last navigable port on the River Yangtse, killing 600 Chinese soldiers. Once Japan was at war with the USA all offensive use of CW was stopped, for fear of retaliation, though Louis Allen relates that a German-invented gas bomb, filled with prussic acid, was employed by the Japanese against British armour during the *Burma campaign (see *Burma: The Longest War*, London, 1984, p. 301).

During the war employing chemicals against plants was regarded as part of biological warfare, though nowadays it would be regarded as part of CW. A chemical compound, isopropyl phenyl carbamate, was developed in the UK in 1942 which would destroy crops and another, calcium-2-methyl-chlorophenoxy-acetate, which would kill root crops. But Churchill decided not to manufacture either as they would take too long to produce in bulk. The data were given to the USA, which in mid-1945 considered spraying Japanese rice crops with ammonium thiocynate. See also SCIENTISTS AT WAR.

Harris, R., and Paxman, J., *A Higher Form of Killing* (London, 1982).

Chennault, Maj-General Claire L. (1890–1958), US Army officer who served as a pilot in the *First World War and as chief of US Army Air Corps fighter training afterwards. He was sufficiently unorthodox to maintain, against the accepted wisdom of the day, that bombers needed the support of fighters (see AIR POWER). In 1937 he was retired because of hearing problems and accepted a post to train Chinese pilots in *Chiang Kai-shek's air force who were to be equipped with American aircraft to fight the Japanese (see CHINA INCIDENT). In November 1940 he returned to the USA to recruit American pilots and maintenance staff who became the nucleus of the *American Volunteer Group (The Flying Tigers) which fought the Japanese in China and in the *Burma campaign. It never numbered more than 200 aircraft, but Chennault's training made it very successful in combat.

In April 1942 Chennault was recalled to active service and was promoted brig-general (a rank he already held in the Chinese Air Force). From July 1942 he commanded the newly formed China Air Task Force (Fourteenth USAAF from March 1943), which controlled all Army Air Force units in China, and this organized the air ferry known as the *Hump which flew supplies into China from India over the Himalayas. In October 1942 he gained Roosevelt's attention—and the necessary *matériel*—when he asserted that with 12 heavy and 30 medium bombers flying from Chinese bases he could 'accomplish the downfall of Japan'. This proved illusory (and many of Chennault's bases were overrun by the Japanese ICHI-GŌ offensive which started in 1944) while he became increasingly involved in arguments over the allocation of resources with *Stilwell who commanded US forces in the *China–Burma–India theatre. In July 1945 he resigned in protest against the proposed disbandment of the joint Chinese–American wing of the Chinese Air Force.

Chennault, C., *Way of a Fighter* (New York, 1949).

Cherwell, Lord, see LINDEMANN.

Chiang, Madam (b.1900). The marriage of *Chiang Kai-shek in 1927 to the American educated and Christian Soong Mei-ling, sister of T. V. *Soong, represented the alliance between Chiang's victorious faction of the Kuomintang (KMT) and Shanghai finance and industry, as well as bringing international connections and acceptance. Madam Chiang was a woman of distinction, who combined charm, intuition, intelligence, beauty, and courage, all of which she used to effect in attracting support, particularly foreign support, to her husband's regime. To her finer qualities must be added a quick temper and considerable hauteur, more readily apparent to the Chinese than to most foreigners.

With the start of the *China Incident in July 1937, Madam Chiang, who at some risk to herself had played an important role in the resolution of the Sian incident (see CHIANG KAI-SHEK) acquired new prominence. She organized work on behalf of China's war orphans (see also CHILDREN), for which she received large sums of money from all over the world, and was involved in the establishment of co-operatives, war work among China's women, care for the wounded, children's education, and the rehabilitation of the homeless. In this she was greatly aided by a publicity campaign targeting official and private organizations throughout the democracies. Inevitably, however, propaganda notwithstanding, all this effort hardly scratched the surface of China's suffering.

A Lt-colonel in the Chinese air force, and for a time its commander, Madam Chiang was also honorary commander of the *American Volunteer Group, or Flying Tigers, in which capacity she championed the views of its commander *Chennault with her husband. Her relations with her husband's Allied Chief of Staff, Lt-General *Stilwell were less happy, but without her mediation the break between Chiang and Stilwell would probably have come sooner.

The acme of Madam Chiang's wartime career was reached with her triumphant visit to the USA from November 1942 to May 1943. Speaking to packed rallies across the country, addressing Congress, her face adorning the cover of *Time* Magazine (its editor, Henry Luce, with his China-missionary background, was one of her strongest supporters), she achieved a virtual apotheosis in the eyes of the American public. She brought China's war with Japan to the USA, and *inter alia* ensured that a reluctant Treasury could no longer delay a large and much needed bullion shipment to China. That her petulant behaviour in private exasperated Roosevelt was not widely known at the time.

As the war approached its end and the inefficiency and corruption of Chiang's KMT government became impossible to ignore, Madam Chiang alone was not enough to ensure continued foreign sympathy, and her political importance diminished accordingly. She had played a significant role in China's struggle, but more than ever it was apparent that her influence had been far greater on foreigners than on her own people. See also WOMEN AT WAR.

Hahn, E., *The Soong Sisters* (London, 1942).
Seagrave, S., *The Soong Dynasty* (New York, 1985).

Chiang Kai-shek as war leader. Generalissimo Chiang Kai-shek (1887–1975), President of the Republic of China and C-in-C of the Chinese armed forces, was appointed supreme commander of the China theatre (see CHINA–BURMA–INDIA THEATRE) by Churchill and Roosevelt in December 1941. In December 1936, in what became known as the Sian incident, he was kidnapped by rebel army officers in the city of Sian (Siking). They wished to force him to abandon his campaign of suppression against the Chinese Communist party; to form a united front with the communists and all other patriotic forces; and to lead China in a war of resistance against Japan whose occupation of *Manchukuo and further encroachment into Chinese territory were soon to culminate in the Marco Polo Bridge Clash and the start of the *China Incident. When Chiang stubbornly refused to treat with the rebels, preferring, as he saw it, death to dishonour, some were prepared to kill him. Others, however, including the communist leader *Chou En-lai, believed that despite the role he had played in the past, only Chiang was capable of leading the whole nation against the Japanese, and eventually a compromise was reached which allowed Chiang to return to the capital in safety, with the communists agreeing to incorporate themselves, at least in theory, into the national army under the generalissimo's command. The widespread and largely spontaneous rejoicing which followed Chiang's return to Nanking seemed to confirm that he was indeed the leader which China needed for the war of resistance.

It was not true, as many (particularly on the left) argued at the time, that Chiang was prepared to appease the Japanese virtually indefinitely. On the contrary, from the mid-1930s and with the assistance of German officers (first General Hans von Seeckt, then General von *Falkenhausen), he had been working hard to train and equip an effective army. He replaced the one-time Soviet instructors at the Whampoa military academy with 30 Germans and the purchase of German arms was arranged through their connections. Between 1936 and early 1937 Chiang and his senior officers, together with their German advisers, worked out a plan of strategic retreat, which involved a fighting but orderly evacuation of most areas north of the Yangtze River. Shanghai would be the pivot for a move upriver, if necessary as far as Chungking.

Behind this plan lay two basic strategic considerations. First, Chiang was convinced, correctly, of China's military and industrial inferiority *vis-à-vis* Japan. Second, he expected that a combination of casualties and overstretched supply lines would steadily weaken the Japanese. Moreover, they would be forced to carry the burden of controlling and governing an area that might (and in the event did) considerably exceed that of Japan itself, both in territory and population. Chungking, in the distant western province of Szechwan, was thought to be a viable economic base from whence his National, or Kuomintang (KMT), government could play a prolonged waiting game. It was hoped that the enemy would eventually realize they had been drawn out to the end of a limb, and that there was nowhere they could go but back.

Chiang genuinely believed that war with Japan would eventually become inevitable, and he was prepared to fight it. However, quite apart from building up his armed forces and his industrial base, he also saw a united home front as a necessary prerequisite for successful resistance. This meant not only holding together, and sometimes fighting, the disparate collection of politicians and military leaders whose loyalty to the KMT government was frequently tenuous in the extreme, but more particularly, eradicating the communists. Chiang saw the latter as a disease of the heart, whereas the Japanese were only an external disorder which would eventually go away, however distressing it might be at the time. Yet he paid more attention to the physical elimination of the communists and their supporters than to the underlying social and economic conditions which were their seed-bed. Critics of the regime were struck by the contrast between the bloody suppression campaigns against fellow Chinese, on the one hand, and such phenomena as the failure to counterattack against Japanese aggression in Manchuria in 1931, the failure to support the courageous Nineteenth Army in Shanghai during the Japanese attack there in the spring of 1932, the signing of the Tangku truce in 1933, and the Ho-Umezu agreement of 1935. These could all be explained by the concept of trading space for time. However, this policy was not well understood, and it was not in the nature of Chiang or of his government to go to great lengths to explain it. It was also true, however, that the communists, who wanted active battle against Japan as a stepping-stone to their own victory, did not want the policy to be understood, and devoted great and successful efforts to this end.

China's war of resistance against Japan began with the Marco Polo Bridge incident on 7 July 1937. Once again, Chiang and many of his colleagues would probably have much preferred to postpone the conflict and make concessions to Japan. But because of the pressure of the united front that had been formed following the Sian kidnapping, they finally felt compelled to resist. Thus Chiang was forced into a war which he did not believe he was yet ready to fight: a war that would prove equally disastrous both to Japan and to the KMT.

These reservations notwithstanding, during the first two years of the war Chinese determination to resist was largely unbroken, and Chiang Kai-shek became the heroic symbol both at home and abroad of that resistance, which surpassed all Japanese expectations. In Shanghai the Chinese forces obeyed their orders to hold out for six weeks and, in the hope of involving the western powers, with their International Settlement and substantial interests in the city, either as mediators or combatants, Chiang decided to postpone the retreat for at least another week. In all, the battle for Shanghai lasted from 13 August to 9 November 1937. When the retreat came, what was to have been an orderly evacuation turned into a near riot, with each man for himself; but as the Chinese armies moved further inland the Japanese lost their chance to force them to surrender, and thus their hopes for an early victory.

Japanese frustration and anger at Chinese resistance resulted in the rape of Nanking. Chiang has been criticized for making a stand in the indefensible capital rather than behind it, from which equal time could have been bought with far less loss of life. During the battle for Shanghai, no preparations had been made for the defence or evacuation of the city. But quite apart from Nanking's symbolic importance, Chiang's aim was to engage world attention, and possibly foreign involvement, because of the presence of the embassies. The fate of the city certainly had a major impact on the way Japan was viewed in the west and further steeled Chinese determination to resist.

Following the fall of Nanking, the Japanese failed to encircle the Chinese at Hankow, the next stop upriver. After Hankow fell, Chiang's German advisers were dejected, seeing no alternative but surrender. Chiang, however, was quite unmoved, and his armies subsequently made a successful defence at Changsha and several other important cities. By the time Chiang had established his wartime capital in Chungking, the Japanese had had to abandon their advance and set about consolidating their territorial gains. Even in territory they occupied, pockets of resistance continued, especially near Hsüchow, where Chinese troops won a major battle at Taierhchwang. In June 1938 Chiang implemented a *scorched earth policy by ordering the dynamiting of the Yellow River dykes.

However, once Chiang had established his wartime capital in Chungking, and as the war stabilized and changed its nature, corruption and demoralization set in at an alarming rate, and the problems and weaknesses of Chiang's leadership became increasingly obvious. With a virtual stalemate on the ground, both communists and nationalists were able to turn their attention to their abiding mutual enmity, and the New Fourth Army incident of January 1941, in which KMT troops destroyed a communist HQ unit, marked the effective end of the united front. Chiang became increasingly reluctant to use his best troops against the Japanese, particularly following the entry of the UK and USA into the war against Japan. For much of the later years of the war, some half a million KMT troops were employed in sealing off Southern China from the communist armies in the North, and the best equipment was hoarded for the inevitable showdown with the communists after the Japanese had been defeated by the Western Allies.

Despite his appointment as Supreme Commander of Allied Forces in the China theatre, Chiang had little interest in the war outside China except as it affected his own position. General *Brooke observed of him at the Cairo conference (see SEXTANT) that he had no grasp of war in its larger aspects, but was determined to get the best of all bargains. Chiang was not the only Chinese whose response would have been that China had been fighting the Allies' war alone for two years, and that a debt was owed. But such an attitude did not serve to make him more popular with Allied leaders, or, increasingly, with the US Congress, though his wife (see CHIANG, MADAM) made a triumphant visit to the USA which brought large financial and propaganda rewards to China. His notoriously bad relationship with his Allied Chief of Staff, Lt-General *Stilwell (see also CHINA–BURMA–INDIA THEATRE), added to this (although it has to be said that Stilwell was a poor diplomat, despite his excellence as a soldier), and Chiang's prickliness and meddling detracted from the only positive contribution played directly by Chinese troops outside China, in the *Burma campaign.

A major point of disagreement between Chiang and Stilwell concerned the use of *air power. The former accepted fully the argument of Maj-General *Chennault who commanded the Fourteenth USAAF in China, that he could defeat both Japanese and communists with air power alone. In the event, the Japanese Chekiang-Kiangsi offensive, which was launched in May 1942, proved, as Stilwell had expected, that the air force could not even halt the Japanese advance on its own bases. Victory had to be won on the ground. Chiang, however, was neither willing nor able to make the changes that would have been necessary to achieve such a victory, and the reasons for this are instructive.

To defeat the Japanese in conventional warfare, it would have been necessary to train and equip a modern army. This had been begun under the German advisers, but the war came well before more than a small proportion of Chiang's forces could have been called modernized, and it was these that he was now keeping in reserve. Stilwell had shown in both Burma and China itself that, properly led and equipped, Chinese troops were more than a match for the Japanese. But these conditions were rarely met, and as the war dragged on, the condition of the common soldiers deteriorated more than ever. Conscripts were treated like criminals, and even a nationalist supporter such as Liu Yutang conceded in 1945 that the army had lost the support it had enjoyed from civilians in 1937–8 before the stabilization of the front. Yet to reform the army from the base up, and to improve the conditions from which the common soldiers came and would be asked to fight for, would have involved the very social revolution which Chiang was seeking to avoid.

In fact Chiang, aloof and reserved at the best of times, was often surprisingly ignorant of actual conditions. He surrounded himself with a ring of men not much less ignorant than himself, and certainly corrupt (which he was not), who gave him a highly distorted view of what was happening. He rarely went to see for himself, and real supervision from the top was notably lacking. His minister of war and chief of staff, Ho Ying-chin, a man with little modern military knowledge, kept the army loyal through manipulation of cliques and control of supplies and funds. When this situation resulted in a plot by young officers to rid the army of their corrupt and inefficient seniors, Chiang's only response was to execute 16 of the young generals and arrest 600 officers involved in the plot. He took no action against those at whom the plot was aimed, for the latter were all his own confidants.

Even had he wished to do so, however, the very nature of his power base would have made such changes virtually impossible. As the US diplomat John Service wrote in a memorandum, Chiang 'has achieved and maintained his position in China by his supreme skill in balancing man against man and group against group, by his adroitness as a military politician rather than a military commander, and by reliance on a gangster secret police'. Accordingly, he became a prisoner of the complex of interests riddling the top levels of China's military structure. He was unable to be too free with the armies under the war zone commanders, and exercised undisputed control only over the ten armies which came directly under the central government. He also had to guard against any other general becoming too powerful, which meant that success was not always rewarded.

It was, of course, his genius as a military politician which had made him indispensable to the Sian kidnappers, for only he could bring together such a diverse group of interests. Only Chiang could have won over his erstwhile enemies, the Kuanghsi warlords, who numbered amongst themselves Li Tsung-jen, the victor of Taierhchwang. But Chiang could only hold the balance, not weld them into a single force. And, characteristically, he did not allow Li to follow up his victory, thus considerably reducing its effect. Stilwell had similar experiences.

The limitations of Chiang's success as war leader were never clearer than at the time of Japan's *ICHI-GŌ offensive, phase one of which was launched in April 1944, and phase two in June, when, despite their reverses in the Pacific, the Japanese were able to strike further into China than ever before. Yet, despite the disastrous situation, Chiang was probably not unhappy to see the force of the offensive directed against the dissident south-west. Central government troops were not engaged. The widely hated and corrupt KMT General Tang En-po, who had fled before the Japanese advance, was subsequently rewarded by Chiang with the command of fourteen US-equipped divisions, and entrusted with disarming the Japanese in the wealthy lower Yangtze-Shanghai region following the Japanese surrender.

At the end of the war, the Chinese had not been defeated, but neither had they defeated the Japanese. Moreover, by having virtually abandoned North China, and having in large part lost the hearts and minds of the people in the areas controlled by his own forces, Chiang, who had always equated strength with armament, ignoring organization, motivation, leadership, and basic care of his own troops and civilians, virtually ensured that he would lose the civil war he had always known would be inevitable. On the other hand, it was under his leadership that China had fought Japan single-handed for over two years, and for the rest of the war tied down a million Japanese troops who could not be used elsewhere. Apart from his skills as a military politician, this was achieved in large part by what his erstwhile Australian adviser William Henry Donald described as his hardheaded, unyielding, and uncompromising stubbornness.

Flawed as he was, Chiang was not devoid of positive attributes as a leader, hence the recognition even by his enemies that he had an essential role to play. He faced many difficulties, of which those posed by the Japanese were only a part. He lacked, however, the qualities which would have enabled him to override those difficulties and entitled him to be ranked as one of the great war leaders. RICHARD RIGBY

Botjer, G., *A Short History of Nationalist China, 1919–1949* (New York, 1979).
Boyle, J. H., *China and Japan at War, 1937–1945* (Stanford, Calif., 1972).
Tuchman, B., *Stilwell and the American Experience in China, 1911–45* (New York, 1970).

Chief of the Imperial General Staff (CIGS), formal title of the head of the British Army who was also a member of the British *Chiefs of Staff committee and of the *Combined Chiefs of Staff. In September 1939 the CIGS was *Ironside. He was succeeded in May 1940 by *Dill who was replaced by *Brooke in December 1941.

Chiefs of Staff (COS) committee, principal British inter-service body which gave advice on operational strategy to those directing the war and issued instructions to its commanders in the field when a strategy had been formulated. Once the USA entered the war the COS formed the *Combined Chiefs of Staff committee with its US counterpart, the *Joint Chiefs of Staff. The COS committee then became solely responsible for operational strategy in the *South-East Asia Command and for *Middle East Command.

Originally constituted in 1923 to co-ordinate defence and advise the Committee of Imperial Defence (CID) on strategy, the COS committee was later reinforced by two sub-committees for Joint Planning and Joint Intelligence (see UK, 8), and these remained the most important of the sub-committees which proliferated during the war years. On the outbreak of war it started reporting to the war cabinet which replaced the CID (see UK, 3). It then comprised Air Chief Marshal *Newall, Admiral *Pound, and Field Marshal *Ironside, with Maj-General *Ismay, as its secretary. *Dill replaced Ironside in May 1940 and Ismay, now Chief of Staff to Churchill in his capacity as minister of defence, became Churchill's representative on the committee. *Portal replaced Newall in October 1940, *Brooke replaced Dill in December 1941, and Admiral *Cunningham replaced Pound in October 1943. The members took turns in the chair, but after chairing it from December 1941 Brooke became its permanent chairman in March 1942.

*Mountbatten, appointed adviser on *Combined Operations in October 1941, attended COS meetings if Combined Operations matters were being considered, as did his successor, Maj-General Robert Laycock. But after his appointment as Chief of Combined Operations, Mountbatten became a *de facto* member, attending whenever 'major issues' or any 'special matter' which directly concerned him were under discussion.

When Churchill became prime minister in May 1940 he put the committee under his own control in his capacity as minister of defence, and he sometimes presided over its meetings which were held at least once daily. Committee members accompanied him to all the major Allied conferences (see GRAND ALLIANCE) and with his support and guidance they increasingly determined British strategy. In time they exerted an influence previously unsurpassed by any British military committee, and though Churchill sometimes opposed them he never overruled them. See also UK, 7.

Bramall, E., and Jackson, W., *The Chiefs* (London, 1991).

children were the victims of the Second World War to an extent quite unknown in previous conflicts. In Germany and occupied Europe many were victims of the Nazi **Lebensborn* and *euthanasia programmes, and it has been estimated that 1.2 million Jewish children died in the *Final Solution. (Only 11% of Jewish children living in Europe in 1939 survived the war.) But before it started the Refugee Children's Movement set up what became known as the *Kindertransporte*. It arranged for German and Austrian children—whose lives were at risk, whose parents were willing to part with them, and whose expenses could be guaranteed—to travel to the UK; and from November 1938 to September 1939 nearly 10,000 children, 9,000 of them Jews, were transported by train to safety.

Children were also victims of Soviet policies. According to Irene Wasilewska (*Suffer Little Children*, London, 1946) the Polish authorities calculated that about 140,000 children were deported to the USSR after Poland was divided between Germany and the Soviet Union in October 1939, of whom about 40,000 subsequently died and 85,000 never saw their homeland again. Many of those children in occupied Europe who did survive faced a bleak future: in 1945 there were 13 million abandoned children; Poland had one million orphans, Czechoslovakia 50,000, France 250,000, and Hungary 200,000; in Greece one child in eight was an orphan.

The number of children who were involved in the actual fighting was not insignificant, especially when their country was *in extremis*. In Moscow in July 1941 the *war photographer Margaret Bourke-White recorded that 'children patrolled the streets at twilight to warn householders who allowed threads of light to leak through their blackout curtains. It was the special function of children to help keep sandbags and water pails constantly filled in case of incendiary raids' (*Shooting the Russian War*, New York, 1942, p. 62). In the occupied parts of the USSR children reconnoitred German positions and worked with the partisans. They were such efficient scouts that Field Marshal *Kluge ordered that 'special vigilance should be exercised with regard to little boys, members of the Soviet Children's organization, the "Pioneers", who snoop around everywhere. Anyone of them caught on the railway line is to be shot on the spot.' A British *war correspondent, Alaric Jacob, related in his book (*A Window in Moscow*, London, 1946) that he met boys aged 13 and 14, who had worked with partisan units and killed with them, and several had been awarded *decorations. Resistance movements in other parts of occupied Europe also used children: boys, some as young as ten, fought with *Tito and the partisans in Yugoslavia; others were used as couriers; in Belgium young children helped resistance workers by noting down the movement of German vehicles. In April–May 1945 Japanese schoolchildren, sometimes armed only with swords, fought on *Okinawa at the same time as 5,000 *Hitler Youth, some only 12, were opposing the Red Army during the fall of *Berlin, an experience only about 10% of them survived.

For every child who was killed or wounded in combat many more died, or were maimed, by bombing. The Allied raids on *Hamburg in July 1943 killed 5,586 children, and several thousand—it is not possible to be more exact—were the victims of the *atomic bombs at *Hiroshima and *Nagasaki in August 1945. Of those who survived the blasts, many subsequently suffered long-term effects from radiation. Horrific damage was also done to unborn children; of 169 exposed *in utero* in Hiroshima, there were 33 cases of microcephaly.

To avoid the bombing both sides evacuated children from cities. In Germany a programme called Kinderlandverschickung (sending children into rural areas) set up about 9,000 camps for children in the country. In July 1941 80,000 women and children were ordered out of Moscow, but in *Shooting the Russian War* Margaret Bourke-White wrote that this was never officially announced as evacuation. Instead 20,000 schoolchildren were said to have gone to the Arctic regions for scientific research and another 50,000 had gone on an expedition to central Asia to undertake geographical surveys. Such was the confusion that some children never saw their families again. In Japan, 15,000 children were evacuated from Hiroshima before the atomic bomb destroyed it, and at the start of the *Finnish–Soviet war in 1939, 9,000 Finnish children, followed by 55,000 more during the next years, were sent to safety in Sweden.

But it was the British who evacuated the largest

As some combatant powers found themselves *in extremis*, so they called upon **children** to help in the war effort. This photograph, taken in May 1943, shows Japanese schoolboys of the Koga National School in Ibaraki prefecture saluting their instructor before starting military drill.

numbers. Under a government scheme, about 4 million adults and children were moved from the bigger cities, and another 2 million were evacuated privately. The first evacuees left on 1 September 1939 and during the next days 827,000 unaccompanied children and 524,000 mothers with pre-school children left the cities. But the *phoney war followed this exodus and by early 1940, 80% had returned to their homes. A further evacuation did not take place until the *Blitz began that September, and this was followed by another from London in mid-1944 when the *V-weapons became operational. British children were also sent to Canada and the USA by their parents. In London, the American committee for the Evacuation of Children, formed by American businessmen, had the names of 35,000 children whose parents had requested their evacuation. But transatlantic travel was hazardous—77 children died when the liner *Arandora Star*, en route for Canada, was torpedoed in 1940—and adequate convoy facilities were rarely available; only 2,000 eventually found American foster homes.

Though the bombing of civilian targets killed many children, and evacuation often inflicted considerable distress on those who survived, the young of unoccupied countries suffered less than those who were forced to live under Nazi rule. In western Europe Jewish children were usually deported with their parents to the *concentration camps. Many were hidden or adopted into other families to avoid this fate, though some families went into hiding together (see FRANK, ANNE). Non-Jewish children were also regularly deported for committing minor offences and many suffered *internment with their parents.

It was in eastern Europe that children, especially Jews, felt the full force of Nazi rule. They suffered a massive disruption of family life, for even if parents survived the fighting, bombing, starvation, or reprisal executions, they were divided, often for ever, from their children by *forced labour and the concentration camps. *Nazi ideology corrupted childhood, and often brought it to an abrupt end because, to survive, a Jewish child had to act and work like an adult. 'Children of tender years were invariably exterminated,' the commandant of *Auschwitz testified after the war, 'since by reason of their youth they were unable to work . . .'

Though the teaching they received was often distorted, non-Jewish children in occupied western Europe were allowed to continue their secondary education. But in those eastern territories absorbed into the Greater Germany the school system was replaced with institutions which only taught, in German, the most basic curriculum, and in the Polish General government (see POLAND, 2(b)), and in the occupied parts of the USSR, all schools above the primary level were closed and their equipment destroyed. 'For the non-German population of the East,' *Himmler stated in May 1940, school should consist 'in teaching simple arithmetic up to 500, the writing of one's name, and that God has ordered obedience to the Germans, honesty, diligence, and politeness. I do not consider an ability to read as necessary.' This policy led (as it did with Jewish pupils who were often banned from school altogether) to clandestine classes being held. In Warsaw alone, 8,000 matriculation certificates were secretly issued during the war years. Play, too, was restricted. Jewish children were forbidden bicycles, the use of local parks, or visits to the theatre or cinema. The laws became draconian and a child of 14 could be given the same punishment as an adult. In some parts of Poland children as young as 12 were eligible for forced labour: in Greece the age was 16, in Yugoslavia 17, and in France it was 18 for boys and 21 for girls.

German children were also the victims of Nazi ideology. Compulsory enrolment in the Hitler Youth and its offshoots encompassed about 80% of those eligible, and its regimentation inculcated a fanaticism among its members to which even the most ardent adult Nazi found it difficult to aspire. However, a significant percentage of those who were not members of the Hitler Youth rebelled against the regime and were persecuted for doing so. There were two main groups. Neither could be classed as mere hooligans; nor did they represent an organized resistance against the regime. The Edelweisspiraten (Edelweiss Pirates) were mostly working-class city youths aged between 14 and 18 in non-skilled jobs, though their leaders were sometimes older. They beat up Hitler Youth patrols, wrote anti-Hitler graffiti, and sang anti-Nazi songs. In Cologne-Ehrenfeld they helped *deserters, raided military depots, and assaulted Nazi Party members, and in November 1944 twelve of them were publicly hanged. The second group, the Swing-Jugend (swing youth), were mostly middle-class youngsters who listened and danced to jazz, condemned as decadent by the Nazis. They wore English clothes, spoke English, aped English mannerisms, and liked singing English songs such as 'We'll hang out our washing on the Siegfried Line'. Some of their leaders were sent to concentration camps but, as with the Edelweiss Pirates, the *Gestapo never managed to eradicate them entirely.

Juvenile delinquency rose nearly everywhere during the war years. In Belgium, France, and the Netherlands the number of cases brought to trial almost tripled, while in Norway they increased six times, from 5,016 in 1939 to 30,152 in 1944. In unoccupied countries such as the UK and the USA the figures were not so dramatic. Nevertheless, figures for the UK show an increase from 55,511 cases in 1936 to 73,620 in 1945. In the USA, where wartime conditions bred *v-girls and the *zoot-suit riots, and where new words such as 'teenager' and 'bobby-soxer' described the young, the statistics varied. Delinquency rose in the large cities, but fell in rural areas. It affected secondary education which in any case suffered a sharp decline, as American youngsters preferred work to study. Between 1941 and 1945 there was a decline of about 17% in enrolments, while the numbers of those aged from 14 to 17 who had a job rose from just over a million in 1940 to two million, or 29.6% of that age group, in 1944.

Dwork, D., *Children with a Star* (New Haven, Conn., 1991).
Halls, W., *Youth of Vichy France* (Oxford, 1981).
Johnson, B. (ed.), *The Evacuees* (London, 1968).
Macardle, D., *Children of Europe* (London, 1949).
Sosnowski, K., *The Tragedy of Children under Nazi Rule* (Poznań, 1962).
Turner, B., *And the Policeman Smiled* (London, 1990).

Chile was the most democratically minded of all the South American states, and basically one of the most pro-Allied. But it refused to sever relations with the main Axis powers despite accepting the recommendations and resolutions of the *Rio conference of January 1942. As a result, *Lend-Lease agreements went unsigned and the country came under considerable pressure to stamp out the activities of Nazi agents based there who were reporting on the movements of Allied shipping. Eventually, on 20 January 1943, a break with the main Axis powers was narrowly accepted by the Chilean Senate, but the government maintained its refusal to declare war on Germany. However, on 12 February 1945 it declared war on Japan and two days later signed the *United Nations Declaration. See also LATIN AMERICA.

CHINA

For the fighting in China, see CHIANG KAI-SHEK, CHINA–BURMA–INDIA THEATRE, and CHINA INCIDENT.

1. Introduction

The *China Incident, or Sino-Japanese war, which began with a minor skirmish at the Marco Polo Bridge near Peking on 7 July 1937, was the true beginning of the Second World War. It merged with the global struggle after the Japanese attack on *Pearl Harbor in December 1941 and led to fundamental change within China and in East Asia: the destruction of the Japanese empire, the triumph of the Chinese Communist Party in 1949 and the flight of *Chiang Kai-shek's Nationalists to Taiwan, deep involvement of the USA in Asia, and the re-emergence of the USSR as a major force on the Pacific rim. After Pearl Harbor, as the *Pacific war unfolded, the USA came to play an increasingly important role in Chinese affairs, both directly and indirectly. British and Commonwealth forces were also heavily engaged in this phase of the struggle, particularly in the *China–Burma–India theatre of operations. Finally, at the very end of the war, the USSR belatedly entered the war against the Japanese, stripped *Manchukuo (Manchuria) of its industrial base, and signed favourable treaties with China.

China's struggle with Japan and its participation in the Second World War was not, in fact, a single war but several conflicts nested one within the other like the intricately carved ivory spheres found in a Chinese antique shop. Until Pearl Harbor, the most encompassing sphere was war between China and Japan. But within this overarching conflict, two Chinas fought against Japan, not just one: the Chinese Nationalists or Kuomintang (KMT)—the official party-government of China under the leadership of Chiang Kai-shek—and the Chinese Communist Party (CCP) symbolized by *Mao Tse-tung. Although the two parties were nominally allied in a united front against Japan, the CCP in fact headed a state within a state: it ruled its own territory, commanded its own military forces, and determined its own policies.

The next inner sphere, indeed, was the struggle between the nationalists and the communists, as each sought to increase its legitimacy, influence, and territorial control at the expense of the other. This struggle began in the 1920s and is best known by the Long March of 1934–5 where communist survivors of an offensive by Chiang's forces retreated 9,600 km. (6,000 mi.) to the remote inland province of Shensi. By 1939 political rivalry was increasingly giving way to armed conflict at the local level, but because of the containing effect of the war between China and Japan, neither party dared initiate an open rupture, and so this incipient civil war remained congealed until after Japan's defeat.

Sometimes neglected because masked by other layers of conflict were the several Chinese regimes organized by the Japanese, and the puppet armies they put into the field against both the nationalists and the communists. The most significant of these collaborators—the Chinese equivalent of *Quisling or *Laval—was *Wang Ching-wei, a former colleague and bitter rival of Chiang Kai-shek who went over to the Japanese side in late 1938 (see also COLLABORATION). These forces were more numerous than effective, and they often changed sides as the fortunes of war and self-interest dictated. But when compelled by Japanese superiors, when they saw easy opportunities for expansion, or when they were cornered, the puppet armies were not a negligible force. At the most local level, puppets, bandits, secret societies, and local self-defence forces formed a shifting kaleidoscope of violence and counter-violence. Nationalists, communists, and Japanese variously sought their allegiance, their neutrality, or their destruction.

Finally, on 7 December 1941, an even larger sphere came to surround all of these struggles. With the attack on Pearl Harbor, the China Incident became a part of the Pacific war and merged fully with the global struggle of the Second World War. This changed the complex dynamics of all the conflicts contained within it, and injected the USA deeply into China and Chinese politics.

During the Second World War, the USA became heavily involved in China, first by assisting its efforts to survive and continue resistance against Japan, second by measures designed to make China politically a member of the *Grand Alliance and militarily a more effective combatant, and third by seeking to mediate the increasingly threatening tension between the nationalists and the communists, as a precondition to China's intended role in post-war East Asia.

At the outbreak of the China Incident in July 1937, the USA was still isolationist in outlook. Although the public felt sympathy for China, few believed that US national interests were at stake or that morality required direct action. Following the beginning of the European war in September 1939, although US government and popular attitudes became more internationalist and global, it was not until the spring and summer of 1941 that the USA took more positive steps: military pilots were permitted to join the newly-organized *American Volunteer Group, a military mission was sent to China, which was declared eligible for *Lend-Lease assistance, and the US began training Chinese pilots at a base in Arizona.

Even before the formal US entry into the Second World War, Roosevelt and Churchill had agreed that top priority had to be the survival of the UK and the war in Europe, with Asia and the Pacific area taking a back seat (see ABC-1 PLAN). Within Asia itself, China and the China–Burma–India theatre came to take second place to the trans-Pacific, *island-hopping strategy that had proved successful by late 1943. China's strategic significance therefore dwindled, a trend exacerbated by the increasingly passive and often inept performance of the Chinese nationalists. China remained important as an arena in which about one million Japanese troops were tied down and as a symbol of what the USA hoped would be the centre of a friendly, free, and democratic East Asia.

2. Domestic life and war effort

In 1937, on the eve of war with Japan, China was the most populous nation on earth—an estimated 480 million of which about 85% lived in rural areas (see Map 20), most as peasants. By contrast, in the great coastal and riverine cities—Peking, Tientsin, Shanghai, Nanking, Hankow, Canton—some of the elements of modern nationhood were taking shape. There, too, was over 80% of China's modern industry (an industrial census enumerated about 4,000 factories in China; although some were large, modern plants, many others were hardly more than workshops). Foreigners were also mainly concentrated there, in what were known as the 'treaty ports'. There were more than two dozen of these major coastal or riverine commercial and industrial cities where Europeans, Americans, and Japanese had been granted special privileges under a whole series of treaties, agreements, and protocols known collectively as 'the unequal treaties', which had been imposed upon China by superior force, mainly in the 19th century. The largest of these treaty ports was Shanghai, followed in importance by Tienstin, Canton, and Hankow.

Beyond the littoral, with its veneer of modernity, lay the hinterland, hardly touched by the 20th century. Overall, China was an extremely backward nation. In 1937, the rail network in all of China proper totalled only about 12,000 km. (7,500 mi.) less than that of the state of Illinois, or Japan's 20,000 km. (12,500 mi.). Gross domestic product in 1933—a depression year, but the only year for which detailed estimates have been made—totalled about US$9 billion, compared with US$40 billion in the USA, with one-quarter the population. Japan had seized Manchuria in 1931, thus depriving China of nearly one-third of its industry and a fifth of its foreign trade. Literacy was perhaps 20%; only about 550,000 students were enrolled, nationwide, in secondary education;

fewer than 20,000 attended the 30 or so universities and colleges throughout China.

Among those Chinese aware of the rising tension with Japan, the outbreak of war, however fateful, was greeted initially with a kind of relief and enthusiasm. Yet life in China during eight years of war was a cruel overlay upon the ordinary harshness experienced by most people in China most of the time.

There were, of course, the normal horrors of war: combat, bombings, armies of occupation, economic dislocation, blockade, and so forth. But there was more. As the nationalists retreated westwards, they sought to deny to the Japanese the fruits of victory by carrying out a *scorched-earth policy.

Beginning with the attack on Shanghai in August 1937 and symbolized above all by the 'rape of Nanking' in December, the Japanese pioneered the strategy of war against a civilian populace that came to be used by all nations in the Second World War. They initially visited these inhumanities mostly upon the cities of central China, where the nationalists were strongest, in the hope of terrorizing the populace into submission and of forcing Chiang Kai-shek's government to accept a dictated settlement. But in less spectacular ways the Japanese sought, throughout the war, to coerce Chinese civilians living in their zone of occupation or operations into acquiescence, obedience, and divorce from the forces of resistance. In areas their ground forces could not reach, the Japanese used the powerful new weapon of *air power, as in the sustained saturation bombing of Chungking throughout much of 1939 and 1940.

Against guerrilla forces, particularly communist-led guerrillas who often blended into the peasant population, the Japanese carried on ruthless campaigns until, late in the war, they could no longer sustain such operations. During 1940, these operations were of two sorts. The first, rapid search-and-destroy forays into communist-controlled bases, sought unsuccessfully to engage communist forces and eliminate their headquarters. The second were 'cage-and-silkworm' tactics, designed to deprive the communists of their vaunted mobility by containing them within 'cages' of which the major transportation routes were the bars, then to nibble inwards from these perimeters, like silkworms consuming a mulberry leaf. These latter tactics threatened the communist bases in northern China with slow strangulation, and in August 1940 the Eighth Route Army, commanded by P'eng Te-huai, undertook a major campaign to break the bars of these cages, the so-called 'Hundred Regiments Offensive'. Initially successful, the campaign called forth a brutal Japanese response and a change of tactics. From late 1940 to 1943, the Japanese carried on mopping-up campaigns which no longer sought to distinguish civilians from guerrillas. These operations were often known, on both sides, as 'three-all' campaigns: kill all, burn all, loot all.

In Japanese-occupied areas, above all in the major cities of eastern China from Peking south to Canton, the occupiers enforced a host of onerous and humiliating requirements upon the subject population, including bowing to Japanese soldiers when passing them in the street.

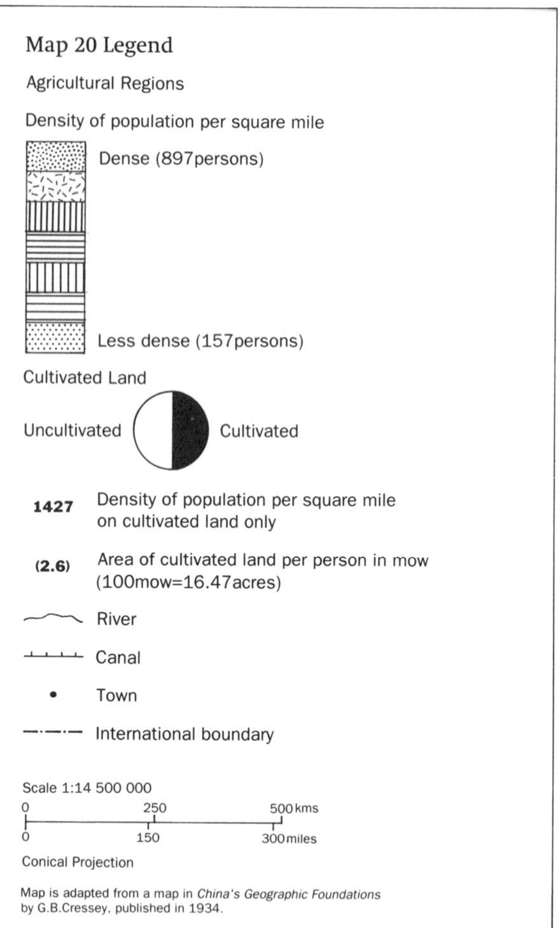

The outbreak of war set off massive migrations, often involving enormous hardship, away from areas being overrun by Japanese armies. Calls went out to transport whole schools and factories—machinery and all—to the interior, and if these attempts failed to create viable war industries, such heroic efforts were inspiring none the less. In one of the great movements of modern times, an estimated 12 million people made their way westwards into the fertile but backward provinces of western China (called 'Free China' or 'The Great Rear Area'), areas least touched by the 20th century and a central government. This migration included some 450 factories and 12,000 technicians.

While most of the evacuations followed the nationalist government, a smaller but significant movement took place into the communist-controlled areas in the barren reaches of north-western China. This stream included

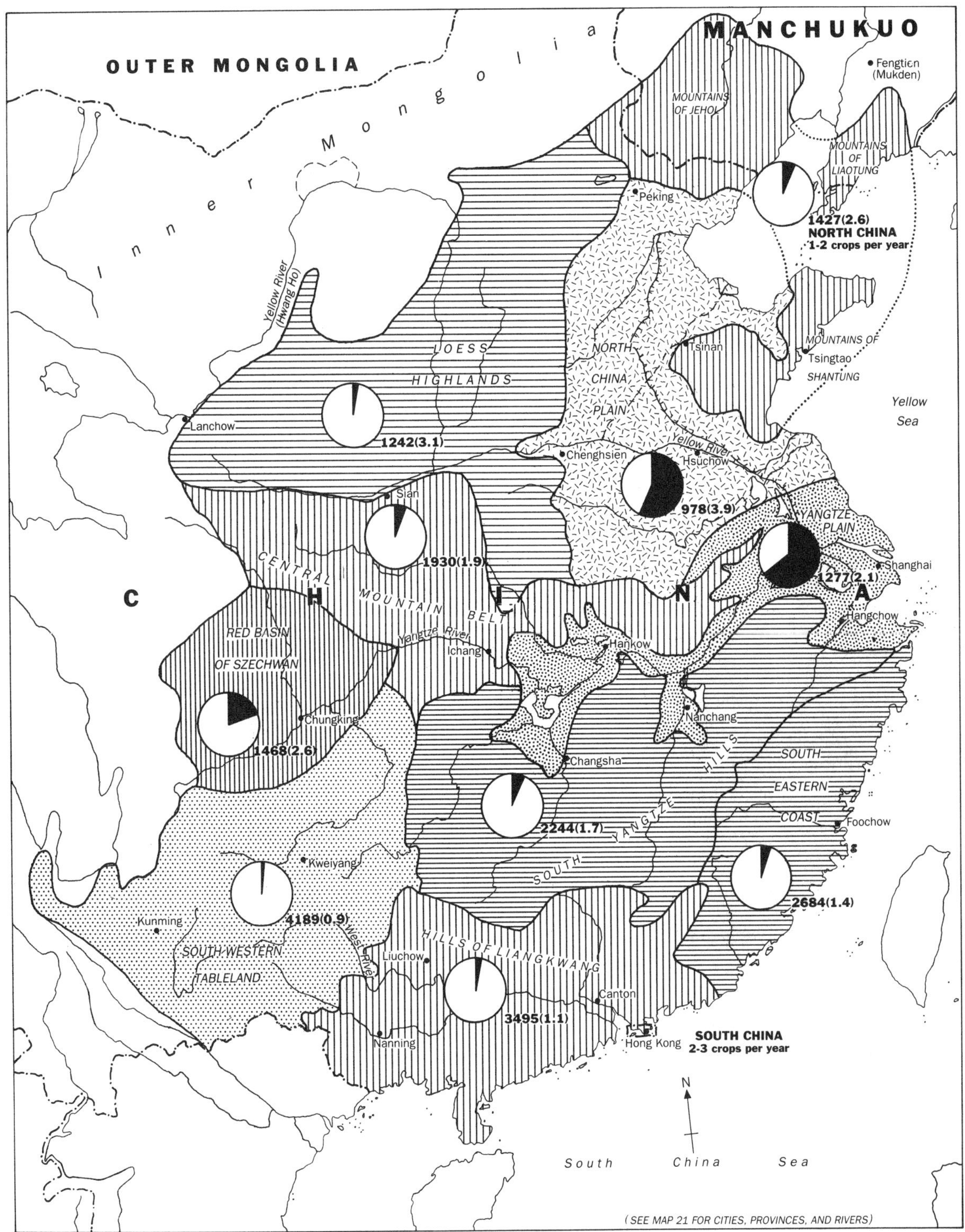

20. **China**: Density of population and percentage of cultivated land

China, 2, Table 1: Value of note issue in terms of pre-war prices, 1937–45 (amount and value in millions of yuan)

End of the period	*Amount of note issue of government banks*	*Average price index*	*Value of issue in terms of pre-war notes*
1937, July	1,455	1.04	1,390
1938	2,305	1.76	1,310
1939	4,287	3.23	1,325
1940	7,867	7.24	1,085
1941	15,133	19.77	765
1942	34,360	66.2	520
1943	75,379	228	330
1944	189,461	755	250
1945, August	556,907	2,647	210
1945, December	1,031,932	2,491	415

Source: Fairbank, J. K. and Feuerweker, A. (eds.), The *Cambridge History of China*, Vol. 13, Part 2 (Cambridge, 1986).

some of the most articulate and radical of China's student leaders and young intellectuals.

Despite the size of these migrations, much larger numbers, of course, remained behind and made the best of their lives under Japanese occupation. As in the occupied zones of Europe and the USSR, there was extensive collaboration—voluntary or compelled—with the invaders. In these areas, where open shows of defiance were ruthlessly punished, resistance had a meaning different from that in nationalist- or communist-controlled regions.

And everywhere in China, for tens of millions of peasants, life went on as it had for generations past memory, except that now and then occasional new threats of disaster were added to the familiar perils of drought, flood, insects, the tax collector, and uniformed or ragtag groups of predators foraging through the countryside. A disastrous famine in Honan province during the summer of 1943, caused partly by drought, partly by the inexorable grain requisitions of the provincial government and nationalist army, and partly by corruption and inattention regarding relief measures, took hundreds of thousands of lives. So enraged and desperate were the Honan peasants that they turned on their own army, disarming and shooting many nationalist soldiers.

Although the outbreak of war at first released much patriotic and selfless energy, the long years of war took an increasing toll on the population of China at all levels. In a seemingly endless struggle, fatigue, war weariness, and self-interest became more and more evident. Corruption, incompetence, personal evasion of the burdens of war, and individual enrichment were not limited to the areas of nationalist rule, but they were more prevalent and visible there than in the communist areas.

With the retreat to the interior and with most imports and industrial production lost, both revenues and supplies were drastically reduced. The Chinese government resorted more and more frequently to the printing press in order to finance its war effort. As a result, both the nationalists and the communists experienced the beginnings of a severe inflation (see Table 1). By 1940 in nationalist-controlled regions, prices were doubling every year; between January and August 1945 alone, prices rose by 250%. Real income of the professional classes had sunk by 1944 to 10% of pre-war levels. Workers were affected also (about 50%); farmers and rural workers, who could rely on subsistence and who benefited from rising prices, maintained about 90% of their pre-war income, meagre though it was for most of them.

Sharp inflation also occurred in the communist-controlled zones, but its effects were mitigated by extensive reliance on a subsistence economy and a commodity exchange system whereby salaries, taxes, and so on were provided in kind. Cash was used mainly for incidentals and non-essentials, when available.

Economic distress was felt in the Japanese-occupied areas, too, particularly in the cities; as in other areas of China, peasants suffered a smaller proportional decline from their already low pre-war standards than did city dwellers. Although the Japanese sought to control supplies and prices, their efforts were only partially successful and black markets flourished in nearly all commodities, from basic foodstuffs to lavish luxury goods. But at the same time, the Japanese and the collaborationist regimes sought to rebuild the economic infrastructure and productive capacity of the areas they controlled, if only the better to exploit them. By 1943 or so, much of this capacity had been restored in both central and north China. The railway network had actually been improved over its pre-1937 condition.

3. Government

Government in wartime China fell into the same untidy three-way division that characterized the country during the Second World War: the National government, the collaborationist or puppet regimes organized by Japanese forces, and the areas ruled by the Chinese Communist Party.

(a) National government

The National government, headed by Chiang Kai-shek, was the internationally recognized government of China. Located in Nanking at the outbreak of war in 1937, it was soon forced to move 650 km. (400 mi.) up the Yangtze to Hankow. As Japanese forces threatened Hankow—it fell in October 1938—the seat of government was again moved, this time 965 km. (600 mi.) further west to Chungking, well-protected by mountains and behind the formidable Three Gorges of the Yangtze river. The National government was organized on lines laid down by Sun Yat-sen, before his death in 1925. In theory and in practice, this regime was a one-party government. With Sun Yat-sen's approval, the party, the Kuomintang (KMT), had been organized along centralist and Leninist principles by advisers of the Communist International (see COMINTERN) during the early 1920s. According to Sun's doctrine, one-party rule would continue until the Chinese people were educated for democracy, at which time constitutional rule would be established, by mechanisms not clearly specified.

Also according to Sun's theory, the National government comprised five major branches, or Yuan: executive, legislative, judicial, control, and examination. Of the five branches, the Executive Yuan was overwhelmingly the most powerful, and was directly controlled by the Central Executive Committee of the KMT, which was to its political party what the Politburo was to the communist parties, a small inner group of influential figures under the dominance of the authoritarian leader. The powers of the Legislative and Judicial Yuan were narrowly circumscribed and often ignored.

The Nationalist Party, or KMT, was designed to be both hierarchical and authoritarian. Centralism took priority over democracy; institutionalized linkages with all segments of the Chinese population were weak; and supreme leadership was incarnated in the person of Chiang Kai-shek. Factional politics were rampant, there were many parallel organizations and bodies—one under the government, one under the party—and, despite his position of authority, Chiang had constantly to manipulate various interest groups within government, party, and army. Factions were to some extent encouraged by Chiang, who could thus weaken all potential rivals and prevent any coalition from challenging him. In his exercise of power, and particularly in his handling of international relations, he was powerfully assisted by his American-educated wife, Madam *Chiang, by his brother-in-law T. V. *Soong, and by other prominent members of the Soong family. Finally, although Chiang Kai-shek headed both party and government, the true source of his power lay in his control over the military apparatus (see below).

When the National government was driven westwards, it lost those regions of China over which its rule had been most secure and where its economy, by Chinese standards, was most highly developed—the provinces of central and eastern China centred on the lower Yangtze river and Shanghai. In these areas, the nationalists were able to maintain some forces behind Japanese lines, but no functioning government. In the rest of 'Free China', the National government had only shallow roots and often had to make compromising adaptations to the local power structure: petty warlords, heads of semi-secret societies, landlords, influential merchants. This was true even in the agriculturally rich but economically and socially backward Szechwan province.

Shortly after the outbreak of the war, the National government formed an advisory body called the People's Political Council (PPC), composed of 200 members, including representatives of the Chinese Communist Party, leaders of small splinter parties, and prominent non-party public figures. The PPC served as a sounding-board for a fairly wide spectrum of public opinion, some of it critical of the National government and the KMT. As this tone became more strident during the early 1940s, the National government convened the PPC less and less often, and increasingly circumscribed its agenda. And, of course, as an advisory body, the PPC had no executive or legislative authority.

A number of these small splinter parties and public figures began to form an independent coalition in 1939. At first this coalition tried to buffer relations between the KMT and CCP, which were now coming into frequent and sometimes bloody conflict. This role continued during the following years, but also broadened to form a so-called 'Third Force', which in hopeful moments imagined that it might become influential on the Chinese political scene. In 1944 the group formed itself into the Chinese Democratic League. But the coalition was never solid, its tiny parties lacked broad public constituencies, it had (and desired) no access to military power, and it was frequently harassed by the KMT. Meanwhile, the communists were content to let the Democratic League voice its criticisms of the National government and thus help to discredit it. The hopes of the more optimistic members of the Democratic League, shared by some US observers including General *Marshall, were thus quite unrealistic.

(b) Japanese rule and Japanese-sponsored governments

During the war, tens of millions of Chinese lived, at one time or another, under Japanese control. Most prominently, this included all those in the great cities of China's eastern seaboard, from Peking south to Canton and in such inland cities as Nanking and Hankow.

Japanese rule in China was founded on the coercive power of its armed forces, exercised through various civil affairs sections and branches. In large cities and along corridors containing major rail lines, this often involved direct rule by military authorities, but in the hinterland a Japanese governing presence was much more superficial and incomplete. One important part of their efforts was to compel existing municipal and local administrations to keep functioning under their authority, meanwhile appointing collaborators and weeding out resisters. The Japanese also made use of traditional Chinese forms of collective security, in which designated groups of Chinese citizens were sternly held responsible for assigned tasks and for the behaviour of each member of the group. In their efforts to exploit the Chinese economy for coal, cotton, foodstuffs, and other resources, the Japanese established or licensed semi-official trading companies to manage commerce in these and other commodities.

The Japanese efforts to set up collaborationist governments were undertaken by the major military commands: by the *Kwantung Army, which had long had responsibility for Manchukuo (Manchuria) and Inner Mongolia; by the North China Area Army (NCAA); and by the Central China Expeditionary Army (CCEA). These commands worked separately and sometimes in rivalry with one another, and the Chinese puppet governments they sponsored reflected these same traits.

In addition to the puppet government of Manchukuo, which had been in existence since 1932, both the NCAA and the CCEA sought to establish Chinese governments. The NCAA's entry, established in December 1937, was called 'The Provisional government of the Republic of China', and was headed by a little-known and lightly regarded banker and fiscal bureaucrat named Wang K'o-min. This government, staffed by conservative or opportunistic nonentities, lacked legitimacy not only in the eyes of the Chinese, but also in the eyes of its Japanese sponsors.

The CCEA meanwhile inaugurated the 'Reformed government of the Republic of China' in March 1938, seated in Nanking, China's pre-war capital. At first much inferior to its northern counterpart, it became more important when the Japanese induced Wang Ching-wei to defect in December 1938. Unlike his northern counterpart, Wang was a well-known political figure. An associate of Sun Yat-sen with longer credentials than Chiang Kai-shek, Wang had sometimes been his uneasy colleague but more often his unsuccessful rival. In the 1930s he became increasingly pro-Japanese, believing that a Sino-Japanese accommodation was necessary to peace, stability, and elimination of the Chinese communists. Wang's dramatic departure from Chungking rocked Chinese opinion.

After more than a year of unpleasant negotiations with the Japanese authorities, the Reformed government was overhauled and Wang became its president. As in the north, the CCEA faced the contradiction between its desire to form an effective pro-Japanese government and its compulsion to exercise direct control. It resolved this

China, 3, Table 2: Wartime expansion of the Chinese Communist Party

1937	40,000
1940	800,000
1941	763,447
1942	736,151
1944	853,420
1945 (Seventh Congress)	1,211,128

Source: Fairbank and Feuerweker.

contradiction by the fiction of the former and the fact of the latter. Though proclaiming the opposite, the Japanese viewed their Chinese collaborators with contempt and mistrust, and were unwilling to allow them the independence and authority that might have gained them some legitimacy in China. Further compromising the puppet governments were sporadic Japanese efforts, at least throughout 1940, to seek a deal directly with Chiang Kai-shek.

These Japanese-sponsored regimes therefore never took root in China. Like their French and Norwegian counterparts, they were largely discredited from the start, but they nevertheless commanded some resources, exercised some delegated authority, and became a symbol of betrayal.

(c) Chinese Communist government

The territories governed by the Chinese Communist Party constituted an *imperium in imperio*. One part of that imperium lay within the territory nominally controlled by the KMT government; the remainder was created behind Japanese lines during the course of the war. The CCP grew rapidly during these years, as shown in Table 2; expansion was most rapid from 1937 to 1940, then levelled off until a second spurt in 1944 and 1945.

As war clouds gathered in 1937, the CCP acknowledged the legitimacy of the nationalists and promised to end its efforts to subvert Chiang Kai-shek's regime. In return, the nationalists agreed to call off their civil war against the communists and to form a united front with them against the Japanese. Thus, in a strictly legal sense, the communist regime became a legalized regional administration (rather than an outlawed rebellion), functioning under the overall authority of the National government. Although CCP leaders publicly embraced this status, in private they considered themselves not only sovereign but morally superior to the nationalists. From the beginning, the CCP was determined to preserve its freedom of action and to prevent the nationalists from exercising any influence whatever upon its organizational and territorial control. The principal constraint on its behaviour was the desire to prevent an open rupture or a nationalist capitulation to Japan.

Structurally, communist rule bore some resemblance to that of the nationalists. Both were one-party, Leninist regimes dominated by powerful and highly symbolic leaders. Like the KMT, the CCP was the dominating leg of the tripod which also included its government apparatus and its military establishment. The party exercised control through its own political rules and through interlocking membership at all levels.

Factions also existed within the CCP, but they were much less pervasive and divisive than in the KMT; by 1940 at the latest, Mao Tse-tung's leadership was unquestioned, and his coalition contained many able and powerful leaders: Liu Shao-ch'i, *Chou En-lai, Teng Hsiao-p'ing, Peng Te-huai, and many others. Where Chiang Kai-shek held his position by manipulating various factions, often setting them against each other, Mao dominated his principal rivals, reducing them to impotence and co-opting their ablest followers. As a result, Mao's power was more solidly based within his regime than was Chiang's. Furthermore, despite many problems and setbacks, the CCP was much more closely linked to the populations under its influence than was the KMT.

During the China Incident and throughout the Second World War, the headquarters of the Chinese communist movement was located in Fushih, a dusty, out-of-the way *hsien* (county town) in northern Shensi province, where the survivors of the Long March had found haven in 1935. During the war, the area came to include portions of two adjacent provinces, Kansu and Ningsia, and the general name for this large base area was Shen-Kan-Ning. Sparsely populated (about 1.5 million inhabitants) and poverty-stricken, Shen-Kan-Ning was the only CCP-controlled region which lay beyond the reach of Japanese armies. From Fushih, Mao and his colleagues sought to control a far-flung and decentralized movement. All other regions under communist rule or influence were behind the lines of furthest Japanese advance.

Immediately following the outbreak of war, CCP armies and political workers moved eastwards and began the process of organizing local governments, linking up with pockets of spontaneous anti-Japanese resistance, and re-establishing contact with local party members who had lived a hunted and underground existence up to the war. As noted above, an initial period of rapid expansion (until 1939) was followed by about three years of desperate hardship (1940–3), before a second wave of expansion that coincided with the weakening of Japan's capacities in China (1944–5).

Part of the communist response to the years of hardship was a whole series of interrelated and quite sweeping reforms: the *cheng-feng* or ideological and organizational 'Rectification Campaign' of 1942 and 1943; the campaign for 'crack troops and simple administration'; the *hsia-hsiang* (to the villages) movement; intensified rent and interest reduction; determined efforts to increase and diversify production and the co-operative movement. These policies were applied most systematically to the Shen-Kan-Ning base and much more unevenly in other base areas, but their cumulative effect helped the CCP to survive, to deepen and consolidate its hold on rural society, and to emerge from this period prepared for whatever opportunities might present themselves.

Eventually, the CCP claimed to have governmental authority in a total of sixteen base areas behind Japanese lines, stretching from Manchukuo to Canton. The most important of these were in north China, with only slightly less important bases in central China; the two so-called bases in the far south were quite insignificant (see Map 21).

The pace at which the CCP was able to set up anti-Japanese resistance bases varied greatly according local conditions. It was easier to establish and maintain them in mountainous, remote terrain than on the more densely populated plains, where their opponents were stronger and where better transport facilities gave them superior mobility. Major railway lines, heavily fortified and patrolled by the Japanese, puppets, and unwilling nearby villagers, often marked the boundaries between one base and another.

Nor were these bases contiguous areas of uniform communist rule. Instead, they were fluctuating archipelagos of influence, islands of firm control surrounded by semi-consolidated zones which gave way in turn to guerrilla territory and no man's land, and finally to zones of strong Japanese or nationalist control. Nevertheless, so far as possible, each base was organized hierarchically, from its central base area government down through regional administrations to districts and villages. In practice, because of the dispersed nature of these bases and the difficulties of communication, lower level bases had to function with considerable discretion and latitude.

In the anti-Japanese bases, penetration and the establishment of control by the communists proceeded through a typical sequence, with much unevenness, frequent repetition, and varying degrees of thoroughness. Not all bases completed all the following stages. (1) Arrival and initial penetration; linkage with local communists and/or anti-Japanese activists. During this phase, communists were willing to work with a very wide spectrum of local society, while identifying those elements most likely to co-operate fully. Land and other resources of 'traitors' were subject to confiscation. (2) Preliminary organization; takeover of local government, reduction of disorder, linkage of local community welfare with resistance led by the CCP. Anti-Japanese contributions were solicited and sometimes enforced against the more affluent, in order to finance local government and the CCP and to demonstrate to rich and poor alike that a change was taking place in local power relations. (3) Reorganization of local government, including the establishment of popularly-elected assemblies, which had no statutory power but served as a valuable sounding-board and as a symbol of the CCP's version of democracy, i.e., active participation, rather than the power to make decisions. Further involvement of villagers into popular organizations aimed at assisting the military (including recruitment), improving

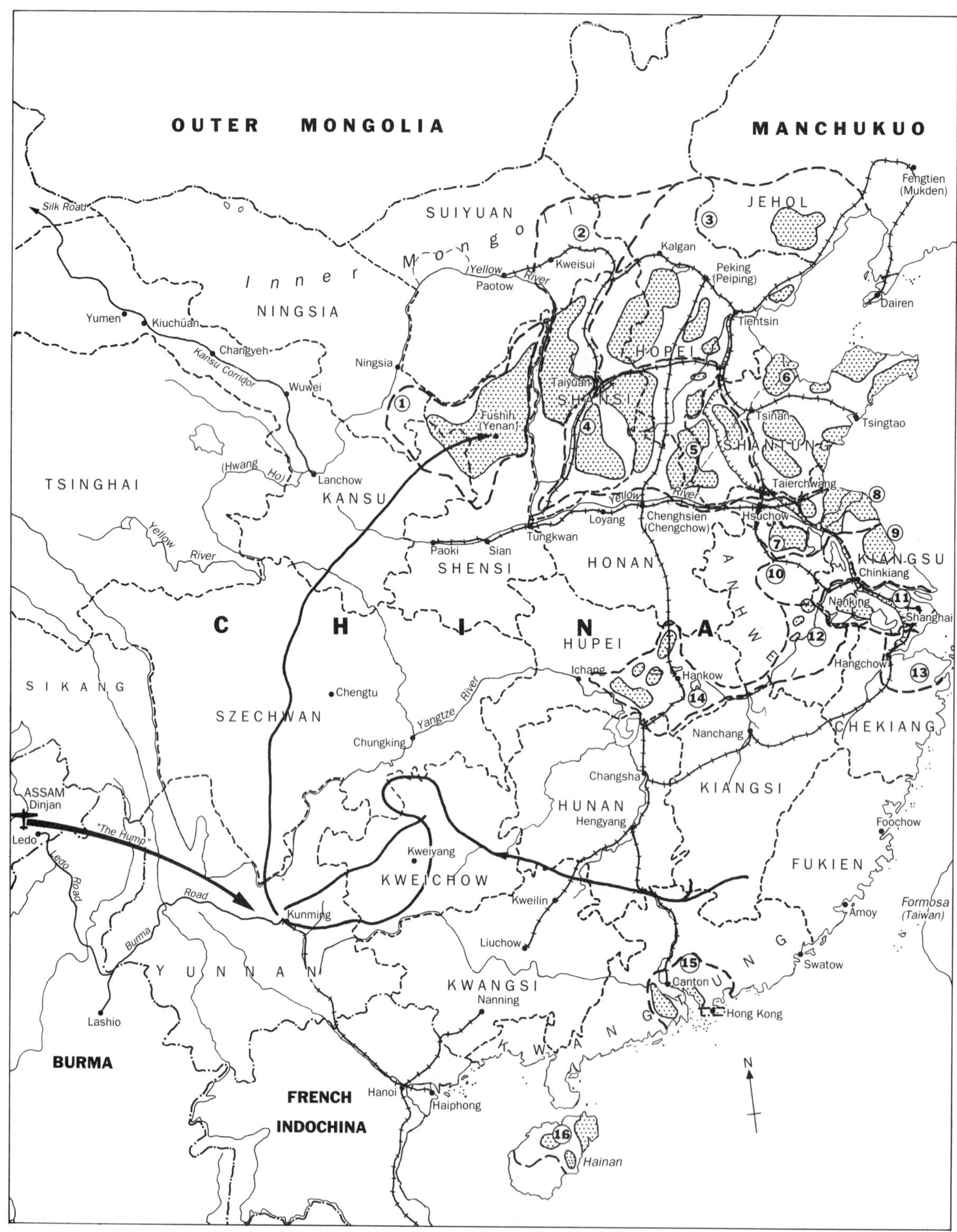

21. **China**: Provinces, principal cities and rivers, and areas claimed by the Communists in 1944

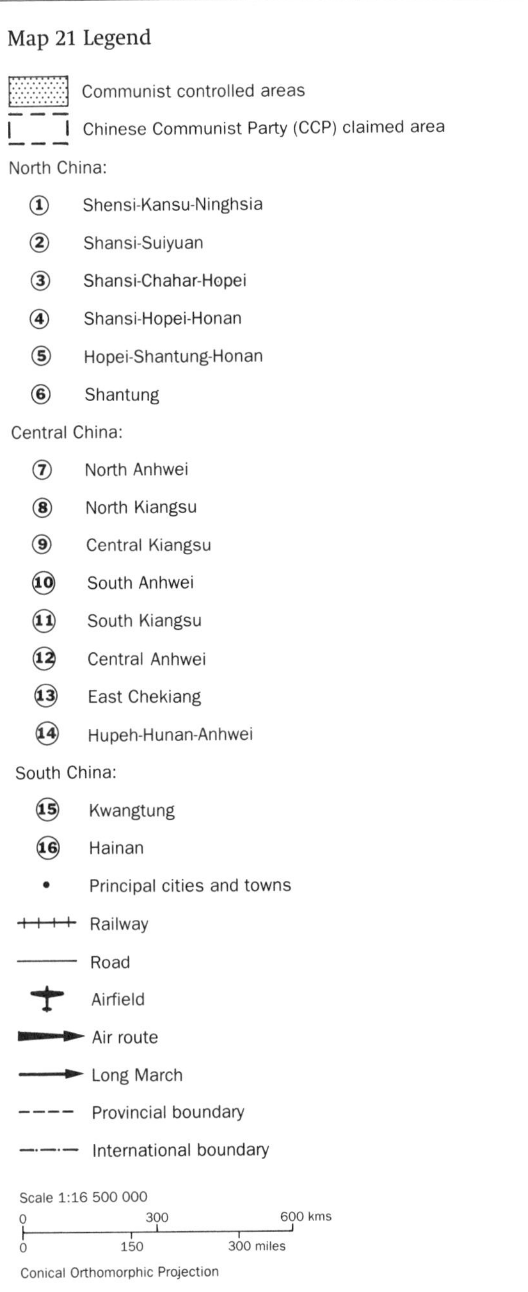

production, maintaining local order, and so on. Programmes of rent and interest reduction were instituted, and were coupled with guarantees that these reduced amounts would in fact be paid, with regularization of the tax system, and with the imposition of a steeply progressive tax.

Following the CCP's second wave of expansion late in the war, Mao Tse-tung claimed that a population of 96,000,000 lived under communist rule. This is a highly misleading figure because the estimate includes all areas of communist influence—consolidated, semi-consolidated, and guerrilla. But even allowing for Mao's exaggeration, the CCP succeeded during the war in vastly expanding its political structure and in penetrating local society. Perhaps more important still, the party felt confident that it had developed the techniques to expand further and had gained extensive experience as a functioning government.

4. Armed forces and Defence forces

The armed forces in China during the Second World War were, like so much else in China during those years, a kaleidoscope. Each major political regime maintained its own separate military apparatus. In addition, the Japanese organized extensive Chinese puppet forces.

Apart from these more or less conventional armed forces were many others. Provincial or regional armies of indeterminate and shifting loyalty sought mainly to survive, but would fight when it served their interests or could not be avoided. At the local level, self-defence forces tried to protect their villages from bandit gangs, while sometimes practising banditry themselves on neighbouring villages. Nationalists, communists, and Japanese alike sought to enlist these provincial and local forces, which were a kind of free-floating resource. They often bore formal unit designations which belied their ragtag and unstable nature.

At all levels, the Chinese understood that possession of military power equated to political power, the size of the former determining the amount of the latter. This perspective, shared by Chiang Kai-shek and Mao Tse-tung alike, contrasted with western, especially US, views that military affairs and politics are essentially separate spheres. The difference in outlook was a rich source of misunderstanding and controversy after the merging of the China Incident with the Second World War, following the attack on Pearl Harbor.

Chiang and Mao both soon recognized that Japan would eventually be defeated by the Allies, especially by the USA, without a major Chinese effort. This recognition grew ever clearer as the war progressed. Both Chiang and Mao also knew that a post-war showdown for control of China was a virtual certainty. Therefore, each sought to use the war against Japan to create the best possible conditions for the coming contest. This strategy suggested avoidance of fruitless, self-destructive combat against the Japanese, but it required survival and it implied enough fighting, or the appearance of fighting, to maintain domestic and international credibility.

(a) Nationalist armed forces

The core of nationalist power, dominated by Chiang Kai-shek, had always depended upon his control of the military. With the outbreak of war, the National government delegated virtually complete power to the National Military Council (NMC), of which Chiang was, to quote the NMC, chairman and sole authority: 'The chairman of the National Military Council, shouldering the full responsibility of national defence, shall have supreme command of the land, naval, and air forces, and shall direct the people of the nation.'

The NMC, functioning independently of party or government control, exercised fairly direct command over the Central Armies which were more or less patterned on a German model as German advisers were the principal source of military assistance available to Chiang's government in the 1930s. They were the best and most loyal of the forces available to the nationalists, though reckoned inferior by western or Japanese standards. At the beginning of the war in 1937, the Central Armies numbered about 300,000 men and included an even more élite group called 'The Generalissimo's Own'. Trained under German advisers, armed with German-made automatic weapons and mortars, the 80,000 men in these élite divisions constituted the core of Chiang Kai-shek's military modernization programme.

Surrounding these core units was a heterogeneous coalition as diverse in their loyalties as they were in their equipment, training, and combat capabilities. In 1937, these forces numbered perhaps 1,200,000. Thus the nationalists began the war with a total armed force of about a million and a half.

The best of their units, including a large part of the Generalissimo's Own, were lost during the first year of the war, particularly in the heroic three-month defence of Shanghai (August–November 1937), the fall of Nanking (December 1937), and the Japanese advance on Hankow (October 1938). Although all Chinese statistics are notoriously unreliable, the nationalists lost perhaps a million men during the first year of combat (killed, wounded, missing, or deserted). The losses were made up partly by incorporation of miscellaneous regional units and partly by conscription.

As the nationalists traded space for time, the Japanese strategic advance into central and southern China gradually slowed and then stopped. A war of offensive movement gave way to a war of attrition. One by one all avenues of access to the outside world were closed off, with the sole exceptions of the nearly impassable *Burma Road in the south-west and the long overland route from the USSR through Central Asia and the Kansu corridor. Over this latter track came substantial aid to China—all to the nationalists, none to the communists—during the first two years of the war, until Stalin realized the urgent need to husband his resources against Germany and to moderate any action which might provoke Japan into offensive operations in Siberia. By 1940, Soviet aid had all but dried up, and the Burma Road was sporadically closed by the British, in response to Japanese pressure.

By the summer of 1941, China was included under the *Lend-Lease Act passed in March. Some of this aid went to improving the load-carrying capacity of the Burma Road, some to supplies transported over it. By November 1941, the road was carrying about 15,000 tons per month; even so, Lend-Lease supplies were piling up on the docks in Rangoon. This traffic was ended in early 1942, when the Japanese seized the Burma segment of the road during their invasion of that region. It was not reopened until early 1945.

After the establishment of the China–Burma–India theatre, China's only external source of supplies was by air, over jungles and a rugged spur of the Himalayas, between north-eastern India and Kunming. This was the perilous 800 km. (500 m.) *Hump route, over which a gradually increasing trickle of supplies entered China. In all of 1942 this route carried only 5,250 tons; not until January 1944, had the flow risen to a monthly rate of nearly 15,000 tons, about the same as that over the Burma Road in late 1941. The larger part of these supplies, however, went to US forces (especially air forces) operating in China. In a situation of great scarcity and urgent needs, many bitter disputes concerned the allocation of Hump tonnage.

By this time, military supplies costing about $200 million were stockpiled in India, awaiting the opening of a surface route into China; much more was in the pipeline. The surface route, named the *Ledo Road (later the Stilwell Road), was finally pushed through in January 1945. Ironically, after so much effort, the road was made unnecessary by the Japanese surrender seven months later, in August.

For most of the war, therefore, the nationalist military had to rely overwhelmingly on what the broad hinterland of China could provide. Since industry in the interior was woefully undeveloped, the nationalists used plentiful manpower in an effort to compensate for other deficiencies. By 1939, these forces had very little motorized transport, or such other standard weapons of modern warfare as medium or heavy artillery, anti-tank weapons, and so on. As to aviation, the nascent Chinese Air Force had been almost totally destroyed by mid-1938. For a time, Soviet pilots and planes flew over China; then the P40s of *Chennault's Flying Tigers. Finally, after 1942, the USA assisted China with pilot training and planes to rebuild a Chinese Air Force (to defend Chungking and the Chengtu B29 base) and a Chinese Air Task Force (to protect the Hump air route from India). Both were minimally operational, but neither was very effective.

Furthermore, all aspects of military enterprise—including conscription, training, equipment, combat utilization, medical treatment—became increasingly corrupt and incompetent. One US military observer likened a nationalist recruiting sweep to a plague of locusts or epidemic disease, except, he noted, that unlike natural disasters, recruiters decimated the healthiest and most able-bodied males in the population. As war weariness grew and as inflation both measured and helped to produce economic disaster, the situation rapidly deteriorated. The result was an army of impressive size, but with very low capabilities. It is astonishing that these forces could fight at all, yet they did, even occasionally with bravery, and they somehow survived.

China, 4, Table 3: Chinese casualties, 1937–45

Year	Killed	Wounded	Missing	Total
1937 (July to Dec)	125,130	242,232	–	367,362
1938	249,213	485,804	–	735,017
1939	169,652	176,891	–	346,543
1940	339,530	333,838	–	673,368
1941	144,915	137,254	17,314	299,483
1942	87,917	114,180	45,070	247,167
1943	43,223	81,957	37,715	162,895
1944	102,719	103,596	4,419	210,734
1945	57,659	85,583	25,608	168,850
TOTAL	1,319,958	1,761,335	130,126	3,211,419

Source: Lloyd Eastman, *Seeds of Destruction: Nationalist China in War and Revolution, 1937–1949*, p. 136.

The principal exception to this picture of the nationalist armed forces were the units trained and equipped by the USA under the 'Thirty Division Plan', a target which was never achieved. By the end of the Pacific war nationalist forces numbered 300 divisions, with a nominal strength of 10,000 men per division, but many were seriously undermanned. Massive amounts of military aid were already in the pipeline and continued to flow to China after August 1945. By 1941 the Nationalist Army totalled 5.7 millon men, and from 1937 to 1945 the government drafted just over 14 million. The officer corps, which numbered 90,000 in 1937, was increased to 180,000. Casualties were high (see Table 3), especially amongst the officer corps (54,000 annually according to the Japanese).

(b) Chinese Communist armed forces

The growing threat of Japanese invasion brought about a rapprochement between the nationalists and communists and the so-called Second United Front. Looking on the surface like a broad-based merger of erstwhile enemies, in fact the two regimes remained quite separate. In the nationalist interpretation, the communists had proclaimed an end to sedition, pledged to integrate themselves with the nationalists, and promised to accept the orders of the recognized government of China. The language of agreements widely publicized by the communists themselves supported this interpretation.

The nationalists designated CCP forces in north China as the 'Eighteenth Group Army' and authorized the formation of three divisions, each placed under the overall control of nationalist commanders heading the territorial war zones into which China was divided. In 1938, the nationalists also authorized the formation of smaller units known collectively as the 'New Fourth Army' in the lower Yangtze region.

Despite all this public posturing, the CCP asserted time and again in classified statements that it would never under any circumstances permit nationalist authority over its territorial bases or its armed forces. Like the nationalist armed forces, the military structure of the communists was controlled by the party through a Military Affairs Committee attached to its Central Committee. Throughout the war, this committee was chaired by Mao Tse-tung.

The CCP's military structure comprised three interlinked levels: regular forces, local forces, and militia. In north China, the regular forces were the Eighth Route Army (the CCP's much more commonly-used designation for what the nationalists called the Eighteenth Group Army); in central China the CCP controlled the New Fourth Army. Only a few small communist-led guerrilla units were active in south China.

These regular forces were full-time outfits available for duty anywhere that the party directed. These were the best-trained and least badly equipped forces available to the CCP. By comparison with most nationalist units of the Central Army, their training and morale were better, but their equipment was more limited. Artillery and mechanized transport were entirely lacking; communications were primitive; *logistics depended mainly on what was locally available, what could be captured, or what could be smuggled from occupied China. It was expected that Eighth Route Army men would perform political and economic work as their military duties permitted, and a strict code of conduct was enforced to prevent the looting, raping, and other crimes that so often went with Chinese armies of whatever persuasion. The communists were fairly successful in changing the image of the army in the eyes of the Chinese rural population.

Ostensibly the Eighth Route Army was divided into three divisions (the 115th, the 120th, and the 129th) authorized by the nationalists. Within a few months after the start of the war in 1937, all three divisions had moved behind Japanese lines in Shansi and Hopei provinces. There they linked up with or organized self-defence forces—always assuring communist leadership—and collaborated in the work of setting up regional anti-Japanese bases. With about a year's lag, the New Fourth Army sought to do the same in central China.

As Table 4 shows, the first couple of years of the war

China, 4, Table 4: Wartime expansion of Eighth Route and New Fourth Armies

	Eighth Route Army	*New Fourth Army*	*Total*
1937	80,000	12,000	92,000
1938	156,700	25,000	181,700
1939	270,000	50,000	320,000
1940	400,000	100,000	500,000
1941	305,000	135,000	440,000
1942	340,000	110,960	450,960
1943	339,000	125,892	464,892
1944	320,800	153,676	474,476
1945 (April)	614,000	296,000	910,000

Source: Fairbank and Feuerweker.

saw a rapid expansion in both the Eighth Route Army and the New Fourth Army. This expansion went far beyond what had been authorized by the nationalists, just as did the CCP's territorial expansion. To avoid obvious provocation, the CCP held to the original three divisions, meanwhile organizing these new forces in units given many different names: training detachments, regiments, dare-to-die corps, and so on.

During the middle phase of the war, little further expansion took place, for two reasons. First, the rapidity of previous expansion now dictated a period of consolidation and qualitative improvement. Second, the pressure of Japanese 'pacification campaigns' and nationalist efforts to restrict the communists both inflicted numerous casualties on these armies. Finally, during the last months of the war, another phase of rapid expansion took place, mainly through wholesale reclassification of local forces as regular forces. By August 1945, Mao could claim regular forces of nearly one million, supported by local and militia forces of two million or more.

Local forces, like the regulars, were full-time units whose members were, in the communist phrase, 'withdrawn from production'. In total numbers, local forces varied between 25% and 40% of the strength of regular forces. They also differed from regular units in that they served only in their home regions, and were not available for assignment elsewhere. This made military service more tolerable to many, for the principle of community defence was widely accepted. Their equipment was even more rudimentary than that of the regulars, and they had less extensive training. In combat, they served as auxiliaries and second-line forces. They organized most of the pre-battle logistics and much of the post-battle rehabilitation. They assisted the local populace with defensive and survival preparations. Finally, they could deal with any unrest or resistance that might occur within their assigned territories.

The militia was a part-time force charged with a wide range of duties and organized at the village level, but supervised from higher echelons. Every able-bodied male between the ages of 15 and 50 was liable for service as needed. In local affairs, the militia enforced public safety and could be employed against recalcitrant landlords or occasional bandits. In support of local and regular forces, they provided detailed intelligence, guides, porters; they helped arrange for billeting or hiding full-time soldiers; they provided stretcher evacuation for the wounded.

This tripartite military structure was not only adapted to functional and territorial differences, it also served as a ladder of recruitment. Rather than enlisting soldiers directly into the Eighth Route or New Fourth Armies, most served first in the militia and/or the local forces. This enabled the CCP to avoid the worst abuses of press-gang conscription as practised by the nationalists; it also provided basic training for new recruits, and it was more acceptable to rural populations.

(c) Collaborationist armed forces

Puppet forces were organized directly by the Japanese and by the collaborationist governments established under Japanese sponsorship. Some of the puppet armies were formed, by a combination of threats and promises, from already existing, semi-organized armed groups: army stragglers, separated from their parent units; local self-defence or secret society forces; bandit gangs.

Other elements of puppet armies were recruited from peripheral nationalist forces (i.e., those other than the Central Army). After 1939, when stalemate and undeclared semi-truce characterized much of the central China Front, the line between nationalists and puppets was quite blurred. Some local commanders did the bidding of either side without scruple, according to their calculations of survival and self-interest.

The communists also claimed that the KMT sanctioned the defection of units under its command to the Japanese if the alternative was destruction, either by the Japanese or by communist forces. The notion was that later on these forces would changes sides once again and be available for anti-communist action. The CCP sarcastically called this tactic 'curveball patriotism'. Although the nationalists strenuously denied the charge, some affiliated forces did in fact surrender to the Japanese and then later return to the nationalist side without punishment for their defection.

It is therefore virtually impossible to estimate the size of puppet armies in China. One estimate for the early 1940s puts those nominally commanded by Wang Ching-wei's Nanking government at about 900,000. Puppet forces in north China may have been equally large. But whatever their size and location, they were viewed with contempt and mistrust by their Japanese masters. Only if directly ordered and constantly watched could puppet forces carry out orders; otherwise they were unreliable. Although puppet forces did not constitute a significant independent force, they were nevertheless a wild card affecting all other players.

5. Intelligence

In China, the collection and use of intelligence was generally divided between the military and the political, with different agencies responsible for the two kinds of information. Problems of overlap, duplication, and rivalry were common. Each military structure—nationalist, communist, Japanese—contained its own military intelligence apparatus. Because of the size of the China theatre and the dispersed nature of operations, the various field commands had much responsibility for their own intelligence. On the political side, the principal intelligence agencies of all three major contestants were concerned primarily with internal security and were held close to the centres of power. Not surprisingly, the Japanese had the best-organized intelligence service. They relied on their military intelligence apparatus in the field, but in the major cities the *Kempei—the much-feared military police—exercised stern control and sought to intimidate the Chinese populace into passivity and compliance.

The nationalist intelligence apparatus was centred in two agencies with the same name—the Bureau of Investigation and Statistics—but one was attached to the government's Central Executive Committee (BIS/CC) and the other to the party's Military Affairs Commission (BIS/MAC). Needless to say, Chiang Kai-shek maintained tight control over both. The former (BIS/CC) was charged primarily with the collection and analysis of political intelligence concerning all non-KMT activity, especially that of the CCP and its sympathizers. In contrast, the BIS/MAC, which was headed by the much-feared General Tai Li, collected military as well as political intelligence, and, unlike its civilian counterpart, it was also assigned operational missions—covert operations, spreading of disinformation, infiltration of target groups, sometimes even assassination. Like BIS/CC, BIS/MAC concentrated heavily on the Chinese communists, but also operated in such tightly-held Japanese areas as Shanghai and Peking.

Despite the presence of the eccentric American code-breaker Herbert O. Yardley in China, no cryptanalysis of any consequence was achieved by the nationalist Chinese.

In early 1942, US naval intelligence, at first in the person of one mid-level officer, began collaboration with BIS/MAC and Tai Li. Out of this collaboration came SACO, the Sino-American Co-operative Organization. Later in the year, the newly organized *Office of Strategic Services entered the scene. The result was a good deal of institutional and personal acrimony. Despite these rivalries, small groups of Americans and Chinese set up weather (see also METEOROLOGICAL INTELLIGENCE), radio, and intercept stations; collected military and political intelligence; assisted in the rescue of downed pilots; and undertook sabotage. Most of these and other activities were carried out behind Japanese lines.

The CCP's internal security agency was euphemistically called the Social Affairs Department, and was directly responsible to the Central Committee; in practice this meant it reported to the Political Bureau and to Mao Tse-tung. For most of the war, it was headed by Kang Sheng, who had lived in the USSR for several years, presumably learning his trade from the *NKVD. (In 1980 he was posthumously denounced and expelled from the CCP, mainly for his actions during the Cultural Revolution.) Political intelligence and related operational assignments outside the CCP were the charge of the United Front Work Department, also directly responsible to the Central Committee. Although its most important target was the KMT, it was also active among the uncommitted splinter parties that in 1944 formed the Democratic League (see GOVERNMENT, above), and in dealing with individuals and groups at the local level.

6. Culture

Cultural life in wartime China suffered many of the same hardships and deprivations that characterized every aspect of life during these eight terrible years. Creative artists of all kinds were among those whose lives were most adversely affected, and the Chinese people had little energy or money to spend on such creations as they might produce. Even the most basic material resources—paper, printing equipment, and ink, for example—were in desperately short supply and of poor quality. Yet somehow a heroically stubborn cultural life survived, in Free China, in the communist-controlled areas, and under Japanese occupation. Despite such adversity, a suprising volume of writing, drama, and graphic material was produced, most of it for popular consumption. Patriotism, nationalism, and support for the war effort were the watchwords everywhere, except under the Japanese, where the expression of such sentiments brought cruel punishment. But even in occupied China, veiled and indirect expression of these themes could be sensed.

One of the most tangible expressions of this spirit was the determination of three of China's most prestigious universities from the Peking–Tientsin area—Peking, Yenching, and Nankai universities—to keep alive the flame of higher education and academic integrity by moving far inland, beyond the reach of the Japanese. These universities eventually transported themselves to Kunming, capital of Yunnan province, over 2,000 km. (1,245 mi.) from Peking, where they merged to form the Southwest Associated University. There they carried on throughout the war, despite enormous difficulties, hardships, and eventually harassment by nationalist authorities angered by the critical independence exhibited by many students and faculty members.

In Free China, cultural life was concentrated mostly in a few major cities: Chungking and Chengtu, in Szechwan province, and Kunming and Kweilin. In Chungking, the nationalist authorities encouraged but also supervised the media, including journalism, literature, drama, and art. In time, they also came to censor it. Chengtu was somewhat less restrictive. The nearest thing to intellectual and cultural freedom existed in Kunming and Kweilin, where sympathetic provincial authorities for a time provided insulation from KMT censors and secret police. In 1944, Kweilin was overrun by the Japanese during Operation ICHI-GŌ, and as the war came to a close, a heavy-handed nationalist influence grew more menacing in Kunming.

Early in the war, considerable numbers of students and left-wing intellectuals made their way to the communist-controlled areas, above all the Fushih area. They raised the cultural level of this backward region, but they also brought with them the critical stance and independence of mind they had exercised—with the party's approval—in Shanghai, Peking, Siking (Sian), and elsewhere. Although they enthusiastically supported the party's general programme, the bolder among them dared to point out the gap between ideals and actualities—the dark side of life in Siking—just as they had in Shanghai.

Mao Tse-tung sought to end this bourgeois individualism during the Rectification Campaign of the early 1940s. In his lengthy 'Remarks at the Fushih Forum on Literature and Art' (May 1942), he decisively rejected the notion of art for art's sake, insisting instead that all literature and art expresses the interests of a social class, either of the people or of their oppressors. He called upon intellectuals to obey the CCP, to drop their arrogant ways and self-centred concerns, to learn instead from the workers, peasants, and soldiers—to use their vocabulary and to create for them. (The ideas underlying Mao's position remained more or less orthodox in Communist China, despite being repeatedly challenged; they were most crushingly applied during the Cultural Revolution, 1966–76, and were revived after the Tiananmen Square episode in June 1989.) Many intellectuals did, in fact, go to the rural areas and shape themselves to this populist mould, but writers who could not or would not follow Mao's dicta were silenced and sometimes imprisoned.

Cultural life in Japanese-occupied cities was thin indeed. In Shanghai, between 1937 and the end of 1941, the International Concession area was a zone free of direct Japanese control because it was administered by the UK and the other treaty powers. Called Solitary Island in the sea of Japanese occupation, it provided a perilous haven for those who would speak out against Japan, despite the real danger of abduction or assassination. After Pearl Harbor, this solitary island was entirely engulfed by the Japanese occupation.

Writers and artists, like the general public, had to choose between collaboration, passivity or escapism, and a deeply concealed attitude of resistance; some sought to reconcile the first two modalities with the third. For most, these issues took a lower priority than the daily struggle for family and individual survival.

However difficult it may be to assess how much the average peasant or worker was affected by the cultural production of these years, most of those who created it were profoundly influenced by their wartime experiences. Excepting those who remained in China's occupied cities, the eyes of writers and artists were opened to China's vast hinterland, to the peasantry, and to the minority peoples of the interior. They experienced a deepened sense of nationalism, if not always complete loyalty to one of the major political parties. For hundreds of millions of Chinese, the Second World War was a defining experience. LYMAN P. VAN SLYKE

Boyle, J. H., *China and Japan at War, 1937–1945* (Stanford, Calif., 1972).

Eastman, L. E. (ed.), *The Nationalist Era in China, 1927–1949* (Cambridge, 1991).

—— *Seeds of Destruction: Nationalist China in War and Revolution, 1937–1945* (Stanford, Calif., 1984).

Van Slyke, Lyman P., *The Chinese Communist Movement: A Report of the United States War Department, July 1945* (Stanford, Calif., 1968).

China–Burma–India theatre (CBI), a general geographic reference, designating the intersection of East Asia, South-East Asia, and South Asia insofar as they were linked together in the struggle against Japan. But CBI also referred loosely to the military commands of various nations which existed within this geographic region and for a time was the name of a specific American military command structure.

The command structures came initially from the *ARCADIA conference held in Washington in December 1941. Churchill and Roosevelt agreed, *inter alia*, upon a joint command for South-East Asia. This was *ABDA Command under *Wavell's overall command. Separate from and nominally co-equal to ABDA Command was the China theatre, of which *Chiang Kai-shek was named Supreme Commander. Symbolically, this status represented an Allied desire to provide moral support to China, in recognition of four years of lonely, unaided combat against Japan (see CHINA INCIDENT). But it was also anomalous because it did not integrate China or Chiang Kai-shek into ABDA Command, or any larger Allied structure, on the grounds that Chiang would never agree to foreign authority over any part of China.

After initial hesitation, the US war department nominated the unenthusiastic Lt-General *Stilwell to be the senior American commander in the region. Stilwell knew China better than any field-grade officer in the US Army, and spoke Chinese fluently. His appointment reflected the confusion of the early months after *Pearl Harbor and the complexity of the region to which he was sent. He was simultaneously 'Commanding General of the United States Army Forces in the Chinese Theatre of Operations, Burma, and India', and 'Chief of Staff to the Supreme Commander of the Chinese Theatre', i.e. Chiang Kai-shek. But since the American forces were a part of ABDA Command, he also served under Wavell, whose jurisdiction included Burma. Furthermore, Stilwell was to have direct command over Chinese forces assigned to operations in Burma, originally three armies (a total of ten divisions, perhaps 80,000–100,000 men). Then and later, however Stilwell had great difficulty exercising this authority in the face of Chiang Kai-shek's frequent interference.

In February 1942, following the fall of *Singapore and the Japanese invasion of Java, ABDA Command was abolished. Thenceforth, the Pacific was an American responsibility, the British were in charge from Singapore to Suez, and Chiang Kai-shek remained Supreme Commander of the China theatre. Wavell continued to exercise overall command in India and Burma (see Map F). As part of this restructuring, Stilwell formed a Headquarters, American Armed Forces: China, Burma, and India. The new command embraced a small pre-existing American Military Mission to China (AMMISCA) and the *American Volunteer Group of Maj-General *Chennault, later a part of Tenth Army Air Force and eventually of Fourteenth Army Air Force.

This command structure lasted until the autumn of 1943, when it was replaced, after several false starts, by what seemed to be a more integrated *South-East Asia Command (SEAC) and operational control of British forces fighting in Burma passed from C-in-C India (*Auchinleck since June 1943) to it. SEAC's Supreme commander was *Mountbatten and Stilwell was named his deputy commander. The China theatre, under Chiang Kai-shek, remained independent of SEAC, though Stilwell's role as Chiang's Chief of Staff was supposed to provide liaison and co-operation among the various parties.

Unfortunately, SEAC was not much more effective than its predecessor, and for the same reasons: there was little agreement as to policy goals and strategies to be pursued (see AXIOM MISSION). The Chinese expression 'same bed, different dreams' fits the situation well. Nor were these tensions and disagreements limited to relations among the Allies, for they existed within the forces of each of the three nations as well, particularly within the US CBI command.

Keenly aware of its own severely strained military assets, the UK gave high priority to protecting India and to defusing an Indian nationalism that threatened collaboration with Japan. The UK saw Burma primarily in terms of these priorities, rather than as an avenue to the strengthening of a China in whose wartime utility and post-war capacities it had little confidence. Yet at the same time, Churchill sought to accommodate Roosevelt's much more sanguine view of China, of which the campaign to recover Burma was a central component. British support for the *Burma campaign was thus by turns half-hearted and determined.

Stilwell, who had long held anglophobic views, believed that the British were more interested in maintaining their empire in India and Burma than in engaging Japan; he was convinced that the British exercised undue and baneful influence over Roosevelt; and he disliked intensely what he viewed as smug and patronizing British formality. He was obsessed with the recovery of Burma. Strategically, he believed that China could become an important theatre and an important contributor in the war against Japan only if its armies could be markedly improved. To the extent that improved effectiveness required massive infusions of heavy equipment, he believed that a secure overland route to China from India was absolutely essential. Such a route—it became known as the *Ledo Road when it was begun—could only go through Burma.

In trying to create a professional, apolitical military force in China, patterned along western lines, Stilwell—despite his deep knowledge of the country—significantly misread the fundamentally political nature of Chinese armies: personal control of core armies was Chiang Kai-shek's major asset, both to maintain his supremacy during the war and to contest the communists after it. Stilwell believed that the Chinese Army required top-to-bottom reorganization, with an end to corruption, incompetence, and political interference. Since such reforms would have threatened his personal control over the armed forces, Chiang never undertook them, always delaying, promising to do so later when conditions were more suitable, and occasionally hanging out a little window dressing in order to keep American aid flowing into his hands. This oblique stonewalling infuriated Stilwell and goaded him into ever angrier outbursts.

Stilwell's belief in Burma's importance was predicated on his estimate that China would be a major theatre of war. But as 1942 turned into 1943, this estimate grew more and more out of touch with reality. The trans-Pacific *island-hopping strategy became more and more apparently the means for defeating Japan from the air and eventually, it was presumed, through *amphibious warfare landings. This approach rendered China a sideshow, important mainly for tying down about one million Japanese troops and preventing their deployment elsewhere. With China thus marginalized, the recovery of Burma became less urgent. Unlike Chiang Kai-shek and the Chinese communist leader, *Mao Tse-tung, both of whom understood the implications of Japan's eventual defeat (mainly by the USA and elsewhere than in China), Stilwell remained unshaken in his effort to make China a major combatant. He therefore remained determined to recover Burma. This obsession with Burma had personal dimensions as well. He sought to avenge the humiliating defeat suffered in early 1942, when vastly superior

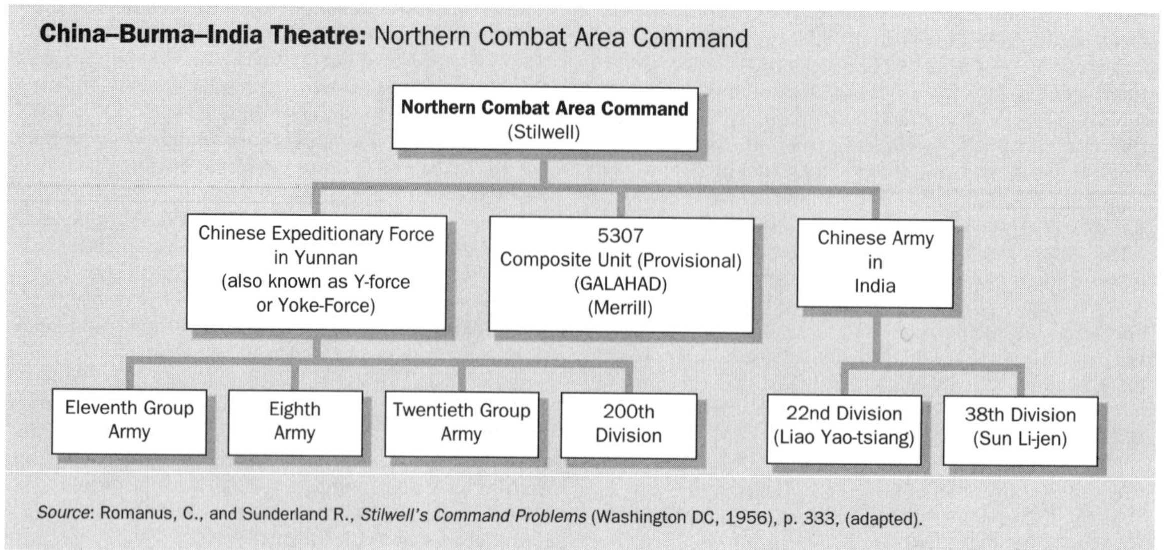

Source: Romanus, C., and Sunderland R., *Stilwell's Command Problems* (Washington DC, 1956), p. 333, (adapted).

Japanese forces drove scattered Allied units—British, American, and Chinese—from the region. During the retreat, Stilwell had refused the air evacuation offered to his headquarters detachment, and insisted on walking out at the head of his soldiers. 'We got a hell of a beating', he said at the time, and he was determined to even the score.

Stilwell had another point to make. He believed that nationalist Chinese troops—considered worthless by the Japanese, by most of the Allies, and even within China—could be the equal of the finest soldiers in the world, if they were properly fed, trained, supplied, and officered. Burma was to be the proving-ground for this belief, an irrefutable example of the effectiveness of the reforms which Stilwell advocated throughout the Chinese armed forces.

A training centre was established at Ramgarh in north-eastern India, to which Chiang Kai-shek reluctantly assigned two divisions (see Chart) with Chinese officers serving under US command. From December 1943 these divisions fought under Stilwell on the Northern Front (called Northern Combat Area Command by the Americans) alongside American and British units in the Burma campaign, and they largely vindicated Stilwell's confidence in them. But Chiang Kai-shek never again trusted the commanders who led these units.

Plans, dating back to pre-Pearl Harbor days, were also in place to help equip and train an initial 30 Chinese divisions. In one form or another the 'Thirty Division Plan', as it was known, remained an integral part of US efforts to invigorate the Chinese Army, but was never fully implemented.

Within the American CBI command, Stilwell and Chennault were at perpetual loggerheads. Both strong characters little given to compromise, they also disagreed on important policy issues. One of these had to do with the allocation of slender resources available to them and to China. With the loss of Burma in the spring of 1942, the *Hump air route was the only link between China and the outside world. However, what this could provide was but a drop in the bucket of China's immense needs. Conflict over the allocation of Hump tonnage was perpetual: Chiang Kai-shek wanted full authority over what was sent and who got it, Stilwell wanted most of it to go on a quid pro quo basis to reformed army units, and Chennault argued that it be allocated to the air forces under his command.

Underlying these controversies over Hump tonnage were fundamental differences in strategic outlook. Chennault believed that *air power was a much more rapid and cost-efficient means of making war against Japan than the foot-slogging ground war envisaged by Stilwell. During 1942 and 1943, huge gangs of Chinese labour were building airfields in the south-eastern province of Kwangsi and in the inland province of Szechwan. From these bases, Chennault argued, Japanese forces throughout China could be gravely damaged and Japan's essential sealanes from South-East Asia to its Home Islands interdicted—but only if he was given the lion's share of Hump tonnage. This view appealed to Chiang Kai-shek, since it implied that his own forces could avoid not only major combat with Japan but also the reforms Stilwell was urging upon him. Meanwhile, Stilwell dismissed Chennault's vision as chimerical. He doubted aviation's capacities, independent of other branches; and he argued that as soon as air power began to hurt them, the Japanese would simply march in and take the air bases of south-east China—unless there was a strong and committed Chinese Army to defend them. Stilwell's gloomy prediction was borne out in mid-1944, during Japan's last great offensive in China, the *ICHI-GŌ campaign, when all the airfields were captured without significant Chinese resistance.

The deficiencies revealed by ICHI-GŌ led to a crisis in Sino–US relations during the summer and early autumn of 1944. Roosevelt, thoroughly exasperated, urged Chiang Kai-shek in harsh terms to undertake sweeping political and military reforms and to place an American commander (presumably Stilwell) in direct command of the Chinese Army. Patrick J. Hurley (1883–1963) was sent to China as Roosevelt's personal representative, with the mission of smoothing over the crisis and mediating the growing tensions between the Chinese communists and the nationalists.

Chiang temporized in meeting Roosevelt's demands, meanwhile objecting to Stilwell's continuing presence in China. In the upshot, Stilwell was recalled to the USA and the more tactful *Wedemeyer replaced him. By October 1944, both Stilwell and Chennault were gone. Except for some cosmetic reforms, Roosevelt's demands were allowed to lapse. Patrick Hurley then became US ambassador to China.

As a part of these changes, CBI in a formal sense came to an end in October 1944, when it was divided into the India–Burma theatre and the China theatre. Wedemeyer took command of US forces in China and served as Chiang's Chief of Staff. Stilwell's deputy, Daniel I. *Sultan, was made Commanding General of US forces in the India–Burma theatre, and, under Mountbatten, he directed the fighting on the Northern Front as head of the Northern Combat Area Command. Yet the familiar acronym CBI had become so well-established that it survived all these changes in formal structure.

Ironically, even as the Burma campaign was finally moving forward successfully, the China theatre was becoming less important militarily, if not politically. It was now utterly clear that Japan would be attacked from the maritime approaches, and perhaps from a staging area somewhere along the north China coast. In late 1944, Japanese forces were cleared from northern Burma, and near the end of January 1945, the first vehicles rolled along the Ledo Road, now renamed the Stilwell Road. During the last months of the war, Allied forces further secured the Burma base and rapidly increased the carrying capacity of the Stilwell Road. In China, Wedemeyer offered advice and assistance to Chiang Kai-shek and encouraged action that would prevent the transfer of Japanese troops from China to more active combat theatres and to the Home Islands.

Politically, Hurley's efforts to mediate the growing tension between the nationalists and the communists had failed badly. He later claimed to have been sabotaged by the state department and the embassy staff in China. But Hurley, whose ignorance of China was matched only by his overweening self-confidence as a negotiator, misread the nature of both parties and badly underestimated the deep antipathy with which they viewed each other.

With the Japanese surrender, the various command structures under the broad rubric 'CBI' were one by one decommissioned. American concerns had now grown to embrace the post-war role of China. The USA was deeply committed to Chiang Kai-shek and his regime, a regime over which it had limited influence but from which it could not detach itself. The contest between the nationalists and the communists hung in fateful balance. At the war's end, the USA was in a position to influence but not to determine the outcome, a position that had evolved from the military and political circumstances of which CBI was a major part. LYMAN P. VAN SLYKE

Romanus, C. F., and Sunderland, R., **China–Burma–India Theater**, 3 vols. (Washington, DC, 1953–9).

Tuchman, B., *Stilwell and the American Experience in China, 1911–1945* (New York, 1970).

White, T. (ed.), *The Stilwell Papers* (New York, 1948).

China Incident (*Shina jihen*), term employed by the Japanese to refer to the conflict between Japan and China which broke out in July 1937 (see Map 22). The expression remained in use until the attack on *Pearl Harbor in December 1941, after which the fighting in China became part of the 'Greater East Asia War' (Dai Tōa Sensō); it was rarely used thereafter. The expression provides insight into the mentality with which Japanese leaders viewed their efforts in China and, indirectly, into the policies they chose. The Chinese, whether nationalists or communists, never used it; to them, the war was from the start the 'War of Resistance Against Japan' (*k'ang-Jih chan-cheng*). Westerners, describing this conflict as the Sino-Japanese war, generally mean the eight years of hostilities between the two powers—1937–45—the period covered here.

This was not the first time Japanese had used the word *jihen* (incident) to characterize events in China. It was employed as early as September 1931, when their *Kwantung Army fabricated a pretext to seize Manchuria and establish the puppet state of *Manchukuo. This was the 'Mukden Incident', or, as the sphere of Japanese action broadened, the 'Manchurian Incident'.

Long before these incidents, elements of pan-Asianism had begun to manifest themselves in Japanese strategic thinking. On one level, the notion implied a leadership mission for Japan within Asia, above all in Korea, Manchukuo, and at least parts of China. In this vision, Japan intended to play the same sort of civilizing mission that European imperialist powers had earlier and elsewhere arrogated to themselves. Less altruistically, such a view justified Japanese exploitation of the resources and markets of East Asia. From quite early in the 20th century, most Japanese had come to believe that national interests—prosperity, security, perhaps survival itself—required a strong position on the Asian mainland. How best to protect or extend those interests spawned many serious controversies and conflicts within the Japanese polity, but few disagreed with the underlying premiss.

On another level, pan-Asian thinking gradually took on a racial coloration, an anti-imperialist Asia for the

Japanese troops fighting in the streets of Shanghai during the **China Incident**.

Asians mentality—led by the Japanese, of course. This sentiment grew as Japan advanced on the resource-rich colonial areas of South-East Asia: French Indo-China, the Netherlands East Indies, and (after Pearl Harbor) the Philippines. This thinking crystallized in the notion of the *Greater East Asia Co-prosperity Sphere, which became a central feature of Japanese ideology in the late 1930s and 1940s. From an ultra-nationalist Japanese perspective, therefore, what lay below the surface of events was a sense of virtual entitlement: Japan had the right, the duty, the obligation to carry out its will in China and elsewhere.

Six years after the Mukden Incident (see MANCHUKUO), on the night of 7 July 1937, some shots were fired at a Japanese detachment—commanded by the future Lt-General *Yamashita—on manoeuvres near the Marco Polo Bridge, a few kilometres south-west of Peking. No one was injured; one Japanese soldier was initially declared missing, but later returned to his unit. Who fired the shots is not known, even now. This minor skirmish was less serious than many other collisions that had taken place in north China as the Japanese sought to expand their influence in the Peking–Tientsin region. On such occasions, these episodes were usually settled by negotiations in which, after posturing on both sides, the Chinese acquiesced to a modified set of Japanese demands.

On this occasion, hard-liners in the Japanese government, particularly in the army and above all in the aggressive and semi-autonomous Kwantung Army stationed in Manchukuo, and in the units stationed in the Peking–Tientsin region, were determined to force a more comprehensive settlement than they had thus far achieved. Hence, they spoke of the 'north China incident' (*hokuShi jihen*). Such a forward policy was opposed by gradualist leaders, and by navy commanders suspicious of army dominance in policy circles. Within the army itself, a lonely voice of moderation was that of Ishiwara Kanji, head of the General Staff's Operations Division. Ishiwara foresaw the likelihood of a costly and protracted involvement in China, from which it would be impossible to withdraw and which would inflict costs upon Japan far in excess of any advantages gained. He and a few others argued that to get bogged down in China would make it more difficult for Japan to cope with her true adversary, the USSR. In the weeks that followed, Japanese policy toward China see-sawed several times, but generally moved towards greater mobilization and tougher demands.

On the Chinese side, meanwhile, local authorities in the Peking–Tientsin area were sufficiently intimidated to accept Japanese terms, while trying to retain as much room to manoeuvre as possible. But in Nanking the nationalist leader, *Chiang Kai-shek, was no longer willing to follow a policy of acquiescence. Although he did not seek a complete rupture with Japan, his patience was growing thin, and he realized that further appeasement might well fatally damage his credibility in the face of an increasingly aroused Chinese nationalism.

On this occasion, therefore, actions on both sides led not to eventual compromise, but to an irregular and not altogether intended escalation. Ishiwara was first ignored, then muffled, and finally silenced by removal from his post. Japanese Navy leaders, recognizing the drift of events, pressed for strong action not in north China, the army's bailiwick, but in the Shanghai region where their influence predominated, and where the flames of Chinese nationalism burned the hottest. In Shanghai itself Japanese residents and Japanese businesses were increasingly at risk; on 9 August, two Japanese marines (a lieutenant and a seaman) were killed by Chinese soldiers. As Japanese mobilization proceeded rapidly, Chinese attitudes also hardened.

On 14 August 1937, the Chinese military undertook what they intended to be a pre-emptive air strike against Japanese warships gathering in the Whangpu river facing the Shanghai waterfront. The Japanese responded at once, and these events marked the true beginning of the Sino-Japanese war. Over the next few weeks, with the battle in Shanghai ferociously joined and Japanese forces fanning out along the railway lines of north China, the Japanese dropped references to 'the north China Incident' and began speaking of 'the China Incident'.

In all these variations, incident had at least three layers of meaning. First, of course, was the euphemistic impulse, the desire to cover a harsh and complex reality with a verbal fig-leaf. Indeed, 'the China Incident' has taken its place alongside such other indirections as 'the *Final Solution' and 'the Korean police action' as classic examples of Orwellian rhetoric.

Second, 'incident' implied that the Chinese would once again capitulate, as they had often done in the past. Japanese military officers, in particular, were dismissive not only of Chinese military capabilities but also of the willingness of the Chinese people to come together in unified resistance. They believed that a salutary, no-nonsense exercise of military prowess would quickly bring the Chinese to terms. The hard-liners discounted Ishiwara's dire predictions, believing it wholly unlikely that much time or energy would be required to bring the Chinese to heel; for such a quick operation, the word 'incident' seemed quite adequate. But as T. V. *Soong, a leading Chinese statesman and Chiang Kai-shek's brother-in-law, noted at the time.

> The Japanese military still hold to their preconceived ideas about the Chinese Army. They think that if you hit us once, we will surrender and do what you want. The Chinese Army has studied hard since the Manchurian Incident ... It knows that it is stronger, and it has the confidence that it won't be beaten this time. So, the Japanese Army underestimates the Chinese Army, and the Chinese Army overestimates itself. Here is where the great danger lies (see Boyle below, p. 67).

Third, by referring to the 'China Incident' the Japanese avoided legal difficulties that might stem from a formal declaration of war. For example, an incident might be treated in any of a variety of ways—by negotiation, by military pressure, by tacit understanding, by piecemeal arrangement with local authorities—all of which would be more difficult or impossible if a state of war were acknowledged. In the international sphere, a declaration of war might suggest to the international community that it observe strict neutrality and suspend strategic trade with both sides. If the USA were to abide by its own *Neutrality Acts, it would have had to cut off a large part of Japan's essential imports, especially oil, iron, and steel.

In dealing first with the 'north China incident' and then with the 'China incident', Japan in fact tried four approaches: direct military action, negotiation with representatives of Chiang Kai-shek's government, mediation by a third party, and efforts to establish puppet regimes (see also COLLABORATION). All these efforts, including military operations, were bedevilled by inconstancy of purpose and goals, factional differences and rivalries within Japanese policy circles, and the inveterate Japanese habit of humiliating those Chinese whom they sought to enlist as collaborators.

From the Marco Polo Bridge episode onwards, various Japanese actors were in contact with Chinese counterparts. While Chinese authorities in the Peking–Tientsin area were conciliatory, hardline Japanese were convinced that Chiang Kai-shek's government in Nanking had to be made a party to any solution satisfactory to them; they would not be put off by local arrangements that could later be repudiated. Meanwhile, moderate elements were secretly floating a much more generous arrangement before Nanking's eyes. This initiative, known as the Funatsu Plan after the quasi-private Japanese emissary who carried it, never got off the ground: it was not wholly satisfactory to Nanking, and it was pre-empted by more aggressive Japanese moves.

During the heroic and bloody defence of Shanghai, from August until early November 1937, no serious efforts at negotiation were attempted. But when the fall of Shanghai and an offensive thrust aimed at Nanking failed to produce the capitulation upon which Japanese leaders had counted, another effort was made to terminate the conflict. To this end, the Japanese enlisted the assistance of Germany, in the persons of its ambassadors to Japan and China, Herbert von Dirksen and Oskar Trautmann respectively. A mediated solution was congenial to Germany, which had become one of China's principal trading partners (especially for military

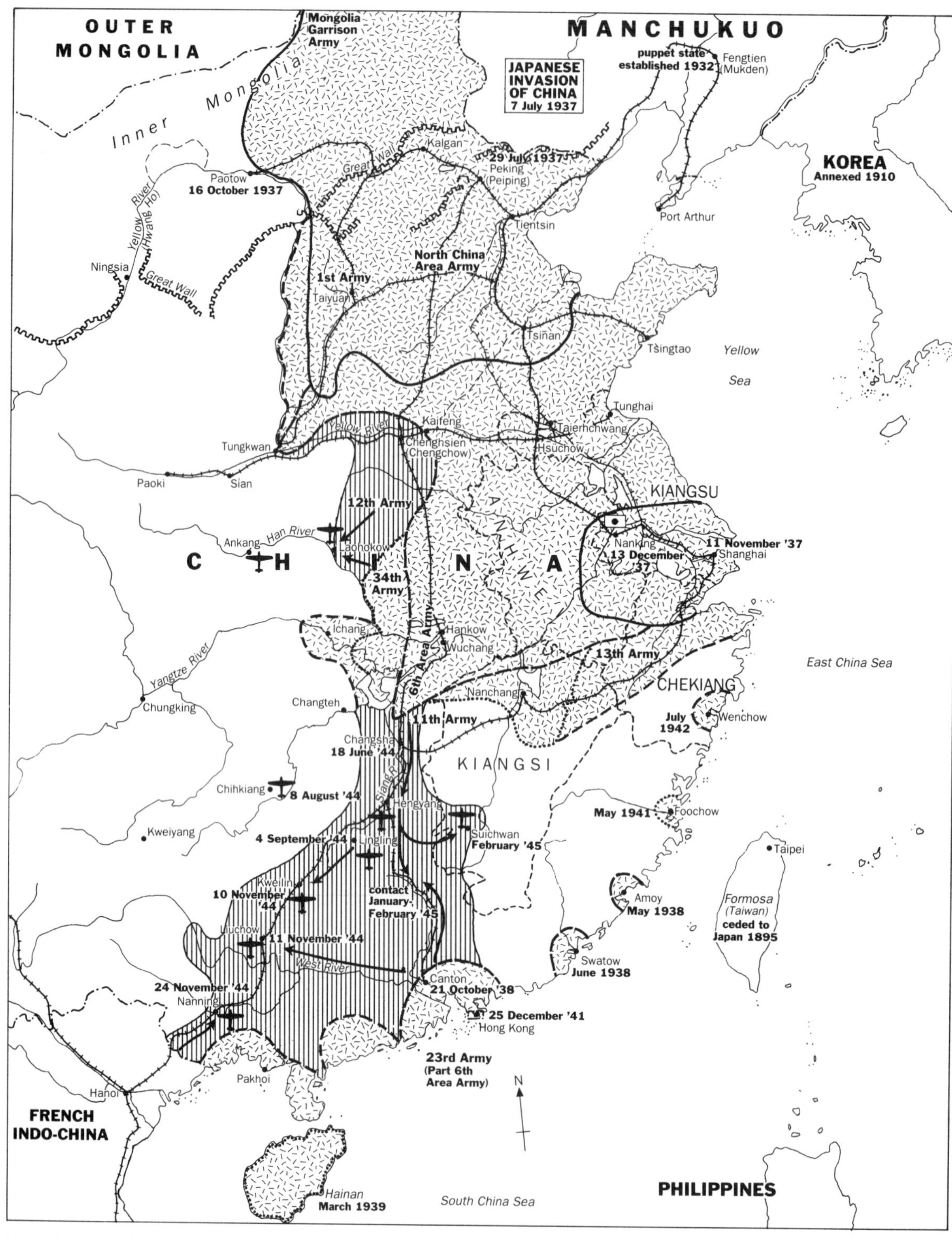

22. **China Incident**, 1937–45

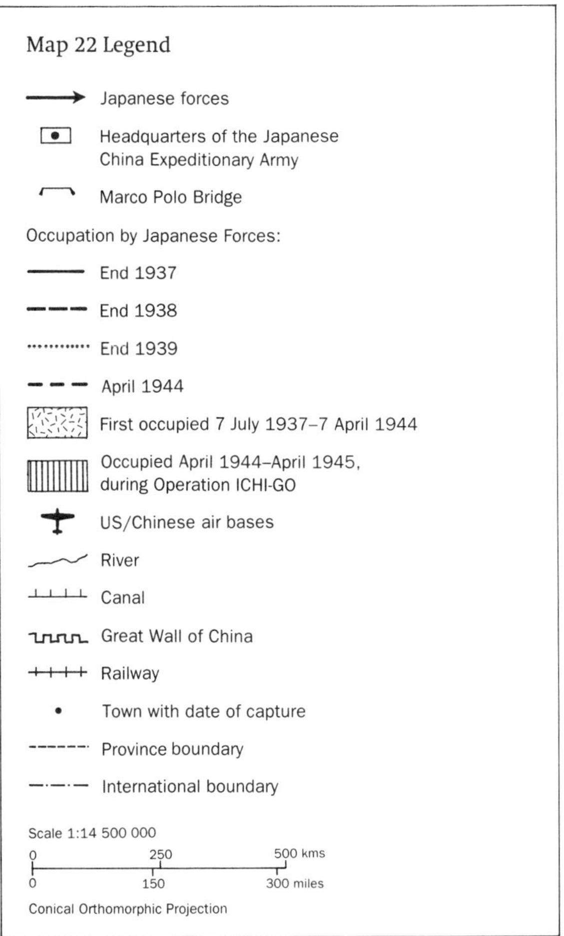

hardware) and which preferred that Japan pose a threat to the USSR, rather than become distracted in China.

In October, an inner circle of senior Japanese government figures dusted off the Funatsu initiative, under which the territorial and administrative integrity of China proper was more or less affirmed, in return for *de jure* recognition of Manchukuo, acceptance of a pro-Japanese regime in inner Mongolia, and termination of all anti-Japanese action by the Chinese government and populace. Sino-Japanese relations were to be 'adjusted' in ways satisfactory to Japan. Joint anti-communist operations were also dangled before Chinese nationalist eyes. These terms were secretly communicated to Trautmann in early November, and he relayed them to Chiang's government. Chiang delayed his response for about a month, while waiting to see if international pressure would be brought to bear on Japan. When no such pressure was forthcoming, Chiang acknowledged these terms as a basis for negotiation.

Meanwhile, however, the Japanese Army, unaware of this peace initiative, continued to drive toward Nanking. When army authorities learned of it, they immediately insisted on more stringent conditions, which made Chinese acceptance much more difficult and compromised the credibility of both Trautmann and the Japanese who had put the offer together.

If this were not enough, Nanking fell to the victorious Central China Expeditionary Forces on 13 December. The conquering forces then engaged in a days-long orgy of killing, rapine, pillage, and looting that became known as 'the rape of Nanking'. The combination of increasingly harsh terms and Japanese atrocities assured the failure of negotiations, which nevertheless dragged on until early January 1938.

The failure of the Trautmann mediation effort also marked a change in Japanese policy. Hard-line leaders were now calling the shots and they were infuriated with Chiang Kai-shek for refusing to fulfil their predictions of surrender. On 16 January 1938, the Japanese government issued a statement known for its operative phrase: *aite ni sezu* (no further dealing) with Chiang. From this point, the Japanese effort was to combine military pressure with the creation of an alternative Chinese regime (or regimes)—puppet governments, in short, which would do as they were told (see CHINA, 3(b)).

In Manchukuo and north China, such regimes already existed but were viewed with contempt by both their Japanese overlords and the Chinese whom they were supposed to govern. In short, the Japanese were unable to resolve the central paradoxes of puppet regimes generally: how to combine obedience with credibility, submission with authority, and dependence with the capacity for effective governance. Japan's most serious effort to create an alternative to Chiang Kai-shek's government was undertaken by the Tokyo and the military authorities in central China. This involved the defection of *Wang Ching-wei, a major political figure and rival to Chiang Kai-shek, in late 1938. But the eminence of the collaborator was no proof against the factional infighting and uncertainty of purpose that plagued nearly every Japanese initiative in China.

By the summer of 1940, while negotiations with Wang Ching-wei were still hanging fire—various Japanese factions remained at odds concerning how much authority to delegate to his Reformed Nationalist government, and what resources to place at his disposal—one more overture was made to Chiang Kai-shek. This was Operation KIRI, a series of conversations between covert and unofficial representatives carried on in Hong Kong.

Japanese motivation for Operation KIRI stemmed partly from the assessment that Wang Ching-wei was unlikely to live up to (or be permitted to live up to) the rosily unrealistic expectations that followed his stunning defection from the Chinese side. Further, it was now clear that Ishiwara's predictions had been accurate: Japan was endlessly and expensively bogged down in China, while tensions with the USSR and the USA were growing. According to this reasoning, the only hope for a timely resolution of the China Incident was to deal once again with Chiang.

For his part, Chiang was prepared to listen without committing himself. By the summer of 1940 the war had dragged on for three years, the outbreak of war in Europe meant that no international assistance would be forthcoming from that quarter, the USSR was scaling back its assistance to China, and the USA was only gradually changing its isolationist stance—with greater concern for the UK and Europe than for Asia. Thus, China was in a desperately beleaguered and isolated position. Chiang may also have understood that his conversations with Japan (through surrogates, of course) would compromise further the efforts to create a functioning collaborationist government under Wang Ching-wei.

But the same dynamics that had scuttled earlier efforts spelled defeat for Operation KIRI as well. The Japanese sponsors of this initiative had to keep it secret from hard-liners in the army and elsewhere, knowing the certainty of their opposition. Exposed as they were, they had no room for genuine negotiation with Chiang's representatives; nor could they be sure whether or not Chiang was genuinely interested or was simply on a fishing expedition. KIRI, like its predecessors, was probably never viable; in any case, it died a premature death in the autumn of 1940.

During this initial period of the war, by far the heaviest blows of Japan were directed against Chiang's KMT Army, as Tokyo sought first to force Chiang into a negotiated settlement, then later to replace his government with a more pliable puppet regime. At first with no intention of waging a costly, protracted war of attrition in China, Japan found that once engaged it was impossible to extricate itself.

Chiang's forces, though more numerous than the Japanese, were no match for them. Apart from one notable victory—the battle of Taierhchwang, in April 1938 which delayed a Japanese advance on Hsüchow by about six weeks—the nationalists were in constant retreat. China was soon almost entirely isolated from the outside world, and the nationalist government was forced to move from Nanking to Chungking in the agriculturally rich but socially backward province of Szechwan. By mid-1940, the Japanese advance had lost momentum and the central China Front lapsed into stalemate. The 'point-and-line' pattern of Japanese occupation was set during this period: garrison the cities and larger towns, together with the main lines of communication linking them. Neither the Japanese nor their puppet forces could occupy the vast Chinese countryside, though they often campaigned through it in search of guerrillas.

For China's communists (see CHINA, 3(c); 4(b)), this first phase of the war was a period of rapid but rather superficial expansion behind Japanese lines, where they were able to organize or absorb local forces. Territorial bases were established in north China by their Eighth Route Army and began functioning as semi-popular political regimes under the control of the Chinese Communist Party (CCP), which later began such reforms as rent and interest reduction. The situation in central China was more fluid, but by the end of this period, the communist-led New Fourth Army was creating similar base areas in Anhwei and Kiangsu provinces.

At first, United Front relations between the KMT and the CCP enjoyed apparent cordiality, then progressively declined, as the KMT contrasted their own disastrous reverses with the rapid growth in communist influence, growth which far exceeded that which it had authorized.

Between mid-1940 and the attack on Pearl Harbor in December 1941, the Japanese established the Wang Ching-wei puppet government in Nanking (see CHINA, 3(b)) and continued their military operations. But now these military operations were designed mainly to consolidate and exploit the territories previously occupied. This meant a virtual stalemate along the front with the Chinese nationalists, but tough military actions against the communists, whose main areas of strength lay behind Japanese lines, well within 'occupied' territory.

This period of the war was the start of the most difficult years for the CCP, since both the KMT and the Japanese were now vigorously opposing them. By late 1939, the KMT had thrown a tough blockade around the headquarters base area of Shen-Kan-Ning containing the capital town of Fushih. Chilly formality at the top covered bloody conflict in areas contested by the armies of the two parties, as the one sought to continue its expansion, the other to halt it. During the summer and autumn of 1940, these clashes grew more intense, with the CCP defeating nationalist forces in Anhwei and Kiangsu provinces. The following January, KMT armies took revenge by decimating their rival's headquarters unit in what is known as the 'New Fourth Army Incident'. In the presence of the Japanese threat, both sides pulled back from further large-scale operations, but continued grim tactical operations against each other. Meanwhile, Japanese pressure was an even more critical challenge, as the invaders sought to pacify and economically exploit occupied China. Mopping-up campaigns, which had begun in the spring of 1940, were intensified after the CCP's Hundred Regiments Offensive in August, which attacked the Japanese along their rail and road network of north China. In this, the largest and most prolonged offensive undertaken by the Chinese communists during the war, almost 400,000 Chinese troops were involved in the three-month campaign (August–December 1940). Most of the battles were designed to disrupt Japanese communications and transport lines, and at the same time to prevent these lines from being fortified and used as the bars of cages confining the communists to ever smaller and more fragmented base areas. After initial communist victories, the Japanese brought up powerful reinforcements and took a heavy toll of their opponents; and, alarmed by the growth of communist power, subsequently set about their cruellest and most thoroughgoing efforts to remove this thorn in their side.

By this time, Japan had military forces numbering more than a million men tied up in China. They were divided into three territorial commands, each of which had considerable autonomy in the field and influence in policy circles back in Tokyo; co-ordination among them was less common than rivalry and independent action. There were the Kwantung Army in Manchukuo; the North China Area Army headquartered in Peking; and the Central China Expeditionary Forces centred on Shanghai. These commands, led by hard-line and narrowly militaristic officers, controlled the puppet regimes functioning in their respective zones. What had been envisioned in 1937 as an operation of quick decision had by 1941 become a massively and divisively institutionalized conflict with no end in sight.

Following the Japanese attack on Pearl Harbor the Sino-Japanese conflict merged fully with the Second World War. In the following two years CCP-controlled territories and populations were cut nearly in half, and very difficult conditions prevailed elsewhere. In May 1942, for example, the Japanese launched a 100,000-strong offensive into the Chekiang and Kiangsi provinces during which they employed *biological warfare. The offensive was mounted to avenge the *Doolittle raid on Tokyo the previous month, and to capture local airfields. But it was also a punitive expedition of exceptional severity—no fewer than 250,000 Chinese were slaughtered before the Japanese withdrew in September—which Chiang's KMT forces could do nothing to prevent.

Throughout 1942 and 1943 the USA could provide little direct material assistance to China. But the strategic import of American involvement—that Japan would eventually be defeated, mainly by the Americans—was understood with increasing clarity by both Chiang Kai-shek and *Mao Tse-tung. Furthermore, the contours of US recognition and support of Chiang and the nationalists as the permanent legal authority in China were emerging more firmly.

From early 1944 the brunt of the war fell on the nationalists again, allowing the CCP to move forward once more, reaching and then exceeding its high-water marks of expansion early in the conflict. Japan was so increasingly drained by its losing struggle against the USA that it could no longer continue costly and ultimately fruitless efforts to eliminate communist influence. Furthermore, its last great offensive of the war (ICHI-GŌ), which took place from April to December 1944, before being called off in May 1945 when Japan itself became threatened, was directed at the nationalists, exposing the continuing weaknesses of their forces and rendering effective anti-communist measures all but impossible. By now, too, CCP action and Japanese mopping-up campaigns had all but obliterated nationalist forces operating behind Japanese lines.

ICHI-GŌ cut a broad swathe southwards across central and south China, opening up a continuous line of communication with French Indo-China, capturing the air bases in the south-east from which US planes were harassing Japanese forces and sinking Japanese ships, and pressing inland towards Chungking. The collapse of nationalist resistance was both complete and revealing. It destroyed the last remnants of hope among China's western allies that the country could play an active role against Japan; China was now seen as important only in its capacity to tie down about a million Japanese troops and possibly as a staging-ground for attacks upon or invasion of the Japanese home islands, the latter perhaps involving a landing somewhere on the north China coast.

By August 1945, then, China had not so much won the war as survived it. Survival was achieved at a staggering cost in human suffering and death on a scale surpassed, perhaps, only by the losses in the Soviet Union, but we will never know how to give accurate measure to this suffering as statistics are unreliable or missing. Chinese military casualties (killed and wounded) can reasonably be estimated at well in excess of five million, counting both nationalists and communists; Japanese military casualties may have been a tenth as many. As the Japanese pioneered the strategy of making total war, later adopted by all combatants, civilian casualties—those directly attributable to both military action and to such indirect causes as starvation and disease—were even larger, perhaps 10–20 million. What had begun with the smallest of skirmishes at the Marco Polo bridge led to eight years of massive and futile carnage. LYMAN P. VAN SLYKE

Boyle, J. H., *China and Japan at War, 1937–1945: The Politics of Collaboration* (Stanford, Calif., 1972).
Duus, P. (ed.), *The Cambridge History of Japan*, Vol. 6: *The Twentieth Century* (Cambridge, 1988).
Morley J. W. (ed.), *The China Quagmire: Japan's Expansion on the Asian Continent, 1933–1941* (New York, 1983).

Chindits, name given to Brigadier *Wingate's 'Long Range Penetration' (LRP) groups who fought behind Japanese lines (see Map 19) during the *Burma campaign while being supplied and supported from the air. It was a corruption of the Burmese word *chinthe*, the winged stone lions which guard Buddhist temples and which were used as the Chindits' insignia. The main principles of Chindit operations were surprise, mobility, and the employment of aircraft in the role of support artillery.

But Wingate's theories also countered Japanese tactics of cutting lines of communication by infiltration and then attacking from the rear. Since his groups were supplied totally by air, there were no lines of communication to cut and no rear to attack. Instead, it was the Japanese who would be infiltrated and whose communication and supply lines would be severed. To deal with such incursions the Japanese, in Wingate's phrase, would have to drop their fists by withdrawing front-line troops, thereby laying themselves open to a knock-out blow from conventional forces.

Long Range Penetration, therefore, was intended to be part of a co-ordinated strategy, not just an isolated incursion behind the Japanese lines. But when General *Wavell, then C-in-C India, told Wingate that, apart from an attack towards Akyab in the Arakan, no offensive was possible, Wingate still urged that he should proceed. His argument was that the only way to convince the many sceptics of the feasibility of such operations was to undertake one. Wavell relented but gave Wingate specific tasks.

In forming his new force, 77th Infantry Brigade, Wingate had abandoned the conventional battalion formation. Instead he divided his units, which comprised the 13th Kings Liverpool Regiment, 3/2nd Gurkha Rifles, No. 142 Commando Company, and the 2nd Burma Rifles, into eight self-contained columns, each made up of four patrols of four sections. But to accomplish the tasks assigned to him by Wavell, Wingate divided his force into two groups for the operation (LONGCLOTH) which was launched in February 1943. One of them was to cut the railway south of Wuntho before it marched 400 km. (250 mi.) across Japanese-occupied northern Burma to rendezvous with the second group, under Wingate. This cut the railway further north near Nanken before crossing the Irrawaddy river. Both groups then combined to sever the Mandalay–Lashio railway, but the country was unsuitable for guerrilla warfare and hard fighting ensued. On 24 March 1943, after attempting to recross the Irrawaddy, Wingate ordered his columns to disperse and find their own way back to Burma. This took many weeks and out of the 3,000 troops involved only 2,182 returned. All had marched at least a thousand miles, some much more.

LONGCLOTH was evaluated as being of no strategic value; but after the war it emerged that it had at least encouraged the Japanese to believe, incorrectly, that they could apply the same principles when they launched their *Imphal offensive in March 1944. Valueless or not it was a great morale booster and the British press seized on it as if it were a victory. Churchill had Wingate recalled and took him to the Quebec conference in August 1943 (see QUADRANT) where Wingate won over Roosevelt and the US *Joint Chiefs of Staff to his theories of 'deep penetration'. He obtained not only the necessary backing to train a new force of Chindits, officially called Special Force, but liberal American aid in the form of a 3,000-strong LRP Group (see GALAHAD) and the *Air Commando. But it was only the impending Japanese Imphal offensive, and not one undertaken by the Allies, that created the right military situation for Wingate's new operation (THURSDAY). As part of a deal to obtain co-operation, Wingate relinquished control of GALAHAD to *Stilwell, whose Chinese forces began advancing into northern Burma from north-east India at the end of 1943. But his new force still comprised six brigades totalling 20,000 men which included the all-British 70th Division, 4/9th Gurkha Rifles, and troops from British West Africa. Each brigade was made up of four small battalions and each battalion was organized into two columns. Its immediate task was to attack from the rear the communications of the 18th Japanese Division to facilitate Stilwell's advance and to create a situation that might encourage *Chiang Kai-shek's forces to advance from China into Burma. But Wingate's vision encompassed far more than that. He was convinced that, by committing his reserves, he could bring about the destruction of *Mutaguchi's Fifteenth Army during its *Imphal offensive by severing its supply lines.

The 1st Brigade entered Burma from India on foot in February 1944 to attack Indaw. The airlifting of the balance, in gliders, started on 5 March 1944, while the Air Commando, which carried out the airlift, also established, with RAF help, air superiority. A road/rail block (WHITE CITY) and two strongholds around airstrips (BROADWAY and ABERDEEN) were established and attacks on Japanese lines of communication began to draw off Japanese troops and aircraft which should have been taking part in the Imphal offensive.

Before his plans had time to bear fruit Wingate was killed in a plane crash on 24 March. He was succeeded by one of his brigade commanders, Walter Lentaigne, who was not a Wingate enthusiast and on 9 April the Chindits' role changed to supporting Stilwell under whose direct command they came on 17 May. The war they now fought was a conventional one, for which they were wholly unsuited. Stilwell, intent on capturing *Myitkyina, kept them in the field much longer than originally planned without adequate supplies or air support (the Air Commando was disbanded on 1 May). Only 25 men out of one Chindit force of 1,350 Gurkha Rifles eventually remained fit to fight, while another force was withdrawn without orders by its brigadier to avoid it being wiped out. By the time the last Chindits were airlifted to India on 27 August casualties had amounted to 3,628 killed, wounded, or missing.

Although training commenced for a new Chindit offensive, Special Force was dissolved in February 1945.

Bidwell, S., *Chindit War*, (London, 1979).
Carfrae, C., *Chindit Column* (London, 1985).
Fergusson, B., *Beyond the Chindwin* (London, 1945).

Choiseul, a Japanese-occupied Solomons island which was raided by US marines in October 1943 as one of the feints to distract the Japanese from US landings on *Bougainville. The marines withdrew after a week but early in 1944 a *Special Operations Australia patrol aided by New Zealand Air Force squadrons began harassing the 700-strong Japanese garrison, which withdrew in mid-1945. See also PACIFIC WAR.

Chou En-lai (1898–1976), Chinese revolutionary who, despite his middle-class background, was an early member of the Chinese Communist Party and became its organizer in Europe while studying in Paris. He returned to China in 1924, took part in the Long March to Fushih (Yenan) with *Mao Tse-tung and then became the party's principal negotiator with *Chiang Kai-shek's Nationalist Party during the *China Incident. He was prime minister of the People's Republic of China from 1949 to 1974.

Christison, Lt-General Sir Philip (1893–1993), British Army officer who commanded the 15th Indian Army Corps, part of *Slim's Fourteenth Army, in the Arakan during the *Burma campaign. The stubborn defence of his troops during the *Admin Box battle foiled Japanese plans to draw off British reserves before the Fifteenth Japanese Army launched its *Imphal offensive in March 1944. He was knighted in 1944.

Chuikov, General Vasili (1900–82), Soviet army officer who served as a military adviser to *Chiang Kai-shek from 1927 to 1929, then commanded the Fourth Army which occupied eastern Poland in the *Polish campaign. He was commander of the Ninth Army in the *Finnish–Soviet war and was promoted lt-general in June 1940. But the Ninth Army was defeated by the Finns and Chuikov was banished to China in December 1940 as Soviet Military attaché. In March 1942 he was appointed commander of the First Reserve Army (later Sixty-Fourth Army) and that September took command of the Sixty-Second Army defending *Stalingrad. 'We shall either hold the city or die there,' he stated and became known to his men as 'General Stubbornness'. He remained in command of the Sixty-Second Army (renamed the Eighth Guards Army in April 1943) which he led until the end of the war, taking part in the *liberation of eastern Poland and in the fall of *Berlin where he received the surrender of the city's garrison. See also GERMAN–SOVIET WAR.

Shukman, H. (ed.), *Stalin's Generals* (London, 1993).

Churchill as war leader.
Winston Spencer Churchill (1874–1965) possessed talents which, like those of his famous predecessor William Pitt, were peculiarly fitted to war. Character and experience provided him, uniquely among the 'Big Three' (see GRAND ALLIANCE), with an awesome armoury of knowledge, ideas and first-hand observations of war which worked along with simple but powerful political instincts. He was a strategist in every fibre of his being, though he did not always adhere to the classical principles he liked to cite in defence of his pet schemes. His earlier life was in many ways an ideal preparation for the task he undertook on 10 May 1940 and he embarked upon the war with a self-confidence which was entirely justified. 'I thought I knew a great deal about it all,' he later wrote, 'and I was sure I should not fail.'

1. Background and preparation
Between 1895 and 1898 Churchill experienced the world of late Victorian soldiering, first in Cuba and then with the Malakand Field Force before finally taking part in the battle of Omdurman. He also saw 'modern war' at first hand in South Africa (1899–1902) and then on the Western Front in 1915–16. These two kinds of experience blended to produce what the wartime chiefs of staff often found an infuriatingly simple 'front soldier' mentality together with an acute awareness of the role of modern technology in war (see MD1, for example). His tenure of most of the major offices of state, but most importantly his time as First Lord of the Admiralty (1911–15), gave him invaluable insights into the conduct of war at the highest levels, which he pondered deeply during the inter-war years, and an enormous fund of practical experience which together were to influence the way he ran the war from 1940 onwards.

The *First World War taught Churchill the importance of avoiding any repetition of the bitter and disastrous split between civilian ministers and military leaders—the 'frocks' versus the 'brasshats'—which, he thought, had bedevilled the conduct of that war. Sure political control and an effective machinery for collaborative decision-making were the legacies the Great War bequeathed to its successor. The Admiralty's reluctance to introduce convoying until April 1917, and its subsequent success, encouraged him to be sceptical of professionals and reinforced a natural tendency to think that in military matters the experts were often wrong and the politicians frequently right. His profound disappointment at the unimaginativeness of generals such as Haig and Robertson helped, in the Second World War, to sustain his faith in unconventional soldiers such as *Wingate and those who were out of favour like *Hobart, as well as these who were out of date (*Keyes, for example). His admiration for Marshal Foch's 'obstinate combativeness' found its echo in the varying treatment he accorded to Air Chief Marshal *Harris, General *Wavell, General *Auchinleck, Admiral *Cunningham, and General *Montgomery. In short, Churchill handled his commanders in the later war very much on the basis of general views formed in the earlier one.

Churchill ended the First World War with a body of firm strategic beliefs which he carried over into 1940 and, although keenly aware of the importance of applied science in war (see OPERATIONAL RESEARCH, for example), he remained convinced that nothing really altered these strategic principles; on 5 September 1939 he remarked that he did not believe the 'essential elements' of war would be altered by the air arm. A devout navalist, Churchill was and ever remained a convinced proponent of *amphibious warfare. The stress he laid on amphibious operations came from a broad conception of strategic manoeuvre and a conviction of the value of putting pressure on an opponent at varying points on his strategic periphery where his communications would be most stretched. It also came from his conception of the war as being divided between a 'main' theatre, where final victory must be won, and 'subsidiary' theatres where it was legitimate to take a 'war gamble'.

These ideas reappeared repeatedly during the Second World War—not least because of Churchill's propensity to recycle a strategic plan to meet a new situation—as did his broad strategic conception of how to conduct large-scale, multi-theatre war. 'Tendencies,' he told the House of Commons on 15 November 1915, 'are far more important than ... episodes.' Sensational victories were not

The British prime minister, Winston **Churchill**, at the QUADRANT conference in Quebec, August 1943. He is seated on the right, hat in hand. Also seated are the Canadian prime minister, Mackenzie King (left), and President Roosevelt. Behind them (left to right) are General Arnold, Air Chief Marshal Portal, Field Marshal Brooke, Admiral King, Field Marshal Dill, General Marshall, Admiral Pound, and Admiral Leahy.

necessary in order to win the war; rather the enemy should be worn down, premature offensives on the main front avoided, machines used as substitutes for manpower, and manoeuvre employed also to reduce slaughter.

Churchill learned much more from the First World War; his inter-war study of his ancestor John, Duke of Marlborough, merely confirmed his sense of the special problems of coalition warfare and of the paramount importance of integrating Allied military efforts. One further aspect of that experience would have a critical influence on the way in which Churchill fought the Second World War: his use of intelligence. Churchill had first realized the value of well-organized field intelligence during his service with Kitchener in the Sudan in 1898. From November 1914, with the three main German naval codes in Admiralty hands, he saw at first hand how intelligence might be integrated into operations—and how its insights could be squandered. While at the Admiralty he read every individual 'flimsy' (decoded signal) and he continued to read intercepts as a cabinet minister after 1918, attaching the highest importance to them. Although out of office, he was given intelligence material after 1931 with the express permission of Ramsay MacDonald and his successors. As a result, Churchill entered the Second World War convinced of the crucial importance of *signals intelligence warfare and of the need to co-ordinate multiple intelligence agencies to achieve maximum operational benefits. His possession of knowledge which his generals frequently lacked reinforced his inclinations to urge them into action.

Much of the Churchillian character had been evident during the First World War: the mixture of romanticism and pragmatism, an adamantine persistence and perseverance, enormous fecundity of mind, and great courage and humour. Less in evidence were its darker sides, which included insensitivity and a tendency unjustly to hound those—especially in the middle ranks—who upset him and his calculations. To achieve his purposes, he used during the Second World War an arsenal into which he had not reached before. 'His battery of weapons,' Admiral John Godfrey, war-time director of Naval Intelligence, recalled, 'included persuasion, real or simulated anger, mockery, vituperation, tantrums, ridicule, derision, abuse and tears.'

2. First Lord of the Admiralty, 1939–40

On 3 September 1939, at the age of 64, Churchill returned to the Admiralty after an absence of 24 years. The signal 'Winston is back' went round the fleet. At once he went into action, ordering the fitting of *radar to all naval vessels (denied all but three of them by pre-war economizing), instituting a convoy system, arming merchant ships, improving the defences of the anchorages at Rosyth and Scapa Flow and urging the construction of cheap anti-submarine escort vessels. Enthusiastically but unrealistically, he urged that 40 divisions be readied within the next twelve months (Churchill was a member of the Land Forces Committee which made recommendations to the war cabinet about policy; characteristically he dissented from them!). Also, embarking on what was to be a long-running but fruitless enterprise, he urged that Turkey be drawn into a Balkan Front.

Whilst galvanizing the navy into activity, Churchill also began to draw on the seemingly inexhaustible reserves of his strategic imagination. Plans to float mines down the Rhine (ROYAL MARINE) and to move British battleships into the Baltic the following spring (CATHERINE) were either launched too late or came to nothing. However his suggestion that Norwegian waters be mined was the first step in a series of events which led to the defeats at Narvik and Trondheim the following spring (see NORWEGIAN CAMPAIGN). Churchill's intention was to tighten the naval blockade of Germany by ensuring that Swedish iron ore (see Sweden, Table) no longer found its way to the Reich via Narvik and the North Sea. When, on 30 November 1939, the *Finnish–Soviet war began, the opportunity beckoned to send an expeditionary force to assist the Finns by way of Norway and Sweden. In his eagerness to cut off Germany's Scandinavian ore supplies and to disregard the rights of neutrals in the process, and in his enthusiasm for fighting what he called 'the opposite, though similar, barbarisms of Nazidom and Bolshevism', he was exhibiting his strategic impulsiveness at its worst. The landings in Norway, first called off when the Finns sued for peace in March 1940 and then resuscitated when the Germans unexpectedly occupied Denmark and parts of Norway on 9 April 1940, were ill-planned, poorly controlled, and confused from first to last. Churchill bore a heavy share of the responsibility for this failure, which he privately acknowledged after the war, and was lucky to escape censure. He was saved by the start of the German offensive in the west on 10 May (see FALL GELB) and his appointment as prime minister the same day.

While still First Lord of the Admiralty, Churchill, although happy to be in operational control of the most active of the three services, was soon deeply unhappy with Neville *Chamberlain's methods of running the war. A small war cabinet, attended by the three service ministers and the Chiefs of staff (who did not have a vote), had been set up, but after a meeting on 21 September, at which the military resisted the notion of extending the war into the Balkans, Churchill suggested to Chamberlain that the politicians might meet without the servicemen being present. Chamberlain's response was to set up the ill-fated Military Co-ordination Committee under the chairmanship of Lord Chatfield, minister for the co-ordination of defence, which comprised the three service ministers and the minister for supply, assisted by the service chiefs. This merely added another layer to the decision-making structure without enhancing political authority, as Churchill soon found out. Chatfield resigned on 3 April 1940 and after a week in the chair Churchill told Chamberlain that the committee needed the weight of prime ministerial authority to achieve anything. The Norwegian campaign demonstrated its weaknesses.

One event of great significance occurred during Churchill's first weeks at the Admiralty. Early in October 1939 he received a letter from Roosevelt, dated 11 September, inviting the First Lord to keep the president 'in touch personally with anything you want me to know about . . .' After gaining war cabinet approval on 5 October, Churchill replied. In the next seven months the two exchanged a handful of messages about naval matters, Churchill signing himself 'Former Naval person'. Thereafter the correspondence increased dramatically until, on Roosevelt's death, the two leaders had exchanged 1,949 written messages and telegrams, a figure which testifies to the central importance of the USA in Churchill's policy. From the outset of the war he banked on American aid; gradually, he won it.

3. Prime minister

(a) 1940–1

When Churchill became prime minister on 10 May 1940—by uncharacteristically staying silent and permitting Lord *Halifax to offer to serve under him without reciprocating—he was at once absorbed in the rush of events which led, six weeks later, to the fall of *France. His immediate reactions were, naturally enough, shaped by visions of static fronts, lines of resistance and the careful deployment of reserves, operational methods which no longer fitted the Wehrmacht's timetable. His emotional response to France's plight took the form of aid (particularly aeroplanes) and the somewhat bizarre offer of Anglo-French union; but sheer military realism, in the shape partly of advice from Air Chief Marshal

*Dowding and partly of innate good sense, ensured that he never risked bringing the UK down with France. By 24 June, Churchill and the British people and empire stood all but alone. This position did not worry the prime minister unduly for he had a massive and unshakeable conviction in final victory in what he saw as a Manichaean struggle between the forces of civilization and of barbarism. The road to that victory, however, was neither obvious nor easy.

On succeeding Chamberlain, Churchill moved swiftly and purposefully to simplify and re-vitalize the organization for making high-level strategic decisions. Appointing himself minister for defence, with the king's approval, he set up a Defence Committee comprising two panels for operations and supply, though as the war went on he substituted it for the former 'staff conferences' at which he and the chiefs of staff debated strategy without the company of the service ministers. To service his needs as strategic co-ordinator of the war, he took over the military section of the war cabinet secretariat under its head, Major-General *Ismay. Ismay's formal position was as the premier's principal staff officer and personal representative on the Chiefs of Staff committee; in practice, he soon became an indispensable go-between and with his small team, headed by Colonels Leslie Hollis and Ian Jacob, became what Churchill called his 'handling machine'.

As part of the process of building a war machine, Churchill reconstructed his team of service heads. He saw no reason to change the First Sea Lord he had inherited, *Pound, a workaholic who was prepared to tolerate a good deal of prime ministerial interference in naval detail and who often failed either to stand up to Churchill or to protect his subordinates. *Dill replaced *Ironside as *Chief of the Imperial General Staff (CIGS) in May 1940. The partnership was an unhappy one, partly because of Dill's reserved temperament and partly because he differed with Churchill over the relative importance of Egypt and the Far East. On Christmas Day 1941 he was replaced by *Brooke, who had the mixture of resilience and combativeness necessary to restrain the frequent flights of Churchillian fancy, and who took over the chairmanship of the chiefs of staff committee in March 1942. In the summer of 1940 the retiring Chief of Air Staff, *Newall, was replaced by *Portal who, possessing considerable intellectual powers, an aloof personality, and a capacity for hard work, soon earned Churchill's respect. Together this troika provided the professional ballast which was essential if Churchill's strategic imagination was to remain tethered to reality.

After the immediate likelihood of invasion had passed, Churchill told the Defence Committee not to worry if they could not see how victory would be achieved, as during the First World War such a question could not have been answered as late as August 1918. Behind this insouciance, however, lay a clear political and strategic conception of how to fight and win the war. That vision was formulated and refined during the years 1940–1 and Churchill never really departed from it thereafter.

Politically, Churchill's dominant objective was to woo the USA to support the UK and entangle it so closely in the war that eventually it must become a belligerent. The *destroyers-for-bases deal he negotiated from May to August 1940 was the first step, and although in concrete terms the bargain undoubtedly favoured the USA, the spirit of co-operation in which it was struck was an important step along the road to alliance. In December 1940 a dramatic letter from Churchill highlighted the UK's near-bankruptcy, prompting Roosevelt to introduce *Lend-Lease, vital for the UK's war effort. Increasing collaboration reached its first climax in August 1941 when the two leaders met at *Placentia Bay, Newfoundland, and signed the *Atlantic Charter. Churchill regarded the charter, which was cast in general terms, as an interim statement of war aims; more cynically, one member of his government saw it as 'mainly a dodge to get the US a little bit further into the war'. As part of his scheme to entangle the USA in a *de facto* military partnership, Churchill was prepared to cede the Pacific to America, thereby virtually handing over Britain's Far Eastern policy. Given the calls on the UK's meagre resources, he had little choice but to do so.

By October 1940, Churchill had devised the broad outlines of a strategy to defeat Hitler. In the immediate future only bombing offered a way to weaken Germany; but beyond that he envisaged a three-stage war in which bombing and blockade in 1940 were followed by medium-sized amphibious operations in 1941 and larger-scale attacks at a number of points on the European coastline in 1942. The details of this picture changed as the war developed—the entry of the USSR into the war in June 1941, for example, meant that Britain no longer had to rely on indirect methods of weakening the German war machine—and the dates moved back, but the essence remained the same. Germany had to be weakened by a combination of internal and external pressures before the *coup de grâce* could be delivered from points on the continental periphery.

Marshal *Graziani's half-hearted attack on Egypt on 13 September 1940 (see WESTERN DESERT CAMPAIGNS) and the Italian attack on Greece the following month (see BALKAN CAMPAIGN) dictated the first major steps in Churchill's war. As the corner-stone of the imperial arch which stretched to India and the Far East, the Middle East had to be defended. Churchill was more than willing to wage a large-scale war there, for as well as offering the military opportunity to invade Sicily or Sardinia and put pressure on Italy, success might persuade *Vichy France to change sides and Spain to remain neutral. Early victories won by Lt-General *O'Connor in the Western Desert were reversed after *Rommel's arrival in February 1941; and Wavell's disastrous adherence to the plan to intervene in Greece helped seal his fate as C-in-C Middle East. Armed with *ULTRA decrypts, in some of which Rommel gave a deliberately misleading picture of his position to his superiors, Churchill prodded first Wavell and then his successor, Auchinleck, to attack and was displeased when the latter refused to do so until late autumn.

In purely military terms, the first half of 1941 was not a good time for Churchill. The sinking of the **Bismarck* in May lightened the gloom a little, but the battle of the *Atlantic proved worrying. However, the entry into the war first of the USSR and then of the USA wholly changed the picture. In December 1941 Churchill rushed to Washington to propose a major Anglo-American campaign in North Africa (GYMNAST) in 1942 as the first step in his strategy to crush the European Axis.

(b) 1942–3

The USA's entry into the war, Churchill wrote on 12 December 1941, 'makes the end certain'. More immediately it offered him the chance to dominate Allied strategy. America had yet to mobilize its war machine, a task which would take some two years; in the meantime, the UK had both a strategy and an active operation (CRUSADER) which seemed about to defeat Rommel. At the *ARCADIA conference (22 December 1941–14 January 1942), Roosevelt accepted both Churchill's proposal for an immediate campaign in North Africa and his long-term strategic outline for Anglo-American landings in Europe in 1943 and the possible liberation of the continent in late 1943 or 1944.

Almost immediately, Roosevelt's generals objected. Churchill's favoured indirect strategy—they christened it 'periphery pecking'—was out of tune with their preference for a massive concentrated thrust directly into the heart of Germany and their immediate wish to relieve pressure on the USSR. In April, Churchill apparently accepted the American alternative—a small preliminary landing in France in 1942 (SLEDGEHAMMER) followed by the main invasion (ROUND-UP, later *OVERLORD) in 1943—but by July he was refusing to countenance the earlier operation. His reasons were sound: SLEDGEHAMMER, which would have to be largely British, would be no more than a pin-prick because of lack of *landing craft and equipment, and the German position was still far too strong for there to be any reasonable hope of success. Having promised the Soviets a Second Front in Europe in 1942, and without SLEDGEHAMMER, Roosevelt had no choice but to fall in with Churchill's North African strategy. The TORCH landings which began the *North African campaign took place on 8 November 1942 and Axis forces were finally cleared from North Africa six months later after a stiff last-ditch resistance. In American minds, the first seeds of doubt about Churchill's commitment to a major European land campaign had been sown.

Although Churchill showed great skill in managing his relations with Roosevelt over strategic questions, he was able to dominate Anglo-American strategy in 1942 more by default than through having secured complete consensus. Over diplomatic issues the differences between Roosevelt and himself became more quickly apparent. Churchill's general conception of the post-war structure of Europe was vague; but as a practical politician he recognized the benefit of acknowledging the USSR's claims to its June 1941 frontiers, even though this ran counter to the Atlantic Charter. Roosevelt emphatically disagreed, preferring to leave all territorial questions to a peace conference, so Churchill dropped the proposal. However, the disagreement was symptomatic of a growing divergence between the two men over international affairs.

Churchill's relations with his other great ally, Stalin, were quite unlike those with Roosevelt. From the moment that Germany attacked the USSR he showed a readiness to put aside his deep loathing of *communism to support a fellow combatant. *Beaverbrook's mission to Moscow (see THREE POWER CONFERENCE) in September 1941 had adopted a policy of 'aid without strings' and Churchill continued to set great store by keeping the supply lines to the USSR open. Lend-Lease to the Soviet Union became an important substitute for a European Second Front and territorial agreements, but the Allies were for various reasons unable to reach the goals agreed in the aid protocols. The disaster to one of the *Arctic convoys, PQ17, in July 1942 forced the UK to suspend them, and in August Churchill flew to Moscow to explain that TORCH was to be the substitute for a European Second Front that year. Aid to the USSR by sea was further curtailed by the North African and *Sicilian campaigns, and by the U-boat successes in the Atlantic. Churchill always remained acutely conscious of this and of the fact that the Soviets were bearing the brunt of the fighting, and repeatedly chided his generals by pointing out that there were 185 German divisions on the Russian Front.

By 1943 Churchill had been carrying the burden of war leadership for three years, yet a never-ending stream of memoranda and instructions still poured from his pen, directed at improving the war effort at every level from the most exalted to the most humble. One example can stand for them all. On 19 April 1943, six days after the announcement of the *Katyń Forest massacre, and while deeply absorbed in military events in North Africa and Burma, Churchill found time to complain to the minister of agriculture that 'you have discontinued the small sugar ration which was allowed to bees, and which is most important to their work throughout the whole year.' His personal concern for efficiency at every level was one of the most striking features of Churchill's style of war leadership. In pursuit of this goal he insisted that memoranda should be written on no more than a single sheet of paper and frequently demanded 'action this day' of subordinates when he felt that bureaucracy was dragging its heels.

Churchill drove himself hard but drove his subordinates harder, for they had to fit into the rhythm of his working day. The early part of the morning he frequently spent in bed or in his dressing-gown reading and dictating, before settling down to a round of meetings and discussions. No matter what the circumstances he almost always found time for a two-hour nap in mid-afternoon, from which he emerged refreshed and reinvigorated. Early evening business was followed by a lengthy dinner, at which he conversed with relish with his staff and invited guests, and then for preference by the screening of a film: his taste was for patriotic and romantic costume dramas. It was often nearly midnight before agnostic military leaders were challenged to debate and defend their views, which were on occasion completely opposed to the prime minister's, and well into the small hours of the morning before they crawled gratefully into bed. Churchill assisted himself not merely by controlling the working day but by selecting loyal and able personal assistants, such as John Colville and John Martin, who ran his private office, and Desmond Morton, his personal link with the intelligence community upon whose output he placed such heavy reliance.

The dispatch of the **Prince of Wales* and *Repulse* to Malaya in 1941 was an ill-fated intervention in Far Eastern strategy, and during 1942 Churchill took little hand in it as British forces evacuated Burma and then dealt with the 'Congress Revolt' in India (see INDIA, 3). At the Casablanca conference in January 1943 (see SYMBOL) he committed Britain to an amphibious operation on the Arakan coast of Burma aimed at recapturing Rangoon (ANAKIM) devised by Wavell in India. It was beyond Britain's strength and resources at that time, and as an alternative the British planners suggested CULVERIN, a landing on northern Sumatra. Churchill seized it with alacrity. It matched his preference for amphibious operations; it would force the Japanese to disperse their forces and launch a strong counter-attack; and it presented an attractive alternative to a bloody land campaign to recapture Burma.

At Casablanca, Churchill and his chiefs of staff succeeded in persuading a reluctant American delegation to accept a 'follow-on' strategy in the Mediterranean, immediately involving the invasion of Sicily (HUSKY). At the same conference, and with Churchill's foreknowledge and concurrence, Roosevelt announced the goal of *'unconditional surrender'.

At the Washington Conference in May 1943 (see TRIDENT), Churchill encountered the same objections to his Far Eastern strategy as his preference for operations in Italy and the Adriatic would soon confront: that such an attack would be costly, ineffective, and directed against a secondary objective. Distrustful of the fighting capacity of the Indian Army, Churchill stuck to CULVERIN throughout the summer and autumn of 1943 against the opposition of the Americans and the doubts of the British planners in *South-East Asia Command.

At Washington Churchill was forced to agree to an invasion of France in May 1944. Thereafter through the autumn he pressed insistently for operations in central and northern Italy and the Balkans and against the *Dodecanese Islands, even at the cost of delaying OVERLORD. His strategy, which aroused increasing American ire, had changed: initially founded in military perceptions, it was now increasingly fuelled by political considerations as the prospect of Soviet control of the Balkans began to loom. He made further efforts, all fruitless, to entice Turkey into the war immediately and, in an attempt to shape global strategy to his own ends, opposed proposals for a landing on the Andaman Islands off Burma (BUCCANEER), which both British and American staffs favoured, in order to have enough naval craft for his favoured Mediterranean ventures. Finally, he manoeuvred to avoid the presence of a Soviet delegate at the first Cairo conference in November 1943 (see SEXTANT) which preceded his meeting with Stalin at Teheran (see EUREKA) since he would simply 'bay for a second front'.

(c) 1944–5

By the end of 1943 the balance of authority in the Anglo-American alliance had passed from Churchill to Roosevelt. This was the inevitable result of the enormous expansion of American productive power: by 1943 the USA was producing three times the British volume of munitions and providing up to half Britain's requirement of tanks, landing craft, and transport aircraft. Churchill felt the consequences of this shift at Teheran, when Stalin added his voice to that of Roosevelt and expressed a decided preference for OVERLORD rather than extending the Italian Front north to the Po and across the Adriatic. Although the conference ended with expressions of unanimity and personal esteem, Churchill was now to grow increasingly out of step with his two partners in strategic matters.

On 23 January 1944 the prime minister took the chair at the first of a series of weekly meetings to review the progress of OVERLORD planning. This characteristic concern for detail did not, however, mean that he had abandoned his Mediterranean gambit. His deeply rooted preference for a 'flanking strategy' produced proposals for operations in Norway (JUPITER) and in Turkey and the Aegean should OVERLORD fail: and between June and August he struggled vainly to have the planned landings in southern France (see FRENCH RIVIERA LANDINGS)—also agreed at Teheran—abandoned in favour of forcing the Germans out of northern Italy and driving on *Trieste. These proposals, which confirmed American convictions that Churchill's strategy was founded in a determination to maintain and safeguard the interests of the British Empire at all costs, were in considerable part an impulsive and pragmatic reaction to German decrypts which exposed the vulnerability of enemy positions on the Po. They were also the consequence of a new element in Churchill's thinking: a belief that political considerations which were now emerging ought to exert a major influence on strategy.

By 1944 Churchill had realized that the advance of the Red Army would settle the political status of areas such as the Baltic States regardless of the niceties of international law. There was an unresolved ambivalence in his attitude towards the Soviet Union and the prospects for post-war co-operation: on the one hand he loathed communism as anti-democratic and irreligious, while on the other he professed to believe that the Soviets respected the West and were prepared to work with it. This view was partly the product of a delusion that Stalin was personally a reasonable man but was frequently the victim of pressure from hard-liners in the Politburo. Ever a pragmatist, Churchill moved to keep Greece out of the Kremlin's sphere of influence, proposing in May 1944 that Britain take the lead there in return for a reciprocal Soviet dominance in Romania. This grew into the 'percentages agreement' of October 1944 (see TOLSTOY) and reflected a realist's view of the shape of post-war European relations.

More immediately, Churchill grew increasingly concerned over the failure to shape Allied military strategy so as to diminish the area of post-war Soviet control in central and south-eastern Europe. This was why he pressed the case for a major effort in Italy in August 1944: by forcing a passage north-east towards Vienna, the West might avoid Yugoslavia and Austria falling under Soviet sway. For the same reason he opposed *Eisenhower's 'broad front' strategy in Europe and, in April 1945, the supreme commander's order not to advance on Berlin but to move instead towards Leipzig and Dresden. His foresight failed to convince an American leadership which divorced strategy from policy and which set great store by Roosevelt's belief that he could deal with Stalin on a personal basis. On 30 April 1945, after Roosevelt's death, Churchill urged President *Truman to liberate Prague and western Czechoslovakia, but the new American leader proved as resistant to his logic as his predecessor had been.

Although Churchill had reluctantly to accept American—and Soviet—strategic preferences in the west, he obdurately refused to do so in the east. He greeted Stalin's announcement at Teheran that the USSR would enter the war against Japan with elation because it eliminated the need to commit additional British forces to the *Burma campaign. His professional advisers favoured either making a substantial naval contribution to the *Pacific war or what became known as the 'middle strategy'—combined Anglo-Australian operations in the south-west Pacific under *MacArthur. Churchill refused to countenance either course. Instead he pushed CULVERIN for all he was worth, despite the revelation that its enormous shipping requirements would delay it until March 1945, largely for political reasons: if Britain merely provided a subsidiary naval force and trailed along 'at the heels of the American fleet', it risked losing control of Malaya to some American-inspired world organization. Relations between Churchill and his chiefs of staff came as close to breaking-point over this issue as they ever would and in March 1944 Ismay warned him of the possibility of resignations.

Paradoxically, Churchill's eastern strategy was undermined by events just when his western strategy was being devised to take advantage of them. The speed of the American advance in the Pacific in the summer of 1944 turned Sumatra into a backwater; and the successes of *Slim's army in Burma made the 'middle strategy' an irrelevance. Nevertheless, Churchill stuck obstinately to CULVERIN and at the Quebec conference in September 1944 (see OCTAGON) made an offer of the British fleet (see TASK FORCE 57) to assist the Americans in the Pacific hoping that it would be refused. Then he would be free to launch his much-favoured and economical amphibious attack on Sumatra. Roosevelt's immediate acceptance of the offer brought his strategy to a complete halt.

Churchill attended his last conference with Roosevelt at Yalta in February 1945 (see ARGONAUT). It was symptomatic of Britain's position in the partnership that Roosevelt kept from him the terms under which the USSR agreed to enter the Pacific war. By now the enormous complexity of any post-war settlement was clearly apparent, with disputes over Poland (towards which Churchill was sympathetic but exasperated as the government-in-exile refused to make territorial concessions he regarded as inescapable), over the zonal division of Germany (see also ALLIED CONTROL COMMISSIONS), over the scale and type of reparations to be extracted from a defeated Germany, and a host of other problems. On 12 April 1945 Roosevelt died. His successor, Harry S. Truman, continued his predecessor's policy of distancing American policy from British influence. Less than a month later, on 7 May, came the news of Germany's surrender. Churchill drank a toast to the chiefs of staff in celebration; they did not reciprocate. He gave notice of a general election and in July, in the midst of the Potsdam conference (see TERMINAL), returned to the UK and electoral defeat. What appeared to be popular ingratitude was more a gesture of support for the Labour Party, which had thought about the peace, than of disapprobation for a leader who had concentrated on winning the war.

4. Retrospect

The explanation for Churchill's successes as war leader lies as much in the organization which sustained him as in his personal qualities. Those qualities should not be belittled, however. Churchill was for many an emblematic figure, a portly British bulldog whose 'V for Victory' signs expressed in a cheekily vulgar way a determination not to succumb to Hitler. His emotional loathing of Nazism and his deep attachment to democracy and the monarchy fuelled his actions and inspired his oratory. They were balanced by an understanding of the importance of careful thought and rational analysis. If any risks were to be run, then they would at least be well-calculated ones.

Churchill's concern for efficiency was as evident on the battlefield as in the office. He prodded his generals, his admirals (less so his airmen) and his bureaucrats mercilessly. Lord Cherwell (see LINDEMANN)—'the Prof'—

and his personal statistical office provided some of his ammunition. Ismay and his staff ensured that, notwithstanding the mercurial energies of their master, the military machinery ran as smoothly as possible. They were a 'winning team', as were the chiefs of staff after December 1941, and the pairings of *Alexander and Montgomery in the Western Desert and Alexander and Harding in Italy. Churchill was not disposed to share his leadership with other politicians: the Dominions were never offered full partnership at the highest levels and his service ministers were never more than civil administrators. He was disposed to share it with professionals whose business was war. His success as a war leader rests on the fact that he was an enormously gifted amateur strategist—and that, ultimately, he acknowledged as much. JOHN GOOCH

Gilbert, M., *Finest Hour: Winston S. Churchill 1939–1941* (London, 1983).
—— *Road to Victory: Winston S. Churchill 1941–1945* (London, 1986).
Jacobsen, M., 'Winston Churchill and the Third Front', *Journal of Strategic Studies*, 14 (1991), 337–62.
Lewin, R., *Churchill as Warlord* (London, 1972).

Ciano di Cortellazzo, Count Galeazzo (1903–44), Mussolini's son-in-law and heir apparent, who served as his country's foreign minister for seven years. He 'combined irresponsibility, fecklessness, vanity, and the snobbery of the newly rich with a political judgement keener in many respects than that of Mussolini, deep family feeling, apparently genuine religious conviction, and physical courage' (M. Knox, *Mussolini Unleashed*, Cambridge, 1982, p. 47).

A lawyer by training, Ciano worked as a journalist before entering the foreign service in 1925. In 1930 he married Mussolini's daughter Edda, and promotion followed rapidly. In 1935, at the outbreak of the war with Abyssinia, he was minister for press and propaganda (but left to become a bomber pilot) and the following year he was appointed minister for foreign affairs. Initially he supported the Rome–Berlin axis but later changed his mind, for he feared German expansionism and was opposed to Italy's throwing in its lot with Hitler. He became convinced that Germany would eventually lose any war it started, that Italy was in no position militarily to support it, and that he must form a Balkan bloc to thwart any German move into the Mediterranean. He therefore opposed the *Pact of Steel, signed in May 1939, and, after the Nazis had occupied the rump of Czechoslovakia in March 1939, he proposed and directed the invasion of Albania the following month as an appropriate response to Hitler's aggression. When war broke out in September 1939 he exerted his influence to keep his country neutral, but he had no power base of his own, nor a feasible alternative policy to war. After Mussolini pledged himself to Hitler in March 1940, when they met at the Brenner Pass, Ciano told Sumner *Welles, whom Roosevelt had sent to Europe to investigate the possibilities of peace, that he was still 'determined to do everything within his power to keep Italy from getting into the war'. But Hitler's sweeping victories in May–June 1940 not only reinforced Mussolini's determination to enter the fray and take what pickings he could, but also altered Ciano's perception. On 10 June, dressed as a major in the Regia Aeronautica, he handed the Allied ambassadors Italy's declaration of war; on 23 June he and *Badoglio negotiated the Franco-Italian armistice which was signed the next day; and on 27 September he signed the *Tripartite Pact. Throughout the summer he urged an invasion of Greece, which he considered had an 'unneutral' attitude; when it was eventually mounted, from Albania in October, the conflict was known as 'Ciano's war', and its failure brought him immense unpopularity with the Italian people.

In January 1941, when Mussolini tried to placate the Italian public by sending many of his ministers, and other high officials, to the front, Ciano spent three months with a bomber squadron based at Bari. He returned to his post in April 1941, but his role was now reduced to not much more than that of a messenger. However, Mussolini's fate was too closely tied to his son-in-law to dismiss him and Ciano remained as foreign minister until the radical cabinet changes of February 1943 when he was appointed ambassador to the Holy See. He was part of one of the conspiracies to overthrow Mussolini and voted for Dino *Grandi's motion in the Fascist Grand Council that July which resulted in his father-in-law's dismissal. In August, after the Germans had occupied those parts of Italy not in Allied hands, he was tricked into delivering himself into the hands of the *Gestapo and was sentenced to death at the *Verona trials and executed.

Muggeridge, M. (ed.), *Ciano's Diaries, 1939–1943* (London, 1947).

CICERO, codename for the German spy, Elyeza *Bazna.

CIGS, see CHIEF OF THE IMPERIAL GENERAL STAFF.

cinema, see culture section of major powers: see also HOLLYWOOD.

CINCPAC and CINCPOA, see NIMITZ.

cipher machines, see ENIGMA, GEHEIMSCHREIBER, PURPLE, SIGABA, and TYPEX.

circuses, cross-Channel sorties by combined formations of RAF fighters and bombers. Their primary objective was to bring the Luftwaffe to battle after the battle of *Britain had been won, and later to force the Germans to increase their fighter strength in the west at the expense of the Eastern Front. Sometimes as many as 300 fighters were employed, using perhaps just six bombers as bait. The results were poor, with the RAF losing more aircraft than the Luftwaffe. See also RHUBARBS.

Civil Air Patrol, formed in December 1941 from US civilian pilots ineligible for the armed forces through age or infirmity, who flew privately-owned light aircraft. It undertook fire patrol, rescue work, and freight carriage, and its anti-submarine coastal patrol squadrons were of a very high order. Though initially employed only for spotting submarines or survivors, the larger aircraft were later armed with a depth charge (see ANTI-SUBMARINE WEAPONS) or two bombs. In April 1943 the patrol became an auxiliary of the US Army Air Forces, but its members, who were unpaid, remained civilians and their aircraft their private property. By June 1943 it numbered 75,000 personnel, 10% of whom were women. See also USA, 4.

civil defence, see under appropriate section of major powers.

Clark, General Mark (1896–1984), flamboyant US Army officer whose Fifth Army captured Rome during the *Italian campaign.

A third-generation soldier, Clark served in France during the *First World War and was wounded there. In June 1942 he went to the UK to command the 2nd US Corps and then became, under *Eisenhower, Deputy Supreme Commander for the *North African campaign landings that November. Before they took place he landed secretly from a submarine to meet pro-Allied French officers and two days after the landings he began negotiations for a ceasefire with the French authorities. The terms earned him criticism at the time but his exploits brought him fame as well. The same month he was promoted lt-general, the youngest in the US Army, and was then appointed commander of the Fifth Army which was part of *Alexander's Fifteenth Army Group which fought the Italian campaign.

The Fifth Army was activated in January 1943 and was initially responsible for holding French Morocco and Algeria and maintaining internal security there. In September 1943 Clark commanded the *Salerno landings, during which he personally led, at a critical moment, a unit that repelled a German tank attack. He captured *Naples on 1 October, but in the fighting which followed Clark was unable to break through the German *Gustav Line and reach Rome. To break this deadlock he launched the *Anzio landings behind the line in January 1944 and at the same time attempted to break through it at *Monte Cassino. Then, in an attempt to link up with the landings, Clark attacked across the River Rapido, a fruitless operation which cost 2,100 lives in 24 hours, and for which he was much criticized. He was also criticized for his obsession with taking Rome ahead of the British. During the Allied operation (DIADEM), launched in May 1944, Clark made straight for the Italian capital instead of encircling the Tenth German Army as instructed. He took Rome on 4 June 1944, but it was an empty gesture for the Germans were able to withdraw and take up new positions on the *Gothic Line. In July 1944 the Fifth Army had to supply some of the forces for the *French Riviera landings and as replacements Clark received the Brazilian Expeditionary Force (see BRAZIL) which, along with the other Allied forces in Italy, suffered the gruelling fighting and heavy causalities that eventually brought the campaign to a halt by Christmas.

Lt-General Mark **Clark**, commander of Fifth US Army, photographed at Siena during the Italian campaign.

In December 1944 Clark succeeded Alexander as Army Group commander, was promoted four-star general the following March, and personally received the surrender of German forces in Italy a few days before the end of the war. Though he was regarded by some as conceited and ambitious his talent was not disputed. Eisenhower rated him the best trainer, organizer, and planner he had ever met, and said he was energetic, forceful, and loyal.

Blumenson, M., *Mark Clark* (London, 1985).

Clark Field, attack on, Japanese air raid on principal US air base in the Philippines on 8 December 1941 (see PHILIPPINES CAMPAIGNS). It was as big a military disaster for the USA as the Japanese attack on *Pearl Harbor which preceded it by some hours.

Taking off from Formosa, 108 bombers of the Eleventh Japanese Air Fleet, escorted by 84 fighters, attacked Clark Field and a fighter base at Iba, both of which were situated on the Philippines main island, Luzon. Half the 35 B17 *Flying Fortresses at Clark Field—the most powerful American striking force in the Far East—56 fighters, and 30 miscellaneous aircraft were destroyed. Many others were damaged, installations were burnt out, and 80 men were killed and more than 150 wounded. In one stroke the Japanese had overcome the main obstacle to their expansion southwards.

General *MacArthur, the US commander in the Philippines, was first informed of Pearl Harbor at 0330 on 8 December 1941. Manuel *Quezon, the president of the Philippines, later remarked that the general 'was convinced for some strange reason that the Philippines would remain neutral and would not be attacked'. MacArthur's air commander, Maj-General *Brereton, twice requested permission to bomb Japanese airfields on Formosa—though MacArthur later denied that he had—and an attack was eventually authorized at 1100, but the raid was then deferred until an air reconnaissance mission had been completed. As Brereton later pointed out, if the raid had been authorized immediately the bombers would have been airborne when the base was attacked. The Japanese were, in fact, fearful of an immediate raid on their Formosa airfields: they knew the Americans must have been alerted by the Pearl Harbor raid: and fog, which prevented their force from leaving at dawn as planned, did not lift until 1015.

However, when other Japanese aircraft were first sighted, at 0900, the bombers were ordered into the air in case Clark Field was attacked. But as the Japanese force despatched to destroy the bombers was approaching northern Luzon the B17s received the all-clear signal and were ordered to land to prepare for the Formosa raid.

Shortly after 1130 reports began coming in of the Japanese force heading for Clark and Iba. At 1145 a warning was dispatched but was apparently never received; a radio warning also failed; and a telephone call had no effect. Fighter squadrons were scrambled from other bases to intercept, but all the aircraft at Clark were on the ground when the Japanese bombers arrived at about 1230. Three fighters managed to take off, and they, helped by others, shot down six or seven Japanese fighters, but the bombers were unscathed. The anti-aircraft defences proved totally inadequate. Only one in six shells exploded and those that did were well below their targets.

After the war, MacArthur, his chief of staff, Maj-General Richard Sutherland, and Brereton all issued conflicting accounts of the disaster. No answers were found as to why authorization to attack Formosa had been delayed; why warnings to Clark Field of the Japanese attack had been either ignored or had failed to arrive; why the bombers had not been dispersed; and why they had been there anyway when it was known how vulnerable the base was to air attacks from Formosa.

Clark Kerr, Sir Archibald (1882–1951), Australian-born diplomat who was appointed British ambassador to China in 1938. In March 1942 he succeeded Stafford *Cripps as ambassador to the USSR, in which post he attended several of the Allied conferences (see GRAND ALLIANCE). He was knighted in 1935.

CLARION, codename for Allied air operations mounted on 22 and 23 February 1945. Their objective was to mobilize all available Allied air power over Germany and to attack those military communications and transportation targets which had so far escaped damage. Most were located in small towns which had never been bombed and it was hoped that the wide-reaching nature of the operations would bring home to the German people the hopelessness of their position. The Joint Intelligence Committee (see UK, 8) later concluded it had done little to affect Germany's will to resist, though not all post-war assessments agreed with this judgement. See also STRATEGIC AIR OFFENSIVES, 1.

Clayton Knight committee, Canadian-based organization formed in September 1939 to recruit US pilots into the Royal Canadian and Royal Air Forces. It was supervised by Air Vice-Marshal Billy Bishop, a *First World War Canadian fighter ace, who appointed Clayton Knight, an American and a fellow First World War pilot, to run it. At first the committee had to work covertly as under the *Neutrality Acts an American could lose his citizenship if he fought in the armed forces of a belligerent power. These laws were soon relaxed, but contacts were mostly made by word of mouth and with discreet newspaper advertisements. A recruitment office was opened initially in New York, and when the flow of volunteers increased after the German offensive in the West in May 1940 (see FALL GELB), others were opened. By the time the US entered the war in December 1941 about 10% of RCAF pilots were American volunteers and 92% of the *Eagle Squadrons were recruited through the Clayton Knight committee. By then it had handled 50,000 applications and had accepted 6,700 volunteers.

CNR, see NATIONAL COUNCIL FOR RESISTANCE.

Coastal Command, see UK, 7(d); see also AIR-SEA RESCUE.

Coastal Picket Patrol, formed in May 1942 as part of the US Coast Guard Auxiliary. It was made up of motor boats, auxiliary yachts, and other small craft which were used for rescue work and spotting hostile submarines off the eastern seaboard and in the Gulf of Mexico. Its official Coast Guard title, Corsair Fleet, was little used, and it was generally known to its amateur and Coast Guard personnel as the 'Hooligan Navy'. It was ineffective and was disbanded in October 1943. See also USA, 4.

Coast Watchers were used by both sides to report on the movement of their opponent's shipping. By far the best known were those raised by the Royal Australian Navy after the *First World War as the Islands Coastwatching Service to watch the long unguarded coastline of Australia and neighbouring islands in case of war. In September 1939 Lt-Commander Eric Feldt was given the task of completing the network and by mid-1941 he had established more than 100 stations equipped with transmitters. These covered 4,000 km. (2,500 mi.), from the western borders of Papua to the New Hebrides. Many running these stations had to be evacuated before the

Japanese arrived, but the reliability of their information led to an expansion of the service and by March 1943 the Solomon Islands had a chain of them. Feldt codenamed their activities FERDINAND after Walt Disney's bull, which did not fight but sat under a tree smelling flowers, a reminder that it was not a Coast Watcher's duty to fight, 'but to sit circumspectly and unobtrusively, gathering information'. Mostly, they followed their orders but if threatened by Japanese patrols they, with the help of loyal local people, had no hesitation in destroying them—and frequently did so.

The Coast Watchers were mostly drawn from Europeans who had settled on the islands, and all, including the one woman operator, were eventually given a service rank in an attempt to give them some protection if captured. When the organization expanded it also included service personnel from Australia, New Zealand, the USA, and the Solomon Islands Protectorate Defence Force, as well as native civilians.

In July 1942 Coast Watchers in *MacArthur's *South-West Pacific Area became part of the newly formed *Allied Intelligence Bureau (AIB) but those in the *South Pacific Area remained part of the Australian Naval Intelligence. Though complicated, this chain of command worked well as Feldt was put in charge of both areas. He was therefore able to feed information to both AIB and the South Pacific Area commander.

As American plans to land on *Guadalcanal in the Solomons matured the information sent by Coast Watchers stationed in the area became increasingly useful. Details of Japanese strengths and movements, and regular reports on weather patterns (see also METEOROLOGICAL INTELLIGENCE), all helped the landings succeed when they took place on 7 August 1942. Two Coast Watchers acted as guides for the landings on Tulagi and once US marines were ashore there and on Guadalcanal other Coast Watchers on Bougainville transmitted vital warnings of Japanese air attacks mounted from New Britain and New Ireland. In the months of bitter fighting for Guadalcanal that followed these agents operated such a vital warning system that the US commander of the South Pacific Forces, Admiral *Halsey, later said that it was Coast Watchers who saved Guadalcanal and that Guadalcanal saved the South Pacific.

During the Guadalcanal campaign a base radio station was established there so that outlying Coast Watchers could report their information direct. Other Coast Watchers were also inserted on Vella Lavella and Choiseul to report Japanese shipping movements. During the Japanese build-up in October 1942 to recapture Guadalcanal they were able to send detailed reports which helped thwart the intended offensive.

Coast Watchers and their indigenous helpers also organized an invaluable rescue service. One on Kolombangara rescued the future US president, Lt John F. Kennedy, after his *PT boat was sunk, while the list of airmen rescued from various islands was an impressive one: Guadalcanal 6, Isabel 28, New Georgia 22, Rendova 8, Vella Lavella 31, Choiseul 23. The Coast Watcher on Segi Island had Japanese airmen rescued, too, and had his local helpers deliver them to him bound hand and foot. They also charted safe water for American supply ships that ran up the north-east New Guinea coast between Milne Bay and Buna; gave early warnings of air attacks when New Britain was invaded; helped organize guerrilla actions behind Japanese lines; and at *Hollandia mounted a pre-invasion reconnaissance. But by October 1944 only isolated, and impotent, pockets of Japanese remained where the Coast Watchers had been operating, and the service, which had suffered a high casualty rate, was disbanded. Many of its members received American or British *decorations.

The Japanese also used coast watchers. The name was used, too, to describe agents organized by *MI6, to watch German naval movements off the Norwegian coastline; and by those organized by *MI5 to watch neutral Eire's western coastline for U-boats which might try to rendezvous with supply ships in isolated coves.

Feldt, E., *The Coast Watchers* (Melbourne, 1946).
Lord, W., *Lonely Vigil* (London, 1978).

codenames were allotted by both sides to all operations and to anything which needed the cloak of *secrecy—conferences, new weapons, and so on. In the UK they were allotted by the *Inter-Services Security Board.

Codenames were also used by the Allies to identify Japanese aircraft as their Japanese designations were often impossibly long and incomprehensible to Allied personnel. In 1942, *South West Pacific Area Command allocated a name to each aircraft, for reporting and descriptive purposes. Fighters and small float planes were allotted boys' names such as 'Oscar' and 'George'; bombers, transport aircraft, and flying boats had girls' names such as 'Betty' and 'Mabel'; and general purpose and training aircraft had the names of trees.

Churchill was particularly interested in codenames and in a minute to General *Ismay, dated 8 August 1943, he stated that 'Operations in which large numbers of men may lose their lives ought not to be described by code-words which imply a boastful and over-confident sentiment, such as "Triumphant", or, conversely, which are calculated to invest the plan with an air of despondency.' He added that they ought not to be frivolous, nor should they be ordinary words, such as 'smooth' or 'flood', which might cause confusion, nor the names of living people.

codes and ciphers are often used interchangeably for a way of making a message—usually a radio message sent in Morse code—incomprehensible to anyone not possessing a method of turning it back into plain language. But, strictly speaking, a code substitutes groups of two or more numbers or letters for the words, phrases, or sentences which make up the message. A cipher substitutes a letter or number for each letter of the message, or transposes them (hence substitution or transposition ciphers). However, the Royal Navy had its own definition of codes and ciphers, the former being used by ratings, the latter by officers.

Code books and cipher books were used to scramble and unscramble the messages, but cipher machines were also used, and were faster (see ENIGMA, GEHEIMSCHREIBER, PURPLE, SIGABA and TYPEX). See also BLETCHLEY PARK, MAGIC, NAVAJO INDIAN CODE TALKERS, ONE-TIME PAD, SIGNALS INTELLIGENCE WARFARE, and ULTRA.

Colditz, a castle built in Saxony, Germany, in 1014. It was, variously a prison, a lunatic asylum, and a temporary *concentration camp before becoming a *prisoner-of-war camp (**Oflag* IVC) in 1939 for Polish and French officers. Because it was regarded as totally secure and as the war progressed it was used to confine difficult prisoners of many nationalities who were inveterate escapers. It contained many well-known characters such as Lt Airey Neave, Wing Commander Douglas Bader, General *Komorowski, and Lt-Colonel David Stirling (see SPECIAL AIR SERVICE). Altogether there were more than 300 escape attempts but only 30 succeeded.

Reid, P., *Colditz: The Full Story* (London, 1984).

Cold War. Although the term was not generally used until the 1950s, historians of the Cold War have traced its origins to the strains of the *Grand Alliance from 1941 onwards.

Both Churchill and Roosevelt agreed that the western powers must sink their differences with Stalin for the duration of the war against Germany: and western propaganda went to great lengths to conceal the crimes of their Soviet ally. Stalin's contribution to the Allied war effort was so immense that he could flout the *Atlantic Charter almost at will, and could gain acceptance of the Soviet viewpoint on many issues where there would otherwise have been no agreement. Even so, there were several conflicts of interest where the Anglo-Americans were unwilling to yield to Soviet claims. One was in Persia, which western oil companies had targeted for post-war developments; another was in Poland whose independence had been guaranteed in 1939.

Stalin, for his part, was careful to bide his time and to avoid an open breach. The Soviet Union received huge shipments of *Lend-Lease war materials from the West; and Moscow was paranoid about the (unlikely) possibility of the western powers changing sides and joining Germany in an anti-Soviet crusade. All three partners of the Grand Alliance were fearful of a split until both Japan and Germany had been forced into *unconditional surrender.

At the end of the war, the Red Army's advance across the states of eastern Europe made Soviet control there a reality, irrespective of western wishes. But before absorbing them completely into the communist bloc, Stalin again played a waiting game in the hope that US troops would be taken home within two years as Roosevelt had once indicated. As a result, despite growing tensions over the joint administration of Germany (see Map I), western and Soviet officialdom maintained an uneasy truce to the end of 1946. Relations began to deteriorate after the blatant manipulation of the elections, by the communists, in Poland in January 1947, and reached breaking-point after the announcement of the Truman Doctrine and of Marshall Aid later that year.

Once Stalin could see that the Americans were not going to withdraw from Europe, he had no further cause for restraint. The communist coup in Prague, in February 1948, and the Berlin blockade launched an era of hostility which never broke into open warfare but which lasted for 40 years. See also DIPLOMACY. NORMAN DAVIES

collaboration

See also under GOVERNMENT section of the occupied powers discussed here; see also CHANNEL ISLANDS.

1. Introduction

In wartime, collaboration assumed meanings that went far beyond its neutral dictionary definitions of 'co-operation' or 'unity of effort' (*OED*). It was almost always used in the pejorative sense of 'working with the enemy' or 'assisting the occupying power'. On the Allied side it became a synonym for treasonable or hostile activity, so that to call people collaborators was to express strong disapproval for their actions.

It is important to recognize, therefore, that collaboration, like *heroism, *liberation, and *occupation, is a subjective concept which depends on the loyalties of those who use it. One side's 'collaborator' was the other side's 'ally' or 'auxiliary' or 'friendly assistant'. Those denounced by the western Allies as collaborators were naturally viewed by the Axis powers in a favourable light.

The problem was particularly complex in those countries of eastern Europe which were forcibly occupied both by the USSR and by the Nazis. As the USSR was part of the *Grand Alliance, it has been the convention in the UK and USA to restrict 'collaborators' to persons who worked for the Nazis. From an impartial point of view, however, there is every reason to extend the term to those who chose to work for the Soviets; and when Germany was occupied by the Allied powers at the end of the war, Germans who seemed to co-operate over-zealously with the occupation regime stood to be regarded as collaborators by their compatriots.

However, for the purposes of this entry the term 'collaborator' has been restricted to describe co-operation with an Axis occupying power, though section 3 does touch on collaboration with the USSR.

NORMAN DAVIES

Collaboration was often severely punished by the inhabitants of German occupied countries after they had been liberated by the Allies. Here a French girl has her head shaved for having relations with a German soldier. The photograph was taken on 29 August 1944.

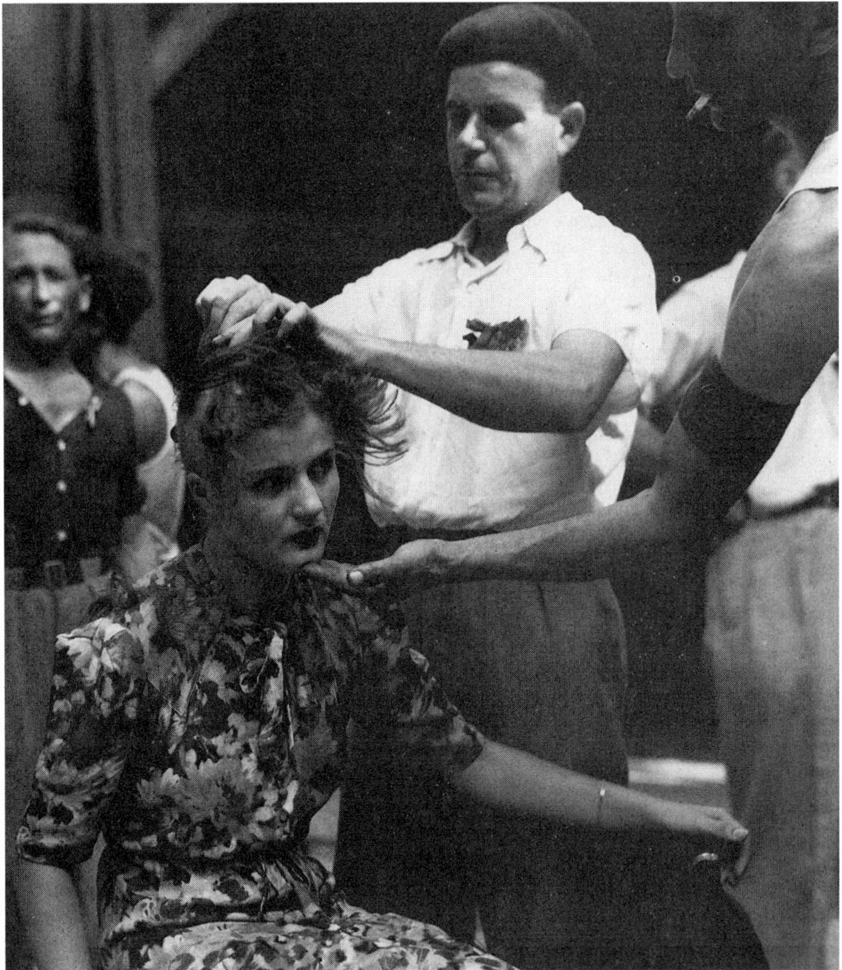

2. Western and Northern Europe

The term collaboration was first used, in its wartime sense, after the memorable meeting between Hitler and *Pétain at Montoire-sur-le-Loir on 24 October 1940. Six days later Pétain declared on French radio that 'collaboration had been envisaged between our two countries' and that he 'accepted it in principle'.

It was the formal acceptance of this political principle that gave rise to the modern definition of collaboration, and that lead, unfortunately, to numerous historical misconceptions and misinterpretations. Collaboration was initially seen as a political arrangement between two nations: the victorious one which had occupied foreign territory, and the loser which tried to preserve as much independence as possible. This narrow definition automatically excluded all other forms of co-operation between victor and vanquished, which were then left open to moral judgement and in most cases moral condemnation.

Collaboration can take numerous forms, and apply to many different cases: political (often ideological), economic, social, or cultural. Naturally collaboration depended upon the aims, the quality, and the actual course of the occupation. Looking at the map of Nazi-dominated western and northern Europe from 1939 to 1945, there was a great variety of political and administrative structures, ranging from military administration, as in Belgium until 1944, to civil administration, as in Norway and the Netherlands, to a retention of sovereignty, as in Denmark until August 1943. The French case initially offered four different forms of political and administrative structures.

During the war, each occupied country developed its own patterns of behaviour, but there were also signs of similar, comparable, reactions among the populations. This was particularly true for the first part of the war, when the Axis powers seemed to be heading for a quick, decisive victory. Under the impact of German military successes by *blitzkrieg, the prevailing attitude in most western and northern European countries hovered between a cautious waiting approach, a form of playing for time (*attentisme*), and a growing willingness to come to terms with the supposedly victorious power in the interest of maintaining law and order; thereby accepting that the political and military situation had been totally transformed in favour of German supremacy in Europe. Such apparent accommodation was in no way equivalent to the kind of notorious collaboration by some fascist groups or individuals, later associated with the names of *Quisling, *Mussert, and *Laval, and with such organizations as the *Milice, but was simply a matter of carrying on with routine functions and the needs of daily life.

In Belgium, where, after the war, 53,000 men and women were convicted of collaboration, officials used the phrase *la politique du moindre mal*, the policy of doing the least harm, to cover the ways in which they tried to accommodate themselves to the Germans' demands: giving way when they had to, holding out for old-established ways when they could. A similar policy was adopted in several areas, as far apart as the Baltic states, the Netherlands, and Salonika, by the elders of the Jewish community in the earliest stages of coming to terms with Nazi rule; they were bitterly undeceived in the end (see FINAL SOLUTION).

Some motives for accommodation were soon eclipsed by motives for collaboration, specific to the individual institutions and organizations concerned. An example of this is the so-called 'New Order' (see GERMANY, 4) debate among Dutch, Belgian, and French industrialists and high-ranking civil servants. This debate related to the anticipated collective re-orientation of national industries to the political and economic realities that the Third Reich sought to create: the dismantling of national economic systems, the development of new spheres and methods of production, the reorganization of social systems, and the possible restructuring of the administrative sector after the removal of parliamentary control. This discussion was ultimately dominated by fear of economic and social chaos, and concern for the maintenance of industrial production and jobs, even though rudiments of the political accommodation of the first phase of the occupation continued to be apparent.

Economic collaboration provides a test case for demonstrating the ambiguity of arguments and attitudes during the occupation period. There were entrepreneurial as well as more general economic reasons for ensuring the continuity of production and intensive economic co-operation with Germany. These included an interest in maintaining companies as viable entities; a desire to safeguard invested capital—including its potential future proceeds—from possible seizure by the occupying power; and the aim of preventing the penetration of the national economy by German big business. The closure of factories could lead to the dismantling and sequestration of machinery, of goods, and of whatever *raw materials were still available. Moreover, the workers who lost their jobs in this process had to face the prospect of being sent to Germany as *forced labour. A high level of industrial production, on the other hand, provided a tolerable livelihood and relative security for many employees. Besides, those goods and finished products which were not intended for export to Germany would benefit the local population.

But there was more to all this than just the aim of maintaining production and keeping enterprises alive. In most of occupied western and northern Europe all major industries increased their output and indeed their profits during the first two years of occupation; some entrepreneurs were able to expand even during the later periods of the war, when general economic decline had become obvious. In some countries, the process of modernization intensified and the monopolization of industries increased as the result of measures taken by the German occupying authorities in co-operation with larger companies and industrial groups. There was certainly something seductive for many businessmen and politicians about linking their country with a vibrant, renovated European economy, as a near-equal partner. However, the reality was quite different. In economic terms the German 'New Economic Order', had it ever been fully established, would have been a large-scale structure organized for, and run on, the principles of the crudest kind of colonialism. So long as the war lasted, Germany's economic policy towards the occupied territories of Europe can be summed up in two terms; exploitation and colonization.

The co-operation of native fascists with the Nazi invaders can be regarded as the classic case of collaboration during the war. In no other case is the range of collaborationist behaviour more clear; nowhere is it more starkly revealed that both the prospects and the limits of collaboration were always linked with the interests of the occupying power. In most cases the demarcation line between Nazi occupation policy and fascist collaboration was very thin, where they did not actually overlap as a result of ideological identification. Collaboration with the occupying power was thus regarded, although perhaps with differing degrees of intensity and conviction, as an ultimate objective; either as a long-term, unlimited co-operation with Nazi Germany or (for a small radical section of the fascist movement) as a total absorption into a future Germanic empire, to be created under the auspices of *Himmler's *SS. The wartime fascist collaborators held rather diverse convictions, which allowed some of them, at times, to appear to be social revolutionaries and modernizers. Yet despite their progressive rhetoric and youthful-sounding slogans of revolution and socialism, these 'revolutionary fascists' remained strongly reactionary and largely anti-modernist.

Fascist collaboration certainly contained an element of historical continuity, although opportunism and political, even personal, corruption also became dominant features. But the element of continuity also applied to other practitioners of collaboration who, like

Marshal Pétain in France, viewed close co-operation with Germany as providing the only operational basis for their policies. The French political scene during the occupation was a logical and to a large extent inevitable consequence of the political events and constellations of the 1930s. What has been called Vichy's 'pluralistic dictatorship' began with Pétain's reactionary-patriarchal regime (1940–2), was followed by Laval's authoritarian-technocratic rule (1942–4) and ended with *Darnand's openly fascist system (1944). Yet despite different motives and diverse approaches, all the protagonists of the *Révolution Nationale* (see FRANCE, 3(c)) agreed that there was no alternative to collaboration with the Third Reich.

However, in every case the potential, as well as the limits, of political collaboration were subordinated to the interests of the occupying power. Nazi Germany was not interested in creating a genuine fascist state in France or elsewhere. The occupation authorities regarded political collaboration (and, incidentally, any other form of it) first and foremost as a useful means of achieving their own goals. Concessions were only temporary, and never constituted any real change of policy.

Hitler made it quite clear that there would be no anticipation of a future political design for Europe. The much-acclaimed European idea was left to propagandists such as *Goebbels who sought to save Europe from Bolshevism in a crusade. The hopes of political collaborators for genuine co-operation with Germany were brushed aside. Native fascist parties and their leaders in most occupied countries, who had constantly demanded a share of power, were reduced to mere puppets and useful tools in the administration, and economic exploitation, of their respective homelands. Quisling in Norway, Mussert in the Netherlands, *Doriot and *Déat in France, to name but a few, all had to realize that Germany's European policy and Hitler's New Order had served one purpose only: to establish and strengthen Germany's superior power and to give it maximum support for conducting the war. There never was a real chance for European partnership for all the right-wing, authoritarian and fascist parties and movements. In this respect Hitler remained a true follower of the nationalistic ideas of the 19th century. He always put the emphasis of his 'Germanic Empire of German Nations' on the word 'German'.

But only a few of the fascist leaders and their supporters were prepared to draw the right conclusion. Most of them remained faithful followers of the Third Reich—even if they promised themselves that after the war things would be totally different—even if they were already politically and morally corrupted to such an extent that they saw no possible escape for themselves. Some were not willing to give up their dreams of a peaceful fascist new order in Europe that easily. The Dutch fascist leader Anton Mussert continued to bombard Hitler with his grandiose ideas about a possible 'League of Germanic Peoples' in Europe in which the 'Greater Netherlands' would take second place after Germany. The last memorandum arrived in November 1944. Hitler did not even bother to read it. GERHARD HIRSCHFELD

Hirschfeld, G., *Nazi Rule and Dutch Collaboration. The Netherlands under German Occupation, 1940–1945* (Oxford, 1988).
—— and Marsh, P. (eds.), *Collaboration in France. Politics and Culture during the Nazi Occupation* (Oxford, 1989).

3. Central and Eastern Europe

(a) Baltic States

When Estonia, Latvia, and Lithuania were invaded and annexed by the USSR in 1940, the invasion was greatly facilitated by the activities of local communist agents who subverted the existing governments and participated in the formation of pro-Soviet regimes. These communists and fellow-travellers, who helped to destroy their countries' independence, were widely held to be collaborators.

In 1941, when German forces invaded the Soviet-occupied Baltic states, many units from the former military and police forces were turned over to German command, and were sent to serve on the Eastern Front. Some of these units also participated in Nazi repressions and in the mass murders of Jews. However, since fighting against the USSR was generally considered a patriotic duty, assisting the Germans was not so widely condemned as aiding the Soviets. No forms of independent politics were permitted in the *Ostland, so there was no question of political collaboration, but the Waffen-SS was able to recruit several divisions of volunteers for purely military duties.

When Soviet forces returned in 1944, all persons who had worked for the Germans in any capacity, willingly or unwillingly, were treated as collaborators and subjected to repression. NORMAN DAVIES

(b) Poland

Polish history books tend to take pride in one of the few countries which was free of collaborators. In reality various forms of collaboration took place, though on a smaller scale than elsewhere. Very few Poles sympathized with either the Soviets or the Nazis.

In the *Polish campaign of September 1939, the invasion of Poland was assisted by various groups of citizens. In the west, some elements of the German community (see VOLKSDEUTSCHE) formed a *fifth column which was organized in advance to assist the Wehrmacht. In the east, a minority of Poland's Belorussian, Ukrainian, and Jewish population welcomed the arrival of the Red Army and took a lead in repressions and in the organization of the Soviet regime. Since Stalin had purged the Polish Communist Party in 1938, killing most of its leading members after luring them to the USSR, there were very few party members available to assist in the process of communization. But a handful of individuals such as Wanda *Wasilewska, who was escorted at her request from the Nazi to the Soviet-occupied zone of Poland, were active in the Soviet service.

During the German occupation the Nazis took no steps to set up any form of Polish political organization, so there was no scope for political collaboration. It was the only country where no attempt was made to recruit Waffen-SS divisions, although large numbers of Poles were forcibly conscripted into the Wehrmacht from regions, such as Silesia or Posnania, that were directly annexed to the Reich.

In the General government (see POLAND, 2(b)), units of the former Polish 'Blue Police' continued to serve under German command, as did Jewish police formations in the *ghettos instituted by the Nazis. In conditions of extreme terror, where the entire economy was directed to Germany's war effort, all Poles who did not escape abroad, engage in sabotage, or join the resistance were obliged to collaborate. Even in the *concentration camps it was possible to exact a measure of collaboration from those who were prepared to serve as *Kapos* or 'trusties', or to work in the **Sonderkommando*.

In 1943–5 large numbers of Poles were mobilized by the Soviets, either to fight under Soviet command (see BERLING'S ARMY, for example) or to join the cadres of the nascent communist dictatorship. Their motives were extremely varied, but in the eyes of patriotic opinion they were generally considered collaborators.

NORMAN DAVIES

(c) USSR

Collaboration was not a negligible phenomenon during the first phases of the *German–Soviet war. But a distinction must be drawn between the populations of the Soviet Union's 1921 territory and those 're-integrated' into the Soviet Union only in 1939–40 (see Map 107) and also between (Great-)Russians and other nationalities. In the newly incorporated areas the German soldiers were greeted as liberators. Collaboration was widespread even in areas of the Ukraine which had always been part of the Soviet Union—not surprisingly, after the horrors of Stalin's policy of collectivization imposed during the 1930s. Among the nationalities of the Caucasus, along the Volga (even where German troops never set foot), and among the Crimean Tatars sympathy for the Germans was obvious. Great Russians often seemed indifferent and not openly hostile to the Germans, but the inclination to collaborate was limited and the nature of the German occupation soon reduced it further. Ukrainian nationals often joined German auxiliary police forces and the growing partisan movement (see USSR, 8) forced German acceptance of this. Some Ukrainian units also acted as guards in extermination camps (see OPERATION REINHARD) and, against the express orders of Hitler, regular units were formed from Soviet subject nationalities (see SOVIET EXILES). By the end of 1941 the Wehrmacht was employing captured Cossacks against the partisans, while the most spectacular case of collaboration was that of the Soviet army general *Vlasov, who fell into German hands in July 1942.

As the Red Army advanced westwards, recapturing areas held by the Germans, tens of thousands of real or supposed collaborators were sent to the *GUlag. In 1943 alone, when the Nazis still held vast parts of the USSR *Beria reported to Stalin that *NKVD troops had arrested 931,549 people for checking (582,515 civilians, 349,034 soldiers), of whom 80,296 (probably there were more) had been detained as 'spies, traitors, members of punitive squads, deserters, bandits and similar criminal elements'. With the extension of liberated areas during 1944 hundreds of thousands of Crimean Tatars, Kalmyks, Meskhetian Turks, Chechens, Ingushi, Balkars, and Karachai were deported on Stalin's orders and dispersed over the eastern territories. Beria spoke of 650,000 Chechen, Ingushi, Kalmyks, and Karachai alone, in whose deportation 119,000 officers and troops of the NKVD, NKGB, and *Smersh took part. Not surprisingly, members of Vlasov's army and others who fought with the Germans were harshly dealt with: large numbers of their officers were shot. The others were sent to camps in Asiatic Russia. Particularly tragic was the experience of roughly 5.5 million Soviet citizens repatriated after the war, of whom 2.3 million were handed over on the basis of agreements concluded at the Yalta conference (see ARGONAUT), often against their will. The core of the repatriated were 2.1 million *Ostarbeiter* ('labour from the east'; see FORCED LABOUR) and about a million *prisoners-of-war. The *Ostarbeiter* had mostly not gone to Germany voluntarily. None the less, half of all those repatriated were condemned to hard labour.

HEINZ-DIETRICH LÖWE

4. Balkans

Of the Balkan states, Romania and Bulgaria formally sided with the Axis during the Second World War, Greece and Yugoslavia with the Allies, while Albania had already been reduced to the status of an Italian protectorate. Under the dictatorship of Marshal *Antonescu, Romania fought alongside Germany in the war against the USSR from June 1941 in order to recover the territories it had lost to the Soviet Union a year earlier under the terms of the second *Vienna award. Antonescu was also indirectly fighting for Northern Transylvania, hoping that Romania might recover what it had lost to Hungary under the same award, and fearing that it could well lose the rest if it did not continue in the war. Although Romania's animosity was directed against its Soviet neighbour, most Romanians sympathized with the western Allies. In August 1944, King Michael was able to carry out a coup which removed Antonescu and brought his country over to the side of the Allies.

Bulgaria hardly participated in the war. Once Greece and Yugoslavia had been defeated, it was allowed to occupy Thrace and Macedonia, which satisfied nationalist opinion. Under the personal rule of King Boris, who died in August 1943, it resisted German pressure to commit troops to the Eastern Front, which would have conflicted with traditional feelings towards Russia, and managed to resist most measures demanded against its Jews. The appearance of the Red Army on the Danube a year later and a Soviet declaration of war eventually brought an end to the pro-German alignment.

Albania had been run since 1939 as a protectorate of Italy with a client regime. It was used as a base for operations against Greece and Yugoslavia, and rewarded with territories. The Albanian population of the annexed areas welcomed the Italian occupation which gave them the opportunity of paying off old scores against Serbs. The Germans, after they had taken over from the Italians, continued to give ostentatious support to the Albanian acquisition of Kosovo and were thus able to recruit an SS Division there.

Greece and Yugoslavia were kept under a harsh occupation regime shared out between Germany, Italy, and their allies. A collaborationist administration was appointed in Athens, organized in the first instance under General Georgios Tsolakoglou, who considered it his primary duty to assure political order until the end of the war. As resistance increased, with Greeks fighting each other as well as outside enemies, and once the Italians had left, the collaborationist government set up Security Battalions to fight against the communist insurgents. Equipped by the occupation forces and active in the Peloponnese, these units also attracted recruits from other resistance groups that had been the victims of the communists.

Yugoslavia was partitioned between Germany, Italy, and their satellites. The Ustašas were allowed to set up a greater Croatian state. As a party-state under *Pavelić, the Independent State of Croatia took its place among the satellites of the Axis, formally declared war on the Allies, set up its own armed forces, and sent troops to the Eastern Front. It established a reign of terror that sought to exterminate Serbs and Jews, causing a mass rising of its Serbian-populated areas and shocking its protectors. The Italian military had to intervene to contain the insurgency, but they could only do so by coming to terms with many of the Serbian rebels. There as well as in Montenegro, where the Italians had failed in their attempt to set up a client state and made non-aggression arrangements with some of the insurgents, these local Serbian bands manoeuvred between increasing dependence on the Italian Army and nominal allegiance to General *Mihailović's movement in their fight against the communists.

In southern Slovenia, which had been annexed to Italy, as communist partisans increasingly alienated the peasantry, the traditional parties organized village guards. These were gradually pushed into collaboration as they came to depend on the Italians for arms. The Germans, after they had taken over from the Italians, set up a native administration under General Leon Rupnik, who was allowed to turn what remained of the village guards into an anti-communist Home Guard.

Serbia was one of the areas of the Balkans under direct German military administration. At the end of August 1941, in an attempt to keep the area quiet by indirect means, a government was appointed under General Milan Nedić, who accepted the task in the hope that collaboration might prevent Serbia from disappearing entirely from Hitler's 'New Europe' (see GERMANY, 4), and to provide a refuge for persecuted Serbs from other regions. He was authorized to organize a Serbian State Guard into which gendarmes were enrolled, but most of them would in due course turn out to be auxiliaries of Mihailović's resistance rather than of the occupation. The only reliable collaborators the Germans could find in Serbia were the adherents of the small pro-Axis movement of Dimitrije Ljotić, who were formed into a Serbian Volunteer Corps which was used in operations against Mihailović's organization. STEVAN PAVLOWITCH

5. Far East

The problems of collaboration with the Japanese had few parallels with those in western Europe, but had some similarities with those posed in eastern Europe where the evils of one kind of *occupation were replaced only by the evils of another. While Japanese rule was quite as ruthless as that imposed by Germany or the Soviet Union, it was based on a different premise. With the exception of China (see CHINA, 3; CHINA INCIDENT; and MANCHUKUO); Thailand, where the government initially welcomed collaboration to avoid usurption of its powers; and the Philippines, which was self-governing but had yet to achieve full independence, the territories occupied by the Japanese were not sovereign states but colonies. There could therefore be no cases of a sovereign nation trying to treat with the occupying power, as Pétain attempted to do—though it is interesting to note that in French Indo-China the Japanese did allow the colonial government to remain in place for most of the war, thus allowing it to collaborate by continuing to exploit the country's resources, but for Japan's benefit not France's. Otherwise it was a matter of the colonial powers being ousted by the Japanese who then imposed their own form of colonialism (see GREATER EAST ASIA CO-PROSPERITY SPHERE) under the guise of Asians liberating economically exploited colonies belonging to fellow Asians. As such they were almost universally welcomed by the indigenous populations whose leaders genuinely believed at first that the Japanese were true liberators who had come to give them their political and economic independence. In varying degrees and on a varying time scale they were disabused of this notion. Even when the Japanese did grant a population its independence, as in Burma and the Philippines, it was purely nominal and ended, in the case of Burma at least, with some of its leaders siding, in a kind of counter-collaboration, with the old occupying power in order to oust the new one (see BURMA INDEPENDENCE ARMY).

Overall, Japanese talk of being fellow-Asians did not conceal the contempt they felt for all nationalities except their own and often their attitude was infinitely worse than the superiority of the white sahibs they had replaced. In the streets of Singapore the local citizens were required to bow whenever they passed a Japanese sentry, and the heads of recalcitrant Malays were exposed on planks to impress passers-by that the newcomers meant business. This was not an atmosphere in which collaboration in its broader sense could be expected to flourish.

So though the premiss for occupation, and therefore the attitude of the native population towards collaboration, was different, the end result—economic exploitation—was the same. Nevertheless, the Japanese did create, sometimes deliberately, sometimes not, the right conditions for the eventual independence of the countries they occupied. For when they overran the American, British, and Dutch controlled areas of South-East Asia, they also set out to eradicate European and American influence and civilization altogether. In this, at least, all the local populations collaborated. It certainly assisted the Netherlands East Indies in their struggle to throw off the Dutch yoke—a struggle that resolved into the Republic of Indonesia in 1949—that the local population were able to watch their white masters being humiliated in Japanese *internment camps; and that the Japanese encouraged the Indonesian nationalist movement and set up a satellite Indonesian government (see JAVA). Equally, Japanese occupation created a new situation in Malaya. There, the old forms of administration were eradicated and the formation of a resistance movement against the Japanese was used to gain post-war independence, while in French Indo-China Japanese exploitation, and then occupation, led to local support of the *Viet Minh which spearheaded the long post-war fight for an independent Vietnam. Thus, collaboration in the Far East did, indirectly, often achieve the goal its indigenous populations sought. M. R. D. FOOT

Collins, Lt-General Joseph L. (1896–1963), US corps commander, nicknamed 'Lightnin' Joe' from the lightning-bolt identification flash of the 25th Infantry Division which he commanded on *Guadalcanal, and then during the *New Georgia campaign. He later built a deserved reputation as one of the war's most aggressive Allied commanders. He led the 7th US Corps from the Normandy landings in June 1944 (see OVERLORD) right up to the time of Germany's surrender the following May. During the *Normandy campaign he captured Cherbourg, spearheaded the breakout at St Lô, and blocked the Germans at Mortain, and under the command of *Montgomery—who much admired him—led the Allied counter-attack during the *Ardennes campaign. *Bradley said he had unerring tactical judgement with just enough bravado to make every advance a triumph.

Collins, J., *Lightning Joe* (Baton Rouge, La., 1979).

Colmar pocket, German bridgehead west of the Rhine and south of Strasbourg, about 80 km. (30 mi.) square. It was held by remnants of the Nineteenth German Army at the end of 1944, which endangered *Eisenhower's plan of closing up to the river all along the length of his front before launching the *Rhine crossings. These remnants also threatened the overstretched line of *Devers's Sixth Army Group (see FRENCH RIVIERA LANDINGS) whose First French Army commanded by General de *Lattre de Tassigny failed to eliminate them. On 7 January 1945 German forces broke out and struck northwards towards Strasbourg as part of a concerted offensive to recapture the city. They were eventually halted, but it took until 9 February 1945 for the pocket to be eliminated by the 21st US Corps and de Lattre's 1st Corps. The Allies suffered 18,000 casualties, but the Germans, by stubbornly refusing to withdraw, lost nearly twice as many.

Colombia took a pro-Allied stance from December 1941 by severing diplomatic relations with the main Axis powers. War was declared on Germany in November 1943 after a number of Colombian ships had been sunk, and signed the *United Nations Declaration in January 1944. See also CARIBBEAN AT WAR.

Comando Supremo, common term for the Italian High Command, properly called Stato Maggiore Generale (STAMAGE), the Supreme General Staff. Marshal *Badoglio headed STAMAGE from its inception in June 1925 until December 1940 and except for the period June 1925–February 1927, when it included the Army General Staff, it consisted only of his small secretariat. STAMAGE theoretically co-ordinated the armed forces. In practice, Mussolini allowed Badoglio such powers only during crises, even then hobbling him with political interference.

Between November 1933 and July 1943, Mussolini served as war, navy, and air minister, rejecting suggestions for a defence ministry and a combined general staff. In 1934 he made each service under-secretary simultaneously that service's chief of staff. This arrangement allowed Mussolini to control each service yet permitted each to develop separate war plans that failed to support Mussolini's plans for Mediterranean conquest. Meetings between Badoglio and the service chiefs in the spring of 1940 failed to resolve these contradictions.

In the six months following Italy's intervention in the war, the service chiefs and major operational commanders reported directly to Mussolini, excluding STAMAGE from major strategic decisions. Mussolini further diluted Badoglio's authority by appointing General Ubaldo Soddu, already army under-secretary, to the new post of deputy head of STAMAGE in June 1940. The consequent confusion and Mussolini's strategic incompetence helped create the disasters of October–December 1940 (see BALKAN CAMPAIGN, SIDI BARRANI, and TARANTO). Seeking scapegoats, Mussolini replaced Soddu with General Alfredo Guzzoni on 29 November 1940 and substituted General *Cavallero for Badoglio on 4 December. Cavallero departed to command in Albania, where the Italians were fighting Greek forces in the Balkan campaign leaving Guzzoni as effective head of

STAMAGE. Guzzoni reduced Mussolini's involvement in military matters but clashed with Cavallero over direction of the fighting in Albania.

After Cavallero returned to Rome on 18 May 1941, Mussolini dismissed Guzzoni, and expanded STAMAGE into a genuine Comando Supremo for the army with some authority over inter-service planning. Comando Supremo acquired its own intelligence service and established liaison with industry and the foreign ministry. Cavallero became Mussolini's chief military adviser, ended his interference with subordinate army commands, and accompanied him to meetings with Hitler. But Mussolini excluded Cavallero from his meetings with the navy and air chiefs and the Wehrmacht representatives in Rome.

Cavallero reoriented Comando Supremo to co-ordinate air, sea, and land operations in the Mediterranean aimed at the conquest of the Middle East. But the setbacks of 1940–1 left Italy dependent on German support and Comando Supremo planning subordinate to German strategy even though German forces in the Mediterranean theatre, including those of *Rommel, officially came under Comando Supremo's control. Mussolini informed Cavallero on 30 May 1941 of imminent German attack on the Soviet Union and of his determination to participate. Thus the Mediterranean would become only a secondary theatre and Italy's mobile ground forces would be divided between Libya (see WESTERN DESERT CAMPAIGNS) and those fighting on the Eastern Front. Comando Supremo sent three divisions to take part in the *German–Soviet war in July 1941 (see ITALY, 5(b)). A year later, it sent seven more. At the time of *El Alamein, the Italians had eight understrength divisions in Egypt but ten well-equipped divisions near *Stalingrad.

Following the fall of Tripoli to *Montgomery's advancing Eighth Army after the second El Alamein battle, Mussolini replaced Cavallero with General *Ambrosio on 1 February 1943. Comando Supremo retrieved what forces it could from the Balkans and Ukraine, while rushing reinforcements to the fighting in Tunisia (see NORTH AFRICAN CAMPAIGN). Meanwhile, Ambrosio urged Mussolini to leave the war. After the *Sicilian campaign landings in July 1943, when Mussolini continued resisting such entreaties, Comando Supremo fulfilled King *Victor Emmanuel's orders to overthrow Mussolini on 25 July 1943. Six weeks later, after Italy switched sides, Comando Supremo plans to defend Rome from the Germans collapsed when the king, government, and Ambrosio fled the capital. Reconstituted thereafter, Comando Supremo came under the command of Marshal *Messe on 18 November 1943 and it controlled the small forces the Allies allowed Italy until the end of the war.

BRIAN R. SULLIVAN

Combat Air Patrol (CAP), a standing airborne patrol positioned so it could intercept enemy aircraft at the greatest possible distance from their target.

combat team, see USA, 5(b).

Combined Bomber Offensive (CBO). At the Casablanca conference in January 1943 (see SYMBOL) it was decided to support Maj-General *Eaker's plan to launch a combined bombing offensive against Germany, with the British bombing at night and the Americans by day. *Portal was given the task of co-ordinating it and on 21 January the *Combined Chiefs of Staff (CCS) issued the Casablanca Directive. This stated that the objective of the CBO was 'the progressive destruction and dislocation of the German military, industrial and economic system, and the undermining of the morale of the German people to a point where their capacity for armed resistance is fatally weakened.'

Despite being planned in four phases between April 1943 and April 1944 the CBO only really started when the POINTBLANK Directive, which amended the Casablanca Directive, was issued by the CCS in June 1943. While listing various categories of targets, it gave absolute priority to the destruction of German fighters, and the factories where they were built, as the Normandy landings (see OVERLORD) could not be launched until air supremacy was achieved. The Quebec conference of August 1943 (see QUADRANT) upheld this high priority while abandoning attacks on German morale as a means of achieving that purpose.

POINTBLANK resulted in air offensives against *Berlin, *Hamburg, and the *Ruhr, and raids on *Schweinfurt and elsewhere, but the heavy losses sustained, and doubts about their efficacy, helped create a crisis of confidence in the CBO. Raids deep into Germany were stopped by the Americans until long-range fighters became available and good weather ensured that any losses sustained would be justified by the results, conditions which were not fulfilled until February 1944. Following the six-day operations mounted then—called *Big Week—the Luftwaffe ceased to defend its air space automatically and was incapable of mounting an effective counter-attack during OVERLORD that June.

German fighter production increased throughout the CBO, and continued to do so until September 1944. What gained the Allies air supremacy over Normandy was the inability of the Germans to train sufficient fighter pilots because of a shortage of fuel, and the inferior performance of those who were trained which enabled US long-range fighters to cause heavy losses amongst them. It remains a matter of conjecture whether the CBO would have achieved more if, as was done later, it had attacked the German synthetic oil industry. See also STRATEGIC AIR OFFENSIVES, 1.

Combined Bureau, Middle East (CBME), British Army–RAF cryptanalytical organization, an outpost of the British government's Code and Cypher School at *Bletchley Park, which was formed at Heliopolis, a Cairo suburb, in November 1940. Before that time work on Italian ciphers had been carried out by Bletchley, but after

Italy entered the war in June 1940 the decrypts often took too long to reach those who had to act on them. Bletchley continued to work on Italian high-grade ciphers while CBME mostly worked on lower-grade ones, but it did break the Italian Air Force's high-grade cipher in East Africa, after it had been changed in November 1940. This proved invaluable to the British fighting the *East African campaign as did CBME's subsequent ability, with the help of an outstation in Nairobi, Kenya, to break every lower-grade code and cipher used by the Italians in East Africa. From March 1941 CBME handled the inward flow of selected *ULTRA intelligence from Bletchley and from June 1941 decrypted the hand ciphers used by the *Abwehr in Turkey, and later by the Abwehr and Sicherheitsdienst (see RSHA) in the Balkans, the Aegean, and North Africa. It was closed in March 1944.

Combined Chiefs of Staff (CCS) committee, supreme Anglo-American military authority which comprised the US *Joint Chiefs of Staff (JCS) and the British *Chiefs of Staff (COS). It advised Churchill and Roosevelt (and their successors) on military strategy, and implemented the strategic decisions taken by them (see GRAND ALLIANCE). In its executive capacity, the committee controlled operational strategy in the battle for the *Mediterranean and European theatres, and in the battle of the *Atlantic, and held general jurisdiction over grand strategy policy in all other theatres where operational strategy was controlled by the COS or JCS alone. In issuing directives to its supreme commanders the committee normally acted through the chiefs of staff of the country that provided the commander, and these in turn acted through the head of the service to which the supreme commander belonged.

The decision to form the committee was made at the Washington conference in December 1941 (see ARCADIA). It sat in Washington, the British COS being represented by a Joint Staff Mission headed by General *Dill and then by General Maitland *Wilson. A combined office, secretariat, and planning staff ensured close co-operation in what General *Brooke, an early sceptic of any joint prosecution of the war, was later to call the most efficient organization 'that had ever been evolved for co-ordinating and correlating the war strategy and effort of the Allies'.

A number of sub-committees were constituted as the war progressed (see Chart). The most important were the Combined Intelligence Committee and the Combined Planning Staff, the British elements of these working under the Joint Staff Mission. More controversial was the decision at ARCADIA to pool the entire munitions resources of the two countries, and to form civilian Joint Boards in London and Washington, under the committee's direct control, to advise on their distribution.

Despite sharp differences, which sometimes caused heated arguments, the committee worked because its members shared common beliefs, a common language (though it was not *that* common) and because at first both powers were making an equal contribution. By the time this equality ceased—in the closing months of the war the US contribution to the war effort was still increasing while that of the UK was declining—the committee was working smoothly, and retained sufficient impetus to continue its work until the end of the war. In any case, during this last phase, the committee's influence diminished for the Americans, now predominant, were content to leave local strategy in the hands of the supreme commanders and discouraged any British contribution that might question this approach. A British suggestion that the committee should be retained when peace returned was never taken up.

The committee, chaired by the president's representative on the JCS, Admiral *Leahy, met in Washington DC on a weekly basis with the Joint Staff Mission being in daily, sometimes hourly, contact with the COS in London. The COS and JCS also accompanied their respective heads of government to the series of conferences that took place throughout the war, and out of the total of 200 CCS meetings 89 were convened during these conferences.

Combined Operations, British nomenclature for *amphibious warfare and the first British organization to have an inter-service headquarters.

Though attacks from the sea had been mounted by the British for centuries they had no establishment which specialized in amphibious warfare until the Inter-Services Training and Development Centre (ISTDC) was opened in May 1938. This began examining the problems inherent in landing on a defended beach and prototypes of *landing craft were built which proved their worth during the *Norwegian campaign and at *Dunkirk.

In June 1940 Churchill called for a policy of raiding occupied territory and the adjutant-general of the Royal Marines, Lt-General Alan Bourne, was appointed 'Commander of Raiding Operations on coasts in enemy occupation, and Adviser to the *Chiefs of Staff (COS) on Combined Operations'. ISTDC and six independent companies of commandos which had been raised for the Norwegian campaign were put under his command, but in July Churchill decided to replace him with *Keyes, a 68-year-old admiral of the fleet.

Keyes, whose title was 'Director of Combined Operations', immediately declared his independence by removing his staff from the Admiralty and setting up Combined Operations Headquarters (COHQ) in Richmond Terrace in central London. He founded the Combined Training Centre at Inverarary (others were later established in Egypt and India), saw to it that more landing craft were built, and was the driving force behind the expansion and training of the commandos. But he did not co-operate easily; he wanted COHQ to be an operational headquarters, not limited, as the COS required, to the study of the inter-service problems which amphibious warfare posed and the development of suitable landing craft and technical aids. In October 1941,

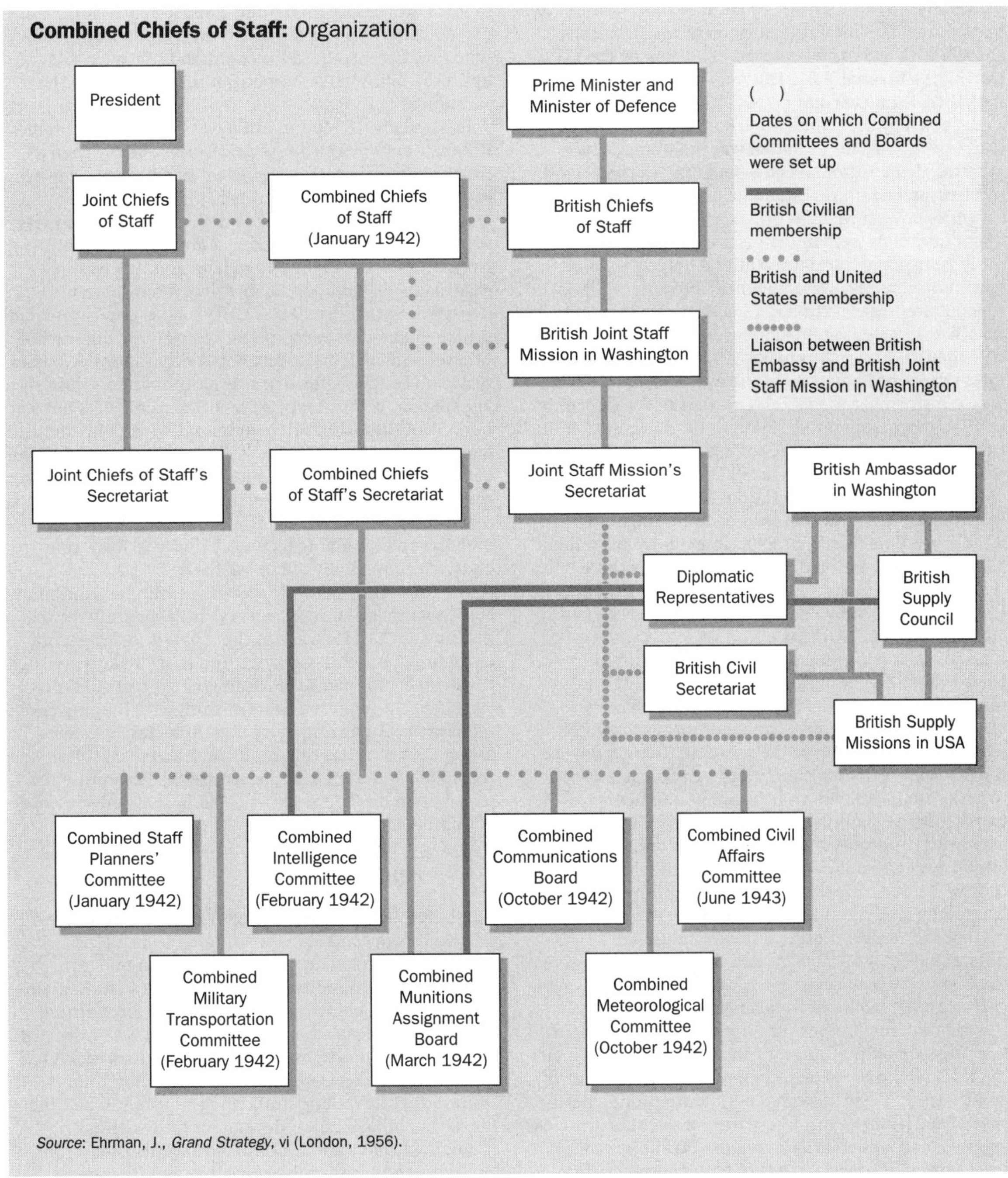

Source: Ehrman, J., *Grand Strategy*, vi (London, 1956).

after a new COS directive changed his title from 'Director' to 'Adviser' he stepped down and Churchill replaced him with *Mountbatten who was promoted to commodore.

Mountbatten was vigorous, young, and brimful of charm; 'Handsome and breezy, like Brighton at its best,' as one observer has described him. He also possessed great tact, not Keyes's forte. Churchill, whose protégé he was, ordered him to start a raiding programme, but told him that his main objective was to plan the return of Allied forces to occupied France, that his HQ was being created to be on the offensive, and that he was to give no thought for the defensive.

Initially only an 'adviser', by January 1942 Mountbatten had become the 'mounting authority' for all raids, though they had to be approved in outline by the COS. During the first half of 1942 a number were mounted, including *Bruneval and *St Nazaire, and several were undertaken by the *Small Scale Raiding Force.

In March 1942 Mountbatten was promoted to vice-admiral. He had also the equivalent rank in the two other services, and a new title, Chief of Combined Operations (CCO). He now sat with the COS as a full member whenever major questions were under discussion whereas previously he had had the right to attend only when matters within his directive were under review.

Soon after his elevation to CCO, Mountbatten had nine US officers, including Brigadier-General *Truscott, seconded to COHQ, thus making it the first international inter-service headquarters of the war. Another decision was to dismember the ISTDC. One part now came under COHQ's newly appointed Director of Experiments and Developments (later Director of Experiments and Operational Requirements, or DXOR). The other part became the Combined Operations Development Centre which in August 1942 was absorbed into the newly established Combined Ops Experimental Establishment (COXE) in North Devon. DXOR was helped by three remarkable scientists, Geoffrey Pyke (see HABBAKUK), J. D. Bernal, and Solly Zuckerman. Sharing secrets with civilians was, like COHQ itself, a previously unheard-of innovation and initially this trio had difficulty in extracting the right questions from service officers requesting their advice. Pyke expressed his frustration by quoting G. K. Chesterton's character Father Brown: 'It isn't that they cannot see the solution: they cannot see the problem'; but eventually all three scientists were able to make an invaluable contribution to the many questions that amphibious warfare posed. COXE, too, was very much involved in solving problems and both establishments could count among their achievements the *MULBERRIES, artificial harbours built for the Normandy landings (see OVERLORD), and the best methods for waterproofing vehicles and tanks, for unloading stores on a beach, and for piping petrol across the Channel (see PLUTO).

Though the landings on *Madagascar in May 1942 showed that amphibious training was on the right lines the *Dieppe raid that August revealed severe deficiencies in amphibious techniques when assaulting a defended coastline. As a result research began into producing specialized landing craft whose fire power could give close support to troops making an opposed landing; schools were started for the clearance of beach obstacles, for beach parties, and for beach pilotage (see COMBINED OPERATIONS PILOTAGE PARTIES); a headquarters ship with adequate signals equipment was designed to command amphibious operations; and a permanent force of landing craft was created to act as a nucleus for any future raid (see FORCE J). By April 1943 COHQ's staff had grown from 23 to more than 350 and it controlled 89 landing ships (LSI), more than 2,600 landing craft, and 50,000 men. This was too much even for Mountbatten who now decentralized his command. With his full approval, all his naval responsibilities reverted to the Admiralty.

In August 1943 Mountbatten was appointed Supreme Commander of *South-East Asia Command. By then an Anglo-American staff (see COSSAC) had been already been established for several months to plan the cross-Channel assault on occupied France, and several COHQ planners were part of it. Mountbatten had always argued for Normandy as the best place to land and this was eventually agreed upon. By the time Mountbatten departed, in October 1943, COHQ had become a valuable source of knowledge about amphibious operations. The COS were divided on its future but eventually decided to retain it though reduced in size. Mountbatten's successor, Maj-General Robert Laycock, reported to the COS but was not one of them, though he often sat with them and still had direct access to Churchill. He retained control of the commandos and responsibility for small-scale raids, but these he now had to clear with COSSAC. He also remained responsible for the assault training of British troops overseas and for giving technical advice to force comanders who were obliged to ask for it.

The Normandy landings were the ultimate fruition of Mountbatten's planning, energy, and ingenuity during his time as CCO. He was not there to witness them but on 12 June Churchill signalled him that: 'Today we visited the British and American Armies on the soil of France. We sailed through vast fleets of ships with landing craft of many types pouring more men, vehicles and stores ashore ... we realise that much of this remarkable technique and therefore the success of the venture has its origin in developments effected by you and your staff of Combined Operations.'

Fergusson, B., *The Watery Maze: The Story of Combined Operations* (London, 1961).

Combined Operations Pilotage Parties (COPP), British Navy and Army personnel who, aided by infra-red equipment, canoes, and conventional and midget submarines, reconnoitred beaches before a landing took place and then helped guide the landing force ashore. The *North African campaign landings in November 1942 (TORCH) were guided ashore with techniques which had been pioneered by Lt-Commander Nigel Clogstoun-Willmott while raiding in the *Aegean Islands, and the formation of COPP, an independent unit within *Combined Operations, followed. However, Clogstoun-Willmott and his team had been banned from going ashore before TORCH and the lack of knowledge about the beaches resulted in some landing craft beaching at unsuitable points with resultant heavy losses of vehicles and equipment. This mistake was not repeated and COPP teams later went ashore to reconnoitre the beaches for the *Sicilian campaign landings (where they lost several men), *Salerno, and Normandy (see OVERLORD). They also operated before the *Rhine crossings and the crossing of the River Elbe during the battle for *Germany, and in the Far East.

comfort women. In January 1938, after the Japanese Army had moved into China (see CHINA INCIDENT), a system of brothels was opened there for Japanese troops. This was done partly to control venereal disease (see MEDICINE), but also to prevent a recurrence of events in Nanking in December 1937 when Japanese troops pillaged the city, raping and massacring its inhabitants. Later the system, only made legal by the Japanese Diet in August 1944, spread to other Japanese-occupied areas such as Burma. The brothels were called *ianjo* (comfort houses) and the *ianfu* (comfort girls) who staffed them were recruited for 1,000 yen each. After this had been repaid (at two yen per soldier) they were, in theory, free to return home, but most were forced into prostitution. A number of nationalities were involved, including Japanese (for officers only), and it has been estimated that between 100,000 and 200,000 girls (some as young as 12) and women were recruited for the system, or for *forced labour, most of them from Korea. In January 1992 the Japanese prime minister apologized in person to South Korea's National Assembly for Japan's role in abducting Korean women, some of whom later that year began a legal action against the Japanese government for compensation.

COMINCH, see KING, ADMIRAL ERNEST.

Comintern, the Communist International, founded in 1919. During the Second World War the veteran Bulgarian communist Georgi Dimitrov was secretary general to its Executive Committee. The *Nazi–Soviet Pact of 23 August 1939 imposed on it a change of policy so revolutionary that it called into question its very basis. Its role as the representative of world communist parties, who in their turn were supposed to represent a sophisticated and class-conscious proletariat, sharply declined.

For a short time after the outbreak of war, the Comintern sections, that is the communist parties, like those of France, the UK, and Germany, maintained their anti-fascist policy. Soon, however, they were forced to adopt a new approach when the non-aggression pact resulted in co-operation between the Soviet Union and Nazi Germany. The Comintern, for so long subjected to the interests of Soviet policy, followed suit. While in the first weeks of war communists argued that both belligerent camps pursued imperialist aims and that there was nothing to chose between them, by early October 1939 the Comintern was echoing *Molotov's and *Ribbentrop's call for a negotiated peace and blaming the UK and France for the continuation of the war. Other Soviet moves were also approved: in a statement on 11 November 1939 the Comintern applauded the annexation of eastern Poland. Also the Comintern's hatred of the social democratic parties could now be openly ventilated. The Soviet secretary of the Comintern, Dimitry Manuilsky, wrote in the spring of 1940 that never before had the liquidation of social democracy 'been so acute an immediate practical task as it is at the present time'. Although there is some indication that after the fall of *France in June 1940 the Comintern became more critical of Germany, speaking of Hitler as the new Barbarossa, it had, by then virtually ceased activity. On 1 May 1941 it no longer issued its customary May Day manifesto.

It was not until the Germans attacked the Soviet Union in June 1941 (see BARBAROSSA) that the Comintern reversed its policy of the past two years and called for a united front against German *fascism. It thus resurrected the Popular Front policies of the Seventh Congress of the Comintern of 1935. Under the new circumstances of Soviet participation in the *Grand Alliance against Germany the existence of the Comintern was no longer necessary. But it was not until 15 May 1943, after the fortunes of war had changed decisively in favour of the Allies, that the Comintern was dissolved. The resolution of the presidium of the Executive Committee of the Comintern gave as the reason for this move the increasing divergence and even contradictions in individual societies, and the differences in the degrees of consciousness and organization of the working class in various countries. Moreover communist parties were now expected to act as the dynamic elements in broadly based anti-fascist coalitions. The decision was to be ratified by the individual sections, a foregone conclusion; even before such ratification, Stalin, in an interview with Reuter's correspondent on 28 May, stated that the dissolution strengthened the unification of all freedom-loving nations against Hitlerism and exposed the lie that 'Moscow' wanted to intervene in other nations and to 'Bolshevize' them. The formal dissolution took place on 8 June 1943, after 31 replies had been received approving the decision. These included the replies of the most important parties and no objections were received from the other 35 member sections of the Comintern. The statement was signed by Dimitrov on behalf of the presidium of the Executive Committee. The measure was purely cosmetic; Moscow continued for many years yet to direct the policies of communist parties outside the USSR. H. HANAK

Braunthal, J., *History of the International, 1919–1943*. Vol. 2 (London, 1967).
Claudin, F., *The Communist Movement From Comintern to Cominform* (London, 1975).
Degras. J. (ed.), *The Communist International, 1919–1943. Documents. Vol. 3, 1929–1943 (London, 1971).*

Commando Order, issued on Hitler's instructions on 18 October 1942, after a British *Small Scale Raiding Force operation against the Channel Islands had resulted in German prisoners being shot while illegally bound. More than a thousand Canadian *prisoners-of-war were put in shackles as retaliation—the British replied in kind—and

Hitler ordered that any commandos or parachutists captured by the Wehrmacht on similar raids were to be handed over to the Sicherheitsdienst (see RSHA), implying that they were to be shot.

commandos, see UK, 7(e).

commissars. 'Political commissar' is a term that was widely used both in Germany and elsewhere to designate officers of the political departments established within the Soviet Army and in other communist-led forces. It is an inexact translation of the Russian 'politicheskii rukovoditel' or 'politruk' (political director).

Political departments of the Soviet type were created not merely to indoctrinate the troops but above all to ensure that all military command structures were directly controlled by the Communist Party. They operated a separate hierarchical organization which existed alongside and within the army's own cadres, supervising and directing the work of all military personnel.

Political officers received separate, intensive training at the party's own academies. When assigned to a military unit, they received a military rank and wore military uniform; but they continued to report to their political superiors. From the army's point of view, they were parasites who could not be subjected to the normal procedures of military discipline. Their approval had to be sought before any military order could be issued. Their displeasure could summon up the representatives of the security organs (see NKVD) and the instant arrest of any soldier. They served at every level from the General Staff to the lowliest platoon; and in every unit where they served, they ran party cells whose activist members acted as guardians over the rest of the soldiers.

All senior Soviet generals were required to work in the presence of a political officer who shared the same quarters, slept in the same room, and countersigned all orders. It is fair to say, therefore, that no Soviet military commander could exercise effective command over the formations which he nominally led. The political officers, not the soldiers, were the Red Army's true commanders.

Leading political officers were given high military rank, and wielded immense power. Men such as Nikita Krushchev (1894–1971) or Leonid Brezhnev (1906–82) emerged from their wartime service at the very top of the Soviet system.

The Political departments gave the Soviet Communist Party a degree of control over the army to which the Nazi Party in Germany could never aspire. Unlike the Wehrmacht, which retained a modicum of control over its own affairs, the Red Army was comprehensively deprived of any form of independent identity.

Hitler's notorious 'Commissar Order' of 1941, which authorized the immediate killing of all captured Soviet political officers, contravened all the conventions regarding the proper treatment of *prisoners-of-war. But it was aimed realistically at the element which ran the Soviet war-machine. There is some controversy over the extent to which it was carried out. See also USSR, 2 and 6(a).

NORMAN DAVIES

Committee to Defend America by Aiding the Allies, bipartisan organization formed in May 1940 by Republican, William Allen White (1868–1944). It was the first to fight American isolationism at a national level and to combat the *America First Committee. But it was non-interventionist and refused to accept funds from the steel industry, armaments manufacturers, or international bankers, all of which were thought by the public to encourage nations to fight wars. It helped the public acceptance of the *destroyers-for-bases agreement and *Lend-Lease, was influential in obtaining the nomination of a non-isolationist Republican candidate, Wendell *Willkie, and was arguably the most important factor in bringing about Roosevelt's re-election in November 1940. See also FIGHT FOR FREEDOM.

Commonwealth, see PHILIPPINES and UK, 5.

Commonwealth prime ministers' conference, held in London from 1 to 16 May 1944. It was the only wartime meeting of its kind and was so-called because the independent Dominions were, by then, commonly known as the British Commonwealth. Present were the prime ministers of Australia (*Curtin), Canada (Mackenzie *King), New Zealand (*Fraser), South Africa (*Smuts), and Southern Rhodesia, and there were two representatives from India. There were wide-ranging discussions on the war and a comprehensive appraisal of the position and future prospects of the British Empire. See also UK, 5.

communism, the generally accepted name for the ideology of Marxism–Leninism, and for the regimes based upon it. Though communists call themselves 'socialists', their movement had little in common with non-communist forms of socialism, or with earlier forms of communism in history, including Christian communism.

Although several conflicting brands of communism were to develop after the Second World War, in 1939–45 the Communist Party of the Soviet Union (CPSU) entirely dominated the movement, and was the only such party to have taken control of a state. During the war, therefore, the main distinction to be made was between the Soviet 'Centre' in Moscow and its numerous dependent non-ruling communist parties which operated, often illegally, in most countries of the world (see COMINTERN).

Marxism–Leninism—the version of Marxism propagated by V. I. Lenin (1870–1924), the founder of the Soviet state—did not regard other brands of Marxism and Socialism as legitimate. It accepted the basic philosophical tenets of Marx's historical materialism, whilst laying special emphasis on the theory and practices of political power. Lenin was most concerned with the role of a disciplined élite or political army, called 'The Party': with the dictatorship to be exercised over society and over all state institutions: and with the 'class war' to be waged in the name of the proletariat. By giving total power to the party, he put the interpretation of Marxism at the mercy of party controllers and censors, who soon subordinated all serious philosophical matters to the immediate requirements of the regime.

The CPSU traced its roots to Lenin's faction within the illegal, pre-revolutionary Russian Social Democratic Labour Party (RSDLP). This faction, which was heavily outnumbered by socialist rivals both inside and outside the RSDLP, had taken the name of *Bolsheviks* or 'majoritarians' at one of the few meetings where it was appropriate. Having seized power in Petrograd in October 1917, it suppressed the Provisional government that had earlier overthrown Tsarism, and moved swiftly to eliminate all other political organizations in areas under its control. It adopted the name of Communist Party (Bolsheviks) in 1918. Having emerged victorious in the Russian Civil War of 1918–21, it reconquered most of the republics which had taken the opportunity to declare their independence and forced them into a new empire of its own making—the Union of Soviet Socialist Republics or USSR (1923–91). (To avoid confusion, the central organs of the CP (b) were often referred to as the 'All-Union Communist Party' as distinct from the subordinate republican, regional branches of the organization.) The formal title CPSU was not adopted until 1952.

Soviet communism underwent several fundamental changes in the inter-war period. Under Lenin, it had sought to act as the avant-garde of an international revolution which theoretically would break out in western Europe especially Germany, but never did. Having been heavily defeated in Poland in 1920, in its one concerted attempt to export revolution by means of the Red Army, it was obliged to modify the extreme coercion of 'war communism' and from 1921 to adopt the compromise of a New Economic Policy. Under Josif Stalin, General Secretary from 1922, it abandoned the primacy of Lenin's internationalism, and, with the slogan of 'Socialism in One Country' gave priority to making the USSR a first-class economic and military power. To this end, no means were spared. Stalin first removed then killed all members of the former Bolshevik leadership. From 1929, he introduced a Command Economy based on central planning, Five Year Plans, heavy industry, collectivized agriculture, and re-militarization. From 1934 he introduced a series of campaigns of mass terror, the 'Purges' which accelerated from the elimination of specified groups within the party and the army (see USSR, 6(a)), to the random destruction of large sections of the population. In ideological matters, he revised chauvinistic Russian nationalism and grafted it onto a vulgarized brand of Marxism–Leninism. The Russian nation was now awarded a 'leading role' among the other Soviet peoples parallel to that of the party within the state. Stalinism was formalized by the constitution of 1936.

The principal opposition to Stalinism within the Marxist–Leninist camp came from Leon Trotsky (1879–1940), sometime commissar for foreign affairs and for war. Trotsky advanced a theory of 'permanent revolution', and strongly opposed the growth of the all-mighty Soviet bureaucracy. Exiled in 1927, he was assassinated by a Stalinist agent in Mexico in 1940.

The Stalinists promoted a coherent body of political beliefs, of organizational methods, and of psychological traits. As 'builders of socialism', they laid emphasis on the collective aspects of political life, minimizing the rights and interests of individual citizens. To this end, they launched the cult of Stalin as the *Vozhd* (leader). They invented the system of parallel party organs to control all state institutions (a practice subsequently common also to *fascism); and within the vast security apparatus of the OGPU/*NKVD they maintained élite internal military forces answering directly to the party leadership. Ironically they were ultra-nationalists, frequently believing in the special mission of the USSR within the world and of the Russian nation within the USSR. They saw unswerving loyalty to the party as the highest virtue, and took special pride in their privileged status above ordinary citizens. In return, they were conditioned to pay extravagant flattery to 'the higher organs', to obey orders implicitly, and to bear all impositions and humiliations without protest. In the 1930s and 1940s they saw hundreds of thousands of their fellow members liquidated, without a murmur of opposition. Like the followers of fascism, they thrived on the paranoia which was eternally seeking enemies 'within and without'.

In many ways, therefore, the onset of the Second World War suited the purposes of Soviet communism very well. It seemed to justify the state of psychological war which Stalinism had imposed during the 1930s; it provided the total conflict which the ideologists had always demanded; and it revealed a real enemy that everyone could understand and fight. The Soviet Union performed better in wartime than in peacetime. Stalin's appeal for a 'Great Patriotic War', together with his wartime reconciliation with the Orthodox Church (see RELIGION), touched deep chords within the popular Russian nationalism which he had earlier sought to foster.

Though Stalin had laid special emphasis on the internal reorganization of the USSR, Soviet communism never resigned from its aspirations to world supremacy. In this, it presented the fascists with one of their principal *raisons d'être*. Hitler, in particular, was wedded to the notion of a death struggle against 'Jewish Bolshevism'.

In the 1930s, the Soviet party's main instrument for co-ordinating international subversion, the *Comintern, was grievously weakened by the Purges. In the period of the Popular Fronts after 1935, Stalin preferred alternative methods; and in 1943, the Comintern was dissolved. Even so, the task of training communist cadres to take over occupied countries was not abandoned. *Tito, who had been trained in Moscow before the war, was unique in spending the whole war fighting in his native country: but in 1944–5 a string of Soviet agents, such as the German W. Ulbricht (1893–1973), the Pole B. Beirut (see LUBLIN COMMITTEE), and the Czechoslovak K. Gottwald (1896–1953), were produced with all the requisite staffs to take over their countries as soon as the Red Army moved in.

NORMAN DAVIES

concentration camps

See also GULAG; see Map 31 for sites of principal concentration camps.

Concentration camps were one of the most important instruments of terror in Nazi Germany. Forecast by Hitler as early as 1921, they were first employed in 1933. At first German political opponents of National Socialism became 'persons in protective custody', to be joined from 1939 by people from all German-occupied territories. 'Protective custody', a measure employed by the Nazi police organizations, was detention without trial which gave no consideration to the due process of law.

1933–4

Immediately Hitler came to power in January 1933 the *SA (Sturmabteilung, or Storm Detachment), the paramilitary organization known as the Brownshirts, created several hundred small detention centres in cellars and other places. Then in March they set up the first larger camps at Nohra in Thuringia and Oranienburg in Prussia, while the *SS and Bavarian Political Police opened the *Dachau camp the same month. By that autumn the Prussian state concentration camps of Sonnenburg, Lichtenburg, Börgermoor, Esterwegen, and Brandenburg were established, as was the Sachsenburg camp in Saxony. Between March 1933 and August 1934 up to 80,000 people were imprisoned.

In May 1934 the SS took over the running of the concentration camps from the SA. Most of the original camps were closed and Heinrich *Himmler, the head of the SS, appointed the former commandant of Dachau, Theodor Eicke, as Inspector of Concentration Camps with the job of reorganizing them. Eicke closed the last SA camps, standardized the administration of the others, and established the SS Death's Head formations, the concentration camp guards. From then on Eicke's Concentration Camp Inspection Office was responsible for the conditions in the camps while incarcerations and releases were effected by the *Gestapo, which maintained its own Political Division in each camp. By June 1935 there were just five camps with approximately 3,500 prisoners: Esterwegen (322), Lichtenburg (706), Moringen (49 women), Dachau (about 1,800), and Sachsenburg (678).

1935–9

In 1935 Hitler approved the expansion of the SS *Death's Head formations and the construction of five new large camps. Preventive Gestapo raids, especially against communists, but also against so-called 'anti-social' persons such as gypsies and persons with a minor criminal record as well as professional criminals, led to a significant increase in the number of prisoners. Thus, on 1 November 1936 there were already 4,761 prisoners, and after the pogroms against the German Jews of November 1938 more than 50,000, but by April 1939 these numbers had decreased again, to 21,000. In addition to 'combating enemies of the state' the concentration camps now had a further, initially secondary, task: exploitation of the *forced labour of their prisoners. New camp sites were now no longer selected solely by previous criteria such as seclusion and good transport routes, but also for their proximity to SS factories.

The first of these new large camps arose in *Sachsenhausen near Berlin in July 1936. This took in the prisoners from the former Esterwegen camp and from the end of 1936 to the end of 1938 the numbers of prisoners there rose from 2,000 to exceed 8,000. In the summer of 1937, *Buchenwald camp was set up near Weimar in Thuringia, and the camps in Sachsenburg and Lichtenburg were closed. Buchenwald was planned for 3,000 prisoners at first, later for 12,000. At the same time the Dachau camp was considerably expanded. Following the Anschluss (union) of Austria with Germany in the spring of 1938, *Mauthausen camp was set up near Linz. A decisive factor in the choice of this site, as for *Flossenbürg camp which was built at the same time, was the proximity of large stone quarries in which the prisoners were forced to work, often until they dropped. For female prisoners, who were initially confined in Moringen and later in Lichtenburg, the *Ravensbrück camp was built to accommodate several thousand prisoners. These projects completed Eicke's system of concentration camps; after this he commanded the SS Death's Head Division until his death on the Eastern Front in 1943; he was succeeded in November 1939, by Richard Glücks, who retained the position of Inspector of Concentration Camps until 1945.

A standard concentration camp such as Dachau was divided into five departments. Department I comprised the commandant and his staff; Department II was the Political Department, headed by a Gestapo officer; Department III, headed by a senior SS officer, was responsible for camp conditions and for selecting of SS Block Leaders and key inmates who exercised unlimited authority in the camp. Department IV was the administration; and Department V was the medical staff. The guard units, the SS Death's Head formations, were in a separate chain of command and were only under the tactical command of the camp commandant. From 1940 all concentration camps were part of the Waffen-SS.

1939–41

With the German invasion of Poland (see POLISH CAMPAIGN) the number of prisoners in the camps rose dramatically. New camps were built at Neuengamme near Hamburg (1940), at Stutthof near Danzig (1941), at Gross-Rosen near Breslau (1941), and at Natzweiler in Alsace (1941). *Auschwitz near Cracow and *Majdanek near

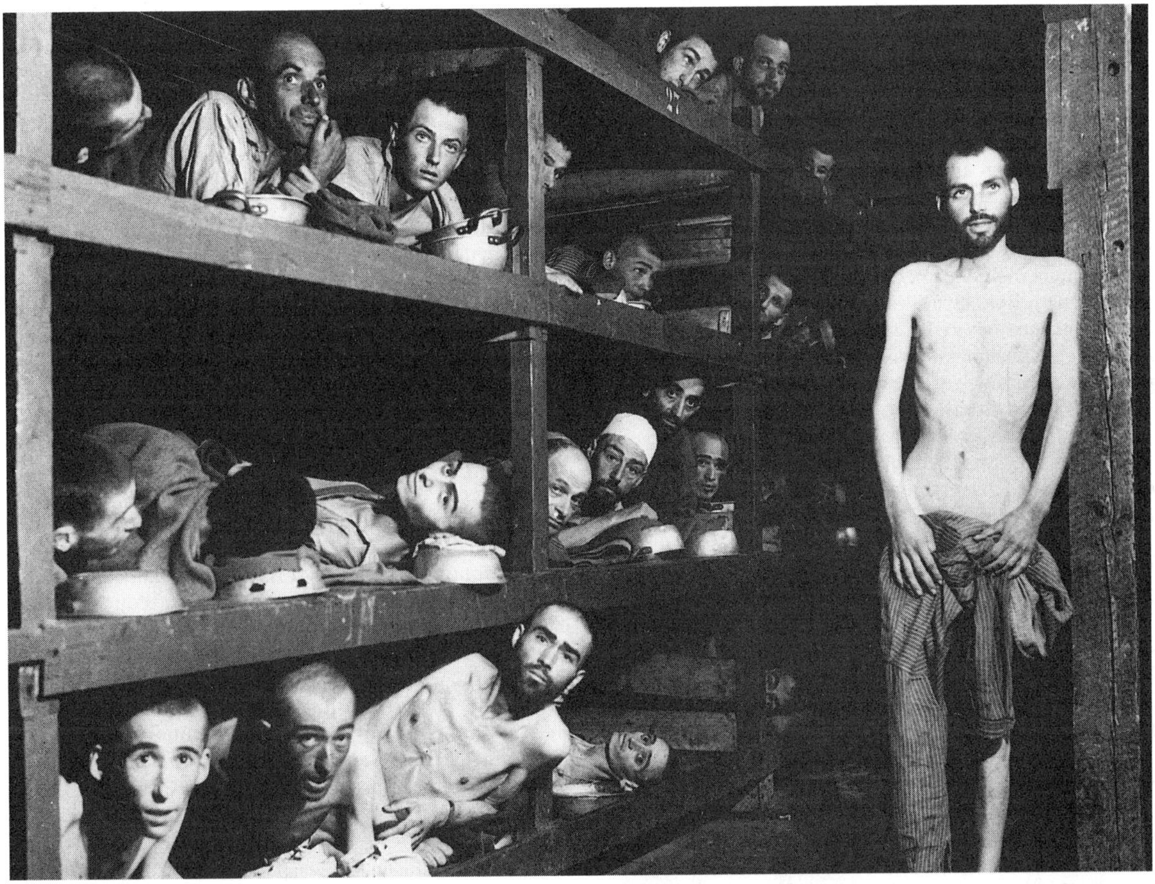

Victims of the Buchenwald **concentration camp**.

Lublin, first planned as prisoner-of-war (POW) camps, later became both concentration and extermination camps. Not included among the concentration camps were the extermination camps of *Operation REINHARD in which from the end of 1941 the mass murder of hundreds of thousands of European Jews began.

1942–4

The prisoners, of whom only a minority were Germans by now, no longer worked in SS factories, but provided slave labour for the entire German armaments industry. Himmler wanted to set up factories in the camps, but was not able to prevail against the armaments minister, Albert *Speer, who preferred a number of small camps near munitions factories. In the following years well over 1,000 satellite camps were set up.

This new phase also made itself apparent in the organization of the camps. In March 1942 the Concentration Camp Inspection Office was integrated as Group D into the SS Main Office of Economy and Administration directed by Oswald Pohl. From then on, the factories ordered prisoners directly from Group D, and the concentration camps charged the firms for the slave

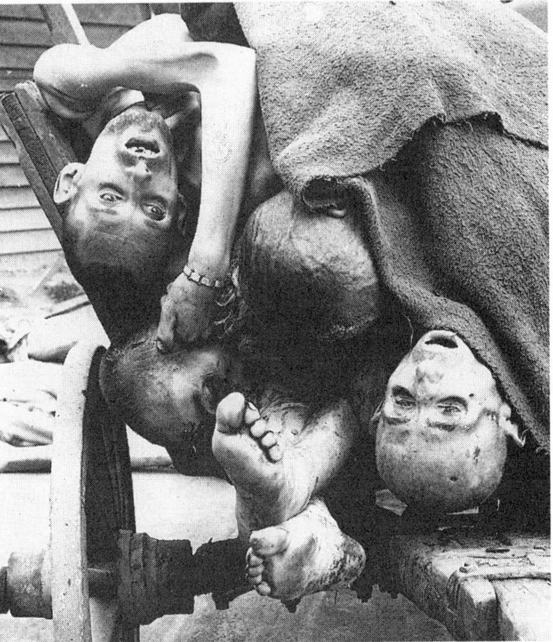

labour, the money being collected by the SS for the Reich ministry of finance.

After the invasion of the Soviet Union in June 1941 (see BARBAROSSA) the number of prisoners increased again. Following Hitler's *Commissar Order, thousands of Soviet officers were murdered in the camps, more than 22,000 in Sachsenhausen and Buchenwald alone. Several thousand other Soviet enlisted men and officers starved in the winter of 1941–2 in specially isolated barracks which were given the cryptic name 'POW work camps'. Some camps included special enclosures (*Sonderlager*) for prominent prisoners. Stalin's son was imprisoned in Sachsenhausen before his murder, as were the former Austrian chancellor Kurt von Schuschnigg, Hitler's would-be assassin Georg Elser, and some prominent Allied POW in Dachau.

In a few camps, especially in Auschwitz and Dachau, the SS and the Luftwaffe conducted medical experiments on inmates which were generally fatal (see MENGELE and MEDICINE). The SS also selected sick inmates in all camps under the codename 'Aktion 14 f 13' who where then killed with poison gas as part of the *euthanasia programme.

In 1942–3 other camps were taken over by the SS as concentration camps. These included ones at Riga, Kauen, and Vaivara in *Ostland as well as the *Krankenlager* (sick camp) *Bergen-Belsen used exclusively for Jewish prisoners. At the same time from 1942 to 1944 more than a million Jews were murdered with the gas *Zyklon-B in Auschwitz-Birkenau.

In 1944 the network of concentration camps reached its zenith. Parts of the armaments industry were moved below ground. Flossenbürg prisoners produced aircraft for Messerschmitt underground, and Neuengamme prisoners set up gigantic factory complexes in the caves of Porta Westfalica. In October 1944 the *Dora-Mittelbau camp near Nordhausen in the Harz mountains, until then a satellite command of Buchenwald, was converted into an independent camp. Here, components for the *V-weapons were produced under unimaginable conditions.

Since 1939 the number of registered camp prisoners had risen from 25,000 to 60,000 (end of 1941), 98,600 (July 1942), more than 200,000 (May 1943), to about 225,000 (August 1943). From July 1942 to June 1943 alone, more than 110,000 died in the camps, which does not include the prisoners executed or brought into the camps for execution. This corresponds to a death rate of over 10% which, after a temporary decrease at the end of 1943, was to climb still higher in 1944–5. Malnutrition and hunger, epidemics, and mass murder marked daily life in the camps. On 15 January 1945 the SS had 511,537 male and 202,674 female prisoners registered in the concentration camps.

1944–5

The last phase of the concentration camps was characterized by chaos and mass death. In July 1944 Majdanek was liberated by Soviet troops. The closer the Allied forces came to the German border, the more frantically the SS attempted to herd prisoners from the threatened areas into the middle of Germany. In January 1945 probably more than 60,000 prisoners were sent on forced marches towards Dachau, Buchenwald, Gross-Rosen, and Mauthausen. At least 15,000 of them died or were shot on the way. In all camps, especially in Sachsenhausen and Ravensbrück, many weak prisoners were singled out to be killed with injections or gas. About 7,000 prisoners of the Neuengamme camp were put on ships in the Bay of Lübeck which were then attacked and sunk by British aircraft. Buchenwald was liberated on 11 April 1945, Bergen-Belsen on 15 April, and Dachau on 30 April. The pictures of the people whom the American and British troops found there, starving or dead, revealed the full extent of the Nazi terror to the world at large for the first time. In Bergen-Belsen alone, 34,000 people died between February 1945 and the liberation, after which another 13,000 died by the end of June 1945 despite all the medical efforts of the British troops. Auschwitz, Bergen-Belsen, Buchenwald, and Dachau became synonyms for the inhuman dictatorship of National Socialism.

The number of prisoners and dead in the concentration camps can only be estimated approximately. Altogether, there were 1,600,000 registered prisoners and 450,000 deaths are documented, though a number exceeding 600,000 dead is more probable. However this does not include the victims of the *Final Solution in Auschwitz-Birkenau, Chelmno, and Majdenek, and in the extermination camps of Operation REINHARD.

JOHANNES TUCHEL

Kogon, E., *The Theory and Practice of Hell: The German Concentration Camps and the System Behind Them* (New York, 1950).
Pingel, F., *Häftlinge unter SS-Herrschaft. Widerstand, Selbstbehauptung und Vernichtung im Konzentrationslager* (Hamburg, 1978).
Tuchel, J., *Konzentrationslager. Organizationsgeschichte und Funktion der 'Inspektion der Konzentrationslager' 1934–1938* (Boppard, 1991).

Coningham, Air Marshal Sir Arthur (1895–1948). Born in Australia but brought up in New Zealand, Coningham served as a soldier in Samoa and Egypt before being invalided home and discharged on medical grounds in April 1916. He immediately sailed to England, was commissioned in the Royal Flying Corps, became a distinguished fighter pilot and squadron commander, was decorated three times and accepted the nickname 'Mary' (derived from 'Maori'), to which he answered for the rest of his life.

After the *First World War he confirmed his reputation as a pilot and leader in the UK, Iraq, Egypt, and the Sudan. In 1925 he earned a fourth decoration by leading the first east–west flight across Africa (from Cairo to Kaduna in Nigeria and back): 10,460 km. (6,500 mi.) in 24 days.

As commander of Fourth Group in Bomber Command, from July 1939 to July 1941, he attracted the attention of *Tedder (head of Middle East Air Command) who summoned him to Egypt to command what became the

*Western Desert Air Force. His leadership before, during and after the vital second battle of *El Alamein was critical to the eventual defeat of *Rommel. Coningham initiated and developed methods of co-operation with the British Eighth Army which were adopted by the US war department in July 1943: air and land power were recognized as 'co-equal and interdependent forces', neither of them 'an auxiliary of the other'. After leading Allied air forces in Tunisia, Sicily, and Italy in 1943, he was among the outstanding commanders gathered in England to prepare for the Normandy landings (see OVERLORD) and headed the Second Tactical Air Force which accompanied the Allied armies from Normandy to Berlin. He retired in 1947 and was killed in an aircraft accident in January 1948. VINCENT ORANGE

Orange, V., *Coningham* (London, 1990).

conscientious objectors (COs). Contrary to expectations during the anti-war reaction of the late 1920s, COs were too few to affect the war effort of any of the combatants during the Second World War; but their numbers, treatment, and behaviour revealed much about the countries which produced them.

COs differ from the generality of 'draft-dodgers' in that their refusal to be conscripted is both avowed and principled. The first COs were members of Protestant sects such as the Mennonites which were so small, intransigent, and idiosyncratic that by the late 19th century even Russia and Germany did not bother to force them to bear arms, though they were required instead to contribute either a tax or non-combatant service. As late as the *First World War, when most liberal states first made provision for conscientious objection, their procedures still favoured members of 'historic peace churches', and offered only conditional exemption. Admittedly, in the UK the law not only recognized all religious objectors—and, even more remarkably, ethical and political ones too—as eligible for CO status, but also provided for unconditional exemption; yet in practice local tribunals often refused to implement these uniquely generous provisions. As a result every liberal state found itself in confrontation with two new types of CO which appeared as significant minorities for the first time during the First World War: those from outside the historic peace sects, and 'absolutists' who refused alternative service. Their sufferings helped to publicize their claim that all sincere objectors had a general right to be exempted, unconditionally where appropriate.

By the Second World War the toleration of COs had begun to be recognized as a touchstone of mature liberalism. The Axis powers prided themselves on refusing to recognize conscientious objection, as did the Soviet Union, which boasted that its previous limited provision had produced no takers; and neither the new states of east-central Europe nor the Catholic countries of western Europe such as France and Belgium catered for COs. There is insufficient evidence to guess the numbers imprisoned or executed for nevertheless attempting to sustain a conscientious objection in such states.

However, in the Protestant-liberal cultures of North America, Australia, New Zealand, the UK, the Netherlands, and Scandinavia, COs were treated better than in the First World War. For example, the USA widened its recognition from historic peace sects to all objections arising from 'religious training and belief', and also introduced a scheme for Civilian Public Service. Its COs numbered approximately 100,000 (0.0029% of those required to register for military service, compared with an estimated 0.0023% in the First World War). Even so, the USA stopped short of either recognizing political objectors or exempting unconditionally; Civilian Public Service was mostly carried out in prison-like camps; and in addition 6% of COs were gaoled. The UK was again most generous, its tribunals now applying the law more fairly than in the First World War: unconditional exemptions were granted to 6.1% of COs (compared with less than 0.003%); alternative service was permitted in ordinary civilian jobs; and less than 10% of COs suffered spells in prison (compared with about 33%). Its total of COs was nearly 60,000 or 1.2% of those called up, an average concealing a steep decline from a peak of 2.2% in the *phoney war (compared with 0.125% of those either volunteering or conscripted in First World War). Although their numbers increased, the UK's Second World War COs had even less influence than their predecessors: generous treatment embarrassed most into co-operative behaviour, though a few complained about repressive tolerance.

MARTIN CEADEL

Barker, R., *Conscience, Government and War* (London, 1982).
Prasad, D., and Smythe, T., *Conscription* (London, 1968).
Sibley, M. Q., and Jacob, P. E., *Conscription of Conscience* (Ithaca, NY, 1952).

consequences of the war. The Second World War ended in both major theatres in acts of total and undeniable capitulation. Victors and vanquished were plain for all to see. The chief aggressors, Germany and Japan, were devastated, numbed, and occupied. The conventional cruelties of war, including the massive problem of *refugees, were compounded by the peculiar horrors of the German *concentration camps and the Japanese *prisoner-of-war camps, which now became public knowledge. The aggressor states were condemned for starting war and vilified for what they did in war. Their power and their good name were destroyed. But not for long. The war in the west was won by Allies who had so little in common that their alliance was precarious at the moment of victory and turned rapidly into open and armed hostility. Germany (or most of it) and Japan were quickly restored to the good graces of their western conquerors and to positions of power in the world.

The *Cold War was not a foregone conclusion of the World War. There were on both sides hopes of an enduring alliance between the western democracies and the Soviet Union and co-operative ventures in wartime—in, for example, the field of intelligence—which made those hopes not ridiculous. But there were also deep distrusts and myths. The *Grand Alliance was made by Hitler when in June 1941 he invaded the USSR (see BARBAROSSA) and six months later declared war on the USA in fulfilment of a promise to Japan. This adventitious alliance, although crucial for the defeat of Germany, was less than wholehearted and neither the exigencies of war not its camaraderie brought much mutual knowledge or understanding. The Allies' armed forces and their states of mind operated in disconnected spheres and at the war's end they confronted one another across a divided continent and with largely mythical ideas about one another's capabilities, intentions, and ambitions. In the USSR, which had suffered even more than Germany and was the one major state to be ruled after the war by an unregenerate pre-war figure, Stalin gave the first importance to securing his battered and enfeebled country by turning central and eastern Europe and as much of Germany as he could get hold of into an exclusive zone, a satellite empire. He was right to think that the capitalist West hated his communist system but wrong to suppose that, even with a monopoly of nuclear weapons, the USA intended to attack it. Even more preposterously wrong was the American fear that the Soviet Union, whose overpowering military successes against Germany were better advertised than its post-war prostration, intended to advance further into western Europe or towards the Mediterranean, or possessed in satellite communist parties instruments capable of subverting western democracies. The USA, besides misinterpreting Stalin's capabilities (as in wartime it had exaggerated his bonhomous sagacity), adopted anti-communism as a political principle. Since communists were not confined to Europe, this ideological stance was potentially global, more so than the World War which engendered it.

Europe, the first department of the Cold War, was sharply sundered by the Second World War. Those parts of the continent reached by Stalin's armies, whether wartime enemies or allied with the USSR—roughly, old *Mitteleuropa* and the northern Balkans—became parts of a new Soviet empire, but an empire virtually isolated in the world economically as well as politically. Since Stalin was left with no allies and made no friends, his international scene consisted only of satellites and enemies, and he treated the former with the harshness of a beleaguered, ageing, and suspicious tyrant. His experience in war, when victory had been won after the closest shave with total defeat, confirmed his authoritarianism, his ingrained urge to assert his personal dictatorship over opponents and supposed opponents, and his imperviousness to any criticism of an economic and administrative system in which incompetence and corruption proliferated. The war prolonged this system in the Soviet Union and extended it to half of Europe, ruled by Stalin until his death in 1953 and by successors of his stamp until 1985. Within this empire endemic conflicts were smothered but not resolved.

In western Europe fear of Germans was replaced by fear of the Soviets but not extinguished. Hence two separate developments: against the Soviet Union a Euro-American alliance, against a German resurgence radically new political and constitutional ideas. Both these developments marked the ending of the old European states system—the first by enlisting the USA into that system as a quasi-European power, and the second by abrogating the sovereignty of the state as an overriding political principle. The USA became in effect a European power, reversing the American retreat from Europe after the *First World War and belying Roosevelt's dictum at the Yalta Conference in February 1945 (see ARGONAUT) that all American forces would quit Europe within two years. Within a short space US dominance of the new alliance, the North Atlantic Treaty Organization (NATO), coupled with the extension of the Cold War to Asia and the consequent strain on American resources in Europe, precipitated the rehabilitation of (western) Germany. Unlike the Soviet Union, the USA had friends and allies; but they were weak. They were suffering from post-war exhaustion and, to American eyes, the perennial European inability to make common cause. Through the Marshall Aid Plan—started in 1947 by General *Marshall who was now US secretary of state—the USA furnished them with massive economic aid for the restoration of their battered but nevertheless resourceful economies, accompanied by hints about the virtues of union or federation.

But the NATO alliance created in 1949 seemed inadequate without a German component and the USA brought about in two steps a major reversal of alliances: first, tacitly abrogating the alliance with the Soviet Union (its collapse was dramatized by the Berlin blockade and the allied relief by airlift in 1948–9) and then pressing the NATO allies to accept western Germany as a partner in arms. Quickly revived by American aid and by its own exertions, western Germany was more transformed by post-war economic and psychological recovery than it had been cast down by military defeat and destruction. The ensuing years of plenitude and widespread international acceptance made the new Federal German Republic what the Weimar Republic had never been after the 1914–18 war: a success. The Federal Republic escaped Weimar's political and economic instability and its pariah status and became, unlike all previous German regimes, a functioning civilian and parliamentary democracy, feared by few. The war had wrecked German power only temporarily. Perhaps it had done more for the German mood or temper, rendering a new Germany no longer as menacing as the Third Reich or the Second.

Even before the end of the war and the impact of a more preoccupying Soviet threat, some among Germany's neighbours were reflecting on the German problem. German economic strength, soundly based in resources, education, and skills, would revive. This revival was not only inevitable but, for those who traded with Germany, highly desirable, even essential. But how could a prosperous German state be prevented from dominating other nations, or making war on them? The aftermath of the First World War had shown the inadequacy of the conventional answer to this question. After 1919 Germany had been hamstrung by limitations on its armed strength and by massively punitive reparations. But these measures served only so long as Germany remained weak; they did not keep it weak, and their failure led to the policy of appeasement which, by making the wrong concessions at the wrong time to the wrong people, failed to buy goodwill or to prevent another war. For Europeans this second war was the Second German War, and although Germany lost it there was little reason in 1945 to suppose that Germany would not one day be capable of fighting yet again. A new antidote to German power had to be found. One war had evoked a commonplace response. Two wars in a single generation stimulated a bolder one.

A system of individual sovereign states invited competition, including armed competition, between the states; in Europe such a system would be dominated by the German state. So the system must be changed. This, in the minds of its first authors, was the germ of the European Community. The state as supreme authority would be replaced by an association of states, in which the several states' adversarial proclivities would be muted, the self-interest of the strongest would tend to coincide with the interests of its less powerful associates, and Germany's will and capacity to economic power would be gratified by co-operation rather than domination: the capacity to dominate would be tempered and countered by the benefits of co-operation. Given the simultaneous division of Europe into two parts by the Cold War this experiment—the most astonishing change in Europe for a thousand years—came to be pursued in a restricted and so more manageable area. Stalin therefore, by occupying central and eastern Europe and taking them out of political circulation, contributed as much as Hitler to the conception and inauguration of the European Community. It was a war baby.

The consequences of the defeat of Japan were less complex than the reordering of Europe. Uniquely among major combatants Japan fought alone, while against Japan the USA fought the *Pacific war with relatively minor, if nevertheless significant, aid from the UK, Australia, and New Zealand. The war begun by the Japanese attack on *Pearl Harbor in December 1941 developed into a duel in which the mastery of the Pacific passed to the USA. In China war (see CHINA INCIDENT) did not restore the rule of *Chiang Kai-shek's nationalists over the entire country but widened the rift between it and the Chinese Communist Party which became in 1949 the government of China. Yet chaos, the ruling condition of China since the previous century, was only moderately and briefly abated. The USSR, pledged at American insistence and impelled by self-interest to enter the war against Japan on the Asian mainland, was deprived of any substantial gain by the abrupt ending of the war by American air and nuclear power (see ATOMIC BOMB). It acquired four Kurile islands and southern Sakhalin from Japan and ensured the bisection of Korea by a joint occupation which turned the country into two separate states—an uncovenanted consequence of the war which, in a remote quarter, assumed unexpected importance when the invasion of south Korea from the north became the first stroke in the extension of the Cold War to Asia. In South-East Asia the Japanese conquests of 1941–2 were undone, but European imperialism was not restored in spite of attempts of varying intensity by the Netherlands, France and the UK to resume their sway. The principal consequence of the French attempt in French Indo-China was the involvement of the USA, first by financing the French war and then by deploying American forces of all arms at sea and on the Asian mainland in vain support of anti-communist regimes in south Vietnam.

For Japan itself the war was a calamitous but brief setback in a rise to power which, after the Meiji restoration in 1868 and by way of wars against China in Korea in 1894 and Manchuria in 1931 (see MANCHUKUO), had become progressively militaristic as the chiefs of the modernized armed services arrogated to themselves the authority and prestige once enjoyed by the shoguns. Their defeat entailed, besides occupation and virtual dictatorship by the USA, deeper constitutional and psychological changes. These included shedding militarism and the divine colouring of the monarchy and their replacement by a vigorous and aggressive commercialism which made Japan the economic wonder of the second half of the century and ensured that defeat did not entail demotion or the renunciation of a world role. Unlike the proverbial leopard, Japan changed its spots. But a change of integument is by definition not deep and although Japan was quickly reconciled with the USA it remained uneasy in its relations with China, the USSR, and South East-Asian states. Japan's pre-war schemes for a *Greater East Asia Co-prosperity Sphere had been perverted by militarism from beneficial co-operation to self-regarding domination; and although Japan's defeat changed the nature of its thrust in international affairs from guns to yen the war in Asia—unlike the Pacific war against the USA—left a legacy of mistrust which Japan's Asian neighbours found it more difficult to forget than did the inviolate and only briefly humiliated Americans.

The war which began in 1914 had been called simply the Great War, but when a second came along both were designated World Wars. Both were world-wide or nearly so in the sense that men and (in the later case) women came from all quarters to fight in it. But in another sense the sobriquet was misleading, for the involvement of most of the world—most of Asia and virtually all Africa—came about through the domination of alien rulers and at their orders: British, French, German, Turkish, Dutch, and more. The people of Asia and Africa fought, not on their own initiative, but because they belonged to somebody: on the outbreak of the Second World War the viceroy of India declared the country at war without consulting any Indian. This state of affairs was destroyed by the war, which greatly accelerated the dissolution of alien empires outside Europe. The Japanese ousted European rulers from South-East Asia and post-war attempts to reverse this verdict failed. In India, Burma, and Ceylon the British felt impelled actually to do what they had been talking of doing for generations: resign. The mandate system in the Middle East—a see-through imperialism invented after the First World War—was abrogated, in the case of France during the war, in the British case soon after it and in spite of victory (see NATIONALISM). Most surprisingly the wave of decolonization spread into Africa. In that continent the direct impact was as volcanic as anything in the history of the continent. Within 20 years of the war's end most of Africa—and within 30 years all of it—consisted of independent sovereign states where, before the war, there had been only three (see Map H). The speed of this conversion was entirely unexpected. It was a consequence of the dissolution of the British and other empires in Asia which turned the sluggish tide of decolonization into a flash flood (see ANTI-IMPERIALISM). The example of Asia was picked up by Africans, while on the European side empire ceased to seem a natural and indefeasible fact. The happier aspect of this rush to liberation was a considerable, if not universal, atmosphere of mutual goodwill. The less cheerful aspect was the unpreparedness of the new states in terms of economic independence, professional services, political institutions, a ruling class, and a governing ethic. This huge transfer of authority and responsibility was not only gratifying to the liberated peoples and their well-wishers. It also transformed the nature of international politics.

Before decolonization vast areas of the world had been the private property of a few foreign states (see Maps D and E). The politics of these areas, in so far as they were allowed any, were either adjuncts of the politics of the metropolitan proprietors or strictly limited affairs. After decolonization these areas became sovereign states whose numbers exceeded the number of existing sovereign states and whose peoples made demands on the rest of the world. In the time of the *League of Nations and in the first years of the United Nations (UN) international affairs had been preponderantly about war and peace. In the new world created by the dissolution of empires a majority of members of the UN was less concerned about world order than about terms of trade, economic development, and the transfer of economic resources; and, complementarily, large areas once private preserves became fields of opportunity for all who were minded to go up and down in the world, make money in it, or seek strategic vantage points. The proliferation of sovereign states, promoted by the Second World War, turned the world into an open world, all the more accessible owing to the contemporary revolution in the technologies of communication from aircraft to the fax machine.

For the Middle East both world wars were European wars which spilled over into western Asia. The first caused the collapse of Ottoman Turkish rule, raised hopes of an Arabia for the Arabs, but ended with the implantation of British and French rule in choice areas. Where, between the wars, Arabs ruled, their rule was fragmented among new states and fostered a secular particularism at odds with the traditional Arab aspiration for a unified Arab realm within the House of Islam (Darul-Islam). In the second war the French were removed (mainly by the British), German and Italian plans were thwarted (also by the British), and the British themselves departed soon afterwards, their war-weariness constituting a large part of the abandonment of their attempts to keep Palestine peaceful and British. But the second war, like the first, introduced a new obstacle to Arab ambitions in the shape of the state of Israel. Hitler's barbarous treatment of the Jews within his grasp (see FINAL SOLUTION) had turned the comparatively marginal Zionist movement into an unstoppable Jewish migration which succeeded by force of arms in evicting all the British and half the Arabs from Palestine. This affront to Arab emotions, coupled with Israel's militancy—in self-defence or in fulfilment of Zionism's biblical fundamentalism—made the Middle East more unsettled after the war than it had been between the wars, while it became also more important for outsiders than ever before owing to the wartime and post-war discovery of new oilfields and the failure of other sources of energy to challenge oil's leading role in satisfying the world's rocketing demands for energy.

Every great war in modern times (and some in ancient) has stimulated attempts to reinforce and extend international law and to improve international mechanisms for the settlement of disputes without resorting to hostilities. After the Second World War eminent surviving German and Japanese civilian and military figures were arraigned on criminal charges before international tribunals (see FAR EAST WAR CRIMES TRIALS, NUREMBERG TRIALS, and WAR CRIMES). The purpose of these proceedings was to apply established law on war crimes, to probe the state of the law on military aggression by states and statesmen, to establish the criminality of certain crimes against humanity (in the context of war), and in all these matters to assert the personal accountability of responsible individuals. A by-product of the trials was the production of copious official documentation on recent history. Separately, but complementarily, statesmen addressed the questions of creating an international organization capable of preventing war or at least some wars, and of devising improved mechanisms and rules for the resolution of disputes by means other than war and for the management of change peacefully instead of by violence or not all.

Inevitably each new venture in international regulation has been devised on the basis that previous attempts have been inadequate. The League of Nations created after the First World War was by 1939 widely discredited, and yet a few years later the UN was created in its place (see SAN FRANCISCO CONFERENCE) and very much in its image. The reasoning of the founders of the UN was that the League had failed on account of flaws in its constitution which were identifiable and corrigible. These were believed to be, in the main, two: the League's limited membership and its limited corporate powers. The principal members and guardians had been the surviving European Great Powers—the UK and France—which were expected to carry the burden of maintaining order in the world at a time when their powers were in decline: the USA, already the world's greatest power, was never a member of the League. The Covenant of the League did not forbid members to have recourse to war; members engaged themselves merely to certain preliminary moves designed to obviate the resolution of a dispute by war but, provided these moves were made, hostilities remained a legitimate instrument of state power. Attempts in the 1920s to make the rules more stringent were defeated by those members which preferred the powers they knew (and possessed) to new and untried international machinery.

The Second World War gave internationalism, if only briefly, a fresh edge. The founders of the UN hoped to remedy the League's defects by giving its successor more members and more powers. Both the USA and the Soviet Union, the world's emerging superpowers, joined at the start and by the UN Charter all members renounced the right to make war except in very restricted (but loosely defined) circumstances. The Charter transferred the right to make war from the state to the international association of states, a step or stride which, while symptomatic of the emotions induced by war, proved to be at least premature—partly because the *Cold War turned the UN into a forum for international dispute rather than conciliation, and partly because opinion at large was unprepared for so drastic an abrogation of the exercise of sovereignty. If the Second World War promoted the creation of a UN of ambitious scope, the Cold War neutered it, opinion in the more powerful states gave little support, and after a few years the tripling of the UN's membership through decolonization distracted its efforts between the management of international disputes and the installation of a more equitable world economic order. While the UN's founders thought of it first and foremost as an embryonic police force, its later recruits required it to give more attention to succouring poor countries in economic distress.

Of attitudes to war itself it is difficult to judge without subjective generalization. Like all modern wars the Second World War was waged by states and endured by individuals. It horrified people but left them sceptical about the chances of preventing more wars. Fifty million dead; as many maimed incurably in limb or mind; uncountable millions flung anonymously from the homes of their fathers, from one country to another, including ten million Germans from lands between the Oder and the Volga where their age-old presence had been an unsettling factor in half Europe; the invention of weapons of horrifying destructiveness applied to indiscriminate mass bombing which culminated in two nuclear bombs dropped on the two Japanese cities of *Hiroshima and *Nagasaki—all these things confirmed popular revulsion against war but, perhaps because this revulsion was no new thing, did little to alter popular assessments of war as an intrinsic element in the human condition. Although the scale might be new, the phenomenon was not.

Yet three items of special significance and some novelty may be pinpointed. On the morrow of the war's end the most encompassing fact, besides peace itself, was the instrument which clinched it—the *atomic bomb. This fearful weapon was accepted as something more than the latest step in the science of destruction, for it provided man with a capacity hitherto reserved to God, the power to destroy all life on earth. Yet at the same time the magnitude of the destructiveness of the nuclear weapon, coupled with the moral and theological issues which it raised, obscured the fact that its usefulness for military or political ends was slight. In the half-century after the war a dozen or more states acquired the knowledge and in some cases the resources to make nuclear weapons and some 100,000 warheads were manufactured. Yet none was used, largely because their use would have been profitless. This strange uselessness of the most potent weapons greatly inflated the element of bluff in the conduct of international affairs. A second item of special significance was the development during the war of *photographic reconnaissance and intelligence which, when allied after the war with the ability to put satellites into orbit round the earth, provided states with information about each other's capacities, activities, and deployments of unprecedented scope and detail. The alliance of photography with rocketry neutralized the secretiveness which had been a major factor in preparations for war. Thirdly, the Second World War gave a boost to a kind of warfare which had existed only in the interstices of international war and on the fringes of international law: war waged by groups which were less than states but more than gangs. Resistance movements in Europe and anti-colonial liberation movements in Asia won an honourable status by operations which in other circumstances would be denounced as criminal. These movements were specially adept at enlisting popular emotions of righteous indignation as well as patriotic fervour and in professionalizing a do-it-yourself approach to warfare which, while it might be welcome to regular commanders and to governments in a crisis, were less welcome when peace returned and states strove to reassert their monopoly of legitimate violence.

The Second World War reformulated an old question in a new context: the question of the uses of power. The punch of the powerful state was hugely enhanced by the

This scene of a winter **convoy** in the north Atlantic conveys the extreme hardships endured by the crews of the merchant ships and their escorts.

introduction of the nuclear weapon, or so it seemed. At the same time the number of such superstates was much reduced, to two by most computations or, on a more rigorous calculation, to one alone. For the USA the experience of war was unique. Americans knew plenty of personal pain and grief, but their country was inviolable and it prospered. The USA, which entered the war as the strongest state in the world, ended the war as a state in a class of its own, raised to a pre-eminence not seen for many centuries. This gift of invincible might carried with it opportunities and temptations, responsibilities, expectations, and hazards, notably in maintaining order in the international community and stability in the international economy. At this level the outcome of the war made the world seem, for a moment, simpler.

PETER CALVOCORESSI

Gaddis, J. L., *The Long Peace. Inquiries into the History of the Cold War* (Oxford, 1987).
Iriye Akira, *The Cold War in Asia* (Eaglewood Cliffs, NJ, 1974).
Mortimer, E., *Faith and Power. The Politics of Islam* (London, 1982).

convoys. (See also ARCTIC CONVOYS.) Though of ancient origin, convoys—defined by the British official naval historian as 'one or more merchant ships sailing under the protection of one or more warships'—were reintroduced into modern maritime warfare by the British in 1917 and proved an effective counter-measure to submarine attacks.

During the Second World War the convoy system was employed by all combatant nations that had access to deep water, but Germany ran only coastal convoys, and what *raw materials it managed to obtain from the Far East were transported in *blockade runners. Italian convoys were also coastal or trans-Mediterranean and a total of 4,385 were run to supply the Axis forces fighting in the *Western Desert and *North African campaigns. These delivered 84.6% of the 2.84 million tons of supplies and fuel carried by them, a remarkable feat given that they were often fiercely attacked and their escorts sustained high losses (see FORCE K).

The third main Axis power, Japan, relied almost entirely on raw materials from overseas, yet it woefully neglected its merchant fleet and the Japanese Navy, conditioned and trained to take the offensive, made almost no preparations to protect it before war broke out in the Far East. As a result, merchant ships sailed alone, or three or four would be escorted by one destroyer. Sporadic, and largely unsuccessful, efforts were made to build sufficient escort vessels, but an efficient shipping protection organization did not exist until the end of 1943; and it was not until March 1944 that a proper convoy system, where between ten and twenty merchant ships were adequately escorted, was introduced. This dramatically reduced losses and also increased the losses of US submarines, but it came too late and by the end of the war 90% of Japanese merchant shipping over 500 tons had been sunk.

The Allied situation was quite different: convoys, particularly those around which the battle of the *Atlantic was fought, were at the heart of their war effort. Broadly, they fell into three main groups: regular ones which used the same assembly port; those mounted for 'one/off' operations such as the North African campaign landings; and the 'Operational Convoys' for troopship movements which seldom exceeded four ships, usually requisitioned passenger liners. (The really fast liners such as the *Queen Mary* and *Queen Elizabeth* almost always sailed alone as their speed was their best protection.) Each convoy route had a two-letter code such as ON or HX. A third letter, 'F', 'M', or 'S', which signified its fast, medium, or slow components, was also sometimes added as was the number of times that particular convoy had been run. On some routes the number started again at 1 after 99 had been reached.

Early in the war westbound convoys were escorted only a certain distance into the Atlantic before dispersing to sail independently to their destinations while their escorts made rendezvous with an eastbound convoy. But in May 1941, with Iceland in use as an Allied base, convoys began to be escorted right across the Atlantic, though the mid-Atlantic *air gap took much longer to close.

Fast convoys often took evasive action by zigzagging, but slow ones rarely did so as it caused too much confusion to the convoy. Instead, they sometimes took 'evasive' courses, changes of between 20° and 40° from the correct course which were followed for a number of hours. To combat air attacks, and to harry the long-range German Focke-Wulf Kondor aircraft which acted as reconnaissance for the U-boats, makeshift efforts were made to give air cover (see CAM SHIPS, FIGHTER CATAPULT SHIPS, and MAC SHIPS), before escort carriers were introduced.

Initially, only ships which steamed between 9 and 15 knots (under 13 from November 1940 to June 1941) were put in convoy, the rest sailing independently, and it was among this latter group that German *auxiliary cruisers, U-boats, and *German surface raiders claimed most of their victims. With the exception of convoys attempting to break the siege of *Malta (see below) during the long drawn-out battle for the *Mediterranean, the ratio of losses of independently routed ships to those in convoy remained about 80:20 throughout the war, which showed just how effective the convoy system was. Troop convoys were always given strong escorts, but early supply convoys only had a single escort, often an *armed merchant cruiser. Later, when U-boats became the main menace in the Atlantic, it was calculated that the minimum number of escorts a convoy needed was three, plus the number of ships in the convoy divided by ten. It was also found that doubling the escort quadrupled U-boat losses for every ship sunk from that convoy, provided the escort had no other duties. In late 1942 *operational research calculated that larger convoys were statistically safer than small ones, the perimeter of an 80-ship convoy being only one-seventh longer than that of a 40-ship convoy. This revelation increased the size of convoys to such an extent that in the summer of 1944 one group of 187 ships crossed the Atlantic.

Besides being involved in the vital Atlantic convoys, and in the essential Arctic convoys to the USSR, the British ran crucial ones to sustain their position in the Middle East and the Mediterranean. Before the fall of *France in June 1940 the French Navy escorted the homeward bound (HG) Gibraltar convoys and patrolled off the African coastline. However, when France capitulated, and Axis *air power and submarines had closed the Mediterranean to all but the fastest British convoys, Freetown in Sierra Leone became an important assembly port and command HQ for the regular 'WS' convoys which had to use the long route via South Africa to Suez. These convoys, codenamed with the initials of Churchill, the British prime minister who had ordered the first in June 1940, took reinforcements and supplies for the troops fighting in the Western Desert campaigns. Once Japan had entered the war the same codename was given to high priority convoys destined for Singapore, Australia, and India.

Sometimes fast convoys through the Mediterranean had to be risked. Losses were high—about three times the rate in the Atlantic—and were invariably the occasion for fleet actions. One (TIGER) which comprised five heavily escorted merchantmen took urgently needed tanks to the Middle East in April 1942; another, the famous PEDESTAL convoy of August 1942, fought its way to Malta. But of the 55 ships which sailed for Malta in convoy between August 1940 and August 1942, 22 were sunk, 11 were forced to turn back, and only 22 arrived.

These statistics, and Malta's desperate situation, encouraged the use of fast merchantmen sailing alone. Unlike other convoy routes, this improved the odds, and of the 31 ships which sailed independently during this time only nine were sunk and only one had to turn back. In May 1943, at the conclusion of the North African campaign, the Mediterranean was reopened to normal Allied convoys. These were crucial to maintain the *Sicilian and *Italian campaigns, and they were run at intervals of nine or ten days.

However, while the Mediterranean remained closed to all but the fastest ships, the increased distance of sending the 'WS' convoys via the Cape—from under 4,800 km. (3,000 mi.) to nearly 20,800 km. (13,000 mi.)—stretched British shipping resources so much that in November 1941, when 20,000 troops needed conveying to the Far East, there were no ships to transport them. The USA, then still neutral, agreed to take them, and its entry into the war, and the construction in large quantities of its *Liberty ships, gradually reduced the strain on British shipping resources.

When the USA first entered the war its navy was short of escort ships. Though it could have done so, it did not immediately adopt the convoy system off its eastern seaboard. Instead the US Navy used patrols—including amateur ones (see CIVIL AIR PATROL and COASTAL PICKET PATROL)—to combat U-boats, and even employed *Q-ships, but 82 ships were lost between January and April 1942 along the eastern seaboard alone before a partial convoy system, called the 'bucket brigades', was started. Ships, escorted by whatever was available, made short daylight-

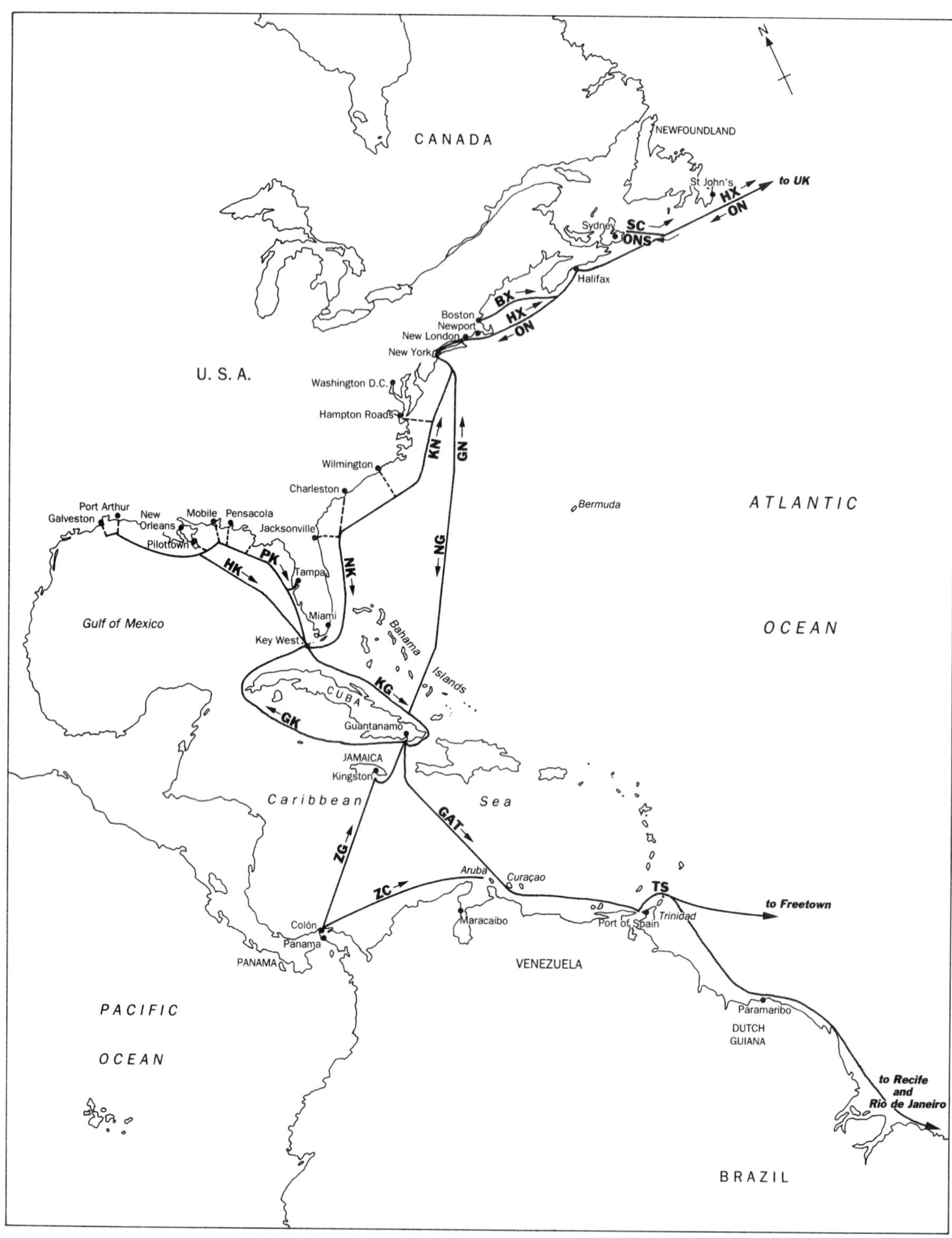

23. Interlocking **convoy** system off US eastern seaboard, 1941–2

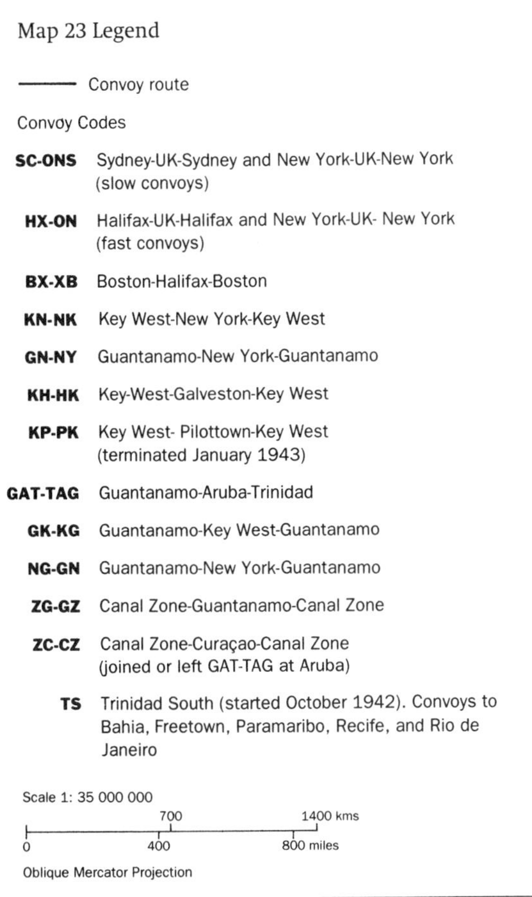

only inshore voyages to guarded anchorages. But this incurred serious delays, sinkings continued, and it was not until what was known as the Interlocking Convoy System (see Map 23) became operational that losses were drastically reduced. With this system ships were run almost like trains. All 'local' convoys were fed into two 'express' convoy routes, Key West–New York–Key West (KN–NK) and Guantanamo–New York–Guantanamo (GN–NG), with the 'express' convoys being timed to arrive at New York just before the departure of Atlantic convoys. After it was first introduced, between Hampton Roads and Key West, on 14 May 1942, it was quickly extended in either direction. Instead, U-boats concentrated in the Caribbean and the Gulf of Mexico, and between May and September 1942 they sank over a million tons of shipping there, a statistic the official US naval historian merited printing in italic. But by October the system had been extended into these areas, and to Brazil, and its efficiency was soon proven by the fact that of the 9,064 ships which sailed in 527 of its convoys between 1 July and 7 December 1942 only 39, or less than 0.5%, were sunk.

Winton, J., *Convoy* (London, 1983).

Cooney teams. Eighteen three-man French *Special Air Service teams dropped into Brittany on the night of 7/8 June 1944 to cut rail links with Normandy after the Allied landings there (see OVERLORD). One of their successes was to prevent the German 3rd Parachute Division being moved out of Brittany by rail.

Cooper, (Alfred) Duff (1890–1954), British Conservative politician, a front-line fighting soldier in the *First World War, who resigned as First Lord of the Admiralty when the *Munich agreement was signed. He served as minister of information, 1940–1. A great francophile, he was British minister in Algiers from December 1942 to November 1944, then British ambassador in Paris.

Cooper, D., *Old Men Forget* (London, 1954).

Coral Sea, battle of, first-ever major naval action between *carriers and the first in which the opposing ships never sighted one another. It was fought from 4 to 8 May 1942 during the *Pacific war between units of the Japanese and US navies which were attempting, respectively, to establish and to prevent a Japanese landing at Port Moresby, Papua. It was, like many battles, much influenced by the weather (see METEOROLOGICAL INTELLIGENCE).

In overall control of the Japanese forces was Vice-Admiral Inoue Shigeyoshi whose three invasion convoys were assembled at *Truk and *Rabaul. The largest convoy was destined for Port Moresby while the others were to establish seaplane bases on Tulagi Island and in the Louisiades. Protecting the convoys was a covering force, commanded by Rear-Admiral Gotō Aritomo, which comprised the light carrier *Shōhō*, four heavy cruisers, and one destroyer; and a striking force, commanded by Vice-Admiral Takagi Takeo, which consisted of the fleet carriers *Shōkaku* and *Zuikaku*, two heavy cruisers, and six destroyers.

The Japanese anticipated the Americans would intervene, and they planned to catch any attacking force in a pincer movement while the main invasion force slipped into Port Moresby. If what the Japanese called Operation MO succeeded, Australia would be isolated and within the range of Japanese aircraft. However, the US Pacific Fleet's C-in-C, Admiral *Nimitz, had been alerted early to the Japanese invasion by *ULTRA intelligence and had assembled two carrier task forces around the fleet carriers *Lexington* and *Yorktown*, and a task force of Australian and US cruisers under a British naval officer, Rear-Admiral John Crace.

The Tulagi invasion force landed unopposed on 3 May, but the next day its ships were attacked by aircraft from *Yorktown* and a destroyer was beached and several smaller vessels sunk. Two days later the three Allied task forces assembled 400 miles south of *Guadalcanal under the command of Rear-Admiral *Fletcher aboard *Yorktown*, and sailed north-west to intercept the Port Moresby invasion transports and Tagaki's carriers. At dawn on 7

May Fletcher ordered Crace to forge ahead to intercept the transports, and then turned north to where he supposed Tagaki to be. However, inaccurate air reconnaissance guided *Yorktown*'s attack group not on to the carriers but on to the invasion convoy's escort, and the threat of their presence was enough to make the convoy withdraw to await the outcome of the main battle. The attack group from *Lexington* then found *Shōhō* and, aided by *Yorktown*'s aircraft, sank her with the loss of only three planes. Meanwhile Crace, when he heard the convoy had turned back, withdrew.

Fletcher, now without air cover and highly vulnerable to attack, only learned after midday that, quite contrary to his expectations, the Japanese carriers were somewhere astern of him and had sunk two of his ships. For Tagaki, like Fletcher earlier, had been misled into • launching air strikes against a subsidiary target—a tanker and its escorting destroyer which Fletcher had ordered to drop astern the previous night.

Next morning, 8 May, the two sides located each other and launched all-out strikes. In the air they were almost equal in numbers, 121 Japanese to 122 American aircraft, but the Japanese types were superior to their American equivalents. The first American attack, from *Yorktown*, damaged *Shōkaku*. Aircraft from *Lexington* also hit her and she turned north trailing smoke, but *Zuikaku* was not even located. Meanwhile, Japanese aircraft were attacking the American carriers with devastating success. Their strike group contained a better balance of different types of aircraft than the Americans', and these were more accurately directed on to their targets. Too few American aircraft could be launched to defend the carriers; *Lexington* was hit by bombs and torpedoes, and had to be sunk after a generator spark set off a huge explosion. *Yorktown*, too, was damaged, but the Japanese failed to seal their victory by pressing home their attack. The battle, therefore, though a tactical success for Tagaki, was a strategic failure for Inouye who was later criticized for not persisting with the invasion of Port Moresby after Crace had withdrawn.

The loss of *Lexington* was a severe blow to the Americans, but neither *Shōkaku*, because of damage, nor *Zuikaku*, because her aircraft strength was so depleted, was able to take part in the critical battle of *Midway the following month, an absence that helped tip the scales there in favour of the Americans.

Corregidor, fortified island situated 3.2 km. (2 mi.) off the *Bataan peninsula, part of the Philippines island of Luzon. After elements of Lt-General *Homma's Fourteenth Army had landed on Luzon in December 1941 (see PHILIPPINES CAMPAIGNS), and had established themselves there, the US Army commander, Lt-General *MacArthur, declared Manila an open city, ordered his army to withdraw into the Bataan peninsula, and then withdrew his HQ to Corregidor. On 11 March he handed over command to Lt-General *Wainwright and left for Australia.

Corregidor, only 5.6 km. (3.5 mi.) long and 2.4 km. (1.5 mi.) wide, was the Gibraltar of the east. It was stocked to feed 10,000 men for a six-month siege, was heavily fortified, and had an intricate tunnel system which protected vulnerable elements such as the hospital from air attack. Along with three other, smaller, fortified islands nearby, its position in Manila Bay denied to the Japanese the use of the finest harbour in the Orient.

Heavy Japanese air raids and artillery fire damaged Corregidor's surface installations, but caused no critical damage or excessive casualties. But after Bataan fell, on 9 April 1942, Japanese artillery massed there, and almost constant air raids destroyed beach defences and all but three of the guns. So intense was the bombardment that the island's topography was altered: cliffs collapsed, woods were obliterated, and the shore road was blown into the sea. The island lay 'scorched, gaunt, and leafless', when men of Homma's 4th Division landed there on the night of 5 May. In fact the assault miscarried and only about 800 men out of 2,000 reached the shore, but these established a beachhead, tanks and artillery were landed, and the 11,000-strong garrison suffered heavy casualties. By morning the Japanese were almost into the tunnel system, which held 1,000 wounded, and Wainwright surrendered.

Corsica, French Mediterranean island occupied by the Italians in November 1942. On 11 September 1943, after Italy had surrendered, the Germans began transferring their garrison from Sardinia there and on 15 September an *SOE-trained French battalion landed at Ajaccio to help the Italian garrison (7th Army Corps) and the 20,000-strong local *maquis, harass the Germans. By then Hitler had already ordered the evacuation of Corsica, too, which took place from the port of Bastia. The German defensive line was pierced there on the night of 29/30 September, during which action the Germans killed 500 Italian troops, but their withdrawal was completed on 4 October.

COSSAC, acronym derived from the title Chief of Staff to the Supreme Allied Commander, a position held initially by Lt-General Frederick Morgan. It was also commonly used as the name for the organization headed by Morgan.

The decision to appoint a chief of staff was taken at the Casablanca conference in January 1943 (see SYMBOL) so that planning for an invasion of the Continent in 1944 could proceed, and the nucleus of an operational HQ could be established for the Supreme Commander designate. Morgan was appointed in March and set up his HQ in Norfolk House, St James's Square, in central London, with an Anglo-US staff. His directive called for him not only to plan the invasion, but for his Ops B section to implement a *deception scheme (COCKADE) that would keep the Germans alert for landings in 1943. Three such schemes were operated as part of COCKADE: landings on the Brest peninsula (WADHAM), an attack on Norway from Scotland (TINDALL), and landings in the Pas-de-Calais (STARKEY). Morgan also had to prepare plans

(RANKIN) to invade immediately if the circumstances merited it.

COSSAC's outline plan to land in Normandy (see OVERLORD) was approved at the Quebec conference in August 1943 (see QUADRANT) and the detailed planning for it was then passed to the staff of the commanders of land, air, and sea forces taking part. Morgan, who was given increased powers, now became the driving force for OVERLORD, and for the many tasks related to it. These included such matters as intelligence, *subversive warfare, *meteorological intelligence, the preparation of prefabricated harbours (the *MULBERRIES), the installation of cross-Channel fuel lines (see PLUTO), and civil affairs. The last of these caused such heated discussions between London and Washington that Morgan remarked that 'there were plenty of affairs but the difficulty was to keep them civil'.

In December 1943 *Eisenhower was appointed Supreme Commander. As he wanted Lt-General Bedell *Smith as his chief of staff, Morgan became one of Smith's three deputies at Eisenhower's Supreme Headquarters Allied Expeditionary Force (see SHAEF) which absorbed nearly all COSSAC's staff when it was formed in February 1944. Morgan, Eisenhower later wrote, made D-Day possible.

Morgan, F. E., *Prelude to Overlord* (London, 1950).

Cossacks, see SOVIET EXILES AT WAR.

Costa Rica declared war on the Axis powers in December 1941 and was the first American state to declare war on Japan, anticipating the declaration of the USA by a few hours. It was one of the original signatories of the *United Nations Declaration. The USA established an emergency air base there. See also LATIN AMERICA.

Counter Intelligence Corps (CIC). US Army counter-espionage and security organization which, until 1 January 1942, was called the Corps of Intelligence Police. It was the American equivalent of the British Field Security Police and there were detachments in every US theatre of operations. Its name became widely known during the 1980s when it was revealed that after the war it had employed Klaus *Barbie.

Courland Peninsula. (see Map 24). This part of Latvia became an enclave for German forces during the last months of the *German–Soviet war.

By the summer of 1944 the Baltic States were becoming a strategic backwater, but they remained significant to Stalin's war aims and what was left of Hitler's. Wanting to legitimize by conquest Soviet possession of the area, which he had seized in 1940 as a result of the *Nazi–Soviet Pact of August 1939, Stalin had attached two of his three Baltic *fronts* (army groups) to the first phase of the summer offensive, although it was aimed south-westwards towards Warsaw and Berlin. Marshal *Vasilevsky co-ordinated the Baltic *fronts*, turning them north-eastwards against German Army Group North, which still occupied Latvia and Estonia. Hitler, engaged in convincing himself that the alliance against him was about to break up and Stalin would then offer terms, dismissed two commanding generals of Army Group North during July, when they argued that their 400,000 troops could not hold its 506 km. (400 mi.) line that stretched north to the River Narva 100 km. (62 mi.) west of Leningrad, and finally called in General *Schörner, a specialist in last-ditch battles.

First Baltic *front*, having by then covered close to 500 km. (310 mi.), broke through to the Baltic coast west of Riga on 31 July. This feat resulted in the *front* commander, General I. Kh. Bagramyan, being made a Hero of the Soviet Union (see DECORATIONS), but Schörner counter-attacked in mid-August and opened a corridor 35 km. (22 mi.) wide along the coast. Vasilevsky thereupon paused a month to regroup and rebuild. On 14 September, when the Baltic *fronts* plus Leningrad Front, under Marshal *Govorov, resumed the offensive with a superiority of 2:1 in troops, nearly 3:1 in armour, and over 6:1 in aircraft, Schörner, realizing at once that the odds were hopeless even for him, proposed a phased withdrawal. Hitler, claiming that Stalin had put out peace feelers, jeopardized the front in Estonia by withholding his approval for four days.

Aware by the end of the month that Schörner would be able to hold the corridor east of Riga long enough to get his troops through, Vasilevsky ordered Bagramyan to redeploy his armour for a thrust due west towards Klaipeda (Memel) on the Lithuanian coast. Schörner's rearguard cleared the corridor on 13 October, but the army group was isolated in Courland, Soviet tanks having reached the coast north of Klaipeda the day before. Nevertheless, the army group's position was much improved as the open sea on the west and the Bay of Riga on the east protected the flanks and rear of its 170 km. (105 mi.) front. On the Soviet side, Vasilevsky returned to his regular duties as chief of the General Staff; Headquarters, Third Baltic *front* was taken out; and Govorov took over the co-ordination of the three remaining *fronts*.

Schörner proposed to open another corridor as soon as he could be resupplied, but on 16 October, three Soviet armies attacking his neighbour, Army Group Centre to the south, drove across the East Prussian border and sent a psychological shockwave through Germany. Thereafter, far from getting help himself, Schörner had to give up several divisions to help regain the lost German soil.

By November, the Klaipeda gap had opened to 160 km. (99 mi.), too great a distance for Schörner to have crossed without abandoning Courland, which Hitler would not have countenanced in any case. In early January 1945, Hitler refused to let the General Staff evacuate the army group, which then still had well over 300,000 troops, to strengthen German defences against the impending Soviet Vistula–Oder offensive. He contended there would be no gain because a greater number of Soviet troops

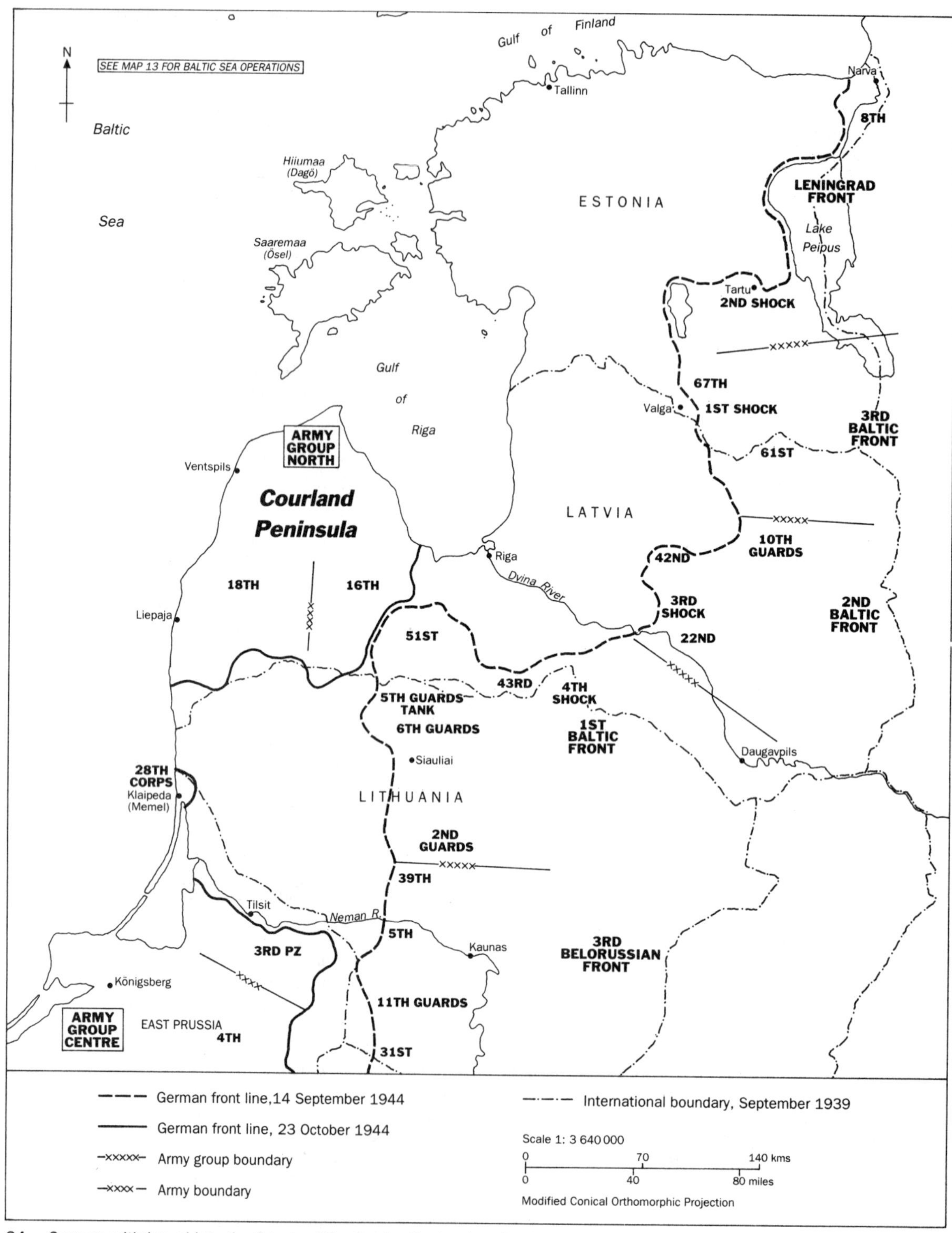

24. German withdrawal into the **Courland Peninsula**, September–October 1944

would be freed. However, disasters on the approaches to Berlin late in the month compelled him to take out divisions—and to replace Schörner with General Lothar Rendulic and transfer Schörner to the main front.

Stalin gave an ironic validity to Hitler's contention. Determined to destroy Army Group Courland (as it was renamed in January 1945) before the war's fast approaching end arrived, he ordered massive two-week-long attacks in January, February, and March, but none succeeded in more than denting the German line. In April, Hitler told the new army group commander, General Karl Hilpert, who had just relieved Rendulic, that he would have to hold out 'until the turn that has occurred in every war has taken place.' By then, Stalin was wholly engrossed in what he took to be a race with his western Allies for possession of Berlin. Between 1 May, the day after Hitler's suicide, and the afternoon of 8 May, when a surrender to Marshal Govorov took effect, German naval vessels evacuated 18,000 men. Hilpert, 41 other generals, and 189,000 officers and troops became Soviet *prisoners-of-war. EARL ZIEMKE

Coventry, industrial city in the British midlands attacked on the night of 14/15 November 1940 by German bombers employing, for the first time, their *Pathfinder Force, KG100, and the X-Gerät beam system (see Map 29) for finding their target (see ELECTRONIC NAVIGATION SYSTEMS).

*ULTRA intelligence and prisoner-of-war information forewarned the British of a major Luftwaffe operation (MOONLIGHT SONATA) against a number of their cities. These included Birmingham, Coventry, and Wolverhampton, but the information was not correlated and there were also indications that the targets might be in London and the south of England. In any case, it was impossible to tell which would be attacked first and the *ENIGMA signals giving their direction to the stations emitting them were not broken in time. By 1500 on the day of the raid the beams were found to intersect over Coventry, but electronic counter-measures (see ELECTRONIC WARFARE) failed to work as the jammers were incorrectly set. The fact that Coventry was to be the target that night was passed on to RAF Fighter Command but 'British counter-measures proved ineffective: of the 509 bombers the German Air Force dispatched to Coventry, 449 reached the target and only one was certainly destroyed' (F. H. Hinsley, *British Intelligence in the Second World War*, Vol. 1, London, 1979, p. 318). This failure probably hastened the scheduled departure of *Dowding from Fighter Command and from it grew the myth that Coventry was left to the mercy of the Luftwaffe in order to protect the secret of ULTRA.

Twelve armaments factories and much of the city centre, including the 14th-century cathedral, were destroyed, and 380 people were killed and 865 injured.

Cowra prison camp, *prisoner-of-war (POW) compound established in New South Wales, Australia, where in August 1944 about half the 2,223 Japanese POW in Australia were being held. According to an Australian officer at Cowra, the Japanese did not understand the *Geneva Convention and were amused by the humane treatment accorded them under its terms. It convinced them, the officer said, that the Australians were morally and spiritually weak, and on the night of 4/5 August 1944 several hundred broke out of the camp. A total of 234 Japanese were killed or died by their own hand and a further 108 were wounded. Three Australian guards were killed and another three wounded before order was restored and the Japanese recaptured.

Crerar, General Henry (1888–1965), Canadian artillery officer who as a lt-general was appointed Chief of the Canadian General Staff in 1941. He was therefore responsible for the dispatch of Canadian troops to *Hong Kong just before its fall and for the difficult task of expanding the Canadian Army at a time when there was considerable controversy over conscription (see CANADA, 3).

In 1942 he was appointed to command the 2nd Canadian Division and the following year briefly commanded the 1st Canadian Corps fighting in the *Italian campaign. When *McNaughton was recalled to Canada at the end of 1943, Crerar was appointed C-in-C of the First Canadian Army in his place, and in this capacity led it in the *Normandy campaign as part of *Montgomery's Twenty-First Army Group. Montgomery was not impressed with him and when, on one occasion, Crerar was unable to attend an important conference, Montgomery threatened to dismiss him, which he had no power to do. Early in the critical 85-day *Scheldt Estuary battle, which started in September 1944, Crerar had to go to the UK for medical treatment and he was replaced by *Simonds, the 2nd Canadian Corps commander, whose reputation stood high with Montgomery. But Crerar returned, was promoted general in November 1944, and led his army, which included American, Belgian, British, and Polish troops as well as Canadians, in some of the most crucial operations during the battle for *Germany.

Crete, battle for, fought on this Greek island (see Map 25) in May 1941 between German paratroopers and Allied troops who had retreated there after the *Balkan campaign. The battle began on 20 May when airborne troops of General *Student's Fliegerkorps 11 began landing at both ends of the island.

It was hoped to hold Crete as a possible base from which to bomb the Romanian oilfields at *Ploesti, but the island's geography made a strong defence of it almost impossible. Most of the 35,000-strong British, Commonwealth, and Greek garrison had just escaped from Greece. It was not a single, coherent formation and was only lightly armed. Transport, artillery, and signals equipment were scarce or non-existent, while RAF

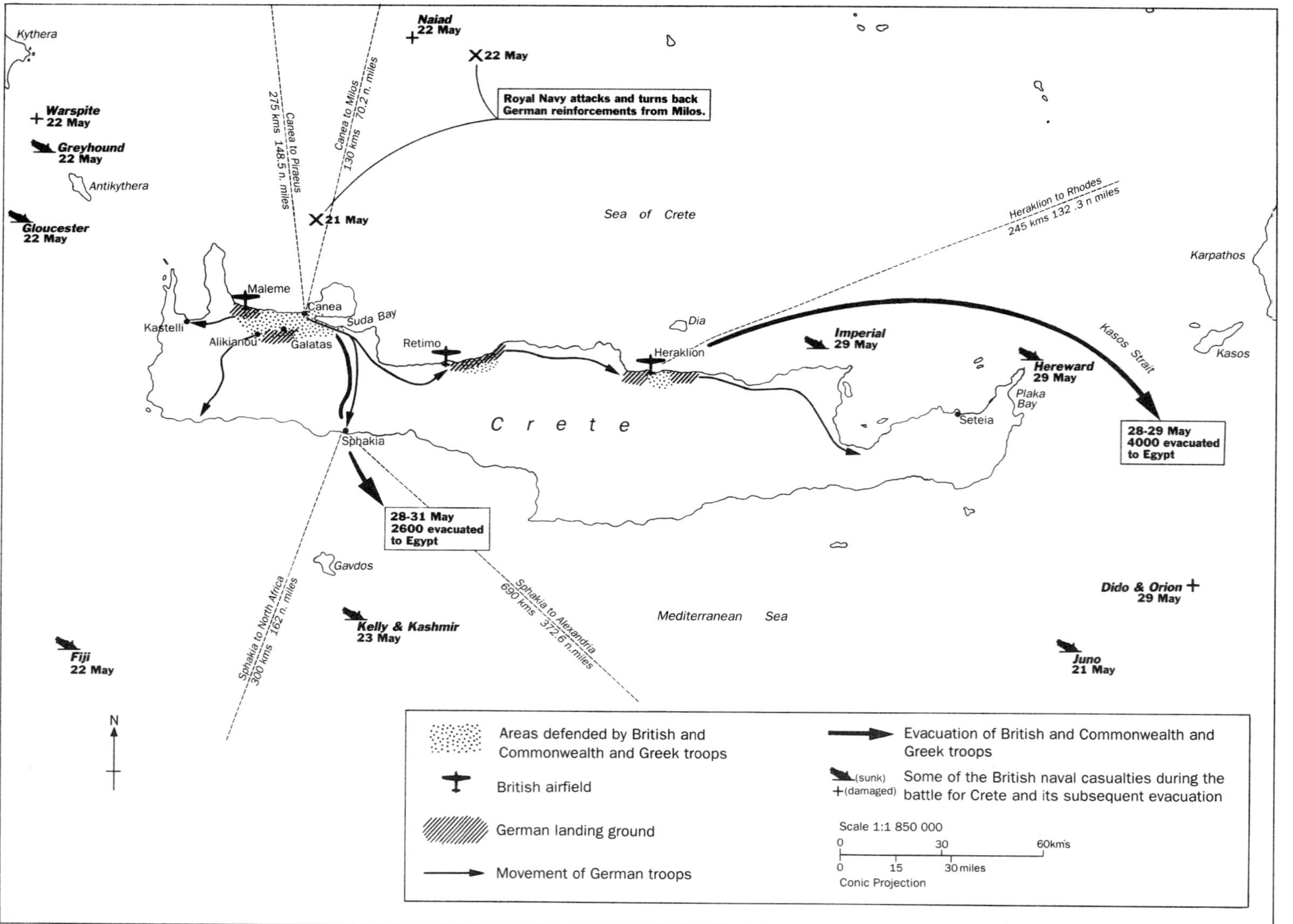

25. Battle for **Crete**, May 1941

Battle for Crete: German forces landed on Crete 20–23 May 1941

May	*Maleme Galatas Suda Bay*	*Retimo*	*Heraklion*	*Total*
20	6,030	1,500	2,000	9,530
21	1,880	0	120	2,000
22	1,950	0	0	1,950
23	3,650	0	400	4,050
TOTAL	13,510	1,500	2,520	17,530

Source: Freyberg, P., *Bernard Freyberg VC* (London, 1991).

support had been reduced to a handful of aircraft which exposed British warships to German dive-bombers.

The appreciation by the Joint Intelligence Committee (see UK, 8) foresaw an equally balanced German assault from both the air and the sea and the island's commander, Lt-General *Freyberg, made his dispositions accordingly and as best as his scanty resources allowed. However, the German plan (MERKUR), which was not part of the Germans' original operation for occupying Greece, depended on the airfields at Maleme, Heraklion, and Retimo being taken immediately, so that mountain troops could be landed, with reinforcements being sent by sea from the island of Milos. It nearly failed, for the Germans had wildly underestimated the garrison's strength and *ULTRA intelligence, which 'rarely gave so complete and accurate a forecast again' (R. Bennett, *Ultra and Mediterranean Strategy, 1941–1945*, London, 1989, p. 56), revealed in good time details of the plan. In particular, it showed that Freyberg's thinly-spread defences were inadequate to hold Maleme airfield.

Contrary to what some historians have written, Freyberg's biographer states that the general was privy to ULTRA; and that, as the success of MERKUR depended on seizing the airfields, he wanted the defences of Maleme airfield reinforced, but was expressly forbidden from doing so to prevent any possibility of the ULTRA secret's being compromised (see P. Freyberg, *Bernard Freyberg VC*, London, 1991). Consequently, the airfield was seized on 21 May, and a mountain regiment was then landed there. Although air and sea attacks dispersed or sank the German reinforcements sent from Milos, and the defences at Heraklion and Retimo caused heavy casualties, the loss of Maleme airfield proved crucial. A delayed counter-attack failed to recapture it and German air reinforcements were then quickly increased (see Table). As pressure on the perimeter around Canea mounted the situation deteriorated rapidly and on 26 May Freyberg reported that his position was hopeless. The next afternoon, after permission had been granted to evacuate, he ordered a retreat to Sphakia on the opposite side of the island. The defenders around Heraklion were evacuated by British warships without incident, but those holding Retimo airfield could not be contacted and eventually had to surrender.

Luftwaffe air attacks wreaked havoc during the evacuation around Sphakia. In fact, so severe were naval losses—three cruisers and six destroyers sunk, seventeen other ships damaged—that the evacuation had to be abandoned after the night of 30 May, and 5,000 men were left behind. Most of these were captured. A few joined the Cretan resistance. This continued, with help from *SOE, to harass the occupying forces (which included the kidnapping of a German general) until the Germans withdrew in 1944. Until Italy surrendered in September 1943, the Italians occupied the eastern provinces of Siteia and Lasitho. The Germans occupied the rest of the island.

British and Commonwealth troop losses on Crete amounted to 1,742 killed and missing, 2,225 wounded, and 11,370 captured, while the Royal Navy had 2,000 men killed and 183 wounded. But the Germans, too, had been badly mauled. Their casualties, estimated at about 7,000 killed, were so severe that they never again mounted a major airborne operation against enemy-occupied territory.

Kokonas, N., *The Cretan Resistance, 1941–1945* (London, 1993).
Macdonald, C., *The Lost Battle: Crete 1941* (London, 1993).
Psychoundakis, G., *The Cretan Runner* (London, 1955).

Crimean landings, see BLACK SEA.

Cripps, Sir (Richard) Stafford (1889–1952), British lawyer and Labour politician who served as ambassador to the USSR from 1940 to 1942 before returning to become Lord Privy Seal and a member of the war cabinet. During 1942, in which he headed a mission to India to negotiate that country's post-war independence, Cripps began to have doubts about the higher direction of the war. His proposal to form a war planning directorate was really a criticism of Churchill, who later called the proposed body 'a disembodied Brains Trust'. He would have nothing to do with it; Cripps resigned, and was replaced by *Morrison.

Cripps's cold manner, dogmatic socialism, and austere disposition did not endear him to everyone, least of all to Churchill, but he had a brilliant brain, and was too valuable to lose. Churchill persuaded him to become minister of aircraft production, a post he retained until the end of the war. He was knighted in 1930.

Croatia, see YUGOSLAVIA.

Cuba, a Caribbean island, had been independent since 1902, but the USA retained naval bases there and reserved the right to intervene in Cuban domestic affairs. Under President Fulgencio Batista (1901–73), who ruled the country from 1940 to 1944, it declared war on Japan (9 December 1941) and on Germany and Italy (11 December 1941), and took various anti-Axis measures. This included the capture of a German agent, Heinz Luning, the only spy to be executed in *Latin America during the war. In August 1942 compulsory registration for military service began but no one was sent overseas. Cuba exported tobacco, sugar, and coffee to the USA, and additional US bases were established there. See also CARIBBEAN AT WAR.

culture, see under culture section of major powers.

Cunningham, Lt-General Sir Alan (1887–1983), British Army officer, younger brother of Admiral *Cunningham, and from November 1940 commander of the British forces in Kenya which in 1941 helped win the *East African campaign. In August 1941 he was appointed commander of the British and Commonwealth Eighth Army, newly formed to fight *Rommel in the *Western Desert campaigns. But following the launch of the British CRUSADER offensive in November 1941, which provoked the hard-fought *Sidi Rezegh battles, he was dismissed when the C-in-C Middle East, General *Auchinleck, was forced to intervene personally. He spent the rest of the war in administrative posts. He was knighted in 1941.

Cunningham, Admiral Sir Andrew B. (1883–1963), British naval officer who, from October 1943, served as First Sea Lord and as a member of the British *Chiefs of Staff and the *Combined Chiefs of Staff committees.

In September 1939 Cunningham, as an acting admiral, was C-in-C of the British Mediterranean Fleet. From the outset his policy was to maintain British naval supremacy, a crucial factor in winning the battle for the *Mediterranean. His air strike at the Italian fleet in *Taranto in November 1940 was a master stroke and whenever possible he brought the more powerful Italian Navy to battle and invariably bested it, notably at *Cape Matapan. With the entry of German *air power into the Mediterranean theatre he suffered severe losses, particularly during the evacuation of *Crete and in the siege of *Malta. In January 1941 he was confirmed in his rank and from June to October 1942 he served in Washington as head of the British Admiralty delegation. But staff work was not his forte and he was pleased to be appointed Allied Naval Commander Expeditionary Force for the *North African campaign landings in November 1942. In January 1943 he was promoted admiral of the fleet and appointed C-in-C Mediterranean, serving as the Allied Naval Commander for the *Sicilian campaign landings in July 1943 and at *Salerno that September. The Italian *armistice, which coincided with Salerno, was the occasion for his most famous signal to the Admiralty: 'Be pleased to inform their Lordships that the Italian battle fleet now lies at anchor beneath the guns of the fortress of Malta.'

After *Pound's death Cunningham was appointed First Sea Lord and it was in no small measure due to him that NEPTUNE, the assault phase of the Normandy landings (see OVERLORD), was successfully mounted in June 1944; also under his aegis a British fleet, the largest ever assembled, operated in the *Pacific war (see TASK FORCE 57).

Affectionately known by his initials 'ABC', Cunningham was the very picture of a fighting admiral, with piercing blue eyes, ruddy complexion, and an infallible memory for old shipmates. He was a man of indomitable spirit; when, during the evacuation of Crete, one of his staff remarked that fighting the Luftwaffe was like butting one's head against a wall, he replied: 'What you have forgotten, you miserable undertaker, is that you may be loosening a brick.' He was knighted in 1939. In September 1945 he was raised to the peerage, and retired the following March. See also SEA POWER.

Cunningham of Hyndhope, *A Sailor's Odyssey* (London, 1951).

Curtin, John (1885–1945), Australian Labour politician who was federal prime minister from October 1941 until his death in July 1945.

Leader of his party from 1935, Curtin nearly won the general election of 1940, though he himself was only saved from defeat in his Fremantle constituency by a parcel of votes sent by Australian troops fighting in the *Western Desert campaigns. In October 1941 *Fadden's coalition government was defeated and Curtin became prime minister, though Labour lacked a majority in the Senate and largely relied upon the votes of independent members for a majority in the House of Representatives. In June 1943 Curtin defeated a motion of censure by just a single vote and until the general election that October, in which his party won a large overall majority, he had his difficulties in retaining power. Many of his problems derived from his own party as much as from the opposition, some feeling he was betraying fundamental socialist principles for a doubtful greater good. During the *First World War Curtin had risked imprisonment when he had opposed conscription. As prime minister, his fiercest political battle came in January 1943 when anti-conscription members of his party opposed his proposal to use Australian conscripts in the *New Guinea campaign, but he won in the end. Two months later, when there were strikes on the Sydney wharves he threatened the dockers with the call-up if they did not return to work.

But though his domestic politics were sometimes fraught, his guidance of his country at a critical period in its history was firm and forthright. In his New Year's message of 1942 he stated that 'without any inhibitions of any kind, I make it quite clear that Australia looks to America, free of any pangs as to our traditional links or kinship with the United Kingdom. We know the problems with which the United Kingdom is faced; we know too that Australia can go and Britain can still hold on.' When this caused some consternation he also made plain Australia's and his own loyalty to the Crown which he described as being 'at the very core' of the country's being.

In February 1942 he ordered total mobilization of all Australia's resources for war and by April had fought for, and obtained, what he hoped would be Australian participation in the higher direction of the war through membership of the *Pacific War Council. He had also, rightly, opposed Churchill by insisting on the return of Australian troops from the Middle East, and negotiated a close association with the USA in prosecution of the war. Little known at first outside Australia, Curtin commanded immediate attention when he participated in the *Commonwealth prime ministers' conference in March 1944. See also AUSTRALIA, 3.

Curzon Line, see POLISH–SOVIET FRONTIER.

Cyprus. This eastern Mediterranean island, under British protection from 1878 and a British colony from 1925, was used mainly for training and resting Allied troops, as a base for aircraft covering convoys, and for small operations against the Aegean Islands.

Cyrenaica, eastern province of the Italian colony of Libya. See WESTERN DESERT CAMPAIGNS.

Czechoslovakia, democratic republic which in 1938 had a population of over 14 million. This was made up of 10 million Czechs and Slovaks, and some 3 million Germans (see VOLKSDEUTSCHE), the balance being Hungarian (700,000), Polish (60,000), and Ukrainian (500,000) minorities. The German population, called Sudeten Germans, were largely a geographically compact group occupying the country's western, northern, and southern rim whose land, Sudetenland, had been given by the *Versailles settlement of 1919 to Czechoslovakia, a new state which had been carved out of the remains of the Austro-Hungarian empire after the *First World War. Despite its disparate people. Czechoslovakia was a working democracy that contained one of Europe's most important armaments industries. But the *Munich agreement, and other factors, had undermined the will of its million-strong, relatively well-equipped army to resist when the Germans occupied the rump of the country in March 1939.

For Czechoslovakia, the Second World War effectively began with the signing of the Munich agreement in September 1938, when Britain, France, Germany, and Italy called for the cession of the Sudetenland to German control. The Czech government, under the leadership of President Edvard *Beneš, accepted this crowning act of the British and French diplomacy of appeasement rather than resist the dismemberment of Czechoslovakia.

The territorial changes in the months following the Munich agreement were considerable. In the west, Sudetenland proper, with its heavily fortified borders, was incorporated into Germany while Poland seized the small industrial and mining border district of *Teschen (Těšín in Czech, Cieszyn in Polish), where the Polish minority lived. In the east, Slovakia, ruled by the Slovak People's Party, became a vassal state of Germany; Hungary acquired pieces of southern Slovakia and Ruthenia; all that remained of Czechoslovakia was Bohemia and Moravia which was occupied by the Wehrmacht on 15 March 1939 (see Map C). Hitler then established the Protectorate of Bohemia and Moravia with Baron von *Neurath named the Reichsprotektor. This retained the Czech governmental institutions but subordinated them to German administrators. After the Czech Army was disbanded, Dr Emil Hácha, the powerless president, was allowed a small militia for ceremonial purposes.

The German occupation of the Czech lands was considerably less harsh than the treatment meted out to Poland, the USSR and Yugoslavia. In Czech society it was the middle class which bore the brunt of Nazi persecution while the Jews became victims of the *Final Solution. German policy was to court industrial workers and peasants who generally benefited from better wages and market conditions. The German authorities allowed one political organization the Narodni Sourucenstvi (National Co-operation) headed by General Rudolf Gajda, a Czech fascist.

Protests against German rule occurred as early as October 1939. On the anniversary of the independence of Czechoslovakia, university students took to the streets in Prague. This act of defiance led to the closure of Czech universities and the execution of nine students. Organized *resistance against the German occupation was slow to develop and it was not until early 1940 that disparate underground organizations were merged into the ÚVOD—Ústředni vedení odboje domácího, or Central Leadership of Home Resistance. The most spectacular act of resistance was the assassination of Reinhard *Heydrich who had replaced von Neurath and German reprisals for his death resulted in the destruction of the villages of *Lidiče and Ležáky with almost all their populations.

Despite the assassination of Heydrich, and the increasing burden of oppression borne by the Czech people, the level of resistance was relatively low. The Czech underground organization was more important for the intelligence it provided the Allies than for its active resistance to the Nazi occupation. But in May 1945 the *Prague rising helped the advancing Red Army enter the Czech capital.

The less oppressive character of occupation in the Czech lands was not the product of any German benevolence but simply a means to the end of maximizing economic exploitation of Bohemia and Moravia. Long-term German plans envisaged the deportation and elimination of the bulk of the Czech population. During the war, more than 350,000 people perished as a result of Nazi oppression.

However, the Czechs' political and military activity conducted abroad played a crucial role in keeping alive the idea of a Czechoslovak state. In October 1938, Beneš went abroad with the view of launching a Czechoslovak political organization when suitable circumstances arose. With the outbreak of war in September 1939 Beneš formed the Czechoslovak National Committee in Paris which received French and British official endorsement in October–November 1939. The fall of *France in June 1940 led to the transfer of Beneš's political activities to London and by the summer of 1941 he was leading a Provisional government of Czechoslovakia which received full recognition from the Allied powers.

The diplomacy of Beneš aimed at the re-establishment of Czechoslovakia after the war. A major success was the British and Free French repudiation in August–September 1942 of the Munich agreement and its territorial changes. Beneš also made some half-hearted attempts at confederation with Poland in 1942 until Soviet objections put an end to this project.

Relations with the USSR were the centrepiece of Beneš's foreign policy. In general, he mistrusted the western powers after Munich and wanted to ensure Czechoslovakia's security through an alliance with the Soviet Union and to this end he signed a *Czech–Soviet Treaty of Alliance on 18 July 1941. Beneš understood that the only way he could return to Czechoslovakia lay in co-operation with Stalin. He reckoned that his return would ensure the preservation of democracy, but in the end he miscalculated, just as he had at the time of the Munich crisis.

Czechoslovak military activity abroad consisted of air and land forces formed in the UK and the Soviet Union. In the UK, a Czechoslovak armoured brigade exceeding 5,000 men was formed which served in the *Normandy campaign. Four Czech squadrons flew with the RAF: Nos. 310, 312, and 313 were equipped with fighters, while No. 311 was a bomber squadron. The transfer of important members of the Czechoslovak intelligence service in 1939 to London proved to be among the most valuable military contributions to the Allied war effort (see THÜMMEL, for example).

As a result of the Soviet–Czechoslovak rapprochement in 1941, military units were formed on Soviet territory, (see SVOBODA). By the summer of 1943, the First Czechoslovak Parachute Brigade had been formed there and numbered approximately 2,500 men, most of whom were Ukrainians from Czechoslovakia. In 1944, a Second Czechoslovak Parachute Brigade was formed from captured Slovak *prisoners-of-war and saw action in the Slovak rising in August 1944 (see SLOVAKIA). Czechoslovak army units in the USSR eventually evolved into the 1st Czechoslovak Army Corps which distinguished itself in bloody fighting to force the Dukla Pass in Soviet operations to cross the Carpathians. Complementing the army units was the 1st Czechoslovak Fighter Regiment which also saw action in the Slovak rising and eventually evolved into the 1st Czechoslovak Air Division.

PAUL LATAWSKI

Korbel, J., *Twentieth Century Czechoslovakia: The Meanings of Its History* (New York, 1977).
Kulka, E., *Jews in Svoboda's Army in the Soviet Union: Czechoslovak Jewry's Fight Against the Nazis During World War II* (New York, 1987).
Mastny, V., *The Czechs Under Nazi Rule: The Failure of National Resistance 1939–1942* (New York, 1971).
Seton-Watson, H., *The East European Revolution* (New York, 1968).

Czech–Soviet Treaty of Alliance, concluded in July 1941 when the Soviet government recognized the Czech *government-in-exile of *Beneš and, along with the UK and USA, conferred on Czechoslovakia the status of an Allied fighting power. A military agreement followed in September 1941 in which the Soviet government granted funds to arm and maintain Colonel *Svoboda's Czech forces in the USSR. A treaty of friendship, mutual assistance, and post-war co-operation was also concluded in December 1943.

D

Dachau, 19 km. (12 mi.) north of Munich, was one of the first Nazi *concentration camps, opened in March 1933 as a correction camp. Of the 225,000 said to have been incarcerated there between 1933 and 1945, 31,950 are officially said to have died but the total was almost certainly more. When liberated it was found to contain such well-known personalities as the Austrian Chancellor Kurt von Schuschnigg, as well as prominent Germans such as *Halder, *Schacht, and *Niemöller. In November 1945 a *war crimes trial of the commandant, 40 guards, and one doctor, was held in the camp, and those responsible for the *Malmédy massacre were also tried there. About 500 medical experiments were carried out on inmates in 1941 and 1942. They included malaria trials and experiments on the reaction of a person being immersed in cold water for long periods.

Dakar expedition. After the fall of *France in June 1940 the possibility that the Germans might threaten British *convoys routed via the Cape of Good Hope, by establishing themselves in this French West African port, alarmed the British. Various preventive measures were discussed, and an Anglo-French expedition was proposed which would first land Free French troops around the port, in the hope that they would not be opposed by the forces of the *Vichy French government holding it. Maj-General N. Irwin was appointed the expedition's land commander and Vice-Admiral John Cunningham its sea commander.

Although intelligence—which was otherwise inaccurate or non-existent—indicated that de *Gaulle, who accompanied the expedition, would not be welcome, 4,200 British and 2,700 Free French troops left Liverpool on 31 August 1940. While the expedition was at sea a Vichy French cruiser squadron slipped unopposed out of the Mediterranean (see NORTH, ADMIRAL). Its mission was to support Vichy forces in *Gabon and to return the French Cameroons to the Vichy fold, but en route it put in to Dakar causing great consternation. Churchill wanted to cancel the operation, but was dissuaded from doing so by the commanders on the spot. The Vichy squadron tried to leave on 19 September, before the operation began, but was chased by Allied warships. Two cruisers managed to return to Dakar, two others were escorted to Casablanca.

Instead of the imposing armada that Churchill had imagined Dakar residents would wake to, fog blanketed the area when the operation was launched on the morning of 23 September. Free French officers were landed by air and boat to negotiate the port's peaceful transfer, but they received a hostile response as did an advance landing party. The battleship *Richelieu* and the port's batteries opened fire, badly damaging a British cruiser and an old battleship. Desultory firing continued for two days amid fog, smokescreens, and increasing confusion, before the operation was eventually abandoned.

Breaches of security in London by the Free French had alerted the Vichy government to the expedition, but its ultimate destination had remained unknown. However, a broadcast by de Gaulle as the Allied force arrived off the port gave Dakar's governor-general plenty of warning. There is no truth in the story that the governor, down to his last few rounds of ammunition, was drafting a surrender letter when the expedition withdrew. If it had been true, it would be difficult to know whether it would have completed, as the historian F. H. Hinsley has succinctly commented (in *British Intelligence in the Second World War*, Vol. 1, London, 1979, p. 158), 'a tale of avoidable errors or closed a list of unavoidable misfortunes'.

Marder, A., *Operation 'Menace' and the Dudley North Affair* (Oxford, 1976).

Daladier, Edouard (1884–1970), French politician who became a radical socialist deputy for his native Vaucluse after the *First World War. In 1933 he became prime minister for the first time and was serving in that position for the third time when, with *Chamberlain, he signed the *Munich agreement in September 1938. His government's failure to support the Finns in the *Finnish–Soviet war led to his resignation in March 1940, but he then served as minister of war, and later as minister for foreign affairs, when *Reynaud succeeded him. In August 1940 he was arrested by the *Vichy French regime and interned in a fortress in the Pyrenees. At the *Riom trial in February 1942 he was arraigned with others on charges of 'causing the defeat of France'. The trial was discontinued but he was still kept in prison—first in Vichy France and, from April 1943, in a *concentration camp. He was one of the few Third Republic politicians who was able to pursue a post-war career in politics but never again held any post of prominence. See also FRANCE, 3(a).

Dalmatian Islands. Situated off Yugoslavia's Adriatic coastline, the larger ones were garrisoned by Italian troops after the end of the *Balkan campaign in April 1941 and were taken over by the Germans after Italy surrendered in September 1943. One of the exceptions, *Vis, became an Allied stronghold.

Dalton, (Edward) Hugh (1887–1962), British Labour politician who served as minister of economic warfare in Churchill's coalition government which involved him in forming *SOE. In February 1942 he became president of the board of trade and did much to improve the coal industry and ease the fuel crisis.

Daluege, Kurt (1897–1946), *SS and police Obergruppenführer (general) and an early Nazi supporter. In June 1936 he was appointed to head the newly formed

*Orpo, which incorporated the state uniformed police and which he thoroughly Nazified. Known within the SS for his stupidity—his nickname was 'Dumm-Dummi'—he was appointed deputy Reichsprotektor of Bohemia and Moravia in May 1942 after *Heydrich's assassination. *Neurath, who was still officially Reichsprotektor, resigned in August 1943, and the same month Daluege was replaced by *Frick. After the war he was executed by the Czechs for his involvement in the *Lidiče massacre.

Dam Busters, nickname of the RAF's 617 Squadron, an élite unit formed in March 1943 to breach dams in the Ruhr, Germany's primary industrial area. The Möhne and Sorpe provided a large proportion of the Ruhr's water needs while the Eder, the largest target, helped maintain the navigable waters of the river Weser and Mittelland Canal. To destroy them a canister-shaped bomb was invented by Barnes *Wallis that had to be dropped only 18 m. (60 ft.) above the water. It then bounced on the water to reach its target and rolled down the dam's wall before exploding.

The raid was mounted on the night of 16/17 May 1943. Eight of the nineteen participating bombers were lost and their commander, Wing-Commander Guy Gibson, was later awarded the Victoria Cross (see DECORATIONS). The Möhne and Eder dams were breached, but the Sorpe was not. Though there was much flooding and dislocation of civilian life, industry in the Ruhr was hardly affected and by October the dams had been repaired.

Wallis's bomb was never used again but, with its reputation for *precision bombing established, the squadron, using special *Tallboy bombs, was later employed in raids against the German battleship *Tirpitz* and other targets. See also AIR POWER and BOMBS.

Brickhill, P., *The Dam Busters* (rev. edn., London, 1977).
Cooper, A., *The Men who Breached the Dams* (London, 1982).

Dansey, Sir Claude (1876–1947), assistant chief of the British Secret Intelligence Service, *MI6, from 1939 to 1945. He served in intelligence in Africa (1900–9), was recruited into MO5, the forerunner of *MI5, in 1914 and ran English port security, and worked for MI6 on a freelance basis during the 1920s before being appointed head of its Rome station in 1929. In 1936 he was dismissed, ostensibly under a cloud, but really to set up, using commercial cover, the 'Z' Organization. This paralleled MI6's organization on the Continent whose operations Dansey suspected the Germans had penetrated. During the war he acted as the *éminence grise* to the head of MI6, *Menzies. Although he had a great gift for rubbing other secret staff officers up the wrong way, he had several successes in persuading the *governments-in-exile to provide him with *spies in Europe. He also supervised the work of *MI9 and was notorious for his total discretion. He was knighted in 1943. M. R. D. FOOT

Danzig, free city of (Polish: Gdańsk). Area of 1,950 sq. km. (754 sq. mi.) lying astride the estuary of the Vistula basin. Although its geographical location made it historically and economically Poland's natural outlet to the Baltic Sea, its population of 400,000 was overwhelmingly German with only 6% being Polish. It thus became part of Hitler's *casus belli* in launching the *Polish campaign in September 1939.

The *Versailles settlement of 28 June 1919 made it an autonomous political unit, known as the Free City of Danzig (see Map A). This complicated political arrangement transferred the city's sovereignty to the *League of Nations; placed it within Poland's customs frontier and its foreign policy under the control of the Polish government; and provided it with political institutions modelled on the Weimar constitution.

The creation of this city state satisfied neither Germany nor Poland. Danzig's German inhabitants wanted the city to be part of Germany. For both the Weimar Republic and Nazi Germany, it became a central German *irredenta* in the east. For Poland, the denial of outright control of what was its historic outlet to the sea compromised its secure access to the Baltic. The development of Gdynia, a nearby fishing village in the *Polish corridor, into a major Baltic port reflected Polish concerns. A bad political compromise, the creation of the Free City of Danzig provided a flashpoint for German–Polish rivalry and as such helped to precipitate the Second World War. It was occupied at the start of the Polish campaign and incorporated into the Third Reich. PAUL LATAWSKI

Kulski, W. W., *Germany and Poland: From War to Peaceful Relations* (Syracuse, NY, 1976).
Mason, J. B., *The Danzig Dilemma: A Study in Peacemaking by Compromise* (Stanford, Calif., 1946).

Danzig corridor, see POLISH CORRIDOR.

Darlan, Admiral (Jean) François (1881–1942), French naval officer who served as minister of marine and then as foreign minister and vice-premier in the *Vichy government.

Darlan was influential in building up the French Navy between the wars and was promoted admiral (the navy's highest rank) in 1939 when he assumed command of all French naval forces. He supported France's *armistice with Germany, agreed in June 1940, but assured the British that his forces would never fall into German hands. He issued specific instructions for the French fleet to be scuttled should the Germans attempt its seizure, which they eventually did (see FRENCH FLEET, SCUTTLING OF); but the British, doubting Darlan's ability and perhaps his will to keep it out of German hands, seized or sank what ships they could (see MERS-EL-KÉBIR), an action which intensified Darlan's anglophobia.

After serving as minister of marine in *Pétain's first government he became one of the ruling triumvirate before replacing Pierre-Etienne Flandin (1889–1958) as foreign minister in February 1941. He was also appointed vice-premier, minister of information, and minister of the interior while remaining minister of marine; and in August 1941 he added the portfolio of minister of defence to his posts, an accumulation of formal power which not even *Laval, Vichy's arch collaborator, ever achieved. He soon proved as keen as Laval to collaborate with the Germans, and was even more willing to co-operate with them militarily. After meeting Hitler in May 1941 he and the German ambassador, Otto Abetz, initialled the *Paris Protocols which gave the Germans significant military concessions in Africa and the Middle East. Darlan's attempts to obtain better terms from the Germans failed miserably. The protocols remained unratified and Darlan was replaced by Laval in April 1942, though he remained C-in-C of the armed forces and Pétain's official successor.

By chance he was in Algiers when the *North African campaign landings took place on 8 November 1942 and he assumed command of the Vichy French forces opposing them. After extensive negotiations with the Americans, and with his own government, he arranged a general ceasefire on 10 November. He then agreed to work for the Allies and was appointed high commissioner for French North Africa. In performing this *volte face*, wrote an early biographer, 'he betrayed the Germans, he betrayed Pétain, he betrayed France' (G. Mikes, *Darlan: a Study*, London, 1943). In vain did the Vichy government assure the Germans that Darlan was acting illegitimately: Hitler ordered his troops into the unoccupied zone of France and into Tunisia. Darlan was assassinated on Christmas Eve by a young French royalist, who, though trained by *SOE, was not acting on its orders. He was executed two days later.

Coutau-Bégarie, H., and Huan, C., *Darlan* (Paris, 1989).

Darnand, Joseph (1897–1945), French *First World War hero who became an early *prisoner-of-war during the Second World War. He escaped and was made head of the Légion Français de Combattants in the Alpes Maritimes. In the summer of 1941 he instituted the fascist Service d'Ordre Légionnaire whose oath read: 'I swear to struggle against democracy, against de Gaulle and the Free French, and against the Jewish plague.' In January 1943 this organization provided personnel for the French *Milice which helped the Germans in their fight against the *Maquis and other French resistance groups (see also FRANCE, 9). Unlike other *Vichy paramilitary organizations it was allowed to recruit throughout France and the ruthlessness with which it tried to suppress the French resistance soon made it notorious. Darnand, by now an officer in the Waffen-*SS, became the Milice's secretary-general and in February 1944 he was also appointed the Vichy government's secretary of state for internal affairs. He moved with the government to Belfort; then to Sigmaringen in Germany where he was a member of *Doriot's Committee for French Liberation; and finally to Italy where he fought the partisans. After the war he was brought to trial and executed.

Darwin, raid on. Before landing on the *Netherlands East Indies island of Java, on 1 March 1942, the Japanese disrupted the Allied Command's communications and supply route with Australia by raiding this northern Australian port. The strike force—four fleet carriers and an escort force which included two battleships—was under Vice-Admiral *Nagumo, the same officer who had struck at *Pearl Harbor. After arriving in the southern part of the Timor Sea at dawn on 19 February 1942, he launched 71 dive-bombers, 81 torpedo bombers, and 36 fighters against Darwin. These, co-ordinating with 54 bombers based on Japanese occupied territory in the Netherlands East Indies, achieved complete surprise and blew up an Australian troopship and a freighter discharging ammunition. The airport was then destroyed and the town was bombed and machine-gunned, starting several fires, before the raiders concentrated again on the shipping. One US destroyer was sunk and another damaged. Eight other ships were also sunk, many valuable stores and more than 200 lives were lost, and 18 aircraft were destroyed. The raid led to a panic flight of military personnel and civilians into the interior.

Nagumo lost only one aircraft and the Japanese subsequently thought they had used, in the words of Nagumo's biographer, Captain Matsushima Keizō, a sledgehammer to break an egg. Darwin was also subsequently raided on many occasions, but never with such devastating effect.

D-Day, Anglo-American staff term for day of any operation; particularly 6 June 1944, the date of the Allied landings in Normandy (see OVERLORD). D stands for day.

DD tanks, see AMPHIBIANS.

Déat, Marcel (1894–1955), French socialist politician who, after the German occupation of Paris, edited there the pacifist newspaper *L'Œuvre*, in which he initially denounced *Pétain's *Vichy government. However, he was converted to Nazi beliefs and later became a supporter of *Laval, Pétain's prime minister and arch-collaborator. In February 1944 he was appointed the Vichy government's labour minister, but he was so loathed by Pétain that he ran his ministry from Paris. He moved with the government to Sigmaringen in southern Germany and at the end of the war found refuge in an Italian monastery where he remained until his death.

death camps, see OPERATION REINHARD; see also CONCENTRATION CAMPS.

Death's Head Corps (Totenkopfverbände) were *concentration camp guards. Commanded by Theodor Eicke, in November 1939 they were formed into the Tokenkopf Division which became part of the Waffen-*SS.

deception is only a longer word, also from the Latin, for feinting, which is as old as combat and far older than war. The ancient Chinese military strategist, Sun Tzu, laid down long ago in his book *The Art of War* that all war depends on it. Great commanders always use it, casting threats in one direction or several to draw their enemies' reserves away from another, in which they intend to strike. So much is this a matter of routine that when, on 10 January 1940, a German light aircraft force-landed at Malines-sur-Meuse in Belgium, carrying a staff officer who failed to burn properly the draft he had with him of the German plan to strike through the Ardennes for the Channel ports (see FALL GELB), the British and French intelligence staffs took for granted that the papers had been planted on them, and could not possibly be true.

Deception in 1939–45 took the form of ploys run by intelligence staffs, for operational purposes. Their necessary bases lay in sound security, which would keep any deceptive plan secret, coupled with sound intelligence—both about the opposing side's situation, and about his reactions to the plan as it developed. Their object was always to make the other side act, or refrain from action, on some mistaken assumption.

Visual deception—camouflage (derived from the French verb *camoufler*, to make up for the stage)—was common to all the warring nations. Sven Nolan's film *Sieg im Westen* included shots of German soldiers traversing the Ardennes with branches in their steel helmets that became world-famous. Major factories and power stations, all over Europe, were dazzle-painted to confuse pilots making low-level air attacks; so were some warships to confuse U-boat attacks as to the range, course and length of their intended victims; by the middle of the war, the factory workers hardly noticed the dazzle-painting any more, so used to it had everybody become. Camouflage of gun positions in the field, and of ships in harbour, soon became automatic, and in the *zone libre*, the area of France nominally controlled by the *Vichy government, army vehicles were disguised as agricultural machinery (see FRANCE, 7). Dummy aircraft—occasionally, whole dummy airfields—were erected by both sides. Close ground observation could spot these at once, and *spies might be able to report accordingly; only a very good dummy airfield would stand up to repeated air *photographic reconnaissance. The RAF and the Luftwaffe both cherish the anecdote of the dummy airfield that was attacked with wooden bombs.

In the UK a department of the air ministry, called Colonel Turner's, specialized in simulating dummy airfields after dark, by breaches of the *blackout that was such a curse to civilians; and it quickly advanced to simulating dummy ports as well. This worked so well that a German air raid aimed at Portsmouth, a naval base in the south of England, early in 1941 and claimed by *Goebbels as a success, in fact attacked nearby rural Hayling Island instead; total casualties amounted to three cows killed.

Even more sophisticated was the camouflage employed above a sprawling US aircraft plant at Burbank, California, over which a 'suburb' was constructed by *Hollywood set makers. The entire factory was covered by netting and canvas on which was painted the continuation of local roads. Along these 'roads' were placed canvas houses and the area around them were 'planted' with trees and shrubs. Fake cars, laundry lines, and gardens were all added while air ducts provided ventilation for the workers in the factory.

During the *New Georgia campaign in the *Pacific war the Japanese concealed the construction of an airfield at Munda on New Georgia island by rigging cables to the top of the trees they needed to clear to make a runway. They then cut the trunks away leaving the treetops suspended in the air while they began working on the airstrip underneath. This ingenious piece of camouflage hid the airstrip from photo reconnaissance flights and the Americans only discovered it twelve days before it was completed.

The Soviets were equally ingenious in hiding Moscow's most important buildings from German air attacks at the start of the *German–Soviet war. The façade of the Great Palace was concealed behind a net covered with green branches; the golden onion domes of the Kremlin were painted battleship grey and its walls were given a camouflage covering of yellow, black, cream, and orange paint; Moscow's squares were painted to give the illusion from the air of rooftops and buildings; and huge backdrops from the Bolshoi Theatre were hung on the exteriors of office buildings.

In Egypt, Jasper Maskeleyne—who before the war had been a partner in Maskeleyne and Devant, celebrated conjurors in London's West End—devised canvas screens that could be fitted over tanks or guns, to make them look like lorries. He invented an inflatable submarine, and bettered it with an inflatable battleship to confuse Axis reckonings of the Royal Navy's order of battle. Such devices had to be inflated overnight, for it would have been ruinous to the ploy if a chance air reconnaissance had photographed a half-inflated warship.

Maskeleyne did his work under the superintendence of Brigadier Dudley Clarke, whom *Wavell had spotted in Palestine in 1936 as an officer likely to take sound charge of deception. Clarke, a regular gunner much involved with the earliest commandos, ran deception in the Mediterranean from December 1940 till the end of the war. His tiny, highly secret unit, codenamed A Force, exercised a far-reaching impact, mainly through Clarke's leading idea: that the enemy should be encouraged to believe that the Allied forces were a great deal stronger than in fact they were. For cover A Force provided training in escape (see MI9) and for its deception work it had a number of bodies known as Thirty Committees which ran *double agents (see also XX-COMMITTEE).

By turning round some *double agents, and setting up some simulated wireless traffic, Clarke gradually succeeded in persuading his German and Italian opponents that the British and Commonwealth forces actively engaged in the *Western Desert campaigns were about half as large again as in fact they were; and moreover that imaginary forces lay to the east of the desert Eighth Army, in the Levant and in Mesopotamia, posing a substantial threat to the Axis hold on the Balkans if

Turkey entered the war on the Allies' side. By the end of 1942 Ninth and Tenth Armies on which this deception was based were almost wholly notional— their real strength hardly amounted to a single fighting division— but they impressed the enemy high command as real.

Another successful form of deception carried out by the British in the western desert involved the planting of deliberately bogus documents. The Germans discovered maps in abandoned British vehicles which had been left there on purpose to mislead them: most famously in late August 1942, when a scout car, with a dead officer inside, was abandoned in a minefield in front of the German 90th Light Division. Found in the wreck was a map (called a going map) of the surrounding sand dunes, showing soft areas as hard and hard areas as soft. A few days later the *Africa Korps tried to probe round *Montgomery's left at *Alam Halfa, using the going map; and got badly entangled in soft sand, in easy range of the 4th Armoured Brigade's anti-tank guns.

Clarke's masterpiece came in the autumn of 1942, when dummy pipelines across the desert, among other measures, succeeded in deceiving *Rommel into the belief that *Montgomery's Eighth Army would not attack him till November, and would then go for his right flank; so that he was on leave in Germany when the second battle of *El Alamein began on 23 October with an onslaught on his left.

J. F. C. Holland who, among his other achievements, was largely responsible for the formation of MI9, *SOE, and the Independent Companies which preceded the commandos, had already, early in the war, sent E. S. Coombe from his irregular warfare branch of the War Office (MIR) to found the *Inter-Services Security Board, which issued codenames for all operations of war and thus became, as Holland had intended, a suitable point from which deception could be organized centrally. Admiral J. H. Godfrey, the director of Naval intelligence, was also much interested in the subject and installed Ewen Montagu in a section of his *Naval Intelligence Division called 17M from which Montagu could look after deception securely.

Clarke's successes in the Near East were such that in 1941 Churchill was persuaded to set up the London Controlling Section, the smallest but not the least important of the British wartime secret services, which, under Colonel J. H. Bevan, ran deceptive affairs from the cellars of Great George Street, below the underground cabinet war rooms. It worked under the direct supervision of the *Chiefs of Staff, in daily consultation with their joint planning staff. American officers were brought in to work with the section's small staff as necessary; so was Montagu's small team of experts; and when *COSSAC was formed in March 1943 it contained a deception Section, Ops(B), which also worked closely with it.

By an extraordinary, probably unique chance, the Allies were able, through the skills of their decipher staffs (see ULTRA, 1), to assess quite accurately how far the other side had been deceived: which plots had been seen through and which were working properly (see MINCEMEAT, for example). Hence the success of FORTITUDE in 1944, which, with its associated ploys, was co-ordinated by an enlarged Ops(B) now part of COSSAC's successor *SHAEF. Commanded by an ex-A Force officer, Colonel H. N. Wild, Ops(B) supervised all deception operations within SHAEF's area of command.

FORTITUDE, to which the double agents of the XX-Committee made a notable contribution, succeeded in persuading both Hitler and the German general staff that the Normandy landings in June 1944 (see OVERLORD) were a feint: that the real attack was going to be delivered in July on the beaches south of Boulogne by General *Patton's notional First United States Army Group (FUSAG) stationed in Kent and Essex. FUSAG's real strength was confined to a few mobile wireless units broadcasting messages to simulate many divisions' activity, supported by dummy invasion craft which supplemented the real ones in east coast ports. Clarke's doctrine of inflating the opponent's estimate of one's order of battle was thus vindicated: FORTITUDE convinced so many great personages at the German High Command (OKW), Hitler included, that hardly a soldier in the Wehrmacht was moved from the right bank of the Seine to the left in June 1944. By 1 July Montgomery had too firm a foothold ashore to be dislodged; and Patton, now leading the newly formed Third US Army, could be fed into real battle on the far right flank of the Allied landing (see NORMANDY CAMPAIGN).

Deception, as employed by the British and Americans, was that rare device, a merciful instrument of war: it saved scores of thousands of lives, on both sides, by a real economy of force. But it was also extensively used by the Red Army which had no scruples when it came to preserving lives. Soviet staff manuals laid stress on the importance of deception, and divided it into strategic, operational, and tactical levels. The Soviet military encyclopedia defined deception (*maskirovka*) in 1978: 'The means of securing combat operations and the daily activities of forces; a complexity of measures, directed to mislead the enemy regarding the presence and disposition of forces, various military objectives, their condition, combat readiness and operations, and also the plans of the command... *maskirovka* contributes to the achievement of surprise for the actions of forces, the preservation of combat readiness and the increased survivability of objectives.'

The Germans were capable of mounting extended deceptions themselves—the whole Nazi regime was founded on bluff. They achieved surprise, to a remarkable degree, at the opening of their invasion of the USSR on 22 June 1941 (see BARBAROSSA). Cover for this operation had been that the main threat was still against the UK; and it succeeded wonderfully. Stalin ignored British warnings (and indeed warnings from his own spy, *Sorge) that it was impending. BARBAROSSA delivered a salutary shock to the Soviet general staff, which thereafter was always looking out for opportunities of springing surprises itself. Like Napoleon before him, Hitler had bitten off more than he could chew when he invaded the USSR. The vast spaces of the Eastern Front, none of which could instantly be crossed, made it all the more important and useful to divert his reserves into the wrong places. The Soviet authorities, consciously or not, followed Dudley Clarke in misleading the Germans about their order of battle, largely by the use of dummy wireless traffic supported by camouflage devices to mislead the Luftwaffe's air reconnaissance. Moreover they made a rule of making all their main troop movements by night, much harder for an enemy to perceive at that time.

The extremely secretive nature of communist society was also a help to them; villagers who had spotted dummy constructions in their immediate neighbourhood were not going to gossip about them. Besides, Stalin enforced the strictest secrecy where high-level planning was concerned. One major operation was prepared in detail by its commander, aided by only two staff officers; and as little as possible was ever put down on paper. This minimized opportunities for spies, maddening though it has proved for historians. The Soviet experience in fact can be held to illustrate the point that security can be even more important than sound intelligence in working a deception plan.

The first major deception the Soviets sprang on the Germans was in the winter of 1941, when they conjured up three hitherto unsuspected armies to drive the leading Wehrmacht forces back from the outskirts of Moscow. In the first half of 1942 they produced very much more substantial tank forces than the Germans had expected; some of their tank armies, known already to German intelligence, were wrongly believed only to be of brigade strength. That autumn, though the Germans realized the Soviets were bound to counter-attack somewhere in an attempt to relieve *Stalingrad, they succeeded in bringing off an attack in a wholly unexpected quarter. Again, in the summer of 1944 the Germans took for granted that the Red Army would advance into the Balkans; it struck westward instead, flummoxing them once more and costing them 350,000 men. Moreover the Soviets succeeded, in the summer of 1945, in convincing the Japanese that they were still far from ready to engage in major operations in the Far East: a grand stroke of politico-military deception. M. R. D. Foot

Cruickshank, C., *Deception in World War II* (Oxford, 1979).
Glantz, D. M., *Soviet Military Deception in the Second World War* (London, 1989).
Howard, M., *British Intelligence in the Second World War*, Vol. 5: *Strategic Deception* (London, 1990).
Maskeleyne, J., *Magic—Top Secret* (London, 1949).
Masterman, J. C., *The Double-Cross system in the war of 1939 to 1945* (London, 1972).

Declaration on Liberated Europe, issued at the Yalta conference in February 1945 (see ARGONAUT). It committed the UK, USA, and USSR to establishing free elections and democratic governments in the countries they had liberated, and reiterated the three leaders' belief in the principles stated in the *Atlantic Charter. It was immediately flouted by Stalin, who established a minority communist government in Romania in March 1945.

'Signing the Declaration was from the Soviet point of view a grave diplomatic blunder. This was not because the Declaration had any chance of stopping the Soviet Union consolidating its position in Eastern Europe but because the Declaration laid down standards for Eastern Europe, and Stalin's subsequent violation of these standards exposed him ... to persuasive charges of bad faith and of breaking the Yalta accords', A. Schlesinger, *Roosevelt's Diplomacy at Yalta*, 1989, quoted in R. Edmonds, *The Big Three*, London, 1991, p. 418. See also GRAND ALLIANCE.

decorations and orders. Besides issuing *campaign medals, every combatant nation awarded decorations for gallantry to the members of its armed services, and to civilians, especially resistance workers. These normally took the form of a cross or a circular medallion, suitably inscribed, which was suspended from a coloured ribbon. Each decoration had a ribbon with its own distinctive colour combination and pattern. Decorations always took precedence over campaign medals and when wearing undress uniform they were worn as strips of ribbon, usually on the left breast but sometimes on the right.

With the exception of Japan and the USSR, orders were normally awarded for distinguished services, not for gallantry. They mostly took the form of stars worn on the breast or suspended by neck ribbons. Sometimes an order also came with a sash.

It is only possible here to list the most common decorations and orders of the principal combatant powers, and the descriptions are not definitive. Although the descriptions of them are in the past tense most Allied ones are still awarded.

Belgium. Existing awards on the outbreak of war included the Order of Léopold, which had civil, maritime, and military divisions each with five classes, the Order of the Lion, and the Décoration Militaire, the last being awarded in two different versions, for bravery and for meritorious services. New ones introduced after the start of the war included the Croix de Guerre, which could be awarded to civilians as well as to all service personnel, was worn immediately after Belgian orders, and was almost identical to the one issued for the *First World War; and the Medal of the Armed Resistance.

France. Existing awards included France's highest, the Légion d'honneur, and the Médaille Militaire. New ones included the Free French Order of the Liberation for those giving exceptional service in the liberation of France. It was highly regarded and worn immediately after the Légion d'honneur. Other decorations included two variations of the Croix de Guerre, 1939–45—one for troops serving with de *Gaulle and the Free French, the other for those serving under General *Giraud—two resistance medals, and the Medal of Liberated France which was awarded to French or Allied personnel who made a notable contribution towards the liberation of France.

The *Vichy French government also awarded two types of Croix de Guerre, one of which was for those who fought in the *German–Soviet war against the USSR.

Germany. All existing military orders and decorations for bravery were abolished after the First World War. The Order of the Iron Cross, originally a Prussian decoration, was reinstated by Hitler on 1 September 1939 with four grades: Grand Cross, Knight's Cross (Ritterkreuz), 1st Class, and 2nd Class. It was necessary to hold the Iron Cross, 2nd Class before being awarded the Iron Cross, 1st Class, but exceptionally they were awarded together. The Grand Cross was awarded only to *Göring. As the war progressed higher grades of the Ritterkreuz, which was worn round the neck, were added. These were Oak Leaves (introduced 3 June 1940), Oak Leaves and Swords (21 June 1941), Oak Leaves, Swords, and Diamonds (29 December 1944), the last only being awarded once.

Other new decorations included the War Merit Cross (KVK) and the German Cross (DK), the latter bridging the gap between the Iron Cross, 1st Class, and the *Ritterkreuz*.

The KVK had five grades: the Gold Knight's Cross and Silver Knight's Cross—both of which were worn at the throat—1st and 2nd Class, and the War Merit Medal. All except the War Merit Medal, which was awarded only to civilians, could be with or without swords, those with swords being awarded to those showing outstanding merit or bravery, but not in action, while those without were awarded to civilians for a wide range of services.

The DK came in two classes, silver and gold. The gold was awarded to those who already held the Iron Cross, 1st and 2nd Class; and the silver to those who already held the KVK, 1st and 2nd Class, and who continued to show distinction in military leadership, but not in the face of the enemy.

The Order of Merit of the German Eagle had seven classes and was awarded only to foreigners.

Italy. Existing decorations included the Medal for Military Valour, Maritime Valour, and Aeronautical Valour, in gold, silver, and bronze, and the Cross for War Merit, which became the 4th grade of the Medal for Military Valour. The Order of the Roman Eagle, instituted in March 1942, was awarded to foreigners only, and came in five classes: Grand Cross (gold and silver), Grand Officer, Commander, Officer, and Knight. There were also silver and bronze Medals of the Order.

Japan. Existing awards included the Order of the Chrysanthemum (seldom awarded to anyone outside the Royal Family and foreign heads of state), the Order of the Rising Sun, the Order of the Sacred Treasure, and the Order of the Golden Kite. The Order of the Rising Sun was awarded in eight classes to civilians and military personnel for distinguished services. Higher than any of the eight classes was the Order of the Rising Sun with Paulownia Flowers which was seldom awarded to anyone below the rank of admiral, general, or ambassador. The Order of the Sacred Treasure was also awarded in eight classes, to women as well as men and to foreigners, for rendering excellent services. The Order of the Golden Kite was conferred on military personnel of any rank in recognition of outstanding service of bravery. It was awarded in seven classes and carried with it a grant. With it was also awarded a medal which came in two classes: **Shukun Ko** (first class) and **Shukan Otsu** (second class). **Shukun Ko** came in seven grades, **Shukun Otsu** in six. The grades awarded depended on the rank of the recipient. Individuals and units were also awarded a citation (**Kanjo**) for bravery or distinguished services which was highly regarded.

Netherlands. Existing awards included Military Wilhelms Order, the highest Dutch honour for gallantry, and the Order of the Netherlands' Lion. New awards included the Bronze Lion, which ranked next to the Military Wilhelms Order and could be awarded to a civilians as well as military personnel, and to foreigners; the Bronze Cross, which ranked below the Bronze Lion; the Cross of Merit; the Flying Cross; War Commemorative Cross, to which was added bars for certain actions; Resistance Star, East Asia; and, high in the order of precedence; the Resistance Cross.

Norway. Existing awards included the Royal Order of St Olaf, St Olaf's Medal, with oak leaves for subsequent citations, and the Medal for Heroic Deeds. New ones included the War Cross, with swords for additional citations; the War Medal, with which were worn up to three stars for additional citations; and King Haakon VII's Freedom Cross and Freedom Medal.

Poland. Existing awards included the Order of the Polonia Restituta and the Order Virtuti Militari, both of which came in five grades, the highest grade of the Virtuti Militari being the equivalent of the British Victoria Cross or the US Congressional Medal of Honor; the Cross of Valour; and the Cross of Merit. New ones included the Order of the Grunwald Cross and the Partisans' Cross.

UK. Existing awards included Britain's highest for gallantry, the Victoria Cross (VC), which could be awarded to all service personnel. (During the Second World War only one man won it twice, Captain Charles Upham, one of three ever to have done so.) The British Empire Medal (BEM) could also be awarded to all service personnel, and to civilians, for 'meritorious service'. Any officer, normally above the rank of major (or equivalent), could be awarded—or more correctly admitted to—the Distinguished Service Order (DSO), and its award to a more junior officer often indicated that the recipient had narrowly missed being awarded the VC. Less senior army officers and warrant officers were awarded the Military Cross (MC); less senior Royal Navy Officers and warrant officers the Distinguished Service Cross (DSC); and less senior RAF officers and warrant officers the

Distinguished Flying Cross (DFC) and Air Force Cross (AFC), the last for bravery not in the face of the enemy. The AFC could also be awarded to civilians.

Non-commissioned service personnel from any of the services could be awarded the Distinguished Conduct Medal (DCM), though those of the navy and air force could only be awarded it when under army command, and the Conspicuous Gallantry Medal (CGM). Naval other ranks were awarded the Distinguished Service Medal (DSM); army other ranks (and occasionally other ranks from the other two services, women as well as men) were awarded the Military Medal (MM); and RAF other ranks the Distinguished Flying Medal (DFM) and the Air Force Medal (AFM), the last being for bravery not in the face of the enemy. The AFM could also be awarded to civilians.

A Mention in Dispatches was recognized by an oak leaf on the ribbon of the 1939–45 War Medal, or on the ribbon of the campaign star relating to action for which the recognition was won.

New awards included the George Cross (GC), which took precedence over all other decorations apart from the VC, and the George Medal (GM). Both were primarily for civilians, or, as in the case of *Malta, civilian populations, for great acts of bravery. British Commonwealth and colonial forces, and those controlled by the various *governments-in-exile fighting alongside the British, were awarded the same decorations.

Further awards of the same decoration were shown by a bar on the ribbon of the cross or medal. Hence the phrase 'he received a bar to his DSO', meaning he had been awarded it for the second time. Members of the Merchant Navy were also awarded certain decorations awarded to personnel of the Royal Navy.

The British also awarded different grades of various orders to service personnel and to civilians for distinguished and meritorious service, but not normally for gallantry in action. The most commonly awarded were those of the military and civilian divisions of the Order of the British Empire, which were awarded to Allied troops and civilians as well as to British citizens. This came in five grades: Knights (or Dames) Grand Cross (GBE), Knights (or Dames) Commander (K or DBE), Commanders (CBE), Officers (OBE), and Members (MBE). Other Orders often awarded during the war included the Order of the Bath and the Order of St Michael and St George, both of which came in three grades.

USA. Existing awards included America's highest, the Congressional Medal of Honor. Next in rank came the Army and Navy Distinguished Service Cross, then the Army, Navy, and Coast Guard Distinguished Service Medal; the Silver Star; the Distinguished Flying Cross; and the Purple Heart which was awarded to anyone wounded in battle or to the next of kin of a person killed or who subsequently died of wounds. Second or subsequent awards of the Purple Heart were denoted by a gold star (navy and marines) or oak-leaf cluster (army and air force). The Soldier's Medal was awarded to army, navy, National Guard, and reservist personnel for 'heroism not involving actual conflict with an armed enemy'.

New awards included the Legion of Merit, awarded, like an order, in four degrees, Chief Commander, Commander, Officer, and Legionnaire. It could be awarded to anyone, US or foreign, distinguished in performing outstanding services to the USA, but American personnel only wore the badge of the Legionnaire which took precedence immediately after the Silver Star. Other new awards included the Medal for Merit, a civilian decoration presented to US and foreign civilians for the performance of outstanding services to the USA; the Bronze Star Medal (not awarded for aerial combat); and the Medal of Freedom, which was awarded to any person, apart from US service personnel, for meritorious services outside the USA. It came in four grades: gold palm, silver palm, bronze palm, and without palm, the last being awarded only to US citizens.

Awards for units were also introduced during the war, the highest being the Presidential Unit Citation. Units not qualifying for this could be awarded the Distinguished Unit Citation (army), the Navy's Unit Commendation (navy), or the Outstanding Unit Award (air force). These awards, a ribbon framed in metal, were worn by the personnel of the unit over the right breast pocket, though the personnel of those awarded to British units wore the emblem on the left shoulder.

USSR. Decorations were divided into three categories: Highest Titles of Distinction, Orders of the USSR, Medals of the USSR. The custom of awarding two or more identical medals, both, or all, of which were worn by the recipient, made Soviet citizens among the most decorated in the world.

The Highest Title of Distinction was Hero of the Soviet Union, awarded for a personal deed of heroism. Recipients were also given the Gold Star Medal, only awarded to a Hero of the Soviet Union, and the highest decoration in the USSR, the Order of Lenin, which could also be awarded on its own for outstanding service over a stipulated period of time. The title Hero of the Soviet Union, and the decorations, could be awarded up to three times to a single recipient.

Other existing awards included the Order of the Red Banner for outstanding courage on active service, though from 1944 it could also be awarded for long service to officers and NCOs, and also collectively to units and schools; and the Order of the Red Star, awarded individually to any rank and collectively to units for outstanding services in defence of the USSR, in both peace and war.

New orders included the country's highest military order, the Order of Victory, awarded to members of the High Command for successful operations involving one or more *fronts* (i.e. army groups); the Order of Ushakov and the Order of Nachimov, both orders in two classes for naval officers; the Order of Glory, in three classes, for junior officers and other ranks in the army and air force;

the Order of Suvorov, awarded to commanders at all levels for outstanding leadership resulting in victory; the Order of Kutuzov, awarded to commanders of army groups and independent *formations for successful operations which caused heavy losses to the enemy; and the Order of Bogdan Khmelnitski. The last three orders all came in three classes, the first class being awarded to the most senior officers, the second to less senior, and the third to those at regimental level and below, though the Order of Bogdan Khmelnitski was also awarded to those in the partisan forces and the third class could be awarded to other ranks as well as junior officers.

Existing medals for bravery included the Medal for Valour and the Medal for Battle Merit, both for all ranks, the latter being also awarded to officers and NCOs for long service. New ones included the Ushakov Medal and Nachimov Medal, both of which were awarded to naval ratings and petty officers; and the Partisan Medals, 1st and 2nd class.

Purves, A., *The Medals, Decorations, and Orders of World War Two* (Polstead, Suffolk, 1986).

defence forces, see in relevant section of major powers.

de Gaulle, see GAULLE, DE.

degaussing was employed to give shipping protection against magnetic mines. To neutralize the magnetism of a ship's steel hull it could be 'wiped', momentarily discharging an electric current through a copper cable wound around its hull, a process which had to be repeated at regular intervals. Alternatively, cables could be permanently placed around the outside of a ship's hull or inside it. It was so-named after Karl Gauss who discovered the properties of magnetism. See also MINE WARFARE, 2.

Degrelle, Léon (1906–94), leader of a group of young Belgian Catholics who formed the anti-democratic Rexist movement in the 1930s. An ebullient, charismatic figure, he opted for *collaboration after the German invasion of Belgium in May 1940 (see FALL GELB). In 1941, he formed and served in the Légion Wallonie which fought with the Wehrmacht on the Eastern Front. He negotiated the Légion's transfer to the Waffen-*SS in 1943 and was awarded several military *decorations, including the Iron Cross with Oak Leaves. He fled to Spain in 1945 where, despite being condemned to death *in absentia* by a Belgian court, he lived in exile until his death.

MARTIN CONWAY

de Guingand, Maj-General Sir Francis (1900–79), British Army officer who served as *Montgomery's Chief of Staff during the *Western Desert campaigns and during the fighting in north-west Europe which followed the Normandy landings in June 1944 (see OVERLORD).

After serving as military assistant to the secretary of state for war, *Hore-Belisha, which gave him valuable insights into the highest level of politics and military affairs, de Guingand served in the Middle East where *Auchinleck, C-in-C Middle East, made him director of military intelligence and then brigadier, General Staff, at Eighth Army HQ. De Guingand did not feel qualified for either appointment, but both showed him to be the perfect staff officer. That August he became chief of staff to Montgomery, whom he had known since the 1920s, when Montgomery took over command of Eighth Army. De Guingand's role as a foil to Montgomery was a vital one and his diplomacy and tact helped palliate Montgomery's abrasiveness. Though both claimed the credit for some critical decisions what mattered was that the right ones were mostly made. After the war Montgomery treated de Guingand shabbily, and de Guingand never forgave him. He left the army in 1946 and became a successful businessman and author. He was knighted in 1944.

De Guingand, F., *Operation Victory* (London, 1947).

de Lattre de Tassigny, General, see LATTRE DE TASSIGNY.

demography of the war.

1. The human disaster

The demographic disaster of the Second World War can never be precisely measured. All that can be done is to present some very rough estimates of military losses, civilian deaths arising from wartime policies, including the Nazi extermination of the Jews (see FINAL SOLUTION), and civilian deaths resulting from other war-related causes.

The epicentre of military action, and therefore, of military losses, in the European war was the *German–Soviet war. Perhaps 10 million Soviet servicemen died in the period 1941–5, the vast majority in the war against Hitler. Approximately three-quarters of all German losses, or roughly 3 million men, also occurred on the Eastern Front.

This level of casualties had never before been registered in the history of armed conflict. In other theatres of operation, statistics for military losses were of an order of magnitude that had been registered in the *First World War. In the *China Incident alone approximately 2 million Japanese servicemen died, and a somewhat higher total—perhaps 2.5 million men—died in the Chinese armies arrayed against them. This is approximately the level of losses suffered by Germany, and by the UK and France, in the First World War.

Some casualty totals were higher in the Second World War than in the First. US losses were three times as high. Other countries, for instance Italy and Romania, suffered about the same levels of military loss in both conflicts, while French losses were significantly lower in 1939–45 than in 1914–18.

The extermination of 6 million Jews, the majority of whom had lived in Poland or the Soviet Union, was a

Demography, Table 1: Approximate war-related deaths of major combatant nations in the Second World War

Country	*Military losses (000s)*	*Civilian losses (000s)*	*Total losses (000s)*
I. Axis			
Germany	4,500	2,000	6,500
Japan	2,000	350	2,350
Italy	400	100	500
Romania	300	200	500
Austria	230	144	374
Hungary	160	270	430
Finland	84	16	100
TOTAL	7,674	3,080	10,754
II. Allies			
USSR	10,000	10,000	20,000
China	2,500	7,400	10,000
UK	300	50	350
Yugoslavia	300	1,400	1,700
USA	274	–	274
Czechoslovakia	250	90	340
France	250	350	600
Poland	123	4,000	4,123
Canada	37	–	37
Bulgaria	32	3	35
Albania	28	2	30
India	24	13	37
Australia	23	12	35
Greece	20	430	450
New Zealand	10	2	12
Belgium	10	78	88
South Africa	7	–	7
Netherlands	6	204	210
Luxembourg	5	–	5
Norway	2	8	10
TOTAL	14,201	24,042	38,343

Approximate total war-related deaths

Military	22,000
Civilian	
died in concentration camps	12,000
died through bombing	1,500
died in Europe from other war-related causes	7,000
died in China from other war-related causes	7,500
TOTAL	28,000
TOTAL LOSSES	50,000

Notes: Casualty statistics are notoriously unreliable. Frumkin provides substantially lower estimates for Germany, Austria, Czechoslovakia, and higher estimates for Poland. Urlanis's estimates for the USSR are higher than those of the other two scholars, and the Americans, Singer and Small, produce higher estimates for American war deaths. It may be a rule that the nationality of the scholar tends to yield higher estimates of war casualties for his or her own nation.

Soviet losses are especially problematical. In 1946 Stalin produced a figure of 7 million which, it was supposed, covered military and civilian losses; in the 1960s, under Khrushchev, it became 'in excess of 20 millions'; by the early 1990s some estimates had increased this to 25–27 million; and the most recent estimate for indirect losses—which includes those unborn—is some 48 million (see J. Erickson & D. Dilks (eds.), *Barbarossa: The Axis and the Allies*, London, 1994, p. 258).

If battle casualties are uncertain, civilian casualties are impossible to verify. Concentration camp mortality, or the human costs of resistance or insurrectionary warfare in Europe, must remain conjectural, and the figures provided reflect those conjectures.

Estimates for Asian casualties are even more uncertain. Chinese data are very sketchy and, given the magnitude of the disaster, likely to remain so. The notional estimate of 350,000 Japanese civilian war-related deaths is almost certainly too low. What is left out is the long-term effects of nuclear bombardment, and the deaths due to it which occurred ten or twenty years after 1945.

Sources: Urlanis, B., *Wars and Population* (Moscow, 1971); Frumkin, G., *Population Changes in Europe since 1939* (New York, 1951); Singer, J. D., and Small, M., *The Wages of War* (New York, 1972).

Demography, Table 2: Approximate net shifts in civilian population of some European nations during and after the Second World War

Country	*1939–45 (000s)* In	Out	*1946–7 (000s)* In	Out	*Net movement (000s)*
I. Axis					
Germany	7,500	4,600	7,200	600	9,500
Italy	1,400	1,500	680	350	230
Romania	450	700	80	–	–170
Austria	385	150	310	33	512
Hungary	180	170	200	225	–15
Finland	12	14	1	3	–4
TOTAL	9,927	7,134	8,471	1,211	10,053
II. Allies					
UK	–	500	–	413	87
Yugoslavia	–	350	90	180	–440
Czechoslovakia	15	1,025	160	1,915	–2,765
France	3,900	3,710	282	50	422
Poland	–	6,900	1,500	2,300	–7,700
Bulgaria	60	110	–	–	–50
Greece	80	60	–	–	20
Belgium	–	30	96	–	66
Netherlands	146	150	172	130	38
TOTAL	4,201	12,835	2,300	4,988	–10,322
III. Others					
Denmark	268	68	42	184	58
Finland	12	14	1	3	–4
Ireland	–	79	–	13	–92
Sweden	128	39	50	19	120
TOTAL	408	200	93	219	–82

Notes: The data are useful only to indicate the scale and relative weight of population movements in the two periods 1939–45 and the turbulent two years following the war. The same order has been used as in Table 1. In and out migration have been separated wherever possible. Where conflicting sources exist, the lower figure has always been chosen. Summary figures are used where only total migratory flows have been estimated.

The USSR has been omitted for two reasons. The first is the massive distortions introduced by boundary shifts, in which over 20 million people were forcibly incorporated into the USSR by 1945. The second is the statistical vagueness or unreliability of official Soviet sources. These make the rough guesses incorporated in the data on other European countries appear to be paragons of precision.

The totals for net movement must be treated with great care. The least that can be said is that it is likely that outside the USSR, over 20 million European civilians migrated at least once across 1939 boundaries after the outbreak of war and before 1947. That figure probably would be doubled should an attempt be made to estimate migration into and out of the Soviet Union.

The margin of error that must be accepted for these rough guesses is no doubt a substantial one. But whatever cautionary note is added, it remains clear that the migratory flows during and after the Second World War within Europe were at least as great as and probably greater in magnitude than any other in the history of the Continent over such a short period.

Sources: Urlanis, B., *Wars and Population* (Moscow, 1971); Frumkin, G., *Population Changes in Europe since 1939* (New York, 1951); Singer, J. D., and Small, M., *The Wages of War* (New York, 1972).

direct outcome of the Second World War. The Nazis made genocide a prime instrument of state policy for the first time in history. The *concentration camp system also claimed millions of non-Jewish victims, though their murder was not part of the same plan as that devised to rid Europe of Jews for ever.

It was not only in the Final Solution that the boundary between civilian and military targets in warfare was obliterated. In Asia, as throughout occupied Europe, disease, famine, and indiscriminate bombardment of civilian populations produced a parallel human disaster, the dimensions of which can never be fully known. The bare outlines of this catastrophe are presented in Table 1. Over half of the 50 million men, *women, and *children who perished in the Second World War were civilians.

2. Recovery and resettlement

The demographic repercussions of the war in terms of fertility and migration were profound. Mobilization and military losses changed the sex ratio of many populations, in particular that of the USSR, reducing marriage and birth rates dramatically. But despite the slaughter,

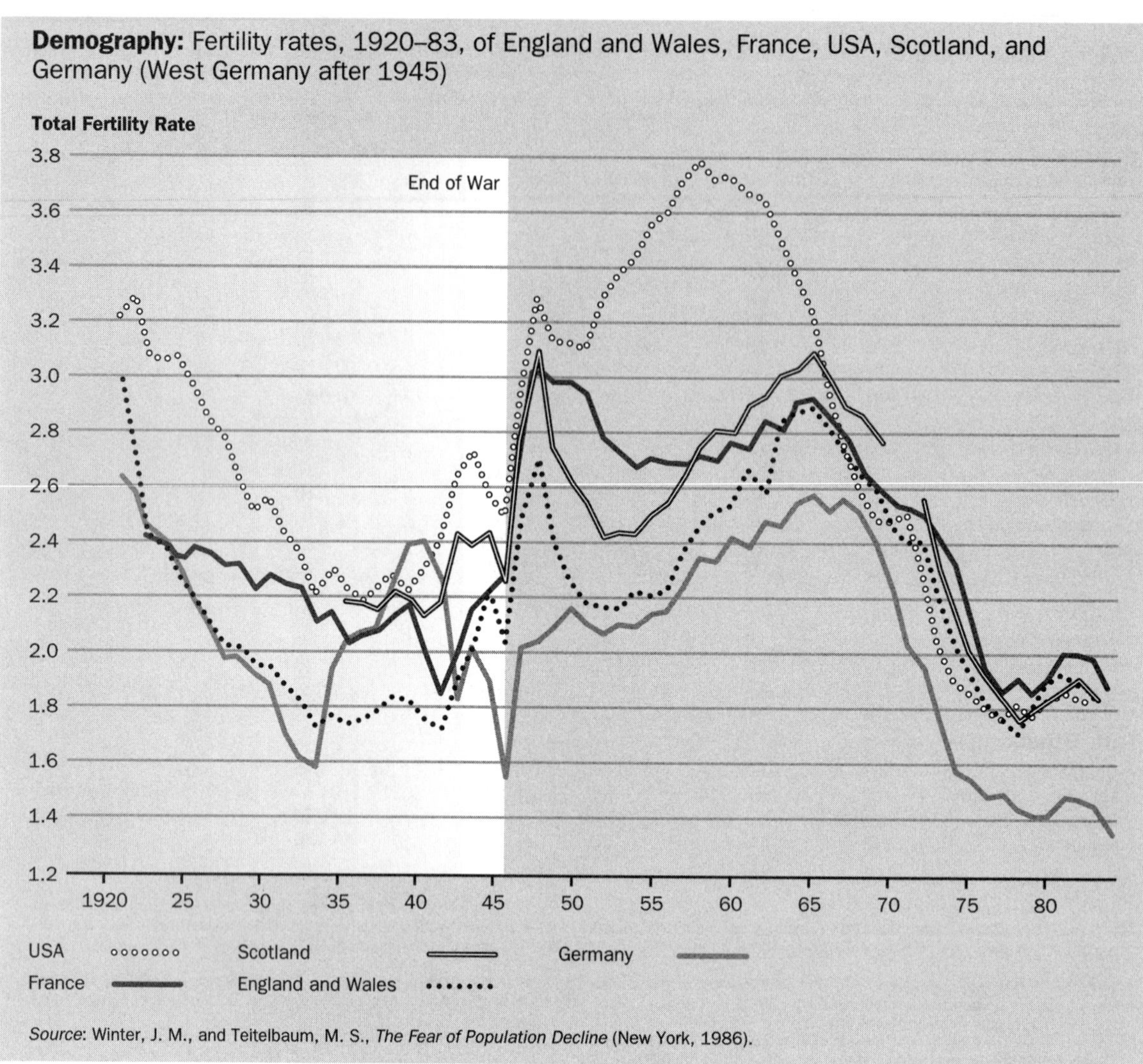

there is evidence of a the rapid recovery of population dynamics in many countries during and after the war (see Graph).

The war also produced powerful migratory shock waves as Table 2 shows. First, the flight of civilians out of the front lines was a constant feature of life (see REFUGEES). Secondly, there occurred, both during and after the war, the expulsion of millions of civilians and the resettlement of the survivors far from their homes (see DEPORTATIONS). The dislocating effects of the 1939–45 war had repercussions on the ethnic and nationalities mix of many regions, storing up explosive material for conflicts still unresolved today. J. M. WINTER

Anderson, B. A., and Silver, B. D., 'Demographic consequences of World War II on the non-Russian nationalities of the USSR', in S. Linz (ed.), *The Impact of World War II on the Soviet Union* (London, 1988).

Frumkin, G., *Population Changes in Europe since 1939* (New York, 1951).

Milward, A., *War, Economy and Society 1939–45* (London, 1977).

Singer, J. D., and Small, M., *The Wages of War 1816–1965. A Statistical Handbook* (New York, 1972).

Urlanis, B., *Wars and Population* (Moscow, 1971).

Dempsey, General Sir Miles (1896–1969), British Army officer who was a staunch supporter of *Montgomery and one of his ablest commanders. He commanded the 13th Infantry Brigade, which took part in the counterattack at Arras during the fighting which preceded the fall of *France in June 1940, and then covered the *Dunkirk evacuation; Eighth Army's 13th Corps during the *Sicilian and *Italian campaigns; and Montgomery's Second Army in north-west Europe. He was knighted in 1944.

Denmark. Neutrality had been the hallmark of Danish foreign policy since 1815, and from the time of the loss of the Duchies of Schleswig and Holstein in 1864, and increasingly so from the rise of the Third Reich, Denmark fell within Germany's sphere of influence, a fact recognized and accepted by the Great Powers including the UK, Denmark's primary trading partner. Scandinavian unity having failed during the late 1930s, Denmark was alone among the Scandinavian countries in accepting, in the spring of 1939, Hitler's offer of a non-aggression pact, and the *Nazi–Soviet Pact of August 1939 completed its isolation. However the pact did guarantee Denmark's right to trade with other nations and before the German occupation in April 1940, Germany did not interfere directly with Anglo-Danish trade. After the occupation nearly all Denmark's exports went to providing Germany with 10% of its consumption of meat, butter, and eggs.

Denmark was a democratic monarchy—Frederik IX (1899–1972) was king throughout the war—with a population of 3.85 million. Pacifism was widespread and after the *First World War a general belief in disarmament dominated Danish politics and the coalition government of social democrats and social liberals, which was led from 1929 to 1940 by Thorvald Stauning (1873–1942). The Danish military establishment was not held in high regard by the population, but the rise of the Nazis in Germany after 1933 led to a change in the attitude of the social democrats and the defence act of 1937 permitted some modernization of the Danish armed forces. But in April 1940 the army's strength was a mere 14,000 men under arms, 8,000 of whom had only been drafted during the previous two months. The small navy, which depended largely upon Copenhagen's coastal defences and mines for defending Danish territory, only had two coastal defence vessels (built in 1906 and 1918), and a total of 3,000 men. The air forces, divided between the army and the navy, possessed about 50 aircraft, mostly obsolete. The two services, traditional rivals for domination of the plans for defending the country, weakened all attempts to establish unity in the High Command and in the government.

Intelligence reports of Germany's intention to invade Denmark reached the Danish government as early as 4 April 1940. (Admiral *Canaris, head of the *Abwehr, had deliberately allowed the information to be leaked to the Danish military attaché in Berlin in an attempt to humiliate the Führer.) But their contents were contradictory and were not believed; it was not until 8 April that any attempt was made to strengthen Danish forces in Copenhagen and in the south of Jutland near the border with Germany. As a result the German attack, launched at 0415 on 9 April, was totally successful. The Danish Army did resist for a few hours in North Schleswig but the navy, which had not even been put on the alert, did not fire a shot and allowed a German troopship to enter Copenhagen harbour unmolested. At 0500 the Germans launched the first ever parachute operation (see also AIRBORNE WARFARE) when they attacked the unarmed fortress of Madnesø south of the island of Zealand, and soon after the important airport of Aalborg in the north of Jutland. At 0600, after Copenhagen had been occupied, the Danish government ordered a ceasefire and, under protest, accepted the German occupation of the country. Until 29 August 1943 the government tried to maintain the illusion of neutrality in an attempt to prevent the Germans from interfering in Danish administration, justice, education, and so on.

The German occupation of Denmark was a result of Operation WESERÜBUNG that had Norway as its prime target (see NORWEGIAN CAMPAIGN). Denmark was no more than a stepping-stone for German troops, but throughout the war the country remained crucial for Germany's access to, and control of, Norway. As a consequence of the decision taken on the morning of 9 April 1940 the government retained power, the law courts and police continued to be under Danish control, and even the armed forces were allowed to continue functioning, though on a reduced scale.

The day after the occupation began the opposition parties joined a national administration on condition that Stauning acknowledge that it was his government which had agreed to capitulate. Censorship of the press and radio, and a ban on political demonstrations, were introduced. In the first months of the occupation it was feared that the small Danish Nazi Party would use the opportunity to seize power, and right-wing groups attacked the parliamentary system. The majority of the Danish population, however, supported the coalition. A new government was formed on 8 July 1940 which included three non-parliamentarians; the most notable of them, Erik Scavenius, became foreign minister. He had successfully filled that post during the First World War and he took the line that, in order to keep the country's administration in Danish hands, it was necessary to show the Germans that the Danes were willing to co-operate. Without doubt, most Danes supported this line for a long time, at least until those turning-points of the war, the second battle of *El Alamein and the battle for *Stalingrad.

This policy of collaboration presupposed that the Germans would honour their undertakings given on 9 April 1940 that they had no intention of interfering with the internal affairs of Denmark. However, during the years of *collaboration, 1940–3, the Germans broke the guarantees they had given again and again, by demanding military equipment, the removal of awkward ministers and politicians, and so on. They also pressed for Denmark's more active support of the German war machine. As a result, about 100,000 Danish workers were urged by the Danish authorities to go to Germany to prevent the Germans from conscripting them. Also, following the invasion of the USSR in June 1941 (see BARBAROSSA), the government was forced to ban the Communist Party and accept recruitment for a Danish

Free Corps to fight on the Eastern Front. Later, in November 1941, Denmark was obliged to join the *Anti-Comintern Pact, though Scavenius did manage to extract some concessions. These obliged Denmark only to act against communists within its own borders and accepted that under no circumstances would the country be drawn into the *German–Soviet war.

In 1942 growing tension led to the recall of the German minister and his replacement by a Nazi functionary, Werner Best; and a hardline army officer, Lt-General Hermann Hanneken, was given command of all German troops in Denmark. Best was instructed by Hitler to 'rule with an iron hand', but he stopped short of ordering Best to take complete control. Hitler wanted a compliant administration which could ensure stability and order in Denmark and ensure continuity in the flow of Danish agricultural goods to Germany. Best took a conciliatory line and for a period succeeded in securing collaboration from the Danish government which Scavenius now led. In March 1943 he even allowed elections to be held, in which 89.5% of the electorate voted, the highest ever, and of these 94% voted for one of the coalition parties working with Scavenius. But, despite this massive vote for the policy of collaboration, the general awareness that the Germans were losing the war led to strikes and a rise in sabotage. Encouraged by *SOE and by *BBC propaganda a general stiffening of *resistance against the occupation became widely marked in all parts of the Danish population.

In August 1943 Best was ordered by *Ribbentrop to force the government to declare a state of emergency, but this it refused to do. Instead, it resigned and on 29 August 1943 the Germans took over the country's administration. Influential citizens were arrested and when Danish military establishments were attacked naval personnel sank their ships in Copenhagen harbour or escaped to Sweden. The most powerful warship, *Niels Juel*, was bombed by the Germans and scuttled by its crew in Isefjord in north-west Zealand.

Following these events the country was administered by an unofficial board of the heads of the civil service departments under Niels Svenningsen, the civil service head of the foreign ministry. But from June 1944, when the Danes organized a spontaneous general strike in Copenhagen as a protest against German brutality, the feelings of the majority of the Danish population were represented by the Frihedsradet (Freedom Council). This was established on 16 September 1943 to organize internal resistance, which had been fostered by SOE from September 1941 onwards, when the first British-trained Danish agents had been parachuted into the country. The council's authority was never questioned. It consisted of an SOE member and seven representatives of the more important underground groups such as BOPA (Borgerlige Partisaner, or Bourgeois Partisans, a name which concealed the fact that the organization was communist-dominated) and Holger Danske (the name of a legendary Danish hero). One of the council's most important functions was organizing an illegal *press, which by 1944 was publishing 254 newspapers with an annual circulation of 11 million copies; and in the months preceding the Normandy landings of June 1944 (see OVERLORD) local groups under its command sabotaged railway lines in Jutland, which may well have had an adverse influence on the movement of German troops from Norway after D-Day. The council also established an important intelligence network and this enabled the first detailed description of the V-1 flying bomb (see V-WEAPONS) to be transmitted to London after one had fallen on the Baltic island of Bornholm during a test flight.

Forewarned by Best's anti-Nazi shipping attaché, G. F. von Dückwitz, and with the help of all sections of the population, including the distinguished Danish physicist Niels *Bohr, the council was also responsible for organizing the escape of 5,500 Jews to Sweden in one night when the Germans started rounding them up on 1 October 1943. Only 472 were were caught, and deported to *Theresienstadt: of these 52 eventually died (see FINAL SOLUTION). The Danish resistance movement was hard pressed by the *Gestapo. Many leaders were arrested and the movement escaped probable collapse only because three Gestapo HQ were bombed by the RAF to destroy the Gestapo's records and to allow the escape of their prisoners (see SHELL HOUSE RAID).

From the beginning Danes outside Denmark were actively involved in the war. The Danish minister in the USA, Henrik Kauffmann, declared himself an independent representative of Danish interests that were outside German control and in this capacity he signed a treaty in April 1941 which gave control of the Danish colony of Greenland to the USA. The Faeroes, another colony, were occupied by British troops in April 1940, as was Iceland in May after it had declared temporary independence from Denmark. Later, US troops took over the occupation of Iceland which declared itself an independent republic in 1944. At the time of the occupation of Denmark 230 of its merchant ships, amounting to 1.2 million tons and crewed by about 6,000 seamen, were outside home territorial waters. Most of these joined the Allied merchant navies and served aboard ships in the *convoys around which the battle of the *Atlantic was fought and in the *Arctic convoys; altogether 1,500 Danish seamen lost their lives and 60% of the fleet was lost. By 1944 two minesweepers, manned by Danish sailors, had formed the nucleus of a Danish section within the Royal Navy and about a thousand other Danish exiles served in the British or US armies, in SOE, or in the RAF.

The number of active Danish saboteurs probably never exceeded 800, but an increasing number of potential resisters were trained for a possible Allied invasion or a sudden German capitulation, and in Sweden a 5,000-strong Danish Brigade, formed from Danish refugees, stood by to intervene if this occurred. By May 1945 the total strength of the internal resistance movement was about 40,000, which included a number of service officers and policemen. The latter had been forced to go underground after the Germans disbanded the police force, which they regarded as untrustworthy, in September 1944 and arrested and deported 2,000 of its members. From that time until the end of the war the country was without a police force and civil patrols had to be formed to control crime.

The German capitulation at *Lüneburg Heath on 4 May 1945 included Denmark and the resistance movement took control of the country the following day. However, the German commandant on Bornholm refused to surrender and on 7 and 8 May Soviet aircraft bombed the towns of Rønne and Neks, killing few people but causing much damage. On 9 May Soviet warships arrived at Rønne and the Germans then surrendered, but Soviet troops remained on the island until April 1946. After the war 34,000 collaborators were arrested and punished.

CLAUS BJØRN

Petrow, R., *The Invasion and Occupation of Denmark and Norway, April 1940–May 1945* (London, 1974).

Dentz, General Henri-Fernand (1881–1945), military governor of Paris in 1940 and, after the fall of *France in June 1940, *Vichy high commissioner in Syria. He led a mixed military force with considerable success during the *Syrian campaign against Australian, British, and Free French forces in June–July 1941. Infringements of the *armistice—Allied prisoners were evacuated from Syria after it had been signed on 14 July—led to his temporary *internment. In 1945 he was condemned to death for high treason. His sentence was commuted but he died in prison.

deportations. In democratic countries, deportation is usually regarded as a legal procedure affecting individuals who have committed an offence such as illegal immigration. In totalitarian states, however, deportation was a phenomenon affecting thousands or even millions of innocent people who could be arbitrarily removed from their homes by administrative means. They were sent to distant locations, often in conditions of the utmost degradation and danger, and with little pretence of legality. During the Second World War, it was practised in this sense on a wide scale both by the Nazis and especially by the Soviets. It also applied in Canada and the USA to residents of Japanese origin (see JAPANESE-AMERICANS and JAPANESE-CANADIANS).

For the Nazis, deportation was an important aspect of resettlement, labour, and security policies, particularly in the occupied zones of eastern Europe. It first became evident in November 1938 when some 30,000 Jews holding Polish passports were summarily expelled from Germany, and deposited in the no man's land between border posts on the German–Polish frontier.

Following the invasion of Poland in September 1939, some thousands of Poles and Polish Jews were forcibly deported to the General government (see POLAND, 2(b)) from other Polish territories, such as the Wartheland, which had been annexed to the Reich. In this instance, in an attempt to eliminate the so-called *Polish corridor, the deported Polish population was replaced by ethnic Germans brought from the Baltic States in agreement with the USSR.

Nazi resettlement policy in the east envisaged the systematic Germanization of whole provinces either within or contiguous to the Greater Reich. To this end, the Jewish population was to be killed, either by executions on the spot or by deportation to the death camps (see OPERATION REINHARD) while the Polish or Ukrainian population was to be removed to make way for in-coming Germans. The Jewish part of the policy was given priority (see FINAL SOLUTION). But several large-scale rural clearances were undertaken, notably in 1943 in the *Zamość region where some 300 Polish villages were destroyed. Old-established German communities living deep in Ukraine were broken up, and their inhabitants relocated further west. Similar methods were used in Croatia by the fascist *Ustašas* intent on 'de-Serbianizing' districts of mixed settlement.

Nazi labour policy required the despatch of between 5 and 6 million men and women, mainly from Poland and Ukraine, to work on farms and in factories in the Reich. In the initial stages, it was possible to recruit a certain number of these *Ostarbeitern* (eastern workers) on a voluntary basis, but they were increasingly deported as *forced labour.

Nazi security policy frequently resorted to deportation as a method for controlling troublesome districts. Selected groups and individuals might simply be expelled, or deported to the concentration camps. At points of maximum tension, as in the *Warsaw rising in 1944, the *SS resorted to random arrests and mass deportations as a means of terrorizing the population.

Mass deportations by the Soviet authorities took place before, during, and after the Second World War. They were a standard feature of the Great Terror and of the Purges, as they were of Soviet policy towards the population of all countries occupied by the Red Army. They may be classified in a number of categories descending from 'free exile' to penal sentences with hard labour (see GULAG). All were conducted by legal fictions, which ignored the innocence of the victims, and by almost total disregard for human life. Because of the vast distances and extreme climatic conditions, the journey to distant destinations in Siberia or the Far East could be no less lethal than the sentence itself. Men, women, and children were forced to travel for weeks and months on end, packed standing into sealed and unheated railway trucks. Large numbers died on the way. So-called 'free exiles' could often fare worse than convicts through being abandoned without food or shelter on the snowbound or drought-ridden steppe. The longest journeys to Magadan or Kolyma in eastern Siberia involving arctic sea jouneys in the holds of prison ships, and forced marches could last a whole year. In 1936, in expectation of war, the Soviets deported about 500,000 Poles to Kazakhstan from the frontier zone in Belorussia and Ukraine.

In 1939–41, during the currency of the *Nazi–Soviet Pact, massive deportations took place from eastern Poland, the Baltic States, Finland and Moldavia (see BESSARABIA). *NKVD officials arrived in each of the newly occupied districts armed with detailed lists drawn up in advance in Moscow. Their deportation orders were taken to apply not only to the persons named, but to all their family members as well. As a rule, the menfolk would be arrested first. A little later the families would then be given 30 minutes to pack their belongings, and would be sent under armed guard to a collection point, on the (false) pretext of joining the men. In this way, three vast convoys took some 1.5 million Polish citizens from eastern Poland alone.

Thanks to the Polish–Soviet Treaty of 1941 (see POLAND, 2(e)) the surviving Polish deportees were granted an 'amnesty' (for crimes never committed). Many thousands left the USSR via the Middle East, or even by walking across the Himalayas to India, and many then joined *Anders' Army. They constituted the only large group ever to make eye-witness reports of the GUlag to the outside world. But their stories were suppressed by Allied wartime censorship, and when told, were widely disbelieved.

After the German invasion of the USSR in June 1941 (see BARBAROSSA) the populations of the industrial cities in the Ukraine were forcibly evacuated to the Urals and western Siberia in circumstances barely distinguishable from deportation; and Stalin, who had always regarded the possibility of *collaboration by non-Russians with an invader as quite high, wreaked his vengeance upon suspected collaborators by deporting them when the Red Army reoccupied their homelands. The Germans showed sympathy, in particular, for the national aspirations of the north Caucasian, Crimean, and Kalmyk peoples. During the two and a half years of German occupation the Crimean Tatars were able to reopen mosques and establish Islamic committees and Tatar units were used against Soviet partisans in the Crimea. In the autonomous republic of Kalmykia a cavalry corps was raised and it, too, operated against Soviet partisans (see also SOVIET EXILES AT WAR). In the Karachayevo-Cherkas oblast a Karachai national committee was formed and enjoyed some autonomy, and a Cossack region, also with a degree of autonomy, was set up in the Kuban in October 1942. When the Red Army reoccupied these areas whole nations, including party members, were deported and accused of collaboration. In November 1943 over 60,000 Karachai were deported from Stavropol krai. The deportation of the Kalmyks began in December 1943 and by the following February over 90,000 had been sent east. In February 1944 it was the turn of the Chechens, Ingushi, and Balkars from the Checheno-Ingush and Kabardino-Balkarian autonomous republics who, in April 1944, were deported to the Soviet republics of Kazakhstan and Kirgizia, and the Checheno-Ingush republic and the Karachayevo-Cherkas oblast were dissolved (both were reconstituted in 1957).

Over 190,000 Crimean Tatars were deported in May 1944. Armed Tatar groups resisted deportation but they were no match for the NKVD. Also deported from the Crimea were 37,000 Bulgarians, Greeks, and Armenians found guilty of collaborating with the Germans. In November 1944 86,000 Turks, Kurds, and Khemshins (Muslim Armenians) were deported from Georgia to Kazakhstan, Uzbekistan, and Kirgizia. About 3.5 million, from 52 nationalities, were deported to the Soviet east between 1940–6. Of these about a million were moved from November 1943 onwards. Possibly about a quarter died en route. Chechens and Ingushi were deported even though only a fraction of their autonomous republic had been occupied by the Wehrmacht. *Beria personally supervised the deportations. Resources were extracted from the military effort to ensure that the deportees were sent packing. Stalin's inhumanity was to cost the Soviet Union dear. While in Kazakhstan and Central Asia the various clans, especially the Chechens, collaborated to survive and thus were born the networks which were later to control the black market in Moscow and elsewhere. The nationality conflicts in the north Caucasus in the 1990s were a direct result of the deportations, since many of those who returned after 1956 did not recover their homes and property.

At the end of the war, with the consent of the western Allies, the remaining German population of the Sudetenland, East Prussia, Pomerania, Posnania, and Silesia, was deported to West Germany. These German *Vertriebenen* (Expellees) were officially classified euphemistically as 'repatriates'. Their numbers have been the subject of controversy, but may well have been in the range of from 5 to 8 million. Their homelands in the east were repopulated by Czechs and Poles, many of whom had been repatriated from lands annexed by the USSR. In 1947, about 500,000 Ukrainians were forcibly deported from the Breszczady region of south-east Poland, mainly to destinations on the Baltic or in former East Prussia.

Taken together, the total number of Europeans subject to deportation cannot have been less than 20 million. Mortality rates among them cannot be determined for certain. At the worst, in the wartime Soviet Union, they could have been as high as 50%.

Mass deportation was one of the hallmarks of totalitarian practice. In several countries, it transformed demographic and ethnic structures out of all recognition (see DEMOGRAPHY). It is one of the features which rendered the wartime experience in Eastern Europe so much more traumatic than anything encountered in the west (but see also REFUGEES). NORMAN DAVIES/MARTIN MCCAULEY

depth charges, see ANTI-SUBMARINE WEAPONS.

Déricourt, Henri (1909–62), French airman, pre-war *V-man for the Nazi security service, the Sicherheitsdient or SD (see RSHA). He may then have been recruited by *MI6, which knew of his SD connection, brought to London in September 1942 to join *SOE's French Section, and in January 1943 was sent to France as an Air Movements Officer. He was ordered to return in February 1944 after he was suspected of betraying SOE's PROSPER network to the SD. An SOE tribunal found his treachery 'not proven' but he was not allowed to return to France until after the war when he was tried there for his wartime activities. He was found not guilty, and though it is now clear that he did betray some colleagues, he was not ordered to do so by MI6 as part of any *deception plan. He was killed in an air crash in French Indo-China.

Desert Air Force, see WESTERN DESERT AIR FORCE.

desert campaigns, see WESTERN DESERT CAMPAIGNS.

deserters were commonplace on both sides, and women deserted as well as men. Those men who deserted while in combat theatres mostly came from the ground forces, as those fighting in the air or at sea had less opportunity to abscond. They were often *prisoners-of-war (POW) as these were especially vulnerable to pressure to join the opposing side. Whole formations—the *Indian National Army and the contingent led by General *Vlasov, for example—were largely composed of deserters.

During the *German–Soviet war desertion was rife in the Red Army. One in sixteen Soviet POW were found to be deserters. The American, British, and French figure was one in 4,962. But deserters joined the Red Army, too. Much of the Hungarian Army deserted to it around *Budapest towards the end of 1944, and before the *Kursk battle in July 1943, 186 'hiwis' (auxiliary helpers drawn from Soviet POW) defected back to the Soviet side with valuable intelligence.

Another formation which deserted *en masse* was the Burma National Army (see BURMA INDEPENDENCE ARMY) when, in March 1945, it abandoned the Japanese to fight under British command. Even Japanese soldiers, taught to die rather than surrender, deserted and did so in increasing numbers as the war progressed. The authors of *Soldiers of the Sun* (M. and S. Harries, London, 1991, p. 359) give the figures of 669 desertions in 1939, when the Japanese were fighting in the *China Incident, which by the first half of 1944 had increased to 1,085.

Men mostly deserted alone or with a few companions. Some of the 3,000 Poles who deserted from *Anders' Army when it arrived in Palestine subsequently joined Jewish resistance organizations (see STERN GANG and IRGUN) which fought the British, but American and British deserters, with the exception of the *British Free Corps, did not generally take up arms against their own side. But they often preyed on it and in the Middle East and Italy they formed gangs which survived by hijack, hold-ups, and pilfering from Allied transport and supply dumps.

In the American and British armies deserters were almost always infantrymen. Most of them were very young and a high percentage had psychological problems (see MEDICINE) or low intelligence. More than 100,000 deserted from the British Army in the course of the war. In May 1942, General *Auchinleck, disturbed by the number of deserters during the *Western Desert campaigns, recommended the reintroduction of the death penalty, which was refused. One British divisional general, Maj-General James Elliot, remarked on the very high level of what he called battle absenteeism. This was higher than the numbers killed in certain actions and sometimes even higher than those wounded. 'It was at times,' he wrote, 'common for some 20 men in a battalion to become Battle Absentees in a given section. About 400 men were Battle Absentees in the average division in 1943–4 in a period of six months. When it is realized that these men came almost entirely from the rifle companies of infantry battalions, the numbers became serious' (quoted in A. Millett and M. Williamson (eds.), *Military Effectiveness*, Vol. 3, London, 1988, p. 100).

The US Army, which had a total of 40,000 deserters, did have the death penalty but it was only enforced on one occasion. The Americans preferred if possible to charge deserters with the lesser offence of being absent without leave which is why, along with the fact that the US Army saw no fighting until mid-1942, US Army figures for desertion were lower than the British ones.

In Germany desertion was regarded as an offence against both the Führer and the *Volksgemeinschaft* (national community) and it also sometimes involved the offence of *Wehrkraftzersetzung* (subversion of the war effort). In April 1940 Hitler issued guidelines which prescribed death as being the normal punishment (see GERMANY, 3). It has been estimated that about 35,000 members of the Wehrmacht were accused of desertion during the war, resulting in about 22,750 death sentences of which at least 15,000—perhaps many more—were carried out. This astonishingly high figure can be largely explained by the extreme measures imposed by German commanders on their troops during the last months of the war. For example, the commander in *Courland, General Lothar Rendulic 'ordered "flying courts-martial" created to scour the rear areas. Every soldier not wounded, picked up outside his unit area, was to be tried and shot' (E. Ziemke, *Stalingrad to Berlin*, Washington, DC, 1968, p. 433).

destroyers-for-bases agreement. On 15 May 1940 Churchill, in a personal message to Roosevelt, made clear the desperate situation in which the UK found itself. Amongst other requests he suggested the USA lend Britain 40 or 50 destroyers as a stopgap until warships under construction in the UK were completed. Roosevelt's reply was negative, saying that Congress, whose approval would have to be sought, would probably be unwilling to circumvent the *Neutrality Acts. However, Churchill continued to press for the destroyers and once Roosevelt had been nominated for a third term as president in July 1940, as well as being assured of the UK's determination to continue the war (for example, see BRITAIN, BATTLE OF, and MERS-EL-KÉBIR), he became more positive. There was considerable negotiation as Churchill was reluctant to link leasing bases with receiving the destroyers, while Roosevelt wanted some kind of guarantee that the British fleet would not be surrendered or scuttled. He also insisted on a formula which did not need the permission of Congress. The question was eventually resolved on 2 September when the British ambassador, Lord Lothian (1882–1940), and Cordell *Hull, the US secretary of state, exchanged letters. Lothian's did not mention the destroyers, and Hull's only mentioned them in passing. As a result of this exchange, the USA acquired 99-year leases on bases in the British West Indies (in the Bahamas, Jamaica, St Lucia, Trinidad, Antigua, and British Guiana). They were also given two more, in Newfoundland and Bermuda, but the terms of all the leases were not settled until March 1941 and by the end of 1940 the British had acquired only 9 of the promised 50 destroyers.

Deutsches Afrika Korps, see AFRIKA KORPS.

De Valera, Eamon (1882–1975), Eire's Taoiseach (prime minister) and minister for external affairs from 1932 to 1948, and president of the *League of Nations from 1932.

The Irish Free State was officially proclaimed in 1922, and when De Valera came to power ten years later he distanced his country from the UK though, wanting reunification with Northern Ireland (see UK, 4), he remained within the British Empire. However, when war came he declared Eire's neutrality; refused the British use of the treaty ports whose return to Irish control he had negotiated in 1938; introduced severe measures against the *Irish Republican Army; and persuaded the British government to withdraw conscription in Northern Ireland. Throughout the war he resisted British, and later US, pressure to join the Allies. But despite sending congratulations to Subhas Chandra *Bose on the formation of his Japanese-sponsored Provisional government of Free India, and expressing his condolences in person to the German ambassador in Dublin when Hitler committed suicide, he was essentially pro-Allied and allowed the British many concessions.

Longford, Earl of, and O'Neill, T., *Eamon de Valera* (London, 1970).

Devers, General Jacob (1887–1979), US Army officer whose administrative ability led to quick promotion. By May 1943 he was commanding *ETOUSA with the rank of lt-general and at the end of 1943 he became Maitland *Wilson's deputy supreme commander in the Mediterranean. He commanded Sixth Army Group from 15 September 1944 until the end of the war (see FRENCH RIVIERA LANDINGS). His mixed force of Seventh US Army under Lt-General *Patch and First French Army, commanded by General de *Lattre de Tassigny, drove through southern France into southern Germany, and he was promoted four-star general in March 1945. But his handling of the *Colmar pocket did not enhance his reputation with *Eisenhower who, in an evaluation of his field commanders, rated him only 24th.

Dewavrin, Colonel André (b.1911), regular French engineer officer, taught at St Cyr in 1939, survived the *Norwegian campaign of April–June, 1940 and joined de *Gaulle and the Free French in June 1940. He took the codename PASSY and became head of the French secret services in London, the *Bureau Central de Renseignements et d'Action. Dewavrin undertook two missions into France by parachute, one with Brossolette and *Yeo-Thomas in the autumn of 1943 to solve problems raised by arrest of *Moulin, the other into Brittany in August 1944. He was head of the French secret service 1945–6. A loyal Gaullist, opposed to *Vichy but otherwise non-political, he was distrusted by the communists.

M. R. D. FOOT

DIADEM, see ITALIAN CAMPAIGN.

Dieppe raid, undertaken, predominently by Canadian troops, primarily to test the defences of this German-occupied French port. Launched on 19 August 1942, it was the biggest such operation of the war.

Originally codenamed RUTTER, the raid was planned by a British organization, *Combined Operations Headquarters, and by GHQ Home Forces which delegated its authority to Lt-General *Montgomery, then C-in-C South-Eastern Command. Under Montgomery's chairmanship the raid became a frontal assault without a heavy preliminary air bombardment and the Command's 2nd Canadian Division under Maj-General J. H. Roberts was nominated to undertake it after Canadian pressure to allow its troops to see action. Bad weather then caused its cancellation on 7 July 1942. Montgomery recommended this should be 'for all time', and shortly afterwards he left to command the Eighth Army in the *Western Desert campaigns. However, the Chief of Combined Operations, Vice-Admiral *Mountbatten, revived it under a new codename, JUBILEE, an unprecedented decision if only because of the security risks involved.

JUBILEE was mounted from five different English ports between Southampton and Newhaven with a force of 4,963 Canadians, 1,075 British personnel, and 50 US Rangers. The naval force, organized into 13 groups, totalled 237 warships and landing craft, including 8 destroyers some of which gave fire support to the landings, the employment of battleships in the confines of the English Channel having been ruled out. Air support was also inadequate, the air ministry having opposed the diversion of heavy bombers from the *strategic air offensive against Germany. However, 66 of the participating 74 squadrons from 9 Allied nations, commanded by Air Vice-Marshal *Leigh-Mallory, were fighter formations in the hope, fulfilled, that the Luftwaffe would be brought to battle.

Intensive *photographic reconnaissance had revealed most of the defences—though not the gun positions in the headland cliffs that were to cause such slaughter—but intelligence was lacking on other essentials. Little was known about the strength of the positions or the whereabouts of German command posts; the beach gradients had to be calculated from a holiday snapshot; and the German order of battle was incorrectly assessed.

At dawn flank attacks by commandos and Canadian troops were launched along a ten-mile front. These were, from west to east: on the coastal battery near Varengeville (No. 4 Commando); on Pourville (South Saskatchewan Regiment and later Queen's Own Cameron Highlanders of Canada); on Puys (Royal Regiment of Canada); and on the coastal battery near Berneval (No. 3 Commando). The local garrison apparently had no foreknowledge of the raid but the defenders at Puys and Berneval were soon alerted when at 0348 a small German convoy exchanged fire with part of the landing force. (The Admiralty had twice warned the naval force commander that the convoy was in the area, signals which he apparently never received.) As a result the vital element of surprise, upon which the planners had gambled, was lost. Only a handful of men from No. 3 Commando landed, but they made the battery temporarily inoperable by sniping at its crew. At Puys the Canadians' difficulties were compounded by being landed late. They were unable to move off the beaches and suffered heavy casualties. However, No. 4 Commando landed without being fired on and stormed the Varengeville battery, the only unit to capture all its objectives. At Pourville, too, the South Saskatchewan Regiment beached without coming under fire. But some were landed in the wrong place, fatally delaying the vital seizure of high ground to the east, though a few did achieve their objectives. The Queen's Own Cameron Highlanders of Canada were landed on the same beach 30 minutes later as planned and some penetrated further inland than any other troops that day, but German reinforcements soon forced them back.

Half an hour after these flank attacks had been launched, at 0520, the main frontal assault was mounted by the Royal Hamilton Light Infantry, the Essex Scottish Regiment, and tanks of the 14th Army Tank Regiment under the cover of smoke screens laid by aircraft. The infantry landed on time, but the lightness of the support fire allowed the German defenders to recover quickly and a fatal delay in landing the supporting tanks destroyed the impetus of the troops and few managed to reach the town. Only 15 of the 27 tanks which landed managed to cross the sea wall and these were soon halted by roadblocks.

Worse was to come as inaccurate information led Roberts to reinforce disaster by ordering two of his floating reserve units ashore. Les Fusiliers Mont-Royal, landed under the port's cliffs, were soon pinned down; and the Royal Marine 'A' Commando was only saved from total disaster by its commanding officer who turned back some of its landing craft before being mortally wounded.

Withdrawal from the beaches began under heavy fire at 1100 and was completed by 1400. Of the 4,963 Canadians who had taken part, 3,367 were killed, wounded, or taken prisoner, though 4,056 eventually survived. British casualties amounted to 275. The Royal Navy lost one destroyer and 33 landing craft, and suffered 550 casualties. The air battle was equally disastrous, the RAF losing 106 aircraft, the Luftwaffe only 48 of the 945 committed. German ground casualties were just 591.

The fiasco of Dieppe was created by a complex web of political and military pressures on Churchill and the British *Chiefs of Staff at a critical juncture of the war. Domestic, and Soviet, demands for a Second Front to relieve German pressure on the USSR; inter-service disputes for the allocation of scarce resources; US expectations, aroused by British promises of action; Churchill's insistence on offensive measures, and his elevation of the inexperienced, malleable—and ambitious—Mountbatten to ensure some; all these, and more, contributed to an uncontrollable impetus to launch an operation that, with hindsight, was never viable.

The Chiefs of Staff may well have acquiesced in JUBILEE because it was a lesser evil than some other plan Churchill might have foisted on them; and the fact that no written record survives of their having approved it has led to speculation, almost certainly unfounded, that Mountbatten proceeded without their authorization. However, he certainly kept its remounting under a cloak of excessive secrecy, denying his own second-in-command, the three service intelligence chiefs, and the *Inter-Services Security Board any knowledge of it.

Lessons were learned, in particular the need for heavy bombardment as the preliminary to any major landing. But JUBILEE is not now seen by all historians as being an essential prerequisite to any full-scale invasion of France. Some now regard it as an unjustified gamble which, without adequate air or sea support, had no chance of success. See also AMPHIBIOUS WARFARE.

Villa, B., *Unauthorized Action: Mountbatten and the Dieppe Raid* (Oxford, 1990).

Dietrich, General Josef ('Sepp') (1892–1966), early Nazi Party supporter and a close associate of Hitler for whom he formed a special bodyguard (*Leibstandarte*) in 1933. Despite having no advanced military training—he had been an NCO in the *First World War—Dietrich successfully commanded this bodyguard when it was formed into a Waffen-*SS formation, Leibstandarte Adolf Hitler, which took part in almost every campaign the Germans fought and eventually became an SS Panzer Corps. In December 1944 he commanded Sixth Panzer Army (later Sixth SS Panzer Army) which played a crucial role in the *Ardennes campaign and which later fought in Hungary and Austria, where its failure led to his dismissal. Hitler called him 'simultaneously cunning, energetic, and brutal', and in July 1946 a US military court gave him a life sentence for the *Malmédy massacre. He was released in 1955, but was again imprisoned for nine months by a West German court in 1957.

Messenger, C., *Hitler's Gladiator* (London, 1988).

Dietrich, Otto (1897–1952), press chief of the Nazi Party from 1931 to 1945, and from 1938 also *Goebbels's state secretary in the ministry of propaganda. Imprisoned in 1945, he was released in 1950.

Dill, Field Marshal Sir John (1881–1944), British *Chief of the Imperial General Staff (CIGS) from May 1940 to December 1941, and then the representative of the British *Chiefs of Staff committee in Washington.

After a brilliant career in the *First World War, which he ended as a brigadier-general, Dill was appointed to command the 1st British Corps in September 1939. He was promoted general the following month, but his corps saw no action before he was recalled in April 1940 to become Vice-CIGS. He succeeded *Ironside as CIGS the following month and it was his misfortune to preside over a disastrous period in British military history. He was plagued by ill health, failed to see eye-to-eye with Churchill, who nicknamed him 'Dilly-Dally', and after being promoted field marshal was obliged to retire in December 1941 to make way for *Brooke.

The same month he accompanied Churchill to Washington and stayed on to head the British Joint Staff Mission there and to be the representative on the US *Joint Chiefs of Staff committee for the minister of defence (Churchill) and the British Chiefs of Staff. His health improved and he soon became one of the crucial figures in cementing Anglo-US relations. His tact and persuasiveness became renowned, and he won the trust and friendship of Roosevelt and the US Chiefs of Staff. Roosevelt commented when he died in November 1944 that he was 'the most important figure in the remarkable accord which has been developed in the combined operations of our two countries.'

He was buried in Arlington cemetery, the only foreigner to be honoured in this way, and was posthumously awarded the American DSM (see DECORATIONS). He was knighted in 1937.

diplomacy. On the outbreak of hostilities, diplomatic missions in enemy countries close down and the diplomats depart. But diplomacy continues to flourish in wartime; diplomatic business becomes, if anything, more urgent. Foreign ministries continue sending out directives and receiving reports; traffic in coded messages becomes brisker; the couriers go on carrying diplomatic bags, if necessary by different routes.

In addition, as belligerent countries concentrate on the conduct of war, neutral states start to play a more significant role in diplomacy. Their missions are sometimes requested to represent the interests of the combatants, and strategically placed neutral countries become meeting-points as well as escape routes. Switzerland and Sweden provided the meeting-ground for diplomats as well as *spies in the Second World War; while Portugal became the gate through which *refugees streamed out of Europe.

The establishments of the foreign ministries in both Allied and Axis countries had grown everywhere before the war; the ministries became clearing houses for many different kinds of foreign business, propaganda, and *economic warfare among them. The diplomats were often consulted on the consequences of military strategies, without having a decisive voice in such matters; they became so overburdened with paperwork that the clarity of their judgement sometimes suffered.

It may be that diplomacy played a less significant role than it had done in the *First World War. From 1914 to 1918, war leaders relied on diplomats to make up for military weakness on crucial occasions. The most striking example was the belief, held in Berlin, that diplomacy would help reduce the war from two fronts—in the west and in the east—to a single-front engagement. In the Second World War diplomatic dilemmas tended to be resolved by military action. For example, Japan, an ally of Germany, was fighting China (see CHINA INCIDENT), which was being aided by the USSR, when the *Nazi–Soviet Pact of August 1939 was concluded; Japan's conundrum was resolved by the German attack on the USSR in June 1941 (see BARBAROSSA), just as the era of US isolationism was brought to an end by the Japanese attack on *Pearl Harbor.

Improved *radio communications strengthened the growing preference of heads of government for keeping in touch directly with each other, and the position of diplomacy also changed for other reasons. The Germans under Hitler and, before them, the Soviets after the Bolshevik revolution, had begun using other means than diplomacy to keep in touch with the outside world. Lenin (1870–1924) and Stalin had the *Comintern at their disposal, which gave Soviet foreign policy a second string. Equipped with a less appealing ideology than *communism, Hitler learned how to use the Nazi Party, in conjunction with the Germans outside the Reich (see VOLKSDEUTSCHE), as vigorous players in the international field.

The network of diplomatic agreements, with which Hitler entered the war, was both ideological and contradictory. Co-operation between Germany and Italy, the two leading fascist states in Europe, had been initiated as early as 1936. It was anchored in a loose accord, which became known as the Rome–Berlin Axis. The *Anti-Comintern Pact between Germany and Japan was concluded a few months later, towards the end of 1936: Italy acceded to the pact in November 1937. On 22 May 1939, Italy strengthened its understanding with

Germany by a more formal alliance, which became known as the *Pact of Steel, and on 27 September 1940 the *Tripartite Pact, which was meant to lay down the foundations of the New Order both in Europe and in Asia, was signed in Berlin by Germany, Italy, and Japan; it was subsequently joined by the smaller states in eastern Europe which had come under the influence of the Reich.

Hitler's *Polish campaign, and then the attack on the USSR, were launched without formal declarations of war. German diplomats had less opportunity than they had, say, in the First World War to be active in the search for potential allies. Hitler placed more reliance on military occupation, both in Scandinavia and in the Balkans, than on diplomatic persuasion.

Nor did the diplomacy of Hitler's foreign secretary *Ribbentrop look coherent. Until the invasion of the Soviet Union, the Nazi–Soviet Pact had been in place, in stark contradiction to the Anti-Comintern Pact. The first signal was sent from Moscow in May 1939, when *Molotov replaced *Litvinov in the commissariat of foreign affairs, and the policy of collective security lost its main Soviet exponent. Hitler, on the other hand, wanted a guarantee of Soviet neutrality before he attacked Poland; a late approach from London to Stalin could no longer prevent his agreement with the Germans.

The New Order for Europe (see GERMANY, 4) had first begun to take shape when, during the years of the economic slump, Hjalmar *Schacht, Hitler's minister of finance, created the dependence of the agrarian economies in the Balkans on the Reich. Other steps towards the New Order were taken by aggressive moves, both military and diplomatic, including the annexation of Austria and the *Munich agreement. From Hitler's point of view, these were mere frontier rectifications, intended to correct some of the injustices of the old order in Europe, created by the peace treaties (see VERSAILLES SETTLEMENT). Others followed when the *Vienna awards—a result of Hungarian diplomacy—ceded to Hungary certain Czechoslovak territories (1938) and then northern Transylvania which belonged to Romania (1940).

By the time of the second Vienna award, the spring and summer campaigns of 1940 had made Hitler the master of a great part of continental Europe. Stalin, alarmed by the speed of Hitler's advance in the west, intensified his effort to improve the position of the Soviet Union on its western border. The negotiations with Finland concerning a mutual assistance pact which included territorial and diplomatic concessions to the USSR, failed, and, in November 1939 the *Finnish–Soviet war began. It cost the Soviet Union its seat on the *League of Nations (14 December 1939) but helped it to gain about 12% of Finnish territory, by the Treaty of Moscow made on 12 March 1940. Lithuania, Latvia, and Estonia were also absorbed by the USSR, after communist coups carried out between 15 June and 16 August. On 23 June, Stalin informed his German partners that he would like to have Bukovina in addition to Romania's Bessarabia, because it contained a Ukrainian population. This claim was too much for Hitler, who decided to block further Soviet advances. Nevertheless, the humiliation of Romania was not yet at an end. The Treaty of Craiova, on 23 August, handed over southern Dobruja to Bulgaria, a territory which it had lost in the second Balkan War in 1913. Hitler agreed to guarantee Romania's territory, which had been diminished by about a third within two months, only after the second Vienna award.

The New Order was created by diplomacy out of economic need, historical resentment, and military aggression. Propaganda put on it whatever gloss it possessed, while the requirements of the industries of the Third Reich at war helped to give the New Order some kind of cohesion. In the Auswärtiges Amt (foreign office) as well, the diplomats were distracted by an increased agenda, and by the new methods of dealing with the world outside the Reich.

Only a small part of the conquered territories suffered outright annexation. Several countries came under German military administration, including occupied France, Belgium, and, in 1941, Greece and Yugoslavia. Norway and the Netherlands, on the other hand, were placed in the care of civilian commissioners. Denmark enjoyed an exceptional status under the royal family, which decided to stay in Copenhagen after German occupation. The formula for the Nazi rule of Slav territories, through imperial pro-consuls, had first been tested in the Protectorate of Bohemia and Moravia before the outbreak of war; it was then used in Poland and, finally, in the occupied territories of the USSR.

The New Order in Europe also contained Hitler's allies on approval: in addition to Italy, they were Finland, Slovakia, Hungary, Romania, and Albania, which had been annexed by Italy in March 1939. Italy entered the war on 10 June 1940: its place in the New Order was never secure. The theories of Hitler's philosophers of race allowed that fascist Italians might be sound ideologically, but they questioned their racial purity. The Germans had encouraged Mussolini's involvement in the *Spanish Civil War so as to distract his attention from south-east Europe, where German diplomacy was becoming increasingly active. When the Italians received German military support for their failing ventures in the Balkans, it was clear that their role in the New Order could never be prominent. The day before the invasion of the USSR, Hitler dictated a long letter to Mussolini in which he said that he had never felt at ease in a partnership with Moscow. This was the first Mussolini knew of Hitler's intention and it is not known whether he felt relieved to hear that the great ideological rift in Nazi foreign policy was about to be mended at last.

On the Allied side, policy co-ordination was the key issue of British and French diplomacy: the *Supreme War Council was created soon after the outbreak of the war; an agreement not to conclude a separate peace was signed in the spring of 1940. Otherwise, British and French interests were hard to reconcile. The British assumed that the war would last at least three years, and they put their faith in the effectiveness of a naval blockade. The French, on the other hand, intended to move the war as far away as possible from their border.

It was in Scandinavia that the French and the British interests promised to be reconciled and where successful diplomacy could have proved harmful to Germany's interests. Iron ore mined in northern Sweden was an important source of supply for German industries, and most of it passed through the Norwegian port of Narvik. On 16 September 1939, the British government declared that an attack on Norway would be regarded as equivalent to an attack on the UK. Various schemes for mining Norwegian territorial waters were considered in London. The context of Allied diplomacy in Scandinavia changed after the USSR started the Finnish–Soviet war on 30 November; the joint Franco-British plans to help Finland and to stop the traffic in Swedish ore came to almost nothing. The desire of the Swedish and Norwegian governments to maintain their neutrality, as well as their reluctance to provoke the Soviets, frustrated the plans of the Supreme War Council before Finnish resistance came to an end.

On 8 April 1940, the Admiralty in London announced that a minefield was being laid in Norwegian territorial waters; on 9 April, the Germans launched their *Norwegian campaign, occupying Norway's principal ports, including Narvik and Oslo. The *phoney war had drawn to a close: after the occupation of Norway and Denmark, the Wehrmacht turned against the Netherlands, Belgium, and Luxemburg (see FALL GELB). The French front was penetrated in the middle of May and, on 14 June, the Germans entered Paris.

British opinion did not consider the fall of *France to have also been the defeat of the UK; for more than a year, however, the country would stand, with its empire, all but alone against an opponent in control of a large part of continental Europe. In the long term, the task of diplomacy was to help the UK survive the isolation; and, eventually, to break out of it. In the short term, the diplomats must try to limit the consequences of defeat.

When the Dutch C-in-C ordered his troops to resist the Germans, Lord *Halifax asked the Dutch foreign minister to let the state of hostilities continue, without negotiating with the Germans. The Dutch royal family came to London, while *Léopold III chose to stay in Belgium. The Belgian politicians, including Paul Henri Spaak (1899–1972), assured the foreign office on 28 May that they would also fight the war to the end. The continuity of the Dutch and Belgian *governments-in-exile provided a spark of hope for the future.

About midnight on 21 June, the new French government under *Pétain received the German terms. In a symbolic act, the *armistice was signed in the same railway dining car, in the forest of Compiègne, in which the Germans had signed their capitulation in 1918. The threat that the UK would suffer the same fate as France came and went, as the Germans failed to invade; but after the entry of Italy into the war the policies of neutral Spain and Turkey became decisive for the British position in the Mediterranean. It was assumed in London that the Spanish leader, *Franco, was looking forward to the defeat of the Allies: yet he did not want a clear-cut victory of the Axis either, because he feared that it would strengthen the position of Italy in the Mediterranean.

Late in September, it seemed that the Wehrmacht would move against Spain rather than the UK. On 23 October Hitler travelled to the Spanish border to meet Franco, who refused to make military concessions to Germany and succeeded in keeping Spain out of the war. In a conversation with *Eden in May 1941, the Spanish ambassador said that, as long as the UK held Suez, Franco would resist the Germans and argue that there was little point in closing down one end of the Mediterranean while the other remained open.

The Turks, on the other hand, concluded a treaty with the UK and France on 28 September 1939. After the fall of *France, they argued that they were no longer bound not to intervene in the case of aggression in the Mediterranean. They did, however, declare that they would remain non-belligerent. The British expected more of the Turks, especially after the Italian attack on Greece, launched on 28 October 1940, which began the *Balkan campaign. The aim of the foreign office was to get Turkey to co-operate with Yugoslavia and go to war with Bulgaria if Bulgaria allowed the Germans to cross its territory. The British knew that the Germans would not allow the Italians to suffer defeat in Greece; and that, on 17 November, Bulgaria's King Boris (1894–1943) visited Hitler. But the Turks were not in a heroic mood, while the foreign office (though less than the prime minister) tended to understate the effect in the Balkans and the Near East of the appearance of British military weakness.

Until the end of 1941, the effort to assure the USA that the UK was worth backing in the war took the foremost place in London. Roosevelt, re-elected on 5 November 1940 for his third term as president, was resolved to keep the USA out of the war in Europe; but, equally, he did not want the UK to suffer defeat. In the UK's hour of greatest need, Churchill's relations with Roosevelt were conducted with tact and a great sureness of touch. In a letter to the president early in December 1940, the prime minister concluded that if the president was convinced 'that the defeat of Nazi and fascist tyranny is a matter of high consequence to the people of the United States and the Western hemisphere, you will regard this letter not as an appeal for aid, but as a statement of the minimum action necessary to achieve our common purpose'. On 17 December, Roosevelt made a reference to the possibility of 'leasing' war material to the British. The question remained of how the UK would pay for such material: the answers were contained in the *Lend-Lease Bill, introduced in the Congress on 10 January 1941. The Bill underwrote the US intention that the UK should not lose the war through the want of material means.

After Germany's entry into the Balkan campaign in

April 1941, the second phase of hostilities was about to open. When the USSR and then the USA were drawn into the conflict by aggressive German and Japanese moves, the continuities between the First and the Second World Wars became clearer. The latter was, of course, concerned with the maintenance in Europe of the status quo established after the First, or with its reversal. After 22 June 1941, when the Germans invaded the USSR (see BARBAROSSA), the combination of the east and the west of Europe against its centre was renewed. There again arose the concern, in London, that the USSR might conclude a separate peace with Germany, and Stalin, after the Bolsheviks' experience of the civil war and the western powers' intervention in it, was deeply suspicious of his allies.

Though the emerging alliance against Hitler was less tied together by diplomatic conventions than had been the alliance against Germany in the First World War, much more time was spent on the design of the post-war world. One of the impulses for the special interest in the future was the presence of several governments-in-exile in London; as well as of communist émigrés in Moscow. But the main contrast between the two World Wars soon emerged. In the First, the Russian steamroller, after initial advances, was put into reverse; in the Second, the Red Army, after severe setbacks, advanced into the centre of Europe. This profoundly altered the strategic context of diplomacy in the Second World War and a new diplomatic agenda started to be drawn up.

However, the two wars remained linked, for the governments-in-exile as much as for the leaders of the Great Powers, by political memories as well as by personal connections. Ignacy Paderewski (1860–1941), who had delighted President Wilson with his accomplished interpretations of Chopin on the piano, and who became the first prime minister of Poland after the First World War, emerged again as the president of the Polish National Council in France. Władysław *Sikorski, who had also taken part in the reunification of Poland, and who served a term as prime minister in 1922–3, became the head of the Polish government-in-exile in London. Edvard *Beneš, who had helped Tomas Masaryk (1850–1937) achieve the recognition of Czechoslovakia by the Allies in 1918, was assisted by Masaryk's son, Jan, to overcome diplomatic hurdles during the war.

The west Europeans in London, including the Scandinavians, in the main shared in the British foreign office's assumption that the states of continental Europe would return to approximately the same position as they had occupied before the war. The east Europeans, on the other hand, believed that they must maintain strong links with the west after the end of the war. Before June 1941, General Sikorski had assumed that his country was at war with the two partitioning powers, Germany and the USSR. The Poles expected the situation of 1918 to be repeated. They believed that the USSR would have no say in the making of peace and that western influence would again prove decisive in the making of post-war order.

Whereas political refugees came to London as a result of the war in Europe, Moscow had become a centre of foreign communists between the two wars. The first wave arrived after the suppression of the regime of Béla Kun (1886–1939) in Hungary in 1919; and among the last arrivals were the leaders of the Communist Party banned in post-Munich Czechoslovakia. Though the ranks of the exiles had been depleted in Stalin's purges, those who survived played significant roles in the politics of their countries during and after the war.

The Bulgarians provided the Comintern with its secretary general, Georgi Dimitrov; among the Germans, Wilhelm Pieck came to Moscow from exile in Paris and Walter Ulbricht (1893–1973)—another member of the KPD Politburo—arrived from Prague. Ana Pauker (1893–1960), a Romanian communist, and Matyás Rákosi, a member of Béla Kun's short-lived Soviet government in Hungary, also sought asylum in Moscow. Bolesław Bierut (see LUBLIN COMMITTEE) came after he had been threatened with arrest in Poland; and Klement Gottwald (1896–1953) headed the last group of communist migrants, when the Communist Party of Czechoslovakia was banned shortly after the Munich agreement.

In an unexpected move, on 15 May 1943, the Comintern asked its member countries to dissolve the organization. Stalin distrusted international socialism, especially when he was unable to manipulate it; and he had turned to other means of exerting Soviet influence abroad, more acceptable outside the USSR than the Comintern. A few weeks after the German invasion, a Panslav congress took place in Moscow. It aimed to unite the Slavs in resistance against Hitler, and call into play political forces outside the Comintern; three similar congresses followed in Moscow, as well as a conference of American Slavs in Detroit in April 1942.

Differences between the policies of exile communities in Moscow and those in London soon emerged. Moscow for instance advocated acts of sabotage and the organization of partisan warfare at a level of intensity and sacrifice which Beneš, for one, was unwilling to allow. It was nevertheless Beneš who regarded Stalin as a person with whom the Czechoslovaks—as well as the other Allies—could do business, while virtually the whole Polish emigration resisted such an idea. The British foreign office tried hard to help the Poles come to an agreement with the USSR: after great difficulties, a treaty was signed between them on 30 July 1941.

The Soviets renounced the Nazi–Soviet Pact and its associated treaties on the insistence of the Poles, who assumed that Moscow thereby acknowledged Poland's claim to its pre-war territories in the east. General Sikorski put the matter bluntly to *Maisky, the Soviet ambassador in London: he said that he would not consider returning to a territorially diminished Poland after the war. In December 1941 Sikorski travelled to Moscow, for an extraordinary meeting with Stalin. At a time when the Wehrmacht had a spearhead within sight of Moscow, Stalin told the Poles, in a tense moment, 'We will conquer Poland and we will give it back to you.' Sikorski and Stalin signed a declaration of friendship, but Soviet–Polish relations did not prosper (see POLAND, 2(e)). The policies of exiled governments, of the Poles especially, gave the British foreign office an unusual, close-up view of Soviet diplomacy. A new field of foreign relations was opened up, which became the matrix of the post-war division of Europe. Before BARBAROSSA, the foreign office had disagreed with the views of Stafford *Cripps, its ambassador in Moscow. Cripps argued that the Soviets were more concerned with the possibility of the UK's constructing an anti-Soviet combination after the war than with the policies of a victorious Germany. At that time, the foreign office wanted the Soviets to remain at least neutral in Europe—as neutral to the UK, that is, as they were to Germany—and, in Asia, to renew, or continue, their assistance to China against Japanese aggression. In return, the British were prepared to recognize Soviet acquisitions in the Baltic and in other parts of Eastern Europe, and they were ready to make an offer of commodities required for the USSR's defence.

The foreign office persisted in this policy of helping the Soviets, especially after Eden succeeded Halifax as foreign secretary, and on the day BARBAROSSA was launched Churchill broadcast an offer of assistance to the Soviet Union. An agreement between the two countries was signed on 12 July 1941, and concerned the two points suggested by Stalin. It was an undertaking by the UK not to conclude an armistice except by mutual consent; and a promise to offer the USSR material support.

Early in the autumn a British delegation, headed by Lord *Beaverbrook travelled to Moscow together with the Americans, led by Averell *Harriman (see THREE-POWER CONFERENCE). It did not provide Stalin with the assurance, especially in the matter of military assistance, he had expected. An unfriendly message from Stalin reached London on 11 November; it elicited the promise from the prime minister that he would travel to Moscow with military experts soon, and that the UK would declare war on Finland, Hungary, and Romania.

As far as the future of Europe was concerned, the return to the status quo in the area west of the River Rhine was never questioned in the British foreign office; it was the future of Germany, and of the territory lying between Germany and the USSR, that came under review. As early as November 1940, a 'confederation' between Poland and Czechoslovakia was declared under the sponsorship of the foreign office; it was further explained in January 1942. In July 1941, Sikorski told Eden that the Yugoslav leaders favoured the creation of two federal blocks; one was to be grouped around Poland, the other around Yugoslavia. The Greeks in London were also in touch with the Yugoslavs on the possibility of forming a union in the Balkans.

As the alliance against Hitler broadened, the scope for diplomatic activity became less. In the Far East, as China began to drift into civil war, the Americans went on the offensive against the Japanese in the Pacific; the British and the Americans—with French and Polish assistance—fought the *North African and *Italian campaigns but all the Allies (except China) became equally engaged only in Europe north of the Alps. It was there that the Big Three showed they had more power at their disposal than any combination in history. Confronted with this *Grand Alliance, *Goebbels's propaganda transformed the idea of the New Order in Europe into the concept of **Festung Europa*.

While the future of Europe moved to the top of Allied diplomatic agenda, the strategic context of the main agenda item changed. Beneš, sensitive as ever to the underlying shifts of diplomacy, visited Washington in May 1943, so as to secure Roosevelt's support for a new and comprehensive treaty between Czechoslovakia and the Soviet Union. Beneš described Stalin as a benign leader, anxious to reform his country; the president thought the view novel and acceptable, and hinted that the treaty could be a model for similar treaties for countries bordering the Soviet Union. The British foreign office was more reserved about the idea: Eden suggested that the Czechoslovak treaty would put the Poles at a disadvantage in their relations with Moscow.

Late in the autumn of 1943, Beneš travelled to Moscow. He was open with the Soviets, and gave Stalin a valuable second opinion on the intentions of the Allied leaders. He assured Molotov that the British government had agreed to the expulsion of the Germans from Czechoslovakia, and that all German property there would be confiscated and nationalized. He opened up the perspective before Stalin of an alignment between social and national revolution, not only in Czechoslovakia but in other countries of eastern Europe as well. He suggested that the new Polish prime minister, Stanisław Mikołajczyk, was the Polish leader most likely to come to terms with the Soviets and told Stalin how important it was that the USSR should share in the occupation of Hungary.

Meanwhile, in London, the concern, with the changing balance of power in Europe grew. On 9 September 1944, five days after the landing of the *British expedition to Greece, Churchill arrived in Moscow for the *TOLSTOY conference to discover Stalin's plans for eastern Europe. He offered to bring Mikołajczyk and his foreign minister, Tadeusz Romer, to Moscow at short notice. They landed at Moscow airport in the evening of 12 October, Mikołajczyk making the long trip for the second time in ten weeks. He still feared the incorporation of Poland into the USSR, and was uncertain about Polish frontiers. The need to resist Hitler had united the Poles; now, the emergence of a powerful USSR started cruelly to divide them.

Stalin helped to advance the interests of the Poles in Moscow, though he neither liked nor trusted them; and most of them were survivors of a party decimated in his purges. The defeat of the *Warsaw rising had put the London Poles into a weak position, though Mikołajczk kept on refusing to give up the eastern territories of Poland, beyond the Curzon Line (see POLISH–SOVIET FRONTIER). After Churchill and the Polish delegation left in October 1944, Stalin was compelled to rely on the Polish team in Moscow.

Stalin regarded the British plans, outside the unresolved Polish question, as being out of touch with reality. As far as he was concerned, Churchill's plan for a Danubian federation, or for a second German state based on Vienna, belonged to the same category of vague aspirations as did the earlier federal plans considered by the Polish, Yugoslav, Greek, and Czechoslovak politicians in London. Churchill had suggested that Poland, Czechoslovakia, and Hungary should form a group which would become a customs union. Stalin replied that the eastern peoples would first want to build up their national life, without restricting their rights by combining with others.

In the concluding phase of the war, diplomacy tended to be transacted at the very top of the Allied hierarchy. Meetings of the Big Three in particular exercised magnetic power over diplomatic business. Items such as the definition of war aims, proposals for the organization of post-war security in Europe, the design for an international organization (see SAN FRANCISCO CONFERENCE), were often handed down to specialized committees and came to occupy most of the time of the diplomats. Chance remarks of the Allied leaders sometimes tended to assume the quality of self-fulfilling prophecies. At the Yalta conference in February 1945 (see ARGONAUT), Roosevelt suggested that the military zones of occupation might be the first step to the dismemberment of Germany: as they indeed proved to be.

In any case, Europe was being divided in other ways. The *Allied Control Commissions in the liberated areas of Europe caused new disputes, in which military and diplomatic concerns overlapped. In Italy, Soviet delegates on the commission complained of being downgraded to the status of observers. In Romania, Bulgaria, and Hungary, on the other hand, western missions came to occupy similar positions. Nevertheless, when on 19 January 1945 the head of the US mission to Bulgaria learned, in a roundabout way, of the agreement between Churchill and Stalin on the division of influence on Bulgaria, he was convinced that the Soviets were in fact being more generous to his mission than they were obliged to be.

Moscow's aim was to break the power of the conservative military and bureaucratic élites in the defeated countries of south-eastern Europe; the power, that is, of the men who had brought those countries to side with Germany in the war. Western officers on the Allied Control Commissions found it hard to understand the extent of the upheaval brought to the region by German ascendancy. In opposition to the growing Soviet influence, they found their friends and informants among the people who were committed to the anti-communist cause. As early as the summer of 1944, the US state department was in possession of a great deal of information, from local sources in south-eastern Europe, concerning the Soviet threat to the region. It seems that the last great campaign by Goebbels's propaganda machine, which focused on the growing rift between the western Allies and the Soviet Union, made its mark.

At the time of the meeting of the Big Three at Yalta, the western partners held different views on the future uses of Soviet military power. Roosevelt assumed that the USSR had no imperial ambitions, while Churchill's view was less sanguine. He believed that Stalin not only planned expansion: he had opted for the tsarist form of imperialism. The terms of Soviet entry into the war against Japan were settled by Roosevelt alone with the Soviets; and, indeed, one of the conditions concerned the restoration of the rights lost by the USSR at the Treaty of Portsmouth, on the conclusion of the Russo-Japanese war in 1905. Roosevelt's other omphalic concern was the establishment of a world security organization, and it helped to explain why he was less concerned than Churchill about the extension of the Soviet influence to the small states of eastern Europe. Roosevelt believed that they would find safety inside the new organization; just as the peacemakers after the First World War had assumed that the minorities in central and east Europe would be safe in the care of the League of Nations.

It was easier to make a general agreement on reparations at Yalta—awarding the USSR half of the German liability—than it was to come to specific terms on Poland. An accord was reached on the Provisional Government of National Unity, committed to hold general elections soon. The eastern frontier of the new Poland was fixed to run along the Curzon Line, while the question of the western border was left open, with a reference to 'substantial accessions of territory in the north and west' (see ODER–NEISSE LINE). The Polish government in London, on learning of the terms, described them as the fifth partition of Poland.

Late in June 1945, the Moscow commission succeeded in cobbling together a compromise cabinet, with Bierut at its head, to rule the new Poland. This was long after Stalin's suggestion that the model of Yugoslavia could be used for Poland had ignited Churchill's anger. *Tito had marginalized the six members of the Yugoslav government who had come from London, including Ivan Subaš, the leader of the Croat Peasant Party. Churchill believed that Stalin had disregarded the fifty–fifty agreement on Yugoslavia that they had made at the TOLSTOY conference and that Tito was well on the way to a dictatorship.

After Roosevelt's death on 12 April and Churchill's electoral defeat in the summer, Stalin was the last survivor of the Big Three at the Potsdam conference in July 1945 (see TERMINAL). President *Truman had initially thought that he could come to terms with Stalin, and that he should not side with the UK against the Soviets, before other voices from the state department started reaching him. The agreement at Potsdam recommended the application of the principles of the UN Charter to post-war problems, and attempted to prevent Germany from ever again becoming a threat to world peace. The Oder–Neisse line became the western border of Poland; and provisions were made for the creation of the Council of Foreign Ministers and for the conclusion of peace treaties with the former enemy states, Italy, Bulgaria, Finland, and Romania. Finally, Article XIII recognized that the transfer of German minorities from Poland, Czechoslovakia, and Hungary would have to be carried out. By then, many of the *Volksdeutsche* from eastern Europe had been on the move for a long time (see DEMOGRAPHY and DEPORTATIONS).

Clement *Attlee knew even less about the development of the *atomic bomb than did Stalin: it had been first tested successfully before the Potsdam meeting, and exploded over *Hiroshima a week after its conclusion. Truman casually mentioned to Stalin at Potsdam that a weapon of unusual force had been developed: Churchill was certain that Stalin had no idea of the significance of the president's remark. At Potsdam, a new era of diplomacy opened. Z. A. B. ZEMAN

Shlaim, A., *Britain and the Origins of European Unity, 1940–1951* (Reading, 1978).
Woodward, E. L., *British Foreign Policy in the Second World War*, 5 vols. (London, 1962).
Zeman, Z. A. B., *The Making and Breaking of Communist Europe* (Oxford, 1991).

direction finding, see ELECTRONIC NAVIGATION SYSTEMS, HUFF-DUFF, and PIP-SQUEAK.

displaced persons, see REFUGEES; see also DEMOGRAPHY.

dive-bombers, see BOMBERS, CARRIERS, and FIGHTERS.

Dnieper, River. At Orsha, 450 km. (280 mi.) west of Moscow, the River Dnieper, already a broad stream, turns sharply southwards and, widening and deepening as it goes, flows towards the Black Sea. At Vitebsk, 80 km. (50 mi.) to the north on the other side of a low divide, the western River Dvina makes a similar turn towards the Baltic Sea. The Dnieper is the natural defence line closest to the Soviet western frontier and the only one west of Moscow; but as such, it posed strategic problems for the Soviet Union. It lies deep in Soviet territory, particularly in the south where a great eastward bend bisects the Ukraine. The west bank is significantly higher than the east—by a hundred metres or more in the Ukraine; and the Vitebsk–Orsha gap offers the best route of approach to Moscow.

In June 1941, when Germany invaded the USSR (see BARBAROSSA), all the Soviet fortifications, such as the *Stalin Line, and *fronts* (army groups), were positioned well to the west of the Dnieper. Owing to Stalin's, and so the army's, commitment to a forward strategy that would carry the war into any invader's territory, the river figured in the Soviet plans only as the line along which successive waves of reserves would assemble before moving westwards to join the battle as it progressed beyond the border. The German objective in BARBAROSSA was to demolish the Soviet main forces in front of the Dnieper and thus prevent their either attempting a stand behind the river or staging an orderly retreat beyond it.

On the direct route to Moscow, the *German–Soviet war did not develop at all as Stalin and his generals had expected. By the fifteenth day, 6 July, one German panzer group was closing in on Vitebsk and another was positioned to cross the Dnieper south of Orsha. In the meantime, in accordance with the original plan, five Soviet armies had arrived, and Marshal *Timoshenko had deployed them to hold the line of the upper Dvina and Dnieper rivers and the gap between them. But after regrouping and beating off counter-attacks, the panzer groups struck eastwards again on 10 July, one pushing into the gap along the left bank of the Dvina, the other driving across the Dnieper towards *Smolensk, which it took on 16 July. The capture of Vitebsk, Orsha, and

Map 26 Legend

→ British Dodecanese operation
- - → German operations
—·—·— International boundary, 1939

British and German landings

1 10 September Italian garrison surrenders to British raiding party
2 12 September Germans seize island from Italian garrison. 2–19 October SBS patrols on island
3 17 September SBS land. 7 October SBS defeat German attack. 12 October SBS withdraw
4 24 October Germans repulse LRDG attack
5 13 September British army garrison established
6 3 October German landings on south and north coasts, parachutists land on airfield. 4 October island in German hands
7 By end of September British observation posts established here and on a number of other islands such as Stampalia. 4 October LRDG withdraw from Calino
8 22 September British army garrison established. 12 November German landings. 16 November British garrison surrenders
9 16 September British force arrives, garrison established later. 17–23 November British garrison evacuated

Scale 1:3 000 000
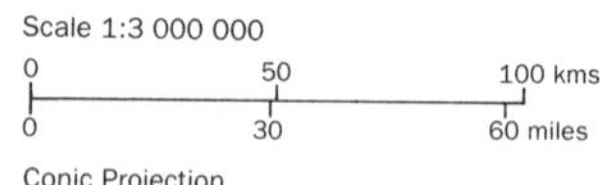

Conic Projection

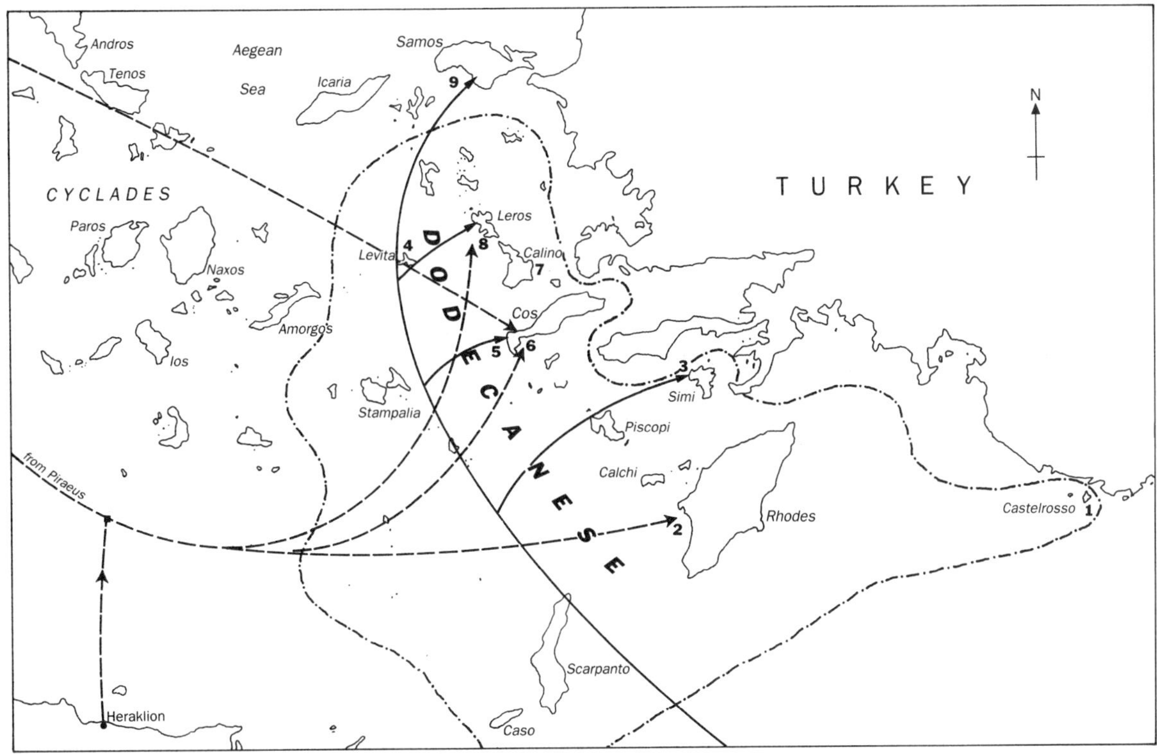

26. **Dodecanese Islands campaign**, October–November 1943

Smolensk opened the road to Moscow and also brought the German armour into position to thrust southwards behind the Dnieper. In August, two panzer groups, one from the north and another that crossed the river below *Kiev, cleared the entire Dnieper line.

The Dnieper re-entered German and Soviet strategy in the spring of 1943. Hitler, knowing he could not manage another massive drive eastwards and facing a growing threat of a Second Front in western Europe, proposed to build an 'East Wall', a fortified line that could be held with relatively small forces until an Anglo-American invasion had been defeated. The Dnieper was to be the central bastion, but the German armies retreating to it in the late summer of 1943 found that no actual work had been done and the line was riddled with Soviet bridgeheads (see ENGINEERS, 1). EARL ZIEMKE

Dodecanese Islands campaign, fought on and amongst this group of Italian islands in the Aegean Sea off Turkey's south-western Anatolian coastline as part of the battle for the *Mediterranean. As the name implies, there are twelve main islands but Rhodes and *Castelrosso (now Kastellorizo) are usually also recognized as being part of the group. The Italians had an air base on Rhodes, the strategic key to the area, an airfield on Cos, and a seaplane base and naval batteries at Leros, while the Germans had an air base on Scarpanto.

On the day Italy surrendered, 8 September 1943, a British officer parachuted into Rhodes to persuade the 30,000-strong Italian garrison to round up the 7,000 Germans on the island. Instead, the Germans attacked the Italians who immediately succumbed. At Churchill's behest a British infantry brigade was then dispatched to the area by the C-in-C Middle East Command, General Maitland *Wilson, to join the *Long Range Desert Group and Special Boat Squadron (see SPECIAL BOAT SECTION) which, transported by British-manned caiques belonging to the *Raiding Forces' Levant Schooner Flotilla, were already at work there.

By early October nearly 4,000 British troops were dispersed amongst eight of the islands and the Aegean island of Samos to the north. But with Allied forces heavily committed in the *Italian campaign it was impossible to gain air superiority and the Germans were determined to maintain their grip on the area. On 3 October they attacked Cos and the British force there quickly surrendered.

Churchill ignored advice to withdraw. He was determined, against US wishes, to pursue a Balkan offensive that might bring Turkey—which claimed sovereignty of the Dodecanese—with its 40 divisions into the war on the Allied side. He therefore insisted that Leros and Samos be held at all costs, and that the invasion of Rhodes was still to be attempted, as it was impossible to continue holding the former without the latter. Leros was reinforced and by early November it contained half the 5,000 men now concentrated on the islands. On 12 November the Germans assaulted the island and overran the British garrison. The remaining British forces were then withdrawn from the area, except for Castelrosso. It was, commented the only *war correspondent on the spot, 'a disaster as big as *Dieppe'.

The British lost 5 battalions, some 4,800 men, and of the 6 cruisers and 33 destroyers (7 of which were Greek) committed to the campaign, 4 cruisers were damaged, 6 destroyers sunk and 4 damaged, while 2 submarines and 10 small coastal craft and minesweepers were also sunk. Of the 288 British aircraft which took part, and which flew 3,746 sorties, 113 were lost. German casualties totalled 1,184 men and 15 small landing craft and ferries.

After the war the Dodecanese were ceded to Greece.

Holland, J., *The Aegean Mission* (London, 1988).

Doenitz, see DÖNITZ.

dogfight. Term used for aerial duels between fighters; see FIGHTERS, 2.

Dohnanyi, Hans von (1902–45), longstanding anti-Nazi, and Dietrich *Bonhoeffer's brother-in-law, who was a pre-war judge of the German Supreme Court in Leipzig. He was recruited into the *Abwehr as a **Sonderführer* and became the deputy to Colonel *Oster, one of the most active conspirators against Hitler. It was Dohnanyi who wrote the *X-Report, compiled to encourage a military *coup d'état* against Hitler. He employed Jews as agents abroad to keep them out of the hands of the *Gestapo and financially compensated Jews whose property had been confiscated. These activities led to his arrest in April 1943, and though often avoiding interrogation by continually infecting himself with diphtheria, he was executed in April 1945. See also GERMANY, 9 and SCHWARZE KAPELLE.

domestic life, see domestic life section of major powers and under name of countries.

Dominions, see UK, 5.

Dominican Republic, with Haiti, makes up the Caribbean island of Hispaniola (see CARIBBEAN AT WAR). It declared war on the Axis powers in December 1941 and was an original signatory of the *United Nations Declaration. It sold its sugar crop to the USA and the UK, and helped the USA patrol its coastline. See also LATIN AMERICA.

Dönitz, Grand Admiral Karl (1891–1980), gifted German C-in-C U-boats, then C-in-C of the German Navy from January 1943 to April 1945, and finally Hitler's chosen successor to lead Germany.

Dönitz entered the German Navy in 1910 and commanded U-boats in the Mediterranean during the *First World War. While trying out a new tactic—a surface night attack—on a convoy in October 1918, he penetrated the destroyer screen unobserved and sank a merchantman. Between the wars he rose to the rank of commodore and in 1935, when the London Naval Agreement allowed Germany to build submarines (see VERSAILLES SETTLEMENT), Hitler—who had a fervent admirer in Dönitz—made him Commander of U-boats.

The agreement permitted the construction of 70 U-boats, but by September 1939 only 56 had been built, no more than 22 of which were capable of operating in the Atlantic. But 1,168 were eventually constructed, and by employing them in wolf-packs, a concept he introduced and which he closely controlled, Dönitz caused severe Allied shipping losses. Brilliant, too, was his reversal of the universally acknowledged role of the submarine—attacking by daylight while submerged—by employing them in surface night attacks as he had himself done in 1918.

His planning and direction of the U-boat attack on the British battleship **Royal Oak* in Scapa Flow in October 1939 brought him promotion from commodore to rear-admiral, and further promotions came in 1940 (vice-admiral) and 1942 (admiral). In January 1943 he replaced *Raeder as C-in-C of the German Navy while remaining C-in-C of U-boats, and was promoted grand admiral. Though promoted largely beyond his capabilities (as shown by his handling of Axis naval forces in the battle for the *Mediterranean, his failure to bring about a reversal of German fortunes in the battle of the *Atlantic, and an increasing propensity to indulge in hare-brained schemes), Dönitz's loyalty to the Führer never wavered. Before Hitler committed suicide on 30 April 1945 he nominated Dönitz to succeed him and he ruled Germany as president until he was arrested on 22 May 1945. At the *Nuremberg trials he was tried for issuing the order to sink the **Laconia*. He was acquitted, but was found guilty of two other charges and given a ten-year sentence.

Carver, M. (ed.), *The War Lords* (London, 1976).
Dönitz, K., *Memoirs* (London, 1959).

Donovan, Maj-General William J. (1883–1959), head of the US *Office of Strategic Services (OSS), an energetic and inspiring, if sometimes erratic, commander whose physical stature earned him the nickname 'Big Bill'.

A lawyer by profession, Donovan finished the *First World War as one of the two most decorated American officers (*MacArthur was the other). In July 1940, at the request of the head of *British Security Co-ordination (BSC), William *Stephenson, he was sent by Roosevelt to the UK where he was briefed on the functions of British clandestine and intelligence organizations, met Churchill, and was given a tour of airfields and military sites. His report helped convince Roosevelt that, despite the pessimistic reports emanating from the US ambassador in London, Joseph Kennedy (1888–1969), the UK would not capitulate.

Though a Republican, Donovan became Roosevelt's Co-ordinator of Information (COI) in July 1941, a first attempt by the Americans to centralize their espionage activities. In this capacity he liaised closely with BSC and established vital Anglo-American ties in security and intelligence matters. In 1942 the Office of COI became the OSS, the forerunner of today's Central Intelligence Agency (CIA), and Donovan then reported to the US *Joint Chiefs of Staff.

doodlebug, one of the nicknames the British gave to the German flying bomb or V-1. See V-WEAPONS.

Doolittle raid. After the Japanese attacked *Pearl Harbor in December 1941, Roosevelt pressed the US *Joint Chiefs of Staff to retaliate. But the only way bombers could reach Japan was from a carrier which, if it was to escape detection, had to operate beyond the range of Japanese air and sea patrols. It was thought that these patrols did not operate more than 800 km. (500 mi.) from Japan, beyond the range of normal carrier aircraft. Instead, 16 USAAF B25 bombers were loaded aboard the carrier *Hornet*, the maximum number that could be carried as they were too big to stow below. They were manned by volunteers who, under their commander, Colonel James Doolittle (1896–1993), trained by taking off from an air strip marked to the exact dimensions of the flight deck. But they never practised taking off from a real carrier.

Hornet sailed from San Francisco Bay on 1 April 1942, and was joined by Vice-Admiral *Halsey's Task Force 16 on 13 April. The plan was for the bombers, each of which was armed with four 500 lb. (225 kg.) *bombs, to fly to Chuchow airfield in China after the raid, some 1,600 km. (1,000 mi.) from the target.

Before dawn on 18 April, while still 1,100 km. (700 mi.) from Tokyo, Halsey's force detected Japanese patrol boats by *radar. Halsey altered course to avoid them but another alerted Tokyo before it was sunk, forcing the decision to launch the bombers immediately instead of at night as planned. One attacked Kobe, another Nagoya, while a third, scheduled to bomb Osaka, dropped its bombs instead on Yokosuka naval yard and Yokohama. A fourth was forced to land at Vladivostok, but the other twelve arrived over Tokyo at noon, just as a mock air raid was being completed by Japanese planes. This lessened the psychological impact of the raid on the local population but helped the bombers escape, and not one was lost over Japan. About 50 people were killed and 100 houses damaged. The bombed areas were cordoned off from civilians who, by and large, remained unimpressed. However, the uncomfortable thought that Japan was more open to air attack than had been supposed did not escape Japanese officialdom, which lost considerable face by the raid, and earlier objections to Admiral *Yamamoto's plans to bring the US Pacific fleet to battle at *Midway promptly ceased.

After the raid, the bombers either crash-landed in China or their crews bailed out, and all but 9 of the 80 crew members involved survived. However, some were captured by the Japanese occupation forces in China (see CHINA INCIDENT) and because civilian buildings had been accidentally hit—and a school machine-gunned—three were subsequently executed after a show trial; another died in prison. The greatest number of casualties caused by the raid were Chinese, as the following month the Japanese launched their Chekiang-Kiangsi offensive in China, both as a revenge for the raid and to capture the local airfields to prevent another.

The raid, of little consequence militarily, gave a much needed fillip to American morale. US Army Air Forces historians subsequently credited Roosevelt with the idea, but there is no documentation to prove this. The navy's C-in-C, Admiral *King, said it came from his operations officer. See also STRATEGIC AIR OFFENSIVES, 3.

DORA (1). Codename for a Nazi concentration camp called Mittelbau KL which supplied *forced labour for the subterranean *Nordhausen factory in the Harz mountains 240 km. (150 mi.) south-west of Berlin. Its inmates, deported from all over Europe, enlarged an existing sodium sulphate mine into a huge network of tunnels and galleries where *V-weapons were constructed. The two main tunnels were nearly 3.2 km. (2 mi.) long and there were 46 other tunnels 200 m. (220 yd.) long and 9 m. (30 ft.) high. On average 100 men died every day during the construction of the factory. In all 60,000 people were deported to DORA; half died.

Michel, J., *Dora* (London, 1979).

Dora (2), name of a German siege gun.

DORA (3), codename of Sándor Radó, head of the *Rote Drei.

Doriot, Jacques (1898–1945), ex-communist French politician who by 1939 had become fervently pro-Nazi. One of the principal collaborators during the German occupation of France (see COLLABORATION, 2), he formed the Légion des volontaires français contre le bolchevisme (French Volunteer Legion against Bolshevism) and fought with it during the *German–Soviet war for several periods from September 1941 to January 1944. After the Normandy landings in June 1944 (see OVERLORD), he led those opposing de *Gaulle and the Free French and the Allied occupation of France, forming for this purpose the Committee for French Liberation at Sigmaringen in southern Germany when the *Vichy government was forced to move there. He was killed in his car in Germany, probably by an Allied aircraft.

Dorman-Smith, Lt-General Eric E. (1895–1969), British staff officer of marked originality; a brilliant thinker who was unable to suffer fools gladly. He was a friend of the military theorist Basil Liddell Hart, who thought him excellent, and of Ernest Hemingway, who nicknamed him 'Chink' and made him the hero of his novel *Across the*

River and into the Trees. During 1929–36 he helped mechanize the army; he also suggested the beret for tank crews and helped design battle dress. He was director of military training in India, 1938–40, then commandant of Haifa staff college. While at Haifa he helped *O'Connor plan his first victory in the *Western Desert campaigns (see SIDI BARRANI). Then he worked in various capacities for the C-in-C Middle East, *Auchinleck, who in May 1942 appointed him deputy chief of staff with the rank of maj-general. As Auchinleck's principal operations officer, he planned the first battle of *El Alamein (July 1942), arguably as much a turning-point in the Western Desert as the second, but when Auchinleck was replaced in August 1942 Dorman-Smith's career—which had always been sufficiently contentious to make him enemies—disintegrated. He commanded a brigade in the UK; became unemployed; returned to his substantive rank of colonel; and was finally removed from command of a brigade in the *Italian campaign in August 1944. He retired to Ireland where he changed his name to O'Gowan and became a military adviser to the *Irish Republican Army. M. R. D. FOOT

Greacen, L., *Chink* (London, 1989).

double agents are *spies who secretly transfer their allegiance to an enemy secret service which uses them to confuse its foes. For example, in February 1942 an early *SOE agent in the Netherlands, hunting for a lorry to remove supplies from a parachute drop, met a Dutchman who ran a small transport firm, whom he engaged. The Dutchman told the *Abwehr, who supervised not only that parachute drop, but hundreds more, thus entrapping almost all of SOE's effort into the Netherlands for eighteen months (see ENGLANDSPIEL). Similarly, a Welsh nationalist was recruited as a spy by the Abwehr before the war. When the war broke out in 1939 he went to his local police station; made his first radio report to Germany from Wandsworth gaol; and helped *MI5 to capture every one of the agents the Abwehr sent to the UK, all through the war (see XX-COMMITTEE). An early escape line (see MI9) in north-eastern France was shattered when one of its organizers, an English sergeant, on being arrested, gave away 50 of his colleagues to the *Gestapo, with whom he worked until 1944.

A Frenchwoman who helped a Franco-Polish intelligence circuit in France in the winter of 1940–1 (**Interallié*) was arrested and became a double agent overnight. She drove round Paris with one of her captors, an Abwehr sergeant, pointing out members of her circuit whom they passed in the street. See also TRIPLE AGENTS.
M. R. D. FOOT

double-cross system, see XX-COMMITTEE.

Douglas, Air Chief Marshal Sir (William) Sholto (1893–1969), British airman and *First World War fighter ace who subsequently worked as a commercial pilot before rejoining in 1920 what by then had become the RAF. By 1938 he had risen to the rank of air vice-marshal and during the battle of *Britain served as deputy chief of air staff. He was, contrary to Fighter Command's C-in-C, *Dowding, a proponent of the 'Big Wing' (see FIGHTERS, 2) and, as he was then the only fighter pilot among the senior members of the air staff, his influence was considerable. The Big Wing was introduced; in November 1940 he succeeded Dowding with the rank of air marshal; and, besides opposing the German *Blitz, he tried to retain the initiative by carrying out fighter sweeps across the Channel (see CIRCUSES and RHUBARBS). He was promoted air chief marshal and in January 1943 was appointed AOC Middle East, a post he held for a year before succeeding *Slessor as C-in-C Coastal Command. He was knighted in 1941 and promoted Marshal of the Royal Air Force in January 1946.

Dowding, Air Chief Marshal Sir Hugh (1882–1970), C-in-C of British Fighter Command which fought the battle of *Britain.

A regular officer in the Royal Artillery, Dowding ended the *First World War as a brigadier-general in the Royal Flying Corps, and was commissioned into the newly formed RAF. By 1936 he was C-in-C of the new Fighter Command where he spent the next four years preparing the UK's air defences which included improved communications and the erection of the vital chain of *radar stations around the southern coasts of England.

After doggedly resisting the dispersal of his precious fighter squadrons during the *Norwegian campaign and in the fighting which preceded the fall of *France, Dowding, in July 1940, delayed his retirement till October at the request of the Chief of Air Staff. It was as well he did, for the RAF was soon faced with a critical fight for air superiority which the Germans had to have if they were to invade (see SEALION). Though the battle of Britain was fought tactically by the Fighter Groups, and by the radar operators who guided them to their targets, no one understood better than Dowding how to command this intricate and delicate form of defence. It was his tight control of the battle and his careful husbanding of his resources, both human and technical, that enabled his fighter pilots—his 'chicks' as he called them—to win the day.

Nevertheless, Dowding and his strategy had their detractors, and his aloof personality perhaps attracted criticism. One of his Fighter Group commanders, *Leigh-Mallory (No. 12 Group), was not a Dowding admirer, while another, *Park (No. 11 Group), was, and these two clashed over the employment of the 'Big Wing' tactics (see FIGHTERS, 2) Leigh-Mallory espoused. Dowding said later he was at first unaware of this dispute and he certainly did nothing to settle it. But as one modern commentator has remarked: 'C-in-Cs have to know. That is what it is all about.' An air ministry meeting in October 1940 stipulated that 'Big Wing' formations could be used

Air Chief Marshal **Dowding**.

'in suitable operations over the 11 Group area', and protests by Dowding and Park were ignored.

Dowding was replaced as C-in-C Fighter Command on 24 November 1940. This was perhaps hastened by Fighter Command's failure during the *Coventry raid, but the manner in which it was done, and the fact that he was given no immediate recognition of his achievements, have been roundly criticized ever since. Dowding said he merely had a telephone call saying he was to be relieved immediately, but he was in fact first told by the minister of state for air in a personal interview. He initially refused a request to go to the USA on behalf of the ministry of aircraft production, but was eventually persuaded by Churchill. The visit was not successful, nor was his appointment to the air ministry to scrutinize air establishments, and in July 1942 he retired at his own request.

Nicknamed 'Stuffy' from his days at the Staff College, Camberley, Dowding had an austere, withdrawn personality. His vision, necessarily, was a narrow one and he was no politician, but his dedication to his task was total. In 1943 he became Baron Dowding of Bentley Priory, the name of his old Fighter Command Headquarters. He was knighted in 1933. See also AIR POWER.

Carver, M. (ed.), *The War Lords* (London, 1976).
Collier, B., *Leader of the Few* (London, 1957).

DPs (displaced persons), see REFUGEES and DEMOGRAPHY.

DRAGOON, see FRENCH RIVIERA LANDINGS.

drama, see culture sections of major powers.

Dresden, raid on. This historic German city was the scene of what was perhaps the most controversial episode in the *strategic air offensive against Germany. Capital of Saxony and situated on the River Elbe, Dresden was particularly noted for its splendid architecture and its manufacture of fine china. It had little heavy industry and up until early 1945 had only been attacked once from the air, a small raid by the Eighth US Army Air Force in October 1944.

In January 1945 the British air ministry drew up a plan THUNDERCLAP for attacks on Berlin and population centres in eastern Germany. This was to take advantage of the recently launched Soviet offensive westwards from the Vistula (see GERMAN–SOVIET WAR, 11) and add to the growing chaos in Germany by disrupting the flow of *refugees fleeing in the face of the Soviet attack. At the same time, the western Allies wished to demonstrate to the Soviets at the forthcoming Yalta conference (see ARGONAUT) that they were giving them the support of their heavy bombers, and, indeed, at Yalta the Soviets specifically requested help in this form. In the meantime, *Spaatz and *Harris, commanding the Anglo-US bombing forces, had received orders for THUNDERCLAP to be put into action, and the first operations of it were US daylight attacks on Berlin and Magdeburg on 3 February, Chemnitz and Magdeburg again on the 6th, and Magdeburg yet again on 9 February.

Air Chief Marshal Harris's intention had been to strike Dresden first, but weather conditions were initially unfavourable. On 13 February they showed improvement, although not good enough for the original plan of an initial US attack during the day. That night, however, RAF Bomber Command despatched 796 Lancaster bombers and 9 Mosquitoes from the UK. These attacked Dresden in two waves three hours apart, dropping 1,478 tons of high explosive *bombs and 1,182 tons of incendiaries which started a *firestorm. Such was the weakness of the air defences that only six Lancasters were shot down, although a further three crashed on friendly territory on the way home. The following day, 311 US B17 bombers also struck the city, adding to the extensive damage caused by the RAF. In all, some 50,000 people, including many refugees, are reckoned to have lost their lives and much of the city was devastated.

At a *SHAEF press briefing two days later it was revealed in 'off the record' comments that the aims of THUNDERCLAP were to bomb large population centres and prevent relief supplies from getting through. An Associated Press *war correspondent immediately filed a story that the Allies had resorted to terror bombing in

The devastation of **Dresden** after it was raided in February 1945.

order to seal Hitler's doom and this set in train a number of embarrassing questions on both sides of the Atlantic on the morality of this form of attack. Eventually, even Churchill, who had been a wholehearted supporter of THUNDERCLAP, went so far as to comment to the British *Chiefs of Staff that 'the destruction of Dresden remains a serious query against the conduct of Allied bombing.' Harris, however, remained unrepentant, commenting on Churchill's objection that he did not regard 'the whole of the remaining cities of Germany as worth the bones of one British Grenadier'. Even so, Dresden remains the prime example cited by those who condemn the morality of 'city busting' as practised by the Anglo-US bombing forces and was still a matter of contention in 1992 when a statue of Harris was unveiled in London. See also AIR POWER and STRATEGIC AIR OFFENSIVES, 1).

CHARLES MESSENGER

Irving, D., *The Destruction of Dresden* (London, 1963).
McKee, A., *Dresden 1945: The Devil's Tinderbox* (London, 1982).
Messenger, C., *'Bomber' Harris and the Strategic Bombing Offensive, 1939–1945* (London, 1984).

Duce (leader), title adopted by Mussolini and copied by *Franco, Hitler, and Subhas Chandra *Bose.

DUKW, see AMPHIBIANS.

Dulles, Allen W. (1893–1969), US lawyer and diplomat who was head of the *Office of Strategic Services in Europe from November 1942. He operated from Berne in Switzerland and was in contact with members of the German resistance against Hitler in the *Abwehr and the German foreign office. His most important coup was to use a clerk, Fritz Kolbe, to feed him copies of 1,500 German foreign office cables, which among other information, helped unmask the German agent Elyeza *Bazna (see also SPIES). His other successes included establishing an intelligence network in southern France and being the intermediary in the negotiations for the *unconditional surrender of all German forces in northern Italy (see also WOLFF) before the end of the war.

Dumbarton Oaks conference, held at a Harvard University centre near Washington DC when delegates from 39 nations met to discuss the framework for a new global security organization as outlined in the *Four-Power Declaration. Because the USSR was not then involved in the war in the Far East, it was held in two phases, the first between 21 August and 28 September 1944, the second between 28 September and 7 October when the Chinese delegation replaced the Soviet one. The conference issued a twelve-chapter set of guidelines for the formation of a United Nations organization (see SAN FRANCISCO CONFERENCE), a Secretariat, and an International Court of Justice. It was agreed that the United Nations organization would comprise a General Assembly and a Security Council. The Council would have executive powers and would comprise five permanent members—China, UK, USA, USSR, and, when a legitimate government had been formed, France—and six other members who would be elected on two-year terms by the General Assembly. Left unresolved were the USSR's demand for a seat for each of the sixteen Soviet republics and the use of the veto in the Council. See also DIPLOMACY.

Dunkirk, evacuation from, the rescue of British, French, and other Allied troops from this northern French port during the fighting which led to the fall of *France in June 1940. Numbers vary, but the British Admiralty calculated that a total of 338,226 men were taken off between 26 May and 3 June, though all their heavy equipment and transport was lost. Between 850 and 950 ships and small craft (again, official figures vary) were employed in the evacuation. These were co-ordinated by the Vice-Admiral, Dover, Vice-Admiral *Ramsay, and his staff working from a room buried in the cliffs which had once housed a dynamo; hence the operation's codename (DYNAMO).

There was much misunderstanding and friction between the French and the British at all levels, for initially they were in Dunkirk for different purposes, the *British Expeditionary Force (BEF) to be evacuated, the French to form a stronghold. The British at first failed to tell their allies that they intended to evacuate their troops and were, indeed, urging them to fight on. During the first days French troops were not allowed to embark—on one occasion at least they were fired on by British troops—and parity of numbers was only reached by the evacuation of 53,000 Frenchmen on the last two nights after all the British troops had been taken off.

Around 28,000 non-essential British personnel had already been evacuated when DYNAMO officially started on 26 May. Discipline among these rear echelon troops was not always good. Those controlling the queues on the beaches often did so with revolvers drawn, and on occasions sailors used their oars as clubs to prevent their small boats being swamped. The gently shelving beaches made evacuation laborious and the major effort was soon switched to the harbour's east mole, from where two-thirds of those rescued were eventually embarked. Later, when the front-line troops arrived and the operation was properly organized the rate of evacuation increased and was more orderly.

The Channel was exceptionally calm. The shortest route that avoided the numerous sandbanks took the rescue ships across to Calais and then up the coast to Dunkirk. This meant the ships were not only shelled but had the Luftwaffe directed against them, so two more northerly routes were also used, though one later had to be abandoned because of attacks by submarines and *E-boats.

The Luftwaffe attacked in force whenever the weather (which did not favour it), the RAF, and its strained *logistics allowed. It soon reduced the town of Dunkirk to rubble, but the resulting pall of smoke was a useful cover for those embarking. The RAF's resources nearly reached breaking-point. Heavily outnumbered—177 aircraft were lost during the nine days of the evacuation—its pilots made an outstanding contribution to DYNAMO's success. 'Wars are not won by evacuations,' Churchill told parliament on 4 June. 'But there was a victory inside this deliverance, which should be noted. It was gained by the Air Force.'

On 29 May, the day the evacuation was announced to the British public, boats from the Small Vessels Pool—privately owned power craft between 9 m. and 30 m. (30–100 ft.) long—started taking troops from the beaches to the waiting ships. These were some of the famous 'Little Ships', but appeals for their numbers to be swelled were not always answered. The Rye fishing fleet refused to go, as did some lifeboat crews, but additional civilian crews with their boats did volunteer once the evacuation was made public. One firm sent its lighters, the London County Council dispatched its hopper barges, and the Port of London nine of its tugs which towed Thames sailing barges behind them.

The other main source of civilian volunteers was retired service personnel. One ex-officer, on his day off, lifted more than 200 troops off the beaches with his motor launch, delivered them to the ships offshore, and then returned to work the next day. On such stories was founded the 'Dunkirk spirit' which boosted civilian morale and helped involve the population in the crusade against Hitler.

On 1 June the Luftwaffe wrought havoc among the rescue ships. Three destroyers and a passenger ship were sunk and four other ships were badly damaged. As a result, Ramsay banned daylight sailings though the shrinking perimeter still contained British troops. Some units retired without orders to do so. Officers were told to shoot anyone moving back, and this, according to some eyewitnesses, did occur. Evacuation continued that night and the next, but at dawn on 2 June all British warships were withdrawn and the last remnants of the BEF were evacuated by a civilian ferry. Ships returned that evening to pick up French troops but, through no fault of their own, failed to do so. This caused such a political furore that Ramsay was ordered to send in his ships again the following night and, amid scenes of great confusion and with Germans on the outskirts of the port, 27,000 more Frenchmen were evacuated.

That an effective perimeter could be formed around Dunkirk, and so many men rescued, was due to several factors: the ideal nature of the countryside for defensive purposes; the orders of Army Group 'A's C-in-C, General von *Rundstedt, for the panzers not to cross the Aa Canal, issued on 24 May and confirmed by Hitler against the wishes of the army's C-in-C, General *Brauchitsch; the gallant defensive battle fought by the First French Army at Lille; and the superb efforts of the British and French navies supported by the RAF and ably organized by Ramsay. Of these factors Hitler's confirmation of Runstedt's order was the most controversial and the French Army's stout resistance at Lille the least recognized. Hitler, intent on eliminating the French armies guarding Paris, wanted to conserve his armour and saw no reason to launch it against the remnants of a force he had been assured the Luftwaffe would, in any case, destroy. Shortly afterwards he left the decision to advance in Rundstedt's hands, a decision the latter withheld for another 48 hours. They were hours, it has been argued, that lost Hitler the war.

Harman, N., *Dunkirk: the Necessary Myth* (London, 1980).
Turnbull, P., *Dunkirk: Anatomy of Disaster* (London, 1978).

Dutch East Indies, see NETHERLANDS EAST INDIES. But see DUTCH WEST INDIES.

Dutch New Guinea, see NETHERLANDS EAST INDIES.

Dutch West Indies, the Caribbean territories of Curaçao, which included the Northern Islands and the islands of Aruba and Bonaire, and Dutch Guiana. In 1922 it was declared an integral part of the Netherlands but only a tiny minority of the colony's 5.8 million inhabitants were enfranchised. After the Netherlands were occupied in May 1940 British and French troops garrisoned Curaçao. The French troops later withdrew and US troops took over the garrison in early 1942.

As it was difficult for oil tankers to enter Maracaibo Bay, Venezuela sent oil to be refined at Curaçao, which at that time had the world's largest oil refineries with a capacity of 480,000 barrels a day. Dutch Guiana was the world's largest producer of bauxite and in November 1941 Roosevelt dispatched troops to safeguard it for the US aluminium industry. See also CARIBBEAN AT WAR.

Dyle Line, allied defensive position in Belgium which, according to General *Gamelin's Plan D, was to be occupied and held by Allied forces if the Germans attacked. It ran southwards along the River Dyle to Wavre, and then to the Franco-Belgian border. In March 1940 Gamelin ordered that it also be extended northwards to Breda and the River Maas in the Netherlands so that Allied forces could join up with the Dutch Army in the event of a German attack. But Gamelin's plan had been foreseen by Hitler and on 10 May 1940 the Germans made their main thrust through the Ardennes (see FALL GELB) where the French had thought the terrain was too difficult for tanks to traverse. The line had hardly been occupied when the Allies, which included the *British Expeditionary Force, were forced to withdraw to avoid being trapped, and the evacuation from *Dunkirk and the fall of *France quickly followed.

Eagle Day, see ADLERTAG.

Eagle's Nest, see BERCHTESGADEN.

Eagle Squadrons, three US volunteer units which served with the RAF from 1940 to 1942. The 240 pilots who joined these formations before the USA entered the war were violating the US *Neutrality Acts and could have lost their citizenship. Some were already in the UK or France at the outbreak of war in Europe in September 1939, but most smuggled themselves into Canada before or after recruitment by the *Clayton Knight committee which provided 92% of the flying personnel for the squadrons.

The original initiative came from a London-based American businessman Charles Sweeny, who in June 1940 proposed to the air ministry that he find recruits for an 'American Air Defence Corps'. This was approved and funds were raised by the Sweeny family from donors who included the American heiress Barbara Hutton.

The first Eagle Squadron, No. 71, was formed in September 1940 and became operational in January 1941, three of its founding members already having seen combat in the battle of *Britain. The following July No. 121 became operational, and No. 133 that August. All three flew Hurricane, and then Spitfire, fighters. In October and November 1941, No. 71 accounted for more German aircraft than any other Allied unit and all three saw action over France and England, including the *Dieppe raid. Some pilots also served in *Malta and the Far East.

Numerous *decorations were awarded to members of the Eagle squadrons. Two eventually became major-generals in the USAAF to whose jurisdiction the squadrons were transferred in September 1942 to become the 4th Fighter Group of Maj-General *Eaker's UK-based Eighth USAAF.

Haugland, V., *Eagle Squadrons* (New York, 1979).

Eaker, Lt-General Ira C. (1896–1987), US Army Air Force officer who, under *Spaatz, commanded 8th US Bomber Command based in the UK and led the first American bomber raid in Europe, on Rouen, on 17 August 1942. In December 1942 Spaatz assumed control of the Allied Air Forces in the *North African campaign and in February 1943 Eaker became commander of an expanded Eighth US Army Air Force based in the UK. He was a forceful proponent of daylight *precision bombing, and helped plan the *Combined Bomber Offensive (also known as the Eaker plan), but the disastrous raid on *Schweinfurt, in October 1943, showed that his confidence in the ability of his bombers to protect themselves, when flying beyond the range of escorting fighters, was not well placed. At the end of 1943 he replaced *Tedder as C-in-C of Allied Air Forces in the Mediterranean, was promoted lt-general, and flew on the first *shuttle bombing raid mounted by the Fifteenth USAAF. In April 1945 he returned to the USA to become deputy commander of the Army Air Forces, an administrative post he held until he retired in 1947. See also STRATEGIC AIR OFFENSIVES.

EAM (Ethnikon Apeleftherotikon Metopon, or National Liberation Front), the political wing of the communist-dominated Greek guerrilla organization, ELAS. It was a coalition of five socialist parties and the Communist Party. See GREECE, 3(c); 6.

East African campaign (see Map 27). Soon after Italy entered the war on 10 June 1940, Italian forces, which had been occupying Abyssinia since 1936, captured the outposts of Karora, Gallabat, Kurmak, and Kassala, all on or near the borders of Sudan, as well as Moyale on the border of Kenya; and in August they occupied the Protectorate of British Somaliland, the first British colony to fall into Axis hands.

From the start the British were outnumbered. By August 1940 there were more than 92,000 Italian and 250,000 Abyssinian troops under arms; the British had only 40,000, nearly all of whom had been raised locally. The Italians also had more tanks, and they had 323 aircraft against the British total of just over 100. But, cut off from any reinforcement or supply, the Italians, commanded by the Duke of Aosta, soon fell into a defensive frame of mind. They failed to take the initiative even when events favoured them, and their ground forces became split between the conflicting tasks of fending off the British and suppressing Abyssinian rebels, or Patriots as they were called.

British strategy for the campaign was worked out at a conference in Khartoum at the end of October 1940. This was attended by Anthony *Eden, General *Smuts, the exiled emperor of Abyssinia, *Haile Selassie, and the C-in-C Middle East, General *Wavell. At the conference it was agreed that the C-in-C Sudan (Maj-General William Platt) would use the 5th Indian Division to attack Gallabat in November and Kassala the following January and that the C-in-C Kenya designate, Lt-General *Cunningham, would assess the possibilities of attacking Kismayu in Italian Somaliland the same month. It was also agreed that *Haile Selassie should receive greater aid to help regain his country once the Patriots, who were being aided and trained by an *SOE-inspired military mission (no. 101), had secured a sufficiently large area within it to which he could safely return. It was also recognized that the emperor would need a military adviser who would help train the local forces being raised to support him, and Major *Wingate, while remaining subordinate to the military mission's commander, Colonel D. A. Sandford, was appointed to this position the following month.

Platt's attack on Gallabat, carried out by Brigadier *Slim's 10th Indian Infantry Brigade, was launched on 6 November. It was intended to clear a route into Abyssinia,

East African campaign

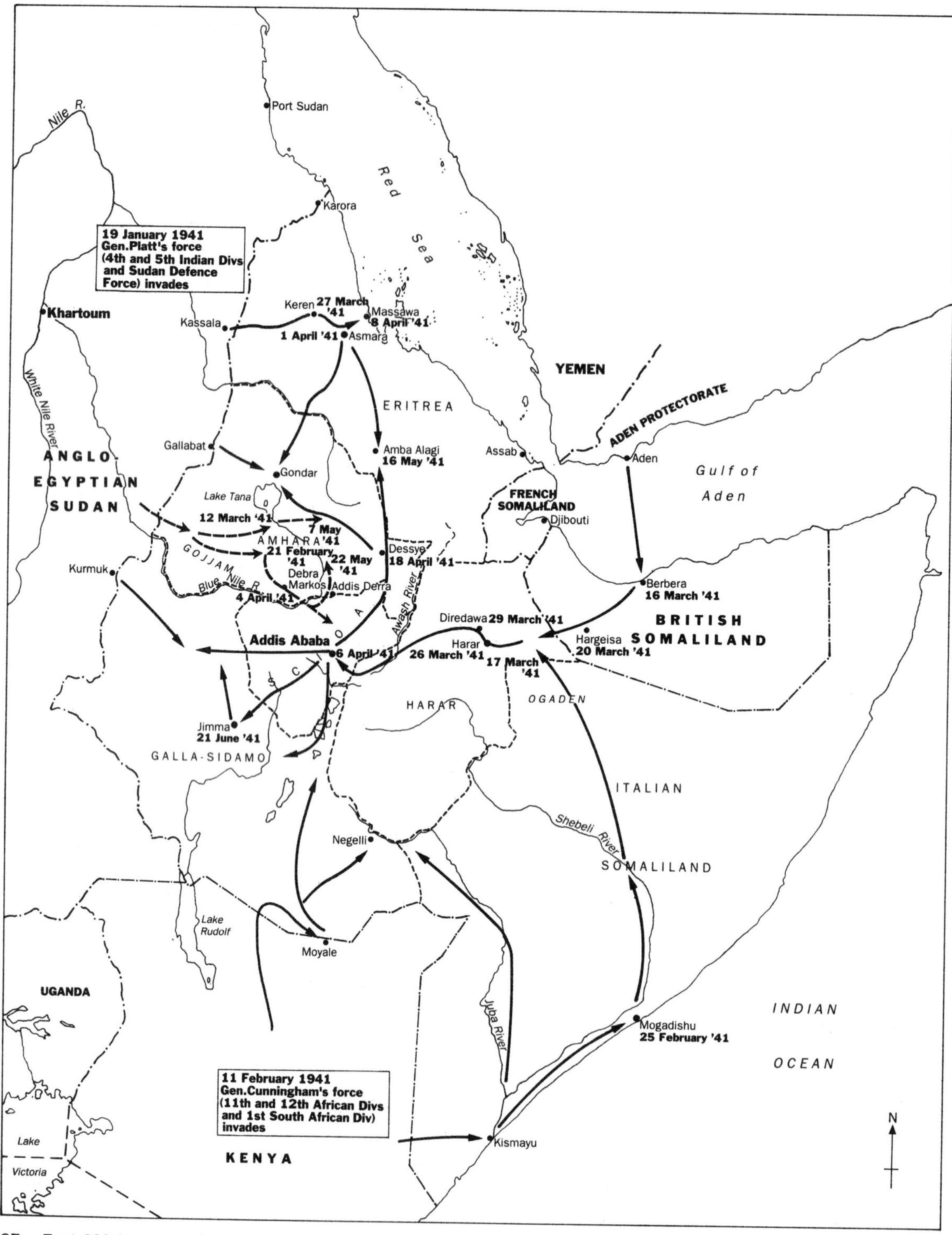

27. **East African campaign**, January–May 1941

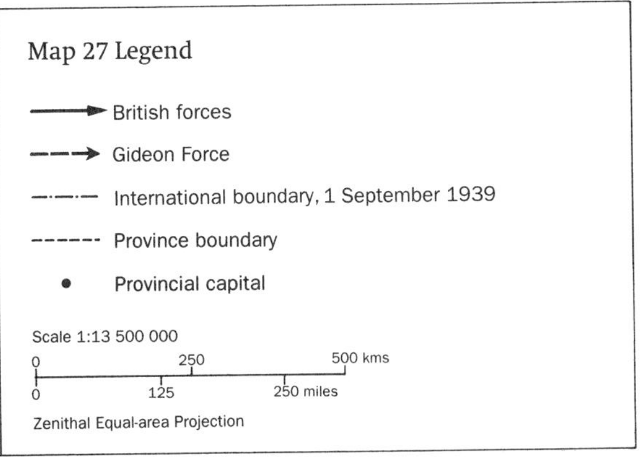

but though Slim succeeded in capturing the frontier post he was then driven back by heavy air attacks. However, the overall British position was not as desperate as the numbers arrayed against them might have indicated, for the Italians did not take advantage of their superior strength and stayed on the defensive. Three other factors also began to work for the British: in November 1940 the government Code and Cypher School at *Bletchley Park broke the Italian Army's high-grade cipher in East Africa; and the same month the Italian Air Force's replacement cipher was broken by the *Combined Bureau, Middle East (CBME). So complete and detailed was the intelligence now provided by CBME, and by one of its outposts in Nairobi, that the Cs-in-C in Cairo had on their desks the Italians' plans and appreciations as soon as they had been issued. The flow was so comprehensive and contained so much advance information that it was judged unnecessary to attach signals intelligence units to the forces that were to attack into Abyssinia.

The third factor was equally decisive. In December 1940 British forces had their first victory in the *Western Desert campaigns when they defeated the Tenth Italian Army at *Sidi Barrani, and this was followed by another at *Bardia the next month. The demoralized Aosta requested, and was granted, permission to withdraw from the Sudanese frontier. This information, quickly decrypted, enabled Platt to start his offensive on 19 January 1941, three weeks earlier than originally planned. His Indian troops, led by Maj-General Noel Beresford-Peirse, were soon in hot pursuit of the retreating Italians and in the battle of the Lowlands they cut off the withdrawal of the 41st Colonial Brigade, capturing its commander, his staff, and 700 others.

General Luigi Frusci, the Italian commander in Eritrea, was now ordered by Aosta to make a stand in ideal defensive country south-west of Keren. To help him Aosta gave him one of his best units, the Savoia Division and it took Platt, who was reinforced by the 4th Indian Division, weeks of hard fighting in the mountains to break Frusci's resistance. It was 27 March before his forces entered Keren and 1 April before they entered Asmara. Though far from being the last, Keren proved to be the decisive battle of the campaign. Italian losses included 3,000 killed; British casualties amounted to 536 killed and 3,229 wounded.

With the British approaching the port of Massawa the six Italian destroyers stationed there left to raid Port Sudan, but were attacked from the air. Two were scuttled and the other four sunk, and on 8 April Massawa surrendered after a joint attack by Indian and Free French troops, the latter having joined the British forces from *Vichy-governed French Somaliland after the fall of *France.

While Platt was striking into Eritrea, Cunningham began his operations by harassing the Italians with raids from Kenya. He had at his disposal about 77,000 troops which included contingents from British East Africa (33,000), British West Africa (9,000), and South Africa (27,000), and which were supported from the air by six South African squadrons. Early in January he sent units of the 1st South African Division and an East African brigade into the Abyssinian province of Galla-Sidamo, hoping that the Patriots there would openly rebel. This did not happen and, though Moyale was recaptured on 18 February 1941, Cunningham's advance eventually petered out. However, his other attack along the coast, launched by two East African divisions on 11 February, met with startling success. The Italians immediately started withdrawing beyond the River Juba so that by 14 February the first objective, Kismayu, was captured. After overcoming light opposition at the Juba, Mogadishu was taken and Cunningham then struck northwards towards the Abyssinian town of Harar. To help shorten his supply lines a small force from Aden, supported by Royal Navy ships, took the port of Berbera in British Somaliland on 16 March. There was little opposition and the Protectorate was soon back in British hands; a West African brigade, after a series of brief skirmishes, then entered Harar on 26 March and the country's capital, Addis Ababa, on 6 April.

In a matter of eight weeks Cunningham's troops had covered 2,735 km. (1,700 mi.) and had defeated a large proportion of the forces under Aosta's command for the loss of 501 British casualties and 8 aircraft. But even more spectacular was the success of Wingate's small group of men. Initially in charge of special units ('Operational Centres') for training the Patriots, Wingate, now a lt-colonel, was the given the task of securing a stronghold in Gojjam for the emperor with a small band of local troops he christened *Gideon Force. But he also intended to accomplish a much more ambitious plan with this force: to return the emperor to his throne. Through a mixture of brilliant guerrilla tactics and sheer bluff, he eventually achieved his objective and after receiving the surrender of an Italian-controlled army of African troops at Debra Markos on 6 April the emperor re-entered his capital on 5 May. Wingate then pursued the remaining Italian forces in the area, undertaking a series of actions which culminated in the surrender of 1,100 Italian and 7,000 colonial troops at Addis Derra on 20 May. But he had been, to say the least, evasive about his movements and had exceeded his orders, and later he was virtually relieved of his command.

While Wingate was employing his guerrilla tactics, for which he was later to become famous during the *Burma campaign (see CHINDITS), the pincers of the two main British forces closed on Aosta's mountainous retreat at Amba Alagi. On 20 April Aosta rejected a call to surrender and for the next 25 days British forces and the Patriots attacked the fortified peaks one by one, pressing the Italians into a smaller and smaller perimeter. His troops finally exhausted, Aosta surrendered on 16 May 1941, but this still left isolated Italian forces in Galla-Sidamo, and at Gondar and Assab, and these were not all rounded up until November.

Besides providing the perfect example of the cryptographers' war, giving a welcome boost to British morale, and releasing vital forces for the Western Desert campaigns, the success of the East African campaign had important strategic consequences. With the Red Sea and Gulf of Aden coastlines cleared of Axis forces, Roosevelt was able to declare on 11 April 1941 that these areas were no longer combat zones. US ships were therefore able to proceed to Suez, thus helping to relieve the enormous strain on UK shipping resources. See also LAND POWER.

Mockler, A., *Haile Selassie's War* (Oxford, 1984).

East China Sea, battle of, the last important air–sea battle of the war which was fought in April 1945 when the giant 64,000-ton Japanese battleship, *Yamato*, accompanied by one cruiser and eight destroyers left Japan to attack US forces then invading *Okinawa. For the *Yamato* it was virtually a suicide mission, for she had only enough fuel aboard for a one-way voyage and without air cover she had little chance of surviving. On the night of 6/7 April the Japanese commander of the force, Vice-Admiral Ito Seüchī, diverted into the East China Sea so as not to approach Okinawa directly, but he was spotted next morning and attacked by 380 US aircraft from *Task Force 58. All the Japanese warships, except four destroyers, were quickly sunk. See also PACIFIC WAR.

Eastern Solomons, battle of. This took place in August 1942 during the *Pacific war and was one of several encounters between the Japanese and US navies off *Guadalcanal. *Yamamoto's Japanese Combined Fleet lost one light carrier and had a seaplane tender damaged, while the American fleet carrier *Enterprise* was badly damaged. The Americans lost 20 aircraft and the Japanese 60 in a battle notable for the caution employed on both sides.

Eben Emael fortress, a series of concrete and steel emplacements, situated on the Albert Canal north of Liège, which in May 1940 guarded the bridges at Briedgen, Veldwezelt, and Vroenhoven, immediately west of Maastricht. They were garrisoned with 700 men and were a linchpin of the Belgian defences at the start of the German offensive in the west on 10 May 1940 (see FALL GELB) which preceded the fall of *France. They seemed impregnable, but 78 German engineers of the Koch Assault Detachment landed on top of the fortifications in gliders. Using hollow charges (see EXPLOSIVES), the engineers destroyed some emplacements, and kept the garrison cowed, while German airborne forces captured the bridges. The next day the 223rd Infantry Division arrived and captured the remaining fortifications. The Koch Detachment lost just six men killed and twenty wounded.

E-boat, or Enemy boat (also *Eilboot*, or boat in a hurry), was the Allied designation for the German *Schnellboot* (fast boat). A high-speed craft armed with two torpedo tubes, it was the equivalent of the American *PT-boat and the British *MTB.

economic warfare

1. Introduction

The phrase 'economic warfare' does not seem to have come into common use until the 1930s and it has no unambiguous definition. In its broadest sense, the term could cover almost any phase of war in which economic weapons are used, but essentially it can be defined as the economic proceedings taken by a government to achieve its own purposes against another power.

Economic blockade is sometimes used as a synonym for economic warfare, and for the UK and USA, as the world's greatest naval powers during the war, it was inevitable that a naval blockade would constitute the corner-stone of any Anglo-American economic strategy against the Axis powers. But economic warfare during the Second World War had a broader meaning and in the summer of 1939 the mission of the British ministry of economic warfare was described as follows in its official handbook:

> The aim of economic warfare is so to disorganize the enemy's economy as to prevent him from carrying on the war. Its effectiveness in any war this country may be engaged in will vary inversely with the degree of self-sufficiency which the enemy had attained, and/or the facilities he has, and can maintain, for securing supplies from neighbouring countries, and directly with the extent to which (1) his imports must be transported across seas which can be controlled by His Majesty's ships, (2) his industry and centres of storage, production manufacture and distribution are vulnerable to attack from the air, and (3) opportunities arise for interfering with his exports originating from his territories.

Economic warfare therefore was not simply naval blockade, but also involved such diverse actions as diplomatic negotiations with neutral countries and the bombing of industrial targets. It also covered the employment of any means by which a country's production capacity could be effectively reduced, and it is significant that the British sabotage organization *SOE

(Special Operations Executive) came under the political aegis of the minister of economic warfare.

On the Axis side the phrase was hardly used, and the concept played little or no part in Axis strategy. With the battle of the *Atlantic the German submarine fleet certainly implemented a wide-ranging campaign against merchant shipping supplying the UK, and the *Blitz was partially directed against British ports, but neither was part of a greater strategic plan, nor were they co-ordinated with any programme aimed at undermining Allied economies.

2. Allied goals and organization

In his official British history of the subject (see below) W. N. Medlicott formulated Allied goals as: (1) a drastic limitation of German imports from non-European sources; (2) to create an encirclement neurosis, which would have an adverse impact on German political and military strategy; (3) a direct hampering of the Axis armament efforts through raw material shortages; (4) an indirect hampering of the Axis wartime economy by additional strains on transport and manpower; and (5) the strengthening of neutral resistance to Axis powers, both by economic aid and by threats of retaliation.

In addition to this list, the Allies also tried to secure vital *raw materials and products from neutral countries which might otherwise all have gone to Germany, the ultimate aim being to deprive Germany of aid from neutral sources. Wherever possible, control was exercised at the source of the materials, in order to prevent goods from being shipped to Germany and techniques devised during the *First World War were developed and refined to achieve this. Lists of goods which were considered of strategic value to the Axis were published, and proclaimed as contraband. The contraband list was wide, and embraced practically all commodities that could be considered of economic value in wartime. Furthermore, compulsory navicerts were supplemented by ship warrants, which were issued when a ship's owner agreed to comply with British regulations. Without this document no facilities were provided by or at British ports. Blacklisting was also used whereby firms which were blacklisted were denied the essential materials they needed to continue production. For example, it was employed against the important Swiss engineering firm of Sulzer in 1943, in order to force the company and the Swiss government to reduce Sulzer's exports of machinery to Germany. The blacklist also led to a new trade agreement which was less favourable to Germany.

In the UK the ministry of economic warfare, with a sphere of activities planned since 1936, was set up at the outbreak of war in September 1939. The experiences of the First World War were of great importance in the formulating of its programme. In the USA the board of economic warfare, a counterpart to the British ministry, was set up in 1941 (it was later renamed the office of economic warfare, and still later, the foreign economic administration). A close collaboration developed between the two organizations especially after *Pearl Harbor, when the American trade embargo against Japan merged with the British one against Germany. The US Government's economic offensive relied heavily on the control of foreign funds. It also licensed exports to neutrals, instituted a proclaimed (black) list, and undertook preemptive buying of scarce items essential to the Axis war effort. The London and Washington blockade committees had members in each other's capital.

Close though Anglo-American collaboration was, the two Allies were not always in agreement over the carrying through of economic warfare, especially where the politics of blockade were concerned. The fact that representatives of the USA became partners in an organization that was already functioning created some difficulties. To some extent, the more cautious British and the more aggressive American attitudes were a result of the fact that the USA entered the war more than two years after the UK. The Americans regarded blacklisting firms, or the threat of doing so, as a form of pressure, and were more active and less considerate about it than the British. They also had a more positive conception of the possibilities of economic warfare, unhampered as they were by the precedents of past wars or the compromises of two years of defeats. The British had in general a greater respect for neutrals, and feared that if they adopted over-forceful measures they would damage their post-war international trade.

3. Relations with neutral states

Before the USA entered the war its *Office of the Co-Ordinator of Inter-American Affairs helped combat Nazi commercial influence in neutral South America (see also LATIN AMERICA AT WAR), and once it became a combatant it was practically impossible for Germany to import any commodities from South America or anywhere else outside Europe, except by *blockade runners from Japan. But Germany's trade with neutral neighbours in Europe presented a more difficult problem for the Allies to handle. There were in fact only six countries on the continent of Europe that remained at peace during the war: Liechtenstein (then of no economic importance), Spain, Portugal, Sweden, Switzerland, and (until the last weeks) Turkey.

At the start of the war, the UK negotiated war trade agreements with neutral countries such as Belgium, Sweden, Norway, the Netherlands, and Denmark which precluded re-exports and limited shipments to 'normal' pre-war levels. It was necessary to negotiate carefully with those neutrals on whom the UK itself was dependent for certain imports, and when Germany stood at the height of its military successes, British negotiators had little leverage. If too much pressure were applied, or a blockade was too complete, neutrals could easily be driven into the German camp. Later in the war, as success on the battlefields shifted, it became more and more possible to persuade neutrals to limit deliveries to Germany. For instance, the export to Germany of iron ore and ball-bearings from Sweden, manufactured goods from Switzerland, chrome ore from Turkey, and wolfram ore from Portugal and Spain were all curtailed. But until as late as 1944 neutral states did largely maintain their pre-war pattern of trade, balancing it between the combatant Great Powers, and therefore providing small, but very important, supplies to the German war economy.

4. Impact of economic warfare

At the outbreak of war, knowledge in the UK of German resources and storage capacity was fairly limited and inaccurate. Many investigations of Axis resources had been pure guesswork. The temptation to be optimistic, or to hope for a quick solution, was sometimes strong, especially among Americans and many incorrect assumptions were made (see below regarding German ball-bearings production). This over-optimistic Allied view was due in part to a mistaken estimate of the achievements of blockade in the First World War, and to the fact that the German economy in the 1930s had shown many weaknesses. Economic targets were selected from an interplay of intelligence information, knowledge of pre-war economic conditions, decisions by the military forces and diplomatic services about what was feasible, and actual changes in the strategic situation.

In Germany on the other hand there had been economic growth during the later part of the 1930s and a programme of self-sufficiency had been prepared. Synthetics were developed, and substitute products used, in a partly successful attempt to replace essential imports such as petroleum, certain alloy materials, and rubber. It had also been possible to build up some stocks of raw materials, arms, and munitions, especially of products which had to come from non-European sources. Germany's economic position in 1939, and during the next three years of war, was far stronger than Allied experts had believed possible. On the other hand, no fundamental change of the German economy, to prepare for a long and exhausting war, had really taken place. It was only partially mobilized for war in 1939; not until 1943 was it adjusted to meet the demands of a large-scale war of attrition in the face of the vast combined output of the UK, the USSR, and above all the USA. Germany's original concept of the war had been a series of *blitzkriegs, so rearmament had taken place rather in width than in depth; more extensive preparations for war had not been thought necessary. The rapid and successful campaigns in 1939–41 put no heavy demands on the German economy and Germany, less isolated than it had been during the First World War, could draw on supplies from a large area, particularly after it had overrun most of the European continent and Italy had entered the war as its ally. Most countries in Europe therefore came well within the German *Grossraumwirtschaft* (wider economic sphere) which made a total economic blockade impossible and rendered the Allied naval blockade only partially successful. One of the most serious blows to its effectiveness was the signing of the German–Soviet trade agreements which arose out of the *Nazi–Soviet Pact of August 1939. These made possible not only imports of corn and raw materials from the USSR, but also a land transport link to the friendly power of Japan. Meanwhile, the Germans had managed to find substitutes for almost every product of which they were deprived.

However, Hitler's fear of the consequences of the Allied blockade played a part in his invasion of the USSR in June 1941 (see BARBAROSSA), involving Germany in a two-front war which ultimately proved disastrous for it. The need for a victory in the USSR to free Germany from the menaces of the blockade was expressed by Grand Admiral *Raeder on 26 August 1942 at a Führer's conference: '1. It is urgently necessary to defeat Russia and thus create a *Lebensraum* which is blockade-proof and easy to defend. Thus we continue to fight for years.
2. The fight against the Anglo-Saxon sea powers will decide both the length and the outcome of the war, and could bring England and America to the point of discussing peace terms.'

So the fear of blockade, the encirclement neurosis mentioned by Medlicott, may have been more important than the blockade itself in bringing Germany to its ultimate defeat.

From 1943 onwards air bombardment of economic targets, particularly in western and central Germany (see STRATEGIC AIR OFFENSIVES, 1) was increasingly important in reducing the enemy's economic strength. The bomber forces came under the command of the RAF and the USAAF, but the ministry of economic warfare had an important role in selecting targets for them. RAF long-range bombers were used against civilian targets and thus eliminated the distinction between combatant and non-combatant personnel, placing factory workers in dangers as mortal as those faced by infantry.

However, Allied bombing policy lacked consistency. Targets were not attacked long enough nor often enough.

Economic warfare, Table 1: German production of finished ball-bearings per thousand of pieces

	1943	*1944*	*1945*
Jan	7,189	6,866	6,891
Feb	7,285	5,662	4,594
Mar	8,576	5,165	
Apr	7,623	3,909	
May	8,567	5,168	
June	7,896	6,716	
July	8,379	7,080	
Aug	7,600	7,547	
Sep	8,130	8,565	
Oct	7,216	8,775	
Nov	8,082	8,496	
Dec	7,634	7,865	

Source: Webster C. K., and Frankland A. N., *The Strategic Air Offensive against Germany 1939–1945*, iv., p. 505.

Economic warfare, Table 2: Index of German armaments production (January–February 1942 = 100)

Year	*Total prodn.*	*Weapons*	*Tanks*	*Air-craft*	*Munitions*
1941	98	106	81	97	102
1942	142	137	130	133	166
1943	222	234	330	216	247
1944	277	348	536	277	306
Jan '45	227	284	557	231	226

Source: Wagenfuhr, R., *Die deutsche Industrie im Kriege 1939–1945*, pp. 178–81.

The Germans also took counter-measures: factories were moved underground, machines were protected, and component parts were stored away from factories. Ball bearings provide one example. The Swedish firm SKF delivered important quantities of high-quality ball bearings to Germany; but a combination of Allied diplomatic action in Sweden and bombing of the town of *Schweinfurt, where the German ball-bearing industry was concentrated, did not succeed (see Table 1). Deliveries of ball-bearing steel and machines from Sweden were hard to control; the ball-bearing factories were difficult to hit; and even when the factories were damaged, the machines continued to work. Moreover, Allied intelligence had assumed that the Schweinfurt factories worked triple shifts; in fact they ran on single shifts until *Speer took over. As a last resort the Germans could fall back on accepting a lower quality product.

In general, it can be said that the bombing raids only became really effective after the back of the German defensive system had been broken—late indeed in the war. Up to the autumn of 1944, Germany succeeded in increasing production; until 1945 such basic industries as steel and coal as well as the armaments industries (see Table 2) were relatively unaffected by Allied economic warfare. The only real shortages that resulted from Allied bombing were of oil and aviation fuel and this undoubtedly speeded up the process of defeating Germany, as did successive losses of territory acquired during the war.

In Japan, by contrast, the country's strategic economic weakness was obvious. Japan's dependence on imports from overseas for the essential basic materials of modern industry, and even for a vital margin of food, had provided the basis even before the war for Anglo-American planning for economic warfare. Japan, like Germany, could demonstrate economic expansion; but during 1943 sinkings of its merchant ships (see JAPAN, 7) began to have effect, and by 1944 imports of essential raw materials had dropped sharply. Nor did Japan have the opportunity to obtain necessary supplies from neighbouring occupied or neutral countries.

The blockade of Japan was a task for naval and air forces, operating on the long and vulnerable passage from South-East Asia to the home islands; in the end they succeeded in this task. Almost cut off from the vast resources conquered at the start of the war, the Japanese economy was on the brink of ruin when the nuclear blasts at *Hiroshima and *Nagasaki gave the knock-out blow.

5. Conclusion

Economic warfare did have its tactical successes, and it played a role in the Allied victory. But it also fell far short of the extravagant hopes that had been placed on it, and a study of its effects is more a study of failures than of successes. Faced with the realities of war, its weapons proved less effective than pre-war strategists had hoped. One cause of the failure was that its tools were not as efficient as had been supposed. Both individual and national economies, and the international economy as well, were more complex than Allied plans for economic warfare had foreseen.

Until the summer of 1944, German and Japanese production continued to rise steeply; and by the time they began to fall, many other causes than economic intervention were at work. While it can be said that economic warfare undoubtedly had an effect in weakening Germany's war potential and war-making capacity, and contributed to Germany's ultimate defeat, it was not at any stage a decisive factor, nor did it alone cause the downfall of Germany.

The case of Japan was rather different. Lacking adjacent neutrals from whom supplies could be drawn, and vulnerable to interference with its shipping routes by air and sea attack, it was seriously affected by the traditional blockade tactics which were of only limited use against Germany. See also WORLD TRADE AND WORLD ECONOMY.

MARTIN FRITZ

Gordon, D. L., and Dangerfield, R., *The hidden weapon. The story of economic warfare* (New York, 1947, repr. 1976).
Medlicott, W. N., *The Economic Blockade*, 2 vols. (London, 1952–9).
Milward, A. S., *War, Economy and Society 1939–1945* (Berkeley, Calif., 1977).
Wagenfuhr, R., *Die deutsche Industrie im Kriege 1939–1945* (2nd edn., Berlin, 1963).

Economic Warfare, Ministry of, see UK, 8.

economies, see domestic life sections of major powers; see also ECONOMIC WARFARE and WORLD TRADE AND WORLD ECONOMY.

Ecuador was defeated in a war with Peru in 1941, losing valuable territory. Peace was patched up at the *Rio conference in January 1942 at which Ecuador announced it was severing diplomatic relations with the three main Axis powers. It allowed US bases on the Galapagos Islands, declared war on Japan, but not Germany, on 2 February 1945—backdated to 7 December 1941—and signed the *United Nations Declaration. See also LATIN AMERICA.

Eden, (Robert) Anthony (1897–1977), British Conservative politician who became foreign secretary in Churchill's coalition government in December 1940.

Eden fought in the *First World War, ending it as the youngest brigade major in the British Army. In 1923 he became MP for Warwick and Leamington, a seat he held until 1957 when, as prime minister, he resigned and was subsequently raised to the peerage as the Earl of Avon.

A man of great charm and elegance, Eden was also extremely hardworking and his political ability soon brought him high office. In December 1935 he became foreign secretary in Baldwin's third government. However, when *Chamberlain succeeded Baldwin in 1937 Eden soon found that while they both agreed that Hitler and Mussolini had to be appeased, in the sense of 'bringing peace, settling strife, etc.', he was not in accord with Chamberlain's methods or timing. In February 1938 he resigned, and in the House of Commons debate which followed the *Munich agreement that September abstained from voting. But though Churchill was later to link their names together as if they had been pursuing a common cause, Eden was not at that time a supporter of Churchill—indeed, they were rivals as possible candidates for the prime ministership had Chamberlain been forced to step down at that time.

In September 1939 Eden was made secretary of state for the Dominions without a seat in the cabinet. When Churchill became prime minister in May 1940, he was appointed secretary of state for war, a post which carried cabinet rank but no seat in the war cabinet. Nevertheless, Eden's influence was considerable and during that critical year he made many decisions which, if they had been wrong, could have been catastrophic. He was a strong supporter of *Dill, *Brooke, and *Wavell, when Churchill was less certain of their talents as generals. Wavell's early victories in the Middle East were a personal vindication of Eden's judgement and when, in December 1940, he became foreign secretary with a seat in the war cabinet it was soon accepted that if anything happened to Churchill it would be Eden who would succeed him. During the war he travelled widely, visiting Moscow several times and he accompanied Churchill to all the major conferences with the exception of Casablanca (see SYMBOL), where foreign secretaries were excluded.

Despite the cordiality of their remarks about one another in their respective memoirs, the relationship between Eden and Churchill was not always a harmonious one. They clashed in particular over the Polish *government-in-exile and de *Gaulle and the Free French, Eden championing the former against the USSR and the latter against the Americans. He objected strongly to the *Morgenthau Plan, a stance which led to a public row with his prime minister; and on one occasion, in 1942, it seems that he seriously considered trying to oust Churchill. But after the war Churchill said that Eden had always been his mainstay. See also DIPLOMACY.

Barker, E., *Churchill and Eden at War* (London, 1978).
Eden, A., *Memoirs: The Reckoning* (London, 1965).
James, R. R., *Anthony Eden* (London, 1987).

Eder, Möhne, and Sorpe dams, see DAM BUSTERS.

EDES (Ethnikos Dimokratikos Ellinikos Syndesmos, or National Republican Greek League), a non-communist Greek guerrilla organization. See GREECE, 6.

Edwards, Air Marshal Harold (1892–1952), Royal Canadian Air Force officer who, from November 1941 until the end of 1943, was based in London and carried out his political directive to form squadrons within the RAF composed entirely of Canadian personnel. This included the formation of the all-Canadian 6th Group of Bomber Command. See also CANADA, 6(d).

Egypt, having been occupied by the British since 1882, became a British protectorate in 1914. The protectorate was ended in February 1922 by a declaration of independence under which the country became a constitutional monarchy with universal male suffrage. However, pending negotiations, responsibility for four matters—defence, the security of the empire's communications, the protection of foreign interests and of minorities, and the Sudan—still rested with the British government. This rendered independence almost meaningless, and even after the signing of the Anglo–Egyptian Treaty of August 1936, the year when King Farouk (1920–65) ascended the throne, the British still retained certain rights. These included the right to continue to defend the Suez Canal, a vital artery to Australasia and British Far East possessions, until the Egyptian Army—which, on the outbreak of war, comprised eleven infantry battalions, one regiment of light tanks and another of armoured cars—was capable of doing so. A clause in Article 7 of the Treaty, which the UK invoked on 1 September 1939, stated that in the event of war the king would give 'all the facilities and assistance in his power, including the use of ports, aerodromes, and means of communication'. In effect, this resulted in the country's virtual occupation by British forces. Alexandria was the main base of the British Mediterranean fleet throughout the war and the HQ of the C-in-C, *Middle East Command, was situated in the capital, Cairo.

At the start of the war, the Egyptian prime minister, Ali Mahir, led a coalition of independents and Sa'adists which had been formed from an anti-British wing of the Wafd nationalist party. Ali Mahir became military governor of the country, which was divided into four military districts, martial law was proclaimed, strict monetary and economic measures and censorship were imposed, German nationals were arrested, and diplomatic relations with Germany were severed. But Ali Mahir was basically pro-Axis, as was Farouk, and Egypt did not declare war on Germany. Diplomatic relations were also severed with Italy in June 1940, when Italy entered the war, but again Ali Mahir refused to declare war. He acted only reluctantly against Italian citizens and property in Egypt, and ordered Egyptian Army frontier guards not to fire on Italian troops.

Farouk was no constitutional monarch. He wielded considerable political power and he was popular with his people, but his country was occupied by the British and real power lay with the British ambassador, Miles Lampson. On 23 June 1940 Farouk was forced by the British to dismiss Ali Mahir, and it was not until this had happened that the Italian legation staff left the country. The opposition Wafd party, though nationalists, wished to co-operate with the British and the British wanted it to form a government, but Farouk, whose power the Wafdists had tried to curb, opposed this. Instead, a compromise prime minister, Hasan Sabri, was appointed who continued to hedge his country's bets. On 17 September 1940 Italian troops invaded Egypt (see WESTERN DESERT CAMPAIGNS) but, despite an earlier declaration that it would declare war if the country were invaded, the Egyptian government maintained a state of non-belligerency. The Italians were subsequently driven back by the British, but air raids on Alexandria caused alarm—650 civilians were killed in one during June 1941—and the shortage of foodstuffs spread internal discontent.

In November 1940 Sabri died and was replaced by Husayn Sirry, whose coalition government the Wafdist opposition refused to join. During that winter domestic conditions deteriorated sharply. There was a severe shortage of basic commodities, the black market flourished, and the introduction of rationing failed to cure the problem. The government then restricted the amount of land that could be cultivated for cotton so that more food could be grown, but so acute was the shortage of bread in January 1942 that some Cairo bakeries were stormed by hungry mobs.

The same month a crisis developed when two ministers resigned, the British forced the government to sever relations with *Vichy France, and Farouk, who had not been consulted, accused the government of infringing his royal prerogative. Axis forces in the desert were now approaching Egypt and amid cries from demonstrators in the streets of 'Forward *Rommel; long live Rommel', Sirry resigned on 2 February. The British insisted that Farouk ask Mustafa al-Nahhas, head of the Wafd, to form a government, but the king wavered and prevaricated. British troops and armoured cars then surrounded the royal palace and Lampson demanded Farouk's abdication. Instead, Farouk accepted a Wafdist government under Nahhas, a decision that was shortly afterwards endorsed by a general election.

Nahhas was firmly pro-British. Ali Mahir was put under house arrest in April 1942 and when *Rommel's Axis forces advanced into Egypt in mid-1942 Nahhas interned suspects and closed the Royal Automobile Club of Egypt where pro-Axis sentiments were openly expressed by the more fashionable members of society. Throughout 1942 anti-British sentiment remained strong, especially in the Egyptian Army whose one-time chief of staff, Aziz al-Masri, was a prominent supporter of the Axis cause, and pro-Axis sympathizers and agents (see KONDOR MISSION) were constantly trying to undermine the British war effort. But in November *El Alamein was fought and won and the war moved away from Egypt. However, despite the antagonism of Farouk, who twice tried to dismiss him, and twice had to be dissuaded by the British, Nahhas remained in power until October 1944. By then the British had lost interest and Farouk replaced him with the Saadist leader Ahmad Mahir. In February 1945 Mahir, who had just obtained parliament's approval to declare war on Germany and Japan, was assassinated, and it was his successor who made the declaration of war on 26 February, allowing Egypt to become a founding member of the United Nations (see SAN FRANCISCO CONFERENCE).

The rise of *nationalism in the country became more marked once an Axis invasion—viewed, despite anti-British sentiment, with some trepidation—was no longer a possibility; after further negotiations and Farouk's abdication in July 1952, the last British troops left Egyptian soil in 1954. See also ANTI-IMPERIALISM.

Cooper, A., *Cairo in the War, 1939–1945* (London, 1989).
Vatikiotis, E. J., *The Modern History of Egypt* (rev. edn., London, 1980).
Warburg, G., *Egypt and the Sudan: Studies in History and Politics* (London, 1985).

Eichelberger, Lt-General Robert L. (1886–1961), US Army officer who served under *MacArthur during the *Pacific war. His most notable contributions were at *Buna during the *New Guinea campaign, which MacArthur told him to take, 'or not come back alive'; on *Biak Island, where he turned the battle around in five days; and during the battle for Manila in March 1945 when he was commanding the newly formed Eighth US Army in the second *Philippines campaign. Altogether he planned and executed 52 *amphibious warfare landings in the *South-West Pacific Area.

Eichelberger, R., *Our Jungle Road to Tokyo* (London, 1951).

Eichmann, Adolf (1906–62), *SS Obersturmbannführer (lt-colonel) who from the autumn of 1941 headed the *RSHA's Section IV B4, the Race and Resettlement Office, which administered the mass extermination of European Jewry (see FINAL SOLUTION). He attended the *Wannsee conference in January 1942 and in March 1944 he conducted negotiations with the *Jewish Agency, through an intermediary, to exchange Hungarian Jews, whom he was deporting to *Auschwitz, for merchandise or cash (see BRAND). At the end of the war he escaped recognition and eventually emigrated to Argentina. In 1960 he was kidnapped by Israeli agents, put on trial in Israel, and hanged.

Pearlman, M., *The Capture and Trial of Adolf Eichmann* (London, 1963).

Einsatzgruppen were mobile killing squads of the *RSHA's Sicherheitspolizei and Sicherheitsdienst. First employed in Austria in March 1938, seven of these units followed behind German forces during the *Polish campaign in September 1939. They murdered Poland's élite—aristocrats, the intelligentsia, priests—and many Jews were arbitrarily killed while the rest were herded into *ghettos. Five *Einsatzgruppen* totalling 3,000 men also followed the Wehrmacht during its invasion of the USSR in June 1941 (see BARBAROSSA) with orders to kill systematically all Jews and Soviet political commissars. By November 1941 perhaps as many as 600,000 Jews had been liquidated. *Einsatzgruppen* were also used against Soviet partisans (see USSR, 8), though these operations were often a cloak for helping to implement the *Final Solution, and it was planned that six should be used in the UK (see BLACK BOOK) should the German invasion, condenamed *SEALION, be successful. See also GERMANY, 4.

Headland, R., *Messages of Murder* (London, 1992).

Eire, name from 1937 of the Irish Free State whose Dominion status was steadily eroded by its Taoiseach (prime minister), Eamon *de Valera, during the 1930s. In 1938 the British agreed to relinquish the ports of Cóbh, Castletown Bere, and Lough Swilly, the use of which they had acquired by treaty, but de Valera kept his country technically within the British Empire in the hope that when he achieved his most important political goal, of reuniting Northern Ireland with Eire, contact with the Crown would not be entirely severed.

When war came de Valera declared a state of emergency—the war years became known in Eire as 'The Emergency'—and he also declared the country neutral, the only member of the British Empire to remain outside the conflict. He formed the Department for Co-Ordination of Defensive Measures under Frank Aiken and introduced severe measures to curb the activities of the illegal *Irish Republican Army (IRA) whose sporadic acts of violence could, de Valera feared, provoke the British into infringing Eire's neutrality.

The British, anxious to use the treaty ports again, hinted at the possibility of the reunification of Northern Ireland with Eire if the latter entered the war. But de Valera maintained his neutral stance, knowing that it reflected the true feelings of the majority of Eire's 2.9 million population. Eire was not only not willing to fight, it was not ready to: in September 1939 the regular Irish Army totalled only 7,494 men, its Air Corps had four effective fighters, and the Irish Naval Service only two patrol boats. The UK did provide some *matériel*, but neither it nor the USA was willing to supply large quantities of arms unless de Valera abandoned his policy of neutrality.

But when the question 'Who are we neutral against?' was raised the answer could only be Germany, for the British were allowed to infringe Eire's air space and pursue U-boats into its territorial waters, while from 1942 Allied air crews of crashed aircraft were sent to Northern Ireland instead of being interned. However, these concessions did not prevent the British also making unauthorized infringements of Eire's neutrality; as did the Germans who landed *Abwehr agents to contact the IRA. Both Hitler and the British considered invading Eire and once the Americans were in the war, and had troops based in Northern Ireland, de Valera was concerned that they might cross the border. Certainly the Irish Army, which, swelled by auxiliary forces, eventually grew to an inadequately armed 250,000, was as alert for an invasion from Northern Ireland as it was for one from occupied France, and though there was military co-operation with the British—the W-Plan covered a move south by the British Army from Northern Ireland in the event of a German invasion of Eire—mutual suspicion pervaded Anglo-Irish relations. When the Germans accidentally bombed a Dublin suburb, most of those on the ground thought the British had raided them; and when two South Africans and an Indian on an Abwehr espionage mission were captured, it was initially assumed they were British *spies. For their part the British were convinced, wrongly, that de Valera permitted Axis agents to roam at will and allowed U-boats to refuel and revictual in remote southern inlets.

Churchill considered Eire's position unforgivable. He threatened to employ 'weapons of coercion' if the UK were not allowed use of the treaty ports, so essential, he considered, if the battle of the *Atlantic was to be won. But though the Atlantic *convoys brought supplies for Eire as well as the UK, de Valera remained adamant. Coercion followed in the form of economic sanctions, though these were carefully disguised as genuine shortages. As the UK provided most of Eire's imports, and controlled the movements of Irish merchant shipping, the effect of sanctions was felt immediately, though they were not as severe as some US government officials would have wished. By 1943 the weekly tea ration in Eire per person was three-quarters of an ounce while in the UK it was two ounces, coal had disappeared from domestic hearths, and private motorists had no petrol. But de Valera remained doggedly neutral to the end. Despite constant Allied pressure—which culminated in March 1944 when Eire was totally isolated to prevent any leakage about the forthcoming Normandy landings (see OVERLORD)—he refused to expel Axis diplomats, and when Hitler committed suicide he went in person to the German Legation to express his condolences.

During the war 124,500 men and 58,000 women left

Eire for Northern Ireland or the UK. Of these 38,544 volunteered for the British armed forces, a figure which included 7,000 *deserters from the Irish Army, and several thousands more already living in the UK also joined up. In 1948 Eire became the Republic of Ireland.

Fisk, R., *In Time of War* (London, 1983).

Eisenhower, General of the Army Dwight D. (1890–1969), US Army officer who served as supreme Allied commander in the Mediterranean and then throughout the fighting in north-west Europe.

One of seven sons of poor Mennonite parents, Eisenhower was born at Denison, Texas, and was commissioned into the infantry from West Point military academy. Despite all his efforts to obtain a posting to France during the *First World War he remained in the USA and was given the task, as a 28-year-old major, of building from scratch the army's first tank corps. By 1918 he was commanding 10,000 men. After serving in Panama, he passed top of his class from Leavenworth, the US Army's staff college, attended war college in Washington, and served on the staff of General John Pershing (1860–1948) before joining *MacArthur's staff in the Philippines.

When war broke out in Europe in September 1939 Eisenhower, whose relations with MacArthur were less than cordial, insisted on returning to the USA, and after a short stint as a regimental executive and then as a battalion commander became, in quick succession, chief of staff of 3rd Infantry Division, of 9th Army Corps, and then of Lt-General Walter Krueger's Third Army. He was promoted colonel in March 1941 and brigadier-general that September, and within a week of *Pearl Harbor he was summoned to Washington by *Marshall to be deputy chief of the War Plans Division. After a reorganization this became the Operations Division which he headed with the rank of maj-general until June 1942 when he was appointed commanding general of the European Theatre of Operations (see ETOUSA). Once in London he quickly assessed that the British were right in refusing to launch a cross-Channel operation that year and when the invasion of French North Africa (see NORTH AFRICAN CAMPAIGN) was agreed upon instead, Eisenhower became the obvious choice to lead it.

What immediately marked Eisenhower out as a military supremo was his ability and determination to make the Alliance an everyday working reality. He demanded, and received, a harmony amongst his Anglo-US staff at his *Allied Forces HQ which reflected his own cheerful, outgoing disposition. He did not mind somebody being called a son-of-a-bitch, he remarked on one occasion, but he was damned if he would have them being called a British son-of-a-bitch or an American son-of-a-bitch.

He survived his political baptism of fire in dealing with the complex situation that confronted him in Algiers after the North African landings in November 1942, but then barely survived his military one in Tunisia. Before the landings he had never heard a shot fired in anger, his US forces were inexperienced, his command structure was uncertain—and made more so by French intransigence—and his front nearly came unravelled at *Kasserine Pass in February 1943. But incompetent commanders were fired and the right ones appointed, and in May 1943 the Axis forces in Tunisia surrendered.

Still only a substantive lt-colonel, Eisenhower was promoted four-star general in February 1943 and served as the Allied commander for all the major operations in the Mediterranean theatre throughout that year. He made his mistakes—both the *Sicilian campaign and *Salerno showed the cautiousness of Allied strategy and the failure to grasp opportunities when they were offered—but his experiences there, he wrote later, 'reaffirmed the truth that unity, co-ordination and co-operation are the keys to successful operations.'

In December 1943 the Mediterranean became a unified command and Eisenhower was appointed its supreme commander, but in January 1944 he was appointed supreme commander of the Allied Expeditionary Forces for the Normandy landings that June (see OVERLORD). Roosevelt picked him for this task because he was, the president believed, the best politician among the military men.

One of Eisenhower's most critical battles was fought before the invasion of occupied Europe even took place. He insisted against opposition from the commanders of the two strategic air forces that their aircraft be diverted from the *strategic air offensive against Germany to bomb German lines of communication in France, and he noted in his diary on 22 March 1944 that if the matter was not resolved to his liking immediately, 'I will request relief from this command.' A compromise was achieved and by 6 June, the date of the landings, French rail traffic in the area had been cut to one-third of its January 1944 level; after the landings the strategic air forces, still under Eisenhower's direction, helped to minimize German counter-attacks, and then paved the way for the break-out that eventually came in August.

The *Normandy campaign was fought by *Montgomery, *Bradley, and *Patton. But it was Eisenhower who accepted the risk of launching the US airborne divisions on the invasion's right flank against the advice of his air commander, *Leigh-Mallory, who predicted 70% casualties; it was he who, once the Allies had broken out of their Normandy bridgehead, ordered the pursuit of the retreating Germans as far as possible as quickly as possible despite the problem of supplying his armies (see RED BALL EXPRESS); and it was he who insisted on the broad-front strategy (see OVERLORD) that is now almost universally accepted as having been the correct one. But he erred in his judgement when, after taking personal control of the land battle on 1 September 1944, he endorsed Montgomery's strategy to seize a bridgehead beyond the lower Rhine at Arnhem (see MARKET-GARDEN) instead of insisting that the approaches to Antwerp were cleared first (see SCHELDT ESTUARY). The conception of

MARKET-GARDEN was Montgomery's, but the ultimate responsibility for it lay with Eisenhower. That their ideas of what it could achieve were so markedly at variance is perhaps a reflection of the intense temperamental and professional differences that divided the two men, differences which brought Montgomery perilously close to being dismissed. Yet it was Eisenhower who unwittingly brought about this state of affairs with his passion (not too strong a word) for trying to find—indeed insisting upon—a consensus, the middle view. It was a stance that infuriated not only Montgomery but at different times Bradley and Patton, too.

The crisis created by the German *Ardennes campaign, launched in December 1944, was also Eisenhower's responsibility in that he had failed to predict it. He acknowledged this, but he reacted quickly to the situation and made the right decisions to counter it: hold *Bastogne, launch Patton northwards, give Montgomery temporary command of the battle. At this time his determination that 'my mannerisms and speech in public speech would always reflect the cheerful certainty of victory' was shown to best advantage. At a meeting to discuss the crisis he remarked that 'the present situation is to be regarded as one of opportunity for us and not of disaster. There will be only cheerful faces at this conference table.'

'As a strategist,' one of his biographers, Stephen Ambrose, has written (*Parameters*, June 1990), 'the highest art of a commander, he was far more often right than wrong. He was right in his selection of Normandy as the invasion site, right in his selection of Bradley rather than Patton as First Army commander, right in his insistence on using bombers against the French railway system, right to insist on a Broad-Front approach to Germany, right to see the Bulge as an opportunity rather than a disaster, right to fight the major battle west of the Rhine. Eisenhower was right on the big decisions. He was the most successful general of the greatest war ever fought.'

Promoted five-star general in December 1944, Eisenhower succeeded Marshall as US Army chief of staff after the war. He retired in 1948 but subsequently commanded NATO forces between 1950 and 1952, and then served as US president between 1953 and 1961. The image sometimes portrayed of him as a simple, pleasant, Midwest farmhand is a partial one. He was simple in the sense of being without guile and in having a rigorous code of honour, but his famous grin—which one British general calculated was worth an army corps in any campaign—disguised a formidable intelligence, just as his amiability hid an inner toughness and self-assurance.

Ambrose, S., *The Supreme Commander* (New York, 1970).
Butcher, H., *Three Years with Eisenhower* (London, 1946).
Eisenhower, D. D., *Crusade in Europe* (New York, 1948).

El Alamein. This Egyptian desert railway halt, situated about 95 km. (60 mi.) west of Alexandria, gave its name to two different encounters between Allied and Axis forces during the *Western Desert campaigns.

The first, and some say erroneously named, was a defensive battle fought by the British and Commonwealth Eighth Army from 1 to 4 July 1942. Commanded by General *Auchinleck, the Eighth Army prevented *Rommel's Panzer Army Africa (renamed German–Italian Panzer Army, 25 October 1942) from breaking through its defensive lines near Ruweisat Ridge when Rommel made a penultimate bid to conquer Egypt and seize the Suez Canal. It is still a matter of debate whether Auchinleck, aided by *ULTRA intelligence and *Dorman-Smith, was at last able to gain the initiative; or whether Rommel had simply run out of steam.

Rommel tried to break through again, and failed, at *Alam Halfa in September. Then in the second El Alamein battle, the Eighth Army, now commanded by Lt-General *Montgomery, fought successfully between 23 October and 4 November 1942 to pierce Rommel's defences, forcing him to retreat into Tunisia.

Unlike most previous Western Desert battles, this second battle was a set-piece affair against static defences with no turnable flank, and lack of fuel and transport (see LOGISTICS) prevented Rommel from practising the mobile warfare of which he was a master. Instead, before going on sick leave on 23 September (he returned on 25 October), he ordered his defences strengthened by laying half a million anti-tank mines. Within these main minefields smaller ones, comprising anti-personnel devices, were laid. The Germans called them 'the Devil's gardens', and they caused Montgomery's attack serious delays. Rommel also 'corseted' the weaker Italian units with German formations and formed his armour into six groups positioned to counter-attack any breach of his defences.

Besides being critically short of fuel, Rommel was outgunned and outmanned by the British:

	Eighth Army	*Panzer Army Africa*
Men	195,000	104,000 (including 50,000 Germans)
Infantry battalions	85	71 including 31 German
Medium tanks	1,029	496
Anti-tank guns	1,451	800
Field and Medium artillery	500	908
Aircraft	530	350 (+150 from elsewhere)

Montgomery's plan (LIGHTFOOT) was to breach Rommel's northern defences by employing four infantry divisions of *Leese's 30th Corps on a 16 km. (10 mi.) front (see Map 28). Paths would be cleared through the minefields to enable the two armoured divisions of Lumsden's 10th Corps to pass beyond the infantry's bridgehead, a line codenamed OXALIC, to a line (PIERSON) running south-east from Kidney Ridge. There they would take up defensive positions against any German armoured attack, and would not go on to the offensive until the infantry battle—the 'crumbling' process as Montgomery called it—had been won.

By attacking in the more heavily defended northern

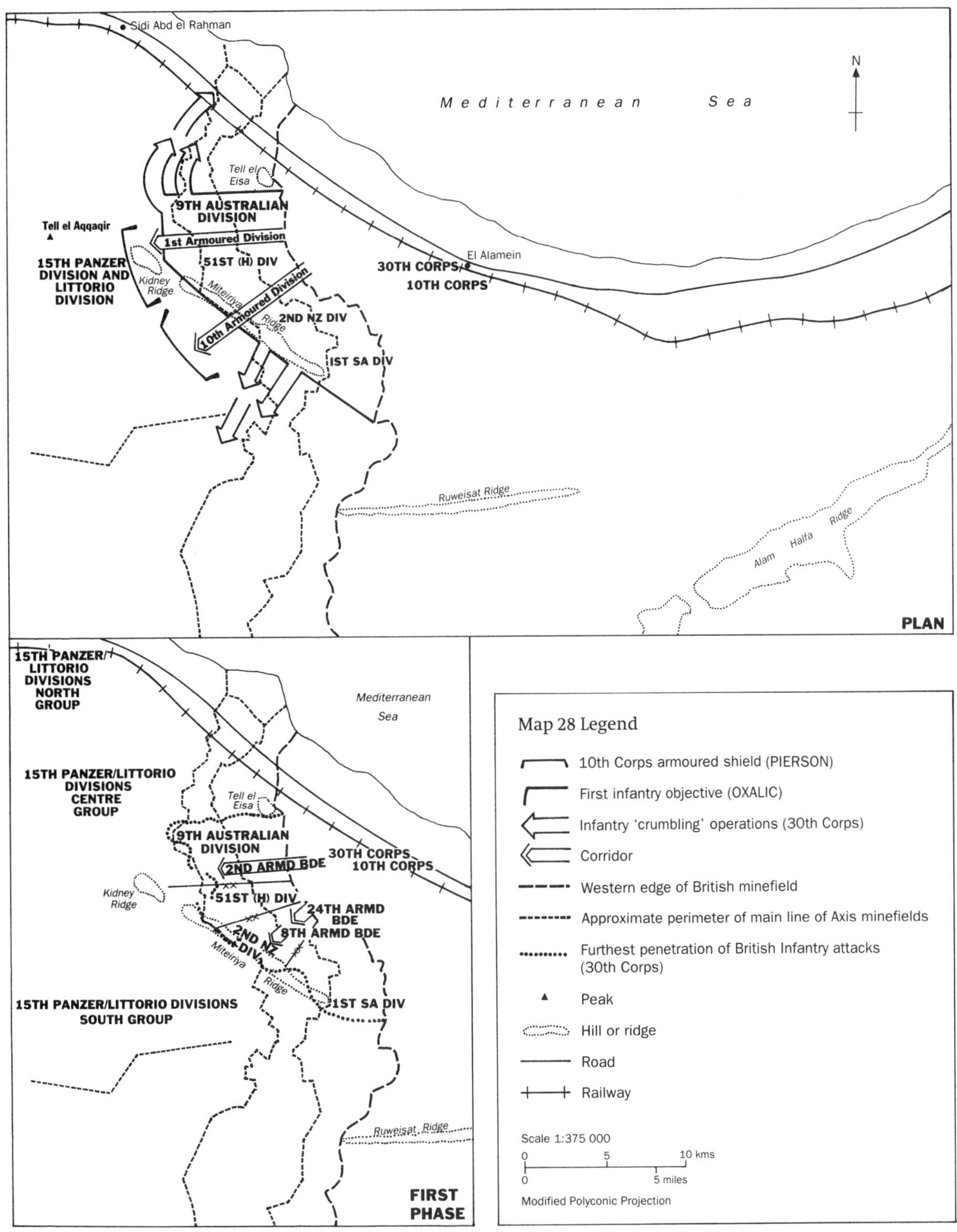

28. Plan for second battle of **El Alamein**, October–November 1942, and its first phase

sector, and by laying on elaborate *deception plans and diversionary attacks in the south with 13th Corps, Montgomery achieved initial surprise. His plan envisaged three stages of the battle: the break-in, the 'dog-fight' which would last about a week, and the break-out.

But the break-in, begun during the night of 23/24 October before a rolling barrage (see ARTILLERY, 2) from 882 guns, was slowed by the depth of Rommel's defences, and Lumsden's armour only reached OXALIC on the first day. However, 9th Australian Division took a key feature (Point 29) in their northern sector and began developing a salient while 1st Armoured Division attacked two centres of resistance (SNIPE and WOODCOCK) either side of Kidney Ridge. Rommel launched fierce counter-attacks there, but these were contained, and constant Allied air attacks and concentrated artillery bombardments (both features of the battle) aided the infantry's 'crumbling' of his forces. Meanwhile the Australians continued to push out their salient, and this siphoned Rommel's best troops away from where Montgomery was about to unleash a second attack (SUPERCHARGE) while it also 'uncorseted' the Italians.

But the process was slow, and Churchill became agitated when divisions were withdrawn from the front for SUPERCHARGE. This was launched on the night of 1/2 November by the New Zealand Division, and other infantry units, north of Kidney Ridge and south of where Rommel's élite units had now been drawn. This cleared the way forward for the armour and Rommel, after his forces had suffered further attrition, decided the battle was lost and that he must save his mobile troops by withdrawing to Fuka. He warned Hitler on 2 November that his army was without fuel and faced annihilation—a signal which, thanks to ULTRA, was in Montgomery's hands the next morning—but when, in a second signal, he said a withdrawal had begun Hitler ordered him to stand fast. Rommel tried to do so but, once started, the process could not be reversed. A night attack by the 51st Highland Division overran its objectives and at dawn on 4 November it found Tell El Aqqaqir abandoned. At midday Rommel's defences caved in and that evening Hitler gave him permission to withdraw. But by then Rommel's defeated army had started its headlong retreat across Libya during which Montgomery netted 30,000 *prisoners-of-war. Allied casualties during the battle had amounted to 13,560.

El Alamein was the climax of the Western Desert campaigns and one of the turning-points of the war; the victory, as intended, influenced the French to co-operate in the *North African campaign after initially opposing the landings there.

Hamilton, N., *Monty: The Making of a General, 1887–1942* (London, 1981), *ad fin.*

Strawson, J., *El Alamein: Desert Victory* (London, 1981).

ELAS (Ethnikos Laikos Apeleftherotikos Stratos, or National People's Liberation Army), the communist-controlled Greek guerrilla organization. See GREECE, 6.

Elba, Italian Mediterranean island situated between Corsica and the coast of Italy which was seized by the Germans after Italy's surrender in September 1943. On the night of 16/17 June 1944 the 9th French Colonial Infantry Division, some 2,000 *Goums, and a *bataillon de choc* (a commando-style unit) commanded by Lt-General Henri Martin, landed from Corsica under cover of the guns of British warships. The island was then overrun in what proved to be a costly and unnecessary operation—the French suffered 1,000 casualties. But as Hitler had ordered their evacuation too late, 2,000 of the garrison's 2,700 troops were captured; and it did exacerbate German fears of yet another Allied landing behind their lines (see SALERNO and ANZIO) as they withdrew northwards during the *Italian campaign.

electronic navigation systems, post-war term for what in the Second World War were known as radio navigation systems. The term embraced all radio and *radar systems used to assist with general navigation and/or target location and attack. Although these systems were used predominantly by aircraft, the same or similar systems were sometimes fitted to ships.

For the crews of bombers flying over land by day and through clear skies, navigation using ground features was a relatively simple matter. But if they had to fly over long stretches of sea, or above cloud, or at night, accurate navigation was considerably more difficult. Hence the need for electronic navigation aids to assist crews to find and bomb their targets. Accurate bombing requires no more care than extremely accurate navigation, so anything that assists the one also assists the other.

The 1930s had seen a rapid development in radio navigational techniques, spurred by the need for airlines to maintain schedules despite changeable weather. At the beginning of the Second World War most bombers were fitted with radio direction finders, which gave bearings of radio beacons on the ground. For flights to a point in the vicinity of the beacon, i.e. by an aircraft returning to base after a mission, the method was adequate and it would continue in use throughout the war. But the radio bearings became steadily less accurate as the distance from the beacon increased, so simple direction finding was of little use when trying to navigate to targets more than 320 km. (200 mi.) from the beacon.

Something better was needed, and the Germans were the first to develop it. Before the war the Luftwaffe developed Knickebein, a device similar in operation to the radio range system employed by airliners to navigate between special ground beacons. The ground transmitter radiated a so-called *Lorenz beam, which in fact comprised two overlapping beams with Morse dots transmitted in one and Morse dashes in the other; where the beams overlapped the dots and the dashes interlocked to produce a steady note lane much finer than either of the beams that produced it. Knickebein employed a huge directional aerial nearly 100 m. (315 ft.) across and 30 m. (100 ft.) high, supported on bogies running on a circular railway track to enable it to be aligned accurately on the target. The device produced a steady note lane only 0.3° wide and operated on one of three frequencies—30, 31.5, or 33.3 MHz. The signals were picked up using the standard airfield approach receiver fitted to all Luftwaffe twin-engined bombers and its use required no specialized training for the crew apart from normal instrument flying.

When using Knickebein to attack a target, the bomber crew flew along the steady note lane from one transmitter, and released the *bombs as they passed through the steady note lane from a second transmitter which crossed the first at the bomb release point. Using transmitters situated in France, the Netherlands, and Norway, the Luftwaffe could align two or more beams over any target in the UK. With the system their bombers could attack with an accuracy of about 1 km. (0.6 mi.) without the crews needing to see their target. Knickebein worked well enough against area targets, until the RAF got to hear about it and jammed it to the point of uselessness (see ELECTRONIC WARFARE).

All German multi-engined bombers could use Knickebein. In addition, for use by a specially trained night precision bombing *Gruppe* (established at about 30 aircraft), the Luftwaffe developed a more accurate beam bombing system codenamed *X-Gerät* (X-apparatus). *X-Gerät* operated on frequencies in the 66 to 74 MHz band and employed Lorenz beams similar to those used by Knickebein, but there were four instead of two: one beam to mark the approach to the target, and three cross-beams (see Map 29). Used in conjunction with a special clock, *X-Gerät* would release the bombs automatically when the aircraft reached the previously computed bomb release point. When the RAF learned of *X-Gerät*, it built and deployed jammers designed to counter the system.

The third of the German beam systems, the *Y-Gerät*, employed only a single ground station. The bomber approached its target by flying along a complex beam, and to measure the distance along the beam the ground station transmitted a separate ranging signal which the aircraft picked up and re-radiated. Operators at the ground station were then able to compute the position of the aircraft with considerable accuracy and, when it reached the bomb release point, they ordered the crew to release the bombs. So long as it could operate without hindrance the *Y-Gerät* was very effective, but once the method of operation was known to the British it proved relatively easy to jam.

It is easy to make light of the German beam systems, and their failure in the face of counter-measures. But it should be remembered that for the first two and a half years of the war they were far in advance of anything in service in any other nation. The significance of the German systems falls into relief if we consider how badly the RAF Bomber Command performed without such aids. If the accuracy of the German night raids on the UK during the period was mediocre, that of the RAF on Germany was miserable. In mid-1941, *photographic

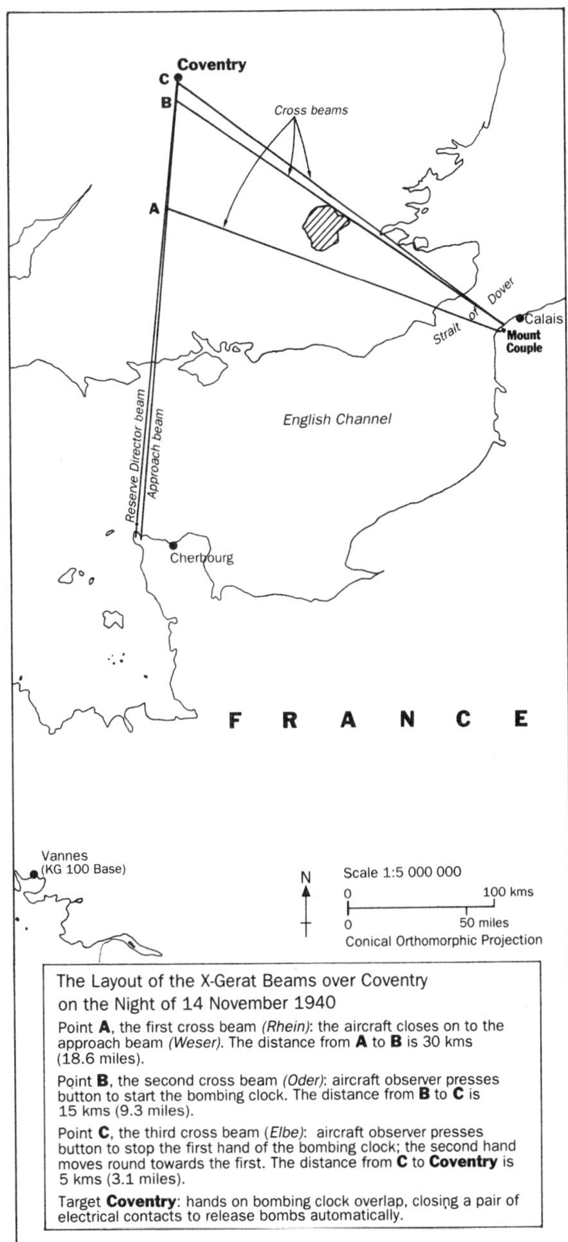

29. **Electronic navigation systems**: Dispositions of the *X-Gerät* beam for the raid on Coventry by KG100, 14/15 November 1940

reconnaissance revealed that only one in three of RAF crews placed their bombs within 8 km. (5 mi.) of the aiming point (see BUTT REPORT). For the Ruhr area, which was almost continually enshrouded in industrial haze, the figure was one in ten. As Churchill chided his chief of air staff: 'It is an awful thought that perhaps three quarters of our bombs go astray . . . If we could make it half and half we should virtually have doubled our bombing power.'

The revelations provided a mighty impetus for the development of electronic navigational systems in the UK. The first to go into service, early in 1942, was GEE. This system employed three ground transmitters working in concert, to radiate a complex chain of pulses in a predetermined order. Using a special receiver, the aircraft navigator could measure the differences in the time of arrival of the various pulses. He then read off his position from a special map. Because the distances from the transmitters were much greater, GEE was not so accurate over Germany as Knickebein had been over the UK. Nevertheless there was a marked improvement in bombing accuracy—until the Germans showed that they too could play the jamming game.

Early in 1943 the RAF introduced its first radar precision bombing system, called Oboe (see Figure) because its pulses sounded similar to the musical instrument. This device exploited the fact that radar can measure the range of an aircraft with considerable accuracy (though it is somewhat less accurate in measuring bearing). The system employed two ground stations. One tracked the aircraft as it flew along an arc of constant range running through the target, and passed correction signals if the aircraft deviated from this arc. Meanwhile the second station measured the range along the arc, and when the aircraft reached the previously-computed bomb release point the release signal was broadcast. The aircraft carried a pair of repeater-transmitters which amplified the range and track signals before returning them to the ground stations; these airborne repeater-transmitters were small and light and they fitted easily into a small aircraft. Under operational conditions Oboe was extremely accurate. Its main disadvantage was that the curvature of the earth limited its use to the area within about 450 km. (280 mi.) of each of the ground transmitters, which, of course, had to be located in friendly territory. A further problem was that a pair of ground transmitter-receivers could control only one bomber at a time during its bombing run and that might last up to ten minutes. Nevertheless, an arc of 450 km. (280 mi.) from the east coast of England took in all of the important Ruhr industrial area in Germany and that was where the device came into its own. Oboe was fitted to Mosquito pathfinder aircraft which marked the targets for the main force of bombers. The Germans found the device difficult to jam, especially in its later short-wavelength versions and they were so impressed with it that they copied the principle for their Egon system which was used to attack targets in the UK during the early months of 1944.

The British GEE-H and the American Shoran systems were essentially similar to Oboe, but their transmissions were initiated from, and the computations were made in, the bomber. The ground stations had only to repeat back the pulses and could thus handle scores of aircraft simultaneously.

All these electronic aids employed ground transmitters, which meant they were unusable at distances of more than 450 km. (280 mi.) from the furthest transmitter. For bombers to attack accurately at greater distances, a system was required that was independent of the ground stations. Early in 1943 the development of the *cavity magnetron enabled the RAF to introduce such a system into service: the *H2S centimetric radar. H2S was, for its time, an extremely advanced type of radar which scanned the ground beneath the aircraft. The returning echoes came strongest from built-up or mountainous areas, less strongly from open countryside and least strongly from areas of water. By displaying the echo signals on a cathode-ray tube it was, therefore, possible to produce a fairly good representation of the terrain which could be compared with a map. Initially the size and weight of the H2S installation limited its application to heavy bombers. Effectively the maximum range of the device was the same as the maximum radius of action of the aircraft carrying it. Bombing accuracy depended on the nature of the terrain around the target. Coastal targets usually produced very distinctive echoes on the radar. Other targets, especially those inland and surrounded by broken terrain, produced less distinct echoes and were more difficult to find.

H2S in its Mark I, II, and III versions served the RAF until the end of the war. A few were delivered to the USAAF where they were fitted into B17s and B24s. Later the USAAF produced its own version of the radar, the H2X, which was used in very large numbers for bombing through cloud. In 1944 the B29 bomber appeared fitted with the APS-20, the most advanced ground mapping radar of the period. The Germans developed their own, but too late for it to be used operationally.

No survey of navigation devices is complete without mention of the German Sonne system which became operational in 1943. The Sonne ground station radiated a complex fan of beams on frequencies in the 300 KHz band, and gave bearings of unprecedented accuracy out to a distance of about 1,600 km. (1,000 mi.). The beauty of the system was that an aircraft or ship needed only a standard communications receiver to receive the signals. The radio operator tuned in to the appropriate Sonne station, counted the number of dots or dashes heard, and referred these to a special map to read off the bearing. The cross of two such bearings produced a 'fix'.

The Luftwaffe set up Sonne stations along the Atlantic coast of Europe, from Norway down to the west coast of Spain, and on the Eastern Front. Once the method of operation of the system was known to RAF intelligence, its accuracy and simplicity made a profound impression. Over the *Western Approaches the device was far more effective than any comparable system available to the Allies. The RAF produced copies of a captured German Sonne map and, renamed Consol, the system was used by aircraft of Coastal Command. In fact it was of more use to the Allies than to the Luftwaffe, for by that stage of the war there was relatively little German air activity over the coastal areas. After the war the original German

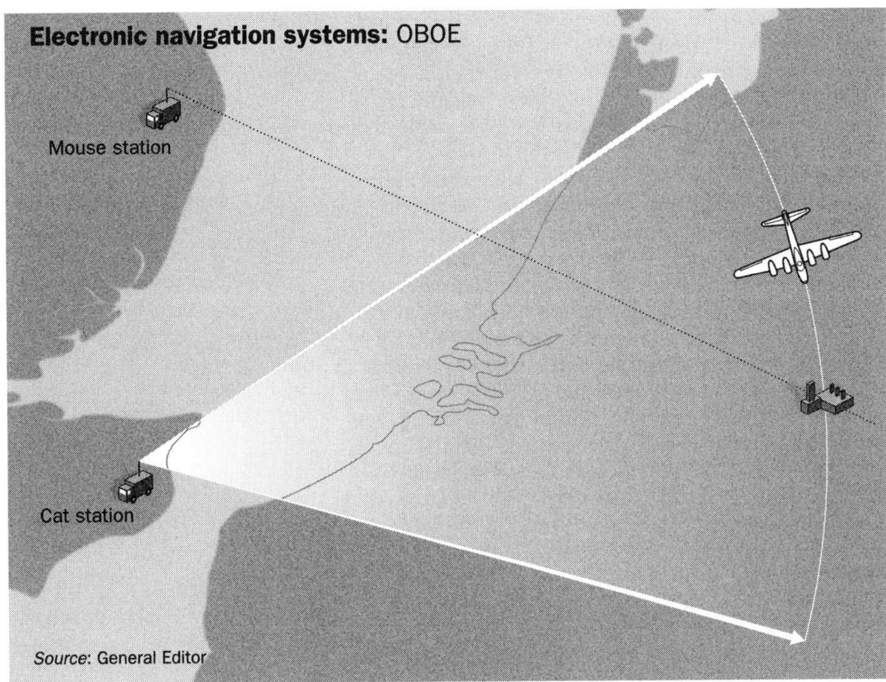

Source: General Editor

transmitters set up at Brest in France, at Stavanger in Norway, and at Lugo and Seville in Spain were kept in operation, and a captured transmitter was set up at Bushmills in Northern Ireland. Two transmitters were set up in the USSR, as were two more in the USA operating on a slightly altered system. The system continued in use for many years after the war, clear proof of the soundness of the original Sonne concept. See also EUREKA (2) and STRATEGIC AIR OFFENSIVES. ALFRED PRICE

Price, A., *Aircraft versus Submarine* (London, 1973).
——*Instruments of Darkness* (London, 1967).

electronic warfare, post-war term for what in the Second World War were known as radio counter-measures and radio counter-counter-measures. Radio counter-measures were those measures taken to counter an enemy's *radar and radio systems. Radio counter-counter-measures were those measures taken to reduce the effectiveness of the enemy counter-measures. Although these techniques were used predominantly by and against aircraft, they were also employed on a much smaller scale in land and naval warfare.

The first occasion on which radar jamming was employed in action was during the battle of *Britain when, in September 1940, the Luftwaffe attempted to neutralize the Chain Home early warning radars (20 to 52 MHz band) along the south coast of England. A ground station was set up at Mont Couple near Calais and employed a number of Breslau spot-noise jammers. The Breslau jamming caused some difficulties to the British radar operators, but at no time was it so serious that the plotting of incoming German formations was degraded to the point where they were able to avoid interception.

Meanwhile the RAF was building up its own jamming organization, No. 80 Wing, to counter the recently discovered Knickebein beam navigation system (see ELECTRONIC NAVIGATIONAL SYSTEMS) employed by the Luftwaffe. The first jammers were hastily improvised by modifying hospital diathermy sets into low-powered transmitters. But soon afterwards a purpose-built jammer, code-named ASPIRIN, was designed and built to counter Knickebein.

ASPIRIN radiated Morse dashes on the German beam frequencies. The dashes were superimposed on the German signals, but not synchronized with them. Some accounts have stated that No. 80 Wing deliberately bent the German beams, making the bombers release their *bombs almost to order. There were certainly wartime rumours to this effect, but it did not happen. The idea of beam-bending was seriously considered, and it was technically feasible, but such was the urgency of the programme to counter Knickebein that there was no time for such refinements. It is possible that on occasions the British dashes and the German dots did come together to produce some sort of bent beam, but there was never any deliberate re-aligning of the Knickebein beams. As a result of the ASPIRIN jamming, the German navigational system never achieved anything like its full potential.

In the autumn of 1940 a scientist in British intelligence, R. V. Jones, discovered that the Luftwaffe was using a new electronic navigation system, the *X-Gerät* (X-apparatus), which operated on a higher frequency than Knickebein (66 to 75 MHz) and was considerably more accurate (see Map 29). A suitable jammer was built, codenamed

BROMIDE, and by mid-November 1940 the first few had been rushed into service. The third of the German beam navigational systems to be employed over the UK during the *Blitz in 1940 and 1941, the *Y-Gerät*, was similarly countered by the DOMINO jammer. With the deployment of bomber units in preparation for the invasion of the USSR in June 1941 (see BARBAROSSA), large-scale night bomber attacks on Britain (the Blitz) came to an end.

The next major incident in the jamming contest occurred on 12 February 1942, when the German Navy sailed the battle-cruisers **Scharnhorst* and *Gneisenau* through the English Channel to Germany (see CERBERUS). As part of the elaborate preparations for the operation, one or more jammers were set up on the north coast of France to counter each radar on the south coast of England. Just before the warships came within range of the British radars, the jammers were switched on simultaneously. The jamming caused considerable confusion and slowed the British reaction, and as a result the German warships had passed through the strait of Dover before the first attacks were launched against them. The attacks were unsuccessful.

As part of the air defences for the German homeland, the Luftwaffe set up a chain of Himmelbett night fighter control stations, employing Freya (125 MHz) and Würzburg and Giant Würzburg (both on 570 MHz) radars (see KAMMHUBER LINE). Night fighters were fitted with Lichtenstein radar (490 MHz). The main early warning radars were the Wassermann and Mammut (both of which operated in the 125 MHz band). In December 1942 RAF bombers began employing the MANDREL spot-noise jamming transmitter to counter Freya, Mammut, and Wassermann. The effect of the jamming was to slow the German defensive reaction during attacks, and it reduced the loss rate of bombers. The Luftwaffe replied by widening the frequency band used by the early warning sets, to dilute the effect of the jamming. The RAF replied by increasing the power and frequency coverage of MANDREL and, later, bombers were fitted with two or more jammers. The battle between MANDREL and the German early warning radars continued throughout the rest of the war.

In 1943 the RAF introduced a new type of countermeasure, WINDOW: strips of metal foil released from aircraft (called 'Chaff' in the USA, *Düppel* in Germany and *Giman-shi* in Japan) to jam the Würzburg, Giant Würzburg, and Lichtenstein radars. WINDOW was first used on a large scale on 25 July, when each of the 746 aircraft attacking *Hamburg released large quantities of foil. The appearance of so many false targets on the radar screens saturated the defences and only 12 aircraft, 1.6% of the force involved, were lost. That was about one-quarter the loss rate usually suffered during attacks on this heavily defended target.

During the autumn of 1943 the US strategic bomber forces in Europe also began employing radar countermeasures to reduce losses. The main target of their jamming was the Würzburg radars used for anti-aircraft fire control. The APT-2 CARPET, a spot-noise jammer, was first used in action in October 1943 and brought about an immediate reduction in losses. A couple of months later, the US bombers began to use 'Chaff' in addition to noise jamming, to counter German radars.

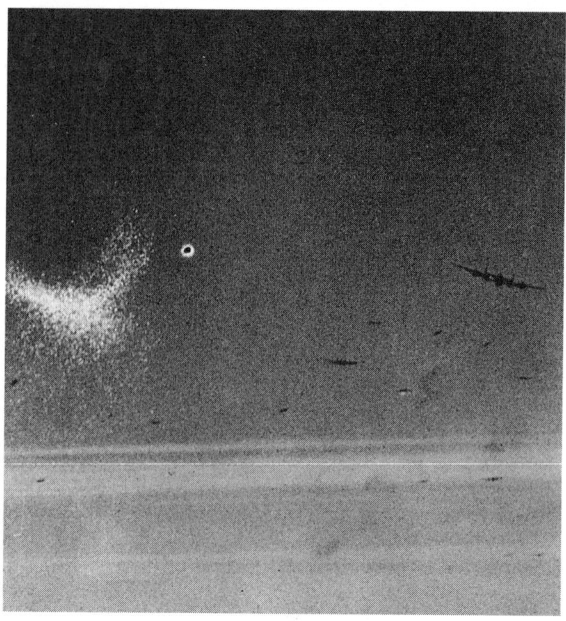

Electronic warfare was employed by both sides to deceive the radar defences of their opponents. Here, WINDOW (seen on the left of the photograph) is being dropped by Lancaster bombers during a raid on Essen, 11 March 1945.

To reduce the vulnerability of Würzburg to 'Chaff' and electronic noise jamming, the Germans launched a crash programme to modify the radar. One anti-Chaff modification (NUREMBERG) provided an audio output so that the operator could hear the propeller modulation of the returning echo pulses and so track the target aircraft through 'Chaff'. Another system (WÜRZLAUS), was a crude form of moving target indicator. To avoid the jamming from CARPET the band of frequencies used by WÜRZBURG was progressively widened, until by the end of the war it ran from 475 to 585 MHz. CARPET was modified to meet each change, as soon as it was discovered. It has been estimated that 'Chaff' and noise jamming used together reduced the effectiveness of 'WÜRZBURG-controlled *Flak by about two-thirds.

During the winter of 1943–4 the German night air defences were reorganized and new and modified equipment was introduced. For a time it was possible to overcome the most serious effects of the jamming and regain the initiative. A new radar for night fighters was introduced, the SN-2 (90 MHz), which because of its lower frequency was unaffected by the type of WINDOW released by British bombers. With an effective airborne radar again, the German night fighter force achieved a dramatic run of successes culminating on the night of 30 March 1944, when 94 bombers were shot down out of a force of 795 attacking *Nuremberg. But three months later the RAF captured a Junkers 88 night fighter complete with SN-2 radar. Flight tests of the captured fighter revealed that SN-2 was vulnerable to 'Rope' (long lengths of foil, which unreeled or unfolded during its fall) and, from the summer of 1944, it suffered the same fate as its predecessor.

The Normandy landings in June 1944 (see OVERLORD) represented the greatest seaborne invasion in history. For this giant set-piece battle the stakes were high, and a massive counter-measures operation was set in motion to neutralize the dense chain of radar stations built into the German *Atlantic Wall. First, ground direction-finding stations in southern England pinpointed the positions of the radar stations. Then fighter-bombers flew some 2,000 sorties against these targets. Finally, on the night of the invasion, an enormously powerful barrage of ship-borne and airborne jamming was turned on the surviving radars. Two squadrons of modified bombers flew up and down the line of the River Somme jamming on the German fighter control frequencies; their aim was to prevent German night fighters west of the line receiving instructions from their control stations to the east of it.

While the invading fleets headed for the landing areas on the coast of Normandy, two 'ghost' fleets headed towards Le Havre and Boulogne (Operations TAXABLE and GLIMMER, respectively). In fact these 'fleets' contained no full-sized ships; the illusion was created by aircraft flying carefully-planned orbits and releasing large quantities of WINDOW. Each 'ghost' fleet involved eight aircraft divided into two waves, with 3 km. (1.8 mi.) between individual aircraft and 13 km. (8 mi.) between each wave of four. The two waves of aircraft flew a series of oblong patterns measuring 13 km. long and 3 km. wide, maintaining their formation. During the long legs of the orbits, when the planes were flying towards or away from the coast, they released one bundle of WINDOW every five seconds; that is to say, one bundle per 400 m. (438 yd.) flown. In this way the planes laid out a vast field of WINDOW measuring 25 km. by 22 km. (16 mi. by 14 mi.), with no gaps larger than the discrimination limits of the German Seetakt coast-watching radar. Each orbit took seven minutes and at the end of each the formation moved forward 1.6 km. (1 mi.). The whole vast field of WINDOW thus appeared to move towards the coast of France at 15 km/h (8.5 knots)—realistically like an actual invasion fleet. To add realism to the operation, other aircraft flew near the WINDOW droppers radiating noise jamming. But the positions of these aircraft had been carefully chosen so that German radars watching the area would just see the 'ghost' fleet through chinks in the jamming.

German records revealed that the defenders were forced to tie down large numbers of troops during the crucial initial hours of the invasion, and send reconnaissance aircraft and patrol boats to scour the coast to the east of the Somme, before the 'ghosts' were exorcized. The level of confusion on the night of the invasion was so great that the only German radar to pass plots on the real invading ships went unheeded. The first positive indication of them, which the Germans did believe, came not from radar but from observers on the eastern side of the Cherbourg peninsula who heard the rumble of ships' engines. No conceivable counter-measures effort could possibly have achieved more.

During 1944 the RAF formed a new unit, 100 Group, to support night bombing operations. The group operated five squadrons of specialized jamming aircraft: B17 Fortresses, B24 Liberators, Halifaxes, and Stirlings. It also operated six squadrons of Mosquito night fighters, which were to serve as escorts for the bombers, and eventually built up its strength to about 250 aircraft. Special equipment was necessary to enable the Mosquito crews to find German aircraft in the darkness, in a sky full of friendly ones. One such device (SERRATE) homed on emissions from the German fighters' radars. Another device (PERFECTOS) fitted to the Mosquitos transmitted interrogating pulses on the German *IFF (Identification Friend or Foe) frequencies. When German aircraft replied, the signals appeared on a screen showing its range and bearing. Several German aircraft were shot down following PERFECTOS contacts.

In the *Pacific war, as in Europe, the use of electronic counter-measures had become firmly established by 1945. Despite early research into the *cavity magnetron, at that stage of the war Japanese radar technology was at roughly the same position as that of the Germans had been in 1941; airborne radar for night fighters was still at the trials stage and the early warning and fire control radars were relatively crude. Nevertheless, so long as the radars remained unjammed, Japanese anti-aircraft guns could have caused serious losses to B29 units attacking the Japanese homeland. To counter them, the US bomber force hurled a massive jamming capability built to 1945 standards of technology.

During daylight attacks the B29s flew in tight formations with each aircraft radiating jamming and dropping 'Rope' to counter the Japanese fire control radars; in this way there was a high degree of mutual screening between the aircraft in each group. During the night attacks the bombers radiated jamming and dropped 'Rope' in the same way but, because the aircraft were more scattered, there was far less mutual screening between bombers. To overcome this problem a few B29s were fitted out as specialized jamming aircraft, to cover the night raiders. These aircraft, nicknamed 'Porcupines', had their bomb racks removed and in their place each carried up to eighteen separate jamming transmitters and almost a ton of 'Rope'. During attacks, the 'Porcupines' orbited the target area and jammed the defensive radars.

In the face of such a concentrated barrage of counter-measures, the ill-equipped Japanese radar system collapsed. During operations against Japan the B29s' average loss rate from the enemy defences was 0.8%, a remarkably low figure and the more remarkable considering that, in terms of anti-aircraft guns, the Japanese cities were by no means weakly protected. The great conurbation of Tokyo, Yokohama, and Kawasaki, for example, was defended by more than 500 anti-aircraft guns. The defenders' problem was not lack of fire-power, but lack of effective fire control due to the jamming.

What was the effect of the various electronic counter-measures on the course of the Second World War? The neutralization of the German radio beam systems, in 1940 and 1941, undoubtedly played an important part in enabling the UK to survive the heavy night attacks of the Luftwaffe. And without the successful anti-radar attacks and the jamming effort, the fight to secure the beachhead in Normandy in June 1944 would certainly have been far bloodier.

The value of the jamming support given to the RAF and the US strategic bombing forces cannot be assessed accurately, because it is impossible to calculate how many more bombers would have been shot down had there been no protection from jamming. Probably the jamming cover for the night attacks saved the RAF something of the order of 1,000 bombers and crews during the course of the war. The USAAF bombers made most of their attacks by day, when the enemy fighters and A-A gunners could usually engage visually and jamming was less effective; nevertheless, there are grounds for believing that the use of electronic counter-measures saved about 400 US heavy bombers and their crews over Europe, plus a further 200 of those attacking targets in Japan.

Only twice during the Second World War did the use of electronic counter-measures bring about the complete collapse of an air defence system. The first was when WINDOW was introduced with such effect during the attack on Hamburg in July 1943, though within a few months the Germans had recovered from its worst effects. The second was during the spring and summer of 1945, when American bombers effectively countered the primitive Japanese radars by the use of 'Rope' and noise jamming. For the rest of the war the effect of the counter-measures was a continual, if less spectacular, reduction in losses by something in the order of one-sixth. See also STRATEGIC AIR OFFENSIVES and TINSEL.

ALFRED PRICE

Price, A., *Blitz on Britain* (London, 1977).
—— *Instruments of Darkness* (London, 1967).

element C were steel gate-like structures erected by the Germans on likely invasion beaches in north-west France to prevent *landing craft from running ashore. They were 2.75 m. (9 ft.) wide and nearly the same high, and weighed 1.5 tons.

El Salvador declared war on the Axis powers in December 1941 and was an original signatory of the *United Nations Declaration. The country spent most of the war in domestic upheaval. See also LATIN AMERICA.

engineers use their skills to help their own army live, move, and fight, and to impede the efforts of the opposing side's engineers. Before 1939 they worked largely with pick and shovel, artisan tools, *explosives, locally found materials, and conscripted labour. In the Second World War, however, their capacity to affect the course of operations was increased dramatically by the introduction of mobile earth-moving machinery—bulldozers, scrapers, graders, and excavators; by the development of rapid bridging equipment such as the Bailey bridge; by the mass-production of anti-tank and anti-personnel mines; and by the manufacture of pre-fabricated surfacing materials for the rapid construction of all-weather airfields.

The needs of armies for engineer help increased equally dramatically: the weight and numbers of military vehicles far exceeded the pre-war design capacity of most roads and bridges, even in Europe; *logistics became increasingly complicated as the tonnage of supplies to be carried multiplied; the scale of theatres of operations and of battlefields expanded inexorably in step with the return of mobility to the land battle and the addition of the air dimension; and the ever increasing needs of air forces for airfields and fuel supplies, threw a new load on engineer resources. The scale on which engineers worked can be illustrated by the fact that during the *Burma campaign alone the Allies built 407 airstrips, 1,300 bridges, and thousands of kilometres of roads which included the *Ledo Road, the Tamu Road from Imphal to Kalewa, via Palel and Tamu, and the Tiddim road from Imphal to Kalewa, via Tiddim and Kalemyo.

Engineer units constituted an average of about 12% of most field armies in the Second World War. They were divided broadly into two components: about one-third were field or combat engineers, organic to divisions and corps, who worked in the combat zone, each division having the equivalent of an engineer regiment (800–1,200 men); and the balance were lines of communication engineers, trained and equipped for major engineering tasks throughout the theatre of war. (Electrical and mechanical engineers, employed on repair and recovery of vehicles and equipment, formed part of the logistic organization of armies and were not classed as military engineers.) In addition, there were specialized engineering organizations at national level, set up to undertake strategic tasks: the *Todt Organization, which constructed major German fortifications and U-boat bases, using *forced labour; the American *Seabees, employed to construct forward operating base facilities in support of *amphibious warfare operations in the *Pacific war; and the equivalent Japanese organizations, which used *prisoners-of-war as labour on major engineering projects such as the infamous *Burma–Thailand railway. The USAAF, unlike other air forces, did not leave the construction of airfields to army engineers. Instead, it formed its own self-contained engineer aviation battalions (27 officers, 761 men to each battalion) which eventually totalled nearly 118,000 engineers.

Lightly equipped parachute engineer battalions were also formed to build emergency airstrips after an amphibious landing.

1. Field engineers

Field engineers had four principal tasks:

In defence they helped protect their formations by constructing field fortifications; digging in major weapon systems; strengthening natural barriers like river lines; and creating artificial obstacles such as minefields and anti-tank ditches.
In withdrawal they delayed the advance of the opposing side by demolishing roads, railways, and airfields; by scorched earth operations; and by random mine-laying and booby-trapping.
In attack they helped the assault forward by breaching natural and artificial obstacles; by destroying fortifications impervious to artillery fire and air attack; and by clearing routes forward through the battle zone.
In advance they opened up routes forward by bridging water obstacles and dozing through dry ones; by mine and booby-trap lifting; and by clearing roads through the rubble of bombed towns and villages, or making diversions around them.

In addition they had the logistic tasks of supplying water to forward troops, and of constructing or renovating living accommodation for them when this was needed, particularly during winter.

The Second World War saw the rapid development of techniques by field engineers in the combat zone.

(a) Fortifications

When the war started in 1939 both sides in Europe were placing great faith in the steel and concrete fortifications and obstacles of the *Maginot and *Siegfried Lines on the Franco-German frontier, already built by civilian contractors under the supervision of military engineers and almost regardless of cost. Neither was ever fully tested in battle because the Maginot was outflanked by the German *blitzkrieg through the Low Countries in June 1940 (see FALL GELB); and the Siegfried could not be manned properly by the weakened Wehrmacht when the Allies crossed the German frontier in the autumn of 1944.

In the Far East, the Americans placed similar faith in the efficiency of steel and concrete in the defence of *Corregidor in the Philippines, and the British did so to a lesser extent in *Singapore. Both fell relatively easily to the Japanese.

Although fixed fortifications can deter assault, they have one exploitable weakness: their immobility. An attacker can examine them in detail, devise special equipment and methods for breaching them, and do so by concentration of effort at the weakest point. For instance, the key to Belgium's defences, Fort *Eben Emael, was captured by the Germans in May 1940 by the novel use of gliderborne assault engineer troops, landing inside the fortress and using hollow charges (see DEMOLITION, below) to neutralize the defences.

On the Eastern Front Soviet engineers had few equals when it came to turning whole towns and villages into fortresses and they showed great ingenuity during the *German–Soviet war. Houses were converted into blockhouses, cellars became strong-points and bunkers, and sewers were used for communications and for infiltrating behind German lines. So strongly and skilfully were the defences constructed that only street-fighting, which included 'mouse-holing'—moving from house to house by blowing holes in the party walls—and the use of *flame-throwers, overcame them. As a consequence it was common for Soviet and German engineers to be in close combat against one another.

The most successful defensive lines in the Second World War were those constructed by field engineers during operations in positions where the front had already begun to congeal. The best examples were the Soviet defences in front of *Moscow and *Leningrad in 1941, and the German *Gustav Line in Italy, based upon *Monte Cassino, in 1943–4. Winter weather contributed to the successful consolidation of these lines.

Nevertheless, pre-planned strategic defence lines still had value in forcing attackers to manoeuvre and concentrate. Lines constructed after the outbreak of war comprised a mix of reinforced concrete bunkers, gun emplacements, and anti-tank obstacles, usually built by civilian contractors under military supervision, and field works—trenches, anti-tank ditches, barbed wire, and minefields—constructed and laid by field engineer units. Examples of these were the anti-invasion beach defences of southern England in 1940–1; Hitler's much vaunted *Atlantic Wall in 1943–4; the German *Hitler and *Gothic Lines built during the *Italian campaign in 1944; and the Japanese defences of their fortified islands in the Pacific in 1943–5.

The stalemate of trench warfare, which engulfed all fronts in the *First World War, was hardly known. The lethal combination of machine guns and barbed wire had been neutralized by the advent of the tank, and in their place came the lavish use of anti-tank and anti-personnel minefields, but these could only hinder and not stop a determined attacker as was shown at the second battle of *El Alamein in October 1942 and during the Normandy landings in June 1944 (see OVERLORD).

(b) Demolition

In the face of the German blitzkrieg, the Allies' standard demolition equipments and techniques, inherited from the First World War, were soon shown to be too slow and inefficient during their enforced withdrawals in the *Norwegian campaign and in the fighting which preceded the fall of *France in June 1940; in the *Balkan campaign in 1941; and in the Burma campaign in 1942. In consequence, Rapid Demolition Devices (RDD) were developed by the British, in which speed rather than economy of explosives was the primary consideration. The principle of

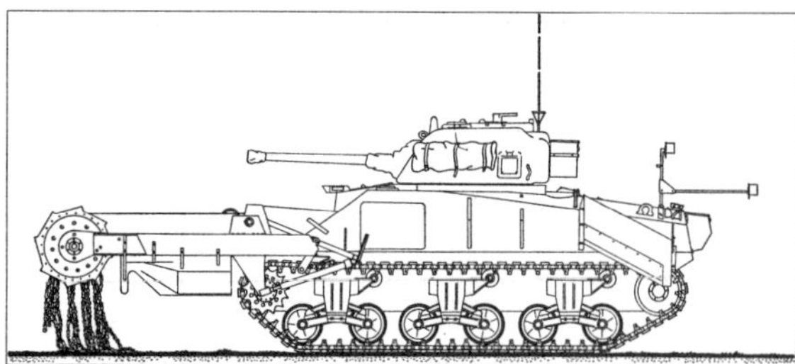

Engineers, Figure 1: Sherman Crab Mark I flail tank. In some operational theatres these tanks were called Scorpions not Crabs.

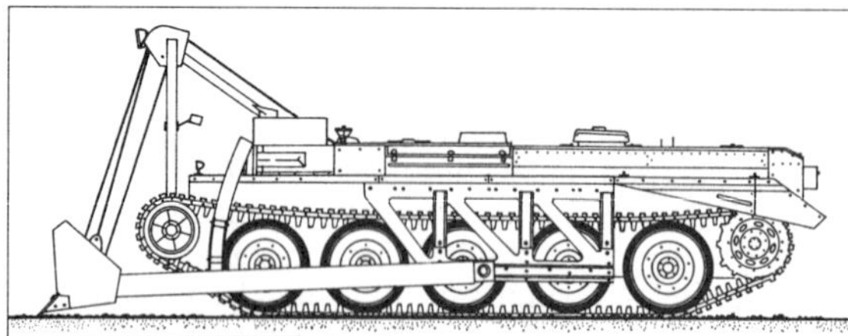

Engineers, Figure 2: Centaur tank-dozer.

the hollow charge was used in the 'Beehive' device (see EXPLOSIVES), which punched a deep hole into masonry, thus eliminating the tedious process of pneumatic drilling when placing borehole charges. The same principle was used for linear-shaped charges, called 'Hayricks', for cutting the steelwork of bridges or reinforcing bars in concrete structures. And crates of bulk explosive, which could be slid rapidly off the backs of vehicles, were designed to sever bridges. Plastic explosive, which could be quickly and easily moulded to fit tightly round targets of any shape, was also introduced. RDD were not available before the Allies went over to the offensive at the end of 1942, but they were further developed for combat engineers to attack the concrete defences in Hitler's Atlantic Wall and the fortified Channel ports.

The German withdrawal operations after the tide turned against them in 1943 were on a far larger scale than the earlier Allied retreats and lasted far longer. Their engineers had ample opportunity to refine their demolition and *scorched earth techniques. Their long withdrawal in Italy, which started from *Salerno in the autumn of 1943 and ended in the Po valley in the spring of 1945 (see ARGENTA GAP), was a classic demonstration of the use of explosives, booby-traps, and mines to delay a more powerful opponent. Almost every bridge and culvert on Italy's north/south roads, and on all the many river lines, were not only blown, mined, and trapped, but were usually covered by the tanks or self-propelled guns of their rear guards to impose increased delay.

(c) Mines

For the types of mine used on land, and the techniques developed for laying and clearing them, see MINE WARFARE, 1. Mine warfare was fought by opposing field engineers in all theatres of war, but most intensively in the deserts of North Africa and on the Russian Front where natural obstacles were scarce.

As in naval mine warfare (see MINE WARFARE, 2), there was a constant battle between the engineers on both sides as new types of mines, fuzes, and laying techniques were devised by the defenders to defeat the advances in detection and clearance methods of the attackers.

(d) Assault Engineering

Engineer troops, using explosives and obstacle crossing devices, have always played a major role in attacking fixed defences, but in the Second World War this role was carried a step further by the British development of armoured assault engineer units. They were equipped with five main types of modified tanks:

(i) Flail tanks were developed first. They were designed to clear lanes through minefields, using a rotating drum, fitted to the front of the tanks, which flailed the ground with weighted chains to explode any mines in their path. They were first used with success at El Alamein (Figure 1).
(ii) Tank-dozers tanks fitted with bulldozer blades for filling in ditches and road craters, and clearing away other obstacles under fire (Figure 2).
(iii) Arks: turretless tanks, decked over and fitted with movable ramps, front and rear, which could drive into an obstacle and lower their ramps, thus providing bridges for tanks and other vehicles to cross over their backs (Figure 3).
(iv) Bridge-laying tanks these carried scissors-type bridges nested on their backs, which could be opened up to their full length and lowered hydraulically over gaps without the crews leaving their armoured protection.
(v) AVREs (Armoured Vehicles Royal Engineers): tanks fitted with demolition guns, firing 18 kg. (40 lb.) projectiles, carrying 12 kg. (26 lb.) explosive charges and nicknamed 'flying dustbins'; and equipped with special fittings to allow them to carry a variety of engineer devices such as fascines for ditch crossing, frames holding made-up demolition charges for breaching concrete obstacles, and dozer blades for rubble clearance. They were also fitted with side doors so that crews could get out to place demolition charges by hand if need be (Figure 4).

For the Normandy landings the armoured engineer units were grouped in the specialized 79th Armoured Division under Maj-General 'Hobo' *Hobart, who was charged by Churchill with developing ways of overcoming the Atlantic Wall defences. Armoured engineers were also employed in Italy in the autumn of 1944, breaching the Gothic Line and crossing the successive river lines in the Romagna during the Allied advance towards the Po valley.

US and Soviet engineers used several very similar equipments, but the Germans and Japanese did not: they were on the defensive by the time the requirement was recognized.

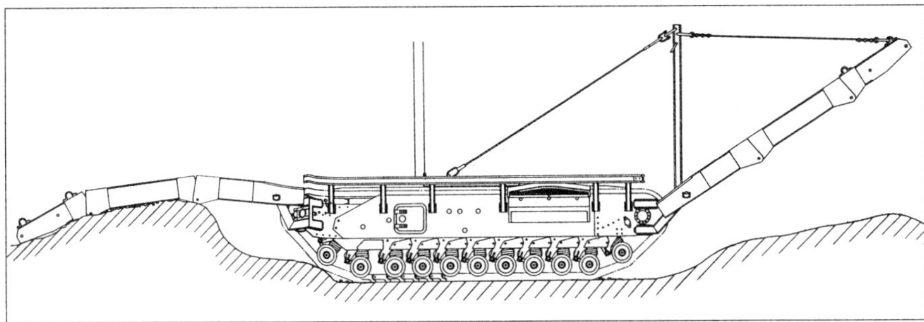

Engineers, Figure 3: Churchill ARK Mark II tank.

(e) Bridging

Significant strides were made during the war in speeding up military bridging. The greatest success came with the invention of the British Bailey bridge by Sir Donald Bailey of the Military Engineering Experimental Establishment at Christchurch, Dorset (Figure 5).

The Bailey bridge girders were constructed from a series of identical steel lattice panels held together by high-tensile pins at their four corners. Each girder could be doubled or tripled for extra length and strength, and could be given up to two extra storeys for very large spans. The roadway was supported on lateral transoms, carried on the lower chords of the panels, and the whole structure was launched on rollers, using a counter-weight, over the gap to be spanned. It was first deployed operationally during the *North African campaign in Tunisia towards the end of 1942, and became the main dry bridging equipment of the Allied armies.

For bridging rivers, two distinct families of floating bridges were developed. The British and the Soviets retained the traditional wooden pontoons to support their bridges, while the Germans, Americans, and Japanese favoured more vulnerable, but easily transported, inflatable rubber floats. The British used their Folding Boat Equipment (collapsible wood and canvas boats, carrying an easily constructed roadway) for vehicles up to 9 tons, and Floating Bailey (Bailey bridging carried on pontoons) for loads up to 70 tons. The Americans used Treadway bridges, which consisted of linked wheel tracks carried on various sizes of pneumatic pontoon, depending on the load to be carried. Sections of most floating-bridge equipments could be modified for use as rafts.

The British lagged in one aspect of river-crossing equipment. They relied on flimsy canvas folding boats, paddled by hand, to carry assaulting infantry across rivers to establish bridgeheads, whereas other armies used powered light alloy or pneumatic storm boats.

River-crossing techniques of the Western Allies during the Second World War were brought to their apogee during their successful *Rhine crossings in March 1945, by which time the speed and efficiency of Soviet engineers in developing bridgeheads across their rivers had also been proven as a German Army Group South report of September 1943 illustrates: 'During the retreat across the *Dnieper on either side of Kiev, German engineers and bridging formations built seven bridges in a sector 650 km. (400 mi.) long over which the German troops were to withdraw. The Soviets, on the other hand, constructed in short time 52 bridges and foot-bridges across 400 km. (250 mi.) of the river.'

(f) Route Clearance

In the First World War, the countryside beyond the pulverized area of the front line was almost untouched by war and presented few problems to advancing troops once they had broken through. This was far from so in the Second World War. Routes forward were not only

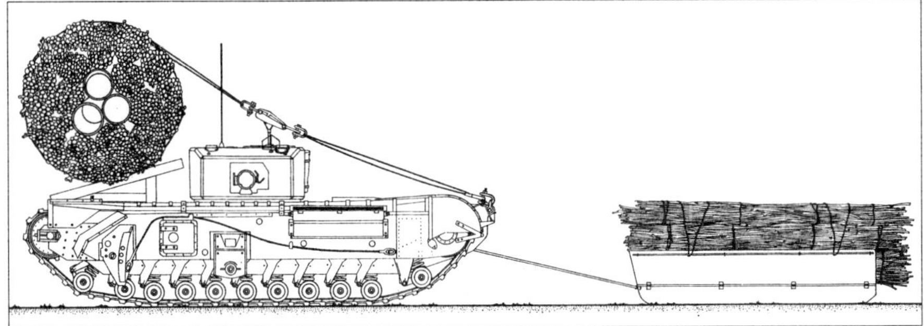

Engineers, Figure 4: Churchill AVRE Mark II tank carrying a fascine and towing another on an AVRE sledge.

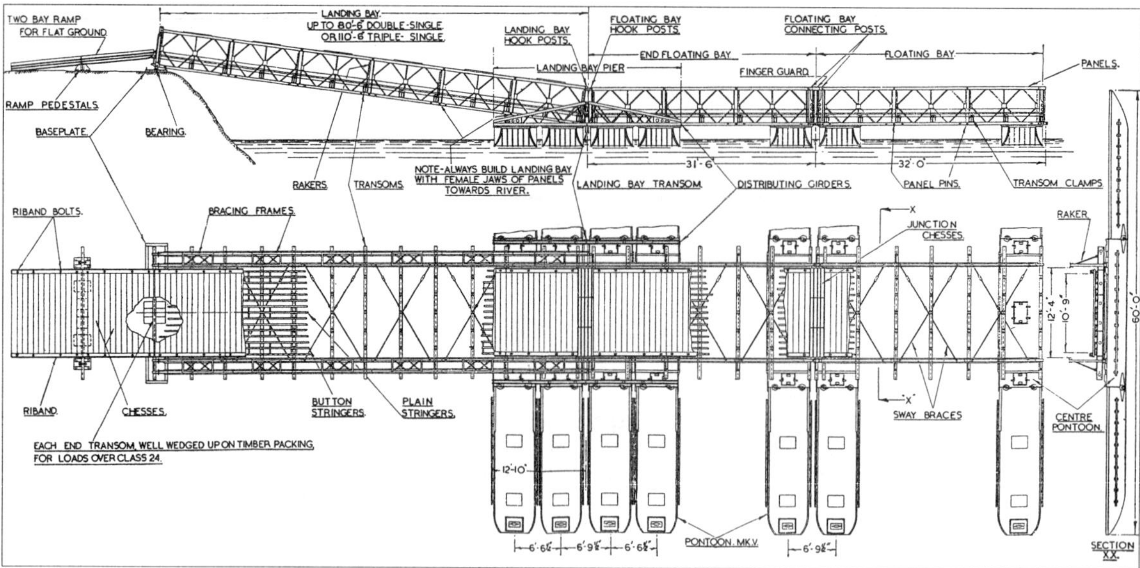

Engineers, Figure 5: Bailey floating bridge.

obstructed by the other side's demolition and mine-laying operations, but also by the destruction of towns and villages by the air forces. Such was the damage done that all field engineer resources often had to be concentrated upon opening up just one route forward per division. Once winter weather set in and mechanized armies became roadbound, the ability of their engineers to keep routes open became a limiting factor in operations.

2. Lines of communication engineers

Lines of communication engineer units were largely recruited from civilian firms with specialist engineering skills. They fell into four broad categories:

Construction units for construction and maintenance of roads and bridges; of airfields; of fuel and water pipe lines; and of accommodation for personnel and logistic installations such as hospitals, store depots, and workshops.

Electrical and mechanical units for the reconstruction of damaged electric power installations and water supply systems, and provision of power and water in base areas.

Railway units for the repair and operation of essential railway systems.

Port operating and construction units for the development of base ports after naval clearance of sea mines and sunken ships in their approaches.

Most engineer work on the lines of communication required large labour forces. The western Allies depended upon recruiting local civilian labour and raising military pioneer units, but the Axis powers and the Soviets used conscripted labour and *prisoners-of-war for labour-intensive engineer work like road and airfield construction.

In the initial phases of the Second World War only the Germans and Japanese were confronted with lines of communication problems, because the Allies were in retreat. Nevertheless, Axis logistic difficulties were never limiting: the speed and success of their operations were such that the infrastructure of the countries overrun was left unscathed and could be used as the basis for expansion to meet increased military requirements.

In the USSR, however, the Germans were faced with the complex railway operating problem of changing from standard to broad gauge at the frontier. They also had to deal with the paucity and poor quality of the Soviet road network. Even the few good roads did not have strong enough foundations to withstand the pounding of German military traffic in the wet weather of autumn before the freeze, and in the thaw conditions of the spring. The Japanese, although needing less logistic support, found monsoon conditions in Burma equally restricting.

When the western Allies turned to the offensive in the autumn of 1942, it was a very different story. Amphibious warfare operations in both the *Mediterranean and Pacific theatres of war needed the establishment of bases and airfields on a vast scale, involving a massive effort by their communications engineers; and, as they advanced through North Africa, Sicily, and Italy, and from island to island in the Pacific, they had to overcome the devastation caused by the slow and deliberate Axis withdrawals, while at the same time building up whatever civilian logistic infrastructure remained to meet their military requirements.

The greatest Allied engineer effort of all came with the invasion of Normandy in June 1944. It was the equivalent of moving a city the size of Chicago, USA, or Birmingham,

England, across the storm-swept English Channel to a green-field site in France under battle conditions, and supplying it with all the resources needed to fight at high rates of operational intensity. Four engineering feats stand out:

(*i*) The design, construction, placing, and operation of the artificial harbours (see MULBERRIES) on the Normandy coast through which the two Anglo-American Army Groups were supplied with 40% of their requirements until the severely damaged port of Cherbourg was captured and reopened (60% was landed over the beaches).
(*ii*) The rapid construction of airfields in the beachhead from which air cover and offensive tactical air support was provided (23 were built in the British sector alone).
(*iii*) The laying of the *PLUTO pipelines across the Channel, which supplied the Allied air forces and armies with fuel.
(*iv*) The subsequent support of the Allied advance across France and into Germany, despite the damage done to communications by the interdiction operations of the Allied air forces and the demolitions carried out by the retreating German Army.

In the same time frame, German engineers were achieving extraordinary feats of ingenuity and improvisation in maintaining the flow of essential requirements to the Eastern, Mediterranean, and Western fronts in the face of devastating Allied air attacks on their transportation system, which were only second in priority to oil targets in the Allied *strategic air offensives. No vital rail links were ever severed for very long, including the highly vulnerable Brenner Pass line into Italy. WILLIAM JACKSON

Englandspiel (*Spiel*, game), codename for German Sicherheitsdienst (see RSHA) counter-intelligence operation, called NORDPOL (North Pole) by the *Abwehr, which, between March 1942 and November 1943, deluded *SOE into believing their network of agents in the Netherlands had not been penetrated. It was probably the best-known *Funkspiel* (radio game) the Germans played, but far from being the only one.

By March 1942 six SOE and eight *MI6 agents had been landed in the Netherlands; five of them had been captured, two from SOE and three from MI6. One of these, an SOE radio operator named Hubert Lauwers, was used by Lt-Colonel Hermann Giskes, the head of the *Abwehr in the Netherlands, and by Major Josef Schreieder of the RSHA's Sicherheitsdienst to transmit messages to London.

This was an eventuality both SOE and MI6 had allowed for by issuing each agent with a security check, usually a deliberate spelling mistake. When Giskes had, earlier in the month, tried to start a *Spiel* using one of the captured MI6 operators he had failed to get any response from London because the operator, Willem van der Reyden, had not revealed his security check.

But when Lauwers' message arrived without his security check in place the head of SOE's Dutch section, Major Charles Blizard, accepted it as authentic, and began passing messages to Lauwers which, of course, fell into German hands. This resulted in all but two of the remaining agents being arrested. One of them, a radio operator called Hendrik Jordaan, denied having a security check and refused to send any messages. So when a German operator transmitted a message in his name it, too, failed to contain the correct security check. But again Blizard ignored the warning and compounded his error by signalling Jordaan to instruct his new operator in the use of his security check, which only resulted in Jordaan being forced to reveal it.

Giskes and Schreieder were now able to pick up every agent whose arrival was announced to Lauwers and Jordaan and this gave them another three radio links. It also resulted in the capture, on 27 June 1942, of George Jambroes and his radio operator, who were involved in 'Plan for Holland', the blueprint for a 1,000-strong Dutch resistance network. This had been drawn up by SOE in collaboration with Colonel M. R. de Bruyne, head of special operations for the Dutch *government-in-exile, and it was later expanded by de Bruyne's 'Plan B' which envisaged a 10,000-strong resistance network.

To help implement these plans a further 27 agents were dropped by SOE between September 1942 and May 1943, as were nine others on different missions. All were captured, enabling Giskes and Schreieder to increase their contact with London to seventeen different links. At least four of the messages transmitted to London by these links excluded the security checks of their operators, and Lauwers also tried to reveal his predicament by twice using the word 'caught' as the jumble of letters that, as a security measure, preceded and ended all messages. But despite these attempts to warn London, Blizard, and his successor from February 1943, Major Seymour Bingham, continued to transmit messages to the captured agents.

Early in 1943 Bingham, and then de Bruyne, did begin to have doubts about the Dutch network but neither acted when in June a message—admittedly rather garbled—was received from a Dutch resistance leader that eight agents had been 'arrested weeks ago'. And when, during the summer, Giskes and Schreieder faked a series of sabotage attacks in the Netherlands it apparently assured Bingham that his agents were still free and working successfully.

In November 1943, the same month as the RAF demanded an investigation into the loss of so many aircraft during Dutch clandestine missions, the Dutch legation in Berne reported that two of the captured agents had escaped to Switzerland. Though they revealed the existence of the *Funkspiel*, Bingham remained unconvinced anything was amiss, especially when the Germans radioed London that the two agents had not really escaped at all but had been returned to the fold as *double agents. When the two escapers eventually arrived in the UK in February 1944 the authorities, erring on the side of caution, imprisoned them. By then, however, the Joint

Intelligence Committee (see UK, 8) had concluded that penetration of the Dutch network had probably occurred and further communications with it were forbidden. On 1 April 1944 Giskes and Schreieder themselves broke off communication with a final mocking message. Although *Englandspiel* had been a great tactical success for them it had not produced the great strategic secret they had been seeking: the date and place of the Allied invasion of France (see OVERLORD).

Englandspiel not only cost the lives of 54 agents—most of whom suffered terrible deaths in *concentration camps—but those of a number of other Dutch civilians and about 50 RAF personnel. It also caused havoc in two French resistance networks when, through information received by the *Funkspiel*, Giskes was able to penetrate their organizations. As a result at least 132 people lost their lives and many others were arrested.

After the war there was a Dutch parliamentary commission of investigation, but it discovered neither treachery nor duplicity.

ENIGMA, codename for the cipher machine, developed from a design patented by a Dutchman, H. A. Koch, in 1919 from which *ULTRA intelligence was derived. Dr Arthur Scherbius, a Berlin engineer, marketed it in 1923; by 1929 he had been bought out by the German Army and Navy, which used different versions of it. So, in turn, did the Luftwaffe, the *SS, the *Abwehr, and the Reichsbahn (German state railways). The machine seemed to the Germans wholly unbreakable: even in its simplest form, for every letter it sent there were hundreds of millions of possible solutions. They forgot how few letters there are in the alphabet; they forgot that no letter could stand for itself; and they forgot that the machine had no number-keys, so that figures had to be spelled out. These gave their potential opponents toe-holds enough. The Poles were reading some ENIGMA traffic as early as 1932, the French in 1938, the British in 1940; with startling results.

M. R. D. Foot

Bloch, G., *Enigma avant Ultra* (Paris, 1988).
Kozaczuk, W., *Enigma* (tr. C. Kasparek, London, 1984).

An early three-rotor **ENIGMA** cipher machine belonging to the Imperial War Museum, London.

Eniwetok Atoll. Five US Army and Marine battalions landed on this Pacific atoll, part of the *Marshall Islands, on 17 February 1944 after the main US objectives in the Marshalls had been seized. The three main islands, Engebi, Parry, and Eniwetok, were defended by about 3,500 Japanese. They were attacked in quick succession, while aircraft of *Spruance's US Fifth Fleet raided *Truk to prevent any Japanese retaliation from the air. All resistance ceased six days later.

The capture of Eniwetok ended any hope Japan had of reinforcing *Wake Island or the bypassed atolls in the Marshalls. It also brought US aircraft within range of the Caroline Islands, and gave the US Navy a vast anchorage and an ideal staging base for further *amphibious operations in the *Pacific war.

ENSA (Entertainments National Service Association), the British organization for entertaining members of the armed forces wherever they happened to be. Its American equivalent was the United Services Organization.

Eremenko, General Andrey (1892–1970), Red Army officer who was part of the top Soviet command echelon when the Germans invaded the USSR in June 1941 (see BARBAROSSA) and remained there to the finish. Stalin never deemed him worthy of a marshal's star, and he did not receive one until 1955, two years after Stalin died. Nevertheless, his career during the *German–Soviet war was more representative of Soviet command performance than *Zhukov's, for instance.

He lost the greater part of his first *front* (army group), Briansk *front*, in October 1941 (see BRIANSK–VYAZMA). After recovering from wounds he took over the Fourth Shock Army in early 1942, made a deep thrust behind German Army Group Centre, but did not reach his objective, the main German supply line. Recovered again from wounds, he distinguished himself commanding Stalingrad *front*, which defended *Stalingrad from August to November 1942, but Stalin did not esteem defensive successes. His mission in the counter-offensive was to regroup his armies and seize Rostov-on-Don. A German counter-attack threw him off stride, and the quarry escaped him.

Throughout 1943, apparently doing penance, he commanded Kalinin (later First Baltic) *front* in a secondary sector. After briefly commanding an army in the Crimea in early 1944, he went to Second Baltic *front*, where he participated for a year in the slow-moving contest for the Baltic States (see COURLAND). In February 1944, Stalin transferred him to Fourth Ukrainian *front*, thereby giving him a chance of becoming a marshal if he could make himself the liberator of Czechoslovakia; but his route, through the Carpathians, and the season prevented that. EARL ZIEMKE

Eritrea was an Italian East African colony from which Italian forces invaded Abyssinia in October 1935, after which it became part of Italian East Africa. During the *East African campaign British and Commonwealth troops overran it and the British remained there until 1952 when it was handed over to Abyssinia (Ethiopia).

escape and evasion, see BRITISH ARMY AID GROUP, MI9, and MIS-X.

escort carriers, see CARRIERS.

espionage, see SPIES.

Estéva, Admiral Jean-Pierre (1880–1951), *Vichy French Resident-General of Tunisia. He made no attempt to resist the German occupation of the French colony in November 1942 at the start of the *North African campaign and was subsequently tried for failing to do so and condemned to life imprisonment. He was released in 1950.

Estonia, the smallest and most northerly of the three Baltic States, started the Second World War as an independent republic and ended it as an involuntary component of the USSR.

In 1939, Estonia (capital Tallinn) was ruled by the nationalist dictatorship of the Peasant Party of K. Päts. As in Latvia, the regime was motivated by fears of Soviet agitation and of the influence of dispossessed German landowners. Estonia was a member of the *League of Nations. Its independence had been established by a treaty signed with the USSR in January 1920, and was guaranteed by the Soviet–Estonian Non-Aggression Pact of 4 May 1932.

However, the *Nazi–Soviet Pact of August 1939 secretly assigned Estonia to the Soviet sphere of influence. As a result, Moscow demanded the conclusion of a Treaty of Friendship and Co-operation, which permitted the stationing of Soviet troops on Estonian territory. This treaty, signed on 28 September 1939, was activated in June 1940. The entry of the Red Army was soon followed by subversive agitation against the Estonian government; by widespread killings and arrests; by fraudulent elections conducted by Soviet security organs; and by the declaration of an Estonian Soviet Socialist Republic that was formally admitted to the Soviet Union on 6 August 1940.

The first Soviet occupation (June 1940–July 1941) was a time of mass terror, when all Estonia's native institutions were destroyed. The German population was deported to Germany.

The German occupation (July 1941–1944) saw Estonia incorporated into the Reich Commissariat *Ostland. Estonian police and military units were formed under German command, and served in the front line round *Leningrad. An Estonian Waffen-*SS Division was recruited. The small Jewish community was deported and killed (see FINAL SOLUTION).

The second Soviet occupation, which began in January 1944, was accompanied by a renewed wave of terror, and by forced collectivization of the peasantry.

Estonia's population was much diminished by *deportations and repressions and by the loss of the German and Jewish elements. It was replenished by a post-war influx of Russians. NORMAN DAVIES

Ethiopia, see ABYSSINIA.

ETOUSA (European Theatre of Operations, United States Army) was the administrative HQ for the build-up of US troops in the UK (BOLERO). Initially commanded by Maj-General *Eisenhower, it was later commanded by Lt-General Frank Andrews and, after he had been killed in an air crash, by Lt-General *Devers. In January 1944 ETOUSA and the HQ of the US Services of Supply were amalgamated under the latter's commanding general, Lt-General John Lee, who also became deputy theatre commander for supply and administration.

EUREKA (1), codename for the Allied Teheran conference held from 28 November to 1 December 1943 to co-ordinate future strategy between the western Allies and the USSR (see GRAND ALLIANCE). Present were Churchill, Roosevelt, Stalin, and their diplomatic and military advisers. It was the first time the three leaders had met together. Stalin confirmed that the USSR would join in the war against Japan once Germany had been defeated. He stressed the importance of mounting an invasion of France to relieve pressure on Soviet forces fighting in the *German–Soviet war, and added that the *French Riviera landings would be an essential adjunct to it. Roosevelt and Churchill then announced their decision that the Normandy landings would be launched in May 1944 (they were later delayed until June: see OVERLORD), and a delighted Stalin agreed to mount a full-scale offensive to coincide with them. It was also agreed to co-operate in devising joint deception schemes (see BODYGUARD).

After the main decision, the timing of OVERLORD, had been taken, subsequent discussions centred on bringing Turkey into the war, the future of Poland and Finland, the post-war division of Germany, and support for *Tito and the partisans in Yugoslavia.

Eureka (2), a navigation beacon, used by the RAF, *SOE, and Anglo-American airborne forces. An aircraft or small boat equipped with Eureka's answering device, called Rebecca, could find it precisely (see Figure).

Eureka (3), a *Higgins boat.

Europe, Declaration on Liberated, see DECLARATION ON LIBERATED EUROPE.

European Advisory Commission, established by the UK, USA, and USSR in London in late 1943 after an agreement to form it had been reached at the *Moscow conference that October. Its terms were to formulate surrender terms for Germany and its Axis satellites, and it drew up the arrangements for the post-war occupation and control of Austria and Germany (see ALLIED CONTROL COMMISSIONS which were discussed at the Yalta conference (see ARGONAUT) in February 1945 and at the Potsdam conference (see TERMINAL) that July. It also considered any questions on the liberation of Allied countries which were submitted by any of the governments of the three participating powers.

European Theatre of Operations, see ETOUSA.

euthanasia programme, Nazi organization for the systematic killing of mentally and physically handicapped children and adults which was officially launched in 1939.

Like many phenomena of the Third Reich, the roots of the so-called 'euthanasia' programme lay in the radical and ruthless way in which German society was developing even before Hitler came to power in 1933. Among the many German victims of the Allied food blockade during the *First World War were numerous inmates of mental homes who were neglected by the authorities and their families, and during these years about 100,000 mentally ill people died of diseases caused by hunger and lack of hygiene. This massive number of deaths, while creating problems for those who had to cope with them, did free hospital and nursing resources to help the army medical service cope with 60,000 military neurological cases created by the fighting. But the horrors of trench warfare also resulted in so many out-patients needing psychiatric and psychological care that the army's medical organization was overwhelmed. When the war was lost, hundreds of thousands of forlorn and desperate men were left to roam the streets. These men were accused by right-wing Germans of being responsible for Germany's collapse, and it was alleged that many of the more unstable radical agitators were drawn from among them.

This traumatic experience of mental illness by a nation already under stress had a profound influence on *Nazi ideology. Applying anthropological, political, and military criteria, the Nazis—and their conservative allies—classified the population into 'superior' and 'inferior' human beings. In their eyes the 'inferior' group profited by war. They argued that while the élite were being lost on the battlefields, those who had psychological defects survived in disproportionate numbers because they were not front-line soldiers. The so-called destruction of army, state, and society by the psychologically sick in 1918, and the rapid post-war increase of inmates in mental hospitals, were considered sufficient evidence that modern warfare created a situation where the least able, not the fittest, survived. In 1929 Hitler publicly stated that in his opinion the best way of improving the German race, and creating a generation which would win the next war, was to eradicate 700,000 'inferior' *children; and, to restore the quality and toughness of the German race, his first legislative act on coming to power in January 1933 was to order the sterilization of the carriers of hereditary mental diseases. In the following years the criteria for this treatment were gradually extended to all those categorized as 'inferior' human beings and, ultimately, between 300,000 and 400,000 Germans were sterilized.

However, during the first six years of the Nazi regime there were those who were so morally opposed to its ideology that they prevented Hitler taking any further steps towards murder. They succeeded in doing this by enforcing an interpretation of the criminal law which led to an explicit ban on the killing of mentally handicapped members of the national community (the *Volksgemeinschaft*). Nevertheless, in 1935, Hitler reached an agreement with the Nazi Doctors' Command (the Reichsarzteführung) for the 'worthless' to be murdered once war had created the opportunity to carry out this programme. With this agreed, propaganda about the advantages of 'mercy killing' was started—which eventually culminated in the famous film *Ich klage an!* ('I accuse')—and early in 1938 the 'workshy' and 'anti-social' elements of the population began to be rounded up and put in *concentration camps.

In the summer of 1939 Hitler assigned his assistant Philipp Bouhler to the 'mercy killing' operation, a task which broke all the laws and regulations of the Third Reich and which was detested by the majority of Germans in both peace and war. Knowing how it was regarded by the public, Bouhler formed a secret organization with headquarters at 4 Tiergartenstrasse in Berlin. Its codename, T.4, originated from this address, and those who manned its departments called the work which they carried out 'the action'. By arguing that early psychiatric casualties of the coming war would need adequate treatment (something the Army demanded, anyway, after its experiences in 1918), and that those civilian

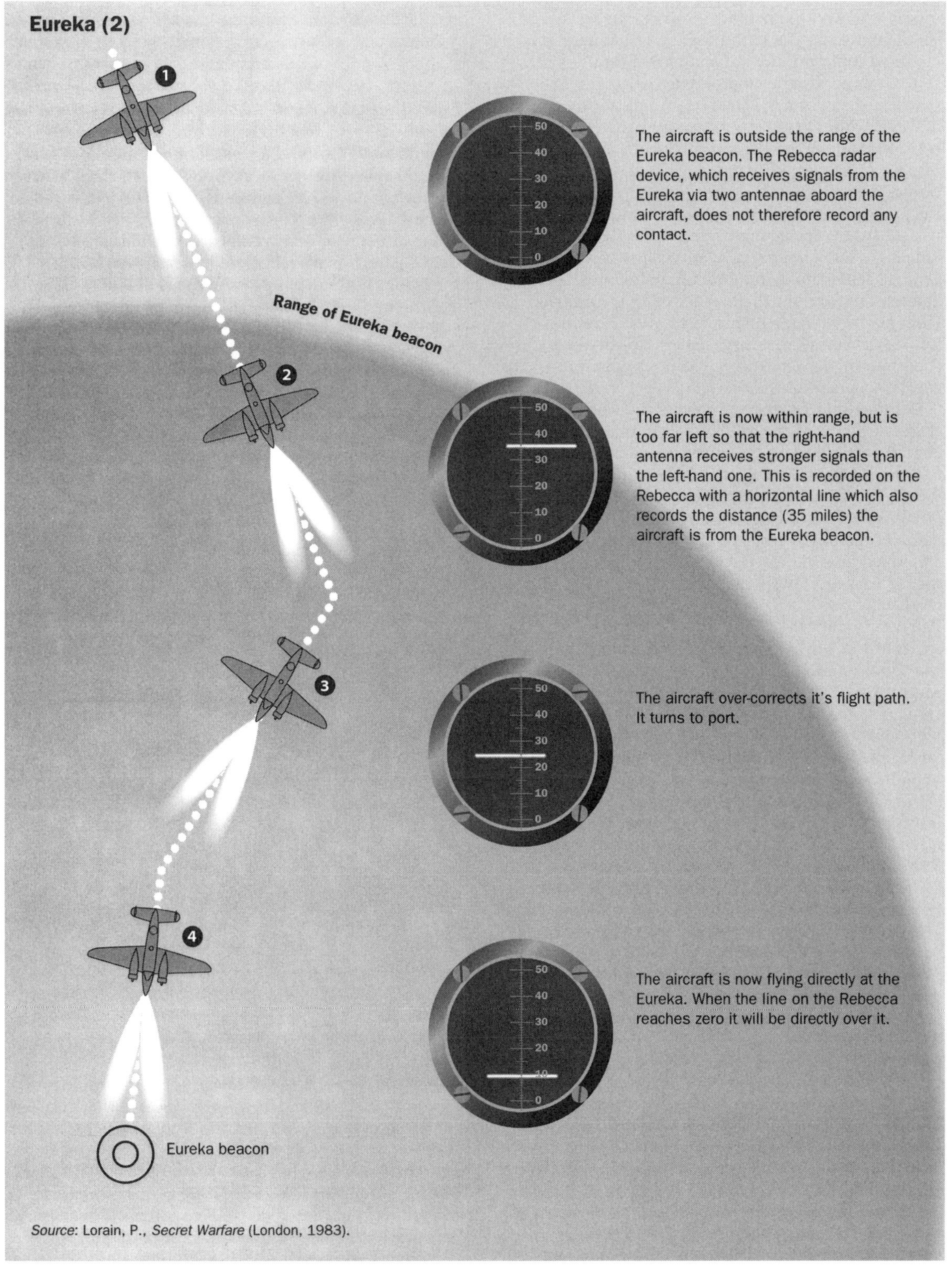

Source: Lorain, P., *Secret Warfare* (London, 1983).

insane who were too poor to afford private treatment should not suffer the same cruelties as before, T.4 obtained sufficient medical and nursing staff to kill 70,000 insane patients. It proceeded to organize the search, registration, concentration, and transportation of them, while at the same time deceiving concerned relatives, and the companies with whom the victims were insured, as to their ultimate fate. Those selected were transferred to hospitals run by doctors sympathetic to the aims of T.4, and consultants in them decided which patients were capable of working and which should be killed. The latter were sent to special institutions at Grafeneck, Hadamar, Bernburg, Brandenburg, Sonnenstein, and Hartheim where they were gassed. From January 1940 to August 1941, 70,237 insane or senile Germans were 'disinfected' in this manner and thousands more were shot by *SS units who wanted their accommodation for themselves.

Despite the strict secrecy in which T.4 worked, and the threats which met any enquiries from the public, the church authorities, or the courts, this mass murder came to light in August 1941. By that time T.4 had accomplished its objectives. When a courageous sermon by the bishop of Münster enraged the public against the killings, Hitler casually agreed that they should cease; but this did not stop the killing of 'inferior' Germans. In general the food rations in mental hospitals were reduced to the 1914–18 level which produced a level of suffering similar to what had occurred during the First World War. Though many specialists in gassing were transferred to implementing the *Final Solution there were still enough to kill, in what was called Aktion 14 f 13, some 20,000 concentration camp inmates who were diagnosed by T.4 doctors to be mentally deficient. Also, about 20,000 misshapen and 'mongoloid' babies, and infants suffering from certain hereditary defects, were transferred to special hospitals (*Kinderfachabteilung*) where they were secretly killed by injections or overdoses of drugs. In other hospitals affiliated to T.4, doctors and nursing staff sympathetic to its aims killed another 20,000 patients in an operation codenamed Aktion Brandt. Occasionally, severely wounded soldiers were also 'redeemed' by Aktion Brandt, and the army, eager to prevent a recurrence of the unstable conditions in 1918, was a silent accomplice in Aktion 14 f 13 as it conveniently annihilated the so-called 'left-wing neurotics' who had been sent to concentration camps after army punishment battalions had failed to discipline them.

When, in 1941–2, German morale began to decline, those who committed even the smallest offences were judged by both the civilian and the military courts as 'inferior', and therefore of jeopardizing the war effort (*Wehrkraftzersetzung*), and innumerable Germans accused of this offence paid for it with their lives (see also GERMANY, 3). In fact, during the war years beliefs based on the 'mercy killing' programme became all-pervading. In 1943, for example, Admiral *Dönitz, when he refused to revoke the death sentence on a condemned soldier, stated that the man's asthma was far from being a reason for clemency because it endangered the *Volksgemeinschaft*.

WOLFGANG PETTER

Evatt, Herbert V. (1894–1965), Australian lawyer and influential Labour politician who became Attorney General and minister of external affairs in John *Curtin's Labour cabinet formed in October 1941. Of an independent turn of mind and 'a granite personality', he retained his post throughout the war and represented his country in the British war cabinet, in early negotiations with the US government—where he 'upset the American assumption that Australians were a sort of Englishman' (K. Tennant, *Evatt: Politics and Justice*, Sydney, 1970, p. 142) —and, to great effect, at the *San Francisco conference in April 1945 where the United Nations was officially founded. He helped write the UN charter, led Australia's delegation at the UN (1946–8), and was UN president in 1948–9. See also AUSTRALIA, 3.

Crockett, P., *Evatt: A Life* (Melbourne, 1993).

explosive motor boats (EMBs) were operated by the Germans, Italians, and Japanese, all with heavy losses. The one-man crew of the 5 m. (17 ft.), 51 km/h (32 mph) Italian MTM (Motoscafi da Turismo Modificati, or modified touring motorboats) and the German 5.75 m (19 ft.) *Linse* (lentil) bailed out before the impact of the boat hitting its target triggered a fuze which detonated the *explosives. The MTM's rudder was locked before it was abandoned, but the *Linse* was guided by radio on to its target by a control boat (see also GUIDED WEAPONS). MTMs sank the British cruiser *York* in Suda Bay, *Crete, in March 1941 and they were also used to attack Valletta harbour during the siege of *Malta, and the *Anzio landings. *Linsen* were claimed to have sunk twelve ships off the Normandy beachhead (see OVERLORD), but elsewhere EMBs rarely sank anything.

The Japanese Navy's *Shinyo* (sea-quake), with different marks varying between 5.1 m. (16.7 ft.) and 6.5 m. (21.3 ft.) in length, and the Japanese Army's 5.6 m. (18.4 ft.) *Maru-ni* (capacious boat) which employed depth charges (see ANTI-SUBMARINE WEAPONS), were both suicide craft. They had limited success when US forces invaded the Philippines (see PHILIPPINES CAMPAIGNS), and when they were employed at *Okinawa, and elsewhere. See also TENTH LIGHT FLOTILLA and GERMANY, 6(e).

O'Neill, R., *Suicide Squads* (London, 1981).

explosives were mostly based on TNT (trinitrotoluene) because it melts before it explodes and can therefore be poured into *bombs and shells. It is relatively insensitive to shock, a vital factor when firing shells, and cannot be exploded without a detonator. It was used by both sides. When eight parts of TNT were mixed with two parts of ammonium nitrate, which the Axis often did to conserve their stocks of TNT, the result was called amatol.

The synthetic pentaerythritol tetranite, or PETN, was

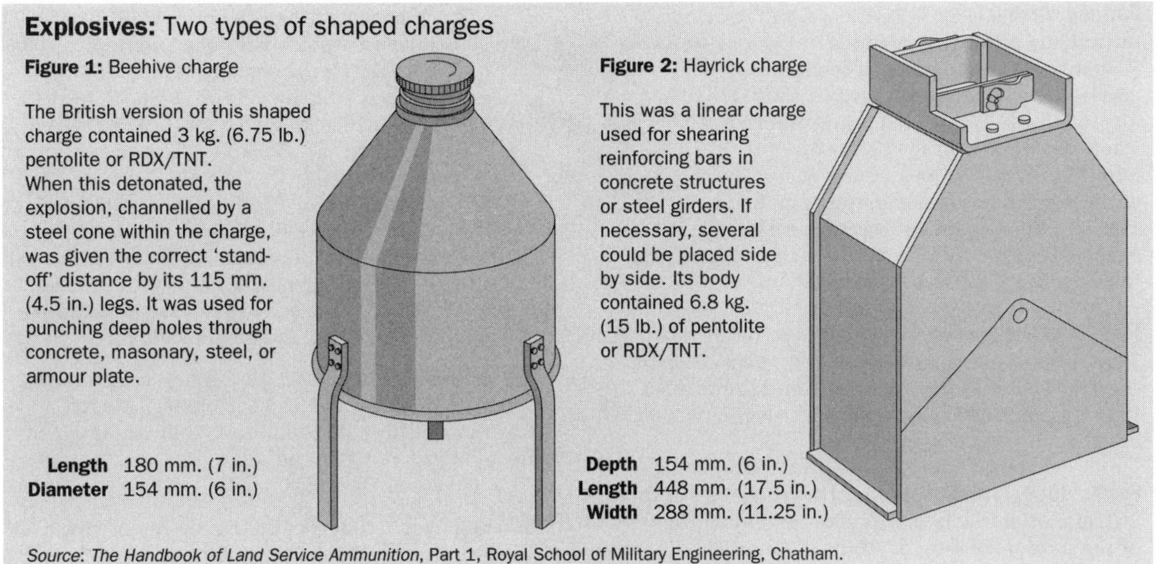

Source: *The Handbook of Land Service Ammunition*, Part 1, Royal School of Military Engineering, Chatham.

also employed by both sides. Too sensitive to use alone, when mixed 50/50 with TNT it made pentolite which was used extensively in detonators, and hand grenades. Picric acid or lyddite (trinitrophenol), used in the Japanese explosive *shimose*, and tetryl (trinitrophenylmethylnitramine) were also highly sensitive, the latter having a higher shattering effect (brisance) than TNT. When mixed 70/30 with TNT, tetryl became tetrytol, used by the Allies for demolition and in mines.

Cyclotrimethylene-trinitramine, called cyclonite by the Americans, RDX (Research Department Explosive) by the British, T4 by the Italians, and hexogen by the Germans, was very powerful but was also too sensitive to use alone. The British desensitized it by mixing it with beeswax for shells (Composition A); with TNT and beeswax for bombs (Composition B); and with plasticizing oil for demolition work (Composition C), this last commonly becoming known as plastic explosive, a British invention. The *Tizard mission took these formulae to the USA in 1940 where they were subsequently produced in large quantities. However, US ordnance officers were wary of the sensitivity of Composition B, which made it unsuitable for *skip bombing.

When, in October 1943, Lord Cherwell (see LINDEMANN) alerted Churchill to the fact that German *bombs were more effective than their Allied counterparts because of the aluminium they contained, Composition B was replaced by titronal, a mixture of TNT and aluminium powder which increased a bomb's power by 50% or more. This realization also led to the production of minol, a mixture of aluminium and amatol, that could devastate an area 80% larger than TNT alone. Minol was also used in depth charges (see ANTI-SUBMARINE WEAPONS) as was torpex, a mixture which contained 40% RDX, 37% TNT, and 18% powdered aluminium which was 50% more powerful than TNT alone.

The power of some explosives was further increased by the shaped, or hollow, charge (see Figures 1 and 2). Although the principle had been known since 1900, it was not until the Second World War that both Germany and the UK developed it simultaneously. Moulding an explosive around a cone concentrated its shock waves and increased its power by up to fifteen times. This also made effective such *rocket weapons as the bazooka and panzerfaust but it was also used to increase the potency of plastic explosives, and even semi-armour-piercing bombs. German engineers used hollow charges very effectively when storming the *Eben Emael fortress in May 1940. See also ENGINEERS, 1(b).

extermination camps, see OPERATION REINHARD; see also CONCENTRATION CAMPS.

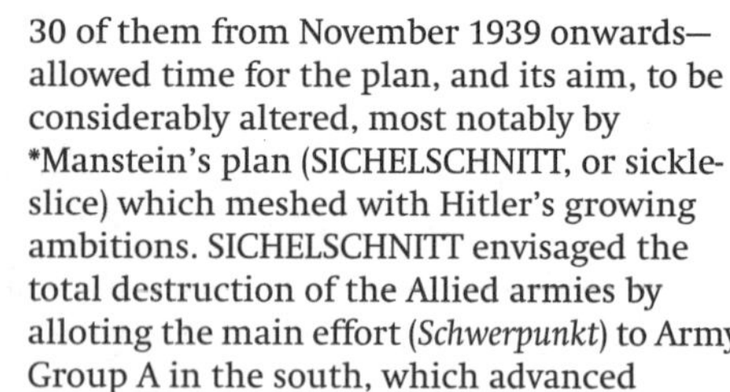

Fadden, Arthur (1895–1973), leader of the Australian Country Party, which in September 1939 was part of a coalition government with Robert *Menzies' United Australia Party. He acted as prime minister when Menzies was in the UK for three months during 1941 and succeeded him when Menzies was forced to resign in August 1941. But his government was soon defeated and was replaced by John *Curtin's Labour government that October. See also AUSTRALIA, 3.

Faeroe Islands, a Danish colony since 1380 consisting of 22 Atlantic islands situated halfway between Iceland and the UK. The British occupied them on 12 April 1940 following the German occupation of Denmark. They became self-governing in 1948.

Faith, Hope, and Charity were the nicknames of three British Gloster Gladiators, obsolescent biplane fighters. At the start of the siege of *Malta in June 1940 they were the only air cover the island had. Originally there were four, found in crates aboard the carrier *Glorious*, but one was destroyed almost immediately. They became the symbol of Malta's—and the UK's—determination to survive, and to win the battle for the *Mediterranean, but only Faith did so.

Falaise pocket, see NORMANDY CAMPAIGN.

Falkenhausen, General Alexander von (1878–1966), German Army officer who was *Chiang Kai-shek's military adviser during the 1930s. After Belgium and France were occupied in 1940, he became the German military governor of occupied Belgium and northern France, a post he held until June 1944. His regime, compared to others in occupied countries, was a lenient one and he was eventually recalled because of the lack of reprisals against the Belgian *resistance. He was also peripherally implicated in the July 1944 plot to kill Hitler (see SCHWARZE KAPELLE) and he was arrested and sent to *Dachau. In 1951 he was sentenced to twelve years' hard labour by a Belgian court for executing hostages and for sending Belgian Jews to *Auschwitz, but was released shortly after because it was recognized that he had also shielded many Belgians from the *SS.

FALL GELB (Operation Yellow), codename for the German offensive in the west which started on 10 May 1940 and culminated in the fall of *France the following month. Hitler initially employed just under 119 divisions for it and had committed a further 23 by the end of the campaign (see Table).

In its original form FALL GELB had the limited aim of destroying a large proportion of the forces which would oppose the German offensive and of gaining access to parts of the Belgian and French coastline to speed the defeat of the UK. Postponements of the offensive—nearly 30 of them from November 1939 onwards—allowed time for the plan, and its aim, to be considerably altered, most notably by *Manstein's plan (SICHELSCHNITT, or sickle-slice) which meshed with Hitler's growing ambitions. SICHELSCHNITT envisaged the total destruction of the Allied armies by alloting the main effort (*Schwerpunkt*) to Army Group A in the south, which advanced through the supposedly impenetrable Ardennes, instead of to Army Group B in the north. As a result, the Allied advance to the *Dyle Line ended in a hasty withdrawal, the *Dunkirk evacuation, and the fall of France.

FALL WEISS (Operation White), German codename for Hitler's attack on Poland on 1 September 1939 (see POLISH CAMPAIGN). He committed 54 divisions which were launched partly on the bogus pretext that Polish troops had attacked *Gleiwitz radio station.

FANY, acronym of the First Aid Nursing Yeomanry, a British women's ambulance unit formed in 1907. It was later renamed the Women's Transport Service but its volunteer members remained known as FANYs. During the war they served as drivers and welfare workers; many worked for *SOE, notably as wireless operators and cipher clerks, and 73 were trained as agents. Of these, 22 were sent into France, and 7, including Violette *Szabo, were caught and did not survive. See also WOMEN AT WAR.

Popham, H., *FANY* (London, 1984).

Far East Combined Bureau (FECB), a British inter-service intelligence organization formed in Hong Kong in 1935. Its radio intelligence facilities included *radio finger printing, several *(huff-duff) stations, a *Y service station, and a naval and military cryptanalysis section. In August 1939 it moved to Singapore, but once Japan entered the war in December 1941 its army and RAF sections returned to their respective services, and it virtually ceased to exist. However, the name continued to be used for the organization's largest section, the naval one, which was moved to Colombo, Ceylon. In March 1942, this station intercepted and partially deciphered a signal which indicated the Japanese Navy intended raiding Ceylon (see INDIAN OCEAN). The section then went with *Somerville's Eastern Fleet to Mombasa (Kilindini) in Kenya but returned to Colombo in 1943.

The FECB's records were probably destroyed and opinions vary as to how much the Bureau contributed to breaking the Japanese Navy's JN-25 cipher (see ULTRA, 2). According to one authority (D. Horner, *High Command: Australia and Allied Strategy, 1939–1945*, Sydney, 1982, p. 225) the British supplied the cipher's key to the US Navy in 1940, and the official historian of British intelligence confirms that sufficient progress had been made in breaking the cipher to enable the British to monitor the Japanese fleet's main movements (see F. Hinsley *et al.*, *British Intelligence in the Second World War*, Vol. 1, London, 1979, p. 53 n). However, this ability was lost when the

FALL GELB: German divisions on the Western Front on 10 May 1940

Grouping	*No.*
Army Gp. B (Bock)	
Eighteenth Army (Küchler)	10 1/3 (1 armd. div.)
Sixth Army (Reichenau)	19 (2 armd. div.)
TOTAL	29 1/3
Army Gp. A (Rundstedt)	
Fourth Army (Kluge)	13 (2 armd. div.)
Twelfth Army (List)	10
Armoured Group Kleist	8 1/3 (5 armd. div.)
Sixteenth Army (Busch)	13
TOTAL	44 1/3
Army Gp. C (Leeb)	
First Army (Witzleben)	13
Seventh Army (Dollmann)	4
TOTAL	17
Available to Army High Command (incl. 7th Air Div.)	28 (3 brigades)
GRAND TOTAL	118 2/3 (3 brigades)
Reserves employed by the end of June	23
TOTAL NUMBER OF DIVISIONS PARTICIPATING IN THE CAMPAIGN IN THE WEST	141 2/3 (3 brigades)

Source: Deist *et al.*, *Germany and the Second World War*, Vol. 2 (Oxford, 1990).

Japanese altered the key prior to their raid on *Pearl Harbor.

Far East war crimes trials, were conducted by the Allies in the Far East following the defeat of Imperial Japan. They had been foreshadowed in the Potsdam Proclamation of 26 July 1945 (see TERMINAL) which declared, 'stern justice shall be meted out to all war criminals, including those who have visited cruelties upon our prisoners'. However, the scope of the trials was broadened when, on 19 January 1946, General *MacArthur, the supreme commander for the Allied Powers, announced the formation of the International Military Tribunal for the Far East (the IMTFE, in Tokyo), to try Japanese charged 'with offenses which include crimes against peace'. The IMTFE's writ reflected the Allied decision, reached at the London conference that previous summer, that the post-war trials in Europe and the Far East would involve not only conventional *war crimes, including in particular brutal atrocities against Allied *prisoners-of-war, but also the more fundamental crime of waging aggressive war itself.

Thus, there were two kinds of war crimes trials in the Far East: the Tokyo trial, the Pacific counterpart to the *Nuremberg trials, and a great many regional hearings that were mainly concerned with conventional war crimes.

1. The Tokyo war crimes trial

The proceedings of the IMTFE, which lasted from 3 May 1946 to 4 November 1948, were held in the former Japanese Army Ministry building in Tokyo. The court consisted of eleven justices. Two of them, Radhabinod Pal of India and Delfin Jaranilla of the Philippines, were from countries which achieved independence after the war. The president of the court, appointed by MacArthur, was Sir William Webb of Australia. The chief prosecutor was Joseph B. Keenan of the USA, who was appointed by President *Truman.

Teams of Japanese and American attorneys defended the 28 Japanese military and civilian leaders, categorized as class A war criminals, who were on trial (see Table). The best-known defendant was General *Tōjō. The rest included thirteen generals, a colonel, three admirals, five career diplomats, three bureaucrats, one politician, and an ultranationalist (Ōkawa Shumei) who was soon declared unfit to stand trial for reasons of insanity. During the trial, two of the defendants, Admiral Nagano Osami and *Matsuoka Yōsuke, a former foreign minister, died.

While one objective of the Tokyo trial was to punish Japanese élites convicted of war crimes and thereby demonstrate to the Japanese people the authority of the occupation and the justice of the Allied wartime cause, a greater historic purpose was to put an end to war for all time by rendering sacrosanct the principle that waging aggressive war was a crime in international law. In this latter respect the charter governing the Tokyo trial, published on 26 April 1946, was deliberately based on the Nuremberg Charter.

In brief, the Tokyo Charter defined 'crimes against peace' to encompass conspiracy to wage, and the waging of, aggressive war, whether or not war had been declared, 'in violation of international law, treaties, agreements

Far East war crimes trials: Verdicts and sentences

Count	*1*	*27*	*29*	*31*	*32*	*33*	*35*	*36*	*54*	*55*	*Sentence*
Araki Sadao	G	G	A	A	A	A	A	A	A	A	Life imprisonment
Doihara Kenji	G	G	G	G	G	A	G	G	G	O	Hanging
Hashimoto Kingorō	G	G	A	A	A				A	A	Life imprisonment
Hata Shunroku	G	G	G	G	G		A	A	A	G	Life imprisonment
Hiranuma Kiichirō	G	G	G	G	G	A	A	G	A	A	Life imprisonment
Hirota Kōki	G	G	A	A	A	A	A		A	G	Hanging
Hoshino Naoki	G	G	G	G	G	A	A		A	A	Life imprisonment
*Itagaki Seishirō	G	G	G	G	G	A	G	G	G	O	Hanging
Kaya Okinori	G	G	G	G	G				A	A	Life imprisonment
Kido Koichi	G	G	G	G	G	A	A	A	A	A	Life imprisonment
Kimura Heitarō	G	G	G	G	G				G	G	Hanging
*Koiso Kuniaki	G	G	G	G	G			A	A	G	Life imprisonment
Matsui Iwane	A	A	A	A	A		A	A	A	G	Hanging
Minami Jirō	G	G	A	A	A				A	A	Life imprisonment
Mutō Akira	G	G	G	G	G	A		A	G	G	Hanging
Oka Takasumi	G	G	G	G	G				A	A	Life imprisonment
*Oshima Hiroshi	G	A	A	A	A				A	A	Life imprisonment
Satō Kenryō	G	G	G	G	G				A	A	Life imprisonment
Shigemitsu Mamoru	A	G	G	G	G	G	A		A	G	7 years imprisonment
Shimada Shigetarō	G	G	G	G	G				A	A	Life imprisonment
Shiratori Toshio	G	A	A	A	A						Life imprisonment
Suzuki Teiichi	G	G	G	G	G		A	A	A	A	Life imprisonment
*Tōgō Shigenori	G	G	G	G	G			A	A	A	20 years imprisonment
*Tōjō Hideki	G	G	G	G	G	G		A	G	O	Hanging
Umezu Yoshijirō	G	G	G	G	G			A	A	A	Life imprisonment

Key:
Blank –Not indicted on the count.
G –Guilty.
A –Acquitted.
O –Charged but no finding made by the Tribunal.
* –separate text entry.
Count 1 –The over-all Conspiracy.
Count 27–Waging war against China.
Count 29–Waging war against the United States.
Count 31–Waging war against the British Commonwealth.
Count 32–Waging war against the Netherlands.
Count 33–Waging war against France.
Count 35–Waging war against USSR at Lake Khassan.
Count 36–Waging war against USSR at Nomonhan.
Count 54–Ordering, authorizing, or permitting atrocities.
Count 55–Disregard of duty to secure observance of and prevent breaches of Laws of War.

Sources: Chart taken from Horwitz, 'Tokyo Trial', Appendix C, *International Conciliation*, No. 465 (November 1950), p. 584. Minear, R. H., *Victor's Justice: The Tokyo War Crimes Trial* (Princeton, 1971) who took it from above source.

or assurances . . .' The charter also covered conventional war crimes and 'crimes against humanity', including 'murder, extermination, enslavement, deportation, and other inhumane acts . . . or persecutions on political or racial grounds in execution of or in connection with any crime within the jurisdiction of the Tribunal . . .'. In contrast to the regional trials of class B and C war criminals (see below), at Tokyo all the defendants were indicted for having committed 'crimes against peace', in addition to the other charges which applied variously in individual cases. Indeed, 36 of the 55 counts comprising the Tokyo indictment pertained to 'crimes against peace'.

The defence challenged the indictment, arguing that 'crimes against peace' and more specifically, the undefined concepts of 'conspiracy' and 'aggressive war', had yet to be established as crimes in international law; in effect, the IMTFE was contradicting accepted legal procedure by trying the defendants retroactively for violating laws which had not existed when these alleged crimes had been committed. Moreover, the defence insisted that there was no basis in international law for holding individuals responsible for acts of state, as the Tokyo trial proposed to do. Finally, the defence attacked the notion of 'negative criminality', by which the defendants were to be tried for failing to prevent breaches of law and war crimes by others, as likewise having no basis in international law.

These challenges exposed the highly controversial

nature of the Tokyo trial. However, despite their validity and after much legal argument, they were all rejected by the court which upheld the indictment as it stood, on the debatable grounds that various legal precedents existed for 'aggressive war', 'conspiracy', and the responsibility of individuals for acts of state and negative criminality. This ruling echoed the Allied consensus at the London conference, especially concerning the issue of 'aggressive war'. Here, the Allies distinguished aggressive war from war waged for self-defence which had been recognized by the 1928 Pact of Paris (see KELLOGG–BRIAND PACT) as the right of every sovereign nation. Yet this consensus itself was rather new. As recently as 1944, it may be noted, the USA, UK, and the Netherlands had judged that it was not a war crime for individuals to participate in the planning and waging of aggressive war.

The Tokyo trial was very controversial for other reasons, too. First, the selection of defendants was somewhat arbitary in that before the trial 250 Japanese officials had been arraigned on suspicion of war crimes, of whom 28 were indicted as a representative sample of the country's pre-war and wartime leadership. The main criterion used in selecting them was the belief, expressed by one of the prosecution lawyers, that 'No person was to be included as a defendant unless the evidence used against him was so strong as to render negligible the chances of acquittal.'

Quite apart from the manifest expediency of this criterion, it was arguably inapplicable to certain defendants, such as the former foreign minister *Tōgō Shigenori, who was known to have worked assiduously for peace both in 1941 and again in 1945. What is more, certain individuals who might have been expected to stand trial in Tokyo were exempted. The most famous was Emperor *Hirohito, in whose name Japan had gone to war. MacArthur exempted him lest his trial provoke widespread Japanese resistance to the occupation. General Abe Nobuyuki and Admiral Yonai Mitsumasa, both former prime ministers, and a number of other key government leaders, were also conspicuously absent.

A second source of controversy concerns the justices. The competency of at least two of them was in doubt, for one was not a judge in his own country (China) and the other, from the USSR, understood neither English nor Japanese, the official languages of the court. As for the principle of judicial impartiality, since the justices all came from countries that had suffered at the hands of the Japanese, they could not have been expected to be unbiased. Two justices were especially open to doubts on this point by virtue of their own experience: Jaranilla had survived the *Bataan death march and imprisonment by the Japanese, and Webb had been prominently involved in investigating conventional Japanese war crimes in the New Guinea campaign. At the end of the trial, Jaranilla would stand out among the justices for arguing that the final sentences were too lenient in several instances.

Third, numerous legal procedures used at the Tokyo trial were plainly suspect. To illustrate, the rules of evidence were relaxed to include such indirect prosecution evidence as hearsay, diaries, unsworn statements, affidavits that could not be verified unless witnesses took the stand, and so forth. Then, too, the rules of evidence were applied inconsistently by the court and more often to the advantage of the prosecution than the defence. Another questionable procedure was the practice whereby a simple majority vote of the court would decide the fate of the accused when the final judgement was rendered.

Fourth, the prosecution's endeavour to prove that from the late 1920s onwards the defendants had participated in a grand conspiracy for aggressive war in seeking to dominate the Asian-Pacific region imposed a grossly simplistic interpretation upon the complex history of the pre-war period with which few historians would agree. Besides the fact that it never defined 'conspiracy', this interpretation virtually ignored both the many clashes over foreign policy questions which had marked the acute struggle for power within Japan and the essentially *ad hoc* nature of Japanese expansionism. Moreover, the conspiracy interpretation rigidly negated the distinct possibility that, as Tōjō and other defendants claimed, Japan's decision in 1941 had been to wage defensive war in reaction to American economic sanctions. Instead, the majority of the court all too easily assumed that the right of self-defence could not explain Japanese motives in 1941 or at any other time in the history of the alleged Japanese 'conspiracy'.

Accordingly, the final judgement found all but two of the defendants 'guilty of conspiracy to wage aggressive war' and all of them were convicted on other charges, the number ranging from one to many counts depending upon the individual in question. Seven, including Tōjō, were sentenced to death by hanging. Their executions were carried out on 23 December 1948 after MacArthur had reviewed and approved the verdict and after the United States Supreme Court had ruled, in considering a defence appeal, that it had no jurisdiction to review the IMTFE judgement. In the case of Hirota Kōki, a career diplomat and former prime minister who was the only civilian executed (primarily for having allegedly failed to prevent Japanese atrocities during the *China Incident), he was sentenced to death on the basis of a narrow six to five majority vote. The other six went to the gallows after a seven to four majority vote in each instance. Of the remaining defendants, sixteen were sentenced to life imprisonment; *Tōgō Shigenori, to twenty years' imprisonment; and Shigemitsu Mamoru, a former foreign minister, to seven years' imprisonment, although he would be released by MacArthur in 1950.

Significantly, although eight justices supported the final judgement, three—Pal, Henri Bernard of France, and B. V. A. Röling of the Netherlands—recorded dissenting opinions. Pal's was the most comprehensive in finding all the defendants innocent on all counts. He denied that a conspiracy had been established and that aggressive war was a crime in international law, to cite only two of his objections. In addition, the majority opinion was divided on specific points. For instance, Webb opposed the death sentence, unsuccessfully, arguing that none of the defendants should be executed since the emperor, under whose formal authority they had acted, had been exempted from trial.

Soon after the trial, all those who had been arraigned but not indicted were released. Six of the convicted defendants subsequently died in prison. On 7 April 1958, the others were set free by the Japanese government after its appeals for clemency to the signatories of the 1951 *San Francisco peace treaty had been approved, as Article 11 of the treaty had stipulated. Because Article 11 also stated Japan's acceptance of the IMTFE judgement, and the results of other Allied war crimes trials in the Far East, the Japanese government subsequently felt under no obligation to pursue the matter of Japanese war crimes. As a consequence, in post-independence Japan, in contrast to Germany, there have been no further prosecutions relating to the Second World War. This, and the fact that the Tokyo trial enabled the Japanese people as a whole to let their leaders take responsibility for the catastrophe of war, possibly explains why they, unlike the German people, have not fully confronted the question of whether they themselves shared in that responsibility, at least in the moral sense of complying with their government's war policies.

The Tokyo war crimes trial remains the subject of great debate even today. Above all, the version of history based on the seriously flawed conspiracy interpretation, which so conveniently suited the victorious Allies, has been justifiably criticized both in Japan and elsewhere. But in over-reacting to the 'Tokyo trial' interpretation, some revisionists, including Japanese, have recently posed equally simplistic counter-interpretations which go too far in the opposite direction of justifying Japanese expansionism. Interpretative swings of this sort still impede a balanced understanding of the origins and causes of war in the Asian-Pacific theatre.

2. The class B and C regional trials

The published proceedings, exhibits, and other documents of the Tokyo trial are invaluable for research on such varied topics as the political history of pre-war and wartime Japan, the fragmented, collective nature of Japanese decision-making, Japanese wartime operations and policies in occupied territories, and Japanese complicity in the widespread sale of opium and other narcotics as a source of wealth and means of social control in wartime Asia. Similarly, the records of the more than 2,000 Allied regional war crimes trials comprise a rich source of information on the conduct of the war by Japanese units in the field, and specifically, their treatment of *prisoners-of-war (POW).

The USA, the UK, China, the USSR, Australia, New Zealand, Canada, France, the Netherlands, and the Philippines all held military courts, some of which continued to operate until 1951, to try Japanese indicted for the murder or brutal ill-treatment of POW and civilians, for theft of property and the like, and for 'crimes against humanity' as broadly defined by the Tokyo Charter. Class B defendants (including certain Korean and Taiwanese, as well as Japanese, prison guards, for example) were accused of having committed such crimes themselves; class C defendants, mostly senior officers, were accused of planning, ordering, or failing to prevent them.

In some cases, only one defendant stood trial. In others, defendants were tried in groups. To cite an albeit rather extreme example, in one of the Australian trials held in the South Pacific, there were 93 defendants. Overall, of the 5,700 class B and C defendants, roughly 3,000 (the statistics are somewhat inexact) were convicted and sentenced to imprisonment for varying terms; 920 were convicted, sentenced to death, and executed. The high rate of convictions reflects the dark reality that, as has been estimated, while 4% of Anglo-American POW died in German camps, as many as 27% died in Japanese camps, not counting the many other European and Asian nationals who also perished there.

In general, the regional trials were less controversial than the Tokyo trial and sentences were commonly reviewed, often with death commuted to life imprisonment. Nevertheless, there were important exceptions. The trial of General *Yamashita by an American military commission in Manila, beginning in late October 1945, was especially controversial.

The principal accusation against Yamashita was that he had failed in his duty as commander of Japanese forces in the Philippines to prevent them from committing brutal atrocities. The defence acknowledged that atrocities had been committed but contended that the breakdown of communications and the Japanese chain of command in the chaotic battle of the second *Philippines campaign was such that Yamashita could not have controlled his troops even had he known of their actions, which was not certain in any case. Furthermore, many of the *atrocities had been committed by Japanese naval forces outside his command. However, the court found him guilty as charged and sentenced him to death. The sentence was appealed to MacArthur, who upheld it. It was then appealed to the Philippines Supreme Court and the United States Supreme Court, both of which declined to review the verdict. Thus, Yamashita was executed on 23 February 1946.

Among the many valid criticisms of this trial are the following. The commission of five officers lacked combat experience and formal legal training. With many Filipinos perhaps understandably anxious to make Yamashita pay for their sufferings during the Japanese occupation, the intensely emotional atmosphere of the trial rendered it extremely difficult for the court to judge the case objectively. The court admitted hearsay and other forms of evidence which the defence could not reasonably challenge and defence counsel complained they were given insufficient time in which to prepare their case. Because the well-known Yamashita was the first Japanese to be tried by the Allies for war crimes, MacArthur wanted a swift trial and a guilty verdict to establish a precedent for the approaching trials in Tokyo and elsewhere in the Far East.

Much the same controversy attended the trial in Manila, commencing in late December 1945, of Lt-General *Homma, who, in addition to other charges, was held responsible for the notorious Bataan death march of 1942 after the surrender of US troops in the Bataan peninsula. Homma claimed he had been aware of the march but not of the high casualty rate, for which he blamed Japanese officers under his command. He was executed on 3 April 1946 after the United States Supreme Court upheld his conviction and death sentence.

Mention should also be made of the Soviet trial at Khabarovsk in Siberia, which began in December 1949. In this case, twelve Japanese defendants who had served in the Japanese Army Unit 731 were accused of carrying out germ warfare experiments on live POW in Manchuria (see BIOLOGICAL WARFARE). All were found guilty and sentenced to imprisonment. The controversy which arises from the Khabarovsk trial is that the USA, although in a position later to bring to trial other Japanese involved in the infamous activities of Unit 731, chose not to do so. The records of the experiments were kept secret, presumably for use in classified American research. In this context and others, the history of the post-war trials clearly merges with the early history of the *Cold War.

STEPHEN LARGE

Hosoya, C., Andō, N., Ōnuma, Y., and Minear, R. H. (eds.), *The Tokyo War Crimes Trial: An International Symposium* (New York and Tokyo, 1986).
Minear, R. H., *Victors' Justice: The Tokyo War Crimes Trial* (Princeton, 1971).
Piccigallo, P. R., *The Japanese on Trial: Allied War Crimes Operations in the East, 1945–1951* (Austin, Texas, 1979).
Pritchard, R. J., and Zaide, S. M. (eds.), *The Tokyo War Crimes Trial: The Complete Transcripts of the Proceedings of the International Military Tribunal for the Far East*, 22 vols. (New York, 1981).

fascism is a generic name for a particular brand of totalitarian regime, several of which made their appearance in Europe between 1922 and 1936.

The name, taken from the Latin *fasces*, the ceremonial bundle of rods and an axe carried before magistrates in ancient Rome, symbolizing the power and unity of the Roman imperium, was coined by Mussolini, whose National Fascist Party was the first such group to gain power. In a general sense, it can be taken to include the National Socialists of Adolf Hitler in Germany, the Falangists in Spain, *Salazar's regime in Portugal, the Ustašas in Croatia, and the Iron Guard and Arrow Cross parties in Romania and Hungary respectively. It also had its adherents, such as the *British Union in the UK, Action Française in France, and the Falanga in Poland, where it never became the dominant political force.

Though as a doctrine fascism has no coherent political programme, the fascists of the 1920s and 1930s shared a number of political beliefs, or organizational methods, psychological traits, and common enemies. Fear of anarchy and of Bolshevik insurrection were elements common to all forms of fascism and important in attracting the support of the middle classes and petty bourgeoisie. Fascists were all ultranationalist, fervently believing in the special mission and often the racial superiority of their nation. They all laid emphasis on the collective life of the nation and its destiny, minimizing the rights and interests of individual citizens.

The climate in which fascism arose favoured also the emergence of charismatic politicians or military commanders, and fascist parties developed the cult of the all-powerful national 'leader'—Duce, Führer, or Caudillo—and they gave monopoly powers to their own ruling party. Like the communists, they established a system of parallel party organs whose function was to control all institutions of the state; and they raised élite forces—such as the Nazi *SS—whose first tasks were to defend the party and to subordinate the regular army to it. A façade of popular elections and legislative assemblies was usually maintained; but through rigged electoral commissions, subservient courts (see PEOPLE'S COURT), police terror, and, in extreme forms, *concentration camps, fascists were able to eliminate most effective active opposition. They paid great attention to education, to youth movements (see HITLER YOUTH), and to the techniques of modern propaganda; and hence to rallies, processions, films, uniforms, the subservience of all forms of art, and social regimentation of all kinds.

By these means, fascists were able to create a social ethos marked by conformism, hostility to outsiders, routine violence, contempt for the weak, and extreme hatred of dissident opinions. They believed themselves to be building a new social order, dominated by a new sort of human being. As a result, in the more radical variants, they had no truck with the conservative traditions of the church (see RELIGION) or the army. The political evils against which their crusade was directed were liberal democracy and, above all, *communism.

Some western political scientists, strongly influenced by fascism's enmity with communism, have generally classified it as a radical right-wing movement (in this, they followed the original communist analysis). In fact this classification is misleading: fascism was a brew of both right-wing and left-wing elements, the particular mix varying from country to country and from phase to phase. Fascism was not so much the opposite of communism as its rival, offering an alternative radical vision for rebuilding the world through violence.

However, the fascist movement was anything but homogenous. The Italian Fascisti, for example, possessed a distinct, left-wing socialist element, as did the German National Socialists up to the Röhm Purge of 1934; the Spanish Falangists did not. The Nazis made *anti-Semitism a central theme in their philosophy, as did the Iron Guard; the Fascisti and the Falangists were much less concerned with it. Both the Italian and the

Romanian fascists worked within the framework of a monarchy, whereas the Nazis overturned all pre-existing state structures. The Falangist party had close ties to the Catholic Church, and saw itself as the latest stage in Spain's thousand-year Christian crusade. Mussolini's Fascist Party was largely indifferent in religious matters once it had made peace with the Vatican through the Concordat of 1929. Hitler's fascists, in contrast, were ostentatiously pagan and anti-Christian (but see GERMAN CHRISTIANS), losing no opportunity to publicize their allegiance to the ancient German gods and the Wagnerian legends.

Inevitably, perhaps, the hysterical nationalism which was inherent in each branch of the fascist movement excluded the possibility of true harmony among them, and the Axis powers did not display any great degree of common 'fascist' purpose during the war. *Franco, the Caudillo of Spain, remained coldly aloof from Nazi designs throughout the war. He rebuffed Hitler outright at their one and only meeting at Hendaye in June 1940; and Spanish assistance to Germany was limited (see BLUE DIVISION and SPANISH LEGION). In Portugal, Salazar followed Franco's lead. Mussolini was less than enthusiastic about Nazi activities in the first stage of the war. Later on, the Germans deeply resented the need to rescue the Italian fascists from their misconceived and ill co-ordinated *Western Desert and *Balkan campaigns. The wholesale massacre of Italian soldiers, and of Italian prisoners in Germany, after Italy surrendered in September 1943 was evidence of this resentment (see also GARIBALDI DIVISION).

Fascism did inspire a measure of public support in many countries of wartime Europe, so long as it was seen to be fighting a successful anti-communist war. The number of French, Flemish, Dutch, Scandinavian, Yugoslav, and Baltic volunteers recruited by the Waffen-SS was impressive (see also SOVIET EXILES). But the success, such as it was, came from essentially negative motives. Fascism was saturated with hatred, which could only be channelled into effective action so long as it could feed on triumphs over enemies real and imagined.

NORMAN DAVIES

FBI (Federal Bureau of Investigation), see USA, 6.

Fermi, Enrico (1901–54), Italian-born Nobel Prize physicist who, after the Italian government had adopted *anti-Semitic laws in 1938, emigrated to the USA because his wife was Jewish. In 1934 he had discovered that metal became much more radioactive when bombarded with neutrons slowed down by water or paraffin, and these early experiments became one of the vital keys to unlocking the secrets of nuclear power. After working on slow neutron bombardment with another émigré physicist, Leo *Szilard, at New York's Columbia University, he directed the first controlled release of nuclear energy. This experiment, which took place in a squash court at the University of Chicago in December 1942, confirmed that an *atomic bomb was possible. See also SCIENTISTS AT WAR.

Fernando Po raid. British operation undertaken by *SOE's Maid Honor force. The name came from the Brixham trawler the force used to hunt for possible U-boat hideouts in the Gulf of Guinea, West Africa. In January 1942 it raided the Spanish island of Fernando Po in two tugs and towed away three Axis merchantmen. See also SMALL SCALE RAIDING FORCE.

ferry pilots were those who flew aircraft from the factories to the air bases. Many pilots were civilians—and some were women—though both the RAF had its Ferry Command and the USA its *Air Transport Command. See also AIR TRANSPORT AUXILIARY, ATLANTIC FERRY ORGANIZATION, and WASP.

Festung Europa (Fortress Europe) was the phrase used in German propaganda that set out from the autumn of 1942 to assure the German population, and to warn the Allies, that any invasion of Nazi-dominated Europe would be shattered on an impenetrable shield of defences. Though parts of the *Atlantic Wall were formidable, the destruction of Army Group Centre by the Red Army and the Normandy landings in June 1944 showed just how false this propaganda was; and, as Roosevelt pointed out, the fortress had no roof, so the Germans were always vulnerable to Allied air power.

Fezzan campaigns, incursions into, and then the crossing of, this Italian-held desert in Libya by de *Gaulle's Free French forces commanded by Colonel *Leclerc. These comprised *Tirailleurs Sénégalais and Chad infantry, and the camel-mounted Groupe Nomade de Tibesti, supported by radio and navigational units of the *Long Range Desert Group (LRDG); and, initially, by fourteen bombers of what later became the *Lorraine Squadron. Their successes prevented the Italians from interfering with the *Takoradi Air Route.

Chad, from which these campaigns were launched, was the only Free French territory adjacent to Axis soil (Italian-owned Libya). In de Gaulle's view, if the British were forced out of Egypt, which seemed likely in 1941, it could be of pivotal importance in defending the rest of colonial Africa, and he was therefore eager to take the offensive in the area. After Major Jean d'Ornano of the Chad garrison had been killed during the first Free French-LRDG raid into the Fezzan in January 1941, Leclerc replaced him. Based at Fort Lamy, he took Kufra in March 1941; raided Italian outposts around the Fezzan capital, Murzouk, the following February; and then in December 1942 sent in 3,250 men and 1,000 vehicles supported by twelve aircraft to destroy all Italian resistance around Murzouk, which was occupied on 12 January 1943. The force then overcame stiff opposition at Mizda, captured on 22 January, before entering Tripoli on 26 January, having covered 2,575 km. (1,600 mi.) since leaving Chad.

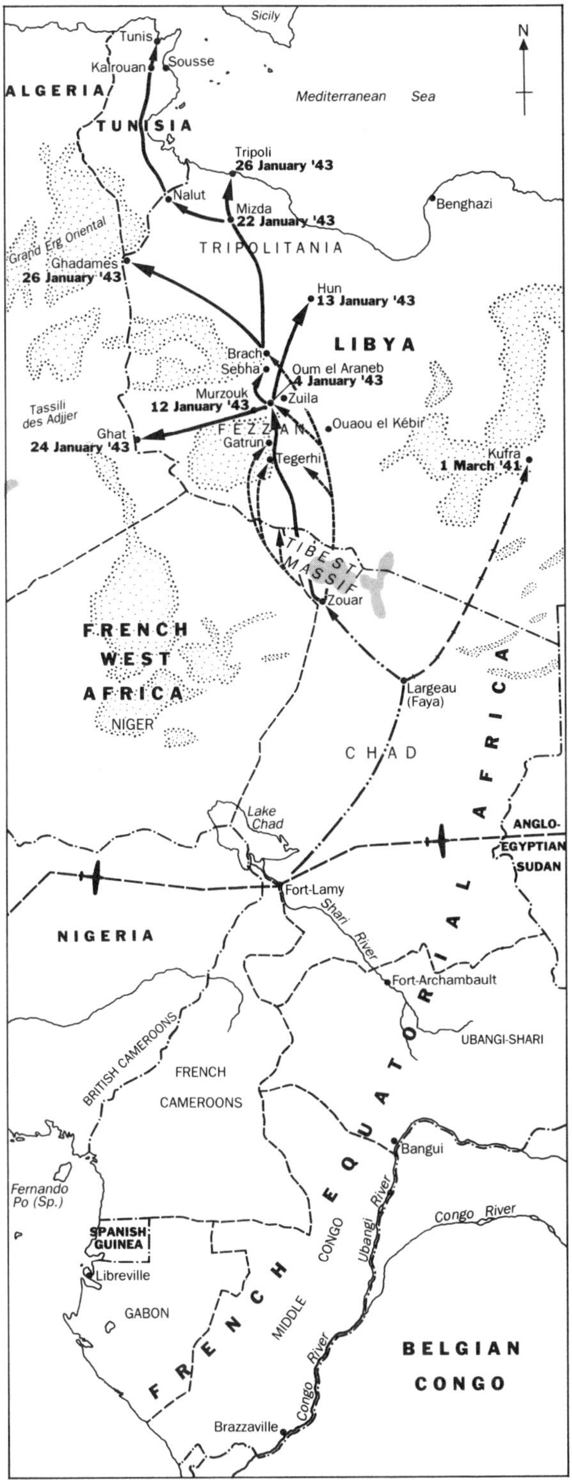

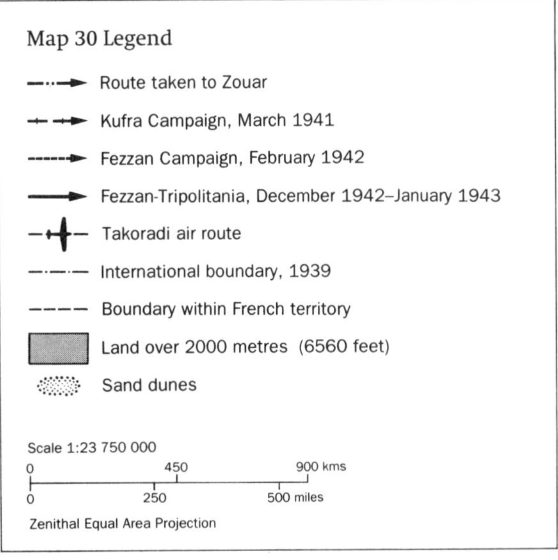

30. **Fezzan campaigns**, 1941–3

Leclerc and his men then became part of *Montgomery's Eighth Army and were known as 'L' Force.

FFI (Forces françaises de l'Intérieur), formed in February 1944 from nearly all the various French resistance groups (some communist ones stayed outside it) and commanded from London by General *Koenig. They initially contained about 30,000 lightly armed men, most of whom were in contact with *SOE or *Office of Strategic Services teams, but by the time of the Normandy landings in June 1944 (see OVERLORD), they had risen to 200,000. Some FFI bands attacked the Germans prematurely (see VERCORS), but during the *Normandy campaign, with the aid of *Jedburgh and *Sussex teams, they cut railway lines and telephone communications, and harassed German reinforcements. *Eisenhower said they were worth several divisions to him.

During the *French Riviera landings in August 1944, FFI bands were even more effective. Small groups in Toulon and Sète thwarted German attempts to destroy harbour facilities and larger ones later helped the invading Allied armies capture Grenoble in seven days when the planners had estimated it would take ninety. In September 1944, FFI groups began to be trained, armed, and integrated with First French Army, commanded by General de *Lattre de Tassigny, which, as Armée B, had taken part in the landings. A total of more than 137,000 from all over the country eventually entered its ranks, taking the place of North African troops (see TIRAILLEURS) who were returned to North Africa.

fifth columnists was a phrase waiting to be coined, as in modern warfare fears about subversion from within went back at least as far as the Franco-Prussian war of 1870. It first appeared in 1936 when a *Spanish Civil War Nationalist general told Republicans defending Madrid that, besides having four armed columns outside the capital, he had a fifth inside waiting to rise and fight for him.

German propaganda intensified the rumours that fifth columnists were at work undermining the morale and defences of the countries which the Nazis wished to conquer. Right-wing sympathizers and minority German groups (see VOLKSDEUTSCHE) were particularly suspect. A well-known *war correspondent wrote that Norway had fallen (see NORWEGIAN CAMPAIGN) thanks to 'bribery and extraordinary infiltration by Nazi agents and treason on the part of a few higher Norwegian civil and military personages'; the role of parachutists, when the Netherlands was invaded in May 1940, linked them immediately to fifth column activities; and British newspapers alleged that fifth columnists were at work in the UK supported by the *Peace Pledge Union among others. In the UK many anti-Nazi *refugees suffered *internment in the panic which ensued about fifth columnists, as they did on the Continent where a number of totally innocent people were shot as suspects during the fighting that preceded the fall of *France. Fifth column rumours also swept Moscow after the Germans launched their offensive against the USSR in June 1941 (see BARBAROSSA). It became impossible to buy a street map, or obtain street directions, and anyone using a torch—or even lighting a cigarette—at night was liable to be arrested on suspicion of signalling to German aircraft.

In fact, fifth columnists were largely a myth. The *Volksdeutsche* did play a substantial role in the Sudetenland and in Yugoslavia during the *Balkan campaign and an organized one in the *Polish campaign. The activities of the *Abwehr also helped fuel the rumours of fifth column activities. But virtually all the deeds of treachery with which fifth columnists were accused—and which spurred the formation of *SOE—were figments of the imagination. Nazi sympathizers and *spies certainly existed in all the conquered countries, but they played a minimal role in those countries' downfall.

Jong, L. de, *The German Fifth Column in the Second World War* (London, 1956).

fighter-bombers, see BOMBERS, 2, and FIGHTERS.

fighter catapult ships were three merchant ships and an old seaplane carrier which the British Admiralty converted to catapult fighter aircraft into the air to protect *convoys. They became operational in April 1941. Unlike the *CAM and *MAC ships, they were considered to be part of the Royal Navy and therefore flew the White Ensign. See also CARRIERS.

Fighter Command, see UK, 7(d); see also BRITAIN, BATTLE OF, and DOWDING.

fighters. (For examples of carrier fighter aircraft, see CARRIERS, 2; for fighter-bombers when employed as dive-bombers, see BOMBERS, 2.)

1. Design and development

The crucial elements necessary for a successful fighter design were speed, manoeuvrability, ceiling (see Table 1), range (see Table 2), and armament. These aspects were all interlinked, and improving one could usually only be achieved to the detriment of another. Only technical developments such as the introduction of the monoplane; external fuel, or drop, tanks; the jet engine; and rockets (see ROCKET WEAPONS) enabled designers to build fighters that could keep pace with the strategic and tactical demands of the war to outfight their opponents (speed and manoeuvrability), destroy enemy bombers (ceiling and armament), escort their own bombers for greater distances (range and armament), and act as effective 'aerial artillery' to support their side's land forces (armament and manoeuvrability).

By 1939 it was apparent that biplane fighters had reached the limits of their design potential. All the nations about to become involved in the Second World War had by then examples of the new generation of fighters, either in service, or about to enter production. These were single-engined, low-winged monoplanes, usually with enclosed cockpits, retracting undercarriages, and a fixed forward firing armament. Germany and the USSR had their Messerschmitt 109 and I16 Rata respectively—both types were used in the *Spanish Civil War on opposing sides—while the UK had introduced the Hurricane and Spitfire. Monoplane fighters were also in service in France and Italy, although Italy persevered with biplanes longer than most nations. The USA had the Curtiss P36 Hawk fighter, later developed into the useful P40 Tomahawk and Warhawk series. Japan also had radial engined all-metal fighters though two of its existing major types had fixed undercarriages. However, about to enter service was the Japanese Navy's A6M Zero which had remarkable manoeuvrability, exceptional range, and a retractable undercarriage.

Between the wars British fighters had been designed as bomber interceptors; they carried enough fuel in internal tanks for this role, and had (for 1939–40) a heavy armament of 8 x .303 in. (9 mm.) machine guns, then considered adequate to deal with unarmoured bombers. Other nations, notably France, Germany, Japan, and the USSR used mixed cannon and machine-gun armament, while the USA preferred the 0.5 in. (12.7 mm.) heavy machine-gun. During the battle of *Britain the Luftwaffe fitted armour into its aircraft; the Royal Air Force responded by fitting cannon in its Hurricanes and Spitfires, and these became operational late in 1940.

Some nations also developed twin-engined fighters, usually two-seater aircraft, and many of these later became successful night fighters as they were sufficiently large to accommodate the necessary *radar equipment with its operator. The first twin-engined fighter to see

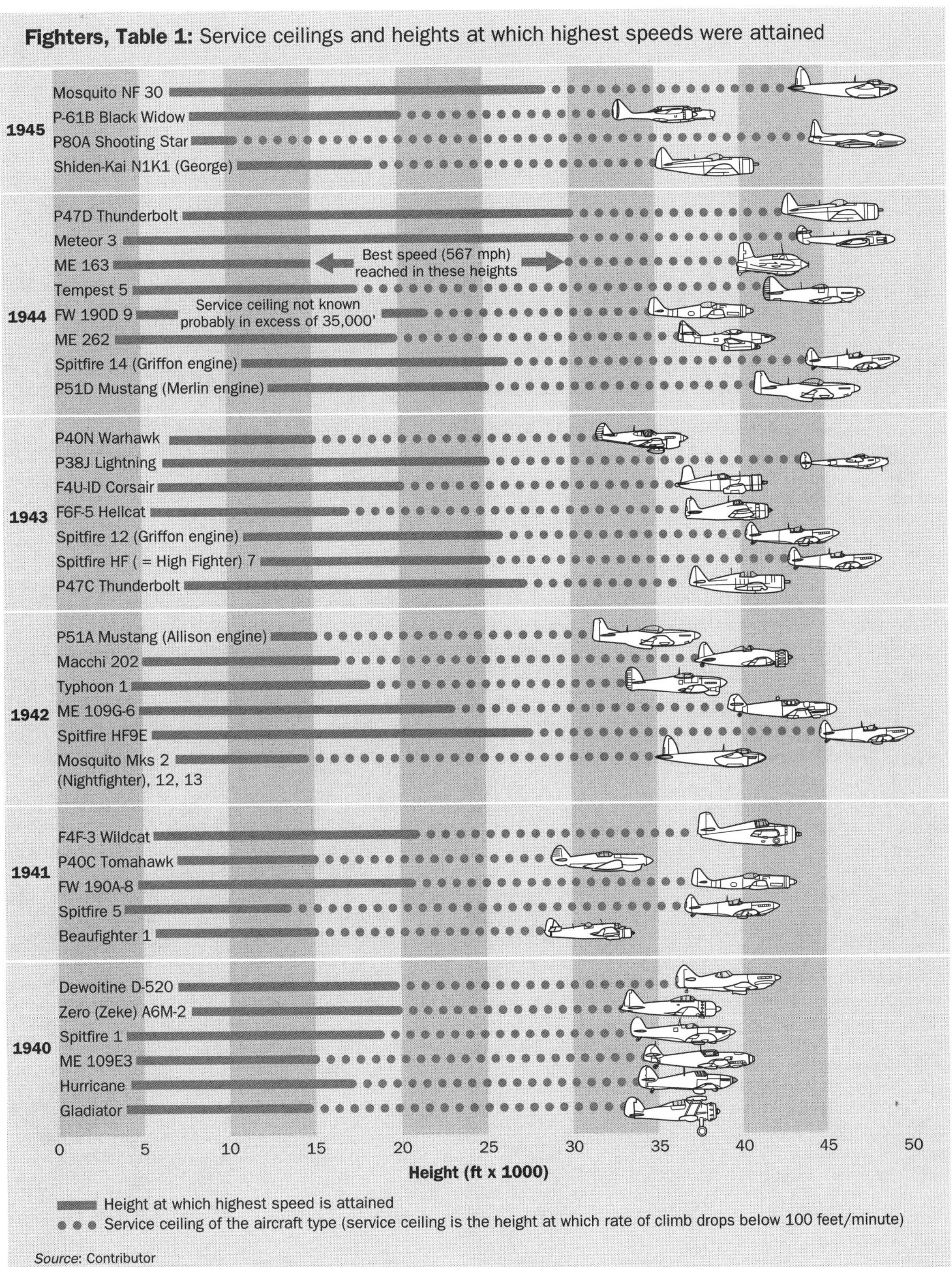
Fighters, Table 1: Service ceilings and heights at which highest speeds were attained
1945
Mosquito NF 30
P-61B Black Widow
P80A Shooting Star
Shiden-Kai N1K1 (George)
1944
P47D Thunderbolt
Meteor 3
ME 163
Best speed (567 mph) reached in these heights
Tempest 5
FW 190D 9
Service ceiling not known probably in excess of 35,000'
ME 262
Spitfire 14 (Griffon engine)
P51D Mustang (Merlin engine)
1943
P40N Warhawk
P38J Lightning
F4U-ID Corsair
F6F-5 Hellcat
Spitfire 12 (Griffon engine)
Spitfire HF (= High Fighter) 7
P47C Thunderbolt
1942
P51A Mustang (Allison engine)
Macchi 202
Typhoon 1
ME 109G-6
Spitfire HF9E
Mosquito Mks 2 (Nightfighter), 12, 13
1941
F4F-3 Wildcat
P40C Tomahawk
FW 190A-8
Spitfire 5
Beaufighter 1
1940
Dewoitine D-520
Zero (Zeke) A6M-2
Spitfire 1
ME 109E3
Hurricane
Gladiator
0
5
10
15
20
25
30
35
40
45
50
Height (ft x 1000)
Height at which highest speed is attained
Service ceiling of the aircraft type (service ceiling is the height at which rate of climb drops below 100 feet/minute)
Source: Contributor

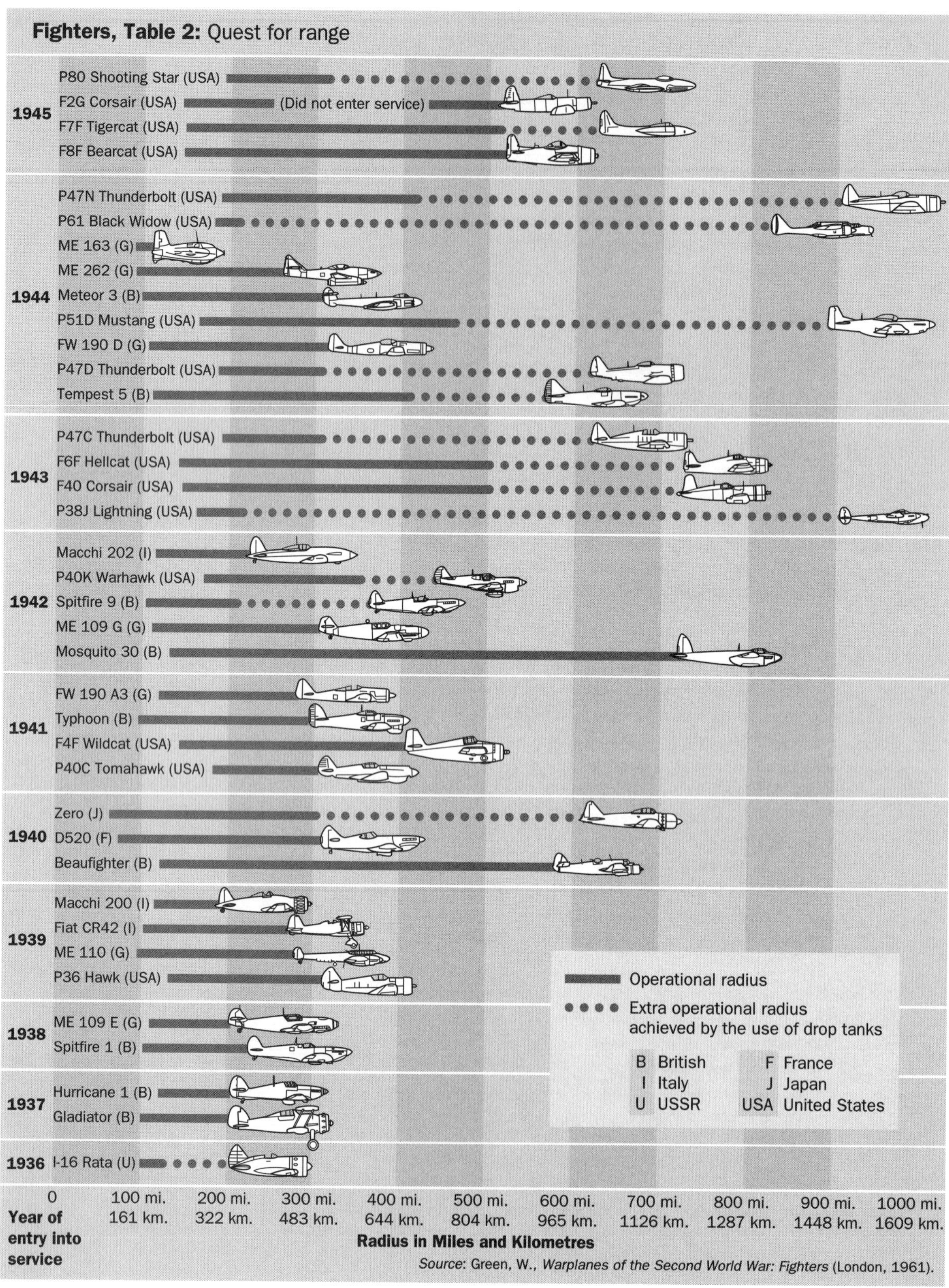

Source: Green, W., *Warplanes of the Second World War: Fighters* (London, 1961).

operational service was Germany's Messerschmitt 110. It was somewhat slower and less manoeuvrable than the nimble Hurricanes and Spitfires which opposed it in 1940, but later in the war it proved to be a successful night fighter, as did a fighter development of the German Ju88 bomber. The British developed the twin-engined Beaufighter and Mosquito—both of which also became successful night fighters—and the USA produced the twin-engined single-seater P38 Lightning. Only the USA produced a purpose-built night fighter, the P61 Black Widow. This was heavier than many medium bombers, and for a large twin-engined fighter had remarkable manoeuvrability.

As the war progressed, the quest for higher speed, and above all, greater operating radius became apparent. The original aircraft types of each nation were improved; engine power output was increased. All the combatant nations introduced newer designs which incorporated where possible the lessons of the earlier war years. New engines were used in some cases; for example, the British developed the Rolls-Royce Merlin into the Griffon, which was installed in later Spitfires.

Second generation fighters then appeared, such as the RAF's Typhoon, later further refined as the Tempest. In Germany, the Focke-Wulf 190, with its powerful BMW801 radial engine, became operational in 1941, and was used in several roles. To counter high-flying bombers, the RAF introduced high-altitude versions of the Spitfire, and a specially adapted example in the Middle East claimed a victory at 14,630 m. (48,000 ft.).

The US Army Air Forces introduced in April and December 1943 respectively the P47 Thunderbolt and the Merlin-engined P51B Mustang which, in late 1943 and mid-1944, extended the radius of fighter operations, and relieved pressure on the beleaguered US bomber formations in daylight raids over Europe during the *strategic air offensives. The later longer-ranged P51D Mustang—an excellent aircraft incorporating a laminar flow wing section (see Figure 1), an all-round-vision blister canopy, and an armament of 6 x 0.5 in. (12.7 mm.) machine guns—flew against and defeated the defending German fighter forces over their own bases. The P51D fitted with external underwing fuel, or drop, tanks had an operating radius of 965 km. (600 mi.) and could reach Poland and Czechoslovakia from bases in England. If bombs or rockets were fitted instead of external fuel tanks, it was very effective at strafing ground targets, and as a dive-bomber it was far better than the vaunted German Junkers 87 Stuka. By the cessation of hostilities in the *Pacific war it was regularly flying operations from *Iwo Jima to the home islands of Japan, a distance of some 1,045 km. (650 mi.).

The Japanese manufactured a number of outstanding fighters, some of which were on a par with anything the western powers produced, but by 1944 their pilots were so poorly trained they were unable to handle them properly. The Japanese Army Air Force, which was much influenced by the aerial clashes in Manchukuo in the 1930s (see JAPANESE–SOVIET CAMPAIGNS), developed short-range tactical aircraft for cold-weather operations. They were therefore unsuited, as indeed were their pilots, for combat in the Pacific war and they mostly operated in the *Burma campaign and in China (see CHINA INCIDENT). Though the Third Air Army did take part in the *Malayan and *Philippines campaigns, and other Japanese Army Air Force formations took part in the *New Guinea campaign, it was the Japanese Navy's air arm which bore the brunt of the fighting in the Pacific.

Fighters, Figure 1: Wing sections compared

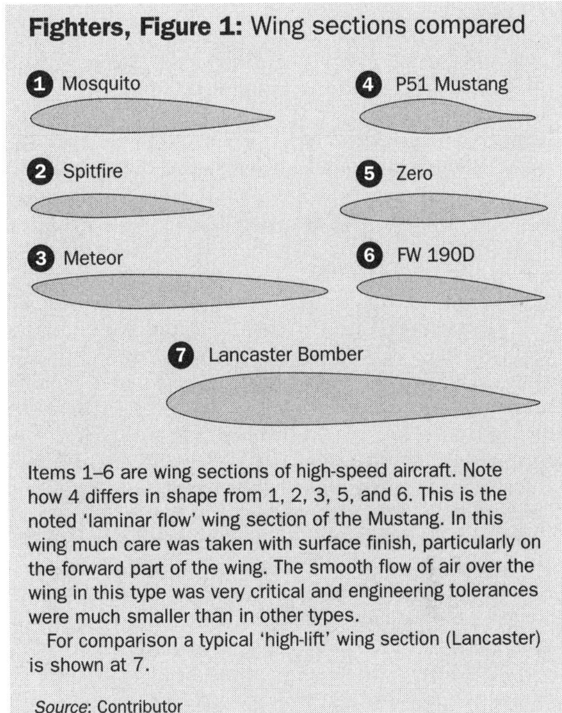

Items 1–6 are wing sections of high-speed aircraft. Note how 4 differs in shape from 1, 2, 3, 5, and 6. This is the noted 'laminar flow' wing section of the Mustang. In this wing much care was taken with surface finish, particularly on the forward part of the wing. The smooth flow of air over the wing in this type was very critical and engineering tolerances were much smaller than in other types.

For comparison a typical 'high-lift' wing section (Lancaster) is shown at 7.

Source: Contributor

Numerically, one of the most important Japanese Army Air Force fighters was the Hayabusa of which three models (1941, 1942, 1944) were built. All three models were armed with two 12.7 mm. (0.5 in.) machine guns; the Hayabusa III had a top speed of 560 km/h (348 mph) at 6,000 m. (19,685 ft.). However, this aircraft was, like its Japanese Navy contemporary the Zero, very lightly constructed, making it extremely vulnerable to the heavier armament of opposing Allied fighters; and, by comparison with Allied fighters, it was seriously undergunned.

Faster but less successful, because they frequently developed mechanical trouble, were the two models (1943, 1944) of the Hien; the Hien I, armed with two 12.7 mm. machine guns and two 20 mm. (0.8 in.) cannon, had a top speed of 650 km/h (405 mph).

Of the second generation fighters the Japanese Army pinned their hopes on the Hayate to turn the tide against US air power. This high-altitude interceptor fighter was developed in April 1944 as 'the ultimate fighter for the Great East Asia War'. The Model V (1945), which had an air-cooled engine, a top speed of 590 km/h (366 mph) at 6,400 m. (21,000 ft.), and an armament of two 20 mm. cannon and two 12.7 mm. machine guns, was specifically designed and developed for intercepting the US B29 bombers which raided Japan from Saipan. They were capable of climbing to 11,500 m. (37,730 ft.) while the Ki-102Ko, of which only 25 were built, could reach 13,000 m. (42,650 ft.).

The Japanese Navy's A6M Zero—by far its most successful fighter of which there were a whole succession of models—first came into service in 1940 and was operated from land bases as well as from *carriers. It was of exceedingly lightweight construction and therefore had excellent manoeuvrability. During the first six months of the Pacific war, its remarkable operating radius of 965 km. (600 mi.) came as an unpleasant surprise to the Allied air forces. Of the early Allied fighters only the F4F Wildcat could oppose it on anything like equal terms.

The Japanese Naval Air Force also introduced entirely new fighters, in addition to improving its Zero fighter. The best of these was the Shiden, a landplane development of a *float-plane fighter (a type used only by the Japanese). Introduced late in 1944, the Shiden of all Japanese fighters most nearly approached the western concept of a late war fighter. It was used by the Japanese in the closing months of the war mainly to intercept US B29 bomber raids during the strategic air offensive against Japan.

Both the Japanese Army and Navy had a number of promising aircraft designs (fighters, bombers, and attack aircraft) at the end of the war. Because of production difficulties caused by shortage of materials and air raids, many of these were in prototype form or had only been built in small numbers. There was also a shortage of skilled technicians in the Japanese aircraft industry because many aero-engineers had been conscripted into the army.

The first use of fighter-bombers—which were simply fighters converted to carrying bombs—occurred in 1940 when German Messerschmitt 109s bombed airfields and other objectives in South-East England. The Focke-Wulf 190 was also successfully used in fighter-bomber operations against targets in southern England, and on the Eastern and Italian fronts.

On the Allied side, Hurricanes, Spitfires, P40 Warhawks, Typhoons, P51 Mustangs, P47 Thunderbolts, F6F Hellcats, and F4U Corsairs were all successfully used as fighter-bombers. In the case of the Typhoon, effective use was also made of rockets, especially against German tanks in the *Normandy campaign, and P47 Thunderbolts were highly effective in a dive-bomber role in support of the US Army in 1944–5.

However, by the time the war in Europe ended in May 1945, the day of the single seat, piston-engined fighter had almost run its course; all the air forces had advanced designs or extremely fast refinements of existing designs which either saw limited service in the closing months of the war, or entered service soon thereafter. Some promising designs appeared only as prototypes and were not built in quantity.

The trend in new fighter aircraft was the jet fighter; both the RAF and the Luftwaffe had examples in squadron service, in the Meteor and Me262 respectively. Both these became operational in 1944; both were low-wing twin jet monoplanes. The US Army's Shooting Star jet fighter was just too late to see wartime squadron service. The Germans also made operational the radical Me163, a tailless all-wing design with a liquid-fuelled rocket motor used in short bursts to get above Allied bomber formations. In level flight under power it was extremely fast (950 km/h or 590 mph), but its fuel only lasted about twelve minutes and it was then flown as a *glider.

Piston engines of the Second World War were of two types, air-cooled radial engines and liquid-cooled in-line engines. The cylinders in radial engines were arranged in one or more rows round the crankshaft like the points of a star, and these engines were cooled by the air flowing over the cylinders and crankcase as the aircraft flew through the air. In in-line engines the cylinders were in rows parallel to the crankshaft, and these engines were invariably cooled by a water-glycol mixture and a radiator. Most in-line engines were of a 'V' configuration, for example, the Rolls-Royce Merlin was of a V-12 layout.

Piston engines, like aircraft, were subject to continuous development. The incomparable British Rolls-Royce Merlin fitted in Hurricanes and Spitfires during the battle of Britain was rated at 1,030 hp; by 1942 the Merlin Mark 66 fitted in the Spitfire 9 developed 1,720 hp. A refinement, the Rolls-Royce Griffon, which equipped late Spitfire variants, developed over 2,000 hp. Versions of the Merlin equipped many Allied aircraft types, including the American P51D Mustang. Merlins for the Mustang were built in the USA by the Packard Motor Company, and, apart from the Mustang, went into Canadian-built Lancasters and Mosquitos.

The American forte was the air-cooled radial engine; the Pratt and Whitney R-2800 18-cylinder (in two rows) engine fitted in P47 Thunderbolts and P61 Black Widows was rated at over 2,200 hp. The same engine powered the F6F Hellcat and F4U Corsair naval fighters.

The Germans produced two outstanding engines, the inverted V-12 Daimler Benz 601–603–605 series, and the powerful BMW 801 fourteen-cylinder two-row radial. The DB601 of 1940 fitted in the Me109E developed 1,100 hp; the late war DB605 produced about 1,500 hp when fitted in the ME 109G. The BMW 801 powered the Focke-Wulf 190, producing about 1,700 hp.

Japanese aero-engines tended to be somewhat less powerful than their Allied counterparts, but with the lighter construction of many of their aircraft, this was not deemed by the Japanese to be a disadvantage. However, by 1944 they had produced the powerful Homare engine, which powered the Shiden fighter.

Fighters, 1, Table 3: Major land-based fighter/fighter-bomber types

Type	*Span*	*Length*	*All-up weight*[a]	*Power plant*	*Armament (cannon/ machine guns)*	*Bombs and rocket weapons (max)*[b]	*Optimum performance*	*Radius*[c]	*Crew*	*Year of entry into squadron service*
France										
Dewoitine D520	10.3 m (33 ft 5 in)	8.8 m (28 ft 8 in)	2,786 kg (6,129 1b)	1 x Hispano-Suiza 910 hp	1 x 20 mm (0.78 in) 4 mg	–	530 kph @ 5,791 m (329 mph/19,000 ft)	499 km (310 mi)	1	1940
Morane-Saulnier MS 406	10.7 m (34 ft 9 in)	8.2 m (26ft 11 in)	2,727 kg (6,000 lb)	1 x Hispano-Suiza 860 hp	1 x 20 mm 2 mg	–	486 kph @ 4,877 m (302 mph/16,000 ft)	402 km (250 mi)	1	1939
Germany										
Focke-Wulf 190 A–8	10.6 m (34 ft 5 in)	8.9 m (29 ft)	4,432 kg (9,750 1b)	1 x BMW 801 2,100 hp	4 x 20 mm 2 mg	450 kg (990 lb)	656 kph @ 6,400 m (408 mph/21,000 ft)	402 km	1	1941
Focke-Wulf 190 D–9	10.6 m	10.3 m (33 ft 5 m)	4,850 kg (10,670 lb)	1 x Junkers Jumo 231A 1,770 hp	2 x 20 mm 2 mg	400 kg (880 lb)	685 kph @ 6,400 m. (426 mph/21,000 ft)	4,8 km (260 mi)	1	1943
Junkers S8 C–6 (night fighter)	25.3 m (65 ft 10 in)	14.5 m (47 ft 1 in)	11,875 kg (26,125 lb)	2 x Junkers Jumo 211J 1,410 hp	3 x 20 mm 3 mg forward firing, 1 mg rearward firing; 2 x 20 mm upward (optional)	–	500 kph @ 6,096 m (311 mph/20,000 ft)	1,609 km (1,000 mi)	3	1940
Messerschmitt 109E	9.9 m (32 ft 4 in)	8.7 m. (28 ft 4 in)	2,510 kg (5,523 lb)	1 x Daimler-Benz DB601 1,100 hp	2 x 20 mm 2 mg	250 kg (550 lb)	566kph @ 3,750 m (354 mph/12,300 ft)	322 km (200 mi)	1	1939
Messerschmitt 109F	10 m (32 ft 6 in)	8.9m.	2,752 kg (6,054 lb)	1 x Daimler-Benz DB601 1,300 hp	1 x 20 mm 2 mg	250 kg	628 kph @ 6,706 m (390 mph/22,000 ft)	354 km (220 mi)	1	1941
Messerschmitt 109G	10 m	9.1 m (29 ft. 8 in)	3,159 kg (6,950 lb)	1 x Daimler-Benz DB605 1,475 hp	2 x 20 mm 2 mg	455 kg	623 kph @ 7,010 m (387 mph/23,000 ft)	483 km (300 mi)	1	1942
Messerschmitt 110 C–5	16.2 m (53 ft 4 in)	12.2 m (39 ft 8 in)	6,955 kg (15,300 lb)	2 x Daimler-Benz DB601 1,100 hp	2 x 20 mm 4 mg 1 mg (rear)	1,000 kg (2,200 lb) or 4 air-to-air rockets	563 kph @ 7,010 m (350 mph/23,000 ft)	850 km (528 mi)	2	1939
Messerschmitt 163B	9.4 m (30 ft 7 in)	5.7 m (18 ft 8 in)	4,318 kg (9,500 lb)	1 x Walter rocket motor, thrust 1,705kg. (3,750 lb)	2 x 30 mm (1.17 in) 24 x R4M rockets	–	949 kph @ 6,096 m (590 mph/20,000 ft)	limited	1	1944
Messerschmitt 262A	12.6 m (41 ft)	10.7 m (34 ft 9 in)	6,409 kg (14,100 lb)	2 x Junkers 004 jet, thrust 900 kg (1,980 lb)	4 x 30 mm	–	869 kph @ 6,096 m (540 mph/20,000 ft)	526 km (420 mi)	1	1944
Italy										
Fiat CR 42	9.8 m (31 ft 10 in)	8.4 m (27 ft 3 in)	2,410 kg (5,302 lb)	1 x Fiat A74 840 hp	2 mg	2 x 100 kg (220 lb) bombs	428 kph @ 3,962 m (266 mph/13,000 ft)	507 km (315 mi)	1	1940
Fiat G50(bis) (Major production variant)	11.1 m (36 ft 1 in)	8.3 m	2,527 kg (5,560 lbs)	1 x Fiat A74 840 kp	2 x 12.7 mm mg 0.5 in	–	469 kph @ 4,316 m (291 mph/14,160 ft)	496 km (308 mi)	1	1938 (early version saw service in Spain)
Macchi C200	10.7 m	8.3 m (26 ft 11 in)	2,598 kg (5,715 lb)	1 x Fiat A74 870 hp	2 mg	273 kg (600 lb)	502 kph @ 4,480 m (312 mph/14,700 ft)	434 km (270 mi)	1	1939
Macchi C202	10.7 m	8.9 m (29 ft 1 in)	3,016 kg (6,636 lb)	1 x Mercedes-Benz DB601 (built under licence by Alfa-Romeo)	4 mg all 12.7 mm (0.5 in)	273 kg	595 kph @ 5,029 m (370 mph/16,500 ft)	386 km (240 mi)	1	1941
Reggiane Re 2001 (Caproni)	11.1 m	8.2 m	3,287 kg (7,231 lb)	1 x Alfa-Romeo 1,175 hp	2 x 12.7 mg 2 x 7.7 mg	up to 2 x 160 kg (353 lb) bombs	539 kph @ 4,316 m (335 mph/14,160 ft)	528 kms (328 mi)	1	1942
Japan: Navy Land-based Fighters. *See entry on codenames										
Japan (navy) Kawanishi NIK2-J Shiden *('George')	12.1 m (39 ft 4 in)	9.4 m (30 ft 8 in)	4,109 kg (9,039 lb)	1 x Homare 21 1,990 hp	4 x 20 mm 2 mg	500 kg (1,100 lb)	594 kph @ 3,000 m (369 mph/9,840 ft)	1,166 km (725 mi)	1	1944
Mitsubishi J2 M2 Raiden ('Jack')	10.9 m (35 ft 5 in)	10 m (32 ft 8 in)	3,955 kg (8,700 lb)	1 x Kasei 23A 1,820 hp	4 x 20 mm	114 kg	597 kph @ 5,791 m (371 mph/19,000 ft)	523 km (325 mi)	1	1944

Fighters, 1, Table 3: *(cont.)*

Type	*Span*	*Length*	*All-up weight*[a]	*Power plant*	*Armament (cannon/ machine guns)*	*Bombs and rocket weapons (max)*[b]	*Optimum performance*	*Radius*[c]	*Crew*	*Year of entry into squadron service*
Japan: Army Fighters										
Nakajima KI-43 Hayabusa ('Oscar')	10.9 m (35 ft 5 in)	9 m (29 ft 3 in)	2,670 kg (5,874 lb)	1 x Nakajima HA 115 1,130 hp	2 x 12.7 mm mg	500 kg (1,100 lb)	515 kph @ 5,944 m (320 mph/19,500 ft)	805 km (500 mi)	1	1941
Nakajima KI-84 Hayate ('Frank')	11.3 m (36 ft 10 in)	10 m (32 ft 7 in)	4,179 kg (9,194 lb)	1 x Nakajima HA45 1,900 hp	2 x 20 mm 2 mg	455 kg	624 kph @ 5,944 m (388 mph/19,500 ft)	1,448 km (900 mi)	1	1944
Kawasaki K161 Hien ('Tony')	12.1 m (39 ft 4 in)	9 m (29 ft 4 in)	3,477 kg (7,650 lb)	1 x Kawasaki HA40 1,175 hp	2 x 20 mm 2 mg	455 kg	560 kmh @ 4,999 m (348 mph/16,400 ft)	885 km (550 mi)	1	1943
Poland										
PZL 11C	10.8 m (35 ft 2 in)	7.6 m (24 ft 9 in)	1,800 kg (3,960 lb)	1 x PZL (built) Bristol Mercury 645 hp	4 mg	2 x 12.3 kg	389 kph @ 5,486 m (27 lb) bombs	402 km (242 mph/18,000 ft)	1	1934
UK										
Beaufighter MK1 (night fighter)	17.8 m (57 ft 10 in)	12.7 m (41 ft 4 in)	9,455 kg (20,800 lb)	2 x Hercules 1,590 hp	4 x 20 mm 6 x (7.8 mm) (0.303 in) mg or 8 rockets	(later versions) 227 kg (500 lb)	520 kph @ 4,572 m (323 mph/15,000 ft)	1,207 km (750 mi)	2	1940
Mosquito 2	16.7 m (54 ft 2 in)	12.6 m (40 ft 11 in)	8,636 kg (19,000 lb)	2 x Merlin 23 1,635 hp	4 x 20 mm 4 x .303 in mg	(some versions) 455 kg or 8 rockets	655 kph @ 8,534 m (407 mph/28,000 ft)	1,287 km (800 mi)	2	1942
Gladiator 1	9.9 m (32 ft 1 in)	8.4 m (27 ft 5 in)	2,159 kg (4,750 lb)	1 x Mercury 840 hp	4 x .303 in mm mg	–	407 kph @ 4,420 m (253 mph/14,500 ft)	322 km (200 mi)	1	1936
Meteor 3	13.2 m (43 ft)	12.7 m (41 ft 3 in)	6,045 kg (13,300 lb)	2 x Derwent jets, thrust 909 kg (2,000 lb)	4 x 20 mm	–	788 kph @ 9,144 m (490 mph/30,000 ft)	483 km	1	1944
Hurricane 1*	12.3 m (40 ft)	9.8 m (31 ft 11 in)	3,000 kg (6,600 lb)	1 x Merlin Mk3 1,030 hp	8 x .303 in mg	(later versions) 455 kg	521 kph @ 4,877 m (324 mph/16,000 ft)	322 km	1	1937
Typhoon 1	12.8 m (41 ft 7 in)	9.8 m	5,182 kg (11,400 lb)	1 x Sabre Mk2 2,180 hp	4 x 20 mm	909 kg or 8 rockets	652 kph @ 5,486 m (405 mph/18,000 ft)	483 km	1	1941
Tempest 5	12.6 m	10.4 m (33 ft 8 in)	6,136 kg (13,500 lb)	1 x Sabre Mk2 2,200 hp	4 x 20 mm	–	700 kph @ 5,182 m (435 mph/17,000 ft)	965 km	1	1944
Spitfire 1*	11.3 m	9.2 m (29 ft 11 in)	2,629 kg (5,784 ib)	1 x Merlin Mk3 1,030 hp	8 x 303 in mm mg	–	587 kph @ 5,791 m (365 mph/19,000 ft)	402 km	1	1938
Spitfire 5	11.3 m	9.2 m	3,084 kg (6,785 lb)	1 x Merlin 45 1,470 hp	2 x 20 mm 4 x .303 in mg	227 kg	602 kph @ 3,962 m (374 mph/13,000 ft)	402 km	1	1941
Spitfire 9	11.3 m	9.6 m (31 ft 4 in)	3,409 kg (7,500 lb)	1 x Merlin 61 1,720 hp	2 x 20 mm 2 x .5 m (12.8 mm) mg	455 kg	669 kph @ 8,230 m (416 mph/27,000 ft)	724 km (450 mi)	1	1942
Spitfire 12	9.9 m (32 ft 1 in)	9.8 m	3,364 kg (7,400 lb)	1 x Griffon 3 1,735 hp	2 x 20 mm 4 x .303 in mg	1 x 227 kg bomb	632 kph @ 5,486 m (393 mph/18,000 ft)	402 km	1	1943
Spitfire 14	11.3 m	10 m	3,864 kg	1 x Griffon 65 (8,500 lb)	2 x 20 mm 2,050 hp	455 kg 2 x .5 in mg	721 kph @ 7,925 m	644 km (448 mph/26,000 ft)	1	1944
* took part in the battle of Britain										
USA										
Bell P39D Airacobra	10.5 m (34 ft)	9.3 m (30 ft 2 in)	3,727 kg (8,200 lb)	1 x Allison V-1710 1,150 hp	1 x 37 mm (1.44 in) 6 mg	227 kg	579 kph @ 4,572 m (360 mph/15,000 ft)	805 km	1	1941
Curtiss P36C Hawk	11.5 m (37 ft 4 in)	8.8 m (28 ft 6 in)	2,732 kg (6,010 lb)	1 x Pratt & Whitney R1830 Twin Wasp 1,200 hp	1 x .5 in (12.8 mm) mg 3 x 3 in (7.7 mm) mg	–	500 kph @ 3,048 m (311 mph/10,000 ft)	362 km (225 mi)	1	1938
Curtiss P40C Tomahawk	11.5 m	9.8 m (31 ft 9 in)	3,663 kg (8,058 lb)	1 x Allison V-1710 1,150 hp	2 x .5 in mg 4 x .3 in mg	– –	555 kph @ 4,572 m (345 mph/15,000 ft)	740 km (460 mi)	1	1940
Curtiss P40N Warhawk	11.5 m	10.2 m (33 ft 4 in)	5,182 kg (11,400 lb)	1 x Allison V-1710 1,200 hp	6 mg	682 kg (1,500 lb)	552 kph @ 4,572 m (343 mph/15,000 ft)	805 km	1	1944
Lockheed P38J Lightning	16 m (52 ft)	11.6 m (37 ft 10 in)	9,818 kg (21,600 lb)	2 x Allison V-1710 1,425 hp	1 x 20 mm 4 mg	727 kg (1,600 lb) or 10 rockets	666 kph @ 7,620 m (414 mph/25,000 ft)	1,818 km (1,130 mi)	1	1941
Lockheed P80A Shooting Star	11.9 m (38 ft 11 in)	10.6 m (34 ft 6 in)	6,364 kg (14,000 lb)	1 x General Electric J33 jet, thrust 1,750 kg (3,850 lb)	6 mg	909 kg or 10 rockets	882 kph @ 3,048 m (548 mph/10,000 ft)	1,062 km (660 mi)	1	1945

Fighters, 1, Table 3: *(cont.)*

Type	*Span*	*Length*	*All-up weight*[a]	*Power plant*	*Armament (cannon/ machine guns)*	*Bombs and rocket weapons (max)*[b]	*Optimum performance*	*Radius*[c]	*Crew*	*Year of entry into squadron service*
North American P51AA Mustang	11.4 m (37 ft)	9.9 m (32 ft 3 in)	4,818 kg (10,600 lb)	1 x Allison V-1710 1,200 hp	4 mg	455 kg	579kph @ 3,050 m (360 mph/10,000 ft)	805 km	1	1942
North American P51B Mustang	11.4 m	9.9 m	5,091 kg (11,200 lb)	1 x Packard-Merlin V-1650 1,620 hp	4 mg	455 kg or 6 rockets	708 kph @ 9,144 m (440 mph/30,000 ft)	1,126 km (700 mi)	1	1943
North American P51D Mustang	11.4 m	9.9 m	5,500 kg (12,100 lb)	1 x Packard- Merlin V-1650 1,695 hp	6 mg	909 kg or 6 rockets	700 kph @ 7,620 m (435 mph/25,000 ft)	1,287 km	1	1944
Northrop P61 Black Widow (night fighter)	20.3 m (66 ft)	15 m (48 ft 11 in)	17,277 kg (38,000 lb)	2 x Pratt & Whitney R-2800 2,250 hp	4 x 20 mm 4 mg (when turret fitted)	1,820 kg (4,000 lb)	589 kph @ 6,096 m (366 mph/20,000 ft)	1,529 km (950 mi)	3, or 2 when turret not fitted	1944
Republic P47D Thunderbolt	12.5 m (40 ft 9 in)	11.1 m (36 ft 2 in)	7,955 kg (17,500 ft)	1 x Pratt & Whitney R-2800 2,535 hp	8 mg	682 kg or 10 rockets	685 kph @ 9,144 m (426 mph/30,000 ft)	1,126 km	1	1944
Republic P47N Thunderbolt	13.1 m (42 ft 7 in)	11.1 m	9,409 kg (20,700 lb)	1 x Pratt & Whitney R-2800 2,800 hp	8 mg	682 kg or 10 rockets	740 kph @ 9,144 m (460 mph/30,000 ft)	1,287 km	1	1945
USA: navy										
Vought F4U-4 Corsair	12.6 m (41.5 ft)	10.4 m	6,668 kg (14,670 lb)	1 x Pratt & Whitney R-2800 2,450 hp	6 mg	909 kg or 8 rockets	718 kph @ 7,986 m (446 mph/26,200 ft)	1,207 km	1	1945
Goodyear F2G-1 Corsair (development of F4U-4)	12.6 m	10.3 m	7,010 kg (15,422 lb)	1 x Pratt & Whitney R-4360 3,000 hp	4 x mg All US mg .5 in (12.7 mm) except where shown	909 kg or 8 rockets	693 kph @ 4,998 m (431 mph/16,400 ft)	1,529 km	1	–
USSR										
Lavochkin LA-7	9.9 m (32 ft 2 in)	8.6 m (27 ft 11 in)	3,407 kg (7,495 lb)	Shvetsov M-82 1,775 hp	3 x 20 mm	2 x 50 kg (110 lb) bombs or 6 rockets	644 kph @ 4,998 m (400 mph/16,400 ft)	483 km	1	1943
Polikarpov I-16 Rata (type 24)	9 m (29 ft 6 in)	6.2 m (20 ft 1 in)	2,055 kg (4,520 lb)	Shvetsov M-62 1,000 hp	2 x 20 mm 2 mg	6 rockets	525 kph (326 mph) @ sea level	354 km	1	1935
Yakolev YAK-9U	10.1 m (32 ft 10 in)	8.8 m	3,175 kg (6,985 lb)	1 x Klimov M107-A 1,650 hp	1 x 20 mm cannon, + 2 x 12.7 mm mg	2 x 100 kg (220 ib) bombs	667 kph @ 4,998 m (415 mph/16,400 ft)	925 km (575 mi) at a speed of 390 kph (242 mph)	1	1945
Yakolev YAK-9D	12.3 m	8.6 m	3,206kg (7,055 lb)	1 x Klimov M105 1,260 hp	1 x 20 mm 1 x 12.7 mm mg	– –	584 kph @ 4,998 m (363 mph @ 16,400 ft)	708 km (440 mi)		1943

[a] Maximum weight permissable for take-off
[b] Bombs and rockets could not be carried together
[c] Maximum radius attainable using droptanks, in which case no underwing weapons could be carried, Figure shown is distance from which an aircraft could return to base after a short combat at extreme range.

Source: Contributor.

Producing 1,990 hp, the Homare was lighter and of a smaller diameter than any other major wartime radial engine, but it was handicapped by unreliability and production difficulties caused by B29 air raids on factories producing it.

E. A. MUNDAY

2. Tactics

As in the *First World War, fighter tactics depended on an aircraft's speed, armament, manoeuvrability, rate of climb, and turning ability, and on a pilot's quick reactions and his use of sun and cloud. Surprise remained the trump card. As one US pilot remarked, 'The guy you don't see will kill you': four out of five fighters shot down during the war never saw their assailant.

The major advance between the wars was the introduction of radio telephony (see RADIO COMMUNICATIONS) into most major air forces. This enabled ground control stations—which in the UK possessed an early form of radar—to direct fighters on to their targets early, allowed flight leaders to organize their pilots quickly for an attack while airborne, and warned pilots when enemy aircraft were above and behind them. In the RAF code-words were introduced (see BANDIT and BOGEY) to aid brevity of speech and eliminate ambiguity, and fighter squadrons were given identity call signs to minimize confusion.

In September 1939 RAF Fighter Command's tactical training was based on the theory that the air threat to the UK would be hordes of German bombers, flying in close formation and not escorted by fighters since these could not reach the UK's shores from airfields in Germany; apparently those who assessed the threat did not take into account the possibility that nearer airfields might become available. *Dogfights, it was held, were a thing of the past and rigid air fighting tactics were introduced which, by a series of complicated and time-wasting manoeuvres, aimed at bringing the greatest number of guns to bear against the bombers. The RAF's fighting unit was the tight vic, or V-formation, of three fighters, and squadron training was based on six types of formation attacks against unescorted bombers. These set-piece attacks were useless in air combat. Tactically the German Fighter Arm was well ahead of the RAF's Fighter Command because their young fighter pilots, such as Mölders and *Galland, had, since 1936, gained valuable tactical experience in the Spanish Civil War and had devised the perfect fighter formation, known as the *Rotte*. This was based on just two aircraft, which flew some 180 m. (200 yd.) apart. The main responsibility of the number two, or wingman, was to guard his leader from an attack from his quarter, or from behind, while the leader navigated his small force and also covered his wingman. The *Schwarme*, two pairs of aircraft, was a development of the *Rotte*, and when in 1941 the RAF eventually copied the Luftwaffe and adopted this pattern, it was called the 'finger-four' because the relative positions of the fighters was similar to a plan view of the finger tips. The Luftwaffe adopted it and it is still used today. For some reason the *Western Desert Air Force did not employ it until the summer of 1942.

Despite the lessons of the brief air fighting which preceded the fall of *France in June 1940 the British began the battle of Britain using the wretched three-plane vics. Tactically, however, the Luftwaffe failed to take advantage of the RAF's radar gap at low level or to destroy its tall radar masts—ideal targets for their Stuka dive-bombers—and as the fighting intensified able leaders such as Malan, Bader, and Broadhurst adopted looser and more manoeuvrable formations. This meant that RAF fighters began to meet the angular German Me109 fighters on better terms when they began escorting the bomber formations. Different tactics were also then adopted against the bombers themselves. One was for the fighters, flying line abreast, to approach the bombers head-on. This minimized the time in which the fighter escort could intervene and often broke up the bomber formation. Another was the Big Wing proposed by Bader. He argued that a large formation attacking simultaneously was more effective than the same number of aircraft arriving separately, and that it was better for morale. The three-squadron (later five) Duxford Wing was formed but the theory was never particularly successful because of the time it took to form up. After the battle of Britain, Fighter Command tried to retain the initiative by luring the Luftwaffe to battle over France (see CIRCUSES and RHUBARBS), but this was unsuccessful, too.

The Soviet Air Forces also retained tight vics of three at the start of the *German–Soviet war in June 1941 (see also BARBAROSSA), but some squadrons soon copied the German *Schwarme* and began to fly eight fighters in two loose sections of four. They did not have radar to help find German formations. Few fighters carried radio-telephones and the leader had to control his pilots by visual signals. They lacked gunnery training and opened fire too far from their targets. When separated from their companions they seemed to lack confidence and initiative; they fought better together. Here and there an aggressive Soviet fighter pilot was encountered and a number took the sometimes suicidal course of ramming (the Soviet Air Forces recorded 270 *tarans*, or rams, during the course of the war). But the rank and file seemed reluctant to engage German bombers closely and broke off their attack too soon. They failed to stop the Stukas. When attacked by German fighters they went into the defensive circling manoeuvre learned in the Spanish Civil War, and they tried to escape at low level. But by 1944 the steadily improving qualities of Soviet fighter pilots and their equipment, and their crushing numerical superiority, had gained them command of the air over the whole front.

Early in the Pacific war the Japanese also flew the traditional three-fighter formation, known to them as a *Shotai*, and flew them in vics, in echelons, or in a loose, staggered trail; and, as was common practice elsewhere, they weaved in the air to check behind them. *Chennault's Flying Tigers (see AMERICAN VOLUNTEER GROUP) used the 'section and stinger' formation against the Japanese whose vics could be more easily lured into combat against a two-aircraft section, and they were then 'bounced' by the 'stinger' hiding above. By the end of 1943, however, and flying a new generation of fighters such as the Shoki (codenamed TOJO by the Americans), the Japanese Army Air Force had adopted the 'finger-four'.

The Japanese Navy's Zero fighter had an infinitely superior performance to its early opponent, the US Wildcat, and US pilots, who had already adopted the 'finger-four', had to rely on teamwork to survive. During the *Guadalcanal campaign a US Navy pilot, Lt-Cdr John Thach, flew two pairs of fighters abreast, the pairs being separated by about 365 m. (400 yd.). Each pair looked out for the other. When an attack was made on one pair the other pair broke towards them to engage, and the pair being attacked broke towards the pair protecting them (see Figure 2). This scissors effect, or Thach Weave as it came to be called, meant the attacking Zero was faced with a head-on attack or was forced to break off his own attack in a straight line which gave the inferior Wildcats a chance to shoot it down.

As the Americans gained the ascendancy in the air war, Japanese fighter pilots staged fake dogfights to lure Allied aircraft to break formation, or performed aerobatics to distract the attention of Allied pilots while an attack was put in from another direction. Towards the end of the war when American superiority became overwhelming the Japanese formed *Taitari* (ramming) units as the only means of countering US B29 superfortresses engaged in the strategic air offensive against their country.

In Europe the Luftwaffe introduced new fighter tactics to counter the USAAF's daylight raids and those mounted by RAF Bomber Command at night (see also WILDE SAU and ZAHME SAU). Against the RAF they included the *von*

Fighters, Figure 2: Thach Weave

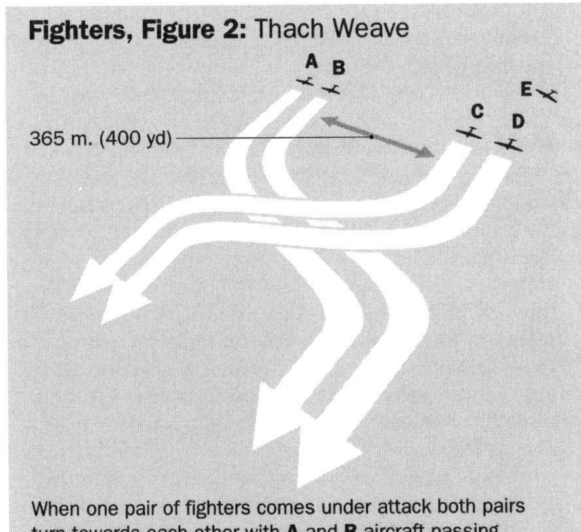

When one pair of fighters comes under attack both pairs turn towards each other with **A** and **B** aircraft passing beneath **C** and **D**. By performing this scissors tactic the attacking Japanese aircraft **E** was left with two choices: he could follow his intended victims as thay broke right, which meant he would be vulnerable to an attack by the other two fighters, or he could break off his attack. If the latter the US fighters simply resumed their original course with the positions of the two sections reversed.

Source: Spick, M., *Fighter Tactics* (London, 1983).

unten hinten (from under and behind) and the *schraüge Musik* (slanting jazz music) which were used after an initial contact with a bomber had been made by radar. In the first the fighter approached from beneath and behind; in the second a fighter, specially armed with upward-firing cannon mounted in the roof of its cockpit, was used. In both the fighters were able to rake unseen the bomber's vulnerable belly, a form of attack which caused heavy Allied casualties during the *Nuremberg raid of March 1944.

By trying to prove the soundness of their long-held doctrine of using heavily armed but unescorted bombers, the Americans suffered some appalling losses during 1943. But once this doctrine had been abandoned and the long-range Mustang fighter was operational the Luftwaffe were faced with insuperable problems. Their more formidable twin-engined fighters could destroy the US bombers but were no match for the more manoeuvrable American fighters; while the lighter German fighters, capable of dogfighting the US escorts, lacked the fire-power to destroy the bombers. One answer was the heavily armed, and heavily armoured, version of the Focke-Wulfe 190 fighter, nicknamed the *Sturmbock* (battering ram). These engaged the US bombers from behind at close range and rammed them as a last resort. They were used in a *Gruppe* of three *Staffeln* of twelve aircraft each, escorted by more than sixty specially adapted, lighter fighters. These *Gefechtsverbände* (battle formations) inflicted some severe losses, but American numerical superiority eventually won the day and by January 1945 they had practically ceased to operate. By then the German jet fighter, the Me262, was operational and its speed (870 km/h or 540 mph) made it all but immune to attack. It attacked in the old tight vic, or *Kette*, by diving at top speed through the fighter screen and continued under the bomber formation before climbing back up to attack it from behind. Allied fighter pilots had no adequate tactic against the Me262 except to 'bounce' it, catch it taking off or landing, or involve it in a dogfight where its poor rate of turn made it vulnerable. But the Germans had too few of them and they became operational far too late to have any effect on the war in the air. JOHNNIE JOHNSON

Green, W., *Famous Fighters of the Second World War*, Vols. 1 and 2 (London, 1957).
— *Warplanes of the Second World War: Fighters*, Vols. 1–4 (London, 1961).
Johnson, J. E., *Full Circle* (London, 1964).
Robertson, B., *Spitfire—The Story of a Famous Fighter* (Letchworth, Herts, 1960).

Fight For Freedom, organization formed in April 1941 to mobilize American public opinion for intervention in the European war. Fight For Freedom Inc. (FFF) advocated a more positive programme of intervention than the *Committee to Defend America by Aiding the Allies, from which it broke away. FFF did not specifically call for a declaration of war, but it urged repeal of all *neutrality laws, authorization for the navy to attack German submarines, and legislation to allow US troops to be sent overseas. Although it never rivalled in its short existence before *Pearl Harbor the growth and mass membership of the Committee to Defend America or *America First, FFF reflected the growing militancy of a significant portion of American élite opinion. WALDO HEINRICHS

Fiji, a British Pacific islands colony, was used as a base for New Zealand and US troops. Out of a population of about 220,000, then divided almost equally between indigenous and Indian Fijians, some 11,000 men served in the armed forces during the *Pacific war. At peak strength they numbered 8,513 (6,371 indigenous Fijians; 1,878 Europeans, including 808 New Zealanders; and 254 Indian Fijians). The indigenous Fijians raised three infantry battalions, two of which garrisoned *Guadalcanal and other Solomon islands, and they fought on *Bougainville with distinction. Fijians, along with men from Tonga and the Solomons, were also members of First Commando Fiji Guerrillas which fought in the *New Guinea campaign with the Americans, who knew them as the South Pacific Scouts.

films, see in culture section of major powers; see also HOLLYWOOD, SUBVERSIVE WARFARE, and WAR PHOTOGRAPHERS.

Final Solution (*Endlösung*), was the term used for the murder of six million Jews during the Second World War. These Jews were citizens of every pre-war state in Europe. Their Jewishness had been defined by the German Nuremberg Laws of 1935 as any person with one Jewish grandparent. Many were Jews only by the Nazi definition; in their own eyes they were Germans, Frenchmen, Belgians, Dutchmen, and so on. A number had been practising Christians for several generations.

When Hitler came to power in 1933 the Jews under German control numbered just over half a million. Hitler and his Nazi Party were pledged to create a Germany in which the German Jews would be set apart from their fellow-Germans, and denied their place as an integral part of German life and culture. The concept of racial purity was paralleled with the stimulation of racial hatred, to create the image of the German Jew as different, alien, and dangerous.

The first measure based upon this *Nazi ideology was the expulsion of German Jews from many hundreds of villages and small towns in which they lived and worked, and in which their ancestors had lived for many centuries; the first record of Jews in the Rhineland precedes the Hitler era by more than a thousand years. This first solution of what the Nazis called the 'Jewish Question' (Judenfrage) was to make hundreds of municipalities 'Jew-free' (Judenrein). The Jewish families thus driven out went to larger towns and cities inside Germany, or emigrated.

Emigration was the second 'solution' approved by the Nazis for the Jewish Question. From 1933 until the outbreak of war in 1939, the official policy of the German government permitted, and even encouraged, emigration (see Map 32). The property of the Jews who left, their shops, their livelihoods, their homes and their furniture, became part of the spoils of racism. Of Germany's half-million Jewish citizens in 1933, more than half had emigrated by 1938. Of these, more than 100,000 found refuge in the USA, 63,000 in Argentina, 52,000 in the UK, and 33,000 in Palestine.

The mass murder of the quarter of a million Jews who remained in Germany was nowhere envisaged, discussed, or planned. Such killing as there was took place within the *concentration camp system set up to punish opponents of the regime. In the years 1933 to 1938 fewer than a hundred Jews were among several thousand German citizens murdered in concentration camps (principally at *Sachsenhausen, *Buchenwald, and *Dachau).

With the annexation of Austria in March 1938 and of Bohemia and Moravia in March 1939 (see CZECHOSLOVAKIA) the number of Jews under German rule increased by another quarter of a million. Still there was no policy of mass murder. Such violence as there was remained on a relatively small scale. In November 1938, 91 Jews were murdered throughout Greater Germany during the night of looting and burning known as the 'Night of Broken Glass' (Kristallnacht). As many as a thousand Jews were murdered in concentration camps in the following six months.

In the eyes of the German government, the 'solution' to the increased number of Jews within the Reich remained emigration. More than 100,000 of Austria's 160,000 Jews now emigrated; most of them to the UK, the USA, and Palestine, to which they took their talent in many professions, including *scientists, doctors, writers, and musicians.

Emigration depended not only on the German willingness to let Jews leave, but also on the willingness of other states to take them in. Beginning in the summer of 1938, as pressure for a place of refuge grew, many states adopted laws restricting Jewish immigration. Another problem for the Jews who left Germany was that they could not know which countries would remain safe; the tens of thousands of Jews who found refuge in France, Belgium, and the Netherlands, for example (as did the German-Jewish girl Anne *Frank and her family), could not know that the countries which took them in would, in due course, be overrun by Germany.

With the German invasion of Poland in September 1939 (see POLISH CAMPAIGN), a further million and a half Jews came under German rule. During the murder in the streets of more than 10,000 Polish civilians in September and October 1939, an orgy of slaughter unprecedented in Europe in the 20th century, 3,000 Polish Jews were among those killed; some of them were forced into synagogues and then burnt alive. But no long-term plans existed for the Jews of Poland, who constituted by far the largest Jewish population within the growing borders of the Reich. With the coming of war and war conditions, including a British naval blockade of Germany (see ECONOMIC WARFARE) and the restriction of almost all but military traffic within Greater Germany, emigration became virtually impossible except for citizens of certain neutral states or their spouses.

Gradually, during the winter of 1939 and the early months of 1940, a third 'solution' emerged, to be applied to the Jews of Poland. They would be expelled from several thousand localities in which they had lived hitherto, and made to live in restricted areas. A medieval concept, that of the *ghetto, was revived. But whereas in medieval times the ghetto, such as the one in Venice, was a centre of Jewish creativity, under the Nazi scheme it was a place of confinement and poverty.

From the spring of 1940 Jews throughout German-occupied and annexed Poland were driven out of the towns and villages in which they had lived for centuries, and sent to specially-designated areas in certain towns. They were also driven out of many parts of the principal cities, such as Warsaw and Łódź, in which they had lived hitherto, and were forced into an area which was too small for their numbers, often lacking adequate sanitary facilities, and deliberately so. The food ration imposed upon them was even smaller than that imposed upon the non-Jewish inhabitants of Poland. Anyone trying to leave

31. **Final Solution**: Sites of death and concentration camps, and estimated numbers murdered from each country

Final Solution

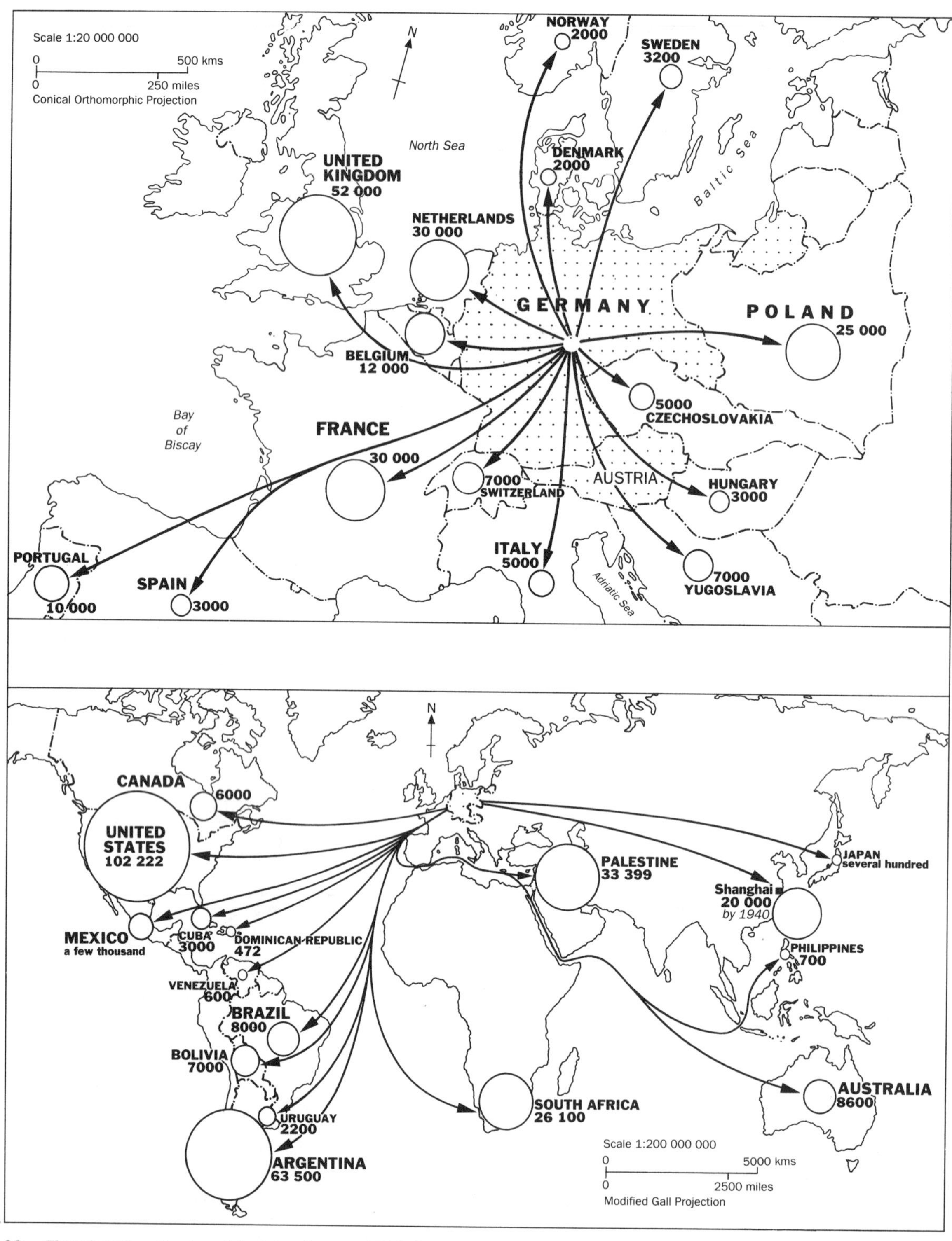

32. **Final Solution**: Exodus of Jewish refugees, 1933–8

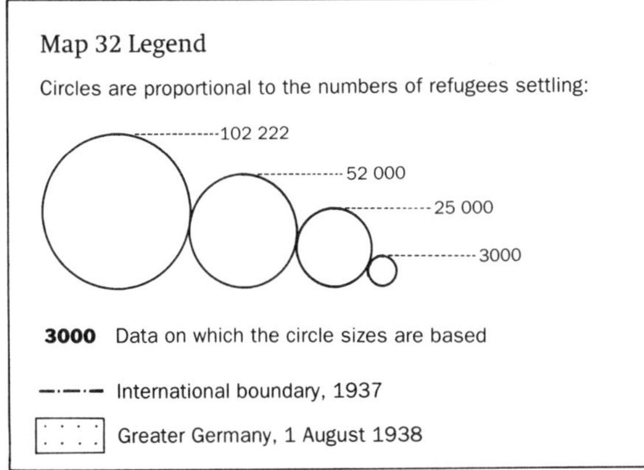

the ghetto, or trying to smuggle food into the ghetto, faced execution.

By April 1941 ghettos had been enforced throughout German-occupied Poland. By June the death toll from starvation had reached 2,000 a month in the Warsaw Ghetto (where half a million Jews were confined), and 800 a month in the Łódź Ghetto (where a quarter of a million were confined). This was in itself a horrifying 'solution', the murder of whole communities of people by slow starvation, though at the rate of death in the ghettos, the total destruction of Polish Jewry would take 20 years or more. No other solution was then in prospect. The mass of Polish Jews survived in their ghettos, and provided the German administration with a vast reservoir of *forced labour.

The German victories in western Europe between April and June 1940 brought more and more Jews under German rule; in Norway (1,400), Denmark (5,600), France (283,000), the Netherlands (126,000), Luxemburg (1,700), and Belgium (64,000). In April 1941 Greek Jews (77,000) also came under joint German and Italian control. These western European and Balkan Jews were subjected to civic disabilities, and obliged to wear a yellow badge on their clothing to identify them (another medieval practice revived). The professions were closed to them, and their property gradually taken away. But their lives were safe; indeed, a few could still emigrate, and did so; others were able to flee for safety to neutral Switzerland, Spain, Portugal, and Turkey.

In June 1941 the German Army invaded the Soviet Union (see BARBAROSSA). Immediately following the troops were special killing squads or **Einsatzgruppen*, whose orders were to murder Jews in every locality. This was the fourth 'solution' after expulsion, emigration, and ghettoization. It led, within six months, to the murder of as many as a million Jews. The aim of the killing squads was to eliminate Jewish life altogether. In hundreds of small villages in what, up to 1939, had been eastern Poland, Lithuania, Latvia, and Estonia, and in western Russia, this destructive aim was fulfilled within a few hours. The killing was made easier by the active participation of local police and para-military groups, especially in Lithuania and the Ukraine. In Bessarabia, Moldavia, and parts of southern Russia, the killing was carried out by Romanians.

In cities with large Jewish populations, thousands were murdered within a few days; at Kiev, a total of 33,000 Jewish men, women, and children were killed in three days, having been taken to Babi Yar, a ravine on the outskirts of the city, and machine-gunned. Tens of thousands of Jews were shot down in ditches, gravel pits, and fields near every town and village in the vast area through which the Germans advanced in the summer and autumn of 1941.

These killing places, some of them pre-war beauty spots, quickly became synonymous with mass murder: Ponar near *Wilno, Kaiserwald near Riga, the Ninth Fort at Kovno, the Ratomskaya ravine at Minsk, and the Drobitsky ravine at Kharkov were five of the most terrible. Other cities with large Jewish populations, such as Kishinev and Odessa, were likewise the scene of massive slaughter.

By October 1941 each of the four 'solutions' so far put into practice was still in effect. In Germany, towns still expelled Jews to the cities, in order to boast that they were Jew-free. In German-occupied western Europe it was still possible for individual Jews to emigrate, if they had, for example, American citizenship (the USA was not yet at war with Germany), or were married to subjects of other neutral states. In German-occupied Poland, more than two million Jews were still confined to ghettos, many of them forced to work in factories manufacturing clothing for the German Army. In former Czechoslovakia, a so-called 'model' ghetto was established, on 10 October 1941, in the 18th-century fortress at *Theresienstadt. Jews were deported there from Prague, Brno, and several hundred other towns and villages in Bohemia and Moravia.

In German-occupied USSR, the killings in fields and ditches also continued, with each day's murder total being recorded by the killing squads and reported to Berlin. On 24 October 1941, for example, 4,000 Jews were taken from Wilno to Ponar and murdered there during the following three days; according to the precise statistics submitted by the killing squad as a matter of routine to Berlin, the murdered Jews included 885 *children.

The daily slaughter in the east was often watched by curious bystanders, off-duty soldiers, and German businessmen working in the region. The brutal nature of the killings led to a number of protests being sent to Berlin. One protest, dated 27 October, was forwarded to Berlin by Wilhelm Kube, the commissioner-general of Belorussia (whose headquarters were in Minsk) with the comment 'To have buried alive seriously wounded people, who then worked their way out of their graves again, is such extreme beastliness that this incident must be reported to the Führer.'

Even as these protests reached Berlin, a fifth solution was under discussion there. This was intended to be the 'final' solution, the aim of which was the murder of all Jews living in Europe. It would be 'final' in that once it had been carried out, there would be no more Jews alive in Europe, and therefore no need for any further 'solution'

Since the German annexation of Austria in March 1938, the bureaucratic aspects of the emigration of Jews had been entrusted to a small government department in Berlin, the 'Central Office for Jewish Emigration', headed by an *SS officer, Adolf *Eichmann. In the autumn of 1941, Eichmann was put in charge of a new department, the 'Race and Resettlement Office', a section of the *RSHA's Amt IV, and was entrusted with the task of preparing the mechanics of the final solution. In an official letter to the German foreign office about an emigration application from a Jewish woman who wished to move from Germany to the unoccupied zone of France, he explained (on 28 October 1941) that the application had to be turned down 'in view of the approaching final solution of the European Jewry problem'

Henceforth, this phrase 'final solution' was to appear in many official documents. The 'solution' itself was as follows: Jews living throughout Europe, whether confined in the Polish ghettos or still living in their own homes in western Europe, were to be rounded up (wherever possible this was to be done by French, Dutch, Belgian, or other local police), detained locally in special holding camps, and then deported by train to distant camps in which they would be murdered by gas. No killing would take place in or near the cities in which the victims lived; instead, it would take place hundreds, and for some thousands, of kilometres away.

During the autumn of 1941 experiments were made on Soviet *prisoners-of-war, and also on Jews, to find out the most expeditious method of murder by gas; the one in which the victims would have the least warning, if any, and in which the least number of operatives would be needed. Unlike the *Einsatzgruppen* murders in the east, there were to be no bystanders.

Central to this plan were the elements of secrecy and deception. 'Deportation' was to be called 'resettlement'. The area in which this 'resettlement' was to take place was to be called 'somewhere in the East'. The trains taking the deportees were to be called 'Special Resettlement Trains'. The nature of the camps was to be kept secret, even from those who had to drive the trains to within a few kilometres of them.

Two methods of mass murder were devised. The first was by means of gas vans in which the deportees would be taken as if on a journey to a labour camp, but would in fact be killed by exhaust fumes during the short drive from the station to the camp itself. The second was by means of specially-designed gas chambers, into which they would be taken as if for a shower, and inside which, once the doors were locked, they would be killed by gas (see ZYKLON-B). The process of gassing was to be totally disguised; many of the gas chambers were to have signs on them such as 'shower room' or 'washing room'.

The camp sites chosen for the reception and murder of the deported Jews were in remote areas, four in German-occupied Poland and one in occupied USSR. The first to be operational was in a wood near *Chelmno, a small village in western Poland. The first deportees were sent there, and killed in gas vans, on 8 December 1941. On that day 2,300 Jews were murdered at Chelmno. In the coming months, at least a thousand were killed each day, most of them brought by train from the Łódź Ghetto and the towns around Łódź, until as many as 400,000 had been killed.

On 20 January 1942, six weeks after the start of the daily deportations and gassings at Chelmno, a group of senior German civil servants gathered at a villa near Berlin, in the suburb of Wannsee, to co-ordinate the activities of the various government departments, including the state railways, the foreign office and the 'Race and Resettlement Office', all of whose active co-operation was needed to carry out the deportation of Jews from throughout Europe. Statistics were prepared for the *Wannsee conference by Eichmann, giving the number of Jews whom it was hoped would be rounded up and deported. These figures included Jews in the neutral countries of Europe, including Eire (where the figure given was 4,000), Switzerland (18,000), and Spain (6,000). Also included on the Wannsee list were the Jews of Britain, estimated by Eichmann at 330,000. All were to be brought into the net of deportation and destruction.

Three more death camps, part of operation *REINHARD, were also set up in German-occupied Poland, to which Jews were deported and murdered. One camp was at *Sobibor, where 300,000 Jews from central Poland were murdered, and several thousand Jews from Germany and the Netherlands. Another camp was at *Belzec, where, beginning in March 1942, 600,000 Jews from western and eastern Galicia, including Cracow and Lwów, were murdered, as well as 1,500 Poles, killed for trying to help Jews. The third camp was at *Treblinka, where at least 700,000 Polish Jews were murdered, including half a million from the Warsaw Ghetto, from which the first deportations took place on 22 July 1942. Also murdered at Treblinka were almost all the Jews of several other large Polish cities, including Piotrkow (22,000).

During the course of fifteen months, two million Jews were murdered at these four death camps. A further million had been murdered by the *Einsatzgruppen* in the east. As a result of this systematic killing, the Jewish populations of Poland, the Baltic States, and the USSR as far east as the Caucasus, had been almost entirely destroyed by the beginning of 1943. The few Jews still alive in those regions worked in *forced-labour camps, at specific tasks needed by the German Army.

The Final Solution, so effective in the east, was also intended to include all the Jews of western Europe. Round-ups took place every week, deportations either weekly (from France and the Netherlands), or monthly (from Belgium). All those who were rounded up were deported by train to the east. Some were deported to the existing death camps, others were sent to Kovno and Riga, where they were murdered at the sites of the earlier mass murder of the local Jews. At Riga, gas vans were used.

Among the Jews deported to Treblinka and murdered were 8,000 from Theresienstadt and 12,000 from 23 Balkan Jewish communities in distant Macedonia and Thrace; they traced their origins to the expulsion of the Jews from Spain in 1492. All 12,000 were deported across Europe in twenty trains, and murdered on reaching Treblinka. Other Jews, possibly as many as 250,000, and including 22,000 from Theresienstadt, were deported from western Europe to Maly Trostenets, a small village outside the Belorussian city of Minsk, where they were killed in gas vans similar to those used at Chelmno and Riga. Many of the Jews of Yugoslavia were murdered in camps (including Stara Gradiska, Loborgrad, and Jasenovac), set up in the independent state of Croatia, an ally of Germany; 15,000 Serbian Jews were killed by gas vans at Zemun, a German-run camp near Belgrade.

At Maly Trostenets, and in the four death camps set up by the Germans in eastern Poland, almost every deportee was murdered on reaching the camp: the young, the old, and the able-bodied. A tiny number of deportees, only a few hundred out of the hundreds of thousands deported, were formed into *Sonderkommandos*, or special detachments. They were kept in a special section of each camp, under heavy guard, and forced to take the bodies of those killed to pits where they were buried or burned; or to sort out the clothes of those who had been murdered for shipment back to Germany. These slave-labourers were then murdered in their turn.

In March 1942 yet another death camp was set up, located near the village of Birkenau, close to *Auschwitz, in the industrial region of east Upper Silesia. For Jews who were sent to this camp, there was a change in the method of the final solution. The region, rich in coal, was part of German-annexed Poland. Several hundred German factories had been relocated here; they, and the existing coal mines, required slave labour on a substantial scale. Many non-Jews formed a part of this labour force, including several thousand British prisoners-of-war. But the need for even more manpower had become urgent, as Germany approached its third year at war, and had still failed either to conquer the USSR or to invade the UK.

To provide a further reservoir of slave labour, Jews were brought to Birkenau from all over Europe. Unlike the murder system already in operation at the existing death camps, not every deportee to Birkenau was murdered. While all children, all old people, and the sick, were taken from the deportation trains and sent straight to the gas chambers, several hundred able-bodied men and women from each deportation train (sometimes as many as 500 in a train with a thousand deportees) were separated from those about to be killed, and had a serial number tattooed on their forearm; at least in the short term their lives were spared; they were sent to barracks from which they would go each day to their slave labour tasks.

The camp at Birkenau consisted of a large area of wooden huts and brick barracks, and two (later four) gas chambers, attached to which were crematoria in which the bodies of those murdered were burned almost at once. Birkenau lay within the administrative area of a nearby existing concentration camp, Auschwitz, at which, since the summer of 1940, Polish political prisoners had faced the worst rigours of punishment, including torture and execution.

Some Polish Jews had already been among the victims at Auschwitz. But Birkenau was established for Jews alone, and with a view to continuing the Final Solution, already so effective elsewhere, by the murder of at least half of those who arrived in each deportation train. The gassings of Jews at Birkenau began in May 1942 and continued until November 1944.

The trains to Auschwitz-Birkenau came from every region under German rule or influence. Usually there were a thousand deportees in each train. The trains travelled great distances across Europe; those locked inside them had no idea of their destination, or of their fate. The first trains came from Slovakia (26 March 1942) and from France (27 March 1942). In both instances, local police, Slovak and French, carried out the task of rounding up Jews, assembling them, and putting them on the trains. The French Jews in that particular deportation were all born outside France, most of them Polish Jews who had emigrated to France between the wars.

During two and a half years, without respite or interruption, trains brought Jews to Auschwitz-Birkenau from as far north as Norway, as far west as the Atlantic coast of France, as far south as Rome, Corfu, and Athens, as far east as Transylvania and Ruthenia. Among the large Jewish communities murdered almost in their entirety at Birkenau were those of the Greek city of Salonika (more than 40,000 murdered), the Polish city of Białystok (more than 10,000), the Greek island of Corfu (1,800), and the Aegean island of Rhodes (1,700). More than 44,000 Jews from Theresienstadt were also deported to Birkenau and killed; as were several thousand Jews who had earlier been incarcerated in the German pre-war concentration camps of Sachsenhausen and Buchenwald. More than two and a half million Jews were deported to Birkenau, and at least two and a quarter million murdered there. In addition to those taken straight from the trains to the gas chambers, at least three-quarters of the slave labourers were among the victims, toiled to death, killed by sadistic guards, or sent to the gas chambers when they fell sick.

The aim of the Final Solution was to murder all the Jews of Europe. In this it failed, despite the terrifyingly high death toll. In June 1944 the Anglo-American forces landed in Normandy (see OVERLORD), and the Red Army was on the border of eastern Galicia. Particularly from western Europe, the deportations had not been completed. From France, 83,000 Jews had been deported and murdered, but 200,000 were still alive, many of them sheltered from deportation by their fellow French citizens. From Italy, 8,000 Jews had been deported to their deaths, but 35,000 were still in Italy at the end of the war, and thus survived. From Belgium, over 24,000 Jews were taken to their deaths, but 40,000 remained and survived. Elsewhere, the ratio of survivors to those murdered was much worse. Only 20,000 Dutch Jews remained undeported; 106,000 were deported and killed. Of Yugoslavia's Jews, 60,000 were killed, and only 12,000 survived. From Greece, 65,000 were taken to their deaths, and only 12,000 survived.

Details of the killings of Jews reached the West only in fragments (see KARSKI and NOWAK, for example). Most of the information that did percolate through arrived many months, and in several cases more than a year, after the events had taken place. Publicity was given to the details as they emerged, but publicity could not halt the killings, which were taking place deep in the heartland of German-occupied Europe, far beyond the range of Allied bombers, and almost three years before the Allied armies were able to advance into central Europe. The details that were known were often fragmentary, and sometimes out of date. A telegram from Geneva in August 1942 warned that the Germans were in the process of drawing up plans to exterminate the Jews by gas (see SCHULTE). In fact, those plans had already been in operation for eight months.

In the autumn of 1942 news of the deportations from France was widely publicized in the British newspapers, and universally denounced. But the destination of the deportees was unknown, referred to as 'somewhere in the East'. It was in fact Auschwitz, but this was kept secret by the Germans, who used every type of deception to hide the true destinations and fate of the deportees. Details of the killing of Jews at Auschwitz II (Birkenau) did not reach Geneva, London, and New York until the summer of 1944, a full two years after the killings had begun. International protest against the deportation and killing of Hungarian Jews was then effective, but only because the tide of war had turned, and Allied aircraft could at last reach Budapest. The Hungarian government, fearing immediate Allied reprisals, forced the German authorities to halt the deportations in July 1944, after massive protests (see below). Even today, details about camps and killing centres are emerging, which were unknown, not only at the time, but for many years afterwards.

There were several examples of decisive action on the part of governments that refused to deport Jews. All 50,000 Bulgarian Jews survived the war because King Boris and the Bulgarian parliament refused the German request to send them to the camps in Poland. In Denmark, with the encouragement of King Frederik IX (1899–1972) almost all 5,500 Jews were taken during a single night by small boats across the narrow water to neutral Sweden, and safety. After the first fifteen deportees from Finland had been murdered, the Finnish government rejected all German pressure to deport the remaining 2,000 Jews, many of whom were refugees from Germany and Central Europe.

Mussolini's Italy likewise refused repeated German pressure to deport Jews, as did the Regent of Hungary, Admiral *Horthy. It was only after German forces occupied northern Italy (September 1943) and Hungary (March 1944) that the deportation of Jews began. After 400,000 Jews had been deported to their deaths from Hungary to Auschwitz-Birkenau, within the space of three months, Horthy, under pressure from Pope *Pius XII, from King Gustav V of Sweden (1858–1950), and from the western Allies, demanded a halt to any further deportations. More than 300,000 Hungarian Jews were thereby saved; though several thousand were subsequently murdered by Hungarian Fascist gangs such as the Arrow Cross (see HUNGARY, 3), others were saved from the gangs by the intervention of several foreign diplomats in Budapest, including the senior Swedish representative in the city, Raoul *Wallenberg.

Like each of the captive peoples of Europe, the Jews were subjected to all the rigours of occupation, as well as the total isolation imposed on the ghettos. Nevertheless, their resistance to deportation was widespread. Best known is the *Warsaw rising of April 1943. Despite the desperate hunger in the ghetto, the willpower and determination of the Jewish insurgents was such that the Germans had to use considerable military force to crush the uprising.

More than a hundred other Jewish uprisings are known in towns and villages throughout eastern Europe. There were also acts of defiance in every death camp. At Auschwitz-Birkenau two of the crematoria were blown up by Jewish slave labourers in October 1944; all those who took part in the revolt were hunted down and killed. Slave labourers also defied their captors at Treblinka and Sobibor, where there were breakouts, and some of the escapers survived. Other Jews managed to escape from the ghettos into the forests, and to join, and even to form, partisan units, harassing German lines of communication, and trying to protect small groups of women and children who had also escaped. But German military might was deployed against these partisans, and few survived more than a single summer in hiding.

Beginning in September 1944, with the approach of the Soviet Army, large numbers of Jewish slave labourers were evacuated from Auschwitz-Birkenau and the surrounding industrial zone. Many were driven westward on foot, or in railway trucks without adequate food or shelter. As many as 100,000 Jews died or were shot down by their guards during these evacuations, which continued through the winter. The marchers were sent to central Germany, to build and to work in vast underground factories, and at other slave labour projects intended to help halt the advance of the western Allies, who by January 1945 had reached the Rhine. Many of those on the death marches were toiled and beaten to death in these factories and the camps attached to them (one of the most notorious was Mittelbau-*Dora). Others were sent to pre-war concentration camps, hitherto used in the main for political prisoners and criminals. In these camps they were the object of sadistic cruelty and neglect.

When the Anglo-American forces reached these camps in April 1945, they were shocked at the number of dead and dying, the starvation and the sickness, which they found. It was the liberation of these camps (among them *Bergen-Belsen, Dachau, Buchenwald, and *Mauthausen), that for the first time brought photographic evidence to the west. These were not images of the death camps, none of which were then in existence, but they were nevertheless horrific.

An estimated 300,000 European Jews survived the camps and death marches. Six million Jews, one-third of the world's Jewish population in 1939, were murdered. Most of the survivors left Europe for the USA, South America, Canada, Australia, the UK, and Palestine. There they sought to rebuild their lives, learn new languages, start new families, and live with the continuing torment of the memory of mass murder, and the destruction of their own loved ones and communities.

In many countries, museums and memorials have been set up to remember the victims of the Final Solution, which is known in Yiddish as the Destruction (*Churban*), in Hebrew as the Catastrophe (*Shoah*), and, more generally, as the Holocaust. Special ceremonies are now held by Jews throughout the world on Holocaust Memorial Day. The anniversaries of *Kristallnacht*, and of the Warsaw Ghetto uprising, are also widely commemorated.

In the immediate aftermath of the war, several dozen camp commandants and functionaries were executed, some on the spot, others after trials. Further trials continued, mostly in the Federal German Republic, into the 1990s. In 1988, legislation was passed in Canada and Australia to bring to trial perpetrators of mass murder; in 1991 the British parliament approved similar legislation. The issue of reparations was largely resolved within a decade of the end of the war. On 10 September 1952, in Luxemburg City Hall, Israel and West Germany (both of them states which had been created after the war) signed the Luxemburg Treaty, under which the West German government agreed to pay substantial sums of money both to Israel and to Jewish organizations, as reparation for 'material damage' suffered by the Jews at the hands of the Nazis. Communist East Germany refused to participate in this agreement, but in 1990 the newly-established non-communist government of East Germany (subsequently merged with that of West Germany) agreed in principle to the payment of reparations to surviving Jewish victims of Nazi persecution.

Several thousand Jews were saved from deportation and death by non-Jews who, at the risk of their own lives, hid and helped them. On 19 August 1953 the Israeli parliament passed a law making it the duty of the State of Israel to recognize the work done by non-Jews in saving Jewish lives during the war. An expression of honour, 'Righteous among the Nations', was awarded, in the name of the Jewish people, to every non-Jewish person or family who had risked their lives to save Jews. Evidence of such action has to come initially from one of those who were actually saved. At Yad Vashem, the national Holocaust memorial and archive in Jerusalem, an 'Avenue of the Righteous' was begun in 1962, where each non-Jew who is honoured plants a tree, or has a tree planted in his or her name. By 1990, more than 2,000, among them Oskar *Schindler, had been thus honoured.

A substantial literature about the Final Solution exists, much of it published in the 1980s, and in large part the testimony of survivors. Several ghetto diaries and chronicles have been found and published, including the mass of material assembled in the Warsaw Ghetto by the historian Emanuel *Ringelblum and his circle, all of whom perished during the war. Further volumes of the recollections of survivors are published every few days; each one adds something to our existing knowledge of the fate of an estimated ten thousand Jewish communities throughout Europe, whose lives, and also whose life and culture, was destroyed between 1939 and 1945.

MARTIN GILBERT

Dobroszycki, L. (ed.), *The Chronicle of the Lodz Ghetto, 1941–1944* (New Haven, 1984).
Gilbert, M., *Atlas of the Holocaust* (rev. edn., London, 1993).
—*Auschwitz and the Allies* (rev. edn., London, 1991).
—*The Holocaust, The Jewish Tragedy* (rev. edn., London, 1988).

Finland, which had gained independence from the Russian Empire in 1917, was engaged in the Second World War from November 1939, when attacked by the USSR (see FINNISH–SOVIET WAR) to March 1940, and from June 1941, when it joined the Germans to invade the USSR (see BARBAROSSA), to the *armistice of September 1944. Finland then fought another campaign until April 1945 to drive the Germans out of northern Finland.

The Finns fought the Soviet invasion of 30 November 1939 united in defence of their freedom and believing in the rightness of their cause. Political, social, and linguistic divisions were submerged in what was known as the 'Winter War', as exemplified by co-operation between the right-wing Civil Guard and the socialists and between trade unions and employers. High morale left the nation unprepared for the harsh territorial losses of the Peace of Moscow of 12 March 1940; bitterness was widespread. Intense Soviet pressure and painful adjustments marked the period March 1940–June 1941. Fears of a Soviet take-over were increased by popular unrest provoked by the Finnish–Soviet Peace and Friendship Society, eventually banned by the government in December 1940 when Risto *Ryti became president, a post he held until replaced by Marshal *Mannerheim in August 1944. Isolation and fear contributed to the government's decision to join Germany and on 26 June 1941 it announced that the USSR had commenced operations against Finland, but this new 'Continuation (of the Winter) War' failed to arouse mass enthusiasm despite conviction of the injustice of the Peace of Moscow.

The right seized the opportunity to crush Bolshevism and annex Soviet eastern Karelia, but the social democrats distanced themselves from an occupation policy designed to further a Greater Finland. Parliamentary influence on government declined during the war period. *Censorship and emphasis on German might made the likelihood of eventual German defeat difficult to accept even by some political leaders; open advocates of peace were characterized as unpatriotic. Yet the strain of protracted war and economic hardship caused considerable war-weariness which made even the severe armistice of 19 September 1944 generally acceptable.

Finland was economically ill-prepared for war in 1939 with slender stocks of essential supplies. Rationing was controlled by the ministry of public welfare, established in September 1939. Only coffee and sugar were rationed during the Winter War but grain, butter, milk, and meat followed in 1940, and potatoes and tobacco in mid-1942. Rations were lowest in the autumn of 1942: 150 gr. (5 oz.) of fats and 200–300 gr. of meat a month, with manual workers getting 250–425 gr. of flour a day; a light worker received 1,000 calories daily and a heavy worker 2,000 calories. Unrationed food and allotment produce provided essential supplementation. A black market, absent during the Winter War, flourished later despite heavy penalties. Substitutes were introduced, but real coffee was acutely missed. Textiles and leather goods disappeared and clothes and shoes made of substitute materials quickly wore out.

About 100,000 Finns were evacuated from border areas of Karelia before the Winter War. All Finns left the areas ceded to the Soviet Union and 430,000 people, over half from farms, had to be resettled in March 1940. The Rapid Resettlement Law of June 1940 aimed to create 35,000 farms by expropriating land already under cultivation. About 275,000 refugees returned to Karelia from 1942 after its reconquest, but had to flee again in 1944. The number of displaced persons then reached 450,000.

Resettlement, relief, and defence caused a massive rise in state expenditure just when important customs revenues collapsed. Additional income tax and new property, wealth, and turnover taxes were imposed; there were voluntary and compulsory loans. But taxation never covered more than 70% of state expenditure and currency issue fed inflation despite high taxation.

Prices were uncontrolled until October 1940 apart from rationed foods, causing suffering to agricultural producers. Rents were controlled from summer 1940. Wage control began in February 1941, the permitted average increase being two-thirds of the rise in the cost of living. Those on the lowest incomes maintained their position best. Compulsory labour service began in October 1939 and was extended in 1942, but skilled labour was scarce. Strikes were prohibited in May 1941.

The war transformed the structure of Finnish trade and reduced its value by two-thirds. The important British market for timber was cut off. From 1941 Germany and German-occupied countries absorbed 80% of Finnish exports (notably copper, nickel, and timber) and provided 85% of imports (chiefly grain, fuel, fertilizers, and war materials). Lost farms, poor summers, and shortage of labour and fertilizers reduced grain production to two-thirds of its pre-war level. Dependence on Germany for grain and fuel complicated withdrawal from the war.

The Second World War reduced the size of Finland by 12%. Growth in the population (3,620,000 in 1938) was checked: 89,000 military personnel and 2,700 civilians were killed. Austerity continued. Nevertheless, there was no Soviet occupation. Finland's political and administrative institutions and social and economic system survived. Independence, for which the country had fought, was saved. J. E. O. Screen

Kirby, D. G., *Finland in the Twentieth Century* (London, 1979).

Finnish–Soviet war, also known as the 'Winter War', was a direct consequence of the *Nazi–Soviet Pact of August 1939 which assigned Finland to the Soviet sphere of influence. On 5 October Finland was requested to send a delegation to Moscow and between 12 October and 9 November three rounds of talks were held with Stalin and *Molotov. Stalin wanted to strengthen the defences against an attacker coming through Finland by moving the frontier on the Karelian isthmus some 70 km. (43.5 mi.) further from Leningrad, and against a naval attack through the Gulf of Finland by taking Finnish islands in the gulf and leasing the port of Hanko for 30 years as a military base to close the entrance to the gulf. He also wanted frontier rectifications on the Arctic Ocean to strengthen the defences of Murmansk and in return offered Finland territorial compensation in Soviet Karelia.

Finland had secured independence after 1917 and experienced a civil war between Reds and Whites in which the Bolsheviks had assisted the defeated Reds. The basis of Finland's foreign policy was that the USSR was an implacable enemy which sought to reverse that defeat and that any significant concession to Soviet demands would encourage further encroachments on independence. Although Stalin showed a genuine readiness to bargain at the Moscow talks, Finland would not compromise. Stalin fell back on an alternative plan: the Leningrad military district would mount a full invasion of Finland. Serious resistance was not anticipated because Finnish workers would welcome the Soviets as liberators and refuse to fight: to encourage them a Finnish Peoples' government was formed by communist exiles led by O. W. Kuusinen to collaborate with the invasion.

After a contrived frontier incident at Mainila, on 26 November 1939, war began on 30 November with a general Soviet advance over the frontier and air raids on the interior (see Map 33). The Finnish Army of 1939 had ten divisions and some special units. It was inadequately equipped, short of automatic weapons despite its own Suomi machine pistol developed for forest warfare, had not received the planned heavy *mortars, and had only 36 pre-1918 guns for each division. It was short of

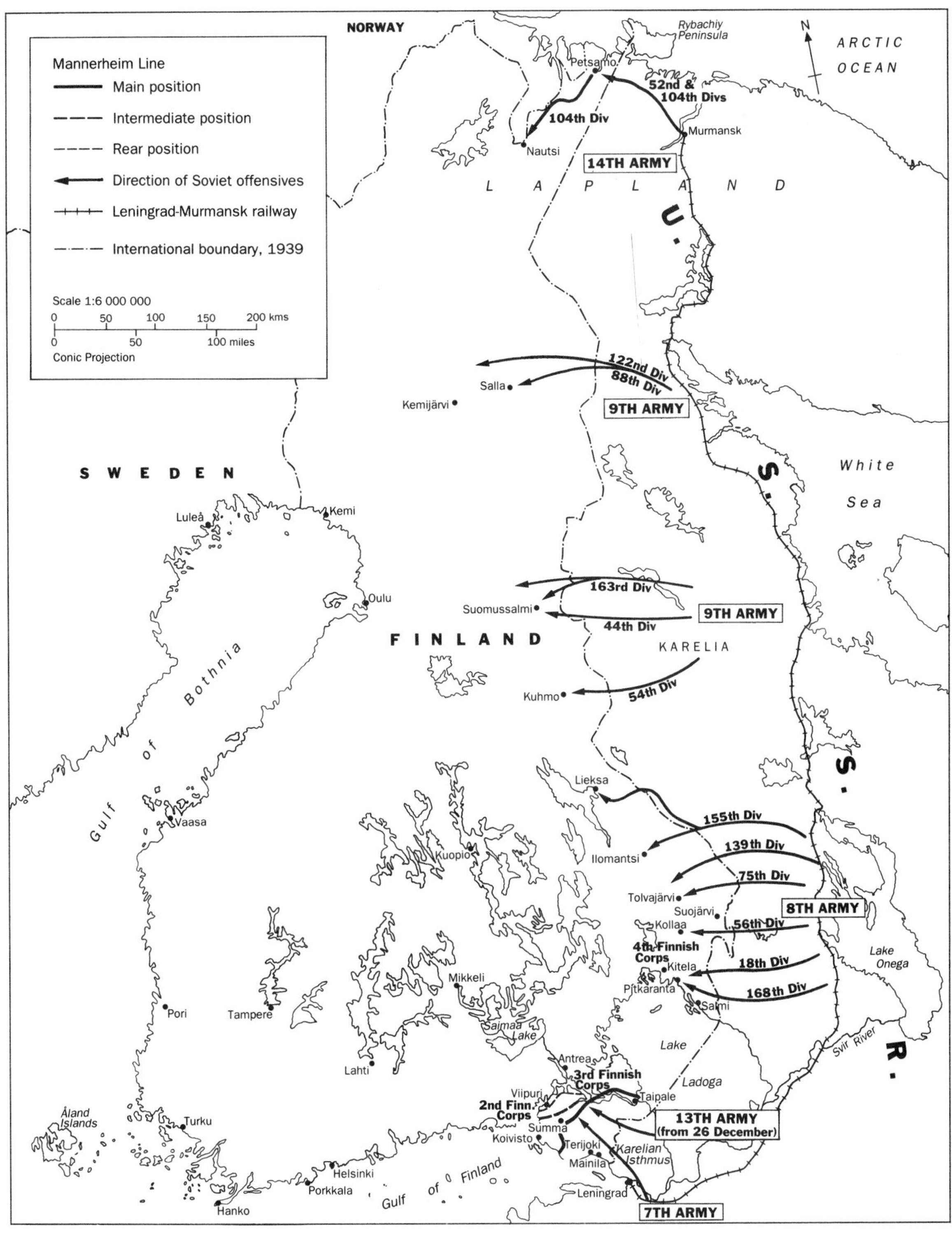

33. **Finnish–Soviet war** First Phase, November 1939

uniforms, tents, radios, and shells. But the soldiers had been trained intelligently to operate in forest terrain, in both summer and winter conditions, could move freely in the wilderness, using skis for mobility in snow, and were strongly motivated to defend Finland's recently-won independence against aggression. Further, the period of negotiation had allowed the Army to mobilize undisturbed and move into position. The frontier was some 1,000 km. (620 mi.) long but most of it trackless wilderness, impassable to a modern army. This allowed the Finnish commander, Marshal C. G. *Mannerheim, to concentrate six divisions along the 65 km. (40 mi.) Mannerheim Line, a prepared system of defences which stretched across the Karelian isthmus. It consisted of field works reinforced at the most vulnerable points by 44 modern concrete bunkers, with automatic weapons but no anti-tank guns or artillery. Two divisions were posted between Lake Ladoga and Ilomantsi to protect the rear of the isthmus: the rest of the eastern frontier was crossed by a handful of poor roads, each guarded by special battalion-sized units. The strategic plan was to hold these positions long enough for outside assistance to arrive.

During the war, the Red Army used 26 divisions, comprising 1,200,000 men, lavishly equipped with motor transport and artillery and supported by 1,500 tanks and 3,000 aircraft. But communications and supply problems prevented the whole force being deployed at once. It was weakened by defective training and tactical leadership, partly a result of Stalin's purges, and was badly prepared for winter warfare, lacking white camouflage clothing, adequate anti-frost protection for equipment, and ski-troops for a campaign fought almost entirely in sub-arctic weather. On the isthmus General *Meretskov commanded the Seventh Army with twelve divisions and a tank corps: north of Ladoga was the Eighth Army with six divisions, on its right the Ninth Army with five divisions, and, at Murmansk, the Fourteenth Army with three divisions. The Soviet superiority in manpower at the front was about $2\frac{1}{2}$:1 and the plan was for a quick general advance on all fronts leading to the total occupation of Finland.

The Soviet advance up the Karelian isthmus ended in stalemate on the Mannerheim Line: despite repeated heavy assaults it remained intact everywhere and the Finnish reserves were not drawn in. Soviet material superiority was of no avail: Soviet aircraft could inhibit Finnish movements by day, but the hours of daylight were few, and their long-distance attacks on towns and communications, against light defences, caused little strategic damage and cost more than 800 aircraft destroyed. The tanks were potentially dangerous to the Finnish infantry who had no experience of armoured warfare and little proper anti-tank equipment. But after some early panics they improvised weapons, notably the *molotov cocktail which was very effective, as the tanks tended to operate in isolation from their infantry and could be hunted down after dark. The Soviet infantry used mass-assault tactics that ended in heavy losses.

After 27 December the Soviet forces broke off action on the isthmus. North of Lake Ladoga the Soviet deployment had been larger than the Finns had anticipated and Mannerheim had to use part of his strategic reserve to stabilize the front which, by 9 December, he managed to do. But on the three crossing-points on the eastern frontier improvement of communications on the Soviet side enabled them to advance in divisional strength and more of the Finnish reserve was needed to halt them; while the Murmansk troops easily overran the Petsamo area, cutting Finland off from the Arctic Ocean, but did not penetrate further south.

As soon as hostilities began a new government was formed in Finland to seek peace but the Soviet Union rejected all approaches on the grounds that it only recognized Kuusinen's Peoples' government, now established on Finnish soil at Terijoki. Finland appealed to the *League of Nations for help: the USSR was expelled and all League members urged to support Finland. Since Germany sympathized with the Soviet Union all aid, whether equipment or volunteers, had to reach Finland through Norwegian ports. This caused such delays that almost no volunteers got into action and much *matériel* remained in Norway. Only Sweden, by straining the limits of neutrality, was able to supply substantial quantities of weapons and two battalions of volunteers in time to be used in the fighting. This meant that the value of the foreign aid to Finland was as much moral as material.

From late December, the Finns counter-attacked along the Eastern Front: facing road-bound Soviet columns, they moved ski troops through the forests to outflank and cut off the invading forces which were split up into isolated hedgehog positions which could be worn down individually. Spectacular victories were secured by Colonel P. Talvela at Tolvajärvi where, by 24 December, the Soviet 139th and 75th divisions were destroyed, and by Colonel H. Siilasvuo at Suomussalmi, where by 5 January he had destroyed the 163rd and 44th divisions: all the heavy equipment was captured and then used by the Finnish Army. But although the Soviet advance on the Eastern Front was halted for the duration of the war, surviving hedgehog positions could not be eliminated and these tied down substantial Finnish forces. Further, these spectacular tactical successes deluded even the Finnish leadership into thinking that the war was winnable, whereas strategically their effect was marginal. But politically they forced a change in Soviet policy, for in January the Soviet leaders signalled a willingness to negotiate with the government in Helsinki and tacitly to abandon the Kuusinen government. Contact between the two sides were continuous after 29 January, but the Finns felt strong enough to bargain. They were encouraged when, on 5 February, France and the UK approved a plan to send an expedition to Scandinavia, ostensibly to help Finland, in reality to seize the Swedish iron-ore mines (see also RAW MATERIALS) and open a Second Front against Germany in Scandinavia: but to do this they needed a request for assistance from Finland.

Militarily the Soviet command was reorganized: General S. K. *Timoshenko took command of a North-West Front: the Seventh Army was reinforced by a new Thirteenth Army of nine divisions and an armoured brigade. Intensive training was implemented to develop close co-operation of infantry, armour, artillery, and aircraft. On 1 February a fresh assault on the Mannerheim Line began: the defences were subjected to continuous bombardment, followed by combined infantry and armoured probes with close air support. The line broke at Summa on 11 February, the decisive factors being the sheer physical exhaustion of the defenders and shortages of ammunition for their artillery. Finnish counter-attacks failed to restore it and on 15 February the Finns retreated to an intermediate position of field works, wire, and tank obstacles, prepared since the outbreak of war. Soviet forces began to threaten this position by 18 February and after a pause for regrouping, broke it on 25 February. There remained a rear position, anchored on Viipuri: Soviet forces began to attack it on 3 March, and also launched troops and tanks over the sea-ice west of Viipuri (Vyborg), which secured a threatening bridgehead behind the line. When fighting ceased, the rear position had been penetrated and only a major strategic retreat could have won a respite for the Finns. On 9 March, Mannerheim advised the government to make peace.

Soviet terms were defined on 23 February: in addition to Hanko, the whole Karelian isthmus, including Viipuri and the north shore of Ladoga were demanded: the Petsamo area would be restored to Finland. The Finnish government procrastinated while it sought military intervention by Sweden, which was refused, and it then explored the Anglo-French offer to intervene, but judged it insufficient. A delegation flew to Moscow and signed the treaty of Moscow on 12 March 1940. Hostilities ceased the following day. Finland made peace because the war was lost without substantial outside assistance. The Soviet reason for making peace, when total victory was in reach, can only be surmised. Probably Stalin wanted freedom of manoeuvre for forthcoming developments in the European war and was nervous about Anglo-French intentions.

The USSR lost 200,000 dead and much *matériel*, but the worst loss was international credibility. World opinion overlooked the final successes and generally underrated Soviet military capacity. Further, in May 1940, the Supreme Military Soviet ordered a general reorganization of the forces in the light of wartime experience, which paid off in 1941. Finland lost 25,000 dead, a tenth of its territory and had to absorb 400,000 refugees.

The national will to survive enabled Finland to sustain these burdens and by June 1941 it had built a new, sixteen-division army, with adequate modern equipment. Germany provided much of the equipment because Hitler's plans to conquer the USSR assumed that Finland would co-operate. The Finns reacted positively to Hitler's covert approaches and in June 1941, in what was known as a continuation of the Winter War, mobilized for their own war of revenge, while in Lapland four German divisions were ready to attack Murmansk. This operation failed, but the Finnish Army regained the lost territories and advanced into Soviet Karelia to the line of Lake Onega and the River Svir. They stopped there and remained on the defensive into 1944.

Finland had joined the German attack on the USSR (see BARBAROSSA) in expectation of total German victory: after *Stalingrad its leaders realized this would not happen and sought to withdraw from the war. But intermittent negotiations broke down in February 1944 and the USSR decided to force Finland to surrender. On 9 June 1944 a massive offensive on the isthmus achieved an immediate breakthrough and drove the Finns back beyond Viipuri: Mannerheim was compelled to abandon the Onega–Svir positions: emergency help had to be purchased from Germany by an undertaking not to make a separate peace and the front was stabilized in early August, roughly on the line of the 1940 frontier. The Soviet command needed resources for other fronts and allowed Finland to renege on the promise to Germany and conclude the *armistice of 19 September 1944. This restored the 1940 frontier, substituted Porkkala for Hanko as the Soviet base and imposed heavy reparations on Finland. At that price Finland, alone among Germany's eastern partners, saved herself from Soviet occupation and survived the war with its sovereignty and western democratic society intact. ANTHONY UPTON

Mannerheim, C. G., *The Memoirs of Marshal Mannerheim* (London, 1953).
Tanner, V., *The Winter War* (London, 1957).
Upton, A. F., *Finland 1939–40* (London, 1974).

firestorms were sometimes created by intensive bombing raids on a city's built-up areas. It is a natural process for a fire to draw in air to consume its oxygen. When many buildings were ablaze during a heavy raid great heat was generated, and the convection the fires caused by sucking in air disseminated sparks and burning debris which started other conflagrations. The more fires the greater the heat and the greater the convection until, in a matter of seconds, all the fires could coalesce into one massive inferno which created hurricane force winds coming from every direction, and temperatures of 800°C.

The first firestorm occurred in the early hours of Wednesday 28 July 1943 during an RAF raid on *Hamburg and was created not only by the intensity of the bombing but by the mixture of explosives and incendiaries used, and by the high natural temperature and low humidity. Within an hour of its happening the Hamburg Fire Department recorded the incident by coining the word *Feuersturm* to describe it. It affected an area of 22 sq. km. (8.5 sq. mi.) and either asphyxiated or burnt to death about 40,000 people. Firestorms also occurred in raids on *Dresden, Kassel, and Tokyo (see STRATEGIC AIR OFFENSIVES, 3).

First Special Service Force, see USA, 5(f).

First World War. The first world war of the twentieth century raged from 1914 to 1918. Every statesman and senior commander in the Second World War vividly remembered the first; all major policies were influenced by it.

The conflict began in July 1914 with an Austro-Hungarian attack on Serbia. Russia indicated such strong support for Serbia that Germany declared war on Russia, and on Russia's ally France; the German war plan involved an immediate invasion of neutral Belgium. The UK therefore entered the war also, against Germany, in defence of the Belgian neutrality that all the European Great Powers had long guaranteed. By mid-August 1914 there was a European civil war raging, with Germany and Austria-Hungary ('the Central Powers') allied against the 'Triple Entente' of Russia, France, and the British Empire ('the Allies'). Most of Belgium was quickly overrun by the Germans, in circumstances that gave rise to a series of atrocity stories—enough of which were later proved untrue to delay Allied acceptance during the Second World War that the *Final Solution was actually happening.

Encounter battles in north-eastern France soon led to a tactical stalemate: a vast fortress line of trenches, well wired in, called the Western Front, stretched from the North Sea to the Swiss frontier. In an effort to break the stalemate, Churchill (then First Lord of the Admiralty) instigated an attack on the Dardanelles, which was ill-managed, and after eight months' bitter fighting failed. No doubt, Churchill's knowledge and appreciation of the Royal Navy's Intelligence Division's work on the decryption of German signals during the First World War alerted him to the potential value of *Bletchley Park at the start of the Second.

The Western Front stalemate was catastrophically expensive in men and in munitions for both sides. British generals in 1939–45 never forgot how many of their own contemporaries had been killed there, and were extra anxious to avoid another national bloodbath. It also bred a defensive frame of mind which led to dependence on the *Maginot Line and a total inability to cope with the mobile warfare the Germans fought in 1939 and 1940.

German attempts in 1915 to break the stalemate by the use of poison gas, then a new weapon, only encountered Allied retaliation in kind; the fact that *chemical warfare was not employed during the Second World War was due to the mobility of the combatants, not for any reasons of morality. The stalemate was broken at last in August 1918 by Allied artillery and infantry working in combination with the newly invented tanks. Artillery barrage fire, brought to new heights of concentration in 1942–5 (see ARTILLERY, 2) was invented on the Western Front in 1915 by, among others, *Brooke.

Japan had entered the war beside its then ally the UK at the end of August 1914, and Japanese warships operated as far west as the Mediterranean; the Japanese army stayed in Asia.

Italy, previously Germany's ally, came in against it in 1915, opening a southern front in the Austrian Alps. Turkey and Bulgaria joined the Central Powers; Romania, in 1916, joined the Allies—and was swiftly defeated. Greece tried to remain neutral, but French and British troops fought Turks and Bulgars on Greek soil round Salonika, 1915–18, and Greeks fought Turks in Asia Minor in 1920–2. There was more movement on the Eastern Front than on the Western; Russia retired from it in 1917 after two successive revolutions, liberal in March and communist in November, had sapped the will to fight, and was crippled by civil war until 1922.

At sea, there was only one main fleet action, the battle of Jutland (31 May–1 June 1916), after which the German fleet hardly put to sea again. A German U-boat offensive almost starved out the British in 1917, but *convoys defeated it, and U-boat depredations brought in the USA also on the Allied side (but as an 'associated', not an allied power) in April 1917. (Roosevelt was then assistant secretary to the US Navy, much concerned with the U-boat war.) The near disastrous delay in organizing convoys in the First World War ensured they were quickly introduced at the start of the Second.

Air operations were still in their infancy. *Portal, *Harris, and *Göring all took an active part in them. Lighter-than-air craft proved vulnerable to fighter attack, and were rarely used again in war (but see BLIMPS); though no effective counter to airborne bombing by heavier-than-air craft was developed.

Turkey, Bulgaria, and Austria-Hungary surrendered in turn in the autumn of 1918. In the west, the German Army was beaten in the open field by an Anglo-French army under a French C-in-C, Foch, with the prospect of unlimited American reinforcements to back it. An armistice was signed at Compiègne in November 1918; fighting at once stopped. A peace congress in Paris produced the Treaty of Versailles, signed on 28 June 1919 as part of the *Versailles settlement; although reviled as excessively harsh in Germany, it was much milder than the peace the Germans had imposed on defeated Russia at Brest-Litovsk on 3 March 1918. Germany's defeat produced a belief on the part of most Germans that the soldiers at the front had been 'stabbed in the back' by subversives who had betrayed their country. This obsession created a social environment in which the seeds of such organizations as the *euthanasia programme and the *People's court were allowed to take root long before the Nazis ever came to power. M. R. D. FOOT

FISH, see GEHEIMSCHREIBER.

Flak, a contraction of *Fliegerabwehrkanonen* (anti-aircraft artillery), meant German anti-aircraft fire.

flame-throwers. Flame, a weapon of antiquity, was re-introduced in the *First World War and was kept in use afterwards. In 1940 it was adopted by the UK as an anti-

Flame-throwers were used by both sides. They were particularly useful to US forces for destroying otherwise invulnerable Japanese bunkers during the Pacific war. This photograph of two US marines attacking a Japanese defensive position was taken in February 1945 during the fighting for Iwo Jima.

invasion measure, largely in the form of the 'flame fougasse', a drum of inflammable oil which could be launched by an explosive charge to land on a road so as to form a block. The much-talked-of 'burning sea', in which oil was floated on the sea and ignited, had been tried in pre-war days and proved to be less successful than anticipated, though it was a useful propaganda device.

The man-carried flame-thrower was used by all armies, though perhaps the greatest use was by the Americans and Japanese in the *Pacific war, where flame was the ultimate weapon to flush opponents out of *foxholes and bunkers. These devices were simple canisters of flame-throwing fluid (thickened gasoline) with a tank of pressurized nitrogen to propel the liquid some 45 m. (50 yds.). It was ignited as it left the launcher. The fear of fire was such that any man seen carrying a flame-thrower was an immediate target and was generally protected by a party of riflemen.

The British pioneered the use of flame-throwers on vehicles, developing the 'Wasp', mounted on a Bren gun carrier, and the 'Crocodile' mounted on a Churchill tank. Similar devices were then developed by the American and Canadian armies. With larger capacity fuel and nitrogen tanks, these weapons could project the flame further and for a longer duration. They were particularly valuable during the Normandy Landings (see OVERLORD), using flame to neutralize pillboxes and similar obstacles, and they continued to be used throughout the campaign in north-west Europe. IAN HOGG

Fleet Air Arm, see navy sub-section of ARMED FORCES section of relevant major powers.

Fleet Train, term used to describe the supply and repair ships that supported Allied warships during the *Pacific war. *Convoys would sail from the US west coast to an intermediate port where ships of the Fleet Train would load supplies, ammunition, and fuel and transport them to the ships in operational areas. When the British Pacific Fleet was formed at the end of 1944 (see TASK FORCE 57) it had to rely heavily on American help, as sufficient merchant ships could not be spared from supplying the UK. By August 1945 the British Fleet Train comprised 92 ships. See also LOGISTICS.

Fletcher, Vice-Admiral (Frank) Jack (1885–1973), US naval officer, nicknamed 'Black Jack', whose reputation for over-caution during early naval battles in the *Pacific war eventually cost him his command. In December 1941 his controversial decision to refuel delayed his task force's arrival at *Wake Island and enabled the Japanese to invade the island unopposed. His forces did turn back the Japanese invasion force during the *Coral Sea battle in May 1942, though he sustained heavier losses than he inflicted, and he was unlucky to have his flagship sunk under him at *Midway in June, as much of the credit for victory went to *Spruance who took tactical command of the battle. But at *Guadalcanal in August 1942 his precipitate withdrawal of his carrier forces left the US Marines isolated ashore, and his tactics during the *Eastern Solomons battle the same month were equally cautious. In October 1942 he was posted to the north Pacific, but took part in the invasion of *Okinawa in April 1945.

FLIVOS, contraction of *Fliegerverbindungsoffiziere*, Luftwaffe liaison officers at German Army headquarters, down to divisional level. They played vital roles in securing army–air co-operation in each *blitzkrieg in 1940–2; thereafter, unconsciously, they were most useful to the Allies. They sent frequent reports of order of battle in an *ENIGMA cipher that was comparatively easy to break and which therefore gave significant aid to those at *Bletchley Park in providing *ULTRA intelligence.

M. R. D. FOOT

float planes, known generically to the British as seaplanes. More than 70 types of this maritime aircraft—often specially designed, but sometimes just land aircraft with wing floats attached—were flown by 11 combatant countries for short-range reconnaissance, *air-sea rescue operations, gunnery observation, and attacking shipping with torpedoes. The Japanese even had a fighter float plane, the Kawanishi Shiden, from which a successful land version was developed.

France produced sixteen types, the USA twelve, while Germany had eleven, the best of which was the German Heinkel He115. More than 400 of these were built for reconnaissance, laying mines, and attacking shipping. The smaller, catapult-launched, single-engined Arado was operated from German warships, and from some German *auxiliary cruisers, for spotting and observation. Other German types included the Dornier Do22 (also supplied to Greece and Yugoslavia), the Heinkel He59, used for air-sea rescue operations, and the Blohm and Voss Ha139. Japan also produced eleven types, including the single-engined Aichi E13AI, codenamed JAKE, three of which were catapulted from cruisers to reconnoitre *Pearl Harbor before the attack on it on 7 December 1941.

The most famous British type was the seaplane version of the Fairey Swordfish (for details see CARRIERS), affectionately known as the 'stringbag'. Virtually obsolescent when the war began, it proved so reliable that it continued to serve throughout it, and outlived the Albacore designed to replace it. *Warspite*'s Swordfish observed her gunfire during the Second *Narvik battle and a less well-known type, the Fairey Seafox, observed the fire of the cruiser *Ajax* during the battle of the *River Plate. The *Norwegian campaign spurred the British into fitting floats to their successful Spitfire fighter. From this evolved the Supermarine Spitfire IX which had a top speed of 606 km/h (377 mph), the fastest seaplane of the war. See also FLYING BOATS.

Flossenbürg, Nazi *concentration camp which was opened in May 1938 near the Bavarian town of that name. It was small compared to some—about 65,000 are said to have been incarcerated there at various times—but during the last fourteen months of the war 14,000 died or were executed there. They included several dozen Allied agents, two conspirators against Hitler, *Canaris and Hans *Oster, and the German pastor Dietrich *Bonhoeffer. It was liberated on 4 May 1945 by US troops.

flying boats were employed by all the major combatants for long-range maritime patrols and *air-sea rescue. Unlike *float planes, flying boats land on the water on their fuselage as well as on their wing floats.

For short-range patrols the Italians used the single-engined Cant Z501 Gabbiano and the French the single-engined Lioré 130. For long-range reconnaissance the French employed the Breguet 521 Bizerte. The Luftwaffe operated the Blohm and Voss 138, easily distinguishable by its twin tail booms, and the Dornier Do24 as transports during the *Norwegian campaign and later for air-sea rescue. Dornier Do24s were also built for and by the Dutch. The few that escaped to Australia after the Japanese invaded the *Netherlands East Indies in early 1942 were acquired by the Royal Australian Air Force and designated A49s. The Germans also built the Blohm and Voss BV222 Wiking, the largest wartime flying boat. Intended originally for commercial purposes this six-engined aircraft could carry 92 fully-equipped troops and was used for ferrying men across the Mediterranean, and for long-range maritime reconnaissance.

The British operated several types of flying boat at the start of the war, including the Saro London and Lerwick, the Short Singapore, and the pusher-engined Supermarine Walrus Mk I. This last was catapult-launched from warships for reconnaissance and observation, or undertook land-based patrol duties. It proved highly reliable and versatile. 287 were manufactured by Supermarine and 453 of the Mk II by Saunders-Roe, but in 1944 it began to be superseded by the more powerful Sea Otter.

The most successful British flying boat of the war was

the Short Sunderland; its operational prowess became legendary, especially after it was armed in May 1942 with depth charges (see ANTI-SUBMARINE WEAPONS) filled with Torpex (see EXPLOSIVES). Five marks, totalling 741 Sunderlands, were produced and by 1945 the RAF had equipped 28 squadrons, including Australian and Canadian ones, with it. Predominantly employed for long-range maritime reconaissance in the battle of the *Atlantic—28 U-boats were sunk by Sunderlands—it was operational just about everywhere over sea. Later versions were so well armed, and armoured, that the Luftwaffe called them *Stachelschwein* (porcupine), and when one was attacked by eight German aircraft in June 1943, it shot down three and damaged the other five.

Very successful, too, was the Japanese Kawanishi H8K1/4, codenamed EMILY by the Allies, which superseded the Kawanishi H6K1/5 long-range maritime reconnaissance aircraft (MAVIS) in 1943. It was the fastest flying boat used by any combatant country and 167 were built; they proved to be exceptionally well armed and armoured, and were treated with the greatest respect by Allied pilots during the *Pacific war.

Pride of place, however, must be given to the ubiquitous twin-engined Consolidated Catalina flying boats, or PBYs as the US Navy initially designated them. Uncomplicated to operate, simple to maintain, and above all dependable, they proved popular with the armed services of several countries including Australia, New Zealand, and the UK. Several hundred were manufactured under licence in the USSR, which also produced its own short-range Beriev and Chetverikov flying boats. The British ordered 50 PBYs in September 1939 and dubbed them Catalinas (after the island off the Californian coast), a name the US Navy, having ordered 200 for the *Neutrality Patrol, also adopted in 1941. An amphibian version was manufactured in Canada, where it was called the Canso, and the Dutch employed them in the Netherlands East Indies against the Japanese. Several variations were introduced and altogether 3,290 were manufactured. One, piloted by an American, sighted the **Bismarck* during her last sortie, while others kept track of the Japanese fleet before the battle of *Midway, hunted down *Tokyo Express destroyers amongst the Solomon Islands, and played a variety of invaluable roles in just about every maritime operational theatre.

Other successful US flying boats included the Martin Mariner—more than 1,200 were produced—and the four-engined Consolidated Coronado. Intended to complement the Catalina, the Coronado had an impressive record against U-boats (ten were sunk between June 1942 and September 1943) but it was then superseded by the land-based Liberator. American civilian clipper flying boats were requisitioned as long-distance transports and were used by both Churchill and Roosevelt to fly to various Allied conferences (see GRAND ALLIANCE). The huge Hughes A4 eight-engined 'Spruce Goose', though designed for wartime use as a cargo carrier, did not fly until 1947.

flying bombs, see V-WEAPONS.

Flying Fortress, US B(oeing)17 bomber which gained its nickname from its heavy defensive armament (see Figure). When the B17 began to be delivered in 1937 it was the first four-engined, all-metal, monoplane bomber to come into service with any air force. It allowed for the theory of high-altitude *precision bombing to be given practical application. In December 1941 four squadrons were stationed in the Philippines but nearly all were destroyed on the ground (see CLARK FIELD). It was the USAAF's principal bomber in its *strategic air offensive against Germany and targets in other European countries. The B17A and B17B were prototypes which never saw combat. The last type, the B17G, production of which started in 1943, was manufactured in the largest quantities, 8,680 being built by the Boeing, Douglas, and Lockheed-Vega plants. See also BOMBERS.

Flying Tigers, see AMERICAN VOLUNTEER GROUP.

Force 133, *SOE organization based in Cairo and later in Bari which controlled the liaison officers attached to the Balkan guerrilla groups such as *EDES, *ELAS, and *Tito's partisans.

Force 136, see SOE.

Force 266, Allied organization formed out of *Force 133 and staffed by *SOE and the *Office of Strategic Services, responsible for supplying *Tito's partisans and *Mihailović's *cetniks*. It controlled a number of Allied units on Vis, an island off the Yugoslavian coast, and also ran training camps for those entering Yugoslavia to help the partisans. It was absorbed into Force 399 of the *Balkan Air Force HQ when it was created in June 1944.

forced labour. Serfdom was not abolished in Russia till 1861, slavery in the USA not till 1865; but thereafter it was presumed to have vanished from every part of the world that claimed to be modern and civilized, though it remained endemic in parts of South-West Asia and Central Africa. However, Stalin introduced it into the USSR in the 1930s, as an unpublicized part of the industrial revolution he conducted there (see GULAG); and once the *Pacific war had started the Japanese used slave labour to build the *Burma–Thailand railway.

But by far the most systematic use of forced labour was employed by the Nazis. In 1944, 7.1 million foreign civilians and *prisoners-of-war (POW) were registered as part of the workforce in the territory of 'Greater Germany'. There were also about 500,000 mainly foreign prisoners in *concentration camps, so that at that particular time, in the entire economy of the Reich, over 24% of workers and employees were foreigners who had, to a large extent, been brought to work in the Reich by compulsion (see Table 1). The National Socialist employment of foreigners between 1939 and 1945 thus

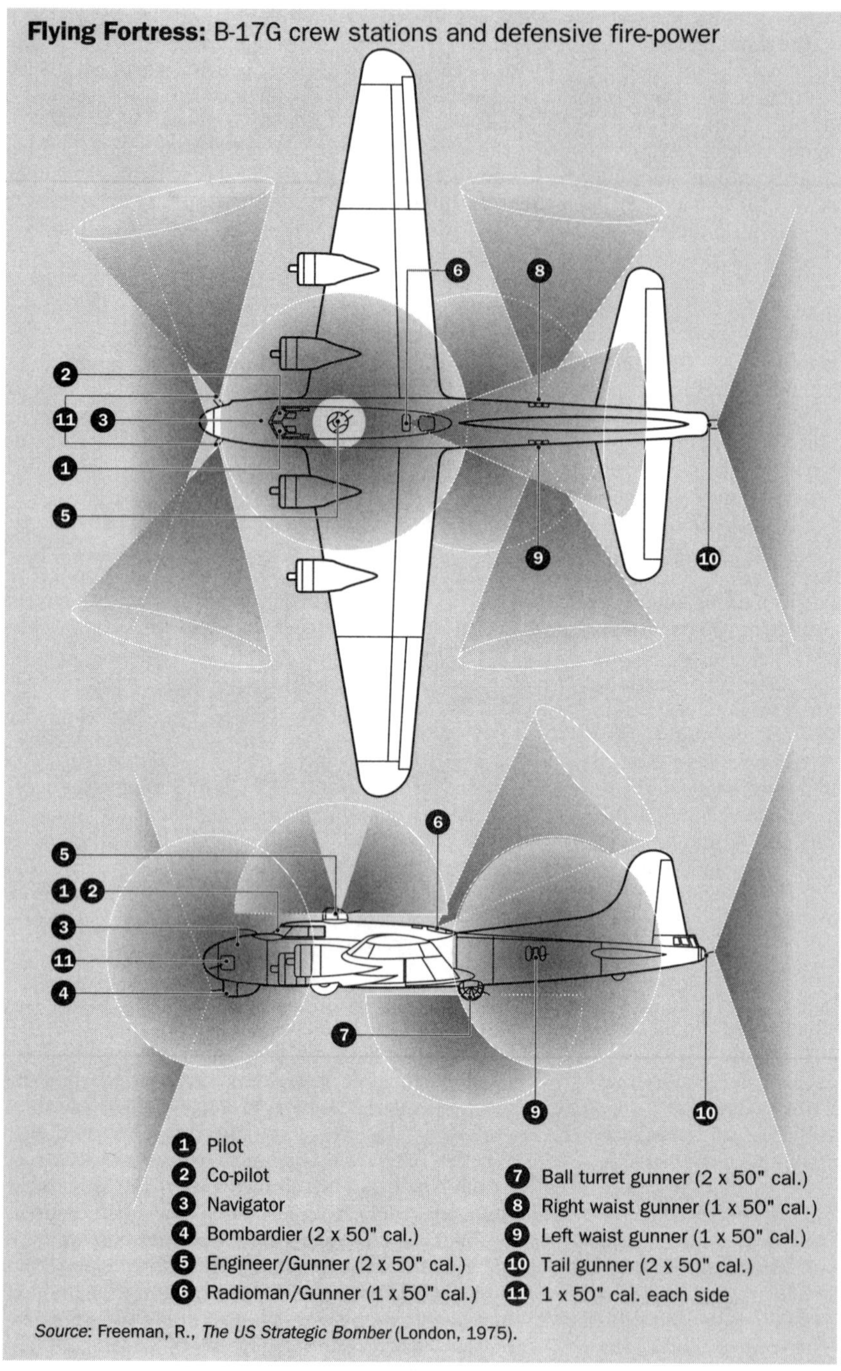

Source: Freeman, R., *The US Strategic Bomber* (London, 1975).

became the most important case in history of a large-scale, use of forced labour since the end of American slavery in the 19th century. It had, however, been neither planned nor prepared for by the Nazi leadership.

Shortly before the beginning of the war, a memorandum of the department for the defence economy of the Wehrmacht stated that, as far as the expenditure for arming their forces was concerned, preparations for the war had encountered three main problems: foreign exchange, certain *raw materials, and labour. For foreign

Forced labour, Table 1: Foreign workers in the German war economy, 1939–45

	1939	*1940*	*1941*	*1942*	*1943*	*1944*
Agriculture						
Germans	10,732,000	9,648,000	8,939,000	8,969,000	8,743,000	8,460,000
Foreign civilians	118,000	412,000	769,000	1,170,000	1,561,000	1,767,000
Prisoners-of-war	–	249,000	642,000	759,000	609,000	635,000
All foreigners	118,000	661,000	1,411,000	1,929,000	2,170,000	2,402,000
Foreigners as a % of all employed	1.1%	6.8%	15.8%	21.5%	24.8%	28.4%
All except Agriculture						
Germans	28,382,000	25,697,000	24,947,000	23,298,000	22,278,000	21,340,000
Foreign civilians	183,000	391,000	984,000	1,475,000	3,276,000	3,528,000
Prisoners-of-war	–	99,000	674,000	730,000	954,000	1,196,000
All foreigners	183,000	490,000	1,658,000	2,205,000	4,230,000	4,724,000
Foreigners as a % of all employed	0.6%	1.9%	6.6%	9.5%	19.0%	22.0%
Total economy						
Germans	39,114,000	35,345,000	33,886,000	32,267,000	31,021,000	29,800,000
Foreign civilians	301,000	803,000	1,753,000	2,645,000	4,837,000	5,295,000
Prisoners-of-war	–	348,000	1,316,000	1,489,000	1,563,000	1,831,000
All foreigners	301,000	1,151,000	3,069,000	4,134,000	6,400,000	7,126,000
Foreigners as a % of all employed	0.8%	3.2%	9.0%	12.8%	20.6%	24.0%

Source: Contributor.

exchange and raw materials a solution was found: following the *blitzkrieg campaigns the resources of the Reich were to be successively increased through the reserves belonging to the countries overrun. This policy had already proved successful in the case of Austria and Czechoslovakia, and was to be confirmed once again in the period 1939 to 1941. The question of labour was more difficult, because it involved, apart from economic aspects, security, and above all, ideological factors. There was a shortage of around 1.2 million workers in the Greater German Reich: a further rise in this number was to be expected after the outbreak of war.

Two possibilities were considered: either large numbers of German women could take their place in the economy, as they had done during the *First World War, or workers could be imported on a large scale from the countries that were to be conquered. But both options were rejected. During the First World War, the conscription of German women had led to considerable political destabilization and dissatisfaction inside the country. Moreover, it would have constituted a flagrant violation of the National Socialists' programme regarding women and social policies. But to bring millions of foreign workers, particularly Poles, to work in the Reich conflicted strongly with the ethnic principles of National Socialism, according to which the mass employment of aliens inside the Reich would be a threat to the purity of blood of the German people (see NAZI IDEOLOGY). The decision was reversed only after the beginning of the war when, compared with the drafting into essential services of German women, employing foreigners seemed to be the lesser evil. It was believed that the risks entailed by the latter could be contained more easily by using repressive measures.

About 300,000 Polish POW who had fallen into German hands after the *Polish campaign were very quickly put to work, mainly in agriculture. A massive recruitment campaign was also started, continuing a long tradition of employing Polish farm workers in Germany. As time went on increasingly harsher methods were adopted and from the spring of 1940 recruitment developed into a regular manhunt inside the so-called General government (see POLAND, 2(b)), where workers were drafted by age group and people were rounded up by raids on cinemas, schools, and churches. By May 1940 more than one million Polish workers had been brought into the Reich in this way.

Nevertheless, the so-called *Poleneinsatz* (employment of Poles), was still perceived as offending against the racial principles of National Socialism. The national and political dangers arising therefrom, as *Himmler stated in 1940, were to be counteracted by suitably stringent measures. Accordingly, a vast system of repressive regulations was brought to bear on the Poles. They had to live in hutted camps (which, in the countryside, soon proved to be impossible), received smaller wages, were not allowed to use public facilities (ranging from express trains to public baths), nor attend German church services; they had to work longer hours than Germans and were obliged to wear a badge—the 'Poland-P'—pinned to their clothing. Outside work, contact with Germans was forbidden; any Pole involved in sexual relations with German women was punished by public execution. In order to protect 'German Blood' it had also been decided that at least half of the civilian workers recruited must be women.

For the German authorities *Poleneinsatz* was, by and large, successful. They managed, within a short time, to bring a large number of Polish workers into Germany against their will, and to establish, within the Reich, a hierarchy dividing society into two classes based on racial criteria.

By May 1940 it was already obvious that even the recruitment of Poles could not satisfy the need for labour in the German economy. So more than a million French POW were brought into the Reich as workers, during and soon after the fall of *France. Furthermore, an extensive recruitment drive was carried out in the occupied territories to increase manpower. For each of these new groups of people special regulations were passed, though, compared with those applying to the Poles, these were definitely less harsh as regards treatment, wages, accommodation, and so on. In this way a graduated system of national hierarchies developed, a scale on which the then so-called 'guest workers' from allied Italy were placed at the top and the Poles at the bottom.

By far the greater part of the foreign civilian workers and POW acquired during the 'blitzkrieg phase'—up to the summer of 1941—were employed in agriculture. Foreigners did not play an important part in industry, which had set its sights on retrieving its German workers from the army soon after the end of this phase. At the same time, the ideological reservations of the party and the authorities, against extending the employment of foreigners, were so great that it was decided to freeze the number of foreigners at the level of spring 1941, at just under 3 million. This policy worked so long as a long war of attrition could be avoided.

However, in the autumn of 1941 an entirely new situation arose. The German armies fighting in the *German–Soviet war had already suffered their first defeat outside Moscow and a quick end to the war was now out of the question. Instead, German munitions production had to adjust itself to a war of attrition which meant considerably increasing its capacity. But a massive wave of call-ups reached even the workers in the armaments factories, who had been exempt until then, and the efforts made to replace them from occupied western European countries could not close the gap. Only the use of manpower from the USSR would be able to provide an effective solution, but the employment of Soviet POW, or civilian workers, in the Reich had been explicitly ruled out before the beginning of the war and continued to be strongly opposed by Nazi leaders. Also, the first newsreels showing the war on the Eastern Front had begun to appear, creating antipathy to the employment of Soviet citizens among the German population. As the Sicherheitsdienst (see RSHA), reported: 'People are worried about what we intend to do with these "animals" in the future. Many of our countrymen believe that they should be radically exterminated. Caused partly by acts of terror perpetrated by escaped Russian prisoners-of-war, a certain fear is spreading that these alien types, with their strange build and features, could enter the territory of the Reich in large numbers and even be given employment.'

For Soviet POW, the consequences of this decision were disastrous. Since the German war economy did not apparently need them, millions were abandoned to their fate in the mass camps in the hinterland of the German Eastern Front. More than half of the 3.3 million POW taken by the Germans up to the end of 1941 froze to death, died of starvation or exhaustion, or were murdered. Altogether, up to the end of the war, of the roughly 5.7 million in German custody, 3.5 million lost their lives.

The decision soon had to be reversed, but by then the vast majority of the Soviet prisoners were no longer available for employment. Of the 3 million POW taken only 160,000 had, by March 1942, arrived to work in the Reich. Hence a new drive to recruit Soviet civilian workers became a matter of urgency for newly appointed 'Plenipotentiary for Employment', *Sauckel, who performed his task efficiently and with boundless brutality. In barely $2\frac{1}{2}$ years, more than 2.5 million civilians were deported from the USSR by the employment staff of the Wehrmacht to become slave workers in the Reich—20,000 people a week.

Although created by the needs of the war economy, the employment of Soviet citizens again offended against the ideological principles of National Socialism. Parallel to the developments at the start of the *Poleneinsatz*, this offence was compensated for by a system of repression and discrimination directed against Soviet civilian workers, which, in its harshness, far exceeded what the Poles had been subjected to. The reasoning of the authorities could be described in these terms: if employment of Soviet citizens in the Reich was inevitable, then the least one could do was to treat them badly.

Inside the Reich, a whole new world of camps had sprung up. In the big towns as in the countryside, there were foreigners' camps on every corner. In Berlin alone there were about 500. Altogether there may have been more than 20,000 in the Reich. About 500,000 Germans were drafted into the organization controlling foreign workers, from camp managers to foremen in charge of foreigners in a factory. The living conditions of the various groups of foreigners followed a strict national system of classification, regimented down to the smallest detail. While the workers from the occupied western territories, and the so-called friendly countries, did mainly have to live in camps, they received the same wages and rations as Germans in comparable posts, and had the same conditions of work. But *Ostarbeiter* (workers from the East), especially Soviet workers, were a great deal worse off. Their rations were so poor that within weeks of arrival they were often severely undernourished and unfit for work.

In the early summer of 1942 a large number of businesses were quick to report that *Russeneinsatz* (employment of Russians) was not an economic proposition, because effective employment required not only better food and sufficient rest periods, but also the training of forced labour for particular kinds of work. In the case of the French workers, measures for improving their conditions had resulted, after a relatively short time, in their output reaching almost the same level as that of the Germans. Conditions, particularly those of Soviet workers, varied a great deal, from one industrial plant to another and from camp to camp. They were generally better looked after in agriculture than in industry, but even there the differences in treatment and in their rations were evident, specially after the end of 1942. Effective and widespread improvement in their conditions did not come until after the defeat at *Stalingrad at the beginning of 1943, when a far-reaching campaign was started that involved linking rations to performance at work. Simultaneously, improved job training brought about a considerable improvement in performance. Allotting skilled tasks to the foreigners, however, was bound to have repercussions on their relations with German workers. Hence the authorities saw to it that the regulations they issued ensured that Germans kept their positions of privilege in relation to all foreigners, but especially the Russians, in all areas of employment. Germans automatically held a superior grade to *Ostarbeiter*; in some firms the German workers who had to provide initial training for the *Ostarbeiter* were given a special rank.

An extract from the report of an official from one of the ministries, who, in 1943, visited various *Ostarbeiter* camps in Berlin illustrates what the situation of Soviet slave workers in Germany was actually like:

> Despite the official rations *Ostarbeiter* are entitled to, it has been reliably established that the meals in the camps are as follows: In the morning, half a litre of turnip soup. At lunchtime, on the worksite, one litre of turnip soup. At night, one litre of turnip soup. Also, *Ostarbeiter* are given 300 gr. about 10 oz of bread per day. In addition, they receive, per week, 50 to 75 gr. [about 1.8 to 2.5 oz] of margarine, 25 gr. [about one ounce] of meat or meat products, which are distributed or withheld according to the whim of the camp leader. Large amounts of these rations get corruptly distributed. But the biggest scourge in the camps is tuberculosis, which is also spreading rapidly among minors. In the context of the *Ostarbeiter*'s health and sanitary situation, it has to be emphasized that the factory medical insurance schemes will not allow their German and Russian doctors to give any medicine whatsoever to the *Ostarbeiter*. Those suffering from tuberculosis are not even isolated. Sick workers are forced to remain at work by beatings, because the camp authorities doubt the competence of the doctors in attendance. I am not aware of the reason why the German authorities imported a large number of children from the Eastern Territories. It is a fact, however, that many *children between the ages of 4 to 15 are in the camps, and that they have neither parents nor relatives in Germany. Most of the children are sick and the only food they get to build up their strength is the same watery turnip soup as the older *Ostarbeiter*.

The employment of foreigners in Germany had by now become accepted as a fact of wartime life, and in view of their own personal worries, for most Germans the fate of the foreign workers was of precious little interest. Their employment was by no means restricted to major industries, but covered, apart from the administration, the entire economy: from small farms to metal workshops with six employees, up to the Reichsbahn (state railway), local authorities, and the large arms factories, as well as many private households which employed a total of 200,000 Soviet maids, who were much in demand because they were cheap. In the summer of 1944 there were 7.8 million foreigners employed in the Reich: of these, 5.7 million were civilian workers and just under 2 million POW. Of these 2.8 million came from the USSR; 1.7 million from Poland; 1.3 million from France—altogether there were at that time people from nearly 20 European countries employed in the Reich (see Table 2). More than half of the Polish and Soviet civilian workers were women, below 20 years old on average—the typical slave worker in Germany in 1943 was an 18-year-old schoolgirl from Kiev. Thus 26.5% of all those employed in the Reich were foreigners; 46% in agriculture, almost 40% in industry, about 50% in the core armaments industry, and up to 90% in individual concerns that had a large proportion of unskilled labour.

However, from the beginning of 1944 it became apparent that even these quite considerable numbers of workers could no longer meet the labour requirements, particularly those of the big armaments projects. But the recruitment of workers was slowing down, especially from the USSR and attention therefore turned to the only organization that still had at its disposal a considerable potential of labour: the *concentration camps of the *SS. In the first few years of the war the employment of prisoners from concentration camps had not played a part in the war economy, though since 1938 the SS had its own industrial enterprises, mainly quarries, brickworks, and repair shops, and nearly all prisoners were drawn into some kind of slave labour. But even in this situation, the concept of work as punishment, 'education', or 'revenge' was still upheld. In practice, it led even before 1939, and more so afterwards, to the extermination of those groups of prisoners who held a low rank in the political and racial hierarchy of the Nazis. It was only in the spring of 1942 that the SS began to send more prisoners into armaments work. Yet the volume of arms production in the concentration camps remained extremely low, their productivity being around 17% compared with the rest of the economy. In the debate between the various factions of the SS, the idea of punishment and extermination, as opposed to work and productivity, found continued support. This was due to the mass deportation of Soviet manpower into Germany,

Forced labour, Table 2: Principal nationalities, of foreign civilian workers and prisoners-of-war, their numbers, and the industry in which they worked, August 1944

	Agriculture	*Mining*	*Metal*	*Chemicals*	*Building*	*Transport*	*Total*
Belgians							
TOTAL	28,652	5,416	95,872	14,029	20,906	12,576	177,451
Civilians	3,948	2,787	86,441	13,533	19,349	11,585	137,643
Pris.-of-war	24,704	2,629	9,431	496	1,557	991	39,808
as % of all Belgians workers	16.1	3.0	54.0	8.0	11.8	7.0	100%
French							
TOTAL	405,897	21,844	370,766	48,319	59,440	48,700	954,966
Civilians	54,590	7,780	292,800	39,417	36,237	34,905	465,729
Pris.-of-war	351,307	14,064	77,966	8,902	23,203	13,795	489,237
as % of all French workers	42.5	2.3	39.0	5.0	6.2	5.0	100%
Italians							
TOTAL	45,288	50,325	221,304	35,276	80,814	35,319	468,326
Civilians	15,372	6,641	41,316	10,791	35,271	5,507	114,898
Pris.-of-war	29,916	43,684	179,988	24,485	45,543	29,812	353,428
as % of all Italian workers	9.7	10.7	47.3	7.5	17.3	7.5	100%
Dutch							
Civilians	22,092	4,745	87,482	9,658	32,025	18,356	174,358
as % of all Dutch workers	12.7	2.7	50.2	5.5	18.4	10.5	100%
Soviet							
TOTAL	862,062	252,848	883,419	92,952	110,289	205,325	2,406,895
Civilians	723,646	92,950	752,714	84,974	77,991	158,024	1,890,299
Pris.-of-war	138,416	159,898	130,705	7,978	32,298	47,301	516,596
as % of all Soviet workers	35.8	10.5	36.7	3.9	4.6	8.5	100%
Poles							
TOTAL	1,125,632	55,672	130,905	23,871	68,428	35,746	1,440,254
Civilians	1,105,719	55,005	128,556	22,911	67,601	35,484	1,415,276
Pris.-of-war	19,913	667	2,349	960	827	262	24,978
as % of all Polish workers	78.1	3.9	9.1	1.7	4.7	2.5	100%
Citizens from the Protectorate of Bohemia and Moravia							
Civilians	10,289	13,413	80,349	10,192	44,870	18,566	177,679
as % of all Citizens from the Protectorate	5.8	7.5	45.2	5.7	25.3	10.5	100%
TOTAL	2,499,912	404,263	1,870,097	234,297	416,772	374,588	5,799,929
Civilians	1,935,656	183,321	1,469,658	191,476	313,344	282,427	4,375,882
Pris.-of-war	564,256	220,942	400,439	42,821	103,428	92,161	1,424,047
as %	43.1%	7.0%	32.2%	4.0%	7.2%	6.5%	100%

Source: Contributor.

which had started at that time, and by supplying the war economy with labour, had taken the pressure off the concentration camps.

It was not until the late autumn of 1942 that, at the instigation of *Speer, a new system was introduced in which prisoners from concentration camps were loaned to private businesses in groups of 500, to be housed in external concentration camps specially constructed in the towns. However, this system was slow to develop; in the summer of 1943 only about 100,000 registered prisoners from concentration camps were put to work in this way. Even by the spring of 1944 the armaments ministry was working on the assumption that only 32,000 concentration camp prisoners had actually been placed in the private arms industry.

Another source of forced labour to which the Nazis turned was the Jews. From the end of 1941 the political aim of the National Socialist leadership had been their extermination (see FINAL SOLUTION), not their employment, and the short-term and dangerous—in the racial and political context—use of them as workers had been discouraged. Up to 1944 most had been sent to the death camps (see OPERATION REINHARD), even those who held positions of prime importance in the war economy and despite strong objections and protests from various authorities and firms. Nor, with few exceptions, of which the best known is the construction of the IG Farben works at *Auschwitz, in which 25,000 prisoners died, had those Jews who had escaped immediate extermination been employed long-term in the German arms industry. However, from early 1944, the acute shortage of labour—and the fact that National Socialism had virtually achieved its aim so far as the Jews were concerned—brought a change in policy. Jewish prisoners, including those inside the Reich, were now given work in SS enterprises; in industries that had been relocated to underground sites; and in private businesses, especially those linked to the major industries.

By August 1943 it had been decided, by the highest echelons of the leadership, to start production of the V-2 rocket (see V-WEAPONS), which was to be carried out in underground sites using prisoners from concentration camps. The number of deaths was enormous, particularly during the construction phase of the site in the autumn and winter of 1943–4. The work was simple but physically demanding; it was easy to replace prisoners. Lack of food, pressure of work, and bad living conditions were the reasons for the high death rate, which did not begin to fall until the camp's living quarters were completed and production had started. But by that time, only a few weeks after arrival, the prisoners were worn out.

Projects of this kind, which required tens of thousands, if not hundreds of thousands, of men working three shifts a day, could only be operated using concentration camp prisoners, as only the SS still had reserves of manpower on that scale. But it was not long before even these reserves were insufficient to handle the amount of work required, and in April 1944 Hitler ordered that for shifting armaments and building large bunkers 'the required number of about 100,000 men was to be supplied by suitable contingents of Jews from Hungary'.

By the spring of 1944 the number of work groups of the external units of the concentration camps had grown rapidly (to about 1,600); the list of German industrial concerns that employed prisoners of concentration camps and Jews kept increasing and comprised hundreds of otherwise reputable firms. At the end of 1944 the total number of prisoners from concentration camps (Jewish and non-Jewish) was about 600,000 of whom 480,000 were reported to be actually fit for work. According to the estimates of the Wirtschafts und Verwaltungshauptamt (principal office for economic and administrative affairs), of the SS, about 140,000 of them had been assigned to the underground depots, about 130,000 to the building projects of the *Todt Organization, and about 230,000 were employed in private industry.

The living and working conditions of the concentration camp prisoners varied considerably. They depended on the type of employment, the position of the individual worker in the racial hierarchy of the SS, and not least on the attitude of the management, as well as that of camp leaders, supervisors, and junior and senior foremen. The Jewish prisoners, separated in special teams, suffered the worst conditions. As a general—but very guarded—statement, it could be said that those who were employed in the arms production industry proper had better chances of survival than the prisoners who worked for the concerns owned by the SS, for the big building projects, and especially in the construction of underground production sites. Where building projects and the underground projects were concerned, speed was of paramount importance. For the prisoners, the consequences were appalling, compounded as they were by poor rations, unhealthy subterranean accommodation, the breakneck pace of work, and above all by the endless stream of new prisoners arriving in the often already overcrowded camps. Towards the end of 1944 the life expectancy of prisoners was limited to an average of a few months. Here, a man was worth no more than the amount of physical strength he could muster for the duration of a few weeks. For the hundreds of thousands of people in these camps, work was synonymous with extermination.

When considering the historical significance of the *Ausländereinsatz* (employment of foreigners), there is enough evidence to show that, by the beginning of 1942 at the latest, the German war economy had no alternative but to rely on foreign forced labour. Only the *Ausländereinsatz* enabled Germany to maintain a level of rationing that was the highest in all the European powers involved in the war. Last but not least, it was the foreign workers who contributed to that gigantic surge in growth and modernization that Germany experienced during the war years, a growth that formed part of the foundation for the rapid upward trend of the economy after 1948.

Most of the foreign workers who survived, described as Displaced Persons (see REFUGEES), returned to their home countries immediately after the end of the war. But for the civilian and prisoner-of-war workers from the USSR, May 1945 brought no end to their suffering. After repatriation to their country they were accused, by the Stalinist authorities, of collective *collaboration, and subjected to harsh repression. Quite a number of them were again locked up, often for years, in the GUlag. Their names have not yet been rehabilitated. ULRICH HERBERT

Herbert, U., *Fremdarbeiter. Politik und Praxis des 'Ausländer-Einsatzes' in der Kriegswirtschaft des Dritten Reiches* (Berlin and Bonn, 1985).

Homze, E. L., *Foreign Labour in Nazi Germany* (Princeton, 1967).
Seeber, E., *Zwangsarbeiter in der faschistischen Kriegswirtschaft* (Berlin (DDR), 1964).

Force H was a powerful British naval squadron, really a small fleet, formed at Gibraltar on 28 June 1940. Initially it was commanded by Admiral *Somerville (later by Rear-Admiral E. N. Syfret and then Vice-Admiral Algernon Willis). Though it had its base at Gibraltar it was an independent operational command, which was soon to cause confusion (see NORTH, ADMIRAL). It was created to fill the vacuum left by the French fleet after the fall of *France and to ensure that that fleet did not fall into German hands (see also FRENCH FLEET, SCUTTLING OF). It was involved in the hunt for the **Bismarck* and in the *Madagascar landings, and took part in nearly every naval action and *amphibious warfare landing during the battle for the *Mediterranean before being disbanded in October 1943.

Force J, British *amphibious warfare assault force formed from *landing craft used in the *Dieppe raid of August 1942. It was based on the Isle of Wight off southern England and used by *Combined Operations for training. Most of its landing craft were employed in the *North African campaign landings in November 1942. By the end of 1943 it had virtually ceased to exist, but it was revived as the naval assault force which landed troops on *JUNO beach during the Normandy landings in June 1944 (see OVERLORD).

Force K, British naval squadron which operated during the battle for the *Mediterranean to attack Italian *convoys supplying Axis forces fighting the *Western Desert campaigns. Formed in October 1941 during the siege of *Malta—the island was its base—it destroyed two convoys before a minefield off Tripoli crippled or sank three of its cruisers and a destroyer after the first battle of *Sirte in December 1941. The force was reconstituted in January 1943 after the siege of Malta had been lifted.

Force Viper, British force of 107 Royal Marines which from February to May 1942 patrolled the Irrawaddy and Chindwin rivers during the Japanese advance at the start of the *Burma campaign.

Formations and units

In the armed services of all nations there are and always have been several levels of command so that forces can be effectively ordered and controlled. The global nature of the Second World War meant that hostilities took place in several geographical theatres and this added to the number of levels. Thus, at the very top, national leaders directed the war, operating through their uniformed chiefs of staff. Theatres of war had commanders-in-chief, who controlled the land, naval, and air forces operating in that theatre. *Eisenhower, as Supreme Allied Commander Europe, received his directives for the Normandy landings in June 1944 (see OVERLORD) from the Anglo-American *Combined Chiefs of Staff and operated through his single service commanders—*Ramsay for the Allied navies involved, *Montgomery (land), and *Leigh-Mallory (air). Each service, however, had its own command level terminology.

Formations, Chart 1: Nomenclature of formations and units. The strength figures represent establishment strength and in practice they were often much lower.

Formation or Unit	*Symbol (British)*	*Average approx size (no of men)*	*Rank of Commander (British)*
Army Group	XXXXX ☐	400,000	Field Marshal
Army	XXXX ☐	150,000	General
Corps	XXX ☐	40,000	Lieutenant General
Division	XX ☐	12,000	Major General
Brigade	X ☐	2,500	Brigadier
Battalion	II ☐	750	Lieutenant Colonel
Company	I ☐	120	Major/ Captain
Platoon	••• ☐	35	Lieutenant/ 2nd Lt
Section	• ☐	10	Corporal

Source: Contributor

1. Armies

The normal levels of command are shown in Chart 1. Starting at the top, an army group consisted of 2–5 armies, but was not used by all countries. The Soviet term for an army group was a *front*. During the early part of the *German–Soviet war the Soviets operated an additional command level, the Theatre, or Main Command for Strategic Direction, which was interposed between *Stavka, the General Staff in Moscow, and the *fronts*. Three of these existed, but the concept was abandoned by summer 1942. The Japanese also did not employ army groups as such, but defined this level of command in terms of general armies, most of them having a geographic title, which commanded two or more area armies, roughly the equivalent of a western army (see Japan, Chart 2). Thus, the Southern Army directed

Twenty-Fifth Army in the overrunning of Malaya and Singapore, Fifteenth Army in its invasion of Burma, and Fourteenth Army's landings in the Philippines.

All nations employed armies and it was at this level that specialized roles began to be reflected in their titles. Both the Germans and the western Allies during the 1944–5 campaign in north-west Europe had airborne armies. In the Anglo-American case the First Airborne Army supervised the airborne operations during the Normandy landings, *MARKET-GARDEN, and the *Rhine crossings, but the German Third Parachute Army fought solely as infantry. The Germans also had the Twentieth Mountain Army, which fought in northern Finland and Norway. In addition, they had a number of panzer armies, which began to be created from the end of 1941 onwards to reflect formations made up largely of tanks and mechanized/motorized infantry. In 1945 the Germans also had two *SS armies, Sixth and Eleventh. The Red Army, too, formed Tank Armies, but also had Shock and Guards Armies. Shock Armies were strengthened formations employed in breakthrough operations, while Tank Armies were used to exploit them. The 'Guards' prefix was an honorific granted to armies which had distinguished themselves in action and were thereafter used as élite troops in especially difficult situations. The Japanese, on the other hand, only had conventional formations. Area Armies were responsible for a particular operational area and had overall charge of whatever formations were deployed in it. For example, the Burma Area Army both oversaw the operations conducted by several Japanese armies against the British and was responsible for the internal security of the country. A Japanese Army performed the same function as a British or American corps as it commanded a number of divisions. However, the Chinese armies which fought in the *Burma campaign only equated in size to an American or British division.

Except for the Japanese, the armies of all combatant nations comprised 2–5 corps, and what were called Army Troops, mainly additional artillery, engineers, and logistics units, which were directly controlled by the army. A corps was like an army in miniature, but varied greatly in size. A Red Army Tank Corps, shown in Chart 2, was on the small side, equating more to an American or British division. Indeed, it had no divisions in it, being built around brigades. In the conventional corps the number of divisions varied up to a general maximum of five. The most common type of division was the infantry division (known as a Rifle Division in the Red Army), and Table 1 shows the composition of a US infantry division in terms of numbers of men and weapons in July 1943 and January 1945. In action it would often have additional elements—tanks, anti-aircraft guns, tank destroyers—attached to it. In a Japanese division, commanded by a lt-general, the infantry elements were under an Infantry Group HQ commanded by a maj-general, who might have other elements assigned to him for specific missions.

The British and Dominion divisions were essentially made up of two or three brigades. In the divisions of other armies they were termed regiments. The exception

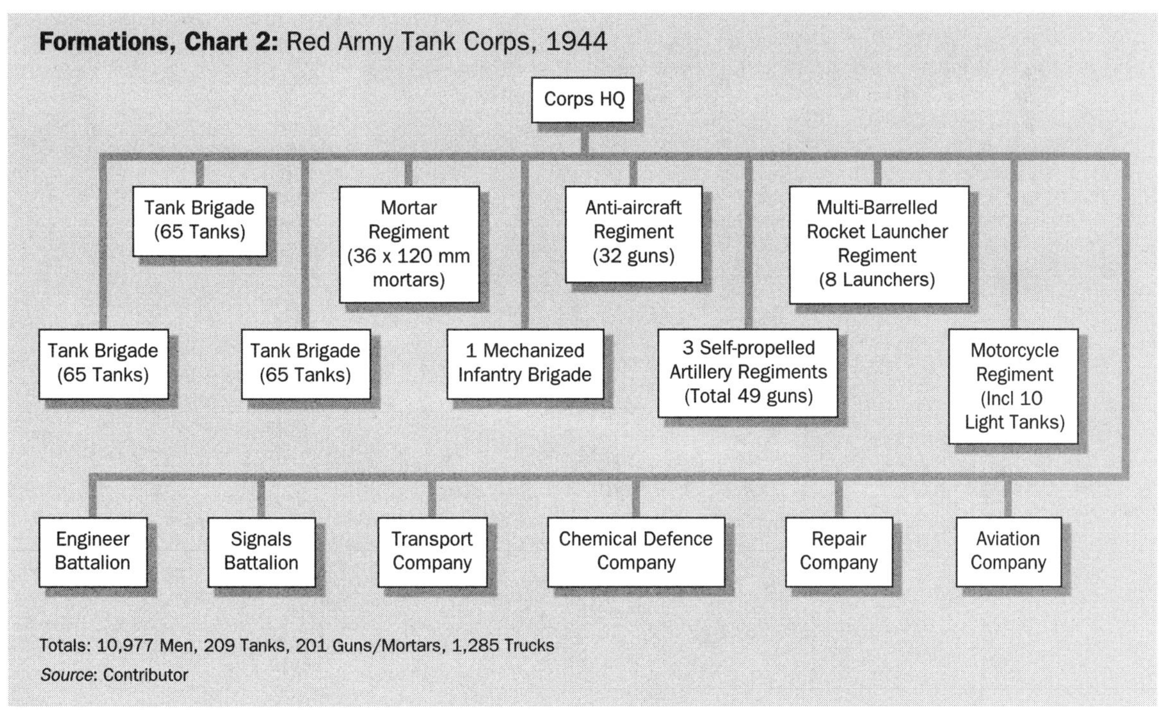

Formations, Chart 3: Infantry Battalion Organization

Commanding Officer: Lt-Colonel (A)

Battalion Headquarters
Second-in-Command/Executive Officer (B), Chief of Staff, Operations Officer, Intelligence Officer, Defence Platoon

Headquarters Company
Company Headquarters
Signals Platoon
Transport
Administrative Services:
Clerical
Medical
Supply

Heavy Weapons/ Support Company (C)
Company Headquarters
Medium Mortar Platoon (D)
(6 Mortars),
Machine Gun Platoon (E)
(6 medium/heavy machine-guns)
Anti-tank Platoon
Anti-aircraft Platoon (F)
(4 or 6 anti-tank guns) (G)
Pioneer Platoon (H)

Rifle Companies (3 or 4, each)
Company Headquarters:
Company Commander (J),
Second-in-Command
Sergeant-major/senior sergeant
(company adjutant)
Quartermaster/supply sergeant
Signallers, orderlies, clerk, and storeman

Rifle Platoon (3, each)
Platoon Headquarters:
Platoon Commander (K)
Platoon Sergeant
Signaller, runner, orderly
Light mortar team (L)
Light Anti-tank team (M)

Rifle Section/Squad (3, each)
Section Commander
Riflemen
Light machine-gun team

Established strength: between 685 and 1240 (N)

Notes:

(A) Sometimes a major. By the end of the war, German, Japanese, and Soviet battalions were commanded by captains or lieutenants.

(B) In American battalions the second-in-command was the battalion chief of staff; in British and Commonwealth battalions, the adjutant.

(C) At the outset of war, some armies had their heavy weapons in headquarters company.

(D) Equipped chiefly with 3 in. (81 or 82 mm.) mortars. See also (F) and (G), below.

(E) British Commonwealth battalions disposed Bren carrier platoons as the commanding officer's fire-power reserve, but were provided with Vickers MMG in, for example, jungle and mountain fighting.

(F) Not all armies had such a platoon established. In any case, all elements were responsible for disposing light machine-guns for anti-aircraft fire if under threat of air attack. The British fielded machine-gun battalions and divisional support battalions with machine-guns and heavy (i.e. 120 mm.) mortars.

(G) These were variously armed, e.g., the German, 37 mm., 42 mm., and 50 mm., the Soviet 45 mm., British 6-pounder. Some armies, including the German and Soviet, disposed specialist anti-tank companies and heavy mortar companies, manned by infantrymen, in their regiments.

(H) Capable of simple field engineer skills, including laying, detecting, and lifting mines. Not all armies included such sub-units.

(J) Company commanders were captains in most armies; from 1943 in the British infantry, majors.

(K) Almost universally, a lieutenant (or second-lieutenant) command. By the middle of the war, many platoons were commanded for periods by sergeants owing to officer casualties.

(L) (M) In the US Army, each rifle company had a heavy weapons platoon including two 60 mm. mortars and two medium machine-guns.

(N) German, Japanese, Soviet and French battalions were smaller than those of British and Commonwealth battalions, much smaller than US battalions, whose rifle companies were almost twice the size of all others, and whose supporting elements were more numerous. However, by the end of the war, Axis units were often down to 300 all ranks, Allied units to 500.

Source: General Farrar-Hockley

Formations, Table 1: Organic composition of US Infantry Division, 1943–5 (aggregate strengths; principal equipment)

Unit	*15 July 1943*	*24 January 1945*
Entire Division	**14,253**	**14,037**
Division Headquarters	**158**	**166**
Infantry	***9,354***	***9,204***
Regiment (three)	3,118	3,068
Hq. & Hq. Company	108	104
Band	–	–
Service Company	114	111
Anti-tank Company	165	159
Cannon Company	118	114
Battalion (three)	871	860
Hq. & Hq. Company	126	121
Heavy Weapons Company	166	160
Rifle Company (three)	193	193
Field artillery	**2,160**	**2,111**
Hq. & Hq. Battery, Division Artillery	114	114
Band	–	–
Light Artillery Battalion (three)	509	497
Headquarters Battery	132	126
Service Battery	77	74
Firing Battery (three)	100	99
Medium Artillery Battalion	519	506
Headquarters Battery	115	112
Service Battery	77	76
Firing Battery (three)	109	106
Anti-tank Battery	–	–
Auxiliary units	**2,074**	**2,046**
Reconnaissance Troop	155	149
Engineer Battalion	647	620
Medical Battalion	465	443
Quartermaster Company	193	186
Ordnance Company	147	141
Signal Company	226	239
Military Police Platoon	73	106
Division Headquarters Company	110	104
Band	58	58
Miscellaneous	–	–
Attached medical	**494**	**497**
Infantry Regiment (three)	135	136
Division Artillery	57	57
Engineer Battalion	17	17
Quartermaster	–	–
Special Troops	15	15
Attached chaplain	**13**	**13**
Principal armament		
Rifles, cal 30	6,518	6,349
Automatic rifles, cal 30	243	405
Machine-guns, cal 30	157	211
Machine-guns, cal 50	236	237
Mortars, 60-mm	90	90
Mortars, 81-mm	54	54
Anti-tank rocket launchers	557	558
Anti-tank guns, 37-mm	–	–
Anti-tank guns, 57-mm	57	57
Guns, 75-mm.	–	–
Howitzers, 75-mm	–	–
Howitzers, 75-mm, self-propelled	–	–
Howitzers, 105-mm	54	54
Howitzers, 105-mm, self-propelled	–	–
Howitzers, 155-mm	12	12
Vehicles, all types (except boats and aircraft)	**2,012**	**2,114**

Source: Greenfield, K., Palmer, R., and Wiley, B., *US Army in WWII: The organization of Ground Combat Troops* (1947).

Formations, Table 2: Strength of a tank battalion. Organizations were frequently changed as the war progressed.

Nationality	*Year*	*No. of tanks*	*Remarks*
France	1940	34	Heavy tank battalion.
Germany	1944	90	Actual strength was usually only 50% of this.
Italy	1942	52	
Japan	1942	57	
UK	1942	61	
USA	1943	70	
USSR	1941	36	

Source: Contributor.

to this was the US armoured division during the latter half of the war. This had three tank and three infantry battalions, which for operations were apportioned to three headquarters elements known as combat commands.

Brigades and regiments within divisions usually consisted of three battalions of the same type, with infantry regiments often also each having an anti-tank gun company and a light howitzer company. An exception to the 'rule of three' was that British and Dominion armoured brigades had three tank and one motorized infantry battalions. Those armies which did not have divisional brigades, did employ brigades elsewhere. The Red Army, as we have seen, had tank and mechanized brigades within its tank and mechanized corps. Early in the war it also deployed independent tank brigades. Other nations also had independent brigades which had their own artillery, engineers, and logistical units. The Japanese termed them Independent Mixed Brigades, while the British called them Brigade Groups.

The brigade was the lowest formation; those below it in the command structure—battalions, companies, platoons, etc.—were known as units and sub-units. This meant that while battalions might be moved between brigades, parts of battalions never were, except on occasion very temporarily for particular operations. Confusion, not least to Axis intelligence, was created by the fact that the British almost alone called their reconnaissance, tank (as did the Japanese), artillery, and engineer battalions 'regiments'.

Chart 3 shows the organization of a typical infantry battalion. Changes during the war were primarily concerned with strengthening the heavy weapons element. Tank battalions varied in strength from nation to nation and during various phases of the war, as Table 2 shows. They were also made up of companies and platoons (British—squadrons and troops). Field artillery battalions generally comprised three batteries each of 6–8 guns, but medium and heavy artillery battalions had only 12–16 guns.

2. Navies

Naval organizations were much simpler than those of armies. At the highest level was the Fleet, which was responsible for a particular operational area, including all naval shore installations. In the Royal Navy and Dominion navies, fleets were broken down into squadrons and flotillas. The former were made up of larger warships by type—battle squadrons (battleships), aircraft carrier squadrons, cruiser and light cruiser squadrons—while the latter, also by type, represented smaller warships—destroyers, submarines, motor torpedo boats. A squadron would consist of 4–6 ships, while a flotilla had 6–12. Escort vessels (destroyers, frigates, corvettes) operated in escort groups of 4–8 ships.

The US Navy took a more flexible approach. Its fleets formed Task Forces, which were tailored for specific operations. They, in turn, would be made up of Task Groups, which equated to British squadrons, and further sub-divided into Task Units. Thus, when the British Pacific Fleet came under American command in the spring of 1945 its fighting portion was designated *Task Force 57 and the *Fleet Train Task Force 112. The German Navy followed the British system, although squadrons tended to be built round one major warship. The Japanese reflected US practice in forming *ad hoc* forces and groups.

3. Air forces

Both the Soviets and the Japanese organized their air forces on army lines and they were part of either the army or the navy. They had air armies and the Soviets also used air corps. Both had air divisions and air regiments, with a regiment consisting of four squadrons (Japanese—companies), each of on average 12 aircraft. The German Luftwaffe had its *Luftflotten* (air fleets), which also had corps and divisions, but thereafter had a singular organization (see GERMANY, 6(d)). The British, too, had a unique system (see UK, 7(d)). The Americans had a mixed organization. An army air force had under it a number of commands, reflecting its various roles. Thus for the Normandy landings the Ninth US Army Air Force had Ninth and Nineteenth Tactical Air Commands, Ninth Bomber Command, and Ninth Troop Carrier Command. The Eighth US Army Air Force, which was primarily a strategic bombing formation, subdivided its Eighth Bomber Command into bombardment divisions, but most Commands were divided into Groups each of which had a number of squadrons (see USA, 5(c)).

CHARLES MESSENGER

Mollo, A., *The Armed Forces of World War II: Uniforms, Insignia and Organisation* (London, 1981).

Formosa. So-called by the Portuguese who visited it in 1590 (Port. *formosa*, beautiful), this island off the China coast, with a five-million population, had been ceded to Japan by China in 1895. At the start of the *China Incident the Japanese launched attacks against the Chinese mainland from it, and on US air bases on Luzon (see CLARK FIELD) at the start of the first *Philippines campaign in December 1941. At the Cairo conference in November 1943 (see SEXTANT) it was pronounced that the island had been stolen from China and would be returned to it, which it was.

Forrestal, James V. (1892–1949), US banker who, from June 1940, served as one of Roosevelt's special administrative assistants before being appointed to the newly created post of under-secretary of the navy that August. As deputy to James *Knox, Forrestal's responsibility was the US Navy's wartime procurement programme. He travelled extensively to combat areas and after succeeding Knox in May 1944 he became the first secretary of the navy to land under fire when he visited US forces on *Iwo Jima in April 1945.

In many ways he was a man of contradictions and he was slow to make decisions, but the navy flourished under his skilled administration. That he was the sole survivor of Roosevelt's cabinet in the administration of President *Truman shows his political acumen, but he always thought of himself as an investment banker and always listed his address in Washington as 'temporary'. In July 1947 he became first US secretary of defense.

Forschungsstelle (research post). This German intelligence unit, situated in the Netherlands and, from the autumn of 1944, in Bavaria, was able to intercept and unscramble transatlantic telephone conversations. Many of them were routine calls between minor officials but it also intercepted the conversations of *Halifax, *Harriman, *Eden, *Hopkins, and those between Churchill and Roosevelt. Nothing of real substance seems to have been gleaned by the unit from any of these conversations, presumably since those involved supposed that the line might be insecure. See also RADIO COMMUNICATIONS and SOURCE K.

FORTITUDE, see DECEPTION.

Foulkes, Lt-General Charles (1903–68), English-born but Canadian educated Canadian Army officer who rose from being brigade major with the 1st Canadian Division in September 1939 to commanding the 2nd Canadian Division during the *Normandy campaign. From November 1944 he commanded the 1st Canadian Corps in the *Italian campaign and then in north-west Europe where he accepted the surrender of German forces in the Netherlands. In May 1945 he returned to Canada as the Canadian Army's Chief of General Staff. See also CANADA, 6(a and b).

Four Freedoms. Having won a third term as US president in November 1940, Roosevelt became more openly pro-Allied, and on 6 January 1941 he espoused, in a speech to Congress, four essential human freedoms: freedom of speech; freedom of worship; freedom from want; and freedom from fear. In world terms this last freedom meant a global reduction in armaments so that no nation could commit an act of aggression against another. Two of his points, freedom from fear and from want, were mentioned as desirable objectives in the *Atlantic Charter.

Four-Power Declaration, signed at the *Moscow conference on 30 October 1943 by the UK, USA, USSR, and, on American insistence, by China. It restated the determination of the signatories to stand by the *United Nations Declaration, reiterated the call for *unconditional surrender of the Axis powers, and recognized the need to establish an international organization 'for the maintenance of international peace and security', and to ensure the rapid and orderly transition from war to peace. See also GRAND ALLIANCE.

foxhole. Unlike a *slit trench, this was dug by infantrymen to hold only one or two men.

FRANCE

For the fighting in France, see FRANCE, FALL OF, after this entry; for details of the activities of the Free French, see DE GAULLE.

1. Introduction

The declaration of war against Germany at 1700 on 3 September 1939 by the government of Edouard *Daladier was received by the French with a mixture of surprise, consternation, and resignation. Mobilization had been ordered the day before, and the war credits had been unanimously voted. Even if there was no overt enthusiasm for war, 76% of a public opinion poll in July 1939 had supported the notion of force if Hitler tried to seize *Danzig. Contrary to claims later made by the Vichy government (see below), defence expenditure under the Popular Front had risen faster than other public spending, and under Daladier in 1938–9 the defence budget was trebled. Daladier, unlike *Chamberlain, brought back no illusions after signing the *Munich agreement, though the foreign minister, Georges Bonnet, was a fervent advocate of a settlement with Germany. The population, which stood at 41.18 million in 1936, had suffered terrible losses in the *First World War (for losses in the Second see Table 3 at the end of this entry), and the French public was receptive to pacifist ideals in the 1930s, though national pride in the victory of 1918 remained high and no current of defeatism swept through France in September 1939. However, there was bewilderment at the shift of government policy from peace to war, and a feeling that France was too subservient to British foreign policy; there was also a lack of any motivating war aim. The emphasis was on defence.

After eight months of what was soon called the *drôle de guerre* (see PHONEY WAR), France was invaded on 10 May 1940 and staggeringly defeated in under six weeks. *Reynaud, who had replaced Daladier on 20 March, resigned on 16 June. With the Germans already well south of Paris and the government evacuated to Bordeaux, the new premier, Marshal Philippe *Pétain, aged 84, called on the French to lay down their arms. He negotiated an *armistice first with Germany and then with Italy (which had declared war on France on 10 June but without any military successes). From June 1940 to the Allied invasions of June and August 1944 (see OVERLORD and FRENCH RIVIERA LANDINGS), France was subjected to German, and partially Italian, occupation, but until November 1942 there was an unoccupied zone in the south. From this zone Pétain led a government centred on the spa town of Vichy and created a new *État* (State). The regime became increasingly identified with *collaboration and collapsed at the *liberation of France, when the Allied forces, de *Gaulle and the Free French, and the widespread resistance movements within France (see below), all joined to drive out the invader. In August 1944 a Provisional government under de Gaulle took power. It was formally recognized by the Allies in October 1944, and France ended the Second World War as one of the victorious powers.

2. Domestic life, economy, and war effort

Following the *Nazi–Soviet Pact, much of the first four months of the war against Nazi Germany was spent by press and public in calls for action against *communism and Soviet Russia. The fate of the Finns in the snows of the Winter War (see FINNISH–SOVIET WAR) preoccupied the popular magazines such as *Match*. On the German Front the daily communiqué was *rien à signaler* ('nothing to report'), and people began to complain of being badly informed. The broadcasts of the minister of information, the playwright Jean Giraudoux, were too abstract, and the large numbers who heard Paul Ferdonnet broadcasting for Germany on Radio Stuttgart and proclaiming that 'the British would fight to the last Frenchman', felt that Germany was winning the propaganda war (see SUBVERSIVE WARFARE). French posters promised, '*Nous vaincrons parce que nous sommes les plus forts*' ('We shall win because we are the stronger') and few people doubted this. They were also reassured by Daladier's promise in December 1939 that French blood would not be needlessly split. But once the Germans had crossed the Meuse, the pattern of poor information produced a rash of rumours which fuelled the panic of the population. Marc Bloch in *L'Etrange Défaite* ('Strange Defeat') was one of many to look back on the *drôle de guerre* and accuse the authorities of not respecting the public's right to know.

In the general mobilization workers had been taken out of vital factories and sent to the front, so that peasants should not once again bear the brunt of the war. Production immediately slumped, so that two million workers were brought back and specially assigned to the armaments industry. Rural attitudes hardened against this decision. Nothing, however, prepared town or country for the mass exodus of population provoked by the German invasion. This civil disaster is inseparable from the military fall of France. It was the biggest migration of people seen in Europe since the Dark Ages. In the hot sun of May and June, broken by fierce thunderstorms, between 8 and 10 million people fled from their homes (see also REFUGEES). Hundreds of *children were separated from their parents, hundreds of lives lost in the low-level strafing by the Luftwaffe. The experience was a nightmare. In the depths of despair people welcomed Pétain's cease-fire. Acceptance of his sacrificial gesture, when he pledged to give himself to France (*le don de ma personne*), produced a cult of the Marshal which assumed religious proportions, though the veneration for his moral leadership did not translate into equal support for the Vichy government. Pétainism as a popular force survived until 1943 or after, but the public had lost any early hopes in Vichy by the winter of 1941–2. Where Pétain appeared to unite, Vichy divided.

Pétainism and Vichy did not monopolize people's choice, and as more and more people chose to adopt attitudes, or undertake actions, of *resistance, this too became a determinant in their lives. It is difficult, therefore, to generalize about the war effort or the economy. For some it was a matter of working resentfully for the Germans, for others it was a question of maintaining a distinct French economy, and for still more it was undermining German economic demands (see Tables 1 and 2) by strikes, go-slows, non-co-operation and sabotage (see SUBVERSIVE WARFARE), and of diverting resources to the Resistance. Vichy extended rationing and state control of prices and labour, and *comités d'organisation* were entrusted with the day-to-day running of the economy within the framework of a labour charter which banned all national trade unions and instituted a corporate system of industrial relations based on the individual firm. At the top, economic technocrats produced a ten-year plan in 1942, which gave priority to the agricultural sector, in line with expectations of the French role within the German-dominated New Europe (see GERMANY, 4). All such planning was vitiated by acute shortages of materials and labour due to German controls and the absence of 1,600,000 men in *prisoner-of-war camps. By 1943 Germany was taking 40% of France's total industrial output, including 80% of its vehicle production. At least 55% of the government's revenue

France, 2, Table 1: German requisitions. Percentage of French output.

Corn	13%
Hay	19
Meat	21
Fish	30
Potatoes	2
Sugar	1
Tobacco	7
Beer	10
Champagne	56
Spirits	25
Wood	50
Coal	29
Mineral ores	74
Steel	51
Bauxite	50
Aluminium	75
Rubber	38
Sulphuric acid	36
Vegetable oils	40
Wool	59
Cotton	53
Flax	65
Copper	67
Cement	55

Source: Contributor.

France, Table 2: German orders to French industry. Percentage of total orders.

Aeronautical	67–100%
Automobile	68
Electrical	43
Shipbuilding	78
Chemical	33
Rubber	62
Woollen	28
Cotton	15
Hosiery	16
Building and public works	72
Quarrying	55

These figures have been arrived at by comparing different sets of official statistics. Given the disparities within these statistics, all figures have to be treated with caution.

Source: Contributor.

went to meeting the costs of occupation, set at 20,000,000 marks per day, with an imposed exchange rate devaluing the franc by 20%. France became the most important source of *raw materials, foodstuffs, and manufactured goods for the German economy, totalling goods and services roughly equivalent to a quarter of Germany's gross national product.

Within this economic subjection, labour was forced to play a substantial part. Service in Germany was introduced by Vichy on a nominally voluntary basis in June 1942: it became an obligatory duty imposed on all male workers of national service age by the promulgation of the Service du Travail Obligatoire (STO), the Compulsory Labour Service, on 16 February 1943. This law was the single biggest spur to public resistance, and the popular revolt against STO severely undermined the forces of law and order. Nevertheless more than 600,000 men were sent to Germany, and a larger number was drafted into French mines and industries deemed essential to the Germans, such as bauxite and aluminium, or engaged in construction works such as the *Atlantic Wall, run by the *Todt Organization.

Shortages (*la disette*) and making-do (known as *le système 'D'* from *débrouiller*, to manage), were the staple features of everyday life. Only 65% of pre-war coal production was achieved; industrial production fell to 38% of 1938 levels; agricultural productivity was reduced by 30%, and the average cost of living went up by 270%. A notional calorie intake set at 1,200 a day was an insufficient diet, and even that was rarely obtained by the poorer sections of society who could not afford black market prices. By early 1942 Vichy faced the constant threat and reality of food riots and demonstrations, led by women whose earning power had been curtailed by Vichy's hostility to working mothers. Peasant producers alienated the towns by refusing to sell at the uneconomic prices enforced by Vichy, but they also undermined German requisitions and in many areas became an integral part of the *Maquis. In the citrus fruits and wine-producing areas of the south, where the climate made it impossible to cultivate extra vegetables, there was both urban and rural deprivation, while in the north there was the added scourge of Allied bombing. This began in earnest on 3 March 1942 with a raid on the Renault factories in the suburbs of Paris which cost 623 lives, exceeded by the raid on Nantes on 16 September which killed 1,150. The French ultimately lost more than 60,000 in Allied raids—about the same number as the British lost to German air attacks—but the context was one of a violent upsurge in German deportations, repression, and reprisals from 1942 to 1944, including the brutal deportation of more than 75,000 Jewish men, women, and children (see FINAL SOLUTION).

The liberation brought ecstatic scenes throughout France and nurtured hopes of radical change, but there were still the same, or even worse, problems of shortages and underproduction. The French war effort continued with less than half the railways in use, moribund industrial plant, the franc at a sixth of its 1939 strength, and a quarter of all buildings damaged or destroyed. Needing urgent help in resettlement were a million homeless families, the survivors of the camps and over a million homeless families, the survivors of the camps and over a million returning prisoners of war, the population of Alsace-Lorraine, which had to be reintegrated, and refugees from all the battle zones. De Gaulle's Provisional government (see GOVERNMENT (d) below) set up *comités d'entreprise* to stimulate production, and nationalized the northern coal mines and the Renault car works, but they had to continue unpopular requisitioning of food and strict rationing during an unusually long winter, which made the festive rejoicings of the liberation seem a little premature. On the domestic front the war had largely been a struggle for personal survival, finally, but not completely, subsumed in the collective struggle of the resistance. The humbling subjection of loss and defeat, and the ambiguities resulting from the *occupation, could not as easily be assimilated.

3. Government

(a) Pre-armistice

In March 1940 Daladier's policy of caution—not just towards Germany but also towards helping the Finns—was rejected as inaction, though at home he had made a move against the USSR by dissolving the Communist Party and arresting hundreds of its members. This persecution did much to keep party loyalties alive in clandestine survival and create an important training-ground for later resistance.

Daladier's successor, Paul Reynaud, appeared more belligerent than he actually was, and policy did not radically change. He was confident in France's long-term superiority, backed by the resources of the empire (see EMPIRE, below). The unreality was shattered by the rapid German advances, and ironically the men brought in to stiffen French resolve, General *Weygand as C-in-C, and the venerable Marshal Pétain, became the focus for a group in the cabinet which decided the war was lost. They prepared the way for an armistice, rejecting last-minute ideas of continuing government from either Brittany or North Africa, favoured by Reynaud, and the idea of a Franco-British union, improbably dreamed up in London to prevent a French surrender.

Caught in the exodus of population and administrators, the government had trailed south to Bordeaux, while town halls were vacated with scant regard for the fate of people left behind or overtaken by the Germans. Posters produced by the German forces played on the theme of an 'abandoned people', and Pétain quickly decided that the institutions of the Third Republic had failed the country both before and during the crisis. His broadcast of 17 June made no attempt to blame the army leaders for the defeat, and the armistice was negotiated against a background of political recrimination. Technically it was the last government of the Third Republic which signed the armistice and organized the vote in the National Assembly on 10 July 1940 which gave full powers to Pétain. The overwhelming mandate by senators and deputies (569 votes to 80) allowed Pétain to promulgate the first constitutional acts of a new state, and it is with his regime that the armistice became associated. The acts carried a vague promise of ratification by the nation and it was on the basis of this slender gesture to democracy that many republican stalwarts voted for the Marshal. It was only seven days after the British attack on the French fleet at *Mers-el-Kébir, and the politicians were meeting at Vichy, only a short distance from the heavy German presence on the demarcation line. The vote was a turning inwards under the shock of the débâcle and the feeling of being betrayed by the UK which, once again, was perceived as *l'Albion perfide*. There was also a genuine belief that Pétain had saved France from an even greater disaster. It was the beginning of the cult of Pétainism, which gave him a personal ascendancy of mythic proportions.

(b) The Occupiers

The armistice was signed in a staged re-enactment of 1918, with the Germans imposing many of the same conditions which had humiliated them after the First World War. The French Army was reduced to 100,000 men, occupation costs were set astronomically high, and France was divided into several different zones of occupation (see Map 34). The French lost the industries of the Nord and Pas-de-Calais which came within the zone attached to direct German rule from Brussels, and the main *zone occupée*, covering the north and west of the country, contained most of France's industrial wealth and the majority of its population. Paris became the seat of the German Military Administration (Militärbefehlshaber in Frankreich) and the capital bristled with German checkpoints, street signs, and Nazi insignia. Every large town had its *Feldkommandantur* and sizeable forces billeted on the population. The armistice made no mention of Alsace and Lorraine, but they were annexed outright by Germany as the first spoils of war, and administered by Nazi **Gauleiters* as part of the Reich. Intense Germanization followed, together with the expulsion of the part of the population considered implacably French, and the mobilization of young men into the German Army.

The Germans used the demarcation line between the *zone occupée* and the *zone libre* to regulate the flow of goods and people, forcing the French in the south to keep the millions of refugees for two or three months while they established an efficient occupation in the north. It allowed them to appear organized and generous in the facilities provided, and subsequent collaboration with the Germans, or *attentisme* (waiting on events), often started with the perception of the occupiers as disciplined and correct. Subsequently many local German commanders extended their reputation for decency by opposing the infiltration of the *Gestapo, but by 1942 its presence was everywhere, and General Karl Oberg was officially invested as head of its operations in France on 28 April 1942 by *Heydrich himself.

German propaganda and cultural control were mediated through the Propaganda-Abteilung and the German embassy in Paris, from which Otto Abetz (1903–58), a francophile Nazi, divided and ruled among the French collaborationist and fascist groups in the capital, and kept in touch with Vichy through the regime's own ambassador to the occupying forces, Ferdinand de Brinon. Abetz's sociability and patronage were central to the projection of a New Europe, crusading against Bolshevism and democracy under Nazi leadership, a vision whose realization in France was disputed by Fritz *Sauckel and Albert *Speer in their competing spheres of labour and production. Sauckel tried to bleed France of all the workers he could transfer into German factories, while Speer undercut his position by keeping substantial numbers in France, employed within his rationalized plan for a new European economy.

By mid-1942 the ideological presence of the Germans was stamped by intensified punishment, repression, and racial persecution. A system of hostage-taking, torture, and executions dominated the German response to resistance attacks, and in 1943–4 this oppression spread to reprisals on whole villages. A hideous norm was set on the night of 1 April 1944 with the massacre of 86 civilians in the village of Ascq near Lille, after an explosion halted a German troop train, but caused no casualties. After the Normandy landings there were massacres at Tulle (99 men hanged), at *Oradour-sur-Glane (more than 600 villagers shot/burned alive), and in the villages of the *Vercors (scores of villagers killed after the defeat of the Maquis). Few areas of France did not experience some *atrocities in the last months of the occupation, the crimes against civilians being perpetrated partly in revenge for resistance actions, partly as punishment for the unwillingness of local officials to intensify the hunt for resisters. In the last six months of

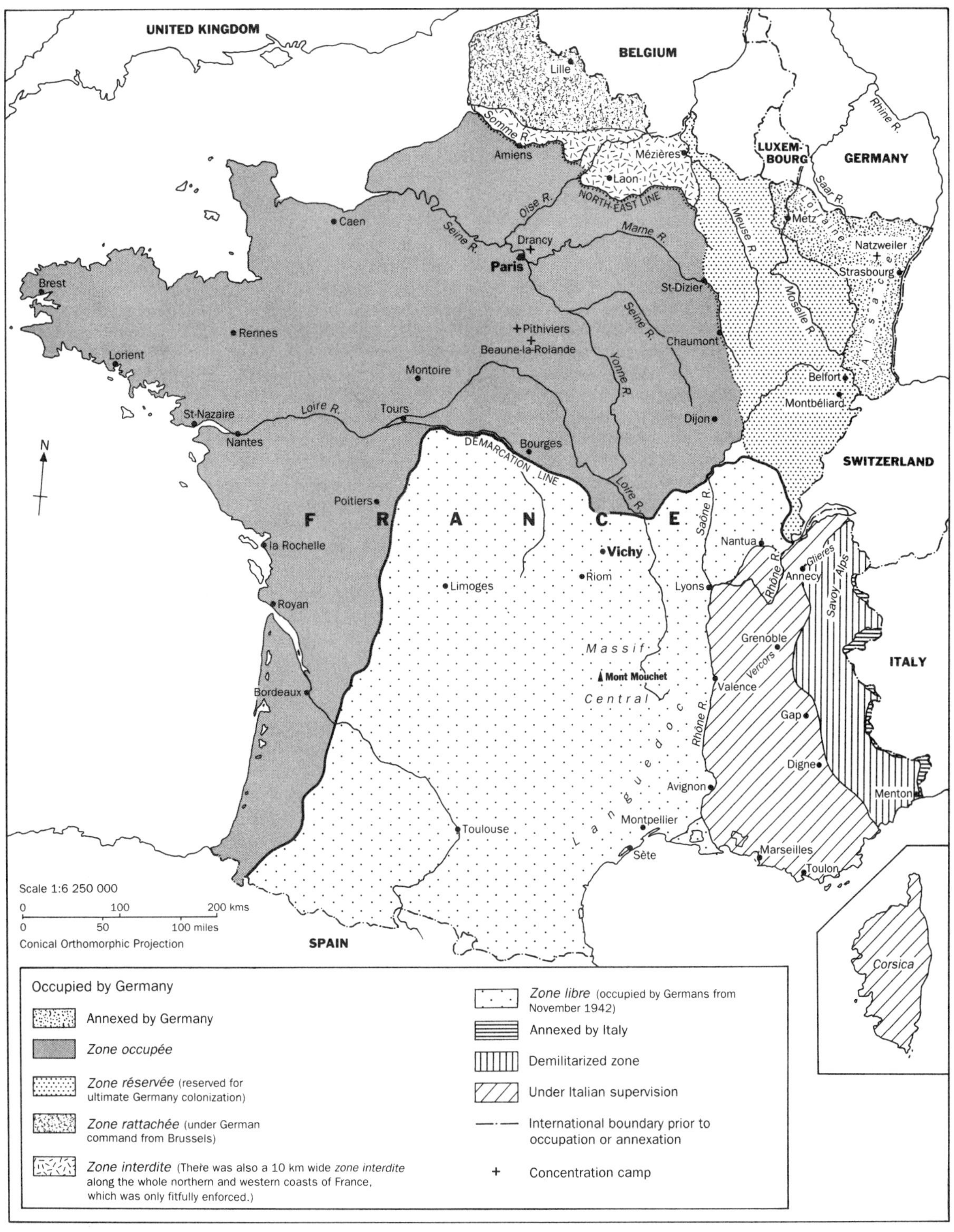

34. Division of **France** after the Armistice, June 1940

the occupation, the Germans encroached on more and more areas previously designated as Vichy spheres of government and by mid-1944 German resources for controlling France were at breaking-point, raising the issue of how Germany could possibly have governed France for four years without the co-operation of Vichy.

This co-operation, or collaboration, was at its height in 1942 when Germany extended the Final Solution to France. A savage hunt for Jews in Paris on 16–17 July 1942 led to appalling scenes of inhumanity when more than 13,000 children, women, and men were herded into the Vélodrome d'Hiver and brutally 'sorted' in the camps of Pithiviers, Beaune-la-Rolande, and Drancy before being deported to the death camps in the east (see OPERATION REINHARD). French police and authorities provided much of the information, assisted in the round-up, and staffed the intermediate camps, and in the Vichy zone carried out similar deportations during August. Ironically it was fascist Italy, in its zone of occupation in south-east France, which provided administrative protection for hunted Jews. Only the premature announcement of Italy's change to the Allied side prevented the escape of thousands of Jews from Nice in the autumn of 1943. The immediate German occupation of the town exposed them to ruthless pursuit and deportation.

(c) The Vichy regime

The spa town of Vichy was envisaged only as a stopping place before a projected return of government to Paris. Archives have shown that Pétain had peace with Germany in mind when he made his overtures for an armistice. In the event he led the new regime from Vichy's Hôtel du Parc for over four years, prefacing the government's decrees with the monarchical formula 'Nous, Philippe Pétain . . . '.

Vichy's rule covered both major zones, but in the *zone occupée* it was subject to the German authorities in Paris. In the *zone libre* it had complete executive power within the restrictions of the armistice.

Vichy was an authoritarian state, patriarchal and messianic, its break with the Republic encoded in a new triad, *Travail, Famille, Patrie*, (work, family, fatherland). It corresponded to the nationalist values which Charles *Maurras had advocated since his opposition to the Dreyfusards in the 1890s, extolling the traditions of old, provincial France, the need to return to rural life (*retour à la terre*), the sanctity of the family with the woman's place in the home (*la femme au foyer*), the benefits of corporatism in industry, and the exclusion of those seen as internal enemies, specifically Jews, Freemasons, and communists. On these principles Vichy launched a moral programme to rejuvenate France by youth organizations, a revived role for the Catholic Church in education, good works known as *l'œuvre du Maréchal*, and the healthy pursuit of sport and the outdoor life. Presented in the form of a *Révolution Nationale* (National Revolution), this ideological offensive was not entirely to the liking of the occupying Germans, who mistrusted its patriotic potential, and several of Vichy's institutional initiatives were banned from the occupied zone. These included the Légion française des Combattants formed of soldiers from both wars, but soon open to all devotees of the National Revolution; the Chantiers de la Jeunesse (youth work camps), compulsory for men aged 20; and the Compagnons de France, a voluntary youth formation.

It is the mixture of autonomy and constraint which needs to be stressed. Vichy was not installed by the Germans as a puppet regime. It was the result of choices and preferences by French politicians who had rejected parliamentary rule (and who included certain dissidents of the Left), and by national figures from the armed forces, high finance, and industrial management who claimed they could salvage France from the wreckage of defeat.

Vichy represented a plurality of aims and motivations, but from the start it was a divisive and punitive regime, acting under the illusion that the widespread veneration for Pétain indicated a similar consensus for its political and social programme. If there was a consensus it was merely a product of the shock and disorientation of the defeat and it did not extend far beyond the winter of 1940–1. By then Vichy had swept away the elected local councils, replaced the mayors of the larger towns with its own nominees, abolished the national structure of trade unions and the federation of employers, reduced all Jews to second-class citizens or worse by two racially-based laws, the *Statuts des Juifs*, and stepped up the persecution of communists. The Freemasons had dissolved their lodges under government pressure, and state employees in all professions were subject to dismissal for left-wing associations. It was the purge of the Popular Front, for which over half of France had voted in 1936. Vichy appeared as a force not of national integration but of political retribution. Its outsiders, mainly immigrant Jews, were interned in camps, first used by Spanish refugees, in the south-west, and a General Commissariat to oversee all Jews and liquidate Jewish businesses was entrusted to Xavier Vallat, who was not pro-German but had introduced anti-Semitic bills throughout the 1930s. In May 1942 his place was taken by Louis Darquier de Pellepoix, an open and venomous racist and advocate of deportation.

Much of the logic behind the armistice had derived from a conviction that France stood alone. The sense of having escaped from the defeat with some measure of national sovereignty and territory intact encouraged Vichy ministers, and particularly Pierre *Laval, the vice-premier, to pursue further negotiations with Germany to improve the position of France in what was presumed to be a new European constellation dominated by Germany. It was not expected that the UK would survive a German attack, and no credence was given to General de Gaulle's appeal of 18 June. He was judged to have deserted the French Army and was sentenced to death *in absentia*. Laval was a tough negotiator and manipulator, an activist in diplomacy in which he pushed at the frontiers of constraint. As an index of his readiness for co-operation, he offered the occupiers the French shares in the Bohr copper mines in Yugoslavia and eased the transfer of the Belgian gold reserves into German hands. He was rewarded by an unexpected meeting with Hitler on 22 October 1940, followed by a second meeting at the small railway station of Montoire two days later. Pétain too came to Montoire, and the handshake of victor and vanquished took on immediate symbolic value. Little was agreed at the meeting, but Pétain used the term 'collaboration' to set up expectations of a two-way process of mutual benefit to France and Germany, which the French public greeted with the first signs of unease. They were momentarily reassured when Pétain sacked Laval on 13 December 1940, for outdistancing other ministers in his approaches to the Germans. In fact Laval's ultimate successor, the anglophobe Admiral *Darlan, came closer to a military commitment to the German cause than any minister either before or after, until the use of the *Milice in the military suppression of the resistance in the last year of the occupation. In May 1941, Darlan offered Hitler the use of French bases in Syria (see SYRIAN CAMPAIGN), and brought back from *Berchtesgaden proposals for a form of joint action in the Middle East, which were known as the *Paris protocols. Pétain refused to sign and Darlan backed down, his 'grand design' against the UK reduced to provocative use of the French fleet to accompany merchant shipping between North Africa and metropolitan France. In so doing he cultivated a special relationship with the USA, whose ambassador to Vichy, Admiral *Leahy, accepted Darlan's assurances that the French fleet and colonies would not be surrendered to the Germans. Darlan used the channel of the US embassy to warn the UK against any interference with French merchant convoys, and in May 1941 indignantly accused it of piratical acts and the seizure of 167 ships. Once the USA moved towards greater commitment to the British cause, Darlan was forced to offer Washington concessions in the French waters of the Caribbean while hiding them from the increasingly exigent Germans. It was evidence of Darlan's success that Leahy stayed on in Vichy after the entry of the USA into the war, and was not recalled by Roosevelt until Laval's return to power in April 1942. American respect for Darlan later became the dynamic in US attitudes towards the rivalry between de Gaulle and first Darlan, then *Giraud, in North Africa after the Anglo-American landings in November 1942 (see NORTH AFRICAN CAMPAIGN). Darlan had remained as commander-in-chief after his loss of power to Laval, and he was in Algeria at the time of the landings. His understanding with the Americans eased the change to the Allied camp. Pétain initially instructed Darlan to resist in the name of French neutrality, but was said to have approved after the event. He now had the opportunity to join Darlan in North Africa, but refused to do so, reaffirming his sacrificial duty to remain in France.

In response to Sauckel's demand for French labour, Laval had set up a 'relief' scheme with the Germans by which one prisoner-of-war would be returned for every three skilled workers who volunteered for work in Germany. It was a typical Laval initiative, offering the Germans a concession in order to avoid something worse, and Laval erected his strategy into a 'shield philosophy' protecting France from the possible rule of a *Gauleiter*. But it was not just manipulation: the volunteer prisoner relief scheme (*la Relève*) was announced by Laval with the statement that he wished for a German victory to prevent the spread of Bolshevism across the continent. These words of 22 June 1942, broadcast to the nation, announced an ideological partnership with Germany, which his collaboration in the deportation of immigrant Jews from the southern camps in August more than confirmed. It was the darkest point of Vichy government. He surrendered thousands of families who believed they had found asylum in France, insisting that they 'must all go' including the very youngest children. Many Jews were found hiding-places in rural areas by humanitarian and resistance action, but the deportations were not halted.

The German occupation of the *zone libre* on 11 November 1942 destroyed any last vestige of the revivalism of 1940. The programme of the National Revolution had fallen short of its own ideals, and now Vichy lost its armistice army and its fleet (see FRENCH FLEET, SCUTTLING OF). It was under mounting pressure from Sauckel that Laval, on 16 February 1943, made the STO compulsory, but the creation of the Milice in January was part of Vichy's own internal move towards a more active partnership with Germany in the repression of resistance. The agreements between the head of the Gestapo in France, General Karl Oberg, and the secretary-general to the Vichy police, René Bousquet, were a cornerstone of this partnership. At local level scores of Vichy administrators and gendarmerie marked their opposition to the new measures by obstructionism and covert support for those on the run. As an administrative unity, Vichy was disintegrating. In January 1944, the accession to ministerial power of *Darnand, head of the Milice, and Philippe Henriot, the effective propagandist on Vichy radio, signalled a further acceleration of repression. On 20 January special courts martial were instituted to expedite the trial of resisters, and armed mobile police (Groupes Mobiles de Réserve) and Milice fought alongside German troops against strongholds of the resistance. Neither Pétain nor Laval ever accepted a co-belligerent status with the Germans in the international war, but both accepted the co-ordination of internal warfare against the resistance. It was not civil war; the repressive forces of Vichy were a very small minority of the French. But it was the final submission of Vichy to the occupiers, and with the liberation of France the government of Vichy, including a protesting Pétain, were taken under German protection to the castle of Sigmaringen on the Danube. From there they went into exile or returned to be judged as traitors by post-liberation courts. Vichy legislation was declared null and void.

The regime has left a legacy of shame, ambiguity, and

recurrent controversy, now known as the 'Vichy syndrome'. Certain of its social policies, such as improved antenatal provision, and its cultural interest in rural traditions are often traded against its negative achievements, and it is acknowledged that most local administrators did try to minimize the impact of the German occupation, and did not promote the Milice. In its first three years Vichy stood opposed to the collaborationist groups of Paris run by Jacques *Doriot (Parti populaire français) and Marcel *Déat (Rassemblement national populaire), and initially refused to give national status to the 3,000 French who fought with the Germans on the Eastern Front in the LVF (Légion des Volontaires français contre le Bolchevisme). But Déat became minister of labour in March 1944, and the LVF was partly legitimated by a change of name. Vichy's racial deportations and internal repression corresponded closely to German demands, and at the very least it can be said that Vichy played a supporting role in the history of Nazism.

(d) Post-occupation government

The structures of government which took power at the Liberation had been meticulously planned by the Gaullist resistance well over a year before Vichy finally collapsed. The pivotal role was that of the Commissaires de la République, who took the place of Vichy's regional prefects and who mediated the decisions of de Gaulle's Provisional government to the Comités Départementaux de Libération composed of local resistance notables. The euphoria and aspirations of the local resistance made these committees the focus for ideas of social change and democratic renewal, but de Gaulle was determined to reconstitute the French state from the top, and his own rejection of the defunct Third Republic and his insistence that worthy resisters should head the new structures of power satisfied many people's desire for change.

Conflicts of aims were, however, not infrequent, and certain commissaires, notably Raymond Aubrac in Marseilles and Yves Farge in Lyons, became identified with the more radical resistance pressures, while the centres of Toulouse and Limoges seemed to threaten overall Gaullist control by their responsiveness to movements of popular power and idealism. Had the Provisional government been more narrowly based it might have provoked even wider protests, but it was representative of most strands of the resistance and included two communists, Charles Tillon, the leader of the Francs-Tireurs et Partisans Français or FTPF, being one of them. The Provisional government was the *French Committee for National Liberation renamed, and in the transfer from Algiers to Paris had lost none of its claims to speak for both the Free French and the internal resistance: Georges *Bidault, the internal leader of the *National Council for Resistance was appointed by de Gaulle as foreign minister, and a socialist, Adrien Tixier, who had been outside France throughout the occupation, as minister of the interior, a crossing of roles which symbolized the unity of the liberation. Recognized by the UK and USA on 23 October 1944 (it had been recognized by the USSR in 1941), the Provisional government defused much of the tension at local level by three major, but controversial, moves. In the first place it rationalized the *ad hoc* process of *épuration* (the purge of collaborators) through the institution of Special Courts of Justice, in which the number of acquittals rapidly came to exceed the convictions; secondly it undermined the status of the Maquis groups by fusing them into the regular army, and thirdly it demobilized and disarmed the local resistance police, the *milices patriotiques*, and created its own new police force the Compagnies républicaines de sécurité (CRS). The Communist Party made no attempt to foster revolutionary ideas, but rather consolidated its popular respectability as the party martyred in the resistance ('le parti des fusillés'), and agreed that national elections should be postponed until the return of prisoners and deportees. Municipal elections (in which women voted for the first time) were held in April–May 1945 and confirmed both the success of resistance individuals and the return of party politics, and when elections to a Constituent Assembly followed in October, over 80% of the seats went to the parties of the Left. The voters had overwhelmingly repudiated the right-wing ideology of Vichy, and in an accompanying referendum they also rejected any return to the Third Republic. They were far less united on what kind of a regime the Fourth Republic should be.

4. Empire

When war broke out the empire was considered one of the main reasons for French optimism (see Map D for French Empire in September 1939). It furnished comforting images of world power, economic resources, and vast reserves of military potential. At the mobilization in August and September 1939, twelve divisions were created from the Armée d'Afrique (see ARMED FORCES (b), below), seven divisions of North African infantry, one Moroccan division, and four African divisions, and by June 1940 some 80,000 colonial troops were deployed on the European stage, the *Tirailleurs from Senegal being considered by the French public as invincible warriors. After the fall of France the Germans treated the black soldiers as racial inferiors, and ordered that the bodies of those killed in the fighting should be left where they fell. (Many were secretly given decent burial by French civilians, a humanitarian act which often represented the first impulse to resistance). It is curious, therefore, that the Armée d'Afrique was allowed to continue and even to expand in the autumn of 1940, and Vichy made much of its diplomacy which had protected the integrity of the empire. It stood firm against any colonial pact with either the Allies or the Free French, and within the colonies the values of Vichy and the leadership of Pétain were enthusiastically embraced by most of the French settlers and governing authorities. Vichy rule was distant, but present, in the protectorate of French Morocco, and the mandates of Syria and the

Lebanon, fervent and popular in Senegal (see FRENCH WEST AFRICA) under Governor-General Pierre Boisson, authoritarian and punitive under Vice-Admiral *Robert in the French West Indies, strongly Pétainist under General Weygand in Algeria, and effectively coexistent with the Bey Ahmed in the protectorate of Tunisia, until the new Bey Moncef placed himself at the head of the nationalists in June 1942. Vichy's hold was weakest over *French Indo-China where Admiral Jean Decoux was forced to concede air and naval bases to Japan in a steady loss of French power, culminating in the deposition of the French governor by the Japanese military command in March 1945.

Well before that date Vichy's imperial pride was undermined from within when the poorer black regions in French Equatorial Africa opted for the Free French and General de Gaulle in August 1940, a crucial strategic and moral secession initiated by the black governor of the Chad, Governor Félix Eboué. In the French West Indies black opposition to the contemptuous rule of Admiral Robert began to look to the Free French, and the Pacific colonies of Tahiti, New Caledonia, New Hebrides, and the Marquesas all sided with de Gaulle as did the few remaining French colonial enclaves in India, the Chinese treaty port of Kwangchowan, and, after they had been occupied by the Free French in December 1941, *St Pierre and Miquelon. But it was the TORCH landings in North Africa in November 1942 which decisively ended Vichy's colonial and imperial power, and took the French empire once more into the war on the Allied side. The transition for Senegal, Algeria, Morocco, and Tunisia was facilitated by the presence of Admiral Darlan and the leadership of General Giraud, so that the alternative for Pétainist officers of submission to Gaullism or continuing opposition to it was avoided. In *Madagascar the Vichy authorities had tried to resist British invasion, but by September 1942 the British were in a position to hand it over to de Gaulle. Soon after, the Réunion Islands went over to the Gaullists, followed by French Somaliland which was starving under the British blockade.

By the end of 1942 Vichy had lost its Armistice Army, its fleet, and then its Armée d'Afrique and its empire. But the re-entry of colonial armies into the war against Germany, and the presence of many individuals as volunteers with the Free French, kept the colonies within the orbit of French national and imperial power. De Gaulle in 1944 had more reason than Pétain in 1940 to regard the empire as his underlying strength. His debt to the peoples of black Africa was later to play a role in shaping his relative success in the process of decolonization. At the same time, the reaffirmation of Empire (see BRAZZAVILLE CONFERENCE), as France came back into the war as a full belligerent, also accounts for the failure of France to reconsider its imperial assumptions in the most divided of its overseas territories, French Indo-China and Algeria. The new Algerian statute of 7 March 1945 merely perpetuated the rule of racial discrimination, and when a revolt broke out in Kabylia in May, it was crushed with great brutality. Another war of liberation loomed, in which the Algerian people would claim the mantle of resistance.

5. Civil defence

Civil defence was attached to the ministry of war in liaison with the army's anti-aircraft posts which defended many French towns, and depended on volunteers formed in the Association des Volontaires de la Défense passive. Towns were divided into sectors, sectors into *îlots* (blocks) each with its *chef* (head) who supervised all aspects of air raid protection. In November 1938 the possession of gas masks was made compulsory, but on 1 September 1939 only a third of the numbers needed were available, though this had doubled by May 1940. The new phrase *mobilisation des civils* (civilian mobilization) in 1938 was popularized in 600,000 copies of a short guide to civil defence. After the first air raid warning in Paris on 2 September 1939, volunteers enlisted in their thousands. The death penalty was prescribed for anyone caught in the act of pillage during a raid. Several thousand small fines were imposed during the *drôle de querre* for pacifist or defeatist remarks. Sandbags protected Notre-Dame's sculptured porch, and works of art were put in the vaults of the Banque de France or sent away to provincial châteaux. Women's employment was accelerated, and 20,000 extra nurses were enrolled in Paris. Children had been evacuated from the northern and eastern frontiers, but a normal start of the school year, and inaction on the front, prompted many parents to bring them back. After the German invasion a psychosis of fear fuelled extravagant beliefs in treason and *fifth columnists, of which there was little hard evidence. Lone motorcyclists were the prime suspects. The massive exodus of the population made it impossible to defend bridges and roads, and local civil defence was in no way equipped to do so.

6. Armed forces

(a) High Command

The massive fortifications and subterranean defences of the *Maginot Line embodied the military thinking of the general staff, whose strategic ideas were based on the lessons of the First World War and not on the immediate evidence of the *Spanish Civil War, nor on the notions of mechanized mobility enshrined in de Gaulle's book *Vers l'armée du métier* ('Towards a Professional Army') which was published in 1934.

Preparations in terms of conscription had been reduced between 1928 and 1935, when the length of military service was only one year. In March 1935 it was raised to two, but the vast bulk of the mobilized reserve in 1939 came from those trained in the one-year period, with a resulting shortage of combat skills. There had been considerable recruitment in the colonies under the energetic direction of Georges Mandel (1885–1944). The fleet, the fourth most important after the UK, the USA, and Japan, was also cast in a defensive role, its strategy

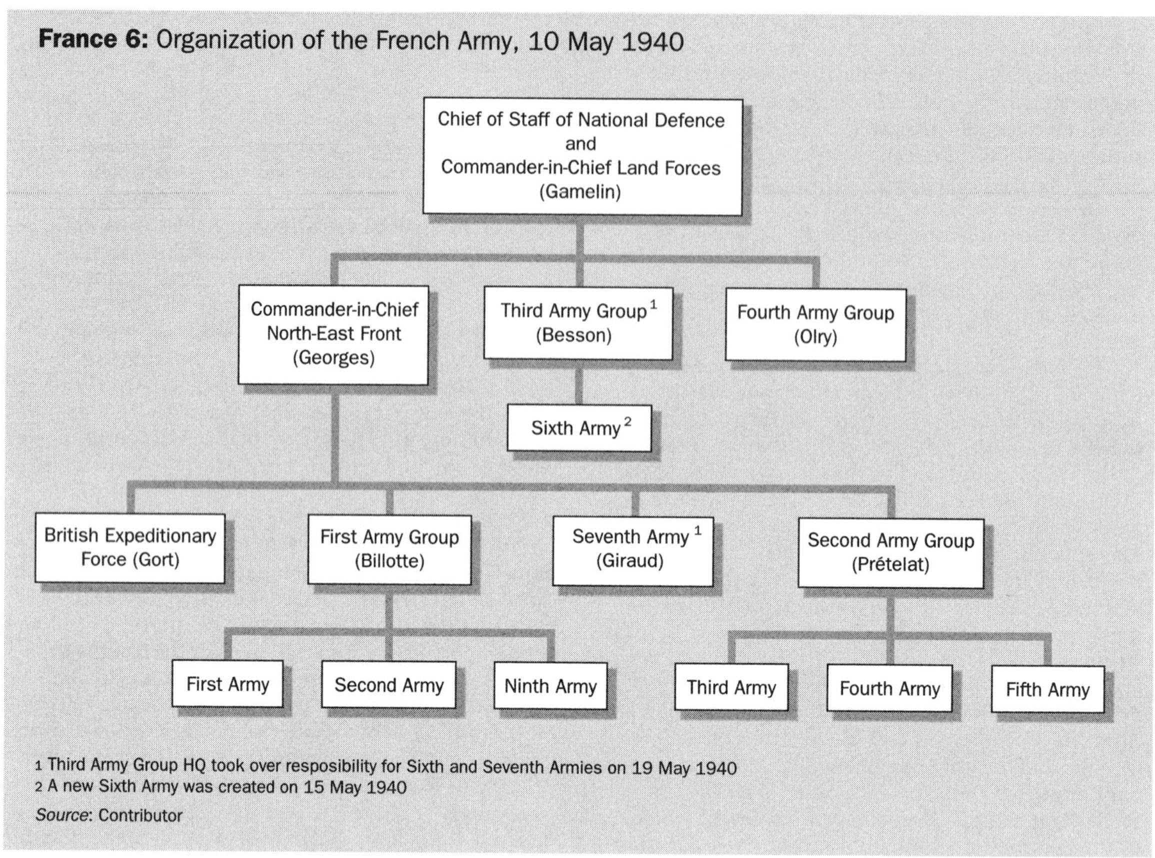

France 6: Organization of the French Army, 10 May 1940

1 Third Army Group HQ took over resposibility for Sixth and Seventh Armies on 19 May 1940
2 A new Sixth Army was created on 15 May 1940
Source: Contributor

linked closely to British dominance in the Atlantic and North Sea. The air force, which only became an independent force in 1934, was continually subjected to pressure from the army to subordinate its operations to the land war. In May 1940 the legacy of peacetime left it under-prepared, ill-equipped, and poorly organized for modern war.

In August 1939, in preparation for joint hostilities against Germany, the French and the British formed a *Supreme War Council, but this was not an operational HQ. The previous month Chamberlain had suggested forming a joint general staff, but the C-in-C of the French Army, the 68-year-old General *Gamelin, was not interested in this proposition. Instead, the *British Expeditionary Force was placed under the command of General Alphonse Georges, who as commander of the North-East Front became, in effect, Gamelin's commander in the field, while Gamelin acted as a kind of supremo (see Chart), not only of the ground forces in metropolitan France but overseas as well. However, he had no direct control of either the air force or the navy. His successor, General Weygand, was appointed Chief of the General Staff of National Defence and C-in-C of all theatres of operations (land, sea, and air) on 19 May 1940, but never exercised his powers. There was no equivalent of the British Chiefs of Staff committee and liaison between the military and their civilian masters was inadequate.

This command system, exacerbated by a mutual antipathy between the two principal protagonists, proved a recipe for disaster, for Georges was responsible for fighting a battle according to plans drawn up by Gamelin with an army which Gamelin had moulded to his own concepts. As a result, once the Germans launched their offensive in the west (see FALL GELB), no one was certain who was actually controlling the battle and this confusion was compounded by the proliferation of headquarters and an inadequate communications system. Gamelin had his command post at Vincennes on the outskirts of Paris while Georges had his main HQ at La Ferté-sous-Joarre some 65 km. (40 m.) east of the capital but spent much of his time at his command post— and residence—at Bondons, 19 km. (12 m.) away. A third, Grand General HQ, commanded by a *major général* (chief of staff), was situated at Montry 32 km. (20 m.), east of Vincennes and south-west of La Ferté, and the C-in-C of the Air Force, General Joseph Vuillemin, had his HQ at a fourth place, St. Jean-les-deux-Jurneaux, near La Ferté; while Admiral Darlan's French naval headquarters was at Maintenon, south-west of Paris.

Montry contained the four Bureaux of the French High Command: First (personnel and organization), Second (intelligence), Third (operations), and Fourth (transport and services). The staff officers of three of them had to divide their time between Montry and La Ferté. The staff of the Fourth Bureau remained at Montry which meant Georges had no immediate access to it. The telephone network was totally inadequate and there was no teletype service between these HQ or between any of them and the armies in the field. Most despatches were sent by motor bike but as several riders were killed in accidents or ended up in a ditch this must have proved as unreliable as the telephone. Consequently, it took six hours for the Army to tell the Air Force which targets it wanted attacked and Gamelin later calculated that it took 48 hours for one of his orders to arrive and be executed by those in the field.

(b) Army

This fell into three groupings: the Armée Métropolitaine, Armée d'Afrique, and the Troupes Coloniales. In theory, each was raised to defend its own territory. The Armée Métropolitaine, underpinned by regular cadres, was a conscript army whose task was to defend metropolitan France. The Armée d'Afrique garrisoned Algeria, Tunisia, and French Morocco and it included a number of white European-only units such as the Foreign Legion and *Zouaves as well as the conscripted *Spahis and *Tirailleurs—drawn from the indigenous population—and the irregular *Goums and Compagnies Sahariennes (camel companies). The Troupes Coloniales, which defended France's other colonies, contained the white-only Colonial infantry and Colonial artillery regiments, mostly volunteer only, and Tirailleurs formed from men from those colonies which had French subject status. In practice, units from both colonial armies were also stationed in France while recruits in the Armée Métropolitaine sometimes had to serve in North Africa if not further afield. In September 1939 over 38% of France's infantry were North African Tirailleurs and it was men from the two colonial forces which largely comprised the Free French forces which so distinguished themselves in the *North African and *Italian campaigns—particularly at *Monte Cassino—and during the fighting which followed the *French Riviera landings.

Seen at the time, the French army mobilized in September 1939 and totalling just under 5 million soldiers, was thought by many—among them Stalin—to be the best in the world, heavily armed and well-equipped and led by highly acclaimed veterans of the victorious army of 1918. Churchill believed that the UK would be safe behind the French army, and the French themselves knew that they had a further two million possible soldiers available in the Empire. Any reconstruction of 1940 must remember that a German attack across the Ardennes and the Meuse was thought to be a military impossibility, even when the French secret services told the High Command of its imminence. In most comparisons of men, material and arms, France was the equal of Germany, and seemed well poised to resist a long drawn-out war. It was the German superiority in the operational deployment and use of tanks and planes that made these comparisons in retrospect look irrelevant.

Of the 94 French divisions at the front or in reserve, 63 were infantry—30 regular, the rest reserve divisions formed around a cadre of regulars—seven were motorized infantry, three were light mechanized, five were cavalry, 13 were attached to the fortifications, and three were heavy armoured. Of the latter, two were assembled in January 1940 and the third composed during March. An improvised fourth was partly constructed in May after the German breakthrough.

Under General Gamelin, the Land Forces C-in-C, who was replaced on 19 May by Weygand summoned from the Middle East, was the North-East Front commanded by General Georges; General Giraud's Seventh Army in the coastal region; General Pierre Billotte's First Army Group, which defended the front from Maulde to the western end of the Maginot Line; General Prételat's Second Army Group and General Besson's Third Army Group which held the Alsace-Lorraine frontiers from Longuyon to Basle; and the Fourth Army Group, under General Olry which held the Alpine Front. The heavy armoured divisions were in reserve, as were two of the motorized infantry divisions, and more than half of the French tanks were spread among the infantry divisions, General Estienne's 'assault tank' having been renamed 'accompanying tank' in the 1930s. The total number of tanks was estimated at over 3,000 on 10 May 1940, and the quality was high, with the Char B tank one of the best war machines of 1940 and the Somua 35 fast for its 20 tons. When all armoured vehicles are taken into account, the French numbers were almost identical to the Germans', though they suffered generally from poor deployment, slower speeds, and insufficient *radio communications equipment. French artillery was superior in numbers (10,700 against 7,378) but not in quality, for half the French pieces were the obsolescent 75 mm. (2.9 in.) First World War field gun while the Germans had the modern 105 mm. (4 in.) gun. More importantly, the French utilized their artillery no better than their aircraft and tanks. It was geared to static warfare and was almost entirely horse-drawn; much of it was paralysed on the roads during the exodus of civilians.

*Anti-tank weapons were thought to be ultimately decisive in open battle, and yet France was still short of such weaponry in May 1940, despite accelerated production during the *drôle de guerre*. Anti-aircraft guns were only taken seriously after 1935, it being presumed that fighter planes were the best defence against enemy aircraft. In September 1939 there were only 325 20 mm. (0.78 in.) and 25 mm. (0.98 in.) machine-guns and cannon out of a planned total of 5,043; 1,696 40 mm. (1.5 in.) and 75 mm. (2.9 in.) cannon out of 2,036; and 16 90 mm. (3.5

in.) anti-aircraft guns for the army's Défence Aérienne du Territoire out of 480. In May 1940 ammunition of many kinds was in short supply, particularly for anti-aircraft and anti-tank guns.

On the Alpine Front which was under Gamelin not Georges, the Fourth Army Group of two mountain divisions and one conventional infantry division were defending well-fortified positions. They had very few anti-aircraft guns and only one small group of fighter planes. Commanded by the energetic General Olry, they faced Italian troops who outnumbered them by seven to one and had considerable air support. Despite intensive bombing these frontiers were successfully held during the battle of the Alps from 20 to 25 June 1940.

After the fall of France in June 1940, the armistice brought a reduction of the army in metropolitan France to 100,000 and a total demobilization of the air force. Military eyes turned to North Africa, where the Armée d'Afrique was authorized to expand to 127,000 after the Royal Navy's attack on Mers-el-Kébir and the *Dakar expedition. Under first Weygand and then General *Juin, it built up to a figure of almost 225,000 including troops from French West Africa and those repatriated after engagements against Free French and British forces in the Syrian campaign. It was heavily armed with modern weapons, and the officers were fiercely attached to Pétain. A direct take-over by de Gaulle at the time of the Allied landings in North Africa (TORCH) in November 1942 would have been unthinkable.

In France the Armée de l'Armistice, by comparison, was only permitted light weapons and its transport was reduced to horses and bicycles. Its eight divisions were stationed at provincial centres in the *zone libre*, but a small number of the abler officers took the opportunity to leave and found a role in different branches of the resistance. Those who were left merely decorated the parades and politics of Vichy. The prisoners-of-war in Germany were not forgotten. Of the two million rounded up during the defeat and kept in transit camps, some 1,600,000 were transported into the Reich. It was the major duty of Vichy's Légion des Combattants to look after their families, most of whom were in the rural areas of France, hence Laval's hope that the *Relève* scheme (see GOVERNMENT (c), above) would find favour among the peasantry. Despite the scheme almost a million were still in Germany at the liberation, mostly used as workers for German agriculture and industry and thus exposed to Allied bombing.

The result of TORCH was to make the troops of North Africa available to the Allies, while in France the armistice army was dissolved by German order on the invasion of the *zone libre*. For several officers this was the decisive break with the Vichy regime, General de *Lattre de Tassigny making for the mountains before being arrested and then escaping to North Africa, and General Giraud taking up the leadership of the Armée d'Afrique. After Darlan's assassination Giraud became military leader in Algeria, disputing authority with de Gaulle. Under his command the Armée d'Afrique's victories in Tunisia in May 1943 ranked with those of the Free French fighting with *Leclerc at Kufra (see FEZZAN CAMPAIGNS) and General *Koenig at *Bir Hakeim. Giraud obtained an agreement with Roosevelt at the Casablanca conference in January 1943 (see SYMBOL) which envisaged the creation of eleven French divisions. Only eight were formed, three of them armoured, one of which, the Second, integrated troops from French equatorial Africa under General Leclerc, a fervent Gaullist and opposed to Giraud's lingering attachment to the principles of the National Revolution. Although outmanoeuvred by de Gaulle at the end of 1943, Giraud's military role continued until he resigned in April 1944, and the Armée d'Afrique distinguished itself in the *Italian campaign (see FRENCH EXPEDITIONARY CORPS).

It was de Lattre and not Giraud who was given the French command of Armée B in the *French Riviera landings on 15 August 1944, Leclerc's division having been diverted to take part in the *Normandy campaign within *Patton's Third US Army. Koenig was given command of the armed resistance, formed into *FFI (Forces françaises de l'Intérieur), which were effectively organized from the spring of 1944 onwards. The immediate achievement of the FFI, the Free French, and the Armée d'Afrique was to vindicate the right of the French to govern their own liberated country, and Leclerc's contribution to the liberation of Paris and de Lattre's to the liberation of the south brought external and internal resistance together. The FFI, however, resented the way in which the resistance was demobilized by the provincial government between 19 and 24 September 1944, leading to the loss of status and individuality of the Maquis resistance units which had been formed from the grass roots. In all, 120–140,000 from the FFI enlisted as regular soldiers, to which must be added those left to harass the 'Atlantic pockets' of Royan, La Rochelle, St Nazaire, and Lorient, where the Germans held out with superior heavy armaments. The main bulk of the reconstituted French armies, which fought as part of *Devers's Sixth Army Group, as the First French Army, liberated Alsace in cruel winter fighting before crossing into the south of Germany and sharing in the Allied victory, marked by the presence of de Lattre at the German capitulation. The winter hardships severely tested the endurance of the colonial troops who had fought through Tunisia and Italy, and it became a point of honour in later years for Africans and Algerians to remind the French that a major role had been played in the liberation of France by troops from the Third World. The Martiniquan writer Frantz Fanon (1925–61) and the Algerian nationalist Ahmed Ben Bella (b.1916), were both decorated in the Italian campaign.

By May 1945, France possessed eighteen divisions with a top-heavy officer corps from which many of the ex-FFI leaders retired. Their hopes of a new, democratic army had gone. The French armed forces had achieved everything except their own structural reform.

(c) Navy

The French fleet, whose C-in-C was the highly respected and capable Admiral Darlan, was calculated at over 660,000 tons in 1939—the fourth largest in the world—a new navy having been built in the five years before the war which absorbed 27% of the military budget. Many of its warships were new and though they lacked modern equipment such as *radar and *SONAR, they were mostly manned by professional, long-service officers and seamen. Between October 1939 and June 1940 the fleet's warships worked with the Royal Navy on convoy escort duties and acquitted themselves with distinction during the *Norwegian campaign and the *Dunkirk evacuation. They also rescued thousands of British soldiers from the Brittany ports. Unlike the French Army, the navy's morale and command communications remained intact during the fall of France and all French warships and merchant ships were removed in good time from ports threatened by the German advance. These included the new battleship *Richelieu*, which was still undergoing acceptance trials when she escaped from Brest to Dakar on 18 June, and her sister ship *Jean Bart*, which had to be removed from her dock at St Nazaire in an unfinished condition and was sailed to Casablanca. Two old battleships, eight destroyers, three submarines, and some smaller vessels went to Portsmouth and Plymouth; the two modern battle-cruisers *Strasbourg* and *Dunkerque*—as powerful as any battle-cruiser the Germans had afloat—six destroyers, two older battleships, and a seaplane carrier sailed to the Algerian naval base of Mers-el-Kébir; six cruisers went to Algiers; and many of the survivors of the French fleet of 80 submarines (24 had been sunk) found refuge in Bizerta. These apart, most of the smaller vessels went to Toulon; a squadron commanded by Vice-Admiral Godfroy, of a battleship, four cruisers, and three destroyers, which had been working with Admiral *Cunningham's Mediterranean fleet remained at Alexandria; and there were also a few minor warships in the French West Indies.

Under the terms of the armistice with the Germans the French fleet should have been deactivated, but because of the British attack on it at Mers-el-Kébir on 3 July 1940 this was not enforced and was only partly carried out. Ships in British ports were taken over—one French officer on board the submarine *Surcouf* was killed during this operation—and their crews were interned. Later, the crews were given the opportunity of being repatriated to Casablanca. Most accepted, but those who remained formed, with their ships, the nucleus of the Free French Navy and later in the war *Richelieu* served with the British Home and Pacific fleets (see TASK FORCE 57).

Those ships which stayed under Vichy control remained largely quiescent. But naval aircraft bombed Gibraltar in retaliation for Mers-el-Kébir; a squadron of French cruisers was sent to support Vichy forces in French Equatorial Africa but were turned back by the British (see NORTH, ADMIRAL); *Richelieu* and other naval units helped repel the Anglo-French Dakar expedition in September 1940; French warships supported Vichy forces during the Syrian campaign in mid-1941 and the British attack on Madagascar in May 1942; and *Jean Bart* defended Casablanca in November 1942 when US forces landed there at the start of the North African campaign. By that time most of the surviving warships not at Alexandria or under British command were at Toulon where they were sunk by their crews before the Germans could seize them (see FRENCH FLEET, SCUTTLING OF).

(d) Air force

The air force was under the overall command of General Joseph Vuillemin who, to give him his due, served a High Command which had a very restricted notion of modern *air power—at a lecture in 1939 Gamelin was heard to remark that there was no such thing as a battle of the air, there was only the battle on the ground—and whose command system was complex and confused. As a result of a pre-war struggle, Vuillemin had been left with direct control only over the general air reserve. In February 1940 an air co-operation force on the North-Eastern Front was created under General Tétu, who was subordinate both to Vuillemin and to General Alphonse Georges, the theatre land commander; his command was in turn subdivided into zones of aerial co-operation corresponding to those of the army groups on the North-Eastern Front. An organization which appeared sensible in theory turned out to be disastrous in practice: operational commanders received orders from at least three different sources and available fighter aircraft were scattered right along the front and could not be concentrated to meet the main enemy thrust.

The inadequacy of the air force in respect of equipment in May 1940 was in part the result of the unresolved struggle with the army during the inter-war years over whether it should exercise an independent strategic role in war or concentrate on tactical co-operation with the army. After an ill-judged attempt to build an all-purpose aircraft (the BCR) between 1933 and 1936, specialized fighters were developed which were obsolescent by the time they went into combat: the Morane 445, the main French fighter, was 80 km/h (50 mph) slower than the Me109 and only fractionally faster than the Do17 bomber. As with the land army, the French Air Force was caught in the middle of a rearmament programme on 10 May 1940: of a total of 2,200 planes, less than half were modern types—610 fighters, 130 bombers, and 350 reconnaissance aircraft. They were annihilated by a combination of German **Flak* and the Luftwaffe.

There are many puzzling features about the French Air Force in 1940. One that has been seen as particularly damning was that Vuillemin ended his war with more aircraft than he had at the start. In fact, this is a tribute to the herculean efforts of the French aircraft industry in the rushed rearmament programme which began on the eve of the war: at the end of 1938 it produced 40 planes a month, a year later 300 a month, and 500 in May 1940. Some of these aircraft were incomplete, but in any case

Vuillemin could make little use of them because of a crippling shortage of pilots, of whom he had only 700 to fly the 637 front-line fighters available when the war in the west began. The mass of conflicting evidence about the air force produced at the *Riom trial during the war and at the post-war parliamentary commission of enquiry aimed more at self-exculpation than at an explanation of the air force's performance in the battle for France.

7. Intelligence

In 1939 the hub of French intelligence and counter-espionage was the Deuxième Bureau, directed by Colonel Rivet, and responsible to the minister of war and to the Commander-in-Chief. When war was declared the Cinquième Bureau took over counter-espionage, reinforced by the police brigades of the Surveillance du Territoire (internal security) set up in March 1937. Arrests for espionage quadrupled in 1937, and the numbers doubled in 1938 and 1939. In 1940 they spiralled to a figure above 1,200 in response to national anxieties about the fifth column. Officers were pulled in two potentially different directions in the last years of the 1930s; by individual involvement in the right-wing subterranean organization known as the Cagoule (hooded men) determined to purge the army of presumed communist infiltration; and by the official pursuit of German and Italian agents. The ambivalence was perpetuated into the occupation.

The Free French set up their own intelligence service in London, the *Bureau Central de Renseignements et d'Action (BCRA), while at Vichy, Rivet and the head of counter-espionage, Captain Paul Paillole, by-passed German restrictions by setting up cover organizations under names of rural conservation and works (*Travaux Ruraux*). Their tightrope between resistance and Vichy involved a double game that was particularly ambivalent for Rivet whose Vichy role involved uncovering *menées antinationales* (subversive activities), interpreted to mean any action destabilizing the Vichy regime. Vichy kept two secret files, known as S and S1 listing people to be arrested immediately there was any major disturbance. On these lists figured communists, Spanish republicans and other anti-fascists, and many 'notorious Gaullists'. In Nice one intelligence officer, Captain Beaune, took this repressive role to the limit, becoming the intelligence arm of Darnand's Milice. Both Rivet and Paillole penetrated German security and sent valuable information to the Allies, which led to the arrest and torture of over 300 intelligence officers by the Germans after their invasion of the southern zone. The two men crossed to Algiers, where their activities, which included running a double cross committee (see XX-COMMITTEE), continued under Giraud, before eventually, against their will, being fused with the BCRA into the Direction générale des services spéciaux (General Directorate for Special Services), attached to de Gaulle and directed by Jacques Soustelle.

Similar in its secret intentions to Rivet and Paillole's cover operations was Commandant Mollard's camouflage of army vehicles, masquerading as an agricultural machinery business. The vehicles hidden in rural depots were found by the Germans after November 1942, but several hundred had been shipped clandestinely to North Africa.

Finally, internal information under Vichy was provided by the secret Service du Contrôle Technique (Technical Control Service) which censored post and telephones on a vast scale. It was brought under the direct authority of Laval from August 1942, and its brief radically changed from monitoring public opinion to control, linking surveillance to repression. The Free French set up their own alternative postal censorship in Algiers, but this did not reveal the existence of the Vichy system.

8. Merchant marine

At the outbreak of war France had the seventh largest merchant fleet in the world, with 502 ships over 1,600 tons, many of which were on short haul duty from North Africa. In peacetime Germany and Poland had supplied over one-third of French coal, carried by rail and canal, but once the war started this had to be imported from the UK by sea. The task revealed that the French fleet available was too small; there were few neutral ships on hand and a belated Anglo-French agreement on shipping matters was not negotiated until December 1939. The drastic coal shortage remained unsolved. Other imports by sea were also inadequate, rising no higher than 50% of French needs in the period September 1939 to June 1940.

After the fall of France the 2.6 million tons of the French fleet began to be sequestered. The British requisitioned some 400,000 tons found in British and Dominion ports, and attempted to put pressure on Vichy by blockading the straits of Gibraltar. The effects were mitigated by the strength of French shipping in the Mediterranean, but Vichy propaganda accused the British of trying to starve the French people. By 1942 almost a quarter of French pre-war shipping was serving the Allied cause, with the Free French operating their own merchant navy, manned where possible by French crews who numbered approximately 3,000 officers and men by 1942. In a sample six months from September 1941 this fleet carried 590,000 tons of supplies for the Allies. In addition several French luxury liners were converted into troop carriers: the *Île de France* (41,500 tons) transported more than 300,000 troops both in the Indian Ocean and from Canada to Britain. The most prestigious liner, the *Normandie*, at 83,000 tons the largest in the world, was requisitioned in the USA, but fell foul of a mysterious fire and sank in the Hudson river. Other liners, celebrated on the routes of the Far East, entered Free French service, the *Maréchal Joffre* escaping from Manila just as the Japanese occupied it. After the success of the Allied North African campaign, French ships seized by the Allies in African ports were allowed to continue to fly the French flag in the Allied cause, and ten French coasters took part in the *Sicilian campaign. However, when the *zone libre* was overrun in November 1942, the Germans and Italians seized, and shared, nearly 290,000 tons of French shipping, by which time the Japanese had also acquired some 20 French merchant ships, mostly from the ports of Saigon and Yokohama.

9. Resistance

At the origin of resistance lay numerous acts of individual defiance and dissidence (see SOURCE K, for example). They were marked by their isolation from each other and by a huge range of aspirations. There were small ad hoc actions 'to annoy the Germans' (*narguer les Allemands*), which were as spontaneous as giving occupying troops wrong information in the street. At the other end of the scale there was no shortage of grand designs, of which de Gaulle's appeal of 18 June 1940 was an example. His was a pioneering voice outside France, though not widely heard at the time, and there were similar lone voices, or tracts, within France which carried the same message: that the war must go on, but clearly by different means. Jean Texcier, a civil servant in the ministry of commerce, wrote a series of tracts called *Conseils à l'occupé* ('Advice to the Occupied') in July 1940; General Gabriel-Roger Cochet of the French Air Force wrote another series called *Tour d'Horizon* ('General Survey'); Captain Henri Frenay, who escaped from a transit prisoner-of-war camp, set out his plans for a whole network of intelligence, propaganda, and armed struggle in the autumn of 1940; Bertie Albrecht used her social work, sanctioned by Vichy, as a cover for collecting and distributing information; Emmanuel d'Astier left the navy and came together with Jean Cavaillès, a philosophy professor, Lucie Aubrac, a history teacher, and others to work out ideas for a 'Dernière Colonne' (last column) to continue the fight; Agnès Humbert helped produce the first journal called *Résistance* at the Musée de l'Homme in Paris; Marie-Madeleine Fourcade started intelligence work from her youth centre in Vichy; individual communists, notably Charles Tillon in Bordeaux, Georges Guingouin, a schoolteacher near Limoges, Joseph Pastor in Marseilles, and Auguste Lecœur in the mining area of the Nord, all found ways of breaking out of the confusion caused in the Communist Party by the Nazi–Soviet Pact, and defied party directives when their activity was discouraged. All these, and many others, envisaged and initiated exactly what resistance eventually became, an alternative France, made up of diffuse personalities, professions, and skills.

Such early diversity, and the growth of defiance from below, gave resistance an intractable complexity which was difficult to organize and control from above. It did not spring ready-armed from the strategic planning of an army headquarters or a political party. It was civilian-based, even where individual army personnel were involved, and the civilians brought to it a wide variety of personal experience, from an intimate knowledge of the Pyrenees which enabled British pilots to escape, to the technicalities of typesetting which lay behind the clandestine press.

The individuals involved were initially a very small minority within France.Their first task was to convince others. Necessarily resistance was counter-information. Clandestine publishing was action; distributing a news-sheet was organization and recruitment. Newspapers became synonymous with movements: *Combat*, *Franc-Tireur*, and *Libération (sud)* in the south, *Défense de la France*, *Libération (nord)*, and *La Voix du Nord* in the north. The Communist Party, while still subservient to the Nazi–Soviet Pact, had reissued *L'Humanité*, and once the pact was dead after Hitler's invasion of the USSR in June 1941 (see BARBAROSSA), the party emerged officially from its period of neutrality and followed its dissident individual members into anti-German activity. The communist-based Front National was the only movement in 1941–2 to be organized across both zones. No other party structures survived the 10 July vote in Vichy, which handed the government over to Pétain, though a group of socialists re-formed in the winter of 1940–1 and brought out their clandestine newspaper, *Le Populaire*. Catholics and Protestants in Lyons combined to issue the foremost Christian journal of Resistance, *Cahiers du Témoignage Chrétien* ('Journal of Christian Testimony'). Copies of *Défense de la France* ran to over 400,000 in January 1944, and most other large papers had print runs of 100–150,000.

Armed action was rare at the start, though a flamboyant royalist, Jacques Renouvin, created *groupes francs* (irregulars) in the area of Montpellier and used explosives against collaborators. It was the embryo for the eventual Armée Secrète (AS) attached to Combat, and other *groupes francs* developed an urban style of guerrilla activity, alongside the communist-run Francs-Tireurs et Partisans (FTP), which had grown out of early sabotage action pioneered by Albert Ouzoulias in the Paris region. The miners' strike in the Nord in May 1941 showed that collective confrontation was possible, but workers found sabotage far more effective. The railway workers (*cheminots*) were able to co-ordinate action over considerable distances, and Résistance-fer (railway resistance) became a major force, well equipped and financed, for example, in the Languedoc, by Tony Brooks, one of many *SOE agents parachuted from London. Recruiting professional workers to resist in their jobs became a distinctive branch of resistance called Noyautage des Administrations Publiques (Infiltration of Civil Administration) as did Action ouvrière (workers' action), which specialized in industrial sabotage. The movements had their own intelligence sections and networks of liaison agents, most of whom were women who were able to travel more inconspicuously than men, often carrying arms and ammunition as well as messages and tracts. All resistance depended on infrastructures of anonymity, and for that reason the names of many essential resisters went unrecorded except at local level.

It was the more secretive networks (*réseaux*) of intelligence and escape which forged the first working links with the British or the Free French in London. The

Free French network Confrérie Notre Dame (Brotherhood of Our Lady), whose main agent was 'Colonel Rémy' (Gilbert Renault), grouped together volunteers who had started their resistance with highly amateur attempts to send photographs of German troop movements to London. The British-financed network Alliance originated with the conspiratorial Georges Loustaunau-Lacau who had contacts in the French secret services. After his arrest it was run by Marie-Madeleine Fourcade with direct links with British intelligence (see SPIES). Other networks with codenames were implanted by SOE whose F section set up, funded, and armed countless local resistance groups between 1942–4. These carried out acts such as the sabotage of the Peugeot factory, organized by Harry Rée at Montbéliard, which saved lives that would otherwise have been lost in Allied air raids. SOE, *MI6, and the Free French BCRA operated independently in France, not without some organizational rivalries, but all dependent on British money and French volunteers.

Resistance activity at several points appeared likely to polarize between communists and Gaullists, though the FTP and the Front National were far from exclusively communist in composition, and many non-communist resisters were wary of too close a control by de Gaulle. In January 1943 Pierre Brosselette, Christian Pineau, and finally Jean *Moulin succeeded in bringing non-communist resistance together in the Mouvements Unis de la Résistance (MUR) in the south, and a Co-ordinating Committee in the north. Although the communists were outside the MUR they were involved in Moulin's last achievement before his arrest on 21 June 1943, the creation of the *National Council for Resistance (CNR), which set out a post-liberation charter of sweeping political and social change. Both the MUR and the CNR acknowledged de Gaulle as leader of the resistance, but at all levels the vitality of the internal movements was maintained. Moulin was very much de Gaulle's envoy: his successor at the head of the CNR, Georges Bidault, came from the resistance within France.

With the creation of the Maquis in the course of 1943, independence and diversity were yet again at the centre of the resistance experience. The German occupation of the whole of France forced increasing numbers of resisters, anti-fascists from many countries, and victimized groups into the search for safer hiding-places which only the forests and hills could provide. The revolt of thousands of workers against labour deportation (STO) intensified this need and provided a youthful influx into the resistance. The percentage of *réfractaires* (STO evaders) who went into the Maquis varied from 5% in some areas to 50% in others, but the popular revolt against STO sustained the Maquis everywhere. Both the Armée Secrète, now within the MUR, and the FTP, created their own Maquis groups, most remaining small and mobile, but some gathering thousands into entrenched positions in the Savoyard Alps and in the centre of the Massif Central. It was in the Glières in March 1944, Mont Mouchet in early June, and the Vercors in July that the Maquis faced overwhelming force of arms, mounted by Germans and Vichy armed police, backed by the Milice who specialized in the rooting out of Maquis sympathizers in the villages. The losses were heavy, particularly in the Vercors where Allied reinforcements were expected to the very last telegram sent by the desperate Maquis leaders. Elsewhere Maquis groups perfected mobile guerrilla tactics of harassment, sabotage, and ambushes, inspired by the news that Corsica had been liberated by these very tactics in September 1943, aided by shock troops from the Armée d'Afrique. Arms were always insufficient, though Allied parachute drops of weapons and crucial supplies proliferated in the spring of 1944. The FTP received few direct drops; their policy of immediate action by all possible means had gained them many recruits within France, and dramatic successes, but their activism did not always conform to Allied strategy which moulded Maquis action round the plans for the Normandy landings.

The Maquis did not monopolize armed action, which accelerated in the towns, too, in late 1943. In Paris the immigrant communist workers' organization, Main-d'œuvre immigrée (MOI), launched more than 40 raids on German installations and personnel between June and November before the leading group, run by Missak Manouchian, an Armenian, was betrayed and decimated. The Germans tried to pillory them as foreign criminals through a poster, *l'affiche rouge*, which carried their photographs. For many French this was the way they learned with gratitude that Jews and immigrants were an integral part of French resistance. Their role was all too easily marginalized after the war.

After February 1944 all armed Resistance was, in principle, was brought within the FFI, and during the Normandy landings British, American, and French agents joined with the internal resistance to execute support plans codenamed Green, Violet, and Blue to immobilize railways, telephones lines, and electrical power in the areas behind the German lines. In the south-west, Maquis and other units crucially delayed the *SS division Das Reich on its way to Normandy, and after the French Riviera landings in mid-August, the Alpine Maquis cleared a path for the invading French and Americans. The cost throughout France was the death, torture, or deportation of more than 90,000 resisters, both men and women, and the deaths of thousands of people in German reprisals.

The Resistance liberated the Savoyard Alps, the south-west and much of the centre of France as the Germans retreated, and played an equally major role in the liberation of Paris (see PARIS RISING). The manner of liberation reflected both the diversity of the resistance and the variables in the nature of collaboration. The purging (*épuration*) of collaborators was accompanied in some places by the arbitrary settling of scores, but the incidence of such acts declined substantially with the appointment of the Special Courts of Justice. In all, executions by the resistance before and after the liberation amounted to just over 10,800, according to the official figures. The variance in the nature and aims of the liberation committees formed in each *département* kept certain localities in a state of unsettled expectancy until the Provisional government consolidated its control. At its head General de Gaulle had staged a triumphant entry into Paris, where he maintained that the Republic had never been constitutionally abolished. Women were empowered to vote by an ordinance of 5 October 1944, and the resistance Union des femmes françaises looked set to become a force in post-liberation politics. Yet, like almost all resistance movements, it was soon subsumed in the return of party politics. The resistance did not become a single, coherent, and innovative political organization. For some it seemed as if a vital opportunity to create a new France had been missed. But a new Catholic democratic party did have its origins in resistance, the Mouvement républicain populaire headed by eminent Catholic resisters, and they played a pioneering role in shaping a new economic and political alignment within Europe, with visions of European unity which had been nurtured by the common opposition to Nazism across occupied Europe. The success of resistance was also marked in French standing after the war. Despite being excluded from the Yalta conference (see ARGONAUT), France was invited to be one of the five permanent members of the United Nations Security Council and to have its own zone of occupation in defeated Germany (see ALLIED CONTROL COMMISSIONS). For individuals, at both national and local level, a resistance past became a touchstone of personal merit, and the little-known monuments scattered throughout the French countryside and in the backstreets of towns testify to the fact that the history of the French resistance was the story of very ordinary people.

10. Culture

At all levels the culture of occupied France was responsive to the ambiguities of the situation. People interpreted a single play, film, or song in diametrically opposed ways, looking for nuances in expression, double meanings, and covert intentions. The reopening of the Paris night clubs, music halls, and the racecourse at Longchamp, could be interpreted as a servile acceptance of the German presence, or the robust reassertion of a distinctive French way of life; '*Notre Espoir*', sung by Maurice Chevalier in 1941, was first taken as Pétainist and later sung in expectation of the liberation; the patriotism of Charles Péguy's writings was claimed by both Vichy and the resistance, as was the historical legacy of Joan of Arc. Was it the English or the invaders who were her enemy? Films like Marcel Carné's *Les visiteurs du soir* and Jean Grémillon's *Le ciel est à vous*, plays like Jean Anouilh's *Antigone* and Henry de Montherlant's *La Reine Morte*, and the novel *Pilote de Guerre* (*Flight to Arras*) by Antoine de Saint-Exupéry were all products of the period, received with rival enthusiasms by Vichy sympathizers and by resisters. Certain intellectual and cultural institutions, such as the Ecole des cadres (staff academy) at Uriage or the artists' association Jeune France, started as expressions of Vichy but developed independently in the opposite direction. The revival of regional folklore and culture was given high priority by Vichy, but it also had its place in the local nature of the Maquis. The hills and valleys of the Cévennes, for example, were valued for their distinctive culture by Jean Chiappe, the collaborationist prefect of the Gard, but the Cévenol traditions of the Camisards, and Protestant culture, sustained every act of resistance. The poet Pierre Seghers exploited the limits of hidden meanings in his annual editions of *Poésie* which had started as collections of war poetry *Poétes casqués* ('Poets in Helmets'), in 1939; and literary journals such as *Confluences*, founded by René Tavernier in 1941, and *Fontaine*, run by Max-Pol Fouchet from Algiers, carried the process to even finer shades of cultural ambiguity.

Radio and cinema were increasingly important, at a time when gatherings, dances, and festivals were progressively banned, but both were caught up in the fundamental polarities of the time. Radio-Paris was repudiated as pro-German ('*Radio-Paris ment* (tells lies), *Radio-Paris est allemand*' ran the popular refrain), and listeners to the *BBC programme '*Les Français parlent aux Français*' valued it as much as relief from an unrelieved diet of German and Vichy martial music, as for its overt resistance message. The cinema was a place to express opinions by catcalls at the German newsreels, a place to keep warm in winter, and a place to drop resistance leaflets from the balcony as the lights went down. Film stars filled the pages of the illustrated magazines, although photographs of Danielle Darrieux, Suzy Delair, Albert Préjean, and others leaving for a goodwill visit to Germany in March 1942, fuelled contempt, not adulation.

It was a productive time for both film-makers and playwrights, with houses full and involvement high. Alongside Carné and Grémillon were younger directors, Robert Bresson, Henri-Georges Clouzot, and Claude Autant-Lara who produced work of quality. Carné's *Les Enfants du Paradis* was the aesthetic triumph of 1944. New plays by Jean-Paul Sartre, Albert Camus, Montherlant, and Anouilh were an indication of theatrical vitality. Provincial theatre companies flourished, in one of which, *La roulotte* ('the caravan'), Jean Vilar made his début. A vogue for the classics met the prescribed aesthetics of Vichy, but also allowed the portrayal of moral choices, heroines and heroes, the dark side of the gods, and the concept of destiny. They offered both escape and commitment. The popular singers—Tino Rossi, Charles Trenet, Suzy Solidor, Maurice Chevalier, André Claveau, Léo Marjane—provided an easy charm and an appearance of life as usual, with the occasional poignant hint of nostalgia or yearning for better days. The same could be said of the Académie Goncourt which continued its prize-givings almost as if nothing had changed.

Survivalism, in fact, was something of an art in itself,

reaffirming for some the role of artist as observer. Picasso, for example, contrived to live peacefully and creatively in Paris. His representation of the horror of war in *Guernica* is echoed in several of his works during the occupation, and due to the antagonism of the Spanish leader, *Franco, and accusations of communism and decadence from Germany, he was not allowed to exhibit. But he was not molested by either Vichy or the *Gestapo. In similar ways, Jean Cocteau continued his own style of life, though not without an aura of compromise. Open to the bizarre in every day events he eventually saw the strange poetic quality of the BBC's coded messages to the Resistance, and he used them to great atmospheric effect in his imaginative film, *Orphée* (1950).

But there was also culture without equivocation. Collaborationist writers such as Robert Brasillach, Lucien Rebatet, Pierre Drieu la Rochelle, Alphonse de Château-briant, and Alain Laubreaux, the anti-Semitic Céline, and the media entrepreneur Jean Luchaire, dominated the cultural and publication scene patronized by Otto Abetz, the Nazi ambassador in Paris. The literary talent of these figures gave their versions of *fascism both individualism and panache and the post-liberation purges struck hard at these intellectual allies of the Nazi presence, confirming the significance of their cultural contribution. At the other end of the polarity, Resistance literature in clandestine editions was revealed at the liberation to have been surprisingly prolific. Editions de Minuit, founded in 1941 by Vercors (Jean Bruller) and Pierre de Lescure produced some twenty titles, the first of which, *Le Silence de la Mer* by Vercors, astounded the small circle of its readers by the quality of the product and the sensitivity of its story. In 1942 a resistance Comité National des Ecrivains (Writers' National Committee) began to publish two cultural reviews, *Les Lettres françaises* and *Les Etoiles*, and the poetry, above all of Louis Aragon and Paul Eluard, expressed the emotional depth and clarity of the resistance commitment. With paper and printing ink not easily available the poem and the song carried the clandestine struggle forward with precision and brevity. The RAF dropped thousands of copies of Eluard's poem 'Liberté' into France, and Emmanuel d'Astier brought the most potent of Resistance songs, 'Le chant des partisans', from London in September 1943. With words by Joseph Kessel and Maurice Druon, and a Russian melody adapted by Anna Marly, it was sung everywhere at the liberation, rivalling in popularity the jazz of Django Reinhardt and Glenn Miller's 'In the mood' to which everyone danced in the rediscovery of freedom.

In everyday life the curfew imposed by the Germans led the French to read more books and write more letters than ever before. Sport, notably athletics, flourished under the aegis of Jean Borotra, the ex-Wimbledon champion and Pétain's crusading minister of sport, whose admiration for Englishness eventually took him into opposition and led to his deportation. As a paean to the outdoor life, Vichy culture took people into the countryside. If they returned with a few mushrooms and a kilo of potatoes it was worth it. But harm was done. For years after the liberation rural values were equated with Vichy. It was eventually the emergence of a new regionalism and the culture of ecology which perhaps marked the final post-war break with the legacy of Vichy France.

RODERICK KEDWARD

France, Table 3: The human losses. Deaths.

Military	
1939–40	92,000
1940–5	58,000
FFI in 1944	20,000
Alsace-Lorrainers conscripted into German Army	40,000
TOTAL	210,000
Civilian	
Bombings	60,000
Resistance losses and German atrocities	60,000
Executions	30,000
TOTAL	150,000
Prisoners and deportees	
Prisoners-of-war	40,000
Racial deportees	100,000
Political deportees	60,000
French workers in Germany	40,000
TOTAL	240,000
GRAND TOTAL	600,000

Source: Contributor.

Azéma, J.-P., *From Munich to the Liberation 1938–44* (Cambridge, 1984).
Kedward, H. R. *In Search of the Maquis* (Oxford, 1993).
—*Resistance in Vichy France* (Oxford, 1978).
Marrus, M. R., and Paxton, R. O., *Vichy France and the Jews* (New York, 1981).
Paxton, R. O., *Vichy France. Old Guard and New Order* (New York, 1972).
Rousso, H., *The Vichy Syndrome. History and Memory in France since 1944* (Cambridge, Mass., 1991).
Sweets, J. F., *Choices in Vichy France* (New York, 1986).

France, fall of (see Maps 35 and 36). On 9 May 1940, the eve of the German offensive in the west, Hitler proclaimed to his assembled general staff: 'Gentlemen, you are about to witness the most famous victory in history.' Like an oriental despot, he gave a gold watch to his chief meteorologist for predicting good weather the following day. He deserved it: 'Göring's weather', essential to the success of the campaign, continued virtually without break over the next three critical weeks. Leaving Berlin that night, Hitler took exceptional security measures. The 'Führer Special' train first headed north, then under cover of darkness swung west to take Hitler

German troops entering Paris on 14 June 1940 during the German campaign which led to the **fall of France**.

to his battle headquarters at Münstereifel, close to the Belgian Ardennes.

At dawn the following morning the Wehrmacht, invaded the three neutral nations of Luxemburg, Belgium, and the Netherlands. An astonishing gamble had been embarked upon. More than to almost any other single factor its success was due to a series of accidents that had imposed radical changes on the original German strategic plan (see FALL GELB), which General von *Manstein converted from what had been an unimaginative blueprint into one of inspired daring. It involved an advance into northern Belgium and the Netherlands which would act, in the admirable simile of the British writer on military strategy, Basil Liddell Hart, 'like a matador's cloak' waved at the *British Expeditionary Force and the powerful French forces in Flanders, and draw them north-eastwards in Belgium. The main blow (*Schwerpunkt*) would then be delivered just north of where the *Maginot Line ended, through the rugged and densely forested country of the Ardennes, which the Germans knew the French general staff considered impassable and which had, therefore, been covered with only inferior forces. Once this breakthrough had been achieved, the panzers would burst out into the flat plains of northern France and race for their objective, the Channel coast, which would effectively cut the Allied armies in two.

The forces at the disposal of the two opposing sides were roughly equal (see Table), but while only just over 29 divisions were allocated to *Bock's Army Group B, which was waving the 'matador's cloak' in the north, just over 44 divisions were concentrated under *Rundstedt's Group A in the south—including virtually all the élite, fast-moving panzer divisions. *Leeb's Army Group C, with 17 divisions, was used to press against the Maginot Line in the south to keep French forces there pinned down. Part of Rundstedt's panzer force was *Guderian's armoured spearhead aimed at Sedan, while protecting the northern flank of the breakthrough was the 7th Panzer Division, commanded by the 48-year-old Brigadier *Rommel. Although Guderian had left his men in no doubt that the English Channel was their ultimate objective, few of the Wehrmacht commanders shared Hitler's remarkable self-assurance about the outcome.

On the other side of the lines, matters were in the hands of the French C-in-C, General *Gamelin, operating a tangled chain of command (see FRANCE, 6(a)) from his convent-like GHQ at Vincennes outside Paris. As un-

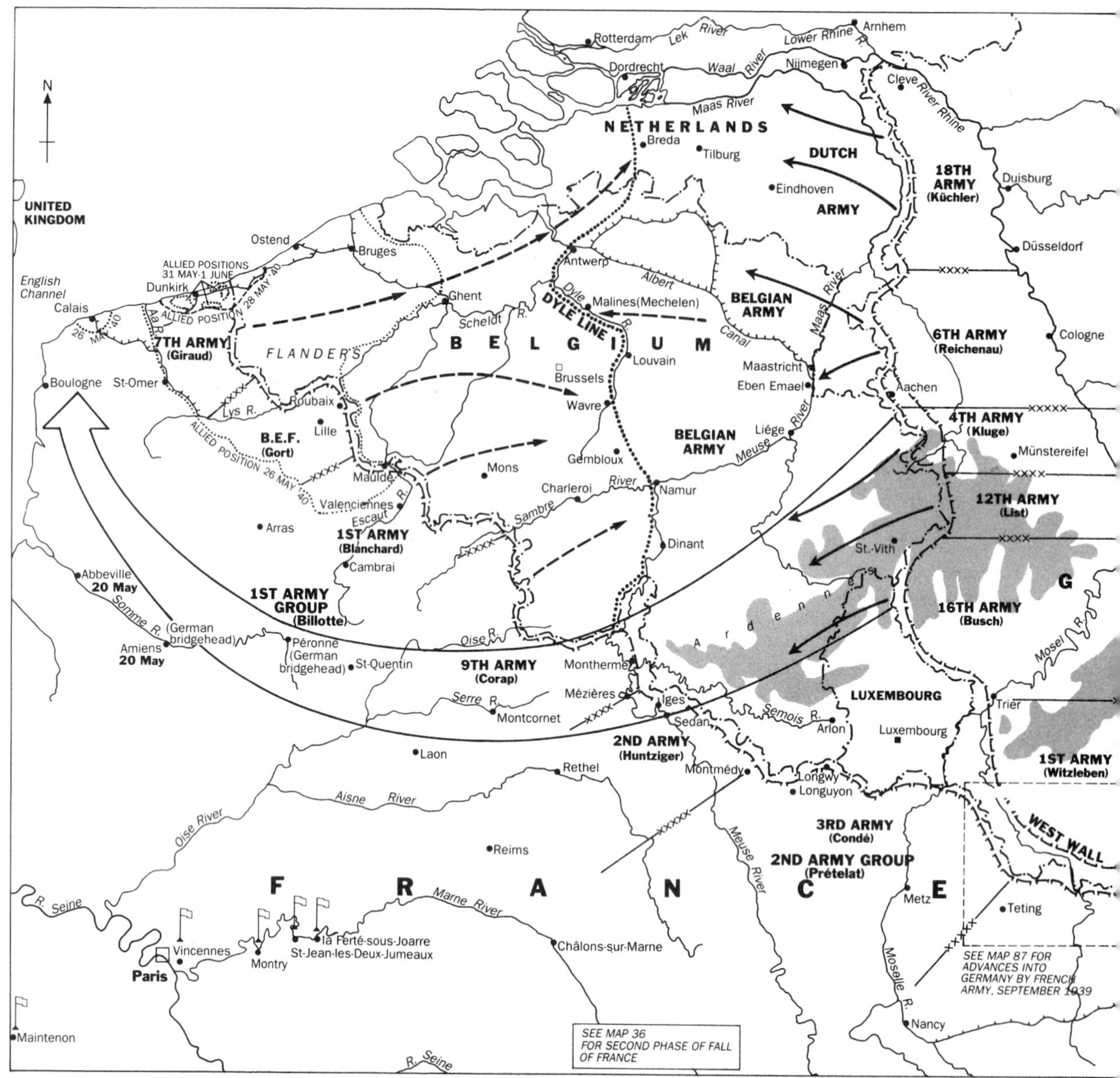

35. **Fall of France**: first phase, 10–31 May 1940

impressive a commander as Gamelin was, in October 1939 he had come close to predicting the eventual direction of the main German thrust. Nevertheless he allowed himself to father the Allied 'Plan D', whereby immediately Germany invaded Belgium, 33 of the best British and French divisions would rush eastwards to the *Dyle Line—just as Hitler had foreseen they would.

The key French sector between Namur and Sedan was held by General André Corap's Ninth and *Huntziger's Second Army, immobile and of poor quality and their morale not enhanced by eight months of *phoney war. No fewer than 30 French divisions were pinned down unprofitably behind the Maginot Line; while Gamelin's last mobile reserve, Giraud's Seventh Army, had late in the day been committed to make a mad dash to Breda, to lend a hand to the Dutch if they were attacked. Thus before the battle was even joined the famous French 'mass of manoeuvre'—their reserves—was virtually non-existent.

The French Army was powerful on paper; it had more tanks than the Germans, and some that were better, but it had not yet fully developed the concept of massing

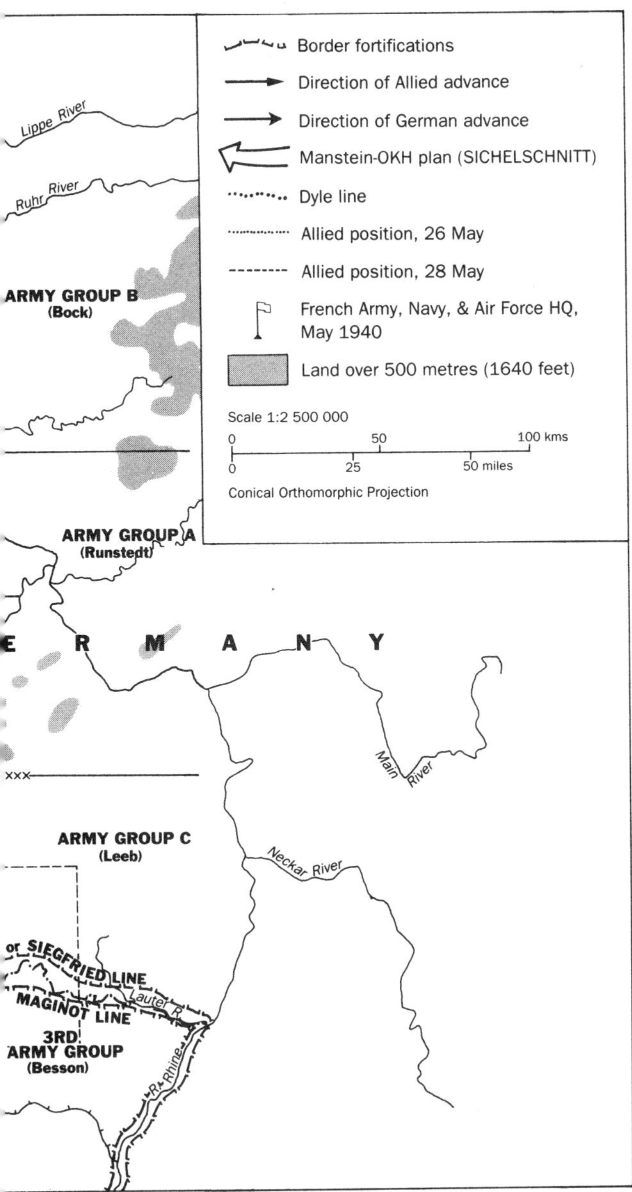

them in the way with which the Germans had already triumphed in the *Polish campaign. Part of its tank strength was instead spread out thinly and ineffectually—ready, like a lot of small corks, to plug holes in the line. Yet the Wehrmacht too had flaws of which its leaders were well aware; the élite panzer divisions were few in number, while the bulk of the army comprised second-rate infantry divisions, often dependent upon horse transport (see ANIMALS), which would have been deeply vulnerable to a flank attack by a determined armoured force.

The British contribution in France amounted to ten front-line divisions (one of which was in the Saar), its smallness the butt of German propaganda broadcasts. A modest support airforce was also sent to France, but the valuable Spitfire fighter was held back for the defence of the UK. There were virtually no tactical attack bombers of any value. It was in the air that the Allies were at their greatest disadvantage, with the French air force largely equipped with inferior machines which, like French armour, were poorly deployed (see FRANCE, 6(d)). In contrast, the German Luftwaffe was designed and trained for a single clear-cut purpose—to be an integral part of the German offensive machine. Its fleets of medium bombers were ready to wreak havoc behind the enemy's lines; while its dive-bombers (the Stukas or Junkers 87s) gave direct support to the advancing tanks and infantry (see BLITZKRIEG).

The first revelation of the full deadliness of the attack came with the news of the fall of *Eben Emael, supposedly the world's strongest fortress and linchpin of the Belgian defences (see BELGIUM, 4). Forty-eight hours later the Netherlands had virtually collapsed (see also NETHERLANDS, 4). Meanwhile, unseen and almost unopposed the great phalanxes of von Rundstedt's armour advanced through the supposedly impassable Ardennes. Their worst problems were the vehicle jams on the inadequate forest roads. Stretching back 80 km. (50 mi.) east of the Rhine, the advancing columns were protected by a massive and constant umbrella of fighters. A few well-placed bombs on these roads could have seriously impeded the advancing tanks, but Allied eyes were focused on the attack they had expected in the north.

By nightfall of Whit Sunday, 12 May, seven panzer divisions stood on the east bank of the Meuse all the way from Dinant (Rommel) to Sedan (Guderian). Still French military intelligence failed to recognize the danger, reckoning (as usual, on the basis of *First World War experience, which still constituted much of Franco-British military doctrine) that the Germans would require at least five or six days to concentrate before they could force a river crossing. This erroneous judgement was passed on to and shared by London. At 1830 hours on 13 May, by which time Guderian was already across the Meuse, Churchill was telling the war cabinet that he was 'by no means sure that the great battle was developing'.

The previous evening, encouraged by his successful advance on Sedan, Guderian had agreed with his immediate superior, General von *Kleist, that he would attack at once, even though one of his three panzer divisions had not yet emerged from the forest. Guderian was promised maximum air support, in particular from the dive-bombers of General Wolfram von Richthofen's Eighth Flying Corps, and the attempt to cross the Meuse was ordered for 1600 hours next day.

Towards midday on 13 May, about 1,000 aircraft struck Huntziger's Second Army opposite Sedan. Casualties were not in fact great, but the terror caused by the Stukas was: 'The gunners stopped firing and went to ground';

France, fall of: Forces available to the powers involved in the German invasion, 10 May 1940

I. Army

	Divisions	Guns	Tanks
France	104[a]	10,700	3,063[a]
Britain[b]	10	1,280	310
Belgium	22	1,338	10
Netherlands	8	656	1
TOTAL	144	13,974	3,384
Germany	141	7,378[c]	2,445[d]

II. Air Force (estimates only)

	Fighters	Bombers	Reconnaissance planes	Total aircraft
France	637	242	489	1,368 [e]
Britain[b]	261	135	60	456
Belgium	90	12	120	250
Netherlands	62	9	50	175
Britain (home-based)	540	310		850
TOTAL	1,590	708	719	3,099
Germany (total)	1,736	2,224	700	5,446
Germany (operational 4 May 1940)	1,220	1,559	535	4,020

[a] North-eastern front alone, including reserves and one Polish division
[b] Forces transferred to the Continent, see BRITISH EXPEDITIONARY FORCE
[c] Excluding Norway and east
[d] Total available
[e] Operational aircraft with front-line formations in metropolitan France

Source: Maier, K. A. *et al*, *Germany and the Second World War*, Vol. 2 (Oxford, 1994).

wrote one French general; 'the infantry cowered in their trenches . . . their only concern was to keep their heads well down.' Meanwhile the Messerschmitt squadrons circled over the battle front, pouncing on any slower French fighter that tried to interfere. Assault troops of the German 1st Panzer Division, attacking immediately downstream from Sedan against the base of the vulnerable Iges peninsula, created the first usable bridgehead. By nightfall 1st Panzer infantrymen had fought their way up the Meuse's southern escarpment, through the French main and secondary defence lines. The division now held a bridgehead on the south bank 4.8 km. (3 mi.) wide and 6.4 to 9.6 km. (4–6 mi.) deep.

French attempts to neutralize this dangerous pocket on 14 May were too slow and too late. In the afternoon, when there was still an opportunity to drive a powerful wedge into the exposed eastern flank of 1st Panzer Division, the French threw away their 3rd Armoured Division, full of spirit and eager to attack, through sluggish deployment and slow refuelling arrangements. When the division could still have attacked with some effect, the order was suddenly countermanded and its precious armour dispersed by the new local corps commander who strung it out in a series of weak defensive positions. The same day the Allies dispatched all available tactical bombers, the greater part of them obsolete British Fairey Battles, to destroy 1st Panzer Division's pontoon bridge. They pressed home their attack heroically, but never concentrated in sufficient numbers to overwhelm the excellent anti-aircraft defences. Losses were disastrous, and the bridge remained intact. On this day, Allied offensive *air power in France was broken and the campaign was effectively decided on the next. For the French wasted the whole of it in preparing, and then abandoning, a counter-attack by the dispersed 3rd Armoured Division instead of attacking Guderian's southern flank which he had exposed the previous afternoon when he had swung his panzers sharply westwards towards the English Channel.

Unfortunately for the French, the Sedan sector also happened to lie right on the hinge between two armies, Huntziger's Second and Corap's Ninth, which greatly increased the difficulties of command for the defenders. Having dealt a crippling blow to Huntziger's forces, Guderian's tanks pushed westwards where the Ninth Army was now in complete disarray as Rommel's tanks had penetrated its rear positions 6.4 km. (4 mi.) across the Belgian Meuse. Corap, a broken man, ordered his army to withdraw but Giraud, who replaced him, found by the end of the day that there was nothing to command—just an open gate, 100 km. (62 mi.) wide, for the Germans to pass through, which Huntziger widened further when he was forced to pull back his hard-pressed army south-eastwards.

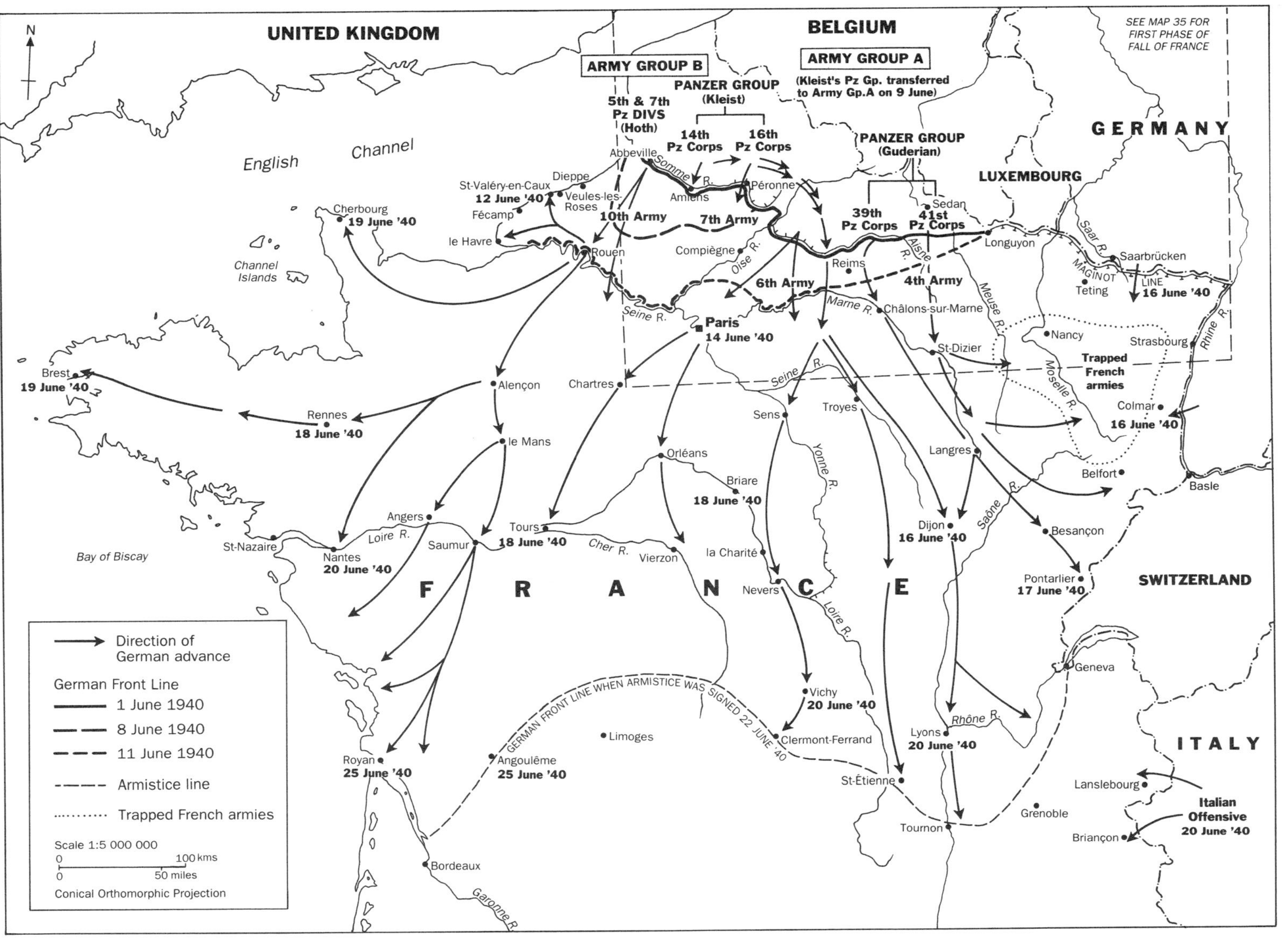

36. **Fall of France**: second phase, 1–22 June 1940

On 16 May Churchill made his historic sortie to Paris; where Gamelin dumbfounded him with the admission that there was no *masse de manœuvre*. *Reynaud, the prime minister, declared the battle was lost, while outside 'venerable officials' stocked bonfires of the Quai d'Orsay archives. As the German thrust to the sea began, the French High Command remained disastrously in the dark as to the enemy's real objective, Paris or the Channel.

The French attempted one more local offensive action, towards Montcornet with a hastily assembled 4th Armoured Division. Though courageously led by Colonel Charles de *Gaulle, it was soon repulsed. Yet, growing nervous of their easy success, the German High Command had already imposed two separate halts on Guderian's panzers on the 15 and 17 May. A well co-ordinated counter-thrust against the German columns might have had considerable effect; but the Allies no longer had the ability to co-ordinate any such an action. Gamelin's replacement as commander-in-chief by 73-year-old General *Weygand on the evening of 20 May contributed nothing except two days' delay in mounting a pincer movement against the vulnerable 'Panzer Corridor'.

On 19 May, Guderian's 2nd Panzer Division reached the Channel near Abbeville, having advanced 320 km. (200 mi.) in ten days. The élite of the French and British forces were now trapped in a vast pocket, with their backs to the sea, and the northern armies suffered additional disarray when their commander, General Pierre Billotte, died as the result of a car crash. A limited British tank attack southwards from Arras on 21 May achieved a success which made a strong impression upon Rommel; but then, seeing no French follow-up, the British Expeditionary Force withdrew to *Dunkirk.

With Kleist's victorious armour massed against the southern perimeter of the Dunkirk pocket on 24 May, ready to push forward for the kill, Hitler made a historic error of judgement: he issued his much-criticized 'Halt-Order'. Aided by some of the earliest *ULTRA intercepts which revealed this order, the *Dunkirk evacuation began. Why ULTRA was unable to do the more to influence the course of the French campaign by revealing the true objectives of the German offensive can be explained briefly as follows: first, many of the crucial German orders were transmitted over secure land-lines, not by radio; secondly, the intercept system at *Bletchley Park and its French equivalent was in its infancy, so that too little information usually arrived too late; finally however, as Ronald Lewin remarks (in *Ultra Goes to War*, London, 1978, p. 67) '... if your enemy, having won strategic surprise, attacks with irresistible power and panache, then the best of intelligence ... tends merely to confirm the inevitable.'

On 28 May the Belgians surrendered; and on 3 June the British completed the 'miracle' of Dunkirk, a deliverance only made possible by the sacrifice of the French and Belgian rearguard forces—a fact not generally appreciated in the UK at the time.

The Wehrmacht was free to mop up the French Army, now fighting alone. After Dunkirk, it became largely a matter of marching for the Germans, who now wheeled southwards to face the French forces which had dug themselves in on the line of the Somme and the Aisne—the so-called 'Weygand Line'. Fighting with often greater tenacity than they had shown on the Meuse, though against hopeless odds, the French resisted the first German onslaught on 5 June. But the 'Weygand Line' was a line in little more than name, and once the Germans had broken through it there was nothing to stop them. On 14 June Paris fell, undefended; the French armies holding the redundant fortifications of the Maginot Line were taken in the rear; Italy administered its infamous 'stab in the back' (though it was ineffectual and barely affected the campaign); and on 22 June France was forced to agree to a humiliating *armistice—signed in the same railway carriage where Marshal Ferdinand Foch (accompanied, among others, by Weygand) had accepted the German surrender of 1918.

The brilliantly improvised German operational plan for the attack in the west had succeeded beyond all dreams. France—with losses estimated at 90,000 dead, 200,000 wounded, and 1.9 million taken prisoners or missing—had been utterly defeated in six weeks for a cost of 29,640 German dead (army and air force) and a total casualty figure of 163,213. But the Germans had no provisions for following up a French collapse; and while they gorged themselves on their triumph, and on the delights of Paris, the RAF spent the unexpected respite in bracing itself for the battle of *Britain in which it was to rob Hitler of final victory.

ALISTAIR HORNE

Bond, B., *France and Belgium, 1939–1940* (London, 1983).

Gunsberg, J., *Divided and Conquered: The French High Command and the Defeat of the West, 1940* (London, 1979).

Horne, A., *To Lose a Battle, France 1940* (London, 1969, new edn., 1990).

Shirer, W. L., *The Collapse of the Third Republic* (London, 1970).

Franco-Soviet Treaties. The USSR recognized the French provisional government in 1941 and on 28 November 1942 signed an agreement with the Free French agreeing to assist all those who rejected the *Vichy government's policy of *collaboration with the Germans. On 10 December 1944 the two countries signed a 20-year treaty of alliance and mutual assistance. This bound both to fight until total victory had been achieved and not to make a separate peace with Germany.

Franco y Bahamonde, General Francisco (1892–1975), Fascist *Caudillo* (leader) of Spain who, despite having received extensive German aid in the *Spanish Civil War (1936–9), refused to join the Axis and would not permit the passage of German troops through Spain to attack Gibraltar. He was a deft negotiator—Hitler remarked after a protracted encounter with him in October 1940 that he would prefer to have three or four teeth extracted than suffer another meeting with him—and managed to keep the exhausted Spain neutral. His principal fighting contribution to the Axis cause was to allow volunteer army and air units to fight on the Eastern Front (see BLUE DIVISION and SPANISH LEGION).

Cozier, B., *Franco: A Biographical History* (London, 1967).

Francs-Tireurs et Partisans, see FRANCE, 9.

Frank, Anne (1929–45), member of a German Jewish family who fled to the Netherlands in 1933 to escape Nazi persecution. After the occupation of the Netherlands they hid for two years in an Amsterdam house, but were betrayed in August 1944 and sent to *Bergen-Belsen. Only her father survived and he subsequently found the diary his 14-year-old daughter had kept while in hiding. It was published in 1947—its English title was *The Diary of Anne Frank* (1952)—and it became a world-wide bestseller. See also CHILDREN.

Frank, Hans (1900–46), Hitler's legal adviser who was made Bavarian minister of justice when Hitler came to power in January 1933, and minister without portfolio in 1934. After the *Polish campaign of September 1939, when Poland was divided between Germany and the USSR, Frank was appointed to rule the rump, the General Government (see POLAND, 2(b)). He declared it would be treated like a colony, and that its people would be 'slaves of the Greater German Empire'. The initial lengths to which he went to accomplish this brought protests from a few German Wehrmacht officers. They were ignored, and in the following years Frank imposed on the Poles the most brutal and degrading consequences of *Nazi ideology: the *Final Solution, **Lebensborn*, and *forced labour. He pleaded guilty at the *Nuremberg trials, and was sentenced to death and hanged.

Fraser, Admiral Sir Bruce (1888–1981), British naval officer who served as Third Sea Lord from 1939 to 1942. He then became second-in-command of the Home Fleet and succeeded *Tovey as its C-in-C the following year. When illness forced *Pound to resign as First Sea Lord in September 1943, Churchill offered Fraser the post. Fraser replied that he would, of course, serve wherever he was sent, but that while 'I believe I have the confidence of my own fleet, *Cunningham has that of the whole navy'. Churchill agreed and Cunningham was appointed. However, Fraser soon received the recognition he deserved when, in December 1943, he sank the German battle-cruiser **Scharnhorst* off North Cape; from this battle he later took the title Lord Fraser of North Cape. In November 1944 he was appointed C-in-C of the new British Pacific Fleet (see TASK FORCE 57) and eventually served as First Sea Lord between 1948 and 1951. He was knighted in 1941.

Humble, R., *Fraser of North Cape* (London, 1983).

Fraser, Peter (1884–1950), son of a Scottish cobbler, served as New Zealand's prime minister from 1940 to 1949. After emigrating to New Zealand at the age of 26 he was, by September 1939, deputy prime minister in Michael Savage's Labour government. But Savage (1872–1940) was a sick man and it fell to Fraser to put his country on to a war footing after New Zealand had declared war on Germany at midnight on 3 September 1939. In March 1940 Savage died and Fraser became prime minister. Though sometimes vetoed proposals for the disposition of New Zealand troops, he proved to be a staunch supporter of the Allied cause and was in regular personal contact with Churchill and Roosevelt, attending war cabinet meetings when in London. In 1944 he was voted back into office, though with a reduced majority. He was a strong supporter of the United Nations and was present at its foundation at the *San Francisco conference in April 1945. See also NEW ZEALAND, 3.

Free French, see DE GAULLE AND THE FREE FRENCH.

Freisler, Roland (1893–1945), Nazi judge who became state secretary in the ministry of justice in 1934, and from 1942 presided over the *People's Court (Volksgerichtshof) in Berlin. After he had tried and had executed many of the conspirators in the July 1944 bomb plot against Hitler (see SCHWARZE KAPELLE), he was killed in an air raid in February 1945 while presiding over the trial of two members of the German resistance, Frau Hanna Solf and her daughter. The bomb also destroyed all the evidence against them and they survived the war.

French Cameroons were that part of the German West African colony of Cameroon which had been mandated to France after the *First World War. Its commissioner, Richard Brunot, tried to repudiate the French *armistice with Germany after the fall of *France in June 1940, but a nominal *Vichy regime took over until Major *Leclerc eatablished control there for de *Gaulle and the Free French with a bloodless coup in August 1940.

French Canadians, concentrated in the province of Quebec, constituted some 3 million of Canada's population of just under 11.5 million people in 1939. French-speaking Canadians resolutely opposed a major Canadian contribution to the Second World War. Their attitude was grounded in history and bolstered by memories of racial injustice and political slights. British imperial sentiment had no appeal in francophone Quebec, and *nationaliste* leaders, who had opposed participation in the Boer War and any contribution to imperial defence, insisted that the Dominion's duty was limited to defending Canadian territory. The burning resentment engendered by events of the *First World War, when Quebec's opposition to conscription had been overridden and a coalition government formed without French-speaking representation, inevitably coloured attitudes to the new war.

The Liberal government of Mackenzie *King, strong in Quebec, had shaped its pre-war foreign and defence policy with a constant eye on French Canadian sensitivities, and the prime minister managed to bring a united Canada into the hostilities by promising a war of 'limited liability' and pledging that his government would not impose conscription for overseas service. That satisfied the Quebeckers, who had few objections to voluntary enlistment. But after the fall of *France, the government, through the National Resources Mobilization Act 1940, put conscription for home defence in place; 'the first bite at the cherry', some said. By early 1942, pressures for 'total war' in English Canada led the government to seek release from its no-conscription pledge of 1939 in a plebiscite. English Canada voted overwhelmingly to free the government (e.g. 82% in Ontario); responding to a skilful campaign by La ligue pour la défense du Canada, however, Quebec said 'no' by 73% to 27%, with most of the 'yes' vote coming from English-speaking Canadians. Stunned by the result, King limited himself to putting enabling legislation through parliament. Not until the autumn of 1944, with the whole Canadian Army in action and infantry reinforcement scarce, did the government send conscripts, of whom under 40% were French-speaking, overseas. The popular reaction in Quebec was fierce but brief, and the King government's narrow re-election in June 1945 was largely achieved thanks to Quebec's support.

Domestic politics aside, French Canada's military effort in the war was substantial. In contrast to the First World War, when perhaps no more than 15–20,000 enlisted, from its 1941 population of 699,000 men between the ages of 18 and 45, Quebec sent 12,404 into the Royal Canadian Navy (RCN), 24,768 into the Royal Canadian Air Force (RCAF), and 138,269 volunteers and conscripts into the army. Part of this enlistment was English-speaking, of course, but francophones in other provinces also volunteered. As recruits were not categorized by language, no firm statistics exist, but estimates are that upwards of 150,000 francophones served, and served well. No French-speaking army officer in field command rose as high as major-general, but there were many brigade and battalion commanders of distinction, and several francophone infantry units such as Le Royal 22e Régiment, Le Régiment de la Chaudière, and Les Fusiliers Mont-Royal created fine fighting records. One RCAF squadron, the Alouette, was also largely French-speaking, but in the RCN and RCAF most of the French speakers were scattered.

J. L. GRANATSTEIN

Granatstein J. L., and Hitsman, J. M., *Broken Promises: A History Of Conscription In Canada* (Toronto, 1976).

Stacey, C. P., *Arms, Men And Governments: The War Policies Of Canada 1939–1945* (Ottawa, 1970).

French Committee for National Liberation (Comité Français De Libération Nationale, or CFLN), formed in Algiers in June 1943 with the arch-rivals *Giraud and de *Gaulle as joint chairmen.

Of the other five original members, General *Catroux, René Massigli, and André Philip supported de Gaulle, while General Alphonse Georges and Jean *Monnet were Giraudists. Other nominees, mostly Gaullists, soon joined them, including two members of the French resistance. All agreed that until the committee could transfer its powers to a future provisional government, 'it undertakes to restore all French liberties, the laws of the Republic, the Republican regime, and entirely to destroy the arbitrary regime of personal power imposed today on the country.' Roosevelt, who disliked de Gaulle, ordered *Eisenhower's HQ in North Africa to deal direct with the French military authorities, and not through the CFLN. This boosted Giraud's standing, but he was no politician and by October de Gaulle had wrested control of the CFLN from him, and Giraud confined himself to military matters. By May 1944, when the committee announced itself the provisional government of the French Republic, Giraud had resigned from the committee, and as C-in-C. But though it began to be consulted by the western Allies on military matters, they still refused to recognize it as the French provisional government. And inspite of pressure from de Gaulle—and despite the fact they accepted the CFLN after the Normandy landings (see OVERLORD) as the *de facto* administration for liberated France—the Allies, on Roosevelt's insistence, continued to withhold recognition until October 1944. See also FRANCE, 3(d).

French Equatorial Africa, federation of French colonies comprising Middle Congo, Chad, Ubangi-Shari, and Gabon. Chad's Guyanese governor, Félix Eboué, declared for de *Gaulle and the Free French in August 1940, and the same month Free French sympathizers seized control in the Middle Congo whose capital, Brazzaville, was also the administrative centre for Ubangi-Shari and Gabon. The last, after rallying temporarily to the Free French cause, altered its allegiance when *Vichy French Forces arrived. It eventually fell to Gaullist and British troops in October 1940 (see GABON CAMPAIGN) and Eboué was established in Brazzaville as governor-general of what was called the Equatorial Federation. See also BRAZZAVILLE CONFERENCE.

French Expeditionary Corps (Corps Expéditionaire Français), which fought with the Allies during the *Italian campaign, was formed by amalgamating Frenchmen who had rallied to de *Gaulle and the Free French with the officers and men of the French regular army who had been stationed in North Africa when France collapsed in 1940; with volunteers from the French colonial empire; and with conscripts just called up. They had a further stiffening, as well, of men who had managed to escape from France. Not much time had been given to weld them into a single fighting force, from such disparate military origins, but they had a forceful commander-in-chief in *Juin, who reported no troubles over morale.

The corps included among its infantry *Tirailleurs *Spahis, and *Goums from France's Armée d'Afrique (see FRANCE, 6(b)). The Americans provided a good deal of their equipment, including artillery. Most of the non-caucasian troops, who composed over half the force, came from peasant families and were used to hardship; this made them the more formidable as soldiers through an Italian winter.

Juin was senior to the American General *Clark, but was prepared to serve under his orders; the French corps, which had an average strength of 110,000, formed part of Clark's Fifth US Army, of which it normally formed the right wing, adjoining the British Eighth Army. It took a prominent part in the fighting round *Monte Cassino, and the strong German position there was eventually turned with critical help from part of the French force, the 4th Moroccan Mountain Division; experience in the Atlas Mountains turned out to be useful for war in the Apennines. The French also captured Siena, the Tuscan capital, in July 1944.

Most of the corps was withdrawn from Italy, reinforced by a further 50,000 men, and, as Armée B, placed under a new commander, de *Lattre de Tassigny, to take part in the *French Riviera landings in August 1944.

M. R. D. FOOT

French fleet, scuttling of. Under the terms of the Franco-German *armistice of June 1940 the French fleet, apart from those units needed for the security of French colonies, was to be demobilized under German and Italian control. However, after the British bombardment of French warships at *Mers-el-Kébir in July 1940, the order was only partially implemented by the reduction of some crews; so that when the survivors of Mers-el-Kébir, and other warships which had left for North Africa to escape the Germans, rejoined the French squadron at Toulon the French fleet remained a powerful entity.

Following the *North African campaign landings by the Allies in November 1942 Hitler ordered the occupation of *Vichy France on 11 November and on 19 November, after some hesitation and complicated negotiations with the French, the seizure of the fleet. In Toulon at that time were about 80 warships totalling 200,000 tons (a third of the fleet's tonnage in 1939) which included two modern battle-cruisers, *Strasbourg* and *Dunkerque*, and the battleship *Provence*. German forces attacked the dockyard at dawn on 27 November and were fired on by the French. Five submarines then managed to escape, but the rest of the fleet was scuttled by their crews before the Germans could find their way to them, thus fulfilling the pledge given by Admiral *Darlan to the British in June 1940 that the ships would never fall into German hands intact.

French Forces of the Interior, see FFI.

French Indo-China comprised the French protectorates of Cambodia, Laos, Annam, Tongkin, and the French colony of Cochin-China, the last three being previously known as Vietnam, as they are now. Except in Cochin-China, which was ruled directly by the French, the original royal houses remained in place, though subordinated to a French governor-general. All but a fifth of the 25 million inhabitants, mostly Buddhists, lived in Vietnam.

By February 1939, when the Japanese seized Hainan Island from China (see CHINA INCIDENT), their threat to French Indo-China and its 40,000 Europeans had become substantial. Appeals to the French government brought few reinforcements, but extra finance enabled General *Catroux, who had been appointed governor-general in August 1939, to raise the local army to 100,000 which included 20,000 Foreign Legion troops. In June 1940 the Japanese demanded the presence of a military mission in the country to ensure the closure of the Haiphong–Yunnan railway, the principal route for supplying *Chiang Kai-shek's Nationalist Chinese forces fighting the Japanese (but see also BURMA ROAD). Catroux, despite his increased forces, felt he was in no position to oppose them. The new *Vichy government disagreed and replaced him with Vice-Admiral Jean Decoux (1884–1963), but when the Japanese made further demands Decoux was ordered to negotiate not to fight.

In fact, the Japanese had no desire to replace the French administration so long as they had full access to French Indo-China's resources, and these they proceeded to acquire with a mixture of threats and astute diplomacy. On the day Decoux signed one agreement, 22 September 1940, the Japanese, feigning ignorance of it, attacked from southern China. They captured two Tongkinese towns and killed more than 800 French troops before expressing their regrets over the 'mistake', and withdrawing. They even turned a French naval victory against Thailand, which claimed Laotian and Cambodian border territory, into a defeat when they forced the French to sign a peace treaty in May 1941 which gave Thailand the territories it wanted. In July 1941, after their demands for bases had been met, the Japanese occupied Saigon and entered Cambodia.

By the end of 1941 Decoux, outgunned, outmanoeuvred, and browbeaten, ostensibly ruled an Indo-China which had become part of the *Greater East Asia Co-Prosperity Sphere, was garrisoned by 35,000 Japanese troops, and was having its industrial and agricultural wealth systematically stripped. Rice—Indo-China was the world's third largest grower of it—corn, coal, and rubber were all shipped to Japan or put at the disposal of the Japanese garrison, and all local enterprises were obliged to work for the Japanese. The economic chaos that followed led to inflation and shortages which caused immense hardship. And when the Japanese garrison became isolated from external supplies, troops used rice needed by the population for fuel, and planted rice fields with jute and cotton to obtain the textiles they needed.

As a result between 1.5 and 2 million people died of starvation in Tongkin in 1945.

Though Japanese policy was to retain the French administration, the Japanese Army did its best to undermine it. But as long as the Japanese could extract what they wanted the French, underpinned by the police and the army, retained their power over the local population. Decoux tried to improve relations with them, but also ensured they could not challenge him politically. A nationalist insurrection in Tongkin in September 1940 was therefore suppressed with great severity, as was one by the communists in Cochin-China that November. Of all the factions working for independence from the French, only the communist guerrilla organization the *Viet Minh, aided by the American *Office of Strategic Services, managed to build up an effective internal organization after its formation by *Ho Chi Minh in May 1941. From 1943, with US support, the Viet Minh also attacked from China into Tongkin, and by October 1944 had established its own administration in its northern areas.

By early 1945 Decoux had become subject to a body organized by de *Gaulle and the Free French. Called the Free French Council of Indo-China, this decided that confrontation with the Japanese, not collaboration, was the best way of retaining the country for France. The *Kempei were quickly alerted to Free French resistance and the Japanese, fearing US invasion after Manila fell in February 1945, decided that Decoux's administration and his forces had to be neutralized. On 9 March 1945 Decoux, after refusing a Japanese ultimatum to put his forces under Japanese command, was arrested and the French garrisons surrounded, and in the fighting that followed about 1,700 French troops were killed or simply massacred.

The Japanese now persuaded the Emperor of Annam, Bao Dai (b.1913), to declare Annam and Tongkin independent, which he did on 11 March 1945, though the Japanese retained control in Cochin-China until they ceded it to Bao Dai on 16 May. King Sihanouk of Cambodia (b.1922) was cajoled into declaring his country independent on 13 March, but the King of Laos, Sisavangvong (1885–1959), who was friendly with the French, proved more obdurate and did not declare his country's independence until 8 April—the day after Japanese troops had arrived in his capital. Bao Dai formed a Vietnamese government under Tran Tong Kim, but this soon resigned when it proved incapable of sending sufficient rice to those starving in Tongkin. On 13 August, *Ho Chi Minh, the communist leader of the Viet Minh, formed the National Liberation Committee of Vietnam which assumed power when the Japanese surrendered on 15 August. Five days later Hanoi was in Viet Minh hands; Bao Dai's abdication and assistance (he became the administration's supreme adviser) were obtained; and on 2 September the Democratic Republic of Vietnam was declared.

Throughout the war Roosevelt's policy was to ensure that the French did not regain colonial power in Indo-China. After the Cairo conference in November 1943 (see SEXTANT), at which Roosevelt's offer to hand over French Indo-China to China had been refused by Chiang Kai-shek, the president raised the possibility of an international trusteeship. This led to an agreement at the Potsdam conference in July 1945 (see TERMINAL) in which China temporarily occupied Vietnam north of the 16th parallel and troops of *South-East Asia Command occupied the rest. However, French colonial rule was soon re-established in South Vietnam, Laos, and Cambodia, and though the Chinese were eventually persuaded to withdraw from North Vietnam, the French then became committed to the long, bitter, and fruitless struggle against the Viet Minh which ended in Dien Bien Phu (May 1954) and defeat. See also ANTI-IMPERIALISM and NATIONALISM.

French Morocco, vast French North African protectorate of 6.25 million inhabitants, including 187,000 Europeans, whose sultan, Mohammed Ben Youssef, declared his support for France when the war started in September 1939. Its French resident-general, General *Noguès, opposed the US landings at Casablanca in November 1942 (see NORTH AFRICAN CAMPAIGN), but remained at his post until the *French Committee for National Liberation replaced him in June 1943 with Gabriel Puaux who kept the country under French control, despite the sultan's efforts to gain independence.

Moroccan *Tirailleurs took part in the fighting which preceded the fall of *France in June 1940 and eight regiments of *Goums and Tirailleurs were formed to fight in the North African campaign. Some of these also fought in the *Italian campaign, distinguishing themselves at *Monte Cassino, and with de *Lattre de Tassigny's Armée B during the *French Riviera landings in August 1944, and in the fighting that followed.

French National Committee (Comité National Français), see DE GAULLE AND THE FREE FRENCH.

French Riviera landings, undertaken, after much Anglo-American wrangling, on 15 August 1944 by *Patch's Seventh US Army formed for the task, and supported by naval and air forces of the two Mediterranean Cs-in-C, Admiral John Cunningham and Lt-General *Eaker.

The operation, initially condenamed ANVIL and later DRAGOON, was originally conceived as a feint to draw off German troops during the Normandy landings (see

An RAF photographic reconnaissance aircraft recorded this scene of devastation shortly after the scuttling of the **French fleet** at Toulon in November 1942. Two cruisers of the Suffren class are still ablaze; the battle-cruiser *Strasbourg*, on the extreme right, has settled on the seabed. Most of the sunken and half-sunken warships in the middle of the picture are destroyers.

OVERLORD), but at the Cairo conference in November 1943 (see SEXTANT) the Americans proposed a major landing in the south of France, and at the Teheran conference (see EUREKA) which followed Stalin backed them (see also GRAND ALLIANCE). But when German forces were drawn away from Normandy by the *Anzio landings in Italy and by the threat of a French Riviera landing, and *logistics made it impossible to launch DRAGOON simultaneously with OVERLORD, Churchill and the British *Chiefs of Staff argued vigorously against mounting it. They urged that, instead of depleting the forces in the *Italian campaign, which were supplying nearly all DRAGOON's manpower, all available resources should be committed to making a strategic thrust—perhaps aided by an Istrian peninsula landing—from Italy into Austria. This added dimension to the threat already facing Germany from west and east would, they argued, be of more help to *Eisenhower's Normandy campaign than DRAGOON, and might also end the German occupation of the Balkans.

But *Eisenhower, who had no major port available to him in Normandy, was eager to have Marseilles and other nearby ports through which supplies, and the numerous divisions still in the USA, could be landed. The US *Joint Chiefs of Staff, who regarded the Italian campaign as a sideshow, supported Eisenhower, as did Roosevelt—who, as always, was suspicious of Churchill's ambitions in the Balkans. Eventually Churchill gave way, though at the eleventh hour he was still urging that the basic military tenet of concentration of effort be upheld by landing DRAGOON's forces at Bordeaux.

DRAGOON came under the overall control of Maitland *Wilson, Supreme Allied Commander in the Mediterranean, whose deputy, *Devers, supervised the operation on his behalf. The initial assault, between Cannes and Hyères, was undertaken by *Truscott's 6th Corps of three US divisions (see Map 37). To guard his flanks the French Groupe de Commandos and the American First Special Service Force (see USA, 5(f)) landed on his left and an ad hoc Anglo-American division, the First Airborne Task Force, was dropped at Le Muy on the right. The initial assault was followed up by seven French divisions of General de *Lattre de Tassigny's 256,000-strong Armée B (renamed First French Army on 19 September) which included troops from the *French Expeditionary Corps and substantial forces from France's Armée d'Afrique (see FRANCE, 6(b)).

Opposing Patch's Seventh US Army were ten German divisions of General *Blaskowitz's Army Group G, of which only three were positioned near the landing beaches, while the Luftwaffe could only muster 200 aircraft against the 2,000 Allied ones gathered on Corsica and Sardinia. Immediately before the landings, the coastline was extensively bombarded by the 5 battleships, 21 cruisers, and 100 destroyers of the Western Naval Task Force under Vice-Admiral Kent Hewitt. In addition to this Task Force, which carried out the landings, aircraft from seven British and two US carriers supplemented those of the Twelfth Tactical Air Force which harassed the Germans throughout the campaign. In total 887 warships and 1,370 landing craft participated in DRAGOON.

The German beach defences and mines were formidable, but the preliminary air attacks and the heavy naval bombardment, and the lack of German manpower, ensured there were few Allied casualties on landing; and, with the Allied armies in northern France on the offensive (see NORMANDY CAMPAIGN), Hitler was soon forced to order the withdrawal of his forces in the south. So once ashore and through the defensive crust Patch's task became one of pursuit and entrapment of the retreating Germans. Truscott, emboldened by *ULTRA intelligence that no large-scale attack by German forces in Italy was planned against his exposed right flank, struck north-west for Avignon and north towards Sisteron while the French made for Toulon and Marseilles. These two ports had been designated fortresses by Hitler and were heavily defended, but the French, whose troops included *Goums and *Tirailleurs, fought with great *élan* and by 28 August both had surrendered. With de Lattre's 2nd Corps now operational on Truscott's eastern flank, his 1st Corps crossed the River Rhône and headed northwards.

By the end of the month the Americans were beyond Valence and Grenoble, though tough resistance by the experienced 11th Panzer Division at Montélimar had allowed a large part of Blaskowitz's Nineteenth Army to escape from the entrapment Patch had planned for it. Lyons fell on 3 September, Besançon on 7 September, and Dijon was liberated on 11 September by the 2nd French Corps and French Forces of the Interior (see FFI). As the 6th Corps drove the Germans back towards their frontier Patch again tried to trap them before they reached the Vosges, but again they escaped his grasp.

From 10 September Truscott's troops began to link up with elements of *Patton's Third US Army and on 15 September all DRAGOON forces passed from Wilson's command to Eisenhower's. At the same time they were now designated Sixth Army Group. The Group's air support was the newly formed First Tactical Air Force (12th Tactical Air Command and, from October, the First French Air Force). By the end of September 6th Corps had managed to cross the Moselle, but by now it had outrun its supplies and had, too, run out of steam. Beyond the Moselle lay the forested hills of the Vosges and for the next six weeks 6th Corps managed to move forward only 25 km. (15 mi.), rather less than the 650 km. (400 mi.), it had covered between mid-August and the end of September. The French, too, were immobilized while they replaced some of their Tirailleurs with FFI detachments. However, the remnants of Nineteenth Army were thinly spread along a winter defensive line and when Devers attacked on 13 November de Lattre's 1st Corps drove through the Belfort Gap and reached the Rhine a week later. This feat threatened the Germans' lines of communication and forced their withdrawal, which eased the way forward for a reinforced 6th Corps, now

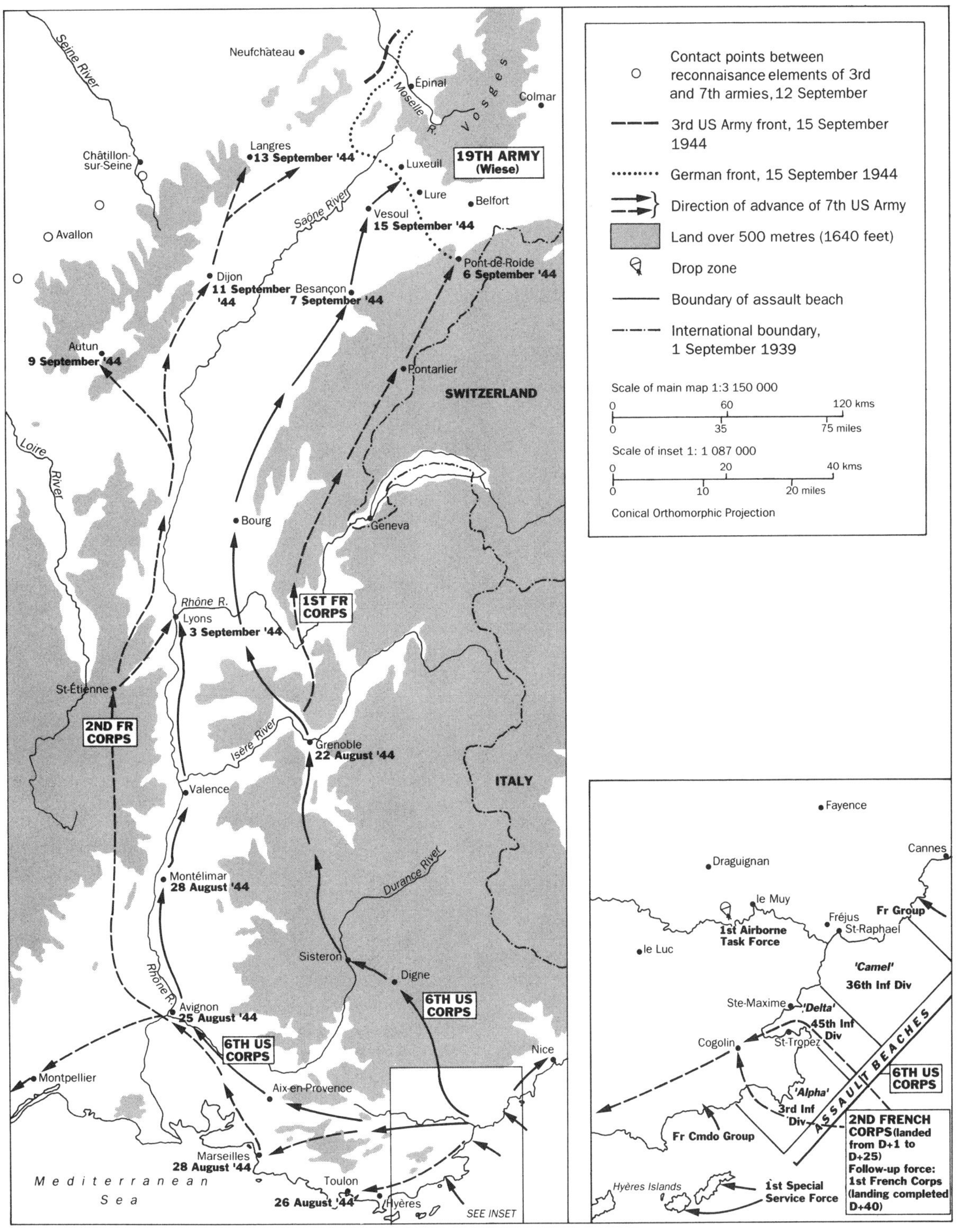

37. Allied **French Riviera landings**, 15 August 1944, and advance northwards

commanded by Maj-General Edward Brooks, and for the 2nd French Corps.

At the height of the Allied crisis that surrounded the German *Ardennes offensive, which began on 16 December 1944, two of Devers's divisions were ordered to support Patton's counter-thrust into the southern flank of the German advance, and de *Gaulle was warned that Allied forces might have to withdraw from Alsace and Lorraine. The French fiercely opposed abandoning these newly liberated areas to the Germans and vowed to defend Strasbourg themselves if the Americans withdrew from the city. This caused a furore, but Churchill supported de Gaulle. Eventually a compromise was reached, enabling Strasbourg to be defended successfully when, on 7 January 1945, a powerful German attack was launched from north of the city and from the *Colmar pocket to the south. The battle raged for two weeks before the German offensive petered out and there then remained only the impediment of the Colmar pocket before Sixth Army Group was able to cross the Rhine and take its part in the battle for *Germany.

Despite Churchill's forebodings—fulfilled in that the Germans remained undefeated in Italy until the last week of the war—DRAGOON was a considerable achievement. For the loss of 4,000 French and 2,700 US casualties the Allies had captured 57,000 Germans; and by October the southern French ports were handling over a third of the 1.3 million tons of US supplies which reached Europe that month. Without them the supply crisis that hit the Allied armies that autumn—critical until the *Scheldt Estuary battle was won—could have been insurmountable.

Lattre de Tassigny, J. de, *History of the French First Army* (London, 1952).

French Somaliland, French East African colony which commanded the strait between the Gulf of Aden and the Red Sea. It was originally part of Somalia which had been divided between France, Italy (see ITALIAN SOMALILAND), and the UK (see BRITISH SOMALILAND) at the end of the nineteenth century. After the fall of *France in June 1940 its governor sided with the *Vichy regime, but the army commander there, General Paul Gentilhomme, took his troops to fight alongside the British during the *East African campaign. The British blockaded it and in December 1942 it joined de *Gaulle and the Free French.

French West Africa, federation of the French colonies of Senegal, Mauritania, Niger, Upper Volta, French Sudan, French Guinea, Ivory Coast, Dahomey, and French Togo, the last being part of Togoland mandated to France after the *First World War. This vast area of 4.8 million sq. km. (1.85 million sq. mi.) was inhabited by about 16 million people, and, when war started, it sent some 65,000 African soldiers overseas, many becoming *prisoners-of-war during the fighting which preceded the fall of *France in June 1940.

Senegal's capital, Dakar, was the third largest port in the French Empire and the base of the *Vichy-appointed high commissioner for Black Africa (French West and French Equatorial Africa), Pierre Boisson. He was, in effect, only the governor-general of French West Africa as French Equatorial Africa rallied to de *Gaulle and the Free French. Boisson's policy of neutrality, especially after the abortive *Dakar expedition in September 1940, was supported by the local population, and was strictly applied to both sides. However, in November 1942, after the *North African campaign landings, he declared his support for Admiral *Darlan, and his resignation was quickly accepted by the *French Committee for National Liberation in June 1943. It replaced him with Pierre Cournarie, and Boisson was imprisoned; he died in captivity in 1947.

French West Indies, the Caribbean territories of Martinique, Guadeloupe, and French Guiana, each of which had its own governor. The population of 616,000 enjoyed universal suffrage to elect members of the local legislature, and representatives sat in the French Assembly. However, after the fall of *France in June 1940 the *Vichy representative, Vice-Admiral *Robert, whose powers extended beyond the French West Indies to *St Pierre and Miquelon, suspended democracy. The British then imposed a blockade which restricted trade with France and the USA and prevented the movement of French warships at Martinique, and of French gold which had been shipped there. Consequently, little food could be imported and it was difficult to export the principal products, sugar and rum.

When the USA entered the war it took over the blockade and in March 1943 it manoeuvred French Guiana into declaring for General *Giraud, both to prevent the colony joining de *Gaulle and the Free French, and to obtain base rights and facilities there. But Robert would not change his allegiance and on 30 April the USA broke off diplomatic relations with him. Local resistance groups eventually pressured Robert into resigning on 30 June 1943 and he was replaced by a Giraudist, who was later replaced by a Gaullist. See also CARIBBEAN AT WAR.

Baptiste, F., *War Cooperation and Conflict: The European Possessions in the Caribbean, 1939–1945* (New York, 1988).

Freyberg, Lt-General Sir Bernard (1889–1963), British-born, but New Zealand raised, commander of the New Zealand Division which fought in all the *Mediterranean campaigns. In May 1941 he commanded the mixed British, Commonwealth, and Greek forces on *Crete. After the war his handling of the island's defences was often criticized on grounds which a biography published in 1991 argues were largely unjustified (see P. Freyberg, *Bernard Freyberg VC*, London, 1991).

A trained dentist, Freyberg fought with the Naval Division during the *First World War before transferring to the army, and was awarded the Victoria Cross and two

DSOs (see DECORATIONS). Forced to retire in 1937, he was recalled when war broke out and was given command of the New Zealand Expeditionary Force, later known as the New Zealand Division. He was promoted lt-general in 1942, but his command only occasionally swelled to that of a corps. He produced one of the toughest, most hard-hitting combat formations of the war at whose head he won two more DSOs. He was not a disciplinarian because he considered camaraderie and self-respect were more effective. 'You cannot treat a man like a butler,' he would say, 'and expect him to fight like a lion.' Orders were made as suggestions and officers and men were on first-name terms. When *Montgomery remarked that his troops did not salute much Freyberg replied: 'If you wave to them they'll wave back', and one of his officers said of him: 'he's as simple as a child and as cunning as a Maori dog.' He was knighted in 1942 and served as New Zealand's governor-general from 1946 to 1952.

Frick, Wilhelm (1877–1946), German lawyer who as an early supporter of Hitler and a dedicated Nazi bureaucrat drew up the Nuremberg Laws in 1935 (see ANTI-SEMITISM). As Reich minister of the interior between 1933 and 1943 he implemented social measures against German Jews (see FINAL SOLUTION) and against opponents of Hitler's regime. In August 1943 he was appointed Reichsprotector of Bohemia and Moravia, though Karl Frank, promoted from state secretary to minister of state, wielded the real power. He refused to testify at the *Nuremberg trials, but was sentenced to death and hanged.

Friedeburg, Gen-Admiral Hans von (1895–1945), German commander of U-boats under *Dönitz whom he succeeded as C-in-C of the German Navy on 3 May 1945. The next day, on *Lüneburg Heath, he surrendered to *Montgomery all German armed forces in the Netherlands, Denmark, and north-west Germany. On 8 May he signed the surrender of all German forces in eastern Germany to the Soviets at Karlshorst, near Berlin. That night he also became a signatory of the document which *Jodl had signed at *Eisenhower's HQ at Reims the previous day for the surrender of all German forces on all remaining fronts. Two weeks later Friedeburg committed suicide.

Fritsch, General Baron Werner von (1880–1939), German Army officer who served as a staff officer during the *First World War. He was promoted maj-general in October 1932, and lt-general and C-in-C of the army in February 1934.

In January 1938 a trumped-up charge of homosexuality was brought against him which coincided with the marriage scandal of the minister of war, Field Marshal *Blomberg. The plot, almost certainly instigated by *Göring, but which also involved *Himmler and *Heydrich, was quickly seized upon by Hitler as a chance to establish his own ascendancy over the army. A week after he dismissed Blomberg he demanded, and received on 3 February, Fritsch's resignation. At his military trial Fritsch was found not guilty, but he was not reinstated.

At the outbreak of war Fritsch returned to his old regiment and was killed in the attack on Warsaw during the *Polish campaign.

frogmen, rubber-suited swimmers equipped with underwater breathing equipment and fins for their feet. They were primarily used to attach *limpet mines to moored ships, bridges, and so on and also for clearing underwater obstacles with plastic *explosives. The Italians pioneered this form of attack, but frogmen were also employed operationally by the Americans, British, and Germans.

Originally, the Italians envisaged frogmen as 'underwater infantry' who would walk in Indian file along the bottom of the sea towards their targets. However, it was soon found that swimming, or riding astride *human torpedoes, was a more practical way of progressing and they were used extensively by the *Tenth Light Flotilla.

The Americans developed Underwater Demolition Teams during the *Pacific war for reconnaissance purposes and for clearing the way for their landing craft and *amphibians through natural and man-made obstacles. They were first used operationally in the *Marshall Islands, and during the *French Riviera landings 41 teams of 11 men each were deployed. The British first used similar units during the Normandy landings in June 1944 (see OVERLORD) when they were known as LCOCUS (Landing Craft Obstacle Clearance Units).

The Japanese also trained a number of frogmen called *Fukuryu* (crouching dragon) to attack the expected American invasion fleet with impact-fuzed charges mounted on stout poles, but they never had to be used in this suicidal role.

Führer (leader), title adopted by Hitler and copied from Mussolini who called himself by the same word in Italian (il duce). *Goebbels, who had suggested it, made its use compulsory in the Nazi Party from 1931. When Hitler combined the offices of chancellor and president in 1934, Führer und Reichskanzler became his official state title.

Funk, Walther (1890–1960), German finanial journalist who joined the Nazi Party in 1931, and from 1933 was state secretary of the ministry of propaganda and chief of the government's press office. He was Minister of Economic Affairs from 1937 to 1945, and, from 1939, President of the Reichsbank. At the *Nuremberg trials he was given a life sentence but was released in 1958.

'funnies', nickname for British armoured vehicles of Maj-General *Hobart's 79th Armoured Division which had been specially adapted for breaching, or bridging, obstacles. See ENGINEERS, 1.

FUSAG, see DECEPTION.

G

Gabon campaign, fought between *Vichy French forces and those of de *Gaulle's Free French when the latter invaded the French Equatorial African colony of Gabon on 12 October 1940 from the French Cameroons and the Middle Congo. The governor had initially opted to join de Gaulle but then reversed his decision and when Free French troops, led by Major *Leclerc, threatened invasion Vichy troops were rushed by sea from Dakar and a naval squadron sailed from Toulon (see NORTH, ADMIRAL). The invading columns met determined resistance from the garrison of four battalions of *Tirailleurs Sénégalais but on 7 November the two columns linked up around Libreville. The next day a ground, air, and sea attack was launched on the city but the defending forces fought well and it took another four days to capture. The UK viewed the campaign unenthusiastically and no British troops were involved on the ground, though a Royal Navy sloop did force the surrender of the single Vichy submarine in the area.

GALAHAD, codename for US volunteer force, otherwise known as Merrill's Marauders, which fought the Japanese in the *Burma campaign. It comprised three battalions, totalling about 3,000 men, each being divided into two combat teams. The force was given training with the *Chindits, with whom it had originally been raised to co-operate. Then, employing Chindit tactics, it was used by *Stilwell between March and August 1944, in conjunction with his First Chinese Army, to try to outflank and then trap the Japanese in northern Burma.

The unit's nickname—coined by a *war correspondent but never used by its members—came from its leader, Brig-General Frank D. Merrill, its official title being '5307 Composite Unit (Provisional)'. Among its ranks were Sioux Indians and *Japanese-Americans who were the backbone of the élite intelligence and reconnaissance platoons. Appointed by Stilwell, whose friend and chief of staff he was, Merrill, a cavalryman, had no infantry experience. He had two heart attacks while in command and the unit was mostly led by his second-in-command, Colonel Charles Hunter.

After a series of brilliant outflanking movements GALAHAD, working with Chinese units and levies from the Kachin hill tribes, captured the airfield at *Myitkyina in northern Burma on 17 May 1944, but by that time the original force, worn down by disease and exhaustion, had practically ceased to exist. Stilwell, determined to capture Myitkyina itself, reinforced GALAHAD with untrained troops and hurried the sick and wounded back into action. The town eventually fell on 3 August, though by then the few survivors had been withdrawn.

When the campaign was over, the unit was disbanded, amidst some acrimony, and its remnants were then accepted into the US infantry as the 475th Regiment. Altogether, its members had fought in 5 major and 30 minor actions and had received precious little praise from Stilwell for their tenacity. However, they eventually received the recognition they deserved—a Presidential Unit Citation, 6 Distinguished Service Crosses, 4 Legions of Merit, and 44 Silver Stars (see DECORATIONS). See also CHINA–BURMA–INDIA THEATRE.

Galland, Lt-General Adolf (b.1912), German Luftwaffe officer who served in Germany's Kondor Legion fighting on *Franco's side during the *Spanish Civil War. He then led a fighter group during the battle of *Britain, becoming for a time the Luftwaffe's leading ace and shooting down 103 aircraft. He was appointed commander of the Fighter Arm in November 1941, making him, at 29, the youngest general in the German armed forces. Having come into increasing conflict with Hitler and *Göring, in January 1945 he was dismissed. He then took command of a squadron of Me262 jet fighters, but was shot down on 26 April 1945 and became a *prisoner-of-war.

Gamelin, General Maurice-Gustave (1872–1958). General Joseph Joffre's operations officer on the Marne in 1914, Gamelin enjoyed a meteoric rise in the French Army. His ascent owed as much to his front-line command of a brigade, a division, and then a corps in the *First World War as to his talent for staff work and knack of making political friends in high places. Successfully pacifying the Druze tribes in Syria during the 1920s, Gamelin vaulted over many senior officers to become chief of the French army staff in 1931, and then C-in-C designate in January 1935, on the retirement of General *Weygand.

Open-minded and professionally innovative, Gamelin raised the cry to refurbish the French armed forces and face the challenge of Nazi Germany. An enthusiastic republican, he gained the confidence of the left-wing Popular Front government which won the 1936 elections. Fashioning a close partnership with *Daladier, the Radical Party leader and Popular Front defence minister, Gamelin supported a 14 billion franc rearmament drive initiated by the Popular Front in September 1936. He held progressive views on mechanization and air support for ground operations, but his efforts were hindered by the officer corps' caution and the French economy's weaknesses. In 1937 and 1938 realistic exercises were curtailed because of equipment shortages and bitter disputes over doctrine with the apostles of strategic bombing who controlled French *air power.

On learning of the *Nazi–Soviet Pact in August 1939, Gamelin told Daladier—by this time prime minister—that France could and should wage war if Hitler invaded Poland. But he also warned that neither France nor her British ally would be ready for many months to try to win a war. Furthermore, he overestimated Polish ability to resist Germany and he expected the neutral Belgians to join the Allies when hostilities began. On both these counts his judgement was seriously awry. The swift defeat of the Poles in the *Polish campaign restricted Gamelin to a strategic and operational defensive in the west and saw him oppose risky strategies to carry the war to Germany via Scandinavia or the Balkans. During the *phoney war of 1939–40 he strove single-mindedly to tighten Anglo-French co-operation and build a larger British Army on the Continent.

Belgium proved the weak link in the Allied lines as well as in Gamelin's thinking. The Belgian frontier was not sealed with *Maginot Line fortifications, since a military accord had linked Paris and Brussels from 1920 to 1936. With British acquiescence, Gamelin therefore planned in November 1939 to advance the Allied left flank on to shorter defensive lines inside Belgium (see DYLE LINE). He added a variant to this manoeuvre in April 1940, instructing his general reserve, the motorized Seventh Army, to respond to a German attack by dashing from the Channel coast to Breda in the southern Netherlands. Gamelin sought to offset superior German numbers through incorporation of the Dutch into Allied dispositions. In practice this plan fatally removed his mobile reserve from the scene of the German mechanized breakthrough on the Meuse between 12 and 15 May 1940. His deployments thus bore much responsibility for the disaster which then overtook the Allies, leading to the *Dunkirk evacuation and the Franco-German *armistice of 22 June.

Gamelin has been widely stigmatized as 'the man who lost the battle of France'. Yet he transformed the peacetime French Army from the skeletal framework he inherited in 1935 to the modernized and rapidly rearming force of 1939–40. His successes, however, had been bought through accommodating republican politicians whom his fellow generals, such as *Pétain and Weygand, despised. When the republican authorities, unnerved by the onrush of the panzers, dismissed Gamelin on 19 May 1940, they opened the gate for the anti-republican authoritarians. These preferred a cease-fire and internal order to resistance and possible insurgency. Gamelin had refitted the French forces so that they *could* fight, but had not fully gauged the character and tempo of the war they *would* fight. For all that, unlike Weygand and Pétain, Gamelin was not among the Third Republic's 'grave-diggers'. A fairer epitaph would acknowledge his key part in ensuring that France could and did choose the path of resistance and honour in September 1939.

MARTIN S. ALEXANDER

Alexander, D. W., 'Repercussions of the Breda Variant', *French Historical Studies*, VIII, 3 (Spring 1974), 459–88.

Alexander, M. S., *The Republic in Danger: General Maurice Gamelin and the Politics of French Defence, 1933–40* (Cambridge, 1992).

—'Maurice Gamelin and the defeat of France', in B. Bond (ed.), *Fallen Stars. Eleven Studies of Twentieth-Century Military Disasters* (London, 1991).

Gunsberg, J. A., 'Coupable ou non? Le rôle du général Gamelin dans le défaite de 1940', *Revue Historique des Armées*, 4 (1979), 145–63.

Le Goyet, P., *Le Mystère Gamelin* (Paris, 1976).

Gammon bomb, British hand grenade (no. 82) used primarily by British airborne forces, one of whose members, named Gammon, invented it. It was simply a bag with a detonator which was usually filled with plastic *explosive and its great advantage for paratroopers, who were limited in what they could carry, was that the filling could be tailored to suit the task in hand. See also GRENADES.

Gandhi, Mohandas K. (1869–1948), Indian political and spiritual leader whose non-violent efforts to free his country from the British resulted in his imprisonment during most of the war. He passionately believed in achieving his political ends by means which went beyond passive resistance—a phrase he disliked—and he chose instead the word 'Satyagraha' (from Sanskrit *satya*, truth or love, and *agraha*, firmness or force) to describe the non-violent resistance practised by his followers.

Gandhi, an English-trained lawyer by profession, was born at Porbandar in Gujarat. After living in South Africa, where he began his life of fighting injustice—whether caused by racism, imperialism, or caste—he returned to India in 1915. By 1921 he controlled the policies of the Indian National Congress (see INDIA, 3) and declared that 'my life is dedicated to the service of India through the religion of non-violence which I believe to be the root of Hinduism'.

He was soon known to millions as Mahatma (great soul) and he gave them hope and a degree of self-respect. He adopted the dhoti (loincloth) as his usual garb, and his spinning-wheel, which he used daily, became an emblem of his belief in the importance of simplicity. Between the wars his crusade against the inherent injustices of imperial rule led to several terms of imprisonment. Though he left the Congress Party in 1934—not all its members agreed with his beliefs—he retained a controlling influence on it. In 1940 he briefly resumed its leadership before Congress, seeing an opportunity to obtain immediate independence if it supported the British, temporarily rejected his policies. However, when the negotiations failed the party again embraced him and Gandhi then organized a selective satyagraha which had resulted, by the end of 1941, in more than 23,000 arrests. But Gandhi was always pro-Allied, spoke out against the Axis, and tried to minimize any inconvenience to the British war effort.

This confrontation was halted when Japan entered the war. Gandhi fervently believed that India would remain unscathed by the conflict if only the British would relinquish power. But Congress again favoured negotiations with them and once more it abandoned Gandhi's non-violent stance. In March 1942 a mission headed by Stafford *Cripps arrived in India with an offer of post-war independence. When this failed to find a solution Gandhi began his 'quit India' movement. However, even *Nehru, one of his most faithful followers, could not stomach his assertion that if the Japanese did invade they must only be confronted by total non-co-operation not by force.

By August 1942 a full-scale civil disobedience campaign seemed imminent, Congress leaders were imprisoned, and Gandhi was interned. The communal violence which followed was blamed on him, an accusation Gandhi rejected by starting a three-week fast, his preferred form of personal protest. He just survived it and was eventually released from *internment in May 1944 having spent a total of 2,089 days in Indian prisons and another 249 in South African ones. He was assassinated while attempting to halt, by fasting, the communal violence that had followed India's independence.

Gandhi was one of the most remarkable men of his age whose power over his people transcended politics, and whose saintliness and simplicity of purpose brought him the adoration of the masses and the bewildered respect of those who ruled his country.

Brown, J., *Gandhi. Prisoner of Hope* (New Haven, 1989).
Fischer, L., *The Life of Mahatma Gandhi* (London, 1951).
Gandhi, M. K., *An Autobiography. The Story of My Experiments with Truth* (London, 1949).

GARBO, see PUJOL.

Garby-Czerniawski, Wing-Commander Roman (1910–85), Polish Air Force pilot who headed the Franco-Polish **interallié* resistance network which was betrayed to the Germans by Mathilde *Carré in November 1941. To save other *interallié* members from execution he agreed to become an *Abwehr agent in the UK. He was allowed to escape to Spain, and from there he made his way to the UK where he became a *triple agent (codenamed BRUTUS) by working for the *XX-Committee. He helped pass vital *deception plans which contributed towards the success of the Normandy landings in June 1944 (see OVERLORD), but he ceased being used by the XX-committee in January 1945 when the trial of Carré in France threatened to compromise him.

Garibaldi Division, perhaps the most important Italian Army formation to fight with the Balkan partisan movements after the *armistice of September 1943 brought the Italians over to the Allied side. At that time the Italians had 27 divisions, amounting to over 600,000 troops, in Yugoslavia, Albania, and Greece, excluding those on the Aegean and Ionian islands. Only a part of these forces resisted the Germans. Those who did lost some 3,000 dead in a few days, many of whom, including 5 generals and more than 200 officers, were shot immediately after being captured. The bulk of the Italian troops were interned in Germany; a few thousand succeeded in crossing the Adriatic to southern Italy, while others joined up with Yugoslav, Albanian, and to a lesser extent Greek partisans and continued to fight.

Of the 14 divisions which had garrisoned Yugoslavia, the Taurinense Division (13,000 Alpine troops) and the Venezia Division (10,000 infantry) in particular fought as organized *formations against the Germans while at the same time maintaining their cohesion in the face of pressure from *Tito's partisans, who wanted to disarm them or break them up into small groups. The Italians were aided by the fact that the Venezia Division possessed powerful radio sets with which it was able to maintain permanent contact with the legal Italian government, from which it received aid. On 2 December 1943 these two divisions joined with a number of smaller units to form the Garibaldi Division under Italian command. Tito's lieutenants were initially able to restrict its combatants to 6,000; the remaining troops were organized into eleven battalions of 'labourers', who were then gradually called upon to replace the division's battle losses. The division, which was partially supplied by Italian aircraft of the *Balkan Air Force, fought alongside Tito's forces in a number of battles including the liberation of Belgrade in October 1944. It was repatriated in March 1945, although other smaller Italian Partisan forces continued to fight in parts of Yugoslavia. These included five battalions operating in Slovenia, and the four battalions of the Italian brigade employed in Bosnia, then in the *liberation of Belgrade, and finally that of Zagreb (May 1945). Approximately 10,000 of the Italian troops operating in the partisan armies of Yugoslavia, Albania, and Greece were killed or went missing in action. Of these, more than 3,000 died and a comparable number went missing in Yugoslavia alone.

LUCIO CEVA (Tr. John Gooch)

Gauleiter, from *gau*, an old Frankish term for a political district, and *leiter*, manager. See GERMANY, 3.

Gaulle, Brig-General Charles de and the Free French. During the night of 16/17 June 1940 the French government just formed by Marshal *Pétain asked Germany for an armistice. On 18 June de Gaulle (1890–1970), broadcasting from London, declared that the war had not been decided by the fall of *France, and that the flame of French resistance must not be extinguished. Four years later he returned to France and formed a new French government. Between those two events, de Gaulle and the Free French movement which he founded played a significant part in the political and military history of the Second World War and a decisive role in the history of France.

This was essentially the achievement of one man. What had prepared de Gaulle for the remarkable quest on which he embarked in 1940. Born in Lille on 22 November 1890, the son of a professor he was brought up as a Catholic and a patriot, with a profound conviction of the greatness of France. He entered the army as an officer cadet in 1909, and served as an infantry officer during the *First World War. He was wounded three times, and taken prisoner in March 1916—an event which at least had the merit of keeping him alive in a war in which junior infantry officers suffered extremely heavy casualties. After the war his career in the army was not distinguished, but he made some mark as a controversial writer on strategy and military theory, notably in two

Brig-General de **Gaulle** at victory celebrations which followed the liberation of Paris in August 1944. On his left is General Bradley, commander of US Twelfth Army Group. Behind him is General Koenig. Behind Bradley is André Le Troquer, the French Commissioner for Liberated Territories.

books, *Le Fil de l'epée* ('The Edge of the Sword', 1932) and *Vers l'armée de métier* ('Towards a Professional Army', 1934), in which he advocated the creation of a career army based on powerful and mobile armoured forces. He promoted his ideas through the press, and by securing a political patron in Paul *Reynaud.

His ideas met with little success, and in 1937 he was simply the commander of a tank regiment. When war began in September 1939 he commanded armoured units in the Fifth Army; but when Reynaud became prime minister in March 1940 he was rapidly appointed to command 4th Armoured Division, then in the process of formation. He led his new division in battle at Laon (17–20 May) with some success, and fought another action at Abbeville during 28–30 May. On 1 June he was promoted to brig-general, thus attaining the rank which became so firmly attached to his name. On 6 June Reynaud, trying to strengthen his government, appointed de Gaulle as under-secretary for national defence, a post which he held for only ten days. At the beginning of June 1940, therefore, de Gaulle was the most junior general in the French Army and a junior minister in the French government. It did not look a strong base.

During his few days as a minister, de Gaulle visited London and met Churchill for the first time (9 June); and he also attended Reynaud's last two conferences with Churchill in France (11–12 and 13 June). During these meetings he made a strong impression on the British prime minister—a matter of crucial importance in the next few days.

Late on 16 June Reynaud resigned and was replaced by Pétain, who at once asked for an armistice. On Reynaud's resignation de Gaulle ceased to be a minister, and he was smuggled out in an RAF aircraft to the UK. On 18 June he made his *BBC radio appeal to Frenchmen to continue the fight, which was only permitted on the personal intervention of Churchill. Then, after some days of hesitation, the British government recognized de Gaulle on 28 June as 'the leader of all free Frenchmen, wherever they may be, who rally to him in support of the Allied cause.' This was followed on 7 August by an agreement on the organization of Free French forces, whose financial costs would be met by the British government. The Free French movement had begun. Its four-year life may be examined in three parts: its uncertain start, from June to December 1940; a time of troubles and consolidation, from January 1941 to January 1943; and a final phase of success and homecoming, 1943–4.

The British government gave its support to de Gaulle in June 1940 in the hope that he would attract a significant following, and that he would win over a large part of the French Empire to continue the war (see FRANCE, 4). Neither of these hopes was fulfilled in the short run. De Gaulle's only means of influence was the radio: he broadcast on the BBC six times at the end of June, and another six times in July, but met little response. No significant political or military figure joined him, and the empire remained loyal to Pétain's *Vichy government. In mid-August the Free French army comprised only 140 officers and 2,100 other ranks. But at the end of August there was a change. The colonies of French Equatorial Africa, were won over by the daring actions of Boislambert, *Leclerc, and de Larminat, with the help of Félix Eboué, the governor of one of the colonies, Chad. These territories were economically poor and far distant from the centre of war in Europe, but they formed a vital territorial base: a starting-point in more than one sense, for it was from Chad that Leclerc's tiny force set off early in 1941 to capture the Libyan oasis of Kufra (see FEZZAN CAMPAIGNS)—the beginning of the long march which was to end at Strasbourg in 1944.

These successes were followed by the débâcle of the *Dakar expedition in September 1940. It was a humiliating failure, and its consequences for de Gaulle and the Free French might easily have been fatal. Churchill could have cast all the blame on de Gaulle; but instead he went out of his way to emphasize his confidence in him. De Gaulle himself was briefly plunged into despair, but rallied quickly, sailing on to Duala in the French Cameroons and spending the next two months touring Equatorial Africa and restoring the confidence of his movement.

It was from this base that de Gaulle launched two vital initiatives in autumn 1940. One was military: the capture of Libreville, the capital of Gabon, from its Vichy garrison in November (see GABON CAMPAIGN). This was a useful gain in itself, but even more important because it was carried out despite British reluctance and non-co-operation. It was a gesture of military independence. The other was political: the Brazzaville declaration and ordinances of 27 October. In the manifesto de Gaulle declared that a true French government no longer existed: the body at Vichy which claimed that title was unconstitutional and subject to the Germans. 'It is therefore necessary that a new authority should assume the task of directing the French effort in the war. Events impose this sacred duty upon me. I shall not fail to carry it out.' De Gaulle also announced the creation of a Council of Defence for the Empire. The ordinances made clear that decisions would be taken by de Gaulle, after consultation when appropriate with the Council of Defence. These proclamations were followed on 16 November by an 'organic declaration' setting out the legal case for regarding the Vichy government as unconstitutional. On the same date de Gaulle declared his confidence in the future by founding the Order of Liberation (see DECORATIONS), whose members were to form a distinguished company. The British were not consulted about any of these actions, which amounted to an assertion of political independence and legitimacy.

By the end of 1940 the balance sheet of the Free French enterprise was modestly favourable. On the debit side, numbers were small, and most of the empire had remained loyal to Vichy. The credit side showed a firm territorial base, crucial British support, and determined steps towards independence. Moreover, de Gaulle had secured the valuable adherence of General *Catroux, formerly governor-general of French Indo-China, who had joined the Free French in September 1940. The future of the movement depended on the answers to two great questions. How could the tension between the principle of Free French independence and heavy practical reliance on the UK be resolved? And could de Gaulle's claim to embody the true France achieve solid support either from the empire or from within France itself? The next two years were to be a time of troubles, but they saw some progress on both these fronts.

The main trouble faced by the Free French was a series of imperial quarrels with the British. Of these the first, longest, and most bitter arose in Syria and the Lebanon. In May 1941 the Vichy government gave permission for German aircraft to use Syrian airfields to support a rising against the British in Iraq. The British commander in the Middle East, General *Wavell, scraped together enough British, Australian, and Free French forces to invade Syria and the Lebanon. The *Syrian campaign began on 8 June; the Vichy commander, General *Dentz, asked for an *armistice on 18 June; and terms were eventually agreed on 14 July. These terms (negotiated by General Maitland *Wilson for the British, with the agreement of General Catroux for the Free French) proved completely unacceptable to de Gaulle, on two counts: first, authority over the Levant states was transferred straight from the Vichy French to the British, with no reference to the Free French; and second the Vichy troops were to be sent home as quickly as possible, without allowing the Free French any opportunity to win them over. During the protracted negotiations, de Gaulle had anticipated trouble and had withdrawn from Cairo to Brazzaville, whence he denounced the terms unequivocally. He then flew back to Cairo to tell the British minister of state, Oliver Lyttelton (1893–1972), that unless the armistice was revised to meet his wishes he would remove the Free French forces in the Middle East from British command. The cease-fire terms were rapidly 'interpreted' to allow the Free French to seek recruits among the Vichy forces (some 6,000 men agreed to come over), and Lyttelton assured de Gaulle that the UK recognized the historic interests of France in the Levant.

This phrase highlighted the heart of the problem. It was de Gaulle's unshakeable intention to maintain the French Empire in its entirety. The British, who were normally willing and indeed anxious to fall in with this objective, made an exception in the Middle East, where they were under pressure from Arab nationalism, and insisted on a guarantee of independence for Syria and the

Lebanon. In the circumstances, even de Gaulle was compelled to accept this in principle, but in practice he adopted every possible expedient to delay independence and to maintain French control. This political problem was made worse by bitter personal friction between de Gaulle and Maj-General Edward Spears, the principal British representative in the Levant, who had previously been one of de Gaulle's leading supporters. The Levant proved a running sore in Free French relations with the British for the whole wartime period.

The fate of *Madagascar produced a similar, though less severe, dispute. The sweeping victories of the Japanese in South-East Asia early in 1942 aroused fears that they would strike across the Indian Ocean, and in May of that year a British expedition landed at the port of Diégo-Suarez, at the northern tip of Madagascar, to pre-empt a possible Japanese strike there. The British commander entered into negotiations with the Vichy governor-general to reach an agreement which would remove the need to occupy the whole island. De Gaulle was offended on two counts: that the operation was mounted without even informing the Free French; and because he rejected any dealings with the Vichy authorities. He had a fierce set-to with Churchill on these questions; but on this occasion the quarrel died away as the British went on to conquer the whole island and then (in November 1942) turned over its administration to the Free French.

Relations between the Free French and the British were also plagued by three successive *affaires Muselier*. First, Vice-Admiral *Muselier, the commander of the Free French naval forces, was arrested by the British in January 1941 on false charges of conspiring with the Vichy government. On de Gaulle's intervention he was quickly released, but the incident left its mark, demonstrating the dependence of the Free French on what amounted to little more than the whims of the British. Then in September 1941 Muselier himself took part in a move to displace de Gaulle as leader of the Free French, in which he acted with the connivance of a number of British officials and with at least the knowledge of the prime minister. In the event Muselier overreached himself, and de Gaulle was able to win over Churchill in support of his authority; but again the affair left a bitter aftertaste. Finally in March 1942 Muselier attempted to secede from de Gaulle's command, taking the Free French fleet with him. This time he had the support of A. V. *Alexander, the First Lord of the Admiralty, and briefly that of the war cabinet. De Gaulle stood fast, the British climbed down, and it was Muselier who left the Free French organization. But at one point de Gaulle went so far as to write a 'political testament', to be published in the event of his arrest by the British—a clear sign both of the vulnerability of his position and of his determination to stand firm.

In these difficulties with the British, where could de Gaulle turn for support? In June 1942, during the Madagascar crisis, he enquired whether the Soviet government would give him refuge if he had to break with the British; but it is doubtful if this was a serious prospect. In the latter part of 1941 he had made approaches to the Americans, and in November that year *Lend-Lease was extended to the Free French, which diminished his dependence on the British for supplies. But relations with the Americans were always difficult, partly because the USA maintained good relations with Vichy, and partly because Roosevelt conceived a strong personal animus against de Gaulle, whom he refused to accept as the representative of France. For his part, de Gaulle was suspicious of American encroachments on the French Empire, especially in the Caribbean (see FRENCH WEST INDIES). All in all, the Free French had little to hope for from the USA and they caused an extra irritant to the Roosevelt administration when, in December 1941, they occupied the French colony of *St Pierre and Miquelon.

In these circumstances, it was crucial for the Free French that they found a source of support in their own country. For a long time de Gaulle's movement was virtually cut off from France itself, and the first resistance groups grew up spontaneously. During 1940–1 de Gaulle, managed to send a few agents into France to report on the situation there, but it was not until 1942 that effective two-way traffic was established by his intelligence services (see BUREAU CENTRAL DE RENSEIGNEMENTS ET D'ACTION) and leaders of the resistance began to reach England—Christian Pineau, François Faure, Pierre Brossolette, Emmanuel d'Astier de la Vigerie, Henri Frenay, André Philip. Drawing on their advice, de Gaulle emphasized his attachment to democracy, reiterated his determination to accept the will of the French people when it could be freely expressed, and also declared himself in favour of some form of social security, which opened the way for him to appeal to left as well as right in France. He thus enhanced his claim to be a national leader, attracting support across the political spectrum. In this process of forging links between de Gaulle and the resistance, and of drawing the diverse resistance groups (including the communists) together, the key role was played by Jean *Moulin who made his way to London in October 1941. He met de Gaulle at the end of November, the two men struck a remarkable accord, and they agreed to make an attempt to unite all the resistance movements into one broad organization recognizing de Gaulle's leadership.

These links with the resistance in France gave de Gaulle a new authority. His movement was no longer made up of *émigrés* (always a dangerous charge), nor solely dependent upon the empire. While these changes were in progress, he received another fillip in the shape of military success. At the end of May and beginning of June 1942 a Free French brigade under General *Koenig fought a successful action in defence of *Bir Hakeim, in the Libyan desert. It was not a big battle—only some 5,500 French troops took part—but as so often with the Free French it was its symbolic value which counted. It is striking, but not wholly incongruous, that the battles of

*Stalingrad and Bir Hakeim are each commemorated by the name of a station on the Paris Métro: both were psychological turning-points, though of a vastly different kind and scale.

Bir Hakeim was the signal for de Gaulle, in June 1942, to change the name of his movement from 'Free France' to 'Fighting France', which doubtless made a useful point at the time but has not endured in the public mind. In any case, behind the name lay the question of what it represented. Repeatedly the Free (or Fighting) French were referred to as a movement: but where were they moving to? There can be no doubt of de Gaulle's answer: towards becoming the government of France. That was the purpose of the Brazzaville declaration in 1940. In September 1941 de Gaulle went further down the same road by forming a *French National Committee, whose members held titles amounting to ministerial portfolios—for the economy, finance, foreign affairs, and so on. It was the framework for a government under the cover-name of a committee, though its recognition as such by other governments, except the USSR, was still far off.

At the end of 1942 and beginning of 1943, indeed, there occurred events which endangered all these advances by the Free French. In November 1942 the Americans and British landed in French North Africa (see NORTH AFRICAN CAMPAIGN). To ease the path of the invasion, the military commanders (with the support of their governments) reached agreements with Admiral *Darlan, minister of marine in Pétain's government, C-in-C of the French armed forces, and a leading advocate of *collaboration with the Germans. In these events de Gaulle and the Free French were disregarded. They had not been informed, still less consulted, about the plans to invade North Africa; and the Darlan deal threatened their whole position. If the Americans and British had continued to support Darlan, it was at least possible that the liberation of France would end in a Vichy restoration. That particular danger was removed when Darlan was assassinated on Christmas Eve 1942; but the Allies, and especially the Americans, accepted in his stead General *Giraud, an officer with strong links with Vichy, so that a similar prospect was revived. The political future of the Free French was still in the balance.

At the Casablanca conference in January 1943 (see SYMBOL), de Gaulle was put under the strongest pressure to accept a new French organization in North Africa in which he would be subordinate to Giraud, who would be the principal among three co-presidents of a new committee and also C-in-C of French forces in Africa. But de Gaulle resisted all coercion and blandishment. He permitted himself a brief and unconvincing handshake with Giraud for the benefit of photographers; and the two generals held a meeting which ended with an enigmatic Gaullian communiqué: 'We have met. We have talked.' In fact, de Gaulle evaded at Casablanca the subordination to Giraud which the Americans, and at that time also the British, tried to impose upon him.

The last stage of the great journey of the Free French, which ended with their emergence as the government of France, filled most of 1943 and 1944, and comprised four sets of events, each embodying a struggle. There was a political conflict in Algiers, in which de Gaulle prevailed over Giraud; the difficult amalgamation between the armed forces of Free France and the Vichy army of North Africa; a dispute with the Americans and British over the administration of liberated France; and a struggle to ensure that de Gaulle's authority was accepted within France by the resistance groups, especially the communists. The last of these is a matter for the story of events within France. The others form the culmination of the epic of the Free French.

The main outline of the de Gaulle–Giraud contest stands out clearly, despite some obscure detail. At the end of April 1943 Giraud made a vital concession by waiving his claim to leadership in whatever organization was to be set up, and accepting partnership instead. On 30 May de Gaulle moved his headquarters to Algiers, and in June agreement was reached on the formation of a *French Committee For National Liberation (CFLN), at first made up of seven members, with de Gaulle and Giraud as co-presidents. Then de Gaulle speedily strengthened his position by doubling the size of the committee and including a majority of his own supporters. A sharp crisis in June about the military functions of the CFLN was resolved by the end of July by de Gaulle becoming sole chairman of the committee with Giraud as C-in-C—but under a Committee of National Defence, whose chairman was again de Gaulle. De Gaulle thus outmanoeuvred Giraud, and at the same time survived an attempt by Roosevelt to get rid of him. In November 1943 de Gaulle removed Giraud from the CFLN altogether; and finally in April 1944 completed the process by assuming command of the armed forces. Giraud vanished from the scene, virtually without trace. It was a triumph for de Gaulle's strong will and his deft political footwork. He owed much also to the help of the British, who for most of 1943 had supported him against Giraud—and against the Americans.

On the issue of the amalgamation of the two armies de Gaulle showed a willingness to compromise which was not always reckoned to be his most prominent characteristic. The problem was deep-seated. The Free French army had been founded on the rejection of established authority, and its soldiers were imbued with an independent, almost a freebooting spirit. Its numbers were small (no more than 50,000 in all at the end of 1942), but some of its units had a proud fighting record and shared the battle honours of the British Eighth Army. The armies of North and West Africa, on the other hand, had remained loyal to established authority in Vichy; their numbers were large (some 230,000 at the end of 1942, with more in reserve); and they had stood idle for over two years. The two forces were thus in marked contrast with one another, their differences neatly embodied in the names of the *hadjis* (those who had made their pilgrimage with the Free French) and the *moustachis* (after the symbolic moustache of the orthodox regular). Yet for France to make a substantial military contribution to the defeat of the Axis the amalgamation of the two was vital. The Free French could provide the spirit, the army of North Africa the numbers—and also one of the best professional officers in the army, General *Juin. Here lay a key problem, for Juin had been a faithful servant of Vichy, and had even taken part in a mission to *Göring led by Jacques Benoist-Méchin, a leading collaborator. In principle de Gaulle always insisted on the out-and-out rejection of Vichy; but on this matter he chose to compromise. After Juin had fought successful actions against the Germans in Tunisia at the end of 1942, de Gaulle wrote him a warm letter of congratulation. The difficult amalgamation of the two armies was begun as far as possible on equal terms. There emerged Juin's *French Expeditionary Corps, which fought with distinction in the *Italian campaign, and de *Lattre's First Army, which took part in the invasion of southern France in August 1944 (see FRENCH RIVIERA LANDINGS). The French Army was back in action, no longer in brigade strength as at Bir Hakeim, but on a large scale.

Free France thus assumed the political shape of the Committee For National Liberation and the military shape of a large army. There remained the last crucial step: to become the acknowledged government of France. De Gaulle pursued this objective relentlessly. In November 1943 he set up a Consultative Assembly to mobilize the widest possible range of support, and to fulfil some of the functions of a parliament. He pressed on with preparations to take over the work of government when the liberation of France took place. In January 1944 *Commissaires de la République* were nominated to replace the prefects in liberated areas. Their instructions were categorical: 'You represent the government to the people, and not the people to the government'. They were not to share power with the resistance groups. In a speech to the Consultative Assembly on 27 March 1944 de Gaulle referred to the CFLN as the provisional government of France; and on 3 June an ordinance published by the committee formally claimed that title.

This claim had yet to be accepted by the Americans and the British, whose forces had to play the major role in the liberation of France; and it also remained to be seen how far the resistance groups would acknowledge the authority claimed by the CFLN. These matters were resolved during the summer of 1944. The question of the administration of liberated areas was still unresolved when the Allied armies launched the Normandy landings on 6 June (see OVERLORD). In principle the Allied authorities intended to establish a system of military government; but in practice, fully engaged in a great battle, they were glad to work with the administration introduced by the CFLN. De Gaulle himself landed in France on 14 June, installing his Commissaire de la République at Bayeux and making much of his welcome by the population. On his return to England he declared that the provisional government was an accomplished fact, which the Allies would now accept. This proved to be true. The British had long favoured acceptance of the CFLN as the best practical means of administering liberated France, but had been unable to overcome the dogged opposition of Roosevelt to such a step. The establishment of de Gaulle's authority, and the obvious co-operation of the resistance groups in northern France, changed the position rapidly. In July de Gaulle visited Washington and was warmly received, with Roosevelt announcing publicly that he was ready to treat the CFLN as the *de facto* authority in liberated France. Then on 23/24 October the USA formally recognized de Gaulle's administration as the provisional government, and the British followed rapidly.

Before then de Gaulle had received his own recognition from the people of Paris. On 26 August 1944 he walked down the Champs Elysées to the acclamation of a vast crowd, and then went on to Notre Dame, where he stood unmoved when a sudden fusillade broke out inside the cathedral. It was the formal entry of a great Frenchman into the capital city. The mission of France Libre was complete, and the work of a new French government was about to begin.

What had de Gaulle and the Free French accomplished? In military terms, they ensured that French forces never dropped out of the war, and in 1944 took a real part in the *liberation of their own country. In world affairs, French sovereignty and the potential role of France as a European power were constantly maintained. France emerged from the ordeals of defeat, *occupation, and profound internal divisions with a greater degree of cohesion and stability than anyone would have predicted in 1940. For those who started with so little, it was no small achievement. De Gaulle served as his country's president until January 1946 and again from 1958 to 1969. P. M. H. BELL

Kersaudy, F., *Churchill and de Gaulle* (London, 1981).
Lacouture, J., *Charles de Gaulle*, Vol. 1: *The Rebel 1890–1944* (London, 1991).
Ledwidge, B., *De Gaulle* (London, 1982).

Gazala, battle of, fought from 26 May to 17 June 1942 when *Rommel attacked the British and Commonwealth Eighth Army's Gazala Line west of his immediate objective, *Tobruk. By doing so he pre-empted a British offensive to drive him out of Libya before the planned start of the *North African campaign that November.

Though technically excellent, the line was based on the concept of static defence. The Eighth Army, then commanded by Lt-General Neil Ritchie, was grouped in defensive strong-points, or 'boxes', with its armour committed piecemeal to their defence. *ULTRA intelligence revealed Rommel's intentions to attack, and when, but gave no indication of his plan to outflank the line by a hook round the most southerly strong-point, *Bir Hakeim. This movement, combined with a frontal assault by Rommel's Italian troops in the north, achieved surprise and at first worked well. But Rommel's intelligence had underestimated British strength and Axis forces, troubled by the length of their supply lines and by the new Allied Grant tank, were brought to a halt on 29 May after some of the fiercest armoured battles of the *Western Desert campaigns. Rommel then withdrew to an area which became known as the 'Cauldron' and Ritchie, thinking he was disengaging, failed to mount an effective counter-attack immediately. This allowed Rommel to reorganize his forces, re-establish his supply line, and send his 90th Light Division to overrun Bir Hakeim. Its fall on 10 June, after Rommel had defeated another attack on him in the Cauldron, turned encirclement into a strong salient deep in the British defences, and on the night of 12/13 June he forced the retreat from a defensive box (KNIGHTSBRIDGE) which made the Gazala Line no longer tenable and opened the way to Tobruk. *Auchinleck vainly ordered Ritchie to form a new defensive line; by 16 June there were no Allied *formations west of Tobruk, which fell on 21 June. Huge quantities of supplies and two battalions of retreating infantry were captured; and a few days later Rommel inflicted another defeat on the Eighth Army at *Mersa Matruh.

Gazala was the nadir of British fortunes in the Western Desert and revealed the inadequacy of those in command; it cost Ritchie, and eventually Auchinleck, their jobs. See also LAND POWER.

GEE, see ELECTRONIC NAVIGATION SYSTEMS.

Geheimschreiber (secret writer), German name for a non-Morse cipher machine. Its encoded messages were transmitted by a teleprinter which used the Baudot-Murray code where patterns of holes on the teleprinter's paper tape represent the letters of the alphabet. The teleprinter translated the transmissions into pulses which could be automatically converted back into a plain language message at the receiving end. They were beamed point-to-point between German stations first detected by the British in 1940 and a number of military links, most of them on the Eastern Front, had been identified by 1942.

Work on decrypting the messages, known to the British by the codename FISH, began at *Bletchley Park in the middle of 1942. Unlike the *ENIGMA cipher machine, which had three, four, or five rotary wheels, the *Geheimschreiber* had as many as ten which made the cipher much harder to break. Nothing of much value was therefore achieved until new machines were devised during the following months to help decrypt the signals. Because of its completely experimental nature, the first of these was known as 'Heath Robinson'; it was succeeded by Colossus I and then by Colossus II, the latter being now recognized as the first electronic digital computer. Colossus II came into operation just in time to decrypt messages between the German High Command (OKW) and C-in-C West on 6 June 1944, the day the Normandy landings were launched (see OVERLORD), and subsequently produced much valuable information.

FISH was used between senior headquarters, and gradually replaced ENIGMA transmissions at these levels. It was classified as *ULTRA intelligence and handled in the same way, and because those signals released into the public domain carry no external marks of their origin it is at present impossible to distinguish between those derived from FISH and those derived from ENIGMA.

RALPH BENNETT

Geneva Conventions, International agreements which sprang from the founding of the Red Cross in Geneva in 1863. The first, signed in 1864 and eventually agreed to by 48 states, dealt solely with the 'Amelioration of the Wounded in the Armies in Field' in a few simple sentences. The second, signed in 1906, widened the original convention, extended its protection to those who treated the sick and wounded, and to the treatment of wounded and sick *prisoners-of-war. The third, signed in 1929, further extended the earlier conventions and, for the first time, incorporated a separate convention on the rights and treatment of prisoners-of-war which updated, and superseded, the 1907 *Hague Convention on the treatment of prisoners. Among the 97 articles were items which delineated the work of the *International Red Cross Committee and the Red Cross generally; established that sick and wounded combatants had to be respected and cared for whatever their nationality; and that the personnel, buildings, equipment, and transport used to succour them should be marked with a red cross to give them immunity from attack—though this only applied if they were part of the medical services of the armed forces of a belligerent. In 1939 the conventions had not been ratified by several states, most notably Japan and the USSR.

A protocol which prohibited the use in war of asphyxiating, poisonous, and other gases, and of bacteriological methods of warfare (see BIOLOGICAL and CHEMICAL WARFARE), was also signed in Geneva by 29 countries in June 1925, with the USSR signing in 1928. The USA adhered to the protocol in 1925 but did not ratify it until January 1975. The current Geneva Conventions were signed in 1949.

George VI (1895–1952), British king who inherited the throne after his elder brother Edward VIII (see WINDSOR) abdicated in 1936. A shy man who had to wrestle with a bad stammer, he and his family became a symbol to the British public of the struggle for freedom. He worked tirelessly to boost the morale of the armed forces and civilians alike and refused to allow either himself or his family to be evacuated at the height of the invasion scare in 1940. He suffered a personal tragedy when his youngest brother, the Duke of Kent, a 39-year-old RAF officer, was killed in an air crash on 25 August 1942.

German-American Bund. Formally organized in March 1936 by a German-born engineer, Fritz Julius Kuhn, this was one of several US groups promoting closer cultural and political ties between German Americans and their homeland. Although the Bund drew many of its members from organizations that were part of the Federation of German-American Societies, it differed from other groups because of the intensity of its pro-Nazi and anti-communist sentiments during the years preceding the Second World War. Attracting a small minority of Americans of German ancestry, the Bund's membership, which at its peak may have totalled more than 20,000, was concentrated in eastern and Midwestern cities containing substantial numbers of German immigrants. The organization opposed racial intermixture, atheism, *communism, Jewish financial interests, and labour movements, and promoted Aryan culture. As Nazism became increasingly unpopular among the American public, including the majority of German Americans, the Bund tried to obscure its allegiance to *Nazi ideology, claiming it had no official ties to Nazi Germany and stressing the Americanism of members.

In many cities the Bund organized massive rallies characterized by calls for pro-German national policies, displays of swastika banners, uniformed marchers, and other forms of Nazi pageantry. The most visible of these rallies were in New York City, where the group held gatherings at Madison Square Garden. The Bund also promoted its views through its national newspaper, *The Free American and Deutscher Weckruf und Beobachter*, and through many programmes aimed at young people. Bund camps were a popular arena for Bund members to congregate. The camps' stated aim was to restore a sense of German community, but the inculcation of Nazi ideology was an additional intent of Bund leaders. Camp Siegfried on Long Island and Camp Nordland in New Jersey were the largest camps, containing restaurants, pools, recreational facilities, and streets named after Nazi leaders.

Although it stressed its non-partisan affiliation, the Bund participated in American politics by urging its members to vote against Roosevelt in the 1936 election because of his leftist inclination and 'preference for the Jewish element'.

The Bund's pro-Nazi reputation prompted widespread criticism as American public opinion turned increasingly against Germany. In particular, the OD (Order Service) attracted much public scrutiny. The OD claimed to be a guard unit needed to preserve order at Bund meetings. Their uniforms—grey shirts and black ties—resembled the German *SS uniforms, prompting public concern that the OD was a subversive, paramilitary organization. Leftist groups often demonstrated outside its meetings, and by the late 1930s, some German American groups were denouncing the Bund's efforts to speak for the entire ethnic group. New York Congressman Samuel Dickstein organized opposition to the Bund and called for a congressional committee to investigate pro-German, subversive activities. In 1937, the House Committee on Un-American Activities launched an investigation of the group. Also in that year, Attorney General Homer S. Cummings initiated an FBI investigation of the Bund camps to determine if they were illegal but could find no violations.

Despite the proliferation of investigations and public criticisms levied against it, the Bund continued to defend its activities and struggled to maintain its membership. Leaders attributed external attacks on their organization to a Jewish–Communist conspiracy or to anti-German hysteria similar to that which occurred in the *First World War. As more states outlawed displays of *swastikas and aspects of the organization, the Bund responded with futile efforts to recruit more members and to prove their American loyalties. Bund leaders forbade the flying of their storm flag, altered the OD uniform to make it appear less like the SS, and publicly pledged their allegiance to the Constitution, claiming that their civil rights were being violated. But as Hitler's aggressive expansionist policies strengthened popular sentiments against Nazi Germany, the Bund lost more and more support from German Americans. Bund leaders encouraged their members to support neutrality and blamed the deepening international crisis on 'Jewish warmongers'.

In 1939, the Bund's recruitment efforts were severely undermined when its Führer, Fritz Kuhn, was convicted of embezzling the group's funds. He was replaced by Wilhelm Kunze, who failed to keep the Bund together and escaped to Mexico in 1941 amid internal turmoil in the organization. His successor, George Froboese, committed suicide soon after assuming office. Afterwards, the Bund lost members, and its remaining chapters disbanded when Germany declared war on the USA in December 1941. A few members were later prosecuted or deported for their pro-Nazi activities.

CLAYBORNE CARSON/STEPHANIE BROOKINS

Bell, L. V., *In Hitler's Shadow: The Anatomy of American Nazism* (Port Washington, NY, 1973).

German Christians came in a variety of guises. The Nazi accession to power in January 1933 stirred nationalistic sentiments among many Protestants in Germany. Pastor Joachim Hossenfelder, leader of the pro-Nazi Faith Movement of German Christians, revealed that his supporters had 'the swastika on our breasts and the cross in our hearts'. More sophisticated theologians developed elaborate reconciliations of 'German faith' and 'Christian faith', in some cases making the Old Testament virtually redundant. Beyond their specific ranks, however, there was a widespread wish that Protestants should not stand outside the apparently new-found unity of the German nation. It was time to form a national Lutheran Reich Church. In July 1933 a new constitution was forced through. The Reichsbishop, elected in September, was Ludwig Müller, an army chaplain and fervent admirer of Hitler. The victory looked complete. There was an 'Emergency League' formed by pastors opposed to these developments, but its opposition was hampered by differences in its ranks. However, the Barmen Declaration of 1934, inspired by the Swiss theologian Karl Barth, declared false the view that the church was 'an organ of state'. Even so, in many parts of the country, 'German Christians' were in control: indeed, the 'German Christian' synthesis remained a factor in German church life until 1945. Its influence, however, was weakened latterly not only by opposition from other church circles but also from those Nazis who preferred straightforward paganism to any kind of Christianity. See also RELIGION.

KEITH ROBBINS

German–Soviet Treaty of Friendship, Co-operation, and Demarcation; see NAZI-SOVIET PACT.

German–Soviet War

For a more detailed discussion of the first six months of the German–Soviet war, see BARBAROSSA. For the contributions of Germany's allies in the war see BLUE DIVISION, FINNISH–SOVIET WAR (*ad fin*), HUNGARY, 5, ITALY, 5, ROMANIA, 4, and SPANISH LEGION. For Soviet preparations for war and reactions to BARBAROSSA, and for details of Soviet armed forces involved in the war, see USSR, 4 and 6. See also UKRAINE.

The German–Soviet war, known in the USSR as the Great Patriotic War, ranks as the greatest armed conflict ever fought on a single front. Statistically and strategically, it dominates the Second World War. For most of four years, on average, more than 9 million troops were continuously engaged. The German forces, with Finnish, Hungarian, Italian, and Romanian support, advanced 2,000 km. (1,240 mi.) into Soviet territory; and the Soviet forces counter-marched 2,500 km. (1,550 mi.) to Berlin. Germany at no time had less than 55% of its divisions committed. The cost in lives was horrifying. The accepted figures have been 5.5 million German and 20 million Soviet military and civilian dead, which together represent about half the total for the Second World War. Of those, 13.6 million Soviet and 3 million German dead in the military category alone account for over two-thirds of the world total. However, researchers in the former USSR have projected Soviet losses in the range of 26 or 27 million (see D. Volkogonov, *Stalin, Triumph and Tragedy*, London, 1991, p. 505).

In contrast to the other theatres of war, where independent air and naval operations figured prominently, the German–Soviet war was conducted predominantly on the ground. With few and brief exceptions, the Soviet and German air forces concentrated on ground support. The Soviet Air Force, which was an integral part of the Red Army, flew 93% of its missions within 50 km. (31 mi.) and did 80% of its bombing within 10 km. (6.2 mi.) of the front. Soviet naval operations, when they could be undertaken at all, were confined to the coastal waters of the *Black and *Baltic seas, and to making a minor contribution to escorting the *Arctic convoys.

1. Blitzkrieg rampant (June–September 1941)
Before dawn on 22 June 1941, three German army groups, 3.05 million men, 3,350 tanks, and 2,770 aircraft, attacked across the Soviet border (see Map 14). The German ambassador in Moscow delivered a declaration of war six hours later. Along the line Warsaw–Moscow, Army Group Centre under Field Marshal Von *Bock conducted the main effort with two field armies and two panzer groups, the latter actually armies though not yet so designated. *Leeb's Army Group North and *Rundstedt's Army Group South, aimed towards Leningrad and Kiev respectively; each had two field armies and one panzer group. The plan (BARBAROSSA) set rapid destruction of the Soviet forces as the primary objective, and staff studies had predicted a victory in eight to ten weeks.

Since early in the year, the Soviet General Staff had been putting into effect MP-41, a mobilization plan, and Plan 9, a defence plan. Concurrently, Stalin, concerned about weaknesses disclosed during a war-readiness conference in December 1940, had engaged in desperate diplomatic manoeuvres to buy time. Following a practice taken over from the tsarist army, the Red Army had divided the western frontier into strategic areas which, in wartime, would become *fronts*, i.e., army group sectors (see table for a list of Army *fronts*). Two, North-West and West *fronts*, were situated between the Baltic coast and the Pripet marshes and two, South-West and South *fronts*, between the marshes and the Black Sea. All had been moved up to several hundred kilometres west of the heavily fortified *Stalin Line by border changes in 1939–40 after the USSR occupied eastern Poland (see NAZI–SOVIET PACT). Plan 9 assumed that the economic resources of the Ukraine would be the principal and Moscow the secondary German objectives. Consequently the deployment, 2.9 million men (plus half a million or so in a strategic reserve), 10,000 tanks, and 7,500 aircraft, assigned 75% of the troops and nearly 90% of the tanks and aircraft to the West and South-West *fronts*. Stalin refused to authorize a war alert until late on 21 June, but two assumptions embedded in Plan 9 also significantly impaired the response to the invasion: that the length of the front and the masses of troops involved precluded a *blitzkrieg against the Red Army; and that two to three weeks' hiatus would intervene between the outbreak of war and the first concerted operations.

Early morning attacks on the Soviet air bases gained the German Air Force absolute air superiority on 22 June. During the day, in keeping with Plan 9, the Soviet acting C-in-C, Marshal *Timoshenko, ordered the *fronts* to stand fast and mount counter-attacks. By then, Bock had launched his panzer groups in deep thrusts through the West Front line.

By 29 June, Bock's two panzer groups had completed a double encirclement around *Bialystok–Minsk that would yield more than 300,000 prisoners and continued eastwards without waiting for the infantry. Timoshenko thereupon assumed command of West *front* and with five

A German motorized column under attack by Soviet aircraft during the early weeks of the **German–Soviet war**.

reserve armies, undertook to hold the line of the upper Dvina and *Dnieper rivers and the gap between them. Against this more determined resistance, the panzer groups crossed the rivers in the second week of July and took *Smolensk, the historic gateway to Moscow, on 16 July. Army Group Centre was now 359 km. (220 mi.) from Moscow, Army Group North had a spearhead 100 km. (62 mi.) from *Leningrad, and Army Group South had one on the outskirts of *Kiev.

The tide of *prisoners-of-war, approaching three-quarters of a million as encirclements around Smolensk were mopped up, convinced the German Army C-in-C Field Marshal *Brauchitsch and his senior generals that Stalin would sacrifice the Red Army to defend the Moscow region, which constituted the ethnic Russian heartland and contained the most highly developed Soviet industrial complex. Hitler, who had insisted all along that Germany had to get the Ukrainian land and mineral resources and the Caucasus oilfields, was not prepared to seek a decision at Moscow before these were within easy reach. On 29 July, he therefore ordered Brauchitsch to stop Army Group Centre at Smolensk and divert the panzer groups off its flanks to assist Army Groups North and South. While the generals argued in vain for continuing the advance on Moscow, the panzer groups rested and refitted; and on 25 August, *Guderian's Second Panzer Group, on the southern flank of Bock's Army Group Centre, wheeled south and headed towards Romny, 200 km. (125 mi.) due east of Kiev.

When Second Panzer Group crossed the River Desna, the last natural obstacle in its path, Rundstedt sent *Kleist's First Panzer Group on a northward strike out of a bridgehead on the Dnieper at Kremenchug, 260 km. (160 mi.) downstream from Kiev. Before and after the encirclement closed, near Romny on 16 September, Stalin refused to let South-West *front* abandon Kiev, the cradle of the Russian state, and as a consequence sent 665,000 men into German captivity. Hitler rewarded the two panzer groups with advancement to full army status. On 29 September, in one of many such actions then taking place on occupied Soviet territory, an *SS detachment killed 33,000 Jewish civilians in the Babi Yar ravine outside Kiev (see also FINAL SOLUTION). While the battle for Kiev was going on, Army Group North secured a foothold on the south shore of Lake Ladoga, thereby starting the 900-day siege of Leningrad by cutting the city off from land contact with the interior; however, heavy Soviet counter-attacks in the Smolensk area confined Bock's other panzer group, Third Panzer, to a modest advance.

In August, assuming as he always had that the only reliable authority was his own, Stalin named himself Supreme C-in-C, made the General Staff his planning and executive agency, and formed a seven-member military group, the *Stavka, to share responsibility with him. The *commissar system gave him a tight hold on the military leadership; but owing to the purge of the late 1930s, many officers in the senior and middle grades occupied commands beyond their levels of competence. The August break in the German offensive and subsequent turns away from Moscow fortuitously enhanced Stalin's stature as a war leader and helped get him firm offers of British and American assistance which resulted in the *Three-Power conference in September.

2. To the gates of Moscow (October–December 1941)
Hitler informed Brauchitsch on 6 September that the main effort would be restored to Army Group Centre for a two-pronged thrust past Moscow (TYPHOON), which was to be completed 'in the limited time before winter'. Bock would regain Hoth's Third Panzer Group from Army Group North and Guderian's Second Panzer Army from Army Group South and would also get Hoepner's Fourth Panzer Group and air reinforcements from Army Group North; Leeb would push his front north-eastwards around Lake Ladoga to make contact with the Finnish Army on the River Svir, and Rundstedt would drive east towards Kharkov and south to the Crimea.

TYPHOON began on 2 October against West *front*, initially under Lt-General *Konev, and Briansk *front*, under Maj-General *Eremenko. Marshal *Budenny had Reserve *front* (five armies) deployed on a line halfway between Smolensk and Moscow. Within a week, Bock's armour had locked nine Soviet armies, the bulk of West and Briansk *fronts*, in the *Briansk–Vyazma pockets. Thereafter, Third and Fourth Panzer Groups on the north and Second Panzer Army in the south began developing wide sweeps aimed past Moscow that could envelop the whole Moscow region east to the River Volga. On 10 October, Stalin formed the Kalinin *front* under Konev from West *front*'s northern armies. He then combined Reserve *front* and those armies of West *front* directly in front of Moscow and gave command of them to General *Zhukov with orders to hold a north–south line centred on Mozhaisk, 100 km. (62 mi.) west of Moscow; the US military attaché, among others, reported that Soviet resistance appeared close to its end.

The threats in the centre and in the south, where Timoshenko had taken over the shattered South-West *front*, were drastically affecting war production. The Moscow and the Donets basin industrial complexes were being dismantled (see USSR, 2) reducing coal, iron, steel, and aluminium capacity by over 60%. Ball bearing output was down 95%. The first British Arctic convoy carrying aid had left Scapa Flow in late August, but could hardly make a difference.

On 18 October, Hoepner's Fourth Panzer Group pushed past Mozhaisk. It should have been there four or five days earlier, but rain had softened the unpaved Russian roads, and within two or three days neither tanks nor infantry could overcome the deepening mud. The rain, a regular feature of the Russian autumn, stopped operations on both sides from Lake Ladoga to the Sea of Azov, and the front did not begin to stir again until the end of the first week in November.

Stalin used the respite to begin setting up nine reserve armies behind the Volga and bring in reinforcements for Zhukov's West *front*. He had an extensive rail network, while Bock had just one line. The German dream of a single-season victory disappeared in the mud. In a speech broadcast on 8 November, Hitler called blitzkrieg an 'idiotic word', and declared himself ready to carry the war into 1942 and beyond. The army group commanders, with misgivings, accepted the advice of General *Halder, the Chief of the Army's General Staff (OKH), to advance as far as they still could before deep winter set in.

To tighten the grip on Leningrad, Leeb took Tikhvin on 8 November. Rundstedt, on Hitler's insistence, sent Kleist's First Panzer Army towards Rostov-on-Don. Bock, no longer expecting to get more than a close-in encirclement of Moscow, resumed TYPHOON on 15 November over now frozen ground.

For twelve days the blitzkrieg appeared to be getting back on track. One Soviet army collapsed under the first attack, and Fourth Panzer Group easily overran another. Third Panzer Group took Klin on 23 November and reached the Moscow–Volga Canal due north of Moscow on 27 November. Guderian, the Second Panzer Army commander, managed a 42 km. (25 mi.) advance on 18 November and had his spearhead near Kashira, 100 km. (62 mi.) south-east of Moscow by 24 November. Alarmed, Stalin demanded diversionary counter-attacks at Tikhvin and at Rostov-on-Don, which First Panzer Army had taken on the 21 November.

Early on 29 November, after a week's stay in Berlin, Hitler returned to his headquarters in East Prussia to confront ominous developments. Rundstedt had refused to cancel an order permitting a retreat from Rostov. Hitler dismissed him. Two new Soviet armies were slowing Third and Fourth Panzer Groups to a crawl, and Guderian was stopped short of Kashira. On 3 December, Leeb warned that he would not be able to hold Tikhvin if Bock could not keep pressure on Moscow. During the following nights the temperature around Moscow dropped to −34 °C (−29 °F) and lower. In paralysing cold that congealed lubricants in the German vehicles and weapons, Zhukov counter-attacked on the morning of 6 December.

Having not bothered to build a solid front while they were on the move, the German armies could neither dig in the frozen ground nor close the gaps between them. Halder pronounced it the 'greatest crisis in two world wars'. Bock declared that the front could rip apart at any hour. Hitler appeared at a loss until, on 18 December, he ordered all officers to compel the troops to 'fanatical resistance' in their positions and prohibited evasive movements. A day later, he dismissed Brauchitsch and himself took command of the German Army. See also MOSCOW, BATTLE FOR.

3. Stalin's general offensive (January–May 1942)
The 'fanatical resistance' order came too late to prevent Army Group North's withdrawal from Tikhvin or Centre's from the close approaches to Moscow, but that in no wise mitigated the crisis. Leeb's front around Leningrad was becoming more vulnerable, and Zhukov had in mind to push Army Group Centre all the way back to the line from which TYPHOON had started. Army Group South had finished its retreat from Rostov in good order; but the Soviet Black Sea Fleet, taking advantage of the Germans being tied down around *Sevastopol, began landing three armies—which formed the Crimea *front* in January—on the Kerch peninsula at the eastern end of the Crimea on 26 December (see BLACK SEA). To impose his will on the generals, Hitler sent Bock home on sick leave, and relieved Guderian and Hoepner, when Bock protested against, and the others actually challenged, the 'fanatical resistance' order.

In its New Year's Day 1942 edition, *Pravda*, citing Stalin who attributed the German advances entirely to the temporary effects of surprise, predicted victory in 1942. On 5 January, Stalin called together the Stavka, of which Zhukov and Timoshenko were members, and disclosed that he and the General Staff had worked out a plan for a general offensive. It would put nine *fronts* in action along the whole line from Leningrad to the Crimea. The scope was ambitious: to liberate Leningrad in the north, the Donets basin and the Crimea in the south, and to make another German attack towards Moscow impossible in the centre.

Zhukov, co-ordinating Kalinin, West and Briansk *fronts*, was to encircle and destroy Army Group Centre in a single, massive double envelopment, which was to close at Smolensk. Deep frost made even rivers and swamps readily passable for tanks and artillery, and Hitler kept movement restricted on the German side. By early February, Zhukov had armies operating as far west as Smolensk. The German front had come to look like a badly frayed lace doily, but Zhukov's lower commands were insufficiently adept at sustaining concentrations over long distances and their thrusts degenerated into amorphous bulges. Bock's successor, Field Marshal von *Kluge, managed to hold open the Warsaw–Smolensk–Moscow road, and the railway, east to Vyazma, where rail lines running north to Rzhev and south to Briansk enabled his armies to sustain a semi-contiguous 350 km. (220 mi.) front.

A similar pattern emerged in the north and south. Volkhov *front*, which had been formed under *Meretskov in December, created a large bulge in the German lines south of Leningrad, and North-West *front* carved out another south of Lake Ilmen, but the German positions around Leningrad held. South-West *front* put three armies across the River Donets at Izyum before the Germans sealed off the bulge. Crimea *front* took the Kerch peninsula, but German forces on the Crimea blocked its western exit.

By March, when the spring thaw stopped all operations for several weeks, Stalin knew his general offensive had failed to rule out another German summer offensive. After having been quiet on the subject during the winter, he opened a diplomatic and press campaign for a Second Front in western Europe; and he told the Stavka that Soviet forces would go over to an 'active defence' after the thaw. Subsequently, he added that it would also be necessary 'to strike several actually nine pre-emptive blows over a wide front'.

These pre-emptive blows, by keeping masses of Soviet troops engaged in vulnerable positions, enabled the Germans to terminate the war's first year with some showpiece successes. Against Crimea *front*, which had been under orders to take the offensive, the German commander on the Crimea, General von *Manstein, earned his marshal's baton with a swift stroke on the Kerch peninsula (8–19 May) that demolished Crimea *front* and brought in more than 170,000 prisoners. On 12 May Timoshenko, now co-ordinating South-west and South *fronts*, launched an enveloping thrust towards *Kharkov out of the Izyum bulge, but within two weeks the Germans blocked the Donets crossings, and he lost a quarter of a million men. In the last week of June, Army Group North sealed off the Volkhov *front*'s bulge south of Leningrad and destroyed *Vlasov's Second Shock Army.

4. Hitler's resurgence (June–September 1942)
On the whole, Hitler came through the winter rather well: the troops had not lost confidence in him; he had preserved a front of sorts within 150 km. (95 mi.) of Moscow; and he had brought the army completely under his control. However, he was having to contend with a severe reduction of means for the next summer's campaign. In July 1941, anticipating that the forces in the Soviet Union could be reduced by about two-thirds before winter, he had cut army weapons, ammunition, and equipment production. He had rescinded the cuts in January 1942; but the production pipelines would not reach full volume again until August. Meanwhile, the Soviet general offensive had kept consumption high, and the cold had imposed heavy attrition in weapons and vehicles. Another BARBAROSSA was out of the question but in any case, he thought, perhaps not necessary.

In April Hitler issued the directive for the summer campaign (Operation BLUE). He set the main—and only major—effort in the south, where Army Group South would be split into Army Group B, on the left in the sector from Kursk to Izyum, and Army Group A, on the right between Izyum and Taganrog. He gave Bock (whom he had reluctantly recalled) B, with Second, Sixth, Fourth Panzer, and Hungarian Second Armies. A, with First Panzer, Seventeenth, Eleventh, and Romanian Third Armies went to Field Marshal List. Eighth Italian and Fourth Romanian Armies were stationed in the Army Group A rear area pending later decisions on their employment. Assuming that Stalin had used up most of his reserves during the winter, Hitler set destruction of the remaining Soviet reserves and capture of the

Caucasus oilfields as the strategic objectives; and he specified three phases (BLUE I–III) in which the army groups would converge on Stalingrad, encircling the Soviet forces as they went. Thereafter, with Army Group B covering it on the Don and the Volga rivers, Army Group A would drive south into the Caucasus.

Stalin was not as badly off as Hitler thought. He had 5.5 million troops 'in action' in late June, and he now had ten field armies and one tank army in the Stavka reserve. (Hitler had 3.5 million German and, counting the 400,000 strong Finnish Army, about a million other Axis troops.) Stalin was also getting enough new production to start building air and tank armies, the latter a recently conceived answer to the panzer armies. On the other hand, he was not as ready as he thought to meet the attack. He believed Moscow would be Hitler's objective, and he had the reserve armies stationed accordingly. At the front, Kalinin and West *fronts* had nineteen armies and a tank army ranged against Army Group Centre. Opposite Army Groups B and A, part of Briansk, South-West and South *fronts* had fifteen armies and a tank army. Briansk *front*, with five armies and a tank army, was the strongest, but three of its armies and the tank army were deployed against Army Group Centre. South-West and South *fronts* were not yet recovered from the disaster in the Izyum bulge.

BLUE I, expected to take about three weeks, began on 28 June with an Army Group B strike along the Briansk–South-West *front* boundary towards Voronezh and the River Don. Maj-General *Golikov, commanding Briansk *front*, did not dare attempt a counter-attack that might jeopardize Moscow, and Timoshenko's South-West *front* reacted lamely. On 6 July, having been delayed more by rain than by Soviet resistance, Fourth Panzer took Voronezh, and Sixth Army reached the Don.

During the day on 6 July, Stalin, for the first and only time in the war, authorized a strategic retreat and Sixth Army, heading south and east the next day, had nothing but bare steppe ahead of it. Two days later, Fourth Panzer Group, now upgraded to army status and under the command of Hoth launched into BLUE II with Kleist's First Panzer Army. What had been planned as a set-piece encirclement degenerated into a mêlée. They cut through masses of fleeing Red Army men, but before their points met near Millerovo five days later, many more had escaped than were being captured. Hitler, who had moved his headquarters to Vinnitsa, in the Ukraine, accused Bock of having misdeployed his armour in the first place, dismissed him and appointed General Maximilian von Weichs in his place.

Nevertheless, the campaign, a whole month ahead of schedule, was developing splendidly. Soviet resistance and German losses had both been negligible. There being no pockets to clear, the infantry, except for Second Army which was getting heavy counter-attacks in the Voronezh area, had as yet hardly seen action. Hitler ordered the panzer army commanders Kleist and Hoth to sweep south to Rostov and keep *Malinovsky's South *front* from escaping across the lower Don. This they did and it soon disintegrated. Hoth had two Fourth Panzer Army corps approaching the River Chir 175 km. (105 mi.) west of Stalingrad. Those Hitler assigned to Sixth Army, ordering its commander, General *Paulus, to make a fast thrust to Stalingrad. Paulus, whose whole previous command career had been as a staff officer, was eager to prove himself on the battlefield.

Meanwhile, Stalin, whose own service as a commissar in Stalingrad (then Tsaritsyn) during the Civil War (1918–20) had given him a high opinion of the city's strategic significance, had concluded that the purpose of the German advance into the Don bend was to gain positions for a northward drive towards Moscow like one the White general, Anton Denikin (1872–1947) had made in 1919. Timoshenko's South-West *front* was temporarily disbanded on 12 July and with its staff, which was practically all that was left of it, Stalin activated Stalingrad *front*, giving it three reserve armies and orders to defend the city.

On 23 July, Army Group B completed the Rostov operation, which brought in a modest 83,000 prisoners; and Sixth Army, after crossing the Chir, encountered Stalingrad *front*'s main line 140 km. (87 mi.) west of Stalingrad. Hitler issued a new strategic directive that night. In it, declaring the initial missions 'substantially completed', he cancelled BLUE III and put two separate operations in its place: EDELWEISS, in which Army Group A would advance through the Caucasus and take the oilfields at Maikop, Grozny, and Baku (the last over 1,200 km./745 mi. from Rostov) and HERON, in which Army Group B would seize Stalingrad and extend down the Volga to Astrakhan. It would also be necessary, he added, to finish off Leningrad before the summer ended; therefore, Manstein and his staff, together with five infantry divisions and siege artillery he had used in the break into Sevastopol in early July, would be diverted to Army Group North.

How difficult sustaining offensives in two directions would be was apparent within a week. Against scattered resistance from the remains of six Soviet armies that had escaped across the Don, Army Group A advanced swiftly; but keeping it on the move necessitated a 50% cut in Sixth Army's fuel and ammunition allocation just as it was meeting stronger resistance. When Hitler added weight to HERON by sending Hoth's staff with a panzer and an infantry corps towards Stalingrad, List protested that EDELWEISS was being jeopardized.

Stalin, who remembered well how the tsar's armies had dissolved in 1917, faced a similar peril: in its fourth week, the strategic retreat was becoming a rout. When First Tank Army went into action against Sixth Army, many of its crews abandoned their tanks, and the army had to be disbanded on the spot. Marshal Budenny, regarded as an inspiring leader, had been appointed to command North Caucasus *front*, which was activated briefly (May–September 1942) and absorbed the remnants of South *front*, but he was having no success in stemming the retreat. On 28 July, Stalin had to make the somewhat dangerous admission that discipline was breaking down and announce drastic punishments for officers and men who did not stand and fight.

Sixth Army gave Stalin more cause for concern on 7 August by destroying the better part of an army on the Don east of Kalach and taking 50,000 prisoners. Thereafter, Paulus received enough fuel and ammunition to launch a 90 km. (56 mi.) dash from the Don to the Volga on 21 August. In two days, behind waves of dive bombers, a panzer corps broke through to the Volga 15 km. (9 mi.) north of Stalingrad. Next, Paulus built a screening line between the rivers and drove south to secure contact with Fourth Panzer Army on 2 September. It looked then as if the finale was close at hand, and Paulus sent Hitler a plan for going into winter quarters.

Guided by flame and smoke from burning oil wells (see SCORCHED EARTH POLICY), First Panzer Army took Maikop on 9 August, concluding the first phase of EDELWEISS. Henceforth, First Panzer would direct its whole weight east towards the Caspian Sea, and Seventeenth Army would push south through the mountains to the Black Sea coast. Although Stalin's order to stand and fight was not markedly affecting Soviet performance, EDELWEISS began to lose momentum. Hitler had decided that, until the issue was resolved at Stalingrad, the city had to be the main objective, and had therefore shifted fuel and ammunition priorities to Sixth Army, and Paulus's drive to the Volga later in the month drew off practically all of Army Group A's air support.

By the second week in September, Sixth and Fourth Panzer Armies were tied down in Stalingrad. First Panzer Army had been stalled for nearly three weeks, and Seventeenth Army was having to contend with snowstorms in the mountains. Hitler had the choice of either reducing the commitment at Stalingrad, by letting Paulus and Hoth go over to the defensive, or stopping EDELWEISS short of its objective. He rejected the first because the contest for Stalingrad had drawn world-wide attention. The second, which would have constituted an admission that his strategy was bankrupt, he buried in a spate of charges against his generals. On 9 September he removed List from the Army Group A command without naming a successor and informed Halder that his term as chief of the Army General Staff was at an end.

5. The turning-point (September–December 1942)
On 27 August, Stalin recalled Zhukov, who had been co-ordinating pre-emptive strikes against Army Group Centre through the summer, appointed him deputy supreme commander, and sent him out to organize a counter-attack at Stalingrad. Stalin could construe the deputy supreme commander's role any way he pleased but, for the moment, he was manifestly feeling an urgent need to give greater scope to military professionalism than he had in the past. Recently, he had rehabilitated the long-prohibited word 'officer' and authorized several medals for officers only; and he was preparing to relieve the officers from subordination to political commissars.

Stalin was responding to the most serious crisis of the war—and of his entire 15-year rule. His losses were immense: half of the European Soviet Union, 71% of the nation's iron, 63% of its coal, potentially over 80% of its oil (see also USSR, 2). On the other hand, the very important central industrial region east of Moscow had survived, as had also the Urals and Kuzbass basin regions. Munitions output was rising. During the summer, 5 tank armies with 700 tanks apiece (to a panzer army's 600) and 15 air armies with between 200 and 1,000 aircraft each were activated, and Stalin still had 10 field armies in reserve. But performance was a problem at the command as well as the troop level. Although the raw power was there, Zhukov would need much skill and more luck to exploit it effectively.

Hitler, knowing victory was out of the question, had to contemplate another winter campaign. The General Staff calculated that a hundred fresh Soviet divisions would be deployed by 1 November while the German forces would be 18% under strength. Army Groups North and Centre had solid fronts. To anchor a front over 1,000 km. (620 mi.) long on the Don and Volga rivers, Army Group B had two strong-points: Second Army at Voronezh, on the upper Don, and Sixth and Fourth Panzer Armies 500 km. (310 mi.) to the south-east, around Stalingrad. To screen the gap between them on the Don General von Weichs, the army group commander, had deployed the Second Hungarian and Eighth Italian Armies, both unproven, and was given Third and Fourth Romanian Armies, which had already failed several tests. Army Group A was stalled in the Caucasus Mountains 600 km. (372 mi.) south of Stalingrad.

On 12 September, the first German troops entered Stalingrad, and Stalin, whose concern for world opinion was as great as Hitler's ordered that the city, or at least some part of it, be held no matter what the cost, until a counter-offensive (URANUS) could be launched (see Map 98). It began on 19 November and the Romanian armies collapsed under the first assaults. Five days later, Soviet armoured spearheads closed an almost perfect double envelopment east of the Don crossing at Kalach. Paulus asked for permission to break out, which he could have done at that time, being well supplied with ammunition and fuel. Instead, Hitler created Army Group Don, which comprised the encircled Sixth Army, Hoth's Fourth Panzer Army, and the two Romanian armies, and this he gave to Manstein with an order to restore contact with the pocket. Although the full effect of this decision would not become apparent for some weeks, the war had reached its strategic turning-point. See also STALINGRAD, BATTLE FOR.

6. Retreat and recovery (January–March 1943)
On 1 January 1943, South-West *front*, which had been reconstituted in October 1942, was surging past Millerovo towards the River Donets; Don *front* took over the line around the Stalingrad pocket; and Stalingrad

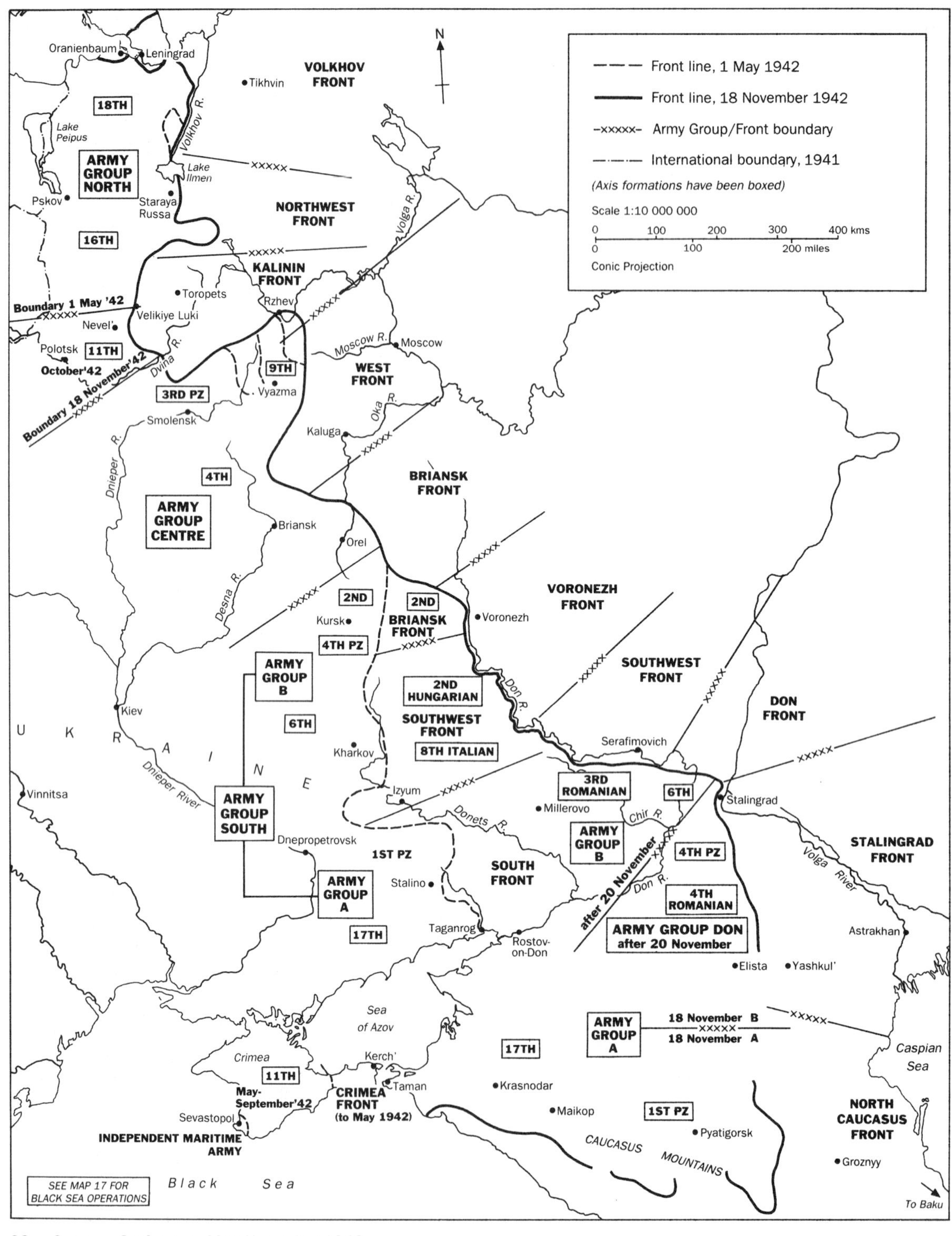

38. **German–Soviet war**, May–November 1942

front (now renamed South *front*) had three armies which it aimed south-westwards towards Rostov along the left bank of the Don. On 10 January, Don *front* set about systematically carving up the Stalingrad pocket and on 31 January, the day after he had been promoted field marshal, Paulus surrendered. In the north, Leningrad and Volkhov *fronts* attacked on 12 January and, in a week, opened a corridor 10 km. (6.2 mi.) wide along the Lake Ladoga shore. On 13 January, Voronezh *front* began an offensive against the Second German and Second Hungarian armies that in twelve days demolished the Hungarian Army and liberated Voronezh. On 15 January, Kleist, to whom Hitler had given command of Army Group A in late November, asked for instructions on withdrawing from the Caucasus. Hitler did not respond until 27 January. By then, South *front* was 50 km. (31 mi.) from Rostov, and except for First Panzer Army which withdrew via Rostov-on-Don, Kleist had to take the army group into a bridgehead on the Taman peninsula. Paulus's surrender at Stalingrad lent enormous psychological impact to an already decisive Soviet victory.

Stalin issued a congratulatory order of the day to the Red Army on 25 January, giving the troops the slogan: 'Onward to defeat the German occupationists . . . '. Zhukov had become a marshal a week earlier, the first to be appointed in the war. *Vasilevsky, until then Chief of the Soviet General Staff, though only a lt-general, received his marshal's star a month later, and Stalin himself also donned the uniform of a marshal.

Hitler proclaimed a 'total war' to defend Europe against an invasion 'out of the steppe'. In a tacit concession that he might not be competent to run the whole war alone he recalled Guderian, whom he had dismissed in December 1941, and made him inspector-general of armour; but he refused out of hand to consider relinquishing command of the army. The conversion to total war came too late, for up to 1942, he had still counted on a short campaign. But Stalin now had more than 6 million troops at the front; and in 1942, Soviet war production had surpassed Germany's by 24,000 to 4,800 in armoured vehicles and 21,700 to 14,700 in aircraft. The one clear superiority the Germans retained was in performance on the battlefield. Generally, probably even at Stalingrad, they imposed heavier losses than they took; and though Soviet performance became vastly more effective under Zhukov and Vasilevsky, and others with talent who were coming to the fore, there were not enough of them to ensure consistency even at the *front* and army levels.

Soviet confidence soared in late January. A German stand east of the River Dnieper seemed impossible. It seemed likely that Army Groups Don and A could be prevented from ever reaching the river, and Army Group Centre had become vulnerable. Lt-General Nikolai Vatutin, the South-West *front* commander, devised an operation (LEAP) to lock Army Group Don into the Donets basin. LEAP began on 29 January, when a mobile group of tank corps crossed the Donets east of Izyum and drove south towards Mariupol on the Sea of Azov. On 2 February, Zhukov and Vasilevsky launched Voronezh *front* into a two-pronged operation (STAR), designed to go south-west past Kharkov towards the Dnieper and north-west via Kursk towards Smolensk. Elements of Don *front* under General *Rokossovsky, being brought north-west from Stalingrad, would take over the northern prong on 15 February and, becoming Central *front*, complete the thrust behind Army Group Centre.

Voronezh *front* took Kursk on 8 February, Kharkov on 15 February, and had spearheads approaching the Dnieper crossings at Dnepropetrovsk and Zaporozhye on 18 February. Rokossovsky activated Central *front* in a sector north-west of Kursk on 15 February, but because the railway's capabilities had been overestimated, his redeployment from Stalingrad took another ten days. LEAP ended on 18 February, when First Panzer Army demolished Vatutin's mobile group; nevertheless, South-West and Voronezh *fronts* were across the Donets everywhere north and west of Slavyansk.

On 11 February, Hitler removed Headquarters, Army Group B, attached Second Army to Army Group Centre, and reinstated Army Group South under Manstein, giving him responsibility for everything between Belgorod and the Sea of Azov. Manstein had a solid 162 km. (100 mi.) front on the River Mius north of Taganrog, which had been built during the previous winter, but nothing worth the name on the remaining 275 km. (180 mi.) to Belgorod. But he had some assets as well: strong air support, a legacy of the effort to hold Stalingrad; three fresh panzer divisions, acquired from Army Group B; and Hitler's permission, given on 19 February, to airlift 100,000 troops out of the Taman bridgehead. He also had a master of mobile tactics in Hoth, whose Fourth Panzer Army staff he shifted from the Mius line to Dnepropetrovsk.

In the last week of February, disregarding the spring thaw which was beginning to soften the ground, Hoth attacked northwards with two panzer divisions and a promise of several more to be acquired later. Although the thaw's full onset in March slowed the advance, it retained enough momentum to reach Kharkov on 11 March. The Soviet Command, intent on getting behind the Donets, left Belgorod exposed, and two panzer divisions running on a railway embankment took it on 18 March.

After he began his projected drive to Smolensk on 25 February, Rokossovsky had to contend with both the thaw and a frustrating change in the situation. On 1 March, Army Group Centre entered into a phased withdrawal from the Rzhev salient (BUFFALO), which even Hitler had to admit no longer posed a credible threat to Moscow. By 23 March, when BUFFALO stopped on a line from Velizh to Kirov, Army Group Centre had cut its frontage by nearly 400 km. (248 mi.) and freed enough strength to keep Rokossovsky in check. The winter's departure left three concentrations of forces, two German and one Soviet, in exposed positions. After BUFFALO, Army Group Centre's front south of Kirov

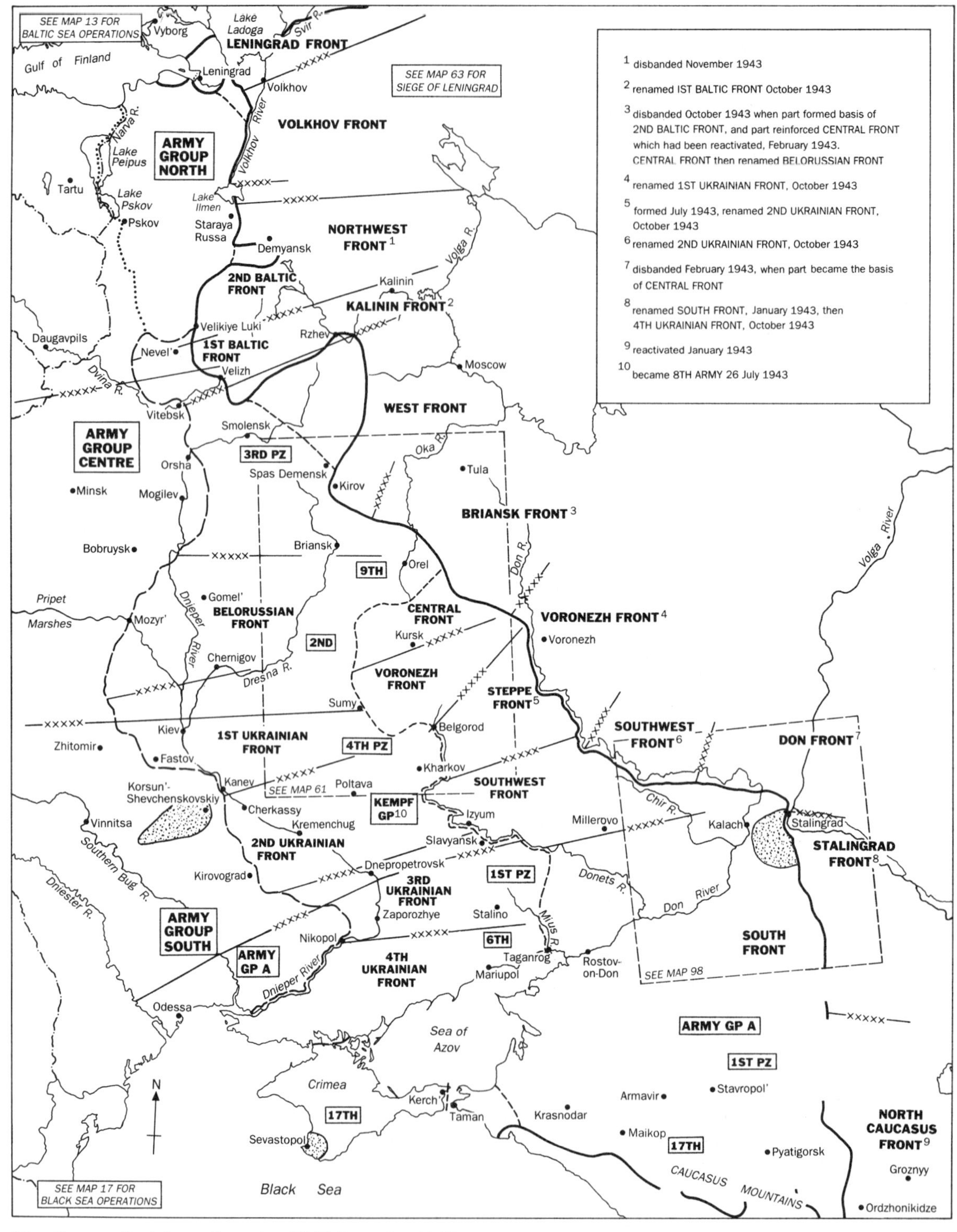

39. **German–Soviet war**, November 1942–December 1943

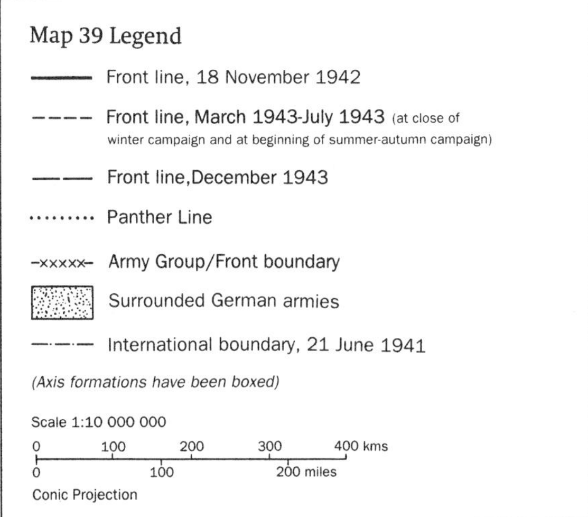

projected eastwards, forming a salient around *Orel. Army Group South's line around Belgorod and Kharkov formed another; and in the 162 km. (100 mi.) gap between them, Central and Voronezh *fronts* occupied an oblong bulge east of Kursk.

7. To the Dnieper (April–December 1943)
Hitler regarded the coming summer as a period of strategic retrenchment. He expected to take the initiative again, but on a reduced scale. An Anglo-American attempt to create a Second Front in Europe was becoming likely, and he had over half a million unreplaced troop losses from the winter. At the front, he had 3.07 million German troops, slightly more than in June 1941, but Stalin had 6.6 million. On the other hand, the Kursk bulge presented an opportunity to make an impressive showing, and means were available. BUFFALO had yielded a surplus army, Ninth Army, which under General *Model had, for fourteen months held the hottest spot on the Eastern Front, the line around Rzhev. Fourth Panzer Army had acquired three new SS panzer divisions, the first divisions to be fully equipped with Panther and Tiger tanks. Through the spring, on Hitler's orders, Manstein and Kluge organized an operation (CITADEL) to pinch off the Kursk bulge.

Stalin, Zhukov, and Vasilevsky also concentrated on Kursk. Uncertain as to how they would fare in summer, they decided to leave the first move to the Germans and planned two operations to be brought into play later: one (KUTUZOV) against the Orel salient, the other (RUMYANTSEV) against the Belgorod-Kharkov salient. By mid-May, they had five *fronts* at the ready and one in reserve in the Orel–Kursk–Kharkov sector (see Map 61).

The prolonged, uneasy quiet ended on 5 July, when Model's Ninth Army launched CITADEL by striking south, and Fourth Panzer Army north, towards Kursk. Although neither succeeded in shaking itself loose, Fourth Panzer was coming close to a breakthrough by 12 July. Zhukov then launched KUTUZOV against the north face of the Orel salient, and Fifth Guards Tank Army entered the battle against Fourth Panzer. Coincidentally, on 12 July, American and British forces began advancing out of beachheads they had taken on Sicily two days earlier (see SICILIAN CAMPAIGN). On 13 July, Hitler told Kluge and Manstein that CITADEL was cancelled. He said he had to use the SS panzer divisions to hold Italy. He then gave Model command of Second Panzer as well as Ninth Army with an order to restore the front around Orel. He agreed to let Manstein keep his offensive going long enough to establish a claim to a victory of sorts but changed his mind four days later and ordered the SS panzer divisions out of the front.

Model lived up fully to his reputation as 'the lion of the defence' until 25 July, when Hitler, reacting to Mussolini's arrest that day, warned Army Group Centre that it would have to give up two dozen divisions. Thereafter, Model went over to a phased withdrawal similar to BUFFALO. Voronezh *front*, Steppe *front* under Konev, and South-West *front* under Malinovsky began RUMYANTSEV on 3 August. On 5 August, Model gave up Orel; Vatutin took Belgorod; and Stalin, in a special order of the day, declared that the 'German legend' of Soviet inability to wage a successful summer campaign had been dispelled. See also KURSK, BATTLE OF.

Actually, a full-scale summer offensive would not be possible for some weeks yet, because Model kept three *fronts* tied up until 17 August and Manstein did likewise with three more until 23 August, when he evacuated Kharkov. But a major doubt had been resolved, and that was immediately reflected in the conduct of the war. Stalin no longer gave Zhukov and Vasilevsky as much of a free hand as he had since September 1942, and he imposed a virtual ban on planned encirclements. The ban, to which he permitted few exceptions thereafter, was not purely arbitrary. Of five encirclements attempted after Stalingrad, the last being KUTUZOV, none had been completed. Stalin's solution was to revert to a form of tactics first used against the White General Denikin in 1919: a broad, frontal attack employing massive 'cleaving blows' to shatter the opposing front and drive it back.

At the end of August, on a 1,000 km. (662 mi.) line from Army Group Centre's northern boundary at Nevel to Taganrog, eight Soviet *fronts* were developing nineteen parallel thrusts toward the River Dnieper. The strongest were west of Kursk and Kharkov, where Central, Voronezh, and Steppe *fronts* (which became Belorussian and First and Second Ukrainian *fronts* on 20 October) had the advantage of their build-ups for the Kursk battle. On 8 September, Hitler approved a limited withdrawal behind the Dnieper; but from the outset that was impossible because Army Group South had to concentrate on reaching five widely separated crossing-points where there were bridges: Kiev, Kanev, Cherkassy, Kremenchug, and Dnepropetrovsk. Between those, Soviet armies had open access to the river and sent their troops across on anything that would float, oil drums, timbers, straw wrapped in ponchos. The resulting race for the right bank evolved in early October into a contest for possession that, by December, gained First Ukrainian *front* a large bridgehead around Kiev and Second Ukrainian *front* another embracing Cherkassy, Kremenchug, and Dnepropetrovsk. By then, Army Group Centre had lost Smolensk and the southern half of the Dnieper Line in its zone. Kleist's Army Group A had a reconstituted Sixth Army ranged along the Dnieper below Nikopol and Seventeenth Army isolated in the Crimea. Stalin could meet Roosevelt and Churchill at the Teheran conference from 28 November to 1 December (see EUREKA), as a supreme commander whose armies had been successful in all seasons.

8. 'Clearing the Soviet land' (January–May 1944)
Goaded by repeated complaints from Manstein, Kluge, and others that half the German Army was fighting in the east while the other half was scattered around western Europe waiting for invasions that did not come, Hitler issued a strategic directive on 3 November 1943. The danger in the east, he conceded, was great; but a greater danger, an Anglo-American landing, was looming in north-west France (see OVERLORD). In the worst case, Germany could still afford to lose large stretches of territory in the east. In the west, however, the distance to Germany's vital centres was far shorter; therefore, the Eastern Front would have to make do with its existing means until after the landing had been repulsed.

In mid-December, Stalin held a joint meeting of the Politburo, the State Defence Committee (see USSR, 4), and the Stavka to review the plan for the coming winter. At that point, the Soviet forces had recovered over half the territory the Germans had occupied since June 1941. The plan projected operations in the north, centre, and south to retake the remainder, at least up to the pre-1939 boundaries. The main effort would be in the south, where the four Ukrainian *fronts* (the Third being the former South-West *front* and the Fourth the former South *front*), possessed massive superiority in troops and material.

On 14 January 1944, Leningrad, Volkhov, and Second Baltic *fronts*—the last having been formed the previous October from two of the Briansk *front*'s armies—attacked around and south of Leningrad. Because keeping a hold on the city no longer served any purpose and his two armies were weakened by transfers to the south, Field Marshal Georg von Küchler, who had superseded Leeb as the Army Group North commander in January 1942, proposed to retreat by stages to the PANTHER Position, a prepared line along the River Narva, Lake Peipus, and Lake Pskov 270 km. (117 mi.) to the rear. Hitler first agreed, then changed his mind and demanded that the front be kept where it was. Stalin declared Leningrad liberated on 27 January, when Volkhov *front* crossed the Moscow–Leningrad railway. In three more days, Küchler's line broke into four parts. On 31 January, Hitler replaced Küchler with Model, who manoeuvred the parts for four more weeks before taking them into the PANTHER Position when the spring thaw halted operations.

The offensive in the centre failed to materialize. First Baltic (formerly Kalinin), West, and First Belorussian (formerly Belorussian) *fronts* made three starts but only minor gains in January, February, and March.

Zhukov, co-ordinating the First and Second, and Vasilievsky, with the Third and Fourth, had trouble getting the four Ukrainian *fronts* back into motion. The weather was party responsible. Freezes alternated with thaws that hampered movement, although less on the Soviet than on the German side, because the Soviet forces were by then equipped with American-built six-wheel-drive trucks. Defective preparation was the more immediate problem. First Ukrainian *front* opened an attack out of its bridgehead on 24 December, but Konev's Second Ukrainian *front* was not ready until 5 January. Third and Fourth Ukrainian *fronts* made a poor start on 10 January and had to be stopped the next day to be put through a reorganization that could not be completed before the end of the month.

On 11 February, knowing that Konev could not advance while his neighbours on the left were stalled, Zhukov proposed, and Stalin approved, encircling six German divisions (56,000 troops) lodged on a 60 km. (37 mi.) stretch of the Dnieper between the Soviet bridgeheads. In slow motion, through mud, snow, and rain, Konev and Vatutin laid two rings round the divisions by 3 February, but 30,000 German troops broke out on 17 February. Although Stalin ordered an artillery salute in Moscow and rewarded Konev with a marshal's star, it is doubtful that he became converted to the encirclement.

However, the operation at Korsun Shevchenkovsky, as it is called, provided an opportunity to declare the winter campaign victoriously completed and initiate a fresh start. On 29 February, Third and Fourth Ukrainian *fronts* completed their original January missions, and the Headquarters of the Fourth Ukrainian *front* went out of the line with two armies to organize a drive into the Crimea. First and Second Ukrainian *fronts* opened a spring offensive on 5 March. Zhukov, who had taken Vatutin's place after Vatutin was badly wounded a week earlier, and Konev mounted two massive parallel thrusts, each spearheaded by three tank armies. On 20 March, Kleist had to let Sixth Army withdraw to avoid being cut off between the Bug and Dniester rivers. Five days later, Manstein ordered First Panzer Army to break out of a pocket Zhukov had formed. Hitler objected strenuously in both instances. On 30 March, he called in Kleist and Manstein, the commanders of Army Group A and South, awarded them the Swords to their Knight's Crosses of the Iron Cross (see DECORATIONS), and told them he no longer needed master tacticians, only generals who could 'get the last ounce of resistance' out of their troops. On leaving, they passed their replacements, Field Marshals Model (Manstein's) and *Schörner (Kleist's). Both had been promoted a day earlier, Schörner's ruthless generalship as a corps commander having brought him to Hitler's notice.

Model and Schörner had little time to practise their skills before 17 April when the Soviet offensive ended on a line from the south-western tip of the Pripet marshes to the foothills of the Carpathians and the lower River Dniester. The Crimea, where the Soviet attack did not begin until 7 April, gave Schörner a better opportunity. Although he did not believe the Crimea was worth the effort, he kept the battle going until 12 May, when 27,000 troops out of what had been a 150,000-man force boarded ships off the beach at Sevastopol.

9. In the main direction (June–August 1944)
Until May 1944, Hitler's strategy had served him moderately well. Much territory had been lost, and his troop strength in the east was down to 2.2 million, but the front at its closest point was 900 km. (560 mi.) from Berlin. Of a dozen panzer divisions activated during the winter ten had gone to the west, only two to the east. Moreover, the Soviet spring offensive appeared to indicate that Stalin proposed to exploit the Anglo-American attempt at establishing a Second Front to realize his hegemonic ambitions in south-eastern Europe. Hitler and the Army General Staff therefore concluded that Army Group South Ukraine (formerly Army Group A) would be the principal and Army Group North Ukraine (formerly Army Group South) the secondary Soviet targets in the coming summer. The Army Group North and Centre areas, they believed, posed operational problems, particularly for armour, that the Soviet commands had not yet mastered.

In early May, Zhukov relinquished his *front* command and returned to Moscow to work on an operation (BAGRATION) against Army Group Centre, which the Soviet offensives against its neighbours had enclosed in a deep embayment centred on Minsk. The final plan Stalin approved later in the month, committed 2.4 million troops, 5,200 tanks, and 5,300 aircraft, double the troops and more tanks and aircraft than had been used in KUTUZOV and RUMYANTSEV together. First Baltic and First, Second, and Third Belorussian *fronts* (the last two having been formed from West *front*) were to direct nine thrusts inwards towards Minsk. In the second phase, Second Baltic and First Ukrainian *fronts* would join in on the flanks, and the advance would proceed westwards along the whole line between the Dvina and the Carpathians. In mid-June, whatever doubts he may have had about the Anglo-American landing being by then resolved, Stalin set 23 June as the starting date.

At Army Group Centre, Field Marshal *Busch, who had replaced Kluge in October 1943, had 700,000 troops. In May, transfers to Army Group North Ukraine cost him nine-tenths of his tanks, half his tank destroyers, a third of his heavy artillery, and a quarter of his self-propelled assault guns. Not a virtuoso in his own right, Busch relied on Hitler's guidance and regarded himself as an instrument of the Führer's will. Adopting a device Hitler had originated during the past winter, Busch designated Vitebsk, Orsha, Mogilev, and Bobruysk as 'fortresses' whose garrisons of several divisions each were to resist 'to the last man'. On 23 June, taking the attack to be preliminary to the offensive against Army Group North Ukraine, Hitler demanded a rigid defence, and Busch complied.

In four days, Busch committed all his reserves without slowing the Soviet thrusts anywhere. The 'fortresses' were all isolated. Third Panzer Army having had to abandon five divisions in Vitebsk, was helplessly adrift. Fourth and Ninth Armies were struggling to extricate themselves from the marshes along the River Beresina. Busch proposed to form another rigid line north and south of Minsk; but on 28 June Hitler, now aware that something more than passive compliance was required, gave Model command of the army group. In good part as a result of his having mightily encouraged the initial misassessment, Model had reserves at hand but not close enough by to have an effect before the first phase of BAGRATION ended east of Minsk on 5 July. At that point, Fourth Army had lost 130,000 out of its original 165,000 troops, First Panzer had lost a similar number, and Ninth Army had collapsed.

In the second phase, First Belorussian *front* turned west towards Warsaw, and Second and Third Belorussian *fronts* headed towards East Prussia and into Lithuania. First Ukrainian *front* came in on 13 July, striking via *Lwów (Lvov) towards the Vistula. Model manoeuvered his army groups backwards as gradually as the circumstances allowed, building cohesion as they went. When the Soviet pressure subsided in mid-August, he had a front a hair's breadth outside the East Prussian border and on the Vistula. First Belorussian and First Ukrainian *fronts* each held a bridgehead on the river.

On the north flank, the second phase became converted into an independent operation after 18 July when all three Baltic *fronts* (the third having been activated the previous April) went on the offensive against Army Group North. Schörner, whom Hitler sent to take command four days later, stabilized the front in August on a serrated line that preserved contact with Army Group Centre through a corridor 27 km. (18 mi.) wide along the Baltic coast west of Riga. After an attempt to pinch off the corridor failed in September, First Baltic *front* turned west in October and drove from Shaulyay to the coast at Klaipeda (Memel). Schörner then had to evacuate Estonia and eastern Latvia, taking the army group through the corridor and into isolation on the *Courland peninsula. Finland, which had depended on German aid shipped from Estonia, signed an *armistice on 2 September.

10. The 'march of liberation' (August–December 1944)
On 20 August 1944, along the Romanian border, Second and Third Ukrainian *fronts* opened the first in a train of operations to 'liberate' south-eastern Europe that would not be completed until three days after the war itself had ended. Stalin, looking towards the post-war order in the region, was making a political, not a military, decision when he ordered these moves. Hitler, also thinking

German–Soviet War

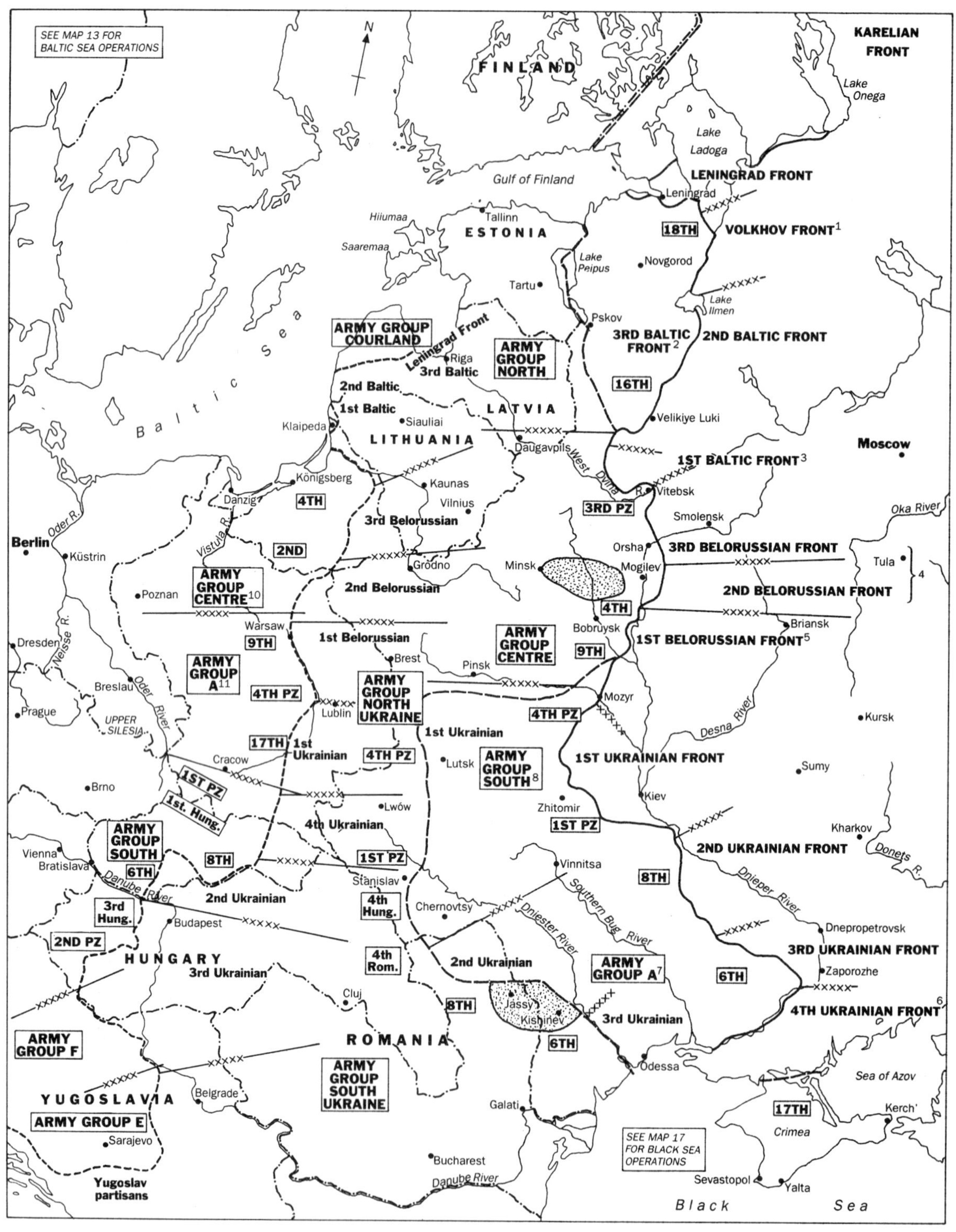

40. **German–Soviet war**, December 1943–31 December 1944

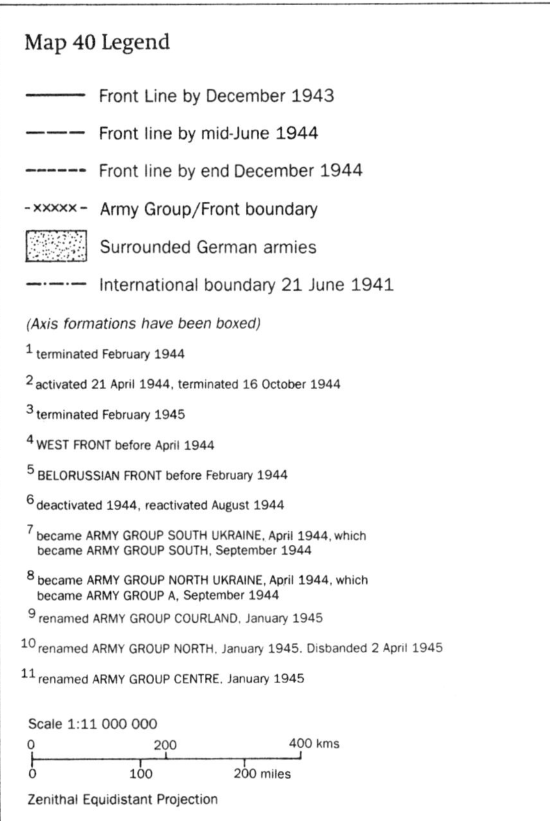

politically, envisioned a clash of Soviet and British interests that would split the alliance against him.

Romania surrendered on 23 August; but Bulgaria, nominally at war with the Western Powers although not with the USSR, created an apparently unexpected complication by attempting to secure a Soviet alignment and negotiate an armistice with the British and Americans. Stalin, regarding the potential outside involvement with deep suspicion, declared war on 5 September and diverted Third Ukrainian *front* into Bulgaria on 8 September. A day later, Bulgaria requested and was granted an *armistice, but Third Ukrainian *front* stayed on until the end of the month to show 'fraternal' support for a communist government being installed in Sofia.

The excursion into Bulgaria, a slow start Fourth Ukranian *front* made at crossing the Carpathian mountains into Slovakia, and a coup engineered by Hitler (see HUNGARY, 3) that prevented a Hungarian surrender enabled Army Group South Ukraine (renamed South in late September) to regain its balance somewhat after reaching Hungary. In November, Army Group South secured a tie-in with the German South-eastern theatre, which was responsible for Yugoslavia, Albania, and Greece. Weichs, the theatre commander, had 600,000 mostly limited service troops spread out from *Trieste to Crete, but after beginning to evacuate Greece in late October, he could cover Army Group South's right flank. On the left, in November, Army Group A, formerly North Ukraine, provided support against Fourth Ukrainian *front*. Throughout November the fighting centred on *Budapest, which Hitler and Stalin regarded as a prestige objective comparable to Stalingrad. Meanwhile, Stalin was having to concentrate on his main line of advance once more; and on 30 December, after Budapest had been brought under siege, he suspended the march of 'liberation'.

11. Stalin victorious (January–May 1945)
Stalin reserved the final operations to himself. In November 1944, after telling Zhukov that henceforth the Supreme C-in-C and the General Staff would handle all strategic planning and co-ordination, he shifted Rokossovsky to Second Belorussian *front* and posted Zhukov to First Belorussian *front*, which was to have the distinction of taking Berlin. Zhukov lost his seat on the Stavka but remained first deputy commander-in-chief, probably as a nominal counterpart to General *Eisenhower. In February 1945, Stalin gave Vasilevsky command of Third Belorussian *front* and appointed General Alexei Antonov, a routinely competent officer, to replace him as chief of the General Staff.

The plan, as completed in late 1944, was direct and simple: to end the war in approximately 45 days by driving from the Vistula to the Oder in 15 days and thence to the Elbe in another 30. First Belorussian and First Ukrainian *fronts* would bring 2.2 million troops to bear against Army Group A, which had about 400,000. Against Army Group Centre, Second and Third Belorussian *fronts* would employ 1.6 million troops to take East Prussia and clear the Baltic littoral.

The heaviest single offensive of the Second World War began on 12 January 1945. In three days, the Soviet *fronts* developed two dozen parallel thrusts, the two most powerful of them out of the Vistula bridgeheads, in which Zhukov and Konev had assembled 10:1 overall superiorities. Hitler gave Schörner command of Army Group A on 16 January—but even his formidable methods were unavailing—and on 23 January put Heinrich *Himmler in command of the newly activated Army Group Vistula. By 3 February Zhukov's and Konev's armies were on the River Oder from Küstrin, 65 km. (35 mi.) east of Berlin, to the Czechoslovak border. The offensive was about a week behind schedule, mainly owing to a sudden thaw in late January.

During the Yalta conference, held from 4 to 9 February, (see ARGONAUT), Stalin apparently decided that a quick victory was not in the Soviet interest. For the rest of the month and through March, he allowed the offensive to degenerate into random skirmishing. Rokossovsky and Vasilevsky pressed slowly through West Prussia and East Prussia. Zhukov diverted two tank armies and a field army north-eastwards to assist Rokossovsky. In February, Konev advanced across the Oder towards Dresden, went about halfway, stopped on the River Neisse, and turned to

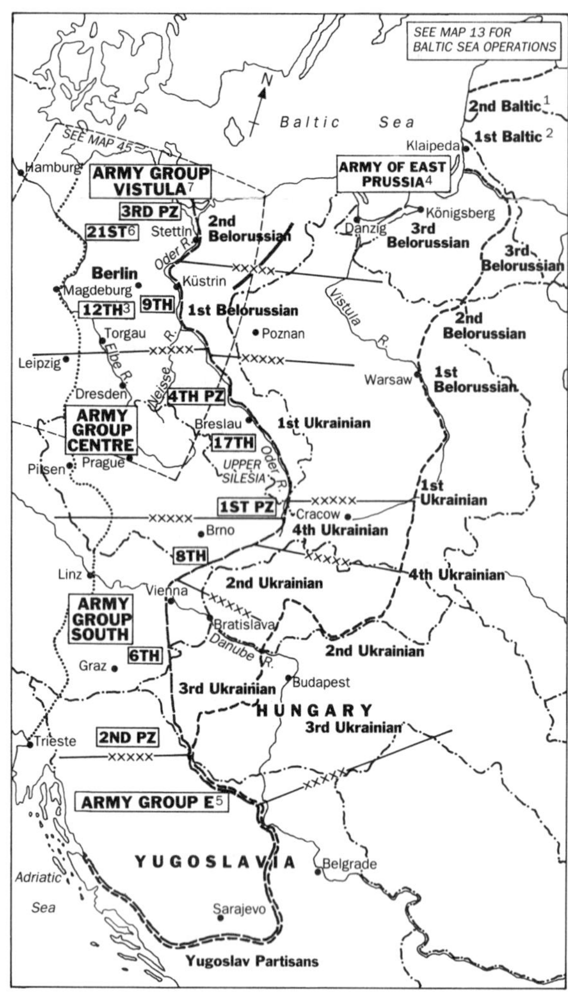

41. **German–Soviet war**, 1 January 1945–May 1945

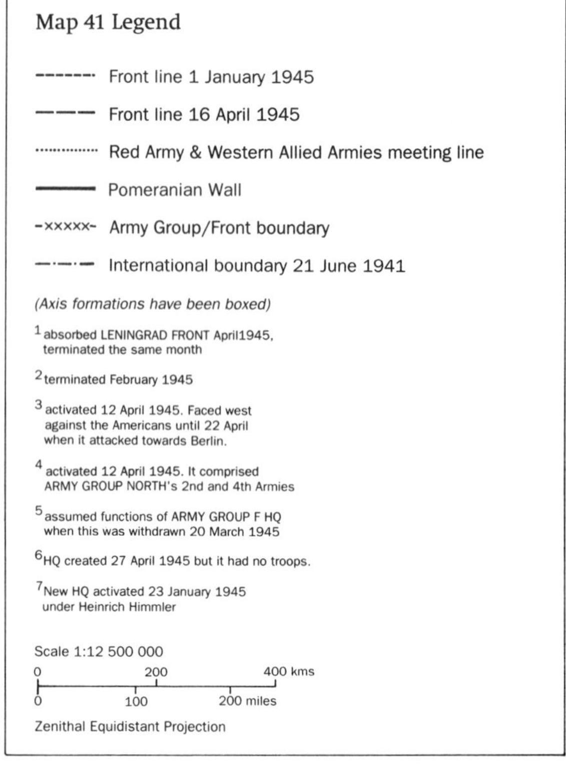

chipping away at Upper Silesia in March. Second and Third Baltic *fronts* kept pressure on Army Group Courland (North, renamed January 1945) but not enough to prevent Hitler from withdrawing divisions for the Oder front.

The prolonged hiatus in Stalin's advance gave Hitler his first opportunity since CITADEL to execute an offensive on the Eastern Front. Except at Budapest, where the fighting did not end until 13 February, the Soviet *fronts* in Hungary had stayed on the defensive through January and February and into March. On 15 January, Hitler had decided to send the Sixth SS Panzer Army, which had been the main force in the *Ardennes campaign against the Americans, to Hungary, where he expected another Soviet attack. Owing to the weather, the condition of the railways, and efforts by the generals to change his mind, the army did not arrive until late February. By then, Hitler had concocted an operation (AWAKENING OF SPRING) that was, like CITADEL, designed mainly to create an impression; and Second and Third Ukrainian *fronts* were, on Stalin's orders, preparing to resume the march of 'liberation'.

The offensive, which the Soviet commands expected and which the German commands and troops considered a pointless waste of effort, ran fitfully, on Hitler's insistence, for ten days. On 16 March, Second and Third Ukrainian *fronts*, the one on the north, the other on the south, attacked along the course of the Danube towards Vienna. On 7 April, Hitler sent General Lothar Rendulic, who had proved himself a worthy successor to Schörner in Courland, as C-in-C Army Group South to defend Vienna or convert it into another Budapest. The front was then at the southern outskirts of the city. Rendulic kept the battle going another five days, but withdrew towards the mountains on the north and west on 13 April.

While Stalin had his forces engaged elsewhere, the situation in central Germany underwent what was, from his viewpoint, an alarming change. In February, the Americans and British had been stalled on the line they had held before Hitler's Ardennes offensive. At the end of March, one British and five American armies were across the Rhine, and the Americans were encircling the Ruhr. On 31 March, Stalin threw First and Second Belorussian *fronts* into a fast redeployment, the object of which was to bring Zhukov into position for a frontal sweep to and beyond Berlin while Rokossovsky and Konev advanced to the Elbe on his flanks. Hitler had Army Group Vistula

German–Soviet war: Soviet army *fronts* and their commanders, 1941–5

North *front*		
Activated on basis of		
Leningrad Military District		24 June 41
	M. M. Popov	June–Aug 41
Divided 23 Aug 41 into:		
Karelia *front*	V. A. Frolov	Sept 41–Feb 44
	K. A. Meretskov	Feb–Nov 44
Staff placed in reserve		
and troops redeployed		15 Nov 44
and		
Leningrad *front*	M. M. Popov	Aug–Sept 41
K. E. Voroshilov	Sept 41	
	G. K. Zhukov	Sept–Oct 41
	I. I. Fedyuninsky	Oct 41
	M. S. Khozin	Oct 41–June 42
	L. A. Govorov	June 42–July 45
Redesignated headquarters,		
Leningrad Military District		24 July 45
North-west *front*		
Activated on basis of		
Baltic Special Military District		22 June 41
	F. I. Kuznetsov	June–July 41
	P. P. Sobennikov	July–Aug 41
	P. A. Kurochkin	Aug 41–Oct 42 and June–Nov 43
	S. K. Timoshenko	Oct 42–Mar 43
	I. S. Konev	Mar–Jun 43
Terminated		20 Nov 43
West *front*		
Activated on basis of		
Western Special Military District		22 June 41
	D. G. Pavlov	June 41
	S. K. Timoshenko	July–Sept 41
	I. S. Konev	Sept–Oct 41
	G. K. Zhukov	Oct 41–Aug 42
	V. D. Sokolovsky	Feb 43–Apr 44
	I. D. Chernyakhovsky	Apr 44
Divided 24 April into:		
Second Belorussian *front*		
Using staff of former North-west *front*		
	I. Ye. Petrov	Apr–June 44
	G. F. Zakharov	June–Nov 44
	K. K. Rokossovsky	Nov 44–June 45
Reorganized as		
Headquarters Northern Forces		10 July 45
and		
Third Belorussian *front*		
Under the former West *front* Staff		
	I. D. Chernyakhovsky	Apr 44–Feb 45
	A. M. Vasilevsky	Feb–Apr 45
	I. Kh. Bagramyan	Apr–Aug 45
Staff withdrawn to reserve		15 Aug 45
South-west *front*		
Activated on basis of		
Kiev Special Military District		22 June 41
	M. P. Kirponos	June–Sept 41
	S. K. Timoshenko	Sept–Dec 41 and Apr–July 42
	F. Ya. Kostenko	Dec 41–Apr 42
Disbanded		July 42
Reconstituted		Oct 42
	N. F. Vatutin	Oct 42–Mar 43
	R. Ya. Malinovsky	Mar 43–Oct 43
Renamed 20 Oct 43:		
Third Ukrainian *front*		
	R. Ya. Malinovsky	Oct 43–May 44
	F. I. Tolbukhin	May 44–June 45
Reorganized as		
Headquarters, Southern Forces		June 45
South *front*		
Activated		25 June 41
	I. V. Tyulenev	June–Aug 41
	D. I. Ryabyshev	Aug–Oct 41
	Ya. T. Cherevichenko	Oct–Dec 41
	R. Ya. Malinovsky	Dec 41–July 42
Disbanded		28 July 42
Stalingrad *front*		
renamed South *front*		Jan 1943
before becoming		
Fourth Ukrainian *front*		October 1943
Reserve *front*		
Activated behind		
West *front*		30 July 42
	G. K. Zhukov	Aug–Sept 41
	S. M. Budenny	Sept–Oct 41
Terminated and merged into		
West *front*		10 Oct 41
Central *front*		
Activated		24 July 41
	F. I. Kuznetsov	July–Aug 41
	M. G. Efremov	Aug 41
Terminated (sector and		
troops transferred to		
Briansk *front*)		25 Aug 41
Reactivated from parts		
of Don *front*		
renamed Central *front* Feb 1943		
Briansk *front*		
Activated		16 Aug 41
	A. I. Yeremenko	Aug–Oct 41
	G. F. Zakharov	Oct–Nov 41
	K. K. Rokossovsky	July–Sept 42
	F. I. Golikov	Apr–July 42
	K. K. Rokossovsky	July–Sept 42
	M. A. Reiter	Sept 42–June 43
	M. M. Popov	June–Oct 43
Transferred four armies to Central *front* 10 Oct 43, and the HQ and two armies were shifted northward to become the basis for:		
Second Baltic *front*		
	M. M. Popov	Oct 43–Apr 44
	A. I. Eremenko	Apr 44–Feb 45
L. A. Govorov	Feb–Mar 45	

German–Soviet war (*cont.*)

Terminated and troops transferred to Leningrad *front*		1 Apr 45
Volkhov *front*		
Activated to take over Leningrad *front* left wing		17 Dec 41
	K. A. Meretskov	Dec 41–Apr 42
and	June 42–Feb 44	
Deactivated		Apr 42
Reactivated		June 42
Terminated and troops transferred to Leningrad *front*		15 Feb 44
Transcaucasus *front*		
Activated on basis of the Transcaucasus Military District		23 Aug 41
	D. T. Kozlov	Aug–Dec 41
Renamed 30 Dec 41:		
Caucasus *front*		
	D. T. Kozlov	Dec 41–Jan 42
Renamed:		28 Jan 42
Crimea *front*		
	D. T. Kozlov	Jan 42–May 42
	S. M. Budenny	May–Sept 42
Terminated 1 Sept 42 and merged into:		
North Caucasus *front*		
Activated		20 May 42
	S. M. Budenny	May–Sept 42
Terminated 1 Sept 42 and merged into:		
Transcaucasus *front*		
Reactivated on basis of the Transcaucasus Military District.		15 May 42
	I. V. Tyulenev	Sept 42–Aug 45
North Caucasus *front*		
Reactivated		24 Jan 43
	I. I. Maslennikov	Jan–May 43
	I. Ye. Petrov	May–Nov 43
Reorganized as the Independent Coastal Army		20 Nov 43
Kalinin *front*		
Activated		17 Oct 41
	I. S. Konev	Oct 41–Aug 42
	M. A. Purkayev	Aug 42–Apr 43
	A. I. Yeremenko	Apr–Oct 43
Renamed 20 Oct 43:		
First Baltic *front*		
	A. I. Yeremenko	Oct–Nov 43
	Kh. Bagramyan	Nov 43–Feb 45
Terminated and merged into Third Belorussian *front*		24 Feb 45
Voronezh *front*		
Activated to take over forces on left wing of Briansk *front*		7 July 42
	F. I. Golikov	July 42
	and	Oct 42–Mar 43
	N. F. Vatutin	July–Oct 43
	and	Mar–Oct 43
Renamed 20 Oct 43:		

First Ukrainian *front*		
	N. F. Vatutin	Oct 43–Mar 44
	G. K. Zhukov	Mar–May 44
	I. S. Konev	May 44–May 45
Reorganized as Headquarters, Central Forces		10 July 45
Stalingrad *front*		
Activated on basis of former South-west *front* staff		12 July 45
	S. K. Timoshenko	July 42
	V. N. Gordov	July–Sept 42
Divided 7 Aug 42, the left wing becoming:		
South-east *front*		
	A. I. Yeremenko	Aug–Sept 42
(In a renaming South-east *front* became Stalingrad *front* and Stalingrad *front* became Don *front*)		27 Sept 42
Stalingrad *front* (continued)		
	A. I. Yeremenko	Sept–Dec 42
Redeployed and renamed:		1 Jan 43
South *front*		
	A. I. Yeremenko	Jan–Feb 43
	R. Ya. Malinovsky	Feb–Mar 43
	F. I. Tolbukhin	Mar–Oct 43
Renamed 20 Oct 43:		
Fourth Ukrainian Front.		
	F. I. Tolbukhin	Oct 43–May 44
Disbanded and staff placed in reserve		16 May 44
Reactivated		6 Aug 44
	I. Ye. Petrov	Aug 44–Mar 45
	A. I. Yeremenko	Mar–July 45
Reorganized as Headquarters Carpathian Military District		10 July 45
Don *front* (Stalingrad *front* until 27 Sept. 42)		
After		27 Sept 42
	K. K. Rokossovsky	Sept 42–Feb 43
Staff and one army redeployed 15 Feb 43 to become basis of:		
Central *front*		
	K. K. Rokossovsky	Feb–Oct 43
Renamed 20 Oct 43:		
Belorussian *front*		
	K. K. Rokossovsky	Oct 43–Feb 44
Renamed 17 Feb 44:		
First Belorussian *front*		
	K. K. Rokossovsky	Feb–Nov 44
	G. K. Zhukov	Nov 44–June 45
Reorganized as Occupation Forces in Germany		10 June 45
Steppe *front*		
Activated on basis of the Steppe Military District in the Kursk area		10 July 43
I. S. Konev		Jul–Oct 43
Renamed 20 Oct 43:		

German–Soviet war *(cont.)*

Second Ukrainian *front*		
	I. S. Konev	Oct 43–May 44
	R. Ya. Malinovsky	May 44–June 45
Placed in reserve		10 July 45
Third Baltic *front*		
Activated to take over left wing of Leningrad *front*		21 Apr 44
	I. I. Maslennikov	Apr–Oct 44
Terminated. Troops shifted to Leningrad and other two Baltic *fronts*		16 Oct 44

Source: Contributor.

(now commanded by General Gotthard Heinrici) opposite Rokossovsky and Zhukov and Army Group Centre (A, renamed in January) on the Neisse and the Czechoslovak border. The German situation was better than it had been two months earlier, but Hitler no longer had the troops and *matériel* to achieve a solid build-up.

Nevertheless, the final blow proved unexpectedly difficult to deliver. After three days, Rokossovsky and Konev had to divert the better parts of their forces towards Berlin. As a result, the British and Americans were able to advance well to the east of the lower Elbe. Konev made contact with First US Army on 25 April at *Torgau on the Elbe, but did not reach Dresden until 8 May. To avoid capture, Hitler killed himself on 30 April and the surrender of its garrison on 2 May completed the fall of *Berlin.

Hitler had named Grand Admiral *Dönitz to succeed him as head of state and C-in-C of the armed forces. From his headquarters in Flensburg, on the Jutland peninsula, Dönitz sent representatives to Eisenhower's forward headquarters in Reims, where they signed an *unconditional surrender on all fronts at 0241 on 7 May. Stalin refused to accept the Reims surrender and demanded a second signing, which took place in Berlin shortly before midnight on 8 May.

The German troops still fighting in Courland and East Prussia surrendered on 8 May. Army Group Centre, however, was temporarily denied that privilege. Stalin had a bit of unfinished business, the 'liberation' of western Czechoslovakia, and he had awarded the honour of taking *Prague to Konev; but Konev could not get his tank armies redeployed from Berlin until 6 May. After a slow start on 7 May, in the next three days, First, Second, and Fourth Ukrainian *fronts*, with 1.7 million troops, plunged towards Prague, forcing Army Group Centre into a pocket east of the city, where it surrendered on 11 May. See also LAND POWER.

EARL ZIEMKE

Erickson, J., *The Road to Stalingrad* **(London, 1975)**

—— *The Road to Berlin* **(London, 1983)**

Minasyan, M. M. (ed.), *The Great Patriotic War of the Soviet Union* **(Moscow, 1974).**

Seaton, A., *The Russo-German War 1941–1945* **(New York, 1970).**

Ziemke, E. F., *Stalingrad to Berlin* **(Washington, DC, 1968).**

German surface raiders (see Map 42). Under the Anglo-German naval agreement of June 1935 the German naval C-in-C, Grand Admiral *Raeder, could have built up to a tonnage equalling 35% of British surface warship strength, which could have been achieved by 1940. But because Hitler assured him there would be no war before the mid-1940s, Raeder adopted a longer-term strategy which would have enabled him to outbuild the British fleet (see GERMANY, Table 11). Consequently, the German Navy, although modern and well equipped, was below the strength permitted by the 1935 agreement when war started.

Because of this disparity, Raeder's policy was to avoid confrontation. Instead he planned to attack British merchant shipping routes, not only with his three pocket battleships, which were designed for just this task, but with his other heavy surface units, too (see Table). By this means he hoped to disperse the Royal Navy's superior strength and, with the help of Dönitz's U-boat fleet and the German *auxiliary cruisers, cut the supply lines upon which the British depended to wage war effectively.

The campaign of the German surface raiders suffered an early blow when one of the pocket battleships was tracked down in December 1939 and forced to scuttle herself (see RIVER PLATE). But in November 1940 another pocket battleship, *Admiral Scheer*, successfully attacked an Atlantic convoy (see JERVIS BAY), and subsequently sank a number of ships in the North and South Atlantic, and in the Indian Ocean; and the heavy cruiser *Admiral Hipper*, after being driven off when she attacked a convoy on Christmas Day 1940, sank seven ships in an unescorted convoy during a second sortie in February 1941. Both warships were then able to return to port safely under cover of the raiding operations then being mounted by the two German battle-cruisers **Scharnhorst* and *Gneisenau*. These had already made several sorties (see RAWALPINDI, for example) without sinking any merchant ships, but from 23 January to 22 March 1941 they sank or captured 22 merchantmen totalling 115,622 tons and managed to dislocate completely the British convoy cycle before returning to port. This was the peak of the surface raiders' success. After the battleship **Bismarck* was sunk in May 1941 while trying to implement Raeder's strategy, Hitler ordered the other surface raiders to be concentrated in Norwegian waters (see CERBERUS) where their purpose was to threaten the *Arctic convoys and to guard the coastline against invasion. See also TIRPITZ.

German surface raiders

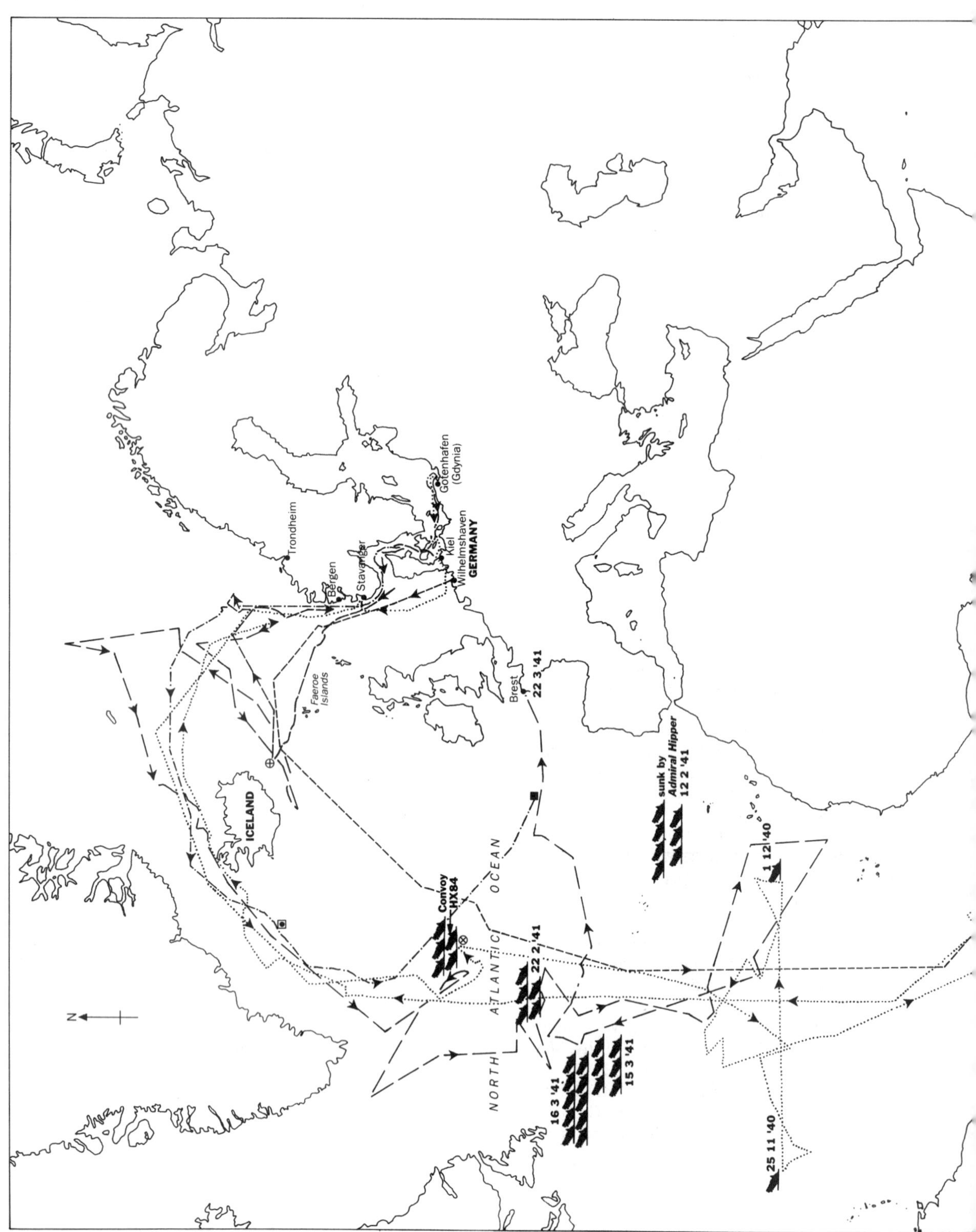

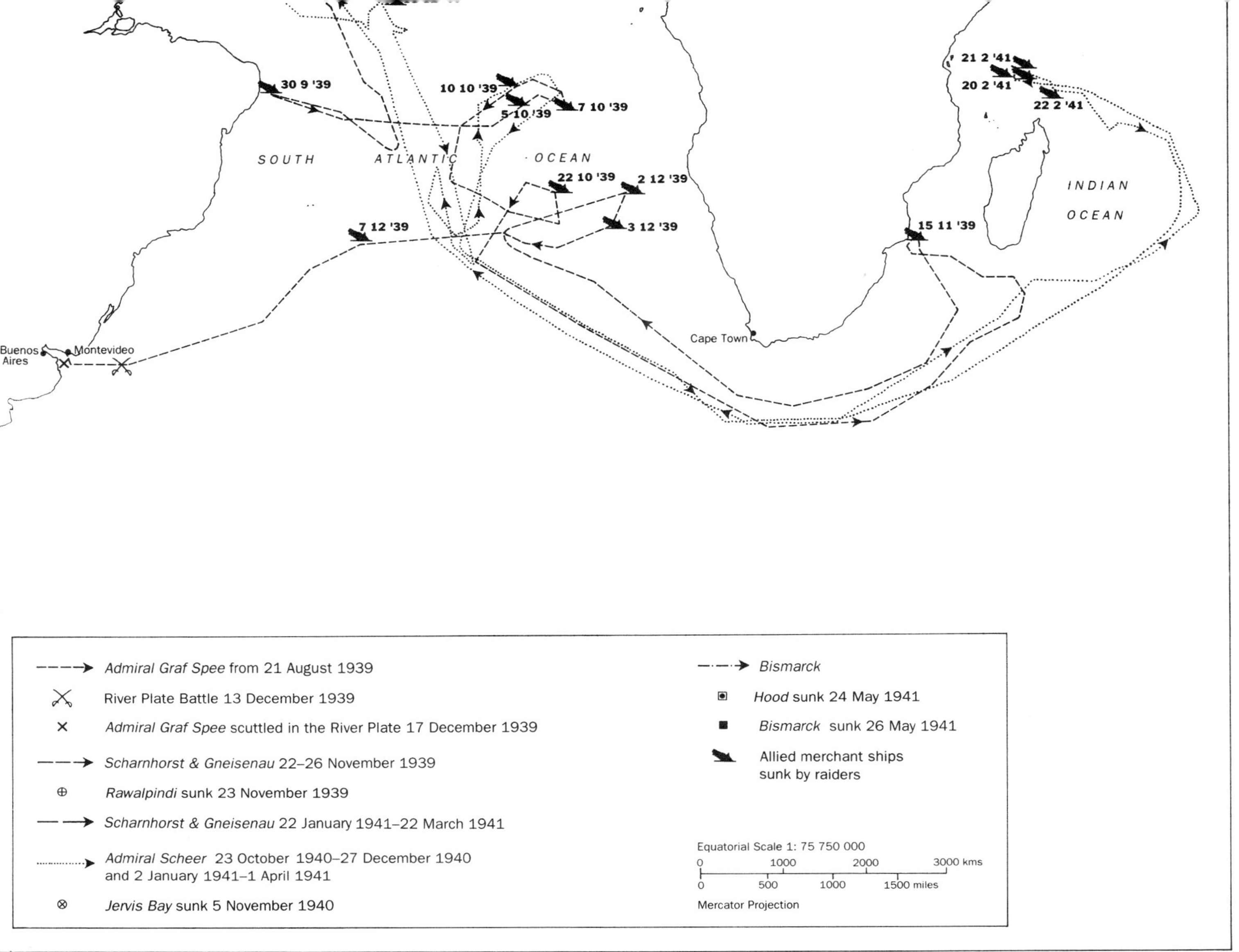

42. Operations of **German surface raiders**, 1939–41

German surface raiders

German surface raiders, 1939–41

Name	Description	Launched	Standard displacement tons	Armament excluding light A-A guns	Aircraft carried	Horsepower 000	Duration of sortie sailing/ termination date	Shipping sunk or captured No.	G.R. tons	Operating areas	Speed knots	Endurance nautical miles	Damage incurred in action, ultimate fate
Deutschland renamed *Lützow* 1940	Pocket battleship	May 1931	12,000	6 x 279 mm (11 in) 8 x 150 mm (5.9 in) 6 x 100 mm (4.1 in) HA 8 T. tubes	2	57	Aug 1939 15 Nov 1939	2	7,000	N.W. Atlantic	28	21,000	11.4.40 (torpedo), 13.6.41 (torpedo-bomber), 3.5.45 (bombs) and blown up in Swinemünde
Admiral Graf Spee	Pocket battleship	June 1934	12,000	6 x 279 mm 8 x 150 mm 6 x 100 mm HA 8 T. tubes	2	57	Aug 1939 17 Dec 1939	9	50,000	S. Atlantic and Indian Ocean	28	19,000	13.12.39 (gunfire), 17.12.39 blown up and sunk in the River Plate
Admiral Scheer	Pocket battleship	April 1933	12,000	6 x 279 mm 8 x 150 mm 6 x 100 mm 8 T. tubes	2	57	23 Oct 1940 1 April 1941	16	99,059	N. Atlantic, S. Atlantic and Indian Oceans	28	19,000	9.4.45 bombed and sunk in Kiel
Admiral Hipper	Heavy cruiser	Feb 1937	12,000	8 x 203 mm (8 in) 12 x 100 mm 12 T. tubes	3	132	30 Nov 1940 27 Dec 1940	1	6,078	N. Atlantic	32.5	6,000	8.4.40 damaged when rammed by *Glowworm*, 31.11.42 (gunfire), 3.5.45 bombed and sunk in Kiel
							1 Feb 1941 13 Feb 1941	7	34,000	West of Biscay			8.6.40 hit by torpedo, 24.7.41 by bomb, 12.2.42 by two mines, 26.12.43 sunk by guns and torpedoes in the Arctic
Scharnhorst *Gneisenau*	Battle cruisers	Dec 1936 Oct 1936	31,000	9 x 279 mm 12 x 150 mm 14 x 100 mm HA	4 (each)	165	23 Jan 1941 22 Mar 1941	22	115,622	N. and Central Atlantic	31.5	10,000	9.4.40 (gunfire), May 1940 (mine), 26.6.40 (torpedo), 6.4.41 (torpedo-bomber), 11.4.41 (bomb), 12.2.42 (mine), 26/27.2.42 (bomb), 1.7.42 paid off
Bismarck	Battleship	April 1939	42,000	8 x 381 mm (15 in) 12 x 150 mm 16 x 100 mm HA	4	138	21 May 1941 27 May 1941	0	0	N. Atlantic	30	8,100	27.5.41 sunk by guns and torpedo-bombers in the Atlantic
Prinz Eugen	Heavy cruiser	Aug 1937	14,600	8 x 203 mm 12 x 100 mm 12 T. tubes	3	132	21 May 1941 1 June 1941	0	0	N. Atlantic	32.5	6,000	23.4.41 (mine), 2.7.41 (bomb), 23.2.42 (torpedo), handed over to Allies and sunk after atomic tests

Sources: Roskill, S. W., *The War at Sea*, Vol. 1 (London, 1954) and Ruge, F., *Sea Warfare* (London, 1957).

GERMANY

For the fighting in Germany, see GERMANY, BATTLE FOR, which follows this entry.

1. Introduction

The academic debate about Germany's responsibility for the Second World War is altogether different from that on its contribution to the *First World War. Most historians accept that it was Hitler, the dominant figure in German politics between 1933 and 1945, who unleashed the war in Europe in September 1939. However, they have had a heated debate on his role within National Socialist Germany. Some historians have argued that he was 'master in the Third Reich', others have termed him 'a weak dictator'. To understand the course of development in the twelve years of the Third Reich it is necessary to look for a synthesis of Hitler's intentions and Germany's impersonal structures rather than to stress the contrast between them. Only when we give as much historical attention to the war years as to the period before 1939 can we arrive at an adequate explanation of Hitler's personal significance in the Third Reich. From 1938 the German state was nothing but the personal and absolute fiefdom of Hitler according to the 'leadership principle'. He occupied more than a mere functional role within a polycratic system of rule. As Führer, Hitler was Leader of the nation, the people, and the Nazi movement. In this capacity, he acted as chief executive, chief legislator, supreme judge, and supreme commander of the armed forces. Moreover, he was the self-proclaimed supreme ideological leader of the officer corps (10 February 1939) and commander-in-chief of the army (from 19 December 1941). The state was held together by Hitler's authority, and by the personal loyalty and ideological commitment of the leaders at the various levels below him. His charismatic leadership was strengthened by feuds among his followers which he could resolve as sole and final arbiter. Another necessary component was the 'Hitler Myth', the public image of his heroic and unerring leadership and the German people's acceptance of it. None the less, 'to designate Hitler as the central agent of a policy of destruction on a European scale is very far from absolving the German society of his time from its responsibility for that policy' (see Stern below, p. 17). The post-war tendency to separate the Führer from his followers and the Wehrmacht from its supreme commander does not help an understanding of the Third Reich at war.

Historians have long suggested that the causes of the rise of National Socialism were the refusal to accept the verdict of 1918, resentment against the terms of the *Versailles settlement (see Map A), the profound consequences of the economic crises, discontent with democracy and the Weimar Republic's policy of compromise with the victors, as well as German military traditions and the glorification of the First World War as a communal experience. These factors, together with revisionism and nationalism, anti-Bolshevism and *anti-Semitism, all had a socially unifying effect in Germany. To these explanations should be added the fact that the two armament programmes initiated in 1928 and 1932 by the Reichswehr (the German army and navy), with all that these implied, played into Hitler's hands and were major assets in his domestic and military policy of reorganizing German society for war. They were the nucleus of a future, much larger people's army based on compulsory conscription, thereby favouring an authoritarian leadership which could revitalize the military spirit of the population.

Hitler was a revolutionary and a racist. He saw history as an interracial struggle and believed that conflict 'in all its forms' was inevitable and the 'father of all things'. It determined the life of individuals and nations. He thought that races could be graded on a scale of merit and that the struggle for survival would be a permanent one until the 'more worthy' German people had proved their claim to world mastery. Peace was desirable only as an opportunity to prepare for war. In this ideological context, war took on a special meaning for Hitler. It was not only the 'highest expression of the life force' of a people, but also a legitimate and inevitable tool in the hands of German statesmen for acquiring sufficient *Lebensraum* (living space) by which the nation's future would be secured racially, economically, and militarily. War was not a moral issue but the physical means to a social end: the survival of the superior Germans. In this new kind of war there would be no distinction between the Home Front and the combat zone. The full force of the fighting German people would strike all national and racial enemies within and without the Reich. There would be no legal restraints.

Hitler's programme was no detailed blueprint for action, but *Lebensraum*, although an amalgam of various elements, did mean something concrete. It meant war, conquest, annihilation, and reshaping German and European society. It was not only anti-Semitism that directed Nazi genocide: the full range of racial victims—Jews, gypsies, blacks, Slavs, and the German mentally handicapped (see EUTHANASIA PROGRAMME)—must be acknowledged in order to see how the war, *Nazi ideology, genocide, and German social policy were interconnected. The war acted as a stimulant to the extension of racial policies, and the link between grand strategy and racial politics in the war policy of the Third Reich makes it impossible to separate the Wehrmacht from its political leadership.

As a social revolutionary, Hitler envisaged a biologically homogeneous German people led by a new civilian and military élite. The creation of a national and social *Volksgemeinschaft* (national community) out of a German society riven by divisions of class, religion, and ideology, was to be accomplished according to 'racial principles'. The new leadership cadres of the party and the armed forces would be created from the purest elements of the German race 'through a heroic selection process' which would evaluate their character and performance. The goal was to have soldierly leaders and political soldiers. This selection process would be accompanied by the ruthless elimination of all ideological and biological enemies and so-called 'asocials' in order to purify the *Volksgemeinschaft*, thus giving it a greater cohesion for war. The reorganization of the German people into a 'community of blood and destiny' would be supported by the infusion of a common 'world view' (*Weltanschauung*). Education was seen as an important means for instilling a new collective mentality. It was the task of the Nazi Party to educate the *Volksgenossen* (national comrades), young and old, to view war as normal, to secure their loyalty to the fatherland and their willingness to fight for its honour. During their military service they would be further instructed by 'the great educational institution of the nation', the Wehrmacht. There was no individual right to liberty or the pursuit of happiness: 'Public need comes before private greed'. Yet the concept of a *Volksgemeinschaft*, a truly integrated society without social barriers, even at the price of freedom, became a force for social integration. It gave many Germans a sense of purpose and national pride. The Weimar Republic had failed to satisfy a psychological need for solidarity, idealism, and self-sacrifice in Germany. This new element in National Socialism bound many people to the Führer.

Today we have immense difficulties in coming to terms with the revolutionary process which Hitler set in train in Germany. It is uncomfortable to discover anything at all positive in him. Yet his egalitarian drive, which undoubtedly created favourable conditions for social mobility and advancement through merit and achievement, appealed to hundreds of thousands of Germans. The war accelerated this process. For example, the army not only commissioned officers from the ranks, but in November 1942 eradicated all formal educational barriers for officer candidates. The fullest consequences of Hitler's social revolution became manifest after the war in the Federal Republic, which speedily developed into one of the most egalitarian and forward-looking states in Europe.

In the years before 1939 no one talked more about peace than Hitler himself. This was necessary in order to conceal from the public and the world the comprehensive programme of educational and military remilitarization which was the foundation for a long-range policy of aggression. When Hitler decided, on 5 November 1937, to achieve his goal of expansion by force in a shorter period and learned that there was a widespread fear of war among the German population, he ordered the propaganda apparatus to turn off the 'pacifist record' and prepare the nation psychologically for war. The blame for what was to come was to be placed on other countries. However, there was no great enthusiasm for war among ordinary German people. When Hitler declared that 'we have been returning fire at the Poles since 5.45 a.m.', the Germans reacted with sober realism and 'reluctant loyalty'. Even *Goebbels's formidable propaganda effort could not make the Germans like war, although the armed forces' successes eased his task. Moreover, in counteracting complaints between 1939 and 1944, he could rely on the information the *SS secretly collected about the mood and attitude of the German population in the so-called 'Reports from the Reich'. The dazzling victory over France in 1940 had profound effects on Germany. The Führer reached the height of his popularity, and the war almost became a patriotic crusade. Hitler and the Germans, in and out of uniform, formed a bond which was stronger than ever. Even a fervent anti-Nazi like Ulrich von Hassell was carried away by the fall of *France. The encirclement of the Sixth Army at *Stalingrad (1942–3) was to become the turning-point of public morale—the news of its destruction was a shock—yet Goebbels kept spirits up on the Home Front by creating a mood of endurance among the German population. He used the mass bombing (see STRATEGIC AIR OFFENSIVES, 1) and the demand for *unconditional surrender to stir up hatred against the Allies and stiffen morale, although, they also made the German people think that defeat might be on the way. Still, as a consequence of the attempt on Hitler's life on 20 July 1944 (see SCHWARZE KAPELLE), there was a short-lived upsurge of support with proclamations of loyalty. When, in the last year of the war, endurance changed to apathy, personal survival became more important than the national interest. Yet there was no mass resistance or sabotage. Terror and patriotic tenacity cannot be the only explanations for this phenomenon. There was also a consciousness of responsibility for the brutal force Germany had used in Europe and for the Nazi crimes.

2. Domestic life, war effort, and economy

On the eve of war, Germany covered an area of 586,238 sq. km. (226,288 sq. mi.) and had a population of 79.5 million (see Map C). By the summer of 1941, the Greater German Reich—which had come into being by formal

Germany, Table 1: Reich's (pre-war territory) labour force, 1939–44 (figure for 31 May each year in millions)

	1939	*1940*	*1941*	*1942*	*1943*	*1944*
Agriculture	11.2	10.7	10.7	11.2	11.3	11.2
Industry & Transport	18.6	16.4	16.8	15.9	16.9	16.2
Commerce	4.6	4.0	3.6	3.2	3.1	2.9
Administration	2.7	2.5	2.5	2.6	2.4	2.3
Military Administrtion	0.7	0.9	1.7	1.1	1.4	1.4
Domestic workers	1.6	1.5	1.5	1.5	1.4	1.4
TOTAL	39.4	36.0	36.2	35.5	36.5	35.4

Source: Contributor/Overy.

annexation (of Danzig, large slices of Poland, and small ones of Belgium), by extension of German civilian administration (over Alsace and Lorraine, Luxemburg, Białystok, and parts of Northern Slovenia), together with the Protectorate of Bohemia and Moravia (see CZECHOSLOVAKIA) and the General government of Poland (see POLAND, 2(b))—covered an area of 891.403 sq. km. (344,080 sq. mi.) with a population of some 116 million.

At the outbreak of the war, Germany's workforce (see Table 1) encompassed 39.1 million Germans (24.5 million men and 14.6 million women) plus 300,000 foreign workers. Unemployment was virtually non-existent, having fallen to only 63,000. The armed forces had mobilized some 4.528 million men. The exempted personnel amounted to 1.87 million (9 December 1939). There was no fresh recruitment of women into the factories. On the contrary, the Nazis resisted for ideological reasons the armed forces' demand for compulsory work service for women and they paid married soldiers generous allowances. After the outbreak of war, many female industrial workers married and stayed at home. Thus in May 1941, there were almost 440,000 fewer women in the workforce than in May 1939 (see Table 2). By the end of 1939 the armed SS stood at 277,000 men, including the various police branches with reinforcements, the *Death's Head units with replacements, and the 23,000 in the militarized formations such as the Waffen-SS. Together with an additional 300,000 men who were with various unarmed supporting services like the air defence, about 6 million men were mobilized for the internal and external security of the Third Reich in 1939.

Germany, Table 2: German women (pre-war territory) in the native German workforce, 1939–44 (%) (figure for 31 May each year)

1939	37.4	37.1
1940	41.2	39.9
1941	42.4	38.9
1942	45.9	40.6
1943	48.6	40.4
1944	50.7	40.6

Source: Contributor/Overy.

Historians of Nazi Germany have only recently shifted their focus from Hitler and Nazi politics and turned their attention to the German people and to social questions. From 28 February 1933, the day after the Reichstag was destroyed by fire, everyday life in Germany was shaped by a perpetual state of emergency and by a dictatorial regime that (after 1 September 1939) murdered millions of its racial and ideological enemies. Yet human beings are bundles of paradoxes. Thus reminiscences by steel workers in the Ruhr reveal that 'the image of National Socialism was characterized principally not by terror, mass murder and war but by reduction of unemployment, economic boom, tranquility and order.' (R. Bessel (ed.), *Life in the Third Reich*, Oxford, 1987, p. 97). This evidence points to the fact that day-to-day reality itself was a contradiction and paradox. Just as the regime was populist and authoritarian, opportunistic and ideological, persuasive and propagandistic, the German people saw the coexistence of participation and opposition, servility and heroism in its own society. Never quite certain of the cohesion of the *Volksgemeinschaft* they had proclaimed, the Nazis relied on a carrot-and-stick approach, combining bribes and threats, savage penalties and calls for decency, to keep German society in its grip. Yet the grip was never complete. The *Gestapo which kept a watchful eye over the Germans and the foreign workers, was a small secret police force largely of career policemen (32,000 full-time employees in 1944) with relatively few fanatical Nazis. With the aid of denunciations, the Gestapo could effectively police the Third Reich, their measures ranging from intimidation, preventive detention, and 'protective custody' in *concentration camps to summary execution.

Hitler charged the SS with safeguarding the state 'by every means'. The SS was the executive within the Nazi Party and it ruled Germany after September 1939 when it completed the amalgation of all the state's various branches of the police with its own police and intelligence units into one single organization. With it, the *RSHA (Reichssicherheitshauptamt or Reich Security Main Office), and his personal deputies in the military districts, the Higher SS and police leaders, *Himmler established for himself a monopoly over internal security. He considered the Home Front as a theatre of war and was not prepared to share his power with the judiciary or have his executive power checked by judges. A violent policy of repression was only part of the motivation behind the principles of state security. As with the mass killings (some 70,000 until August 1941) of those Germans 'unworthy of life' (see EUTHANASIA PROGRAMME), organized by Philipp Bouhler, chief of the party's leader chancellery, and Dr Karl Brandt, Hitler's *Begleitarzt* (personal surgeon), the SS used the war as an opportunity to take new and radical steps to purge Germany of social outcasts as well as of its political and biological enemies. Thus, the Gestapo considerably intensified its arrests of political opponents before the operations against France and the USSR.

The Nazis considered the Jews their foremost enemies and persecuted them from 1933 (see FINAL SOLUTION). They took new discriminatory measures against the German Jews after the outbreak of war, when many Polish Jews had already been killed or herded into *ghettos. The first deportation of German Jews occurred in October 1940 (to Gurs in southern France), six months after gypsies had been deported into occupied Poland. On 1 September 1941, Jews in the Reich were forced to wear a yellow badge sewn to their clothing and one month later the transports began to roll to Łódź, Kovno, and Riga from such big cities as Berlin, Breslau, Cologne, Frankfurt, Prague, and Vienna. Tens of thousands were murdered soon after their arrival. In early December 1941 the death camp at *Chelmno opened, by which time at least 900 Soviet prisoners of war had already been killed at *Auschwitz with *Zyklon-B gas. This was the final step in the systematic annihilation of the Nazis' racial enemies, Jews, gypsies, Slavs, and the mentally handicapped, in Germany and occupied Europe.

Gleichschaltung (regimentation and conformity) was progressively applied to every aspect of life in Germany. From 1933 onwards, the Nazis converted the federal Weimar Republic into a unitary state, smashing all independent parties, agencies, or organizations, and tying all groups and interests to their party. They also purged and organized German society hierarchically according to the racial and leadership principle. They demanded involvement in one or more of the innumerable organizations run by or affiliated with the party. Despite the irritations of this pressure towards uniformity and conformity, the constant drill and coercion, these activities created group comradeship, leisure activities, and mobility which brought a certain liberation from the traditional family and church authority and the confines of village or town life. Membership of the German Labour Front (DAF), headed by *Ley, was compulsory for all employers, craftsmen, and workers. By 1942, it had about 25 million members and was run by 40,000 functionaries. The various branches of the agricultural economy, and the co-operatives,

Germany, Table 3: Government expenditure (bn RM)

	military	*civil*
1939–40	38.0	20.0
1940–1	55.9	24.1
1941–2	73.3	28.2
1942–3	86.2	37.8
1943–4	99.4	30.6

Source: Contributor/Overy.

producers, and distributors, were organized through mandatory membership in the Reich Foodstuffs Corporation with about 15 million members by the end of 1939. Membership in the Deutsches Jungvolk (ages 10 to 14 years) and in the *Hitler Youth proper (ages 14 to 18) was compulsory for boys, while young girls were compulsory members in the Jungmädelbund (ages 10 to 14) and Bund Deutscher Mädel (BDM, ages 15 to 18). The armed forces wanted to use the German youth between 14 and 18, an estimated 2.7 million male and 2.6 million female youngsters, for auxiliary military service, but this demand was rejected by the Nazis for ideological reasons and fear of unrest. However, young men between 18 and 25 were obliged to spend six months in the Reich Labour Service (RAD) the mass of which came under Wehrmacht jurisdiction on the eve of the war. Labour service was followed by military conscription. There was voluntary labour service for young women between 18 and 25. The service period for these 'work maidens' lasted 26 weeks as a rule, and at most 50,000 could participate in the programmes. The Nazi Party itself had had some 850,000 members in January 1933. By September 1939 this had increased to more than 4 million members with 150,000 officials and by January 1943 the party numbered 6.5 million.

'German history will never see a repetition of November 1918', Hitler declared on 1 September 1939. This remark was aimed at both the conduct of war and domestic policies. This time there would be neither capitulation nor revolution. The trauma of 1918 was the experience that formed the Nazi leadership's thought and action in the domestic sphere. Their fear of unrest kept the sacrifices which Hitler had demanded from the Germans in his address at the beginning of the war to a minimum. On the material side, the Nazis faced a challenge on the Home Front which included management of the economy, allocation of manpower, and provision of food, adequate working conditions, and fair wages. On the spiritual side, it involved justifying the war morally, making the people believe that their sacrifices were necessary, and assuring them that their hardships were equitably shared.

German industry was subordinate to the requirements of the Nazis. Political conformity and economic efficiency were its primary motives. Rearmament and

Germany, Table 4: Military output

	1939	1940	1941	1942	1943	1944	1945
Aircraft	8,295	10,247	11,776	15,409	24,807	39,807	7,540
Aero-engines	3,865	15,510	22,400	37,000	50,700	54,600	–
Tanks		2,200	5,200	9,300	19,800	27,300	–
Munitions (000 t)		865	540	1,270	2,558	3,350	–
Automatic weapons (000s)		171	325	317	435	787	–
Heavy artillery and anti-aircraft guns (000s)		6	30	69	157	361	–

Source: Contributor/Overy.

autarchy had been the goals since 1933 and were merely accelerated from 1936. Germany did not have a defined overall *blitzkrieg strategy in 1939, so there was no such thing as a 'blitzkrieg economy'. As far as armaments were concerned, the war in Europe began three to four years prematurely for the armed services. Hitler mobilized both sectors of the German economy, the armament factories and the civilian industries, after 3 September 1939 (see Tables 3, 4, and 5 for government expenditure, and military and industrial output). Yet there was no total economic mobilization to counter the probability of attrition in a long war. The peacetime war economy (from August 1936) was followed—though some historians disagree—by a peace-like wartime economy. By and large, business as usual prevailed. Only in mid-1944 did the government introduce a series of prepared measures that covered food rationing, the freezing of prices and wages, and the regulation of working conditions. Since Germany had already accumulated stocks of *raw materials and had adequate food supplies, and necessary commodities could, until 22 June 1941, be imported from the USSR, the first years of war scarcely affected the standard of living (see Table 6 for consumption per capita). The regime met civilian demands by producing consumer goods and by keeping the individual food rations substantially higher than in the First World War. In the spring of 1942 the food rations had to be reduced (see Table 7). At the same time the British began their mass bombings of such cities as Lübeck, Rostock, Bremen, Düsseldorf, Cologne, and Essen, the last two with *thousand-bomber raids. Together with the failure of the assault against the USSR (see BARBAROSSA) and the entry of the USA into the war, the mass bombings demonstrated to the Germans that the blitzkrieg era was over. Germany was now forced to fight the industrial, total war which Hitler, the Nazis, and the military had long sought to avoid. Reluctantly they began to mobilize Germany for this new type of war, economically, militarily, and psychologically.

For a long time Germany did not possess a single central administrative authority for its war effort. The Council of Ministers for Reich Defence under *Göring, which had been formed on 30 August 1939, could have played a useful role in co-ordinating civilian, industrial, and military requirements, but it had disbanded after six meetings as Göring had not wanted to come into conflict with Hitler's political prerogatives. Later, Fritz Todt (see TODT ORGANIZATION), when minister of armaments and munitions, tried to initiate a reorientation of the German war effort and its administration, but it was his successor Albert *Speer who, from 1942 to 1944, took complete control over the whole war economy with Hitler's backing. Before then, four separate military agencies and after March 1940, the ministry of armaments and munitions had borne responsibility for the equipment of the armed forces. Only Hitler's top priority directives had set levels of arms production or mediated the competing demands of labour allocation and military replacement. Speer established a central planning board and a system of 'organized improvisation' to mobilize the economy for total war (see SPEER PLAN). Through the better management of this board, together with the massive closing down of small firms and the redistribution of skilled labour, there was a better use of

Germany, Table 5: Industrial output

	1939	1940	1941	1942	1943	1944
Steel (m t)	23.7	21.5	31.8	32.1	34.6	28.5
Coal (m t)	204.8	247.9	248.3	264.2	268.9	249.0
Lignite (m t)	211.6	226.8	235.1	248.9	252.5	260.8
Synthetic oil (m t)	2.2	3.3	4.1	4.9	5.7	3.8
Synthetic rubber (000 t)	22	40	69	98	117	104
Aluminium (000 t)	199.4	211.2	233.6	263.9	250.0	245.3

Source: Contributor/Overy.

Germany, Table 6: Consumption in Germany per capita, 1939–44 (1938 = 100)

1939	95.0
1940	88.4
1941	81.9
1942	75.3
1943	75.3
1944	70.0

Source: Contributor/Overy.

resources and a higher output in armaments. Yet the so-called Speer miracle, which was able to answer the Allied bombing offensive with a considerable increase of Germany's war production in 1943 and 1944, was not realizable without the ruthless exploitation of human and material resources from occupied Europe.

Another reaction to the failure of blitzkrieg was the centralization of labour management in March 1942, with *Sauckel as plenipotentiary. He found a decisive answer to German manpower problems resulting from the high personnel casualties on the Eastern Front (see GERMAN–SOVIET WAR). He met German labour shortages by increasing the use of *prisoners-of-war and *forced labour, especially from the western parts of the USSR. This influx of foreign workers replaced Germans who were being called up for military service at the front and reduced the demand on German women workers. As a result of the various so-called Sauckel actions and other measures after January 1943, both the distribution of German manpower between the armed forces and the war economy and the composition of the workforce in May 1944 show a different picture from that at the beginning of the war. The 1944 workforce totalled 28.6 million Germans: 14.1 million men (including 6.2 million exempted personnel) and 14.5 million women, and 7.1 million foreign workers (5.3 million forced labour and 1.8 million prisoners-of-war), a figure which, by August 1944 had reached 7.8 million. The armed forces comprised 10.6 million men, while in June 1944 the Waffen-SS stood at 594,443 men (including many foreigners; see SS, table of SS divisions). The high number of 6.2 million exempted Germans in the war economy points to the fact that foreign labour was no substitute for skilled German labour. Yet together with ideological taboos on the part of the Nazis, the exploitation of foreign labour helped to compensate for the lack of male German labour without substantially raising the number of German female workers. Another source of industrial labour in 1944, especially in the underground factories for aircraft production, was the *concentration camp inmates. Their number rose tenfold during that year, from 30,000 to over 300,000. Bringing forced labour within his administrative control had been the reason which Himmler used in March 1942 to place the concentration camps under the newly formed central office of the SS in all economic and administrative matters, headed by SS-Obergruppenführer (lt-general) Oswald Pohl.

The conditions for the millions of foreign workers in Nazi Germany were by no means identical. They varied not only according to the workers' skills, but above all according to their racial rating. *Ostarbeiter* (eastern workers) were the worst treated, Russians even worse than Poles, because they were considered racially inferior to the Danes or French. Even if they were not worked to death like the concentration camp inmates, their physical health was ruined. Almost without exception, Germans became foremen or warders over foreign workers in those sectors of the war industry that still relied mainly on manual skills and where the quota of foreign workers amounted to over 70%. The Nazis' ruthless exploitation of the human and material resources in occupied Europe enabled them to raise the food rations for the German people. By the end of 1943, nutrition was nearly the same as in 1939.

The summer of 1944 marked an important turning-point in Germany's war effort. The catalyst for this change was the abortive plot against Hitler's life on 20 July, following which, Hitler ordered full mobilization for total war and appointed Goebbels as his plenipotentiary. This appointment paralleled Himmler's taking over of the Replacement Army (see 6(b), below) and the reform of the armed forces' structure. At the same time, the SS and the judiciary increased their brutal grip on the German population. These and other measures ensured that the Germans went on fighting. The high level of endurance and sacrifice also had a reverse side. They increased the attrition rate and guaranteed that the final defeat of National Socialist Germany would be more terrible.

3. Government and legal system

Germany had already become a centralized state ruled by one party before 1939, and parliamentary democracy and political parties had long been overturned. The general process of *Gleichschaltung* (forcing people to conform) concentrated the effective political and military power in the hands of Hitler to a degree unknown in Germany since the days of Frederick the Great. There were no checks and balances to Hitler's dictatorship: 'The will of the Führer is law.' It is not easy to bring light into the jungle of authorities and functions which grew and changed under the impact of war and the dynamism of the Nazi movement. There was a deliberate contra- and juxtaposition of state and party institutions with overlapping functions, while at the same time, special political agencies often hampered the unity of executive measures. This form of Nazi rule has been described as 'organized chaos'. Yet the combination of state and party functions in a personal union favoured both the party's increasing power over the machinery of the state and Hitler's dictatorship. Recent historical scholarship on the period reveals that the outbreak of war represented a watershed in Nazi ideological policies. It speeded up the final transformation of a constitutional state, based on the rule of law, into a police state, with oppression the only means of ruling. The war helped to alter the dualism of state and party in favour of the latter.

Nazi Germany was a unitary state but its national and local administration was a maze. Hitler had no interest at all in establishing a firm governmental system: since life was a permanent struggle for survival between races, nations, and individuals, institutions should not remain static but fluid. The dynamic process within the Third Reich was determined by three principles: leadership, loyalty, and character. In its racial conflict, Germany was to be led, not administered. So it was not surprising that behind the monolithic façade of the Reich, relations between party and state as well as within each body were in fact fierce power-struggles. The actual power of key individuals varied according to their personal drive, ability, and relationship to Hitler. There were old comrades like Ley and Wilhelm Kube, and new managers like *Bormann, *Heydrich, Todt, and Speer who combined ideological conviction and enthusiasm with competence. The leadership principle was hostile to a government which governed by talking and working together, hostile to co-ordination and shared responsibility. Since there were no such bodies as a war cabinet or joint chiefs of staff, or a committee system, it was only in Hitler's hands that the threads came together.

He was in a unique position, commanding the machinery of party and state by both claiming personal allegiance and espousing hierarchy as the source of order and compliance. The institutional character of the Reich was thus transformed into a kind of feudalism. What mattered to Hitler, whether acting as party leader, or Reich Chancellor, or Supreme Commander, was the obedience of his lieutenants and the compliance of his followers. He was in full command of the Third Reich, especially its conduct of war, moving his seat of government between Berlin, *Berchtesgaden, and his various military headquarters, including the WOLF'S LAIR at Rastenburg in East Prussia and WEREWOLF near Vinnitsa in the western Ukraine.

Hitler was served by five different chancelleries or secretariats, the principal ones being those for administration under Hans-Heinrich Lammers, for the party under Bormann (from 1941), and for military affairs under *Keitel. These offices were not concerned with policy-making, but operated under Hitler's direct authority drafting laws, decrees, directives. Yet all the regional party leaders, the **Gauleiter*, and the commanders-in-chief of the three armed services had direct access to him. Another way Hitler imposed his authority was to give orders to the principal lieutenants for inner security and racial matters (Himmler), propaganda (Goebbels), foreign affairs (*Ribbentrop), and economy (Göring, later Todt and Speer). They in turn ruled via their staffs and lieutenants. This becomes especially visible in the way Himmler fulfilled some of his various functions. His direct deputies within the Reich and the occupied territories were the higher SS and police leaders, while at the same time he had an effective staff for security matters under Heydrich and later *Kaltenbrunner or able lieutenants like Hans Jüttner for the Waffen-SS.

Yet another way Hitler ruled was via special agencies or envoys for various tasks, which Hitler established either by intention or of necessity. The nomenclature varied between Plenipotentiary, Reich Commissioner, and Inspector-General. To name only a few, there were those for administration, economy, housing, labour, racial matters, total war, and water and energy. The increasing accumulation of state and party offices by a few persons helped to erode the dualism of state and party and effectively furthered personal decisions over the different steps of administration. To demonstrate this peculiar feature of Nazi Germany, it is not enough to

Germany, Table 7: German food rations 1939–45, for one adult (weekly ration, in grams)

A. Bread	
Sept 1939	free
Jul 1940	2,400
Apr 1942	2,000
Oct 1942	2,125
May 1943	2,412
Sept 1943	2,475
Oct 1944	2,525
Feb 1945	2,225
Mar 1945	2,225
Apr 1945	900
B. Meat	
Sept 1939	550
June 1941	400
Apr 1942	300
Oct 1942	356
May 1943	437
Jan 1944	362
Mar 1944	362
Feb 1945	156
Apr 1945	137
C. Fats	
Sept 1939	310
Jun 1941	269
Apr 1942	206
May 1943	215
Jan 1944	218
Mar 1944	218
Jan 1945	156
Feb 1945	156
Mar 1945	190
Apr 1945	75

Source: Contributor/Overy.

point to Hitler's various powers. Goebbels, for example, was a regional party leader and a Reich defence commissioner, he was in charge of the party's and state propaganda, steered the Reich's cultural affairs, and became Plenipotentiary of Total War. Himmler was not only the supreme leader and judge of all the various SS branches, but also became Reich Commissioner for the Strengthening of German Nationhood (i.e. for racial matters) in October 1939 and Reich Minister of the Interior in August 1943. He could thus successfully combine the security of Germany, within and without, with racial goals. In 1944–5, Himmler seized military power, when he became commander-in-chief of the **Volksgrenadier* and commander of the Replacement Army. He was also made responsible for the Wehrmacht's reorganization and for the military command of the Volkssturm (see 5 below). He even twice took command of an army group in the field.

The regional structure of the Greater German Reich in 1941 comprised 42 *Gaue* party districts (see Map 43), but 39 state components (*Reichsgaue, Länder,* and Prussian provinces) and 18 military districts, including the Protectorate of Bohemia and Moravia. Demands from the interior ministry for a unified administration were never met because Hitler deliberately wanted to postpone the structural reform of the Reich until Europe's final racial reorganization. On the regional level, there was an institutional linkage between party and state functions. On 1 September 1939 fourteen *Gauleiter* were appointed as Reich defence commissioners, and two more after the defeat of Poland. They were made responsible for a uniform handling of all defence matters in their respective districts and the commanders of the corresponding military districts were stripped of their powers. This decision had formidable consequences for civil—military as well as party—state relations within the Third Reich. In matters of dispute it was the party that finally decided what belonged to Reich defence and what did not. These *Gauleiter* established defence committees to advise them on such issues. While the High Command (OKW) failed to get its armaments inspectors on this body, Himmler's deputies in the military districts (the higher SS and police leaders) were present. On 16 November 1942, all 42 *Gauleiter* were elevated to Reich defence commissioners. Thus they combined state powers with party loyalties which became particularly important in July and September 1944, when the Allies were approaching Germany proper and Hitler had to decide who was to be in command in a particular zone of operations. At that time, the army commander's authority was reduced to the immediate combat zone while the executive power within the main and rear area rested with the chosen Reich defence commissioner guided by Himmler. In this way, the party controlled the army.

In 1940, there were 2,199 law courts under 198 higher courts (*Oberlandesgerichte*). In addition, there were the supreme civil (*Reichsgericht*) and military courts (*Reichskriegsgericht*), 55 so-called Special Courts and the *People's Court (for civil, military, and political crimes). The legal system in the Third Reich was a contradiction of the rule of law. The judiciary's function of controlling the activities of the police was turned on its head by Hitler giving Himmler unlimited powers for state security. Justice was no longer able or willing to guarantee life and freedom to the individual. The judiciary, like the police, was part of the public security organization, an instrument of Hitler's will to discipline and purge society. As the police authority was deliberately not put under the control of law, it could prosecute and pass verdicts. The resulting lawlessness of the police (which even Hans *Frank complained about in August 1942), was by no means unprincipled. Since racism was the fundamental tenet of the Nazi revolution, the highest legal maxim was the life of the nation. The 'spirit of National Socialist law' is best revealed by the concept of the 'sound feeling of the people' and by the instruction of 1936 to interpret the laws on the basis of Nazi *Weltanschauung*.

In both substance and procedure, the Nazis tightened up the law generally and the criminal law in particular. After the outbreak of war, the government issued a series of decrees and principles to ensure the security of the Reich, its people, and its war effort. These included regulations against listening to foreign radio stations and spreading information obtained from them, against violation of the food rationing and consumption restrictions, against criminal offences committed under cover of the wartime *blackout, and against critical remarks about the progress of war. Many more offences became punishable by the death penalty than before September 1939. *Freisler, later president of the People's Court, considered himself one of Hitler's political soldiers and spoke of the Special Courts as 'the tank arm of the legal system' (24 October 1939) or on 21 February 1940 as the 'courts-martial of the home front'. From 1941, the judiciary began to receive political directives from its ministry, and on 1 October 1942, Minister Otto-Georg Thierack began to offer 'guidance' with his infamous 'Letters to the Judges' (*Richterbriefe*). Many judges shared his belief that there was a deterrent value in draconian verdicts; many were motivated by political considerations and applied harsh penalties because of the offender's antisocial attitude rather than because of the actual offence, although not all judges easily condemned men and women to the block and the gallows. From the summer of 1944, when Germany was being fully mobilized for total war, the judiciary had to support this goal, although many responsibilities had already been given to the police. Almost 198,000 men and women were in prison on 9 December 1944, including 15,774 Poles in detention camps. Although the statistics of the criminal courts are incomplete, almost 15,500 death sentences were passed between 1933 and 1944, of which over three-quarters were carried out.

For the first time since the First World War, a system of military law was established for the armed forces

43. *Gaue* of the Greater **German** Reich, 1942

in January 1934. They were given back the traditional right to try their own offenders and award their own punishments for crimes against both the military and the civil code. The task of military justice was to maintain the discipline of the troops and thereby their fighting power. It had been common among soldiers, former military lawyers, and Nazis to view the system of military justice in the First World War as a weak instrument for keeping up morale. The procedures had taken far too long and too few death sentences had been passed and executed. The Nazis intended military law to be adapted to their political aims, fitted into the requirements of a *Volksgemeinschaft* fighting for its survival and executed 'in the Name of the German People'. A soldier's personal guilt in violating a rule or an order was important, but his offence or crime was also to be seen as damaging the people.

In preparation for the coming war, a new anti-sedition decree was issued in 1938. It contained the infamous offence of *Wehrkraftzersetzung* (subversion of the war effort) and specified the death penalty for persons who attempted to persuade military personnel to refuse to obey orders or anyone who tried to undermine the war effort. This *Verordnung gegen Volksschädlinge* (Decree against Enemies of the People), which was issued by the Council of Ministers for Reich Defence on 5 September 1939 served the same purpose on the civilian side. Military courts also linked *deserters to *Wehrkraftzersetzung* and saw them as offending against the people and its leader. Courts martial were composed of one professional judge and two soldiers of equivalent rank to the accused. The decision to confirm or annul a sentence passed by a court martial rested with the army commanders, the service chiefs, or with Hitler as the supreme commander. During the trial the judges were free from any directives by military commanders, but their function was disciplinary rather than judicial. Maintaining military discipline at all costs increased in urgency as the war progressed, with deserters deemed to be undermining the war effort and offending both the people and their leader. In 1943, there were more than 1,000 military courts and more than 3,000 military lawyers. Wehrmacht statistics reveal that 9,732 persons were executed up to the end of 1944. Yet military courts worked up to May 1945, especially the newly established mobile *Fliegendes Standgericht* ('flying courts-martial'). A total figure of at least 21,000 executions has been estimated.

On 17 October 1939, the SS could introduce its own penal code as a form of military justice, applying it at first only to its own armed formations, the Waffen-SS and the police units in the field. By the summer of 1942, all the police branches and foreign auxiliary units, roughly 636,000 men, had been brought under this penal code. Himmler, the supreme judge after Hitler, ordered that 'none of the legal profession should ever become chief of an SS-court' (26 August 1942) and 'lively personalities' were preferred. At the end of 1943 there were 31 permanent courts and 20 in the field, with a total of 204 judges. Between 1939 and 1944, SS courts executed 1,001 men.

4. New Order

Germany dominated great parts of Europe between 1939 and 1945. How far was its rule also purposeful? Hitler had a Grand Design, but it was more of a vision than a plan. Although he was motivated by the urge to acquire *Lebensraum* for the German people and establish a new European order on a racial basis, Hitler was pragmatic. He was more interested in winning the war and exploiting the conquered territories than in establishing a New Order in Europe prematurely and thereby arousing resistance among the occupied or dependent countries unnecessarily. As Goebbels put it on 26 October 1940: 'If anyone asks me what do you really want, I cannot give him an answer. That depends on the circumstances. It depends on how much we want and how much we can get. We want living space. Yes, but what does that mean? We will provide a definition after the war . . . When this war is over we want to be masters in Europe.'

Hitler summed up his imperialistic and racial objectives in the euphoria of global triumph during the summer of 1941. During a five-hour meeting on 16 July, he told Bormann, Göring, Keitel, Lammers, and *Rosenberg: 'We must make of the newly-acquired Eastern areas a Garden of Eden.' Hitler did not want the 'final settlement' of Europe which he had already initiated to be obvious to everyone. 'We can nevertheless take all necessary measures—shooting, resettling, etc.—and we shall take them . . . In principle we have now to face the task of cutting the giant cake according our needs, in order to be able, first, to dominate it, second, to administer it, and third, to exploit it . . . Never again must it be possible to create a military power west of the Urals . . . *We must never permit anybody but the Germans to carry arms!*' Hitler admired the British for their effective colonial rule, and wanted to create a German India out of the eastern areas. He said: 'What distinguishes the Englishman is his constant and consistent following of *one* line and *one* aim. In this respect we must learn absolutely from him.'

Hitler was not interested in a unified administration, favouring a pragmatic, working solution until final victory would give him the freedom to decide on a concrete 'New Order' in Europe. This attitude did not hinder the resettlement of **Volksdeutsche* (ethnic Germans), deportations and annihilation of racial enemies, and the creation of rough administrative structures for the German-dominated area which were already in progress. The Nazis graded peoples and countries racially and according to their behaviour towards Germany. Hitler's decision on their place in Europe depended on whether or not they were essential components of the new Germanic Empire. The historian Hans Umbreit summarized the New Order which had emerged up to the end of 1941. He considered Croatia and Slovakia satellite, but not occupied, states. He also regarded Austria, Sudetenland, *Memelland, and Eupen-Malmédy not as occupied areas since the great majority of the population welcomed the invading German forces or their later annexation. In those territories, naturally, there were minorities that were persecuted or felt themselves as being occupied. In contrast, Umbreit classed large, annexed slices of Poland as occupied territories since the vast majority of their population was not German and resisted the Nazi policy of degradation, deportation, exploitation, and persecution.

The pattern of German power in occupied Europe was as follows:

I. The extension of the Reich administration with some special arrangements over:

1. formally annexed territories under Reich governors or heads of Prussian provinces (*Oberpräsidenten*): Danzig-West Prussia, province of Poznań (Wartheland), south-eastern Prussia, and eastern Upper Silesia,
2. those territories under heads of the civil administration which were increasingly treated as parts of the Reich, but had not yet been formally incorporated: Alsace and Lorraine, Luxembourg, parts of Northern Slovenia (Untersteiermark, the occupied parts of Krain and Carinthia), Białystok.

II. Territories where civil administrations or civil supervisory authorities were established:

1. countries which had been put under German protection with a Reich Plenipotentiary: Denmark (from August 1943) and Hungary (from March 1944),
2. countries with Germanic populations that were intended for incorporation into the eventual Great Germanic Reich under Reich commissioners: Norway, the Netherlands, and Belgium (from July 1944),
3. German settlement areas the colonization of which had already been planned or begun: the Protectorate of Bohemia and Moravia, the General Government of Poland, the Reichskommissariate for *Ostland and *Ukraine.

III. Areas where military administration was a military necessity, or because of lack of interest in the territory concerned:

1. Military commanders: Belgium (before July 1944), France with the Channel Islands, and the south-east (Serbia, Salonika and the Aegean Islands, southern Greece with Crete),
2. Commanders of army groups and armies in the rear area of the zone of operations: Soviet Union.

In imposing this new order in Europe, Hitler had a concept of *Lebensraum* which was an amalgam of racial superiority, autarky, living space, and world politics. Thus, the new kind of war that he unleashed in September 1939 meant conquest *and* annihilation. All the German measures taken behind the front line were both part of the war effort and part of his wider scheme of reorganizing Europe demographically and economically. Exploitation of human and material resources in the occupied countries helped the Germans to sustain the war. Although the Wehrmacht's attitude to the indigenous population was a mixture of insecurity, racial arrogance, and naïve trust in the methods of force, Hitler did not see the military as an instrument in the racial struggle before the war against the USSR began. The SS played the key role in the racial and repressive policies. Himmler's deputies all over occupied Europe were the higher SS and police leaders and they were a law unto themselves. The executioners of German racial policy were the **Einsatzgruppen* which were deployed in both Poland and the USSR, the *Orpo and a specially formed unit, the Kommandostab Reichsführer-SS, used only in the USSR. In September 1939, the foremost target of the *Einsatzgruppen* was the Polish intelligentsia. Heydrich officially defined the role of these mobile killing squads as 'combating all Reich and state enemies behind the front line troops'. Significantly, this task paralleled that of the SS within Germany. In June 1941, Heydrich ordered these squads to carry out the elimination of both the biological and ideological manifestations of 'Jewish Bolshevism'.

It is very likely that we shall never know the exact number of Soviet prisoners-of-war (POW) who were killed following political or racist criteria. Apologists estimate several tens of thousands, other assessments begin at 140,000 and go up to 600,000 POW who were handed over to the SS for these reasons. Historians also debate the overall figure of Soviet POW who died while they were under the armed forces' control. These numbers range from 1.68 million to at least 2.53 million and up to 3.3 million, out of a total of 5.7 million prisoners taken between 1941 and 1945. Behind this controversy over the extent of the mass deaths is a debate over its causes. It would be grossly misleading to explain the great rise in mortality, which began in September 1941, solely by the circumstances in the areas of war operations, for 47% of the prisoners who died up to the spring of 1942 died in camps within the Reich. The mass deaths among Soviet prisoners must be ascribed to the German policies of exploitation which were influenced by the trauma of 1918 and by racial considerations. The Nazis condemned millions of POW and large parts of the Soviet population to death by starvation and endemic diseases in order to feed the Wehrmacht and the German population. In its magnitude this crime is comparable to the mass murder of the Jews. By the spring of 1942, when the Final Solution was just getting under way, some two million Soviet POW had already died, significantly more than the number of Jews who had been shot by the SS squads or starved to death in the disease-ridden ghettos of Poland and Russia. The Nazis' change of attitude toward their Soviet POW in October 1941 was caused not by moral considerations but by the necessities of war, chiefly the labour shortage in the German war economy. The sudden increase in their value resulted not only in an improvement in the German treatment of Soviet prisoners as workers, but the German armed forces began to use them as armed auxiliaries (see SOVIET EXILES AT WAR). This is a great contrast to Hitler's attitude earlier in 1941.

The details of Germany's coercive measures varied in practice from one occupied country to another, but Hitler decided the overall pattern and the SS and the armed forces carried it out. The start of the German–Soviet war also marks a turning-point in this regard. The SS and the armed forces did not use terror, the principal means of domination, indiscriminately. Confronted with incipient communist resistance in France, when German military personnel were assassinated, Hitler saw the opportunity 'to exterminate everyone who opposes us' (16 July 1941) and to export the Nazis' ideologically inspired policy of repression from the USSR into the other occupied countries, and even into the Reich itself. The distinction between guilt and innocence was abolished as thousands were put under preventive arrest and transferred to concentration camps. Many were immediately shot, not because of what they had done but because of what they were: Jews, communists, 'similar riff-raff', 'mischiefmaking clerics', or anti-German nationals. A growing range of orders to carry out this policy, the most prominent being those of 27 August 1941 (Heydrich), 16 September 1941 (Keitel), 7 December 1941 (Keitel's *Night and Fog Decree), and 30 July 1944 (Hitler's *Bullet Decree), could not eliminate the growing armed resistance to German occupation in Europe. On the contrary, as terror tactics increased collaboration dwindled. The growing number of concentration camps and their inmates corresponded inversely with the Reich's deteriorating situation. In September 1939, there had been about 25,000 inmates in six camps. By March 1942, there were just under 100,000 in 15 camps. The peak of 20 concentration camps, with an additional 165 branch labour camps, was reached in April 1944. Four months later, there were 524,286 prisoners. In January 1945, 714,211 inmates were guarded by approximately 40,000 men. See also WORLD TRADE and WORLD ECONOMY.

5. Defence forces and civil defence

In German air strategy, offence dominated over defence. The belief that the bomber would always get through, and that an active air defence by fighters and anti-aircraft artillery was not sufficient, forced the German government to prepare for the worst. Since August 1934 the towns were secretly classified into three categories depending on their value for the war economy. 106 towns fell into the first category and means for the construction of air raid shelters were allocated. 201 of secondary rank had to rely on enlarged emergency measures, the rest on self-protection. This policy clearly favoured the maintenance of production. Following the law of 26 June 1935, a large-scale programme of passive aerial defence was established under the auspices of the Reich's Air Defence League (Reichsluftschutzbund). The nation was to be hardened against air attacks, although the Nazis and the Luftwaffe shared the assumption that the German *Volksgemeinschaft* was more disciplined than democratic societies. By 1939, 12 million Germans had joined the League, 70% of them women. Since passive aerial defence ranked tenth among national priorities, only 2,046 public air raid shelters had been built in Berlin by September 1939. This meant that less than 2% of Berliners were protected against air attacks.

Civil Aerial Defence (Ziviler Luftschutz) was viewed as a component of the country's military defence, led by a working group in Luftwaffe's general staff and mobilized on 1 September 1939. Yet it had to take a back seat. The anti-aircraft artillery was to be the decisive element in the Reich's active air defence. It mobilized more than 300,000 men to operate 7,813 guns, the majority deployed in the West. The demand for soldiers fit for front-line duty increased during the war, so too did the Luftwaffe's conscription of schoolboys of the Hitler Youth (between 16 and 18 years of age) to man the anti-aircraft guns. Their numbers rose from 24,000 in 1940 to 92,500 in 1945.

While the assumption of victory prevailed, the Luftwaffe made no step towards a central command for air defence, and initiatives to activate passive aerial defence remained half-hearted despite the fact that bombing attacks had become a reality, even in Berlin. It was the beginning of mass bombing in 1942 which forced Germany to rethink its air strategy and to develop a satisfactory command and tactical relationship between day and night fighters. Not before the end of 1943 did a unified, *radar-based system of air intelligence and communications emerge. Every step towards improving aircraft and aerial defence was grudgingly made. By that time, there were still no more than 400 fortified air raid shelters (*Luftschutzbunker*) in Berlin which gave only 20,000 people protection against air bombings. The air warning systems in those towns not thought to be in direct threat from Allied strategic bombing were altered to minimize interruption to production. Despite this, Cologne was warned 1,122 times although these alarms were followed by only 262 attacks. Moreover, Hitler lost confidence in Göring and his Luftwaffe, and the Party's authority over passive aerial defence measures increased. By February 1945, the Luftwaffe's relevant staff became a component of the OKW.

On 25 September 1944, Hitler established the Deutscher Volkssturm, a German civil defence force. The name was created from *Volks*wehr (people's defence) and Land*sturm* (landstorm). Symbolically, Hitler published his secret decree on 18 October, the anniversary of the great victory over Napoleon at Leipzig in 1813, the so-called 'Battle of the Nations'. With Germany a nation in arms, the Nazis wanted to put themselves in the tradition of the Prussian reformers. Yet the call for the Volkssturm did not arouse the same popular enthusiasm as in 1813. Its function as a final resort was too obvious.

Authority over this German home defence force was mixed. It was organized and politically led by the party under Bormann, but commanded by Himmler in his capacity as commander-in-chief of the Replacement

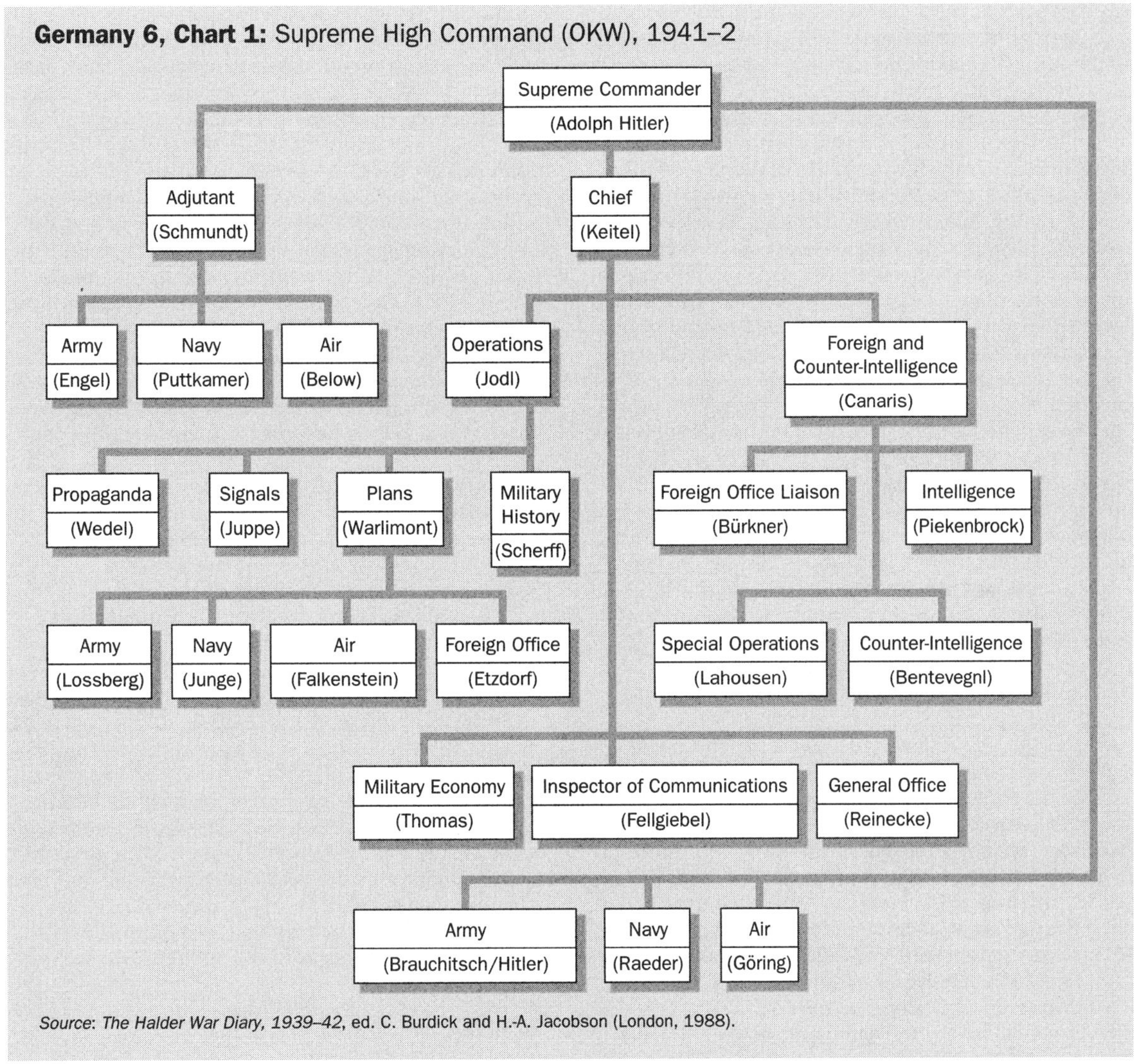

Source: *The Halder War Diary, 1939–42*, ed. C. Burdick and H.-A. Jacobson (London, 1988).

Army. After Hitler's decree, both men signed the principal orders. As their chiefs of staff they named Helmuth Friedrichs and Gottlob Berger respectively. Yet in military matters, Berger relied more on the higher SS and police leaders than on the Replacement Army's chain of command and also tried to keep the responsible regional party leaders aloof. For this new home guard to defend the fatherland, all German males between 16 and 60 were liable for service in four levies of men born between 1884 and 1928 to make a planned strength of 6 million. This estimate seemed realistic to the Nazis, since in May 1944, there were still 6.2 million exempted men in the German workforce. Since labour had priority, training in anti-tank and infantry combat was undertaken for four hours on Sundays. The drafted men had to bring their own uniforms, and arms and ammunition were scarce. By the time the Red Army reached German soil in 1944–5, the Volkssturm was deployed in the front line. The total of casualties is unknown: 175,000 were listed as missing in action after the war.

6. Armed forces and special forces

(a) High Command

Overall direction of the German armed forces, collectively termed the *Wehrmacht* (defence power), was retained by Hitler himself as *Führer und Oberster Befehlshaber* (Leader and Supreme Commander) *der Wehrmacht*. Up until 1938 there had been a war ministry, with *Blomberg as minister, and he had exercised the high command function. The ministry was dissolved after Blomberg's disgrace, and Hitler set up the Oberkommando der Wehrmacht (OKW, or Wehrmacht High Command) as the means through which he would direct the war (see Chart 1). He appointed Keitel as chief of staff and *Jodl to run the operations section, posts that they would hold throughout the war.

Apart from being titled Supreme Commander, Hitler was able to exert a tight personal grip on the conduct of the war for a variety of reasons. He was largely able to keep the officer corps bound closely to himself through exploiting the traditional Prussian military code of Honour, Duty, Loyalty. This was especially so after Hindenburg's death in August 1934, when Blomberg made all the officer corps swear an oath of personal loyalty to Hitler. By the same token, the Prussian military code, under which the senior officers had been brought up, had made them inward-looking and discouraged involvement in the wider issues of strategy. Thus, while they were expert at the operational and tactical levels, their understanding of strategy, as Hitler would often remind them, was imperfect. He, on the other hand, had an almost messianic conviction of his own skill as warlord, laying down the strategy to be followed through a series of directives which were transmitted through the OKW. Furthermore, as the war went on, he increasingly involved himself in the minutiae of operations, especially on land. This was partly because of his self-conviction, but also because he trusted his generals less and less to obey his directives to the letter.

Another aspect in Hitler's favour was that the Wehrmacht seldom spoke with one voice. The single service commanders-inchief had direct access to Hitler, leaving the OKW as merely his military mouthpiece rather than the co-ordinator of views. His overall policy of divide and rule applied as much to the Wehrmacht as to all other fields of government, and the individual service chiefs merely represented the vested interests of their own service, which were often at variance, as illustrated by the debate between the army and navy over the projected invasion of the UK in 1940 (see SEALION). Yet, such was Hitler's all-pervading dominance, that by the second half of the war their audiences with him became merely another forum for him to lay down his views rather than for them to advise him.

The Wehrmacht also laboured under another significant disadvantage, that of over-rapid growth. When Hitler came to power in January 1933 the German armed forces were still bound by the restrictions of the Versailles settlement, which forbade conscription, limited the army to 100,000 men and the navy to 15,000 men, and prohibited an air force, though there was no ban on rocket development (see V-WEAPONS). Bent on the creation of strong armed forces in order to support his territorial ambitions, Hitler initially lacked the trained manpower. The last intake of trained conscripts was the class of 1900, which had to be called to the colours in 1918, and these were now middle-aged. Consequently, the Wehrmacht had to rely initially on those classes born during the First World War, the so-called white years, which had seen a significant drop in the birthrate. Even so, by the outbreak of war in 1939 Germany had more than 4.5 million men under arms, including those in training.

As the war progressed, military commitments grew and casualties mounted, so the Wehrmacht was increasingly forced to reduce exemptions, to comb out men for combat duty, and to cast its recruiting net wider. The enlistment age was gradually reduced from 21, increasing reliance placed on recruiting inhabitants from the occupied territories of Europe, firstly ethnic Germans (see VOLKSDEUTSCHE), then Soviet citizens (see SOVIET EXILES AT WAR), and others who together by the end of the war represented as much as 10% of the army's strength. Table 8 shows the annual wartime strengths of the Wehrmacht.

Closely allied to the manpower problem was that of arms and equipment. The procurement system was unable to keep pace with the expansion of the armed forces, and matters were not helped by the fact that even after Hitler had gone to war in September 1939 he refused to put his country on to a true war economy. The result was that all three armed services suffered serious equipment shortfalls.

In the light of these difficulties it is perhaps surprising that the Wehrmacht was able to perform as well as it did during almost six years of war. Much of the reason lies in the German character, especially in its traditions of industry, resilience, discipline, and self-confidence. The

Germany, 6, Table 8: Wartime strength of the Wehrmacht (millions)

Year	*Army*	*Navy*	*Air Force*	*Waffen-SS*	*Total*
1939	3.74	0.122	0.677	0.023	4.522
1940	4.37	0.19	1.1	0.125	5.762
1941	5.2	0.404	1.545	0.16	7.309
1942	5.75	0.57	1.9	0.19	8.41
1943	6.55	0.78	1.7	0.45	9.48
1944	6.51	0.81	1.5	0.6	9.42
1945	5.3	0.7	1.0	0.83	7.83

(Figures after 1942 are approximate)

Source: Contributor/Overy.

Germany, 6, Table 9: Total losses of the Wehrmacht, 1 September 1939–31 January 1945

Causes of loss	*Total*	*Army*	*Navy*	*Air Force*
Dead through enemy action	1,810,061	1,622,561	48,904	138,596
Other causes	191,338	160,237	11,125	19,976
Wounded	4,387,701	4,145,863	25,259	216,579
Missing	1,902,704	1,646,316	100,256	156,132

Source: Bundesarchiv-Militärarchiv, RM 7/810 D, OKW/WFSt/Org (V b) Nr. 743/45 v. 17.3.1945. The Army figures include Waffen-SS, Air force field divisions and volunteer formations. The 'missing' figures include many more dead, probably a ratio 1:1. The 'navy' figures do not include January 1945. Reliable estimates of the losses after 31.1.45 speak of 500,000.

Allied policy of unconditional surrender also discouraged many from laying down their arms until there was no other option open. Total losses are shown in Table 9.

(*b*) *Army*

For Waffen-SS, see SS. In line with many continental European nations, whose land frontiers are much longer than their coastlines, the army (*das Heer*) traditionally enjoyed primacy among the German armed forces. Before the outbreak of war the German Army was headed by the C-in-C, General von *Brauchitsch, and the Oberkommando des Heeres (OKH, or Army High Command), with *Halder as chief of staff (see Chart 2). Below OKH were six *Heeresgruppen* (army groups), each of which controlled a number of *Wehrkreise* (military districts). The *Heeresgruppen* were primarily concerned with training, but on mobilization they formed army groups and some of the army HQ, the remainder being formed from the *Wehrkreise* HQ. The only exception to this was HQ Army Group South, which was formed from Arbeitstab von Rundstedt (Working Staff von *Rundstedt), which was set up in late spring 1939 to carry out the detailed planning for the *Polish campaign. The reason for this was that the existing mobilization plans only called for two army group commands, one in the west and the other in the east, but it was realized that Poland would require two army groups and to form the additional HQ from a *Heeresgruppe* would mean having to recast the complete mobilization plan.

On mobilization the OKH was split into two parts. OKH Main, headed by Brauchitsch, consisted of the operations, intelligence, organization, and training departments and was deployed into the field. A quartermaster general was also appointed to advise the C-in-C on supply matters and there was OKW representation in the fields of 'air matters', communications, and transport. OKH Rear remained in Berlin and was responsible for co-ordinating the second echelons of the staff branches in OKH Main and those departments not represented in it. When Hitler sacked Brauchitsch in December 1941 and took the post of C-in-C himself, the status of OKH became even more reduced. It was left with merely the day-to-day conduct of the war on the Eastern Front, while OKW (the High Command) assumed direct responsibility for all other theatres. It should, however, be stressed that from June 1941 onwards the Eastern Front was the primary theatre of operations and never less than 60% of the army was deployed there.

Another part of the OKH second echelon was the Replacement Army (Ersatzheer), which was set up under the command of General Friedrich Fromm and took over command of the *Wehrkreise*, which remained in place as administrative organs, and some functions of the former war ministry. The *Wehrkreise* had a number of replacement regiments, each dedicated to a particular division, the divisions themselves being recruited on a regional basis. The replacement regiments provided the recruits with their basic training and then delivered them to their divisions in formed bodies, as *Marsch* (marching) battalions or companies. Here they joined divisional replacement battalions, where they completed their training before being posted to combat units. This system worked well during the early part of the war, but after that, as the fighting intensified, especially on the Eastern Front, it proved too elaborate and broke down under the increasing strains placed on it.

Also included under Fromm's command were the various inspectorates. These looked after the particular interests of their arm or service and included those of panzer (armoured) troops, infantry, artillery, engineers, signals, and medical services. The only change in this respect came in February 1943 when Hitler made *Guderian, as inspector-general of panzer troops, directly answerable to himself, giving him the status of independent army commander.

The Field Army was organized at the highest level into army groups, and then armies and army corps. At the end of 1944 there were no fewer than 11 army group commands controlling 26 armies, including six panzer, one mountain and one Luftwaffe parachute. The division, however, was the basic building block and, with its regional recruitment and reinforcement system, was the nearest that the German Army of 1939–45 came to the British regimental system (see UK, 7(b)). At the outbreak of war these consisted of Panzer, Light, Motorized, Cavalry, Jäger, Infantry, and Mountain divisions. The majority of these categories were on a war footing by midsummer 1939 and could be fully mobilized within twelve hours. The infantry divisions, however, were classed in terms of 'waves' (*Wellen*), based on speed of

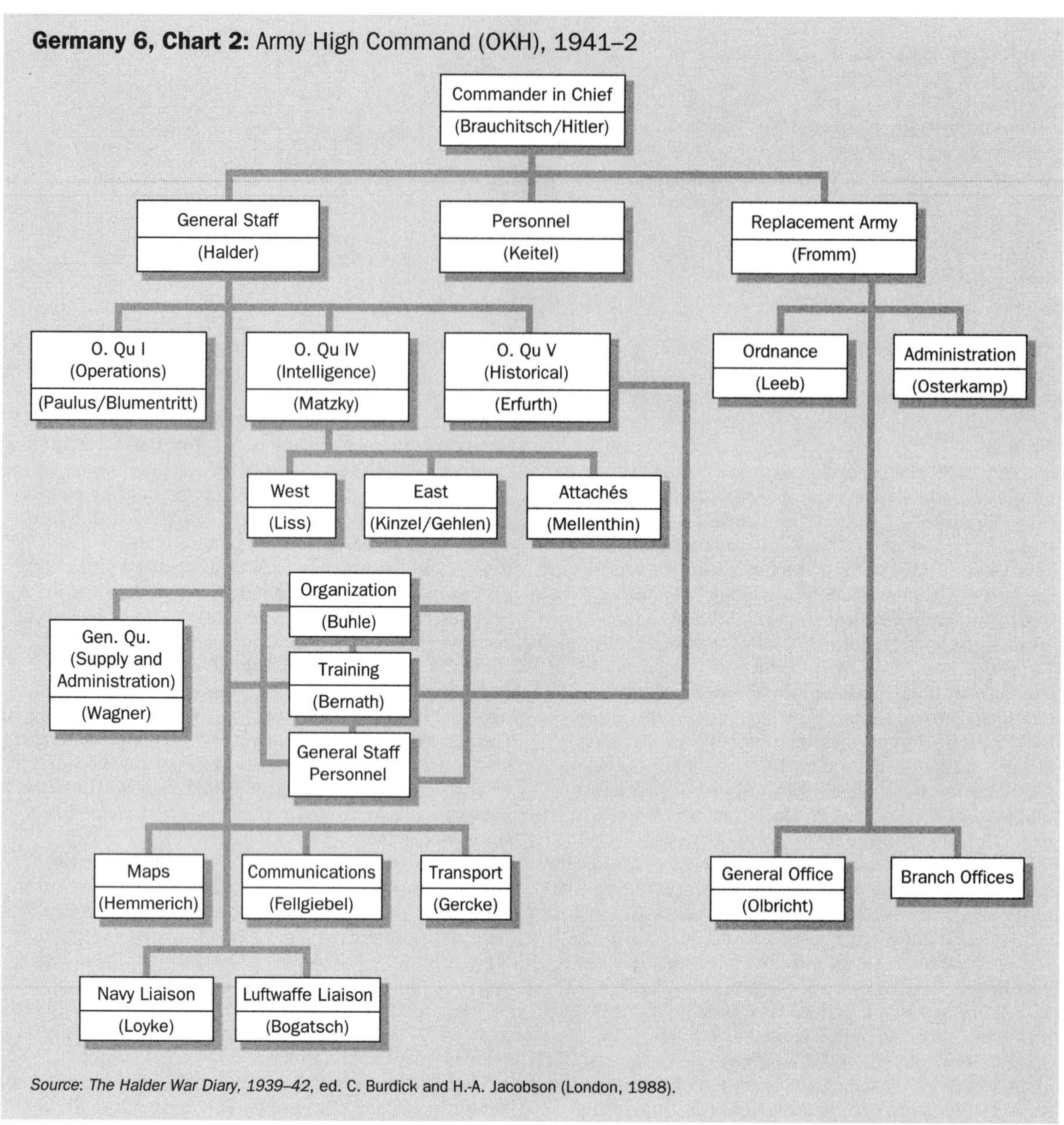

Source: *The Halder War Diary, 1939–42*, ed. C. Burdick and H.-A. Jacobson (London, 1988).

mobilization, organization, and fighting quality. Thus, on 1 September 1939 there were four waves. Wave 1 represented the 35 infantry divisions of the standing army, Wave 2 was 16 divisions formed from reservists, Wave 3 was 21 divisions made of reservists with only limited training and older men, the *Landwehr*, and Wave 4 was 14 divisions formed from reinforcement battalions from the standing army. During the war a total of no fewer than 33 waves were activated. Table 10 shows the strength of the army in terms of divisions at the outbreak of war and in early 1945.

Table 10 does not take into account the fact that as the war progressed a significant number of divisions were disbanded or totally lost. Thus, after the fall of France in June 1940, Hitler ordered seventeen divisions to be disbanded, believing that the war was virtually at an end. They were not reactivated, and fresh divisions were formed for the invasion of the USSR in June 1941. On the other hand, Hitler was sometimes loath to remove divisions from the order of battle even after they had been totally destroyed. Thus the 20 divisions lost at Stalingrad at the beginning of 1943 were immediately

Germany, 6, Table 10: Strength of the German Army in terms of divisions

Division Type	*1939*	*1945*
Panzer (armoured)	6	31
Motorized (later Panzer Grenadier)	4	13
Light (armoured)[a]	4	–
Cavalry	(one bde)	2
Infantry	86	176
Jaeger (light infantry)	2	11
Mountain	3	10
Volksgrenadier	–	50
Airlanding	1	1
Coastal Defence	–	4
Security[b]	–	6
TOTALS	106	304

[a] These comprised motorized infantry and a tank battalion but were later converted to Panzer divisions by increasing the number of tanks at the expense of infantry.
[b] Formed to guard installations. They did not therefore have, like other divisions, integral artillery.

Source: Contributor.

resurrected as skeleton cadres. Most were sent to France to re-form and all were in action once more, in the *Italian campaign, and on the Eastern Front, by that autumn. Increasing casualties meant, however, that although there were more divisions their individual strength became less. Thus, the infantry division of 1939 had a strength of 17,734 men, but this had fallen to 12,700, including more than 1,700 'Hiwis' or auxiliary helpers (see SOVIET EXILES) by 1944. The lower figure applied especially to the *Volksgrenadier* divisions which began to be raised in that year. Ad hoc temporary formations were also formed for particular operations. These *Kampfgruppen* (battle groups), named after their commanders, usually consisted of elements of all combat arms and were of reinforced battalion size.

The parallel increases in losses and numbers of divisions also accentuated the problem of weapons and equipment supply. Much of this was certainly equal to and in some fields superior to that of the Allies, but increasingly there was not enough to go round. Thus, unlike the western Allies, the German Army was never able wholly to motorize its transport and placed much reliance on the horse-drawn variety throughout the war (see ANIMALS). It also had to use captured equipment to make good shortfalls, an early example being the use of Czech tanks to equip panzer divisions raised after the *Polish campaign. Its weapons procurement system also pursued too many diverse projects, and the upshot of all this was that the diversity of weapons placed much strain on the supply system.

A further problem under which the German Army laboured was in its relations with the SS and Luftwaffe, which again, reflected Hitler's overall divide and rule policy. The Luftwaffe, apart from being responsible for parachute forces, also had field divisions and even a panzer division. It also controlled the bulk of the anti-aircraft artillery (*Flak*) arm. All these elements came under the army's operational control in the various theatres of war, but the Luftwaffe chain of command remained in place, which could, and did, give rise to conflict. A classic example of this was during the *Normandy campaign in 1944 when the Luftwaffe refused to allow the army to use their 88 mm. anti-aircraft gun batteries in an anti-tank role.

The army's relationship with the Waffen-SS was even more singular. During the early campaigns there was frustration at the SS troops' lack of discipline and the army's inability to bring them to account for it, because this was Himmler's preserve, and also jealousy that Waffen-SS divisions were generally better equipped. As the war went on, however, the army came to admire the fanaticism with which the Waffen-SS fought and its formations were often used as 'fire brigades' sent to hold critical points of the line. On the other hand, many of its leading commanders, such as 'Sepp' *Dietrich, lacked the necessary military education and, in order to make them more effective, a number of staff officers were transferred from the army to the Waffen-SS. More problematical were the SS *Einsatzgruppen* and SS police battalions, and their murderous activities on the Eastern Front. Though they operated within the army's area of responsibility the military commanders had little control over them, and such was the straitjacket in which Hitler had bound them, that his generals made little complaint.

In spite of all these difficulties, the German Army of 1939–45 did enjoy some significant advantages. The first was in the excellence of its staff work. Its senior commanders had been largely members of the élite of the old Prussian Army, the Grosser Generalstab (Great General Staff). Even though the 1919 Versailles terms had forced its dissolution, its traditions lived on, and a new generation of first-class staff officers began to be produced when

Hitler reopened the old Kriegsakademie (War Academy) in Berlin in 1935. Clarity of thought and precision were the hallmarks of the German staff officer.

Allied to this was the German system of conducting operations. In comparison with the British and US armies, German subordinate commanders were given considerable latitude. The key was that they fully understood what their superiors were aiming to achieve and that all their actions were in furtherance of this purpose. Concise written orders and maximum use of radio during a battle enabled commanders to identify their individual critical points and to make considerable use of their own initiative. This concept of *Auftragstaktik* (mission-oriented tactics) was one of the major ingredients of the successful blitzkrieg campaigns of 1939–41.

Finally, the German soldier at all levels was imbued with the *Führer*, or leadership, principle. This was an aspect of the training system which had been developed during the 1920s. Each soldier was encouraged to think two grades of command above himself. Consequently, if his immediate commander was put out of action he was more than capable of immediately assuming his mantle and carrying on with fulfilling the mission. It was perhaps this, more than anything else, which kept the German Army as an effective fighting machine until the very last weeks of the war.

(c) Navy

Hitler's navy began to take shape in 1935. Its title was changed from Reichsmarine to Kriegsmarine, but more important was the Anglo-German Naval Treaty of the same year. By permitting Germany to have a surface fleet 35% the size of the Royal Navy's and 45% of its submarine strength—and parity would be acceptable if Germany sacrificed tonnage in surface types—the UK formally recognized that Germany had finally thrown off the shackles of the Versailles settlement. Hitler also saw in this treaty confirmation that war between the UK and Germany was not likely and the initial shipbuilding programmes were merely designed for war against France or the USSR. In early 1938, however, Hitler suddenly changed his mind. War with the UK and France was now more than possible and the Kriegsmarine had to prepare for it.

There were two schools of thought on how this should be achieved. One, under Grand Admiral *Raeder, bargained on the bulk of the Royal Navy's being deployed in foreign waters and believed that a force of modern battleships and cruisers, even restricted in numbers by the terms of the Ango-German Naval Treaty, would more than match the British Home Fleet. The other, led by Admiral Dönitz, a First World War submarine ace now in charge of the U-boat arm, argued that priority should be given to undersea warfare against Britain's maritime trade. In the event, Raeder's case won, as much as anything on the grounds that anti-submarine measures, such as *ASDIC, had apparently made underwater vessels obsolete. The result was Plan Z (see Table 11), which was approved by Hitler in January 1939 and was a shipbuilding programme designed to create a large surface fleet, but not before 1944.

Consequently, the navy was even less ready for war in September 1939 than the other two services. Its total active strength was 2 battleships, 3 pocket battleships, 1 heavy and 6 light cruisers, 21 destroyers, 12 torpedo-boats (see E-BOAT), and 57 U-boats. Yet, although totally outnumbered by the fleets opposing it, it remained a force in being until the very end of the war, especially its U-boats in the battle of the *Atlantic.

A significant reason for this success was that the Kriegsmarine was a more streamlined organization than the army or the air force. Raeder and, from 1943 onwards, Dönitz were much more commanders-in-chief in their own right as professional longservice seamen than Göring was of the Luftwaffe. They also had the advantage that Hitler, the First World War soldier, understood little of naval affairs and, for the most part, recognized this and did not meddle as he did with the army. The one major exception was his furious criticism of the surface fleet after the failure to intercept a British Soviet-bound *Arctic convoy on the last day of 1942, which brought about Raeder's resignation and Dönitz's appointment as C-inC.

The navy's supreme headquarters was the Oberkommando der Marine (OKM) in Berlin. The equivalent of the Army General Staff was the Seekriegsleitung (SKL). The OKM headed by the chief of staff and its key departments covered operations, armaments, administration, and ship construction. Directly subordinate to the OKM came the operational commands, which, like those of the Royal Navy, were a mixture of geographic and fleet commands. On the outbreak of war the former consisted of Naval Group Commands (Marinegruppenkommando) East and West, and Naval Stations (Marinestationen) North Sea and Baltic. Naval Group Command East was responsible for the defence of the Baltic and West initially for the German Bight and North Sea. After the fall of France, however, Naval Group Command West transferred its HQ to France and controlled operations in French Atlantic waters. At the same time Naval Group Command North was set up to cover the German Bight, North Sea, and Norwegian waters. All three had a number of subordinate territorial commands. The two naval station commands, on the other hand, were solely responsible for coastal defence and all training, including recruits. In order to man the coastal guns the navy had its own artillery regiments and also manned *flak* regiments covering ports and other key coastal areas.

The fleet itself was divided into three basic categories, the High Seas Fleet (Flottenstreitkräfte), the Security Forces (Sicherungsstreitkräfte), and U-boats. The first was headed by the Fleet Commander (Flottenchef), of whom there were five during the war. (One, Admiral Günther Lütjens, went down with the **Bismarck* in May 1941.) The Fleet Commander controlled all battleships, cruisers,

Germany, 6, Table 11: Raeder: The 'Z-Plan' long-term production plan for the German Navy, 1939–47 (excludes experimental and auxiliary vessels)

	Number of units to be completed by:									
Ship category	*1939*	*40*	*41*	*42*	*43*	*44*	*45*	*46*	*47*	*Final target*
Battleship Type H	–	–	–	–	2	6	6	6	6	6
Battleship Types *Gneisenau* and *Bismarck*	2	2	3	4	4	4	4	4	4	4
Pocket Battleships[a] Type *Deutschland*	3	3	2[b]	1[c]	3	3	3	3	3	3
Battle Cruisers Type P	–	–	–	–	3	3	8	8	10	12
Aircraft Carriers	–	1	2	2	2	2	2	3[d]	4	8
Heavy Cruisers	2	5	5	5	5	5	5	5	5	5
Light Cruisers Type M[e]	–	–	–	3	3	4	5	8	12	24
Scout Cruisers	–	–	–	2	6	9	12	15	20	36
Destroyers	22	25	36	41	44	47	50	53	58	70
Torpedo Boats	8	18	27	35	44	54	64	74	78	78[f]
U-Boats										
Atlantic	34	52	73	88	112	133	157	161	162	162
Coastal	32	32	32	32	33	39	45	52	60	60
Special Purpose	–	–	6	10	16	22	27	27	27	27

[a] Armament of *Scharnhorst* and *Gneisenau* to be upgraded 1941–2. [b] *Scheer* to be converted 1941. [c] *Spee* and *Deutschland* to be converted 1942. [d] First two carriers to be followed by smaller type. [e] Five light cruisers of *Köln* and *Leipzig* class, plus [f] twelve torpedo boats of *Möwe* and *Wolf* class, from 1942 to be relegated for training purposes.

Source: Bekker, C., *Hitler's Naval War* (London, 1974).

destroyers, torpedo-boats, fast attack craft, *auxiliary cruisers, and supply and training ships. Each of these categories had its own flag officer, although elements of his command, especially where the smaller types were concerned, were often placed under the operational control of other commands and task forces. The Security Forces were primarily concerned with the defence of coastal waters and encompassed minesweepers, patrol and coastal defence boats, submarine hunters, and escorts. They were organized into eleven security divisions (*Sicherungsdivisionen*) covering all coasts controlled by the Germans, except for Norway, whose coasts were covered by the Coastal Security Unit (Küstensicherungsverband).

Lacking the surface strength to make a direct challenge to the Royal Navy, the main thrust of German naval strategy from the outset was to cut the UK's sea communications, thus reflecting the Dönitz school of thought. True, during the early part of the war the High Seas Fleet did play a significant role in this (see GERMAN SURFACE RAIDERS) and the deployment of its capital ships, notably the **Tirpitz*, to northern Norway remained a serious threat to the Allied Arctic convoys until late in the war, but very quickly the emphasis switched to the U-boat arm. Thus Plan Z was quickly torn up, with no major warships being commissioned after early 1941, when the *Tirpitz* came into service. Instead, from May 1943, ship construction was primarily devoted to the production of submarines, with the target rising to 40 per month. The only surface ships to be built were a few destroyers and torpedo-boats.

The U-boat arm grew from 57 boats at the beginning of the war to a peak strength of 445 in early 1944, with more than 1,100 commissioned during the war years. The overall organization controlling them grew in consequence until it represented an armed service within a service. Initially, Dönitz, as flag officer for U-boats, had his HQ at Wilhelmshaven and it consisted of two main branches, operations and organization. The former controlled operations in all theatres of war, while the latter dealt with training, weapons, supplies, and personnel, with construction the responsibility of a special office within the OKM. There were also three flag officers appointed to look after organizational, but not operational, aspects in the main U-boat theatres of operation, the Atlantic, Norway, and the Arctic, a fourth being appointed later for the Central theatre.

After the fall of France and the subsequent setting up of U-boat bases on the French Atlantic coast, Dönitz transferred his HQ to Paris and then to Lorient. The status of the operations branch was also raised to that of a command (Ubootsführung). It was run throughout the war by Admiral Eberhardt Godt, who in March 1943 was promoted to Befehlshaber für Unterseeboote (Operationen) (BdU Ops, or C-in-C for Submarines (Operations)). At the same time the U-boat HQ was moved back to Berlin because Dönitz, by now supreme commander of the navy, wanted to maintain direct control.

The U-boats themselves were organized in operational flotillas, each based on a particular port and usually numbering up to 20 boats, of which at least half were at sea at any one time. The flotilla commander, however, only had responsibility for his boats when they were in port or in coastal waters, and answered directly to the U-boat theatre command in which the flotilla was based. There were also a number of training flotillas, since the U-boat arm, unlike the surface navy, was responsible for training its crews. These were based in the north German ports.

Unlike most other navies, the Kriegsmarine did not have its own air arm, mainly because Göring was categorical that all fighting aircraft, whatever their role, were his responsibility. Even if Germany's one aircraft carrier laid down, the *Zeppelin*, had entered service, her aircraft would probably have still belonged to the Luftwaffe. Where Luftwaffe units did undertake maritime operations, as in the battle of the Atlantic, in the battle for the *Mediterranean, and off the coast of Norway, it was usually under air force command; few units were ever placed directly under naval command, and then only very grudgingly. Indeed, air-sea co-operation was generally poor, as Göring refused to give maritime operations more than a very low priority.

(d) Air force

The Luftwaffe, unlike the other two branches of the Wehrmacht, was purely a Nazi creation, since the 1914–18 air arm had been part of the army and an air force had been forbidden under the Versailles terms. It also had Göring, a member of Hitler's inner circle, at its head. Consequently, it was generally looked on much more favourably by the hierarchy than were the other two armed services.

Hitler also initially saw the Luftwaffe as a more important tool than the army or navy for achieving his territorial ambitions. He was much influenced by the theories of the omnipotence of *air power which were dominant at the time and conceived the Luftwaffe as a *Risikoflotte* (risk fleet) which could be used as a threat to force Germany's neighbours to concede its demands. It had, however, to grow quickly in order to match neighbouring air forces, especially, from August 1938, those of France and the UK. The Luftwaffe displayed an impressive rate of numerical expansion in terms of aircraft, but these were one- and two-engine types, designed for waging short, decisive wars. Although long-range heavy bombers were developed, they never went into full production and lack of a true strategic bomber was to prove a significant weakness.

The Luftwaffe also suffered from serious organizational weaknesses at the top. Göring, besides being C-in-C, was also Reich aviation minister and controlled air matters through the Reichsluftfahrtministerium (Reich Aviation Ministry). This consisted of two elements. The first was the office of the secretary of state for air, Erhard *Milch, who dealt with all aviation matters other than operations and was also inspector-general of the Luftwaffe. But there was also the Luftwaffe chief of staff, for much of the war until his suicide in 1943, Hans *Jeschonnek, who headed the operations, intelligence, quartermaster's, organization, training, and signals branches. However, he only had direct access to Göring on operational matters. The situation was made worse by the fact that Jeschonnek had no control over personnel, this office being directly under Göring's control, or supply and procurement, whose head, *Udet, reported to Milch, although after Udet's suicide in 1941 Milch took direct control over this office. Personal emnity between Milch and Jeschonnek did not help. Not until mid-1944 was the organization made less cumbersome, with a Luftwaffe High Command (Oberkommando der Luftwaffe, or OKL) being established and aircraft procurement transferred to Speer's armaments ministry, as it was for the other two armed services, and Milch's post was eliminated. But then it was too late; the damage had been done, not just in shortfalls in aircraft procurement, but also in delaying for too long the Luftwaffe's switch from an offensive to a defensive posture. Indeed, it was not until the very end of the war that the chief of staff was formally recognized as Göring's principal deputy and won comprehensive control over the Luftwaffe.

Because of Göring's standing within the Nazi hierarchy, for much of the war Hitler allowed him to run the Luftwaffe with little interference. He surrounded himself with a collection of young, inexperienced, and sycophantic staff officers, and often accepted their over-optimistic reports rather than the more realistic ones submitted by his chief of staff. By mid-1944, however, he had begun to lose interest and Hitler increasingly concerned himself in Luftwaffe affairs, which made the situation even worse.

The operational Luftwaffe was organized in *Luftflotten* (air fleets). These were multi-role formations, with aircraft of all types. Initially there were four *Luftflotten* (Nos. 14), each covering part of the Third Reich, but as the war progressed their sectors were expanded and three additional *Luftflotten* (5, 6, and Luftflotte Reich) were formed, the last specifically for the defence of Germany. Each *Luftflotte* consisted of a number of *Fliegerkorps* (flying corps). The next operational command level below this was the *Fliegerdivision*, but this was often made directly subordinate to the *Luftflotte*. Both this and the corps contained a number of *Geschwader*, which equated to a Group in the RAF. These were designated by type: *Kampfgeschwader* (KG) (bomber), *Jagdgeschwader* (JG) (fighter), *Nachtjagdgeschwader* (NJG) (night fighter), *Stukageschwader* (StG) (dive-bomber), *Zerstoerergeschwader* (ZG) (destroyer, usually Me110 formations), and *Lehrgeschwader* (LG) (operational training). These in turn controlled 3–4 *Gruppen* (groups), equating to an RAF Wing, with each *Gruppe* commanding 3–4 *Staffeln* (squadrons), a *Staffel* consisting of 12 aircraft. In September 1939, the Luftwaffe comprised 302 *Staffeln* with 2,370 operational crews and 2,564 operational aircraft (bombers, dive bombers, and fighters).

Each *Luftflotte* also had its own signals branch and a branch that controlled the anti-aircraft artillery (*Flak*) within its geographical area of responsibility (see DEFENCE FORCES, above). It also had control of a number of *Luftgaue*, administrative commands responsible for airfields, personnel and *logistics, and training.

The air defence of Germany itself became the responsibility of Luftflotte Reich, which had some unique features. For a start, instead of being multi-role like the other *Luftflotten* it merely had day and night fighters under the control of Fliegerkorps 12, which for much of the war was commanded by General Josef Kammhuber, architect of the *Kammhuber Line, set up to protect Germany from Allied bombers. Another unique aspect of this branch of the Luftwaffe was that it was the only part of the Wehrmacht to employ women in uniform, apart from nurses, although they were not members of the Wehrmacht as such. In order to release able-bodied men serving in home-based flak units for combat duty, 100,000 women auxiliaries (*Helferinnen*) were called up in 1944 to serve in the air warning service, and in the telephone and teletype departments.

There were two other significant parts of the Luftwaffe. The first was the *Fallschirmjäger*, or parachute arm. Creation of this was personally instigated by Göring in 1936 and two years later a complete division, Fliegerdivision 7, had been formed and was used to capture *Crete. In 1943 this was redesignated 1st Fallschirmjäger Division and by early 1945 nine more such divisions had been raised. They were never used in the airborne role, but fought under army command both on the Eastern Front and, as part of the First Parachute Army, in north-west Europe and Italy.

Göring, an empire builder like the other members of the Nazi hierarchy, also created conventional ground divisions. This was as a result of his plea to Hitler in 1942 not to order surplus Luftwaffe personnel to be transferred to the army (a move which would, so he claimed, taint their 'fine National Socialist attitudes'). Altogether, 21 Luftwaffe field divisions were formed, but passed to army control in November 1943. They were generally of inferior quality to their army counterparts and many were destroyed during the Soviet offensives on the Eastern Front. In contrast, the Hermann Göring Panzer Division, which was raised exclusively from volunteers, fought well in the *North African, *Sicilian, and Italian campaigns.

Eventually the Luftwaffe lost the war in the air not so much through inferior aircraft or lack of aircraft—indeed, production peaked, as it did in almost all sectors of the German war industry, in 1944—but through increasing lack of fuel. Not only did this force the grounding of many aircraft, but it also increasingly cut into the flying hours of trainee aircrew. That problem was aggravated by a growing shortage of instructors as more and more were required to replace casualties in combat units. By mid-1944 they were receiving just half the amount of training of their American and British counterparts and in early 1945 all flying training was virtually halted. Thus the quality of aircrew *vis-à-vis* their opponents also declined and further contributed to eventual defeat (see BIG WEEK for example).

(e) Special forces

Although the Germans were the first combatant nation to employ special forces during the war, they never used them to the same extent as the British. This was largely because the military hierarchy had an inbred distaste for this type of unit, especially those not wearing uniform. The main impetus behind them throughout the war was therefore the intelligence organizations of the Wehrmacht and the SS, the *Abwehr and the Sicherheitsdienst or SD (see RSHA). While the SD created incidents such as the one at *Gleiwitz on the Polish border to justify a German invasion, special Abwehr units, manned by ethnic Germans, attacked key targets just across the border in order to assist the progress of the invading forces. These units would eventually become the *Brandenburg Division, the largest of the German special force *formations. The SS also formed a number of units, and, took over the Abwehr's interest in them after the dismissal of Admiral *Canaris in 1944. Some, such as the Jagdverbände, were employed on anti-partisan operations, while others, led by Otto *Skorzeny, the leading German exponent of special operations, were responsible for such exploits as the arrest of the Hungarian dictator Admiral *Horthy.

The navy developed its own special forces during the second half of the war. These were the so-called K-Units (*Kleinkampfverbände*) of *explosive motor boats, *human torpedoes, *frogmen, and *midget submarines which operated against Allied shipping during the *Anzio and Normandy landings (see OVERLORD), but with scant success. The Luftwaffe, too, had its Kampfgeschwader 200, (see KG 200), which included among its roles the insertion of agents behind Allied lines, often using captured Allied aircraft. During the last months of the war the Luftwaffe, in desperation, also created storm detachments to destroy Allied bombers by ramming them, and another organization formed during this last period was the *Werewolves, designed to operate as partisans in areas of Germany overrun by the Allies.

In summary, German special forces failed to capitalize on a promising start. They became too much an organ of the Nazi Party and were used more for its own ends than to help fulfil strategic military objectives. The bulk of them were also not formed until the tide had turned against Germany, by which time it was too late for them to have much effect.

7. Intelligence

Intelligence about real or potential adversaries was ostensibly given high priority in the Third Reich, with many state, party, and Wehrmacht agencies collecting it. Yet the fragmentation of the German intelligence organization displays a lack of intelligence. Each agency worked for itself, and though the various departments of the Wehrmacht's intelligence and counter-intelligence organization, the *Abwehr, worked in relative harmony, there was otherwise much rivalry and duplication of effort and little exchange of information. The fact that the intelligence establishment was not collegial cannot solely be blamed on Hitler's order of 11 January 1940, which forbade anybody to receive more information than was necessary for the execution of his tasks. There was no single high-level committee which controlled the various collecting agencies and evaluated their findings. The separate channels of information flowed together only in the mind of Hitler.

Although Hitler was the ultimate consumer of intelligence, and made good use of it at the tactical and operational level, he was not the only one who absorbed it selectively, fitted facts to his preconceptions, and disregarded uncomfortable information. Moreover, intelligence estimates of Allied capabilities and intentions were often influenced by deeply held values on the part of the intelligence officers. The lack of co-ordination of German intelligence until the last year of the war clearly reflects the peculiarities of the Führer state. In addition, intelligence was considered by the Wehrmacht as less important than leadership. Intelligence was subordinate to operations, subsumed under tactics. It was not intelligence that earned victory but men, fire, and will. This traditional, dismissive, attitude to intelligence changed only reluctantly and partially during the late years of the war when the Wehrmacht was forced on to the defensive and when good information about Allied intentions had to make up for military weakness.

After September 1939, intelligence services existed mainly within three areas of society: the SS, government ministries, and the Wehrmacht.

The SS, an organ of the Nazi Party, had a domestic and foreign intelligence service, the Sicherheitsdienst (SD). After the establishment of the RSHA the SD's foreign intelligence arm became its Department VI under Heinz Jost. His more prominent successor, from June 1941, was Walter *Schellenberg who, after the RSHA acquired control of the Abwehr in 1944, commanded an enlarged department of 12 groups and 48 desks.

There were two government intelligence services: the foreign ministry's branches for spying (after 1941), deciphering, and monitoring press and radio; and Göring's Forschungsamt (research department) which was linked to the State of Prussia and which also broke codes, intercepted diplomatic, commercial, and radio messages, and tapped telephones (see FORSCHUNGSSTELLE). Though it was successful in staying out of power struggles with the other intelligence agencies, the Forschungsamt's importance diminished when, during the war, the need for tactical and operational information grew. Several military agencies provided this kind of intelligence, three of which belonged to the OKW under Keitel. Firstly, there was the Abwehr whose field units went into the army's zone of operations and into occupied countries, while stations (*KO*) were created in allied or neutral countries. For BARBAROSSA the Abwehr established a forward headquarters, *Stab Walli*, outside Warsaw from where it directed all secret operations against the USSR until the spring of 1942. It was then placed under the control of the OKH's Foreign Armies East (see below). Secondly, economic intelligence was handled by the relevant unit of the OKW's war economy and armament office under General Georg Thomas but the information it provided was more useful as a basis for the office's estimates than as a guide for decision-making at the top. Thirdly, there was OKW's signals organization.

Although *signals intelligence was the most important source of information at the tactical and operational level during the war, the competent and innovative Chef des Wehrmachtnachrichtenwesens (Chief of Armed Forces Signals Service), General Erich Fellgiebel, has received little attention. He not only directed the signals communication group with its cryptographic branch (*Chi*) within the OKW, but he was also the head of army signals communications (1939–44) and plenipotentiary for signals in the Third Reich (after October 1940). Yet neither the signals organization of the Replacement Army nor the inspector for signals was subordinate to him. For army radio intelligence, Fellgiebel had ten fixed stations and eight mobile units (*Horchkompanien*) attached to higher command staffs at his disposal in 1939. *Horchkompanien* became an integral part of blitzkrieg warfare when the system was upgraded after the Polish campaign. In fact, Fellgiebel's signals intelligence became the most important source for the estimates of the opponents' situation which were drawn up by the OKH's Foreign Armies branches. Other sources utilized for the current development, order-of-battle, and command structure of Germany's adversaries on the ground were *photographic reconnaissance and prisoner-of-war interrogation.

Fellgiebel's signals service co-operated with the Luftwaffe's own radio intelligence and cipher unit which was part of the third section of the Luftwaffe signal communications service. It was directly subordinated to the chief of staff, not to the intelligence branch of the Luftwaffe's operations staff. The radio intelligence units carried out reconnaissance, deception, camouflaging, and jamming as well as radar observation and their findings were directly streamed to the intelligence and operations officers of the higher command staff. It has been said that 70–80% of useful tactical information stemmed from radio intelligence. The first substantial co-ordinated operation in radio screening and jamming between the air force and the navy was conducted during the breakout of *Gneisenau* and *Scharnhorst* through the English Channel in February 1942 (see CERBERUS). The navy's signal intelligence unit, *B-Dienst, part of the naval staff's Third branch (Nachrichten, or signals), did gain numerous successes of its own, especially during the battle of the Atlantic.

In the Wehrmacht, intelligence was not evaluated by

one highlevel body within the High Command (except for a small unit created by the OKW operations staff under Jodl in January 1943 and enlarged in 1944), but by each of the three services separately. Within the Army High Command (OKH) two branches of the general staff—the Third, Fremde Heere West (FHW, or Foreign Armies West), and the Twelfth, Fremde Heere Ost (FHO, or Foreign Armies East)—evaluated intelligence. FHW was responsible initially for the armies of western Europe, the UK, the upper Balkans, and the *Western Hemisphere after *Pearl Harbor. Its head until 1943 was Colonel Ulrich Liss. FHO dealt with the armies of Poland, Scandinavia, the lower Balkans, Africa, the USSR, the Far East, and the USA until December 1941. It was directed by Lieutenant-Colonel Eberhard Kinzel up to the spring of 1942, then Colonel Reinhard Gehlen took over. He reorganized the branch, giving the Soviet section pride of place and was successful in upgrading operational intelligence once the Wehrmacht's need for reliable information on the Red Army became essential for maintaining its defensive stance.

The Luftwaffe's supposedly central intelligence agency was the Fifth branch of the general staff, Fremde Luftwaffen (Foreign Air Forces), which was run by Colonel Josef 'Beppo' Schmidt until October 1942. Since intelligence did not enjoy high prestige in the air force, the work was not centralized. Instead of co-operation, there was much rivalry and friction between the various branches that had to do with different pieces of intelligence: signals, economic, technical, or photographic. Information on radar, for instance, was evaluated by ten agencies. Thus, the Fifth branch was not an evaluating centre, but, like the naval staff's Third branch, which also played a minor role in coordinating and evaluating intelligence, was just one of the many units that distributed intelligence to the general staff for assessment.

The German forces in the field, air, and on the seas likewise had their own units at the various command levels which collected and authenticated data, the *Ic* (Army and Air Force) or *A3* (Navy). Thus, evaluated intelligence came to the top levels by these well-established sub-organizations. These intelligence officers, whose responsibility also included troop welfare, propaganda, and censorship, were *de facto* subordinated to the operations officer or chief of staff. There were general staff officers, experienced in intelligence, only at higher levels.

It has been said that what is important is not the form of organization but the continuity of information, and the organizational maze of German intelligence did not greatly impair its tactical usefulness. Yet strategic underestimation took place in the first years of the war which shaped its course. In addition to the scarcity of reliable data, the tendency to underestimate the Allies stemmed from the deeply held conviction of German superiority in leadership and offensive capabilities, and, in the later years of the war, reliable information was not acceptable to those people who refused to believe in the possibility of a German defeat.

8. Merchant marine

Since the maintenance of sea communications was not as vital for Germany as for the UK, the German merchant fleet did not gain the same significance. Only the shipping of Swedish ore through the Baltic and Romanian oil along the Danube were important. From 1939 to mid-1941, the British blockade (see ECONOMIC WARFARE) was successfully offset by Soviet supplies. Later in the war, the merchant fleet was used for Wehrmacht transport. In 1939, when it consisted of 4.5 million gross tons, it came under the control of the navy until May 1942 when *Gauleiter* Karl Kaufmann of Hamburg was named Reich Commissioner of Shipping. Before the war began all merchant ships on the high seas had been given sealed orders about what to do in case of hostilities and on 25 August 1939, they were instructed by radio to open them. Up to 9 April 1940, 76 ships totalling 463,122 tons managed to return to home ports, 28 totalling 171,822 tons scuttled themselves, 25 ships totalling 109,422 tons fell into British and French hands, 15 ships totalling 73,178 tons were sunk, and 200 ships totalling 829,568 tons sought refuge in neutral ports.

By the end of the war, the Allies had sunk 3 million tons of German shipping while 176 merchant ships totalling 337,841 tons had been constructed. Approximately 3,000 German merchant seamen lost their lives during the war. Ten merchant ships were used as armed merchant raiders, or *auxiliary cruisers, and a few were employed as *blockade runners between Japan and Germany. Auxiliary cruisers sank, up to the end of 1941, nearly double the tonnage that the navy's capital ships had sunk in its campaign against Allied shipping in the Atlantic.

9. Resistance

Judgement on Hitler's German opponents is not easy, historically or historiographically. Given the peculiarities of the Nazi state and the lack of an active non-conformist tradition, there could be no unified mass resistance movement in Germany. Since Nazism did not exist in a vacuum, resistance was carried out by a qualitatively and sometimes quantitatively outstanding minority, but it could not topple the regime: this was done by losing the war.

Courageous opponents of Nazism emerged from all walks of life and with a mixture of motives and aims. The outbreak of war both hindered and helped the opposition. On the one hand, it became more difficult to differentiate between Germany and Nazism, to choose between compliance and conscience. Hitler's military triumphs were applauded. The victory over France was a defeat for the opposition and the fight against Bolshevism was not unpopular. Moreover, any resistance had to take place in great secrecy, because even a hint of criticism of the German conduct of the war became a capital crime after 1 September 1939. Under the watchful eyes of the Gestapo and its informers, organized political opposition on any scale was virtually impossible. It is no coincidence that so many members of the Schwarze Kapelle plot to kill Hitler were kinsmen.

On the other hand, the war opened up new possibilities for using military channels as a means to organize resistance. By and large, however, the senior officer corps' inaction was more striking than their action. Only a few were able to make up their minds that their oath of obedience had become meaningless and to act against their supreme commander. The increasing number of defeats on all fronts after 1942–3 helped the conspirators to win sympathisers for their cause. More were prepared to follow suit after someone else had successfully attempted a *coup d'état*. A Berlin joke of 1944 reflects the attitude of the general public: 'I'd rather believe in victory than run around with my head cut off.'

*Historiography tries to define different forms of resistance to Nazism: political opposition, social non-conformity, and ideological dissidence. They can be shown by institutions or individuals. None of those episodes of resistance that history remembers aroused a mass movement against the regime. The 'White Rose' was a group at Munich University in 1942–3—its nucleus consisted of the students Sophie and Hans Scholl, Willi Graf, Christoph Probst, Alexander Schmorell, and Professor Kurt Huber—which used pamphlets to arouse a university movement against the regime. They were denounced by the university beadle on 18 February 1943, tried with their friends, and executed. The abortive attempt to assassinate Hitler by Colonel Claus Schenk von Stauffenberg on 20 July 1944 was the last effort to avert catastrophe. The regime used this plot as a pretext to execute almost 5,000 opponents, whether implicated or not, and to persecute the families of the conspirators. The majority of Germans repudiated the attempt on the Führer's life, and the Nazi Party reached the height of its power in the aftermath of the plot.

Many names are not honoured in the resistance literature. Hundreds of courageous Germans from all strata of society, of all ages and beliefs, who voiced opposition or simply refused the social and ideological conformism and were killed will remain unknown, their deeds unrecorded in the surviving documents. Because they were isolated, their moral heroism deserves our admiration.

In fact the organizations of the labour movement were the first to oppose the Nazis actively after 1933, before all later forms of resistance from the clergy, the military, the bureaucracy, former politicians, students, youth groups, and other individuals. The Gestapo was unable to break completely the resistance of communists and social democrats who agitated underground. The first attempt on Hitler's life, on 8 November 1939, was undertaken by Johann Georg Elser, acting on his own initiative. Luck was with Hitler. Elser's bomb exploded fifteen minutes after the Führer had left the beer hall in Munich. Elser was executed at *Dachau on 9 April 1945, the day on which more famous German resisters were hanged in *Flossenbürg: Pastor *Bonhoeffer, Admiral Canaris, Maj-General *Oster, and the Army Judge-Advocate Karl Sack.

Both Germanies needed a past they could admit to after the downfall of Hitler's tyranny. Both states chose to appropriate the legacy of the resistance, and thereby overrated it. The Adenauer government emphasized especially the attempted assassination of Hitler on 20 July 1944. By viewing this military–civilian conservative opposition to Hitler as the 'other Germany', whose blood had cleansed 'our German name of the shame which Hitler cast upon it' (Federal President Theodor Heuss), and whose sacrifice was seen as a true gift to the (West) German future, Bonn's leaders had to downplay its less democratic features and to overlook the fact that some of those who tried to kill Hitler had been among those who had helped him to rearm Nazi Germany. Ulbricht's East German government chose to appropriate the legacy of the communist opposition to Hitler's regime, to magnify its impact, and to select a few members of the military–civilian conservative resistance as patriots who took part in the 'class war against German imperialism'. It was not until the late 1960s that historians on both sides of the Wall began to take a new look at Hitler's enemies, to define forms of resistance, abolish political distortions, and include all the various groups of resisters, even the *Rote Kapelle and the captured soldiers who worked for the downfall of Nazi Germany under Soviet leadership as members of the National Committee for a Free Germany and the Association of German Officers. (See also PAULUS.) The men, women, and adolescents of the resistance saved the honour of the German people; but their courage should no longer be used as an alibi for the compliant attitude of the great majority.

10. Culture

One of the main purposes of the Nazi regime was to exert an ideological influence on German culture. In order to control all creative activity, its production and distribution, Goebbels, on 1 November 1933, established the Reich Chamber of Culture (Reichskulturkammer), nominally a public corporation but closely controlled by his propaganda ministry. It was composed of five chambers, each under its own president, responsible for literature, cinema, music, theatre, and the fine arts, while two others were responsible for press propaganda and, until 1939, broadcasting. During the war, military censorship underpinned the censorship imposed by the chambers.

As many as 5,000 scholars and artists, as well as dozens of *scientists, fled persecution by the Third Reich. A large proportion of these were writers, for both popular writing and serious literature were 'purified' as the Nazis sought to eliminate political dissent and what they termed 'Jewish influences'. Many prominent and independent-minded writers, as well as Jewish ones, were silenced or exiled as a result of measures undertaken by the police and SS, and those who were spared persecution were compelled to become members of the Reich Chamber of Literature (Reichsschrifttumskammer). Membership of this body, which was refused to literary critics such as Erich Kästner, required a certificate of political and racial clearance which was issued by the propaganda ministry. Publication of books and articles, other than those classified as scientific, was made contingent on membership of the Reichsschrifttumskammer. They were not censored, though publishers reflected official standards and reviews in official Nazi periodicals determined a bookseller's willingness to stock an author's work.

Although great works which were of suspect but not obviously Jewish origin, like the novels of Thomas Mann, were printed until wartime shortages of paper prevented it, the bulk of German literature celebrated 'heroism' in situations which ranged from the war novels of Ernst Jünger to commonplace stories of the simplest kind. Novels dealing with great historical personalities were both fashionable and ideologically welcome and skilled authors who could manipulate the Nazis' inability to analyse art were able to incorporate subversive themes into such works, thereby presenting their readers with disguised criticisms of racialism (Reinhold Schneider, *Las Casas vor Karl V.*, 1938) or the lack of legal rights (Werner Bergengruen, *Der Grosstyrann und das Gericht*, 1935). Run-of-the-mill writers—from Erwin G. Kolbenheyer, the Third Reich's star author, to the political mystery writer Hans F. Blunck (first president of the Reichsschrifttumskammer)—used the novel or short story as a crypto-history of their own day, praising the moral values which the party had decreed were eternal.

Poetry of an acceptable kind was in particular demand by the Nazi Party, and Hitler fêted its most acceptable practitioner, Heinrich Anacker. Reviewers tried hard, especially in poetry, to counter the worst of the kitsch which was widely produced to satisfy the Nazi cultural system. Literature of other kinds was published only in translation and then in order to demonstrate that in the world outside 'negative' Jewish influences were perverting art: thus the American pessimist Theodore Dreiser was much recommended and Somerset Maugham was widely read. These involuntary cultural links between Germany and the outside world were severed in 1943 when the pressures of war reduced all literature to propaganda of one type or another.

The Nazis regarded the cinema as the most important medium through which to govern German culture, and it was one of the main areas of activity of the Reich propaganda ministry. Screenplays, actors, directors, and even particular scenes were decided personally by Goebbels—occasionally even by Hitler. Everyone involved in film production and distribution was required to join the Reich Chamber of Films (Reichsfilmkammer) where they were subject to racial and political control. When war broke out Goebbels completed the construction of his cinematic empire by buying up the last few independent companies and incorporating them into the state-owned UFA group. This gave him control over all newsreel rights, thereby allowing him to ensure that the images of war presented to the public accorded with the needs of the regime.

The German cinema, now completely centralized, became Goebbels's most effective indirect instrument of cultural warfare. Of the 1,100 films made between 1933 and 1945 about 15% were direct propaganda, most famously exemplified in the work of Leni Riefenstahl. German techniques in this field were so highly developed that British cinema critics recommended imitating them. Skilful documentation of the war demonstrated, as Goebbels ordered that it should, 'the severity and greatness' of the conflict while simultaneously carefully concealing its horrors. Well-made and widely-disseminated films propagated hatred for the British (*Ohm Krüger*, 1941), anti-Semitism (*Jud Süss*, 1940), acceptance of the euthanasia programme (*Ich klage an*, 1941), or identification with German heroes (*Bismarck*, 1940; *Der grosse König*, 1942). However the main goal of German cinema was, as Goebbels said, simply 'to keep our people happy because that is of strategic importance too.' Hollywood-standard colour films like *Gone With the Wind* were never equalled in Germany, but sumptuous medieval costume dramas such as *Stern von Rio* (1940) and *Münchhausen* (1943) vied with popular musicals which picked up contemporary trends such as *Wunschkonzert* (1940), based on a radio programme and seen by 20,000,000 people. The vast majority of German films did not deal with the war in any form but depicted common human problems and pleasures or were merely escapist entertainment through the enjoyment of which the audience could forget the war for a few hours.

As a result of the great importance which the Nazis attached to the cinema its top stars enjoyed high salaries and a degree of racial tolerance unequalled anywhere else in the Reich. The mass of propaganda or entertainment films also allowed the occasional production to step outside officially-countenanced norms (*Der Postmeister*, 1940) and offered the kind of aesthetic complexity which had given German cinema its international reputation. After 1943–4 film production was considerably reduced as the urgent needs of the war necessitated the transfer of skilled personnel to the armed forces or the armament industries; however, a broad spectrum of output was sustained to the last and in the final months of the war both the philosophical *Unter den Brücken* and the monumental and patriotic *Kolberg* were produced.

Two closely associated cultural fields were broadcasting and music. Music was thought to exercise a particularly strong influence on the general public's frame of mind. Cheap radio sets (*Volksempfänger*) were produced in vast numbers in order to supplement printed with spoken propaganda. No sooner had the war started than the propaganda ministry began a campaign to take control of all programme planning, a goal it achieved in October 1941. Two musicians with international reputations, the composer Richard Strauss until 1935 and later the conductor Peter Raabe, presided over the Reich Chamber of Music (Reichsmusikkammer), ensuring that unwanted and especially Jewish music was neither composed nor performed and making judgements on borderline cases. Control over music broadcasting was also exercised by the Reich propaganda ministry which, for example, encouraged the performance of works by the Hungarian composer Franz Lehár, even though he had married a Jewess, because Hitler liked his tuneful operetta style.

However hundreds of composers, performers, teachers, and critics of music were not fortunate enough to enjoy the Führer's admiration and were excluded from practising their art for political or racial reasons. As contemporary musical creativity was stifled, concert performances fell back on the great heritage of classical German music, though composers like Mahler or Mendelssohn who were Jewish were excluded from the official repertoire.

Progressive music disappeared, but swing and jazz remained borderline cases, castigated by the Nazis as Jewish or 'nigger' music but tolerated because otherwise the soldiers listened to foreign broadcasts (see also CHILDREN). Dance music was governed by a policy which tried to take into account both the seriousness of the military situation and the widespread desire for diversion; permission and prohibition alternated in a random sequence. During the war German broadcasting emphasized marches and popular songs, thereby simultaneously presenting the war and allowing people to forget it. The highlight of the week's listening was the Sunday request programme *Wunschkonzert*, introduced by Heinz Goedecke, which united front and homeland by passing on personal messages and playing music of all kinds, thereby 'awakening the experience of national community in many thousands' as one report observed. The melancholy ballad 'Lili Marlene', suppressed after the German defeat at Stalingrad, best represented the 'present-and-forget the war' combination and became the top international song of the period (see also MARCHING SONGS).

The development of German theatre was similar to that of music in several respects. Artistic and avant-garde writers who were Jewish or left-wing were eliminated; classical or trivial pieces monopolized the stage; and alongside the established patronage of state or community was introduced that of Robert Ley's mass Nazi organization Kraft durch Freude (Strength through Joy) which became predominant during the war. New plays, other than operetta and musicals, followed the lines drawn for literature and paradigmatically demonstrated in *Schlageter* (1933), the heroic work of Hanns Johst, president of the Reichsschrifttumskammer. Political enthusiasm ranked higher than ability and many secondrate writers like Heinrich Zerkaulen, whose miserable *Admiral Brommy* received standing ovations in 1941, were able to score great successes. More honest theatrical managements preferred to stage Goethe, Schiller, Kleist, and even Shakespeare, though all other 'enemy' playwrights were banned in 1939–40.

Even in the Third Reich and in wartime, politically motivated pieces soon proved to be evanescent. Performances sponsored by Robert Ley declined rapidly during the war as he ceased sending workers to the theatre and organized soldiers' entertainments instead. The Reichstheaterkammer, as well as executing its political function, succeeded in protecting its members until, in 1942, it had to start closing theatres and shifting personnel to armaments production. Thereafter its main problems were war profiteering by actors who demanded extravagant salaries and avoiding bombing zones for such performances as were put on. In August 1944 all German theatres were closed.

The last of the five Reichskulturkammer sections was the Reichskammer der bildenden Künste, which supervised painting and sculpture. Its president, Adolf Ziegler, was a painter who specialized in naturalistic female nudes. He fought the Weimar avant-garde, whom he called 'pacemakers of international Jewry' and he eliminated modernism and experimentalism by excluding painters such as Paul Klee or Max Beckmann who practised such styles, and Jews such as the popular impressionist Max Liebermann. Sculpture presented the regime with less of a problem since it was in the main a public art concerned with producing memorials.

In 1937, on Hitler's orders, Ziegler organized an exhibition of 'decadent art', which he defined according to political or racial and not artistic criteria—though he had a very high regard for the Jewish artist Franz Lenbach. Hitler's artistic criterion was classicism, therefore German fine arts fell back to pre-art-deco standards and were enthusiastically applauded by the broad mass of the population which was weary of Weimar's non-naturalism. German painting declined because the Reichskulturkammer's commissioner for design, Hans Schweitzer, allowed art to degenerate into mere illustration. The great moment for Nazi painting came when war broke out: it at once abandoned its favourite style, the 'blood-and-soil' genre, for pictorial representations of the heroic aspects of the struggle which photography was not able or not solemn enough to reproduce.

Hitler, who had started out on careers both as an architect and as a painter, was particularly concerned to impose his tastes on the fine arts. He wished, for instance, to change the Austrian city of Linz where he had spent his youth into the world's centre of art. Until his last days he sketched grand buildings and splendid streets of a future Linz leading to a giant gallery of art which he expected to become an adequate memorial to himself. In order to raise an appropriate stock of works, German *Kunstraub* commissions looted much of the classical heritage of European art. The Linz project, apart from the robberies committed by Göring and other corrupt potentates, deprived Europe of about 22,000 works of art (see LOOT).

Finally, something must be said about all those artists

who chose, or were forced, to leave the Third Reich. The creativity of many had already declined before they left, or they had fallen silent altogether. But others, particularly musicians, artists, and those from the world of theatre and the cinema, assimilated well into their new environments. The 500 actors and directors who went to *Hollywood—Marlene Dietrich, Peter Lorre, Billy Wilder, and Fred Zinnemann among them—became willing contributors to the wartime output of American films; and Walter Gropius's Bauhaus school of architecture integrated so well into the American architectural scene, that when it was reimported into Germany after the war it was thought to have originated in the USA. However, many exiled writers endeavoured to uphold the continuity of non-Nazi German culture in opposition to the Nazi's Reichskulturkammer, and in this they were not unsuccessful. Thomas Mann, Anna Seghers, Franz Werfel, Robert Musil, and Hermann Broch, for example, all continued to create timeless works of literature, while others—Klaus Mann with *Mephisto* (1936); Berthold Brecht with *Furcht und Elend des Dritten Reiches* (1938) and *Mutter Courage und ihre Kinder* (1939)—reflected contemporary experience.

JÜRGEN FÖRSTER
CHARLES MESSENGER (Armed Forces)
WOLFGANG PETTER (Culture)

Domestic life, government, law

Bessel, R. (ed.), *Life in the Third Reich* (Oxford, 1987).
Burdick, C., and Jacobsen, H.-A. (eds.), *The Halder War Diary 1939–1942* (Novato, Calif., 1989).
Burleigh, M., and Wippermann, W., *The Radical State: Germany 1933–45* (Cambridge, 1991).
Calvocoressi, P. *et al.*, *Total War* (2nd edn., London, 1989).
Förster, J., 'The Dynamics of Volksgemeinschaft. The Effectiveness of the German Military Establishment in the Second World War', in A. R. Millett and W. Murray (eds.), *Military Effectiveness*. Vol. III: *The Second World War* (Boston, 1988).
Freeman, M., *Atlas of Nazi Germany* (New York, 1987).
Hildebrand, K., *The Third Reich* (London, 1984).
Kershaw, I., *The Nazi Dictatorship* (London, 1985).
Militärgeschichtliches Forschungsamt (ed.), *Germany and the Second World War*; 4 vols. (Oxford, 1990–4).
Noakes, J., and Pridham, G. (eds.), *Nazism 1919–1945*. Vol. III: *Foreign Policy. War and Racial Extermination* (Exeter, 1988).
Rebentisch, D., *Führerstaat und Verwaltung im Zweiten Weltkrieg* (Stuttgart, 1989).
Rich, N., *Hitler's War Aims*, 2 vols. (London, 1973–4).
Stern, J. P., *Hitler. The Führer and the People* (Berkeley, Calif., 1975).

Armed forces

Absolon, R., *Die Wehrmacht im Dritten Reich*, 5 vols. (Boppard, 1968–88).
Cooper, M., *The German Air Force 1933–1945: An Anatomy of Failure* (London, 1981).
Lucas, J., *Kommando: German Special Forces of World War Two* (London, 1985).
Mallmann Showell, J. P., *The German Navy in World War Two* (London, 1979).
Murray, W., *Luftwaffe* (London, 1985).
Salewski, M., *Die deutsche Seekriegsleitung*, 2 vols. (Frankfurt am Main, 1970–5).
Seaton, A., *The German Army 1933–45* (London, 1982).
Van Creveld, M., *Fighting Power: German and US Army Performance, 1939–1945* (London, 1983).

Culture

Boeschenstein, H., *The German Novel 1939–1945* (Toronto, 1949).
Gray, R., *The German Tradition in Literature 1871–1945* (Cambridge, 1965).
Hinz, B., *Art in the Third Reich* (London, 1980).
Hoffmann, C., *Opposition Poetry in Nazi Germany* (Berkeley, Calif., 1962).
Hull, D., *Film in the Third Reich* (Berkeley, Calif., 1969).
Lane, B., *Architecture and Politics in Germany 1918–1945* (Cambridge, Mass., 1968).

Germany, battle for (see Maps 44 and 45). On 15 January 1945, when Hitler returned to Berlin from the headquarters he had used during the *Ardennes campaign, he knew his military options were exhausted. Henceforth, he could only hope for a 'Miracle of the House of Brandenburg' like that of 1763 in which the death of the Russian Empress Elizabeth had split a European coalition against Frederick the Great and saved him from a total defeat in the Seven Years War. The alliance against Hitler was indeed coming under great strain, but not over concerns from which he could profit. Nazi Germany's fate was sealed. The war was about to become a contest for shares in the victory, and the German capital, symbol of German militarism and expansionism, was regarded as the grand prize (see BERLIN, FALL OF).

1. Clearing the Rhineland

Though they had fought their first major battles on German soil as early as the previous autumn (see AACHEN and HUERTGEN FOREST), there was grave doubt that *Eisenhower's armies were credible contenders in a race for Berlin on 28 January, the day they reoccupied the line they had held before the Ardennes offensive. *Zhukov's First Belorussian and *Konev's First Ukrainian *fronts* (army groups) were closing to the River Oder, 65 km. (35 mi.) east of Berlin, at high speed; and the Soviet plan called for the city to be taken and the River Elbe reached in a maximum of 30 more days.

On 1 February, meeting at Malta before the Yalta conference which was held from 4 to 9 February (see ARGONAUT), the *Combined Chiefs of Staff approved Eisenhower's plan for a final offensive. It delegated the main effort to *Montgomery's Twenty-First Army Group, which would employ First Canadian, Second British, and Ninth US Armies in a drive to and across the *Rhine north of the Ruhr and thence over the North German plain to Berlin. The remaining armies, three American and one French, after completing the clearing of the Rhineland, would develop as strong a secondary thrust south of the Ruhr as could be managed without impairing support for Montgomery's effort. To assist the Soviet forces, who had no heavy bombing support of their own, the chiefs also approved a bombing offensive by Bomber Command and Eighth US Army Air Force against rail centres in eastern Germany.

The bombing began almost at once and reached its peak intensity in night and day raids on *Dresden on 13 and 14 February. The first (see VERITABLE) of two operations to bring Montgomery's armies to the Rhine began on 8 February. It was launched out of the Nijmegen salient created by *MARKET-GARDEN and involved the British and Canadians in some of the most difficult fighting of the campaign when they had to clear the *Reichswald forest. The second (see GRENADE) was to have started two days later, but German engineers had destroyed the floodgates on several dams, which kept the River Ruhr flooded in front of the Ninth US Army until 23 February. Thereafter, Twenty-first Army Group pushed steadily towards the Rhine. General *Bradley's Twelfth Army Group, First and Third US Armies, joined in on the right on 3 March. On 7 March, First Army, by a stroke of luck that was to have far-reaching effect, captured the Ludendorff railway bridge at *Remagen. By 10 March, Montgomery's and Bradley's lines were on the river from the Dutch border upstream to Koblenz.

Joined on the north by *Patton's Third US Army, *Devers's Sixth Army Group, Seventh US and First French Armies, began clearing the Saar and Palatinate on 15 March. The Third US Army seized a bridgehead at Oppenheim, near the confluence of the Rhine and Main rivers on 22 March, and all German resistance west of the Rhine ended three days later.

Meanwhile, Stalin had prolonged the race for Berlin. At Yalta, when Roosevelt and Churchill opposed shifting the Polish border west to the *Oder–Neisse Line, he had told them that then it was better 'the war should continue a little longer, although it would cost Russia much blood, so that Poland could be compensated at Germany's expense' (W. S. Churchill, *Triumph and Tragedy*, London, 1953, p. 370). Through February, while Hitler withdrew divisions from the Western Front to defend Berlin, Zhukov, was stopped on the Oder; Konev crossed the Oder and moved towards Dresden, but stopped at the River Neisse on 21 February; and then in March, both busied themselves in Pomerania and Upper Silesia, taking territory planned for transfer to Poland.

2. The Ruhr pocket

Bradley had instantly grasped the opportunity the Remagen Bridge offered for an enlarged American role in the advance beyond the Rhine. Eisenhower, having his obligation to the combined interest to consider, had evinced some restraint. Nevertheless, he had allowed the bridgehead to be expanded and on 18 March approved Bradley's plan for VOYAGE, an American operation south of the Ruhr that would be a counterpart to PLUNDER, Montgomery's advance on the north.

On 24 March, Montgomery's armies crossed the Rhine at Wesel. For the three previous days, Bomber Command and Eighth USAAF had devoted virtually their entire strengths to strikes at road and rail junctions around the crossing zone. First US Army began VOYAGE on 25 March. *Kesselring, who had assumed command of the German Western Theatre on 10 March, had three army groups: H, downstream from Düsseldorf; B, between Düsseldorf and Koblenz; G, Koblenz to Karlsruhe. He had 55 weak divisions; Eisenhower had 85, all at full strength, and overwhelmingly superior air power. Army Group B, sandwiched between the Allied bridgeheads, was the actual first target of VOYAGE and PLUNDER.

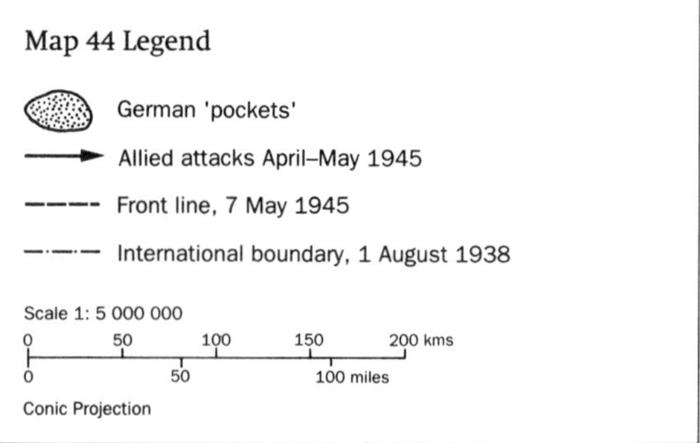

On 27 March, Montgomery issued his order for the breakout from the Wesel bridgehead, and First US Army reached Marburg, 110 km. (68 mi.) east of the Rhine, where it was to turn north behind Army Group B. A day later, Eisenhower changed the strategic plan. Telling Montgomery that Ninth US Army would revert to Bradley's control after it and First US Army had encircled Army Group B, he directed Montgomery to protect Bradley's north flank while Twelfth US Army Group made the main thrust towards the Elbe along the Erfurt–Leipzig–Dresden line.

When First Army made contact with Ninth US Army at Lippstadt on 1 April, Hitler resorted to a device he had used on the Eastern Front, notably at *Stalingrad: he declared the entire Ruhr a fortress, placed it directly under his control and forbade any attempt to break out. *Model, the Army Group B commander, had earned his field marshal's baton as a defensive specialist, but the Ruhr, once the heart of the munitions industry, could no longer sustain even his two armies. He shot himself on 17 April, and 317,000 of his troops were taken prisoner.

3. To the Elbe

Eisenhower's change of plan gave his American generals a victory in a long-standing and latterly acrimonious rivalry with Montgomery. It also aligned his American armies on easterly and north-easterly courses across central Germany that bypassed the entire south between the Rhine and the Czechoslovak border and raised, in Eisenhower's and Bradley's estimation, a danger of prolonged, vicious fighting after the war ended on the main fronts. The idea of a so-called *'National Redoubt' in the Bavarian and Austrian Alps, probably suggested by Swiss doctrine, had no concrete evidence to support it but appeared entirely consistent with the Nazi mentality. Were Hitler and his most fanatical troops to make such a

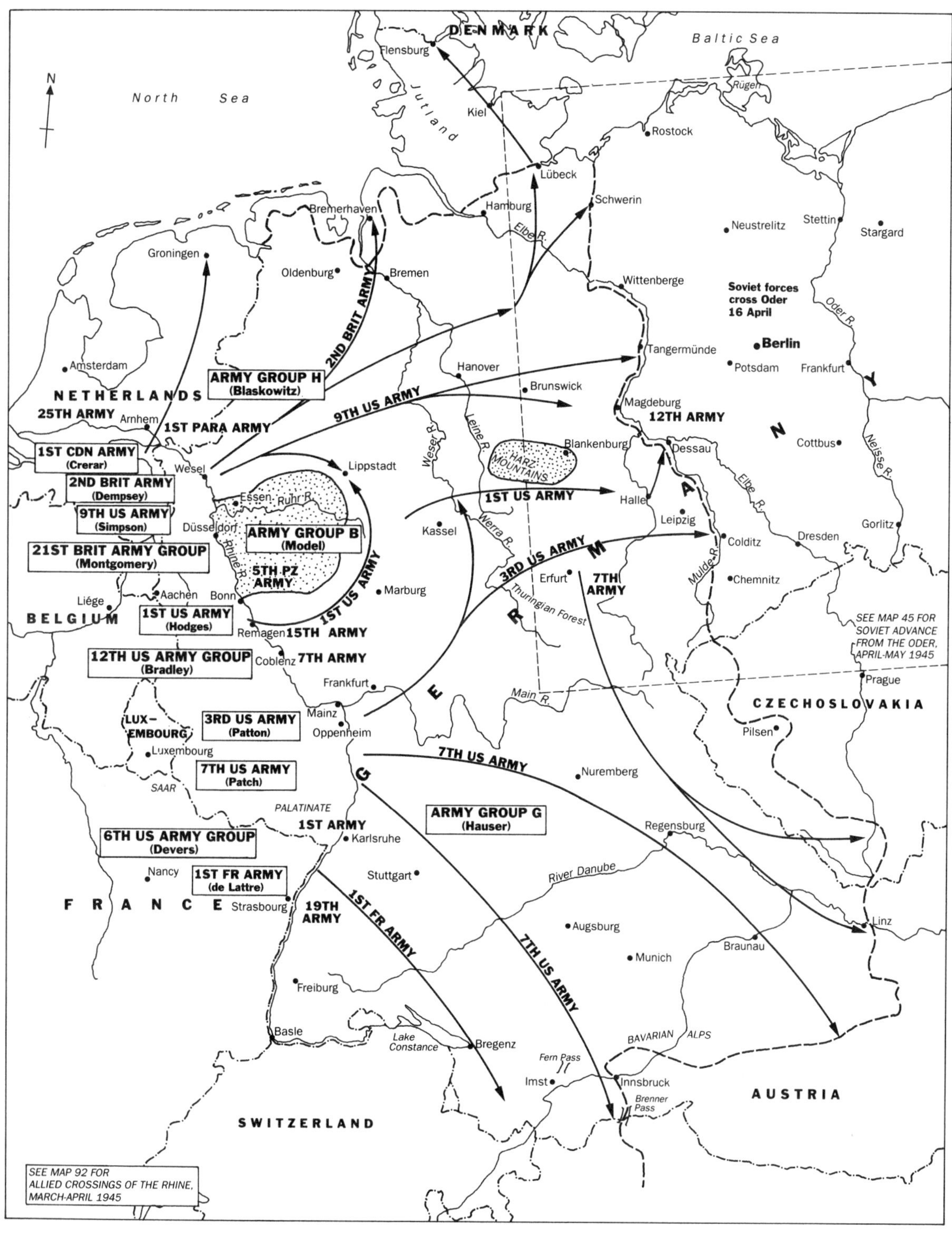

44. **Battle for Germany**: Allied advance from the Rhine, April–May 1945

Germany, battle for

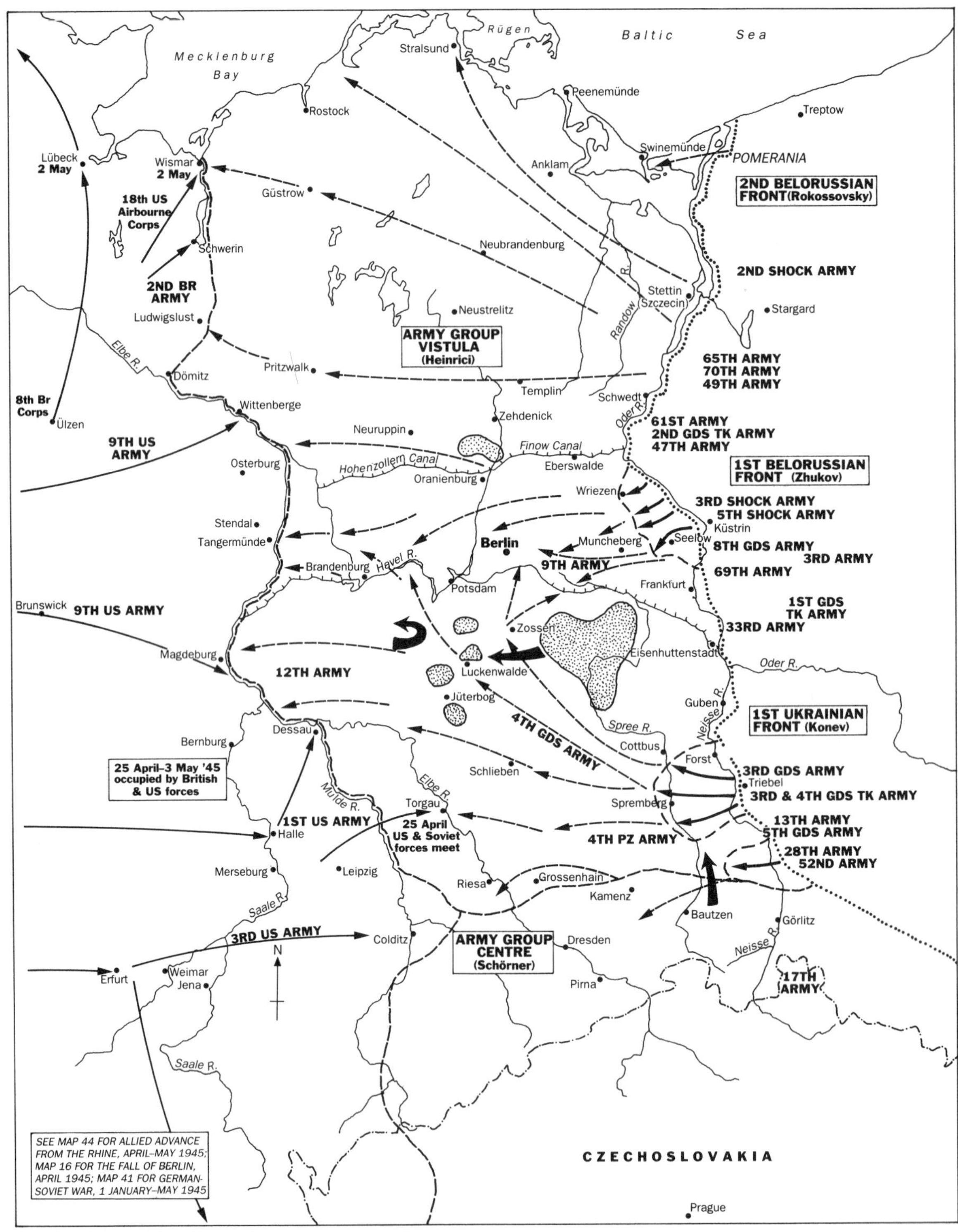

45. **Battle for Germany**: Soviet forces advance from the Oder, April–May 1945

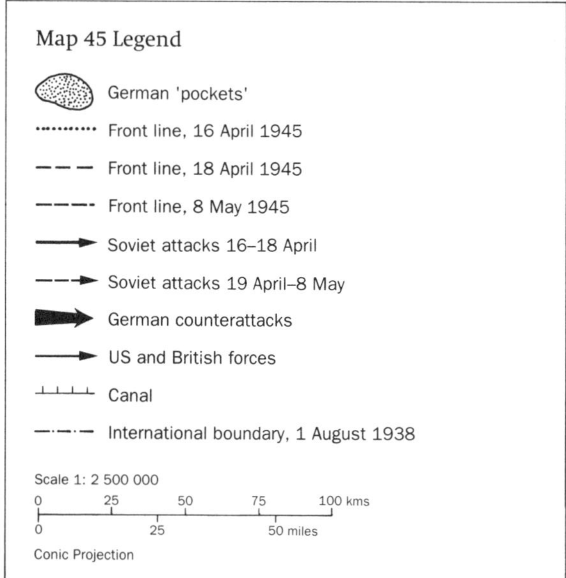

last stand, they could tie down American forces scheduled for transfer to the *Pacific war.

On the day he communicated the changed plan to Montgomery, Eisenhower also sent a message to Stalin, in which he proposed an arrangement for his and the Soviet forces' meeting. The Yalta conference had divided Germany into occupation zones (see also ALLIED CONTROL COMMISSIONS), but those were not to come into being until a state known as ECLIPSE—German collapse or surrender—was reached. To Stalin, Eisenhower stated that he wished to make a junction with Soviet forces along the Erfurt–Leipzig–Dresden axis, which would be his main line of attack because he believed the German government ministries were being moved to that area.

The first response came from Churchill and the British *Chiefs of Staff, who attempted to have the message stopped on the ground that Eisenhower was intruding into the inter-governmental sphere. Churchill also argued that Berlin had not lost either its military or its political significance, because the Germans would keep fighting as long as it held out; and he added that leaving the city to the Soviets would allow them to claim the lion's share of the victory. When the US *Joint Chiefs of Staff supported Eisenhower on all points, the British accepted his reassurance that the decision on Berlin was not irrevocable.

Eisenhower's message reached Stalin on 31 March. For him, the contents were no doubt a shock: not only were Erfurt, Leipzig, and Dresden deep in the designated Soviet zone, but he could not bring himself to believe Eisenhower would go for Dresden, which was further east, and not for Berlin. That night he had Zhukov and Konev in Moscow working on a hasty redeployment for a massive strike to Berlin. He replied blandly to Eisenhower, saying he agreed fully that Berlin had lost its strategic significance. Three days later, however, he dispatched an explosive note to Roosevelt. His 'military colleagues', he asserted, had solid evidence that the Americans and British had made a deal with the Germans whereby, in exchange for easier armistice terms, the Germans would open their Western Front to them while stiffening their resistance to the Soviet forces in the east.

The Ruhr pocket tied down two First and one Ninth Army corps and after it closed Kesselring had a great gap 200 km. (125 mi.) wide in his centre. But Hitler's 'stay put' order had denied Army Group B any further influence on the war, thereby lending an ironic validity to Stalin's charge as coherent defence was now impossible.

Against sporadic resistance, Eisenhower allowed the advance to continue as a pursuit on a broad front. Cities, rivers, and terrain features such as the Harz mountains and Thuringian forest, which could provided temporary rallying-points for the defence, barely kept the war alive, while masses of prisoners marching rearwards signalled its imminent demise. However, the absence of rail transport east of the Rhine posed some problems for the supply services, although the Ninth, First, and Third US Armies had the advantages of operating in the gap, and were, therefore, able to narrow their fronts slightly as they progressed eastwards, the Second Canadian and First British Armies had to fan out northwards and eastwards on widening fronts.

By 7 April, First British and Ninth, First, and Third US Armies had crossed the approximate halfway mark to the Elbe, the line of the Weser and Werra rivers. The Third Army was at Erfurt on 10 April, and by 12 April the Ninth Army was closing to the Elbe between Wittenberg and Magdeburg. By then, all three American armies were inside the Soviet zone. On 12 April, Bradley instructed First Army to stop short of Dresden, on the western tributary of the Elbe, the River Mulda, and await the Soviet contact there.

4. Victory in Europe

In a cable sent to *Marshall, the US chief of staff, on 15 April, Eisenhower said that in view of his and the Soviet forces' relative positions, it would be foolish to push on towards Berlin. Thereafter, the debate on how the race should have ended was in the hands of memoirists and historians. Zhukov and Konev began the Soviet Berlin offensive on 16 April. On that day also, the Allied air staffs declared a victory in the strategic bombing offensive and terminated it.

On 19 April, Second British Army reached the Elbe upstream from Hamburg, and First US Army took Leipzig. Three days later, Third and Seventh US and First French Armies opened the drive to eliminate the supposed National Redoubt. Since the stop on the Mulda did not apply to reconnaissance, First Army sent parties across the river, and one of those made contact with Konev's troops at *Torgau on the Elbe on 24 April.

After the Soviet Berlin offensive began, Churchill

expressed great concern to Washington that Denmark would fall into the Soviet sphere. The British zone extended east of Jutland to Lübeck, but Montgomery doubted that he had the strength to get there in time. Had the Soviet attack resulted, as planned, in a fast, crushing sweep to the Elbe, he would certainly have been right but German resistance was tying down all of Zhukov's and most of Konev's, strength around Berlin. On 29 April, Montgomery crossed the Elbe with the 18th US Corps supporting him on the right. Second British Army reached Lübeck on 2 May, and 18th Corps took Wismar and made contact with Soviet units there a day later.

In Berlin, on 30 April, Hitler designated Grand Admiral *Dönitz his successor as chief of state and C-in-C of the armed forces and then killed himself. Dönitz attempted, by piecemeal surrenders to the British and Americans, to give the forces on the Eastern Front time to escape westwards. On 4 May he surrendered the Netherlands, Denmark, and north-western Germany to Montgomery (see LÜNEBURG HEATH).

On 6 May, the fighting ended for the American armies. The Soviet forces completed their advance to the Elbe and the Mulda opposite the Ninth and First Armies. In the south, the National Redoubt having proved to have been an illusion, Third Army made contact with Soviet troops at Linz, and Seventh Army linked up with Fifth US Army at the Brenner Pass. Third Army also took Pilsen, which placed it in position for an advance to Prague, but Eisenhower acceded to an urgent request from the Soviet General Staff not to go beyond Pilsen.

Dönitz's emissaries arrived at Eisenhower's forward headquarters (see SHAEF) in Reims on 5 May to seek either a separate surrender to the Americans or a phased one that would allow more time to the troops on the Eastern Front. Eisenhower let them be told he would not grant anything but a simultaneous *unconditional surrender on all fronts. General *Jodl, who had been Hitler's chief military adviser, came a day later and after being given the same answer, with a threat that Eisenhower would close all his fronts to German military and civilians if the negotiations were not completed promptly, signed the unconditional surrender at 0241 on 7 May. It specified that all German forces were to cease operations and movements at 2301 on 8 May.

Churchill and *Truman declared 8 May *V-E Day, but Stalin, suspecting treachery, refused to accept the Reims signing as valid and demanded another, which took place in Berlin half an hour before midnight on 8 May, so that 9 May became the Soviet V-E Day. But Konev was then in the midst of a massive operation to take Prague (see GERMAN–SOVIET WAR, 11); consequently, Soviet operations did not end until 11 May. In the event, both surrenders proved to apply to the German military but not the civil government, and that omission, the Dönitz government having been abolished, had to be corrected on 5 June in a declaration by the four occupying powers.

EARL ZIEMKE

Ellis, L. F., *Victory in the West*, Vol. II (London, 1968).
Pogue, F. C., *The Supreme Command* (Washington, DC, 1954).
Wilmot, C., *The Struggle for Europe* (New York, 1952).

germ warfare, see BIOLOGICAL WARFARE.

Gestapo, acronym derived from Geheime Staatspolizei (State Secret Police), the organization with which *Göring replaced the Prussian political police in 1933. In 1936 it became a branch of *Heydrich's security police (see SIPO), which remained within the ministry of the interior, but in September 1939, when the *RSHA (Reichssicherheits-hauptamt) was formed as a main office of the *SS, it became its department (*Amt*) IV.

ghettos. The Nazis first established ghettos in which Jews were compelled to live after the *Polish campaign in September 1939. Until this time, Nazi policy towards the Jews within the frontiers of the enlarged Third Reich sought to disenfranchise them, strip them of their property, and compel them to emigrate. *Anti-Semitism had, from the start, been a central feature of *Nazi ideology, serving to bind together the disparate aspects of Nazi doctrine. Of the hostility of the inner core of Nazis to the Jews and of their desire to root out Jewish influence, there can be no doubt. Some dispute has, however, arisen as to whether Hitler aimed, from an early date in his political career to 'solve' the 'Jewish problem' by mass murder, or whether the exigencies and the opportunities created on the Eastern Front led to the *Final Solution. Certainly, as early as January 1939, speaking in the Reichstag, he threatened: 'If the international Jewish money power in Europe and beyond again succeeds in enmeshing the peoples in a world war, the result will not be the Bolshevization of the world and a victory for Jewry, but the annihilation of the Jewish race in Europe.'

Nazi policy towards the Jews in occupied Poland was laid down by Reinhard *Heydrich on 21 September 1939, even before the final Polish defeat. Heydrich was head of the *RSHA (Reich Main Security Office), a central body which had, in that month, been created under the control of the *SS to unite the state and party police. Heydrich's directives stated that Jews were to be expelled from the areas directly annexed to the Reich (Upper Silesia, Wartheland, the part of western Poland which had been annexed to Germany, and the area around Danzig), with the exception of Łódź. They were to be concentrated in the General government (see POLAND, 2(b)), as the remainder of German-occupied Poland was designated. In order to control them more easily, they were to be forced to live in 'ghettos' which would be administered by Jewish councils (Judenräte) which would be 'fully responsible in the literal sense for the execution of all orders'. This was to prove a thankless task. Some representatives of the Jewish élite accepted functions on the Jewish councils, hoping in this way to mitigate the harshness of Nazi rule and save at least some of the Jews under their care. They have been severely criticized for their role, particularly in the period when the Nazis deported the bulk of the inhabitants of the ghettos to death camps. But it should be borne in mind that at this stage the Germans had not yet adopted their 'final solution'. Thus attempts to save a remnant of the Jewish people, a policy as old as the diaspora, had a certain rationale at a time when the ghettos, which were in fact at the same time prisons and *forced labour camps, had achieved a certain stability.

The first ghetto was established in Piotrkow on 8 October 1939. In February 1940, a ghetto was created in Łódź, which, before the war, had contained the second largest Jewish community in Poland. Here, more than 165,000 Jews were forced into an area of less than 4 sq. km. (1.5 sq. mi.), which was sealed off from the rest of the city in May 1940. In 1940, ghettos were set up in almost all Polish towns with a significant Jewish population. It took some time before a ghetto was established in Warsaw (see WARSAW RISINGS), but in October 1940 the Germans issued an order creating one, which in November was cut off from the rest of the city by a wall, imprisoning over 400,000 people. After the invasion of the USSR in June 1941 (see BARBAROSSA), ghettos were established in most towns with a substantial Jewish population occupied by the Germans, including *Wilno, Riga, *Lwów, and Minsk as well as in many smaller urban centres.

Conditions in the ghettos were deliberately kept harsh. By 1941, the daily food ration for a Jew in Warsaw was as low as 184 calories, compared to 669 for a Pole and 2,163 for a German. Their inhabitants were subjected to sustained terror and forced labour and many died as a result of the terrible conditions they were forced to undergo. Higher casualties were only prevented by large-scale food smuggling, which was, for the most part, tolerated by the Germans. Yet, in spite of the harshness of the treatment they were experiencing, many Jews hoped that if they made themselves useful to the German war effort, some of them would survive the war. This was, in fact, a cruel illusion, fostered by the Nazis in order to facilitate the achievement of their goals. From mid-1941, Nazi policy towards the Jews had taken a very ominous turn. The invasion of the USSR was accompanied by the notorious *Kommissarbefehl* (commissar order), empowering German commanders to shoot out of hand any Soviet *commissar who fell into their hands. As a first step, **Einsatzgruppen*, mobile killing squads, were set up, which followed the advancing German troops and were entrusted with the task of murdering Jews, along with communist officials. It was at this time that the fateful decision was taken, in which Hitler was almost certainly personally involved, to 'solve' the 'Jewish problem', by mass murder.

From the spring of 1942, Jews were deported from the ghettos of Poland, Belorussia, the Ukraine, and the Baltic States to the death camps of *Chelmno, *Sobibor, *Belzec, *Treblinka, and *Auschwitz, where they were killed by gassing. Subsequently Jews from the rest of Europe, where ghettos were not established, were to share their fate. More than 4.5 million people perished in this way. The last of the ghettos to be destroyed was that of Łódź, whose leadership had managed up to that date to prevent the murder of the remnant of its population by producing uniforms for the German Army. Initially the Germans were able to carry out the deportations, making use of the SS, their own police, Polish and Jewish police, and the Jewish councils without much resistance. As it became apparent what fate was in store for the Jews, movements aiming to oppose deportation by armed resistance began to develop. Given the vast disparity of forces, resistance of this sort could only have a symbolic character. Armed opposition to the Nazis was offered in the Warsaw, Białystok, and Minsk ghettos. In many others armed formations were created which engaged in armed resistance in the countryside after the destruction of the ghettos. See also RINGELBLUM and THERESIENSTADT.

ANTONY POLONSKY

GI, nickname for a US soldier. It stood for Galvanized Iron (garbage cans), General Issue, or Government Issue. For GI Bill of Rights, see USA, 3.

Gibraltar, a rocky promontory which is part of the southern Spanish coast, has been a British colony since 1704. Following the fall of *France in June 1940, it was, until 1943, the only Western Allied stronghold on the continent of Europe. In 1939 about 20,000 Gibraltarians lived there, over 16,000 of whom were evacuated to North Africa and then mostly to the UK.

Hitler had plans (ISABELLA-FELIX), thwarted by the Spanish dictator, General *Franco, to capture Gibraltar so as to close the western entrance to the Mediterranean. *Force H, and the British Naval Contraband Control Service which searched all neutral merchantmen, operated from Gibraltar, and *convoys started from there. These played a crucial role during the siege of *Malta in supplying the island. For this reason Gibraltar attracted air attacks by Italian bombers, and its shipping made it a favoured target for sabotage raids mounted by the *Tenth Light Flotilla. It was also raided by *Vichy French bombers in retaliation for the Royal Navy's attack on *Mers-el-Kébir in July 1940. It was an invaluable haven for escaping Allied personnel (see MI9), and the chairman of the *XX-committee called it, from the intelligence point of view, 'one of the most difficult and complicated places on the map', for its closeness to pro-Axis, though neutral, Spain made it vulnerable to constant surveillance by *Abwehr agents.

A total of 40 km. (25 mi.) of tunnels, containing supply and ammunition dumps, workshops, and living quarters, were bored into the Rock, and *Eisenhower's HQ was situated there for the *North African campaign landings in November 1942. The excavated rubble was used to extend an airstrip into the sea, and this was completed in time for 600 aircraft to be packed on to it, which were used to give cover to the landings.

Gibson Girl, the first US portable radio transmitter (SCR-578), modelled on a German *air-sea rescue transmitter, which from mid-1942 onwards became part of the air-sea rescue equipment for ditched crews. Later models provided a crew's position from bearings 1,600–2,400 km. (1,000–1,500 mi.) away. The antenna was raised by a kite or balloon. The name came from the radio's hourglass shape which was reminiscent of the waist of the young women drawn by the artist Charles Dana Gibson in the late 1890s. See also RADIO COMMUNICATIONS.

Gideon Force, British *SOE force which comprised 50 officers, 20 British NCOs, 800 men from the Sudan Frontier Battalion, and 800 semi-trained Abyssinian troops. It was formed, and named, by Lt-Colonel *Wingate at the start of the *East African campaign in January 1941. It achieved its objective of establishing a base for Emperor *Haile Selassie in the Abyssinian province of Gojjam and then escorting him back to his capital, Addis Ababa. With it Wingate fought a guerrilla campaign of great skill and daring.

Gilbert and Ellice Islands, British western Pacific colony situated south-south-east of the *Marshall Islands and north-east of the Solomon Islands. Besides the sixteen atolls of the Gilberts and the nine islands of the Ellice group the colony included Ocean (see NAURU), Fanning, Washington, Christmas, and Phoenix islands. The Japanese occupation of the Gilberts during the *Pacific war was a constant air threat to the US–Australia sea route. US Marines mounted the *Makin Island raid in September 1942 and seized *Tarawa the following November. The more southerly Ellice Islands were never occupied by the Japanese but US forces were based there from October 1942.

Giraud, General Henri-Honoré (1879–1949), French Army officer who commanded the Seventh French Army, and then the merged Seventh and Ninth Armies during the fighting which led to the fall of *France. He was captured and held in Germany, but in April 1942 made a daring escape to unoccupied France, a feat which made him a hero in his country and an assassination target for the *Gestapo.

But though he was brave, and active in pushing through the re-equipment of his forces by the Americans, Giraud was arrogant and lacked any political sense. To ensure their fidelity to the Allied cause, the Americans wanted him to assume command of all French troops in North Africa after the proposed *North African campaign landings in November 1942. Giraud agreed, provided neither de *Gaulle nor the British were involved, and it was understood—by Giraud at least—that he would command the operation. When he learned otherwise he initially refused to co-operate and when he eventually did so his fellow officers in North Africa refused to accept his authority. He then raised a volunteer French army to fight alongside the Allies and after *Darlan's assassination in December 1942, Giraud replaced him as high commissioner in French North Africa, while still continuing as C-in-C of all local French forces.

De Gaulle and Giraud were rivals, but at the Casablanca conference in January 1943 (see SYMBOL), Churchill and Roosevelt demanded that the two work together. This took time to negotiate but resulted in their becoming joint chairmen of the *French Committee for National Liberation established in Algiers in June 1943. Giraud, however, was no match for de Gaulle politically. By November 1943 he was off the committee and in April 1944 his position as C-in-C was abolished. He was offered the post of inspector-general but chose to resign. No one, as one writer has commented, appeared sorry, or even noticed, that he had departed.

Gleiwitz radio station, raid on, faked assault by 'Polish' troops on a German radio station 1.6 km. (1 mi.) from the Polish border which became one of Hitler's pretexts for launching the *Polish campaign in September 1939. The attack was organized by *Heydrich and was led by an *SS Sturmbannführer (major), Alfred Naujocks. With eight men, all dressed in the uniform of the Polish regular army, Naujocks stormed the radio station on the evening of 31 August and immobilized its staff. Listeners to the station heard shots and then an announcement in Polish that it was time for the Poles to attack Germany. Before they left, the attackers, as evidence of Polish brutality against the civilian population, killed a *concentration camp inmate they had specially brought with them for this purpose. His body was shown to foreign *war correspondents as proof of the attack.

glider bombs, see GUIDED WEAPONS.

gliders, engineless aircraft used to carry airborne troops, tanks, artillery, and supplies. They were usually towed singly, but sometimes in pairs, behind specially converted bombers. Made of wood, or constructed from a tubular steel frame covered with fabric, they were towed to their targets and then released to glide down to a predetermined landing area.

The USSR pioneered gliders for military purposes, and glider units were formed there during the mid-1930s, but during the *German–Soviet war the Soviets used them only to supply their partisans. Germany was the first to employ them to transport troops, and was the only Axis country to do so, though Japan did develop a glider assault force. To acquire suitable military personnel, gliding was fostered by the Nazis as a sport between the wars, and the DFS230 'attack glider' was developed. It was this type which, at the start of the German offensive of 10 May 1940 (see FALL GELB), was used to capture the Belgian *Eben Emael fortress and the three vital bridges across the River Meuse. The Germans also used gliders to seize the Corinth Canal bridge in Greece during the *Balkan campaign and then for the airborne invasion of *Crete. The heavy losses incurred during this last operation turned Hitler against large-scale airborne assaults, but the Germans continued to use gliders in smaller operations. They were used to deliver supplies on the Eastern Front; *Skorzeny employed them in his daring operation to liberate Mussolini; and they were also used to attack French resistance fighters in the *Vercors. The Germans built the largest glider of the war, the 24-ton Messerschmitt 323. Called the Gigant (Giant) it could carry 200 fully equipped men, but it needed three aircraft, or two welded together, to tow it and though 200 were built they never proved satisfactory.

The Allies developed several types, notably the British 30-man Horsa, the larger Hamilcar, which could carry a light tank, and the American Waco. The British first used gliders, against *Vemork, in November 1942. But their first large-scale use by the Allies took place at the start of the *Sicilian campaign in July 1943 when 69 gliders out of the 137 used landed in the sea. More successful was their use by the *Air Commando which, in March 1944, landed some of the *Chindits by glider behind Japanese lines in Burma. This led to their being employed in large numbers to place Allied airborne troops on the flanks of the Normandy landings in June 1944 (see OVERLORD). They were also used successfully during the *French Riviera landings that August; during operation *MARKET-GARDEN in September 1944 where more than 2,500 gliders delivered British, Polish, and US units to their targets at Arnhem and elsewhere; and when British and US units were dropped beyond the Rhine in March 1945 during the battle for *Germany.

Attempts by the Americans to develop an amphibious glider for the US Marine Corps in the *Pacific war were curtailed, and the only use made of American gliders used in that theatre was when seven landed supplies and jeeps in northern Luzon (see PHILIPPINES CAMPAIGNS) in June 1945. They were also similarly employed in the last phase of the *Burma campaign. See also AIR POWER.

Mrazek, J., *The Glider war* (New York, 1975).

G-men, or government men, were FBI agents (see USA, 6).

Goebbels, Josef (1897–1945), Nazi minister of propaganda from 1933 until he committed suicide in the Führerbunker on 1 May 1945.

Born in the Rhineland town of Rheydt of Catholic working-class parents, Goebbels was awarded scholarships and then a university grant (which he refused to repay until taken to court). After reading for a degree in philology he completed a doctorate at Heidelberg in 1921. He started to write—articles, plays, a novel—but could not find employment. He became involved in politics and soon fell under Hitler's spell. In 1926 he was made Berlin's **Gauleiter*, and in 1930 the Nazi Party's propaganda chief, conducting a series of successful election campaigns that led to Hitler becoming Chancellor. It was he who introduced the greeting **Heil Hitler!* between party members in Berlin and also the name *Führer, making its use compulsory. It is no exaggeration to say that he created Hitler's public image, not merely as a political leader but also as saviour of his people.

In March 1933 Goebbels entered Hitler's second cabinet to head the new Reich Ministry of Information and Propaganda which was also responsible for the arts. He created the Reich Chamber of Culture (see GERMANY, 10) which regulated every aspect of creative life and purged from it anyone who was a Jew or who failed to applaud the Third Reich. This led to the mass emigration of the country's most talented novelists, dramatists, and musicians. But it was as a propagandist for Hitler and *Nazi ideology that Goebbels excelled. He grasped the enormous possibilities of disseminating the Nazi message by radio and saw to it that the manufacture of inexpensive sets was encouraged. He was a brilliant speaker and soon drew huge radio audiences, and in 1935 he began the world's first regular television service, a closed circuit one restricted to Berlin.

Once the war started, Goebbels developed radio propaganda services against Germany's enemies—including the use of American and British broadcasters (see, for example, 'AXIS SALLY' and JOYCE)—the sweeping victories of the early years greatly simplifying his task. His propaganda machine worked to undermine the morale of Polish and French troops, encouraged the belief that *fifth columnists were at work, and built up the image of generals such as *Rommel. But when he distorted events—such as his version of the sinking of the liner **Athenia*—it fooled no one, and as a civilian surrounded by military men, whom he mostly loathed, it seemed early in the war as if his star was on the wane. He turned to making propaganda visits at home and abroad, planning new public projects, and initiating collection drives for the war effort. When the Allied *strategic air offensive against Germany became more intense he toured the towns and cities, organized motorized units which brought relief to their bombed-out populations, and worked on improving the morale of their inhabitants, all of which helped to restore his popularity. And when disaster struck at *Stalingrad in January 1943, he played it up, seeking by such reverses to drive the German people into the 'total war' he now advocated.

Goebbels was a victim of his own propaganda; his loyalty to his leader was total. Right to the end he managed to maintain Hitler's public image as a true German who sacrificed himself for the good of his people. After the July 1944 bomb plot to assassinate Hitler (see SCHWARZE KAPELLE) he acted promptly to control the situation in Berlin by assuming military command of the city. This act of loyalty gave him the power he had long sought and for which he had constantly intrigued. Hitler appointed him 'Reich Plenipotentiary for Total War', which made him, after Hitler and *Himmler, the most powerful person in the Third Reich. He introduced the 60-hour week, shut down all forms of entertainment, and raised special battalions from the medically unfit.

In April 1945 he entered the Führerbunker with his family. He witnessed Hitler's marriage to Eva *Braun and was named the Reich Chancellor in Hitler's political testament. But the day after Hitler committed suicide he had his children killed, and he then had his wife and himself shot by an orderly.

Unlike most of the other leaders of the Nazi Party, Goebbels was a man of some intellectual stature. He was unprepossessing in appearance, and suffered from a club foot. Neither stopped him from being a womanizer (one scandalous liaison in the late 1930s threatened his marriage and his career), but his disability embittered him and from it probably stemmed his basic cynicism and contempt for mankind.

Heiber, H., *Goebbels* (London, 1973).
Reimann, V., *The Man who Created Hitler* (London, 1977).
Trevor-Roper, H. (ed.), *The Goebbels Diaries: The Last Days* (London, 1978).

Goering, see GÖRING.

GOLD, codename for assault beach in British sector on which the British 50th Infantry Division disembarked at the start of the Normandy landings on 6 June 1944 (see OVERLORD). By the end of that day 24,970 troops had landed there. It lay between Port en Bessin and the River Provence east of Mt Fleury in the Baie de la Seine. One of the two artificial harbours (see MULBERRIES) was installed there, at Arromanches.

Golikov, General Filip (1900–80), Soviet Army officer who commanded the Sixth Army when it occupied eastern Poland during the *Polish campaign, and in the *Finnish–Soviet war in which he distinguished himself. In July 1940, when *Timoshenko was appointed Defence Commissar in place of *Voroshilov, Golikov became his deputy and head of Military Intelligence (see GRU). In that capacity he must take much of the blame for the Soviet Union's incorrect assessment of German intentions before and after they launched their invasion of the USSR in June 1941 (see BARBAROSSA), which included ignoring the warnings of the Soviet agent Richard *Sorge. However, this débâcle did him no visible harm and in July 1941 he was chosen by Stalin to lead a three-month *Lend-Lease mission to London and Washington. In October 1941 he was appointed to command the Tenth Reserve Army which took part in the successful counter-offensive outside Moscow that December. He was then given command of the Briansk *front* (army group) but failed to hold Voronezh during the German summer offensive (see GERMAN–SOVIET WAR, 4) and was dismissed. He then served in an unspecified capacity around *Stalingrad before returning to his post as deputy defence commissar in April 1943.

Shukman, H. (ed.), *Stalin's Generals* (London, 1993).

Gona, battle of, fought in mud and swamp during the *New Guinea campaign when Allied troops attacked a Japanese defensive perimeter on Papua's northern coast on 16 November 1942. The perimeter, 18 km. (11 mi.) long, protected a beachhead established by the Japanese the previous July. While two regiments of 32nd US Division attacked *Buna and Cape Endaiadere at its south-eastern end two brigades of 7th Australian Division attacked it around Gona village and, with a third US regiment, Sananada Point.

After two months' hard fighting on the *Kokoda trail the Australians were debilitated by disease and lack of food (see also MEDICINE). The numbers defending the perimeter had been grossly underestimated and the division's 25th Brigade took more than 200 casualties in three days. On 28 November it had to be relieved, as did 16th Brigade which had been struggling towards Sananada. Eventually, with the help of two extra battalions, 21st Brigade, which had relieved 25th Brigade, entered Gona on 8 December. The Australians had 750 casualties, but there were more as fighting around the perimeter continued, and Sananada Point was not finally cleared until 21 January 1943.

Göring, Reichsmarschall Hermann (1893–1946), C-in-C of the Luftwaffe who was also, from 1939 until April 1945, Hitler's chosen successor.

The son of a former governor of German South-West Africa, Göring was born in Rosenheim, Bavaria. A regular infantry officer, he started flying in October 1914, won Germany's highest decoration, the Pour le Mérite, and ended the war as commander of the famous Richthofen Squadron. He joined the Nazi Party in 1922 and became commander of Hitler's bodyguard. Wounded during the beer hall putsch of November 1923, he became addicted to the morphine he was given to ease his pain, and for several years drifted in and out of mental institutions.

In May 1928 he became a Nazi Reichstag deputy and was elected its president in August 1932. When Hitler became Chancellor in January 1933, he was immediately appointed minister of the interior for Prussia, becoming president of Prussia that April. From this power base he quickly established the Nazi system of repression, founding an auxiliary police force (*Hilfspolizei*); the first two *concentration camps, Oranienburg and Papenburg, for political opponents; the state secret police, soon to be known by the acronym *Gestapo; and his own intelligence agency (see GERMANY, 7).

In January 1933 he was also appointed Reich commissioner for aviation (Reich minister of aviation from May 1933). With *Milch, *Kesselring, and others, and in defiance of the *Versailles settlement, he began building the Luftwaffe whose C-in-C he officially became in March 1935. Though incompetent where economics were concerned, he became Hitler's special commissioner for the four-year economic plan in 1936 and in the following year replaced *Schacht as minister of economic affairs (November 1937–February 1938). He also acted as Hitler's

Undated photograph of Hermann **Göring** addressing the Reichstag.

roving ambassador and troubleshooter, and in 1938 was promoted field marshal. Remembering those early years, Hitler later said of him that he was 'ice cold in times of crisis,' and added: 'I've always said that when it comes to the crunch he's a man of steel—unscrupulous', while the foreign minister, *Neurath, told the British ambassador: 'Göring is regarded as the real Fascist in the Hitler party.'

By 1939 the Luftwaffe was the world's strongest air force. When Warsaw refused to surrender during the *Polish campaign of September–October 1939 Göring bombed it into submission, and Hitler awarded him the Grand Cross of the Iron Cross (see DECORATIONS), the only person ever to receive it. In the spring of 1940 the Luftwaffe also excelled in the *Norwegian campaign and during the fighting which led to the fall of *France in June 1940.

In July 1940, when he was promoted Reichsmarschall, Göring was at the height of his powers. As the war progressed his prestige and influence gradually declined, though his popularity with the German public, who regarded him with bemused affection, surprisingly did not. However, his plan to destroy RAF Fighter Command was unsuccessful (see ADLERTAG); the Luftwaffe lost the battle of *Britain; proved incapable of supplying the Sixth German Army when it was cut off at *Stalingrad; and failed to prevent the Allied *strategic air offensive, or to retaliate effectively. Perhaps more importantly he made serious errors of judgement—he was adamant, for example, that the entrance of the USA into the war would have little effect—and his incompetent handling of the country's war economy steadily isolated him from the centre of power and more and more alienated those who had to implement his directives. His energy, so unflagging before the war, came only in sporadic bursts, and he took increasing refuge in his narcotic addiction, in the fantasy world of his various luxurious homes, or in travelling aboard his lavishly equipped private train. In this he shuttled from one European city to another, acquiring the art treasures (see LOOT) which so obsessed him, or visiting the Führer's headquarters where he fawned on Hitler and was treated with increasing, if covert, contempt by Hitler's cronies, and with exasperation and fury by Hitler himself. Though Hitler, who could be quite sentimental, retained a degree of faith in his old comrade, Göring was steadily eclipsed by his rivals for power and became progressively hemmed in by the multiplying intrigues against him.

In April 1945 Hitler gave him command in the south of Germany and on 23 April Göring, not unreasonably under the circumstances, suggested he assume power as Hitler was trapped in the capital. However, Hitler reacted furiously. He had Göring arrested and named *Dönitz his successor as head of state. In the hands of the *SS until 6 May, Göring managed to give himself up to the Americans the next day and was eventually arraigned at the *Nuremberg trials. Weaned from his drugs and much thinner, he defended himself vigorously. But in July 1941 he had signed the decree that had empowered Reinhard *Heydrich to 'make all necessary preparations ... for the overall solution of the Jewish problem' (see FINAL SOLUTION), and this alone was sufficient for him to be sentenced to death. He escaped execution by taking cyanide from a phial which he had somehow managed to conceal or which had been smuggled in to him.

Göring's corruptness and megalomania were exacerbated by his morphine addiction. Suborned by riches and power, his personality degenerated into a physical and mental grossness that became as legendary as his magpie obsession for collecting works of art, his elaborate uniforms, and his grotesque, bejewelled appearance.

Irving, D., *Göring* (London, 1989).
Overy, R., *Goering: 'The Iron Man'* (London, 1984).

Gort, Field Marshal Lord (1886–1946), born John Vereker, Gort inherited an Irish viscountcy at sixteen. A *First World War hero—holder of the Victoria Cross, three DSOs, and the MC (see DECORATIONS)—he was appointed *Chief of the Imperial General Staff (CIGS) in 1937. At the war office he was, as one of his staff officers commented, 'a fish out of water', and his relations with the war minister, *Hore-Belisha, were strained.

On 3 September 1939 he was delighted to be appointed C-in-C of the *British Expeditionary Force (BEF) whose existence and readiness were largely due to him. His courage during the fighting which preceded the fall of *France in June 1940 is undisputed, but he had never commanded anything larger than a brigade and it has been said that his appointment was beyond him intellectually. Nevertheless, he acted decisively, and on his own responsibility, when, on 25 May 1940, he plugged the gap about to be opened by a German pincers attack on the Belgian Army withdrawing northwards. By doing this, instead of obeying orders to attack southwards (the *Weygand plan), he made the *Dunkirk evacuation possible and saved the BEF from certain annihilation. He wanted to stay with his troops on the beaches, but, when ordered by Churchill, he handed over his command to *Alexander and returned to England on 1 June. After some months as inspector-general of training, he was appointed C-in-C Gibraltar in April 1941 and then of *Malta the following May. He successfully led the island's defence with such *élan* that in 1943 he was promoted field marshal. He left Malta in 1944 and finished the war as high commissioner and C-in-C in Palestine. He was knighted in 1940.

Colville, J., *Man of Valour* (London, 1972).

Gothic Line, series of German defences in the Apennines held during the *Italian campaign. It was thus named in April 1944, but two months later Hitler changed its name to the Green Line. The Allies called it the Pisa–Rimini line, though it actually ran from north of Lucca on the west coast to south of Pesaro on the east coast of Italy. The Allies broke through it in September 1944.

Goums were originally *gendarmerie*, small groups of irregular volunteers recruited from the indigenous population of French Morocco. However, like the *Spahis, they later gave their name to regular units which became part of France's Armée d'Afrique (see FRANCE, 6(b)). They evolved into specialized units (part-mounted, part-infantry, each about 200 strong), trained as mountain troops to police their own territory. In September 1939 there were 126 Goums of which 57 were regulars. Four were used against the Italians on the Tunisian–Libyan border before the fall of *France. After the *armistice, the French resident-general of Morocco, General *Noguès, contravened its terms by expanding them and keeping them secretly trained and properly armed. Following the *North African campaign landings in November 1942 four regiments of *goumiers* (Groupements de Tabors Marocains, or GTM) were formed. Two fought with the Allies in Tunisia, one fought with *Patton in the *Sicilian campaign, and one helped liberate Corsica. Then, as the 2nd and 4th Moroccan Infantry Divisions numbering some 10,000 men, they formed part of the *French Expeditionary Corps in the *Italian campaign, distinguishing themselves during the final battle for *Monte Cassino. From August 1944 they fought in de *Lattre's First French Army which, took part in the *French Riviera landings (as Armée B) and then in the battle for *Germany. They were very highly regarded as savage fighters, but they also inflicted their savagery on the civilian populations they encountered in Sicily and Italy.

Clayton, A., *France, Soldiers and Africa* (London, 1988).

government, see in government section of major powers and under name of country.

Government Code and Cypher School, see BLETCHLEY PARK.

governments-in-exile were formed in the UK and elsewhere by representatives of Allied countries overrun by the Axis. They were recognized in the normal way by the Allied powers, who exchanged diplomatic missions with them (most of them came to be headed by ambassadors), and they sent envoys to such meetings as the *San Francisco conference which founded the United Nations. Many of these governments controlled part of their own armed forces, formed in the UK, and had some control over resistance forces in their home countries.

When Poland was overrun by Germany and the USSR in September 1939, the government of the Polish republic—which had foreseen such a catastrophe—escaped, through Romania to Paris, where it established itself until the fall of *France the following summer forced it on the move again, this time to the UK. Even before the Poles had settled in London, King Haakon VII of Norway (1872–1957) and Queen Wilhelmina of the Netherlands (1880–1962) had arrived there, each accompanied by a cabinet. The Grand Duchess of Luxemburg moved on from London to Canada, leaving her prime minister and officials in London.

These first exiles were joined in the autumn of 1940 by the Belgian cabinet, whose King *Léopold III had stayed behind in Brussels. They too became a government-in-exile, sustained by the economic resources of the Belgian Congo. The Dutch and the Norwegians, similarly, had not only their gold reserves but also the resources of their merchant marine, as financial support; to which the Dutch added much of the network of an already large international airline, KLM.

Two more kings went into exile in the spring of 1941, when the Wehrmacht overran Yugoslavia and Greece during the *Balkan campaign. The young King Peter II of Yugoslavia (1923–70) moved to London, with his cabinet; he had protracted difficulties in exerting any real influence in his kingdom. King George II of the Hellenes (1890–1947), a close relation to the British King *George VI, moved first to Cairo, also with his cabinet; then, leaving them in the Near East—they went to Jerusalem—to London, to be near his cousins. His cabinet moved for a time to Johannesburg in South Africa, but then returned to Cairo where he sometimes rejoined them.

The Czechoslavak president, Edvard *Beneš, much distressed by the *Munich agreement, resigned soon after it, and went to teach sociology in Chicago. He returned to London in 1939, and was recognized in 1941 as the head of a Czechoslovak government-in-exile, which managed with British help to assassinate *Heydrich.

*MI6, usually operating through Colonel *Dansey, found it useful to co-operate as closely as *SOE did with these exiled bodies; several of them produced useful volunteer intelligence organizations in their homelands, as well as more or less well organized secret armies, standing by to help an Allied invasion. Moreover, though he was not recognized as the head of a government-in-exile by the British or the Americans until October 1944, General de *Gaulle had been active in London from 17 June 1940 as head of the Free French movement; the Soviets had recognized him as early as September 1941. His followers too provided Dansey as well as SOE with many volunteers; and *Eden said to him, only half in jest, when he came to leave London, that he had been more trouble to the British than all the other regimes in exile put together. He moved his headquarters from Carlton Gardens, London, to Algiers in May 1943, and by the end of that year had established himself, rather than *Giraud, as the undoubted leader of anti-*Vichy Frenchmen.

*Pétain, who had proclaimed himself head of the French state (state, not republic) in July 1940, himself became head of a government-in-exile in August 1944, when Vichy became untenable by the Germans; they moved him to Sigmaringen in south Germany, the seat of the Catholic branch of the Hohenzollern family whose Protestant cousins had ruled the Second Reich. This was a nominal arrangement—Pétain made no further attempt to exercise any authority in France.

There were also two governments-in-exile from Asia: President *Quezon escaped from the Philippines to form one in Washington, and the governor of Burma got away to Simla, where he headed the ghost of a regime which had no impact on events. See also government sections of occupied European countries mentioned in this entry.

M. R. D. Foot

Govorov, Marshal Leonid (1897–1955), taciturn Soviet artillery specialist who, after the German invasion of the USSR in June 1941 (see BARBAROSSA), commanded *Zhukov's Fifth Army during the defence of *Moscow in October–November, and in the Soviet counter-attack that December. He was promoted general and was given command of the Leningrad *front* (Army Group) in June 1942, remaining in that post until the end of the war. In January 1943 he succeeded in opening a corridor into the besieged city of *Leningrad, raised the siege completely in January 1944, and later overran the Baltic States. He was promoted Marshal of the Soviet Union in 1944.

Graf Spee, see RIVER PLATE.

Grand Alliance, term coined by Churchill to describe the association of nations, in particular the UK, USA, and USSR, which came together to fight the Axis powers in the Second World War. The title was a conscious reference to the alliance which had defeated Louis XIV of France in the War of the Spanish Succession, 1701–13, under the leadership of Churchill's ancestor the first Duke of Marlborough.

The Alliance did not assume its final form until two and a half years after the war in Europe had begun, when the German attack on the Soviet Union on 22 June 1941 (see BARBAROSSA) and the Japanese attack on the US fleet at *Pearl Harbor on 7 December precipitated those two non-belligerents reluctantly into the conflict. The relationship between London and Washington had however been progressively closer ever since the summer of 1940, when Roosevelt had realized that a Nazi Germany dominating Europe would ultimately threaten the USA. The passing of *Lend-Lease legislation in March 1941 had already made the USA 'the arsenal of democracy'; providing the UK not only with war supplies but also with naval escorts for the *convoys which transported them across the Atlantic. The USSR, however, before it was attacked, had been even more hostile to the western 'imperialist' powers than to Nazi Germany, with whom it believed itself to be on good terms. The two totalitarian powers had divided Eastern Europe between them in the *Nazi–Soviet Pact, signed by *Molotov and *Ribbentrop in August 1939, and Stalin had provided Hitler with economic assistance up to the moment of the invasion.

Once the USSR was in the war, however, the need to sustain its military effort was always a major consideration in British and American strategy; if only because victory in the east would release the full strength of the German Army and make invasion of the European continent from the west virtually impossible. It was for this reason that Churchill and Roosevelt, while they were together at the *Placentia Bay conference, cabled Stalin to suggest the *Three-Power conference. Yet relations between the USSR and its western allies were dogged by ideological hostility and cultural differences which complicated still further the task, difficult enough in itself, of getting help to a country isolated by its enemies from the west and by vast distances and poor communications in all other directions. The USSR therefore very largely fought its own war (see GERMAN–SOVIET WAR), giving to allies, whose intentions it never ceased to mistrust, the minimum information about its capabilities and plans.

When Germany attacked the USSR in June 1941 the UK had already been at war for almost two years—ever since, in implementation of the guarantee to Poland (see POLAND, GUARANTEE OF) the British declaration of war on 3 September 1939. It had not been alone in doing so. In addition to the forces of the British Commonwealth and Empire, whose independent white dominions rapidly declared war on their own account, there was an apparently powerful continental ally in France, with whom the UK had already co-ordinated its strategic plans.

These plans were based on two highly optimistic assumptions. The first was that *economic warfare would be successful because the German economy was already overstretched by military preparations, and so would be vulnerable to the economic pressure of naval blockade and direct, if discriminate, attack on her industries by the heavy bombers of the RAF. The second was that France would, with British help, be able to sustain a successful defence along its frontiers for however long was needed to build up sufficient military strength to invade a Germany already fatally weakened by blockade, bombardment, and, it was hoped, political dissension.

All these assumptions proved wrong. The German economy was not overstretched. The Germans indeed did not begin total mobilization on the scale introduced by the British in 1939 until early in 1942. They were able, by dominating or conquering their neighbours in Eastern Europe, to evade the effects of blockade. It took the RAF three years to develop the techniques and capacity to inflict serious damage on German industry (see STRATEGIC AIR OFFENSIVES, 1). Above all, the German army with its *blitzkrieg technique, had developed operational skills that enabled it to slice through the defences of the Western allies in May 1940, resulting in the fall of *France, as rapidly as they had those of Poland during the *Polish campaign in September 1939, and impose a total hegemony over the European continent, threatening the UK with its own weapons of air bombardment and blockade.

Nevertheless the general principles for Anglo-French strategy in the summer of 1939 continued to guide British strategic planning throughout the war. Germany was to be isolated and worn down to the point when a military offensive would stand a good chance of success. In 1940–1 such a prospect seemed remote: British strategy had to be almost entirely defensive; the only offensive weapon available was RAF Bomber Command, on whose capabilities and performance exaggerated expectations were placed. Having warded off the German invasion threat of summer 1940 (see SEALION) and survived the bombing of its cities in the winter of 1940–1 (see BLITZ), the UK could do little more than defend the sea lanes across which came the supplies from North America that enabled it to survive. In the Middle East, early successes against the Italians had held out further false hopes of clearing the shores of North Africa and building up an alliance of Greece, Yugoslavia, and Turkey to contain German expansion in south-east Europe. But here again the speed and decisiveness of German operations in the *Balkan and *Western Desert campaigns in the spring of 1941 threw British forces back on the defensive.

Desperate as the position appeared, neither the Soviet nor even the US entry into the war appeared unmixed blessings for the UK. No one in the west, in the summer of 1941, expected the USSR to survive the Nazi onslaught which might then, the British feared, continue through Persia to the Middle East and even India. Nevertheless help had to be found for the USSR, and supplies badly needed by the UK itself had to be sent round the dangerous route of the North Cape in *Arctic convoys decimated by German naval and air forces based in Norway. As for the Japanese attack on Pearl Harbor on 7 December 1941, although it brought the USA into the war as an open ally, it also brought in Japan as an open enemy; and Japan was in a position to do more immediate damage to British interests in the Far East than was a still largely unmobilized USA to provide countervailing help.

Japan's entry into the war and invasion of South-East Asia brought about the nightmare situation with which the British *Chiefs of Staff had warned throughout the 1930s that the UK would be unable to cope: war with major adversaries in western Europe, East Asia, and the Mediterranean. The British had constructed a major naval base at *Singapore, and it was hoped that, in the event of war with Japan, a fleet would be available to sail there to command the surrounding seas. As it was, only two capital ships could be spared from the European theatre, the **Prince of Wales* and *Repulse*, and they were promptly sunk by Japanese aircraft. With the US Pacific fleet also eliminated by the Pearl Harbor attack, there was nothing to stop the Japanese from landing forces in the *Philippines, the Malay pensinsula (see MALAYAN CAMPAIGN), and the *Netherlands East Indies and overrunning them within a matter of weeks.

Hitler, by fulfilling his alliance obligations to Japan and declaring war on the USA, removed all ambiguity about the situation (see also AXIS STRATEGY AND CO-OPERATION). The Americans found themselves full belligerent allies of both the UK and the USSR. This situation had been to some extent anticipated by the US Joint Board, the predecessors of the US *Joint Chiefs of Staff formed in February 1942. As early as November 1940 they had agreed that if the USA found itself at war with both Germany and Japan, they should stand on the defensive in the Pacific and give priority to the European theatre, where the major threat lay (see RAINBOW PLANS).

When in December 1941 Churchill and his military advisers attended the first Washington conference, (*ARCADIA) to co-ordinate the strategy of the Alliance, a bare two weeks after the attack on Pearl Harbor, there was still little inclination to depart from this decision. Nor were the members of the US Joint Board as yet in a position to dissent very strongly from the proposals presented to them by their British colleagues. These involved for 1942 the continued containment of Germany by closing and tightening a ring around it through maximum aid to the USSR and the conquest of the entire North African coast; together with bombing, blockade, and subversion. This, they hoped would clear the way for a return to the Continent in 1943 either across the Mediterranean or from Turkey into the Balkans, or by landings in western Europe. In the Far East, only such positions would be maintained as would safeguard vital interests and deny to Japan access to *raw materials vital to its continuous war effort. The latter task was entrusted to *ABDA Command under General *Wavell, which was, however, to disintegrate two months later when the Japanese completed their conquest of South-East Asia.

The conference also established the mechanism through which the Alliance would operate. The *Combined Chiefs of Staff committee was set up in Washington consisting of the American and British chiefs of staff sitting together, serviced by a Combined Secretariat and Combined Staff Planners. The British Chiefs of Staff were to be represented in their absence by the heads of the Joint Staff Mission which the British had already established in Washington; in particular by Field Marshal *Dill, who had recently been replaced as *Chief of the Imperial General Staff by General *Brooke. In addition Combined Boards were set up to co-ordinate shipping, raw materials, and war production. All these were located in Washington, which became effectively the capital of the Alliance.

Within a few weeks the US Joint Chiefs of Staff were becoming increasingly unhappy with the strategy they had accepted in December 1941. For one thing the speed and success of the Japanese advance was making even minimal resistance in the *Pacific war far more costly than had been anticipated; a cost which was to rise sharply during the summer when US forces tried to stem the tide in the Solomon Islands at *Guadalcanal. Secondly the Soviet Union, in spite of a brilliant recovery in December 1941, was again coming under severe pressure. The British strategy seemed to the Americans altogether too vague and leisurely. In February Major-General *Eisenhower, then chief of the war plans division in the war department, presented General *Marshall, chief of the army staff, with radical proposals for a landing in France in 1942, and for a sufficient build-up of US forces in the UK to make possible a large-scale invasion in 1943.

There now appeared that fundamental difference in national strategic concepts that was to underlie Anglo-American differences for the next two years. The American concept was simple. Commanding as they did overwhelming resources, the only problem they foresaw was how to get them to the Continent in order to engage the bulk of available German forces, defeat them decisively in battle, and pursue them in Napoleonic style to Berlin. For the Americans there seemed no strategic problem that numbers and technology could not cure.

The British, always short of resources, could not afford to think so boldly. Further, they had had bitter first-hand experience of the quality of the German armed forces. They therefore emphasized the need, first, to wear down German military strength by all possible means before engaging in confrontation, and secondly, to force maximum dispersion on the German armies so that the Allies would be able to get ashore and then engage with a favourable ratio of forces. To the British the Americans appeared naïve, to the Americans the British seemed timid; neither judgement was entirely unfair. The Americans were reluctant to learn from the experience of an ally for whose military performance to date they had little respect, while the British generals were not going to risk the lives of their men on the scale they had themselves experienced in the *First World War. British tactics as well as strategy tended to err on the side of caution, American on the side of rashness. It was a difference that not only bedevilled strategic planning but led to friction in every theatre, and at every level of command.

The British refused to undertake a premature landing on the coast of France in 1942, but in April 1942 they accepted in principle the American long-range strategy: the build-up of forces in the UK in 1942 (BOLERO) in preparation for a major landing in France in 1943 (ROUNDUP). It was a strategy, however, that failed to satisfy Roosevelt. Conscious of the growing public pressure for action in the Pacific, concerned at the plight of the USSR, and aware also that Congressional elections were due in November, he insisted that US forces should be engaged in action somewhere in the European theatre before the end of the year. With a landing on the French mainland ruled out, the only remaining option was one that Churchill had proposed the previous December; a landing in French North Africa (GYMNAST; later TORCH), to join hands with British forces advancing west from Egypt, thus clearing the Mediterranean and 'closing the ring'. Marshall and Eisenhower accepted this plan only with the greatest reluctance. Not only would it make ROUNDUP logistically impossible in 1943, but it would create an open commitment in the Mediterranean and make it more difficult to resist the pressure for a transfer of resources to the Pacific. Further, it would delay help to the hard-pressed USSR, as Churchill had to explain to Stalin on an awkward visit to Moscow in August 1942.

Nevertheless Eisenhower accepted command of the Allied forces and the TORCH landings which began the *North African campaign took place on the coast of North-West Africa on 8 November 1942. Simultaneously at the other end of the Mediterranean the British and Commonwealth Eighth Army under General *Montgomery finally defeated the German–Italian forces opposing them at the second battle of *El Alamein. Thanks to stubborn German resistance in the Tunisian mountains the Allies did not finally clear the shore of North Africa until May 1943. Even then, six months after the TORCH landings, the future course of Allied strategy was still undecided.

The Combined Chiefs of Staff met for the second time, together with Churchill and Roosevelt, at Casablanca, in January 1943 (see SYMBOL). The Americans once again pressed for a landing in France in 1943, failing which, they indicated, they would have to transfer substantial forces to the Pacific. The British on the other hand urged what became known as 'the Mediterranean strategy'. By continuing operations in the battle for the *Mediterranean, argued Churchill and General Brooke, they would bring pressure to bear on the weakest element in the enemy alliance, Italy, thus forcing the Germans to detach forces both from the Eastern Front and from the defences of north-west France. The Soviets would then be helped in the most direct way possible, while the German defences in France would be weakened in preparation for a full-scale attack, if not in 1943 then certainly in 1944. General Marshall, reluctantly accepting that a 1943 invasion was now out of the question, acquiesced to the extent of agreeing to an attack on Sicily once the African coast was cleared. Beyond that he was not prepared to go.

A further meeting therefore had to be held in Washington in May 1943 (see TRIDENT), during the closing stages of the fighting in North Africa. Opinions had now hardened on both sides. Churchill, elated with the successes of the British forces in North Africa, urged that the war should now be carried across the Mediterranean into Italy itself, whose collapse would transform the strategic situation. The US Joint Chiefs of Staff, on the other hand, insisted that nothing should now be allowed to interfere with the invasion of north-west France planned for 1944. Eventually it was agreed that the invasion (now meaningfully renamed *OVERLORD) should be firmly scheduled for 1 May 1944; that seven of Eisenhower's divisions should return from the Mediterranean to the UK to take part in it; but that with his remaining forces Eisenhower should mount such operations as he considered necessary to knock Italy out of the war. The invasion of Italy as such was not specified. But the landings in Sicily on 10 July (see SICILIAN CAMPAIGN) led to a collapse of Italian resistance so complete that even if it had not resulted as it did in the overthrow of Mussolini and secret overtures for surrender, the move into Italy itself would have been almost a foregone conclusion. With General Marshall's blessing, therefore, Eisenhower landed one of his armies across the straits of Messina at *Reggio di Calabria on 3 September (BAYTOWN) and landed the other at *Salerno, south-east of Naples, six days later.

Meanwhile attention had to be given to the problems of the Far East. Although the priority given to the European theatre remained in principle unchanged, the Combined Chiefs of Staff had agreed at Casablanca that adequate forces should be allocated to the Pacific and Far Eastern theatres, with the object of maintaining pressure on Japan, retaining the initiative and attaining a position of readiness for a full-scale offensive against Japan as soon as Germany was defeated. Japanese expansion had already been checked, primarily by the decisive naval battle at *Midway fought from 4 to 7 June 1942. At Casablanca it was possible to begin planning a counter-offensive.

In the Far East even more than in Europe Allied planning was complicated by different strategic concepts—indeed, different strategic objectives. Both the UK and the USA were of course concerned with the ultimate defeat of Japan, and the British accepted that in bringing about that defeat they could play only a very secondary role. But the ultimate objective of the British, especially of Churchill, was to recover the imperial possessions—Burma, Malaya, Hong Kong, Singapore—from which they had been so humiliatingly evicted. Churchill, an imperialist to his fingertips, declared that he had not become the king's First Minister in order to preside over the liquidation of the British Empire. But the USA had certainly not gone to war to preserve it. Even British rule in India, already threatened by the activities of the Congress Party (see INDIA, 3), was openly disapproved of by Roosevelt.

Indeed Roosevelt did not see the British as his principal allies in the Far East at all. That role was played by China under General *Chiang Kai-shek, with whom the USA had a close 'special relationship'. It was, after all, in an attempt to deter Japan from conquering China (see CHINA INCIDENT) that the USA had imposed on Japan the crippling trade restrictions which made the Japanese try to seize the resources of South-East Asia, thus precipitating the Pacific war. For Washington the initial objective was therefore to rescue China; partly as an obligation of honour—one of which the skilful and attractive Madam *Chiang Kai-shek constantly reminded the American people—but also because at this stage of the war, it was generally accepted that air, naval, and military bases in China would be needed for mounting an invasion of Japan and so securing her defeat.

By 1942 Japan controlled the entire Chinese coastline. In American eyes therefore, the best contribution the British could make to the war in the Far East was to restore land communications between the outside world and the besieged Chinese government by reopening the *Burma Road. Until this was done all help for Chiang Kai-shek had to be airlifted from north-east India over the *Hump, some of the worst flying country in the world. The British on the other hand regarded the Chinese military potential as negligible and were unimpressed by Chiang either as a political or as a military leader, an opinion which he himself helped to reinforce when he attended the Cairo conference in November 1943 (see SEXTANT). Far from wishing to attack overland through villainous campaigning country, British preference was for amphibious operations south-east across the Indian Ocean to reconquer their old possessions; Burma, Malaya, Singapore. Unfortunately for the British not only were these operations of little interest to the USA, but they competed for the same resources for *amphibious warfare that were needed in the Pacific and the European theatres.

At Casablanca the Americans agreed to provide resources for a seaborne attack on Rangoon (ANAKIM) as a step in opening the Burma Road, and sketched out their own plans for the Pacific. Their two-pronged strategy was already becoming apparent. In the central Pacific, Admiral *Nimitz's amphibious forces would advance from Midway to seize *Truk in the Caroline and *Guam in the Mariana Islands; while in the south-west Pacific, General *MacArthur was to squeeze the Japanese out of the fortress they had established at *Rabaul in the

Bismarck Archipelago, in preparation for a further offensive.

By the time of the TRIDENT conference in May 1943, it was clear that no resources would be available for ANAKIM. The Burma Road could be opened, if at all, only by an overland offensive. For this the British were far from ready: the most they were prepared to undertake was a limited offensive in Upper Burma to safeguard the air route, over which it was hoped that greatly increased aid could now be flown. In the Pacific the lines of the two-pronged attack became clearer, with MacArthur's line of operations being extended up the northern shores of New Guinea towards the Philippines. But the possibility was recognized, for the first time, that American control of the seas in the Western Pacific might force Japan to surrender before its territory was invaded.

It was further agreed at the first Quebec conference in August 1943 (see QUADRANT) that a new Allied command structure should be created, in succession to the ill-fated ABDA, to control operations in South-East Asia—*South-East Asia Command. The commanders appointed to head it indicated the inchoate breadth of its responsibilities. The Supreme Allied Commander, Admiral *Mountbatten, was an expert on amphibious warfare, and his appointment reflected British, especially Churchillian, aspirations to a seaborne reconquest of the Malay peninsula. His deputy, the American Lt-General *Stilwell, also held the post of chief of staff to Chiang Kai-shek, and indeed commanded American-trained Chinese forces in the field (see CHINA–BURMA–INDIA THEATRE). The only place where their interests overlapped was Burma. Since adequate resources for any amphibious operations could not in any case be made available until the war had been won in Europe, attention for the next year was therefore focused on operations in this most inaccessible and unfriendly of regions. As operations there had to be supplied almost entirely from the air, and since the aircraft capable of doing so were also required to supply China over the Hump, strategic decisions usually boiled down to the allocation of these machines; decisions which, because of their political delicacy, could often only be taken in Washington. In any event the forces available in the theatre were insufficient to effect any change in the strategic situation for another year to come. When this did happen it was to be as a result not of an Allied but of a Japanese initiative.

Meanwhile in Europe the collapse of Italy in September 1943 at the start of the *Italian campaign seemed to the British to open up a huge range of dazzling possibilities. Not only did they foresee a rapid German withdrawal at least to the Pisa–Rimini Line (see GOTHIC LINE), but the Balkan peninsula and the Aegean Islands, which had been largely garrisoned by Italian troops, now seemed wide open to Allied penetration. But the opportunities quickly vanished. The speed with which the Germans disarmed and replaced their former allies, Hitler's determination to retain the economic resources of the Balkans, and the unimpressive performance of the Anglo-American forces in southern Italy convinced the German High Command that they could contain the Allied advance in the mountains south of Rome. The Allied forces thus rapidly found themselves faced with the prospect of a gruelling campaign up the length of a peninsula ideally suited to the needs of defence. Undeterred, Churchill and the British Chiefs of Staff now pressed for a revision of the strategic concept agreed at TRIDENT so as to make possible the maintenance of continuing pressure in the Mediterranean; even if it meant that the invasion of France would have to be deferred.

The Americans, however, were adamant. Having fought hard for an agreed date for OVERLORD—1 May 1944—they were not now going to abandon it. Nor would they reconsider their demand that seven divisions should be transferred from the Mediterranean theatre to the UK, to take part in the operation. They were unimpressed by the British arguments, that only by maintaining pressure in the Mediterranean could they bring continuing help to the USSR and prevent the Germans from strengthening their forces in France to an extent that would make landings impossible. They saw them rather as a specious excuse for a reluctance, on the part of a military and political leadership which remembered the First World War, to engage in any frontal attack against the Wehrmacht; that, and also cover for an ill-defined 'Balkan strategy'.

A myth was propagated by some British and American journalists after the war (in particular Chester Wilmot and Hanson Baldwin) that the British had a long-term politico-military strategy derived from historical experience, which consisted in evading a direct frontal approach against the Germans' defences and using the flexibility of sea power to attack them at a point where they were ill-prepared and where the greatest political advantages might be reaped. Such advantages, so this thesis ran, were available in south-east Europe, where stalwart resistance movements were already alive in Greece and Yugoslavia, and where military operations might bring Anglo-American forces into central Europe before it fell into Stalin's hands. It has been argued that this was the real objective of Churchill's strategy. In the aftermath of the war, after the famous 'Iron Curtain' had descended from Stettin to *Trieste, it was seen as a great opportunity missed, and the US Chiefs of Staff were sorely blamed for it.

In fact the British had no such long-term strategy. Before the summer of 1943, it is true, this Balkan option had not been excluded, and was in fact being urged by the British High Command in Cairo (see MIDDLE EAST COMMAND) where close links were maintained with resistance movements in the Balkans. But the decisions at TRIDENT finally ruled it out, and the opening of the Italian campaign drew in all available forces in the Mediterranean. At Churchill's urging the *Dodecanese campaign was mounted in September 1943 in which an attempt was made to seize the Dodecanese, but the

Americans refused to divert forces to help the operations, and speedy German reaction foiled the British attempt at a *coup de main*. Allied *deception operations did indeed maintain a highly credible threat of an invasion of the Balkans by an imaginary Twelfth British Army, but in reality all that was intended was continuing help to the resistance movements on an ever-increasing scale. As for the Soviets, it was not until the summer of 1944 that their advance into eastern Europe was seen as a political or a military threat to the west. In 1943 the western Allies looked forward to it with eager anticipation.

By the autumn that advance was well under way. In November 1942–January 1943, simultaneously with Allied victories at both ends of the Mediterranean, the Soviet victory at *Stalingrad had thrown the German armies on to the defensive. In July, simultaneously with the invasion of Sicily, the Red Army destroyed German armoured strength in the battle of *Kursk (CITADEL). By the end of September they had reached the *Dnieper, and at the beginning of November they broke across it at *Kiev. With the ring now seriously tightening around Germany, the time had come for the western Allies to co-ordinate their strategy with that of the USSR. At the end of November, Roosevelt and Churchill for the first time met Stalin at the Teheran conference (see EUREKA) in order to do so.

The British and the Americans arrived in Teheran with their differences unsettled, and Stalin had effectively to adjudicate between them. These differences had been exacerbated by an American proposal that, after the capture of Rome, the Italian campaign should be virtually closed down and Mediterranean forces concentrated on an invasion of the South of France to coincide with OVERLORD. The Americans had no problem in enlisting Stalin's support for their view that OVERLORD should be the main operation for 1944 to which all other operations, whether in the Mediterranean or elsewhere would be secondary; though whether Stalin accepted this on purely strategic grounds or in order to give himself a free hand in eastern Europe must remain uncertain.

So the *French Riviera landings (ANVIL) were decreed. Churchill's continued pleas for operations in the Aegean were overruled, but it was agreed that the advances in Italy should be continued to the Pisa–Rimini Line. Most important of all, Stalin announced his intention of entering the war against Japan once the war in Europe was over. Since the US Chiefs of Staff still at this stage believed that the defeat of Japan could only be brought about by operations launched from the mainland of Asia, and since that mainland was still occupied by the bulk of the Japanese Army, this announcement came as a considerable relief to them.

Though they bowed to the views of their two major allies and confirmed their acceptance of OVERLORD for May 1944 (Generals Eisenhower and Montgomery and their staffs being transferred from the Mediterranean to take charge of the operation), the British continued to argue against ANVIL. The stubbornness of German resistance along the River Garigliano, and the failure of the Allied attempt to circumvent it by their landings at *Anzio in January 1944 (SHINGLE) led to ANVIL being postponed from May to July, but Churchill remained deeply unhappy with the idea of withdrawing some eleven divisions from a theatre where their presence might make a decisive difference to one where they could not. His discontent boiled over when at last, in May, the Allies broke through the German defences with operation DIADEM and surged forward to capture Rome on 4 June.

Once again, as in the previous September, glittering possibilities opened up. The Pisa–Rimini Line now appeared to Churchill far too modest an objective, as it did to General *Alexander, the Allied C-in-C in Italy. Alexander put forward far-reaching proposals, contingent on his retaining the ANVIL divisions, for an offensive that would break through the Gothic Line between Pisa and Rimini, overrun the plain of Lombardy, and thence strike north-east into Austria via the Ljubljana gap. The morale of his forces, reported Alexander, 'was irresistibly high ... Neither the Apennines nor even the Alps should prove a serious obstacle to their enthusiasm and skill.'

Needless to say, Churchill gave these proposals his strongest support, but the Americans would have nothing to do with them. OVERLORD had been successfully launched on 6 June without the simultaneous landings in the South of France originally demanded; but the Americans insisted that those landings (now renamed DRAGOON) should still be mounted so as to open up additional supply facilities for the advance on Germany. Churchill continued to plead for a change of plan, but in vain: the DRAGOON landings took place, against minimal German resistance, on 15 August.

Meanwhile at the end of June the Red Army had opened a massive offensive along the entire length of their front. By August they had crossed the Polish frontier. But the *Warsaw rising, the apparently deliberate inactivity of the Soviet forces while the Germans crushed the insurrection, and Stalin's refusal to provide facilities for Allied air forces to drop supplies, opened the first serious rift in Allied unity and sharply diminished western enthusiasm at the prospect of the Red Army liberating eastern Europe.

For Churchill, and some later critics of Allied strategy, this seemed to provide tragically belated justification for his arguments against ANVIL. But the possibility that Alexander could have achieved all he promised, even if he had been left with ANVIL divisions, was remote. The terrain north-east of Venice is ideally adapted to defence, as the Italians had found to their cost in the First World War. Quite possibly, however, the Allied armies, had they not been weakened, might have broken through into the Po valley and liberated northern Italy before the winter. As it was, Alexander just failed to break through the German defences north of Pisa and Rimini, and the offensive bogged down until the following spring. Meanwhile Italian resistance forces in Lombardy, which had risen in September in response to overoptimistic Allied appeals, were crushed by the Germans as ruthlessly as had been the Poles, and felt no less bitter a sense of betrayal.

In September 1944 indeed, with the German forces broken in the *Normandy campaign and streaming back to their own frontiers, the Allies were confident that the war would be over by the end of the year—an overconfidence which played a large part in the check their forces received at Arnhem (see MARKET-GARDEN). Despite Churchill's insistence at the second Quebec Conference (see OCTAGON), held just before MARKET-GARDEN was launched, that the UK take a larger role in helping to defeat Japan, it was a matter of considerable importance for the British that the war should not drag on for another year. They had reached the end of their resources, demographic as well as economic, and their dependence upon the USA was becoming absolute. For the Americans there was no such urgency. Having landed five armies in France, the Supreme Allied Commander, General Eisenhower, was prepared to use them all in a prolonged strategy of attrition on a broad front. His subordinate, Field Marshal Montgomery, however, urged a more decisive strategy in which British forces would spearhead a drive on Berlin. The dispute rumbled on through the winter, and though Mongomery's approach understandably found strong support in London, in Washington the Combined Chiefs of Staff, equally understandably, refused to interfere with Eisenhower's conduct of operations.

The toughness of German resistance throughout the winter provided some justification for Eisenhower's view, that the only way to overcome it was by a process of grinding attrition in which Allied *matériel* could make its superiority felt. By the end of March 1945 that attrition had done its work. The Allied armies surged across the *Rhine, and found little resistance beyond it.

Meanwhile the Red Army had driven deep into eastern Germany, and by the end of February it stood along the line of the Oder and the Neisse rivers, 60 km. (37 mi.) from Berlin. Eisenhower now planned to drive deep into central Germany in the direction of Leipzig in order to cut off the *'National Redoubt' that he believed Hitler to be preparing in the Alps. Indeed he informed the Soviets that he intended to do so. Montgomery made a last appeal for a drive on Berlin, with the full support of Churchill and the British Chiefs of Staff. In the political confrontation that was now developing between the USSR and the western Allies, Berlin seemed a prize of the highest importance. But Marshall again supported Eisenhower, and Roosevelt, now a dying man, did not overrule him. Roosevelt in fact died on 12 April, leaving a political vacuum in Washington in these final critical weeks. When two weeks later Churchill urged Eisenhower to speed his advance into Czechoslovakia in order to occupy *Prague, Marshall vetoed the proposal. 'Personally,' he said, in a phrase that haunted him ever after, 'I should be loath to hazard American lives for purely political purposes.'

Although he spoke as a soldier, Marshall in fact probably expressed the views of the bulk of the American, and perhaps of the British, people. The Soviets were still greatly admired allies—they had borne the brunt of the fighting and without their sacrifices victory would have been impossible. A military confrontation with them, in which Allied lives might have been placed at risk, in order to gain a few more miles of territory would have been very difficult to justify before a war-weary public opinion. In any case boundaries between the Allied zones of occupation (see ALLIED CONTROL COMMISSIONS) had already been drawn up when Stalin, Churchill, and Roosevelt had held their second 'Summit' meeting at Yalta in February 1945 (see ARGONAUT)—boundaries which left Berlin deep within the Soviet zone (see Map I).

Most of the business at Yalta was concerned with the settlement of Germany, Europe, and the United Nations, once the war was over, and so falls outside the ambit of this article. One event of strategic importance did, however, take place: Stalin reaffirmed his intention of entering the war with Japan three months after the conclusion of the war in Europe, and a secret agreement was reached on his price for agreeing to do so (see KURILE and SAKHALIN ISLANDS).

By this time events in the Far East had moved swiftly. In the Central Pacific, Admiral *Nimitz's forces had cleared the *Marshall and *Mariana Islands and in October 1944 had destroyed what was left of Japanese sea power in the battle of *Leyte Gulf. General MacArthur's forces, leapfrogging up the northern coast of New Guinea, had at the end of January 1945 landed in the Philippines. In the *Burma campaign, however, the Japanese themselves had taken the initiative in March 1944 with an attack on the British bases at *Kohima and *Imphal. They were held and thrown back in disorder the following June. In October *Slim's Fourteenth Army followed on their heels with an offensive which was to capture *Mandalay in March and Rangoon in May 1945: the Burma Road at last stood open.

Ironically it was no longer needed. In April 1945 US forces landed on *Okinawa in the Ryūkyū Islands, bringing the whole of Japan within fighter as well as bomber range. Tight blockade from the sea and continual battering from the air now made the defeat of Japan without the need for invasion a serious possibility. Nevertheless planning for the invasion continued, and it was agreed that British naval, land, and air forces should take part. Though bases were no longer required on the Asian mainland, Soviet intervention was still needed, to mop up the large Japanese Army stationed there. Plans for these final operations were discussed at the last Allied summit meeting at Potsdam in July (see TERMINAL); a meeting which also issued a joint declaration calling upon Japan to surrender and at which President *Truman informed Stalin that the USA 'had a new weapon of unusual destructive force'. Stalin replied 'that he was glad to hear it and hoped that they would make good use of it against the Japanese'. On 6 August the first *atomic bomb was dropped on *Hiroshima. Two days later the USSR declared war on Japan. On 14 August Japan accepted the Allied demand for *unconditional surrender.

The Potsdam conference was terminal not only for the war but also for the Grand Alliance. Roosevelt was dead, Churchill was voted out of office while the conference was actually in progress, and Stalin had already begun the process of insulating the USSR and its conquests from Western influence that would lead directly to the *Cold War. The USA terminated Lend-Lease to the UK, as to all its other allies, and the two governments quarrelled bitterly over the terms of the loan that was to take its place. Disagreement over the treatment of Germany, over British access to the results of joint nuclear research, and over British policy in Palestine was rapidly to destroy the old wartime camaraderie. But the Grand Alliance had served its purpose. In spite of all differences and disagreements, it had held together as effectively and functioned as efficiently as any in the history of war.

MICHAEL HOWARD

Butler, J. R. M. (ed.), *History of the Second World War, Military Series: Grand Strategy*, 6 vols. various authors (London, 1956–76).
Matloff, M., and Snell, E., *United States Army in World War II: Strategic Planning for Coalition Warfare 1942–44*, 2 vols. (Washington, DC, 1953–9).
Feis, H., *Churchill, Roosevelt, Stalin: the War they Waged and the Peace they sought* (Princeton, 1957).

Grandi, Count Dino (1895–1988), Italian undersecretary, then minister, of foreign affairs from 1925 to 1932 before being appointed ambassador in London. He was too moderate for Mussolini's liking and in July 1939 he became minister of justice. In early 1941 he was sent to the Albanian Front (see BALKAN CAMPAIGN) when Mussolini abruptly mobilized his ministers and high officials to try to restore public morale. This caused considerable rancour and Grandi later said that it was at the front that he planned with others the resolution which led to Mussolini's downfall in July 1943. He was offered, but refused, the governorship of Greece, and in February 1943, despite his earlier 'grovelling protestations of loyalty to the regime' (M. Knox, *Mussolini Unleashed*, Cambridge, 1982, p. 268), he was dismissed from the cabinet. That July he tabled the motion at the Fascist Grand Council which led to Mussolini's deposition and arrest. He fled abroad before the *armistice with the Allies was declared in September 1943 and was subsequently refused re-entry into Italy. In his absence he was sentenced to death at the *Verona trials and after the war was acquitted by a commission enquiring into fascist crimes. He lived in Brazil before returning to Italy in 1973.

Grand Slam bomb, British bomb developed by Barnes *Wallis. At 22,000 lb. (10,955 kg.) it was the heaviest bomb used in the war creating a crater 9.1 m. (30 ft.) deep and 37.7 m. (124 ft.) wide. Wallis's proposal for it early in the war had been rejected by the air staff, but after his success with his cylindrical bomb in May 1943 (see DAM BUSTERS), work was started on the Grand Slam. The *Tallboy, a smaller version, became operational in June 1944, but the Grand Slam was not used operationally until March 1945. Altogether, 41 were dropped by the Dam Buster squadron (617) on bridges and viaducts in Germany. See also BOMBS.

Graziani, Marshal Rodolfo (1882–1955), Italian Army chief of staff who served as a minister in Mussolini's Italian Social Republic (see ITALY, 3(b)), and proved to be the most reliable fascist of Mussolini's senior army officers.

Graziani finished the *First World War as the army's youngest colonel and by 1928 he was commanding all Italian forces in Tripolitania. In 1930 he became vice-governor of Cyrenaica and commanded a harsh campaign against the rebellious Senussi tribesmen, sealing the Egyptian border with a wire fence and imprisoning the nomadic population in camps. In early 1935 he was appointed military governor of Italian Somaliland and commanded the troops that invaded Abyssinia that October. The following May he succeeded *Badoglio as governor-general and viceroy in Abyssinia. After brutally suppressing the local population, which led to a general revolt, he left Abyssinia in January 1938 and after passing two years in virtual retirement was appointed army chief of staff in October 1939.

In June 1940, when the governor of Libya, Marshal Italo Balbo (1896–1940), was accidentally shot down and killed by his own anti-aircraft batteries, Graziani replaced him as commander of Italian forces in Libya, retaining his position as the army's chief of staff. Having been ordered to attack, in September 1940 he reluctantly moved his forces into Egypt. However, he had only got as far as *Sidi Barrani when he was decisively beaten by *O'Connor's Western Desert Force in December 1940. He was defeated again at *Bardia and *Tobruk, and was finally driven out of Cyrenaica following the defeat of the remains of his forces at *Beda Fomm in February 1941. He then pleaded a nervous breakdown and retired to private life. A board of enquiry was established to investigate his conduct, but though it reported adversely no action was taken. During the life of Mussolini's Italian Social Republic in northern Italy he served as defence minister and Mussolini's chief of staff and instigated repressive measures against Italian partisans. After the war he was sentenced by an Italian court to nineteen years' imprisonment but was released in 1950.

Great Britain, see UK.

Greater East Asia Co-prosperity Sphere. The Japanese language does not make a clear distinction between 'great' and 'greater'. When describing the war they fought between 1941 and 1945—the Allies called it the *Pacific war—the Japanese, in their English-language coverage of the war directed at the peoples of the conquered territories, generally used the phrase 'Greater East Asian War' (*Dai To-A senso*). Like the earlier British use of 'Great Britain' and the German one of '*das grosse deutsche Reich*', the words implied the idea of expansion and expansionism; but it also had an extra connotation, suggesting 'freeing the peoples of Asia from colonialism and imperialism', which satisfied the Japanese claim to be fighting a war of liberation in Asia.

This fact is relevant to any consideration of the Greater East Asia Co-prosperity Sphere (*Dai To-A kyoeiken*) which was a part of the ideological underpinning of the Greater East Asian war. To the Japanese the phrase did not convey a message of imperialism or expansion so much as one of co-operation, and it was part of a doctrine which began to be propounded midway through Japan's war with China (see CHINA INCIDENT), and before the outbreak of the Pacific war in December 1941, in order to explain and rationalize its relationship with the peoples of Asia. It amounted to a statement of Japan's war aims at their most favourable and was intended to give heart to the Japanese people, and to enlist the support of the populations of countries occupied or about to be occupied by the Japanese armies. As a slogan, it tried to rally those in Japanese-occupied areas against imperialism and colonialism, and to encourage them to mobilize with Japan both in the war and in the peace that would follow. The emphasis on mutual prosperity increased as the scope of the war extended.

However, the idea of a Greater East Asia Co-prosperity Sphere was being refined in Japanese minds for most of the 1930s. When the momentous decision was taken to sanction the setting up of a new state in Manchuria in 1932 (see MANCHUKUO), there was already a debate among Japan's leaders about the way Japan should react to its continental neighbours. One of the initiators of the Manchurian Incident, which precipitated the Japanese occupation of Manchuria, founded the Concordia Association in July 1932 in an attempt to combine economic objectives, such as promoting agriculture and industry, with pan-Asian concepts of racial harmony. In his view, the new Manchukuo should be regarded as a model for Sino-Japanese co-operation with equal opportunity for Chinese, Mongols, and Koreans alike (Korea was then a Japanese colony). It was a blueprint for benign intentions, though the reality was that Japan brought about an economic and defensive amalgamation of Manchuria with Japan.

Shortly after war broke out between Japan and China, in July 1937, the ideas of the Concordia Association surfaced afresh. In two declarations on 3 November and 22 December 1938, the then prime minister, Prince *Konoe, spelled out the doctrine of a New Order for East Asia, a doctrine which was linked to proclamations about the New Order in Europe being issued in Germany and Italy which were, by this time, Japan's partners in the *Anti-Comintern Pact of November 1936 (see also AXIS STRATEGY AND CO-OPERATION). The notion, still a vague one, was that Japan had a mission to eradicate European and American imperialism, and also the influence of *communism, from East Asia. It created the idea of a bloc consisting of Japan, Manchukuo, and China whose object would be to keep out alien influences. It was a challenge to the world powers interested in China and did not appeal to China's leader, *Chiang Kai-shek, who continued his stubborn resistance to Japan's invasion of his country.

The German occupation of the Netherlands and the fall of *France in June 1940 made their East Asian colonial possessions (see FRENCH INDO-CHINA and NETHERLANDS EAST INDIES) vulnerable—the Netherlands East Indies was an important source of oil which Japan badly needed—and on 29 June Arita Hachirō, the foreign minister, announced in a radio broadcast that the bounds of the New Order were being extended to take in South-East Asia. When Konoe returned as prime minister in July, he reiterated his views about the New Order, promising 'increasingly to bind ourselves economically to Manchukuo and China and to proceed to South-East Asia'. Shortly afterwards a policy statement laid down that Japan should strive for world peace, based on *Hakkō ichiu*—literally, 'eight points of the compass under one roof', but meaning a spirit of universal benevolence—and that it should aim for a New Order in Greater East Asia centred on Japan, occupied China, Korea, and Manchukuo. The notion of the Co-prosperity Sphere was thus announced and in November 1940 it was adopted as a national objective; but there was still a large element of vagueness because of the emphasis given to phrases such as 'New Order', 'the great spirit', and 'the Imperial Way', which were undefined and had a peculiarly Japanese meaning. The concept was still far short of a blueprint and could hardly be the basis of a firm alliance in wartime.

The Co-prosperity Sphere was partly a response to world events and partly a retaliation to the economic sanctions the USA was imposing on Japan in an effort to stop its aggression in China. After the attack on *Pearl Harbor in December 1941, and more especially on the British colonial territories of Hong Kong and Malaya the same month, the bounds of the sphere had to be further defined. In a policy statement to the 79th Diet on 21 January 1942 the new prime minister, General *Tōjō, referred to Japan's conviction about the mutual benefits to be derived from coexistence and co-prosperity based on a common goal, with Japan as 'the core, the kernel, whereby all states and peoples of Great East Asia will be enabled to find their true place (in the world)'.

In this speech Tōjō seemed to be reflecting ideas formulated by a body called the Total War Research Institute which had close relations with the army and the cabinet. In January 1942 the institute prepared 'the draft plan for the establishment of the Co-prosperity Sphere', which seemed to influence the thinking of the government. Here for the first time we have an attempt at a definition of the sphere. The document divided it into three areas: the Inner Sphere (Japan, Manchukuo, North China, the lower Yangtse valley, and the Soviet Maritime area); the Smaller Co-prosperity Sphere (including the Inner Sphere, plus Eastern Siberia, China, French Indo-China, and the **Nanyo** or South-East Asia; and the Greater Co-prosperity Sphere (including the Smaller Sphere, plus Australia, India, and various island groups in the Pacific Ocean area). It was the Smaller Sphere which would be developed in the immediate future, but it was envisaged that it would require at least 20 years to complete, after which there would be a gradual extension to the construction of the Greater Sphere, though this 'presupposes the need for another great war in the future'.

It will be clear from this definition that, while the doctrine was sweeping, it was also imprecise. It represented long-range thinking, and had little relation to practical realities, but Tōjō at least made a move in the right direction when he established the Greater East Asia ministry in November 1942 which inevitably led to a greater concentration on pan-Asian thinking and propaganda. This move by Tōjō also amounted to a vote of no confidence by him in the foreign ministry which was relieved of many of its diplomatic functions, especially over Japanese-occupied areas. The administrative structure of these had been worked out in Tokyo in a hasty way in November 1941 when it was agreed that they would be largely under military control, though a large number of civilian bureaucrats followed the occupation forces (army and navy). But even when the Greater East Asia ministry took over it had only limited involvement.

The military occupation administration showed considerable variation from place to place, and from time to time, partly because of the changing character of the war itself and partly because of the swift changes amongst those in command. The Netherlands East Indies was divided between the army and the navy, with the army being responsible for the military administration of North Borneo, Java, and Sumatra, as well as for Hong Kong, the Philippines, British Malaya/Singapore, and Burma; while the navy set up similar administrative structures for Celebes, Dutch Borneo, the Moluccas, and the Lesser Sunda Islands, as well as for New Guinea, the Bismarck Archipelago, Wake Island, and Guam.

It is generally agreed that the short-lived administration of the sphere was not a success. It was undermined by lack of clear thinking on the part of the military, by army–navy rivalry (which prevented the creation and independence of an Indonesian state at the same time as Burma and the Philippines were given their nominal independence in August 1943) by jealousy within factions of the army, and by personal antipathy between Tōjō and General *Yamashita, the victor of the *Malayan campaign, as well as between Yamashita and Field Marshal *Terauchi, the supreme commander of all Japanese forces in South-East Asia. The bureaucrats, who were subordinate to the military, were preoccupied with red tape, and were driven by jealousies and by their inability to cope with problems of corruption.

Not even the Greater East Asia Conference, which was held in November 1943 to rally Japan's partners to oppose the Allied offensives, had any positive effect on a deteriorating situation. The conference was held in Tokyo and was attended by representatives of *Wang Ching-wei's Nanking government, Thailand, Manchukuo, the Philippines, and Burma. Subhas Chandra *Bose, the leader of the Provisional Government of Free India, also attended but purely as an observer. On the final day the delegates signed a joint declaration 'undertaking to co-operate towards prosecuting the Greater East Asian war to a successful conclusion and liberating their region from the yoke of British–American domination'. It also mentioned the establishment of co-prosperity; mutual recognition of each other's independence; abolition of racial discrimination; and the need to develop the resources of the region. It claimed to be speaking for the hundreds of millions of the masses of South-East Asia, but as the tide of the naval war had already turned it was widely regarded as an unrealistic piece of propaganda.

As the war progressed, and particularly after Burma and the Philippines were ostensibly granted their independence, the contradictions within the sphere became more obvious. On the one hand the notion of co-prosperity, which was still being promoted, seemed rather threadbare when it was placed alongside the economic adversity which most parts of Japan's far-flung empire were increasingly suffering; on the other, the notion of an effective wartime coalition was not very convincing in the face of Allied counter-offensives which were launched initially against the sphere's territories rather than Japan itself. The battle of *Midway in June 1942 cost Japan its command of the seas and it was unable to supply the outer reaches of the sphere or to draw produce from them in safety (see Table). Factors such as the shortage of foodstuffs and supplies, inflation, and the loss of jobs began to exist everywhere, though the impact varied from place to place. This led to anti-Japanese activities, sometimes communist in origin, sometimes nationalist, and from around the end of 1943, as the prospect of a Japanese victory became less likely, there were increasing signs of resistance to its policies which, by 1945, drove the Tokyo government to varying, sometimes diametrically opposed, reactions. In French Indo-China in March 1945, for example, it clamped down harshly, while in August it behaved relatively generously to the Indonesian nationalists.

If we try to sum up the thinking underlying the sphere, it is evident that it covered a multiplicity of ideas. The one of mutual economic co-prosperity should have carried a wide appeal to the Chinese and other traders in South-East Asia. The problem was whether the concept could be credible because of the sharp contrast between the developed economy of Japan and the underdeveloped economies of all other countries in the sphere. Was it

Greater East Asia Co-prosperity Sphere: Raw materials imported by Japan from GEACS, 1940–5

Except for oil, the figures, in thousands of tons, are for raw materials taken from Korea, Manchukuo, Formosa, north and central China. The figures in brackets are for amounts taken from Nanyo territories (South-East Asia). Oil, per thousand barrels, is for both zones.

	1940	*1941*	*1942*	*1943*	*1944*	*1945*
Coal	6,535 (431)	6,109 (350)	5,967(421)	5,036 (145)	2,635 (...)	548 (...)
Bauxite	(275)	(150)	(305)	(909)	(376)	(16)
Iron ore	1,944 (3,288)	3,359 (2,136)	4,485 (215)	4,027 (271)	2,057 (96)	314 (27)
Scrap iron	17 (75)	16 (49)	38 (9)	19 (16)	18 (...)	12 (...)
Lead	8 (8)	9 (9)	9 (2)	16 (8)	17 (–)	4 (...)
Tin	(11)	(6)	(4)	(27)	(24)	(4)
Zinc	... (1)	2 (3)	5 (3)	7 (3)	6 (1)	3 (...)
Phosphoric ash rock Phosphoric acid salt	17 (118)	55 (80)	56 (286)	56 (181)	66 (24)	23 (...)
Dolomite magnesite	410	506	469	438	287	66
Salt	1,270 (20)	1,342 (27)	1,477 (7)	1,394 (31)	989 (–)	387 (...)
Oil	22,050	3,130	8,146	9,848	1,641	...
Rice	445 (1,144)	792 (1,436)	1,102 (1,528)	279 (857)	709 (74)	151 (–)
Natural rubber	(28)	(68)	(30)	(40)	(28)	(17)

Source: US Strategic Bombing Survey: *Collapse of the Japanese Wartime Economy.*

not merely a scheme to give the Japanese raw materials under the guise of a nominal co-prosperity? Another of its ideas was the linguistic-radical-religious links which existed between many of the constituents of the recently-acquired Japanese empire. Japan was clearly appealing to a regional mentality and to pan-Asian sentiments. As the communiqué of the Greater East Asia Conference had stated, it was intended to unite the sphere on the basis of racial equality within Asia. While the Japanese may have hoped that this would be a sentiment which would commend itself to Chinese both at home and overseas, it carried little weight with them. At a third level it acted as a rallying cry for the eviction of outsiders from the area. It was therefore a call for pan-Asianism and for the removal of imperialist or colonial traces from the Asian region. No doubt this attracted a range of followers, but it seems likely that such a following was limited because of the failure of the economic aspects of the sphere.

In all these respects the implementation of the sphere was at variance with the doctrines which it propounded. The realities of its existence grew out of the New Order. But the New Order doctrine was harsh and was linked to the rhetoric of Hitler and Europe. By contrast, the ideals of the sphere were milder, some would say more seductive. Some scholars such as Professor Akira Iriye have compared the Greater East Asia joint declaration of November 1943 to the *Atlantic Charter. There was a 'feel-good factor' for those associated with it, though there was also an element of political propaganda as it set out Japan's war aims in the most attractive way possible, and as the war went sour for Japan, the sphere took on in the minds of Japanese an element of idealism. It offered a sort of cushion against impending defeat. They could say to themselves: 'even if we are defeated, East and South-East Asia will never be the same again', and the sphere's proponents could feel they had at least responded positively to some of the forces like *anti-imperialism which were coming to the fore in these areas, and in the USA.

But the sphere did not contribute much to the Japanese war effort and the fact that Tokyo failed to hold together the countries belonging to it showed that it was rather more potent on paper than it proved on the ground. The partnership between Japan and its satellite states was illusory. It is doubtful if either side gained much from it and its doctrine cut little ice with those who suffered from the Japanese occupation and who soon found the doctrine it propounded to be bogus. See also COLLABORATION, 5.

IAN NISH

Beasley, W. G., *Japanese Imperialism, 1894–1945* (Oxford, 1987).
Jones, F. C., *Japan's New Order in East Asia: Its Rise and Fall, 1937–1945* (Oxford, 1954).
Morley, J. W. (ed.), *The Fateful Choice: Japan's Advance into South-East Asia, 1939–41* (New York, 1980).
Myers, R. H., and Peattie, M. R. (eds.), *The Japanese Colonial Empire, 1895–1945* (Princeton, 1986).

Great Patriotic War, see GERMAN–SOVIET WAR.

GREECE

For the fighting on the Greek mainland, see BALKAN CAMPAIGN

1. Introduction

Greece, an independent kingdom with a population of 7,345,000 (1940), was drawn into the Second World War as a result of the Italian invasion launched from Albanian territory on 28 October 1940. This began the *Balkan campaign and was followed by a German invasion in April 1941, the exile of the king, George II (1890–1947), and the Axis occupation of the country. Athens, the capital, was liberated on 18 October 1944 by a *British Expeditionary Force and the rest of Greece soon afterwards, but the travails of war, resistance, and occupation were to be prolonged by a savagely fought civil war from 1946 to 1949. Just as Greece had been on a war footing for much of the period between the outbreak of the First Balkan War in October 1912 and the defeat in Asia Minor of its forces by the Turkish nationalists in September 1922, so the entire decade of the 1940s was to be blighted by the war and its bitter aftermath.

2. Domestic life and war effort

From the outset of the occupation Greece was systematically plundered of its economic resources, principally foodstuffs and *raw materials, which were shipped off to Germany. The requisitioning of food led to immediate shortages. Moreover, German insistence that the *Quisling government pay the full costs of occupation gave rise to inflationary pressures that led to one of the highest rates of inflation in recorded history. At the time of the Italian invasion in October 1940 an *oka* (1.3 kg., or nearly 3 lb.) of bread cost 10 drachmas. By the time of the liberation in October 1944 the price was 34,000,000 drachmas.

During the dreadful famine of the winter of 1941–2 some 100,000 people died as a result of malnutrition. So appalling, indeed, was the situation that the British government, under pressure from the government-in-exile (see below) and the US administration, agreed to a partial lifting of the blockade. From the summer of 1942 onwards, the *International Red Cross was able to distribute relief supplies in sufficient quantity to prevent a recurrence of the worst horrors of the previous winter. The catastrophic effects of famine and inflation were compounded by forced Bulgarianization, with the importation of Bulgarian immigrants into the Bulgarian-occupied territories of Western Thrace and Eastern Macedonia, and by the systematic destruction of the once flourishing Jewish community of Salonika. Out of a total population of some 70,000, fewer than 10,000 Greek Jews survived the *occupation (see also FINAL SOLUTION).

Such privations by no means broke the spirit of the people. As early as the night of 30/31 May 1941 the Nazi *swastika was torn down from the Acropolis. This symbolic act was followed by sporadic acts of sabotage and passive resistance, which soon developed into more organized forms of armed *resistance (see below).

The problems that confronted the government-in-exile when it returned to Greece in October 1944 were truly formidable. The economy was shattered; food was in short supply; disease was rife and the distribution of relief was made additionally difficult by the disruption of communications. Inflation continued to accelerate. The only currency to retain confidence was the gold sovereign, which had been shipped into Greece in large quantities by the British authorities to finance resistance activities. Alongside the economic hardships of the great mass of population, the black market flourished and those with access to money could freely purchase food and imported luxury goods. There remained, too, the pressing problem of what to do about collaborators and those who had belonged to the German-equipped, collaborationist, and anti-communist 'security battalions'.

3. Government and legal system

(a) Pre-occupation government

From the foundation of the independent state in the early 1830s, the UK, with France and Russia one of the original 'Protecting Powers', had exercised a preponderant influence over the external affairs of Greece. None the less, the British government turned down the offer made in 1938 by the dictator General Ioannis Metaxas (1871–1941) of a formal alliance. In April 1939, however, following the Italian occupation of Albania, the UK and France undertook to guarantee the integrity of Greece and Romania provided they resisted aggression. Moreover, despite the adoption of some of the external trappings of *fascism by Metaxas, and notwithstanding the high degree of German penetration of the economy, Greece's external relations, in part as consequence of the pro-British proclivities of King George II, remained oriented towards the UK.

On the outbreak of the Second World War in September 1939, Metaxas sought to maintain Greek neutrality, while being prepared to give some low-level assistance to the British war effort. Hitler had sought to dominate south-east Europe through economic and political means. Mussolini, on the other hand, was determined to make territorial gains at the expense of Yugoslavia and Greece. In the summer of 1940, the Italian dictator adopted an increasingly menacing stand towards Greece, authorizing the torpedoing of the Greek cruiser *Elli* stationed off the island of Tenos on 15 August. This and other provocations were followed by the presentation by the Italian ambassador in the early hours of 28 October of a calculatedly unacceptable ultimatum. Metaxas, authoritarian, unpopular, and unrepresentative though he was, captured the national mood in a dignified rejection of the ultimatum. (After the war 28 October was declared a national holiday as *Okhi* ('No!') day.) The ultimatum was followed three hours later by the Italian invasion of northwest Greece. This was quickly repulsed, with Greek forces capturing a substantial area of southern Albania before the advance ground to a halt in atrocious weather.

Shortly before his death on 29 January 1941, Metaxas refused Churchill's offer of ground troops for he was still hopeful of securing some accommodation with Italy through German mediation. However, in secret talks at the royal palace of Tatoi on 22/23 February between Alexandros Koryzis, the new prime minister, King George II, and the C-in-C General Alexandros Papagos (1883–1955) on the Greek side and Anthony *Eden, the British foreign secretary, Field-Marshal *Dill, the *Chief of the Imperial General Staff, and General *Wavell, the C-in-C Middle East, on the British, it was agreed to dispatch an expeditionary force, composed largely of Australian and New Zealand troops.

A misunderstanding occurred at the Tatoi meeting which was seriously to diminish such chances as existed of a successful combined resistance to an increasingly imminent German invasion. The British participants were under the impression that Papagos had agreed to an immediate withdrawal of Greek forces from the fortified Metaxas Line on the Bulgarian frontier to the natural defensive line of the Aliakmon River in Western Macedonia, there to link up with the British expeditionary force. Papagos, with reason in the light of the available evidence, understood such a withdrawal to be contingent on the prior determination of Yugoslavia's willingness to resist the Germans.

The delay critically impeded resistance to the German invasion, (MARITA) launched on 6 April 1941. In the chaos of the invasion, Koryzis committed suicide. Emmanouil Tsouderos, Koryzis' successor as the legitimate prime minister, was in office for only three days before withdrawing with King George and the rest of the government to Crete on 23 April as resistance to the invading German forces collapsed.

(b) Government under occupation

General Georgios Tsolakoglou, in command of the Western Macedonian Army, had negotiated an unauthorized *armistice. He subsequently became prime minister of a collaborationist government, to be succeeded by Konstantinos Logothetopoulos and Ioannis Rallis.

The Italians were the principal occupying power, until the Italian armistice in September 1943, but the Germans controlled key areas that were important from an economic and strategic point of view, while the Bulgarians were permitted to occupy most of Western Thrace and part of Macedonia (see Map 46).

(c) Government-in-exile and post-occupation government

Official British policy, and Churchill in particular, favoured the restoration of King George II, whereas the resistance, communist-controlled or not, that soon came into existence was overwhelmingly republican in orientation. This created a serious dilemma for British policy-makers. The British military authorities were in general anxious to maximize the anti-Axis military effort with little regard for the political consequences, while the foreign office was primarily concerned with ensuring a postwar Greece that was well-disposed to British interests, preferably monarchist, and certainly not communist.

This contradiction was present from the outset and the situation was further complicated by the fact that relations between the two principal resistance movements within Greece, the National People's Liberation Army (ELAS) and the National Republican Greek League (EDES), were poor and co-operation minimal. In the winter of 1943–4 fighting broke out between the two organizations but a truce was negotiated between them in February 1944; the Communist-dominated political wing of ELAS, the National Liberation Front (EAM), created a Political Committee of National Liberation (PEEA) whose function was to administer the large areas of rural Greece under its control.

Although PEEA was careful not to claim that it constituted a rival government, it clearly posed a threat to the government-in-exile, whose influence within Greece was marginal throughout the period of the occupation. Within days of the establishment of PEEA, mutinies broke out in the Greek armed forces in the Middle East, the leaders of which demanded the creation of a government of national unity based on PEEA. An incensed Churchill ordered the forcible suppression of the disorders but not before they had provoked a profound crisis within the government-in-exile. This resulted in the veteran liberal politician and staunch anti-communist George Papandreou (1888–1968), becoming prime minister. Seeking to isolate the left, he organized a conference in Lebanon in May 1944 to which he invited representatives of all political parties and resistance groups. EAM, ELAS, PEEA, and the KKE (Communist Party) all sent delegates, but only two were communists, despite the power, deriving from genuine popular support reinforced by terror, wielded by the far left in the country. EAM/ELAS, by now by far the most powerful political and military formation in occupied Greece, was to disown the concessions made by its delegates in Lebanon. Instead it demanded control of key ministries and the removal of Papandreou from the newly formed government of national unity.

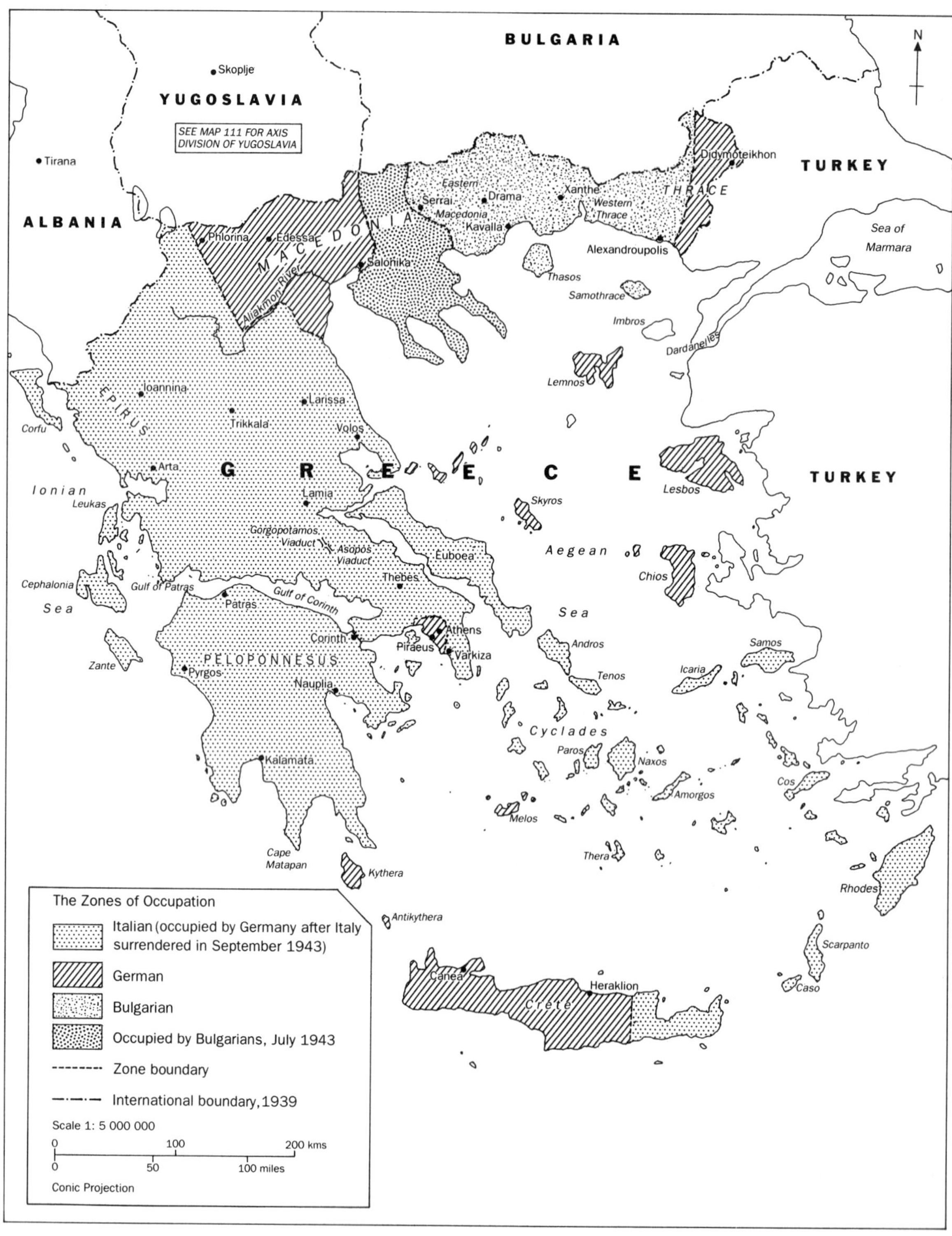

46. Axis occupation zones after the defeat of **Greece**

The deadlock was to be resolved, unbeknown to the principal protagonists, by high-level horse-trading between Churchill and Stalin. Churchill, in the early summer of 1944, had become obsessed with preventing the communist tide that he foresaw would follow in the wake of the Red Army's drive through eastern Europe from reaching Greece, which he looked upon as a vital link in the protection of the UK's imperial communications. For this reason, in May 1944 he offered to accept Soviet preponderance in Romania in exchange for British preponderance in Greece, a deal that was subsequently widened to include Bulgaria and Yugoslavia in the 'percentages agreement' that he negotiated with Stalin in Moscow in October 1944 (see TOLSTOY). In this the 'percentage' of British interest in Greece and, conversely, of Soviet interest in Romania was put at 90%.

This agreement was to overshadow all subsequent developments in Greece. Churchill's understanding with Stalin may indeed—although there is no direct evidence—explain EAM's sudden abandonment at the beginning of August 1944 of its uncompromising line towards Papandreou and the government of national unity. Only a week earlier a Soviet military mission, headed by Colonel Grigori Popov, had parachuted to ELAS headquarters. It has been speculated that Popov brought instructions to EAM to co-operate, or at least indicated that Stalin was indifferent to the fate of the Greek left and that, for this reason, the communist leadership of EAM felt that it had to make some accommodation with a Britain that appeared likely to be the predominant power in Greece after the liberation as it had been before the war.

Be this as it may, EAM now agreed to enter the Papandreou government on the original terms that had been agreed in the Lebanon in May, though these did not reflect the strength of the EAM/ELAS power base in Greece. Six EAM nominees entered the government in relatively junior positions and, even more significantly, ELAS, together with the much smaller EDES, agreed to place its armed forces (some 60,000 strong) under the command of Lt-Gen Ronald Scobie, the commander of the small (smaller than Churchill would have wished) *British expedition to Greece which accompanied the Papandreou government's return on 18 October 1944. This was recognized as the legitimate government by the Allies and was ultimately backed up by British arms. Moreover, Churchill had prevailed upon King George not to return with his government. As the last of the German forces withdrew from Greece, harassed by guerrilla units and by British raiding forces, Papandreou and his government were greeted with overwhelming enthusiasm. Yet within less than three months the legitimacy of the government of national unity was to face a fierce challenge in the communist insurgency of December 1944; Papandreou was ousted from the premiership; and King George was forced to agree at last to the creation of the regency that he had so long resisted.

The reasons for this turn of events are complicated and controversial. The most pressing and, at the same time, the most intractable problem was the question of the demobilization of the guerrilla formations and their replacement by a national army that would underpin the authority of the Papandreou government. Throughout November 1944, Papandreou and the left-wing ministers in the government were engaged in protracted negotiations over the demobilization issue. Amid charges and counter-charges of lack of good faith and in a climate of mounting tension, the left-wing ministers resigned from the government on 2 December and EAM called a general strike for 4 December, to be preceded by a mass demonstration in Syntagma Square, in the centre of Athens, on Sunday 3 December.

The mistakes and miscalculations of those involved, the left-wingers, the national government, and the British, all contributed to the creation of a situation that was moving rapidly and seemingly inexorably towards a tragic climax. Thousands of pro-EAM demonstrators converged on Syntagma Square, and, at the height of the demonstration, in circumstances that are still not wholly clear, panic-stricken police opened fire, leaving some fifteen dead and many more wounded. The shooting provoked attacks by ELAS on police stations and within a few days ELAS and British troops were locked in bloody street fighting. Churchill, who for some time had made it clear that he did not flinch from the prospect of outright confrontation with EAM/ELAS, cabled Scobie, the British military commander, that he should treat Athens as a conquered city which must be held even at the price of bloodshed. The leaking of this telegram in the American press contributed to the policy of ostentatious neutrality adopted by the US administration throughout the fighting in December 1944. The Soviets likewise stood aloof from this vicious conflict, unique in the Second World War, between erstwhile allies.

The small number of British troops in the capital were rapidly thrown on to the defensive and before long controlled only a small area of the city centre. With the inflow of reinforcements, which could be ill spared from the *Italian campaign, the military tide began to turn. The communists' motives in launching the December insurgency still remain unclear. If bent on an outright seizure of power there were a number of curious features in their tactics, notably their decision (apart from an irrelevant attack on the forces of EDES in Epirus) to restrict the fighting to Athens despite their effective *de facto* control of much of the rest of the country. It seems that they were not so much after outright power as the de-stabilization of the Papandreou government and ousting him from office, for he was clearly perceived as the principal obstacle to any attempt by the left to achieve power through constitutional or quasi-constitutional means.

Whatever the motives behind the insurgency, it was characteristic of Churchill's obsession with Greek affairs that, to the astonishment of his staff and with the war in the west still far from over, he made the impulsive decision to fly with Eden to Athens on Christmas Eve 1944 in an effort to negotiate a settlement. Not even Churchill's great prestige could effect a deal but he was now aware of the pressing need to establish a regency and, on his return to London, pressured King George into appointing Archbishop Damaskinos as regent. In early January Papandreou was replaced as prime minister by the seemingly more conciliatory General Nikolaos Plastiras. The insurgency was essentially suppressed by military means, in which British control of the air was vital.

A ceasefire, negotiated on 11 January 1945, was followed by a political settlement at Varkiza on 12 February. Given the bitterness of the December conflict, the terms imposed on the left were not as oppressive as might have been expected. ELAS had to give up its arms but EAM and the KKE remained legal organizations and the government undertook to purge the administration, security battalions, and police of collaborationist elements and to hold a plebiscite on the monarchy, to be followed by elections. The peace that appeared to have been secured by the Varkiza agreement proved, however, to be illusory. A succession of weak governments proved incapable of holding in check the anti-communist backlash that followed the December 1944 insurgency. Moreover, with the KKE itself vacillating between a policy of seeking power, or a share of it, through constitutional means, and preparing for further armed conflict, the country slithered towards chaos. The liberation of the country from Axis occupation proved to be the prelude to a bitterly fought civil war (1946–9) which was to set back the process of post-war reconstruction for a further five years.

4. Armed forces

(a) Army

In 1940 the Greek Army totalled 18 divisions. Except for its heavy guns, which were inferior, it had more efficient artillery than the Italians and more machine-guns, but it had only one pitifully equipped motorized division and virtually no tanks. In October 1940 at the start of the *Balkan campaign four first-line divisions opposed six Italian ones on the Albanian border. But Italian divisions 12,000–14,000 strong were smaller than Greek ones (18,500 strong) and the Italians were soon driven back, though they had air superiority. By mid-November the Greeks had numerical superiority on the front where eventually eleven infantry divisions, two infantry brigades, and one cavalry division opposed fifteen Italian infantry divisions and one tank division. Other Greek divisions manned the Metaxas, or Nestos, Line, which protected Salonika, and, with British forces, the Aliakmon Line. Casualties during the Balkan campaign amounted to 13,408 killed and 42,485 wounded. About 9,000 escaped to Crete, others fled through Turkey to Egypt. These constituted the 18,500-strong Royal Hellenic Army in the Middle East which came under British command and which eventually formed three brigades, an armoured car regiment, an artillery regiment, and the *Greek Sacred Regiment, made up solely of officers. One brigade fought at the second *El Alamein battle before being withdrawn, but the rest, apart from the Greek Sacred Regiment, saw little active service as the army was riven by politics. After the mutiny of April 1944, which precipitated a confrontation with British forces, much of it was interned. The rest were used for non-operational duties, though 2,500 of those regarded as more 'reliable' were formed into the Third Mountain Brigade which subsequently fought with distinction in the Italian campaign. There it became known as the Rimini Brigade, and it helped the British quell the ELAS insurgency in Athens in December 1944.

(b) Navy

In October 1940 the Greek Navy comprised 200 officers and 2,700 men. The fleet consisted of an ancient 10,000-ton cruiser, a flotilla of 6 modern and 4 old destroyers, 13 old torpedo boats, 6 submarines, and 30 miscellaneous craft. Its submarines sank 18 Italian ships from Adriatic convoys, but in April 1941 many Greek warships were sunk by German aircraft. Twelve, including the cruiser, three new destroyers, and three submarines escaped to Alexandria, and these subsequently operated under overall British command. By April 1944 the numbers had risen to several thousand men, some of whom manned destroyers handed over by the British. Five ships, which joined the *mutinies of April 1944, were stormed by Greek seamen loyal to the government-in-exile. Eleven seamen were killed, others were wounded, and many were subsequently interned.

(c) Air Force

The Army and Navy Air Forces comprised about 3,000 men. These flew and maintained a miscellany of about 300 aircraft, many of them obsolete, and they made no impact on the Italians. There were too many aircraft types, few spare parts, no replacement aircraft, and a dearth of forward airfields because of the country's rugged terrain. Too few personnel escaped for an independent air force to be formed but eventually three Greek squadrons (nos. 13, 335, and 336) were raised as part of the *Western Desert Air Force.

5. Merchant marine

At the outbreak of war the substantial Greek Merchant Marine consisted of 577 ships, totalling 1,837,315 tons. Of these 334 were sunk through Axis action, 32 were seized by the Axis powers, and 63 were lost for other reasons. Total tonnage lost amounted to 1,346,502, 71% of the total. Two thousand seamen lost their lives and a further 2,500 were wounded, losses which had a disproportionate impact on the relatively small number of Aegean islands from which crews were recruited.

6. Resistance

Small guerrilla bands, whose activities provoked savage reprisals, came into existence as early as the summer of 1941. The main initiative in organizing more co-ordinated resistance was taken by the Communist Party (KKE) which, paradoxically, was to emerge as the major political force in occupied Greece. Paradoxically because, riven by factional disputes and obliged by the *Comintern to espouse the unpatriotic cause of an independent Macedonia, the KKE had been a marginal political force during the inter-war period.

The Metaxas dictatorship had, however, left behind a political vacuum which was perpetuated by the occupation. This enabled the KKE, with much greater experience of clandestine activity than the bourgeois politicians, adroitly to exploit their inadequacies, want of vision, and lack of organization. It was thus able to project itself with some conviction as the only valid instrument of change and progress in the war-ravaged country. Once Hitler had launched the invasion of the Soviet Union in June 1941 (see BARBAROSSA), the KKE abandoned its hitherto ambiguous line towards the war, and took the lead in organizing a mass resistance movement. In September 1941 the National Liberation Front (EAM), nominally a coalition of a number of small left-leaning parties, was founded. From this the traditional party leaders stood wholly aloof. From the outset the KKE kept a tight grip on EAM, even if the bulk of its rank-and-file membership (estimates of its size range between 500,000 and 2,000,000) was not communist. A number of offshoots of EAM came into existence, the most important of which was the Ethnikos Laikos Apeleftherotikos Stratos (ELAS, the National People's Liberation Army), which was founded in December 1941 as the military arm of EAM. In the early summer of 1942 the first ELAS guerrilla band under the able but ruthless leadership of Ares Veloukhiotis (the pseudonym of Athanasios Klaras) took to the mountains. There it was joined by another resistance group, the Ethnikos Dimokratikos Ellinikos Syndesmos (EDES, the National Republican Greek League), commanded by General Napoleon Zervas (1891–1957). This was non-communist but, like EAM/ELAS, was republican. Other small resistance groups came into being but the royalist presence in the resistance was minimal.

The potential of guerrilla resistance was realized when, on 25/26 November 1942, detachments of ELAS and EDES, armed and co-ordinated by a British sabotage team parachuted in by *SOE, destroyed the Gorgopotamos viaduct which carried the Salonika–Athens railway line, perhaps the most spectacular act of sabotage anywhere in occupied Europe up to that time. It had originally been intended that the British team would be withdrawn. Now, however, it was ordered to remain in Greece to assist in the co-ordination of resistance activity. The Gorgopotamos operation was to prove the only instance of co-operation under a unified command between ELAS and EDES during the occupation. At best relations between the two organizations were uneasy, at worst they degenerated into internecine fighting, as ELAS sought to consolidate its hold over all resistance activity with an eye to the inevitable power struggle on liberation. British fears as to the ultimate political objectives of EAM led to a conscious effort during the early months of 1943 to build up EDES as a counterweight to EAM/ELAS. In the course of this process Zervas, the leader of EDES, was induced to make a statement of support for King George II.

Military necessity, however, was soon to lead the British to switch from a policy of containment of ELAS to one of co-operation. *Deception schemes in connection with the invasion of Sicily in July 1943 (see SICILIAN CAMPAIGN) made it imperative to lead Hitler, already obsessed with the idea of an Allied landing in the Balkans such as had occurred during the First World War, to expect the opening of a front in Greece. These deceptions required large-scale sabotage activity, which could only be carried out in co-operation with ELAS, given its domination of the resistance. Accordingly, in July 1943, the 'National Bands' agreement was negotiated. In return for an undertaking not to molest rival resistance organizations, EAM/ELAS was given a predominant role in the Joint General Headquarters that was set up in free mountain Greece with the object of co-ordinating all resistance activity under the aegis of the *Middle East Command. The diversionary sabotage of the summer of 1943 achieved some notable successes, including the blowing-up of the Asopos railway viaduct by an SOE team. Hitler was duly deceived into transferring two crack divisions to Greece.

But the 'National Bands' agreement was in effect for only a short time before a major crisis developed in relations between the resistance organizations in Greece and the British diplomatic and military authorities, the government-in-exile, and King George II in the Middle East. It was occasioned by the arrival in Cairo in August 1943 of a guerrilla delegation, accompanied by Brigadier E. C. W. Myers, the commander of the British military mission. As was the case with the guerrilla Joint General Headquarters, the delegation was dominated by representatives of EAM/ELAS. The arrival of the guerrillas represented possibly the only opportunity during the occupation of creating a unified resistance movement. But the chance of reaching agreement between the resistance forces within Greece, the government-in-exile, the king and the British—the principal source of logistical support for the resistance and who recognized the king and the Tsouderos government as the embodiment of constitutional continuity—was bungled by the British authorities.

The guerrilla delegates had two basic demands. Firstly, they wanted the king to declare unambiguously that he would not return until a plebiscite had voted in his favour. Secondly, they wanted to take charge of three key government portfolios in those areas of Greece that they already effectively controlled. Both demands were refused and the guerrilla delegation returned to the mountains in September convinced that the British were prepared to impose the monarchy by force if necessary. Within a matter of weeks, internecine fighting, with many of the characteristics of a civil war, had broken out between ELAS and EDES, with the former accusing the latter of collaboration. The British sought to staunch the fighting by cutting off supplies to ELAS, but this move was largely negated by the fact that ELAS secured the lion's share of the arms and equipment of the Italian forces in Greece following Italy's armistice with the Allies on 9 September. Eventually, the truce of February 1944 led to a ceasfire and delineated the respective operational areas of ELAS and EDES, with the latter being restricted to Epirus in north-western Greece. RICHARD CLOGG

Fleischer, H., *Im Kreuzschatten der Machte: Griechenland 1941–1944* (Frankfurt, 1986).

Hondros, J., *Occupation and Resistance: the Greek agony* (New York, 1983).

Mazower, M., *Inside Hitler's Greece. The Experience of Occupation, 1941–44* (New Haven, 1993).

Woodhouse, C. M., *The Struggle for Greece 1941–49* (London, 1976).

Greek Sacred Regiment, commando-type unit formed in August 1942 by officers of the Royal Hellenic Army who had escaped to Egypt after the *Balkan campaign. About 300 enlisted as soldiers and it was the only Greek unit to be regularly employed operationally. It was the regiment's third incarnation, having been formed first in 370 BC, and then again in 1821 to fight for Greece's freedom. It became part of the *Special Air Service, then of *Raiding Forces which harassed the Germans during the *Dodecanese campaign, and was also used by the British to quell the ELAS rising in Athens in December 1944 (see GREECE, 3(c)).

Greenland, the world's largest island, was a Danish colony. Its two sheriffs decided to join the Free Denmark movement started by the Danish minister in Washington, Henrik Kauffmann, after Denmark had been occupied by the Germans in April 1940. They repudiated the Danish government and governed the island themselves, and a Greenland Commission was set up in the USA to handle Greenland's trade. In April 1941, Kauffmann signed a treaty with the USA which allowed American air bases to be built on the island. The USA accepted responsibility for the military security of the island and the west coast was protected by US Coast Guard patrols. But the east coast was too remote, so sledge patrols were started there, its handful of members becoming the Greenland Army. These patrols were involved in the 'Weather War' (see METEOROLOGICAL INTELLIGENCE) which was fought when the Germans established weather stations there.

Howarth, D., *Sledge Patrol* (London, 1957).

Greer, US destroyer which was attacked by a U-boat 200 km. (125 mi.) south-west of Iceland on 4 September 1941. She was not damaged, but Roosevelt called the attack 'piracy' and warned that if any German or Italian warships entered waters being protected by the US Navy they did so at their own risk. This ended the US Navy's predicament of trying to protect large stretches of water during the battle of the *Atlantic without having the authority to shoot, and from that time Germany and the US were opponents in a *de facto* war there.

Greim, Field Marshal Robert Ritter von (1892–1945), Luftwaffe chief of personnel in 1939 who subsequently commanded a number of fighter groups before taking command of a *Luftflotte* (air fleet) on the Eastern Front during the *German–Soviet war. Summoned to the Führerbunker, on 25 April 1945 he was told by Hitler that he had succeeded *Göring as C-in-C of the Luftwaffe and was promoted field marshal. He committed suicide soon after Germany's surrender.

Ritter is a German hereditary knighthood.

GRENADE, operational codename for a drive made by Lt-General William H. *Simpson's Ninth US Army in February 1945 as part of *Montgomery's Twenty-First Army Group operations to close up to the River *Rhine during the battle for *Germany. The plan was for Simpson to strike north from the Roer valley and link up with the First Canadian Army's Operation *VERITABLE. He was forced to postpone his attack for two weeks because the Germans had flooded the Roer valley, but when he did launch it on 23 February it caught the Germans with their attention concentrated on VERITABLE. Consequently he was able to link up with the Canadians at Geldern on 3 March, having reached the Rhine opposite Düsseldorf the previous day. At a cost of 7,500 US casualties, half those of VERITABLE, Simpson inflicted 16,000 on the Germans and captured 29,000 prisoners. CHARLES MESSENGER

grenades were used by infantrymen to lay smoke, penetrate armour and reinforced concrete, and in close-quarters fighting. Some types were thrown; others were fired from a discharge cup fitted to a rifle or pistol. Anti-personnel grenades were mostly made of cast iron or plastic which fragmented when the *explosives they contained were detonated by a time fuze. The US M9A1 armour-piercing rifle grenade was especially effective and infantrymen often preferred it to the bazooka (see ROCKET WEAPONS) as it did not entail carrying an extra weapon. Both the British egg-shaped 36M hand grenade, known as the Mills bomb, and the standard German Steilhandgranate 39, popularly, called the 'potato masher' or stick grenade because of its wooden handle, dated back to the *First World War. See also GAMMON BOMB and STICKY BOMB.

Gromyko, Andrei (1909–89), Soviet economist who joined the diplomatic service in 1939 and became a protégé of *Molotov, the foreign minister. In 1943 he became the Soviet ambassador in the USA, a post he held until 1946. He led the Soviet delegation at the *Dumbarton Oaks and

*San Francisco conferences, and attended the *Grand Alliance conferences at Yalta (see ARGONAUT) and Potsdam (see TERMINAL). He served as Soviet foreign minister from 1957 to 1985.

Grossraum (great space). Originally an economic term, this was Hitler's theory for the Greater Germanic Estate which was to comprise continental Europe from the Atlantic to the Urals. But what it stood for was more important than its boundaries. Those who lived within it were to be moved around to fit the concept of centralized planning where each country was told what to grow and manufacture, and was provided with the labour to produce it. It was where the Nordic races were to live, with a Greater Germany at the industrial and economic apex, and the Slavs and inferior races at the base, a theory which became reality with the formation of *Ostland. See also NAZI IDEOLOGY and GERMANY, 4.

Grot-Rowecki, see ROWECKI.

Ground Force Replacement System, US Army organization formed in the European Theatre of Operations (*ETOUSA) in January 1944 to replace casualties during the fighting in north-west Europe. The average combat replacement, or anyone returning to combat duty after being wounded, made four stops on his way to the front line: at the reception depot in the UK or France where he normally only stayed overnight; the intermediate depot where his processing began and where, during a 48-hour stay, he was given a rifle and any necessary equipment; the forward depot; and finally the forward battalion which assigned him to a particular sub-unit. There was one forward depot for each army formation with one forward battalion to support each front-line corps. The system controlled a pool of 70,000 men, 54,800 of them infantrymen. However, by September 1944 there was such an acute shortage of infantrymen that the system had to retrain as many as 14,400 men in the infantry role. In December 1944, when it was realized that the term 'replacement' was having a deleterious affect on morale, the system was renamed Ground Force Reinforcement Command.

Ground Observer Corps, see USA, 4.

GRU (Glavnoye Razvedyvatelnoe Upravleniye), the Main Intelligence Directorate of the General Staff of the Red Army, has a history which goes back to 1918. In the period immediately before the outbreak of the *German–Soviet war it had, like the *NKVD, suffered severely in the purges. Indeed the head of the organization, air force General I. I. Proskurov, who had fought with distinction in Spain, was shot in June 1940, apparently because of his doubts about the wisdom of Stalin's German policy (see NAZI–SOVIET PACT). Under his successor, General *Golikov, the GRU revived, although Golikov did not dare to disabuse Stalin of his belief that intelligence of aggressive German intentions was merely 'English provocation'. From October 1941 to March 1942 the organization was headed by General A. P. Panfilov, who was also shot. Panfilov had been effective head from July 1941 when Golikov went to the UK and the USA as part of a military *Lend-Lease delegation. Indeed, Golikov was the only head of the GRU to receive public exposure and in 1961 became a Marshal of the Soviet Union. Panfilov's last wartime successors were I. I. Ilyichev to the summer of 1943 and finally F. F. Kuznetzov to April 1946.

The task of the GRU was to collect strategic, technical, and military intelligence. During the Second World War it may also have been active in sabotage behind German lines and co-operation with partisan units. However, intelligence activity at the front was the responsibility of army commanders and conducted by them through intelligence departments (Razvedyvatelnyi Otdel, or RO) although it was integrated and closely supervised by the GRU. Although there is little evidence of co-operation with *SMERSH, which was founded in April 1943, the two organizations had great success in penetrating the German military structure on the Eastern Front. Together with the NKVD it was active in foreign intelligence although as the weaker institution it was probably subject to the NKVD. Richard *Sorge in Japan, and in Germany and German-occupied Europe, Leopold Trepper, Arvid Harnack, Rudolf von Scheliha, and Harro Schulze-Boysen, all members of the *Rote Kapelle, were some of the more spectacular agents recruited by the GRU, but its most important network was the *Rote Drei which operated from Switzerland. H. HANAK

Akhmedov, I., *In and out of Stalin's GRU: A Tatar's Escape from Red Army Intelligence* (London, 1984.)
Glantz, D. M., *Soviet Military Intelligence in War* (London, 1990).
Villemarest, P. de (in collaboration with C. A. Kiracoff), *GRU, le plus secret des services soviétiques, 1918–1988* (Paris, 1988).

Guadalcanal campaign (see Map 47). This was, following the first *Philippines campaign, the first real test of land strength between Japan and the USA in the *Pacific war. The bloody and protracted struggle for this steamy, malaria-ridden, rain-sodden Solomon Island began on 7 August 1942.

The operation came under the overall command of Vice-Admiral Ghormley (1883–1958), C-in-C *South Pacific Area (see Map F), and was commanded tactically by Vice-Admiral *Fletcher. US naval victories in the *Coral Sea and at *Midway had given the Americans the opportunity to mount the campaign, its purpose being to prevent a further Japanese advance southwards which would have severed the lines of communication between Australia and the USA.

Three fleet carriers and a powerful escort of warships protected Rear-Admiral *Turner's amphibious force as it landed 19,000 men of the reinforced 1st Marine Division commanded by Maj-General Alexander Vandegrift (1887–1973). Except on the twin islets of Gavutu-Tananbogo, two of seven nearby islands also being occupied (see TULAGI),

Japanese casualties after the battle of the Tenaru River which was fought in August 1942 during the initial stages of the **Guadalcanal** campaign.

the marines met little opposition. But the landings were hurriedly conceived and executed to pre-empt a Japanese occupation, and to capture a partially-built Japanese airfield before it became operational. They flouted basic *amphibious warfare doctrine by failing to secure lines of communication and isolate the landings from Japanese attack. Additionally, little was known either about the British-owned island—available maps of the area proved hopelessly inaccurate—or the Japanese order of battle.

Japanese reaction to the landings was swift. Aircraft and a strong naval force under Vice-Admiral Mikawa Gunichi were immediately dispatched from *Rabaul. An early warning by a *Coast Watcher of the bombers' approach prevented much damage, but before dawn on 9 August Mikawa surprised and defeated an Allied screening force off *Savo Island. The landings then under way remained unscathed, but when Fletcher, who felt vulnerable to air attack, withdrew his carriers the next day the partially unloaded transports were forced to leave too. This left the marines without vital reserves and essential supplies, and until the nucleus of the *Cactus Air Force arrived on 20 August they remained virtually isolated and highly vulnerable.

The Savo island battle gave the Japanese superiority at sea and they immediately began to land troops of their

Seventeenth Army to wrest Guadalcanal from the marines. But throughout the campaign their commander, Lt-General Hyakutake Haruyoshi, not only repeatedly committed his men piecemeal—an error he could sometimes not avoid as they were brought from all over Japan's *Greater East Asia Co-prosperity Sphere at different times—but greatly underestimated the marines' strength. So it was symptomatic of his tactics and approach that, on 18 August, only part of the Ichiki Detachment was used to attack the marines' defensive perimeter around the airfield; and in what became known as the battle of Tenaru River—it was really the River Ilu—the whole Japanese force, some 900 men, was wiped out.

In the following months many more desperate land actions were fought to defend the airstrip (Henderson Field) but gradually the marines widened their perimeter as other units, which included 2nd Marine Division, reinforced them. But initially they only received *Seabees to keep the airfield operational while the Japanese used the *'Tokyo Express' to pour in infantry and supplies, though Cactus Air Force patrols soon forced it to operate only at night.

The Table shows how both sides built up their forces on the island, the dates being some of the most critical of the campaign.

In their efforts to reinforce and support their men ashore both sides fought several critical naval actions and the struggle for supremacy on land was contingent on the outcome of the one being fought at sea. In the *Eastern Solomons battle on 24 August the Japanese won a tactical victory, though the Americans delayed the landing of the Kawaguchi Brigade and the balance of the Ichiki Detachment. Six days later the fleet carrier *Saratoga* was torpedoed and so badly damaged that she had to return to the USA. Then on 15 September submarines sank another carrier, *Wasp*, and badly damaged the new battleship *North Carolina*; and though in the battle of *Cape Esperance, fought on the night of 11/12 October, the Americans partially avenged these losses, it seemed that command of the sea was slipping from them. However, on 18 October 1942 Ghormley was replaced by the more aggressive Vice-Admiral *Halsey and from that time the US Navy—although it suffered several more tactical reverses, which included the battles of *Santa Cruz and *Tassafaronga—slowly gained the upper hand.

Guadalcanal: Build-up of Japanese and American forces during the campaign to take Guadalcanal

	Japanese	*American*
7 August	2,200	10,000
20 August	3,700	10,000
11 September	9,000	11,000
12–20 October	22,000	23,000
12 November	30,000	29,000
1 December	25,000	40,000

Source: Contriutor.

Both the balance of the Ichiki Detachment and the 3,000-strong Kawaguchi Brigade were eventually landed at night well to the east of the marines' beachhead, and on 12 September another concerted effort was made to break through the American lines. But the three-pronged attack failed, though in the main action known as the battle of Bloody Ridge (or Edson's Ridge), fought against a Raider battalion, some Japanese came within 900 m. (1,000 yds.) of the airfield.

In early October the Sendai Division landed around the mouth of the River Matanikau to the west of the airstrip and this, and the bombardment by battleships of the Japanese Combined Fleet which almost obliterated Henderson Field and its aircraft, heralded a third major Japanese offensive. But when it started, on 23 October, it was badly co-ordinated and the marine garrison, recently reinforced by 3,000 men of the *Americal Division, repulsed it.

In mid-November a final effort was made to swing the land battle in Hyakutake's favour by dispatching, under heavy naval escort, the veteran 38th Division in eleven transports, an operation which resulted in a three-day sea action known as the battle of Guadalcanal. The first clash, on the night of 12/13 November, lasted just 24 minutes and was one of the fiercest ever fought. The Americans lost six ships and the Japanese three, including one battleship. This prevented another bombardment of Henderson Field by the Japanese battleships, but that night their cruisers shelled it heavily. Nevertheless, the Cactus Air Force was still operational the next morning and this wrought havoc amongst the Japanese landing fleet. One cruiser was sunk and three others damaged before the marine pilots turned on the transports sinking seven. That night there was another clash at sea. The Japanese lost another battleship and one destroyer while the Americans lost three destroyers with one battleship badly damaged. The four remaining transports were beached to get their troops ashore, but were bombed and destroyed the next morning.

This naval battle proved to be the climax of the struggle for the island. The Japanese continued to send supplies and reinforcements, and to bombard Henderson Field, but at the beginning of 1943 mounting American superiority forced them to form a new defensive line on islands further north. From that time the dwindling Japanese forces on the island received only essential supplies by submarine (see also BLOCKADE RUNNERS), and the 'Tokyo Express' was almost abandoned.

During December 1942 the 1st Marine Division was relieved by the 25th US Infantry Division and Maj-General *Patch, commanding the 14th US Corps, replaced Vandegrift. By early January, with his corps now totalling about 50,000 men, Patch went on to the offensive. The Japanese, cut off from supplies or reinforcements,

Guadalcanal campaign

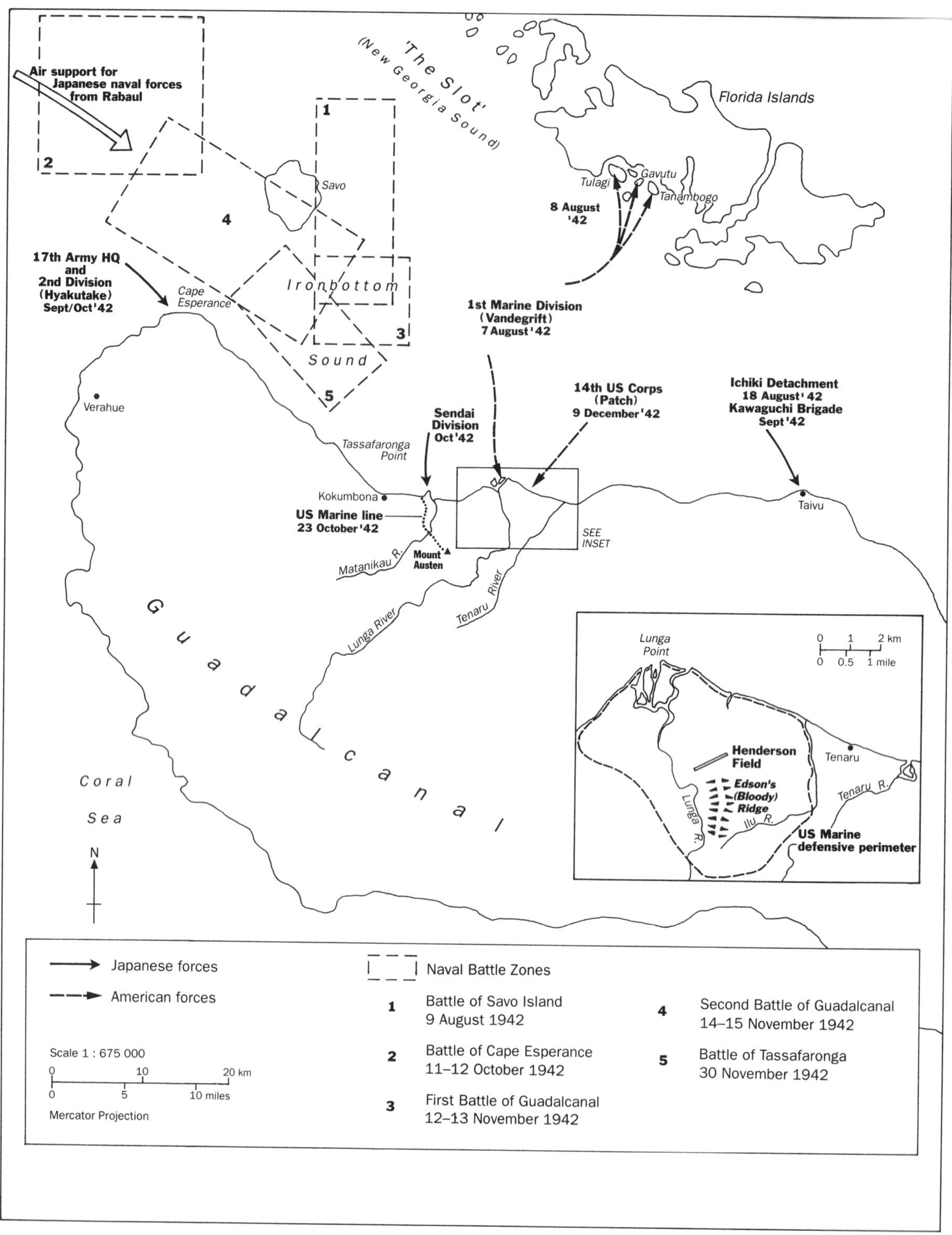

47. **Guadalcanal campaign**, August 1942–January 1943

continued to fight bravely. But at the end of January the survivors were ordered to withdraw to Cape Esperance where, in a brilliantly executed operation the Americans knew nothing about, some 13,000 men, including Hyakutake, were ferried in barges at night to waiting destroyers.

Seven major naval battles, with the determination of the Cactus Air Force pilots in the air and the marines ashore, combined to bring eventual victory for the Americans. The cost had been heavy—6,111 US army and marine casualties, including 1,752 killed, and substantial naval losses—but Guadalcanal is now seen as a major turning-point in the Pacific war from which Japan never recovered.

Coggins, J., *The Campaign for Guadalcanal* (New York, 1972).
Tregaskis, R., *Guadalcanal Diary* (New York, 1962).

Guam. The largest of the Pacific Marianas, this island, ceded to the USA in 1898, was occupied by the Japanese at the start of the *Pacific war and put under navy administration. In July 1944 it was recaptured by Maj-General Roy Geiger's 55,000-strong 3rd US Amphibious Corps. Guam contains some of the Pacific's most difficult terrain in its 55 km. (34 mi.) length, and at the time it possessed the only adequate water supply in the Marianas, and the best harbour. It was therefore vital to the Americans as an advanced base to begin the second *Philippines campaign and to permit US aircraft to start the *strategic air offensive against Japan. The landings by the 3rd Marine Division and the 1st Provisional Marine Brigade, with 77th Infantry Division in reserve, were delayed until 21 July because Saipan had taken longer than expected to capture; and because approaching Japanese surface forces had first to be defeated (see PHILIPPINE SEA).

The delay enabled the Japanese garrison of 19,000 troops to construct the most formidable beach defences, a way through which had to be cleared by underwater demolition teams (see FROGMEN). But the delay also allowed US support forces to deliver the most meticulous, intensive, and prolonged air and sea bombardment the Japanese received during the Pacific war. As a result, Japanese resistance was sporadic and uncoordinated, and 10,646 were killed, ten times the US losses. But the survivors kept fighting and it took three weeks to occupy the whole island. Mopping-up operations continued throughout the remainder of the war, and beyond it: the last Japanese soldier hiding there did not surrender until 1972.

Guatemala declared war on the Axis powers in December 1941, and was an original signatory of the *United Nations Declaration. US bases were established there and Guatemala's production of quinine and hemp was useful to the Allied war effort. See also LATIN AMERICA.

Gubbins, Maj-General Colin McV. (1896–1976), British irregular soldier, born in Yokohama. He was an artillery officer throughout the *First World War, then served in north Russia, acquiring Russian, and in Ireland, 1919–22. Between the wars he had staff and intelligence appointments in India and the UK. In 1938 he joined MI(R), a predecessor of *SOE, and he was chief of staff of the British military mission to Poland in the summer of 1939. Gubbins commanded independent companies, the forerunners of the commandos, during the *Norwegian campaign, April–June 1940, and formed secret stay-behind parties who were to have disrupted rear areas of the German UK invasion force (see SEALION). He joined SOE in November 1940, in charge of training and operations, and became its mainspring; from September 1943 he was its executive director. Having once got its resources organized, he was glad to place them at disposal of local Cs-in-C.

He was a small, spare, wiry man, highly intelligent, with unusual gifts of persuasion and leadership. Although he was sometimes outmanoeuvred by *Dansey, he showed unexpected gifts of diplomacy in his dealings with *governments-in-exile, and strong leadership when it came to inspiring those who worked with him in SOE. He retired in January 1946, when SOE was disbanded, and died in the Western Isles of Scotland from which his family derived. M. R. D. FOOT

Wilkinson, P. A., and Astley, J. B., *Gubbins and SOE* (London, 1993).

Guderian, General Heinz (1888–1954), German Army officer who, after an early training in *radio communications, and active service during the *First World War, propounded in the 1930s the revolutionary theory that tanks were the primary weapon of a concentrated attack to which all other arms should be subordinated (see BLITZKRIEG). In 1935 he laid the foundations for three panzer divisions; he published his theories of tank warfare in a book (*Achtung Panzer*, 1937); and in November 1938 was promoted lt-general and appointed to a new post, Commander of Mobile Troops.

He commanded 19th Panzer Corps during the *Polish campaign in September 1939, and in the fighting which preceded the fall of *France in June 1940. Both campaigns proved that the combination of tanks, dive-bombers, and motorized infantry (Panzer Grenadiers) produced the swift, overwhelming, annihilating striking power that characterized the blitzkrieg Guderian espoused, and he was promoted general. Initially, this combination also worked during the German invasion of the USSR in June 1941 (see BARBAROSSA): Guderian's 2nd Panzer Group swept towards *Moscow and then, on Hitler's orders, into the Ukraine where his forces helped surround huge Red Army forces at *Kiev. His Group was rewarded with Army status by a delighted Hitler, but Guderian was critical of the Führer's failure to take advantage of initial German successes by striking straight for Moscow, as he had advised. These criticisms, and the fact that he was preparing to withdraw his army from its exposed position, led to his dismissal on 20 December.

He languished without an appointment for over a year before Hitler recalled him in March 1943 as Inspector-General of Armoured Troops, an appointment which made him chief of the Panzer Command. Before the July 1944 bomb plot to kill Hitler (see SCHWARZE KAPELLE) he was asked to join the conspirators, and though loyalty stopped him he kept the plot to himself. In its aftermath he was a member of the 'Court of Honour' which expelled those officers involved in the plot, so that they could be handed over to the *'People's Court'. He was made chief of the Army General Staff (OKH), but had such bitter arguments with Hitler that on 28 March 1945, after flatly contradicting Hitler to his face, he was sent on sick leave.

Guderian, H., *Panzer Leader* (London, 1952).
Macksey, K., *Guderian* (London, 1992).

guerrilla warfare, see in resistance section of relevant major powers and under names of relevant countries.

guided weapons. For the purposes of this entry, a 'guided weapon' is an unmanned weapons system the path of which can be steered during its travel, either automatically or remotely, to increase the chances of it striking the target.

The first guided weapon to see action during the Second World War was the US-built 'Mark 24 Mine', a deliberately misleading codename applied to an air-dropped torpedo fitted with an acoustic homing head and designed for attacking submerged submarines. It was first used on 12 May 1943, when a Liberator of No. 86 Squadron RAF dropped one into the swirl left by U-456 as it dived in the North Atlantic. The weapon followed the U-boat for about two minutes, then detonated against it causing severe damage. The following day the boat was finished off by Allied warships. Between then and the end of the war the 'Mark 24 Mine' destroyed about a dozen enemy submarines.

The German Navy developed its own acoustic homing torpedo, for use by U-boats against Allied convoy escorts. Codenamed the ZAUNKÖNIG (wren)—the British called it the GNAT—it first saw action on 20 September 1943 when it caused serious damage to the Royal Navy frigate *Lagan*. After a brief initial spell of success, Allied warships were equipped with the 'foxer' device, a towed noisemaker, which lured homing torpedoes safely away from them. Thereafter ZAUNKÖNIG became ineffective and its use was discontinued.

Also during 1943, the Luftwaffe introduced two separate types of air-dropped radio command guided weapon for use against enemy ships: the Henschel Hs293 glider bomb, and the Fritz-X guided bomb. The Hs293 resembled a small aircraft with a wing span of 3.1 m. (10 ft. 3½ in.) and carried a 500 kg. (1,100 lb.) warhead in the nose. After release from the carrying aircraft (usually a Dornier 217 or Heinkel 177), a rocket motor accelerated the weapon to maximum speed of about 600 km/h (375 mph) then cut out. The missile coasted on, steered to the target by an observer in the nose of the aircraft operating a joystick controller linked to a radio transmitter. The Hs293 became the first airborne guided missile to sink an enemy ship, after one struck the Royal Navy sloop *Egret* off northern Spain on 27 August 1943 and caused her magazine to explode.

The Fritz-X was a free-fall bomb weighing 1,400 kg. (3,100 lb.), fitted with fixed cruciform wings midway along the body and movable control surfaces at the tail. Its radio guidance system was similar to that used by the Hs293. Released from high altitude, the bomb achieved a velocity sufficient to penetrate the deck armour of a battleship. First used during a Luftwaffe attack on Italian warships on their way to surrender to the Allies on 9 September 1943, two of them hit the battleship *Roma* and she blew up with heavy loss of life. The specifications of these bombs became known to the Allies through *MAGIC intelligence.

The US Army Air Forces developed a weapon similar to the Fritz-X, codenamed the AZON, a 454 kg. (1,000 lb.) bomb fitted with radio guidance equipment. The weapon was first used in action in February 1944, and it scored hits on locks in the River Danube and the Avisio viaduct in northern Italy. Later it was used with considerable success against bridge targets in the *Burma campaign.

Another US guided weapon that saw operational use was APHRODITE, a war-weary B17 or B24 bomber fitted with 11,340 kg. (25,000 lb.) high explosive charges and equipment to transmit television pictures of the target. Radio-guided on to targets by 'mother' aircraft, the explosive bombers were used against targets in Europe. The twin-engined TDR assault drone, used by the US Navy in the *Pacific war, operated on a similar principle. Near the end of the war the US Navy's Bat anti-ship missile entered service. This unpowered glider weapon was fitted with a 454 kg. (1,000 lb.) warhead, and carried to within range of enemy ships by a PB4Y-2 Privateer aircraft. The *radar of the parent aircraft was used to illuminate the target, and the missile homed on the source of the reflected signals using its semi-active radar homing head.

Finally, and to illustrate the breadth of the 'guided weapon' genre, there was the German Goliath weapon that can best be described as a self-propelled remote-controlled demolition charge. First used against the *Anzio beachhead in February 1944, the tracked vehicle resembled a miniature *First World War tank 1.75 m. (5 ft. 9 in.) long. It weighed 285 kg. (628 lb.) and carried an 80 kg. (176 lb.) high explosive charge. Electrical steering signals from the control unit were passed via wires unreeled by the weapon as it headed for the target. The Goliath was powered by a Zundapp petrol engine and had a maximum speed of 20 km/h (12 mph). See also EXPLOSIVE MOTOR BOATS.

ALFRED PRICE

Gunston, B., *Rockets and Missiles* (London, 1979).
Price, A., *Aircraft versus Submarine* (London, 1973).

Guingand, see DE GUINGAND.

GUlag, Russian acronym for Main Administration of Camps', a branch of the *NKVD dedicated to the running of Soviet slave labour camps. By extension, the term is also used to describe the network of camps over which the GUlag presided.

Together with ordinary gaols and zones of administrative exile, the camps constituted the core of the Soviet system of repression. The inmates, both men and women, would usually have passed a brief period of arrest and interrogation before being sentenced *in absentia* to a fixed period of 8, 10, 12, or 25 year's hard labour. They could expect their sentence to include a further period of 'free exile' outside the camp. The vast majority did not live to see the end of their sentences. Many succumbed during the initial journey in penal convoys, which took them in sealed cattle wagons or river barges to the most distant and inhospitable regions of the country. The average life expectancy within the camps was one winter. For all practical purposes, to be sent to the GUlag was equivalent to a death sentence.

The first camps had been set up shortly after the October Revolution of 1917 and were used in the civil war from 1918 to 1920. In the late 1920s Stalin expanded their staff, their powers, and functions with the inception of forced-rate industrialization and forcible agriculture collectivization. The system came into its own with the so-called Great Terror, with the most intensive spate of incarceration occurring from 1936 to 1938. But the camp system of mass slave labour was maintained thereafter, and the arrest of innocent Soviet citizens continued to be a widespread practice. During the campaign of 'dekulakization', as also in the later stages of the Great Terror, the Soviet security services had frequently resorted to mass shootings as they did in the *Katyń forest. But the relative decline of the Terror after 1939, together with the increased demand for labour, restored the GUlag's primacy.

Information about the GUlag began to be brought to the West during the late 1920s by some of the few who had managed to escape. In 1930 the US Treasury Department imposed an embargo on Soviet pulpwood and matches, largely on the basis of evidence that slave labour had been used in their manufacture. In the UK the Anti-Slavery Society launched an enquiry which concluded that prisoners were being used as *forced labour in the lumber camps and there were grim accounts of their working conditions. These stories were reinforced by the Poles of *Anders' Army when they left the USSR in 1942. They were the largest group of people to come to the West with first-hand evidence of the GUlag, and they brought with them NKVD documents relating to the Poles' imprisonment in the camps and their subsequent release—evidence which had never been seen in the West before.

The start of the Second World War in September 1939 gave Stalin his chance to occupy Estonia, Latvia, Lithuania, eastern Poland, and eastern Romania, where vast numbers of arrests took place. The terror machinery set up already in the USSR was geographically redeployed by the NKVD troops under the leadership of *Beria.

Soviet repressive policy had a brutal underlying rationale. Many of the victims belonged to the military, political, professional, and cultural élites, especially in the newly-occupied areas. Stalin intended to remove all real and potential influences which obstructed the imposition of a Stalinist political structure and ideology.

Conditions in the GUlag were inhuman. Prisoners were forced to toil on a starvation diet and under extreme, climatic rigours. Non-fulfilment of demanding norms was punished by the reduction of rations, and minor breaches of discipline by beatings and shootings. The Soviet novelist Alexander Solzhenitsyn, himself an inmate of the GUlag system, calculated that the death rate from malnutrition, disease, and exhaustion during the war years reached 1% per day. It was not unusual for those few prisoners who served their term to be refused release on the grounds that they were *a fortiori* the most useful workers.

Most camp prisoners underwent a worsening of their conditions after Germany's invasion of the USSR on 22 June 1941 (see BARBAROSSA). Hitler's occupation of Ukraine and parts of the Volga region created difficulties of food supplies: and the GUlag population was compelled to bear the collective brunt of the crisis. Even the planned ration for prisoners, below the minimum for subsistence as it was, was not fully delivered. The death rate in camps doubled in 1941 and quintupled in 1942 over the previous period.

Forced labour was directed to vital national projects: the construction of railways, factories, and flats in climatically harsh areas; the mining of gold and coal; the felling of forests. Without slave labourers, Stalin's industrial economy would have fallen well short of its goal. But even Stalin and Beria had to recognize wartime priorities. It is reckoned that up to a million prisoners received early release from captivity during the *German–Soviet war. In some cases, high-ranking officers re-entered the Red Army with their previous ranks restored. Otherwise they were enlisted into units carrying out the most dangerous offensive duties. The decline in the number of camp inmates was reversed from the beginning of 1944 when victory was all but certain and captured enemy soldiers and repatriated Soviet *prisoners-of-war entered the GUlag.

The largest camp complexes were located near to mineral resources in the most northerly latitudes. One, in the district of Vorkuta, consisted of some thirty compounds scattered round the frozen coalfield of northern Russia. 'In Vorkuta', the historian Robert Conquest has written of the area (*The Great Terror*, London, 1968, p. 334), 'it is below zero Centigrade for two-thirds of the year, and for more than 100 days the *Khanovey*, or "wind of winds", blows across the tundra ... few would be alive after a year or two'. Another in the gold-mining

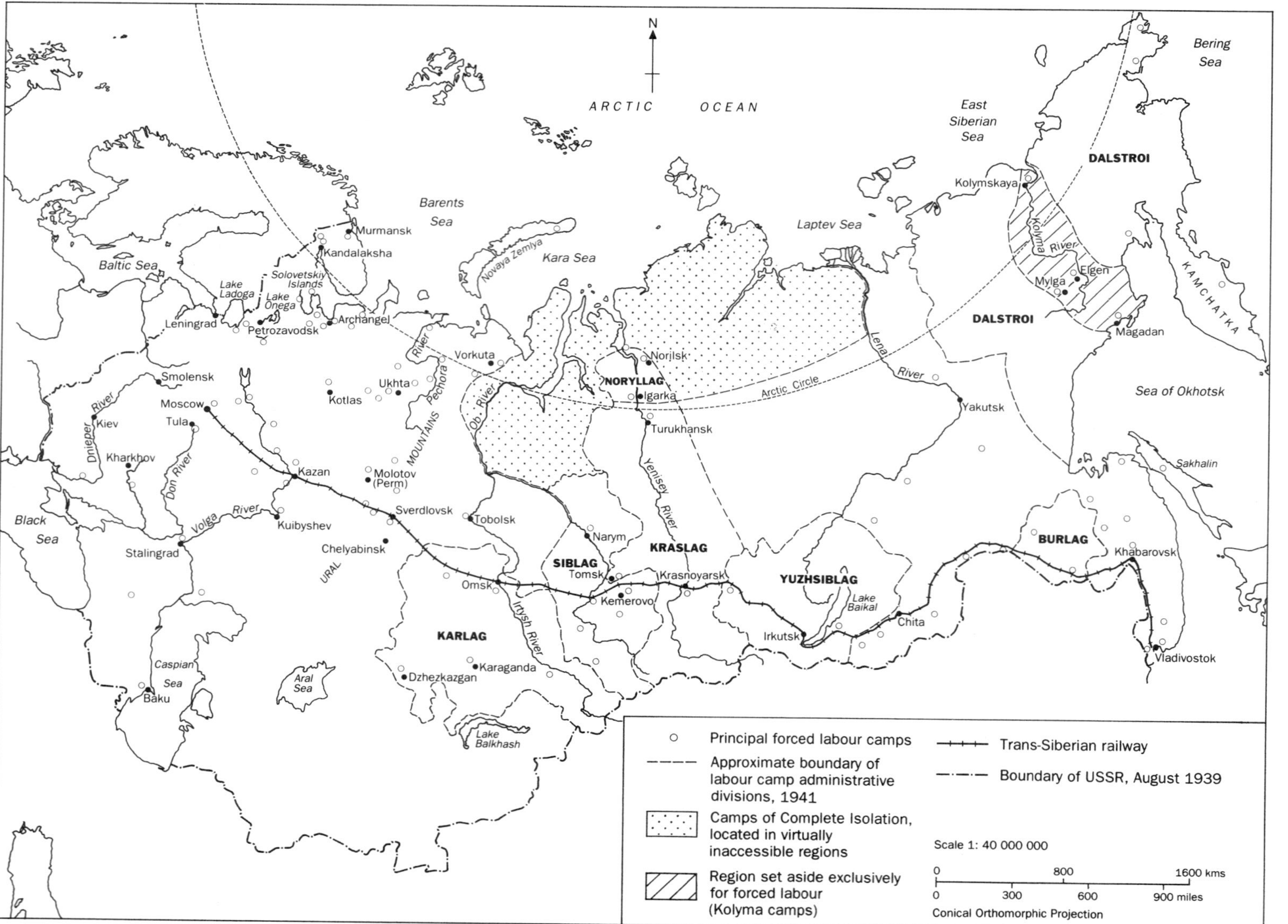

48. **GUlag** system showing approximate boundaries of camp administrative divisions, 1941

district of Kolyma in north-east Siberia covered an area similar to that of the UK. (Its victims outnumbered those of *Auschwitz.) A major collecting centre was sited at Magadan on the Pacific coast. In between them existed what Solzhenitsyn called an 'archipelago' of hundreds of lesser transit camps, project centres, and feeder stations.

A member of Anders' Army, imprisoned at Kolyma, later reported that: 'there were about 5,000 prisoners, 436 of them Poles. About seven to eleven men died daily from famine and exhaustion, from beatings at work and from frost, and when the frost reached minus 68 degrees centigrade, more died from so-called thermic shock. Of all the Poles, only 46 remained with me, the rest starved to death or died from exhaustion. In March 1941, a new prisoner arrived at the Komsomoles mine in Kolyma, a Russian and former chief of the local N.K.V.D in northern Kamchatka, Tchukotka Peninsula, where there are lead mines. In conversation with him I learned that in August 1940 a boat had arrived at Tchukotka carrying 3,000 Poles, mostly military and police personnel. All these Poles who arrived in Tchukotka were sent to the lead mine, and their working parties were purposely sent to the worst galleries. Poles working in these mines suffered from lead poisoning, and about 40 died daily. Before he left about 90 per cent of the Poles had died. In 1941 Georgians and Kazaks were received to replace the Poles. Up to the time of my departure from Kolyma, July 7th, 1942, no Poles had returned from Tchukotka.' (Quoted in W. Anders, *An Army in Exile*, London, 1949, p. 73).

The scale of the GUlag's operation beggars belief. At the end of the Great Terror in March 1939, up to 10% of the Soviet population may have found themselves in the camps. The historian Robert Conquest has estimated one million deaths per annum during the war years that followed. By the time of Stalin's death in 1953 the total number of victims of the GUlag probably exceeded 20 million. Revised estimates based on Soviet records have been eagerly awaited since the collapse of the USSR in 1991.

Comparisons with German and Japanese practices are instructive. The Nazis disliked arresting Germans unless they were political opponents, Jews, homosexuals, gypsies, or mentally disturbed individuals. The Japanese repressed fellow Japanese only in cases of proven political or moral delinquency (see TOKKŌ). Stalin was the sole war leader who kept millions of fellow-citizens deprived of the means to life without giving any reasons for their repression.

At the end of the war in the Far East in August 1945 hundreds of thousands of Japanese were also interned in the GUlag. Within two weeks of the Red Army overrunning Manchukuo (see JAPANESE–SOVIET CAMPAIGNS), Japanese troops and civilians in Manchukuo, North Korea, Sakhalin, and the Kurile Islands were organized into 569 labour gangs, each about a thousand strong; and by late August 1945, 639,635 Japanese (including 575,000 soldiers belonging to the *Kwantung Army) had been interned. The soldiers were put in about 2,000 prisoner-of-war camps located in eastern Siberia, Outer Mongolia, Central Asia, and the southern (Rostov) and western (Moscow) parts of the Soviet Union. The camps were built by the POW themselves, and 80% were in Siberia where the temperature dropped to 30–40 °C below zero in winter time. Lack of winter clothes, fuel, food, and medicine took a toll of more than 60,000 men, about 10% of the internees, in eleven years of internment. Many of them were buried without markers, their whereabouts unknown to this day.

Japanese POW were mobilized in forced labour of all sorts such as mining coal, cutting timber, constructing railways, roads, and buildings, and working as labourers in farms, factories, and wharves. The construction of the Bam railway (second Siberian railway) and the Ulgar railway (350 km. long, connecting the first and second Siberian railways) was so harsh that under every railway sleeper there lay the body of a Japanese soldier. It is no exaggeration that Japanese POW helped the USSR's post-war reconstruction.

Soviet administrators and some turncoat Japanese imposed a production quota, according to which food was rationed. Exerting themselves to achieve the quota, hundreds of POW died of exhaustion.

Soviet authorities brain-washed Japanese internees by organizing in each POW camp a 'Friendship Association'. Prisoners were required to read propaganda material, which promoted class struggle and attacked the Japanese social class structure. Leaders of this brain-washing campaign were radicals who held real power in the POW camps, and they often served as informers betraying fellow POW who were unsympathetic to communist doctrine and uncooperative with Soviet officials. Those opposed to *communism were held back from repatriation, which began in late December 1946. By 1950 just over 530,000 had been repatriated. This left some 3,000 Japanese still held in prisons. As a result of negotiations between *International Red Cross representatives of both countries and of Stalin's death, repatriation resumed in December 1953. With the normalization of Japan–Soviet diplomatic relations in October 1956, the remaining 1,049 prisoners were repatriated in December.

The Japanese government and private organizations set up by former POW continued to press the Soviet government for details about the deaths of prisoners and the locations of some 780 burial grounds, information which was in part supplied by the then Soviet president, Mikhail Gorbachev, when he visited Japan in April 1991.

AKASHI YOGI/NORMAN DAVIES/ROBERT SERVICE

Buca, E., *Vorkuta* (London, 1976).
Conquest, G. R. A., *Kolyma: The Arctic Death Camps* (London, 1987).

Gustav Line, series of German defensive positions north-west of Naples held during the *Italian campaign and completed in early 1944. Originally it was a fall-back, or switch, line for the *Bernhardt Line. At its western end it covered the gap between the sea and the end of the Bernhardt Line near Minturno; inland it broke off from the Bernhardt Line north-east of Castelforte, ran west of the Garigliano, and Rapido rivers, incorporated *Monte Cassino, and then ran east of S. Biagio, before rejoining the Bernhardt Line at Alfedina. When the Gustav Line was completed the Bernhardt Line also came to be known as the Gustav Line, and, with the *Hitler Line, was known to the Allies as the Winter Line.

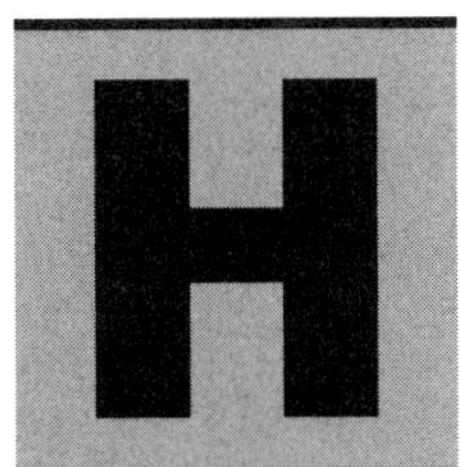

H2S, codename for centimetric British airborne *radar device which displayed for bomber navigators the type of area (water, open country, conurbations) they were flying over. It was one of the war's most successful *electronic navigation systems. In his book *Most Secret War* (London, 1978, p. 319), R. V. Jones relates how the codename originated from a remark—'it stinks!'—made by *Lindemann, Churchill's scientific adviser, referring to the reason given to him for a delay in developing the device. The remark subsequently led to researchers giving the radar the codename H2S (the chemical formula for hydrogen sulphide, the gas which comes from rotten eggs). When Lindemann then asked what the codename meant one bright individual replied: 'Home Sweet Home', which is the usual explanation of its meaning.

The Germans called it the 'Rotterdam Gerät', as the first set that fell into their hands came from an aircraft that had crashed near that city. By July 1944 they had produced a similar set, the 'Berlin Gerät', but it came too late for offensive use.

HABBAKUK, British codename for the construction of a 600 m. (2,000 ft.) carrier from 1.7 million tons of frozen sea water mixed with sawdust. It was the idea of Geoffrey Pyke, a *Combined Operations scientist who called the material Pykrete. A successful 18 m. (60 ft.) prototype was produced in Canada and Pykrete was successfully demonstrated by *Mounbatten (who fired a revolver at it) at the Quebec conference in August 1943 (see QUADRANT). It was never developed, but detractors of Combined Operations thought the scheme far less crazy than the *MULBERRIES, the artificial harbours constructed for the Normandy landings (see OVERLORD).

Lampe, D., *Pyke, the Unknown Genius* (London, 1959).

Hácha, Emil (1872–1945), elected president of Czechoslovakia in November 1938 after *Beneš resigned because of the *Munich agreement which gave Czechoslovakia's Sudetenland to Germany. Hácha was mercilessly bullied by Hitler. His country was dismembered and he spent the war as the powerless president of the Reichsprotectorate of Bohemia and Moravia, all that remained of it. He died in prison awaiting trial for high treason.

Haganah (defence), clandestine, paramilitary organization formed in Palestine in 1920 by Jews to protect themselves against Arab attacks. The more militarist Haganah B was formed from it in 1931, but in 1937 this split, half returning to Haganah, the other half forming the more extreme *Irgun. The Arab revolt of 1936–9 changed the Haganah from a collection of local defence bands into an army structure which its political master, the *Jewish Agency executive, used to organize illegal immigration and control extremists. The British, who governed the mandated territory of Palestine, nearly destroyed the Haganah in 1940, but in 1941 it began to form special independent units (Palmach) from its members. These were used in British military operations such as the *Syrian campaign, but the British never legalized the organization. Its wartime hoarding of arms, and the formation of an intelligence branch, paid dividends during post-war confrontations with British and Arab forces, and with Jewish extremists.

Hague Conventions, international agreements signed in 1899 and 1907 which codified the conduct of war including the prohibition on acquiring *loot. Unlike the *Geneva Conventions of 1864 and 1906, which dealt with the treatment of the sick and wounded on land, they dealt primarily with the methods of waging war, with the outlawing of certain weapons, the qualifications of belligerents, and the rights and duties of neutrals. The 1899 Conventions, agreed by 26 countries, specifically banned the employment of expanding bullets—called 'dum-dum' bullets after the Indian factory which made them for the British Indian Army—and of asphyxiating gases; gave some protection to civilian populations; extended the 1864 Geneva Convention to those fighting at sea; and one included articles on the treatment of *prisoners-of-war who were not sick or wounded.

The 1899 Conventions were updated in 1907 and new ones were adopted. These included: the need to declare war so that there was 'previous and explicit warning' or 'an ultimatum with a conditional declaration'; the status of merchant ships of belligerent powers when war was declared; and the conversion of merchantmen into warships. One also prohibited the discharge of projectiles and explosives from balloons.

That part of the Hague Convention which covered the treatment of prisoners-of-war was eventually replaced by the 1929 Geneva Convention.

Haile Selassie (1891–1976), Emperor of Abyssinia who was exiled in 1936 after the Italian occupation of his country. In May 1941 he was escorted back to his capital by *Wingate during the *East African campaign and he thereafter struggled to ensure his country's independence from British domination. He was deposed in 1974.

Hainan Island, a Chinese possession situated 480 km. (300 mi.) south of Hong Kong. The Japanese, as part of their move southwards during the *China Incident, persuaded *Wang Ching-wei, the leader of the Chinese puppet government in Nanking, to allow them to occupy it in February 1939 to establish air and naval bases, and their seizure of it threatened nearby French Indo-China. It was on Hainan that the original 30 *Thakins of the *Burma Independence Army were trained before the army's formation in December 1941. After the war it was returned to China.

Haiti, which shares the Caribbean island of Hispaniola with the Dominican Republic, declared war on the Axis powers in December 1941 (see CARIBBEAN AT WAR), and was an original signatory of the *United Nations Declaration. The USA undertook to patrol Haitian waters and install manned coastal batteries. Haiti sold its sugar crop to the USA and the UK, but an ambitious programme to grow rubber, funded by the USA, was a failure. See also LATIN AMERICA.

Halder, General Franz (1884–1972), anti-Nazi German Army officer whose talent as a staff officer during the *First World War led to promotion to maj-general in 1936, to lt-general in February 1938, and to his succeeding *Beck as chief of the Army's General Staff (OKH) in September 1938.

Halder was a practising Christian (a Protestant) from a Bavarian family with ancient military traditions, but his initial determination to use his position as chief of staff to oppose the Nazi regime was never converted into action. His first opportunity came during the Czechoslovakian crisis of 1938 (see ORIGINS OF THE WAR). *Brauchitsch, the army's C-in-C, refused to act, but there were others who were prepared to stop Hitler leading Germany into a war for which the army was not prepared. In the event it was the *Munich agreement which saved Hitler; interviewed in 1969, Halder pointed his finger at his British interlocutor and said: 'it was your prime minister, your prime minister who ruined our hopes by giving in to Hitler!' (quoted in C. Barnett, *Hitler's Generals*, London, 1989, p. 105).

Halder's expertise as a staff officer taught him the importance of mobility in warfare. It was a lesson he did not apply to Hitler's satisfaction when planning the proposed invasion of Czechoslovakia in September 1938—perhaps he was distracted from his task by the proposed *coup d'état*—but he scored a notable success when he orchestrated a swift victory in the *Polish campaign in October 1939.

However, he viewed with horror the decision to launch a western offensive in the autumn of 1939 and for weeks contemplated plans to assassinate Hitler. But caught between Hitler's demands and those of the conspirators, his nerve broke—indeed, a fellow officer reported him as suffering a complete nervous collapse—and he ordered the cancellation of another *coup*.

By the time the offensive was launched in May 1940 the General Staff's plan had been altered to incorporate *Manstein's bolder stroke (see FALL GELB). Halder, by now unenthusiastic about overthrowing Hitler, was converted late to this plan but afterwards claimed it was his. That it worked so well, and led to the fall of *France the following month, was one of the German General Staff's greatest achievements—and Halder's.

However, the General Staff's plan for the invasion of the USSR in June 1941 (see BARBAROSSA) proved less successful. Although it produced stunning early victories, Halder's intelligence staff had miscalculated the Red Army's strength and therefore the possibility of a swift campaign. When this became clear Halder could not prevent Hitler imposing his own plans on the General Staff, and even when Brauchitsch was dismissed in December 1941 Halder deemed it his duty to the army to remain at his post. But as soon as Hitler's offensive into the Caucusus became bogged down (see GERMAN–SOVIET WAR), Halder was made the scapegoat; in September 1942 he was dismissed, and was not re-employed.

Halder was not directly involved in the July 1944 bomb plot against Hitler's life (see SCHWARZE KAPELLE), but he and his family were arrested when it failed, and he was imprisoned in *Flossenbürg and then *Dachau. After the war he served with the US Army's Historical Division for fourteen years, and in 1961 was given the Meritorious Civilian Service Award, the highest US civilian award for services to the state (see also DECORATIONS).

Burdick, C., and Jacobsen, H.-A. (eds.), *The Halder Diary, 1939–1942* (London, 1988; ed. version of three-volume *Halder Diaries*, ed. H.-A. Jacobsen, 1962–4).

Halfaya Pass. Situated near the Egyptian–Libyan border, this gap was one of only two exits through a defensible escarpment which narrowed the coastal plain to a bottleneck south of Sollum in Libya. This made it one of the most disputed pieces of ground in the *Western Desert campaigns. *Rommel's *Afrika Korps captured it on 27 April 1941 and recaptured it after it was retaken during a British advance mounted that May (BREVITY). The pass then became an anchor point for a powerful German defensive line that ran through Hafid ridge to Sidi Azeiz. It was successfully held by Rommel's remarkable military cleric, Major Wilhelm Bach, when the British launched their next offensive in June 1941 (BATTLEAXE) and, despite being isolated, he continued to hold it when a third British offensive was launched that November (CRUSADER). He was finally forced to surrender in January 1942. Rommel then retook the pass after the *Gazala battle in June 1942, but it was successfully stormed by New Zealand infantry in November 1942 after the second battle of *El Alamein.

Halifax, Lord (1881–1959), British Conservative politician born the Hon. Edward Wood, fourth son of the second viscount Halifax. He became Lord Irwin on his appointment as Viceroy of India (1926–31) and inherited his father's title in 1934. He supported appeasement and tried to forward it when he met Hitler (and *Goebbels, to whom he took a liking) in November 1937, and he continued to pursue it when he became foreign secretary in February 1938. But in September his attitude changed, and to *Chamberlain's consternation he opposed Hitler's Bad Godesberg terms (see MUNICH AGREEMENT). Later he described the Munich agreement as a 'hideous choice of evils', supported rearmament, and negotiated the guarantee of Poland (see POLAND, GUARANTEE OF). Such was his stature that he was Chamberlain's—and King *George VI's—first choice as prime minister in May 1940.

But he refused the post: he was no military strategist and probably calculated he could restrain the impulsive Churchill better by serving under him. In December 1940 Churchill, politically strengthened by early victories in the *Western Desert campaigns, was able to remove him, and he was appointed British ambassador to Washington, though he remained a member of the war cabinet. Initially, the Americans did not care for his aristocratic mien, nor his self-confessed *anti-Semitism, but once the USA was at war he became both popular and successful. He was granted an earldom in 1944 and remained at his post until 1946.

Roberts, A., *The Holy Fox: A Biography of Lord Halifax* (London, 1991).

Halsey, Admiral William ('Bull') (1882–1959), US naval officer who graduated from the Naval Academy in 1900 after an indifferent career as a student. Between the wars he became a qualified pilot and by 1940 he was a vice-admiral and the most senior carrier admiral in the Pacific. His carriers were away from *Pearl Harbor when the Japanese attacked and as an advocate for taking the offensive as quickly as possible—which earned him the permanent loyalty of *Nimitz, his C-in-C—he led his carrier task force on an acclaimed series of daring raids against Japanese-held Pacific islands during the first two months of 1942. He stayed in the public eye for the rest of the war.

Promoted Commander of Carriers, Pacific Fleet in April 1942 he launched the *Doolittle raid on Tokyo, but missed the *Midway battle through sickness. His combat aggressiveness brought him command of the South Pacific Force in October 1942 at a critical time in the *Guadalcanal campaign, and his forces there engaged the Japanese in key naval actions that eventually secured the island for the Americans. He was promoted admiral in November 1942 and throughout 1943 and early 1944 continued as *South Pacific Area commander directing the American offensive in the Solomons (see Map 83).

In September 1944 he took up sea command of Third Fleet (Fifth Fleet when commanded by *Spruance) which covered the American landings on Leyte the following month (see PHILIPPINES CAMPAIGNS). The Japanese, playing on Halsey's pugnacious, impulsive temperament, nearly accomplished their goal of destroying the landings by luring him north to attack *Ozawa's decoy carrier fleet, and in the battle of *Leyte Gulf which followed only the efforts of the much smaller Seventh Fleet averted disaster. His judgement was also questioned when he took his fleet into two typhoons in one of which three destroyers were lost. But it was aboard his flagship, the battleship *Missouri*, that the Japanese surrender ceremony took place on 2 September 1945 in Tokyo Bay and that December he was promoted Fleet Admiral.

Appropriately nicknamed 'Bull', Halsey's rugged appearance underlined his toughness and readiness to fight. He was universally liked and admired, but his natural aggressiveness worked against him at Leyte Gulf and a large question mark remains over his abilities as a planner and an administrator.

Halsey, W., and Bryan, J., *Admiral Halsey's Story* (New York, 1947).
Potter, E. B., *Bull Halsey* (Annapolis, Md., 1985).

Hamburg air offensive. Employing WINDOW for the first time, to confuse German *radar defences (see also ELECTRONIC WARFARE), the RAF committed over 3,000 bombers to four *area bombing night raids on this German port: 24, 27, and 29 July and 2 August 1943. Additional nuisance raids were mounted and the US Army Air Forces also launched daylight raids on 25 and 26 July.

The second night attack, which used high explosive and incendiary bombs alternately, caused the first man-made *firestorm which affected an area of 22 sq. km. (8.5 sq. mi.). It rendered helpless the city's fire-fighting force and altogether it is estimated that the raids killed 44,600 civilians and 800 servicemen, compared with the wartime total of 60,595 British civilians killed in German raids. It reduced half the city to rubble and nearly two-thirds of what remained of the population had to be evacuated.

Although the raids were aimed primarily at the civilian population, 580 industrial and war production firms were destroyed or damaged and the British Bombing Survey Unit concluded that the loss of war production was equivalent to the city's normal output over 1.8 months. The U-boat yards were not badly damaged, but it was estimated that as many as 27 U-boats were never built because of the raids. Output returned to 80% of normal within five months, but full recovery was never achieved.

The introduction of WINDOW forced the Germans practically to abandon the *Kammhuber Line of air defences and begin using the highly successful *Wilde Sau night fighter tactics. See also STRATEGIC AIR OFFENSIVES, 1.

Middlebrook, M., *The Battle of Hamburg* (London, 1980).

hand grenades, see GRENADES and VEMORK.

Harriman, (William) Averell (1891–1986), US diplomat who served as Roosevelt's special envoy to the UK and the USSR. The son of a multimillionaire, Harriman began his public career in 1934 and altogether it spanned four Democratic presidents and 35 years. A first-class administrator and an excellent negotiator, he served briefly in the US Defense Department in 1940 before being sent to the UK as the administrator of that country's share of *Lend-Lease. 'I want you to go to London,' Roosevelt instructed him, 'and recommend everything that we can do, short of war, to keep the British Isles afloat.'

He took part in the *Placentia Bay conference in August 1941 and that autumn accompanied *Beaverbrook to the *Three-Power conference in Moscow to arrange Lend-Lease for the USSR. Harriman's position in the UK was even more important than that of the US ambassador, John Winant, for he appealed to Churchill more than Winant did and the prime minister knew he was close to Roosevelt, whom Harriman had known since childhood.

He was appointed US ambassador to Moscow in October 1943 and held the post until 1946.

Harriman, W. A., and Abel, E., *Special Envoy to Churchill and Stalin, 1941–46* (New York, 1975).

Harris, Air Chief Marshal Sir Arthur (1892–1984), C-in-C of British Bomber Command from 1942 to 1945, who earned the nickname 'Bomber' because of his fervent support for *area bombing.

During the *First World War Harris was a bugler with the 1st Rhodesia Regiment before joining the Royal Flying Corps, and in 1918 became a squadron leader in the newly formed RAF. In September 1939 he was given command of No. 5 Bomber Group before serving for six months as deputy chief of the Air Staff and then as the head of the first RAF delegation in Washington. During his absence heavy daytime losses, and then wildly inaccurate night raids, led to the suspension of long-range sorties and the transfer of Bomber Command's C-in-C, Air Chief Marshal Richard Peirse (1892–1970), to India. Harris became Bomber Command's new C-in-C in February 1942 and was promoted air chief marshal shortly afterwards.

Harris had witnessed London burning during the *Blitz and believed incendiaries would destroy a city more effectively than high explosive *bombs. He proved this with early raids on Lübeck and Rostock and then displayed the effectiveness of his methods with one bold stroke. In May 1942, he risked the entire structure of Bomber Command by gathering together the maximum number of available bombers, from training units as well as all operational ones, and devastated Cologne in the first of the *thousand-bomber raids. Only 40 bombers were lost, new tactics were learned (see BOMBERS, 2), and though subsequent raids of the same size were not as successful British morale was boosted by the first one, and that of Bomber Command restored, and his methods were backed by increasing bomber production.

New *electronic navigation systems and the *Pathfinder force brought further successes for Harris in 1943. But his raids on *Berlin, beginning in November 1943, were at variance with the spirit of the POINTBLANK Directive (see COMBINED BOMBER OFFENSIVE), issued the previous June, which made selected industries the priority targets. At first there was support for his continuing belief that area bombing alone would destroy Germany's will to fight, but heavy losses, combined with mounting evidence that German morale remained unbroken, steadily eroded it. Eventually the policy brought him into direct conflict with *Portal and with Churchill, when, during the last winter of the war, he continued to pursue it.

Harris was an outstanding leader, and he inspired the total confidence of most of those under him. But his stubbornness during the last months of the war, in continuing to allocate the preponderance of his forces to a policy no one else believed could singlehandedly achieve victory, caused resentment after the war and some obloquy. He had been knighted in 1942 but was ignored by *Attlee's government in the victory honours list of January 1946, and his request for a special *campaign medal for Bomber Command was refused. However, on his resignation from the RAF in 1946 he was promoted Marshal of the Royal Air Force and when Churchill returned to power in 1951 Harris was offered a peerage. This he refused but accepted a baronetcy (1953). See also AIR POWER.

Carver, M. (ed.), *The War Lords* (London, 1976).
Saward, D., *Bomber Harris* (London, 1984).

Hart, Admiral Thomas C. (1877–1971), commander of US Asiatic fleet based at Manila from 1939. In January 1942, by which time his fleet had withdrawn to the *Netherlands East Indies, he was appointed *ABDA Command's naval commander (known as ABDAFLOAT) but was replaced the following month by Vice-Admiral C. Helfrich of the Royal Netherlands Navy.

Leutze, J., *A Different Sort of Victory: A Biography of Admiral Thomas C. Hart* (Annapolis, Md., 1981).

Havana conference, pan-American meeting held in July 1940 to discuss neutrality and economic co-operation. The principal topic was the protection of peace in the *Western Hemisphere. The USA, traditionally opposed to the transfer of territory in the Americas from one European power to another, feared that European colonies in the area might be converted into 'strategic centres of aggression' if any were acquired by the Axis. The delegates from Argentina, Brazil, Chile, Peru, Uruguay, and the USA therefore agreed, by the Havana Act, that there should be a collective trusteeship of any territory which was in danger of becoming such a centre. The Act also decreed that such territories should subsequently have the right to determine their own futures, which did not please the British, French, or Dutch governments. It was never invoked but Cordell *Hull, the US secretary of state who led the US delegation, accused de *Gaulle and the Free French of contravening it by occupying *St Pierre and Miquelon that December.

heavy water, see ATOMIC BOMB, 1 and VEMORK.

Heil Hitler! *Heil* ('hail' or 'long live') was a traditional word of acclamation in Germany; the crowds shouted *Heil Hitler!* when Hitler was released from prison in 1924. The Nazi Party first used it during a parade in 1925 in conjunction with the Nazi salute which Hitler had adopted from the Italian fascist salute. When *Goebbels became *Gauleiter of Berlin in 1926 he made it the compulsory greeting between party members.

Heisenberg, Werner (1901–76), German nuclear physicist who won the Nobel Prize for Physics in 1932 as one of the principal architects of quantum mechanics. He was no lover of the Nazis but, he said after the war, his intense patriotism prevented him from leaving his country during the 1930s when he became the leader of the Uranverein, the German project to make an *atomic bomb. He later averred he did what he could to prevent the manufacture of an atomic device, a claim which has been questioned, but which is supported by a biography published in 1993. He was arrested by the leader of the *Alsos mission to Germany in May 1945 and was briefly interned. See also SCIENTISTS AT WAR.

Powers, T., *Heisenberg's War: The Secret History of the German Atomic Bomb* (London, 1993).

helicopters were developed by several combatant countries but only Germany, which ordered the production of two types, the Kolibri (humming-bird) and the heavier Drache (kite), and the USA, where the Sikorsky company built several hundred, used them operationally. Allied air raids prevented all but a handful of German helicopters ever taking to the air but the Americans used some for rescue operations in the *Burma campaign from April 1944 and the US Coast Guard employed others on *air-sea rescue work.

Henlein, Konrad (1898–1945), leader during the 1930s of the Sudeten German Party, the Sudetenland's equivalent of the Nazi Party. This received both its funds and its orders from Germany. Henlein's agitation for autonomy from Czechoslovakia for the German minority there (see VOLKSDEUTSCHE), and his other demands on the Czech government, precipitated the political crisis which led to the *Munich agreement in September 1938 which handed over the Sudetenland to Germany. In October 1938 Henlein was appointed the Sudetenland's *Gauleiter, but he wielded little power and many of his supporters were subsequently eliminated by the Nazis. He committed suicide in an Allied *internment camp before he could be brought to trial.

heroism, which is defined in the *Oxford English Dictionary* as 'exalted courage, intrepidity, or boldness', can be observed in the conduct of all the armies in the Second World War and numerous *decorations were awarded by both sides for it. It was also evident in the conduct of civilians, especially in such dire events as the siege of *Leningrad, the *Warsaw risings, or the fire-bombings of *Dresden or Tokyo. Some writers have contrasted the 'quiet heroism' of individuals like Janusz Korczak, who chose to accompany orphans to the death camp of *Treblinka without protest, with the more conventional bravery of soldiers.

However, there is a marked tendency for heroism to be discussed in subjective, one-sided terms. Many commentators have reserved 'heroism' for the actions of their own side in the war, while conceding that the enemy side showed only 'fanatical courage' or 'suicidal bravery'. In the USSR, where the Second World War remained the focus of official propaganda to the end, state censorship always insisted on confining heroism to the ranks of the Red Army, never letting it to be mentioned with reference to the Wehrmacht.

For Allied commentators, there is a problem in assessing the conduct of totalitarian armies, where brutality and genocide were often practised as a matter of policy, but where individual heroism could also be evidenced. Such are the moral overtones, it is sometimes hard to accept that members of the Nazi *SS, for example, could be both heroic and genocidal. Whether Japanese *kamikaze pilots are judged heroic or not often depends more on political loyalties than on the cool analysis of their motives. Historians have a special problem in explaining extravagantly heroic conduct among Soviet soldiers, many of whom went to their death with the shout *Za Stalina!* on their lips at a time when the Soviet dictator was destroying millions of his own people. How could such a hated regime exact such selfless service?

The conventional answer is sought in the realm of Soviet and particularly Russian patriotism, which the regime could effectively invoke once the USSR was invaded. But this is hardly sufficient given the Soviet Army's high numbers of *deserters. An equally plausible explanation may lie in the unprecedented climate of fear which surrounded Soviet soldiers both in their homes before conscription and in their units. Young men who grew up in the 1930s amidst the mass killings, collectivization, and purges, knew that they would be sent into combat in waves of unprotected infantry, with the guns of the enemy ahead and the guns of the *NKVD behind. For them, a last act of bravado or of sacrifice for their comrades, promised blessed relief. NORMAN DAVIES

Hertzog, General (James) Barry (1866–1942), South African politician who founded the National Party in 1913 which fought, *inter alia*, for the equality in South Africa of the Afrikaans language with English. In 1924 he made a pact with the Labour Party which made him prime minister and in 1933 entered into a coalition with *Smuts's United Party. Hertzog remained prime minister, but there was increasing conflict between the two leaders over his dealings with Nazi Germany. He resigned in September 1939 after his motion for South Africa to remain neutral was narrowly defeated in parliament. He was replaced by Smuts, and retired from politics in December 1940.

Hess, Rudolf (1894–1987), Hitler's entirely devoted Nazi Party deputy who, from March 1939, was second in line to the chancellorship after *Göring.

Born in Alexandria, where his Bavarian father owned an export firm, Hess was educated in Germany from the age of fourteen before he entered the family business. During the *First World War he served in the same regiment as Hitler, was wounded twice, received a commission, and joined the German Air Force. After the war he went to Munich, fell under Hitler's spell, and became a close confidant of the future Führer. In 1923 Hess took part in Hitler's attempted Munich putsch and they subsequently shared a cell in Landsberg prison where Hitler dictated most of **Mein Kampf* to him, and to it Hess added the concept of **Lebensraum*.

However, after Hitler assumed power in January 1933, Hess's influence within the party steadily diminished. He was elected to the Reichstag and became a minister of state, but was never considered Hitler's successor. In fact, as Hitler continued on his triumphal way, Hess must have begun to feel unappreciated, a feeling which was intensified by the advent of war. It is therefore possible that he had a desperate desire to re-establish himself in Hitler's eyes and that it was this desire that partly caused him to undertake the bizarre mission to the UK for which he is best known. But he also enjoyed dabbling in foreign affairs and after trying, but failing, to make contact with British intermediaries on the Continent, he must have decided to present his plan—whereby the UK and Germany would ally themselves against the USSR—in person.

On the evening of 10 May 1941 he flew from Germany to Scotland in a twin-engined Messerschmitt 110, his third attempt to make the flight, and parachuted to the ground, as planned, near the country seat of the Duke of Hamilton. He hoped the duke, whom he had met, would arrange for him to meet King *George VI to discuss his peace terms. When he was captured he did not reveal his identity until he met the duke. In due course the British diplomat Ivone Kirkpatrick arrived and identified him. Hess then explained that he had come to negotiate peace.

If a conversation partly overheard by one of Hess's adjutants is to be believed, Hitler was aware of his deputy's scheme, though whether he took it seriously is another matter. It was almost certainly not authorized, for when Hitler heard what Hess had done he flew into a rage and was quick to follow Hess's suggestion, in a letter written before he left, that if his mission failed he could be disowned as being insane.

Hess certainly appeared unstable to those who interrogated him in the UK. Once Churchill had decided to have nothing to do with him, and to treat him as a prisoner-of-state, he was put into the care of psychiatrists and he twice made feeble attempts at suicide. The British press speculated wildly about his flight, but no hint of his peace plans reached a public which, at that particular juncture of the war, might have been receptive to them. He was kept first at a Scottish military hospital, Buchanan Castle; then in the Tower of London; then, until June 1942, at Mytchett Place near Aldershot, and finally at a former hospital, Maindiff Court, at Abergavenny, South Wales. At the *Nuremberg trials he was found guilty of war crimes, sentenced to life imprisonment, and incarcerated in Berlin's Spandau prison. Before a prisoner could be freed, his release had to be agreed by the four main Allied powers. By 1966 only Hess remained in Spandau but the Soviets refused to free him. When he died the prison was demolished. It was officially confirmed that he had committed suicide by strangling himself with an electric cord, but some believe he was murdered.

A number of stories, partly fuelled by the British government's refusal to release all the relevant files, have grown up around Hess and his mission. One of them, that it was not Hess who flew to Scotland but a double, has been disproved. Another, that Stalin believed that Hess's mission was to negotiate an Anglo-German attack on his country and somehow received a transcript of an interview between Hess and *Beaverbrook during which Hess proposed just that, might explain the Soviets' vindictiveness towards him.

Though diagnosed as a psychopath and then as suffering from hysterical amnesia—which he later said he faked—no one ever considered Hess clinically insane.

Gabel, C., *Conversations Interdites avec Rudolf Hess* (Paris, 1988).
Hess, W., *My Father Rudolf Hess* (London, 1986).
Schwarzwäller, W., *Rudolf Hess* (London, 1988).

Heydrich, Reinhard (1904–42), *SS Obergruppenführer (lieutenant-general) who was head of the *RSHA (Reichssicherheitshaumptamt, or Reich Security Main Office), *Himmler's deputy, and a leading proponent of the *Final Solution.

The son of a Dresden music teacher, Heydrich was born at Halle and in 1922 joined the German Navy. He served for a time under Admiral *Canaris, whose rival intelligence organization, the *Abwehr, Heydrich later constantly schemed against. However, in 1931 he was forced to resign from the navy after a scandal involving the daughter of a shipyard director. The same year he joined the Nazi Party and then the SS through whose ranks he rose quickly to become an SS lieutenant-general in July 1934.

In 1932 he established the intelligence department (Sicherheitsdienst, or SD) of the SS, and in 1934 took command of the Prussian *Gestapo in Berlin. Two years later he was appointed to command the newly formed security police (Sicherheitspolizei, or *Sipo), a forerunner of the RSHA. Though the Sipo remained within the ministry of the interior, this gave Heydrich nationwide control of the Gestapo and of the criminal police (Kriminalpolizei, or *Kripo). As head of the Gestapo he instituted a merciless persecution against any religious or cultural group which he deemed to be enemies of National Socialism. He built up dossiers not only on communists, Jews, and other enemies of the regime, but on his rivals for power; he helped engineer the downfall of Field Marshal *Blomberg and General *Fritsch in 1938, and organized the fake attack on the *Gleiwitz radio station which triggered the German attack on Poland on 1 September 1939.

In September 1939 the RSHA was created as a new branch of the SS and Heydrich was given command of it. As the RSHA not only contained the SD but had the

Gestapo and Kripo transferred to it from the ministry of the interior, he now had the complete secret police apparatus under his direct control. With it he organized the herding of Polish Jews into *ghettos and the deportation eastwards of those living in Germany and what had been Austria, and from the annexed areas of Poland. In July 1941 he was ordered by *Göring to find 'a total solution of the Jewish question'; death camps began to be constructed specially for the destruction of the Jews—an undertaking that was to be called *operation REINHARD in his honour—and on 20 January 1942 he convened the *Wannsee conference where it was decided how best to implement the last stages of the Final Solution. By then he had been Deputy Reichsprotektor of Bohemia and Moravia (see CZECHOSLOVAKIA) for about four months and on 27 May 1942 he was fatally wounded by Free Czech agents who had been trained in the UK by *SOE and parachuted into the country. He died a week later and his death led directly to the *Lidiče massacre.

Though the very picture of blond Aryan handsomeness, Heydrich was reputed, wrongly, to be half-Jewish, a rumour which probably fed his sense of inferiority. His blue-eyed good looks, athletic prowess, arrogant mien, and musical talent hid a neurotic personality which was deeply divided, uncertain, and treacherous.

Aronson. S., *Reinhard Heydrich und die Fruhgeschichte von Gestapo und SD* (Stuttgart, 1971).
MacDonald, C., *The Killing of SS Obergruppenführer Reinhard Heydrich* (London, 1989).

Higgins boats were wooden 11 m. (36 ft.) infantry *landing craft built for the US Marines by Andrew Higgins, a New Orleans boatbuilder. Also known as Eurekas, they were originally constructed for civilian use and had considerable power for their size. They could be retracted easily from a beach and a later version, which the British used in the *Dieppe raid, had a ramp in the bows. During the *North African campaign landings in November 1942 their wooden hulls proved to be too vulnerable, and they were withdrawn from operational use. See also AMPHIBIOUS WARFARE.

Himmler, Heinrich (1900–45). Son of a Catholic schoolmaster, who was Nazi head of the *SS from 1929 to 1945, and Germany's minister of the interior from 1943 to 1945.

Born in Munich, Himmler trained as an officer cadet at the end of the *First World War without seeing active service, then studied at Munich's technical college where he obtained an agricultural diploma. He worked as a fertilizer salesman then as a poultry farmer, joined the Nazi Party in 1925, served as a deputy **Gauleiter*, became deputy leader of the SS in 1927 and its head in January 1929, and was elected a member of the Reichstag the following year.

Using his position as head of the SS, Himmler now began to build a state within the state. At first he concentrated on expanding the organization (by January 1933 it numbered 53,000), then on establishing its autonomy within the Nazi Party, and lastly on ensuring its dominance in every sphere of state security and domestic policy. It was his vehicle for translating *Nazi ideology into action and as early as March 1933, the same month as he became head of the Munich police, he established Dachau, one of the first Nazi *concentration camps, and later founded the **Lebensborn* organization. By 1936 he had manoeuvred himself into a position where he was not only head of the SS but of a newly unified nationwide police.

In October 1939 he was given total control of the annexed parts of Poland and within a year more than a million Poles and 300,000 Jews had been pushed eastwards to be replaced by **Volksdeutsche*. He then became Reich Commissioner for the Strengthening of German Nationhood, to oversee all racial matters, and in August 1943 was appointed minister of the interior in which post he oversaw the *Final Solution, administered the system of *forced labour, and authorized the medical experiments of SS doctors.

The July 1944 bomb plot against Hitler (see SCHWARZE KAPELLE) further strengthened Himmler's hand (though he behaved with extreme deviousness during the crisis) and the army was obliged to accept him as Fromm's successor as C-in-C of the Replacement Army (see GERMANY, 6(b)); and despite his lack of military experience in January 1945 he was even given command of the newly-activated Army Group Vistula, though he was soon replaced by General Gotthard Heinrici. During the last months of hostilities Himmler, who had for some time suspected the eventual outcome of the war, realized that it was now lost for Germany. He ordered a halt to the Final Solution and by various methods attempted to start peace negotiations with the Allies. But his grip on reality was beginning to slip for he really believed the Allies would endorse him as Germany's new leader once Hitler had been deposed and peace restored.

Just before he killed himself, Hitler, on learning of Himmler's latest efforts to contact the Allies, via Count *Bernadotte, dismissed him from all his posts and ordered his arrest. When *Dönitz became head of state Himmler offered his services, which were declined. After Germany surrendered Himmler tried to escape in disguise, but was captured and on 23 May 1945 killed himself with poison.

Smelzer, R., and Zitelmann, R. (eds.), *The Nazi Elite* (London, 1992).

Hirohito (1901–89) was Emperor of Japan from 1926 until his death. His role in relation to the Second World War is still highly controversial. In Allied wartime perceptions, as the supreme ruler of Japan he was the paramount symbol of Japanese nationalism, and the personification of Japan's participation with Germany and Italy in a 'fascist conspiracy' to dominate the world. The belief that Hirohito had led Japan into the war prompted demands after it ended that he be tried as a war criminal (see also FAR EAST WAR CRIMES TRIALS).

A quite different, and more accurate view, based mainly

Japan's Emperor **Hirohito**, at Tokyo central railway station. This picture was taken shortly after the official Japanese surrender had taken place in September 1945.

on research in the primary Japanese sources of the period, is that Hirohito personally opposed armed conflict with the Allies, that he was peripheral to his government's decisions in 1941, and that he was instrumental in bringing about Japan's surrender in 1945.

1. Japan's decision for war, 1941

As head of state Hirohito was technically responsible for Japan's final decision to start hostilities at the Imperial Conference on 1 December 1941, six days before the attack on *Pearl Harbor which began the *Pacific war. It is also the case that during hostilities Hirohito, in military uniform and astride a white horse, frequently exhorted his troops and the nation to prevail in battle. For most Japanese, he was a living god, as propounded in the myths of State Shintō, and the conflict was a holy war fought in his name.

However, in reality, Hirohito reigned but did not rule. The sweeping civil and military prerogatives ascribed to the emperor by the Meiji Constitution of 1889—itself a confused amalgam of absolute and limited or constitutional monarchy—had long since been delegated to his ministers of state and the army and navy chiefs of staff. Like the British monarch, at most he had 'the right to be consulted, the right to encourage, and the right to warn', but not, in practice, the right to govern. In keeping with the traditional role of past emperors, Hirohito's main function was to legitimize the policies of his government by formally declaring them as the 'Imperial Will'. This he did simply through his silent attendance at the strictly ceremonial Imperial Conferences (*gozen kaigi*) which routinely followed the Liaison Conference (*renraku kaigi*) where, without the emperor present, leading civilian and military officials decided national policy. That the emperor would ever veto a decision arising from the Liaison Conference, or the cabinet, was unthinkable in pre-war Japan.

His actual powerlessness was all the greater by virtue of the fact that by 1940 the military had achieved political hegemony as a consequence of Japan's evolution into a 'national defence state' (*kokubō kokka*) since the Manchurian Incident of 1931 (see MANCHUKUO). This enabled the military not only to dominate the Liaison Conferences but also to manipulate the symbolic authority of the emperor so that imperial sanction of military policies would be automatic, through the ritual bestowal of the Imperial Will. There was, then, much irony in the remark of the prime minister, General *Tōjō Hideki, at the end of the fateful Imperial Conference of 1 December 1941 that 'Once His Majesty reaches a decision to commence hostilities, we will all strive to repay our obligations to him' (by winning the war). Everyone present knew that the government, not the emperor, had decided upon war at the previous Liaison Conference of 27 November. The Imperial Will for war did not reflect the emperor's personal will in 1941.

Possessing considerable influence, as distinct from effective power, Hirohito had, in 1940 and 1941, privately endeavoured to avoid war with the Anglo-American powers by working behind the scenes at court, just as he had tried, without success, to avoid war with China in the Manchurian Incident and, again, in the *China Incident which commenced in July 1937. From the time of his visit to the UK as crown prince in 1921, he had always believed that peaceful co-operation with the UK and the USA should be the cornerstone of Japanese foreign policy. It was on this account that he had opposed, to no avail, the *Tripartite Pact, signed on 27 September 1940, and the stationing of Japanese troops in French Indo-China, which also began that month. Whereas the government had held that these initiatives would help deter the USA from opposing Japan's New Order in Asia (see GREATER EAST ASIA CO-PROSPERITY SPHERE), Hirohito feared they would provoke greater American hostility towards Japan, resulting ultimately in war.

The application of American sanctions, in particular the embargo on oil exports to Japan on 1 August 1941, justified this apprehension. Accepting the military's argument that the Japanese–American negotiations in

Washington (see USA, 1) could not be prolonged indefinitely lest Japan lose the capacity to defend the empire, the Liaison Conference of 3 September determined that Japan should commence war in October if the USA remained unshakeably opposed to the New Order in Asia. This deadline on *diplomacy impelled Hirohito to warn the government of the folly of war at an Imperial Conference on 6 September. Breaking the convention of imperial silence on such occasions, he read aloud a poem written by his grandfather, Emperor Meiji, which he said expressed his personal wish for peace. The gesture, at best an indirect warning, did not dissuade the government ministers from their chosen course, however. It took the political crisis attending the resignation of the prime minister, Prince *Konoe Fumimaro, and his cabinet, on 16 October, to erase the deadline, with Hirohito's blessing.

Although hostilities were averted at that time, renewed pressure from the military caused the Tōjō government on 2 November to impose a new deadline: the decision for war would be taken by the end of the month if the Washington negotiations were still deadlocked. Though now becoming resigned to war, Hirohito continued in vain at court to press for Japanese diplomatic concessions, to prevent it. However, once the 'Hull note' of 26 November from the US secretary of state, Cordell *Hull, which was regarded as an American ultimatum, had completely unified the government, Hirohito had no choice but to give ritual sanction to its decision to commence hostilities with the Imperial Will on 1 December. The government's otherwise belligerent Imperial Rescript of 8 December, informing the Japanese people that war had begun, did at least express Hirohito's genuine personal regret that 'it has been truly unavoidable and far from Our wishes that Our Empire had now been brought to cross swords with America and Britain'.

Thus, despite his public image of great power and unassailable authority, Hirohito was politically impotent to prevent the Tōjō government from launching a major war. Moreover, he was as peripheral to two other related developments as he had been to the decision for war itself. First, President Roosevelt's last-minute message to the emperor on 8 December, Japan time, was rejected by Tōjō, not by Hirohito. Second, Japan's final note to the USA, in effect a declaration of war, was not delivered by Japan's envoys in Washington until after the Pearl Harbor raid had commenced, despite the emperor's strong wish that it be communicated in advance of the attack, to conform with international norms. Although he had been informed of plans for the attack that autumn, he had not been personally involved in war preparations, as these had always been, and would remain, the exclusive responsibility of the general staffs.

It should be emphasized, however, that while Hirohito had no real political responsibility for the decision to go to war, this does not mean that he was an uncompromising pacifist. Like the men who committed Japan to total war in 1941, he was a nationalist who had accepted the legacy of empire as a legitimate fruit of Japan's historic quest for wealth and power. He wanted peace but not peace at all costs, if the price for peace was the liquidation of the empire. This is perhaps why he seems fatalistically to have accepted the apparent inevitability of war in late 1941, especially after the earlier imposition of American sanctions.

Another important factor in his reluctant compliance with the decision to make war was his long-standing wish to emulate the British model of constitutional monarchy. He was determined to refrain from interfering with the policies decided upon by his government for fear that otherwise Japan would succumb to 'the bane of imperial despotism', as he often put it. It was the particular misfortune of Hirohito that this self-imposed political constraint, bred of his constitutional idealism, unintentionally assisted those who upheld the public fiction of the emperor as absolute monarch. The result was that he had perforce to sanction a decision he himself opposed. His closest court advisers, notably Kido Kōichi (1889–1977), the Lord Keeper of the Privy Seal, contributed to this fiction by keeping Hirohito above the political fray of decision-making in order to preserve the traditional transcendental authority of the emperor.

Nor was Hirohito, for reasons of personality and temperament, the kind of man who would forcefully resist the tide of war. Conditioned by the rigid precedents and protocol of court life to play the symbolic role expected of him, and more at ease as a scientist in his laboratory studying marine biology than in the rough give and take of politics, he was less a leader than a follower of Japan's road to belligerency.

2. Japan's decision to surrender, 1945

In many pre-war discussions with General *Sugiyama and Admiral Nagano Osami (1880–1947), the army and navy Chiefs of Staff respectively, Hirohito had repeatedly questioned whether Japan had the material means to carry out their proposed policies. While he was pleased by Japan's early conquests in the war, it is not surprising that as early as 1942 he fervently urged Tōjō to negotiate an end to the conflict, believing that Japan, overextended on land and at sea, was unlikely to endure a prolonged war of attrition.

As the war continued, and as Japan fell on to the defensive, Hirohito's desire to have it ended was well known to civilian and military leaders alike. Yet given the determination of the military to continue fighting, it required a combination of three developments for Hirohito to be able to end the war: the coalescence of a 'peace party' strong enough to support imperial intervention; a prime minister who would assist the emperor in this endeavour; and the obvious deterioration of Japan's position in the war to the point where surrender was absolutely necessary to save the nation and the monarchy from obliteration.

This combination did not materialize until the spring

of 1945. By then a 'peace party', including former prime ministers, diplomats, and members of the imperial family, had been formed. In Admiral *Suzuki, formerly a Grand Chamberlain, Japan had a prime minister who could co-operate closely with Hirohito in orchestrating an imperial intervention. By then, also, the Allied blockade and incessant bombing (see STRATEGIC AIR OFFENSIVES, 3), and the loss of the *Philippines and *Okinawa, clearly signified the nation's impending defeat.

Whether Hirohito could have intervened sooner than he did and thereby spare Japan the trauma of *atomic bombs being dropped on *Hiroshima on 6 August and *Nagasaki on 9 August, not to mention the USSR's declaration of war on 8 August, is doubtful. Hirohito himself favoured acceptance of the Allies' Potsdam Proclamation of 26 July (see TERMINAL) demanding the immediate *unconditional surrender of Japan's armed forces. But the government's decision at the behest of the military to ignore the demand held sway, resulting in the calamitous events of early August. On 9 August, with the government completely immobilized by conflict between advocates of surrender and the military, Suzuki took the unprecedented step at an Imperial Conference of asking the emperor to decide the issue.

Whereas in 1941 his self-image as a constitutional monarch had prevented him from interfering with the government's unanimous decision for war, the imminent destruction of Japan now resolved him to state his desire to surrender. Even then a second imperial intervention was required to end the war, at the decisive Imperial conference of 14 August, after the military had continued to reject surrender without clear Allied assurances that the monarchy would be retained. In an Imperial Rescript broadcast the next day Hirohito urged the nation to 'endure the unendurable' of defeat. Unlike 1941, the Imperial Will for peace, which the people obeyed, represented the emperor's personal will.

3. The aftermath of war

The war had resulted in immense suffering and loss of life throughout the Asian-Pacific region. Many *atrocities had been committed by Japanese forces against Chinese civilians and Allied *prisoners-of-war and civilians in conquered territories. Hirohito had been informed of some of these outrages, but his attempts to end them went unheeded. Perhaps it was the thought that he was morally, though not politically, responsible for a war which Japan had fought so destructively in his name that caused Hirohito, in his meeting with General *MacArthur on 27 September 1945, to offer to take personal responsibility for everything Japan had done in the war. MacArthur, however, refused the offer, intending instead to use Hirohito's residual authority to assist the democratic reform policies of the occupation. For example, the imperial promulgation of a new constitution, in effect from 3 May 1947, stripped the emperor of all theoretical powers and redefined him as a 'symbol of the state and of the unity of the people, deriving his position from the will of the people with whom resides sovereign power'. Similarly, after the occupation proscribed State Shintō to demystify the emperor, Hirohito repudiated his so-called divinity in an Imperial Rescript on 1 January 1946. Since, as a scientist, he had never believed in the myth, he was glad to take this symbolic step, which also reflected his long-held desire to function as a secular constitutional monarch. He also undertook extensive post-war tours around Japan, to bring the monarchy closer to the people.

Hirohito was therefore not tried for *war crimes. Rather, he co-operated with the occupation in helping to adapt the monarchy to democracy along the lines of constitutional monarchy in the UK. he continued to encourage this evolution of the Japanese imperial institution for the rest of his life. Yet Hirohito never fully justified his role in the war. When he died on 7 January 1989 after a reign of 64 years (the longest on reliable record in Japanese history), many people around the world still condemned him as a war criminal. A small minority in Japan did so, too, although Japanese public opinion polls from 1945 onwards consistently indicated strong popular support for him. STEPHEN LARGE

Large, S. S., *Emperor Hirohito and Shōwa Japan: A Political Biography* (London, 1992).

Titus, D. A., *Palace and Politics in Prewar Japan* (New York, 1974).

Hiroshima, Japanese city, situated some 800 km. (500 mi.) from Tokyo, on which the first operational *atomic bomb was dropped at 0815 on 6 August 1945 (see NAGASAKI for the second). Nicknamed 'Little Boy'—a reference to Roosevelt—the bomb was 3 m. (9 ft. 9 in.) long, used uranium 235, had the power of 12.5 kilotons of TNT (see EXPLOSIVES), and weighed 3,600 kg. (nearly 8,000 lb.).

Much discussion by a Target committee had preceded the decision to make Hiroshima the first target. To be able to assess the damage it caused, and to impress the Japanese government with the destruction it was expected to wreak, it was necessary to choose a city that had not yet been touched by the USAAF's *strategic air offensives. Kyoto was also considered but its unrivalled beauty ruled it out.

The bomb was delivered by a US B29 bomber, nicknamed Enola Gay, from the Pacific island of Tinian. Dropped by parachute it exploded about 580 m. (1,885 ft.) above the ground, and at the point of detonation the temperature probably reached several million degrees centigrade. Almost immediately a fireball was created from which were emitted radiation and heat rays, and severe shock waves were created by the blast. A one-ton (900 kg.) conventional bomb would have destroyed all wooden structures within a radius of 40 m. (130 ft.). Little Boy destroyed them all within a radius of 2 km. (1.2 mi.) of the hypocentre (the point above which it exploded). The terrain was flat and congested with administrative and commercial buildings, and the radius of destruction for the many reinforced concrete structures was about 500 m. (1,625 ft.), though only the top stories of

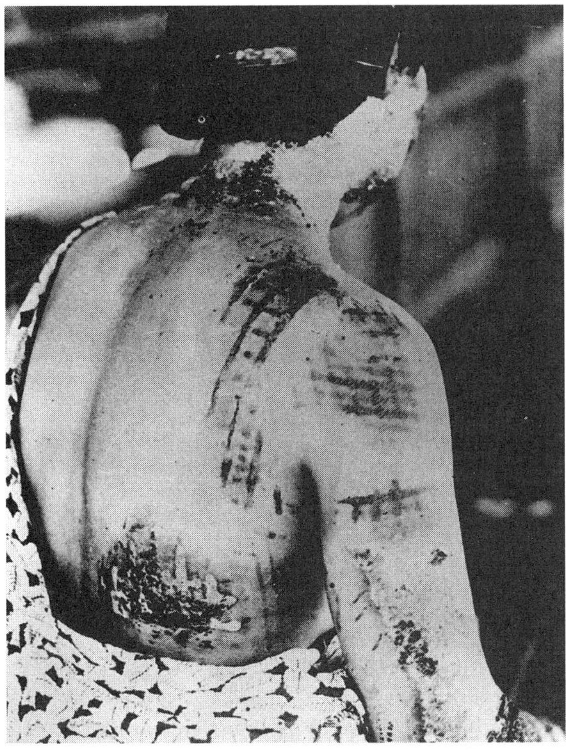

A victim of the atomic bomb which was dropped on **Hiroshima**, 6 August 1945. The pattern of her kimono has been imprinted on her skin by the flash of the bomb.

earthquake-resistant buildings were damaged or destroyed. Altogether an area of 13 sq. km. (5 sq. mi.) was reduced to ashes and of the 76,000 buildings in the city 62.9% were destroyed and only 8% escaped damage.

Within 1.2 km. (.74 mi.) of the hypocentre there was probably a 50% death rate of the 350,000 people estimated to have been in Hiroshima at the time. Hiroshima City Survey Section estimated a figure of 118,661 civilian deaths up to 10 August 1946 (see Table). Add to this a probable figure of 20,000 deaths of military personnel and the current figure—for people are still dying as a result of the radiation received—is in the region of 140,000. Among those who survived, the long-term effects of radiation sickness, genetic and chromosome injury, and mental trauma have been catastrophic, even unborn *children having been stunted in growth and sometimes mentally retarded.

Committee on Damage by Atomic Bombs in Hiroshima and Nagasaki, *Hiroshima and Nagasaki: The Physical, Medical, and Social Effects of the Atomic Bombings* (London, 1981).

historiography. The movement of the war from memory into history is still far from complete. Many participants still survive, and help to keep the memory green. There is also a legacy of film and sound archive, which combines with the impact of feature films and documentaries on popular understanding to ensure that the perception of historical writings about the years 1939–45, and the audience for this history, are shaped by non-academic influences to an unusual degree for any historical subject. Since this war was even more 'total' than the *First World War, with an unparalleled mobil-

Hiroshima: Total number of civilian casualties due to the atomic bomb dropped on Hiroshima up to 10 August 1946

Distance from Hypocentre (km)	*Killed*	*Severely Injured*	*Slightly Injured*	*Missing*	*Not Injured*	*Total*
Under 0.5	19,329	478	338	593	924	21,662
0.5–1.0	42,271	3,046	1,919	1,366	4,434	53,036
1.0–1.5	37,689	7,732	9,522	1,188	9,140	65,271
1.5–2.0	13,422	7,627	11,516	227	11,698	44,490
2.0–2.5	4,513	7,830	14,149	98	26,096	52,686
2.5–3.0	1,139	2,923	6,795	32	19,907	30,796
3.0–3.5	117	474	1,934	2	10,250	12,777
3.5–4.0	100	295	1,768	3	13,513	15,679
4.0–4.5	8	64	373		4,260	4,705
4.5–5.0	31	36	156	1	6,593	6,817
Over 5.0	42	19	136	167	11,798	12,162
TOTAL	118,661	30,524	48,606	3,677	118,613	320,081

Source: Hiroshima Shiyakusho, *Hiroshima Genbaku Sensaishi* [RHAWD] (Hiroshima, 1971), Vol. I.

ization of *women and non-combatant men for war work, the range and types of sub-histories which it has stimulated are broader than for any previous conflict.

Moreover, it was a war where *secrecy abounded. As these secrets are revealed, with the slow passage of time and the relaxation of rules about what must never be spoken of at all, the dimensions of war history expand, so that more and more aspects of the struggle call for serious coverage.

This they often do not at first receive. In the affluent western world, commercial pressures have encouraged the diversification of historical and pseudo-historical writing about the war. There is not only a buoyant market for memoirs and anecdotal accounts of everyday wartime life, either in the armed forces or on the home fronts, but also a keen public appetite for sensation, readily filled by accounts of derring-do, some of them much more accurate than others. The continued closure of wartime files, maintained because of bureaucratic ineptitude or from genuine concern that a nation's security might be endangered if too much became public too soon, or from delicacy about revealing intimate details of wartime private lives, has had an unanticipated result: it has promoted a flourishing industry of speculation and distortion. Several world best-sellers on supposed secret service affairs are historically beneath contempt. The line between fact and fiction has become so hard to draw that a new use has been found for the word 'faction', to describe the conflation of the two.

Moreover, in recent decades many professional academic historians have moved away from the traditional concentration on diplomatic, political, and military history towards a greater interest in exploring the history of everyday life. Some of their academic studies have embraced parts of German-occupied eastern Europe where, until recently, political pressures discouraged realistic accounts of life under Nazi rule.

Wartime emotions and enmities have still not entirely waned. Even those born since 1945 are shaped by the war's impact on their relatives. It is not only in the UK that faces and symbols from the war remain living images in popular culture, often evoked and instantly recognizable.

A main difficulty for the historian is the work of sensationalists, who get hold of part—often only a small part—of some astonishing exploit, write it up in a best-seller, and leave the reading world with a distorted view of what actually happened. Let one instance suffice.

More than 20,000 British and American participants knew something, from their own war work, about the successes the Allies had with decipher during the war (see MAGIC and ULTRA); for nearly 30 years, not one of them spoke out in public. In 1967 a French journalist, Michel Garder, devoted a section of his *La Guerre Secrète des Services Speciaux Français 1935–1945* to the French end of the ULTRA story, although without actually naming the *ENIGMA machine cipher. *Bertrand, head during the war of French decipher and by 1967 a retired general, was so furious at what he thought were Garder's inaccuracies that he persuaded the French security authorities to let him put out a correct version which was published in Paris early in 1973. In it even he nodded: he swallowed whole the Polish cover story for the Poles' advances into ENIGMA, without realizing what they had not cared to tell him. When Bertrand's book appeared, Group Captain F. W. Winterbotham, who had helped organize the distribution of ULTRA material round the British High Command, persuaded the British authorities in turn that he might now be allowed a word, and published *The Ultra Secret* in 1974. This made an immediate newspaper and television sensation, parts of which echo to this day (see COVENTRY). Not until 1978 did Ronald Lewin's *Ultra goes to war* get the facts more or less right; and not till 1988 did the second part of the third volume of Sir Harry Hinsley's magisterial official history of *British Intelligence in the Second World War* put the available record quite straight.

Since the natural trend of all historical scholarship is revisionist, there has been a steady divergence between what academic historians have studied, argued, and written about controversial issues and the popular conclusions long since established. Most of these conclusions were determined by the impact of wartime propaganda and, in the defeated states, by reaction against it (often under the influence of Allied re-education campaigns). The first wave of writing about the war took the form of journalistic accounts, and of memoirs by participants; of these last the flow goes on.

Only Churchill, de *Gaulle, and Queen Wilhelmina of the Netherlands (1880–1962), of the warring heads of governments, left substantial memoirs of the war years. As a fluent non-academic historian, Churchill, naturally enough, sought to set his own account of his struggles from the anti-appeasement stage to victory in the form of a history of the whole war, not merely as the memoirs of one of its protagonists. The six volumes of his *The Second World War* appeared from 1948 to 1954, and apart from their historical value, which remains larger than some of his critics allow, at first served as a political tool to re-establish the reputation that had been diminished by his electoral defeat in 1945. De Gaulle, too, used his *Mémoires de Guerre* (3 vols., Paris, 1954–9) as a weapon in the post-war politics of France. Queen Wilhelmina's *Eenzaam maar neet alleen* (The Hague, 1959, translated in London the following year as *Lonely but not alone*) was slighter, though interesting.

Apart from *Goebbels and *Ciano, who kept copious if self-serving diaries, no other leading political figures on either side left any substantial literary legacy. (*Molotov's posthumously published memoirs reiterate his well-known public stance—of 1945, of course, not of 1940.) Despite recurrent efforts to forge diaries by Mussolini (who did actually keep one, but it has never been found) or Hitler, neither they nor Stalin left any account either of their *diplomacy or of their strategy. The post-war publication of official correspondence between

Roosevelt, Churchill, and Stalin gives many insights into their relationship, the extent to which they co-operated, and the origins of post-war tensions.

As is usual with military memoirs, most are written by the victors: execution, suicide, or death in action removed most of the key Axis commanders (e.g. *Rommel and *Yamamoto) before they could go on record for posterity. Memoirs of statesmen and generals have been accompanied by recollections by the lower ranks, and followed by oral history undertaken by younger historians (many of whom forget how important a source oral history was to Thucydides, the greatest master of the trade). Much recent work is damaging to the reputations of wartime heroes, and is more concerned with personal foibles than with strategic acumen, or lack of it.

Official histories, some inordinately long and some inordinately dull, but a few of fascinating interest, have been produced in quantity, particularly by the British and the Americans. The British histories now cover grand strategy, in six volumes edited by Sir James Butler (1956–76); all the main land campaigns; the war at sea; the war in the air; the intelligence front; and, in several volumes, the home front. Sir Michael Howard's volume on *Strategic Deception* (1990) and W. K. Hancock and Margaret Gowing's *British War Economy* (1949) are perhaps the most notable.

S. E. Morison published a fifteen-volume *History of United States naval operations in World War II* (Boston, Mass., 1947–62) and followed them up with a single-volume summary, *The two-ocean war* (1963). W. R. Craven and J. L. Cate dealt in seven volumes with the history of the USAAF (Chicago 1948–58). Forrest C. Pogue, the biographer of *Marshall, has supervised several valuable histories of land campaigns.

Some of the most striking American books about the war have dealt with tactics rather than strategy, such as Charles B. Macdonald's *Company Commander* (1947) or Stephen E. Ambrose's *Pegasus Bridge* (1984). Mention must also be made of a few books of direct recollection which can still make the reader's hair rise on the back of the scalp: George Millar, *Horned Pigeon* (1947) and *Maquis* (1945), F. Spencer Chapman, *The Jungle is Neutral* (1949), Peter Kemp, *No Colours or Crest* (1958), R. V. Jones, *Most Secret War* (1978), and Sándor Radó, *Codename Dora* (1977). Similarly, Terence O'Brien's trilogy *Chasing after Danger* (1990), *Out of the Blue* (1984), and *The Moonlight war* (1987) gives a more vivid account of what the air war felt like to a pilot than is to be found in many official memoranda.

Soviet and eastern bloc historians have had to write under very different conditions from their western counterparts. In the USSR particularly, accounts of the war soon had to be expressed in almost mythical form: the defeat of Nazi aggression and the sufferings inflicted on the Soviet people by the Germans became the Great Patriotic Struggle which legitimized the regime more than anything else in its history. Embarrassment about the *Nazi–Soviet Pact of August 1939 prevented any serious diplomatic history of the origins of the war from appearing in the USSR. Even after the dissolution of the Soviet Union, only a few titbits of information appeared; up to its demise no serious history of that period had been attempted (or permitted?). The biography of Stalin by Dmitri Volkogonov, published in 1991, adds many new details about its subject's life, but it contributed little to the study of his role in the strategy of the Soviet armed forces or the diplomacy of international relations that was not already published in the West.

In Yugoslavia, and still more in Albania, the war represented the legitimizing spirit of the post-war regime. As in the USSR, official historians have been torn between emphasizing the heroism of communist partisans, fighting not only the foreign invader but also local anti-communist forces, and wishing to play down the divisions among the people during the war. Whereas in France, for instance, the study of *collaboration and *resistance, and the many shades of both, has become a major historical industry, in Yugoslavia the bitterness of the internecine fighting still marks the study of the problem, and plays its part in the country's difficult present. Milovan Djilas's wartime memoirs still ring with the ferocious certainties of civil war, despite all his later loss of faith in *communism.

The perception of the Second World War as a European civil war, lucidly illustrated in John Lukacs's *The Last European War: September 1939/December 1941* (1976), gave rise to two major public historical disputes in the 1980s.

In the UK, Nikolai Tolstoy campaigned to publicize the forced repatriations of Soviet citizens (see SOVIET EXILES AT WAR), Yugoslavs, and others by the British occupation authorities in Germany and Austria at the end of the war. Many other historians took up the question, without getting involved (as Tolstoy did) in legal battles.

In Germany, the West Berlin historian Ernst Nolte published in 1986 a 700-page study, *The European Civil War*, in which he argued that the Second World War should be seen as an ideological civil war which was the culmination of the impact of the Bolshevik revolution in 1917. *Fascism should be seen as a counter-revolution, with Hitler, particularly, bent on destroying the Marxist–Leninist USSR, but also having learned from Stalin's terroristic methods. Some historians objected to Nolte's comparisons between Nazis and communists, feeling that this reduced in significance Hitler's *Final Solution against European Jewry. Others thought Nolte's argument too narrowly focused on Germany and the USSR: after all, had not the west European states, the USA and Japan all had a major role to play in the origins and nature of the war? Nolte's work was typical of a recent trend among historians towards re-emphasizing ideological issues in the study of the war, after a period when economic and other allegedly 'real' issues had predominated. Debates about the morality of individual allied operations, such as the bombing of *Dresden (13 February 1945) or the dropping of the first *atomic bombs on Japan, are similarly at the borderline between history and moral philosophy.

Civilians in the war have been the subject of much

recent study in the West. Of course, there was a very great difference between the conditions of life for civilians in occupied and in unoccupied Europe. Popular historians have studied the impact of war, rationing, and other restrictions on the private lives of men and women from 1939 to 1945. Despite the obvious divergences in regime, the conclusion seems to be that both in the UK and in Germany, for instance, the effect of the war was to loosen traditional moral constraints, especially about extra-marital sex. Studies of popular entertainment in Germany and the UK also indicate how far the same transatlantic influences made themselves felt on the dance floor. Some historians have seen the origins of post-war problems, such as juvenile delinquency, in the wartime years when fathers at the front could no longer play their traditional disciplinary role (foreshadowing the spread of divorce and of single-parent families in the West).

Of general histories of the war there are now many, which vary greatly in size and in quality. One can be picked out as surpassing the rest: the second edition (1989) of *Total War* by Peter Calvocoressi, Guy Wint, and John Pritchard. In this edition (the first came out in 1972) Calvocoressi was able to state that he had been an intelligence officer at *Bletchley Park during the war, and to incorporate directly into his text some of the insights into the war's conduct that he had picked up from having been privy to ULTRA traffic at the time.

The continuing boom in all manner of publications about the war shows no signs of abating. The study of historical writings about it has now itself become a specialized field; there is plenty of room for criticism of previous historians' efforts. The collapse of the USSR in 1991, and the new techniques of oral and popular history, offer the chance for yet more fresh materials to come to light; while irresolvable debates on decades-old controversies will no doubt continue.

MARK ALMOND/M. R. D. FOOT

Hitler as war leader.

No leader played so large a part in the national war effort of his country as Adolf Hitler (1889–1945). His ideas on foreign policy and military strategy dominated German public affairs in the late 1930s and throughout the war. As Führer (leader) of the German people and supreme commander of German forces, he was responsible for making the major decisions in home affairs and war policy. His views were almost impossible to challenge, yet his increasingly wayward and irrational leadership was largely responsible for Germany's complete defeat in 1945. By the end, like Napoleon, he trusted no one to take even the smallest decisions. Germany's fortunes during the war were bound to the whims and convictions of a leader incapable of fulfilling the vast tasks he set for himself; a leader whose vindictive and obsessive personality launched Europe and the world on war, and almost destroyed the European Jews.

Hitler's uninhibited role as war leader stemmed from the nature of the dictatorship he established in Germany after 1933. His rule began as chancellor in a multi-party cabinet. Within two years he fused the offices of chancellor and president to become the Führer; all other political parties were banned and Hitler ruled with emergency, dictatorial powers. In 1937–8 he dispensed with many of his erstwhile conservative supporters, promoted Nazi Party leaders to prominent positions in the state and, in February 1938, assumed Supreme command of the armed forces. This move permitted him to fuse together in one individual direct responsibility for strategy, military planning, and state policy in general. No major affairs of state could be conducted without approval from Hitler's chancellery, or from the office of the Supreme Commander (OKW).

He brought with him a particular style of leadership. He deliberately sought to construct what has been called the 'myth of the Führer', a popular belief that he could single-handedly carve out Germany's destiny, that he stood above party as a genuine national leader. A corollary of this myth was acceptance of him as supreme decision-maker. Skilful propaganda drew widespread popular support, even from those who had previously opposed him. The collective endorsement of his image as the saviour of Germany made opposition or criticism difficult to pursue. By the late 1930s he had succeeded in stifling avenues of policy of which he disapproved; his own views came more and more to dominate German strategy.

Hitler's ideas shaped the nature of his leadership, and the nature of German foreign policy and war-making. He believed that in political life will power, intuition, and conviction were more important qualities than rational evaluation and shared responsibility. Though he recognized the importance of luck, or providence as he usually called it, and opportunity, he saw his own political success as a product of his iron determination and fanatical belief in his mission. He saw himself as someone who took great risks that paid off; as someone who would never admit the impossible. Leadership required above all, he once remarked, 'perseverance and fanatical tenacity'. The more successful his political career, the more convinced he became of his providential calling and his power to overcome all obstacles.

Hitler saw his mission as the salvation of Germany and the building of a new European, even world, order with Germany at its core (see GERMANY, 4). In foreign policy he formulated the view early on that Germany should not merely reverse the terms of the *Versailles settlement, but should transcend them by creating a German-dominated Europe and carving out 'living-space' or **Lebensraum*, for Germany in the east. At first he hoped to achieve this in agreement with the British Empire, but by 1937 he saw the UK too as an enemy of German destiny. By the late 1930s he saw Germany's role in more grandiose terms, aiming for world power even at the expense of eventual conflict with the UK and the USA. To achieve Germany's bid to become a super-power Hitler recognized that it was necessary to establish domestic

Hitler at the Munich conference, September 1938. With him (left to right) are the British prime minister, Neville Chamberlain, the French prime minister, Edouard Daladier, Mussolini, and the Italian foreign minister, Count Ciano.

political and social unity. This was to be achieved by a combination of terror and propaganda, and by the isolation of internal enemies, the Jews in particular (see FINAL SOLUTION). It was also necessary to build up German economic resources. Hitler was convinced on the evidence of the *First World War that a healthy economy was essential if a major war was to be waged with any success, and if the danger of a collapse of the Home Front was to be averted. From 1936 onwards he personally authorized the transformation of the German economy to meet the needs of war, setting higher and higher goals for rearmament and insisting on the preparation of the economy and workforce for total mobilization. In May 1939 he told his generals: 'The idea of getting out cheaply is dangerous. There is no such possibility.'

Hitler began his plan for Germany slowly, waiting for his political power to be secure, and for the economy to recover. Step by step he undermined the Versailles settlement. In 1935 he declared German rearmament; in 1936 he re-occupied the de-militarized zone of the Rhineland; in March 1938 he forced political union with Austria, land of his birth; in September 1938 he bullied the western states into giving him the German areas of Czechoslovakia (see MUNICH AGREEMENT). This series of bloodless victories won him widespread domestic support and fed his growing sense of invincibility. German expansion also provided essential material resources without which, as Hitler always recognized, it would be impossible to build up sufficient military strength. By 1939 he was convinced that the Versailles signatories would no longer oppose further German expansion eastwards, and that the smaller states of eastern Europe, Poland, Romania, Yugoslavia, Hungary, would become economic and political satellites of Germany. Between July 1938 and January 1939 he authorized large new armaments programmes for all three services, which were designed to make Germany the major military power in Europe by the mid-1940s. It was then that the struggle for German ascendancy would begin in earnest.

During the course of this gradual extension of political influence in eastern Europe, Hitler met with resolute opposition for the first time. Poland refused to become a satellite state, or to hand back the German areas lost in 1919 (see Map A). Hitler's reaction was typical of his behaviour later in the war: he immediately ordered the armed forces to prepare for an attack on Poland to punish the Poles for their obduracy (see POLISH CAMPAIGN). He sent German forces into the rump of Czechoslovakia in March; trade treaties were signed with Romania and Yugoslavia; a non-aggression treaty was signed with the USSR in August 1939 (see NAZI–SOVIET PACT). The object was to isolate Poland and to defeat it in a rapid campaign in the early autumn. Hitler remained convinced throughout that the western states would not actively intervene, but only make gestures of defiance. Despite widespread and public evidence that the UK and France would fight for Poland, Hitler based his judgement on what he perceived as the weak will of his potential enemies. Here, too, he eschewed serious evaluation in favour of conviction. Despite growing misgivings among his advisers and military leaders, who knew that Germany was not yet ready for major war, Hitler insisted throughout the crisis that the war could be localized. This was the first, and in some ways the most important, strategic misjudgement of Hitler's foreign policy career. In September he found himself at war with the UK and France over an issue that he had assured all his subordinates could be solved without the intervention of the Great Powers.

Once again his reaction was typical. He was thrown into a rage by the western declaration of war and immediately ordered the armed forces to begin planning for a winter offensive against France to 'beat her to pulp'. For almost the last time Hitler was prevailed upon by his military commanders to accept that Germany was simply not yet ready to wage such a campaign, though in the end only bad weather finally convinced him. Later in the war he accused his generals of missing a golden opportunity to exploit the lack of French preparation and the poor state of British assistance.

During the last months of 1939 Hitler personally supervised much of the planning for a spring offensive and ordered the full conversion of the economy to war in order to meet the much enlarged production programmes finally approved in December. He gave top priority to production for the 1940 campaign, at the expense of development programmes for military output in later years. He was not prepared to accept a defensive stance, but resolved to defeat the western powers in one single and decisive offensive blow. The generals were sceptical of such an assault, which they assumed the western powers would anticipate. Hitler talked of an attack through the Ardennes forest, but not until General von *Manstein produced a detailed operational plan for such a thrust (see FALL GELB) did Hitler seize on the idea and insist on its prosecution against all warning and advice. The plan was almost undone by fears that the UK might occupy Scandinavia and outflank German forces, but here too Hitler insisted, against expert advice, that Norway could be occupied at low cost to pre-empt the British and pave the way for the attack in the west. In both the *Norwegian campaign and the fall of *France he played a central part in deciding on strategic and operational priorities.

In both cases Hitler's judgement was vindicated. This was only partly due to the nature of the strategic conception, which carried great risks. Weaknesses and poor preparation on the Allied side, and the high fighting skills and operational competence of German forces produced victory against general expectations. If Hitler's caution and *Göring's ambition had not combined to give the British time to evacuate their forces at *Dunkirk, the victory would have been complete.

By the summer of 1940 Hitler had achieved domination of the continent. The German people thought the war was over, but Hitler saw both opportunities and dangers in the situation created by victory. He offered the UK the opportunity to make peace, though on his terms, a move designed to free him for the possibility of conflict in the east. As early as July 1940 it became evident to Hitler that his war with the west was being used by Stalin as a lever to increase Soviet influence in eastern Europe, and he began to explore the prospect of a pre-emptive strike against the USSR the following spring. He reasoned that his forces would be better prepared than the Soviets, and that war would provide the downfall of the chief ideological enemy and provide large material resources at the same time. These resources would be necessary to hold down the German empire and, if necessary, to confront the increasingly hostile USA.

Against his expectations, the UK refused the peace offer, and Hitler half-heartedly explored the prospect of an invasion instead (see SEALION). But his eyes were now turned to the USSR as the failure of the Luftwaffe to defeat the RAF in the battle of *Britain inclined him more and more to tackle the problem in the east first. By September the invasion plans were postponed, though he ordered the bombing of Britain to continue. This was partly a violent response to the bombing of Berlin by the RAF, partly a final attempt to get the British to see things his way and sue for peace. It was a poorly-thought-out gambit, which succeeded only in strengthening British resolve, thoroughly alienating American public opinion, and wearing down the Luftwaffe to a point where it could barely field more aircraft against the USSR in 1941 than it had had for the Polish campaign. While the *Blitz continued, Hitler ordered the armed forces to prepare for *BARBAROSSA, the invasion of the USSR. To meet the demands of the campaign he laid down in July 1940 extensive new plans for the economy and the armed forces. He demanded an army greater than all enemy armies put together—180 divisions, 20 of them armoured—and substantial increases in army output. He planned to take the USSR by surprise and to knock out its armed forces in six months.

During the war Hitler withdrew from much of the day-to-day running of the Home Front. Decisions were taken by his chancellery chief, Hans Lammers, or his secretary, Martin *Bormann, although any major ones would be passed on to Hitler for final approval. He concerned himself much more with military and technical issues, or with foreign policy (see AXIS STRATEGY AND CO-OPERATION), which he discussed in his military headquarters, or on his special train, complete with offices and bedrooms. For relaxation he spent time going over the plans and architects' models for the rebuilding of Berlin and other German cities. He became increasingly cut off from contact with the outside world; his evenings were devoted to a small circle of cronies to whom he delivered monologues on any subject that caught his fancy. He took seriously his pledge made at the outset of the war that he would live a frugal and abstemious existence as long as the war lasted. Usually he wore simple military dress.

In the spring of 1941 Hitler terminated air attacks on the UK and prepared for an assault on the USSR in May. Exactly as a year before the programme was interrupted by fears of British intervention on the German flank, this time in the Balkans. British assistance to Greece was followed by a Yugoslav army revolt which overthrew the pro-Hitler regime. Hitler realized that unless the situation in the Balkans could be stabilized BARBAROSSA might be compromised and ordered the armed forces to improvise an assault on Yugoslavia at short notice. In April Yugoslavia was defeated and British forces ejected from Greece (see BALKAN CAMPAIGN). German paratroopers captured *Crete in May and drove Allied forces out of the Balkans and Near East, leaving the way clear for an attack on the USSR a month later than planned. On 22 June German forces began the assault and within weeks drove far into Soviet territory. Hitler once again looked beyond the immediate task. He ordered war production to shift from army weapons to air and naval equipment for the renewed attack on the UK, and in case conflict developed with the USA. He also began to involve himself much more in the domestic war economy. Dissatisfied with the level of output achieved for BARBAROSSA, during the summer and autumn of 1941 he ordered greater rationalization and streamlining of the economy to meet the additional demands for war *matériel* issued in July. In December 1941 he issued a decree on production designed to compel the armed forces to reduce the complexity of their weapons and to open the way to greater mass production. In February 1942 he appointed his architect Albert *Speer to reorganize the war economy to make the fullest use of Germany's industrial resources (see SPEER PLAN). From then on he intervened directly in the war economy and in questions to do with the technical development of weapons through regular Führer conferences with Speer.

Hitler's growing involvement in the details of economic life matched an increasing intervention in military affairs. He never trusted the regular staff officers in the army, whom he regarded as unadventurous and pessimistic. His well-known dislike of professional expertise, and his growing belief that he was, like Frederick the Great, a natural strategist and military leader, increased his conviction that he knew better than the generals what was possible. When the German campaign in Russia finally bogged down in the winter mud, and Soviet forces began to counter-attack around *Moscow, Hitler insisted against his military advisers that the line should be held firm at all costs. On 19 December 1941 he finally decided to take over command of the army directly. From then on he became not only supreme commander but *Feldherr*, leader of the armies in the field. At this critical juncture in the war he chose to increase his responsibilities rather than reduce them.

This decision was taken against a sudden deterioration in Germany's international position. In December Japan attacked the USA at *Pearl Harbor and Hitler surprised his entourage by declaring war on the USA on 11 December. This placed Germany at war with the major economies of the world, with the USSR and the UK undefeated. In retrospect the decision seems perverse, but by this time Hitler could see that the USA was giving the UK and the USSR all the help it could short of actual war, and the German Navy was even engaging American ships in the battle of the *Atlantic. Hitler had a limited and superficial view of the USA. He considered Roosevelt an 'imbecile' and American foreign policy as mere *Bluffpolitik*. When he declared war he believed that Japan would keep the USA occupied while he completed the defeat of the USSR. With Soviet economic resources under his control, he would then confront the Anglo-Saxon states. In practice December 1941 marked a turning-point for Hitler: German forces suffered their first major defeat, in the *Western Desert campaigns; German armies came to a halt before Moscow; and Hitler now faced a combination of the other major powers whose material resources vastly outweighed those available to Germany.

For the next nine months, under Hitler's direct leadership, German armies reached their fullest extent, from the frontiers of Egypt to the lower reaches of the Caucasus mountains. These final successes owed as much to the fighting skills of German forces as they did to any strategic or tactical insight of Hitler's. Indeed it was Hitler who insisted against his staff's advice to place the main emphasis on the southern flank when fighting began again in the *German–Soviet war in the spring of 1942. His object was to seize Soviet oil supplies, although it turned out later in the year that hardly any preparations had been made in Germany to exploit the oil once it had been captured. The summer saw rapid advances into and beyond the Crimea, but it left the Germans seriously overstretched and allowed Soviet forces to regroup and choose their place of engagement. At the point where Hitler was at his most confident of final victory, the Allies planned to turn the tide. The victory at the second battle of *El Alamein began the long retreat from North Africa; at *Stalingrad the Soviet armies began their planned assault to break the Southern Front; in Morocco and Algeria Allied forces landed to secure the southern Mediterranean (see NORTH AFRICAN CAMPAIGN). Hitler's reaction was to insist on a general policy of no retreat. The result was the loss of the North African armies and a great deal of Axis shipping in the attempt to keep *Rommel supplied. In Russia the result was the defeat of German forces at Stalingrad, where Hitler insisted that his soldiers hold fast even when an orderly retreat might have been possible. When the crisis worsened in December, Hitler accepted Göring's promise that German armies in the city could be supplied from the air: the result was heavy loss of aircraft as well. He refused to accept operational reality, arguing instead that willpower and racial character would overcome physical handicaps. The defeat at Stalingrad set the pattern for the rest of the war. Hitler blamed the morale and attitude of his forces for the capitulation and was horrified when the commanding officer at Stalingrad, Field Marshal *Paulus, did not commit suicide.

For the next two years Hitler presided over the long retreat, in Italy, across the whole Soviet front, and, after the Normandy landings, in June 1944 (see OVERLORD), in the west as well. German forces fought with great skill, but were worn down by the sheer array of strength that Hitler's strategy had brought down upon them. Hitler made the task harder by insisting on holding the existing line wherever possible rather than carrying out strategic withdrawal. Effective resistance was also undermined by the difficulty local commanders experienced in getting clear orders from a supreme commander simply overburdened by the tasks he faced. Hitler's real interest lay in the conflict in the east. In the west he underestimated Allied strength and fighting power, and lack of contact with the situation there led to a confused and ultimately ineffective German response. He was also prepared to gamble on secret weapons which he felt sure would turn the tide of the war. He was convinced that the *V-weapons would not only compel the Allies to end the bombing of Germany, but might even end their invasion. He placed a similar reliance on the development of the jet aircraft. He insisted, against the advice of air force leaders, that the new jets should be used as fighter-bombers rather than fighters, holding up the development programme significantly and reducing what tactical impact the new aircraft might have had. None of the wonder weapons was capable of turning the tide of the war, as any serious strategic evaluation would have shown.

By 1944 many German military and political leaders wanted an end to the war. In July 1944, frustrated by what they saw as Hitler's frivolous destruction of German forces and the German state, a large number of senior officers conspired to assassinate Hitler and sue for peace (see SCHWARZE KAPELLE). The failure of the assassination attempt convinced Hitler that, despite all the problems faced by German forces, fate had saved him in order to salvage German fortunes from the wreckage. These delusions fuelled his determination to fight to the death. The grip that party fanatics had on German society made it difficult to challenge the Führer's determination to wage a bitter total war rather than admit defeat. As the war went on, Hitler vented his anger against those he blamed for Germany's situation. He was obsessed with the defeat in 1918, and was determined that no internal social crisis or dissent should weaken his war effort. He gave the internal machinery of repression under *Himmler, head of the *SS, free rein against 'saboteurs' and 'traitors'. Convinced that the Jews were the chief enemy of Germany's ambitions, he waged a war against them as well as the Allies; the more bitter and prolonged the conflict Germany faced, the more savage Hitler's *anti-Semitism became. Although the operational aspects of the Jewish genocide were undertaken by others, there can be no doubt that Hitler was the inspiration for the escalation of violence against European Jews. He demonstrated the same cynical brutality, the same moral blindness, against any group or individual who crossed his prosecution of the war effort. The slow hanging of the conspirators in the July plot was filmed for his own viewing.

In the last year of war Hitler even turned against his own forces, blaming them for cowardice or incompetence and dismissing anyone who dared to argue with him. Though his chief lieutenants either tried to urge an end to the war or seek one themselves separately, Hitler refused to consider such a course. In the last months he clung to the expectation that Providence would again come to his assistance. In December 1944, ignoring his generals' advice once more, he decided on one final offensive stroke in the Ardennes to drive a wedge between the British and American forces. His idea was to create such confusion and demoralization on the Allied side that the alliance would break up and he could concentrate on his war in the east. The failure of the so-called 'Battle of the Bulge' (see ARDENNES CAMPAIGN) was transformed in Hitler's mind into a successful spoiling action and his delusions were pandered to by soldiers terrified of his vindictiveness, but equally fearful of Soviet victory. When Hitler heard the news of Roosevelt's death in April 1945 he saw it as a sign that Germany's fortunes would revive, as had those of Frederick the Great following the death of the Russian Empress Elizabeth in the Seven Years War. Only in the final stages of the conflict did he come to realize that the war was lost. In its last days he blamed the Germans for not playing the role he had assigned for them in history: 'If the German people loses this war, it will have proved itself not worthy of me.' On 30 April 1945, with Soviet forces close and the fall of *Berlin imminent, he committed suicide.

Hitler's leadership exerted a fundamental influence on the course and nature of the war. At all the major turning-points it was his decision to seize the initiative: the invasion of Poland; the assault on France; the proposed invasion of England; the attack on the Soviet Union, and the declaration of war against the USA. No one else could have made these decisions, for Hitler exercised a form of dictatorial authority based on the wilful desires and intuitive judgements of a single person. By those around him this could be interpreted as a strength rather than a weakness. Hitler did take risks, and did stick with unrelenting determination to a course of action once he had decided on it. His style of leadership required this kind of single-mindedness and egotism. He saw himself as indispensable to the war effort. In August 1944 he told his staff that since 1941 it had been his task 'not to lose my nerve, under any circumstances'. He remained convinced that without his 'iron will' Germany would not win the 'struggle of the peoples' that his ambition and arrogance had generated. Under these circumstances he possibly achieved more than he might have done, given the obvious weaknesses in his style of leadership and decision-making, and his increasingly irrational and self-deluding view of the world. Singleness of purpose and a messianic self-belief infected those around him, and infused his whole strategy. Even at the end of the war dispirited generals recorded how an interview with Hitler could revive belief in Germany's cause.

In practice much of Hitler's early *diplomacy and military successes rested on the slow or divided response of other states to the unorthodox or unexpected. The illusion of strong leadership could be maintained in the light of others' weaknesses. Hitler depended, much more than he would concede, on the high fighting skills of German forces (which had little to do with Hitler) and the mistakes and ineffectiveness of the forces opposing them. Hitler and the propaganda machine made a great deal of victory in conflicts which were always heavily loaded in Germany's favour—against Poland for example. Hitler failed to defeat the major states he confronted: the UK, the USSR, and the USA. Only the defeat of France, in which he took a decisive role in choosing the campaign plan and urging his forces on to achieve its aims, could be viewed as a success in these terms. From 1942 onwards, when Hitler identified himself more closely than ever with the direction of the war, the weaknesses of leadership by willpower and intuition became manifest.

The early military successes masked the basic strategic misjudgements that characterized Hitler's leadership. In 1938 he failed to recognize how strong resistance from the west would be in his conflict with the Czechs; he made the same mistake a year later over Poland. In late 1940 he hesitated between a British and an eastern strategy; in 1941 he greatly underestimated the strength of the USSR and the UK's willingness to prosecute the war. In December 1941, with two major enemies still undefeated, he took on the USA, dividing Germany's forces damagingly and provoking a coalition of very great material and manpower resources. At every turn he justified his strategy in terms of the racial feebleness or moral inadequacy of his opponents. By extension, he believed that German forces could achieve more than the material balance might allow because they were invigorated by the justness of their racial cause. He consistently used the alleged qualitative superiority of German soldiers and weapons as a factor in Germany's favour when faced with states that relied on mere mass and quantity.

Such views might well have been modified by some effective system for the evaluation of strategy or the discussion of policy. In practice Hitler eschewed war by committee. He listened to advice when he needed it, or searched out detailed information. But in both military affairs and state policy there was no war cabinet, no chiefs of staff committee, no forum where strategy, operations, and diplomacy could be weighed up, investigated, and recommended. Much of the operational planning was conducted by the staffs of the separate services, whose standards of staffwork were very high. But the office of the supreme commander had no high-level planning staff, and liaison officers from the three services were usually relatively junior. As the war went on Hitler interfered with the processes of staff evaluation to such an extent that it became difficult (and dangerous) for officers to suggest or promote alternatives. The war effort was governed throughout its course by War Directives which came from Hitler himself. There were 74 directives in all, the first on 31 August 1939, the last, an order to the soldiers on the Eastern Front on 15 April 1945 to fight to the death against 'the last assault of Asia'. The directives combined general strategic considerations with detailed operational instructions. They provided the whole war machine with the drift of Hitler's thinking; they were unalterable, and binding on everyone.

The high-level conduct of the war was therefore inordinately influenced by Hitler's own strategic and tactical preconceptions and intuitions. He was by preference an army leader. He understood very little about naval power and was little interested in naval solutions. The navy was starved of resources and its leaders found it difficult to persuade Hitler that it had much of a role until submarine warfare began to bite in 1942–3. Grand Admiral *Raeder's attempt in 1939–40 to get Hitler to agree to a naval and air blockade of the UK broke down on Hitler's innocence of naval strategy and Göring's refusal to collaborate. Hitler was also much less at home with air strategy. He toyed with the idea of strategic bombing, but did little to throw his weight behind it. The Blitz on Britain persuaded him that bombing an enemy economy did not achieve very much, and he assumed for a long time that Allied bombing was a mere terror tactic, which could be countered by yet more terror. No serious attempt was ever made by Hitler to integrate German air power into a broader strategic framework. He was slow to authorize an effective defence force, and remained hostile to the views of air leaders who in 1943 and 1944 wanted to concentrate on fighter aircraft for defence against bombing, at the expense of the fighter-bombers and medium bombers needed for the front. He remained wedded to a tactical conception of air power. Yet in 1944, as the bombing increased in intensity, he turned on the air force for not having done more to halt the bombing offensive. He advocated the use of V-weapons as an alternative to *air power, strengthened the anti-aircraft forces, and threatened the Luftwaffe with disbandment. The result was widespread demoralization in the Luftwaffe and an end to the effective prosecution of the air war.

Hitler's primary interest was the German Army in which he had served as a corporal in the First World War. He had a very straightforward view of the army's function: to annihilate the enemy in great blows and sweeps, to prosecute the offensive at every opportunity, and to brook no retreat. Doubtless some of this conception stemmed from his understanding of the First World War. But it made it difficult for his generals to operate in adverse situations, or to think defensively, or to retreat in good order. Hitler simply would not brook the abandonment of territory once gained, or the notion of surrender against overwhelming odds. In a speech in December 1944 he said: 'In my life I have never learned to know the word "capitulation".' Generals did withdraw and stand on the defensive, risking his anger. The success of the long retreat and the rearguard engagements in 1944 and 1945 came despite, rather than because of, Hitler. There remained scope for ignoring what emanated from supreme headquarters, where Hitler was all too often immersed in details.

The Führer's concern for the minutiae of operations or of technology was well known. He took pride in his ability to remember instructions or specifications which his staff could not recall in front of him. He gave the impression to others of an extraordinary, if amateur, grasp of the most complex technical issues. This facility helped to boost the image of the omnicompetent leader. There is no doubt that he was fascinated by technical questions, particularly in the field of army weapons, but his interest was that of the enthusiatic amateur, absorbed by novelty and distinction but unable to grasp wider strategic or technical issues (the support he gave to the rocket programme, which achieved very little, was a prime example). Hitler's judgement was all too often flawed by his excessive concern for detail, all the more so given the sheer range of responsibilities that he took upon himself. His reluctance to delegate or share responsibility led to failures of discrimination and evaluation, and to an uneven distribution of effort. One man, even Hitler, could not hope to devote sufficient weight to all the affairs, major and minor, that required his attention. This problem lay at the core of the 'Führer-state': the more responsibility the leader assumed, the more his subordinates shunned decision-making, and the greater still became his responsibility.

Hitler was not an easy leader to follow. He imposed demands on his subordinates which were difficult, if not impossible, to fulfil scrupulously or with a clear conscience. The German war effort produced a stream of prominent suicides—the Luftwaffe's Ernst *Udet and Hans *Jeschonnek, the army Field Marshals Rommel, *Model, and von *Kluge; and so on. Hitler demanded exceptional levels of loyalty, and in return remained loyal to his party comrades appointed to tasks far beyond their competence. The Luftwaffe lacked a serious commander-in-chief for much of the latter period of the war, but Hitler resisted all recommendations for Göring's dismissal. For a great many officials and soldiers during the war Hitler's leadership was a constant source of friction and frustration—there were resignations as well as suicides—but what is surprising is the extent to which Hitler was able to retain the active support of those who ran the war effort. The support ran thinner as the war went on, but however grudging the endorsement or acquiescence, residual support for Hitler lasted until the very last months of conflict. It was retained partly through the sheer force of his personality, partly through the structural pressures in German government and society that made conformity desirable and penalized dissent. He had also become by the start of the war a symbol of German revival and national renewal. Loyalty to him became the test of patriotism and social allegiance in general. In the end he spurned that loyalty. He stubbornly refused to end his quest for the New Order when Germany clearly faced disaster, and blamed the German people for their failure to grasp their racial destiny. Hitler bore the responsibility for that failure. It was he who deliberately provoked war, who exulted in conquest, and who, without a shred of remorse, brought his country down in flames around him. See also GERMANY, 1.

RICHARD OVERY

Carr, W., *Hitler: a study in personality and politics* (London, 1978).
Kershaw, I., *Hitler* (London, 1991).
Lewin, R., *Hitler's Mistakes* (London, 1984).
Trevor-Roper, H. (ed.), *Hitler's War Directives 1939–1945* (London, 1964).

Hitler Line, German defensive line held during the *Italian campaign. Hitler ordered its construction in November 1943 as a fall-back, or switch, line for the *Bernhardt Line, and to defend the Liri valley. It ran from Terracina on the west coast of Italy, to Fondi, through the Aurunci mountains, to Pontecorvo, Piedimonte, and Monte Cairo. In January 1944 its name was changed to the Senger Line when the Allies appeared to be threatening its safety and, thereby, Hitler's prestige. With the Bernhardt and *Gustav lines it was known to the Allies as the Winter Line.

Hitler Youth (Hitlerjugend), Nazi organization for young men aged from 14 to 18 which was founded in 1922. From 1929 it also embraced the League of German Maidens (Bund deutscher Mädel, or BdM) for the same age group and, from 1931, two organizations for the 10–14 age group, the German Young People (Deutsches Jungvolk) for boys and the Young Maidens (Jungmädelbund) for girls. Girls from 18 to 21 became part of the BdM called Glaube und Schönheit (Faith and Beauty). The boys joined the State Labour Service in which they served for six months before joining the German armed forces (Wehrmacht) or the *SS, with which the Hitlerjugend was closely linked and for whom a Hitlerjugend Division was formed within its combat wing, the Waffen-SS, in 1943.

Members of the Hitler Youth were required to be, according to Hitler, 'slim and slender, swift as greyhounds, tough as leather, and hard as Krupp steel'. The organization was a mainstay of the Nazi regime and its influence, which became all-pervasive in Germany, was extended into occupied countries. Baldur von Schirach (1907–74), who ran it from 1931 to 1940, increased its membership from 2.3 million at the end of 1933 to 7.7

million by 1939. It was made a state organization in April 1933 and membership became compulsory in 1940. When in the summer of 1940 Schirach was appointed state governor of Vienna, he was succeeded by Artur Axmann (b.1913).

As the Hitler youth grew its power and influence grew with it. It was a propaganda machine for inculcating *Nazi ideology into the young; it dominated the schools and formed the Patrol Service (Streifendienst), which functioned as a kind of junior *Sipo; and as the war progressed the youthful loyalty of its members was ruthlessly exploited. At twelve a boy was trained in the use of a rifle and machine gun and at fourteen he attended a military training camp for a month. From 1943, 15–17-year-olds manned anti-aircraft guns and youngsters performed many civil defence duties, such as fighting fires, patrolling the streets, and digging tank traps. They were an especial menace to shot-down Allied airmen. During the last months of the war the Hitler youth also became an important part of the Volkssturm (see GERMANY, 5); during the battle that led to the fall of *Berlin, Axmann committed young teenagers to front-line combat in which few survived; and a number were enlisted into the abortive *Werewolves guerrilla organization. See also CHILDREN.

Rempel, G., *Hitler's Children* (Chapel Hill, NC, 1989).
Sosnowski, K., *The Tragedy of Children under Nazi Rule* (Poznań, 1962).

'Hiwis' or *Hilfswillige* (voluntary helpers), see SOVIET EXILES AT WAR: OSTTRUPPEN.

Hobart, Maj-General Sir Percy (1885–1957), British tank commander. Born in India of Ulster parentage, he became a Royal Engineer officer in 1904, fought in the Mohmand campaign in 1908, and in the *First World War was decorated at Neuve Chapelle in 1915 and won the DSO in Mesopotamia in 1916. He was distinguished for energy and conversational brilliance, and for disregarding orders he knew to be bad. Foreseeing the predominance of tanks, he joined the Royal Tank Corps in 1923 and was an instructor at Quetta staff college until 1927. In 1934 he demonstrated the efficacy of *radio communications in *tank warfare and in 1937–9 he formed and trained 7th Armoured Division. He then retired but was rescued by Churchill from corporal's rank in the Home Guard to form 11th Armoured Division. He also formed 79th Armoured Division, of vehicles specially designed for opposed landings, such as the Flail and Crocodile tanks (see ENGINEERS, 1) and, led it, with heavy casualties and marked success, through the Normandy landings (see OVERLORD) and beyond. He was knighted in 1943. M. R. D. FOOT

Macksey, K., *Armoured Crusader* (London, 1967).

Ho Chi Minh (1890–1969) means 'he who enlightens'. He was leader of the Communist Party of French Indo-China who was originally known as Nguyen Ai Quoc (Ai Quoc, 'dedicated patriot'). In May 1941 he formed with other parties a League for the Independence of Vietnam (Vietnam Doc Lap Dong Minh Hoi, soon shortened to *Viet Minh) in southern China from various nationalist groups. Its aim was 'the union of all anti-fascist forces in the struggle against French and Japanese colonialism until all Vietnam is liberated'. Ho was not violently anti-French but he wanted them out of his country, and he knew that the independent regime for which he had been fighting for over two decades would have to be a democratic one to attract international support. However, the Chinese Nationalist leader, *Chiang Kai-shek, did not trust Ho and in 1942 he imprisoned him. He was released after fifteen months and then, with American aid, his forces struck into northern French Indo-China. They were aided in the field by the *Office of Strategic Services, whose operatives were impressed with Ho's personality. 'If I had to recall one quality of this old man sitting on his hill in the jungle,' said one of them, 'it would be his sweetness' (See L. Allen, *The End of the War in Asia*, London, 1976, p. 113). On 13 August 1945 Ho formed a provisional government, the National Liberation Committee of Vietnam, and on 2 September he declared a Democratic Republic of Vietnam. In April 1946 he became president of an autonomous Vietnam within French Indo-China, but fighting subsequently broke out between his forces and the French that eventually led to the French defeat at Dien Bien Phu in 1954. See also ANTI-IMPERIALISM.

Hodges, General Courtney H. (1887–1966), US Army officer who commanded the First US Army during most of the *Normandy campaign and in the fighting in north-west Europe which followed.

Hodges failed his exams at West Point Military Academy and joined up as a private. He was commissioned in 1909, was twice decorated during the *First World War, and rose to become chief of the Infantry School at Fort Benning. In March 1944 he was appointed *Bradley's deputy at First US Army and took over its command that August when Bradley's Twelfth Army Group was formed. Hodges, a taciturn man with an innate dislike of publicity, was a first-rate general and he led his army through some of the toughest fighting in north-west Europe: it captured *Aachen, took the brunt of the German attack at the start of the *Ardennes campaign, seized the bridge at *Remagen, and eventually linked up with the Red Army around *Torgau. He was promoted general in April 1945.

Holland, see NETHERLANDS.

Hollandia, colonial administrative centre on the northern coast of Dutch New Guinea which was occupied by the Japanese in April 1942 at the start of the *New Guinea campaign. They built it up into an important air and naval base before units of three of *Alamo Force's US infantry divisions (24th, 32nd, and 41st) landed there, and at Aitape, 200 km. (125 mi.) to the south-east, on 22 April 1944.

This first step in *MacArthur's drive towards the Philippines was commanded by Lt-General *Eichelberger and ultimately 217 warships and 80,000 ground troops were employed. It meant bypassing Wewak and Hansa Bay, which the Japanese had deployed their Eighteenth Army to defend, and leaping some 800 km. (500 mi.) from the nearest Allied base in the Australian mandate of New Guinea. This feat was only made possible by *ULTRA intelligence. Because of it the Hollandia operation has been cited 'as perhaps the classic example of the application of intelligence from codebreaking to operational planning in World War II' (E. Drea, *MacArthur's ULTRA*, Lawrence, Kans., 1992, p. 121).

The prior destruction of Japanese *air power at Hollandia by Lt-General Kenney's Fifth US Army Air Force left the Japanese with only 25 serviceable aircraft and neither landing at Hollandia or Aitape was seriously opposed. The inland airstrips were seized in three days and the area was secured by 6 June with minimal losses. On 10 July 1944 the Eighteenth Army counter-attacked at Aitape, but documents captured by *Allied Intelligence Bureau patrols, and then ULTRA intelligence, gave ample warning for the US perimeter to be reinforced and for 11th US Corps, commanded by Maj-General Charles Hall, to be formed to defend the front along the Driniumor river. The battle that followed lasted until 25 August. The US defensive line was temporarily pierced, but the Eighteenth Army was virtually destroyed, losing 9,000 men out of the 20,000 committed.

Hollywood, the world's movie capital, offered the American—and British—public escape from the war and at the same time tried to build a popular consensus behind the war effort. The war suffused cinemas, from government promotional films, to newsreels (which, before television, were the public's primary visual source of news), and features. Average weekly attendance in the USA soared to 100 million people—three-quarters of the population—and profits reached record levels.

Films attracted government regulation of their content that was unprecedented, before or since, in American media. The *Office of War Information (OWI) closely monitored the studios' output. It issued a lengthy manual for the studios ('Will this picture help win the war?' was the ultimate question by which to judge a movie) and tried to steer producers to the war themes it favoured. OWI officials read the screenplays of most major pictures as production went forward, offered suggestions (sometimes gratefully received and sometimes angrily rejected), on occasion went so far as to write dialogue, and reviewed finished films. Although lacking censorship power, OWI achieved considerable influence through patriotic persuasion and through its liaison with the Office of Censorship, which held Hollywood's vital foreign market by the throat.

The studios tried to remould attitudes about enemies and allies to fit the war's political viewpoint. A top priority was revising the image of the USSR, most strikingly in Warner Brother's *Mission to Moscow*, based on the memoirs of Joseph E. Davies, the American ambassador to Moscow from 1936 to 1938. Converting the USSR into a worthy democratic ally, *Mission to Moscow* invented a pleasant land of plenty, cast the dreaded secret police as harmless comic gumshoes, reverently portrayed Stalin as an ominiscient world statesman, and even endorsed the discredited Kremlin line that the massive purges of the 1930s had been necessary to root out *fifth columnists. Controversial politics and dull entertainment, *Mission to Moscow* became a *Cold War embarrassment.

China and the UK were easier to bend to propaganda needs, although the results often proved misleading. Allies became Americans with quaint customs and mildly different looks. Representations of China followed Hollywood's well-worn formula of warm-hearted, condescending exoticization. *Dragon Seed* starred Katharine Hepburn, made up with slanted eyes. China had to be shown as a modern, unified nation. At OWI's insistence peasants' mud huts were transformed into neat little brick houses 'with a considerable feeling of civilization about them'. Hollywood's Chinese were likeable, loyal fighters, but always overshadowed by the Americans.

The British excited American admiration. *The White Cliffs of Dover*, based on Alice Duer Miller's mawkish and hugely popular poem of the same title, perpetuated a sentimental identification with Britain. The biggest hit about the British was *Mrs Miniver* (1942), which reassured audiences that the UK had the will to win and was democratizing the class system, which rankled with many Americans.

The USA, too, was painted in warmly idealized tones. Hollywood and the OWI collaborated to show a unified nation, happily mobilized for victory to its smallest details. A woman who hoarded 127 tubes of lipstick was shamed by her housemates in *Tender Comrade*. Screeching tyres were slashed from Preston Sturges's screwball comedy *Hail the Conquering Hero* so as not to undermine rubber conservation drives. Industrial disputes gave way to labour–management co-operation for the war effort in King Vidor's paean to capitalist industry, *An American Romance*. Racial discrimination, the biggest blot on American democracy in a war for the *Four Freedoms, was harder to cure: OWI settled for occasional positive roles for blacks in films such as *The Ox-Bow Incident* and Alfred Hitchcock's *Lifeboat*. Blacks sometimes got a better break on the screen than in real life; *Bataan* featured a racially integrated combat unit when none existed in the real army for democracy (see also AFRICAN AMERICANS AT WAR).

The ultimate expression of the home front, David O. Selznick's lavish *Since You Went Away*, invoked every wartime cliché. A husband leaves for war, his nervous wife takes a job as a welder in a bomber factory, her

Hollywood actress Marlene Dietrich entertains US troops.

daughter postpones college to work as a nurse, the black maid works overtime for no pay, a wimpish young man attains manhood and dies valiantly in battle, and dad returns to the cosy home in the suburbs on a snowy Christmas Eve. Selznick reassured Americans that they could cope with death, domestic disorder, and changing sex roles, and everything would be put back to normal after the war.

Combat movies offered the irresistible combination of vivid action, exotic locations, and clearly defined heroes and villains. Early combat films made the battle front seem scarcely more deadly than a football game. Only towards the end of the war did Hollywood begin to come to terms with reality, most notably in *The Story of G.I. Joe*, based on dispatches by the *war correspondent Ernie Pyle. *The Story of G.I. Joe* avoided the false heroics of most combat pictures. Death was a lottery and another firefight loomed up the road. Hollywood typically reassured audiences that the war was rational and that military service promised upward mobility after the war.

The enemies wore black hats, but with important differences. OWI insisted that the war was with Hitler and the Nazis, not the entire German people. Hollywood's Nazis were appropriately ruthless, though the moviemakers, like most of the public, could not allow themselves to contemplate the Nazis' utter depravity. Even in serious treatments of Nazism such as *The Hitler Gang* *anti-Semitism was barely acknowledged. But the distinction between good (if duped) Germans and bad Germans was an uneasy one. Howls of protest greeted the inclusion of a sympathetic young German army lieutenant in *The Moon is Down*.

Hollywood granted the Japanese no sympathetic individuals; they were always a mass, fanatically devoted to the war-mongering emperor. They were 'prints off the same negative', according to Frank Capra's *Why We Fight* films for the army. While the Germans fought a recognizable war, the Japanese were depicted as little better than jungle animals.

By 1944 the cycle of war pictures had begun to wane. Like Europeans earlier in the war, Americans no longer wanted fictional re-enactments. Escape took the form of musicals, such as *Going My Way* with Bing Crosby, a story of two priests which swept the Oscars in 1944, and Judy Garland in *Meet Me In St Louis*, with its nostalgic return to 1904. 'Elegant shockers', such as *Double Indemnity* and *Murder, My Sweet*, put violence in a familiar domestic context. Religious pictures, such as *Song of Bernadette*, offered divine reassurance. In 1945 Darryl F. Zanuck campaigned for internationalism with *Wilson*, a tedious effort to sanctify Woodrow Wilson (1856–1924), the US president from 1912 to 1920, as a prophet of world peace, but a public tired of war savoured what had always been Hollywood's preferred product: escape.

CLAYTON R. KOPPES

Koppes, C. R., and Black, G. D., *Hollywood Goes to War: How Politics, Profits, and Propaganda Shaped World War II Movies* (New York, 1987).

Holocaust, see FINAL SOLUTION.

Home Army, see POLAND, 4.

Home Guard, see UK, 6.

homing torpedo, see GUIDED WEAPONS.

Homma Masaharu, Lt-General (1887–1946), Japanese Army officer who, by May 1942, had completed the capture of the *Philippines from *MacArthur's US and Filipino forces.

The son of a wealthy landowner, Homma was born on Sado Island off the north-west coast of Japan. A gifted, cultured man, more westernized than his army colleagues and not at all bound, as most of them were, by the *Bushidō code, he passed out top of the Military Academy, had two tours of duty with the British Army, and by 1935 was a major-general. He took part in the *China Incident before being appointed to command Fourteenth Army for the invasion of the Philippines in December 1941. This took much longer than the 50 days allowed by Imperial Japanese Headquarters and after the last American forces had surrendered, on *Corregidor, Homma neither expected nor received congratulations. He was recalled to Japan in August 1942 and remained unemployed throughout the remainder of the war. In January 1946 he was tried by the US Military Commission for being responsible for the many *war crimes committed by his men, one of which was the *Bataan Death March. Homma claimed he had never heard of this dreadful event, but this did not save him and he was executed by a firing squad. See also FAR EAST WAR CRIMES TRIALS.

Honduras declared war on Germany in December 1941 and was an original signatory of the *United Nations Declaration. Its usefulness to the Allied war effort was confined to committing its small air force to search for hiding places and refuelling points for German U-boats operating in the Caribbean. See also LATIN AMERICA.

Hong Kong. This British colony, situated in southern China, contained in its 1,035 sq. km. (400 sq. mi.) a population of about 1.4 million, almost all of them Chinese. Japanese *spies had been at work there for many years and had obtained accurate intelligence on the British defences, troop dispositions, and communications. A Japanese invasion from occupied China (see CHINA INCIDENT) was not unexpected; the colony had simply been told to hold out for as long as possible. But lacking any possibility of reinforcement—and with help from *Chiang Kai-shek's army failing to materialize—resistance from its inadequately armed 12,000-strong garrison was brief.

The principal British defensive line was just 5 km. (3 mi.) north of Kowloon in the Leased Territories. Manned by three battalions of Indian and Scottish troops, it was too long for the numbers available to defend it. Another three battalions were deployed on Hong Kong island; two were Canadian—the first Canadian troops to see action in the war. Local artillery and volunteer defence units were the only other ground forces available to the garrison's commander, Maj-General Christopher Maltby, and his air and sea support were pitifully inadequate: seven obsolescent aircraft, one destroyer, eight *MTBs, and four gunboats.

Early on 8 December 1941 Japanese bombers destroyed all seven aircraft at Kai Tak airfield and the Japanese Twenty-Third Army's 38th Division, commanded by Lt-General Sano Tadayoshi, crossed the Sham Chun river into the Leased Territories. By the evening of 9 December it had reached the main defensive line and that night took an important redoubt. This made the overextended British positions untenable and forced Maltby to evacuate the mainland.

After Maltby's hasty withdrawal to Hong Kong island, completed on 13 December, Sano immediately began to bombard it, and heavy air attacks were also launched. These badly damaged the destroyer and two MTBs, and caused bad fires in the central business district, Victoria. Though most of the civilian population had responded to a call to resist the Japanese, some civil unrest and banditry followed, and a number of Chinese unsuccessfully attacked an important anti-aircraft position. An attempt by Sano's troops to cross the island on 15 December was repulsed, but three nights later they landed in strength between North Point and Aldrich Bay. They quickly penetrated inland, splitting the defending forces. MTBs tried to stem the tide, by attacking boats carrying Japanese reinforcements, but Japanese air superiority was complete and naval losses were heavy. Nevertheless, resistance was so stiff that on 20 December Sano was forced to halt temporarily to reorganize, but by 24 December the surviving defenders were exhausted, and water and ammunition supplies were short. On the afternoon of Christmas Day a cease-fire was arranged and that evening the governor surrendered the colony unconditionally to Sano's army commander, Lt-General Sakai Takashi.

Japanese casualties amounted to 2,754; the garrison's were 4,400 including 800 Canadians. A few of the defenders escaped, including those who formed the *British Army Aid Group, but most became *prisoners-of-war. Some Indian troops joined the *Indian National Army; white civilians suffered *internment; and the colony remained in Japanese hands as part of the *Greater East Asia Co-prosperity Sphere for the remainder of the war.

Hoover, (John) Edgar (1895–1972), director from 1924 of the US Bureau of Investigation—later called the Federal Bureau of Investigation, or FBI (see USA, 6)—a post he retained until he died.

Having accumulated responsibility for *Western Hemisphere intelligence matters, Hoover was authorized by Roosevelt in 1940 to form his Special Intelligence Service which operated agents in Latin America to monitor Nazi activities.

Though officially exonerated, the FBI was part of the general failure of US intelligence preceding the Japanese attack on *Pearl Harbor in December 1941. It was a débâcle for which Hoover was quick to blame others. The moral rectitude with which he had earlier viewed the British double agent Dusko *Popov has been assessed as part of this failure, but Hoover did pass to naval intelligence the Pearl Harbor questionnaire that the Germans had given Popov; and there is no reason why Hoover should have thought it anything but an indication of yet another potential sabotage operation.

After 1941 he concentrated on keeping the US free of *spies and saboteurs, and in ensuring no other intelligence organization encroached upon his territory. He was eminently successful in achieving the former, but suffered a serious bureaucratic defeat when the *Office of Strategic Services was formed in 1942, and he conducted a running feud with its head, Colonel *Donovan, for the remainder of the war.

Powers, R., *Secrecy and Power: The Life of J. Edgar Hoover* (New York, 1987).

Hopkins, Harry L. (1890–1946), US politician and diplomat who acted as Roosevelt's, and then *Truman's, special envoy during the war.

Hopkins was born in Iowa and as a young man was involved in social work in New York. A detached retina disqualified him from military service and in 1917 he worked for the American Red Cross in New Orleans. After the war he worked in welfare which eventually led to his appointment as director of the New Deal Federal Emergency Relief Administration when Roosevelt became president in 1933. He was appointed secretary of commerce in December 1938 but was plagued by the digestive disorders which eventually killed him, and resigned in August 1940. In January 1941 he visited the UK as Roosevelt's 'special representative' to catalogue Britain's military *Lend-Lease requirements and it was during his six-week stay there that he established a close working relationship with Churchill. 'Churchill is the gov't in every sense of the word,' he wrote to Roosevelt. '... I cannot emphasize too strongly that he is the one and only person over here with whom you need to have a full meeting of minds' (quoted in R. Edmonds, *The Big Three*, London, 1991, p. 211). In March 1941 he was given responsibility for the whole Lend-Lease programme, and by the time he relinquished this post to *Stettinius that August he was being called assistant to the president or, as someone dubbed him, 'Roosevelt's own personal foreign office'.

In July 1941 he again went to London, to prepare for the *Placentia Bay conference, before flying on to Moscow to meet Stalin, and Roosevelt subsequently accepted his recommendation that the USSR should be included in Lend-Lease. During that year he also worked as the president's special representative in the complicated negotiations with the British over Lend-Lease. He subsequently became Roosevelt's aide at nearly every major Allied conference and was the personal link not only between the president and his fellow members of the *Grand Alliance but with his military leaders, which enabled the White House to dominate every aspect of America's conduct of the war. His final mission before he resigned in July 1945 was to Moscow in May to try to solve the problem of a provisional Polish government (see POLAND, 2(d)), and over the Security Council's voting procedures at the *San Francisco conference.

Hopkins was an outstanding representative of Roosevelt's views and he commanded the respect of both Stalin and Churchill, his highly valued bluntness leading the latter to say that if Hopkins were ever elevated to the peerage he should take the title 'Lord Root of the matter'. For much of the war he was one of Roosevelt's closest advisers and confidants. From May 1940 until November 1943 he lived in the White House and became part of the president's family. Frequent ill-health, and a temporary drop in Roosevelt's esteem after he left the White House, did not prevent him making a major contribution to his country's policies during the war years.

McJimsey, G., *Harry Hopkins* (Cambridge, Mass., 1987).
Sherwood, R., *The White House Papers of Harry L. Hopkins*, 2 vols. (London, 1948–9).

Hore-Belisha, Leslie (1893–1957), British Liberal politician who was a reformist secretary of state for war from 1937 until January 1940, and a member of *Chamberlain's war cabinet. His ruthless modernization of the army, his introduction of a field force (see BRITISH EXPEDITIONARY FORCE), his doubling of the Territorial Army in March 1939, his insistence on bringing in conscription, and his organization of anti-aircraft defences proved he was in the van of those striving to prepare the country before it was too late. But his sharpness of mind and tongue, the employment of the military strategist, Basil Liddell Hart, as an adviser (see LAND POWER), and perhaps *anti-Semitism (Hore-Belisha was a Jew), led to personality clashes with General *Gort and other senior officers. His alleged interference in military matters and his brash assertiveness motivated Chamberlain to offer him another post; instead, he chose to resign.

Horrocks, Lt-General Brian (1895–1985), British Army officer who served as a battalion commander in *Montgomery's 3rd Division during the fighting which led to the fall of *France in June 1940. He went on to become a highly successful corps commander under Montgomery in the *Western Desert and *North African campaigns. Before the *Sicilian campaign he was severely wounded during an air raid but in August 1944 he was appointed to command 30th Corps of *Dempsey's Second British Army which played a critical role in *MARKET-GARDEN and in the battle for *Germany.

Horrocks, B., *et al.*, *Corps Commander* (London, 1977).

'Horst Wessel', see MARCHING SONGS.

Horthy de Nagybánya, Admiral of the Fleet Miklós (1868–1957), Austro-Hungarian Empire hero of the *First World War who subsequently turned to politics. Hungary technically became a monarchy again in January 1920, but the heir to the throne was not asked back. Instead, Horthy assumed the title of Regent and ruled as a virtual dictator. Though he tried to resist excessive German pressures during the 1930s, and to maintain cordial relations with the western nations, his fear of *communism drove him into the fascist camp. In November 1940 he joined the *Tripartite Pact. Hungarian forces took part in the German attack into Yugoslavia in April 1941, an act which caused Horthy's prime minister to commit suicide. In June 1941 Horthy declared war on the USSR, and in December 1941 he declared war on the western Allies. But as the war progressed he became less and less anxious to be involved in it, and in March 1944 the Germans, antagonized by his attempts to negotiate with the Allies, occupied Hungary. *Eichmann then began implementing the *Final Solution on Hungarian Jews by deporting them to *Auschwitz, but in July Horthy, under pressure from various western sources, was able to bring these deportations temporarily to a halt. On 15 October 1944, with the Red Army on his doorstep, Horthy publicly requested an *armistice but the next day the Germans forced his abdication (see SKORZENY), imprisoned him in Germany, and put a fascist regime into power. It was decided not to prosecute Horthy at the *Nuremberg trials and he retired to Portugal.

Hot Springs conference was held at Hot Springs, Virginia, USA, on food and agriculture and was the first United Nations conference (the second established *UNRRA and the third was held at *Bretton Woods in July 1944). It took place from 18 May to 3 June 1943 and led to the creation of the Food and Agriculture Organization.

Howe, Clarence D. (1886–1960), US-born Canadian businessman who, after entering parliament as a Liberal in 1935, became minister of transport in 1936 (where he helped create what eventually became Air Canada) and then minister of munitions and supply in April 1940 with almost dictatorial control of Canadian industry. He ran the country's war production programme brilliantly and in 1941 alone got it to produce more armaments than had been manufactured during the whole of the *First World War. He also chaired the *Canadian Mutual Aid Board and in 1944 headed the new department of reconstruction, overseeing the freeing of the economy from government control.

howitzers, see ARTILLERY, 1.

'Hubal', pseudonym of one of the earliest Polish partisans, Major Henryk Dobrzański (1896–1940). He refused to surrender at the end of the *Polish campaign in October 1939 and spent the winter carrying out guerrilla operations against the Germans until he was caught and killed in April 1940. See also POLAND, 4.

Huertgen Forest, battle of. Clearance by *Hodges's First US Army, started in September 1944, of three evergreen woods, the Wenau, Huertgen, and Roetgen at the start of the battle for *Germany. Situated in a 80 sq. km. (50 sq. mi.) triangle bounded by the German towns of *Aachen, Düren, and Monschau, the German defenders holding the woods were thought to threaten Hodges's right flank and rear. The battle continued until December, and was one of the worst US reverses in north-west Europe.

The area was thickly laced with mines, barbed wire, and concealed pillboxes with interlocking fields of fire, and among the dark, damp, thickly-wooded forest the Americans lost all their normal advantages of mobility, fire power, and technological superiority. It became an infantry slogging match in which accurate German mortar and artillery fire, bursting at treetop level, had devasting results.

Initial attempts to clear the forest lacked concentration of effort. First one regiment tried on a broad front, then two, then one division and then another. Finally two divisions were thrown into the gloomy, shell-blasted woods, and snow and incessant rain added to the casualties. The 9th US Division attacked first and had 4,500 casualties in advancing 3 km. (1.8 mi.); its replacement, 28th US Division, suffered 6,184 with little to show for it. The 4th US Division, which relieved it, attacked on 16 November as Hodges's 7th US Corps launched an offensive south of Aachen. But by the time it emerged from the forest at Gey on 1 December it had had 6,053 casualties, while 8th US Division and an armoured regiment, thrown in to help clear the forest, suffered about 5,200 before gaining the Roer plain from Bergstein.

'huff-duff' was the Allied nickname for HF/DF (High Frequency/Direction Finding) equipment which measured the direction of radio transmissions so that bearings from two or more could fix the transmitter's position. It played a vital part in combating U-boats in the battle of the *Atlantic, and during the *Pacific war it detected the approaching Japanese fleet before the *Philippine Sea battle.

Hull, Cordell (1871–1955), US lawyer who was secretary of state in all Roosevelt's administrations.

Born in a rented log cabin in Tennessee, Hull studied law before being elected to the Tennessee state legislature at the age of 21. In 1906 he won a Democratic seat in the House of Representatives which he held, with the exception of two years, until he was elected to the Senate in 1930. He resigned from the Senate to become secretary of state in March 1933, a position in which he served for twelve years. Throughout this time, Hull was dominated by Roosevelt who often by-passed him in matters of wartime foreign policy. None the less they were basically in accord, particularly in their dislike of de *Gaulle and of colonialism.

Hull was not interested in the organization of the state department, but he was a canny politician whose rigid morality made him a hardliner in international affairs. From 1939 Roosevelt's main interest lay in Europe and Hull had little influence on early decisions and policies connected with helping the UK in the war against Germany and Italy. Roosevelt, however, left to him the business of negotiating with Japan (see also USA, 1) and in the spring of 1941 Hull began a series of meetings with the Japanese ambassador, Admiral Nomura Kichisaburō, at which he took an uncompromising stance against Japanese aggression in China (see CHINA INCIDENT) and French Indo-China. While these meetings were in progress Hull was being kept fully informed of Japan's attitudes and decisions through *MAGIC intelligence and by early November 1941 he knew from decrypts that the Japanese government had imposed a deadline on the negotiations. On 7 November Hull warned the cabinet that Japan might attack at any moment and on 26 November he responded to Japanese offers of a *modus vivendi* with a ten-point plan which required the withdrawal of all Japanese armed forces from China and French Indo-China. The Japanese regarded this as an ultimatum and after further negotiations the attack on *Pearl Harbor was launched on 7 December 1941.

Nomura's last meeting with Hull took place after Hull knew of the attack. Hull received Nomura and another diplomat, Kurusu Saburō, icily and after scanning the fourteen point message they had delivered remarked that in all his 50 years of public service, he had never seen such a document that was more crowded with infamous falsehoods and distortions. As the Japanese, who did not know of the attack, withdrew in confusion, Hull muttered: 'scoundrels and piss-ants'.

Following Pearl Harbor, Hull and his staff drew up the *United Nations Declaration which was signed on 1 January 1942 by the Washington representatives of those nations then at war with Axis forces. He was also closely involved in formulating the document which by 1943 had become known as the 'Charter of the United Nations'. This charter was the basis of US proposals at the *Dumbarton Oaks conference and led Roosevelt to call Hull 'the father of the United Nations'.

Roosevelt did not want Hull at any of the major Allied conferences, although he did attend the *Moscow conference in October 1943 and created a deep impression there by his friendly and dignified behaviour. But political feuding and overwork left him exhausted; in October 1944 he collapsed and spent seven months in hospital. He was awarded the Nobel Peace Prize in 1945 and was appointed a delegate to the *San Francisco conference of April 1945, at which the United Nations was officially founded, but was too ill to attend.

Hull, C., *The Memoirs of Cordell Hull*, 2 vols. (New York, 1948).

human torpedoes were used primarily by the Italians, who pioneered them, but also by the British, Germans, and Japanese.

The 6.7 m. (22 ft.) Italian Maiale (pig) had a detachable explosive nose and a two-man crew who sat astride the torpedo wearing rubber suits and oxygen equipment. Taken close to their targets by specially adapted submarines, they crippled the British battleships *Queen*

Human torpedoes: The Marder

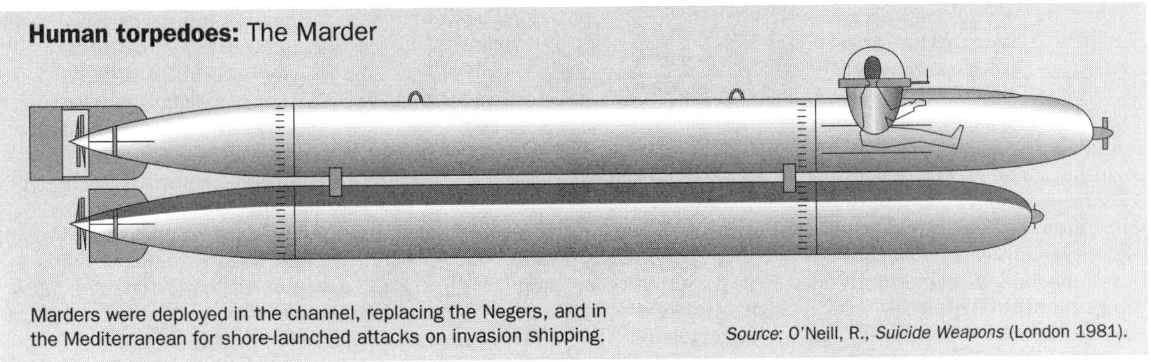

Marders were deployed in the channel, replacing the Negers, and in the Mediterranean for shore-launched attacks on invasion shipping.

Source: O'Neill, R., *Suicide Weapons* (London 1981).

Elizabeth and *Valiant* in Alexandria harbour on 19 December 1941, and they also attacked shipping in Malta, Algiers Bay, and Gibraltar.

The British 7.6 m. (25 ft.) Chariot, modelled on the Maiale, was developed to attack the German battleship **Tirpitz*, but the operation, mounted in October 1942, failed when the two Chariots, slung under a *Shetland bus fishing boat, broke adrift close to their target and sank. However, attacks on Italian shipping in Palermo and elsewhere were more successful.

The 7.6 m. one-man German Mohr (Moor) comprised two electrically-propelled torpedoes clamped together vertically, the upper one having a tiny plexiglass-covered cockpit instead of a warhead. It was slow, could not dive, and the torpedo had to be released close to the target. First used against shipping during the *Anzio landings in January 1944, and later during the Normandy landings that June (see OVERLORD), results were negligible and losses very high. A development of it, the Marder (pine marten), was equally unsuccessful (see Figure).

The Japanese human torpedoes, known as *Kaiten* (conger), were Long Lance *torpedoes enlarged to include a compartment for the crewman and a conning tower. Transported by specially adapted submarines, they were first used at Ulithi atoll in November 1944, sinking a US fleet tanker. They were also used at *Iwo Jima, *Okinawa, and elsewhere, but suffered a high loss rate and had few successes.

O'Neill, R., *Suicide Squads* (London, 1981).

humint, human intelligence, as opposed to sigint, or signals intelligence. See SPIES.

Hump, the, name given to the air route organized by the India–China Wing of US *Air Transport Command which supplied US forces in China and *Chiang Kai-shek and his army. In April 1944 it also airlifted 18,000 Chinese troops to India to participate in *Stilwell's advance during the *Burma campaign.

Once the Chinese coastline had been sealed by the Japanese (see CHINA INCIDENT), and Burma captured so that the *Burma Road could not be used, the only method of supplying the Chinese was to airlift supplies across a series of mountain ridges (Patkai, Kumon, and Santsung), some 4,500 m. (15,000 ft.) high. The route was from Dinjan, and nearby airfields, in India's eastern Assam to Kunming, a distance of about 800 km. (500 mi.). It often involved flying at an aircraft's maximum ceiling, with icing, violent turbulence, and monsoon weather, all of which combined to make it an extremely hazardous task.

The route was inaugurated in July 1942 when 82 tons of supplies were airlifted to China and it first exceeded 1,000 tons a month that December. However, the urgent needs of Chiang Kai-shek and Stilwell's *China–Burma–India theatre for fuel, ammunition, and general supplies, soon led to a rapid expansion. In July 1943, 2,916 tons were flown in; in July 1944, 18,975 tons; and in July 1945, the peak month of the whole operation, 71,042 tons. In total 650,000 tons of supplies—the equivalent of the cargo of 70 *Liberty ships—were airlifted to China and at its peak the Wing employed more than 22,000 service personnel, 47,000 civilians, and more than 300 aircraft. Losses in aircraft and crew were heavy. In January 1945, for example, when 44,000 tons of supplies were airlifted, there were 23 major accidents which caused the loss of 36 lives.

HUNGARY

1. Introduction

Hungary's support for the Axis can only be understood in the light of its experiences at the end of the *First World War. By the Treaty of Trianon (see VERSAILLES SETTLEMENT) in 1920, Hungary lost over two-thirds of its territory to Romania, Czechoslovakia, Yugoslavia, and Austria. Before 1914 its population was almost 21 million, of whom roughly half were ethnic Magyars; after Trianon the population was fewer than 8 million, and the boundaries of 1920 stranded some 3 million Magyars within the successor states. Rightly or wrongly, the affront offered to Hungary's national sentiment meant that it was almost inevitably inclined to side with whichever great power promised help in revising the treaty.

There were other factors which made alliance with the Axis likely. Hungary's brief experience of communist dictatorship, the Soviet Republic of 1919, left a deep-rooted fear of Bolshevism amongst the upper and middle classes, which reinforced traditional fears of Russian pan-slavism. The prominent role played by Jews in the Republic also fuelled *anti-Semitism, in a country where Jews were already highly visible, numbering over half a million even after Trianon. Some 2–300,000 refugees from the successor states flooded the country after 1920, most of them middle class, nationalist, and embittered; they formed a fertile breeding-ground for a new type of right-wing radicalism. Hungary's sizeable minority of ethnic Germans (see VOLKSDEUTSCHE), and their preponderance in the officer corps, engendered a sympathy for Germany which was shared by many of the right-wing radical movements.

After 1933 Hungarian governments made clear their interest in association with Nazi Germany. The first fruit of this policy was the cession of southern Slovakia to Hungary in the wake of the *Munich agreement in 1938, followed by the reoccupation of Carpathian Ruthenia in 1939, on the final partition of Czechoslovakia. In 1940, under German pressure, Romania returned northern Transylvania to Hungary. Henceforward Hungarian leaders were mesmerized by the fear that, if they did not co-operate with the Germans, Romania might be allowed to take back this territory. It was to guard against this possibility that Hungary joined the *Tripartite Pact in November 1940. And in April 1941, when Hitler launched his invasion of Yugoslavia across Hungary, the latter was rewarded with additional Magyar-populated territory (see Map 49).

These territorial gains gave Hungary a powerful reason for throwing in its lot with Germany when Hitler invaded the USSR in June 1941 (see BARBAROSSA). In addition, the conviction was widespread that it was in Hungary's interests for Germany to eliminate the joint threat of pan-slavism and *communism, and that Germany was bound to win. The official pretext for Hungary's declaration of war on 27 June, however, was the mysterious bombing of Kassa in northern Hungary, which has not been adequately explained to this day. The Hungarian government claimed the bombing was the work of the Soviet Air Force; but no convincing reason has ever been offered as to why the Soviets, then under attack by the Germans, should gratuitously bomb Hungary. The general assumption was that the aircraft involved were disguised German machines, although no evidence has emerged to prove this. The fact remains that it was the Germans who stood to gain most by forcing Hungary into the war, since they thus ensured access to the oilfields of neighbouring Romania, already a German ally.

2. Domestic life and economy

Hungary between the wars was still a predominantly agricultural economy, with 55.8% of the population in 1920 deriving its living from the land. It was also a class-bound, inegalitarian society, dominated by a numerous gentry, where over half the arable land belonged to some 10,000 landowners. These large estates were dependent on the labour of the 1.5 million landless agricultural workers, many of them living in conditions of extreme poverty. In the towns the middle classes and, to a certain extent, the growing industrial proletariat, had profited from Hungary's post-war reconstruction boom, only to experience renewed economic difficulties in the 1930s. This insecurity increased the appeal of the right-radical parties.

Traditional markets and resources were lost at the end of the First World War, although much of the agricultural and industrial wealth was retained. The country was heavily dependent on exports of grains, especially wheat, and was drawn irresistibly into the German economic sphere of interest. By 1939 Germany took 52.2% of Hungary's exports, and provided 52.5% of its imports, reflecting the growing interest of the Nazis in south-eastern Europe generally, as a source of foodstuffs and *raw materials as well as a market for German manufactures. During the war the principal Hungarian exports to Germany were livestock, wheat, corn and flax, bauxite, manganese ore, oil, and charcoal. In addition Hungarian industry produced ammunition and, from 1941, aircraft, including Messerschmitt 109s and 210s. Exports of wheat fell off substantially after 1941, however, owing to a succession of poor harvests. The real economic surprise of the war was Hungary's emergence as an important oil producer. From the start of commercial exploitation, in 1938, production rose rapidly: in 1942, Germany imported 125,418 tons from Hungary; in 1943, 203,629 tons. As the war turned against the Reich, Hungary became, next to Romania, its most important source; this fact influenced the Nazi occupation of the country in March 1944, and Hitler's determination to hold on there for as long as possible in 1944–5.

German occupation, paradoxically, limited Hungary's value as an economic partner. The costs of occupation, mass deportation of Jews (see FINAL SOLUTION), and intensive Allied bombing (see STRATEGIC AIR OFFENSIVES, 2) all reduced production. From October 1944 the country itself was a theatre of war, and by April 1945 almost 40% of the national wealth, in the shape of crops, rolling-stock, infrastructure, housing, and so on, had been destroyed.

3. Government

Hungary was a kingdom without a king. In 1920 the Hungarian parliament repealed all legislation passed since the revolution of 1918, thus effectively restoring the monarchy. The Habsburg royal family, however, was not welcomed back; instead a Regency under Admiral *Horthy was installed. Horthy, as *de facto* head of state, had wide powers. He was C-in-C of the armed forces, whose officers swore an oath of personal allegiance to him. He appointed and dismissed the prime minister, could dissolve parliament, and had a veto over legislation. Horthy's position during the war was crucial since, although deeply conservative, he resisted until quite late in the day an openly fascist government.

Politics in inter-war Hungary revolved around the struggle between the conservative Unitary Party and the rising right-radical movements. The system set up in 1919 gave only 27.5% of the population the vote, there was open balloting in rural constituencies, and the party in power was more or less enabled to fix elections. Dissent was tolerated, but the government was essentially

49. **Hungary**'s territorial acquisitions, 1938–41

oligarchical. By the late 1930s governments were an uneasy mix of conservatives and right-radicals. In response to pressure from extreme right-wingers, such as Ferenc Szálasi's Arrow Cross movement, attempts were made at land redistribution, anti-Semitic laws were passed limiting the property Jews could hold, and closer relations were sought with Germany. Subservience to Germany, in turn, made it even harder to ignore the views of the Arrow Cross, after 1939 the second largest party in parliament and the openly pro-German officer corps.

The Arrow Cross was only the most prominent of a number of such factions, all openly fascist and drawing support from a wide social spectrum including the industrial working class. Arrow Cross ideology, like Nazism, relied on an authoritarian, chauvinist populism, appealing to Hungarians' yearning for a 'just' society, but also to primitive notions of an order based on the power of the strongest or, in Szálasi's words, a 'brutally realistic étatism'. Since Szálasi regarded the Hungarians, with the Germans and Japanese, as one of the world's three chosen peoples, it was with full Arrow Cross backing that the government of László Bárdossy (April 1941–March 1942) found itself forced into declaring war on the USSR. By December 1941 Hungary was also at war with the UK and the USA.

War with the western Allies represented a defeat for Horthy and the conservatives, who were convinced it lessened Germany's chances of defeating what they regarded as the real enemy, the USSR. Bárdossy's successor, Miklós Kállay (March 1942–March 1944) therefore pursued a 'see-saw policy' which sought to limit Hungary's military involvement, without provoking German retaliation. After the military disaster of *Stalingrad in January 1943, Hungary was briefly permitted to take a back seat on the Eastern Front, but it was no easier to resist German demands for raw materials and for further restrictive measures against the Jews. Kállay's inconclusive negotiations with the western Allies for Hungarian withdrawal from the war merely confirmed the suspicions of Hitler, who was kept informed by pro-German figures in Kállay's own cabinet. On 19 March 1944 German forces occupied the country. Horthy was browbeaten into appointing an unambiguously pro-German government under General Döme Sztójay, and a Reich plenipotentiary was installed to ensure Hungarian compliance.

For several months this puppet government strove to satisfy its masters. Anti-Nazi parties were suppressed, and a new army sent to the front. Deportation of the Jews, hitherto resisted, was now implemented under *SS supervision: between March and July 1944 some 400,000 people, mostly from outside Budapest, were sent to *Auschwitz. The realization of what was happening to these victims, coupled with Romania's switch from the Axis to the Allied cause, appears to have led Horthy to make a stand. The deportations were stopped, and a new government under General Géza Lakatos appointed on 29 August. Most significantly, Horthy finally accepted that *armistice negotiations would have to be conducted with the USSR, within whose sphere of influence Hungary fell. The Hungarian–Soviet preliminary armistice concluded on 11 October, and Horthy's broadcast announcing it four days later, were the signal for a Nazi-inspired coup (see SKORZENY). Horthy was removed and an Arrow Cross government under Szálasi installed. The Szálasi regime, however, could do little to influence events, and after the fall of *Budapest in February 1945 its writ hardly ran beyond the German-occupied west of Hungary. In the meantime a Soviet-sponsored provisional government had already been formed at Debrecen on 21–22 December.

4. Defence forces and civil defence

It was not until mid-1942, with the regular forces committed to the Eastern Front and the government obsessed by the fear of a Romanian attack, that plans were laid for a Home Army of some 220,000 men. Such plans suffered from the same problem afflicting the front-line units, the shortage of manpower and above all *matériel*. The Germans, moreover, while agreeing to make good Hungary's equipment losses at the front, refused to supply the Home Army. Their suspicions had some foundation, since the Home Army rapidly became the Hungarian government's excuse for not sending more troops to the front. The result was that neither the defence force nor the front line was adequately equipped. There is no evidence that the Home Army played any serious role in stemming the Soviet offensives of 1944–5.

5. Armed forces

Despite rearmament Hungary was hopelessly ill-equipped in 1941. The regular army consisted of 9 army corps, comprising 27 brigades or light divisions (the terms were interchangeable in Hungarian usage) of two regiments each. Since the effective strength of a regiment was 4,000 men, total infantry strength was 216,000. There were also two cavalry brigades and two motorized brigades. None of these units was prepared for a modern war. The infantry relied on rifles which frequently jammed, and lacked anti-tank guns. Tanks to begin with were Italian Ansaldo light armoured vehicles, with fixed turrets. Later Hungary produced its own Toldi and Turán tanks, but these were never up to date; in 1941 only 190 were in service, and only 440 were made by 1944. There were hardly enough vehicles for the motorized brigades, let alone the whole army; even in 1943 the army had only a third of the motor transport it needed. Of an air force, on paper, of 302 machines, only 189 were operational in March 1941, and were in any case obsolete.

The so-called Mobile Corps, under General Ferenc Szombathelyi, accompanied the German Seventeenth Army on its advance into the Soviet Union in July and August 1941. It was only partially motorized, being made up of the two motorized brigades, a cavalry brigade and ten Alpine battalions, six of which were mounted on bicycles. Partly because the Red Army was continually retreating, the Mobile Corps reached the River Donets before being withdrawn at the insistence of the Hungarian government, having taken casualties of under 1,000 men. Lightly armed units were retained behind the front to deal with partisans.

German pressure led to the commitment of a much larger force in 1942. The Second Army, commanded by General Gusztáv Jány, comprised three infantry corps (the 3rd, 4th, and 7th) and the 1st Armoured Corps. Including the (mainly Jewish) forced labour battalions of perhaps as many as 50,000, it totalled some 250,000. The Second Army took part in the offensive of General Maximilian von Weich's Army Group B in the Ukraine between 28 June and mid-September, reaching the Don and suffering losses of 21,621 officers and men. It was already apparent that both infantry and armoured units were vastly outclassed by the Soviet forces, which resulted in a pervasive sense of inferiority and loss of morale.

In the aftermath of Stalingrad the Second Hungarian Army was effectively destroyed. Stationed opposite the Soviet Don *front* to the south of Voronezh, it was attacked on 12 January 1943 by forces three times as strong, and overrun within a matter of days. There were no reserves, and the already depleted Hungarian light divisions were probably extended over too long a sector for their numbers. But the greatest single cause of the Voronezh disaster was undoubtedly the inadequacy of Hungarian equipment. Despite urgent pleas for anti-tank guns in particular, the German High Command had only begun to remedy these deficiencies, and the Hungarians still lacked the heavy-calibre pieces needed to stop Soviet armour. It is hard not to conclude that the Germans themselves were largely responsible for the failure of their allies. Casualty figures are still disputed, but vary between 106,000 and 190,000 including the majority of the forced labour battalions, who perished in the retreat.

Voronezh confirmed the Hungarian government's desire to keep its army out of the fighting as far as possible, and throughout 1943 the Hungarian presence at the front was confined to nine light divisions used as occupation forces. The German occupation of March 1944 was in part designed to end this reluctance, as the Soviets advanced westwards. Reorganized in larger, 'mixed' divisions of 15,000 men, the Hungarian regular Army made what was in effect its last stand between April and October 1944. By the end of July the Soviets had reached the Carpathians; by 22 September they had broken through into the Hungarian Plain. The confusion surrounding the Arrow Cross coup in October did little to encourage the front-line troops, and there was a steady increase in defections with, on occasion, whole battalions pulling out of the line and simply melting away. The units still fighting now did so under close German supervision, and of the new units planned by the Szálasi regime only the 'St László' Division and the Hunyadi SS Armoured Grenadier Division ever saw action. After the fall of Budapest, some Hungarian forces retreated into Austria with the Germans, but for most the war was over by mid-February 1945.

6. Intelligence

Hungarian intelligence was served by the counter-intelligence department of the ministry of defence, and the State Security Centre of the interior ministry. Neither office seems to have made any significant contribution to the Axis war effort; on the contrary, the Germans mistrusted them. The most notable achievement of military intelligence was an entirely negative one: a report at the end of 1942, the eve of Voronezh, concluded that the Soviet Army was still incapable of mounting any large-scale offensive.

7. Merchant marine

Hungary's numerous river craft, especially oil tankers, were of strategic importance, as shown when the Germans removed 487 of the 489 vessels available in the winter of 1944–5. There were also, in 1941, six Hungarian ocean-going ships, two of which were chartered by the Luftwaffe, and four leased as supply ships in the *Black Sea.

8. Resistance

Serious resistance in Hungary only emerged in the summer of 1944. Political opposition was in any case muted, and the few anti-war demonstrations were dealt with by mass arrests. The most likely focus of resistance, the Communist Party, was banned and, even disguised as the Peace Party after July 1943, most of its activity consisted of distributing leaflets. Britain's *SOE made contact with the Kállay government in March 1943, but the results were disappointing. To requests for industrial sabotage, the Hungarians replied that this would only provoke a German occupation. The occupation, when it came, made genuine resistance only marginally more popular. SOE sent a total of six missions into Hungary after March 1944, but all were either captured or forced to pull out. Partisan activity sprang up on a piecemeal basis, with some Hungarians joining the rising in Slovakia in July 1944, or liaising with *Tito in the south. It was not until early November that a multi-party Committee of Liberation was formed to organize armed resistance; this was promptly betrayed to the *Gestapo and most of its members arrested. Thereafter Hungarian resistance made little practical contribution to German defeat.

9. Culture

The counter-revolution of 1919, and the political oligarchy which followed it, led many of Hungary's most gifted citizens to emigrate. Those who remained often retreated into a world of fantasy or symbolism, such as the first writer of psychological novels in Hungarian, Sándor Marai. Poetry, in the hands of Árpád Tóth or Mihály Babits, became more a matter of form than of intelligibility. Writers of novels set in a fabulous world of tycoons and big business, remote from contemporary Hungarian reality, were the most enduringly popular. Socialists who stressed the struggle of the poor, like the poet Attila József, were a minority voice. So too were the glorifiers of rural values, like the novelist Zsigmond

Móricz or the explicitly anti-Semitic Dezsö Szabó. Gyula Illyés, whose classic *People of the Puszta* appeared in 1936, saw the rural masses as the true heart of Hungary, the improvement of whose condition was essential for democratic reform.

Popular music was a mix of gypsy tunes, Pest operetta, jazz, and whatever sentimental ditty was the rage. Artistically Béla Bartók (who emigrated in 1940) and Zoltán Kodály dominated the scene. Kodály's work was largely an adaptation of traditional folk music, as in his *Marosszék Dances* (1944). Bartók, while also relying on folk themes, was more modern in his treatment, seeing in what he preferred to call 'peasant music' a primitive beauty transcending national boundaries. The fine arts reflected the chasm between establishment and artistic community. Some of the most famous Hungarian artists, such as the photographer-painter László Moholy Nagy or the painter Lajos Tihanyi, lived abroad. Those favoured by the regime still tended towards the neo-Gothic in architecture and sculpture, and an academic historicism in painting. Only towards the end of the inter-war period, after some of the émigrés returned, could the modernist influences apparent in Hungarian art before the First World War begin to reassert themselves. IAN ARMOUR

Fenyo, D., *Hitler, Horthy, and Hungary: German-Hungarian Relations, 1941–1944* (New Haven, Conn., 1972).
Juhász, Gyula, *Hungarian Foreign Policy 1919–1945* (Budapest, 1979).
Macartney, C. A., *October Fifteenth: A History of Modern Hungary 1929–1945*, 2 vols. (Edinburgh, 1956–7).

Huntziger, General Charles (1880–1941), French Army officer who commanded the Second French Army during the fighting which led to the fall of *France in June 1940. De *Gaulle thought him brilliant and wanted him to become the Allied C-in-C instead of *Weygand when *Reynaud replaced *Gamelin on 20 May. He led the French delegation at the *armistice negotiations with the Germans and in September 1940 *Pétain made him minister of war, and then C-in-C of *Vichy ground forces. He was killed in an air crash.

HUSKY, see SICILIAN CAMPAIGN.

Husseini, Hadj Amin el- (1897?–1974), pro-Axis Mufti (a Muslim religious official who issues Islamic law rulings) of Jerusalem from 1921 who led the Arab revolt in Palestine during the 1930s. Forced to flee in 1937 he eventually reached Iraq where he worked closely with *Rashid Ali against British influence in the Middle East. After Rashid Ali's revolt against the British failed in April 1941, the Mufti ended up in Germany working as a propagandist and as recruiter of Muslim volunteers for the German forces. See also ANTI-IMPERIALISM.

Hyde Park Declaration, economic agreement between Canada and the USA which was signed by Roosevelt and Mackenzie *King on 20 April 1941 at Hyde Park, the American president's home on the Hudson River. It was designed to help ease Canada's financial problems in aiding the UK's war effort. The simple six-paragraph document stated that Canada and the USA would provide each other with the *matériel* each was best able to produce; and that if Canada required American component parts for equipment and munitions needed by the UK, they could be acquired by the UK under the terms of *Lend-Lease.

Iceland had been a free and sovereign state under the king of Denmark since 1918, and its foreign relations in 1939 were still handled by Denmark. Whoever controlled Iceland commanded the North Atlantic sea lanes and the naval exits into the Atlantic from Europe, and it proved an invaluable Allied air and escort base during the battle of the *Atlantic.

On the outbreak of war in September 1939 Iceland maintained its neutral stance and when Germany invaded Denmark in April 1940 it declared temporary independence from Denmark. Initially it refused British protection for fear of provoking German retaliation, but in May the British landed there to pre-empt the Germans, though they guaranteed not to interfere with the country's internal affairs. Canadian troops followed and in July 1941 Iceland came under US protection when the island was defined as being part of the *Western Hemisphere. The same month, at the request of the Icelandic government, US forces relieved the British garrison which was needed elsewhere. Iceland declared itself an independent republic in 1944. During the war British staff officers always referred to it, on Churchill's orders, as Iceland (c), because early in the war one of them had sent a ship to Ireland instead.

ICHI-GŌ, see CHINA INCIDENT.

IFF (Identification Friend or Foe) was a device fitted to aircraft to enable ground *radar defences to identify them as friendly. British ones made the radar echoes from a friendly aircraft appear on a radar screen as a distinctive elongated blip. The device was usually switched on when the aircraft was about 65 km. (40 mi.) from the British coast. British bomber crews thought, incorrectly, that it could also jam German radar and they liked to keep it on when bombing Germany. In fact, doing so helped German fighters to be vectored on to them, and it took the *MI6 scientist R. V. Jones some time to prove what a dangerous practice it was. See also PIP-SQUEAK TRANSMISSIONS.

Ilsley, James (1894–1967), Canadian Liberal politician who served in Mackenzie *King's wartime cabinet, initially as minister of national revenue and then as minister of finance. His expertise in economics, which gained him tremendous prestige during the war years, enabled the Canadian government, through *Canadian Mutual Aid, to offer financial help to several Allied countries, particularly the UK. He was not close to the prime minister, but King noted that he was 'absolutely indispensable, not only to Canada but to the war effort of the United Nations.' (J. Pickersgill and D. Forster, *The Mackenzie King Record, vol. 1: 1939–1944*, Toronto, Ontario, 1960, p. 650). See also CANADA, 3.

Imphal offensive (see Map 50). This was the turning-point of the *Burma campaign when, in March 1944, *Mutaguchi's Fifteenth Japanese Armyattacked from Burma into India. Mutaguchi's primary objective was to pre-empt an offensive by *Slim's Fourteenth Army by destroying Slim's supply bases at Imphal. But Mutaguchi also wanted to gain a foothold for his *Indian National Army (INA), hoping to precipitate a revolt in India. To make the British commit their reserves before launching this offensive, Lt-General Kawabe Masakazu (1886–1965), the Japanese Burma Area Army commander, struck into the Arakan in February 1944, precipitating the battle of the *Admin Box.

Outnumbered, out-gunned, and without air superiority, Mutaguchi's offensive relied on speed and tactical surprise. It was a desperate gamble which nearly paid off. For though Slim was expecting, indeed hoping for, a Japanese offensive as a necessary preliminary to advancing himself—and had planned a withdrawal to the Imphal plain to fight on ground of his own choosing if one came—Mutaguchi still achieved tactical surprise because Slim had miscalculated the timing of the offensive and its strength.

To draw Slim's reserves away from the objectives of his other two Japanese divisions, Mutaguchi had his 33rd

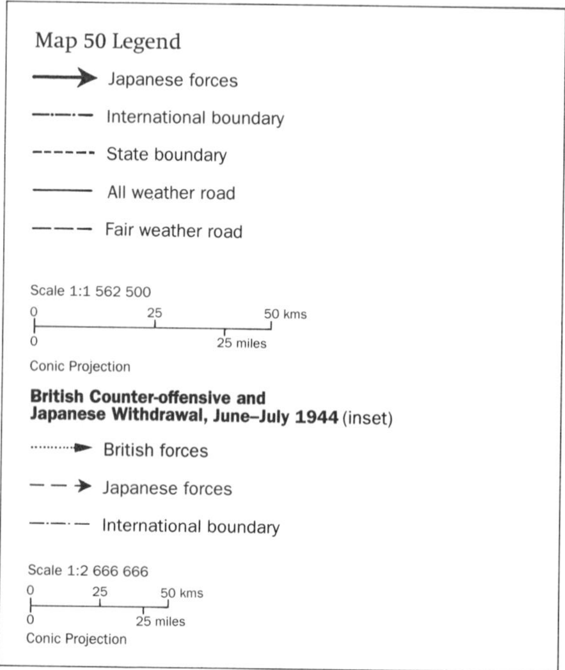

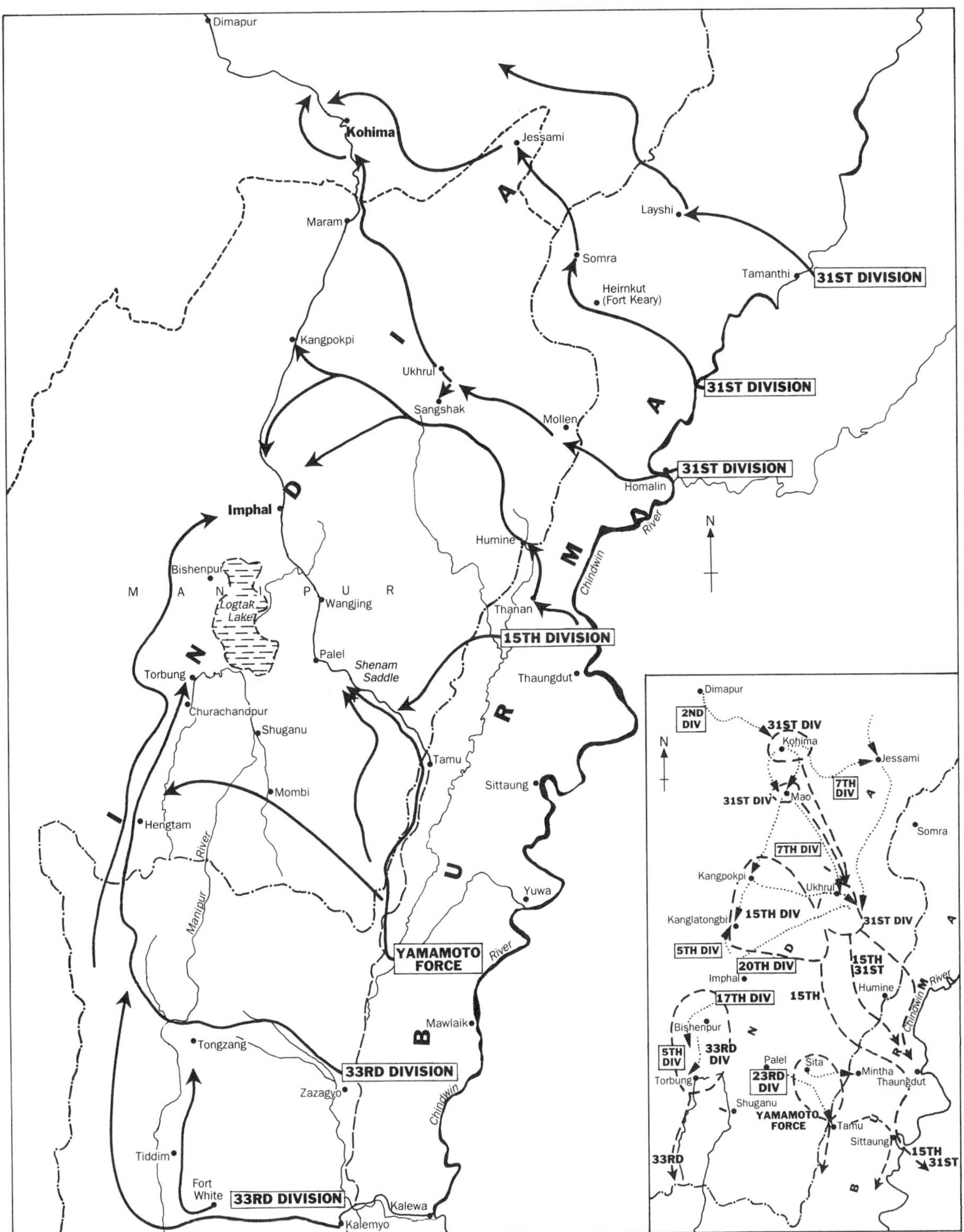

50. Japanese offensive against **Imphal** and Kohima, March 1944

Division strike first, from the south, on 7 March. Part of this nearly trapped Slim's 17th Division at Tiddim, forcing it into a fighting retreat, while another part, Yamamoto Force, fought to destroy the 20th Division around Tamu but was eventually stopped at Shenam Saddle. A week later Mutaguchi's 15th Division, which attacked in the centre, and his 31st Division, which formed the northern part of the Japanese pincer, poured across the River Chindwin. But the Japanese Arakan offensive had been launched, and defeated, too quickly and this allowed two of Slim's divisions (5th and 7th) to be airlifted from there to Imphal. As the first men began landing on 19 March the Japanese were only 48 km. (30 mi.) away.

Slim had made another miscalculation, too. He had expected an assault on *Kohima, to the north-west of Imphal, because its capture would sever Imphal's supply route from Dimapur, his main supply base. But he had estimated that the terrain was too difficult for the commander of the 31st Division, Lt-General Satō Kotuku, to deploy more than one regiment; in fact, Satō brought forward his whole division. After a bloody curtain-raiser with the 50th Indian Parachute Brigade at Sangshak the division's infantry group reached Kohima on 3 April.

Nine days later Mutaguchi's 15th Division cut the Kohima–Imphal road at Kangpokpi. Soon it was overlooking the defensive positions of Slim's 4th Corps and was only 10 km. (6 mi.) from them. But the Japanese were exhausted from road-building. They also lacked the necessary firepower and were defenceless against Slim's tanks, which the divisional commander had been told not to expect; in the desperate fighting which followed, Slim's 5th and 23rd Divisions gradually broke this Japanese stranglehold. But with his supply road cut, Slim had to start being supplied by air, an extraordinary achievement by the RAF's Third Tactical Air Force which, during the course of the four-month battle, moved prodigious amounts of men and supplies, including over 4.5 million litres of petrol (one million gallons), 12,000 reinforcements, 13,000 casualties, and 6.35 million kg. (14 million lb.) of rations.

Mutaguchi's *logistics were even more dire. He knew that insufficient supplies could be brought forward through the jungle and he had gambled on capturing Imphal quickly to obtain what he needed from the British supply dumps there. So when the town's defences held, and both the 17th and 20th Divisions escaped destruction, Mutaguchi decided to exceed his orders by striking at Dimapur which contained everything he needed. But this plan was thwarted by the cautious Kawabe and as Slim slowly stabilized the battle front during April and May, so Mutaguchi's situation became more and more desperate. His men—though not the INA—fought with great bravery. But Satō's withdrawal, against orders, from Kohima on 31 May, and his earlier refusal, or inability, to detach part of his division to aid 15th Division's attack on Imphal, undermined the whole offensive. Meanwhile the arrival of monsoon weather in mid-May, as well as disease and malnutrition, hampered Mutaguchi's force's movements and reduced their numbers. Slowly the battle turned in Slim's favour, the Dimapur–Imphal supply road was reopened on 22 June, and on 18 July Kawabe and Mutaguchi agreed that no further offensive operations were possible. Mutaguchi withdrew across the Chindwin, but Slim's forces followed on his heels and the withdrawal became a rout.

Imphal was an unmitigated disaster for the Japanese. Out of 85,000 fighting men, 53,000 became casualties (the British had 17,000), including 30,000 killed, while hundreds more died of disease, malnutrition, and exhaustion. Not one tank or heavy weapon was saved, and 17,000 mules and pack ponies perished. The Japanese in Burma never recovered and the INA never achieved the foothold in India it so desperately sought.

Evans, G., and Brett-James, A., *Imphal* (London, 1962).

Inayat Khan, Noor (1914–44), *SOE operative who, under the codename MADELEINE, worked for the organization's CINÉMA network in Paris from mid-1943. Half-Indian, half-American, she was born in the Kremlin and was living in Paris when war broke out. She went to the UK and served as a WAAF wireless operator before receiving a commission and joining SOE. She was betrayed in September 1943 and after spending nearly a year in prison in chains she was sent to *Dachau and shot. She was posthumously awarded the George Cross (see DECORATIONS).

incendiary bombs, see BOMBS.

INDIA

1. Introduction

India (population in 1941, 318.7 million) was crucial to the global Allied war effort and strategy. To a greater extent even than during the *First World War, it became a source of fighting men, money, *raw materials, and key manufactures. Because this was a worldwide war, it stood also as a geographically strategic hinge: facing Africa and the Middle East, it confronted a possible Axis thrust from the west; to the east the Japanese drive through South-East Asia to India's own borders from 1942 physically imperilled its north-eastern territory and eastern seaboard. So significant was the subcontinent that when the UK faced invasion at home the viceroy and the secretary of state for India thought it might provide an alternative imperial capital; and later India and its resources made it possible for the Allies to drive back through Burma and into South-East Asia (see BURMA CAMPAIGN). To the Americans there was a further dimension to India's role, as the base for the *Hump air supply route to China.

Because India was under direct British imperial rule (except for the French enclaves of Pondicherry, Mahé, Karikal, Yanam, and Chandernagore, and the Portuguese one of Goa) it was not a free agent in relation to the war. The UK expected the subcontinent's resources to be placed at the disposal of metropolitan Britain and its allies, assuming as it had for three-quarters of a century, that India had a vital role to perform for the UK, not least in imperial finance and defence. Consequently in September 1939 Lord Linlithgow (1887–1952), who was India's viceroy from 1936 to 1943, simply declared that India was at war with Germany. Although this procedure was constitutionally correct, his failure to consult broadly with leaders of Indian public opinion was politically disastrous. For at least 20 years the British had recognized that the country could not be governed autocratically and had made constitutional provision for the incorporation of articulate, educated Indians into the administrative and decision-making structures of the Raj. Ironically, much Indian opinion was broadly sympathetic to the Allies and their war aims. Among the western educated, many had been to England or were steeped in British history and literature and prized the values of liberalism, democracy, and the rights of small and suppressed nations, however much they criticized imperial practice in India. Few had any sympathy with the values and aims of the Axis powers. Jawaharlal *Nehru, for example, was caught between hatred of imperialism and fascism equally, and eager to find a way of supporting the Allied war effort without buttressing imperial rule. A small section of India's politicians, personified by M. K. *Gandhi, were on principle opposed to violence and were consequently hostile to Indian involvement in any war. A tiny number in India and abroad, like Subhas Chandra *Bose, supported the Axis powers and hoped to use the war to overthrow the Raj. Most ordinary people knew little of the war in its early stages, given poor communications and low literacy levels; though from 1942 they began increasingly to suffer from inflation and acute shortages.

2. Domestic life, economy, and war effort

India's massive war-time mobilization of people and resources in a predominantly agricultural society had a profound effect on its economy and the lives of its people. This was particularly so because, even though the British government would ultimately pay for much of the military effort, payment on the spot had to be made by the government of India. The solution to this short-term problem was a mixture of increased direct taxation, loans raised within India, and an expanded money supply. (The total money supply was Rs. 317 crores [crore = 10 million] in August 1939 and Rs. 2,190 crores in September 1945.) Purchasing power was increased by new money, but goods available to the civilian population were paradoxically reduced because of the diversion of India's expanded product to the war effort, the decrease in exports and the disruption of communications. The result was inflation, particularly severe once the Japanese campaign was under way. (See Tables 1 and 2.) The cost of living index had risen, from a base of 100 in mid-1939, to 168 by 1942–3 and by 1945–6 stood at 231. Control of inflation and direction of the economy towards war ends involved the government in intervention on an unprecedented scale. Taxation to provide revenue and absorb excess purchasing power, savings schemes, controls on share issues, licensing of new industrial ventures, requisitioning of manufactures for the army, and ultimately price control, food rationing, and official control of food and grain marketing changed irrevocably the relationship of the government to the economy. Weary civilian administrators took on an unprecedented range of duties to control the economy, a burden which contributed to the near-collapse of the civilian government by the end of the war. India may thus have been able to swell the war effort; but it could not feed its own people or save them from severe shortages of goods. The worst catastrophe was the food crisis which began in 1942 and culminated in the Bengal famine of 1943. This was the result of the failure of harvests, the loss of the Burmese rice supply, disruption of transport because of

India, Table 1: Indices of relative price movements, 1939–44 (August 1939 = 100)

	Rice	*Wheat*	*Cotton manufactures*	*Kerosene*
December 1941	172	212	196	140
December 1942	218	232	414	194
December 1943	951	330	501	201
December 1944	333	381	285	175

Rationing was introduced during 1944.

Source: Tomlinson, B. R., *The Political Economy of the Raj, 1942–1947. The Economics of Decolonization in India* (London, 1979), p. 94.

the primary needs of the war effort, but above all the inability of the government to break down regional barriers to free movement of food and to organize distribution efficiently and fairly. It was only with great difficulty that General *Wavell, who became viceroy in October 1943, was able to extort even the most minimal help in terms of grain from the Allies, despite the magnitude of the crisis and its potential political as well as military repercussions, even though stocks were available in Canada and Australia for example. Helping to feed Indians meant taking urgent shipping space away from the direct war effort; and in Whitehall's calculations starving Indians came second in priority. Probably more than 3 million people perished in this greatest calamity to befall India for decades. In the longer term India's economy was left with increased industrial potential, though this was mainly in the sectors which had produced strategic goods. It is estimated that between 1941 and 1946—which included the years when it was a supply base for Commonwealth, Chinese, and American forces as well as its own troops in the re-taking of Burma—India produced £286.5 million worth of materials, and for US forces in India alone nearly £130 million worth of supplies. Industrial products included guns, ammunition, machine tools, aircraft supplies, armoured vehicles, surgical instruments, chemicals and drugs, and textiles. It also sent food and made an extensive contribution to shipbuilding and repairing. In India itself 200 airfields were constructed, 130 new hospitals were built, railways and ports were expanded, new depots and camps were set up, and new roads constructed in the difficult north-eastern border lands. However, no general break-through in industrialization occurred, because of the effects of government control, shortages of capital goods, and lack of skilled manpower. In relation to the UK, India was by the end of the war a creditor rather than a debtor, having accumulated sterling balances in London of more than £1,300 million on account of Indian local expenditure in the war effort.

3. Government and resistance

India's huge mobilization for war took place in the context of, and contributed to, a break in the trend away from autocratic imperial rule to governance by political consultation and partnership with Indians which had been apparent since before the First World War. The British ruled two-thirds of the subcontinent directly, leaving the remainder under the control of India's surviving princely families who were none the less firmly subordinate to the British. In 'British India' a viceroy (crown representative from 1858) answerable to the secretary of state for India in Whitehall, who was in turn answerable to the British crown and parliament, presided over an executive council and an administration divided into provinces, each with a governor, and manned by a civilian cadre of generalist administrators, the Indian Civil Service (ICS). But in the early years of the 20th century, autocracy had been increasingly mellowed by pragmatism, in the face of growing Indian political opinion and national aspiration, a sophisticated élite of English-speaking professional men, and the uncomfortable recognition that even if in the last resort the army could buttress British rule, tranquil and economical governance, as required by the British parliament and taxpayer, depended on engaging the collaboration of Indians in administration and decision-making. The result was a series of constitutional reforms and conventions which culminated in the Government of India Act, 1935. This gave domestic autonomy to provinces which had been ruled by governors working in co-operation with Indian ministers responsible to the local legislatures, expanded the franchise to the provincial and central legislatures, and placed Indian politicians who could mobilize the electorate in positions of considerable power in Delhi and particularly in the provincial capitals. The ICS, once almost totally British, was steadily Indianized by a conscious recruitment policy, well before the Indianization of the officer corps of the army during the war.

The political organization which most articulately and systematically voiced nationalist demands and proved able to mobilize the admittedly small electorate was the Indian National Congress, founded in 1885. From a scrupulously loyal meeting of subjects of the empire it had become between the two world wars the largest pan-Indian force demanding independence. Its tactics ranged from outright co-operation in the reformed legislatures to varieties of non-violent civil disobedience under the guidance of Gandhi, whose spiritual and national vision, strategy of withdrawal of vital co-operation from government, and ability to appeal to a far broader Indian audience, drew to him Indians who were in no sense revolutionary in social or political terms but yearned for their country to have independence from imperial rule.

At the outbreak of the war in Europe in September 1939 Congressmen were in active co-operation with the British, manning the political structures at all levels, learning the procedures of democratic government, and beginning to play a constructive part in government and in the badly-needed processes of social and economic change. The 1935 Act had envisaged an even greater relaxation of control in Delhi, leading ultimately to Dominion status (see UK, 5) once India's princes joined the British provinces in a federation. Certainly the British retained considerable control, particularly over finance and defence; but this was imperial rule of a very different order and feel compared with the years before the First World War. But all this co-operation, and the hope for a future federation, were shattered by the war. Reversion to an older form of imperial control enabled the British to mobilize India for the war, but ultimately it destroyed the Raj.

Congress was internally divided between those committed to non-violence and those who wished to help the Allies at the price of major political concession by the British. From late 1939 to August 1942 Congress's internal debates interlocked with attempts by the British to achieve a new system of co-operation with Indian politicians. The first attempt in October 1939 collapsed, and Congress withdrew its men from all the provincial ministries and the governments they had helped to run, forcing the administration back on the provincial governors' emergency powers of direct rule. In the subsequent year Congress moved towards civil disobedience and, having rejected yet another constitutional offer, embarked on a Gandhian plan of individual protest against the war which was more symbolic than threatening to the structures of the Raj, thus unifying Congress and avoiding repression. The stalemate was broken at the turn of 1941–2 by the entry of the USA into the war, and then the fall of *Singapore in February 1942, followed in March by the fall of Rangoon. Now the British were in grievous danger in India itself, and vulnerable to American criticisms of imperialism and disquiet in their refusal to apply the *Atlantic Charter to India. However, the presence of Churchill as prime minister worked against any radical rethinking of imperial policy towards India; he was profoundly and unrelentingly hostile to Indian national aspirations and fiercely proud of India's imperial role. He only moved in order to soothe American critics and to moderate Indian opinion when it was absolutely necessary to do so.

In March 1942 the cabinet sent Stafford *Cripps to try to achieve a new pattern of co-operation with Indian political groups. The basis of such agreement would be the promise of an electoral body after the war to fashion a new constitution for India, even one that presupposed complete independence, and immediate participation of representative Indians in the viceroy's Executive Council. Despite the genuine advance on the offers made in 1939 and 1940, Congress rejected the plan and the mission ended in bitterness and recrimination. Two major issues dividing Cripps and Congress were whether Indians should have control over military matters during the war, and whether the viceroy would function with his ministers with cabinet-style collective responsibility. From the point of this breakdown, the Raj took no further political initiatives, content to rule where possible with the co-operation of non-Congress groups which would form provincial ministries, or to rely on its constitutional powers for official rule in emergency or in the event of a breakdown in constitutional government. For its part

India, Table 2: Indices of goods available for civil consumption in India 1939–40 to 1945–6 (1938–9 = 100)

	1939–40	*1940–1*	*1941–2*	*1942–3*	*1943–4*	*1944–5*	*1945–6*
Rice	109	92	103	97	121	111	104
Wheat	95	101	91	92	103	97	108
Other cereals	105	116	106	121	118	107	na
Sugar[a]	162	121	86	106	123	95	97
Tea[b]	122	115	93	226	173	31	na
Cotton piece-goods[b]	96	88	84	60	82	81	84
Iron and steel[b]	100	na	81	40	63	63	80
Cement	62	49	47	16	57	55	141
Paper and pasteboard	95	80	59	33	30	39	58
Kerosene	103	97	86	54	42	47	61
Wool manufactures[a]	100	26	31	13	4	18	37

[a] annual pre-war average = 100
[b] in calendar years (viz. 1939–40 = 1939); 1938 = 100

Source: Tomlinson, B. R., *The Political Economy of the Raj*, p. 97.

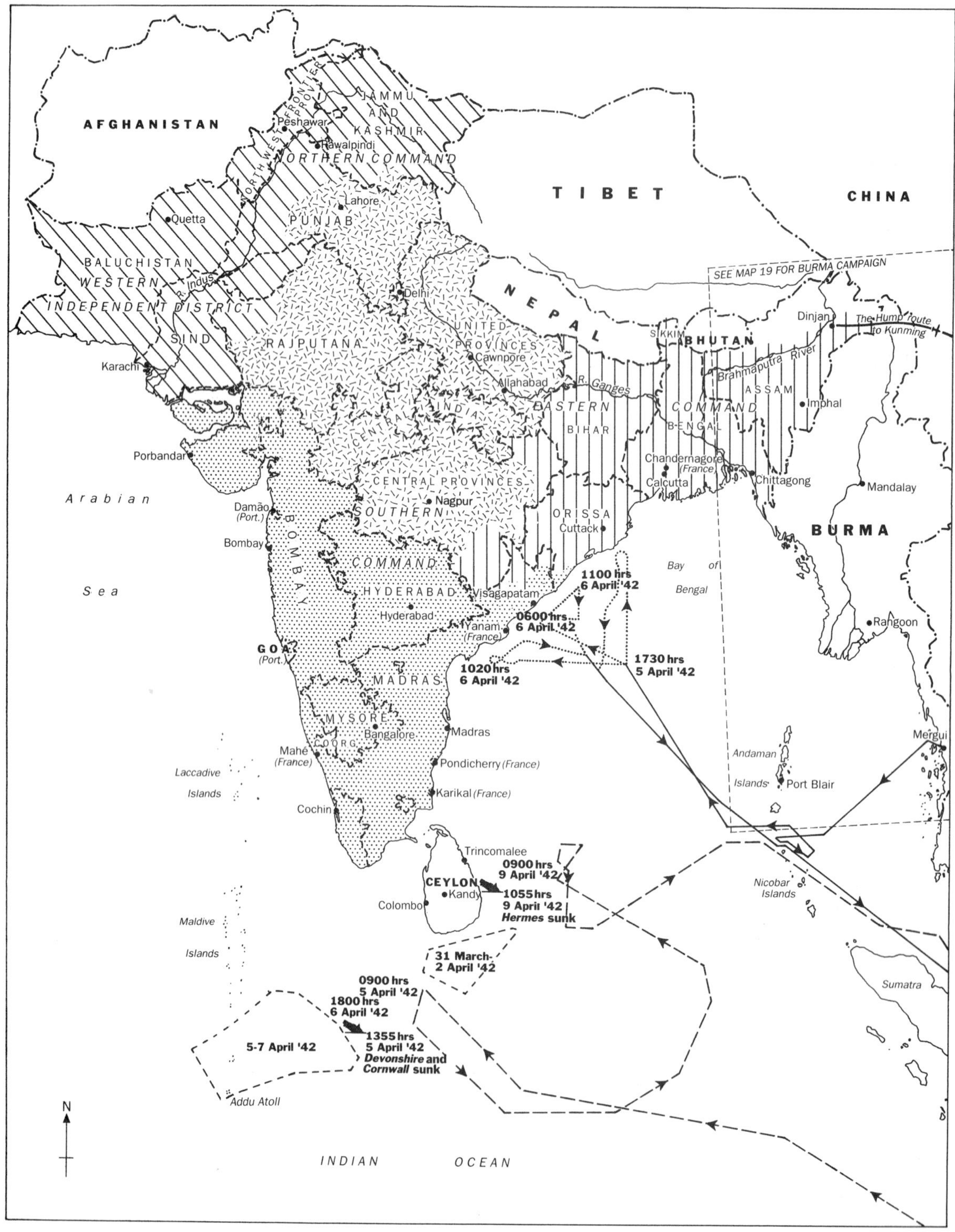

51. Change of command areas in **India** and Japanese attack into Indian Ocean, April 1942

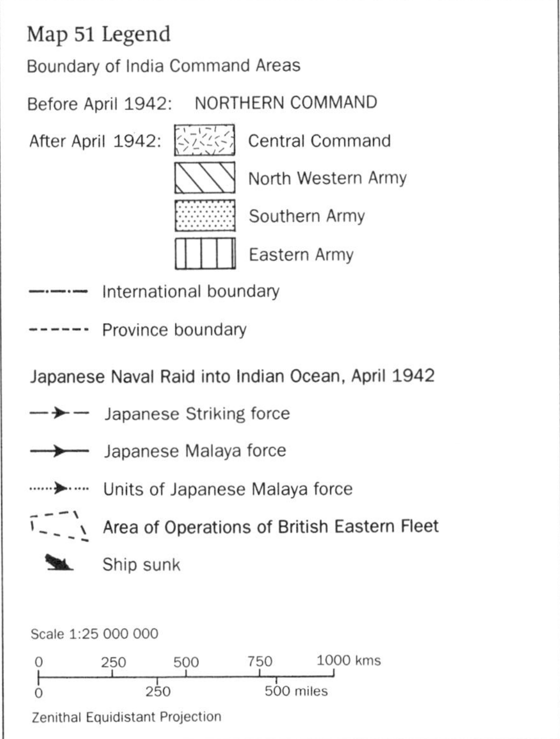

Congress moved towards outright rebellion in the 'Quit India' movement of 1942. Many in Congress were still profoundly uneasy about such a total break with government and negation of constitutional co-operation, and fearful of Japanese invasion if the British were further weakened or India collapsed into disorder. But Gandhi ingeniously devised a formula demanding that the British leave, thus making India less desirable to a potential Japanese invader, yet agreeing that Allied troops should stay on Indian soil for India's defence. Even he hoped for last-minute talks with the viceroy, as had so often happened in the past on the verge of conflict between Congress and government. Instead the government, interpreting the challenge as a mortal betrayal when the empire was in danger, used its draconian emergency powers to ban Congress, break up its organization, and imprison its leadership within hours of the 'Quit India' resolution. Many Congressmen remained incarcerated for the duration of the war, though Gandhi was released in 1944 on grounds of extreme ill-health and frailty. Ironically Congress was in collision with a regime which had abandoned the strategy of *collaboration and was prepared to use force at its hour of greatest danger: at no other time when Congress had clashed with the Raj had the authorities so many troops at their disposal and such a fixity of moral purpose. Bereft of the central leadership which opposed violence and terrorism, and allowed no time for careful planning, the movement disintegrated into localized movements directed by lower-level activists, and was rapidly crushed, with only a sporadic underground still active in 1943. Even so, the destruction and disruption were on a far greater scale than in any of the earlier civil disobedience movements, as was the government's repressive action. Bombay, Eastern United Provinces, and Bihar were the worst affected areas, the last being a particular danger because it imperilled communications with Bengal and Assam which were vital for defence against the Japanese. Government property, post offices, and railways were the prime targets. More than 50 battalions of troops were in turn deployed in suppression, over and above the police force.

In the long term this breakdown of political co-operation was of profound significance, confirming the effects of war on the subcontinent, and on the relations of its peoples with each other and with the British. The experience of 'Quit India' and imperial repression made convinced nationalists of virtually all politically articulate and active people. By 1945 few Indians would have countenanced the survival of the Raj. Congressmen were able to weld themselves on their release into a more powerful and popularly-rooted political party which could far more realistically claim to speak for India's people when they demanded independence. Yet a tragic fissure had also opened up in public life which led eventually to the partition of the subcontinent in 1947 into a secular but predominantly Hindu India and Muslim Pakistan. Muslim unease about Congress priorities and values, and some sectarian violence, had been apparent well before 1939. Yet even by that date Muslims were not a united community with a corporate strategy and a single voice. The British need to seek co-operation in the war effort, and to quieten the predominantly Muslim regions which produced most recruits for the army, and Congress's political self-denying strategy, encouraged the growth of the *Muslim League, under the leadership of M. A. Jinnah (1876–1949), with his call for Pakistan, or a separate homeland for a Muslim nation. In the August offer of 1940 and the Cripps offer of 1942, the British made it plain that no minority would be forced into a unitary independent India. This gave Jinnah and the League a bargaining status which they used with consummate skill. Yet it must be acknowledged that when war ended Muslims were still profoundly divided by region, and few had any precise idea of what Pakistan might mean in practice.

The war also spelled out conclusively that the end of the Raj would come rapidly when hostilities ended. Cripps had made this clear; on that there could be no going back. For not much longer would there be Indians who would co-operate in the imperial structures, and even the loyalties of Indian ICS men were cruelly divided. Further, the war effort had irrevocably weakened the whole imperial machine, despite the temporary reversion to authoritarian government and the apparent

India, Table 3: Defence expenditure in India, 1939–45 (in Rs. crores: 1 crore = 10,000,000)

	1939–40	*1940–1*	*1941–2*	*1942–3*	*1943–4*	*1944–5*	*1945–6*
Chargeable to India	49.54	73.61	103.93	267.14	395.86	458.32	395.33
Chargeable to HMG (London)	–	53.00	194.00	325.48	377.87	410.84	374.53
TOTAL	49.54	126.61	297.93	592.62	773.73	869.16	769.86

Source: Tomlinson, B. R., *The Political Economy of the Raj*, p. 93.

ease of repressive control from 1942. *Wavell, as viceroy, noted the running-down of the administration, and the increasing age and weariness of its members, who had received no new Indian or British recruits during the war. In his view once the war ended, British power to control events had almost disintegrated—a weakening compounded by the dangers of sectarian strife among the civil population, but even more dangerously in the army which ultimately was the bedrock of British power. It would have needed a massive injection of money, manpower, and resources to re-establish British rule; and for this the British public had no stomach, eager rather to welcome its soldiers home and to set about the task of domestic reconstruction.

Another factor was that India, compared with its contribution in the earlier years of the century, had declined in economic value to the UK; and Britain was for the first time India's debtor rather than creditor as a result of the war effort and India's vast sterling balances. In such a situation there could be no reassertion of empire. The end of the Raj in India was also highly significant for the future of Britain's relations with its other colonies and its attempts to construct patterns of world-wide defence. The protection of India and routes to India had been at the heart of imperial expansion in Africa and the Middle East; once India was independent the strategy of expensive imperial control in those areas lost its rationale. India might have been crucial to Allied victory: but the experience of war as it impinged on India helped to demolish the empire and to force the UK to find a new world role after 1947.

4. Armed forces

(a) Army

The Indian Army was a professional volunteer army with a proud tradition, but still in 1939 largely officered by British men who made it their career. It was under the control of a British C-in-C who was also a central figure in the government of the Raj because internal and external security were of paramount importance to British rule. (During the war the most important figures to hold the position of C-in-C were *Auchinleck and Wavell. From October 1943 Indian troops were also under *Mountbatten, the supreme commander of *South-East Asia Command.) However, the need to govern India economically, the wish to conciliate Indian political opinion, and the increasing pressure of Indian politicians over the Indian central budget meant that in practice the Indian Army had become by the outbreak of war old-fashioned in equipment and attitudes, large enough to provide for little more than India's own defence and internal security. In the knowledge of impending war the British planned a rapid and much-needed modernization of the army; and a new agreement was reached between London and Delhi in November 1939, laying down the relative military expenditure of the metropolitan government and the dependency. Basically, India was to pay for its own defence while the UK would pay for modernization, capital outlay for industrial expansion for the war effort, and all costs not deemed essential to India's own interests. Between 1939 and 1946 the UK's share amounted to nearly £1,400 million—for the first time in the Indo-British relationship the UK paying something like a market price for India's contribution to imperial defence. The rise in the government of India's own military expenditure reflected in part the rapid and dramatic increase in the size of the Indian Army (see Table 3).

The C-in-C India was the commander-in-chief of all three services and also the defence member of the viceroy's Executive Council. Directly under him came the Defence Department (War Department from July 1942), the link with the civilian government, the army's GHQ at Delhi, and the HQ of the other two services.

In April 1942, to counter a possible Japanese invasion of India from Burma, the C-in-C India, Wavell, restructured India's defences by abolishing the army's three independent commands (Northern, Eastern, and Southern), and Western Independent District, and replacing them with a new structure (see Map 51). This comprised Central Command, and three armies: North-Western, Southern, and Eastern. It was Eastern Army which attacked into the Arakan in December 1942 and which, in October 1943, became *Slim's Fourteenth Army. In mid-November 1943 the operational responsibilities of GHQ Delhi and air force HQ were transferred to South-East Asia Command (SEAC).

The pre-war Indian Army was structured along British Army lines and had similar regimental traditions. But it was almost feudal in its outlook and personal loyalties, and its rapid expansion—which meant the absorption of a largely uneducated mass of volunteers who reflected

India, Table 4: Indian armed forces recruit intake by provinces and states, 3 September 1939 to 31 August 1945

		Indian States			
Province	*British Territory*	*State*	*Intake*		*Total*
Assam	19,702	Minor States	567	567	20,269
Baluchistan	2,154	Minor States	840	840	2,994
Bengal	171,252	Minor States	4,621	4,621	175,873
Bihar	93,533	Minor States	2,777	2,777	96,310
Orissa	8,142	Minor States	4,254	4,254	12,396
		Hyderabad	22,334		
Bombay	107,117	Kolhapur	7,272	51,482	158,599
		Minor States	21,876		
C.P. & Berar	48,172	Minor States	1,262	1,262	49,434
Coorg	973	–	–	–	973
Delhi	8,058	–	–	–	8,058
		Cochin	20,142		
		Mysore	12,912		
Madras	475,984	Pudukottai	2,856	117,448	593,432
		Travancore	81,291		
		Minor States	247		
N.W.F.P.	95,541	Minor States	7,573	7,573	103,114
		Jammu & Kashmir	65,362		
		Jind	7,907		
Punjab	617,411	Kapurthala	7,154	137,140	754,551
		Nabha	7,063		
		Patiala	30,012		
		Minor States	19,642		
		Alwar	9,518		
		Bharatpur	4,544		
		Bikaner	5,431		
Rajputana	12,418	Jaipur	17,232	77,466	89,884
		Jodhpur	11,627		
		Mewar (Udaipur)	5,069		
		Minor States	24,045		
Sind	9,853	Minor States	622	622	10,475
United Provinces	352,797	Tehri Garhwal	2,646	7,964	360,761
		Minor States	5,318		
Miscellaneous	24,323	–	–	–	24,323
TOTAL INDIAN	2,047,430	–	–	414,016	2,461,446
NEPAL	–	–	–	120,280	120,280
GRAND TOTAL	2,047,430	–	–	534,296	2,581,726

Notes: Above figures include the following:
(i) R.I.N. 28,972[a] (iii) N. Cs. (E) 613,930
(ii) R.I.A.F. 52,845[a] (iv) Civilians 8,980[b]

[a] Intake after 1–2–42 only. Prior to this date personnel were enlisted direct and not included with figures rendered by military recruiting authorities.
[b] Recruited for Ordnance Factories early in the war but not shown separately in return.
Separate details of recruitment from Indian States were not available before July 1942. In order to arrive at the above figure the total intake during the period September 1939 to June 1942 was adjusted on the ratio of actual recruitment between British Territory and Indian States over the period 1–7–1942 to 30–9–1943.

the country's multifarious races, castes, creeds, and languages—created enormous difficulties which took time to overcome. In 1939 it totalled 205,000 Indians, 63,469 British troops, and 83,706 troops from the princely states (see Table 4). But though the other ranks were overwhelmingly Indian, there were very few Indian officers—396 out of 4,424—and the army's complement of officers for its size was half that of the British Army. Despite British insistence (against the legislature's wishes) that it garrison areas of British interest (such as the Anglo-Iranian oilfields), as well as defend India, it was poorly equipped. In September 1939 its cavalry regiments were still mounted; the infantry was without mortars and anti-tank guns; and there was a serious shortage of

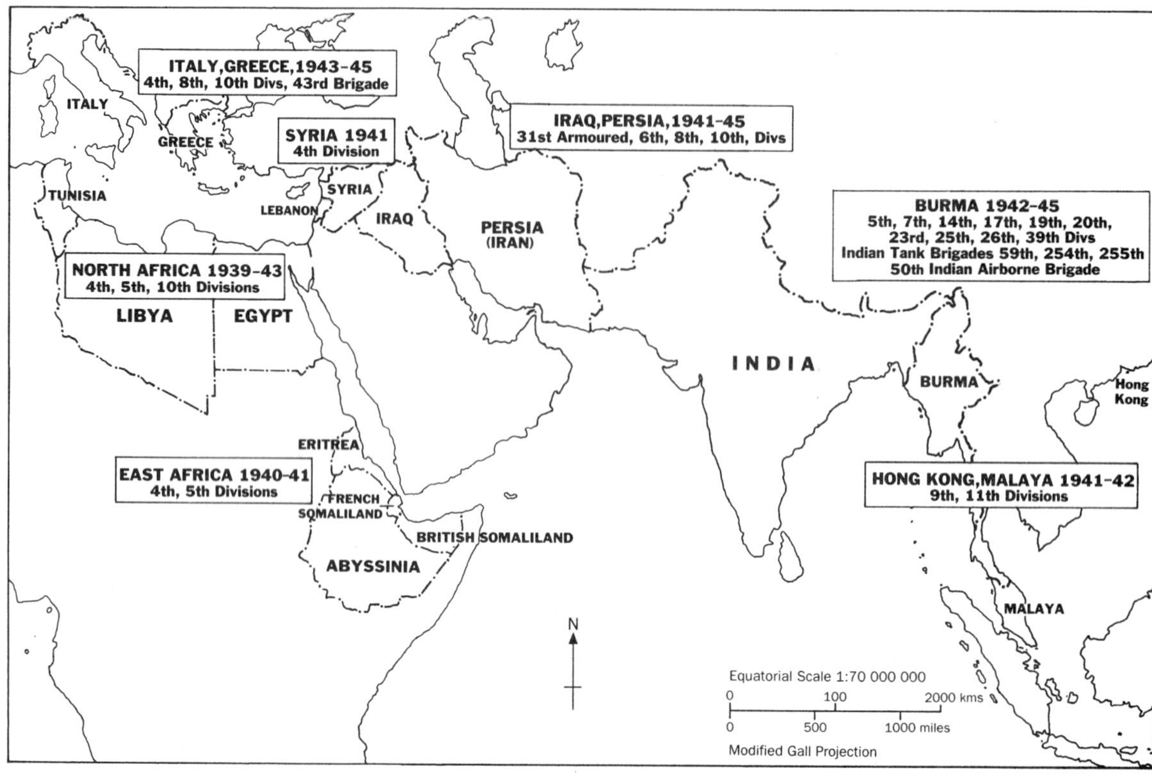

52. Battlegrounds of the **Indian** Army, 1940–5

transport, and of modern signals and engineering equipment.

Four *animal transport companies participated in the fighting that led to the fall of *France in June 1940 and thereafter Indian troops fought in many theatres (see Map 52). In particular, they fought and won the Burma campaign, where they also took part in the two *Chindit operations (out of one million troops commanded by SEAC, 700,000 were Indian).

As men were called to fight, so women increasingly came into the military effort in a wide range of non-combatant support roles as the famous WAC(I)s—the Women's Auxiliary Corps (India). Founded in April 1942, the corps was over 10,000 strong two years later, providing not only a crucial element in India's war role but also giving those involved, Indian and British women alike, a revolutionary expansion of social and professional opportunities compared with their previously circumscribed worlds and limited expectations. Most women served in the army, and a few in the air force, but there was also a naval wing which was renamed the Women's Royal Indian Naval Service in March 1945, though it remained part of WAC(I).

Although morale in the army was problematic before the arrival of Mountbatten as SEAC's invigorating supreme commander, most Indian troops never wavered in their loyalty to India's imperial rulers. The Axis-controlled *Indian Legion and *Indian National Army were never significant military forces, partly because of their numbers, but also because the Axis powers were ambivalent and discouraging about their status and role.

By the end of the war the army's infantry battalions had increased from 113 to 268, and the total numbers, which included 8,300 Indian and 34,500 British officers, had risen to 2,500,000, the largest volunteer army in history. Its casualties amounted to 24,338 killed and more than 64,000 wounded, nearly 12,000 were missing, and nearly 80,000 had been taken prisoner.

(b) Navy

The Royal Indian Navy, only inaugurated in 1934, expanded from 1,708 men in September 1939 to 30,478 in July 1945. From 1939 it assumed responsibility for India's coastal defence, when India no longer contributed to Commonwealth naval defence, and increasingly it became involved in operations and convoy work as far afield as the Mediterranean and the Atlantic. At the start of the war it comprised just 8 small coastal vessels; by its end it had 10 sloops, 3 frigates, 4 corvettes, 17 minesweepers, and a number of smaller warships, and it also had a landing craft wing of 41 boats. In 1940 only one officer in four joining the RIN was Indian; by 1945 this position was almost exactly reversed.

(c) Air force
The Royal Indian Air Force, begun in 1933, expanded from 1,628 men in 1939 to 1,638 officers and 26,900 other ranks in 1945. At the start of the war it did not even have one complete squadron; by 1945 it had nine, three fighter reconnaissance, two ground attack, two light bomber, and two fighter. A shortage of suitable recruits meant that RIAF squadrons also contained RAF personnel, but the number of Indian officers rose from just 14 in September 1939 to 1,375 in September 1945, nine of whom held the rank of wing commander or above.

5. Intelligence
India was the centre for several intelligence organizations. Force 136, the Far East section of *SOE, had its HQ there; the British codebreaking organization at *Bletchley Park had an outstation, the Wireless Experimental Centre, at Delhi, which contributed to the Allied successes in decrypting Japanese Army codes (see ULTRA, 2); and there was also a branch of the Combined Services Detailed Interrogation Centre at Delhi, where Japanese prisoners were interrogated. Tactical military intelligence gathering during the Burma campaign was mostly undertaken by *V-Force personnel.

JUDITH BROWN

Brown, J. M., *Gandhi. Prisoner of Hope* (London, 1989).
Greenough, P. R., *Prosperity and Misery in Modern Bengal: The Famine of 1943–44* (Oxford, 1982).
Tomlinson, B. R., *The Political Economy of the Raj 1914–1947. The Economics of Decolonization in India* (London, 1979).
Voigt, J. H., *India in the Second World War* (New Delhi, 1987).
Ziegler, P., *Mountbatten. The Official Biography* (Glasgow, 1985).

Indian Independence League, the political and propaganda wing of the *Indian National Army which, with Major Fujiwara Iwaichi's F. Kikan organization (see JAPAN, 6), it helped found. A branch of the League was in existence in Tokyo in 1937 and one was formed by a Sikh missionary, Giani Pritam Singh, in Bangkok before the start of the *Malayan campaign in December 1941. Pritam Singh, who had previously organized the anti-British Independent League of India in Bangkok, worked with Fujiwara to undermine the morale of Indian troops during the Malayan campaign and the fall of *Singapore, and to recruit them into the League. After June 1942 the League was the only political organization allowed by the Japanese in Malaya, where it helped alleviate the problems of the Indian community. Other branches quickly sprang up throughout South-East Asia and Subhas Chandra *Bose became its president in July 1943. When Bose founded the Provisional government of Free India in October 1943 it remained in being.

Indian Legion, precursor of the *Indian National Army formed in 1941 by the Indian revolutionary Subhas Chandra *Bose from Indian *prisoners-of-war captured during the *Western Desert campaigns to further his cause for an independent India. Out of 15,000 prisoners 4,000 volunteered. They finished training in December 1942 and three battalions of 1,000 men each were formed, but they were officered by Germans who gave their orders in German. In early 1943 Bose left Germany for Japan to try to realize his ambitions for an independent India and two months after his departure the Legion mutinied as its members wished only to fight the UK, not the USSR. Ten men were shot out of hand and the battalions were then absorbed into the German Army, becoming Infantry Regiment No. 950 which was posted to France. In the summer of 1944 the regiment was absorbed into the Waffen-*SS and its survivors were subsequently put on trial by the British at the Red Fort in Delhi.

Indian National Army (INA), formed by Pritam Singh's *Indian Independence League and Major Fujiwara Iwaichi's F. Kikan (see JAPAN, 6) in February 1942 from Indian Army *prisoners-of-war (POW) captured in the *Malayan campaign and the fall of *Singapore. Later it also included a women's unit, the Rani of Jhansi Regiment, which was named after an Indian heroine of the 1857 Indian Mutiny and was led by a woman doctor from Singapore, Laxmi Swaminathan. The INA (Azad Hind Fauj) failed militarily but not politically, for its existence was influential in gaining India its independence in 1947.

Fujiwara and Pritam Singh worked together during the Malayan campaign to sap the morale of the badly organized Indian troops and to recruit them into Pritam's organization. One POW recruited into the League, a Sikh captain called Mohan Singh, became the INA's first commander and he and Fujiwara spoke of an independent India to a vast throng of Indian prisoners in Singapore where the INA was inaugurated in February 1942. Out of some 60,000 Indian prisoners, about 20,000 volunteered, but in December 1942 Singh, who had become suspicious of Japanese intentions in India, was arrested and the INA was virtually disbanded. However, in June 1943 it was reconstituted when the Indian revolutionary, Subhas Chandra *Bose, took command of it.

Bose wanted the INA to spearhead a Japanese thrust into India as this would result, he predicted, in rebellion against the British. The Japanese were sceptical. They preferred the INA fragmented into small units attached to Japanese formations, employed in sabotage and propaganda and used as guides and interpreters, a role in which they had some success in the *Admin Box battle during the *Burma campaign. A compromise involved some 7,000 INA troops being attached to Japanese units during the *Imphal offensive into India while the rest were used as auxiliaries.

But even the fighting elements of the INA were poorly equipped and trained, and their morale was suspect. During the Imphal offensive more men surrendered or became *deserters than were casualties, and the rest fought no better at *Meiktila when *Slim's Fourteenth Army advanced into Burma. Near Pyu the entire 1st Division of 3,000 men surrendered without firing a shot, as did the 5,000-strong INA garrison at Rangoon. Total casualties amounted to 400 killed and 1,500 dead from other causes, a small loss compared to the 11,000 Indian prisoners-of-war who died in Japanese hands.

After the war, INA survivors were put on trial by the British, and became heroes to many of those who sought India's independence. See also INDIAN LEGION.

Lebra, J., *Jungle Alliance: Japan and the Indian National Army* (Singapore, 1971).

Indian National Congress, political party founded in 1885 to embrace all religions and factions in India. By 1939 it had become the main Hindu political group with a membership of nearly 4.5 million, but its Muslim support had been eroded by the *Muslim League. See also INDIA, 3.

Indian Ocean raid. Having incapacitated the US Pacific Fleet at *Pearl Harbor and supported the invasions of *New Britain and the *Netherlands East Indies, Vice-Admiral *Nagumo's carrier striking force sailed into the Indian Ocean in March 1942 to attack Ceylon (see Map 51). Opposing this Japanese incursion was Admiral *Somerville's British Eastern Fleet, which included five elderly battleships, three carriers, and five cruisers. While Nagumo mounted bombing raids on the island with his aircraft, Vice-Admiral *Ozawa led a smaller number of ships (MALAYA FORCE) into the Bay of Bengal where he destroyed 23 merchantmen, 20 of them in one day, and also bombed the Indian towns of Cocanada and Vizagapatan which caused little damage but much panic. Simultaneously, Japanese submarines added to the toll by torpedoing 32,000 tons of Allied shipping off India's west coast.

Two of Somerville's carriers were new, but his battleships were too old to keep up with them. He therefore planned a pre-emptive night attack that gave some protection from the 300 aircraft of Nagumo's five carriers. From *ULTRA intelligence Somerville expected the attack on 1 April. When that date passed he had to divert his main force to his secret base at Addu Atoll in the Maldive Islands, to refuel and replenish its water supplies, and he sent the small carrier *Hermes*, two cruisers, *Dorsetshire* and *Cornwall*, and the Australian destroyer *Vampire*, to Ceylon for repair and escort duties. On 4 April, while at Addu, Somerville heard that Nagumo had been sighted 565 km. (350 mi.) to the south-east of Ceylon and though he immediately dispatched his ships there he was too late to pre-empt the attack.

Ceylon's Colombo harbour, Nagumo's first target, had been mostly cleared of shipping, but his aircraft, when they raided it on 5 April, sank a destroyer and an *armed merchant cruiser. They also destroyed 27 British aircraft for a loss of 9 of their own. Other Japanese aircraft then sank *Dorsetshire* and *Cornwall* after the two cruisers had left Colombo to rejoin Somerville. Realizing that his carrier aircraft, notably inferior to the Japanese, were unable to protect his battleships, Somerville sent the latter to the Kenyan port of Kilindini (Mombasa) in British East Africa and warned the Admiralty that he could only 'create diversions and false scents, since I am now the poor fox'. However, Nagumo's air reconnaissance failed to find what remained of the British fleet, though on 9 April his bombers raided another Sinhalese port, Trincomalee. These caused widespread damage, and more aircraft and shipping losses, including both *Vampire* and *Hermes*. But luckily for the British the Japanese had not planned to stay, and after this raid both Nagumo, who had lost just seventeen aircraft, and Ozawa withdrew.

Indo-China, see FRENCH INDO-CHINA.

infantry warfare. In 1939 infantry were still the largest single component of an army. Their organization, doctrine, and equipment were heavily influenced by the experiences of the *First World War; indeed, many weapons of that war, and earlier, were still in service. The most important of these were the bolt action rifle and the machine gun, and hand *grenades and *mortars. But as the war progressed the bolt action rifle was increasingly supplemented, or replaced, by carbines and by a variety of other automatic and semi-automatic firearms (see SMALL ARMS for types of weapons used by infantrymen) and by portable anti-tank arms (see PIAT and ROCKET WEAPONS). More importantly, *anti-tank weapons organic to infantry units were disposed in specialist platoons in all armies; and, with the exception of the Red Army, *radio communications were introduced at least down to the level of rifle companies. The infantry's traditional roles persisted: to seize and hold ground; and to deny ground to an enemy. The evolution of trench lines from a network of individual *slit trenches was still envisaged in British, French, and American doctrine. Some believed that infantry machine-guns, behind barbed wire and mines and supported by *artillery and *anti-tank weapons, were still invincible.

The battalion (see FORMATIONS AND UNITS, Chart 3) remained the operational unit, which fought collectively in brigades or regiments—this latter term being used in the international as distinct from the British sense, that is, a formation of three battalions, similar to a brigade—within infantry divisions. The evolving mechanized formations disposed motorized infantry, mounted to maintain the pace of armour (see TANKS), and specialist units such as machine-gun battalions and heavy mortar and anti-tank companies. Otherwise, infantry marched unless contingencies demanded otherwise. The transport of infantry divisions in some national armies, for example, that of Germany, was horse-drawn throughout the war (see ANIMALS).

Germany had concentrated its mobility in armoured or mechanized divisions (see BLITZKRIEG). The success of these in the *Polish campaign and the fall of *France showed that conventional infantry defences could readily be broken by mobile striking power, suggesting that tanks had supplanted infantry as the decisive

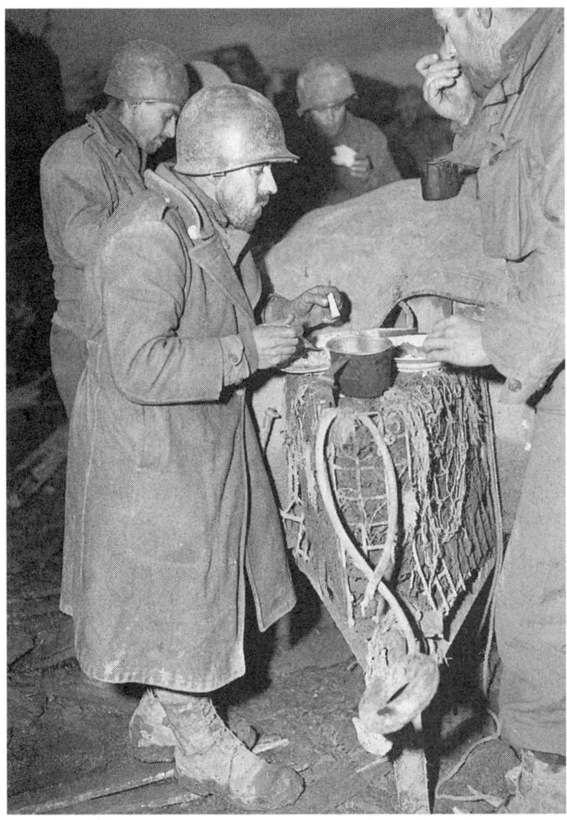

Infantry warfare nearly always produced the highest rate of battle fatigue and casualties. Here, exhausted US Army infantrymen snatch a meal during the Huertgen Forest battle, September–December 1944.

fighting arm. Subsequent campaigns showed that this belief was ill-founded. Infantry were inevitably the primary arm in jungle operations, in mountains, and in some phases of winter warfare before heavy snow packed down. Even in open country, where armour could develop sweeping manoeuvres, infantry frequently provided the means of breaching enemy defensive positions. They were essential in holding key ground and, between offensives, maintaining covering lines.

In the *Western Desert campaigns, British tanks and infantry worked successfully as a team against the Italians. However, by early 1942, after struggles with the Germans, British armoured commanders had come to regard the infantry as an appendage. Motor battalions were needlessly hazarded, left to hold ground, for example, without adequate anti-tank defence, a mistake *Montgomery corrected when he took command of the Eighth Army in August 1942. He demonstrated the value of infantry strongholds, when they were properly supported, to inhibit enemy armoured thrusts. Later, he employed his infantry offensively at night to break open Axis defences for the launching of armour. Much of his success was due to using the potential of each fighting arm to best advantage.

German commanders employed this principle from the outset of the war. Though the quality of their tanks and anti-tank guns was generally superior, their early victories owed much to judicious grouping and regrouping of armour and mechanized infantry. They enhanced their gains by expecting junior commanders to seize local initiatives.

The Japanese succeeded in winning all the opening rounds of 1941–2 with inferior numbers. Their infantry leadership was seasoned after ten years of fighting in China (see MANCHUKUO and CHINA INCIDENT), but they had no experience of jungle warfare. In 1941, after an intense study of requirements, they converted five infantry divisions to this role. Their mastery of movement and navigation in dense foliage was enhanced by the quality of their junior leaders, the hardihood of all ranks and their capacity for night attacks. Shock frontal action, using light tank support, and the frequent encirclement of their opponents, cutting off their retreat, carried the Japanese infantry to triumphs in the *Malayan and *Burma campaigns, and in the *Netherlands East Indies. Similar tactics were successful in the first of the *Philippines campaigns and the tactic of encirclement was not overcome by the Allies until they had developed the technique of supplying their troops from the air (see CHINDITS, for example).

These early reverses obliged the Allies to analyse their weaknesses as they mustered huge forces for counter-offensives. The British infantry began this after *Dunkirk. They concluded that while their basic principles were sound, command procedures were ponderous, battalions were not mentally and physically attuned to combat, and their organic anti-tank capability was inadequate.

From brigade level downwards, battle procedures were sharpened. 'Battle drills' were instituted within battalions to inculcate the responsibilities of each member down to the rifleman and light machine gunner. Tactical doctrine was widely revised. For example, the sound principle that a commanding officer laid out his defences on his machine-guns was amended; in open country he was to lay them out on his anti-tank resources. The battle drills obliged rifle companies and even platoons to organize all-round defence of their positions; and to practise frequently the simple manoeuvres of 'fire and movement' in attack from the rifle section upwards. New standards of physical fitness led to greater energy in fieldcraft, in alertness for observation, and in strength to carry and use effectively the range of infantry weapons. Live rounds were introduced into certain field exercises; given sensible precautions, commanding officers were excused occasional casualties. The quality of training was raised by forming 'Battle Schools' for leaders to develop expertise and initiative. A new range of training pamphlets, using cartoons and sketches as much as words to illustrate lessons, was issued widely. Those officers who could not adjust adequately to the new dynamics were replaced. The average age of commanding officers fell by 1943 from 40 to 30 years.

The tactical lessons learned by British, Australians, and New Zealanders in Europe and Africa were circulated among the other Allies. Some were adopted by the USA as the small US Army began its huge expansion programme in 1942. But scale there necessitated individual training en masse; a single infantry instructor would take a class of as many as 200 men at a time. Comprehension levels were thus patchy, performance often indifferent. The American command system tended, moreover, to centralize authority. Battle experience remedied some of these weaknesses but at some considerable cost. Surprisingly, losses due to poor defences did not persuade American infantry to dig *'foxholes' as a matter of routine in exposed areas. S. L. A. Marshall in his book *Men Against Fire* (New York, 1947) records that no more than a quarter of US infantrymen, in whichever theatre they fought, actually fired their weapons during a battle. This was due to the low status of the junior non-commissioned officer in a rapidly and hugely expanded US Army—though not in the US Marine Corps. His responsibility was minimal, and training as a fire team leader or section/squad commander inadequate. The contrary was true in, for example, the German and British armies in which junior NCOs were specially selected, trained, and accustomed to responsibility and respect. In the Japanese Army, ardour for combat was instilled during training to the point that it was not uncommon for junior officers to be borne prematurely into an assault by their men.

By 1944, however, infantry expertise was rising among the Allies in many environments. Experience had been gained, for example, in street fighting, exemplified by the struggle for *Stalingrad. Commanders learned that cities absorbed great numbers of infantrymen. Among buildings, struggles were at close quarters; success more than ever depended upon the resolve and enterprise of company and platoon commanders. The grenade and machine carbine were key weapons in this type of fighting. By 1944, the techniques of mountain warfare had also been learned by the Allies while forcing a way forward through the Apennines during the *Italian campaign. Mules were required to supply remote positions, and when these were on precipitous heights, infantrymen in reserve turned porter for their comrades in the line. In summer, water supply was a particular problem. Men shaved in their tea or coffee dregs.

Winter conditions in Italy were severe but tolerable in comparison to those on the Eastern Front where Soviet infantry were used to attack on winter nights, often en masse. In summer and autumn they maintained defensive lines in the same way as their German counterparts, from which armoured forces made grand sorties. These lines were highly developed with deep bunkers behind trench networks. Approaches were obstructed by anti-tank and anti-personnel mines and barbed wire, and covered by anti-tank guns and machine-guns. Even in 'quiet times', local attacks to capture points of advantage were frequent. Casualties dwindled during deep winter for armoured units but not for the infantry. Battlefield promotions to commissioned ranks were commonplace among Red Army battalions.

In the *Pacific war, as in the Mediterranean and Europe, a comprehensive organization was developed for *amphibious warfare. Infantry were required to assault across beaches to secure bridgeheads. Portable *flame-throwers had been developed for use against fortifications and bunkers. They were valued notably by US Marine Corps and Army infantry rooting out obdurate Japanese defenders in beach and jungle strong-points.

During the closing stages of the war, the availability of fire-power from artillery and air support, and the extension and refinement of weapons and equipment eased the Allied infantrymen's burden considerably, as the lack of these contributed to the defeat of their opponents. Road and air transport had improved supply in Europe and the Far East respectively. Operational efficiency and co-operation between all Arms was greater than in any previous conflict. It is noteworthy that five years later in Korea, and in the development of NATO (North Atlantic Treaty Organization) forces, many lessons learned had to be rediscovered, not least the need for infantry and armour to work as a team.

Anthony Farrar-Hockley

Hayasi, H., *Kogun: The Japanese Army in the Pacific War* (Quantico, Va., 1959).
Kippenberger, H., *Infantry Brigadier* (London, 1949).
Slim, W., *Defeat into Victory* (London, 1956).
Werth, A., *Russia at War* (London, 1964).
Zaloga, S., *The Polish Campaign* (London, 1985).

Inönü, Ismet (1884–1973), president of Turkey from 1938 to 1950, and successor of Turkey's first president, Mustafa Kemal Atatürk (1881–1938), whose policies of secularizing the country he continued. His success in maintaining the country's neutrality almost throughout the war, despite intense pressure from both the Axis and the Allies, 'must be regarded,' wrote an obituarist, 'as one of the most skilful operations of its kind.' As part of the *economic warfare they were waging against Germany, the Allies persuaded Inönü in 1944 to cut down on Turkish exports of chrome to Germany, which helped to deprive Hitler of this much-needed strategic *raw material. That August Inönü broke off diplomatic relations with Berlin and in the following February declared war on Germany so as to allow Turkey to attend the *San Francisco conference, the founding meeting of the United Nations, although no Turkish forces saw active service.

Intelligence, see for example ABWEHR, COUNTER-INTELLIGENCE CORPS, KEMPEI, MI5, MI6, RSHA, SECURITY INTELLIGENCE MIDDLE EAST, SPIES, TOKKŌ, and the Intelligence section of major powers. See SIGINT for examples of signals intelligence entries; see also SIGNALS INTELLIGENCE WARFARE.

interallié was the Franco-Polish intelligence circuit founded in Paris in the autumn of 1940 by Roman *Garby-Czerniawski, a Polish pilot who had escaped from the defeat of Poland. He secured touch with the Polish *government-in-exile in London; of which the intelligence branch worked in close co-operation with *MI6. *Interallié* produced some useful naval intelligence from agents in Brest and other ports, data about Luftwaffe installations in northern France that were useful to the RAF, and indications of the eastward shift of German forces in the first half of 1941, in preparation for *BARBAROSSA.

The network collapsed in the autumn of that year. The wireless operator was caught by direction-finding, at his set in Montmartre; Mathilde *Carré who was arrested with him promptly became a *double agent; most of their companions were rounded up. The Germans used *Interallié*'s wireless to feed disinformation to the Admiralty about **Scharnhorst* and *Gneisenau*'s readiness for sea (see CERBERUS). They also believed they had made a double agent out of Garby-Czerniawski, whom they allowed to escape to England; where he at once turned *triple, and proved a useful channel for the British *XX-committee. M. R. D. FOOT

Garby-Czerniawski, R., *The Big Network* (London, 1961).

Inter-Allied Services Department, see SPECIAL OPERATIONS AUSTRALIA.

International Labour Organization, agency of the *League of Nations which remained active when the League became moribund. Its objectives were the improvement of working conditions world-wide by democratic means, the promotion of social progress, and ending colonial exploitation. The USA, though it never joined the League, became a member in 1934 and others who resigned from the League retained their membership of the ILO. Two members of the *Rote Drei espionage network worked at its head office in Geneva.

International Monetary Fund, see BRETTON WOODS CONFERENCE.

International Red Cross Committee, body based in Geneva comprising not more than 25 Swiss citizens who, with the Red Cross societies of individual countries and the League of National Red Cross Societies, make up the International Red Cross. It was started in 1863 when a committee of five 'for succouring the wounded' was organized in Geneva by a Swiss, Henri Dunant, who was much influenced by the work of Florence Nightingale in the Crimean war and by the scenes he had witnessed after the battle of Solferino in 1859. Following the committee's first meeting national societies were founded in many countries, the first *Geneva Convention was signed in 1864, and the Geneva branch developed into the International Committee.

The Red Cross flag, the Swiss flag reversed, came to be universally acknowledged as a sign which should protect ships, hospitals, medical personnel, and ambulances from attack. Though it was emphasized that the cross had no religious significance, the Turkish government later adopted a red crescent, the Iranians used a red lion and sun, and the Israelis a red Star of David.

In September 1939 the committee placed itself at the service of all belligerent countries 'to contribute,' it stated in a letter, 'in a humanitarian way, in its traditional role and with all its resources, towards lessening the evils brought by war.' It organized a central agency for information about *prisoners-of-war (POW), transmitting 120 million messages; arranged the exchange of sick and wounded POW, and of medical personnel; forwarded 36 million parcels to POW; co-ordinated unofficial relief measures; and its delegates made thousands of inspection visits to POW and *internment camps. It arranged that interned civilians received the same treatment as POW, but the Jews in *concentration camps were beyond its help, for those running the German Red Cross were active Nazi Party supporters who, in line with Hitler's *Night and Fog Decree, ensured that no information would be given about any prisoners in these camps.

The committee had no powers of compulsion with countries such as Japan and the USSR, which were not parties to the 1929 Geneva Convention. But it used the bargaining point of reciprocity when negotiating with powers to uphold the Geneva Conventions regarding prisoners, and it also carried moral weight in the world community. By the end of the war it had 145 permanent delegations, all Swiss. They were mostly doctors but also included lawyers, engineers, and businessmen, who would liaise with the Red Cross societies of the countries they were in.

internment of civilian nationals belonging to the opposing side was undertaken with varying degrees of severity by all the belligerent powers, though in Brazil some Japanese communities remained unmolested and even managed to improve their lot. Internment was also usually the fate of the armed forces personnel of combatant nations who, through the hazards of war, accidentally found themselves in a neutral country, and the Germans interned a number of prominent politicians of occupied countries, some of them in *concentration camps.

The *Geneva Conventions did not cover non-combatant enemy aliens. However, at the start of the war the *International Red Cross Committee obtained from belligerent countries an agreement that interned civilians, including merchant seamen, should have the same protection as *prisoners-of-war. It was therefore sometimes better for civilians to be interned as their camps were inspected, and they received mail, food parcels, and other forms of relief, while those who merely suffered restrictions of their freedom did not have these advantages. In Italy, for example, enemy aliens were banished to small mountain villages where sufficient food and warm clothing were hard to obtain. Not for nothing were they known as *isolati*.

In Germany and the UK only those thought to constitute a danger were immediately interned when war was declared in September 1939, the remainder being allowed to return to their own countries. However, in France male refugees from Germany and what had been Austria were interned immediately and when the Germans launched their May 1940 offensive (see FALL GELB) fear of *fifth columnists led to a wave of arrests, some quite unjust, in Belgium, France, and the Netherlands, resulting in the dispatch of trainloads of civilians to internment camps near the Pyrenees. After the fall of *France, when these countries had been overrun by the Germans, male civilians of Allied countries were confined to internment camps, or Ilags (*Interniertenlager*), in France and Germany, but most women remained free. However, in the Channel Islands German policy was much harsher, and in 1942–3 2,350 men, women, and children who had not been born there were sent to internment camps in Germany.

When war broke out special tribunals in the UK classified all enemy aliens into three categories. Those in 'A' (569) were interned as a possible security risk, those in 'B' (6,782) were subject to certain restrictions, while those in 'C' (66,000) remained without restrictions, 55,457 of this last category being recognized as *refugees from Nazi oppression. But in May 1940 rumours about fifth columnists altered the perception the British had of aliens in their midst. The home secretary, John Anderson (1882–1958), urged on by the press and the military, had every male alien between 16 and 70 removed from designated 'protected areas' around most of the coastline, and all German and Austrian nationals living there were interned. Internment of all 'B' category male Germans and former Austrians, aged 16–60, followed and after France fell nearly all 'C' category males were also interned.

Many internees in the UK were confined to camps on race courses, or in partially completed housing estates, or were sent to the Isle of Man. But some were shipped abroad and when one ship, the *Arandora Star*, was torpedoed 661 people died. When the surviving internees reached Canada genuine refugees initially had to live with Nazi supporters. Internees were also shipped to Australia in the *Dunera*, and these suffered humiliating conditions and treatment, many having their possessions stolen or thrown overboard by their British guards.

This mass internment and deportation caused an outcry in parliament and from August 1940 internees began to be released. By February 1941 more than 10,000 had been freed and by the following summer only 5,000 remained in the camps. Many of those released subsequently served with the British armed forces.

Within the first few days of Japan and the USA entering the war in December 1941 some 3,846 Germans, Italians, and Japanese had been arrested in the USA as 'dangerous enemy aliens'—though the criteria used by the FBI (see USA, 6) to label them thus remain unknown to this day—and *Japanese-Americans were later forced to move from the West Coast and were interned inland as were *Japanese-Canadians. In the Philippines Japanese civilians were not well treated—five were killed by their Filipino guards after an air raid—which resulted in American civilians receiving similar treatment when they were interned in the Philippines after Japanese occupation of the islands. But until the treatment of interned Japanese-Americans became known the 12,500 US citizens in Japanese-occupied countries were often ignored. Very few lost their liberty entirely, and in Shanghai Americans still retained their legal rights, but by March 1943 all citizens of Allied countries had been interned.

The number of British and Dutch civilians trapped by the Japanese invasion of European colonies far outnumbered American internees and Japanese treatment of them was immediately harsh. There were 30,000 Dutch internees in Java alone; 3,250 British in Hong Kong's Stanley peninsula camp, and another 4,500 in Singapore, including about 300 children; while those civilians, about 1,500 or so, who fled from Singapore by boat were eventually interned on Sumatra. As with so many prisoners-of-war in the Far East, many did not survive their ordeal. See also WOMEN AT WAR.

Collar, H., *Captive in Shanghai* (Oxford, 1990).
Gilman, L. and P., *'Collar the Lot!'* (London, 1980).
Pearl, C., *The Dunera Scandal* (Sydney, 1983).

Inter-Services Security Board, British intelligence organization established in February 1940 to be responsible for the security of, and *deception for, British war plans to intervene in the *Finnish–Soviet war. It came under the Joint Intelligence Committee (see UK, 8) and comprised representatives from *MI5, *MI6 and all three services. At the end of 1941 when the London Controlling Section was formed to control strategic deception its brief was confined to such matters as issuing *codenames and controlling the distribution of classified documents and maps. But it remained the co-ordinating body for the security of all operations and when *Mountbatten failed to inform it of the *Dieppe raid its powers were strengthened. It subsequently co-ordinated security precautions for such operations as the *North African campaign landings and *OVERLORD.

intruder operations, night fighter sorties to shoot down bombers when they were at their most vulnerable, that is, taking off or landing. See also FIGHTERS, 2.

Ionian Islands. Six of these Greek possessions, Corfu, Paxos, Leucas, Ithaca, Cephalonia, and Zante, are situated off the western coast of Greece. The seventh, Cerigo, is off the southern coast of the Peloponnese. They were occupied by the Italians after the *Balkan campaign and the garrisons of the largest ones—Corfu, Leucas, Cephalonia, and Zante—were all overwhelmed by the Germans after the Italian *armistice in September 1943. On Cephalonia the Italians resisted strongly until they ran out of ammunition. More than a thousand were killed in the battle and subsequently thousands more were shot out of hand.

IRA, see IRISH REPUBLICAN ARMY.

Iran, see PERSIA.

Iraq, a former Turkish province under the Ottoman Empire, was a British mandate until 1932 when it gained full independence and joined the *League of Nations. However, the 1930 Anglo-Iraqi Treaty reserved for the British important strategic, economic, and diplomatic privileges which caused resentment and unrest. These included a commercial interest in the Mosul and Kirkuk oilfields, which in 1940 produced 2.5 million tons of oil, and the right to pass troops through the country and to maintain air bases near Basra and at Habbaniya.

By September 1939 the country was ruled by a regent, Emir Abdullah, with a government headed by the pro-British Nuri es-Sa'id. He wished to declare war on Germany, but nationalist factions wanted to extract concessions from the British first. Eventually Nuri followed Egypt's lead and merely broke off diplomatic relations. In March he was replaced by *Rashid Ali but remained in the government as foreign minister.

Rashid Ali was the political mouthpiece of a pro-Nazi military junta, known as the Golden Square, and for a time Iraqi sentiment was openly pro-Axis—for example, diplomatic relations with Italy were not broken off—with Rashid Ali intriguing against the British. But in January 1941, following successes by *Wavell in the *Western Desert campaigns, he resigned and his replacement moved against the Golden Square. A military coup followed, the regent fled, and on 3 April 1941 Rashid Ali became prime minister again. Encouraged by hints of Axis aid, he refused the British their rights under the Anglo-Iraqi Treaty to move troops through the country and Iraqi troops surrounded the British air base at Habbaniya, some 40 km. (25 mi.) west of Baghdad. German aircraft were flown via Syria to help support the Iraqi Army, and some did intervene in the fighting in mid-May. The *Vichy French authorities in Syria also supplied *matériel*, but it was soon obvious that the Germans had moved too slowly and the Iraqis too fast. Indian troops were landed at Basra and a 5,800-strong British relief force (HABFORCE), which included 1,500 men of the Arab Legion from Transjordan, moved into Iraq (see Map 102). The Iraqi army of five conscript divisions was no match for the invading forces. The small Iraqi Air Force of 56 mostly obsolete aircraft was quickly destroyed and within a month Habbaniya had been relieved, Baghdad surrounded, and an *armistice signed. The regent returned and in October 1941 Nuri became prime minister of a pro-British administration which declared war on the Axis in January 1943. See also ANTI-IMPERIALISM.

Ireland, see EIRE and UK, 4.

Irgun (Irgun Zvai Leumi, or National Military Organization). Jewish organization, also called Etzel, which was formed in Palestine in 1937 by extremist elements of *Haganah B to undertake reprisals for Arab attacks. After May 1939 it also carried out sabotage and bomb attacks against British targets to show its dislike of British immigration policies. But once the war started it declared a truce and its leader, David Razi'el, was killed in Iraq while on a mission for the British. This, and the formation of the *Stern Gang, which split its ranks, left it temporarily immobilized. But in the USA, after the *Bermuda conference of April 1943, members founded the Emergency Committee for the Rescue of European Jews which drew wide publicity. In December 1943 Menachem *Begin, a member of *Anders' Army temporarily stationed in Palestine, assumed the leadership of Irgun. He cut all ties with the Haganah and, in a campaign for an independent Jewish state, resumed attacks on British installations and police stations, obtaining funds by extortion and intimidation. The *Jewish Agency eventually neutralized the Irgun, but a post-war revival of its activities included blowing up part of Jerusalem's King David Hotel in July 1946.

Irish Republican Army (IRA), formed during the *First World War to fight the British for Irish independence. It continued to fight them after 1918 to make Eire a republic and to coerce them into leaving Northern Ireland (see UK, 4).

In January 1939 the IRA started a bombing campaign on the British mainland which continued until heightened security stopped it at the end of the year. On both sides of the Irish border the police acted promptly against the IRA when the war broke out. Many IRA suspects were interned, and an IRA raid on an army magazine in Dublin resulted in a further round-up. In August 1940 the organization's chief of staff, Sean Russell, died while returning to Eire from Germany in a U-boat and in 1941 his successor, Stephen Hayes, was accused by the leader of the IRA in Northern Ireland of being an informer. He was kidnapped and tortured by the IRA, but managed to escape; this led to a loss of public sympathy and the capture of the remaining IRA leaders.

In February 1939 the *Abwehr sent an agent to discuss co-operation between the Germans and the IRA, and an IRA member then travelled to Germany three times to seek arms and financial assistance. To the annoyance of the German minister in Dublin, who knew that aiding and abetting subversion by the IRA could only help the Allied cause, several more Abwehr agents did arrive with radio transmitters and funds during the course of the war. All were captured and virtually nothing was gained by either party, one agent describing the IRA as rotten at its roots.

Iron Cross, see DECORATIONS, GERMANY.

Iron Guard, military wing of the Romanian fascist movement, the Legion of St Michael. It briefly shared power with *Antonescu in 1940 before being suppressed. See also ROMANIA, 3.

Ironside, Field Marshal Sir Edmund (1880–1959), British army officer who served as *Chief of the Imperial General Staff (CIGS) from 3 September 1939 to 27 May 1940.

In 1938 Ironside became governor of Gibraltar, expecting it to be his last post before retirement. But in May 1939 the war minister, *Hore-Belisha, appointed him Inspector General of Overseas Forces and on 3 September Ironside succeeded *Gort as CIGS. He soon proved as temperamentally unsuited to this task as his immediate predecessor, whose dislike of Hore-Belisha he shared. He chafed at the government's inactivity during the *phoney war and supported plans for cutting off German iron ore supplies that precipitated the ill-fated *Norwegian campaign. His assessments of Hitler's plans in the west, and the Allies' ability to counter any offensive, were inadequate and he proved unequal to the task of pleasing Churchill when the latter became prime minister on 10 May 1940. He was replaced by *Dill and made C-in-C Home Forces, a post he held for under two months before he was succeeded by *Brooke, promoted field marshal, and retired. He was knighted in 1919 and created a baron in 1941.

Keegan, J. (ed.), *Churchill's Generals* (London, 1991).
Macleod, R., and Kelly, D. (eds.), *The Ironside Diaries* (London, 1962).

island hopping was a technique developed by US forces in the *Pacific war in which Japanese island garrisons were bypassed and isolated. It was also used with great effect in the *New Guinea campaign at *Hollandia.

Ismay, General Hastings (1887–1965), British Army officer who served as Churchill's chief of staff in his capacity as minister of defence. He handled the relationship between Churchill and the British *Chiefs of Staff with great aplomb and Churchill trusted him totally. His position was unique and he spent, as he said, 'the whole war in the middle of the web'. He was promoted lt-general in 1942 and general in 1944. He was never knighted but was created a baron in 1947.

The Memoirs of Lord Ismay (London, 1960).

Itagaki Seishiro, General (1885–1948), Japanese Army officer born in Iwate prefecture, who graduated from the military academy and the war college (*Rikugun daigaku*). After regimental service, he became assistant military attaché in China. By 1930 he had been promoted to chief of staff of the *Kwantung Army in which capacity he plotted, along with Colonel Ishiwara Kanji, the Manchurian Incident which was planned to give Japan greater control over the area (see MANCHUKUO). After the establishment of Manchukuo, in whose creation he was again a key figure, he became senior adviser in the military administration. Following a period as divisional commander, he joined the first cabinet of Prince *Konoe as war minister in 1937.

When Japan became involved from July 1937 onwards in the *China Incident, Itagaki became the minister responsible for the campaign in central China which by the middle of 1938 had reached stalemate. As a result, Konoe offered the resignation of his government in January 1939, but Itagaki stayed on as war minister under the successor prime minister, Baron Hiranuma Kiichirō (1867–1952). In this capacity he fought for Japan to enter into a military alliance with Germany but felt betrayed by the *Nazi–Soviet Pact of August 1939, which led to the resignation of the government. Itagaki was then posted to the China Expeditionary Army as its chief of staff where he served until July 1941 when, as a full general, he became C-in-C of Japanese forces in Korea. In mid-1945 he became commander of the Seventh Area Army in Malaya where he surrendered on behalf of the Southern Expeditionary Armies on 12 September 1945. He was subsequently tried at the *Far East War Crimes trials, sentenced to death, and hanged. IAN NISH

Italian campaign (see Maps 53–5). This period of the war has never ceased to excite harsh judgements. It was a hurried and improvised attempt to exploit the Axis collapse in the *North African campaign by carrying the war to the northern shores of the Mediterranean. The initial decision to strike at Sicily was agreed upon at the Casablanca conference in January 1943, (see SYMBOL), but a definite agreement to invade Italy was not secured until the second Washington conference in May (see TRIDENT). Once the Axis forces had surrendered in North Africa, the Allies had to be seen to be doing something to continue Germany's defeat on land. The only alternative was to bring the Allied troops, flushed with victory, home to the UK, an immensely complex task which would have left these experienced forces in unjustifiable idleness for twelve months.

The strategic logic underlying the employment of Allied forces in the Mediterranean basin appeared overwhelming to the British *Chiefs of Staff, especially the *Chief of the Imperial General Staff (CIGS), General *Brooke. The aim of an Italian campaign was to distract German forces from France and the Eastern Front. It would prepare the ground for *OVERLORD (the landings in Normandy) and perhaps contribute to a decisive Axis defeat in the east. At TRIDENT the British chiefs declared that 'the Mediterranean offers us opportunities for action in the coming autumn which may be decisive ... If we take these opportunities, we shall have every chance of breaking the Axis and of bringing the war to a successful conclusion in May 1944'. But their plan at this

Monte Cassino town, with the monastery above it, which was the scene of some the most bitter fighting during the **Italian campaign**.

stage was to get an army north of Florence in the shortest possible time to strike at Germany's vulnerable southern flank. They did not envisage fighting up every inch of the Italian peninsula.

Because of American scepticism, the eventual decision to invade was hedged about with qualifications. At the operational level, the aim of the Italian campaign was never clearly stated. All planners were agreed that speed and surprise were of the essence, but this would be achieved by the most hazardous and intricate of all military operations—*amphibious landings. They agreed, too, that adequate tactics would have to be improvised in a mountainous theatre of war quite unsuited to mobile warfare. These contradictions led to a great deal of muddle and miscalculation. The problems emerged clearly during the *Sicilian campaign of July 1943 (HUSKY) which ended with the Germans making an orderly withdrawal across the strait of Messina.

Sicily set the scene for the Italian campaign. Despite Allied command of the air and excellent intelligence, the Germans always escaped to fight another day. The invasion of the mainland was delayed by haggling over whether the Italian peace terms were consistent with the doctrine of *unconditional surrender announced at Casablanca. The Germans moved sixteen divisions into Italy during this interlude. The Allied invasion plan envisaged a pincers movement across the straits of Messina, with landings near *Reggio di Calabria by the Eighth Army (BAYTOWN) and a landing by the Fifth US Army south of Naples at *Salerno (AVALANCHE). The former was an object lesson in over-insurance, as the crossing was unopposed; the latter a careless, complacent scramble. Once the news of the Italian surrender was announced on the evening of 8 September, Allied troops expected the Salerno landing at 0330 the next morning to be unopposed. Instead, they were almost driven into the sea for, as at the start of the Sicilian campaign, the available force was spread over too wide an area. The beachhead only survived because the German counter-attack was too weak to destroy it. But

Salerno convinced Hitler that the strategy advocated by *Kesselring, commander of Army Group C defending Italy, was correct: every inch of ground should be contested, and orders were issued for the construction of the *Gustav Line south of Rome.

Each battle thenceforth sought to break gaps in the German defences; the campaign was transformed into a remorseless, attritional grind. A foretaste of the great battles of *Monte Cassino was savoured during the frustrating fighting on the banks of the Garigliano and Sangro rivers in the autumn. 'I don't think we can get any spectacular results', Montgomery reported to Brooke, 'so long as it goes on raining; the whole country becomes a sea of mud and nothing on wheels can move off the roads.' But both the weather and the terrain were to deteriorate as the winter wore on. The four great battles of Cassino (12 January–18 May 1944) brought to a head all the muddles and contradictions of the Italian campaign. Alexander, commanding the two Allied armies, was given no operational aim or timetable to fulfil it. His attacks were uncoordinated and often too weak for a decisive breakthrough. The Allies consistently underrated the defensive skill of the Germans. Central Italy was ideal defensive terrain, and because of the hard rock the attacking troops could not dig in. At Cassino, the Allies were drawn into fighting a battle of attrition under the most disadvantageous circumstances on ground not of their choosing—a battle they were neither mentally nor materially equipped to fight.

The first battle of Cassino resembled the *First World War battle of the Somme in even more appalling conditions and Mark *Clark, who command the Fifth US Army, showed an obstinacy worthy of Haig in insisting that attacks on the 2nd US Corps front north of Cassino town continue long after any chance of breaking through had disappeared. But Clark's persistence was justified by the need to break through and relieve the 6th US Corps at the *Anzio bridgehead. Anzio (SHINGLE), launched in January 1944, was another improvised amphibious operation. Its aim was never thought through. Alexander expected its commander, Lucas, to drive for the Alban hills, cut enemy communications south of Rome, and permit the Fifth Army to breach the Gustav Line and advance up the Liri valley. Lucas, taking advice from Clark, thought it more prudent to strengthen his defences. Anzio was isolated and beleaguered. The strategic design was reversed. Clark renewed his offensive to take the strain off troops whose landing had been calculated to relieve the Fifth Army. The first battle of Cassino cost the Fifth Army 16,000 casualties for just over 11 km. (7 mi.).

Alexander had never been very confident of Clark's ability, and for the second battle he turned to the Eighth Army, now commanded by General *Leese. A newly organized New Zealand Corps, commanded by *Freyberg, was entrusted with the breakthrough—an improvised force organized on the principle that the senior New Zealand divisional staff should double up their duties.

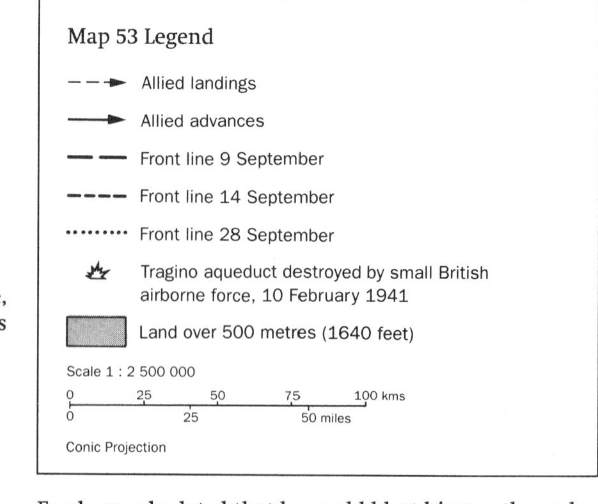

Freyberg calculated that he could blast his way through the outlying German defences—the *Hitler Line. A massive artillery bombardment was supplemented by aerial bombing, which destroyed the 6th-century Benedictine monastery overlooking the town. But the most vexed issue underlying Freyberg's tactics was not whether the monastery should have been bombed at all, but why this experiment in air–ground co-operation was so incompetently executed. After the aerial attack an entire day was wasted before the ground attack was thrown in. Movement on the ground was hampered by the bomb damage. There were no distractions launched on other parts of the Fifth US Army front. The method was crude and bull-headed. Indeed, the third battle was a repeat performance of the second: 1,060 guns supported by medium and heavy bombers. Again, the advance was halted because of the appalling conditions on the ground. Due to an extraordinary blunder the ruined monastery, now an ideal defensive site for the Germans, was omitted from the list of targets. The courage, endurance, and sacrifice of the troops was not compensated for by any significant advance. The weight of firepower only added to, rather than detracted from, the problems of topography that hamstrung the Allies.

Such problems could not be overcome merely by deploying overwhelming strength in the air. By the end of the first month of the Italian campaign, the Allies had secured complete aerial superiority. Increasingly, this would reflect a very marked American dominance. In that time, the United States Army Air Forces had flown two-thirds of the sorties and dropped 70% of the bombs. The operations of the Mediterranean Allied Strategic Air Force, commanded by Maj-General Nathan F. *Twining and comprising the Fifteenth US Army Air Force and No. 205 Group RAF, demonstrated the limitations of air superiority. In part this was a function of terrain. Tactical bombing in mountainous country was much less effective than on the open plains of north west Europe. The Germans withdrew twice—after Sicily and Salerno—

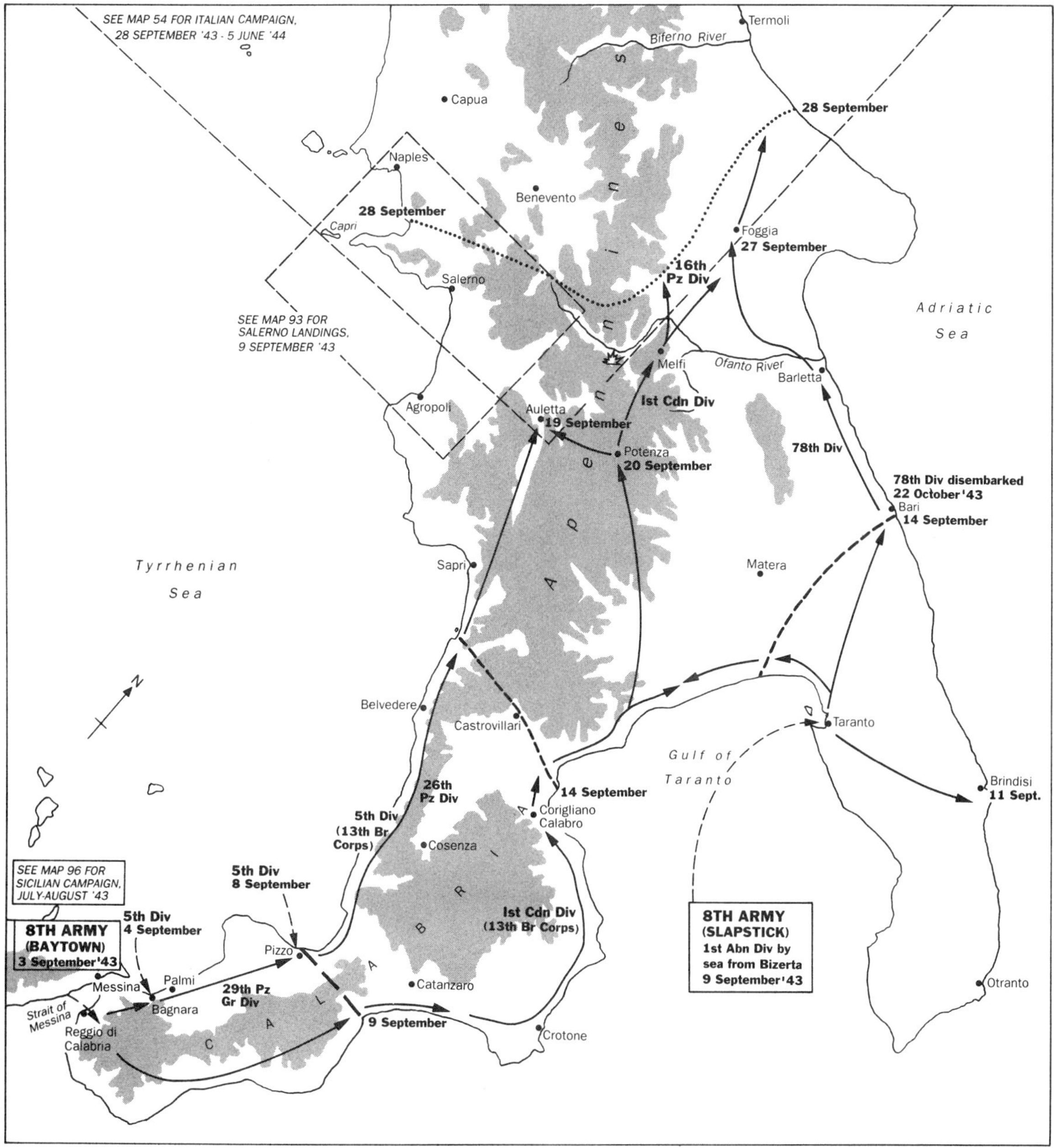

53. **Italian campaign**: advance of British Eighth Army, 3–28 September 1943

in the face of air superiority and showed a certain immunity to it. This did not prevent the formulation of STRANGLE, an attempt to force the Germans to withdraw from the Gustav Line by interdicting their lines of communication. Indeed Twining's British deputy, Air Marshal *Slessor, wrote that he was forced to admit that the plan was not working, that is, to 'make it impossible by the end of April [1944] for the Hun to maintain an army of seventeen divisions south of Rome'. After the fiasco of the bombing at Cassino, when co-ordination between ground and aerial forces was conspicuous by its absence, Slessor also concluded 'that the immediate battlefield is not the place to use the bomber, *even the fighter-bomber.*' This was perhaps too pessimistic. It was only towards the end of the campaign that the interdiction began to work—the scarcity of petrol reduced

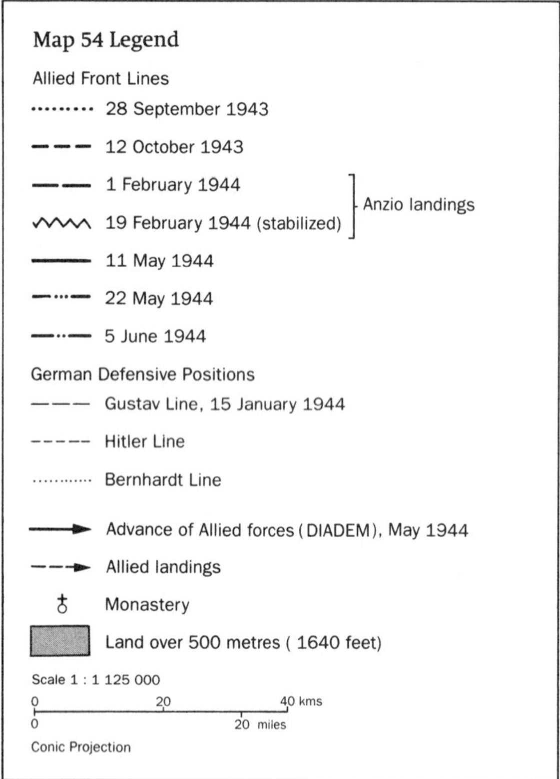

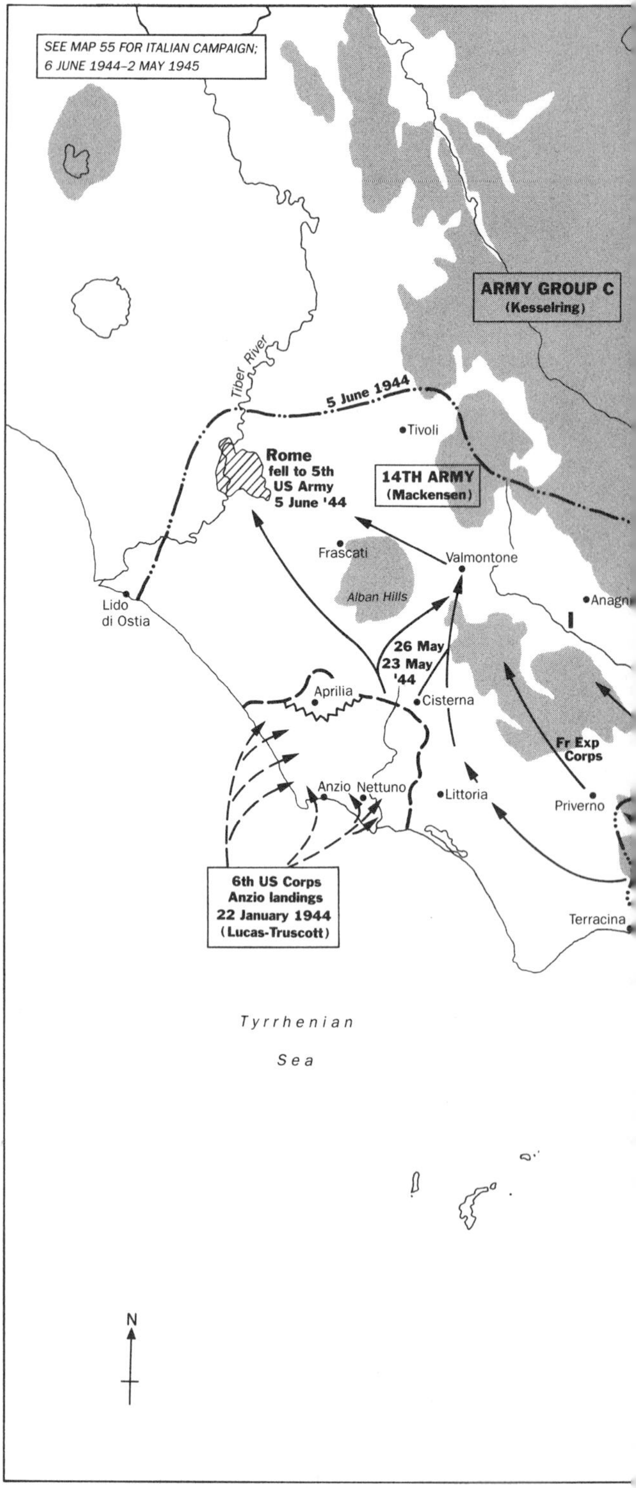

54. **Italian campaign**, 28 September 1943–5 June 1944

the value of armoured reserves, and after 21 March the Brenner Pass remained permanently closed. Such a development underlines a general conclusion, namely that no matter how enormous the level of air superiority, it normally can be no substitute for progress in operations on the ground; and success here demands skilful planning and tight co-ordination.

The fourth battle of Cassino was embodied in Operation DIADEM which culminated in the fall of Rome. At long last Alexander's group of armies would be employed like an army group and not a miscellaneous string of corps. The Gustav Line was breached by a two-fisted punch mounted by both armies and the 6th US Corps would break out towards Valmontone in the German rear. The operational aim was now at last spelt out—the destruction of the German Army south of Rome. Kesselring was tricked into expecting further amphibious landings and kept his reserves well back. A massive artillery bombardment opened the offensive at 2300 hours on 11 May 1944. Leese likewise held his reserves back and the fresh 13th Corps ruptured the Gustav Line in a set-piece attack. The breakthrough was completed by the 2nd Polish Corps seizing Monte Cassino and the astonishing feat of the *French Expeditionary Corps (FEC) in overrunning the *Hitler Line. Kesselring committed his reserves too late in the Liri valley. Alexander monitored these movements closely through

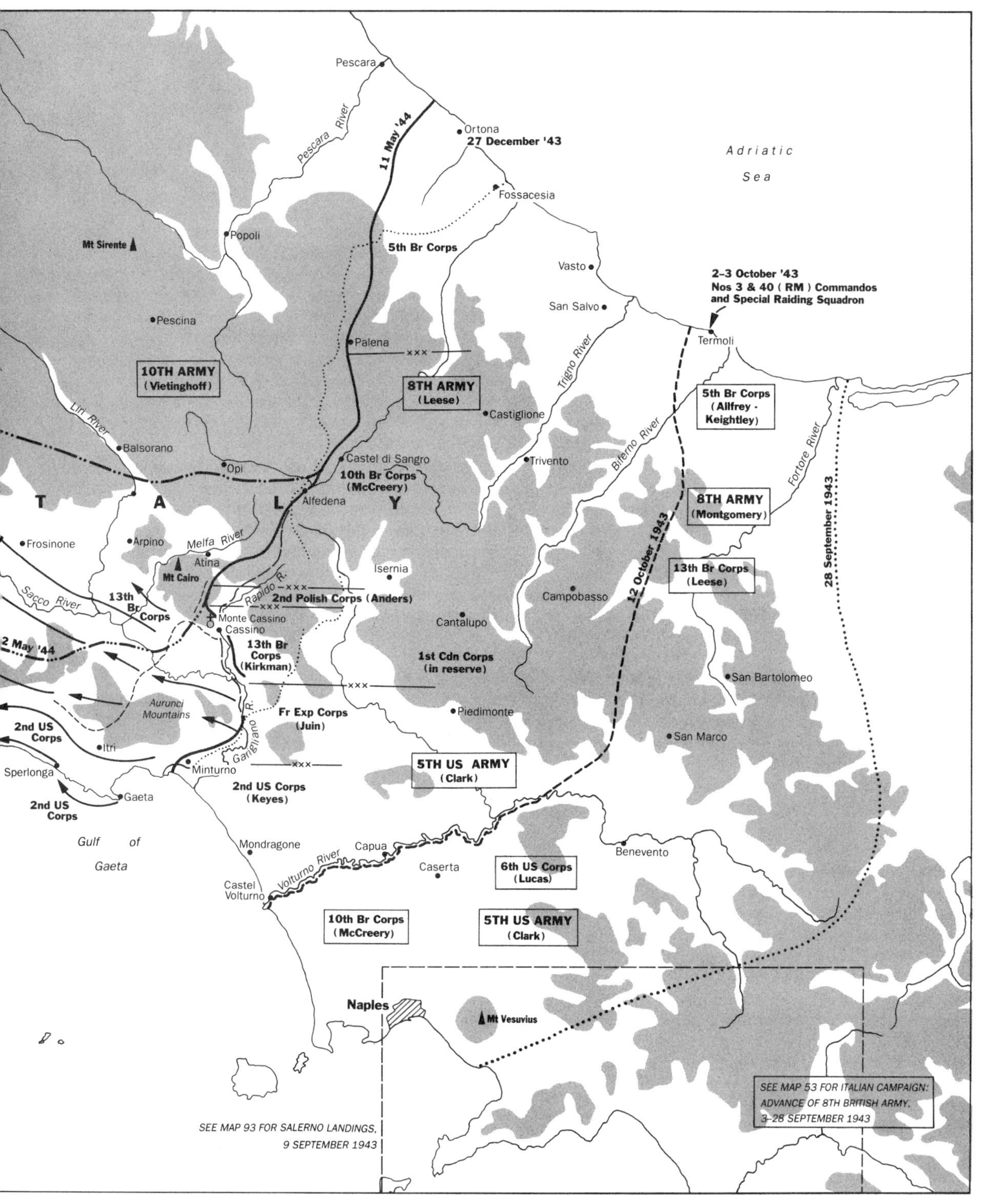
Pescara
Pescara River
11 May '44
Ortona
27 December '43
Adriatic
Sea
Fossacesia
Popoli
Mt Sirente
5th Br Corps
Vasto
2–3 October '43
Nos 3 & 40 (RM) Commandos
and Special Raiding Squadron
San Salvo
Pescina
Palena
Termoli
10TH ARMY
(Vietinghoff)
8TH ARMY
(Leese)
Trigno River
5th Br Corps
(Allfrey - Keightley)
Liri River
Castiglione
Biferno River
Fortore River
Balsorano
Castel di Sangro
Trivento
Opi
10th Br Corps
(McCreery)
T A L Y
Alfedena
8TH ARMY
(Montgomery)
28 September 1943
12 October 1943
Frosinone
Arpino
Melfa River
Atina
Mt Cairo
Isernia
13th Br Corps
(Leese)
Sacco River
13th Br Corps
Rapido R.
2nd Polish Corps (Anders)
Campobasso
Monte Cassino
Cassino
Cantalupo
2 May '44
13th Br Corps
(Kirkman)
1st Cdn Corps
(in reserve)
San Bartolomeo
Aurunci Mountains
Fr Exp Corps
(Juin)
Piedimonte
2nd US Corps
Garigliano R.
San Marco
Itri
Minturno
5TH US ARMY
(Clark)
Sperlonga
2nd US Corps
(Keyes)
Gaeta
2nd US Corps
Gulf of Gaeta
Mondragone
Capua
Benevento
Volturno River
Caserta
6th US Corps
(Lucas)
Castel Volturno
10th Br Corps
(McCreery)
5TH US ARMY
(Clark)
Naples
Mt Vesuvius
SEE MAP 53 FOR ITALIAN CAMPAIGN: ADVANCE OF 8TH BRITISH ARMY, 3–28 SEPTEMBER 1943
SEE MAP 93 FOR SALERNO LANDINGS, 9 SEPTEMBER 1943

*ULTRA intelligence and on 23 May ordered the Anzio break-out. The victory seemed complete, but could it be exploited?

DIADEM was the last opportunity for seizing a decisive victory in Italy. But all Clark's thoughts were concentrated on revelling in the glory of seizing Rome and denying it to the British. He issued orders altering the direction of his Fifth US Army's advance towards Rome even before it had arrived in the area of Valmontone. A gap opened up between the Allied armies as Clark moved away from the decisive point—closing the rear of the German Army. But even after the fall of Rome on 4 June, Alexander's second pursuit ordered three days later was wooden and hesitant. He gave the impression of preferring to close up to the next German defensive position—now identified by ULTRA as the *Gothic Line—rather than to destroy German forces in the open. This failure in the pursuit was the most marked feature of the western Allies in the Second World War.

After DIADEM the Italian campaign assumed a secondary status and six divisions (including the expert mountain troops of the FEC) were withdrawn for the *French Riviera landings. Efforts were made to replace some of these troops with Italians. An agreement had been reached with the Italian government substituting an enlarged force of six battle groups for the moribund Italian Corps of Liberation (CIL), originally formed in April 1944. This newly equipped force was to take the field between October 1944 and January 1945, but that proved too optimistic. By October 1944 only two of the battle groups had received any equipment. Bands of Italian partisians also launched guerrilla raids, though Alexander discounted their military value. On 1 July 1944 General John Harding, Alexander's chief of staff, estimated that Army Group C comprised 18–21 divisions and the Allied armies in Italy 14 infantry and 4 armoured divisions. Alexander was now ordered to close up to the River Po. Subsequent operations would develop in three stages: securing bridgeheads over the Po; gaining the line Padua–Vicenza–Verona; and finally, crossing the Piave to capture the Ljubljana gap. The first stage envisaged a central thrust which would entrap the Tenth German Army against the south bank of the Po. On 4 August Leese urged Alexander and Harding to meet him at Orvieto airfield. He persuaded them that an offensive (OLIVE) should be concentrated on the Adriatic coast. He believed that the going was better for armour north of Pesaro than in the steep mountains of the northern Apennines. This attack also had the major advantage for Leese of being distant from the Fifth US Army: there would be no doubt as to the nationality of the victor. But in persuading Alexander to adopt this change, Leese was repeating earlier errors in not utilizing the full resources of an army *group*.

Leese, moreover, was wrong in his tactical calculations. The many rivers flowing west–east proved to be as great a barrier as the mountains. The time lost in reorganizing the Allied forces brought heavy autumnal rain which

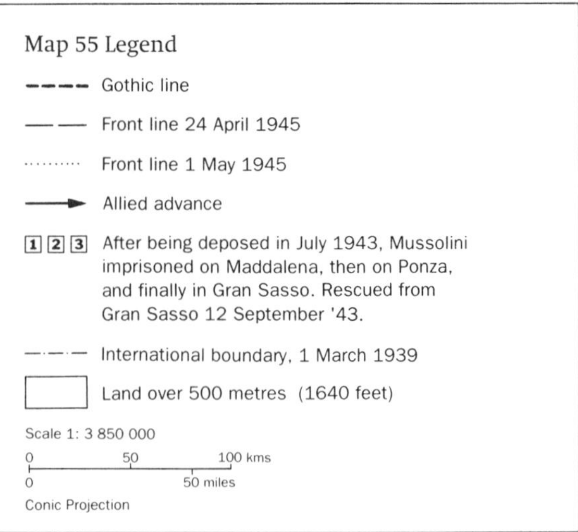

swelled their waters. The operation was not a failure, but it was not a conspicuous success either. Progress through the Gothic Line was satisfactory until the weather broke on 3 September, and clouds of dust were turned into glutinous mud. Even though Leese broke out into the Romagna by 20 September, the Eighth Army, after a year spent in the Italian mountains, had forgotten how to fight a fluid, mobile battle.

The lack of success of OLIVE confirmed *Marshall, the US chief of staff, in his view that Italy was an expensive sideshow, but Alexander refused to be downhearted. In December 1944 he resuscitated his grandiose scheme for an attack through the Ljubljana gap, driving on Vienna. But his ambitious goals only increased American suspicions of Britain's motives in enlarging operations in Italy. Marshall was inclined to believe that the British were trying to strengthen their imperial position in the Mediterranean; such suspicions made British attempts to modify American strategy in north-west Europe more difficult. After the Yalta conference in February 1945 (see ARGONAUT), Alexander, now Supreme Commander in the Mediterranean, was instructed by the *Combined Chiefs of Staff merely to pin down the maximum number of German divisions in Italy while the Nazi collapse in the west continued apace. Alexander sought to fulfil this directive by annihilating the German armies before they could retire behind the Alpine barrier. In GRAPESHOT he at last achieved his goal of destroying the German army group now commanded by General Heinrich Von Vietinghoff (1887–1952). *Argenta fell to the Eighth Army and both Allied armies joined hands fittingly at Finale nell'Emilia on 25 April. A cease-fire followed on 2 May 1945.

Allied casualties during the campaign were 188,746 for the Fifth US Army, 123,254 for the Eighth Army. German casualties were probably 434,646 (including 214,048 missing). The process of attrition was therefore not self-

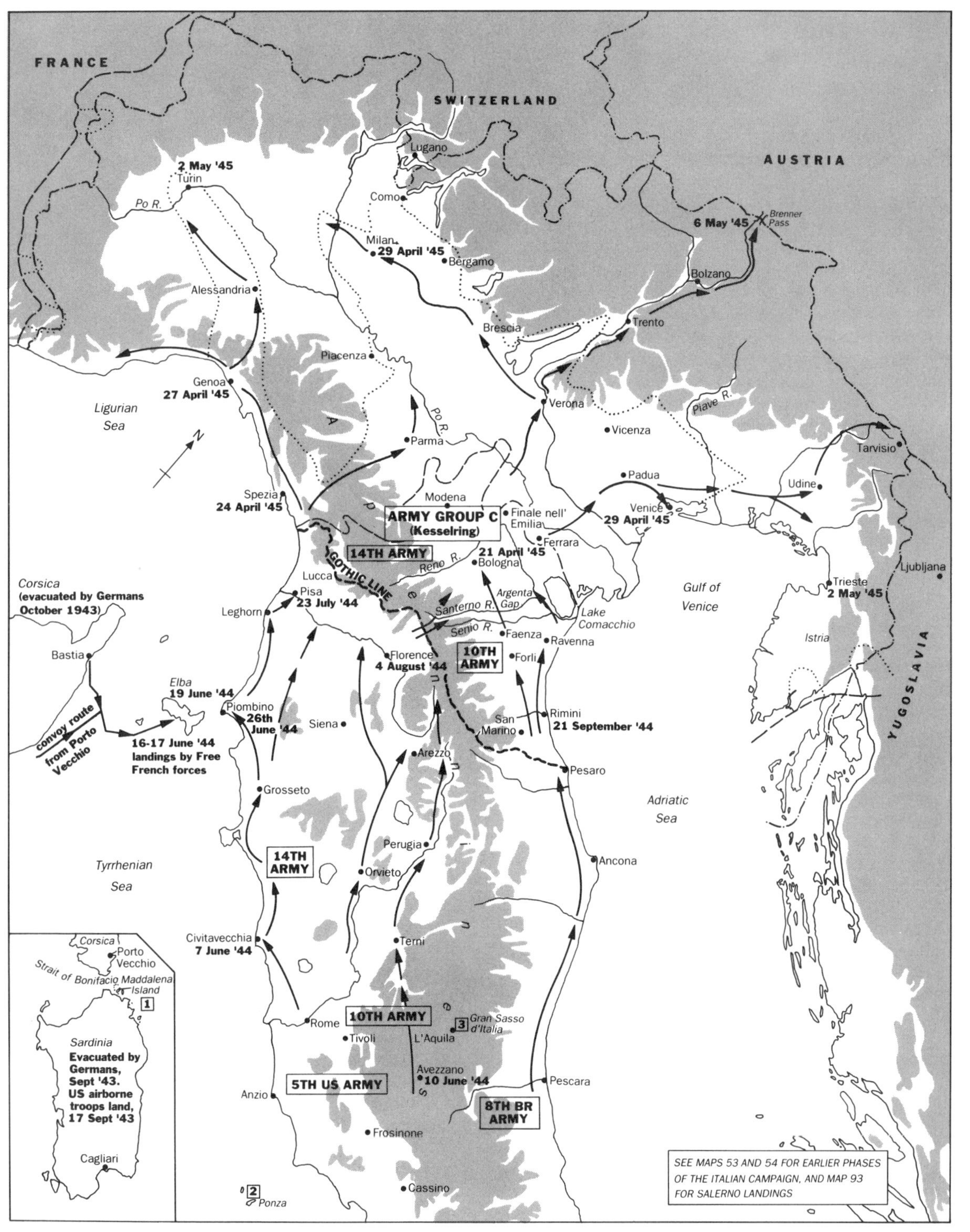

55. **Italian campaign**, 6 June 1944–2 May 1945

defeating. But perhaps the most impressive aspect of the campaign had been Kesselring's skill as a defensive commander deprived of the initiative and facing overwhelming air superiority. As to the contribution of the Italian campaign to the Allied victory, the record is mixed. Contrary to early British expectations, it had no appreciable impact on the Eastern Front. As for OVERLORD, it provided a valuable proving-ground for gaining experience in amphibious landings and tied up more than 20 divisions. Nevertheless, the campaign was a distraction for the Allies, too. Hitler was able to muster 26 new divisions for the *Ardennes campaign without drawing upon forces in Italy. The Italian campaign became an object lesson in the constraints imposed by scarce resources and the tensions of waging coalition warfare. BRIAN HOLDEN REID

Graham, D., and Bidwell, S., *Tug of War: The Battle for Italy, 1943–45* (London, 1986).

Reid, B. H., 'The Italian Campaign, 1943–45', in J. Gooch (ed.), *The Decisive Campaigns of the Second World War* (London, 1990).

Italian East Africa (Africa Orientale Italiana) was a federation of Italian East African colonies formed in 1936, comprising Eritrea, Italian Somaliland, and Abyssinia which had been occupied by Italy that year. It had six provinces (see Map 27) the governors of which were responsible to the governor-general (*Graziani and then the Duke of Aosta) in Addis Ababa. In 1941 it was overrun by Allied troops during the *East Africa campaign.

Italian Somaliland, Italian colony, part of Somalia, which had been divided between France (see FRENCH SOMALILAND), Italy, and the UK (see BRITISH SOMALILAND) at the end of the nineteenth century. Italian forces under *Graziani invaded Abyssinia from there in October 1935 and it became part of Italian East Africa after the Italian occupation of Abyssinia was completed in 1936. It was overrun by Lt-General Alan *Cunningham's Commonwealth and colonial troops, who advanced from Kenya in February 1941 during the *East African campaign.

ITALY

For the fighting in Italy, see ITALIAN CAMPAIGN and SICILIAN CAMPAIGN.

1. Introduction

A united kingdom under the constitutional monarchy of the House of Savoy, Italy had a population of 42 million in 1936. From 1861 until the advent in 1922 of the fascist regime and Mussolini's dictatorship, it was a parliamentary democracy with universal male suffrage since 1913. To its colonies (Libya, Eritrea, Italian Somaliland, the Dodecanese Islands) the fascist regime added Abyssinia in 1936 and Albania in 1939, so that *Victor Emmanuel III, the sovereign since 1900, was also emperor of Abyssinia and king of Albania.

Mussolini moved into the Nazi orbit, first by means of a friendship between accomplices in 1936, then with the *Pact of Steel in 1939, and finally by intervening in the war against the UK and France on 10 June 1940 (see also AXIS STRATEGY AND CO-OPERATION). The central problem of the dictatorship lay in the relationship between the popular masses upon whom *fascism had been inflicted and those sections of the bourgeoisie which had actively favoured it. The recipe—which was subsequently imitated beyond the Alps—involved the anaesthetizing of social conflict by means of a permanent mobilization of the masses in a fever of grandeur aimed at imperial expansion. Once this had taken place social problems would be resolved by means which were for the moment still invisible in the glowing light of the future.

The accent therefore had to fall on external action by the state, but of itself this did not require immediate and exact foreign policy choices. In part fascism built its strength on memories of slights to Italian national pride, still smarting from the humiliation meted out by Abyssinian forces at Aduwa in 1896, more recently from their defeat by an Austro-German army at Caporetto in 1917—not to mention the slender rewards of victory in 1918. However, international opportunities were blocked by Anglo-French dominance of the *League of Nations which guaranteed the peace treaties of 1919 (see VERSAILLES SETTLEMENT); Italian imperialism more or less lapsed up to 1933, apart from some verbal tempestuousness on Mussolini's part and an attempt at violent action against Corfu in 1923 which was quickly abandoned.

The pragmatic and juridical construction of the fascist state (see GOVERNMENT, below) was opposed courageously but to little effect by the clandestine remnants of the old political opposition (liberals, Catholics, and communists) and by new groups such as the liberal-democratic Giustizia e Libertà (Justice and Liberty). These domestic opponents were marginalized by a variety of means which included prohibition, intimidation, violence by the police and fascist squads, and finally imprisonment. Meanwhile the colonial territories inherited from pre-fascist Italy—Eritrea, Somalia, and Libya—were 'pacified' with the usual ferocity of colonial powers. In lieu of foreign policy successes, which were for the moment unattainable, government propaganda trumpeted the successes of the everyday administration and public works such as the reclamation of the Pontine marshes near Rome. Neither the recalcitrant masses of workers and peasants nor the bulk of the middle classes were much enamoured of the regime, although the bourgeoisie appreciated its maintenance of public order, the outlawing of strikes, and the keeping down of workers' wages.

The chance to pursue an active foreign policy came with German rearmament. The military conquest of Abyssinia in 1935–6 was the regime's greatest visible success. That the victory had been won despite the opposition of the 52 states in the League of Nations, led by the UK, was a cause of some pride. Opposition to the move, bland in substance but dramatic in form, in the shape of the arrival of the British Home Fleet in the Mediterranean, was astutely blown up for domestic purposes. On the evening of 9 May 1936 Mussolini appeared on the floodlit balcony of the Palazzo Venezia and proclaimed to a vast crowd the 'reappearance' of the old Roman Empire. This theatrical gesture seemed finally to reconcile to fascism some of those forces which, in pre-war liberal Italy, had at times pursued similar goals, albeit with greater prudence and less of an uproar. Moreover, just as the colonial policy of the years 1886–96 had kindled hopes in the starving masses of the south, so once again the myth of empire had its brief moment of popularity among the poor peasants of that region. But reality shattered these dreams quickly and even more bitterly than had been the case 40 years earlier: then it had been possible to emigrate, albeit at the cost of some hardship and risk, but now even that possibility was closed. The poorest Italians had no other means to earn a few lire than to enlist as 'volunteers' in the forces Mussolini was now sending to Spain to fight others as poor as themselves.

Historians differ in their interpretations of Mussolini's policy thereafter: his abandonment of the defence of the European status quo (Locarno 1925, the Four-Power Pact 1933, the reaction to the assassination of Dolfuss 1934, the Stresa Front 1935); his ever closer links with Germany, not only in the *Spanish Civil War but also in abandoning the defence of Austrian independence in 1938; his open hostility to France and the UK, save for momentary alignments with the 'appeasers' (January 1937, November 1938, the *Munich agreement, the visit of *Chamberlain and *Halifax to Rome in January 1939); the occupation of Albania, the Pact of Steel with Germany (April–May 1939) and the failure to intervene in the war alongside his ally in September 1939. In fact Mussolini's words and deeds were so contradictory as to justify many interpretations. This is not surprising when we consider the character and intellectual baggage of the man, soaked in Nietzschean and Sorelian sediments. His urge to dominate was manifest both in his socialist anti-war stance and his anti-German interventionism in 1914, and in his later promotion of war as an end in itself and noisy proclamation of a battery of different objectives.

It is probably not particularly important to establish whether Mussolini's true intention was to pursue a 'pendulum' policy, oscillating between Nazi Germany and the western democracies and selling himself to the highest bidder, or whether his choice of Hitler remained fixed, although subject to moments of doubt and worry. What is certain is that the convergence of Fascist Italy and Nazi Germany was not unnatural. Fascism and National Socialism shared much common ground: nihilistic violence, humiliation of their adversaries, imperialism, biological planning (the campaign for births) and finally racism. Fascism was not intrinsically anti-Semitic but from the outset it practised racism and colonial extermination; therefore no special exertions were necessary when, in 1938, Mussolini decided to persecute the Jews in tune with the German alliance.

The German victories in the spring of 1940 triggered a decision by Mussolini in which the wish to profit from Nazi power was mingled with the illusion of competing with it. Had Mussolini aligned himself with the democracies at any moment they would have accepted him and perhaps compensated him well, though not to the same extent as the power of Germany would allow; moreover, an alliance with the democracies would not have accorded him the super-hero status created by the German–Italian propaganda chorus—a newspaper could at any time have criticized him or ridiculed him in a caricature. As for internal consensus, although it did not diminish it became of greater concern to the regime from 1938 onwards. Intervention in Spain lasted too long; Germany gave cause for anxiety; the anti-Jewish measures were unpopular in one of the few European countries which lacked any tradition of *anti-Semitism; and a policy of anti-bourgeois repression angered the educated classes without gaining fascism any sympathy from the proletaraiat.

In 1938–9 anxiety about the future touched the crown, the upper bureaucracy, and the class which controlled the economy. They might have tried to change things had not Hitler, by showing himself able to crush as prestigious a power as France in only a few weeks in 1940, appealed to their sense of 'realism'—a feeling which had little to do with morality or with a well-balanced cultural life. Behind the 'realists' and a handful of fanatics stood the masses, muddled by propaganda and ready to acclaim successes, but preoccupied by the dangers and sacrifices which fell chiefly on them, just as they had during the First World War.

In June 1940 the small minority of Italians who were radically opposed to war were in exile abroad, in prison, banished to offshore islands, or reduced to silence and, if young, obliged to fight. Many feared for the future of those same western democracies (France and the UK) which, until directly threatened, had been so ready to praise Mussolini. But the sufferings of war and the humiliations of defeat rebounded on all Italians whatever their private thoughts.

2. Domestic life, economy, and war effort

The war cut deeply into domestic life in Italy. Apart from the foolish prohibition of dancing, both in public and in private, which was imposed at the outset, Mussolini sought to maintain the appearance of normality. As a result restrictions, when they belatedly came, were too harsh. In the autumn of 1941 tram services shut down at 10 p.m. and theatres closed early; however, *blackout was not adapted until the summer of 1943 and then at varying times. In Rome, on moonlit nights even the miserable blue-coloured public lighting was switched off. At the end of 1941 petrol-driven motor cars were forbidden, but some public and private transport continued to run throughout the war, fuelled by methane from the Po valley.

From 1939 sugar and soap were rationed, and coffee was unobtainable. Fats were not rationed until the autumn of 1940, and other foodstuffs the following autumn though that did not mean that they were easy to find in the interim. Newspapers were limited to four pages, later reduced to two. One pair of shoes or a few articles of clothing could be purchased each year, but not both. Food intake was reduced to below 1,000 calories a day: 200 grams (7 oz.) of bread a day (later reduced to 150), and 400 grams of meat, 500 grams of sugar, and 100 grams of olive oil a month. Only those engaged in heavy physical labour were allowed more. Such a drastic diet, together with an absence of controls, the impossibility of pooling grain, and the fact that most urbanized Italians had lived in cities for only a few generations and maintained close connections with the countryside, meant that a well-organized black market flourished. Only those people with money could take advantage of it, though sometimes—even in illegal trading—there was a social equalizing and poorer quality food was sold at lower prices. Up to September 1943 the official price level never rose above 273 (1938 = 100); but on the black market bread reached 797, butter 1,054, and olive oil 1,387. Repeated increases in salaries and wages were absorbed by inflation; but even in the north, which was separated from the south after the autumn of 1943, inflation stayed at reasonable levels until May 1945.

As far as paying for the war was concerned, fiscal impositions contributed little except for tax on the exchange of goods and consumption, a policy which affected everyone but especially the working classes and minor employees. Otherwise fiscal pressures and new taxation (such as property taxes) failed because of the difficulties of assessment and also because, once introduced, they opened the doors to avoidance and evasion. A decisive contribution was made by the war loans to which the banks (which were owned by the state) had to subscribe and which also attracted private savers until 1942.

The state budget displayed fearsome deficits: from 29.4 billion lire in 1939–40, the deficit increased to 64.5 billion in 1940–1, 84.8 billion in 1941–2 and 109.8 billion in 1942–3. Circulation of paper money quadrupled between 1940 and 1943, while in Germany it doubled and in the UK it was less than double.

In order to assess Italy's military strength and its influence on the conduct of the war it is necessary to look back to the pre-war era. Notwithstanding fascist propaganda and a shrill foreign policy, the Italian economy and civil life remained semi-developed until the outbreak of war. Twenty years of fascism saw the average per capita earnings of 42,000,000 Italians increase very little, so that they only equalled those of the UK and the USA at the start of the 19th century and of France about 1850. Moreover, there were great inequalities in per capita income between north and south. Public works (land reclamation, roads, and railways), state aid to heavy industry (e.g. assistance to shipyards provided by modest naval rearmament in the 1920s), and the natural development of some sectors such as electricity and synthetic fabrics were not enough to compensate for the drying-up of emigration, now down from 600,000 a year to 60–70,000, which had made possible the development Italy had enjoyed before the *First World War.

The entire fascist period was characterized by low incomes and unemployment, which was severe after the crisis of 1929 but less grave after partial rearmament began in 1935. The official figures for 1934 showed 961,000 unemployed (of whom 750,000 were in industry and commerce), approximately 10.7% of the male work force. From 1935–6 salary increases were largely absorbed by increased prices, while industrial profits grew: net interest relative to capital invested rose from 1.38% in 1932 to 5.74% in 1935 and 7.28% in 1936. Unemployment among the educated remained high. In 1919–20 of 53,670 university students only 33% were studying engineering, science, and mathematics; this percentage collapsed in 1939–40 to 13.6% of a university population of 85,535. Even in 1935, more than 50% of engineering graduates were unemployed. National illiteracy levels in 1931 amounted to 17%. The development of some areas of northern Italy was not typical of the whole: half the active population were engaged in small-scale agriculture and even in 1938 more than half of average family expenditure went on food. The regime preached the virtues of ruralism and sustained the uneconomical 'battle for grain' which sought to achieve self-sufficency by the inefficient transformation of pasturage into grain-producing areas with high duties and premiums.

The great crash of 1929 led to protectionism through the increase of customs barriers and an internal monopoly policy in which the domestic market was divided according to fixed quotas. Legal cartels—which existed alongside illegal or semi-legal ones—set prices according to the costs of marginal producers, assuring the others of excess profits. Laws passed in 1933 and 1937 required official authorization before new industrial plant could be created or existing plant expanded. Many manufacturers who at first opposed these measures soon perceived their advantages. To halt competition they put in many requests for new plant, the mere existence of which allowed official bodies (within which the big industrial trusts had their own men) to reject genuine applications as unnecessary duplication. The system could also be distorted in other ways: once a producer had gained a place in the consortium which controlled his area of production he enjoyed guaranteed advantages which were independent of the costs or quality of his product. Naturally, the consolidation of monopoly positions—which were at their greatest in military manufacturing—did not encourage the inventiveness, speed, and research indispensable for true economic progress. Instead it led to backwardness and provincialism.

Italy was poorly off for *raw materials. In 1938 it produced one million tons of hard coal (and had to import another 12,000,000 tons each year) compared with 47,000,000 tons produced by France, 186,000,000 tons by Germany, and 230,000,000 tons by the UK. It produced 2,300,000 tons of steel in comparison with more than 6,000,000 in France, more than 10,000,000 in the UK, and 23,000,000 tons in Germany. A total lack of petroleum stimulated the development of the electricity industry: in 1939 Italy produced more than 15,000,000 kWh, compared with more than 22,000,000 kWh in France, almost 36,000,000 kWh in the UK, and 61,380,000 kWh in Germany. Shipbuilding enjoyed some expansion, but production in 1939 amounted to only 135,000 tons against a productive capacity of 300,000.

The automobile industry was good but small; in 1939 it produced 71,000 vehicles (of which only 12,000 were commercial), against 227,000 in France (45,000 commercial), 445,000 in the UK (104,000 commercial), and 338,000 in Germany (63,000 commercial). In that year there were 372,000 vehicles on Italian roads, compared with 2,269,000 in France 2,527,000 in the UK, and 1,656,000 in Germany. The modest scale of the automobile industry affected the armed forces by limiting the numbers of drivers and mechanics available.

The aircraft industry enjoyed a wholly unjustified reputation founded largely on international record-breaking, which did not entail comparisons of series-manufacturing capacity or of originality of design. Italian aero engines, in particular, were poor copies of foreign models.

Military expenditure, which had been effectively held in check between 1922 and 1926, began to increase and in 1935–9 it reached a level equivalent to 89.5% of that of the UK and 22.8% more than that of France. This figure is particularly striking when it is related to an Italian national income which was less than half that of France and less than a quarter that of the UK. The enormous costs of conquering and 'pacifying' Abyssinia, of intervention in Spain, and of the occupation of Albania absorbed 77 billion lire out of a total of 116 billion allocated to the armed forces and the colonies between 1935 and 1940.

Costs were inflated by the need to import primary materials and to use high-cost national industries which, after Mussolini proclaimed economic autarky in 1936, charged very high domestic prices for their products. Synthetic petrol cost four times as much as imported petrol; and the costs of Italian steel and coal were respectively double and triple those in the UK, while metallurgical products were between 50 and 100% dearer. It has been calculated that if the battleship *Littorio* (built between 1934 and 1940) had been constructed in France it would have cost only half as much. In 1935–6 automobiles cost 18–20 lire/kilogram to manufacture, as compared to 17 lire/kg. in Germany, 11–12 lire/kg. in the UK, and 6–8 lire/kg. in the USA. However, salaries were on average 56% of those paid in Germany and 27% of those paid in the USA.

In order to assess the state and character of Italian military strength in the Second World War, it is necessary to examine the evolution of relations between state and industry, as well as within industry itself, during the fascist period and in comparison with the First World War. Between 1915 and 1918 the growth of Italian industry and the results on the battlefield (e.g. 12,000 guns, 79,000,000 shells, 12,000 aeroplanes, 37,000 machine guns) was a consequence not only of assistance from the Entente in the shape of raw materials and loans but also of the efficiency of the office of under-secretary for armaments and munitions (which subsequently became a ministry) under General Alfredo Dallolio (1853–1952), who shared out orders and raw materials for the army and the navy between some 1,500 factories and 600,000 workers under a disciplined system of industrial mobilization. However, although appreciating such measures as the forbidding of strikes, industry accepted Dallolio's strict controls only under sufferance and in 1918 subjected him to a trial from which he emerged victorious but embittered. Big business would have preferred to deal individually with each of the armed services; and they, divided as they were by rivalries and intolerance, had no desire to combine in their dealings with industry.

Thus when fascism came to legislate on these matters after 1923–5, a tacit understanding grew up between industry and the three armed forces (the air force had become an independent arm in 1923). A system of 'civil mobilization' involving six ministries in addition to the armed forces, the militia, and the Fascist Party, was overseen by the old Supreme Commission for Defence, a

Committee for Civil Mobilization (CMC), a permanent secretary, and in time some 20 other offices with thousands of functionaries. Their different spheres of authority were so varied, so minute, and so extensive that it is simpler to note not what they had but what they lacked, which was fundamental power over the orders given to industry; here each of the three armed forces acted independently.

Since everything had officially to be controlled by the state, a National Council for Research (CNR) was set up in 1923, under the chairmanship in its early days of Guglielmo Marconi (1874–1937). Although on paper the CNR possessed very extensive powers, it does not seem to have interested itself very much in the preliminary results of experiments in nuclear fission, carried out by Enrico *Fermi in 1934, or later in *radar or jet engines. Dallolio chaired the CMC, aware of the inadequacy of his powers but probably hoping that at a suitable moment Mussolini would reinforce them. This occurred in small part when in 1935, as a consequence of the Abyssinian crisis, the General Commissariat for War Production (COGEFAG) was set up and given to Dallolio under the 'direct and exclusive' authority of the Duce. However, all purchasing orders remained within the sphere of authority of the armed forces. Even the limited powers of COGEFAG, which related chiefly to the distribution of raw materials, aroused protests from the navy, an example of the strength of sectional interests in fascist Italy.

Dallolio's thoughts on the problem of artillery equipment were disregarded. He had hoped to stimulate high-quality output by building a pilot plant at Terni the workforce of which would in due course become instructors for others. However, in 1929 the army preferred to pursue the ideal of a gigantic programme of complete re-equipment, amounting to 15,000 guns and 58,000,000 rounds of ammunition, which was approved in principle but remained a paper scheme owing to lack of money. When, in 1938, alarmed by the possible consequences of his foreign policy, Mussolini wanted to undertake a serious rearmament programme he had to meet the wishes of industry and above all of the two leading manufacturers, Ansaldo and Terni (which had in the meantime been taken over by the state), who obtained an advance against losses of 15% of the value of future orders for plant renewal. The way was opened to what could have been the achievement of a major programme of artillery rearmament by 1943–5.

Dallolio retired in August 1939, aged 87, and was replaced by General Carlo Favagrossa who, with the same powers but less prestige, was unable to impose his personality on the industrialists. They had begun to replace old plant, but the military preferred to use raw materials for armoured vehicles rather than artillery (save only for the 90 mm./3.5 in. anti-aircraft gun and the 47 mm./1.8 in. anti-tank gun, which was inferior to the British two-pounder). As a result large factories such as OTO, equipped to manufacture artillery but not tanks, remained almost unoccupied whilst Ansaldo, which made both, had too much work. More far-sighted programmes which aimed only at what was strictly necessary, like updating the gun-carriages of the huge stock of First World War artillery (much of which was good Skoda-built stock), would have produced better results in terms of both economy and efficiency. As for rearmament of the infantry, which had begun in the early 1930s, its outcome was by no means perfect but no worse than that of other countries; here the greatest problem was the lack of training, notwithstanding the succession of wars and expeditions in which the country had been engaged since 1935.

Until 1923 there were few changes in the nature of industrial capital; thereafter while some munitions manufacturers were taken over by the state (such as the Cogne steel works in 1923), many large firms fell into the hands of the banks which had financed them. However, from 1929 onwards the banks failed to match the time limits on ordinary credits with the needs of industrial credit and, faced with the prospect of major collapses, radical public intervention became necessary. Between 1933 and 1937 the state debarred the banks from owning industrial property, reformed them, and restricted them to ordinary credit operations while itself taking over a majority shareholding in industry and starting to finance and administer it through the Institute for Industrial Reconstruction (IRI). This body controlled most of the arms-producing metallurgical, armaments, and ship-building firms and, when other sections of industry are taken into account, represented the most extensive experiment in state control outside the USSR.

However, appearances of unity were deceptive: in reality each IRI enterprise developed its own policy like a private company while at the same time enjoying the benefits of public ownership (the impossibility of bankruptcy, guaranteed work, and so on). The IRI industries should, at least in theory, have respected not only state laws but also the rules of the market-place. They did not. Even in the 1920s the main manufacturers of artillery (Ansaldo, Terni, and others, all still at that stage private companies) operated cartels to keep prices high. Similar practices, which touched the limits of legality and damaged the military administration, continued after the advent of IRI. Corruption was widespread and included state enterprises: in 1933–4 Ansaldo (a member of IRI) and Fiat (privately owned) reached an agreement to exclude other companies from the construction of tanks.

It was this oligopoly, along with the political weakness of the army, which produced the situation whereby up to 1939 Italy had built only the small CV3 tanks of three tons, without *radio communications, with poor visibility, and carrying only two machine-guns. The disastrous inefficiency of these machines, which were derived from the British Carden Lloyd tank of 1928, was demonstrated in Abyssinia and Spain; even so, up to September 1943 Fiat and Ansaldo only manufactured medium tanks of 11, 13, 14, and 15 tons (some in a self-propelled gun version). The M11 has been called the worst tank of its day and the various versions of the M series were all inferior to British Cruiser tanks in armament, weight of armour, and especially in speed.

After the early disasters of the *Western Desert campaigns, culminating in *Beda Fomm (February 1941), Italian tank troops of the Ariete Division learned to use the mediocre M13s more effectively and combine them with artillery, producing some successes during the battles of the British CRUSADER offensive in late 1941. The tanks themselves received some savage criticism: *Rommel said they would 'make one's hair curl'. As a minimum improvement, engines were requested that matched those of the British Cruisers whose speed allowed them to withdraw whenever necessary. The war ministry tried to interest other companies in manufacturing tanks, hoping to improve their quality. The army proposed adopting a Czech tank which Skoda were ready to make, and licences were obtained to build Panzer III and IV models; but all these attempts failed, and after tortuous manoeuvrings the army had to accept Fiat–Ansaldo products. The company even refused requests to adapt their tanks by using Fiat aero engines. In fact there were engines in store, or mounted on aeroplanes such as the Fiat CR42 biplane and Fiat G50 which were by now useless in combat, derived from the Liberty, Continental W670, and Wright Continental R975 engines which the British and Americans adapted for use on their Cruisers, Grants, and Shermans. But rather than use others' products, Fiat preferred to improve its own versions.

Competition was by no means the whole story. Italian aviation adopted different aeroplanes according to the outcome of public competitions; but the best aeroplane did not always win, a phenomenon not unknown outside Italy. The custom developed of asking small companies to produce perhaps 40 or 50 examples of a model so that all the manufacturers were able to survive. This system, which had some logic in peacetime, was continued during war. The smallest companies were sometimes requested to manufacture aeroplanes which were not of their own design but were thought useful. However it was not possible to compel Fiat to build Macchi 202 or 205 fighters; the company promised its own G55 which was not ready until the eve of the *armistice in September 1943, to the benefit not of Italy but of Germany, and meanwhile continued to produce its outdated CR42s and G50s.

Among the many reasons for the inferiority of Italian warplanes was the fact that in 1927 a law supported by Italo Balbo (1896–1940), Mussolini's minister of aviation from 1929 to 1933, had deprived the technical branch of the air force of the authority to choose prototypes and had passed that power to an office (the Direzione Generale) from which technical experts were excluded in favour of ministerial cronies. The air engineering branch continued to voice its opinions on the quality and defects of prototypes, as in the competition in 1939 in which it recommended the Re2000 fighter. But the Direzione Generale made the choices, and in 1939 it preferred the inferior Fiat CR42 and G50.

The quality of naval armaments was influenced not only by very high costs but by scientific backwardness in respect of *radar and radio communications in general and by the excessive 'tolerance' allowed in shells, which had disastrous effects on naval gunfire. However, many deficiencies derived from defective strategic concepts (up to 1935 and in part afterwards the standard of comparison for the Italians was the French Navy) and from a tendency to fake the results of trials, according to which the navy claimed to be able to reach speeds much higher than were really possible. In addition, rivalry with the air force hindered the development of aircraft carriers. Finally there was much hidden mismanagement. For example, a large fleet of outdated submarines was built (113 by 1939) while between 1935 and 1938 midget submarines, which became the most effective arm of the Italian Navy, were neglected (see TENTH LIGHT FLOTILLA).

The widespread assumption that Italy's shortage of raw materials was the primary cause of its defeat is therefore incorrect. Certainly Italy had no Ruhr or Caucasus and just as this prevented it from becoming a Great Power *ab origine* so it would also have made its effects felt had Italy's war continued much beyond September 1943. Metallurgical output was modest; but in September 1943 the Germans seized three times as much steel as was available in 1940. It would not have been possible between June 1940 and August 1943 to armour more than approximately 3,054 tanks of all types, which was the maximum number that the small monopoly plants could have built. If more tanks had been provided than was actually the case, but only in variants of the M series, the problem of poor quality which was not tackled until 1942 would not have been ameliorated. The need, until then, was not for more tanks but for better ones.

Much the same is true of the artillery: some 7,000 guns were provided for the army between June 1940 and June 1943, and they would have had a much greater effect had not 51% been the 47 mm. model which was inferior to every British anti-tank gun. The 60–65,000 motor vehicles supplied to the army between spring 1940 and spring 1943 would have been far from insignificant if they had been concentrated in North Africa instead of being scattered between the Eastern Front, the Balkans, and France. The modest increase in warships between 1940 and 1943 (a battleship, 3 light cruisers, 5 destroyers, 16 torpedo boats, and 39 submarines) represented an increment to a not inconsiderable force but one which was hamstrung by technical and scientific inferiority, a lack of aircraft carriers, and by the adoption of economic rather than military criteria.

Between January 1940 and April 1943 the aeronautics industry manufactured 10,545 aircraft (4,510 fighters, 2,063 bombers, 1,080 reconnaissance planes, 468 transports, 1,769 trainers, and 655 of various minor types); monthly production amounted to 271 machines in 1940, 292 in 1941, 235 in 1942, and 241 in 1943. The 8,000 aircraft sent to the Mediterranean up to mid-1942 would have represented a serious problem for the Allies had they included more modern bombers than the S79 and Fiat BR20 and rather more than the 250 to 300 Macchi 202 and Re2001 fighters which were the only ones able to compete with the Curtiss P40 and the Hurricane.

Had more petroleum been available, Italian tank forces might have had a more timely and less disastrous training than that which they received on the field of battle. However, it would have been difficult before the war to convince the High Command of the pressing need for training, a need which (as the *Balkan campaign showed) was felt even by the infantry, who had received many of the 16,800 *mortars and 125,000 machine guns produced between 1939 and 1943. It is possible to imagine that with more coal and rubber supplies the temporary closures of factories in wartime would not have been necessary. But such impediments did not have dramatic effects on the quantity of vital arms produced until at least mid-1942. After that time, Anglo-American and Soviet production would have crushed Italy as it subsequently crushed Germany.

However it is difficult to imagine a rational and calculated use of raw materials, whether abundant or not, when the state lacked the power to impose the necessary changes in production upon industry. The defeat of Italy occurred before the point was reached at which her lack of raw materials became the determining factor.

The material costs of the war were considerable: on average, 8% of industrial plant was destroyed (25% in the engineering sector and 16% in textiles); 2,000,000 rooms were destroyed out of a total of 36,000,000 (the worst damage being suffered in the cities); and the railways were especially badly hit (60% of railway engines and 50% of goods wagons destroyed), along with automobiles (90% of lorries, 30% of buses, and 50% of motor cars) and ports and merchant shipping (which were reduced by some 90%). Shipbuilding and metallurgical manufacturing capacity was reduced by half; 5,000 bridges were destroyed; and heavy losses were suffered in the agricultural sector, productivity falling by 60% with serious damage to 770,000 hectares of cultivated land and 67,000 hectares of woodland and the destruction of 135,000,000 vines and fruit trees.

3. Government and legal system

(a) Up to 25 July 1943

The triumph of the fascist movement in 1922 was the product of three years of political instability which was caused by the end of liberal hegemony, signalled in the 1919 elections, and by the absence of any accord between the two major parties, the socialists (from whom the communists seceded in 1921) and the Catholics. The 'red' agitation, which culminated in the occupation of the factories in September 1920, was overcome by violence by the squads of the Fasci di combattimento founded by Mussolini in 1919. These fascist squads, or *squadristi*, were aided by elements of the armed forces and by some sections of liberal society, who nursed the illusion of being able to use them as an instrument to combat the 'red' threat. After a lengthy period of ungovernability the armed fascist movement occupied the key points of the state without any real resistance, and this provoked the king in October 1922 to invite Mussolini to form a cabinet. The fascist government had the support of parliament and, as visible proof of its alliance with crown and armed forces, it had as ministers for the army and navy the victors of the First World War, General Armando Diaz and Admiral Paolo Thaon di Revel. The transformation from democracy to fascist regime took place between 1925 and 1926 after the political crisis of 1924, during which crown and army supported Mussolini when he might have been unseated by the wave of anger following the assassination of the Socialist leader, Giacomo Matteotti, by fascists.

By the eve of the Second World War, the transformation was long established. Mussolini, as well as being Duce of fascism, was head of government and responsible only to the king. Ministers were responsible to him and not to parliament, which lacked power and was nominated by fascist organizations with the approval of rigged plebiscites which were themselves abolished after 1934. Mussolini nominated the members of the Fascist Grand Council, which he alone could call together in secret session to debate specific issues or so that he could learn their opinions on the most important topics of the moment. Among these, according to a law of 1928, were the powers of the crown and the succession to the throne—a warning of some significance to the ruling house of Savoy. However Mussolini declared war on the UK, France, the USSR, and the USA without ever consulting his Grand Council.

Local administration was nominated and directed from above. There were no other parties apart from the fascists and there was no freedom of speech. The press, and subsequently the cinema and the radio, were controlled by an under-secretary of state's office (which became a ministry in 1935). The secret police (OVRA) operated without restrictions, using informers, wire-tapping, and intercepting mail. Opponents of the regime were tried by a special tribunal formed from officials of the fascist militia. Working through provincial commissions, the government could put anyone into political confinement, which meant exiling them to the most isolated localities on the mainland or to one of the small islands in the south. There were no trials and sentences were decided and prolonged arbitrarily. The death penalty was re-introduced for both civil and political crimes. Workers' and owners' organizations were 'fascistized' and conflicts of authority resolved through the so-called 'corporations'. Schools, universities, and leisure organizations were also 'fascistized'. The youth movement Gioventú Italiana del Littorio (GIL), later imitated in Germany by the Nazis, controlled young males between the ages of 6 and 21, using uniforms, rifles, and the trappings of the military to inculcate ideas of discipline. GIL was divided into the Figli della Lupa, for those from 6 to 9, Balilla from 10 to 13, Avanguardisti from 14 to 17, and Giovani Fascisti from 18 to 21. There were also two female sections, the Piccole Italiane (9–14) and the Giovane Fasciste (15–17). The appearance of consensus was organized through mass rallies, sports, gymnastics, hikes, and camps and orchestrated according to a liturgy derived in part from Bolshevik models and in part from the inventions of the celebrated soldier-poet Gabriele D'Annunzio (1863–1938).

Despite all this control absolute totalitarianism, in the sense of absorbing within the state every morsel of national life, was never attained. Many institutions which predated fascism were not replaced by party structures, not only because Mussolini had perforce to rely on elements such as the Catholic Church, the crown, the upper bourgeoisie, and the higher levels of the state bureaucracy which were difficult to bring within the ambit of party hegemony, but also because of calculations which were, at least in the short term, quite astute. Mussolini imposed his personal dominance on a balance between the old and the new without allowing the forces on either side to claim him. In general he preferred to entrust himself to the old state structure and to traditional economic forces and gain their trust, allowing them a good deal of autonomy in exchange for noisy servility. Dictatorship often meant high-level mediation, and was least controlled in the field of foreign policy where even before fascism the economic establishment had intervened only rarely and then never directly.

The many fascist organizations, which were always multiplying and expanding, served two main purposes. Above all they were a potential threat, a social wild card which only the Duce could tame or unleash. Then, and increasingly as time went on, they acted as a form of social outlet—a means of employment and profit for the great and the humble. The characteristics of fascist dictatorship, which was both cunning and compromising, were evident too in its military organization, perfect for the exercise of power but ruinous in terms of combat effectiveness.

The fascist militia or 'Blackshirts', established in 1923 to absorb the *squadristi*, was a typical compromise. Astutely, Mussolini made the militia into a bogey for his opponents but also an opportunity for many ex-officers who had been unemployed since 1918. After 1924, during the early years of the fascist regime, the militia owed its loyalty not merely to Mussolini but also to the king. On paper is was the 'armed guard of the revolution'; in practice it was the worst face of the armed forces. Its members, old soldiers who had already seen service, were disliked by the army because they were paid slightly more. Between 1940 and 1943 a proportion of conscripts were directed into the militia, which thereby lost its volunteer character (see 5(c) below). Militia officers were usually of the lowest quality and when, during the Abyssinian war, militia divisions were created they were given regular army commanders, as well as regular artillery. During the Spanish Civil War, and notwithstanding its political character, the role of the militia was subordinated to that of the army, especially after the defeat at Guadalajara in 1937. The militia had no influence on the younger officers coming into the army and it produced no new military concepts. No real parallels can be drawn between the fascist militia and Hitler's Waffen-*SS, just as there were only superficial points of resemblance between the fascist squads and the Freikorps in the years immediately after the First World War.

In 1940–1, despite military defeats and the collapse of fascist prestige, there still prevailed among the Italian population a feeling of apathy and a sense of inevitable German supremacy. The somewhat artificial Balkan 'conquests' seemed to prefigure the future status of Italy as a satellite of the Third Reich. But by the spring of 1942, despite the successes of the Axis and the Japanese, the mood had changed. The German defeat before *Moscow in December 1941, US intervention in the war, and the increasing shortages of food combined to create a feeling that in the long run Germany must lose. Among the economic élite the fear spread that the USSR would interpose between the defeat of Germany and the Anglo-Saxon victory with consequences which would be felt both inside and outside Italy. Lower down the social scale, a revival of sympathy for communism was accompanied by an awareness of the power of the USA, something which decades of emigration had fixed firmly in the popular consciousness.

Scheming between Marshal *Badoglio and Princess Maria José of Savoy, the daughter-in-law of King Victor Emmanuel, to make contact with the British and Americans began in August 1942; by that time the most cunning leading fascists such as *Grandi and Giuseppe Bottai were also trying to get into the crown's good books. Old, and new, parties began to be active underground. In the summer of 1941 the Communist Party rebuilt its rank and file and the clandestine edition of its newspaper *L'Unità* appeared the following year. In July 1942 the Party of Action was formed as heir to the democratic 'Justice and Liberty' group whose leader, Carlo Rosselli, had been assassinated in France in 1937 on Mussolini's orders. Catholics, too, reorganized in what would become the Christian Democrat party, and exiles were active abroad: in Toulouse secret accords between the socialists and 'Justice and Liberty' were reached in 1941 and a liberal and republican congress took place in Montevideo on 27 August 1942.

The turning-point came in 1942–3 with *Stalingrad, the bloody defeat of the Italian Army on the Eastern Front, and the American landings in North Africa. The RAF bombing of northern Italian cities led to a flight from the towns into the countryside which gave rise, on trains and in factories, to a freedom of discussion not seen or dared for years. All strata of society were affected by these changes. Some soldiers and politicians, anticipating the wishes of the crown, sought contact with the Allies, but were obstructed by what seemed to Italians to be an ambiguous posture. Churchill never departed from his theme that 'one man alone, Mussolini' was responsible for Italian disasters, but in January 1943 the British foreign secretary, Anthony *Eden, rejected feelers put out via Switzerland for unseating the Duce.

At first industrialists were interested in the ferment among the fascist leaders, not only because of the opportunities it offered for personal survival but also because of the possibility of political reincarnation. In November–December 1942 Alberto Pirelli, the rubber magnate, recorded in his diary the mixture of euphoria and animus being shown by Bottai, Dino Grandi, Galeazzo *Ciano, and Luigi Federzoni, and by Giuseppe Volpi 'who has hopes of succeeding Mussolini'. Very shortly afterwards Pirelli saw the possibility of a different outcome when, on 26 March 1943, he talked with Cardinal Luigi Maglione, a close collaborator of Pope *Pius XII, who spoke of the communist threat and of resolving the situation not by means of discredited fascist relics but through 'the monarchy, the crown, the church, the army and the leaders of the economy'.

Mussolini appeared indecisive and impotent. He urged Hitler to make a separate peace with the USSR in December 1942 and April 1943, and tried to distract public opinion by changing his entourage: the head of the *Comando Supremo was replaced on 31 January 1943, and Ciano, the foreign minister, and other members of the government were sacked on 5 February. In fact, the Duce was living from day to day and had completely lost his willpower. He failed to grasp the significance of the major strikes which took place in Milan and Turin in February 1943 (after Amsterdam, the first in Hitler's Europe); and after the Allied landings in Sicily he agreed to the calling of the Fascist Grand Council (which had not met since 1939) on 24 July, even though he knew it was likely to be hostile. The meeting was requested by Grandi, Bottai, Ciano, and others who hoped that the king would get rid of Mussolini and put them in power, possibly under a military presidency.

The meeting lasted well into the night and witnessed a noisy quarrel which left Mussolini isolated. In fact the king, after long hesitation, had just accepted a military plan masterminded by Vittorio *Ambrosio, the new head of the Comando Supremo, to arrest Mussolini as he left a royal audience, after which he could be replaced with Marshal Badoglio. The vote of the Grand Council offered the king the cover of constitutional legitimacy for this move: Mussolini was arrested on 25 July and secretly transported to a series of hideaways at Ponza, La Maddalena, and then in the mountains of Gran Sasso. (See Map 55.)

(b) From 25 July 1943

Badoglio immediately formed a government of soldiers and technocrats which excluded any of the conspirators on the grand council. Popular demonstrations in support of the change were tolerated for a few days and then viciously repressed when they crossed the boundary of political demonstration and began to demand social reforms and immediate peace, which made them immediately suspect in German eyes (100 were killed, 536 wounded, and thousands arrested, chiefly in Turin, Milan, Reggio Emilia, and Bari). Badoglio was backed by the army, the church, and the leading economic elements. Many fascist leaders hid, fled to Germany, or took refuge in neutral countries; but Enzio Galbiati, head of the fascist militia, and Carlo Scorza, secretary of the party, quickly adapted to the new conditions. After the initial period of repression anti-fascists cautiously regrouped and gradually succeeded in freeing some political detainees, including communists: more than 3,000 were freed and most became the core of the resistance (see below).

Badoglio wanted to negotiate secretly with the Allies while holding the Germans at arm's length and hoped to make an *armistice coincide with a major Anglo-American landing backed by Italian troops. Apparently the Germans played along in order to win time to reinforce their forces in Italy, which were increased from six divisions in July to eighteen in September with four more on their way. At meetings in Bologna and Treviso, Ambrosio and Raffaele Guariglia (at that time foreign minister) tried vainly to resist these reinforcements which were officially described as being for the common defence. Also the dealings with the Allies were compromised as a result of mistakes and improvisations by the Italians who hoped for an Allied landing of fifteen divisions—more troops than the British and Americans had in the whole of the Mediterranean and more than they were able to land in Normandy the following year (see OVERLORD).

On 3 September the 'short' armistice terms were signed at Cassibile. General *Eisenhower, the Allied supreme commander, agreed to send an airborne division to aid in the defence of Rome but the Italian general staff said they were unable to take the measures necessary to secure a landing for it. The clandestine negotiators, who reached Rome at considerable risk on 7 September, had therefore to return with the message that help could not be accepted. The armistice was announced on 8 September. While the Allies landed at *Salerno, against fierce German resistance, Badoglio and the general staff fled south, abandoning millions of soldiers without any orders. There were a number of heroic episodes. On Cephalonia the Acqui Division held out against the Germans from 15 to 22 September; 1,250 Italian troops died in the battle and a further 4,750 were subsequently shot. On Leros, aided by the British, the Italians held out until November 1943. In Rome the High Command used only a few of the available troops, but the Granatieri (grenadier) Division, with the armoured cars of the Montebello Regiment (of the Ariete Division) and aided by armed civilians, put up a stiff defence of Porta San Paolo. Nevertheless within only 24 hours the Italian Army disintegrated. Some 650,000 soldiers were deported to

Germany. The fleet reached Malta, en route losing the modern battleship *Roma* to German *guided weapons. The air force saved perhaps 400 planes and the army 16 divisions (7 of them coastal divisions) which were located in the far south and Sardinia.

After September 1943 Italy became a country fought over by foreign powers. National political organizations were shaped by military events: in the south, the Badoglio formula under close Anglo-American supervision and in the north the creation of the Italian Social Republic (RSI), or Saló Republic, under German domination and led by Mussolini, who had been freed by *Skorzeny. This return to the past, which used Gargnano on Lake Garda as its headquarters, was immediately challenged by a popular armed revolt co-ordinated by the clandestine Committees for National Liberation (see RESISTANCE, below). The resistance movement opposed not only the Germans and the fascists but also—with the exception of a few moderate groups—the monarchical regime which seemed to be prevailing in the south.

The RSI made much of the supposedly republican and socialist origins of fascism, reviving the name of Mazzini and accusing the monarchy, the generals, and the industrialists of betrayal, the latter after having enjoyed 20 years of preferential treatment. Mussolini's speeches on German radio on 18 September, and at the congress which met at Verona in November 1943, were revolutionary tirades on the decadence of the monarchy, the enforced nationalization of industry, and the need to fight alongside the German ally. Mussolini thought to demonstrate his 'Roman' character by having Ciano and those 'traitors' of the Grand Council on whom he could lay hands shot on 11 January 1944 (see VERONA TRIALS).

At first support for the RSI and enlistment into the military forces headed by Marshal Graziani (which included much of the Tenth Light flotilla commanded by Prince Borghese) was quite considerable, due to a combination of fear, disorientation, the desperation of old fascists who had been compromised, and a certain determination on the part of the young not to abandon at a time of misfortune a system which they had applauded while it was successful. However it rapidly became apparent that the Germans saw the RSI as no more than a tool of occupation. The provinces of Trento, Bolzano, Belluno, Gorizia, Trieste, and Pola passed under direct German administration (see Map 56). The country was systematically plundered, beginning with the gold in the Bank of Italy (see also LOOT). More than 100,000 workers were deported to Germany, while a special German office took over control of Italian industry solely for the benefit of the German war, completely disregarding Mussolini's 'socialization'. The workers showed their lack of enthusiasm for Mussolini's belated socialism and for measures nominally taken on their behalf by going on strike: more than 500,000 downed tools in Turin and Milan in November 1943 and March 1944, Conscription, attempted by the RSI, raised a few units, including four divisions which were trained in Germany, but pushed tens of thousands of young men into the burgeoning ranks of the partisans.

Important though the partisan war was, it is important not to overlook the non-fascist political developments both in the north and in the south, which were of great significance for Italy's post-war development. In the south the king and Badoglio, supported by the Allies and especially by the British, moved against the anti-fascist parties who opposed them (for the most part republicans) and who, like Count *Sforza, were generally disinclined to reach a compromise with the old ruling classes. This split risked compromising the small share in military operations which the Allies were prepared to allow the Italian forces in the south.

The situation persisted until April 1944 when, after the USSR had recognized Badoglio on 14 March, and Palmiro *Togliatti had arrived back in Italy from the USSR as Stalin's agent, the communists decided to collaborate with the king. Their sole condition was that Victor Emmanuel would step down once Rome was taken, naming his son *Umberto as his 'lieutenant', and that the future of the monarchy would be decided once the war was over. The arguments over this move (known as the 'Salerno turn-around') still persist today. Togliatti undoubtedly obeyed Moscow's orders, following a united front policy and breaking up the cohesion of the anti-monarchist bloc, as well as angering intransigent elements in his own party. On the other hand, the 'turn' was a realistic move. From the communists' point of view, dreams of revolution did not mesh with Anglo-American predominance and it was more important to integrate the party into post-war politics. From the national point of view, this ended the immediate struggle and created a common body of anti-fascist feeling which lasted into the *Cold War and beyond.

The formation of a government which included the main parties of the Committees for National Liberation, under the leadership first of Badoglio and then, from June 1944, of Ivanoe *Bonomi, won support from the Allies and the Soviets, thereby allowing the artful Badoglio the opportunity sometimes to play one side off against the other.

4. Defence forces and civil defence

Until the end of the 19th century, the Italian alpine and maritime frontiers were defended by a combination of permanent fortifications and fixed artillery. After the First World War, new corps and new specialist bodies were formed to fulfil these tasks (and the new duty of anti-aircraft defence): these included the Frontier Guard (Guardia alla Frontiera, or GAF), made up of nine regiments of artillery and one of infantry as well as a number of smaller detachments, which was divided among eleven army corps districts as well as being assigned to special defensive zones. In addition there were specialist militia units which included MILMART (Milizia Marittima Artiglieria), or coastal artillery and DICAT (Difesa Contraerea Territoriale), the country's anti-aircraft command which had many machine-guns and, by 1940, consisted of some 200 batteries armed at times with good guns but lacking fire directors. In 1940–3 these units, along with some 400 battalions of territorial and coastal troops, were divided among the fifteen regional army corps commands. The whole was commanded by a chief of staff for territorial defence, responsible sometimes to the war minister and sometimes to the army chief of general staff. In addition to these forces, all military units which were permanently or temporarily stationed in command districts were available for territorial defence duties. Fortified naval bases and selected tracts of coastline had special defences.

This organization was extended and strengthened during the war, partly by adding to fixed units and partly by stationing mobile units in such a way as to secure the defence of the most threatened zones, commencing in 1940–1 with the major islands. Gradually the islands and the peninsula itself were divided into military districts allocated to the various armies (Sixth Army in Sicily, Seventh Army in the far south, Fifth Army for a large part of the Tyrrhenian coast and Sardinia). The exact number of troops involved is impossible to determine but by the summer of 1941 it exceeded half a million. This figure increased to approximately 1,500,000 men when the 25 to 30 mobile divisions stationed in Italy were also taken into account; these included units assigned to armies in the course of formation, those preparing to go to the Eastern and African fronts and those earmarked for special duties such as the planned landings on Corsica and Malta, as well as the Fourth Army which was stationed on the French frontier. In the summer of 1941, 350 anti-parachutist groups (Nuclei anti Paracadutisti, or NAP) were also created and spread throughout the country. Formed from army units, and sometimes from the fascist militia, they numbered 20–35 men each and were equipped with a lorry and sometimes with bicycles and motor cycles. These units seem to have done good service; and their creation avoided the need to have recourse to the *carabinieri* (see 5(c) below) and security guards as had happened when a group of British parachutists had successfully been hunted down and eliminated in the Calabrian region (see TRAGINO).

The most important innovation, however, was the publication of regulations for the defence of the maritime frontier in the autumn of 1941, following which 20 divisions and ten coastal brigades were created in the succeeding 12 to 16 months. A protective cordon of units comprising infantry, machine-gun detachments, old artillery, and extremely primitive communications was set up, starting with the most exposed zones (Sicily and Sardinia). These divisions and brigades, which eventually amounted to more than 600,000 men after absorbing pre-existing units with similar functions, were assigned to the various armies garrisoning the peninsula. Their task was to delay any attempted enemy landing for long enough to allow the mobile units stationed in the interior to intervene. The structure, sensible enough in itself, would have functioned well had the armament and communications of the coastal units been better and had the interior forces consisted of strong armoured and motorized forces; however, most were infantry divisions, moderately well equipped but at best only transportable by motor vehicles in relays. Their artillery was mostly of pre-First World War vintage; and their transport, a motley collection of mules, horses, bicycles, motor cycles, and a few lorries, belonged in a museum. Given this state of affairs, it is remarkable that some of the coastal units in Sicily (for example, the 202nd Division) gave the Anglo-American forces such a good run for their money at the start of the *Sicilian campaign, albeit briefly.

Anti-aircraft defences were allocated to different localities according to available resources. Many of these locales were simply 'spotting zones', with personnel equipped only with a pair of binoculars and a telephone. More effective were the improvised arrangements made at the time when the RAF launched its major raids on the northern cities from autumn 1942 to summer 1943 (see STRATEGIC AIR OFFENSIVES, 2). Since the British bomber formations almost always flew over Switzerland, Italian diplomats and consuls there were able to telephone warnings to military commanders who then had sirens sounded. The air force took no part in anti-aircraft defence: it exercised autonomous control over fighter interceptions, which were almost always launched on the return routes.

The fact that, from 1941 to 1943, there were never less than a million and a half men stationed in Italy, a figure which eventually rose to over two million, raises a number of important issues. For one thing, Italy never had any equivalent to the British Home Guard. The only comparable body of which any traces remain is the National Union for Anti-Aircraft Protection (Union Nazional Protezione Antiacrea, or UNPA), whose activities involved fining those who broke the *blackout regulations and collaborating with the fire brigade in putting out incendiaries and helping the population during and after bombing attacks. Finally it is worth noting that in order to maintain the appearance of normality, Mussolini authorized large public works programmes as late as 1942. None was ever completed, but some were begun using valuable concrete which the military had requested for coastal fortifications.

5. Armed forces and special forces

(a) High Command

From 1925 Mussolini was minister for all armed forces, save for a brief interlude between 1929 and 1933. He acted through three under-secretaries who were almost always also chiefs of staff of their respective branches of the armed forces. These officials, who enjoyed a large measure of autonomy in exchange for public servility to the Duce, were generally switched every three years or so. This system gave Mussolini the advantage of dealing with each of the armed forces separately; for him this advantage outweighed the consequent inefficiency and lack of co-ordination. The post of chief of general staff of the armed forces (see COMANDO SUPREMO), created by laws of 1925 and 1927, was held by Marshal Badoglio, one of the heroes of 1918. He was a meticulous, professional soldier but one whose mind was entirely closed to modern ideas, and he was little more than a figurehead.

Badoglio, who had no staff to head, acted as an adviser to the Duce and could only correspond with the chiefs of staff of the three arms through their respective ministries—which almost always meant going through Mussolini. He lacked any real powers but served to calm the anxieties of the crown and the public who, ignorant of the true state of affairs, saw him at the head of the armed forces and trusted him. Badoglio accepted this role and also took on other lucrative tasks: he was governor of Libya 1929–33 and commanded in Abyssinia in 1935–6. In 1938 Mussolini, wishing to give himself high military rank (notwithstanding his legal powers, he was still only a sergeant in the light infantry, or *bersaglieri*), passed a law making himself and the king 'first marshals of the empire'. In 1940, on the eve of war, he persuaded the king to delegate overall military command to him personally.

As supreme commander, Mussolini was assisted by Badoglio, chief of the armed forces general staff, whose powers in relation both to the Duce and the three services were ill-defined. At the end of 1940 Badoglio was replaced by Ugo *Cavallero who completely reformed the post in June 1941 (see below), before being replaced by Vittorio Ambrosio in 1943. The navy and the air force were both commanded by chiefs of staff who also retained the powers of ministerial under-secretaries (Mussolini himself being the minister in both cases); they were respectively Admiral Domenico Cavagnari (replaced in December 1940 by Arturo Riccardi and in 1943 by Raffaele De Courten) and General Francesco Pricolo (replaced by Rino Corso Fougier in 1941 and Renato Sandalli in 1943). From November 1939 the posts of chief of staff and under-secretary of the army, which had previously been combined, were separated and given respectively to Marshal Rodolfo *Graziani and General Ubaldo Soddu. Soddu, who in June 1940 also became deputy chief of the armed forces general staff (and therefore Badoglio's deputy), briefly commanded the Italian troops in the Balkan campaign before being retired in December 1940. The post of deputy chief of the armed forces general staff was abolished by Cavallero as part of his reforms, while the under-secretaryship of war was held first by General Antonino Squero (1941) and then by General Antonio Sorice (1943). Despite being put in command of Libya after the death of Marshal Balbo on 28 June 1940, Graziani remained the army chief of staff until march 1941, aided as deputy chief of staff by Mario Roatta who himself assumed the post in 1941, being succeeded in January 1942 by Vittorio Ambrosio and in February 1943 by Ezio Rosi; finally in June 1943 Roatta returned once more.

This complex pyramid, complicated from the first months of the war by shifts in function and authority both in Rome and at the various military fronts, encouraged Mussolini's—and Ciano's—natural tendencies to intervene at all levels of the hierarchy with verbal, written, and telephoned orders which were often contradictory.

In the winter of 1940–1, disasters on land and at sea put an end to the 'parallel' war which Mussolini had hoped to win with only indirect German assistance. Hitler now intervened directly in the battle for the *Mediterranean, not to win the conflict there but only to help his ally. Rommel's small but highly effective force stabilized the position in Libya while large German forces overawed Romania and Bulgaria and by June 1941 had conquered Yugoslavia, Greece, and Crete. In Germany's wake, Italy gained large but unpacified territories in Dalmatia, Slovenia, Croatia, Montenegro, and Greece.

The substantial Italian forces detached to the Balkans from 1941 onwards were naturally involved in the anti-partisan campaigns, which were especially bitter in Yugoslavia, as were the units in France although to a much lesser extent. Alongside the excesses of these campaigns should be set the fact that the *Garibaldi Division fought with *Tito and the partisans and that the Italian military authorities saved some 600,000 Croatian Jews from the *Ustašas* and as (in 1942–3) protected approximately 240,000 French Jews from capture by the Germans and the *Vichy police.

While the bulk of the German forces then turned on the USSR in June 1941 (see BARBAROSSA), and were employed almost exclusively on the Eastern Front until the summer of 1944, there began for Mussolini what was called—though not by him—the 'subaltern war', which aimed at currying favour with Germany. With the end of the Balkan campaign, which was at once followed by a guerrilla war, the structure of the Italian High Command settled down a little. Cavallero had replaced Badoglio in December 1940 but until May 1941 he had remained in Albania commanding the Italian Forces fighting the Greeks. He then returned to Rome and set up a real Supreme Command, somewhat larger and better organized than Badoglio's which even by December 1940 had numbered only a few more officers than the 26 of the previous June. He was unable to make himself the only intermediary between Mussolini and the armed forces because the heads of the navy and the air force, who as under-secretaries were part of the government, continued to deal directly with the Duce. However he did improve inter-service collaboration and he tried to improve protection for naval traffic with Libya, now being held to ransom by the British thanks to *ULTRA intelligence. However his efforts to improve the quality of Italian equipment were still hampered by inefficiency and vested interests (see DOMESTIC LIFE, above).

(b) Army

From 1937 the organizational target was an army of 126 divisions (see Graph for numbers actually achieved, and

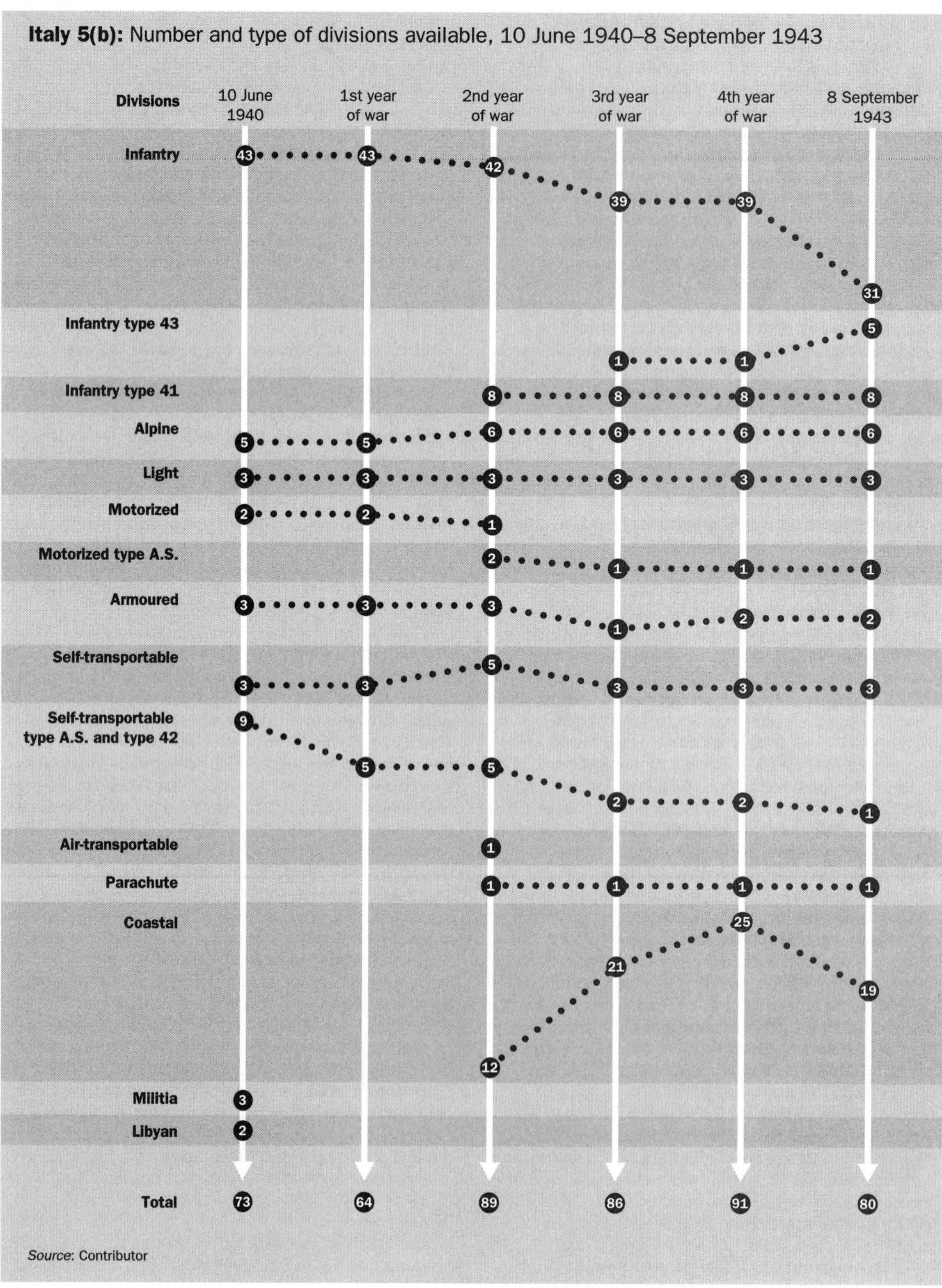

Source: Contributor

type). These *formations—called 'binary' divisions as they had two regiments of three battalions each instead of the previous three of three—were really mixed brigades which included two regimental batteries of pack artillery of eight 65 mm. (2.5 in.) guns and two of 81 mm. (3.1 in.) mortars (12 guns), a divisional battalion of 81 mm. mortars (18 guns), a divisional regiment of artillery of 24 75 mm. (2.9 in.) guns and 12 100 mm. (3.9 in.) guns (all horse-drawn or pack) and sometimes in addition an anti-tank company of eight 47 mm. (1.8 in.) guns (not self-propelled), one anti-aircraft company of eight 20 mm. (0.8 in.) machine-guns and a somewhat shabby force of fascist Blackshirts (two small battalions).

The so-called 'self-transportable' divisions had a regiment of truck-drawn artillery and could move their infantry on specially assigned trucks. Motorized divisions had three motorized regiments (six battalions in all), and motorized artillery. Light divisions (*celeri*) consisted of two regiments of cavalry, one of *bersaglieri* on trucks, motor cycles, and bicycles, and a regiment of artillery which was partly horse-drawn and partly motorized. Armoured divisions had one regiment of infantry consisting of 184 light tanks, a regiment of *bersaglieri* (two battalions in trucks, the third on motor cycles) and a regiment of motorized artillery of 24 75 mm. guns. Alpine divisions consisted of two regiments of *alpini* and a regiment of artillery of 24 75 mm. pack guns. Anti-aircraft and *anti-tank weapons were slightly increased in the motorized and light divisions, while in the armoured divisions only the 20 mm. guns were doubled in number. Alpine divisions had neither anti-aircraft nor anti-tank guns. Colonial divisions could be transported by truck but had particularly antiquated weapons.

Infantry divisions functioned as 'attack columns', which were easily self-transportable, to create and exploit any tactical opportunity, and control both of the movement of individual divisions and of the medium calibre guns was retained by army corps headquarters. Replacement of the First World War artillery was planned to start only in 1942–3. Automobiles were few and tanks, other than the 24 very poor M11s in Abyssinia and another 72 quickly sent to Libya, were always the feeble CV3 (see GOVERNMENT, above). Radio communications were generally backward, and no tanks were equipped with radios. The so-called 'binary division' can fairly be criticized because it served chiefly to increase the number of generals in the army. However, during the war almost every army lightened its divisions and Italy had to do so in the *Western Desert campaigns in 1941–2, diminishing the infantry component yet further by increasing anti-tank and anti-aircraft units. The failure of the binary division in the Balkan campaign of 1940–1, which was fought in First World War style, was due above all to the fact that Mussolini had just sent 600,000 men out of a total force of 1,100,000 on leave for political reasons and, not wanting to recall them, filled the divisions with untrained men who were unfamiliar even with basic infantry weapons.

On 10 June 1940 the army numbered 1,600,000 men (600,000 overseas and 1,000,000 in Italy, to whom a further 100,000 were added during the summer), with 19,500 regular and 37,000 reserve officers. Excluding Italian East Africa, which had a separate organization, it comprised 26 army corps: one armoured, one self-transportable, one light, one alpine, and 22 ordinary corps. There were 73 divisions in the army: 3 armoured, 2 motorized, 3 light, 5 Alpine, 43 marching infantry, and 17 'self-transportable'. Of these, 14 self-transportable divisions (including 3 Blackshirt and 2 colonial divisions) were in Libya (Fifth and Tenth Armies), 5 in Albania (1 armoured, 3 infantry, and 1 Alpine), one infantry division was in the *Dodecanese and the remaining 53 divisions were in Italy.

These forces were divided into three army groups. Army Group West (commanded by Umberto of Savoy, Prince of Piedmont) contained the First Army under General Pietro Pintor and the Fourth Army under General Alfredo Guzzoni and numbered 22 divisions, four of them Alpine. Army Group East (commanded by General Camillo Grossi) comprised the Second Army under General Ambrosio, the Sixth Army, the Po, under General Mario Vercellino, and the Eighth Army under the Duke of Bergamo. Army Group South (commanded by Marshal Emilio De Bono) was composed of the Third Army under General Carlo Geloso, two army corps scattered on the larger islands, and the Albanian command. The Seventh Army (commanded by the Duke of Pistoia) formed a general reserve. Outside Italy there was an Aegean Islands Command under General Cesare Maria de Vecchi, while in Libya first Balbo and then Graziani commanded the Tenth Army under General Mario Berti and the Fifth Army under General Italo Gariboldi which amounted to fourteen infantry divisions, three of which were Blackshirts and two were colonial divisions.

During the course of the war the army groups and armies were frequently dissolved and reconstituted with varying shapes and contents. During 1940–1 the three army groups and First, Third, Sixth, and Eighth Armies were dissolved and a special army group was created for the Balkan campaign comprising two new armies, the Ninth under General Vercellino and then Alessandro Pirzio Biroli, and the Eleventh under General Geloso. After May 1941 they garrisoned Albania and Greece respectively. Yugoslavian territory was occupied until 1943 by the Second Army commanded by General Ambrosio, then Roatta, and finally Mario Robotti with a special corps in Montenegro under Pirzio Biroli. The Fourth Army under General Vercellino was stationed on the French frontier and in November 1942 occupied large areas of Vichy France. The Eighth Army, reconstructed in 1942, was sent to the Eastern Front (see below), while the Sixth Army under General Guzzoni, now with a very different composition, was in Sicily at the time of the Allied landings in July 1943. After the destruction of the Tenth Army in the Western Desert campaigns and the dissolution of the Fifth Army in Libya in 1941, Italian forces operated alongside Rommel's divisions only up to corps level; commanded first by Gariboldi and then by General Ettore Bastico, they included an armoured corps (commanded successively by Generals Gastone Gambara, Francesco Zingales, Ettore Baldassare, and Giuseppe De Stefanis). In 1942 these corps were incorporated into Rommel's German–Italian Panzer Army. This in turn was transformed into the First Italian Army in Tunisia (though it retained the German forces) and this force, under the orders of General (later Marshal) *Messe fought bravely at *Mareth, Wadi Akarit, and Enfidaville during the last phase of the North African campaign. Meanwhile other Italian troops fought in Tunisia under the command of the Fifth German Army.

In June 1940 some 30 divisions (First, Fourth, and Seventh Armies and part of Sixth Army), under the command of Prince Umberto, the heir to the throne, attacked through the French Alps with little success. Then 40 divisions were concentrated in the Veneto (the three regions of Venezia, Venezia Tridentina, and Venezia Giulia) for an attack on Yugoslavia, but this was forbidden by Hitler in August 1940. In the Western Desert Marshal Graziani, who had taken over command after Marshal Balbo had been shot down over Tobruk by Italian anti-aircraft fire, advanced 100 km. (62 mi.) into Egypt, using 72 M11 tanks alongside his infantry columns, but was subsequently defeated at *Sidi Barrani, *Bardia, and *Beda Fomm.

From Italian East Africa, where the Duke of Aosta commanded 352 obsolescent aircraft, and 91,000 Italian and 200,000 native troops (divided into 2 divisions, 29 colonial brigades, and 34 other battalions), excursions were made into the Sudan and Kenya (see EAST AFRICAN CAMPAIGN), and British Somaliland was captured. But by mid-1941 these early victories had been turned into defeat.

Despite these commitments, Mussolini still had sufficient resources to take part in the *German–Soviet war, even though the Germans had not initially asked for Italian assistance. An army corps made up of three divisions (Torino, Pasubio, and 3rd Light) was sent to the Eastern Front in 1941 and, under the command of Messe, fought well both on the offensive (at Petrikowka on the *Dnieper, Stalino, and elsewhere) and on the defensive (in the Donetz basin). In 1942, this time at Germany's request, Italian forces were greatly expanded. The Eighth Army, now under the command of Gariboldi (Messe was repatriated in October 1942), now had a further seven divisions in addition to the original three: Ravenna, Cosseria, Sforzesca, and Vicenza (infantry), and Julia, Tridentina, and Cuneense (Alpine) as well as some Blackshirt units. In total the force, which had numbered 60,000 under Messe, now amounted to 220,000 men. The air component, which in 1941 had amounted to some 90 fighter, reconnaissance, and transport planes, was expanded in 1942 by the addition of more modern fighters (MC202s), several reconnaissance and bomber squadrons (twin-engined Fiat BR20s), and other transport aircraft. Most importantly, the very few modern heavy and anti-tank guns went to the Eastern Front—36 of the 48 available 149 mm. (5.8 in.) guns, all 12 210 mm. (8.1 in.) howitzers and the only 36 75 mm. (2.9 in.) guns—as well as over 16,000 motor vehicles, more than would have been necessary to motorize all the Italian forces in North Africa. The Italian Army advanced to the Don where it was partially destroyed by the Soviet counter-offensive at *Stalingrad which crushed the entire German southern wing of the front. Some *midget submarines and small surface units of Italy's most successful special forces unit, the Tenth Light Flotilla, had a number of successes in the *Black Sea, and on Lake Ladoga during the siege of *Leningrad. But it was the employment of the Italian land forces on the Eastern Front which helped to frustrate a sketchy and ill-thought-out Mediterranean strategy pursued by the Axis in the spring of 1942.

In fact the *matériel* destined for the Eastern Front was collected together at a time when the efforts of the Italian fleet and German U-boats, together with the temporary air reinforcements granted by Hitler, would have allowed the shipment of more stores to Libya for several months. At the same time preparations were made during the siege of *Malta for an amphibious attack on the island, in which the crack Folgore Parachute Division and a number of other, better adapted, units were scheduled to take part. All this was in vain when, after the capture of *Tobruk on 21 June 1942, Hitler abandoned the Malta project in favour of pursuing the retreating British forces deep into Egypt. The epilogue occurred at *El Alamein in October 1942, where the Italians sacrificed the Trento, Bologna, Brescia, and Pavia infantry divisions, the Folgore parachute division, the Sabratha Division (lost at the end of July), and most of the two armoured divisions (Ariete and Littorio).

By this stage, with the German failure in the east, which also shook the Italian Army, and with the North African landings heralding the start of the North African campaign, the Axis Mediterranean strategy had become simply one of survival. Fierce resistance was put up in Tunisia to this end, resulting in the loss of the last armoured division (Centauro), the Giovani Fascisti and Trieste infantry divisions (formerly motorized, they had survived Siwa and El Alamein respectively), and a number of other units initially destined for Malta (Pistoia, La Spezia, and Superga). Also destined for Malta was the Livorno Division which instead fought bravely in Sicily in July and August 1943. If the 20 coastal divisions, which were of little account, are subtracted from the 90 divisions—now totalling about three million men—which existed in 1943, along with the remnants of the 10 divisions lost on the Eastern Front, 10 lost in Sicily (of which 6 were coastal divisions), and the 40 or so divisions divided between the Balkans and France, there remained only about 15 divisions, some of whom opposed the German occupation after the armistice on 8 September 1943 and later fought with the Allies. In fact, despite Anglo-American lack of enthusiasm, Italian participation in the *Italian campaign grew. Until the summer of 1944 the Italians were only permitted a 'motorized group' (a reinforced regiment), which fought at *Monte Cassino, and the Italian Corps of Liberation (equivalent to a division) which operated chiefly in the Adriatic sector.

However, the transfer of some Allied forces from Italy for the *French Riviera landings in August 1944 forced *Alexander to arm six Italian divisions, of which four were used, although they were called 'combat groups' and not allowed to combine into a single corps for fear of political repercussions. The soldiers who made up these 'groups' (which were deployed from January to April 1945 in the front between Bologna and the Adriatic) fought bravely and at some cost: 1,868 died, 5,187 were wounded, and 443 were listed as missing, mostly killed.

To these losses, and those of 8 September 1943 (19,000 dead and wounded) may be added those suffered in the war against the Allies: some 200,000 dead (80,000 on the Eastern Front, more than 50,000 in the Balkans, 20–22,000 in Africa, some 40–50,000 at sea, in the air and in minor episodes), a larger but unknown number of wounded, and more than 600,000 taken prisoner. Even today there are no exact figures, but it is reasonable to estimate the total number of dead, including those who fell in the partisan war and the victims of Allied bombing, reprisals, German *deportations, and so on, at above 300,000.

(c) Fascist Militia and Carabinieri

By 1940 the fascist militia or Blackshirts amounted to 177 legions (39 of which were attached to infantry divisions of the army while another six formed three divisions in Libya), as well as about 200 battalions (of which 132 were territorials and 30 were in Italian East Africa), and a number of specialized units which included DICAT anti-aircraft units (22 artillery legions with 228 batteries and 4,206 machine-gun squads) and MILMART coastal artillery (see DEFENCE FORCES, above). Discounting militia units with non-military roles (roads, forests, post and telegraph), there were in Italy and its colonies more than 300,000 Blackshirts. The militia divisions in Libya were comparable to the 'self transportable' infantry divisions of the army. In addition, the fascist organizations formed battalions of fascist youth, some of whom were incorporated into the army and performed well in the Western Desert and in North Africa from the autumn of 1941 until May 1943.

The *carabinieri*, founded in Piedmont in 1814, came under the war ministry for their organization and equipment and under the interior ministry for their employment. They functioned as military police and sometimes formed combat units. There were also two other less important police forces: the public security police and the customs police (*guardia di finanza*). In 1940 the *carabinieri* amounted to 7 brigades, 28 territorial legions (the equivalent of militia regiments), one school, one pupil legion, and a number of overseas detachments in East Africa, Libya, Albania, and Egypt. It had also formed three administrative divisions, and by the summer of 1943 numbered 156,000 men.

(d) Navy

The Italian Navy was every bit as fiercely independent as the air force. As its head, Admiral Cavagnari served as chief of staff and under-secretary for seven years—an exceptionally lengthy period of command during the fascist regime. Its 6 battleships (2 modern and 4 re-built), 19 cruisers (7 of 10,000 tons), its 100 smaller surface vessels (which included three *auxiliary cruisers), and 113 submarines were built on the basis of two erroneous suppositions: that Italy's enemy would be France alone and that the First World War naval battle of Jutland would remain the eternal model for all naval actions. The 168,614 officers and men of the Italian Navy in June 1940 (a number which had risen to 259,000 by August 1943) formed a separate body, perhaps better trained than the two other services but still a long way behind other navies in respect of its technical development. Leaving aside the lack of radar and *ASDIC and the absence of aircraft carriers, it may be noted that naval gunnery put a premium on muzzle velocity and range rather than on accuracy, that speeds reached during trials could not be maintained on active service due to poor sea-keeping ability, and that night fighting was regarded as an improbability. Supplies of oil were limited from the start, amounting to only 1,700,000 tons which had been stockpiled before the war started and which, from the summer of 1941 onwards, had to be supplemented by a monthly supply from Romania. More serious was the attitude that large and expensive warships should not be risked lest Italy end the war without a navy. It was almost as though the naval High Command wanted to preserve its fleet even at the cost of losing the war.

It was this outlook, and not any lack of courage, which led to no risks being taken in the summer of 1940 when fuel was still abundant but peace seemed close at hand. However the fleet was employed at the end of 1941 and during the first half of 1942, despite the shortage of fuel, when Malta and the situation in the Western Desert made it inescapable. It was once again kept from danger in 1942–3 when, with peace looming, conserving a navy seemed more important than making a grand gesture; by this time, a shortage of light shipping exacerbated the problems of lack of fuel and air cover. Paradoxically, it was the British—the defenders, not the aggressors—who attacked first when they raided *Taranto on 12 November 1940. Three Italian battleships were disabled by their antiquated Swordfish biplanes and the prudence with which Cavagnari had restrained his admirals during the summer, directing their operations from the navy staff war room at admiralty headquarters in Rome, went for nothing. Taranto cost Cavagnari his job (he was replaced by Admiral Arturo Riccardi), but the more determined deployment of surface vessels terminated in disaster at *Cape Matapan (28 March 1941).

The most notable Italian achievements in the war at

sea were attained by small submarine units; by torpedo bombers operating against the Malta *convoys, especially during August 1942; and by Tenth Light Flotilla attacks on warships and merchant ships in British harbours at Alexandria, Suda Bay, and Gibraltar.

All in all, the navy performed well in supplying Italian troops in Libya for three years despite British intervention from Malta and above all the effects of ULTRA intelligence from the summer of 1941. The sacrifice of both men and ships was considerable: some 15,000 of the 33,859 men in the navy died and over 800,000 tons of merchant shipping was lost (see below). But when regarded in aggregate terms the results of this effort were remarkable: 91.7% of the 206,202 men and 84.6% of the 2,844,698 tons of stores and fuel sent to North Africa were landed there. Many more men were transported by plane, although capacity was limited by the need to carry fuel for the return trip. However, although the loads successfully carried by sea and air were large in percentage terms, they were much less than what was needed. Traffic was protected partly by mining the Sicilian straits and the confines of Tripoli using German mines; this contributed to the partial destruction of *Force K in December 1941.

By the time of the armistice of September 1943 the navy had preserved six battleships and nine cruisers after sacrificing many smaller ships and submarines—the latter taking part in the battle of the *Atlantic from 1941. Having possessed about 680,000 tons of shipping at the start of the war, to which were added 136,234 tons of new construction and 62,453 tons of seized foreign shipping, the navy had lost 334,757 tons (265,392 tons of surface shipping and 69,365 tons of submarines). Three cruisers, 11 destroyers, 6 torpedo boats, 15 smaller vessels, and 11 submarines had been sunk by gunfire; a battleship, 6 cruisers, 11 destroyers, 7 torpedo boats, 7 smaller ships, and 41 submarines had been sunk by aerial or naval torpedoes. The battleship lost was the *Cavour*, damaged at Taranto and not fully repaired by 8 September 1943. Aerial bombing accounted for 2 cruisers, 9 destroyers, 10 torpedo boats, and 98 smaller vessels. Mines sank 6 destroyers, 12 torpedo boats, 12 smaller ships, and 3 submarines. Finally a cruiser, 7 destroyers, 6 torpedo boats, 66 smaller ships, and 20 submarines were lost to unknown causes.

(e) Air Force

The Italian Air Force, the pride of fascism and greatly overrated by outsiders, comprised 23 flights of land bombers, 2 flights of naval bombers, 1 group of dive-bombers, 1 assault flight, and 2 combat groups; 6 flights, 8 groups, and 2 squadrons of fighters; 56 reconnaissance squadrons and 2 colonial groups. In all, these formations amounted to 1,753 front-line aircraft, of which only 900 were modern machines. The Fiat CR42 biplane fighters, which were even inferior to the British Gloster Gladiator biplane, and the bombers dating from 1936 which had operated in Spain, were counted as 'modern'. Not all planes had radios and aerial intercommunications did not exist until well into 1942; few planes were equipped for night flying and torpedo bombers were not yet organized. The theories of strategic bombing propounded by General Giulio Douhet (1869–1930) were paraded by the air force, but only to justify its complete independence from the other services, an independence which prevented the manufacture of aircraft carriers and destroyed any hopes of air–navy collaboration. Germany's apart, Italy's was the only major navy which did not control its own aviation.

Between 8 and 15 July 1940, 490 triple-engined bombers attacked British naval squadrons in the Mediterranean using level-flight bombing tactics. Their *bombs—50 kg. (110 lb.), 100 kg. (220 lb.), and a few 250 kg. (550 lb.)—were too small to have any effect even when, as happened only rarely, they hit their target. The pilots were brave but they did not have the same level of training as their opponents. Some squadrons bombed Gibraltar and even the Persian Gulf. When 200 planes were transferred from Italy to Belgium to take part in the *Blitz against the UK, 20% of the force was lost or damaged in error during its flight over friendly territory. However, by the end of 1941 some fighter squadrons, flying Macchi 202s fitted with German Daimler Benz engines, began to show evidence of their effectiveness. Before then torpedo bombers had been introduced and pilots, operating slow and large S79s and S84s, attacked British convoys sailing to Malta with great tenacity in 1941–2, sinking or damaging a number of mechantmen and warships, among them the battleship *Nelson* (27 September 1941). But by the summer of 1943 the Italian Air Force numbered fewer than a hundred modern fighters and perhaps a thousand more older planes which were almost valueless.

(f) Special Forces

Amid their dreams of greatness, the Italians had forgotten the insidious means by which they had achieved their naval successes with light motor torpedo boats and *human torpedoes during the First World War. Neglected until 1930 and then revived in 1940, too late to make a major impact when Italy entered the war, this type of operation, mounted by Tenth Light Flotilla, was especially suitable for employment by an under-developed country because it was economical in everything but courage. However, despite the valour of its crews, the novelty of its equipment, and the efficiency of its organization it had to wait many months for its first successes.

The Italians also operated a number of other special forces. The 10th Arditi Regiment's two battalions were trained in sabotage, either as parachutists or using jeeps, the former having some success when US aircraft were attacked on Benina airfield near Benghazi in June 1943. The Sahara companies, a rare example of effective co-operation between the Italian Air Force and the army, were under the command of air force officers. Used to defend the southern regions of Libya, they were eventually bested by *Leclerc's French troops in the *Fezzan campaigns. Other special units included the San Marco Landing Regiment, the Monte Cervino Alpini Ski Battalion, and the Libyan Carabinieri Parachute Battalion.

6. Intelligence

Neither the Italian High Command nor Mussolini, who retained direct personal responsibility for the preparation and co-ordination of the armed forces, ever understood the importance of a single unified system of military intelligence which was both authoritative and properly resourced. In consequence, both in peace and in war Italy had a number of intelligence services whose respective areas of competence were never clearly defined and which were riven with bitter rivalries, at considerable cost to their efficiency and credibility. (It should be noted that reliable studies of them are few since their archives remain closed.)

The most important agency was SIM (Servizio Informazioni Militari), a branch of the army. Technically the most efficient at intercepting and decrypting enemy communications, it was active both inside Italy and abroad but lacked overseas centres and spy networks. In the years before the Second World War SIM had shown a marked propensity to play a political role under the wing of Galeazzo Ciano, being extremist in the Spanish Civil War and anti-German in the period 1939–40. In 1940 it numbered 150 officers, 300 non-commisioned officers, and 400 other ranks. Alongside SIM there existed other military intelligence agencies: naval intelligence (Servizio Informazioni Segrete, or SIS) was very efficient, while air force intelligence (Servizio Informazioni Aeronautica, or SIA) was of minor significance. In addition overseas theatres of operations—East Africa, Libya, the Aegean, and Albania—each had its own autonomous military intelligence service.

Inside Italy intelligence functions were also carried out by the *carabinieri* (see 5(c) above) which, besides acting as military police, also operated against general crime and political opposition and furnished SIM with many of its personnel; and by the police, the fascist regime's preferred instrument in the suppression of opposition and the maintenance of order. The intelligence services of minor branches of the regime such as the fascist militia and the customs police (*guardia di finanza*) also played a part in counter-espionage. The ministry of foreign affairs, the governor of Albania, and the Italian African police also had their own intelligence services which dealt in part with military matters.

There was no co-ordination whatsoever between all these arms. Mussolini never acknowledged the necessity for such co-ordination since his own role as dictator was strengthened by rivalry between various organs of the state. The inefficiency of the military intelligence services was therefore only one facet of the general lack of military preparation for war. The extent to which the Comando Supremo, the Italian High Command, underestimated the importance of an up-to-date intelligence service is evident in the fact that SIM was dismembered in April 1940 as a consequence of a power struggle within the army, counter-espionage being detached from it until 1941. As a consequence of this situation SIM's evaluations of the strength of Allied forces in 1940 were vague and inaccurate and almost always greatly overestimated their powers. In any case Mussolini's decisions were always made without taking any account of the findings of his intelligence services. His decision to attack Greece in October 1940 was taken as a result of information from political and military sources in Albania that the Greek Army was about to disband; in fact SIM had contrary information which was more accurate but it was not consulted by Mussolini and the military chiefs, nor did it seek to challenge the dictator's decision.

Though their co-ordination and their influence on politico-strategic decision-making did not improve during 1941–2 the organization and general efficiency of the Italian intelligence services did (see below for two examples). However their work continued to be of marginal importance in the Mediterranean, not only because of the lack of co-ordination and therefore of general credibility but also because of the complete absence of any modern concept of intelligence in either the military and political hierarchy or among the secret services themselves. SIM and the other intelligence services were expected to provide concrete information in a restricted frame of reference, and not to incorporate it into an overall analysis of the strategic situation and of enemy strength, tasks which the operational command kept to itself. The main objective of the secret services remained the brilliant coup rather than the systematic collection and correlation of every scrap of information about the opposing side. As a result their work failed to make a major impact; the operational commands took whatever account of intelligence they thought fit in the absence of any synoptic intelligence appreciations. Overall, the organization and the activities of the Italian military intelligence services showed a cultural backwardness at all levels, since they were generally limited to traditional espionage and police-style counter-espionage and never developed the sophisticated role that intelligence work acquired in the UK and the USA.

A few examples of SIM's work are significant. In April 1941 it succeeded in penetrating the Yugoslavian radio communications system, thereby generating much confusion and disinformation. In so doing it helped to prevent a sudden attack on Italian troops in Albania who would have had to improvise a hasty deployment in the Scutari region with units switched from the Greek Front. More important was the successful microfilming of an American cipher, known as the *Black code, in Rome in September 1941. For six months, between 18 December 1941 and 29 June 1942 (when SIM was commanded by General Cesare Amé), the daily situation reports on the Eighth Army transmitted by the American Colonel

Bonner Fellers from Cairo to Washington were deciphered and passed to the Germans in Rome who then re-ciphered them and transmitted them to Rommel using the *ENIGMA machine.

This episode raises some questions about the range of the ULTRA Intelligence derived from the British decipherment of ENIGMA radio messages. How did this escape being noticed for a good six months? For a long time some British writers claimed that the leak came to light on 9 July 1942 following the capture at El Alamein of documents belonging to a German advanced tactical radio interception unit. This does not seem credible since the leak had already been identified by the British on 29 June. Probably this explanation was one of those cover stories not infrequent in matters where national security is involved.

Among Italian intelligence failures was the exaggeration of the size of British and French forces in the Mediterranean in the spring of 1940. It has been claimed that the basis for this deception was an understanding between Badoglio, Ciano, and the then commandant of SIM, General Giacomo Carboni, to dissuade Mussolini from entering the war. However, even after war had been declared Badoglio insisted that Italian strategy be tailored to this 'fact'. This was not the only time that SIM exaggerated the size of Allied forces; there were at least two other such episodes. The first related to Anglo-American forces in the Mediterranean in the spring and summer of 1943. The second, in August–September 1943, had to do with the German detachments deployed around Rome, which were credited with a tank strength approximately ten times larger than was actually the case. By this time SIM was once again under the command of General Carboni, who had taken up the post on 18 August 1943.

Italy, 7: Merchant shipping lost during hostilities

	Ships over 500t.	*Ships under 500t.*
1940	186,631 t.	4,326 t.
1941	714,410 t.	20,935 t.
1942	522,082 t.	16,834 t.
1943 (to August)	767,734 t.	39,755 t.
TOTAL:	2,190,857 t.	81,850 t.

Source: Contributor.

7. Merchant marine

In 1939 the Italian merchant fleet (counting vessels of over 100 gross tons) amounted to 3,448,543 tons. It was thus some 16% larger than the French and Dutch fleets and fifth in size after the British (over 21,000,000 tons), the USA (over 12,000,000 tons), the Japanese (over 5,500,000 tons), and the Norwegians (over 4,800,000 tons). The greatest loss was inflicted on it by Mussolini on the afternoon of 10 June 1940 when, in order not to miss the 'historic moment', he declared war, forgetting that there were 218 Italian ships totalling 1,215,000 tons in neutral or enemy ports outside the Mediterranean. This figure represented 35% of the total fleet and more than 50% of the losses due to the war, and was never made good.

Not all of what remained could be used to transport men and supplies to Libya, various Mediterranean islands, and Albania: many liners could not be used because of their excessive draught, among them the *Rex* (51,000 tons) and the *Conte di Savoia* (48,000 tons). Other passenger ships were used, however: conversion of the *Augustus* and the *Roma* into aircraft carriers (re-named the *Aquila* and the *Sparviero*) began in 1941 but was not finished by the time the armistice was signed in September 1943. In all, 597 ships (over 500 tons) totalling 2,190,857 tons were lost in the Mediterranean and the Red Sea along with another 1,278 ships (under 500 tons) amounting to 81,850 tons (see Table).

Out of a total loss of 2,272,707 tons, surface units sank 6.4%, submarines 36.5%, planes 33.9%, mines 6%, 9.5% scuttled themselves, and 7.7% sank due to natural or unknown causes. Over 800,000 tons of shipping of all types was lost on the routes to Libya and Tunisia; and the tonnage sunk while in port, although it cannot be ascertained with accuracy, was undoubtedly very high. Between June 1940 and September 1943 Italian shipyards produced 305,733 tons of shipping of all types. Figures for captured shipping incorporated into the Italian fleet are not complete. The main gain in the Mediterranean was represented by the 289,210 tons (of ships over 500 tons) seized from the French after Axis forces occupied the whole of France in November 1942 and shared between Germany and Italy.

Losses suffered between 9 September 1943 and 8 May 1945 can be calculated only for ships entered in the Italian Naval Register and do not include foreign ships incorporated into the Italian fleet. They amounted to 220 ships of over 500 tons, totalling 888,853 tons, and 994 smaller ships amounting to 88,049 tons. It is impossible accurately to identify the proportions lost to different causes, but it seems likely that most were scuttled to avoid seizure by the Germans: many liners, including the *Rex* and the *Conte di Savoia*, were sunk for this reason.

8. Resistance

Following the German occupation of northern Italy, the Committees for National Liberation (CLN) from Tuscany northwards functioned as clandestine local and regional governments, forming the backbone of an event which was without precedent in Italian history: a patriotic and political war in which bourgeois élites, workers, and peasants fought alongside one another. As was perhaps inevitable the myth of the resistance, which spread beyond the geographical and social boundaries of the area, combined with the international post-war situation to create a great many misconceptions.

The earliest bands were formed of soldiers who refused to obey the Germans and Mussolini's Italian Social Republic (RSI); many were men who at the armistice found themselves far from their homes and could only live outside the law. Ferocious German repression (as at Boves in Piedmont on 19 September 1943) and Nazi-fascist persecution of those who had helped thousands of Allied prisoners or groups of Jews whom the SS were hunting down, led to a rapid expansion of what was initially a spontaneous phenomenon. A measure of popular anti-German feeling which went back to the Risorgimento and the First World War was revived, especially by the survivors returning from the Eastern Front who had direct experience of German arrogance and of the systematic ferocity with which they had treated the Soviet population. Finally, military call-up by the RSI and the search for labour by the *Todt Organization also played their part: men did not care to work for Germany and sheer survival then dictated that they fight against her.

In the cities resistance was organized by the political parties, above all the communists: it ran the gamut from military sabotage to attempts to assassinate the supporters of the 'new fascism' (some of them small fry, others well-known such as the philosopher Giovanni Gentile), and to acts which not everyone supported, such as the killing of 32 German soldiers in Rome which in turn triggered the *Ardeatine massacre.

The war in the mountains was almost entirely in party hands. The largest groups were the 'Garibaldi' (communist) and 'Justice and Liberty' (Party of Action) formations, but there were also some autonomous apolitical groups, sometimes monarchist, socialist ('Matteotti'), or Catholic ('Green Flames'). However by no means all the leaders or followers in partisan bands owed their loyalty to the parties with which their names were associated; motivated by patriotism and nationalism, they made up the base on which the Italian resistance rested.

The Allies dropped supplies and missions (see also BALKAN AIR FORCE) to aid a movement which had already assumed a size and a character somewhat different from their own preference for a net of saboteurs on the lines of the French resistance. There was no lack of saboteurs, but from the spring of 1944 the mountain groups began to swell in size and by the autumn they numbered over 100,000 men. Aided by geography (the Alpine and Apennine valleys radiate from the main communication centres), these bands created military difficulties for the Germans, the seriousness of which is only now becoming fully apparent with the release of Wehrmacht documentation. Then there were the 'republics', vast tracts of land occupied by the partisans and governed by the CLN which restricted the area under RSI control to the plains. These 'republics' stirred up a violent reaction on the part of the Germans and the fascists—some, such as Ossola on the Swiss border, because of their political significance and others, such as those in Liguria and Emilia (Bobbio, Oltrepò, and so on) or in Piedmont (Langhe, Monferrato, Cuneese after the French Riviera landings), because of their military importance.

The political unity which prevailed in the south was reflected in the north. From June 1944 all the partisan forces (Voluntary Freedom Corps, or CVL) were co-ordinated into a collective command structure; at its head was the moderate General Raffaele Cadorna (parachuted in from the south), with two joint deputies, Luigi Longo (communist) and Ferrucio Parri (Party of Action). The second winter in the mountains was the worst. The Allied push came to a halt 15 km. (9.3 mi.) outside Bologna and, in a radio announcement which was also heard by the Germans, Alexander announced the suspension of operations for the winter, an error which the communists subsequently, but incorrectly, claimed had been a deliberate ploy by the British to rid themselves of politically inconvenient allies. Nevertheless, the Nazis and the fascists, who had already undertaken bloody reprisals against the civilian population (see MARZABOTTO MASSACRE), then unleashed a terrible offensive against the Italian resistance (see Map 56) making considerable use of Soviet troops—chiefly two Cossack cavalry divisions (see SOVIET EXILES AT WAR) and 162 infantry division commanded by General Oscar Ritter von Niedermayer. The CVL lost almost all the territory it had formerly controlled, its forces were decimated, and the population suffered terrible reprisals. But in February 1945 the great Soviet victories, followed later by those in the west, revived the movement, which acted vigorously and with considerable military effect.

The partisans knew nothing of the inconclusive surrender negotiations being conducted in Switzerland with SS Lt-General *Wolff. By now the 'republics' had been recreated and at the first signs of the Allied spring offensive the partisans began operations which liberated Genoa, Milan, Turin, and other northern cities on 25–26 April 1945, ahead of the Anglo-American forces. The final act was the shooting of Mussolini and the leading fascists after negotiations for their surrender to the resistance, using the Archbishop of Milan, Cardinal Schuster, as an intermediary, had failed. The CLN became the *de facto* government of the north and put itself forward as spokesman for the Allies and the government in the south. As was inevitable, victory vastly increased the number of partisans, though in fact their formations in the mountains were weaker on the eve of liberation than they had been the previous autumn (70–80,000 men).

The Italian resistance, of whom some 40,000 died (including the victims of reprisals), was one of the strongest in Europe. Its military successes did not, however, eradicate its internal divisions, of which the most significant was the split between the democrats and a Communist Party which, while highly intellectual and flexible, always remained subservient to the wishes of Moscow. Furthermore, notwithstanding popular

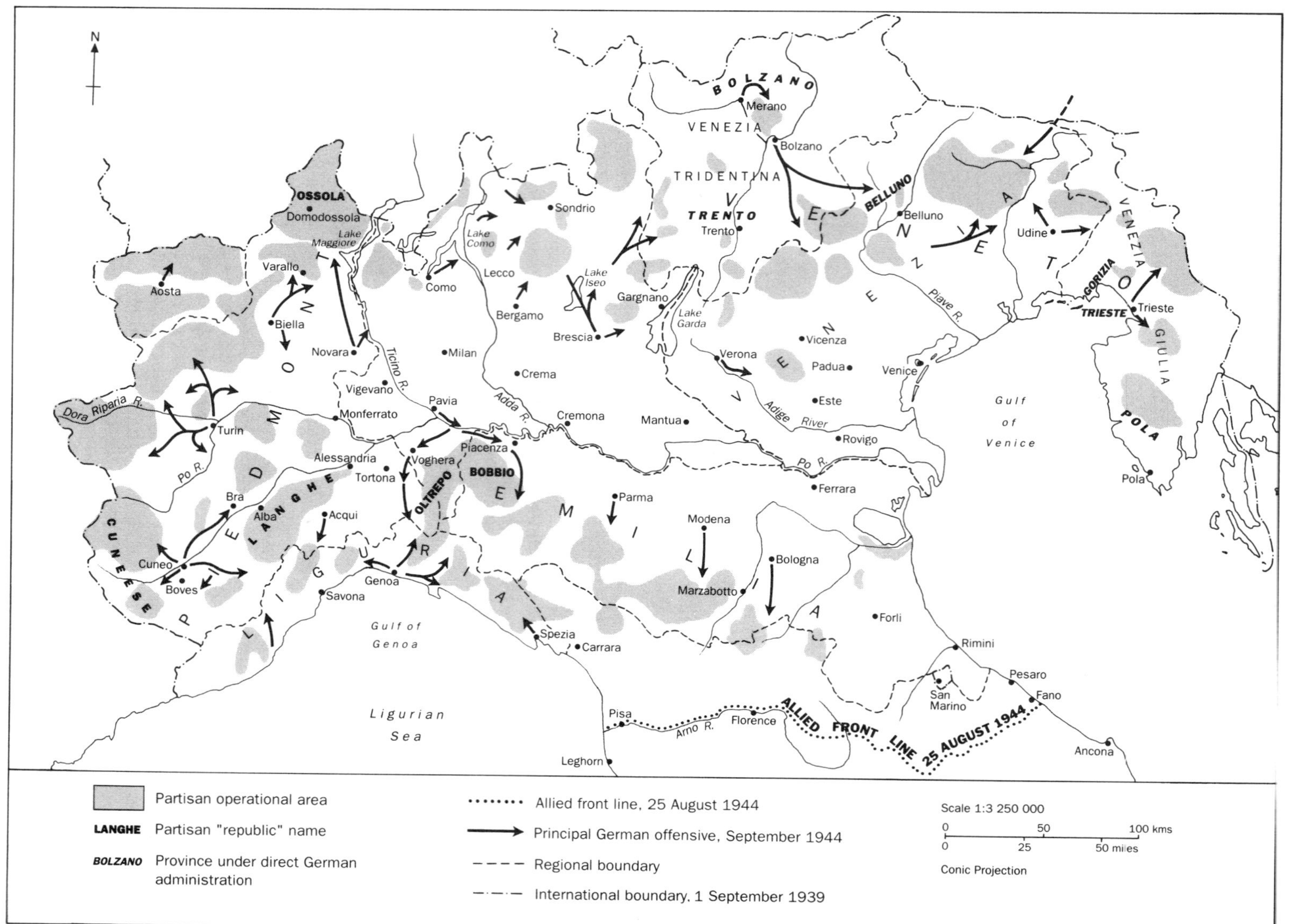

56. German offensive against Partisans in Northern **Italy**, September 1944

participation, the resistance was a minority activity which had a limited impact on Italian secular backwardness which was so strongly in tune with the reactionary conservatism sustained by the Catholic Church and by the structure of agriculture and industry.

On foreign policy the resistance had no impact. Neither the Anglo-Americans nor the Soviets accorded it any importance and the punitive nature of the peace treaty and its enforcement were shaped by the *Cold War and not by any recognition of the efforts of the Italian partisans. The resistance itself, Italy's detachment from Nazi Germany in 1943, and before that the struggles of the anti-fascists, were mistakes or pointless risks in so far as the Second World War witnessed a clash of powers which differed from what had occurred before only in terms of size. In fact, everything which had not been shattered by the time that the Cold War started (such as the *Franco dictatorship, *Hirohito's throne, and German rearmament), had a prosperous future. The resistance and the fight against fascism were regarded as obligatory by the minority who, in Italy as elsewhere, saw the upheavals which culminated between 1939 and 1945 in a world war as moral and political issues, but not necessarily national struggles. The few Italians who were ashamed of the alliance between their government and Nazism were part of the many who had fought against that government.

9. Culture

Before the war education, culture, and the arts were superficially 'fascistized'. The Accademia d'Italia, set up in 1929 in imitation of France, never had any real prestige or significance although it numbered among its members a few men of real merit. Some, among them the philosopher Benedetto Croce and the playwright Roberto Bracco, refused to join it. In 1931 only thirteen university professors (out of a total of 1,200) refused to take a political oath of loyalty and forfeited their chairs; but those who took the oath did not teach from a fascist perspective if they were not themselves already fascists. Thus levels of moral and scientific learning remained high, as exemplified in the work of the jurists Piero Calamandrei and Arturo C. Jemolo, the philosophers Guido De Ruggiero and Guido Calogero, the historians Adolfo Omodeo and Federico Chabod, and the men of letters Concetto Marchesi and Luigi Russo.

The two reforms of secondary education (by Gentile in 1923 and Bottai in 1939) did not solve the problem of graduate unemployment, which was the result of an imbalance between education and the labour market. In different ways both sought to focus demand on professional and general education, discouraging access to those schools which could lead on to university. They failed because the social response was to reject this pattern of education and to continue to seek access to the universities. Nevertheless under Gentile's system the upper schools were of solid merit, although it is doubtful whether they would have maintained their standards had not Bottai's reforms been broken off due to the collapse of fascism. Bottai still had time to apply the racial laws to education, throwing out more than 200 teachers and some 5,000 Jewish students.

Failing to 'fascistize' the schools as a result of popular resistance to change, the regime had to limit itself to setting up a youth organization alongside them which sought to militarize all those between the ages of 6 and 21. This manufactured consensus was often so clumsy as to make fascism look ridiculous, while similar organizations for civil servants and workers (*dopolavoro*), with their trips, tours, films, and other functions, had a modest success, especially among the young.

All in all, though, fascism seemed to live from day to day without any deep foundations. Although it obsessively proclaimed its intention to last it did nothing to organize its own renewal, either at the centre or on the fringes. Thus no mechanism of succession to Mussolini existed and nothing was done to ensure that a genuine fascist technocracy, public or private, was created. There were transfers to and fro between party and technocracy, especially at the higher levels, but no institutions existed which could select and shape new political cadres and thereby compensate for the failure of the state educational system to produce such people.

In culture and the arts the war both accentuated existing trends and created new ones. The few opposition intellectuals who were at liberty included Croce, whose philosophical review *La Critica* had 3,000 subscribers in 1943. Alberto Moravia stayed on in Italy, though affected by the racial laws; in 1929, as a young man, he had published the nonconformist novel *Gli indifferenti*. Among those working in exile or abroad were the historian Gaetano Salvemini, the conductor Arturo Toscanini, and writers and scholars such as Ignazio Silone, G. Antonio Borgese, Lionello Venturi, and Emilio Lussu. The writer, Lauro de Bosis died in an aircraft in 1931 after having dropped anti-fascist leaflets on Rome. In 1937 the historian Nello Rosselli was murdered in France by fascist thugs, along with his brother Carlo. Antonio Gramsci died in prison that same year; and among those who worked from prison or confinement were the economists Ernesto Rossi and Pietro Grifone, the music critic Massimo Mila, and the painter Carlo Levi.

By and large, however, Italian intellectuals (save for a few fanatical fascists) switched between periods of support for and detachment from the regime, deluding themselves that by doing so they kept their work above everyday events; examples include the poets Giuseppe Ungaretti and Salvatore Quasimodo, the playwright Luigi Pirandello, and the painter, Giorgio Morandi. The words of the famous poet Eugenio Montale, written in 1925, certainly did not apply everywhere and to everyone:

> For this alone can we tell you today:
> What we are not, what we want not.

On the other hand, in a totalitarian regime any speaking out was immediately suspect. With the outbreak of war opposition journals appeared, among them *Oggi*, edited by Mario Pannunzio and Arrigo Benedetti and suppressed in 1942, and *Primato*, actually produced by the minister for public education Bottai, an expert at playing the double game who combined flirting for moderation with a background as boss of a gang of fascist thugs. The list of contributors to *Primato* includes many noteworthy intellectuals; some were anti-fascists, such as Luigi Salvatorelli, Cesare Pavese, and Sergio Solmi, others non-fascist, among them Montale, Umberto Saba, Cesare Zavattini, and Giaime Pintor who later died in the resistance.

The parts played by Pavese, an anti-fascist, and Elio Vittorini, a left-wing fascist, were particularly important. It was through their efforts that American literature (Faulkner, Dos Passos, Saroyan, Steinbeck, Melville, Gertrude Stein, and others) was translated and distributed through Italy. It was work which encouraged doubt, dissent, criticism, and renewal, carried out under the noses of fascist censors who were too ignorant to recognize its subversive character. Both deserve to be remembered not only as translators but as authors. Whatever may be said about their dependence on American models, they found tones which today can be interpreted as alarm calls. Thus in the allusive voyage of *Conversazione in Sicilia* (Vittorini, 1941) 'abstract furies' and the invocation of 'new duties' were based on the desperate wretchedness of Sicilians and on a mythical America, a 'heavenly kingdom on earth' where everyone ate several times a day. Much of the Italian literature, poetry, criticism, and historiography of subsequent decades was genetically linked to the war: examples include Pavese, Massimo Mila and Carlo Levi, Vittorio Sereni, Giorgio Bassani, Italo Calvino, Beppe Fenoglio, and Franco Venturi.

In the world of music the operatic style of the 19th century came to an end with Puccini's *Turandot* (1924), and during the war composers destined to influence future generations such as Giorgio F. Ghedini, Luigi Dallapiccola, and Goffredo Petrassi (the latter two working with the twelve-tone scale) managed to continue producing work. Jazz, which was banned by fascism, had little influence on the mediocre Italian light music of the day. Regional folk music persisted, but aroused no particular interest.

There was much noteworthy activity by architects,

This photograph—taken on Mt Suribachi during the fighting for **Iwo Jima** in February 1945—was a posed shot. A much smaller flag had been raised hours earlier while fighting was still in progress on the mountain. This did not prevent it from becoming one of the most famous war photographs ever taken.

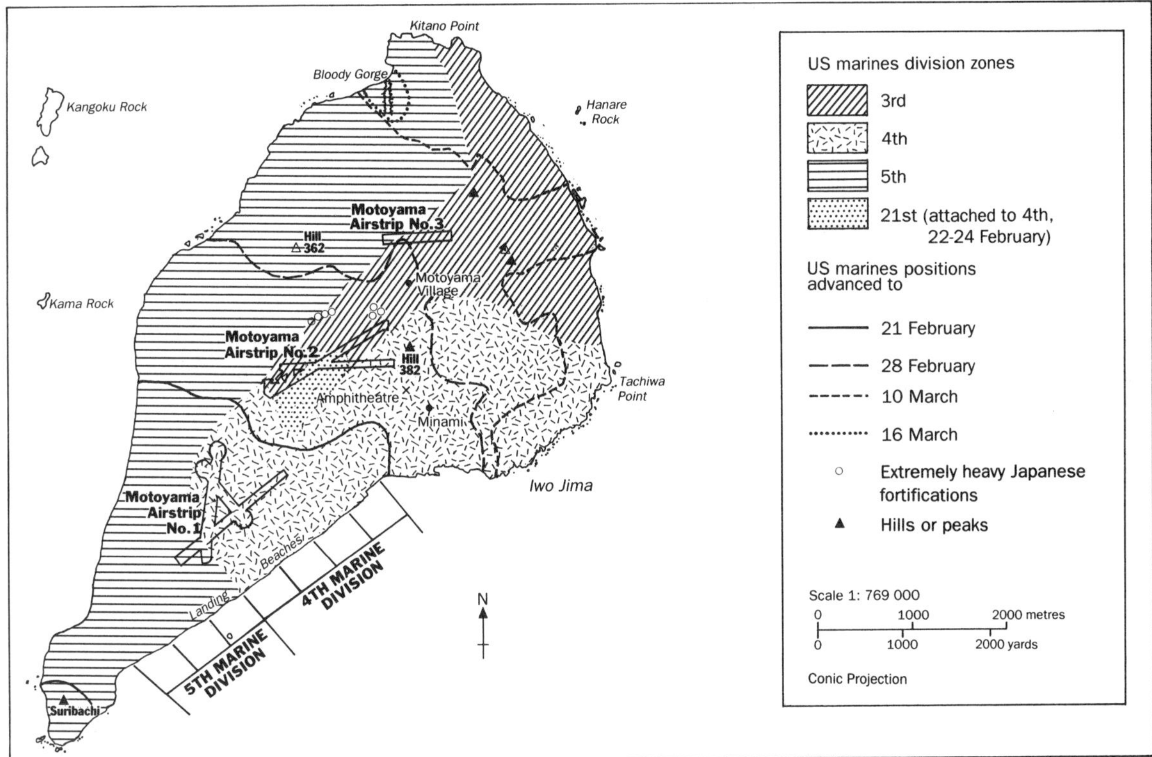

57. Battle for **Iwo Jima**, February–March 1945

painters, and sculptors. Leaving aside the vexed question of which of the contemporary schools they belonged to, an incomplete list would include: Giuseppe Terragni, Edoardo Persico, Marcello Piacentini, Carlo Carrà, Giorgio Morandi, Giorgio de Chirico, Arturo Tosi, Felice Casorati, Alberto Savinio, Filippo De Pisis, Ottone Rosai, Renato Birolli, Renato Guttuso, Bruno Cassinari, Giacomo Manzù, Marino Marini, and Alberto Viani.

Despite fascist censorship, the war stimulated a renaissance in film-making (examples include Luchino Visconti's *Ossessione*, made in 1942, and Vittorio De Sica's *I bambini ci guardano*, made in 1943) which exploded in 1944–5 with the first breath of freedom and opened the era of neo-realism. Early post-war products of this cinematic flowering include Roberto Rossellini's *Roma città aperta* and *Paisà* and De Sica's *Sciuscià*, *Ladri di biciclette*, and *Umberto D.* Its rapid spread world-wide was a sign that Italy had emerged from her period of tyranny and suffering and that one of the world's oldest civilizations still had new things to say. LUCIO CEVA

GIORGIO ROCHAT and LUCIO CEVA (Intelligence)
(Tr. John Gooch)

Knox, M., 'The Italian Armed Forces, 1940–1943', in A. R. Millett and W. Murray (eds.), *Military Effectiveness*, Vol. III (Boston, 1988).
—— *Mussolini Unleashed* (Cambridge, 1982).
Lamb, R., *War in Italy: 1939–45* (London, 1993).
Mitchell, B. R., *European Historical Statistics, 1750–1950* (New York, 1975).
Sullivan, B. R., 'The Italian Armed Forces, 1918–1940', in Millett and Murray, op. cit., Vol. II.
On the Italian historiography of the Second World War, see also MUSSOLINI, note at end.

Iwo Jima, the best-known battle of the *Pacific war, a classic example of *amphibious warfare, and a vital objective to give more air bases for aircraft taking part in the US *strategic air offensive against Japan.

Iwo Jima (sulphur island), 8 km. (5 mi.) long, is one of the Volcano Islands, a volcanic pear-shaped piece of land 1,045 km. (650 mi.) south-east of Tokyo. It contained three airstrips and was a vital link in Japan's inner ring of defences. At the southern end lay Mt Suribachi, a 150 m. (500 ft.) extinct volcano, and volcanic ash at the northern end made *foxholes too hot to live in. The whole place stank of sulphur and the terrain, full of rocky ridges, caves, and deep ravines, was a honeycomb of concrete and steel. 'It is probable that no other given area in the history of modern war has been so skillfully fortified by nature and by man' (J. Isley and P. Crowl, *US Marines and Amphibious War*, Princeton, 1951, p. 486).

On 19 February 1945 the 4th and 5th Marine Divisions of 5th Amphibious Corps, with 3rd Marine Division in reserve, landed on the island after a preliminary naval bombardment and 72 days of continuous air strikes which had, however, only encouraged the defenders to build ever-deeper bunkers. Altogether 60,000 marines, commanded by Maj-General Harry Schmidt, were committed to an operation which eventually absorbed 800 warships, 110,000 men ashore, and another 220,000 afloat.

The US Navy gave the marines a rolling barrage (see ARTILLERY, 2) and this helped them advance 320 m. (350 yd.) inland without severe casualties. As at *Peleliu, the garrison of 22,000 Japanese army and naval troops, commanded by Lt-General Kuribayashi Tadamichi, made little attempt to prevent the marines from landing. Instead, part of Kuribayashi's forces attacked them once they were ashore, with concentrated flanking fire that proved deadly, but most of the defenders remained under cover inland.

The first airstrip near the landing beaches was taken on the second day and Mt Suribachi and the second airstrip on the fifth, but the hardest fighting, to break through Kuribayashi's two remaining fortified lines, was still to come. One fortified feature, Hill 382, caused so many casualties that it became known as 'The Meat Grinder' and on one day alone five Congressional Medals of Honor (see DECORATIONS) were awarded to men of 5th Division. The Japanese fought with astonishing bravery and made their last stand in a rocky canyon which became known as 'Bloody Gorge'. It was only 650 m. (700 yd.) in length but it took ten long days to eradicate its occupants. Capturing Iwo Jima had been expected to take 14 days. It took 36, by which time over a third of the marine force— 5,931 killed, 17,372 wounded—had become casualties.

JAPAN

1. Introduction

By July 1937, when undeclared war broke out between China and Japan, the so-called *China Incident, Japan was a strong, technologically advanced country with a population of 70 million. About 14 million Japanese were engaged in agriculture, 7.5 million in manufacturing, and 5 million in commerce. Some sectors of Japanese industry had reached the highest world standards but this applied mainly to consumer products: cotton piece goods, silk goods, toys, matches, and so on. The textile industry employed 38% of the total labour force, while machinery, vehicles, tools, and chemicals together employed some 30%. From the Manchurian crisis of 1931 onwards (see MANCHUKUO) a perceptible militarization of the economy took place. Japan's free market economy was replaced by government control and planning. Electricity and oil were brought under state control in 1934–6. Rice production was controlled from 1936 onwards and rationing was introduced in 1939 when the government gained the power to purchase the total rice crop. In order to prepare for military campaigns overseas it was necessary to develop the heavy and chemical industries rapidly, using male manpower rather than the female labour used in the textile factories. By the end of the 1930s the country had been largely converted from a free market, with some guidance from an efficient bureaucracy, to a controlled war economy.

But Japan was not financially ready for total war. The 1920s had been a harsh time for the country: the recession following the *First World War had led to a banking crisis in 1927, agricultural collapse, and complaints of over-population. As a country dependent on foreign trade, Japan also suffered from the world depression of 1930–2 during which both exports and imports declined. That the economy recovered was due to the skills of the minister of finance (1931–6), Takahashi Korekiyo. By initiating a Keynesian spending policy before Keynes, he enabled Japan to recover from the worst aspects of the depression earlier than the UK or USA.

Japan faced in two directions: towards the continent of Asia and towards the Pacific Ocean, and especially the western Pacific. This created difficulties for strategic planning at a time when the army and the navy were not only gaining increased political power over the civilian governments of the day but were in open confrontation with one another over sharing out the defence budget. This problem became more marked after the London Naval conference of 1930 when the naval general staff expressed extreme dissatisfaction with the treaty that emerged—they tried unsuccessfully to prevent its ratification—and in December 1934 Admiral Okada Keisuke's cabinet announced the obligatory two years' notice of Japan's unilateral withdrawal from it. Then in January 1936 the Japanese delegates at the Second London Naval Conference withdrew (see VERSAILLES SETTLEMENT) leaving Japan free to build without restrictions from 1937 onwards.

This increasing assertiveness on the part of the naval leadership led to the adoption of what was known as the southern strategy, that is expansion into South-East Asia. In February 1936 there was a general election, the results of which displeased the army: and junior officers planned a *coup d'état*, occupying the government district of central Tokyo and assassinating the home and finance ministers (the so-called '26 February incident'). The army was by this time becoming increasingly worried by reports of growing Soviet forces marshalling on the borders of Manchukuo, while the navy was preoccupied with making sure that its legitimate claim for appropriations should not be overlooked because of increased army demands. During April the navy negotiated with the army general staff over the need for a southern strategy.

Eventually a new Imperial Defence policy was worked out and approved by the emperor on 29 May 1936. But the debate over national policy and the financial needs for new weapons systems persisted throughout the summer. Eventually after a Five Ministers' conference it was agreed that there should be expansion both on the continent and towards the south. This was in the nature of a compromise between the two services, leaving open the question of whether Japan would contemplate moving north or south. But the navy's desire for a southern initiative now enjoyed equal prominence with the army's continental ambitions which had been the essence of defence planning hitherto. This implied an accommodation rather than a reconciliation of wills: the army did not share the navy's thinking found in the phrase *Hokushu nanshin* ('Stay put in the north; advance to the south').

From July 1937 onwards Japan was to be fully stretched by the needs of the military campaign in north and central China. The army opposed the navy's demand for a southern front, though the navy seized the opportunity of seizing some islands in the neighbourhood of Amoy and Hong Kong. However, the army's invasion of China did not bring the Chinese to the negotiating table, and, from 1938 onwards, distinguished figures in the army general staff did not favour a further extension of lines of communication in central China, especially as there was evidence that the Soviet Union was supporting the Chinese war effort and might strike against Manchukuo at any moment. Frontier incidents such as the one at Nomonhan in August 1939 (see JAPANESE–SOVIET CAMPAIGNS) seemed to confirm this fear.

When the European war broke out, there was the possibility that the Germans would call on Japan to support the Axis by implementing the southern strategy in some form. But though Japan had entered into the *Anti-Comintern Pact with Germany in 1936, the navy had consistently opposed its being converted into an alliance. Moreover, the Japanese were deeply resentful of the *Nazi–Soviet Pact of August 1939, of which Germany had given them no advance notice. As a result Japan declared its strict neutrality. However, after the fall of *France in June 1940, the arguments for a German alliance and for an advance into Dutch and French colonies in South-East Asia were heard again. The navy's leaders generally opposed these ideas from their fear of Anglo-American naval co-operation, but in September 1940 Japan joined with Germany and Italy in the *Tripartite Pact. By this time the army had withdrawn its resistance to a southern advance, while the new naval leaders took the view that, if it meant war with the USA, they would need time to make appropriate preparations. Both services were agreed that the best chance of severing the supply routes that were supporting China's war effort (see BURMA ROAD) was to move in to southern China and South-East Asia. Japan therefore occupied the northern part of French Indo-China during the summer of 1940, and in July 1941, instead of attacking the Soviet Union as Stalin had feared, moved into southern French Indo-China.

By the summer of 1941 Japan had therefore added substantially to its earlier empire in the north which comprised Sakhalin south of the 50th parallel, acquired in 1920; Korea, a colony since 1910; Formosa, Japan's oldest colony having been acquired in 1895; and it also had an alliance with the puppet state of Manchukuo which had been created in 1932. From Formosa it had also moved southwards by occupying the Chinese-owned Hainan Island in February 1939 and the strategically placed Spratly Islands the following month. As mediator in the frontier dispute between Thailand and France, Japan also enjoyed a close relationship with the Thai military leadership. In this way it was able to locate air bases and establish naval stations which would be invaluable if war occurred.

In negotiations which were under way in Washington during the summer of 1941 (see USA, 1), Japan was asked by the USA to withdraw all its military forces from China and French Indo-China. The Japanese replied ambivalently while preparations for war were continued by General *Tōjō's cabinet, and in November 1941 the army and navy were able to reconcile their positions on the southern advance by agreeing 'to seize the initiative with a sudden attack on the Philippines and Malaya while opening operations at the same time elsewhere'. This last, a veiled reference to the attack on *Pearl Harbor, was the navy's precondition for embarking on the southern strategy. There were also to be subsidiary operations against *Guam, *Hong Kong, and *British North Borneo, and measures for the 'stabilization' of Thailand, especially if the UK were to invade southern Thailand while Japan was still preparing for operations.

Japan, 2, Table 1: Military budget and total expenditures, 1931–40 (in millions of yen)

Fiscal Year	*Military Budget*	*Total Expenditures*	*Military Budget as % of Total Expenditures*
1931	434	1,477	29.4
1932	733	1,950	37.6
1933	873	2,225	39.2
1934	955	2,163	44.2
1935	1,032	2,206	46.8
1936	1,105	2,282	48.4
1937	3,953	5,521	71.6
1938	6,097	8,084	75.4
1939	6,417	8,952	71.7
1940	7,266	11,033	65.9

Sources: War, Navy and Finance Ministries, from Cohen, J., *Japan's Economy in War and Reconstruction*, (Minneapolis, 1949, repr. Westport, Conn., 1973).

Thus the Greater East Asian war of December 1941 unfolded into its two separate sectors: the South-East Asian theatre, starting with the highly successful *Malayan campaign, the invasion of the *Netherlands East Indies, and the *Burma campaign; and the Pacific theatre, starting with Pearl Harbor and extending to the islands in the central and southern Pacific. IAN NISH

2. Domestic life, economy, and war effort

Following Japan's conquest of Manchuria in 1931, the Japanese government successfully encouraged planned industrial development and modernization, a process which was helped by the existence of the large conglomerates, the Zaibatsu, which combined mining, shipping, manufacturing, and banking activities. Textiles experienced relative decline but heavy industry grew rapidly, accounting for 73% of industrial production at the end of 1941 compared with 58% at the start of the China Incident in July 1937. Increasing numbers of workers left the land to work in urban factories so that the percentage employed in agriculture dropped from 48% in 1930 to 42% a decade later. Of even greater significance was the creation and expansion of distinctly modern sectors of military production. The motor vehicle, aircraft, and shipbuilding industries expanded rapidly and were sustained by army and navy expenditure which, by 1938, absorbed 75% of Japan's national budget (see Table 1). To support this increase in public spending bank credit was expanded and large deficits became a lasting feature of national accounting. Very high inflation was the result and the retail price index rose from 100 in 1936 to 175 in 1940. During the same period the UK's rose to 125 and that of the USA to just 101.

Even more crucial was Japan's increasing dependence on imported *raw materials to sustain this expansion. Oil, bauxite, tin, rubber, and nickel—all essential to its military industries—could not be provided by Manchukuo, nor was Japan self-sufficient in them itself (see Table 2). In 1936 two-thirds of Japan's oil was imported from the USA, while rubber and tin had to be purchased from European colonies in South-East Asia. Soon new Japanese oil refineries were built, the production of synthetic petroleum was attempted, and national stockpiling began. However, none of these measures could prevent Japan's growing dependence upon international shipping, and the oilfields, mines, and plantations of South-East Asia.

Similarly, the domestic sources of Japan's food supplies depended on small-scale, non-mechanized farms. By 1941 the cultivation of arable land had just about reached its maximum possible expansion—even golf courses were ploughed up—but in that year Japan needed to import 22% of its rice, 72% of its soyabeans, and 82% of its sugar. The line between adequate supplies and starvation was a very thin one, but domestic rice crops and imports kept the population adequately fed until the shipping blockade and *strategic air offensive during the last year of

Japan, 2, Table 2: Dependence on imports of industrial raw materials

Commodity	*Percent Self-Sufficient in 1936*
Iron Ore	16.7
Pig Iron	93.8
Steel	62.2
Scrap Iron	–
Copper	63.2
Lead	8.2
Tin	28.8
Zinc	38.9
Bauxite	–
Finished Aluminium	40.6
Nickel	–
Sulphuric Acid	14.1
Crude Oil	20.2
Coal	90.9
Crude Rubber	–
Salt	31.3
Phosphate rock	12.0
Raw cotton	–

Sources: Japan's Dependence on Imports, Special Study No. 28, Mitsubishi Keizai Kenkyu Kyoku (in Japanese), (Tokyo, 1938), p. 11.; From Cohen.

the war disrupted supplies and brought quite severe shortages and some malnutrition.

When undeclared war broke out between Japan and China in July 1937—the China Incident—Japanese civilians showed little spontaneous enthusiasm. Not only was it a distant conflict, but Japanese aims were largely undefined. Soon Japan's leaders sought to remedy this popular indifference by promoting a major programme of spiritual or psychological mobilization. In October a National Spiritual Mobilization Central League was established which organized lectures, distributed pamphlets, and encouraged visits to important patriotic shrines. The League's local sub-committees reinforced these activities by providing psychological support for the families of servicemen going to the front. Soldiers were sent off amid flags, banners, and martial music, and later more subdued ceremonies were held to receive the ashes of the fallen. Groups of housewives also showed their patriotism by making 'thousand stitch belts' which were reputed to protect their wearers from bullets and the Chinese winter cold.

Alongside the encouragement of patriotic enthusiasm the government took increasingly severe measures against any signs of political or social dissent. In December the renowned Christian scholar Yanaihara Tadao was driven from his position at Tokyo Imperial University and more than 400 left-wing activists were arrested, accused of conspiring to establish a popular front.

Parallel with morale building and political discipline

the government shaped economic policies designed to increase military production and national efficiency. As early as 1936 Japan had instituted a 'quasi-wartime economy' and in August 1937 the ministry of commerce and industry took new powers to encourage the creation of cartels and enforce obedience to industry-wide agreements. Further powers were provided by the Foreign Trade Adjustment Law. This enabled the government to ban the import of foreign luxuries and 'unnecessary' products, and prevent the export of goods and materials which were essential for military production. A new planning body was also established to integrate production and prepare new legislation for the control of the economy. In late October the existing Cabinet Planning Office and Resources Bureau were merged to form the Cabinet Planning Board, which soon began the drafting of a National General Mobilization Law. When this wide-ranging law was presented to the Diet (the Japanese parliament) in February 1938 a handful of conservative members criticized it as unconstitutional, but it was soon approved and provided the legal foundation for a network of wartime rules and regulations which would control almost every aspect of economic life.

Government intervention was further extended by the creation of the Industrial Patriotic League, which aimed to replace conventional union activity with 'Industrial Patriotic Associations' promoting labour–management co-operation. The League's slogans were 'Family Harmony' and 'The Plant as One Family', and by 1939 almost three million workers and managers had been drawn into these company organizations.

In addition to economic and political policies designed to promote industrial efficiency the cabinet shaped social policies to improve the nation's physical and psychological health. In January 1938 a Welfare Ministry was founded to improve the physical fitness of potential recruits to industry, agriculture, and the armed forces. In contrast, philanthropic organizations which could be construed as 'hotbeds of left-wing thought', such as Tokyo Imperial University's 'Settlement', were promptly closed.

Although Japan's diplomatic links with Nazi Germany and fascist Italy still remained issues of serious controversy, government policies increasingly aimed to promote pro-German and pro-Italian feeling among Japanese civilians. In the summer of 1938, 30 members of the *Hitler Youth were entertained in Japan. A Japanese youth delegation visited Germany and Japan's most popular female entertainers, the Takarazaka Girls' Opera Group, sailed for a goodwill tour of Germany and Italy.

By the end of 1938 broad government strategies increasingly impinged upon the details of Japanese daily life. Fuel shortages brought charcoal-powered buses on to Tokyo's streets, and restricted the opening hours of public bathhouses. Cotton goods were increasingly replaced by textiles made of a blended 'staple fibre', and wood and bamboo often replaced metal in the manufacture of kitchen utensils.

In 1939 not only did the China Incident absorb increasing numbers of Japanese troops but a protracted campaign against Soviet forces on the Manchurian border (see JAPANESE–SOVIET CAMPAIGNS) reinforced demands for the creation of a yet more disciplined society. In March a new national committee gave a fresh impetus to spiritual mobilization; in April attendance at ideological evening schools was made compulsory for boys outside conventional education; and in May martial arts were added to the junior school curriculum. Even more dramatic were prohibitions on women having permanent waves, and restrictions on the opening hours of restaurants, bars, and dancehalls. Discipline and 'spirituality' were further intensified on 1 September 1939 when the first day of every month was declared 'Public Service for Asia Day'. This somewhat euphemistic term described days when citizens carried out 'labour service', neon signs were extinguished, and *sake* (rice wine) was removed from public sale.

Throughout 1939 economic controls affected an increasing range of daily necessities. Rice distribution was brought under government regulation. The price of sugar was fixed by civil servants, and in October the price of many goods was frozen at their 18 September level. By December even the distribution of charcoal was subjected to government ordinance. Despite this fine mesh of official regulations, Japan's consumer economy still proved difficult to control. The October price freeze was impossible to enforce and black marketeering became an established feature of city life. Perhaps the strangest product of the new, supposedly moralistic economy, was the appearance of scrap metal dealers on annual lists of Tokyo's wealthiest citizens.

By 1940 government slogans, rules, and prohibitions may have appeared all-pervasive but the possibility of war with the western powers stimulated a new wave of petty controls. Attempts to create a more patriotic and disciplined culture soon reshaped what remained of popular pleasure and entertainment. Singers with western stage names were compelled to adopt more Japanese equivalents; traditional story-tellers were ordered to purge salacious or criminal content from their stories; and cigarettes with English names such as Cherry or Golden Bat were converted into more 'patriotic' brands.

But for most Japanese, food and clothing remained their most pressing concerns. These were subjected to further restrictions and rationing procedures. In June, rice, salt, sugar, and soy sauce were distributed against coupons in six major cities, and five months later the system was extended to the entire country. In these months the manufacture of silk clothing and neckties was forbidden and in November an austere national people's uniform was launched for civilians of both sexes.

The imposition of orthodox conduct was most marked in the policies of the home ministry which was the most powerful agency of domestic administration. The newly founded Imperial Rule Assistance Association was designed to provide a Japanese equivalent of the Nazi

Party, but it proved an ineffective structure. In contrast the home ministry successfully brought all voluntary and quasi-voluntary neighbourhood and hamlet associations under local government control. In later years all would hold meetings at centrally determined times, listen to identical radio broadcasts, and support savings and salvage campaigns according to government order.

At the beginning of 1941 the army minister, General Tōjō, placed a new emphasis on the training of children and young people for a role in the new National Defence State Structure. On 16 January the government created the Greater Japan Youth Corps which was to integrate its training programme with those of conventional schools, and in April junior schools were drastically changed. Renamed People's Schools (*kokumin gakko*—a literal translation of the Nazi *Volkschule*), these eschewed such democratic concepts as liberalism and individualism, and replaced so-called 'intellectualism' with 'the union of mind and body'. A new five-subject curriculum sought to 'refine an imperial nation', and placed increasing emphasis on collective acts, such as regular bowing towards the imperial palace. Even more dramatic was the introduction of semi-military 'national defence sports' into outdoor school activities. Institutions of secondary and higher education were also subjected to powerful military influences. In late August military training experts were attached to all universities and, soon after, the academic year for universities, higher schools, and technical colleges was shortened in the interests of military service and the war economy.

The dominance of military priorities in national life was also apparent from the steady deterioration of many civilian services. Virtually all group travel was forbidden. Third class sleeping-cars disappeared from the national railways and dining-cars became very scarce delights. The communications ministry even forbade the sending of greetings or condolence telegrams.

As relations with the western nations deteriorated, anti-Western propaganda became more bitter. Its most common theme was Japan's encirclement by the ABCD League (America, Britain, China, and the Dutch). This was a strange emotional fabrication, but the public's increasing xenophobia received serious justification when, on 15 October 1941 one of Japan's most distinguished journalists, Ozaki Hotsumi, was arrested on a charge of transmitting secrets to the USSR; and three days later a raffish German journalist, Richard *Sorge, was seized for participating in the same spy ring. These dramatic events gave added strength to government appeals for vigilance, and popular fears of aliens and dissidents.

During the first months of the *Pacific war a rapid series of victories aroused public enthusiasm and assisted the government in consolidating its so-called 'new order'. In January 1942 the Great Japan Imperial Rule Assistance Youth Corps was established to create an ideologically aggressive youth movement and four months later the Imperial Rule Assistance Political Association was founded to include virtually all members of both houses of the Diet. This policy of amalgamating similar groups into new inclusive organizations was further extended with the creation of the Great Japan Women's Association—which, it has been claimed, had more than 19 million members—the Great Japan Martial Arts Association, and the Japan Publications Culture Association. This process reached its climax with the integration of all neighbourhood associations into the Imperial Rule Assistance Association.

Yet victories and organizational changes could not prevent the appearance of new shortages and greater austerity. In January 1942 gas and cooking salt were subjected to systems of rationing and 37 Ginza restaurants were closed after participating in black market activities. By the end of the year a network of local foodstuff corporations had been organized to distribute staple foods to neighbourhood associations; these grassroots organizations were to play a vitally important role in the distribution of rice and basic foods to individual families.

Shortages of consumer goods reflected the dominance of military priorities in the national economy, but in late 1942 problems in military production began to trouble Japan's leaders. Initially Japan had expected a short war and its economic plans had been based upon this erroneous premiss. Indeed the first year of war was a time of surprising complacency. Not only was little attention paid to the production of essential ships such as tankers and ocean freighters, but little attempt was made to stimulate the overall growth of the economy. Even more marked was the inefficiency of government planning agencies. The cabinet planning board could draft detailed plans, but it had no authority to impose them upon particular industries or private companies. This power was left in the hands of individual ministers. In late 1941 pre-war cartels had been replaced by a series of industrial control associations which were to organize production and distribution in particular sectors. The Transfer of Administrative Authority Law soon gave these associations additional powers, but industrialists rather than ministers or civil servants controlled these organizations. As a result the government's wishes could still be thwarted by industrial leaders.

By March 1943 Japanese forces had suffered important defeats at *Midway and *Guadalcanal and Tōjō (prime minister from October 1941) took increased powers to direct the economy. Now maximum emphasis was placed upon five industrial sectors: coal, steel, light metals, ships, and military aircraft (see Table 3). At the same time army/navy *rivalries were increasingly seen as serious impediments to effective planning. Simultaneously a high-level study of aircraft production revealed that 45% of Japan's aluminium supplies was being sold on the black market, or being used for the manufacture of pots, pans, or other inessentials. In the face of these discoveries and a worsening military situation Tōjō brought about an administrative revolution. The ministry of commerce and cabinet planning board were abolished and a new

Japan, 2, Table 3: Production of matériel[c]

Type	*1941*	*1942*	*1943*	*1944*	*1945*
Medium tanks (14–17 tons)	495	531	554	294	89[a]
Light tanks	529	634	232	48	5[a]
Self-propelled guns		26	14	59	48[a]
Armoured cars	88	442	615	725	105[a]
Fighters[b]	1,080	2,935	7,147	13,811	5,474
Bombers	1,461	2,433	4,189	5,100	1,934
Reconnaissance aircraft	639	967	2,070	2,147	855
Battleships	1	1			
Aircraft carriers	5	6	3	4	
Cruisers	1	2	2	1	
Destroyers	9	9	15	31	6
Submarines	11	22	40	37	22

[a] April–July 1945
[b] total annual aircraft production, including fighters, bombers, reconnaissance aircraft, trainers, flying boats, gliders, etc., was 5,088 (1941) 8,861 (1942), 16,693 (1943), 28,180 (1944), and 11,066 (1945)
[c] For production of merchant ships, see section 7, below

ministry of munitions was created. Furthermore a new transportation ministry replaced the previous communications and railway ministries. The main aims of these radical changes were the effective control of aircraft production and the creation of integrated land and maritime transport policies. However, the attainment of these vital objectives was partially undermined by continued military interference.

Such drastic changes inevitably made further inroads into what remained of normality or semi-normality in Japanese civilian life. Middle-school education was reduced from five to four years, limits on the working hours of women and minors were waived, and cloth shortages led to restrictions on the sleeve length of traditional dress and a prohibition on the manufacture of double-breasted suits. But perhaps the most striking changes were those which revealed a serious reappraisal or abandonment of values which had, hitherto, been central to Japanese life. Tōjō had viewed the traditional domestic role of *women as a major strength of the nation, but in September 1943 unmarried women under the age of 25 were conscripted into a labour volunteer corps. A powerful symbol of Japan's crisis was a large-scale ceremony at the Meiji Shrine Stadium on 21 October 1943 to bid farewell to thousands of university students who were to join the imperial army and navy. Even Japan's precious intellectual élite was no longer immune from the hazards of modern war.

Despite the organizational difficulties of Japanese economic planning, 1943 and 1944 saw remarkable achievements in some spheres of war production. These successes did not result from the utilization of raw materials from conquered territories, for Allied submarines controlled the southern seas. Instead, rapid increases in production were based on plundering raw material stockpiles, reducing civilian production, and the desperate employment of an emergency workforce. Perhaps Japan's greatest success was in aircraft production. In 1943 it produced 16,693 aircraft and in 1944 28,180, representing a remarkable advance on the 5,088 planes which had been manufactured in the first year of war. However this was a once-and-for-all achievement, for when stockpiled raw materials had been exhausted many factories were left with spare capacity and an under-used labour force. Soon, fear of American bombing ushered in measures which caused further interruptions to production. In an attempt to preserve large numbers of strategic factories machinery was dispersed to mountain and rural regions—often by means of primitive ox-carts and other improvised transport. In many cases, machinery was relocated in damp caves and underground chambers where corrosion soon ruined sophisticated equipment.

For Japanese civilians temporary industrial achievements brought little reward; shortages multiplied and the fabric of city life was eroded by new scarcities and further restrictions. On 20 April 1944 all Tokyo kindergartens were closed. In August sugar rations were suspended and in the autumn passenger trains were drastically reduced to permit the transport of larger quantities of military equipment. Even worse, food shortages led to wild dogs roaming the streets of Tokyo. Some were even killed and marketed for human consumption.

While the Japanese government now prepared to resist an Allied invasion, American bombing of Japan's cities began in earnest. At first B29 raids sought to destroy defined industrial targets, but on 9 March 1945, 334 B29 Superfortresses launched a low-level incendiary attack on northern Tokyo. Within hours 40 sq. km. (15.4 sq. mi.) of the city were destroyed and tens of thousands of civilians were killed. This raid demonstrated the total inadequacy of Japan's defences and stimulated a vast process of urban flight. During the last months before surrender more than 10 million city dwellers—two-thirds of them women and children—fled to the countryside. Increasingly pessimistic rumours circulated among civilians and Korean immigrants were accused of guiding American bombers to their targets.

Now a complex of economic forces began the final dislocation of Japan's economy and society. Food shortages drove workers to the countryside to buy rice and vegetables, and industrial absenteeism rose to unprecedented heights. Simultaneously, blockade made the importation of food and raw materials from Korea virtually impossible; even ferry links between Japan's two principal islands, Hokkaido and Honshu, were interrupted by bombing; and soon the process of aerial destruction was extended to virtually every significant provincial town and city in Japan.

Government spokesmen continued to talk of discipline, duty, and resistance, and fortune tellers were officially instructed to produce optimistic forecasts, but the Soviet declaration of war on 8 August, and nuclear attacks on *Hiroshima and *Nagasaki brought a swift acceptance of Allied terms. At first little changed. Special police (see TOKKŌ) continued to trail potential dissidents, and political prisoners remained in gaol, but soon fear of the 'devilish' enemy brought new policies and patterns of behaviour. Thousands of wives and daughters were sent into the countryside for fear of American molestation, while the government instructed local authorities to establish brothels to satisfy the anticipated desires of the occupiers. Much of the army which had been prepared to resist an Allied invasion was rapidly demobilized and ministers now urged citizens to turn their attention to national reconstruction and peace. Indeed, soldiers were instructed to avoid any actions which might produce friction with American units. By the time US forces arrived, and the war was formally ended on 2 September, Japanese society was mentally and physically disarmed.

GORDON DANIELS

3. Government

To outsiders, wartime Japan appeared to be a fascist totalitarian state ruled by a military dictatorship. Thus, the prime minister, General Tōjō, who held office from 18 October 1941 to 18 July 1944, was often likened to Hitler. Yet the reality was quite different, for Tōjō inherited a complex political system which he found impossible to master.

This complexity originated in the contradictory, dual, nature of Japan's constitutional monarchy, as defined by the 1889 Meiji Constitution. On the one hand, the constitution located sovereignty in the emperor and attributed to him executive, legislative, and military prerogatives so extensive as to make him virtually an absolute monarch who, being 'sacred and inviolable', possessed supreme authority as 'head of the Empire'. Yet on the other hand, the constitution also contained articles which significantly limited him by delegating the exercise of his prerogatives, for example, to the cabinet in the case of his executive powers, to the bicameral parliament, or Diet, where his legislative powers were concerned, and to the military, with respect to his powers of 'supreme command' and military administration.

The net effect of this ambiguous blend of absolute and limited monarchy was that emperor *Hirohito reigned but did not rule. Rather, his primary political function was formally to legitimize policy decisions reached by his government and in performing this role, he was advised at court by the Lord Keeper of the Privy Seal, the Grand Chamberlain, and other officials who generally kept him neutral as a transcendental symbol of national unity. Inevitably the various institutions established by the constitution, which exercised his prerogatives in actual practice, engaged in acute sectarian rivalry to have their respective, and often conflicting, policies ratified by the 'Imperial Will'.

Ostensibly, national policy was made by the cabinet, which was responsible not to the Diet but to the emperor, who appointed the prime minister on the recommendation of his court advisers, including especially, from 1940, the lord keeper of the privy seal, in consultation with the informal conference of 'elder statesmen' made up of former prime ministers (Jūshin Kaigi). However, the cabinet's position was weak *vis-à-vis* the military; and the central bureaucracy, which implemented the policies of the foreign, finance, home, and other cabinet ministries, constituted a conservative and increasingly assertive political force in its own right. In addition, the co-operation of the Diet was required to legislate policy. But the mainstream, conservative parties—the Minseitō and Seiyūkai—which together dominated the lower House of Representatives as a consequence of national elections, did not always comply. Their formal powers were limited, essentially to budgetary review. The even more conservative upper House of Peers, composed of hereditary nobles and appointed officials, acted as a check on the lower house. A multiplicity of other institutions, some civilian, some military, also tried to influence policy formally or informally. They included: the privy council; business and labour interest groups; the military Reservists' Association; the Board of Field Marshals and Fleet Admirals; the Supreme War Council, which included the last-named board, and the service ministers and chiefs.

The conflicts inherent in this system of élite pluralism had proved manageable until they were greatly intensified by the crises of the early 1930s, particularly the great depression and the 1931 Manchurian Incident (see MANCHUKUO). Furthermore, the system as a whole was weakened by a deepening ultranationalist reaction, especially on the part of radical dissidents within the armed forces who aspired to install a military dictatorship. Had one of the planned or attempted *coups d'état* perpetrated by radical young officers been successful, such a dictatorship might well have resulted. However, once these attempted coups, culminating in the rebellion of 26 February 1936, were repressed, the army chose to rely on gradual penetration and subtle manipulation of the government to increase its leverage over the bureaucratic, non-party, cabinets which followed the Seiyūkai party administration of Inukai Tsuyoshi upon his assassination in May 1932.

The army was able to do so mainly because there was widespread support for its plans to build a powerful, self-sufficient, 'national defence state' (*kokubō kokka*) in a context of perceived foreign threats to the empire. Two additional factors assisted the army's political ascendancy. First, while the Meiji Constitution had given Hirohito the right of supreme command, over which the cabinet had no control, in practice the military, and in particular the army general staff office, used the so-called 'independence of the supreme command' and the direct access of the chief of staff to the throne, to usurp this imperial prerogative, as had been done, for example, in the Manchurian Incident earlier. Notably, this continued to be the case after the control of combat operations was broadly assumed by Imperial General Headquarters (see 5(a), below); revived in November 1937 during the early stages of the China Incident, this institution, which also included the army and navy ministers, was dominated by the army and navy chiefs of staff.

Second, through an arrangement whereby the service ministers were required to be generals and admirals on active service rather than in the reserves, in 1936 the army acquired the ability to cause the fall of a given cabinet simply by withdrawing or refusing to provide an army minister. This 'veto', which made the cabinet all the more subservient to the army's priorities, was applied on several occasions in pre-war Japan when the cabinet, including even administrations headed by military men, proved incapable of obtaining the Diet's support for specific national defence measures.

That the army found it necessary to abort cabinets in this way suggests the extent to which the Minseitō and Seiyūkai parties were anxious to preserve as much political influence as possible, notwithstanding their general support of a 'national defence state'. In retrospect, their resistance to political centralization favouring the military was natural. Having formed the government for most of the period 1918–32, the parties resented their loss of power.

The China Incident, which started in July 1937, dramatically intensified the process of building a 'national defence state'. In March 1938, Prime Minister Prince *Konoe and his cabinet negotiated the support of the Diet for the enactment of a National Mobilization Law which gave the government comprehensive wartime controls over manpower, resources, production, transportation, wages, and prices. Similarly, in August that year, Konoe launched a 'spiritual mobilization' campaign to whip up public support for what had already become a military stalemate in China. As part of this campaign, various patriotic front organizations, typified by the National Defence Women's Association, increased their activities. Another example of mobilization occurred under Konoe's successor, Hiranuma Kiichirō, who took office in January 1939, when the Diet enacted the Major Industries Association Ordinance in August 1939. The ordinance was intended to enhance the government's economic controls through the formation of compulsory cartels in strategic industries. However, no single organ was established to supervise the cartels, and control was divided among several ministries.

The army and the 'revisionist bureaucrats', who wanted greater centralization of state power, were frustrated by the need for the government to negotiate with the parties for their support in the Diet. Accordingly, a new national unity front, the Imperial Rule Assistance Association, or IRAA, was founded on 12 October 1940, with Konoe, who had returned as prime minister that July, as its ex-officio president. The existing parties were then pressured to dissolve themselves voluntarily and join the IRAA, just as labour unions and business organizations were pressured to merge into a new Industrial Patriotic League. But contrary to expectations in some quarters that the IRAA, as a Nazi-type organization, would strengthen the hand of the government, it proved to be little more than a sounding-board for the government's defence agenda. The Diet members of the former Minseitō and Seiyūkai parties, the bureaucracy, and indeed the army itself, were prepared to support the IRAA only insofar as it did not compromise their respective powers and interests.

Hence, prior to Tōjō's appointment as prime minister, the Japanese political system was a balance between competing élites, with the army's predominance more hegemonic than dictatorial because of its need to forge co-operative working relationships with other élites. However, this system was further complicated by the many divisions that existed within the government concerning defence priorities and the role of Japan's growing military power in the critical area of foreign policy. In addition to acute civil–military rivalry, debates on these issues reflected conflict between, and within, the army and the navy, and tensions between the general staff and field commanders who frequently undertook operations that had not been authorized by the government.

Since the army and navy general staff offices conducted operations without cabinet control, the cabinet itself could not make foreign policy decisions with any confidence in the military's compliance. Therefore, during the China Incident, when both general staff offices became the Imperial General Headquarters, the Liaison Conference (Renraku Kaigi) was established to co-ordinate the military and civilian branches of government in decision-making. It usually included the prime minister, the service ministers, the foreign minister, and sometimes the finance minister from the cabinet and, representing Imperial Headquarters, the army and navy chiefs and vice-chiefs of staff and numerous bureau chiefs who served as secretaries. This extra-constitutional body, which was numerically dominated by the military, quickly superseded the cabinet as the centre of Japanese decision-making. Its meetings were often prolonged by heated disagreements but once decisions were made, they were then automatically sanctioned by the emperor when the members of the Liaison Conference met him formally in subsequent Imperial Conferences (Gozen Kaigi). After this, the cabinet conferred its endorsement, again as a matter of routine, whereupon decisions became official national policy.

All major foreign policy decisions in the pre-war period, including, for example, the decision to enter the Tripartite Pact and advance south in 1940, and the decisions leading to the Pearl Harbor attack in December 1941, were taken in this labyrinthine institutional setting. While in each case the military had its way, it should be emphasized that decision-making involved the often laborious process of negotiating a collective consensus of all the participants. Thus, while power was highly centralized, it was also significantly fragmented and although the military dominated the government, its leadership was by no means absolute. Because these conditions continued to prevail in Japan throughout the Second World War, the long-standing aim of a totalitarian 'national defence state' was never achieved.

When Konoe's clash with the military over the question of war or peace caused him to resign in October 1941, he was replaced by Tōjō on the recommendation of the emperor's advisers, with a mandate to continue final preparations for war with the Anglo-American powers in the expected event that further negotiations in Washington, would fail to prevent war. Tōjō served concurrently as army minister to bolster his own position, and to co-ordinate better civil and military administration. Until mid-February 1942 he also served as home minister. Apart from Admiral Shimada Shigetarō, the navy minister, most other members of his cabinet were civilian bureaucrats.

The onset of war in Asia and the Pacific made this a war cabinet but Tōjō did not proclaim a state of emergency. Rather, he relied upon the Diet, which continued to function throughout the conflict, to enact wartime legislation. Thus, in the spring of 1942 he called a general election in order to strengthen the Diet's co-operation with his administration. A list of approved, pro-government, candidates was prepared and they were duly elected. Remarkably, however, a small minority of non-listed independent candidates, including such outspoken critics of Tōjō as the conservative Nakano Seigō and the liberal Ozaki Yukio, were also elected that year. Some of these men refused to join a new parliamentary body, the Imperial Rule Assistance Political Association, which was formed as an offshoot of the IRAA, soon after the election. Although the wartime Diet co-operated with the government, Nakano, Ozaki, and others often publicly criticized Tōjō for having amassed too much personal power.

Ozaki was arrested, convicted (of *lèse majesté* during the recent election campaign) and sentenced to imprisonment, although he was subsequently pardoned. Nakano, too, suffered police harassment for his bold advocacy of Tōjō's dismissal and ultimately committed suicide, in 1943. More broadly, Tōjō used the Special Higher Police the Tokkō, the Military Police, known as the *Kempei, and the courts to suppress known and suspected 'thought criminals' who allegedly threatened the state and Japan's war effort. In addition to the 1925 Peace Preservation Law, aimed mainly at the communists, other laws, such as the Special Emergency Act of December 1942, greatly extended the state's authority to carry out sweeping arrests. Yet the number of prosecutions for illegal dissent was lower than might be expected; at the end of the war there were only 2,500 political prisoners in detention. Torture was seldom used, more subtle forms of persuasion to elicit confessions being preferred. The scale and severity of repression in wartime Japan did not compare with that exercised by the *Gestapo or the *NKVD in the USSR.

During the tenure of Tōjō's administration, bureaucratic centralization proceeded rapidly. The home ministry, which was responsible for internal security, also strengthened its control over neighbourhood associations (*tonarigumi*) which had been organized to conduct civil defence drills, distribute rations, and maintain public order. The home ministry likewise gained control of the IRAA and the army-backed Young Men's Corps, which had been founded in early 1942 in the expectation, which proved futile, that it would evolve as a Nazi-style organization. Similarly, the new Greater East Asia ministry, founded in September 1942, all but eclipsed the foreign ministry by assuming responsibility for Japan's wartime relations with Asia.

Furthermore, a new Special Wartime Administrative Law, passed in March 1943, empowered the prime minister to direct various ministries concerning war-related economic production and, relatedly, Tōjō also personally took charge of the ministry of munitions, established eight months later. His new powers generally reflected the further encroachment of the military in government; the cabinet planning board, established in 1937, and similar agencies, were increasingly dominated by the army despite their putative civilian status.

Politically, Tōjō was still obliged to orchestrate a wartime coalition of Japan's competing élites. His augmented powers still proved insufficient to overcome the intractable problem of army–navy rivalry which constantly obstructed Japan's conduct of the war. Although Tōjō was army minister, he had no control over the navy. Overall, he was as frustrated by the independence of the Imperial General Headquarters as his predecessors had been.

He therefore took the unprecedented step of assuming yet another post, that of army chief of staff, on 21

February 1944, with navy minister Shimada Shigeru serving concurrently as navy chief. But this belated attempt to co-ordinate the services fell short of establishing a unified command and as Japan's position in the war sharply deteriorated, Tōjō was increasingly vulnerable to a growing coalition of former prime ministers (the jūshin), diplomats, and imperial princes who regarded his removal as the first step to ending the war. Finally, after the fall of *Saipan on 7 July 1944, he was forced to resign, along with his cabinet, on 18 July.

If, with all his powers, by virtue of the concurrent posts he held, Tōjō could not impose control over the war effort, it was unreasonable to expect that his successor, General *Koiso Kuniaki, who held only the post of prime minister, could do so. When he took office, Koiso was urged by the emperor and his advisers to improve army–navy relations as the most urgent priority. To accomplish this, a new, more streamlined, war cabinet, the Supreme Council for the Direction of the War, was established in August 1944, to replace the former Liaison Conference as the principal centre of decision-making.

Consisting of the prime minister, the service ministers, the chiefs of staff, and the foreign minister, the Council proved somewhat more effective. But Koiso's personal influence on its deliberations was insignificant and the political divisions that had plagued the Tōjō cabinet remained. Above all, little was done to solve the ever-growing dilemma of army–navy rivalry, exemplified by the operational discord between, and within, the two services that contributed to heavy Japanese losses in the second of the two *Philippines campaigns. As another calamitous defeat, on *Okinawa, loomed, and with American planes bombing Japan at will in their strategic air offensive, Koiso resigned on 5 April 1945, vainly recommending that only a powerful government combining the cabinet and the supreme command could possibly save the empire.

However, the structure of the government was not changed under Koiso's successor, Admiral *Suzuki Kantarō, whose cabinet is notable for the predominance of naval, rather than army, officers and for the inclusion of former party politicians. Whereas it would have been possible to declare martial law and rule arbitrarily, the government preferred still to depend upon the Diet to legislate new bills related to the final defence of Japan in the last desperate stages of the war. On 12 June 1945, for instance, the Diet legislated that most adults, including women, had to join a so-called Volunteer Fighting Corps and a separate wartime emergency measure bill was passed which gave the government authority to do virtually whatever was necessary to hold the economy and society together. Even at this point, though, the Diet obliged the government to consult with it in implementing national policies.

Like Koiso, Suzuki was permitted by the military to attend the meetings of Imperial Headquarters but inter-service co-operation remained elusive. While the military persisted in its determination to carry on fighting, a 'peace party' centred primarily on the *jūshin* and the imperial court manoeuvred behind the scenes to bring the conflict to a close before the country was completely destroyed.

In this polarized context, the issue of continued war or surrender was to be settled by the Supreme Council for the Direction of the War. But its proceedings were completely deadlocked between those who wanted to fight to the finish and those who advocated surrender on the terms set forth by the Allies in the Potsdam Proclamation of 26 July 1945 (see TERMINAL). When the government could no longer function in resolving this impasse, it took the unprecedented intervention of Emperor Hirohito, at Suzuki's invitation, to break the deadlock and end the war, with the result that the emperor announced Japan's termination of hostilities on 15 August 1945. On that day, Suzuki resigned, taking official responsibility for the defeat. He was replaced by Prince Higashikuni Naruhiko (1887–1990) the first imperial prince to serve as prime minister, who had the task of managing the country's transition into the post-war occupation.

It is striking how little the experience of total war altered the Japanese system of government. The Meiji constitutional order remained intact; the emperor's role was largely confined to legitimating policies decided upon by his government, as his predecessors had always done; despite the façade of central controls, power was diffused among different competing élites, with the Diet continuing to function pretty much as it had functioned before the war; and transitions from one wartime administration to the next were relatively smooth and unmarked by bloodshed. Basically, in these respects, the government operated quite effectively. But its great defect was the independence of the supreme command which, more than any other single factor, had led Japan down the path to war and contributed to the lack of co-ordination that might have facilitated the war effort.

Japan's wartime regime was repressive but it was not a fascist regime in the sense found in Europe. Its ideology, combining traditional communitarian values and loyalty to the emperor, was deliberately projected as uniquely Japanese and altogether unrelated to European fascism. The various experiments with Nazi-type organizations were distinctly unsuccessful.

Did the wartime government have the public trust even though it was scarcely accountable to the public? Perhaps it did, at least early in the Pacific war, although many Japanese may have gone along with it less out of conviction than from the perceived necessity to conform to the dictates of the state. But this trust did not survive the conflict. Rather, the widespread disillusionment of the people with a government that had waged a catastrophic war made them generally receptive to the reforms of demilitarization and political democratization which were soon introduced by the occupation.

STEPHEN LARGE

4. Defence forces and civil defence

Although Japan held its first air raid drill in July 1928, little serious attention was devoted to civil defence until the eve of the China Incident. On 5 April 1937 the government promulgated the Air Defence Law which proclaimed broad principles of policy and made prefectural governors responsible for local civil defence. Two years later the home ministry established auxiliary police and fire units which were largely based upon traditional volunteer associations. Civil defence was further encouraged by the founding of the Great Japan Air Defence Association and the Great Japan Fire Defence Association, nationwide bodies which sponsored publicity and training, and provided financial aid to local citizens' groups.

Even after Pearl Harbor most civil defence preparations remained the responsibility of local officials and bitter inter-ministerial rivalries obstructed the formation of integrated policies. Even more damaging were the military assumptions which formed the basis of civil defence planning. Army and navy commanders claimed that Japan would never face large-scale air attacks, and that limited preparations would suffice to protect her major cities. In April 1942 the *Doolittle raid penetrated Japan's air defences, but it was ineffective and seemed to confirm rather than challenge the premisses of government policy.

These complacent attitudes remained largely unchanged until November 1943, when news of Allied victories and the bombing of German cities gave a new urgency to civil defence policy. Symbolic of this new mood was the creation of the Air Defence Headquarters under the minister of home affairs. This new organization attempted to co-ordinate policies between rival ministries and initiate new lines of action. By this time large numbers of trench shelters had been constructed; now these were roofed, and local authorities were urged to excavate public tunnel shelters in cliffs and hillsides. Tunnel shelter construction was further encouraged by government offers of large subsidies to prefectural and city governments.

In late 1943 the central government also began drafting formal plans for the evacuation of non-essential personnel from the Tokyo, Nagoya, Osaka, and north Kyūshū conurbations. Initially, Prime Minister Tōjō opposed such schemes as he feared that they would fragment families and undermine national morale. However his reservations were gradually overcome by his desire to preserve the next generation for future wars. Old people, mothers, and children were encouraged to move to the homes of friends and relatives in the countryside. In cases where this was impossible junior school pupils from the third to the sixth grade were to be evacuated, as classes, with their teachers. In the summer of 1944 thousands of city teachers visited parents to persuade them of the virtues of school evacuation and by August more than 333,000 children had travelled to rural villages. Here they lived in inns, temples, and public halls, and despite homesickness and meagre rations, continued their education with tolerable success. A further 459,000 children travelled with their parents to the homes of country relatives.

A further wave of evacuees was precipitated by radical fire prevention policies. In 1943 the government began the destruction of thousands of dwelling houses to create fire-breaks; this destruction soon drove more than 343,000 city dwellers to rural areas, or to temporary accommodation near their workplaces.

Besides these ambitious evacuation policies the government also encouraged local training for expected incendiary raids. In every town and city 'block associations' and neighbourhood groups donned padded clothing and practised 'bucket relays' and other primitive methods of fire-fighting. Equally important was the 'air defence oath' which urged citizens to stand their ground in the face of incendiary or high explosive *bombs. Such training was understandable but suicidal, for by 1945 Japan's anti-aircraft batteries and fighter squadrons were obsolete and could offer no challenge to modern, high-flying bombers. When large-scale incendiary raids began on 9 March radio warnings effectively mobilized fire brigades and civil defence workers but neither could control the *firestorms which swept across northern Tokyo. In the aftermath of this catastrophe the evacuation of third to sixth grade pupils was made compulsory, and first and second grade pupils were urged to leave all major cities. Within a month 87% of children in these groups had reached sanctuaries in the country.

As American bombers devastated city after city thousands of medical personnel and civil defence workers ignored orders and fled. For millions of urban Japanese escape to the country now constituted the only effective form of 'civil defence'. Government rules, plans, and preparations were soon rapidly overwhelmed by a mass unplanned exodus to the safety of provincial villages. The country's defence forces never had to be employed operationally and would have proved equally ineffective if they had been.

In January 1945 Imperial General Headquarters (see ARMED FORCES (a), below) formulated a Homeland Operations Plan in preparation for an expected Allied invasion. Army and navy leaders planned large-scale military resistance and Prime Minister Koiso sought to reinforce these efforts by drawing millions of citizens into auxiliary activities. On 23 March the cabinet formally decided to establish People's Volunteer Units (Kokumin Giyūtai). These were to consist of both men's and women's sections, and were to be organized on the basis of school, workplace, or locality. Volunteers were to assist the army, navy, and police in such diverse tasks as military construction, evacuation, transport, food production, air defence, the repair of roads and buildings, and the maintenance of public order. In May and June the government gave further encouragement to the growth of the volunteer movement by dissolving the Imperial Rule Assistance Association and other patriotic societies

Japanese women practising civil defence drill in the Meiji Gaien stadium, Tokyo, **Japan**, November 1943. Many of them are wearing hooded air raid shrouds.

(see GOVERNMENT, above) and encouraging their members to join the new volunteers.

As the danger of invasion grew the government moved to transform many of the new groups into fighting units. On 23 June a new volunteer military service law created the People's Volunteer Combat Corps (Kokumin giyū Sentōtai) to be raised from men aged from 15 to 60 and women aged from 17 to 40. These citizen forces were planned as city or prefectural federations, appropriate for flexible local defence. They were under the control of local governors and the prime minister acted as the corps' C-in-C. By this time modern weapons were almost unobtainable and tens of thousands of volunteers were trained with simple staves and bamboo spears. Government propagandists now advocated 'The Glorious Death of One Hundred Million' to 'Defend the National Polity' but the *atomic bomb attacks brought surrender before an invasion, and on 2 September 1945 all People's Volunteer organizations were dissolved and their activities ended. GORDON DANIELS

5. Armed forces

Two military codes regulated the behaviour of Japanese servicemen: the Imperial Rescript to Soldiers and Sailors (Gunjin Chokuyu) and Instructions for the Battlefield (Senjinkun). The former was read every day by servicemen, particularly in the army, and copies of the latter were distributed to everyone on active duty.

The Gunjin Chokuyu, first issued in 1882, stressed that the armed forces were directly responsible to the divine figure of the emperor (see RELIGION) and laid down five principles to guide a serviceman's conduct: loyalty, propriety, valour, righteousness, and simplicity. Loyalty called for absolute obedience to the emperor and propriety demanded the acceptance of orders from a superior as if they had come direct from the emperor.

The Senjinkun was issued on 8 January 1941 in the name of General *Tōjō, who was then war minister. This enjoined absolute obedience to orders and forbade any retreat ('A soldier must never abandon the field to the enemy, even at the risk of his life') or surrender ('A soldier must never suffer the disgrace of being captured alive').

These codes, and *Bushidō, led to what western observers have called 'fanatical' resistance (see also HEROISM), to suicidal **banzai* charges, to many soldiers shouting 'Long Live the Emperor' as they died, and to some refusing to surrender even after the war had ended. Lieutenant Onoda Hiroo, for instance, ordered to undertake guerrilla warfare on Lubang Island in the Philippines, refused to give himself up until 1974.

(a) High Command

The Meiji Constitution (1898–1947) declared that 'the Emperor has the supreme command of the Army and Navy', but it was Imperial General Headquarters (IGH) that directed Japanese forces during the war (see Chart 1). The prime minister became an ex-officio member in March 1945 but civilian control of IGH was minimal (see GOVERNMENT, above).

In peacetime both general staffs were responsible to their respective ministries, but after the start of the China Incident in July 1937 IGH was formed and the two staffs were then known as IGH, Army Section, and IGH, Navy Section. However, the sections remained independent of each other and there was no unified command system such as the US *Joint Chiefs of Staff, though the formation of IGH was an attempt to create one. No one co-ordinated the two staffs nor was there anyone to act as an arbiter, or final decision-maker, when a disagreement occurred.

By 1941 IGH, Army Section, or Army High Command,

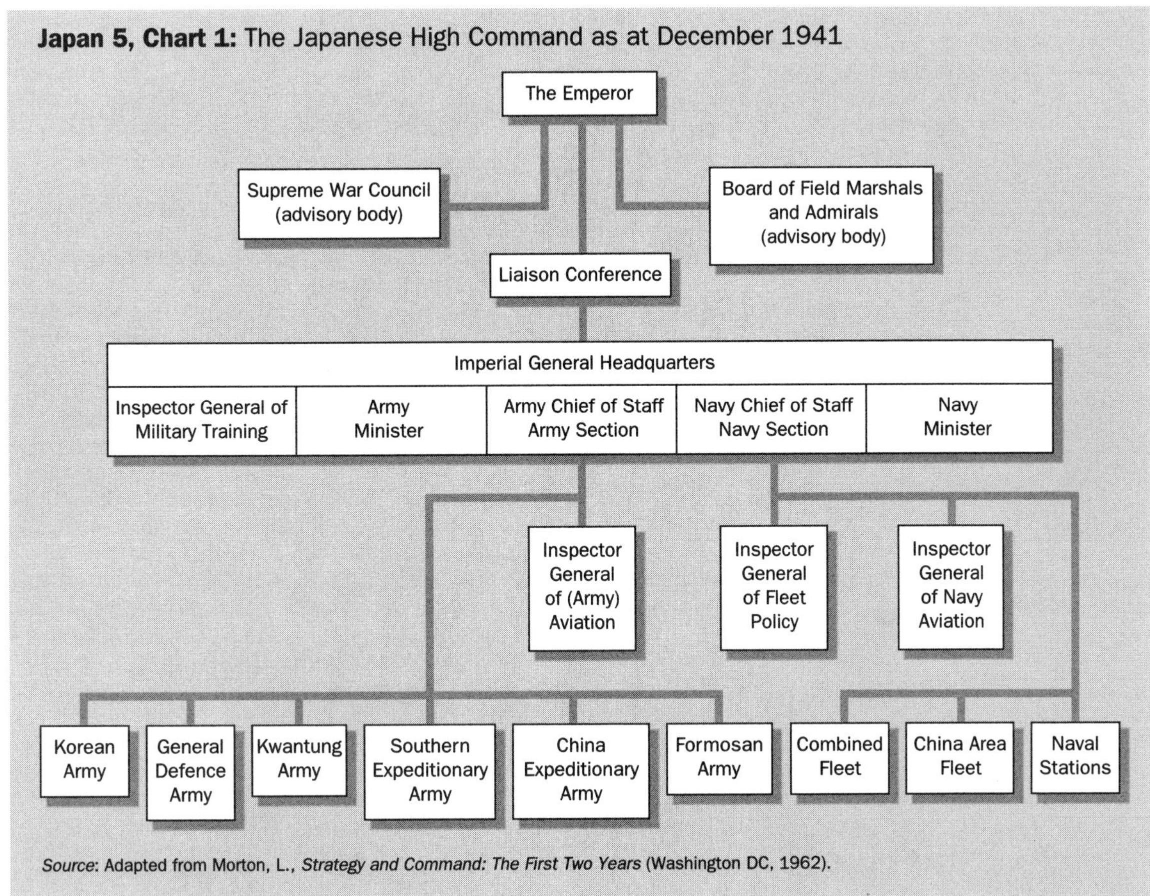

was headed by General *Sugiyama Hajime (later succeeded by General Tōjō and then General Umezu Yoshijirō), who was assisted by a deputy chief. The Navy High Command was headed by Admiral Nagano Osami (later succeeded by Admiral Shimada Shigeru and then Admiral *Toyoda). Each section had its own bureaux for operations, intelligence, and *logistics. The operations bureau, particularly in the army, always attracted the top staff officers, a tradition which led to intelligence and logistics being underrated. Indeed, it is no exaggeration to say that Japan lost the Pacific war because staff officers neglected intelligence.

Other factors also hindered the efficiency of IGH. The conservative seniority system stifled the promotion of talented staff officers. Neither Shimada nor Sugiyama was particularly able, but because of the seniority system each occupied the highest post in their respective services for part of the war. The training of staff officers ignored strategy and war theory in favour of tactics. It also created an élite officer corps where a network of personal relationships, founded on paternalism, made it difficult to discipline subordinates and where the principle of reward and punishment failed to apply. This was tolerated by both high commands though it functioned to the detriment of the system as a whole.

Both sections of IGH frequently failed to clarify their strategic or operational objectives. As a result, staff officers, especially in the field armies, resorted to *dokudan senkō* (complete operational freedom) and *gekokujō* (where junior officers defied their seniors), and they often seemed incapable of formulating strategies based upon scientific reasoning. Anyone who argued rationally or advised prudence could be accused of cowardice, and the superiority of spiritual power over material strength was always being emphasized.

This attitude led to the High Command neglecting to improve weapons and mechanize the army. Infantrymen were armed with rifles made in 1905 which had been hardly improved since that date. The navy's emphasis on rigorous training, which in itself was excellent, retarded the development of such modern technology; and though it developed the outstanding Zero fighter it failed to give its pilots adequate protective armour because it wanted to promote offensive thinking. This inability to

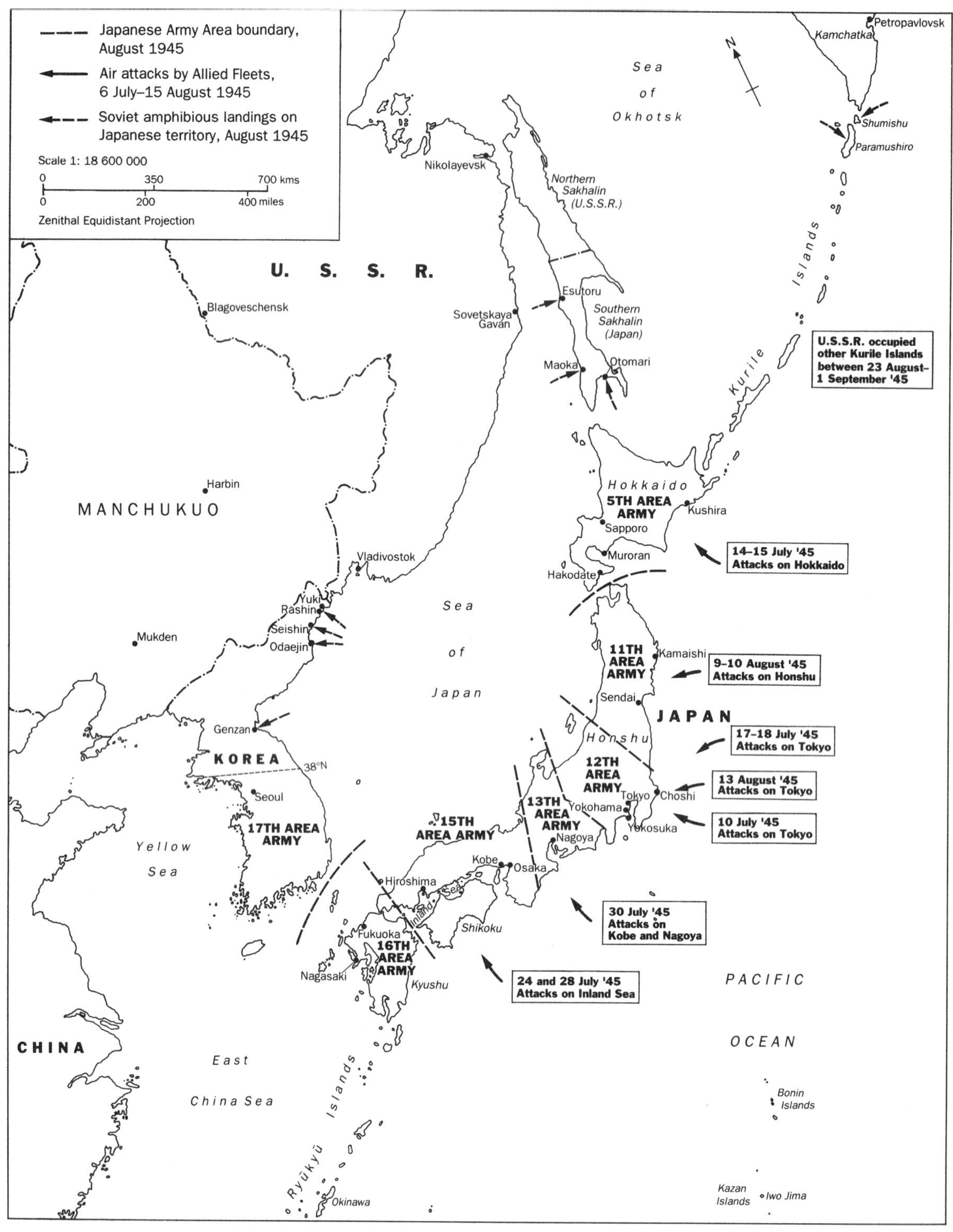

58. **Japan** under siege, July–August 1945

use a scientific approach needlessly cost the lives of hundreds of thousands of Japanese servicemen.

Senior Japanese commanders and staff officers of both services were good at planning surprise attacks for defeating an adversary in a short and decisive battle, but they hardly gave a thought to the problems of a protracted war. Neither Nagano nor Sugiyama, when questioned by the emperor in September 1941, had a long-term strategy. They staked all on rapidly smashing the US Navy and compelling Roosevelt to negotiate a peace on adverse terms.

Despite its weaknesses and defects, the Japanese High Command in its short history should be given some credit for building up its armed forces to equal those of western powers, and for creating, despite its weaknesses, a professional officer corps.

(b) Army

The Imperial Japanese Army (IJA) was run by a triumvirate: the Inspectorate General of Military Training, the War Ministry, and the General Staff (see HIGH COMMAND, above). The Inspectorate General of Military Training was primarily concerned with the administration of the military academy, the war college, and other service schools. The war ministry dealt with politico-military affairs, budget, personnel, mobilization, and ordnance, and had under it Central Shipping Transportation (until July 1942 when it came under the direct control of the IJA's Chief of Staff) and the HQ of the departments of armour, army aeronautics, fortifications, fuel, and arsenal administration.

The peacetime standing army comprised 17 divisions in addition to the Korean Army, the Formosan Army, and the *Kwantung Army in Manchukuo. Between 1937 and 1941 this number was increased to 31 divisions to reinforce the China Expeditionary Army fighting in the China Incident, and to prepare for the invasion of South-East Asia, and the Kwantung Army was also increased, from 5 to 13 divisions. The *Indian National Army and the *Burma Independence Army, raised with Japanese help, fought alongside the IJA in the Burma campaign; and volunteer armies (*giyūgun*) were raised in Java and elsewhere, but these were merely auxiliary forces for bolstering Japanese coastal defences.

The IJA's command structure (see Chart 2) embraced a number of general armies, area armies, and armies. Armies were formed from two or more divisions, which were the basic fighting formation. The wide variety of tasks imposed on the IJA demanded flexibility in its divisions. By 1939 the standard one was the B (*Otsu*) type, with a total strength of 20,000 men. This had three infantry regiments and one engineer, one transport, and one artillery regiment (36 guns), plus a reconnaissance unit (in Manchukuo often cavalry, which the Japanese retained throughout the war), and service troops. There were also the A (*Kō*) and C (*Hei*) type divisions. The former (29,000 men) operated in China and Manchukuo and had extra artillery, larger infantry battalions, and, often, a tank battalion; the latter (13,500–15,000 men), used for garrison and anti-guerrilla duties, had just two brigades of two infantry battalions.

Independent Mixed Brigades, first used in China, had between three and six infantry battalions (each 750–900 strong) with artillery, signals, and engineer units attached. When used in the Pacific war they had extra artillery and four to eight battalions as well as specialist anti-aircraft and anti-tank units. Commanded by a major-general, their strength varied between 3,100 and 6,000 men. Scaled-down versions, Independent Mixed Regiments, were used to defend Pacific islands.

Special Detachments (*shitai*), all-arms forces of brigade strength, were often raised for special missions. They were sometimes named after their commander (e.g. the Ichiki Detachment on Guadalcanal), and sometimes according to where they operated (such as the South Seas, which landed at Guam and then on New Guinea, and the North Seas, which started the *Aleutian Islands campaigns). They were normally formed and controlled by army or area army commanders, but also directly from Imperial General HQ.

Up to August 1939 the Japanese used their armour only to support their infantry, but the battle of Nomonhan (see JAPANESE–SOVIET CAMPAIGNS) changed their perception of how it should be employed. Nevertheless, the first Japanese armoured division was not ready for service, in Manchukuo, until 1943. Before then their armour operated in tank groups (*sensha dan*) of three or four tank regiments (80 tanks each) from which tank companies (12 tanks) were detached to operate with infantry if required.

Both the IJA and the navy had parachutists. The army's basic unit was what was known as the Raiding Regiment (*teishin rentai*). This contained about 600 parachutists and was part of a Raiding Group (*teishin dan*) which had two parachute regiments, two squadrons of transport aircraft to carry them, and a glider regiment.

The nature of the Pacific war led the IJA to being widely involved in seaborne operations and administration. Two divisions, 5th (Samurai) and 11th, were specially trained in *amphibious warfare, of which the IJA had, from earlier conflicts, long experience. Though supported by the navy, all large landings were conducted by the IJA (but see WAKE ISLAND), and it was army *engineers who, between the wars, developed the necessary landing craft—including the bow ramp which the Americans and the British were to copy—shipping facilities, and complete operational techniques.

Once it had occupied so many far-flung islands the IJA was obliged to supply and reinforce its garrisons. Central Shipping Transportation's Shipping and Transport Command controlled three Water Transport Commands (whose code, when broken, provided early *ULTRA intelligence) which in turn controlled a network of island anchorages and the shipping using them. It also commanded Shipping Artillery Regiments (*senpaku hōhei rentai*), Shipping Regiments (*senpaku kōhei rentai*), which

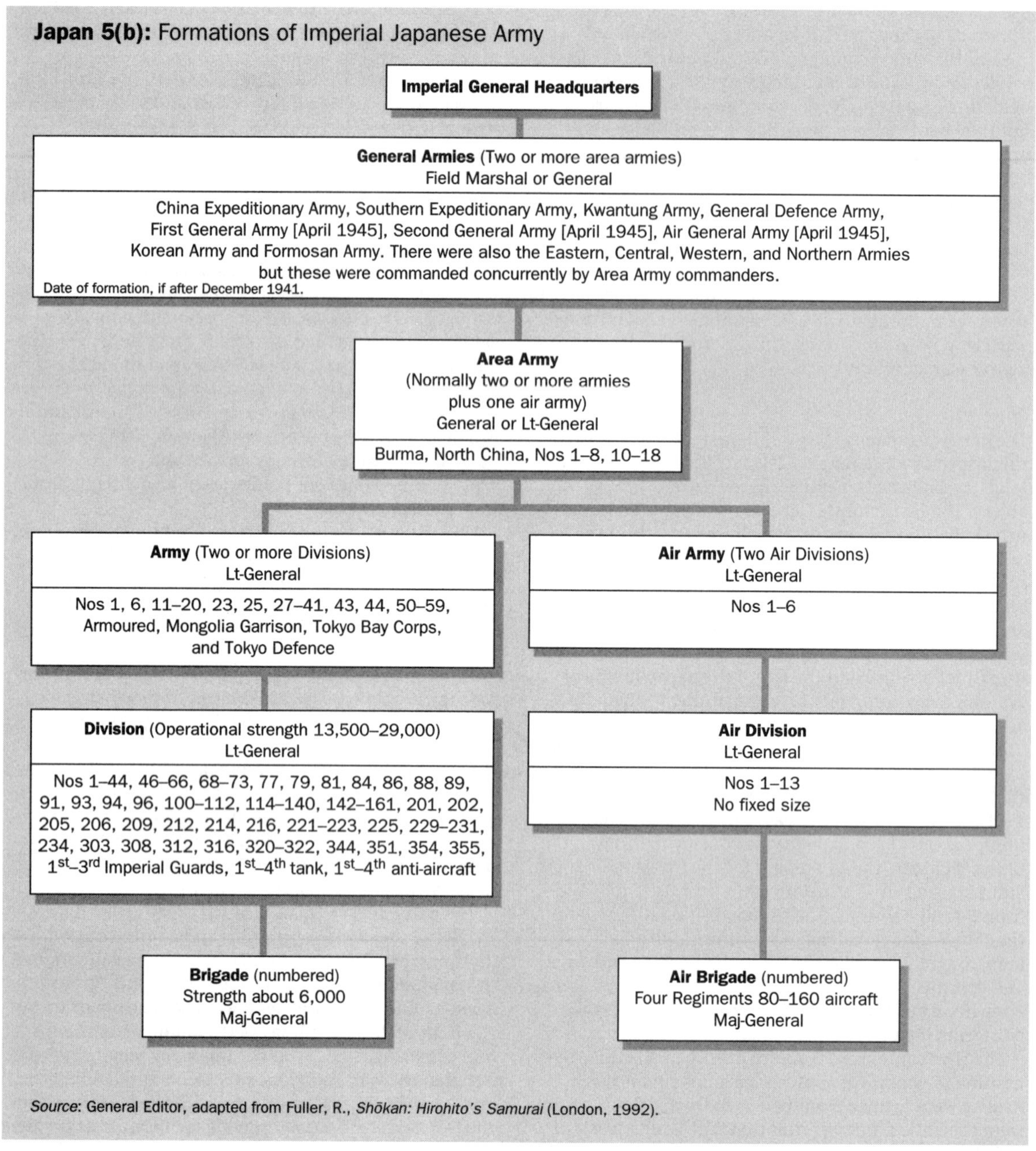

were similar to the US *Seabees, and Shipping Communications units (*senpaku tsūshintai*), which mounted amphibious operations.

In 1943 several mobile seaborne brigades (*kaijō kidō ryodan*) of three reinforced infantry battalions were raised, to each of which was permanently attached a 1,500-strong shipping engineer regiment, which was called a 'sea transport unit'. These brigades were intended as mobile reserves for IJA island garrisons but were, in fact, only used in a static defence role.

By the end of the war the IJA was even operating its own escort carriers to protect its *convoys with Army Air Force aircraft. But its air force was mostly employed in Manchukuo and China, or on larger land masses such as New Guinea, as its short-range aircraft were not suitable for the Pacific war nor were its pilots trained for flying long distances over water. The basic air force unit was the Air Group (*sentai*), which had three squadrons or companies (*chūtai*) of nine to twelve aircraft. Above the Group was the Air Brigade (*hikōdan*), which had three fighter, light bomber, or heavy bomber groups, and a reconnaissance unit. Two or three Air Brigades formed an Air Division (*hikōshidan*) and two or three divisions an Air Army (*kōkūgun*). First, Second, and Third Air Armies were created in June and July 1942; the Fourth in July 1943; the Fifth in February 1944; and the Sixth in August 1944.

In December 1941 IJA troops were deployed as shown in Table 4 and supporting them were 151 squadrons, based mostly on Formosa, or in French Indo-China, Manchukuo, and China. Hostilities began with landings by the Twenty-Fifth Army in southern Thailand and northern Malaya. These were followed by the Fourteenth Army landing on Luzon Island at the start of the second of the two Philippines campaigns; Twenty-Third Army's attack on Hong Kong; Fifteenth Army's invasion of Burma from Thailand; and several amphibious operations launched by Sixteenth Army in the *Netherlands East Indies. General Terauchi, based at Saigon, took overall charge of these operations as commander of the Southern Expeditionary Army.

In China the 3rd, 6th, 34th, and 40th divisions of the Eleventh Army, based at Hankow, attacked Changsha, and in May and June 1942, after the bombers participating in the Doolittle raid on Tokyo landed at Chinese-held air bases, the China Expeditionary Army ordered the Eleventh and Thirteenth Armies to attack Kuomintang army air bases at Lishui, Yüshan, and Chuchow. The Thirteenth Army advanced westwards from Hangchow while Eleventh Army advanced eastwards, and by early June the Kuomintang armies were driven out of the Chekiang-Kiangsi district. These operations apart, the fighting in China was minimal until the ICHI-GŌ offensive of 1944.

The first phase of the war ended with victories beyond Japanese expectations. But just as the IJA was readjusting to prepare for a protracted war and to consolidate an impregnable defensive perimeter in occupied South-East Asia, an Allied counter-offensive, beginning with the landing of US Marines on Guadalcanal in August 1942, upset its strategy. The Seventeenth Army, formed in May to take Port Moresby, was forced to divert its divisions (38th and 51st) to Guadalcanal to support 2nd Division, where they incurred serious losses. To deal with this serious situation Eighth Area Army was formed under General Imamura Hitoshi at Rabaul. This controlled Eighteenth Army, formed at the same time at Rabaul as Eighth Area Army to take over the *New Guinea campaign, and the Seventeenth Army, which was relieved of the Guadalcanal operations to defend the rest of the Solomon Islands. But these changes, delayed by squabbles within the Army High Command, were too little and too late, and Guadalcanal was eventually evacuated in February 1943.

As the Allied counter-offensive intensified, the Army High Command was compelled to deploy additional troops. During the first half of 1943 the Eighteenth Army's 20th and 51st Divisions, which had originally been intended for Guadalcanal, were sent with the Eighteenth Army's 41st Division to fight in the New Guinea campaign, and 6th Air Division was dispatched to support Eighth Area Army's operations there. In late June 1943 Eighth Area Army's air power was further augmented by deploying the newly created 7th Air Division, and in July Fourth Air Army was created to control the two air divisions. By July the main forces of Eighth Area Army had been deployed for the defence of eastern New Guinea, while Seventeenth Army co-operated with Eighth Fleet to defend the central and northern Solomon Islands (see BOUGAINVILLE, for example).

In the meantime, Terauchi had transferred his HQ from Saigon to Syonan (Singapore) and had created the Palembang Defence Army, supported by Third Air Army's 9th Air Division, to defend the Palembang oilfields; the Borneo Garrison at Kuching, Sarawak, mainly to establish a military government; the French Indo-China Garrison at Saigon in French Indo-China; and a garrison at Bangkok. In March 1943 the Twenty-Fifth Army was transferred to Bukittinggi, Sumatra.

To strengthen the defensive perimeter in the eastern part of the Indonesian archipelago, the Southern Expeditionary Army deployed, after October 1942, 48th Division for the defence of Timor, Sumba, and Lombok, and ordered a contingent of 5th Division to occupy islands in the Banda Sea. To control these two divisions, and to consolidate the area's defences, the Nineteenth Army was formed in January 1943. Supporting it was the Third Air Army's newly organized 7th Air Division, though this was transferred to New Guinea shortly afterwards. Additionally, 54th Division, organized in Himeji, Japan, was transferred to the Sixteenth Army to defend the Lesser Sunda Islands. In November 1943 the defensive perimeter north of Australia was strengthened further by transferring Second Area Army, commanded by General *Anami, and Second Army (36th and 46th Divisions) from Manchukuo and putting the Nineteenth Army under Anami's command.

Following signs of an Allied counter-offensive in Burma the Army High Command, in March 1943, hastily organized the Burma Area Army under the command of Lt-General Kawabe Masakazu, which had a strengthened Fifteenth Army under Lt-General *Mutaguchi as its core. It also commanded the newly created 31st Division at Bangkok, 25th Independent Brigade in Malaya, 124th Regiment from Guadalcanal, and howitzer and engineer regiments from central and southern China, and 15th Division from Nanjing, though this was not up to full strength until after October 1943. By the time of Mutaguchi's *Imphal offensive in April 1944, the Twenty-Eighth and Thirty-Third Armies had also been created from these forces.

In response to the reinforcement of Allied naval forces

Japan, Table 4: Deployment of ground forces, December 1941

Locations	*Names of Commands*	*Attached Divisions*	*Nos of Brigades or Equivalents*
Japan			
Tokyo	General Defence Army HQ		
Tokyo	Eastern District Army HQ	52nd	4
Osaka	Central District Army HQ	53rd, 54th	3
Fukuoka	Western District Army HQ		3
Sapporo	Northern District Army HQ	7th	1
Korea			
Seoul	Korean Army HQ	19th, 20th	0
Formosa			
Taipei	Formosan Army HQ[a]	0	0
Manchukuo			
Hsinking	Kwantung Army HQ	10th, 28th, 29th	1
Mutankiang	Third Army HQ	9th, 12th	4
Pehan	Fourth Army HQ	1st, 14th, 57th	5
Tungan (Mishan from 1943)	Fifth Army HQ	11th, 24th	4
Hailar	Sixth Army HQ	23rd	1
Chi-ning	Twentieth Army HQ	8th, 25th	4
Hsinking	Kwantung Defence Army HQ		5
China			
Nanking	China Expeditionary Army HQ		
Peking	North China Area Army HQ	27th, 35th, 110th	5
Tayuan	First Army HQ	36th, 37th, 41st	3
Tsinan	Twelfth Army HQ	17th, 32nd	3
Changchiakow	Mongolia Garrison HQ	36th, Cavalry Group Corps	1
Hankow	Eleventh Army HQ	3rd, 6th, 13th, 34th, 39th, 40th	2
Shanghai	Thirteenth Army HQ	15th, 22nd, 116th	5
Canton	Twenty-Third Army HQ	38th, 51st, 104th	1
South-East Asia			
Saigon	Southern Expeditionary Army HQ	21st	1
Kao-hsiung	Fourteenth Army HQ	16th, 48th	1
Saigon/Haiphong	Fifteenth Army HQ	33rd, 55th	0
Tokyo, Saigon	Sixteenth Army HQ[b]	2nd, 38th, 48th	1
Sanya (Hainan I.)	Twenty-Fifth Army HQ	Imp. Guard, 5th, 18th, 56th	
Bonin Is	Nankai Detachment HQ		

[a] There was no standing army of division strength in Formosa in December 1941 excepting a garrison army consisting of a few infantry regiments (including an air regiment) and a few artillery battalions. Formosa served as a staging station for troops before deployment elsewhere in China and South-East Asia. In September 1944, the Formosa Arm was reorganized as the 19th Area Army composed of the Thirty-second Army (24th, 26th, 62nd Divisions), 9th, 12th, 50th, 66th, 71st Divisions. Its defence area covered Formosa and the Ryukyu Islands.

[b] The Sixteenth Army, when organized in November 1941, was located in Tokyo, and its troops were assembled in phases at Saigon via Kaohsiur Formosa during the period between late December 1941 and January 1942. The 38th Division after completing the campaign in Hong Kong joined with the Sixteenth Army on 14 February to capture Palembang, Sumatra, and 48th Division after capturing Manila joined on 1 March to attack eastern Java.

Source: Contributor.

in the Indian Ocean, and an expected further increase in their power, the Southern Expeditionary Army created 24th Independent Mixed Brigade in Tenasserim and 29th Independent Mixed Brigade in Thailand and dispatched a contingent of the Twenty-Fifth Army's Imperial Guards Division in Sumatra to the Andaman and Nicobar Islands. Furthermore, at Terauchi's request, the Army High Command authorized the deployment of 4th Division to Sumatra, the reorganization of two garrisons into the 27th and 28th Independent Mixed Brigades, and the deployment of 53rd Division to Malaya in November as a reserve force under the Southern Expeditionary Army Command. To complete the defensive perimeter in the Indian Ocean, the Twenty-Ninth Army was formed at Taiping (northern Malaya) in January 1944, and the 35th and 37th Independent Mixed Brigades were placed under its command.

Before US naval forces launched their counter-offensive across the Central Pacific in November 1943, the Army High Command deployed the home-based 52nd Division to islands scattered in the central Pacific. Detachments were thinly spread out on *Tarawa and *Makin in the Gilbert Islands, Kwajalein and *Eniwetok in the *Marshall Islands, and on many other islands, but they were insufficient to halt the American drive and were all eventually overrun or bypassed. In a further attempt to halt the American advance and establish an invincible defensive perimeter in the Central Pacific the Army High Command created, on 18 February 1944, the Thirty-First Army, which came under the command of Vice-Admiral *Nagumo's Central Pacific Fleet based at Saipan. It comprised 52nd Division at Truk; 14th Division in the Palaus; 43rd Division, which was mobilized in Nagoya and transferred to Saipan in the Mariana Islands; 29th Division, which was transferred from Manchukuo to Guam; and 109th Division, which was formed in Kōfu and dispatched to Iwo Jima.

To counter any further northern offensive by US forces, after these had recaptured Attu in the Aleutian Islands campaigns in August 1943, the Army High Command upgraded the North District Army at Sapporo to become the Fifth Area Army and formed Twenty-Seventh Army. This covered Hokkaido, the Kurile Islands, and Sakhalin with 42nd Division, mobilized at Sendai in February 1944, and 7th Division based at Obihiro, Hokkaido. Reinforcing the Fifth Area Army further were 91st Division, 69th Independent Mixed Brigade, and 3rd, 4th, and 43rd Brigades in the Kurile Islands, 77th Division at Kajiki in Western Hokkaido, the Sakhalin Mixed Brigade, 1st Air Division at Sapporo, and rear echelons of 7th Division.

In March 1944 all the armies deployed in South-East Asia were integrated under the Southern Expeditionary Army. Its HQ was moved to Manila in May 1944, commanding an area which stretched from the western part of New Guinea to Burma. Under its command were: the Second Area Army at Amboina, which included the Second Army (Western New Guinea) and Nineteenth Army (Banda Sea); Seventh Area Army based in Singapore, which comprised the Sixteenth Army (Java), Twenty-Fifth Army (Sumatra), Twenty-Ninth Army (Malaya), and the Borneo Garrison Army (upgraded to Thirty-Seventh Army in September 1944); the Burma Area Army, which commanded Fifteenth Army in north Burma, Twenty-Eighth Army in west Burma, and Thirty-Third Army in east Burma; the Fourteenth Army in the Philippines (upgraded in September 1944 to Fourteenth Area Army under General *Yamashita); the French Indo-China Garrison Army (upgraded to Thirty-Eighth Army in December 1944); the Thai Garrison Army (upgraded to Thirty-Ninth Army in December 1944); Third Air Army (Malaya); and Fourth Air Army (the Philippines).

Expecting that the next decisive battle would be on the Philippines, and that air power would play a crucial role, the Army High Command strengthened the Southern Expeditionary Army's air force with 2nd and 4th Air Divisions, which were transferred from Manchukuo. The Fourteenth Army, which until early 1944 had consisted of only 16th Division and 30th and 33rd Independent Mixed Brigades, was also reinforced from May 1944 with six more divisions and three Independent Mixed Brigades, but with the exception of two divisions these forces were hastily mobilized, poorly equipped, and badly trained.

With the situation worsening in the central Pacific, the Army High Command restructured the General Defence Command to bolster the defence of mainland Japan and the nearby Ryūkyū islands. In the spring of 1944 the Eastern, Western, and Central District Armies, Formosan Army, Korean Army, and various air formations, including the First Air Army, were put under the General Defence Command and Thirty-Second Army was created to defend the Ryūkyūs with its 9th, 24th, and 62nd Divisions stationed on Okinawa.

By July 1944, US Central Pacific forces had driven a wedge into the empire's inner perimeter of defence, seizing Saipan and Guam, thereby forcing Tōjō's resignation from all of the offices he held, including chief of staff. In Burma, too, Japanese forces had taken a beating with the ill-fated Imphal offensive turning into a rout.

The second Philippines campaign began in October 1944. The Thirty-Fifth Army (1st, 16th, 26th, 30th, 100th, and 102nd Divisions, and 18th, 54th, and 55th Independent Mixed Brigades), supported by the Fourth Air Army, fought until it was annihilated, with Fourth Air Army pilots resorting to *kamikaze attacks. By February 1945 organized resistance by the Fourteenth Area Army had virtually ceased.

After the fall of the Philippines, US forces took Iwo Jima and Okinawa after very bloody struggles and prepared for landing operations in Japan's mainland. These were scheduled for Kyūshū in November 1945 and to the east of Tokyo in January 1946. Waiting for the invasion were 1,900,000 troops organized into 53 divisions (of which 40 were newly mobilized between January and July 1945), 23 independent mixed brigades, 3 security brigades, and 2 tank divisions.

By August 1945 the IJA had raised 170 infantry, 13 air, 4 tank, and 4 anti-aircraft divisions. These totalled 2,343,483 men of whom 1,439,101 either perished or were counted as missing in action, and 85,620 were permanently handicapped through injuries. Akashi Yogi

(c) Navy

The Imperial Japanese Navy (IJN) emerged from the First World War as the world's third largest sea power. This was duly acknowledged in the Washington naval arms limitation conference of 1922 at which the Americans, with some British support, restricted Japanese capital ship tonnage to 60% of their own. Subsequently, Japan constructed aircraft carriers and more powerful cruisers than its western counterparts, and infringed the capital ship tonnage limit, so that by 1939 the IJN was a very formidable force.

The IJN, which was much influenced by the Royal Navy, had a higher status than the army; its officer corps, trained at the Naval Academy (Etajima) and the Naval War

Japan, 5(c), Table 5: IJN strength in ships on 7 December 1941

	Existing Strength		*Under Construction*	
Classification	*Number of vessels*	*Tonnage*	*Number of vessels*	*Tonnage*
Battleships	10	301,400	2	128,000
Aircraft carriers	10	152,970	4	77,860
Heavy cruisers	18	158,800	–	–
Light cruisers	20	98,855	4	42,700
Destroyers	112	165,868	12	27,120
Submarines	65[a]	97,900	29	42,554
Others	156	490,384	37	57,225
TOTAL	391	1,466,177	88	375,459

[a] Twenty-one of these boats were obsolete and of little value.

Source: Hattori Takushirō, *The Complete History of the Greater East Asia War* (Washington DC, 1953).

College (Meguro), was socially and intellectually part of Japan's élite. But a purge during the early 1930s removed some of the IJN's best officers. Consequently, Admirals Oikawa Koshirō and Nagano Osami, who held the posts of navy minister and chief of the naval general staff in 1941, were second-rank admirals and were noted for their tendency to accept the view of army leaders and their own, more hawkish, juniors. Additionally, the IJN's rivalry with the army caused major strains, in budgetary and strategic terms, and this further weakened the Naval High Command. However, during the 1930s the IJN supported army operations on the Chinese mainland, and in doing so it acquired valuable experience in the use of naval air power. This support role continued during the Pacific war, which taxed its capabilities for an independent strategic role, particularly from 1943 onwards.

Japanese naval strategy was predicated on the assumption that the USA, because of its industrial might and greater resources, would be able to maintain a larger fleet. However, by utilizing the IJN's advances in air power, and developments in submarine and torpedo technology, and by using the Pacific mandates, the Caroline, Mariana, and Marshall Islands as bases, IJN planners developed a strategy of attrition which would erode this superiority. Basically, they envisaged luring the US Pacific Fleet to a 'decisive' battle. While attempting to reach across the Pacific at Japan, the US fleet would be whittled down until the two main battle fleets reached something approaching parity. Then, with the IJN able to operate from its own bases, but with US lines of communication and supply overextended, a 'decisive' battle would be fought and won.

In 1934 Japan abrogated the naval treaty agreements and began a construction programme which included, besides a number of aircraft carriers, the keels of two Yamato class battleships, the most powerful *warships ever built. A rapid expansion of the IJN's air force was also planned, so that by December 1941 the navy had available, besides a powerful surface fleet and submarine force (see Table 5), a front line strength of about 1,750 fighters, torpedo-bombers, and bombers, and some 530 flying boats and float planes for reconnaissance missions. Oil, the lack of which eventually crippled the IJN, had been stockpiled to provide a two-year reserve.

The steady accretion of such powerful forces, the emphasis on fighting spirit which had been fostered to counter treaty-imposed deficiencies, and a purge in 1934 which resulted in major commands at sea being given to over-aggressive officers created an overweening superiority complex in the IJN. This feeling of invincibility—the 'victory disease', as some called it after the victories of Pearl Harbor and the fall of Singapore—led to the IJN making such major errors as extending Japan's defensive Pacific perimeter beyond the range of land-based air cover, failing to ensure an adequate training programme for replacement pilots, sacrificing defensive armour in its ships and aircraft in favour of speed and offensive power, neglecting the protection of convoys, and ignoring such vital technological advances as *radar and *ASDIC.

Despite these obvious drawbacks—to which should be added its external conflicts with the army and internal ones that hinged on the relative superiority of the battleship and air power—the IJN was, by 1941, a highly disciplined, well-trained and powerfully armed force. Only 20% of the lower deck were conscripts; its 'Long Lance' oxygen-fuelled *torpedoes were the most advanced in the world; its gunnery out-ranged any opponent; its navigators were skilled; and its air power was highly developed. In night fighting, its superior night binoculars, pyrotechnics, and highly trained lookouts, gave it a definite edge over its opponents, as the Allies (who, in their assessment of the IJN, had been just as arrogant as the IJN was in its outlook) found to their cost off *Savo Island and in other night actions during the Guadalcanal campaign.

Describing the IJN's various fleets, task forces, strike forces, and special units has defeated western and Japanese naval historians. But broadly speaking virtually all the IJN's warships except the China Fleet were organized administratively into fleets which were all part of the Combined Fleet commanded by the highest ranking naval officer afloat (Admiral Yamamoto, then Admiral *Koga, and finally Admiral Toyoda). In December 1941 these were the First (Battle), Second (Scouting Force), Third (Blockade and Amphibious Force), Fourth (Mandates Fleet), Fifth (Northern Fleet), and Sixth (Submarine) Fleets, and two air fleets, the First (carrier aircraft) and Eleventh (land-based aircraft). Home Naval Stations at Kure, Sasebo, Maizuru, and Yokosuka had the responsibility of patrolling home waters and, almost incidentally, of escorting convoys. Their counterparts outside the home islands (Manchukuo, Korea, Formosa, Hainan Island) were Naval Guard Stations.

From the administrative fleets various task forces were formed. In December 1941 these comprised the Main Body under Admiral Yamamoto; the Striking Force under Vice-Admiral Nagumo; the Southern Force under Vice-Admiral *Kondō; a South Seas Force under Vice-Admiral Inoue Shigeoyoshi; a Northern Force under Vice-Admiral Hosogaya Boshiro of one cruiser squadron; and a Submarine Fleet under Vice-Admiral Shimizu Mitsumi of 26 submarines. It was the Striking Force which undertook the Pearl Harbor raid and the Southern Force which covered the landings which began the Malayan campaign. The First Air Fleet provided the aircraft for Nagumo's fleet carriers which carried from 63 to 72 aircraft each; Eleventh Air Fleet, of three air flotillas, was based mostly on Formosa and in French Indo-China. This supported Southern Force and came under Kondō's command.

Once the colonies of the western powers had been occupied, the Seventh (Korean Straits), Eighth (Rabaul), and Ninth (New Guinea) Fleets were formed as well as another six air fleets (Second, Third, Fifth, Tenth, Twelfth, and Thirteenth), and naval troops (Naval Base Corps, Special Naval Base Corps, and Naval Garrison Units) were used to garrison ports and defend island harbours and anchorages. There were also area fleets (North-East, South-West, South-East, China, Central Pacific Area, and so on) which were combined administrative commands. For example, Vice-Admiral Kusaka Jinichi, commander of the Eleventh Air Fleet at Rabaul, was also commander of the South-East Area Fleet which made him responsible for the Eighth Fleet and all naval forces in the Bismarcks, Solomons, and New Guinea.

By August 1943 the principal fleets and the names of the tactical forces formed from them were as follows:

Fleet	*Tactical Title*
First	Battleship Force
Second	Diversion Attack Force
Third	Striking Force
Fourth	Inner South Seas Force
Fifth	Northern Force
Sixth	Advance Expeditionary Force
Eighth	Outer South Seas Force

In November 1943, in response to increasing US submarine attacks, a General Escort Command was formed, but the numbers of vessels allotted to it were inadequate and losses continued to mount. In March 1944 the IJN underwent a radical reorganization and the Combined Fleet was redesignated the First Mobile Fleet (Dai Ichi Kidō Kantani) which became First Mobile Force for tactical operations such as A-GŌ. First Mobile Fleet included practically all surface warships, its Second Fleet consisted largely of battleships, and its Third Fleet of carriers.

The Sixth Fleet, based in the Marshall Islands, was assigned a vital role in the IJN's strategy: its submarines, working with the surface fleet, were to help whittle down the US Pacific Fleet as it moved westwards. Between 1925 and 1940 three types of submarine were developed, but emphasis was placed on the largest, the long-range Kaidai type. This type had various I-class boats which were heavily armed, and 36 of them carried one or more seaplanes. It was these which carried out the few attacks that were made against the North American mainland. In February 1942, I17 penetrated the Santa Barbara Straits, north of Los Angeles, and fired ten rounds at the shore. In June 1942, I26 fired seventeen rounds at a naval wireless station on Vancouver Island, Canada. Other attacks included two on Australia (Port Gregory and Newcastle) and one on the Cocos Islands. At the other extreme midget submarines, which could be carried by I-class submarines, were constructed from 1938, but these failed at Pearl Harbor and had little success when they attacked *Sydney harbour in 1942. After Pearl Harbor the submarine force fell from favour, and the fact that it continued to be used in its original role, instead of attacking Allied merchant shipping, made it largely ineffective.

The IJN's role in amphibious warfare was mainly one of supporting the army. However, it did have its own offensive, as well as defensive, naval troops which were employed in amphibious operations such as Wake Island, for example. They were named after the naval station where they were trained (e.g. Kure) and were called Special Naval Landing Forces. From one of these were raised two battalions of paratroops (Yokosuka 1st and 3rd Special Naval Paratroops), some of whom helped capture *Timor.

The IJN's air force took the brunt of the air fighting during the Pacific war. Thanks to its strongest proponent, Admiral Yamamoto, it was well equipped and trained. With the Zero (codenamed ZEKE by the Allies) it had a fighter that outclassed anything the Allies were flying in 1941 and it also had the excellent Mitsubishi (NELL, BETTY, and KATE) and Yokosuka (JEAN) bombers, and one of the war's best flying boats in the Kawanishi (MAVIS). Initially, its pilots were superbly trained: those who took part in the Pearl Harbor attack had a minimum of 300 hours' training and an average of 800 (British Fleet Air Arm pilots at that time had, at most, 150 hours). Apart from the First and Eleventh Air Fleets, six other Air Fleets were formed (Second, Third, Fifth, Tenth, Twelfth, Thirteenth) during the war. Often commanded by the

Cs-in-C of area fleets, they were divided into two or more Air Flotillas (commanded operationally by the Air Fleet C-in-C) which had two or more Air Groups of 50–150 aircraft each.

Pearl Harbor and the sinking of the *Prince of Wales* and *Repulse* were a major boost to supporters of air power within the IJN, and Admiral Nagumo's victory over the British Eastern Fleet off Ceylon (see INDIAN OCEAN) in April 1942 was a further argument in their favour. But though the *Coral Sea battle the following month was a tactical victory for the IJN, it was a strategic one for the Allies; and, having goaded the US fleet to a decisive encounter at *Midway, the IJN was stripped of all its initial advantages by losing its four key carriers and, more importantly, a massive number of seasoned and irreplaceable pilots.

The series of naval actions in the Solomons during 1942 and 1943 slowly eroded IJN strength and it became locked into a war of attrition for which it was neither materially nor mentally equipped; and the lack of an adequate training programme for replacement pilots resulted in the débâcle—dubbed the 'Great Marianas Turkey Shoot' by the Americans—in which 243 Japanese carrier aircraft, piloted by raw recruits, were lost in the *Philippine Sea battle of June 1944. As a consequence of this battle, the IJN was so bereft of its air component that by the time of the *Leyte Gulf battle in October 1944 it could only use its remaining carrier strength as a lure; and by the last months of the war it could resort only to kamikaze attacks, to the use of such suicide weapons as the *human torpedo, *explosive motor boat, and *Baka bomb, and to the deployment of *Yamato* that led to the battle of the *East China Sea. This pointless sacrifice of its last super-battleship was final proof that, by early 1945, the once proud Imperial Navy was finished as a fighting force and its few remaining units, immobilized by lack of fuel, were sunk at Kure in July.

Out of the total of 451 surface warships and submarines in commission during the war, 332 had been sunk by the time Japan surrendered and only 37, or 8.2%, remained operational.

IAN GOW

6. Intelligence

Historically, the Japanese were well versed in intelligence matters. Military intelligence had played an important part in Japan's victory over China in 1895; army *spies had reported on Russian preparations and naval operators had intercepted Russian fleet signals during the Russo-Japanese war of 1904–5; and during its Siberian intervention in the early 1920s the Imperial Japanese Army (IJA) had formed 'Special Service Organizations' (*tokumu kikan*) to gather intelligence on the Soviet guerrillas it was fighting, and to foster sabotage and subversion (*bōryaku*).

The Japanese foreign ministry had its own separate political intelligence agency, which appears to have relied on journalists, businessmen, and the like, but military and naval attachés in diplomatic posts were also proficient at intelligence-gathering. They had budgets to employ spies, who were sometimes appointed to consular posts, and purchase information, and they could also engage in sabotage and subversive activities. So assiduous were they at this type of work that although their ciphers were eventually broken—army attaché ciphers began to be resolved by the Americans in the spring of 1943, and, after a lapse of six years naval attaché ciphers were re-entered in 1944, mainly by the British—it has been suggested that they became the best spies the Allies had inside occupied Europe.

Before the start of the Pacific war Japanese signals intelligence (sigint) also made significant contributions to Japanese knowledge of its potential, and actual, opponents. For example, some simpler UK and US diplomatic systems were broken from the early 1930s, and US state department radio traffic and the British Interdepartmental code and Administrative code (used by the Admiralty as well as by the Foreign Office) were penetrated. Additionally, the IJA broke the Diplomatic code used by the Chinese mission in Tokyo; traffic analysis and direction-finding units of the Imperial Japanese Navy (IJN) could, and did, track individual warships of the US Pacific Fleet across the Pacific; and close monitoring of local Hawaii radio stations helped reveal the names of US warships in port prior to the attack on Pearl Harbor.

The Japanese also had long-standing organizations for internal security and counter-intelligence, this being one of the responsibilities of the Kempei (law police), a branch of the army founded in 1881, and of the Tokkō (known as thought police) which had been formed in 1911.

However, contrary to what many thought at the time, Japanese intelligence during the Pacific war proved to be, in nearly every respect, inadequate. The reason was partly one of attitude—once hostilities had begun, intelligence work failed to appeal to the Samurai spirit—and partly one of lack of co-ordination, co-operation, and organization. There was no formal combined intelligence structure, either for overt (*jōhō*) or covert (*chōhō*) activities, and the profound difference in the strategic outlook of the two services exacerbated their traditional rivalries in intelligence as in other matters. These antagonisms were so intense that within Imperial General Headquarters (IGH) the intelligence bureau of each service remained totally separate, with an exchange of intelligence but no central analysis of their joint product, and both services remained opposed to the principle of civil control over either of them. Excessive zeal, especially in the army, led secret organizations to trespass outside strictly intelligence functions, both in covert operations and in political decision-making. Moreover, each service devoted a substantial part of its resources to trying to discern the real intentions of the other. Meticulous inter-service agreements had to be worked out before each campaign; the strains on national strategic capabilities were enormous.

These handicaps, combined with the Japanese predilection for the decisive battle and offensive thinking, led to intelligence units, both at IGH and in the field, often being largely ignored and frequently undermanned. 'The American section of the General Staff's Intelligence Bureau was not set up until 1942 and even then it had only three permanent officers' (see Harries [below], p. 320) and intelligence units in the field were hurriedly formed and inadequately staffed. For instance, the commander of the Army Air Force's 4th Air Intelligence Detachment, formed in November 1942 and sent to New Guinea, was the only person trained in intelligence.

The intelligence departments of both services ran Special Service Organizations. From the period just before Pearl Harbor the sigint and undercover desks of the Naval Staff were brought together under the head of the Naval Intelligence Department so that attaché, agent, and decrypt sources could be combined more effectively, and this became known as the Chūō Kikan (Special Service Headquarters). The IJN also had special service organizations, called *kaigun tokumu bu*. These operated in occupied territories administered by the IJN and were present in most major ports in China and South-East Asia—even among local fishing fleets—but the IJA's were more numerous, larger, and more powerful. Several schools were set up to train officers in secret warfare, of which the Nakano school, formed in 1938, became the best known. Later, civilian specialists (*bunkan*), who wore uniform but with different badges of rank, were also employed.

Before a country was occupied the function of a Special Service Organization included espionage, propaganda, and *fifth columnist activities; afterwards it helped in internal security, counter-espionage, and pacification. Economic exploitation was also an important task (not often appreciated in the literature), especially after 1940, when increasingly scarce sources of raw materials were sought out, and heroin and other drugs were bartered for strategic mineral supplies. Except in Sumatra, where Kikan personnel worked directly with the intelligence unit of the highest IJA formation on the island, the Kikan became part of the military administration and liaised closely with the administration's councillors' department (*komon-bu*) or the chief administrator (*shishei chokan*).

Special Service Organizations covered every aspect of clandestine warfare and many spawned large subnetworks of their own. Dozens were formed during the course of the war. One, the Nami Kikan, was set up in May 1944 to detect landings by enemy agents on the coastline of occupied territories and, with the help of fishermen, to report on the movements of Allied shipping, but in May 1945 it became a sabotage organization. Another, the Ibaragi Kikan, was formed in March 1945 to counter the activities of the communist resistance in Malaya. A third, the Matsu Kikan, based in Timor and led by a graduate of the Nakano school, Captain Yamamoto Masayoshi, landed a reconnaissance patrol in northern Australia in January 1944 which stayed ashore for four days.

The best known were the Minami Kikan, which organized the Burma Independence Army, and the F Kikan (F stood for its leader, Major Fujiwara Iwaichi, and for freedom and friendship) which recruited the Indian National Army. It was Fujiwara who, before the war, fostered the *Indian Independence League and who dispatched various teams ahead of, or with, the Japanese forces invading South-East Asia. They had various objectives, such as to subvert Indian troops during the fighting and to sow propaganda amongst the local populations. In this they had some success. F Kikan was replaced by Colonel Iwakura Hideo's Hikari Kikan (Lightning Organization), which assumed the task of liaison with the Indian National Army, and when Iwakura later became chief of staff at Twenty-Eighth Army in Burma he created a number of intelligence and reconnaissance units, some of which penetrated British lines. The Hikari Kikan changed names several times as it increased in size and one of its tasks included infiltrating agents into India for espionage, sabotage, propaganda, and subversion. Perhaps there were as many as 600 of these so called JIFs (Japanese inspired fifth columnists), but they achieved very little.

However, supporters of intelligence such as Fujiwara and Iwakura were few and far between, and the use of intelligence in the field was more the exception than the rule. For example, Lt-General Mutaguchi, who commanded Fifteenth Army in northern Burma—in which Fujiwara served as both intelligence and operational staff officer—preferred to rely on *seisho* (spirit) for victory.

In the field of sigint the Japanese had three distinct organizations: the IJA's Central Special Intelligence Department (Chūō Tokushu Jōhō Bu), the IJN's Special Service Section (Tokumu Han), and the foreign office's Cryptographic Research Section (Angō Kenkyū Han). The IJN, like the Germans (see B-DIENST), read British instructions to their convoys until 1942, and thereafter managed to keep close track of these, and most surface warship movements, by traffic analysis and air reconnaissance. The known facts about what army sigint teams accomplished are sparse because little, if any, documentation survives. But it has been claimed that 95% of China's codes were deciphered by Japanese cryptographers; that radio messages of US Army Air Forces units in China and Burma, some encoded by machine cipher, were successfully broken, as were those of the British intelligence-gathering unit *V-Force; and that the radios of captured Allied agents were used to dupe those who had dispatched them (see SPECIAL OPERATIONS AUSTRALIA, for example). However, none of this activity appears to have led to any decisive victory in the field, though in the case of the Chinese codes it definitely aided Japanese formations to counter the moves of the Chinese Army during the latter part of the Burma campaign. Certainly, Japanese signals intelligence failed to achieve anywhere near the same level of success as that achieved by the Allies with their MAGIC and ULTRA intelligence, as is shown by the title of Professor Iwashima Hisao's book on the subject, *Japan's Total Defeat in the Intelligence War* (*Jōhōsen ni kanpai shita Nihon*), which was published in 1984.

As it was deemed a disgrace to be made prisoner, there was no Japanese equivalent of *MI9, which trained Allied personnel in counter-interrogation techniques. Japanese prisoners were rarely of a high enough rank to know anything of long-term value, but those who did talked freely.

Finally, the Japanese were not alone in sometimes allowing crucial intelligence to fall into the hands of a potential, or actual, opponent (see AUTOMEDON, for an example, which proved of immense value to the Japanese), but their lapses often proved invaluable to the Allies. For instance, after the *Bismarck Sea battle in March 1943, the current Japanese Army List, which detailed the names and assignments of all IJA officers, was found aboard a lifeboat; following the Saipan landings in 1944, US forces captured seven tons of documents of which 60% had some intelligence value; and the careless burial in New Guinea of the codebooks of the IJA's main code resulted in ULTRA intelligence which gave *MacArthur a critical edge in the New Guinea campaign. John Chapman

7. Merchant marine

Japan made a late start in joining the industrialized economies of the world but by the First World War her shipping industries had already made up much of the lost ground. Thus by 1910 the Japanese merchant fleet consisted of 1,146,977 million tons and was third in size after the UK's (over 13 million tons) and Germany's (3 million tons). This success was only partly emulated by the Japanese shipbuilding industry owing to the lack of efficient steel producers and a viable engineering sector but, even so, in 1914 it was able to complete 86,000 tons. This was sufficient to place it in sixth international position but it was a long way behind the UK's output of 1,680,000 tons.

Further progress was made during the period 1914–18, but both the operating and building sides of the industry fell back sharply in the early post-war years. As a result production was down to only 48,185 tons in 1925. This caused great consternation in Tokyo and led to demands for additional state aid. The replacement of the 'liberal' administrations of the 1920s by the more militaristic governments of the early 1930s then saw a series of measures designed to make production more attractive. These included 'Scrap and Build' schemes, a 'Superior Ship Building Promotion' scheme, and the guarantee of profitable freight rates. The effect of these incentives can be seen in the steady increases in output which followed: 147,118 tons in 1934, 217,461 tons in 1936, and 423,039 tons in 1938.

With a few notable exceptions many of these vessels were less advanced and more expensive than those produced in the west, so it was not possible for any to be exported. Thus although Japan was able to compete on the profitable New York routes with its sophisticated motor vessels, it also held its own at the bottom of the market against Greek owners by utilizing sub-standard tonnage with poorly paid crews. These tactics enabled the fleet to grow in spite of the world depression but its average age gradually increased and much was characterized by only moderate quality and efficiency.

The opening of hostilities in China following the Manchuria Incident in 1931 led to both sides of the shipping industry being subject to increasingly tight government control. These moves towards a quasi-war footing led the shipping companies to develop a self-regulating system (*kaiun jiji renmei*), but as the demands of the state intensified the degree of autonomy steadily declined. Then in mid-1941 the government initiated a plan called the *Senji Kaiun Kanri Yoko* (Outline of War-time Shipping Control). The first part of the resulting legislation came into effect in March 1942, so that all steamships over 100 tons and sailing vessels of over 150 tons were requisitioned. This was quickly followed by the establishment of the *Senpaku Uneikai* (Shipping Committee) which then acted as the sole employer of all of Japan's merchant seamen. The actual ship operations were, wisely, left to the shipowners and this ensured that practical men of experience—mainly from NYK, OSK, Mitsui Bussan, Yamashita Kisen, Kawasaki Kisen, and Tatsuuma Kisen—were responsible for all aspects of organization. During the course of the war the ever increasing shortage of tonnage (see Table 6) led to further attempts to improve efficiency, such as the reduction of the number of shipping companies from 350 in 1941 to 90 by the end of 1943.

The shipbuilding sector also moved under the control of the state and after 1937 all construction had to be authorized by the government. These regulations were further extended by the *Zosen Jigyo Ho* (Shipbuilding Industry Law) in 1939 and thereafter a broader view was taken in an effort to maximize total production. Six designs for 'standard' ships were adopted and there can be no doubt that this simplification of the product mix did much to raise output, even though the vessels concerned were of inferior quality in many respects. A further difficulty was that one-third of capacity was already being used for naval construction in 1941 and conflict arose between those who wished to give further priority to this need and those who wanted to increase the building of merchant ships. The establishment of the Zosen Tosei Kai (Shipbuilding Control Association) and the Keikaku Zosen (Programmed Shipbuilding Scheme) helped to rationalize the system, but the conflict with the naval authorities was only resolved when the Imperial Japanese Navy, whose concept of the decisive battle and a short war had led to its neglecting the need to enlarge and protect the country's merchant fleet, was made responsible for all shipbuilding in February 1943.

In December 1941 when Japan became involved in war

Japan, 7, Table 6: Japanese merchant shipping during the Second World War

Period	*Tonnage captured or salvaged*	*Tonnage built*	*Total gain*	*Tonnage lost*[a]	*+ or –*	*Tonnage available*
8 Dec 41	–	–	–	–	–	5,996,657
8 Dec 41–31 Dec 42	672,411	272,963	945,374	1,123,156 (241 ships)	–177,782	5,818,875
1 Jan 43–31 Dec 43	109,028	769,085	878,113	1,820,919 (434 ships)	–942,806	4,876,069
1 Jan 44–31 Dec 44	35,644	1,699,203	1,734,847	3,891,019 (969 ships)	–2,156,172	2,719,897
1 Jan 45–15 Aug 45	5,880	559,563	565,443	1,782,140 (701 ships)	–1,216,697	1,503,200[c]
	822,963	3,300,814	4,123,777	8,617,234 (2,345 ships)[b]	–4,493,457	

The table excludes all ships of less than 500 tons gross weight.

[a] Of this the tanker tonnage lost was:

8 Dec 41–31 Dec 42	9,538	(2 ships)
1 Jan 43–31 Dec 43	169,491	(23 ships)
1 Jan 44–31 Dec 44	754,889	(131 ships)
1 Jan 45–15 Aug 45	351,028	(103 ships)
TOTAL	1,284,946	(259 ships or 15% of total losses)

[b] In addition 1,966,521 tons of naval shipping (687 ships) were sunk, making the total tonnage lost 10,583,755.

[c] Of this tonnage only some 557,000 was operable.

Source: Woodburn Kirby, S., *The War Against Japan* (London, 1969), Vol. V, p. 475.

with the western Allies its merchant marine amounted to about six million tons plus a million tons of coastal and fishing vessels, many of which were constructed of wood. The vast extent of Japan's early conquests made this tonnage totally inadequate for its needs and many expedients, such as the building of the *Burma–Thailand railway, were adopted to save shipping space. With the aid of a workforce which rose from 80,161 in 1936 to 287,799 in 1944, construction was steadily increased and 3,300,814 tons were completed from December 1941 to August 1945. During this period the technical aspects of production changed very little and there was no widespread acceptance of developments like block construction and welding which were being pioneered by the Kaiser Corporation in the United States (see LIBERTY SHIPS).

A further 822,963 tons were either captured or salvaged by the Japanese during the war, but the total additions to the fleet were insufficient to offset the severe losses inflicted principally by American submarines and aircraft. Japan's failure to introduce convoys at an early stage was undoubtedly a significant factor in these sinkings which rose from just over 1 million tons in the first year of hostilities to nearly 4 million in 1944 and to a total of 2,345 ships, totalling more than 8.5 million tons over the whole period. As a result when Japan surrendered on 15 August 1945 its merchant marine had been reduced to 1.5 million tons, only 557,000 tons of which was still in seagoing condition.

With the benefit of hindsight it is clear that two of Japan's most important wartime weaknesses were its shortage of oil and the limited size of its merchant navy. These two major constraints on its freedom of action can both be illustrated by reference to the role played by its oil tanker fleet. This consisted of only 42 vessels amounting to 356,000 tons in 1941 and although many more were built during the war they were always in short supply. From the beginning they were made a prime target and the fact that 259 tankers of 1.3 million tons were sunk by Allied action was undoubtedly extremely significant in reducing Japan's capacity to wage an effective war.

PETER DAVIES

8. Culture

For most Japanese artists and intellectuals war began on 7 July 1937 when Japanese and Chinese forces exchanged fire at the Marco Polo Bridge near Peking. Fighting soon spread across north and central China and Japanese publishers and government organizations mobilized literary celebrities to raise national morale. In August and September prominent writers were dispatched to the front and produced vivid, if highly censored, accounts of Japanese campaigning. Among these literary chroniclers perhaps the most successful was Hino Ashihei whose trilogy *Wheat and Soldiers*, *Earth and Soldiers*, and *Flowers and Soldiers* became best-sellers.

Four years later Japan's attack on Pearl Harbor aroused near-mystical delight among Japanese writers. Intense patriotism and anti-colonialism united authors from right to left, and in May 1942 virtually all professional writers joined the Japan Literature Patriotic Association (Nihon Bungaku Hōkokukai). This government-sponsored organization included eight sections embracing novels, drama, general poetry, *tanka* (31-syllable verse), *haiku* (17-syllable verse), the history of Japanese literature, the history of western literature, and literary criticism; it was headed by the veteran writer Tokutomi Sohō. In April 1943 its first conference discussed 'The Creation of a Literature of the Annihilation of America and England' and a month later the association produced a new variant of the popular anthology *Poems by One Hundred Poets* entitled *Patriotic Poems by One Hundred Poets*.

Writers were also mobilized for pan-Asian propaganda in the Greater East Asian Writers Congress (Daitōa Bungakusha Taikai). The congress included authors from Japan, Korea, Formosa, China, Manchukuo, and Mongolia, and held wartime conferences in Tokyo and Nanking. These Japanese-dominated gatherings repeatedly emphasized such themes as anti-westernism and Asian solidarity, and promoted the Japanese language as the new life-force of East Asian culture.

As in the China Incident, writers were frequently sent abroad to produce reportage and spread knowledge of Japanese civilization. Visits to South-East Asia brought contact with unfamiliar cultures, and writers responded with reflective fiction and propaganda. Ozaki Shirō's *Cumulus Clouds* described American defeats from a Filipino viewpoint while Ibuse Masuji's *City of Flowers* recounted the adventures of Japanese propagandists in occupied Singapore; arguably the most effective short work of this genre was Takami Jun's *Nowkana*, an account of Japanese difficulties with Indian cooks and servants, which unconsciously echoed European colonial writing.

One of the most remarkable literary products of the war years was a vast outpouring of nationalistic poetry, particularly in the traditional *tanka* form. But such works as Noguchi Yonejirō's 'Slaughter them, the English and Americans are our enemies' were too direct and emotive to attract discriminating readers.

Wartime dramatists also sought to utilize traditional forms to present pan-Asian and anti-Western themes to domestic audiences. A medieval-style *nō* play was produced to commemorate the capture of Rangoon, and traditional farces (*kyōgen*) were written to excoriate Western imperialism. A typical one was *Treasure Island* in which greedy English and American devils were attacked by swarms of bees and driven into the sea.

As Japan's fortunes declined official censorship tightened, and one of Japan's most distinguished writers became a victim of it. In January 1943 the élite magazine *Chūō Kōron* began the serialization of Tanizaki Junichirō's novel *The Makioka Sisters*, but after two instalments, publication was banned. This major work contained no criticism of official policy, but its subject, pre-war middle-class life, was considered too frivolous for a nation at war.

Throughout eight years of hostilities Japanese writers showed little overt resistance to government policy. Many sincerely believed in Japan's cause, and non-co-operation would have closed all doors to work and publication. Nevertheless, one writer of independent means, Nagai Kafū, abstained from all public pronouncements and confined himself to acid criticisms of the government in his private diary.

Newspapers and magazines were equally powerful cultural influences on public opinion (see also PRESS). In earlier times the Japanese press had a vigorous tradition of exposing public corruption but the China war brought a tightening net of government controls. Although all editors spontaneously supported the war effort, daily *censorship was imposed by the press sections of the army and navy, and of the foreign, home, and Greater East Asia ministries. In addition the Cabinet Information Bureau, the quasi-official news agency Dōmei, and the press department of Imperial Headquarters carried out effective programmes of news management. These organizations blacklisted some authors, approved others, and imposed news bulletins and commentaries on national and provincial newspapers.

In the early months of war when Japanese armies won sweeping victories there was little need for deception or distortion in the projection of daily news, but in 1942 the catastrophe of Midway was reported as a victory, and in the following year Japanese forces were said to have carried out a 'sideways advance'. In contrast the European conflict was described with relative objectivity, and Japanese readers were clearly aware of the declining fortunes of their allies in Rome and Berlin. Similarly, Japan's domestic difficulties were often analysed with surprising frankness. No journalist ever criticized the government's ultimate objectives but inefficiency and mismanagement were frequently attacked; food distribution, local administration, air raid defence, and industrial management were all targets of editorial criticism. Even more remarkable were admissions of glorious defeats and occasional criticisms of the conduct of war. In May 1943 the annihilation of Japanese forces on Attu in the Aleutian Islands campaigns was openly reported, while in February 1944 the *Mainichi Shimbun*'s naval correspondent attacked the army's preparations for an Allied invasion in an article entitled 'Bamboo Spears are Not Enough'. The author was soon conscripted into the army but even Prime Minister Tōjō did not dare to close a national newspaper with several million readers.

Although Japan's illustrious 'general magazines' had far fewer subscribers than daily newspapers, their influence and intellectual character made them deeply suspect in the eyes of official censors. In September 1942 a contributor to *Kaizō* was arrested for praising Soviet policies towards minority peoples and, soon after, the editor and his senior staff were compelled to resign. Further arrests and four deaths under torture followed, and in 1944 both *Kaizō* and *Chūō Kōron* were closed.

In contrast with the UK, where painting as a means of communicating the horrors of war produced a number of great works of art, Japanese painters played a relatively minor role in their country's wartime culture. In April 1942 many of Japan's most important artists were commissioned to travel to South-East Asia to paint battle scenes and other war subjects, but there is little evidence that these works exerted a major influence on public opinion. Instead, bringing the visual impact of the war to the Japanese public was largely left to the cinema.

By 1937 Japan had a highly developed film industry which was dominated by two powerful companies, Tōhō and Shōchiku, and a number of important documentary producers.

Like publishers, film companies saw the war in China as a subject of profound public interest and newsreel cameramen were posted to the front to cover the fighting. Soon Tōhō, Shōchiku, and their satellites began producing feature films set against the background of the China campaign. Many roughly-made productions were unsuccessful but such films as Tasaka Tomotaka's *Five Scouts* recreated the ordeal of combat with sombre accuracy. The most highly acclaimed film of this genre was Tasaka's rendering of the novel *Earth and Soldiers* which described a unit's physical and emotional endurance in the Hangchow campaign. Another common cinematic theme was Japan's mission in China and the building of Sino-Japanese co-operation. Watanabe Kunio's *Vow of the Desert* showed co-operation in highway building and a Sino-Japanese romance, while Fushimizu Osamu's *China Nights* featured a tender relationship between a Japanese naval officer and a Shanghai orphan. Efforts were also made to reinforce Japanese links with Nazi Germany by encouraging a major co-production. Arnold Fanck's *The New Land* attempted to explain the cultural mainsprings of Japanese conduct; but despite fine photography it failed to attract Japanese audiences.

By 1939 Japan was increasingly attracted to Nazi methods of film propaganda and a Film Law was passed modelled upon German legislation (see GERMANY, 10). This established pre-production censorship, government control of film distribution, restrictions on the import of foreign films, and the compulsory showing of newsreels. In 1940 government controls were further extended with the forced amalgamation of all private newsreel companies into the Nippon News Film Company (Nippon Nyūsu Eigasha).

Japan's attack on British, Dutch, and American territories at the start of the Pacific war brought new cinematic opportunities. Cameramen recorded not only impressive victories but also the exotic scenery of Malaya, Burma, and the Philippines which added to the novelty of documentary productions. In the early months of war newsreels were far more popular than ever before and the Japanese armed forces shot lengthy documentaries chronicling recent conquests; the army's *Malaya War Record*, *Burma War Record*, and *Victory Song of the Orient* were widely shown in schools and community centres, as well as in conventional cinemas.

As victories became fewer the government attempted to maintain public morale by reconstructing earlier successes in major feature films. In 1942 the navy encouraged the production of the first such work, *The War at Sea from Hawaii to Malaya*, and later examples depicted the capture of Hong Kong and Singapore. Like most countries at war Japan also deployed history or quasi-history in the cause of propaganda. Stories of samurai self-sacrifice such as *Chūshingura*, and depictions of Western imperialism, notably *The Opium War*, attracted large audiences in both Japan and South-East Asia. As Japan's situation became critical film-makers were pressed to create civil defence documentaries, and feature films relevant to increased production. In 1944 and 1945 air raid precautions were the subject of several instructional films while the young Kurosawa's *The Most Beautiful* depicted women workers in an optical lens factory. By the final months of war film stock had become extremely scarce and new productions were shorter and fewer than in earlier years. In addition American bombing destroyed hundreds of cinemas.

Although film may have been the most sophisticated wartime medium, radio was perhaps the most flexible. The Japan Broadcasting Corporation (NHK) had been founded in 1926 and by 1937 over a quarter of Japanese were licence holders. In peace and war the Japanese government saw radio as an important vehicle of education and propaganda; entertainment occupied only a minor place in broadcasting schedules.

During the China Incident news bulletins were extended and ministers and civil servants regularly explained government objectives over the radio. More original were special programmes which linked troops at the front with their home towns and prefectures. In these years radio ownership spread rapidly, and the armed forces became an increasingly powerful voice in determining broadcasting policies.

By the time of Pearl Harbor wartime schedules had been carefully prepared and news was supplemented by ministerial speeches, and readings from patriotic and anti-western works such as Ōkawa Shūmei's *A History of American and British Aggression in Asia*. Particularly impressive were attempts to deepen national resolve by transmitting cultural programmes of high quality. This trend began in 1939 with the broadcasting of Yoshikawa Eiji's historical novel *Miyamoto Musashi*, continuing with talks on such subjects as Zen Buddhism and traditional flower arrangement. By 1944, when it was clear that monotonous exhortation was achieving little, a new radio strategy was adopted which attempted to raise morale by increasing and improving entertainment programmes.

'Sensuous' western melodies had already been banned, but European classical music now occupied a significant place in NHK schedules. Such operas as *The Marriage of Figaro* and *Tannhäuser* were broadcast and attracted large audiences. An even more impressive example of quality entertainment was a star-studded radio production of the famous *kabuki* (music and dance) play *Kanjinchō* on

New Year's Day 1945. This provided a significant fillip to national morale when economic and social conditions were declining rapidly; but in the final months of war the production of radio sets fell, and their repair was rendered increasing difficult by shortages of valves and components.

Although music could not convey complex and detailed propaganda messages it was viewed as an important element in Japanese ideological policy. As early as 1937 the authorities aimed to create a Japanese equivalent of the Nazi 'Horst Wessel' song (see MARCHING SONGS) and organized a national competition for suitable words for Setoguchi Tokichi's 'Patriotic March'. This composition was jaunty rather than military and became popular throughout Japan and South-East Asia. Further marches followed and songs from successful films such as *Earth and Soldiers* and *China Nights* achieved widespread popularity. Throughout the war special songs were composed to commemorate victories and inspire national support for vital campaigns. Yet despite official attempts to emphasize national and patriotic elements in Japanese musical life European classical music remained widely popular and orchestral concerts continued until June 1945.

Despite its superficial orientalism Japanese cultural propaganda employed themes which were also used in Allied films, books, and broadcasts. Historic victories, national solidarity and diligence were emphasized by both democrats and proponents of authoritarian ideals. Ironically, Japan's centralized mass media were used by American occupiers to spread democracy in the post-war years. GORDON DANIELS

Domestic life, economy, and war effort

Cohen, J. B., *Japan's Economy in War and Reconstruction* (Minneapolis, 1949, repr. Westport, Conn., 1973).

Havens, T. R. H., *Valley of Darkness. The Japanese People and World War Two* (New York, 1978).

Johnston, B. F., *Japanese Food Management in World War II* (Stanford, Calif., 1953).

Government/Culture

Berger, G. M., *Parties out of Power in Japan, 1931–1941* (Princeton, 1977).

—— 'Politics and mobilization in Japan, 1931–1945', in P. Duus (ed.), *The Cambridge History of Japan*, Vol. 6: *The Twentieth Century* (Cambridge, 1988).

Maxon, Y. C., *Control of Japanese Foreign Policy: A Study of Civil–Military Rivalry 1930–1945* (Berkeley, 1957; repr. Westport, Conn., 1975).

Shillony, B.-A., *Politics and Culture in Wartime Japan* (new edn., Oxford, 1991).

Defence forces and civil defence

United States Strategic Bombing Survey *Field Report Covering Air Raid Protection and Allied Subjects in Kyoto* (Washington, DC, 1947).

—— *Final Report Covering Air Raid Protection and Allied Subjects in Japan* (Washington, DC, 1947).

Armed forces/Intelligence

Allen, L. 'Japanese Intelligence Systems', *Journal of Contemporary History* (October, 1987).

Barker, A. J., *Japanese Handbook, 1939–1945* (London, 1979).

Chapman, J., 'Japanese Intelligence 1918–1945', in C. Andrew and J. Noakes (eds.), *Intelligence and International Relations 1900–1945* (Exeter, 1987).

Drea, E., *MacArthur's ULTRA: Codebreaking and the War Against Japan* (Lawrence, Kans., 1992).

Francillon, R. J., *Japanese Aircraft of the Pacific War* (London, 1970).

Fujiwara Iwaichi, *F. Kikan: Japanese Army Intelligence Operations in Southeast Asia during World War II* (Hong Kong, 1983).

Harries, M. and S., *Soldiers of the Sun* (London, 1991).

Hashimoto Mochitsura, *Sunk. The Story of the Japanese Submarine Fleet, 1942–45* (London, 1954).

Hayashi Saburo, and Coox, A. D., *Kogun: The Japanese Army in Pacific War* (Quantico, Va., 1959).

Marder, A., *Old Friends, New Enemies*, 2 vols. (Oxford, 1981–90).

Stripp, A., *Codebreaker in the Far East* (London, 1989).

Merchant marine

Chida, T., and Davies, P. N., *The Japanese Shipping and Shipbuilding Industries: A History of their Modern Growth* (London, 1990).

Davies, P. N., 'Japanese Merchant Shipping and the Bridge over the River Kwai', in C. G. Reynolds (ed.), *Global Crossroads and the American Seas* (Missoula, Mont., 1988).

Japanese-Americans. The war led to profound changes in the status of Japanese-Americans in the USA. For members of the American-born Nisei (second) generation, it brought about a major test of the assimilationist aspirations that led Japanese-Americans to believe that they could gain acceptance as US citizens. Despite the Japanese Exclusion Act of 1924, the passage of laws restricting land ownership by aliens, and the hostility of groups such as the Native Sons and Daughters of the Golden West, by the time of the Japanese attack on *Pearl Harbor, Japanese residents had become well established in the economies of Hawaii and California. As the USA mobilized for war, the Japanese-American Citizen's League reflected a widely-shared desire among Nisei to affirm their loyalty to the country. Nevertheless, during the war they would be singled out for unprecedented forms of discrimination. Military exigencies became a justification for forced relocation of Japanese-Americans, citizens as well as resident aliens, living on the West Coast, a policy which was also adopted by Canada (see JAPANESE-CANADIANS). Before the end of the war, the relocation programme had been suspended. Nisei soldiers, including some former internees, distinguished themselves while serving with US forces in the European and Pacific theatres.

At the time of the Pearl Harbor attack in December 1941, the territory of Hawaii contained the nation's largest concentration of Japanese-Americans. More than 150,000 Hawaiians, 37% of the total population, were of Japanese descent. Initially attracted during the late 19th century by employment opportunities in Hawaii's sugar plantations, ethnic Japanese remained an essential part of the islands' workforce as the USA began wartime mobilization. Because of their importance in the territory's economy and their long-established presence in a cosmopolitan society with a large non-white population, Japanese-Americans in Hawaii had not endured the kind of intense racism that was directed against Asian immigrants on the US West Coast.

Japanese-Americans being moved from the US West Coast, 1942.

Hawaiian civilian and military authorities, as well as the islands' newspapers, were generally more willing than their mainland counterparts to play down rumours of sabotage by disloyal Japanese. Recognizing that federal investigation had not confirmed these rumours and that martial law controls made subversive activity less threatening, authorities were concerned about the potential economic impact of anti-subversive programmes that were targeted at all residents of Japanese descent. General Delos Emmons, Hawaii's military governor, resisted Navy Secretary Frank *Knox's effort to evacuate Japanese residents of Oahu, and the reluctance of Emmons and other Hawaiian leaders to fan wartime fears of *fifth column activity led to a policy of limited relocation which involved the internment of only about 1% of the Japanese resident in Hawaii.

Japanese-Americans on the mainland were treated far worse than those in Hawaii. At the outbreak of war, about 120,000 Japanese lived on the West Coast, most of them in California. Unlike the Japanese in Hawaii, they had endured intense discrimination that included restrictions on land ownership. Moreover, California had been a centre of anti-Asian activism that culminated in exclusion legislation preventing further immigration from Asia. Although Roosevelt received no reliable reports that Japanese-American citizens represented a subversive threat, he and other national political leaders agreed to the demands of western whites that they be removed from the West Coast.

Viewed differently from German-Americans (see GERMAN-AMERICAN BUND) and Italian-Americans, Japanese residents were singled out for special treatment. On 19 February 1942, Roosevelt signed Executive Order 9066 empowering military authorities to relocate residents of 'military areas'. On 2 March 1942, Lt-General John L. DeWitt, head of the Western Defense Command, declared California, Oregon, and Washington strategic areas from which all residents of Japanese descent should be excluded. Forced to settle their personal affairs immediately, more than 110,000 Japanese-Americans on the West Coast (64% of whom were American citizens) were forced to abandon homes and businesses and live in one of ten relocation centres.

The well-publicized involvement of Japanese-American troops in the war effort (including about one thousand volunteers from the internment camps) was an important step towards overcoming exclusionist sentiments. The isolated cases of anti-military agitation (there were no proven cases of Japanese involvement in sabotage or espionage) among Japanese-Americans received far less publicity than the valour demonstrated by Japanese soldiers. The 100th Battalion composed of Hawaiian Nisei fought in the *Italian campaign of 1944 and suffered such a high rate of casualties that they were called the 'Purple Heart Battalion'. The survivors were later integrated into the 442nd Regimental Combat Team, which continued to sustain heavy casualties during 1944 and 1945. The unit won many commendations for valour, including a Congressional Medal of Honor (see DECORATIONS).

The Supreme Court initially upheld the relocation policy, but found in the 1944 case of *Endo* v. *United States* that the detention of persons whose loyalty had not been questioned was unconstitutional. Even after the evacuation order was rescinded and the internment camps closed during 1944 Japanese residents continued to encounter discrimination, but the distinguished record of Japanese soldiers and the wartime disruption of traditional Japanese social life encouraged the eventual integration of Nisei and Sansei (third generation) Japanese into the American mainstream. See also INTERNMENT and LATIN AMERICA AT WAR.

CLAYBORNE CARSON

Daniels, R., *Asian America: Chinese and Japanese in the United States since 1850* (Seattle, Wash., 1988).
—— *Concentration Camps USA* (New York, 1971).
Takaki, R., *Strangers from a Different Shore: A History of Asian Americans* (Boston, 1989).

Japanese-Canadians. The first Japanese came to Canada in 1877 and, although neither the Japanese nor the Canadian government encouraged the flow, by 1941 there were 23,000 people of Japanese origin in Canada, almost all living in British Columbia. Hard-working and slow to integrate, they stirred fears of the 'Yellow Peril' which increased exponentially as Japan turned expansionist in the 1930s. A Special Committee on Orientals, appointed in 1940, ordered registration of Japanese-Canadians and barred them from military service. There were, however, no plans for their evacuation from the coast or internment in event of war with Japan, though Canadian and American officials discussed the need for co-ordinated action at the *Permanent Joint Board on Defense. After *Pearl Harbor and the fall of *Hong Kong, British Columbian fears increased, political and military leaders called for action, and on 14 January 1942, Ottawa decided to move Japanese male nationals of military age inland. As Allied defeats continued, the pressure mounted; on 24 February, following the signing of an executive order by Roosevelt, which empowered the military to remove *Japanese-Americans from the US West Coast, the government ordered evacuation of all Japanese-Canadians, men and women, citizens and aliens. Over the next months, their property confiscated, Japanese-Canadians were moved to inland communities, often very rough. Men worked on road gangs, though before long labour shortages led Ottawa to encourage them to move eastwards to Central Canadian manufacturing plants. Evacuation resisters, along with Japanese patriots, were interned. On 4 August 1944, Ottawa decided to

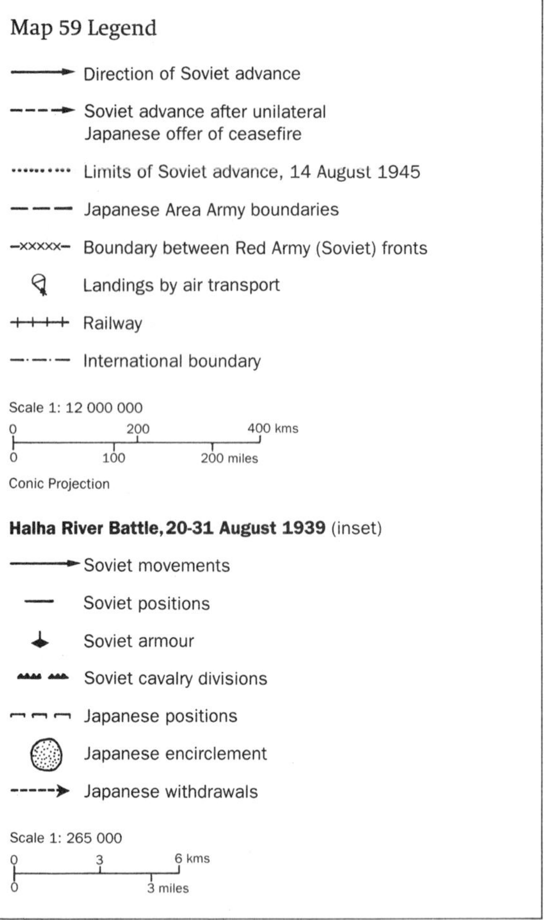

repatriate 'disloyal' Japanese-Canadians to Japan and later to include those voluntarily seeking to return; after protests, 3,964 went. The remainder established new lives east of the Rockies. See also INTERNMENT.

J. L. GRANATSTEIN

Adachi, K., *The Enemy That Never Was: A History of the Japanese Canadians* (Toronto, 1976).
Roy, P., *et al.*, *Mutual Hostages: Canadians and Japanese during the Second World War* (Toronto, 1990).

Japanese–Soviet campaigns and relations, 1939–45. Japan fought two major campaigns against the USSR, in 1939 and in 1945 (see Map 59). In between, the two countries maintained an uneasy truce.

Japan's conclusion of the *Anti-Comintern Pact with Nazi Germany in 1936 and its aggression the following year which started the *China Incident increased tension between the two countries. This precipitated a number of border disputes between the USSR, and/or Soviet-backed Outer Mongolia, and Japan-backed Manchukuo, garrisoned by the *Kwantung Army, which escalated from May 1939 onwards to include Soviet bombing raids on

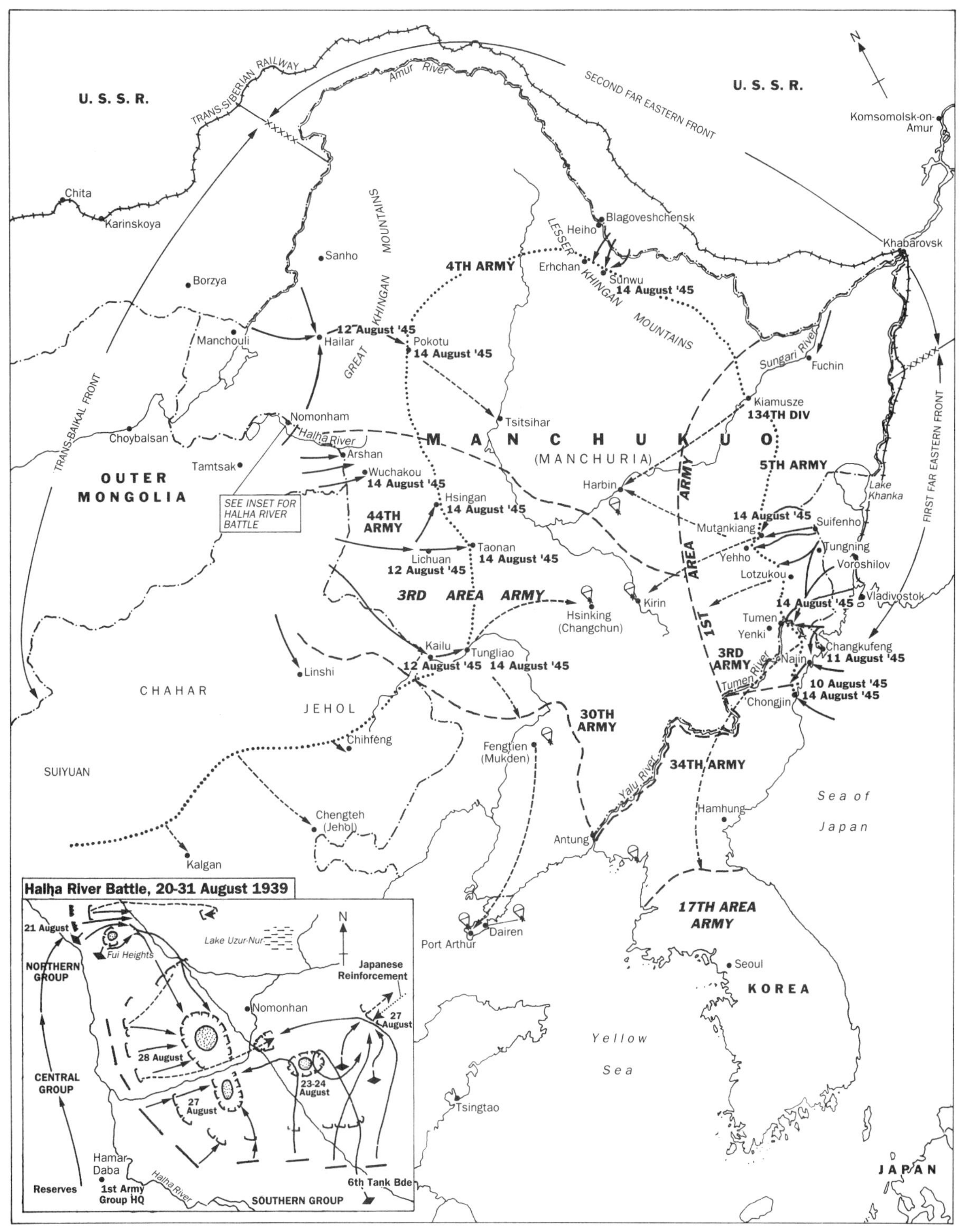

59. **Japanese–Soviet campaigns** in Manchukuo, 1939 and 1945

Manchukuo, and Japanese air attacks on Mongolia which were not authorized by the Army General Staff in Tokyo, and which culminated in a Soviet offensive in August 1939. Never before had aircraft been used on such a large scale and 'from 28 May onwards the numbers multiplied until at last 150–200 or more aircraft were engaged in a single battle' (A. Sella. 'Khalkhin-Gol: The Forgotten War', *Journal of Contemporary History*, 18, 1983). On 2 July Japanese infantry of the Kwantung Army crossed the River Halha into Mongolia but were stopped, as were Japanese tanks. Reinforced with artillery the Kwantung Army tried again on 23 July, but were again checked. However Stalin, concerned that the Japanese were aiming to cross into Soviet territory and cut the Trans-Siberian railway—the only means of transporting troops to and from the Far East—sent General *Zhukov to reorganize Soviet forces into the newly formed First Army Group and launch a counter-offensive. Zhukov arrived in early June and began gathering a powerful force (35 infantry battalions, 20 cavalry squadrons, 500 aircraft, and 500 of the new and powerful T34 tanks) which outnumbered anything the Kwantung Army could put into the field. These preparations he carefully disguised by sending easily deciphered radio messages which indicated he was concerned only in defence (see also SIGNALS INTELLIGENCE WARFARE), but on 20 August he launched a massive surprise offensive (known to the USSR as the Kalkhin-Gol, or River Halha, battle, and to the Japanese as the Nomonhan Incident, after the border post where the Red Army crossed into Western Manchukuo) that in ten days reached objectives 30 km. (18.6 mi.) beyond the Khalka. 'Zhukov's essential achievement lay in combining tanks, artillery, aircraft and men in an integrated offensive for the first time in modern war. By 31 August the Russians had completed what they described as the most impeccable encirclement of an enemy army since Hannibal beat the Romans at Cannae. The 23rd Division of the Kwantung Army was virtually wiped out, and at least 18,000 Japanese were killed' (P. Snow, 'Nomonhan—the Unknown Victory', *History Today*, July 1990).

There was a general feeling among Japanese leaders that as long as the China Incident lasted, Japan was in no position to engage in an all-out war with the USSR. But there is no doubt that Japanese middle-grade officers in the Kwantung Army were prepared to step up the scale of fighting and were eager to strike a heavy blow at the Soviet Army.

The *Nazi–Soviet Pact, signed on 23 August 1939, convinced Japanese leaders that the Soviet–Japanese balance of power had shifted against Japan. They started every effort to end hostilities through diplomatic channels. Whilst the outbreak of the European war in September 1939 convinced Moscow of the need to come to an agreement with Japan. Soviet and Japanese diplomats in Moscow arranged a cease-fire that became effective on 16 September, and agreed to the establishment of a joint committee to deal with demarcation of the border between Outer Mongolia and Manchukuo. The total killed in this first Japanese–Soviet clash reached a total of 30,000.

As Japanese military operations bogged down in China and relations with the USA deteriorated rapidly, Japan in turn hoped for an agreement with Germany and the USSR which would improve its international position. Following the signing of the *Tripartite Pact in September 1940, Japan proposed a non-aggression pact with the USSR and concluded the Soviet–Japanese Neutrality Pact on 13 April 1941 in Moscow. However, the outbreak of the *German–Soviet war in June 1941 forced Japanese decision-makers to reconsider Japan's relations with the USSR. A series of meetings was held to decide whether Japan should join in the attack on the USSR or stay out of the war. Foreign Minister *Matsuoka Yōsuke favoured the former course, but the majority of civil and military leaders at an Imperial Conference on 2 July opted to await developments. At the same time, they decided to try to build up the Kwantung Army rapidly to facilitate an attack on the Soviet Far East Army when a favourable situation presented itself. Although the rapid build-up of the Kwantung Army continued, the Army General Staff finally decided in August not to start operations against the Soviet Army that year.

When Japan attacked the USA that December (see PEARL HARBOR), Washington asked for air bases in the Soviet Far East, but Moscow refused, fearing a confrontation with Japan. Thus the Neutrality Pact remained in effect precariously through most of the *Pacific war, even while Japan and the USSR were fighting desperately against each other's allies, for it shielded them both from a dreaded two-front war. With the deterioration of its military position Japan sought to remove any incentive for the USSR to enter the Pacific war. Efforts by the Japanese foreign ministry to dispatch a special envoy to Moscow to broker a peace agreement between Germany and the USSR came to nothing, as did attempts to engage the Soviets in deliberations which might improve Soviet–Japanese relations. On 5 April 1945 Moscow gave Japan formal notification of its intention not to extend the Neutrality Pact beyond its 25 April 1946 expiration date.

Unaware of the promise Stalin had made at Yalta in February 1945 (see ARGONAUT) to enter the Pacific war within three months of Germany's surrender, the Japanese government tried to obtain Soviet mediation in bringing hostilities to a close as Japanese military leaders agreed that the USSR was likely to continue to want to avoid hostilities with Japan. According to the Army General Staff estimate, the aim of the USSR would be to seek to secure a greater voice in post-war Asian affairs and would therefore prefer to have the Pacific war sufficiently prolonged to exhaust both Japan and the USA before making diplomatic moves at the final stage. On 7 August the Japanese foreign minister, *Tōgō Shigenori, finally instructed Ambassador Sato Naotake in Moscow to seek an immediate audience with Foreign Minister Vyacheslav *Molotov to determine the Soviets' attitude towards acting as a mediator, but the next day, at 1700 hours, Molotov informed Sato that the USSR had declared war on Japan, effective on 9 August.

In the months following the surrender of Germany in May 1945 the Soviet Army in the Far East, commanded by Marshal *Vasilevsky, had been doubled from 40 to 80 divisions. By August more than a million troops, backed by 5,000 armoured vehicles, 26,000 guns and mortars, and 5,000 aircraft, were poised to attack and two hours after Sato's meeting with Molotov, just before midnight in East Asia, a massive offensive was launched against the Japanese forces in Manchukuo and in the Korean peninsula. The seizure of the Kurile Islands and southern Sakhalin also constituted part of the Soviet continental campaign. About 39% of the Soviet forces were contained in Marshal *Malinovsky's Transbaikal *front* (army group) which struck from Mongolia while the First and Second Far Eastern *fronts* attacked from the north and east. Everywhere they heavily outnumbered the depleted Kwantung Army, some 267,000 strong with another 143,000 in reserve. Soviet *deception plans led the Japanese into miscalculating both where the main attack would come from, and when it would be launched, and within six days the 40 Japanese divisions had been neutralized, though some troops continued to resist strongly in the north and east up to and beyond Emperor *Hirohito's announcement of Japan's surrender. The overwhelming nature of the Soviet offensive caused very high casualties among the Kwantung Army. More than 80,000 were killed, while the Soviets lost 8,219 dead and 22,264 wounded.

As a result of the USSR's entry into the war and its participation in the Postsdam Declaration (see TERMINAL), Japanese leaders came to share the notion that Japan had no choice but to accept the Declaration unconditionally. In this sense, the Soviet entry into the war had a greater effect on the decision by Japanese leaders to end the Pacific war on 14 August than the dropping of *atomic bombs on 6 and 9 August.

Immediately after the end of the war, more than 500,000 Japanese soldiers, officials, and other residents in Manchuria and Korea were arrested by the Soviet Army and were detained in Siberia (see GULAG).

HATANO SUMIO

Japanese–Soviet Treaty, April 1941, see JAPANESE–SOVIET CAMPAIGNS AND RELATIONS, 1939–45.

Java, principal island of the *Netherlands East Indies, rich in rubber, tin, and oil (see also RAW MATERIALS), where, despite Dutch repression, *nationalism had developed considerably between the wars. The Japanese Sixteenth Army, commanded by Lt-General Imamura Hitoshi, swiftly conquered the island in March 1942 and a military administration, quite benign under Imamura, was established there. What remained of the 250,000-strong Dutch population who had not fled were interned, and while the administrative infrastructure was nominally turned over to the Indonesians, the Japanese held nearly all the key positions. An auxiliary military force, called Peta (Pembela Tanah Air, or Defenders of the Homeland), some 35,000 strong by 1944, was raised by the Japanese. They also recruited 25,000 military auxiliaries, or *hei-ho*, and started a number of organizations which ranged from auxiliary police to the 50,000-strong Jibakutai (self-explosion corps) whose members, armed with nothing more than bamboo spears, were pledged to die defending their country.

As elsewhere in South-East Asia the Indonesians at first welcomed the Japanese as liberators from their colonial masters. But this welcome soon turned to frustration when the Japanese imposed their own form of colonial rule. Initially they encouraged division amongst the country's different social, religious, and racial factions, but later replaced this traditional policy of 'divide and rule' with one of attempting to unite the people to oppose any Allied invasion. After much pressure from nationalists, the Indonesians were allowed to form a political association in March 1943. Called Pusat Tenaga Rakjat (Centre of People's Power), or Putera, it was ostensibly a stepping-stone towards independence, and was led by a four-man committee with the nationalist *Sukarno as its chairman. When it failed to live up to Japanese hopes of using it to maintain Japanese domination, it was dissolved in February 1944 and replaced by the more broadly based Jawa Hōkōkai (People's Service Association), though Sukarno remained at its head. After more prevarication, and spurred by a Peta revolt against them in February 1945, the Japanese took steps towards conceding Java's independence. But on 16 August, before this could be announced, Sukarno was kidnapped by radicals of a youth organization called Angkatan Muda (Young Generation). They argued that independence must be seized from the Japanese, not granted by them, or the Allies would not recognize it, and proposed attacking the occupiers that night. This was averted when the Japanese on the island urged Sukarno to declare independence which he did the next day. In the weeks, months, and years which followed the Indonesians fought the Japanese, then the British, and finally the Dutch, until in November 1949 the government of the Netherlands recognized Indonesia's independence and its control of all the Netherlands East Indies except Dutch New Guinea (see Map H).

Friend, T., *The Blue-Eyed Enemy: Japan Against the West in Java and Luzon, 1942–45* (Princeton, 1988).

Java Sea, battle of, series of naval encounters fought off this *Netherlands East Indies island between Japanese and Allied warships. The initial battle, on the afternoon and night of 27 February 1942, was the first fleet action of the *Pacific war and one of the last that was not fought totally at night until the battle of *Leyte Gulf in October 1944.

The Japanese, who called the first encounter the Naval Battle off Surabaya, had already captured much of the

Netherlands East Indies and had isolated Java before launching, under the overall command of Vice-Admiral Ibo Takahashi, two invasion forces against the island. The 41 transports of the eastern force, bound for Surabaya, were covered by Vice-Admiral Takagi Takeo's four cruisers and fourteen destroyers. They were opposed by a mixed *ABDA Command force of five American, British, Dutch, and Australian cruisers and nine destroyers commanded tactically by a Dutchman, Rear-Admiral Karel Doorman. In theory the two forces were evenly balanced, but the Allied force was a makeshift one and Tagaki's ships had more fire-power and the superior Long Lance *torpedoes. Communications between the Allied ships were poor or non-existent, there was no common system of fire control, and Doorman had never previously fought a fleet action. Anticipating a night action he had left his ships' reconnaissance aircraft ashore. This badly hampered them, and the lack of air cover generally was a crucial factor in their defeat. The British cruiser, *Exeter*, was damaged and forced to withdraw to Surabaya, two Dutch cruisers and three destroyers were sunk, and Doorman was killed. Tagaki, whose caution throughout the action later earned him much criticism, had one destroyer damaged.

The next night the two surviving Allied cruisers from the battle, the Australian *Perth* and the US *Houston*, while withdrawing from the area through the Sunda Strait, found the other Japanese invasion fleet at anchor 65 km. (40 mi.) west of Batavia. They sank two ships and damaged three others before the Japanese covering force of three cruisers and nine destroyers arrived and sank them. The same evening *Exeter* and two destroyers left Surabaya in an attempt to escape to Ceylon. But the next morning, 1 March, soon after the Japanese began their landings on Java, they were spotted by air reconnaissance, intercepted, and sunk.

The only Allied warships to survive these actions were four US destroyers which had withdrawn early and which subsequently managed to slip through the Bali Straits and reach Australia.

Van Oosten, F. C., *The Battle of the Java Sea* (Annapolis, Md., 1976).

Jedburgh teams, groups of three uniformed men—an Englishman, an American, and a Frenchman—dropped into France at the time of the Normandy landings on 6 June 1944 (see OVERLORD), and for the following ten weeks. Drawn from *SOE and the *Office of Strategic Services, they acted as a staff for local French resistance units. They helped to ensure that the French resistance was co-ordinated in the best interests of Allied strategy, and that it was kept supplied with arms. Each team comprised two officers and one sergeant wireless operator who were trained leaders in guerrilla tactics, and in demolition. In all, 93 teams were dropped, 21 of whose members were killed. Jedburgh teams were also used, with Dutch personnel, during *MARKET-GARDEN in September 1944 to co-ordinate the efforts of the Dutch resistance, and in Norway.

jeep, four-wheel-drive vehicle which the US Army Chief of Staff, George *Marshall, said was the USA's greatest contribution to modern warfare. *Eisenhower believed it was one of the three tools which won the Allies the war (the Dakota aircraft and *landing craft were the other two). Early prototypes were made by several companies but Willys-Overland won the initial contract in July 1941 to build 16,000 at a cost of $739 each. By the end of 1945, 653,568 had been manufactured many of them for the *Lend-Lease programme. The name probably came from the initials GP (General Purpose), but perhaps from a comic-strip character called Eugene the Jeep.

jerry cans were German metal petrol containers, so-named by the British forces fighting in the *Western Desert campaigns because 'Jerry' was their nickname for the Germans. They were far superior in construction to anything the British possessed and after the first ones were captured by the *Long Range Desert Group in 1941 they became much sought after. A *Combined Operations HQ staff member eventually persuaded the British to start manufacturing them.

Jervis Bay, British 14,000-ton *armed merchant cruiser sunk by the German pocket-battleship *Admiral Scheer* on 5 November 1940 (see Map 42) during the first phase of the battle of the *Atlantic. The German warship attacked one of the westbound Atlantic *convoys, HX84, which *Jervis Bay* was escorting. The encounter lasted only 22 minutes but the British ship's resistance allowed all but five of the convoy to escape. See also SEA POWER.

Jeschonnek, General Hans (1899–1943), chief of the Luftwaffe General Staff from February 1939 who was an ardent admirer of Hitler. At least initially, he was also a willing subordinate of *Göring, though his relationship with Göring's deputy, *Milch, was poor. He was an enthusiastic supporter of the dive-bomber which was one of the foundation stones of the *blitzkrieg, but he neglected the other forms of *air power in which a protracted war soon involved the ill-prepared Luftwaffe. He failed to support the development of a strategic air force—he had no enthusiasm for the He177, the Luftwaffe's only four-engined bomber—or an air transport command, choosing instead to concentrate on medium bombers. He saw no reason to increase the production of fighters so that his ability to counter the Allied *strategic air offensive against Germany was quite inadequate. When this offensive began to gather pace, and after the failure to supply the beleaguered troops at *Stalingrad by air, an operation Jeschonnek had sanctioned, Hitler increasingly turned on Göring, and Göring increasingly blamed Jeschonnek. On 18 August 1943, the day after the Americans had bombed *Schweinfurt and the British *Peenemünde, he prepared a paper aimed at discrediting Göring. He then wrote a note which said, 'I can no longer work together with the Reichsmarschall. Long live the Führer!', and shot himself.

jet aircraft, see FIGHTERS.

Jewish Agency, the official organization for forming a Palestinian national home for the Jews which worked with the British, the mandatory authorities in Palestine. It was really a quasi-government for the Jews and its president from 1935, David Ben-Gurion (1886–1973), worked with an executive of eight who functioned virtually as cabinet ministers. When a chief of staff was appointed for the *Haganah in 1939 he reported to Ben-Gurion.

The Agency was sceptical of early reports of the extermination of the Jews in Europe (see FINAL SOLUTION). But at the end of 1942, when the facts became incontrovertible, it made them public, appealed to the Allied powers to try and stop the killings—which resulted in the *Bermuda conference—and contributed financially to a series of largely fruitless rescue attempts, the best known of which was the deal to exchange Hungarian Jews proposed by *Eichmann in 1944 (see also BRAND). During the course of the war the Agency's emissaries in neutral countries, particularly Turkey, helped arrange the flight of some thousands of Jews to Palestine, sometimes with tragic consequences (see PATRIA and STRUMA).

Jodl, General Alfred (1890–1946), German Army officer who served as chief of the Operations staff of the German High Command (OKW) throughout the war and was, therefore, one of Hitler's closest military advisers.

Born in Würzburg, Bavaria, Jodl fought as an artillery officer during the *First World War. In 1932, as a major, he was appointed to the operations branch of the Truppenamt, the clandestine replacement for the German General Staff which had been forbidden by the *Versailles settlement. He then became leader of the National Defence Branch of the Armed Forces Office, and in October 1938 was given command of an artillery unit in Vienna, before returning to Berlin in August 1939 to become chief of OKW's Operations staff under his father-in-law, *Keitel.

A prudent, impassive, and cautious man who preferred persuasion to confrontation when dealing with Hitler, Jodl was promoted straight to lt-general from brigadier in July 1940 and in January 1944 was promoted general. He remained a loyal, but far from servile, supporter of Hitler to the end, and though, as the war progressed, his judgement sometimes faltered, he retained the Führer's confidence. On 7 May 1945 he signed at Reims the *unconditional surrender of all German forces on behalf of the German government and was found guilty of war crimes at the *Nuremberg trials and hanged. A German de-Nazification court exonerated him in 1953.

John, Otto (b.1909), anti-Nazi German lawyer employed by Lufthansa airlines who, from 1942, was in touch with British intelligence. After the July 1944 bomb plot against Hitler (see SCHWARZE KAPELLE) he fled to Lisbon and was then taken to the UK where he was employed to broadcast propaganda over the 'Soldatensender Calais' radio station (see SUBVERSIVE WARFARE).

John, O., *Twice Through the Lines* (London, 1972).

Joint Chiefs of Staff (JCS) committee, principal US inter-service body which formed the *Combined Chiefs of Staff (CCS) committee with its UK counterpart, the British *Chiefs of Staff (COS). Under the American president, it was responsible for operational strategy in the *Pacific war, for co-ordinating operations in China with Allied strategy in the Far East, and, as part of CCS, with operational strategy elsewhere.

At the time of the Washington conference in December 1941 (see ARCADIA) the principal US inter-service committee was the Joint Board, comprising the service chiefs, their deputies, and the heads of the War Plans Division and air arms of the two services. However, with the formation of the CCS it became necessary to form an American body that matched that of the COS. This was formally constituted in February 1942 as the JCS committee. On it sat the Army Chief of Staff, General *Marshall, Admirals *Stark and *King, and Lt-General *Arnold, the commanding general of the US Army Air Forces. When Stark departed the following month for London as C-in-C US naval forces in Europe, his position as Chief of Naval Operations, the US Navy's senior post, was merged with that of King as C-in-C of the US Fleet.

In July 1942 Roosevelt, after it was pointed out to him that there was no American equivalent of Lt-General *Ismay—Churchill's representative on the COS committee and his chief of staff in Churchill's capacity as minister of defence—appointed Admiral *Leahy the committee's chairman and his chief of staff, an appointment unprecedented in American history. However, Leahy's functions were different from Ismay's, who was not a COS committee member, and his influence within the committee, dominated by Marshall and King, was limited. Under Leahy's chairmanship the committee remained unchanged throughout the war, and it became the apex of the US executive command structure below which lay numerous joint committees which dealt with every aspect of waging the war. Unlike the COS committee, which was integrated into the British cabinet committee system (see UK, 3), it was responsible directly to the president in his capacity as C-in-C US armed forces. Because of this it was given more scope—and in turn tended to give more to its field commanders—than its British counterpart; but it was occasionally overruled by its political master which the COS committee never was. See also USA, 5, and GRAND ALLIANCE.

Hayes, G. P., *The History of the Joint Chiefs of Staff in World War II: The War Against Japan* (Annapolis, Md., 1982).

Joint Intelligence Committee, see UK, 8.

Joubert de la Ferté, Air Marshal sir philip (1887–1965), British air force officer who served as air adviser to *Combined Operations and then as Assistant Chief of Air

Staff responsible for the practical application of *radar in the RAF. Its subsequent vital role in the UK's contribution to the air war was largely due to his early recognition of its potential. In June 1941 he was promoted air chief marshal and appointed C-in-C of Coastal Command, a post he had held before the war. His principal task was combating the U-boat in the battle of the *Atlantic. Up to that time Coastal Command had shared in the destruction of only two U-boats; by February 1943 when he relinquished his command it had sunk 27. He reduced the mid-Atlantic *air gap significantly; centralized his command to maximize the use of scarce resources; saw the introduction of the Torpex filled depth-charge (see EXPLOSIVES and ANTI-SUBMARINE WEAPONS) and an accurate low-level bombsight with which to deliver it; and, after initially rejecting it, encouraged the development of the Leigh Light (see SEARCHLIGHTS). But he was a controversial figure whose battles with the Admiralty over the employment of air power at sea eventually resulted in his being appointed Inspector-General of the RAF before virtual victory in the Atlantic was achieved. He retired in October 1943 but was almost immediately recalled to serve in *South-East Asia Command as one of *Mountbatten's deputy chiefs of staff. He was knighted in 1938.

Joyce, William (1906–46), born in Brooklyn, New York, of an Irish-American father and an English mother. In 1909 the family moved to Eire and in 1922 to the UK, where Joyce obtained a first class honours degree in English Literature. He joined the British Fascist Party (1923), the Conservative Party (1925), and the British Union of Fascists (1933)—where he became *Mosley's deputy—before founding in 1937 the openly pro-Nazi British National Socialist League.

Travelling on a British passport, falsely acquired in 1933, he fled to Germany in August 1939 to escape *internment and began working for the German English-language radio station. He soon established himself as a scriptwriter and broadcaster, but he was not the original 'Lord Haw-Haw', this sobriquet, which Joyce adopted later, having initially been given by a British journalist to another German propaganda broadcaster—probably Norman Baillie-Stewart—first heard in April 1939.

Joyce became a naturalized German citizen in September 1940. But during his trial for treason a ruling established that he had still owed allegiance to the Crown while his British passport remained valid, and on these grounds he was found guilty and hanged.

Selwyn, F., *Hitler's Englishman* (London, 1987).
West, R., *The Meaning of Treason* (London, 1949).

Juin, General Alphonse (1888–1967), French Army officer who served the *Vichy regime after the fall of *France before commanding the *French Expeditionary Corps (FEC) which fought with the Allies during the *Italian campaign.

Juin, Algerian-born, was a classmate of de *Gaulle's at

Marshal **Juin**, commander of the French Expeditionary Corps in the Italian campaign.

the French military academy at St Cyr, but he did not join the Free French until mid-1943. As a brigadier-general he commanded the 15th Motorized Infantry Division which took part in the stubborn defence of Lille during the fighting which preceded the fall of France in June 1940, and which enabled so many to escape from *Dunkirk. In June 1941 the Germans were persuaded to release him to join General *Weygand in North Africa where he was promoted maj-general and put in command of all French troops in French Morocco. When Weygand was recalled to France in November 1941, Juin was promoted lt-general and became Commander, Land Forces North Africa.

After the landings which started the Allied *North African campaign in November 1942, Juin joined the Allies and commanded the French land forces (five divisions, mostly *Tirailleurs and *Spahis, and a light mechanized brigade) which fought in Tunisia. In February 1943, when his forces became the 19th French Corps, he was promoted general and withdrawn to form the FEC. However, he still retained the right to intervene in French operations when he thought necessary, and did so very positively during the German advance through the *Kasserine Pass. Before moving with the FEC to Italy in November 1943, he acted as resident-general of Tunisia and in that capacity he was obliged to remove the Bey of Tunis, a political move with which he strongly disagreed, but his opposition to the Nationalist leader, Habib *Bourguiba—Juin did not believe the North African territories were capable of self government—led to Bourguiba fleeing the country. During his nine months as commander of the FEC he reverted, at his own request, to the rank of lt-general. In July 1944 he became chief of staff of French National Defence and after the war served as C-in-C Land Forces Central Europe for the North Atlantic Treaty Organization. He was promoted a Marshal of France in May 1952.

Clayton, A., *Three Marshals of France* (London, 1992).

JUNO, codename for assault beach in British sector on which the 3rd Canadian Division disembarked during the Normandy landings of 6 June 1944 (see OVERLORD). It lay between the River Provence and St Aubin sur Mer in the Baie de la Seine. By the end of the day 21,400 troops had landed there.

Kaltenbrunner, Ernst (1903–46), the son of an Austrian lawyer who followed in his father's footsteps in 1921 when he began studying law at Graz. He joined the Austrian Nazi Party in 1930 and the Austrian *SS in 1933 and headed this organization, then proscribed in Austria, from 1937. After the Anschluss (Germany's annexation of Austria in March 1938) he was appointed higher SS and police leader (Hoherer SS und Polizeiführer) in Vienna and in January 1943 was selected by *Himmler, to whom Kaltenbrunner gave his total loyalty, to head the *RSHA, the Reich Main Security Office of the SS, which gave him control of elements of the Nazi apparatus such as the *Gestapo and the methods of extermination for the *Final Solution. He was, therefore, responsible for *atrocities on an enormous scale and his character fitted his deeds. In February 1944 his organization absorbed the *Abwehr, the erstwhile head of which, Admiral *Canaris, remarked that Kaltenbrunner had cold eyes and 'murderer's paws', and his power grew to such an extent that he became a close confidant of Hitler. He was chosen by the Allies to represent the SS in the dock at the *Nuremberg trials, and was sentenced to death and hanged. The novelist Evelyn Waugh who was at the trials noted that Kaltenbrunner was the only one among the accused who looked an obvious criminal.

Black, P., *Ernst Kaltenbrunner: Ideological Soldier of the Third Reich* (Princeton, 1984).

kamikaze pilots (*kamikaze* means 'divine wind'), Japanese who deliberately crashed their aircraft on to their targets. At first they were volunteers whose sense of honour, or *Bushidō, enabled them to embrace this form of attack eagerly, but conscripts proved to be equally enthusiastic. The Japanese developed a number of suicide weapons (see BAKA BOMB, EXPLOSIVE MOTOR BOATS, HUMAN TORPEDOES, and MIDGET SUBMARINES), but the kamikaze pilot was the only effective one and he did nothing to improve the morale of those he targeted.

Early in the *Pacific war, Japanese aircraft occasionally crashed on Allied warships, but it only became a deliberate policy when, on 19 October 1944, Vice-Admiral Ōnishi Takijinō suggested forming a kamikaze force to attack American carriers supporting US landings in the second of the *Philippines campaigns, an idea enthusiastically received and quickly adopted.

The first officially recognized kamikaze attack was made on the Australian cruiser *Australia* on 21 October 1944, though the aircraft may have crashed unintentionally. But the aircraft which attacked US ships on 25 October, sinking an escort carrier during the battle of *Leyte Gulf, were undoubtedly kamikazes.

Ordinary combat aircraft were used, later modified to carry heavier bombs. At first aircraft were crashed with these attached but later the bombs were often released before impact. Kamikaze attacks reached their zenith during the American invasion of *Okinawa in April 1945 when massed suicide sorties, called *kikusui* (floating chrysanthemums) by the Japanese, sank 36 ships and landing craft, and damaged 368. It has been estimated that 5,000 kamikaze pilots died.

The Japanese were not the only ones to train suicide pilots (see FIGHTERS, 2 and KG200).

A **kamikaze** pilot being seen off by schoolgirls during the battle for Okinawa in April 1945.

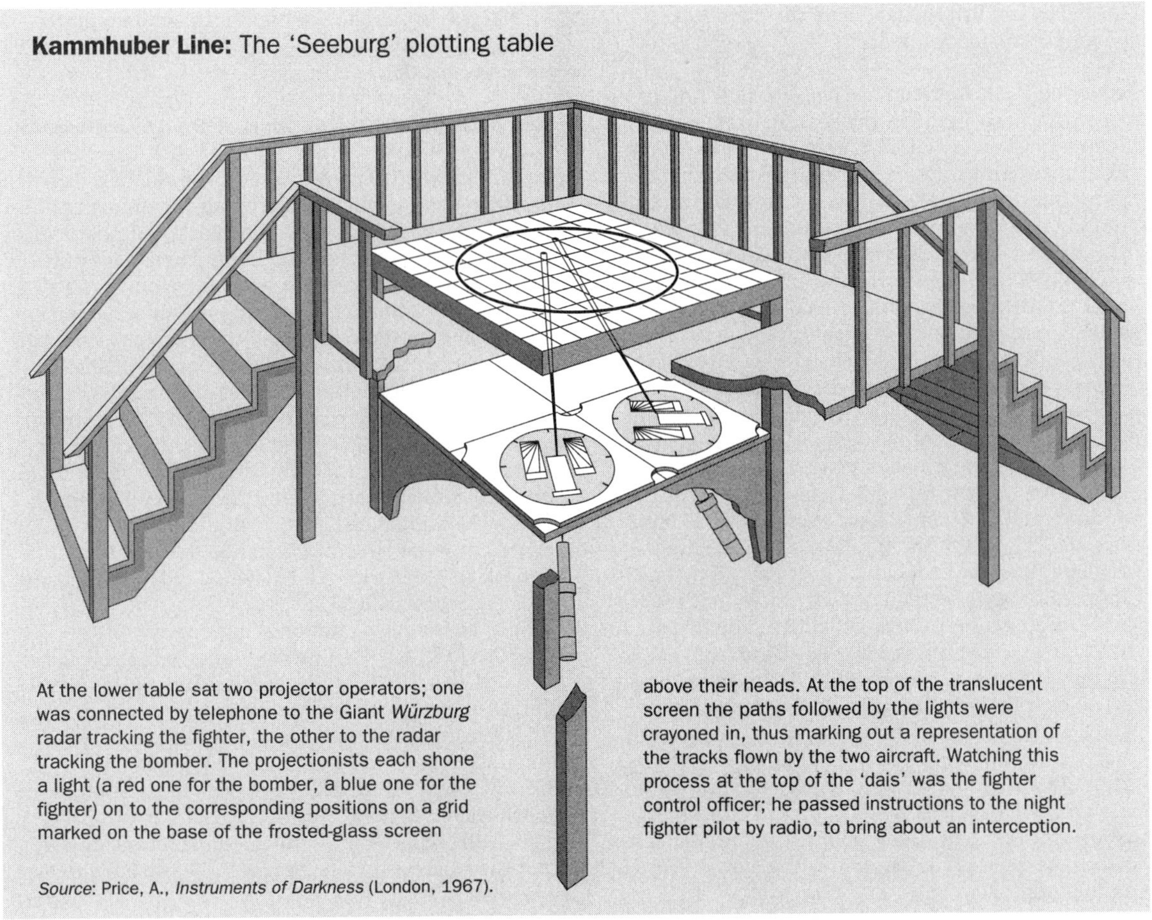

Kammhuber Line: The 'Seeburg' plotting table

At the lower table sat two projector operators; one was connected by telephone to the Giant *Würzburg* radar tracking the fighter, the other to the radar tracking the bomber. The projectionists each shone a light (a red one for the bomber, a blue one for the fighter) on to the corresponding positions on a grid marked on the base of the frosted-glass screen above their heads. At the top of the translucent screen the paths followed by the lights were crayoned in, thus marking out a representation of the tracks flown by the two aircraft. Watching this process at the top of the 'dais' was the fighter control officer; he passed instructions to the night fighter pilot by radio, to bring about an interception.

Source: Price, A., *Instruments of Darkness* (London, 1967).

Kammhuber Line, Allied name for German defence system organized by General J. Kammhuber in the summer of 1940 to intercept RAF bombers taking part in the *strategic air offensive against Germany. Originally there were three zones, each of which had anti-aircraft and *searchlight units, and two *radar sets which controlled night fighters circling a radio beacon while waiting to be directed on to their targets. This proved highly successful and was expanded into a system called *Raumnachtjagd* (sector night fighting, or box system). This consisted of a series of overlapping defensive areas, or 'boxes', each of which had radar sets and a control officer who directed the fighters on to their targets with the help of a plotting table (see Figure). These defensive boxes stretched from Denmark to beyond Paris. In some places there were two rows of them near the coast and, to protect certain German cities, a further one inland. However, in July 1943, during the *Hamburg raid, British bombers used WINDOW to block the radar (see ELECTRONIC WARFARE), and by the time of the *Peenemünde raid in August the line had almost been abandoned and nearly all the German fighters had adopted a new tactic (see WILDE SAU).

Karski, Jan (b.1914), pseudonym of Jan Kozielewski, an emissary between the Polish Socialist party and the Polish government-in-exile in London. In November 1942 he reached London with details of the *Final Solution. Having entered *Belzec disguised as a guard, he gave an eyewitness account of it in action to, among others, *Eden and Roosevelt. When he described the fate of European Jews to Judge Felix Frankfurter in New York, the judge's reply was typical of western reaction to the news of the Final Solution, which others had already reported (see NOWAK, RINGELBLUM, and SCHULTE): he said he did not believe him. When Frankfurter was assured that Karski was telling the truth he replied: 'I did not say this young man was lying. I said I cannot believe him. There is a difference.' Because of Karski's evidence the Polish government-in-exile made a formal appeal to the Allied governments. On 17 December, these issued a declaration condemning 'this bestial policy of cold-blooded extermination', and held the *Bermuda conference the following April.

Kasserine Pass, battle of (see Map 60). In February 1943, at a crucial stage in the *North African campaign, *Rommel's German–Italian Panzer Army, and Arnim's Fifth Panzer Army, launched a counter-stroke to prevent *Eisenhower's Allied forces from reaching the central Tunisian coast and splitting the Axis forces in two. The first phase of this offensive forced the withdrawal of Allied forces to the Western Dorsale mountains, which protected the Allied flank in Tunisia; and to guard the passes which bisected them were the inexperienced reserves of Lt-General Lloyd Fredendall's 2nd US Corps.

A miscalculation, caused by the difficulties of interpreting available *ULTRA intelligence, led to the British land commander, Lt-General Kenneth Anderson, deploying the main Allied reserves further north, leaving only a mixed force to guard the pass. It was made up of one battalion of Colonel Robert Stark's 26th US Infantry Division, elements of the 19th US Combat Engineer Regiment, the 33rd US Field Artillery Battalion, the 805th US Tank Destroyer Battalion, and a battery of the French 67th African Artillery. During the first night of the battle these units were reinforced by a battalion from 6th US Armored Infantry Regiment, and by a mixed British force rushed forward from Thala. This miscellany of units proved quite inadequate to cope with an *Afrika Korps assault group which was reinforced by part of Arnim's 10th Panzer Division. When Rommel's intentions became obvious Fredendall told Stark to take command at Kasserine and 'pull a Stonewall Jackson.' Stark managed to keep the Germans at bay on the first day, 19 February, but that night Rommel switched his attack north-westwards, and by the next afternoon his assault group, with additional support from an Italian armoured division and infantry, was through the pass and heading for Tébessa, while the 10th Panzer Division struck out for Thala. By that time Fredendall's command system was, as one official historian has remarked, a tangled skein of misunderstanding, duplication of effort, overlapping responsibility, and consequential muddle. However, the Germans were also in some confusion. Rommel and Arnim had conflicting strategies, so that Kasserine was only one of three uncoordinated attacks, and after the breakthrough occurred, Rommel was ordered by *Comando Supremo to attack towards Le Kef, where the Allied reserves were, instead of towards Tebessa. Heavy fighting continued the next day in the rain storms which fell throughout the battle, but on 22 February Rommel, deterred by the poor terrain for mobile operations, by increasing Allied opposition, and by Arnim's lack of co-operation, called off the offensive.

Although a great shock at the time, and an unfortunate misjudgement by Allied intelligence, the US defeat around Kasserine had no long-lasting adverse effect on Allied strategy, and by 24 February the pass had been reoccupied. But losses of men and *matériel*—and confidence—was high. Eisenhower therefore replaced Fredendall with *Patton, and he also replaced his chief intelligence officer.

Katyń massacre. During the Nazi–Soviet partition of Poland in 1939, more than 180,000 Polish *prisoners-of-war fell into Red Army hands. Ordinary soldiers were sent to labour camps, officers were separated and sent to three special camps: Kozelsk (near Smolensk), Starobelsk (near Kharkov), and Ostashkov (Kalinin district). They numbered 15,000 in all and included a large number of reservists, as well as customs officers, police, prison guards, and military police. All three camps were under *NKVD control and all prisoners were subjected to detailed interrogations and Soviet propaganda.

In the course of April and early May 1940 convoys of prisoners under NKVD guard left the three camps for unknown destinations. Daily lists of those who were to travel were telephoned through from the NKVD in Moscow. Rumours had previously circulated that the prisoners were going to be sent home. Those leaving Kozelsk travelled through Smolensk and were unloaded at a small town called Gniezdovo.

Once Polish–Soviet diplomatic relations were re-established in July 1941 (see POLAND, 2(e)), the Polish authorities immediately began to search for officers to staff the new Polish units being formed on Soviet soil (see ANDERS'S ARMY). Captain Józef Czapski, a former inmate at Starobelsk, was charged with the task of locating them. Despite the personal intervention of the Polish leader, General *Sikorski, the Soviet authorities denied any knowledge of the missing officers, claiming that they had been released under the general amnesty extended to Poles.

In April 1943 the Germans released the news that they had discovered a number of mass graves in the Katyń forest near Smolensk, which they believed to be those of Polish officers murdered by the NKVD. The victims had all had their hands wired behind their backs and had been shot in the back of the head. It was later confirmed that the 4,400 bodies were those of prisoners from the Kozelsk camp. The discovery of the graves led to dramatic repercussions in the diplomatic field. When the Polish government in London approached the *International Red Cross in Geneva with the suggestion that an international commission examine the graves (a move earlier suggested by the Germans) the Soviet government broke off diplomatic relations with the Poles. An international team of experts found no documents on the bodies dated later than April 1940—which pointed to Soviet guilt for the crime. Moscow subsequently organized its own commission of enquiry. The Soviet line was that following the German invasion of the USSR (see BARBAROSSA) the Polish officers had fallen into the hands of the Germans, who had massacred them in the late summer of 1941.

In July 1946 those conducting the *Nuremberg trials pointedly refused to apportion blame for the Katyń

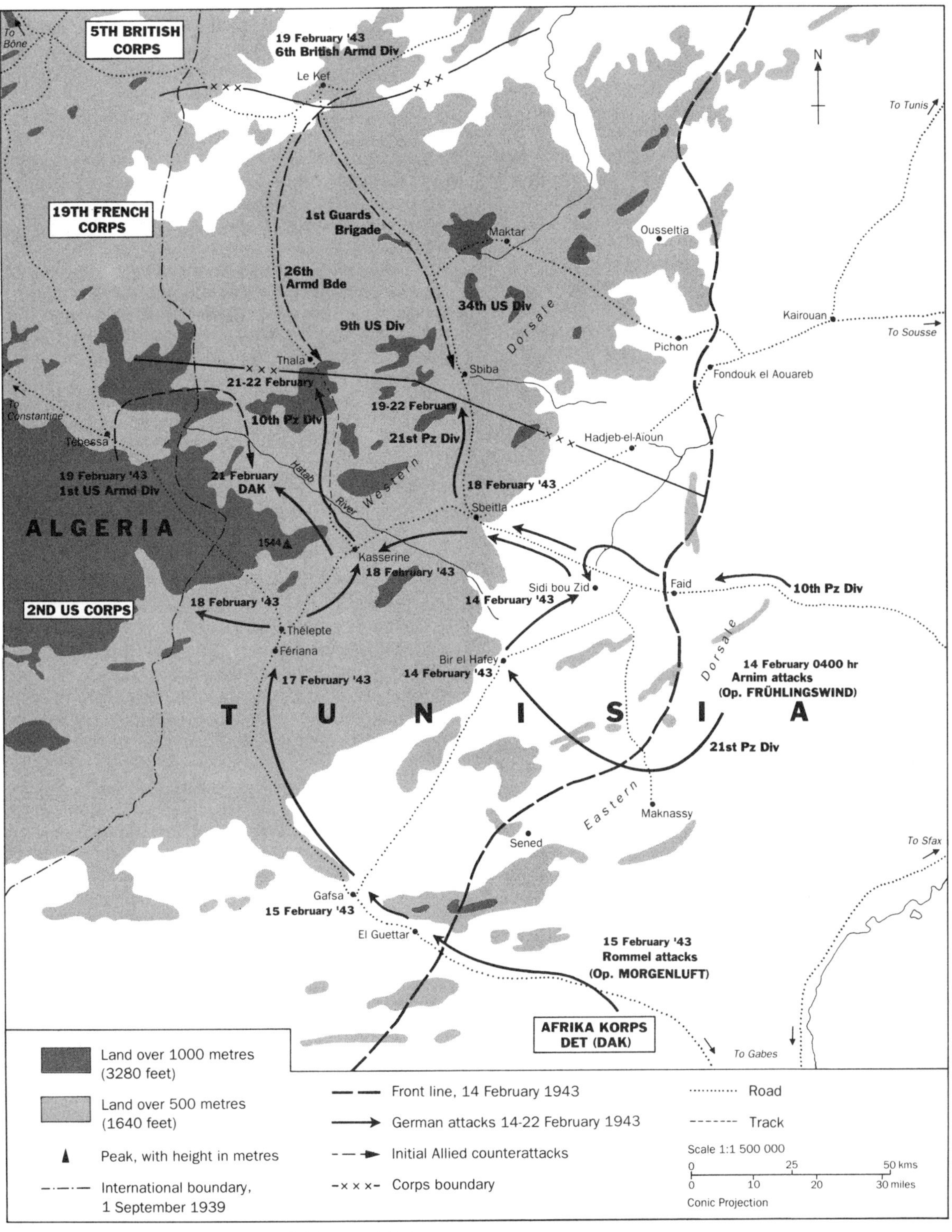

60. **Battle of Kasserine Pass**, 14–22 February 1943

massacre, despite Soviet attempts to portray it as yet one more Nazi atrocity. In the west and in Poland there was a widespread belief that the NKVD had committed the crime. In April 1990, on the 50th anniversary of the date it was committed, an official Soviet announcement confirmed that the NKVD had been responsible. The prisoners from the three camps had been handed over to NKVD boards in Smolensk, Kharkov, and Kalinin for execution. In the summer of 1990 two further mass graves were found at Kharkov and Miednoye (near Kalinin). Just over two years later, in October 1992, the Russian president, Boris Yeltsin, handed over documents to the Polish authorities which proved beyond doubt that the crime had been carried out under the direct orders of Stalin and the Soviet Politburo. See also ATROCITIES and KHATIN. KEITH SWORD

Czapski, J., *The Inhuman Land* (London, 1951).
Zawodny, J. K., *Death in the Forest: the Story of the Katyn Forest Massacre* (London, 1971).

Kearny, US destroyer attacked and torpedoed by U-boats in October 1941 while escorting North Atlantic convoys. She became the first American warship to be damaged in the undeclared war between Germany and the USA which was part of the battle of the *Atlantic. Several seamen lost their lives, which resulted in key sections of the *Neutrality Acts being repealed.

Field Marshal **Keitel** signing Germany's surrender, 8 May 1945.

Keitel, Field Marshal Wilhelm (1883–1946), German Army officer who, as head of the German Armed Forces High Command (OKW) from 1938 to 1945, ratified the *unconditional surrender of Germany on 8 May 1945. He was Hitler's closest military adviser as well as being one of his greatest admirers. 'He had ambition but no talent, loyalty but no character, a certain native shrewdness and charm, but neither intelligence nor personality' (J. Wheeler-Bennett, *The Nemesis of Power: The German Army in Politics, 1918–1945*, London, 1964, pp. 429–30).

Keitel, a professional soldier, served as an artillery officer on the Western Front during the *First World War and then as a staff officer. From 1926 to 1933 he was head of the organization branch of the Truppenamt, the clandestine replacement for the German General Staff which had been banned by the *Versailles settlement, and from 1935 to 1938 headed the Armed Forces Office (Wehrmachtamt), being promoted during this time to maj-general and then lt-general. In February 1938 he became head of the newly formed OKW and that November was promoted general. He personally conducted the French armistice negotiations after the fall of *France in June 1940 and was promoted field marshal the following month.

Keitel was second only to Hitler in the military hierarchy, but was despised by his contemporaries who nicknamed him 'Lakaitel' (*Lakai*, lackey). From being 'an honourable, solidly respectable general,' as one of Hitler's entourage described him, 'he had developed in the course of years into a servile flatterer with all the wrong instincts' (A. Speer, *Inside the Third Reich*, New York, 1970, p. 244). Hitler said he was 'as loyal as a dog' and refused to countenance his chief adjutant's wish to replace him. The relationship between them was finally sealed when in July 1944, after the bomb planted in Hitler's HQ had exploded (see SCHWARZE KAPELLE), Keitel, against all convention, rushed to embrace Hitler, exclaiming: '*Mein Führer*, you're alive, you're alive.' He subsequently presided over the Court of Honour which expelled from the army those officers implicated in the assassination plot so that they could be turned over to the *People's Court.

In his slavish devotion to Hitler, Keitel went far beyond the bounds of his military duty. On 6 June 1941 he signed the *Kommissarbefehl*, Hitler's order that all Soviet *commissars be shot once the invasion of the USSR (see BARBAROSSA) had got under way, and in July 1941 he signed an order which began the *SS reign of terror in German-occupied Soviet territory. He was also responsible for the *Night and Fog decree, for encouraging German civilians to lynch captured Allied airmen, and for other acts against humanity. For these crimes he was arraigned at the *Nuremberg trials, found guilty, and hanged.

Keitel, W., *The Memoirs of Field Marshal Keitel* (London, 1965).

Kellogg–Briand Pact, signed in 1928 by 65 states—almost every state then existing, including all the Great Powers of the day—renouncing war as an instrument of national policy. Its formal originator was the French statesman

Aristide Briand (1862–1932); it was also named after Frank B. Kellogg (1856–1937), the cornflakes millionaire and United States secretary of state, who led the main negotiations for it. Within a dozen years, it had been broken by Japan, Italy, Germany, and the USSR among others of its signatories. M. R. D. FOOT

Kempei, Japanese equivalent of the military police of many armies, but they had intelligence and other security functions too. They were founded in 1881 as a branch of the army under the Provost Marshal General, who in turn was directly responsible to the minister of war. They were therefore both part of the army and endowed with a surveillance function over it. The Kempei headquarters was divided into a general affairs section and a services section, the first being responsible for policy, personnel, records, discipline, and 'thought control' in the armed forces, the second for supply, organization, and training of police units, security, and counter-espionage.

Kempei wore army uniform, with a distinguishing armband bearing the characters *ken* (law) and *hei* (soldier), usually black on white but occasionally red on khaki. Officers were armed with sword and revolver, other ranks with bayonet and pistol. For special duties they could wear civilian clothes. In pre-war Japan they were responsible to the minister of war for normal military duties, to the minister for home affairs when they assisted the civil police, and to the minister of justice for duties concerned with the administration of the law. They had wide powers of arrest, both within and without the armed services. Outside Japan, in Manchukuo, Korea, and later in the occupied territories of South-East Asia and the Pacific, they were responsible to the local commanders-in-chief, but also reported back to their own headquarters.

Kempei, Table 1: Geographical distribution of Kempei personnel

Japan	10,679
Taiwan	745
Korea	1,927
Kwantung Army	4,946
North China	4,253
Central China	6,115
South China	1,094
French Indo-China	479
Singapore	362
Malaya	758
Thailand	937
Burma	540
Philippines	829
Sumatra	387
Java	538
Borneo	156
South Seas	89
5 Field Kempei	520
6 Field Kempei	163
8 Field Kempei	207
10 Field Kempei	163
Other	150

Source: Contributor.

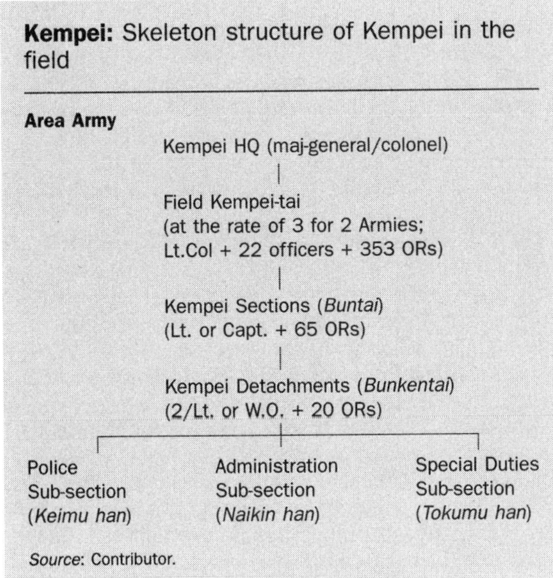

Their duties were surveillance over military discipline, security enforcement, protection of military areas, and the prevention and detection of crime among troops. They could award and execute field punishment. During campaigns they were used to round up stragglers, to patrol railway stations and ports, and to supervise dumps and depots. Their standard of education and physique was, as a rule, higher than that of the normal soldier. Other ranks were volunteers, and officers were transferred from other arms and permanently assigned to the Kempei. They were trained in special schools, usually for a year, though in wartime the period was reduced to six months. There were Kempei training establishments in Tokyo and Seoul (Korea), and in 1942 a Kempei school was set up in Singapore to serve the Southern Regions. Kempei operated in static roles in Japan and in base areas in Manchuria, Korea, and north China. In the field, the organization was different (see Chart). Field Kempei Units (*yasen kempei-tai*) operated under the Area Army C-in-C, usually under the command of a maj-general or colonel. The duties of Field Kempei were wider than those in Japan. They were responsible for liaison with local communities in occupied territory, for the requisition of food and supplies, recruiting native labour, and organizing reconnaissance and espionage networks behind Allied lines. They were also involved in the issue of travel permits and identity papers, the detection of subversive anti-Japanese thought and activity, countering Allied propaganda, the supervision

Kempei, Table 2: Kempei involvement in war crimes

War crimes overall	
Incidents	2,230
Personnel	5,551
Kempei crimes	
Incidents	619
Personnel	1,534
Kempei sentences	
Death	447
Confirmed	317
Executed	312
Life Imprisonment	125
Other	1,050
Not guilty	49

Source: Contributor.

of hotels, post offices, canteens and depots, and the prevention of theft of military stores.

In 1937 the Kempei numbered around 315 officers and 6,000 other ranks, most of whom were NCOs. At the time of Japan's surrender in August 1945, their total in all areas numbered 36,037, distributed as shown in Table 1.

After the surrender Kempei reinforcements were conscripted in order to provide security details for national shrines such as Ise and Atsuta, often as many as 2,000 men per shrine, but on 30 October 1945 they were demobilized.

The scope of their duties, and the ruthless brutality with which they carried them out, made comparison with the *Gestapo obvious. The use of beatings and torture was widespread, and in the pursuit of *chian iji* (the maintenance of order) they acquired a fearful and unsavoury reputation. In the immediate post-war period, many Kempei were tried and convicted for crimes against the civilian populations of occupied territories (see also FAR EAST WAR CRIMES TRIALS). Table 2 gives some idea of the proportions involved. LOUIS ALLEN

Otani Keijirō, *Kempei* (Tokyo, 1973).
Sleeman, C., and Silkin, S. C. (eds.), *Trial of Sumida Haruzo and Twenty Others (The 'Double Tenth' Trial)* (London, 1951).
Zenkoku Kenyūkai (All-Japan Kempei Old Comrades' Association), *Nihon Kempei Seishi* ('Authentic History of the Kempei', Tokyo, 1976).
— *Nihon Kempei Gaishi* (Unofficial accounts of Kempei History, Tokyo, 1983).

Kenya, see BRITISH EAST AFRICA.

Kerr, Archibald, see CLARK KERR.

Kesselring, Field Marshal Albert (1885–1960), German Luftwaffe officer who, from December 1941 to November 1943, was C-in-C South, then C-in-C South-West, before being appointed C-in-C West Europe in March 1945.

Born in Marktsheft, Bavaria, Kesselring served on the army General Staff during the *First World War and by 1932 was a colonel. The following year he was appointed chief of the Reich aviation ministry's administrative office and was, therefore, among those who founded the Luftwaffe. In June 1936 he was appointed the Luftwaffe's Chief of Staff with the rank of maj-general and was promoted lt-general in 1937. In 1938 he was appointed C-in-C of the First Air Fleet which he commanded during the *Polish campaign. He then became C-in-C of the Second Air Fleet during the fighting which led to the fall of *France in May 1940 and its success led to his promotion to field marshal that July. Almost as successful was his decision to direct his bombers against British airfields during the battle of *Britain, a tactic that very nearly brought the Germans victory. After his air fleet had supported Army Group Centre during the German invasion of the USSR in June 1941 (see BARBAROSSA) he was appointed C-in-C South with the task of establishing Axis air and sea superiority in the Mediterranean. This ostensibly gave him control over all axis forces, including *Rommel's Panzer Army Africa fighting in the *Western Desert campaigns. As all Axis forces there already came under the Italian High Command (see COMANDO SUPREMO), his position called for a good deal of tact and persuasion, but he was more thwarted by Hitler and Rommel than he was by the Italians.

After the surrender of all Axis troops in Tunisia in May 1943, which ended the *North African campaign, Kesselring became C-in-C South-West. At the start of the *Sicilian campaign in July 1943 he moved swiftly to bolster the Italian forces on the island by moving 14th Panzer Corps there; and then, without authority, arranged the extrication of German forces across the strait of Messina, a superbly executed withdrawal. But his brilliance and versatility in a post where politics confused so many issues were really best displayed when the overthrow of Mussolini in July 1943 was followed by Italy's surrender that September. He not only occupied central and southern Italy with exemplary speed, but ruthlessly disarmed the Italian forces and contained the Allied landing at *Salerno.

On 21 November 1943 he was appointed C-in-C of Army Group C and with it organized an outstanding campaign of attrition and delay that badly hampered the Allied *Italian campaign. In October 1944 he was severely injured in a road accident and returned only briefly to his command before succeeding *Rundstedt in north-west Europe in March 1945.

A man of immense authority and cheerful disposition—he was known to his troops as 'smiling Albert'—Kesselring was one of Hitler's outstanding generals whose image has been darkened by his harsh and brutal orders concerning the fate of Italian soldiers after the Italian surrender. His military achievements were all the more remarkable for the fact that he had risen to such a high

Field Marshal **Kesselring**.

position without the command experience or specialized training normally associated with such an appointment. In May 1947 he was sentenced to death by a British military court in Venice for ordering the execution of hostages. Churchill, among many, thought this too severe and he appealed to the then British prime minister, Clement *Attlee, to intervene. The sentence was commuted to life imprisonment and in 1952 Kesselring was released because of poor health.

Kesselring, A., *The Memoirs of Field Marshal Kesselring* (London, 1953).
Macksey, K., *Kesselring: the Making of the Luftwaffe* (London, 1978).

Keyes, Admiral of the Fleet Sir Roger (1872–1945), retired British *First World War hero of the Zeebrugge raid and a member of parliament who served as Churchill's envoy to King *Léopold of the Belgians during the fighting which led to the fall of *France in June 1940. In July 1940 Churchill, a friend, made him director of *Combined Operations. Keyes fostered the commandos and was a vociferous supporter of aggressive action, but was inclined to be overly bellicose. He was replaced by *Mountbatten in October 1941 after he had disagreed with a directive from the British *Chiefs of Staff that altered his title to 'Adviser'. He was knighted in 1918 and created a baron in 1943.

KG200 was a German air force unit formed in February 1944 to undertake special operations. By November 1944 it comprised four groups: I/KG200 received its orders from the Sicherheitsdienst (see RSHA) and employed a variety of aircraft, including a few captured US bombers, for special missions; II/KG200 comprised the Mistel (mistletoe) piggy-back aircraft, and some escort and pathfinder bombers; III/KG200 was equipped with specially adapted Focke-Wulf 190 fighters which never became operational; and IV/KG200, the maintenance and training group which also contained about 80 men called Totaleinsatz (total effort) who had volunteered for suicide missions.

Almost no documentary evidence remains about KG200 and its activities, but the unit's historian describes a number of hare-brained schemes which envisaged the use of the Totaleinsatz, including the attempted assassination of Stalin (ZEPPELIN) and experiments with piloted V-1s (see V-WEAPONS), codenamed REICHENBERG, in which the test pilot Hanna Reitsch was involved. Hardly more effective, but at least proven to work, were the piggy-back aircraft: fighters clamped on top of pilotless bombers filled with explosives. These were developed to attack long-range targets with maximum destructive power. Using the bomber's engines to reach the target, the fighter's pilot had sufficient fuel to return to base after releasing the bomber on to its target. They were employed in March 1945 to attack bridges across the river Oder.

Stahl, P., *KG200: The True Story* (London, 1981).

Kharkov, battles of. The fifth largest Soviet city and main administrative and railway centre in the eastern Ukraine, Kharkov acquired the unique distinction of having been the object of five battles and changing hands four times during the *German–Soviet war. During the first phase of the war (see BARBAROSSA), on 24 October 1941, after a slow approach against stiffening Soviet resistance, the Sixth German Army took the city, its last major objective in that year's campaign, and stopped a week later 40 km. (25 mi.) to the east, on the River Donets.

Although meanders reduced the river's defensive value, particularly south of Kharkov where it made a deep westward bend, the front remained reasonably stable through the winter; and Hitler decided to begin his 1942 summer offensive there. On its side, the Soviet General Staff (see STAVKA), under orders from Stalin to mount 'pre-emptive blows' in all threatened sectors, devised a complicated plan calling for five armies to cross the Donets 120 km. (75 mi.) south-west of Kharkov and carve out a bulge large enough to engulf the city. The execution, begun on 12 May 1942, fell to Marshal *Timoshenko's South-West *front* (army group). After driving his armies in deep, on 17 May Timoshenko committed two tank corps to complete the advance to Kharkov; but on that day the Sixth and First Panzer armies launched converging thrusts along the Donets from the north and south. Timoshenko stopped the tanks 25 km. (15 mi.) short of Kharkov on 20 May, too late to bring them into play against the German spearheads, which trapped his armies in an encirclement three days later.

At the end, on 28 May, Timoshenko had lost over a quarter of a million troops and 1,200 tanks.

On 11 February 1943, late in the Soviet post-*Stalingrad offensive, two armies belonging to General N. F. Vatutin's Voronezh *front* crossed the Donets east of Kharkov; and Hitler ordered three SS panzer divisions to hold the city as a fortress, which by his definition meant to the death. On 16 February, encircled and having to contend also with an uprising in the city, the divisions disregarded Hitler's order and broke out to the south. After driving south 186 km. (115 mi.) to link up with General Hermann Hoth's Fourth Panzer Army, the SS divisions reversed course and were back on 9 March bent on restoring their honour. Disobeying an order from Hoth to bypass Kharkov, they plunged straight in on 11 March and in three days of exceedingly vicious fighting swept through the city. Encouraged by the victory, on 13 March, Hitler issued a directive for Operation CITADEL in which Kharkov would provide the staging area for the southern arm of an offensive to pinch off the *Kursk salient.

The Soviet defensive success at Kursk in July 1943, and the immense quantities of troops, tanks, and aircraft assembled for the battle, enabled 14 Soviet armies, at least 1.5 million troops, to go over to the offensive on 3 August. Kharkov, now the northern anchor of the whole German front in the Ukraine, was the first objective; and against it, *Konev's Steppe *front* launched four armies. After repeated refusals, Hitler allowed Kharkov to be evacuated on 22 August 1943. EARL ZIEMKE

Khatin, one of many villages in Belorussia, which in 1941–4 were the scene of massacres perpetrated by German forces in reprisal for partisan activity. It was selected by the Soviet authorities after the war as the site of Belorussia's national war memorial, presumably to confuse public awareness concerning the *Katyń massacre.

NORMAN DAVIES

Kiev encirclement. During the opening phase (see BARBAROSSA) of the *German–Soviet war, the point of *Kleist's First Panzer Group reached this Soviet city's outer defensive ring on 11 July 1941 and then, to avoid the hazards of street fighting, turned south along the River *Dnieper, having advanced 400 km. (248 mi.) in 18 days. Nevertheless, Lt-General M. P. Kirponos's South-West *front*, four armies well equipped with artillery and armour, was doing relatively well—disappointingly so for Hitler, who regarded the Ukrainian land and resources as his most important objectives. German Army Group South, having just one panzer group, had not yet managed an encirclement, and Kirponos's armies were still intact. By the first week in August, Army Group South was closing to the Dnieper downstream from Kiev, but South-West *front* was in position to accomplish an orderly withdrawal to the east bank. Stalin, believing Kiev and the river line to the south could be held, was sending up two more armies and other reinforcements.

Meanwhile, Hitler had decided, to his generals' intense dismay, to stop the advance towards Moscow east of Smolensk and divert General *Guderian's Second Panzer Group southwards behind the Dnieper. After a short refit, Guderian wheeled south on 25 August. Kleist pushed north out of a bridgehead at Kremenchug on 10 September, and the two spearheads met near Romny, 200 km. (124 mi.) east of Kiev, six days later. Since Kirponos's armies had not been in the path of the advances, they stood a good chance of breaking out, but Stalin forbade the attempt. The Germans' final prisoner count reached 665,000. EARL ZIEMKE

Kimmel, Admiral Husband E. (1882–1968), C-in-C of the US Pacific Fleet which was attacked in *Pearl Harbor by the Japanese on 7 December 1941. He was relieved of his command, found guilty of dereliction of duty, and retired. In 1944 a naval court of inquiry cleared him, but the post-war Congressional inquiry did not, though it said that he was guilty of errors of judgement, not dereliction of duty.

Kindertransporte, see CHILDREN.

King, Admiral Ernest J. (1878–1956), C-in-C of the US Fleet who was assessed by the official US Navy historian as being 'the Navy's principal architect of victory' and 'undoubtedly the best naval strategist and organizer in our history.'

Born in Ohio of Scottish parents, King served in destroyers during the *First World War and on the staff of the commander of the Atlantic Fleet's Battleship Force. Besides having a ruthless, driving personality, he was a man determined to master every aspect of his profession and between the wars he became both a submariner and a naval aviator. By 1938 he was a temporary vice-admiral, but the highest appointment in the navy seemed denied to him when *Stark became Chief of Naval Operations (CNO) in 1939.

The war in Europe gave him new opportunities and in December 1940 he was offered command of the Atlantic Squadron, which, though a demotion, he accepted. (In the war-plans safe of his flagship he found just one file, covering possible hostilities with Mexico.) Restoration to three-star rank followed shortly afterwards and in February 1941 the Atlantic Squadron became the Atlantic Fleet and King was appointed its C-in-C with the rank of admiral. During this time he conducted the undeclared sea war with Germany in the Atlantic (see GREER and KEARNY for example) with such skill and aggression that after the USA entered the war in December 1941 Roosevelt appointed him C-in-C of the US Fleet (COMINCH). The president had complete faith in him and called him the 'shrewdest of strategists'. But he never allowed King to reorganize the Navy Department, a long-running saga in which King was continually thwarted, nor did he always take King's advice (see TASK FORCE 57).

In March 1942 Stark went to London as C-in-C US naval forces in Europe and the post of CNO was combined with that of COMINCH, though the two organizations remained separate and distinct. The same month Roosevelt approved King's proposals for a Pacific offensive, a strategy summed up by King as: hold Hawaii; support Australasia; drive north-westwards from the New Hebrides. He pursued it with such vigour that Churchill called the Pacific 'King's pet ocean', and by January 1943 it produced a resounding victory on *Guadalcanal which was one of the turning-points of the *Pacific war. Credit must also be given to him for the US Navy's part in winning the battle of the *Atlantic which his creation in May 1943 of the US anti-submarine Command, Tenth Fleet, helped bring about.

Unlike *MacArthur, King never objected to the 'Germany first' policy (see RAINBOW PLANS and ARCADIA), but he did object to the Pacific theatre being ignored or neglected, and often said so very bluntly. This caused disagreement, and sometimes acrimony, at several Allied conferences, but none the less he retained a good relationship with, and even deferred to, the army Chief of Staff, General *Marshall.

Two-thirds of King's time was devoted to the business of the US *Joint Chiefs of Staff and to that of the *Combined Chiefs of Staff. That he devoted only one-third of his time to running the greatest fleet in history says much for his ability to delegate and for the quality of his staff. He was not interested in details, but concentrated on broad principles. His mind, as one obituarist put it, 'was of Olympian simplicity'.

As a boy, King was much influenced by his father's upright and inflexible character. It made him single-minded and uncompromising, and he was not known for his geniality. He had the greatest contempt for civilians and said that they should be told nothing until the war was over, and then only who had won. His weaknesses, according to a US Naval Academy professor, were 'other men's wives, alcohol, and intolerance', and one of his daughters said of him: 'He is the most even-tempered man in the Navy. He is always in a rage.' But to those who measured up to his exacting standards he was considerate and generous, and by the end of the war he had mellowed sufficiently, when Japanese overtures to surrender became insistent, to send a message to *Nimitz, the C-in-C Pacific Fleet, which began: 'This is a peace warning.'

He was promoted fleet admiral in December 1944, and stepped down to CNO when, on his recommendation, COMINCH was abolished after the defeat of Japan. He retired on 15 December 1945. See also GRAND ALLIANCE.

Buell, T., *Master of Sea Power* (Boston, Mass., 1980).
King, E., *Fleet Admiral King* (New York, 1952).
Larrabee, E., *Commander in Chief: Franklin D. Roosevelt, His Lieutenants, and Their War* (New York, 1987).

King, (William) Mackenzie (1874–1950), Canadian Liberal politician who served as Canada's prime minister throughout the war.

After losing his seat in the 1911 general election, King was offered a post with the Rockefeller Foundation in 1914, and spent most of the *First World War in the USA. But he retained his interest in Canadian politics—he ran for election in 1917 and lost—and in 1919 was elected leader of the Liberal Party. He became an MP again and, two years later, prime minister. Between the wars he had two periods in opposition and showed himself during this time to be a staunch supporter of an autonomous and increasingly independent Canada and, as one mark of this, he allowed a week to elapse before bringing Canada into the war. Once the two major political parties had pledged themselves against conscription for overseas service, his decision that Canada should enter the war had the support of both sides in parliament, and in the 1940 general election he obtained a record majority.

One of his first, and most important, acts after Canada became a belligerent was to bring about the *British Empire Air Training Scheme—'I suppose no more significant Agreement has ever been signed by the government of Canada,' he noted in his diary—and throughout the war he worked closely with both Churchill and Roosevelt to maximize Canada's war effort. Before the USA became a belligerent he was a convenient conduit between the two statesmen in such delicate negotiations as the *destroyers-for-bases agreement and he also helped to smooth some early differences between them. His relationship with Roosevelt produced the *Ogdensburg agreement in 1940 and the *Hyde Park Declaration the following year, and he strongly backed the UK war effort with economic assistance (see CANADIAN MUTUAL AID) as well as men and *matériel*—the English Channel, he said, was Canada's first line of defence.

In 1942 a plebiscite was held in Canada on whether the government should be released from its pledge not to send conscripts overseas. When French-speaking Quebec (see FRENCH CANADIANS) voted 'no' King saw that the question of conscription for overseas service could split the nation and spent the next two years cleverly avoiding its introduction. Eventually, in November 1944, in a fruitless effort to avoid it, he ruthlessly replaced *Ralston, his minister of national defence. But conscription had to be introduced anyway by Ralston's successor, General *McNaughton, when an agreement was reached that 16,000 men conscripted for home defence should be sent overseas. This compromise caused bitterness amongst the French-Canadian population and the resignation of one of his cabinet, Charles *Power. But King's government remained intact and in June 1945 he won a general election, though with a greatly reduced majority. When he eventually retired in 1948 he had served continuously as prime minister for thirteen years.

By the end of the war King had established himself as a respected elder statesman who had done much to ensure Canada's independence and stature. A lifelong bachelor and a devout Presbyterian, he was not a man who kindled affection in others and his ponderous speeches were notorious, but he kept Canada united at a vital period in her history. See also CANADA, 3.

Pickersgill, J., and Forster, D., *The Mackenzie King Record*, 2 vols. (Toronto, Ontario, 1960–8).

Kippenburger, Maj-General Howard (1897–1957), New Zealand Army officer who led a battalion, and later a brigade, in *Freyberg's New Zealand division which fought on *Crete and in the *Western Desert and *North African campaigns. He then commanded the 2nd NZ Division in the *Italian campaign where he lost both feet. He was one of the official war historians of the New Zealand forces.

Kippenburger, H., *Infantry Brigadier* (Oxford, 1949).

Kleist, Field Marshal (Paul L.) Ewald von (1881–1954), German Army officer who during the *First World War served as a staff officer and at the front, and who rose to command Army Group A during the *German–Soviet war.

Promoted lt-general in August 1936, Kleist retired in February 1938, but was recalled the following August to command 22nd Corps, part of *List's Fourteenth Army. The corps performed well in the *Polish campaign and in February 1940 Kleist was given command of three panzer corps (including *Guderian's 19th Corps) which played the crucial role in the Germans' western offensive of May 1940 (see FALL GELB).

Kleist was promoted general in July 1940 and his First Panzer Group, as his command was now designated, invaded Yugoslavia in April 1941 (see BALKAN CAMPAIGN) and was part of *Bock's Army Group Centre when the USSR was invaded that June (see BARBAROSSA). The group's success around *Kiev delighted Hitler who redesignated it First Panzer Army in October 1941 when it was transferred to Army Group South (Army Groups A and B from July 1942). In May 1942 Kleist, in temporary command of what was to become Army Group A (First Panzer Army and Seventeenth Army), played a major role in the *Kharkov battle of May 1942, before returning to command the First Panzer Army which spearheaded the German thrust towards the Caucasus that summer. When this offensive petered out List, the commander of Army Group A, was sacked and Hitler took direct control himself, but on 21 November gave command of it to Kleist. By then the position of Army Group A, isolated in the Caucasus, was precarious indeed.

But Kleist proved equal to the task of avoiding encirclement and destruction, and in February 1943 he was promoted field marshal as a reward for his generalship. His attitude towards the local population did much to ensure his Army Group's survival during this time. The previous September he had remarked on the vast hordes of people in the occupied areas, and had added: 'We're lost if we don't win them over.' He therefore ignored Hitler's orders to treat them as *Untermenschen* (subhumans) and had on his staff experts who advised him on how best to gain their co-operation. Many in the occupied areas were anti-Stalinist and when sympathetically treated they joined the Germans in their tens of thousands (see DEPORTATIONS and SOVIET EXILES AT WAR).

Kleist remained in the Kuban until September 1943 before being allowed to withdraw across the Kerch straits to the Crimea (see BLACK SEA). But his clashes with Hitler over the conduct of the war culminated in Kleist's threatening to override Hitler's orders if he were not allowed to withdraw his depleted forces from behind the River Bug. Having no alternative, Hitler acquiesced. But he abhorred the field marshal's policy of treating local populations humanely, his open disdain for the Nazis, and his independent outlook, and on 30 March Kleist was dismissed, and went into retirement.

In 1946 Kleist was tried in Yugoslavia for war crimes and was given a fifteen-year sentence. Two years later he was extradited to the USSR and was charged with alienating local Soviet populations 'through mildness and kindness' (C. Davis, *Von Kleist: From Hussar to Panzer Marshal*, Houston, Texas, 1979, p. 26), and spent the rest of his life in a Soviet prison.

Mitcham, S., *Hitler's Field Marshals and their Battles* (London, 1988).

Kluge, Field Marshal Günther (Hans) von (1882–1944), German Army officer who served as a staff officer during part of the *First World War, was severely wounded at Verdun in 1918, commanded the Fourth Army from 1939 to 1941, was C-in-C Army Group Centre in the *German–Soviet war from December 1941 until October 1943, and C-in-C West from July 1944 until he committed suicide on 8 August.

Born into an aristocractic Prussian military family, by 1936 Kluge had risen to the rank of lt-general and the following year he took command of Sixth Army Group which became Fourth Army when war broke out. When Hitler threatened to invade Czechoslovakia, Kluge was part of a plot, which came to nothing, to arrest him and form an anti-Nazi government (see SCHWARZE KAPELLE).

Torn between his dislike of the Nazis and his pride in the new German Army, Kluge led the Fourth Army during the *Polish campaign with tremendous panache. However, when he heard that Hitler was planning to attack westwards he protested, but this did not stop his Fourth Army being given the task of attacking through the Ardennes during the German offensive that culminated in the fall of *France in June 1940. By then Kluge was the master of the *blitzkrieg and the brilliance of his campaign brought him promotion to field marshal in July 1940.

When Hitler launched his invasion of the USSR in June 1941 (see BARBAROSSA) Kluge's Fourth Army played a prominent role in the offensive of *Bock's Army Group Centre which reached the outskirts of *Moscow that autumn, and in December 1941, when Bock went on sick leave, Kluge replaced him as C-in-C Army Group Centre. A group of Staff officers planning Hitler's overthrow now took Kluge into their confidence, but he was ambivalent and indecisive. In October 1942 he accepted 250,000

Reichsmarks from Hitler for his exemplary conduct in the war; vetoed a plan to arrest and shoot Hitler when the Führer visited him in March 1943 (see SMOLENSK ATTENTAT); and faithfully complied with Hitler's orders during the abortive offensive against the *Kursk salient in July 1943.

In October 1943 Kluge was badly injured when his car overturned. He returned to duty on 30 June 1944 and on 2 July replaced *Rundstedt as C-in-C West whose forces were fighting the *Normandy campaign. All Kluge's old feelings of ambivalence now returned, for he soon realized that Hitler had misled him and that defeat was certain. He again flirted with the conspirators planning Hitler's demise; but when the July 1944 attempt to assassinate the Führer failed, his nerve went and he refused to be involved any further. Yet on 15 August, with his troops in desperate straits at Falaise, he apparently left his headquarters to try and contact the Allied commanders. That same day an Allied signal was decrypted asking where Kluge was and this warned Hitler that he might be organizing a cease-fire. It was, Hitler said, 'the worst day' of his life. On 17 August he replaced Kluge with *Model and ordered Kluge back to Germany. But, knowing the fate awaiting him, Kluge committed suicide the next day.

Kluge was one of Hitler's outstanding generals and one of the few he trusted, but love of his country and the army, and his rejection of Nazi methods, deeply divided him and prevented him from acting decisively. Though he was known as '*der kluge Hans*' (clever Hans), his indecision cost him his life and probably cost the country he loved additional suffering.

Mitcham, S., *Hitler's Field Marshals and their Battles* (London, 1988).

Knickebein (crooked leg), see ELECTRONIC NAVIGATION SYSTEMS.

Knox, (William) Franklin (1874–1944), proprietor of the *Chicago Daily News*, and a formidable opponent of Roosevelt's New Deal, who was Republican candidate for the US vice-presidency in 1936. Nevertheless, after the fall of *France in June 1940, when Roosevelt broadened his administration, he appointed Knox secretary of the navy. Attacked by fellow Republicans for accepting the post, Knox said he was an American first and a Republican afterwards. Never afraid to speak out—in October 1941 he said 'we shall lock Nazi Germany up in an iron ring and within that ring of sea power she shall perish'—he was a strong advocate of the two-ocean navy which he did so much to foster, and he reorganized the US Marine Corps to shape them into the potent wagers of *amphibious warfare which they became in the *Pacific war. According to the official US Navy historian, he was one of the best secretaries the navy ever had.

Koenig, Lt-General Marie Pierre (1898–1970), commander of the Western Desert 1st Free French Brigade at *Bir Hakeim which, in June 1942, held off *Rommel's forces for ten days during the *Gazala battle.

Koenig fought with the 13 Demi-Brigade of the Foreign Legion during the *Norwegian campaign and after the fall of *France in June 1940, against the advice of family, friends, and brother officers, he joined de *Gaulle. After taking part in the *Dakar expedition he fought in the *Gabon campaign and was promoted to lt-colonel in December 1940. He then served as chief of staff to General Paul Legentilhomme, the commander of the French forces which fought in the *Syrian campaign of June 1941, was promoted colonel and then brigadier-general, and was given command of the 1st Free French Brigade in the Western Desert.

Bir Hakeim did much to restore French military prestige in the eyes of the world, and the stubbornness of its defence was largely due to Koenig's fighting qualities. He then fought with the Eighth British Army during the remainder of the *Western Desert campaigns and in the *North African campaign. Promoted maj-general in May 1943, he was appointed assistant chief of staff of French ground forces in North Africa that August before moving to the UK in April 1944 to hold three appointments simultaneously: the delegate to *SHAEF of the *French Committee for National Liberation; C-in-C French Forces in the UK; and commander of the French Forces of the Interior (see FFI). He was promoted lt-general in June 1944 and became the military governor of Paris when the capital was liberated (see also PARIS RISING). After the war, he commanded French occupation troops in Germany and was promoted general.

Koga Minechi, Vice-Admiral (1885–1944), Japanese naval officer who served as vice-chief of the Naval Staff from December 1937 to October 1939 when he was succeeded by Vice-Admiral *Kondō. He possessed an agreeable and calm personality, but he was a battleship man who underestimated modern air power and had a reputation for being over-cautious, a trait revealed by his handling of the Japanese Combined Fleet when he succeeded Admiral *Yamamoto as C-in-C in April 1943. He was apparently killed when his aircraft disappeared in fog on 31 March 1944.

Kohima, battle of, fought for this small town in Assam, eastern India, during Lt-General *Mutaguchi's *Imphal offensive launched from Burma in March 1944. Situated 1,220 m. (4,000 ft.) up in the Naga hills, Kohima commanded Imphal's supply road from Dimapur which Mutaguchi ordered Lt-General Satō Kotoku's 31st Division to sever. When the threat became clear *Slim, the British commander, ordered the town's small garrison, led by Colonel Hugh Richards, to be hurriedly reinforced by one of 5th Indian Division's brigades. Part of it joined the garrison while the balance, which included its artillery, a decisive factor in the battle, formed a defensive box nearby.

At 0430 on 5 April Satō's 58th Regiment launched the first attack. The Dimapur–Imphal road was quickly cut and both Kohima and the defensive box were surrounded. Supplies were air-dropped, but the defenders were holding such small areas that many of them went astray. The Kohima garrison clung to several hills around the town, but one by one they were overrun. The defensive box was relieved on 14 April, but for those defending Kohima the situation became increasingly desperate. By 18 April, when the relief force broke through, only one position, Garrison Hill, remained in their hands. In some of the war's fiercest fighting—where tiny areas such as the district commissioner's tennis court were contested for weeks—Satō was then gradually driven back by Lt-General *Stopford's 33rd Corps, which had been hurriedly brought forward from India. Instead of sending part of his division, as ordered, to help take Imphal, Satō committed all of it at Kohima—something Slim had not thought possible because of the terrain—but on 31 May, lacking reinforcements or supplies, and again against orders, Satō started to withdraw.

Kohima was a small action in terms of numbers involved, but the casualties were high and the consequences far-reaching. Total Japanese losses were around 6,000; British and Indian casualties, including three brigade commanders killed, came to 4,000. Satō's withdrawal, taken, he said, to save his division 'from a meaningless annihilation', was later called 'premeditated treason' by the Japanese intelligence officer, Fujiwara Iwaichi. It undermined Mutaguchi's offensive and helped Slim turn it into a rout.

Koiso Kuniaki, Lt-General (1880–1950), Japanese Army officer who succeeded *Tōjō as prime minister in July 1944 after serving as chief of staff of the *Kwantung Army in Manchukuo (1932–4), minister of overseas (colonial) affairs (1939–40), and then from mid-1942, governor-general of Korea. But he was, as one Japanese diplomat remarked, 'utterly ignorant of the realities of the military situation' (quoted in P. Calvocoressi *et al.*, *Total War*, London, 1989, p. 1178 n.), and made no attempt to work with his deputy prime minister, Admiral Yonai Mitsumasa, a former prime minister who was striving for peace. Koiso eventually resigned in April 1945 after his unrealistic negotiations to split China from her western Allies were leaked, and the Japanese Army had rebuffed his suggestion that he should also become war minister. He was succeeded by *Suzuki Kantarō and died in prison after being given a life sentence at the *Far East War Crimes Trials. See also JAPAN, 3.

The so-called 'Golden Stairs', near Imita Ridge, was a particularly treacherous part of the **Kokoda trail** as the steps were greasy with mud and many of the logs which battened their edges were broken.

Kokoda trail, 1,610 km. (100 mi.) jungle track over Papua's precipitous Owen Stanley mountains, 4,000 m. (13,000 ft.) high, which divide the southern coast—where Papua's capital, Port Moresby, is situated—from the north. It was named after a hill station at its northern end from where a track led to *Buna on the northern coastline. Marked on Japanese and Australian maps as a passable route, which it was not, it was fought over by Australian and Japanese troops during the *New Guinea campaign.

Kolombangara, battle of. This naval action was fought during the *Pacific war near the Pacific island of that name on the night of 12/13 July 1943. It took place when the US Navy's Task Force 18 attempted to surprise Japanese *Tokyo Express transports carrying reinforcements during the *New Georgia campaign. It was a repeat performance of the battle of *Kula Gulf the previous week, both clashes showing that the US Navy still did not have the Japanese Navy's expertise in night actions. The Americans used *radar to track their opponents but the Japanese had new radar detector equipment which gave them early warning of the Americans' presence. The flagship of the Japanese commander, Rear-Admiral *Tanaka, was sunk under him but torpedoes from his other ships sank one Allied destroyer and severely damaged three cruisers, and the troops disembarked on the island as planned.

Komandorski Islands, battle of, Japanese–US naval action fought on 26 March 1943. The battle occurred about 1,600 km. (1,000 mi.) south of the Komandorski Islands, which lie in the northern Pacific between the Aleutians and the Kamchatka peninsula. Vice-Admiral Charles McMorris's US task group of one heavy cruiser, one light cruiser, and four destroyers was patrolling to prevent any Japanese reinforcement of Attu and Kiska during the *Aleutian Islands campaigns when it intercepted two fast merchantmen escorted by Vice-Admiral Hosogaya Boshiro's more powerful force of two heavy cruisers, two light cruisers, and four destroyers. McMorris, after failing to catch the merchantmen, fought a retiring action. Hosogaya's flagship was damaged but only a smokescreen prevented the loss of McMorris's heavy cruiser brought to a halt by Japanese gunfire. But Hosogaya, short of fuel and ammunition, was forced to withdraw after nearly four hours of fighting without accomplishing his mission to reinforce the Japanese garrisons, and he was transferred to the retired list the following month. A daytime surface fleet action in which carriers took no part it was, according to the official historian of the US Navy, unique in the *Pacific war.

Kommandobefehl, see COMMANDO ORDER.

Kommissarbefehl, see COMMISSARS.

Komorowski, Lt-General Count Tadeusz (1895–1966), Polish cavalry officer who, after fighting in the *Polish campaign, initially commanded the Union for Armed Struggle (Związek Walki Zbrojnej, or ZWZ), the Polish Home Army from February 1942, in the Cracow area. He then became its deputy commander, and finally, after *Rowecki had been captured in July 1943, its commander. After ordering the start of the *Warsaw rising of August 1944 he was captured but survived imprisonment in *Colditz. After the war he went into exile in the UK. He added 'Bor' in front of his name as his *nom de guerre* was 'General Bor'.

Bor-Komorowski, T., *The Secret Army* (repr. Nashville, Tenn., 1984).

Kondō Nobutake, Admiral (1886–1953), pro-German Japanese naval officer who served as vice-chief of the Naval Staff from October 1939 to October 1941. As C-in-C of the Combined Fleet's administrative Second Fleet, he commanded Southern Force which exercised control over all naval, naval air, and *amphibious warfare operations during the Japanese attacks on Malaya, the Philippines, and the *Netherlands East Indies. He also oversaw the *Indian Ocean raid in April 1942 and his warships participated in the attempt to take *Midway in June 1942, in many of the night actions off *Guadalcanal, and in the *Leyte Gulf battle in October 1944. A gunnery specialist and an able staff officer, his excessive caution prevented him from being a successful fighting admiral.

Kondor mission, German *Abwehr espionage operation in Egypt undertaken in May 1942 by two German nationals, Johannes Eppler and his wireless operator Hans Gerd Sandstetter. In an operation codenamed SALAAM the Hungarian desert explorer Captain Ladislaus de Almaszy drove them from the Gialo oasis to Assiut in Egypt where they caught a train to Cairo, Eppler's birthplace.

The desert journey was a remarkable achievement but what followed is the kind of story which gives *spies a bad name. Much has been written about Eppler's mission but the official files are less dramatic. They show that though the Germans' desert journey was detected by *ULTRA intelligence, its purpose was not known until two wireless operators, detailed to receive Sandstetter's messages, were captured during the *Gazala battle of June 1942. Documents with the operators indicated the mission's presence in Egypt, but there is no mention in the official files of the key to Standstetter's code—Daphne du Maurier's novel *Rebecca*—which figures in nearly every written account of the mission.

The agents were sheltered by a belly-dancer, Hekmat Fahmy, on her houseboat where her English officer lover—away in the desert—had left a map of the *Tobruk defences. But the map was out of date and anyway Sandstetter was unable to make contact on his transmitter after Fahmy installed them on a nearby houseboat. This failure, compounded by the Abwehr's mistake in giving them English currency, soon turned the mission into a farce, and their efforts to change the money, as well as their 'riotous living', eventually attracted attention. A watch was put on their houseboat and on the chauffeur-driven car they used to meet their contacts, two of whom were a future Egyptian president, Anwar el-Sadat (1918–81), and a German called Viktor Hauer, who worked in the Swedish legation. But the houseboat was only raided, on 25 July, when a contact of Hauer's apparently revealed to the British that the two men on the houseboat were Germans, and it was only when they were interrogated that their connection with Almaszy's journey was established.

The two agents were treated as *prisoners-of-war, the chauffeur and Fahmy were let off with a caution, and the other participants were interned or deported, except for Hauer who disappeared.

Eppler, J., *Operation Condor* (London, 1977).

Konev, Marshal Ivan (1897–1973), Soviet Army officer who acted as a military *commissar during the civil war before becoming part of the officer corps in 1924.

Konev, not entirely without reason, regarded *Zhukov as his nemesis. In 1937–8, he commanded the Soviet special force stationed in Outer Mongolia, but in 1939 it was Zhukov who was given command of the Halha River (Khalkin-Gol) operation (see JAPANESE–SOVIET CAMPAIGNS). In October 1941, during the initial phase (see BARBAROSSA) of the *German–Soviet war, Stalin divided West *front* (army group), which Konev had commanded for a month, giving him the armies on the outer right flank as Kalinin *front* and Zhukov the main force in the Moscow sector. Thereafter, he was Zhukov's junior partner until August 1942, when Stalin returned him to West *front* after Zhukov left to take charge at *Stalingrad.

The action shifted south in the winter, and Konev was out of it until July 1943, when, according to one biographer, 'his hour struck'—faintly. He commanded Steppe *front*, which was the reserve in the *Kursk battle but, together with Voronezh *front* and under Zhukov, became part of the main force in the ensuing Soviet summer, winter, and spring offensives. In October, Voronezh became First and Steppe became Second Ukrainian *front*; and in February 1944, apparently to boost him to Zhukov's level of celebrity, Stalin gave Konev a marshal's star. In May 1944, Konev inherited the strategically more important First Ukrainian *front* after Zhukov, who had commanded it in person since March, departed.

However, he had still not fully emerged from Zhukov's shadow. In the 1944 summer offensive, he played the accompaniment to Zhukov's bravura performance against German Army Group Centre, and his role in the 1945 offensive was initially to have been the same. His hour did not strike resoundingly until 17 April, when Stalin ordered him to drive towards *Berlin because Zhukov was having trouble crossing the River Oder, and he therewith acquired a share in the victory there.

Three days after *V-E Day, Konev gained a more doubtful distinction as the liberator of *Prague, and in July 1945, Stalin named him Soviet high commissioner for Austria. In July 1946 he was appointed first deputy armed forces minister and commander-in-chief of the ground forces to succeed Zhukov, who, after having held those posts briefly, was being sent off to vegetate in out-of-the-way military districts. EARL ZIEMKE

Konoe Fumimaro, Prince (1891–1945), Japanese politician from the noble line of Fujiwara who served as prime minister, during two critical times in Japan's war with China (see CHINA INCIDENT). The eldest son of a prominent politician, he was born in Tokyo and lost his parents at an early age. He studied philosophy first at Tokyo and then at Kyoto universities, and as a prince of the blood became a member of the upper house of Japan's parliament (Diet), the House of Peers, in 1916, and accompanied Saionji Kinmochi (1849–1940), Japan's plenipotentiary, to the Paris Peace Conference in 1919 (see VERSAILLES SETTLEMENT). At that time he published a famous article, 'I reject the peace principles dictated by Britain and the United States'. In 1933 Konoe became president of the House of Peers and gradually came into association with the military leaders.

He became prime minister for the first time in June 1937 and led the country through the early stages of the war in China which saw many military victories, but he and his foreign ministers then failed to capitalize on these by entering into negotiations with *Chiang Kai-shek's Kuomintang government in China. In November 1938 he announced his scheme for a new order in East Asia (see GREATER EAST ASIA CO-PROSPERITY SPHERE) in which Japan would play the leading part. In the following January, Konoe who had come under great criticism for failing to resolve the China problem diplomatically in spite of the military successes, resigned in frustration, but formed a second cabinet in July 1940. Almost immediately he set about forming the Taisei Yokusankai (Imperial Rule Assistance Association), a semi-fascist organization which was intended to contrive a merger between political parties (see also JAPAN, 3). His cabinet entered into the *Tripartite Pact with Germany and Italy in September but early in 1941 it took steps to enter into negotiations with the USA (see USA, 1). His foreign minister, *Matsuoka Yōsuke, decided to visit Japan's European allies and concluded a Neutrality Pact with the USSR on his return journey (see also JAPANESE–SOVIET CAMPAIGNS). The contradictions between these various policies led to divisions within the cabinet and to its resignation in July in order to get rid of Matsuoka. Konoe's third cabinet was then formed with a new foreign minister and this concentrated on peace negotiations with the USA. When these did not succeed and the Washington authorities froze Japanese funds, Konoe offered to visit the USA for direct talks with Roosevelt. The proposal was rejected and the cabinet resigned in October; Konoe rejoined the imperial court as an adviser. Towards the end of the war Konoe feared a communist revolution and advocated bringing hostilities to a speedy conclusion in order to preserve the imperial family. After the war, when the question of war guilt was under discussion, he was taken into custody by the Allies but committed suicide in prison on 16 December 1945 before he could be arraigned at the *Far East War Crimes Trials. IAN NISH

Nish, I. H., *Japanese Foreign Policy, 1869–1942* (London, 1977), ch. 11, 12.
Yoshitake Oka, *Konoe Fumimaro: A Political Biography* (Tokyo, 1983).

Korea became, against the wishes of its population, a Japanese protectorate in 1905 and was annexed by Japan in 1910 when the king was forced to abdicate. Resistance to Japanese occupation increased after 1919 and from 1925 onwards was mostly controlled by a number of communist factions outside and within Korea.

The Japanese wrought an industrial revolution in Korea and in 1937 a process of assimilating the 23.5 million population began after a Japanese general, Minami Jiro, had been appointed governor-general the previous year. The Korean language and literature were banned from schools, and Koreans were even ordered to change their names to Japanese ones. In 1938 a 'volunteer' system began conscripting Korean youths; in 1939 Korean labour began being employed overseas; and in 1942 conscription for the Japanese Army was started. The nationalists and communists in China also raised army units from Korean patriot groups who had taken refuge there. Those who joined the nationalists were formed into a single military force in 1941, headed by Yi Pom-sok, and one of its units took part in the *Burma campaign. The communist bands, based at Siking in north-west China, were led by Kim Il-sung, North Korea's first post-war political leader.

As the war progressed Japanese exploitation of Korea increased. The country was stripped of its rice production, cattle were confiscated, and metal objects of all kinds were seized for the war effort. This exploitation caused unrest, forcing the Japanese to increase their military presence in the country, from 46,000 troops in 1941 to 300,000 by 1945. By the end of the war 2.6 million Koreans were engaged in forced labour in Korea and 'thousands of sociopathic Koreans were recruited to serve in the ranks of the repressive police. Korea became a slave-labor camp under armed guard' (R. Whelan, *Drawing the Line: the Korean War 1950–1953*, London, 1990, p. 22). Some 723,000 Koreans were also sent overseas as were tens of thousands of women who were forced to act as *comfort women for Japanese troops. Many Koreans were sent to work in Japan and by January 1945 made up 32% of the labour force there. Perhaps as much as a quarter of the total casualties at *Hiroshima were Koreans.

At the Cairo conference in November 1943 (see SEXTANT) it was agreed by China, the UK, and the USA that Korea should become independent 'in due course'. With this Stalin concurred and at the Yalta conference in February 1945 (see ARGONAUT) a form of trusteeship, first raised by Roosevelt with *Eden in early 1943, was discussed between the major powers, but was never implemented.

After the USSR declared war on Japan in August 1945 (see JAPANESE–SOVIET CAMPAIGNS), Soviet forces mounted a number of small *amphibious operations north of the 38th Parallel (see Map 58) and the Soviet Twenty-Fifth Army advanced into Korea from China. As agreed with the USA (which had suggested the 38th Parallel as a dividing line), the Soviets then occupied north Korea while General John Hodge's 24th US Corps, which landed on 8 September from Okinawa, occupied south Korea. Syngman Rhee (1875–1965), who had been associated with an ineffective Korean provisional government formed in China in 1919, became president of the Republic of Korea in 1948.

Cumings, B., *The Origins of the Korean War* (Princeton, 1981).

Kosciuszko Division, see BERLING'S ARMY.

Krebs, Lt-General Hans (1898–1945?), German Army officer who was appointed the last head of the German General Staff on 29 March 1945 when Hitler dismissed *Guderian. On 30 April Hitler committed suicide and the next day Krebs left the Führerbunker during the battle which led to the fall of *Berlin and crossed Soviet lines to meet General *Chuikov. But any hope he had of some form of capitulation other than *unconditional surrender were soon dashed. Krebs returned to the bunker where *Bormann and *Goebbels were among those waiting to hear the result of his mission. He said he was going to commit suicide and almost certainly did so, but his body was never found.

Kreisau circle, German political resistance group called after an estate owned by its leader, Count Helmut von Moltke. See SCHWARZE KAPELLE.

Kriegsmarine, German Navy. See GERMANY, 6(c).

Kripo, or Kriminalpolizei (criminal police), was the German state criminal investigation branch. In 1936, when *Himmler embarked on a reorganization of the police it became, with the *Gestapo, a branch of the newly formed Sicherheitspolizei, or *Sipo (security police), which was headed by Reinhard *Heydrich. When the *RSHA (Reichssicherheitshauptamt) was formed in September 1939 it became the RSHA's Department (Amt) V.

Kula Gulf, battle of, naval action in the *Pacific war which was fought off Kolombangara Island in the Solomons on the night of 5/6 July 1943. US warships, forewarned by *ULTRA intelligence, tried to prevent Japanese destroyer transports (see TOKYO EXPRESS) from landing troops and supplies on the island during the

*New Georgia campaign. This they failed to do for though they sank one of the destroyers, they were slow to engage, and one US cruiser was sunk.

Kulmhof, see CHELMNO.

Kuomintang, *Chiang Kai-shek's Nationalist Party of China. See CHINA, 3(a).

Kurile Islands. These extend south of the USSR's Kamchatka peninsula to Hokkaido, Japan, and form the boundary between the Sea of Okhotsk and the Pacific Ocean. They are made up of more than 30 islands, and in the Soviet view are judged to include the four islands of Etorofu, Kunashiri, Shikotan, and the Habomai, which are immediately adjacent to Hokkaido, and which Japanese usage calls 'the northern territories'. The Kuriles were administered as part of Hokkaido after the Treaty of St Petersburg in 1875, but were later the subject of dispute between Japan and the Russian Empire.

Soviet seizure of the Kuriles (see Map 58) as part of a campaign that opened on 9 August 1945 (see JAPANESE–SOVIET CAMPAIGNS) was based on the secret Yalta agreements (see ARGONAUT). At Yalta, the USA and UK agreed that the Kurile Islands would be handed over to the USSR, in return for Soviet entry into the *Pacific war. They were formally declared Soviet territory in September 1945 and from 1947 administered as part of the Sakhalin district. The Japanese population of the four islands was forcibly expelled.

The Japanese government defined the four islands of 'the northern territories' as inalienable Japanese lands and made repeated calls for their retrocession. Japan's claim was based on the assertion that they do not form part of the main Kurile chain which was the subject of the dispute with tsarist Russia and which Japan renounced in the *San Francisco Peace Treaty of 1952. They were never in Russian possession before 1945, and had always constituted an integral part of Japan.

The USSR, which did not sign the peace treaty, took the position that under a series of international agreements all the Kurile Islands legitimately became part of its own territory. When the then Soviet president, Mikhail Gorbachev, visited Japan in April 1991, he agreed that 'the northern territories' should be subject to negotiation, and discussions concerning their status were begun.

HATANO SUMIO

Kurita Takeo, Vice-Admiral (1889–1977), Japanese naval officer, a torpedo specialist, best described as a sea dog as he spent much of his career afloat. As a rear-admiral he commanded 7th Cruiser Squadron which helped cover the Japanese invasion force for Malaya and Thailand in December 1941 (see MALAYAN CAMPAIGN). He subsequently took part in the conquest of the *Netherlands East Indies and commanded the Close Support Force during the *Midway battle in June 1942. Before the *Leyte Gulf battle in October 1944, during which he led the First Striking Force, he had his flagship sunk under him and was then forced by a shortage of fuel to disengage from the much weaker US force screening the US landings just when victory seemed assured.

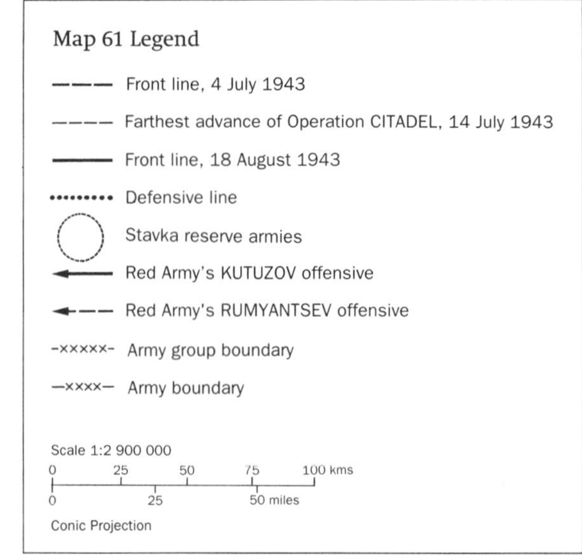

Kursk, battle of. In the Soviet view, Kursk was the decisive turning-point of the *German–Soviet war, the point after which the Soviet forces permanently held the initiative. In fact the battle confirmed but did not decide that: Hitler and his generals knew it beforehand. The most they expected was to extract psychological leverage from a precarious, strategically insignificant advantage, as Hitler put it, to 'light a bonfire' that would impress the world and possibly intimidate the Soviet Command.

The 1942–3 winter campaign left a westward bulge 190 km. (118 mi.) wide and 120 km. (75 mi.) deep in the front around Kursk, an important rail junction some 800 km. (500 mi.) to the south of Moscow. Inside were five Soviet armies. On the north, von *Kluge had shortened the German Army Group Centre's front and had an army, Ninth Army, to spare. On the south, *Manstein's Army Group South had acquired three almost new SS panzer divisions. In Germany, Panther and Tiger tanks, somewhat superior to the Soviet T34/85 and KV85, were coming into quantity production. On 15 April, Hitler ordered Kluge and Manstein to be ready by 4 May to start an operation (CITADEL) that would pinch off the bulge. On 6 May, he postponed the offensive until mid-June, later telling his tank expert, *Guderian, that thinking about CITADEL made his stomach turn over.

Stalin, his deputy as Supreme Commander-in-Chief, Marshal *Zhukov, and Chief of the General Staff, Marshal *Vasilevsky, regarded the bulge as an entering wedge for their first summer offensive but were not certain Hitler could not still contrive a surprise as he had in the two previous summers. They decided to reinforce the *fronts*

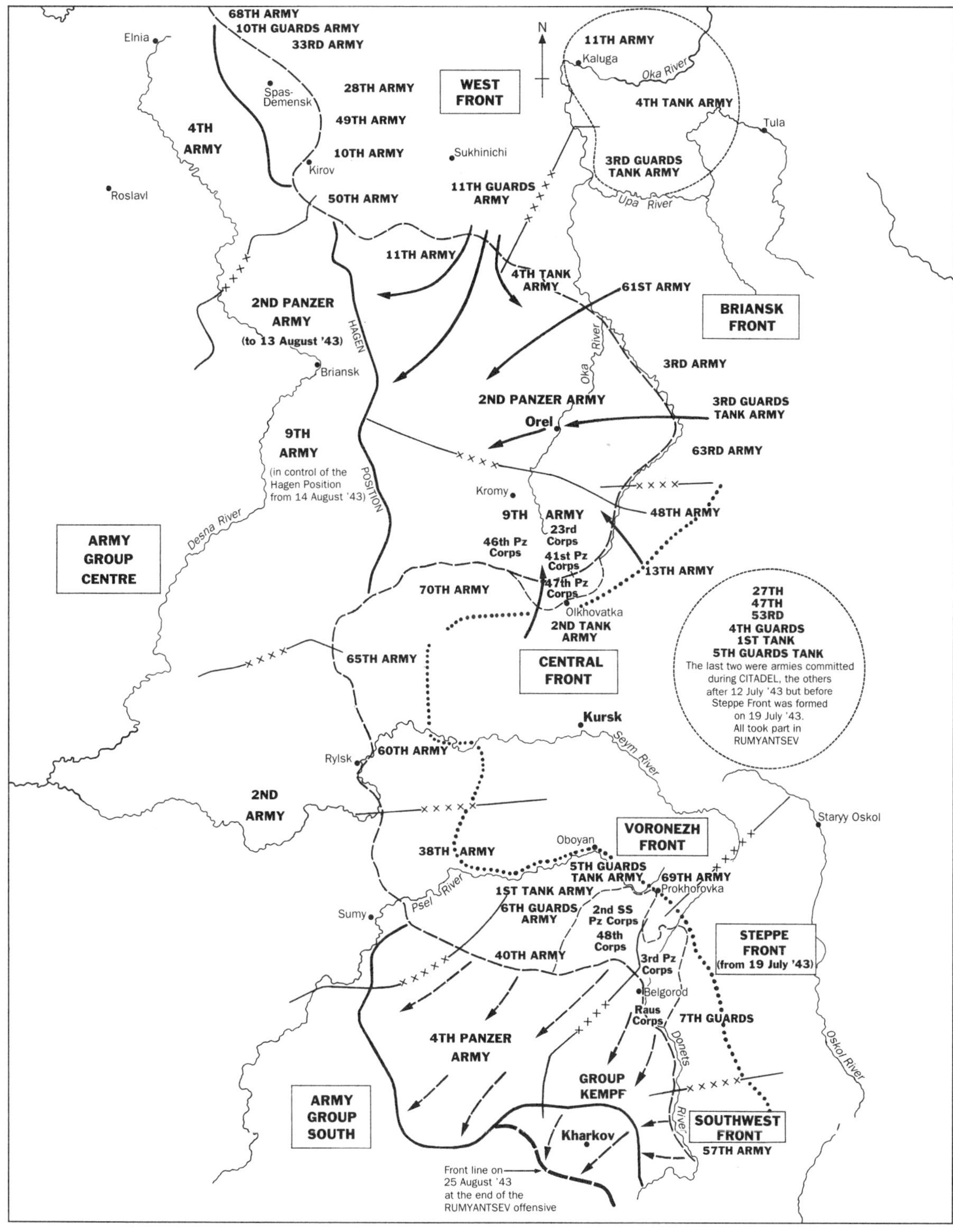

61. **Kursk**: operations CITADEL, KUTUZOV, and RUMYANTSEV, July–August 1943

(army groups) holding the bulge, *Rokossovsky's Central *front* on the north and Vatutin's Voronezh *front* in the south, and let Hitler have the first move.

Hitler finally let CITADEL start on 5 July. The forces—in the north Ninth Army under *Model, in the south Fourth Panzer Army under General Hoth and Army Detachment 'Kempf' under Lt-General Werner Kempf—numbered about 700,000 troops, 2,400 tanks, and assault guns, and 1,800 aircraft. Rokossovsky and Vatutin had a total of 1.3 million troops, 3,400 tanks and assault guns, and 2,100 aircraft. The 105-day interlude since the winter fighting ended had given them time to ring the bulge with six belts of three to five trench lines; and, to the east, there were six armies in a *Stavka reserve. By 1 August they were all deployed against the Belgorod–Kharkov Salient where, Konev's Steppe *front* having taken over on Vatutin's left, an offensive (RUMYANTSEV) was launched on 3 August.

Model's three panzer corps had the village of Olkhovatka, about a third of the way to Kursk, as their first objective. By nightfall on the second day, they had covered 21 km. (13 mi.) and were approaching Olkhovatka. Rokossovsky then committed his reserves, Second Tank Army and a tank corps, forcing the panzer corps into a battle of attrition reminiscent of the *First World War. On 9 July, Model told Kluge that a breakthrough to Kursk was hardly any longer to be expected.

Hoth made his northward attack west of the River Donets with two panzer corps and Kempf his east of the river, thereby achieving the only element of surprise in the entire operation. Vatutin had his heaviest deployment east of the river, while Hoth was conducting the main effort with 48th and 2nd SS Panzer Corps, the best equipped in the German Army at that time. Vatutin still had Hoth outnumbered in tanks, but he entered the battle on the wrong foot.

Hoth's initial objective was Oboyan, halfway to Kursk and just inside Vatutin's last trench line. In two days, Hoth's attack gained 20 km. (12 mi.) on a 40 km. (25 mi.) front. Although Vatutin committed the First Tank Army and a tank corps from the Stavka reserve, Hoth went another 15 km. (9 mi.) by 11 July. The next day, 2nd SS Panzer Corps crossed the last trench line and at Prokhorovka, 35 km. (22 mi.) south-east of Oboyan, encountered the Fifth Guards Tank Army, which had been part of the Stavka reserve. The ensuing mêlée involving some 1,200 tanks, three-quarters of them Soviet, became the largest tank battle of the war.

The events of 12 July around Kursk combined with Anglo-American landings on Sicily two days earlier (see SICILIAN CAMPAIGN) to extinguish Hitler's bonfire. The 2nd SS Panzer Corps inflicted more damage than it received, but the relative Soviet advantage increased. Kluge had to take two panzer divisions plus artillery and rocket launchers from Model to counter a Soviet attack that threatened the Ninth Army's rear. And the Americans and British advanced out of their beachheads on Sicily. Insisting that he had to have 2nd SS Panzer Corps, which he rated as the equivalent of 20 Italian divisions, to deal with an invasion of Italy, Hitler cancelled CITADEL on 13 July; and what was left of the initiative passed to the Soviet Command.

Soviet histories treat the battle as including also the subsequent elimination of the *Orel and *Kharkov salients in late July and August 1943. Since the total forces then committed numbered 4 million men, 13,000 armoured vehicles, and 12,000 aircraft (three-quarters of them Soviet), the Kursk battle thereby becomes one of the largest of the whole war. EARL ZIEMKE

Manstein, E. von, *Lost Victories* (Chicago, 1958).
Zhukov, G. K., *Memoirs of Marshal Zhukov* (London, 1971).
Ziemke, E. F., *Stalingrad to Berlin* (Washington, DC, 1968).

Kutno, battle of, the Polish Army's one successful counter-attack during the *Polish campaign. Launched south-eastwards from the river Bzura on 9 September 1939, the Poznań Army, commanded by General Tadeusz Kutrzeba, struck the flank of General *Blaskowitz's advancing Eighth German Army and destroyed one of its divisions. This forced the withdrawal of German troops besieging Warsaw, giving the capital's defenders time to prepare their defences. It also forced the Germans back about 16 km. (10 mi.) before air attacks and reinforcements from the Tenth German Army checked the attack, and by 14 September the Poles were again on the retreat.

Kuwait was an independent Arab sheikhdom under British protection from 1914 to 1961 which was ruled by Sheikh Ahmad from 1921 to 1951. Oil deposits were found in the late 1920s and early 1930s but drilling stopped during the war.

Kwantung Army, Japanese formation which policed what had been the Russian South Manchurian Railway zone in the Chinese province of Manchuria following Japan's victory in the Russo-Japanese war of 1905. During the 1930s, one of its more dubious enterprises was to develop *biological warfare which it employed during the *China Incident and possibly during the first *Japanese–Soviet campaign of August 1939. Given independent status in 1919, the army became a highly political organization during the 1920s and attracted the best and most ambitious Japanese officers. It was always an influence in the development of Manchuria, and from 1928 it played an increasingly assertive role there. In September 1931 a number of officer conspirators within the army organized the Mukden, or Manchurian Incident, the alleged sabotage of the Mukden–Port Arthur railway line. As a result of it the Kwantung Army (against the wishes of the Japanese government and its commander, Lt-General Honjō Shigeru) overran Manchuria by defeating the numerically stronger armies of the local Chinese warlords. It then created the puppet state of Manchukuo with the emperor, *Pu-Yi, at its head and added Jehol, a part of Inner Mongolia, to its conquests. General Minami Jiro, now the Kwantung Army's commander, became the

Japanese ambassador to Manchukuo which he effectively governed with little reference to Tokyo.

The ambitions of the Kwantung Army's officers did not end there. A truce was signed with China in 1933, which created a buffer zone in North China, but Kwantung Army agents began fostering independent movements and Japanese influence there, which helped kindle the China Incident in July 1937. However, Japan still regarded the USSR as its primary opponent and the Kwantung Army was involved in several border incidents with the Red Army. These culminated in the first Japanese–Soviet campaign of August 1939 in which the Kwantung Army was severely rebuffed and had one division almost entirely destroyed. By August 1945, when it again faced the Red Army, it had grown to 24 divisions and 12 brigades (267,000 men with another 243,000 in reserve), but it was inadequately equipped, trained, and supported—for example, there were just 50 front line aircraft—and was of low morale. It therefore proved nowhere near strong enough to stem what one historian has described as 'an awful invasion, one of terrible massacre, incredible speed, confusion and panic' (P. Calvocoressi *et al.*, *Total War*, London, 1989, p. 1193). Japanese casualties amounted to 80,000 dead, and 594,000 officers and men, including 148 generals and about 20,000 wounded, were taken prisoner (see GULAG).

Laconia, armed 20,000-ton British liner torpedoed in the South Atlantic 400 km. (250 mi.) north-east of Ascension Island on 12 September 1942. She had aboard 2,771 men, women, and children, including 1,800 Italian *prisoners-of-war. Once aware of the prisoners, the U-boat captain started rescue operations. *Vichy French assistance was requested from Dakar in French West Africa and the U-boat captain signalled in English that any rescue ship would be given immunity from attack. This message was received at the British base at Freetown, Sierre Leone in British West Africa, but not by the US air base on Ascension. On 15 September Freetown informed Ascension of the sinking, but not of the rescue operation still under way. Freetown then requested air cover for British ships proceeding to the scene and a Liberator bomber, dispatched the next morning, found the U-boat collecting survivors in readiness for the rendezvous with French ships from Dakar. Though the U-boat was displaying a large Red Cross flag (see INTERNATIONAL RED CROSS COMMITTEE), and was towing four lifeboats, the bomber was ordered to attack. It missed the U-boat but the rescue operation was immediately abandoned and eventually the French rescued most of the 1,111 survivors. The attack caused additional loss of life among the survivors and prompted the German U-boat C-in-C, Grand Admiral *Dönitz, to issue what became known as the 'Laconia Order' which forbade the rescue of crews of sunken ships. At the *Nuremberg trials the prosecutor failed to have Dönitz convicted for issuing the order after Fleet Admiral *Nimitz confirmed the US Navy had pursued a similar policy in the *Pacific war.

landing craft and landing ships were specialized vessels employed in *amphibious warfare. The Allies built them in large quantities (see Table), but they were always in short supply.

In 1939 landing craft were small open boats, some of which had ramps fitted in their bows. They were carried aboard landing ships, which were either specially constructed or converted from their peacetime role, and ferried the landing force and its transport and supplies from the landing ships to the beaches. Later, in the *Pacific war, where great distances were involved, this 'ship to shore' method remained the system of attack. But for the European theatre much larger landing craft were developed by the western Allies for 'shore to shore' landings where the landing force was carried direct from the port of embarkation to the beaches.

In 1914 the British built special landing craft for use in the Baltic, in 1916 the Tsarist Navy operated a landing ship in the Black Sea, and during the 1920s the US Marine Corps began developing suitable craft for amphibious landings. But during the 1930s the Japanese, experts in amphibious warfare, were far ahead of other nations in designing both craft and ships. During the *China Incident they employed the world's first specially constructed landing ship for amphibious landings at Tientsin—the *Shinsu Maru*, 8,108 tons, 144 m. (472 ft.) long, designed along the lines of a factory whaling ship. They also used the small Dai-Hatsu type, the first landing craft to be built in quantity with a ramp in its bows, a design the British and the Americans copied in the late 1930s.

However, as the war progressed, landing craft and landing ships were primarily developed by the UK and USA to undertake the amphibious operations so central to their strategy, and they eventually constructed 60 different types, many by mass production methods. But in mid-1940, when Churchill ordered *Combined Operations to be formed, the British had only a handful of Landing Craft, Assault (LCA), which carried an infantry platoon, and Landing Craft, Mechanized (LCM), designed to ferry ashore a single tank or vehicle; while in the USA only the *Higgins boat was in operational use.

To carry landing forces on early raids such as those on the *Lofoten Islands the British converted three cargo

Landing craft: UK and US landing ships and craft. Overall war production for use in all theatres

	1939–42	*1943*	*1944*	*1945 (six months)*	*Totals*
UK					
Landing Ships	–	3	–	21	24
Major Landing Craft	281	442	418	123	1,264
Minor Landing Craft	644	1,017	887	319	2,867
TOTALS	925	1,462	1,305	463	4,155
USA					
Landing Ships	62	344	862	305	1,573
Major Landing Craft	620	479	1,356	31	2,486
Minor Landing Craft	6,276	13,898	15,988	6,362	42,524
TOTALS	6,958	14,721	18,206	6,698	46,583

The above totals exclude merchant ships built or converted for employment as HQ ships, troopships, and so on. Over 2,500 of the landing ships and landing craft built in the USA and listed above were transferred to the UK under Lend-Lease and were part of the Royal Navy until the end of the war.

Source: Ellis, L. F., *Victory in the West*, Vol. I, p. 514 (London, 1962).

LSM **landing craft** approaching Iwo Jima, prior to the landings there on 19 February 1945. Mt Suribachi is in the background.

liners, designated Landing Ship Infantry (Large), or LSI(L), and some cross-Channel ferries, designated LSI(M)s. Later, specially designed landing ships like the Landing Ship, Stern-chute (LSS) and the Landing Ship, Gantry (LSG) were constructed. The Americans used purpose-built landing ships for amphibious warfare which they called Auxiliary Personnel Attack Ships (APA), which carried their assault troops, and Attack Cargo Ships (AKA), which carried their minor landing craft and supplies. They also built fourteen of the British-designed Landing Ship, Dock (LSD) a direct successor of the *Shinsu Maru*. The LSD flooded its hold to discharge landing craft or *amphibians from its stem.

With 'shore to shore' cross-Channel raids in mind the first British Landing Craft, Tank (LCT) was launched in November 1940. There were eight different marks of this versatile craft which varied in length between 34 m. (112 ft.) and 68 m. (225 ft.) The Mk4, designed specifically for the shallow-grade beaches used during the Normandy landings (see OVERLORD), carried six medium tanks. It was mass produced in the USA and became the Allies' basic vehicle-carrying landing craft.

The *Dakar expedition showed the need for an ocean-going tank landing ship that could keep convoy with the LSI(L)s. As a stopgap three shallow-draught Maracaibo oil tankers, which could each carry eighteen Churchill tanks, were converted into Landing Ships, Tank (LST). One was used at *Madagascar in May 1942, and all three were employed for the *North African campaign landings (TORCH) in November 1942, where it became obvious that many more were needed to put armour and troops speedily ashore in quantity. TORCH also revealed the inadequacy of the wooden Higgins boat and this soon began to be replaced with steel-built types like the Landing Craft Vehicle Personnel (LCVP).

To solve the problem of producing LSTs in quantity the Americans adopted the design of the first purpose-built British one which the Maracaibo conversions had inspired and this became the 91 m. (300 ft.) 2,286-ton LST Mk2. Over a thousand were built and they played a central role in all major amphibious landings in Europe, from the *Sicilian campaign (HUSKY) onwards. In the Pacific war they were first employed during landings on *Bougainville, but over the great distances involved they proved too slow to stay in convoy. Instead, an American version, the 62 m. (203 ft.), 12-knot Mk7, known as the Landing Ship, Medium (LSM), began to be built in 1944.

Another important US design was the prefabricated 48 m. (158 ft.) Landing Craft, Infantry (Large) which could accommodate 200 men for a 48-hour voyage. Its bow, unlike other landing craft, did not become a ramp; instead two gangways were lowered either side of it. Used for the first time during HUSKY, the LCI(L) was acquired under *Lend-Lease by the British and by the USSR. A smaller, wooden version, the LCG(S), was built by the British but it proved vulnerable under fire during OVERLORD in which 2,470 landing craft were employed in the assault phase alone.

Landing craft were converted for a variety of uses, from

hospital ships to those equipped to render emergency repairs. One was even converted into a miniature carrier for launching two spotter aircraft during HUSKY. But the most essential type for a successful assault became the close fire support craft: LCTs were converted into Landing Craft, *Flak (LCF), Landing Craft, Gun (Large) (LCG(L)), and the LCT(R) which fired banks of rockets (see ROCKET WEAPONS). The *Dieppe raid had revealed that these were a fundamental necessity after the lightly armed early versions of the Landing Craft, Support (LCS) had proved ineffectual against the German defences. They proved invaluable when first deployed during HUSKY and were first used in the Pacific during landings on *New Britain in December 1943. Rocket ships based on the LSM hull were also constructed, and by March 1945, when *Okinawa was invaded, these LSM(R), armed with 1,040 rockets which could be reloaded in 45 minutes, had attained the fire-power of some pre-war cruisers.

land mines, see MINE WARFARE.

land power. With one significant exception—the *atomic bomb—land power exerted the decisive influence in the Second World War that it had generally done throughout the ages. Ultimate victory was still fundamentally achieved, in spite of what some sailors and airmen might argue, through the infantryman (see INFANTRY WARFARE) with his rifle and bayonet, helped by other forms of land power such as *engineers, *tanks and *artillery, occupying the opposing side's territory.

The nature of land warfare during 1939–45 cannot be understood without considering the experience of the *First World War. The bloody deadlock of trench warfare cast a long shadow, and no nation, least of all the Germans, wished to repeat that experience. If general war in Europe was to occur again, and for much of the inter-war period most people fervently believed that it would not, it must be of short duration, and they hoped that that technological development of the late 19th century, the internal combustion engine, would help make this possible. By 1914 it had already been adopted for military use in the form of armoured and staff cars, and the lorry. By the autumn of 1918 the tank, developed initially by the British as a means of breaking through heavily fortified trench systems, was becoming a decisive weapon, its main limitations being mechanical unreliability and relative low speed. Even so its performance on 8 August 1918, the first day of the battle of Amiens, and the first major action in the Allied counter-offensive on the Western Front which would bring the war to an end three months later, caused Erich von Ludendorff (1865–1937), the German chief of staff, to note that it was 'the Black Day for the German Army'. The Germans, too, employed tanks during 1918, in small quantities, but they also developed an effective method of restoring mobility to a deadlocked battle field. This was through their storm troops who were trained to penetrate weak points in the defences and, bypassing strong opposition, which would be reduced by follow-up troops, make for the enemy's rear.

The move away from static warfare also affected artillery which between 1914 and 1918 was the dominant weapon on land. While the artillery barrages of 1939–45 seldom matched those of the Western Front in duration, the importance of this weapon was by no means reduced. Technical developments during the latter half of the First World War had made artillery much more responsive and accurate. Between the wars and during the Second World War itself the accent was on improving mobility and flexibility, especially when it came to providing intimate close support for the forward troops. Thus guns tended to be lighter and more manoeuvrable than their 1914–18 counterparts and were adapted for every theatre and form of war, from self-propelled guns to support armoured formations to guns which could be parachuted to operate with airborne troops. *Radio communications, too, enhanced the flexibility of artillery to bring down quick, accurate and highly destructive fire and was a vital, and sometimes revolutionary, ingredient in all forms of land warfare between 1939 and 1945.

The general reaction to the armistice in November 1918 was one of relief and the conviction that the slaughter of the past four years had been 'the war to end all war'. Most British professional soldiers considered it an aberration and yearned to return to what they termed 'real soldiering', defending the frontiers of empire. Yet there were a few who recognized the influence of technology on warfare during 1914–18 and were prepared to look to the future of warfare rather than merely turn the clock back. Initially at the forefront was Colonel J. F. C. Fuller, who had been chief of staff of the British Tank Corps in France. He argued that the tank had restored mobility to warfare and enabled the pendulum to swing back in favour of attack as the stronger form of war. Furthermore, the armoured fighting vehicle (AFV) had the potential to increase dramatically the pace of operations. He was quickly joined by Captain B. H. Liddell Hart, who had turned to journalism after being invalided from the British Army. His starting-point was the concept of the Expanding Torrent, which was a plea to commanders at all levels to position their reserves so that, by rapid deployment, they could best influence the sector in which the most success was being achieved. He went on to develop the idea of the Indirect Approach. This argued that the strategy of 1914–18 was fatally flawed in being based entirely on the defeat of the other side's army. A more effective and subtle approach was to paralyse the opposing command, control, and communications systems. This could be achieved by threatening from several directions and launching high-speed, rapier-like strikes at operational headquarters and communications centres. Mechanized forces were the means of achieving this, and they brought in their wake a new form of *mine warfare.

Some official note of the apostles of mechanized warfare was taken in the UK, sufficient to create an

Land power: Soviet tanks burning before the German front line during the German advance towards Stalingrad in the autumn of 1942.

experimental mechanized force during the latter half of the 1920s, but the concept of a fully mechanized army was still only a distant dream. None of the victorious nations of the First World War wished to spend more than the very minimum on defence. In Europe the crippling costs of the war meant that public spending was at a premium, while the USA, which also created a small experimental mechanized force at the end of the decade, had the money, but perceived no real threat to itself, having reverted to its traditional isolationist policy. The tank had been one of the weapons specifically banned to the defeated nations because it was seen as an aggressive weapon. For the victors, too, determined as they were to prevent a future war through the *League of Nations and disarmament agreements, large tank forces were politically unacceptable.

Military conservatism also baulked at mechanized forces. Some soldiers went so far as to claim that the tank was merely a product of trench warfare, which itself could never occur again. Others, especially cavalrymen, saw in the tank a threat to their beloved horses. Some, too, especially infantrymen and artillerymen, feared that their own arms would be taken over by it. Indeed, Fuller had begun to propose an 'all tank' army, with infantry merely being the occupiers of the territory that the tanks had overrun. It was at this point that Liddell Hart began to diverge from Fuller's views. He believed that infantry still had a significant role to play and began to look more in terms of what the Soviets later termed the Combined Arms Army. As far as the official view went, the tank's primary role remained support of the infantry in the attack.

The French who, given their horrific casualties during 1914–18, had most to fear from another major conflict in Europe, adopted an entirely different concept. In contrast with the pre-1914 view that the French soldier, with his singular *élan*, performed best in the attack, they took the doggedness of the *poilu* in defence at Verdun in 1916 as their guide. Germany, although militarily emasculated, remained the prime threat in French eyes. In order therefore to deter any future attack the decision was made in 1927 to construct a fortified belt, the *Maginot Line, along the Franco-German border.

The Germans, although denied modern weapons and restricted by the *Versailles settlement to a 100,000-man long service army, took a deep interest in the mechanization debate. In spite of their military disadvantages, they had two bonuses. Firstly, the disbandment of the old army meant that they could start afresh and develop new concepts. Also, through secret clauses in the 1922 Treaty of Rapallo, they were able to send officers to the USSR for training in modern warfare in exchange for giving the Soviets technological advice, so that by the time Hitler came to power in 1933 the groundwork for both the Luftwaffe and Germany's panzer arm had been completed. The Soviets also created, after considerable debate as to the shape it should take, a new Red Army. By the early 1930s, led by its chief of staff Marshal Tukhachevsky (1893–1937), the Red Army had developed the concept of Deep Thrust. Once the opposing side's defences had been penetrated, swiftly moving mechanized forces would create local encirclements and then, in conjunction with airborne and airmobile forces (see also AIRBORNE WARFARE), enter the pursuit phase. Emphasis was on all-arms mechanized forces. By the mid-1930s the Red Army had developed, in the form of mechanized corps, a larger AFV fleet than any other nation. Close behind was the German Army, which formed its first three panzer divisions in 1935.

It was Hitler himself who first coined the term 'lightning war' or *blitzkrieg. His own experience on the Western Front convinced him that if he had to resort to war to attain his ends it would have to be short. In the meantime the Wehrmacht had to be rapidly expanded, but the resultant demands on German industry were severe and Germany's armed forces could not have everything they wanted. Thus, while the navy was forced to concentrate on surface vessels at the expense of submarines and the Luftwaffe on large numbers of medium bombers as opposed to four-engined, long-range types, the army gave priority to armoured fighting vehicles. This meant that at the outbreak of war in 1939 the bulk of Germany's land forces consisted of infantry divisions dependent largely on their feet and horse-drawn transport (see ANIMALS).

The Western democracies, once they realized that war with Germany was possible, began to rearm. In the UK priority went to the Royal Navy and RAF. The army began to create two armoured divisions, one in Britain and the other in Egypt, but, unlike the Germans, concentrated primarily on motorizing transport. Thus, by 1939 the horse, apart from one cavalry division sent to Palestine, had been removed from the order of battle. France continued to rely on the Maginot Line as the bulwark of its defence, although in 1933 Colonel de *Gaulle wrote a book entitled *Towards a Professional Army.* He proposed that a 100,000-man career armoured army should be superimposed on the existing conscript force in order to act as a shield against surprise attack. Little notice was taken of the book in France where the concept of a regular army was anathema to the left-wing politicians in power. Besides which, a large armoured force implied offensive operations, to which the French military establishment was totally opposed. Mechanized reconnaissance formations were raised, but the tank remained primarily wedded to the infantry. One of the false lessons from the *Spanish Civil War was that the anti-tank gun (see ANTI-TANK WEAPONS) had outstripped the tank. This served to reinforce the belief that the tank could not be allowed to operate outside these two roles (infantry support and reconnaissance) unless the opposing side had first been broken by other means.

The Red Army also suffered, albeit indirectly, from the Spanish Civil War. Flying in the face of Tukhachevsky's doctrine, they had attempted to use tanks on their own, with disastrous results. Consequently, the lesson they drew was that tanks could only survive if used in close support of infantry. Stalin's purges were getting under way at this time and he used this failure as an excuse to liquidate Tukhachevsky and two-thirds of the Red Army's senior commanders (see USSR, 6(a)). The mechanized corps were broken up and tanks dispersed in small brigades among the infantry. Only the Far Eastern Army survived reasonably intact and Tukhachevsky's doctrine was proved effective during the clashes with the Japanese on the Outer Mongolian border with Manchukuo in August 1939 (see JAPANESE–SOVIET CAMPAIGNS). Little notice was taken of this experience in Moscow and the effect of the purges would be sorely felt during the 1939–40 *Finnish–Soviet war.

The German blitzkrieg in the *Polish campaign of September–October 1939, and in the fighting which culminated in the fall of *France in June 1940, stunned both the vanquished nations and the neutral Americans. Poland, of course, was in an impossible position; the fighting spirit of its troops could not compensate for lack of modern weapons and long and awkwardly shaped borders which committed its army to a largely linear defence. Even so, the campaign, short as it was, did produce some sobering lessons for the Germans. During the early days a certain hesitancy in the panzer divisions meant that higher panzer commanders needed to lead very much from the front and to make maximum use of the flexibility which radio communications, with which every tank was equipped, gave them. The German High Command revealed a nervousness over allowing the armour to get too far ahead of the marching infantry and putting itself in danger of being cut off. It was also realized that more panzer divisions than the six employed in Poland would be needed to overcome the western Allies.

The *phoney war, which witnessed a winter-long tussle between Hitler, who wanted to strike westwards as soon as possible, and his generals, who wanted to delay until their forces were properly organized, should have been beneficial to the Allies, but was not. True, the seven months' pause gave them time to mass more troops, but their strategy and posture were fundamentally flawed. The Allied Plan D, which called for a move of the left-wing armies into Belgium, was designed to counter a repeat of the 1914 von Schlieffen wheel. The original German plan, with its limited objective of providing a shield for the Ruhr and gaining sufficient territory in the Low Countries and northern France to wage sea and air war against the UK, had some similarities to the 1914 concept, but when amended to mounting the main thrust through the Ardennes, it exposed the right flank of the northern Allied armies (see FALL GELB). Besides which, the French and British had had no opportunity to view the River *Dyle positions because of Belgian neutrality. The Allied command, control, and communications structure was cumbersome and although they had more tanks, these were mostly dispersed along the front and could only be committed piecemeal.

Yet the Germans were not without their problems. High Command nervousness over the panzer formations getting too far ahead of the follow-up infantry and risking being cut off was even more apparent than in Poland, and resulted in the famous 'Halt Order' in front of *Dunkirk. Within the panzer divisions themselves, the wear and tear to crews and tanks during the dash to the Channel was also a cause of worry. Nevertheless, the Germans were so successful because, as in Poland, the pace of their operations was such as to numb the Allied High Command and to make it incapable of effective reaction, let alone wrest the initiative from the attacker (see also FRANCE, 6(a)).

In the immediate aftermath of the French campaign the decision was made to raise the existing three British armoured divisions to seven, manpower and availability of tanks being the only brakes at the time. The USA, too, reacted on similar lines, forming an Armored Force with a projected strength of no fewer than 50 divisions. What had also been especially impressive about the German performance was the close air support provided by the Luftwaffe to the panzer formations. Luftwaffe officers equipped with ground-to-air radio travelled with the Panzer Divisions (see also FLIVOS) and this meant that air support was highly responsive. Indeed, the Ju87 Stuka dive-bomber was used as aerial artillery (see also BOMBERS, 2). Before the war, jealous of the independent status of the RAF, the British air ministry accorded low priority to ground support. The machinery for employing air support on the battlefield did not exist and such air assets as were available were used, as they were in most other air forces, for reconnaissance, artillery spotting, and interdiction (attacks behind the battle area). The events of May 1940 forced a radical reconsideration and the result was the formation of teams to carry out the same role as the Luftwaffe ones with the panzer divisions.

The *Western Desert campaigns were where the British close air support system was fully developed. It was also undoubtedly the 'cleanest' land campaign of the war in terms of low civil population density, the openness of much of the terrain, and the way in which both sides observed the laws of war. The desert also, at least on the surface, gave the opportunity for armour, the dominant land weapon, to manoeuvre like fleets at sea just as the tank pioneers of the First World War had envisaged. *Rommel's handling of his armour proved to be more imaginative than that of the British. In defence he used it to draw the British tanks on to his anti-tank guns, especially the 88 mm. (3.4 in.), more powerful than any existing tank gun. The German formation of *ad hoc* all-arms battle groups (*Kampfgruppen*) in fluid tactical situations, something which had become doctrine common to all theatres in which the German Army was engaged, was also prominent. The British tended to be more rigid in their approach, but did recognize with experience that their armoured formations needed a better balance between tanks and infantry. Dominating all during the campaign in the desert was the question of *logistics. The rapid and long advances by both sides overstrained supply systems and eventually brought these advances to a halt. Attempts to use the numerous ports along the Libyan coastline in order to shorten the supply lines were often frustrated by the withdrawing side's destroying the port facilities. Eventually the tide turned in favour of the British, largely because the Axis sea routes across the Mediterranean were successfully interdicted. *Montgomery was able to take advantage of his material superiority at the second battle of *El Alamein, but was also careful to ensure that his pursuit of Rommel was logistically supportable. Some commentators have accused him of being over-cautious, but he was only too aware of the supply problems that his predecessors had experienced.

In Hitler's eyes the Western Desert campaigns were never more than a mere sideshow; he had only become involved in order to prop up his Italian ally. In contrast, from July 1940 until the end of 1941 the battle for the *Mediterranean was the only theatre in which British land power was actively engaged against the Axis. However, during much of this time British forces fought not just in Egypt and Libya, but also in the *East African, *Syrian, and *Balkan campaigns, as well as on *Crete, and in Iraq and Persia, and at times these additional commitments severely stretched resources.

From June 1941 the *German–Soviet war dominated land warfare in Europe, and, indeed, the war in the northern hemisphere. War on the Eastern Front, as earlier great captains—Gustavus Adolphus, Charles XII of Sweden, and Napoleon—had previously discovered, was much influenced by two factors, space and climate. Moscow, the USSR's capital, lay 965 km. (600 mi.) from the east Prussian border, but to the east again the Soviet Union extended for a further 16,000 km. (10,000 mi.). The weather is bounded by the spring thaw and the autumn rains, and the German planners recognized that the objectives of Moscow, Leningrad, and the Ukraine had to be gained before the rains arrived (see also METEOROLOGICAL INTELLIGENCE). As it happened, the spring thaw came late in 1941 and this, together with the foray into the Balkans—another spectacular demonstration of blitzkrieg—delayed the starting date. Nevertheless, the German armies had major initial advantages in that Stalin refused to place his forces on alert until it was too late and the Red Army was in the midst of a major reorganization as a result of its poor showing in the war against Finland.

The summer of 1941 proved the high-water mark of the German blitzkrieg machine, with the Panzer Divisions gaining spectacular successes. At the same time it also showed up the German Army's main weakness, namely that the bulk of it still consisted of infantrymen relying on their feet. This meant that at times the German armour was as much as two weeks' marching time ahead of the main mass. Inaccurate maps were also a problem and often the tanks were merely directed by the smoke and dust produced by Stuka attacks on Soviet positions. Hitler increasingly interfered with the day-to-day conduct of operations and his decision to remove the armour from Army Group Centre in July 1941 and pass it to the flanks meant that valuable weeks were lost in the drive on *Moscow. When the advance did resume the autumn rains slowed it and by the time the ground had hardened again with the onset of winter the Soviets had gained a valuable breathing-space. All this, and the strain placed on the logistical system by the autumn rains, left the Germans dangerously extended, both in front of Moscow and at Rostov, gateway to the Caucasus, and they lacked the clothing and other means to combat the severe Russian winter. The Soviets took advantage of this and their successful counter-attacks in front of Moscow and at Rostov marked the beginnings of the reorganized Red Army. This reformation was reinforced during the summer 1942 campaign in the south when instead of allowing themselves to be surrounded the Soviet *fronts* (army groups) withdrew in the face of the German thrusts.

*Stalingrad, besides being the turning-point of the war on the Eastern Front, was also a reminder that an ancient form of land warfare, the siege, was by no means obsolete. Indeed, the Germans had successfully besieged both Odessa and *Sevastapol on the Black Sea in 1941, but they failed against Leningrad, which held out for two and a half years before being relieved in January 1944. The British, too, had been besieged in *Tobruk during 1941, and in the latter part of the war Hitler declared several towns and cities *Festungen* (fortresses), which were expected to hold out to the last man (see BRESKENS POCKET and BRESLAU FESTUNG, for example). During the campaign in north-west Europe the French Channel and Atlantic ports were so designated, and St Nazaire and Dunkirk did not surrender until the end of the war.

Although the Red Army made significant territorial gains during the winter of 1942–3, it was not until after the abortive German attacks on the *Kursk salient in July 1943 that the Soviet counter-offensive really got under way. Stalin's strategy was to strike blows all along the front. As soon as one began to run out of momentum another attack would be mounted elsewhere, never allowing the Germans to reinforce threatened sectors from elsewhere on the front. The Soviet version of blitzkrieg drew on the German concept, but also on the Tukhachevsky doctrine in which major attacks were preceded by aggressive reconnaissance and accompanied by highly concentrated artillery barrages. Increasing emphasis was placed during the preparatory phase on *deception measures (*maskirovka*) in order to achieve surprise. Once a breakthrough was imminent mobile groups, consisting of armoured formations, would be deployed. Their object was to reach the depth of the defences, seizing key terrain and disrupting command and control in order to facilitate the advance of the main body. Where defences were especially strong, the Soviet forces would be echelonned, with the first echelon achieving the break-in of the first line and the second being passed through it to deal with the depth defences. By 1945 they had developed the offensive art to a high degree and gave a spectacular demonstration of it in their overrunning of the Japanese *Kwantung Army in Manchukuo in August 1945 (see Map 59).

The *North African campaign, in Tunisia during the winter of 1942–3 brought the US Army into the European war for the first time. Inexperience resulted in some early reverses (see KASSERINE PASS), but by the end of the campaign the necessary lessons had been learned. The closer terrain of Tunisia, compared with that of the Western Desert, and the realization that the same situation would be encountered when the continent of Europe was re-entered, caused the western Allies to reconsider their policy over armoured formations. There was a reduction in the number to be raised and more infantry were included in them.

Tunisia and Sicily (see SICILIAN CAMPAIGN) favoured the defender and Italy, with its numerous mountains and lateral river lines, did so even more (see ITALIAN CAMPAIGN). The Germans' defence was tenacious, as evidenced by the fighting at *Monte Cassino, and when they did withdraw it was always to another prepared defensive line. Not until the very end did the Allies enjoy the rapid advances of other theatres, but then Allied strategy dictated that the Italian campaign was never meant to be decisive, but was fought to tie down as much German fighting strength as possible to prevent it being deployed in north-west Europe.

Following the Normandy landings in June 1944 (see OVERLORD) German resistance was also bitter and this in spite of the overwhelming Allied air supremacy and naval gunfire support for which the Germans quickly gained a healthy respect. But their failure to prevent the Allies from consolidating their beachheads—brought about largely by Hitler's refusal to release the theatre panzer reserves in time and the successful interdiction campaign by Allied *air power and the French resistance prior to invasion—proved fatal for them. The panzer formations were committed piecemeal and found themselves having to assist the infantry in the line rather than being used for counter-strokes. To Hitler, voluntarily surrendering ground, even if it made sound military sense, was anathema, which meant that the armour could not be sufficiently concentrated to strike a decisive blow, and pressure on the Eastern Front made infantry reinforcements hard to come by. Thus the fighting in Normandy became a matter of wearing down the German strength, but it was not until the beginning of August that the Allies began to break out (see NORMANDY CAMPAIGN).

The Allied drive across France during August 1944 was spectacular, but was eventually halted by the logistic brake. Hitler's *Festung* policy meant that all supplies still had to come through Normandy and eventually the supply lines (see RED BALL EXPRESS, for example) became overstretched and the armies began to run out of fuel. Not until the *Scheldt Estuary was cleared and the port of Antwerp opened at the end of November were the Allied logistics put on a sound footing once more. It was the supply situation which in part provoked the argument between Montgomery and *Eisenhower over the narrow versus broad front strategy (see OVERLORD). On the surface the debate appeared to be between sound military sense and political expediency; but, even if Montgomery's gamble at Arnhem had been successful (see MARKET-GARDEN), it is questionable whether his proposed narrow thrust past the Ruhr and then on to Berlin would have succeeded. By early September the Germans were beginning to recover, as they demonstrated during the fight for Arnhem, and Montgomery's resultant exposed flanks would have been very vulnerable to counter-attack. As it was, the fighting during the autumn of 1944 was bitter and protracted. Hitler's own gamble in launching the *Ardennes campaign in December caught the Allies momentarily off-balance, but it could not conceivably do more than delay the inevitable by more than a few weeks, especially once the Red Army had begun its offensive across the Vistula in January 1945.

Although the German–Soviet war was the dominant example of the use of land power during the war—the navies of the opposing sides only played an insignificant part while their air forces had an important, but subsidiary, supporting role—mention must be made of *amphibious warfare as an essential adjunct of the western Allies' employment of land power. The Anglo-French experience in the Dardanelles in 1915 had convinced the major powers that large-scale landings on hostile shores were not an operation of war and at best only lip-service was paid to the subject during 1919–39. Indeed, it was only in July 1940 when the Germans were confronted with the realization that cross-Channel invasion (see SEALION) might be the only way to force a British surrender that serious attention began to be devoted to amphibious warfare. As it was, they recognized that air supremacy over the beaches was an essential prerequisite to success. Similarly, the British and Americans quickly appreciated that the Axis could not be defeated without re-entering the continent of Europe and this could only be done from the sea. Hence Anglo-US strategy in Europe and in the battle for the Mediterranean was geared from the outset to this end. The British, recognizing from past experience the necessity for air, sea, and land elements to work closely together, termed amphibious warfare *'Combined Operations', establishing a special directorate for it, whose head was for a time accorded similar status to that of the naval, army, and air force chiefs. While the Americans agitated for a cross-Channel invasion of France sooner rather than later, the British preferred a more indirect approach. The *Dieppe raid of August 1942 proved if nothing else that a successful landing would take time to prepare. In the meantime, the Allied expertise in mounting amphibious operations grew with the TORCH landings which began the North African campaign and the invasions of Sicily and Italy, and the experience gained in the Mediterranean helped to ensure the success of OVERLORD in June 1944.

The *Pacific war was influenced by amphibious operations to an even greater extent than Europe, for obvious reasons. By the end of 1943, however, the overall Allied demand for *landing craft and other specialized amphibious shipping was outstripping supply and strategic priorities had to be laid down. This meant that the Burma and Italian theatres suffered at the expense of the Pacific and north-west Europe, thus limiting the options open to the Allied commanders in each. But while OVERLORD represented the largest amphibious operation in history the projected Allied invasion of Japan, if it had had to be mounted, would have been just as crucial and significantly greater in scope.

At the outset of the war against Japan, the speed of the Japanese advance took the British and Americans by surprise, primarily because they had totally underestimated Japan's military capabilities, not the least of which was their expertise in amphibious warfare. *Hong Kong, the *Philippines, and Allied island possessions in the Pacific and South-East Asia were lost largely because they could not be given the necessary sea and air support in time, but in the *Malayan and *Burma campaigns, and in the fall of *Singapore, it was Japanese land power which proved to be decisive. The British and Dominion troops had carried out little jungle training and assumed that the Japanese would rely on the roads. Instead, though they did have some tanks (and in Malaya they made good use of bicycles), they constantly outflanked Allied positions by using the jungle, despite not having any experience of operating in those conditions. And their rate of advance was rapid because the Japanese soldier required much less to support him than his western counterpart and hence had a much smaller logistical tail.

By late summer 1942 the tide had begun to turn in the Pacific war thanks to the Allied naval successes at sea (see MIDWAY, for example) and the frustration of the Japanese landings in the *New Guinea campaign. The Allied troops, however, had to learn how to both defeat the Japanese and master the jungle. The former was partly achieved by developing the technique of supplying ground forces from the air (see CHINDITS); the latter was accomplished through the setting up of special jungle warfare training centres which helped to instil the necessary confidence. Allied air and maritime supremacy proved to be crucial in the Pacific, and the former was also true in Burma, especially in the context of resupply. By the end of 1943 the British, under *Slim's tutelage, had learned not to be panicked into precipitous withdrawals when their flanks had been turned—inevitable since it was impossible to create cohesive defensive lines in the jungle—but to stand and fight and encourage the Japanese to wear away their strength in attacks on specially fortified positions which were resupplied from the air and were, therefore, immune to the Japanese speciality of infiltration and then severance of supply lines. These 'boxes', as they came to be known, first proved their worth during the battle of the *Admin Box in the Arakan in February 1944, while air supply was invaluable at *Kohima and *Imphal in April.

Once the tide had turned in Burma and the Pacific the *Bushidō spirit of the Japanese soldier came to the fore. Many Japanese continued to fight on when their situation was hopeless and preferred to employ the **banzai* charge or commit suicide to surrender. This was why it took so long to capture *Mandalay and to subdue such islands as *Iwo Jima and *Okinawa, and it was the Allies' belief that, given this obduracy, the invasion of Japan would be very costly. This perception influenced the decision to use the atomic bomb, which brought about Japan's surrender before ground troops set foot on its mainland.

The Second World War was unique, as regards land warfare, in the variety of the terrain and climate in which it was waged. Mountain, jungle, and desert, intense heat and extreme cold all required specialist skills and these were often employed as much in a battle with the elements as against the other side. At times, especially in the North African desert and on the Russian steppes, armour was able to operate in the way that the pre-war theorists had envisaged, striking swiftly. Yet in other theatres and conditions, such as Italy during the winters of 1943–4 and 1944–5, the fighting became as static as the Western Front during 1915–17. On balance, though, the pace of operations was faster than it had been during 1914–18, not only because of wider use of the internal combustion engine, but also because of the great strides made in radio communications since 1918, which made the passage of information and hence reaction times very much more rapid.

In spite of the improvements in weaponry and ancillary military equipment, however, the Second World War produced no radical new lessons for land warfare. It mainly served to reinforce old and well-proven maxims. In particular the principle of war, co-operation, took on an even sharper aspect. No one weapon was predominant, but victory usually went to the side which best combined its infantry, armour, and artillery and enjoyed air superiority. In addition, an army might possess more technically sophisticated equipment, but this was of little advantage if it lacked the necessary additional logistic resources to support its operations. Finally, the war showed that land power could never be decisive on its own. It had to have the support of air and, at times, *sea power as well.

CHARLES MESSENGER

Keegan, J., *The Second World War* (London, 1989).
Messenger, C., *The Art of Blitzkrieg* (rev. edn., London, 1991).

Latin America at war. Apart from the battle of the *River Plate and the Caribbean, where 1,200,000 tons of shipping were lost to U-boats in 1942, the actual fighting took place elsewhere, and Japan's defeat at *Midway in June 1942, followed by Allied *North African campaign landings that November, marked the end of any serious military threat to the area. The Panama Canal, and Brazil's north-east (the 'hump' of land closest to Africa), which were the key elements in the defence of the *Western Hemisphere by the USA, were now safe from attack. Afterwards they became, Brazil especially, important transit points for men and equipment to other combat theatres (see TAKORADI AIR ROUTE, for example). For Latin Americans, losses of life and property were small, though by 1944 many were actively engaged in combat theatres. The Brazilian Expeditionary Force served ten months in the *Italian campaign, which included heavy fighting; the Mexican 201st Fighter Squadron saw action on Luzon in October 1944 (see PHILIPPINES CAMPAIGNS). In fact 250,000 Mexican nationals served in US forces, of whom 1,000 died, the most from any Latin American country.

Militarily, the actual course of war in Latin America fitted US war planning, which since 1938 had envisaged Germany, not Japan, as the main strategic threat (see also RAINBOW PLANS). In 1939, the US defence perimeter was extended to Brazil and northern South America but did not include the Southern Cone. The fall of *France in June 1940, coupled with the possibility that Britain's navy would be lost, prompted a series of military staff discussions with Latin American nations to secure bases and to develop joint defence plans. Even Japan's attack on *Pearl Harbor failed to shake this strategy: winning the war against Germany had priority.

Hemispheric defence was from the beginning an Atlantic defence, and this set the context for Latin America's war. The air bases and a few naval stations from Mexico to Peru saw little action in defence of the Panama Canal. By contrast, the arc of air and naval bases from the Caribbean to Brazil was used extensively in the anti-submarine campaign and to deny German access to food and *raw materials in the South Atlantic. This explains why Brazil, the headquarters of US Army forces South Atlantic, received $366,000,000 in military equipment, the lion's share (three-quarters) of all the *Lend-Lease aid sent to Latin American nations from late 1941 onwards. By contrast, Mexico received only $39,000,000 in Lend-Lease equipment, the bulk of which was used to bolster internal security, a contrast in which geography played a large part.

The war's impact also depended on the extent to which each nation was able to advance its own national interests. To be sure, this took place in the context of a lengthening US reach, starting with the Lima foreign ministers' conference of 1938, which launched the principle of collective security and laid the groundwork for subsequent agreements on hemispheric defence (see PANAMA, RIO, and HAVANA CONFERENCES). Later collective security was broadened to include not only arms, but also the financing of capital goods and commodity purchases, and military training missions and cultural exchange. By 1943, as the military threat waned, these became more important along with the deepening impact of US business methods and popular culture among Latin American élites and middle classes.

For the USA, Latin America was the early proving-ground for its emergence as a new superpower, seeking security and influence through a modern alliance system rather than the traditional, and failed, policies of intervention in the Caribbean Basin. For Latin American nations, the war marked the emergence of Brazil, Mexico, and Venezuela as rising regional powers, the leaders in terms of wealth, coherence, and prestige. By contrast, Argentina and to a much lesser extent Chile (because it was far from any military theatre) suffered a relative decline. It is these political and economic changes that are perhaps the most interesting aspect of the war in Latin America. Furthermore, the war affected the ways urban labour and the middle classes were being incorporated into politics and the state, in effect accelerating social changes under way for at least a generation.

Brazil bargained hard and successfully for arms and industrial equipment, including the famous Volta Redonda steel works and the beginnings of an oil industry, in return for the air bases Washington required. By 1942, it had priorities to receive equipment, both military and civilian, that hard-pressed US planners were loath to grant, save for the country's political and strategic importance. President Getúlio Vargas had already played a German card (arms and barter trade) with skill to secure advantages from Washington. In 1941 he moved to the status of a close wartime ally despite almost total dependence on the US for energy, spare parts, and markets. Thanks to US arms, Brazil achieved military superiority over its rival Argentina and sent a fighting force abroad. Such was Brazil's prestige that Roosevelt sought a permanent seat for it on the new United Nations Security Council, a move the USSR and UK blocked, to Canada's and France's relief, in 1945 at the inaugural *San Francisco conference. (Brazil did receive the first non-permanent seat.) Meanwhile, labour was embraced by the strong state apparatus; the foreign debt was written off; and Brazil's emergence as an economic power in a special relationship with the USA had begun.

As long as the Royal Navy stayed intact, Argentina held only minor strategic status on the southern shipping routes but this facilitated its following an independent policy. Self-sufficient in petroleum, and with British markets for its beef also intact, Argentina refused to join the US-sponsored Petroleum Pool, and other commodity supply and purchasing agreements. (The US-sponsored Petroleum Pool supplied gasoline, fuel oil, and derivatives to all of Latin America except Argentina, which adhered to a policy of resources nationalism and refused to join. The Pool used rationing and price controls to allocate supplies and protect the area against economic collapse which might result from disruption by enemy action and the competing requirements of the Allied war effort.) Much to Washington's annoyance, it pursued instead a traditional rivalry with the US; retained a military purchasing mission in Germany until 1944; and stayed neutral until March 1945. Some of the officer corps was pro-Nazi, but public opinion was not. If anything, the military looked to settle old scores with Chile or with the UK over the Falklands/Malvinas Islands. For its part, the US misread Argentine neutrality and blundered into boycott and confrontation, which in turn eased the rise of Juan Perón (1895–1974) and his wife Eva (1919–52), populists and nationalists who in 1945 brought the working class into power with them under redistributive economic policies that, as it happened, could not long be sustained. Wartime earnings were squandered on consumption and the purchase of the decrepit British-owned railways.

Mexico predicated its wartime alliance upon the settling of private economic claims, notably by the British and American oil companies whose fields and refineries had been expropriated at the instigation of Mexican oil workers in 1938. Eager to comply, Washington provided loans and credits in the November 1941 settlement, which in turn rapidly cleared the way for military co-operation. (With no strategic interests at stake, the UK did not settle until after the war.) Staff talks had in fact begun in 1940, but Mexico co-operated only passively until the settlement. Although Mexico never became the close ally that Canada did in 1940—there was no *Permanent Joint Board on Defense with Mexico, although the USA wanted one—basing and transit rights were granted. The Export-Import Bank facilitated the purchase of equipment for Mexico's steel industry and foreign debts stretching back to the *porfiriato* (the presidency of Porfirio Díaz at the turn of the century) were paid off. Industrialization through import substitution was reinforced, as were ties between the two private sectors. The revolution was said to have matured. Meanwhile and not unrelated to these developments, tough laws designed to root out Nazi sympathizers were used by the state to curb dissent and stayed on the books for years.

For its part Venezuela emerged from the war with a flourishing petroleum industry and the principle of sharing royalties 50–50 with the foreign oil companies, something which the young oil minister, Juan Pablo Pérez Alfonzo (who became the father of OPEC—the Organization of Petroleum Exporting Countries), obtained just after the war in December 1945. Ironically, the first enabling legislation had been drawn up by US advisers in 1943 when oil prices were relatively low. (Iran followed suit in 1949 and by the mid-1950s all the world's oil exporting countries had adopted Venezuela's 50–50 tax initiative.) By then the road to a petroleum-based economy and its problems was well established. However, oil wealth also facilitated the emergence of Acción Democrática, the reformist party under Rómulo Betancourt, and labour's allegiance to democratic pluralism.

If, in hindsight, Venezuelan profit-sharing was a milestone in Third World resource management and control, pro-Nazi political and economic movements, labelled collectively as the *fifth column and much discussed at the time, have declined in historical importance. Fascist tendencies appealing to the middle classes and the right did appear in places: the Movimiento Nacionalista Revolucionário under Victór Paz Estenssoro in Bolivia, the nationalist government of Arnulfo Arias in Panama, the Francoist *sinarquistas* in Mexico, the statist Grupo de Oficiales Unidos (to which Perón belonged) in Argentina. But APRA, the more established radical party in Peru, developed a more favourable view of the USA, which for its part saw Nazi manipulation behind all of these movements. German agents were few and easily rounded up; populations of German descent, as in southern Brazil and Chile, were easily monitored or cowed.

In any case, the structures of collective regional security under US leadership, which culminated in the Act of *Chapultepec in March 1945, were not fertile ground for fascist movements, especially after *Stalingrad. The rise of Soviet power and the great wartime alliance gave space to communist parties in Latin America, and they presented what at that time still seemed an alternative way to incorporate labour and the middle classes in a workable economic system. For the US, there was not much of a leap from leading the alliance against *fascism to post-war anti-*communism. But it can now be seen that nationalism and social change under capitalism, broadly defined, were more important than fascism or communism in Latin America during the Second World War. JOHN D. WIRTH

Di Tella, G., and Watt. D. C. (eds.), *Argentina Between the Great Powers, 1939–46* (Oxford, 1989).
Humphreys, R. A., *Latin America and the Second World War*, Vol. 1 1939–1942, Vol. 2 1942–1945 (London, 1981–2).
McCann, F. D., *The Brazilian Alliance, 1937–1945* (Princeton, 1973).
Stetson, C., and Fairchild, B., *The Framework of Hemisphere Defense The U.S. Army in World War II, The Western Hemisphere*, Vol. 1 (Washington, DC, 1960).

Lattre de Tassigny, General Jean-Marie de (1889–1952), French Army officer who commanded the 14th Division which fought well at Rethel during the fighting which preceded the fall of *France in June 1940. As a maj-general, then a lt-general, he served the *Vichy French government, commanding French troops in Tunisia between September 1941 and September 1942. However, he was imprisoned by the Vichy government when he resisted the German occupation of Vichy France in November 1942, though he was in fact simply carrying out the secret orders of the C-in-C French forces, Admiral *Darlan. A charge of treason was dropped, but he was given a prison sentence of ten years for abandoning his post. At the fourth attempt he escaped and was flown, with *SOE help, to the UK where he joined de *Gaulle's Free French forces. In December 1943 he flew to North Africa, was promoted general, and was given command of what was to become Armée B. His forces captured *Elba in June and some became part of the *French Expeditionary Corps. This force fought with the Allies in the *Italian campaign until July 1944 before being returned to de Lattre for the *French Riviera landings in August 1944 in which Armée B took a leading role.

In September Armée B was renamed the First French Army and de Lattre remained its commander in the fighting which followed (see COLMAR POCKET, RHINE CROSSINGS, and GERMANY, BATTLE FOR). During these months de Lattre's army absorbed about 137,000 members of the French Forces of the Interior (see FFI) and these gradually replaced some of his North African troops which were repatriated. In May 1945 he signed Germany's surrender on behalf of France but was replaced by *Koenig as C-in-C French Army of Occupation in Germany by de Gaulle that August. He was posthumously promoted a Marshal of France.

Clayton, A., *Three Marshals of France* (London, 1992).

Latvia (capital Riga), the middle one of the three Baltic States, started the Second World War as an independent republic and ended it as an involuntary component of the USSR.

In 1939, Latvia was ruled by the nationalist dictatorship of the Peasant Party under K. Ulmanlis. It was a member of the *League of Nations whose independence had been established by a treaty signed with the USSR in August 1920, and was confirmed by a Treaty of Guarantee signed on 9 March 1927. But as in Estonia, the regime was motivated by fears of Soviet agitation and of the influence of dispossessed German landowners and the *Nazi–Soviet Pact of August 1939 secretly assigned Latvia to the Soviet sphere of influence. As a result, Moscow demanded the conclusion of a Treaty of Friendship and Co-operation, which permitted the stationing of Soviet troops on Latvian territory. This treaty, signed on 5 October 1939, was activated in June 1940. The entry of the Red Army was soon followed by subversive agitation against the Latvian government; by widespread killings and arrests; by fraudulent elections conducted by the Soviet security organs (see NKVD); and by the declaration of a Latvian SSR that was formally admitted to the USSR on 5 August 1940. This first Soviet occupation, from June 1940 to July 1941, was a time of mass terror, when all of Latvia's native institutions were destroyed. The German population was deported to Germany.

The German occupation, which lasted from July 1941 to April 1945 and which followed the German invasion of the USSR (see BARBAROSSA), saw Latvia incorporated into the Reich Commissariat *Ostland. Latvian police and military units were formed under German command, and served on the Eastern Front. A Latvian Waffen-*SS Division was recruited, the large Jewish community was concentrated, especially in the Riga *ghetto, and killed.

The second Soviet occupation took place in stages in

1944–5 because the Wehrmacht's Army Group North was cut off in the *Courland peninsula and did not surrender until 8 May 1945. It was accompanied by a renewed wave of terror, and by forced collectivization of the peasantry. Latvia's population was much diminished by the *deportations and repressions, and by the loss of the German and Jewish elements. It was replenished by a post-war influx of Russians that soon stood to become an absolute majority. NORMAN DAVIES

Laval, Pierre (1883–1945), *Vichy French politician who initiated and pursued the policy of *collaboration with the Germans.

A working-class lawyer, Laval became the Socialist Party's youngest deputy in 1914. He later became an 'independent socialist', drifted to the right politically, and during the 1930s formed three administrations. At this time, he was no supporter of Hitler and the abortive Hoare–Laval Plan (December 1935), which was designed to give Mussolini much of what he wanted in Abyssinia, was part of his effort to align France with Fascist Italy to contain German expansionism. When the British repudiated it he resigned, and remained in the political wilderness until the war he had bitterly opposed brought him back into government on 25 June 1940 as minister of state and vice-premier in *Pétain's government.

Laval now became, as he put it, 'the official receiver for our bankrupt country'. He ushered in the new constitution that made Pétain head of state with dictatorial powers, and was named his official successor. He immediately tried to establish a Franco-German accord, and by arranging for Pétain to meet Hitler at Montoire in October 1940 he ensured that Pétain would rubber-stamp his policy of collaboration, which he expected to bring concessions from the Germans. However, none was forthcoming and in December 1940 Pétain manoeuvred him into resigning.

When neither of his successors proved competent negotiators with the Germans, and having recovered from a wound inflicted in Paris by a would-be assassin the previous August, Laval was recalled by Pétain in April 1942 to head the Vichy government. He now wielded unprecedented power for he was also given the ministries of foreign affairs, interior, and information. In June 1942 he broadcast an appeal for Frenchmen to work in Germany (see also FRANCE, 2) and then stated that, to avoid *communism establishing itself everywhere, 'I wish for a German victory.' He failed to prevent the Germans from taking over unoccupied France after the Allied *North African campaign landings in November 1942—which resulted in Pétain's being forced to give him the power to issue decrees and laws—but he still persisted in his policy of trying to extract concessions through collaboration long after the Germans had lost interest, hinting that France might declare war on the Allies and suggesting the formation of a French force to reconquer North Africa. By then Franco-German relations had deteriorated into mutual suspicion and recrimination. Laval, always supremely confident, remained certain that his policy would succeed, but the more he tried to come to a working arrangement with the Germans the more they demanded, and the more his countrymen came to hate and despise him for his collaboration. His negotiations during 1943 to hand over foreign Jews living in France, and to provide French workers for Germany, only increased this hatred—though it has been said in his favour that by sacrificing some he saved a larger number. Pétain, who loathed him, tried twice more to remove him.

By early 1944 the Germans were dictating the composition of the Vichy government, and, sandwiched between firm Nazi supporters such as Marcel *Déat on the one hand and the ever-increasing power of the resistance on the other, Laval saw his policy collapsing about him. In August 1944, after he had failed to resurrect the Third Republic, he was ordered by the Germans to Belfort, on the Franco-German border, and then to Sigmaringen in southern Germany, with his government.

In May 1945 a German aircraft flew him to Barcelona where he was told war criminals were not wanted. 'But I am a peace criminal,' he protested. In July he flew to Austria but was handed over to the French who sentenced him to death after what has been described as 'a disgracefully unfair trial' (P. Calvocoressi *et al.*, *Total War*, London, 1989, p. 329). Minutes before his execution he took cyanide but survived it to face the firing squad. See also FRANCE, 3(c).

Kupferman, F., *Laval* (Paris, 1987).
Warner, G., *Pierre Laval and the Eclipse of France* (London, 1968).

Layforce. British Commando force commanded by Lt-Colonel Robert Laycock which comprised Nos. 7, 8, and 11 (Scottish) Commandos, Nos. 50 and 52 Middle East Commandos, and the *Special Boat Section. It was formed in the Middle East in February 1941. For security reasons 7, 8, and 11 were renamed A, B, and C Battalions, and 50 and 52 became D Battalion. A and D Battalions were captured in *Crete; four troops of B joined the *Tobruk garrison; and C fought in the *Syrian campaign. Layforce was disbanded in August 1941 and its remnants became No. 3 Troop of the newly formed *Middle East Commando under Laycock.

League of Nations, founded in 1919 as part of the *Versailles settlement at the end of the *First World War, was intended to be a world-wide peacekeeping organization. Its principal founder was Woodrow Wilson (1856–1924), president of the USA; but, for reasons primarily of American internal politics, the US Senate did not ratify the treaty in which the League's covenant was first set out, and the USA was never a member. Germany did not join until 1926, and left in 1934—an early indication by Hitler that he did not agree with world peace; and not till after Germany left did the USSR join. The League therefore lacked the membership of several important world powers, and never exercised the full influence envisaged for it by its founders.

Moreover Mussolini twice defied it—over the comparatively trumpery Corfu incident of 1923, and over his invasion of Abyssinia in 1935; and Japan defied it in Manchuria in 1931 (see MANCHUKUO). Although its members all undertook, in article 10 of its covenant, 'to respect and preserve as against external aggression the territorial integrity and existing political independence of all Members', this did not stop many of them from embarking on further pacts of mutual assistance, limited to particular areas; which in turn reflected badly on the good faith of their adherence to article 10. Article 16 provided for immediate economic and social, and potential military, sanctions against any member that committed any act of aggression; but when it came to the point, in Manchuria and in Abyssinia, little economic or social and no military action was taken. The League was, in short, as was said of Prohibition in the USA, 'an experiment, noble in motive' that turned out too ideal for the real world.

It provided a useful forum in the 1920s for international debates and for attempts to arrive at a general understanding about disarmament; and various subsidiary organs, such as the (still existing) *International Labour Organization, were of substantial use in promoting welfare over much of the world's territory. The colonial possessions of Germany and Turkey, both defeated in the First World War, were parcelled out in League of Nations mandates among the victorious powers; some of these became independent, as had been Wilson's intention, in the 1930s (for example Iraq), while others (like Palestine) were still under the control of their mandatory power in 1939 (see Maps D and E). League inspections of them had ceased by that date.

The last political act of the League was to expel the USSR, in December 1939, in response to the Soviet invasion of Finland (see FINNISH–SOVIET WAR). Thereafter the League entered a state of suspended animation and was replaced in 1945 by the United Nations, with a different constitution and a more comprehensive membership (see SAN FRANCISCO CONFERENCE). M. R. D. FOOT

Walters, F. P., *A History of the League of Nations*, 2 vols. (Oxford, 1952).

Leahy, Admiral William D. (1875–1959), US Navy officer who, during the *First World War, struck up a lifelong friendship with Roosevelt, the then assistant secretary of the navy. Promoted rear-admiral in 1927, Leahy became chief of Naval Operations in 1937, at that time the US Navy's highest post, before retiring in 1939 to become governor of Puerto Rico. In 1941 he became Roosevelt's ambassador to *Vichy in France and had the difficult and controversial task of trying to minimize the Vichy government's *collaboration with Germany.

He was recalled in April 1942 and in July 1942 was appointed the president's chief of staff and chairman of the US *Joint Chiefs of Staff. In these capacities he became one of Roosevelt's closest advisers and accompanied him to all the major Allied conferences (see GRAND ALLIANCE). He proved to be a skilled bureaucrat, a realist, and a moderating influence. Along with Roosevelt he disliked de *Gaulle, but he also distrusted the president's policy of concessions to the USSR. After Roosevelt died, Leahy was retained by *Truman but wielded less influence with him. He became the first fleet admiral in 1944 and retired in 1949.

Leahy, W. D., *I was There* (New York, 1950).

lease-lend, see LEND-LEASE.

Lebanon, French mandate whose governor sided with the *Vichy government after the fall of *France in June 1940. The country was conquered by British and Free French forces in July 1941 during the *Syrian campaign, the mandate was terminated, and Lebanon's future independence was announced by the Free French authorities. But it was only finally achieved in 1946 after wartime public disturbances and the threat of armed intervention by the British on the side of the nationalists. Lebanon was a founding member of the *Arab League.

Lebensborn, a neologism meaning 'fountain of life', was a Nazi programme organized by *Himmler to increase the birthrate of 'racially sound' babies.

The Lebensborn Registered Society was formed in December 1935 with the objective of caring for the wives, fiancées, and girlfriends of members of the *SS and the police, and special maternity homes were established for this purpose in Germany, and later in certain occupied countries. To encourage a higher birthrate publicity for contraception was forbidden in Germany and abortion was severely punished. Illegitimacy was no longer stigmatized and unmarried mothers were given all the rights of married women. Most of the girls using the homes belonged to the Bund deutscher Mädel (League of German Girls), the female part of the *Hitler Youth organization. They were taught that motherhood was the highest form of service to the Third Reich and were encouraged to become pregnant by SS men who, married or not, were relieved of any responsibility for their progeny. The total number of births in Lebensborn homes is believed to be about 12,000. Some mothers chose to keep their babies, but most were adopted by 'racially sound' parents. Those born physically or mentally handicapped were sent to a special institution where they did not survive (see EUTHANASIA PROGRAMME).

Another aspect of Lebensborn was the importation of Aryan-looking *children from occupied countries who were then placed by the society with German families or in special schools. This process of acquiring 'racially valuable' children started as early as 1940 when it was agreed with Himmler to deal with those aged under six, though later, in certain cases, they were accepted to the age of twelve. They were initially taken to transit camps where they were given German names and identity papers, and taught the rudiments of the language and of *Nazi ideology. This usually took six months, and they were then placed with suitable families. Most came from families whose parents had been deported or liquidated but often they were just picked up in the street by the *Sipo, SS personnel who were trained to assess likely candidates, or by women who belonged to the Nazi Welfare Association (Nationalsozialistische Volkswohlfahrt, or NSV) which dealt with children too old to be handled by the Lebensborn organization. At the *Nuremberg trials it was revealed that the Wehrmacht had been involved in kidnapping 40,000–50,000 children during the *German–Soviet war and that another 50,000 were taken from Ruthenia. About 200,000 Polish children, including thousands from the *Zamość region, were thought to be 'racially useful' and were sent to Germany for adoption, and many Yugoslav children suffered the same fate. Of those abducted, 80% never returned.

Henry, C., and Hillel, M., *Children of the SS* (London, 1976).

Lebensraum (living space), term used by the Nazis as a slogan for German expansionism, particularly eastwards. Originally conceived by *Hess, when he and Hitler were in prison together in 1924, it was propounded by Hitler at a secret meeting with *Blomberg, *Neurath, and his three service chiefs which took place in November 1937. Hitler reiterated what had always been his policy: the security and expansion of the German people. He rejected colonies as a method of expansion and said that the necessary living room had to be found in Europe, and that, contrary to his public pronouncements, force was going to have to be used to obtain it as soon as the right opportunity occurred.

Also present was Hitler's military adjutant, Colonel Friedrich Hossbach, who, against Hitler's orders, took notes of what Hitler said and later turned them into a document which became known as the Hossbach Memorandum. This meeting was revealed to the world at the *Nuremberg trials and the memorandum is one of the most important documentary pieces of evidence for Hitler's determination to wage war. See also GERMANY, 1.

Lebrun, Albert (1871–1950), French politician of the Republican left who was first elected president in 1932 and was the last president of the Third Republic. He was re-elected in 1939, appointed Marshal *Pétain prime minister in June 1940 when Paul *Reynaud resigned, but resigned himself on 11 July 1940 and was replaced by Pétain, who took the title not of *Président* but of *Chef d'Etat*.

Leclerc, Lt-General Philippe (1902–47), pseudonym of a French Army officer, Captain Viscount Philippe de Hauteclocque, who joined de *Gaulle and the Free French in the UK after the fall of *France in June 1940. De Gaulle promoted him major and sent him to rally colonies in French West Africa and French Equatorial Africa to the Free French, and in August 1940 he organized bloodless coups in the French Cameroons and Middle Congo, and later led French colonial troops (see TIRAILLEURS) in the *Gabon campaign. Based at Fort Lamy in Chad, he was promoted colonel, then brigadier-general (August 1941) while directing the *Fezzan campaigns which culminated in his men fighting their way north to join the British and Commonwealth Eighth Army outside Tripoli in January 1943.

After fighting successfully in southern Tunisia during the *North African campaign, Leclerc was promoted maj-general in August 1943 and his forces became the nucleus of the 2nd French Armoured Division (2ème Division Blindée). This new formation also included officers and men from the *Vichy French forces in French North Africa and it was only Leclerc's strength of character that moulded such a disparate force into a first-class fighting unit.

After his division landed in France on 29 July 1944 it fought in the *Normandy campaign and the battle for *Germany with *Patton's Third US Army. It captured Le Mans and Alençon, and was, on *Eisenhower's orders, the first Allied formation to enter Paris (see also PARIS RISING) where Leclerc took the surrender of the German garrison. He then helped capture Strasbourg, was promoted lt-general, and fought with the Third Army all the way to *Berchtesgaden. In May 1945 de Gaulle sent him to the Far East as C-in-C French Forces and it was he who signed the Japanese surrender on behalf of the French nation. He died in a plane crash in North Africa and was posthumously made a Marshal of France in 1952.

Clayton, A., *Three Marshals of France* (London, 1992).

Ledo Road, 770 km. (478 mi.) long India–China supply road and oil pipeline built through the mountainous area of northern Burma. It ran from Ledo (situated in India near the northern border with Burma) to *Myitkyina in northern Burma, then Bhamo, and finally to Muse where it connected with the *Burma Road that had been built to Kunming in China. It took 17,000 Allied *engineers and $148 million to build it, and was one of the major engineering feats of the war. Construction started in December 1942 at the insistence of the USA, which was eager to support *Chiang Kai-shek's forces fighting the Japanese in China (see CHINA INCIDENT), whose supplies were by then restricted to the tonnage being flown in by the *Hump air route. Lt-General *Stilwell's Northern Combat Area Command offensive between October 1943 and August 1944 cleared the Japanese from northern Burma (see BURMA CAMPAIGN), but it soon became apparent that the road would not be ready in time to be of much strategic use. It was completed in January 1945 when its name was changed by Chiang Kai-shek to the Stilwell Road. See also LOGISTICS.

Leeb, Field Marshal Wilhelm, Ritter von (1876–1956), anti-Nazi German officer who fought with great bravery during the *First World War. An authority on defensive

Lt-General **Leclerc**, commander of the 2nd French armoured division which fought with Patton's Third US Army in north-west Europe.

warfare, he rose quickly in rank and by 1934 was a lt-general. Hitler found him 'an incorrigible anti-Nazi' and he was one of sixteen high-ranking German army officers forced into retirement in January 1938.

However, during the Czechoslovakian crisis of August 1938 (see ORIGINS OF THE WAR) Leeb, who had been promoted general on retirement, was recalled and given command of Twelfth Army, part of which occupied the Sudetenland after the *Munich agreement. He then went back into retirement, but was again recalled in September 1939, this time to command Army Group C which faced the *Maginot Line from Luxembourg southwards.

From the time Hitler first proposed a western offensive in the autumn of 1939 (see FALL GELB) Leeb bitterly opposed it. He argued that if the Germans were to violate Belgium's neutrality again every civilized country would turn against them. He therefore supported *Halder's proposed coup against Hitler, and tried to persuade the Cs-in-C of the other two army groups to join in resigning with him, but without success.

When FALL GELB was finally launched on 10 May 1940, Leeb's defeat of the French in Alsace-Lorraine brought him promotion to field marshal that July. Army Group C became Army Group North for the German invasion of the USSR in June 1941 (see BARBAROSSA) and despite slow progress on occasions—Leeb was unaccustomed to handling panzer formations—by September he was close to capturing *Leningrad. But then Hitler ordered him to starve it into surrender instead, 'one of the greatest tactical blunders of the war' (S. Mitcham, *Hitler's Field Marshals and Their Battles*, London, 1988, p. 141). In January 1942, after the Red Army had launched a large counter-offensive against his Army Group (see GERMAN–SOVIET WAR, 3) Leeb requested permission to withdraw from the Leningrad area in order to shorten his lines of communication and establish a coherent defensive line. Hitler refused and Leeb asked to be relieved. This was granted, and he was never re-employed. In October 1948 he was sentenced by an Allied military court to three years' imprisonment for minor war crimes. Ritter is a German hereditary knighthood.

Leese, General Sir Oliver (1894–1978), British Army officer who commanded 30th Corps in the British and Commonwealth Eighth Army from August 1942 to December 1943, taking part in the *Western Desert, *North African, *Sicilian, and *Italian campaigns. *Montgomery, whom Leese succeeded as commander of the Eighth Army in December 1943, thought him first class and Leese's successes in Italy—which included breaking through the *Gustav Line at *Monte Cassino and later breaching the *Gothic Line—bore out this judgement. In November 1944 Leese took over Eleventh Army Group, which controlled the British and Commonwealth forces fighting in the *Burma campaign, and became *Mountbatten's C-in-C Allied Land Forces South-East Asia. He was critical of Mountbatten's prosecution of the campaign and was dismissed, perhaps unjustly, in July 1945 over the posting of *Slim away from Fourteenth Army. He was knighted in 1943.

Ryder, R., *Oliver Leese* (London, 1987).

Leigh Light, see SEARCHLIGHTS.

Leigh-Mallory, Air Marshal Sir Trafford (1892–1944), British airman who was C-in-C of the Allied Expeditionary Air Force during the Normandy landings in June 1944 (see OVERLORD).

After serving in the British Army and then the Royal Flying Corps during the *First World War, Leigh-Mallory was commissioned into the newly formed RAF in 1919. By 1938 he was an air vice-marshal commanding No. 12 Fighter Group which, during the battle of *Britain, defended the Midlands. When requested, it supported *Park's No. 11 Fighter Group defending south-east England. But Leigh-Mallory's methods, in particular his support for 'Big Wing' tactics (see FIGHTERS, 2), were controversial and this led to increasing differences between Leigh-Mallory on the one hand and Park and *Dowding, C-in-C Fighter Command, on the other. These continued after Dowding was replaced in November 1940 and to end them Park was replaced by Leigh-Mallory in December 1940; and Leigh-Mallory then pushed for 'Big Wing' offensive operations over France, which, with hindsight, were of doubtful value (see RHUBARBS and CIRCUSES).

In July 1942 Leigh-Mallory was promoted acting air marshal and in August commanded the air operation covering the *Dieppe raid. In November 1942 he was appointed C-in-C Fighter Command and the following December was confirmed as C-in-C Allied Expeditionary Air Force for the Normandy landings with the rank of air chief marshal, a post in which he unhappily found himself sandwiched between *Tedder on the one hand and *Coningham on the other. His job of co-ordinating the tactical air forces was finished by October 1944, and the following month, while flying to take up a new appointment as AOC-in-C *South-East Asia Command, his aircraft crashed and he was killed. He was knighted in 1943.

LeMay, Maj-General Curtis E. (1906–90), the US Army's youngest two-star general who took a leading part in the *strategic air offensive against Japan and was one of the war's most innovative air tacticians (see also BOMBERS, 2).

LeMay joined the US Army Air Corps in 1928 and by October 1942 was a colonel commanding a bomber group in the UK. Besides being a strict disciplinarian, he was a tactician who thrived on new ideas (see PATTERN BOMBING, for example). He was promoted brigadier-general in September 1943 and maj-general before he took command of the Twentieth USAAF's 20th Bomber Command in the *China–Burma–India theatre in August 1944. The 20th Bomber Command flew supplies from India into China, over the *Hump air route, and bombed Japan with the new B29 Superfortresses that were based in India and staged through Chinese airfields.

In January 1945 LeMay took command of Twentieth USAAF's 21st Bomber Command which mounted raids on Japan from its base on the Mariana Islands. LeMay changed their tactics from high-level precision attacks with high explosive bombs to low-level incendiary raids in specially-lightened B29s. This important tactical innovation had a devastating effect and on the night of 9/10 March, 25% of Tokyo was destroyed in a *firestorm. In July 1945 LeMay was given command of Twentieth USAAF and in August became chief of staff to *Spaatz when the latter formed the USAAF's Strategic Air Forces in the Pacific.

Lemay, C., and Kantor, M., *Mission with LeMay* (New York, 1965).

Lend-Lease, or lease-lend, was the programme by which the USA provided the bulk of its aid to nations fighting Germany, Italy, and, eventually, Japan during the Second World War. In lieu of credits and loans, the US Government supplied to over 38 nations whatever goods were certified by President Roosevelt as 'in the interest of national defense'. The only legal limitations were his own judgement, and the need for Congressional appropriations to pay for the goods. Repayment was to be as 'the President deems satisfactory', an extraordinarily broad grant of authority (both quotations from the text of the legislation).

The need for a scheme like Lend-Lease lay in the experience of the USA in the aftermath of the *First World War. Whatever the facts, Americans perceived European actions after that conflict as a rejection of US leadership. That frustration, combined with the international crisis of the great depression, made Americans reluctant to get involved in Europe's political crises—even adamantly against doing so—a policy popularly labelled 'isolationism', but better called nationalism.

In the midst of the economic collapse of the 1930s, and as Mussolini and Hitler began to threaten the status quo, Congress constructed a series of legislative barriers designed to prevent the nation from being drawn into a European war by greedy industrialists and bankers as had supposedly happened in 1917. The *Neutrality Acts initially

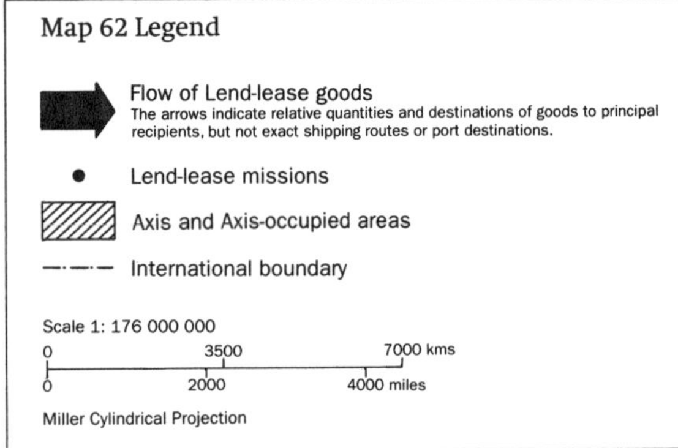

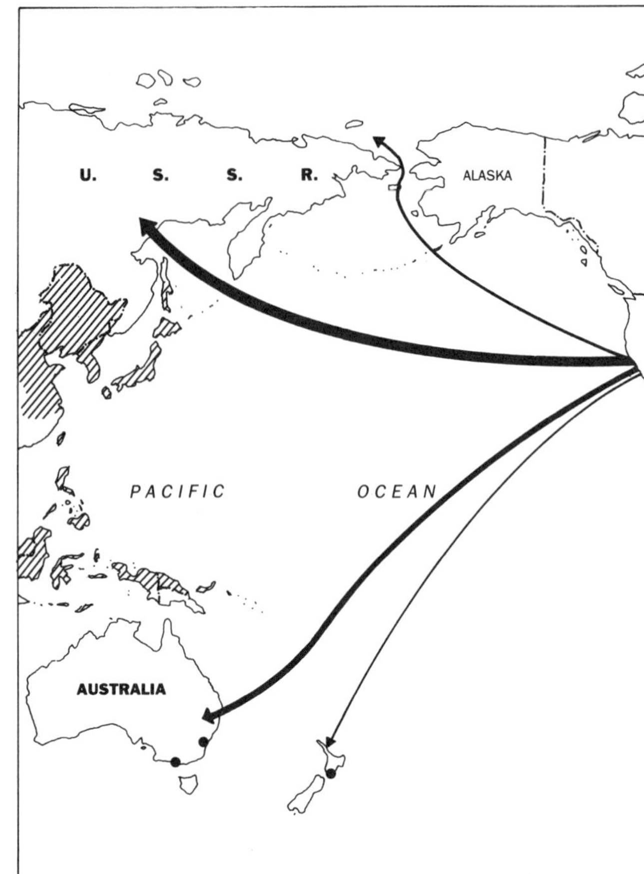

62. Flow of US **Lend-Lease** material to principal recipients, 1 September 1943

prevented belligerents from purchasing war materials in the USA, while the Johnson Debt-Default Act prohibited nations from borrowing money if they had not paid all their First World War war debts—something only Finland had done. By the time hostilities began in Europe in 1939, Roosevelt and his closest advisers had privately chosen sides, but saw no need to move the nation towards intervention, particularly in the face of intense domestic opposition. As a result, the neutrality laws were modified enough to permit nations at war to buy even military goods, but only on a strict (pay) cash-and-carry (them in your own ships) basis. British and French preparedness benefited, as did the American economy.

But cash was in increasingly short supply in the western European 'democracies.' The depression had seen a collapse of international trade, a situation that worsened with the disruption of war. Then, in June 1940, the French surrender left the UK facing Germany and Italy alone. Preparing to combat an invasion of the British Isles as well as defending key positions in North Africa and the Middle East strained British financial resources to the limit, and beyond.

But Americans, even Roosevelt, found it difficult to believe that the vast British Empire was short of cash. Not until Churchill instructed treasury officials to open the books to the Americans did Roosevelt and his treasury secretary, Henry *Morgenthau Jr., conclude that the UK had to have some kind of credits, loans, or subsidies. After all, Roosevelt and most Americans still hoped to avoid all-out involvement in the war, but that depended on the UK's success—or at least survival.

Substantial American aid to the UK faced two hurdles. The Johnson Debt-Default Act seemed small, even silly, in the shadow of German militarism, but Americans remained embittered by their First World War experience and viewed the refusal of the Europeans to pay their debts as a serious breach of faith. Underlying that resentment was the fear that aid would bring the nation into war rather than help to avoid it. One of Roosevelt's advisers told him: 'It seems to me that we Americans are like the householder who refuses to lend or sell his fire extinguisher to help put out the fire in the house that is right next door' (Kimball [see below], p. 77). But anti-interventionist Senator Burton Wheeler warned that 'you can't put your shirt-tail into a clothes wringer and then pull it out suddenly while the wringer keeps turning' (ibid., p. 58).

Events suggest that both were correct—the USA was being shortsighted in not helping put out a fire that might spread, yet that help once extended constituted an economic declaration of war that virtually ensured American involvement. But in the autumn of 1940, Roosevelt still temporized. Public opposition to intervention, inadequate military preparedness, and a sneaking suspicion that the expected German invasion of England (see SEALION) would succeed all blended to make him cautious. He had stretched presidential authority as far as he dared, or wanted, with the *destroyers-for-bases agreement and special government loans to expand American war production plants. Yet British officials, from the ambassador to treasury representatives, came to Washington with their hands out. 'Britain's broke,' warned the British ambassador, Lord Lothian (1882–1940), and Morgenthau agreed. Assets

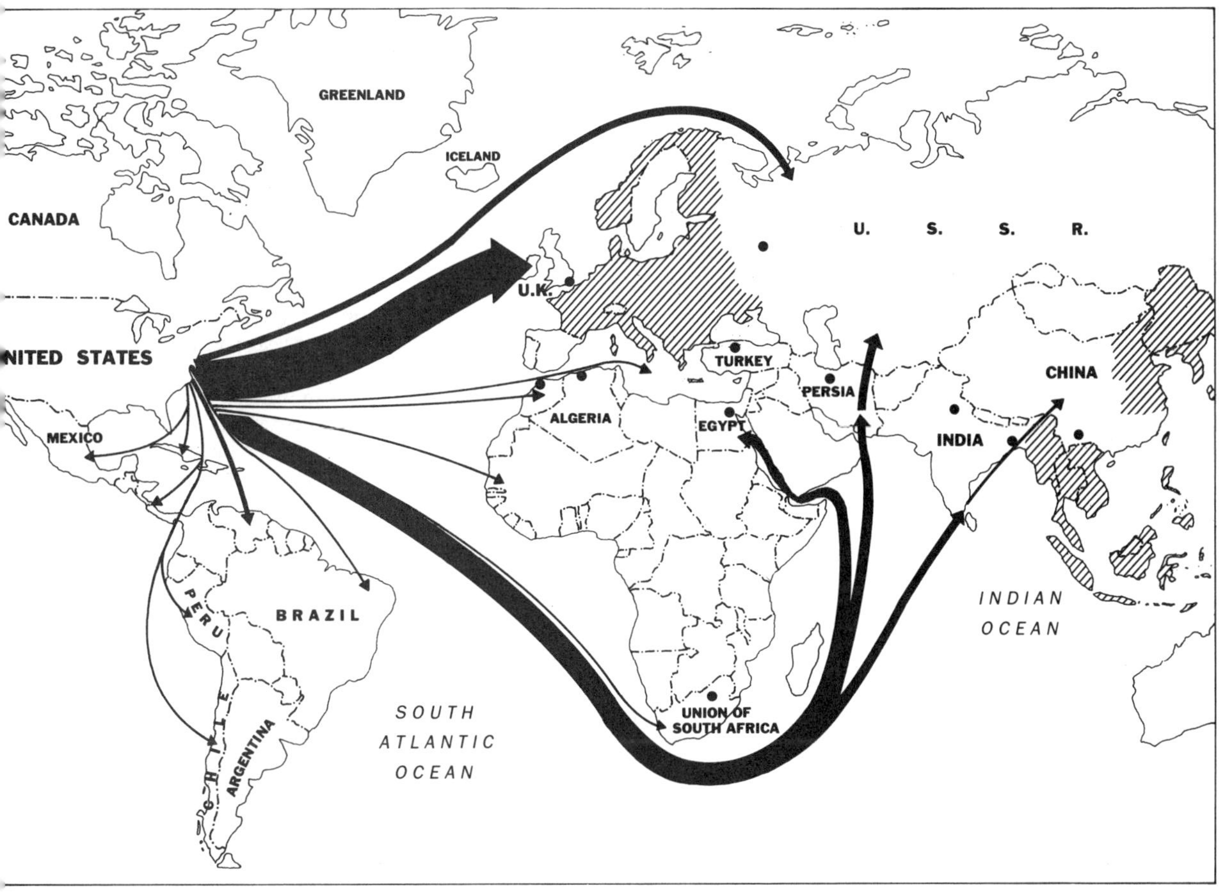

such as India, the Suez Canal, and post-war trade prospects did not translate into cash. Churchill, while writing one of his histories a year earlier, had summed it up: 'Money—above all, ready money. There was the hobble which cramped the medieval kings; and even now it counts somewhat' (*The Birth of Britain*, London, 1956, p. 474).

By early December 1940, Roosevelt was ready to act. SEALION had been postponed, rumours had surfaced of a German move towards the Balkans and the USSR (though the British insisted they were still Hitler's primary target), and full American aid held out the promise of success without having to send American troops to fight in Europe. The president instructed his cabinet to come up with a solution, then left for a short Caribbean cruise. Churchill, by then in regular telegraphic correspondence with Roosevelt, added his eloquent plea: 'You may be assured that we shall prove ourselves ready to suffer and sacrifice to the utmost for the Cause, and that we glory in being its champion. The rest we leave with confidence to you and to your people, being sure that ways and means will be found which future generations on both sides of the Atlantic will approve and admire.' Grand phrases aside, the prime minister promised a fight to the end if only (and perhaps only if) the Americans would provide the wherewithal.

Ten days later, on 17 December, at a carefully planned presidential press conference, the fire-hose analogy resurfaced as Roosevelt suggested a way to give the UK that wherewithal, without calling it loans, credits, or subsides. He claimed he had a new idea that would get 'rid of the silly, foolish old dollar sign', proposing that the USA should lend its garden hose to help its neighbour put out the fire—and if the hose were damaged in the fight, then there would be 'a gentleman's obligation to repay in kind' instead of an invoice for the dollar amount.

A few days later, on 29 December, Roosevelt put Churchill's grand if unrealistic commitment into specific terms, arguing that the USA should become the 'Arsenal of Democracy'. Secretary of War Henry *Stimson warned that 'we cannot permanently be in the position of tool-makers for other nations which fight', but Americans seemed comforted by the thought of protecting their security without having to go to war. The unlikelihood of the UK having the strength to defeat Hitler (as opposed to merely surviving) was raised only by the so-called isolationists, who were already tarred as unrealistic appeasers or even as pro-Nazi (see AMERICA FIRST COMMITTEE).

Putting the fire-hose concept into legislation was the treasury department's job, though Roosevelt attached two broad guidelines. First, the debate in and out of Congress was to appear full and unrestricted—though that did not mean full candour on his part. The president needed broader public support as he moved to aid the UK, and only a 'Great Debate' would give him the mandate he sought. Second, Roosevelt wanted a bill that gave him the widest possible latitude to decide what nations to aid, what goods to send, and what to ask as repayment.

He got pretty much what he wanted. The debate over H.R. 1776 (so numbered by the Parliamentarian of the House to make it sound more patriotic) was long and full, and served to heighten public awareness of the geopolitical crisis in Europe. Congress did require that Lend-Lease appropriations be made annually and that regular reports be submitted, thus establishing some semblance of oversight. But administration spokesmen refused to discuss the possibility of military intervention or even the need to use US warships to convoy Lend-Lease goods—a refusal that was as much a matter of indecision within the government as it was a desire to avoid the issues. Opponents unsuccessfully tried to prohibit aid to the USSR and attached a meaningless statement that the legislation did not authorize convoying, but on 11 March 1941 the bill passed easily in a vote that generally followed party lines, as Democrats overwhelmingly supported the president.

At that point, Lend-Lease took on two separate lives. The first was as an extraordinary aid programme that supplied the sinews of war to the *Grand Alliance and others; the second was what is best called the politics of Lend-Lease. The programme was a remarkable success as a straightforward subsidy for US allies. As American war production expanded in what was truly an economic revolution, Lend-Lease provided the means and organization to deliver the goods. The Office of Lend-Lease Administration (OLLA, officially created in August 1941), briefly headed by Roosevelt's alter ego Harry *Hopkins, and then by businessman and later secretary of state Edward *Stettinius, handled its task with great enthusiasm and reasonable efficiency. As with so much in the Roosevelt administration, initiative was more important than official channels, and OLLA took charge.

The *logistics of Lend-Lease delivery were as crucial to the programme as production, and a good deal more difficult. The physical task of delivering hundreds of thousands of tons of goods was staggering. Merchant ships carried the bulk of the *matériel* from the USA in *convoys, much of it to British ports for trans-shipment to its final destination. Shipments to the USSR were usually taken by the *Arctic convoys from the UK to Murmansk in the north, or from the USA to the Persian Gulf and thence by a new rail line built from Persia into the USSR. Lend-Lease aircraft were flown across the Atlantic, usually ferried by civilian pilots—some of them women (see ATLANTIC FERRY ORGANIZATION); those heading for the USSR or the Middle East were ferried across central Africa (see TAKORADI AIR ROUTE) though some were flown from Alaska across the Bering Strait. Lend-Lease for China as well as for Anglo-American forces fighting in South and South-East Asia went through Indian ports, which proved serious bottlenecks that required the expansion of rail and road facilities. At the outset, Lend-Lease was limited by two factors: US production could not meet the demands of the American military, and merchant shipping was in very short supply. By 1943, both those limits were overcome as shipments reached $10 billion that year and $11 billion the next.

After the Normandy landings in June 1944 (see OVERLORD), a second set of limits began to affect the programme. Stettinius had relied on the justness of his cause in the bureaucratic infighting of wartime Washington, but by 1944, OLLA had been absorbed into the Foreign Economic Administration, a vast, inchoate organization with little sense of purpose or *esprit de corps*. Moreover, both the state and treasury departments reasserted their power as the time came for post-war planning. Coincidentally, Congressional support for huge Lend-Lease appropriations began to slip as Americans thought more and more about conversion to peacetime pursuits.

Whatever the programme's problems, Lend-Lease was a rousing success. A precise dollar figure cannot be determined since the value of the dollar changed during the war, and the worth of services and technological transfers can only be estimated. But between $42 and $50 billion of aid-food, military goods, oil, industrial production, and services-went to America's wartime allies (see Tables 1 and 2). The UK, the original beneficiary, and its empire received about half that total, the USSR, about $10 billion, France (mostly de *Gaulle's Free French movement) some $3.5 billion, and China over $2 billion—the latter a relatively small amount because of a combination of hazardous supply routes (in particular the *Hump air route), a weak Chinese military performance, and shifting US military priorities in the Pacific. Irrespective of sheer quantity, much of the aid was crucial to the war effort. Lend-Lease trucks helped put the Red Army on wheels as it rolled across eastern Europe; Lend-Lease munitions armed soldiers from North Africa to New Guinea; Lend-Lease food helped maintain the Home Front from London to New Delhi. In addition, some $8 billion of 'reverse' Lend-Lease—mainly technology transfers, and *raw materials from the British and French empires—went to the USA.

Even while Lend-Lease functioned as an aid and exchange programme, it took on its second life—as a political programme. Almost as soon as the bill became law, state department officials began to use it as a lever to force broad changes in the world's political economy. Repayment was to be in concessions, not kind. The American position surfaced during the *Placentia Bay

Lend-Lease, Table 1: Lend-Lease aid in millions of dollars

	Monthly			*Cumulative from 11 March 1941*		
	Goods	*Services*	*Total*	*Goods*	*Services*	*Total*
1943						
January	627	55	682	7,175	1,760	8,935
February	656	41	697	7,831	1,801	9,632
March	663	24	687	8,494	1,825	10,319
April	720	63	783	9,214	1,888	11,102
May	716	74	790	9,930	1,962	11,892
June	954	77	1,031	10,884	2,039	12,923
July	1,018	32	1,050	11,902	2,071	13,973
August	1,114	147	1,261	13,016	2,219	15,235
September	1,121	76	1,197	14,137	2,294	16,431
October	1,028	73	1,101	15,165	2,368	17,533
November	971	105	1,076	16,136	2,473	18,609
December	1,300	77	1,377	17,436	2,550	19,986
1944						
January	1,214	45	1,259	18,650	2,595	21,245
February	1,124	226	1,350	19,774	2,821	22,595
March	1,406	224	1,630	21,180	3,045	24,225
April	1,266	18	1,284	22,446	3,063	25,509
May	1,160	239	1,399	23,607	3,301	26,908
June	1,212	150	1,362	24,819	3,451	28,270
July	1,308	82	1,390	26,127	3,533	29,660
August	1,009	156	1,165	27,136	3,689	30,825
September	1,116	82	1,198	28,252	3,771	32,023
October	1,048	97	1,145	29,300	3,868	33,168
November	856	39	895	30,156	3,907	34,063
December	1,254	65	1,319	31,410	3,972	35,382
1945						
January	997	179	1,176	32,407	4,151	36,558
February	1,407	55	1,462	33,814	4,206	38,020
March	993	- 41[a]	952	34,807	4,165	38,972
April	902	68	970	35,709	4,233	39,942
May	846	33	879	36,555	4,266	40,821
June	886	314	1,200	37,441	4,580	42,021

[a] Negative figure results from adjustment to reflect downward revision in ship charter rates.

Source: 'Twentieth Report to Congress on Lend-Lease Operations (on the period ending 30 June 1945)' (US Government Printing Office, 1945).

conference, but the 1941–2 negotiations for a Master Lend-Lease Agreement with the UK set the tone. The state department insisted that their ally open its markets, at home and in the empire, to unrestricted American trade and commerce. With the UK so dependent on the USA for both wartime and post-war economic help, the British negotiator, John Maynard Keynes, had to acquiesce. The Imperial Preference System (special trade and tariff privileges among members of the British Empire) was the initial target, but the concept was pursued in conferences on the international wheat market, post-war civil aviation, and the monetary agreements made at *Bretton Woods.

Lend-Lease to the USSR posed special problems from the outset. Roosevelt, wary of domestic criticism and aware that no significant aid could arrive before the 1941 battle for Moscow was decided, waited over four months after the German invasion in June 1941 (see BARBAROSSA) to declare the USSR eligible for Lend-Lease, although he provided symbolic aid before that (see also THREE-POWER CONFERENCE). American strategists knew that only the Red Army could defeat Hitler on the ground, and Lend-Lease helped do just that. It constituted only about 7% of what the USSR itself produced during the war, but did allow the Soviets to concentrate their production where they were most efficient.

But Lend-Lease to the USSR was, for Roosevelt, much more than just a wartime aid programme. It was an integral part of his aspiration to make the Grand Alliance an educational experience for the suspicious, wary Bolsheviks who had remained outside the mainstream of international relations. Lend-Lease would demonstrate the benefits of the American system, help convince Soviet leaders that the liberal democracies could be trusted,

Lend-Lease, Table 2: Lend-Lease aid — by category

	Cumulative to 1 July 1945	*Per cent of Total Aid*
Goods Transferred		
Munitions		
Ordnance	$1,291,672,000	3.1
Ammunition	2,652,458,000	6.3
Aircraft	4,967,466,000	11.8
Aircraft engines, parts, etc.	2,543,882,000	6.1
Tanks and parts	3,542,997,000	8.4
Motor vehicles and parts	2,074,751,000	4.9
Watercraft	3,618,336,000	8.6
TOTAL	20,691,562,000	49.2
Petroleum products	2,184,730,000	5.2
Industrial materials and products		
Machinery	2,180,020,000	5.2
Metals	2,069,780,000	4.9
Miscellaneous materials and manufactures	4,407,914,000	10.5
TOTAL	8,657,714,000	20.6
Agricultural products		
Foods	5,094,724,000	12.1
Other agricultural products	811,742,000	2.0
TOTAL	5,906,466,000	14.1
TOTAL TRANSFERS	37,440,472,000	89.1
Services Rendered		
Rental of ships, etc.	3,268,092,000	7.8
Servicing, repair of ships, etc.	570,433,000	1.4
Production facilities in USA	634,210,000	1.5
Miscellaneous expenses	107,572,000	.2
TOTAL SERVICES	4,580,307,000	10.9
TOTAL DIRECT AID	42,020,779,000	100.0
Consignment to US commanding generals for subsequent transfer under Lend-Lease	788,603,000	

Source: as Table 1.

and put Americans and the people of the USSR in close contact with each other—what a later president called a people-to-people programme. That put the USSR in a special category for Lend-Lease aid. Presidential policy called for promising to give the Soviets almost everything they requested, which caused misunderstandings and resentment when either US production, German submarines, insufficient shipping resources, or the requirements of other theatres made it impossible to deliver.

Despite public statements during the war by Stalin praising US aid, American diplomats in Moscow created a minor incident when they complained that the Soviets did not give the USA credit for its Lend-Lease aid. That episode foreshadowed the deterioration of the image of Lend-Lease in the USSR from a popular and successful aid programme into another *Cold War argument. At the end of the war, the *Truman administration required payment for non-military supplies to the USSR, especially a large number of ships. The initial estimate of the bill was $2.6 billion. The Soviets rejected the amount, and eventually agreed to negotiate. But the discussions came to nothing as one or another Cold War consideration prevented a settlement. Finally, in June 1990, in the glow of *glasnost* and with the USSR eager to qualify for US credits (still illegal under the Johnson Debt-Default Act until the USSR paid its Second World War 'debts'), a repayment agreement was reached. At the same time, Soviet historians began to revise their earlier dismissal of the significance of Lend-Lease for the Soviet war effort.

Once the tide of war had changed and attention began to focus on the shape of the post-war world, some in the USA began to accuse the UK of using Lend-Lease to husband its own resources and thus gain a competitive edge. Such charges fell on receptive ears, for Americans retained their suspicions of British guile and belief in the UK's opulence. Even Roosevelt insisted that one had to drive a hard bargain with one's closest ally. White Papers outlining restrictions on the re-export of Lend-Lease goods were followed by arguments over Lend-Lease for post-war reconstruction (Stage II Lend-Lease). Whatever vague promises of post-war Lend-Lease Roosevelt made at the Quebec conference in September 1944 (see OCTAGON)—allegedly in return for Churchill's agreement to the *Morgenthau Plan for Germany—Truman, fearful of Congressional opposition and ignorant of the ramifications of his action, abruptly halted Lend-Lease on the day the Japanese surrendered, 15 August 1945. It was a petty, sordid ending to what Churchill had called 'the most unsordid act'.

But that does not eclipse its significance as an immensely successful wartime aid programme, one that set the stage for the US foreign aid programmes that followed. Lend-Lease was designed to deliver America's economic strength to the war effort without leaving behind a residue of war debts and recriminations. Despite a bad after-taste in both the UK and the USSR, it worked. See also CANADIAN MUTUAL AID and WORLD TRADE AND WORLD ECONOMY. WARREN KIMBALL

Dobson, A. P., *US Wartime Aid to Britain, 1940–1946* (New York, 1986).
Herring, G. C., *Aid to Russia, 1941–1946: Strategy, Diplomacy, and the Origins of the Cold War* (New York, 1973).
Kimball, W. F., *'The Most Unsordid Act': Lend-Lease, 1939–1941* (Baltimore, Md., 1969).
Stettinius, E. R., Jr., *Lend-Lease: Weapon for Victory* (New York, 1944).

Leningrad, siege of. In all likelihood, a million or more non-combatants died during the 900-day siege of this Soviet city, making it a frightful human disaster by any standard (see Map 63). The USSR's allies regarded the siege—which was actually not a siege but a blockade deliberately imposed to wipe out the city and its population—as the ultimate test of Soviet steadfastness and determination to fight and win the *German–Soviet war, and Stalin and Hitler waged a personal power struggle over it.

On 22 June 1941 the Germans invaded the USSR (see BARBAROSSA). On 8 July, at Shlisselburg, the old fortress

A street scene in 1942 during the 900-day siege of **Leningrad**. A couple pull a body along Nevski Avenue to the communal burying ground.

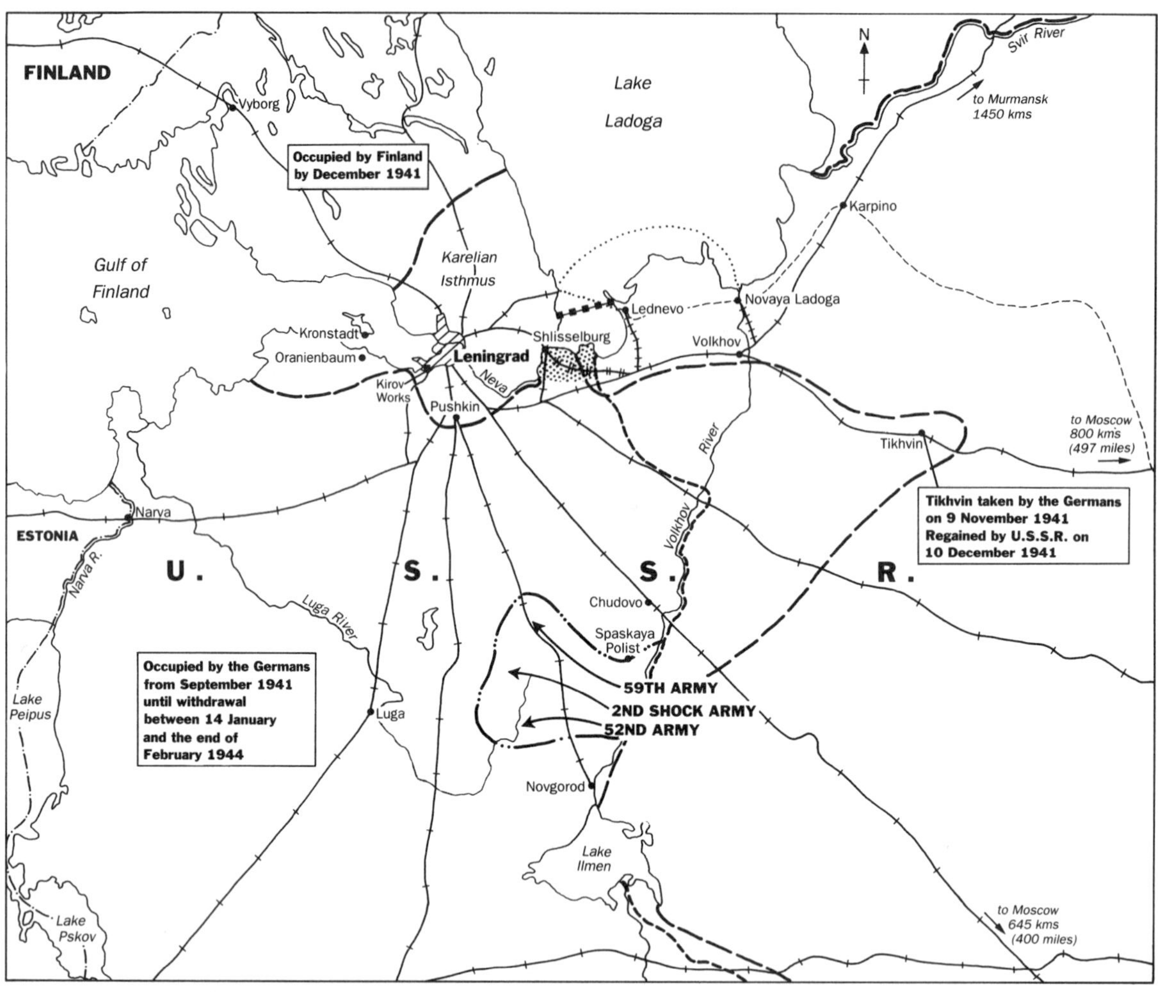

63. **Siege of Leningrad**, 1941–4

guarding the point at which the River Neva flows out of nearby Lake Ladoga, the German Fourth Panzer Army severed Leningrad's land contact with the Soviet interior. To the north, Finnish forces were advancing east and west of the lake toward the River Svir and Leningrad. Field Marshal von *Leeb, the Army Group North commander, believed his troops and the Finns together could take the city in short order. But complications were developing: the Finns refused to commit themselves to going beyond the Svir or their pre-1940 boundary 40 km. (26 mi.) north of Leningrad, and Leeb lost the Fourth Panzer Army staff along with half of its tanks to the Moscow offensive. Moreover, Hitler ordered the city and its whole population to be obliterated by bombing, shelling, starvation, and disease and prohibited a surrender from being accepted, were one to be offered. Leeb then settled in for an indefinite stay on two lines, one around the Oranienbaum complex of forts that included Kronstadt, the other just close enough to Leningrad to bring the entire city within artillery range. On the south shore of Lake Ladoga, German fronts facing east and west 18 km. (11 mi.) apart formed what the Germans, from its narrow, elongated shape, called 'the bottleneck'.

In mid-October, on Hitler's insistence, Leeb began with misgivings a wide, 250 km. (155 mi.) sweep around the lake to make a junction with the Finns on the Svir. On 8 November, his armour, over-extended and much depleted, took Tikhvin, about halfway to the Svir. As the railway centre controlling access to the Ladoga shore, Tikhvin briefly attained strategic prominence alongside Moscow and Rostov-on-Don. In December, certain of victory at *Moscow, Stalin poured reinforcements northwards, and on 18 December, Hitler had to allow Leeb to withdraw his troops to the River Volkhov and the line of the 'bottleneck'.

Winter came early that year, and was exceptionally cold. Leningrad, always entirely dependent on outside sources for food, coal, and oil, had suffered from

Map 63 Legend

- Front line 1 December 1941
- Front line 6 January 1942 (after retreat from Tikhvin)
- Front line 22 February 1942
- Soviet attack
- Railway existing in 1941
- Railway built 1941–42
- Railway built under German shellfire, 1943–44
- Oil pipelines and electric cables laid on the bottom of the lake, May 1942
- Road built between 9 November and 6 December 1941 (maximum speed, 32 kms/day)
- Soviet motor routes over lake ice (for evacuation and supplies during the winters of 1942 and 1943)
- Area regained by the USSR January 1943 (the bottleneck)
- International boundary, 1 September 1939

Scale 1:2 750 000

0 25 50 75 100 kms

0 25 50 miles

Conic Projection

breakdowns in the distribution system before, most recently during the 1939–40 war with Finland, but never on the scale it was about to experience. Although the city had been in acute danger after mid-July, nothing had been done about evacuating the people or industrial plants, even though removing the factories was standard practice everywhere else (see USSR, 2). The Hermitage Museum's art works had been shipped out in secret, and not all were removed in time. The Leningrad party chief, Andrei Zhdanov, who ostensibly ranked next to Stalin in the hierarchy, and Marshal *Voroshilov, whom Stalin had appointed to defend the city, had been afraid to do anything that might be construed as defeatist. Consequently, along with Leningrad *front* (army group) and the Red Banner Fleet in the *Baltic Sea, they had 2.5 million civilians to feed. In November, the civilian ration fell to the starvation level. Thereafter, those who managed to come by a few frozen potatoes, some glue or linseed oil, a share in a dead horse or stray dog, counted themselves fortunate.

Lake Ladoga afforded a 'lifeline' to the interior—by boat in summer, by a road across the ice in winter—but it could not reliably sustain even a minimum ration and could not mitigate the fuel shortage at all. Initially, freight had to be unloaded east of Tikhvin and trucked 280 km. (175 mi.). The German retreat from Tikhvin did not show a substantial result until February 1942, when the railway was rebuilt, and German bombing and shelling combined with the weather to keep the lake-crossing hazardous at all times.

Death, from hunger, cold, and reduced resistance to illnesses, none of which could be treated, was commonplace in Leningrad. It could also come suddenly and violently from the tooth-and-nail struggle for survival, or from German bombs and artillery shells. The supply trucks carried evacuees on their return trips, which, in unheated vehicles, must have been the last journeys for many. The dead, hurriedly buried in mass graves when spring came, were perhaps never counted. According to Soviet figures, 850,000 persons were evacuated between January and July 1942 and 7–800,000 remained in the city, which leaves 850–950,000 unaccounted for.

On 7 January 1942, Stalin, emboldened by the victory at Moscow, launched General *Meretskov's Volkhov *front* on an offensive to demolish the 200 km. (120 mi.) German front facing east between Lake Ladoga and Lake Ilmen. After a ragged start, Meretskov managed to open a narrow gap north of Lake Ilmen, through which *Vlasov's Second Shock Army made a 62 km. (37 mi.) advance to the northwest before being halted by the thaw in March. Although the change in seasons shifted the advantage to the Germans, Stalin refused to let the army withdraw and lost it in June, when the Germans closed the gap.

Hitler's first directive for the 1942 summer campaign called for complete isolation of Leningrad when an adequate force became available, and Army Group North planned an operation (NORTHERN LIGHTS) along with half a dozen similarly tentative ventures. In late July, Hitler revised the directive. Leningrad, he said, would have to be destroyed and the whole area between Lake Ladoga and the Baltic coast occupied before the end of September in order to release Finnish troops for an operation against the Murmansk railway. He would be sending, he added, five divisions, large-calibre siege artillery, and aircraft used recently to reduce the *Sevastopol fortress. On 24 August, after the German army group commander, then Field Marshal Georg von Küchler, had repeatedly protested that the solidly-built city could neither be blasted nor burned to the ground, he turned NORTHERN LIGHTS over to *Manstein, who had commanded at Sevastopol.

On 27 August, Meretskov directed a powerful strike against the eastern face of the 'bottleneck'. When it was stopped, on 4 September, Hitler sent in Manstein and his five divisions for a counter-attack. While Meretskov, intent on getting going again, poured in troops, Manstein took up positions at the mouth of the bulge and, on 25 September, locked two Soviet armies and two corps in a 10×6 km. (6.2×3.7 mi.) pocket, and two weeks later, Hitler, concerned about the coming winter, cancelled NORTHERN LIGHTS.

While the lake was ice-free, surface vessels kept the lifeline in operation, and pipelines and electric cables were laid under the water. The German Navy brought in *E-boats, the Italian *Tenth Light Flotilla operated *midget submarines, and the Luftwaffe stationed Siebelferries, catamaran-type anti-aircraft gun platforms, on the lake, but they arrived late and the summer ended before effective tactics were devised. During the summer, enraptured audiences in the UK and the USA listened for the first time to the sombre tones of Dmitri Shostakovich's Seventh Symphony, dubbed (though not by the composer) 'the Leningrad' (see also USSR, 10).

In October 1942, Leningrad *front*, which had thus far not possessed an offensive capability, began receiving enough reinforcements, including tanks and artillery, to raise its strength from three to four armies. On 12 January 1943, General *Govorov, the *front* commander, and his colleague on the east, Meretskov, mounted simultaneous assaults (Operation SPARK) on both sides of the 'bottleneck'. Their points met east of Shlisselburg on 19 January, and Moscow celebrated the breaking of the blockade with artillery salvos. The Germans recovered, however, and held the gain to a corridor 10 km. (6.2 mi.) wide. On 7 February, a train steamed into Leningrad after having passed through the corridor and crossed the Neva on track laid over the ice. The line, although it was exposed to artillery fire and had to be repaired daily, operated continuously thereafter. In the city, random bomb and shell explosions were an equally continuous reminder that liberation had not yet been achieved.

In October 1943, the German Army Group North planned an operation (BLUE). Its front had not changed since January, but the fighting elsewhere was draining away its divisions. On the other hand, as the only army group not embroiled in the Soviet summer offensive, it had time to build its share of an 'East Wall' which Hitler had belatedly projected. This ran on the line of the River Narva–Lake Peipus–Lake Pskov, 120 km. (72 mi.) east of Leningrad. BLUE was to be a phased retreat. In December and January, Hitler took more divisions from the group but refused to commit himself to BLUE; and on 14 January, when Meretskov and Govorov hit with at least 2:1 superiority in troops and 4:1 in tanks and aircraft, he ordered all existing positions to be held. The Leningrad environs thereupon became the scene of one of the war's hardest fought and, for the German soldiers, most pointless battles. Pushkin, where a tower on Observatory Hill had given artillery spotters a direct view into the city, fell on 24 January. Three days later, after the Leningrad–Moscow railway had been cleared, Stalin declared the blockade broken, and that night the city's anti-aircraft batteries fired victory salvos while the battle rumbled on the western horizon. EARL ZIEMKE

Meretskov, K. A., *Serving the People* (Moscow, 1971).
Pavlov, D., *Leningrad 1941* (Chicago, 1965).
Salisbury, H. A., *The 900 Days* (New York, 1969).

Léopold III (1901–83), King of the Belgians between 1934 and 1951 who personally commanded his army when the Germans invaded his country in May 1940 (see FALL GELB). Against the wishes of his cabinet, he surrendered unconditionally to the Germans on 28 May 1940 and then declared himself a prisoner-of-war (he was in fact interned in the palace of Laeken). He was much reviled because of this, and because he refused to leave Belgium with his ministers, who later formed a *government-in-exile in London. But he twice travelled to Germany to confront Hitler about improving his people's lot and on 7 June 1944 was deported with his family to Germany. He lived in Switzerland until July 1950, returning only after three-fifths of his people had voted for him to do so. But the socialist government then in power resigned in protest and rioting followed, and the following July he abdicated in favour of his son, Baudouin. See also BELGIUM, 2.

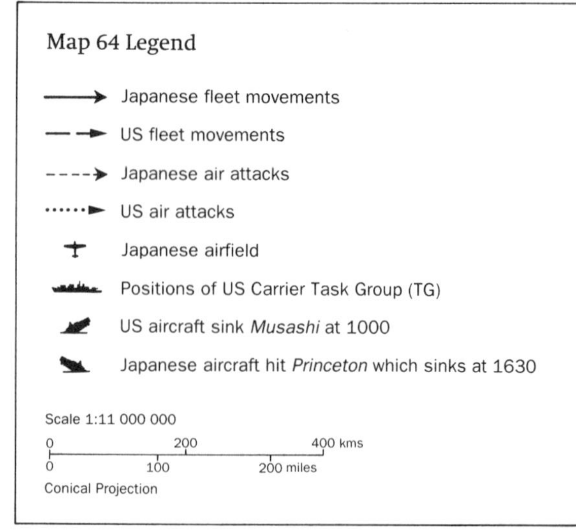

Keyes, R., *Outrageous Fortune* (London, 1984).

Ley, Robert (1890–1945), early and fervent Nazi supporter who in 1933 created the sham trade union known as the Nazi German Labour Front (Deutsche Arbeitsfront, or DAF).

Ley, the son of a prosperous farmer, was born at Niederbreidenbach east of Cologne. He fought in the army and the flying corps during the *First World War and was badly wounded. After completing his university degree he obtained a well-paid job but soon detached himself from bourgeois society to become a devoted Nazi Party member. Appointed a **Gauleiter*, he was quick to show his skill as an agitator and Jew-baiter, and in May 1933, on Hitler's orders, he organized the obliteration of the free trade unions and replaced them with the DAF, which embraced both employers and employees. Its function, which it performed with marked success, was to educate all working Germans to the Nazis' way of thinking, and to abolish industrial and class conflict by improving the workers' lot.

DAF's growth, economically and numerically, soon

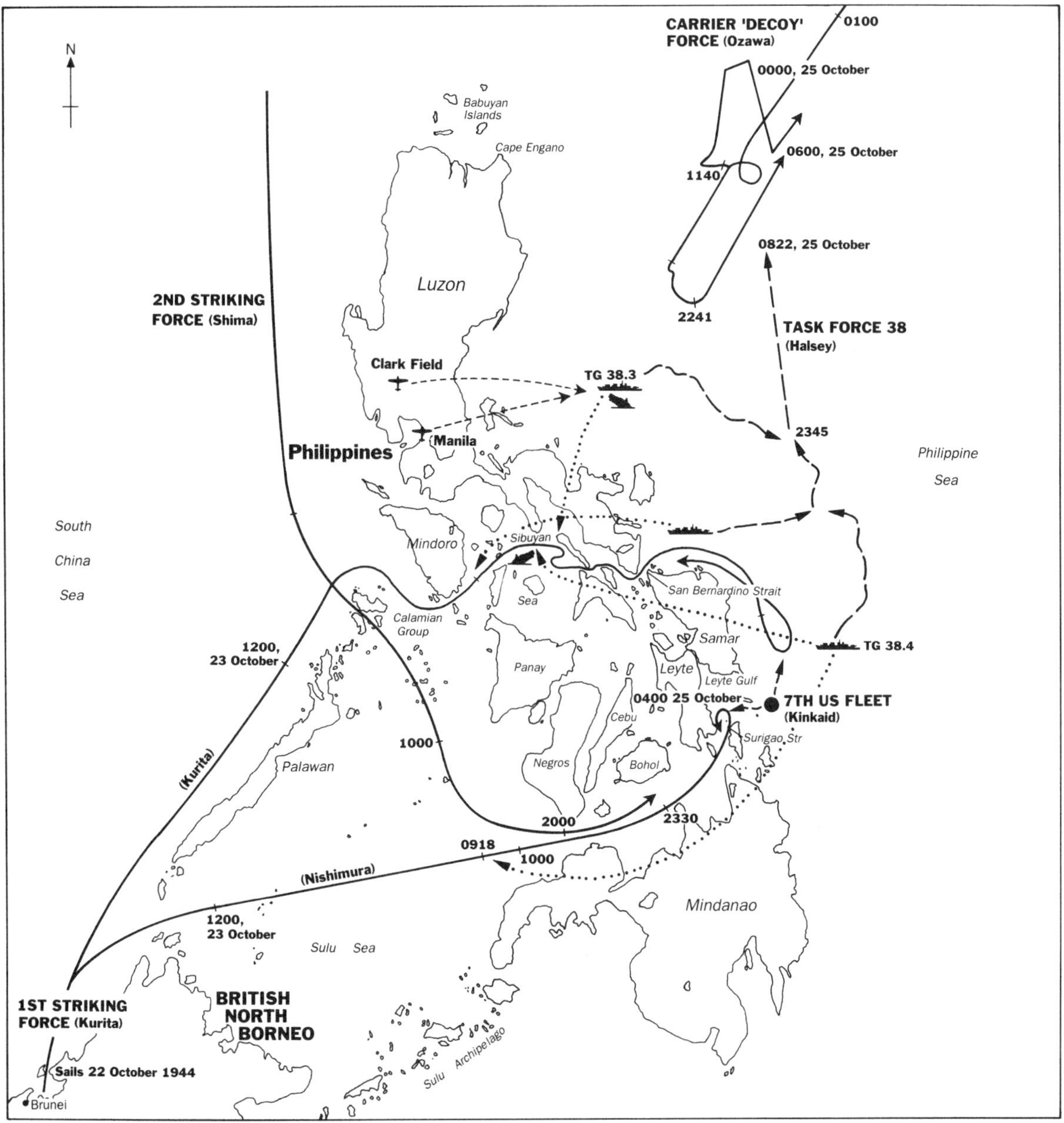

64. **Battle of Leyte Gulf**, October 1944

made it a powerful conglomerate with tentacles stretching into welfare, insurance, and housing, as well as into such political functions as wage bargaining and working conditions. One of its most successful ventures was its leisure organization, Strength Through Joy (Kraft durch Freude, or KdF), which offered workers lavish holidays and gave them, as Ley put it, 'the best of the best in food for the soul, mind, and body'.

By 1938 DAF had become so powerful, and Ley's ambitions so grandiose, that the union threatened to overshadow party and government, but once Germany was at war its importance inevitably declined as did Ley's career. He was charged with formulating the post-war social agenda and with controlling German housing. One became irrelevant; the other a disaster once the *strategic air offensive against Germany had got into its stride. Nevertheless, he remained a fervent supporter of Hitler and his regime until the end. He committed suicide before he could appear at the *Nuremberg trials.

Smelser, R., *Robert Ley, Hitler's Labor Front Leader* (Oxford, 1988).

Leyte Gulf, battle of, series of naval actions during the *Pacific war which took place on 24/25 October 1944 when Japanese naval forces attempted to destroy US landings on the Japanese-occupied Filipino island of Leyte (see PHILIPPINES CAMPAIGNS). It was the biggest naval battle ever fought and saw the introduction in numbers of *kamikaze pilots (see Map 64).

Once the C-in-C of the Japanese Combined Fleet, Admiral *Toyoda, knew where the Americans intended to land he implemented the SHO-GŌ (Victory Operation) Plan. This envisaged Admiral *Halsey's much more powerful Third US Fleet which included 16 carriers, being lured north out of the way while a pincers movement crushed both the landing forces and Vice-Admiral Thomas Kinkaid's smaller Seventh US Fleet guarding them. It nearly worked, for a change in the key of the Japanese naval code (see ULTRA, 2), and strict adherence to radio silence, denied the Americans any foreknowledge of Toyoda's plans.

In tactical command of this, the last throw of the dice for the Japanese Navy, was Vice-Admiral *Ozawa. His Mobile Force contained nearly all the warships Japan had left afloat including the two giant 72,800-ton battleships *Yamato* and **Musashi*, five other battleships, and sixteen cruisers. It was divided into two striking forces, commanded by Vice-Admiral *Kurita and Vice-Admiral Shima Kiyohide, and Ozawa's decoy force, which included four carriers. Ozawa's task was to lure Halsey northwards while the two striking forces formed the pincer. Part of Shima's force, along with some of Kurita's ships commanded by Vice-Admiral Nishimura Shōjō, was ordered to penetrate the Gulf via Surigao Strait, while Kurita himself approached via San Bernardino Strait. The rest of Shima's force was employed in escorting re-inforcements to Leyte, and this later lost two ships to US aircraft.

Halsey's Third Fleet comprised Vice-Admiral Marc Mitscher's Task Force 38 (see TASK FORCE 58) which was protected by Vice-Admiral 'Chink' Lee's battleships and cruisers. Despite losing the carrier *Princeton* to land-based aircraft three of TF38's four task groups (the fourth had withdrawn to refuel) launched air strikes against Kurita on 24 October as he crossed the Sibuyan Sea. They sank one battleship and damaged other vessels, and made Kurita temporarily reverse course. This caution put him behind schedule, but over-optimistic reports of the damage he had sustained led Halsey to assume that Kurita was no longer a menace. So when Ozawa was sighted he sent both TF38 and Lee north to destroy him.

The trap was set, but one arm of the Japanese pincers soon crumbled when Nishimura, followed at a distance by Shima, entered Surigao Strait that night and was attacked first by *PT boats, then by destroyers, and finally by Kinkaid's battleships and cruisers. Nishimura was killed and eventually only one destroyer from his force survived. Shima prudently retired without fighting, but later lost two ships in air attacks. However, the other arm of the pincer, formed by Kurita's force, which emerged next morning from San Bernardino Strait, was not detected until it encountered one of Kinkaid's escort carrier groups under Rear-Admiral Clifton Sprague off Samar Island. Surprise was mutual, but Kurita, judging American forces in the area to be much stronger than they were, ordered his ships to attack independently. This proved to be an error, for in the battle which followed—the first daylight surface naval action of the Pacific war since the *Java Sea battle in February 1942—two Japanese cruisers were sunk by aircraft, and another was crippled by destroyer's torpedoes. But the heavily outgunned Sprague lost two of his escort carriers (one of them to a kamikaze), two destroyers, and one destroyer escort, and other ships were damaged. The situation appeared desperate when, to the amazement of the Americans, Kurita, plagued by doubt and hesitation, and probably short of fuel, broke off the engagement and retired through the San Bernardino Strait.

When Halsey received Kinkaid's first call for help he ordered one of Mitscher's task groups south to attack Kurita. But bent on totally annihilating Ozawa, whose four carriers had been sunk by Mitscher, he did not detach Lee to block Kurita's escape. However, just when Lee's battleships were within range of the remnants of Ozawa's force, Halsey was forced by Kinkaid's plight to send Lee south. It was a decision he later bitterly regretted. For though a smaller force did pursue Ozawa, sinking two more ships while a US submarine torpedoed another, the Japanese escaped total destruction, while Lee was too late to trap Kurita.

After the war the Japanese navy minister said the Japanese defeat at Leyte was 'tantamount to the loss of the Philippines. When you took the Philippines, that was the end of our resources.' See also SEA POWER.

Falk, S., *Decision at Leyte* (New York, 1966).

liberation. Despite dictionary definitions, liberation is a term which in the context of war is usually employed selectively and subjectively, i.e. for military operations that are approved. Hence, in Allied literature, military operations undertaken by the western Allies or by the USSR are described as 'liberations', while similar operations conducted by Axis forces are described as 'invasions' or 'occupations'. In Axis literature, the roles of 'liberator' and 'occupier' are exactly reversed.

Reality was rather more complicated. The only true touchstone of liberation must be sought in the feelings and attitudes of the supposedly liberated populations. Yet such attitudes were often ambiguous. In many parts of the USSR and eastern Europe, for example, where Soviet and Nazi regimes were equally resented, the arrival of the Red Army or of the Wehrmacht could be felt as a longed-for liberation and a hated occupation at one and the same time. The German advance into the Baltic States in 1941 was welcome to the extent that it put an end to the murderous Soviet occupation of the previous year. Yet it brought terrible impositions and murderous policies of its own. Similarly, the western advance of the Soviet armies in 1944–5 was welcome to the extent that it put an end to the murderous Nazi occupation of the previous years; yet it brought reprisals and totalitarian policies that were no less vicious than those it removed. Liberations that did not liberate are not worthy of the name. See also COLLABORATION and OCCUPATION.

NORMAN DAVIES

Liberia, West African state which in 1847 became, after Abyssinia, Africa's second independent country. Estimates of its population in 1939 varied between 12,000 and 20,000, and mostly comprised descendants of repatriated slaves from the USA. In 1942 a treaty was concluded in which Liberia provided military bases for US forces, and it declared war against Germany and Japan in January 1944.

Liberty ships, mass-produced merchantmen which were constructed in the USA, many by the West Coast Kaiser shipyards. They were described as ships that were 'built by the mile and chopped off by the yard'.

In September 1940 the British ordered 60 ships from the USA which were based on a British plan for a ship of simple design. To speed up the production of this order these vessels were welded, not riveted, and the original plans were considerably modified by the Americans to take this into account. In January 1941 the USA launched its own emergency construction programme of 200 ships based on the modified British design. These 7,126-ton, 11-knot, ships were dubbed 'The Liberty Fleet' and 27 September 1941, the day the first one, *Patrick Henry*, was launched, was called 'Liberty Fleet Day', a name which stuck.

Liberty ships came in several lengths and though most were designed to carry freight (see Figure), troops, or fuel, others were modified for a variety of uses, from hospital ships to floating repair shops and Army Tank Transports ('zipper ships'). American Liberty ships were mostly named after notable US citizens and a total of 2,710 were constructed. One was launched 4 days and 15½ hours after her keel was laid.

Under the *Lend-Lease programme about 200 went to

Liberty ships: Typical Liberty Ship

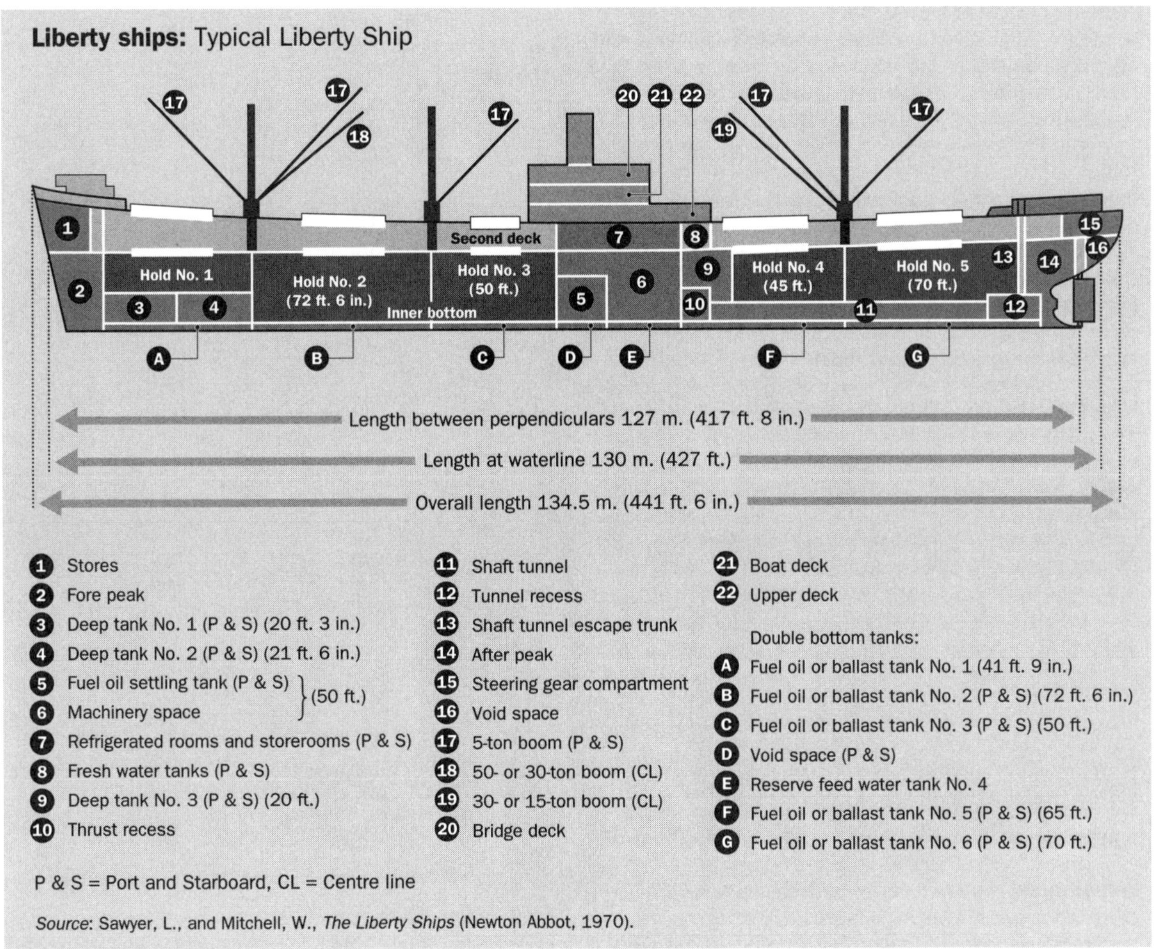

1 Stores
2 Fore peak
3 Deep tank No. 1 (P & S) (20 ft. 3 in.)
4 Deep tank No. 2 (P & S) (21 ft. 6 in.)
5 Fuel oil settling tank (P & S) } (50 ft.)
6 Machinery space
7 Refrigerated rooms and storerooms (P & S)
8 Fresh water tanks (P & S)
9 Deep tank No. 3 (P & S) (20 ft.)
10 Thrust recess
11 Shaft tunnel
12 Tunnel recess
13 Shaft tunnel escape trunk
14 After peak
15 Steering gear compartment
16 Void space
17 5-ton boom (P & S)
18 50- or 30-ton boom (CL)
19 30- or 15-ton boom (CL)
20 Bridge deck
21 Boat deck
22 Upper deck

Double bottom tanks:
A Fuel oil or ballast tank No. 1 (41 ft. 9 in.)
B Fuel oil or ballast tank No. 2 (P & S) (72 ft. 6 in.)
C Fuel oil or ballast tank No. 3 (P & S) (50 ft.)
D Void space (P & S)
E Reserve feed water tank No. 4
F Fuel oil or ballast tank No. 5 (P & S) (65 ft.)
G Fuel oil or ballast tank No. 6 (P & S) (70 ft.)

P & S = Port and Starboard, CL = Centre line

Source: Sawyer, L., and Mitchell, W., *The Liberty Ships* (Newton Abbot, 1970).

the UK and 50, which were never returned, to the USSR. Many were sunk in the *convoys which sustained both countries. The British ships were given the prefix 'Sam', not as an indication of their origin but because it was the initials of their type of construction (Superstructure Aft of Midships).

The speed with which Liberty ships were produced, often by inexperienced workers, resulted in a high percentage of defects and the loss of a number of vessels—one in 30 suffered major fractures. However, some absorbed severe punishment both from the sea and from Axis attack, and one, *Stephen Hopkins*, sank a German *auxiliary cruiser with her single 4 in. (10 cm.) gun.

Sawyer, L., and Mitchell, W., *The Liberty Ships* (Newton Abbot, 1970).

Libya, North African Italian colony which was the battleground for most of the *Western Desert campaigns. Its capital, Tripoli, was the principal port for Axis supplies. Oil had not yet been discovered there.

The two provinces of Tripolitania and Cyrenaica were conquered by Italy in 1912, and the Turkish occupying forces were driven out. In December 1934, after the civilian population had been forcibly pacified by *Graziani, *Badoglio, and others, the two provinces were officially combined into the new colony of Libya. By 1939 the population had grown to 900,000, 10% of whom were Italian immigrants. Most Italians lived in the coastal towns and that year the coastal zone was declared part of Italy. Cyrenaica, Libya's eastern province, saw most of the fighting as Axis forces under *Rommel launched a series of offensives to capture Egypt and the Suez Canal.

When British and Commonwealth troops occupied the larger Libyan towns such as Benghazi the local Arab population turned on the Italian colonists. Libyans served in both the Italian and British forces, though the latter did not use them in combat.

Lidiče massacre, ordered by Hitler on 9 June 1942 to avenge the assassination of the Deputy Reichsprotektor of Bohemia and Moravia, Reinhard *Heydrich, a week earlier. Lidiče, a village near Prague was chosen for its alleged connections with the Czech resistance assassins (see also CZECHOSLOVAKIA). Along with another village, Lezaky, it was razed to the ground. Lidiče's 198 male inhabitants were shot, 184 *women were sent to *Ravensbrück, 11 went to prisons, and 98 *children were abducted (see LEBENSBORN).

Liechtenstein, 160 sq. km. (62 sq. mi.) independent principality, whose citizens speak a German patois, sandwiched between Switzerland and Austria. It remained neutral under Swiss protection, though some of its citizens served in the *SS Wiking Division.

'Lili Marlene', see MARCHING SONGS.

limpet mine, explosive device with magnets which battened it to any steel target. British and Italian *frogmen used them to sabotage shipping, as did Allied *canoeists. Invented by *MD1, more than two and a half million were manufactured in the UK, nearly one million of which went to the USSR. There was also a pocket version, called a 'clam', and two captured ones were used by those trying to assassinate Hitler in March 1943 (see SMOLENSK ATTENTAT).

Lindbergh, Charles A. (1902–74), famous US transatlantic aviator whose visits to German aircraft factories in the late 1930s, and reports on German air power, helped convince the US ambassador in London, Joseph Kennedy (1888–1969), that the UK would be defeated in any war—though they were also a spur to enlarging the US Army Air Corps. An *America First Committee member, Lindbergh refused a cabinet post offered him by Roosevelt as a *quid pro quo* for keeping silent, and he began making radio broadcasts and speeches opposing the president's anti-Nazi policies. Roosevelt became convinced he was a Nazi and once America was at war the Army Air Force refused to have him. Instead, Lindbergh worked as a technical consultant at the *Willow Run Plant and elsewhere. He later flew 50 combat missions during the *Pacific war while serving as a technical adviser for the US Navy's Bureau of Aeronautics.

Cole, W. S., *Charles A. Lindbergh and the Battle against American Intervention in World War II* (New York, 1974).
Mosley, L., *Lindbergh* (London, 1976).

Lindemann, Frederick (Lord Cherwell) (1886–1957), physicist of French Alsatian origin who was Churchill's wartime scientific adviser. Born in Germany, a fact he always resented, Lindemann had been a friend of Churchill's since 1921. Known as 'The Prof', he was such a controversial member of the *Tizard committee that in July 1936 it was dissolved and then reformed so that he could be excluded from it. In 1939 Churchill, then at the Admiralty, made him head of its statistical section and throughout the war his analyses of such subjects as the accuracy of British night bombing (see also BUTT REPORT) had a profound effect on policy-making. In 1941 he was raised to the peerage as Lord Cherwell and in 1942 was appointed paymaster-general. He was never in the war cabinet but his influence on Churchill was said to be greater than that of any of its members. He had his blind spots—notably, he doubted the existence of the German V-2 rocket (see V-WEAPONS)—but he was a strong supporter of research into new weapons, the *proximity fuze being one, the *atomic bomb another; of developing new systems and counter-measures in *electronic warfare; and of improving conventional *explosives. See also H2S and SCIENTISTS AT WAR.

Birkenhead, Earl of, *The Prof in Two Worlds* (official life, London, 1961).
Harrod, R., *The Prof* (memoir, London, 1959).

Lindemans, Christiaan (1910–46), Dutch garage hand called 'King Kong', and a *double agent, ran a successful

Allied escape line (see MI9) from the Netherlands to Paris till March 1944, when he secretly changed sides to rescue his younger brother and a favourite mistress from the *Gestapo. He betrayed several Allied agents to the Germans during the spring and summer of 1944, deceived MI9's local staff, crossing lines again in September 1944; but did not betray the airborne attack on Arnhem (see MARKET-GARDEN), of which he had no prior knowledge, though he passed news to the Germans on 15 September that airborne troops would be used on 17 September to help a British attack towards Eindhoven. He did not obtain this information at Prince *Bernhard's HQ, as some have supposed, as his first contact with it occurred only after MARKET-GARDEN had failed.

M. R. D. Foot

List, Field Marshal Siegmund (1880–1971), German Army officer who commanded the German forces in Austria after the Anschluss of March 1938. Promoted general in April 1939, he led the Fourteenth Army during the *Polish campaign of September–October 1939 and the Twelfth Army during the fighting which culminated in the fall of *France the following June. He was promoted field marshal in July 1940, commanded the Twelfth Army during the *Balkan campaign—which he conducted brilliantly—and from June to October 1941 was C-in-C South-East, commanding German forces in the Balkans. In July 1942 he was succeeded by General *Löhr and then commanded Army Group A in the *German–Soviet war. He was given the task of capturing Rostov-on-Don, and then seizing the Caucasus, but when his offensive stalled (see GERMAN–SOVIET WAR, 4) he was dismissed by Hitler in September 1942, and retired. In 1948 he received a life sentence from an American military tribunal, chiefly for *war crimes in the Balkans and Greece, but was pardoned and released in 1952. He has been judged as one of 'the most neglected and underrated of all of Hitler's field marshals' (S. Mitcham, *Hitler's Field Marshals and their Battles*, London, 1988, p. 203).

literature, see in culture section of major powers; see also HISTORIOGRAPHY.

Lithuania (capital in 1939, Kaunas), the largest and most southerly of the three Baltic States, started the Second World War as an independent republic and ended it as an involuntary component of the USSR.

In 1939, Lithuania was ruled by the nationalist dictatorship of A. Smetona. Unlike Estonia and Latvia, it had enjoyed good relations with Moscow, largely through shared antipathies against Poland. Its main concerns centred on its frustrated claims to *Wilno, the historic capital of Lithuania which had been annexed by Poland in 1922 and whose large Polish majority wished to remain in Poland, and on German claims to *Memelland. Lithuania was a member of the *League of Nations. Its independence had been established by a bilateral treaty signed with the USSR in July 1920, and confirmed by the Soviet–Lithuanian Non-aggression Pact, signed on 28 September 1926 and prolonged in 1934 for a ten-year period to 1944.

Lithuania's vulnerability was underlined in January 1939 when a Polish ultimatum forced an end to the state of war which had formally persisted ever since the start of the dispute over Wilno in 1920. It was fully exposed on 22 March 1939 when German forces seized and annexed Memelland.

The *Nazi–Soviet Pact initially assigned Lithuania to Germany's sphere of influence. But during the invasion of Poland in September, Soviet troops occupied Wilno; and the German–Soviet Treaty of Friendship and Demarcation of 28 September secretly transferred the whole of Lithuania to the Soviet sphere. As a result, Moscow's demands for the conclusion of a Treaty of Friendship and Co-operation with the Lithuanian government in Kaunas were supported by an apparently generous offer—to hand Wilno over in return for permission to station Soviet troops on Lithuanian territory.

However, when the Soviet–Lithuanian Treaty was activated in June 1940, the entry of the Red Army was soon followed by subversive agitation against the Lithuanian government; by widespread arrests and killings; by fraudulent elections conducted by the Soviet security organs (see NKVD); and by the declaration of a Lithuanian SSR that was formally admitted to the Soviet Union on 5 August 1940.

The first Soviet occupation (June 1940–June 1941) was a time of mass terror, when all of Lithuania's native institutions were destroyed. Repressions were also directed against everyone connected with the former Polish state. The German population was deported to Germany.

The German occupation (June 1941–July 1944) saw Lithuania incorporated into the Reich Commissariat *Ostland. Lithuanian police and military units were formed under German command, and served on the Eastern Front. A Lithuanian Division was recruited for the Waffen-*SS. The large Jewish community was concentrated, especially in the *ghettos of Wilno and Kaunas, and then killed. Elements of the Polish Home Army (see POLAND, 4) were active in underground resistance, and participated in the liberation of Wilno.

The second Soviet occupation, which began in April 1944, was accompanied by a renewed wave of terror: by forced collectivization of the peasantry: by the deportation of most remaining Poles: and by persecution of the Catholic Church (see also RELIGION).

Lithuania's population was diminished by at least 25% by the *deportations and repressions, and by the loss of its German, Jewish, and Polish elements, but, unlike Estonia and Latvia, it was not subjected to a major post-war influx of Russians.

Norman Davies

Litvinov, Maxim (1876–1952), Soviet commissar for foreign affairs from 1930 to 1939 who helped win his country's admittance to the *League of Nations in 1934 and represented it there from 1934 to 1938. He was a Jew married to an Englishwoman, and fiercely anti-Nazi. He was replaced by *Molotov in May 1939. In December 1941 he was appointed the USSR's ambassador in Washington, a post he retained until becoming Soviet vice-minister of foreign affairs in 1943.

Local Defence Volunteers, British Army's amateur defence force. Their name was later changed to the Home Guard. See UK, 6.

Lofoten Islands raids, mounted against these Norwegian islands by British commandos on 4 March 1941 and again on 26 December after Norway had been occupied by the Germans the previous year. In the first attack factories producing glycerine were destroyed. More importantly, the current settings for an *ENIGMA machine were found aboard a German armed trawler. This coup enabled the British government's Code and Cypher School at *Bletchley Park to break the German naval ENIGMA traffic (see ULTRA, 1) for the previous month. It also resulted in the capture of two German weather ships (see METEOROLOGICAL INTELLIGENCE) which in turn yielded material that helped Bletchley read the naval ENIGMA traffic for July 1941. The second raid helped divert German attention during another commando operation against *Vaagso.

logistics, an all-embracing term used to cover every aspect of maintaining armed forces in the field. These are normally divided into two main areas, personnel matters and equipment. The Table lists what comes under each. Of these the most important for giving forces immediate sustenance in action are fuel, food and water, and ammunition. The last was so vital that it had its own supply system (see Figure 1).

There are, too, a number of important principles governing logistics. Their operation should be kept as simple as possible and aim for economy of effort. An elaborate and over-complicated system will quickly grind to a halt. It is also vital that the logistical system is flexible: it must be capable of reacting to the unexpected. Another important principle is good co-operation. Many agencies are involved in handling logistics and it is essential that they co-ordinate their efforts. Logisticians also require the ability to anticipate, so that the right supplies are in the right place at the right time. Finally, no operation of war will be successful unless it can be logistically supported (see Figure 2).

The global nature of the Second World War meant that forces, particularly the western Allies and Japan, were often operating at a distance from their home base and were reliant on resupply by sea. Being islands, the UK and Japan were also dependent on maritime communications for maintaining their war economies. In the UK's case, communications across the Atlantic were vital. The *convoys which used these sea lanes carried the *Lend-Lease *matériel* produced by the USA to enable the British war effort not only to be sustained but, during 1940–1 when the UK stood almost alone, to survive. Convoys also brought across the US and Canadian forces deployed to the European and Mediterranean theatres, and their supplies, and took Lend-Lease from the UK to the USSR (see ARCTIC CONVOYS). The importance of the lifeline across the Atlantic had been long recognized by the Germans and in the longest campaign of the war, the battle of the *Atlantic, they tried to sever it. They failed, but the issue remained in doubt until the summer of 1943. In contrast, the US submarine fleet had by the end of 1944 totally throttled the Japanese sea routes between its new possessions in the Pacific and South-East Asia and the Japanese mainland. This proved decisive in that Japan was even more reliant on the import of *raw materials than the UK. The Japanese themselves, however, expended little effort in using their submarines to attack the US Pacific supply routes, preferring to concentrate their efforts on warships. This proved a serious mistake.

Naval operations themselves require a large amount of logistical support. Naval bases are of prime importance, and such ports as Malta and Alexandria in the Mediterranean, *Pearl Harbor in the Pacific, and the German U-boat bases on the French Atlantic coast had much influence on the conduct of the war at sea. Yet naval forces often operated at a considerable distance from their bases, especially in the Pacific and Atlantic. In order to maintain their combat effectiveness increasing reliance was placed on oilers, supply vessels, and repair ships; what the Americans called the *Fleet Train. The Germans also made strenuous efforts to keep their surface raiders and U-boats at sea for the maximum length of time through the use of supply vessels camouflaged as merchantmen and the Mark XIV U-boat, an underwater tanker known as the Milchkuh (milk cow). The Allied success in tracking these down, largely thanks to *ULTRA intelligence, and sinking them, was a contributory factor towards eventual victory in the battle of the Atlantic.

Aircraft, too, could not operate without bases and the extent of their operations was dictated by range. This was especially crucial in the context of close air support for the ground forces. During the *Western Desert

Logistics: The two main areas of logistics

Personnel	*Equipment*
Medical/Hygiene	Ammunition
Reinforcements/ Replacements	Food and water
	Fuel
Discipline	Clothing and equipment
Pay	Maintenance and repair
Welfare	Quartering (barracks and camps)
Prisoners-of-war	Mail
	Salvage

Source: Contributor.

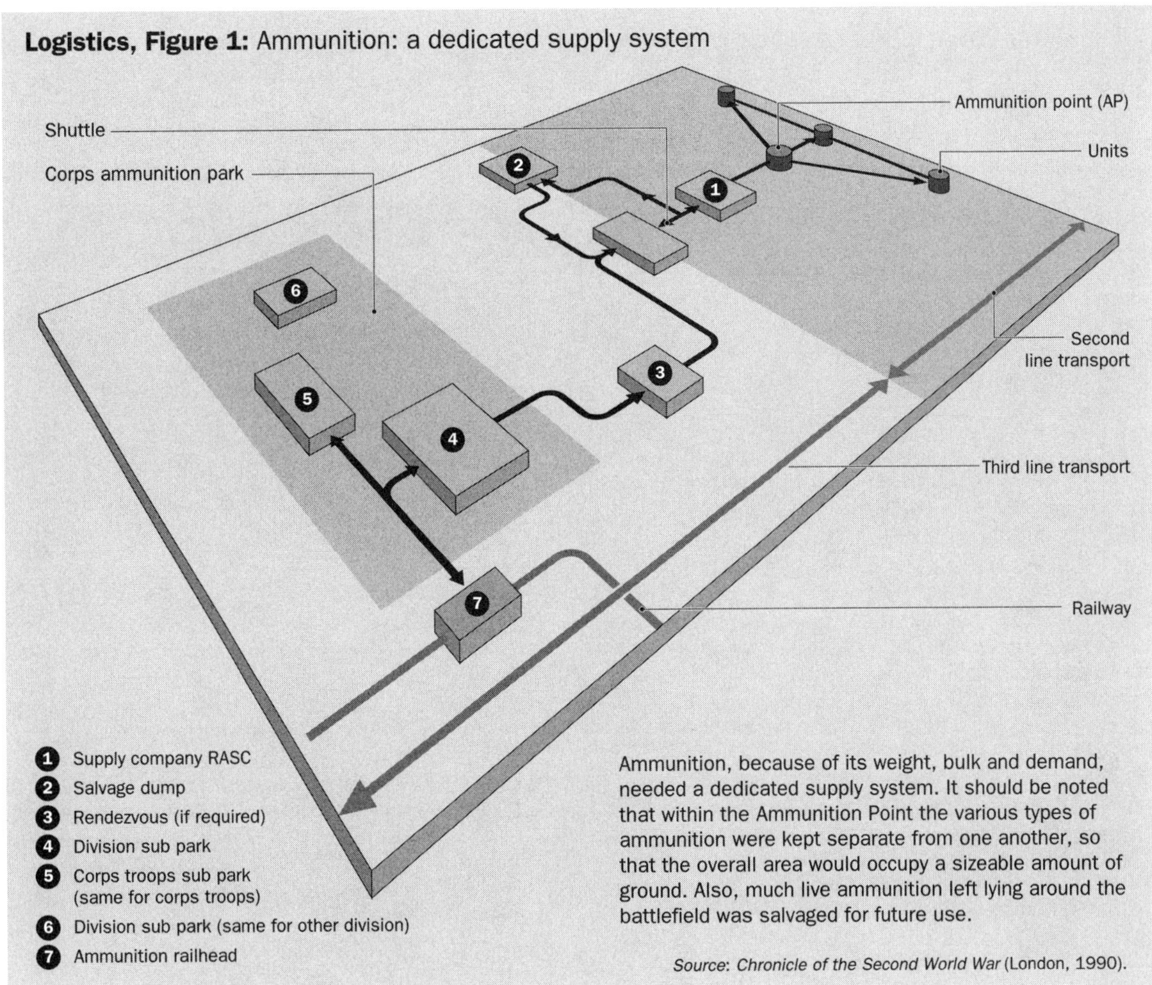

Logistics, Figure 1: Ammunition: a dedicated supply system

Ammunition, because of its weight, bulk and demand, needed a dedicated supply system. It should be noted that within the Ammunition Point the various types of ammunition were kept separate from one another, so that the overall area would occupy a sizeable amount of ground. Also, much live ammunition left lying around the battlefield was salvaged for future use.

Source: *Chronicle of the Second World War* (London, 1990).

campaigns the desert became littered with advanced landing grounds, on which both sides relied heavily. These were stocked with fuel, ammunition, and emergency maintenance facilities to enable fighters and fighter-bombers to operate from as close to the front line as possible. The British, both for South-East Asia and the campaign in Europe, formed RAF Servicing Commandos, whose task was to follow up close behind the attacking troops and refurbish or create airfields for this purpose.

Transport aircraft also played an important role in both resupply and reinforcement. Part of the reason for the German success during the *Norwegian campaign in 1940 and on *Crete in 1941 was the quick seizure of airfields so that they could be used for flying in reinforcements. Similarly, when the TORCH landings took place at the start of the *North African campaign in November 1942, the Germans were able to deploy troops quickly to Tunisia by air. It was perhaps in South-East Asia, however, that air resupply came into its own. For a start, when the Japanese closed the *Burma Road, the highway which ran from Rangoon to Chungking, the only means by which *Chiang Kai-shek could be kept supplied in order to maintain his resistance to the Japanese during the *China Incident, was to fly in stores and equipment from India using the *Hump route over the mountains to Kunming. During the *Burma campaign the jungle and lack of roads were a logistical nightmare for both sides and often the Allies found that aircraft were the only effective means of keeping the front-line troops supplied. This was especially so during the *Chindit expeditions of 1943 and 1944 and the fighting around *Imphal in the spring of 1944. Yet air resupply did have its limitations. *Göring's boast that the Luftwaffe could keep the defenders of *Stalingrad supplied with all their wants proved an empty one, and the Anglo-US attempts to use aircraft to maintain their high-speed advance across France in late summer 1944 did not prevent fuel tanks from running dry. In both cases there were simply not

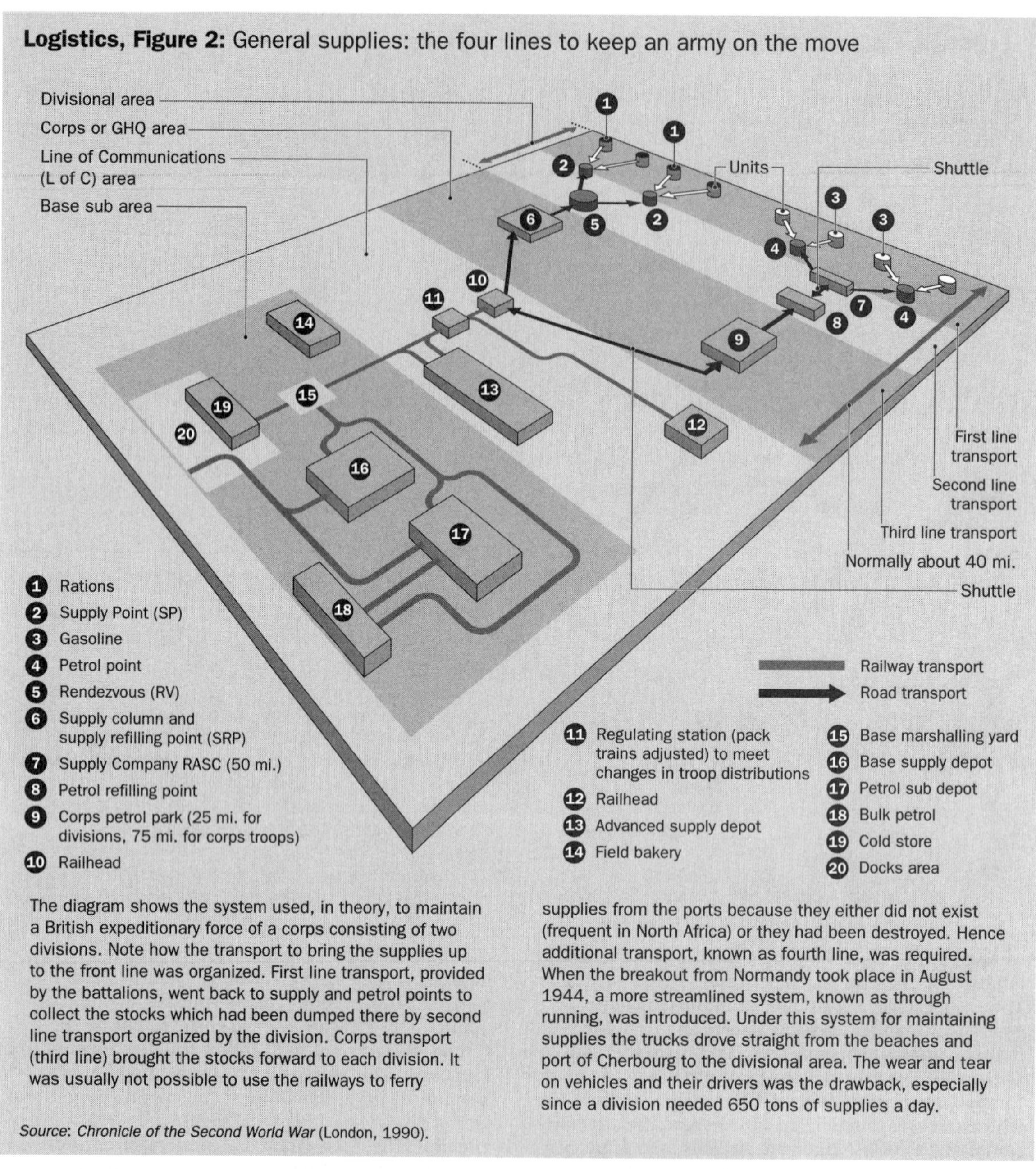

Logistics, Figure 2: General supplies: the four lines to keep an army on the move

The diagram shows the system used, in theory, to maintain a British expeditionary force of a corps consisting of two divisions. Note how the transport to bring the supplies up to the front line was organized. First line transport, provided by the battalions, went back to supply and petrol points to collect the stocks which had been dumped there by second line transport organized by the division. Corps transport (third line) brought the stocks forward to each division. It was usually not possible to use the railways to ferry supplies from the ports because they either did not exist (frequent in North Africa) or they had been destroyed. Hence additional transport, known as fourth line, was required. When the breakout from Normandy took place in August 1944, a more streamlined system, known as through running, was introduced. Under this system for maintaining supplies the trucks drove straight from the beaches and port of Cherbourg to the divisional area. The wear and tear on vehicles and their drivers was the drawback, especially since a division needed 650 tons of supplies a day.

Source: *Chronicle of the Second World War* (London, 1990).

enough transport aircraft available to meet the demand.

Logistics took on a very particular character when it came to *amphibious warfare. Planners had to grapple with two main requirements. First there was the need to keep supplied the troops who carried out the initial landings and established the beachhead. Sufficient stocks had to be built up also within the beachhead itself to maintain the advance once the ground forces broke out of it. The ideal was to land close to a port, but this was not always possible. One valuable lesson learned from the disastrous *Dieppe raid of August 1942 by the planners of the Normandy landings (see OVERLORD) was that the French Channel coast ports were likely to be too heavily defended to guarantee success. Hence their selection of an area well away from towns, but the penalty to be paid was the problem of getting equipment and stores from ship to shore. It was overcome in part by the *MULBERRIES (artificial harbours) and also by *PLUTO. In the Pacific, where the distance from the mounting area to the objective was usually too great for such measures to be practicable, harbours were constructed by US Navy engineers called *Seabees. There was, however, always the temptation to sacrifice surprise in favour of over-caution in building up supplies within a beachhead. A classic example of this was the Allied landing at *Anzio in January 1944. Consequently, the Germans were able to deploy sufficient forces to prevent the early capture of Rome.

Napoleon's often quoted dictum that armies march on their stomachs serves as a reminder that logistics must be at the forefront of a land force commander's mind. Before the coming of the railway and invention of the internal combustion engine armies subsisted largely by foraging, both for food and fuel, the latter, of course, being horse feed. Indeed, armies often had to keep moving in order to survive. Railways were first used to a significant extent as a means of supplying armies during the American Civil War and in 1914 were to be the basis of the German deployment to both the Eastern and Western fronts. The *First World War itself saw mechanical transport slowly begin to take over from the traditional horse-drawn variety, as well as the appearance of the first armoured fighting vehicles, and between the wars the pace of military mechanization reflected that of the world at large. Thus by 1939 some armies, the British and US, had largely forsaken the horse as a means of transport. The continental armies had done so to a lesser degree, especially the Germans, who went to war with a large amount of horse-drawn transport (see ANIMALS), employed with the infantry, while mechanized and motorized formations had mechanical transport supply columns.

*Tank warfare, as exemplified by the high-speed German *blitzkrieg, brought special supply demands which were first revealed during the German march into Austria in March 1938, when the panzer formations involved suffered severely from both mechanical problems and lack of fuel. Steps were taken to improve the supply systems and to make them more responsive to rapidly moving armour, but even so in both the *Polish campaign and in the fighting which led to the fall of *France they became very stretched. The two main problems were supply of fuel and the repair of broken-down vehicles. The faster and longer the advance the greater these problems became. They cropped up again during the Western Desert campaigns where they acted as brake to the swiftly moving offensives conducted by both sides. Time and again these were forced to a halt because supply lines became stretched to the point of breaking. The only way in which they could be shortened was through securing ports. Hence the importance of Benghazi and *Tobruk during the fighting.

However, the logistical problems in the Western Desert paled into virtual insignificance when it came to the war on the Eastern Front. According to the German plan for the invasion of the USSR (see BARBAROSSA), the German armies were expected to carry out an advance of up to 1,300 km. (800 mi.) on a 1,600 km. (1,000 mi.) front in the space of just four months while totally destroying the USSR's military power in the process. Apart from the distances involved, and the high rate of advance to be achieved, the German logisticians were faced with a sparse road network and the need to stockpile massive supplies of fuel, ammunition, food, spare parts, and all the other items needed to maintain a force of over a million men in the field. That the successes of the opening weeks of the campaign were so spectacular were in no small measure due to the efforts of the logisticians, but the coming of the autumn rains changed the situation. Wheeled vehicles stuck in the mud and horse-drawn ones could barely get through. The situation became especially difficult in Army Group South's sector when the retreating Soviets destroyed the bridges over the River *Dnieper. This meant that the railheads, on which the advancing armies were so dependent, could not be advanced east of the river until these were repaired. It was, however, the coming of the snows which really overstretched the German supply system. It was largely for this reason that, in terms of clothing, the German Army initially found itself so ill-equipped to cope with the Soviet winter. It was not, as it is popularly believed, that no provision had been made for it, but that the supply system could not cope with these additional demands.

The Soviet railways played a vital part in the German supply system during the *German–Soviet war and as such became a prime target for the partisans (see USSR, 8). The importance of railways was also recognized by the western Allies and was reflected in their attacks on them, and on road bridges, in Germany and occupied Europe during the last year of the war. In combination with the bombing of oil targets, they eventually brought the German transportation system almost to a complete halt.

The Allies, too, had their problems in supporting highly mechanized armies. A classic example of this was after the break-out from the Normandy beachhead in August 1944 as Hitler employed another means of interdiction by denying the Allies the use of the Channel ports, in much the same way as the British had done against *Rommel with Tobruk in 1941. Consequently, as the Allied armour dashed across France their supply lines, still stretching back to Normandy, quickly became overstretched and, in spite of the efforts of the *Red Ball Express, eventually forced it to halt. This was because, the further they got from their source of supply the more supplies, particularly fuel, the Allies needed to maintain the ever-increasing length of their supply lines and the broadening of their front. The Germans, on the other hand, were in retreat which shortened their lines of supply; by the winter of 1944 a German division needed only 200 tons a day while an Allied one needed 650.

Clearly when warfare was comparatively static resupply

was much easier and smaller quantities were needed. Yet it was often the nature of the terrain which prevented mobile operations and provided its own logistical problems. While air resupply could help overcome these, it was usually necessary to resort to more primitive modes of transport as well. In the mountains of Italy and the jungles of South-East Asia resupply of the front line was often carried out by mules and porters, and during his *Imphal offensive in the spring of 1944 the Japanese Commander, Lt-General *Mutaguchi, took with him hundreds of head of cattle.

Even so, compared to previous wars, the armed forces of the Second World War generally required much more elaborate logistics to be able to operate effectively. Part of the reason, as we have seen, was the faster pace at which operations were conducted and the longer lines of communication. While many of the weapons employed were little different in their technical complexity from those of 1914–18, others, such as *radar and *rocket weapons, required highly specialist logistical support. Indeed, the range of weapons and equipments employed was much more varied and this added to the logistical burden.

There was, however, another aspect, which applied especially to the western nations. Armed forces are a reflection of the societies that spawn them. Western troops, especially the Americans, expected and received a higher quality of life in terms of food, welfare, clothing, and equipment than their Chinese, Japanese, or Soviet counterparts. This contributed to making their administrative machines larger and more complex and also meant that for every soldier in the front line many more men were needed to support him on the lines of communication. While eight soldiers were needed in a European army to keep one fighting, about eighteen were needed to keep one US soldier fighting in the Pacific. Such huge engineering tasks as building the *Ledo Road in Burma and the vast distances involved in shipping supplies across the Pacific undoubtedly contributed to this imbalance, but by contrast the Japanese often employed only one man to keep one soldier fighting. However, this indifference to logistics proved counter-productive for them, and while the Allies employed some of their best brains in its administration Japanese staff officers were only interested in working in their *formations' prestigious operations sections. The Chinese were equally unconcerned, James Lunt noting in his book on the Burma campaign (*A Hell of a Licking*, London, 1986) that much of the Chinese Sixth Army's transportation was by porters, that its logistics were 'virtually non-existent', and that one of its British liaison officers referred to it as 'Genghiz Khan's horde'.

*Manteuffel's view of the advancing Red Army also indicates that the Soviets did not give logistics the same priority as the western Allies or the Germans. 'The advance of a Soviet army is something that Westerners cannot imagine,' he is quoted in Liddell Hart's book, *The Other Side of the Hill* (rev. edn., London, 1951, p. 339; *The German Generals Talk* in the US). 'Behind the tank spearheads roll on a vaste horde partly mounted on horseback. Soldiers carry sacks on their backs filled with dry crusts of bread and raw vegetables collected on the march from the fields and villages. The horses feed on the straw from the roofs of houses—they get very little else. The Russians are accustomed to carry on for as long as three weeks in this primitive way, when advancing. They cannot be stopped as an ordinary army is stopped, by cutting their communications, for you rarely find any supply columns to strike.'

The western soldier's morale was also likely to be more affected if the logistical system broke down, hence the priority given to sustaining it. Morale was also maintained by insisting on high standards of personal hygiene and by the efficient and speedy casualty evacuation systems. Knowledge that if he was hit his wounds would be quickly and properly tended made the soldier much more willing to go into battle. Regular mail from home was also an important consideration, as were the availability of canteens and reasonable leave facilities in overseas theatres, and even the production of forces' newspapers. All these factors played their part and were included to a greater or lesser extent, dependent on nationality and theatre of war, in the logistics machinery.

Yet, however carefully logistical plans were laid, the unexpected could always create problems. One of the dilemmas that both sides had to face was the care of large numbers of *prisoners-of-war (POW) after a victory. The vast pockets created by the Germans in 1941 in the USSR resulted in hundreds of thousands of POW suddenly falling into their hands. It was the same at the end of the war in Germany, and in both cases the victors found themselves with inadequate immediate resources to feed and provide sufficient shelter for their prisoners. The result was that many died, not so much through deliberate neglect but because the logistical system could not cope.

Logisticians have always been regarded by those who do the actual fighting with a certain disdain. Yet, even more than in previous wars, those who waged the Second World War realized only too well the fact that without sufficient logistics support they could achieve little. As the US Navy Chief of Staff, Admiral Ernest *King, is supposed to have remarked in 1942, 'I don't know what the hell this "logistics" is that *Marshall [US army chief of staff] is always talking about, but I want some of it.'

Charles Messenger

Logistics meant ensuring the distribution of supplies in the necessary quantity at the right time. Here a US convoy supplying Chiang Kai-shek's troops ascends a mountain pass into China.

Thompson, J., *The Lifeblood of War: Logistics in Armed Conflict* (London, 1991).
Van Creveld, M., *Supplying War: Logistics from Wallenstein to Patton* (London, 1977).

Löhr, General Alexander (1885–1947), the only Luftwaffe officer besides *Kesselring to become a theatre commander, Löhr was C-in-C of the Austrian Air Force at the time of Germany's annexation of Austria in March 1938. He led the Fourth Air Fleet during the *Polish and *Balkan campaigns and commanded both Fourth Air Fleet and *Student's airborne forces during the capture of *Crete in May 1941. His Fourth Air Fleet then took part in the German invasion of the USSR in June 1941 (see BARBAROSSA) when, supporting *Rundstedt's Army Group South, it contributed substantially to German successes at *Smolensk that August. In July 1942 he was appointed C-in-C South-East, and in January 1943 took command of Army Group E in Greece and the Aegean Sea which inflicted reverses on British forces during the *Dodecanese campaign later that year.

Löhr's forces committed *atrocities on the civilian population during their withdrawal from Yugoslavia in September 1944, and in 1947 he was hanged in Yugoslavia for these war crimes.

London Controlling Section, see DECEPTION.

Longmore, Air Chief Marshal Sir Arthur (1885–1970), Australian-born RAF officer who became C-in-C Training Command in 1939 and helped initiate the successful *British Empire Air Training Scheme. He then served as C-in-C Middle East Air Forces, but he incurred Churchill's displeasure on a number of counts and was summoned to London in May 1941 and replaced by his deputy, *Tedder. He then served as inspector general of the RAF before retiring in 1942. He was knighted in 1942.

Long Range Desert Group (LRDG), British unit formed at the start of the *Western Desert campaigns in June 1940 by Captain Ralph Bagnold who commanded it until August 1941. Equipped with specially adapted trucks, this force reconnoitred behind Axis lines, inserted *spies, provided intelligence, and mounted lightning attacks on Axis fuel dumps, airfields, and garrisons. The first volunteers, New Zealand army personnel, were followed by others from Rhodesia and the UK, and all became expert in driving and navigating across the desert. The group also co-operated with the *Special Air Service and *Popski's Private Army by transporting their personnel to their targets, and it mounted raids with the Free French during the *Fezzan campaigns which started in January 1941. But its most crucial role was to keep a road watch behind Axis lines to check supply convoys. This enabled *ULTRA intelligence to be checked, a task which was described later by *Montgomery's chief-of-staff, *de Guingand, as being the group's most valuable contribution to winning the Western Desert campaigns. An LRDG road watch was also kept during the second *El Alamein battle, which provided a 'window' on the Germans; and during the final phase of the *North African campaign LRDG patrols reconnoitred the route which made possible Montgomery's plan to outflank the *Mareth Line in southern Tunisia in March 1943.

In September 1943 the LRDG moved to the *Dodecanese Islands in the Aegean Sea and suffered heavy losses during the fighting there. In December the New Zealanders were withdrawn and Rhodesians replaced them, and in February 1944 the group entered the *Italian campaign. Initially, one squadron was attached to *Force 266 and the other to the Eighth Army, but from August 1944 both squadrons worked under Land Forces, Adriatic (see BALKAN AIR FORCE), mounting shipping watches, reconnaissance patrols, and raids on Axis forces in Yugoslavia, Albania, the Dalmatian Islands, and Greece during the final phase of the battle for the *Mediterranean.

Owen, D., *Providence Their Guide* (London, 1980).
Shaw, W.B.K., *The Long Range Desert Group* (London, 1945).

Longstop Hill, battle of. This was fought during the *North African campaign, from 22 to 25 December 1942. It was a tactically vital position if the Allies were to capture Tunis quickly. Fought in heavy rain, it was infantry warfare at its worst. First taken by the British, it was lost next day to the Germans by the Americans who failed to retake it. The British retook it on Christmas Eve but then lost the upper part on Christmas morning to German reinforcements. This forced *Eisenhower, who called it 'a bitter decision', to halt his advance on Tunis. 'Christmas mountain', as it came to be called, remained in German hands until 24 April 1943 when the Allies launched their final offensive (VULCAN) to clear Axis forces from Tunisia.

loot is a traditional perk of victorious armies and those fighting the Second World War were no exception. Art treasures have always been particularly vulnerable to any invader. For example, part of the Schliemann collection, the so-called King Priam's Treasure, as well as a number of paintings by Velasquez, El Greco, and other old masters, turned up in Moscow in 1991, having been lost to the world since the fall of *Berlin in May 1945.

But during the Second World War, and in defiance of the *Hague Convention, the Nazis turned looting into an official policy. Works of art—whether paintings, porcelain, sculptures, tapestries, furniture, rare books, or manuscripts—were acquired by a variety of dubious means. In the occupied countries of western Europe (including Austria and, after September 1943, Italy) the purloining of art treasures was often justified on the grounds that they were created by German artists, or were German-inspired, and therefore were only returning to their place of origin. Alternatively, it was argued that a work of art was merely being 'protected', and that it was much better for it to be displayed in Germany, where millions could enjoy it, than hidden away for safety. If the 'legality' of these arguments remained unproven, the work of art was purchased with devalued Reichsmarks.

US Third Army troops examine the painting *Winter Garden* by the French impressionist Edouard Manet, part of a haul of German **loot** found in a salt mine at Merkers in Germany.

In eastern Europe works of art were simply seized, though sometimes a receipt was issued. Museum authorities in Warsaw kept a secret inventory of what had been looted from the city: it amounted to 2,774 paintings of the European school, 10,738 Polish paintings, and 1,379 sculptures. One of the most famous paintings, Raphael's *Portrait of a Young Man*, was never recovered. The *Soviet War News* reported in September 1944 that 34,000 museum pieces, including '14,950 pieces of unique furniture', had been plundered from four palaces around Leningrad; and the 18th-century Amber Room, 46 sq. m. (55 sq. yd.) of carved amber panels, was dismantled and removed from the Ekaterininsky Palace at Pushkin. It also has never been recovered.

To acquire the best of the loot for his proposed museum at Linz (see also GERMANY, 10), Hitler appointed an art expert, Hans Posse, to head Sonderauftrag Linz (Special Operation Linz) based in Munich. Posse had first choice from the art treasures that were looted from Poland, either on *Göring's orders, or by *Rosenberg's ERR (Einsatzstab-Reichsleiter Rosenberg, or Administration Staff Rosenberg). The ERR was established in the Jeu de Paume in Paris after the fall of *France to sell, at artificially low prices, works of art confiscated from Jews. Rosenberg was, in fact, only ERR's titular head: Göring supplied the organization's personnel and transport and, incidentally, took whatever he required for his own art collection if Posse did not want it. What was left went to German institutions. The ERR sent 21,903 items to Germany, which included 10,890 paintings and pictorial works, and 2,471 pieces of furniture. A rival organization was also established by *Ribbentrop. This was a 'Special Service Battalion' of four companies, three of which operated in occupied eastern Europe, to strip libraries, museums, and scientific institutions.

After the war most of the art treasures were tracked down by two Allied units: *SHAEF's Monuments, Fine Arts and Archives teams and the *Office of Strategic Services Art Looting Investigation Unit. Much of the loot was found stored in salt mines at Alt Aussee and Grasleben, or in castles in Bavaria and Austria. Several hundred items, including paintings by Frans Hals, have never been claimed and works by Canaletto, Cézanne, Dürer, Renoir, and Vermeer, to name but a few, have never been recovered.

Another aspect of Nazi loot was the gold they acquired, again by the most dubious 'legal' means, from the central banks of European occupied countries. Altogether, in 1939 terms, they seized $625 million in gold bullion and coins from the central banks of occupied countries, including Austria ($102.7 million), Czechoslovakia ($44 million), the Bank of Danzig ($4.1 million), the Netherlands ($163 million), Luxembourg ($4.8 million), Belgium ($223.2 million), and Italy ($80 million). About $330 millions-worth of gold was eventually found, most of it in a mine at Merkers in western Thuringia, but some of it has never been recovered. However, much of the balance went to neutral countries, primarily Switzerland, as early in the war they all accepted gold in exchange for goods required by Germany. Switzerland, despite Allied pressure, continued to accept the gold until the last months of the war.

Jaeger, C. de, *The Linz File* (Exeter, 1981).
Smith, A., *Hitler's Gold* (Oxford, 1989).

Lord Haw-Haw, see JOYCE.

Lorenz beam, German blind-landing system developed by a German scientist, Dr Hans Plendl, during the 1930s. It was used by civil airlines as well as by the Luftwaffe and the RAF. The principle was later adopted by Plendl to develop the X-Gerät which guided German bombers on to their targets (see ELECTRONIC NAVIGATION SYSTEMS).

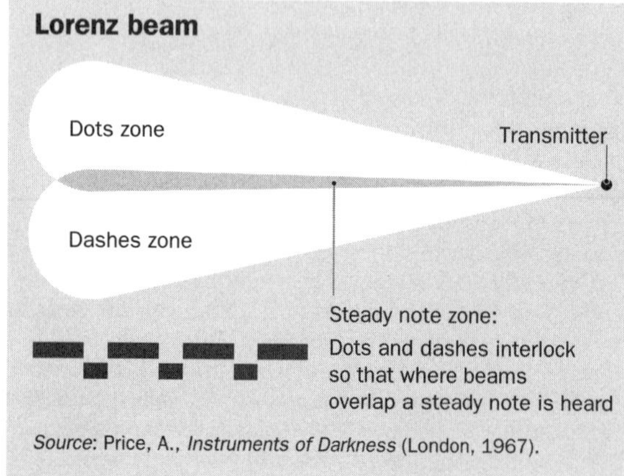

Source: Price, A., *Instruments of Darkness* (London, 1967).

Lorraine Squadron, formed in August 1941 from Blenheim bombers of the first Free French air unit, Groupe de Bombardement No.1, which took part in the *Fezzan campaigns. The three surviving Blenheims of this campaign supported ground troops in the *East African campaign before moving to Damascus where they merged with another Free French wing. Together these became officially known as the Lorraine Squadron, one wing being called 'Metz' the other 'Nancy'. The squadron moved to Libya in November 1941 and in 56 days flew 388 missions supporting Allied troops fighting in the *Western Desert campaigns. One-third of the air crews were killed in these operations. When the squadron was withdrawn the Metz Wing started ferrying duties on the *Takoradi air route while the Nancy Wing was stationed in Palestine for coastal patrols. In December 1942 the squadron went to the UK and was equipped with Boston bombers and later with Mitchell bombers. It became part of the RAF as 342 Squadron and flew low-level missions against targets in the Low Countries and France, supported Allied ground troops during the *Normandy campaign, and undertook raids over Germany. Its casualties included 800 killed.

Lambermont, P., *Lorraine Squadron* (London, 1956).

Lublin Committee. On 22 July 1944 Red Army units crossed the River Bug and occupied Chełm, the first Polish town lying to the west of the line agreed by the *Nazi–Soviet Pact in August 1939. Accompanying the Soviet forces was the 'Polish Committee of National Liberation', a seventeen-member group recruited from among the ranks of the communist National Council for the Homeland (see POLAND, 2(e)) and the Union of Polish Patriots (see POLAND, 4). Its president was the leader of the National Council, Bolesław Bierut (1892–1957), the assumed name of a long-time *Comintern agent.

On the day the committee arrived in Chełm it published its Manifesto to the Polish People (the 'July Manifesto') setting out a political programme, which had clearly been drafted under Moscow's influence. On 26 July the committee moved to Lublin, which had just been captured by the Red Army, where the 'Lublin Committee' signed an agreement with the Soviet government, under the terms of which it received the power to administer those territories liberated by the Red Army which the Soviets acknowledged to be Polish, i.e. those lying west of the Bug (see POLISH–SOVIET FRONTIER). The committee also sanctioned the Soviet annexation of the former Polish provinces east of the Bug and provided for the uprooting of some 4.5 million Poles from these regions. Indeed, it assumed many of the tasks of a legitimate government, enforcing conscription, printing currency, and carrying out land reform.

On 31 December 1944, in response to the 'will of the people', Moscow 'agreed' that the Lublin Committee be transformed into a 'Provisional Government of the Polish Republic'. It was this sham 'government', headed by Bierut, which formed the basis for the Provisional Government of National Unity recognized by the UK and the USA on 5 July 1945. KEITH SWORD

Kersten, K., *The Establishment of Communist Rule in Poland, 1943–1948* (Oxford, 1991).
Rozek, E., *Allied Wartime Diplomacy. A Pattern in Poland* (London, 1958).

LUCY Ring, the name given by the head of the *Rote Drei, a *GRU (Soviet Military Intelligence) espionage network, to the espionage network run by a German communist, Rudolf Rössler, from Switzerland.

According to the most reliable publication on the subject (*Rote Kapelle: the CIA's History of Soviet Intelligence and Espionage Networks in Western Europe, 1936–45*, Washington, DC, 1979), Rössler, who ran a map publishing firm in Lucerne, had four principal German sources: Werther—the most important—Teddy, Olga, and Anna. Between them they provided almost half the messages transmitted by the Rote Drei to Moscow. They may have given their intelligence to Rössler direct; more probably, it went to the Swiss General Staff who passed on to Rössler, via Swiss intelligence, what they wanted Moscow to know.

Before he died Rössler told a confidant who these sources were (though there is no means of knowing if he was telling the truth). Three of them were prominent conspirators against Hitler (see SCHWARZE KAPELLE): Hans Gisevius, an *Abwehr agent stationed in Switzerland; Carl Goerdeler, a former mayor of Leipzig; and a German 'major' who, from what Rössler told his confidant, was probably Maj-Gen Hans *Oster, the Abwehr's second-in-command. The fourth, a 'General Boelitz', has never been identified. Oster was the most likely candidate for Werther.

Contrary to what some publications state, Rössler's intelligence did not include the date of the German invasion of the USSR in June 1941 (see BARBAROSSA) as he was not in contact with the Rote Drei until September 1942, or thereabouts. But according to some sources he was provided with high-level intelligence on the intentions of the German High Command (OKW) which included not always accurate information about the German preparations for the *Kursk battle in July 1943.

In June 1944 Rössler was arrested by the Swiss police, but was released three months later. After the war, he continued to pass high-level intelligence on the western Allies to the Czech authorities until he was caught by the Swiss in 1953 and jailed. See also SPIES.

Luftwaffe, the German Air Force; see GERMANY, 6(d).

Lüneburg Heath, situated some 40 km. (25 mi.) south-east of Hamburg. Here on 4 May 1945, in the presence of *Montgomery, a German delegation led by General-Admiral von *Friedeburg signed the tactical surrender of all German forces in Denmark, north-west Germany, and the Netherlands. This meant, from that date, Grand Admiral *Dönitz, based at Flensburg, was ruling Germany while technically a prisoner-of-war.

Luxemburg, was a Grand Duchy without a standing army. This tiny country of 293,000 people, wedged between Belgium and Germany, was occupied by the Germans on 10 May 1940. Seven of its 87 defenders were wounded while resisting the invasion. Its ruling family and government escaped to the UK, where a government-in-exile was subsequently formed. The population was generally hostile to the Germans, as was borne out by a plebiscite held on 10 October 1941 when 97% of the electorate voted against welcoming the German occupation. This unwelcome result was ignored and all Luxemburgers were declared German nationals and 2,000 German- and Letzteburgesch-speaking Luxemburgers joined the German armed forces. In August 1942 Letzteburgesch (a Low German dialect) was banned and obligatory military service was introduced. When 13,000 Luxemburgers were conscripted a general strike was called, but it was soon broken after 21 strikers were executed and hundreds more were sent to *concentration camps. Altogether 2,848 Luxemburgers died in German uniform, many being shot as *deserters. A number served on the Allied side, mostly in a unit attached to the Belgian Brigade, but also in the RAF, Royal Navy, and as agents in *SOE and *MI6. Resistance workers generally followed the orders of the Belgian resistance and were a vital link in the network which rescued Allied airmen.

US troops entered the country on 10 September 1944 and for the first time in Luxemburg's 50 years of independence a local regular armed unit was raised for guard duties. But the country had to endure the *Ardennes campaign before being finally liberated in February 1945.

During the war 5,259 Luxemburgers lost their lives and the post-war government punished 10,000 for *collaboration.

Lwów was in September 1939 the principal city of south-east Poland, the centre of a region which has been variously known as East Galicia, Eastern Matopolska, or Western Ukraine. Although the city itself possessed a clear majority of Poles, and a large Jewish minority, it was surrounded by districts where Ukrainians predominated; and it inevitably became the target for competing territorial claims. It lay immediately to the east of the demarcation line envisaged by the *Nazi–Soviet Pact; and in September 1939, having been encircled by German forces, it was ceded to the Soviet Union. In the period, 1939–41, when it was annexed to the Ukrainian SSR, it was the scene of brutal repressions, forcible sovietization and the deportation of some 80,000 people, especially former Polish officials and Ukrainian nationalists. In June 1941, when the Wehrmacht was advancing with great rapidity (see BARBAROSSA), the *NKVD shot all 5,000 inmates of the city jail before retreating. On the same day, a group of Ukrainian activists proclaimed an independent Republic of Ukraine, which was immediately suppressed by the advancing Germans. Lwów was then allocated to the General government of Poland as Lemberg, capital of the Distrikt Galizien (see POLAND, 2(b)). In the period of Nazi occupation (1941–4), it saw the construction of a major *ghetto, and of the infamous Janowska Street *concentration camp. The killing of the city's 150,000 Jews was completed by November 1943.

The future of Lwów became a bone of contention between the Allied governments from the time of the Teheran conference (see EUREKA). The western powers were torn between the conflicting claims of the Soviet Union and of the Polish *government-in-exile. According to the original version of the Curzon Line drawn up at the Spa conference in July 1920, Lwów lay on the Polish side of the line (see POLISH-SOVIET FRONTIER). But according to the amended version sent to Moscow, and duly produced by *Molotov at Teheran in November 1943, it lay on the Soviet side; and the Soviet version was allowed to prevail. After the reoccupation of the city by the Soviet Army on 27 July 1944, a new reign of terror commenced. Units of the Polish underground Home Army, which had assisted in the city's capture, were arrested and in part deported. Brutal purges of Polish and Ukrainian activists took place; and in 1946 the bulk of the remaining Polish population were transported en masse to the new Poland. Most of them were sent to repopulate the ex-German city of *Breslau, now Wrocław, in Silesia. Lwów, renamed L'viv (Ukrainian) and Lvov (Russian), escaped serious physical destruction: but its tremendous human losses had to be replaced, largely by migrant Russians. Its fate, trapped between Hitler and Stalin, left no room for the wishes of its citizens; and was mirrored in the parallel experiences of other ex-Polish cities such as *Wilno or Brzesc nad Bugiem (see BREST-LITOVSK).

NORMAN DAVIES

M

Macao, neutral Portuguese colony on the mainland coast of south China. It was not occupied by the Japanese when they overran nearby *Hong Kong in December 1941, but they maintained effective control of it throughout the war.

MacArthur, General Douglas (1880–1964), US Army officer who was one of the most controversial—and the longest serving (1918–51)—generals in the US Army.

The son of an army officer, whose family was both distinguished and aristocratic, MacArthur entered the US Military Academy, West Point, in 1899. He graduated with the highest marks ever received there and by the end of the *First World War was a highly decorated brig-general who had proposed the formation of, and then led, the famous Rainbow Division. His rise continued to be meteoric and by 1930 he was army chief of staff with the temporary rank of general. In 1935 he went to the Philippines, where he had earlier served two tours, to become its military adviser, taking with him a young Major *Eisenhower whom he considered the best staff officer in the US Army.

In 1936 President *Quezon made MacArthur a field marshal in the Philippine Army and he retired from the US Army the following year. However, in July 1941 Roosevelt recalled him to active duty as commander of US forces in the Far East with the rank of lt-general. MacArthur's failure to bomb Formosa—where the Japanese had air bases from which they could, and did, attack the Philippines—immediately after Japan raided *Pearl Harbor has never been satisfactorily explained. Nor have the reasons why, ten hours after the raid, Japanese bombers found US aircraft still on the ground when they raided *Clark Field and another important US air base in the Philippines.

MacArthur's defence of the *Philippines, when the Japanese invaded on 22 December 1941, was also badly flawed and though his withdrawal into the *Bataan peninsula was well executed, his *logistics let him down as insufficient supplies had been stockpiled there. In March 1942, on the president's orders, he made a perilous escape by sea to Australia and on arrival made his famous remark about the Philippines: 'I shall return'. The *Office of War Information liked the phrase but requested it be changed to 'We shall return.' MacArthur refused.

In April 1942, from his HQ in Brisbane, Australia, appalled by the paucity of his forces, he assumed command of what was known as the *South-West Pacific Area (see Map F) which included Australia, New Guinea, and the Netherlands East Indies (except Sumatra). Initially, most of his ground troops were Australians whose fighting abilities he doubted. He doubted, too, the ability of his Land Forces commander, *Blamey, while the Australians regarded McArthur as ignorant of jungle warfare and the problems of New Guinea's rugged terrain (see also AUSTRALIA, 3). By mid-1943 he had sufficient Americans to create *Alamo Force which prevented Blamey commanding US personnel and sidelined Australian troops from the principal campaigns that preceded the recapture of the Philippines.

One of MacArthur's claims to fame in the *Pacific war was the technique known as 'leap-frogging' or 'island-hopping' whereby strong centres of Japanese resistance were bypassed in favour of capturing weaker ones which cost less lives. In fact he was converted late to the idea and wanted to take *Rabaul long after the US *Joint Chiefs of Staff had decided to bypass it—though after the war he claimed it had been his idea. However, once *ULTRA intelligence enabled him to know the strength of Japanese garrisons he did use the technique most effectively. In his presence, his forces landed on the *Admiralty Islands in February 1944, and then, during the *New Guinea campaign, he bypassed Hansa Bay and Wewak and landed further up the coast at *Hollandia in April 1944. But though leap-frogging in his later campaigns saved lives his New Guinea campaign caused fearsome casualties. One Allied serviceman in 11 died during it compared to one in 37 on *Guadalcanal; and the capture of Sananda (see GONA), which he described, with typical hyperbole, as 'mopping up', took three weeks and many casualties.

MacArthur, who disliked Roosevelt and the liberalism he represented, abhorred the policy that Germany had to be defeated before Japan (see RAINBOW PLANS and ARCADIA) and he remained seriously at odds with the Joint Chiefs of Staff over Pacific strategy. He probably got his way to liberate the Philippines, instead of bypassing them as the navy desired, because it suited Roosevelt politically not to oppose his plans. MacArthur, a right-wing Republican with presidential ambitions, was an idol of the American public, and Roosevelt, in election year, found it expedient to show public support for him. Whatever the reasons, MacArthur fulfilled his promise to return to the Philippines when his forces landed on Leyte in October 1944 (see also LEYTE GULF BATTLE) and on Luzon the following January. Later he sent forces to capture the central and southern Philippines without instructions from the Joint Chiefs of Staff, and despite the fact that these islands had no strategic value.

MacArthur had received his fifth star in December 1944, and in April 1945 he took command of all US Army forces in the Pacific. He was designated ground commander for the invasion of Japan and after the Japanese surrender was appointed Supreme Commander, Allied Powers (SCAP). In this post he administered Japan with a surprisingly liberal and democratic hand. In 1950 he was appointed C-in-C of the United Nations forces in the Korean war, but he quarrelled with President *Truman and in April 1951 was relieved of all his commands.

MacArthur's personality was complex, chameleon-like, magnetic, and contradictory. He had an insatiable appetite for publicity, his actions and motives were often suspect, and his communiqués became notorious for

General **MacArthur** wades ashore at Leyte island, October 1944, fulfilling his promise that he would return to the Philippines. This is a posed photograph, as he had already waded ashore without the historic moment being properly recorded.

their boasts and their distortion of the facts. But though he was vain, egotistical, and flamboyant, he was also, to those who knew him well, charming, gracious, and cultured. His real genius as a commander lay in his ability to plan and lead with imagination and boldness. But this genius was flawed by his almost paranoid reaction to criticism, by his flagrant disregard of, and contempt for, many of those in authority above him, and by his gathering officers around him more renowned for their slavish fidelity than their intelligence. As the US army chief of staff, General *Marshall, once remarked to him: 'You don't have a staff, General. You have a court.'

Larrabee, E., *Commander in Chief: Franklin D. Roosevelt, His Lieutenants, and their War* (New York, 1987).
Long, G., *MacArthur as Military Commander* (London, 1969).
Manchester, W., *American Caesar* (Boston, 1979).

McCreery, Lt-General Sir Richard (1898–1967), British Army officer who was *Alexander's chief of staff during the *Western Desert campaigns when Alexander was appointed C-in-C Middle East in August 1942. Alexander thought him that rare creature, a brilliant staff officer and an inspiring commander. He commanded the Eighth Army's 10th Corps at *Salerno and *Monte Cassino during the *Italian campaign. In November 1944 he became the last commander of the Eighth Army when *Leese went to the Far East. He was knighted in 1943.

Macdonald, Angus (1890–1954), Liberal premier of Nova Scotia who became Canadian minister of national defence for naval services in 1940, overseeing the expansion of the Royal Canadian Navy and its escort forces which took part in the battle of the *Atlantic (see also CANADA, 6(c)). An able administrator, he put defence priorities before his party's survival in power during the conscription crisis (see CANADA, 3). In April 1945 he resigned to return to Nova Scotia as premier.

McEwen, Air Vice-Marshal Clifford (1896–1967), *First World War Canadian fighter ace who by 1941 had reached the rank of air commodore. After commanding the 1st (Maritime) Group of the Royal Canadian Air Force (RCAF) in St John's, Newfoundland, he took command in January 1944 of the RCAF's 6th (Bomber) Group in northern England, and his forceful personality improved its morale and its performance. See also CANADA, 6(d).

machine ciphers, see ENIGMA, GEHEIMSCHREIBER, PURPLE, SIGABA, and TYPEX. See also CODES AND CIPHERS.

Maclean, Donald (1913–83), British diplomat and traitor, son of an eminent liberal politician, who became a communist while reading modern languages at Cambridge. He disguised his views to enter diplomatic service where, regarded as a high flyer, he served in embassies in Paris, 1938–40, and Washington, 1944–8, and in the foreign office in between. A useful spy for the USSR, both on diplomatic and on atomic matters, he drank heavily and was bisexual. *MI5 detected his activities but before they could arrest him he defected to Moscow in 1951, with the Cambridge friend Guy Burgess who had recruited him. There he spent the next 32 years writing about international affairs and enduring the system he had advocated. M. R. D. FOOT

Maclean, Brigadier Fitzroy (b.1911), British diplomat and Conservative member of parliament who was Churchill's personal envoy to *Tito and the partisans and head of the British military mission in Yugoslavia from September 1943. He attended the Cairo conference that November (see SEXTANT) and his mission did much to secure British government backing and aid for the partisans. See also BALKAN AIR FORCE.

Maclean, F., *Eastern Approaches* (London, 1949).

Macmillan, (Maurice) Harold (1894–1988), British Conservative politician who was attached to *Eisenhower's *Allied Forces Headquarters (AFHQ) in Algiers during the *North African campaign in 1943 as a political adviser and to *Alexander's AFHQ at Caserta in 1944–5 during the *Italian campaign. As president of the *Allied Control Commission in Italy he acted as the link between Allied commanders, the British government, and the local authorities. British prime minister from 1957 to 1963, he was created Earl of Stockton in 1984.

Macmillan, H., *War Diaries* (London, 1984).

McNaughton, General Andrew (1887–1966), Canadian electrical engineering scientist who devised new artillery techniques during the *First World War and became, according to one British officer, 'probably the best and most scientific gunner in any army in the world'. After the war he remained in the Canadian Army and in 1929 was promoted maj-general and appointed chief of the Canadian General Staff, a post he held until 1935 when he became president of the National Research Council. From December 1939 to December 1943 he was C-in-C Canadian troops in Europe whose size during that time grew from divisional to army strength. McNaughton maintained that his Canadian forces should fight together and disagreed with the piecemeal detachment of some of them to fight in the *Italian campaign. This view brought him into conflict with the Canadian minister of national defence, Layton *Ralston, and when both the CIGS, General *Brooke, and McNaughton's immediate superior, General *Paget, declared him unsuitable to command troops in the field he had little alternative but to resign. He returned to Canada and retired in October 1944 with the rank of general. The prime minister, Mackenzie *King, wanted him to be the country's first Canadian governor-general but when the conscription crisis arose (see CANADA, 3) he offered him Ralston's position in the cabinet. He was sworn in on 2 November 1944 but was unable to find the volunteers needed for service overseas and limited conscription had to be introduced anyway, to which the electorate reacted by rejecting him at a by-election. He also failed to win a seat in the general election of June 1945 and resigned that August.

MAC ships, or merchant aircraft carriers, were merchant ships fitted with a flight deck so that they could, while still carrying their cargoes, launch three or four aircraft to help protect the *convoys in which they were sailing. They were introduced into the battle of the *Atlantic in May 1943 when the lack of escort carriers became acute. Two types were used: 8,000-ton grain carriers and 11,000-ton tankers. Like the *CAM ships, they sailed under the Merchant Navy's red ensign.

Maczek, Lt-General Stanisław (b.1892), Polish Army officer who commanded a motorized brigade in the *Polish campaign. He escaped to the UK, was promoted maj-general, then commanded the 1st Polish Armoured Division which, as part of the First Canadian Army, fought in north-west Europe, notably at Falaise during the *Normandy campaign and in the Netherlands. He was promoted lt-general in May 1945.

Madagascar, capture of. This was undertaken in May 1942 by troops from British East Africa, South Africa, and the UK (see Map 65).

This island 1,610 km. (1,000 mi.) long off the East African coast was a French colony and 34,000 Malagasy soldiers took part in the fighting which preceded the fall of *France. Initially its governor rallied to de *Gaulle and the Free French. But after the British had bombarded the French fleet at *Mers-el-Kébir in July 1940 he resigned and was replaced by a representative of the *Vichy government.

In March 1942 *MAGIC intelligence revealed that Germany was pressing the Japanese to occupy the island. To forestall this the British *Chiefs of Staff decided to capture the naval base of Diégo Suarez situated at the island's northern end. The landing force, in the UK's first major *amphibious operation of the war, was commanded by Maj-General Robert Sturges, and comprised two army brigade groups and No. 5 Commando. They were supported by a strong naval force under Rear-Admiral Neville Syfret. Supported by Fleet Air Arm aircraft the landings, on the opposite side of the

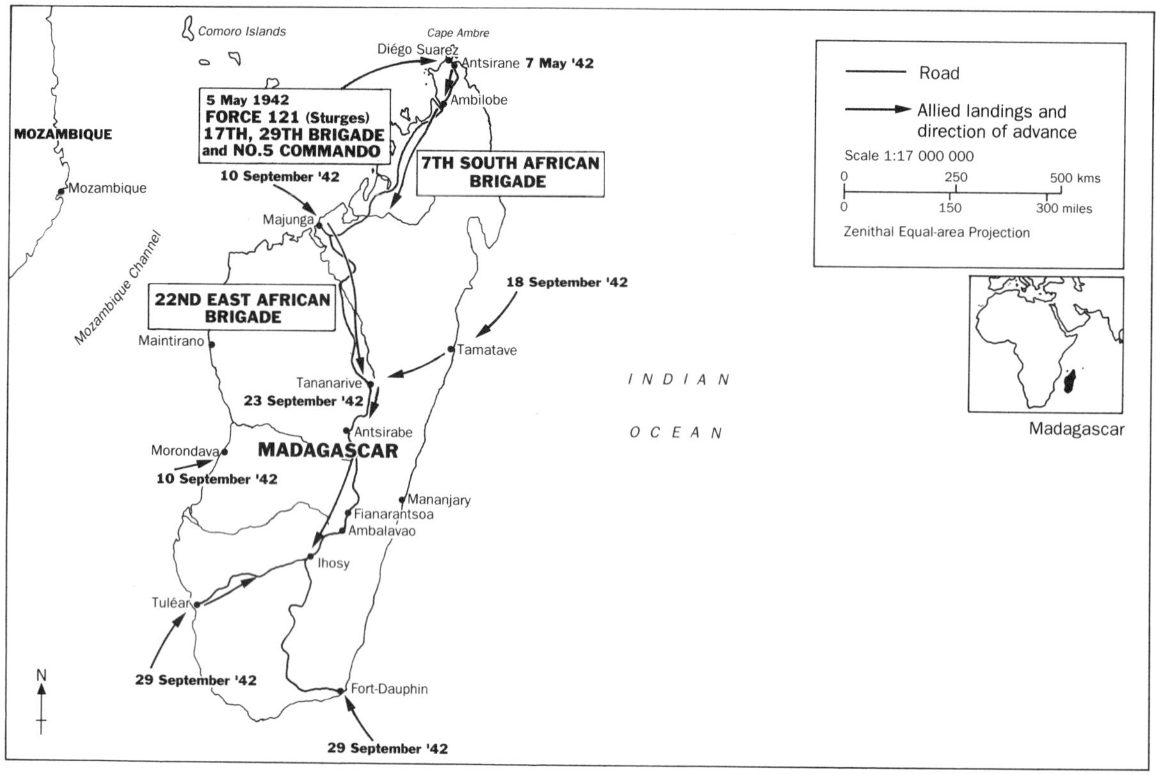

65. Battle for **Madagascar**, May–September 1942

peninsula to Diégo Suarez, took place before dawn on 5 May 1942. Total surprise was achieved, but resistance soon stiffened. However, a night attack on 6/7 May, which coincided with a diversionary raid on Antsirane on the opposite side of the bay, succeeded. In the morning the French defenders in both places capitulated though the governor refused to do so and retreated to the south of the island with his remaining forces.

The original plan had been limited to capturing Diégo Suarez and allowing the rest of the island to remain in Vichy hands. But South Africa's prime minister, General *Smuts, now insisted that other ports be captured as well. Further landings were therefore made at Majunga and Morondava on 10 September, and were followed by others. On 5 November an *armistice was arranged and control of the island passed to the Free French. General Paul Legentilhomme was appointed high commissioner and in May 1943 he handed over the island to a civilian governor-general.

Mafia, criminal organization which originated in Sicily and subsequently spread to mainland Italy and the USA, among other places. Suspecting that members of New York's large Italian community might be feeding intelligence about Allied *convoys to the Germans, in 1942 the US Navy enlisted the help of the Mafia which controlled the workings of the port of New York. As a result, Italian-speaking US Navy officers, who had been given the names of local Mafia members by their US brethren, made contact with with them at the start of the *Sicilian campaign to help gather intelligence. 'The question of the American Mafia's contribution to the liberation of Sicily is clouded with ambiguity and contradiction' (C. D'Este, *Bitter Victory*, London, 1988, p. 627). But the island's liberation was undoubtedly followed by a resurgence of Mafia activity—repressed under Mussolini—as the *Allied Military Government of Occupied Territories (AMGOT), which organized a civilian administration in Sicily and Italy, unknowingly recruited local Mafia members and could not prevent the black market, by which Mafia fortunes were revived, from flourishing.

MAGIC is most commonly known as the American codeword to identify deciphered Japanese diplomatic communications. During the war the word was also used for deciphered Japanese military communications, and, to add to the confusion, all these deciphered messages were classified TOP SECRET ULTRA. While there is overlap in substance as well as designation between the diplomatic and military categories, it is important to preserve the distinction between messages exchanged by the Japanese foreign ministry and its diplomatic posts abroad and those of the Japanese army and navy.

Accordingly MAGIC is restricted here to its more generally understood meaning of diplomatic communications, and Japanese military decipherments are dealt with elsewhere (see ULTRA, 2).

MAGIC included all decrypted messages in Japanese diplomatic codes and ciphers. The most valuable by far were those encrypted by the cipher machine known to the Americans as PURPLE. The cryptanalytical feat of breaking into PURPLE's ciphers was extraordinary. Once in, the Americans were able to read the most secret Japanese diplomatic communications from before *Pearl Harbor to the end of the war. MAGIC supplied no specific warning of the attack on Pearl Harbor or on British and American possessions in South-East Asia, but the cumulative effect of the 1941 messages was the impression of an expansionist Japan ever nearing a decision for war. With MAGIC American officials could in effect peer over the shoulder of the Japanese ambassador in Washington as he sought a diplomatic formula to avoid war in the spring and autumn of 1941 (see also USA, 1).

By way of the Japanese ambassador in Berlin, MAGIC intelligence also provided vital information throughout the war about German plans and operations against the USSR and the western Allies, as well as about Japan's relations with the USSR and its attempts to secure Soviet mediation in ending the war.

The PURPLE cipher machine consisted of two typewriter keyboards connected by a maze of circuits, plugs, and switches. Machine encipherment was an important form of communications security in the Second World War, the most famous example being the German *ENIGMA machine, but it was unusual for Japan and the PURPLE itself was unique. No 'J' machine, called the Type 97 Alphabetical Typewriter (97-shiki O-bun In-ji-Ki) by the Japanese, survived the war, nor are any of the American analogues known to exist. Eyewitness descriptions are few and sparse but offer a rough idea of how the machine worked

In place of rotors, which supplied a sequence of letter substitutions in most enciphering machines, the PURPLE machine used switching gear—stepping switches, to be precise—from the dial telephones of the day. To encipher, the operator pressed the appropriate typewriter key for the plain text letter. This carried current through a plugboard (like an old telephone switchboard), which provided changeable letter substitutions, which served as 'keys' for use on any given day. Thence the current ran through a series of stepping switches. Each of these consisted of a semicircular array, or matrix, of electrical contacts facing a shaft from which projected finger-like conductors, which rotated across the matrix. Each contact and finger stood for a letter of the alphabet. Since the fingers and the matrix were wired differently, each time a typewriter key was pressed a letter substitution occurred. At set intervals the shaft and fingers rotated ahead one or more steps to a new set of contacts, new wiring, and deeper encryption. Then the current passed on to another stepping switch (the PURPLE machine had four) and finally depressed a cipher text key in the second typewriter. Obviously these successive substitutions provided a formidable challenge to cryptanalysts.

Theoretically the possible substitutions by machine cipher were almost endless, millions upon millions. Practically the task was somewhat less daunting. In most cases, including MAGIC, the cryptanalysts found beachheads into the cipher from bureaucratic words and phrases regularly used and available in plain text. Certain forms of address and key words related to the events of the day could be anticipated. In the case of MAGIC, the Japanese foreign ministry made a critical mistake in repeating messages sent in previous encipherment (by the so-called Red machine), so old decrypts could be used to solve PURPLE. Easing the task was the division of the alphabet into two subsets, each group enciphering separately. Keys changed every ten days but within the month varied only slightly and predictably.

In many cases in the Second World War cryptanalysts were assisted by the capture of the other side's code or cipher material or machines but this was not the case with PURPLE. However, American cryptanalysts could get the gist of some enciphered texts from Japanese diplomatic messages delivered to the state department.

Leading the attack on PURPLE was the best American mind in codes and ciphers, William F. Friedman (1891–1969), chief cryptanalyst of the US Army Signal Intelligence Service. A child of Russian-Jewish immigrants, he followed the more prosaic career interests of electrical engineering and plant genetics until 1916 when at the Riverbank Laboratories in Geneva, Illinois, he became intrigued by a project aiming to prove by means of a hidden cipher that Sir Francis Bacon was the real author of Shakespeare's plays. During the *First World War Friedman served in the code room of American headquarters in France and in 1921 returned to the army to spend the next 34 years at the heart of American cryptography.

Modern cryptology, as the authority David Kahn says, is 'saturated with mathematical operations, mathematical methods, mathematical thinking' (see Kahn [below], p. 410). Friedman, though not trained specifically as a mathematician, was expert in statistics and probability, and an authority in applying these to cryptanalysis. In addition he brought to the task of breaking PURPLE mastery of the whole field of cryptology, exceptional intuition, and dogged perseverance. Although his contribution was vital (and so intensive it put him in hospital with a nervous breakdown), this was not a one-man show, for Friedman engaged talented PhDs in mathematics to help him; and the US Army and Navy had made a prolonged effort to gather and train staffs of cryptanalysts, pooling resources and sharing results in the attack on PURPLE.

Beginning in early 1939, the breaking of PURPLE took eighteen months. One hypothesis after another was tried and discarded. A critical breakthrough occurred when a cryptanalyst from naval intelligence, Harry L. Clark, suggested that the Japanese might be using ordinary telephone stepping switches instead of rotors. Laboriously they separated cipher text into segments representing different key settings and then tackled texts in the same key, building out from known letters and words, looking for symmetries in the position of letters, and trying out letters according to the known frequency of their use. Translators filled in missing letters and completed words.

With agonizing slowness at first and then gradually more swiftly the plain text messages emerged. The first message was completed on 25 September 1940, two days before the signature of the Axis *Tripartite Pact. So impressed with the feat was one authority that he referred to the team as 'magicians', hence the codeword MAGIC.

Once the Friedman group understood what kind of a machine enciphered PURPLE and how it must be wired, they constructed a machine to duplicate its functions. By the spring of 1941 four of these machines were at work, one in the Philippines, two in Washington, and one in the UK at *Bletchley Park.

The American gift of a PURPLE machine to the UK—revealing to a foreign power a vital state secret—was the first big step in establishing British–American co-operation and co-ordination in signals intelligence and cryptanalysis. That path, as Bradley F. Smith has shown in his book *The Ultra-Magic Deals* (Novato, Ca., 1993), was painfully slow and tortuous but in the end extremely successful and important in the prosecution of the war. Upon receipt of the PURPLE machine the British began intercepting and decrypting Tokyo's messages to and from its embassies and consulates in Europe and the Middle East. By June 1941 the British had received a second machine for Singapore.

One example to which these machines were put to use was to reveal the treachery of Burma's prime minister, U *Saw. On his way back home from London, after unsuccessful talks about Burma's independence, he visited the Japanese consulate in Lisbon. He assured the consul-general that if the Japanese invaded Burma his people would rise against the British and help the Japanese drive them out (see also THAKIN). The next day Tokyo was apprised of this conversation; the encoded signal was decrypted; and U Saw was arrested further along his journey and spent the rest of the war in *internment.

The flow of decrypts continued until Japan's defeat. The Japanese never suspected that their most secret diplomatic cipher had been compromised. Some messages were deciphered and translated the same day and most within a week; a few in cases of key change took longer, one as long as 59 days. Shortage of translators, in particular those familiar with the forms used in official, telegraphic transmissions, caused delay.

MAGIC was, as the chief of staff of the US Army, *Marshall, said, a 'priceless asset' for the USA and UK and extraordinary measures were taken to keep it secret. Indeed, these precautions were so protective, at least before *Pearl Harbor, that they hampered effective use of the information. Horrified to find a copy of a MAGIC message in a White House wastebin, the army for a time struck the president off its list of recipients. MAGIC was treated with such *secrecy that it was almost impossible to integrate it with other forms of intelligence. In fact before Pearl Harbor there was no national system for correlating and evaluating intelligence from different sources. By the end of the war the distribution system was systematic and comprehensive, the president and high officials receiving the daily 'Black Book', a digest of important MAGIC and ULTRA intelligence from British and American sources.

Although it revealed the imminence of war, MAGIC did not pinpoint Pearl Harbor or other objectives since Japanese diplomats were kept in the dark about military plans. However, a better organized American intelligence system might have been alerted by a message of 24 September 1941, not in PURPLE but a lesser cipher, asking the precise location of warships in Pearl Harbor. But distinguishing Japanese intelligence-gathering for an attack on Pearl Harbor from the mass of information sought by the Japanese on American naval activities throughout the Pacific would have been difficult at best. In the last hours before war, MAGIC did disclose the Japanese intention of breaking off negotiations in Washington and the particular hour this was to occur, 1300 in Washington, dawn in the Hawaiian Islands. Washington officials anticipated an attack somewhere and issued warnings, but missed the Hawaiian connection.

While MAGIC had limited operational value during the war, it was important in reinforcing American and British perceptions of Japanese aggressiveness. Intercepts of June and July 1941 gave an inside view of Japan's coercive diplomacy to secure military bases in southern French Indo-China. They also plainly indicated Japan's interest in further penetration of South-East Asia: Tokyo directed its consuls to find Japanese who knew Malaya, secure maps of the region, and gain information about the *Netherlands East Indies beach defences and the camouflage markings of American planes at Manila. Typical as a preliminary to war were messages ordering Japanese consulates to destroy back files and cipher material. They indicated, too, plans for anti-American propaganda and espionage networks in Latin America and the recruitment of *African Americans as *spies.

MAGIC was also a rich source of intelligence on the European war. While the Japanese foreign ministry had limited access to information about its own military forces, and shared it sparingly with its missions abroad, traffic the other way was heavy: Japanese embassies and legations in German-occupied Europe, Berne, Lisbon, Stockholm, and Moscow provided a stream of information on the tide of battle and German capabilities and intentions. The military and naval attachés in these posts used their own codes but even these in time were decrypted.

The most valuable reports were those of Lt-General *Ōshima the Japanese ambassador in Berlin. As principal representative of Germany's Axis partner, Ōshima had access to the highest German sources including Hitler himself, as well as to leaders of the Wehrmacht. The Germans were not overly generous in sharing secrets with their Japanese ally (see AXIS STRATEGY AND CO-OPERATION), but neither could they leave Tokyo entirely in the dark, so the ambassador's reports were of vital interest to Washington and London.

In early June 1941 Ōshima reported that conversations with Hitler and Foreign Minister von *Ribbentrop indicated, in all probability, an imminent German attack on the USSR (see BARBAROSSA). Although the massing of German forces in the east was impossible to conceal or ignore, British and American intelligence found it difficult to believe that Hitler would actually strike. Rather it was suspected that he was seeking to intimidate Stalin into making large territorial concessions. Ōshima's message was important, though by no means singular, in convincing the doubters of Hitler's real intention.

The course of the swaying tide of battle in the *German–Soviet war was of intense interest to Japan, and Ōshima followed it closely. By way of his deciphered messages the western powers gained confirmation from Berlin that the German drive on *Moscow in the autumn of 1941 was slowing down, and the following spring that the Soviet counter-offensive was ebbing. During the crucial battle for *Stalingrad, word that Japan had rejected a German appeal to attack the USSR encouraged the view in London that the Soviets would hold out. Further examples are: a decrypt of August 1943 reflecting German pessimism during the great battle of *Kursk; and another in January 1944, as the Allied invasion of France approached (see OVERLORD), dwelling on the difficulty Hitler saw in waging war on more than one front.

One of the most valuable contributions of MAGIC was the information Japan's Berlin and *Vichy embassies provided about German defences and troop dispositions against the Allied invasion of France in June 1944. Reports by Ōshima and his naval attaché of tours of the defences in France gave details of the German command structure in the west, the number of divisions in each sector, the composition of the mobile reserve, the nature of the *Atlantic Wall, and warning of underwater obstacles erected against landing craft. The Germans planned to defend at the beachline, said Ōshima, and smash any beachhead with their panzer reserve. As to where the Allied forces would land, and whether the landings in Normandy were to be the only ones, the Japanese confirmed German uncertainty right down to D-Day and beyond (see also XX-COMMITTEE).

Also of great value were decrypts concerning German production, morale, and weaponry. By way of the Japanese, the Allies learned the characteristics of the new German *Schnorchel-type U-boats, and specifications of their radio-guided, air-launched, rocket-propelled, anti-ship bombs (see GUIDED WEAPONS). The growing weight of the Allied *strategic air offensive against Germany was also reflected in MAGIC decrypts. In August 1943 Ōshima told of German plans for increased fighter plane production to counter the raids. By June 1944 the embassy was describing daylight attacks as overwhelming. It reported more than once on severe and possibly fatal bomb damage to oil refineries and synthetic oil plants. The Berlin embassy also correctly predicted, more than once, a German counter-offensive in the west in late 1944, but not where, when, and in what strength (see ARDENNES CAMPAIGN).

MAGIC was only one of many intelligence sources available to the western Allies. It was not always respected or heeded: to some, the Japanese seemed gullible, taken in by German claims. Nevertheless, it provided an extraordinarily valuable supply of operational intelligence both in Europe and in waging the *Pacific war. Its final gift was the revelation to the Americans of Japan's desperate and futile effort to secure Soviet mediation in ending the Pacific war, which clearly indicated Japan's insistence on maintaining the institution of Emperor *Hirohito as a condition for peace.

WALDO HEINRICHS

Heinrichs, W., *Threshold of War: Franklin D. Roosevelt and American Entry Into World War II* (New York, 1988).

Kahn, D., *The Codebreakers* (New York, 1967).

Lewin, R., *The American Magic: Codes, Ciphers and the Defeat of Japan* (New York, 1982). Published in UK as *The Other Ultra*.

Maginot Line, series of highly sophisticated French fortifications (*ouvrages*) constructed between the wars to deter a German offensive into France. Named after André Maginot, the French minister of war who initiated the construction, it ran from Switzerland to the Luxemburg and Belgian borders, and into southern France, where the Italians failed to breach it in June 1940. There were fortifications, too, on Corsica and in Tunisia, but its two most heavily fortified areas were the Metz region between Longuyon and Teting and the Lauter region between the Saar and Rhine rivers. It was a symbol of French defensive thinking, and when the Germans launched their offensive in May 1940 (see FALL GELB) its 400,000 troops performed well and refused to surrender. However, the main German thrust outflanked the line and it was later breached near Saarbrücken and Colmar.

Kemp, A., *The Maginot Line* (London, 1981).

Maisky, Ivan (1884–1975), Soviet ambassador to the UK from 1932 to 1943. During this time he lobbied hard for a Second Front once the *German–Soviet war started in June 1941; negotiated *Lend-Lease for the USSR and mutual assistance pacts with the Polish and Czech *governments-in-exile; and arranged for the Free French *Normandie squadron to fight on the Eastern Front. In 1943 he was made deputy people's commissar for foreign affairs and later attended the Yalta (see ARGONAUT) and Potsdam (see TERMINAL) conferences.

Majdanek, *concentration camp situated on the outskirts of Lublin in Poland. It was built as a *prisoner-of-war camp in late 1941 but grew to become the largest Nazi concentration camp after *Auschwitz. From August 1942, when it was fitted with gas chambers, until July 1944, when the Red Army reached it, it was a death camp (see OPERATION REINHARD) where about 200,000 people were killed. See also FINAL SOLUTION.

Makin Island raid, mounted in August 1942 by a US Special force, *Carlson's Raiders, against the Japanese garrison on this Pacific atoll, the most northerly of the Gilbert Islands. Intended to distract the Japanese from the landings then taking place on *Guadalcanal, it involved transporting 222 men 3,200 km. (2,000 mi.) by submarine. At the time the raid seemed successful, but it prompted the Japanese to reinforce and fortify a nearby atoll called *Tarawa, which cost the US Marine Corps heavy losses in November 1943. See also PACIFIC WAR.

Malaya was the collective name for those states contained in the 1,100 km. (700 mi.)-long Malay peninsula, and Singapore. They comprised the Federated Malay States (Perak, Selangor, Negri Sembilan, and Pahang); the Unfederated Malay States (the northern states of Kedah, Perlis, Kelantan, and Trengganu which had at one time belonged to Thailand); and the Straits Settlements (Penang Island and the territory opposite it, the mainland enclave of Malacca, and Singapore). The Straits Settlements, whose government also administered the Christmas and Cocos-Keeling islands, and the island of Labuan (part of British Borneo), formed a British colony while the other two were, in varying degrees, under British protection.

Malaya in 1939 has been described as tranquil, complacent, and politically backward. The population during the war years was about 5.5 million of whom only 2.3 million were indigenous Malays, the rest being Chinese (2.4 million), Indians (750,000), and 100,000 of other nationalities including the British. Most of the Chinese lived in towns in the Federated States and Straits Settlements, while the majority of the Malays were engaged in agriculture in the Unfederated States.

Apart from the local British businessmen in Singapore and Penang, who had the right to elect representatives to the Straits Settlements Legislative Council, native members of the various legislatures were nominated by the British administration or by the sultans through whom the British ruled. There was a fixed majority of government officials on each legislature, but co-operation and consultation were the general rule and formal voting was rare. There were no political parties as such, though the Union of Young Malaya (Kesatuan Melayu Muda or KMM), founded in 1938, had some influence, as did the illegal Malayan Communist Party (MCP).

Malaya was a valuable asset to the British for it produced 38% of the world's rubber and 58% of the world's tin (see RAW AND SYNTHETIC MATERIALS); so valuable that it was decided not to introduce conscription for fear that it would adversely affect production. As a consequence, when the Japanese invaded on 8 December 1941, the only indigenous forces available of any consequence were the Malayan Regiment, a regular unit, and eight Volunteer infantry battalions.

After the *Malayan campaign and the fall of *Singapore the KMM attempted to achieve their national aspirations for independence through the Japanese, but in June 1942 they were banned and from then on the only political organization allowed was the *Indian Independence League. However, initially, the KMM were allowed to raise a local military force, but hedged their bets by keeping in contact with the nucleus of a guerrilla force which had been trained by the British to operate in the jungle. This force, mostly Chinese members of the MCP who had been trained by *SOE in Singapore before its capture, formed the Malayan People's Anti-Japanese Army (MPAJA) which harassed the occupying forces.

In 1943 SOE and *Special Operations Australia, established contact with the MPAJA and provided it with leaders such as F. Spencer Chapman as well as arms and supplies. The MPAJA claimed after the war that it undertook 340 operations against the Japanese whose records show that they lost some 600 men and 2,000 local police while inflicting 2,900 casualties on the MPAJA. By the end of the war the MPAJA numbered about 7,000.

Singapore became the centre of the Japanese regional military administration (which also included Sumatra) and British civilians were interned in the notorious *Changi prison there. Singapore was regarded as a Japanese colony and was ruled by a mayor, while the states were placed under a Japanese military governor. All western influence was ruthlessly extinguished and replaced by Japanese culture and language, and in October 1943 Thailand was allowed to annex the four northern Unfederated States. For a time the sultans were stripped of their power and the diminution of this traditional influence led to a flowering of genuine Malayan nationalism which the Japanese began to encourage from mid-1943. From this process a new Malay élite emerged and in July 1945 the Japanese formally agreed to promote a Malay nationalist movement. Malay Indians were encouraged to join the *Indian National Army, which was initially based, as was Subhas Chandra *Bose's Provisional government of Free India, in Singapore. However, 60,000 were sent to work on the *Burma–Thailand railway, of whom only 20,000 returned. But it was the Malay Chinese, who had been financially supporting *Chiang Kai-shek, who received especially brutal treatment from the Japanese, and those known to have contributed to the China Relief Fund were executed.

Thousands more were massacred in Singapore when the Japanese overran it and the survivors were pressured to become followers of *Wang Ching-wei's puppet government in Nanking (see CHINA, 3(b)).

There was an acute shortage of food in Malaya during the war years, with rice production falling by a third. Up to 1941 the population had been increasing by 100,000 a year, but by 1945 there was an annual decline of 10,000. Much of the tin production was destroyed in the fighting, but rubber production continued. However, both were soon brought to a standstill because Japanese industry could not absorb what was being produced.

On 9 September 1945 the British resumed control by undertaking *amphibious landings (ZIPPER), with two divisions and one brigade landing south of Port Swettenham and north of Port Dickson. As the Japanese had already surrendered, they were unopposed, but the MCP then clashed with the reinstated colonial government. From 1948 it conducted an armed struggle for independence which was eventually achieved in 1957.

Chapman, F. S., *The Jungle is Neutral* (London, 1949).
Kheng, C. B., *Red Star Over Malaya* (Singapore, 1983).

Malayan campaign. This started on the night of 7/8 December 1941 when elements of the Twenty-Fifth Japanese Army under Lt-General *Yamashita, covered by units of Vice-Admiral *Kondō's Southern Force, invaded northern Malaya and southern Thailand with the fall of *Singapore as their ultimate objective. On the morning of 7 December the Japanese committed the first act of aggression in the *Pacific war when a British Catalina flying boat was shot down by land-based aircraft to maintain the secrecy of the invasion fleet's destination.

Yamashita had four divisions at his disposal but, according to one Japanese writer (M. Tsuji, *Singapore 1941–42: The Japanese Version of the Malayan Campaign of World War II*, Sydney, NSW, 1960) after considering the fighting capacity of the British Army decided that three divisions would be enough. His force numbered 60,000 men, but as late as 26 December 5th Division still lacked one regiment, 18th Division lacked two regiments and its HQ, and the Imperial Guards Division, which had not seen action since the Russo-Japanese war of 1905, was two-thirds under strength. But the infantry was supported by the guns of Vice-Admiral *Ozawa's Malaya Force, by 158 naval aircraft and 459 aircraft of 3rd Air Division, and by 80 tanks, 40 armoured cars, and several regiments of artillery.

By attacking and taking Malaya first, the Japanese were able to assault the great British base of Singapore from the rear, a tactic the defenders were ill-prepared to meet. The British and Indian garrison in Malaya also lacked the mobility of the Japanese on land, they quickly lost control of the sea, and their few air bases were poorly protected.

Instead of coinciding their attack with *Pearl Harbor, as had been intended, the Japanese accidentally started their assault early, with Ozawa's warships beginning their bombardment of Kota Bharu in northern Malaya at 0115. Yamashita's troops then made an unopposed diversionary landing there before others began landing at Singora and Patani in southern Thailand, and during the next 48 hours there were more landings on the northern Malayan coast.

To oppose Yamashita the British C-in-C Far East, Air Chief Marshal *Brooke-Popham, had some 88,600 Australian, British, Indian, and Malay troops, all commanded by Lt-General Arthur Percival. However, he had only 158 aircraft, mostly obsolete types, available for operations in Malaya, and no tanks. Lt-General Lewis Heath's 3rd Corps comprising the 9th and 11th Indian Divisions, and 28th Independent Infantry Brigade, was entrusted with the defence of northern Malaya, while the 8th Australian Division, commanded by Maj-General *Bennett, defended Johore. Two infantry brigades were kept in Singapore with a third in reserve.

A pre-war plan (MATADOR) to occupy the Singora–Patani area of Thailand, to prevent just such a Japanese landing, was not implemented for political reasons; and an alternative, to occupy defensive positions around Jitra, was not ordered until ten hours after the Japanese had landed, a delay which proved disastrous. Because MATADOR was not activated Japanese aircraft were able to operate from the airfields at Singora and Patani, as well as from southern French Indo-China, and these soon wrought havoc amongst forward British air bases where aircraft were often caught on the ground. To add to the defenders' problems the **Prince of Wales* and the *Repulse*, two of the Royal Navy's most powerful warships, were sunk by Japanese aircraft after they had left Singapore to attack the Japanese beachheads.

Yamashita's 5th Division crossed to the west coast; the Imperial Guards Division occupied Bangkok; and elements of 18th Division, the Koba and Takumi Detachments, attacked along the east coast. The 5th Division's advance guard, the equivalent of only two battalions, supported by a tank company, swept aside 11th Division—many of whose poorly-trained Indian troops had never even seen a tank—at Jitra. Though not trained in jungle warfare, the 5th and 18th Japanese Divisions were battle-hardened veterans from the fighting in the *China Incident. They were more mobile than the defenders—they used bicycles on the excellent roads—and were often helped by a compliant Malayan civil population, and they moved south with spectacular speed. Time and again the British were outflanked, sometimes by seaborne landings from small boats, sometimes by attacks through the jungle, and on 11 January 1942, with the help of the Imperial Guards Division which had joined 5th Division on 24 December, the capital Kuala Lumpur fell.

The 3rd corps now withdrew to Johore. A new force, 'Westforce', comprising elements of the 8th Australian and 9th Indian Divisions, was formed under Bennett to halt the main Japanese advance; and nine days later 'Eastforce', comprising 22nd Australian Brigade and other units, was formed under Heath to halt the Japanese

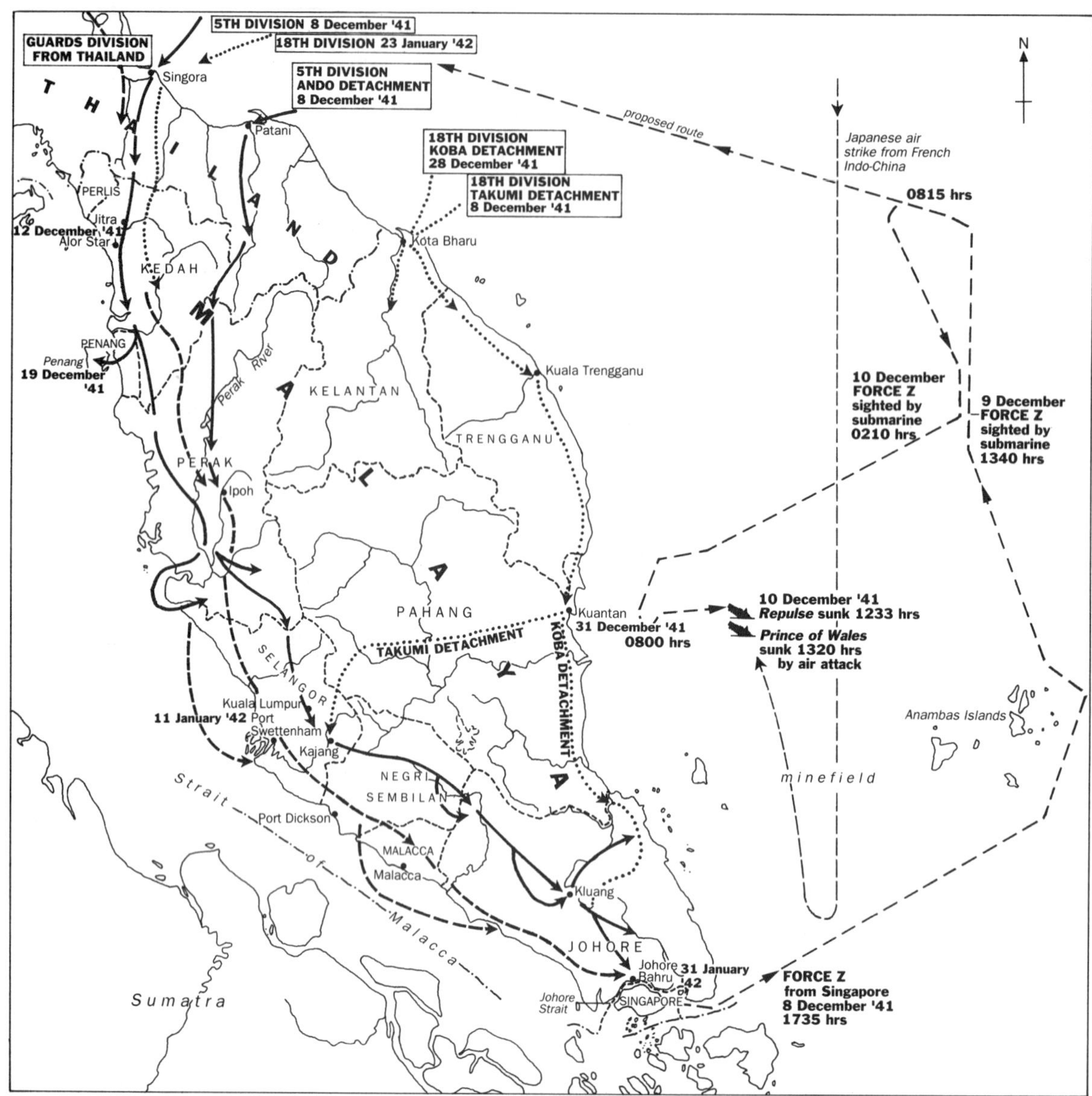

66. **Malayan campaign**, December 1941–January 1942, and sinking of *Prince of Wales* and *Repulse*, December 1941

advance down the east coast. But they were quickly swept aside and by 31 January all British forces had withdrawn to Singapore.

With the fall of Singapore, the Malayan campaign was the Japanese Army's most brilliant campaign of the war. By advancing 965 km. (600 mi.) in 54 days, at a cost of under 10,000 casualties, Yamashita inflicted a crushing and ignominious defeat on the British from which their Far East empire never recovered. British casualties were 38,496, Australian 18,490, Indian 67,340, local volunteer groups 14,382. These casualties totalled 138,708 of whom more than 130,000 were *prisoners-of-war.

Maldive Islands, British colony situated some 965 km. (600 mi.) to the west of Ceylon. The British Eastern fleet used the most southerly of the string of islands, Addu Atoll, as a secret base for its operations. See also INDIAN OCEAN.

Malinovsky, Marshal Rodion (1898–1967), Red Army officer who was an infantry corps commander when the *German–Soviet war broke out in June 1941, and who by the following December had risen to the command of an army group (South *front*). However, a succession of defeats culminated in South *front*'s complete disintegra-

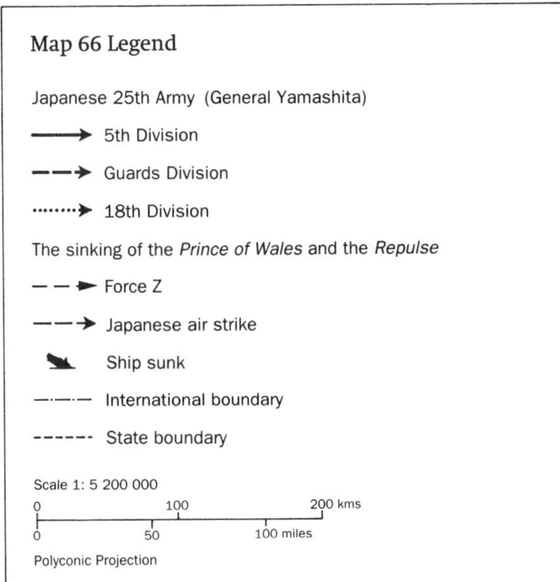

tion in July 1942. The disasters that befell him were probably inescapable, but Stalin did not acknowledge a distinction between misfortune and incompetence. His career might have languished permanently had Stalin not had to call on him to take over the reconstituted South *front* in February 1943 when the commander, General *Eremenko, suddenly fell ill at the height of the Soviet offensive after *Stalingrad.

Subsequently, Malinovsky competently commanded army groups in secondary sectors in the Ukraine and the Danube Basin. In September 1944, after his Second Ukrainian *front* had taken Bucharest, he was advanced to Marshal of the Soviet Union, probably to give him rank befitting the anticipated conqueror also of *Budapest and Vienna. In August 1945, he commanded the Transbaikal *front* against the Japanese *Kwantung Army (see JAPANESE–SOVIET CAMPAIGNS). EARL ZIEMKE

Malmédy massacre, mass execution of US *prisoners-of-war and local civilians which took place at Baugnez near Malmédy in pre-war Belgium on 17 December 1944. It was carried out by *SS Standartenführer (colonel) Joachim Peiper's special *Kampfgruppe* (battle group) which penetrated US lines during the *Ardennes campaign. There were 43 American survivors, but 86 were killed.

After the war, the commander of Sixth SS Panzer Army, General *Dietrich, Peiper, and two others were charged with issuing illegal orders—the massacre had been only the largest of a number of similar incidents—and they and 69 other suspects were incarcerated in *Dachau where their trial began in May 1946.

The prosecution admitted that confessions had been abstracted by threatened execution, false witnesses, and mock trials, but all the defendants were found guilty. Peiper and 42 others were condemned to death; 22, including Dietrich, were sentenced to life imprisonment. Subsequent legal reviews and appeals reduced these sentences and they were further reduced when evidence emerged that the accused had been ill-treated. In March 1949 the Armed Services Committee of the US Senate started an investigation in which Senator Joseph McCarthy, the anti-communist crusader, accused the US Army of *Gestapo tactics and the investigating sub-committee of whitewashing the army's conduct. None of the death sentences was carried out. Dietrich was paroled in 1955. Peiper, released in 1956, was killed in 1976 when his house was fire-bombed. See also ATROCITIES.

Malta, siege of, British Mediterranean island colony with a civilian population of 270,000 which, by refusing to capitulate to intense air bombardment, played a critical role in the battle for the *Mediterranean.

The island's governor (Lt-General William Dobbie and, from May 1942, General Lord *Gort) acted as its C-in-C. It possessed several airfields and the only British harbour between Gibraltar and Alexandria. It was therefore crucial to British air and sea operations against the *convoys supplying Axis forces fighting in the *Western Desert and subsequently in the *North African campaigns. But its proximity to Sicily—95 km. (60 mi.)—and its distance from the nearest British base (1,600 km./1,000 mi.), made it difficult to defend and to supply. Though plans were formulated by the Axis to invade the island, neutralization from the air always appeared a more attractive option. That this was never permanently achieved proved fatal to their Mediterranean strategy.

Malta was first attacked by Italian aircraft on 11 June 1940 when only three obsolescent biplanes (see FAITH, HOPE, AND CHARITY) and inadequate anti-aircraft defences were available to defend it. With the arrival of the Luftwaffe in Sicily, raids intensified between January and April 1941, and in July the Italian *Tenth Light Flotilla launched a brave but unsuccessful attack on the island's Valetta harbour. Hitler's invasion of the USSR in June 1941 (see BARBAROSSA) diverted Luftwaffe units to the *German–Soviet war, but raids were renewed in December with even greater intensity. During January 1942 there were 262, during February 236, and in March and April twice the tonnage of bombs that London had suffered during the *Blitz was dropped on Malta. From 1 January to 24 July there was only one 24-hour period when no bombs fell and air raids became such a permanent feature of everyday life that the civil population led an underground existence. Health standards declined, malnutrition spread, scabies was rife, and that summer there was a typhoid epidemic (see also MEDICINE). Civilian casualties alone from the bombing amounted to 1,493 dead and 3,764 wounded, a high proportion of them *children.

Along with the fighter squadrons flown in to protect the island, it was convoys—and fast merchant ships which ran the Axis gauntlet alone—that saved Malta from

The scene of the **Malmédy massacre** which took place during the Ardennes campaign in December 1944.

capitulation (see Table). But of the 86 supply ships sent to the island between August 1940 and August 1942, either in convoy or independently, 31 were sunk and many others were severely damaged. Mines also caused losses and by April 1942, when the island was awarded the George Cross (see DECORATIONS), Axis minefields had become almost impenetrable and had forced the withdrawal of Malta's one remaining offensive capability, a flotilla of submarines. Food, fuel, and ammunition were now all in desperately short supply and the island was virtually helpless.

On 10 May the German C-in-C South, *Kesselring, reported that Malta had been neutralized, but this statement proved premature as was the diversion of Luftwaffe units to other theatres. Kesselring's misjudgement created a lull the island desperately needed and morale was lifted by the arrival of 61 Spitfire fighters which, unlike an earlier delivery, avoided instant destruction on the ground. These and later fighter reinforcements, combined with the diversion of the Luftwaffe units, brought about a marked decline in raids and by mid-July enough mines had been cleared for the submarine flotilla to return. But for the civilian population the situation remained critical and when a convoy (VIGOROUS) from Alexandria, in Egypt, was forced to turn back in June 1942 the daily calorie rate was cut to 1,500; it was not until the PEDESTAL convoy arrived in August that starvation and inevitable capitulation were once more avoided.

In October 1942 Kesselring, in a final attempt to bring the island to its knees, launched yet another series of intensive air raids. But again he failed and the capture of Cyrenaican airfields in Libya that November after the second *El Alamein battle brought relief and a convoy (STONEHENGE) from Alexandria arrived intact when only twelve days' supply of food and five of aviation fuel

Malta, siege of: Major Malta conveys, 1941–2

1941

Naval forces employed	From West, Jan 1941 Operation 'Excess'			From West, July 1941 Operation 'Substance'			From West, Sept 1941 Operation 'Halberd'		
	No.	*Sunk*	*Dmgd.*	*No.*	*Sunk*	*Dmgd.*	*No.*	*Sunk*	*Dmgd.*
Capital ships	4	–	–	2	–	–	3	–	1
Aircraft carriers	2	–	1	1	–	–	1	–	–
Cruisers	8	1	1	5	–	1	5	–	–
A-A ships	1	–	–	–	–	–	–	–	–
Destroyers	23	–	1	18	1	1	18	–	–
Corvettes	4	–	–	–	–	–	1	–	–
Submarines	3	–	–	8	–	–	9	–	–
Transports and Merchant ships	14	–	–	13	–	2	12	1	–

1 January–31 July 1942

Naval forces employed	From East, Convoy 'M.W.10' (March)			From West, Operation 'Harpoon' (June)			From East, Operation 'Vigorous' (June)		
	No.	*Sunk*	*Dmgd.*	*No.*	*Sunk*	*Dmgd.*	*No.*	*Sunk*	*Dmgd.*
Capital ships	0	–	–	1	–	–	–	–	–
Aircraft carriers	0	–	–	2	–	–	–	–	–
Cruisers	4	–	3	3	–	1	7	1	2
A-A ships	1	–	–	1	–	1	1	–	–
Destroyers	18	3	2	18	2	3	26	3	–
Minesweepers and Corvettes	–	–	–	4	–	1	6	–	1
Submarines	5	1	–	4	–	–	9	–	–
Transports and Merchant ships	4	1	–	6	4	–	11	2	2
No. of Transports and Merchant ships which arrived in Malta	3[a]			2			0		

[a] all sunk after arrival

1 August–31 December 1942

Naval Forces Employed	From West, Operation 'Pedestal' (August)			From East, Operation 'Stoneage' (November)[a]			From East, Operation 'Portcullis' (December)		
	No.	*Sunk*	*Dmgd.*	*No.*	*Sunk*	*Dmgd.*	*No.*	*Sunk*	*Dmgd.*
Capital ships	2	0	0	–	–	–	–	–	–
Aircraft carriers	3	1	1	—	–	–	–	–	–
Cruisers	6	1	2	4	0	1	4	0	0
A-A ships	1	1	0	–	–	–	–	–	–
Destroyers	31	1	0	17	0	0	10	0	0
Minesweepers and Corvettes	8	0	0	–	–	–	–	–	–
Submarines	8	0	0	–	–	–	–	–	–
Transports and Merchant ships	14	9	3	4	0	0	5	0	0
Number of Transports and Merchant ships which arrived in Malta	5			4[b]			5		

[a] Tobruk recaptured 13 November, Benghazi 20 November
[b] The relief of Malta

Source: Roskill, S. W., *The War at Sea*, 3 Vols (London, 1959–1961).

remained. From that time conditions steadily improved, and in May 1943, when Axis forces in North Africa capitulated, the siege was completely lifted. See also FORCE K.

Bradford, E., *Siege: Malta 1940–1943* (London, 1985).
Hogan, G., *Malta: The Triumphant Years 1940–1943* (London, 1978).

Manchukuo ('state of the Manchus') was the name given by the Japanese to the Chinese state of Manchuria—historically a territory disputed by China, Japan, and Russia—after their *Kwantung Army occupied it in September 1931. The occupation took place after what was known as the Mukden (Fengtien after 1932), or Manchurian, Incident, in which the Japanese accused the Chinese of blowing up a railway line which they had sabotaged themselves. A puppet state was established in March 1932 for the 34 million inhabitants, to which the province of Jehol was added the following year and eastern Chahar in 1935. They and the 240,000 Japanese residents in Manchuria—who by 1939 had increased to 837,000—were nominally ruled by Emperor *Pu Yi. But the real power lay with the Japanese commander of the Kwantung Army, while Manchukuo's commerce was dominated by the South Manchurian Railway Company, whose influence and prestige have been likened by one historian to those of a latter-day East India Company. Japan officially recognized Manchukuo's existence in September 1932, but, with the exception of Germany and Italy—and later *Wang Ching-wei's puppet regime in Nanking (see CHINA, 3(b))—few other countries did so. When the *League of Nations condemned the occupation Japan simply left the League.

Japan's huge investment programme modernized Manchukuo's communications and economy, and developed *raw materials such as coal, iron ore, and timber. It soon became a market closed to everyone but Japanese businessmen; Nissan formed the Manchukuo Heavy Industries Development Corporation to exploit the area's natural resources; a five-year industrial plan was introduced; and eventually the country's output was completely geared to Japan's war economy. Also, the Japanese cynically encouraged the production and sale of opium and its more lethal derivatives, heroin and morphine, thereby not only acquiring staggering financial profits but ensuring a quiescent population.

After Manchukuo was annexed the Kwantung Army became involved in many border clashes with the USSR which culminated in the Nomonhan Incident in August 1939 (see JAPANESE–SOVIET CAMPAIGNS). After Japan surrendered in August 1945 Manchukuo was returned to China. See also CHINA INCIDENT and COLLABORATION.

Mandalay, battle of. This was fought in March 1945 between General *Slim's Fourteenth Army and Lt-General Katamura Shihachi's Fifteenth Army during the *Burma campaign.

In April 1942 the Japanese had bombed Mandalay almost flat after which the *Burma Independence Army had moved in. It had been Burma's last independent capital before the British took the country over and its recapture by them, which included fierce fighting to take Mandalay Hill and Fort Dufferin, was more a blow to the prestige of the Japanese and their Burmese collaborators—'who rules Mandalay rules Burma'—than a military disaster.

But the fact that the main Japanese strength was pinned down there, while Slim drove an armoured column into Katamura's vulnerable lines of communication further south at *Meiktila, resulted in a Japanese rout that opened the way to Rangoon for the British.

MANHATTAN PROJECT, abbreviation of MANHATTAN ENGINEER DISTRICT, the codename of the project to construct the necessary buildings and plants for the development of the *atomic bomb in the USA.

Mannerheim, Marshal Baron (Carl) Gustaf Von (1867–1951), Finnish ex-Tsarist army officer who distinguished himself in five wars. During the 1930s he organized the construction of the 'Mannerheim Line' on the Karelian peninsula which impeded the advance of the Red Army at the start of the *Finnish–Soviet war in November 1939. He led the Finnish Army during this campaign and when the Finns subsequently fought with the Germans against the USSR. Having succeeded Risto *Ryti as Finland's president in August 1944, he negotiated the *armistice with the USSR in September 1944 which was followed by a declaration of war against Germany.

Jägeskiöld, S., *Mannerheim* (London, 1986).

Manstein, Field Marshal Erich von (1887–1973), arguably the ablest of Hitler's generals, the master of the mobile battle, and thought by some to be, after Hitler, Germany's most outstanding wartime personality.

The tenth child of a Prussian aristocrat, General Eduard von Lewinski, Manstein took the name of his uncle who adopted him. He served as *Rundstedt's chief of staff in the *Polish campaign of September–October 1939, and during the months which preceded Hitler's delayed offensive in the west he suggested an alternative to the plan which the German Army's High Command (OKH) had made for it (see FALL GELB). Discussions centred on the main effort of the German forces: Manstein wanted it shifted from the northern wing of the front to the southern wing where Rundstedt's Army Group A was to operate. Though he did not know it, some of Manstein's thoughts, which included an armoured attack through the Ardennes, coincided with Hitler's. *Halder, chief of OKH, irritated by Manstein's flow of memoranda urging that FALL GELB should be altered, had him transferred to command the 38th Corps in Stettin. However, this only gave Manstein the opportunity to explain his plan (SICHELSCHNITT, or sickle-slice) to Hitler in person and the 'convergence of Manstein's inspired concept and Hitler's ideas' (H.-A. Jacobsen, *Fall Gelb*, 1957, quoted in K. Maier *et al.*, *Germany and the Second World War*, Vol. 2, Oxford, 1991, p. 247) was further developed by OKH, and resulted in the fall of *France in June 1940.

Manstein soon proved himself not only an able staff officer but an outstanding commander in the field. He commanded 38th Corps during the fighting that led to the fall of France, in which his troops were first across the River Seine, and was promoted lt-general. He was equally aggressive during the German invasion of the USSR in June 1941 (see BARBAROSSA), leading 56th Panzer Corps with such skill—from 22 to 26 June it advanced 320 km. (200 mi.)—that in September he was given command of the Eleventh Army, part of Rundstedt's Army Group South. For Hitler's offensive (BLUE) in June 1942 (see GERMAN–SOVIET WAR, 4) Army Group South was divided into two, A and B. The Eleventh Army became part of Army Group A; and after clearing the Crimea, and defeating a major Soviet counter-attack, Manstein captured *Sevastopol in July 1942 and was promoted field marshal.

In November 1942 Manstein assumed a new command, Army Group Don, which took over the *Stalingrad sector. It included, apart from the Eleventh Army, *Paulus's encircled Sixth Army, which even Manstein was unable to relieve. In February 1943, after Paulus had surrendered, Army Group Don and Army Group B became the reconstituted Army Group South, and with it Manstein retook *Kharkov and Belgorod in March 1943, a brilliant offensive which cost the Red Army 40,000 casualties (see GERMAN–SOVIET WAR, 6). But from that time, except for the offensive to eliminate the *Kursk salient in July 1943, which failed after Hitler had fatally delayed it, Manstein was forced on to the defensive. That September he executed a withdrawal to the River *Dnieper, but his situation remained precarious and though his tactics of giving ground in order to build up reserves inflicted heavy casualties on the Red Army, by mid-February 1944 his forces had been forced into further withdrawals. His dismissal by Hitler followed, on 30 March, and he took no further part in the war.

In 1949 a British military court sentenced him to eighteen years' imprisonment for war crimes in the USSR but he served only four.

Carver, M. (ed.), *The War Lords* (London, 1976).
Stahlberg, A., *Bounden Duty* (London, 1990).

Manteuffel, General Hasso-Eccard von (1897–1978), German panzer general who rose from lt-colonel in 1939 to command of a division during the *North African campaign and then of 7th Panzer Division and the Grossdeutschland Panzer Grenadier division, in the *German–Soviet war. He was promoted lt-general in September 1944 and given command of the Fifth Panzer Army which played a crucial role in the *Ardennes campaign that December. From March 1945 he commanded the Third Panzer Army. This was part of Army Group Vistula which tried to stem the Soviet advance and prevent the fall of *Berlin. By retreating at speed he managed to surrender to the Americans and not to the Red Army on 3 May 1945.

Mao Tse-tung (1893–1976), a founding member of the Chinese Communist Party when it was formed in 1921. In 1934 he was hounded from the Chinese Soviet Republic in Kiangsi Province by *Chiang Kai-shek, and he and his followers, who included *Chou En-lai, then started the 10,000 km. (6,000 mi.) Long March to Fushih in northwest China. It was during this exodus that Mao first gained control of the party apparatus and in Fushih he established a government and social system very different from Chiang's corrupt regime. From this power base he fought both the Japanese (see CHINA INCIDENT) and sometimes Chiang, and by 1945 his troops dominated most of occupied China's countryside. Of all the engagements fought by the Japanese in China, 75% were against Mao's forces.

One of the major figures of the 20th century, who wrought a total revolution in the world's most populated country, Mao has been described as having 'a solid elemental vitality' with the simplicity and naturalness of the Chinese peasant. He was a brilliant speaker who worked tirelessly to teach, enlighten, and indoctrinate. After defeating Chiang Kai-shek in a long-drawn-out civil war he became chairman of the People's Republic of China in September 1949.

maquis is the Corsican name for the local brushwood which resistance fighters on the island of Corsica used for cover. It was also the name given to groups of young Frenchmen who, from the autumn of 1942 onwards, took to the forests and mountains to avoid compulsory labour service in Germany which had been forced upon the *Vichy government by Fritz *Sauckel. Some were only intent on avoiding capture but others, armed and trained by *SOE and by the *Office of Strategic Services, became a formidable part of the resistance movement which so hampered the Germans after the Normandy landings in June 1944 (see OVERLORD) and were so effective after the French Riviera landings that August (DRAGOON). Later many joined General de *Lattre de Tassigny's First French Army in time for the *Rhine crossings and the battle for *Germany. The biggest Maquis base was in the *Vercors. See also FRANCE, 9.

Kedward, R., *In Search of the Maquis* (London, 1993).

marching songs have been sung in all fighting forces to sustain morale, denigrate opponents, and mock higher authority. They were often unprintable and have been part of fighting men's equipment from at least the time of the American Civil War. Some sung in the Second World War derived from earlier conflicts. A variation of a Civil War song, 'John Brown's Body', was sung by Allied paratroopers as 'Glory, glory what a hell of a way to die

. . . And he ain't going to jump no more', while 'A Long Way to Tipperary', popular in the *First World War, was as popular in the Second and was given new words by British troops fighting in the Far East:

It's a long time since I saw Blighty [Britain],
It's a long time ago,
It's a long time since I left Blighty
To fight to Tokyo.

The French had a song, sung to the tune of the German national anthem, 'Deutschland über alles', which mocked the German Army. Marches often involved long halts and British troops, when kept hanging about for no obvious reason, liked to sing, to the tune of 'Auld Lang Syne':

We're here because
We're here because
We're here

and so on *ad infinitum*. But new songs were also written. Those such as 'Bless 'em all', 'You are my Sunshine', and 'Kiss me Goodnight, Sergeant Major' showed that the British preferred humour and sentiment. Soviet marching songs, on the other hand, were often solemn and patriotic. One written for Soviet artillerymen exhorts them 'for our mothers' tears and for our country, fire! fire!' A German one, called the 'Avanti-Schritt' or the 'Italian Forward March', mocks the fighting ability of their Italian allies.

The Nazis had their own marching song. It was written by a storm trooper, Horst Wessel, who was killed in a street fight with communists in 1930. He was made into a Nazi martyr and his words—which were sung to a tune whose source is not known but perhaps came from a Salvation Army song—became second only to 'Deutschland über alles' in importance in Germany. Its tone was blatantly political.

In the USA, Tin Pan Alley produced a stream of songs such as 'This is the Army, Mr Brown', but according to one of America's best fighting generals, Lt-General *Truscott, American GIs did not sing as their fathers had in the First World War. However, while commander of 3rd US Division he had a soldier's ballad, which he had heard, turned into what became a well-known marching song called 'The Dogface Soldier':

I'm just a dogface soldier with a rifle on my shoulder
And I eat a Kraut [German] for breakfast every day.
So feed me ammunition, keep me in the Third Division,
Your dogface soldier boy's Okay.

But the most memorable, and popular, marching song of the war was the haunting German ballad 'Lili Marlene'. Originally composed as a poem in 1915 by Hans Leip, who had been in love with two women, Lili and Marlene, it was made universally known by a German singer, Lale Andersen, early in the war. Leip also set it to music, but it was Norbert Schultze's melody that brought it fame. In translation its sense was somewhat changed but it was as popular with the British Army as it was with the Germans. At the end of the *North African campaign, in May 1943, when the 7th Armoured Division, on its way to the Allied victory parade in Tunis, passed the German 90th Light Division marching into captivity, both columns were singing it.

Murdoch, B., *Fighting Songs and Warring Words* (London, 1990).
Page, M., *Kiss Me Goodnight, Sergeant Major* (London, 1973).

Mareth Line, pre-war French defensive system in southern Tunisia designed to prevent Italian incursions from Libya. Situated a few kilometres south-east of Mareth, it ran from the sea 35 km. (22 mi.) inland to the Matmata Hills. On 19 March 1943, with the *North African campaign in its final phase, the British and Commonwealth Eighth Army, commanded by *Montgomery, began a frontal assault on it from the south while a specially formed New Zealand Corps, under *Freyberg, struck inland to try to outflank it. Defending the line was *Rommel's old German–Italian Panzer Army, now renamed the First Italian Army and commanded by *Messe. When this drove off the frontal assault by Montgomery's 30th Corps, Montgomery, aided by *Long Range Desert Group intelligence that the line could be outflanked inland, reinforced Freyberg. Supported by the *Western Desert Air Force and artillery fire this strengthened left hook broke through the Tebaga Gap on 27 March. It threatened to surround Messe's forces which only escaped when Freyberg was held up outside El Hamma.

Mariana Islands, group of fifteen Pacific islands that stretch in a curve for 800 km. (500 mi.) half way between Japan and the island of New Guinea. The four biggest islands are *Saipan, *Tinian, Rota, and *Guam. Guam was ceded to the USA by Spain in 1898. The others were purchased by Germany and during the *First World War they were captured by Japan to whom the *League of Nations mandated them after 1918. Guam was occupied by the Japanese two days after *Pearl Harbor and Saipan became an important administrative centre for them during the *Pacific war. Operation FORAGER was launched by US forces in February 1944 to capture the whole group, the last, Guam, falling that August. The most northerly of the main islands, Saipan, was 1,930 km. (1,200 mi.) from Tokyo and the islands became the main US base for mounting the *strategic air offensive against Japan.

marines, see under ARMED FORCES, NAVY of UK, USA, and USSR.

Mark Clark, see CLARK.

MARKET-GARDEN, Allied operation conceived by *Montgomery, and launched on 17 September 1944 (see Map 67). It was designed to outflank the German defensive line known as the *West Wall, by establishing a bridgehead across the lower Rhine at the Dutch town of Arnhem. It was hoped that this would place the Allied armies at the threshhold of the Ruhr and possibly bring the war to an early conclusion.

The supreme commander, *Eisenhower, endorsed Montgomery's strategy on 10 September and offered him *Brereton's First Allied Airborne Army. Later, he agreed to divert supplies from other fronts to Montgomery's Twenty-first Army Group, so setting the scene for one of the Allies' most disastrous errors in north-west Europe: the failure to clear immediately the approaches to the vital port of Antwerp (see SCHELDT ESTUARY).

As the codename implied, the operation, commanded tactically by a British Army officer, Lt-General *Browning, was divided into two: MARKET, the employment of airborne troops to seize bridges across eight water barriers; and GARDEN, the advance of *Horrocks's 30th Corps across them. Speed was essential, with Horrocks having to cover in three days the 95 km. (59 mi.) to Arnhem from his starting line on the Meuse–Escaut Canal. To aid the operation the Dutch *government-in-exile called for a railway strike. This brought German military supplies to a halt but also led to German reprisals that caused a terrible famine that winter.

To capture the bridges the 101st US Airborne Division landed between Eindhoven and Veghel; 82nd US Airborne Division dropped around Grave and Groesbeek; and 1st British Airborne Division dropped near those at Arnhem—but not near enough. The initial drop of 16,500 paratroopers and 3,500 troops in gliders was completed with unprecedented accuracy, but from that high point the tactical execution of Montgomery's bold strategy deteriorated.

The remains of two *SS Panzer Divisions, 9th and 10th, were refitting in the area and had just completed an exercise on how to repel an airborne landing. Indications of their presence before the landings had been ignored and their alertness—plus the loss of 1st Airborne Division's armoured jeeps and the capture of a US officer in improper possession of the operational order—put MARKET-GARDEN immediately in jeopardy. It took four hours for British paratroopers to reach the bridges on foot, by which time German resistance was already stiffening. The railway bridge was destroyed and the British, their forces already scattered and pinned down by a stout German defence, were only able to capture the northern end of the road bridge. The final blow came when bad weather delayed reinforcement by the Polish Parachute Brigade. Some were dropped at Driel, but the Germans prevented them from crossing the river.

Stubborn German resistance also delayed the land forces. The 30th Corps was already late when it linked up with 101st Airborne Division near Eindhoven and the construction of a Bailey bridge (see ENGINEERS) at Zon, to replace one destroyed by the Germans, put Horrocks 33 hours behind schedule. The advance of the British 8th and 12th Corps on either side of the narrow corridor being carved out for 30th Corps was also, as Montgomery admitted, 'depressingly slow' and their tardiness exposed 101st Airborne Division to increasingly intense flank attacks which cut the Eindhoven–Nijmegen road ('Hell's Highway') more than once.

The 82nd Airborne Division occupied the Groesbeek Ridge to block any counter-attacks, and captured the bridges leading to Nijmegen, but was then forced to wait for 30th Corps as bad weather delayed its reinforcements. Its arrival gave the Americans the additional fire-power they needed and on 20 September a battalion made the perilous trip across the River Waal in assault boats. Both Nijmegen bridges were soon captured, but it took 30th Corps another 24 hours to start its move to Arnhem. By then the British there had been driven from the bridge, allowing German artillery to move across it and reinforce a roadblock at Ressen which had halted Horrocks's advance yet again. Men were diverted to Driel, but it proved impossible to cross in any strength.

On 25 September the British pulled back their surviving paratroopers to the river for withdrawal that night. Although 2,163 men of 1st Airborne Division, 160 Poles, and 75 men out of the 250 who had managed to cross from Driel escaped, the Germans took more than 6,000 captive, nearly half of whom were wounded. The losses of the two US airborne divisions, which stayed in the line for another two months, totalled 3,532.

Though the attempt to gain a bridgehead across the lower Rhine failed, the Allies retained a valuable salient from which Operation *VERITABLE was launched during the battle for *Germany in February 1945.

Ryan, C., *A Bridge too Far* (London, 1974).

Marrakesh conferences, held in a villa at Marrakesh in French Morocco where Churchill was convalescing. The first two, with Churchill in the chair, were held on 7 and 8 January 1944 to discuss the proposed landings at *Anzio. Those present included *Beaverbrook, Generals *Alexander, *Devers, Bedell *Smith, and Maitland *Wilson, and Admiral John Cunningham. Churchill also conferred with de *Gaulle on 12 January.

Marshall, General of the Army George C. (1880–1959), US Army chief of staff from 1939 to 1945, a member of the *Combined Chiefs of Staff committee throughout the war, and one of the Allies' most outstanding military leaders.

A graduate of the Virginia Military Institute, Marshall was chief of operations for 1st US Infantry Division in France during the *First World War. In 1918 his co-ordination of the movement over three roads of 600,000 men and 2,700 field guns in less than two weeks, earned him high praise and the position of General John Pershing's chief aide between 1919 and 1924.

Between the wars Marshall served in China with *Stilwell and at the Infantry School, Fort Benning, where future generals such as *Bradley, *Collins, and Bedell

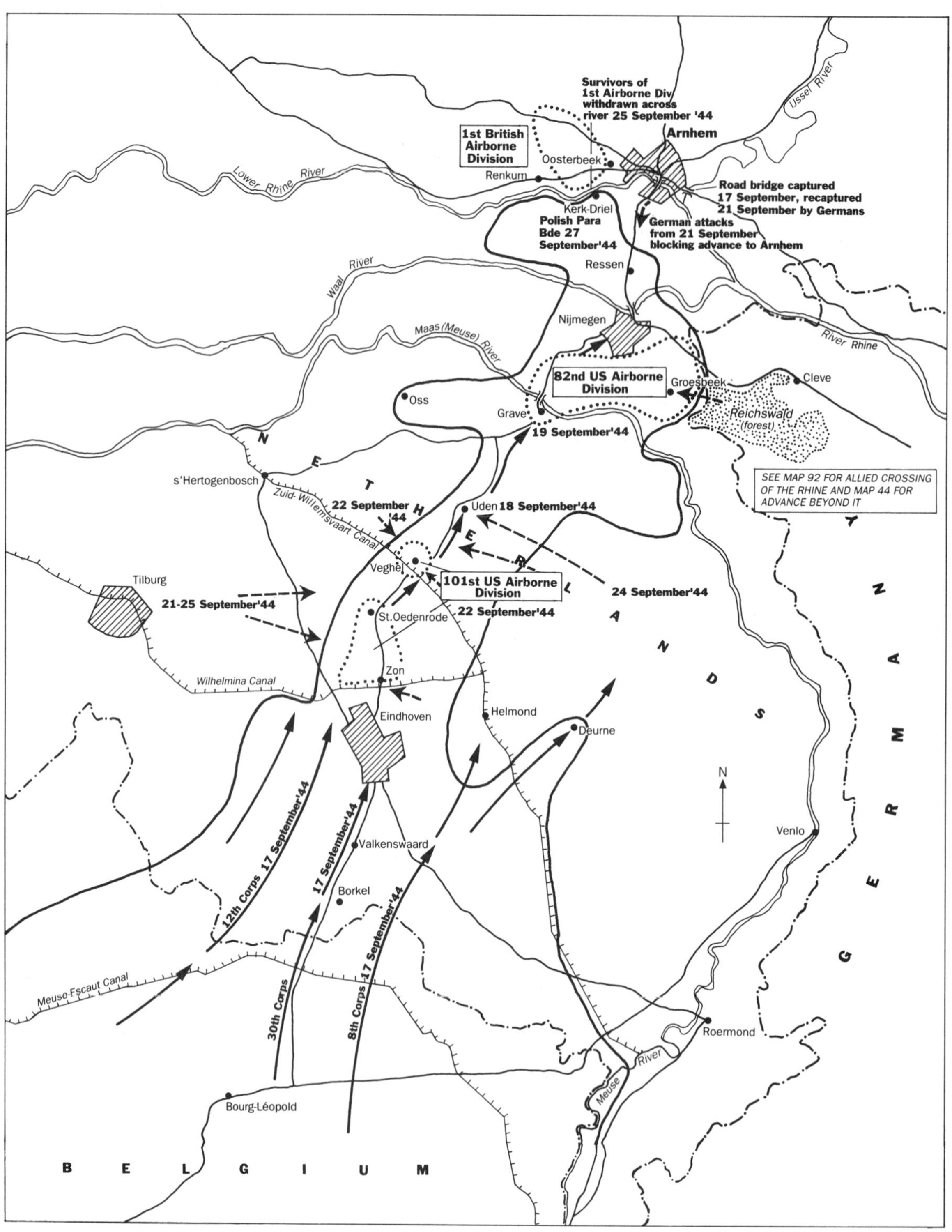

SEE MAP 92 FOR ALLIED CROSSING OF THE RHINE AND MAP 44 FOR ADVANCE BEYOND IT

67. Operation **MARKET-GARDEN**, September 1944

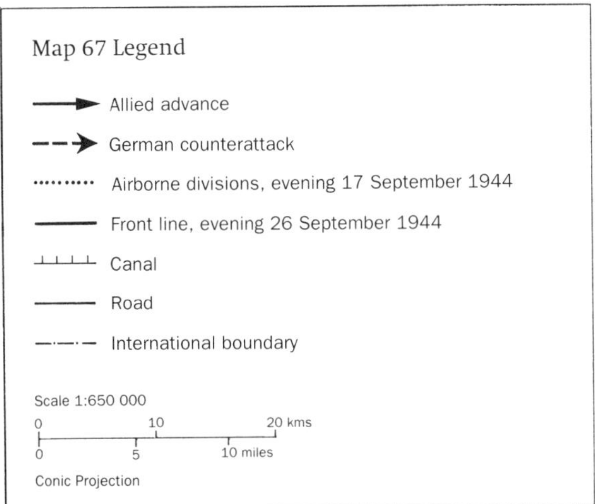

*Smith, were either instructors or students. Promotion was slow—he remained a lt-colonel for eleven years—but in 1936 he was promoted brig-general and in 1938 became chief of the War Plans Division. A few months later he was promoted to deputy chief of staff. During this time his proverbial candour came to the fore at a White House meeting. Roosevelt, while summing up his conclusions, turned casually to Marshall, whom he hardly knew, and said: 'Don't you think so, George?' Marshall replied: 'I am sorry, Mr President, but I don't agree with that at all.' Roosevelt never called Marshall by his Christian name again. Soon afterwards, on the recommendation of his closest adviser, Harry *Hopkins, and of Pershing, he promoted him chief of staff. It proved to be one of Roosevelt's most inspired appointments.

The two men came to trust and respect one another, but their temperaments and work habits were too dissimilar for complete rapport. Marshall worked well with his immediate civilian superior, Henry *Stimson, the secretary for war, and managed a working relationship with the chief of naval operations, Admiral *King, despite the fierce inter-service *rivalries that existed.

Marshall acted as chief of staff for two months before taking up the post on a permanent basis on 1 September 1939 and during this time he started his monumental task of increasing the army's strength, restructuring it, and equipping it for modern warfare, an undertaking for which, with the USA still neutral, he was often denigrated and which he pushed through relentlessly despite the opposition of many including the president. He was his own best liaison man with Congress and with the press, and it was his persuasiveness which resulted in Congressmen agreeing to conscription and then to its extension (see SELECTIVE SERVICE SYSTEM). This enabled him to build the army's strength to 1.8 million by December 1941 and by the time the war ended to 8.25 million. In terms of divisions (90) this proved only just sufficient and he has been criticized for running it so close.

Marshall never seriously wavered from his conviction that Germany must be defeated first (see RAINBOW PLANS) and he was the chief advocate of an early cross-Channel invasion, which caused some quite serious misunderstandings with the British (see GRAND ALLIANCE). He was fiercely opposed to the *North African campaign, correctly supposing that intervention in the battle for the *Mediterranean would not end there and would result in a full-scale invasion of the Continent being delayed. When the British refused to launch an invasion in 1942, despite apparently agreeing to do so earlier in the year, Marshall threatened to shift US resources to the *Pacific war, a bluff which Roosevelt quickly called. At first it was assumed that Marshall would command the Allied forces invading north-west Europe (see OVERLORD)—indeed Roosevelt had insisted he did—but when the moment of decision came the president wavered. He left the decision to Marshall, who declined to make it; then Roosevelt said he could not sleep well at night with Marshall out of Washington, and appointed *Eisenhower instead.

Marshall was promoted five-star general in December 1944, and in November 1945 requested retirement. However, he was soon recalled to civilian duty, became President *Truman's special representative in China, and then agreed to succeed James *Byrnes as secretary of state. He served in that post from 1947 to 1949, inaugurating during that time his famous Marshall Plan (see CONSEQUENCES OF THE WAR) and in 1950 served as secretary of defence until he retired the following year. In 1953 he was awarded the Nobel Peace Prize.

Marshall was an aloof man, whose mere presence inspired confidence. His soft voice covered a sharp temper that could boil over or become icily disdainful. The aura of command that surrounded him was unmistakable but the principle of open discussion regardless of rank was rigorously maintained and encouraged by him. With the promotion and retirement of officers he was totally ruthless. He was not infallible in picking the right men—Fredendall (see KASSERINE PASS), Dawley (see SALERNO), and Millikin (see REMAGEN BRIDGE) were all his choice as corps commanders who had later to be relieved of their commands—but when asked who the army's leaders were going to be he produced a list of those known to him personally or recommended to him by officers he trusted. Besides Bradley, Collins, and Eisenhower, it included *Devers, *Hodges, *Patton, *Eichelberger, *Patch, *Simpson, *Clark, and *Truscott.

Marshall himself thought that his most important contribution to the war was to stand up to Churchill, for it was sometimes left to him to dispose of the prime minister's latest pet project. But Churchill never took this personally and once, after he had dined with Marshall, he turned to his personal physician and said: 'That is the noblest Roman of them all.' When Marshall retired Truman read a citation which said that while millions of Americans had given their country outstanding service, General of the Army George Marshall had given it victory.

Larrabee, E., *Commander in Chief: Franklin D. Roosevelt, His Lieutenants and Their War* (New York, 1987).
Pogue, F., *George C. Marshall: Organizer of Victory* (New York, 1973).

Marshall Islands campaign. This group of 36 Micronesian Pacific atolls includes Kwajalein, the world's largest. During the *Pacific war they formed part of the outer defensive perimeter guarding Japan, to which they had been mandated after the *First World War.

A US marine and army amphibious force of 85,000 combat, garrison, and construction personnel, carried and escorted by an armada of nearly 300 warships and landing craft, invaded the group on 30 January 1944. Reconnaissance troops landed on Majuro Atoll, the first US occupation of Japanese soil, before 4th Marine and 7th Infantry Divisions landed on the inner islands of Kwajalein Atoll, Kwajalein, and the twin islets of Roi-Namur, *ULTRA intelligence having revealed that the Japanese had moved men to the outer atolls in the expectation of landings there. After being neutralized by air attacks, these outer atolls were bypassed and did not surrender until the end of the war, but after *Eniwetok Atoll had been occupied, US forces completely controlled the area.

Despite confusion during some of the landings, the lessons learned at *Tarawa the previous November resulted in a brilliantly executed campaign which proved of immense strategic value. It forced the Japanese fleet to withdraw from *Truk and brought forward the invasion date of the Mariana Islands by 20 weeks.

Mars Task Force, officially designated 5332 Brigade (Provisional), this 3,000-strong US Army unit was a long-range penetration group which fought during the *Burma campaign (see CHINDITS). Activated in India in July 1944 it was commanded by Brigadier-General Thomas Arms and comprised 612th (US) Field Artillery battalion, 124th (US) Cavalry Regiment, 1st Chinese Regiment, and 475th (US) Regiment, the last containing surviving personnel from Merrill's Marauders (see GALAHAD). It took part in Lt-General *Sultan's Northern Combat Area Command offensive, originally launched by *Stilwell from northern Burma in October 1943, one of its principal objectives being to clear the Japanese-held *Burma Road. When this was accomplished, in February 1945, Mars Task Force was withdrawn to China.

Marzabotto massacre. This Italian commune in the province of Bologna had a population in 1944 of 4,200 of whom 650 lived in the main town. Between May and July 1944, following operations against Italian partisans German forces carried out bloody reprisals there destroying 58 houses. Then, in October 1944, elements of the *SS Panzer Division 'Adolf Hitler' arrived under the command of Major Walter Reder who, on 12 August, had burned Santa Anna di Stazzema (Lucca), massacring 560 people. When his operations at Marzabotto ended, on 18 October 1944, nothing remained of the commune and a total of 1,604 men, women, and children and 226 partisans had been murdered. Marzabotto and Santa Anna di Stazzema were awarded the Medaglia d'oro and their names, along with those of other European towns such as *Lidiče and *Oradour-sur-Glane, became symbols of Nazi brutality. After the war Reder was tried, convicted and condemned to life imprisonment. See also ATROCITIES. LUCIO CEVA (Tr. John Gooch)

massacres, see ATROCITIES.

Matsuoka Yōsuke (1880–1946), Japanese ambassador to the *League of Nations at the time Japan left the League in 1933 because of Japan's occupation of Manchuria (see MANCHUKUO). He later served as foreign minister in the critical year from July 1940 to July 1941. Though thoroughly westernized—from the age of thirteen he had been brought up in the USA and he had been to university there—Matsuoka mistrusted both the UK and the USA, and during his time as foreign minister Japan moved irrevocably down the path which led to the *Pacific war. In 1940 he successfully demanded military bases in French Indo-China and the temporary closure of the *Burma Road. The same year he negotiated the *Tripartite Pact with Germany and Italy—which, contrary to his intentions, caused increasingly belligerent US policies—and attempted a solution to the *China Incident by recognizing *Wang Ching-wei's puppet regime (see CHINA, 3(b)). In April 1941, to the astonishment of his government, he signed a non-aggression treaty with Japan's traditional antagonist, the USSR (see JAPANESE-SOVIET CAMPAIGNS). As a result—and, more importantly, because of the China Incident—Japan's hands were tied when Hitler invaded the USSR in June 1941 (see BARBAROSSA). To get rid of him the prime minister, Prince *Konoe, and his whole government had to resign, and it was then reformed without Matsuoka. Arrested at the end of the war, Matsuoka died before he could appear at the *Far East War Crimes Trials.

M.A.U.D. committee, name given to a scientific body, set up in April 1940 and chaired by the British physicist, George Thomson, whose brief was to 'examine the whole problem, to co-ordinate work in progress and to report, as soon as possible, whether the possibilities of producing *atomic bombs during this war, and their military effect, were sufficient to justify the necessary diversion of effort for the purpose' (quoted in R. Clark, *The Greatest Power on Earth*, London, 1980, pp. 91–2). As a sub-committee of the *Tizard Committee for the Scientific Survey of Air Warfare it was at first called the Subcommittee on the U-Bomb, but was given the cover name, M.A.U.D. committee, by Thomson in June 1940 (neither the initials, nor the name they spelt, meant anything). It reported in July 1941 that a uranium bomb was practicable and 'likely to lead to decisive results in the war'. It recommended that the UK develop such a weapon and this led to the formation in October 1941 of a government body, codenamed TUBE ALLOYS, to control all aspects of British nuclear research. However, one of the committee, Patrick *Blackett, recommended that the atomic bomb be developed in the USA; the government acted on his minority report; and the same month the report was handed to the Americans and the following year the *MANHATTAN PROJECT came into being to build a nuclear weapon. See also ATOMIC BOMB, 1.

Mauritius, Indian Ocean island, occupied first by the Dutch and then the French, who called it Île de France, before it became a British colony in 1810. Some of its 400,000 inhabitants, which included 265,000 Indians, volunteered to serve in the Middle East and fought at *Bir Hakeim. Others were conscripted into the Mauritius Regiment which helped garrison Madagascar from the end of 1943. The British used it as a place of *internment for illegal Jewish immigrants to Palestine and its principal product, sugar, was exported to the UK.

Maurras, Charles (1868–1952), influential French political theorist and author, and one of the founders of the royalist right-wing journal *L'Action Française*. A supporter of *fascism and *collaboration with the Nazis he became one of the ideologists behind *Pétain's *Vichy regime. He was arrested in September 1944 and sentenced to life imprisonment, but was released shortly before his death.

Mauthausen was a *concentration camp near Linz in Austria. It also had 60 sub-camps. The main camp was opened in August 1938 and housed Jews from all over Europe. Figures vary but out of the 206,000 incarcerated there at various times 71,000 are said to have perished, either from overwork in the stone quarries and the armaments industries, or from starvation and disease, and it was the destination of all those who fell victim to the *Bullet Decree. When the Americans liberated the camp on 5 May 1945 they found a communal grave containing nearly 10,000 bodies. See also FINAL SOLUTION.

Max organization, putative German *Abwehr espionage network which was said to be based in Sofia, Bulgaria. Its leader was a German Jew, Richard Kauder (MAX KLATT), who worked with two White Russian émigrés, Anton Turkul and Ilya Lang. They claimed to have a network of radio agents among Red Army personnel who belonged to anti-Soviet families (see also SOVIET EXILES). Kauder told the Abwehr that their reports were collated in the USSR and then transmitted to Turkey from where they were sent on to Sofia by radio. The reports gave detailed and accurate information concerning Red Army troop movements and order of battle. German intelligence apparently relied heavily on the organization but post-war Allied investigations have identified Turkul, Lang, and Kauder as Soviet agents. *Counter Intelligence Corps reports released in the 1980s under the US Freedom of Information Act indicate that Turkul was one of the Soviet Union's most effective agents and that one of his aims was to sabotage the use of *Vlasov's army in the *German–Soviet war. See also SPIES.

MD1, or Ministry of Defence 1, was a British department formed in early 1939 to develop special weapons. Though there was no such ministry during the war, there was a minister of defence—Churchill—and MD1, which was headed by Major Millis Jefferis, was directly responsible to the war cabinet. Known to its detractors as Churchill's 'toyshop', it produced 26 new weapons and devices, including the *limpet mine, *sticky bomb, *PIAT, various detonating devices for booby traps, and special equipment used by 79th Armoured Division (see ENGINEERS, 1) during the Normandy landings (see OVERLORD).

Macrae, S., *Winston Churchill's Toyshop* (Kineton, Warwick, 1971).

Medenine, battle of. This was fought on 6 March 1943, during the final phase of the *North African campaign, when *Rommel, by then C-in-C Army Group Africa, struck at forward formations of *Montgomery's British and Commonwealth Eighth Army in southern Tunisia with his three panzer divisions.

To relieve pressure on US forces fighting at *Kasserine Pass in central Tunisia, Montgomery had moved two of his divisions forward from Libya to attack the *Mareth Line's outposts in southern Tunisia. This left the divisions vulnerable and the Axis plan to attack—it was not Rommel's and he disliked it—was for the panzers to advance on Montgomery's flank from the Matmata Hills inland while forces from General *Messe's German–Italian Army put in a diversionary mobile infantry attack from the Mareth Line.

Montgomery's forces were unbalanced to meet so powerful an attack, but *ULTRA intelligence accurately revealed its timing, strength, and direction, and this enabled Montgomery to bring forward reinforcements and construct well-concealed defences of anti-tank guns and infantry before the town of Medenine. The armour remained in reserve: it was employed only once and not one tank was lost. The German armour was driven off and suffered heavy losses.

Although Medenine was a significant Allied victory, it highlighted the dangers inherent in using ULTRA intelligence operationally in such a situation. Rommel was convinced his plans had been betrayed and *Kesselring, the German C-in-C South-West, accused Messe of revealing them. But luckily for the Allies no security enquiry appears to have been made.

medicine. A striking feature of warfare up to 1939 is that, with the exception of the Russo-Japanese war of 1904–5, in which battle casualties were extremely heavy, more service personnel were lost to disease and accidental injury than to hostile fire. In this, the Second World War was little different from previous conflicts, with over two-thirds of admissions to hospital, in both Allied and Axis forces, resulting from sickness and injury not sustained in military action. Among British troops in North Africa, for instance, the average number of admissions from sickness was 564 per thousand and the number of battle casualties only 60 per thousand. In north-west Europe the sickness/casualty ratio among British troops was less marked, with an average of 151 admissions per thousand due to disease against 37 per thousand from hostile fire. The incidence of disease among British troops was highest in the *South-East Asia Command, with an admission rate of 1,118 per thousand from disease (mainly malaria) and 45 per thousand from wounds. But in all theatres the incidence of most diseases and battle casualties was lower than it had been in the *First World War, and for the first time in the history of warfare more service personnel died as a result of wounds sustained in battle than from sickness and disease.

Health, hygiene, and preventive medicine

Table 1 shows dramatic reductions in the incidence of many infectious diseases among British troops in the Second World War as compared with previous conflicts. Note in particular the much lower incidence of diseases such as enteric fever and dysentery. The introduction of preventive inoculation and, since the South African Wars (1899–1902), greater recognition of the importance of sanitary discipline meant that military commanders were by 1939 equipped with the means to keep such diseases under control.

Yet the lessons of the past were not always heeded by the major combatants, and the incidence of disease varied greatly in different armed forces and from one theatre to another. For example, the incidence of diphtheria among Allied troops increased greatly in 1944–5 as they came into contact with reservoirs of infection in the formerly German-occupied territories.

It is also necessary to consider separately the medical fate of servicemen captured by opposing forces. The fortunes of *prisoners-of-war (POW) in Europe were mixed. Axis troops in Allied POW camps and English-speaking prisoners in German camps generally received some medical attention and an adequate diet, usually supplemented by parcels from voluntary organizations (see INTERNATIONAL RED CROSS COMMITTEE). But prisoners of other nationalities, and especially Soviet troops, were often denied both by their German captors. It was among these prisoners that tuberculosis, which thrived in the damp and overcrowded conditions inside POW and *forced labour camps, took its highest toll. Though conditions in German POW camps were often far from ideal from a medical point of view, levels of disease rarely reached those of camps run by the Japanese. In the Far East, undernourishment and malnourishment were common, and the incidence of deficiency diseases such as beri-beri reached staggering proportions. Cholera, dysentery, and malaria also claimed many victims among Allied prisoners in Japanese camps. More than 10,000 of the 12,600 deaths among British POW in the Second World War occurred in the Far East.

Much harder to gauge with accuracy is the medical impact of the Second World War on civilians, since medical records for many countries under Axis occupation are incomplete or unreliable. In the UK, where accurate records of the health of the civilian population were kept throughout the war, sickness and death rates (excluding air-raid casualties) did not exceed peacetime averages to any great extent. Food rationing maintained and, in some cases improved, standards of nutrition, while the Emergency Medical Service directed medical personnel and resources on a national basis according to need. In other European countries, where invasion and German occupation severely disrupted public health and medical services, the civilian population did not fare so well. Neglect of sanitation on the part of the German authorities left much of Europe prey to typhus, diphtheria, and other camp followers of war. It is estimated that cases of epidemic disease, except smallpox and influenza, in continental Europe doubled, and in some cases trebled, during the Second World War (see Table 2 as an example). Typhus, especially, was rampant in eastern Europe and on the Eastern Front, claiming some two million victims.

In many urban areas of occupied Western Europe food shortages led to an increase in deficiency diseases and a general lowering of body weights among *children. In Poland, Yugoslavia, Greece, and the USSR, ruthless requisitioning of foodstuffs pushed the populations of those countries towards starvation. German occupation also saw the extension of the secret *euthanasia programme begun in Germany in 1939 against the incurably ill and the 'mentally deficient'.

Though often denied the civilian populations of occupied Europe, hygiene and preventive medicine usually occupied an important place in the minds of both Allied and Axis commanders. However, there were some important and surprising exceptions; not least the virtual

Medicine, Table 1: Major infectious diseases in the British Army during wartime, mean monthly incidence per 1,000 strength

	1898–1901	*1914–18*	*1944–5*
Venereal disease	2.92	2.48	2.50
Jaundice	0.94	0.08	0.44
Diphtheria	0.01	0.11	0.69
Enteric fever	8.70	1.53	0.01
Dysentery	5.75	0.47	0.22
Pneumonia	0.38	0.42	0.17
Influenza	1.34	0.89	0.27
Scabies	–	–	3.46

Source: Crew, F. A. E., *The Army Medical Services. Campaigns*, Vol. IV, North Western Europe (London, 1962), p. 561.

Medicine, Table 2: Infectious diseases notified in France

	Median 1928–38	1939	1940	1941	1942	1943
Typhoid fevers	5,868	4,373	4,304	7,934	10,612	13,761
Dysentery	73	67	651	250	80	23
Diphtheria	19,893	14,019	13,568	20,018	31,466	46,539
Scarlet fever	18,431	14,640	10,951	11,201	11,980	17,085
Cer.-sp. meningitis	461	328	2,321	1,143	585	406
Poliomyelitis	487	460	342	484	322	1,783
Typhus fever	0	–	3	3	230	4
Smallpox	6	5	5	8	63	5
NOTIFIED CASES	45,219	33,892	32,145	41,041	55,338	79,606
Percentage change from 1928–38		–25	–28.9	–9.2	+22.4	+76.0

Source: League of Nations, *Bulletin of the Health Organisation*, 10, 4 (1943/44), p. 608.

absence of sanitary precautions in the German lines in the *Western Desert campaigns. According to British observers, the German defences at the second battle of *El Alamein were obvious from the amount of human faeces lying on the ground. This lack of sanitary discipline among the otherwise exemplary *Afrika Korps cost it dearly in terms of sickness and its ability to combat the Allied offensive. Dysentery, hepatitis, malaria, and skin diseases were widespread among German troops in the Western Desert, and a German soldier was 2.6 times as likely to be incapacitated by disease as his British opponent. In the two months before the second battle of El Alamein, more than one in five Germans had been stricken by disease, and even élite units such as the 15th Panzer Division were well below strength. It seems likely that the greater awareness of hygiene in hot climates displayed by British combatant officers, as well as those in the medical corps, may be attributed to the British Army's long experience of conditions in Africa and India.

The medical lessons of colonialism also paid dividends for the Allies in the Far East, but in the early stages of the war tropical hygiene was difficult to maintain as the number of service personnel in South-East Asia and the Pacific underwent a vast and rapid expansion. American and Filipino troops defending *Bataan were never issued with mosquito nets and the supply of anti-malaria drugs was insufficient to permit a prophylactic dosage. The consequences were catastrophic. In March 1942 the number of admissions to hospital from malaria rose from 500 to 1000 daily, leaving 75–80% of men in the front line infected with the disease. Medical officers of the British and Indian armies told a similar story. In Burma, annual sickness rates were as high as 1,850 per 1,000 men, malaria being responsible for at least 50% of cases.

Anti-malaria measures traditionally took the form of individual precautions such as mosquito repellants and the prophylactic use of drugs like quinine and mepacrine (atebrin), or more general measures such as drainage of mosquito breeding pools and the spraying of adult insects with insecticides. The high casualty rate suffered by the Allies in the first two years of war spurred research in all these directions. A systematic examination of the value of various anti-malarial drugs was undertaken at the Australian Army Medical Research Unit at Cairns, Queensland, and led to the development of a more effective drug (Paluride) though this did not come into general use until after the war.

The real value of the work at Cairns was that it highlighted the importance of anti-malaria discipline: of ensuring that anti-malaria drugs were taken on a regular basis. From 1943, as these findings came to light, anti-malaria discipline was tightened considerably in Allied units. General *Slim, commanding the British Fourteenth Army in Burma, threatened to sack any regimental officer under his command who failed to see that his troops took their daily dose of mepacrine. Educational campaigns were also conducted to overcome widespread fears that taking anti-malarial drugs led to sexual impotence and other unpleasant side-effects.

Stringent regulations soon made an impression on sickness rates, falling among British and Indian troops in Burma from 1,400 per 1,000 per annum in 1943, to 500 per 1,000 in 1945. But the importance of anti-malaria discipline was apparently not impressed upon officers of the Japanese forces. From March 1945 all Japanese troops captured by the British in Burma were questioned about the incidence of malaria in their ranks and about supplies of quinine. Interrogation revealed the relative neglect of precautions in Japanese lines and an incidence of malarial infection of 30–50%, equivalent to rates of infection among British and Indian troops two or three years earlier. The official historian of British Army medicine in the *Burma campaign concluded that neglect of anti-malaria precautions by the Japanese was 'one of the most important reasons' for the Allied victory there (F. A. E. Crew, *The Army Medical Services: Campaigns*, Vol. 5: *Burma*, London, 1966, p. 647).

In fact Japanese medical services seem not to have

escaped the general Japanese disinterest in *logistics, of which, in common with all armed services, they formed a part. According to Meirion and Suzy Harries (*Soldiers of the Sun*, London, 1991, p. 317), who quote a British expert as saying that Japanese professional knowledge of tropical diseases 'was not of a very high grade', the Japanese did not recognize scrub typhus for a long time. They called it Wewak fever and Hansa fever (see NEW GUINEA CAMPAIGN) and confused it with malaria. Nor did the Japanese medical services offer 'prophylactic injections against tetanus, which left troops highly vulnerable to wounds received in the agricultural land that saw much fighting in Burma and the Philippines.'

Though the control of malaria in the Allied forces may be attributed largely to the vigilance of ordinary combatant officers, important developments also took place in the direction of mosquito eradication. In the three years before the war, the destruction of adult mosquitoes by insecticide had become recognized as one of the most effective anti-malaria measures. Pyrethrum was the active ingredient of most of these insecticides, but since it was extracted from flowers which grew mainly in Italy and Japan, it was necessary for the Allies to try to develop an alternative. The most important of the substances investigated by scientists in the UK and the USA was dichlorodiphenyl-trichlorothane, or DDT, first synthesized by a German chemist in 1874, though it was not until 1939 that its insecticidal properties were discovered. Subsequently, tests were carried out at the London School of Hygiene and Tropical Medicine, and at the Chemical Defence Research Experimental Station at Porton, to determine the extent of its application and its toxicity. The first full-scale use of DDT in a military context was in early 1944 against the body louse during the Naples typhus epidemic where it was credited with bringing the epidemic under control. From then on, DDT was used extensively for de-lousing by both Allied and Axis forces, though it often proved difficult to enforce in armies in retreat and disarray. Later the same year, field trials employing DDT against mosquitoes were carried out in India, and their success led to its extensive use by Commonwealth and US forces in the final stages of the war in the Far East. It was also employed in mosquito eradication by German forces, particularly in the malarious areas of the southern USSR.

The prevention of venereal disease (VD) was equally high on the list of most medical officers and military commanders: in previous conflicts it had been one of the single largest causes of incapacity among troops. By 1939 it was recognized that the success of VD prevention lay in the co-ordination of educational and other efforts between civilian and military agencies. However, the American experience of VD during the Second World War shows that the relationship between the civil and military sectors was often an uneasy one, despite their common aim.

In May 1940 the US Army and the US Public Health Service began an educational campaign to discourage promiscuity among troops by explaining to them the attendant risks of venereal infection. The other key aspect of their strategy was to discourage prostitution by placing red-light districts out of bounds to troops and in some cases closing down those brothels which had been traditionally tolerated by the military authorities. State and Federal laws were enforced and segregated areas of prostitution eliminated, but in many cases line officers refused to co-operate with central directives, and continued to allow their troops to attend nearby brothels. Their behaviour caused an outcry among civil public health agencies and religious groups, which urged the government to exert more control over the military. Although the issue became less prominent after 1942, some military authorities continued to tolerate prostitution under certain conditions.

Overseas, the US Army did even less to discourage prostitution, in fact—as in other Allied forces—prostitution usually received official sanction provided that women and brothels were registered and that prostitutes reported twice weekly for medical inspection. In most of the newly-liberated areas such as French North Africa and Italy, widespread poverty ensured that there was no shortage of women from all classes who were willing to earn their living as prostitutes. According to one observer in North Africa, 'Every community of greater than hamlet size had several registered prostitutes, and the larger cities had hundreds' (T. H. Sternberg *et al*, 'Venereal diseases', in L. D. Heaton (ed.), *United States Army Medical Department: Preventive Medicine in World War Two*, Vol. 5: *Communicable Diseases*, Washington, DC, 1960, p. 206). Where registered prostitution was accepted, military authorities placed most emphasis on prophylaxis—often compulsory—which generally involved the application of antiseptic creams. Prophylaxis was seen by church groups and others in the USA as an implicit endorsement of promiscuity and prostitution, but military authorities had to balance health and morality against the morale of their troops. Few Allied commanders—with the notable exception of *Montgomery, a bishop's son—were prepared to risk discontent and disciplinary problems among their troops for the sake of appeasing the religious lobby at home. The Japanese were more organized, and more ruthless, about controlling VD while maintaining the morale of their troops (see COMFORT WOMEN).

Despite medical safeguards, the incidence of venereal disease rose alarmingly among Allied troops in certain theatres of the war. Troops in the Mediterranean and North African commands showed the highest rates of infection, with an average of 91 and 67 admissions to hospital per 1,000 US troops respectively in 1942–5, compared with 33 per 1,000 in the USA and 23 per 1,000 in the South-West Pacific. However, troops suffering from VD were likely to be returned to duty much faster than in previous wars, thanks to the development of more efficient treatment with sulphonamides and later with penicillin. Among RAF personnel, for example, the length of time before each venereal case was returned to duty fell from 31 days in 1939 to only 18 in 1945, compared with 61 days immediately after the First World War.

The medical sciences

It is ironic that the exigencies of warfare have often produced scientific and technical innovations of great benefit to humankind. There can be few better illustrations of this than the development of penicillin during the Second World War. Until the early 1940s bacterial infections resulting from injury and disease were generally treated with sulphonamide drugs, useful in the treatment of pneumonia, for instance, but largely ineffective when employed against streptococcal infections. The limitations of sulphonamides, and their often unpleasant side-effects, spurred research into the development of new drugs on the principle of antagonism between various species of microbe. In 1939, at the Sir William Dunn School of Pathology in Oxford, Professor Howard Florey began an investigation of the anti-bacterial properties of various substances, including *Penicillium notatum*, first observed by Alexander Fleming ten years before. In May 1940 encouraging results were obtained by Florey and his team in connection with penicillin and streptococcal infections and by 1941 enough evidence had been collected to warrant clinical trials. The tests confirmed that even the most severe bacterial infections could be controlled by penicillin and that it had no harmful side-effects.

However, penicillin could be produced in only minute proportions under laboratory conditions and just one case of severe sepsis might require the processing of up to 2,000 litres (440 gallons) of medium. It seemed that the only way to obtain sufficient quantities of the drug was to enlist the help of industry. But since industrial capacity in the UK was already stretched to its limit, enquiries were made via the Rockefeller Foundation to find a suitable manufacturer in the USA. By 1942 sufficient quantities had been produced by American firms to allow the use of penicillin in the field and in the following year the drug was being used extensively in the treatment of wound infections in North Africa.

The refinement of sulphonamide preparations and later of penicillin had a significant bearing on surgery during the Second World War. Due to the high mobility of armies in the North African desert, it was difficult to operate on wounded men until they had been evacuated to base. Chemotherapy and antibiotics, combined with drainage of the wound and its immobilization, kept the patient relatively comfortable and his wound free from infection until a hospital was reached. More complex surgical procedures such as closure of the wound and skin grafting could take place only when an army's advance was steady and when air superiority ensured constant supplies. For the Allies, these conditions did not occur until the end of the war.

As in former conflicts, surgical techniques themselves evolved to meet the changing demands of warfare. Among the more important developments in 1939–45 were the use of proximal colostomy in cases of injury to the large intestine and improvements in the treatment of burns, such as the saline bath associated with the British doctor A. H. McIndoe. McIndoe's technique, which was not entirely new, involved the immersion of severe limb burns in a bath of flowing saline solution, after which would be applied sulphonamide (later penicillin) powder or cream, and the burns covered with a bandage dressing which was floated off in a subsequent bath. Great strides were also made in anaesthesia—which had progressed relatively slowly in peacetime—with the introduction of 'closed-circuit' or 'local' anesthesia and of new anaesthetics, given intravenously and orally. Local anaesthesia revolutionized thoracic surgery in the combat zone and paved the way for the inception of cardiac surgery after the war.

Wartime medical research illustrates the trend, evident since the First World War, for *scientists to become directly involved in the solution of military problems. The Second World War accelerated this process, with scientists anticipating as well as providing for the needs of the military. One area in which they made an important contribution in this regard was in the field of 'Services Personnel Research', which concerned the safety and efficiency of the armed forces. In the UK, working under the auspices of the Medical Research Council, scientists considered means of protecting service personnel against noise, blast, and the vagaries of climate, and nowhere was such research more important than in the field of aviation medicine. High-altitude flying was a miserable and often perilous experience. Bomber crews were regularly subjected to temperatures of 30–50 °F below zero and flight surgeons estimated that half of all crewmen suffered from the effects of oxygen starvation. Oxygen masks tended to freeze above 6,100 m. (20,000 ft.) and lack of oxygen made men far more susceptible to the cold. Amputations due to frostbite were alarmingly common.

Research into these problems involved close collaboration between British and American scientists. The newly-opened RAF Physiological Laboratory at Cambridge, for example, conducted experiments regarding oxygen installations for high altitude bombers of the US Army Air Forces. This work led to the development of the 'economiser-and-mask' system, a constant-flow apparatus which wasted no oxygen during expiration. At the same time, American scientists developed electrically heated body suits and gloves for high-altitude flying, though their use was restricted and the suits themselves prone to failure. Some progress in aviation medicine were also made in the USSR, but, despite a number of exchange visits organized between Soviet scientists and their counterparts in the West, scientific interchange was limited and the flow of information largely travelled West to East. In Germany, the Forschungsführung der Luftwaffe and other aviation research institutions achieved results which matched those of Allied scientists, except in the development of high-altitude oxygen equipment.

Collaboration between Commonwealth and American scientists also proved successful in the investigation of the cause and spread of serum hepatitis which came to be distinguished from the 'infective' form of the disease. Research into jaundice was stimulated by several severe epidemics among Allied troops in Europe and during the early stages of the *North African campaign. However, such investigations proved difficult because of the unusually long incubation period of the disease. Considering these obstacles, the successful conclusion of hepatitis research was considered at the time to be one of the outstanding medical achievements of the war. Scientists in the UK and USA came to the conclusion that hepatitis was caused by a virus transmitted by contact with contaminated syringes. However, a vaccine against serum hepatitis was not developed until 1969.

Two less well-known aspects of medical science during the Second World War are those related to atomic and chemical weapons research. The development of isotopic tracers during the war was a by-product of the preparation of radioactive and stable isotopes in connection with work on the *atomic bomb. The outbreak of war in Europe also led to the intensification of research into the medical effects of chemical weapons. Though they were never employed in the Second World War, their use was both feared and contemplated by Allied and Axis governments. Researchers at the British Experimental Station at Porton assessed the offensive and defensive capabilities of a range of weapons including mustard gas, phosgene, and chlorine, as used in the First World War, and several new compounds were developed between 1939 and 1945. In order to gain an accurate impression of the effects of these weapons, researchers at Porton were authorized to use human guinea-pigs for some experiments. Volunteers drawn from the Porton research team and from the three armed forces were exposed to mustard gas and various other compounds designed to incapacitate troops.

By this time it was known that hot and sweaty skin was especially sensitive to the effects of vesicants such as mustard gas, and the entry into the war of Japan in December 1941 raised the alarming prospect of these weapons being used in tropical climates. Since it was difficult to simulate such conditions at Porton, two new experimental stations were established: one in Queensland, Australia, the other in southern India. Both made use of human volunteers, many of whom, as at Porton, suffered burns and other severe injuries as a result of their participation. It is a matter of continuing controversy whether or not some volunteers for these experiments were misled or inadequately informed of their probable effects.

We can speak with more certainty, however, about medical experiments carried out in the German *concentration camps. In *war crimes trials conducted after the war, it was a common defence among camp doctors to plead that any medical experiments were conducted with volunteers, yet the testimony of those subjected to these experiments, together with official documentation, shows that the overwhelming majority were carried out on inmates against their will, and in many cases with the willing compliance of camp doctors. These experiments frequently concerned matters of military efficiency such those carried out at *Dachau simulating high altitude flying and those involving exposure to extreme cold. In the case of the former, inmates were forced into decompression chambers, where the pressure was steadily lowered until most died in agony. At other camps such as *Ravensbrück and *Buchenwald the emphasis was on the artificial inducement of, and experimental inoculation against, diseases such as typhus, which had claimed more than 10,000 German lives on the Eastern Front in the winter of 1941–2 (see GERMAN–SOVIET WAR). Nazi doctors also found time to pursue research aimed at 'proving' Aryan racial superiority. At *Auschwitz, the ambitious Josef *Mengele embarked on a study to find evidence for the supposed 'physical degeneracy' of Jews, and there he conducted his infamous experiments on twins and the causes of dual births. Other doctors took advantage of 'human guinea-pigs' among the inmates to complete university doctorates in medicine and genetics.

Casualty evacuation and treatment

Advances in medical science during the war did much to contribute to the recovery rates of sick and wounded service personnel. British casualties in north-western Europe were 25 times more likely to make a full recovery than their predecessors in the First World War, but this improvement was due as much to the more efficient organization of casualty services as it was to advances in medical science. The Allies learned much from defeats inflicted in the early stages of the war. An internal inquiry by the Royal Army Medical Corps in 1941 found its field units insufficiently mobile and not readily adapted to tactical changes on the battlefield. German casualty services were also found wanting during the invasion of the USSR in June 1941 (see BARBAROSSA). The severe Russian winter exposed all existing inadequacies and hindered the evacuation of sick and wounded by air and land. In this first winter of the war against Germany, the Soviets themselves suffered severe shortages of medical personnel and medical supplies.

In other combat theatres air transport was being used to better and better effect and, as the war progressed, the field medical units of the major combatants also became more mobile and more effective. In the Commonwealth armies, the process of evacuation began with regimental stretcher bearers, who conveyed battle casualties to Regimental Aid Posts (RAP). These RAPs were usually makeshift structures such as a ruined cottage or a lean-to of bracken and branches. Next in line was the Casualty Clearing Post (CCP), equipped with a light

A Royal Army **Medical** Corps officer attends a wounded British soldier at an advanced dressing station during the second El Alamein battle, October 1942.

ambulance and two trucks, around which the camp was constructed. Behind this lay the Advanced Dressing Station (ADS), a more permanent affair consisting of six or seven tents. The RAP and CCP were expected to respond almost immediately to an order to move, and the ADS at up to four hours' notice. After 1941, these units were assisted by several specialist formations such as the Field Dressing Station, which resuscitated casualties suffering from shock, and the Field Surgical Unit, a mobile team capable of being directed to any point on the battlefield.

Similar procedures for casualty treatment and evacuation were followed by all the major combatants. Every German infantry division had two medical companies, each of which provided one field hospital, two main dressing stations, and two casualty clearing stations to receive wounded from medical units in the field. In addition, all German medical companies were equipped with a motorized unit. Similarly, by the end of 1942, Soviet field medical units were accompanied by mobile specialist surgical and ophthalmic teams. In the US forces, special 'Replacement Depots' were created to receive, hold, and finally to assign service personnel from hospitals and convalescent centres to appropriate duties.

At the end of the war, Allied commanders were generally satisfied with the level of efficiency attained by their casualty services. At *Iwo Jima, wounded US marines were quickly evacuated by air and sea, and, following the cessation of hostilities in Europe, Montgomery expressed his gratitude to the Allied medical personnel who had evacuated with the minimum of delay some 100,000 troops, greatly improving their chances of recovery.

Casualty evacuation and treatment at sea had also improved by the end of the war. In addition to sick bays on board fighting ships, several vessels were earmarked by the British and American governments immediately before the war for conversion into hospital ships. Hospital ships were of two kinds: those used by the navy as 'floating general hospitals' and those used to convey casualties from land theatres to hospitals in friendly ports. During 1939–45 a total of eleven hospital ships were in service with the Royal Navy, admitting a total of 93,142 patients. But the number of hospital ships was often insufficient, particularly in the later stages of the war in the Far East, giving rise to acrimonious disputes between the British Army and the Royal Navy over the allocation of these vessels. Following their entry into the war, American forces also felt the lack of hospital ships, but by the end of 1943 a number of large, specially-built, and well-equipped hospital vessels came into in service with the US Navy and altogether the US Army had 24 hospital ships (6 of them *Liberty ships) and the US Navy 17.

Two features of casualty evacuation by sea are especially worthy of mention. One was the evacuation of the *British Expeditionary Force from France in May 1940 when several hospital ships joined other vessels in picking up wounded troops from *Dunkirk and other beaches under extremely hazardous conditions. Heavy shell-fire forced several hospital ships to return to England without completing their mission and two—*Wakeful* and *Grafton*—were sunk with the loss of many lives. The other was the use of specially-converted *amphibians and landing craft during the Normandy landings in June 1944 (see OVERLORD) to carry wounded Allied personnel back to hospitals in the UK. Evacuation was somewhat slower than by ship—each crossing taking 26–30 hours—but a continuous shuttle service across the Channel meant that wounded men were evacuated from the beachhead without delay.

A vital component in the treatment of battle casualties in the Second World War was the development of more efficient forms of blood transfusion: many of the improvements in this field were a direct consequence of research conducted in the USA between 1939 and 1945. In December 1939, American scientists announced their discovery that unfiltered blood plasma was a useful substitute for whole blood in transfusion. It was impossible to dry whole blood without destroying the red cells, but plasma could be dried without damaging it and could therefore be stored and transported in all temperatures. The discovery of the rhesus factor in human blood by American scientists also had important implications for blood grouping and, ultimately, for the development of human genetics. But such developments were slow to reach the medical services of the Axis forces. Until 1943 the Germans relied upon a synthetic blood substitute called 'Periston', which most German medical officers interrogated by the Allies admitted was unsatisfactory. It was not until after the capture of dried blood serum from the British at *Tobruk in June 1942 that natural blood substitutes were employed by German medical units.

Once a casualty had been removed from the battlefield, treatment took place in military hospitals or in military wings of civilian hospitals with a number of service personnel in attendance to maintain military discipline. In the UK, where it was expected that large numbers of civilian air-raid casualties would occur soon after the declaration of war, local authorities and the ministry of health were apprehensive about the requisitioning of hospitals for military use. The precedent of the *Spanish Civil War suggested that estimates of high casualties among the civilian population were well founded, and the war cabinet accepted the ministry's suggestion that the army should relinquish its claim on 25 of the 29 general hospitals then under construction. But, though air-raid casualties were far from negligible, they did not occur in the numbers expected, reinforcing the argument of army commanders who had all along stressed the need for more hospital accommodation specifically for military use. Throughout the war, and afterwards, many remained critical of the inadequate hospital provision for military sick and wounded. The allocation of medical resources for civilian or military use was never adequately resolved, but in retrospect it seems unreasonable to have expected the government to have done anything other than plan for the worst of all eventualities. Few at the time disputed the civilian casualty ratio on which the ministry of health and the cabinet based their decision and, in the years leading up to the war, the prospect of a loss of civilian morale and social disorder as a result of air attack loomed large in the minds of all concerned.

While efficient planning enabled the UK to cope with its casualties of war, little could be done with regard to hospital provision in north-west Europe and other battle zones once conflict had begun. In western Germany, in 1945, hospitals were overflowing with sick and wounded from the Allied and German forces, as well as with civilians. On the Eastern Front the situation was even worse, though the expansion of hospital accommodation within the USSR during the war was an astonishing feat. At the beginning of 1941, hospital provisions for wounded Soviet troops were woefully inadequate: in five days, one 200-bed hospital near the front had to cope with more than 5,000 casualties. But by 1944 the Soviets had built more than 1,370 evacuation hospitals with some 664,595 beds, 75% more than in 1940.

Psychiatric medicine

Over one-third of medical discharges from the British and Commonwealth and American armed forces were the result, not of physical injury and sickness, but of psychiatric disorders, which also afflicted some *deserters, More than half the psychiatric disorder cases were diagnosed as 'anxiety neuroses', stemming directly from combat stress (see BATTLE OF THE PIPS for an example of this), or from a multiplicity of sources including separation from families and domestic problems. Other reasons given for psychiatric discharge, in descending order were 'psychoses', 'mental deficiency', and 'psychopathic personality'. Though no major theoretical advances were made in military psychiatry during the Second World War, there were, in the Allied camp at least, significant developments in terms of the mechanism for dealing with psychiatric casualties and in the position of psychiatrists in relation to military administration as a whole.

As the Allied forces became more deeply embroiled in conflict, the value of psychiatrists in maintaining morale and in returning psychiatric casualties quickly to duty was increasingly recognized by officers in the field. During the Western Desert and the North African campaigns, individual army psychiatrists began to develop new methods of forward treatment for nervous exhaustion, and by 1944 these innovations had been incorporated into official procedures for dealing with psychiatric casualties in the Allied forces. Troops suffering from battle exhaustion were generally placed under sedation for 48 hours and removed to a therapeutic environment at a divisional centre. Thereafter, they underwent a period of rehabilitation in which military discipline was reimposed, before being returned to appropriate duties. In north-west Europe, official sources estimate that as many as 65% of British psychiatric casualties were returned to full combatant duty in less than a fortnight.

In the Axis forces there was no comparable system of treatment for battle exhaustion and other psychiatric disorders, though the German Army had a high incidence of psychiatric illness on the Eastern Front. In his book *Hitler's Army* (Oxford, 1991, p. 22) O. Bartov notes that during the Soviet counter-offensive in front of *Moscow in December 1941 'Symptoms of mental attrition caused by fatigue, hunger, exposure, and anxiety' became increasingly prevalent and that there were 'numerous cases of physical and psychological breakdown caused by the wretched living conditions.' The German High Command responded to this crisis after 1942 simply by tightening military discipline as the majority of German military psychiatrists had long insisted that stress breakdowns were military rather than medical problems, resulting from deficiencies in leadership and morale. Treatment generally amounted to indoctrination of the sick or, in extreme cases, electric shock therapy, and the military authorities reacted to all breaches of discipline, regardless of whether these resulted from psychiatric breakdown, with undiscriminating severity. By mid-1944, 107,000 German soldiers had been tried for absence without leave, and a further 49,000 for disobedience. More than 7,000 were executed for desertion and subversion as against only 48 in the First World War. Suicides among German troops also increased markedly at the end of the Second World War, some 10,000 occurring among those undergoing treatment for battle neuroses.

The other important development in military psychiatry in the Allied camp was the introduction of psychological and intelligence testing. Acute manpower shortages in 1941, especially in the skilled trades, led Allied military authorities to consider a more efficient basis for the allocation of service personnel. Some means had also to be devised for detecting and disposing of the many 'undesirable' persons admitted to the armed forces through conscription. Intelligence, aptitude, and 'character' testing provided a rationale for such procedures and opened an avenue to academic psychologists hitherto marginalized by the military and academic establishments. Increasingly, military psychiatry came under the influence of men who saw themselves as social engineers. Whole regiments, such as the British Pioneer Corps, were formed to provide employment for men not considered suitable by virtue of 'low intelligence' or 'inappropriate personality' for the combatant or technical branches of the army. These tests continued to form the basis for personnel selection in the British Commonwealth and American armed forces after the war. In a slightly modified form, they were later introduced for candidates for the British civil service.

Post-war planning

Throughout the Second World War, Allied leaders gave much thought to the problem of reconstruction when victory was achieved. Planning for health administration and medical relief following the *liberation of occupied countries began as early as 1941, when, at an inter-Allied conference in London, it was accepted in principle that these tasks should be the joint responsibility of the Allied nations. As a result, an Allied Post-War Requirements Committee was set up to estimate the immediate post-war needs of various countries under Axis occupation and its work paved the way for the formation of *UNRRA in November 1943. In conjunction with Allied military authorities, civil governments, and voluntary organizations, UNRRA was empowered to co-ordinate and administer the provision of clothing, shelter, health services, and other forms of aid. The Health Division of UNRRA became one of its most important branches, and regional organizations were formed in Europe and the Far East.

In practice, however, the responsibility for health administration fell most heavily on the Civil Affairs Administrations of the liberating armies (see ALLIED CONTROL COMMISSIONS and ALLIED MILITARY GOVERNMENT OF OCCUPIED TERRITORIES). In the final years of the war, training centres were established by the Allied armies to school both service and civilian personnel in various aspects of public administration and to familiarize them with the social and economic conditions of occupied countries. However, it is unlikely that this training would have prepared relief workers for the scale of the problem they actually encountered in the liberated countries. In Germany, the British Army alone had responsibility for some 700 camps containing more than 750,000 displaced persons (see REFUGEES). Typhoid, diphtheria, poliomyelitis, and other diseases were rife among the dispossessed, and de-lousing and other typhus control measures were instituted in all camps under Allied command. However, it was some time before the medical advances which had so markedly improved the lot of servicemen in the Second World War began to touch the lives of those who had been left destitute by five years of conflict and occupation. MARK HARRISON

Copp, T., and McAndrew, W., *Battle Exhaustion: Soldiers and Psychiatrists in the Canadian Army, 1939–1945* (Montreal, 1990).
Green, F. H. K., and Covell, G. (eds.), *Medical Research: Medical History of the Second World War* (London, 1953).
Heaton, L. D. (ed.), *United States Army Medical Department*, 10 Vols. (Washington, DC, 1955–63).

Mediterranean, battle for the. War spread to the Mediterranean basin on 10 June 1940 when Italy declared war on the UK and France (see Maps 2 and 68). Mussolini, who nursed a jealousy of Hitler's spectacular successes in the fighting then going on in France, aimed to establish a 'New Roman Empire' by ruling those parts of the Mediterranean area which belonged to the British and French colonial empires. In pursuit of these aims, he informed Hitler during a meeting at the Brenner Pass on 4 October 1940 that he wanted Corsica, Malta, Tunisia, parts of Algeria, an Atlantic port on the Moroccan coast, and French Somaliland, and to replace the British imperium in Egypt and the Sudan.

Another fascist Mediterranean state, Spain, with whom Germany had signed a Treaty of Friendship in March 1939, also had designs on the British and French colonies and had, as a preliminary, annexed the internationally administered port of Tangier to prevent any move into it by Mussolini. But it was still suffering the ravages of the *Spanish Civil War and was reliant on the Allies for food imports. So when, on 23 October 1940, Hitler suggested to *Franco that he co-operate in a joint attack on the British colony of Gibraltar, the Spanish leader declined.

Opposing Mussolini's grand ambitions were France and the UK. Although France was quickly defeated and reduced to vassal status, with the country divided into an occupied zone and one controlled by the *Vichy government, it still retained some influence. It enjoyed American favour, and still controlled its fleet and its colonies in the area—Algeria (the Mediterranean coast of which formed part of metropolitan France) and the protectorates of French Morocco and Tunisia—and it also retained control of Syria and Lebanon on the eastern littoral through a *League of Nations mandate. As a belligerent, the position of the UK was less secure. Save for a number of small outposts that were crown colonies—the naval bases at Gibraltar and Malta, and the island of Cyprus (which respectively dominated strategic points in the west, central, and eastern Mediterranean)—its position was sustained mainly by informal treaty with Egypt, with Palestine and Iraq being ruled through League of Nations mandates and the former in the throes of revolt 1936–9. However, the British were determined to control the Mediterranean and the strategic routes, via the Suez Canal, to India and Singapore. After the fall of *France the Admiralty, which had depended on the French Navy to secure the Western Mediterranean, contemplated evacuating the eastern Mediterranean and falling back to Gibraltar. This proposal was rejected by Churchill. The Mediterranean was by this date the only theatre in which British forces could engage any of the Axis powers, and in the initial phase, they enjoyed the advantage of engaging a power of the first rank, Italy, whose forces were equipped with obsolescent equipment. Germany regarded the theatre as secondary. The Mediterranean was of interest to Hitler only in so far as it defended the south-eastern flank of his armies fighting the *German–Soviet war, but before this began German units were sent south in order to bolster up Italy's defeated forces in the *Western Desert campaigns. This, in the opinion of the German General Staff (OKH), was a tiresome distraction, *Rommel's 'African Adventure'. Opportunities to destroy British power in this region were missed because of the failure to make more than a fragmentary effort.

Stiffened by Churchill's resolve, the Admiralty created a new *ad hoc* force to fill the vacuum created by the collapse of French power in the western Mediterranean—*Force H, commanded by Admiral *Somerville. In July 1940 the British acted precipitately to reduce the risk of powerful Vichy French warships falling into the hands of the Germans by attacking the French naval base at *Mers-el-Kébir, near Oran in Algeria. This act risked the entire western Mediterranean by bringing Vichy France back into the war on the Axis side. The danger passed slowly, but not before Vichy had signed the *Paris protocols in May 1941 promising to co-operate with Germany in the Middle East and Africa. Air, sea, and land facilities were granted in Syria, and use of Bizerta.

The war on land in the Mediterranean followed a similar pattern to that in France and the Low Countries. A period of masterly inactivity was followed by rapid and crushing movement. The Tenth Italian Army in Libya appeared very imposing on paper: 250,000 men, with a further 350,000 in Abyssinia. The British C-in-C Middle East, General *Wavell, had only 36,000 in Egypt. In September 1940 the Italians invaded Egypt from Cyrenaica, but halted after only 80 km. (50 mi.). The following month Mussolini launched a disastrous invasion of Greece from occupied Albania (see BALKAN CAMPAIGN). The Greek Army put up a spirited defence in the mountain passes, which the Italians lacked the fire-power to dominate; not only were the Italians repulsed but the Greeks advanced into Albania. In this first phase of the Mediterranean war these campaigns were interdependent, activity in one having effects on another. Closely related, too, were the land, air, and sea elements. Victory could not be attained by one side or the other unless the three services worked in intimate co-operation.

The Italian humiliation in Greece, followed closely by the extraordinary success of the British Fleet Air Arm in attacking the Italian fleet in harbour at *Taranto in November 1940, encouraged Wavell in his belief that the Tenth Italian Army should be attacked at *Sidi Barrani and driven back into Cyrenaica. The strategic results of his audacious decision were momentous and did much to shape the war in this region. A mere 31,000 men of the Western Desert Force, commanded by Maj-General *O'Connor, and supported by units of the Royal Navy which bombarded *Bardia and the coastal road, advanced through a gap in the Italian defences on the morning of 9 December 1940. Five Italian divisions were destroyed within two days and *Tobruk fell. This great victory transformed the Mediterranean from a backwater, in which the British forces seemed likely to be crushed by the weight of Italian numbers, into the main British land front where Axis forces could be successfully engaged. O'Connor urged that he be permitted to continue his advance on Tripoli. Wavell refused, thus ensuring that the land war on the southern shores of the Mediterranean would continue.

Wavell's forces were spread very thinly over great distances. Not only was he advancing in Libya, but since January he had undertaken the conquest of Italian East Africa, and the recapture of British Somaliland (see EAST AFRICAN CAMPAIGN) which the Italians had occupied the previous August. After a tenacious defence, the Italians surrendered the Abyssinian capital, Addis Ababa, on 5 April. None the less, securing all these objectives was beyond the resources allocated to Wavell. The secretary of state for India, Leo Amery, was of the view that the occupation of Tripoli was 'the key to any future operations on a serious scale against Sicily, Sardinia, or in the Balkans. It might be the Open Sesame of the whole war and as an operation of surprise might completely disorganize the enemy's plans' (quoted in J. Baynes, *The Forgotten Victor: General Sir Richard O'Connor*, London, 1989, p. 126). There can be little doubt that Amery was correct. But a third priority was now jostling to the top of Wavell's agenda, the need to send troops to sustain Greece against a German threat of invasion.

In 1939 the British government had guaranteed Greek independence along with that of Romania and the ill-fated Poles (see POLAND, GUARANTEE OF). The precedent was not a happy one and the Greeks were reluctant allies. The Greek dictator, General Ioannis Metaxas (1871–1941), refused to make any moves likely to antagonize Germany. After the Italian invasion, all British help therefore had to be covert. On 29 January 1941 Metaxas died and within a month the new Greek government acknowledged that it needed British troops to counter-balance the growing German threat. These could only come from O'Connor's Western Desert Force. Wavell viewed this extension of his commitments with what can only be described as equanimity. When members of his directorate of intelligence in Cairo argued that any Greek expedition would have a poor chance of success, Wavell observed laconically that Wolfe had once described war as 'an option of difficulties'.

The Germans invaded Greece and Yugoslavia on 6 April. The latter was conquered within thirteen days, falling victim to overwhelming military strength, firepower, and command of the air, and British intervention in Greece resulted in disaster, mitigated only by a further naval victory over the Italians at *Cape Matapan on 28 March 1941. The Greek Army of fourteen divisions refused to give up its gains in Albania. The British and three Greek divisions took up position on the Aliakmon Line. A gap emerged between this position and the main Greek Army through which the Germans surged. Within five days they had secured all the important towns; the British retreated to Thermopylae and thence to Piraeus for a repeat performance of *Dunkirk in which the Royal Navy succeeded in performing another 'miracle' in evacuating the troops in face of German aerial superiority. These forces were removed to *Crete which was to be transformed into a bastion to prevent the spread of German power to the southern shores of the Mediterranean. The German invasion of Crete relied heavily on air power—an aerial bombardment to demoralize the defenders followed up by paratroopers who delivered the *coup de main*. This reliance paid off (although only just) and another hurriedly improvised evacuation was organized to bring the remnants of British forces back to Egypt. In a very short passage of time the strategic balance had swung in favour of the Axis once German forces were deployed in the theatre. In February German troops were reported in Tripoli commanded by what British intelligence called 'this obscure general'—Erwin Rommel.

If the full might of the Wehrmacht had been deployed in the eastern Mediterranean in the spring of 1941, British power in this region, fragile and over-extended, would surely have been destroyed. British forces were too weak and poorly equipped to overcome German professionalism. The land campaign in Cyrenaica demonstrated that British generals had quite enough difficulty overcoming Rommel's tiny panzer force in a theatre which OKH regarded as a 'side show'. Before December 1942 German forces in Libya never amounted to more than three divisions compared with 200 on the Eastern Front. Yet by the end of the first week in April Rommel had recaptured Benghazi and Derna. All that Wavell had achieved in three months had been cancelled out in one. This setback, followed by the repulse of a British offensive (BATTLEAXE) in July, led to a strategic stalemate.

During these months Wavell was distracted by the needs of other operations which endangered his rear. The first was the crushing in May 1941 of a pro-Axis coup in Iraq led by *Rashid Ali, prime minister since March 1940. The British then moved to consolidate their rear by securing the Levant in a five-week operation mounted mainly by Free French forces. After the Vichy commander *Dentz surrendered on 14 July 1941, the Lebanon and Syria were granted their independence by de *Gaulle. These events put General *Auchinleck, the new C-in-C of *Middle East Command, who replaced Wavell in July 1941, in a stronger position to concentrate his resources for a major effort in the Western Desert and his first offensive (CRUSADER) illustrates more clearly than any other the interdependent character of the Mediterranean war.

By the autumn of 1941, the plight of *Malta, lying astride Rommel's line of communications, and the only British outpost remaining in the central Mediterranean, was becoming desperate. Blockaded and subject to constant aerial attack, its relief could only be assisted if the Libyan ports, Benghazi especially, fell into British hands. This required the assistance of the navy. The army could only move on these ports under an air umbrella, and to guarantee such cover more airfields in Cyrenaica had to be captured by driving Rommel out of the territory. Consequently, the operations in this campaign revolved around the northern communications centres.

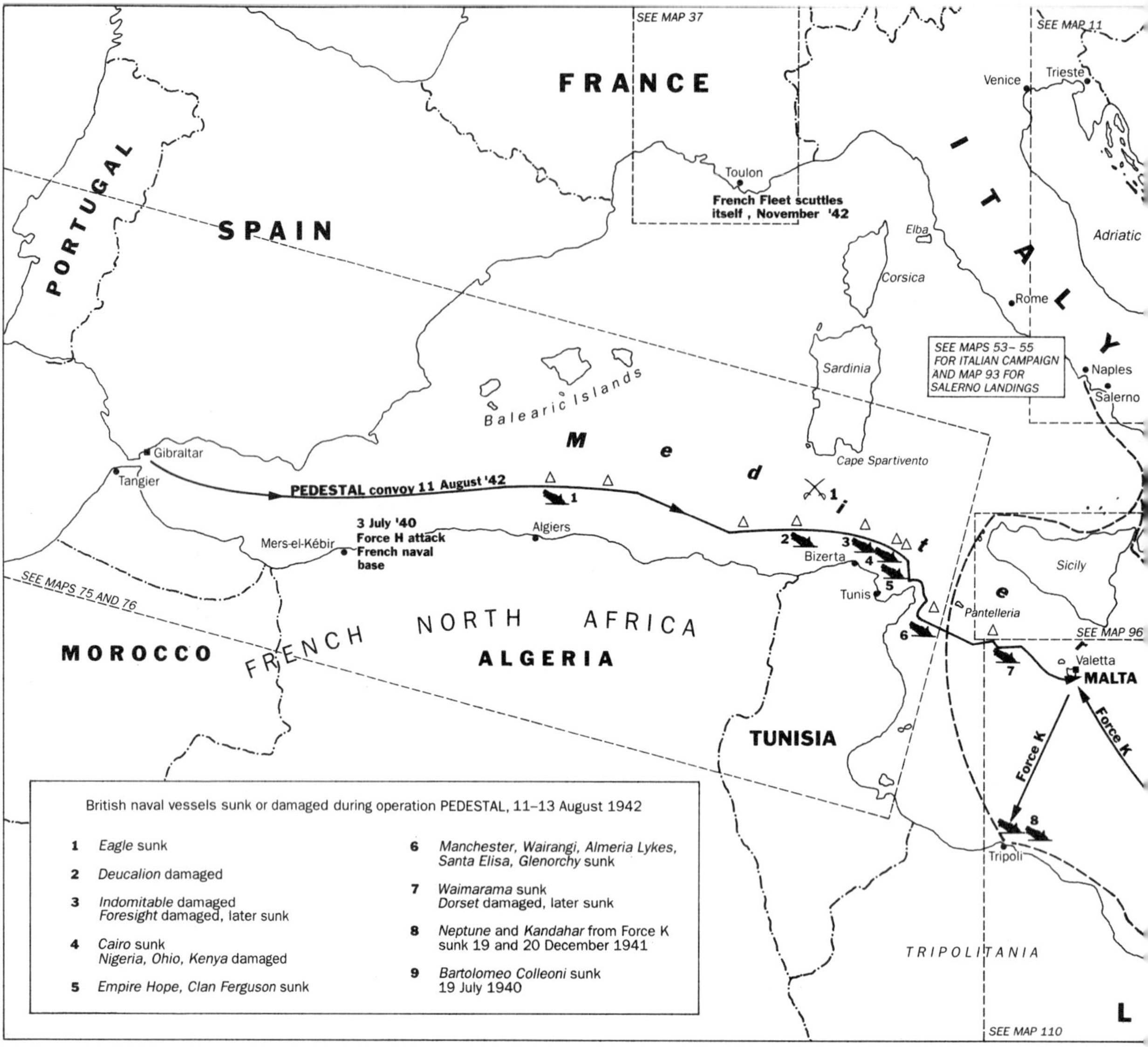

British naval vessels sunk or damaged during operation PEDESTAL, 11–13 August 1942

1 *Eagle* sunk

2 *Deucalion* damaged

3 *Indomitable* damaged
Foresight damaged, later sunk

4 *Cairo* sunk
Nigeria, Ohio, Kenya damaged

5 *Empire Hope, Clan Ferguson* sunk

6 *Manchester, Wairangi, Almeria Lykes, Santa Elisa, Glenorchy* sunk

7 *Waimarama* sunk
Dorset damaged, later sunk

8 *Neptune* and *Kandahar* from Force K sunk 19 and 20 December 1941

9 *Bartolomeo Colleoni* sunk 19 July 1940

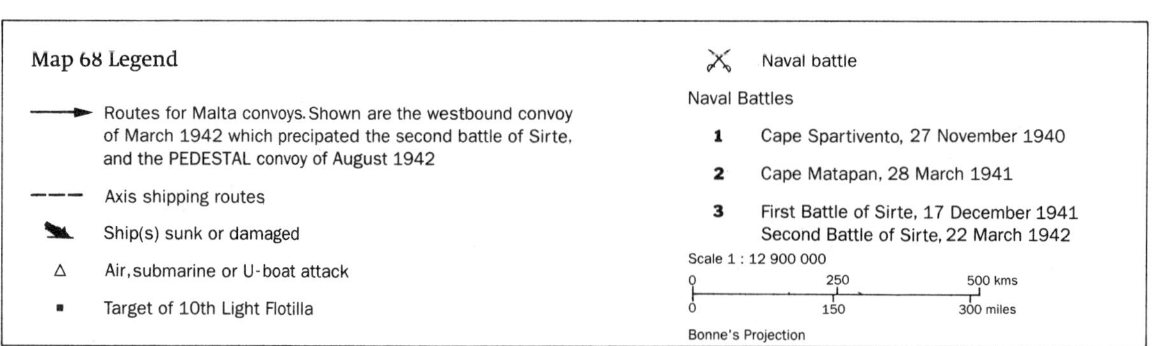

68. **Battle for the Mediterranean**, 1940–3

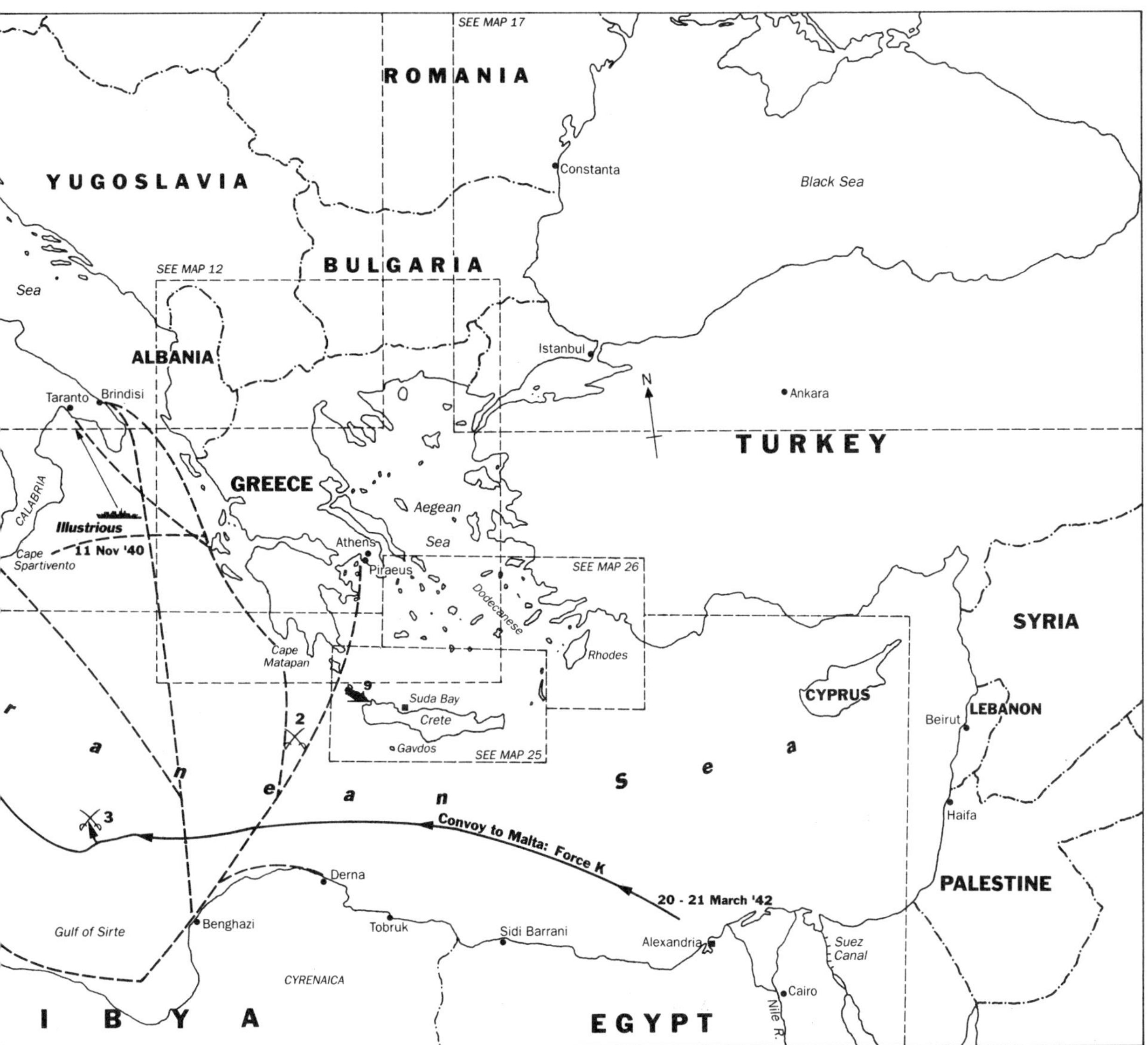

Conversely, Rommel could not drive the British from Alexandria and capture the Suez Canal until his lines of supply (especially of fuel) were freed from a grip exerted from Malta. All of these considerations were determined by *logistics and levels of inter-service co-operation. Consequently, the campaign in the Western Desert developed into a 'pendulum war', one side or the other recovering as it was thrown back on its sources of supply while the opposing side became over-extended.

Here the strategic position of Malta, equidistant from Gibraltar and the Levant, was pivotal. In 1940–1 the Royal Navy could not strike effectively at the Axis convoys supplying Rommel—despite having access to *ULTRA intelligence—because of a shortage of submarines and aircraft. But maintaining a base at Malta was a powerful potential thorn in the Axis side and it was a valuable aid to the ships escorting Allied *convoys. These comprised Vice-Admiral Philip Vian's Fifteenth Cruiser Squadron, which escorted convoys between Alexandria and Malta, from which Force H took them west to Gibraltar. This system was put to the proof when, in December 1941, Fliegerkorps 10 was transferred to Sicily along with eighteen submarines. Air attack on Malta now became unremitting and British sea power was crippled. In the three months October–December 1941, the aircraft carrier *Ark Royal*, the cruiser *Galatea*, and the battleship *Barham* were sunk by air action. Two other battleships, *Valiant* and *Queen Elizabeth*, were disabled by Italian frogmen, the *human torpedoes of the *Tenth Light Flotilla, who attached mines to their hulls in Alexandria harbour. On 18 December *Force K, the only striking force left in the central Mediterranean, floundered into a minefield off Tripoli and, depleted and harassed by incessant air attack, it was withdrawn to Gibraltar. Eight months later it returned escorting a convoy of fourteen merchantmen, of which only five arrived in Valetta harbour, but they included the precious tanker *Ohio* (lashed between two destroyers), whose fuel nourished Malta's beleaguered air defences.

Thus the war at sea and in the air undermined the foundations upon which Auchinleck's success in CRUSADER rested and, in the early months of 1942 Rommel was allowed to build up the resources upon which his spring and summer offensives were wholly reliant. But by the summer of 1942 this equation was reversed. The Allies again tightened their grip on his supply lines and simultaneously improved their own. ULTRA intelligence once more permitted the pinpointing of convoys that could be attacked by Allied submarines or by 'sweeps' from the air. In January–July 1942, 80 ships of 163,000 tons were sunk; in the months August–December 1942 this tally was almost doubled, 150 ships of 276,000 tons being destroyed, and in August 1942 Rommel's monthly stock of supplies dwindled to 6,000 tons.

All the major desert campaigns, especially CRUSADER (November 1941), Rommel's second counter-offensive (January–February 1942), the battle of *Gazala (May 1942), and the first battle of *El Alamein (July 1942), were governed by these factors. If Hitler had allowed Rommel to concentrate his resources on finally eliminating Malta in the summer of 1942, rather than pursuing the British towards the Nile delta, then the Germans might have solved their logistical conundrum. A solution was provided for the British by the decision taken by *Roosevelt that US forces should enter the battle for the Mediterranean. After the fall of Tobruk in June 1942 the British and Commonwealth forces, which had been formed into the Eighth Army the previous autumn, were re-equipped with American tanks. This permitted the substantial build-up of equipment which served as the basis of Montgomery's success in the battle of *Alam Halfa and the second at El Alamein (August and October–November 1942). Throughout the early months of 1943 Allied naval superiority was established, laying the basis for later *amphibious warfare operations in the Mediterranean and strangling Rommel's supply lines. This task was made easier by the transfer of Fliegerkorps 10 back to the USSR. Allied navies now dominated the central Mediterranean.

In deciding to intervene in the Mediterranean, Roosevelt had effectively overruled the advice of his military advisers. The US chief of staff, General *Marshall, argued that it was a theatre of secondary value, and that resources should be concentrated in the UK for the decisive blow that would follow in north-west Europe. Even a small commitment to the Mediterranean, he believed, would grow inexorably. There was something in Marshall's view, but he overlooked the importance of political factors and the necessity for 'blooding' American troops without excessive slaughter. The British had long cherished ambitions to extend the conflict to French north-west Africa, and this was a tempting spot to strike because it was calculated (wrongly) that the Vichy French would not be disposed to fire on American troops. The successful landings of 8 November 1942 that started the *North African campaign (TORCH) signalled a major Allied commitment to the Mediterranean theatre, and Marshall was right in thinking that it would continue to grow. But the success of these amphibious operations and the advance into Tunisia do not justify the argument advanced by some historians that the second battle of El Alamein was a strategic irrelevance. Rommel's army had to be worn down, and if it had been allowed to withdraw intact into the mountain fastnesses of Tunisia, securing a decisive land victory in North Africa would have been rendered immensely difficult.

By the time victory in the North African campaign had been achieved in May 1943 the decision had been taken in principle to invade Sicily, although discussion on the subject at the Casablanca conference in January 1943 (see SYMBOL), where the decision had been made, had hinged around the benefits of a Sardinian alternative which would have provided bases from which to bomb northern Italian cities. To clear the remaining obstacles for the *Sicilian landings, which began on 10 July, the island of *Pantelleria was occupied on 11 June and Lampedusa and Linosa captured. Islands further north, such as *Corsica and *Elba, were also eventually liberated. By then the principle of invading the Italian mainland had been accepted by the Americans at the Quebec conference held in August 1943 (see QUADRANT), in return for a definite commitment by the British to launch the Normandy landings in the spring of 1944 (see OVERLORD), but at that time none of the advocates for a landing in Italy envisaged a prolonged campaign inching its way up the Italian peninsula. In truth, though, the logic of exploiting the victories already won in the Mediterranean was incontrovertible.

None the less, the US chiefs of staff fought a long battle to restrict the numbers of US troops involved in the *Italian campaign which began on 3 September 1943. The Mediterranean, which became a unified command in December 1943, was dominated by the British, and after its first supreme commander, Eisenhower, had departed in January 1944 Maitland *Wilson was appointed supreme commander. The bulk of his troops were British, but this concealed the overall US dominance of the Western Alliance. Whereas the British had dreams of opening up an immense theatre aligning Turkey against the Axis, the USA was only interested in the theatre to the extent that it contributed to OVERLORD. Marshall therefore supported a scheme for an invasion of southern France as this operation (ANVIL, later DRAGOON), would open up a new route of supply for US forces participating in OVERLORD. Unilateral British efforts to extend operations to the eastern Mediterranean, as during the ill-fated *Dodecanese Islands campaign in September–December 1943, merely underlined how important American assistance had been in earlier victories, and from then on operations in the Mediterranean were run down. Seven divisions were withdrawn from Italy in December 1943 and transferred to Britain for OVERLORD. Turkey remained obdurately neutral. Despite the fall of Rome in June 1944, a further six divisions including the *French Expeditionary Corps, were withdrawn for the *French Riviera landings, which went ahead in August 1944 despite impassioned British protests.

In the event it was less British efforts than the arrival of Soviet forces in the Balkans that affected affairs in the eastern Mediterranean. The defection from the Axis of Romania and Bulgaria in August 1944 and the retreat of over-extended German forces from the Balkans, forced the *British expedition to Greece (MANNA) to prevent a communist coup. In the early 1950s an argument was advanced that the sagacious British were more far sighted in envisaging the full extent of the communist threat in eastern Europe after 1945. If greater resources had been placed in the Mediterranean theatre and more support given to *Alexander's ambitious plans to advance on Vienna via the Ljubljana gap, writers such as Chester Wilmot argued, then the West would have been in a stronger position to wage the *Cold War. Much of this is retrospective pipe-dreaming. There were no thoughts in British plans about frustrating the Soviets, only defeating the Germans. In achieving the final defeat of Nazi Germany, the Mediterranean campaigns had a subsidary, if not insignificant, role. They were the decisive proving-ground of Allied forces—allowing expertise to be developed in ground, air–ground, and amphibious operations before the Allies undertook the massive challenge of OVERLORD and the defeat of the Wehrmacht in north-west Europe. BRIAN HOLDEN REID

Hamilton, N., *Monty: Master of the Battlefield 1942–1944* (London, 1983).
Howard, M., *The Mediterranean Strategy in the Second World War* (London, 1968).
Macintyre, D., *The Battle for the Mediterranean* (London, 1964).
Sainsbury, K., *The North African Landings: 1942* (London, 1976).

Meiktila, battle of, four-week encounter fought between Japanese and British forces in February–March 1945 during the *Burma campaign. It was *Slim's greatest strategic triumph of the campaign and took place after his Fourteenth Army crossed the River Irrawaddy in central Burma in pursuit of Lt-General Katamura Shihachi's Fifteenth Japanese Army. To trap Katamura's forces, which were still reeling from the failure of the *Imphal offensive, Slim employed a large-scale *deception plan (CLOAK). This involved, *inter alia*, transmitting radio signals from a bogus HQ, which succeeded in convincing the Japanese that Slim's 4th Corps was about to move on *Mandalay. Slim feinted in that direction, but his main thrust was made by secretly moving the striking force of 4th Corps (17th Indian Division and 255th Tank Brigade) down the Myittha valley and across the Irrawaddy, and then sending his armour racing towards Meiktila, the heart of Katamura's communications and supply network.

The only opposition in the area, the *Indian National Army, was brushed aside. Japanese transport troops, 300 infantrymen who reached Meiktila before the British attacked, and even the wounded, fought bravely, but the town fell to 17th Division on 3 March in what Slim described as 'a magnificent feat of arms'. More than 2,000 Japanese bodies were counted.

With Katamura now embattled around Mandalay the Burma area commander, Lt-General Kimura Hyotaro, reacted swiftly and in strength by ordering Lt-General Honda Masaaki to retake Meiktila with 49th Division and elements of four others. For a time 17th Indian Division was cut off, but it was supplied by air, a brigade was flown in to reinforce it, and Honda failed to break the division's grip on the town. On 28 March 1945 he withdrew after covering Katamura's withdrawal. For a time he stood at Pyawbwe, but once he had been overcome there the way to Rangoon was open.

Mein Kampf ('My Struggle') was Hitler's autobiography-cum-political manifesto. He began dictating the first volume to *Hess when they were both imprisoned after the Munich putsch of November 1923 and it was published in the summer of 1925. A second volume, published in December 1926, was later added to the first volume to become, from 1930, the standard edition. Up to 1930 23,000 copies of the first volume were sold and 13,000 copies of the second. By the end of 1933 the combined volume had sold 1.5 million copies and probably as many as ten million were sold in Hitler's lifetime. Its style is turgid and convoluted, and Hitler later tried to distance himself from it, though he affirmed that 'as to the substance, there is nothing I would want to change.' See also NAZI IDEOLOGY and ORIGINS OF THE WAR.

Memelland, an area on the Baltic sea north of the River Neman which belonged to East Prussia before the *First World War. However, much of its population, particularly those who lived outside the port of Memel, was Lithuanian and under the *Versailles settlement it was detached from Germany and put under French administration. It was then proposed that it become a free state, but in January 1923 it was seized by Lithuanian forces and Memel was renamed Klaipeda. It became an autonomous region within Lithuania until 23 March 1939 when a German ultimatum forced its return to Germany. In 1945 it was returned to Lithuania, by then part of the USSR.

Mengele, Josef (1911–79), German doctor who, from May 1943, was chief medical officer at *Auschwitz. The most notorious of the medical experiments he carried out on the inmates were those on twins—allegedly to find a means of multiplying the German nation—and on one occasion he supervised the sewing together of two gypsy children to create Siamese twins. But he also killed thousands with lethal injections. Because he always took part in deciding who should live and who should die while dressed in an immaculate white medical coat he was known by the inmates as the 'Angel of Death'.

After the war he escaped to Argentina, where in 1960 he narrowly avoided capture by Israeli agents. He then fled to Paraguay. In 1985 human remains were disinterred from a grave in Brazil and genetic fingerprinting subsequently identified them as Mengele's.

Menzies, Robert (1894–1978), Australian lawyer who served as prime minister of his country from 1939 to 1941, and again from 1949 to 1966.

Menzies entered politics in Victoria in 1928 and by April 1939 was the national leader of the United Australia Party. The same month he formed his first administration and, having supported the policy of appeasement, reluctantly led Australia into the war against Germany a few hours after the UK had declared war. Despite having a majority of only one after the general election of September 1940 he went to London in February 1941 in an attempt to alert the British to the Japanese threat. In this he was hardly successful, but in the following two months he helped in some vital decisions by attending war cabinet meetings—including the disastrous intervention in Greece (see BALKAN CAMPAIGN), for which he was heavily criticized in Australia.

In May 1941 he returned to Australia and found his party in disarray. The Labour Party opposed a vote approving his visit to London and in August 1941 he was forced to resign. He was replaced by his deputy, *Fadden, though he continued to serve in the cabinet as minister for the co-ordination of defence, but in October 1941 *Curtin's Labour government was voted into power and Menzies spent the rest of the war in opposition.

'We are all very grateful to you for the courage you showed and the help you gave,' Churchill wrote to Menzies, referring to his time in London; 'I am the gainer by our personal friendship'. He found Curtin much less ready to co-operate. Nevertheless, Menzies was highly critical of how the war cabinet was run and of Churchill's wide-ranging powers. A strong supporter of the British Empire, he wanted an Imperial war cabinet that included the prime ministers of the dominions, but this was opposed not only by Churchill but by the prime ministers of New Zealand and Canada as well. See also AUSTRALIA, 3.

Hazlehurst, C., *Menzies Observed* (London, 1979).
Martin, A., *Robert Menzies: A Life*, Vol. 1 (Melbourne, 1993).
Menzies, R., *Afternoon Light* (London, 1967).

Menzies, Maj-General Sir Stewart (1890–1968), British Army officer who served as chief ('C') of the British Secret Intelligence Service, *MI6, from November 1939 to 1952. Although he had his detractors, most authorities praise his wartime success in expanding and maintaining a diverse empire that included MI6, the government Code and Cypher School at *Bletchley Park, MI6's Radio Security Service, and the communications network of *Special Liaison Units (SLU) which were responsible for delivering *ULTRA intelligence to commanders in the field. Though he had not been Churchill's candidate to succeed Admiral Hugh Sinclair as 'C'—he achieved the post through the backing of Lord *Halifax—Menzies's success was only possible because of his close relationship with the prime minister, which was resented by other directors of intelligence.

Menzies's career in intelligence began in 1915, when he joined the staff of Field Marshal Douglas Haig (1861–1928), and he worked in MI6 between the wars. On becoming 'C' his immediate priorities were to expand Bletchley Park, reinforce the counter-espionage side of his organization, and rebuild the European networks exposed after the *Venlo incident. Colonel Valentine Vivian headed the counter-espionage expansion and Claude *Dansey the intelligence-gathering; though each regarded himself as Menzies's deputy, neither was formally appointed. This lacuna made it difficult for Menzies to absent himself from his post and the burden of work in any case kept him chained to his desk. His liaison with Bletchley Park was initially maintained through Group-Captain F. W. Winterbotham who formed the SLU networks. To these networks and to Menzies's zealous care for ULTRA security must be largely ascribed the preservation of this vital source. By 1945 Menzies, who was decorated by six Allied governments, had brought intelligence to a new peak of effectiveness. His retirement, two years after the normal retiring age, had no connection with the scandal of the treachery of 'Kim' *Philby which broke later. He was knighted in 1943.

ROBERT CECIL

merchant marine, see merchant marine section of relevant major powers.

Meretskov, Marshal Kirill (1897–1968), Soviet Army officer of peasant stock whose training included a spell in Germany in 1931.

In November 1939, when he was the Leningrad Military District commander, Stalin ordered him to launch an impromptu invasion of Finland (see FINNISH–SOVIET WAR). After the ensuing near-débâcle, Stalin, with uncharacteristic generosity, retained him in high positions, making him chief of the General Staff (see STAVKA) in August 1940 and a deputy commissar of defence in January 1941. In the early months of the war with Germany, Meretskov served as STAVKA representative at North-west *front* (army group) and Karelian *front*, both in the Leningrad area. In December 1941, he commanded the army that recovered Tikhvin and thereby preserved Soviet road and rail access to the Lake Ladoga shore east of *Leningrad which enabled a tenuous link with the besieged city to be maintained.

From December 1941 to February 1944, he commanded Volkhov *front* south of Lake Ladoga. His mission, to liberate Leningrad, was a taxing one since the city had acquired profound psychological significance for both sides. In January 1943, he opened a corridor 10 km. (6 mi.) wide along the Ladoga shore, but liberation had to wait until 24 January 1944, after which Volkhov *front* was dissolved.

In June 1944, then commanding the Karelian *front*, Meretskov once more attempted a whirlwind offensive against Finland. His armies, better prepared this time, quickly broke through defences the Finns had worked on for nearly three years but lost momentum thereafter; and in July he had to stop for two weeks to regroup. Two months later the Finns asked for terms, and Stalin agreed to an *armistice on 19 September. In October, Meretskov staged a four-week offensive to dislodge the German Twentieth Mountain Army from the Petsamo area, after which Stalin advanced him to Marshal of the Soviet Union.

In February 1945, after having followed the German retreat to Kirkenes, Meretskov began redeploying his troops to the Vladivostok area, where, as First Far Eastern *front*, they participated in the August war against Japan (see JAPANESE–SOVIET CAMPAIGNS). EARL ZIEMKE

Merrill's Marauders, see GALAHAD.

Mersa Matruh, battle of. This was fought during the *Western Desert campaigns after *Tobruk had been captured by *Rommel's forces on 21 June 1942 and the remnants of the British and Commonwealth Eighth Army, commanded by Lt-General Neil Ritchie, had retreated to this Egyptian port. On 25 June the C-in-C Middle East, *Auchinleck, dismissed Ritchie and took command himself. Rommel's attack the next day, and poor communications and confused orders left the New Zealand Division isolated and 10th Corps surrounded. The New Zealanders, in one of the epic actions in the desert war, broke out at the point of the bayonet and 10th Corps, amidst confused fighting, eventually managed to break out, too. Rommel occupied the port on 27 June while the Eighth Army withdrew once more, this time to *El Alamein.

Mers-el-Kébir, Algerian port where the French fleet was at anchor when on 3 July 1940 it was bombarded by the Royal Navy.

When the *armistice between France and Germany was signed on 25 June 1940, the fate of the powerful French fleet, the fourth largest in the world, was of critical importance to the British. Most of its main units were scattered among various Mediterranean ports, though some were in British ones and a few were in the French West Indies. The warships at the Mers-el-Kébir naval base included the modern battle-cruisers *Dunkerque* and *Strasbourg* (both superior to any German battle-cruiser), two older battleships, and six large destroyers, while seven destroyers and four submarines were at nearby Oran.

The terms of the armistice stipulated that the French fleet would not be used by the Germans or Italians, but would be immobilized under their control, and the *Vichy French navy minister, Admiral *Darlan, had instructed his captains that under no circumstances were their ships to fall into German hands (see FRENCH FLEET, SCUTTLING OF). The full text of this message was not available to the British who, in any case, were concerned about the ultimate fate of these powerful vessels. It was therefore decided that the French fleet must be put permanently out of Hitler's reach, and that the vacuum created by its absence in the Mediterranean should be filled by creating *Force H under Admiral *Somerville.

As a first move all French ships in British ports were seized on 3 July 1940. The same day Force H was dispatched to Mers-el-Kébir where Somerville opened negotiations with Admiral Marcel Gensoul who commanded the French naval forces there. Initially, Gensoul refused to see Somerville's emissary and the negotiations were conducted in writing. The French admiral was given four options:

1. put to sea and join forces with the Royal Navy;
2. sail with reduced crews to any British port where the ships would be impounded and the crews repatriated;
3. sail with reduced crews to a French port in the West Indies where the ships would be immobilized;
4. scuttle his ships within six hours.

The Admiralty also instructed Somerville that should Gensoul refuse all these offers it would allow the ships to be immobilized in their present berths. Given the conditions laid down by the Admiralty, this was an impracticable proposition and so was never mentioned to Gensoul. He was told that if he refused to agree to any of the terms his ships were to be sunk. Gensoul reported the negotiations to the French Admiralty by signalling only that he had been told to scuttle his ships within six hours or force would be used. As a consequence, and not surprisingly, Gensoul was given full authority to resist.

When Gensoul at last agreed to meet an emissary, Somerville, who was profoundly unhappy about using force, delayed taking any action for as long as possible. But while the emissary was still aboard Gensoul's flagship, *Dunkerque*, the French Admiralty sent a plain-language signal ordering all French naval forces in the Mediterranean to move to Oran and to put themselves at Gensoul's disposal. This message was intercepted by the Admiralty which ordered Somerville to proceed quickly before he had to deal with reinforcements as well as with the forces before him.

Somerville's emissary left *Dunkerque* at 1725 having already informed Somerville that Gensoul still refused to comply exactly with any of the four options, and at 1754 Somerville opened fire. The battleship *Bretagne* blew up, several other ships were seriously damaged, and 1,297 lives were lost. *Dunkerque* was only slightly damaged, but was crippled by torpedo aircraft during a second attack on 6 July. *Strasbourg* and six other ships escaped, as did some cruisers stationed at Algiers.

Two days after the bombardment the French battleship *Richelieu*, at Dakar, was attacked by torpedo aircraft from the carrier *Hermes* and damaged, but at Alexandria the British C-in-C Mediterranean, Admiral *Cunningham, persuaded the French admiral to disarm his ships, thus avoiding more bloodshed.

Mers-el-Kébir created great tension between the French and the British. The Vichy government broke off diplomatic relations and French torpedo bombers made a retaliatory raid on Gibraltar. But it clearly showed the world in general, and the Americans in particular, that though apparently on the brink of defeat the British would stop at nothing to win the battle for the *Mediterranean and to achieve eventual victory. See also SEA POWER.

Marder, A., *From the Dardanelles to Oran: Studies of the Royal Navy in War and Peace, 1915–1940* (Oxford, 1974).

Messe, Marshal Giovanni (1883–1968). Italian Army officer who, until October 1942, was commander of the Italian Expeditionary Force, Italy's initial contribution to Axis forces fighting in the *German–Soviet war (see also ITALY, 5(b)). From February 1943 he led *Rommel's former German–Italian Panzer Army, renamed First Italian Army, in Tunisia during the *North African campaign. He defended the *Mareth Line and later held *Montgomery's Eighth Army at Enfidaville, but in May 1943 he surrendered with all Axis forces in North Africa, which did not prevent Mussolini from then promoting him marshal. In November 1943, after Italy's armistice with the Allies in September 1943, he succeeded *Ambrosio as head of the Italian High Command (see COMANDO SUPREMO), but was replaced in 1945.

Messervy, Lt-General Sir Frank (1893–1973), British Army officer whose sanguine but dashing temperament made him one of the most successful British commanders. He led a brigade during the *East African campaign; 4th Indian Division, and then 7th Armoured Division (Desert Rats), during the *Western Desert campaigns; 7th Indian Division in the *Burma campaign, which successfully fought the Japanese during the *Admin Box battle and their *Imphal offensive; and, from December 1944 to July 1945, 4th Corps which defeated the Japanese at *Meiktila, and then entered Rangoon. His last wartime post was as C-in-C Malaya. He was knighted in 1945.

meteorological intelligence was essential to both sides in order to fight with the maximum effectiveness. It is impossible to overstress the importance of the weather in waging war, from launching a tactical attack to deciding when to start hostilities. As an example of the latter, weather conditions were a vital ingredient in the planning of Japan's move southwards in December 1941. War had to begin then, before the north-east monsoon in the South China Sea and the winter gales in the north Pacific reached their full strength, and while the Manchurian winter made Japan's northern flank comparatively safe from its traditional enemy, the USSR. The Japanese carrier force which attacked *Pearl Harbor used bad weather to hide its approach, and at the start of the *Coral Sea battle of May 1942 a cold front, with its associated cloud and poor visibility, concealed *Yorktown*'s carrier aircraft as they approached their targets.

The use by the Japanese of a frontal system to cover their attack on Pearl Harbor resulted in the Americans employing meteorologists lavishly, with the Weather Wing of the US Army Air Forces (USAAF) eventually having more than 4,000 meteorologists in its weather squadrons world-wide. Meteorology was also considered sufficiently important for the *Combined Chiefs of Staff to have their own meteorological committee. 'Weather is a weapon,' one expert is quoted in *The US Army in World War II. The Signals Corps: The outcome* (G. Thompson and D. Harris, Washington, DC, 1966, p. 465). 'If left to chance it may help you and the enemy, hurt both of you, or aid one of you and hinder the other. If it is properly used, the weather can be ... on your side most of the time.'

To be accurate, meteorological intelligence has to be on a world-wide basis, and the German occupation of much of Europe, the Japanese seizure of much of the Pacific during the *Pacific war, and the total secrecy of the USSR, denied large areas of the world to the western Allies during the early part of the war. Once the USSR joined the Allies, in June 1941, some progress was made in obtaining Soviet co-operation, an exchange of weather information being made between some Siberian stations and the USA. This information was far from complete, but certainly helped US operations in the north Pacific such as the *Aleutian Islands campaigns, and was later extended to facilitate the delivery of *Lend-Lease aircraft via the Alaskan–Siberian air route. But it was not until March 1944 that Soviet meteorological intelligence for operations against Germany became available to the West, when a reciprocal agreement was established which obtained data from 100 Soviet weather stations.

Accurate meteorological intelligence was most frequently required by air forces, and both the Americans and the British, apart from flying regular meteorological reconnaissance flights, used airborne meteorologists to fly ahead of their aircraft and report the weather over intended targets. In August 1943 the Germans inflicted heavy losses on American bombers when the fine weather predicted over *Schweinfurt by German meteorologists showed it to be the USAAF's most likely target; and an accurate forecast of fine weather was also the key factor in launching *Big Week in February 1944, which resulted in such heavy losses for the Luftwaffe over Germany. In the *China–Burma–India theatre, the best meteorological intelligence that could at first be obtained for US pilots delivering supplies to China over the *Hump was visual. 'The present system,' one pilot commented, 'is that if you can see the end of the runway it's safe to take off.' But even when proper meteorological intelligence was provided, aircraft continued to be lost in the atrocious flying conditions that prevailed over the Himalayas.

On land meteorological intelligence was needed by artillery units to fire accurately as ballistic adjustments had to be made to allow for wind direction and strength, and atmospheric pressure. It was also essential for launching ground offensives and to judge the condition of terrain. For example, accurate forecasts, as well as a thorough understanding of Lake Lagoda's ice surface, enabled the maximum amount of relief supplies to reach *Leningrad across the lake's ice road during the winter of 1941–2; and an accurately predicted cold snap enabled Soviet tank forces, previously bogged down by rain and impassable roads, to launch a surprise offensive in the northern Caucasus during the winter of 1942.

In March 1943 the Japanese failed to repeat their success of using a weather front to screen their approach by sea when their meteorologists incorrectly predicted that poor visibility would hide from air reconnaissance their troopships taking reinforcements to New Guinea. The error compounded Allied foreknowledge of the operations through *ULTRA intelligence and as a result the Japanese suffered heavy losses to Allied air power in the *Bismarck Sea battle.

Allied amphibious and airborne operations against Lae during the *New Guinea campaign also hinged on specific weather conditions. *MacArthur's air commander, Lt-General George C. Kenney, required clear weather over the area for Allied aircraft, but fog over western New Britain and adjacent straits to hinder Japanese aircraft. Such conditions were not uncommon and though the American and Australian weather teams picked different dates as to when they would occur; Kenney chose the day between them and obtained the weather he needed.

Perhaps the best known example of momentous events hanging on accurate meteorological intelligence was the Normandy landings (see OVERLORD). Allied meteorologists correctly predicted a gap in the poor weather—a prediction helped by information supplied by aircraft and warships specially stationed in the Atlantic—which enabled *Eisenhower to launch OVERLORD on 6 June, while the failure of their German counterparts to predict the gap led to a relaxation of German vigilance. However, German weather reports were certainly accurate when the *Ardennes campaign was launched on 16 December 1944: Hitler stated that meteorological intelligence obtained from U-boats in the Atlantic 'contributed decisively' to the initial success of the offensive because it was started in low cloud which neutralized Allied *air power.

As in so many other fields of scientific endeavour, meteorology developed swiftly during the course of the war. By 1944 the Allies were employing 'sferic' (an abbreviation of atmospherics) equipment which, could take bearings on the lightning a storm caused up to 1,600 km. (1,000 mi.) away, far beyond the range of *radar. Along with a radio direction finder called a Rawin, radar was by then being used to track hydrogen balloons, the basic tool of the meteorologist on both sides. Tracked by theodolite, these balloons indicated the speed and direction of the wind in the upper atmosphere. They were also used to take radiosondes into the upper atmosphere to measure temperature, pressure, and humidity. Lack of atmospheric pressure eventually caused the balloon to burst and the radiosonde, still recording the information, then descended by parachute. By 1944 the Americans had developed a radiosonde which transmitted the information back to its controller.

It was the positioning of meteorological teams employing this equipment, or of automatic weather stations transmitting meteorological information, which caused what might be termed the 'weather war'. This was waged in the Atlantic and Arctic by the Allies against German meteorological teams and weather ships whose information, supplemented by weather flights, was of great assistance to the Luftwaffe opposing the Allied *strategic air offensives in Europe. Meteorological parties were dispatched by the *Abwehr to Greenland, Spitzbergen, and other Arctic islands. Because the British Code and Cypher School at *Bletchley Park had broken the Abwehr's hand cipher, the early parties were all captured, but some later ones, as well as unmanned stations, were successfully established by the German Navy. The teams were all pinpointed eventually, some of them from ULTRA intelligence. ULTRA was also responsible for capturing two German weather ships, both of which yielded vital cryptographic information, but one of the unmanned stations, established on Canada's Labrador coastline, remained unidentified until 1981. On Spitzbergen, where one German team flew daily reconnaissance flights, German and Norwegian meteorologists clashed in a number of running fights. Another German team fought off the Greenland Sledge Patrol before long-range US bombers forced its evacuation months later. Its successor, perhaps because it supplied Bletchley Park with useful ULTRA intelligence, remained unmolested from August 1943 to April 1944, but two others, dispatched to Greenland in August and September 1944, were quickly rounded up by the US Coast Guard.

Stagg, J., *Forecast for Overlord* (Shepperton, 1971).

Mexico was neutral until the USA entered the war in December 1941. It was then quick to sever diplomatic relations with the Axis powers, and to establish defence arrangements, and economic agreements with the USA. When a Mexican tanker was torpedoed in May 1942, the Mexican government declared war and the following month signed the *United Nations Declaration.

Mexico's main, and most important, war effort was to increase its exports of *raw materials, meat, food, timber, and leather to the USA. But it also supplied labour for American farms and railways through the **bracero* programme to relieve the US manpower shortage, and 250,000 Mexicans resident in the USA joined the armed forces, 14,000 of whom saw combat. The Mexican Expeditionary Force helped liberate the Philippines and Formosa, and a Mexican Air Squadron saw action during the last months of the *Pacific war. See also LATIN AMERICA.

MGB stood for Motor Gunboat, a high-speed British Coastal Forces craft. It was bigger and more heavily armed than an *MTB—some were over 30 m. (100 ft.)—and its primary task was to attack small craft such as the German *E-boat and *R-boat. But its speed also made it suitable for *air-sea rescue and clandestine operations. See also WARSHIPS.

MI5, British security service which in the Second World War, as in the First, shared with *MI6 and the Special Branch of the Metropolitan Police the responsibility of evaluating, and advising the British government on, intelligence relating to national security, this being defined as 'the defence of national interests against hostile elements other than the armed forces of the enemy: in practice against espionage, sabotage and attempts to procure defeat by political subversion'.

The dividing line between MI5 and MI6, which went back to the establishment of the two bodies under the war office before the *First World War, was geographical. MI5's responsibility extended to the three-mile limit off the UK and, in co-operation with the local authorities, of the countries of the empire, including Egypt (see SECURITY INTELLIGENCE MIDDLE EAST), while MI6 (the body primarily concerned with collecting intelligence abroad, which was officially named the Secret Service or the Secret Intelligence Service from 1921) was also responsible for national security beyond those limits.

Within the UK MI5 reverted after the First World War to being a small section of the war office charged only with security on behalf of the armed forces, and the Special Branch was made responsible for security as it affected the civilian population. This change was made in response to ministerial, public, and police distrust of the development of a domestic secret service at a time when the increasing prominence of labour organizations, pacifist groups, and communist activists was blurring the distinction between subversion and legitimate disaffection—and when espionage had ceased to be an obvious threat. But the resultant duplication and friction were such that in 1931 MI5 (now officially named the Security Service but also, like MI6, retaining its old title for reasons of custom and convenience) took over the responsibility for evaluating and advising on all intelligence relating to subversion (other than that relating to known Irish and anarchist groups and to the maintenance of public order, which remained in the province of the Special Branch) and to espionage. The responsibility for taking executive action on the intelligence remained with the Special Branch and the chief constables under the authority of the home secretary. As the Security Service, MI5 was also made accountable to the home secretary in view of his constitutional responsibility both for the safety of the state and for the liberty of the subject and the rights of minorities.

With the outbreak of hostilities in September 1939 MI5 perforce delegated its direct responsibility abroad, in Egypt and at British bases, to the military authorities. Otherwise the above arrangements remained unchanged throughout the war. Clashes of jurisdiction with MI6 in the field of counter-espionage revived suggestions that MI5 should either be incorporated into MI6 or should assume responsibility for all counter-espionage, both at home and abroad. But practical experience and constitutional considerations—MI6 was accountable to the foreign office—dictated the retention of a separate security service for British territory.

Disagreements relating to security against the threat of subversion in the UK were less frequent, and they were not clashes about jurisdiction between MI5 and the police but differences of judgement between MI5, supported by the police, and the home office. The earliest of them, and the most prolonged, persisted throughout the first year of the war. The home office, with its concern for the liberty of the individual, was slower to implement against enemy aliens, and the potentially dangerous British fascist and communist organizations, some of the formidable array of emergency Defence Regulations drawn up before the war (under the royal prerogative or by extension of the Official Secrets Acts and the Aliens Restrictions Acts) than MI5, with its responsibility for security, thought advisable; and after the fears let loose by the German offensives in the west in May 1940 (see FALL GELB) had prompted the hasty application of drastic measures during the *fifth column panic of July 1940 (see INTERNMENT), the home office was quicker to relax them than MI5 desired. A similar conflict arose in the last eighteen months of the war: MI5 then pressed to little avail for the exclusion from government service of communists, who had been excluded from the application of the security measures adopted in 1940.

As before, it drew a distinction between known members of the Communist Party, or people known to have close associations with them, and people who, though known to have once had some association, had long since ceased to give grounds for concern. It had no evidence during the war that a few in the latter category who were active on behalf of the Soviet authorities after entering government service included employees of MI6 and MI5 itself (see SPIES).

MI5 naturally kept a watch on known adherents of *Mosley's fascist organization (see BRITISH UNION), and on those who had advocated close Anglo-German friendship before the war began. Among this latter group, one of MI5's undercover women agents found a White Russian refugee woman who had befriended a cipher clerk in the US embassy in London, called Tyler Kent. Kent was strongly opposed to Roosevelt's policy of friendship with the UK, and stole from the embassy texts of telegrams exchanged between Roosevelt and Churchill, which he hoped to be able to release to the public in some way that would ruin Roosevelt's chances of re-election to the presidency in November 1940. Joseph Kennedy (1888–1969), the US ambassador, was persuaded to waive Kent's diplomatic immunity; Special Branch raided Kent's flat, and found the telegrams. The young man was tried *in camera* and sent to prison.

In the arguments preceeding the fifth column panic MI5 had been doubly handicapped. Its staff—some 400 in total, as compared with 800 in 1918—was overwhelmed and its headquarters disorganized by an enormous increase in such mundane if necessary work as the vetting of entrants into government service, the organization of travel controls, and the scrutiny of floods of neurotic reports from the public denouncing aliens and suspected enemy agents. In the second place, it was in the unenviable position of having to assume in the absence of reliable negative evidence that an organized subversive movement, harbouring enemy agents, might be reporting abroad and even waiting for the opportunity to strike. The first handicap largely disappeared in the wholesale tightening up of security procedures effected during the panic by a new security executive set up under an ex-cabinet minister, Lord Swinton: under his supervision its sections were reorganized and its more humdrum duties were decentralized to the chief constables.

At the same time Churchill noticed that MI5 was still headed by Sir Vernon Kell, who had founded it in 1909 and was in the new prime minister's opinion no longer fit for the task. Kell was abruptly retired. For a few months the organization was run by Brigadier 'Jasper' Harker, one of his subordinates, while his successor returned from abroad. This was Sir David Petrie, who had had 36 years' continuous service in the Indian police and thus had every aspect of security at his fingertips. He worked easily with the many newcomers into his department, most of them university dons.

The removal of the second handicap—the dearth of reliable intelligence—did not follow from these steps. It was brought about by developments which coincided with the reorganization, when the morale and the reputation of MI5 were at their lowest ebb. MI5 had fretted over the lack of evidence for an organized fifth column when no such thing existed; but it could not confirm the non-existence before suspects had been interned and could be interrogated. In the same way, the fact that it had detected some 30 cases of attempted espionage before the outbreak of war had only persuaded it that others might have escaped detection and that from the beginning of the war their numbers were increasing (which was not the case). Whatever its faults, complacency was not among them. It was correspondingly quick to exploit opportunities thrown up by the outbreak of hostilities. It used the fact that an *Abwehr agent volunteered his services in September 1939, and a second in January 1940, to introduce to the Abwehr two further *double agents by August 1940. It took full advantage of the fact that from August 1940 the first radio transmissions associated with the Abwehr's plans against the UK were intercepted by the Radio Security Service (RSS) and decrypted by the government Code and Cypher School at *Bletchley Park. With the aid of these two sources, double agents and signals intelligence, it directed the total defeat of the first Abwehr offensive against the UK from September to November 1940, when all but one of the 21 agents who arrived were either immediately captured or immediately gave themselves up; the exception committed suicide.

From this success, as from its equal success in intercepting the agents the Abwehr continued to try to infiltrate into the UK at the rate of some 20 agents a year till the end of 1943, MI5 acquired more double agents. Others were Abwehr employees who from January 1941 volunteered their services; they included the few who, under the codenames TRICYCLE (*Popov), GARBO (*Pujol), and BRUTUS (*Garby-Czerniawski), came to be the most valuable. A similar expansion took place in the signals intelligence provided for MI5 from December 1940, when Bletchley Park cryptographers began to read the main hand ciphers of the Abwehr, and even more so from December 1941, when they mastered the Abwehr's version of the *ENIGMA machine cipher. By then MI5 and MI6 had built up so full a knowledge of the order of battle and operations of the Abwehr throughout Europe (as also, to a lesser extent, in the Middle East and Latin America) that, though remaining a considerable nuisance in areas where effective action against it was difficult to mount (particularly Spain and Gibraltar), the Abwehr presented no threat within the UK for the rest of the war. Indeed, its activities were turned into a substantial liability for Germany by the decision to use the double agents for *deception.

The prime purpose to which MI5 put the intelligence was to advance security by persuading Germany that it was so well served by agents that it need not struggle to develop new methods for infiltrating others. Not until it could be confident that it controlled all agents in the country, and would not fail to detect new arrivals, could MI5 pay serious attention to using the double agents to pass misleading information as part of a sustained programme of strategic deception about the resources and the intentions of the Allies. That point was reached in the middle of 1942. Thereafter, though only as one element in a complex machine directing strategic deception in support of Allied operations from the UK, the London Controlling Section (see UK, 8), and the *XX-committee, MI5 made a crucial contribution to the deception plans by choosing and briefing the double agents. In the Middle East and the Mediterranean parallel machinery for the control of deception was set up under the military authorities, and MI5 played only an advisory role.

Whatever benefit the Allied operations derived from the deception programme, it must be stressed that *suggestio falsi* was of less consequence than *suppressio veri*. Deception could be instrumental in the success of the operations, notably of the Normandy landings in June 1944 (see OVERLORD), only if the Allies were able to conceal their true intentions. They owed their success in achieving this to several considerations, including the general weakness of Germany's intelligence sources, but the check on enemy espionage, in which MI5 played the leading role, and their own meticulous security precautions, which were drawn up and supervised by yet another complex machine, a strengthened *Inter-Services Security Board, with advice from MI5, were among the most important. F. H. HINSLEY

Andrew, C., *Secret Service: The Making of the British Intelligence Community* (London, 1985).
Hinsley, F. H., and Simkins, C. A. G., *British Intelligence in the Second World War*, Vol. 4: *Security and Counter-Intelligence* (London, 1990).

MI6, placed under the British foreign office and officially known as the Secret Intelligence Service from 1921, had the responsibility of gathering foreign intelligence relating to national security (see MI5 for definition). 'C', the chief of MI6, was also responsible for the government Code and Cypher School at *Bletchley Park where the German *ENIGMA and *Geheimschreiber signals were decrypted and which produced the vital *ULTRA intelligence.

While there is general agreement that intelligence had an important part in winning the Second World War, this verdict is associated in most minds with ULTRA, and the official history (F. H. Hinsley *et al.*, *British Intelligence in the Second World War*, 5 vols., London, 1979–91), by concentrating so heavily on this aspect, has put the verdict beyond appeal. This hardly does justice to the role of MI6, nor to the principle that the most reliable intelligence is nearly always that derived from the congruence of different sources. It should also be borne in mind that MI6 also provided the *Special Liaison Units by which ULTRA was communicated to the military headquarters in the field. These units played a vital role in safeguarding ULTRA throughout the war.

The low rating of MI6 at the start of the war was directly due to neglect at the hands of the foreign office and treasury which did not understand that intelligence requires a long-term perspective and cannot be turned on, like a tap, when a crisis impends. This neglect, combined with the intractable problem that MI6 officers faced in trying to penetrate the defences of the totalitarian states of the USSR and Nazi Germany, resulted in a grave deficiency of strategic intelligence immediately before the war and during its early phase. When the purse-strings were at last released in 1938, the head of MI6, Admiral Hugh Sinclair ('C'), made a start by building up his counter-espionage section and creating a new section (D) for sabotage and subversion. One of the new recruits into Section D was the traitor Guy Burgess; but in 1940 he was dismissed for incompetence.

Sinclair's death late in 1939 and his replacement by Stewart *Menzies coincided with the abduction of two of his officers at *Venlo. Their disclosures greatly contributed to the loss of the European networks, so that Menzies found himself virtually starting from scratch. His position was further weakened when Churchill came to power in May 1940, removed Section D from MI6 and incorporated it into *SOE which came under ministry of economic warfare, not foreign office, supervision. The ensuing rivalry between MI6 and SOE for scarce resources, such as transmitters, light aircraft, and coastal craft, was probably unavoidable, but could have been mitigated if both organizations had been answerable to the same cabinet minister. Only in New York, where *British Security Co-ordination was set up in August 1940, was there an effective merger of the activities of MI6, MI5, and SOE.

In September 1941 Section V recruited from SOE the *traitor 'Kim' *Philby, who later ran counter-espionage in the Iberian peninsula and Italy. Section V established a sound working relationship with MI5, especially in the joint exploitation of controlling Axis agents (see XX-COMMITTEE). This exploitation was greatly helped when, in March 1940, the *Abwehr's hand cipher was broken, later followed by its machine ciphers and those of the Sicherheitsdienst or SD (see RSHA). From October 1940 the Abwehr's signals were issued as the ISOS series and the SD's as the ISK series (the initials of the heads of the Bletchley Park sections which decrypted the signals: Intelligence Section, Oliver Strachey, and Intelligence Section, Knox). Later it became common for all German intelligence signals to be circulated as ISOS, regardless of origin or method of encipherment. Both ISOS and ISK were controlled by Section V.

The close collaboration between Section V and MI5 survived the contested transfer to the former in early 1941 of the Radio Security Service (RSS), which listened to German intelligence signals and for any illicit domestic transmissions; but Section V at first imposed a ban on the wider circulation of papers produced by the RSS analysis bureau. This problem was only overcome in the summer of 1943 when responsibility for the bureau was transferred from Section V to Section VIII.

Another effective adjunct to the strength of MI6 was the creation of a scientific section, in which the moving spirit was R. V. Jones. His incorporation in the MI6 air intelligence section, headed by Group-Captain F. W. Winterbotham, meant that links with the air ministry were particularly close and fruitful. Winterbotham was also instrumental in developing *photographic reconnaissance which was taken over by the RAF on the outbreak of war.

Initially, there was a tendency in Whitehall to impute to failure of intelligence-gathering errors and oversights that were more properly attributable to failure of assessment. Thus failure to foresee Hitler's invasion of Norway in April 1940 (see NORWEGIAN CAMPAIGN) and of the USSR in June 1941 (see BARBAROSSA) must be ascribed primarily to defective assessment of such

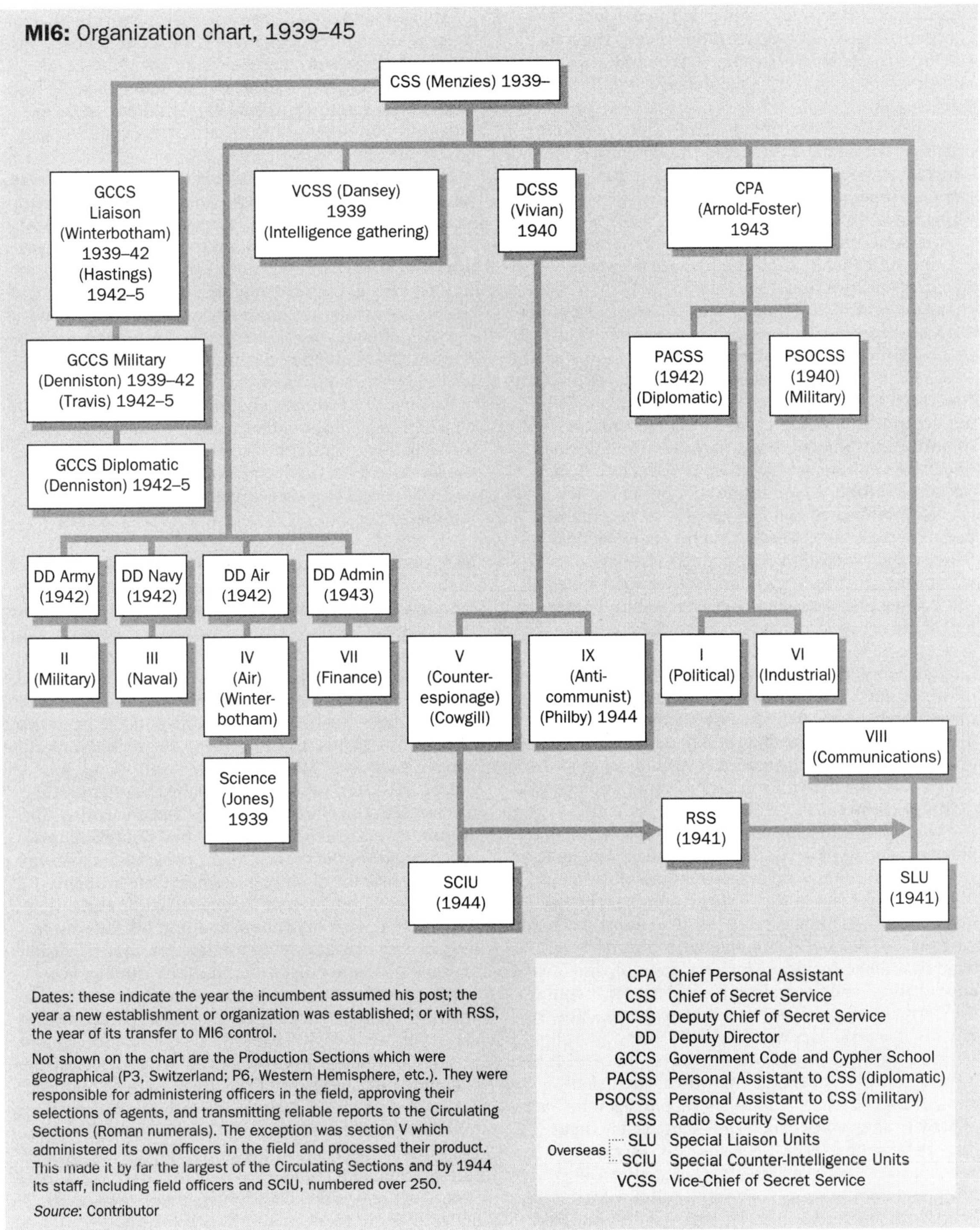

MI6: Organization chart, 1939–45

Dates: these indicate the year the incumbent assumed his post; the year a new establishment or organization was established; or with RSS, the year of its transfer to MI6 control.

Not shown on the chart are the Production Sections which were geographical (P3, Switzerland; P6, Western Hemisphere, etc.). They were responsible for administering officers in the field, approving their selections of agents, and transmitting reliable reports to the Circulating Sections (Roman numerals). The exception was section V which administered its own officers in the field and processed their product. This made it by far the largest of the Circulating Sections and by 1944 its staff, including field officers and SCIU, numbered over 250.

Source: Contributor

CPA Chief Personal Assistant
CSS Chief of Secret Service
DCSS Deputy Chief of Secret Service
DD Deputy Director
GCCS Government Code and Cypher School
PACSS Personal Assistant to CSS (diplomatic)
PSOCSS Personal Assistant to CSS (military)
RSS Radio Security Service
Overseas: SLU Special Liaison Units
Overseas: SCIU Special Counter-Intelligence Units
VCSS Vice-Chief of Secret Service

intelligence—admittedly limited and sometimes contradictory—as MI6 was providing. But as the Joint Intelligence Committee (see UK, 8) acquired greater aptitude, this aspect of the problem came to be better understood.

During 1942, as the Allies began to move over to the offensive, the demand for tactical intelligence grew and here MI6 was able to play a more effective part. 'C' could rely on co-operation with the intelligence services of the Allied *governments-in-exile, of which the Poles and the Czechs, who were permitted to maintain their own lines of communication to their intelligence networks, were the most effective.

The German occupation of *Vichy France in November 1942 weakened the links established there; but the fact that such links persisted damaged co-operation with the Gaullist *Bureau Central de Renseignements et d'action. Nevertheless, clandestine activity in France gained momentum and proved of special value along the Atlantic coast, where U-boats were based and German *blockade runners and *auxiliary cruisers found shelter (see also CANOEISTS). No major landings in Europe could yet be contemplated, but MI6 gave essential help in planning cross-Channel raids, such as those against *Dieppe and *St Nazaire. Ship-watchers (see also COAST WATCHERS), mainly Norwegians, were also installed on the Norwegian coast, where German warships lay in wait for *Arctic convoys, and reports from them enabled attacks to be launched against them by aircraft and *midget submarines. Useful contacts with the German internal resistance (see SCHWARZE KAPELLE) were also maintained in Sweden and Switzerland. But it was difficult to estimate the state of morale in Germany, just as it was the state of the economy. Agents (see SPIES) and informers could locate factories, but could not gauge output accurately.

Two areas in which agents' reports, supplemented by photographic reconnaissance, enabled heavy losses to be kept to a minimum were in the exposure of German *radar defences and in the confirmation that the Germans were developing *V-weapons of an unprecedented kind. As RAF Bomber Command intensified its *strategic air offensive against Germany, it was of vital importance to locate and neutralize the defensive ring round the German heartland (see KAMMHUBER LINE). The raid on *Bruneval, facilitated by MI6 reports, was of special importance in discovering the complexity of these radar defences and in countering them (see ELECTRONIC WARFARE). As regards V-weapons, agents' reports of activity at *Peenemünde had begun to come in as early as November 1939, when the *Oslo report mentioned it. Two years later it seemed increasingly likely that both missiles and rockets of some kind were being built and tested there. As evidence accumulated, much of it coming from conscripted non-German labour, 'C' successfully challenged the persistent scepticism of Lord Cherwell (see LINDEMANN), and in August 1943 major air raids at last took place. These critically delayed production and impelled transfer of research to Blizna, deep in Polish territory. On the French and Belgian coasts launching pads and storage sites for the V-1 were discovered; a single agent identified no fewer than 37. These discoveries, and the air attacks which followed them, averted an untold number of casualties in London and south-east England.

In the run-up to the Normandy landings in June 1944 (see OVERLORD) an agent stole the plans of the *Atlantic Wall; others contributed sketches of 80 km. (50 mi.) of the coastline where the landings were to take place. Even after OVERLORD Section V still had work to do for it formed Special Counter-Intelligence Units which accompanied the armies to France and advanced with them into Belgium and the Netherlands. This was an important task, even though rumours of Nazi *Werewolf packs proved exaggerated.

MI6, which had begun the war at a low pitch, ended it on a high note. Maj-General *Strong was right when in his book *Men of Intelligence* (London, 1970) he described the latter years of the Second World War and the early post-war period as a kind of golden age for British Intelligence.

ROBERT CECIL

MI9, the British escape service, was a semi-secret branch of the military intelligence directorate in the war office, founded in December 1939 at the suggestion of the future Field Marshal Sir Gerald Templer, who was then in charge of security for the *British Expeditionary Force. Its head, Colonel Norman Crockatt, decorated and wounded in the *First World War, combined common sense, courage, and discretion. Having been brought into MI(R), a predecessor of *SOE, by its chief, J. C. F. Holland, he worked under the wing of *Dansey at MI6.

Crockatt's staff were mostly recalled regular officers, like himself; they included a sailor and an airman. The air ministry later regretted that it had not taken up a suggestion that the branch might come under its own control, for many of MI9's customers were airmen. Crockatt settled his headquarters at Wilton Park, Beaconsfield, west of London, and sent his staff out to lecture men in uniform. He was later promoted brigadier, and made a deputy director of military intelligence.

MI9 had several aims: to secure intelligence about the enemy, from repatriated *prisoners-of-war and by coded correspondence with those still in POW camps; to assist prisoners to escape, by advice given beforehand and by smuggling escape gear in to them; to train the armed forces in methods of escape and evasion; and, eventually, to organize groups of helpers abroad to assist escapers on their way home. None of the smuggling was done in *International Red Cross food parcels, on which scores of thousands of prisoners of war depended, towards the end of the war, for their continuing health.

Aircrew undertaking operational flights, or commandos going on raids, were provided by MI9 with purses, each containing some £10 worth of the local currency of wherever they were going, a small hacksaw, and a small compass: this would give them a start in making a getaway. They carried maps printed on silk, for durability and ease of concealment.

Gradually, with heroic help overseas, MI9 was able to build up lines of helpers, who were prepared to undertake the sheltering of fugitives on their way out of occupied territory. These lines worked particularly well in Belgium and France; attempts were also made in the more spacious and more suspicious lands of south-eastern Europe. In the Far East much less could be done, because escapers of Caucasian descent were immediately recognizable as non-natives (but see BRITISH ARMY AID GROUP).

If an escaper or an evader (someone who had never been in enemy hands) was caught while travelling along one of these lines, he had only to produce his identity discs to establish his status as an Allied combatant, covered by the *Hague and *Geneva conventions, and could legitimately expect to be sent, or to be sent back, to a prisoner-of-war camp. His helpers were much more harshly treated: the best they could hope for was a prison sentence, and a great many of them were killed. It was reckoned in MI9 that every one of the 2,000-odd aircrew safely brought out of western Europe to fly again had cost a helper's life. The German security services devoted much effort to trying to break escape lines up; and they ran one or two bogus lines themselves, for the sake of the intelligence they could glean from them about Allied air order of battle.

A grand total of more than 33,000 men from British, American, and British Commonwealth forces got back to the Allied lines after being inside enemy territory, whether as escapers or as evaders. A substantial proportion of them—not recoverable exactly from the surviving statistics—did so with the help, known or unknown, of MI9 or of its American equivalent MIS-X.

Escape stories, many of them hair-raising, form a distinct and distinguished part of war literature. They seldom if ever mention MI9, because it was so secret at the time that few prisoners had ever heard of it. When they mention maps, tools, or wireless sets, without stating a source for them, they can reasonably be supposed to have come from MI9. The author of a best-seller from the First World War, A. J. Evans, who had written *The Escaping Club*, served on MI9's staff. He joined the unit called IS9 (WEA) which accompanied *Eisenhower's armies during the fighting in north-west Europe. IS9 (CMF) was a similar unit working in Italy; IS9 (ME), based in Cairo, covered the eastern Mediterranean and south-east Europe, and provided cover for 'A' Force (see DECEPTION). All three IS9 units came under Crockatt, an early believer in the slogan 'small is beautiful'; the whole of the staff under him did not number as many as 300, but they exercised a disproportionately large influence on the course of the war.

Not only did they make escapes and evasions more easy, as they had been meant to do; they provided for thousands of prisoners-of-war, directly and indirectly, some degree of hope, and thus made prison endurable, whether the men concerned were directly involved in escape projects or no. Whether they also provided a significant body of intelligence remains an official secret.

M. R. D. FOOT

Foot, M. R. D., and Langley, J. M., *MI9* (Boston, 1980).

Middle East Command, British Army HQ activated in Cairo in August 1939 with General *Wavell as C-in-C. Egypt, the Sudan, and Palestine-Jordan, which had all been separate army commands, now came, with Cyprus, directly under Wavell's control. With his naval and air force opposite numbers Wavell formed a High Command responsible to the British *Chiefs of Staff. In early 1940 his fief was extended to include the British land forces in East Africa and British Somaliland, and any that might be dispatched to operate in Turkey, the Balkans, Iraq, Aden, or the shores of the Persian Gulf. His responsibilities were therefore vast. At one time he was fighting three separate campaigns—the *Western Desert, the *Balkan, and *East African ones—as well as commanding the forces being used to quell the revolt in Iraq, and he had quasi-political and diplomatic commitments as well. These burdens were lightened for Wavell's successor, *Auchinleck, with the appointment of a minister of state in the Middle East, who represented the War Cabinet, and the formation, in August 1941, of East Africa Command which came directly under the War Office.

In the autumn of 1941 Middle East forces were reorganized. Two Army commands were created under Auchinleck—troops in Syria and Palestine became the Ninth Army while those in the Western Desert became the Eighth Army—and, on orders from Churchill, the Commandos were reconstituted (see UK, 7(e) for description of special forces in the Middle East). In January 1942 Persia and Iraq were detached from C-in-C India and put under Middle East Command, and the same month the troops there were designated the Tenth Army. From 11 March to 15 May 1942, at the height of the siege of *Malta, the island also came under Auchinleck.

In August 1942, when Auchinleck was replaced by *Alexander, Persia and Iraq were formed into a separate command (see PAIFORCE). In February 1943 Maitland *Wilson succeeded Alexander. By then Middle East Command had become mainly an administrative HQ, though Wilson did mount the abortive invasion of the *Dodecanese. In January 1944 Wilson was succeeded by *Paget who remained in the post until the end of the war.

Middle East Commando, formed in October 1941 from L Detachment (see SPECIAL AIR SERVICE), the remnants of *Layforce (No. 3 Troop) and No. 51 Middle East Commando, and the *Special Boat Section. It was short-lived and was disbanded when Churchill agreed in August 1942 that all special operations should come under the *Special Air Service. Its only operation of note was when, in

December 1941, Lt-Colonel Geoffrey Keyes, the son of Admiral *Keyes, led No. 3 Troop (which also called itself No. 11 Commando) in a raid on what was incorrectly thought to be *Rommel's living quarters. Keyes was killed and was posthumously awarded the Victoria Cross (see DECORATIONS).

midget submarines were employed by the Italians, who had pioneered their use during the *First World War, and by the British, Germans, and Japanese, with varying degrees of success. They were mostly used to attack warships in defended harbours which conventional submarines had little chance of penetrating. The crews of British midgets used *limpet mines, Axis ones mostly *torpedoes.

The British operated three types: variants of the one-man Welman, a cross between a midget submarine and a *human torpedo; the 15.5 m. (51 ft.), 35-ton, four-man X-craft; and the XE-craft, a later development of the X-craft, which were employed in the Far East where their crews cut Japanese communication cables and damaged a cruiser. *SOE's Welman was a failure, but six X-craft altered the balance of *sea power in northern waters when they attacked, and badly damaged, the German battleship *Tirpitz* in September 1943. In April and September 1944 others attacked a floating dock in Norway—which an earlier Welman operation had failed to destroy—and two more were used by *Combined Operations Pilotage Parties to survey the Normandy beaches and then helped guide in the invasion forces in June 1944 (see OVERLORD).

The Germans also operated three types: the 9 m. (29.5 ft.), 6.5-ton Biber (beaver), in which the crewman was apt to be asphyxiated by carbon monoxide from its petrol engine; the 10 m. (34.4 ft.), 11-ton Molch (newt), which attacked Allied shipping off the Normandy beaches during OVERLORD and elsewhere without achieving much; and the more successful diesel-engined two-man 11.9 m. (39 ft.), 14.7-ton Seehund (seal), which sank a number of Allied ships.

In 1941 the Japanese Navy had more than 40 two-man, 24 m. (78.5 ft.), 46-ton Ko-gata (Type A) midget submarines. Five were used, and lost, in the attack on *Pearl Harbor, after being carried there by fleet submarines, and they attacked British warships at Diégo Suarez, Madagascar, in May 1942, damaging a battleship, *Ramillies*, and sinking a tanker. Type As were also used to attack shipping in *Sydney harbour and at *Guadalcanal. The three-man 25 m. (82 ft.), 50-ton Hei-gata (Type C) was employed with Type As during the *Philippines campaigns and elsewhere but with little success. The Japanese also developed two types of suicide midget submarines: the 17 m. (56 ft.), 19-ton two-man Kairyu (Sea Dragon) and the larger, faster 26.2 m. (86 ft.), 60-ton, two- or five-man Koryu (Scaly Dragon) which had explosive charges in the bows or could carry torpedoes.

The Italians had several prototypes but the only operational ones were the four-man CBs which were used in the *Black Sea with some success during the Axis blockade of *Sevastopol. A plan to attack shipping in New York harbour with another type of midget submarine was thwarted by the surrender of Italy in September 1943. See also TENTH LIGHT FLOTILLA, GERMANY, 6(e), FROGMEN, and HUMAN TORPEDOES.

O'Neill, R., *Suicide Squads* (London, 1981).

Midway, battle of. This was fought between Japanese and US carrier forces from 4 to 7 June 1942, and was the first decisive defeat the US inflicted on Japan in the *Pacific war.

In May 1942 Admiral *Yamamoto, C-in-C of the Japanese Combined Fleet, collected a force of 145 warships to invade Midway Island, by then America's most westerly Pacific outpost. His objective was to lure part of the smaller US Pacific Fleet into the northern Pacific by launching the *Aleutian Islands campaigns and then to bring the rest of the fleet to battle, and inevitable destruction, off Midway. If he succeeded, Hawaii was Yamamoto's next target with the USA at some point accepting, or being driven to sue for, a negotiated peace.

Instead of concentrating his formidable forces, Yamamoto was therefore dispersing them, and his plan was so intricate that some of his subordinates requested more time to train for it. He made other mistakes, too. He thought one of the US carriers, *Yorktown*, had been sunk; he was deceived by US radio deception (see also SIGNALS INTELLIGENCE WARFARE) into believing that the Americans' two remaining operational carriers, *Enterprise* and *Hornet*, were nowhere near Midway; he was disastrously late in putting a screen of submarines in place; and a last-minute *photographic reconnaissance of *Pearl Harbor, which would have revealed the US forces gathered there, was cancelled.

But more crucial to the forthcoming battle than any of Yamamoto's errors was the faith the Pacific Fleet's C-in-C, Admiral *Nimitz, put in the still new and untested *ULTRA intelligence which soon revealed that Midway was Yamamoto's chief objective. It enabled Nimitz to place two carrier groups—comprising the 3 carriers, 233 aircraft, and an escort which included 7 heavy cruisers—near Midway before the Japanese submarine screen was in place, and the island was also strongly reinforced. In overall command was Rear-Admiral *Fletcher aboard *Yorktown*, while the other carrier group was commanded by Rear-Admiral *Spruance.

Yamamoto's force was divided into an invasion group with a powerful escort of warships; Vice-Admiral *Nagumo's strike force of 4 carriers with 261 aircraft, 2 battleships, and other smaller escort ships; and a main group built around 3 battleships. The invasion force was sighted first, on 3 June, and was ineffectually attacked by bombers that afternoon. At dawn the next day aircraft from Nagumo's carriers attacked Midway, causing widespread damage. Then at 0715, still unaware of any American carriers in the area, Nagumo decided to rearm the aircraft he had kept in reserve for any American surface forces, and to use them for a second attack on Midway. This proved to be a costly error, for when Spruance's carrier group was eventually sighted Nagumo was unable to launch an immediate strike. But Spruance, though still at extreme range, committed his torpedo bombers immediately the Japanese were sighted. By doing this he caught Nagumo's bombers, which had just returned from Midway, on the decks of the Japanese carriers.

Out of the 41 US torpedo planes launched by Spruance, and later by *Yorktown*, only 6 returned. However, the evasion tactics they had forced the carriers to take prevented additional Japanese fighters being launched, while those already in the air had been drawn down almost to water level by the bombers' low-level attacks. This allowed the dive-bombers that followed to attack almost unopposed, and they soon reduced three Japanese carriers to burning wrecks. The fourth, *Hiryu*, escaped, and in mid-morning she launched a strike at *Yorktown*, causing serious damage and forcing Fletcher to move ship and hand over command to Spruance. Spruance's dive-bombers retaliated and *Hiryu* was so seriously damaged she had to be scuttled. *Yorktown* survived a second attack, but was sunk on 7 June by a Japanese submarine.

Nagumo now announced that his escort was retiring in the face of superior forces, but was ordered by Yamamoto to reverse course and to prepare for a night action. However Spruance, whose mixture of daring and caution was to make him a leading figure in the Pacific war, coolly retired out of range to avoid any contact. It was as well he did so, for Yamamoto's powerful main group (which the Americans knew nothing about) was also approaching Midway at top speed in the hope of engaging him. When it became obvious that Spruance was not going to play his game Yamamoto cancelled the Midway operation and withdrew. Spruance followed, but when air reconnaissance next day failed to find the Japanese he contented himself with launching air attacks on two Japanese cruisers crippled in a collision, sinking one and badly damaging the other.

Thanks to ULTRA intelligence and superior tactics, the Americans inflicted a severe defeat on the Japanese which shifted the balance of *sea power in the Pacific in their favour. It caused the Japanese to abandon the construction of battleships in favour of more carriers, postponed their plans to advance on New Caledonia, Fiji, and Samoa, and delayed their offensive in the *New Guinea campaign.

Prange, W., *Miracle at Midway* (New York, 1982).

Mihailović and the Četniks. A *četnik* was originally a member of an armed band (*četa*) operating against the Turks from Serbian-inhabited territory. In the wars of 1912–18, the *četniks* had been *francs-tireurs* helping the Serbian armies, and in 1941 the popular name was taken up again to describe all sorts of insurgents all over Yugoslavia, including army officers who had not accepted capitulation to the Germans.

The best known was Colonel Dragoljub ('Draža') Mihailović (1893–1946), whose idea was to organize, from German-occupied Serbia, a skeleton secret army to prepare for action to be co-ordinated with the plans of his *government-in-exile and of the Allies. He called it the Yugoslav Home Army, to emphasize the continued legal existence of Yugoslavia, and to end the confusion that arose from the name *četnik*. The spontaneous rising in Serbia which followed on the German invasion of the USSR in June 1941 (see BARBAROSSA) interrupted his plans, and also brought to the surface a rival set of insurgents with other aims—*Tito's partisans. The two fought uneasily side by side until brutal German repression exploded the bubble of popular optimism, relations between them turned to civil war, and, by the end of the year, the revolt had been quelled. Mihailović was generally considered its leader, in spite of his reticence and of the part played by the communists. Although his influence and his accomplishments were greatly exaggerated by Allied propaganda, nothing as important had so far occurred in occupied Europe, and Mihailović, promoted general, was symbolically made army minister in the exiled government in January 1942.

Tito and his partisans left Serbia for Bosnia, and Mihailović went back to his original plan to form a home army, careful to avoid further useless sacrifices. Keeping the base of his organization in Serbia, he removed himself just out of German reach, to northern Montenegro. Following on the Italian repression of the rising in Montenegro, the revolutionary activities of the communists had made the local Četniks willing to settle for 'live-and-let-live' with the occupying army, and in the Italian zone of *Pavelić's fascist independent state of Croatia (NDH) as well, many Serbian rebels had come to terms with Italian commanders in exchange for protection against Pavelić's fascist Ustašas. Nevertheless, all Serbian rebels were anxious to acknowledge Mihailović as a nominal paramount symbol of their distant king and the Allies, to legitimize their authority over the local population.

Mihailović accepted the link, which provided him with intelligence and Italian *matériel*, in the hope that he would be able to destroy the NDH through the Četniks in anticipation of an Allied landing in Dalmatia, but they had already achieved as much as they could, and he never had any real authority over them. He did, however, collect useful data, and carry out sabotage on communications through Serbia, which earned him Allied praise.

Although he had been engaged in only limited direct action against the Germans since the end of 1941, the Allies believed Mihailović to be potentially the most dangerous of all the Yugoslav rebels. However, his strength was weakened in the bloody entanglements of the first half of 1943 when, in expectation of a landing, the Axis, Tito, and Mihailović all acted to safeguard their interests at each other's expense. But when he returned to Serbia that summer, he emerged again to the point where he is estimated to have led the second most active *resistance movement in Europe—after Tito's. Time, however, was against him, for Tito was indeed impressing the British as 'killing the most Germans', and well ahead in terms of mobilization and organization. In December 1943, disappointed in their expectations, the British withdrew what support they had given Mihailović, and eventually, in May 1944, prevailed upon King Peter (1923–70) to appoint a new government which did not include him.

That summer marked the nadir of Mihailović's military action against the Germans, left as he was without supplies and facing the increasing onslaughts of Tito's partisans who were intent on returning to Serbia to link up with the advancing Red Army. Yet he organized the saving of shot-down Allied airmen, hunted down acknowledged collaborators, and continued rail sabotage. At the beginning of September he proclaimed a general mobilization to rid Serbia of its occupation forces. But attacked on three sides—by the Soviets, by the Bulgars who had turned from pro-German occupiers to pro-Soviet liberators, and by the partisans—he soon had to leave Serbia to try and regroup his forces in Bosnia.

In western Yugoslavia the collapse of Italy in September 1943 had deflated the independent Četniks. Most of what remained of them had eventually found their way to the region of Venezia Giulia in north-east Italy and were kept there by distrustful Germans who reinforced them with collaborationist auxiliaries from Serbia after that territory had been evacuated by the Germans and their auxiliaries. In October 1944 this jumble of armed groups wanted Mihailović to join them, so as to reorganize them into an efficient anti-communist force acceptable to the Allies. Mihailović wanted to disperse his troops into guerrilla groups and return to Serbia, but he did not entirely reject the plan, as it offered the possibility of joining with anti-communist forces in Slovenia and with the Anglo-American forces fighting in the *Italian campaign. He sent them the nucleus of a command staff, and left all his men free to go or to stay with him. Many went, but only a few eventually got to Italy, and the plan came to nothing.

Mihailović then set out in April 1945 to return to Serbia to start a resistance movement against the new communist order being set up there. But ambushed and attacked on their way by strong and well-equipped partisan forces, and beset by hunger and disease, the remains of the Yugoslav Home Army soon melted away. Only a few thousand reached Serbia, where they fought a disorganized guerrilla campaign, until Mihailović was captured in March 1946 by communist security troops. His capture marked the final defeat of the losing side in the civil war and after a dramatic trial in Belgrade, he was executed for treason and war crimes on 17 July 1946.

STEVAN PAVLOWITCH

Karchmar, L., *Draža Mihailović and the Rise of the Četnik Movement 1941–42* (New York, 1987).
Pavlowitch, S., *Yugoslavia* (New York, 1971).
Roberts, W., *Tito, Mihailović and the Allies 1941–45* (2nd edn., Durham, NC, 1987).

Milch, Field Marshal Erhard (1892–1972), deputy Reich commissioner for aviation from 1933 who was a prime mover in founding the Luftwaffe.

Born in Wilhelmshaven, Milch commanded a fighter squadron during the *First World War. After it he served with several airlines before joining Lufthansa in 1926, eventually rising to become its chief executive in 1929. Milch was an early Nazi supporter, and when *Göring—who had been receiving Lufthansa's financial support for several years—became Reich commissioner for aviation in 1933 he appointed Milch his deputy. Though Göring only allowed him a free hand for the first two years, it was Milch, as Göring's state secretary, who ran the new air ministry; and by various stratagems, including using Lufthansa as a front, he helped organize the construction of an air force that, kept secret up to 1935, by 1939 was the most powerful in the world.

Milch was commissioned as a colonel in the army in 1933 (the Luftwaffe was not officially formed until March 1935), but his rise was meteoric and by 1938 he was a Luftwaffe general. He commanded 5th Air Fleet during the *Norwegian campaign in April 1940 with great success, and was promoted field marshal that July. He had become inspector-general of the Luftwaffe at the start of the war and in November 1941 took on the technical directorate of the air ministry after *Udet committed suicide. In 20 months he increased German aircraft production 2.7 times, but in June 1944 virtually all military arms production was consolidated under *Speer and Milch's resignation as director of air armament followed. Göring, with whom Milch had long been in dispute, then dismissed him as state secretary but he stayed as inspector-general until January 1945 and was made deputy armament minister by Speer. He was sentenced to life imprisonment at the *Nuremberg trials but was released in 1955.

Irving. D., *The Rise and Fall of the Luftwaffe: The Life of Erhard Milch* (London, 1973).

Milice, or more properly Milice Française, was a 30,000-strong *Vichy French paramilitary police force. It collaborated with the Germans in rooting out Jews for deportation and hunting down the *Maquis and other French resistance groups, and became notorious for its brutality. It was founded in January 1943 from Joseph *Darnand's Service d'Ordre Légionnaire, which had been recruited the previous year from right-wing elements of *Pétain's veteran organization, Légion Française des Combattants. Members had to swear an oath of allegiance to Pétain on their knees after undertaking a night's vigil. Most wore uniform—khaki shirt, black beret, and black tie—but there was a plain-clothes section and it also employed a small number of women (Miliciennes) for clerical work. Its members, known as the Franc-Garde, were divided into two divisions: the younger, fitter element, about 10–12% of the total, served full time while the rest were older non-regulars who could be called upon in an emergency. At first restricted to what had been the unoccupied part of France, from December 1943 they became active over the whole country. A quite separate organization was the much smaller Milice Bretonne which was also active against local Maquis from early 1944.

Mills bomb, see GRENADES.

MINCEMEAT was the codename for a British *deception operation which originated from two members of the *XX-committee.

On 30 April 1943 a British submarine dumped a body off the Spanish coast near Huelva, where the German consul was known to be an efficient spy. The supposed victim of an air crash, it was dressed as a Royal Marines officer with the fictitious name of Major Martin. Attached to its wrist was an attaché case carrying, among other papers, a letter to General *Alexander which conveyed the impression that an invasion of Greece was imminent and that Sicily—the Allies' real objective—was the cover plan for another operation. The cadaver was handed over to the British consul within hours of its discovery, but the attaché case was not returned for some days, and tests in London revealed that the letter had been opened. On 14 May *ULTRA intelligence revealed that the Germans had taken the bait and Churchill, who was attending the *TRIDENT conference in Washington, received a simple message: 'MINCEMEAT swallowed whole.'

MINCEMEAT certainly coincided with Hitler's own fears about landings in the Balkans, and reinforcements were sent there and to Sardinia, troops who could have been used to defend Sicily at the start of the *Sicilian campaign.

Montagu, E., *The Man Who Never Was* (London, 1953).

mine warfare.

1. Land mines

Until 1939 mine warfare on land meant mining and counter-mining under the walls of fortresses or fortified fronts to blow breaches in them. The advent of the tank, which restored mobility to armies by neutralizing the lethal combination of barbed wire and machine-guns, gave the term a new dimension. Anti-tank mines and guns were introduced, bringing naval-style mine warfare into the land environment. But anti-tank mines laid on land could be detected and lifted more easily than at sea, unless they were covered by fire or protected by some other means. Consequently, anti-personnel mines were developed to make mine-lifting hazardous, particularly at night when covering fire was less effective.

The Germans had used a primitive form of anti-tank mine in 1918, consisting of an artillery shell fitted with a pressure fuze, and all armies developed their own versions in the inter-war years. The first anti-tank mines to be used operationally were the Italian bar-mines laid in 1940 during the *Western Desert campaigns. These were 91 cm. (36 in.) long and 12.7 cm. (5 in.) square in cross-section, contained 3 kg. (7 lb.) of explosive, and were actuated by pressure on the lid. Their anti-personnel mines were stick grenades, triggered by either trip-wires or pressure fuzes.

The British developed a small circular and over-complex anti-tank mine to exacting ammunition safety standards, but they had not produced it in quantity before the fall of *France in June 1940. Faced with imminent invasion by German panzer forces, they abandoned stringent safety requirements and adapted a commercial cake tin, filled it with 3.6 kg. (8 lb.) of TNT (see EXPLOSIVES), and fitted it with a simple pressure fuze. The Mark IV, as it was called, was later found to be over-susceptible to blast. It was replaced by the Mark V with redesigned fuzing to make it less vulnerable to explosive clearance devices. The British did not produce an anti-personnel mine, preferring to depend upon covering their minefields by fire.

The Germans developed their excellent circular Tellermine, weighing 8.6 kg. (19 lb.), filled with 5 kg. (11 lb.) of TNT and fitted with a pressure fuze. They also provided themselves with jumping anti-personnel mines, the S-Mine (Springenmine), which was buried with only the small prongs of the trigger mechanism visible. When actuated, a shrapnel-filled canister was blown upwards from the mine's casing, rising to about chest height before exploding with lethal effect. The Teller and S-Mines were first brought into service in the Western Desert campaigns around *Tobruk in 1941.

At the start of the *German–Soviet war the USSR suffered a critical shortage of mines as the Main Military Engineering Administration had been neglected during the 1930s. Also, because mines were defensive weapons, they were not politically acceptable and were thought to be the weapon of the 'weak'. This policy was eventually reversed but in early 1941 the Red Army had only one million anti-tank mines—just over a third of what was required for half a year's operations—and no other types at all. This shortage, exacerbated by having to defend terrain void of any natural defences against tanks, meant that improvised mines had to be made. These often had hardly any metal content, being mainly constructed of wood, glass, or even tarred cardboard, and infantrymen often had to resort to using the *Molotov cocktail against German armour. But once the Red Army had more mines of different types its engineers employed them cleverly and used them in massive quantities. It has been claimed that by the end of the war the Red Army had laid 200 million mines.

Mines were laid in their millions during the war, mostly in the Western Desert campaigns and on the Eastern Front. The density for laying them varied; the British laid their anti-tank mines one for every yard of front. There was less call for them in the Pacific and South-East Asian theatres where jungle conditions inhibited armoured warfare, but the American and Japanese had mines similar to the German versions available. On *Okinawa Japanese minefields held up one US division for a week.

Mines were far easier to lay than to detect and clear. Laying was largely a problem of *logistics, transport, and manpower. All mines had to be dug in by hand as neither side managed to develop a successful mechanical minelayer during the war. They were usually laid in fields some 460 m. (500 yd.) deep in staggered rows, which both reduced a tank's chances of driving through unscathed and made detection and clearance as protracted as possible.

But mines proved two-edged weapons. If minefields were not clearly marked with perimeter wire and warning signs, and their location and layouts accurately recorded, one's own side could blunder into them, and lifting them later could become a dangerous task. Marking minefields, in fact, increased their deterrent value, and made laying dummy minefields an effective ploy (see also DECEPTION).

A struggle between detection and counter-detection, and between clearance and counter-clearance, soon began, just as it did at sea. At first, mines could only be found by laborious prodding with bayonets or metal probes, and they had to be lifted by hand, usually by stealth at night or behind an artillery barrage. By 1942, hand-held electronic mine detectors had been developed, but they were far from reliable.

The bulk of mine-laying, breaching, and clearance was carried out by *engineers. All arms were trained in the rudiments of mine warfare to help them to look after themselves and to reduce calls on engineers. But on the Eastern Front the Red Army—which, especially early on, had rudimentary mine-clearing equipment and a shortage of engineers—was ruthless in using untrained infantrymen to clear a path through a minefield; and it has been said—though it is probably apocryphal—that it was the specific task of *penal battalions to do so by simply walking across them.

The British developed a number of mine clearance devices fitted to tanks such as indestructible rollers and mine ploughs, which were later adopted and adapted by the Americans who called them 'Earthworms' and 'Aunt Jemimas'. The most successful were the flail tanks called 'Crabs' and 'Scorpions'. They were standard gun-tanks fitted with rotating drums driven off their engines, from which weighted chains flailed paths through minefields. The early marks were mechanically unreliable, but they played a useful part in Allied operations from the second battle of *El Alamein onwards (see also ENGINEERS, Figures 1–4).

Blast clearance devices were also developed by the Allies such as explosive-filled steel pipes, called Snakes (see also BANGALORE TORPEDO), pushed through minefields by tanks. Most anti-personnel mines could be cleared by the blast, but some anti-tank mines were left unscathed. Later versions of the German Tellermine were blast resistant, a precaution the British had developed as early as 1941. To combat this the Americans developed a bomb-firing tank (T12) whose missiles exploded above the mines which were detonated by the pressure caused by the explosions.

Mine warfare caused many casualties both on land and at sea. Here a US soldier examines a German 'S' mine which he has just dug up with his bayonet. Called 'bouncing Bettys' by US troops, they jumped into the air after being stepped on so that they exploded level with the midriff.

By 1943 the Axis were beginning to use non-metallic mines to defeat the Allied mine-detectors. They were mostly cheap and easy to produce wooden box mines with plastic pressure fuzes for anti-tank and anti-personnel purposes. The German wooden anti-personnel *Schuh-mine* proved highly successful. It was a wooden box with just enough explosive to take a man's foot off, and yet small enough to be difficult to spot. It maimed many a senior officer looking for an observation point, as well as taking a toll of attacking infantry. The Germans also made greater use of anti-handling devices. For instance, their Tellermine was fitted with screw sockets on the side and underneath to take various types of anti-lifting device, and anti-handling fuzes were issued.

As the pace of German withdrawals quickened in 1944, and their commanders saw less likelihood of returning to an area, they discontinued marking minefields, and mines were sown at random to harass the Allied advance.

While the mine never managed to reverse the success of the tank in restoring mobility to land battlefields, it did reduce the dominance which armoured formations had enjoyed in the early phases of the Second World War.

Between 20% and 30% of all tank casualties were caused by mines. See also LIMPET MINES. WILLIAM JACKSON

2. Sea mines

In use since the 1840s, sea mines were employed by both sides, minefields being laid both defensively for protection and offensively to inflict shipping casualties. About 500,000 mines were laid during the course of the war. They did not sink nearly as many warships, or merchantmen, as did aircraft or submarines—only 6.5% of all Allied merchant shipping was sunk by mines—but their influence on the conduct of the war at sea was great. German mines closed British and US ports for days at a time, and played a major role in imposing the Axis siege of *Malta; a Finnish minefield in the *Baltic Sea crippled the Soviet Red Banner Fleet in August 1941; British mines damaged *German surface raiders in February 1942 (see CERBERUS); and, though it was US submarines which enforced the blockade of Japan, it was minefields laid from the air that finally severed its supply routes.

The moored contact mine was the one most commonly employed by both sides and, despite the introduction of the magnetic, acoustic (sonic), and pressure mines, known generically as influence mines (see below), it remained the biggest hazard because of the huge quantities laid. A spherical ball, it was fitted with horns and filled with 272 kg. (600 lb.) of *explosives. When one of the horns was fractured by contact with a ship's hull a chemical was released which activated the firing mechanism. It was usually laid in waters not exceeding 180 m. (600 ft.) in depth—though the Japanese had ones that could be laid in depths up to 1,100 m. (3,500 ft.)—and was moored by a cable attached to a heavy weight on the sea bottom. It was laid by specialist minelaying vessels but also by a variety of warships, including *auxiliary cruisers.

Influence mines, cylindrical in shape, containing as much as 350 kg. (775 lb.) of explosives, were usually dropped by parachute from aircraft. This meant flying vulnerably low to obtain accuracy, but from January 1944 *radar enabled Allied aircraft to lay them accurately from altitudes of up to 4,600 m. (15,000 ft.). The Soviet Union did not possess influence mines before 1943—which delayed its development of the means with which to sweep them—and Japan never had any of its own though it laid a few captured ones.

From September 1940 onwards the Luftwaffe dropped sea mines by parachute on to British cities with devastating effect. The 1,000 kg. (2,200 lb.) Luftmine, which the British called a land mine, was an ordinary B magnetic mine with a dual fuze; the 1,000 kg. Bombenmine was known to the British Bomb Disposal Service as the 'G' mine.

The Germans and the British had developed the magnetic mine, which was normally detonated on the sea-bed by the magnetic field of a ship's steel hull, during the *First World War. The Germans kept working on its development between the wars but the British only continued to investigate possible counter-measures. The Germans therefore scored a tactical success when they started laying them in September 1939, causing heavy losses. However, for various reasons, their mine-laying operations were halted from early December 1939 until the end of March 1940, and when they were resumed not enough mines were laid to neutralize British shipping.

Churchill's attempts to retaliate against German minelaying, with an operation (ROYAL MARINE) to float small air-dropped magnetic mines down the Rhine, was initially blocked by the French (see PHONEY WAR). When it was finally implemented, after the start of the German offensive in the west in May 1940 (see FALL GELB), it suspended nearly all river traffic between Karlsruhe and Mainz, but had no effect on the German campaign.

In November 1939 the British Minesweeping Service had found a German magnetic mine intact and by mid-1940 had developed a magnetic sweep. Once this had been introduced, the Germans began to use acoustic mines which were detonated by the sound of a ship's propeller acting on a diaphragm within them. But they repeated their error of introducing them prematurely and by November 1940 the first British acoustic sweeps—which magnified sound—were operational.

Mines were swept by specially-built minesweepers, or by converted civilian craft such as trawlers and paddle steamers. The most common equipment for sweeping contact mines in the Allied navies was the Oropesa sweep, so-called after the first ship to use it in 1919. Towed behind the minesweeper this severed the mine's mooring cable with a specially-weighted wire equipped with sharp cutters and a small explosive charge. Once on the surface the mine was destroyed by gunfire. The principal method of destroying magnetic mines was the LL, or magnetic sweep. Two long, insulated, buoyant cables were towed astern of a wooden sweeper and an electric current was run through them to create a magnetic field which detonated the mines. Magnetic coils on wooden barges towed by a tug were also used, as were low-flying aircraft fitted with circular magnetic coils. Less successful were mine destructor ships with large electro-magnets in their bows. The most effective counter-measure was *degaussing which obliterated the magnetic field of a steel hull.

Mine warfare at sea was a constant battle of wits between those laying the mines and those sweeping them. Both sides laid minefields of different types; manufactured mines that were both magnetic and acoustic; and introduced delaying devices which meant sweeping a minefield several times before the mines could be induced to detonate. In 1940 the Germans introduced sweep obstructors which were subsequently copied by the Allies. One was an explosive conical float, which severed the sweep wire before it reached the mine's mooring cable; another used static cutters to perform the same task. But perhaps the simplest and most effective was the introduction of heavy chain moorings which the sweep wires could not sever.

The Japanese surrender ceremony aboard the US battleship ***Missouri***, 2 September 1945. Mr Shigemitsu signs for Japan.

Refinements were continually being made, but the next operational use of a major advance in mine technology did not come until the Normandy landings in June 1944 (see OVERLORD) when the Germans introduced the pressure mine, codenamed OYSTER by the Allies. This device had been conceived by a German naval officer early in the war, but as the Germans could find no antidote they refrained from using it in case the British might find one, learn how it worked, and use it against them, especially in the Baltic's shallow waters. The British, who knew the principle on which it worked—a ship passing above altered the water pressure on the mine, which triggered the firing device—did not deploy it for the same reason.

The Germans were careful not to use the pressure mine operationally until they had plenty of them, and more than 400 were laid off Normandy. They caused considerable losses until one was found and dismantled. This enabled the British to compute the maximum speed at which a vessel could move in different depths without triggering the device, but no other antidote was ever found for it.

Some devices were called mines when they were not. 'Mk24 mine' was the cover name for a US-built acoustic torpedo (see GUIDED WEAPONS). The Long Aerial Mine, a British invention, was a bomb which was dangled in the flight path of German bombers by a wire suspended from a parachute. The Japanese invented a similar gadget. Neither was effective. I. C. B. DEAR

Achkasov, V., and Pavlovich, H., *Soviet Naval Operations in the Great Patriotic War, 1941–45* (Annapolis, Md., 1981).
Elliott, P., *Allied Minesweeping in World War II* (London, 1979).
Lott, A., *Dangerous Sea* (New York, 1960).

Missouri, US battleship on board which was signed Japan's surrender on 2 September 1945. A Japanese plan to bomb it as it entered Tokyo Bay was narrowly averted.

MIS-X, the US equivalent of the British escape and evasion organization *MI9. In China, where it was set up in September 1943, it was known as the Air Ground Air Service, or AGAS, and it took over the work of the *British Army Aid Group in the last months of the *Pacific war.

Mobile Naval Base Defence Organizations (MNBDO), British Royal Marine detachments formed to occupy and defend naval bases overseas. Parts of MNBDO 1 were deployed on *Crete, others mounted Middle East *amphibious warfare raids, and volunteers formed *Force Viper. Units of MNBDO 2 took part in the *Sicilian campaign in July 1943, but both MNBDOs were disbanded in April 1944 to form Commandos and an Anti-Aircraft Brigade, and to become landing craft crew for the Normandy landings that June (see OVERLORD).

Model, Field Marshal Walther (1891–1945), German Army officer whose expertise in defensive warfare during the *German–Soviet war earned him the nickname of the 'Führer's fireman'.

Born near Magdeburg to a Lutheran schoolmaster, Model ended the *First World War as a captain and by November 1940 his talents and drive—'can't that be done faster?' was a favourite phrase of his—had earned him promotion to maj-general. A ruthless man of enormous energy and resourcefulness, he was a strong supporter of Hitler, though whether through conviction or opportunism it is impossible to say. He was one of the very few generals who continually stood up to Hitler and yet managed to survive. He was as popular with his troops as he was unpopular with his staff who despaired of his meddling in tactical detail.

Model's 3rd Panzer Division, as part of *Guderian's Second Panzer Group, led the thrust into the Ukraine when Germany invaded the USSR in June 1941 (see BARBAROSSA), and early successes, and Hitler's high regard for his talents, resulted in promotion to lt-general while commanding a panzer corps during the drive on *Moscow in late 1941. Then in January 1942, in his first task as a 'fireman', he took command of the Ninth Army, threatened with encirclement around Rzhev. He turned potential defeat into a defensive victory and was promoted general. Successive Soviet offensives to dislodge his army from its salient 180 km. (112 mi.) from Moscow failed; and when eventually forced to withdraw, in March 1943, he did so with consummate skill.

Model's prowess now gave him a leading role in CITADEL, Hitler's plan to destroy the Red Army's salient around *Kursk, but he persuaded Hitler to delay the German offensive from May to July 1943 so that he could build up his forces. The pause also gave his opponents time to build up theirs and he must take a large share of the blame that Kursk, the largest tank battle in history, ended in a German defeat.

However, Hitler's faith in him remained undiminished and in January 1944 Model took command of Army Group North which had just suffered a severe reverse when the Red Army raised the siege of *Leningrad. To counter Hitler's ban on retreat, Model introduced his policy of *Schild und Schwert* (shield and sword)—a withdrawal was permissible as part of a planned counter-offensive. It satisfied Hitler and allowed Model to stabilize his front, and on 1 March 1944 he was promoted field marshal, the second youngest in the German Army after *Rommel.

On 30 March 1944 Model became C-in-C Army Group South (Army Group North Ukraine from early April) and in June 1944, while still commanding Army Group North Ukraine, replaced *Busch as C-in-C of the defeated remnants of Army Group Centre. Model pulled back what remained of his forces and by 1 August the Red Army was just 24 km. (15 mi.) from the east Prussian border. But it then ran out of steam and Model, though heavily outnumbered, counter-attacked, destroyed the Second Tank Army, and pushed the Soviets back nearly 50 km. Hitler called him the 'saviour of the Eastern Front' and in August sent him to replace *Kluge as C-in-C Army Group B and C-in-C West.

But by mid-August the *Normandy campaign was beyond redemption for the Germans and by early September Model's forces had been cleared from France. Hitler now recalled *Rundstedt to become C-in-C West, but Model retained command of Army Group B. With it he led a supremely skilful defence which caused the Allies numerous problems during the 85-day *Scheldt Estuary battle and which successfully repelled the Allied airborne attack at Arnhem (see MARKET-GARDEN). He then commanded the *Ardennes campaign in December. When this last gamble failed and his forces, some 325,000 strong, became trapped in the Ruhr pocket during the battle for *Germany, he dissolved his Army Group and committed suicide.

Mitcham, S., *Hitler's Field Marshals and Their Battles* (London, 1988).

Molotov, Vyacheslav (1890–1986), a Bolshevik since before the fall of the imperial monarchy, who rose to high office in Lenin's party in the 1920s, Molotov was People's Commissar of Foreign Affairs for the USSR throughout the Second World War. He had proved himself a ruthless local official in the Civil War, associating himself with the group surrounding Stalin. In 1930 he was appointed as governmental premier, or chairman of Sovnarkom (see USSR, 3) a post he held until May 1941. His record of support for Stalin in the 1930s was unequivocal, and he distinguished himself by bloodthirsty confirmations of sentences of death passed on purge victims.

His appointment as People's Commissar of Foreign Affairs in place of *Litvinov in the summer of 1939 was rightly taken by Hitler as a signal that Stalin's orientation was towards a deal with Germany rather than with the UK and France. Under the direction of Stalin, who had simultaneously assumed the chairmanship of Sovnarkom, Molotov conducted rapid, decisive negotiations with *Ribbentrop; and in August 1939 the two foreign ministers signed the *Nazi–Soviet Pact. As foreign minister, Molotov had a grumpy and unaccommodating style which mystified his diplomatic interlocutors. Yet his family background—he came from a well-to-do family and the composer Alexander Skriabin was his uncle—gave him insight into the ways and attitudes of the foreign embassies. Working closely with Stalin in the state committee of defence, Molotov was a competent and demanding minister.

In public reputation, he had become the second most powerful figure in the Soviet political hierarchy by 1941. He was no less shaken by the German invasion in 1941 (see BARBAROSSA) than was Stalin and German diplomats recorded his anguished complaints about Hitler's treachery. Unlike Stalin, however, he did not immediately buckle under the strain, and it was he who made the first major announcement of the outbreak of the *German–Soviet war to the Soviet public.

Molotov continued to behave as he had always done. The Finns had noted his harsh mode of speech in the negotiations following the *Finnish–Soviet war of 1939–40. He was equally harsh in negotiations with his own allies after the Soviet Union's entry into the war against Germany. Stalin made use of his reputation as a dourly Bolshevik fanatic in the various meetings with western Allied representatives in 1942 as well as at the major conferences of the Allies at Teheran in November 1943 (see EUREKA), Yalta in February 1945 (see ARGONAUT), and Potsdam in July 1945 (see TERMINAL). Molotov was indeed, like Stalin, an ideologically-driven fanatic as well as a bureaucrat. The recovery and subsequent advance of the Red Army in 1943–4, moreover, confirmed his confidence that the future of civilized states and societies lay with *communism and that capitalism's life was drawing to a close.

Molotov was an admirer of Stalin, but feared him also. Stalin even arrested his wife after the war. Molotov lost the post of foreign minister in 1949; and, from 1952, his career fell into eclipse when Stalin criticized him at a Central Committee plenum. On Stalin's death he again became minister of foreign affairs; but he fell out with Nikita Khrushchev (1894–1971) and was pushed down into lowly jobs from 1957 as a member of 'the anti-party group' until his retirement. ROBERT SERVICE

Molotov cocktail, hand-made explosive device, normally a petrol-filled bottle with a piece of rag as a fuze. After the fuze had been lit, the bottle exploded on impact. First employed during the *Spanish Civil War, it was mostly used during the *German–Soviet war by Soviet troops and partisans against German tanks, and was named after the Soviet People's Commissar for Foreign Affairs (above). See also STICKY BOMB.

Molotov–Ribbentrop Pact, see NAZI–SOVIET PACT.

Mongolia had been two separate entities since the 17th century. In 1924 Outer (northern) Mongolia, an independent kingdom since 1911, became the People's Republic of Mongolia, a client state of the USSR, the status quo of which was confirmed at the Yalta conference (see ARGONAUT) in February 1945. Its independence was recognized by China in 1946. Inner (southern) Mongolia, absorbed into the Republic of China in 1911, came progressively under Japanese influence after the Japanese annexation of Manchukuo in 1932. After the start of the *China Incident in July 1937 a Japanese puppet regime was set up in the eastern provinces which later came under the nominal control of *Wang Ching-wei's government in Nanking (see CHINA, 3(b)). See also JAPANESE–SOVIET CAMPAIGNS AND RELATIONS.

Monnet, Jean (1888–1979), French banker and industrialist who was a member of the French Economic Mission in London during the fighting which preceded the fall of *France. With Robert Vansittart of the British foreign office he drafted the declaration of Anglo-French Union which Churchill offered to, but which was declined by, the French cabinet on 16 June 1940. He later became political adviser to General *Giraud in North Africa and was a founding member of the *French Committee for National Liberation. After the war he helped organize the European Economic Community.

Monte Cassino, battles for. A series of four battles fought during the *Italian campaign as the Allies tried to advance on Rome. They took place between January and May 1944 when German Panzer Grenadiers and paratroopers defended the fortified town of Cassino, and Monastery Hill which overlooked it (see photograph, page 573). The area, precipitously steep, rocky, and bleak, was a key part of the German *Gustav Line which barred Lt-General Mark *Clark's Fifth US Army from advancing on the Italian capital via the Liri valley and also prevented relief of the Allied beachhead at *Anzio.

During the first battle, fought in appalling conditions, the *French Expeditionary Corps (FEC) broke through outlying defences on the night of 11/12 January 1944. It then drove towards Atina before being halted, while to the west 2nd US Corps, between 25 January and 12 February, fought desperately to capture and hold vital features adjacent to Monastery Hill. The German commander, Lt-General Fridolin von Senger und Etterlin, later said that the Americans had come 'within a bare 100 metres of success', but in fact they never got within ten times that distance of his main defences.

The second battle was fought by *Freyberg's New Zealand Corps from 15 to 18 February when 2nd New Zealand Division was ordered to attack Cassino railway station, and 4th Indian Division Monastery Hill. The commander of 4th Division thought the Germans might use the 6th-century Benedictine abbey on top of the hill to defend it and requested its destruction. Clark disagreed—he rightly foresaw that the ruins would become an ideal defensive position—but Freyberg insisted and the Army Group commander, General *Alexander, supported him. In fact the Germans, who had told the Vatican they would not use the abbey, did not do so until after its destruction by Allied bombers. The bombing killed many civilians who had taken refuge within it, but not one soldier, and occurred before the Indian Division could take any advantage of the situation that was meant to have accrued from it. The assault failed.

The third battle, much delayed by atrocious weather, began on 15 March. The Indian Division assaulted features below the abbey before trying to take the hill, but made little progress. The New Zealanders again attacked the town of Cassino, this time after a massive air strike and artillery bombardment. But the rubble to which it was reduced helped the defenders rather than those attacking and this assault, too, was soon halted.

The final battle, which took place between 11 and 18 May as part of Alexander's spring offensive (DIADEM), involved the Eighth Army's 13th Corps and the 2nd Polish Corps (see also ANDERS' ARMY) as well as Clark's Fifth Army. The FEC now moved to the Garigliano bridgehead, cut across the Aurunci mountains, which were thought impassable by most, and destroyed the southern hinge of the German defences. Further inland 13th Corps took Cassino town and struck along the Liri valley, but the task of capturing Monastery Hill was given to the Poles. Their first attack was repulsed, two battalions being virtually wiped out, not one man escaping death or injury. A second night attack took two important features but the hill itself remained impregnable. By now, however, the Gustav Line was no longer tenable and late on 17 May the German paratroopers defending the hill reluctantly withdrew; but it took the Poles, whose casualties amounted to about 3,500, time to find anyone with enough strength to climb up and occupy the monastery's ruins.

After the war the Allies insisted they had irrefutable evidence that the monastery had been part of the German defences and it took until 1969 for the Americans to admit that it had not been. A British government investigation into the bombing in 1949 was kept from the public for 30 years when it concluded no such irrefutable evidence existed. Objections to Freyberg being blamed for the bombing were still being voiced in the 1980s.

Ellis, J., *Cassino* (London, 1984).

Montgomery, Field Marshal Sir Bernard (1887–1976), British Army officer whose victory at the second *El Alamein battle in November 1942 made him the war's most successful—and most publicized—British general.

Commissioned into the Royal Warwickshire Regiment in 1908, Montgomery was severely wounded in 1914 and served as a staff officer for the rest of the *First World War. His experiences during those years taught him that, as he saw it, the 'profession of arms was a life-study', and he devoted himself to his profession with an almost religious fervour, determined to win his battles at a minimum cost in human life. Meticulous planning before an operation, the gathering of maximum support to aid his ground troops during it, and a fierce refusal to move until *he* was ready, made him the master of the set-piece battle. To some these were the symptoms of over-caution, but though he was less adept at exploiting a fluid situation—as the pursuit of the defeated Axis forces after El Alamein showed—his advance to Antwerp during the *Normandy campaign, when his two armies covered 320 km. (200 mi.) in one week, was a triumph.

Between the wars he served in India, Egypt, and Palestine, and proved himself a first-rate instructor and an outstanding brigade commander. His ability was unquestioned, but his brusque and abrasive manner aroused hostility which probably hampered his early career. However, in April 1939 he was given command of 3rd Division, part of the *British Expeditionary Force which took part in the fighting that preceded the fall of *France in June 1940, and his demeanour during this crisis so impressed his corps commander, Lt-General *Brooke, that he remained one of Montgomery's strongest supporters throughout the war.

Montgomery's rise was now rapid. Promoted lt-general in July 1940 he commanded 5th Corps, then 12th Corps, and from December 1941 South-Eastern Command, all key appointments. His insistence on training, more training, and more training still, in all weathers, day and night, became legendary, as did his emphasis on physical fitness. When one corpulent colonel protested that he would die if he was forced to run seven miles, Montgomery—teetotal and a non-smoker—replied that it would cause fewer administrative problems if he died in training than on the battlefield.

The death in August 1942 of Lt-General William Gott, Churchill's first choice as commander of the British and Commonwealth Eighth Army then fighting for its life in the *Western Desert campaigns, gave Montgomery his chance. Handed a dispirited, defeated force, he instilled into it the will to win. He was perhaps fortunate that *ULTRA intelligence confirmed that his dispositions were correct when *Rommel attacked at *Alam Halfa, but the second El Alamein battle which started in October 1942 was a personal triumph, the set-piece situation that suited him so well. It earned him promotion to general and a knighthood, but the *North African, *Sicilian, and *Italian campaigns which followed revealed his flaws more than his strengths (it has been remarked that he always seemed to mislay his genius when he met a mountain). However, his interventions during the planning stages of the Sicilian and, later, the Normandy landings (see OVERLORD), improved the assault phases of both immeasurably and may well have prevented disaster.

With OVERLORD—during which he acted as Allied land commander—Montgomery displayed his best qualities. His energy and organizational skills, his ability to grasp the essentials of a problem, and his insistence on simplicity, all contributed to its success. However, his attempts to capture Caen—which somehow became transmuted by him into a deliberate strategy—earned him much criticism and there was talk of replacing him. Eventually the break-out was achieved and France was liberated, but with the Germans in full retreat he made two errors: he failed to move beyond Antwerp to cut off the German forces which had retreated on to the Beveland peninsula, and he then chose to launch *MARKET-GARDEN to gain a bridgehead beyond the lower Rhine at Arnhem instead of clearing the approaches to the *Scheldt Estuary.

However, it was not Antwerp or MARKET-GARDEN that nearly proved Montgomery's undoing, but his astonishing

Field Marshal **Montgomery** after a conference during the Ardennes campaign, 26 December 1944. On his right is General Collins, on his left General Ridgway.

insouciance. His increasing fame fed an egocentricity that made him incapable of understanding that co-operation was the basis of the Allied effort. Once the supreme commander, *Eisenhower, had assumed control of ground operations on 1 September 1944—the day Montgomery was promoted field marshal and reverted to the command of 21st Army Group alone—he became increasingly divisive and fractious, for though he admired Eisenhower the man he judged him incapable of fighting a battle. He rejected Eisenhower's Broad Front strategy in favour of a concentrated thrust into Germany (see OVERLORD); by pursuing this to the verge of dismissal he automatically put himself in the wrong; and by implying at a press conference that it was he who had defeated the Germans during the *Ardennes campaign, he pushed the Americans to the limits of their patience, and perhaps beyond. However, he survived to lead his Army Group in the battle for *Germany and on 4 May 1945 he accepted the surrender of all German forces in north-west Germany, Denmark, and the Netherlands (see LÜNEBURG HEATH). Final victory brought him adulation and high honours, and in January 1946 he was created Viscount Montgomery of Alamein.

Montgomery's utter dedication to his task inspired the total confidence of those who served under him and he had the knack of being able to communicate to the ordinary soldier in the simplest of terms—'we'll hit 'em for six' was one of his favourite phrases. But his almost unbearable conceit and cockiness infuriated many—particularly, but not only, the Americans—and his shortcomings as a man have inevitably coloured assessments of him as a great commander.

Hamilton, N., *Monty*, 3 vols. (London, 1981–6).
Lewin, R., *Montgomery as Military Commander* (London, 1971).
Montgomery, B.L., *Memoirs* (London, 1958).

Morgenthau Plan, scheme for the post-war pastoralization of Germany which was proposed in 1944 by the secretary of the US Treasury, Henry Morgenthau Jr. (1891–1967).

Morgenthau was highly successful—he raised and spent more money than all his 51 predecessors combined, and he took a leading role at the *Bretton Woods conference in July 1944—but his plan should never have seen the light of day. However, at the time Roosevelt's intimate adviser, Harry *Hopkins, was out of favour and Morgenthau's ideas were influential. The plan envisaged Germany being divided into two states, northern and southern, after being stripped of the territory it had acquired. No financial reparations would be demanded, as this would have meant keeping part of Germany's industrial strength operational to pay for them. Instead, all industrial machinery would be dismantled and transported to Allied nations, mostly to the USSR, 'as restitution'. In its original form no help was to be offered, and a deindustrialized Germany was to be left, as one official history comments, 'to stew in her own juice for a long time'.

The president adopted the scheme enthusiastically and asked Morgenthau to present it at the second Quebec conference in September 1944 (see OCTAGON) when Germany seemed on the verge of collape. Though Churchill later said he disliked it, he wanted Morgenthau's agreement for further financial credit, and both he and Roosevelt initialled it. When their advisers strongly opposed the plan it was put on one side, but it remained extant until more realistic policies were adopted at the Potsdam conference in July–August 1945 (see TERMINAL). This made it difficult for *SHAEF's civil affairs division to formulate a policy for the military government of Germany (see ALLIED CONTROL COMMISSIONS).

When the plan was revealed in the American press it was seized upon by German propaganda as evidence of what *unconditional surrender meant, and may have contributed to bolstering German resistance during the last months of the war.

Morocco, see FRENCH MOROCCO.

Morrison, Herbert (1888–1965), British Labour politician and a member of Churchill's cabinet, first as minister of supply, then as home secretary and minister of home security. He created the National Fire Service in the autumn of 1940 and gave his name to the *Morrison shelter, and was a member of the war cabinet from 1941.

Morrison shelter. Named after the British wartime home secretary (above), this bomb shelter was introduced in the autumn of 1941 and was designed to protect a family at home. It comprised a steel plate on legs with wire mesh sides, which could double as a table. It was supplied free to families whose income did not exceed £350 per annum and was sold for £7 to those who earned more. See also ANDERSON SHELTER.

Morshead, Lt-General Sir Leslie (1889–1959), Australian Army officer who acted as garrison commander when his 9th Australian Division held out at *Tobruk from April to October 1941. Both he and his division subsequently played a major role in the second *El Alamein battle in October–November 1942. He later led the same division in the *New Guinea campaign before being appointed to command 1st Australian Corps which, in May 1945, began *amphibious warfare operations against the Japanese in British Borneo and at *Balikpapan and *Tarakan in the Netherlands East Indies. He was knighted in 1942.

Moore, J., *Morshead* (London, 1976).

mortars. A mortar is defined as a weapon which fires only at angles above 45 degrees, and, so far as the Second World War is concerned, is usually interpreted as meaning the light smooth-bore weapons employed by infantry for their own close support. The term is, however, also correctly applied to heavy rifled ordnance of the howitzer class used for coastal defence by some nations, though few ever saw use in 1939–45.

Mortars: Mortar bomb lethal radii.
Based upon standard 1939–45 period HE bombs. Based upon 70° angle of descent, average meadowland.

50 mm/2 in	6 m (19.7 ft)
60 mm	10.5 m (34.5 ft)
80–82 mm/3 in	15 m (49 ft)
107 mm/4.2 in	15 m (49 ft)
120 mm	20 m (65.5 ft)

These figures can be considered the 'worst case'; the actual distribution of splinters resembles a figure eight with the bomb in the centre and the two loops at each side. Very little goes forward or backward, the greatest area of risk being at the side, and that is what these figures represent. The lethal area immediately in front of the bomb is a matter of 4–5 m (13–16 ft) at the most.

Source: Contributor.

Infantry mortars were largely derived from two prototypes, the British Stokes mortar and the French Brandt mortar, both of which were developed during the *First World War. In the 1920s both, but more especially the Brandt, were copied and licensed for manufacture in several countries, so that most of the world's mortars were very similar weapons in similar calibres. They fell into three groups: the light class were of 50–60 mm. (1.95–2.3 in.) calibre, the medium of 81–82 mm. (3.15–3.2 in.) calibre, and the heavy of 100 mm. (3.9 in.) calibre and above. They were almost all of similar construction; a smooth-bore barrel, the end of which rested upon a steel baseplate which spread the recoil shock to the ground and a supporting bipod or tripod which held the barrel at the desired elevation and was provided with adjustments to permit elevating and traversing the barrel.

The projectile, generally called a 'bomb', was usually of tear-drop shape with fins at the tail. The propelling charge was in two parts; the 'primary' charge was a shotgun cartridge in the centre of the tail with a filling of smokeless powder, and the 'secondary' charges were fixed around or between the tail fins in cloth bags or celluloid containers, retained by clips or springs. To load, the bomb was simply dropped down the barrel so that the primary cartridge struck a fixed firing pin. This exploded the primary, which ignited the secondary charge and blew the bomb from the barrel. Some mortars had firing pins which were actuated by triggers.

The US Army was unusual in having a rifled mortar; this demanded a somewhat more complicated bomb in order to allow drop-loading but still take the rifling when fired, but it was of superior accuracy and fired a heavy 107 mm. (4.2 in.) bomb. The German Army used an 81 mm. mortar as their standard until they encountered a much superior 120 mm. (4.7 in.) design used by the Soviets; after putting captured 120 mm. mortars into service they began manufacturing a copy and this generally replaced the 81 mm. as their standard.

The Soviets also used much heavier mortars than any other country, having 160 mm. (6.25 in.) and 240 mm. (9.4 in.) weapons manned by artillery. These were of special design, in which the 160 mm. allowed the barrel to be tipped down to permit muzzle loading and the 240 mm. also tipped the barrel forward but was breech-loaded. Although cumbersome, they were quicker and cheaper to manufacture than conventional artillery pieces.

The British Army used 2 in. (51 mm.), 3 in. (76 mm.) and 4.2 in. (107 mm.) weapons, the latter being operated by artillery regiments in the Burma jungles where the conventional field artillery was not well suited to the terrain (see photo, p. 175). The Japanese used several mortars, largely based on Brandt designs. The celebrated 'knee mortar' was so-called because it could be carried strapped to a man's leg. That it was fired off the bent knee was a myth.

Italy and the USA used licensed versions of the French 60 mm. and 81 mm. Brandt mortars. Since the German 81 mm. was also generally of the Brandt pattern, and since the bombs of all these mortars were similar, it meant that American, Italian, and German bombs could be used in each others' weapons, a fact put to use in the *Italian campaign.

Mortars were heartily disliked by the infantry, since they were quick to come into action and deadly in their effect. Towards the end of the war the British Army had some success in adapting surplus air defence *radar sets to detect a mortar bomb in flight. The trajectory could then be plotted and extrapolated backwards so that its position could be located. This technique was considerably improved upon in post-war years. Ian Hogg

Moscow, battle for. The core of the Russian heartland, the Soviet capital was the centre of the most highly developed industrial complex and of the national railway network, and was the Germans' single most important military objective when they invaded the USSR in June 1941 (see BARBAROSSA). The German General Staff believed Stalin would sacrifice his last manpower and *matériel* reserves to defend it and the surrounding region. Hitler gave higher priority to other objectives, belatedly shifted the main effort towards Moscow, by launching Operation TYPHOON on 2 October 1941, and thereby set the stage for the first and one of the most serious German defeats on land in the Second World War.

On 10 October 1941, Stalin appointed General *Zhukov to command West *front* (army group), eight armies on a 280 km. (174 mi.) north–south line centered on Mozhaisk, 100 km. (62 mi.) west of Moscow. Opposite Zhukov, *Bock's Army Group Centre had, from north to south, Ninth Army, Third Panzer Group, Fourth Panzer Group, Fourth Army, Second Panzer Army, and Second Army. As Soviet armies had smaller establishments than German armies, the forces were numerically about equal, roughly a million men each.

The speed of Bock's advance after the launching of TYPHOON had already aroused apprehension on the Soviet side, and when Zhukov lost his northern anchor,

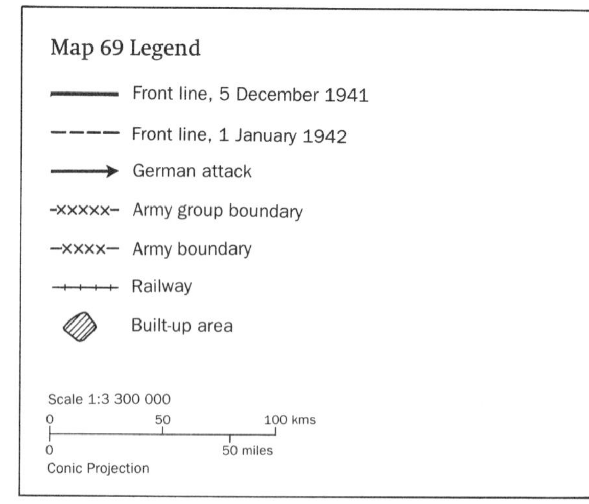

Kalinin, on 14 October and Mozhaisk four days later, panic broke out in Moscow and signs of disintegration appeared in the armies. On 19 October, the city went under martial law and the government offices and diplomatic corps began evacuating to Kuibyshev. But the autumn rains, which turned the unpaved Russian roads into rivers of viscous mud, then began to bring the German advance to a three-week halt. Nevertheless, the Germans spent little effort bombing Moscow, preferring to use the Luftwaffe against Soviet ground forces. According to Soviet sources (which credited Moscow's air defence system for such small numbers), only 229 German aircraft appeared over the capital during the first six months of the war.

During the hiatus, Zhukov restored discipline at the front, and Stalin set about mustering nine reserve armies behind the River Volga. The armies, about 100,000 men each, had to be filled with raw troops, many over-age, under-age, or unfit, but seasoned Siberian divisions were also coming in to act as stiffening. German confidence waned. Wide, deep thrusts past Moscow that would engulf West *front* and possibly end the war before winter could hardly be contemplated. On the other hand, if the city alone were to be surrounded, appearances—and the psychological upper hand—would be preserved. The risk would still be great but, Bock decided, justified by the alternative, which was to sit out the winter 65 km. (40 mi.) or so from Moscow at the end of a single railway line while Zhukov had half a dozen at his disposal.

When TYPHOON resumed, on 15 November, the conditions were better than they had yet been. The ground was frozen solidly enough to support tanks; the summer's dust and insects were gone; and the lowland forests and swamps were giving way to open terrain. A whole Soviet army opposite Ninth Army collapsed on the first day. On 27 November, Third Panzer Group reached the Moscow–Volga Canal 60 km. (37 mi.) north of the city; on its right, Fourth Panzer Group had a division 20 km. (12.5 mi.) outside the suburbs; and Second Panzer Army

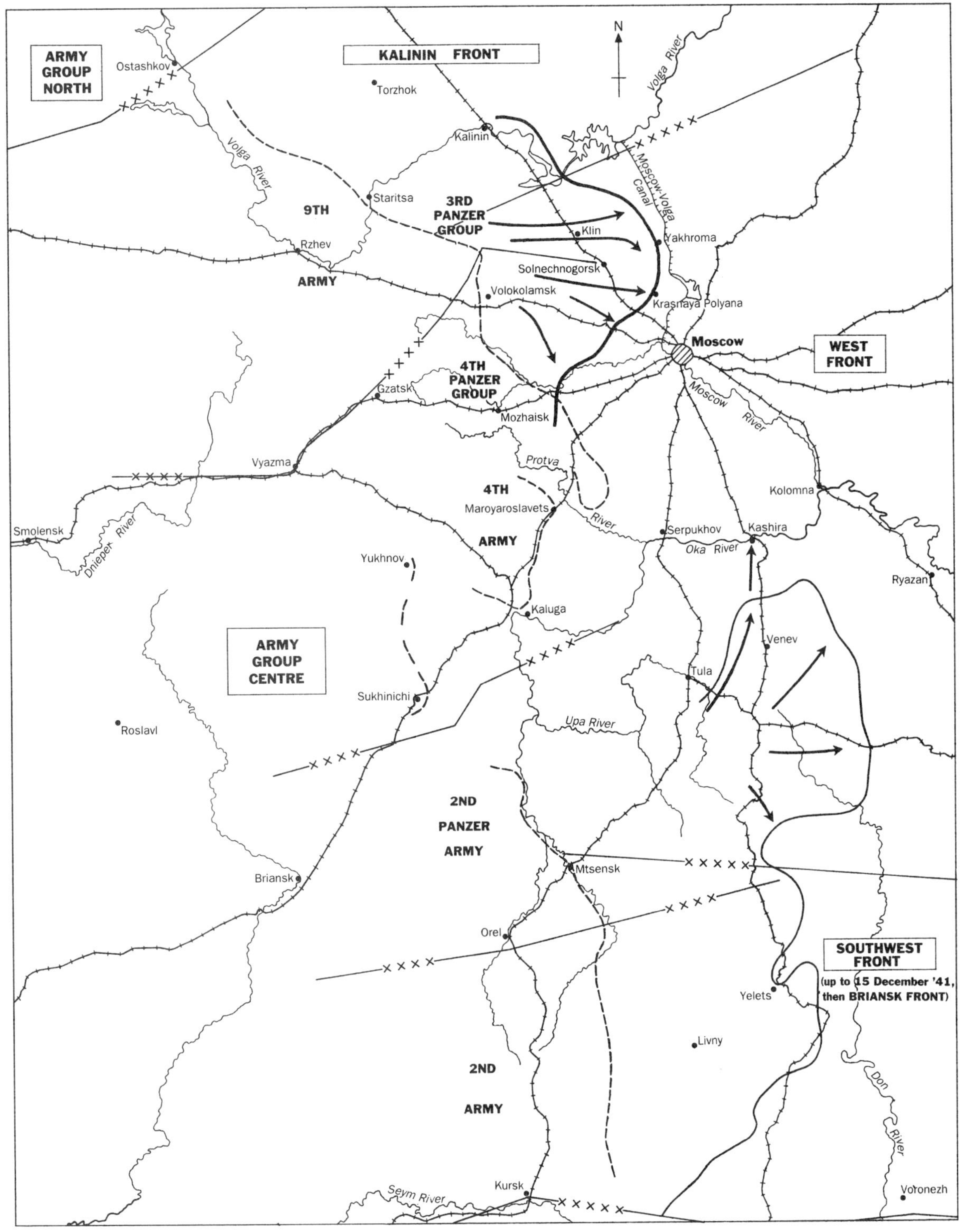

69. **Battle for Moscow**, December 1941–January 1942

had pushed past Tula to Kashira, on the river Oka 100 km. (62 mi.) south-east of Moscow. Stalin apparently considered the situation too precarious to be worth his expending reserves other than odds and ends, and culls from Moscow jails. But Bock was in even deeper trouble: he had no reserves, and the Fourth Army, which was to have formed the western arc of the encirclement, was stalled and acting like a leash holding back both armoured spearheads.

For a week, without making significant gains, the armoured elements kept a tenuous hold on the one advantage they still had, the initiative. On the night of 4 December, after a heavy snowfall, the temperature dropped to −34 °C (−29 °F), immobilizing much of the German equipment and penetrating the troops' ordinary winter dress: Hitler had expected to have withdrawn two-thirds of the troops and vehicles before the severe cold arrived and the winter gear and supplies for the other third had been stored in Poland to avoid clogging the supply lines while the offensive was in progress. On 5 December, Zhukov ordered a counter-attack to begin along the whole front the next day. That night the temperature fell to −40 °C (−40 °F) and in the morning gaps in the German line, which had formerly been covered by mobile patrols, became avenues for the Soviet advance.

Armies from Stalin's reserve rapidly transformed the counter-attack into a counter-offensive. German units trying to engage the Soviet elements behind and between them had to abandon numerous tanks, trucks, and artillery pieces immobilized by the cold. Blizzards blocked the roads and brought down telephone lines. Rear echelon troops retreating westward in full flight were congesting the few open roads. The chief of the German General Staff, General *Halder, pronounced it the 'greatest crisis in two world wars'.

On 16 December, the German salients north of Moscow and north-east of Tula having been eliminated, Zhukov put the counter-offensive into its second phase, a frontal push westwards. On 18 December, Bock requested sick leave, and the German Army's C-in-C, Field Marshal von *Brauchitsch, offered his resignation. Hitler appointed Field Marshal von *Kluge to replace Bock and named himself Commander-in-Chief. He then issued an order to all commands demanding 'fanatical resistance' and prohibiting retreats for any reason. Officers who disobeyed were subject to dismissal or worse. Among the first to go was the Second Panzer Army commander, General *Guderian, until then one of Hitler's favourites.

By 7 January 1942, Zhukov had pushed the German front back to the line from which TYPHOON had resumed in November. He believed he could go the whole way to its starting line east of *Smolensk before the winter ended, but Stalin, seeking a grand encirclement of Army Group Centre, ordered the effort shifted to the flanks. The scope of that venture overtaxed Soviet operational skill, and in the ensuing mêlée, the German commands gradually recovered their equilibrium. When the spring thaw terminated the fighting—and the Soviet initiative—the front was a ragged line, but Army Group Centre still held a solid segment 150 km. (93 mi.) west of Moscow.

EARL ZIEMKE

Seaton, A., *The Battle for Moscow* (London, 1971).
Zhukov, G. K., *Memoirs of Marshal Zhukov* (London, 1971).
Ziemke, E. F., *Moscow to Stalingrad* (Washington, DC, 1968).

Moscow conference, held in October 1943 with a view to improving Anglo-US relations with the USSR prior to the Teheran conference the following month (see EUREKA). It was attended by the foreign ministers of the UK, USA, and USSR, and their military advisers. The Soviet delegation was assured that an Allied invasion of France would take place the following spring (see OVERLORD); a declaration against those responsible for Nazi *atrocities in occupied countries was signed; it was agreed to establish the *European Advisory Commission; a protocol was drawn up on joint Anglo-Soviet action to bring Turkey into the war on the Allied side; and the *Four-Power Declaration (also known as the Moscow declaration) was issued. It was also agreed that after the war Austria should become an independent state again.

A conference was also held in Moscow in August 1942 when Churchill, accompanied by his military advisers and Averell *Harriman, accepted Stalin's invitation to meet members of the Soviet government and to discuss the question of a Second Front.

For the conferences held in Moscow in October 1941 and October 1944 see THREE-POWER CONFERENCE and TOLSTOY. See also DIPLOMACY and GRAND ALLIANCE.

Moscow trials. By the spring of 1945 Poland was occupied by the Red Army. Although the Polish government had formally disbanded the underground Home Army (see POLAND, 4) on 8 February, large numbers of its former soldiers were still being arrested by the communists. On 27 March sixteen leaders of the Polish underground, wishing to clarify the situation, responded to an invitation to talks at Red Army HQ near Warsaw, and they were later flown to Moscow, ostensibly to meet Marshal *Zhukov. Only on 4 May did the Soviet government reveal to the world that the sixteen had been arrested for 'anti-Soviet activities' and collaboration with the Germans. Their show trial took place in Moscow from 18 to 21 June 1945. Most, including General *Okulicki, were found guilty and sentenced to varying terms in jail.

KEITH SWORD

Stypułkowski, Z., *Invitation to Moscow* (London, 1951).
Rozek, E., *Allied Wartime Diplomacy. A Pattern in Poland* (London, 1958).

Mosley, Sir Oswald (1896–1980), British baronet and former member of parliament who founded and led the British Union of Fascists from 1932 (see BRITISH UNION). By 1934 the membership of his party, which included his deputy, William *Joyce, had swelled to about 34,000. He and his wife, along with other union members, were arrested in May 1940 and interned. Both were released in November 1943, by which time their political importance was nil.

Mosley, O., *My Life* (London, 1968).

Moslem League, see MUSLIM LEAGUE.

Moulin, Jean (1899–1943), French resistance leader who, on behalf of de *Gaulle and the Free French, welded the multifarious resistance groups in France into a potent fighting force.

As a prefect of the department of Eure-et-Loire (the youngest prefect in France at that time), Moulin stayed at his post in Chartres when the Germans arrived in the summer of 1940. When they tried to make him sign a report on alleged *atrocities by French colonial troops, he preferred to cut his throat. He survived, but was dismissed by the Germans in November 1940 after refusing to sack left-wing mayors. He moved south, adopted a new identity, and in October 1941 arrived in the UK as the accredited representative of three French resistance movements. He met de Gaulle who made him the delegate in France for his *French National Committee, and on 1 January 1942 he parachuted into the unoccupied part of France with an assistant and a wireless operator. It was envisaged that for some time to come the main resistance role would be propaganda, and during the next fourteen months Moulin did much for the underground press. But he soon realized that arms would eventually be needed and one of his main achievements was to set up organizations which directed the distribution of weapons parachuted into France by *SOE.

Moulin worked at the highest political level (he left leading the resistance in the field to a French general, Charles Delestraint) and there is no doubt that it was through his efforts, formidable charm, and political skill that civil war between the different resistance groups was avoided. 'Moulin, known in France as *Max*, carried in SOE the appropriate field name of *Rex*, for it was he more than any other man—even than de Gaulle himself—who welded the antagonistic fragments of resistance in France into one more or less coherent and disciplined body' (M.R.D. Foot, *SOE in France*, London, 1966, p. 182).

After a short stay in England, Moulin returned to France in March 1943 and formed the *National Council for Resistance, bringing on to it representatives from all the main resistance movements including the communists. On 21 June 1943 he was arrested in Lyons and was severely tortured by the *Gestapo chief there, Klaus *Barbie, but refused to talk. So severe were his injuries that he died while being taken to Germany by train.

Mountbatten, Admiral Lord Louis (1900–79). Born Prince Louis of Battenberg and known as 'Dickie' to his friends, Mountbatten was a great-grandson of Queen Victoria. His father, First Sea Lord in 1914, was driven from office because of his German origins. In 1917 the family name was anglicized and his father became Marquess of Milford Haven. Mountbatten's title was therefore a courtesy one until he was ennobled in 1946 as Viscount Mountbatten of Burma.

During the *First World War, Mountbatten saw action in Admiral David Beatty's flagship and though he later acquired the reputation of being a playboy he was also immensely ambitious: by 1937 he was a captain. In June 1939 he was given command of the destroyer *Kelly* and became Captain (D) of 5th Destroyer Flotilla that September, but his sea career was short, colourful, and unsuccessful. His exploits aboard *Kelly* brought him fame through Noël Coward's film *In Which We Serve*—a production he did much to promote—and the quality of his leadership was never in question. But within a few months he had nearly capsized, had collided with another destroyer, was mined once and torpedoed twice, and was finally sunk by German aircraft off *Crete in 1941 (his ship capsized under full helm at 34 knots). However, his exploits, dashing image, and popularity with the Americans, brought him to the notice of Churchill who, in October 1941, appointed him 'Chief Adviser' of *Combined Operations, with the rank of acting commodore. Then in April 1942, desperate for offensive action, Churchill made him chief of Combined Operations with the rank of vice-admiral (and the equivalent honorary rank in the other two services). He also made him a *de facto* member of the *Chiefs of Staff committee, an extraordinary position for so young a man.

Though they had been planned prior to his arrival, the raids on *Bruneval and *St Nazaire were carried out under Mountbatten's aegis. Some historians now judge that his biggest operation, the *Dieppe raid, should have been cancelled, and his determination to remount it has prompted one of them to comment that he permitted himself to be driven by the ageless forces of hunger for power and prestige. However, at the time, the Dieppe débâcle did him no visible harm and his drive and charm did wonders for the success of Combined Operations Headquarters. In August 1943 he attended the Quebec conference (see QUADRANT) at which it was agreed that he be promoted acting admiral—the youngest in the history of the Royal Navy—and appointed supreme commander of the newly created *South-East Asia Command (SEAC). He took up this position in October, with his headquarters first in Delhi and later at Kandy in Ceylon.

Mountbatten's appointment to SEAC was fraught with difficulties. His US deputy, *Stilwell, behaved deviously (see AXIOM MISSION), his British Cs-in-C questioned his operational jurisdiction over them, the Chinese proved obdurate, and every operational move he proposed was eventually rejected. He was, in fact, a far better diplomat, organizer, and inspirational leader than he was a fighting officer or grand strategist. Early on he identified three areas for improvement which were to have a profound effect on the *Burma campaign: he ordered fighting to continue during the monsoon which resulted in the rout of *Mutaguchi's Fifteenth Japanese Army in June 1944 after the failure of its *Imphal offensive into India; he found solutions which brought a drop in malarial sickness from 84% in 1943 to 13% in 1945 (see also MEDICINE); and he ensured that morale, brought low by neglect and a series of Japanese successes, was restored. He also more than proved his worth during the Japanese Imphal offensive when, contrary to orders but with the backing of Churchill, he diverted US aircraft from the *Hump supply route to airlift two divisions from the Arakan to defend Imphal; and he later refused a request from the US *Joint Chiefs of Staff for the return of other aircraft that were needed to supply *Slim's Fourteenth Army besieged at Imphal.

On 12 September 1945 Mountbatten received the surrender of the Japanese at Singapore, and he remained at his post until May 1946. Honours and awards were showered on him. He was appointed India's last viceroy then first governor-general, and after becoming a viscount was granted an earldom in 1947.

Mountbatten's immense vanity and hunger for publicity and power, coupled with his vaulting ambition and a propensity for realigning the truth, were narrowly outweighed by his colossal energy and charm, and his ability to get things done. He inspired devotion from those he commanded and the grudging admiration of his seniors.

Hough, R., *Mountbatten: Hero of our Time* (London, 1980).
Villa, B., *Unauthorized Action: Mountbatten and the Dieppe Raid* (Oxford, 1990)
Ziegler, P., *Mountbatten* (London, 1985).

Mozambique, see PORTUGUESE AFRICA.

MTB stood for Motor Torpedo Boat, a 21 m. (70 ft.) British Coastal Forces high speed craft armed with two torpedo tubes and small-calibre guns. It was the equivalent of the German *E-boat and the US *PT-boat. Its primary purpose was to attack Axis shipping, but its speed made it suitable for other roles, including *air-sea rescue and clandestine operations. See also WARSHIPS.

MULBERRIES, codename for two artificial ports built to supply Allied troops fighting the *Normandy campaign.

After the *Dieppe raid showed the virtual impossibility of capturing a French port by frontal assault, *Combined Operations Headquarters (COHQ), whose chief, *Mountbatten, had already been minuted by Churchill in May 1942 about floating piers, intensified research into alternative methods of supplying troops ashore. Floating piers (WHALES) with adjustable legs (SPUDS) were developed which were protected by 213 hollow concrete caissons (PHOENIXES), some of which were 61 m. (200 ft.) long, 18 m. (60 ft.) high, and displaced 6,000 tons. To give additional protection from bad weather, and to provide a sheltered deepwater anchorage, 61 m.-long floating tanks (BOMBARDONS) were also built for mooring on the 10-fathom line. Later, five smaller harbours (GOOSEBERRIES), formed from 74 blockships (CORNCOBS), which would shelter small craft before the PHOENIXES were in place, were added to the plan. Two became part of the MULBERRIES, while the other three provided separate shelter closer inshore.

The parts for the two harbours, which comprised 400 units weighing 1.5 million tons, were built all around the UK. They were then towed to the south coast where they were submerged, to avoid being spotted by German air reconnaissance. After the Normandy landings on 6 June 1944 (see OVERLORD) they were towed across the Channel and assembled, an operation which involved, 10,000 men and 132 tugs.

Both harbours—one at St Laurent for the Americans, the other at Arromanches for the British and Canadians—were nearing completion when, on 19 June, a gale drove 800 craft ashore and caused such extensive damage to the MULBERRY at St Laurent that it was decided to abandon it. From then on all supplies—up to 11,000 tons a day which were distributed by the *Red Ball convoys—were channelled through the MULBERRY at Arromanches with its four WHALES. Though only designed to be operational for 90 summer days it remained in use until December 1944.

Hartcup, G., *Codename Mulberry* (Newton Abbot, 1977).

Müller, Josef (1898–1979), anti-Nazi Roman Catholic German lawyer. He was employed in the Vatican from September 1939 where he was used by the anti-Nazi conspirators in the *Abwehr to establish contact with the British government to negotiate peace terms. These purported to be summarized in the *X-report, so-called because Müller was referred to in it as 'X'. He was arrested in April 1943 and was imprisoned in *Buchenwald and then *Dachau, but escaped execution. See also GERMANY, 9.

Munich agreement. After the German annexation of Austria in March 1938, the conquest of Czechoslovakia came next on Hitler's programme for expanding Germany. 'It is my unalterable will,' he laid down on 30 May, 'to smash Czechoslovakia by military action in the near future.' A torrent of propaganda, orchestrated by *Goebbels, asserted the wrongs of the Sudetenland German minority in the Czechoslovak republic, and Hitler ordered his general staff to prepare a plan (FALL GRÜN) for the invasion of Czechoslovakia. A small war at least seemed imminent; it might easily turn into a large one, as both France and the USSR had alliances with Czechoslovakia, beyond that republic's membership of the *League of Nations.

On 12 September Hitler made a violently anti-Czechoslovak speech at a Nazi Party rally at Nuremberg;

Part of the pierhead of the **MULBERRY** harbour at St Laurent which was used to supply US troops after the Normandy landings. It was destroyed by a storm on 19 June 1944.

this was public. D-day for FALL GRÜN was set for 30 September ; this was secret. The British prime minister, *Chamberlain, tried to appease Hitler by travelling to Germany to see him. On 15 September he went by air (he had hardly ever flown in his life before) from London to see Hitler in his mountain eyrie at *Berchtesgaden in the Bavarian Alps. Hitler agreed to defer violent action for the time being. A week later they met again, at Bad Godesberg, on the Rhine a few miles above Cologne; at this second meeting Hitler raised his terms, and pressed also for concessions by Czechoslovakia to Poland and to Hungary. He was much assisted by being able to read, through his decipher staff, most of the messages the British, French, and Czechoslovak diplomats were exchanging among themselves.

On 26 September Hitler made another violent attack on Czechoslovakia in a public speech, cheered to the echo, in a Berlin sports stadium. Next day the Royal Navy was mobilized; German army mobilization was delayed a further 24 hours. Mussolini then proposed a four-power conference which took place in Munich on 29 and 30 September 1938.

The principals present were Hitler, Mussolini, Chamberlain, and the French prime minister *Daladier. The contribution of the USA to the crisis was confined to a message from Roosevelt on 26 September reminding all the European powers concerned of their obligation under the half-forgotten *Kellogg–Briand Pact of 1928 not to go to war with each other. The USSR was not invited; Chamberlain profoundly mistrusted Stalin, who in any case had then hardly any useful armed forces, on account of his great purge of senior officers. Two Czechoslovak diplomats, summoned to Munich, were held overnight under *Gestapo guard, and confronted on the morning of 30 September with what the great powers had decided.

The German Army was to be allowed to take over the German-speaking frontier areas of Czechoslovakia during the first ten days of October with all the installations they contained. Benefits for the Poles and the Hungarians were to follow; and what was left of Czechoslovakia was to be placed under some kind of indeterminate guarantee, never enacted.

On the same morning Chamberlain and Hitler met again, and both signed a declaration that in future their two countries would consult, instead of quarrelling, over any difficulties that might arise between them. This gave Chamberlain reason to revive a phrase of Disraeli's when he got back to London that evening—he said he had brought 'peace with honour'.

Strategic experts continue to argue about whether the year's grace before the Second World War broke out was of more benefit to Germany or to the Allies.

M. R. D. Foot

Wheeler-Bennett, J. W., *Munich: Prologue to Tragedy* (London, 1948).

Mufti of Jerusalem, see HUSSEINI.

Murphy, Robert (1894–1978), US career diplomat who was counsellor in Paris when it was occupied by the Germans in June 1940 and became chargé d'affaires when the *Vichy French government was formed. In 1941 he became the US representative in French North Africa with the rank of minister. He signed an economic agreement there with *Weygand and helped the Allied landings at the start of the *North African campaign in November 1942 by establishing contact with the intelligence network *Agency Africa, accompanied Maj-General Mark *Clark during his secret negotiations with the French military authorities before them. He then acted as *Eisenhower's political adviser during the campaign before being attached to the *Allied Military government of Occupied Territories in Italy. He ended the war as *SHAEF's political adviser on German affairs.

Murphy, R., *Diplomat Among Warriors* (London, 1964).

Murray, Rear-Admiral Leonard (1896–1971), Canadian naval officer who commanded the Newfoundland Escort Force during the battle of the *Atlantic before being appointed C-in-C of the newly formed Canadian North-West Atlantic command in April 1943, thus becoming the only Canadian to command a theatre of war. He retired early because of his alleged failure to control men under his command during riots in Halifax on *V-E Day.

***Musashi* and *Yamato*,** 27-knot Japanese battleships, each 263 m. (863 ft.) in length, with a displacement tonnage of 62,300 which made them the largest warships ever built. Armed with nine 46 cm. (18 in.) guns which fired 1,360 kg. (3,000 lb.) projectiles up to a maximum range of 37,850 m. (41,400 yd.), they could pierce the armour of any US warship whose armaments would also have been outranged. But both became victims of *air power. Though they were part of Vice-Admiral *Kurita's force during the *Leyte Gulf battle in October 1944, where *Musashi* was sunk (it took 19 torpedoes and 17 bombs), they took little part in the *Pacific war. *Yamato* was sunk in the battle of the *East China Sea in April 1945 (it took ten torpedoes and six bombs).

Mitsuru Yoshida, *Requiem for Battleship Yamato* (Seattle, Wash., 1985).

Muselier, Vice-Admiral Émile (1882–1965), Free French naval forces commander, then commissioner for the navy on the *French National Committee, who is credited with being the first to suggest the Cross of Lorraine as the Free French emblem. De *Gaulle found him politically difficult and three months after occupying the French Atlantic colony of *St Pierre and Miquelon in December 1941 he resigned. He later joined General *Giraud in North Africa who appointed him civil and military commander of Algiers.

music, see in culture section of major powers; see also MARCHING SONGS.

Muslim League, All-India, the political organization for Indian Muslims which was founded in 1906 to safeguard their rights. It quickly grew, once Muhammad Ali Jinnah (1876–1949) became its president in 1934, from being only a few hundred strong to being a political force that rivalled *Gandhi's mainly Hindu *Indian National Congress.

Though its Lahore Resolution of March 1940 demanded a sovereign Muslim homeland, there was nothing inevitable during the war years about the creation of Pakistan. However, the British, not wanting to alienate the Muslim community—which provided, especially from the Punjab, valuable recruits for the Indian Army—assured the Muslims that they would not have to be ruled by any post-war independent Indian government if they did not wish it. This undertaking was clarified by the *Cripps mission in March 1942, whose offer of post-war independence for India specifically stated that no part of India would be forced to become part of an independent state if it did not wish to (see INDIA, 3). These promises gave Jinnah useful leverage in the various negotiations which preceded India's independence in 1947.

Soon after the outbreak of war in 1939, the eight Congress ministries in the provinces and the pro-Congress North-West Frontier Provinces ministry resigned. The Muslim League stepped into the vacuum, forming ministries in Assam and Sind, which had had Congress-led coalition ministries, and in the North-West Frontier Provinces, where the pro-Congress ministry of Dr Khan Saheb had held office. By 1944 the League had a membership of about three million and in the 1945–6 election it polled 4.5 million votes, or about 75% of the Muslim vote. It was this dominance of Muslim voters by the League that made Pakistan a reality.

Mussert, Anton (1894–1946), Dutch *Quisling leader and founder of the Nazi Party in the Netherlands who was appointed as the country's leader in 1942. His party, 30,000 strong at the start of the war rose only to 50,000. He was executed in 1946. See also NETHERLANDS, 3(a).

Mussolini as war leader.

Benito Mussolini (1883–1945) worked as a teacher, then a journalist, and fought in the *First World War. In March 1919 he formed the Fasci di Combattimento, the Fascist Party (see FASCISM), which came into power in October 1922 and enabled him to assume dictatorial powers in Italy three years later.

Hitler and **Mussolini** in Munich, 1940.

1. Military policy

As self-styled *Duce* (leader) and head of Italy's government, Mussolini had direct responsibility for Italian military policy for more than 20 years; he was also minister for all three armed services between 1925 and 1929 and again between 1933 and 1943, and was president of the supreme defence commission, minister of foreign and internal affairs and of the colonies, and commandant of the fascist militia (see ITALY, 5(c)) for most of his years of dictatorship. Despite these burdens he never felt the need to equip himself with a personal staff or even a military office which could have provided him with intelligence and advice. Nor did he ever create a proper armed forces general staff: Marshal *Badoglio was named chief of the *Comando Supremo and served in that office from 1925 until 1940, but without possessing any real authority. With a secretariat of only six officers Badoglio's role was a cosmetic one—so much so that he was able to absent himself from Rome as governor of Libya between 1928 and 1932 and again in 1935–6 as commander-in-chief in East Africa. The three armed services, the colonial troops, and the fascist militia all acted under Mussolini's orders with little or no co-ordination to lessen their traditional rivalry.

Mussolini's role in national military policy, although theoretically unlimited, was in practice restricted to fixing the size of the military budget (which at the beginning of the 1930s took approximately one quarter of total state expenditure and was shared between the army, navy, and air force in proportions of 4:2:1) and periodically replacing ministers, their military under-secretaries, and chiefs of staff. He did this not in order to influence the preparations for war but to cement his own position as irreplaceable and all-powerful leader by rotating his minions around the state administration. The armed forces were thus able to operate with full autonomy under their respective leaders, free from any check by a gagged public opinion or from interference by the Fascist Party. This situation was by no means unusual in the fascist regime, since Mussolini always respected the autonomy of those groups which had brought him to power and kept him there: major industries, agriculture, the Catholic Church, and the main state bureaucracy were never 'fascistized' in any depth but instead were given privileges and concessions in exchange for their support.

The armed forces therefore accepted Mussolini with enthusiasm and endorsed his propaganda about the power of the new fascist Italy and his myth of being a great warrior. Membership of the Fascist Party was encouraged by the air force, not encouraged by the army, and discouraged by the navy, but there were no real differences in the degree of their adherence to the regime, although all three armed forces had to submit to the expulsion of Jewish officers in 1938 when previously there had been no discrimination against them. Since Mussolini gave no orders for war preparation and did not enforce any co-ordination between them, the three armed services developed in different directions. The army prepared for a defensive war in the Alps, putting a greater premium on the number of divisions than on their equipment or training. The navy followed its traditional policy of collaboration with the UK, building a large fleet which had some fundamental defects (lack of any naval aviation, inferior guns, and poor performance from a large fleet of submarines). The air force, which lacked any proper industrial base, basked in a sense of superiority which rested on such feats as the transatlantic flight of Italo Balbo (1896–1940) and refused to co-operate with either of the other two services.

2. Power policy

Mussolini's lack of interest in preparations for war, for which, however, he claimed the responsibility and the glory, seems to contrast with the declaration that fascist Italy was now a major power—a claim which was both the main object and the ideological justification of the dictatorship and which was sustained by a noisy and well-organized propaganda campaign. In reality Italy was a medium-rate power, halfway between development and under-development, which could not hope to compete with the great powers of Europe; and Italian industry did not seek imperialist expansion in Europe or Africa but wanted monopoly control of the domestic market and state aid. Mussolini's self-proclaimed policy of power therefore lacked both a solid base and precise objectives. Nor was he really preparing for a European war; what he sought were prestigious coups and the domestic mobilization of the bourgeois and petty bourgeois classes which were the foundations of the regime.

At the military level a genuine power policy would have required much larger sums than those which already weighed heavily on the national budget, together with an energetic initiative by Mussolini to overcome the resistance of the military hierarchies to modernization and co-ordination; but even then there still remained the fact of industrial and technological inferiority. So Mussolini chose a short-term policy. He sought cheap successes which fascist propaganda could then magnify without giving any thought to the growing gap which developed during the 1930s, between an increasingly aggressive and de-stabilizing foreign policy and military preparations which were falling ever further behind those of the great powers.

3. The Abyssinian war

A far-sighted foreign policy would probably have avoided Italy's attack on Abyssinia, which involved very high costs without any economic compensations and meant deploying forces in a distant theatre with vulnerable lines of communication. But Mussolini sought a propaganda coup which would reinforce his domestic popularity at a time of economic difficulty. Therefore, taking advantage of a fluctuating international situation, in which Italy's friendship had become important, he launched in 1935 a campaign the dimensions of which resembled not so much earlier colonial wars as those in French Indo-China and Algeria which were to follow. Almost half a million men, 450 aeroplanes, and unlimited supplies guaranteed the rapid and crushing victory which was required to overcome international opposition and enthuse the Italian masses.

It was Mussolini's 'finest hour': a popular war, a demonstration of Italian military efficiency—in reality more because of the improvisation of a large and modern military operation in a hostile environment than because of the defeat of a desperately inferior opponent—and a clear triumph over the *League of Nations where Franco-British opposition had been largely a façade. His personal stature emerged greatly enhanced. He alone had decided on war and on its extraordinary dimensions, overcoming the considerable hesitations of his military commanders (a precedent which would weigh heavily in 1940) and imposing a command structure in which everyone and everything was his ultimate responsibility. The resulting conflicts of authority, personal rivalries, errors, and waste were masked by an overwhelming Italian military superiority.

In the moment of triumph it was easy to forget the costs. The war continued after 1936 because Abyssinian resistance could never be completely crushed. This in itself was partly Mussolini's fault since he refused for reasons of prestige to collaborate with his new subjects and instead imposed heavy racial discrimination. The new empire represented a self-inflicted wound in the European war which soon followed, absorbing men and resources with no corresponding strategic benefits. Finally, the heavy cost of its conquest (and of the intervention in the *Spanish Civil War which followed) took all the available funds so that nothing was left to match the rearmament of Germany, France, and the UK between 1935 and 1939. In 1935 the armament of the Italian Army was qualitatively equal to that of the French; in 1940 it was still at the same level (new weapons had been introduced but only in token amounts) while the French had made great strides, albeit not enough to resist the German offensive that led to the fall of *France in May 1940. This was the result of Mussolini's power policy, which was beyond the nation's strength. The myths surrounding Italian successes in Abyssinia and Spain, which were never the subject of critical revision, would enjoy only a brief life.

4. The alliance with Germany

The attack on Abyssinia and Italian intervention in the Spanish Civil War contributed to the upsetting of the European balance of power and the approach of world war. Mussolini feared such a war, despite his bellicose utterances, because Italian power would then meet a real test whereas hitherto it had been based on propaganda and bluff. He tried for as long as possible to avoid taking sides: in January 1935 he promised France nine Italian divisions on the Rhine in the event of a German attack; little more than a year later he announced the creation of the Rome–Berlin Axis (a political understanding and not yet a military alliance); in 1938 he signed an accord with the UK for a common Mediterranean policy; at Munich he played the role of mediator and guarantor of peace in Europe (see MUNICH AGREEMENT); in April 1939 he seized Albania as a base for a more ambitious policy in the Balkans, and in May he signed the *Pact of Steel, a political alliance which bound Italy automatically to enter a war provoked by Germany. Almost immediately Mussolini sought to restrict the scope of this alliance, insisting to Hitler that the 'inevitable' offensive against the western democracies must be postponed for several years. The contacts between the Italian and German armed forces did not lead to any strategic co-ordination, to the formation of unified commands, or even to forms of liaison between authorities, either then or later, because Mussolini and Hitler both intended to preserve the maximum freedom of action in relation to their ally despite their written undertakings and the propagandistic claims of the indestructible solidity of the Axis (see also AXIS STRATEGY AND CO-OPERATION).

5. From neutrality to intervention

On the outbreak of war in Europe in September 1939 Mussolini proclaimed Italian neutrality. He had some basis for doing so since Hitler had kept him in ignorance of his plans, but his real reasons were the lack of readiness of the armed forces (which Mussolini and the military leaders now recognized, but without any self-criticism or diminution of their bellicose utterances), the inadequacy of war production, and doubts about whether the fascist regime could succeed in imposing on the population the sacrifices necessary for a long and unwanted war. To quieten public opinion the army, which had been increased to over 1,500,000 men, was largely demobilized between October and November 1939.

There was no way out of the situation: Italy was incapable of waging war at the level of the great powers, but its 'imperial' image, built up by propaganda and by Mussolini's diplomatic successes, meant that it could not remain neutral without being exposed to pressure and retaliation from the belligerents and destroying the prestige of the regime. So strong was the latter consideration that Mussolini preferred to talk of Italian 'non-belligerence' and not of neutrality, which was considered a sign of weakness. The solution agreed to by the entire ruling group, from the king to the military, the fascist hierarchy, and the industrialists, was to trust in Mussolini who, in his genius, could perhaps save Italy and his own regime as he had done in 1935 (a moment which had in reality been much less dramatic).

Military preparation and strategic planning were therefore relegated to second place. Instead Mussolini decided to wager on German might. Italy would enter the war when Germany had gained the upper hand to share in the victory without taking much of a risk or incurring much expense. The moment came with the great German successes during the fighting which led to the fall of France. On 10 June Mussolini announced Italy's intervention in the war; such were his hopes of rapid victory that he was prepared to sacrifice a third of the Italian merchant fleet, taken by surprise outside the Mediterranean when war broke out.

6. The 'parallel war' of 1940

'I need several thousand dead to be able to take my place at the peace table,' Mussolini told Badoglio in justifying Italian intervention in the war. The assumptions underlying the 'parallel war' which he undertook (the term was his own) were clear: it was Germany's task to end the conflict by invading England (see SEALION)—with the symbolic but worthless participation of a small contingent of the Italian Air Force—while Italy had only to undertake a series of territorial conquests, not necessarily to completion, which at the moment of peace would allow her to create an autonomous area of influence alongside that of the Third Reich. The efficiency of the armed forces was therefore a matter of secondary importance: the improvised offensive into the French Alps in June 1940 was condemned to fail but served to establish Italy's right to territorial concessions from France. In the event Italy obtained almost nothing at the *armistice because of Hitler's need for the support of *Vichy France.

A High Command was thus superfluous. The head of the armed forces general staff, Badoglio, had general responsibilities for co-ordination but no concrete powers since the three armed forces and the principal theatre commanders continued to be subordinated directly to Mussolini. The direction and co-ordination of the war were entirely in Mussolini's hands, but he did not feel the need to create a general staff to help him; instead he took pains to make himself commander of the armed forces in the field—a vague and useless title since he already possessed the necessary concrete powers, but one which aimed at reducing the role of the king, *Victor Emmanuel III, who, according to the Savoyard constitution of 1848, was C-in-C of the armed forces. The organization of the country and of industry for war was no less useless: Mussolini's concern not to alarm public opinion was such that the army was only partially mobilized (in June it amounted to fewer than 1,500,000 men) and then practically demobilized in October when 600,000 of the older reservists were sent on leave.

After the French armistice Italy's war unfolded in four theatres. East Africa was cut off from the homeland and after prolonged fighting was lost (see EAST AFRICAN CAMPAIGN); the considerable military forces there were not even capable of crushing the Abyssinian guerrillas, still less of resisting attack by modern British forces in January 1941. The battle for the *Mediterranean was also of little interest to Mussolini: the blockading of maritime traffic was supportable in a short war and precarious Italian control over the central Mediterranean (which was based on aviation that was not prepared for operations at sea) would not have any adverse effects at the peace table.

Much more interesting was Libya where the army, forgetful of its brilliant exploits in the colonial war of the 1920s, had built up divisions of foot soldiers which were in difficulties from the start in the *Western Desert campaigns against the numerically smaller but fully mechanized British divisions. Mussolini asked the Italian commander, Marshal *Graziani, only to advance into Egypt before the Germans invaded England so that he would be in a position to claim the area up to Suez at the moment of the UK's collapse. Graziani met this request in September with a slow advance to *Sidi Barrani where he halted and remained until the British offensive in December broke up his army which was large in size but weak in armaments, training, and organization.

The final theatre on which Mussolini concentrated was the Balkans. The offensive against Yugoslavia had long been prepared, but in August 1940 Hitler had it suspended so as not to disturb his politico-economic penetration into the region. However, Mussolini could not leave the Germans to dominate the whole of the Balkans, and in October 1940 he decided on the spur of the moment to start the *Balkan campaign by attacking Greece from Albania in the belief, for which there was no foundation whatsoever, that he would meet no resistance. The military leaders were taken by surprise but did not oppose the idea and the attack was therefore launched in suicidal circumstances, with forces clearly inferior to the Greeks and the army at home simultaneously being demobilized.

The whole of Greece rose in response, despite the unpopularity of the Metaxas regime; high in morale and initially greater in numbers, Greek forces pushed the Italians back and launched a deep counter-attack into Albania. The Italian forces teetered on the edge of collapse, their command structure and *logistics in tatters, unable to co-ordinate a flow of improvised reinforcements. However most battalions continued to fight despite harsh conditions; and the Greek offensive, which in its turn began to suffer supply difficulties, was halted in December. The reorganization of the Italian front line in the following months was not enough to alter the fortunes of war: a big offensive in March 1941, at which Mussolini himself was present in the hope of harvesting the laurels, met with no success. In the months that followed, the collapse of an exhausted Greece was the result of the descent of the Wehrmacht in force on the Balkans.

7. The 'subaltern war' 1941–3

By the end of 1940 the 'Parallel war' was over. A German victory had receded into the future while, in addition to Italian defeats in north Africa and Albania, half the Italian fleet was sunk at *Taranto in November by torpedo biplanes from the British carrier *Illustrious*. To continue the war Italy now depended on German supplies of fuel and *raw materials, in exchange for which Germany received Italian foodstuffs and labour; in addition, the Italian defeats made it necessary for the Germans to intervene in the Mediterranean. German abandonment of the attempt to invade England allowed the British to take the offensive in the Mediterranean, their principal theatre of operations in 1941–3 after the vital battle of the *Atlantic. But the German–Italian alliance brought neither clear agreements nor true collaboration; Hitler regarded the dispatch of *Rommel's *Afrika Korps and *Kesselring's air force to North Africa as the price to be paid to prevent Italy's collapse and had no strategic plan for a breathing-space. Mussolini had to accept subordination to Germany's interests to save his regime and defend his position—no longer as Hitler's ally but now as the Third Reich's chief vassal.

Mussolini's weakness was partly the result of Italy's economic and industrial inferiority, but chiefly of the failure of the fascist regime which showed itself to be incapable of mobilizing the nation's energies for war—which had always been its main objective. War production rose only a little above peacetime levels and organizational and technological delays mounted: between 1940 and 1943 some 4,000 armoured vehicles and 11,500 mediocre aeroplanes were manufactured, compared to Germany's 20,000 tanks and 25,000 planes and the USSR's 24,000 tanks and 35,000 planes produced in 1943 alone, almost all of superior performance to Italian machines (see also ITALY, 2). Mussolini did not try to impose his will on industry, did not dare to increase taxation very much, did not succeed in organizing the efficient requisition of agricultural production and failed to provide a steady supply of necessities to the Italian citizenry, who were condemned to turn to the black market or starve. Mobilization of the army in 1941 brought 2,500,000 men under arms, more than could be supplied with modern weapons and equipment, so that many of them were employed in worthless tasks. At the same time 960,000 physically fit young men were exempted from service; some on unconvincing grounds which caused public resentment.

Mussolini's intervention in the conduct of operations lessened in comparison to 1940, partly because the new chief of the armed forces general staff, Marshal *Cavallero, took on more concrete responsibilities for the direction and co-ordination of the armed forces than Badoglio (who had been sacked as the scapegoat for the Albanian defeat), but chiefly because the strategic picture had become more settled. Some 650,000 men were posted in Yugoslavia, Albania, and Greece as occupying forces and were much involved in tough campaigns against partisans. The navy wore itself out defending the *convoys which supplied Axis forces in the Western Desert, where continuing Italian support was subordinated to Rommel who evaded Italian control. Even when Mussolini went to Libya in the summer of 1942 so as not to miss the triumphant entry into Cairo which appeared to be imminent, he was unable to make Rommel listen to him. The only strategic decision of any importance taken by Mussolini in these years was the dispatch to the Eastern Front of an Italian army corps at the start of the *German–Soviet war in June 1941 (see BARBAROSSA) and an army in 1942 (see ITALY, 5(b)). The political requirement to defend his position as first vassal of the Reich caused Mussolini to overlook the puzzlement of his military commanders. The decision was a disastrous one because the divisions sent to the Eastern Front could only play a secondary role in a war of such vast dimensions, and in the winter of 1942–3 they were overrun by the great Soviet offensive. The motor vehicles and modern artillery with which they had been equipped might have had a decisive effect in the more restricted theatre of the Libyan desert.

8. Mussolini's fall

The repeated defeats, the Anglo-American intervention in force in the Mediterranean (see NORTH AFRICAN CAMPAIGN), and the great strikes in Milan and Turin in March 1943 signalled the end for Mussolini. Italy's surrender became inevitable and Mussolini was not the person who could obtain it. After long hesitation and in some fear King Victor Emmanuel III, with the support of the army High Command and some of the fascist leaders, dismissed Mussolini on 23 July 1943 and had him arrested. The Fascist Party and its organs were dissolved amid popular celebration. But on the day after the proclamation of the armistice on 8 September 1943 Mussolini was freed by the Germans and placed at the head of the Italian Social Republic (see ITALY, 3(b)), a puppet regime intended to legitimize the German occupation of Italy and demonstrate the continuity of the Nazi–fascist alliance.

Mussolini, who was by now physically exhausted and incapable even of holding the great rallies at which he had excelled, passively accepted his new role. He was a head of state with neither power nor authority and depended entirely on the Germans, unable either to influence the course of the civil war or to protest when the Reich annexed Italian provinces in the Veneto. He was shot on 28 April 1945, while attempting to flee into Switzerland, by partisans carrying out the death sentence imposed on him and on the main fascist leaders by the Italian authorities. His body was transported to Milan and exhibited in Piazzale Loreto—a savage gesture which set the seal on 20 years of dictatorship for which the Italian people had paid dearly and 20 months of bitter civil war.

GIORGIO ROCHAT (Tr. John Gooch)

The output of memoirs and historical works on Mussolini as dictator and military chief in the Second World War is immense. See the contributions on the fascist regime and Italy in the Second World War in *Il mondo contemporaneo*, Vol. I, *Storia d'Italia* (Florence, 1978); *La storiagrafia militare italiana negli ultimi venti anni* (Milan, 1985); and the *Bibliografia italiana di storia e studi militari 1960–1984* (Milan, 1987). See also Deakin, F. W., *The Brutal Friendship* (London, 1962).

Mutaguchi Renya, Lt-General (1888–1966), Japanese army officer, a fervent believer in *Bushidō, whose troops in 1937 fired the first shots of the *China Incident. By March 1938 he was *Yamashita's chief of staff with the rank of maj-general and by August 1940 a lt-general commanding 18th Division which he led during the *Malayan campaign in December 1941. In March 1943 he took command of Fifteenth Army in Burma with which he launched his *Imphal offensive into India in March 1944, having become convinced by the operations of *Wingate's *Chindits that Burma's jungle terrain was passable. His principal task was to prevent *Slim's Fourteenth Army moving into Burma by destroying its supply bases at Imphal, the capital of Manipur, but he was also urged to gain a foothold for the *Indian National Army, part of his forces, as this might result in a general rising in India against the British. Mutaguchi's offensive was the turning-point of the *Burma campaign and in an attempt to prevent it disintegrating he replaced all three divisional commanders. But by then his chance had gone and his withdrawal, begun in June 1944, soon turned into a rout. Under him the Japanese Army suffered its largest and most decisive defeat of the war, perhaps ever, and at the end of the year he was removed from his command and given an administrative post.

mutinies, that is, open revolt by servicemen against their military or political leaders, are as old as war itself. During the Second World War, mutineers, like *deserters, were heavily punished if caught, often by death. When some 800 *Tirailleurs mutinied in Algeria in January 1941, killing French servicemen and civilians, nine of the ringleaders were ceremonially shot before their assembled colleagues, and another 23 were later executed. However, in the Wehrmacht, where there were very many more cases of desertion (13,000–15,000) than of mutiny (442), the former offence was punished more severely, as deserters were often regarded as undermining the will of the people to fight (*Wehrkraftzersetzung*). Under Nazi rule this was a more serious crime than the purely military offence of mutiny, and most mutineers escaped the death sentence.

There was no loss of life when in 1942 Yugoslav forces mutineed against their *government-in-exile. But when Greek army and navy units mutinied in Egypt in April 1944 there were a number of deaths. The British, averse to communist influence in Greece, supported the official Greek government-in-exile and it was this that caused the Greek Armoured Brigade, stationed south of Cairo, and the crews of a number of Greek warships at Alexandria and Port Said, to mutiny. The Greek ships, which were under Royal Navy discipline, were isolated as was the armoured brigade in its camp. The official policy was to avoid force and to starve the mutineers into surrender, but when this failed the Greek government used loyal sailors to recapture some of the ships while others surrendered. There were 20 casualties. On shore the British moved against the armoured brigade which soon surrendered with the loss of one life.

There were several incidents in the USA involving black soldiers and white military police which also led to loss of life (see also AFRICAN AMERICANS AT WAR), and another occurred in the UK in June 1943, at Bamber Bridge camp in Lancashire, which resulted in several black soldiers being court-martialled for mutiny.

The British Army court-martialled 789 servicemen for mutiny. Most of the offences were comparatively trivial in nature, but on two occasions loss of life occurred. In May 1942 fifteen soldiers of the Ceylon Defence Force, prompted by pro-Japanese and anti-European beliefs, mutinied by trying to take over their gun battery on the Cocos-Keeling Islands. They failed, but one loyal soldier was killed and a British officer was wounded, and seven of the mutineers were sentenced to death. Four of the sentences were commuted but three of the guilty were hanged. The second occasion occurred in March 1942 when Indian soldiers garrisoning Christmas Island killed their British officers and NCOs (non-commissioned officers) prior to a Japanese landing there. After the war they were traced and prosecuted, and in 1947 five were sentenced to death. However, when the governments of India and Pakistan made representations against the sentences, the men were given penal servitude for life.

A less serious but well publicized incident was when 1,500 men from the British 50th and 51st Divisions, who had been convalescing from their wounds in Tripoli, were mistakenly put ashore at *Salerno on 16 September 1943 as reinforcements for those who had first landed there on 9 September. The men thought they were rejoining their old units, and when they found they were to join 46th Division 300 refused to leave the beaches. The commander of 10th Corps, Lt-General *McCreery, then appeared, admitted there had been a mistake and said it would be rectified, but the men must follow orders; and 109 did so. The remainder were arrested and three NCOs were subsequently sentenced to death while the others received various prison sentences. However, all the sentences were immediately suspended and the men were returned to their front-line units.

Myitkyina, battle for. The courageous Japanese defence, from May to August 1944, of this northern town in Burma against attacks by the Chinese and US Forces of *Stilwell's Northern Combat Area Command (NCAC). Stilwell's goal of clearing a supply route to China with his First Chinese Army before the monsoon rains began seemed possible when, on 17 May 1944, his force, supported by Merrill's Marauders (see GALAHAD) and *Chindits, took Myitkyina's airfield. But the town itself was quickly reinforced and then superbly defended by Maj-General Mizukami Genzu. After holding out for 79 days against seemingly impossible odds, the garrison's survivors slipped across the River Irrawaddy having lost 790 killed and 1,180 wounded. On 3 August, the day Stilwell's exhausted and demoralized troops took the town, Mizukami committed suicide. Chinese casualties were 972 killed and 3,184 wounded, the Americans, 272 and 955, plus 980 from illness and disease. It was the NCAC's most important battle in the *Burma campaign. See also CHINA–BURMA–INDIA THEATRE.

N

NAAFI, initials of the Navy, Army, and Air Force Institutes which organized canteens and other welfare services for the British armed and civil defence forces.

Nagasaki, Japanese city on which the second operational *atomic bomb was dropped (see HIROSHIMA for the first). Nicknamed 'Fat Man' (a reference to Churchill), the bomb, which used plutonium 239, was dropped by parachute at 1102 on 9 August by an American B29 bomber from the Pacific island of Tinian. It measured just under 3.5 m. (11 ft. 4 in.) in length, had the power of 22 kilotons of TNT (see EXPLOSIVES), and weighed 4,050 kg. (nearly 9,000 lb.). The aircraft's first target was the city of Kokura, now part of Kitakyushu, but as it was covered by heavy cloud the aircraft was diverted to its second target, Nagasaki.

Unlike Hiroshima, Nagasaki lies in a series of narrow valleys bordered by mountains in the east and west. The bomb exploded about 500 m. (1,625 ft.) above the ground and directly beneath it (the hypocentre) was a suburb of schools, factories, and private houses. The radius of destruction for reinforced concrete buildings was 750 m. (2,437 ft.), greater than at Hiroshima where the blast caused by the bomb was more vertical. But because of the topography, and despite the Nagasaki bomb being more powerful, only about 6.7 sq. km. (2.6 sq. mi.) of Nagasaki was reduced to ashes compared with 13 sq. km. (5 sq. mi.) of Hiroshima. Of the 51,000 buildings in the city 22.7% were completely destroyed or burnt, with 36.1% escaping any damage.

Among the 270,000 people present when the bomb was dropped, about 2,500 were labour conscripts from Korea and 350 were *prisoners-of-war. About 73,884 were killed and 74,909 injured, with the affected survivors suffering the same long-term catastrophic results of radiation and mental trauma as at Hiroshima.

Committee on Damage by Atomic Bombs in Hiroshima and Nagasaki, *Hiroshima and Nagasaki: The Physical, Medical, and Social Effects of the Atomic Bombings* (London, 1981).

Nagumo Chuichi, Vice-Admiral (1887–1944), Japanese naval officer who commanded the Combined Fleet's élite carrier striking force (*kido butai*) that attacked *Pearl Harbor in December 1941. He was a torpedo, not an air, specialist and, despite his peacetime reputation for daring, he was too cautious to launch a third attack on the harbour's installations which could have destroyed it as a base. During the first half of 1942 he also took part in the capture of the *Netherlands East Indies, and commanded the highly successful raids on *Darwin and into the *Indian Ocean. But his fortunes then changed, for he was decisively defeated at *Midway in June 1942, and though he won tactical victories in the waters around *Guadalcanal (see EASTERN SOLOMONS and SANTA CRUZ), the battle strength of his forces, and perhaps his own confidence, were steadily eroded, and in 1943 he was relieved of his command and posted to the Mariana Islands. Put in charge of the defences of *Saipan, he committed suicide just before the US invasion of the island in July 1944.

Matsushima Keizō, *Higeki no Nagumo Chūjū* ('The Tragedy of Vice Admiral Nagumo', Tokyo, 1967).

Nankin, 7,131-ton Australian steamer seized by the German *auxiliary cruiser *Thor* on 10 May 1942 off Western Australia. Aboard was mail for Ceylon which included top secret summaries from the Combined Operations Intelligence Centre in Wellington, New Zealand. These referred to *ULTRA intelligence and contained information which could have been obtained only by breaking the Japanese naval cipher. But luckily for the Americans, who used ULTRA intelligence to win the battle of *Midway in June that year, the Germans failed to pass on the summaries to Japan until late August 1942. By then the Japanese had already introduced a new version of the cipher, and apparently thought no further precautions were necessary.

The USA was never informed of the loss of these summaries and great care was taken after the war to cover up their capture. The story was only pieced together when German and New Zealand records were declassified in the early 1980s.

napalm, see BOMBS.

Naples rising. This Italian city had a brief revolutionary past, still vivid in popular memory: when Garibaldi arrived there in 1860, he outfaced the royal garrison, and helped depose the Bourbon King of Naples in the name of a new King of Italy. On 27 September 1943, believing the arrival of Allied troops to be imminent, the populace of Naples rose again. There had been no clandestine preparations. This time the Germans fired back. After four days' massacre, the leading Allied troops reached what was left of the city on 1 October. M. R. D. FOOT

Narvik, naval battles at. This ice-free Norwegian port was vital to the German war effort as Swedish iron ore (see also RAW MATERIALS) was shipped from there to Germany. On 8 April 1940 the British laid mines off West Fjord, the entrance to the port, but any plans they had to occupy it were pre-empted by the Germans who, on 9 April 1940, landed 2,000 troops there from ten destroyers.

The same day a British destroyer flotilla, commanded by Captain Bernard Warburton-Lee, was ordered to Narvik to prevent a German landing. The five destroyers arrived too late to do so, but U-boats guarding the fjord's entrance failed to sight his ships. This, and the protection of heavy snow, helped them to achieve total surprise when they entered the harbour next morning: two German destroyers were sunk and one damaged, and six German merchant ships were also destroyed. However,

Warburton-Lee was unaware that another five German destroyers were in neighbouring fjords and when these emerged the British destroyers were caught between two fires. Warburton-Lee was killed, his flagship had to be beached, two other destroyers were damaged, and a third was sunk. But the German warships, which had also suffered damage, were unable to press home their attack, and the remaining British destroyers escaped.

A few days later, on 13 April, the British battleship *Warspite* and nine destroyers sank the remaining eight German destroyers—stranded at Narvik through lack of fuel—and one U-boat, and a blockade was then imposed to prevent any further supplies reaching the German troops ashore. See also NORWEGIAN CAMPAIGN.

National Armed Forces (Narodowe Sily Zbrojne, or NSZ) was a Polish partisan group whose fascist tendencies led it to break away from the Polish Home Army (see POLAND, 4). In August 1943 its members attacked a communist *People's Guard unit and later murdered several Jews in the Home Army's high command. An agreement for it to rejoin the Home Army then split its leadership. Some of its members fought in the *Warsaw rising of August 1944; others, some 850 strong (the Holy Cross Brigade), escaped with German help to Czechoslovakia. Those remaining in Poland fought security police after the war and their leaders either fled to the West, or were caught and executed.

National Council for Resistance (Conseil National de la Résistance, or CNR), French clandestine organization formed in Paris on 15 May 1943, by the Free French representative Jean *Moulin, whose task it was to create a co-ordinated resistance movement in occupied France. Its sixteen members, plus Moulin, represented all major resistance groups and political parties; eight were from the resistance and six from different political parties active within the resistance, including one from the French Communist Party, and two from the trade unions. The work of co-ordination was carried out by a three-man executive. After Moulin's death in July 1943 Georges *Bidault was elected chairman. The CNR worked with the Forces Françaises de l'Intérieur (see FFI) when they were formed in February 1944.

National Guard, see USA, 4.

nationalism, rise of. Nationalism is a policy of putting the interests of one's own nation before the interests of all other nations, and the common interests of mankind.

From 1939 to 1945 *communism, Nazism, capitalism, colonialism, *anti-imperialism, *fascism, and other ideologies fought it out around the world. But the 'ism' that caused the war, the one that rallied people everywhere to make the necessary sacrifices to carry on the conflict, the one that caused the most difficulties within the Axis and Allied alliances, and the one that had the most staying power, was nationalism.

That this was so is hardly surprising. Nationalism predated all the other 'isms'. Political ideologies come and go; nationalism remains, because it is based on a common heritage, culture, language, and religion. It is usually, although not always, closely aligned with racism, the belief in the superiority of a particular race over all others. Nationalism and racism were synonymous in Germany, Italy, and Japan; they were closely allied in the Russian-dominated USSR; they were only loosely connected in the UK, composed as it was of English, Scots, Welsh, and Irish; they were hardly connected at all in the USA, with its many races, nationalities, and religions.

In the countries of diverse origin and make-up, a reverse racism fed nationalist sentiments—hatred of the enemy race. In the USA, it was fully expressed in the universally used expression 'Jap'. Everything Japanese was despised, even though *Japanese-Americans fought, with honour, for the USA in Europe. And though about one-third of the white population of the USA was German in origin, the Germans too were despised. General *Eisenhower said he was ashamed of his name, and in a letter of 1945 told his wife, 'God, I hate the Germans'. Soviet feelings were, if anything, stronger. As the Red Army prepared to enter Germany, Stalin told his troops in an Order of the Day, 'Remember, in Germany only the unborn are innocent.'

National feelings, always strong, were reinforced during the war by a variety of methods, by all sides. The centralization of power, whether in Berlin or London or Washington or Tokyo or Moscow, combined with newly discovered means of manipulation of the masses, especially through radio and motion pictures, to make it possible for central governments to extol the virtues of the Motherland or the Fatherland, to appeal to the unique natural greatness of the nation's people, and to present the other side as beasts. This propaganda blast, already present in the *First World War, of course, rose to previously unimaginable levels after 1939, thanks in large part to the new technology.

The barrage of nationalistic propaganda, from which none was immune, made a major contribution to the excesses of this, the most savage war ever fought. The bombing of the cities, the use of *atomic bombs against civilians, the slaughter of the Jews (see FINAL SOLUTION), the barbarous conduct of Japanese soldiers in China (see CHINA INCIDENT) and the Philippines, and the other horrors of the war (see ATROCITIES) could not have happened without the constant reiteration of the theme that 'we, us, our side' was all good, while 'they, them, the enemy' was inhuman.

Nationalism fired up and inspired troops around the globe, swelling pride and fanning hatred. It caused jealousies, disagreements, and suspicions among allies,

The atomic explosion over **Nagasaki**, 9 August 1945.

at the expense of the common cause. It often dominated strategic decisions, and always dictated the political bargaining when leaders got together at summit meetings.

A notable feature of the war was that even in the most ideological states, propaganda emphasized not the ideology but the nation. This was true in Nazi Germany, fascist Italy, the capitalist USA, and the USSR, where men died by the millions to defend not communism but Mother Russia.

Another phenomenon: leaders everywhere recognized the power of nationalism and ruthlessly exploited it within their own countries, but in general failed to take advantage of nationalist stresses and strains in the other camp. The most obvious example was Hitler, who again and again showed that while the Germans make excellent soldiers, they are terrible occupiers and even worse politicians. In Poland, Hitler could have appealed to a nationalist sentiment that was at least as anti-Russian as it was anti-German. In France, he could have appealed to a nationalist sentiment that was traditionally anti-British—exacerbated by the British evacuation at *Dunkirk at the height of the fighting which led to the fall of *France in June, 1940 and then by the British attack on the French fleet at *Mers-el-Kébir—and strongly anti-communist.

Instead, Hitler annexed much of the western part of Poland directly to the Third Reich, then created a General Government for the remainder, under the command of governor-general Hans *Frank (see POLAND, 2(b)). His punitive rule aimed at the enslavement of the Poles and the extermination of the Jews, rather than the building of an anti-Soviet army (see SOVIET EXILES) and a genuine Polish nation. In Czechoslovakia, Hitler created the Protectorate of Bohemia and Moravia, first under von *Neurath, then under Reinhard *Heydrich, one of the most notorious of all the Nazi criminals. The result of Heydrich's misrule was to heighten Czech nationalism and increase hatred of all things German.

German policy in central and eastern Europe, and in the occupied parts of the USSR, was based on Nazi racial theory, which held that Jews were not human at all, and that Slavs were **Untermenschen*, or subhumans, who were to be either exterminated or enslaved. In western Europe, the Nazi concept was that there were first- and second-class Aryans (insulting to people such as the Dutch, who were assigned second-class status), a concept that made occupation policy difficult.

In France, the Nazis did seek out those willing to become involved in *collaboration with them (and found many who were willing to help them), and they allowed the government of unoccupied southern France, in Vichy, a certain degree of independence. The Vichy government (see FRANCE, 3(c)), under Marshal *Pétain, did appeal to French nationalism, but with little success, partly because it was so obviously a tool of the Nazis, partly because of the counter-appeal of General de *Gaulle in London. In late 1942, following the Allied invasion of French North Africa (see NORTH AFRICAN CAMPAIGN), the Germans occupied the whole of France and the pretence came to an end.

In the Netherlands, Artur *Seyss-Inquart, an Austrian Nazi, ran the country as Reich Commissioner for occupied Holland. More than 5,000 Dutchmen served in the Waffen-*SS; but many others joined the underground to resist. In Norway the Nazis ruled through a native politician, Vidkun *Quisling, who was Minister President and leader of the Nasjonal Samling (National Union) Party. His pathetic appeals to Norwegian nationalism brought him only scorn; in October 1945 he was tried and executed by the post-war Norwegian government.

Throughout occupied western Europe, the Germans—who claimed to be creating a united Europe—exploited the people in every imaginable way, most directly by sending them to Germany to work as *forced labour in war factories, under appalling conditions. Perhaps never in human history has an occupying force been so hated, or done so much to strengthen the nationalist feelings of the oppressed.

In another irony Hitler, who wanted to kill all the Jews, created a powerful Jewish nationalism that found its fullest expression in the post-war emergence of Israel. In his own perverted way, Hitler did more for Zionism than any Jewish leader had ever managed to do.

Hitler might have attempted to exploit national sentiments in Scotland and Wales, but did not. He did make some clumsy efforts to rouse Irish nationalists to carry on acts of sabotage against the UK (see IRISH REPUBLICAN ARMY), but without much effect.

Most of all in the USSR did Hitler have opportunities to appeal to the nationalism of the subject states, as Alexander the Great had done so successfully in the Persian Empire, or Cortés in Mexico. In 1941 the USSR seethed with nationalist unrest, in the Baltic States (seized by the Soviets in 1939), in the Ukraine, in Moldavia (see BESSARABIA), in Azerbaijan, in Soviet Armenia, in Georgia, and elsewhere. When the German armies marched into those Soviet republics, the people of these disaffected nationalities greeted them with flowers and songs. The oppressed thought they were being freed, only to discover that they had merely exchanged one brutal dictator for another. Soon they formed guerrilla bands to fight behind the lines, against Hitler and for Stalin. Many students of the war believe that it was there that Hitler lost his Soviet gamble.

The Japanese made similar mistakes. Although they proclaimed a *Greater East Asia Co-prosperity Sphere, in which all Asians would be equal, in fact they imposed a system in which some Asians were more equal than others, namely the Japanese. To them other Asians, especially the Chinese, were the *Untermenschen*. In the Philippines, in French Indo-China, in the Netherlands East Indies, the Japanese could have encouraged genuine local rule, closely aligned to Japan, of course, but still independent. They chose, instead, to set up puppet regimes that claimed to be nationalist but fooled no one.

Local armies that might have been raised to fight with some degree of enthusiasm on the Japanese side hardly ever emerged; instead, as in the occupied areas of the USSR, guerrilla bands harassed the Japanese and forced them into man-wasting occupation duties.

In Manchuria, the Japanese did try to exploit a breakaway nationalist sentiment. Manchuria had long been dominated by China, but when the Japanese Army seized it in 1931 they re-named the region the nation of Manchukuo and placed *Pu-Yi (who had abdicated the Manchu throne of China as an infant in January 1912) on the throne. But they treated Pu-Yi with a mixture of embarrassing condescension and brute force, and made no friends for themselves, much less an enthusiastic ally.

In French Indo-China, the Japanese kept the former colonial masters in nominal command. French police and soldiers maintained order, while the Japanese gave the orders. At the very end, in March 1945, the Japanese gave limited encouragement to Vietnamese nationalism by replacing the French with a royal puppet government under the Bao Dai (b.1913) and declaring Vietnamese independence. The only effect was to establish *Ho Chi Minh's communist guerrillas in temporary—and eventually permanent—power.

In the Philippines, it was the former colonial masters who appealed successfully to nationalist sentiment, while the Japanese, who might have presented themselves as liberators, became brutal and hated oppressors. Although there were some collaborators with the Japanese, mainly old men who had been leaders of the struggle against the Americans four decades earlier, far more Filipino activists joined anti-Japanese underground forces. General *MacArthur skilfully utilized Filipino nationalism against the Japanese, helped considerably by a promise the US government had already given to the Filipinos, that they would have full independence on 4 July 1946.

The French had made no such promise in French Indo-China, so there the guerrillas were as concerned with preventing the return of French rule as they were with fighting the Japanese. To a large extent this was also true in the occupied British colonies, though the greatest of these, India, was not overrun by the Japanese. India provided men and materials to aid the British cause. Nevertheless, it was the source of much difficulty for the British, as a result of nationalist sentiment. By the time the war began, the great Indian leader *Gandhi had spent more than 20 years fighting for Indian independence. The Indian Congress Party (see INDIA, 3) demanded independence from the UK as a condition of Indian co-operation in the war. When the country appeared threatened by the Japanese in 1942, Gandhi argued that the Japanese were unlikely to attack a free India, but if they did, he said the attack must be met with the kind of civil disobedience that had been used against the British. He was arrested and undertook one of his famous prison fasts which forced the British to release him from gaol in May 1944, because of his physical frailty.

Indian nationalism was two-sided, and religious in its essence. So long as the Hindus and Muslims had a common British enemy, they could co-operate; when the British granted independence in 1947 the country had to be partitioned into India (mainly Hindu) and Pakistan (mainly Muslim), leading to a civil war that was the bloodiest in history.

The Japanese failed to recognize, much less appeal to, Chinese nationalism. They thought they knew all about China; in fact they knew next to nothing. They wanted to run the country, in their own way for their own benefit, without understanding it. They offered no alternative to *Mao Tse-tung and the communists, or *Chiang Kai-shek and the Kuomintang, other than their own oppression. Mao and Chiang, for their own reasons, did tap Chinese nationalism, but each was more concerned with the triumph of his own leadership and cause than with a genuine Chinese nationalism. Thus they concentrated on struggling against each other rather than co-operating to fight the common enemy. They never did drive the Japanese Army from their country, but they did position themselves for post-war conflict.

Many philosophers, and some politicians, argued at the end of the war that nationalism had to be tempered by regional and world-wide organizations if war were to be avoided in the future. The world could no longer afford the international anarchy that is inherent in the nation-state system. To Americans, this meant the revival of Woodrow Wilson's idea of collective security through the *League of Nations (now succeeded by the United Nations), the creation of regional security through such alliances as the Organization of American States, and the building in Europe of a United States of Europe.

The latter idea had deep roots, going back to the Holy Roman Empire and beyond. It had more recent encouragement; in 1940, on the eve of the fall of France, Churchill (a strong nationalist himself, but the leader of a nation in desperate trouble) proposed a common citizenship for the British and French. This remarkable proposal got nowhere at the time, but it remained in men's minds.

Towards the end of the war, the victors founded the United Nations at the *San Francisco conference. But the members were united in name only. None gave up the sovereign power to make war, conclude treaties, enter into economic, political, or military alliances, or any other of the rights of a nation state.

In Europe, despite the efforts of such men as Jean *Monnet of France and Eisenhower, no union emerged from the ashes. Instead, Europe divided into two camps, the North Atlantic Treaty Organization and the Warsaw Pact. The USA dominated the former, the USSR the latter. These alliances were economic and military; they were not designed to promote political unity. But by the end of the 1980s, some limited and halting steps towards political unity had been taken in western Europe, while in central and eastern Europe the events of the autumn of 1989, and the collapse of the USSR in 1991, demonstrated that the communist attempt to create an international socialist system that would make nationalism a thing of the past had utterly failed.

Nationalism caused the Second World War, it dominated the way the war was fought, it survived the war. Even in those countries where nationalism was most devilish and brought on the worst catastrophes—Germany and Japan—nationalism remained a powerful force. The war showed that nationalism is the most dangerous of all the 'isms', and the most persistent, because it is the most human. See also ORIGINS OF THE WAR.

STEPHEN E. AMBROSE

Fussell, P., *Wartime: Understanding and Behaviour in the Second World War* (Oxford, 1989).
Way, A., *Europe Since 1939* (New York, 1966).

National Redoubt, final Nazi stronghold, so-called by the Allies who probably borrowed the phrase from a redoubt which had been organized in Switzerland. It was said to centre on Hitler's Bavarian mountain retreat at *Berchtesgaden. Allen *Dulles, the head of the *Office of Strategic Services in Berne, warned of its possible existence in September 1944, but this was sceptically received by most intelligence officers. When US troops were diverted away from the drive to Berlin to deal with it, it was found that it did not exist, though Hitler, on 18 April 1945, had, on the spur of the moment, ordered the preparation of a *Kernfestung* (inner fortress) in the Bavarian Alps which, with the Allies on the verge of victory, was totally impossible to achieve.

The myth of a national redoubt also exercised the minds of many *resistance leaders—especially in France and Yugoslavia—and often with disastrous results, as in the *Vercors.

National War Labor Board, US civilian agency established in January 1942 to mediate in labour disputes and regulate wages. It was the successor of the National Defense Mediation Board which had been formed the previous March. Headed by William H. Davis it had twelve members who represented industry, the unions, and the public. More powerful than its predecessor, it was able to impose a solution on a dispute and, if necessary, could call on Roosevelt to seize a business which ignored its decisions. In 1943 the government temporarily took over the coal mines when strikes affected production; and the following year it assumed control of Montgomery Ward, a group of stores and mail-order merchandising concern with 78,000 employees, when the owner refused to follow the War Labor Board's directions in a union dispute.

Nauru and Ocean Islands, situated about halfway between the Marshall and the Solomons groups of Pacific islands. In 1939 Nauru was a British mandate administered by Australia. Ocean Island, situated about 240 km. (150 mi.) east of Nauru, was a British possession administratively part of the Gilbert and Ellice Islands. They had valuable phosphate deposits, a million tons being shipped from Nauru in the year ending June 1940 and half that coming from Ocean. In December 1940 German *auxiliary cruisers sank three phosphate ships and shelled the islands' installations. The Japanese occupied them in August 1942 and about 1,200 islanders were deported to *Truk as *forced labour. See also PACIFIC WAR.

Navajo Indian 'code talkers' were used by the US Marine Corps during the *Pacific war. To encipher and then decipher signals could be fatally time-consuming (see ONE-TIME PAD, for example), but to speak 'en clair' was foolhardy. By employing specially-trained Navajo Indian signallers to speak to one another in a code based on their language—incomprehensible to the Japanese—the marines had a secure and quick means of transmitting vital radio messages during the critical phase of an *amphibious warfare assault. They were especially useful at *Iwo Jima and about 300 of them were deployed in the Pacific theatre. See also RADIO COMMUNICATIONS.

Paul, D., *Navajo Code Talkers* (New York, 1978).

Naval Intelligence Division (NID), the senior naval staff division of the British Admiralty which, unlike its army and air force counterparts, was an operational as well as an administrative centre. The NID had been considerably run down between the two world wars and had also lost its team of cryptographers (Room 40), transferred to the Secret Service as the government Code and Cypher School under the control of the foreign office (see BLETCHLEY PARK). It was organized into 'geographical' sections, each gathering naval information on one country or group of countries, invaluable for the forward planning of major operations in war.

The Abyssinian crisis of 1935 sounded the first alarm bells. The Deputy Chief of Naval Staff sent a memorandum to the Director of Naval Intelligence (DNI) on the need to establish an intelligence centre so that operational intelligence could be transmitted to the fleets and squadrons at sea with the minimum of delay. In June 1937 Paymaster Lt-Commander Norman Denning was selected to organize the creation of an operational intelligence centre (OIC) and to recruit a team to operate it. In January 1939 Rear-Admiral John Godfrey was appointed DNI and, less restricted than his predecessor by treasury limits on expenditure, was able to devote his considerable drive and energy to the expansion of NID as a whole and of OIC in particular in readiness for the war which most recognized was now inevitable. Shortly before war was declared OIC was mobilized and put on a war footing.

Information came to OIC from a variety of sources. A direct telephone and teleprinter link with the network of directional wireless stations provided bearings of all Axis signals which, when plotted in OIC, gave the position of the sender. A similar link with Bletchley Park brought decrypts of signals when cipher breaks were made, and all these within minutes. Advance copies of sighting reports from ships and aircraft arrived direct from the War Registry, the Admiralty department which distributed all signals; and reports from naval attachés in neutral countries (see BISMARCK, for example), and from *spies in occupied countries reached OIC direct from the foreign office (see MI6). Information on Axis merchant shipping came from Lloyds and the Baltic Exchange and there were direct telephone lines to all the main home bases and to the individual commands of the RAF. This internal communications network was amplified by authority for OIC to communicate directly with naval forces at sea so that the fruits of operational intelligence could be received by them as soon as it had been assessed in OIC.

In May 1941 Bletchley Park's cryptographers got the break they needed to penetrate the German U-boat cipher (see ULTRA, 1). The capture in the Atlantic of a weather-reporting trawler and a U-boat provided an undamaged *ENIGMA machine and invaluable ancillary information which led to the breaking of the heavy ship cipher and the Mediterranean ciphers. The text of decrypted signals reached OIC within minutes and, after assessment and precautions to safeguard the source, was passed to the squadron or fleet concerned. With all its sources of information, coupled with the authority to communicate direct, NID was able, for the first time since its formation in 1886, to operate as a modern and efficient intelligence service.

One of Godfrey's most valuable innovations was to set up, in the geography schools at Oxford, the Inter-Service Topographical Department (ISTD), a group of experts from all three services who collected and collated all sorts of information about ports, coastlines, communications and other points of interest to projected invading forces. Without ISTD's groundwork neither the landings which preceded the *North African and *Sicilian campaigns, nor the Normandy landings in June 1944 (see OVERLORD), could have succeeded.

Another important section of NID was 17M which handled the Admiralty's non-operational ULTRA intelligence and provided the naval information being fed to the Germans via controlled *double agents (see XX-COMMITTEE). It was formed in December 1940 and headed by an RNVR officer, Lt-Commander Ewen Montagu, who planned one of the more ingenious *deception operations of the war (see MINCEMEAT). PETER KEMP

Beesly, P., *Very Special Intelligence* (London, 1977).
McLachlan, D. H., *Room 39* (London, 1968).
Montagu, E., *Beyond Top Secret U* (London, 1977).

Nazi, acronym formed from NAtionalsoZIalist, the first word of the official title of Hitler's party, the Nationalsozialistische deutsche Arbeiterpartei, or NSDAP (National Socialist German Workers' Party), which was founded in 1919. See GERMANY, 3.

Nazi ideology. The outbreak and course of the war were profoundly influenced by the ideological outlook of the Nazi leadership. Nazi ideology aimed at the building of a new social order in Germany to prepare the German nation for fighting; it laid emphasis on the racial or biological character of politics; and it contained the view that only through conflict with other races and nations could Germany prove itself worthy to establish a new German empire.

The ideas produced by Nazism were not particularly novel. They were derived from vulgar ideas about race and empire common to the radical right throughout Europe. Nazi thinkers such as *Rosenberg were influenced by contemporary views rejecting democracy and liberal values, and calling instead for rule by a new authoritarian élite of 'supermen'. These ideas were shaped by a widespread cultural pessimism, the belief that bourgeois Europe was doomed and that a new age was beckoning. Nazis shared the view that the world was a Darwinian jungle in which the fittest culture or race survived only through ceaseless struggle against other cultures and races. They were attracted to the popular geopolitical idea that a successful race would only survive in this struggle if it acquired **Lebensraum* (living space). The conquest of additional land would produce a proper balance between population and territory, and halt internal decline. Hitler distilled all this in his book **Mein Kampf*. No other Nazi writer was as influential as Hitler in setting the ideological goals of the movement both inside Germany and for the plethora of small pro-Nazi groups that sprang up in Europe, the Middle East, South Africa, and the Americas (see BRITISH UNION, GERMAN–AMERICAN BUND, and OSSEWABRANDWAG, for example).

The first of these goals was the establishment of a new political and social order in Germany, the so-called 'Third Way' between decaying bourgeois capitalism and the growing threat of radical socialism. Nazis called this new order the *Volksgemeinschaft* (national community). It was distinguished by an authoritarian political system based on the 'leadership principle', where authority flowed downwards from the nation's leader and responsibility upwards from the racial 'followers'. Society was no longer to be a class society but a corporative one, organized in estates and corporations, which would bind people to the national community and create a true sense of Germanness. Everything was to serve the interests of the *Volk* rather than those of the individual. This applied equally to German capitalism: though Hitler respected private property, the economy was to be controlled to serve political ends. The ultimate purpose was to create a community of racially pure Germans, loyal to their leader, who would meet the challenges of Germany's destiny in the historic struggle with other races.

The idea of race was central to the Nazi world view (*Weltanschauung*). Hitler believed that history was a constant process of racial struggle, like the struggle in nature. The main racial enemy was the Jew, who was regarded as the enemy of all races, sapping the vitality of the host nation and producing chaos and misery. The Jew came to symbolize for the Nazis all that they disliked in the world about them, unbridled modernization, international finance capitalism, international *communism. Hitler saw the final struggle between Jew and German as a contest of world-historical proportions, a final reckoning with those responsible for Germany's downfall in the *First World War. He did not exclude struggle with other races too, the Slavs in particular, who were regarded as *Untermenschen* (subhumans), fit only to be ruled by the master race, the *Herrenrasse*. Racial ideology had a number of implications. It led to the *euthanasia programme in Germany, and the pursuit of a violent biological politics, directed against racial 'undesirables', homosexuals, prostitutes, the disabled, the mentally ill. For German Jews it led to their gradual exclusion from public life and the loss of civil rights, and, during the war, to extermination (see FINAL SOLUTION).

The racial view of the world necessarily implied the idea of international struggle as well as internal 'purification'. Nazis hoped to create a new order in world affairs as well as the new order at home. They saw war as a test of racial virility, and conflict with other races as historically inevitable. 'Mankind has grown great in eternal war,' wrote Hitler, 'it would decay in eternal peace.' He believed it was Germany's destiny to transcend the limitations imposed on it by the vengeful Allies in the *Versailles settlement, and to seize its destiny, become the dominant power in Europe, and thence to achieve world power. This ambition required the conquest of 'living-space' for the master race through war against the Slavs in the east, who were led, Hitler believed, by the bitterest enemies of Germandom, Jews and Marxists. 'If we want to *rule*,' he once said, 'we must first conquer Russia.' Hitler saw Germany as a new Roman empire, extending firm rule over the subject races of Europe and Asia. There would be a racial hierarchy within the empire, with Germany at the top. The new imperial cities planned in Berlin, Nuremberg, Linz, and Vienna would demonstrate the triumph of Germanic culture. With Europe conquered in 1941 German leaders began to implement the 'New Order' in Europe, reorganizing the economy to serve German interests, murdering the Jews, and planning the exploitation of living-space in the east (see GERMANY, 4).

Historians are divided on the significance of Nazi ideology. It can be seen as a mere propaganda gloss for a political strategy that was opportunistic or shaped by circumstance. There was always a gulf in practice between ideological aims and social or military reality. The drive to get *women back into the home, for example, could not be reconciled with the labour demands of re-armament. By 1939 there were more women working than in 1929. Popular protest obstructed the euthanasia programme and Nazi paganism. The invasion of the USSR in June 1941 (see BARBAROSSA) had a powerful ideological drive behind it, but its timing was governed as much by changes in Soviet policy in eastern Europe, and the need to acquire additional resources to fight the war in the west.

Nevertheless, there is strong evidence that by 1938, once Hitler had come to dominate decision-making, ideology did come to shape German political and military choices directly. The war against the USSR was an ideological war to smash 'Jewish-Bolshevism'; the extermination of the Jews fulfilled the ideological imperative; a new political order was imposed by force on Germany after 1933, and then on Europe after 1940. From the late 1930s the more radical racists in the Nazi Party gradually assumed a greater political prominence, anxious to put the Führer's wishes into literal effect. Ideological conformity was enforced on the population, and dissent from ideological goals was violently penalized. Ideology supplied a broad frame of reference for the formulation and implementation of Nazi policies; acceptance of ideology became a crude litmus test of loyalty to the regime and the Führer; finally, ideology was used to legitimize wars of conquest and genocide. See also FASCISM. RICHARD OVERY

Jäckel, E., *Hitler's Weltanschauung* (Middletown, Conn., 1972).
Cecil, R., *The Myth of the Master Race* (London, 1972).
Herf, J., *Reactionary Modernism: Technology, Culture and Politics in the Third Reich* (Cambridge, 1986).
Herzstein, R. E., *When Nazi Dreams Come True* (London, 1982).

Nazi–Soviet Pact. As commonly encountered in western history books, this is a somewhat imprecise label that is used to refer both to the German–Soviet Treaty of Non-Aggression of 23 August 1939 and to the broader political settlement between Germany and the USSR which followed it. In the narrow sense, it includes not only the public clauses of the Non-Aggression Treaty, but also the secret protocols which accompanied them. More broadly, it may also be taken to cover the German–Soviet Treaty of Friendship, Co-operation, and Demarcation of 28 September 1939, which modified the earlier agreement and which governed German–Soviet relations until 22 June 1941 when the German invasion of the USSR was launched (see BARBAROSSA). Taken together, these agreements between Europe's two leading military powers set the framework within which the events of the first two years of the Second World War took place.

Many misunderstandings about the Nazi–Soviet Pact have arisen as the result both of the policy of the western powers at the time, and of subsequent Soviet *historiography. In 1939–41, the western powers, which declared war on Germany and Italy, were careful to avoid conflict with the USSR. They were banking on the possibility—which later materialized—that Hitler and Stalin would eventually fall out and that a Western coalition with Moscow against Germany could re-emerge (as during the *First World War). Because of this, many western historians were led to talk of Stalin's 'neutrality' during the Nazi–Soviet Pact. This however, is a very partial point of view, which is arguable even in relation to

Molotov signs the **Nazi–Soviet Pact**, 23 August 1939. Stalin and Ribbentrop (on Stalin's right) look on.

Stalin's attitude towards the West, and is entirely inaccurate regarding Soviet military activities in eastern Europe (see POLISH CAMPAIGN, FINNISH–SOVIET WAR, BALTIC STATES, BESSARABIA, and BUKOVINA). For their part, until as late as 1990 Soviet historians were reluctant to admit to the genuine character of the secret protocols. The existence of the second German–Soviet treaty, of 28 September 1939, was simply ignored.

A Nazi–Soviet rapprochement was in the making from May 1939. Stalin had never completely closed the German option. But when *Molotov surfaced as commissar for foreign affairs in place of *Litvinov, the advocate of collective security with the West, a more energetic approach was being prepared. Direct negotiations began in June under cover of 'trade talks', and were pursued in parallel to the much more leisurely discussions about a possible Anglo-Soviet defence arrangement. By the time that *Ribbentrop, Hitler's foreign minister, flew to Moscow in August, preparations were well advanced.

Both Hitler and Stalin harboured fundamental objections to the *Versailles settlement as imposed by the western powers after 1918. Among other things, both harboured resentments against the independent Poland, which lay between them. Hitler had long ago decided to attack Poland, but could not afford to do so if he would thereby offend Stalin's own ambitions.

The Pact solved not only the immediate Polish conundrum, but also the wider issue of German and Soviet revisionist aims. The essence of the deal was to create two distinct spheres of influence within which each side would be free to operate without fear of interference from the other. Once Poland had been destroyed by joint action, Hitler would be free to attack his neighbours to the west, whilst Stalin would be free to do the same in the east. In this context, the concept of 'non-aggression' was given an especially gangsterish interpretation. The Nazis and Soviets agreed to refrain from aggression against each other, in the full expectation that they could both commit aggression with impunity in other directions.

The main text of the German–Soviet Treaty of 23 August 1939, therefore, can only be fully understood in conjunction with the accompanying protocols, which remained secret until the capture of the Nazi archives in 1945. After discussing 'their respective spheres of influence in eastern Europe', the plenipotentiaries decided for the time being on an 'approximate' line along the rivers Vistula, Narew, and San. The Soviets staked out their claim to the larger part of Poland, to Bessarabia, Estonia, and Latvia, though not at this stage Lithuania. The protocols were to be kept secret. A further 'friendly agreement' was envisaged 'in the course of further political developments'. The expected assault on Poland, for which the Pact was the political starting signal, was not explicitly mentioned (see R. J. Sonntag and J. S. Beddie, *Nazi-Soviet Relations: Documents from the Archives of the German Foreign Office*, Washington, DC, 1948, pp. 78 ff.).

Towards the end of the Polish campaign, on 28 September, the German–Soviet Treaty of Friendship, Co-operation, and Demarcation made important extensions and amendments to the treaty of 23 August. German–Soviet relations were raised to the active plane, especially in the realms of security and propaganda. The Soviets surrendered their claim to a large slice of Poland between the Vistula and Bug in return for Lithuania. Provision was made for joint action against 'Polish agitation' (see KATYŃ).

Much remains to be discovered about the Nazi–Soviet Pact, especially in relation to Soviet policy. Just before the collapse of the USSR in 1991, Soviet historians exploded the myth that Stalin entered the Pact in order to gain time for strengthening the Red Army's defences: the Red Army never adopted systematic defensive positions, even in 1941. Nothing is known for certain of his calculations concerning the likely outcome of Hitler's attack on western Europe, nor of Stalin's intentions in the longer term, once Germany and the Soviet Union had achieved their immediate objectives. If the Soviet military had shared the predictions of the western experts, with whom they held lengthy talks in 1939, it is reasonable to suppose that they would have been expecting an Allied–German conflict on the Western Front to last for three or four years (as in 1914–18). In which case, it may also be within the realm of possibility, as one ex-Soviet officer has suggested, that Stalin was biding his time, to launch a European offensive of his own (see V. Suvorov, *Icebreaker: Who started the Second World War?*, London, 1990). The collapse of the USSR, and the prospect of access to Soviet archives, may finally throw light on these questions, which are vital to any full analysis of the outbreak of war, but which have remained unanswered for more than 50 years. NORMAN DAVIES

Nebelwerfer, see ROCKET WEAPONS.

Nehru, Jawaharlal (1889–1964), Indian lawyer and Congress Party leader who, though he distrusted British policies towards India, was sympathetic to the Allied cause. Though neither he nor Congress was always in tune with their spiritual leader, Mahatma *Gandhi, he supported Gandhi's civil disobedience campaign in 1940. He was arrested that October and sentenced to four years' imprisonment, but was released in December 1941 when the campaign was called off. However, his support of Gandhi's 'Quit India' movement, which followed the failure of the mission led by Stafford *Cripps in March 1942, led to his arrest again, in August 1942, and he was imprisoned until June 1945. He subsequently became India's first prime minister on independence in August 1947. See also ANTI-IMPERIALISM.

Gopal, S., *Jawaharlal Nehru*, Vol. 1: 1889–1947 (London, 1975).

NEPTUNE, codename for the assault phase of the Allied invasion of Normandy. See OVERLORD.

NETHERLANDS

1. Introduction

A democratic kingdom of nearly 9 million people, whose overseas possessions of the Dutch West Indies and the Netherlands East Indies brought it considerable wealth. The Netherlands had never been at war with another state since it was founded—to replace the ancient and warlike Dutch republic—in 1815. By 1939 its politicians and diplomats had become obsessively neutral and no plans for concerted military action were made with any neighbouring state, not even with Belgium.

After war broke out in Europe in September 1939 the Dutch queen, Wilhelmina (1880–1962), joined with King *Léopold III of Belgium in an autumn appeal to France, Germany, and the UK to make peace; which had no effect. Hitler sent the queen a personal assurance that he would continue to respect Dutch neutrality.

The war cost the Netherlands 220,000 lives and the loss of 33% of its gross national product.

2. Domestic life, war effort, and economy

Dutch dairying and horticulture had developed, during the 1920s and 1930s, so far that the country had a large export surplus of butter, cheese, fruit, and vegetables; under the occupation all this was siphoned off to Germany, where it helped the Germans to maintain an agreeable diet and hindered the UK's blockade (see ECONOMIC WARFARE). The German war economists took care to pay for what they took at prices which the Germans could easily afford, while they offered no prosperity to Dutch farmers or gardeners—part of the Germans' usual doctrine of *vae victis*, 'woe to the conquered'. They tried moreover a few large experimental collective farms, as convenient testing-grounds for various Nazi agricultural fads, without bothering to consult the convenience of the landowners.

To conform with what was already happening in Germany, various Dutch professions were Nazified; all Jews in these fields had to abandon their work. The non-Jewish professors in the University of Leyden objected to this measure and the university was thereupon closed down. A great many doctors, architects, lawyers, and so on, sooner than join the appropriate Nazi-dominated body, simply resigned from their jobs, and either lived on what savings they had, or took some quite different employment; or they went into hiding (diving under, *onderduiken*, was the Dutch term).

*Religion had a good deal to do with such decisions. A great many Dutch citizens lived in Calvinist families, with strong traditions of Bible reading and correct conduct; the Roman Catholic minority, though it read the Bible less, was no less concerned with behaving ethically; almost all Dutch Christians abominated Nazism as ungodly, and many Dutch ministers and priests were ready to take risks in anti-Nazi activity. Nazi doctrines and methods were often denounced from the pulpit.

Some 104,000 Dutch Jews were deported to *concentration camps, while 36,000 more saved themselves, or were saved by their neighbours, by going into hiding. One of the deported Jews became world famous after her death—Anne *Frank the schoolgirl diarist, who had been born in Germany and whose father had not moved far enough away from it. She and her family duly dived under; after four years a neighbour gave them away.

Nazi theory held that the Dutch were of Aryan race, close cousins to the Germans, with whom they would in the end become absorbed; meanwhile they would have to put up with being treated strictly, as second-class citizens. Strictness, persecution, deportation were wholly strange to the Dutch, who had regarded themselves as a cultivated, Christian, and easy-going people. Severity used by Nazi gangs at an early round-up of Jews in Amsterdam brought on a great strike in February 1941. Although it was inspired by the local communists (the party had secured 4% of the votes in 1937), every class took part and it spread for a few days to most of the large towns. It was followed by seventeen executions of Dutchmen who were already in prison (fifteen of them, saboteurs from a shipyard downstream of Rotterdam, had done their best to wreck a cruiser under construction for the German Navy). These executions appalled the bulk of the Dutch, who had abolished the death penalty in 1870.

On 17 September 1944, the opening day of the airborne attack on Arnhem (see MARKET-GARDEN), a *BBC broadcast by P. J. Gerbrandy, prime minister of the Dutch government-in-exile (see below), ordered the Dutch railways to come out on strike, which they duly did. The Germans, in retaliation, cut off the movement of food by canal, hitherto regarded as indispensable to feed the large cities in the western part of the kingdom. The winter of 1944–5 is still remembered as the Hunger Winter. In some parts of the country there was at times no food at all, not even sugar beet or tulip bulbs, and 16,000 people died of starvation in one of the most fertile countries in the world—an instance of the absurdities of war.

3. Government

(a) Occupation

The Dutch parliament did not meet during the war, Queen Wilhelmina having taken into exile with her an official whose assent was necessary to the legality of any Dutch law, but this did not deter the Germans from administering the Netherlands as a dependent province of the Third Reich. *Seyss-Inquart headed Reichskommissariat Niederlanden, aided by another Austrian Nazi, also picked personally by Hitler, H. A. Rauter (1891–1949), as head of the *SS and security police. They squeezed everything out of the Netherlands that they could, both food and manufactures, for the benefit of Germany. From government offices in the centre of The Hague, they ran a stern colonial administration, laying down—sometimes in minute detail—what their conquered Dutch subjects were and were not to do.

At the last general election in 1937, 4% of the electorate had supported the Dutch Nazi Party, which grew from 30,000 to 50,000 members during the occupation; but its leader, Anton *Mussert, was given no high place or special treatment by the Germans. He bombarded Hitler with memoranda about the Aryanism and the potentialities of the Dutch, and foresaw a Greater Netherlands which would reabsorb the Flemish-speaking provinces of Belgium at least; but he never received any serious attention from Berlin, where he was regarded as an unimportant puppet. Over 5,000 Dutchmen joined the Waffen-SS, and another 54,000 belonged of their own will to various other Nazi organizations; in a total population approaching 9,000,000, they remained a small minority. The civil service and the police continued to operate more or less as usual; the police did their best not to carry out their instructions from Rauter too promptly or too well.

(b) Government-in-exile and post-occupation government

In spite of Hitler's assurances, the Wehrmacht invaded the Netherlands on 10 May 1940 (see FALL GELB) and three days later the queen boarded a British destroyer. She hoped to continue the battle from Zeeland, in the south-west of the country, but the situation deteriorated so rapidly that she was taken to England instead. The Dutch cabinet, having transferred all its powers to General H. G. Winkelman, C-in-C of the Dutch forces, followed the queen who settled in London. She dismissed her strongly pacific prime minister, D. J. de Geer (who went back home), replacing him in late August 1940 with the minister of justice, P. J. Gerbrandy, who proved combative enough. But the Dutch forces in exile were never strong. Of those who had managed to escape, the airmen became part of 320 Squadron RAF, the army formed the Irene Brigade under Lt-Colonel de Ruyter van Steveninck, which fought in the *Normandy campaign and in north-west Europe, and the warships fought with the Royal Navy.

The queen encouraged her people by frequent broadcasts on Radio Orange and she quickly became accepted, by the occupied Dutch and the Allies alike, as the symbol of Dutch freedom and independence.

In May 1944 the government made an agreement with the British for the formation of a Dutch military government when the country was liberated; and in September, in preparation for the liberation, the government formed the Netherlands Forces of the Interior (Binnenlandse Strijdkrachten, or BS, a phrase borrowed from the French). Under the command of the queen's son-in-law, Prince *Bernhard, this integrated the three main resistance groups in the Netherlands which, in the liberated areas of Zeeland, North Brabant, and Limburg, worked under the Allied armies as an auxiliary force. It was these areas that the Dutch military government, with BS aid, administered and when five Dutch ministers arrived in December they were largely ignored. This forced Gerbrandy to form a more representative government which included representatives from the liberated provinces.

4. Armed forces

(a) Dutch defences and the German invasion

The defensive outlook of Dutch politicians contributed to the swift defeat of their country when the Germans invaded on 10 May 1940. In the past the Dutch had relied on flooding to defend themselves and in 1937 the Dutch prime minister declared that he could stop any invasion by simply pushing a button. This defensive outlook, so similar to the French reliance on their *Maginot Line,

Netherlands

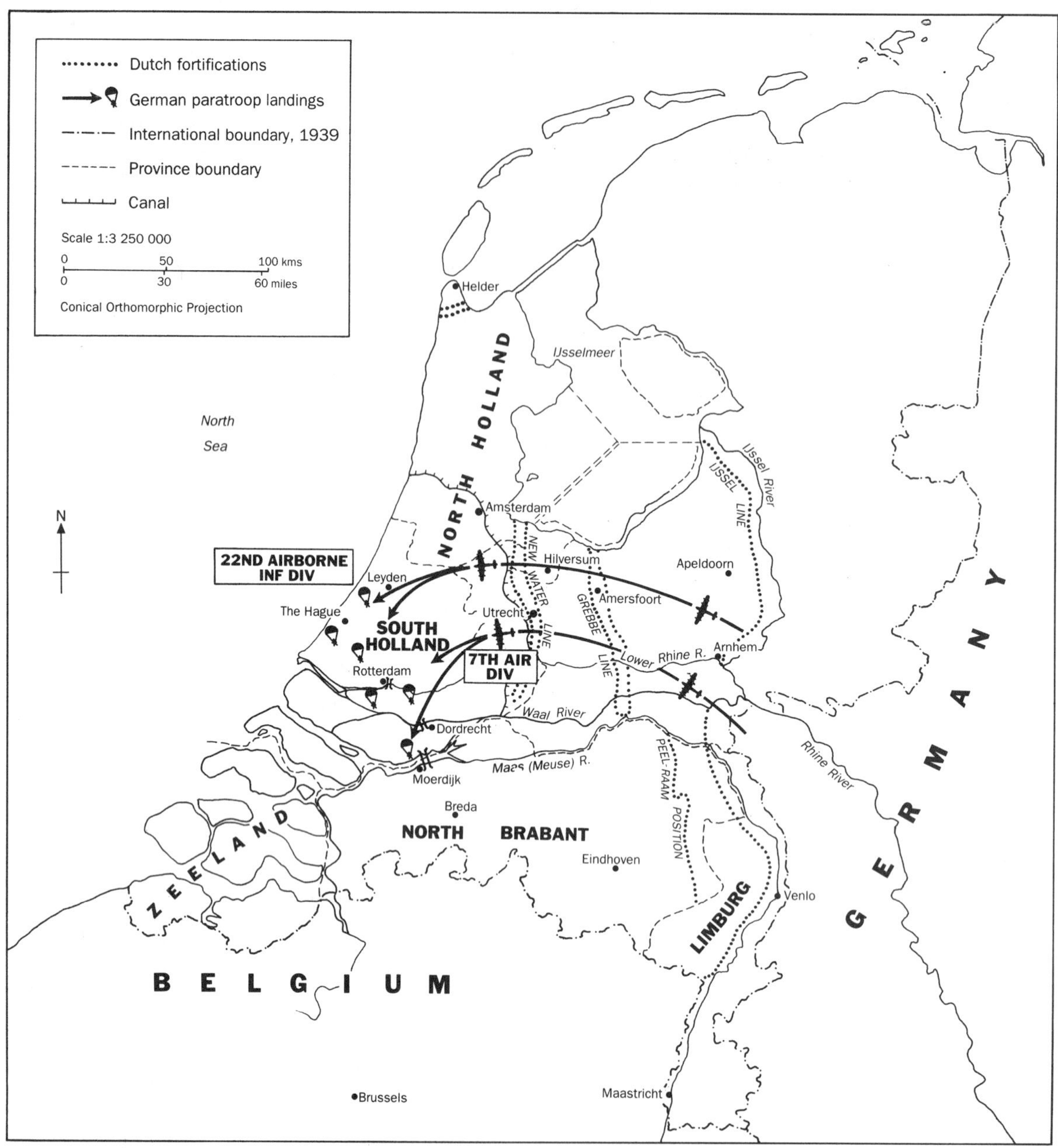

70. **Netherlands:** Dutch defences and German airborne attack, 10 May 1940

made inundations an integral part of the Dutch defences which comprised three indifferently fortified lines: the IJssel, the Grebbe north of the Meuse and the Peel-Raam south of it, and finally, a water line which was a last-ditch defence of 'Fortress Holland' (see Map 70). But the Dutch took no account of the German *blitzkrieg, nor of *airborne warfare.

The Eighteenth German Army quickly overran the IJssel Line and though the two German airborne divisions which were dropped at strategic points in 'Fortress Holland' were hard pressed and received some severe reverses, they could not be eliminated. Those holding the crucial bridge across the Waal at Moerdijk, which gave direct access into 'Fortress Holland' behind the Grebbe Line, held on until the 9th Armoured Division arrived on the third day and advanced on Rotterdam. To the south the Seventh French Army, too weak to intervene, withdrew and left the Dutch isolated. That same evening orders were issued 'to break resistance in *Rotterdam by all possible means' and the next day, 14 May, the city, whose bridges had been stoutly defended by Dutch marines, was heavily bombed and that evening the Dutch capitulated.

(b) Army
Commanded by General H. G. Winkelman, the Dutch Army comprised four army corps of two divisions each and four brigades. These plus a number of smaller units totalled some 400,000 men. This was a sizeable force, but it had not a single tank, and only 26 armoured cars and 656 outdated guns. A strong pacifist movement in the Netherlands (its symbol was a broken rifle) had helped inhibit the army's modernization; lack of operational experience, and parsimony in equipping it properly, left it incapable of effectively resisting the Wehrmacht. Its losses during the fighting were 2,100 dead and 2,700 wounded.

(c) Navy
The small but modern navy was employed primarily to defend the *Netherlands East Indies. It comprised 5 cruisers, 8 destroyers, 24 submarines, 16 minesweepers, and a number of torpedo boats and auxiliary craft. It also had about 50 operational but obsolete aircraft. In May 1940 only one cruiser, one destroyer, and a number of smaller vessels were stationed in the Netherlands. The destroyer was sunk by German aircraft and some of the ships were subsequently scuttled. However, most escaped to the UK and the cruiser subsequently worked with the Royal Navy in the Mediterranean. Nearly all those in the Netherlands East Indies were lost to air attack, or in the battles of the *Java Sea and Sunda straits, but one or two survived to serve with the British Eastern Fleet. The navy had developed an early version of the **Schnorchel*, plans of which fell into German hands, but luckily for the Allies the Germans were slow to develop it.

(d) Air Force
The Luchtvaart Afdeling (Military Aviation Division) of the Dutch Army was created on 1 July 1913, but separate air arms were later formed by the navy and the army in the Netherlands East Indies. To oppose the 1,100 aircraft employed by the Germans on 10 May 1940 the Dutch had just 175, of which only 132 were serviceable and only 72 were modern. They lost 62 of them on the first day and few survived beyond capitulation on 14 May.

5. Intelligence
One of the reasons the Germans gave for invading the Netherlands was that Dutch intelligence was co-operating in an anti-Hitler conspiracy. This claim was not without foundation, for the Dutch chief of intelligence, Maj-General J. W. van Oorschot, turned a blind eye when his cryptanalysts presented him with the wireless traffic—which they had easily deciphered—being exchanged by an agent of *MI6 in the Netherlands with a source in Nazi Germany (see VENLO). This turned out unhappily; the source was not, as MI6 supposed, one friendly to the Allies.

A German source that did turn out to be entirely reliable, but one which was also largely ignored, was Colonel *Oster, deputy chief of the *Abwehr, the German military intelligence organization. An early member of the resistance against Hitler (see SCHWARZE KAPELLE), Oster was a friend of the Dutch military attaché in Berlin, Major G. J. Sas, and kept him informed about German invasion plans. On the evening of 9 May he told Sas that the Netherlands were to be invaded the next morning, but though Sas passed this information on to The Hague many of those guarding the country's strategic points were still taken by surprise.

Once the Dutch government-in-exile had been formed in London it set up a special intelligence service under the queen's secretary, F. van't Sant, which worked with MI6. It was not successful; Sant resigned in the summer of 1941 and a new intelligence organization was formed under Colonel M. de Bruyne, but this also had its problems (see ENGLANDSPIEL).

Until the Japanese invaded the Netherlands East Indies (NEI) the Dutch had a small but efficient code-breaking organization (Kamer 14) in Java. According to one source (see E. Layton *et al.*, *And I was There*, New York, 1985, p. 206) it made inroads into the Japanese naval code (see ULTRA, 2) and into a consular cipher, but did not manage to decrypt Japanese diplomatic messages encoded on the *PURPLE machine cipher (see MAGIC). Layton also quotes the Dutch C-in-C in the NEI, General Hein ter Poorten, as reporting that Kamer 14 had alerted him to the concentration near the Kurile Islands of the Japanese task force that raided *Pearl Harbor, but as all the Dutch records were destroyed there is no means of confirming this.

After the NEI had been overrun by the Japanese both the Netherlands Forces Intelligence Service based in Australia (see ALLIED INTELLIGENCE BUREAU) and the Ceylon-based Korps Insulinde, which was part of *SOE's Force 136, attempted intelligence-gathering operations into the NEI, but with negligible success.

6. Merchant marine
Most of the merchant marine, overseas at the moment of invasion, rallied to the government-in-exile, for which it provided an important source of income. Dutch *schuyts*, coastal sailing barges, were prominent among the little ships at *Dunkirk. Dutch shipping—640 strong, apart from more than 200 small vessels—was of material help to the Allies; nearly half of these ships were lost to German or Japanese torpedoes or mines, at a cost of some 3,000 Dutch seamen's lives. The shipyards near the mouths of the Rhine and Maas were put to work by the Germans to build ships for the German Navy, a task they carried out as badly as they could.

7. Resistance
Several resistance movements developed, including three large ones; some of them co-operated with their local policemen, who were personal friends. The Orde Dienst

(OD), favoured by the government-in-exile, was intended to make sure that the queen's return would be untroubled by left-wing disturbances. All the OD's detailed instructions were sent through *SOE channels in 1942–3, so it could claim few successes: all of them were controlled by the Abwehr's/SD ENGLANDSPIEL. The Raad van Verzet (Resistance Council) and the *knokploegen* (combat groups) did a good deal to help the *onderduikers*, and managed a little useful sabotage; but they were short of arms and explosives. Their efforts were much hindered, as SOE's had been, by the prevalence of *double agents. Moreover, everybody who was anybody in the Netherlands knew everybody else; it was exceptionally hard to keep anything really secret.

From 1942, there were some useful intelligence circuits at work passing data back to England (see SPIES), and the many good Christians, far more numerous than the double agents, made it possible to set up some escape lines. Both the Protestant and the Catholic churches, outspoken as usual in denunciation of Nazi methods, supported a further great strike, in April–May 1943, which was the response to a German attempt to re-arrest thousands of Dutchmen whom they had taken *prisoners-of-war, and then sent home; the strike was brutally put down, at the cost of some 150 lives, but at least the prisoners were not re-arrested. The country's large printing industry made possible an unusually widespread clandestine newspaper service; one journal, *Je Maintiendrai* (the royal family's motto), run by a Dutch reserve artillery officer, Dirk de Loos, circulated in 80,000 copies of each issue (see SUBVERSIVE WARFARE). De Loos was betrayed in 1942 but survived five concentration camps, including *Dachau.

Several thousand young men, due for *forced labour in the Reich, joined the *onderduikers*. Terrain forbade the formation of *maquis, as in France—there was all too little rough country; they either hid in a town, with the connivance of a clerk at the town hall, or pretended to be farm labourers (who were exempt from the labour call-up) in the countryside.

When the Allies entered the Netherlands the three main resistance groups, now amalgamated into the BS, were able to seize a few useful strong-points. They also provided a lot of useful battle intelligence, as First Canadian Army fought its way towards Bremen across the eastern Netherlands in the spring of 1945. At the end of the war the Germans still held the two provinces of North and South Holland. M. R. D. FOOT

Maass, W., *The Netherlands at War* (London, 1970).
de Jong, L., *Het Koninkrijk der Nederlanden in der Tweede Wereldoorlog*, 14 vols. in 29 (The Hague, 1969–91).

Netherlands East Indies (NEI), colony in South-East Asia covering a huge area some 3,660 km. (2,275 mi.) wide by 1,825 km. (1,135 mi.) long, including *Java, Sumatra, Dutch Borneo, Dutch New Guinea, Celebes, western Timor, and Moluccas. It was vital to the economy of the Netherlands, a seventh of its income coming from it. Oil, its most vital product, came mostly from Sumatra (see Table 1); the colony ranked only behind Malaya in tin production, its total output in 1940 being 44,563 tons; and bauxite and coal were also mined. The colony's inhabitants in 1940 totalled an estimated 70.5 million, including one million Chinese. There were also 250,000 Dutch nationals, many of whom suffered harsh years of *internment when the Japanese occupied the area.

Netherlands East Indies, Table 1: Oil production in 1940

Area	*Quantity (000 barrels)*	*Total production in barrels for:*
North Sumatra	7,484	Sumatra 39,755,000
Djambi	9,617	
Palembang	22,654	
Central Java	5,608	Java 6,168,000
Eastern Java	560	
Tarakan	5,433	Borneo 12,522,000
Balikpapan	7,089	
Ceram	664	Ceram 664,000
		Netherlands East Indies 59,109,000

Source: 'Netherlands East Indies', Vol. 2 (Naval Intelligence Division, London, 1944).

After the German occupation of the Netherlands in May 1940, the People's Council in Batavia, the local representative legislative body in Java, remained loyal to the Dutch government-in-exile but became virtually autonomous. In January 1941 the People's Council protested when the Japanese foreign minister referred to the NEI as part of the *Greater East Asia Co-prosperity Sphere and it refused Japan's more extreme demands for its local produce, for unimpeded rights of fishing and prospecting, and for unrestricted access to its ports. Though it did adjust upwards the amount of *raw materials it exported to Japan (see Table 2), the trading relationship quickly deteriorated, and in August 1941, on orders from the Dutch government-in-exile, it stopped supplying oil to Japan.

For the Japanese the NEI was a prize of great significance. Besides the raw materials already mentioned, the area produced rubber, copra, nickel, timber, quinine, and important foodstuffs such as sugar, rice, tea, and coffee. To gain these resources quickly, and before any of them could be destroyed, they deployed the maximum possible forces which attacked the most vital areas almost simultaneously. On 20 December 1941 units of Lt-General Imamura Hitoshi's Sixteenth Army, from Mindanao in the Philippines, attacked Dutch Borneo, Celebes, and the Moluccas, and Japanese paratroops saw action for the first time when they were dropped on a north Celebes airfield on 11 January. The oil-rich centres of Dutch Borneo were also quickly seized, as were important airfields at Kendari (southern Celebes) and Amboina (Moluccas). Paratroops were used again when, on 16 February, another Sixteenth Army invasion force landed at Palembang in southern Sumatra to capture the great oil refinery there, and they were used, too, when Dutch Timor was occupied on 19 February.

Though poorly equipped, the forces in the NEI, aided by American, Australian, and British forces under General *Wavell's *ABDA Command, resisted as best they could. But what air power Wavell possessed was practically destroyed during two raids of 19 and 27 February. In the first of these the Japanese showed their superiority when 23 Navy Zero fighters shot down 40 Allied fighters. At sea, Allied warships caused some damage—US destroyers sank four Japanese transports and a patrol boat off Balikpapan—and delayed the advance momentarily, but Allied naval strength was no match for the Imperial Japanese Navy and was subsequently destroyed (see JAVA SEA).

Overwhelmed everywhere, ABDA Command was dissolved on 25 February and the Dutch governor-general on Java assumed command of the still considerable forces that remained. By then the Japanese had captured their other objectives, and on 1 March they landed on Java in two places and began advancing on Bandung. On 8 March the Dutch capitulated—93,000 men of the Royal Netherlands East Indies Army surrendered—and other Allied units did likewise. The same day Japanese troops from Singapore landed in northern Sumatra and by the end of the month they held the whole island and had begun to land in Dutch New Guinea. Resistance continued in Dutch Borneo and Celebes until October 1942 and the Japanese never conquered all the NEI for the Dutch flag continued to fly over Merauke, the capital of Dutch New Guinea.

Under Japanese rule the territory was reorganized. Sumatra came under the same military administration as Malaya with Singapore as its centre; Java and a number of other islands were also administered by the Japanese Army, but the other two administrative areas, which centred on Borneo (British and Dutch) and on the Celebes, the Moluccas, and Dutch New Guinea, were controlled by the Japanese Navy.

Guerrilla bands operated in some places—Australian units on Timor were particularly effective—and attempts were made to aid them by landing clandestine parties. These were organized by *SOE's Force 136 for Sumatra and by *Special Operations Australia (SOA) and the Netherlands Forces Intelligence Service (see ALLIED INTELLIGENCE BUREAU) elsewhere, but the hostility of the local population and difficult climatic conditions resulted in the eventual capture of practically all of them. However, units landed by SOA prior to Australian landings on British Borneo, at *Tarakan Island, and at *Balikpapan, between May and July 1945, were more successful. See also ANTI-IMPERIALISM and NATIONALISM.

Netherlands East Indies, Table 2: Supplies to Japan in 1940 (000 tons)

Commodity	*Previous quota*	*Japanese demand*	*Supply approved*
Petroleum	600	3,750	1,936
Tin	3	12.5	3
Manganese	–	27	10
Nickel	–	180	150
Bauxite	360	400	250
Rubber	20	30	15
Copra	12	70	20
Palm oil	1	30	12

Source: 'Netherlands East Indies', Vol.2, (Naval Intelligence Division, London, 1944).

Neurath, Konstantin, Baron von (1873–1956), German diplomat who was Germany's foreign minister from 1932 to 1938. Hitler retained him partly to help the democracies accept the assumption of power by the Nazi Party in 1933 and partly to cloak the radical changes going on within Germany. When this no longer proved necessary he was replaced by *Ribbentrop. After the Germans moved into Czechoslovakia in March 1939 Neurath was appointed to govern what remained of it, Bohemia and Moravia, but his lenient rule, and intriguing by the *SS, led to his replacement by Reinhard *Heydrich in September 1941, though he did not officially resign until August 1943. He was sentenced to 15 years' imprisonment at the *Nuremberg trials but was released in 1954.

Neutrality Acts, passed by the US Congress during the 1930s as an expression of American isolationism (see AMERICA FIRST COMMITTEE). The first two (1935, 1936) were temporary, but the third, passed in May 1937, was intended to be permanent. It stated that if any war broke out that threatened US security (as deemed by the president) an arms embargo would be automatically brought into force and any loans or credits to a belligerent would be forbidden. The Act also banned US nationals from travelling as passengers on ships belonging to a belligerent, prohibited the arming of US merchant ships, and included a cash-and-carry provision, which required belligerents wanting non-contraband goods to purchase them for cash and to transport them in foreign ships.

During the first half of 1939 Roosevelt tried, without success, to have the Act amended and when war erupted in Europe that September he issued the proclamation of neutrality that the Act required. But he also summoned Congress for a special session to discuss repealing parts of the Act, and on 4 November a new one was passed. To help France and the UK this allowed the purchase of arms on a cash-and-carry basis—a blow to American isolationists—but continued to forbid loans to belli-

Netherlands East Indies

71. Japanese occupation of **Netherlands East Indies** and British Borneo, December 1941–March 1942

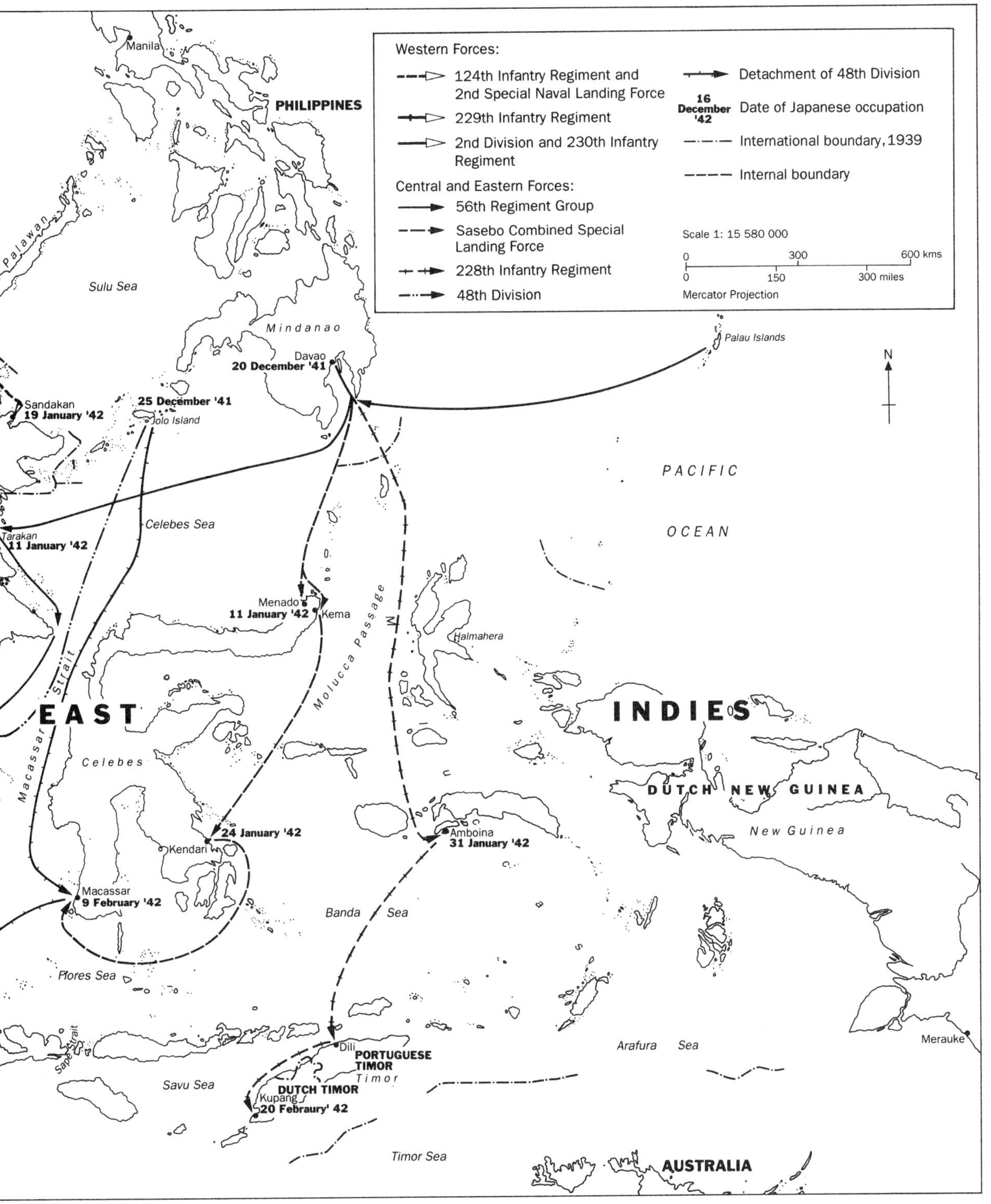

Western Forces:
124th Infantry Regiment and 2nd Special Naval Landing Force
229th Infantry Regiment
2nd Division and 230th Infantry Regiment
Central and Eastern Forces:
56th Regiment Group
Sasebo Combined Special Landing Force
228th Infantry Regiment
48th Division
Detachment of 48th Division
16 December '42 Date of Japanese occupation
International boundary, 1939
Internal boundary
Scale 1: 15 580 000
0 300 600 kms
0 150 300 miles
Mercator Projection
Manila
PHILIPPINES
Palawan
Sulu Sea
Mindanao
Davao
20 December '41
Palau Islands
N
Sandakan
19 January '42
25 December '41
Jolo Island
PACIFIC
OCEAN
Celebes Sea
Tarakan
11 January '42
Menado
11 January '42
Kema
Molucca Passage
Halmahera
Macassar Strait
EAST
INDIES
Celebes
DUTCH NEW GUINEA
New Guinea
24 January '42
Kendari
Amboina
31 January '42
Macassar
9 February '42
Banda Sea
Flores Sea
Sape Strait
Dili
PORTUGUESE TIMOR
Timor
DUTCH TIMOR
Kupang
20 Febraury' 42
Savu Sea
Arafura Sea
Merauke
Timor Sea
AUSTRALIA

gerents. It initially forbade US ships from entering war zones (as defined by the president), or from transporting arms, ammunition, or implements of war to a belligerent, but an amendment later in November allowed armed US merchant ships to sail through the war zone to the UK.

Roosevelt circumvented the Act at least twice: in May 1940 he suggested aircraft be flown to the USA's northern border, which were then pulled across the border into Canada (see also ATLANTIC FERRY ORGANIZATION), and in September 1940 he approved the *destroyers-for-bases agreement. Following the loss of personnel aboard the destroyer **Kearny* in October 1941, key sections of the Act were repealed.

Neutrality Patrol, operated by US Navy and air units. On 5 September 1939 Roosevelt ordered its formation to discourage any warlike activities in waters adjacent to *Western Hemisphere countries. His action was endorsed at the *Panama conference of the American republics later that month and enshrined in the Panama Act which it issued. Belligerents were warned not to conduct hostile operations within 480 km. (300 mi.) of the American continent, Canada and the colonies and possessions of European countries excepted. Though Hitler ordered his navy to avoid incidents in the zone, German warships soon entered it and the British government never admitted any restraint on its operations to pursue them. See also NEUTRALITY ACTS.

Newall, Marshal of the Royal Air Force Sir Cyril (1886–1963), British airman who, as an air chief marshal, served from 1937 to September 1940, as chief of the Air Staff and on the *Chiefs of Staff committee. He supported the government's decision not to bomb Germany during the *phoney war, as he saw no point in provoking retaliation before the RAF could fight on equal terms. He presided over the development of Fighter Command which, under *Dowding, was to win the battle of *Britain, having opposed its expansion in 1939 at the expense of Bomber Command. He was succeeded by *Portal, promoted, and then appointed governor-general of New Zealand, a post he held from 1941 to 1946 when he was created a baron. He was knighted in 1938.

New Britain campaign, fought during the *Pacific war on this island 500 km. (320 mi.) long in the Bismarck archipelago, which was part of the Australian mandate of New Guinea. The mandate's capital, *Rabaul, at the island's eastern end, was captured by Maj-General Horii Tomitaro's South Seas Force on 23 January 1942 and it became a major air and naval base for the Japanese South-East Area.

*MacArthur's offensive to capture Rabaul (CARTWHEEL) was launched in June 1943, but in August it was decided at the Quebec conference (see QUADRANT) to bypass it instead, and in December marine units of *Alamo Force landed at the western end of New Britain to develop air and naval bases to help neutralize it. After initially putting up stiff resistance the Japanese withdrew towards Rabaul and in the following months native patrols led by members of *Special Operations Australia waged a guerrilla war against their outposts. By November 1944, when 5th Australian Division relieved the American garrison, the Japanese were confined to the Gazelle peninsula at the eastern end of the island. Despite scanty air and sea support the Australians started a limited offensive which, when Japan surrendered in mid-August 1945, was found to have bottled up in Rabaul nearly 70,000 troops and 20,000 civilian workers.

New Caledonia, French colony, a Pacific island situated some 480 km. (300 mi.) south-south-east of the New Hebrides, opted for de *Gaulle and the Free French after the fall of *France in June 1940. In August 1940 a pro-*Vichy administration, backed by a French sloop, assumed control. But in September a pro-Gaullist *coup de force* succeeded and the French resident commissioner for the New Hebrides, Henri Sautot, was landed from the Australian cruiser *Adelaide*. Sautot then assumed control and the French sloop was persuaded to leave. During the *Pacific war the island's capital, Noumea, was used as a major US base.

Newfoundland, situated off the eastern coast of Canada and the UK's earliest colony. It was self-governing from 1855 until 1933, when the depression forced its government to step down in favour of British and local commissioners. Its strategic position during the battle of the *Atlantic made it a useful home for the *Newfoundland Escort Force and for bases granted to the USA under the *destroyers-for-bases agreement, while Gander airport was a valuable staging-point for transatlantic flights. Newfoundland remained a crown colony until 1949, when the population voted for confederation with Canada.

Newfoundland Escort Force, Canadian naval force which protected Allied *convoys during the battle of the *Atlantic. It was formed under Commodore *Murray in May 1941 when the British Admiralty requested the Royal Canadian Navy (RCN) to base warships at St John's, Newfoundland, to escort convoys from Newfoundland to a mid-ocean point south of Iceland. It initially comprised 7 Royal Navy (RN) and 6 RCN destroyers, 4 RN sloops, and 17 RCN and 4 RN corvettes, and by the end of that year 78% of the RCN's escort strength was gathered at St John's. It ceased to exist in February 1942 when all escorts became part of the new escort force, though the name was retained for local Newfoundland forces.

New Georgia campaign, fought during the *Pacific war on this group of islands situated in the central Solomons (see Map 83). US forces invaded them as part of an American offensive (CARTWHEEL) to isolate and neutralize *Rabaul, the main Japanese base in their South-East Area.

On 20 June 1943 a Raider battalion (see USA, 5(f)) landed at Segi Point on the main island, New Georgia, and during the next two weeks there were other landings by US Marines and 43rd US Division on Rendova and Vangunu islands, and on western New Georgia, to seize a Japanese airstrip at Munda point. Despite the US Navy's intervention, which resulted in the battles of *Kula Gulf and *Kolombangara, 4,000 reinforcements were successfully dispatched to the commander of the 10,500-strong Japanese garrison, Maj-General Sasaki Noboru. Most reinforced Munda, which became the focus of Japanese resistance, and their night infiltration tactics unnerved the inexperienced US troops. Non-battle casualties, caused by exhaustion and 'war neuroses' (see MEDICINE), increased alarmingly, and when the commander of 14th Corps, Maj-General Oscar Griswold, arrived on 11 July he reported the division was 'about to fold up'. The 37th US Division was brought in, Griswold replaced the worst affected units, and he then launched a corps attack on 25 July. Fierce fighting followed but by 1 August the Japanese, outnumbered and outgunned, had withdrawn inland. This time US Navy destroyers prevented more reinforcements reaching them when, on the night of 6/7 August, they sank three Japanese transports (battle of Vella Gulf).

Munda now became the base of Marine Corps squadrons which supported landings on *Vella Lavella on 15 August. These bypassed and isolated Sasaki's garrison now gathering on Kolombangara after further US reinforcements, elements of 25th US Division, had failed to destroy them on New Georgia. On 15 September Sasaki was ordered to withdraw. In a brilliantly organized evacuation 9,400 men out of the 12,500 on Kolombangara were rescued by landing craft, and the following month those on Vella Lavella were also evacuated.

The campaign proved costly for the Americans who had 1,094 killed and 3,873 wounded with thousands more becoming non-battle casualties. Excluding the fighting on Vella Lavella, 2,483 Japanese bodies were counted. Planned as a one-division operation, the Japanese garrison's 'skill, tenacity, and valor'—to quote the campaign's official US historian—eventually made it one where elements of four had to be used. 'The obstinate General Sasaki,' the same historian concludes, 'deserved his country's gratitude for his gallant and able conduct.'

New Guinea, island which lies north of Australia—the world's largest after Greenland—which was divided into Dutch New Guinea (part of the Netherlands East Indies), the Australian territory of Papua, and the Australian mandate of New Guinea. The Australian mandate comprised the island's north-east quarter and extended to the islands of *Bougainville, Buka, and the Bismarck archipelago which included *New Ireland, the *Admiralty Islands, and *New Britain—at the eastern end of which was the mandate's capital, *Rabaul—and all these were occupied by the Japanese, as was part of the island's northern coastline. In early 1944 an indigenous unit, 1st New Guinea Battalion, was formed in the mandate, and in October this became part of a new Australian Army unit, the Pacific Islands Regiment, which was quickly expanded by the addition of three more New Guinea battalions. These, and the indigenous New Guinea Constabulary, took an active part in the *New Guinea campaign.

New Guinea campaign. This was fought during the *Pacific war on this rugged, jungle-clad, malaria-ridden island, firstly in the Australian territory of Papua, then in the Australian mandated territory of New Guinea, and lastly in Dutch New Guinea (see Map 72). Of great aid to the Allies in one of the fiercest and most unrelenting campaigns of the war were the Papuans and New Guineans who not only formed volunteer infantry battalions (see previous entry), but performed miracles in bringing up supplies, evacuating the wounded, and helping with reconnaissance and intelligence missions.

The campaign started on 8 March 1942 when the Japanese landed two battalions at Lae and Salamaua on New Guinea's Huon Gulf as part of the forces to be deployed to take Papua's capital, Port Moresby, situated on the island's south-western coastline. This gave them control of the Dampier and Vitiaz Straits, and in April they put troops ashore at nine other points. Their seaborne assault on Port Moresby was frustrated by the battle of the *Coral Sea, but as most of the Australian Army was fighting in the *Western Desert campaigns, or had been captured after the fall of *Singapore or in the *Netherlands East Indies, there were only two small Australian forces—one at Kokoda, the other (Kanga Force) at Wau—to oppose an overland advance on the capital by the Japanese from Lae and Salamaua.

However, the battle of *Midway in June 1942 decisively shifted the balance of Pacific naval power towards the USA, and on 2 July the US *Joint Chiefs of Staff directed *MacArthur, the commander of the *South-West Pacific Area, to start a limited offensive to clear the Japanese from the island. As a first move to recapture Lae and Salamaua, MacArthur ordered his small forces across the Owen Stanley range to Papua's northern coast. But the Japanese pre-empted him when, on 12 July 1942, Maj-General Horii Tomitaro's South Seas Detachment landed there to advance on Port Moresby via the *Kokoda trail. This soon drove back the Australian militia battalion sent to reinforce the Papuan Infantry Regiment defending Kokoda, and by 14 August Horii's men were at Isurava with more reinforcements being regularly poured into the Japanese beachhead.

By mid-August two extra Australian battalions were on the Kokoda trail, but neither MacArthur nor his Allied

Australian troops and local guides moving out on patrol in the Huon Peninsula during the **New Guinea campaign**, 15 November 1943.

Land Force Commander, General *Blamey, was aware of the terrible conditions confronting their troops. Overloaded with equipment they staggered up muddy, near-vertical tracks; and air drops, on which they depended, often failed to materialize. As they reached Isurava, Horii, who was having supply difficulties himself, took personal control of the Japanese advance and drove the Australians back, harassing them all the way with ambushes and outflanking movements. Many Australians who were driven off the trail by these tactics simply died in the jungle; and soaked by rain, burdened by their wounded, and worn out by lack of food and by the constant fighting, the rest retreated to Ioribaiwa.

On 30 August MacArthur, concerned not only by events on the Kokoda trail but by the pressure being exerted on Kanga Force around Wau, and by a Japanese landing at Milne Bay on the south-eastern tip of Papua, told the Joint Chiefs of Staff that unless 'moves are made to meet the changing conditions a disastrous outcome is bound to result shortly; it is no longer a question here of preparing a projected offensive...'

But *ULTRA intelligence had disclosed the presence of a Japanese submarine screen off Milne Bay—which indicated that the Japanese intended landing in the area—and this enabled Allied reinforcements (18th Australian Brigade) to be sent to the bay. As a result the 2,000 Japanese of the Special Naval Landing Forces who landed there on the night of 25/26 August 1942 were heavily outnumbered. The troops, a second prong of the Japanese advance on Port Moresby, were reinforced by another 600 on 29 August, but the Australian garrison—aided by US engineers and by two Australian squadrons flying from airstrips built by them—held them off. The Japanese fought bravely but were eventually forced to withdraw, and only 1,200 survived to start re-embarking on 4 September.

However, on the Kokoda trail it looked as if MacArthur might be right. Though the Australians at Ioribaiwa were again reinforced, on 17 September they were forced back to a final defensive position at Imita Ridge. That day MacArthur told *Curtin, the Australian prime minister, that he had lost confidence in Australian troops and recommended that Blamey take personal control in New Guinea. This Blamey did, precipitating a major command crisis with Lt-General Sydney Powell, the Australian commander there, which resulted in Powell's dismissal.

But by then the worst of the crisis was past. For Horii, his hopelessly over-extended supply line now under constant air attack from Lt-General George C. Kenney's Fifth USAAF, had been ordered to withdraw to the Japanese beachhead to conserve supplies and reinforcements required for a final Japanese effort in the *Guadalcanal campaign. Supplies were so short that the Japanese resorted to cannibalism, eating the flesh of prisoners and their own troops. This was a campaign so fiercely fought that few prisoners were taken and fewer survived capture.

The collapse of the Japanese offensive enabled MacArthur to mount his own on their beachhead in northern Papua, now protected by a strongly fortified 18 km. (11 mi.) perimeter. In October 1942 two regiments of 32nd US Division were airlifted or brought by sea to the Wanigela-Pongani area. On 19 November they attacked *Buna and Cape Endaiadere while the Australians, having routed the Japanese on the Kokoda trail, advanced on *Gona and Sananda Point. But the US troops were inadequately equipped and trained and the Australians were exhausted by the fighting on the trail. Both sides suffered from disease, and lack of food and *matériel*, and casualties increased alarmingly in a battle of attrition that amounted to a stalemate. The Australians eventually captured Gona on 8 December 1942 and after a crisis in command which needed the personal attention of the corps commander, Lt-General *Eichelberger, the Americans entered Buna village on 14 December and then, on 2 January, took Buna mission. But it took a further three weeks for the combined forces of the Americans and Australians to eradicate the final Japanese positions at Sananda Point.

About 20,000 Japanese had been involved in this first phase of the New Guinea campaign: probably 12,000 of them were killed or died of starvation or disease. Allied losses were heavy, too: 2,165 Australian and 930 US servicemen were killed, but malaria—the Australians recorded 9,249 cases, the Americans 8,659—caused the most casualties (see MEDICINE). The 32nd US Division was so depleted that retraining and rehabilitation kept it from operational duties for almost a year.

The fighting now shifted north-westwards along the coast and into the Australian mandated territory of New Guinea where the Japanese garrisons at Lae and Salamaua were reinforced in early January 1943 by elements of Lt-General Adachi Hatazo's Eighteenth Army. As a preliminary to another overland advance on Port Moresby, 2,500 Japanese troops were dispatched into the Bululo valley to destroy Kanga Force and capture Wau airstrip. Heavy fighting followed and the Japanese were only thwarted when part of an Australian brigade was flown into Wau airstrip under fire, and fighting in the stench, mud, rottenness, and gloom of the jungle had, by the end of February, driven them back to Mubo.

But having been by now defeated on Guadalcanal the Japanese were determined to hold New Guinea. During the next months the balance of Adachi's army began to be landed along the coast and the Fourth Air Army was created to control an equal expansion of Japanese air power in the area. Despite losing part of his 51st Division in the *Bismarck Sea battle in March, Adachi's build-up continued. He moved his HQ to Lae and by April this controlled 20th Division at Wewak, 41st Division at Madang, and the remaining two regiments of 51st Division in the Huon peninsula, and at Lae and Salamaua.

To oppose these new Japanese forces in the New Guinea mandate, and those in the South-West Pacific Area as a whole, MacArthur regrouped his forces into two main bodies: *Alamo Force, which contained mostly US troops, and the Australians of New Guinea Force. With these, on 29 June 1943, he launched an operation (CARTWHEEL), of which the New Guinea campaign formed a part, to isolate and reduce the main Japanese base of *Rabaul at the eastern end of New Britain.

The increase in Japanese *air power posed a threat to these plans and Fourth Air Army, short of airstrips, concentrated two of its air divisions at Wewak—well beyond the range of Kenney's fighters, with which his bombers must operate or suffer unacceptable losses. But, alerted by ULTRA intelligence to the Japanese build-up, Kenney secretly constructed a forward airstrip 95 km. (60 mi.) west of Lae. It was eventually detected by Japanese *photographic reconnaissance, but too late to prevent nearly 200 US aircraft being launched against Wewak's four airstrips on 17 August 1943. Even at that late date the Japanese had no *radar operating at Wewak and the telephone lines of the air intelligence unit, which spotted Kenney's bombers over Hansa Bay, failed to operate. The result was total surprise and the raid, and another the next day, left only 38 Japanese aircraft operational and three of the four strips out of action.

This devastating operation allowed Allied ground operations on New Guinea to proceed almost unchallenged from the air. Three Australian divisions (3rd, 5th, and 11th), the 41st US Division, and a number of Australian Independent Companies (see AUSTRALIA, 5(e)), started an all-out offensive to defeat Adachi and capture the airstrips needed to attack Rabaul and to support MacArthur's final drive on the Philippines. A successful Allied feint drew Japanese reinforcements from Lae to Salamaua. The 9th Australian Division then made an amphibious landing east of Lae while the 7th Australian Division (which had been airlifted to Nadzab after the airstrip there had been secured by US paratroopers on 5 September) advanced from the north. By 16 September 1943 both Japanese strongholds had been overrun, though about 7,800 Japanese escaped by marching across the mountainous Huon peninsula to Sio.

On 4 October 7th Division, now advancing up the Markham Valley, captured Dumpu, and another amphibious landing by Australian troops enabled Finschhafen to be seized in early October. But severe fighting continued in the Huon peninsula with the 20th Japanese Division fiercely defending the area around

New Guinea campaign

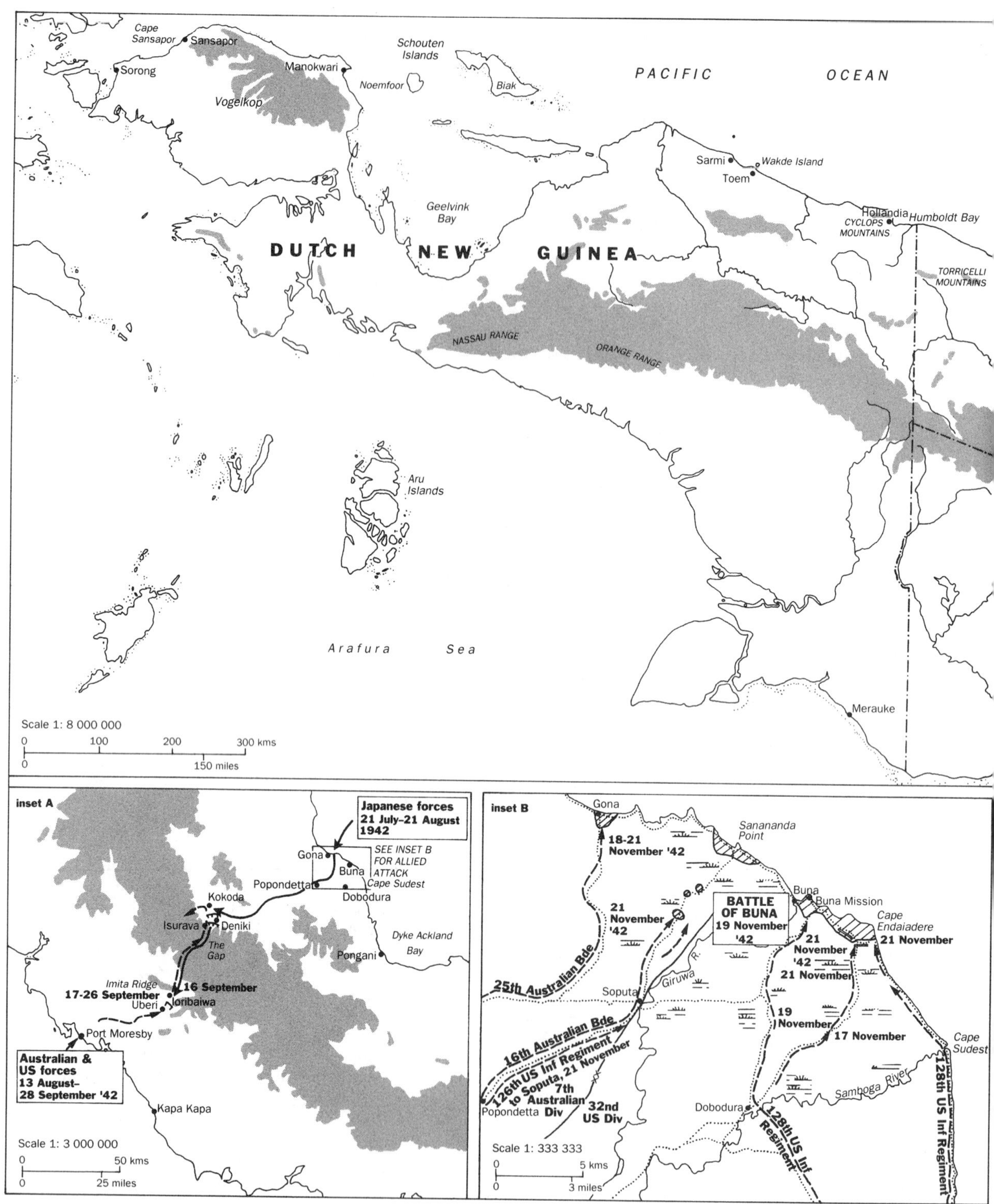

72. **New Guinea campaign**, 1942–5

New Guinea campaign

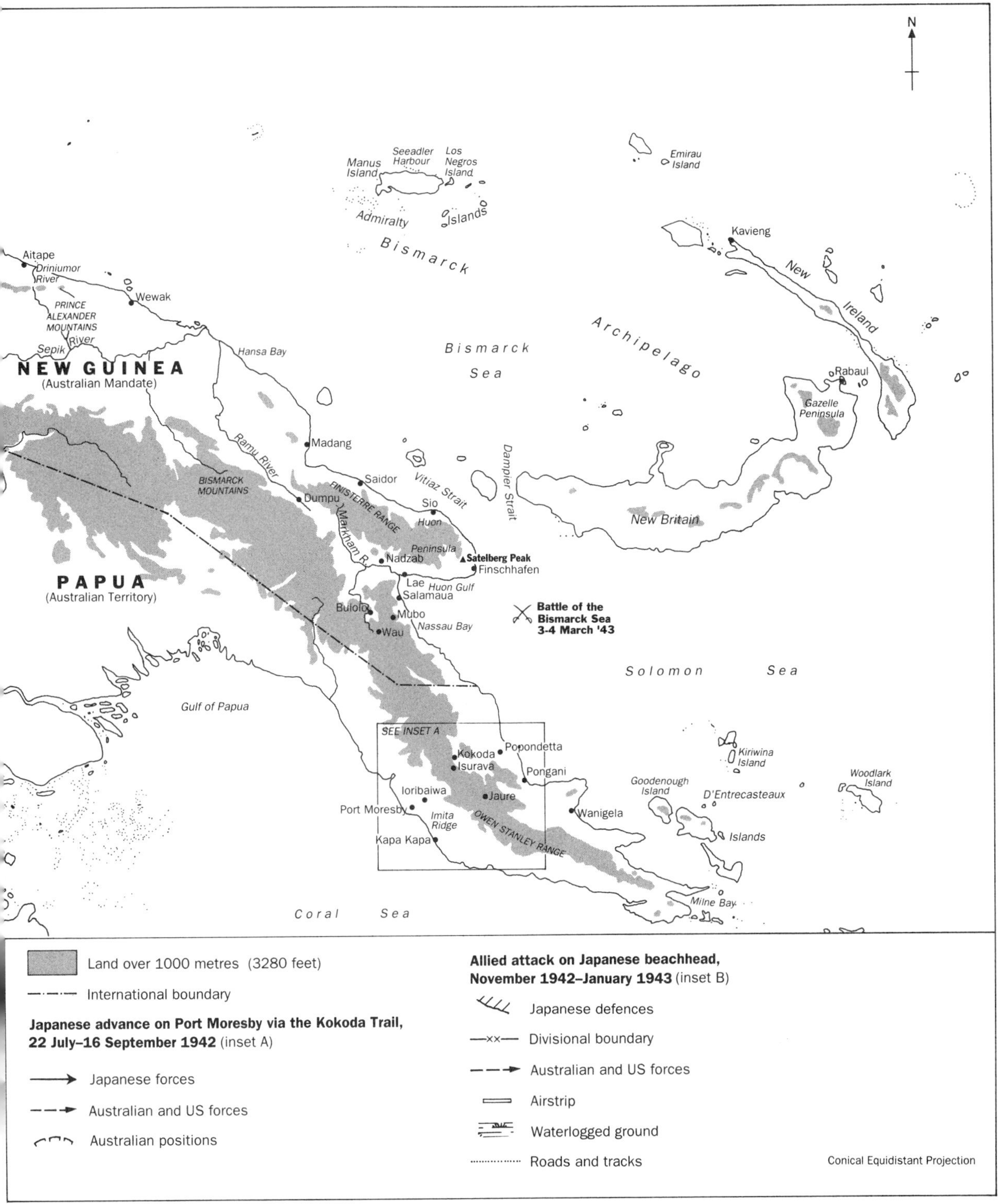

Sattelberg peak. This was not cleared until 8 December 1943 and it took most of that month to clear the peninsula's tip. Then, on 2 January 1944, 32nd US Division, now part of Alamo Force, landed at Saidor, 112 km. (70 mi.) west of Sio, but they failed to cut off the retreating Japanese 20th and 51st Divisions being pursued by the Australians. The 7th Division, advancing along the Ramu valley, also failed when their thrust to the coast was halted by Japanese defending the Finisterre mountains; and it was not until US troops landed further to the west at *Hollandia and Aitape on 22 April 1944 that Adachi's escape route was cut. These landings were the result of ULTRA's greatest contribution to the Allied campaign on New Guinea, for it revealed where Adachi had concentrated his forces, so that MacArthur could bypass and outflank them.

In March 1944 control of Adachi's army passed from Eighth Area Army at Rabaul to Lt-General *Anami's Second Area Army, elements of which had been recently transported to Dutch New Guinea. To deal with these, 41st US Division landed on Wakde and *Biak islands in May and, aided by 6th US Division, had, by 25 June, captured Wakde, and Sarmi on the mainland. In early July another island, Noemfoor, was seized and by the end of the month 6th Division had taken Sansapor on the Vogelkop peninsula, the last Allied landings of the campaign.

To free US troops for the invasion of the Philippines, in October 1944 the Australians began to assume responsibility for all operations on the islands of Bougainville, New Britain, and New Guinea. Eichelberger's troops around Aitape, having virtually destroyed the Eighteenth Army's offensive capabilities when Adachi attacked their perimeter on the Driniumor river in July 1944, were replaced by 6th Australian Division. Supported by an Australian wing of fighter-bombers this attacked along the coast towards Wewak, where Adachi had his HQ, and through the precipitous Torricelli mountains, but by the time Wewak fell on 10 May 1945 the Japanese had already begun withdrawing into the Prince Alexander ranges for a final stand. They were still resisting when the war ended and only 13,500 survived to surrender.

New Hebrides, group of Pacific islands under joint Anglo-French administration during the war, situated west of Fiji and some 480 km. (300 mi.) north-north-east of New Caledonia. They include Espiritu Santo which was used as a major US base during the *Pacific war. In June 1940 the French resident commissioner, Henri Sautot, declared for de *Gaulle and the Free French.

New Ireland, one of the Bismarck archipelago islands and part of the Australian mandated territory of New Guinea. Its capital Kavieng, was only defended by an Australian Independent Company (see AUSTRALIA, 5(e)) when the Japanese landed there on 23 January 1942. It was quickly overrun and Kavieng became an important Japanese base with the island being garrisoned by about 11,000 troops. For this reason it was, like *Rabaul, bypassed during *MacArthur's advance northwards, and Emirau island and *Hollandia were occupied instead. The garrison surrendered at the end of the war. See also PACIFIC WAR.

New Order, see GERMANY, 4; see also GREATER EAST ASIA CO-PROSPERITY SPHERE.

NEW ZEALAND

1. Introduction

Although a small farming country, far from the major battle theatres, New Zealand's contribution to the war was unmatched, proportionately, by any other part of the British Empire. Of its population of 1,630,000 (including 90,000 Maoris) a greater proportion were killed than in any other part of the empire. Its war expenditure by 1943 equalled the UK's as a proportion of national income. Even more important than the provision of military manpower was New Zealand's production of meat, butter, and cheese to feed the UK and, from 1942, US forces in the South Pacific. So great was the strain imposed on this small population by the twin demands of the forces and food production that by January 1944 the prime minister, Peter *Fraser, had to inform Churchill that 'New Zealand has reached the end of its resources of manpower.'

As a self-governing Dominion within the British Empire, New Zealand was not technically a sovereign state in 1939. But shortly before midnight on 3 September 1939 the cabinet made its independent decision to associate New Zealand with the UK's declaration of war upon Germany. Two days later Michael Joseph Savage (1872–1940), then prime minister, affirmed in a broadcast his country's support for the UK: 'Where she goes, we go, where she stands, we stand.' Nevertheless, there was a sombre mood in the land. Many families had lost sons in the *First World War, and the first Labour government (1935–49) had placed great faith in collective security through the *League of Nations. Yet although it was anti-imperialist and anti-militarist in sentiment and enthused by internationalist socialist idealism, it had not neglected defence preparations. Conscious of the country's inability to defend itself it still subscribed to the concept of imperial defence. Its two-cruiser navy was organized as a division of the Royal Navy; the army was based upon providing an expeditionary force of an infantry division and a mounted rifle brigade with a division for home defence; and the air force was based on two long-range bomber squadrons and a scheme of pilot training for the RAF. All three services were trained to operate with British Commonwealth forces. For security in the Pacific reliance was placed on the deterrent power of the British fleet, and New Zealand had contributed £1 million towards the building of the Singapore naval base to facilitate fleet operations in the Pacific when needed.

In 1939 New Zealand was not directly threatened by the war but, because of its economic, cultural, and personal ties, it could not contemplate a world in which the UK lost is pre-eminence both as a market and as a political focus. This involvement sharpened in mid-1940 with the fall of *France, Italy's entry into the war, and Churchill's statement that the fleet could not be sent to the Pacific in the foreseeable future. The outbreak of the *Pacific war in December 1941 induced New Zealand's most urgent phase of preparedness, peaking in the second half of 1942.

2. Domestic life, economy, and war effort

Economically New Zealand had developed as the UK's outlying farm. Its wealth was based on a narrow range of pastoral products—wool, meat, butter, and cheese—which made up over 80% of the value of its export earnings. Before the war, 97% of its food exports went to the UK, which purchased from New Zealand over half its imports of cheese and a quarter of its butter imports. Within two weeks of the outbreak of war the British government contracted for the bulk purchase of all New Zealand's exportable surplus of meat, dairy produce, and wool. In 1942 a second large customer appeared. The US Joint Purchasing Board took a quarter of the export surplus of meat (especially beef) for American forces in the South Pacific. Because of this rising overseas demand for food, domestic rationing of butter began in 1943 followed by meat in 1944. Food production had also to compete for manpower with the armed services. For the 1941–2 harvest season 10,000 troops were assigned to work on farms; in 1943 the Home Defence Forces had to give up 16,000 men, and in 1944 over 9,000 men were released from the army's 3rd Division for civil work, half of whom went to farms. Increases in farm production were achieved through growing mechanization. The number of tractors in the country rose from 9,600 in 1939 to 18,900 by 1946, 11,000 of which had been supplied by the USA under *Lend-Lease. Soon after the end of the war the air force began experiments with aerial top dressing.

There was also a rise in manufacturing, notably shipbuilding. More than 500 vessels were produced, including 13 minesweepers and 12 anti-submarine patrol boats for the navy, 27 fuelling barges and launches for the air force, and more than 300 tug boats, barges, and minor craft for US forces. A surplus of war supplies, including Bren gun carriers, 2-in. mortars and mortar bombs, hand grenades and small arms ammunition, were exported, chiefly to Eastern Group Supply Council, in India.

Apart from having mines laid off some of its ports by *auxiliary cruisers, New Zealand never came under attack, but the war placed major strains on its people as the demands of military mobilization and food production increased. By mid-1942 there were 20,000 US marines in the North Island, preparing for the *Guadalcanal campaign. The presence of the well-paid, friendly, and courteous newcomers was a source of delight to local girls who, by the end of the war, had provided 1,396 *GI brides. Less happily, there were occasional brawls between marines and Maoris.

The Labour government had always said it would conscript wealth before people. Nine days after war was declared voluntary enlistment began for an infantry division which was offered to the UK on 21 November 1939 for service in a vital theatre. But in June 1940 the government took emergency powers to conscript men and over the next five years 306,000 were called up. At the peak of mobilization in September 1942 there were 157,000 in the armed services (of whom 50,000 were serving overseas). This represented half of all males in the 18 to 45 age group and 30% of the normal male work force (see Table 1). At the request of Maori leaders an infantry battalion of Maoris was raised, which fought with distinction with *Freyberg's New Zealand division in the *Balkan campaign, on *Crete, and in the *Western Desert, *North African, and *Italian campaigns. The Maori War Effort Organization, which worked through tribal committees to secure recruits, also took part in valuable social welfare work. Civilian jobs were filled, at first, from a pool of 19,000 unemployed, a legacy of the depression, but by 1942 unemployment was down to only 2,000 and as the demands for military manpower grew the government had to designate certain essential occupations. Direction of labour was introduced and by the end of the war 176,000 has been 'manpowered' into essential work with surprisingly little friction. As the danger declined in the Pacific in the second half of 1942, men were gradually released from military service to work on production. In 1944 the army's 3rd Division, which fought briefly in the Pacific, was disbanded for the same reason.

Apart from those who served in the armed forces (see below), there was an upsurge in the employment of *women in 1942–3, including 35,000 in war manufacturing. Thousands of women also worked in voluntary

New Zealand Table 1: New Zealanders serving in the armed forces, 1939–46

Date	*Total men*	*Estimated per cent of workforce*	*Total including women*	*Total serving overseas*
1939				
Sep	2,570	0.5	2,570	463
Nov	4,081	1	4,081	609
1940				
Feb	12,339	2	12,339	7,649
Aug	43,253	8	43,253	15,392
1941				
Feb	70,704	14	70,705	33,583
Aug	75,168	15	75,755	43,274
1942				
Feb	123,910	24	125,391	48,846
Sep	153,587	30	157,000 (peak)	50,000
1943				
Feb	140,730	27	146,953	60,523
Nov	127,879	25	136,067	70,291 (peak)
1944				
Feb	118,033	23	126,102	69,246
Aug	103,372	20	110,578	55,710
1945				
Feb	91,131	18	97,047	55,500
Aug	84,238	16	89,320	51,889
1946				
Feb	24,294	5	26,499	8,052

Source: Baker, J. V. T., *The New Zealand People at War: War Economy* (Wellington, 1965), pp. 589–90.

organizations co-ordinated by the Women's War Service Auxiliary. The numbers peaked at 75,000 in 1942, mainly in canteens, hospitals, and transport, and there was also a Women's Land Service for farm work. These new opportunities for female employment ended with the war.

The demand for goods and services, as well as severe shortages of imported materials provoked real fears of inflation. One major economic achievement of the war was the government's stabilization policy. After the Court of Arbitration awarded a 5% wage increase in 1940, an Economic Stabilization Conference was called to find ways of fixing costs, wages, and prices so that the war would not allow any one group to benefit at the cost of any other. In August 1941 the prices of 38 essential items—food, clothing, power, and tram fares—were stabilized and on 15 December 1942 a comprehensive scheme was announced. Prices of 110 items, all wages and salaries, and transport rates were pegged at the 15 December 1942 level. Rents were stabilized at the 1 September 1942 level. Increases in incomes were to be tied to a Wartime Prices Index. No increase was permissible until the index went up 2.5%. It did not rise above 1% until 1947, but prices were only held during the war by a variety of interventions such as subsidies, standardization, simplification, and cross-subsidy from non-listed items. By 1945–6 subsidies were equivalent to 2.5% of national income.

War finance proved another wartime economic success. Having been given hard terms by British bankers during the depression, the Labour government determined to finance the war from taxes and internal borrowing. A War Expenses Account was established to isolate war costs. Out of a total war expenditure of £699 million, £476 went on the armed forces (see Table 2). At the peak of the war effort in 1942–4 it cost the equivalent of two-fifths of the country's output. Defence expenditure increased more than 50 times between 1939 and 1944. In 1943 it took 53% of national income. Of war revenues totalling £681 million, £295 million came from loans in New Zealand, £225 million from taxes, and £104 million from Lend-Lease. The country incurred no outstanding overseas debt as a result of the war. Indeed, total indebtedness declined by £45 million over the six years. From a purely bookkeeping point of view, the war achievement has been rated 'admirable, a bargain' (see Taylor [below], p. 1287).

3. Government

Politically, New Zealand was a parliamentary democracy, owing allegiance to the British Crown (represented by a governor-general), but wholly self-governing. Although the Dominion did not become, constitutionally, a sovereign state until the adoption of the Statute of Westminster in 1947, the Crown was advised in all executive matters by a ministry, responsible to the General Assembly made up of the governor-general, the nominated upper house (the Legislative Council) and the lower house (the House of Representatives) elected by all adults aged 21 and over. Elections were normally held triennially and a ministry could only retain power if it had a majority in the house. Party politics were not suspended during the war and there was never an effective all-party coalition as in the UK. The election due in 1941 was, however, postponed until 1943. Throughout the war the first Labour government retained office, led by Michael Joseph Savage until his death in 1940 and thereafter by Peter Fraser, who is still regarded as one of New Zealand's greatest statesmen.

A war cabinet was formed on 16 July 1940, consisting of the prime minister, the minister of finance (Walter Nash), the minister of defence (Fred Jones), the minister of supply and munitions (Dan Sullivan), and two members of the opposition National Party, its leader Adam Hamilton (as minister in charge of war expenditure) and a former prime minister, Gordon Coates (as minister for armed forces and war co-ordination).

New Zealand, Table 2: New Zealand's war finances, 1939–46

	£000s
Expenditure	
Navy	37,086
Army	294,334
Air Force	145,218
Civil (chiefly subsidies)	34,130
Other (including reverse Lend-Lease)	158,756
TOTAL	669,524
Revenue	
Loans	295,402
War Taxes	225,014
Transfers from Consolidated Fund	26,586
Disposal of assets	14,749
Lend-Lease	104,569
Canadian mutual aid	6,103
Miscellaneous	7,609
Rehabilitation receipts	521
Aeroplane fund	163
Fijian Government	169
Profits from Marketing Pool	377
TOTAL	681,262

Source: Baker, *War Economy*, pp. 254–5.

During the most critical phase of the Pacific war, in June 1942, a coalition arrangement was finally attempted. A war administration was created, consisting of seven government and six opposition members. The war cabinet became its executive arm and included the new leader of the opposition, Sidney Holland, as deputy chairman. The arrangement lasted only three months: when opposition members disapproved of the prime minister's handling of a coal miners' strike they withdrew from the war administration. However, Hamilton and Coates put country before party and remained in the war cabinet. In the general election on 25 September 1943 the government lost a few seats but retained a comfortable majority in parliament.

The war induced the opening of New Zealand's first diplomatic relations with foreign powers. Previously, the sole political representative overseas was the high commissioner in London, who had doubled as representative to the League of Nations, and there were consular offices in Sydney, Melbourne, Los Angeles, and New York. After Churchill's statement on 13 June 1940, that the UK could not contemplate sending the fleet to Singapore and that, if Japan took advantage of the European war to strike in the Pacific, the Dominions would have to look to the USA for protection, New Zealand sought diplomatic representation in Washington. A legation was established in 1942 and Walter Nash, minister of finance, became the first incumbent. High commissioners were appointed to Ottawa in 1942 and Canberra in 1943. The first post in a non-English-speaking country was the legation opened in Moscow in 1944. Ever since the late 19th century New Zealand had enjoyed a voice in empire and, thereby, world affairs. From 1941 the main task of diplomacy was to achieve a voice in Washington, where the *Combined Chiefs of Staff became the centre of strategic planning.

4. Armed forces

Although New Zealand turned to the USA as its main protector from 1941, its military co-operation with the UK was not diminished. The largest part of the armed forces continued to serve with British formations, but from 1943 elements of all three services also served under American command in the South Pacific. Balancing contributions to the European and Pacific theatres provided the war's most taxing dilemma.

(a) Army

The army expeditionary force (2nd NZEF) always presented the most formidable demand for manpower. The New Zealand Division (designated 2nd Division from June 1942) represented, as a proportion of the Dominion's population, the equivalent of 25 British divisions. Commanded by Major-General Freyberg, who had been brought up in New Zealand but had served in the British Army, it had the status of a national force by the terms of the general's letter of instructions of 1940. Freyberg was instructed to act under the orders of the theatre C-in-C 'subject only to the requirements of His Majesty's government in New Zealand'. It took eighteen months for 2nd Division to become fully formed. The first echelon (4th Brigade) reached Egypt on 12 February 1940, followed by 6th Brigade on 27 October.

Divisional Signals, the New Zealand Engineers' railway and water supply companies, and the service corps transport units all took part in *O'Connor's Western Desert campaign in December 1940 and January 1941. The second echelon (5th Brigade) was diverted to the UK, where it became part of the covering force in the defence of South-East England facing an anticipated German invasion in the second half of 1940 (see SEALION). After this period of scattered deployment the division finally came together and the next eighteen months, from March 1941 to September 1942, were a time of costly fighting to create the battle-hardened division, which then became part of the spearhead of *Montgomery's Eighth Army. In the disasters in Greece (see BALKAN CAMPAIGN) and Crete and the attempted relief of *Tobruk the division incurred more than 10,000 casualties. During the fighting in the Western Desert in mid-1942 the division's strength was reduced from 20,000 to 13,000 in a month. But from the second battle of *El Alamein in October 1942 to the capture of Tunis seven months later, 2nd Division took part in a series of decisive operations. Thereafter New Zealand's increasing role in the Pacific cast doubts on 2nd Division's future employment in the battle for the *Mediterranean. During 1941 the Women's Army Auxiliary Corps was formed and by July 1943 its numbers totalled 4,600.

New Zealand had taken over certain British

responsibilities in the Pacific Islands. An infantry company had been sent to Fanning Island (the cable station halfway between Hawaii and the Cook Islands) in 1939. A brigade group, known as B Force, went to garrison Fiji in 1940 and at the outbreak of the Pacific war this force was augmented with a second brigade. With a divisional headquarters it became the Second New Zealand Expeditionary Force in the Pacific and was designated 3rd Division from May 1942. With these growing responsibilities close to home, Fraser warned Freyberg early in 1942 that New Zealand might have to follow the Australian example and withdraw from the Mediterranean to concentrate on the South Pacific. But a decision was delayed when the USA took responsibility for Fanning, Fiji, and Tonga and 3rd Division was brought home to New Zealand for training in *amphibious warfare. In June 1942 the American C-in-C *South Pacific Area, Admiral *Halsey, set up his headquarters in Auckland and the 1st US Marine Division arrived in New Zealand. For two years there were 20,000 American troops stationed in New Zealand, while 50,000 New Zealanders served overseas. When the American forces began to wrest the Solomon Islands from Japan, beginning with their assault on Guadalcanal in August 1942, Royal New Zealand Air Force (RNZAF) squadrons were sent in support and 3rd Division became the garrison for New Caledonia. Garrisons were also provided for Norfolk Island and Tonga.

Following the second battle of *El Alamein and the Allied landings in North Africa (TORCH) Fraser asked in November 1942 for the return of 2nd Division but was persuaded by Churchill and Roosevelt that this would be disruptive to shipping. In April 1943 when the British sought to train the division for the proposed *Sicilian campaign Fraser withheld consent and took the question of future deployment to a secret session of parliament in May. Here it was agreed that 2nd Division would remain in the Mediterranean, but that 6,000 long-service troops would have home leave and no reinforcements would be made available for the rest of the year, and that 3rd Division (reduced in size) would stay in the Pacific. Thus 2nd Division fought in the Italian campaign from October 1943 until it was involved in the occupation of *Trieste in May 1945. Meanwhile, in the Pacific, 3rd Division (reduced to two brigades) joined the Americans in the Solomon Islands and its units were used separately in three operations: 14th Brigade relieved US units on Vella Lavella in September 1943 and cleared the Japanese from that island; 8th Brigade landed in the Treasury Islands in October 1943; and 14th Brigade captured Nissan, in the Green Islands, in February 1944, the last two operations being commanded by Maj-General H. E. Barraclough, the divisional commander. At this point, New Zealand's severe manpower problem forced a review of priorities. The matter was put to the Combined Chiefs of Staff in Washington, and after the Quebec conference in September 1944 (see OCTAGON) it was decided to leave a reduced 2nd Division in Italy, disband 3rd Division, and use its men for reinforcements and for domestic production.

(b) Navy

The New Zealand Division of the RN (consisting of the light cruisers *Leander* and *Achilles*, two British escort vessels, and one mine-sweeping trawler) came under Admiralty control on the outbreak of war. *Achilles* played a notable part in the action with the *Admiral Graf Spee* in the battle of the *River Plate in December 1939, *Leander* sank the Italian auxiliary cruiser, *Ramb I* in the Indian Ocean in February 1941 and for several months joined the British Mediterranean Fleet. In September 1941 the Division became the Royal New Zealand Navy (RNZN), which also contained a New Zealand section of the Women's Royal Naval Service whose numbers, by October 1944, totalled 500. The RNZN retained its two 6 in. (15 cm.) cruisers throughout the war but was augmented in strength by 2 corvettes, 16 mine sweepers, 12 anti-submarine patrol boats, and more than 100 harbour defence launches and other minor craft. In naval engagements off the Solomon Islands in 1943 both cruisers were badly damaged, one minesweeper was sunk, and another dented by ramming a Japanese submarine. The cruisers *Achilles* and *Gambia* and the corvette *Arbutus* joined the British Pacific Fleet (see TASK FORCE 57) in operations off Japan in 1945. See also ANZAC AREA.

(c) Air Force

Even more widespread than the army and naval contributions were those of the RNZAF. Apart from manning two reconnaissance squadrons in New Zealand and two in Fiji, the air force's main contribution in the early years of the war was to provide trained air crew for the RAF (see BRITISH EMPIRE AIR TRAINING SCHEME). More than 500 New Zealanders were serving in the RAF in 1939 and crews which were in the UK taking delivery of Wellington bombers formed the nucleus of 75th Squadron, the first Dominion squadron. By the end of the war more than 10,000 New Zealanders were serving in the RAF, either scattered throughout British units or concentrated in seven specifically New Zealand squadrons, six stationed in the UK and one in West Africa. For the defence of Malaya in 1941, the RNZAF sent an airfield construction unit and the pilots for an RAF fighter squadron. But it was in the Pacific that the air force reached its greatest strength. New Zealand squadrons covered operations in the Solomons, staying on after the withdrawal of 3rd Division in 1944 and seven air squadrons and a squadron of radar units operated in the garrison area around Guadalcanal, the New Hebrides, and Fiji. A five-squadron task force operated in the battles for the northern Solomons and early in 1945 there was a ring of four New Zealand air bases surrounding the Japanese base of *Rabaul. Of the RNZAF's total wartime strength of 45,000, one-third served in the Pacific. On the carriers of the British Pacific fleet a quarter of the pilots were New Zealanders. The air force was the first to recruit women into its ranks when the

New Zealand, Table 3: New Zealand casualties, 1939–45

	Deaths	Wounded	Prisoners	Interned	Total
Army	6,839	15,324	7,863		30,026
Navy	573	170	54	3	800
Air Force	4,149	255	552	23	4,979
Merchant Navy	110			123	233
TOTAL	11,671	15,749	8,469	149	36,038

Source: Kay, R., (ed.), *Chronology: New Zealand in the War, 1939–1946* (Wellington, 1968).

Women's Auxiliary Air Force was formed in January 1941, and by August 1943 this had reached a peak of 4,000.

New Zealand's total war casualties—killed, wounded, or taken prisoner—amounted to 36,038 (see Table 3). Of these 11,671 were killed, which represented 6,684 per million of the country's population compared with 5,123 for the UK and 3,232 for Australia. The army lost 6,839 killed and the air force 4,149 including those who died in service with the RAF. Of the 573 naval losses, the largest proportion were sailors serving in the RN. Few families in New Zealand were unaffected.

5. Culture

The isolation, austerity, and boredom induced by war gave some encouragement to cultural developments, which also received a major fillip from the Centennial in 1940 and the arrival of refugees from Europe. As well as a major exposition celebrating the growth of the country's economy and institutions, a centennial orchestra was created, which toured the country. Many new books were published locally, including government-sponsored centennial volumes. There was a retrospective exhibition of New Zealand art. During the war musical life continued to be centred on choirs and chamber music groups in the four main cities and the National Broadcasting Service's string orchestra. Lunchtime concerts, starting in Auckland, were a success, but brass bands and pipe bands represented the most popular musical expression and both flourished. No fewer than 25 bands accompanied the 2nd NZEF, and the RNZAF Band achieved a high reputation. These developments led to the founding of a national orchestra in 1946.

New Zealand writers had become fascinated by problems of national identity in the 1930s and received encouragement after 1934 from the radical fortnightly *Tomorrow* until it was suppressed under wartime emergency regulations in 1940. The *New Zealand Listener*, founded in 1939 to publicize radio programmes, also provided a large readership for poetry and short stories. The Caxton Press, in Christchurch, continued to publish the poetry of Denis Glover, Alan Curnow, and A. R. D. Fairburn. A New Zealand Progressive Publishing Society was formed in 1942 and *New Zealand New Writing*, edited by Ian Gordon, ran from 1942 to 1945. A government sympathetic to the arts founded the New Zealand Literary Fund in 1946.

Artists trained at the Dunedin and Canterbury schools of art and the Elam School in Auckland received encouragement from 'The Group' centred on Christchurch. Rita Angus, Toss Wollaston, and Colin McCahon turned to the New Zealand landscape, which they interpreted in new abstract forms. When the New Zealand Academy of Fine Arts had to vacate the National Art Gallery, taken over for war purposes, it continued exhibiting in a department store in central Wellington where it was more accessible and became more popular. Further popular portrayals of New Zealand were forthcoming from the National Film Unit, started in 1941, which produced in 'Weekly Review' the first locally made newsreels. A further expression of growing self-confidence was the ending of overseas assessment of university degree examinations—a move accelerated by wartime postal delays and even the loss of papers due to enemy action. As in the matters of farm production and military prowess, the war induced considerable advances in the cultural life of New Zealand. W. David McIntyre

Baker, J. V. T., *The New Zealand People at War: War Economy* (Wellington, 1965).
Taylor, N., *The New Zealand People at War: The Home Front*, 2 vols. (Wellington, 1986).
Wood, F. L. W., *The New Zealand People at War: Political and External Affairs* (Wellington, 1958).

Nicaragua declared war on the Axis powers in December 1941. It was an original signatory of the *United Nations Declaration, but was otherwise not involved in the war. See also LATIN AMERICA.

Niemöller, Martin (1892–1984), legendary *First World War submarine commander who became the symbol of German Protestant opposition to the Nazis. He was ordained in 1924 and became a pastor in Westphalia and then in Berlin. Initially he supported the Nazis, but soon began preaching against their excesses and was arrested in 1937. Though acquitted of 'malicious attacks against the State' he spent the next eight years in *concentration camps rather than relinquish his convictions. See also GERMANY, 9 and RELIGION.

Davidson, C., *God's Man: The Story of Pastor Niemöller* (New York, 1959).

Nigeria, see BRITISH WEST AFRICA.

Night and Fog Decree, order issued in December 1941 by Hitler through *Keitel, the head of the German Armed Forces High Command (OKW). Its name came from the common German phrase *bei Nacht und Nebel* ('by night and fog') which implies secret and illicit action. It authorized the execution of any non-German civilian who committed crimes against German forces in occupied countries. Most of those executed under it came from Belgium and France. The order was intended to create a new dimension of fear among the local populace by making its victims simply disappear without trace. No questions about them would be answered nor any knowledge of them confirmed or denied, and they were buried in unmarked graves. Most of those accused under the order were deported to Germany. The *People's Court, which sentenced many of them, often held the proceedings in the prisons where the accused were being held. In correspondence, and on prison camp rolls, the initials NN, which stood for the Latin phrase *non nominatur* (not named), as well as *Nacht und Nebel*, were put against their names. By April 1944, 8,639 NN prisoners had been deported to Germany; the total numbers killed under the decree are not known.

Nimitz, Fleet Admiral Chester W. (1885–1966), US naval officer who succeeded Rear-Admiral *Kimmel as C-in-C US Pacific Fleet (Cincpac) after *Pearl Harbor, a post he retained throughout the war.

Born in Texas of parents of German stock, Nimitz spent most of his early career in submarines and was instrumental in having diesel engines adapted for US Navy use. He achieved flag rank in June 1938 and the next year became chief of the Bureau of Navigation (later Bureau of Personnel), which brought him into contact with Roosevelt, who thought highly of him. To Nimitz, Pearl Harbor was not an unmitigated disaster. The carriers were intact, the base facilities almost untouched, and the battle fleet, though at the bottom of the harbour, was mostly salvageable, which it would not have been if it had fought the vastly superior Japanese forces in deep water. 'It was God's mercy that our fleet was in Pearl Harbor on 7 December 1941,' he said later.

He built up around him a first-rate staff and exceptionally able fighting commanders—*Halsey, *Turner, Marc Mitscher, *Spruance, and the top Marine Corps commanders, Holland Smith (1882–1967) and Alexander Vandegrift (1887–1973). A submariner who chose a submarine as his flagship, Nimitz was a man who liked to attack and to keep constant pressure on his opponents. He ordered Halsey's carrier group to raid the Japanese-held islands in early 1942 and then had him launch the *Doolittle raid that April. The same month, when the Pacific was divided between his navy command and *MacArthur's *South-West Pacific Area command, he became C-in-C Pacific Ocean Areas (Cincpoa), which gave him command of Allied air and land forces in his area as well as all naval ones.

Admiral **Nimitz**.

The battle of *Midway in June 1942 was, with *Guadalcanal, the turning-point in the *Pacific war, and it was planned and executed by Nimitz. *ULTRA intelligence was the key to that battle, and it was Nimitz who, in those early days before ULTRA had proved its true worth, decided the intelligence was valid and acted accordingly. After Midway Nimitz went on to the offensive by landing forces on Guadalcanal in August 1942. By February 1943 it had been cleared of Japanese troops and he then implemented the effective strategy that governed the series of *amphibious warfare landings in the Central Pacific beginning with *Tarawa. Simultaneously, his submarines gradually eliminated the Japanese merchant marine creating a stranglehold on vital supplies that the Japanese could not break and which by August 1945 was total. His forces supported MacArthur's during the landings on Leyte in October 1944 (see PHILIPPINES CAMPAIGNS), and in the ensuing battle *Leyte Gulf the Japanese Navy was practically destroyed. *Iwo Jima and *Okinawa followed, vast operations which

Nimitz commanded from Guam, and he signed the Japanese surrender document on the US government's behalf.

Nimitz was an easy-going, affable man, but he could be tough when necessary, and he was one of the ablest strategists the US Navy ever produced. The Pacific war was a naval war and Nimitz won it in under four years with a fleet that at first had hardly existed (see USA, 5(d)), an astonishing achievement. Promoted to admiral on taking command of the Pacific Fleet in 1941 he became a fleet admiral in December 1944 and in November 1945 was made chief of naval operations when Admiral *King retired.

Potter, E. B., *Nimitz* (Annapolis, Md., 1976).

Nisei, see JAPANESE-AMERICANS.

Nissen hut, prefabricated building made of curved sheets of corrugated iron bolted to a wooden frame. It was invented by a Canadian engineer officer of that name during the *First World War, but was also used extensively during the Second for accommodating troops and storing supplies.

NKGB, see NKVD.

NKVD (Narodnyi Kommissariat Vnutrennikh Del, or People's Commissariat for Internal Affairs) has origins which go back to the beginnings of Soviet power. The All-Russian Extraordinary Commission for Combating Counter-revolution and Sabotage (Vecheka) was founded on 20 December 1917. The Vecheka was disbanded on 8 February 1922 and its functions transferred to the State Political Administration (GPU), although the term 'Chekist' to describe its agents, officials, and functionaries has persisted to the present day. When, the USSR was founded in 1923 the GPU became the OGPU (Unified State Political Administration) and was attached to the Council of People's Commissars. In July 1934, the OGPU was transformed into the GUGB (Main Administration of State Security) and integrated into a newly formed NKVD. During this whole period the powers and competence of the security services increased, so that they became, together with the Communist Party of the Soviet Union (CPSU), the basis on which Soviet power rested and also the basis of Stalin's power. In 1938 L. P. *Beria became head of the NKVD and remained its head and that of its successor organizations until after the death of Stalin in 1953.

In February 1941 the state security organs and the intelligence section, the former OGPU, were separated from the NKVD and a separate People's Commissariat of State Security (Narodny Kommissariat Gosudarstvennoy Bezopasnosti, or NKGB) was formed. But in July 1941, following the German invasion of the USSR (see BARBAROSSA), this decision was reversed. However, in April 1943 the original, pre-war plan was put into operation and the NKVD and NKGB were again split, with the state security organs going to the NKGB. Although internal affairs and state security were now the responsibility of separate commissariats, Beria, who in January 1942 had received the rank of general commissar of state security, equivalent to that of Marshal of the Soviet Union, remained in charge of the security apparatus. One of his lieutenants, V. N. Merkulov, became head of the NKGB. In March 1946 the commissariats became ministries and the NKVD and NKGB became MVD and MGB respectively. Throughout this period Soviet citizens always referred to the security services as NKVD rather than NKGB.

To carry out its functions the NKVD had at its disposal a vast apparatus of agents, internal counter-insurgency and border troops, and units responsible for communications. A Soviet estimate puts the number of NKVD troops during the war at 53 divisions and 28 brigades, not counting border troops, and these played a leading role in partisan warfare (see USSR, 8).

In 1921 border troops numbered 95,000 men. In 1934 they were placed under the authority of the NKVD. On the eve of the German attack they numbered 157–158,000 men, and of these 100,000 were positioned along the western borders of the USSR. Armed only with light weapons, they were exposed to the German onslaught (see BREST-LITOVSK, for example) and suffered heavy losses. The survivors were formed into fifteen infantry divisions and took part in fighting on many fronts, including the battles of *Moscow, *Smolensk, *Stalingrad, and *Kursk. During the course of the war 113,700 border troops were engaged in fighting. Three days after the outbreak of the *German–Soviet war, on 25 June 1941, they were given the task of securing the rear of the Red Army. As such their tasks were numerous: uncovering enemy agents, liquidating small detachments of enemy troops, protecting communications, and arresting *deserters. When the Red Army took the offensive they were charged with mopping-up operations, restoring order and suppressing dissident nationalist forces—in fact with restoring Soviet authority. Their operations did not terminate at the borders of the USSR. They continued their functions with the Red Army in eastern Europe and Germany. Equally important was their activity against Japanese forces when the Soviets went to war against Japan on 7 August 1945 (see JAPANESE–SOVIET CAMPAIGNS). Because of their knowledge of the terrain the border troops mounted the initial attacks. These were successful and enabled the Red Army to move rapidly against the Japanese *Kwantung Army.

The pre-war terror unleashed by the NKVD was neither the first nor the last exercise of mass persecution, mass imprisonment, and mass murder. Even the purge of the officer corps of the armed forces did not cease after BARBAROSSA, but only in November 1941. Under the aegis of the *Nazi–Soviet Pact, the Soviets annexed eastern Poland in September 1939, the three Baltic States and the Romanian provinces of Bessarabia and Northern

Bukovina in June 1940. The elections which followed these annexations and which provided the appearance of overwhelming support for Soviet rule were one way in which the NKVD carried out its task of integrating these territories into the USSR. Another was the liquidation of all those who might be considered a danger to Soviet power. Thus, some one and a half million Poles were transported from their homes, nearly half of whom died. It is estimated that 4% of the population of Estonia and 2% of Latvians and Lithuanians were transported to corrective labour camps, the *GUlags, administered by a NKVD department. The officer corps of those Polish soldiers taken prisoners by the Soviets was massacred, some 15,000 of them shot. In 1943 the Germans discovered the bodies of 4,000 of them in mass graves in the forest of *Katyń, near Smolensk. After BARBAROSSA a similar fate awaited some of the Soviet nationalities. By a decree of 28 August 1941 the Volga Germans living in their own autonomous Soviet Socialist Republic were transported from their homes. The grounds given for this population transfer was that there were among the Germans 'thousands and tens of thousands of diversionists and spies' whom the others had chosen not to report to the Soviet authorities. A similar fate awaited the Crimean Tatars and six other smaller nationalities. The number involved certainly exceeded a million (see DEPORTATIONS).

NKVD and NKGB activity did not spare the other nationalities of the USSR. At the end of the war there were in Germany about two million Soviet citizens who had been taken there as *forced labour. In addition there were over a million *prisoners-of-war, the miserable remnant of the millions the Germans had murdered or starved to death. Willingly or unwillingly all these Soviet citizens, or citizens of areas recently annexed by the USSR, were handed over to Soviet authorities and the majority of them were sent to the GUlag.

The establishment of a foreign intelligence and information department of the Vecheka did not come until December 1920, when a foreign department, (Innostranyi Otdel, or INO) was founded. The gradual establishment of Soviet diplomatic and trading agencies gave the INO the opportunity to gain a foothold abroad, directing its main activity at White Russians in exile, and subsequently the Trotskyists. It can thus be seen as an extension of the NKVD's police activities within the USSR. From 1938 to 1940 it was headed by V. G. Dekanozov, who for part of this time was also deputy foreign commissar and subsequently ambassador to Berlin. His successor until 1946 was P. M. Fitin and it was under him that the INO was raised in status becoming the foreign directorate (Inostrannoye Upravlenie, or INU).

In its intelligence work abroad the NKVD was also closely associated with military intelligence, the Fourth Department of the General Staff, later the *GRU, whose work the NKVD, being the more powerful organization, supervised. It is probable that intelligence activity in Germany and German-occupied Europe, as also in Japan (see SORGE), was the responsibility of the GRU, while it was the NKVD/NKGB which controlled the network in the USA. Perhaps its most spectacular success was in the UK where, through the agency of 'Kim' Philby (see MI6) and other British traitors, it penetrated influential sections of government. It was equally successful in recruiting as agents men involved in research to produce the *atomic bomb. During the war the NKVD/NKGB also had contacts with both *SOE and the *Office of Strategic Services. H. HANAK

Andrew, C., and Gordievsky, O., *KGB. The Inside Story of its Foreign Operations from Lenin to Gorbachev* (London, 1990).
Knight, A. W., *The KGB. Police and Politics in the Soviet Union* (rev. edn., Boston, 1990).

Noguès, General Auguste (1876–1971), C-in-C French forces in North Africa in September 1939 who became so notorious for changing sides during the course of the war that he was nicknamed General 'No-yes'. He became the *Vichy French resident-general of French Morocco and broke the terms of the Franco-German *armistice by keeping his irregular mountain forces, the *Goums, fully armed and trained. His troops and naval forces resisted the US landings in French Morocco at the start of the *North African campaign in November 1942, but he then agreed to serve the Allies. In June 1943 de *Gaulle forced his resignation and he retired to Portugal. In 1947 he was sentenced *in absentia* to 20 years' imprisonment for *collaboration and was arrested in 1956 when he returned to France, but was then released.

Nordhausen, a German underground factory for manufacturing *V-weapons. See DORA.

Normandie Squadron, Free French fighter squadron which, from March 1943, served with the Soviet Army Air Force during the *German–Soviet war. After distinguishing itself in the fighting to clear Lithuania of Germans and in the crossing of the River Niemen it became known as the Normandie-Niemen Regiment. In Soviet aircraft (Yak-9 and then Yak-3) serviced by Soviet technical personnel, it flew more than 5,000 sorties, shooting down 273 German aircraft. The unit was highly decorated and four of its pilots were made Heroes of the Soviet Union (see DECORATIONS).

Normandy campaign (see Maps 73 and 74; for the Normandy landings see OVERLORD). In the spring of 1943 the Anglo-American Allies decided to launch a cross-Channel attack and invade German-occupied Europe on 1 May 1944. The *Combined Chiefs of Staff (CCS) specified certain assets for the operation, codenamed OVERLORD, and Lt-General Frederick Morgan, appointed chief of staff to the as yet unnamed supreme allied commander (see COSSAC), headed a small Allied staff and drew up an outline plan. The document was ready by August, and the CCS, meeting at the Quebec conference (see QUADRANT), approved it despite Morgan's warning of the need for additional resources and more divisions on a wider front to give the landings a better chance of success.

Because the Americans were eventually to furnish 60 divisions for the campaign in western Europe while the British and Canadians together could provide no more than 20, President Roosevelt in December designated General Dwight D. *Eisenhower Supreme Allied Commander of the Expeditionary Forces (see SHAEF). Churchill placed *Montgomery at the head of the Twenty-First Army Group, the top British-Canadian ground command for the crossing and subsequent fighting. Eisenhower invited Montgomery to be his commander of the Allied ground forces for an indefinite length of time, and Montgomery agreed. He served under Eisenhower as did Admiral *Ramsay and Air Chief Marshal *Leigh-Mallory, in charge, respectively, of the Allied naval units and the tactical air forces (those in direct support of the ground forces). Eisenhower's deputy Allied commander, Air Chief Marshal *Tedder, loosely co-ordinated the tactical air and the US and RAF strategic air forces, the strategic air forces being directed by *Spaatz and *Harris.

Allied bombardment preparing for OVERLORD began in January 1944, as planes destroyed bridges, railway yards, and industrial and military targets. In the process, they contributed to a huge *deception plan codenamed FORTITUDE. Its purpose was to persuade the Germans to expect Allied landings in the Pas de Calais, across the narrowest part of the Channel, by a fictitious army group under *Patton, who, the Germans inferred would lead the invasion. There were fake subordinate headquarters and camps, sham equipment and communications; the British also manipulated captured German agents to disseminate false information and employed *ULTRA intelligence to check the extent to which the Germans were swallowing the story (see also XX-COMMITTEE).

In reality, the Allies were planning to land on the coast of the Baie de la Seine. Eisenhower and Montgomery increased the strength of the initial assault. They expanded the amphibious forces from three to five divisions, two British, one Canadian, and two American, to move across five beaches, *UTAH, *OMAHA, *JUNO, *SWORD, and *GOLD; used three airborne divisions, two American and one British, to secure the invasion flanks; and employed certain special operations such as the attack on the strongly defended Pointe du Hoc. They enlarged the frontage to approximately 80 km. (50 mi.), from Ouistreham, Caen's port, on the left, to the vicinity of Ste Mère Eglise, where half the Americans, who were on the right, would be closer to Cherbourg and therefore in a better position to capture this major port. But enlarged assault forces required additional facilities, particularly *landing craft and ships, and, to be sure of having sufficient equipment on hand, the Allies postponed the invasion for a month, setting 5 June, when tidal and weather conditions would be most suitable, as D-Day.

The objective of Morgan's blueprint, what OVERLORD was supposed to accomplish, was to be achieved in three months. After coming ashore, the Allies were to extend inland and take possession of a lodgement area, that part of western France bounded by the Seine and Loire rivers, together with the Paris–Orléans gap that, is, lower Normandy, all of Brittany, and parts of Maine and Anjou. By conquering that region, the Allies would have enough (1) ports to sustain and nourish their augmenting forces; (2) sites for airfields from which to support the ground operations; (3) room to manœuvre to utilize the superior Allied mechanized forces; and (4) space in which to locate headquarters, installations, depots, and the other formations of modern armies. Once in the lodgement area, the Allies would halt and prepare to attack to the German border, then strike towards the Ruhr, the industrial heart of Germany.

The organizations participating in OVERLORD planned in detail how they were to get ashore. The headquarters of *Bradley's First US Army and *Dempsey's Second British Army, together with their subordinate units, trained their men and devised their procedures for the landings. All was in readiness early in June, when a storm arose over the Channel. High winds and driving rain made crossings impossible. Assured by *meteorological intelligence which came from reports from weather stations in Greenland and elsewhere in the west, of a turn for the better, Eisenhower deferred the invasion for 24 hours and set D-Day for 6 June.

Across the Channel, on the Continent, the Germans awaited an invasion but lacked knowledge of its time and place. *Rundstedt, C-in-C in the west, had a mobile theatre reserve force situated in a central location ready to speed to the landing sites and throw the invaders into the sea. Under him, *Rommel, in command of Army Group B, believed it would be impossible to turn the Allies back once they had a foothold. Allied planes had gained complete air superiority and were bound to destroy the central reserve travelling to the beaches to repel the landings. Allied naval gunfire was sure to prevent the Germans from regaining the coast. It was therefore necessary, Rommel believed, to defeat the Allies at the water's edge. To that end he had, from November 1943, directed the construction of the *Atlantic Wall, fortifications which included artillery pieces, pillboxes, underground troop shelters, beach obstacles such as *element C and booby traps.

Rundstedt and Rommel presented their different methods of meeting an invasion to their Führer. Unable to choose which solution he preferred, Hitler tried to implement both with the result that neither commander was satisfied with the means he had received. Rundstedt thought his reserve too small; Rommel's defences were far from finished and, he thought, too weakly manned.

Rommel controlled two armies, the Seventh stationed in Normandy and Brittany, and the Fifteenth in the Pas de Calais, the latter fixed there by the FORTITUDE deception. The Germans were so convinced of an eventual Allied arrival in northern France that, long after

Normandy campaign

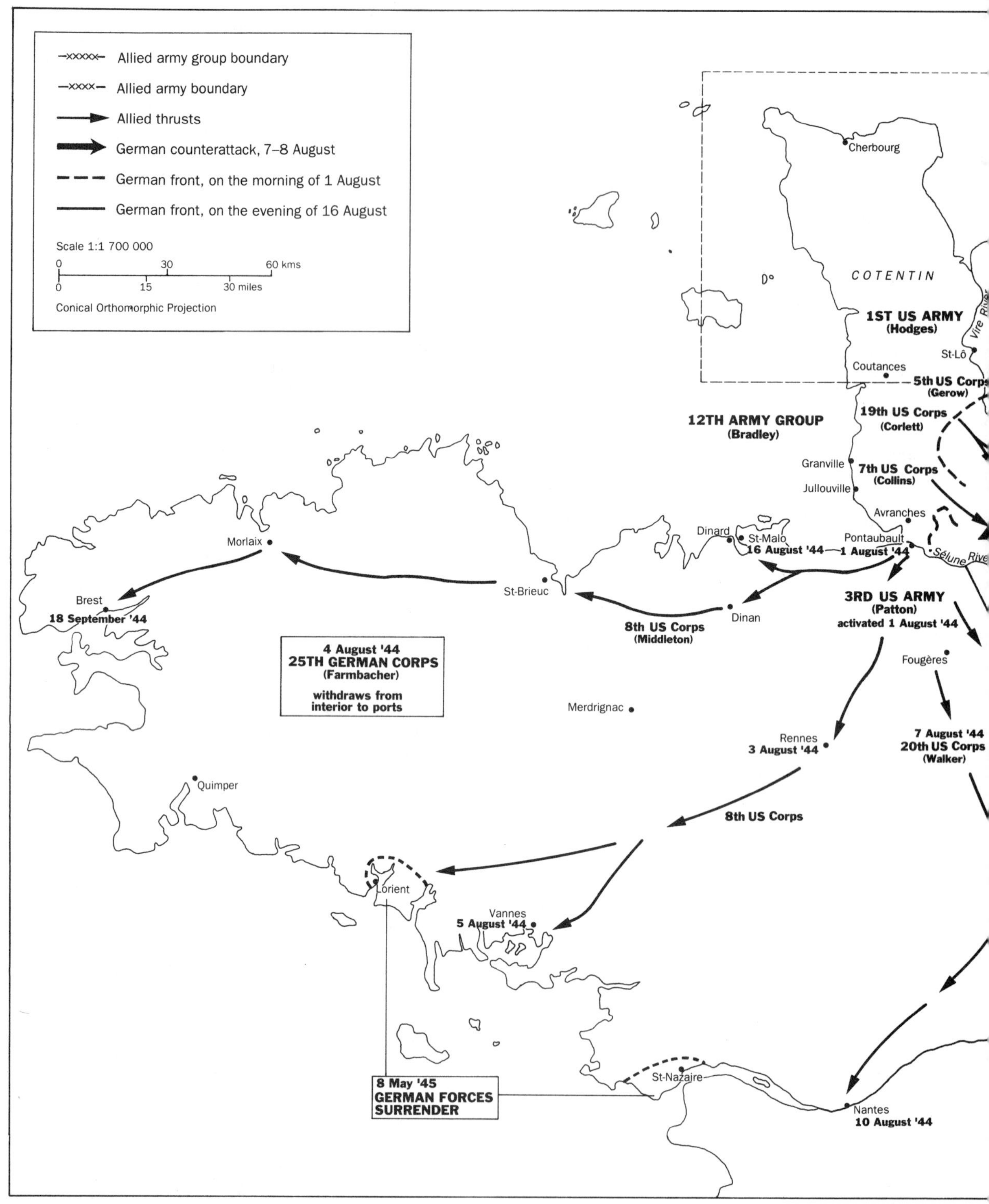

73. Allied advance to the Seine during the **Normandy campaign**, August 1944

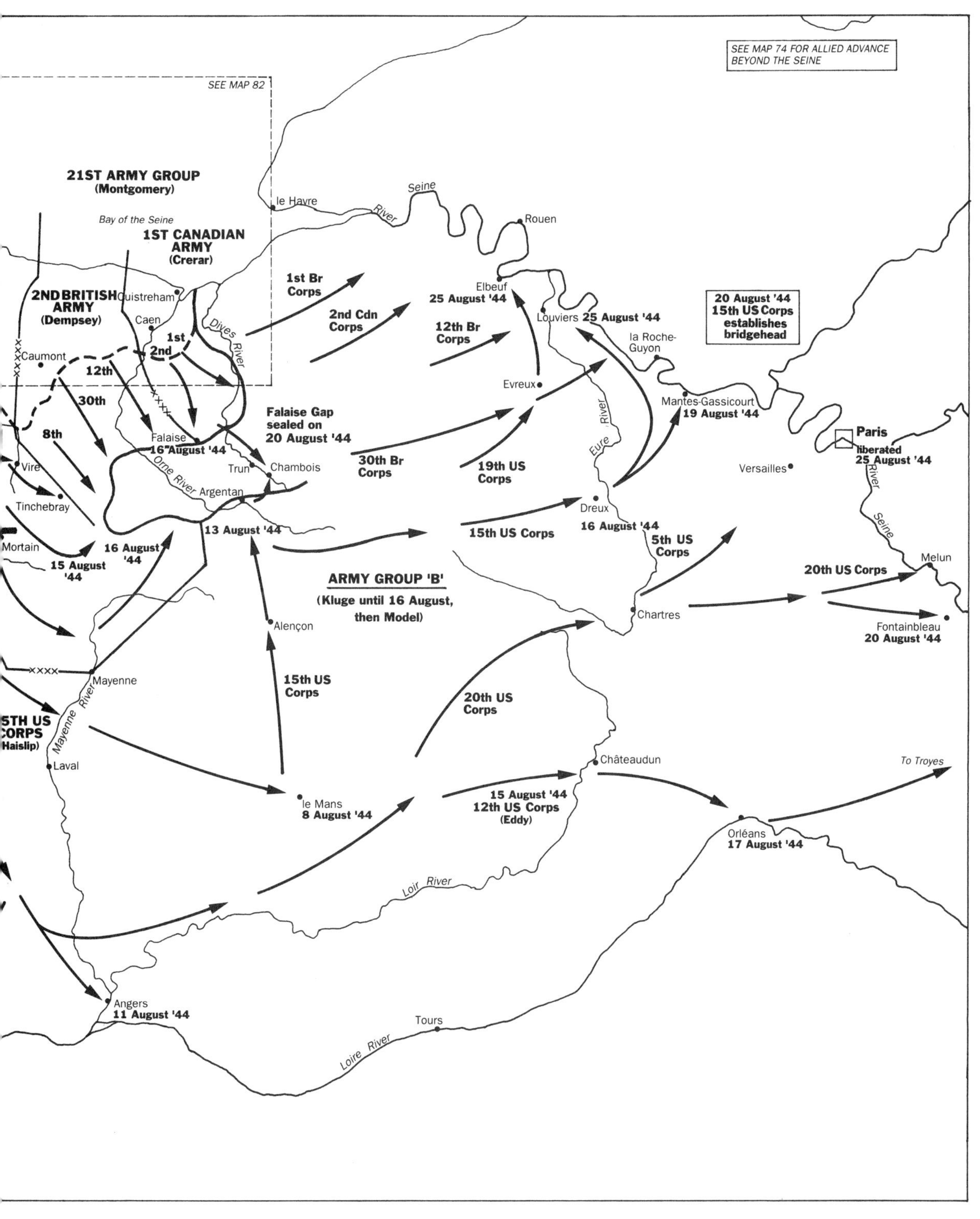
SEE MAP 74 FOR ALLIED ADVANCE BEYOND THE SEINE
SEE MAP 82
21ST ARMY GROUP
(Montgomery)
Bay of the Seine
1ST CANADIAN ARMY
(Crerar)
2ND BRITISH ARMY
(Dempsey)
le Havre
Seine River
Rouen
Ouistreham
Caen
Caumont
1st Br Corps
2nd Cdn Corps
12th Br Corps
Elbeuf
25 August '44
Louviers 25 August '44
20 August '44
15th US Corps establishes bridgehead
la Roche-Guyon
Dives River
1st
2nd
12th
30th
8th
Evreux
Mantes-Gassicourt
19 August '44
Falaise Gap sealed on 20 August '44
Falaise
16 August '44
Paris liberated 25 August '44
Vire
Trun
Chambois
Orne River
Argentan
30th Br Corps
19th US Corps
Eure River
Versailles
Tinchebray
Dreux
16 August '44
13 August '44
15th US Corps
5th US Corps
Seine River
Mortain
16 August '44
15 August '44
Melun
ARMY GROUP 'B'
(Kluge until 16 August, then Model)
20th US Corps
Alençon
Chartres
Fontainbleau
20 August '44
Mayenne
15th US Corps
20th US Corps
Mayenne River
5TH US CORPS
(Haislip)
Laval
Châteaudun
To Troyes
le Mans
8 August '44
15 August '44
12th US Corps
(Eddy)
Orléans
17 August '44
Loir River
Angers
11 August '44
Tours
Loire River

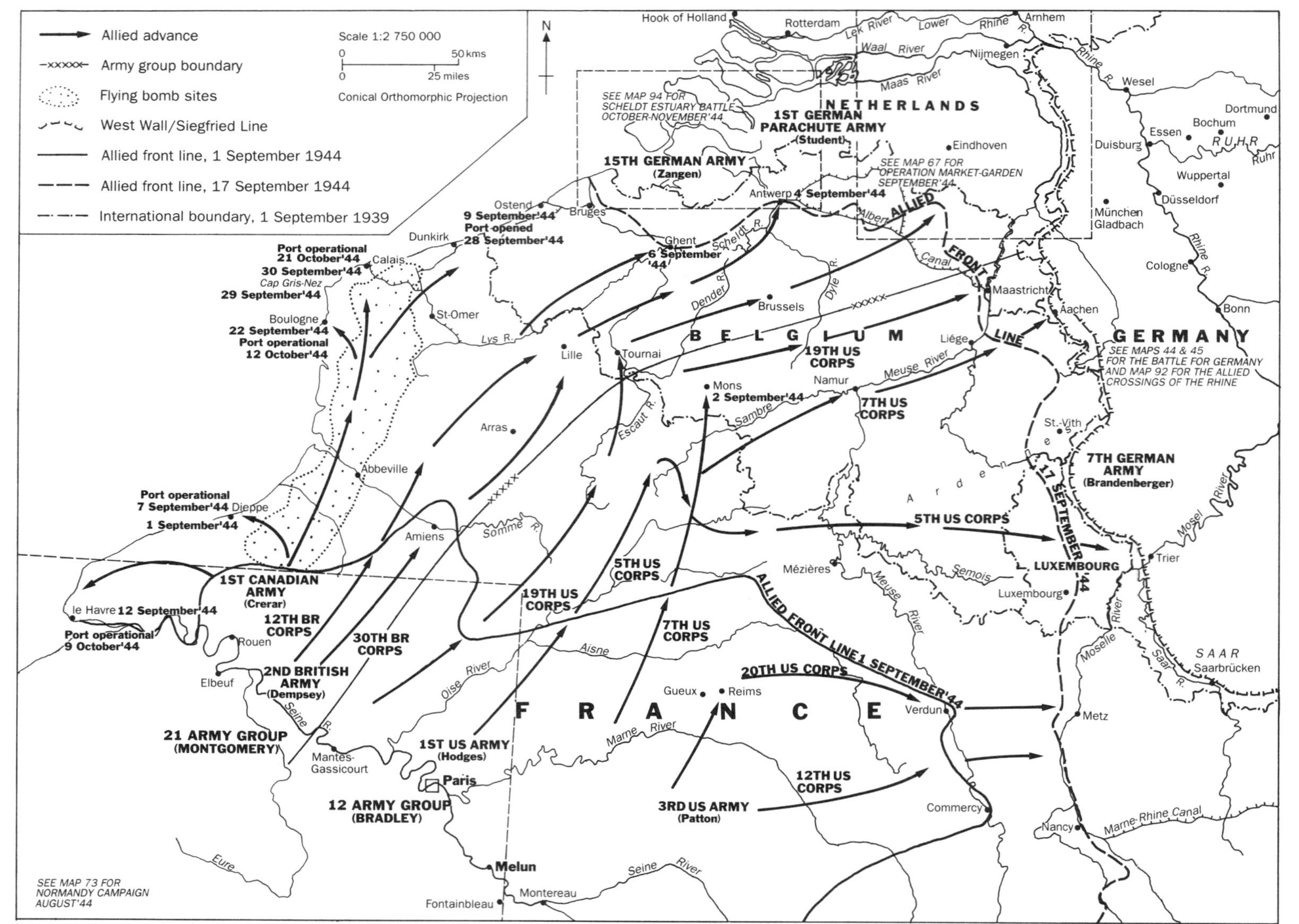

74. Allied advance beyond the Seine during the **Normandy campaign**, August–September 1944

the landings in Normandy, they believed them to be a diversion designed to draw German forces away from the main effort, which was still to strike the Pas de Calais.

German reconnaissance planes and boats were unable to penetrate the Allied screens and see what was going on in the UK, so there was no way of judging the imminence of an Allied descent. The storm sweeping across the Channel early in June persuaded the Germans of the impossibility of a crossing on the 6th.

Meticulously synchronized, the complex parts of OVERLORD unfolded as thousands of ships and planes escorted, protected, and carried Allied soldiers across the Channel and caught the Germans completely by surprise. Allied paratroopers, followed by glidermen, about 23,000 in all, dropped into Normandy and, though widely dispersed in many places, quickly secured the invasion flanks. Ships and boats deposited more than 130,000 soldiers on the invasion beaches, and the troops had relatively little difficulty gaining a foothold, except at OMAHA where a German division had recently moved for training exercises: Allied intelligence became aware of its presence too late for the planners to change the assault zones and not until the early evening of *D-Day was OMAHA in Allied hands. Overall casualties on that date were under 5,000, far fewer than anticipated.

Their coastal defences penetrated, the Germans set into motion a train of events to turn the tables. They strengthened their positions and prevented the Allies from advancing inland. They committed the central reserve, and also tried to bring additional troops from Brittany and southern France—but not from the Pas de Calais—to the combat area. Their aim was to launch a devastating, decisive counter-attack and drive the Allies into the sea.

Sabotage by French *resistance as well as bombings and strafings by Allied aircraft hampered German efforts to reinforce the front. Allied planes caught Rundstedt's central reserve as it was moving and wiped out the headquarters, killing and wounding staff officers and knocking out tanks and vehicles. Damage to railways and bridges delayed German troop movements. Towards the end of June, both Rundstedt and Rommel were privately admitting their inability to mount a concentrated counter-attack or to drive the invaders from the Continent. Summoned to meetings with the Führer on 17 June at Soissons, north-east of Paris, and again on 29 June at *Berchtesgaden, the field marshals requested freedom to order local withdrawals instead of holding stubbornly, as Hitler insisted, to defensive positions. Hitler refused permission and shortly afterwards relieved Rundstedt, replacing him with *Kluge. He also warned Rommel pointedly about what he called defeatism. On 17 July, three days before the attempt on Hitler's life (see SCHWARZE KAPELLE), an Allied plane strafed Rommel's vehicle and sent it crashing into a ditch. Rommel was badly injured, but he was making a miraculous recovery in September when Hitler discovered that he was implicated in the assassination plot and gave him two alternatives: trial by the *People's Court and the inevitable disgrace of his family, or suicide. Rommel chose suicide.

Meanwhile the Allies, in addition to bringing more troops, equipment, and supplies across the Channel, had pushed several kilometres inland. More importantly, they extended laterally along the coast and closed the gaps between their individual beaches, thereby creating a consolidated, stronger, and safer beachhead.

In mid-June, the Americans in the Cotentin drove to the western shore and isolated Cherbourg. Turning north, they fought through the ring of forts protecting the port. By 30 June, they had captured it, as well as the tip of the Cherbourg peninsula. The Germans had thoroughly destroyed the harbour and its machinery, and had scuttled ships to block the marine roadstead, and it took *engineers six weeks to clear the rubble and repair the docks. Only then could the Allies begin to unload cargoes there.

At the beginning of July, a situation resembling a stalemate hung over the front. The Allies had advanced generally about 32 km. (20 mi.) into the interior and were bogged down. Incessant rain and low clouds prevented Allied aircraft and spotter planes from finding and blasting German defenders. A storm in the Channel around 20 June had halted supply operations along the invasion beaches for several days, had severely damaged the two artificial harbours towed across the Channel and installed offshore (see MULBERRIES), one so badly that it had to be abandoned, and had driven hundreds of craft ashore where they broke up. Although more than 800,000 soldiers were on the French side, the build-up of forces on the Continent had fallen behind schedule. Even these numbers found it difficult to obtain space, for the beachhead was one-fifth the size projected by pre-invasion plans, too small to accommodate the organizations in Normandy. Far too few airfields existed. To gain more room, the Allies altered their shipping programme and sent more combat troops and fewer logistical units to Normandy to expand the beachhead.

In the Cotentin, the Americans opened an offensive to the south, hoping to gain first Coutances, about 32 km. ahead, then Avranches, about 48 km. (30 mi.) beyond that, but progress was disappointingly slow and frustrating, measured in metres and high casualties. The bocage, low-lying country with high hedgerows, offered insufficient routes of advance and canalized American movements, which the Germans easily countered. Avranches, even Coutances, seemed as distant as Berlin.

Caen, a D-Day objective, still remained in German hands. British and Canadian troops deployed in a large semicircle around the edge of the city were unable to enter. As long as the Germans held Caen, they denied access to the plain stretching southwards for just over 30 km. (18 mi.) to Falaise, excellent ground not only for armoured warfare but also for constructing airfields. When operation EPSOM, which utilized the newly arrived 8th corps to try and envelop the city, failed at the end of June, Montgomery turned to the strategic bombers for help.

The Allies had already used heavy bombers in a directly supporting role in Italy, once in February against the Benedictine abbey on *Monte Cassino, and again in March against the town of Cassino, but had achieved no success. The importance of Caen led to another attempt. On the evening of 7 July, bombers demolished the city and permitted British and Canadian soldiers to move into the streets. The Germans withdrew from its northern part and, on the other side of the River Orne which flows through the city, re-established defensive positions.

Impressed by this triumph, Bradley thought of applying the technique to help him move ahead at least to Coutances. But first he had to be free of the soggy meadows of the Cotentin and move to higher, drier ground around St Lô so that he could use tanks. He mentioned this notion to Montgomery, who encouraged him. Dempsey then suggested a comparable British effort to reach Falaise. Montgomery at first demurred but later told Dempsey to plan an attack. What Montgomery conceived was a one-two punch, a British blow followed by an American crack. Together they would perhaps pierce the defences, forge ahead, and quickly gain a substantial piece of the lodgement area.

Dempsey's offensive (GOODWOOD) had a less than clear-cut objective. Ostensibly in pursuit of Falaise, it jumped off on 18 July after heavy preparatory bombing, secured the rest of Caen, and gained about 5 km. (3 mi.) down the road to Falaise. The British were about to penetrate the German lines when fierce resistance stopped further progress, and, when a thunderstorm broke on the afternoon of 20 July, Montgomery called off the effort. The British had lost 4,000 men and 500 tanks, more than one-third of the tanks they had in Normandy.

Bradley, who had finally moved his army ahead about 11 km. (7 mi.) after two weeks of heavy fighting, which cost 40,000 casualties, now had the dry ground he needed around St Lô. He was supposed to start his attack (COBRA) on 21 July, but a continuing downpour imposed delay. The weather seemed to clear momentarily on 24 July, and some bombers carried out preliminary strikes. The real bombardment came on the following day, and although it appeared at first to have had little effect, it shattered the German defences. American infantry and armour sped through the opening and headed for Coutances.

Two days later it was apparent that the Americans had demolished the German left flank. Bradley set his immediate sights on Avranches and turned his First US Army headlong to the south. On 30 July, with many German units in the Cotentin falling back in confusion, the Americans seized Avranches, withstood a counter-attack, and went on to capture a still intact bridge at Pontaubault. This was a most valuable acquisition, for it opened the way westwards into Brittany, southwards to the River Loire, and eastwards to the River Seine and the Paris–Orléans gap. Possession of the OVERLORD objective, the entire lodgement area, seemed to be more than likely in the near future.

*Crerar's First Canadian Army headquarters had become operational on the Continent on 23 July under Montgomery and assumed control of the left or easternmost part of the Allied front, its first major objective eventually being Falaise. In the American zone, Bradley turned over the First US Army to Courtney *Hodges and activated and stepped up to command the Twelfth US Army Group. On 1 August, Patton's Third US Army entered the campaign on the right or westernmost part of the Allied line. Thus Montgomery and Bradley each directed two armies, respectively Dempsey's and Crerar's, and Hodges's and Patton's, but Montgomery remained in command of the Allied ground forces pro tem.

Except for a relatively narrow corridor around Avranches, which the Germans were unable to plug, they held firm all along the line elsewhere, exhibiting neither panic nor desperation. Although all the senior commanders thought it time to start at least thinking of eventual withdrawal from Normandy, even from France, Hitler directed them to prepare a large-scale offensive westwards through Mortain to regain Avranches on the Cotentin west coast. Success would re-establish the German left flank and restore a continuous front line. It would also separate the First and Third US Armies and create opportunities for further offensive activity, even to roll up and destroy the Allied right.

Meanwhile, Patton sent a corps westwards into Brittany. In sunny weather, and against hardly any resistance, American troops advanced rapidly. The entire Third Army was supposed to seize the major ports, particularly St Malo, Brest, and Lorient, which were expected to be the main entrances for American manpower and goods arriving directly from the USA. But no more than a corps was needed, for the Germans had fled from the interior to the ports. However, it would take a reinforced division two weeks of heavy fighting to capture St Malo; three divisions more than a month to reduce and take Brest; and one division to isolate and pen up the Germans in Lorient and St Nazaire for the rest of the war. Brittany became a backwater, for the opportunity to drive southwards from Avranches to the River Loire and to swing eastwards to the River Seine and the Paris–Orléans gap was too tempting to disregard. The Allies cast their sights to the east. Starting the movement, one of Patton's corps proceeded southeastwards from Avranches to the successive objectives of Mayenne and Le Mans and reached the latter, 120 km. (74 mi.) away, in less than a week.

That was when the Germans struck Hodges's First US Army when, in the early morning hours of 7 August, they launched what they called their Avranches counter-attack. Parts of four armoured divisions penetrated American lines, retook Mortain, and gained about 11 km. (7 mi.). When daylight came, the tankers pulled off the roads, camouflaged their tanks, dug foxholes, and awaited the inevitable retaliation. Allied planes were out in force, and RAF rocket-firing Typhoons and Hurricanes were particularly effective. Of 70 German tanks estimated in the operation at the start, only 30 remained operable at the end of the day.

Although the Germans continued their pressure in the Mortain area for four more days, they made no further progress. The US infantry division directly involved held stubbornly, the corps commander quickly marshalled nearby organizations to buttress the defences, and about 700 Americans, who had excellent observation over the region from a hill they stubbornly retained, even though German troops surrounded and continuously stormed the place, called down effective artillery fire. These, plus the air effort, stopped what the Americans called the Mortain counter-attack.

Meanwhile, 5 km. (3 mi.) south of Caen, late on 7 August, Crerar opened a major operation. Montgomery had instructed him to cut off some Germans in front of Dempsey's army and also to disrupt the German withdrawal from Normandy that Montgomery expected. To those ends, Crerar mounted a massive and meticulously planned armoured attack preceded by a heavy bombardment. Despite some collisions and confusion in the darkness, the effort moved well and gained several kilometres down the road to Falaise, then ran out of steam at daylight. A Canadian and a Polish armoured division, both untested in combat, tried to recharge the endeavour. All sorts of difficulties, including simple inexperience, lack of co-ordination, and, more telling, a short bombing by Allied planes in close support took the edge off. Although the fighting continued until 10 August, little more was accomplished.

The German attack to the west, the Canadian attack to the south, and the availability of one of Patton's corps at Le Mans, able to attack to the north, gave Bradley an idea. Eisenhower, who was visiting, thought the notion promising, so on 8 August Bradley telephoned Montgomery and proposed to trap the Germans at Mortain. If the Canadians moved south to Falaise and Patton's soldiers north 49 km. (30 mi.) to Alençon, then beyond Alençon for another 45 km. (28 mi.) to Argentan, there would be only 23 km. (14 mi.) separating the Canadian and American forces. Closing the jaws completely would form a pocket and encircle an estimated 21 German divisions west of Falaise and Argentan. Although Montgomery had his eyes fixed on the Seine, he approved Bradley's proposal. The interior armies, Dempsey's and Hodges's, Montgomery specified, would continue their pressure to destroy German cohesion and to herd them into the trap being set by Crerar and Patton.

Consequently, Patton's corps turned north from Le Mans on 10 August and against virtually no opposition drove through Alençon and reached the outskirts of Argentan by the evening of 12 August, thereby threatening a flank attack on the German forces around Mortain and, in addition, menacing most of the German combat formations in Normandy with encirclement. Preparations were under way to capture Argentan and proceed towards Falaise when, in one of the most controversial decisions of the campaign, Bradley halted further movement to the north. Many explanations of his action have been advanced since then, among them the desire to avoid a head-on clash between the Americans and Canadians and the supposed presence of time bombs dropped by the air forces in the territory between the two armies. But the real reason seems to have been concern over a German intention to launch a huge breakout attack against Patton's men in the Argentan area.

The German need to gather forces for this effort led Hitler to acquiesce in some local withdrawals around Mortain on the evening of 11 August, and that brought the battle there to an end. Although the Germans were never able to execute their breakout attack, they built up their southern shoulder and began to send supply and administrative units eastwards through the Argentan–Falaise gap to safety.

The Canadians attacked again on 14 August, and again bombs dropped short disrupted the effort. Still, by the end of the day, the Canadians had moved ahead more than 6 km. (3.7 mi.) down the road and were about the same distance from Falaise. Two days later, they fought their way into the town.

Meanwhile, Patton, upset over being halted at Argentan, persuaded Bradley on 14 August to let him send the bulk of his Third US Army to the east. On the following day, half the corps at Argentan moved towards Dreux, another corps headed for Chartres, and a third drove towards Orléans. Despite a second stop order by Bradley, which temporarily delayed Patton's virtual road march, these objectives were in hand on 18 August. The lodgement area was as good as won.

The Germans, in the meantime, fighting desperately to hold their defensive positions despite the repeated blows from Dempsey's and Hodges's men, finally received permission from Hitler on 16 August to withdraw. He had been shocked by the Allied *French Riviera landings the day before and further upset by the loss of Falaise that day. Most of the combat troops in Normandy, somewhere between 150,000 and 200,000 men, were penned into an enclosure resembling an elongated horseshoe about 65 km. (40 mi.) long and 20–25 km. (12.4–15.5 mi.) wide, much of it under Allied artillery fire and air bombardment. In a carefully organized and highly disciplined movement, which lasted four nights, the Germans withdrew to the east, and by the night of 18 August had reduced the length of the pocket to an area about 9 by 11 km. (5.6 by 6.8 mi.). They were also getting troops out through the Argentan–Falaise gap. The Allies had, by the same date, constricted that opening to 5–8 km. (3–5 mi.).

Montgomery had asked Bradley to eliminate the gap and to close the pocket by sending Americans to meet Canadians and Poles at the small towns of Trun and Chambois. On the evening of 19 August, when American and Polish soldiers made contact in Chambois, they shut the trap. But the Germans, helped by rain and a heavy mist and covered by an attack launched from outside the pocket, continued to escape eastwards for two more days.

The Germans had suffered a grievous defeat. They lost somewhere between 25,000 and 50,000 men who were taken prisoner and another 5,000 to 10,000 killed. The terrain in the Falaise area held the charred and destroyed remains of German weapons, equipment, and vehicles, and the bloated bodies of thousands of dead horses. Those who escaped headed towards the Seine, determined to salvage as many troops and headquarters cadres as they could. They had to deal with additional Allied efforts to cut them off and to block their flight to and across the Seine, but the Germans later characterized these as badly executed and weakly pursued.

On 18 August, Patton had sent the two-division corps at Dreux to Mantes-Gassicourt, 60 km. (37 mi.) downstream from Paris. During the night of 19 August, one division crossed the Seine, the first Allied crossing of the river. This was in conformity with a significant Eisenhower decision. Believing the lodgement area to be as good as taken in about ten days less than the 90 specified by the OVERLORD plan, Eisenhower, contrary to the pre-invasion planning, determined to forgo a halt at the Seine. Because the Germans were so soundly defeated and on the run, so obviously falling back in a large-scale withdrawal, he decided the Allies would instead strike immediately for the German border.

Trying to harass the Germans crossing to the far bank of the Seine, three American divisions pushed down the left or near bank and with great difficulty, because of fierce German resistance to protect their crossing sites, reached Louviers and Elbeuf downstream on 25 August and closed off about 100 km. (60 mi.) of the river to the Germans. The British and Canadian armies also struck hard at the Germans heading for the Seine, attaining its lower reaches at the end of the month. But they too encountered heavy resistance as the Germans fought to guard their crossings. Although the Allies believed all the bridges to be destroyed, between 19 and 31 August the Germans managed, again by marvellous organization and discipline, to get 240,000 men across the Seine, and as these troops streamed across northern and north-eastern France towards Belgium, Luxemburg, and Germany, the Allies launched a pursuit. Patton's Third US Army initiated it on 21 August by crossing the Seine at Melun and Fontainebleau and racing to crossings of the River Yonne at Montereau and Sens. The army rolled through Troyes, and on the last day of the month, as fuel supplies dwindled, then vanished, arrived at the River Meuse and captured bridges at Verdun and Commercy intact. The army was then almost 300 km. (186 mi.) beyond the Seine.

Meanwhile, *Leclerc's French armoured division, included on the Allied troop list specifically for this purpose, liberated Paris on 25 August to the great joy of the inhabitants, of French nationals everywhere, and of untold numbers of people throughout the world (see also PARIS RISING).

Elsewhere, Dempsey's British, Crerar's Canadian, and Hodges's US armies instituted pursuit operations in the last week of August and made spectacular progress. As the month came to an end, Crerar's troops were working up the coast, isolating and reducing the Channel ports; Dempsey's men were heading for Belgium and would soon reach Brussels; and Hodges's units were dashing towards eastern Belgium and Luxemburg. The surge of these armies would come to an end during the second week of September.

To the Allies at the end of August, the war seemed about to be over and won. In consonance with that optimism, the CCS meeting again in Quebec (see OCTAGON) switched some resources originally scheduled for Europe to the Pacific theatre. Nobody seemed to be aware of the supply crisis—the inability to move goods, mainly fuel, from the invasion beaches to the combat troops quickly enough (but see RED BALL EXPRESS)—which was about to shut down offensive operations. That, together with the approach of winter and the German re-establishment of a cohesive line of defence from the Channel to Switzerland, what the Germans called the 'Miracle in the West', would insure continuation of the conflict.

Although Eisenhower's decision on 19 August to cross the Seine at once indicated the end of the OVERLORD operation, a symbolic event closed the Normandy campaign on 1 September. On that day, Eisenhower assumed command of the Allied ground forces, and Montgomery received promotion to field marshal. No one suspected that eight more months of hard fighting lay ahead before the Allies won the war.

For the fighting in north-west Europe from 1 September 1944, see SCHELDT ESTUARY, MARKET-GARDEN, ARDENNES CAMPAIGN, and GERMANY, BATTLE FOR. See also FRENCH RIVIERA LANDINGS. MARTIN BLUMENSON

Blumenson, M., *Breakout and Pursuit* (Washington, DC, 1963).
Bradley, O. R., *A Soldier's Story* (New York, 1951).
D'Este, C., *Decision in Normandy* (New York, 1983).
Eisenhower, D. D., *Crusade in Europe* (New York, 1983).
Hamilton, N., *Monty: Master of the Battlefield* (London, 1983).

Normandy landings, see OVERLORD.

North, Admiral Sir Dudley (1881–1961), British naval officer who was Flag Officer North Atlantic at Gibraltar in July 1940 when Admiral *Somerville's *Force H, which was based at Gibraltar but was not under North's operational command, was ordered by the Admiralty to bombard the French fleet at *Mers-el-Kébir. After the operation North informed the Admiralty how repugnant the operation had been to all concerned. This bluntness earned him a severe reprimand and was almost certainly the true reason why he was subsequently dismissed when, in September 1940, he allowed six *Vichy French warships to pass through the straits of Gibraltar unmolested. The Axis had allowed them to sail from Toulon to reinforce Vichy French forces in *Gabon; and

Meeting of Allied leaders, December 1942, during the **North African campaign**. Left to right: Admiral Darlan, Admiral Cunningham, and General Eisenhower. General Giraud has his back to the camera.

North, whose orders were to avoid incidents with the French Navy, assumed that if the Admiralty wanted them stopped it would have ordered Somerville to act.

In fact, through a series of mishaps and mistakes, the Admiralty was unaware that the French ships had sailed, and their appearance in the Atlantic, just as the Anglo-French *Dakar expedition was about to land in French West Africa, caused great consternation. Though the ships did not affect the outcome at Dakar, and were later intercepted and turned back, North was blamed for failing to take action, and was relieved of his command. After the war powerful voices were raised on North's behalf but the Admiralty refused him a court martial or a public enquiry. However, in 1957 the then prime minister, Harold *Macmillan, stated in parliament that neither North's honour nor his professional integrity had been impugned. He was knighted in 1937.

Marder, A. J., *Operation 'Menace': The Dakar Expedition and the Dudley North Affair* (Oxford, 1976).

North African campaign. This was fought after Anglo-American landings (TORCH) in French Morocco and Algeria on 8 November 1942 and culminated in the capitulation of German–Italian forces in Tunisia the following May (see Maps 75 and76).

The fall of *France in June 1940 left the North African French colonies in the hands of *Vichy French administrations pledged to defend them against all comers. Nevertheless, an early plan for British forces to occupy Tunisia and Algeria (GYMNAST) was based on the hope that the French there would co-operate with any Allied invasion. A later plan (SUPER-GYMNAST), which included American help, was dropped when the British and Commonwealth Eighth Army was forced out of Libya after the *Gazala battle of June 1942, but was soon revived as a more realistic alternative to the immediate invasion of France. Though not the Second Front that Stalin so ardently sought, it had a greater chance of success, required fewer landing craft, and was considered a more suitable baptism of fire for unblooded US troops. It was hoped that the French in North Africa would side with the Allies and to facilitate this realignment General *Giraud, a staunch opponent of Germany, was spirited away from Vichy France by submarine. But his codename, KING-PIN, proved inappropriate: at first he refused to co-operate and then he proved politically ineffectual.

TORCH was primarily an American operation and Lt-General *Eisenhower was appointed C-in-C, Allied Expeditionary Force. His deputy was another American, Maj-General Mark *Clark, as was the Western Air

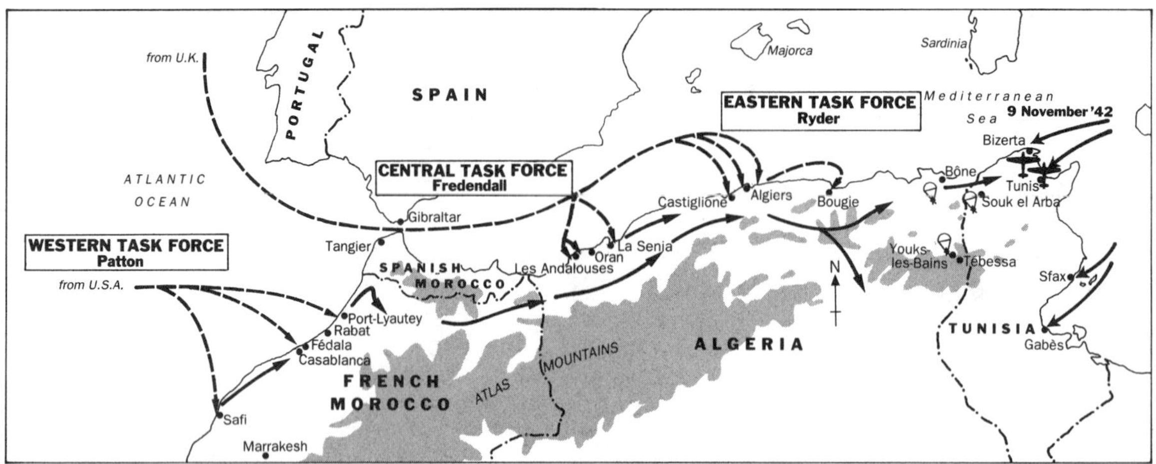

75. **North African campaign** landings, November 1942

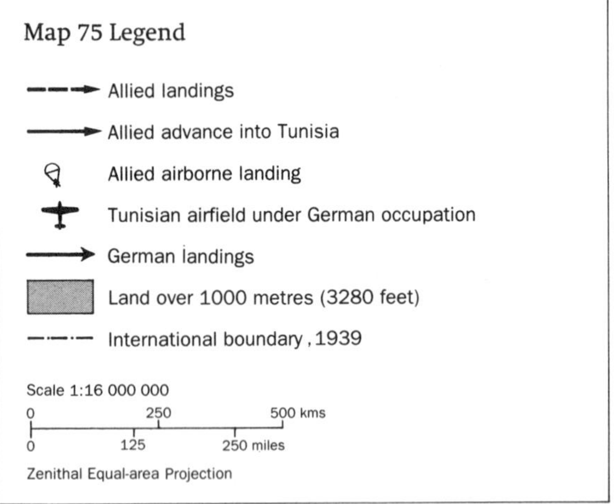

Commander (Twelfth USAAF) Brigadier-General James Doolittle (see also DOOLITTLE RAID); all his other commanders—Lt-General Kenneth Anderson, Admiral *Cunningham, and the Eastern Air Commander, Air Marshal William Welsh (No. 333 Group RAF)—were British. With these officers Eisenhower set out to achieve a truly unified command. In marked contrast to the animosity that prevailed between the two Panzer Army commanders, Arnim and *Rommel, who opposed the Allies in Tunisia, Eisenhower's *Allied Forces Headquarters (AFHQ) 'proceeded,' as he put it, 'as though all its members belonged to a single nation'.

Eisenhower's directive from the *Combined Chiefs of Staff was to gain complete control of North Africa from the Atlantic to the Red Sea starting with landings in Algeria and French Morocco; after taking all of French North Africa, to strike eastwards and take *Rommel's German–Italian Panzer Army in Libya in the rear; and to clear that country of all Axis forces.

In the hope of preventing hostilities with the French, Clark landed secretly near Algiers on 22 October 1942 to meet the pro-Giraud Maj-General Charles Mast, chief of staff of the 19th French Corps. Mast guaranteed that if he was given four days' notice neither the French Army nor the Air Force would resist the Allied landings with any enthusiasm, especially around Algiers, though he could not answer for the navy (which, in the event, resisted strongly).

Three landing places, Casablanca (Western Force, commanded by Maj-General *Patton), Oran (Central Force, commanded by Maj-General Lloyd Fredendall), and Algiers (Eastern Force, commanded by Maj-General Charles Ryder), were eventually chosen, with Western Air Command supporting the two westerly landings and Eastern Air Command those around Algiers. The Western and Central land forces were all American and they later provided formations for 2nd US Corps which fought in Tunisia. As it was thought that the French were more likely to oppose British landings—the British bombardment of the French Navy at *Mers-el-Kébir and the *Syrian campaign had not been forgotten—the Eastern Force initially comprised only a US assault force which was to be reinforced later by British troops. These were then to combine to become, 'by the wave of a wand' as the British official historian of the campaign put it, First British Army, though it only had one corps until early 1943. Its task was to move into Tunisia as quickly as possible, Ryder having handed over to Anderson.

The total number of Allied troops involved in the landings was 65,000, a little more than half the strength of the French forces in North Africa. Some 650 warships were deployed to take and guard the Central and Eastern forces from the UK; Patton's force sailed direct from the USA. The landings, facilitated by good intelligence from *Agency Africa, took place in the early hours of 8 November 1942 and excellent security achieved complete strategic surprise. The toughest opposition was met around Casablanca: landing in the surf proved hazardous and the resident-general, General *Noguès, uncooperative. But Algiers was occupied the same day and Oran two days later—though 1,400 American and 700 French troops were killed in the process.

Initially the political situation was uncertain and complicated. Shortly before the landings took place, Robert *Murphy, Roosevelt's personal representative in North Africa, had informed the C-in-C French Forces, North Africa, General *Juin, that they were about to take place and had requested French co-operation. Juin was willing to co-operate but by chance the C-in-C of the Vichy French armed forces, Admiral *Darlan, was in Algiers and Juin refused to act without his authority. Initially, Darlan refused to countenance French co-operation, but after a day of negotiations, and telegrams to and from Vichy, he ordered Juin to negotiate a cease-fire and US troops entered Algiers that evening. Units were then dispatched by sea and air to secure the ports of Bougie and Bône, and nearby airfields, to support the overland advance into Tunisia.

Negotiations continued with Darlan who, on 10 November 1942, agreed to order a general cease-fire which stopped all fighting in French Morocco and Algeria and saved Casablanca from being stormed. But the political consequences were far-reaching. The Vichy government broke off relations with the USA and accepted the offer of German air support, which resulted in the immediate German occupation of Tunisian airfields. To assuage German anger the Vichy government repudiated Darlan's cease-fire, and when Darlan tried to rescind it he was promptly arrested by the Americans. But the Vichy government's action failed to stop the Germans moving into unoccupied (Vichy) France; Corsica was occupied by the Italians; and Axis troops started pouring into Tunisia with the acquiescence of the French resident-general, Admiral *Estéva.

The occupation of Vichy France released Darlan from his obligations to the Vichy government. After agreeing to co-operate with the Allies, he was appointed high commissioner for French North Africa by Eisenhower. Giraud, who had proved to be a non-starter politically for the Allies, became C-in-C French Forces, North Africa, with Juin under him. Doing a deal with such a notorious Vichyite as Darlan caused a furore, especially in London, but only he wielded the necessary influence to bring his countrymen on to the side of the Allies—though he failed to persuade the French Fleet at Toulon to join him and it subsequently scuttled itself (see FRENCH FLEET, SCUTTLING OF). However, on 24 December 1942, he was assassinated by a French student and was replaced as high commissioner by Giraud, who also remained as C-in-C. By then the French, including Estéva's ground forces in Tunisia, were firmly in the Allies' fold.

By the end of November 1942 the Luftwaffe was harassing the advancing Allies with increasing effectiveness while 17,000 Axis troops had been airlifted or shipped into Tunisia. Initially these troops came under Lt-General Walther Nehring's 90th Corps HQ. When Arnim, who was closely directed by the German C-in-C South-West, Field Marshal *Kesselring, arrived in December, 90th Corps became Fifth Panzer Army with 10th Panzer Division as its main striking force.

Arnim's task was to prevent the capture of Tunis; to stop the Allies reaching the central Tunisian coastline and thereby severing his forces from Rommel, who was then withdrawing into southern Tunisia; and to deepen his dangerously narrow bridgehead. Although Allied troops got within 20 km. (13 mi.) of Tunis, in the short term Arnim accomplished all three objectives. At the northern, coastal, end of the Allied line, Anderson's First Army—thwarted first by 10th Panzer Division's attacks around Tébourba; then by the rain and mud of a Tunisian winter and by inadequate air support; and lastly by the tenacious German defence of *Longstop Hill which blocked the way to Tunis—could only wait for reinforcements and better weather. At the mountainous southern end it was drier, and in mid-January 1st US Armoured Division and part of 1st US Infantry Division (see BIG RED ONE), commanded by Fredendall's 2nd US Corps HQ, gathered there to launch an attack towards the coast. But before this could be mounted Arnim launched his own offensive (EILBÖTE) on 18 January by attacking the poorly armed and equipped French divisions further north which were holding the Eastern Dorsale mountains south of Pont du Fahs.

Allied calculations that German tanks could not operate in this mountainous region soon proved erroneous and the French were thrown into disarray. On 24 January Anderson was given operational control of Allied troops, but by the end of the month all the Eastern Dorsale passes were in German hands and two weeks later the Germans started a new offensive. Arnim took Sidi Bou Zid and then Sbeitla, while some of Rommel's forces entered Gafsa unopposed as the Allies began withdrawing to the Western Dorsale mountains. This withdrawal was completed on 19 February 1943 but in one 48-hour period Fredendall lost two tank, two infantry, and two artillery battalions to Arnim's panzer divisions; and when Rommel struck at the *Kasserine Pass, instead of further north as *ULTRA intelligence had seemed to predict, Fredendall's forces cracked.

Fleetingly the two panzer armies now had the chance to outflank and destroy the Allied forces in northern Tunisia. But Rommel could no longer exercise the independence of command he had enjoyed during the *Western Desert campaigns. Instead of attacking towards Tébessa, as he knew he should, the Italian High Command (see COMANDO SUPREMO) ordered him northwards towards Le Kef and Allied reinforcements—'an appalling and unbelievable piece of shortsightedness' as he later described it. It certainly failed to achieve anything and increasing Allied resistance, the unsuitable terrain for mobile operations, and Arnim's obstructiveness forced Rommel to abandon the offensive on 22 February 1943. The next day he was promoted C-in-C Army Group Africa and handed over command of his German–Italian Panzer Army, which was renamed First Italian

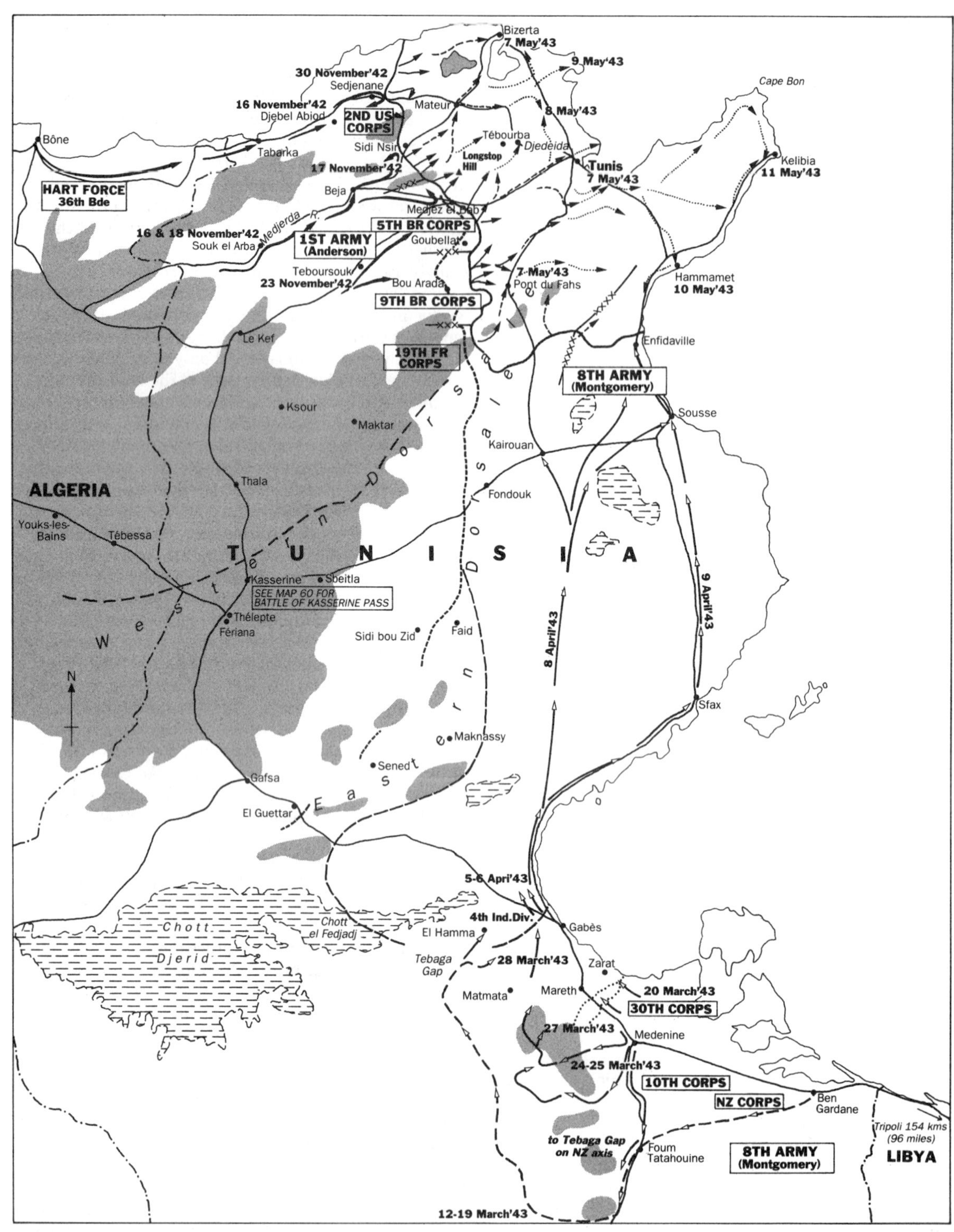

76. **North African campaign**, March–May 1943

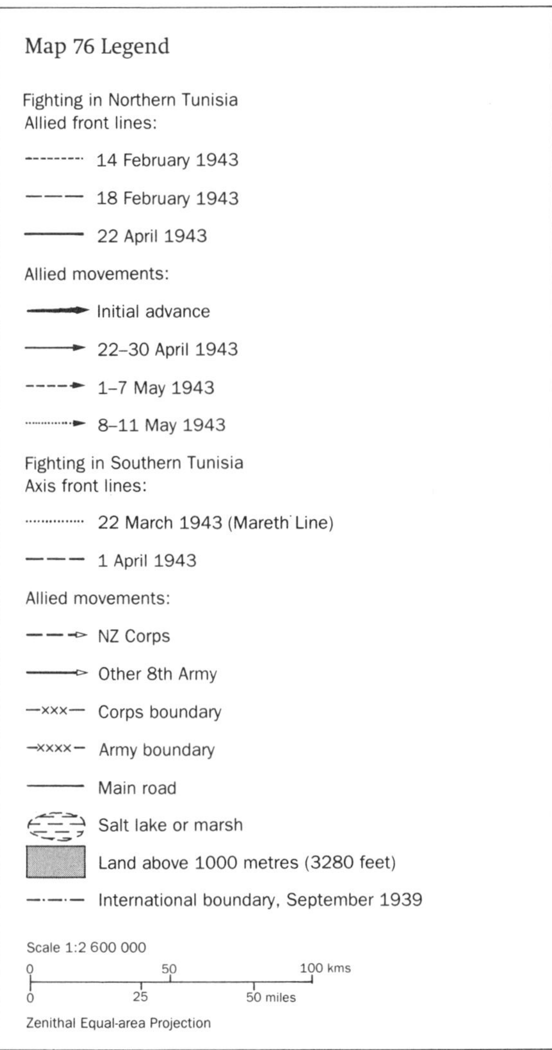

Army, to General *Messe. Then on 28 February ULTRA revealed his plans to use all three of his panzer divisions to attack *Montgomery's Eighth Army which were approaching the Axis *Mareth Line defences in southern Tunisia.

On 20 February, while the fighting at Kasserine was at its height, the decision made at the Casablanca conference the previous month (see SYMBOL), to form Eighteenth Army Group and a unified air command, was implemented. Air Chief Marshal *Tedder became AOC-in-C Mediterranean Air Command and General *Alexander was appointed Eisenhower's deputy and C-in-C of the new group which comprised both armies (First and Eighth) in Tunisia. Two days later the Allies were back at Kasserine, but much confidence had been lost, as well as men and *matériel*, and Fredendall was replaced in March by Patton. Alexander, who had as his directive the completion of the campaign by the end of April 1943, so that the *Sicilian campaign landings could take place before August that year, found the command situation abysmal. He reported that British, American, and French units were all mixed up on the front, especially in the south, that there was no policy or plan of campaign and that, as a result, the Allies had lost the initiative.

The front was quickly reorganized. National sectors were created and the French divisions were re-equipped. Some ground was lost in the north when Arnim, trying to take advantage of the chaos caused at Kasserine, launched a new, and ill-conceived, offensive (OCHSENKOPF), but by 1 April it had all been retaken by the Allies. In southern Tunisia, the Eighth Army rebuffed Rommel at *Medenine on 6 March and three days later Rommel, a sick man, flew to Germany and never returned.

Messe's forces defending the Mareth Line more or less matched Montgomery's in numbers, but the Eighth Army was far better equipped. It also had more tanks and was strongly supported by the *Western Desert Air Force. Even so, Montgomery's frontal assault on the Mareth Line, begun on 19 March, failed. He then outflanked it inland but was unable to prevent Messe withdrawing to another position further north at Wadi Akarit. But with Patton's 2nd US Corps now threatening his flank and rear, Messe's position was critical—as, indeed, was the whole of Army Group Africa's. When one of Kesselring's staff officers commented to Arnim that the Army Group seemed always to be thinking of retreat, squinting over its shoulder, as he described it, Arnim replied bitterly that he was squinting for ships, for he was without food or ammunition, as Rommel's army had been before him. The consequences, he warned, were inevitable.

The inevitable soon occurred. The tourniquet applied by the naval blockade and by the Allied air forces to the Axis forces in Tunisia was now so tight that few supplies or reinforcements were reaching them. On land, an attempt by 2nd US Corps to reach the coast failed, but Montgomery broke through at Wadi Akarit and forced Messe into another withdrawal. Slowly, the Axis began to be pressed into a pocket around Tunis: one of First Army's corps began clearing the hilly country north of the Beja–Medjez el Bab road, while 2nd US Corps, now commanded by Lt-General *Bradley, moved to the northern flank to attack towards Bizerta. These preliminaries accomplished, Alexander launched an all-out offensive (VULCAN) on 22 April 1943. The First Army attacked towards Tunis to envelop Arnim's main force blocking the Medjez–Tunis road; Bradley struck at Bizerta and 19th French Corps advanced towards Pont du Fahs; but Montgomery failed to break through Messe's new positions at Enfidaville, and he remained on the defensive. When VULCAN appeared to be flagging Alexander took Montgomery's advice—and two of his best divisions—to help mount a final assault (STRIKE) by First Army's 9th Corps along the Medjez–Tunis road. Aided by massive artillery and air support this succeeded and

Arnim's defences collapsed, with Tunis, Bizerta, and Pont du Fahs all falling in one day. The two German panzer armies now disintegrated into isolated pools of resistance which were mopped up one by one, the last surrendering on 13 May. The Allies, who had 76,000 casualties during the campaign, took more than 238,000 *prisoners-of-war.

It was argued at the time, especially by the US *Joint Chiefs of Staff, and has been argued by some since, that the North African campaign sidetracked the Allies from their primary task of defeating the Germans by invading France. But given the shaky performance of the Allied command system, and of some troops, it is hard to see how such an undertaking could have been successfully achieved in 1942 or 1943. As it was, US troops under Patton showed their true mettle in the *Sicilian campaign, and the experiences gained from the TORCH landings were put to good use both there and when the Allies landed in Normandy in June 1944 (see OVERLORD). See also GRAND ALLIANCE and LAND POWER.

Jackson, W., *The Battle for North Africa* (London, 1975).
Macmillan, H., *War Diaries* (London, 1984).
Sainsbury, K., *The North African Landings, 1942* (London, 1976).

North Cape, battle of, see SCHARNHORST.

Northern Combat Area Command, see CHINA–BURMA–INDIA THEATRE; also STILWELL.

NORWAY

For the fighting in Norway see NORWEGIAN CAMPAIGN which follows this entry

1. Introduction

When war broke out in September 1939 Norway, a constitutional monarchy with a parliamentary system of government and a population of 3 million, had been fully independent only since breaking out of the union with Sweden in 1905. Its policy was one of neutrality, and its security was believed to rest on the two corner-stones of its geographical situation on Europe's periphery and a trust in automatic protection by British sea power. The experiences of the *First World War had shown the problem of combining neutrality with extreme dependence on foreign trade and on the earnings of one of the world's largest merchant navies. But having somehow come through with its neutrality intact, Norway expected the impending war to follow a similar pattern.

Having practically disarmed during the 1920s, Norway faced the outbreak of war with a minority Social Democratic cabinet which had come to power in 1935 on a programme for ending the economic and social crisis. Both ideologically and for reasons of economy the government had only reluctantly agreed to increase the defence budget during the last two years of peace. Norway thus faced the war with an outdated navy, air forces with few modern aircraft, and an inadequately trained conscript army. Suggestions during the winter of 1939–40 for a national coalition government were turned down by the prime minister, Johan Nygaardsvold.

2. Domestic life under German occupation

Norway's pre-war economy was heavily dependent on external trade. Its exports, mainly products of the fisheries, of forestry, and of mining, were insufficient to pay for imports of foodstuffs and machinery, and the balance was made up by the earnings of the world's fourth largest and most modern merchant navy. The German invasion in April 1940 and the occupation meant that Germany not only took control of Norway's exports but became responsible also for supplying the country with imported food, for most of the merchant navy, requisitioned by the Norwegian government during the Norwegian campaign, served in Allied war transport under control of the government-in-exile (see below).

German long-term plans for the development of the economy of occupied Norway aimed at exploiting the country's resources of minerals and hydro-electric power, especially by expanding its aluminium industry. But from 1942 onwards German economic policy for Norway became reoriented towards meeting Germany's short-term needs directly connected with the conduct of the war, such as the maintenance of the very large German army of occupation (one German soldier for every ten Norwegians). Exploitation of Norway's resources became increasingly ruthless: the standard of living was drastically reduced, with most consumer goods being rationed; one-third of the national income went to pay for the costs of the occupation; one-fifth of Norway's pre-war capital stock was destroyed. In 1944 a *scorched earth policy was applied to the two northernmost counties, by German forces retreating as Soviet troops began the *liberation of that area.

Apart from the economy, the German occupation regime was mild compared with conditions prevailing in eastern Europe. Norwegians had the dubious honour of being regarded by the Nazi regime as a kindred folk—a wayward Nordic tribe that should be led into the Greater German Reich through persuasion. Hence the willingness to let Vidkun *Quisling's Nazi Party have a role in the administration of the country under the watchful eyes of the German Reichskommissariat, even though in pre-war elections or in membership the party never gained the support of more than about 3% of the people. About 40,000 Norwegians were imprisoned or put in *concentration camps by the Germans during the war, 8,000 of those being sent to camps in Germany, where about 2,000 of them—including about 700 Jews—died. A further 500 Norwegians were killed or executed for resistance activities.

The liberation of Norway began with units of the Red Army crossing the border into the county of Finnmark in October 1944, followed by Norwegian troops from the UK and Sweden (see GOVERNMENT-IN-EXILE, below) which gradually took control of the two northern counties. The remainder of the country was held by German forces until *V-E Day, 8 May 1945. The government returned to Norway on 31 May, followed by King Haakon VII (1872–1957) on 7 June—five years to the day after he had left for exile.

3. Government

(a) Occupation Regime

In the evening of 9 April 1940, the day of the German invasion, Quisling attempted a *coup d'état*, announcing the formation of 'a government of national unity'. But it soon became clear to the German authorities that Quisling's attempt to set up a rival government merely stiffened Norwegian resistance to the invaders, and on 15 April a non-political Administrative Council was set up in co-operation with the Supreme Court to deal with civil affairs in the occupied areas. The German Reichskommissar, Josef *Terboven, tried during the summer of 1940 to suspend the exiled king and his government, and to transform the Administrative Council into a government of *collaboration.

Parliamentarians and other public figures in the occupied country, discouraged by the apparent invincibility of the Germans and the feebleness of Allied responses, attempted to establish a *modus vivendi* with the German authorities. An appeal was sent to the king asking him to abdicate in favour of a 'Council of the Realm' to be established in occupied territory. After the king's refusal, the parliamentarians continued to discuss the composition of such a council with the German authorities, and by September a majority of them were recorded as in favour of voting to suspend the king for the duration of the war. The negotiations in Oslo then broke down over new German demands, and on 25 September the Reichskommissar announced his appointment of Nazi Commissioner Ministers to head the various government departments. Also, as local government officials resigned rather than co-operate in the Nazi 'New Order' (see GERMANY, 4), collaborators were appointed in their place. But the lack of suitably qualified personnel from Quisling's party meant that their penetration of elective or administrative bodies was far from complete. As a consequence, many civil servants, members of local councils, policemen, and so on faced the dilemma of either resigning, leaving their functions at the mercy of Nazi-appointed replacements, or carrying on and trying as far as possible to sabotage or at least soften the impact of the New Order.

A final attempt to establish Quisling as a national figure with a semblance of independence occurred on 1 February 1942, when he was formally installed as Minister President. Together with his council of ministers he now made determined attempts to promote the New Order, for instance, through the curriculum of elementary and secondary schools. But a flood of protest letters from parents, and the refusal of a majority of the teachers to co-operate, convinced Terboven that the German authorities had to keep Quisling on a tight rein in order to avoid more widespread unrest. The Reichskommissariat, together with the C-in-C of the German forces in Norway, henceforth kept close control of affairs.

(b) Government-in-exile

At the end of the Norwegian campaign King Haakon VII and the government decided to go into exile in the UK, in order to maintain Norway as a sovereign state and protecct the nation's interests and assets—of which the most important was the merchant navy—in the free world. They brought with them the nucleus of an administration as well as of a navy and an air force.

The king's refusal to abdicate strengthened his position as the symbol of resistance and national unity, and his unflinching support of his cabinet served gradually to dispel the unpopularity of a government blamed for the disasters that had befallen the country in the spring of 1940. Co-operation between the home front and the government-in-exile improved as communications across the North Sea or via Sweden could be established, although sharp disputes flared in 1943 over the question of the respective roles of the government and an increasingly self-confident resistance leadership in the transition from war to peace, and in the shaping of post-war Norway. The king and his government were throughout recognized by Allied as well as neutral states as the legitimate representatives of the sovereign kingdom of Norway, and the earnings of the merchant fleet secured their financial independence. Relations with their main ally, the UK, which had suffered during the *'phoney war' and the Norwegian campaign, steadily improved after the Norwegian government in the autumn of 1940 renounced its pre-war policy of neutrality and isolation in favour of close co-operation with the western powers during and after the war.

Soon after the government's arrival in London it decided to start the build-up of armed forces that were identifiably Norwegian. The navy began with a few older ships based on Rosyth in Scotland as well as a squadron of motor launches in the Channel, before taking over five of the US destroyers obtained by the UK under the *destroyers-for-bases agreement. From this basis the Royal Norwegian Navy grew to a complement of 58 ships and 5,000 men in January 1943. The combined air forces established a training centre in Canada, and fielded their first operational squadron on Icelandic bases in June 1941. Two fighter squadrons and another maritime squadron became operational before the end of 1942. With most of the recruits escaping from Norway across the North Sea, manpower was the limiting factor, which hampered the build-up of land forces. A small brigade was formed in Scotland, in readiness for the liberation, as well as a company of commandos, and an Independent Company which took part in Allied raids on the Norwegian coast and provided agents and instructors for tasks inside the occupied country. All the units were national in character, but served under British operational control in accordance with a treaty defining them as the 'forces of the kingdom of Norway allied with the United Kingdom'.

From 1943 a relaxation of Sweden's neutrality policy permitted the organization of an increasing flow of Norwegian refugees into light infantry forces known as 'police troops', numbering 12,000 in 1945. With an army of 3,500 in the UK, plus nearly 7,000 in the navy and about 2,500 in the air force, the government-in-exile at the end of the war mustered armed forces of about 25,000 men, more than 50 naval vessels, and 59 aircraft.

4. Armed forces

Having practically disarmed during the 1920s and early 1930s, Norway made considerable increases in the defence budget in the final years before the outbreak of the war. But the inevitable time lags of procurement meant that new aircraft, for example, remained on order at the time of the German invasion.

Norway's armed forces were based on conscription, but the period of national service had only been gradually increased from 48 to 84 days. The peacetime organization of the army comprised six divisions, each of which would on mobilization produce a fighting force of one brigade plus various ancillary units. This would on full mobilization provide a field army of 56,000 to protect a land area of 323,000 sq. km. (125,000 sq. mi.). Territorial units plus recruits under training would bring this up to an absolute maximum of 106,000 men. As regards equipment the main deficiencies were in armour, anti-tank, and anti-aircraft weapon systems. The navy, partially mobilized on the outbreak of war in September 1939 to guard Europe's longest coastline, disposed of four new escort destroyers and a new minelayer, two large but outmoded coastal defence vessels, three small pre-1918 destroyers, and about 40 smaller vessels. The coastal forts, partially manned, and the small naval air force, brought the total mobilized manpower of the navy to nearly 5,000 men by the end of 1939. The army air force could muster about 40 aircraft, only 16 of which were modern, and the naval air force 6 modern and about 20 older aircraft. There were 150 aircraft on order.

At the end of the fighting in north Norway in June 1940 those units of the navy and air forces which were able to do so were ordered to leave the country, while the army was demobilized and sent home. The German occupation regime did not foresee any Norwegian armed forces, and officers were allowed to return to their homes against a promise not to take up arms again against Germany. Towards the end of 1940 Quisling brought up the idea of admitting Norwegians to service with the German Army, and in January 1941 the first of a series of special 'Nordic' units, the Standarte Nordland, was officially announced by him. It never reached regimental strength, and was dissolved in 1943. A more ambitious scheme was 'The Norwegian Legion', created under the slogan 'Fight Against Bolshevism'. About 2,000 men served in the Legion, which suffered heavy losses during the *German–Soviet war before being disbanded. Other units intended for Norwegian volunteers were subsequently formed but had to be brought up to strength by volunteers from other occupied countries. Altogether about 5,000 Norwegian citizens did war service on the Eastern Front.

5. Intelligence

At the beginning of the war Norway possessed only the rudiments of an intelligence service in the form of small intelligence bureaus in the Norwegian Admiralty and the Army's General Staff. By July 1940 the foreign ministry in exile in London had established an intelligence section to run agents into occupied Norway in co-operation with the British Secret Intelligence Service (see MI6). In January 1941 this work was transferred to the Norwegian ministry of defence's Intelligence Bureau, which developed sections for co-operation with *MI5, MI6, and intelligence networks in occupied Norway. Particular emphasis was laid on providing operational intelligence about German naval movements on the coast of Norway, and for this purpose more than a hundred radio stations were established, with more than 200 Norwegian agents sent over from the UK.

From 1942 the reorganized Norwegian Defence Command (Forsvarets Overkommando, or FO) in London formed a special section for military intelligence, FOII, mainly for the purpose of systematic intelligence-gathering with a view to the liberation of Norway. By the end of the war FOII had a staff of about 700, and a subsidiary in Stockholm for better liaison with networks in occupied Norway. The largest of those networks, under the name of XU, had about 1,500 agents by the end of the war.

6. Merchant marine

At the outbreak of the Second World War the Norwegian merchant navy was the fourth largest in the world with about 4.8 million tons of mostly modern ships, including almost 20% of the world's tankers. Most of the ships were plying between foreign ports. The invasion on 9 April

1940 gave the Germans control of a number of mostly small ships in Norwegian waters, but the majority—85% of the fleet, or about 1,000 ships—was subsequently requisitioned by the legal Norwegian government for service with the Allies. This fleet was administered on behalf of the government-in-exile by the Nortraship organization from its headquarters in London and New York.

It has been estimated that in the spring of 1942 over 40% of the UK's imports of oil and petrol was transported by Norwegian tankers. Losses during the war amounted to more than 500 ships and more than 3,000 sailors. Thanks to the earnings of the merchant navy the Norwegian government-in-exile was economically independent of the Allies.

7. Resistance

Small, dispersed, and mostly unarmed military resistance groups began to be formed in Norway soon after the end of the Norwegian campaign. During the spring of 1941 contact was established with *SOE in the UK. A central leadership gradually emerged in Oslo, and in October 1941 this Milorg was recognized by the government-in-exile as the fourth arm of the Norwegian armed forces. From 1942 arms and instructors began to flow from Britain, on fishing vessels across the North Sea (see SHETLAND BUS), and later by air drops. Some sabotage actions were carried out, but setbacks through penetration of some networks by enemy agents, as well as the realization that the liberation of Norway would only come as part of a general German surrender, forced a reorientation of Milorg towards a 'force in being' ready to assist during the final liberation of the occupied country. Sabotage, such as the successful action against the heavy water plant at Rjukan (see VEMORK) was therefore carried out mainly by personnel from the Norwegian special forces sent in from the UK. At the time of the German capitulation Milorg, officially named the Home Forces, numbered about 40,000 men.

Civilian or political resistance arose in organized form after the attempts by the occupation regime to take control of the professional associations in 1941. Several of the associations formed clandestine networks to lead their members in the opposition against Nazification of the professions, and their leaders came together in a co-ordinating committee. This committee, working in liaison with a small group of public-spirited citizens which in mid-1941 had established contact with the government-in-exile, gradually assumed the functions of a general staff of civilian resistance, issuing instructions on how to meet the challenge of the New Order. The committee also forged close links with the central leadership, which meant that from the end of 1943 a strongly unified Norwegian resistance movement could work hand-in-hand with the government-in-exile in London.

After the occupation authorities in 1941 requisitioned all wireless receivers in the country, to stop people listening to Norwegian broadcasts from London, the underground press became an all-important means of maintaining morale and a spirit of resistance as well as counteracting the propaganda and bias of the heavily censored newspapers (see also PRESS). There were more than 300 such underground newspapers or news letters, many of them shortlived or appearing at irregular intervals as the people producing or distributing them were arrested. See also RESISTANCE. OLAV RISTE

Andenæs, J., Riste, O., and Skodvin, M., *Norway and the Second World War* (3rd edn., Oslo, 1983).

Nøkleby, B., and Riste, O., *Norway 1940–1945: The Resistance Movement* (4th edn., Oslo, 1984).

Riste, O., *'London-regjeringa': Norge i krigsalliansen 1940–1945*, 2 vols. (Oslo, 1973–9). ('The London Government: Norway in the wartime alliance'): the only comprehensive study of the Norwegian government-in-exile.)

Norwegian campaign. On 9 April 1940 Germany invaded Norway, and after a campaign that lasted two months the German forces had occupied the whole country. The assault is a prime example of a successful strategic and tactical surprise. Another salient feature is the combined use of air, sea, and naval forces—including paratroopers. The success of the enterprise secured German access to Swedish iron ore and other valuable *raw materials from Scandinavia, as well as valuable bases for Germany's submarine warfare in the battle of the *Atlantic and for air-sea operations against the *Arctic convoys to northern Russia (see ARCTIC CONVOYS). But the cost was high, as up to 350,000 German troops were required to occupy the vast, 323,000 sq. km. (125,000 sq. mi.) area and guard the coast against an Allied invasion.

During the *Finnish–Soviet war France and the UK had been preparing an expeditionary force to seize control of the port of Narvik—the only all-weather outlet for Swedish iron ore—under cover of aid to Finland. Rumours about such preparations led the Germans to plan counter-moves which would amount to a full-scale occupation of Denmark and Norway (WESERÜBUNG). The Soviet–Finnish *armistice on 13 March led to the abandonment of Allied preparations, but *Raeder, the chief of the German Navy, persuaded Hitler that WESERÜBUNG should be carried out as soon as possible, before the assembled naval forces had to be dispersed. The final order was given on 2 April, and the first supply ships left port the following day.

In the meantime the Anglo-French *Supreme War Council, giving in to pressure to break the inactivity of the *phoney war, had decided to lay mines on the Norwegian coast to force German ore vessels from Narvik out into the open seas where they could be attacked by the Royal Navy. The mines were laid in the morning of 8 April, by which time minor British forces had also been embarked on warships to counter possible German retaliatory moves against Norway. During that day it gradually dawned on the British Admiralty that a major German operation against Denmark and Norway was on its way, independent of Allied plans.

Norwegian campaign

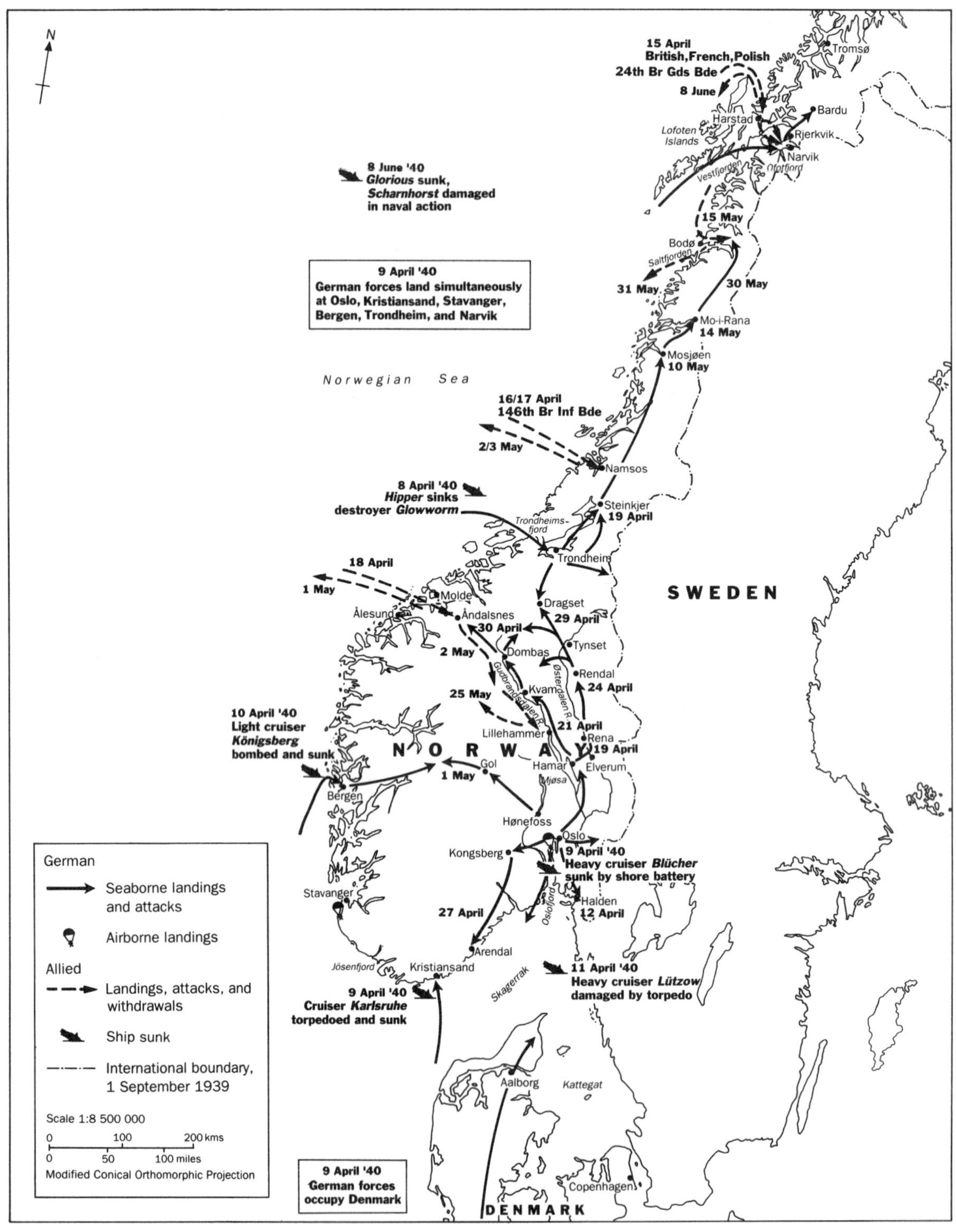

77. **Norwegian camapign**, April–June 1940

The surprise achieved by the Germans was due to three factors: first, the lack of real intelligence clues to the German operational plans and preparations; second, the complete absence in Norway of anything that could properly be called organs for the collection and analysis of military-political intelligence; third, the inability of decision-makers to free themselves from the established perception that a major German assault on Norway was rendered unthinkable by the superiority of British naval power in the area and any small-scale attacks would only be mounted in retaliation against major British violations of Norwegian neutrality. This perception, and particularly its latter component, led to a concentration of attention by Norway on the actions and intentions of the western Allies, and excluded consideration of the possibility that a German assault might occur independently of any Allied move.

A combination of flawed intelligence and strategic prejudice also explains why the British were taken by surprise. Convinced, like the Norwegians, that a major German assault on Norway was impossible in the face of British naval superiority, they were predisposed to interpret incoming reports of large-scale moves of German warships as indicating a break-out into the Atlantic. The success of the German invasion was thus due to a double surprise: the strategic surprise of launching an operation which went contrary to the rules of naval warfare, and tactical surprise in the actual execution of the assault.

The invasion (see Map 77) was carried out through a simultaneous assault on a number of the most important coastal cities, from Oslo in the south to Narvik in the north. Airborne troops were used for the two main airports at Oslo and Stavanger; for the rest the forces were carried on warships, with supplies and reinforcements brought in by merchant ships and aircraft. By the end of the morning the Germans had secured control of such major towns as Kristiansand, Stavanger, Bergen, Trondheim, and Narvik, severely curtailing mobilization efforts in those areas. The partly mobilized navy, with mostly old vessels, and the inadequately equipped coastal forts, were soon overwhelmed by the superior strength of the German Navy. The only serious setback for the Germans occurred in the Oslo fjord, where the vanguard of the invading force, the cruiser *Blücher*, was sunk by the guns and torpedoes of the Oscarsborg fortress.

King Haakon VII (1872–1957) and the government, which at 0530 had rejected a German ultimatum to surrender, profited from the respite provided by the sinking of the *Blücher* to escape to the interior of the country. Initial despair about the futility of an armed struggle against the invader gradually disappeared in the wake of Vidkun *Quisling's attempted *coup d'état* in the evening of 9 April, and of British promises of armed help. A new German ultimatum the following day was turned down, after which the government began to organize a somewhat improvised military resistance.

A new C-in-C, Major-General Otto Ruge, drew up a campaign plan based on a fighting retreat while organizing his forces and awaiting the promised assistance from France and the UK. But Allied assistance was weak, poorly organized, and slow in coming. A fixation on Narvik, and the fear of losses due to German air superiority, led to the abandonment of British plans for a naval assault to reconquer Trondheim in central Norway, and forces landed further south as part of a pincer movement against that city had to be sent to reinforce Ruge's southern front. By the end of April Allied forces had been evacuated from southern Norway, and the remaining Norwegian forces in the area capitulated on 3 May.

The king, the government, and the Norwegian High Command now moved to the Tromsø area in northern Norway. Here substantial Norwegian, French, Polish, and British troops were engaged in trying to eject the Germans from Narvik. Successful actions by British warships on 10 and 13 April (see NARVIK BATTLES) had eliminated the German naval force in the Narvik area, but cautious Allied commanders opted for a gradual advance in difficult terrain towards the town. On 28 May the port was successfully reconquered by French and Norwegian troops, and the German forces under Maj-General Eduard Dietl were pushed back towards the Swedish frontier. But by then the German offensive in the West (see FALL GELB) had forced the Allies to decide to abandon the campaign in Norway. Allied troops were evacuated at the beginning of June, and on 7 June the king and his government departed for the UK and exile.

Of the total losses in connection with the Norwegian campaign the heaviest were suffered by the Germans—about 5,500 men, more than 200 aircraft, and a number of their most modern warships, a loss from which the German surface navy never quite recovered. The British lost nearly 4,500 men, of whom about 1,500 went down with the aircraft carrier *Glorious* and her two destroyer escorts when they were sunk by the **Scharnhorst* on their way back to the UK. About 1,800 Norwegian lives were lost, and French and Polish losses amounted to about 500.

OLAV RISTE

Adams, J., *The Doomed Expedition: The Campaign in Norway 1940* (London, 1989).
Derry, T. K., *The Campaign in Norway* (London, 1952).
Moulton, J. L., *A Study of Warfare in Three Dimensions: The Norwegian Campaign of 1940* (Athens, Oh., 1967).

Nowak, Jan (b.1913), pseudonym of Zdzisław Jeziorański, a courier for the Polish Home Army. As Jan *Karski had before him, he took to London evidence of the *Final Solution, and was the first emissary to arrive after the *Warsaw ghetto rising which started in April 1943. From then until the end of the war he travelled to London and Stockholm five times to contact the UK government and the Polish government-in-exile, and he took part in the Warsaw rising of August 1944.

Nowak, J., *Courier from Warsaw* (Detroit, 1982).

Nuremberg raid, mounted by RAF Bomber Command on 30/31 March 1944; this operation has been described as the greatest air battle in history (M. Middlebrook, *The Nuremberg Raid*, London, 1973). Because of the extended flying time over Germany, and because the visibility was so good—many thought the operation should have been cancelled because of that—German night fighters employed their *Zahme Sau tactics and new SN-2 radar (see ELECTRONIC WARFARE) to great advantage. Of the 782 bombers dispatched, 106 were lost, a crippling casualty rate of 13.6%. Bomber Command had 743 dead or wounded and a further 159 became *prisoners-of-war. The high losses resulted in the bomber-stream method of flying to the target (see BOMBERS, 2) being abandoned. The damage to Nuremberg was minimal and the Germans lost only ten fighters. See also STRATEGIC AIR OFFENSIVES, 1.

Nuremberg trials. The post-war legal proceedings at Nuremberg are best viewed as falling into two closely related categories. The first covers hearings conducted there between November 1945 and October 1946 before an International Military Tribunal (IMT) jointly established by the USA, the USSR, the UK, and France. This action against 22 major German war criminals was complemented by an eleven-power prosecution and judgement of Japanese leaders at the broadly comparable *Far East war crimes trials. The second category embraces a series of 'Subsequent Proceedings', also held at Nuremberg and lasting until the spring of 1949. In them nearly 200 other prominent Nazis were tried before US Military Tribunals which operated within the American zone of occupation (see ALLIED CONTROL COMMISSIONS) under the terms of Control Council Law Number Ten.

The Nuremberg IMT

In the Moscow Declaration, issued after the *Moscow conference in October 1943, Roosevelt, Stalin, and Churchill made clear their determination to punish the principal Nazis, but left entirely vague all questions of procedure. As the war moved towards its close, the desirability of mounting full-scale legal proceedings remained in dispute. Though controversy occurred even in Washington, it was the US government which emerged as the strongest supporter of a comprehensive trial. The British cabinet, on the other hand, tended to oppose this option. It heeded the view of Lord Simon (1873–1954), the Lord Chancellor, that the fate of the German leadership cadre was essentially 'a political, not a judicial, question', and that summary process would provide a simpler (and potentially less embarrassing) solution. Not until May 1945 did the view of the Americans (supported eventually on this issue by the USSR) decisively prevail and the four-power London Agreement, signed on 8 August, two days after the dropping of an *atomic bomb on *Hiroshima, settled the ground rules for a major trial. These were embodied in a charter, which included provision for the establishment of a special tribunal comprising one judge, and one alternate, from each of the signatory states. The members then chose the senior British representative, Lord Justice Lawrence, to preside over what his colleague Norman Birkett called 'the greatest trial in history'.

On 6 October 1945 the prosecutors appointed by the four powers published their joint statement of indictment. With Hitler, *Himmler, and *Goebbels all dead, that document listed 24 others as defendants. However, by the time that the proceedings actually began in November, Robert *Ley had committed suicide and the industrialist Gustav Krupp had been deemed unfit to plead. All the remaining accused (see Table) reached the dock, except for *Bormann who could not be found either alive or dead and was tried *in absentia*. The prisoners had been selected largely to represent the major administrative groupings within the Third Reich. This approach reflected the original American plan to put heavy stress on the need for obtaining declaratory judgements of criminality against certain indicted Nazi organizations. But, once the trial was under way, this theme became subordinated to more directly human issues, concerning especially the degree of responsibility attaching to each of the individual prisoners.

Those in the dock were, in personality and demeanour, a motley crew. *Göring, weaned from drugs and in better mental and physical condition than for some years past, almost revelled in his position of primacy over the others. Certainly he surprised observers by the scope of the shrewdness and intelligence which he brought to bear on his self-justifications, which formed (as the writer Janet Flanner reported) 'the complicated narrative of a brain without a conscience'. As for the leading representatives of the army and navy—*Keitel, *Jodl, *Raeder, and *Dönitz—these were consistent in expressing a defiant pain at having their obedience to military duty interpreted as cause for criminal prosecution. The old conservatives *Neurath and *Papen, together with the banker *Schacht, manifested similar haughty indignation at finding themselves bracketed with a bully like *Frick or a vulgar mediocrity like *Sauckel. The cold brutality of *Kaltenbrunner, leading survivor from the *SS, was starkly evident; so too was that of Hans *Frank, the broken 'butcher of Poland'. The impression made by *Speer on the courtroom was more subtle and confusing, as he sought to project himself as a decent man misled—through the irresistible spell of the Führer, the promptings of youthful ambitions, and the moral tunnel-vision that so readily afflicts the technocrat. There were other defendants such as *Ribbentrop, *Funk, and *Rosenberg who seemed notable principally for their spinelessness; and, as for *Streicher and *Hess, even their sanity stood in question.

Each of the accused was tried under at least two of the four broad headings devised for the indictment. Count One covered the formulation or execution of 'a common plan or conspiracy'; Two, 'crimes against peace'; Three, 'war crimes'; and Four, 'crimes against humanity'. The

The defendants in the dock during the **Nuremberg trials**. They are, front row, left to right: Göring, Hess, Ribbentrop, Keitel, Kaltenbrunner, Rosenberg, Frank, Frick, Streicher, Funk, and Schacht. Behind them are, left to right: Dönitz, Raeder, Schirach, Sauckel, Jodl, Papen, Seyss-Inquart, Speer, Neurath, and Fritzsche.

American prosecuting team concentrated on the first category, and the British on the second; the Soviet and French representatives assumed principal responsibility for establishing guilt under both the remaining headings, dividing their task with reference to offences in eastern and western Europe respectively. Among these counts, the third had the firmest base in precedent. It built upon the efforts of the *Hague and *Geneva Conventions to deal with violations of the laws or customs of war. These were defined under the Nuremberg charter especially in terms of 'murder, ill-treatment or deportation to slave labour or for any other purpose of civilian population of or in occupied territory, murder or ill-treatment of prisoners-of-war or persons on the seas, killing of hostages, plunder of public or private property, wanton destruction of cities, towns, or villages, or devastation not justified by military necessity'.

Count Four constituted a more innovatory extension of Count Three, adapting it to circumstances of total conflict hardly envisaged when the law on 'war crimes' was first evolved. By referring to 'crimes against humanity', the prosecutors intended to convey that the Nazis had descended to quite unprecedented levels of systematized barbarity. As defined by the charter, this offence encompassed 'murder, extermination, enslavement, deportation, and other inhumane acts committed against any civilian population before or during the war, or persecutions on political, racial, or religious grounds in execution of or in connection with any crime within the jurisdiction of the Tribunal, whether or not in violation of domestic law of the country where perpetrated'. Taken together, Counts Three and Four spanned the area where the Nuremberg prosecution was most successful in obtaining verdicts of guilt from the IMT. Here the quantity and scope of the incriminating material, including photographic as well as documentary evidence concerning the extermination camp system (see OPERATION REINHARD), was such as to

The Nuremberg IMT: Defendants, charges, verdicts, and sentences

This listing of defendants follows the order of the indictment. G = Guilty; NG = Not Guilty.

Defendant	*Count 1*	*Count 2*	*Count 3*	*Count 4*	*Sentence*
Hermann Göring	G	G	G	G	Hanging
Rudolf Hess	G	G	NG	NG	Life
Joachim von Ribbentrop	G	G	G	G	Hanging
Wilhelm Keitel	G	G	G	G	Hanging
Ernst Kaltenbrunner	NG	—	G	G	Hanging
Alfred Rosenberg	G	G	G	G	Hanging
Hans Frank	NG	—	G	G	Hanging
Wilhelm Frick	NG	G	G	G	Hanging
Julius Streicher	NG	—	—	G	Hanging
Walther Funk	NG	G	G	G	Life
Hjalmar Schacht	NG	NG	—	—	Acquitted
Karl Dönitz	NG	G	G	—	10 Years
Erich Raeder	G	G	G	—	Life
Baldur von Schirach	NG	—	—	G	20 Years
Fritz Sauckel	NG	NG	G	G	Hanging
Alfred Jodl	G	G	G	G	Hanging
Martin Bormann	NG	—	G	G	Hanging
Franz von Papen	NG	NG	—	—	Acquitted
Artur Seyss-Inquart	NG	G	G	G	Hanging
Albert Speer	NG	NG	G	G	20 Years
Konstantin von Neurath	G	G	G	G	15 Years
Hans Fritzsche	NG	—	NG	NG	Acquitted
TOTAL GUILTY	8	12	16	16	
TOTAL NOT GUILTY	14	4	2	2	

Source: Contributor.

provide the main basis for the twelve death sentences eventually decreed by the judges.

Critics of Nuremberg have often argued, with good cause, that the trial would probably have been tidier and more effective had it concentrated simply on these third and fourth categories of indictment. Counts One and Two certainly proved more awkward for the prosecutors and judges alike to handle. The offence of 'conspiracy'—covering not just the substantive crime but also its preparation, as virtually a separate and additional matter—was based on a concept familiar only to the American and British lawyers involved. The stress placed on it by the trial planners from the USA in particular was such as to encourage at Nuremberg a constant, complex, and fascinating distortion of evidence from both sides. It gave the prosecutors extra motive for exaggerating the overall coherence of Nazi policy-making, while conversely supplying the defendants with added reason to seize every opportunity of overstating the confused nature of their responsibilities and, above all, the scale of their ignorance about what had been happening under the Reich. Viewed thus, the courtroom transcripts often look like the first rough sketch for much later debates between the 'intentionalist' and the 'structuralist' interpreters of such topics as the evolution of Nazi foreign policy or the path towards the *Final Solution. The judges themselves swiftly sensed the difficulties raised by the conspiracy accusation. They eventually ruled that it would be pursued only in respect to the period starting from Hitler's 'Hossbach' meeting of November 1937, at which he reiterated to a group of his followers his intention of nursing a policy of aggressive expansion (see LEBENSRAUM), and only in association with the offences alleged under Count Two.

That area of accusation became the most problematic of all. The indictment defined it as embracing 'the planning, preparation, initiation, and waging of wars of aggression, which were also wars in violation of international treaties, agreements, and assurances'. It listed these wars as the ones launched by Germany against Poland, the UK, and France in 1939; against Denmark, Norway, Belgium, the Netherlands, and Luxemburg in 1940; and against Yugoslavia, Greece, the USSR, and the USA in 1941. But the reference to violations of international law during the preparatory planning of these aggressions meant that Count Two, in close association with the conspiracy charge under Count One, drew the court into tangled issues of historical as well as legal judgement concerning the *origins of the Second World War. The prosecutors felt obliged to contend that various compacts from the inter-war period had indisputably evolved into a legal consensus about crimes against peace, which should now for the first time be enforced through penal sanctions. There was little difficulty in proving Hitler to have been by far the most aggressive actor on the European diplomatic scene during the 1930s. But the formal criminality of his pre-war foreign policies was much more disputable, as Simon (fearful of counter-charges about *ex post facto* legislation) had made amply plain to the British cabinet in April 1945. Pivotal to Count Two was the *Kellogg–Briand Pact for the renunciation of war, signed in 1928 and subsequently ratified by all major and most minor states. This made no reference to penalties, and provided no clear definition of 'aggressive war'. All the same, at Nuremberg the pact was accorded seminal importance. Was it however, as one of the defence lawyers argued, a significance belied by the attitudes and practices of all the main powers as these actually developed through the 1930s?

The record of that decade was indeed littered with complications for the IMT. Prosecutors piously invoked the aims of the *League of Nations, a body to which the USA had never belonged and from which the USSR was eventually expelled. As for the British and French governments, certain aspects of their reaction to Mussolini's Abyssinian invasion suggested some condoning of aggression. While the defendants were repeatedly castigated for not seeing where **Mein Kampf* pointed, the bearing of this criticism upon Allied policy-makers was neglected. As Schacht later wrote in his memoirs, 'How were the German people supposed to realize that they were living under a criminal government when foreign countries treated this same government with such marked respect?' In 1938 Anglo-French protests against the German annexation of Austria had been remarkably tame, and the participation of *Chamberlain and *Daladier in the *Munich agreement left these figures open to the charge of having been accessories (however reluctant) to criminal action. As E. L. Woodward, historical adviser to the foreign office, was still warning the trial planners in August 1945: 'Up to September 1, 1939, His Majesty's government were prepared to condone everything Germany had done to secure her position in Europe.' Even deeper embarrassment was caused by the *Nazi–Soviet Pact on 23 August 1939, and above all by its cynical 'secret protocol' which gave the USSR a free hand to launch its own aggression against eastern Poland, the Baltic States, and Finland. Moreover, once the Nuremberg indictment had included the German attack on Norway (see NORWEGIAN CAMPAIGN), Whitehall was keen to prevent the defence from probing too deeply into discussions of 1939–40 concerning the case for a pre-emptive British landing, if necessary even against Norwegian resistance.

At these points, and at others concerned with the subsequent conduct of the war, the prisoners predictably did whatever they could to discredit the Nuremberg proceedings as mere 'victors' justice'. After the Allies' own *strategic air offensives, the prosecutors found it increasingly awkward to press home charges involving 'wanton destruction of cities'; and, as the judges of the IMT explicitly conceded, the trial soon revealed that Germany's policy of unrestricted *submarine warfare had been broadly matched by Anglo-American practices (see LACONIA). Still wider problems stemmed from the Soviet presence in the courtroom, which meant that one nakedly totalitarian regime—with its own Stalinist record of mass murders and deportations, and of rigged trials (see MOSCOW TRIALS, for example)—was passing judgement on another. In eastern Europe the war had clearly been waged with utter callousness, from both sides. Supremely indicative of this was the *Katyń Forest massacre. Though the USSR insisted on including this slaughter of Poles in the indictment, by the close of the trial it was more than ever evident that the atrocity had been committed not in 1941, as alleged, but in 1940 when the Smolensk region was still under Soviet rather than Nazi control. The tribunal itself made no concluding reference to the matter—a silence which was, in its own way, thunderously loud.

Historians now know, especially from the papers of the principal American judge, Francis Biddle (1886–1968), a good deal about the secret processes by which the fate of the defendants was eventually determined. There was a certain measure of haggling and horse-trading (most notably, to avoid Biddle making public his view that Dönitz should be acquitted on the charges as formulated), but the main impression is one of great care and general fairness within the sometimes compromising framework imposed by the charter. Throughout the trial the judges, guided by Lord Justice Lawrence's robust good sense, had bothered less with flights of jurisprudential theory than with the requirements of practical wisdom. They announced their verdicts and sentences in the courtroom on 1 October 1946. Two weeks later—with Bormann still missing and with Göring's suicide cheating the hangman by a few hours—ten defendants went to the gallows. On last-minute instructions from Moscow the main Soviet judge, General I. Nikitchenko, dissented publicly from the failure to add Hess to that number, and from the three acquittals. He also expressed the view of the USSR that the Reich cabinet, together with the General Staff and High Command, should have been retained on the list of organizations that were finally deemed criminal which included the SS and the 'Leadership Corps of the Nazi Party'.

Those who mounted the Nuremberg trial accepted that much of its success would have to be gauged by the impetus which, in the longer term, it might give to the development of a proper system of international criminal law—one which would enable the world community to take effective judicial action against those who waged aggressive war or pursued genocidal policies. On that topic, much has been spoken since 1945 and very little actually achieved. The biggest difficulty remains the fact that proceedings of the Nuremberg type are attractive to governments only when the identity of victors and vanquished is conveniently settled in advance. In its more immediate aims, however, the

IMT registered a firmer achievement. The trial's imperfections undoubtedly weakened its beneficial impact upon the German public, and gave comfort to those ardent to purvey neo-fascist myths. But far fewer fantasies developed than after 1918, and far fewer than would have been the case had the advocates of summary execution won the day in 1945. On balance, the IMT played a positive role in detailing the horrors of Nazism both before and during the Second World War, and thus in creating better prospects for democratic stability within the emerging Federal Republic. Finally, it needs to be emphasized that the Nuremberg trial, however flawed, gave those who stood in its dock an infinitely better hearing than anyone ever received before a Nazi court, or indeed amidst the infernal conditions of *Auschwitz or *Treblinka where even the pretence of legal forms was so murderously abandoned.

Subsequent proceedings at Nuremberg

The principles and procedures evolved for the main legal action at Nuremberg were also applied, in broadly similar terms, to other *war crimes trials conducted by various Allied powers operating on a more individual basis. Most particularly, Control Council Law Number Ten of December 1945 entitled any of the four forces that were actually occupying post-war Germany (see Map I) to arrange its own zonal prosecutions. Although the Soviet authorities made no use of this specific provision, it did supply the basis upon which, for example, British Military Courts operated at Hamburg, Wuppertal, and elsewhere with regard to defendants such as General von *Manstein. That same inter-Allied agreement also empowered the Americans, as occupiers of Germany's south-eastern zone, to launch a second phase of proceedings at Nuremberg.

There, between November 1946 and April 1949, US Military Tribunals settled the fate of a further 185 defendants. Though the responsibility for prosecution and judgement now rested with a single power, the variety and scale of the offences alleged were sufficient to lead international lawyers to regard these proceedings as the most significant supplement to the work of the earlier Nuremberg court and to that of the Tokyo IMT (see FAR EAST WAR CRIMES TRIALS). The Americans organized the new set of hearings into twelve different trials, whose titles are usually cited in the following shorthand form:

1. *The Medical Case*, charging senior Nazi doctors with having conducted experiments upon the inmates of concentration camps;
2. *The Milch Case*, involving *forced labour and medical experimentation at *Dachau;
3. *The Justice Case*, concerning abuses of legal process within the Third Reich;
4. *The Pohl Case*, directed against SS officers involved in the administration of *concentration camps and of slave labour-programmes;
5. *The Flick Case*, involving industrialists' complicity in the confiscation of Jewish property and in the use of forced labour;
6. *The I. G. Farben Case*, probing similar offences by officials of the leading chemicals manufacturer;
7. *The Hostages Case*, bearing upon ill-treatment of civilians in south-eastern Europe;
8. *The RuSHA Case*, mounted against officials of the SS Race and Settlement Office implicated in the policies of genocide;
9. *The *Einsatzgruppen* Case, concerning SS units responsible for mass murder;
10. *The Krupp Case*, again focusing on the industrial exploitation of slave labour and confiscated property;
11. *The Ministries Case*, directed against officials from the foreign office and other departments who had been engaged in laying the diplomatic, economic, and other foundations for Hitler's 'New Order' (see GERMANY, 4);
12. *The High Command Case*, charging senior military figures with offences against *prisoners-of-war, and against civilians in occupied areas.

Overall, the dozen trials conducted by US military tribunals at Nuremberg resulted in the acquittal of 35 defendants (though some of those later faced German denazification courts) and the release of a further 19 on various other grounds. Death sentences were implemented against 24 of those charged, while 20 were condemned to gaol for life and 87 to shorter terms of imprisonment. MICHAEL BIDDISS

Gilbert, G. M., *Nuremberg Diary* (London, 1948).
Smith, B. F., *Reaching Judgment at Nuremberg* (London, 1977).
Tusa, A. and J., *The Nuremberg Trial* (London, 1983).
Tutorow, N. (ed.), *War Crimes, War Criminals, and War Crimes Trials: An Annotated Bibliography and Source Book* (New York, 1986).

Nyasaland, see BRITISH CENTRAL AFRICA.

OBOE, see ELECTRONIC NAVIGATION SYSTEMS.

Observer Corps, see UK, 6.

occupation. Despite dictionary definitions, 'occupation' is a term which in the context of war is usually employed selectively and subjectively, that is, for military operations that are not approved. Hence, in Allied literature, operations conducted by the western Allies or by the USSR are generally described as *'liberations', whilst similar operations conducted by Axis forces are described as 'occupation' or 'invasion'. In contemporary Axis literature, the roles of 'liberator' and 'occupier' were exactly reversed.

Reality was rather more complicated. Operations by the Allied armies were not always welcome to the local population; and operations by the *Axis powers were not uniformly resented.

In two key instances, however, the Allied powers dropped all pretence of 'liberating' the countries which their armies entered. The Allied policy of *unconditional surrender ensured that Germany and Japan were to be occupied by Allied forces regardless of the wishes of the populations concerned. In these two cases, the term 'Allied Occupation' was both conventional and correct.

NORMAN DAVIES

Ocean Island, see NAURU.

O'Connor, Lt-General Sir Richard (1889–1981), British Army officer who commanded the Western Desert Force which defeated Italian forces during the early *Western Desert campaigns. He was captured in March 1941, but escaped in September 1943 and commanded 8th Corps during the *Normandy campaign. But 'the experience of capture and imprisonment ... had taken its toll, and O'Connor was often only a ghost of his former self' (N. Hamilton, *Monty: The Field Marshal, 1944–1976*, London, 1986, p. 98). In December 1944 he was posted to India and promoted general in April 1945. He was knighted in 1941.

Baynes, J., *The Forgotten Victor* (London, 1989).

OCTAGON, codename for the second Quebec conference held from 12 to 16 September 1944 to discuss future Allied strategy (see GRAND ALLIANCE). Present were Churchill and Roosevelt, and their diplomatic and military advisers. Churchill offered a British fleet (see TASK FORCE 57) to operate with the Americans in the *Pacific war. The president, having earlier overridden Admiral *King's objections, replied that 'the British Fleet was no sooner offered than accepted.' The post-war division of Germany into occupation zones was agreed (see ALLIED CONTROL COMMISSIONS and Map I) and the *Morgenthau Plan for its deindustrialization discussed. It was also agreed that the UK would continue to receive *Lend-Lease as long as the war with Japan continued. See also DIPLOMACY.

Oder–Neisse Line, the *de facto* German–Polish frontier at the end of the Second World War. Running south from the Baltic Sea, it followed the course of the River Oder to the western River Neisse and then along the Neisse to the Czechoslovak border.

At the Teheran and Yalta conferences (see EUREKA and ARGONAUT), the Allied powers agreed in principle to the idea of moving Poland westwards at Germany's expense. The USSR, the UK, and the USA supported this proposal as a means of compensating Poland for its territorial losses to the USSR (see POLISH–SOVIET FRONTIER).

At the Potsdam conference in July–August 1945 (see TERMINAL), the Oder–Neisse Line took its final shape. Although the American and British delegations accepted the line of the Oder, they objected to the western Neisse as the southern part of the boundary. The USSR staunchly supported the westernmost extension of Polish frontiers. Uniquely, the Allied powers invited Polish representatives to present their case for the Oder–Western Neisse Line to the conference.

With the final joint communiqué at Potsdam, the Oder–Western Neisse line became the post-war German–Polish frontier. The onset of the *Cold War and muddled understanding of the political and physical geography of Central Europe by the western powers had produced a frontier with every attribute except legal international recognition. The Allied powers placed German territories east of the Oder–Neisse Line 'under the administration of the Polish state' pending the 'peace settlement'. The communiqué also sanctioned the removal of the German population 'remaining in Poland'. This latter measure, more than any other ambiguous wording in the communiqué, made the Oder–Neisse Line into a permanent frontier. *De jure* recognition eventually came with the German reunification treaty signed in Moscow on 12 September 1990. See also DIPLOMACY.

PAUL LATAWSKI

Kulski, W. W., *Germany and Poland: From War to Peaceful Relations* (Syracuse, NY, 1976).
Szaz, Z. M., *Germany's Eastern Frontiers: The Problem of the Oder–Neisse Line* (Chicago, 1960).

Odessa organization, fictional body alleged to have been founded by Austrian Nazis after the fall of the Third Reich to help those who had committed *war crimes and were wanted by Allied, German, and Austrian prosecuting authorities to escape abroad. Though the organization never existed, there were certain avenues of escape, called ratlines, for Nazi criminals and collaborators (see VATICAN), one of which (Tirol–Rome–Genoa–South America or Near East) was later dubbed the Odessa Route. Odessa was an abbreviation of Organisation der ehemaligen SS-Angehörigen (Organization of former *SS members).

A. STREIM

Oder–Neisse Line

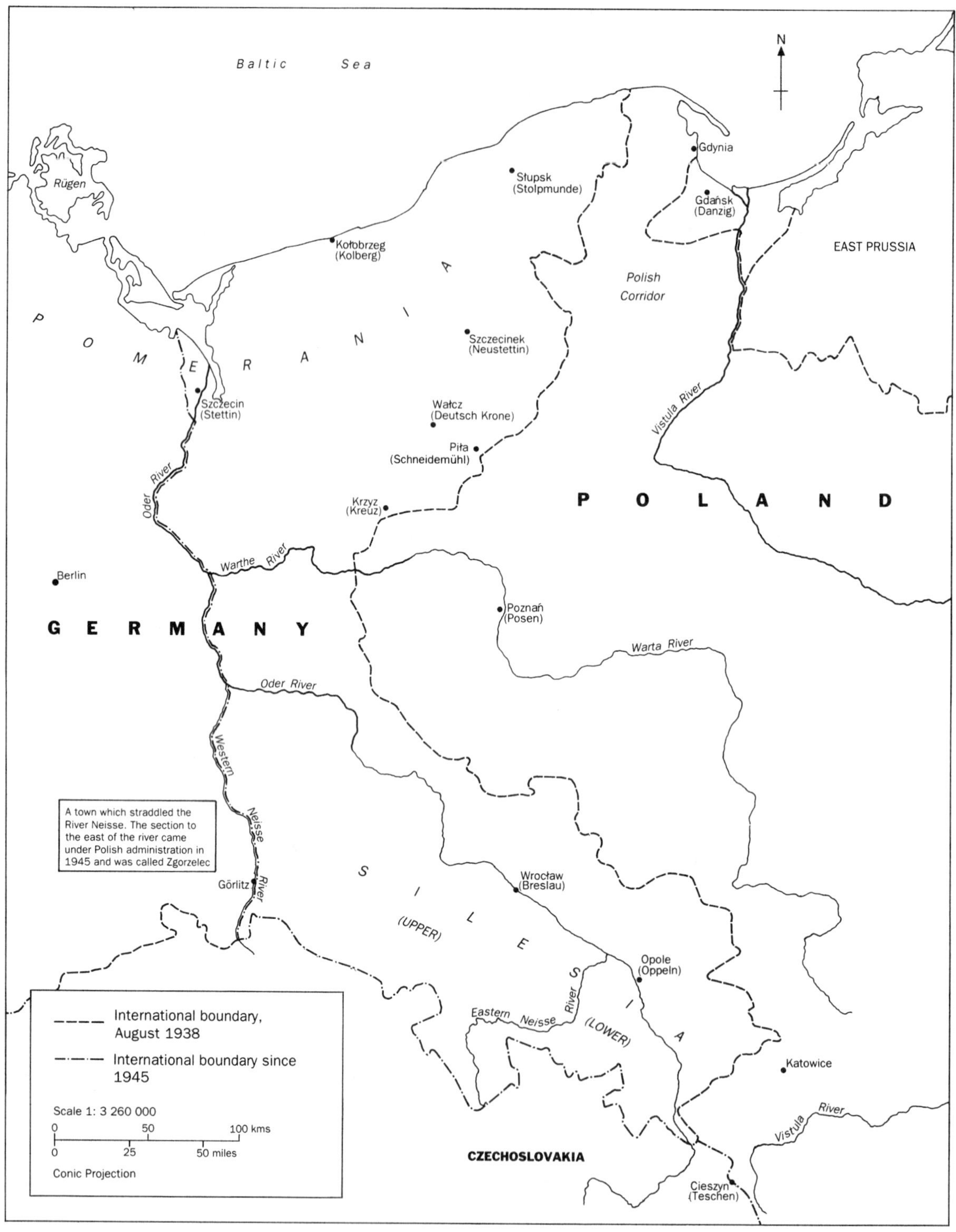

78. **Oder–Neisse Line**

Office of Price Administration (OPA), US civilian agency established under Leon Henderson in August 1941. It was the successor to, and had the same function as, the Office of Price Administration and Civilian Supply, which had been formed under Henderson in April 1941 to prevent spiralling prices, rising costs, profiteering, and inflation. It controlled prices in the shops, issued ration cards to every citizen, froze rents in some areas, and introduced rationing of scarce commodities. Lack of rubber made car owners early victims of its powers, with the sale of tyres being strictly controlled; but petrol was not rationed until December 1942. Sugar was rationed from April 1942, shoes from February 1943, and the OPA made sure that meat rationing was fair when it was introduced in March 1943 by issuing a 40,000-word document on how it should be distributed and sold. But unlike the UK, where rationing laws were strictly enforced, black marketeers and violators of OPA restrictions were lightly dealt with in the courts: only 1.5% of prosecutions resulted in prison sentences. However, in its policy of price control the OPA was much more successful and received full public support. Compared with the UK, where rationing lingered on until the early 1950s, the OPA ended controls swiftly in the USA. On 16 August 1945 it removed them from petrol, fuel oil, and processed foods, and by the end of the year very few remained. See also USA, 2.

Office of Scientific Research and Development (OSRD), US organization which, along with its predecessor, the National Defense Research Committee (NDRC), played a key role in the rapid wartime mobilization of American science and engineering. Established before US entry into the war, by 1945 the OSRD had spent nearly half a billion dollars and accelerated a revolution in modern warfare. From OSRD-sponsored research in university and industrial laboratories came a host of new and improved weapons including *radar and the *proximity fuze that helped create a new electronic environment for war (see also TIZARD). Other contributions included rockets and high explosives; the DUKW (see AMPHIBIANS) and the *weasel; medical advances such as antimalarial drugs, blood substitutes, and the quantity production of penicillin (see MEDICINE). OSRD helped insinuate mathematicians, economists, and other experts into military planning at all levels in the new discipline of *operational research or operations research as it was called in the USA. Its most notorious achievement was the *atomic bomb, a project for which the agency bore primary responsibility until its transfer to the army at the end of 1942. As important, however, as its military work were the institutional precedents it set for the large-scale federal patronage of civilian science 'in the nation's service' that became commonplace in the years after the war.

The NDRC was established by Roosevelt's executive order on 27 June 1940, largely due to the efforts of the engineer Vannevar Bush (1890–1974) of the Massachusetts Institute of Technology (MIT). Initially the committee consisted of Bush himself, who maintained responsibility for high-level policy and liaison; Karl Compton, the president of MIT; James Conant, the president of Harvard; Frank Jewett, the head of Bell Laboratories and president of the National Academy of Sciences; Conway Coe, the commissioner of patents; Richard C. Tolman, a physicist from the California Institute of Technology; Rear Admiral Harold Bowen; and Brig-General George Strong. In its first year, NDRC funded research worth almost $6,000,000 and assigned over 250 contracts. In 1941 it was renamed and its mandate enlarged to include development. The new OSRD included, in addition to the original NDRC, the Committee for Medical Research, the Office of Field Service, and several ancillary panels including the Applied Mathematics Panel under Warren Weaver. By the end of the war it had a staff of more than 1,400 and had issued almost 2,300 contracts worth approximately $500,000,000. OSRD was not the only sponsor of wartime research and development (R&D); its share of the nation's R&D budget was some 30%. It was, however, crucial for the rapid and effective mobilization of civilian science.

OSRD's achievements, which rested on an impressive civilian scientific and industrial base laid down in the early decades of the century, were facilitated by key decisions made early. First, in contrast to the policy of the *First World War, Bush decided to rely on existing private facilities rather than newly built and federally managed laboratories. Second, mobilization was to be managed by civilians familiar with private sector strengths, frequently serving 'without compensation' and thus free of political and bureaucratic ties. Third, the agency would operate contractually, in the manner of the market-place. The contract was doubly crucial to OSRD's wartime achievements, not least of which was the rapid enlistment of private sector leaders and resources. In brief, the contract (and the supervision exercised by OSRD's contract office) both guaranteed centralized control of the agency's programmes and funded them in a manner that respected traditional boundaries between the state and private enterprise. Lastly, Bush committed OSRD to close liaison with the military. That liaison was fraught with tension and hindered by bureaucratic jealousies; but by 1945 the military–civilian co-operation to which OSRD had committed itself was accepted by the armed forces. All in all, OSRD was an effective though ambivalent success. On the one hand, it embodied an older and more conservative belief in limited government and the primacy of private enterprise. On the other, it foreshadowed an era of federal dominance.

The influence of the OSRD on post-war developments was mixed. In November 1944, Bush had been asked by Roosevelt to report, on behalf of his organization, on the requirements of future national science policy. *Science—The Endless Frontier* was delivered to President *Truman in July 1945. In his report Bush argued for the establishment of a new civilian-controlled scientific agency to manage the massive federal support for civilian and military

R&D that post-war national security required. The report was widely read and enormously popular, but its goals were attained only in part and with great difficulty. Indeed, while federal sponsorship grew dramatically in the decade after the war, none of the agencies influenced by the OSRD satisfied the hopes expressed in Bush's report. The Atomic Energy Commission, created quickly in 1946, was narrow in its focus and tightly constrained by the needs of the military and national defence; the National Science Foundation, established in 1950 only after five years of controversy over political accountability, proved modest in scope, budget, and authority; and attempts to unify military R&D in any manner fell victim to bureaucratic squabbles within the military.

In more general ways, however, OSRD's success helped shape a new political economy for American science. Many in the younger and less conservative generation for whom wartime patronage proved addictive welcomed the new linkage between government, national security, and institutional growth. Furthermore, the co-operation between scientists and military men fostered by OSRD survived the war and contributed to the development of the military–industrial–university complex. And not least, OSRD helped convince the military that future security rested on new and improved weapons. The 'Star Wars' defence shield and other federally funded, large-scale, hugely expensive, 'high-tech' weapons systems like the B2 Stealth bomber are only recent examples of a military faith in technology encouraged by the success of OSRD. See also SCIENTISTS AT WAR. LARRY OWENS

Baxter, J. P., *Scientists Against Time* (Boston, 1946).
Stewart, I., *Organizing Scientific Research for War: The Administrative History of the Office of Scientific Research and Development* (Boston, 1948).

Office of Strategic Services. The Office of Strategic Services (OSS) was the approximate US counterpart of the British Secret Intelligence Service, *MI6, and Special Operations Executive, *SOE, with which it co-operated on more or less equal terms throughout the war and after it. It was created by presidential Military Order on 13 June 1942. It functioned as the principal US intelligence organization, in all theatres, for the rest of the Second World War.

Origins

In July 1940, at the personal request of Roosevelt, William J. *Donovan undertook the first of a series of overseas missions to appraise the global military situation and to make recommendations about American intelligence requirements. The USA had, at this time, no central agency responsible for the collection, analysis, and dissemination of information bearing on national security, these functions having been dispersed among the armed services (G-2 and N-2 for the army and navy, respectively), regional desks in the state department, and various other agencies and departments.

On his return Donovan submitted to the president a 'Memorandum of Establishment of Service of Strategic Information' in which he urged that a regular channel of strategic information be created, and predicted that political and psychological factors would play a major role in the war. Roosevelt accepted these recommendations, and in July 1941 appointed General Donovan to the civilian post of 'Co-ordinator of Information' (COI). The COI was instructed to consolidate these tasks, under the authority of the president and the *Joint Chiefs of Staff (JCS).

In its first year the COI grew rapidly under Donovan's aggressive leadership, and claimed the functions of information gathering, propaganda, espionage, subversion, and post-war planning. This led both to an unwieldy organization and to jurisdictional rivalries with other government agencies. On 13 June 1942, the overt propaganda functions of the COI were severed and autonomously constituted as the *Office of War Information (OWI), while the COI itself was reorganized as the Office of Strategic Services.

Organization

The OSS was instructed by the president to 'collect and analyse such strategic information as may be required' and 'plan and operate such special services as may be directed' by the JCS. The streamlined organization of the agency reflected this dual mandate.

The Deputy Director for Intelligence Services, Brig-General John Magruder, was responsible for the activities of four intelligence branches: Secret Intelligence (SI) procured, frequently through unorthodox means, data about Axis and Axis-occupied countries; Counter-Intelligence (X-2) monitored the intelligence operations of other nations, ran *double agents in the field, and evaluated the credibility of foreign nationals offering their services to American officials; the Foreign Nationalities Branch (FN) interviewed refugees and foreign citizens residing in the USA.

The largest of the intelligence branches, corresponding to General Donovan's belief that at the heart of modern intelligence work lay 'good old-fashioned intellectual sweat', was Research and Analysis (R&A). This unit, directed by William L. Langer, a historian from Harvard University, drew heavily upon specialists from the American and refugee academic communities and included a large number of distinguished scholars. The R&A Branch produced analytical reports on economic, political, geographical, and cultural topics pertaining to all theatres of operation, the USSR, and Latin America. R&A also produced a number of highly regarded publications which served as weekly digests that were used throughout the government.

Parallel to the intelligence branches were the operational branches, overseen by a Deputy Director for Strategic Services and Operations. The Special Operations Branch (SO), engaged in acts of physical subversion including sabotage, the support of resistance movements, raiding and other irregular combat missions in support of military and intelligence requirements; the first SO operations were conducted in north-west Africa in late 1942. Morale Operations (MO) conducted psychological warfare including planted rumours, leaflets, and covert or 'black' radio broadcasts directed at the Axis populations (see also SUBVERSIVE WARFARE).

Finally, the highly innovative work of the technical support services of OSS deserves to be mentioned since there was literally no precedent for the actual implementation of the tasks with which the new agency was charged. These included a Research and Development group that devised specialized communications equipment, weapons, and contraband; a Field Photographic Unit whose staff produced a vast array of materials for informational and propaganda purposes; the Interdepartmental Committee for the Acquisition of Foreign Periodicals amassed an enormous body of invaluable primary documentation; the Presentation Branch employed an exceptional group of artists, architects, and graphic designers who worked on projects ranging from the visual presentation of statistical data for the president to the design of the legal chambers in which the *Nuremberg trials were held. The work of the these groups would be felt long into the post-war era, both in intelligence and in a broad range of civilian professions.

The headquarters of the OSS were in Washington, but it also maintained overseas outposts which engaged in information-gathering, liaison activities with Allied intelligence agencies, prisoner-of-war interrogations, and the interviewing of foreign nationals. Chief among the overseas units was the London Outpost, established at the end of 1941 to provide Washington with a listening-post in Europe, to facilitate co-operation between Allied intelligence services, and to serve as a base of operations for intelligence, espionage, and operational activities. Outposts were also created in neutral Stockholm and Berne, and subsequently in Algiers, Rome, Caserta, Paris, Wiesbaden, Salzburg, and finally Berlin. OSS was also active in the Middle East, especially Cairo and Istanbul, and in Asia, where it maintained outposts in Chungking, New Delhi, Kandy, and elsewhere.

Effects

The Office of Strategic Services was designed to be an apolitical service agency, specifically excluded from policy-making roles in Washington and strictly subordinated to the military theatre commanders overseas. These constraints resulted in a limited influence on military and diplomatic policy, and a considerable measure of frustration on the part of agents, analysts, and administrators. However, they also enabled OSS to gain a reputation for disinterested objectivity and to make a number of significant contributions to the war effort. Its principal fields of activity included the following:

North Africa

OSS penetrated North Africa before the *North African campaign started in November 1942 (TORCH), to gather intelligence, identify informants, rally political support, and lay a communications network. These softening-up operations, together with extensive documentation prepared by the Research and Analysis Branch in Washington, were considered to be of exceptional importance in facilitating TORCH. The North African campaign served as the first major test of Donovan's organization (see also AGENCY AFRICA).

Enemy Objectives Unit (EOU)

From the autumn of 1942, a highly trained group of OSS economists, working under the auspices of the Economic Warfare Division of the US embassy in London, developed a programme of strategic aerial warfare based on *precision bombing of selected industrial targets. The concept, designed to cause maximum disruption of strategic supplies, represented an early application of economic theory to military practice. It was applied to a limited extent by the Eighth and the Fifteenth Army Air Forces in Germany, Eastern Europe, and occupied France (see STRATEGIC AIR OFFENSIVES, 1 and 2), and remained a basic strategic concept until well into the nuclear age.

Mediterranean theatre

OSS operational teams and intelligence officers worked in close co-operation with military forces in the North African and *Italian campaigns, and in the Balkans. Between the start of the *Sicilian campaign, in July 1943, and the fall of Rome 11 months later, OSS units conducted missions throughout central and northern Italy in support of resistance activities, frequently in conjunction with *SOE and *MI6. The SI and X-2 Branches engaged in intelligence-gathering activities, and R&A units in Caserta and Rome reported extensively on political, economic, and strategic matters.

Balkans

In mid-1943 Force *266—OSS teams attached to SOE missions—were allowed into Yugoslavia, where they supplied and conducted paramilitary operations with the forces of both *Tito and *Mihailović. Officially, OSS attempted to encourage anti-Nazi resistance from whatever source, whether communist or royalist. In the same period some 300 agents were infiltrated into Greece where they collected intelligence and engaged in extensive subversion. Force 266 was absorbed into the *Balkan Air Force's Force 399 in June 1944. According to one historian (K. Ford, *OSS and the Yugoslav Resistance*, Texas, 1992, pp. 82–4), OSS was, from this date, heavily penetrated by communist sympathizers.

Normandy landings

The OSS operated in close co-operation with the UK's secret services in the period following the Allied invasion of Normandy in June 1944 (see OVERLORD). Specially trained *Jedburgh teams, made up of American OSS and

British SOE officers, and representatives of de *Gaulle's Free French, conducted successful operations in northern and southern France, and OSS members were part of the *Sussex teams which were also dropped into France before OVERLORD. R&A teams followed the advancing armies and set up their own intelligence-gathering activities in newly-liberated territories.

Operation SUNRISE
In November 1942, Allen *Dulles arrived at the OSS mission in Berne, Switzerland, bearing the title 'Special Legal Assistant to the US Ambassador' and an agenda that was simultaneously military (the defeat of Nazi Germany) and political (the neutralization of Soviet influence in the period of post-war reconstruction). In addition to maintaining a far-flung network of agents and informants, Dulles was able to establish contact with representatives of the anti-Nazi resistance in Germany, including leading members of the failed conspiracy of 20 July 1944 (see SCHWARZE KAPELLE). In February 1945, Dulles' office began to receive peace overtures from the German generals through various civilian intermediaries. These led ultimately to negotiations between OSS/Berne and *SS General Karl *Wolff for the surrender of the German armies in north Italy under his command. The German surrender was accepted on 2 May 1945, to the great consternation of Soviet leaders who still feared a separate peace and who suspected OSS of acting to pre-empt communist elements of the Italian *resistance.

Penetration of Germany
One of the signal accomplishments of American intelligence was to achieve the actual penetration of Nazi Germany by OSS operatives. In autumn 1944, in the context of the surprising success of the German counter-offensive in the *Ardennes, the decision was made to activate plans for the penetration of the Reich that had been in preparation almost from the beginning of the war. The OSS Labor Branch, the London Special Operations Branch, OSS Berne, and other units began to identify German and Austrian individuals who had made their way to the west, and to train and equip them for specific missions inside Germany. Following General Donovan's dictum that 'I'd put Stalin on the OSS payroll if I thought it would help defeat Hitler,' exiled communist and socialist party members were the first to be recruited; they were followed by an assortment of labour activists, anti-Nazi *prisoners-of-war, German *deserters, expatriate Poles, Jewish refugees, and at least one White Russian (Youri Vinogradov) who, according to one source (see J. Persico, *Piercing the Reich*, London, 1979), managed to penetrate the command of the German Security Service, the Sicherheitsdienst (see RSHA) in Berlin. Operating at great personal risk, these men and women undertook to report on conditions within the Reich, to evaluate the unexpected tenacity of the German forces, to identify strategic targets and resources, and to promote acts of resistance, sabotage, and subversion. By the following spring OSS had infiltrated a number of agents into Germany and Austria who were operating in virtually every militarily important city in the Reich. The achievements of the teams and individuals who penetrated Nazi Germany varied greatly. Collectively, their greatest significance was probably to provide independent confirmation of Allied intelligence with regard to the evaluation of military targets, political tendencies, and significant personalities in the last months of the war.

Military Occupation, Denazification, and War Crimes
OSS was actively engaged in planning for the post-war governance of Germany and German-occupied territories well in advance of Germany's capitulation (see also ALLIED CONTROL COMMISSIONS). At the end of 1943, R&A was commissioned by the Civil Affairs Division of the War Department to outline the programme for the American military occupation, denazification, and democratic reconstruction of post-war Germany. This massive research project resulted in extensive documentation of German occupation policies in Europe, as well as a series of detailed handbooks and guides for the use of occupation authorities which dealt with every aspect of political, economic, and cultural life. In general, OSS recommendations were considerably more sweeping than the anti-Nazi measures actually carried out.

A related activity was the identification of prominent Nazis to be investigated, detained, or tried for *war crimes. Political and legal theorists in R&A, working in co-operation with the departments of war and justice, helped to devise the set of guidelines used by the American prosecutors at the Nuremberg War Crimes tribunal. The OSS series on 'Nazi Plans for Dominating Germany and Europe', prepared for the use of the War Crimes staff, provided some of the most detailed documentation available on the extent of Nazi criminality, including the extermination campaign against the European Jews (see FINAL SOLUTION).

Asia and the Pacific
In the Asian theatre OSS had to manoeuvre among nationalist, communist, and imperialist interests; these difficulties were aggravated by a reluctance on the part of General *MacArthur and Admiral *Nimitz to allow OSS agents to operate freely. Throughout the region, OSS was subject to the control of American, British, and Chinese military authorities, and never gained much autonomy. However, despite these constraints, OSS units made a number of important contributions to the war in the *China–Burma–India theatre.

The first COI/OSS presence on the Asian mainland was in China where SI and R&A units began gathering intelligence from Chungking in 1942. To this continuing activity was added the OSS component of the multi-service 'Dixie Mission', an American military detachment stationed in the communist capital of Fushih from July 1944, which gathered intelligence and maintained a politically delicate liaison with the Chinese communists.

OSS operations in Japanese-occupied Thailand were paralysed by differences among the Allies over European colonial interests in the postwar configuration of South-East Asia. In October 1944, Free Thai units began to infiltrate Thailand from OSS bases in China and to perform valuable intelligence functions. OSS and SOE were arming, training, and equipping units of the Free Thai underground organization in preparation for an eventual uprising at the time of the Japanese surrender. Following the end of hostilities in Europe a considerable number of experienced OSS units were transferred to China and French Indo-China, where they established contacts with nationalist and communist guerrilla movements. However, in general, OSS operations in the region were marginal to the air and naval campaigns mounted by the conventional military forces.

Elsewhere in the Far Eastern Theatre, an SO combat unit known as Detachment 101 was formed in April 1942, in support of American military objectives in the China–Burma–India theatre.

The rapid advance of Japanese forces through South-East Asia threatened the only remaining supply route to nearly 4 million Chinese forces under *Chiang Kai-shek. With the Pacific Fleet badly damaged at *Pearl Harbor, and the bulk of American air and ground power committed in Europe, General *Stilwell accepted a proposal to conduct intelligence gathering and unconventional warfare activities in Burma. Colonel Carl Eifler was named commanding officer of the proposed detachment; seriously wounded in late 1943, he was succeeded by Colonel William R. Peers.

Operating from a secret base in northern Assam, the unit—initially only 21 strong—raised a considerable force of Burmese nationals whom they trained in intelligence collection and internal propaganda, as well as espionage, sabotage, and harassment operations against Japanese targets. By the end of 1942 Detachment 101 had infiltrated Burma, and by the end of 1943 six bases, staffed by Americans and Kachin guerrilla forces, were operating behind Japanese lines. By the end of the war the detachment fielded some 120 Americans and 10,800 American-trained Burmese guerrillas, and it figured importantly in the eventual recapture of the *Burma Road.

Among its other principal accomplishments, the detachment disrupted Japanese air defences so as to secure the *Hump supply flights and thus maintain the viability of Chinese nationalist forces. Secondly, an estimated 85% of all the intelligence received by Stilwell's Northern Combat Area Command came from Detachment 101 sources. Third, its sabotage and guerrilla activities proved exceedingly costly to the Japanese occupation army, in terms of men, *matériel*, and perhaps morale.

Conclusion

The Office of Strategic Services was terminated abruptly by Executive Order 9620, signed by President *Truman on 20 September 1945 and effective ten days later. Among civilian critics, concerns had been growing about the propriety of a secret intelligence agency within an open society during peacetime. Within the government, OSS was often regarded as an interloper, usurping functions properly belonging to the military services or the Department of State. OSS involvement in political controversies within the French, Yugoslav, Chinese, and German resistance movements, and its efforts to avert a superpower stand-off in the post-war era, gave it a reputation for leftist sympathies which further discredited it in the waning months of the war.

Accordingly, the teams of Special Operations, Secret Intelligence, and Counter-Intelligence agents were mostly disbanded and dispersed throughout the Strategic Services Unit of the war department. Exceptional efforts were made to keep the Research and Analysis Branch intact. Donovan was among many who believed that the experience of Pearl Harbor demonstrated the need for a permanent intelligence apparatus, and argued with little success that the trained specialists he had gathered for this task should not be dispersed. Some R&A personnel were transferred to the Interim Research and Intelligence Service (IRIS) in the state department, but within a few years the majority had returned to academic life.

The Central Intelligence Agency (CIA), created by the National Security Act of 1947 and the successor to the wartime OSS, assumed custody of its records. In 1980 the CIA began the process of transferring the majority of these materials to the US National Archives. BARRY M. KATZ

Chalou, G. (ed.), *The Secrets War: The Office of Strategic Services in World War II* (Washington, DC, 1992).
Katz, B. M., *Foreign Intelligence. Research and Analysis in the Office of Strategic Services. 1942–1945* (Cambridge, 1989).
Smith, B. F., *The Shadow Warriors. OSS and the Origins of the CIA* (New York, 1983).
War Report of the OSS, 2 vols. (New York, 1976).

Office of the Co-ordinator of Inter-American Affairs, originally designated the Office of the Co-ordinator of Commercial and Cultural Relations, was created by Roosevelt in August 1940, with Nelson Rockefeller (1908–79) at its head. Until July 1941, when it became illegal for US firms to deal with pro-Nazi commercial interests, the office combated Nazi commercial influence in Latin America and persuaded US firms by voluntary means against dealing with any pro-Nazi agency. Information was fed to it, via the FBI (see USA, 6), from *British Security Co-ordination and by intelligence missions on the ground.

Office of War Information (OWI), US organization established by Roosevelt in June 1942 under Elmer Davis to disseminate information about the government's policies. Domestically, the OWI also acted as a link between the media and the government and it had a special division for the film industry (see HOLLYWOOD). Unlike its predecessor during the *First World War, the

OWI was not officially responsible for *censorship, and Roosevelt avoided using the word 'propaganda' to describe its function: Davis said his task was primarily educational and that he would tell 'the truth and nothing but the truth'. But what OWI disseminated was bound to be selective and it was accused by Republicans of spreading Democrat values; its information was for ever being disputed by one faction or another. In 1943 the House of Representatives voted to disband its domestic branch. The Senate overturned this decision but the OWI's budget was severely cut.

Oflag, abbreviation of *Offizier-Lager* (officer camp), German camp holding Allied officers. See also PRISONERS-OF-WAR.

Ogdensburg agreement, result of a meeting between Roosevelt and the Canadian prime minister, Mackenzie *King, at Ogdensburg, New York, on 17–18 August 1940, at which it was decided to form a *Permanent Joint Board on Defence. This decision was announced in a short press release—which was well received in the USA and Canada—but there was no formal agreement. The meeting was significant as it marked a concrete US move away from isolationism (see also AMERICA FIRST COMMITTEE) and towards open support for the Allies. See also CANADA, 4.

OGPU, see NKVD.

OKH, initials derived from Oberkommando des Heeres, the German Army High Command. See GERMANY, 6.

Okinawa, capture of. Situated 550 km. (340 mi.) from mainland Japan this principal, and central, island of the Japanese Ryūkyū archipelago was assaulted on 1 April 1945 by four divisions of Lt-General Simon Buckner's newly formed Tenth US Army (see Map 79).

Ninety-six kilometres (60 mi.) long, Okinawa was a vital air base for any US invasion of mainland Japan. For the Americans it was the most costly and complex operation in the *Pacific war, and the last. In sheer magnitude it can only be compared with the Normandy landings (see OVERLORD), with the USA committing a total of over half a million troops and 1,213 warships. The British Pacific Fleet (see TASK FORCE 57) also took part.

Preliminary air and sea bombardments, the occupation of Keise Island and the Kerama Islands, and the clearance of a complicated tangle of beach obstacles by underwater demolition teams (see FROGMEN) preceded the landings. Vice-Admiral *Turner's Joint Expeditionary Force initially put ashore, on Okinawa's western coast, 1st and 6th Marine Divisions of Maj-General Roy Geiger's 3rd Marine Amphibious Corps, and 7th and 96th Infantry Division of Maj-General John Hodge's 24th Corps. Eventually more than 170,000 US servicemen took part in the island's capture.

Okinawa was strongly defended by 77,000 troops of the Thirty-Second Japanese Army and 20,000 Okinawan militia, and even by local children. Their commander, Lt-General Ushijima Mitsuru, relied on *kamikaze pilots to destroy the landings and arranged only a nominal opposition to them. Instead he concentrated almost his entire force inland, around the capital, Naha, and on the northern Motobu peninsula, with the intention of inflicting as many casualties as possible for as long as possible. These tactics, which had been used to a lesser degree on *Peleliu and *Iwo Jima, enabled the marines to take Kadena and Yontan airfields immediately, for 1st Marine Division to occupy the Katchin peninsula by 4 April, and for 6th Marine Division to break through the Ishikawa isthmus defences on 4 April and reach Nago at the base of the Motobu peninsula three days later while 1st Marine Division moved up the east coast to Aha. However, in the south a stalemate developed when 24th Corps encountered the first of Ushijima's immensely strong defensive positions, which were constructed in rugged, cave-riddled terrain that made them largely immune to air or sea bombardment.

Six days after the landings the C-in-C of the Japanese First Mobile Fleet, Admiral *Toyoda, launched his operation TEN-GŌ. Massed kamikaze attacks—called *kikusui* (floating chrysanthemums) by the Japanese—attacked the American invasion fleet and the Mobile Fleet sailed to attack it, too. Between 6 April and 22 June about 1,900 kamikaze sorties caused unprecedented Allied naval casualties, but the Mobile Fleet was destroyed in the battle of the *East China Sea.

Ashore, the marines reached Okinawa's northern tip Hedo Point, in mid-April, and by 20 April 1945 had cleared the Motobu peninsula. Nearby Ie Island was captured by the newly committed 77th Infantry Division, and other offshore islands were also cleared. The marines and 77th Division then reinforced Hodge's corps which, bolstered by the recently landed 27th Infantry Division, had started a major assault on Ushijima's first defensive line on 19 April. This had succeeded and Ushijima, after launching a fierce counter-attack on 4 May, concentrated his forces on a line which ran from Naha through Shuri, the core of his defences, to Yonabaru. Though two badly mauled infantry divisions had to be withdrawn, the extra weight of the marines eventually broke this line. Shuri was abandoned, Naha capitulated on 27 May, and Ushijima fell back on his final defensive position on the Oroku peninsula. Bitter fighting followed, but on 22 June, the day Ushijima committed suicide, Okinawa was declared secure. Of the Japanese garrison only 7,400 survived to become *prisoners-of-war. But the Allies also paid a heavy price for Okinawa. Thirty-six warships and landing craft were sunk and 368 damaged; more than 4,900 seamen were killed and 4,824 wounded. Kamikaze pilots caused the most damage, but some was done by mines, bombs (including the first use of the *Baka bomb) and explosive motor boats. Marines and infantry also suffered heavily, 7,613 being killed, including Buckner, and 31,807 wounded, while 763 aircraft were lost. See also AMPHIBIOUS WARFARE.

Gow, I., *Okinawa 1945* (London, 1986).

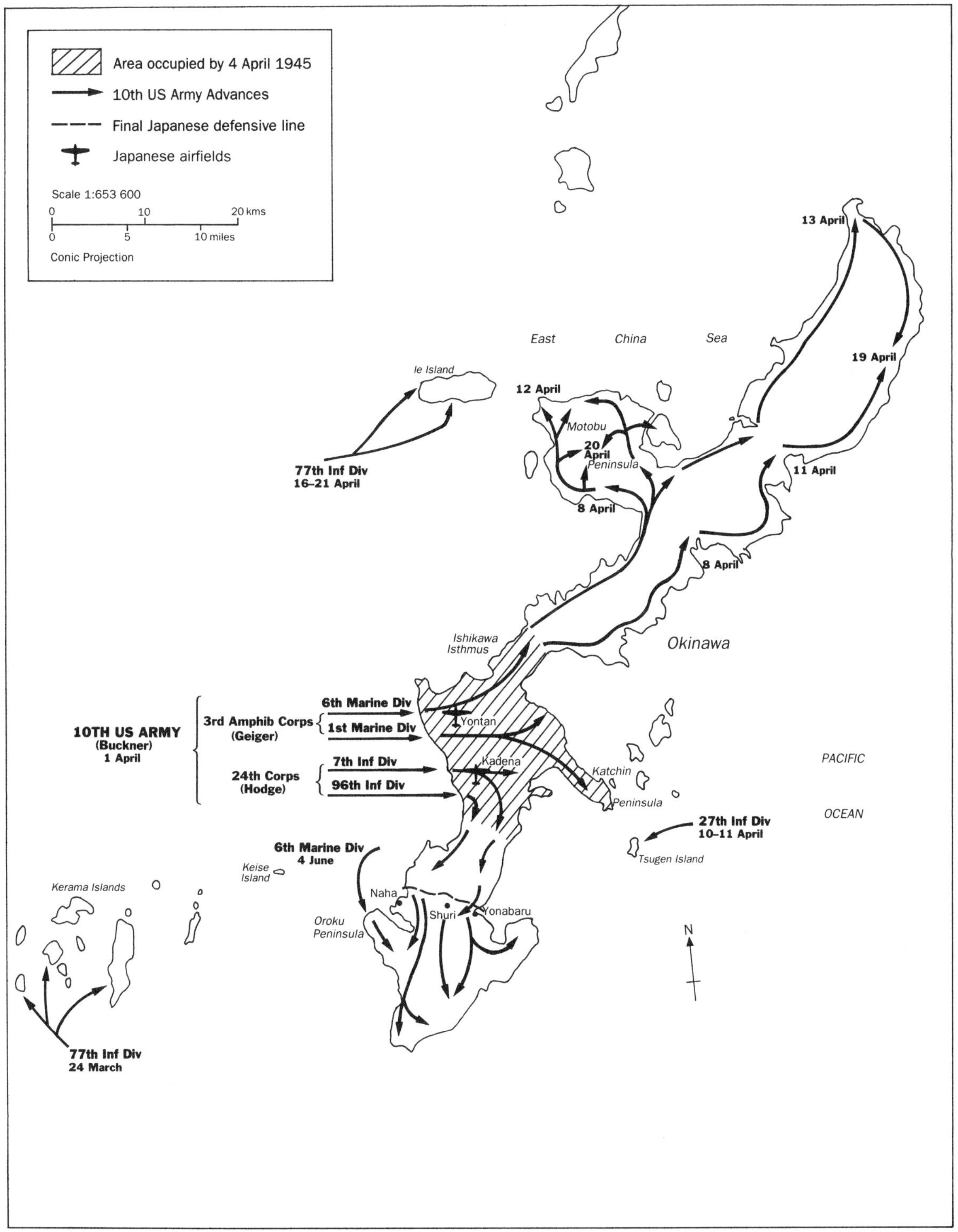

79. **Okinawa** campaign, April–June 1945

Okulicki, Maj-General Leopold (1898–1946?), Polish Army officer who headed the Union for Armed Struggle (Związek Walki Zbrojnej, or ZWZ), the precursor of the Polish Home Army (see POLAND, 4) in eastern Poland when, under the *Nazi–Soviet Pact, it was occupied by the USSR in September 1939. Captured in January 1941 he was imprisoned in Moscow, but was later released and served as chief of staff in *Anders' Army. In September 1943 he joined the Polish Home Army which, as a maj-general, he led from October 1943. In 1945 he was sentenced by the Soviet authorities to ten years' imprisonment, allegedly for conducting activities hostile to the Red Army, and he probably died, or was executed, the following year.

OKW, initials derived from Oberkommando der Wehrmacht, the German Armed Forces High Command which Hitler formed in 1938. See GERMANY, 6(a).

OMAHA, codename for assault beach in American sector of the Normandy landings (see OVERLORD) on which the 1st US Infantry Division (see BIG RED ONE) disembarked on 6 June 1944. It lay between Port en Bessin and the mouth of the River Vire in the Baie de la Seine. By the end of the day 34,250 troops had been landed there, but the Germans nearly prevented the Americans gaining a foothold and caused heavy casualties (about 2,000 against the 200 on *UTAH). One of the two artificial harbours (see MULBERRIES) was installed off OMAHA, at St Laurent, but on 20 June a storm destroyed it.

Oman, independent Arab Sultanate, situated on the south-eastern part of the Arabian peninsula. It was closely tied to the UK by a treaty signed in 1939. Oil deposits there were not discovered in commercial quantities until 1964.

one-time pad, secure method employed to encipher signals for transmission by radio. The sender and receiver used identical pads of tear-off sheets containing information for enciphering and deciphering a signal. The sender indicated which sheet he was going to use and once the message had been transmitted and deciphered both parties destroyed their copy of it. No other copies existed. Although unbreakable, it was a slow and tedious method of communicating and code books or machine ciphers (see ENIGMA, GEHEIMSCHREIBER, PURPLE, and TYPEX) were more frequently used as the war progressed. See also NAVAJO CODE TALKERS and SIGNALS INTELLIGENCE WARFARE.

operational research (OR), the practical scientific study of how well methods and weapons of war work, had been used in earlier conflicts. In the USA it was called Operations Research. Benjamin Franklin is credited with having invented the concept. In 1775 he analysed the cost to the British of the American War of Independence by calculating that 'Britain, at the expense of three millions, has killed 150 Yankees this campaign which is £20,000 a head.' OR had been undertaken for the Royal Naval Air Service during the *First World War. But it was only during the Second World War, first in the UK and then in the USA and the British Dominions, that the necessary establishments and committees were formed to apply it in such that a way that its development 'was one of the chief scientific features of the war' (J. Crowther and R. Whiddington, *Science at War*, London, 1947, p. 91).

In the UK each of the services had its own research sections and the heads of these sections formed an OR committee. *Watson-Watt founded the air ministry's first section to assess the value of *radar to the RAF's Fighter Command and in August 1940 *Blackett, who later became director of OR at the Admiralty, was invited by the chief of Anti-Aircraft Command, General Frederick Pile (1884–1976), to study the effectiveness of radar-directed anti-aircraft guns. The army OR group undertook a time-and-motion study of the most efficient way of laying mines and came up with an idea for warning British troops in the *Burma campaign who were being caught unawares by Japanese night infiltration tactics. The obvious answer to counter this infiltration was a fine wire which lit a signal lamp when broken. Not so obvious was how to discover the wire's correct diameter, as it had to be strong enough not to break accidentally but not so thick that it could be seen. The answer was found by testing different wires on the charladies who scrubbed the floors of the various government establishments. They spent much of their time moving forwards on their knees—much as the infiltrating Japanese must have done—and those wires broken without comment from the charladies were noted by observers.

By 1943 several scores of American, British, and Dominion *scientists were being used in OR, co-operating fully with one another. Researchers took care, as a rule, not to say anything until they felt they had an adequate grasp of the subject, based on actual experience—in combat, if necessary—alongside the weapon or the type of unit they sought to improve. Even so, it was not always easy, especially at first, to get their results accepted, as certain ideas were entrenched and part of service routine. For example, the efficiency of RAF squadrons had always been judged on the percentage of serviceable aircraft they had available. OR showed that this was just a fetish; what really counted was that as many aircraft as possible should be used as often as maintenance allowed, which lowered the serviceability ratio but increased the output. In Australia an OR study carried out on the amount of Japanese shipping sunk by mines laid by Australian aircraft conclusively proved that this method of destroying Japanese supplies was 40 times more effective than if the same aircraft were employed to bomb the supplies after they had been landed and dispersed.

Anti-submarine tactics, for both aircraft and surface craft; tactics for minesweepers; optimum size of *convoys; design of *bombs for aircraft; design of *landing craft; and design of artillery shells were among the subjects that benefited directly from OR reports. *Mountbatten took particular interest in the subject and had three scientists at *Combined Operations to advise him. See also BUTT REPORT and OFFICE OF SCIENTIFIC RESEARCH AND DEVELOPMENT.

Thiesmeyer, L., and Burchard, J., *Combat Scientists* (Boston, 1947).
Waddington, C. H., *Operational Research in World War Two* (London, 1973).

OPERATION REINHARD was the *SS organization which implemented the systematic destruction of 2,284,000 Jews in Poland's General Government and was an integral part of the *Final Solution. Its headquarters was established in Lublin and the operation began in March 1942 when *Belzec started to operate. There were two other OPERATION REINHARD death camps, *Sobibor and *Treblinka, but all three were also used to kill Jews from other parts of Europe. *Chełmno, *Majdenek, and *Auschwitz-Birkenau were extermination camps too, but were not part of the operation.

The organization, led by SS Brigadeführer (brigadier) Odilo Globocnik and SS Hauptsturmführer (captain) Hermann Hofle, was only given its name after the assassination of Reinhard *Heydrich in May 1942 and was so-called in his honour. In his capacity as its commander Globocnik was directly subordinate to *Himmler. His remit included:

1. The planning and co-ordination of deportations from the various districts in the General Government to the death camps;
2. The construction of the death camps and the murder of all those who arrived at them;
3. Collecting all the victims' clothing and valuables.

Globocnik's staff totalled 450, including a number of SS members who had been involved in the *euthanasia programme. These proved to be the most important members of the team as only they had the knowledge and experience in murdering large numbers of people, often by gas. The method evolved was to pump carbon monoxide gas into chambers holding the victims (*Zyklon B gas was not used). The bodies were then buried by the **Sonderkommandos*. When burial proved unsatisfactory crematoriums were constructed and the bodies burnt.

Besides the three death camps the operation included the SS training camp at Trawniki and the SS clothing workshops at Lublin. Trawniki provided training for the guards running the camps and in the $2\frac{1}{2}$ years of its existence between 2,000 and 3,000 of them were given guidance in how to round up Jews, organize their transportation to the death camps, and then to kill them. Most of the guards were **Volksdeutsche*, Red Army *prisoners-of-war who volunteered for the task. Many were Ukrainian. The clothing workshops disinfected, repaired and sorted the clothing of those killed for use in Germany. Personal belongings such as watches and trinkets were distributed or sold to SS personnel, but many valuables—including gold bars and currency—worth millions of Reichsmarks were also collected. The money raised from these acquisitions was used by the Department for *Volksdeutsche*, an SS organization which aided *Volksdeutsche* living in German-occupied European countries, or was acquired by the Reichsbank or the ministry of economics.

OPERATION REINHARD was terminated in December 1943, by which time only a handful of Jews, working in Luftwaffe clothing factories, remained in the General government.

Arad, Y., *Belzec, Sobibor, Treblinka: The Operation Reinhard Death Camps* (Indianapolis, 1987).

operations research, see OPERATIONAL RESEARCH and OFFICE OF SCIENTIFIC RESEARCH AND DEVELOPMENT.

Oppenheimer, (Julius) Robert (1904–67), US nuclear physicist whose outstanding teaching and research abilities quickly established his reputation during the 1930s. In August 1942 the US Army was made responsible for organizing the efforts of British and US physicists towards developing an *atomic bomb and Oppenheimer was asked to set up and administer a suitable establishment. He chose Los Alamos, New Mexico, as the site and it was there that the bomb was developed. For this work he received the Presidential Medal of Merit in 1946 (see DECORATIONS), but in 1954, having opposed the development of the hydrogen bomb on both technical and moral grounds, he was accused of being a communist sympathizer and had his security clearance revoked. See also SCIENTISTS AT WAR.

Oradour massacre. On 10 June 1944, the third company of the first battalion of the Der Führer regiment, attached to the 2nd *SS Panzer Division—a lorried infantry unit—made a detour to Oradour-sur-Glane, a farming village 24 km. (15 mi.) west-north-west of Limoges, on their way from Montauban in south-west France to the Normandy beachhead. They collected all the women and children in the church, and all the men in five barns, interrogated the men briefly, and then set all six buildings on fire, shooting down those who tried to flee. A very few escaped and a very few more had slipped into the fields alongside the village as the Germans arrived. The Germans then looted and burned down the houses, and withdrew, leaving 642 corpses. They lost one officer, killed by a stone that fell off the burning church.

They had found no arms (beyond shotguns), nor any sign of resistance activity, in the village, which had hitherto lain completely outside the military course of the war. No certain motive has ever been established. Revenge has been conjectured, for a popular officer in the division had been abducted by a party from the *maquis the day before; so has trouble over the division's gold reserve, looted in its turn from occupied banks. The officer in charge on the spot, Captain Kahn, was killed in action in Normandy. Long afterwards, several of his underlings—most of them Alsatian conscripts, and so again French citizens by the time they were traced—were put on trial without severe results.

The catastrophe, though unique in France, was not unexampled further east. See also ATROCITIES.

M. R. D. FOOT

Kruuse, J., *Madness at Oradour* (London, 1969).

Oran, see MERS-EL-KÉBIR.

Orel salient. In March 1943, during the *German–Soviet war, just before the spring thaw brought movement to a temporary halt, a pair of adjacent bulges forming an inverted 'S' developed in the Soviet–German front. One, on the north around Orel, was in German hands. The other, around *Kursk, was Soviet-held. The two immediately attracted attention on both sides. Hitler, looking towards an otherwise unpromising summer, devised Operation CITADEL to convert the Kursk bulge into a massive encirclement and deployed General Walter *Model's Ninth Army south of Orel as the northern striking force. Stalin's deputy, Marshal G. K. *Zhukov, planned a similar operation (KUTUZOV) against the Orel salient; and by 5 July, when CITADEL began, he had three army groups deployed there, from north to south, the West, Briansk, and Central *fronts* with a total of fourteen armies arrayed against the German Ninth and First Panzer Armies.

Zhukov began KUTUZOV with three strikes against the north face of the Orel salient on 12 July. Those no doubt figured in Hitler's decision to call off CITADEL on that day, but they were raggedly executed. On 15 July, Hitler gave command in the salient to Model who ordered work begun on a line, the HAGEN position, across its base. Model, whose speciality was defence, had the front almost stabilized at the end of the month, but then Hitler needed to withdraw 24 divisions for transfer to Italy. In a phased withdrawal begun on 1 August, Model manoeuvered his troops back to the HAGEN position, where the last settled in seventeen days later. Zhukov had apparently by then decided the Soviet prospects were better further south.

EARL ZIEMKE

origins of the war. The events which led to the outbreak of the Second World War in Europe and the Pacific followed a well-known path—the *via dolorosa* of mankind in the 1930s and early 1940s. The great economic depression which began in 1929 destroyed the growing economic and political stability achieved during the 1920s and set every great power on the road to economic *nationalism. It provoked, especially in Europe, a sharp rise in political extremism, and notably the advent of Hitler to power in Germany. In Europe, events then moved with accelerating speed. In March 1935 Germany openly proclaimed its rearmament, in defiance of the disarmament clauses of the *Versailles settlement of 1919. In October 1935 Italy invaded Abyssinia, and in the process robbed the *League of Nations of its remaining credibility as a safeguard of international security. In March 1936 Germany occupied the Rhineland, previously demilitarized under the Versailles settlement and the Treaty of Locarno. In March 1938 the Germans first occupied and then annexed Austria. At the end of September 1938 the *Munich agreement accepted German annexation of the Sudetenland, and in March 1939 the remains of Czechoslovakia were broken up, mostly falling under German control. In April 1939 Italian forces occupied Albania. Meanwhile, from July 1936 to March 1939, the *Spanish Civil War was being waged, threatening from time to time to spill over into the rest of Europe. For some three years there was a sense of undeclared war. Then on 1 September 1939 Germany attacked Poland, two days later France and the UK declared war on Germany, and the war was formally under way. Poland was rapidly conquered by Germany during the *Polish campaign, with the USSR joining in from the east. After a pause—the *phoney war—German aggression was resumed, this time at headlong speed. In April the Germans launched their *Norwegian campaign; in May they invaded the Low Countries and France (see FALL GELB); and by the end of June the fall of *France was accomplished. In October 1940 Mussolini opened the *Balkan campaign by attacking Greece; and Germany joined in by invading Yugoslavia and Greece in April 1941. Finally in June 1941 the German assault on the Soviet Union was launched (see BARBAROSSA), and the climax of the long movement towards total European war was reached.

In Asia and the Pacific events followed a similar course. In 1931–2 the Japanese occupied Manchuria (see MANCHUKUO). In July 1937 a clash at the Marco Polo Bridge near Peking led to the *China Incident. Nanking was captured in December 1937, and Canton in October 1938. By the end of 1939 Japan had occupied the whole north-eastern quarter of China, together with all the major ports. In July 1940 the Japanese took advantage of the German victories in Europe by forcing the British to close the *Burma Road, one of the few supply routes remaining to the Chinese; and in September they compelled France to allow Japanese forces to enter northern French Indo-China. In July 1941 this occupation was extended to southern French Indo-China, where the Japanese stood poised for a move southwards. At that point the USA, which since 1939 had imposed limited economic sanctions against Japan, imposed an oil embargo, which was joined by the British and the Dutch and so became virtually total. The Japanese decided to break it by force. On 7 December 1941 they attacked the American fleet at *Pearl Harbor, and elsewhere began a sweeping assault which swiftly overran all the American, British and Dutch colonies in South-East Asia.

The two drives for expansion (German and Italian in Europe, Japanese in Asia) appeared very similar, and there were some links between them (see AXIS STRATEGY AND CO-OPERATION). In November 1936 Germany and

Japan signed the *Anti-Comintern Pact, to which Italy adhered a year later. In September 1940 the three powers concluded the *Tripartite Pact, agreeing to co-operate in establishing their respective 'New Orders' across the world. Taken together, events in the two continents attained such a momentum and revealed such powerful forces at work that an air of inevitability has come to dominate the whole process, and the phrase 'the roots of war' has attained more than a conventional meaning.

Once the search for the roots of an inevitable conflict has begun, there is no shortage of them to be found. Let us look first at Europe, where one root is at once apparent in the profoundly unstable nature of the peace settlements of 1919–20. At the end of the *First World War Germany was defeated but not crushed, mutilated in body through loss of territory and wounded in pride by the so-called 'war guilt' clause of the Versailles settlement, yet still with a large population and great industrial resources. In such circumstances, a war launched by Germany to reassert national pride and predominance was a distinct possibility. At the same time, eastern Europe was completely transformed, on utterly insecure foundations. No fewer than nine new or renewed states came into being at the end of the war: Finland, Estonia, Latvia, Lithuania, Poland, Czechoslovakia, Austria, Hungary, and Yugoslavia. All these states had disputed frontiers. All claimed to be nation states, but nationalities were so scattered across the map that every country contained substantial alien minorities such as the **Volksdeutsche*. Poland and Czechoslovakia were particularly vulnerable in this respect; but everywhere the problems posed by national minorities were almost insoluble, and an appeal to force was always possible.

This does not exhaust the tale of instability in eastern Europe. In 1918 events of a quite extraordinary nature had occurred. First Russia and then Germany had suffered overwhelming defeat within a year, and it was from the wreckage of that double defeat that new states had emerged, from the Baltic to the Carpathians. But these conditions could not last. As Germany and Russia regained their strength the new states would be threatened: they had been built on a sandbank at low tide, and as German and Russian power rose again they were almost bound to be overwhelmed.

The European settlement of 1919–20 presented a bleak and depressing prospect, offering the likelihood of war in various forms: war by Germany to restore its dominance in Europe; war by France or Poland to prevent any such thing; or conflict in eastern Europe arising out of any of its numerous points of friction. It is this dreary vision which has led many observers to claim that the two World Wars were parts of a single whole—a new Thirty Years War. It is surely true that some causes of renewed conflict were embedded in the consequences of the First World War, from which, despite the signing of the *Kellogg–Briand Pact by almost all sovereign states, hostilities of some sort might well arise. But there is a long step from a war of some sort to that which actually developed in Europe between 1939 and 1941. Europe changed a great deal in the period between the wars, notably in terms of ideology, economics, and strategic thought.

It was ideology which produced the most startling changes. Europe in the 1930s was vibrant with ideological conflict, and Italy and Germany were dominated by regimes which proclaimed the virtues of war, dynamism, and expansion. If the doctrines of fascism and Nazism were followed to their conclusion, then war was almost bound to ensue. In the case of Italian fascism, the situation was not too grave, because Italy was not strong enough to sustain a major war; but even so *fascism transformed Italian diplomatic style from a cautious Machiavellianism to an erratic bravado, and from 1935 onwards Italian foreign policy was launched upon a career of almost ceaseless aggression and disturbance. The attack on Abyssinia in 1935, intervention in the Spanish Civil War, the occupation of Albania, attacks on France in June 1940 and Greece in October—all added to the tensions in Europe and extended the area of conflict. Moreover, fascist Italy made common cause with Nazi Germany in the Rome—Berlin Axis; and while there may be doubts about the threat posed by Italy, there can be none about Nazi Germany.

*Nazi ideology pointed plainly towards war. This does not mean that we should accept Hitler's **Mein Kampf* as a blue print or a programme of action in foreign policy. But there were powerful and consistent elements in his thoughts and emotions: living space (*Lebensraum*) for the German people; a racial doctrine directed against both Jews and Slavs; anti-Bolshevism; and a sort of social Darwinism which saw all politics in terms of a struggle for existence. All these pointed towards a great war in the east, where living space was to be found, and where the Soviet Union concentrated Jewish, Slavonic, and Bolshevik enemies into a single whole. If these broad aims of Nazi ideology were seriously pursued, they would lead inevitably to war. Moreover, we must look not only at ideological aims, but at methods. The Nazis applied in foreign policy the tactics which served them so well in their domestic struggles—intimidation, subversion, and deceit, all applied with a malevolent yet inspired boldness. For some time, such methods brought them success without war (as in Austria and Czechoslovakia), but in the long run they produced such revulsion in other countries that they made war certain. A state which behaved in such a way generated total mistrust, so that negotiation became impossible.

Ideological issues, of course, had more than one aspect. The ideologies of fascism and Nazism faced other systems of thought and belief in *communism and liberal democracy, both of which were threatened in their very lives by the advance of fascism. This was no illusion: when war came, the successive victors imposed forms of government and ways of life upon the vanquished. Europe was in the grip of a conflict of values and ideas, which was a profound force in the movement towards war.

When we turn to economics, the position is less clear-cut. The economic interest of many states lay in avoiding war. This was particularly true for the UK, where governments were unwilling to divert resources into armaments, and where it was correctly calculated that all-out war would speedily render the country bankrupt. Moreover, the UK had excellent short-term reasons for maintaining good economic relations with Germany, which in 1938 was the fifth largest customer for British exports. In France, the effects of the depression were felt later than elsewhere, reaching their worst in 1935. The economy continued to stagnate in subsequent years, and France was acutely conscious of its industrial weakness as against Germany. In economic terms, it had every reason to avoid a confrontation with its powerful rival. The Soviet Union was in a different position, with no inhibitions about devoting a large part of its economic efforts to armaments. But collectivization of agriculture, over-rapid industrialization and the purges of the 1930s brought economic dislocation, and the USSR had compelling economic reasons to avoid war. Italy too, despite its belligerent record, suffered from grave weaknesses, and had an economy incapable of sustaining a serious war (see ITALY, 2).

Economic interests, crossing ideological lines, thus generally pointed towards keeping out of war. But from this consensus there was one crucial exception: Germany. The German economy recovered rapidly from the end of 1932 onwards, achieving almost full employment by 1938. From 1935 this recovery was accompanied by large-scale and rapid rearmament. The natural consequence was a sharp increase in imports of *raw materials and food; and imports have to be paid for. By 1938 and 1939 Germany was facing a balance of payments crisis, with neither exports nor foreign exchange available on the scale necessary to pay for its imports. One solution would have been to slow down the pace of rearmament, but Hitler ruled this out. Another was expansion and conquest, which might produce direct results (for example, by annexing Lorraine and its iron ore); or it might work indirectly but very effectively. In May 1940, when Germany was enjoying military success all over Europe and the British and French were powerless, it proved easy for Germany to secure from Romania a highly favourable agreement for the export of Romanian oil. Similarly, after Germany had occupied Norway, it was possible to sign an advantageous agreement with Sweden for the export of iron ore. The German government believed that war could be made to pay, and in the short run this proved correct.

This leads to questions of strategic calculation. It is generally agreed that the Second World War in Europe was not brought about by the generals: in most European countries (including Germany) the professional military men urged caution upon their governments. But while the German generals were conscious of the defects in their forces (the German Army was less strong in depth and less well trained than its predecessor of 1914), the Nazi leaders saw that for a few years between about 1938 and 1941 they had a window of strategic opportunity. The German Army and Luftwaffe were amply strong enough to strike terror among potential enemies, as was successfully achieved by ostentatious displays of air power during the Czechoslovakian crisis in 1938. They were also highly capable of rapid assaults and quick victories (see BLITZKRIEG), as they showed in Poland in 1939 and France in 1940, even if they were not yet ready to wage prolonged war against powerful adversaries. This period of superiority might not last long, and while it existed there was a strong temptation to exploit it.

Thus the picture builds up. A fundamentally unstable European situation, combined with the expansionist drive of Germany (and to a lesser extent Italy), propelled by ideology, economic forces, and the need to seize a fleeting strategic opportunity, make the case for the inevitability of war appear very strong. But it is not yet complete. What of the powers which might have been expected to defend the status quo: France, the UK, and the USSR? All these three powers at best seemed paralysed in face of advancing German expansion, and at worst positively encouraged it. Why was this?

France seemed destined to be an early victim of the German advance, and yet it remained passive. The reasons are not far to seek. The First World war had cost France dear, with some 1,300,000 dead and a calamitous fall in the birthrate during the war, with consequences which worked their way inexorably onwards, culminating in the 'hollow years' of 1935 and 1936, when the numbers of men attaining call-up age for the army fell drastically. France had won the First World War, but could it afford any more such victories? In political terms, the country was suffering from sharp internal conflicts, unstable governments, and a stagnant economy. In foreign policy, France was caught in a dreadful dilemma. If it resisted the growth of German power, it risked a war which could at best only end in a Pyrrhic victory. If it acquiesced in that growth, the best it could hope for was to be eaten last. French ministers might not have been directly acquainted with Mr Micawber, but it is not surprising that they waited for something to turn up.

The UK was at any rate not paralysed. Its governments were stable, and when *Chamberlain became prime minister in 1937 he was determined to pursue an active foreign policy. The basis of that policy was to avoid war if possible (though not at the expense of fundamental British interests), and to secure a lasting European settlement. The policy of 'appeasement', meaning the satisfaction of reasonable German and Italian aspirations by negotiation, arose from powerful motives. We have already noted the economic case for avoiding war, or even rapid rearmament. Behind that, as in France, lay the pressures exerted by memories of the First World War, which no one wanted to repeat. There were also compelling strategic arguments. British resources were overstretched, and in 1937 the *Chiefs of Staff prudently advised that the task of British diplomacy should be to diminish the number of the country's enemies. Three adversaries—Germany, Italy, and Japan—were too many. The economic, psychological, and strategic constraints placed upon British policy were severe; and if a negotiated settlement could be reached with Germany or Italy, it would be reasonable to try for it.

The Soviet Union was not in principle a supporter of the status quo; indeed by its nature and origins it was revolutionary. But in both ideological and territorial terms it appeared threatened by Nazi Germany, and for some time it followed an anti-German course. In 1935 the Soviet Union concluded an alliance with France, while its adjunct the *Comintern proclaimed a policy of Popular Fronts against fascism. In March 1938 the Soviet government proposed a conference of countries opposed to German aggression, only to be ignored by the British and French. In 1939 there were negotiations for a three-power alliance between the USSR, France, and the UK, but the British showed only a half-hearted interest. Finally Stalin opted instead for an agreement with Germany, the *Nazi–Soviet Pact of 23 August 1939, by which Poland was to be partitioned and eastern Europe divided into spheres of influence.

In short, all three potential defenders of the status quo accepted the growth of German power, tried to accommodate it by negotiation, and on occasion even encouraged it. A series of occasions for resistance was allowed to pass by. In March 1936 France permitted Germany to remilitarize the Rhineland unopposed, which has been seen (rightly or wrongly) as the best opportunity to stop Hitler with only limited use of force. In 1938 the UK and France virtually coerced Czechoslovakia into surrendering the Sudetenland. In August 1939 Stalin met the Germans halfway in partitioning eastern Europe. It is salutary to reflect that Munich and the Nazi–Soviet Pact were very similar in their nature and consequences, though the name of Stalin is not usually so closely associated with 'appeasement' as those of Chamberlain or the French foreign minister, Georges Bonnet (1889–1973).

The ultimate consequence of this behaviour by the potential defenders of the status quo was to permit Germany (Italy was less important) to advance so far that it could no longer be resisted except at the cost of a major war. The occasions when the cost might have been smaller, or when Germany might have been deterred without war, passed by. However, this did not mean that Germany would never be resisted. 'Appeasement' did not mean peace at any price for any of its practitioners, who all had fundamental interests which would not be abandoned without a fight. If Germany's drive for expansion continued—as it did—it would certainly at some point be opposed. The questions were when, where, and by whom?

So the case builds up for the inevitability of war; but at the same time the limitations of that case can be discerned. The roots were present, with the potential to grow and bring forth fruit in the shape of a European war. Yet there were also decisions to be made. The idea of decision is inherent in the widely held concept of 'lost opportunities' to check Hitler, in the Rhineland or Czechoslovakia. It is also clear that leading figures changed their minds on occasion, and thus were not completely in the grip of inexorable forces. Hitler himself hesitated in September 1938. Up to 27 September there was every sign that he intended to press ahead with an invasion of Czechoslovakia. German forces were moving up to the frontier, and the assault was set for 30 September. Yet two days before he drew back, and accepted the idea of a conference. For whatever reason—the unreliability of Mussolini, the lukewarm response of the crowds in Berlin, or the mobilization of the British fleet or of the Czech Army—he did not take the final step. In August and September 1939 the story was different. This time Hitler was set on war, and seems to have been determined that no one should cheat him out of it. Thus Hitler, who of all the European leaders was the most fixed upon war, decided against it in 1938 and for it in 1939. Similarly Mussolini decided in September 1939 to stay out of the war, though he was supposedly committed to Germany by the *Pact of Steel; and then in June 1940 he changed his mind and joined in, to make sure of his share of the spoils.

Chamberlain too changed his mind, and indeed his policy. In 1938 he was set on a negotiated settlement with Germany, but by the end of March 1939 he had come to believe that Germany was out to dominate Europe by force, and would have to be resisted, if necessary by war. It would have been possible, and in many ways would have been the logical continuation of previous policy, to permit further German expansion in eastern Europe, but in fact Chamberlain and the British government chose otherwise. The same was true of *Daladier and the French government, though with great reluctance and with heavy hearts.

Thus choices were possible. The significant point about the changes of mind just described is that they all brought war nearer. Only one ruler of a great European power continued to the end to believe that he both could and should avoid war: Stalin. The Soviet Union was forced into the war in June 1941 by the brutal imperative of a German invasion (see BARBAROSSA). All the others decided that a point had been reached at which they must fight. In this process, Poland was the catalyst. In 1939 the Poles were determined not to yield an inch of territory, nor to permit a German take-over of *Danzig. They were prepared to fight rather than give way, and they were astonishingly confident in their power to resist. In Poland, Hitler encountered for the first time an adversary who could not be bullied; and again the element of choice is demonstrated.

Thus the events of 1939 took shape. German expansion had already made great progress, and by the end of March Poland, the UK, and France had decided that any further aggression must be resisted. A pattern of almost geometrical precision then emerged, and war could only have been avoided in one of three ways. First, Germany might have settled for what it had gained already. Second, Germany's potential opponents (especially the UK, France, and the USSR) might have combined in an alliance so formidable that Germany would have been deterred from any further advance. Third, those opponents, singly or together, might have decided to accept the further growth of German power, and make what terms they could. None of these things happened. Germany pressed on. The *Grand Alliance against it did not yet materialize. The Soviet Union struck a bargain with Germany, but Poland, the UK, and France did not. And so war came.

What was it about? It was in a fundamental sense Hitler's war. It is true that in September he found himself in a war which he had not expected, because he had not counted on an Anglo-French declaration of war; but it is more important that he pursued a course which would lead to German dominance in Europe, and which was bound at some point to be resisted. What German dominance meant can be seen by examining the fate of Europe over the next few years. Churchill remarked in the summer of 1940 that those who said they did not know what they were fighting about should stop fighting, and they would see. It was a simple observation, which contained much truth. In practice, Germany's opponents were fighting to protect their own territory, independence, and way of life, and in the long run to overthrow that German dominance which was established over so much of the Continent.

In the Far East, the roots of war are mostly sought in the motives behind Japanese expansion. Among these, one of the most important was economic. Japan was acutely dependent upon foreign trade, and therefore upon the economic and tariff policies of other states. The great depression exposed Japanese vulnerability to outside pressures, and brought home the fact that the country needed secure sources of food, raw materials, and fuel, and also unimpeded outlets for its exports. One way to establish these sources and outlets was by conquest, and by the creation of what was called a *Greater East Asia Co-prosperity Sphere. Another motive which pushed in the same direction was racial—a reaction against western predominance in the Far East, crudely expressed in the slogan 'Asia for the Asians'. Another mainspring of Japanese action, rather in contradiction to this slogan, was fear of China. The Japanese looked with dismay on the possibility of Chinese unification and restoration as a great power, and sought to pre-empt any such development. Finally, there was a strong impulse towards adventure and martial endeavour, to be found particularly deeply-rooted in the officer corps of the Japanese Army, which itself held a commanding position in Japanese society and government.

The 1930s also provided an opportunity—perhaps even a last chance—for Japanese self-assertion and expansion. During that decade, other states with interests in the Far East were prepared to stand back and permit the growth of Japanese power. In 1931–2 there was not the slightest chance that other great powers would combine to oppose the Japanese occupation of Manchuria (see MANCHUKUO). The USA, the UK, and France had only slight direct interest in the province; nor did they have any serious reason to support China, because Chinese nationalism was at the time a greater threat to their commercial interests than any action being taken by Japan. Moreover, all were much preoccupied with their domestic affairs. Only the Soviet Union was seriously concerned about Manchuria, through its common frontier with the province and its stake in the Chinese Eastern Railway; but for overriding internal reasons Moscow chose to accept the Japanese occupation, and even at one stage offered to sell its interest in the railway to Japan.

By the time Japan came to invade China proper in the latter part of 1937 and the following two years, the likelihood of opposition by other powers had if anything diminished. In May 1937 the US Congress placed the *Neutrality Act permanently on the statute book, and the tide of isolationism was running strongly. The UK and France were preoccupied with European affairs, and in the USSR the great purges were nearing their height. Germany, which had for some time provided limited but valuable assistance to China, changed its policy in 1938 and sought closer relations with Japan. Thus the Japanese had a virtually free hand; and in 1940 they were presented with an opportunity which they found simply too good to be ignored. Germany defeated the Netherlands and France—both with large colonial possessions in the Far East; and the UK stood apparently on the brink of defeat. These same events confronted the USA with the alarming possibility of German control of the Atlantic, and drew American attention towards Europe. Japan had a clear field.

In this field of golden opportunities there was only one awkward outcrop of rock. In 1939, at Nomonhan in Outer Mongolia, Japanese forces had fought a stiff battle with units of the Red Army—and lost (see JAPANESE–SOVIET CAMPAIGNS). It was the only serious military check they suffered in this period, and it effectively deterred them from any further northward advance. The main effect, however, was only to enhance the attractions of the south; and in the south Japan pressed on, exploiting the opportunity provided by events in Europe. It occupied northern French Indo-China in 1940, and then moved into southern French Indo-China in July 1941. It was at this point that the pattern of events was broken.

So far, Japanese expansion had been resisted only by the Chinese, whose country was after all being invaded. Other powers had looked on—even the Soviet victory at Nomonhan is not an exception, because it was a battle waged in self-defence. But the occupation of southern French Indo-China was unmistakably the first step into South-East Asia, threatening the American territory of the Philippines, the British colonies of Malaya and Singapore, and the Netherlands East Indies. At that point, in August 1941, the USA imposed an embargo on the export of oil to Japan, an example which was at once followed by the British and the Dutch. This placed Japan in a position in which it would run out of oil within a measurable period. Japanese choices were thus narrowed to two: to negotiate with the Americans under the pressure of the oil embargo, which in effect meant accepting American terms; or to go to war to break the blockade and impose its own control over the whole of the Far East. The terms presented by the Americans during the next few months were Japanese withdrawal from French Indo-China and the whole of China (except Manchukuo), which meant the abandonment of all the gains made since 1937. The furthest the Japanese would go was to offer to withdraw from French Indo-China and to confine their occupation of China to the north, while preserving a special economic position in the whole country. This meant deadlock, and there was no serious doubt as to Japanese action: they would go to war.

The course of these events has left two major questions over which historians continue to ponder: how fixed and determined was Japanese policy; and what were the intentions of the Americans in imposing what proved to be their fateful economic sanctions?

The more closely Japanese policy between 1937 and 1941 has been examined, the less fixed and inevitable does its course appear. In 1937 the Japanese government clearly did not expect the incident at the Marco Polo Bridge to have far-reaching consequences. A local cease-fire was quickly arranged, which was rejected not by the Japanese but by the Chinese leader *Chiang Kai-shek. The Japanese then embarked on a large-scale campaign in China without working out either their objectives or the likely consequences. During 1938 they hesitated as to what policy to pursue. The army High Command first recommended bringing the war in China to an end, and then intensified its operations there. Negotiations were opened with Chiang Kai-shek, but led nowhere. Much the same happened early in 1940, when the government resolved to withdraw large forces from China but ended by sending reinforcements, and further negotiations were begun but not followed up. There were many signs that the Japanese had become involved in a war which they could neither win nor end by negotiation.

There were other signs of uncertainty later in 1940. It was clear that Japan faced a remarkable opportunity: but what was to be done with it? For a time, the Japanese concentrated on cutting China off from the outside world, and so bringing Chinese resistance to an end—that was the main point of occupying northern French Indo-China. But in October and November 1940 Japanese naval commanders were developing strategic aims which pointed southwards, towards the oil resources of the Netherlands East Indies. If Japan were to move in that direction, it would be prudent to avoid trouble with the USSR; and a neutrality agreement with that country was signed in March 1941. In June 1941 the German attack on the USSR plunged the Japanese into further uncertainty. The government and High Command considered three major options: to try for peace with China and an agreement with the USA; to join the Germans in attacking the Soviet Union; and to advance southwards. The conclusion reached, at the beginning of July, was to try a bit of everything: to construct a Greater East Asia Co-prosperity Sphere; to settle the war in China; to prepare for expansion southwards; and to solve the northern problem—whatever that might mean. The first practical step agreed on was the occupation of southern French Indo-China, which as we have seen led to grave consequences.

Examination of Japanese policy-making thus reveals divided counsels and frequent uncertainty. What it does not reveal, however, is any serious willingness to call a halt to expansion. The disputes were usually about whether to advance northwards or southwards, to bite off a lot or a little; and decisions were always in favour of at least one more expansionist move. Thus, while our picture of Japanese policy is more complicated than it once was, the essence remains unchanged.

When we turn to US policy, the puzzle is of a different nature. The Americans in effect accepted the Japanese occupation of large parts of China, and then the northern part of French Indo-China, with only nominal opposition. In 1939 they declined to renew the American-Japanese trade treaty of 1911, and in 1940 they put an embargo on the export of scrap metal to Japan—warning shots, no doubt, but scarcely drastic action. Then, after the occupation of southern French Indo-China, the Americans introduced the most damaging economic sanction in history, and confronted the Japanese with a choice between accepting US terms and running out of oil. Why did American policy change so radically, and why did they impose so tough an economic sanction without realizing that it would in all probability lead to war? To the first question, the likeliest answer is an increasing realization of the nature of Japanese aims, leading to an extremely rigid stance which was in large part a reaction against earlier inactivity. To the second question, answers have varied widely. Some writers have implausibly argued that Roosevelt was deliberately inviting war, as much in the Atlantic as in the Pacific—the so-called back door to war in Europe. It is much more likely that the US government, and Roosevelt in particular, believed that severe economic sanctions together with a tough line in negotiations (see USA, 1) would deter Japan from going to war. American policy was thus based on a disastrous miscalculation, which came home to roost at Pearl Harbor.

The final picture retains a fundamental simplicity. Japan was set on expansion, though its precise course and stages were subject to much uncertainty and debate. For a long time that expansion was accepted by other powers, but in 1941 the USA decided to oppose it by severe economic measures and a demand that Japan should not simply call a halt but retreat to the position before 1937. For the Japanese, this amounted to an impossible surrender. Confident in their military prowess, they preferred to try the arbitrament of war.

Events in Europe and the Far East moved on separate and largely unrelated courses, but they shared a similar pattern. An expansionist great power (Germany in Europe, Japan in the Far East) carried all before it for several years, without serious opposition. Then at a late stage other powers (France and the UK in Europe, the USA in the Pacific) tried to check the course of expansion by an exercise in deterrence, only to find that the only recourse was war. In both cases, historical debate has concentrated on elucidating the motives behind the expansion, the reasons why it was so long accepted, and the question of why it was ultimately resisted. It is from our answers to these questions that we form our views of the origins of the wars.

See also ANTI-IMPERIALISM and NATIONALISM and Introductions to the entries for the major powers.

P. M. H. BELL

Bell, P. M. H., *The Origins of the Second World War in Europe* (London, 1986).
Carr, W., *Poland to Pearl Harbour. The Making of the Second World War* (London, 1985).
Iriye Akira, *The Origins of the Second World War in Asia and the Pacific* (London, 1987).
Watt, D. C., *How War Came. The immediate origins of the Second World War 1938–1939* (London, 1989).

Orpo, or Ordnungspolizei (order police), was the domestic uniformed police in Nazi Germany. During the war it spread to occupied countries and it became more military in character. Armed formations were raised from its personnel and these worked closely with the *SS in the suppression of resistance groups in eastern Europe, the Balkans, and, after Italy's surrender in September 1943, in northern Italy.

Ōshima Hiroshi, Lt-General Baron (1886–1975), Japanese army officer turned diplomat who helped negotiate the *Anti-Comintern and *Tripartite Pacts. As a lt-general he served as ambassador to Berlin in 1938–9 and 1941–5. It was his diplomatic *MAGIC messages that were so helpful to the Allies during the war. He was sentenced to life imprisonment at the *Far East War Crimes Trials but was given parole in 1955.

Oslo report, two letters sent incognito to the British naval attaché in Oslo in November 1939 and forwarded for assessment to the *MI6 scientist, R. V. Jones. They contained descriptions of the German development of various types of armament, including *V-weapons and *radar, and one also included the triggering device for a *proximity fuze which was superior to anything the British had at the time. Jones had no doubt as to the veracity of the letters, but he could find no one else who would take their contents seriously. It transpired that most of the report was remarkably accurate. It helped Jones counter the various German beam systems that guided German bombers on to their targets (see ELECTRONIC NAVIGATION SYSTEMS and ELECTRONIC WARFARE), and as the war progressed Jones took to referring to the letters to see what was likely to appear next.

The identity of the report's author, a German physicist called Hans Ferdinand Mayer who worked for the electronic firm Siemens, remained unknown until 1989 when Jones revealed it in his book *Reflections on Intelligence*, which contains the complete report (pp. 333–7). Because of his anti-Nazi stance Mayer was imprisoned in *Dachau in 1943 but survived the war to become professor of astrophysics at Cornell University in the USA. Jones judged his report the best received from any single individual during the war, Mayer having 'in one great flash ... given us a synoptic glimpse of much of what was foreshadowed in German military electronics' (*Reflections on Intelligence*, London, 1989, p. 275).

OSS, see OFFICE OF STRATEGIC SERVICES.

Ossewabrandwag (Oxwaggon Sentinels), organization officially launched in South Africa in 1939 to preserve the culture and traditions of the Afrikaners, which quickly developed into a neo-Nazi, paramilitary force. At its peak it had 400,000 members and posed a considerable threat to the South African government. Some of its members became *stormjaers* (storm troops) and during the war it committed various acts of sabotage and subversion, and also helped German internees escape. In April 1941 the *Abwehr sent to South Africa a South African Olympic boxer, Robey Liebrandt, in the hope that he would help the Ossewabrandwag start a rebellion, and by the spring of 1943 four other Abwehr agents and radio equipment had been introduced into the country. This enabled the organization to send information to

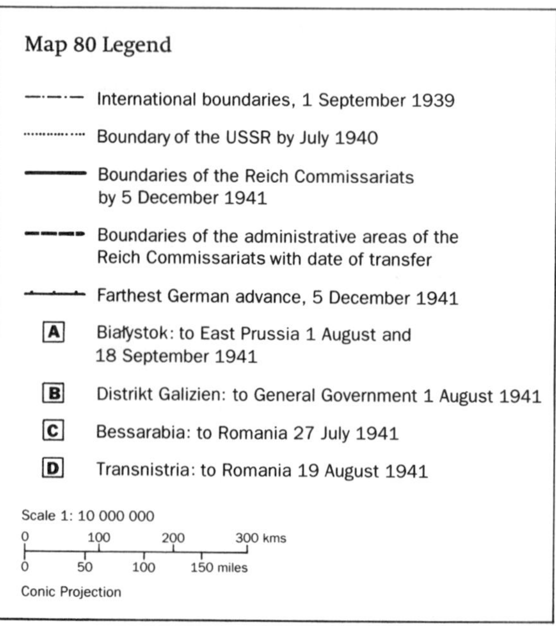

80. **Ostland**: Division by Axis of Soviet territories occupied after BARBAROSSA, June 1941

Germany via the German consulate general who had escaped to Lourenço Marques in Portuguese East Africa, but nothing of any consequence was ever transmitted. The South African prime minister, *Smuts, who always tried to give his opponents sufficient rope with which to hang themselves, refused to allow the organization's Commandant General, J. F. J. van Rensburg, to be arrested, though some of the agents, including Liebrandt, were, and about 2,000 Ossewabrandwag members were interned. In June 1944 the Ossewabrandwag's strength was estimated at 30,000 but by then its political influence was virtually nil.

Visser, G., *OB: Traitors or Patriots?* (Cape Town, 1976).

Oster, Maj-General Hans (1888–1945), anti-Nazi member of the German *Abwehr which he joined in May 1933 after being forced to resign from the German Army because of an illicit love affair. *Canaris had him readmitted to the officer corps and made him his deputy in 1938. Though they were close friends and political allies before the war—when they planned to remove Hitler by a *coup d'état*—Canaris was later alienated by what he regarded as Oster's brand of reckless treachery.

In May 1940, via the Dutch military attaché in Berlin, Colonel J. G. Sas, Oster gave last-minute invasion warnings, mostly ignored, to Norway, Denmark, Belgium, and the Netherlands. The fact that he had the Abwehr's communications network at his disposal, his own extensive ring of agents, and connections in the highest places, make it quite likely that he was the *LUCY ring's most valuable source called Werther. He also used various organizations abroad, which were under Abwehr protection, to help some Jews escape the *Final Solution, and for this he was suspended from duty in April 1943. He was later implicated in the July 1944 bomb plot to assassinate Hitler (see SCHWARZE KAPELLE), and was arrested and executed in April 1945.

Ostland (1), one of the two military Reich Commissariats established under Alfred *Rosenberg as Reich Minister for the Occupied Eastern Territories, the Reich Commissariat Ukraine being the other (see Map 80). It consisted of the Baltic States, parts of Belorussia, and part of eastern Poland (see also GERMANY, 4).

Ostland (2), abbreviation of Ostdeutsche Landbewirtschaftungsgesellschaft (East German Land Development Society), a German agricultural organization created in February 1940 to colonize certain Polish regions, and also parts of occupied France where it concentrated on developing land abandoned by smallholders, Jews, and refugees.

Ostmark was the Nazi name for Austria after the Anschluss in March 1938.

Osttruppen (eastern troops), see SOVIET EXILES AT WAR.

OVERLORD was the overall codename for the Allied invasion of occupied north-west Europe (see Maps 81 and 82). The assault phase of OVERLORD, the Normandy landings and associated operations, was codenamed NEPTUNE.

The Casablanca conference convened in January 1943 (see SYMBOL), gave the initial impetus to planning and executing OVERLORD by agreeing to establish a planning staff, *COSSAC, and to increase the build-up of US troops in the UK (BOLERO). COSSAC, aided by earlier plans for other incursions on to the Continent, sought a suitable landing area in the Low Countries or France which was within range of Allied fighters, where the beach defences could be neutralized, and where the rate of build-up of Allied troops could equal that of the defending German forces. This last depended on the immediate capture of a major port, but as it was supposed that it would take three months to put any port into working order, it was necessary to find firm and sheltered beaches over which the troops ashore could be supplied for at least 90 days, and which had an adequate road network behind them. COSSAC eventually chose the Baie de la Seine, between Le Havre and the Cherbourg peninsula, because it fitted the necessary criteria and was close to a major port, Cherbourg, which could, it was hoped, be captured almost immediately. All supplies were to be landed over the beaches, via artificial harbours (see MULBERRIES), while fuel was to be pumped across the Channel by pipelines known generically as *PLUTO.

This COSSAC plan—it was really a feasibility study—was approved at the Quebec conference in August 1943 (see QUADRANT) at which Churchill requested a 25% increase in the assault force. No firm decision on this request was made until January 1944 when, despite the acute shortage of landing craft, it was decided to expand the assault force from three divisions to eight, three of them airborne.

In February 1944 *SHAEF, the HQ of the Allied Expeditionary Force's Supreme Commander, General *Eisenhower, was activated, and OVERLORD's land, air, and sea commanders (*Montgomery, *Leigh-Mallory, and *Ramsay) produced the NEPTUNE Initial Joint Plan. This incorporated the expanded assault forces, but to have the landing craft available to transport them the *French Riviera landings, planned originally to coincide with NEPTUNE, and NEPTUNE itself, had to be delayed.

Timing was critical. All Allied amphibious operations in the Mediterranean had started under cover of darkness; but, because of the complexity and vastness of the landings, and because air and naval forces could only neutralize the heavily defended coastline in daylight, it was decided to assault after dawn. Other factors limited the landings to about one hour after low water and this, plus the need for the airborne troops to have a full moon, narrowed the first possible days down to 5, 6, and 7 June. The chosen day was 5 June, but the landings were delayed 24 hours because of bad weather (see also METEOROLOGICAL INTELLIGENCE).

To guard the time and place of the landings the most

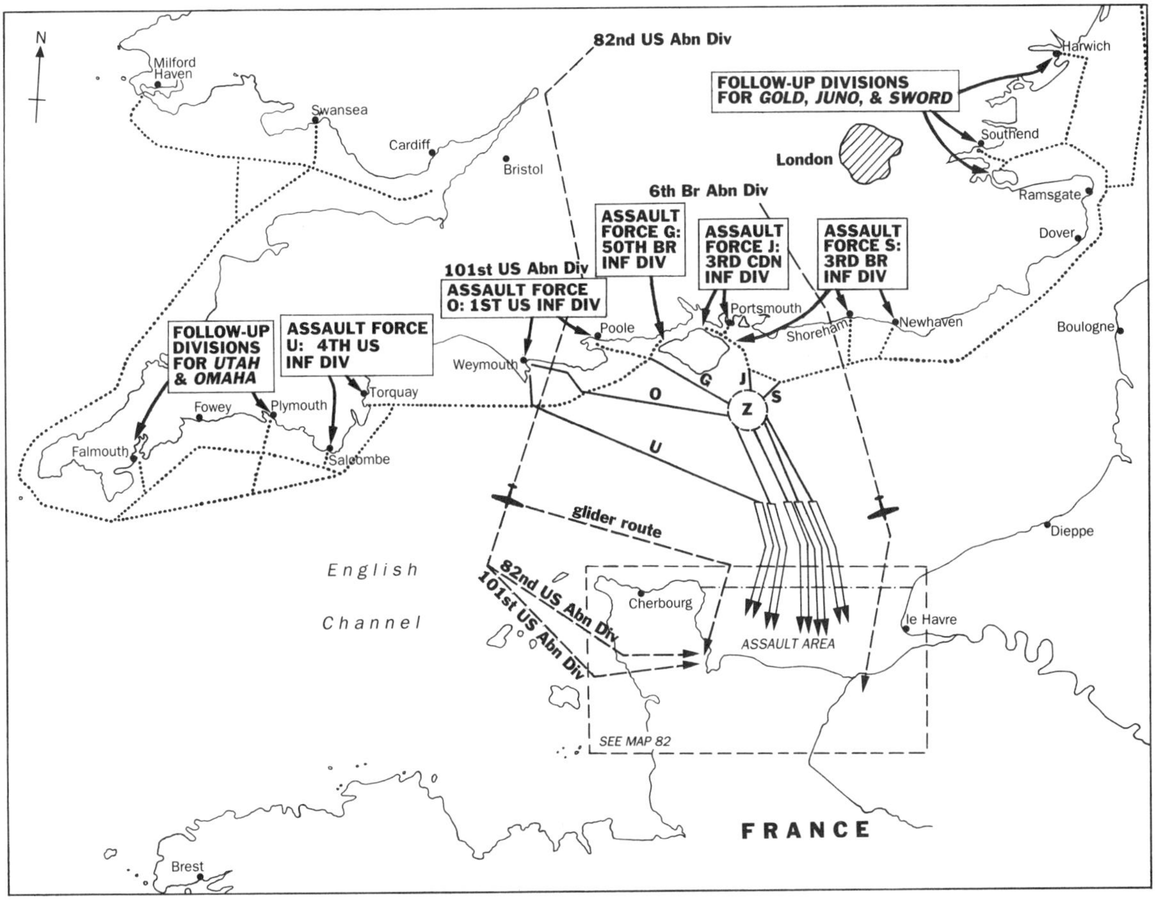

81. **OVERLORD**: Departure points of assault and follow-up divisions for Normandy landings, 6 June 1944

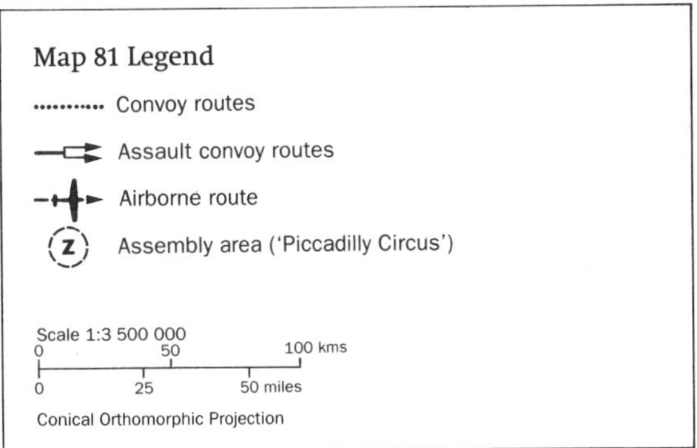

stringent measures were taken to maintain security. All plans relating to them were given the classification of BIGOT and all officers involved in them were said to be BIGOTed, and were forced to follow the strictest of guidelines. Civilian travel between the UK and Eire was stopped and a coastal belt 16 km. (10 mi.) deep, stretching from the Wash to Land's End, and either side of the Firth of Forth, was closed to all but authorized travellers. Neither diplomats nor their couriers were permitted to enter or leave the country and only the Americans and the Soviets were allowed to continue to transmit signals in their diplomatic ciphers. The Polish *government-in-exile also continued sending cipher signals, though neither the USA nor the USSR were told it was doing so. It was allowed to continue because the British could not break the Polish diplomatic cipher and it was thought that if they could not do so, then neither could the Germans.

The Germans were, of course, well aware that the Allies intended to invade, but *deception kept them guessing as to where the landings would be, and, once they had occurred, whether they were a diversionary operation. They were also afflicted by an unsatisfactory command system (see Chart) and conflicting methods of organization. Neither the C-in-C West, Field Marshal von *Rundstedt, nor the commander of Army Group B, Field Marshal *Rommel, had any control over the naval and air forces in France, while the two men held differing views on how any invasion should be defeated. Rundstedt

OVERLORD

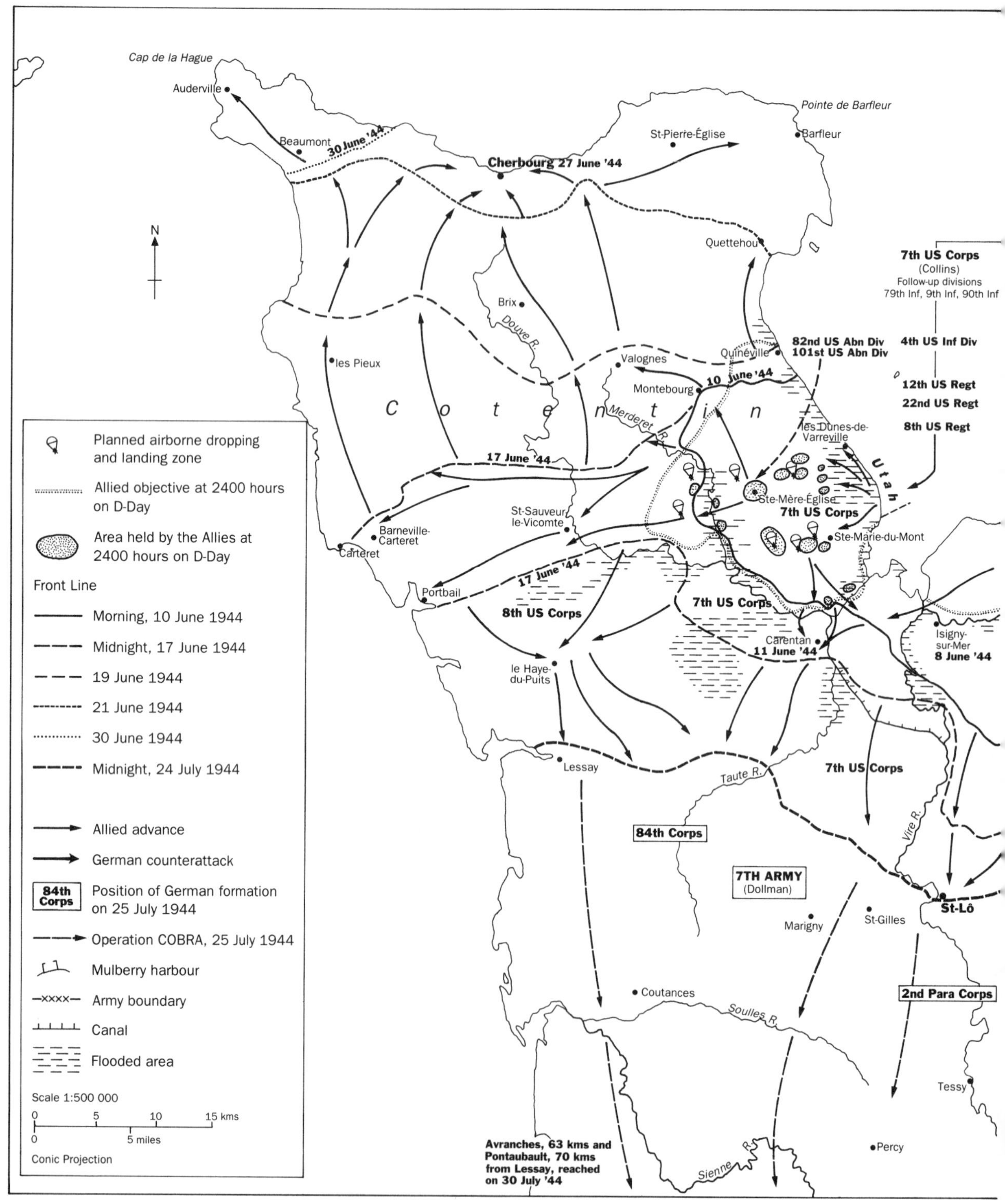

82. **OVERLORD**: Normandy landings and subsequent fighting, 6 June–25 July 1944

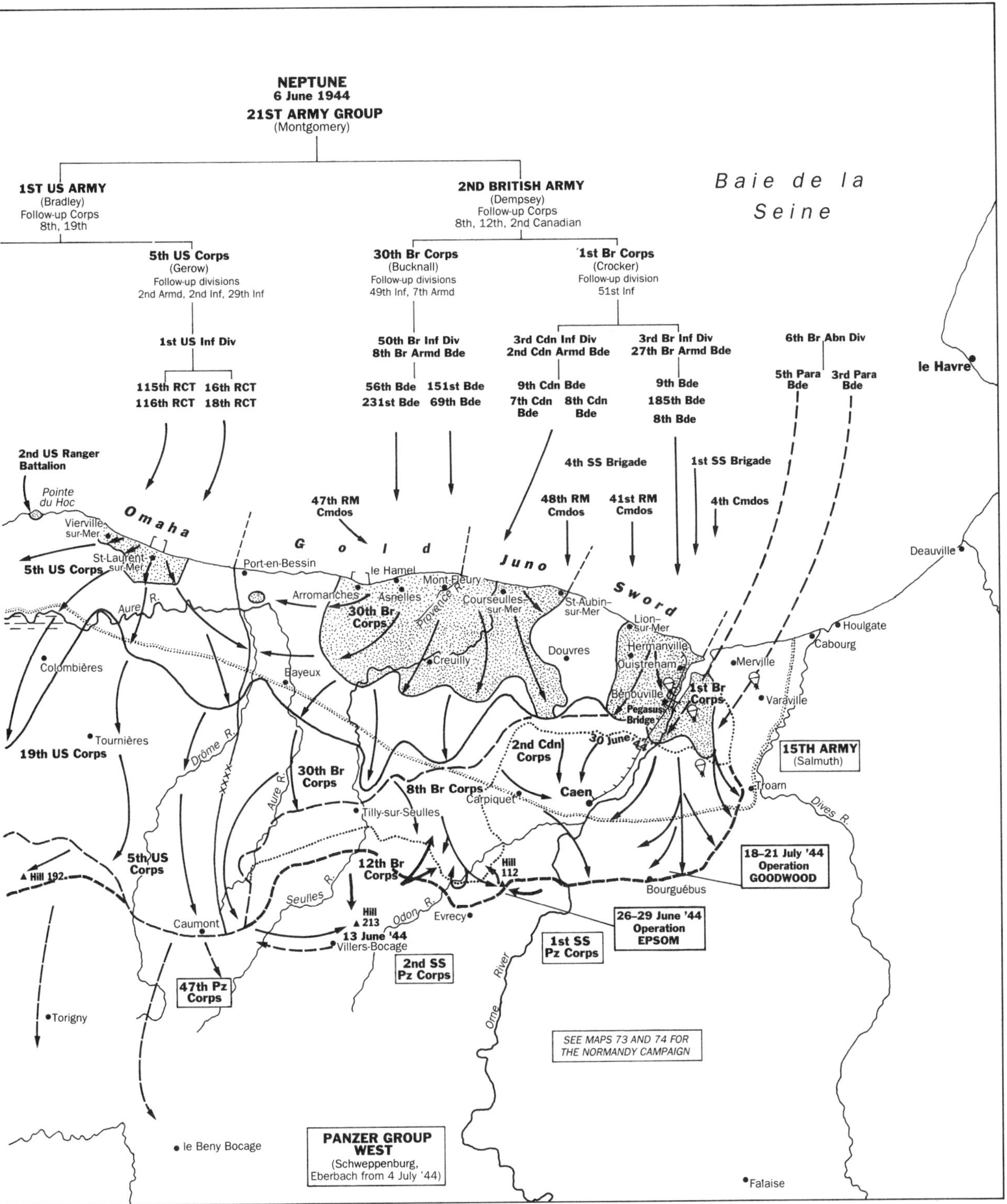
NEPTUNE
6 June 1944
21ST ARMY GROUP
(Montgomery)
1ST US ARMY
(Bradley)
Follow-up Corps
8th, 19th
2ND BRITISH ARMY
(Dempsey)
Follow-up Corps
8th, 12th, 2nd Canadian
Baie de la Seine
5th US Corps
(Gerow)
Follow-up divisions
2nd Armd, 2nd Inf, 29th Inf
30th Br Corps
(Bucknall)
Follow-up divisions
49th Inf, 7th Armd
1st Br Corps
(Crocker)
Follow-up division
51st Inf
1st US Inf Div
50th Br Inf Div
8th Br Armd Bde
3rd Cdn Inf Div
2nd Cdn Armd Bde
3rd Br Inf Div
27th Br Armd Bde
6th Br Abn Div
115th RCT 16th RCT
116th RCT 18th RCT
56th Bde 151st Bde
231st Bde 69th Bde
9th Cdn Bde
7th Cdn Bde
8th Cdn Bde
9th Bde
185th Bde
8th Bde
5th Para Bde
3rd Para Bde
le Havre
2nd US Ranger Battalion
4th SS Brigade
1st SS Brigade
Pointe du Hoc
47th RM Cmdos
48th RM Cmdos
41st RM Cmdos
4th Cmdos
Omaha
Gold
Juno
Sword
Vierville-sur-Mer
St-Laurent-sur-Mer
5th US Corps
Port-en-Bessin
le Hamel
Mont Fleury
Arromanches
Asnelles
Courseulles-sur-Mer
St-Aubin-sur-Mer
Deauville
Aure R.
30th Br Corps
Provence R.
Lion-sur-Mer
Houlgate
Cabourg
Douvres
Hermanville
Colombières
Bayeux
Creuilly
Ouistreham
Merville
Bénouville
Pegasus Bridge
1st Br Corps
Varaville
Tournières
Drôme R.
2nd Cdn Corps
30 June '44
15TH ARMY
(Salmuth)
19th US Corps
30th Br Corps
8th Br Corps
Troarn
Carpiquet
Caen
Aure R.
Tilly-sur-Seulles
Dives R.
5th US Corps
12th Br Corps
Hill 112
18–21 July '44
Operation
GOODWOOD
Hill 192
Bourguébus
Seulles R.
Odon R.
Evrecy
Hill 213
Caumont
13 June '44
Villers-Bocage
26–29 June '44
Operation
EPSOM
1st SS Pz Corps
2nd SS Pz Corps
Orne River
47th Pz Corps
Torigny
SEE MAPS 73 AND 74 FOR THE NORMANDY CAMPAIGN
PANZER GROUP WEST
(Schweppenburg, Eberbach from 4 July '44)
le Beny Bocage
Falaise

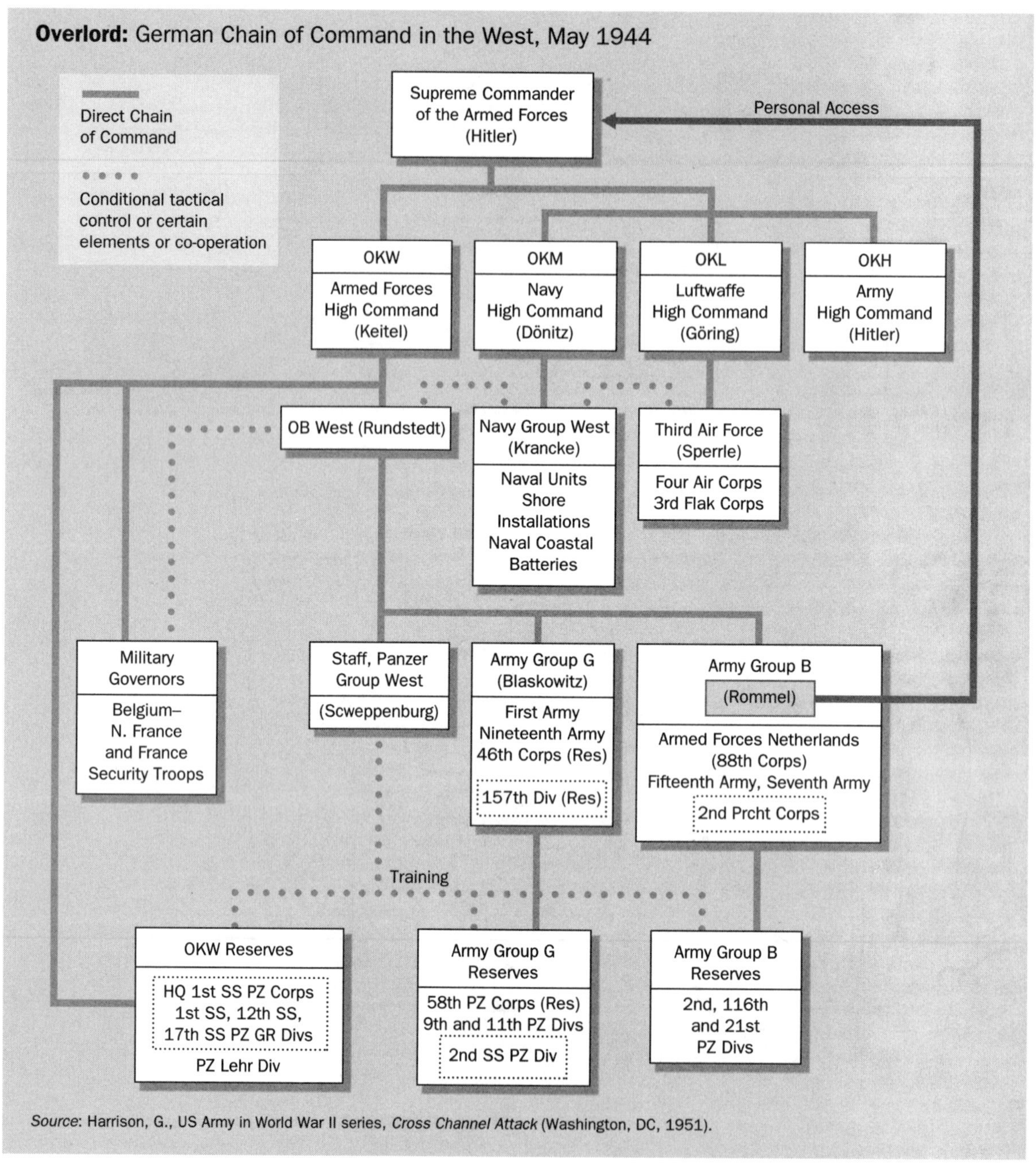

Source: Harrison, G., US Army in World War II series, *Cross Channel Attack* (Washington, DC, 1951).

believed that nothing could prevent the *Atlantic Wall defences from being pierced and that the best hope was to hold a large mobile force in reserve, positioned to strike once the Allies had landed. But Rommel and Hitler were convinced that any invasion had to be beaten on the beaches and that reserves should be positioned close to the most vulnerable places. In the event neither policy was pursued properly and in April the armoured reserves were divided between Rommel and Hitler's Armed Forces High Command, so that Rundstedt had none.

In the first six months of 1944 Rommel strongly reinforced the defences and placed obstacles such as *element C on all large beaches. Extra troops were also brought in so that by the end of May Rommel's two armies (Fifteenth in northern France and Seventh in Normandy) comprised 25 static coast divisions, 16 infantry and parachute divisions, 10 armoured and mechanized divisions, and 7 reserve divisions. But the Third Air Fleet in France remained weak—only 319 of its aircraft operated on *D-Day, though within a week it had been boosted to 1,000—while German naval surface forces amounted to only 4 destroyers in the Atlantic ports and 39 E-Boats between Ijmuiden and St Malo.

Much of Rommel's work to reinforce the Channel coast, and to rush reinforcements to the invasion beaches, was hampered by Leigh-Mallory's tactical air forces, and by the two strategic air forces (Bomber Command and Eighth USAAF) which the *Combined Chiefs of Staff placed temporarily under Eisenhower's command. Between 1 April and 5 June 1944 more than 11,000 aircraft from these Allied air forces flew more than 200,000 sorties in support of the invasion, dropping 195,000 tons of bombs on rail and road communications, airfields, military installations, industrial targets, and coastal batteries and radar positions. Nearly 2,000 were lost, but the bombers wrought havoc with the German communications and supply routes which seriously hampered the reinforcement of those troops trying to contain the Allied bridgehead. The Allied air forces also achieved almost total air supremacy and as the historical staff of the Luftwaffe commented, 'the outstanding factor both before and during the invasion was the overwhelming air superiority of the enemy.'

Another important factor that hampered the Germans before and after the landings was the work of the French resistance. By May 1944 it was calculated that some 100,000 Frenchmen, armed and helped by *SOE and the *Office of Strategic Services, were ready to take orders from the head of the Free French Forces of the Interior (see FFI), General *Koenig. There were, too, some 35–45,000 armed *maquis, though a quarter of these had only enough ammunition to fight for a day. Before and after D-Day special teams (see COONEY, JEDBURGH, and SUSSEX) were dropped to gain intelligence, and to support the French resistance. Sabotage was widespread: the railway system and the Germans' communication network were severely disrupted.

NEPTUNE began just after midnight on 6 June—known then and now as D-Day—when 23,400 British and US paratroopers were landed on the flanks of the invasion beaches. On the left flank 6th British Airborne Division was dropped east of the River Orne, and on the right flank 82nd and 101st US Airborne Divisions were dropped between Ste Mère Eglise, the first village in France to be liberated, and Carentan. Then, starting at 0630, the assault divisions were delivered by five naval assault forces to their beaches, which were codenamed (from west to east) *UTAH, *OMAHA, *GOLD, *JUNO, and *SWORD. Each naval assault force was given the first letter of the codename of the beach on to which it was to deliver its division. There were also two additional naval forces, B and L, which were associated with landing the follow-up troops. Nearly 7,000 ships and landing craft were employed to bombard German positions, land the five Allied divisions, create the two artificial harbours which had to be towed across the English Channel, and counter any German naval attacks. Of the 1,213 naval warships involved 79% were British and Canadian, 16.5% were American, and 4% were Dutch, French, Greek, Norwegian, and Polish. Including the Allied merchant navies, 195,701 naval personnel took part. The Allied Expeditionary Air Forces also played their part, protecting the armada from air attack, bombing German defences, and creating a 'ghost' invasion force which deceived German radar (see ELECTRONIC WARFARE).

Altogether 75,215 British and Canadian troops and 57,500 US troops were landed on D-Day. There were about 4,300 British and Canadian casualties, and 6,000 US ones.

NEPTUNE officially ceased on 30 June 1944, by which date 850,279 men, 148,803 vehicles, and 570,505 tons of supplies had been landed for the loss of 59 ships sunk and 110 damaged. Pressure mines (see MINE WARFARE, 2) caused a substantial number of naval casualties, and a storm on 19 June, which wrecked one of the artificial harbours, caused many more. See also AMPHIBIOUS WARFARE and NORMANDY CAMPAIGN.

Ozawa Jizaburō, Vice-Admiral (1886–1963), Japanese naval officer who in May 1945 succeeded *Toyoda as the last C-in-C of the Japanese Combined Fleet. 'A first class

Vice-Admiral **Ozawa**.

fighting admiral, and the Navy's foremost tactician' (A. Marder, *Old Friends, New Enemies:* Vol. 1, Oxford, 1981, p. 445), he commanded the Malaya Force (Southern Expeditionary Fleet) which covered the Japanese landings at the start of the *Malayan campaign. He was an early supporter of naval air power and it was the aircraft under his operational control which sank Force Z, the **Prince of Wales* and *Repulse*, off the Malayan coast on 10 December 1941. He used the aircraft at his disposal to equally good effect during the conquest of the *Netherlands East Indies and in *Kondō's *Indian Ocean raid in April 1942. He commanded the First Mobile Fleet during the battle of the *Philippine Sea in June 1944 and also played a critical role in the *Leyte Gulf battle in October 1944 when his carriers successfully lured *Halsey's Third Fleet away from protecting the US invasion beaches on Leyte.

Ozawa was a modest man who said little but did not hesitate to speak out if he thought it right. He took no pleasure in the sinking of Force Z, had no interest in glory, and refused promotion to admiral on the grounds that serving his country was more important than rank.

Pacific Military conference, see PACIFIC WAR.

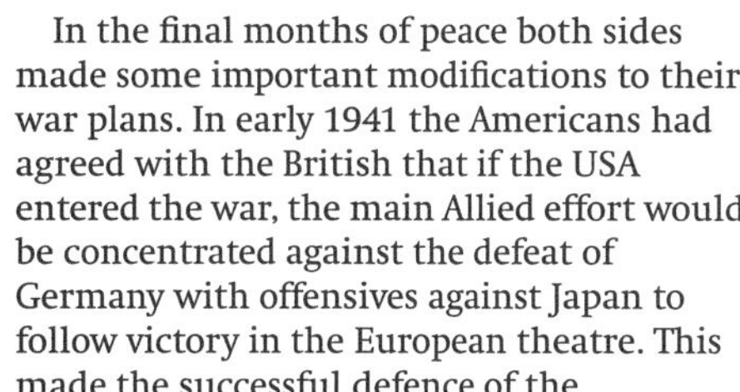

Pacific war (see Map G). The Japanese attack on *Pearl Harbor on 7 December 1941 marked the beginning of one of the largest and most complex wars in American history. Called the Great East Asia War by the Japanese, the land campaigns sometimes approached those in the *Italian and *North African campaigns in size, while in the naval campaigns there were more sea battles and more warships sunk than in all other 20th-century naval wars combined. In size, the theatre of war was immense, stretching from the Aleutian Islands in the fog-bound north Pacific south to tropical Fiji and New Caledonia, from Java in the Netherlands East Indies to Hawaii and Midway in the central Pacific.

Since before the *First World War, Japanese and American strategists had planned and debated the possible course of a Pacific conflict. For the Americans, the principal problem was the defence of the Philippines, thousands of kilometres from the USA but only 320 km. (200 mi.) from Japanese bases on Formosa. The Philippines were well fortified but the US fleet was based at Hawaii on the other side of the Pacific. American war plans, the 'Orange Plans', called for an early offensive 'primarily naval in character', to establish American control of the western Pacific and relieve the Philippines. By the mid-1930s dozens of war games and studies had convinced the planners that a second offensive across the Pacific would be slow and difficult, a matter of years rather than months. Island bases would have to be captured along the way. The army proposed to cross the Philippines off the list. In case of war with Japan, US forces should withdraw to more defensible bases in Alaska, Hawaii, and Panama. The navy refused to give up the idea of an offensive in the Pacific, although they tacitly agreed that the Philippines would almost certainly fall long before relief could arrive.

The Japanese were well aware of the basic course that the Americans were likely to follow and designed their own strategy accordingly. They planned to seize control of the Philippines and Guam at the outset of the war and then wait for an offensive by the US Navy. Their submarines and aircraft would harass and wear down the American fleet as it made its way across the Pacific and the decisive battle would take place close to Japanese bases in the Philippines, the Carolines, or the Marianas, after the fleet had been exhausted and depleted by its long, costly voyage.

The Japanese counted on the superior toughness and morale of their men and intensive training in night fighting to even the odds against the numerically superior American fleet. They had also developed new tactics and instruments of war, notably a new type of oxygen-driven, 24-inch torpedo with a maximum effective range of over 19 km. (12 mi.), and an excellent array of night vision devices.

In the final months of peace both sides made some important modifications to their war plans. In early 1941 the Americans had agreed with the British that if the USA entered the war, the main Allied effort would be concentrated against the defeat of Germany with offensives against Japan to follow victory in the European theatre. This made the successful defence of the Philippines and their early relief appear even more unlikely. However, in July 1941 General *MacArthur, one of the USA's best-known and most distinguished soldiers, was recalled to active service to command the combined US and Philippine Commonwealth forces in the islands.

MacArthur argued that with the large army planned for the Philippines and with modern military equipment, especially the USAAF's new long-range bomber, the B17 *flying fortress, the islands could, for the first time, be successfully defended against a large-scale invasion. Agreeing with MacArthur's reasoning, the war department earmarked some of its most modern weapons and planes for the Philippines. In fact only a small proportion of these had arrived by December 1941, and the Philippine Army was still largely untrained.

Meanwhile the Japanese were also making modifications in their planning. At the outbreak of war, to obtain the oil and other *raw materials they needed, they planned to seize not only the Philippines but Burma, Malaya, Thailand, Borneo, the Netherlands East Indies, and various island bases in the south and central Pacific. Admiral *Yamamoto, C-in-C of the combined fleet, argued that success in such a war would be possible only if the US fleet at Hawaii were destroyed or disabled. The traditional Japanese strategy of lying in wait for the American fleet in the western Pacific was unsatisfactory. The Americans might not come out to fight until they had reinforced their fleet with newly constructed warships, or conversely they might take advantage of the dispersion of the Japanese fleet in South-East Asia to strike quickly across the Pacific. Only an attack on the US base at Pearl Harbor would eliminate the threat.

At Yamamoto's insistence Imperial General Headquarters (see JAPAN, 5(a)) agreed to a raid on Pearl Harbor by all six of the navy's large carriers while the rest of the Japanese offensives went forward. The Japanese planned to seize and occupy a vast area from Burma and Thailand to the Gilbert Islands and *Wake in the central Pacific. The Philippines, Malaya, British North Borneo, and Hong Kong were to be attacked in the first stage of war, followed by the Netherlands East Indies and Burma.

Japanese successes in the first months of the war exceeded even their most optimistic expectations. The attack on Pearl Harbor sank or seriously damaged 6 battleships and 8 other ships, and destroyed almost 200 planes with only light losses to the attackers. During the next few days, Japanese planes destroyed over half of MacArthur's air force on the ground at *Clark Field near Manila and sank the British capital ships **Prince of Wales*

The **Pacific war** was often fought on islands which the Japanese had turned into fortresses. Here, in the first offensive of the American drive across the central Pacific, US marines clear Tarawa of its defenders, November 1943.

and *Repulse* off Malaya. *Hong Kong fell on Christmas Day and *British Borneo was occupied a few days later. In the Malayan campaign the Japanese combined powerful frontal attacks with skilful flanking movements from the sea and through the jungle to push the British defenders down the peninsula. In the first of the two *Philippines campaigns MacArthur's plan for a beach-head defence of the islands quickly collapsed and the American and Filipino forces fell back towards the *Bataan peninsula on the north side of Manila Bay.

The Japanese, obsessed with capturing Manila and expecting the Americans to fight for the capital, allowed MacArthur's forces to execute a skilful withdrawal into Bataan, but without sufficient supplies and food and medicine. They quickly captured Manila and then began withdrawing some of their troops for the invasion of the Netherland East Indies. The remaining troops proved insufficient to overcome the American defences on Bataan. With the Americans too weakened by lack of food and medicine to counter-attack, each side settled into a two-month stand-off. Meanwhile the Japanese pushed British, Indian, and Australian forces in Malaya back to Singapore. After a week of air and artillery bombardment Japanese troops crossed the narrow strait of Johore which separates Singapore from the mainland and, on 15 February, the supposedly impregnable fortress, which had long been seen as the corner-stone of British defences in the Far East, surrendered.

At the time of the fall of *Singapore Japanese forces were already closing in on the Netherlands East Indies. A hastily established Allied *ABDA Command, set up to co-ordinate the defence of South-East Asia, proved incapable of halting the Japanese advance. Allied naval forces defending Java were destroyed in the battle of the *Java Sea on 24 February, and the Netherlands East Indies surrendered on 8 March. Rangoon had fallen to Japanese troops in Burma the day before.

On 3 April, as their troops pursued the British north through Burma towards the border of India, the Japanese opened a new offensive on Bataan with air and artillery reinforcements fresh from Malaya and Hong Kong. By 8 April the American defences on the peninsula had collapsed. The island fortress of *Corregidor in Manila Bay held out for another month before succumbing to Japanese attacks on 6 May. MacArthur had left the Philippines, at the order of Roosevelt, on 12 March vowing 'I shall return.'

With the collapse of ABDA Command at the end of

February the USA assumed almost complete direction of the war in the Pacific. The British tacitly acquiesced in this arrangement; and while the Australians and New Zealanders complained loudly from time to time about the American monopoly, there was very little they could do to change the state of affairs (but see PACIFIC WAR COUNCIL), despite the fact that during 1942 and 1943 they provided a substantial proportion of the forces arrayed against the Japanese in the south Pacific. Indeed, in August 1943, the Australian component of the land forces available in the Pacific (one armoured and nine infantry divisions) was larger than the American one, and in October 1943 their comparative strengths were: Australian land forces 492,000, US land forces 198,000. The Australian air strength was also greater in total but the Americans had more combat squadrons available (59) than had the Australians (43).

It is also interesting to note that, despite the priority given to defeating Germany and Italy, there were, at the end of 1942, more US forces committed to the Pacific theatre than to the European and Mediterranean ones. In the Pacific theatre, including Hawaii, there were eleven American divisions, while in the North African campaign there were only six (a seventh was stationed in the UK). The US Navy, too, had the preponderance of its strength in the Pacific. Only the USAAF had more forces committed to Europe and the Mediterranean (47 groups) than it had in the Pacific and South-East Asia (23 groups), but this imbalance was largely offset by the seaborne air power of the US Pacific Fleet.

The Americans divided the Pacific into two principal theatres (see Map F). MacArthur, having made good his escape to Australia, assumed command of the *South-West Pacific Area, comprising Australia, New Guinea, the Solomons, the Philippines, Borneo, the Bismarck archipelago, and much of the Netherlands East Indies. Most of these territories were, of course, under Japanese control. The rest of the Pacific was left to the navy whose vast domain, the Pacific Ocean Areas, sub-divided into three separate theatres, was entrusted to Admiral *Nimitz, who also commanded the Pacific Fleet. MacArthur and Nimitz received their orders from the US *Joint Chiefs of Staff (JCS), but *King, the chief of naval operations, had a 'direct line' to Nimitz, bypassing the other members of the JCS. This was because King also held the position of Commander in Chief, US Fleet (COMINCH) and thus could issue orders and advice to Nimitz as Commander-in-Chief, Pacific Fleet, through the 'operational' channel. General *Marshall, the army chief of staff, had no such direct line to MacArthur, who himself could not directly command the army, air forces, or fleets under him as Nimitz could command the Pacific Fleet.

The immediate concern of MacArthur and Nimitz was stopping new Japanese offensives in the south and central Pacific. In May 1942 a Japanese invasion force sailed from Rabaul to seize Port Moresby on the south coast of the Papuan peninsula of New Guinea (see also NEW GUINEA CAMPAIGN). The Americans, warned by Japanese messages which they had intercepted and decoded (see ULTRA, 2), had a carrier task force waiting in the *Coral Sea. In the ensuing naval battle, fought entirely by carrier aircraft, the Americans sank the small Japanese aircraft carrier *Shōhō* while the Japanese sank the large carrier *Lexington*, a destroyer, and an oiler. However, the two large Japanese carriers *Shōkaku* and *Zuikaku* lost most of their planes and aircraft and the *Shōkaku* was badly damaged. The Port Moresby invasion force turned back and returned to Rabaul.

Without waiting for the *Shōkaku* and *Zuikaku* to make good their losses, Yamamoto began a much larger operation aimed at the American base at *Midway, an island about 1,600 km. (1,000 mi.) west of Hawaii. The object was to draw out the inferior American fleet and destroy it in a decisive battle after dividing its strength by luring part of it northwards to counter a Japanese invasion which began the *Aleutian Islands campaigns. But the Americans again learned of the Japanese plan through ULTRA intelligence and had their carriers waiting in ambush north-east of Midway, out of range of Japanese search planes.

On 4 June 1942 the Japanese launched a large air strike at Midway and discovered the US carriers only after they were recovering their strike planes and fighting off attacks by bombers from Midway. As the Japanese completed hurried preparations for attacks against the fleet, planes from the US carriers struck. The Japanese lost three of their four large carriers and the fourth later in the day. Japanese planes managed only a single air strike against the Americans which damaged the carrier *Yorktown* which was later sunk by a submarine. The shattering loss of four big carriers in an afternoon ended Japanese hopes for further offensives in the central Pacific.

After the Japanese defeat at Midway, the JCS approved a limited offensive in the South Pacific by MacArthur and Nimitz's forces aimed at the Japanese base at *Rabaul. The first phase of the offensive was to be the seizure of the islands of Tulagi and then *Guadalcanal in the southern Solomon Islands, where the Japanese had recently established a base. At the same time, MacArthur's Australian and US forces were to begin an advance along the north-east coast of New Guinea. But the Japanese forestalled MacArthur by landing almost 16,000 men on the north-east coast of Papua near *Buna and these advanced rapidly south along the *Kokoda trail and across the supposedly impassable Owen Stanley mountains towards Port Moresby, the prize the Coral Sea battle had denied them. Desperate fighting by the Australians finally halted the Japanese on the southern slopes of the Owen Stanleys within sight of Port Moresby.

Meanwhile, on 7 August, the US attack on Guadalcanal had gone forward with little resistance by the unsuspecting Japanese. American marines assumed control of Tulagi and the unfinished airfield on Guadalcanal, which they named Henderson Field after an aviator lost

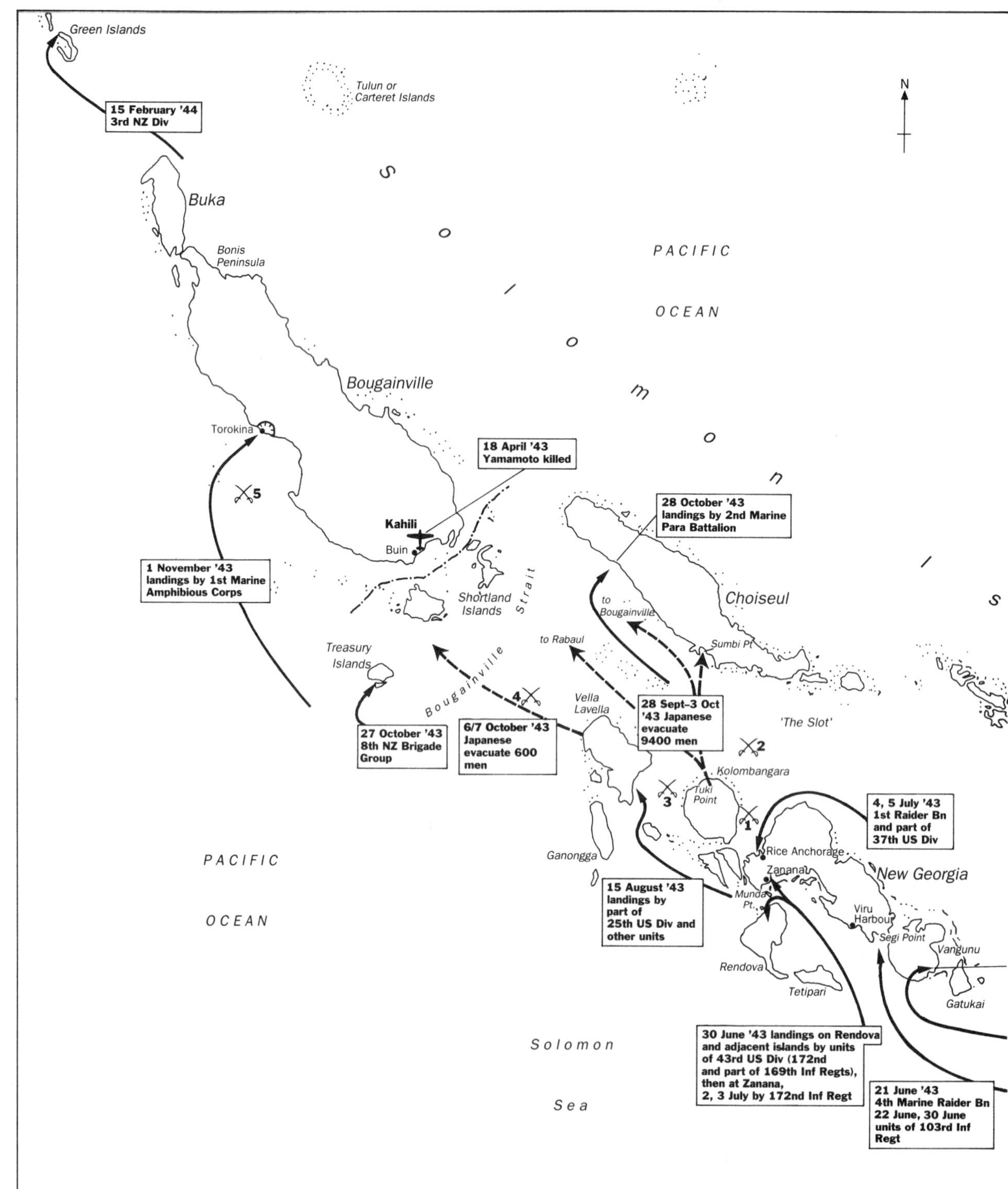

83. Allied landings on the Solomon Islands during the **Pacific war**, February 1943–March 1944

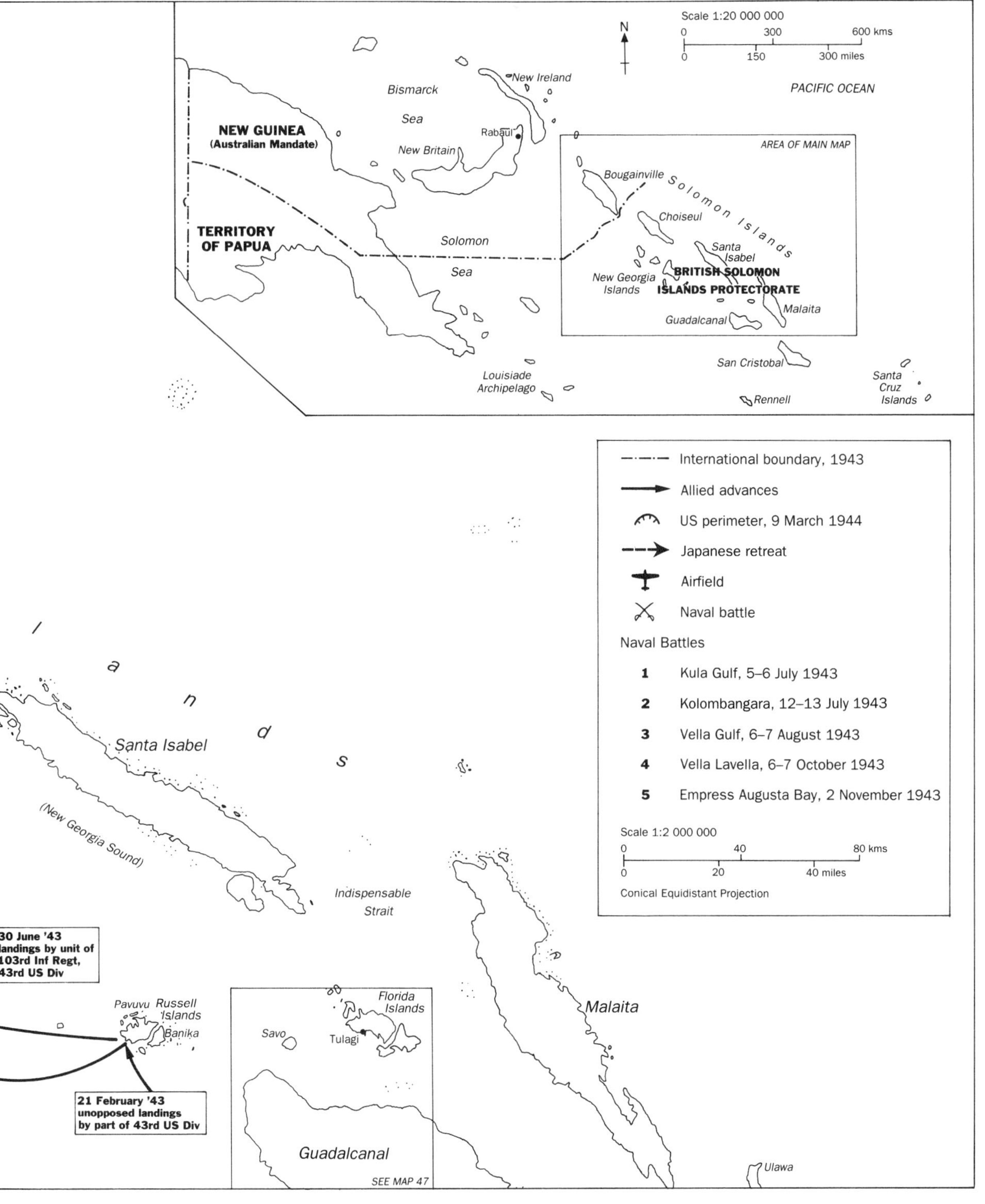
Scale 1:20 000 000
0 300 600 kms
0 150 300 miles
N
PACIFIC OCEAN
Bismarck
Sea
New Ireland
Rabaul
New Britain
NEW GUINEA
(Australian Mandate)
TERRITORY
OF PAPUA
Solomon
Sea
AREA OF MAIN MAP
Bougainville
Solomon Islands
Choiseul
Santa
Isabel
New Georgia
Islands
BRITISH SOLOMON
ISLANDS PROTECTORATE
Malaita
Guadalcanal
San Cristobal
Louisiade
Archipelago
Rennell
Santa
Cruz
Islands
International boundary, 1943
Allied advances
US perimeter, 9 March 1944
Japanese retreat
Airfield
Naval battle
Naval Battles
1 Kula Gulf, 5–6 July 1943
2 Kolombangara, 12–13 July 1943
3 Vella Gulf, 6–7 August 1943
4 Vella Lavella, 6–7 October 1943
5 Empress Augusta Bay, 2 November 1943
Scale 1:2 000 000
0 40 80 kms
0 20 40 miles
Conical Equidistant Projection
l a n d s
Santa Isabel
(New Georgia Sound)
Indispensable
Strait
30 June '43
landings by unit of
103rd Inf Regt,
43rd US Div
Pavuvu Russell
Islands
Banika
21 February '43
unopposed landings
by part of 43rd US Div
Savo
Florida
Islands
Tulagi
Guadalcanal
SEE MAP 47
Malaita
Ulawa

at the battle of Midway.

The Japanese response was not long in coming. Two days after the invasion Admiral Mikawa Gunichi, with a squadron of cruisers from Rabaul, surprised the Allied cruisers and destroyers guarding the landing force in a night attack and the battle of *Savo Island sank four cruisers and badly damaged a fifth without serious loss.

The battle for Guadalcanal soon developed into a six-month slogging match between the Japanese, determined to retake the island, and the Americans, determined to hold it. US possession of the airfield on Guadalcanal gave them a long-term advantage that the Japanese were never able to overcome. In general, they controlled the waters and skies near Guadalcanal in the daytime, while the Japanese ran in supplies and reinforcements at night (see TOKYO EXPRESS). There were a total of seven naval battles in which Japanese superiority in night fighting stood them in good stead. However, US aircraft and submarines tended to even the odds. The Japanese long underestimated the number of Allied troops ashore on the islands and fed in forces piecemeal to deliver uncoordinated attacks on the airfield after exhausting marches through the jungle.

In mid-November the Japanese put together a major effort to capture the island. Battleships and cruisers of the Combined Fleet would bombard Henderson Field while a reinforced division would be brought down to Guadalcanal aboard a fast convoy. But on the night of 12/13 November an American cruiser-destroyer force under Rear Admiral Daniel J. Callahan intercepted the Japanese battleships and turned them back in a desperate night action—known as the battle of Guadalcanal—which cost the US Navy three destroyers sunk and four other ships badly damaged.

The following morning planes from Henderson Field found the Japanese battleship *Hiei* limping away from the battle and sent her to the bottom as well as attacking the transports of the Japanese reinforcement convoy. A second Japanese attempt to bombard Henderson Field the next night was met by two new US battleships, *Washington* and *South Dakota*, and again turned back. The *South Dakota* was damaged and three US destroyers sunk, but the Japanese lost their remaining available battleship and the invasion convoy was decimated by air attacks the following morning.

These actions of mid-November decided the fate of Guadalcanal, although fierce fighting continued for several weeks. In the New Guinea campaign the Japanese effort had been weakened by the need to send reinforcements to Guadalcanal and Australian forces gradually pushed the enemy back to their beachheads near *Gona, Buna, and Sanananda Point on the north coast. Fighting in some of the worst conditions of the war, Allied troops took almost four months to capture the last of these positions in late January 1943.

As American commanders realigned and refitted their forces, and integrated new units and equipment, the Japanese attempted to shore up their defences and plan pre-emptive strikes against the steadily growing Allied forces on their perimeter. No overall plan for the defeat of Japan had yet been agreed upon or even formulated, nor had the American and British High Command agreed about the nature of the Allied effort to be made against Japan before the defeat of Germany.

In January 1943, at the Casablanca conference (see SYMBOL), the Americans proposed that the *Combined Chiefs of Staff agree, in principle, to allocate 30% of Allied resources to the war against Japan. The British refused to commit themselves to any specific formula but did agree that the Americans could go ahead with further offensive moves against Japan designed to retain the initiative. Back in Washington, army and navy strategists held the Pacific Military conference to discuss the implications of the Casablanca decisions and ponder their next move. All three pacific commanders, MacArthur, Nimitz, and Admiral William F. *Halsey, who exercised a quasi-independent command in the South-West Pacific under MacArthur's general direction (see SOUTH PACIFIC AREA), agreed that they lacked sufficient forces to complete the conquest of Rabaul in 1943. They especially wanted more long-range bombers which could reach Rabaul. But the USAAF, eager to begin the combined bomber offensive against Japan, also agreed on at Casablanca, was reluctant to make bombers available for the south Pacific.

In the end, the Pacific commanders did get some additional aircraft and troops, but not enough to meet their requirements for an attack on Rabaul. The JCS, accordingly, modified their objectives to include only an advance up the Solomons (see Map 83) as far as *Bougainville and a parallel advance by MacArthur's forces along the north coast of New Guinea with both approaches converging on Rabaul.

Meanwhile JCS planners had drafted a broad blueprint for an overall strategy for the war against Japan. The plan called for the continuation of MacArthur's and Halsey's advances through the Solomons and along the New Guinea coast towards the Philippines. At the same time, it called for the opening of a new advance across the central Pacific, a region of thousands of tiny islands extending from the Gilberts near the equator north and west through the Marshalls, the Carolines, and the Marianas. This was a route favoured in the pre-war American Orange Plan for war with Japan. It was also the shortest route and one where the growing might of American naval and amphibious forces could be brought to bear most effectively.

At the Quebec conference held in August 1943 (see QUADRANT), the JCS presented to their British colleagues a timetable for their planned two-pronged advance in the Pacific. These drives were to be synchronized with a long-desired but still delayed British advance into Burma. Rabaul was crossed off the list of invasion targets; its neutralization by air was to be completed by May 1944, followed by MacArthur's westward advance towards the Vogelkop peninsula of New Guinea. Meanwhile Nimitz would follow his Gilberts assault with attacks on the Marshalls, Carolines, and the Palaus, all this to be completed by the end of 1944. The JCS failed to specify whether MacArthur's or Nimitz's campaign would receive priority, simply declaring that 'due weight would be given to the fact that operations in the central Pacific promise more rapid advance.'

The long-planned American offensives in the Pacific finally got under way in June 1943 as MacArthur and Halsey's forces moved north and west against Japanese bases in the Solomons and on the New Guinea coast. In all, MacArthur and Halsey planned to carry out thirteen separate and sometimes simultaneous operations to isolate and surround Rabaul.

The capture of *New Georgia, Halsey's first objective in the central Solomons, took over a month of hard fighting. Rather than begin a second slogging match Halsey decided to bypass his next objective, Kolombangara, and seize *Vella Lavella, a little further up the Solomons' ladder, which was lightly defended but within range of Japanese airfields.

Halsey's gamble paid off handsomely. On 15 August, acting with speed and in great secrecy, he put 4,600 troops ashore on Vella Lavella within twelve hours. The large Japanese garrison at Kolombangara was now bypassed and incapable of stemming the American advance. In the months to come both MacArthur and Halsey would employ this island hopping technique to bypass and isolate strong Japanese garrisons and assault weaker ones. The technique, which depended on American control of the air and sea, was to be employed with even more daring over greater distances as the Pacific war progressed.

By December 1943 MacArthur and Halsey's forces had landed on Bougainville and had seized Cape Gloucester at the extreme western end of *New Britain. From these bases and from New Georgia and Vella Lavella Allied planes began a systematic air campaign to knock Rabaul out of the war. By the end of January 1944 its spacious harbour was almost untenable by Japanese ships and by late February all serviceable aircraft had been withdrawn. The strongest Japanese base in the South Pacific had been effectively neutralized and its 100,000-man garrison left to wither on the vine.

The long-contemplated central Pacific drive did not begin until November 1943 and got off to a shaky start with an attack on *Tarawa in the Gilbert Islands. For the assault, Admiral Nimitz had assembled a formidable force in the form of the Fifth Fleet under Vice-Admiral *Spruance, the victor of the battle of Midway. His forces included battleships, cruisers, and almost a dozen new aircraft carriers. With 50 to 100 aircraft each and a formidable array of anti-aircraft guns firing *proximity fuze shells, the carriers had already demonstrated their power in raids against Rabaul in early November.

US planes soon neutralized Japanese air bases near Tarawa and Spruance's battleships and cruisers moved in to pump 3,000 tons of shells into Tarawa in about two and a half hours pausing only briefly for air strikes by Allied planes. Yet Japanese defences, pillboxes of coconut logs and concrete and steel, proved able to withstand much of the bombing and shelling. If marines assaulting Tarawa suffered heavy casualties from the still-active Japanese gunners on the island, casualties greatly increased when their landing craft grounded on a fringing coral reef forcing the troops to wade ashore in the face of heavy fire.

After three days the atoll was secured but the heavy casualties, 3,000 dead and wounded to capture less than 8 sq. km. (3 sq. mi.) of ground, shocked the US public. Spruance and his commanders conducted a thorough critique of the operation which yielded valuable lessons and improved techniques for future *amphibious warfare operations.

The lessons learned paid off well in the second phase of the central Pacific campaign, the assault on the *Marshalls. At the beginning of February 1944, after carrier planes and bombers from Tarawa had crippled Japanese air power in the islands, Spruance's forces struck directly into the heart of the Marshalls seizing Majuro, Kwajalein, and Roi-Namur atolls. These bases fell so swiftly that the US troops were able to attack *Eniwetok atoll at the extreme north-west end of the island chain six weeks ahead of schedule. In the process, Spruance's carrier forces attacked and crippled the principal Japanese central Pacific base at *Truk in the Carolines.

The swift and relatively easy capture of the Marshalls enabled the USA to change the entire Pacific timetable and the assault on the Marianas was set for June 1944, instead of September. MacArthur, fearful of being relegated to a back seat in the Pacific drive, also speeded up his advance. In a daring gamble he seized the *Admiralty Islands two months ahead of schedule, thus completing the encirclement of Rabaul and forcing the Japanese to yield more of the north coast of New Guinea. Then, in April 1944, in their most brilliant campaign of the war, MacArthur's forces 'leaped' 930 km. (580 mi.) to seize the Japanese base at *Hollandia on the north coast of Dutch New Guinea, bypassing 40,000 Japanese troops and turning back a fierce Japanese counter-attack along the Driniumor river two months later. Meanwhile, other elements of MacArthur's forces pushed up to capture the Vogelkop peninsula at the extreme western end of New Guinea and the nearby island of *Biak which the Allies quickly converted into a major air base.

As MacArthur's forces completed their conquest of New Guinea and Spruance prepared to seize the Marianas, the Japanese were suffering even more deadly blows from the cumulative effects of the US submarine campaign. At first dogged by faulty torpedoes and ineffective tactics, US submarines, by late 1943, were taking a heavy toll of Japanese shipping, aided by US signals intelligence (see ULTRA, 2) which directed them to lucrative targets. During 1944 Japan had lost more than 600 ships totalling over 2.7 million tons. It had begun the war with a merchant marine too small to sustain a widespread commitment, and its shipping was steadily whittled away by the conversion of many cargo vessels to wartime use. The limited capacity of Japanese shipyards and the Imperial Japanese Navy's neglect of anti-submarine warfare added to this predicament. As the Allies penetrated further into the empire, merchant ships also came under increasingly frequent air attack. By mid-1944, fuel shortages due to loss of tankers were so great that ships of the Combined Fleet had to be based close to oil wells and refineries.

The American attack on the Marianas in June 1944 struck at the inner ring of Japanese defences. From the islands of *Saipan, *Tinian, and *Guam, the new American super-bomber, the B29, could reach the Japanese home islands. The Combined Fleet, reorganized as a striking force of nine carriers, sallied forth to challenge the invaders. In the ensuing battle, called the battle of the *Philippine Sea, the Japanese succeeded in finding Spruance's carriers first and launching four waves of air attacks while the Americans, who had hung back to protect their landings on Saipan, did not find the Japanese until late the following day. Yet the battle was a disaster for the Japanese whose inexperienced and outnumbered pilots were no match for the American fighters and the blizzard of anti-aircraft fire from the ships screening the US carriers.

Spruance's carriers finally located the Japanese fleet late on the afternoon of 20 June and launched 200 planes at extreme range against the retiring Japanese. They found the Japanese carriers just before dark and sank the *Hiyo* and damaged three others. The large carriers *Shokaku* and *Taiho* had already been sunk by submarines earlier in the battle. US forces secured Saipan on 9 July and Tinian and Guam by the end of the month. In September Nimitz's forces also seized *Peleliu in the Palau Islands after one of the toughest island battles of the war.

The loss of the Marianas brought the fall of the *Tōjō government and Japanese plans for a final all-out defence of the Ryūkyūs, the Kuriles, or the Philippines, with the last-named considered most likely to be the next target. The JCS, however, did not reach their final decision until October. Admiral King argued that Luzon could be bypassed, and American forces operating from bases in the Marianas could strike directly at Formosa or even the main islands of Japan, but MacArthur, was outraged at the thought of leaving any part of the Philippines under Japanese occupation.

Three developments finally settled the argument. Admiral Halsey, now in command of the Task Carrier Forces, raided the southern Philippines during September 1944, and found them to be only lightly defended. Acting on Halsey's report, Admiral Nimitz suggested to the JCS that the previously planned slow and deliberate approach to the Philippines be modified and that US forces strike directly at the island of Leyte. MacArthur quickly agreed, as did the JCS, who set the new date for the Leyte invasion at 20 October 1944.

From that point on events conspired to make a decision in favour of Luzon rather than Formosa all but inevitable. First, MacArthur informed the JCS that the new invasion date for Leyte would enable him to invade Luzon two months ahead of schedule, on 20 December 1944. Formosa could not possibly be attacked so soon. Then Washington planners discovered that the manpower needs for a campaign against Formosa far exceeded the number of troops actually available in the Pacific. By this point, also, Nimitz was urging King to consider an alternative plan: to neutralize Formosa by air attacks, then use the central Pacific forces to seize *Iwo Jima and *Okinawa which would provide far better airfields than Formosa for a final assault on Japan.

Finally, on 3 October, King gave in. The JCS directed MacArthur to invade Luzon on 3 December. Nimitz's forces, after providing naval support to the Philippine invasion, would invade Iwo Jima and Okinawa.

Three weeks after that decision MacArthur and Halsey's forces converged on Leyte. At 1300 on 21 October, with fighting still raging near the Leyte beachhead, MacArthur and the Philippine president, Sergio Osmena, waded ashore. As cameramen filmed the dramatic scene, MacArthur proclaimed, 'People of the Philippines, I have returned.'

While Allied troops fought to extend their beachhead, the largest naval battle in history raged in *Leyte Gulf. The Japanese plan was to use their surviving carriers, now largely denuded of planes, to decoy the main US fleet away from the beaches, allowing two powerful battleship striking forces to converge on the landing forces. The plan came near to succeeding, though at great cost.

While MacArthur's forces began their campaign to retake the Philippines, American forces elsewhere—on Bougainville and New Britain, and in the New Guinea campaign—were gradually replaced by Australian troops to release US troops for the Philippines campaign; and in April 1945 the Australians, with US amphibious help, also started their own offensive to recapture the Netherlands East Indies (see BALIKPAPAN and TARAKAN).

The Americans needed over two months to secure Leyte in the face of determined counter-attacks by Japanese forces reinforced by troops from Luzon, Formosa, and Japan. It was not until early January 1945 that MacArthur's forces landed at Lingayen Gulf on Luzon in the face of fierce attacks by *kamikaze aircraft, to begin the largest ground campaign of the Pacific war. Advancing rapidly, elements of the 1st Cavalry Division entered Manila on 3 February, but the Japanese waged a stubborn defence for almost a month which left the city in ruins. Meanwhile other US forces secured Bataan and Corregidor, and the Eighth Army, under General *Eichelberger, rapidly cleared the Japanese from Palawan, Zamboanga, Panay, Mindanao, and Cebu. By mid-March the Americans had advanced into northern Luzon where grinding battles against the last Japanese defenders continued to the end of the war.

Meanwhile, Nimitz's forces had seized Iwo Jima in another costly island battle, and landed on Okinawa in the Ryūkyūs, the final stepping-stone to Japan itself. The Japanese defence of Okinawa was stubborn and protracted, the most skilful of the Pacific war. Offshore, kamikazes took a heavy toll of the invasion fleet which included the newly formed British Pacific Fleet (see TASK FORCE 57). In Hawaii, Washington, and Manila, American military planners studied the Okinawa campaign and viewed the impending invasion of Japan with apprehension, but both sides were spared this ultimate ordeal when Japan surrendered on 15 August, following the destruction of *Hiroshima and *Nagasaki by *atomic bombs and the entry of the USSR into the war (see JAPANESE–SOVIET CAMPAIGNS). RONALD SPECTOR

MacIntyre, D., *The Battle of the Pacific* (London, 1966).
Spector, R., *Eagle Against the Sun: the American War with Japan* (New York, 1985).

Pacific War Council, two advisory committees formed in London and Washington in February and April 1942 to ensure that Australia, New Zealand, China, and the Dutch and Philippine *governments-in-exile, had a say in the conduct of the *Pacific war. Other members were Canada, the UK, and the USA. Though Australia in particular, wished it, the council had no operational responsibilities, these being exercised by the US *Joint Chiefs of Staff.

Pact of Steel, Mussolini's name for a military alliance between Italy and Germany which was signed in Berlin on 22 May 1939 by the two countries' foreign ministers, *Ciano and *Ribbentrop. It declared that either country would come to the aid of the other if it were attacked and the Italians signed it on the verbal understanding that neither power would provoke war before 1943. Ciano recorded in his diary that Hitler was well satisfied with the Pact, and confirmed that Mediterranean policy would be directed by Italy. However, the Pact's political effect was much reduced by Japan's refusal to join it. See also AXIS STRATEGY AND CO-OPERATION.

Paget, General Sir Bernard (1887–1961), British Army officer who, as a maj-general, fought during the *Norwegian campaign and extricated his troops with skill at the end of it. In 1941 he was appointed C-in-C South-Eastern Command, was promoted lt-general, and then succeeded *Brooke as C-in-C Home Forces, a post he held until July 1943. He then formed and trained Twenty-First Army Group which fought in north-west Europe under *Montgomery, a task Paget performed ably. He served as C-in-C *Middle East Command from January 1944 to 1946. He was knighted in 1942.

Paiforce, officially called Persia and Iraq Command, this British command was formed in August 1942 when Persia and Iraq were split off from *Middle East Command. Its British, Indian, and Polish troops of *Anders' Army—designated Tenth Army—guarded the Persian and Iraqi oilfields, constructed bases, and organized the flow of *Lend-Lease supplies from Persia to the USSR. It was commanded first by Maitland *Wilson and then, from March 1943, by General Henry Pownall, by which time its forces had been reduced to those needed for internal security purposes only.

Palau Islands, a 130 km. (80 mi.) arc of islands, the most westerly of the Pacific Caroline Islands. In September 1944, during the *Pacific war, two of them, *Peleliu and Angaur, were occupied by US forces. This secured the right flank of General *MacArthur's advancing forces and both were later used as air bases to support the US invasion at the start of the second of the two *Philippines campaigns.

Palestine, British mandate in the eastern Mediterranean where one million indigenous Arabs were in open confrontation with the country's 470,000 Jews, mostly immigrants, whose claim for a homeland in Palestine had been acknowledged by the British since the Balfour Declaration of 1917.

In July 1937 the British Peel commission announced the decision to divide Palestine between the Arabs, the British, and the Jews and this pushed the Arabs into what is now known as the Arab Revolt. It was led by Hadj Amin el-*Husseini, the mufti of Jerusalem, but once he had been forced to flee, and other Arab leaders had been interned, the revolt was crushed and Arab political life became paralysed, and remained so throughout the war. But approaching hostilities, and the need for oil, made the British government reverse its policy of partition. In May 1939 it announced its intention of creating a single independent state, to include both Arabs and Jews, within ten years. It virtually prohibited the sale of land to Jews and limited any further Jewish immigration to 75,000 over the next five years. No more immigration would then be permitted without Arab agreement.

The British aim was not only to obtain Arab acquiescence—in which, by and large, it was successful—but to pose the Jews an insoluble dilemma that if they opposed the British in Palestine they would, in effect, be aiding their Nazi persecutors. Not surprisingly, the *Jewish Agency, which worked for the establishment of a Jewish national home in Palestine, opted to co-operate, and the Histradut, the Jewish labour organization, mobilized its agricultural and industrial resources to help the UK's war effort. At first the economy faltered and unemployment rose, but from 1941 war production boosted it considerably. By 1943 63% of the Jewish workforce was employed in the production of *matériel* for the British forces; and during the course of the war Jewish-owned factories tripled from 2,000 to 6,000, 47 new settlements were established, and cultivation was increased by 70%.

When the war started 136,000 Jewish men and women volunteered to join the armed forces. The first unit to see action was a mixed (Arab and Jew) company which served with the Royal Pioneer Corps in the fighting which preceded the fall of *France in June 1940. In October 1940 men from this company became the nucleus of No. 51 (Middle East) Commando which fought in the *East African campaign. When this was disbanded in late 1941 some of its members joined the *Middle East Commando.

It was hoped that a Jewish Legion, similar to the one which had fought in the *First World War, could be formed, but the British, fearing its creation would lead to another Arab rising, refused permission. However, the Jews were determined to fight. Many joined the East Kent Regiment (The Buffs), forming three companies which became known as the Palestine Regiment, and by August 1942 there were 18,000 Palestinian Jews serving with the British forces in the Middle East. About 25% served in the front line and a thousand, of whom only 45 survived, helped defend *Bir Hakeim. Eventually a 5,000-strong Jewish Brigade was formed which from early 1945 fought in the *Italian campaign as part of the British Eighth Army. Between March and September 1944, 32 parachutists were dropped into occupied Europe to help the Jewish populations escape the *Final Solution. Estimates vary, but perhaps as many as 30,000 Jews served in the British armed forces, as did 9,000 Palestinian Arabs. Palestine itself had little direct contact with the war, though during the summer of 1940 the Italians bombed coastal towns killing about 200 people.

Apart from those serving in the British forces, special units called Palmach (*Plugoth Machatz*, or commando strike-force) were formed by the British from the clandestine Jewish army, the *Haganah, to defend the country or to perform acts of sabotage should it be overrun. Some Palmach units were also used for intelligence and sabotage missions in advance of the *Syrian campaign, as guides at its start, and in an abortive attempt to raid the oil refineries in Tripoli. However, once the German threat had passed the British closed Palmach training bases, reclaimed the arms they had distributed, and unsuccessfully demanded the dissolution of those units whose members had not volunteered to serve with the British.

While actively aiding the British, the Haganah openly flouted their authority by using every conceivable method to give sanctuary to as many European and Middle Eastern Jews as possible. This infuriated the British, who saw Jewish immigration as a German tactic to undermine stability in the Middle East, or even as a means of importing *spies. Many illegal immigrants were interned on Mauritius and enforcement of the British immigration policy led to several disasters, including the loss of two ships (the **Patria* and **Struma*) and many of their passengers. In fact, both the British and the Americans, after holding the *Bermuda conference in April 1943, opposed any plans for the mass rescue of Jews from occupied Europe. However, in 1944 Roosevelt did authorize the establishment of the *War Refugee Board and British immigration policy was circumvented to allow the few thousand European Jews who escaped into neutral countries to enter Palestine.

In 1943, Churchill, who considered British policy towards Palestinian Jews 'a gross breach of faith' with them, set up a committee under Herbert *Morrison which recommended its reversal. But this was strongly opposed by Anthony *Eden among others, who understandably feared an Arab backlash, and there the matter rested. The Jewish Agency chairman, David Ben-Gurion (1886–1973), whose desire for confrontation with the British had been outvoted by his executive, now mobilized strong support from American Zionists. In May 1942 these held a conference at New York's Biltmore Hotel, and then issued a manifesto (the Biltmore programme) which demanded Jewish sovereignty over Palestine, so that all Jews who survived the war would have a home to go to. It was ignored.

By 1944 the Jewish Agency had, in the words of the Supreme Allied Commander in the Mediterranean, Field Marshal Maitland *Wilson, arrogated 'to itself the powers and status of an independent government'. But though it strongly opposed the terrorist methods of the more extremist groups, such as the *Irgun and the *Stern gang, it was violence that eventually ended the British mandate and gave birth to the State of Israel on 14 May 1948. See CONSEQUENCES OF THE WAR.

Porat, D., *The Blue and Yellow Stars of David* (Cambridge, Mass., 1990).

Panama declared war on the Axis powers in December 1941 and was an original signatory of the *United Nations Declaration. It co-operated with the USA in protecting the Canal Zone, including the granting of bases, and Panamanian ships and crews took part in the *Arctic convoys. See also LATIN AMERICA.

Panama conference, convened by the USA and 20 other American states on 23 September 1939. The participants divided themselves into three sub-committees to discuss neutrality, the maintenance of peace in the area, and economic co-operation. At the end of its deliberations the conference issued the Panama Declaration which confirmed the neutrality of the participants, banned belligerent submarines from entering their ports, demanded the cessation of subversive activities within their countries, and announced the formation of a maritime security zone which was to extend for 480 km. (300 mi.) either side of the American continent, except for Canada and the colonies and possessions of European states. It was this area that was subsequently policed by the *neutrality patrol. See also LATIN AMERICA.

Pantelleria, small Italian island which lies between Sicily and Tunisia. Its air base posed a threat to the *Sicilian campaign landings, which took place in July 1943, and was needed by the Allies for them. But the island was heavily defended, and a surprise attack was impossible, so *Eisenhower ordered its reduction by air attacks. A British scientist, Solly Zuckerman, produced a scientific bombing plan to subdue the island's defences so that troops could land virtually unopposed, and 14,203 bombs weighing 4,119 tons were dropped on 16 batteries over 6 days. Out of 80 guns, 53 were damaged, and another was destroyed by naval gunfire. Before the first landing craft of the British assault force reached the beaches on 11 June 1943 a white flag had been raised. The Allies captured 11,000 Italians and the only British casualty, Churchill recorded, was one man bitten by a mule.

Panzer, German word for armour, now Anglicized; see TANKS.

Panzerfaust, see ROCKET WEAPONS.

Panzerschiffe (armoured ships), the name given to the three German pocket battleships, *Deutschland* (later renamed *Lützow*), *Admiral Scheer*, and *Admiral Graf Spee* (see also RIVER PLATE).

Papen, Franz von (1879–1969), chancellor of Germany from June to November 1932 who organized Hitler's appointment as chancellor in January 1933, becoming vice-chancellor himself. After serving as ambassador to Austria, where he paved the way for the Anschluss in March 1938, he was appointed ambassador to Turkey, a post he held from 1939 to 1944. He was acquitted at the *Nuremberg trials, and later won an appeal against an eight-year sentence by a German court. 'When all else about him is forgotten,' wrote an obituarist, 'Franz von Papen will be remembered as the man who held his hands for Hitler to leap into the saddle.'

Papua, Australian territory which comprised the south-east quarter of the island of New Guinea.

Most of the *New Guinea campaign was fought in Papua whose tip is divided by the precipitous Owen Stanley mountain range over which wound the notorious *Kokoda trail. In 1940 about 7,200 Australians and Europeans lived in Papua and the neighbouring Australian mandate of New Guinea. Some of these joined the Australian New Guinea Administrative Unit (ANGAU), which administered both territories when civilian government was suspended. Others became *Coast Watchers or joined the Papuan Infantry Battalion, which included volunteers from the warlike Papuan hill tribes and was greatly feared by the Japanese. In October 1944 it became, with the indigenous 1st New Guinea Battalion, part of the Pacific Islands Regiment. Another indigenous force, the Royal Papuan Constabulary, also played an active part in the New Guinea campaign. Papuans also performed a number of important non-combatant roles for those fighting the New Guinea campaign.

Paraguay broke off diplomatic relations with the main Axis powers in February 1942, although as a satellite of its neutral neighbour Argentina, Nazi influences in the country remained unfettered. However, it eventually declared war on Germany and Japan in February 1945 when it also signed the *United Nations Declaration. It exported canned beef to the UK, but otherwise contributed little to the war effort of either side. See also LATIN AMERICA.

paratroops, see AIRBORNE WARFARE.

Paris protocols, agreements negotiated with the Germans by Admiral *Darlan on behalf of the *Vichy French government in May 1941. They granted the Germans, retrospectively, military facilities in Syria, and in Tunisia and French West Africa. In return the Germans agreed to reduce their occupation costs from 20 to 15 million Reichsmarks a day; return some 6,800 French specialists from prisoner-of-war camps for service in North Africa; and ease the restrictions that governed the demarcation line between occupied and unoccupied France. Another protocol recorded that the Vichy government hoped eventually to establish its authority over the whole of the country. The first of four protocols was initialled by Darlan and by Otto Abetz, the German ambassador to France, the others were initialled, on behalf of Germany, by German officers. They represented the high point of French *collaboration, but Darlan's policies resulted in the *Syrian campaign being launched by the Allies; and when he was unable to obtain better terms from the Germans the protocols lapsed and were never ratified.

Paris rising. As the Allied forces engaged in the *Normandy campaign neared Paris, tension in the former capital grew. On 10 August the railway workers came out on strike; on 15 August so did the police—before they heard of the *French Riviera landings that day. Next day the post office workers followed suit except for the telephone operators, who stayed on duty and played an essential background part in what followed.

General Dietrich von Choltitz (1894–1966), who had supervised the destruction of Rotterdam in May 1940 and of *Sevastopol in 1942, commanded some 20,000 German soldiers—mostly garrison troops, but including armoured Waffen-*SS units. The forces of *resistance, few in number, were politically divided: the communists were for immediate action, the Gaullists for caution.

The Gaullists sent a messenger into Paris to explain that the Allied armies did not intend to arrive before the second week in September (it suited *Eisenhower's administrators to let the Germans feed the five million Parisians for as long as possible). Locally, the communists had a majority on the essential committees, and the head of the Parisian committee of liberation, *Rol-Tanguy, decided it was time to strike, even though he only knew of 600 weapons larger than revolvers that his forces could use.

Early on the morning of 19 August he was bicycling past police headquarters on his way to proclaim the

This photograph is probably posed, but such scenes were common enough during the **Paris rising** which took place just before the French capital was liberated in August 1944.

rising when he saw a tricolour hoisted over it, and heard the 'Marseillaise' being sung inside: on an order from de *Gaulle's delegate-general, the judge Alexandre Parodi, the Gaullists had stolen a march on him.

Sporadic street fighting broke out that day all over Paris. In the evening, the police—who had held out in their headquarters but were running low in ammunition, and whose numbers had dwindled from 2,000 to 500, mainly by desertion—were offered a temporary truce while both sides collected their wounded. This was arranged direct with Choltitz by Raoul Nordling, the Swedish consul-general, who was also in touch with Parodi (the telephone here proving invaluable). The truce, spreading over the city, lasted into the next day, but soon broke down.

All over Paris, particularly in the working-class and communist-dominated eastern quarter, the liveliest citizens built barricades in their streets, and the most hot-blooded young men got hold of weapons if they could, and sniped at any stray Germans they could find. Hardly any of the barricades were tank-proof and Choltitz had some tanks, but he hesitated to use them. Hitler ordered him to defend Paris stone by stone; Nordling persuaded him that as an officer, a European, and a Christian he had a duty to disobey orders and preserve it. He could moreover see for himself that the Germans had lost the campaign in France at least, if not the war.

Responsible Frenchmen were anxious that Paris should be spared the fate of *Warsaw, then in the throes of its own disastrous rising. Eisenhower continued to give no orders for the capture of Paris. The *BBC, to shame him into action, published on 23 August a report that the city had already been liberated. That day, Eisenhower and the commander of the Third US Army, *Patton, consented to release the 2nd French Armoured Division, under *Leclerc, from normal duty; Leclerc launched a couple of troops of tanks on Paris, and followed them with the rest of his division as soon as he could. Captain Raymond Dronne led this token force into the heart of Paris, reaching the Place de l'Hôtel de Ville on the evening of 24 August.

Next morning Paris was *en fête*, and Choltitz signed an instrument of surrender, on which Rol's signature preceded Leclerc's. External and internal resistance could jointly claim a victory. M. R. D. FOOT

Dansette, A., *Histoire de la Libération de Paris* (Paris 1946, constantly revised).

Michel, H., *Paris résistant* (Paris, 1982).

Park, Air Chief Marshal Sir Keith (1892–1975), New Zealand airman who commanded an RAF Fighter Group during the *Dunkirk evacuation and then in the battle of *Britain.

From July 1938 to April 1940 Park served as senior air staff officer to *Dowding, the C-in-C Fighter Command, and was then appointed to command No. 11 Fighter Group which comprised about 23 squadrons and was responsible for defending south-east England. Promoted air vice-marshal that July, Park maintained high morale during those critical months by regularly piloting his own Hurricane to visit his stations—he was one of the very few high-ranking air force officers in the world in 1940 able to fly modern fighters. His value lay not only in his leadership but in his ability to adjust quickly to new Luftwaffe tactics. However, his methods conflicted with the 'Big Wing' theory (see FIGHTERS, 2) of *Leigh-Mallory who commanded No. 12 Fighter Group and whose fighters sometimes reinforced Park's. Dowding supported Park, the air ministry backed Leigh-Mallory. In November Dowding left Fighter Command and the following month the argument was settled by Leigh-Mallory replacing Park who was transferred to No. 23 Group, Flying Training Command. But by then the battle had been won.

In January 1942 Park was appointed AOC Egypt and then, in July, AOC *Malta. In January 1944 he became C-in-C RAF Middle East and the following February took up the post of air C-in-C for *South-East Asia Command with the rank of acting air chief marshal. He was knighted in 1942.

Orange, V., *Biography of Air Chief-Marshal Sir Keith Park* (London, 1984).

partisans, see resistance sections of relevant major powers; see also FFI, GARIBALDI DIVISION, HUBAL, MAQUIS, MIHAILOVIĆ AND THE ČETNIKS, NATIONAL ARMED FORCES, PEASANT BATTALIONS, PEOPLE'S GUARD, and TITO AND THE PARTISANS.

passive resistance, see RESISTANCE, 2.

Passy, see DEWAVRIN.

Patch, Lt-General Alexander McC. (1889–1945), US Army commander of the *Americal Division assigned to defend New Caledonia, before taking command of American ground forces on *Guadalcanal in December 1942. He was promoted lt-general in August 1944, and as commander of the Seventh US Army commanded the *French Riviera landings that month. Later, when his Seventh Army was part of *Devers' Sixth Army Group, it helped eliminate the *Colmar pocket, before taking part in the *Rhine crossings at Worms, capturing Nuremberg and then Munich. He died of pneumonia in November 1945.

Pathfinder Force. After the Luftwaffe first used a specially trained force (Kampfgruppe 100) to mark and illuminate *Coventry with incendiary *bombs, to help guide other German bombers on to the city, the British developed a similar method called the *shaker technique to aid RAF Bomber Command during its *strategic air offensive against Germany. In August 1942 the bombers using this method were replaced with four squadrons of Wellington and Stirling bombers commanded by an Australian, Group Captain Donald Bennett. Later, Mosquitoes were mostly used and these flew ahead of the main force to mark the targets for those who were less navigationally experienced.

By the time Bennett's force became operational a new *electronic navigation system called GEE was already being jammed by the Germans (see ELECTRONIC WARFARE) and this, plus the fact that it was not automatically allotted the best crews or the best equipment, initially limited the force's effectiveness. However, once other *electronic navigation systems and target-indicating bombs were introduced bombing accuracy improved dramatically.

To keep the British bomber-stream compact and flying accurately (see BOMBERS, 2) Pathfinders were also used to mark the route, and a senior Pathfinder pilot, called a Master Bomber or Master of Ceremonies, would fly above the target to broadcast advice to the main force.

Bennett, D., *Pathfinder: A War Autobiography* (London, 1958).

***Patria*, sinking of.** After the British Navy intercepted two vessels taking 2,000 illegal Jewish immigrants to Palestine in November 1940 they were transferred to the *Patria* for *internment on Mauritius. The *Haganah, in an attempt to prevent it leaving, accidentally sank it and 250 lives were lost. See also FINAL SOLUTION.

pattern bombing, method devised by Maj-General *LeMay during the Eighth US Army Air Force's (USAAF) daytime *strategic air offensive against Germany in which the entire bombload of a formation was dropped simultaneously. The British had already discovered how inaccurate their bombing was (see BUTT REPORT) and pattern bombing was introduced by the USAAF to increase the statistical probability of more *bombs hitting their target or straddling it, especially when they were being dropped by inexperienced crews. The bombers were led to the target by a veteran flight leader who released a smoke marker when the release point had been reached.

Patton, General George S. (1885–1945), the US Army's most controversial officer whose inspired, and inspiring, leadership won him as many devotees as he lost because of his volatile temperament.

Patton was commissioned into the cavalry in 1909, represented his country at the 1912 Stockholm Olympic Games, took part in the 1916 punitive raid into Mexico, and in 1917 went to France as a captain on the staff of

General John Pershing (1860–1948) where he later rose to command a tank brigade. By April 1941 he was a two-star general and the following January he was given command of 1st Armoured Corps. As commander of the Western Task Force—the equivalent of two divisions—he directed the amphibious operations near Casablanca during the *North African campaign landings in November 1942 and quickly became known as a hard-driving, aggressive combat officer whose offensive spirit was summed up in his method of attack: 'Hold them by the nose and kick them in the rear.' In March 1943, after the disaster at *Kasserine Pass, he took command of the 2nd US Corps which had been defeated there. He always maintained that an army commander did whatever was necessary to accomplish his mission, 'and nearly 80% of his mission is to arouse morale in his men'. In this he succeeded with 2nd Corps, though he later commented he thought it the most difficult job he had ever undertaken. He relinquished his command to *Bradley in April 1943 to plan the *Sicilian campaign in which he commanded Seventh US Army with the rank of lt-general.

In Sicily the Americans came of age as a fighting force and Patton's army, though initially assigned a subsidiary role, took Palermo with a daring armoured thrust and then wound the campaign up by arriving in Messina before the British. However, an inflammatory speech he delivered before the landings was later cited as a contributory factor to the *Biscari massacre and on two occasions he verbally abused and slapped soldiers suffering from combat exhaustion (see MEDICINE). He later claimed he had done it deliberately to jolt the men out of their shocked state, but it became public knowledge and nearly ended his career. However, *Eisenhower, then Supreme Commander in the Mediterranean, declared him too valuable to lose and refused to send him home. He remained for a time in Sicily without a posting before being sent to the UK to command and train the Third US Army for its role in the *Normandy campaign. He also took part in the *deception plan FORTITUDE SOUTH, as commander of the non-existent First US Army Group (FUSAG).

The Third US Army, comprising four corps, was officially activated in France on 1 August 1944. Patton launched a series of spectacular armoured thrusts but the Germans retreated to his primary objectives, the major seaports such as Brest, and prevented their immediate capture. Meanwhile, the break-out of the Allied armies began and on 19 August Patton's forces, helped by emergency airlifts of fuel, put a division across the Seine south-east of Paris and twelve days later they were on the Meuse. *Logistics soon slowed the Allied advance but by November Patton had reached the *West Wall which guarded the German border and on 13 December he captured Metz. Three days later the Germans launched their *Ardennes campaign during which Patton's army executed what has been called one of the most remarkable movements in military history. He turned it northwards and with incredible speed moved it to attack the southern edge of the German counter-offensive, relieving *Bastogne and disrupting the German advance. In March 1945 his army crossed the Rhine at Mainz and Oppenheim, drove into the heart of Germany, and ended the war in Czechoslovakia and Austria. He was promoted four-star general in April 1945 and was hailed as the outstanding American general of the war. But in September 1945, while military governor of Bavaria, he publicly recommended that members of the Nazi Party should be employed in administrative jobs, and he was relieved of his command.

Patton projected toughness, flamboyance, and extrovert aggression, the qualities, he believed, of a successful general. His highly polished boots and the ivory-handled revolvers strapped to his hips were all part of this posturing, as was the profanity of his language. But he was actually a deeply religious, sensitive, and cultured man who wrote poetry, was widely read, and who had many interests. He was audacious and fearless—'old blood and guts' was one of his nicknames—but a thoughtful, meticulous planner as well, a perfectionist. Most remarkable of all, he achieved his well-merited fame, as has been pointed out (R. Nye, in *Parameters*, Winter 1991–2), in just thirteen months of combat command during the Second World War (less than a week at Casablanca, less than 30 days in Tunisia, 38 days in Sicily, 318 days in north-west Europe). He was mortally injured in a car accident in December 1945.

Blumenson, M. (ed.), *The Patton Papers*, 2 vols. (Boston, 1972–4).
Essame, H., *Patton the Commander* (London, 1974).
Patton, G., *War as I Knew it* (Boston, 1947).

Paulus, Field Marshal Friedrich (1890–1957), German Army officer who served as *Halder's deputy chief of the Army General Staff (OKH) and chief of its operations section before commanding Sixth Army at *Stalingrad.

Paulus spent all but the first few months of the *First World War as a staff officer and by the start of the Second had risen to become Chief of Staff to *Reichenau who commanded Tenth Army during the *Polish campaign (renamed Sixth Army after it) and then in the fighting which preceded the fall of *France in June 1940.

Paulus, a great admirer of Hitler, finalized the OKH plan for the German invasion of the USSR in June 1941 (see BARBAROSSA) and in January 1942 Reichenau, who had just replaced *Rundstedt as C-in-C Army Group South, requested that Paulus take over Sixth Army which took part in Hitler's spring offensive into the Caucasus (see GERMAN–SOVIET WAR, 4).

After an uncertain start Paulus had some successes, particularly at *Kharkov in May 1942, and by August was poised to attack *Stalingrad. But his appointment was seen by many as being an ill-advised one considering he had virtually no combat experience. However, by October 1942 he had taken most of Stalingrad but then found himself surrounded. Instead of acting to save his Army, by breaking out when it was possible to do so, he obeyed Hitler's orders to stay put. His promotion to field marshal on 30 January 1943, when capitulation was inevitable, was Hitler's invitation for him to commit suicide—no German field marshal had ever surrendered—but the next day his HQ was overrun, and he and his staff were taken prisoner. During the following days, in one of the turning-points of the whole war, 110,000 German troops, including 20,000 wounded, went into captivity.

After the July 1944 bomb plot against Hitler (see SCHWARZE KAPELLE) Paulus joined the Federation of German Officers (Bund Deutscher Offiziere). This had been formed the previous summer by captured Sixth Army officers as part of the National Committee of Free Germany (Nationalkomitee Freies Deutschland), a Soviet-inspired anti-Nazi propaganda organization of German Communist emigrants. Paulus made a number of propaganda broadcasts which resulted in his family being arrested by the *Gestapo, and he was a witness for the Soviet prosecution at the *Nuremberg Trials. Released in 1953, he became a resident of Dresden in the German Democratic Republic.

Goerlitz, W., *Paulus and Stalingrad* (London, 1963).

Pavelić and the Ustašas. The Ustaša (insurrectionary) Movement was a revolutionary organization that developed in the 1930s to fight by all means for the independence of Croatia. Feeding on the dissatisfaction of most Croats with developments in Yugoslavia, Ustašism emerged after King Alexander (1888–1934) had dispensed with the Constitution in 1929. An extreme-right-wing deputy from Zagreb, Ante Pavelić (1889–1959) went abroad to set up his secret organization. He soon became the symbol of a radical Croatian fringe, turning for support to Italy and Hungary. Fusing Balkan rebelliousness with *fascism and the Nazi cult of authority, action, violence, and race, and operated from abroad, his movement never attracted many supporters in Yugoslavia before the war, but the dissatisfaction on which it fed spread among Croats. It was an Ustaša agent who killed King Alexander in Marseilles in 1934.

The collapse of Yugoslavia in April 1941 (see BALKAN CAMPAIGN) provided the Ustašas with their opportunity. They were allowed by the Axis powers to set up an Independent State of Croatia (Nezavisna Država Hrvatska, or NDH) on 10 April over all the territories inhabited by Croats, thus taking in Bosnia and Herzegovina. All power was in the hand of the movement, under its *poglavnik* (leader) Pavelić.

The NDH took its place among the satellites of the Axis, and declared war on the Allies. It established a conscript army, at best lukewarm in its loyalty to the regime which, for efficient action, had to rely on the Ustaša Militia, the NDH counterpart to the *SS. Satellite Croatia had been planned to fit into Mussolini's Adriatic schemes, and Italy duly annexed a large part of the coast, while Germany's interests were safeguarded by an occupation zone which covered two-thirds of the territory, the rest being the Italian zone (see Map 111).

With its 6.5 million inhabitants, the NDH contained almost as many 'aliens' as 'pure' Catholic Croats, a great majority of whom initially accepted the new regime, even though the Ustašas remained a minority. Muslims were accepted as being Croats of Islamic faith. There were, however, just under two million Orthodox Serbs, who represented a 'problem' to be solved, it was openly stated, by conversion, expulsion, and killing. Ustaša bands were immediately let loose to spread terror among them, starting with the intellectual and social élite, before moving on to mass extermination. Those fortunate or near enough fled to German-occupied Serbia or Italian-annexed Dalmatia. The rest took to the hills.

The Ustašas' action was so ferocious and blatant that their protectors were shocked. Italian troops intervened to halt the massacre, to prevent the Serbs from exacting retribution, and stop the insurgency from spreading to the coast. In spite of—and because of—their ruthlessness, the Ustašas failed in their attempt, and in 1942 had to admit defeat by pretending that the Serbs were henceforth Orthodox Croats. In Bosnia they actually had to come to terms with many of the rebel peasant leaders, which in effect put an end to Ustaša power in most of the Bosnian uplands. Tension with the Italians made Pavelić draw closer to the Germans who, worried by the inherent instability of the Ustaša state, would look closer into its affairs and take over control of its armed forces, as *Tito and the partisans increased their activities. Recent research estimates that one out of every six Serbs in the NDH lost his life during the Second World War, a large majority being victims of Ustaša massacres.

Tito's communist partisan movement had fattened on the anarchy of the Ustaša regime, and as the Germans reduced their hold to essential points in 1944, Pavelić's authority shrank. When the final German withdrawal started, and a parallel partisan advance rolled up what remained of the NDH, the Ustašas, the remnants of their army, and masses of civilians fled to reach Austria and the protection of the western Allies before Soviet and partisan forces cut off their retreat routes. On 9 May 1945 the Yugoslav partisans entered Zagreb. In those early days of May, thousands of Croats were turned back by the British, and summarily executed by the partisans.

Many of the Ustašas escaped, going underground and to safe havens under assumed identities. Pavelić himself eventually reached Argentina, survived an assassination attempt there, and died in Madrid.

STEVAN PAVLOWITCH

Djilas, A., *The Contested Country: Yugoslav Unity and Communist Revolution 1919–1953* (Cambridge, Mass., 1991).
Djordjević, D., and Avakumović, I., 'Yugoslavia', in P. Sugar (ed.), *Native Fascism in the Successor States 1918–45* (Santa Barbara, Calif., 1971).
Pavlowitch, S., *Yugoslavia* (London, 1971).

PBI (Poor Bloody Infantry) was the term Allied infantrymen, who almost always sustained the highest losses in any battle, used to describe themselves. See also INFANTRY WARFARE.

Peace Pledge Union, British pacifist organization founded by Canon Dick Sheppard which encouraged people to claim exemption from military service and urged peace with Germany. Its membership exceeded 130,000 in September 1939 and its newspaper had a circulation of 40,000; in the early months of the war membership probably increased further. A careful watch was kept on the few fascists connected with it, but *MI5 recognized that the vast majority of its members were genuine pacifists and, unlike those of the *British Union, no action was taken against any of its leaders. See also CONSCIENTIOUS OBJECTORS.

Pearl Harbor, attack on, Japanese pre-emptive strike on the US Pacific Fleet's Hawaii base—5,500 km. (3,400 mi.) from Japan—which had been planned by the C-in-C of the Imperial Japanese Navy, Admiral *Yamamoto. It was launched by units of his combined fleet at 0600 on Sunday 7 December 1941 after the Japanese realized that negotiations with the USA over, *inter alia*, their involvement in China (see CHINA INCIDENT) were proving fruitless (see USA, 1).

The striking force, commanded by Vice-Admiral *Nagumo, comprised two fleet and two light carriers; two carriers converted from a battleship and a cruiser; and two battleships, two cruisers, a destroyer screen, and eight support ships. They left Kure naval base between 10 and 18 November 1941, and signals deception (see SIGNALS INTELLIGENCE WARFARE) and strict radio silence meant that the US Pacific Fleet's C-in-C, Rear-Admiral *Kimmel, had no idea where the carriers were. When, on 2 December, he asked his fleet intelligence officer their location, the officer replied he did not know. 'Do you mean to say,' said Kimmel, 'they could be rounding Diamond Head and you wouldn't know it?'

Kimmel's dilemma was a real one. In the event of hostilities he was required to raid the Japanese Marshall Islands, which meant he had to keep aircraft in reserve for long-range reconnaissance of them. In any case he had sufficient aircraft only to cover a 144° sector out from Hawaii. Not unnaturally he concentrated on the sector that covered the Marshall Islands—some 3,250 km. (2,000 mi.) to the south-west and the closest Japanese territory to Hawaii—as it was from them that any Japanese attack could be expected; and it was here that the only three reconnaissance aircraft aloft were patrolling at the time of the attack. But Nagumo approached from the north.

US planners in Washington were also looking the wrong way as they considered the Philippines the most likely area for a pre-emptive Japanese strike. Sabotage and submarines were thought the most likely forms of attack on Hawaii. That the navy department considered an air strike there a remote possibility was confirmed, in Kimmel's eyes at least, by its decision to transfer many of his P40 fighters to Wake and Midway islands to cover bombers being flown to reinforce the Philippines. Because the harbour lacked the necessary depth, the department had also ruled out a raid by torpedo-carrying aircraft, so no nets protected the battle fleet. In fact, the Japanese, who had learned much from the British raid on *Taranto the previous year, had modified their torpedoes to run in shallow water.

On 27 November all US Army and Navy commanders had received a final war warning. But this had not mentioned Hawaii as a possible target, and the island's army commander, Lt-General Walter Short, interpreted it as meaning that any attack on Hawaii would take the form of sabotage. He therefore brought his defences to the highest state of alert for sabotage and informed Washington that he had done so. When he received no reply he assumed that he had interpreted the war warning correctly. Consequently, anti-aircraft batteries around the harbour had no ready ammunition and USAAF aircraft on the ground were easy targets as they were grouped together unarmed on airfields for easier protection against saboteurs. The naval defences, too, were alerted only to sabotage which resulted in the following state of affairs: only one in four of the navy's machine guns was manned, with the ready ammunition being locked in boxes to which only a duty officer had the keys; none of the main or 5 in. (12.7 cm.) batteries was manned; no additional long-range air reconnaissance had been ordered; and one-third of the ships' captains were ashore, as were many of their officers.

Though both Kimmel and Short were undoubtedly culpable for allowing a normal Sunday routine to continue in such circumstances, much of the blame for Hawaii's lack of general preparedness lay in Washington where inter-service and inter-departmental *rivalries were rife. Hawaii's communication intelligence unit, Station Hypo, was unable to read the Japanese *PURPLE diplomatic machine ciphers, the source of *MAGIC intelligence, as the machine originally earmarked for it had been sent to the British government Code and Cypher School at *Bletchley Park instead. Yet Washington, which also had other information about Axis interest in Pearl Harbor (see POPOV), failed to supply Hawaii's commanders with this intelligence on a regular basis. Notably, it failed to supply them with deciphered messages sent to the Japanese consul general in Honolulu which requested his *spies to divide Pearl Harbor into a grid of five areas and detail the ships within them. Five days later a Japanese agent working in the consulate suggested an even more detailed grid. Knowledge of these 'bomb plot' messages, as they came to be called, would have changed radically his estimate of the situation, Kimmel testified after the war.

By 22 November the striking force had assembled at the Kurile island of Etorofu. Four days later it sailed and under cover of a weather front (see also METEOROLOGICAL INTELLIGENCE), which moved at about its speed across the Pacific, it was able to reach a position 450 km. (275 mi.) north of Pearl Harbor without being detected, and Nagumo then launched his aircraft. The first wave, which comprised 49 bombers, 40 torpedo bombers, 51 dive-bombers, and 43 fighters, was followed by a second wave

The devastation in **Pearl Harbor** after the Japanese attack on it, 7 December 1941. The battleship *Oklahoma* has capsized; alongside her is the *Maryland*. Two other battleships, *West Virginia* and *Arizona*, can be seen burning.

of 54 bombers, 78 dive-bombers, and 36 fighters. As the first wave approached Hawaii the clouds parted to reveal the target. This seemed so miraculous to Nagumo and the first wave's leader that both saw in it the hand of divine intervention.

Yamamoto planned that any shipping not sunk in the air attack would be destroyed by sixteen I-type submarines, five of which carried *midget submarines, and at 0645 a patrolling destroyer sank a midget submarine as it tried to enter the harbour. It had been first sighted three hours previously, but its presence was not reported until after it had been sunk. Its presence was never reported at all to the army, a typical example of the lack of inter-service co-operation and of military insouciance, which is the hallmark of the Pearl Harbor catastrophe. However, none of the submarines accomplished anything and that arm of the Japanese Navy consequently suffered a loss of prestige from which it never wholly recovered.

The first contact with the incoming waves of Japanese aircraft was made by the Opana Mobile *Radar Unit, whose operators were under training on Kahuku Point. Their operational hours had been extended after the war warning, from 0400 to 0700, and on that particular morning, between 0645 and 0700, all three radars picked up a reconnaissance *float plane from the Japanese force. Its presence was reported but no action was taken. Then, because the breakfast truck was late, one team of operators kept their set on. This detected the approaching carrier aircraft which was also reported to the inexperienced duty officer. But, because the operators failed to report how many planes they had seen, he again did nothing as a flight of B17 bombers was expected from the same direction.

In harbour that Sunday morning were 70 warships, including 8 battleships and 24 auxiliaries, but the heavy cruisers were at sea with the fleet carriers. Guided on to this target by the music being played by a local radio station, and then by the consul general's bombing grid, the first wave of torpedo and dive bombers attacked the battle fleet, and bombed and strafed the airfields. This first phase lasted until 0825 and was followed, after a lull of fifteen minutes, by high-level bombing attacks on the harbour. Then at 0915 the dive-bombing was renewed before the raiders withdrew at 0945. Six battleships were sunk and the other two were damaged. Three destroyers, three light cruisers, and four other vessels were also sunk or damaged. On the airfields 164 planes were destroyed and another 128 damaged. Altogether, 2,403 servicemen and civilians were killed, and 1,178 wounded. Japanese combat losses were light: 29 aircraft and 6 submarines, 5 of them midgets. But Nagumo, fearing a counter-attack, made a critical mistake by refusing to launch a third wave on the harbour's repair facilities and fuel installations, which would have destroyed Pearl as a base. And though he temporarily wrecked the battle fleet, six battleships eventually returned to active service, as did all but one of the other vessels sunk or damaged. But he permanently wrecked the careers of Kimmel and Short, both of whom resigned the following spring.

Though traumatic, the disaster welded the US nation together for war as few other acts could have done. The Japanese won a significant tactical victory, but brought upon themselves a long-term strategic defeat of awesome proportions. The attack was as much a psychological shock to the USA as a physical one and no less than six wartime investigations, and one post-war Congressional inquiry, were made into the reasons for its success. None revealed the president, or any of his subordinates, guilty of misconduct and so far no evidence has ever come to light that convincingly supports the thesis that Roosevelt allowed the attack to occur in order to bring his country into the war. Nor has any incontrovertible evidence yet appeared that a British intelligence unit, the *Far East Combined Bureau (FECB), was able to read the Japanese JN25 code at that time and that Churchill therefore knew about the attack beforehand. FECB files are said to have been destroyed but refutation of this *canard* can be found in evidence that when, in mid November 1941, the Japanese fleet ceased to transmit radio signals—and therefore could no longer be pinpointed by British radio monitors—the Joint Intelligence committee (see UK, 8) immediately informed Washington of this development. A Dutch intelligence unit at Bandung, Kamer 14, may have been able to decipher part of the code as the Dutch commander in the Far East, General Hein ter Poorten, claimed after the war that it had provided him with intelligence reports that showed Japanese naval concentrations near the Kuriles, but this remains unsubstantiated as all the Dutch files were apparently burned when the Japanese invaded *Java. What seems certain is that signals dispatched before Nagumo sailed contained sufficient information to alert the Americans to the attack, as 188 deciphered after the war were connected to Japanese preparations for it (see F. Park, *Cryptologia*, vol. XV, October 1991).

Equally problematical is the case of what became known as the 'East Winds' signal. Japanese embassies had been warned that if a weather forecast, *Higashi no kaze ame* (east wind rain), was broadcast by Tokyo it would mean that Japanese–US relations were in danger. The potential use of this warning was known to the Americans through MAGIC intelligence and was regarded by the US navy department as being tantamount to a declaration of war if it was issued. It was later stated, though the navy department denied it, that the 'East Winds' message had been broadcast, and intercepted, on 4 or 5 December 1941. The message was logged but all record of it subsequently disappeared. See also PACIFIC WAR.

Layton, E., Pineau R., and Costello, J., *And I Was There* (New York, 1985).
Prange, W., *At Dawn We Slept* (New York, 1981).
Wohlstetter, R., *Pearl Harbor—Warning and Decision* (Stanford, Calif., 1962).

peasant battalions (*bataliony chlopskie*) formed a branch of the Polish partisans organized by the Peasant Party after Poland was occupied by Germany and the USSR in October 1939. Political differences prevented them from subordinating themselves to the main partisan group, Union for Armed Struggle (Związek Walki Zbrojnej, or ZWZ), commanded by Colonel *Rowecki, but these differences were eventually resolved when the Union became the Home Army (see POLAND, 4) in February 1942.

Peenemünde raid, night *precision bombing operation mounted by RAF Bomber Command against the German *V-weapons research station on the Baltic coast. Its existence had first been revealed to the British by the *Oslo report in November 1939, but no action was taken until the bugged conversation of two captured German generals in March 1943, and rumours from other sources, intimated that rocket research was under way there. Churchill's son-in-law, Duncan Sandys, was appointed to lead an investigation, *photographic reconnaissance sorties were flown, and a rocket on a trailer was identified in one photograph by the *MI6 scientist, R. V. Jones.

The raid took place on 17/18 August 1943 only a few hours after the USAAF mounted raids on Regensburg and *Schweinfurt, and a diversionary raid was also made on Berlin. Out of the 596 bombers used, 560 reached the target, which was marked by the *Pathfinder Force.

Opposing this formidable force was an equally formidable one of German fighters using *Wilde Sau tactics. For the first time the fighters were also being guided to their targets by German radio commentaries on the bombers' flight path. This system lacked central control and most of the 213 German fighters which were operational that night were diverted to the Berlin raid. Some did reach the area later, but they were too few and too late to stop the destruction of much of Peenemünde, some of which was caused by 4,000 lb. (1,810 kg.) block-buster *bombs. Nevertheless, the RAF lost 44 bombers and 42 crews (290 men), only three of which were downed by *flak. The Germans lost 12 fighters and their crews, and between 120 and 178 killed in the bombing. One of these was a scientist working on an anti-aircraft rocket projectile and the two-stage A-9 rocket. About 600 inmates of a nearby *forced labour camp also lost their lives from stray bombs.

Although Peenemünde continued to operate on a very

limited scale—and was subsequently bombed three times by the Americans in 1944—much of the work was moved elsewhere. It has been estimated that the raid delayed the V-2 rocket, first used operationally in September 1944, by between four weeks and six months.

Middlebrook, M., *The Peenemünde Raid* (London, 1982).

Pegasus Bridge, post-war name of a bridge that, until 1993, crossed the Orne Canal at Bénouville in Normandy. Its capture by a single gliderborne company of British 6th Airborne Division a few hours before the Normandy landings on 6 June 1944 (see OVERLORD) secured the invasion's eastern flank. Its name came from the division's winged horse insignia.

Ambrose, S., *Pegasus Bridge* (London, 1984).

Peleliu, capture of. One of the Pacific *Palau group, this 18 sq. km. (7 sq. mi.) Japanese-occupied coral island was assaulted by the 1st US Marine Division on 15 September 1944 to protect General *MacArthur's flank as he advanced on the Philippines (see PHILIPPINES CAMPAIGNS).

The landings were preceded by such a heavy three-day naval bombardment that the marines' commander, Maj-General William Rupertus, predicted success in four days. But the Japanese had adopted new tactics. Instead of trying to drive the attackers back into the water, the 10,600-strong garrison, led by Colonel Nakasawa Kunio, largely avoided the bombardment area and beaches, and dug near-impenetrable defences inland. However, this did not stop them immediately inflicting heavy American casualties and though the airstrip fell after eight days the defenders then retreated to prepared positions among the caves on Umurbrogol ridge. These were not reduced until the end of November, and some Japanese did not surrender until February 1945. For the marines, who had to be replaced by 81st Infantry Division in mid-October, it was one of the *Pacific war's bloodiest actions during which they suffered 6,526 casualties, including 1,252 killed. See also AMPHIBIOUS WARFARE.

penal battalions were Red Army punishment units. At the start of the *German–Soviet war there was just one penal battalion to each army, but in May 1942 the numbers were increased so that, additionally, there were between ten and fifteen at the disposal of each *front* (Army Group) commander. They comprised a guard company and three penal companies containing soldiers whose loyalty or courage in battle was in doubt, or who had been found guilty of various offences. They also sometimes contained partisans who had accidentally failed to keep behind German lines. Each battalion was 360 strong, and they included officers who had been stripped of their rank and all decorations. Penal battalions were normally kept in the rear, but when a breakthrough of a German position was to be attempted they were brought forward under guard. Once the heavily armed guard company had positioned itself behind the penal companies the latter were given their weapons and were ordered to attack. If they turned back they were shot. Massed attacks by penal battalions were not uncommon, 34 being used by Marshal *Zhukov on one occasion during the fighting in Belorussia. The few who survived such operations took part in the next one so that eventually all were killed, but they proved a very effective means of clearing the way forward for the élite infantry that followed them. There were also mine clearing and air force penal units. The former were said to have been dispatched across minefields to make a safe path for the following infantry; the latter were air gunners.

Pentagon, Washington HQ of the American armed forces. Work on the building (the name derives from its shape) was begun in mid-1941 and completed in January 1943 at the cost of $83 million. It housed Henry *Stimson, the secretary of defence, the *Joint Chiefs of Staff, and 27,000 personnel, previously scattered around central Washington. See also USA, 5.

People's Court (National Socialist People's Court, in German *Volksgerichtshof*, or VGH), the highest Nazi court for political crimes. These varied in severity, from listening to forbidden radio broadcasts to the attempted assassination of Hitler (see SCHWARZE KAPELLE).

The roots of the People's Court, set up in April 1934, went back to 1922 when the then minister of justice, as the result of a political assassination, abrogated the time-honoured principle of *nulla poena sine lege* (no punishment without law) and the legal system of the Weimar Republic was highly politicized. It was allowed to exist because most Germans fervently believed that the *First World War had been lost because of *traitors in their midst and its creation was predicted by Hitler in **Mein Kampf* when he wrote that 'one day a German national tribunal must condemn and execute several tens of thousands of the criminals who organized and are responsible for the November treason [the armistice which ended the First World War was signed in November 1918] and everything connected with it'.

Otto Thierack was president of the VGH until 1942. He was then succeeded by Roland *Freisler and, finally, by Harold Haffner. Its jurisdiction extended beyond pre-war Germany to the population of Bohemia and Moravia, Poles in annexed territories, and Germans in Alsace-Lorraine and Eupen-Malmédy, and to non-Germans arrested under the *Night and Fog Decree.

The VGH was part of Germany's normal legal system in that those appearing before it were arrested and prosecuted by the police in the normal way. But its courts ignored an elementary rule of justice, impartiality, as it employed judges, both professional and lay, who were committed to the Nazi cause. There was no right of appeal and no trial by jury. Not everyone was found guilty by its courts, but those who were released were simply rearrested by the *Gestapo and sent to a *concentration camp. The Wehrmacht had its own courts, the highest being the Reichskriegsgericht which tried members of the German *Rote Kapelle. Officers implicated in the attempt to assassinate Hitler in July 1944 were expelled from the Wehrmacht so that they could be tried by the VGH.

Figures are unreliable, but an estimated 12,891 death sentences were passed by the VGH between 1934 and 1944, most of them during the latter stages of the war when increased resistance activity, and then Hitler's attempted assassination, greatly added to the numbers. See also GERMANY, 3.

Koch, H. W., *In the Name of the Volk: Political Justice in Hitler's Germany* (London, 1989).

People's Guard (Gwardia Ludowa, or GL) was the armed wing of the Polish Worker's Party (see POLAND, 2(e)).

Permanent Joint Board on Defence, advisory committee formed by Canada and the USA in August 1940 to study joint defence problems. Established by the *Ogdensburg agreement, it comprised two national sections each composed of a civilian chairman, and representatives of the armed forces and foreign service. It was especially influential while the USA was neutral, and is still in existence.

Persia had its name changed to Iran in 1935, but continued to be known as Persia during the war years. In 1940 Persia's oil output was 8.4 million tons which was vital to the British war effort, and the country's strategic importance became increasingly evident during the course of the war. Worried by German advances in the *Western Desert campaigns, and an anti-British revolt in Iraq, the Allies viewed the prospect of further Axis gains in the Persian Gulf oil basin with alarm, and following Germany's attack on the USSR on 22 June 1941 (see BARBAROSSA), they regarded Persia as an indispensable route for sending *Lend-Lease supplies to the Eastern Front. Although the country was officially neutral, its ruler, Reza Shah Pahlavi, and Germany maintained friendly relations, and many German advisers and technicians were involved in different Persian industrial projects: the British estimate of the number of German nationals living in Persia in July 1941 was 2,000–3,000 including about 1,000 men. In 1940–1, Germany was Persia's biggest partner in foreign trade. German *fifth columnists were also active with anti-Soviet propaganda. Reza Shah's negative response to a joint British and Soviet request, made on 21 August 1941, to expel all the German nationals prompted a co-ordinated invasion of the country by the Soviet and British forces on 25 August 1941 (see Map 84). These easily undermined scattered Persian resistance and subsequently Reza Shah abdicated in favour of his 22-year-old son Mohammad Reza Pahlavi, left the country, and died in exile in Johannesburg in July

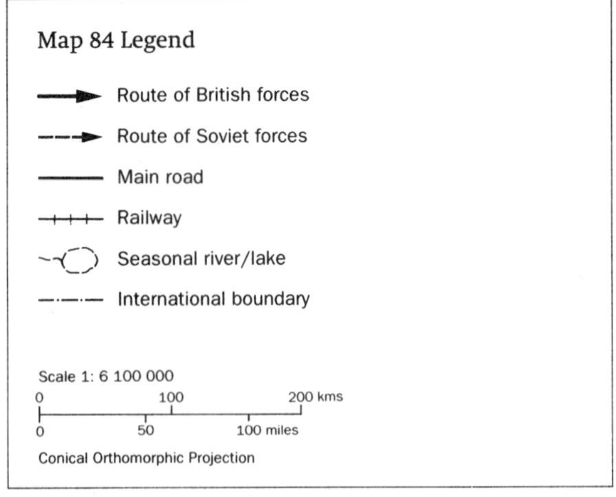

1944. Shortly after Reza Shah's abdication Persia severed diplomatic relations with Germany and Italy and expelled their nationals, and the severing of relations with Japan followed on 12 April 1942. The Allies initially guaranteed Persia's territorial integrity and independence. A Tri-Partite Treaty of Alliance between Persia, the UK, and the USSR, signed in Teheran on 29 January 1942, committed the Allies to leave Persia within six months after the end of the war with Germany and its associates. This was later extended to six months after the end of hostilities with Japan. Following the US entry into the war, these earlier agreements were reaffirmed in the Teheran conference of November 1943 (see EUREKA). The Allies had initially maintained that they would not interfere with Persia's internal affairs. In practice, however, some intervention was inevitable. *Logistics required the use of Persian facilities such as ports, roads, railways, and telecommunications, as well as food supplies and manpower. In sending essential aid to the USSR, the trans-Iranian railway connecting the Persian Gulf to the Caspian Sea played an important role. During the war some 4,159,117 tons of Lend-Lease supplies, or 23.8% of the total aid delivered to the USSR, was shipped through the Persian Gulf. This aid was decisive in further consolidation of the Soviet defences, to such an extent that Persia has at times been referred to as 'the bridge of victory'. See also PAIFORCE.

ALI GHEISSARI

Lenczowski, G., *Russia and the West in Iran, 1918–1948: A Study in Big-Power Rivalry* (New York, 1949).
Millspaugh, A. C., *Americans in Persia* (Washington, DC, 1946).
Skrine, C., *World War in Iran* (London, 1962).
Stewart, R., *Sunrise at Abadan: The British and Soviet Invasion of Iran, 1941* (New York, 1988).

Peru defeated Ecuador in a war in 1941, gaining valuable territory. It made peace with Ecuador at the *Rio conference, held in January 1942, also announcing that it was severing diplomatic relations with the three main

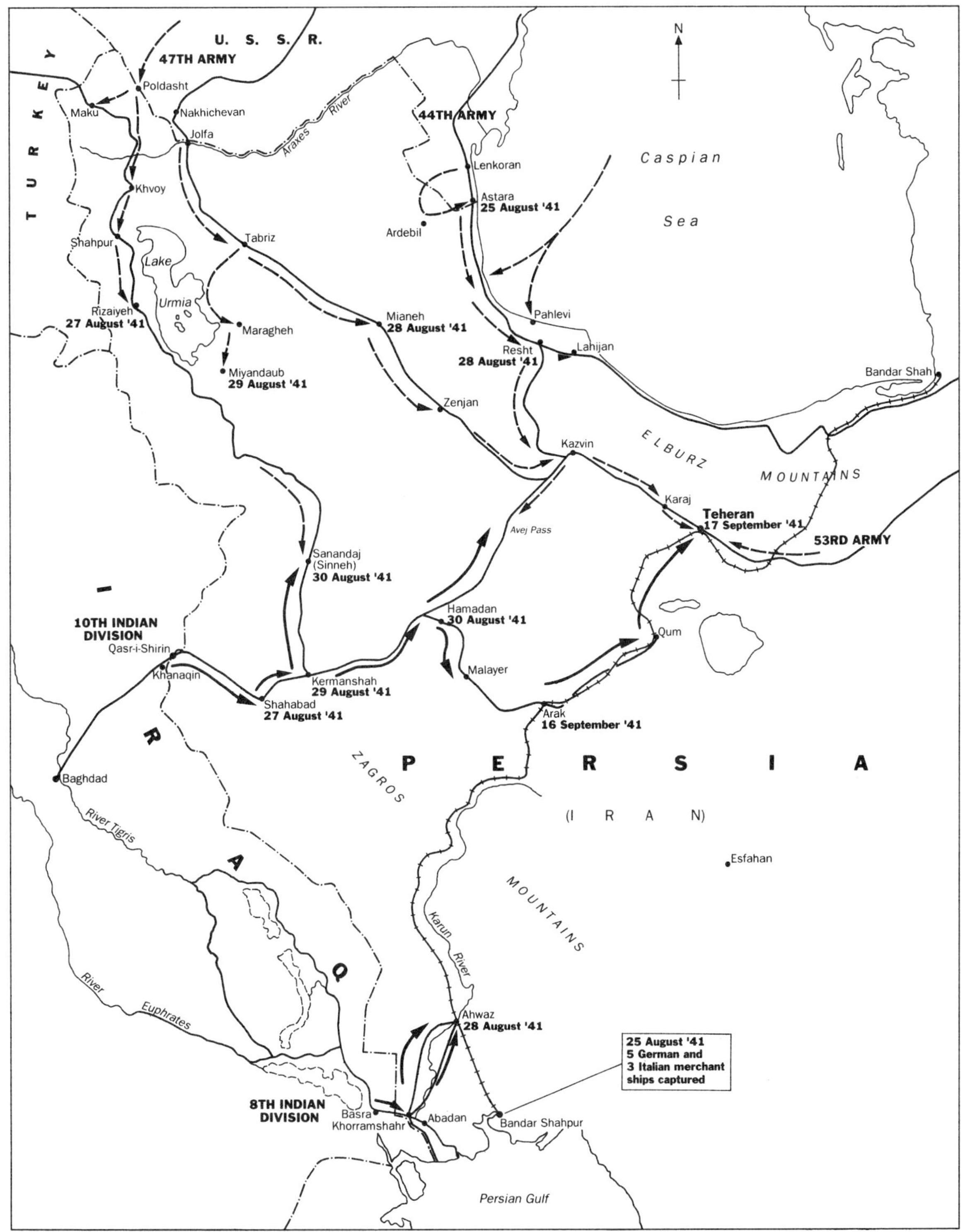

84. Allied invasion of **Persia**, August 1941

Marshal **Pétain** inspecting a guard of honour outside the Sévigné pavilion at Vichy. With him is his vice-premier, Pierre Laval.

Axis powers. It then established strong commercial links with the USA which resulted in the latter receiving a useful flow of *raw materials. In return, the USA provided military and economic aid, and established a base at Salinas. Peru declared war on Japan and Germany on 13 February 1945 and signed the *United Nations Declaration three days later. See also LATIN AMERICA.

Pétain, Marshal (Henri) Philippe (1856–1951), French Army officer who was head of the French *Vichy state from July 1940 to August 1944.

A regular officer born of farmers, Pétain was about to retire as a colonel in 1914 when war catapulted him to high command; and in December 1918, as the victor of Verdun and a public hero, he was made a Marshal of France. On 18 May 1940 the prime minister, Paul *Reynaud, appointed him minister of state and vice-premier to act as a rallying-point for the army and the people. Churchill's liaison officer in Paris, Maj-General Edward Spears, found Pétain infinitely pathetic and that France was fading out, as he put it, on an old man's evocation of a heroic past. There was certainly nothing heroic about Pétain in 1940. He advised seeking an *armistice and immediately began negotiating for one when he replaced Reynaud late on 16 June. On 1 July his government settled in Vichy—the small town in central France which gave its name to Pétain's regime—and ten days later the National Assembly vested all its powers in him as *Chef d'Etat*. Now head of state as well as prime minister, the government he formed, with Pierre *Laval as vice-premier, contained more military men than any ministry since Marshal Soult's in 1832. With the approval of the Germans, it launched, under the slogan of 'Work, Family and Country', a 'National Revolution', and Pétain saw himself, and was seen as, the embodiment of France whose soil he pledged he would never leave.

In October 1940, at Laval's behest, Pétain met Hitler at Montoire to offer *collaboration with Germany. Although Montoire was a disappointment, for which Pétain blamed Laval, France's true predicament was probably not brought home to Pétain until his meeting with *Göring at the end of 1941. When Pétain told the Reichsmarschall that he thought collaboration implied treating between equals, a furious Göring shouted, 'who are the victors, you or us?'

In December 1940, when Pétain dismissed him, Laval called him 'a puppet, a windbag and a weathercock which turns with the wind' (quoted in P. Webster, *Pétain's Crime, The Full Story of French Collaboration in the Holocaust*, London, 1990, p. 74). He certainly swung with whatever breeze last blew on him, but his efforts to blame others for the disasters of 1940 backfired (see RIOM TRIAL). He was as devoted to *secrecy as he was to power, and by intrigue and double-dealing he maintained an aura of aloofness. To the French he stood above the collaboration they quickly came to hate, but there seems little doubt that Pétain must bear his share of the responsibility for such pro-Nazi acts as the deportation of Jews, the execution of hostages, and the formation of the notorious *Milice.

Pétain's substitute for Laval, Pierre Flandin, proved unacceptable to the Germans as, in the end, did Flandin's successor, Admiral *Darlan, and in April 1942 they forced him to have Laval back and to give him increased powers. However, towards the end of 1943 the mounting threat of the French resistance within, and of de *Gaulle and the Free French without, pushed Pétain into overplaying his hand. He tried, unsuccessfully, to replace Laval and though no supporter of democracy he attempted to strengthen his own legitimacy by making the defunct National Assembly his successor, not Laval. The Germans refused to allow it, Pétain virtually went on strike, and he only climbed down when Hitler threatened dire consequences. From that time the make-up of the Vichy government became increasingly dictated by the Germans and after Marcel *Déat joined it in March 1944 Pétain ceased to attend its meetings.

Though the Vichy government was by that time as hated as it was impotent, Pétain himself was still seen by many as the symbol of French unity and was warmly received when he visited Paris in April 1944. On 19 August, when pressed to leave Vichy, he resigned, but was removed first to Belfort and then to Sigmaringen in Germany. In April 1945 he persuaded the Germans to take him to Switzerland where de *Gaulle hoped he would stay. Indeed the Free French leader apparently asked the Swiss to refuse any extradition requests. However, Pétain chose to return to France and was put on trial that July. He put up a stout defence—'Every day, with a knife at my throat, I struggled against the enemy demands'—against a prosecution that hardly bothered to study the available evidence. Inevitably, he was condemned to death, but was reprieved and spent his last years a prisoner on the Île d'Yeu. See also FRANCE, 3(c).

Griffiths, R., *Marshal Pétain* (London, 1970).
Lottmann, H., *Pétain* (New York, 1984).

Phantom Regiment, British signals unit which, as No. 3 British Air Mission, transmitted information during the early months of the war about the front-line positions of Belgian, British, and French troops to the commander of British air units in France. Its initial purpose was to prevent Allied aircraft bombing friendly ground forces. After it was joined by Lt-Colonel G. F. Hopkinson, whose task was to liaise with the Belgians, it expanded, and during the fighting which preceded the fall of *France its highly mobile patrols were able to obtain up-to-date battlefield intelligence which was transmitted direct to Army HQ. It proved a great success and as GHQ Liaison Regiment (Phantom), and later as the Signals Reporting Regiment, operated with forward units in all the Allied campaigns in north-west Europe and in the *Western Desert campaigns. Its F Squadron was attached to the *Special Air Service.

Phantom's system of obtaining battlefield intelligence proved unsuitable in the Western Desert. Instead, the J Service was formed in 1941. This intercepted the *radio communications of friendly forward formations as well as those of the enemy, and relevant intelligence was immediately passed to the operations staff at army HQ. J Service later fought in the *North African, *Sicilian, and *Italian campaigns and was amalgamated with Phantom in 1945. Its US equivalent was the Signals Information and Monitoring unit.

Warner, P., *Phantom* (London, 1982).

Philby, Harold ('Kim') (1912–88), member of British Secret Intelligence Service (see MI6) who, from the early 1930s, worked for the Soviet Intelligence Organization *NKVD and its successor the KGB. His association with other Soviet agents such as Donald *Maclean and Guy Burgess began at Cambridge University, and his friendship with Burgess resulted in his recruitment into *SOE in 1940 as a propaganda expert. In September 1941 he transferred to the counter-espionage section of MI6 and in November 1944 was promoted to head its newly reconstituted section for counteracting Soviet *communism in the post-war world. This was very damaging to British interests because, by initiating plans to penetrate Soviet intelligence defences, he was able to ensure that these would fail; and he also had the opportunity to betray anti-communist resistance, particularly in the Baltic States, and potential Soviet defectors.

The most destructive phase of his spying career ended in 1951 because of his association with Burgess who defected that year. However, nothing had been conclusively proved against him before his own defection twelve years later. In 1968 he wrote his memoirs, *My Silent War*, which contains much disinformation. In particular, his charge that the foreign office and MI6 began, as early as 1943, to divert efforts from defeating the Nazis to menacing Stalin is untrue, and he greatly exaggerated the wartime friction between *MI5 and MI6.

ROBERT CECIL

Philippines (for the fighting in the Philippines, see PHILIPPINES CAMPAIGNS). The Philippines comprise nearly 7,100 islands and islets scattered between Formosa and Borneo with a population in 1941 of some 17 million. In 1937 Tagalog had been selected as the basis for a national language, but the huge number of dialects made communication between the inhabitants difficult and rendered recruitment for the armed forces on a national scale a problem.

The Philippine Army totalled only ten reserve divisions, with a small nucleus of trained personnel, and the navy and air force had only two torpedo boats and 40 aircraft respectively. In July 1941 these forces became part of the newly formed US Army Forces in the Far East commanded by General *MacArthur whose principal fighting force was a US Army formation, the Philippine Division, commanded by Maj-General *Wainwright. The division's fighting elements were 8,000 Philippine Scouts, officered by Americans, a US infantry regiment some 2,000 strong, and a regiment of artillery.

Like several other lesser powers caught in the crush of the war, the Philippines became a battlefield between Axis and Allied forces. Besides being small and inconveniently located (for the peace of mind and body of their inhabitants), the Philippines laboured under the additional disadvantage of being neither entirely independent nor wholly under the control and protection of a great power. When the *Pacific war began in

December 1941, the islands were slightly more than halfway into a projected decade of commonwealth status, during which the government of the American possession was preparing to assume full sovereignty. Since 1935 the administration of President Manuel *Quezon had been working to create a Philippine military establishment that could defend the country against aggression, but the effort was complicated by lack of resources and uncertainty as to whether, if war did occur, the USA would feel obliged to rescue the Filipinos. Although US war plans (the Orange and *Rainbow series) called for a defence of the Philippines, Congressional niggardliness and a widespread American desire to have done with empire and imperial responsibilities precluded successful implementation of the plans.

Consequently, despite last-moment American efforts to strengthen local security, the Japanese air raids of 8 December 1941 against *Clark Field and other installations caught the Philippines unprepared. Within hours the Japanese crippled the islands' air defences; within days they had landed troops and were marching on Manila. Even had Washington at this point wished to make a stand in the Philippines—which it did not, in keeping with its Germany first strategy—the blow the US Pacific Fleet suffered at *Pearl Harbor rendered such an effort out of the question. MacArthur urgently requested reinforcements, but to no substantial avail. At the end of December, he declared Manila an open city and evacuated his headquarters to the rock-fortress of *Corregidor. American and Filipino troops retreated to the *Bataan peninsula, where Japanese forces cut them off, forcing their surrender on 8 April 1942. The Corregidor garrison capitulated on 6 May, following the departure of MacArthur and top officials of the Philippine government, including Quezon.

Filipino responses to the Japanese occupation principally involved variations on the two themes of *resistance and *collaboration. The organized resistance in central Luzon was led by the Hukbo ng Bayan Laban sa Hapon (People's Anti-Japanese Army), or Hukbalahap. The Huk resistance drew both on a long-standing nationalist sentiment, with members trying to oust the Japanese and reclaim control of their homeland just as many Filipinos two generations earlier militantly resisted first the Spanish and then the Americans; and on specific grievances against the Japanese, who treated Filipinos usually with contempt and often with brutality. Organized resistance also sprang up in northern Luzon, where stranded American and Philippine regular troops formed the nucleus of a guerrilla army; in southern Luzon, where government loyalists established an outfit calling itself President Quezon's Own Guerrillas; and in the Visayas and Mindanao. Although the resistance forces, taken together, did not seriously upset Japanese operations through most of the occupation period, they allowed the Philippine *government-in-exile (in Washington) to maintain contact with Filipinos in the islands, and they gathered intelligence that proved very useful in the American reconquest of the country in 1944–5. At the same time, to those for whom such issues mattered, they served as a symbol of national self-respect in the face of intractably unpleasant and doubt-inducing reality.

For most of the Filipino population, however, as for most populations in occupied countries, survival required accommodating the country's new rulers. Before the war some Filipinos had argued that, if it came to such a pass, Japanese rule would be preferable to American, in that the Japanese were fellow Asians, uncorrupted by the racism that commonly tainted American dealings with the Philippines. Japanese military officials made the same argument in January 1942 when they declared American sovereignty in the islands ended and demanded the co-operation of the Filipino populace. One Japanese officer reminded the Filipinos: 'Like it or not, you are Filipinos and belong to the Oriental race. No matter how hard you try, you cannot become white people.' Another added, 'The time has come to assert yourselves as an Oriental people' (see Steinberg [below], p. 49).

The argument from Asian solidarity worked better in theory than in practice: once the oppressive nature of Japanese rule became evident, most Filipinos wished for the good old days of American paternalism. Such collaboration as occurred resulted less from affinity with the Japanese than from fear of the consequences of non-collaboration. As soon as Japanese forces took control of Manila, the Japanese C-in-C in the Philippines, Lt-General *Homma, ordered Filipino civilian officials to remain at their posts and to carry on their duties as before. Failure to do so would be punishable by death.

An inclination to avoid such a fate, as well as a desire to mitigate the harshness of the *occupation, prompted a number of prominent Filipinos to meet Japanese officers for the purpose of establishing a new government for the Philippines. Among the group were Jorge Vargas, the mayor of Manila; Jose Laurel, formerly secretary of the interior and currently acting chief justice of the supreme court; and Claro Recto and Benigno Aquino, leading figures in the ruling (until the Japanese arrived, anyway) Nacionalista party. Some members of the group initially hoped to trade co-operation with the Japanese for Tokyo's recognition of Philippine independence. Others, worried that such a course would open them to charges of sedition against the USA, should the Americans ultimately recapture the islands, recommended the formation of a provisional executive, chosen under the authority of the existing commonwealth government. When the Japanese rejected the latter plan, making clear they would have nothing to do with the American-sponsored commonwealth, Vargas and the rest announced the creation of a provisional council of state, headed by an executive commission, unaffiliated with the pre-existing government.

Until the beginning of 1943 this arrangement satisfied the Japanese, who were more interested in converting the production of the islands to military use than in the niceties of constitutionalism. Tokyo demanded first call on the Philippine rice harvest, which went to feed Japanese soldiers. Cotton plants replaced sugar cane in some areas; where the cane fields survived, the sugar they produced was channelled to the manufacture of fuel alcohol. The Japanese defence ministry commandeered the country's supply of abaca (hemp).

Under the pressure of war and occupation, and torn by the dilemmas of collaboration and resistance, the Filipino people 'lost their social and moral balance,' in the words of two Filipino historians of the period (see T. A. Agoncillo and O. M. Alfonso [below], pp. 466–7). After MacArthur's designation of Manila as an open city, and before the arrival of the Japanese Army, looters sacked stores for goods that were becoming and would remain scarce. Police, disarmed to remove the temptation to shoot at the Japanese, joined in the looting. Throughout the war, profiteering enriched a few at the expense of the many. Corruption in government flourished. Economic dislocation, partly the result of war-closed markets, partly the consequence of Japan's forced changes to the country's production, resulted in widespread malnourishment and disease. In the regions where resistance units operated, guerrilla fighting yielded its usual crop of coercion and reprisal, of opportunism and score-settling.

Early in 1943 Japan indicated an intention to grant independence to the Philippines. The tide of the war in the Pacific was turning in favour of the Allies, and Tokyo hoped a promise of self-government would diminish resistance and free Japanese troops for battle elsewhere. In July 1943 Japanese authorities in Manila called on the leading citizens of the country to draft a constitution for a Philippine republic. The document in question, the Japanese explained, must contribute to the security of the *Greater East Asia Co-prosperity Sphere; in addition, as Prime Minister *Tōjō personally told Vargas, Laurel, and Aquino after summoning the three to Tokyo, the ratification of the constitution must be followed shortly by a declaration of war against the USA. 'It was a shock to all three of us,' Laurel recalled afterwards, 'I silently prayed and said the Pater Noster.' He and the others asked for time to raise the issue with their colleagues in Manila and Tōjō granted the request. For several weeks the Filipino leaders sought to devise a formula that would allow them to steer between the Scylla of present Japanese control, with Tokyo's insistence on a war declaration, and the Charybdis of America's likely return, with Washington's certain displeasure at such a flagrant form of collaboration. In light of the mistreatment of American and Filipino prisoners after the surrender at Bataan, trials of collaborators for *war crimes could not be ruled out.

To this personal consideration was added the fact that the USA would surely not recognize the independence of a Philippine republic founded under Japanese aegis, and might in response delay America's own conferral of Philippine independence, planned for 1946. In the end, the collaborators' decision turned on a belief that the Americans would show greater forgiveness than the Japanese. Asked whether Japan or the USA would make the more vindictive enemy, Laurel, the first and only president of the wartime Philippine republic, answered that Japan would. Accordingly, in September 1944 the Philippine government declared war on the USA.

The declaration made little difference to the course of the fighting. In October 1944, MacArthur, as promised on his departure from Corregidor in 1942, returned to the Philippines. American forces, after landing at Leyte on the eastern side of the Visayas, fought their way to the outskirts of Manila by February 1945. The battle for Manila lasted two weeks and devastated the city and its population. While approximately 1,000 Americans and 16,000 Japanese died, the Filipino dead—by far the greatest portion civilians—numbered more than 100,000. The destruction of buildings, bridges, utilities, and the like in large parts of the city was almost complete.

Meanwhile the pacification of the rest of the Philippines proceeded. The Leyte landing gave encouragement to the various resistance groups, whose activities in turn facilitated the success of the regular American forces. By April 1945 the latter had secured the central Luzon plain, the geographical and political heart of the country. In more remote parts of the archipelago, fighting continued, with diminishing ferocity, until Emperor *Hirohito's August announcement of capitulation to the Allies.

As the war wound to its conclusion, the US government evolved a policy toward the collaborators. Laurel and some high-ranking associates fled the country for Japan (where they eventually surrendered themselves to the American occupation forces there). Most of the rest of those who held positions in the wartime republic, lacking the opportunity if not the desire to flee, stayed behind. MacArthur immediately stamped his influence on policy toward the collaborators, as he would stamp his influence on policy towards defeated Japan. He personally embraced and pardoned Manuel Roxas, a highly visible collaborator but one who throughout the war had maintained touch with the resistance and with the Americans. By treating Roxas as a rescued prisoner rather than as a captured *Quisling—a move that provoked considerable controversy in both the Philippines and the USA—MacArthur set a precedent that led to lenient treatment and swift rehabilitation of the large majority of the collaborators. When Roxas won election to the presidency of the Philippines in 1946, just in time for America's granting of independence, the case against the collaborators collapsed entirely. H. W. Brands

Agoncillo, T. A., and Alfonso, O. M., *History of the Filipino People* (Quezon City, 1967 edn.).
Friend, T., *Between Two Empires* (New Haven, 1965)
Laurel, J. P., *War Memoirs* (Manila, 1962).
Steinberg, D. J., *Philippine Collaboration in World War II* (Ann Arbor, Mich., 1967).

Philippines campaigns (see Maps 85 and 86). The roots of the wartime struggle for control of the Philippines ran back nearly to the turn of the century, when US leaders began to worry about the growing power of Japan. By diplomatic means (the Taft–Katsura agreement of 1905, for example), arms control measures (the Washington conference system of 1922 and after), and military preparations (the strengthening of Philippine forces in the islands in the latter 1930s), Washington sought to shield the Philippines from Japan's southward expansion. After Tokyo's take-over of French Indo-China during the summer of 1941, the US government accelerated its efforts to make the Philippines defensible. Roosevelt issued an executive order integrating its armed forces, which had been autonomous since the creation of the Philippine commonwealth in 1935, into the US military, and the war department recalled General *MacArthur, who had been serving as chief military adviser to the Philippine government, to active duty as army commander for the Far East, with headquarters in Manila.

During the six months before December 1941 MacArthur worked furiously to prepare for the onslaught which seemed increasingly probable. While the Japanese might well not attack the USA directly—or so one could still hope during this period—they appeared unlikely to overlook the Philippines. They evidently intended to push towards the oil and other resources of the *Netherlands East Indies, and they could hardly allow the continued existence of a modest but not insignificant US force on the flank of their route in that direction. MacArthur, suspecting the worst, supervised increases in the size of the American contingent in the Philippines to more than 30,000 troops, and of Filipino active units to more than 110,000. American air power in the islands came to include 35 B17 bombers at *Clark Field, 107 P40 fighters at Clark and other fields on Luzon, and more than 100 additional planes, providing the Philippines with the largest concentration of US *air power in the Pacific. Naval forces in the islands included 3 cruisers, 13 destroyers, more than 40 smaller surface craft, and 29 submarines. In addition, at the beginning of December 1941 a large US convoy carrying 70 warplanes, 600 tons of bombs, 9,000 barrels of aviation fuel, 48 75 mm. (2.9 in.) guns, and several million rounds of ammunition left Hawaii for the Philippines.

The convoy never arrived. On 8 December (7 December east of the dateline) Japanese bombers and fighters based on Formosa attacked the airfields on Luzon. The attack came not entirely without warning: at 0300 (Manila time) a report arrived at MacArthur's headquarters of the Japanese blow against *Pearl Harbor. Subsequent reports confirmed the news, and at 0700 MacArthur received a radiogram from Washington announcing that a condition of hostilities obtained between Japan and the USA and authorizing him to implement war plans against Japan. MacArthur's air commander, Maj-General *Brereton, pressed for permission to launch air strikes against Japanese airfields on Formosa; but for reasons that remain unclear and contentious, gaining MacArthur's approval required more than three hours. The American planes were still on the ground when the Japanese bombers reached Luzon from Formosa shortly after noon.

The first wave of Japanese planes, including more than 50 bombers and three dozen fighters, destroyed two squadrons of American bombers and one of fighters at Clark. A second squadron of American fighters, returning from patrol, met a second Japanese attack group at Iba, 65 km. (40 mi.) north-west of Clark. Only two American planes survived the encounter.

At this point, MacArthur had lost half his air force. Things only got worse during the next several days as Japanese aircraft further ravaged the American air force in the islands and bombed naval installations and ships. By the evening of 13 December, American air power had been so reduced that MacArthur chose to withhold his remaining planes from combat lest he lose them too.

With no air cover, the commander of the American Asiatic fleet, Admiral *Hart, decided to withdraw most of his ships from Luzon to the southern portion of the Philippine archipelago, where they would be beyond the reach of Japanese planes based on Formosa. Of the vessels that remained in the Manila area, the most important were 27 submarines, which were harder for Japanese planes to hit than surface ships and which could more easily run a Japanese blockade if matters came to that.

Soldiers of the Fourteenth Japanese Army began landing in the Philippines even while bombing of the American air and naval bases continued. The first landing took place on Batan Island in the Luzon Strait on 8 December. Two days later Japanese troops landed on the northern coast of Luzon itself. On 12 December a small force from Palau to the east of the Philippines invaded Legaspi in southern Luzon. On 20 December another contingent from Palau landed at Davao on Mindanao.

The primary purpose of these initial landings was to secure advanced air bases for covering the larger invasion that began in earnest on 22 December. Two Japanese divisions came ashore from the Lingayen Gulf and commenced marching south towards Manila; shortly after, a smaller Japanese force landed at Atimonan on Lamon Bay on Luzon's eastern coast and also began pushing towards the capital. It soon became apparent that the aim of Lt-General *Homma, the commander of the Japanese invasion, was to trap the American and Philippine troops defending Manila in a pincers.

American forces in northern Luzon, under the command of Maj-General *Wainwright, initially contested the Japanese advance south along the central Luzon plain, but MacArthur soon recognized that the defenders were overmatched. He proceeded to declare Manila an open city and to direct the evacuation of his headquarters and of the Philippine government to the island fortress of *Corregidor in the mouth of Manila Bay. At the same time he ordered American and

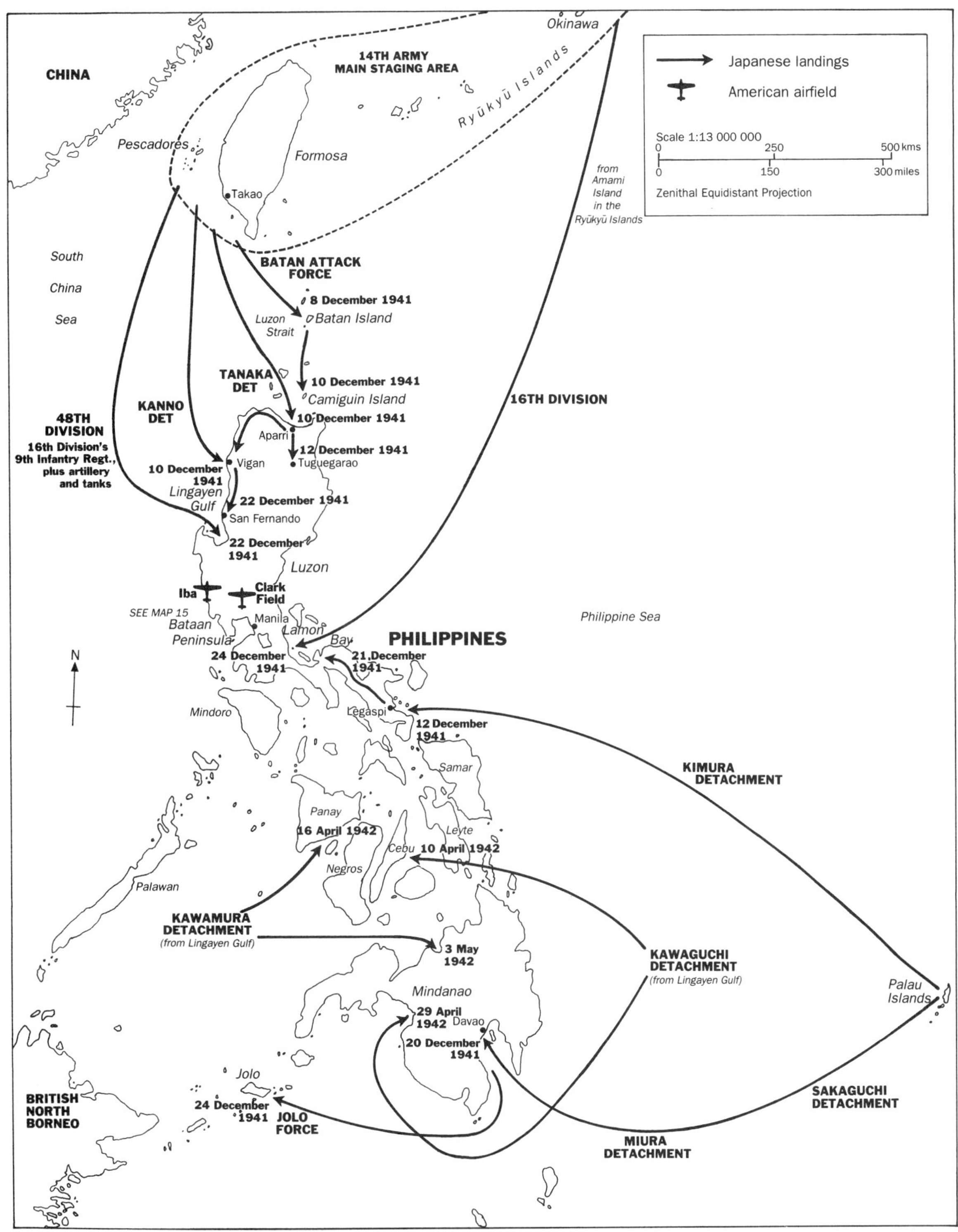

85. First **Philippines campaign**, December 1941–May 1942

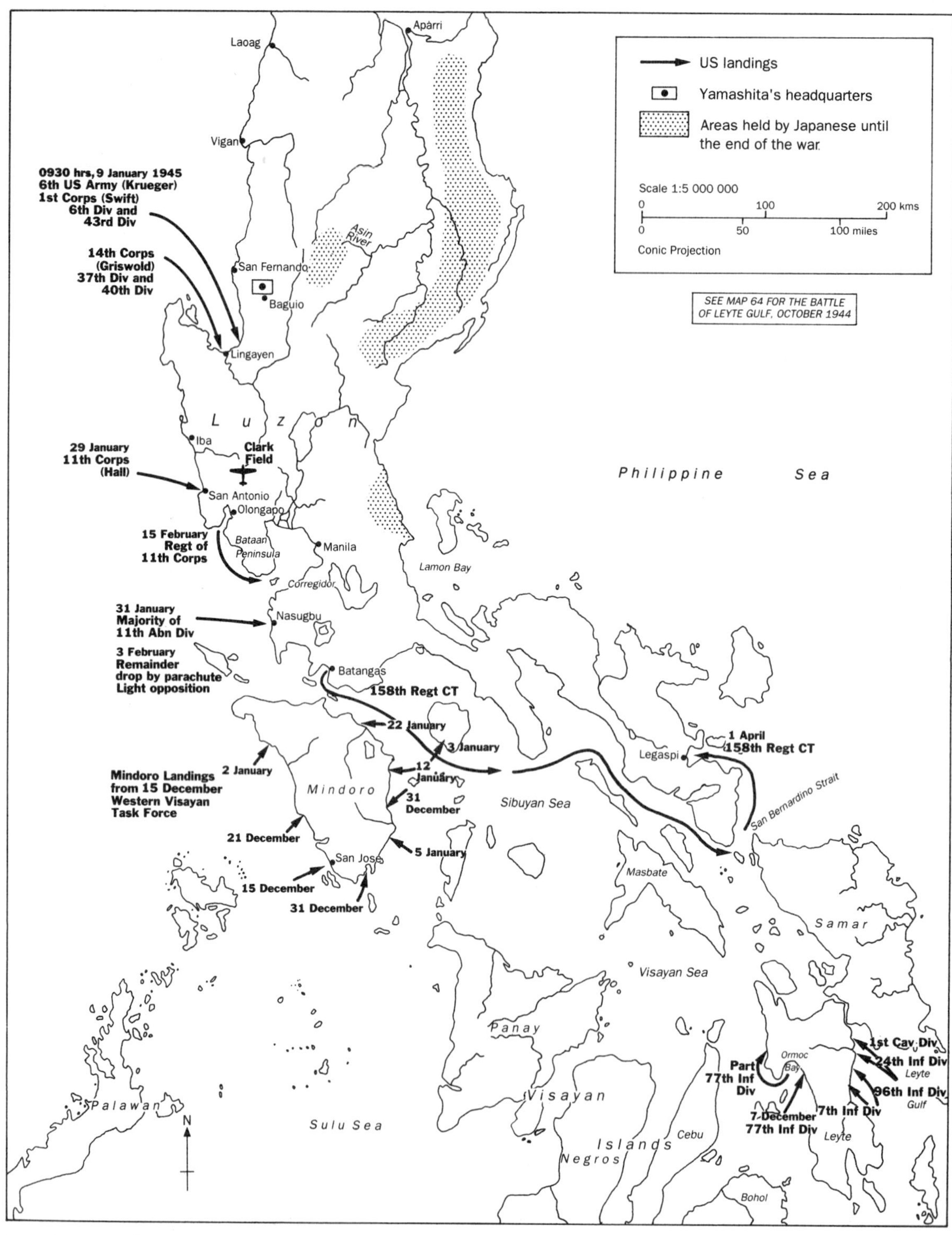

86. Second **Philippines campaign**, October 1944–August 1945

Philippine troops in the area to retreat to the *Bataan peninsula west of Manila Bay.

Leaders in Washington viewed the course of fighting in the Philippines with no little embarrassment, since an American possession was being overrun largely as a result of the parsimoniousness of the US government in the years before the war. But despite a sincere desire on the part of the Roosevelt administration to come to an eleventh-hour defence of the Filipino people, the agreed Germany first strategy (see RAINBOW PLANS) dictated that the USA concentrate its resources elsewhere. Though MacArthur agitated for reinforcements and for swift counter-blows against Japan, Roosevelt refused to take the risks necessary to relieve the Philippine garrison. A small amount of supplies were slipped by submarine past the Japanese ships that now controlled the waters around Luzon, but the major effort required to break through to the Philippines appeared too dangerous. Roosevelt told MacArthur to negotiate the surrender of Filipino troops under his command if and when surrender seemed necessary; as for the US troops, they should hold out as long as there existed any possibility of resistance.

Roosevelt's decision not to attempt to rescue the American and Filipino units on Bataan and Corregidor effectively sealed their fate. The only question was how long they could fight. The answer was: until 9 April for the Bataan forces, and until 6 May for the troops on Corregidor. MacArthur, on Roosevelt's orders, left Corregidor by PT boat on 12 March, and after switching to a B17 in Mindanao continued to Australia.

Between the spring of 1942 and the autumn of 1944, various resistance groups in the Philippines kept up the fight against the Japanese occupiers. The guerrillas included US and Filipino officers and men who had eluded capture, communists and other radical elements, and various individuals outraged by Japan's heavy-handed treatment of the civilian population of the country. The guerrillas did not seriously threaten Japanese control of the islands, but they made the *occupation more costly than it otherwise would have been, they sustained the morale of those who refused to reconcile themselves to the occupation, and they provided intelligence to Allied forces outside the country.

This intelligence proved extremely valuable when the reconquest of the archipelago began. In July 1944, as the Allies fought towards Japan, American officials met in Hawaii to determine how best to tighten the noose around Tokyo. Admiral *King, the chief of naval operations, advocated bypassing the Philippines and moving directly against Formosa. MacArthur dissented vigorously, contending both that the Philippines were strategically vital and that the USA owed a moral obligation to the Filipino people to liberate their home as soon as humanly possible. MacArthur won the argument, and Roosevelt ordered implementation of plans for an invasion of the Philippines.

In September 1944, American carrier-based airplanes started to bomb Japanese airfields in central Luzon. The planes initially achieved a large measure of surprise, and in short order they crippled some 400 Japanese aircraft. Soon the Americans enjoyed effective control of the air over the Philippines, although Japanese reinforcements succeeded in contesting that control.

In mid-October MacArthur orchestrated the gathering of a huge invasion fleet east of the Visayan Islands for the invasion of Leyte Island. The force comprised more than 700 ships carrying hundreds of planes and some 160,000 men. At dawn on 20 October the group's battleships, cruisers, and destroyers announced the main assault with a four-hour barrage against Japanese positions on and behind the beach. At 1000 four divisions went ashore, where they met only light resistance. By evening they had secured a beachhead and captured an airstrip close by.

During the next few days, as the Americans landed more troops and equipment and expanded their foothold, the Japanese dispatched a large fleet of their own towards Leyte. Beginning on 24 October American and Japanese ships fought out the greatest duel in naval history. The battle of *Leyte Gulf ended in a decisive Japanese defeat, virtually assuring American success in the effort to liberate the Philippines.

But success was not quick in coming. General *Yamashita, the recently appointed commander of Japanese forces in the Philippines, dispatched some 50,000 fresh troops to Leyte and, with aircraft flown in from Japan and Formosa, mounted a series of aerial assaults on the American positions on the island. MacArthur responded with a landing at Ormoc on Leyte's west coast, outflanking the defenders and subsequently splitting the Japanese forces in two. As they had done elsewhere in the Pacific, the Japanese fought bitterly and to the last. During the next several weeks 80,000 Japanese troops were killed; fewer than 1,000 surrendered.

By the end of December, American forces had secured Leyte and were looking across the San Bernardino Strait to Luzon. MacArthur sent a task force to Mindoro, with the goal of capturing airfields for use in support of landings on Luzon and of the drive to Manila. The Mindoro landing met only modest resistance, and in a short time the Americans had two airfields operating.

MacArthur, in the hope that Yamashita was expecting an attack from the south, now circled to the north. In the second week of January 1945 he dispatched an invasion force to Lingayen Gulf on Luzon from Leyte. Yamashita was not entirely surprised: Japanese forces detected the invasion fleet moving up the Luzon coast and did significant damage to it. But they were outnumbered and outgunned, the Americans got ashore in good shape, and other, smaller, landings followed.

In the following few weeks, the main US force traced the route the Japanese had traversed three years before in their march against Manila. Like MacArthur in that earlier campaign, Yamashita chose not to make a stand against the superior invading force on the central Luzon plain. Instead he dispersed his units and withdrew towards the mountains.

But, unlike the Americans earlier, the Japanese contested the taking of Manila. The battle for the capital lasted nearly a month and was marked by the heaviest destruction of the war in the Philippines. As Japanese troops shortened their defensive perimeter, they blew up bridges, military facilities, and caches of supplies; in the process, and deliberately, they set fire to many of the city's wood-and-thatch civilian structures. The flames ravaged large areas, killing thousands and displacing tens of thousands more. Though MacArthur forbade air attacks against the city (which had been his home for much of his adult life) heavy artillery barrages by both sides levelled much of what the fires had left standing. By 3 March, when the last Japanese resistance had been suppressed, most of the city was in ruins. Approximately 1,000 American soldiers died in the battle, roughly 16,000 Japanese, and as many as 100,000 Filipinos, nearly all non-combatants.

While the fighting for Manila continued, American forces worked to root out Japanese troops on Bataan and Corregidor, which threatened the approaches to Manila Bay. Retaking Bataan involved heavy casualties, as US officers misjudged the strength of the Japanese defenders, but the job was accomplished by the end of February. Corregidor fell to the joint efforts of marines and paratroops at about the same time. Although the American attackers surprised the Japanese troops holding the fortress, the latter managed to detonate the large stockpiles of munitions they had placed in the island's tunnels. The concussion killed hundreds of Japanese and dozens of Americans, and hurled debris more than a kilometre into the harbour.

The final several months of the *Pacific war saw American regulars and Filipino guerrillas steadily reducing the area controlled by the Japanese. Yamashita, knowing he could expect no help now that the Allies were closing in on the Japanese home islands, fought a capable delaying campaign. He retreated into the rugged terrain near Baguio and required the Americans to fight their way up narrow passes and through precipitous gorges. He gave ground, but not without inflicting sizeable losses and tying down troops that might have been used elsewhere. The war ended in August with Japanese troops still at large along the River Asin.

Recapturing the rest of the Philippine archipelago proceeded more swiftly. The Eighth US Army, led by Lt-General *Eichelberger and benefiting from American air and naval supremacy in the area, conducted *amphibious warfare operations against Japanese positions throughout the southern islands. Although some Japanese troops continued to hold out until August, by June 1945 the most important towns, roads, and airfields were once again in Allied hands. H. W. Brands

Breuer, W., *Retaking the Philippines* (New York, 1986).
Morton, L., *The Fall of the Philippines* (Washington, DC, 1953).
Morison, S. E., *Leyte: June 1944–June 1945* (Boston, 1958).

Philippine Sea, battle of. This, the war's biggest carrier battle, took place in June 1944. It was fought during the *Pacific war between Admiral *Spruance's Fifth US Fleet—whose *Task Force 58, under Vice-Admiral Marc Mitscher, was protecting American landings on *Saipan—and the First Japanese Mobile Fleet commanded by Vice-Admiral *Ozawa.

Admiral *Toyoda, the Japanese fleet's C-in-C, had formulated a plan (see A-GŌ) for the destruction of the US fleet if the Americans invaded Saipan, and on 13 June he ordered it to begin. 'The fate of the Empire rests on this one battle,' he said, echoing Admiral Tōgō Heihachirō's order before the famous Japanese naval victory of Tsushima against the Russian fleet in 1905. 'Everyone must give all he has.'

But A-GŌ had fallen into American hands and when the two groups of Japanese warships were detected by US submarines and Spruance refused to be drawn towards Ozawa, as the Japanese had intended. Instead he waited for the fleet to come to him. In preliminary skirmishes 17 out of the 25 Japanese submarines committed were sunk and Japanese airfields in the area were heavily attacked. All this disposed of A-GŌ's assumption that submarines and land-based aircraft, *shuttle bombing between the fleet and Japanese airfields on *Tinian and *Guam, would destroy at least a third of the Fifth US Fleet before it was brought to battle.

The disparity between the two forces was marked.

	American	Japanese
Carrier aircraft	956	473
Carriers	7	5
Light carriers	8	4
Battleships	7	5
Heavy cruisers	8	11
Light cruisers	13	2
Destroyers	69	28

Despite his inferior strength, Ozawa was confident of victory, for his air reconnaissance spotted the US carrier groups before they spotted him. This enabled him to keep out of range of US aircraft, but still launch his own because the trade winds were blowing to his advantage, and his aircraft had greater endurance and could use airfields to rearm and refuel. But Ozawa had broken radio silence to contact his land-based aircraft and *huff-duff pinpointed his position for Spruance. Although a search failed to find the Japanese fleet US *radar detected the first of Ozawa's four strikes at 250 km. (150 mi.) when it was launched at 0830 on 19 June 1944. As American fighter strength had not been dissipated by attacking the Japanese fleet, and dawn raids had destroyed the last of Ozawa's land-based *air power, the better-trained US pilots—aided by radar and radio intelligence which monitored the voice of the Japanese pilot co-ordinating the attacks—were easily able to break up the Japanese attacks. Out of the 373 aircraft Ozawa dispatched only 130 returned. The fighting then switched to the skies over Guam where the Japanese lost about 50 more.

A Japanese carrier division under air attack during the **battle of the Philippine Sea**, June 1944. The large carrier is the *Zuikaku*.

While this air battle (which later became known to the Americans as 'The Great Marianas Turkey Shoot') was raging US submarines made a notable contribution of their own, torpedoing Ozawa's new flagship, the carrier *Taiho*, and another fleet carrier, *Shōkaku*.

That night Task Force 58, which had so far only lost 29 aircraft, set out in pursuit of the retreating Japanese fleet, and the next afternoon American air reconnaissance caught its first proper sight of Ozawa's force since the start of the battle. Although it was late—which meant recovering his planes at night—and the Japanese ships were at the limit of his range, Mitscher immediately launched a strike of 216 aircraft. This sank the carrier *Hiyu* and damaged two others, and Ozawa, now aboard another carrier, was left with just 35 planes. Only 20 US aircraft failed to return, but 80 more were lost when they ran out of fuel and ditched, or crash-landed on their carriers' decks in the dark. Nearly all the crews were recovered but rescue work delayed any further pursuit which Spruance then abandoned, though he later said he felt he had missed a prime opportunity to destroy what remained of the Japanese fleet. But historians have not judged him harshly, for his overriding responsibility was to protect the amphibious landings on Saipan, and this he successfully accomplished. See also SEA POWER.

Y'Blood, W., *Red Sun Setting* (Annapolis, Md., 1980).

phoney war, US newspaper description of that period of military inactivity which followed the Anglo-French declaration of war on Germany on 3 September 1939. To the British it was also the Bore War—Churchill called it the Twilight War—while the French described it as *la drôle de guerre* and the Germans as the *Sitzkrieg*.

France and the UK honoured their obligations to Poland (see POLAND, GUARANTEE OF) by declaring war, but neither did anything significant to support the Poles militarily. Indeed, they did little to distract Hitler during the five weeks his forces took to complete their *Polish campaign. The French C-in-C, *Gamelin, like the whole French Army, was in a defensive frame of mind. No attempt was made to shell the industrialized Saar, well within the range of French heavy artillery, and Gamelin did little more than probe the German *West Wall around Saarbrücken (see Map 87) where it was reported that captured German soldiers were unaware that France and the UK were at war with their country. This inactivity had a bad effect on the morale of the French Army which was

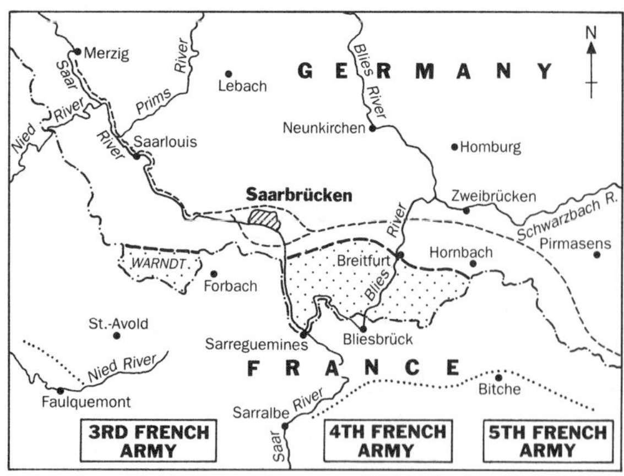

87. **Phoney war**: French offensive into Germany, September 1939

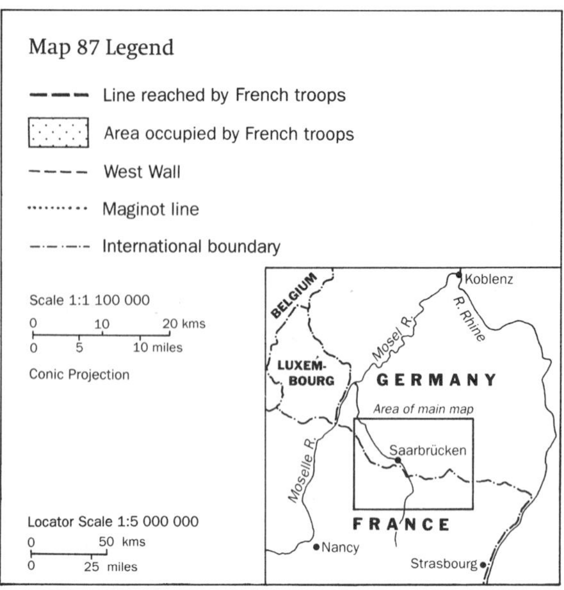

to become only too evident when the fighting started in earnest in the spring.

British policy was equally timid. Retaliatory air raids on British cities were feared, and many politicians were still so dominated by peacetime attitudes that when, on 5 September 1939, Leo Amery asked Kingsley Wood, the secretary of state for air, why an attempt should not be made to set the Black Forest alight (vetoed on the grounds that it conflicted with the spirit of the *Hague Convention) he was told that 'there was no question of our bombing even the munition works at Essen, which were private property' (L. Amery, *My Political Life*, Vol. 3, London, 1955, p. 330). British aircraft were sent to attack German shipping at Wilhelmshaven, but no bombs were dropped on German territory while *Chamberlain was prime minister, and on land the *British Expeditionary Force confined its offensive operations to patrolling. Churchill, first lord of the Admiralty at the time, wanted to float air-dropped fluvial mines down the Rhine, but when the matter was discussed in the *Supreme War Council the French were adamant that this operation (ROYAL MARINE) should not proceed. The French prime minister, *Daladier, told Churchill that the 'President of the Republic himself had intervened, and that no aggressive action must be taken which might only draw reprisals upon France' (W. S. Churchill, *The Second World War: The Gathering Storm*, London, 1948, p. 518). The idea of not irritating the enemy, wrote Churchill after the war, 'did not commend itself to me' (ibid.), but the operation took place only after the Germans had launched their offensive in the west in May 1940 (see FALL GELB).

Only on the open ocean did hostilities immediately become apparent: the liner **Athenia* was torpedoed within hours of war being declared; the British battleship **Royal Oak* was sunk in October 1939; the German pocket battleship *Admiral Graf Spee* was scuttled in December 1939 after the *River Plate battle; and the German *auxiliary cruisers soon made their presence known on the high seas. These events brought home to the British public the intensity of the war at sea, but they had no direct effect on the civilian population, whose mood of determination to meet an immediate attack soon changed to boredom, bewilderment, and resentment at the disruption of the *blackout, rationing, and the evacuation of *children, all of which had been imposed on them for no apparent reason. To increase their irritation more emergency laws were passed in the first two weeks of the war than had been passed in the first year of the *First World War.

Of course the phoney war was not created by the Allies alone. It was encouraged by the Germans, too. The first bombs to be dropped on the UK fell on the Shetland Islands on 13 November 1939, but it was not until December 1939 that the British suffered their first service fatality in France. By contrast 50,000 British servicemen had been lost during the first three months of the First World War. And it was not until 16 March 1940 that the first British civilian was killed, during an air raid on Scapa Flow. Initially, it gave Hitler time to finish the Polish campaign undisturbed and though he then wanted to attack westwards before the end of 1939, the German High Command, which included several conspirators against him (see SCHWARZE KAPELLE), lacked any such enthusiasm. Like many in France and the UK, General *Jodl, the head of operations at Hitler's Armed Forces High Command, thought that the war would die a natural death if the Germans kept quiet in the west. But it was mainly bad weather, not the Führer's opponents, which allowed the phoney war to continue through the first winter of the war, and the Sitzkrieg did not end until Hitler launched his *Norwegian campaign on 9 April 1940. Even then, according to Leo Amery, RAF aircraft were initially ordered not to bomb German-held airfields, only to machine-gun them.

Turner, E., *The Phoney War* (London, 1961).

photographic reconnaissance (PR) was, next to *signals intelligence warfare, the primary source of intelligence during the Second World War. As early as 1938 the commander-in-chief of the German Army, General von *Fritsch, stated that 'the country with the best reconnaissance will win the next war' and it has been said that 'The American armed Services could not take a step and could not fire a shot without photographs and the maps that were created from them.' (S. Moeller, *Shooting War*, New York, 1989, p. 192). In the UK PR was initially developed by Group Captain F. Winterbotham within *MI6, the British Secret Intelligence Service. In September 1938 he approached an Australian businessman, Sidney Cotton, who dealt in a new type of film. Cotton agreed to fly an aircraft fitted with cameras for his business trips to Germany and Italy. Between them they pioneered new techniques in aerial photography which were used to good effect when war came and the RAF assumed control of all PR.

In the light of Cotton's experiments the RAF was quickly forced to abandon its pre-war belief that PR could be undertaken by any competent pilot flying existing aircraft. Instead, they developed the use of fast unarmed aircraft (mainly Spitfires and Mosquitoes) to fly high-altitude sorties which avoided enemy defences. The RAF also adapted armed single-engined fighters for low-level reconnaissance in preference to the vulnerable Lysander light aircraft with which it entered the war. The RAF eventually established a separate PR group, for strategic reconnaissance, and dedicated wings for the tactical role. The tactical wings were allocated mobile processing units to provide rapid interpretation facilities on a large scale—the units of 84 Group alone produced 4.5 million prints between the Normandy landings on 6 June 1944 (see OVERLORD) and the end of the war in Europe.

Interpretation of strategic PR was undertaken by a Central Interpretation Unit (CIU) at RAF Medmenham, later to become an Allied unit (ACIU). When a PR sortie landed the film was developed at the airfield and selected prints were interpreted immediately. The film was then transferred to the ACIU for 'second phase interpretation', where a more detailed general analysis was produced within 48 hours. Third phase interpretation then took place in specialist sections, each of which was trained to look for more specific information on a particular subject, such as airfields.

The interpretation of photographs at the ACIU relied heavily on stereoscopic techniques which reproduced a three-dimensional image from a two-dimensional photograph, by mimicking the human brain's merging of twin images. Each camera was automatically set to take photographs with a 60% overlap of the previous print and two prints could be arranged side-by-side to produce a single image when viewed through a stereoscopic magnifier. The aircraft's forward momentum caused a difference in the angle at which the two photographs had been taken, and this gave the appearance of a 3-D image when viewed through the stereoscope, which was of great benefit in enabling the interpreter to identify objects and pick out important detail. Difficulties caused by the blurring of images on low-level photographs as a result of the aircraft's forward movement were overcome by using cine film in forward-facing cameras with the pilot flying directly at the target.

The vertical cameras in RAF aircraft were usually mounted in pairs at a slight angle to cover twice the ground in one pass and give a 10% sideways overlap. Later in the war forward-facing oblique cameras were mounted on each wingtip to give stereoscopic low-level cover. The RAF was hampered early in the war by having cameras with short focal length lenses, which gave small-scale prints and made interpretation difficult. Gradually bigger cameras were introduced with larger lenses and a greater number of exposures. In 1942 cameras were introduced capable of producing photographs of 1/10,000 scale from 9,150 m. (30,000 ft.): a scale suitable for detailed interpretation.

The intelligence available from the photographs was used in planning by all three services. Bomber Command's operations over Europe relied on PR cover for pre-raid briefings and post-raid assessment of results (see also BUTT REPORT). Later in the war, when oil and transportation targets were being systematically attacked, PR cover was essential. Sorties were also regularly flown on behalf of the navy, to establish the whereabouts of German naval and merchant shipping. During the campaign against the *V-weapons PR provided intelligence on their development, including dimensions, and the location of the launching sites. Between 1 May 1943 and 31 March 1944, 40% of all Allied PR sorties were directed against the V-weapons programme, and a total of 1.25 million photographs were taken. PR also provided vital information on German *radar and anti-aircraft defences for Bomber Command and others. Centralized interpretation, regular coverage, and integration with other intelligence allowed interpreters to identify interesting or unusual developments for further investigation.

When the USA entered the war the Americans quickly recognized the merits of the British system, and adopted it for their own use. Interpretation for the US Army Air Forces (USAAF) strategic offensive was concentrated at Medmenham in an integrated unit. As with other nations in the pre-war period, the USA had short-range reconnaissance units equipped with slow and obsolescent aircraft, and longer range PR was to be undertaken by bomber aircraft equipped with suitable cameras. Drawing on British experience the Americans were quick to adapt the P38 Lightning and P51 Mustang as reconnaissance aircraft. In the *Pacific war, where distances were greater and the opposition less formidable, the USAAF also used reconnaissance versions of the B24 and B29 to provide strategic cover for the war with Japan.

In the two years which followed the Japanese attack on *Pearl Harbor in December 1941, US airmen, using a camera which could take an area 48 by 14.5 km. (30 by 9 mi.) in one shot, mapped 21 million square kilometres (8 million square miles) of the earth's surface. This was done at high altitude, but they also flew at 100 m. (300 ft.) with continuous-strip cameras to map invasion beaches and, using flashlight bombs which generated a billion candlepower, they were able to photograph Japanese movements at night. The results were so detailed that it was possible to identify ships by name and new aircraft types on the ground. So valuable was PR to US forces in the Pacific that the commanding general of the USAAF, General *Arnold, commented that 'a camera mounted on a P38 (Lightning fighter) often has proved to be of more value than a P38 with guns' (Moeller, p. 192).

The Luftwaffe had entered the war with some 80 reconnaissance squadrons, and a similar approach to the Allies. Tactical units were equipped with the Henschel Hs126, similar to the Lysander. Longer-range PR squadrons were equipped with the Dornier Do17F, or the Junkers Ju88D. The Luftwaffe also developed the high-altitude Ju86P, which operated in limited numbers over the UK, the Middle East, and the USSR. The Luftwaffe also followed the Allies in deploying reconnaissance versions of single-engined fighters. However, with the exception of the unarmed but slow Ju86P, the Luftwaffe never adopted the Allied philosophy of removing the armament to increase range and performance, and flying high-altitude profiles. Hence, when air superiority was lost, as it was over the UK, PR was severely restricted or non-existent. This meant a lack of comparative cover, which was dependent on repeated sorties, and the photographs obtained were often of limited value. Once the British produced fighters capable of downing the pressurized Ju86Ps in 1942, Luftwaffe PR in the west became almost totally ineffective.

On the Eastern Front, Luftwaffe long-range PR continued to operate, and utilizing short-range aircraft such as Focke Wulf Fw189s, Fw190s, or Messerschmitt Bf109s, tactical reconnaissance remained effective until much later in the war. However, German PR was hamstrung by organizational weakness. Each *Luftflotte* HQ was responsible for all PR and interpretation in its area, and co-ordination was often poor. Furthermore, although there was a central photographic unit, interpretation was decentralized, and interpreters seldom rose above the rank of senior NCO. As a result interpretation often took the form of searching only for the information which had been specifically requested. Little detailed analysis comparable with the ACIU's third phase interpretation was undertaken and, because of the lowly status of the work, interpreters were frequently unaware of the intelligence available from other sources which would have assisted their interpretation. In addition the Germans tended to use larger and heavier, though technically excellent, cameras, and they never developed the range of cameras and techniques employed by the Allies. German interpreters often worked from negatives, which meant that they could not use stereoscopic techniques and their work lacked detail. Therefore, while tactical and topographical PR was adequate strategic reconnaissance frequently was not. As a result German intelligence in such areas as Allied preparations for OVERLORD, the accuracy of the V-weapon bombardment, and the whereabouts of British capital ships was frequently poor. Misled by their early success, the Germans never developed the philosophy or equipment to emulate British success in the face of enemy air superiority.

In the USSR much emphasis had been laid on the importance of PR in pre-war manuals, but in 1941 the gap between theory and practice proved immense. As with other countries the Soviets rapidly discovered that obsolescent aircraft such as the Polikarpov Po2s were too vulnerable. The first Soviet unit equipped with the more effective Petlyakov Pe2 was not formed until November 1941. German air superiority and poor Soviet aircraft and equipment meant that little effective PR could be performed for some time, and the absence of trained interpreters before April 1942 also severely hampered their efforts.

As the war went on and the aircraft, equipment, and personnel improved, so did Soviet effectiveness. Concentrating almost exclusively on reconnoitring German army dispositions within 800 km. (500 mi.) of the front line, the Soviets concentrated on roads, railways, and military dumps and concentrations. By the later phases of the war such areas on the axes of a Soviet advance would be photographed several times before any attack. Even so progress was slow and the Soviets remained heavily reliant on visual observation. During the *Kursk operations in 1943 only 40% of Soviet reconnaissance flights were capable of taking photographs. However, by the end of the war Soviet PR units were capable of providing effective intelligence. The proportion of PR to visual reconnaissance rose from 10% in 1941 to 87% in 1945 and during the course of the war Soviet pilots photographed 6.5 million square kilometres (2.5 million square miles) of land.

By 1945 PR had become far more advanced both technically and in its ability to provide intelligence. Among the operations to which it contributed vital intelligence were the *Bruneval raid, the *Peenemünde raid, the OVERLORD landings (before which more than 4,500 PR sorties were flown), and the Allied *strategic air offensives. On the Eastern Front first the Germans, and then the Soviets, used it to assess the opposing defences, often with great accuracy. SEBASTIAN COX

Brookes, A., *Photo Reconnaissance* (Shepperton, 1975).

PIAT, or Projector Infantry Anti-Tank, a British hand-held spigot weapon which was developed by *MD1 and went into production in mid-1942 (see Figure). It fired a shaped

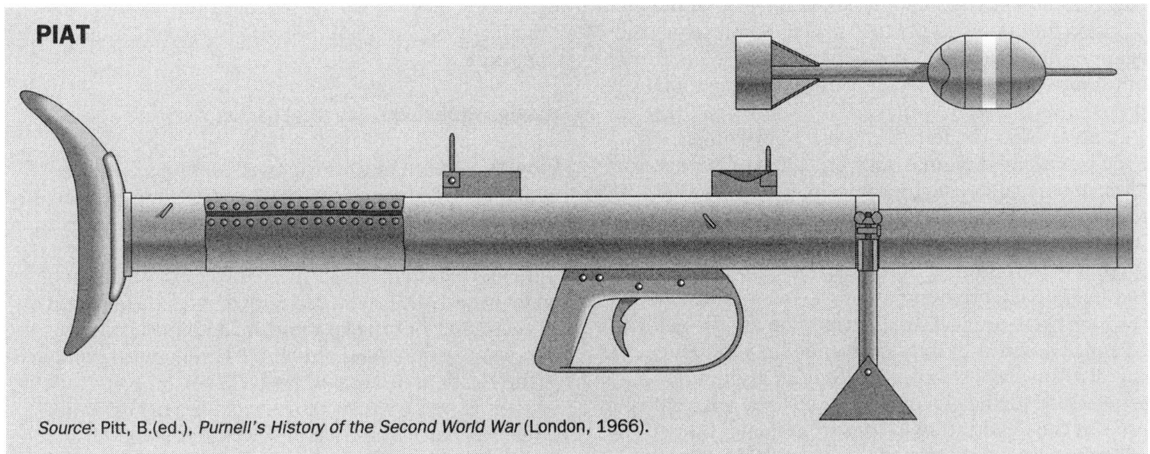

Source: Pitt, B.(ed.), *Purnell's History of the Second World War* (London, 1966).

charge (see EXPLOSIVES) round with fins to stabilize it, and was effective up to 90 m. (100 yd.). See ROCKET WEAPONS for other hand-held *anti-tank weapons.

pip-squeak transmissions, radio signal emitted from British fighters so that their position could be fixed by Fighter Command's direction-finding (d/f) stations. Ground control could then vector the fighters into the correct position to intercept Axis aircraft which had been detected by *radar. The signal was normally emitted by one fighter in each section of three. See also IFF.

Pius XII (1876–1958). Born in Rome, Cardinal Eugenio Pacelli was elected Pope in March 1939, having previously served as papal nuncio in Germany from 1917 to 1930, and as Vatican secretary of state from 1930. His wartime stance remains a matter of controversy, considerably reinforced by Rolf Hochhuth's slanderous but influential play *Der Stellvertreter* (*The Representative*, 1963) in which Pius is accused of having refused to do anything to save the Jews (see FINAL SOLUTION). In more muted criticism, the UK's wartime minister to the *Vatican wrote that the Pope's neutrality had been 'meticulous and seemingly pusillanimous' but that he and his advisers 'reckon in centuries and plan for eternity and this inevitably renders their policy inscrutable, confusing, and on occasion reprehensible to practical and time-conditioned minds' (O. Chadwick, *Britain and the Vatican during the Second World War*, Cambridge, 1986, pp. 315–16).

Three elements are discernible in the wartime pontificate: the traditional Catholic ideological objection to all forms of totalitarian secular power, especially atheistic *communism with which no accommodation was seen as possible; the prime endeavour to stop the war and its attendant horrors by persuading the belligerents to seek a negotiated peace; and, in the face of *atrocities, balancing the good that might come from condemnation of evil against the danger of thereby provoking further horrors—as in fact occurred in May 1943 when the Dutch Catholic bishops, in issuing a pastoral letter condemning the deportation of Jews, provoked the immediate arrest and deportation of Dutch Jews who had been baptized as Catholics, while Protestant Jews were spared.

Pacelli was an experienced diplomat who, as secretary of state, had felt forced to accede to the 1933 concordat offered by the Nazi government. His motive was to secure a legal basis for opposing the subsequent anti-Church measures which he foresaw as clearly as he anticipated Hitler's repeated violations of its terms. He had played a major role in drafting the three encyclicals of his predecessor against *fascism, Nazism, and communism. His efforts to arrange a peace conference before the outbreak of war failed; and repeated calls for peace subsequently were ignored by both sides. Not surprisingly, he later deplored the Allied policy of *unconditional surrender which, no less than Axis ambitions, made a negotiated settlement an unrealistic aim. His very first encyclical, *Summi Pontificatus* (October. 1939), though couched in the traditionally generalized language of the Roman Curia, condemned the political and religious policies of the German and Soviet governments in Poland and the Baltic States.

In early 1940 the Pope allowed Vatican officials, including his own personal private secretary, a German Jesuit, to act as intermediaries between anti-Nazi conspirators and the Allies (see X-REPORT), but to no avail. In 1941 he refused to declare the German invasion of the USSR a crusade (see BARBAROSSA), a stance which did not surprise Hitler but enraged Mussolini. In praising the courageous and influential sermons against the Nazi *euthanasia programme delivered in 1941 by Clemens August von Galen, the bishop of Münster, he maintained that national episcopates and the local clergy were best placed to judge when speaking out would be the effective course. Though strongly urged to do so by the Italians, he refused to condemn the Allied *area bombing which caused such high civilian casualties. The Allies for their part pressed hard for a public condemnation of the *Final Solution and in his 1942 Christmas radio message, and again in June 1943, the Pope deplored it in generalized but unmistakable terms that infuriated the Germans but failed to satisfy the Allies.

In areas where he felt he could achieve something, the Pope was active diplomatically on behalf of *refugees and Jews, in particular using what influence he had with Italy to help Jews in Italian-occupied parts of Yugoslavia, and in July 1944 petitioning Admiral *Horthy to prevent further deportations of Hungarian Jews to *Auschwitz. He supervised a programme for the relief of war victims through the Pontifical Aid Commission and, when Hitler occupied Rome after Italy's surrender in September 1943, the *Vatican City became effectively an asylum for refugees. Nevertheless, in October 1943 he was unable to prevent the deportation of Jews from Rome, though the majority were saved, many being given hiding in Church property and in the Vatican itself. In 1944 as the Allies advanced on Rome during the *Italian Campaign, the Pope made impassioned pleas for the city with its priceless heritage to be spared Allied bombing, and when Rome was liberated in June 1944 he was hailed by the people as 'defender of the city'—though in fact the Allies had refused to give any undertakings. Towards the end of the war, Pius denounced the concept of national collective guilt, whilst emphasizing the need for a proper legal basis for the punishment of individuals. He warned against imposing on Germany a permanent state of subjection without hope of a new future. In June 1945 he uttered an apologia for his policy towards Nazism, claiming that his radio messages had in fact been the only effective way both to uphold moral principles before world opinion and to maintain among German Catholics the ideals of truth and justice in a situation of over-whelming evil and violence (*Acta Apolostolicae Sedis* XXXVII, 159–68). See also RELIGION and DIPLOMACY.

NICHOLAS COOTE

Holmes, J. D., *The Papacy in the Modern World 1914–1978* (Tunbridge Wells, 1981).
Michaelis, M., *Mussolini and the Jews: German–Italian Relations and the Jewish Question in Italy 1922–1945* (Oxford, 1978).

Placentia Bay conference, held from 9 to 12 August 1941 by Churchill and Roosevelt, and their respective advisers. It took place aboard the US cruiser *Augusta* and the British battle-cruiser *Prince of Wales*, as they lay anchored off the Newfoundland coast. The *Atlantic Charter was agreed upon and published; a note was drafted which threatened Japan with joint action if it continued to act aggressively; and a joint telegram was sent to Stalin suggesting the *Three-Power conference. Though the draft note to Japan was a watered-down version of Churchill's original text, Cordell *Hull, the US secretary of state, called it 'dangerously strong' and the one eventually received by the Japanese ambassador was practically meaningless. See also DIPLOMACY and GRAND ALLIANCE.

plastic explosives, see EXPLOSIVES.

Ploesti, Romanian town situated north of Bucharest, which provided as much as 60% of Germany's crude oil supply (see also RAW MATERIALS); about 40 refineries, producing some 400,000 tons of refined petrol annually, were located there. It was first attacked by Soviet bombers on 23 June 1941. It was also raided by 12 US bombers on 12 June 1942, but the best known, and most controversial, raid was the one mounted by 178 US Liberator bombers of the North Africa-based Ninth USAAF on 1 August 1943. By then Ploesti was one of the most heavily defended targets in Europe, and surprise was not achieved as the Germans were reading Ninth USAAF's codes. When the mission's top two navigators were shot down before arriving at the target confusion followed: 54 bombers were lost, 41 of them in action, and 532 of their crews were either killed, wounded, or made *prisoners-of-war. It was the only American air action of the war in which five Congressional Medals of Honor (see DECORATIONS) were awarded.

The raid destroyed 42% of Ploesti's total capacity, but it had only been running at 60% capacity and within weeks was producing at a higher rate than before the raid. However, attacks on the town continued and in April 1944 a campaign was started against it by Fifteenth USAAF based in Italy which, by the time the Red Army arrived there in August, had totally destroyed all its installations.

Dugan, J., and Stewart, C., *Ploesti* (London, 1963).

PLUTO, acronym derived from the phrase Pipe Line Under The Ocean. Experiments began in 1942 by the British HQ, *Combined Operations, to find a means of pumping petrol through flexible pipes laid across the floor of the English Channel. A trial pipe was laid across the Bristol Channel and four pipes, unwound from large drums (CONUNDRUMS) towed by tugs, were laid from the Isle of Wight to Cherbourg when the port was captured after the Normandy landings in June 1944 (see OVERLORD). In January 1945 another 16 pipes were laid from Dungeness to Ambleteuse, delivering up to 4,000 gallons a day. During the assault phase of the Normandy landings (see OVERLORD) petrol was pumped ashore from tankers direct to storage tanks by means of buoyed pipe lines, an operation codenamed TOMBOLA. The British terminus was at Port-en-Bessin, the American at St Honorine.

poetry, see culture section of major powers.

POL stood for petrol, oil, lubricants.

POLAND

For the fighting in Poland in September–October 1939, see POLISH CAMPAIGN.

1. Introduction

Hitler's attack upon Poland was the immediate cause of the outbreak of the Second World War. It remained an occupied country throughout the hostilities and suffered incomparably both from the campaigns which were waged on its soil and from the harsh policies of the occupying regimes. There were more than 6 million casualties in a population of 35 million. Hundreds of thousands of Polish citizens were subject to involuntary uprooting and transfer (see also DEPORTATIONS). The physical damage included more than half a million homes destroyed (see Table 1).

When, on 15 March 1939, German troops marched into Bohemia and Moravia, completing the Nazi annexation of Czechoslovakia, it was only a matter of time before Poland became Hitler's next victim. Within days of the seizure of Prague, German diplomats in their talks with the Poles had renewed their demands for the incorporation of Danzig into the Reich and for an extraterritorial road and rail link with East Prussia. The Poles rejected the German demands. Shortly afterwards the British government offered the Polish foreign minister, Józef *Beck, an alliance. The British move was calculated to warn Hitler against any further aggressive moves in east–central Europe. On 31 March, *Chamberlain, declared that the UK would guarantee Poland's independence and promised aid (see POLAND, GUARANTEE OF). Later in the year, on 25 August, a Mutual Assistance Pact was signed between the two states.

Hitler, enraged by the Poles' defiance and by their decision to turn to the British for support, denounced the 1934 German–Polish Non-Aggression Pact. At the end of May 1939 he outlined to German commanders the plan to attack Poland in order to create **Lebensraum* (living-space) for the German people in the east. Aware that such a move would risk conflict with the UK, and with France which had an alliance with Poland dating from 1921, Hitler attempted to determine what the Soviet position would be if hostilities broke out.

During the summer of 1939 Stalin was courted as an ally both by Berlin and by London and Paris in tandem. In the end Hitler's offer of territorial gains overcame any ideological scruples Stalin may have had. On 23 August the *Nazi–Soviet Pact was concluded in Moscow. Though it was called a non-aggression pact, it was a blueprint for aggression—against Poland and other states. By assuring Hitler that the USSR would not join forces with the Poles and their western allies against him, it effectively paved the way for war.

On the morning of 1 September 1939, without a declaration of war and on false claims that Poland was infringing German territory (see GLEIWITZ), Hitler's forces invaded Poland on a wide front. Pitching superior numbers of troops and armour, and greater mobility, against a stubborn but out-gunned defence, this brought speedy results; and, when Red Army troops crossed into eastern Poland on the morning of 17 September, the Poles' situation, already desperate, became hopeless. Although the Soviet move had been anticipated in secret protocols attached to the Nazi–Soviet Pact, it came as a complete surprise to the Poles and their allies. Poland had a Non-Aggression Pact with the USSR dating from 1932. Confusion was deepened by Soviet claims to be neutral and to be intervening merely to safeguard fellow Slavs—the Belorussian and Ukrainian communities in Poland. Despite Soviet attempts to disguise their aggression, the Polish authorities were to consider themselves in a state of war with the Soviet Union, as well as with Germany, until June 1941.

With the meeting of German and Soviet troops in central Poland, the occupying powers had to give thought to the future shape of the region. Plans for the creation of a residual Polish 'puppet' state were quickly abandoned and the demarcation line originally agreed was changed in Germany's favour. Instead of running along the River Vistula, the line would now run along the River Bug, some 150 km. (93 mi.) to the east. Stalin conceded a large area of central Poland in return for German recognition of a dominant Soviet interest in Lithuania. This new arrangement was sealed in Moscow on 28 September (German–Soviet Treaty of Friendship, Co-operation, and Demarcation), at which time the partitioning powers expressed their determination to combat all forms of Polish resistance and warned Britain and France against prolonging hostilities.

2. Domestic life and government

(a) *Pre-occupation government*

On the eve of the Second Word War the Polish government was controlled by the followers of Marshal J. Piłsudski (1867–1935), the dominant figure in inter-war Polish politics, who had assumed quasi-dictatorial powers following a coup in 1926. After his death, his followers in the so-called 'Sanacja' (the word denotes 'cleansing') regime continued to rule in his name. The four most important political parties—the Christian Democrats (Ch.D.), Peasant Party (SL), the Polish Socialist Party (PPS), and the right-wing National Party (SD)—were all in opposition. On the fringes of political life were the Communist Party (KPP), whose following was extremely small, and the National Radical Camp (ONR), an extreme right-wing grouping hostile to the communists and to the non-Polish minority groups.

President and head of state in 1939 was Ignacy Mościcki (1867–1946), a former colleague of Piłsudski's from his early days with the Polish Socialist Party. The government had a distinctively military flavour; the prime minister was a doctor and professional soldier, General Felicjan Sławój-Składkowski (1885–1962), and the foreign minister was Colonel Józef Beck. The Sanacja regime had become increasingly authoritarian and intolerant of dissent in the course of the 1930s. It monopolized the process of political decision-making and refused to allow other parties any kind of voice. Several of the Sanacja's more determined opponents were jailed. Others went into exile. Even when war was seen to be inevitable, in the spring of 1939, the suggestion by opposition parties that a government of national unity should be formed was rejected by the Sanacja. When war came, Poles were prepared, through love for their country, to rally to the national cause, but in the wake of the September 1939 defeat recriminations were bitter and persistent. The debates and divisions created around the figure of Piłsudski and the Sanacja government continued to bedevil Polish politics into exile.

On 18 September the Polish government crossed the southern border into Romania, where it was interned. Accompanying it were the president, Mościcki, and the C-in-C of Polish forces, Marshal Edward Śmigły-Rydz (1886–1941). The latter ordered his troops to seek sanctuary on the territory of neutral states and try to make their way to France where the Polish Army would re-form.

(b) German occupation

Having partitioned the country (see Map 88), the occupying powers set about imposing their administration on the territory under their control. In the German occupation zone, the western provinces (Silesia, Pomorze, Poznań, most of Łódź and parts of Warsaw, Cracow, and Kielce provinces) were annexed to the Reich by a decree of 8 October and were known as the Wartheland. They accounted for some 90,000 sq. km. (35,000 sq. mi.) and some 9.5 million of Poland's pre-war population. In the remaining area which fell under German control, the Nazis established a 'General government' which was intended as a labour colony of the Reich. It incorporated some 96,000 sq. km. (37,000 sq. mi.) of territory—including the cities of Warsaw, Cracow, Radom, and Lublin—and 12 million inhabitants. The seat of power was established at Cracow and Hans *Frank, a Nazi lawyer, was appointed governor.

The Nazi occupation marked the beginning of almost six years of unspeakable horror for Poles. Indeed the terror began even as Wehrmacht units crossed Polish territory during the September campaign. In the wake of the Wehrmacht, *SS operational units followed in close attendance. Armed with lists of political activists—particularly of those who, almost 20 years earlier, had

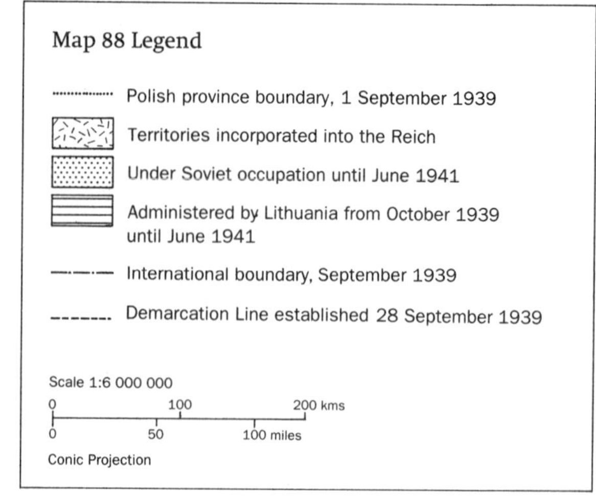

risen against German rule in Silesia and Wielkopolska—the **Einsatzgruppen* carried out summary executions of these and other 'undesirable' elements, including Jews. In Bydgoszcz German *fifth columnists, who aided the Nazi forces by providing intelligence and organizing diversions, took up arms against the Polish garrison, believing that resistance was nearly extinguished. Polish reinforcements swiftly put down the revolt and executed many of its perpetrators, and when the Germans eventually captured the city, they elected to regard this as an unprovoked massacre, and shot thousands of Polish citizens as a reprisal.

This was to be only the first of many thousands of such 'reprisals'. Before Wehrmacht administration of Polish territory ended on 25 October 1939, some 531 towns and villages were burned and 16,376 Poles executed by various branches of the German army and police. Mass murders continued after military activity had ceased, the most notable during the early months of the war being those at Wawer in December 1939, and at Palmiry, where 1,700 Poles were shot between December 1939 and July 1940.

In the Wartheland, Hitler's aim was to eradicate all traces of Polish culture and to Germanize its inhabitants completely (during the 19th century, and until Poland was restored to statehood in 1918, they had been under Prussian administration). This task fell to Heinrich *Himmler, the Reich Commissioner charged with the consolidation of German nationhood. The implementation of his programme involved the forcible expulsion of a million Poles who were considered unsuitable for Germanification. This mass movement took place during the winter of 1939–40 under extremely harsh conditions. Those expelled were moved with few possessions and allowed to take little cash. They were not compensated for the goods, businesses, and property they had left behind, which were taken over by ethnic Germans repatriated from the Baltic States, eastern Poland, or

88. **Poland** under German and Soviet occupation, September 1939–June 1941

Romania. Their transportation, in unheated freight trucks in the cold of winter, resulted in the death of many thousands. Most were moved to the General government area and simply dumped there, although able-bodied menfolk were separated from their families and taken to the Reich as *forced labour. The Poles who remained behind in the Reich areas came under great pressure to Germanize. They were compelled to register as ethnic Germans, for example, and forbidden to use the Polish language. Tens of thousands were forced into military service in the Wehrmacht and more than 200,000 *children were sent to the Reich for Germanization (see LEBENSBORN). Furthermore all visible signs of Polish life and culture were erased: Polish schools, theatres, public libraries, museums, and bookshops were closed down.

In the General government—the reservation which Hitler had earmarked for Poles—German policy in the early days of the occupation was restrained. University courses began normally, theatres opened, newspapers circulated. Only with the appointment of the governor, Hans Frank, in late October did the situation change. On 27 October the mayor of Warsaw, Stefan Starzyński—symbol of the capital's brave resistance—was arrested, and later shot. On 6 November there followed the seizure of 182 members of academic staff of the Jagiellonian University and other higher education institutes in Cracow. They were taken to *Sachsenhausen where many subsequently died. On 9 November street round-ups took place in Lublin.

The closure of universities, schools, libraries, publishing houses, archives, museums was accompanied by the destruction of Polish monuments and the seizure of Polish works of art (see LOOT). The playing of music by Polish composers was banned. The systematic attempts to demoralize the Poles by eradicating their culture were part of a design to reduce them to a subhuman level, fit only for the role of slaves. 'The Poles,' stated Hans Frank, 'do not need universities or secondary schools: the Polish lands are to be changed into an intellectual desert.' However, Nazi policies went beyond eradication of culture. They anticipated the literal extermination of the Poles as a nation and several policies were directed towards this end. Systematic economic exploitation meant that food was in short supply. The diet of the average Pole grew steadily worse and as early as 1941 daily food rations in Warsaw provided a notional 669 calories per day, compared to the Germans' 2,613. (The Jews were allotted a mere 184 calories.) Reduced diet meant starvation and weakened resistance to illness and disease. The flourishing black market, which the Germans found impossible to suppress, was a lifeline for many. A higher minimum age for marriage was set, in an attempt to reduce the birthrate. The deportation of men and women to the Reich to work in German agriculture or industry (some 2 million were taken between 1939 and 1944) had a similar effect in reducing fertility.

The most brutal measures employed to destroy the Poles, though, were the 300 labour and *concentration camps which were established on Polish soil. The camps were often located in the vicinity of factories so that the hapless camp-dwellers, both Christians and Jews, could be utilized as forced labour. By the same logic, they were frequently sited on or near railway lines to facilitate the transport of goods and personnel. Camps such as *Auschwitz and *Majdanek became bywords for the savagery of the Nazi regime, and they housed prisoners from all over Europe as well as Poles.

The Jewish population of Poland was earmarked for especially brutal treatment by the Nazi regime (see also FINAL SOLUTION). There were some 2.5 million Polish Jews in areas controlled by the Nazis. Many tens of thousands more would have fallen into Nazi hands had they not fled before the advancing German troops in 1939 to areas which came under Soviet occupation. From late October 1939, a series of sweeping measures was introduced which struck at the freedom and rights of Polish Jews. Compulsory labour was introduced for those aged between 14 and 60 years. Property rights were first restricted, and then curtailed altogether as Jewish property was confiscated. In January 1940, restrictions on the movement of Jews were introduced. They were herded into *ghettos in major Polish cities, which were sealed off and guarded by police. Inside the ghetto walls life continued after a fashion and Jewish councils (Judenräte) were formed to carry out administrative tasks. Half a million people were concentrated in the Warsaw ghetto alone. Conditions became appalling as supplies of food and medicine dwindled. After October 1941 Jews who were found outside the ghetto risked death, as did Poles attempting to help them. The mortality rate within the ghettos rose and people expired on the street.

Within days of the German attack on the USSR in June 1941 (see BARBAROSSA) all Poland as constituted in September 1939 came under German rule for the first time. In a new administrative division, the south-eastern regions became transformed into Distrikt Galizien with its administrative headquarters at *Lwów, and this was incorporated into the General government. To the east the remaining territories became Reichskommissariats of the Ukraine and *Ostland—the latter incorporating also the Baltic States (see Map 80). Poland was now divided between the Reich (30.8%), the General Government (38.8%), and the eastern Reichskommissariats (30.3%).

In the course of 1941 a change in German policy towards the General government took place. Hitler had decided that it would become a German region and 80% of its Polish population would be expelled. Efforts were made to emphasize the German character of towns such as Cracow, Tarnów, and Lublin and in November 1942 the Germans embarked upon a mass resettlement and colonization operation in the *Zamość region. The situation of Polish Jews also worsened. Almost the entire Jewish population was earmarked for extermination; most were to die in Nazi death camps (see OPERATION REINHARD), although many thousands died when the urban ghettos were eventually liquidated. Attempts made by Christian Poles to help could only be symbolic when measured against the size of the task and the sanctions they faced. By contrast with Nazi occupation policies in western Europe, in Poland whole families risked death if they were detected attempting to conceal a Jew.

(c) Soviet occupation

Whereas the Germans took control of some 188,700 sq. km. (72,800 sq. mi.) of Polish territory with a population of 22 million (18.5 million Poles, 2 million Jews, under a million ethnic Germans), the Soviets took slightly more territory—201,000 sq. km. (77,500 sq. mi.), but with a population of only 13 million (5 million Poles, 4.5 million Ukrainians, 1.5 million Belorussians, and 1.5

million Jews). In the north-east the town of *Wilno and its environs were transferred to Lithuania. But Moscow's largesse was short-lived; only nine months later Wilno, now called Vilnius, and the whole of Lithuania were to find themselves under Soviet rule when the Baltic States were occupied by the Red Army.

In the course of the September campaign, according to Soviet sources, some 200,000 Polish troops were captured by the Red Army. (A further 11,000, interned in Lithuania, were to fall into Soviet hands with the seizure of the Baltic States in the summer of 1940.) Some of the ordinary soldiers—including those of non-Polish origin and those whose homes were in German-held areas—were released and allowed to return home. Thousands of others were held in *prisoner-of-war camps in the south-east of the country, many being employed on construction projects. Most of the officers were taken to camps within the USSR, but few of them survived until the re-establishment of Polish–Soviet relations in 1941. The majority fell victim to *NKVD execution squads at *Katyń forest and other sites.

In the Soviet occupation zone conditions were only marginally less harsh than under the Germans. The entry of the Red Army into Poland had not passed without resistance and where the defending forces had fired on the invaders the Soviets frequently took immediate reprisals, shooting prisoners on the spot. The terror increased in the days immediately following the entry of Soviet troops when military rule was still in force. The commanders of the Belorussian *front* (army group) and the Ukrainian *front*, generals Kovalev and *Timoshenko, authorized the creation of local people's militias or peasants' committees to maintain order. These included in their ranks prisoners the Soviets had released from jail, or else radicalized Poles, Ukrainians, and Jews—many with grudges and their own scores to settle. At risk from random retribution by them were Polish officers, members of the Frontier Defence Corps (KOP), policemen, local officials, judges, prison staffs—anyone, in fact, who having held a responsible position in the service of the Polish state, or else because of his class background, was disliked by the new regime.

Within days the Soviet civilian authorities began to build an administration at all levels which included many Soviet citizens. P. Ponomarenko, first secretary of the Belorussian Communist Party, took over control from his new base in Białystok, whilst his opposite number in the Ukraine, N. Khrushchev (1894–1971), moved to Lwów. The Soviet security agencies, led by the NKVD, established a firmer hold on the territories, and Stalinist terror became more systematically applied, as arrests and disappearances increased.

The formal annexation of the Polish territories took place within five weeks of the invasion. Throughout the Soviet-occupied region 'elections' took place on 22 October. This plebiscite, staged to determine 'the will of the people', was manifestly fraudulent. The list of candidates was selected by the NKVD, threats and pressures were exerted on people to vote, and there was widespread evidence that the results had been falsified. Yet on the basis of this poll, delegates were elected to 'People's Assemblies' of Western Ukraine and Western Belorussia which met at the beginning of November in Lwów and Białystok respectively. The delegates were invited to vote in favour of incorporation into the Soviet Union. Once they had served their purpose the assemblies were dissolved. On 29 November the Supreme Soviet decreed that inhabitants of the annexed territories had acquired Soviet citizenship. The Polish government in London (see below) refused to accept the election result or the steps which followed from it, regarding the Soviet annexation as an act of *force majeure* and protesting vigorously against infringements of international law.

Nevertheless, Moscow henceforth treated the eastern Polish provinces as an integral part of the USSR, and the Soviet authorities felt free to impose their own political, economic, and social system. The Polish złoty was removed from circulation and replaced with the rouble. Savings accounts were frozen and largely confiscated. Large industry, financial institutions, and the mines were nationalized. Free trade was outlawed as 'speculation' and co-operatives and state shops introduced. In the countryside, estates were seized and placed under state control. In the towns, apartments were appropriated for the use of Soviet personnel and their owners were thrown out on to the street. In time, too, Poles in more responsible positions began to lose their jobs, replaced either by members of the local non-Polish communities, or else by Soviet personnel brought in from Minsk and Kiev.

The eradication of Polish political, cultural, and economic influence proceeded in direct proportion to the encouragement of Ukrainian and Belorussian aspirations. There was destruction of Polish monuments, removal of Polish street signs, closing of Polish bookshops, publishing houses, newspapers (although communist newspapers in Polish rapidly appeared). Ukrainian and Belorussian became the languages of school and university, while Russian also became compulsory. Polish history was replaced on the syllabus by the principles of Marxist–Leninism—or the Soviet Constitution. Religious influences were also seen as harmful and were countered. Bans were imposed on the teaching of *religion in schools and on outward manifestations of religious belief such as the ringing of church bells, or the wearing of vestments outside the church. Although religious worship as such was not outlawed, punitive taxes were imposed on the churches and many were forced to close.

Arrests began soon after the arrival of the Red Army and existing prisons were soon too full to cope with the numbers. The Soviets sought to root out the 'enemies of socialism' and found these enemies everywhere—including among the ranks of Polish labour leaders and members of the pre-war Polish Communist Party (KPP). Tens of thousands of prisoners were transported by stages to prisons in the Soviet interior, and then on to the *GUlag or to state farms. In the first half of 1940, hundreds of thousands of Polish citizens were forcibly deported in three mass movements (in February, April, and June). Many of these deportees, estimated to number 1.5 million, were women and children. They included members of the pre-war minorities—Ukrainians, Belorussians, and Jews—although ethnic Poles predominated, and they came from all walks of life: peasants, forestry workers, and artisans accompanied judges, teachers, businessmen, state officials, politicians. Many, particularly the elderly and young children, died in the freight trucks on journeys to Kazakhstan or elsewhere beyond the Urals—journeys which commonly lasted some three weeks. Polish sources estimate that some 30% of those deported died in the Soviet Union before most were released under 'amnesty' in the autumn of 1941.

The German attack on the low countries and France in May 1940 (see FALL GELB) caused a halt to the NKVD's two-monthly cycle of deportations. With the western powers embroiled in the fighting that led to the fall of *France, Stalin decided it was a good time to make further territorial acquisitions—the Baltic States and Bessarabia. This brought more Poles into the Soviet orbit including civilian refugees, military internees, and pre-war Polish residents of Lithuania. However, the Poles in areas controlled by the Soviets were to experience a marginally less repressive regime in the latter half of 1940. Following the unexpectedly speedy collapse of France, the Soviets became concerned about the pro-German sentiments of Ukrainian nationalists and their potential as fifth columnists should Hitler decide to turn his armies eastwards once more. They were also concerned by the resistance of Ukrainian and Belorussian peasants to collectivization.

In eastern Galicia jails began to fill with Ukrainians, and the firmly anti-German Poles were courted. Moves began to revive Polish cultural life and a literary monthly, *Nowe Widnokręgi* ('New Horizons'), was started in January 1941. A number of prominent Poles, including the former premier Kazimierz Bartel were invited to Moscow to be questioned about the mood of the Polish population under Soviet rule. Talks even began with captured Polish officers about the possible formation of Polish units to fight alongside the Red Army. Unfortunately, such moves did not help those who were still in NKVD prisons during June 1941. When the Germans launched BARBAROSSA, the NKVD murdered thousands of Polish prisoners in their cells, rather than allow them to fall into German hands.

(d) Post-occupation

Poland at the end of the war had new borders and was some 20% smaller in area than the pre-war state, but it was not only affected by territorial changes. Its population had also changed. The country had suffered tremendous war losses—more than 6 million, of whom 5,384,000 died as a result of mass terror on the part of the occupying powers—and its population was reduced from a pre-war figure of 35 million to some 24 million. Warsaw alone lost 700,000 people, more than the combined losses of the UK and USA during the war. The intelligentsia suffered disproportionately: Poland lost 45% of its physicians and dentists, 57% of its lawyers, more than 15% of its teachers, 40% of university professors, and more than 18% of its clergy. (See Table 1 for losses of plant and property.)

Poland, 3(d), Table 1: Losses in plant and property in Poland (post-war frontiers) during the Second World War

	in billions of pre-war Zloties	*as % of total*
Residential buildings, furniture and contents, private offices	9.69	30
Culture and art	5.36	43
Education and schools	1.86	60
Health service	0.54	55
Public and local administration, state monopolies, banking, insurance	3.00	60
Transport and communications	9.35	56
Industry, energy, workshops	11.04	33
Trade	7.10	65
Forestry, hunting, fishing	3.58	28
Agriculture, horticulture	5.24	35
Military equipment	5.26	100
TOTAL	62.02	38

Source: Luczak, C., 'Polityka ludnościowi: ekonomiczna hitlerowskich Niemiec w okupowanej Polsce', (Poznań, 1979).

In ethnic and religious terms Poland had become more homogeneous. Hitler's racial policies had destroyed the large Jewish community; the loss of the eastern provinces had removed the large Ukrainian and Belorussian minorities of pre-war days; the German population was expelled. Thus the population of the new Poland was overwhelmingly Polish by ethnic origin and Roman Catholic by religion. But hundreds of thousands of Poles found themselves outside the borders of their homeland, having been scattered by the vicissitudes of war to destinations as dispersed as Mexico, Uganda, India, and Japan. The largest concentration was in Germany and Austria—Poles who had been forced to work for the *Todt Organization or had been forcibly conscripted into the Wehrmacht. There were more than 750,000 Polish displaced persons (see REFUGEES) and *prisoners-of-war in the western zones of Germany alone in the summer of 1945. More than a million Poles from Germany and Austria had been repatriated by the end of that year.

(e) Governments-in-exile

Following the internment in Romania of the Polish president, the government, and the C-in-C, leadership of the Polish cause was temporarily paralysed. On 30 September 1939 President Mościcki transferred his powers to Władysław Raczkiewicz, a former interior minister and marshal of the senate. Raczkiewicz was one of several Poles who found themselves in France at the time of the Polish collapse, or else made their way there in the course of the Polish campaign. His first act as president was to entrust General *Sikorski with the task of forming a government in Paris. Sikorski, once a colleague of the pre-war leader, Marshal Piłsudski, had fallen from favour after the latter's 1926 coup. He had turned to writing on military matters and had spent much of the intervening period in France. While extremely critical of the pre-war Sanacja regime, he was forced to co-operate with a number of figures closely associated with it. Sikorski formed a coalition government of national unity which included moderate representatives of it as well as members of the pre-war opposition; the Peasant Party (SL), the Socialists (PPS), the National Democrats (ND), and the Labour Party (SP). This government was recognized immediately by France and the UK and thereafter by many neutral states. Sikorski concentrated in his hands both political and military power: not only was he prime minister, but he also became minister of war and C-in-C of the armed forces. His main objectives were to ensure the continuity of the Polish state, to build up Polish military forces abroad, and to represent national interests in Allied councils at a time when Poland itself lay powerless.

Sensitive to possible charges that his government lacked a mandate, Sikorski authorized the creation of a National Council (Rada Narodowa) in December 1939. The council was intended as a people's chamber or parliament, which would substitute for the democratic institutions of the homeland. However, the members of the council were appointed, not elected; they consisted of some 20 prominent politicians then in France. The Jewish community in Poland had its representatives, as did the Polish emigration, but—significantly, in view of the Polish government's determined denial of Soviet claims to their eastern provinces—there was no representative of the Ukrainian or Belorussian minorities. Furthermore, the council was a purely advisory body and had no powers to legislate. Its first president was Ignacy Paderewski, the world-renowned concert pianist who had represented the Polish cause at the *Versailles settlement in 1919. For most of its period in France, the Polish government had its seat at Angers.

Sikorski had good contacts in France, but he was little known in the UK. He visited London in November 1939 to confer with members of the British government, and with diplomatic and military staffs. He soon became a respected figure in Allied councils, but despite this the Poles found it difficult to gain treatment as equals. From 1939 onwards, the Polish government found itself in the position of a 'client'—first of France, then of Britain, and later, to some degree, of the USA and the USSR. Lacking a territorial base, it was forced to accept the hospitality of others and became a supplicant for arms, supplies, transport, finance, and so on. Sikorski felt his country's weakness sorely. His determination to build up a sizeable armed force was based on his conviction that increased military power would strengthen Poland's voice in international counsels.

When France fell in June 1940, Sikorski was forced to reorient his policy towards the only remaining power opposed to Hitler—the UK. Through the offices of his ambassador in London, Count *Raczyński, and his personal adviser, Józef *Retinger, Sikorski flew to London to meet Churchill during the French campaign. As a result of their meeting it was agreed that the Polish government would be transferred to London and Churchill gave orders for the Royal Navy to evacuate Polish troops from French ports. The fall of France came as a great shock to Sikorski, who had placed great hopes in his ally. Moreover, the speedy collapse of a military power such as France made the Polish defeat of 1939 seem in retrospect less ignominious. Sikorski's criticisms of the former regime's performance were seen to have been unfair, and it was pointed out that his own performance had not been much better. The bulk of the Polish Army in France had been lost, and Sikorski himself had been incommunicado for days as, in his role as C-in-C, he roamed France attempting to keep up with the rapidly changing military situation and remain in contact with his troops.

Once the Polish government re-established itself in London, Sikorski came under strong pressure to resign. Apart from his poor handling of the French crisis, there was a further reason for his colleagues' discontent. After the fall of France the hundreds of thousand of Poles deported to the Soviet interior formed the one reservoir of manpower that could be used to boost Polish military strength and Sikorski had submitted a memorandum to the British foreign office which contained the suggestion that, in order to defeat Hitler, it might eventually prove advantageous to form Polish military units on Soviet soil. But the memorandum had not been cleared by his own cabinet. Furthermore many Poles at this time were at least as suspicious of Stalin as they were of Hitler. President Raczkiewicz moved to dismiss Sikorski, but when it became clear that the prime minister was supported by the British and that the step might provoke a revolt in Polish ranks, he was forced to back down.

During the twelve-month period between the fall of France and the launching of BARBAROSSA, Poland was, the British Empire apart, the UK's only significant ally in the fight against Hitler, but, with Hitler's attack on the USSR on 22 June 1941, the configuration of forces shifted. The Soviet Union became a key member of the anti-Nazi alliance; an understanding between Soviet and Polish governments became essential and on 30 July they signed the Polish–Soviet Treaty. The pact not only paved the way for a renewal of diplomatic relations, but provided for full military co-operation against the common enemy, Germany. There was agreement that all the Polish citizens held by the Soviet authorities in prisons and in the GUlag would be released under 'amnesty' and that a Polish Army would be formed in the USSR, but although the Soviet government stipulated that its earlier pacts with Berlin had lost their validity, there was no agreement on the question of the *Polish–Soviet frontier. The signing of the agreement, without an assurance on frontiers, led to the resignation of three ministers, General *Sosnkowski, M. Seyda, and the foreign minister, A. Zaleski.

With hindsight, Sikorski's failure to tie Stalin down to an agreement on the frontier issue was a mistake. There were to be few other opportunities to achieve one during the eighteen-month period that the Red Army reeled before the German onslaught and Soviet diplomats spoke from a position of weakness (a further chance was spurned by Sikorski during his Moscow meetings with Stalin in December 1941). By the end of 1942, as the tide of battle turned on the Eastern Front and the Red Army went on to the offensive, any opportunity there might have been to seal an agreement favourable to the Poles was lost completely.

The Polish embassy was soon re-established in Moscow (though within weeks it transferred to Kuibyshev as the German advance threatened the Soviet capital) and Stanisław Kot, Sikorski's minister for home affairs, was sent as ambassador. The embassy set up a network of regional delegates to distribute relief supplies to destitute Polish deportees scattered throughout Soviet territory. At the same time, Poles were flooding from all corners of the USSR to join a new force, *Anders' Army, which was being formed in the southern Urals. But despite a visit by General Sikorski to Moscow in December 1941, Polish–Soviet relations soon began to run into difficulties. The Soviets were reluctant to arm and equip the Polish divisions. They were also reluctant to allow Polish citizens of Ukrainian, Belorussian, and Jewish origin to be recruited, arguing that these had become Soviet citizens. The decision to evacuate Anders' Army during 1942 to British command in the Middle East accelerated the deterioration in relations. Not only did Moscow refuse the Polish government permission to raise further troop formations on Soviet soil, it also began to dismantle the Polish embassy's relief network, and to arrest embassy delegates on charges of spying. Relations finally ruptured irrevocably in April 1943 over the Katyń Forest massacre. The Germans' discovery of some 4,000 bodies in a mass grave near Smolensk helped to explain the disappearance of thousands of Polish officers sought by General Anders during 1941–2. This tragedy for Poland was exploited to the full by the Germans, who sought to rupture Allied unity. Polish requests that the *International Red Cross Committee investigate the affair proved a sufficient pretext for Moscow to break off diplomatic relations with the Poles.

After the break the way was clear for Polish communists (both within Poland and in the USSR) to step up their activities. Stalin had dissolved the pre-war Polish Communist Party (KPP) in 1938 and had liquidated most of its leaders, but following the German attack in 1941 he had sanctioned the creation of a replacement, the Polish Workers' Party (PPR). In December 1941 Polish communists headed by Paweł Finder and Marceli Nowotko, had parachuted into Poland to begin the work of organizing the new party and had made contact with figures such as Władysław Gomułka (1905–82). The PPR formally came into existence on 5 January 1942. Although its support in the early days was thin, it quickly sought to build up its own military resistance organization, the *People's Guard (GL).

In Moscow the Union of Polish Patriots (ZPP) was established under the leadership of Wanda *Wasilewska in March 1943. Not all its members were communists, but all were prepared to bow to the dictates of Soviet policy. Importantly, they agreed to Soviet demands for the Polish eastern provinces and conceded that post-war Poland would be a state allied to Moscow. Immediately following the rupturing of diplomatic relations with the Polish government, Stalin approved Wasilewska's proposal for the creation of a second Polish army on Soviet soil. The new force, *Berling's Army, was be subordinated to the ZPP and through it to the Soviet authorities. The Polish government in London was given no say regarding its formation or its use.

A further blow to the Polish cause fell on 4 July 1943 when the prime minister, General Sikorski, returning from a visit to General Anders and his troops in the Middle East, was killed as his Liberator aircraft was taking off from Gibraltar. He was the one Polish statesman of stature who commanded the respect of the Allies. Henceforth, the political and military wings of the Polish establishment were to be divided—with unfortunate results for Poland. The Peasant Party leader, Stanisław Mikołajczyk (1901–66), who had been Sikorski's deputy, became prime minister, while General Sosnkowski became C-in-C of the armed forces. The two men had different social and political philosophies, and they did not get on. While Mikołajczyk attempted to reach an understanding with Moscow, Sosnkowski distrusted the Soviet politicians absolutely.

The conference of the Big Three powers at Teheran in November 1943 (see EUREKA) had a decisive influence on Poland's post-war fate, yet its representatives were not admitted to the discussions and their views were not aired. The Allies agreed that the Polish–Soviet frontier should follow the 'Curzon Line', which they recognized as Poland's ethnographic border in the east. Thus the USA and Britain conceded to Stalin most of the large area of eastern Poland that he had seized as a result of the Nazi–Soviet Pact in 1939 (see Map 90). Poland, it was agreed, would be compensated at the expense of Germany and the restored Polish state would enjoy 'friendly relations' with the USSR.

By the middle of 1944 the negotiating position of the London Polish government *vis-à-vis* Moscow had become hopeless. It could expect little help from its western allies.

While the USA and Britain wanted a strong Poland which might curb any future German expansionism, they were not prepared to listen to Polish protests against the loss of territory to the Soviets. However, the western Allies—and particularly Churchill—did expect that in return for these territorial gains, the legitimate Polish government in London would be allowed to return to administer the country. But on this matter, too, Stalin's position hardened. Despite British efforts to bring about the restoration of Polish–Soviet relations, the Soviets placed more and more hurdles in their way. In June 1944 *Molotov, the Soviet foreign minister, stated that before diplomatic relations could be restored, certain members of the government who were 'reactionary' and 'anti-Soviet' would have to be removed. The names mentioned included Raczkiewicz, Sosnkowski, and Kukiel the minister of defence. It was clearly impossible for any Polish government to accede to such demands without itself becoming little more than a puppet.

At the end of July 1944 the prime minister, Stanisław Mikołajczyk, travelled to Moscow for talks with Stalin. His aim was to try to put Polish–Soviet relations on a more secure footing, to agree to reform the Polish government with the addition of Polish Workers' Party representatives (see RESISTANCE, below), and to clarify how Polish territory liberated by the Red Army might be administered. Stalin was unwilling to negotiate, arguing that Mikołajczyk should talk to the leaders of the Soviet-backed Lublin Committee. In fact there was little to talk about. Stalin did not need the 'London Poles'; he had his own Polish government in the making, the Lublin Committee, and it was already seeing to the administration of the liberated territories. To make matters worse, while Mikołajczyk was in Moscow, the *Warsaw rising broke out (on 1 August) and Mikołajczyk found himself in the embarrassing position of having to request Soviet help for the insurgents. He returned empty-handed. On 12 October he again travelled to Moscow to attend the *TOLSTOY conference with Churchill and *Eden, who had suggested that Mikołajczyk renew attempts to reach an accommodation with Stalin. The main issue at stake for the Poles in the Moscow talks was, once again, that of the Polish–Soviet border. Since the Great Powers had already come to an agreement on the eastern Polish border at the Teheran conference, the Moscow discussions could only be on points of detail. The British put intense pressure on Mikołajczyk to concede and agree to the Curzon Line. But even a compromise proposal that would have enabled Poland to retain Lwów and the Borysław oilfield was rejected by Stalin. On his return to London, Mikołajczyk failed to persuade his cabinet to accept the Soviet terms and he resigned as prime minister on 24 November. Convinced that the London Poles no longer posed any threat to his ambitions, Stalin authorized the Lublin Committee to transform itself into the Provisional government of the Republic of Poland on 1 January 1945. In the course of the next *Grand Alliance conference at Yalta in the Soviet Crimea between 4 and 11 February (see ARGONAUT), the Allies reaffirmed their 'common desire to see established a strong, free, independent and democratic Poland'. They called for the provisional government to be organized on a broader basis, with the inclusion of democratic leaders from Poland itself and from abroad. The new, reconstituted government would pledge itself to holding 'free and unfettered' elections as soon as possible.

(f) The Communist take-over

In June 1945, Mikołajczyk and a small number of colleagues returned to Warsaw to take up positions in the new Polish government of National Unity (TRJN). The line-up of the new government had been agreed previously in Moscow. Of the 21 ministerial posts, the 'London' Poles received just five—the remainder going to Lublin Committee nominees. The government was headed by Edward Osóbka-Morawski, one of a group of Socialist Party (PPS) members who had decided to throw in their lot with the communists. Mikołajczyk became deputy premier and minister of agriculture. The new government was formally recognized by the UK and the USA on 5 July. Henceforth the Polish government in London, under its new leader, the veteran socialist, Tomasz Arciszewski, was to be the voice of Polish opposition in exile.

At the Potsdam Conference which began on 17 July (see TERMINAL), the western borders of Poland were agreed upon by the Great Powers. Poland advanced its borders at the expense of Germany by over 200 km. (125 mi.) in places, recovering land which had belonged to Polish rulers in the Middle Ages (see Map 78). The German population was expelled from these areas in a massive operation which saw 3.5 million people removed, some under conditions of great hardship. With Stalin having refused to re-establish the pre-war Polish–Soviet frontier, a population transfer of similar scale was carried out in the east following agreements between the Polish provisional government and communist authorities in the Lithuanian, Belorussian, and Ukrainian republics. Hundreds of thousands of Poles were 'repatriated', the majority leaving their homes in what was now Soviet territory. Most of them were taken to the west to colonize the regions freshly acquired from the Germans. Stettin became Szczecin, Oppeln became Opole, and Breslau became Wrocław.

Not all Poles were willing to return to a homeland under communist domination. In May 1945 Polish servicemen and women in the West numbered 250,000 and were dispersed in four main theatres: Germany, Italy, the Middle East, and the UK. Once the western Allies transferred diplomatic recognition to the communist authorities in Warsaw, the troops were faced with a dilemma; should they accept the authority of this new regime and agree to be repatriated? Many, especially those like Anders who had suffered and seen their friends and kin die in the Soviet Union, viewed the communists with hatred and suspicion. Many of those from eastern Poland had, in any case, no homes to return to; they had been absorbed into the USSR. Large numbers wanted to wait until the elections which, they hoped, would throw the communists out of power. The hostility of the Polish communist and Soviet media towards General Anders and other Polish commanders was reflected in the violence of their language and by the later decision to strip him and 75 other senior officers of their Polish citizenship. Eventually, in the autumn of 1946, having become convinced that large numbers of Polish troops were stubbornly opposed to repatriation, the British authorities took steps to bring all units to Britain and demobilize them (see POLISH RESETTLEMENT CORPS).

The elections provided for in the Yalta accords were not held until January 1947 and resulted in a sweeping victory for the communists. They had been preceded by a widespread campaign of political terror and were followed by allegations of electoral malpractice. In October 1947 Mikołajczyk fled to the West, fearing for his life. The western powers were helpless to intervene, and after six years of Nazi occupation, Poland found itself once again under the heel of a powerful neighbour. The first to defy Hitler, it now became the first victim of the *Cold War.

3. Armed forces

The strength of the Polish armed forces in September 1939 was as follows. The army, commanded by Marshal Edward Śmigły-Rydz, amounted to about 280,000 men. There were 30 regular infantry divisions, 11 cavalry brigades, and 2 mechanized brigades, which could be reinforced by some 3 million reservists. The navy, commanded by Rear Admiral Józef Swirski, had 4 modern destroyers, 5 modern submarines, and 23 aircraft, and there was also a small coastal defence force. The air force, commanded by Maj-General J. Zając, had 400 operational aircraft which included 15 fighter squadrons. These forces proved no match for either the German or Soviet ones they faced, and those who could fled abroad.

For Polish forces raised in the USSR, see ANDERS' ARMY and BERLING'S ARMY; for those raised in the West, see below.

(a) Army

By the end of September 1939 some 90,000 Polish troops had made their way out of the country, both in order to evade capture and to prosecute the war from abroad. The majority (70,000) of these troops crossed the south-eastern border into Hungary and Romania, while smaller numbers sought refuge in Lithuania and Latvia. Despite the rapid sealing of the borders by the occupying powers, Poles of military age continued to cross unguarded parts of the frontier and to make their way to the west. In 1939–40 some 43,000 men reached France from Hungary or Romania either travelling overland or else by ship from ports such as Constanta and Split.

The French government's agreement to the formation of Polish military units on French soil had been secured in a Franco-Polish Military Agreement of 9 September 1939, and this was later strengthened (in January 1940) by a military accord. The French immediately provided their guests with a training camp in Brittany—Coetquidan, which became the Poles' main military base in France. Their military headquarters were located at the Hotel Regina in Paris. By 10 May 1940, when the German attack on France was launched, there were some 80,000 men under Polish colours, 42,000 of whom, as active military personnel in France, were subordinated to French operational command and dispersed among French defensive units; this was to have disastrous consequences when the French collapse gathered momentum. During the *Norwegian campaign the Polish Highland (Podhale) Brigade landed at Narvik but, despite the already grave situation in France, it was then ordered to return to Brittany, where it was trapped by the speed of the German advance. The 2nd Rifle Division commanded by General Prugar-Ketling had to cross into Switzerland where it was interned for the duration of the war, but some 20,000 Polish troops were evacuated by the Royal Navy from French ports. They were taken to Scottish ports before being directed to camps on the eastern coast of Scotland and employed in coastal defence work. On 5 August 1940 an Anglo-Polish Military Agreement was signed which regulated the conditions for Polish forces regrouping in the UK. Earlier agreements had been signed concerning the formation of the Polish Air Force (mainly bomber) units in Britain (11 April 1940) and the organization of Polish naval units alongside the Royal Navy (18 November 1939). These Anglo-Polish agreements also applied to Poles serving in military *formations outside the UK, the most notable of these being the *Carpathian Brigade, which served in the *Western Desert campaigns, and Anders' Army which, as 2nd Polish Corps, fought with the Eighth Army in the *Italian campaign.

The Polish High Command was compelled to re-establish itself in London. The C-in-C's staff was headed initially by General T. Klimecki and later in the war (following Klimecki's death at Gibraltar in 1943) by General S. Kopański. The body of troops that was to become the 1st Polish Corps numbered more than 14,000 men in the autumn of 1940. The Corps' 4th Rifle Brigade under Colonel Stanisław Sosabowski became an Independent Parachute Brigade which distinguished itself during the Arnhem operation (see MARKET-GARDEN) and General *Maczek's 1st Armoured Division was also formed from the Corps. This crossed to the Continent in June 1944 and, attached to *Montgomery's 2nd Canadian Corps, took part in the fighting in north-west Europe.

(b) Navy

Ships and personnel of both the Polish Navy and the merchant marine managed to evade German hands in 1939. Many, following prior agreement with the British authorities, had left their home ports before the outbreak of war and made their way to the UK. The most dramatic escape was that of the submarine *Orzeł*, which had initially been interned in neutral Estonia. Despite the confiscation of its armaments and navigation equipment, the *Orzeł* succeeded in making its way out of the Baltic, across the North Sea to a safe haven in Britain. The *Orzeł* was one of two submarines, three destroyers, a training vessel and a supply ship which the Polish naval command had at its disposal in November 1939. In all, 38 ships of the merchant marine also escaped German hands, including the troopships *Baltic*, *Batory*, and *Sobieski*.

The Anglo-Polish Naval Accord provided for co-operation between the British and Polish fleets and for the subordination of Polish units to Admiralty operational control. Polish warships took part in convoy escort duties and in guarding British shores, and the Polish destroyer *Piorun* engaged the **Bismarck* in the north Atlantic during the famous chase which led to the sinking of the German battleship in May 1941. Following the fall of France the Polish navy and merchant marine were merged. Steady recruitment throughout the war period meant that an initial complement of 1,500 men had been increased to 4,000 by 1945. A number of losses were suffered, in the course of the war, including the destroyer *Grom* and the submarine *Orzeł*, but replacement British vessels were found.

(c) Air Force

After the Polish campaign, several Polish squadrons were formed in France and the UK. In France in 1940 the Polish Air Force already had two fighter squadrons, two reconnaisance squadrons, and one bomber squadron. But it was in Britain from 1940 onwards that the Polish air units really began to expand and an Anglo-Polish Agreement provided for the Polish Air Force to be subordinated to RAF command.

Priority was given to fighter squadrons for the defence of Britain against German air attack. The first two squadrons to see service were 302 (Poznań) and the famous 303 (Warszawa) squadron, the latter based at Northolt just outside London. Despite initial reservations, the British soon came to appreciate the skill and courage of the Polish pilots, several of whom had experienced air combat with the Germans in two campaigns already. The Poles played an outstanding role during the battle of *Britain, shooting down a disproportionately high number of German aircraft. Between 10 July and the end of October 1940, 1,733 of all types were destroyed; 203 of these were shot down by Poles, including 110 claimed by 303 squadron alone. The Poles continued to offer a valuable service in many theatres throughout the war (bomber crews took part in the ill-fated operations to drop supplies to the insurgents during the 1944 Warsaw rising). At the end of the war there were some 15 squadrons operational and 19,400 personnel serving in air force ranks.

4. Resistance

Polish resistance to both German and Soviet occupation regimes sprang up spontaneously. In many areas partisan organizations had been formed before the Polish campaign was over. On the night of 26/27 September an underground organization called Service for the Victory of Poland (Służba Zwycięstwu Polski, or SZP) was created in Warsaw, the embattled Polish capital. Under the leadership of General Michał Tokarzewski-Karasiewicz, it subordinated itself to the exiled Polish government in France and slowly set about absorbing and subordinating to its command the myriad local resistance groups which had come into being.

Two factors aided the creation of a resistance movement in Poland. One was the longstanding tradition of underground struggle and revolt, especially against Russian rule. The second factor was the unbridled terror which both occupying forces brought to the country. The Germans in particular, with their vicious policies of exploitation and extermination, left no room for compromise or collaboration with the Polish population.

In January 1940 General Sikorski ordered the creation of an underground army named the Union for Armed Struggle (Związek Walki Zbrojnej, or ZWZ). It absorbed the SZP and was put under the overall command of General Sosnkowski in London. A few months later the exiled Polish authorities created a homeland political Delegature consisting of representatives from the major political parties. The first government delegate was Cyril Ratajski. Whereas the ZWZ was the Polish government's military presence in Poland, the Delegature acted as its political representation.

The military organization was based on officers and soldiers from the Polish services. It could therefore draw on a large reservoir of willing and experienced recruits

Poland, 4, Table 2: Sabotage undertaken by the Polish Home Army during the period 1 January 1941–30 June 1944

Locomotives damaged	6,930
Locomotives delayed in overhaul	803
Transports derailed	732
Railway trucks destroyed	979
Railway trucks damaged	19,058
Transports set on fire	443
Disruptions of electric power in Warsaw	638
Military vehicles damaged or destroyed	4,326
Railway bridges blown up	38
Aircraft damaged	28
Aircraft engines destroyed	68
Petrol storage tanks destroyed	1,167
Tons of petrol destroyed	4,674
Oil wells put out of action	3
Truckloads of wood burned	150
Military warehouses burned	122
Military food storage depots burned	8
Production in factories brought to halt	7
Factories burned	15

Source: Lukas, R. C., *Forgotten Holocaust. The Poles under German Occupation, 1939–1944*, (Lexington, 1986).

who had knowledge of arms, explosives, tactics, and so on, and the ability to mount armed attacks and undertake sabotage (see Table 2 for losses inflicted on the Germans). But the need to counter Nazi propaganda and to boost civilian morale also led to the printing and distribution of newspapers, leaflets, and posters. Intelligence gathering was another important activity. The Poles produced reports for British intelligence of the growing traffic in war materials between the USSR and Nazi Germany. In 1941 they were able to inform the British about the impending German attack on the USSR. Polish intelligence also warned Britain about the danger from the German rocket programme and managed to conceal a whole V-2 (see V-WEAPONS) and preserve the engine for transport to the UK.

When the threat to the Jewish community in Poland became apparent, the underground created a Committee for Aid to Jews (see ŻEGOTA). Underground courts existed which carried out punishment (including the death sentence) on offenders. Furthermore, resistance included maintaining all the normal educational and cultural activities of Polish life which the Germans were so determined to undermine and destroy. Secret schools and university courses existed, artistic pursuits such as the theatre continued, as did scientific activity. It is not difficult to see why the Poles refer to this resistance activity as the 'Underground State'.

Although the Polish High Command was at all times in touch with resistance leaders, communication whether by radio or by courier (see KARSKI and NOWAK, for example) was difficult and the problem was exacerbated in the early period of the war by the country's division into two occupation zones with a tightly controlled frontier. Initially radio communication was maintained with bases in Budapest, Bucharest, and Kaunas. Later, when expanding German and Soviet influence made a presence in these capitals impossible, the bases were re-established in Stockholm and Istanbul. Couriers could be sent overland but after the fall of France this channel of communication became difficult. The Polish section of *SOE, which was formed in the late summer of 1940, did much to help the Sixth Bureau of the Polish general staff develop communications with Poland. From early 1941 most incoming couriers, travelled by air and parachuted into Poland, though the return journey still had to be negotiated by land via either neutral Switzerland or the Middle East.

During the period 1939–41, Poland was divided between Germany and the USSR, at that time allies. The Polish underground aimed, amongst other things, to sabotage the trainloads of war materials which Stalin was supplying to Hitler, in an effort to help him evade the British blockade (see ECONOMIC WARFARE). After the German attack on the USSR, in the summer of 1941, Poland found itself completely under German occupation and to the rear of an operational front line. With the disappearance of the Nazi–Soviet frontier, it became easier to organize resistance activity over the country as a whole. From 1942 onwards, when the ZWZ was transformed into the Home Army (Armia Krajowa, or AK), a strong partisan movement developed in the marshes and forest land of Eastern Poland. It included not only Home Army members, but also Polish communist partisans and Soviet troops stranded by the speed of the Wehrmacht's advance.

The Home Army leaders adopted a restrained policy with regard to armed activity against the Germans. Unwilling to risk heavy reprisals against the civilian population, they played a waiting game, planning for a general rising which would occur when the decisive phase of the war had been reached. A departure from this policy occurred at the end of 1942 when the SS began a massive expulsion of Poles from the Lublin and Zamość region to make way for German colonists. The Home Army sanctioned a 'self-defence' operation against the colonists, and the Germans, realizing their vulnerability, called a halt to the expulsions in February 1943.

The creation by Polish communists of the Polish Workers' Party (PPR) in January 1942 led to the creation of its resistance wing, the People's Guard (GL) which, in 1944, was renamed the People's Army (AL). Although the communist resistance started with a very small membership (some 3,000), they scorned the 'London' camp's calls for restraint and adopted an aggressive policy towards the Germans. They increased sabotage and partisan attacks on the occupying forces, irrespective of the terrible price that the local population often paid in reprisals. Sometimes they clashed with the right-wing *National Armed Forces (NSZ), a partisan group which had broken away from the AK. In the summer of 1943 the Polish underground suffered a grave blow when its commander, General *Rowecki, was betrayed to the Gestapo, arrested, and spirited away to Berlin. He later died in Sachsenhausen concentration camp and his deputy, General *Komorowski, was appointed his successor.

During the autumn of 1943 attempts were made to forge some kind of co-operative working relationship between the 'pro-London' political and military underground and the Polish Workers' Party and its resistance wing. When these collapsed, encouraged by the military successes of the Red Army, the communists took the initiative. On 31 December 1943, only days before Soviet troops were due to cross the pre-war Polish frontier, they formed a National Council for the Homeland (KRN) led by Bolesław Bierut. The KRN had a narrow political base, but it received the support of the Polish communists in Moscow. Its claims to 'represent' the Polish nation were plainly unfounded, but its formation was a warning to the Polish government in London about the way the situation might develop. The non-communist underground (the government Delegature) responded within days by creating, on 9 January 1944, a Council of National Unity (RJN). This 'underground parliament' had representation from four of the major Polish political parties and its formation was an attempt to regain the initiative from the communists. Its declaration, issued in mid-March, had some important proposals concerning economic and social reform in post-war Poland. But the declaration also foresaw an enlarged Poland which not only retained the pre-war Polish frontier in the east, but was enlarged in the north and west at the expense of Germany. This was not a realistic proposition, given the balance of military and political forces at the time.

As early as November 1942, General Sikorski had sent the Home Army commander, General Rowecki, instructions on how his forces should react once Red Army units arrived on Polish territory (see TEMPEST). At the beginning of January 1944, when the Red Army crossed the pre-war eastern Polish border, attempts to co-operate with the Soviets were made by local Home Army commanders and some joint operations did take place, notably in *Volhynia. But more often, the Home Army units were given the option of joining Berling's Army or else of disbanding and in some notorious cases Polish leaders who went to meetings with Red Army commanders disappeared completely (see WILNO).

The Warsaw rising was the Polish resistance movement's final desperate attempt to show that the Poles could be masters in their own house. Beginning on 1 August and lasting for more than two months, it proved a political and military disaster and an estimated quarter of a million Poles died. One of the few positive results was that many of the illusions the western leaders held about Stalin were dispelled. It marked the end of the Home Army as an organization capable of resisting communist domination of the homeland. A further body-blow occurred in March 1945 when sixteen underground leaders, including the Home Army's C-in-C, General *Okulicki, were rounded up by the Soviets and sentenced to various terms of imprisonment at the *Moscow trials. KEITH SWORD

Garliński, J., *Poland in the Second World War* (London, 1985).
Lukas, R. C., *Forgotten Holocaust. The Poles under German Occupation 1939–44* (Kentucky, 1986).
Rozek, E. J., *Allied Wartime Diplomacy: A Pattern in Poland* (New York, 1958).

Poland, Guarantee of. The German occupation of the rump of Czechoslovakia on 15 March 1939 killed the *Munich agreement of the previous autumn, and with it the western policy of appeasement. It also made Poland the obvious next target of Hitler's expansionist policy. Soon after the entry of the German Army into Prague, the Polish government faced renewed demands from Germany for *Danzig as well as extraterritorial road and rail links through the *Polish Corridor. Polish policy resolutely rejected German demands.

Hitler's elimination of the last vestige of Czechoslovakia (see Map C) made a considerable impact on the climate of British public and political opinion, and the British government began rapidly to rethink its policy towards both Germany and the countries of central Europe. British appeasement of Hitler ended when, on 31 March 1939, *Chamberlain offered a verbal guarantee to Poland in a statement before the House of Commons. The prime minister also spoke for the French government in issuing the guarantee.

The verbal guarantee to Poland represented a marked change in British foreign policy which, ever since the end of the *First World War, had resisted security commitments in east and central Europe. The Polish government warmly welcomed British (and French) support: the foreign minister, Józef *Beck, had for some time made an alliance with Britain a central aim of Polish foreign policy.

An extended series of high-level Anglo-Polish discussions followed the British and French guarantees, and culminated in a formal treaty on 25 August 1939. The Anglo-Polish Agreement of Mutual Assistance pledged Britain and Poland to come to each other's aid in the event of hostilities involving a 'European Power'. A secret protocol supplemented the text of the published treaty and it contained some important caveats including the definition of the 'European Power' as being Germany. Although the text of 25 August 1939 pledged British support for Polish independence, it nevertheless carefully avoided any British commitment to the territorial integrity of Poland. In this sense the agreement represented a significant element of continuity with earlier British policy, as the Polish government would find to its cost when war began. PAUL LATAWSKI

Polish campaign. The German invasion of Poland on 1 September 1939 marked the beginning of the Second World War in Europe (see Map 89). Each of the protagonists of the campaign had substantially differing aims. For Germany it was to overturn the *Versailles settlement, destroy Poland, and satisfy territorial irredenta including Upper Silesia, the *Polish corridor, and *Danzig. With the exception of Danzig, none of these territories contained a German majority. For the USSR, Stalin's alliance with Hitler (see NAZI–SOVIET PACT) was to 'liberate' Belorussian and Ukrainian peasants from 'Polish landlords' and to gain time and a territorial buffer against a potentially menacing Nazi Germany. For Poland, the aim was survival in what promised to be a long and costly war.

The immediate political crisis leading to the Polish campaign began in spring 1939 with the German absorption of what remained of Czechoslovakia. Following the occupation of Prague, France and the UK made a verbal Guarantee of Poland (see POLAND, GUARANTEE OF) and Hitler signed the Nazi–Soviet Pact which contained secret clauses for the fourth partition of Poland.

On the eve of the conflict, Germany (and the Soviet Union) enjoyed a significant preponderance of military strength over Poland. In the spring of 1939, the German armed forces mustered more than 100 active and reserve divisions and a cavalry brigade. The most important units

Polish campaign

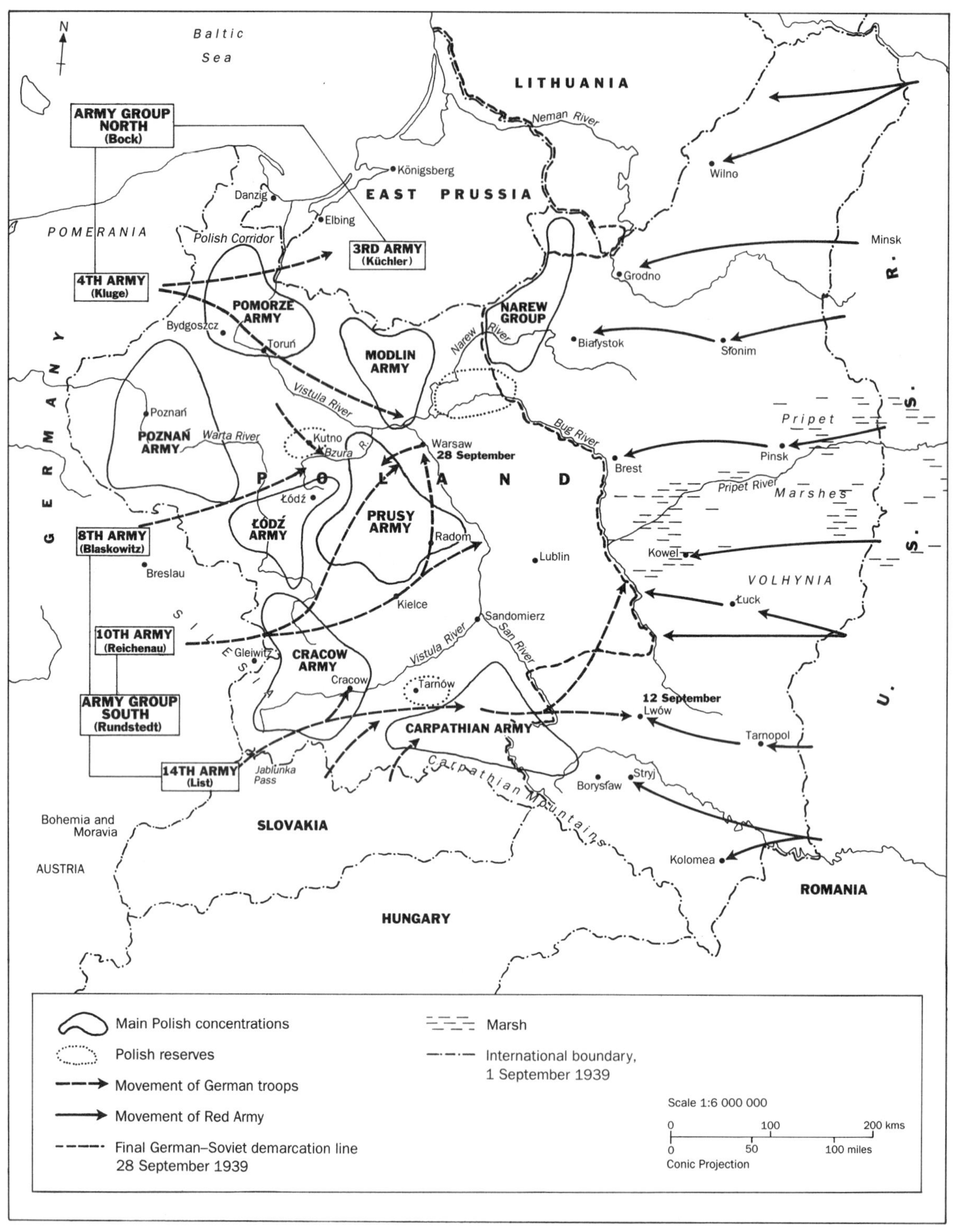

89. **Polish campaign**, September–October 1939

of the Wehrmacht were the 5 panzer divisions (about 300 tanks each), the 4 light divisions (with substantially fewer tanks, these were scheduled to be converted into panzer divisions), and 4 motorized divisions (infantry divisions completely equipped with motor vehicles). The German infantry divisions were more numerous and well provided with artillery and supporting weaponry although they were almost exclusively dependent on horse transport (see ANIMALS). The total manpower of the German armed forces consisted of 2,500,000 trained men, active and reserve.

The Polish Army's peacetime strength in 1939 stood at about 280,000 men in 30 infantry divisions, 11 cavalry brigades, 2 mechanized brigades, and supporting specialist units. The peacetime army could draw on a large pool of nearly 3 million trained and partially trained reservists. Upon mobilization, reservists brought the standing units up to wartime strength and held the potential for fifteen reserve divisions. Some reservists without specific mobilization assignments served in a National Guard-type formation, the Obrona Narodowa.

The disparity in strength was even more evident when comparing German and Polish strength in air and naval forces. The Luftwaffe had more than 3,600 operational aircraft available on the eve of hostilities and deployed more than 1,500 of them: 897 bombers, 426 fighters, and numerous auxiliary types such as reconnaissance and transport in two *Luftflotte*. The Polish Air Force (Lotnictwo Wojskowe) in 1939 had in all approximately 1,900 aircraft and deployed more than 400 of them, including 154 bombers and 159 fighters. German aircraft of virtually all categories were more modern and technically advanced than the obsolescent machines used by the Poles. Only in some categories of bomber aircraft did the Polish Air Force have fully up-to-date equipment.

The German navy possessed an overwhelming superiority in the *Baltic Sea. Available at the outbreak of hostilities were the modern battle-cruisers **Scharnhorst* and *Gneisenau*, 3 'pocket battleships', 2 heavy cruisers, 6 light cruisers, 22 destroyers 43 submarines, and 2 obsolete pre-Dreadnought battleships used as training ships, the *Schlesien* and *Schleswig-Holstein*. The principal units of the Polish Navy consisted of just 4 modern destroyers and five modern submarines.

In terms of military doctrine, the Polish campaign provided the Wehrmacht with an opportunity to test the efficacy of the previously untried *blitzkrieg technique. Although the Polish Army's tactical doctrine was also innovative, by emphasizing manoeuvre and economy of force, the material condition of Polish units made its application an ambitious prospect—Polish cavalry brigades, for instance, were only beginning the process of conversion into mechanized units.

German operational planning for the campaign crystallized in August 1939 under the codename FALL WEISS (Operation White). It envisaged the destruction of the Polish Army west of the Vistula–Narew–San river line by a concentric attack originating from Silesia in the south and Pomerania–East Prussia in the north. General von *Bock commanded Army Group North with the Third Army under Lt-General Georg von Küchler composed of eight infantry divisions, a panzer brigade, and a cavalry brigade in East Prussia and Fourth Army under *Kluge containing four infantry divisions, two motorized divisions, and a panzer division in Pomerania. Both armies had the task of pinching off the Polish corridor at its base. Third Army also had a central role in that it was to drive south towards Warsaw and cut off the line of retreat of Polish forces to the west.

Army Group South in Silesia contained the bulk of the German forces deployed in the Polish campaign. Under the command of General von *Rundstedt, it comprised: Eighth Army under *Blaskowitz, of five infantry divisions; Tenth Army under *Reichenau of six infantry, two motorized infantry, two panzer, and three light divisions; and Fourteenth Army under *List of five infantry, two panzer, and one light divisions. The objective of the Tenth Army's advance was Warsaw, with the Eighth and Fourteenth Armies providing protection on its flanks.

FALL WEISS committed the bulk of the German Army (over 60 divisions) to the Polish campaign, leaving only a screening force in the west. German plans rested on a speedy end to Polish resistance before the French Army could intervene.

Polish planning for a war with Germany began rather late. Although the Polish general staff made some initial studies in 1935, it was not until March 1939 that detailed work began on defence plan 'West', or 'Plan Z' as it would eventually be known. Polish planners correctly anticipated the directions from which the Wehrmacht would attack. Moreover, the Polish military understood that Poland could not conduct a war bereft of allies, but that help would not be immediately forthcoming.

With these assumptions in mind, the Polish general staff adopted a cordon defence in Plan Z that aimed to defend the western areas of the country. Although a plan predicated on a defensive position behind the Vistula–Narew–San river lines would have seemed more prudent, the western regions of Poland were the most populous and economically developed in the country. Political considerations therefore made it impossible to abandon them. Plan Z precluded a local German offensive to seize only the Polish corridor and Upper Silesia and signified Polish resolve to contest every bit of Polish territory, insuring against a repeat of the Anglo-French policy of appeasement of Germany typified by the *Munich agreement.

Polish dispositions under Plan Z were strung out along the length of Polish frontier facing Germany and Slovakia. In the north facing east Prussia was the Narew Group consisting of two infantry divisions and one cavalry brigade commanded by Maj-General Czesław Młot-Fijałkowski. West of the Narew Group and also facing east Prussia was the Modlin Army under General Emil Przedrzymirski-Krukowicz with two infantry divisions and two cavalry brigades. Behind these two formations was a reserve force of three infantry divisions under General Stanisław Skwarczyński.

At the base of the Polish corridor stood General W. Bortnowski's Pomorze Army with five infantry divisions and one cavalry brigade. The Poznań Army, commanded by General Tadeusz Kutrzeba, was the next major formation to the south with four infantry divisions and two cavalry brigades. It stood in the Poznań salient and was supported by a reserve force of two infantry divisions. The Łódź Army occupied the central sector along the Polish–German frontier and consisted of four infantry divisions and two cavalry brigades under General Juliusz Rómmel. Facing Silesia was the Cracow Army with seven infantry divisions, a cavalry brigade, and a mechanized brigade led by General Antoni Szylling.

The Carpathian Army under General Kazimierz Fabrycy covered the southern border with two mountain brigades and was supported by the Tarnów reserve force of two infantry divisions. The general reserve of the Polish armed forces, the Prusy Army, situated just south of Warsaw, was commanded by General Stefan Dab-Biernacki. It contained eight infantry divisions, one cavalry brigade, and a tank brigade. A very weak screening force covered the long Polish–Soviet frontier.

The bombardment of the Polish garrison at *Westerplatte by the German training ship, *Schleswig-Holstein*, anchored in Danzig harbour, signalled the opening of the German attack on Poland in the small hours of the morning on 1 September 1939. Air attacks were launched simultaneously, with military targets, such as airfields, roads, and railway lines, being heavily bombed. The Luftwaffe's weight in numbers gave it immediate air superiority, allowing it to range over the country.

The ground war moved quickly as the German Army broke through the Polish defences in the opening battles. The campaign proceeded in three phases: (1) the opening battles on the frontier, (2) the drive on Warsaw and the one Polish counter-attack, and (3) the elimination of pockets of Polish resistance.

In the north, the German Third and Fourth Armies effected a juncture, cutting the Polish corridor at the base by 3 September. These operations led to the destruction of the Pomorze Army and the withdrawal of the Modlin Army. From Silesia, German Army Group South made initial breakthroughs against the Łódź and Cracow Armies. By 5 September the Polish position was critical, with the British and French declarations of war against Germany offering little hope of relief.

Between 6 and 10 September the Third and Fourth Armies from the north and Army Group South pressed home their initial successes by driving on Warsaw. With their motorized and panzer divisions, the German Fourth Army in the north and the Tenth in the south played a crucial role in the advance and demonstrated the efficacy of the blitzkrieg.

The only serious Polish counter-attack was launched on 9 September by the retreating Poznań Army in a south east direction from the Bzura against the flank of the advancing German Eighth Army. In the three-day battle of *Kutno the Poznań Army destroyed a German division before air attacks and reinforcements from the German Tenth Army checked the Polish attack. The speed of the advancing German armour and the disruption of communications by the Luftwaffe precluded plans for organizing a defence behind the Vistula–Narew–San line; and with the Polish command structure breaking down under the onslaught, the Polish C-in-C, Marshal Edward Śmigły-Rydz, found it impossible to communicate with, let alone direct, his increasingly isolated formations. By mid-September, the German forces from Army Groups North and South met near Brest-Litovsk completing a wide encirclement of Warsaw and the bulk of the Polish armed forces.

In the final phase of the September campaign, the collapse of Polish resistance was accelerated by the entry of the Red Army into eastern Poland on 17 September. What remained of any substantial organized Polish resistance was centred on Warsaw and the fortress of Modlin to the north of the city. After a resolute defence in the face of air and artillery bombardment, and continual pressure from the German Army, Warsaw capitulated on 27 September followed by the Modlin fortress a day later. The last vestige of organized resistance ended on 5 October.

The tally sheet of the September campaign reflects the success of the blitzkrieg doctrine. German casualties in the four-week campaign numbered under 50,000 with 8,082 killed, 27,278 wounded, and 5,029 missing. Polish losses were significantly higher, with an estimated 70,000 officers and men killed and about 130,000 wounded. Some 90,000 men escaped to Hungary, Latvia, Lithuania, and Romania, many of whom made their way to the west.

The September campaign has engendered many myths about Polish ineptness and suicidal heroism. The often repeated stories that the Polish Air Force was destroyed on the ground in the opening hours of the war and that Polish cavalry charged tanks are cases in point. They owe more to historical fiction than to actual events on the battlefield. The Polish armed forces simply succumbed to a more numerous and better equipped foe employing a new and deadly military doctrine. PAUL LATAWSKI

Kennedy, R. M., *The German Campaign in Poland* (1939) (Washington, DC, 1956).

Biegański, W., Kozłowski, E., and Matusak, P. (eds.), *The Policy and Strategy of Poland in the Second World War 1939–1945* (Warsaw, 1975).

Polish corridor, as it was called in German and Anglo-American terminology, was a narrow strip of land of some 15,500 sq. km. (6,000 sq. mi.) which gave Poland access to the Baltic Sea (see DANZIG) and separated east Prussia from Germany proper (see Map 78). Awarded to Poland in the *Versailles settlement of 28 June 1919, the corridor had a mixed population with a Polish majority. Between the wars it was of vital economic and strategic importance to Poland; for Germany, it was a territorial irredenta. In Polish eyes, it formed the bulk of the province of Royal (West) Prussia, seized by the Hohenzollerns in 1772. PAUL LATAWSKI

Fitzgerald, W., *The New Europe: An Introduction to Its Political Geography* (3rd edn., London, 1948).
Kulski, W. W., *Germany and Poland: From War to Peaceful Relations* (Syracuse, NY, 1976).
Mason, J. B., *The Danzig Dilemma: A Study in Peacemaking by Compromise* (Stanford, Calif., 1946).

Polish Resettlement Corps. In the summer of 1945 some 250,000 Polish troops remained in the West serving under British operational command. Large numbers did not wish to return to a homeland under communist rule. They were encouraged to join the Polish Resettlement Corps (PRC), a non-combatant unit of the British Army formed in September 1946 with the purpose of facilitating the transfer of Polish troops to civilian life in the UK. Service in the PRC was for a maximum of two years during which members could learn English and a trade, before seeking employment. Some 114,000 Poles joined the PRC, of whom 20,000 either emigrated or returned to Poland. KEITH SWORD

Sword, K., with Davies, N., and Ciechanowski J., *The Formation of the Polish Community in Britain, 1939–50* (London, 1989).

Polish–Soviet frontier, the source of considerable acrimony between the Polish *government-in-exile in London and the USSR during the Second World War. Why the eventual frontier was chosen can only be understood in the context of earlier attempts to find a solution to this problem.

The *Versailles settlement that followed the *First World War never defined a permanent Polish–Soviet boundary, and its recommendation (8 December 1919) that the line of the River Bug should form a 'provisional minimum frontier' was never implemented. This frontier was then revived at the Spa conference (July 1920), and agreed to by the Poles, as a potential truce line for terminating the Polish–Soviet war, and it was at Spa that it became known as the Curzon Line, so-named after the then British foreign secretary.

However, the Curzon Line remained undefined in eastern Galicia, and though it was agreed at Spa that the truce line there should run where the armies stood when the truce came into effect, the telegram explaining this to Moscow contained a glaring ambiguity. For it simultaneously proposed two lines in eastern Galicia: one to the east and the other to the west of the city of *Lwów.

In any case the line was never implemented, as the truce was soon broken when the Bolshevik armies advanced across it and eventually it was events on the battlefield which determined the boundary between the two countries, with the Treaty of Riga (1921) establishing a frontier considerably east of the Curzon Line. For the Poles this closed the matter, but the signing of the German–Soviet Treaty of Friendship, Co-operation, and

90. **Polish–Soviet frontier**

Demarcation (see NAZI–SOVIET PACT) on 28 September 1939 resulted in a German–Soviet partition of Poland. This established a line mostly to the west of the Curzon Line. In eastern Galicia it followed the part of the Curzon Line mentioned in the Spa telegram that ran to the west of *Lwów.

Later in the war, when negotiations with the USSR began over the future of Poland, Stalin maintained that the line established by the Riga treaty was defunct. At the wartime conferences at Teheran (see EUREKA) and Yalta (see ARGONAUT) the USSR, the UK, and the USA agreed to a revived Curzon Line as the post-war Polish–Soviet frontier. The USSR successfully exploited the ambiguity of the Spa telegram to obtain the Curzon Line which, in its southernmost reaches, excluded Lwów from Poland. The UK and the USA urged the Polish government-in-exile to accept the Soviet version of the Curzon Line in 1944, and in the end the new boundary became a *fait accompli*. PAUL LATAWSKI

Kirkien, L., *Russia, Poland, and the Curzon Line* (London, nd).

Political Warfare Executive (PWE), a British secret service devoted to propaganda and *subversive warfare, formally set up in September 1941 after fourteen months' bitter wrangling between several government departments, open and secret. Most of its staff came from SO1, the propaganda branch of *SOE, into which, in turn, they had moved in 1940 from a semi-secret department of the foreign office, usually called EH after Electra House on the Thames embankment where it had worked in 1938–9. Sometimes EH was called CS, after the initials of Sir Campbell Stuart its head, who returned to business in Canada soon after SOE was formed.

PWE had three political masters at once, an unusual but (as it turned out) not quite unworkable arrangement. They were, in order of importance, the foreign secretary, Anthony *Eden, who decided policy (when he had time); the minister of information, Brendan *Bracken, who ran administration and day-to-day detail; and the minister of economic warfare, Hugh *Dalton, and then Lord Selborne, who had some influence on policy and helped with transport. For cover, PWE used the political intelligence department of the foreign office (PID); it even used PID's writing-paper, which has frequently confused historians.

The service's first executive head was a diplomat, Reginald ('Rex') Leeper (1888–1968), who moved back to diplomacy in 1943. In March 1942 another figure, also nominally a diplomat but with journalistic capacities as well, Robert Bruce Lockhart (1887–1970) was put in over Leeper's head; he had been the first British representative in the USSR, while the Bolshevik revolution raged, and had charm as well as a capacity for leadership. In 1939, EH had moved its main base to the Duke of Bedford's seat at Woburn, some 60 km. (40 mi.) north-west of London; there most of PWE's staff remained. A few of them found it necessary to return to London, and worked in Bush House, Aldwych, beside the offices of the *BBC that worked into Europe: contacts between PWE and the BBC were constant and necessary. While the last word always rested with the speaker actually in front of the microphone, PWE had a large say in forming the outlines of BBC broadcasts into occupied territory. In the second half of the war, PWE helped to formulate such directives as the British issued through this channel to assist the course of actual operations; before then, its tasks were to spread news of how the war was actually going, to keep alive a spirit of resistance, and to counter the daily assertions of *Goebbels on Berlin radio. It had in fact a dual role: to influence German opinion against the Nazis, and to influence opinion in occupied countries against the Germans.

PWE was always aware that the BBC's broadcasts were an invaluable source of news for the clandestine press, to which it sometimes afforded more direct help. A few PWE agents were sent into western Europe, usually through SOE channels, to assist or even to found clandestine newspapers; in times of crisis, they could sometimes arrange for supplies of newsprint and printer's ink to be parachuted in.

Official programmes put out by the BBC were classified as white propaganda; PWE was also much involved in clandestine broadcasting, classified as black, notably through the work of Sefton ('Tom') Delmer (1904–79), a gifted *Daily Express* journalist, and of the equally gifted D. H. McLachlan (1908–71) of *The Times*. It has never been possible to measure how much impact their two stations had.

Equally, no useful measurements have ever been made of the effectiveness of PWE's other main channel of seeking to influence opinion, the dropping of leaflets from the air either over Germany, or over German- or Italian-occupied territories. In the US Army, where PWE's work was termed psychological warfare, still more attention was paid to leaflet-preparation and dropping.

More secretly, thanks to a printing accident PWE was also able to forge German official documents, and try to distribute them. In 1934 the Monotype Corporation had won an international competition to provide new sets of Gothic type for every German government department, and had kept a set of them. This set was shown by chance to Ellic Howe, then a sergeant-major at Anti-Aircraft Command HQ, who at once saw the possibilities. He moved to PWE, where he not only manufactured bogus pamphlets, but produced German *Kennkarten* (identity papers) indistinguishable from genuine ones: a valuable gift to other secret services.

The maverick R. H. S. ('Dick') Crossman (1907–74) played an influential and sometimes useful role in PWE, mainly in its German section, which he headed for over two years; he was close to *Eisenhower's elbow during the Normandy landings in June 1944 (see OVERLORD).

Laughter is a great weapon against tyrants; PWE helped to mobilize it by passing on Churchill's gibes against Mussolini and Hitler, and by light-hearted commentaries on the occasional idiocies of German and Italian propaganda. Moreover, Goebbels had arranged for a twice-daily communique to be sent out to the whole of the German press; of which, by a communications accident, PWE twice daily obtained a copy. This enabled Delmer and other broadcasters to provide such intimate details of current life inside Germany as to persuade their listeners either that they were broadcasting from inside that country, or that the British were miraculously well informed.

In the early *Western Desert campaigns, PWE operated a few front-line propaganda units, armed with megaphones, to try to persuade Italian troops to desert. These came under G. L. Steer, who had distinguished himself as a *Times* reporter during the *Spanish Civil War. The rest of PWE's effort in the Near and Middle East became over-entangled with staff intrigues in Cairo, and was of slight effect.

*Mountbatten, never one to discount publicity, made sure that PWE had every opportunity it wanted in the Far East; but the scarcity of wireless receiving sets in occupied areas, and the extra difficulties of oriental languages, made PWE much less effective in Asia than it was in Europe. M. R. D. Foot

Balfour, M., *Propaganda in War 1939–1945* (London, 1979).
Howe, E. *The Black Game* (London, 1980).
Young, K. (ed.), *The Diaries of Sir Robert Bruce Lockhart* (London, 1980).

Pomeranian Wall, a line of fortifications which was built in 1932–7 along the German (western) side of the so-called *Polish Corridor. It consisted of a series of interlinked tank-traps and artillery emplacements, and stretched for some 120 km (75 mi.) on either side of the town of Schneidemühl (see Map 41). In January 1945 it failed to halt the main Soviet offensive towards Berlin, having been bypassed to the south by forces moving through central Poland. But its defenders posed a serious threat to the Soviet Army's communications, and fought with dogged determination for many weeks. They included two Dutch divisions of the Waffen-*SS who were still holding out at the start of the battle which led to the fall of *Berlin. They were finally overpowered by units of the First Polish Army fighting under Soviet command. Norman Davies

Pope, see PIUS XII.

Popov, Dusko (1912–81), Yugoslav-born British *double agent, codenamed TRICYCLE, who has been described as 'a familiar character in marginal cosmopolitan circles; energetic, raffish, charming, plausible, worldly, full of wonderful schemes, so marvellous that he came to believe them himself' (B. Bruce-Riggs, *Intelligence and National Security*, April 1992, p. 77).

Popov, a Yugoslav commercial lawyer with a German degree, was approached in 1940 to join the *Abwehr. He reported this to the British who used him as a double agent during his business trips to Lisbon and elsewhere. In August 1941 the Abwehr sent him to the USA to form a new spy network and to obtain economic and military intelligence. The full facts are still not known, but it appears there was no high-level assessment of the Abwehr questionnaire, concealed in microdots on four documents, which Popov had with him and which included a number of questions about *Pearl Harbor. One of the reasons put forward for this lack of interest by US intelligence is that J. Edgar *Hoover, the head of the FBI (see USA, 6), disliked and distructed the high-living Popov, but it is equally likely that he thought he was a British plant. Popov later alleged that other relevant information he supplied had also been ignored, but there is no evidence that he ever provided it.

FBI ineptitude in handling the feedback of information to the Abwehr, and German suspicions resulting from it, ended in Popov's returning to the UK in October 1942. He eventually managed to re-establish his credentials with the Abwehr and this enabled him to be used for *deception purposes by the *XX-committee before the Normandy landings in June 1944 (see OVERLORD). After the war Popov was decorated and awarded British citizenship. See also SPIES.

Popov, D., *Spy–Counterspy* (London, 1974).

Popski's Private Army (PPA), British special forces sabotage unit, the smallest independent unit in the British Army. It was formed by a Belgian émigré of Russian extraction, Vladimir Peniakoff, nicknamed 'Popski' by members of the *Long Range Desert Group (LRDG) with whom he initially worked. Officially designated No. 1 Demolition Squadron, it operated in armed jeeps behind Axis lines during the *Western Desert, *North African, and *Italian campaigns. It initially comprised two officers and twelve other ranks, but by December 1943 had expanded to 6 officers and 80 other ranks. After its formation in November 1942 it did much useful work with the LRDG reconnoitring the route for *Montgomery's left hook which outflanked the *Mareth Line in southern Tunisia in March 1943. It was then attached to Lt-General Kenneth Anderson's First Army in northern Tunisia and undertook several raids that destroyed 34 aircraft and 118 vehicles before all Axis forces surrendered in May 1943. When the Italian campaign started in September 1943 the PPA landed at Taranto with the British 1st Airborne Division, and from December 1943 operated for the rest of the war with Italian partisans behind German lines.

Peniakoff, V., *Private Army* (London, 1950).

Portal, Marshal of the Royal Air Force Sir Charles (1893–1971), British airman, known to all his friends as Peter, who, as a member of the British *Chiefs of Staff and *Combined Chiefs of Staff committees, was one of the principal architects of the Allies' victory in Europe.

A dispatch rider at the start of the *First World War, Portal was soon commissioned and then seconded to the Royal Flying Corps in which he served with distinction.

He was commissioned into the newly formed RAF and by 1939 was the air council member in charge of personnel with the rank of air vice-marshal. In September 1939 he was promoted acting air marshal and in April 1940 was appointed C-in-C Bomber Command.

It was soon shown during the *Norwegian campaign and in the fighting which preceded the fall of *France that without adequate fighter protection Portal's forces were of little consequence by day. However, Churchill was much impressed by the energy with which Portal prepared against the impending German invasion of the UK (see SEALION) and by the comparative effectiveness of night raids on German invasion ports and barge concentrations. The vigour with which the RAF struck back at German cities (see STRATEGIC AIR OFFENSIVES, 1) immediately bombs started falling on London also appealed to the prime minister, for though these sorties caused little damage—far less than was thought at the time—they did wonders for morale. They also goaded Hitler into diverting the Luftwaffe from attacking RAF airfields to bombing London, a critical turning-point in the battle of *Britain.

From the start Portal urged that German industrial areas be attacked, not just selected factories or plants, for he knew such precision was, at that time, beyond the capabilities of his aircraft. However, this policy was not accepted until after he had succeeded *Newall as chief of air staff in October 1940 with the rank of air chief marshal. Making this policy work was no simple matter and much of Portal's energies early on were directed to improving *electronic navigation systems and bombing aids, increasing the power of his bombs, and making early experiments in marking targets which led to the formation of the *Pathfinder Force. When the *Butt report of August 1941 showed just how ineffective RAF raids were, Portal proposed a wider use of *area bombing by night, and to implement his new directive in February 1942 he replaced Bomber Command's C-in-C, Air Chief Marshal Richard Peirse (1892–1970), with *Harris. But he always appreciated the advantages of daylight precision bombing; was keen, once the USA came into the war, to establish in the UK an American bomber force that could implement it; and held steadily to the worth of such a force when Churchill, for one, was sceptical of its potential. Ironically, Portal held the view that the long-range fighter, which eventually enabled the daylight bombers to be so effective, would always be outfought by its short-range opponents.

Portal accompanied Churchill to nearly all the *Grand Alliance conferences and was immediately accepted and respected by the Americans who appreciated his calm, measured approach. At the Casablanca conference in January 1943 (see SYMBOL) he was selected by the Combined Chiefs of Staff to co-ordinate the strategic bomber forces of the two nations in a *Combined Bomber Offensive against Germany. In April 1944 the two bomber forces were placed under *Eisenhower's control for the Normandy landings that June (see OVERLORD), but when they reverted to the Combined Chiefs in September, it was decided to concentrate them on precision targets, especially oil plants. However, Harris disagreed with this approach, preferring to pursue the area bombing of German cities. It was a wrangle which remained unresolved. Attacks on German cities continued, including *Dresden, though precision raids did take precedence over them when operational conditions allowed. Only the cessation of hostilities avoided the dismissal of Harris or a great diminution in Portal's authority.

When not attending the Allied conferences Portal fought most of his war from Whitehall, and at the 2,000 or so Chiefs of Staff meetings he later calculated he attended. He did not concern himself with the day-to-day running of the RAF but with the strategic planning of the war. He made mistakes, particularly over Harris and with his initial opposition to long-range fighters, but his friendship with the UK's principal allies, and the confidence Churchill retained in him, were of overriding value to the war effort. He was promoted Marshal of the Royal Air Force in January 1944. Eisenhower later said that he regarded Portal as the greatest British war leader, 'greater even than Churchill'. Described as 'Cold, remote, enigmatic, but obviously of very high intelligence' (J. Terraine, *The Right of the Line*, London, 1985, p. 684), Portal, who had been knighted in 1940, retired from the RAF in 1945 and the same year was created Baron Portal of Hungerford.

Richards, D., *Portal of Hungerford* (London, 1977).

Portugal, the UK's oldest ally which remained neutral throughout the war. Portugal had been a republic since 1910. Its president during the war, General António Carmona (1869–1951), had seized power in May 1926 and in 1932 had appointed *Salazar as prime minister. The country's upper classes admired the Nazis, and were influenced by them, but the Portuguese working people undoubtedly supported the Allies.

In March 1939 Portugal and Spain signed a Treaty of Friendship and Non-Aggression, the Pacto Iberico, and one of the most important, if not the most important, services Salazar made to the Allied cause was the part he played in helping the Spanish leader, General *Franco, resist Hitler's blandishments to join the Axis powers. When the war started, on 1 September 1939, both Spain and Portugal declared their neutrality. By the end of it Portugal, through its co-belligerent status, had qualified as a founding member of the United Nations (see SAN FRANCISCO CONFERENCE), which Spain had not.

Salazar's regime was a right-wing dictatorship but he disliked the Nazis. However, this dislike was tempered by his fear of *communism, and he walked a tightrope to keep his country out of the war. His foreign policy contained two main elements: Iberian solidarity and maintaining the Anglo-Portuguese alliance which dates back to 1374. Neutrality was therefore strictly enforced:

when eleven US aircraft were obliged to land at Lisbon in January 1943 they were impounded and their crews interned. Even after October 1943, when allowing Allied air bases in the Azores made it a co-belligerent, Portugal maintained an outward veneer of neutrality. It was, for example, one of two non-combatant countries (Eire was the other) which flew flags at half-mast after Hitler's suicide in April 1945.

However, strategically situated as it was, Portugal could not escape the effects of the war. Its far-flung colonies (see Map E) in Portuguese Africa, and those of Goa and Portuguese Timor, were of little consequence. But its island dependencies in the Atlantic—the Azores, Cape Verde Islands, and Madeira—were potentially of great strategic importance, and its production of tungsten was vital to both sides. Apart from Spain, and Sweden which produced only one-tenth of Portugal's output in 1941, it was the only European source for this essential *raw material, used for alloying steel, and Salazar's hard bargaining over the export of it to Germany exasperated the Allies. Fearing retaliation from Hitler, after Allied air bases were established in the Azores, Salazar refused to stop his tungsten allocation to Germany. As part of their *economic warfare efforts, intense Allied diplomatic pressure was brought to bear on Portugal with Brazil, a former Portuguese possession, objecting that the tungsten was contributing to casualties among its troops fighting in the *Italian campaign. Salazar was eventually forced to relent, and in June 1944 he agreed to embargo all German tungsten supplies—a tough decision as it meant the loss of £2 million in revenue and 100,000 jobs, a huge cost for such a poor country.

Portugal's capital, Lisbon, was the chief distribution port for *International Red Cross Committee relief supplies to *prisoner-of-war and *internment camps; the main link for civilian flights between the UK and the USA; and a notorious centre for *spies.

Portuguese Africa consisted of Portuguese East Africa (Mozambique) and the Portuguese West African colonies of Cabinda, Angola, São Tomé, and Portuguese Guinea, which, with Portugal, remained neutral. Portuguese East Africa was, for part of the war, a base for German agents working in South Africa (see OSSEWABRANDWAG).

postal history is one of the lesser auxiliary sciences which offers a rich source of information about the Second World War. It encompasses philately, but is more concerned with the collection and analysis of letters, postcards, envelopes, telegrams, and other material which circulated in the postal systems of the era. Hence, in addition to postage stamp issues, which reflect political authority at any particular point, it requires the study of postmarks, of postal *censorship, of addresses and addressees, of correspondents and their correspondence. Since most items of postal history carry a very precise record of the time and place of their posting and delivery, they provide an unusually accurate and penetrating insight into shifting wartime conditions. The categories which most interest war historians include: occupation issues; field post offices; soldiers' correspondence; *prisoner-of-war and *concentration camp correspondence; wartime censorship; refugees and *International Red Cross agencies; propaganda cards; civilian correspondence, especially in occupied zones or from military families; 'underground' postal services; *Judaica*; postal communication with enemy countries via neutral states; illustrated postcards. NORMAN DAVIES

Potsdam conference and Declaration, see TERMINAL; see also GRAND ALLIANCE.

Pound, Admiral of the Fleet Sir (Alfred) Dudley (1877–1943), British naval officer who served as First Sea Lord and a member of the British *Chiefs of Staff committee from the outbreak of war in September 1939.

After serving in the *First World War—he commanded a battleship at the battle of Jutland—Pound became C-in-C Mediterranean in 1936, and then, in June 1939, First Sea Lord when the first choice fell ill. He was promoted Admiral of the Fleet the following month.

Pound was shy, and shunned the limelight. Unlike the other two service departments, the Admiralty was an operational centre and he was overinclined to interfere with the conduct of operations; and, partly through not appointing a Deputy First Sea Lord until 1942, he was badly overworked. There was widespread, though unjust, criticism of him when a German squadron sailed the length of the English Channel in February 1942 (see CERBERUS); and it was Pound's decision to order the *Arctic convoy PQ17 to scatter, with disastrous results. But there were also many notable successes, the sinking of the **Bismarck* in May 1941 and victory in the battle of the *Atlantic, to name but two. Early on, as chairman of the Chiefs of Staff, he was a steadying influence on Churchill with whom he worked closely and to whom, some have argued, he too often deferred. In March 1942 he resigned as chairman, possibly in protest at *Mountbatten's promotion to vice-admiral and his appointment to the committee. But he remained a member under *Brooke, who questioned his effectiveness because of his habit of 'cat-napping' in meetings. Some of those who worked with him have vouched for his vigour and stamina, but there was a question mark over his health. At the Quebec conference in August 1943 (see QUADRANT) he began to feel the effects of the tumour which was to kill him, and he was forced to resign the following month. He had already declined a peerage early in 1943, and he died on Trafalgar Day that year before he was able to receive the high awards that were undoubtedly due to him. He was knighted in 1933. See also SEA POWER.

Power, Charles (1888–1968), Canadian Liberal politician who was appointed minister of national defence for air in Mackenzie *King's government in May 1940 and associate minister of national defence the following month. He guided the development and operation of the *British Empire Air Training Scheme and did much to promote the interests of Royal Canadian Air Force personnel serving in the UK. But as a Quebecker he opposed conscription for service overseas and resigned in November 1944 when it was introduced.

PQ17, see ARCTIC CONVOYS.

Prague rising, part of a general rising against the Germans in Bohemia and Moravia which resulted in the last large-scale fighting in Europe. It began with strikes in nearby towns, and on 5 May 1945 Prague's population rose against the German garrison as Red Army troops of Marshal *Konev's First Ukrainian Front (army group), and Lt-General *Patton's Third US Army, approached from the east and west respectively. The Czech *government-in-exile in London appealed for help from the western Allies but *Eisenhower, who had agreed with the Soviets not to advance beyond a certain point, refused to allow Patton to help. Karl Frank, the real power behind *Frick, the Reich Protector of Bohemia and Moravia, also appealed for reinforcements and *Dönitz sent two divisions to help the garrison, which was without tanks or artillery. But on 8 May these reinforcements were stopped by the 1st Division of General *Vlasov's army which deserted from the German side to help the Czechs. They also cleared the remaining Germans from the capital before withdrawing, the following day Konev's troops entered Prague, and the Germans finally surrendered on 11 May (see GERMAN–SOVIET WAR, 11).

precision bombing is the bombing of specific targets, which the Eighth and Fifteenth US Army Air Forces employed during their daylight *strategic air offensives against European targets. It was something of a misnomer because only a squadron's lead bomber aimed at the target; the others just dropped their bombs as close as possible to those released by the leader (see also PATTERN BOMBING).

When the *Butt report revealed British Bomber Command's failure with precision bombing in 1941 the RAF turned to *area bombing which the Americans also used during their strategic air offensive against Japan. Later in the war, when *electronic navigation systems increased its accuracy, Bomber Command used precision bombing, often with remarkable success.

An example of true precision bombing was the destruction, prior to the Normandy landings (see OVERLORD), of all 24 bridges across the River Seine by aircraft of the Ninth USAAF. One of them, a railway bridge at Vernon, was destroyed by eight fighter-bombers with just eight tons of bombs. See also AMIENS PRISON, DAM BUSTERS, PEENEMÜNDE, and SHELL HOUSE raids.

press. Despite a shortage of newsprint, newspapers and magazines continued to be published in every country during the war years. The civilian press of the belligerents was part of the propaganda war; the armed forces newspapers boosted morale at the front; and the clandestine press of the various resistance organizations in occupied countries played an important part in keeping in contact with the civilian population and disseminating information not otherwise available (for propaganda and underground press see SUBVERSIVE WARFARE).

The number of newspaper titles published diminished in all belligerent nations as the war progressed, as did the size of those which survived, but circulations often increased. In the USA, where 135 newspapers were lost; the circulation of the rest jumped by 10 million to 50 million despite the competition created by broadcasting. UK newspapers increased their circulation from 19 million in 1938 to 24 million in 1945, though most were reduced to four pages. Only *The Times* and the *Daily Telegraph* chose to print six pages and take a 25% reduction in their print run. Germany, which had the largest press in the world in 1932 with 3,362 newspapers, had only 2,200 by 1939 and a mere 779 by 1945. In 1943 alone 950 were closed, including the famous *Frankfurter Zeitung*, and all cities of 100,000 or fewer were limited to a single newspaper. Nevertheless, the total circulation of the survivors increased from 19.8 million in 1939 to 25 million in 1945, 82.5% of it being devoted to Nazi publications. However, by the end of the war German newspapers were just single sheets of official communiqués and obituaries.

Japan, which in 1941 'possessed one of the most sophisticated mass media networks in the world' (B.-A. Shillony, *Politics and Culture in Wartime Japan*, Oxford, 1991, p. 91), did not have party or government newspapers. Most were privately owned and these backed the government for patriotic not political reasons. After the *China Incident began in 1937 they were strictly controlled by long-established *censorship laws and new laws were introduced in 1941. Provincial newspapers began to be amalgamated in 1940 so that they could be controlled more easily, and to save paper. Nevertheless, at the start of the *Pacific war the Japanese press had a daily circulation of 19 million, 'an average of more than one newspaper per household' (loc. cit.).

Censorship was total in Germany and Italy. It was total, too, in the USSR, where 2,700 out of 8,789 publications were lost when the Germans invaded in June 1941 (see BARBAROSSA), and in the occupied countries of Europe. A notable exception was Denmark where the Germans laid down certain censorship guidelines but left them to be implemented by the Danes. German occupying troops could not be criticized but the Danish Nazi Party could be, and was. The general tone of the Danish press did much to foster Danish resistance to the occupation which grew steadily throughout the war.

Of the neutral European countries Sweden had no censorship, but Switzerland was forced by Nazi pressure to introduce a law against anyone publicly insulting a foreign state. The press of both countries reported the deportation of Jews (see FINAL SOLUTION), Swiss newspapers doing so as early as August 1942. (Their plight seems to have been first mentioned in newspapers published in Slovakia in March 1942.) Despite censorship the newspapers of Axis countries were a useful source of information, as were those from neutral countries, and the British *Political Warfare Executive had analysts at the British embassy in Stockholm who read them all; an aircraft flew their reports to London weekly.

Censorship was so strict in Paris before the fall of *France in June 1940 that one paper protested by printing scissors on a blank column on its front page. Censorship was self-imposed in both the UK and USA, but a number of newspapers were forcibly closed on both sides of the Atlantic: Charles Coughlin's *Social Justice* in the USA and the Communist *Daily Worker* (for nineteen months) in London were two examples. The US press spoke out more often against the government than the British did against theirs, and the *Daily Mirror* was severely castigated by other London newspapers, and threatened with closure, when it stepped out of line by doing so. Security was of paramount importance and few reports from *war correspondents escaped the censor. But in June 1942 the *Chicago Tribune* published a report that could have betrayed US knowledge of the Japanese naval code (see ULTRA, 2); and in November 1940 the London *Evening Standard* reported the capture of a German weather party (see METEOROLOGICAL INTELLIGENCE) which might have warned the Germans that their *Abwehr hand cipher had been broken.

Hohenberg, J., *Free Press, Free People: The Best Cause* (New York, 1973).
Olson, K., *The History Makers* (Baton Rouge, La., 1966).

***Prince of Wales* and *Repulse* sinking of** (see Map 66). In an attempt to deter Japan from entering the war, this British battleship and battle-cruiser were sent to Singapore in October 1941. The carrier *Indomitable* should have joined them to provide air cover, but she had been damaged by running aground in the British West Indies. Her absence, and that of other intended components of the force, turned a doubtful political decision into a dangerous enterprise. The ships, designated Force Z, were under the overall command of Admiral Tom Phillips and were at Singapore on 8 December when the Japanese began their highly successful *Malayan campaign. Both ships were deployed immediately with three destroyer escorts to cut the supply lines of *Yamashita's Twenty-Fifth Army which had begun landing in Thailand and northern Malaya. But when surprise could not be achieved, nor cover by aircraft provided, the force turned back.

Phillips was then informed by Singapore that a further landing was taking place at Kuantan, close to his position. Assuming that he had to act on this information, and that air cover would automatically be provided, he altered course to investigate. His assumptions were wrong, and, ironically, he kept wireless silence to maintain a surprise that was never necessary as there were no landings. By failing to signal his intentions, he ruled out the possibility of receiving fighter cover which might conceivably have saved his ships.

The British force was first sighted by a Japanese submarine on 9 December and, though contact was subsequently lost, a second submarine sighted them early next morning and reconnaissance aircraft spotted them at 1015 the next morning. There followed a series of devastating bomb and torpedo attacks by aircraft of Rear-Admiral Matsunaga Sadaichi's First Air Force based in French Indo-China. They attacked at 1115 but Phillips still kept wireless silence and an emergency message, dispatched by *Repulse*, was not sent until 1158, too late for the air cover that was scrambled to help. *Repulse* was sunk first, at 1233, followed by *Prince of Wales* at 1320, and 840 men, including Phillips, lost their lives. Following *Taranto, the day of the invincibility of the surface capital warship had now finally passed. See also SEA POWER.

Marder, A., *Old Friends, New Enemies*, Vol. 1 (Oxford, 1981).
Middlebrook, M., and Mahoney, P., *Battleship* (London, 1977).

prisoners-of-war (POW). The *Hague Conventions of 1899 and 1907 declared that in modern warfare fighting men who laid down their arms were to be decently treated; the *Geneva Convention of 1929 spelled out the details. This last convention was signed and ratified by all the principal warring powers but two. The Japanese signed, but did not ratify; the USSR did not sign at all, for in Stalinist theory no soldier in the Red Army would ever surrender.

Under the Geneva Convention, POW were to be removed promptly from the battle area; if wounded, they were to be given adequate medical care; and they were to be housed and fed no worse than garrison troops of the capturing power. Under interrogation, they were entitled to refuse all information except their name and rank, or their service number. They could practise any *religion and they could correspond with their families and friends; if they escaped, they were to undergo no worse punishment on recapture than a month's solitary confinement. The *International Red Cross committee was to be allowed to inspect the permanent camps in which they were held.

By a long-standing convention among the world's officer class, capture had meant dishonour, but by the mid-twentieth century the changes and chances of war, particularly air war, were such that it might happen to anybody, and the aura of disgrace did not cling so tightly. What no one had foreseen was the scale of the impending problem.

So completely did the Polish and French armies collapse in 1939 and 1940 during the *Polish campaign and the fall of *France that the Germans found themselves with more than 2 million prisoners-of-war on their hands. As the war progressed, they lost more than 4.5 million men as prisoners themselves; and so false, in this respect at any

German **prisoners-of-war** captured in the Ruhr pocket, April 1945.

rate, was Stalinist myth that they captured nearly 5 million members of the Red Army. The *British Expeditionary Force left more than 50,000 prisoners behind after *Dunkirk, and British Empire forces also endured heavy losses in prisoners in the *Western Desert and *Balkan campaigns. The Italians' losses were not small, either; a famous message from the Coldstream Guards in the Western Desert on 9 December 1940 reported that they had had no time to count their prisoners yet, but held 'about five acres of officers and two hundred acres of other ranks'. Some 10,000 aircrew of RAF's Bomber Command survived the destruction of their aircraft to become POW.

Prisoners' fates varied very widely, according to time, place, and nationality. A few units—the Waffen-*SS on the Eastern Front was notorious in this respect—had a rule not to take any prisoners at all. In a few areas of Germany, aircrew who parachuted safely to earth were liable to be lynched by infuriated mobs. American and British POW formed the opinion that the Italians made much less agreeable gaolers than the Germans did; on the other hand, the Germans treated captured Soviet personnel abominably: about five-sixths of the soldiers of the Red Army who were taken prisoner did not survive the war. As the Soviet government had not signed the Geneva Convention, the Germans held that they were not bound by its terms; and they forgot their own obligations under the Hague Conventions (which had been instigated by the last tsar of Russia) and the dictates of common humanity. These men were hardly given food or shelter at all; their officers were, with few exceptions, shot after interrogation, and the rest were left prey to lice and typhus. Those who got the chance volunteered to join General *Vlasov's renegade army—anything to escape from the pit they were in. German policy in this respect was dictated by Nazi racial myth, which held that Anglo-Saxons were Aryans—therefore worthy of respect—while Slavs were only a superior form of cattle.

On a battlefield, POW were of interest to the intelligence officer of the battalion that had captured them, and might be subjected to a brisk interrogation by him, aimed at discovering the unit to which they belonged and anything that was to be found out about the enemy's immediate intentions. They might well be interrogated again, at more leisure, in some rear area. The Luftwaffe established a *Durchgangslager* (transit camp) at Oberursel near Frankfurt-am-Main through which they passed all the aircrew they captured, pumping them as ingeniously as they could for information about air force order of battle. The British had a similar institution at Cockfosters in north London.

Once clear of interrogation, officer POW had nothing to do but wait for the war to end; unless, as many of them did, they plotted to escape. Only one German managed to escape from England back to Germany, and he had to go round by Canada (where he jumped off a train) and the then still neutral USA. A total of more than 35,000 British, Commonwealth, and American fighting men managed escapes or evasions the other way (see MI9).

Those officers who made themselves extra obnoxious to the Germans by escaping repeatedly were liable to be sent, on recapture, to the medieval fortress-castle of *Colditz in Saxony, although even from Colditz it was not impossible for a few extra brave and extra lucky men to escape.

The Geneva Convention forbade work of any kind for officer prisoners and NCO (non-commissioned officer) prisoners were only supposed to do supervisory work. Private soldiers could be made to work (they were to be paid for it, after the war), provided they were not given any tasks of military importance—a rule everyone often found it convenient to forget. For instance, Italian POW in the UK were mostly used as farm workers, thus saving shipping space by reducing the need for food imports. An American prisoner who thought he was being overworked, contrary to the convention, for 14 hours a day seven days a week, complained to his guard who tapped his own rifle and remarked, 'Here is my Geneva Convention.'

The prisoner's worst enemy was usually boredom. Those who were not so intent on escape that they could think of nothing else might spend their time on amateur dramatics, or on educating each other. Food was an incessant preoccupation, particularly in the last winter of the war. Up to then, the Red Cross had provided British and American prisoners, at least, with food and comfort parcels which supplemented their often meagre rations. When *Himmler took over command of the German Replacement Army, and therewith of POW camps, in the autumn of 1944, the supply of parcels dried up.

With the help of Red Cross food and cigarettes, prisoners were often able to get on much closer terms with their guards than Himmler would have approved; it was sometimes possible to bribe or browbeat or blackmail a guard into providing equipment, and even passes, indispensable for a successful escape.

In the closing months of the war in Europe, the Germans tried to move their prisoners about, to keep them out of the way of the advancing armies; this meant that several thousand British and American prisoners were liberated by the Red Army rather than by compatriots. They were all sent out, eventually, through Odessa, but their presence in Soviet hands was a brake on Allied diplomats at the Potsdam conference (see TERMINAL). Stalin insisted on having all the surviving Red Army prisoners back, and all were sent off for a spell in the *GUlag, as a punishment for having been captured.

In South-East Asia, entirely different conditions applied. The Japanese had built up earlier in the century an almost universal conviction that surrender was the unspeakable disgrace, for a fighting man; until very late in the war, hardly any of their troops surrendered unwounded. Consequently they despised the 80,000-odd troops whom they took prisoner after the fall of *Singapore, as well as the captured Dutch inhabitants of the *Netherlands East Indies, and made no attempts to treat them humanely. They were given the minimum of food and shelter to sustain life and were worked hard as well. In particular, work gangs of POW were set down under ferocious guard to construct the *Burma–Thailand railway, through jungle and mountain; about 12,000 of them died while they laboured at this task. See also COWRA PRISON CAMP, FORCED LABOUR, INTERNMENT, OFLAG, and STALAG.

M. R. D. FOOT

propaganda, see SUBVERSIVE WARFARE and POLITICAL WARFARE EXECUTIVE.

proximity fuze, generic term for radio devices which detonated projectiles within lethal range of their targets.

An early version was fitted to British *rocket weapons in 1940 and British research into the fuze was passed by the *Tizard committee to the USA for development the same year. The *Oslo report revealed that the Germans were also working on a similar device but, it seems, they never used any operationally. The Americans called it the VT fuze—VT was just a *codename and did not stand for variable time or anything else. It was placed in the nose of a projectile—which had to be 75 mm. (2.9 in.) calibre or more—and emitted signals which were received back after being reflected from the target. When these reached the right strength the projectile exploded.

One of the war's safest fuzes, it was also one of its most closely guarded secrets. Its operational use was controlled by the *Combined Chiefs of Staff Committee which initially authorized only its use at sea to minimize the possibility of its being compromised. It was first employed operationally in June 1943 when the US cruiser *Helena* shot down a Japanese aircraft during the *Pacific war. British anti-aircraft guns defending London were permitted to use it against the German V-1 (see V-WEAPONS) from June 1944 and during the last week of these attacks it was responsible for their destruction of 79% of their targets. The *Ardennes campaign, which started on 16 December 1944, brought forward the date for its use in north-west Europe by nine days and it contributed decisively to the defeat of this German offensive, artillery air bursts having a particularly devastating effect. It was first employed against land targets in the Pacific during the pre-landing saturation bombardment of *Iwo Jima's defences in February 1945.

psychiatry, see MEDICINE.

PT boat. Officially designated a Patrol Craft Torpedo, this 24 m. (78 ft.) high-speed craft, armed with two torpedo tubes, was the US equivalent of the British *MTB and the German *E-boat. See also WARSHIPS.

Puerto Rico was, like the Virgin Islands, a US Caribbean colony. Air and sea bases were constructed there and conscription was introduced for the 2 million inhabitants when the USA entered the war; 70,000 Puerto Ricans subsequently served in the US armed forces. The island's principal crop was sugar which it produced in greater quantity than the British, Dutch, and French West Indies combined. See also CARIBBEAN AT WAR.

Pujol, Juan (1912–88), Spanish-born British *double agent codenamed GARBO—because the British considered him the best actor in the world—and ARABEL by the Germans.

When Pujol first approached the British to work for them he was rejected. He then approached the Germans, sensibly reasoning that if he was in *Abwehr pay he would become an offer the British could hardly refuse, and tricked the local Abwehr into believing he was sending them messages from England. One happened to be perilously close to the truth and his apparent presence in the UK, revealed by *ULTRA intelligence, caused *MI5 great consternation until his true whereabouts, and his true allegiance, became known, and he was then taken from Portugal to the UK.

In England Pujol was handled by a brilliant case officer, Tomàs Harris. Between them they invented a notional spy ring which comprised fourteen sub-agents and eleven well-placed informers, all of whom the Germans came to accept as real and trustworthy. During the next three years, this enabled the *XX-committee to pass false information to the Abwehr including, most importantly, the *deception plans for the Normandy landings (see OVERLORD). Pujol was so highly regarded by both sides that he was awarded the MBE by the British and the Iron Cross by the Germans (see DECORATIONS).

Pujol. J., and West, N., *Garbo* (London, 1986).

PURPLE, US codename for the Japanese diplomatic cipher enciphered on the Alphabetical Typewriter 97. For details see MAGIC.

Purple Heart, see DECORATIONS, USA.

Pu-Yi (1906–67), puppet ruler of the Japanese-dominated state of Manchukuo from 1932 to 1945. Widely known as Henry, a nickname given to him by his English tutor, he had been enthroned, aged three, as Hsüan T'ung, the last emperor of China, but was deposed by the 1911 Chinese revolution. After the Japanese annexed Manchuria, and renamed it Manchukuo, he eagerly accepted an invitation to become the new state's chief executive, and then its puppet emperor. When the USSR invaded Manchukuo in August 1945 (see JAPANESE–SOVIET CAMPAIGNS) he was captured and imprisoned in Siberia. As a witness, he gave perjured evidence at the *Far East War Crimes Trials before being returned to China in 1950 where he was again imprisoned. Satisfactorily converted to *communism, he was released in 1959 and worked as a gardener in Peking's botanical gardens, and then in the department of historical archives.

Pu-Yi, H., *From Emperor to Citizen, The Autobiography of Aisin-Gioro Pu-Yi* (Oxford, 1987).

QUADRANT, codename for the first Quebec conference held from 17 to 24 August 1943 to discuss future Allied strategy (see GRAND ALLIANCE). Churchill, Roosevelt, and their diplomatic and military advisers were present. They endorsed *COSSAC's outline plan for the Normandy landings (see OVERLORD) and approved the artificial harbours to be used there (see MULBERRIES); raised, for the first time, the possibility of the *French Riviera landings to coincide with OVERLORD; decided to bypass the Japanese stronghold of *Rabaul; and formed a new theatre of war, *South-East Asia Command, with *Mountbatten as its supreme commander. They also considered a scheme to build a huge carrier from ice (see HABBAKUK), listened to Brigadier *Wingate expound his methods of warfare in the *Burma campaign, and agreed to pressure Spain to discontinue supplying tungsten to Germany, and to withdraw its *Blue Division from the *German–Soviet war. Other business included the signing of the secret Quebec agreement by Churchill and Roosevelt. This regulated the procedures for co-operation between the UK and USA regarding the development and production of the *atomic bomb in which it was agreed, *inter alia*, that neither would employ a nuclear weapon against the other; that it would never be used against a third party without mutual consent; and that mutual consent was also required before a third party was given any information that would help that party produce an atomic bomb. See also DIPLOMACY.

Quebec Conferences, see QUADRANT and OCTAGON; see also GRAND ALLIANCE.

Quezon, Manuel (1878–1944) was elected president of the Philippines interim government, known as the Commonwealth, in 1935, and was re-elected in November 1941, but was forced to abandon Manila when the Japanese invaded Luzon in December 1941. He accompanied General *MacArthur to the fortified island of *Corregidor in Manila Bay but on 19 February 1942 was evacuated by submarine. He formed a *government-in-exile in Washington on 14 May 1942, and on 15 November 1943 Roosevelt signed a bill which extended Quezon's term of office until the Japanese had been expelled from the Philippines. After his death he was replaced by Sergio Osmeña.

Quisling, Vidkun (1887–1945), founder of the Norwegian Fascist National Union Party who forged useful links with Hitler and other Nazi leaders during the 1930s. In April 1940, when they invaded Norway (see NORWEGIAN CAMPAIGN) the Germans demanded that he be made prime minister. Initially, this only helped stiffen the Norwegian Government's resistance but in June both it and King Haakon were forced to flee to the UK. At first Quisling was treated sceptically by the Reich Commissioner for Norway, Josef *Terboven, but on 1 February 1942 he became the country's minister-president and began the Nazification of his country, which was rigorously opposed by most Norwegians. When the war ended he was tried for treason and executed. His name has lived on as a synonym for a *fifth columnist, collaborator, or *traitor.

Q-ships, disguised armed Allied merchantmen designed to lure Axis submarines into a surface attack so that they could be sunk by gunfire. They had been used with some success during the *First World War and the US Navy commissioned several in 1942, but they never sank anything. One was torpedoed with the loss of 141 men—a quarter of the total personnel employed on Q-ships—so that statistically they proved to be more hazardous than any other branch of the US armed forces. The British, who called them decoy ships, fitted out eight between October 1939 and March 1940. None ever achieved anything: two were torpedoed and the remainder were withdrawn in December 1940.

Rabaul, port situated at eastern end of New Britain, one of the islands in the Bismarck archipelago. The capital of the Australian mandated territory of New Guinea, it was captured by the Japanese in February 1942 and became the principal air and naval base in their South-East Area, during the *Pacific war. The Allies dropped 20,584 tons of bombs on Rabaul, forcing the garrison to live in specially constructed tunnels and caves. Because it was so heavily defended, early US strategy to capture it was reversed at the Quebec conference in August 1943 (see QUADRANT). Instead, *MacArthur's offensive (CARTWHEEL), which had been launched two months previously, isolated and reduced it from the air (see also NEW BRITAIN CAMPAIGN). By March 1944 all principal Japanese naval and air units there had withdrawn to *Truk, but in August 1945 53,000 army troops, 16,200 naval forces, and 20,000 civilian workers surrendered there.

Raczyński, Count Edward (1891–1993), Polish ambassador in London from 1934 to 1945 who also served as minister of foreign affairs in *Sikorski's *government-in-exile. He signed the Anglo-Polish Treaty in August 1939 which formalized the British guarantee of Poland (see POLAND, GUARANTEE OF) given the previous April, and which brought the UK and France into the war on 3 September 1939. After the war he stayed in the UK and from 1978 to 1984 served as president of the Polish government-in-exile.

radar is an acronym for Radio Detection And Ranging, now embracing a diverse group of systems which employ radio waves to detect the presence or measure the location of distant objects. There exist two essentially different types of radar system, monostatic and bistatic: the former and more common has its transmitting and receiving antennas at the same location, whereas the latter may work with the entire transmitting and receiving systems widely separated from each other. The frequencies utilized by radar sets during the Second World War ranged from 20 MHz to 10 GHz (see Chart). Pulse radars predominated. In a pulse radar energy is transmitted for brief periods of time (of the order of a millionth of a second) separated by relatively long quiescent intervals (generally greater than one-thousandth of a second), during which the echoes from targets can be received and processed.

Between the years 1934 and 1936, radar emerged independently and for military purposes in eight countries: France, Germany, the Netherlands, Italy, Japan, the UK, the USA and the USSR. In most it was first seen as a means of early warning against air attack and as an anti-aircraft gun-laying device (see Table for some of the more notable radar sets).

Three related events, which were very significant for the Allies, were the British discovery of the *cavity magnetron in July 1940, which made centimetric radar possible (see ELECTRONIC NAVIGATION SYSTEMS and H2S); the *Tizard mission to the USA two months later, when the cavity magnetron was disclosed to the Americans; and the setting up of the Radiation Laboratory at the Massachusetts Institute of Technology in November 1940. From an objective global viewpoint, the impact of the work of the Radiation Laboratory, both on the operational uses of radar during the latter half of the war and thereafter on its immediate post-war usage, can hardly be over-emphasized.

The radar programmes in the countries listed above will receive brief mention. These programmes were extensive in the case of the UK (and its Dominions), the United States, and Germany and, to a lesser extent, Japan.

France

A bistatic early-warning system using continuous waves and beat-frequency technique was proposed by Pierre David in 1934 and operationally tested in 1937. In 1939 fixed David radar chains protected naval bases along the English Channel, the Atlantic Ocean, and the Mediterranean, and also the north-eastern approach to Paris. A limited number of early-warning pulse radar equipments were manufactured in 1939 by commercial companies. Mobile early-warning and gun-laying radar sets were employed in France by the *British Expeditionary Force from October 1939 to May 1940.

Germany

Radar in Germany had its origins in the foresight and determination of Dr Rudolf Kuhnold of the German Navy's Signals Research Establishment. In 1934 he set up the company GEMA, which in 1936 produced prototypes of both the Seetakt series of ship-based search and gun-ranging radars operating at 370 MHz and the Freya early-warning sets operating at 125 MHz. Radar development in Germany, while technically successful, did not follow a clear co-ordinated programme. There is no doubt that much work, particularly in microwaves, was curtailed or delayed because of Hitler's edict prohibiting research which could not guarantee early success.

Radar was used for aircraft reporting purposes as early as December 1939 with radar plots being passed directly to fighter and *flak units. The first night-bombing of Germany by the RAF took place on 15 May 1940. It was a prelude to a sustained air defence campaign of almost five years by the Germans in which *searchlights, night fighters, radar—and, for a while, sound detectors—and the Luftwaffe's flak arm played their various roles. General Joseph Kammhuber and the *Kammhuber Line figured prominently in this. The *area bombing raids by the RAF which began in the spring of 1943 radically affected the efficiency of the Kammhuber Line and this ushered in

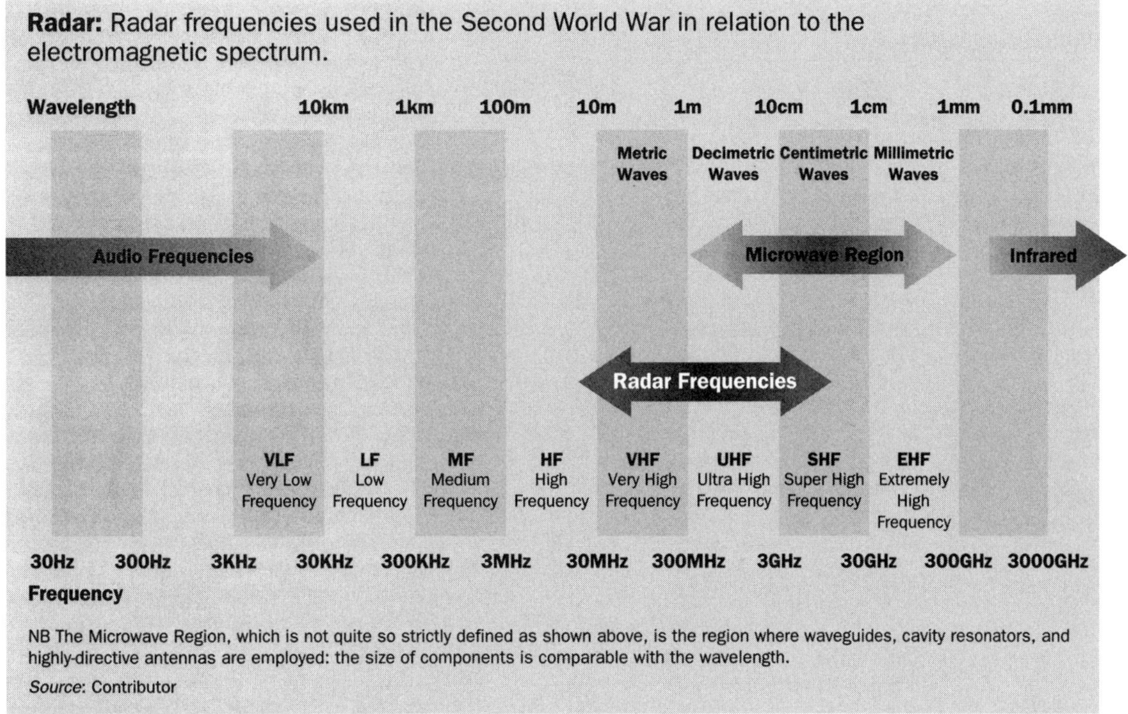

Radar: Radar frequencies used in the Second World War in relation to the electromagnetic spectrum.

NB The Microwave Region, which is not quite so strictly defined as shown above, is the region where waveguides, cavity resonators, and highly-directive antennas are employed: the size of components is comparable with the wavelength.

Source: Contributor

new methods of fighter control and a re-allocation of the areas of control. This period also coincided with the widespread use of radar counter-measures as part of the •electronic warfare being waged by both sides.

Italy

Following observations made in 1933, Guglielmo Marconi built a radar system which he successfully demonstrated to Mussolini and members of the general staff on 14 May 1935. The military authorities enlisted the services of Professor Ugo Tiberio who produced, practically single-handed, a series of experimental sets; the last, EC-3 ter, was completed in 1941 and went into production with the SAFAR company. There appear to have been more than 100 Italian naval radar sets available at the time of the •armistice in September 1943: their potential had not, however, been realized.

Japan

Microwave and magnetron research was carried out from 1933 onwards at the Japan Radio Company and the Naval Technical Research Institute, and experiments were also conducted by Professor Okabe Kinjiro of Osaka University in 1936. The first sets, which went into operation in 1941, were continuous wave, as opposed to pulse, bistatic systems operating in the 40–80 MHz band. Serious work on pulse radars began in 1941. A complete lack of liaison between the army and navy led to great inefficiency and duplication of effort (see RIVALRIES). The navy, from 1941 until the end of hostilities, carried out an extensive programme of design and manufacture of successful land-based, shipboard, and airborne metric and centimetric wave sets. One cannot say that the Japanese radar programme was not good: it just could not equal that of the USA and UK.

Netherlands

In 1936, work on the design of a radar began independently in the Philips Physics Laboratory at Eindhoven and in the physics laboratory of the Dutch armed forces. A few prototypes were built. One of these was operating in The Hague, when the Germans invaded in May 1940.

UK

The unease felt by A. P. Rowe in 1934, when, as assistant to the director of scientific research at the air ministry, he examined the state of Britain's preparedness against air attack, set a chain of events in motion. By 31 May 1935 a basic radar transmitter and receiver, at that time called Radio Direction Finding (RDF), a name the British retained until the middle of the war, were operating at Orford Ness on the east coast on a frequency of 6 MHz. In August and September 1935 the early-warning chain of radar stations which became known as the Chain Home (CH) was planned. In the organization of all this, Robert •Watson-Watt played a leading part. At the outbreak of war, on 3 September 1939, eighteen CH stations were operational and connected to the Stanmore filter room in north London; two more in Scotland were operating locally. This result was achieved after much

Radar: Some notable radars

Function	*Type/Name*	*Frequency*	*Tx Peak Power*	*Pulse Width*	*PRF (Hz)*	*Range km*	*Range miles*
1. Germany							
Early warning	Freya	125 MHz	20 kW	2–3 μs	500	200 km	125 mi
Gun Laying; Ground Control of Interception	Würzburg	560 MHz	8 kW	2 μs	3,750	30 km	18.5 mi
Sea Search	Seetakt FUM022	368 MHz	8 kW	5 μs	500	25 km	15.5 mi
Aircraft Interception	Lichtenstein SN2 FuG 220	91 MHz	2.5 kW	1 μs	937	4 km	2.5 mi
2. Italy							
Naval: Sea Search	EC-3 ter ('Gufo')	500 MHz	10 kW	4 μs	500	25 km (on battleship)	15.5 mi
3. Japan							
Early warning (land and naval)	Type 13	150 MHz	10 kW	10 μs	500	100 km	62 mi
Surface Search	Type 22	3 GHz	2 kW	10 μs	2,500	25 km	15.5 mi
4. UK							
Early warning	Chain Home A.M.E.S. Type 1	22.7–29.7 MHz 42.5–50.5 MHz	200–800 kW	6 μs–25 μs	25; 12 1/2	300 km	185 mi
GCI (Ground Control of Interception)	A.M.E.S. Type 15	209 MHz	100 kW	3 μs; 5 μs; 8 μs	300–540	180 km	112 mi
Gun Laying	G.L.11	54–85 MHz	80 kW	2 μs	1,200	45 km	28 mi
Naval: Air Search	Type 281	90 MHz	350 kW 1 MW	15 μs 2 μs	50	220 km	136 mi
Naval: Sea Search	Type 271	3 GHz	70 kW	1.5 μs; 0.7 μs	500	25 km (on battleship)	15.5 mi
Air to Surface Vessel	ASV Mk11	176 MHz	7 kW	2.5 μs	400	Coastlines 100 km Destroyer 35 km	62 mi 22 mi
Air to Surface Vessel	ASV Mk111[a]	3 GHz	50 kW	1 μs	750	160 km	99 mi
Air Interception	AI MkVII[b]	3.3 GHz	5 kW	1 μs	2,500	5 km	3 mi
5. USA							
Naval: Air Search	CXAM	195 MHz	15 kW	3 μs	1,640	130 km	80 mi
Precise tracking of aircraft	SCR-268	205 MHz	75 kW	3 μs–9 μs	4,098	36 km	22 mi
Early warning	SCR–270	106 MHz	100 kW	10 μs–25 μs	621	230 km	142 mi
Early warning and fighter direction	EW (Microwave Early Warning) AN/CPS-1	3 GHz	1 MW	1 μs	320	380 km	236 mi
Gun Laying (Automatic Tracking)	SCR 584	3 GHz	300 kW	0.8 μs	1,700	Tracking from 29 km	18 mi
6. USSR							
Early warning	RUS-2	75 MHz	70–120 kW			150 km	93 mi

[a] Same as H_2S Mk1 (see ELECTRONIC NAVIGATION SYSTEMS).
[b] Although only about 50 aircraft were fitted with this set, it is of great historical interest as it was the first ever centimetre-wave airborne radar to become operational: it first flew in a Blenheim on 10 March 1941.

Source: Contributor.

The heart of RAF **radar** operations in 1940—the filter room at Fighter Command HQ at Bentley Priory. The incoming German aircraft were plotted on the map and fighters were vectored on to them.

effort and the benefit of air exercises. The effectiveness of the CH system throughout the war, but especially during the battle of *Britain, lay not only in the performance and reliability of the radars but in the efficiency of the personnel in the radar stations, the filter rooms (where information on a raid was evaluated before being passed to the operations room), and the operations rooms.

From 1940 to 1943, the Chain Home coverage was extended to the south-west and west coasts and Northern Ireland. Its capability was added to by the employment of 200 MHz CHL (Chain Home Low) and 3 GHz CHEL (Chain Home Extra Low) stations which were effective against low-flying aircraft: the latter also reported the movements of shipping.

The setting up of the CH network was purposely given priority of resources. Nevertheless, even as early as 1935, most of the later radar developments were given consideration. In 1937, Dr E. G. Bowen carried out successful AI (aircraft interception) tests using a radar fitted in a Heyford bomber and a co-operating transmitter on the ground. This work eventually led to the development of a number of successful ASV (aircraft to surface vessel) and AI radars.

Naval set development began in 1935 and by 1939 an air-warning set, Type 79, operating at 43MHz, was fitted to some of the larger vessels. The fitting of microwave radar to escort vessels in 1942 was an important factor in the war against the U-boats during the battle of the *Atlantic. Serious work on army radars began at the end of 1936. Before the end of the war some 80 types of sets and their variants had been designed.

Before the outbreak of war, a radar programme for the air defence of British overseas ports existed. Part of this programme was implemented in the early days of the war. Radar was employed effectively in early-warning and in fighter interception in the various defensive and offensive campaigns in the Middle East, in the Far East, in the *North African and *Italian campaigns, and in north-west Europe. The period June 1944 to March 1945 saw the bombardment of London and the south-east coast by *V-weapons and radar played a very considerable part in their destruction. See also SCIENTISTS AT WAR.

USA

The development of radar in the USA from its origins to the end of the war can be viewed in two stages. It was born in the USA in the Naval Research Laboratory from observations made in June 1930 by Leo Young and Laurence Pat Hyland which eventually led in 1934 to Robert Page's building of a 60 MHz pulse radar set. A development of this, the CXAM, became available in November 1939. Twenty sets were installed on battleships, aircraft carriers, and cruisers in 1940.

Major William Blair, the director of the Signal Corps Laboratories at Fort Monmouth, New Jersey, promoted radar experiments from 1933 onwards. A simple pulse radar was demonstrated in December 1936. By May 1937, a prototype of the first US Army radar, the SCR-268, was built. A long-range radar, operating at 106 MHz, the mobile SCR 270 and its fixed counterpart the SCR-271, went into service in 1940. About 800 were produced between 1939 and 1944. By early 1942 the Aircraft Warning Service had a chain of SCR-270 and SCR-271 radars protecting the east coast from Maine to Key West and the west coast from Washington to San Diego.

Radar: The ratio of Allied ships sunk to the number of German submarines lost, plotted at three-monthly intervals for the duration of the war. The dates on which ASV Mark II, the Leigh Light, and ASV Mark III were introduced are as shown.

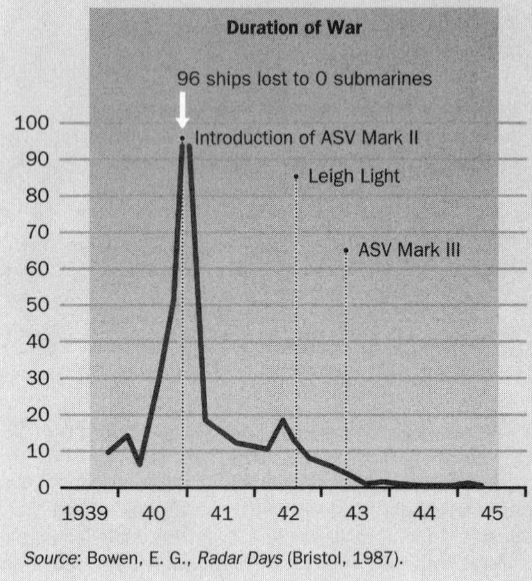

Source: Bowen, E. G., *Radar Days* (Bristol, 1987).

At the time of the Tizard mission and the exchange of information with the UK in 1940, the USA possessed a very solid and developing radar programme though it lacked, perhaps, the urgency engendered by a country threatened by war. The second stage of development was initiated by the setting up of the Radiation Laboratory in November 1940, a direct result of the mission.

USSR

The air defence command, dissatisfied with sound-location, contracted with the Leningrad Electro-Physics Institute to undertake research into the radio detection of objects. The result was the experimental set 'RAPID', a bistatic continuous-wave system, which in August 1934 detected the presence of aircraft up to a distance of 75 km. (53 mi.). Acute political changes occurred during 1937–8 which undoubtedly affected the radar programme, but from February 1942 onwards the state defence committee actively promoted radar. By the end of the war successful naval surface-search and airborne AI sets were being produced.

Radar as a weapon

Radar systems enhanced the capability of air, land, and sea forces in both defensive and offensive roles. The element of surprise in attack became more difficult to achieve. In some operations or battles the use of radar or a particular type of radar was of decisive importance.

The use of the Chain Home in the battle of Britain was an essential factor in the RAF's victory. It was also the first time in history that early warning and control were used in an air battle. In the assault phase of the Normandy landings (see OVERLORD), the chain again played an essential part: its radar coverage was extended by three specially equipped fighter director tenders, which finally hove to off the coast, and by the GCI (ground control of interception) and other sets which were landed on the bridgehead. The landings, involving accurate blind-bombing and naval bombardment of shore targets, and the expeditious movement of a huge air and sea armada, would have been impossible without a heavy involvement of radar.

The Allied *strategic air offensive against Germany went through many phases. Overall, it was by no means a one-sided victory for RAF Bomber Command and the Eighth US Army Air Force. The German radar early-warning system was very effective so that the defences were hardly ever surprised. In the biggest night air battle of the war, on 30 March, 1944, a force of 782 Halifaxes and Lancasters, carrying out a raid on *Nuremberg, suffered 13.6% losses due in large part to the effectiveness of the German night fighters' Lichtenstein SN2 AI sets.

The *Pacific war, which lasted almost four years, was essentially a naval war. American submarines and radar-equipped aircraft inflicted heavy losses on Japanese merchant shipping and tankers. The balance of naval battles, in both defensive and offensive phases of the campaign, was determined largely by the effectiveness of the American Task Forces' radar directed fighters. The 'Great Marianas Turkey Shoot' of 19 June 1944, during the battle of the *Philippine Sea, when nearly 300 Japanese aircraft were destroyed for a loss of 30 American aircraft, was an example of the potency of well-organized radar fighter-control.

One instance where the usage of radar was critical for the Allies and in which the outcome of battle was vital to the whole conduct of the war was the battle of the Atlantic. The submarine war on Allied merchant shipping lasted from the outbreak of hostilities until the defeat of Germany. Losses such as those of June 1942 when 141 ships were sunk, could not have been sustained for long. Many factors apart from radar, including code-breaking (see ULTRA, 1), ship-building potential, *anti-submarine weapon development, and *convoy procedures, denied ultimate victory to the U-boats. The use of radar, particularly the British naval Type 271 microwave set used in escort vessels, proved very successful. At the end of 1940, the ASV MkII was fitted to a variety of aircraft including Wellingtons, Whitleys, Sunderlands, and Catalinas. Later, American long-range aircraft, such as the Liberator, fitted with radar were used in the western Atlantic. At night, the combination of ASV radar which could pick up a surfaced submarine and the

Leigh Light (see SEARCHLIGHTS) which could illuminate it as the aircraft made its final run in before dropping depth charges, proved a deadly weapon. The 200 MHz ASV MkII lost much of its potency due to the Germans' introduction of listening receivers on submarines. However, the advent in March 1943 of the 3GHz ASV MkIII set, which could not be detected, heralded the defeat of the submarines.

The graph starkly and simply illustrates the flow of the U-boat war, focusing on the ratio of Allied vessels sunk to U-boats lost. When the USA entered the war the U-boats moved into American waters and for many months convoy losses rose dangerously high: the peak in the curve for February 1942 illustrates this. SEAN SWORDS

Guerlac, H. E., *Radar in World War II* (New York, 1987).
Burns, R. W. (ed.), *Radar Development to 1945* (London, 1988).

radio beams, see ELECTRONIC NAVIGATION SYSTEMS.

radio communications. (Radio was an American term, the British more commonly using wireless.) During the Second World War radio communications revolutionized how the armed services fought, and they brought a new dimension to clandestine warfare, cryptology, battlefield intelligence, and even to the political conduct of the war as Churchill and Roosevelt were in regular contact by radio telephone (see also FORSCHUNGSSTELLE), and from June 1944 Moscow and Washington were linked by a teleprinter service. Radio telephony (R/T), pioneered as early as 1904, became crucial in controlling a battle on the ground and in the air. Wireless telegraphy (W/T)—used with morse code—remained dominant at sea but was always a useful means of transmission when, because of noise and interference, speech was unintelligible. Field telephones and teleprinters (teletypewriters), using land lines or temporary wire, were also used extensively, especially in the rear areas.

Radio is defined in *The Concise Oxford Dictionary* as 'the transmission and reception of sound messages etc. by electromagnetic waves of radio-frequency'. The first transmission took place in 1892 and by 1901 the Italian Guglielmo Marconi (1874–1937) was regularly transmitting morse code signals to ships at sea and even across the Atlantic. W/T was employed effectively at sea during the Russo-Japanese war of 1904–5 and by the start of the *First World War it had become part of land warfare for rear communications, the Germans being especially well advanced in its use. During the Second World War wireless, offering flexibility and mobility, became in its various forms (see Table) the most important method of military communications. The choice of technical parameters, such as frequency range and transmitter power output, for the different types of sets depended primarily on matching the users' operational requirements with the transmission characteristics of the various frequency bands (see Figures p. 926). The technology necessary for producing successful VHF and FM sets was not fully in place in 1939, but was established by the end of the war.

The size and weight of early equipment, as well as technical difficulties and financial restraints, inhibited the development of radio communications between the wars. The natural conservatism of the military hierarchy had also to be overcome. The chapter on 'Command and Control' in the British *Field Service Regulations*, published in 1935, did not even mention radio; and when, in 1934, the German tank specialist Colonel *Guderian said that he proposed leading his panzer divisions 'from the front—by wireless', the chief of the German General Staff, *Beck, replied 'Nonsense! A divisional commander sits back with maps and a telephone. Anything else is Utopian!' (quoted in K. Macksey, *Guderian*, London, 1975, p. 61).

Despite these obstacles, experimentation did continue. The first demonstration of controlling and manoeuvring a brigade of tanks by R/T took place in the UK in 1931. In 1934 the British armoured warfare expert Brigadier *Hobart was able to demonstrate that R/T was, in principle, the most efficient means of controlling an armoured force down to individual tanks, and the following year a British scientist began developing a circuit which simplified the working of sets in a radio 'net'. (The net consists of a control station working to a group of sub-stations on a common frequency. Net working, if it adheres to strict procedures, prevents excessive use of frequencies and ensures that each station hears all the messages passed over the net.)

However, it was the Germans who first exploited the full potential of radio communications in *tank warfare. The first exercise by a panzer division controlled by R/T was held in 1935. Guderian, who had commanded a radio unit during the First World War, encouraged the development of simple and reliable tank radio for the new type of warfare he was largely instrumental in developing, the *blitzkrieg. Only R/T—though supplemented by the more secure field telephone and teleprinter networks—could control the blitzkrieg effectively. But its essence was not only instant communication and control of forward armoured units but co-operation of all arms in a way never previously envisaged. Radio communications in armoured units were therefore paralleled in artillery and tactical aviation and allowed for intercommunication between them.

By contrast, French radio communications during the fall of *France in May–June 1940 reflected the French Army's lack of preparation for blitzkrieg and the static state of mind with which it tried to counter it. Between the wars French planning had been almost entirely defensive (see MAGINOT LINE) and radio communications in all their forms were given a low priority. Between 1923 and 1939 only 0.15% of the military budget was spent on communications equipment and few resources were alloted to research and development. The French C-in-C, General *Gamelin, 'had nothing more than a telephone and an occasional courier' (A.

Radio Communications: Representative list of military radio sets

Type	Frequency range MHz	Frequency band	Rated transmitter output (watts)	Type of emission	Expected range in kilometres (miles)	Remarks
American						
AN/MRG-1 (incorporating SCR-399)	2.0 to 13.0	HF	2,000	W/T	1,600 (1,000)	Portable. Facilities for high power high speed automatic W/T transmission
SCR-399	2.0 to 18.0	HF	400 (W/T) 300 (R/T)	W/T R/T	1,600 (1,000)	Army mobile high power station
SCR-508	20.0 to 27.9	HF	30	R/T	24 (15)	FM set. Installed in tanks, scout cars, and trucks
SCR-511	2.0 to 6.0	HF	0.75	R/T	4.8 (3)	Manpack and vehicular set
SCR-300	40 to 48	VHF	0.5	R/T	1.6 (1)	FM walkie-talkie
SCR-536	3.5 to 6.0	HF	0.02	R/T	800 m (1/2)	Light weight handie-talkie
SCR-522	100 to 156	VHF	6	R/T	Line-of-sight[a]	Airborne transmitter-receiver 4 pre-set channels
AN/ARC-3	100 to 156	VHF	6	R/T	Line-of-sight[a]	Airborne transmitter
TBS-3	60 to 80	VHF	50	R/T	32 (20)	Surface craft or submarine vessel to vessel inter-communication
TBY-1	28 to 80	VHF	0.5	R/T	1.6 (1)	For use by Marines
British						
Marconi Sender SWB 8	3.0 to 22.2	HF	3,500	W/T	8,000 (5,000)	RN and RAF fixed service transmitter
No. 5 HP	0.2 to 0.6 3.0 to 20.0	LF/MF HF	2,000	W/T	World-wide	Army fixed station
No. 33	1.2 to 17.5	MF/HF	250 (W/T) 65 (R/T)	W/T R/T	1,600 (1,000) (for W/T) 100 (60) (for R/T)	Army fixed or mobile station
No. 19 (A Set)	2.0 to 8.0	HF	12	W/T R/T		Armoured Fighting Vehicle set
No. 46	3.6 to 4.3 5.0 to 6.0 6.4 to 7.6 7.9 to 9.1	HF HF HF HF	1.5	W/T R/T	6.5 (4)	Commando and paratroop set
No. 38	7.3 to 8.8	HF	0.5	R/T	1.2 (3/4)	Infantry manpack set
T1083	0.136 to 0.50 3.0 to 15.0	LF/MF HF	30	W/T R/T	Line-of-sight[a] (at least)	Airborne transmitter
R1082	0.111 to 15.0	LF/MF/HF		W/T R/T		Airborne receiver used in conjunction with T1083
T1143	100 to 124	VHF	5	R/T	Line-of-sight[a]	Airborne transmitter receiver
T1131	99 to 126	VHF	50	R/T	Line-of-sight[a]	RAF ground station transmitter
German						
1.5-kW-LK Sender a	0.1 to 0.6	LF/MF	1,500	W/T	1,000 (600)	Army high power mobile station
1.0-kW-KW Sender b	1.090 to 6.70	MF/HF	1,000	W/T R/T	1,000 (600)	Army high power mobile station
Fu5 SE 10 (includes 10-W-S.c)	27.2 to 33.3	HF/VHF	10	W/T R/T	6.5 (4)	Armoured Fighting Vehicle set

Radio Communications (*cont.*)

Type	*Frequency Range MHz*	*Frequency Band*	*Rated transmitter output (Watts)*	*Type of emission*	*Expected range in kilometres(miles)*	*Remarks*
Feldfu.a1	120 to 156	VHF	0.15	R/T	1.2 (3/4)	Infantry manpack set
Feldfu.h	23.1 to 25.0	HF	0.15	R/T	1.6 (1)	Infantry manpack set
FuG10	3 to 6	HF	40	R/T	Line-of-sight[a] (at least)	Airborne transmitter-receiver
T200 FK 39	3 to 23	HF	200	W/T 100 R/T	(60) with special 'eel' antenna	Communications transmitter for submarine use

[a] Line-of-sight range for standard conditions of atmosphere is approximately 160 km (100 mi) between a ground station and an aircraft at 3,048 m (10,000 ft)

Source: Dr Sean Swords.

Millett, and W. Murray, *Military Effectiveness*, Vol. 2, London 1988, p. 58), and once the battle became fluid communications broke down.

The Japanese and Italian armies were even more poorly equipped when their countries entered the war, with Millett and Murray writing of 'chronically poor' communications in the Japanese Army and 'the utter inadequacy of Italian equipment . . . Italian tank crews suffered without voice radios until 1941. Even after that, no long distance radio that could operate on the move existed' (ibid., Vol. 3, pp. 34, 151–3).

The Red Army, too, lacked modern radio communications. Radio nets only extended down to company level in armoured units, so that company commanders had to communicate with their tanks by hand signal or motorcycle. In 1941 the infantry had to rely mostly on the civilian telephone network and it was not until *Lend-Lease began supplementing what existed that the situation began to improve. Even when they had radios many Soviet commanders disliked using them as they knew that their transmissions could disclose their positions, and in 1943 Stalin had to issue an order which pointed out how essential radio communications were.

The USA, as with so many other technological developments, was quick to put its enormous financial and scientific resources behind the development of all aspects of radio communications. It produced some remarkable portable radio sets, the 2.26 kg. (5 lb.) walkie-talkie (the SCR-536, known then as the handie-talkie), the *Gibson Girl, and the radiosonde, used to obtain *meteorological intelligence, being three examples. Other developments included automatic teleprinters which could transmit messages at a rate of 100 words a minute, and facsimile facilities which could transmit *war photographers' prints halfway round the world in seven minutes.

Despite these advances, radio communications had their disadvantages. In the heat of battle orders given over R/T could be confused or misheard, and technical difficulties were numerous. For instance, not until *Operational Research scientists in Australia investigated the effect of a tropical climate on the operational life of dry batteries was the constant failure of radios in the *New Guinea campaign eradicated.

Security was also a problem. 'Wireless is still untrustworthy and entirely unsecret,' *Dorman-Smith wrote in July 1942 during the *Western Desert campaigns. 'Speak in clear and you give the enemy your plans. Speak in code and you slow everything down. Use cypher and it takes hours encoding and decoding. You pay your penny and you choose your inconvenience' (L. Greacen, *Chink*, London, 1989, p. 215). Even the increasing use of cipher machines, which also speeded up the process of transmission and decipherment, did not guarantee security, as the Allied gathering of *ULTRA intelligence showed. In the *Pacific war US forces overcame the problem to a certain extent by employing *Navajo Indian 'codetalkers'.

Radio communications at sea also suffered from security problems as the relative slowness of ships made them, and their operational intentions, vulnerable to an opponent. This meant that radio silence was imperative until contact with the enemy had been made, though systems were devised of transmitting W/T signals from shore stations which did not entail revealing the position of the receiving ship. However, Allied direction-finding equipment could often pinpoint the position of U-boats, even though the Germans devised a method for abbreviating transmissions to a few seconds (see HUFF-DUFF).

W/T at sea increased in scale during the war years without undergoing any radical changes. In September 1939 the British Admiralty had a world-wide network of seventeen high-frequency radio stations which relayed W/T messages to British warships. By 1945 it had 65, and

Radio communications: Propagation of radio waves

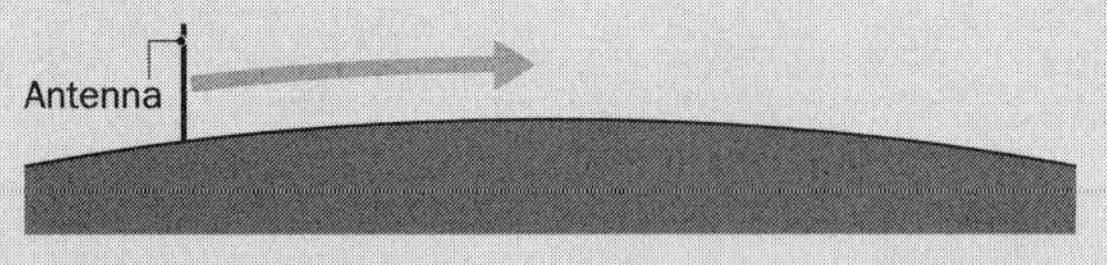

Surface Wave
Present in LF, MF, and HF transmission: with appropriate transmitter power, ranges of thousands, hundreds, and tens of kilometres, respectively, are achievable.

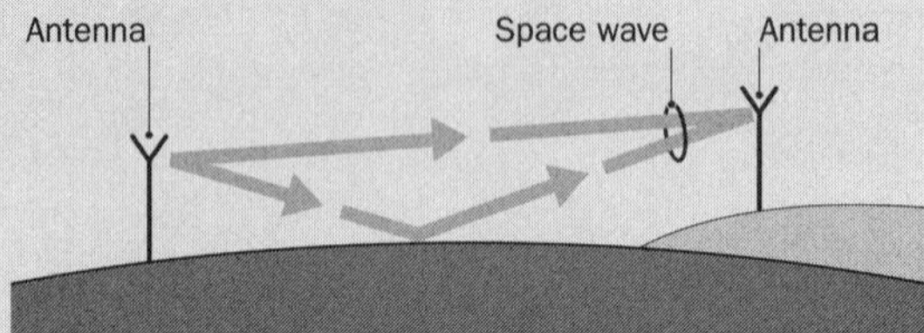

Space Wave
Principal mechanism in VHF/UHF transmission: range restricted by constraints of earth's curvature and height of antennas. Diagram shows the direct and ground reflected components of the space wave.

Sky Wave
The principal component of HF transmission: hundreds of kilometres range possible with modest transmitter powers. The optimum working frequency for the ionospheric conditions that pertain must be ascertained when planning a link.

In HF, in addition to the sky wave, a ground wave component (a combination of surface wave and space wave) is present. This is represented in the diagram by the horizontal arrow. The ground wave does not fade with time of day or season and is useful in fixed or mobile working for communicating over moderate distances. A 'skip zone' may exist between the maximum distance for useful ground wave and the minimum distance at which sky waves are returned to earth.

Radio Frequency Bands of Relevance

Designation	Frequency Range	Corresponding Wavelengths
Low Frequency (LF)	30kHz to 300kHz	10,000 m. to 1,000 m.
Medium Frequency (MF)*	300kHz to 3MHz	1,000 m. to 100 m.
High Frequency (HF)	3MHz to 30MHz	100 m. to 10 m.
Very High Frequency (VHF)	30MHz to 300MHz	10 m. to 1 m.
Ultra High Frequency (UHF)	300MHz to 3GHz	1 m. to 10 cm.

*The portion 1.5 to 3MHz of the MF band is often in army communications considered as part of the HF band.

Source: Dr Sean Swords

also scattered across the world were some 20 stations for intercepting enemy signals (see FAR EAST COMBINED BUREAU, for example) and 69 direction-finding stations. In 1939 a battleship had, typically, eight transmitters and nine receivers; by 1945 it had 16 transmitters and 23 receivers.

R/T became widespread in the western Allied surface navies, though it had been practically unknown at sea before the war, the properties of VHF making it comparatively safe from interception by the enemy. It was the basis for controlling aircraft operating from *carriers, and was also used by convoy escorts during the battle of the *Atlantic, as it was not possible for distant U-boats to intercept VHF transmissions. To prevent a nearby one picking up a conversation, escort groups used a simple voice code which disguised vessels' names, changes of courses, and so on.

In the air the lack of security from which R/T suffered was not usually relevant as the speed of aerial warfare made the information gleaned by the opposing side largely obsolete within minutes (but see PHILIPPINE SEA). Apart from the blitzkrieg, the earliest example of the paramount importance of radio communications in the air was the battle of *Britain. Encouraged by *Dowding (who in 1917 had almost certainly become the first person to be in ground–air voice communication with an aircraft) the basic system for intercepting incoming enemy bombers had been developed during the 1930s. The bombers were tracked by *radar and the intercepting fighters by high-frequency direction finders which locked on to the fighters' *'pip-squeak' transmissions. The bearings of both groups of aircraft were plotted in the sector control room and the fighters were then guided on to the bombers by R/T. The bombers were recognized as enemy aircraft because they did not transmit the correct *IFF signals.

However, by 1937 the HF (high-frequency) wavebands fighter R/T used for ground–air transmission had become unsatisfactory—they were overcrowded and were subject to distortion and interference—and it was decided to develop a VHF (very high frequency) set with air-to-air range of 160 km. (100 mi.) and an air–ground range of 225 km. (140 mi.) at a height of 3,000 m. (10,000 ft.). But the delivery of these sets was delayed and though, by September 1940, sixteen fighter squadrons had been equipped with it the battle of Britain was fought largely with HF sets. The British VHF set, the TR-1143, was copied for US aircraft, and designated the SCR-522.

Air co-operation with ground forces was another sphere in which radio communications played a central role, and as the war progressed, and R/T became more reliable and more portable, radio communications enabled both artillery and aircraft to give close support to infantry and armour. Beginning during the *Italian campaign forward air controllers equipped with SCR-522 radios fed information to artillery fire direction centres from light aircraft while new procedural systems enabled controllers on the ground to call down accurate fighter-bomber air strikes, a form of support quickly adapted by the US Marine Corps in the *Pacific war when the limitations of naval gunfire became apparent. It was brought to a fine art by Lt-General Pete Quesada's Twelfth Tactical Air Force, which supported *Bradley's Twelfth Army Group in north-west Europe, with tanks being specially converted for air–ground co-operation.

Finally, the development of smaller and more powerful radios influenced clandestine warfare as *spies were able to use suitcase-sized transceivers and resistance groups special ground to air R/T sets such as the *S-phone.

Devereux, A., *Messenger Gods of Battle* (London, 1991).
Hallion, P., *Strike from the Sky* (Shrewsbury, 1989).
Hezlet, A., *The Electron and Sea Power* (London, 1975).

radio counter-measures, see ELECTRONIC WARFARE.

radio finger printing, method used by the British *Far East Combined Bureau to identify the radio transmitters of Japanese warships and shore stations. No two operators transmitted in exactly the same way. Their differences could be recorded by displaying their transmissions on a cathode ray tube and using a cine camera, equipped with very sensitive film, to take high-speed photographs of them. A film library was then built up which, with the input from other radio intelligence sources, such as the *'Y' service, 'was, literally, a dictionary of the transmissions of the main H/F [high frequency] sets of all the major Japanese warships and shore wireless stations. Using this dictionary, ships could be identified without the necessity of identifying the call signs which they used from the traffic they handled' (A. J. Marder, *Old Friends, New Enemies*, Vol. 1, Oxford, 1981, p. 359).

Raeder, Grand Admiral Erich (1876–1960), German naval officer who was appointed the German Navy's C-in-C in October 1928 with the rank of admiral, a position he retained until January 1943.

Raeder's immediate ambitions were to build a fleet on a parity with France's, and eventually one to challenge the other major maritime powers. The construction of three *Panzerschiffe* (pocket battleships) was begun—the first was launched in 1931—and 14 months after Hitler came to power, an event Raeder welcomed, Raeder was not only proposing to build, by 1949, a fleet which included 8 pocket battleships, 3 aircraft carriers, and 72 U-boats, but persuaded Hitler to increase the tonnage and armourment of two *Panzerschiffe* then on order (they became the battle-cruisers *Gneisenau* and **Scharnhorst*).

Hitler's repudiation of the *Versailles settlement in March 1935, followed by the Anglo-German Naval Agreement that June, resurrected Germany as a naval power. By then a battleship and an aircraft carrier (never completed) had already been ordered and in the autumn of 1935 Captain *Dönitz was given command of the first submarine flotilla. But Raeder failed to develop any long-term strategy; decisions on the naval construction programme were 'not based on a detailed, structurally well-thought-out plan' (W. Deist, *et al.*, *Germany and the Second World War*, vol. 1, Oxford, 1990, p. 471); and, to gain *Göring's support for the diversion of more resources to implement the Z-plan (see GERMANY Table 11), Raeder shelved plans for an independent air arm.

On 27 January 1939 Hitler signed the directive to divert the necessary resources to the Z-plan and by April, when Raeder was promoted grand admiral, it seemed his goal of building a world-class fleet was attainable. But in September 1939, when the gap between Raeder's grandiose plans and reality had never been wider, Germany entered a war Hitler had assured Raeder would not occur until 1944, and Raeder concluded that his ships 'would only be able to show that they know how to die with honour' (ibid., p. 480).

The circumstances forced Raeder to resort to stop-gap measures and short-term policies from which the navy was never able to extricate itself. Apart from U-boats, all new naval construction virtually ceased. But his strategy of neutralizing British naval superiority by attacking the UK's commercial sea lanes on a global basis with his *auxiliary cruisers was fairly successful at first, and Hitler heeded his advice to occupy Norway—achieved at a considerable cost to the navy—and not to invade the UK (see SEALION). But Raeder's rivalry with Göring left his forces without adequate air reconnaissance or a proper mine-laying capability, and he could not persuade Hitler that an Axis victory in the battle for the *Mediterranean was a preferable option to *BARBAROSSA, for Raeder vehemently opposed invading the USSR while the UK remained undefeated.

In the battle of the *Atlantic Raeder's U-boats gave a handsome return for the resources they absorbed, but the operational results of the larger *German surface raiders were less impressive, and after **Bismarck* was sunk in May 1941 Hitler ordered their withdrawal from the Atlantic and put restrictions on their use. Their redeployment in Norwegian waters threatened the *Arctic convoys, but when the pocket battleship *Lützow* and the cruiser *Admiral Hipper* failed to destroy a convoy in December 1942, Hitler demanded the decommissioning of all major German surface forces. Raeder's resignation, and his appointment as the Navy's inspector-general, followed. His parting words to Hitler were: 'Protect the interests of the Navy, and my successor, against Göring.' He was sentenced to life imprisonment at the *Nuremberg trials, but was released in 1956.

Howarth, S. (ed.), *Men of War* (London, 1993).

Raider battalions, see USA, 5(f).

Raiding Forces, from October 1943, the name of British co-ordinating HQ which formed the *Raiding Support Regiment and had under its command, among other units, the *Long Range Desert Group, Special Boat Squadron (see SPECIAL BOAT SECTION), and the *Greek Sacred Regiment. These all took part in the *Dodecanese Islands campaign that autumn and the last two, and the Levant Schooner Flotilla (Greek caiques manned by British service personnel), became part of the newly formed Anglo-Hellenic Schooner Flotilla when Raiding Forces were reorganized in April 1944.

Raiding Forces was also the name by which the two elements of No. 1 *Special Air Service were briefly known when the regiment was reconstituted after the capture of its commanding officer, David Stirling (1912–90), in February 1943.

Raiding Support Regiment, British special forces unit formed by *Raiding Forces in November 1943. Designed to give heavy weapons back-up to other units in Raiding Forces, it was organized into five batteries: mountain guns, machine-guns, mortars, anti-aircraft, and anti-tank guns. It was stationed on Vis, the nearest of the Dalmatian Islands to Italy, taking part in raids against German-occupied Yugoslavia and supporting *Tito and the partisans there. When the *Balkan Air Force was formed in June 1944 it became part of its ground component, Land Forces Adriatic.

Rainbow Plans, US war plans drawn up for five different scenarios. They were so-called to differentiate them from earlier ones which had coloured codenames. Rainbow 5 was the closest to the situation in which the USA found itself in 1941, in that it envisaged working with the UK to 'effect the decisive defeat of Germany, Italy, or both', while a defensive strategy was maintained in the *Pacific war until success against the European Axis powers was assured. It was based on paragraph D (for Dog) of a recommendation which Admiral *Stark had made to Roosevelt in November 1940. This paragraph, or Plan Dog as it came to be called, was then developed into the Rainbow 5 Plan by Rear-Admiral Kelly *Turner. 'Louis Morton in his *Strategy and Command* volume in the Army histories calls it "perhaps the most important single document in the development of World War II strategy". Its importance lay in its cogent formulation of the Atlantic-first argument, its acceptability to the Army, and its encouragement of close coordination with the British. Henceforward Plan Dog was to be the cornerstone of American politico-military thought.' (E. Larrabee, *Commander in Chief*, NY, 1987, p. 48). See also ABC-1 PLANS.

Ralston, (James) Layton (1881–1948), popular and courageous Canadian *First World War battalion commander who was appointed Canada's minister of national defence in July 1940. He was a great supporter of the Canadian fighting man, and of conscription for service overseas. In 1942 he failed to withdraw a letter of resignation over the issue of overseas conscription, though he subsequently settled his differences with the prime minister, Mackenzie *King. In October 1944 he returned from a visit to Europe convinced that conscription was unavoidable, and his stand threatened to split the cabinet. King attempted to resolve the dispute by offering the defence portfolio to General *McNaughton and forcing Ralston's departure by accepting his 1942 letter of resignation. See also CANADA, 3.

Ramsay, Admiral Sir Bertram (1883–1945), British naval officer who commanded Operation DYNAMO, which evacuated the British Army from *Dunkirk and who served as Allied naval C-in-C for the Normandy landings in June 1944 (see OVERLORD).

During the *First World War Ramsay served with the Grand Fleet and the Dover Patrol before retiring in 1938 with the rank of vice-admiral. In August 1939 he was recalled to become Vice-Admiral Dover, and was knighted on the successful completion of DYNAMO.

In April 1942, Ramsay was appointed naval C-in-C for the invasion of Europe due later that year. When it was subsequently decided to invade North Africa instead (see NORTH AFRICAN CAMPAIGN) objections were raised to an acting admiral on the retired list commanding such a large operation. This led to Admiral *Cunningham's being given command with Ramsay as his deputy, and he subsequently served under Cunningham as commander of the Eastern Task Force during the *Sicilian campaign landings in July 1943. In December 1943 Ramsay returned to London to start planning *NEPTUNE, the assault phase of OVERLORD, and in April 1944 he was restored to the active list with the rank of admiral. The planning and execution of NEPTUNE were superbly handled by him, as was the subsequent build-up of troops and supplies. On

2 January 1945 he was killed in an air crash. He was a tough, modest man, an ideal staff officer, and much admired by all his colleagues.

Rangers, see USA, 5(f).

ranks. In this book, the rank as given in the headword of those servicemen who have a biographical entry is the highest they achieved during the course of the war. *SS ranks have their equivalent British rank in brackets after them: a full list appears in the SS entry. The very highest ranks are, when necessary, translated into English (i.e. *Gross Admiral* is given as Grand Admiral). Otherwise, with one exception, the equivalent British rank has been given for officers (i.e. a German *Generalmajor* is called a brigadier), both in biographical entries and in the text (see Table). The exception is the American, and French, rank of brigadier-general, the equivalent of a British brigadier, which has been retained (in France a brigadier is a non-commissioned rank). The Japanese did not have the rank of brigadier, nor the naval equivalent of commodore.

Apart from the fact that the air forces of some powers were part of the army or navy, and their officers therefore had military or naval ranks, the ranks of the most senior air force and naval officers of the major combatants were equivalent to those in the Royal Navy and Royal Air Force, with the exception that the highest ranks in the Japanese armed forces were general and admiral, field marshal and admiral of the fleet being honorary ranks bestowed by the emperor on rare occasions.

The reader must not infer from the above that all officers of equivalent rank, whatever their nationality, commanded the same size *formations. For example, a Japanese major-general normally commanded a brigade, an American or British major-general a division.

Rashid Ali el-Ghalani (1882–1965), Iraqi lawyer who co-founded the Muslim Brotherhood. This party opposed the Anglo-Iraqi treaty of 1930 which came into force after Iraq became independent in 1932. Backed by the 'Golden Square', a pro-Axis military junta of four colonels who were concerned that the pro-British party, led by Nuri al-Said, might bring Iraq into the war on the British side, Rashid Ali became prime minister, for the third time, in April 1941. He immediately broke the Anglo-Iraqi treaty by refusing the transit of British troops through Iraq and evidence mounted that he was receiving German support via the *Vichy French regime in Syria. In May 1941 his supporters attacked the British air base at Habbaniya, but in the fighting which followed he was forced to flee to Persia. He ended up in Germany as a leading Arab collaborator and propagandist for the Nazis, remaining in exile until 1958. See also ANTI-IMPERIALISM.

Ravensbrück, a Nazi *concentration camp for women and children which was opened in May 1939. Situated 80 km. (50 mi.) north of Berlin, its victims were transported to it from all over Europe. It was built to house 6,000 prisoners, but by October 1944 it contained 42,000 from 23 nations. Of the estimated 133,000 sent to the camp, perhaps as many as 92,700 did not survive. Odette *Sansom was imprisoned in Ravensbrück and Violette *Szabo and Anne *Frank both died there.

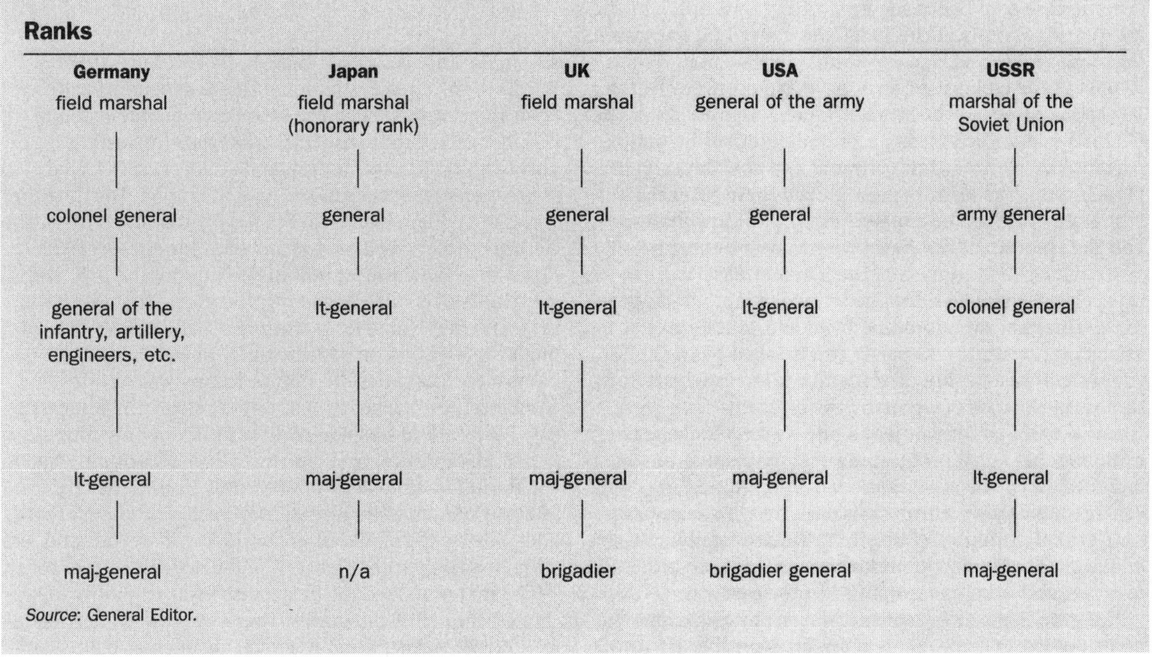

Ranks

Germany	Japan	UK	USA	USSR
field marshal	field marshal (honorary rank)	field marshal	general of the army	marshal of the Soviet Union
colonel general	general	general	general	army general
general of the infantry, artillery, engineers, etc.	lt-general	lt-general	lt-general	colonel general
lt-general	maj-general	maj-general	maj-general	lt-general
maj-general	n/a	brigadier	brigadier general	maj-general

Source: General Editor.

***Rawalpindi*, sinking of.** On 12 November 1939 the C-in-C of the German Navy, Grand Admiral *Raeder, decided to threaten British *convoys by simulating a breakout into the Atlantic by two of his *German surface raiders, **Scharnhorst* and *Gneisenau*. By doing this he also hoped to take the pressure off his pocket battleship *Admiral Graf Spee*, by diverting British warships which were hunting her (see RIVER PLATE). While making this feint the two warships, on 23 November 1939, came upon *Rawalpindi*, a 16,697-ton British *armed merchant cruiser which was patrolling the gap between the Faeroes and Iceland. Although *Rawalpindi* scored one hit, it took *Scharnhorst* only fourteen minutes to sink her.

raw and synthetic materials. One of the key lessons of the *First World War was the importance of having regular and adequate supplies of raw materials to sustain the industrial war effort. There grew up in the inter-war years a body of strategic thinking which saw economic preparation for war and economic mobilization as the foundation for military success. It was widely believed that those powers that controlled access to vital material resources needed for war would have greater staying-power and military capacity. During the war both sides waged *economic warfare to deny these resources to the other, and shortages of certain raw materials became serious as the war went on, particularly for the Axis states. So important were strategic raw materials perceived to be that states with limited natural resources made efforts to find synthetic substitutes for the important materials they lacked. In the end shortages proved critical only for Germany and Japan, under the combined pressure of naval blockade and bombing.

Some case could be made for arguing that much of the international crisis of the 1930s was caused by the search for more secure and sizeable sources of raw materials following the collapse of an open world economy in the 1929 slump (see WORLD TRADE). Japan's aggression in the *China Incident had strong economic motives behind it, particularly control of the mineral and coal deposits of Manchukuo. The Japanese recognized their potentially vulnerable position as a major importer of raw materials, and the creation of the New Order in Asia during the 1930s with the formation of the *Greater East Asia Co-prosperity Sphere was designed to make Japan less open to the threat of sanctions and blockade. Mussolini's attack on Abyssinia was partly conditioned by the belief that it held vast untapped mineral resources which Italy lacked. In the case of Germany the link was clear. From the mid-1930s Hitler wanted to build up a 'blockade-free' economy through a programme of import-substitution and foreign expansion. *Lebensraum* (living-space) in central and eastern Europe was designed to compensate for Germany's limited supply of raw materials by engrossing through conquest the sources of oil, coal, iron ore, and other commodities in the east.

The growing pace of rearmament in the 1930s and the revival of world trade created pressures on the supply of

Raw materials were in short supply even in the USA as the caption for this cartoon—'I'm conserving wool, this bathing suit's painted on'—shows.

raw materials. The USSR and the USA were relatively immune through possession of large continent-wide resources, though even the USA was dependent for a number of key industrial raw materials (including chrome, manganese, nickel, and rubber) on external sources of supply such as the British Empire. For the other states dependence on overseas supply remained high. The UK imported 60% of its raw material supplies in 1938. Japan imported almost 90% of its iron ore in 1938, and two-thirds of its oil. The situation in Germany was in some respects even worse for it was highly vulnerable to blockade and had an insufficiently powerful navy to contest the sea lanes. In 1938 Germany was almost completely deficient in 20 out of 26 'strategic' materials (see Table 1) and had adequate supplies of only four—potash, magnesite, coal, and zinc. The UK not only had the naval power to keep open supply lines to its empire and the USA, but the British Empire as a whole had adequate stocks of 19 out of the 26 key materials and was a major supplier of at least nine for the rest of the world.

The materials needed to sustain a war economy fell into a number of categories. There were those needed to feed heavy industry and engineering such as coal, iron

Raw and synthetic materials, Table 1: percentage of world output in 1938 of key raw materials in the British Empire, USA, USSR, and Germany

Material	*Br. Empire*	*USA*	*USSR*	*Germany*
Bauxite	15.6	7.7	6.1	2.3
Antimony ore	2.1	1.6	0.0	4.1
Chrome ore	37.6	3.6	17.3	0.0
Copper ore	29.8	25.1	4.8	1.5
Iron ore	12.9	20.2	19.5	6.1
Lead ore	35.9	18.7	3.9	5.6
Magnesite	7.4	16.1	0.0	42.6
Manganese ore	36.1	0.8	41.3	8.3
Molybdenum ore	0.2	92.4	0.0	0.0
Nickel ore	87.9	0.4	2.3	0.0
Tin ore	39.2	0.0	0.0	0.2
Tungsten ore	25.2	7.8	0.0	0.0
Zinc ore	29.0	25.1	3.7	11.9
Coal	24.8	29.0	10.9	16.4
Crude petroleum	2.4	60.3	10.6	0.2
Phosphates	9.1	26.8	15.8	0.0
Potash	0.1	9.6	4.1	62.2
Pyrites	8.9	5.4	n.a.	4.2
Sulphur	0.0	78.5	0.0	0.0
Mercury	0.0	11.9	5.2	1.9
Vanadium ore	34.8	27.3	0.0	0.0
Cotton (ginned)	17.0	41.7	13.5	0.0
Rubber	51.9	0.0	0.0	0.0
Silk (raw)	0.1	0.0	3.6	0.0
Wool	45.7	11.5	7.6	1.2
Cobalt ore	45.0	0.0	0.0	0.0
Titanium	72.0	1.1	0.0	0.0

For production of oil and coal, and principle use of key raw materials, see STATISTICS.

Source: Contributor.

ore, copper, lead, zinc; there were materials critical for weapons production, notably bauxite to provide the aluminium for aircraft manufacture; there were materials needed to keep the armed forces moving, oil and rubber; finally there were scarce minerals needed in industrial processes for alloys or specialized equipment, such as tungsten, molybdenum, or platinum. All states had adequate access to some of these, but no state had straightforward access to them all (see STATISTICS Tables 6, 7, 8). The high dependency on overseas supply led some governments well before the war to pursue strategies of autarky, or self-sufficiency, by means of which domestic production would be expanded either through exploiting domestic natural resources more fully, or by finding a synthetic substitute.

In October 1936 Hitler launched a Four Year Plan designed to achieve this goal. Iron ore imports were to be reduced in favour of lower-grade domestic ores; synthetic rubber and oil programmes were established on a scale necessary to satisfy Germany's potential military needs in the mid-1940s. The production of synthetic textiles—forerunners of the man-made fibres developed after 1945—was encouraged to reduce Germany's high dependence on overseas supply of cotton and wool. Synthetics were used for everything from parachutes to uniforms. In the same year Japan's leaders initiated a synthetic oil programme to produce 14 million barrels a year by 1943. In mainland Japan strenuous efforts were made to discover and exploit all available raw material reserves however poor their quality. Neither programme reached the planned goals. Japan lacked the industrial expertise and a sufficiently advanced industrial base to produce what was needed (in 1939 only 0.5% of the synthetic oil plan was achieved). In Germany the programmes were interrupted by the outbreak of war, and though a great deal was subsequently achieved, emphasis was also placed on exploiting captured resources.

The democracies also made preparations for the use of raw materials in wartime. The UK and France set up state-funded programmes to build up stocks of strategic materials in the late 1930s and encouraged the expansion of raw material output in their colonial territories, particularly in Africa, the Caribbean, and Canada. The USA passed the Strategic Materials Act in June 1939 which empowered the bureau of mines to search for all possible sources of scarce materials in the continental USA and to stockpile resources from overseas. By 1941 more than $1 billion had been spent on stocks, and the raw material output of a number of Latin American states was boosted by American investment programmes and generous orders. In this way heavy American reliance on resources from China and south Asia was reduced in favour of supplies from the western hemisphere.

With the outbreak of hostilities in 1939 Germany's worst expectations were fulfilled: the Allied blockade denied it access to overseas markets almost entirely. Economic warfare was initiated across the world to deny resources to Germany, and from 1940 to Italy as well. When Japan refused in 1941 to reverse its military expansion in Asia it became subject to embargoes on key materials, and when this situation precipitated a Japanese invasion of colonial territories in South-East Asia, Japan too was blockaded. Throughout the war Germany, Italy, and Japan had to satisfy their requirements of strategic materials from the new economic blocs conquered in Europe and Asia.

Both these blocs provided very significant supplies; without them the Axis war effort would have been much reduced. German conquests in Europe brought access to Romanian oil, bauxite from Greece and Yugoslavia, Polish coal, manganese from the USSR, and iron ore from France. Thanks to this expansion, supplies of coal were 60% greater in 1944 than in 1936, and supplies of iron ore 140% greater, while Romania provided a large proportion of German oil requirements from 1940 to 1944. In the Japanese case the seizure of Malaya, French Indo-China and the *Netherlands East Indies (NEI) made all the difference to Japan's war effort. The NEI supplied rubber, cobalt, and by 1943 the great bulk of the bauxite needed for Japanese aluminium production. French Indo-China and Malaya provided tin and rubber, the Philippines large amounts of copper. Most important of all was oil. The oilfields seized in the Dutch territories produced nine times as much crude oil by 1943 as all the sources in Japan and China together. Without the supply of oil from southern Asia Japan's war effort would have ground to a halt.

The vulnerability of the Axis economies was exploited wherever possible by the Allies. In 1940 the British and French developed plans to seize the Swedish iron ore fields and to bomb the Soviet oilfields to deny these supplies to the Reich. Neither operation was carried out for fear of the political repercussions, though it was German access to Swedish iron ore that precipitated the *Norwegian campaign in April 1940. When the *strategic air offensive against Germany began in earnest the iron and steel and synthetic oil industries were top targets. In 1944 the destruction of much of Germany's oil producing and refining industries paved the way for the final collapse of Germany's air force and industry, and then of the Reich itself. Against Italy and Japan the western states operated a submarine campaign that created havoc with vital supplies of ore, coal, and oil. In 1944 the Allies sank almost 750,000 tons of Japanese tanker capacity, and supplies of oil from the south virtually dried up. The naval and air assault on Japan's shipping lanes during 1944 and 1945 brought its war economy to the point of collapse (see JAPAN, 7) even without the relentless fire-bombing of Japanese cities.

There were a number of ways in which the Axis tried to conserve strategic materials to meet these threats. Civilian consumption was progressively reduced and resources allocated to war industry and the armed forces. By the end of 1940, 75% of German steel and 80% of all aluminium was allocated to military purposes. Scarce materials were strictly rationed and quotas arranged between the armed forces and industry to make sure that materials went to where they were most needed. Where the shortage was critical, efforts were made to find substitutes, or to find more rational production methods less wasteful of materials. By 1944 46% fewer raw materials were used in the production of the BMW aero-engine than in 1941. From 1942, when the *Speer Plan set up Central Planning, the supply of raw materials was reviewed centrally and supplies granted only to the most efficient firms, with strict priorities. The result of all these efforts was an increase in military production to very much higher levels in 1944 with only modest increases in raw material input. Thanks to increased efficiency and rationing Germany remained 'blockade-free' until bombing reached its peak in 1944–5.

The same course was followed in Japan. Rationing, resource substitution, the collection of scrap metal and rubber and reduction in quality were all used to sustain Japan's war output. The synthetic oil programme slowed down with the conquest of south Asia, but strict control over use of natural oil was imposed on industry and the civilian population. When the tide turned against Japan the failure of the synthetic oil programme was fully exposed. Instead of the 14 million barrels planned, only 1.5 million were produced at the peak. The supply of crude oil collapsed in 1944 and 1945. From 1944 Japan fought from a rapidly shrinking raw material base.

The Allied powers were by no means immune to these problems, but they were in a stronger position than the Axis because they were better endowed with natural resources and had less restricted access to world markets. In 1938 the future Allies produced 57 million tons of steel and 718 million tons of coal to the 31 million tons of steel and 241 million tons of coal of the Axis states. During the war the gap widened through the massive productive effort of the USA (see Table 2). What the British Empire and the USA did not produce from their own resources they were able to buy from overseas. Despite the threat of the submarine most of the world's trade routes were kept open, and new routes established to Africa and the Middle East, while the *Arctic convoys supplied the USSR. The western Allies were able to invest freely abroad in order to build up alternative sources of supply when the collapse in the Far East cut them off from the tin, oil, and rubber of southern Asia.

There was also a much higher level of co-operation between the Allied states in the provision of strategic materials. The UK relied heavily on its empire and on American supplies. The introduction of *Lend-Lease in

Raw and synthetic materials, Table 2: Output of selected raw materials in the USA, 1939–45

Material	*1939*	*1940*	*1941*	*1942*	*1943*	*1944*	*1945*
Coal (mill.tons)	394.8	460.8	514.1	582.7	590.2	619.6	577.6
Iron ore (mill.tons)	51.7	73.7	92.4	105.5	101.2	94.1	88.4
Crude oil (mill.brls)	1,265	1,353	1,402	1,386	1,505	1,677	1,713
Bauxite (000 tons)	375	439	937	2,602	6,233	2,824	981
Chrome ore (000 tons)	4	3	14.3	112.9	160.1	45.6	14.0
Manganese ore (000 tons)	32.8	44.0	87.8	190.7	205.2	247.6	182.3

Source: Contributor.

1941 and the onset of American rearmament led to an unprecedented degree of collaboration between the empire and the USA in assessing future raw material needs and agreeing to their distribution between the various economies. In May 1942 an Empire Clearing House was set up for materials produced in the British colonies and dominions. In January 1942 a Combined Raw Materials Board was set up to oversee the whole raw material effort of the Allies and to decide on allocation with the USSR as well. Nearly 60% of the Lend-Lease supplies sent to the USSR was in the form of agricultural and industrial materials and equipment to meet the urgent need for raw materials after the German invasion in June 1941 (see BARBAROSSA) and the consequent loss of the Soviet Union's western industrial regions. It was even supplied with high-grade aviation fuel which could not easily be produced by the Soviet oil industry. By contrast co-operation between the Axis states was much less evident. For example, Japan was not given the most advanced scientific information on synthetic oil production by the Germans until January 1945. However, Japan and Germany did send supplies to each other via the USSR up to the time of BARBAROSSA and surface *blockade runners continued to run between the two countries until 1944 (see also AXIS STRATEGY AND CO-OPERATION).

In addition to the world-wide control of raw material supplies, the Allies also introduced a range of controls and restrictions at home to conserve raw materials and to divert them to war use. They too found alternative materials, introduced more rational production methods to save on scarcer materials, and exploited domestic supplies more extensively. In the case of rubber, where 98% of American supplies and 87% of British supplies came from South-East Asia, it became necessary to find a synthetic substitute (buna). In a remarkably short space of time the USA was producing more synthetic rubber in a year than had been imported in 1940. The situation in 1942 was nevertheless a difficult one and the gap between consumption and production was met partly from accumulated stocks equivalent to a whole year of pre-war consumption, and partly from a nation-wide collection of scrap rubber which bridged the gap between the collapse of overseas supply and the domestic production of synthetics. Some idea of the sheer scale of the American effort can be seen by comparing American and German output. In 1943 the USA produced 730,000 tons of synthetic rubber, Germany 121,000 tons.

The main threat to Allied supplies of raw materials came not from simple deficiency but from the military actions of the Axis. The battle of the *Atlantic and Axis successes in the *German–Soviet war both threatened in 1942 to undermine the Allied war effort to a dangerous degree. The U-boat menace extended as far as the coastal waters of the eastern USA, and cost so much in the loss of oil tankers (see CONVOYS) that an expensive oil pipeline (the famous 'Big Inch') had to be built from Texas to the industrial centres of the north-east. The threat to British trade was met by a massive shipbuilding programme in the USA (see LIBERTY SHIPS, for example) which was only finally lifted by the defeat of the German submarine fleet in May 1943. The most serious danger was the loss of the UK's oil supply, which by 1942 came almost entirely from the USA and the Caribbean, 65% of it shipped from the eastern seaboard of the USA where it was, at that time, particularly vulnerable to interception by submarines. For the UK there was no alternative source, for it had been decided in the 1930s that synthetic production was too costly, and oil from the Middle East was consumed by Allied forces in Africa and India. From 1942 to 1944 the Allies lost 6.5 million tons of tanker capacity, which was only made good by the addition of 8.5 million tons of tankers from American shipyards. As a result of this effort the supply of oil to the UK rose from a weekly average of 150,000 tons in the spring of 1942 to an average of 350,000 tons a week by the summer of 1943.

The loss of the raw materials of the western USSR was a more serious blow. It was made good partly from western supplies channelled through Siberia, Archangel, and the Persian route, partly by the fuller exploitation of resources in the Urals and Siberia. The Soviet authorities made war production a priority. Where possible civilian production was virtually eliminated, and when necessary Soviet weapons were produced without scarce materials. The irony was that the German conquerors obtained much less from the captured areas than they had hoped. Manganese production was expanded quickly, but the output of coal, iron ore, and other metals revived either very slowly or hardly at all, while the failure of the southern thrust in 1942 meant that Germany never got the oil of the Caucasus. Much of what was extracted in the USSR was used by the German forces there, while transport difficulties, the destruction of facilities by the retreating Red Army when it employed a *scorched earth policy, and a shortage of German engineers to organize the new production, all militated against effective exploitation.

As the war turned against the Axis states the raw material gap between the two sides began to widen. Neutral states which had traded with both sides began to favour the Allies. Latin American governments prohibited exports to the Axis states; Turkey curtailed its supply of chrome to Germany; Spain reduced the flow of tungsten, and so on. By the last months of war the Axis states were compelled to rely on stocks, scrap, and domestic production. Bombing and submarine attack eroded the raw material base through continuous attrition.

By 1945 Japanese imports of iron ore were 3% of the level in 1942, coal imports were 3.3%, bauxite imports 0.3%. As a result the quality and number of Axis weapons deteriorated rapidly and the reduction in strategic supplies for German and Japanese industry was an important factor in the rapid collapse of both countries' resistance in 1945. Richard Overy

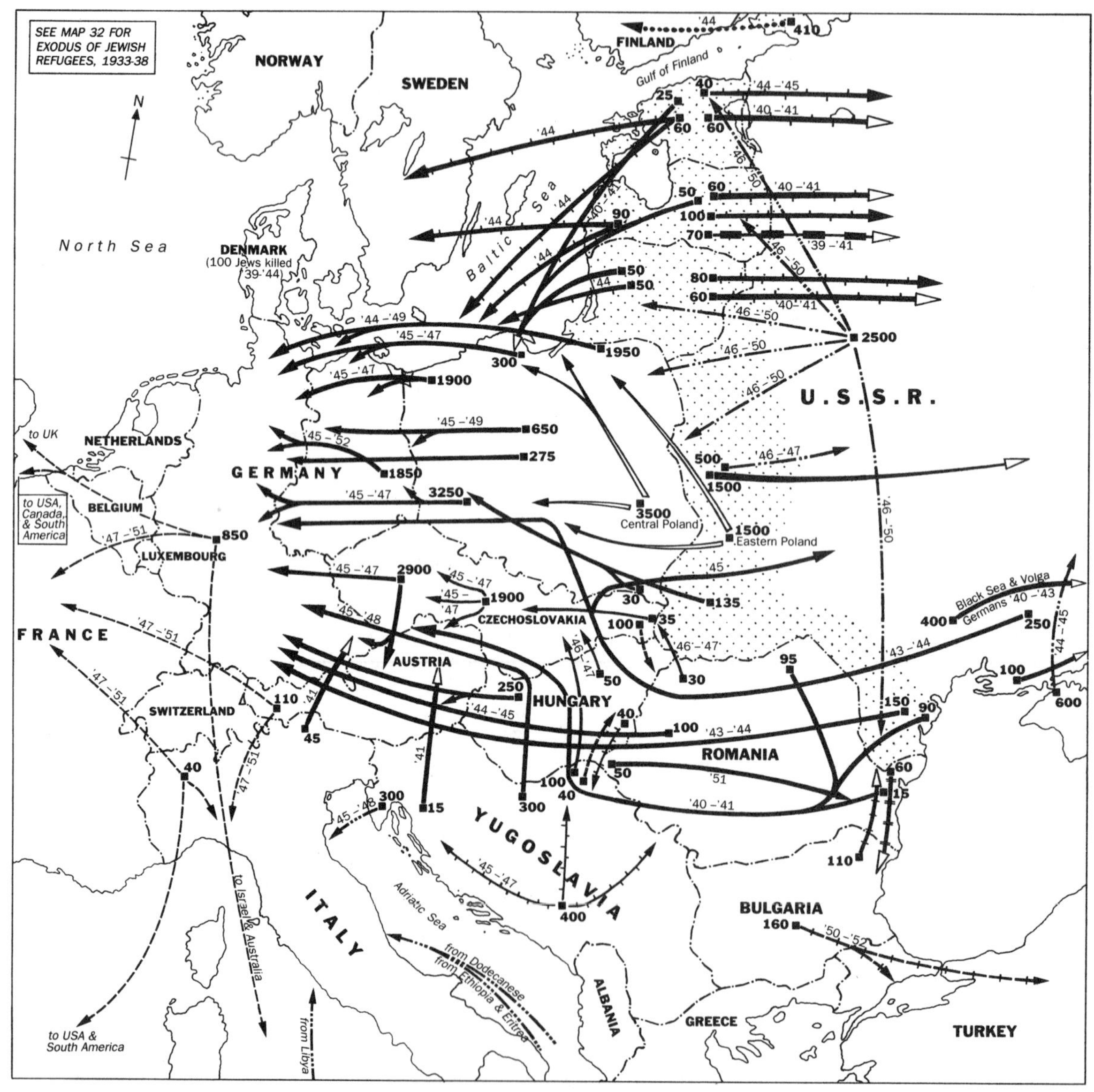

91. Movement of **refugees** through settlement, evacuation, or expulsion, 1939–52

Ashworth, W., *A Short History of the International Economy since 1850* (3rd edn., London, 1975).
Cohen, J., *Japan's Economy in War and Reconstruction* (Honolulu, 1949).
Hurstfield, J., *The Control of Raw Materials* (London, 1953).
Milward, A. S., *War, Economy and Society 1939–1945* (London, 1987).
Vatter, H. G., *The US Economy in World War II* (New York, 1985).

R-boat, or *Räumboot* (sweeping boat), was a German minesweeping, or defensive patrol, craft. It was the equivalent of the British 34 m. (112 ft.) motor launch. See also WARSHIPS.

RDF (Radio Direction Finding), the original name for *radar in the UK. A chain of RDF stations was built along the east and south coasts and helped win the battle of *Britain.

Rebecca, (1) device carried aboard Allied aircraft to receive signals from the *Eureka navigation beacon.

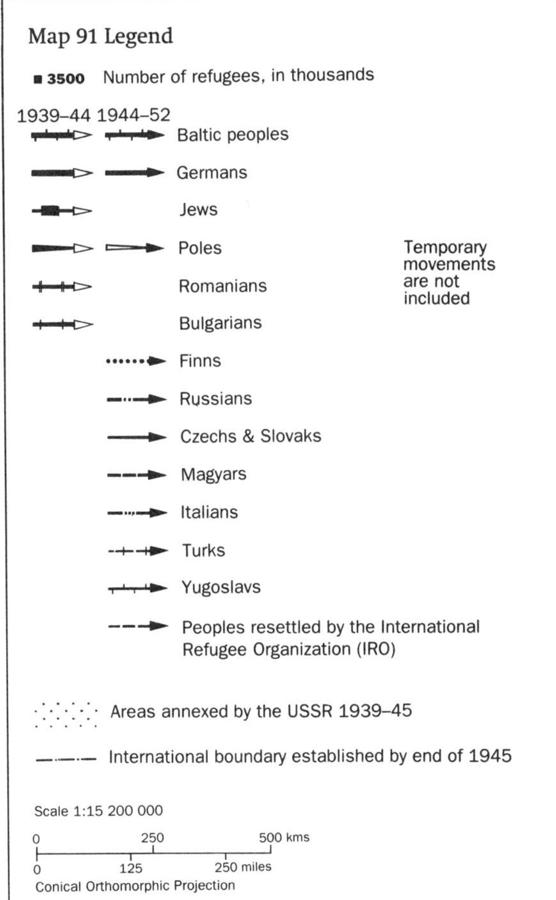

Rebecca, (2) novel by Daphne du Maurier used by the *Kondor mission as the key for their codes.

Red Army, see USSR, 6(b). It officially became the Soviet Army in 1944 but, as it continued to be popularly known as the Red Army, this name has been retained throughout the text.

Red Ball Express, truck convoys used to supply the Allied armies when *Eisenhower decided to pursue the Germans across the River Seine during the *Normandy campaign. It was estimated that 100,000 tons of supplies, excluding POL (Petrol, Oil, Lubricants), would have to be transported by convoys of trucks from the beaches to depots south-west of Paris, a considerable feat of *logistics. A one-way loop highway was introduced between St Lô and Chartres with every available truck using it around the clock. The convoys, whose name derived from railroad slang for fast freight, began on 25 August 1944 and on 29 August 5,958 trucks delivered 12,342 tons of supplies. They ceased on 6 September having delivered 89,939 tons and having consumed 300,000 gallons of petrol a day doing so.

The Red Ball Express was also run from Bayeux to Brussels to supply *MARKET-GARDEN and it was the precursor of several similar operations. Special trains were also used. The Toot Sweet Express, for example, took supplies from Cherbourg to Namur and Verdun.

Red Cross, see INTERNATIONAL RED CROSS COMMITTEE.

Red Orchestra, see ROTE KAPELLE.

refugees were one of the *consequences of the war. From its very first day, a trickle of refugees began: Poles whose houses had been destroyed by German bombs or gunfire, and who set off—on horseback or on foot, perhaps with a cart or handcart or perambulator full of belongings—away from where they supposed the enemy to be. Some headed for distant friends or relatives, some simply took fright and fled. In Belgium and in France in May and June 1940, the trickle became a flood: most of the motorcar-owning population of Brussels, Lille, and Paris fled south-westwards in turn, jamming the roads (to the exasperation of the Allied armies) and subsisting as best they could.

By midwinter 1944–5, with the Allied armies closing in on Germany from east, south, and west, millions of Germans too had become refugees. The upper and middle classes in eastern Germany, in particular, were reluctant to come under the aegis of the advancing communist forces. The peasantry and the urban working class had doubts as well: hordes moved westwards. All over Germany, those who had been compelled to work as *forced labour seized any chance that offered to escape, and became refugees themselves. By the end of the fighting in Europe in May 1945, with the railway system disrupted by bombing, and the road network broken up

The miseries of war are poignantly depicted here as a young German **refugee** weeps over the few possessions saved from his home outside Aachen.

by shellfire and demolitions, with even the German state machine in disarray and many newly liberated territories close to anarchy, refugees could be numbered in tens of millions. Henri Michel, a sober and discriminating historian, reckoned them at about 30,000,000.

The newly founded United Nations organization (see SAN FRANCISCO CONFERENCE) set up the United Nations Relief and Rehabilitation Administration, usually known by its acronym of *UNRRA, to try to resettle those refugees who were outside the boundaries of the USSR, where they were retained as labourers. Bureaucrats labelled them 'displaced persons' (DPs); 'DP camps' sprouted on the edges of large towns all over western and central Europe. Volunteers did what they could—often they could do very little—to provide medical aid, clothing, even elementary sanitation; UNRRA did what it could to collect and distribute aid. It handed out some 25,000,000 tons of food in seventeen different countries in 1945–7.

Gradually, some DPs became reunited with missing members of their own families; some managed to get work; some, lucky ones, were granted citizenship of a new country. The skilled craftsmen among them were welcome enough in states that were trying to reconstruct themselves after the desolation of war; the rest endured, sometimes for years. See also DEMOGRAPHY and DEPORTATIONS.

M. R. D. FOOT

Regensburg–Schweinfurt raids, see SCHWEINFURT RAIDS.

Reggio di Calabria landings, opening move in the Allied *Italian campaign which took place on 3 September 1943 after a preliminary bombardment by warships and heavy air attacks on Axis airfields and communications. Three Canadian brigades crossed the strait of Messina from Sicily to spearhead landings of part of *Montgomery's British and Commonwealth Eighth Army near Reggio di Calabria. Montgomery's objective was to clear the toe of Italy before moving northwards in conjunction with Allied forces landing at *Salerno. The operation was not opposed as the German High Command had concluded that Calabria was expendable.

Reichenau, Field Marshal Walther von (1884–1942), German Army officer who served as a staff officer during the *First World War. As *Blomberg's chief of staff in East

Prussia, he became head of the defence ministry's Wehrmachtamt (armed forces office) when Blomberg became minister of defence in January 1933. Promotion followed quickly and by 1935 Reichenau was a lt-general. He commanded the Tenth Army (renamed Sixth Army) in the *Polish campaign of September–October 1939 and was promoted general before leading it during the fighting which led to the fall of *France. He personally accepted the surrender of King *Léopold and the Belgian Army in May 1940 and was promoted field marshal that July. His Sixth Army, as part of *Rundstedt's Army Group South, performed well during the German invasion of the USSR in June 1941 (see BARBAROSSA) and in September 1941 it took *Kiev. In December 1941 he succeeded Rundstedt, but died of a heart attack the following month. By that time his early approval of Hitler had long turned to scepticism and then distrust.

Reichswald, battle of. The Reichswald is a large tract of forest situated south-west of Cleves. In February 1945, during the battle for *Germany, it was the scene of bitter fighting as *Montgomery's Anglo-Canadian Twenty-First Army Group closed to the Rhine (see VERITABLE). The Germans had constructed no fewer than five lines of defences in the forest and matters were made worse by a sudden thaw, accompanied by heavy rain. Furthermore, the Germans had flooded much of the area, forcing the British and Canadian troops under the command of *Crerar's First Canadian Army to advance on a narrow front. The result was slow progress and heavy casualties, in spite of much use of RAF Bomber Command to bomb objectives before they were attacked. Indeed, the battle bore marked similarities to the Western Front of the *First World War. Not until 9 March was the Reichswald finally cleared. CHARLES MESSENGER

religion. The attitude all religious traditions should adopt towards war has always been a contentious and divisive topic, and the Second World War proved to be no exception. The circumstances in which war should be supported, or whether it should ever be supported, had been a matter of public debate in western Europe, in particular, ever since the *First World War. The extent to which the churches had almost without exception, endorsed national aims in that conflict subsequently became a matter for regret amongst Christian leaders. A commitment to 'peace' became a much more prominent aspect of church life, particularly in the English-speaking world. In England, Dick Sheppard, Charles Raven, and Donald Soper were among those who had declared they would never support any war. In the mid-1930s, the 'Christian Pacifist' option appeared likely to be a substantial section of opinion. Archbishops and bishops, who would not go so far, nevertheless made it clear that peace was so highly prized that every attempt should be made to preserve it. Pacifism, whether 'hard' or 'soft', probably had a greater impact on the British churches than on those of any other European country. It grew out of a Dissenting tradition but now incorporated episcopal members of the House of Lords. Yet by 1939 it was not as potent a factor as had been anticipated. The events of 1938, coupled with an increasing awareness of the nature of Nazism, led many in the churches to feel that war, even if not necessarily 'just' according to traditional doctrine, was nevertheless justified. In consequence, when war came, there was no major cleavage between the majority of church members and government. The pacifist option was followed by only a small minority (see CONSCIENTIOUS OBJECTORS).

However, there was a determination, on the part of both Anglican and Free Church leaders, not to repeat some of the crude statements allegedly made by their predecessors in 1914–18. Paradoxically, it was not easy to maintain the stance of solid but restrained support because it seemed self-evident, at least in 1940, that the war was a struggle to preserve Christian civilization from a National Socialism which was profoundly anti-religious. The inter-war period had seen the tentative development of a (Protestant) ecumenical movement. A celebrated conference on Church, Community, and State, held in Oxford in 1937, had brought together many leaders to discuss these issues. Organizationally and institutionally it was still fragmentary, but an extensive network of supra-national personal contacts had been built up. Church leaders did not want the objectives of the war to become simply national. There was a place in British church life for Christians exiled from Germany. The concept of Christian civilization had a wide appeal, extending beyond those in active membership of any of the churches. It was a term to be found on the lips of a prime minister not otherwise conspicuous for his Christian devotion.

Identification with the term even made possible a degree of collaboration between Roman Catholics and other Christians. Momentarily, in 1940, in the wake of events in France and the establishment of the *Vichy regime, there had been a suspicion, even in high places, that British Catholics were not altogether loyal. The fact that Eire had decided to remain neutral engendered a certain suspicion, for it was known that there were many Catholics there. The government of Northern Ireland found itself in a good position to play the Protestant card, particularly when the geographical location of the province became of increasing importance. In the event, notwithstanding the fact that Catholics clearly did not identify the USSR with the defence of Christian civilization, they did not dissent from the view that Hitler had to be defeated. The dean of Canterbury, Hewlett Johnson, took the Soviet Union and Christian civilization to be synonymous, but that was extreme. There was, nevertheless, a drift in the churches, as the war progressed, towards the left. William Temple, archbishop of Canterbury 1942–4, was a member of the Labour Party and his best-selling *Christianity and Social Order* (1942) reasserted Christianity's claim to have a prophetic public role.

Prominent though Temple was, the most notable British religious figure was George *Bell, bishop of Chichester, a man with wide international and ecumenical sympathies. His willingness to speak publicly against the policy of *area bombing earned him both admiration and enmity in public life. Germany had to be defeated, but it mattered how. Perhaps more than any other figure, he summed up the determination of the British churches, as expressed through prominent figures, to support the war and yet to maintain a certain critical distance. Naturally, there were some who thought the emphasis erred in one direction and others who thought it erred in the opposite direction. One element in this stance was also an awareness of the distance between church life and the concerns and beliefs of the population at large. Service padres during the First World War had realized this at first hand. Chaplains in the Second World War tended to be both more circumspect and sympathetic in their responsibilities. In short, Christian civilization was a capacious category and there was an awareness in many quarters, though perhaps not on the part of Temple's successor, Geoffrey Fisher, that the religion of the British people, as it found expression in the war, did not fit securely and simply into the ecclesiastical or theological categories of the mainline churches.

The generally subdued symbiosis of religion and war which developed in the UK could not be found so readily in other parts of Christian Europe. Hitler's early sponsoring of something called 'practical Christianity' seemed disappointing in its fruits. His sapping of Protestant Christianity had proved extremely divisive in the churches. That there was opposition to him in the churches cannot be doubted, but its basis was not constant. For some, opposition was only justified if there was direct interference in internal ecclesiastical affairs. For others, as the regime consolidated itself, a more wide-ranging and political opposition was justified. Attitudes on these issues reflected highly elaborate Lutheran notions of the respective spheres of church and state. On the Roman Catholic side, the broad strategy had been to try to preserve an institutional life for the church by formal agreements. *'German Christians' emerged who claimed to be able to synthesize the best of National Socialism and the best of Christianity. Many Christians seemed able to reconcile themselves to at least certain aspects of anti-Semitic legislation. Those who could not, like Martin *Niemöller and the archbishop of Münster (who opposed the *euthanasia programme), often ended up in *concentration camps. Many young people had little interest in abstruse theological debate and preferred the religion of the open air.

The war of 1939 therefore produced in Germany a wide variety of reactions, public and private. It was difficult to believe that a victory for Hitler would advance the cause of Christianity. It was equally difficult to believe that the defeat of Germany was desirable. It was almost impossible to believe that the churches had a positive duty to contribute to that defeat. Pacifism, while not absent from the churches, had often been seen as 'Anglo-Saxon', a product of an emphasis on the 'Social Gospel' not congenial in the theological climate in Germany in the 1930s. When the USSR was invaded in June 1941 (see BARBAROSSA), many anguished Christians serving in the Wehrmacht began to feel a little more comfortable about supporting a war that now included the overthrow of godless *communism. However, Hitler himself had largely abandoned the notion that he could enlist the Catholic Church in the front line against Bolshevism. It was difficult for Christians to know whom to trust. Anti-Nazi pastors had often been vehemently critical of the *Versailles settlement in the past. The war could not be supported unreservedly but neither could Germany's enemies. Pre-war friends tried clandestinely to reach out across the chasm, as when George Bell met Dietrich *Bonhoeffer in Stockholm. These were brave gestures, but power lay elsewhere. Pre-war enemies delicately came together in small groups. Christians and Socialists whistled together in the dark. Protestants and Catholics, sundered in the past by political and theological divides, tried to find common ground. Such encounters were always difficult and incarceration was always a possibility. True believers, it seemed, had returned to the catacombs. The most difficult question of all eventually had to be faced. Was it right to take part in an opposition which could have as its objective the assassination of Hitler? The July plot of 1944 (see SCHWARZE KAPELLE) is evidence that some Christians did reach that conclusion. They had to pay the price, either immediately or subsequently. There was also a nagging anxiety. If Hitler was killed, would the German people support a Christian peace?

Here and there, too, individuals displayed heroism in helping all men and women in danger—Christians, Socialists, or Jews. It is not surprising that they were the exceptions. At another level, Roman Catholic bishops and Evangelical church leaders still struggled to maintain some semblance of 'normality' in the institutional life of their respective churches. It might be that otherwise Christianity would simply disappear. Cardinal Bertram, president of the conference of bishops and the last prince bishop of Breslau, felt it his duty to congratulate the Führer every year on the occasion of his birthday. When he heard, after Hitler's suicide on 30 April 1945, that the Führer had fallen at his command post in the Reich Chancellery, fighting against Bolshevism to his last breath, the cardinal ordered a solemn requiem to be held throughout his archdiocese in memory of the Führer and all those who had fallen in the struggle for the German Fatherland. In his prison cell, Dietrich Bonhoeffer meditated on what he thought the war was teaching the Christians of Germany. It would be impossible simply to

Religion: A US soldier contemplates the damage done to a church at Acerno, Italy, September 1943.

reinhabit the old structures as though nothing had happened. He offered some tantalizing thoughts on 'religionless Christianity' for the survivors to puzzle over.

Elsewhere in western and central Europe, neither the British nor the German situation could be precisely repeated. In the mainly Protestant countries of northern Europe—Norway, Denmark, and the Netherlands—German conquest produced a profound shock, particularly since they had all been neutral in the First World War. In Lutheran Scandinavia, Germany had been the cultural and theological home of church leaders. In this unexpected situation should they collaborate and seek what terms they could for their churches? Should they identify with *governments-in-exile, where these existed? Should they become *de facto* the embodiment of national resistance in the absence of the customary institutions? Was it really the job of churches to be so political? But on the other hand, it was undoubtedly the case that they were national churches, virtually coextensive with the population at large. That justified such involvement, indeed it perhaps required it if the church leaders were to retain credibility. Should they simultaneously seek some kind of international mediating role between the UK and Germany with a view to bringing the war to an end? Sweden, close at hand, might facilitate such an enterprise. To these questions there were, inevitably, different answers. To be even more precise, there were different answers from the same people at different times. In the gloom of 1940 things looked different from the picture in 1944. Church leaders wrestled with the balance between prudent pragmatism and what they believed to be moral imperatives. Calvinists in the Netherlands had substantially the same problems but the context of their occupation was not quite the same. In addition, unlike in Scandinavia, historic Catholic/Calvinist differences did not make it possible to mobilize a national/church resistance. We should not ignore, either, sections of the population, among them some church members, for whom the idea of participating as equal partners in the 'New European Order' had attractions.

In Catholic Europe some similar but also some different issues arose. Church and state were separated in France and the clerical/anti-clerical divide had remained a constant aspect of the politics of the Third Republic. In 1940, there was a disposition in high clerical circles and among some *bien-pensants* to regard the catastrophe of the fall of *France in June 1940 as a judgement upon that regime. The spiritual decadence which the Third Republic had embodied had to be remedied. The German victory was not in itself to be welcomed but an opportunity was now to hand in the new regime of *Vichy, underpinned by the ideology of Charles *Maurras and other right-wing Catholics, to make a fresh start. The Papal nuncio discovered 'the Pétain miracle'. The only blemish on *Pétain, apparently, was his 21-year marriage to a divorcée, but ways and means were happily found to legitimize the union. It looked to many as though the regeneration of agriculture and Catholicism could go together. It is true that the initial paeans of praise about Pétain's regime in French clerical circles gave way, subsequently, to more restrained comment and even criticism. The fact that Strasbourg cathedral had been turned into a war museum seemed a little premature, even to the Vichy episcopate, but it is worth noting that even in the spring of 1944 it was the judgement of French cardinals and archbishops that *resistance constituted 'terrorism'. Yet that is not the whole story. More than a thousand priests were deported by the Nazis and some individual bishops were very critical of the Vichy regime. The Protestant minority in the south was not enamoured of the trappings of clerical restoration. It had a certain tradition of fighting in hostile terrain and some of its members revived that link (see MAQUIS). Those Catholics who disliked 'Vichy Catholicism' noted that Charles de *Gaulle went regularly to Mass. The massive deportation of Jews in the summer of 1942 was the first issue on which bishops (of Toulouse and Lyons, for example) openly opposed the regime. Country priests often helped shot-down airmen, and others, who were trying to evade capture, for many were anti-Nazi. The abbé in north-eastern France who sat under his church tower with a sten gun concealed in the folds of his soutane, while an *SOE wireless operator used the tower for a transmission, was only an extreme instance of the general attitude among many of them.

Mussolini did not go regularly to Mass but Italy was a Catholic country. The Lateran Accords of 1929, which regulated the relations between two sovereign states, Italy and the *Vatican, also defined their rights in educational and spiritual matters. Within a few years, Mussolini had been given the papal Order of the Golden Spur and relations between the Vatican and Italy seemed better than at any time since the creation of the Italian state. Papal pronouncements concerning the war in Abyssinia in 1935–6 had been Delphic. The *League of Nations, based in Geneva of all places, had been viewed with suspicion. However, bishops and clergy could be found in 1935 who gave thanks that they were alive at such an epic moment in Italian history. Perhaps 1940 was not quite such an epic moment, but it was inconceivable that the church could have stood out against Italian intervention in the war. Obedience to the state in time of war was ordained by God and was a religious duty. The Pope, *Pius XII, unable to prevent war or persuade the belligerents to negotiate, struggled to retain a sort of detachment in the precarious enclave which was the Vatican. Given that the Pope was Italian and the weight of the Italian presence in the Curia, it was inevitable that the fate of the church in Italy should be close to their hearts—but it had to be subordinated to the needs of the church as a whole.

Vatican *diplomacy confronted two nasty phenomena: German National Socialism and Soviet communism. It was open to persuasion that the former was the immediate danger, but had little doubt that the latter was the long-term danger. Was there a path between Scylla and Charybdis? There were regimes, 'Catholic regimes', which purported to be steering such a course. Josef Tiso (1887–1947), the man most responsible for the creation of 'independent' Slovakia, was a Catholic priest. There had been some relief, in 1939, that the Slovaks had escaped from the Hussite clutches of Prague. Yet the regime Tiso presided over in wartime was oppressive. It was not difficult for Protestants and non-Christians to suppose that the Vatican favoured nominally independent, clerico-fascist regimes which followed the path of *collaboration as a way of avoiding the two unpleasant threats, and they were not persuaded that this new phenomenon was an improvement. The situation in erstwhile Yugoslavia gave them more ammunition. That country's defeat in April 1941 was probably looked upon by most Croats as an opportunity to escape from what had been a Serbian-dominated state. The establishment of the Independent State of Croatia by the Ustaša leader Ante *Pavelić was welcomed by the Catholic Church. Over the coming years this step triggered off a series of vicious and bloody events whose consequences in turn triggered further vicious and bloody events 50 years later. It was the unsurprising conviction of the Catholic bishops that the Catholic Church was the true church and that Orthodox Christians were schismatics. Conversions were to be welcomed. To the dismay of at least some of the bishops, a reign of terror began. Killings took place on a vast scale. Precise figures remain in dispute and so, also, do attributions of responsibility. It would be a mistake to suppose that the scene was witnessed with satisfaction by all church leaders. However, the fact remains that whether in Zagreb or in Bosnia-Hercegovina, emotions ran so deep that national, cultural, and religious allegiances could not be disentangled. The 'European' and 'Catholic' world (as Croats perceived it) clashed with the 'Byzantine' and 'Orthodox' world. There could be no quarter. To suppose that 'religion' was the primary cause of these conflicts would be as naïve as the claim by religious leaders that they could detach themselves, either at the time or later, from the evil consequences of what they supposed to be desirable ecclesiastical objectives.

Elsewhere in the Balkans, and in central Europe, the various fascist occupations resulted in a patchwork of persecution and indifference. Generally speaking, the Italians were less zealous than the Nazis, though ugly campaigns were inflicted on both the Muslims of Albania and the Orthodox of Greece. In Hungary, pre-war religious life, including Judaism, was able to continue until the German occupation of March 1944. In Romania, the *Iron Guard preserved the Romanian Orthodox Church, whilst persecuting the religious minorities.

Echoes of Europe's religious–political conflicts were not absent in the USA where, locally or nationally, the Protestant churches or the Roman Catholic Church reached back into a particular aspect of the European past. Yet it all seemed very far away. In the wake of the First World War, and after the débâcle of the *Versailles settlement of 1919, the main thrust of American Christianity was American. The mainline Protestant denominations were able to combine a fairly comfortable pacifism with the knowledge that the USA would not be involved in a war again anyway. A theologian and political commentator of the stature of Reinhold Niebuhr, who combined a knowledge of the European scene with a firm conviction that the Christian church could not be pacifist, was a rarity. The fact that the USA was drawn into the conflict as a result of *Pearl Harbor made the mobilization of Christian America more straightforward. It offered full scope for what critical commentators called the religion of the American way of life. Notwithstanding the formal separation of church and state, the entire community seemed to subscribe to Judaeo-Christian values, however they might be embodied in any particular church. Such subscription existed alongside an apparently deep divide between Protestants and Catholics. The fact that, from the American viewpoint, the war was occasioned by Japan made it possible for all Christians, from the president downwards, to hope that God would bless America. It was equally the fact, however, that wily Europeans had succeeded in persuading Washington that Europe came first. Roosevelt had already explained to the Pope that the survival of the USSR would be less dangerous to religion, to the church as such, and to humanity in general, than would the survival of what he called the German form of dictatorship. The Pope declined the suggestion that he might associate himself with the signatories of the *Atlantic Charter, though it is conceivable that he would have been impressed by the hymn-singing which accompanied its signature. The arrival of US forces in North Africa in November 1942 and then on continental Europe caused some surprise in the extent to which ordinary *GIs did not seem inhibited in talking about and to God. Cynical Europeans dismissed American 'religiosity'. Was it, they wondered, really important that *Eisenhower's parents were devout members of the River Brethren, a small puritan sect? But as US troops encountered at first hand the godlessness, or the intractable ethnic-religious-political conflicts, of old Europe, they suspected that a dose of straightforward new world religion would be no bad thing.

The war began in 'Christian Europe'. It was waged world-wide largely by countries which conceived themselves to be, or were perceived by non-Christian communities to be, in a general sense Christian. Chaplains were on hand to encourage, console, and bury. Services in the desert or the jungle were the order of the day. Not for nothing was the victor of *El Alamein the son of the bishop of Tasmania. But he was also the grandson of the lieutenant-governor of the Punjab and British Christian soldiers knew from long experience in the Middle East and India that the religious beliefs and traditions of Sikhs, Muslims, and Hindus had to be treated with respect and care. There was always the possibility, too, that the configuration of the conflict might produce situations in which leaders of non-Christian religions might seek to exploit the discomfort of the Christians.

In this respect, however, there was no direct repetition of the problems posed by the Ottoman Empire in the First World war. Although the Mufti of Jerusalem, Hadj Amin el *Husseini, did his best, there was no figure in the Axis camp with whom Muslims could identify in the way some had identified with the Caliph in the earlier conflict. Nevertheless, from an Islamic perspective, the war was an alien imposition fought by outsiders on territory which was part of the Umma of Islam. Problems for the British might enable Arabs—Christian or Muslim—to gain the upper hand against Jews in Palestine. Both in Iraq and in Egypt, there were sections of Islamic opinion who saw that there might be an opportunity to evict the British Christians. How far, if at all, the circumstances warranted or made feasible a jihad or holy war was another matter. In the event, no permanent eviction did take place. The same broad situation existed in India. Here, unlike the Middle East, the explicit use of any religious rallying-cry against the British Raj was likely to prove two-edged, given the religious complexity of the Indian subcontinent. It was as likely to turn Muslim against Hindu as to turn both against the government. Martial Sikhs would not stand idly by. There were already enough signs of the depth of the religious divide which was ultimately to lead to partition. In the event, the British were able to maintain the Indian Army intact as a multi-religious agglomeration. Indeed, the way in which Muslims, Brahmins, other Hindus, Buddhists, Sikhs, and Christians all fought—and ate—together in a communal struggle against a common enemy, irrespective of doctrinal differences, is an interesting, probably unexampled, instance of religious toleration in wartime. Even so, by the end of the war, it was evident that some regiments and their commanders were already positioning themselves for an anticipated internal conflict. Earlier in the war, too, the British were able to take advantage of the fact that their defeat might only precipitate an India under Nazi hegemony. *Gandhi was nevertheless prepared to press his 'Quit India' campaign but did so in the knowledge that another outside power might not be so relatively tolerant of his own religious ideas and the political strategies which stemmed from them.

The extent to which Christianity straddled the war, modifying or reinforcing national struggles in particular circumstances, has already been noted. In the case of Japan religion reinforced the national struggle without the restraint of a universalistic aspiration. The nationalistic appeal of Shinto—which treated the emperor as God, a man directly descended from the Sun Goddess—had helped the cohesion of Japan during its remarkable adaptation and modernization over the previous 50 years. Shinto reinforced already strongly-established national notions of spiritual discipline and physical fitness. The reverence extended to swords, spears, bows, and arrows as symbols of fighting gods did not promote pacifism. Buddhism, which in previous decades had suffered from Shinto intolerance, revived to some extent, though it, too, had a strongly nationalist tone. Small Protestant and Roman Catholic minorities, some 300,000 out of a population of about 80 million, stood at the margins of society, though they were not without influence. Japan therefore appeared to present the most complete example of the religious underpinning of a national effort in war. It was a unity which was frequently criticized outside Japan. There was, then, a certain irony in the fact that it was the 'Christian' west which dropped the *atomic bombs on *Hiroshima and *Nagasaki. When the full implications of that action became apparent, it led Christian theologians increasingly to criticize any attempt to 'Christianize' the west.

In eastern Europe, religious life was subjected to a series of ordeals that were far more severe than anything experienced in the west. At the outset, both atheistic communism and pagan *fascism might have been considered equally hostile to religion. In practice, the pattern of persecution proved to be extremely capricious. Soviet conduct, in particular, turned out to be inconsistent. In 1939–41, the USSR was still in the grip of militant atheism. In the countries occupied by the Red Army at that time, vicious purges took place against religious leaders of all faiths. The Uniate Church in eastern Poland (western Ukraine) was banned. Large numbers of pastors, priests, and rabbis were deported to the *GUlag together with believers. In principle, no religious congregation was permitted to exercise an independent role within the community. However, the *German–Soviet war persuaded Stalin to revise his stance towards religion (see below for religion in the USSR). In consequence, when the Red Army returned to Poland in 1944–5, milder polices were often pursued. The Uniate Church, which had enjoyed a brief resurgence under German occupation, was suppressed once again. But elsewhere, the Soviet authorities were more concerned to force compliant clergy to co-operate, than to destroy them wholesale.

On the other hand, the Nazi authorities treated the Roman Catholic Church in Poland with unbridled hostility from the start. During the *Polish campaign of September 1939, Luftwaffe pilots were specifically ordered to bomb and to strafe churches. On 3 February 1940 the Governor-General, Hans *Frank, noted in his diary: 'The Church is the central assembly point of the Polish spirit . . . I know myself that (it) is the deadly enemy of all Germans in the country.' As a result, the church was reduced to the status of an informal association, directly administered by a department of the *SS.

Initially, the heaviest blows fell on the districts, such as the so-called Wartheland, which were directly incorporated into the Reich with a view to immediate Germanization. The vast majority of parish churches were closed, and their property seized. All seminaries were disbanded. Polish religious art was systematically profaned or became *loot. The higher clergy were arrested *en masse*. The lower clergy, when not murdered on the spot, were often sent to concentration camps: more than 1,500 Polish priests died in *Dachau alone and all the monks of the national shrine at Jasna Gora in Częstochowa perished in *Auschwitz. By the end of 1941, the US State Department reported that only 34 priests out of 828 were left in the archdiocese of Posen. A year later, only 2 churches out of 50 were open for worship in the city of Łódź. The Polish primate, Archbishop Hlond of Gniezno, fled abroad and remained in exile in Rome.

The Catholic Church escaped more lightly in the rump of Poland known as the General Government (see POLAND, 2(b)). There, priority was given to the destruction of Jewry and Judaism (see FINAL SOLUTION); and time ran out before Nazi plans for the Catholic population could be implemented. Almost all the synagogues were burned or otherwise demolished. The Great Synagogue on Tomicka Street in Warsaw, the Polish capital's largest religious building, was dynamited in May 1943. St John's Cathedral met the same fate at the end of 1944. The cardinal-prince of Cracow, Adam Sapieha, was not removed, even when he served Governor Hans Frank a plate of cold porridge, but 8,500 out of 14,000 priests were arrested, of whom roughly half perished. In Distrikt Galizien, the Ukrainian Uniate Church was allowed to revive, subject to supervision; and a few confiscated Catholic churches were handed over to the small Orthodox community. Overall, only an estimated 10% of Polish churches stayed open throughout the war.

The reaction of the Polish church to Nazi and Soviet terror was mixed. The hierarchy, broken by arrests and dismayed by the passivity of the Vatican, had little option but to collaborate. The surviving clergy, however, often worked closely with the Polish Home Army (see POLAND, 4) and other resistance movements, strengthening the bond with the common people that became manifest in the post-war years.

In many parts of eastern Europe, as in the Balkans, national identity was defined by religious allegiance. As a result, hatreds aroused by wartime tensions could sometimes drive smouldering ethnic rivalries into open religious warfare. Some of the worst *atrocities (apart from those committed in Croatia) were in *Volhynia and western Ukraine, where in 1943–4 tens of thousands of Catholics and Poles were murdered by Ukrainian nationalists. In the USSR the Russian Orthodox Church emerged with vigour from the penumbra of state atheism. Reflecting later on the events of the 1940s, a Russian Christian wrote, 'In the old days our army carried its standard into battle with the cry, "For God and the Tsar"; you never heard anyone in the Great Patriotic War cry, "For atheism and Stalin".' In truth, the German invasion of June 1941 (see BARBAROSSA) caused not only a cessation of persecution, but a temporary reversal of Stalin's plan to eliminate the church.

By 1939 this plan had been substantially implemented. Only a handful of churches were open on Soviet territory, four powerless bishops remained in place, the vast majority of clergy were in prison or had been murdered. Religious vitality existed only in the most secret places of an underground church. Yet from 1941 Stalin became almost a patron of the Russian Orthodox Church, while the third of his former subjects who fell temporarily under German occupation promoted a religious revival of remarkable proportions.

One of the mysteries of the German–Soviet war is how the head of the church, Metropolitan Sergel (there was no longer a patriarch), managed to call the Soviet people to a defence of the motherland in a radio broadcast on the very day of the invasion, while Stalin remained silent for a further ten days. Churches began to reopen in many places, with clergy emerging from the catacombs or prison. The church raised the enormous sum of 150 million roubles for the defence fund, equipping the 'Dmitri Donskoi' tank brigade (called after a medieval Christian hero) and a comparable wing of the air force. In the depth of the war (July 1942) the church even managed to produce a lavish volume of 457 pages extolling its own position and glossing over Stalin's persecution.

Nor was all propaganda. Metropolitan Alexei showed immense personal fortitude in staying with the faithful throughout the 900 days of the siege of his city of *Leningrad. There can be no doubt that the church sustained national morale at a time of desperate need.

Stalin gave the church its official reward on 4 September 1943. The aged Metropolitan Sergel returned from Ulyanovsk on the Volga, whither the regime had sent him for his safety. Stalin received him with the few other available senior hierarchs in the Kremlin and a concordat resulted. The patriarchate was restored, with the enthronement of Sergel eight days later. A theological course began in Moscow the next year and it became possible to publish a journal again, albeit under heavy censorship.

Patriarch Sergel died in May 1944. The enthronement of his successor, Metropolitan Alexei, early the next year was attended even by some foreign dignitaries, such as Cyril Garbett (1875–1955), the archbishop of York, who undertook a hazardous journey to demonstrate his church's solidarity. The Russian Orthodox Church was to hold these concrete gains for fifteen years after the war.

In German-occupied territory events moved swiftly. With the removal of the immediate constraints of Stalin's persecution, there was no region which did not experience a religious revival of major proportions. Ukraine was a special beneficiary and it is not surprising that oppressed Christians often welcomed the Germans as liberators who allowed them to restore their lost heritage. This alleged 'collaboration' was unfairly used right up to the age of *glasnost* to attach a stigma to both Orthodox and Uniates.

Before the revolution, the area from St Petersburg west to Pskov had been an Orthodox stronghold, but Stalin had turned it into an ecclesiastical desert. Following the German invasion, it experienced an astonishing religious revival under Metropolitan Sergi (Voskresensky), who was eventually to be murdered in April 1944 in obscure circumstances, either by the Germans or by Stalin's agents. Before this he had led the 'Pskov Spiritual Mission' which saw the reopening of churches everywhere and the gathering of tens of thousands of the faithful every time the liturgy was celebrated. The occupying power even permitted the teaching of religion in schools.

Captured German war archives confirm these facts, but also illustrate that it was not the ultimate policy to gain the allegiance of the people by restoring religious liberty. Indeed, in many places the Germans handled this clumsily and ineffectively. Hitler wanted to bar the churches in the newly occupied lands from playing any political role; he wanted to remove any Soviet influence, which in practice meant helping Ukrainian nationalist church movements financially; and Christian influence was to be reduced by banning any national religious structures. These policies would prepare for the eventual destruction of the churches after the war.

Such was the strength of the religious revival that these policies failed and as the war turned against the Germans they had ever less time to pay attention to such complicated and subtle matters as controlling church life.

As the Red Army drove west towards the end of the war, the Soviets regained territories where the church had made a significant recovery from the devastation of the 1930s. Beyond this, in the lands which had never been Soviet—or only briefly so after the *Nazi–Soviet Pact of August 1939 (western Ukraine, western Belorussia, the Baltic States, Bessarabia)—there were richly flourishing churches (Byzantine Catholics, Orthodox, Lutherans) which had hitherto escaped persecution altogether.

It is one of the ironies of the Second World War that its end found a much more flourishing Christian church on Soviet soil than its beginning.

In all these circumstances no easy audit of religion and the war is possible. Despite some alleviation of the position of churches in the USSR, few were in any doubt that the Stalinist regime remained fundamentally hostile to religion—whether Christianity or Islam. The victory over Nazism in Europe was not therefore a simple one for 'religion' against 'irreligion'. Nevertheless, as the full extent of Nazi atrocities became apparent, there was talk of a Christian counter-attack to redeem Europe from its apostasy. 'Christian Democracy' was one solution, though horror at what had been done by those without religion was tempered by the knowledge of what had also been done in the name of religion. Acts of compassion and mercy were matched by acts of intolerant fanaticism. The universalist claims and aspiration of both Christianity and Islam existed side by side with the reality of ethnic animosity and inter-state conflict. Stalin's brutal question, 'How many divisions has the Pope?' pointed to the fact that the pontiff could only play a hand that was powerless, as the world seemed to understand power.

But perhaps it was not only world Christianity that was powerless to prevent war or end its horrors. What did the conflict say about the power of God? It was a question brought into acute focus by the *Final Solution and has had an enduring resonance among both Christian and Jewish theologians ever since. What kind of God 'allowed' such things to happen? How could the Holocaust be reconciled with notions of God as omnipotent? For unbelievers such questions were meaningless, though it left them looking starkly at a picture of mankind with a capacity for evil which called into question the optimism of the Enlightenment. Christian believers looked more intensely at the picture of a man on a Cross. The capacity to reconcile emerges from a willingness to suffer. Whatever answers might be returned, the questions pointed to a deepening of debate about God, the human race, and the world, taking it far beyond any simple notion that the function of religion in time of war was the bland endorsement of secular objectives and the securing of divine assistance in their achievement. See also ANTI-SEMITISM.

KEITH ROBBINS
NORMAN DAVIES (Poland)
MICHAEL BOURDEAUX (USSR)

Alexeev, W., and Stavrou, T. G., *The Great Revival: the Russian Church under German Occupation* (Minneapolis, 1976),

Fletcher, W. C., *A Study in Survival: The Church in Russia, 1927–1943* (London, 1965).

Holmes, J. D., *The Papacy in the Modern World 1914–1978* (London, 1981).

Scholder, K., *A Requiem for Hitler and Other New Perspectives on the German Church Struggle* (London, 1989).

Remagen bridge, the Ludendorff railway bridge which spanned the Rhine at Remagen near Bonn. On 7 March 1945, during the battle for *Germany, it was captured by an armoured patrol of *Hodges's First US Army, when the Germans failed to destroy it. This gave the Allies a great psychological, as well as military, advantage for it enabled more than 8,000 troops, supported by tanks and self-propelled guns, to cross in under 24 hours. However, the Americans found it difficult to hold their bridgehead and the corps commander was dismissed for his timidity while trying to exploit it.

Hitler was furious at the bridge's capture and replaced *Rundstedt with *Kesselring. The German officer charged with destroying it was, along with four others, summarily shot and V-2 rockets (see V-WEAPONS) were even fired at it, the first and only time they were used tactically. *Model, Kesselring's immediate subordinate, tried, unsuccessfully, to dislodge the Allied bridgehead around it. After five divisions had crossed, the bridge collapsed on 17 March, killing 26, but by then engineers had built pontoon bridges.

***Repulse*, sinking of,** see PRINCE OF WALES.

resistance. In every country occupied by Axis forces there was some degree of resistance to occupation, although, in spite of the myth to the contrary, there was never any continent-wide resistance movement, either in Europe or in Asia; each country reacted according to its own historical experience. At first in some countries almost everybody, in others almost nobody, undertook a task that was always dangerous, always illegal, and always the object of special vigilance by the occupying powers. Experience of occupation brought its own lessons, usually harsh. More and more people joined in resistance everywhere, as the time of *liberation approached.

Resisters came from every class in society. Railway workers in western Europe may be picked out as a single sub-class with an unusually high share of resisters, but even they had collaborators and German staff mixed up among them.

1. Active resistance

Scholars continue to debate about how resisters should be categorized. Three main active tasks stand out: collecting intelligence about the other side (see also SPIES); helping others to escape (see also MI 9); and sabotage of the war effort (see also SUBVERSIVE WARFARE). Sabotage could range from pinprick attacks on individual weapons or machines to full-scale onslaughts on formed bodies of troops. It could extend also to moral sabotage, exercised through clandestine publishing or the circulation of rumour, and might merge eventually into insurrection.

Several Allied secret services such as *SOE were eager to assist in these tasks, sometimes with political objects in mind. On the occupied spot, few resisters bothered about spymasters' rules which laid down that each task was to be undertaken by separate groups. Enthusiasts were prepared to tackle several tasks in a night, or even at once, if they thought doing so would do the occupiers harm. Trained professionals, sent in from outside to curb their enthusiasm, were rare, and to the professional policemen of the Axis security services they were often easy prey. It was natural to talk, even to boast, to one's friends about what one was doing to help get rid of the invaders, particularly in those countries that had no recent experience of being occupied (unlike the Poles). Careless talk of this kind could easily be overheard, and come to the wrong ears. When captured, some former resisters turned *double agent, thus making trouble for their more loyal friends.

Anyone who was in this business for more than a few hours realized how secret it had to be. Sensible resisters wrote down as little as they could, and trusted nobody they had not known well before the war began. *Women were of great use, not only as couriers, but also in the organizing and leading of resistance groups (see WITHERINGTON, for example); this was one of the spheres in which they again proved their right to combatant status and to equality with men.

Courage, swiftness of decision, discretion, patience, and steadiness of purpose were indispensable qualities in a successful resister; to be observant and inconspicuous helped. Above all, resisters (like generals) needed luck.

Sometimes they were able to collect in sizeable bodies, clear of Axis police influence (see MAQUIS, for example), but as a rule they had to have some cover job, in town or country, and conduct resistance work instead of sleeping. Often they became involved with gangs of criminals; for example, they needed first-class forgers to provide them with papers to enable them to pass through control points, which were legion. Black markets, often encouraged by the *Gestapo in German-occupied countries, sometimes involved resisters; sometimes they found themselves robbing tobacconists or banks; criminals occasionally went into resistance, for criminal reasons. Nevertheless, post-war myth has exalted resisters into national heroes and heroines, for the most part, and revisionist history has not dented the myth severely.

See also RESISTANCE section of relevant major powers.

M. R. D. FOOT

2. Passive resistance

Resistance movements in the Second World War assumed some forms which were non-violent in character: strikes, go-slows, demonstrations, nonco-operation, symbolic acts of loyalty to the legitimate government, running underground information services, and hiding wanted people or helping them to escape. These actions have generally attracted less attention than armed struggle, yet they played an important part in the politics of the occupied countries, and contributed to the overall effect of resistance. Often they fall within the category of civil resistance as a political technique: only exceptionally were they a product of a general ethic of non-violence.

In Norway, after the German invasion of April 1940 (see NORWEGIAN CAMPAIGN), resistance came to be headed by two organizations: Milorg, concerned above all with military supplies, training, and co-operation with Allied military forces outside the country; and Sivorg, which (along with many ordinary peacetime organizations) played an important role in organizing civil resistance. The division of labour between these two bodies was never complete, and there was some overlapping of military and civil resistance. From the start of the occupation, the widespread antipathy to the occupying power and its Norwegian supporters was demonstrated in 'cold-shoulder' attitudes and small acts of defiance. From 1941 onwards, various organizations—the clergy, teachers, and others—led extensive non-co-operation against attempts to impose National Socialist ideas and practices. Throughout they stressed that their actions were in accord with international law, especially the 1907 *Hague Conventions. Despite threats and *deportations, their solidarity was not broken, and the power of the regime was effectively limited. The Norwegian Nazi leader Vidkun *Quisling conceded the point when he had to abandon his plan for a 'State Assembly', and, in an outburst in May 1942, said: 'It is you teachers who are to blame ...'

In Denmark, also occupied in April 1940, strikes and demonstrations became widespread, often in conjunction with acts of violent sabotage. In October 1943, when Berlin ordered the arrest of Denmark's several thousand Jews, a tip-off from the German shipping attaché prompted the resistance's escape service to organize their transport across the Sound to Sweden: fewer than 500 fell into German hands.

In the Netherlands, occupied in May 1940, many aspects of the resistance had a civilian character, especially as most of the Dutch realized that in their small and crowded country, with its lack of adequate cover, armed resistance was not likely to be successful. There was no large-scale sabotage, no Maquis, and no armed revolt such as the *Paris and *Warsaw risings. However, there were three mass strikes: in February 1941, against the arrests of Jews; in spring 1943, against a call-up of former prisoners-of-war for *forced labour in Germany; and in September 1944, on the railways, to frustrate German counter-measures against the landings of Allied troops (see MARKET-GARDEN). The Germans took harsh reprisals, especially severe in 1944 when there was widespread famine, and the strikes did not lead to much improvement in German policy, but they did contribute powerfully to a Dutch sense of solidarity.

In France, occupied in June 1940, perhaps the most effective actions in the field of unarmed resistance were those of the railway workers. In the summer of 1944, at the time of the Normandy landings (see OVERLORD), the railways were of very limited use to the German forces: a German survey conceded that it was not so much the damage by Allied air forces, nor the incessant demolitions by those waging subversive warfare, of saboteurs, that made the railways unworkable, as the permanent attitude of non-co-operation and go-slow of the railway staff.

In other Axis-occupied countries non-co-operation in various forms was a significant part of resistance. In one case, Luxembourg, the inhabitants took advantage of a Nazi-organized plebiscite in 1941 to vote 97% against the *occupation. However, where (as in China, Bohemia and Moravia, Poland, the USSR, and Yugoslavia) the occupation regime was especially harsh, and was based upon doctrines of national expansion and racial superiority, non-co-operation generally assumed covert forms: failure to carry out orders efficiently, go-slows, underground activities of various kinds.

In some Axis or pro-Axis countries there were important acts or movements of civil resistance, especially against deportations. For example, in Germany, attempts in Berlin in 1943 to deport Jews who were married to non-Jews met with spontaneous demonstrations, mainly by the wives of those arrested: the deportations were stopped. In Bulgaria in the same year, mass opposition to deportations of Jews led the fascist government to give up its plan to send the Jews of Bulgaria to the death camps (see OPERATION REINHARD).

Before the war or in its early stages, *Gandhi—who led the wartime non-violent resistance movement against the British in India (see INDIA, 3)—Aldous Huxley, and many others in Allied countries had seen non-violent resistance as a possible means of effectively opposing military attack and occupation. The events of 1939–45 suggest that such resistance can indeed have an effect, but that it often operates best in conjunction with armed resistance movements. While non-violent civil resistance sometimes emerged quite early in the war—before the great turning-points of *El Alamein and *Stalingrad—there is no doubt that in many occupied countries it derived strength from the knowledge that the Allied armies were in the field, and from the continued existence of *governments-in-exile. On its own, civil resistance was not capable of dislodging a determined occupying power. However, it did sometimes save lives, significantly modify occupation policy, or assist Allied military operations; and in many countries the fact that there had been widespread civil resistance against foreign occupation maintained national self-respect not only during the war, but also long afterwards. See also CONSCIENTIOUS OBJECTORS.

ADAM ROBERTS

Foot, M. R. D., *Resistance: An Analysis of European Resistance to Nazism 1940–1945* (London, 1977).
Gjelsvik, T., *Norwegian Resistance 1940–1945* (tr. T. K. Derry and C. Hurst, London, 1979).
Halestrup, J., *Europe Ablaze* (Odense, 1976).
Michel, H., *The Shadow War* (tr. R. H. Barry, London, 1972).
Roberts, A. (ed.), *The Strategy of Civilian Defence: Non-violent Resistance to Aggression* (London, 1967).
Sharp, G., *The Politics of Nonviolent Action* (Boston, 1973).
Suhl, Y. (ed.), *They Fought Back: The Story of the Jewish Resistance in Nazi Europe* (London, 1968).

Retinger, Józef (1888–1960), Cracow-born writer who, as a young man, worked tirelessly to regain Polish independence and who, as a consequence, came to know and be highly respected by many European and US politicians and statesmen. During the Second World War he came to be known as the *éminence grise* of General *Sikorski, the head of the Polish *government-in-exile, which resulted in his being involved in wartime diplomacy at the highest level. In 1944, at the age of 56, he parachuted into Poland to contact the leaders of the Polish Home Army (see POLAND, 4) and after the war became one of the foremost proponents of the European community (see CONSEQUENCES OF THE WAR).

Pomian, J. (ed.), *Joseph Retinger: Memoirs of an Eminence Grise* (Brighton, 1972).

***Reuben James*,** neutral US destroyer which was torpedoed by a U-boat 965 km. (600 mi.) west of Eire on 31 October 1941 while helping to escort a convoy during the battle of the *Atlantic. It was the US Navy's first loss of what was virtually a *de facto* war against Germany in the Atlantic, and 115 men died.

Reynaud, Paul (1878–1966), French politician who was a leading member of the Democratic Alliance from 1930 and served as president of the council of ministers (prime minister) during the fighting which preceded the fall of *France in June 1940.

When the more aggressively minded Reynaud succeeded *Daladier as head of the French government on 21 March 1940 (a change which delighted Churchill) he also became foreign minister. On 28 March he made an agreement with the British that neither country would sign a separate peace with Germany and the following month he supported Allied intervention in Norway (see NORWEGIAN CAMPAIGN). Despite the early disasters that befell the French Army when the Germans launched their offensive (see FALL GELB) he announced to the French National Assembly on 16 May that though only a miracle could save France, 'I believe in miracles.'

On 20 May he moved Daladier to the foreign ministry and took Daladier's post as minister of national defence and war while remaining prime minister. The same day he replaced *Gamelin, the C-in-C Allied Forces, with *Weygand and appointed Marshal *Pétain deputy prime minister. But these changes failed to stem the German onslaught and put, as one historian has remarked, too many doves amongst the hawks. Though Reynaud's determination to fight on had one staunch supporter in de *Gaulle—who became Reynaud's under-secretary for war on 5 June 1940—the coalition which Reynaud now led became increasingly defeatist. On 15 June, with the government now at Bordeaux, the cabinet decided to ask the British government to release France from the agreement of 28 March. Reynaud wanted to resign, but was dissuaded. The next day, the British accepted the French request, provided the French fleet was sailed to British ports to be beyond the Germans' reach (see also MERS-EL-KÉBIR). Reynaud then proposed that the army should surrender, but that the government should continue the fight in North Africa. This brought little support from the cabinet and Pétain resigned. Though Reynaud was keen on the idea, Churchill's proposition for indissoluble union between France and the UK was received by the French with an equal lack of enthusiasm. Reynaud then resigned to be replaced by Pétain, who interned him in September 1940, and in November 1942 the Germans imprisoned him in Oranienburg *concentration camp, and later in Itter castle in Austria. After being released by the Americans, he was the principal witness at Pétain's trial. See also FRANCE, 3(a).

Rhine crossings. The River Rhine marked the last major natural obstacle barring the advance of the western Allies during the battle for *Germany in 1945. In spite of *Montgomery's objections, *Eisenhower planned to cross the river on a broad front, with Montgomery's Twenty-First Army Group in the north, *Bradley's Twelfth Army Group in the centre, and *Devers's Sixth Army Group in the south. Before this could be done, however, the approaches to the Rhine had to be cleared. This was the object of the Twenty-First Army Group operations *VERITABLE and *GRENADE and First US Army's Operation LUMBERJACK, all of which were launched in February. Further south, the Third and Seventh US Armies had yet to breach the *West Wall.

First to arrive on the west bank of the river were elements of *Simpson's Ninth US Army opposite Düsseldorf on 2 March, only to find the bridges blown. More success was enjoyed by *Hodges's First US Army to Simpson's south. They stumbled across an intact bridge at *Remagen five days later and their successful seizure of it brought about the dismissal of *Rundstedt, German C-in-C West and his replacement by *Kesselring. On 10 March Twenty-First Army Group had fully closed to the Rhine and Montgomery now began to prepare for a crossing at Wesel, north of the Ruhr. In the south, meanwhile, *Patton's Third US Army and *Patch's Seventh US Army continued to clear the area between the Moselle and the Rhine, while de *Lattre de Tassigny's First French Army reduced the *Colmar pocket.

While every effort was made to reinforce the Remagen bridgehead, the countryside east of the Rhine in this area was not conducive to break-out operations. In any event, to concentrate all his resources here was against Eisenhower's Broad Front policy (see OVERLORD), and he preferred to wait until other bridgeheads had been established. The first of these was achieved on the night of 22/23 March, when Patton, in a lightning move and assisted by *deception measures elsewhere on the river, bounced a crossing at Oppenheim, south of Mainz, catching the defenders, a weakened *Panzergrenadier* division, totally by surprise. The following night, and in marked contrast in its elaborate planning and massive artillery support, came Montgomery's crossings at Emmerich, Rees, Wesel, and Rheinberg (PLUNDER). These were assisted by the dropping of one British and one US airborne division east of Wesel on the morning of 24 March (VARSITY), as well as an RAF Bomber Command attack on the town just before the crossing. During the following few days Third US Army made further crossings at Boppard and near St Goar (night of 24/25 March), both between Koblenz and Mainz; Seventh US Army crossed near Worms (26 March); and the French at Germersheim and Speyer, between Mannheim and Karlsruhe, on 31 March, and at Leumersheim on 2 April.

Thus, in the space of three weeks the western Allies had achieved a number of crossings over the Rhine on a front of no less than 320 km. (200 mi.). Eisenhower's Broad Front strategy had been maintained and the curtain was about to rise on the last act of the war against Germany. As for the crossings themselves, those at Remagen, Oppenheim, and by Twenty-First Army Group represent the three type of operational river crossing—opportunistic, hasty, and deliberate. CHARLES MESSENGER

Ellis, L., *Victory in the West*, Vol. 2 (London, 1968).
Weighley, R., *Eisenhower's Lieutenants: The Campaigns in France and Germany, 1944–45* (London, 1981).

Rhine crossings

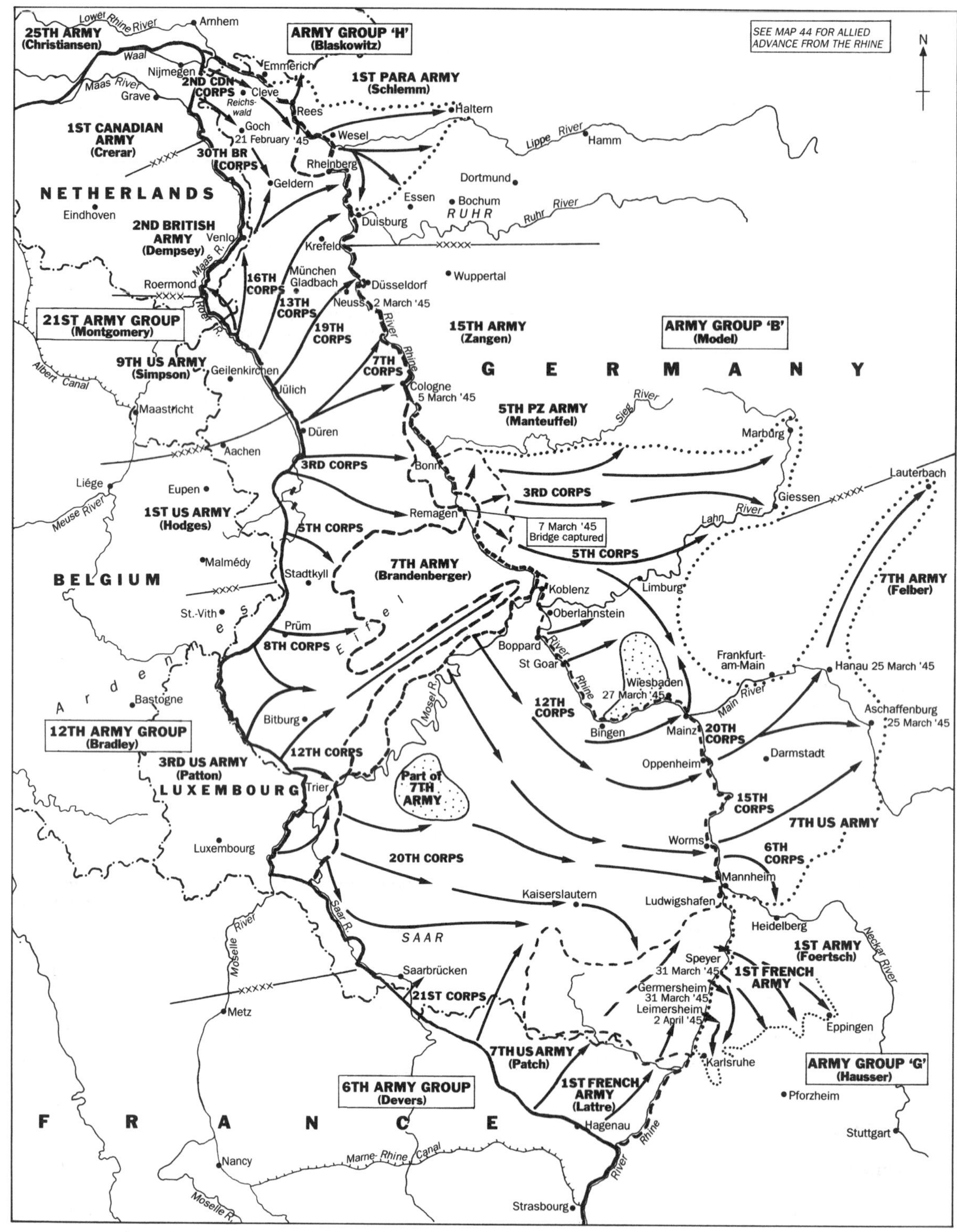

92. Allied **crossings of the Rhine**, March–April 1945

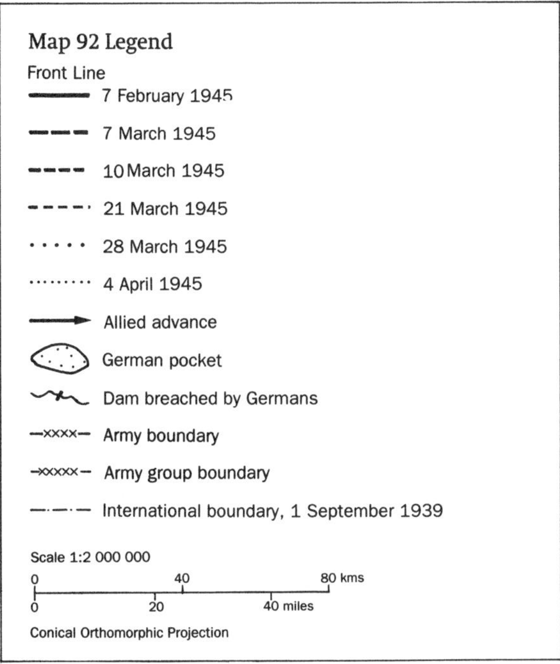

Rhodesias, See BRITISH CENTRAL AFRICA.

rhubarbs were cross-Channel sweeps by RAF fighters which sometimes involved 500 aircraft. Started in December 1940 to bring the Luftwaffe to action, and later to draw some of its strength from the Eastern Front, they proved both ineffective and expensive. See also CIRCUSES.

Ribbentrop, (Ulrich F. W.) Joachim von (1893–1946), German wine salesman who was commissioned and decorated during the *First World War before serving as the Nazi Party's foreign minister from 1938 to 1945. Hitler dubbed him 'greater than Bismarck', though by the end of his career his influence was zero.

Ribbentrop's background was affluent middle-class. He had studied in London and lived in Canada, and spoke English and French. Socially ambitious, he married the daughter of Otto Henkell, a German champagne magnate, in 1920 and in 1925 added the aristocratic 'von' to his name. He dabbled in right-wing politics and a meeting with Hitler, with whom he remained besotted throughout his life, led to his joining the Nazi Party in May 1932. This was very late in the day for someone who was to rise to the top of the Nazi hierarchy (his party number was 1,119,927). But the Ribbentrops, rich and well-connected, were useful to Hitler and it was at their house that the negotiations took place for Hitler to become chancellor in January 1933.

Once in power Hitler asked Ribbentrop to establish an office to advise him on foreign policy and to act as a rival to the German foreign ministry. In April 1934 Ribbentrop was given his first official appointment, 'Plenipotentiary for Matters of Disarmament' and in 1935, with the title of Ambassador Extraordinary of the German Reich on Special Mission, he concluded the Anglo-German Naval Treaty (see VERSAILLES SETTLEMENT). This triumph sealed his immediate future as Hitler's foreign policy adviser and his *Büro* was enlarged to become the Ribbentrop Agency. In September 1936 his friend Heinrich *Himmler made him an honorary *SS-Gruppenführer (maj-general); in October 1936 he took up his post as Germany's ambassador in London; and that November he persuaded Japan to join the *Anti-Comintern Pact. Then, when the foreign minister, von *Neurath, was dismissed by Hitler in February 1938, Ribbentrop replaced him.

Ribbentrop's greatest coup was the *Nazi–Soviet Pact which he signed with the Soviet foreign minister, *Molotov, in August 1939, but once the war had begun his influence waned rapidly. In March 1940 he failed to persuade Mussolini to join the war immediately and was equally unsuccessful with the French and Spanish leaders that October. His attempts to maintain German–Soviet relations were also doomed and discussions with Molotov in November 1940 had an embarrassing conclusion when an air raid interrupted dinner. While in the shelter Ribbentrop returned to his argument for German–Soviet co-operation by saying that Britain had already lost the war. Then why, Molotov asked, are we sitting here?

The Japanese pact of non-aggression with the USSR in April 1941 (see JAPANESE–SOVIET CAMPAIGNS) and finally the German invasion of the USSR that June (see BARBAROSSA) spelled the end of Ribbentrop's involvement in serious diplomacy, and he spent the rest of the war as Hitler's messenger to delinquent allies or to neutral countries. At the *Nuremberg trials it became clear that German foreign office staff had, on Ribbentrop's orders, collaborated in the *Final Solution and for this, and other, crimes he was sentenced to death and hanged. See also DIPLOMACY.

Weitz, J., *Hitler's Diplomat* (London, 1992).

Ringelblum, Emmanuel (1881–1944), Polish historian and Jew who lived in the Warsaw *ghetto and chronicled the fate of Polish Jews under Nazi occupation. He had documentation about *Chełmno smuggled to the Polish *government-in-exile in London which led, in June 1942, to the *BBC making the first public announcement about the *Final Solution (though it was Eduard *Schulte who broke the news in Switzerland in July 1942 that Hitler was pursuing a deliberate policy of exterminating Europe's Jews). During the *Warsaw ghetto rising of April–May 1943 he was captured by the Germans and sent to a *forced labour camp. He managed to escape, was given false papers, and lived in Warsaw as an Aryan, but was eventually discovered and, with his wife and son, was executed. His summaries were found in 1946, and more were discovered in 1950; these were later published as *Notes from the Warsaw Ghetto* (ed. J. Sloan, New York, 1958).

Rio conference, pan-American meeting of foreign ministers held at Rio de Janeiro in January 1942. It followed on the conferences at *Panama and *Havana, and the objective of the USA was to obtain a joint pledge from all Latin American states that those who had not declared war on the Axis powers would do so. Chile and Argentina objected and the US resolution was replaced by one that simply recommended the severance of relations with the Axis. The conference also established an Inter-American Defense Board, which gave *Latin America an involvement in *Western Hemisphere defence, and an Emergency Advisory Committee for Political Defense. This monitored pro-Axis activities, and its investigations brought about Chile's severance of relations with the Axis powers in 1943. See also DIPLOMACY.

Riom trial, held by the *Vichy authorities in the French town of Riom in February 1942 of those alleged to be responsible for the fall of *France in June 1940. They were Léon Blum, the prime minister of the Popular Front government during the 1930s; Edouard *Daladier, who was prime minister from April 1938 to March 1940; the Allied C-in-C, General *Gamelin; the minister for air, Guy La Chambre, who was held responsible for the inadequacies of the French Air Force (see FRANCE, 6(d)); and another minor minister.

Because the head of the Vichy government, Marshal *Pétain, had been minister of war in 1934 and represented the French military establishment responsible for the disaster, the trial was limited to events after 1935. Pétain, who had already declared the accused guilty, hand-picked the judge, but the accused politicians (except Gamelin, who remained silent) quickly turned the prosecution's case to their own advantage and after two months the trial was abandoned, though none of the defendants was freed.

Ritterkreuz, see DECORATIONS, GERMANY.

rivalries. It was natural that German troops working with Italians, or British with Americans, were always anxious that their own nation's methods and turn-out should be superior to their allies'; the feeling was reciprocal. Inter-service rivalry was commonplace, too. In the RAF, all ranks were conscious that their service was the most junior, but the most efficient and the most up-to-date of the armed forces of the crown; while all ranks of the Royal Navy were aware that they belonged to the oldest organized fighting force in the world; and in the British Army everyone knew that without the army the war could not be won. Within each service, inter-unit rivalry was also normal; it was officially encouraged in the navy, by competitions between ships. In the Brigade of Guards, a (later highly distinguished) Coldstream officer was heard to remark that his object on the battlefield was 'teaching those damned Grenadiers how to fight'. Even within units, sub-units strove with each other, to be the best platoon in the company, or the best squadron or battery in the regiment.

All this was good for morale, but rivalries could have a damaging effect on operational efficiency. Inter-service rivalry between the US Navy and the US Army was endemic at the start of the war; *Pearl Harbor was a classic example of how this attitude encouraged the lack of co-operation that hindered the two services before and during the attack. Rivalry led to Mussolini backing the Italian Air Force's refusal to allow a separate air arm for the Italian Navy, with disastrous consequences for the navy's fighting efficiency in the battle for the *Mediterranean. The Imperial Japanese Navy and Army were at such loggerheads that, *inter alia*, Japanese development of *radar was seriously hindered; their respective intelligence departments devoted almost as much time to gathering information about the rival service as they ever did to finding out about the other side. Rivalry also bred lack of trust; allies seldom if ever trust each other entirely. Certainly, Soviet agents kept Stalin better informed about the Americans and the British than about the Axis (see SPIES).

Inter-secret-service rivalry, notoriously, was often especially bitter—as between the *NKVD and the *GRU, or the *Abwehr and the Sicherheitsdienst (see RSHA), or *MI6 and *SOE. Towards the end of the war the Sicherheitsdienst hanged the head of the Abwehr; this was extreme.

M. R. D. FOOT

River Plate, battle of, fought off this South American river on 13 December 1939 between the German pocket battleship *Admiral Graf Spee* and an Allied naval task force. *Admiral Graf Spee*, armed with six 28 cm. (11 in.) guns, was commanded by Captain Hans Langsdorff. She had left Germany with her supply ship **Altmark* before war began and later sank nine ships in the Indian Ocean and South Atlantic before her engines began to malfunction. Langsdorff, anxious to increase his score before steaming to Germany for repairs, returned via the River Plate to intercept a convoy he knew was in that area, a move anticipated by Commodore Henry Harwood, whose Force G was one of eight formed to hunt Langsdorff down. Harwood lay in wait with two light cruisers, *Ajax* and the New Zealand *Achilles*, and the larger *Exeter*. (A fourth cruiser, *Cumberland*, arrived after the battle.) Langsdorff saw the British first and, thinking they were the convoy, he steamed straight at them. In the 80-minute battle which followed Harwood tried to divide the German warship's gunfire by attacking from two directions. But Langsdorff concentrated on *Exeter* which was soon forced to withdraw, and when *Ajax* and *Achilles* were also damaged Harwood disengaged. But instead of driving home his advantage, Langsdorff entered the port of Montevideo in neutral Uruguay that night because, as well as having problems with his engines, his damaged ship was now unseaworthy for the long haul back to Germany. Nevertheless, it is hard to see what he hoped to gain for he was given just 72 hours to leave by the Uruguayan government.

British reinforcements ordered to the scene were not

due until 19 December, but Langsdorff, misled by false British signals and by his gunnery officer's assertion that he had seen the British battle-cruiser *Renown* approaching, assumed they were already in position. Langsdorff was ordered to scuttle his ship if he could not fight his way up river to Buenos Aires but *internment was forbidden him. When the time limit expired on 17 December, he sank his ship in neutral waters and committed suicide. The encounter was greeted by the British as a victory and a much-needed boost for their morale. See also SEA POWER.

Robert, Vice-Admiral Georges (1875–1965), French naval officer who was recalled from retirement in August 1939 to become C-in-C French Atlantic Forces and then, after the fall of *France in June 1940, high commissioner of the French West Indies whose fief included *St Pierre and Miquelon. He was both an anglophobe and anti-Free French, but for trading reasons retained good relations with the USA. In November 1942 Admiral *Darlan, who was by then working for the Allies, wanted him to use his ships against the Germans. He refused, as he did a US request to disarm them. The American blockade that followed caused civil and military unrest and in July 1943 he resigned and was replaced by a *French Committee for National Liberation representative, Henri Hoppenot. In 1947 Robert was condemned to ten years' imprisonment but was freed on appeal.

Robertson, Norman (1904–68), Canadian civil servant who in 1941 became under-secretary of external affairs when O. D. *Skelton died. He regularly attended the Canadian cabinet's war committee and advised on Canadian policy towards the UK and USA; had a hand in the *Hyde Park agreement; ensured that Canada had some voice in controlling the Allied war effort; and played a forceful role in the *San Francisco conference.

Robin Moor, US merchant ship torpedoed by a German U-boat in the South Atlantic on 21 May 1941. Like the German attacks on US warships (see GREER, KEARNY, and REUBEN JAMES), it was an incident which failed to push the USA into declaring war but brought it one step closer to hostilities. Six days later Roosevelt declared an 'unlimited national emergency', and the following month he closed German and Italian consulates. Axis

Rocket weapons of great power and versatility were developed by both sides during the war. This photograph shows US Marine rocket trucks on Iwo Jima firing 4.5 in. rockets.

assets were seized and US merchant shipping was put under naval control. The arming of merchantmen was considered but was not implemented until key sections in the *Neutrality Acts were repealed in November 1941.

rocket weapons (for the German V-2 rocket, see V-WEAPONS). The rocket as a weapon saw little use in the early part of the century, but in the 1930s it began a revival, largely on the grounds of economy. The principal advantage of the rocket is the simple launching device, much cheaper and easier to make than a complex gun; the problem lay in the development of a suitable propellant. In the UK, the development of solventless cordite made possible the manufacture of large sticks of smokeless powder which could be extruded in shapes which gave the desired burning characteristics, and this, coupled with the sudden demand for enormous increases in anti-aircraft weapon strength, led to work on 2 in. (5 cm.) and 3 in. (7.6 cm.) rockets for air defence in the mid-1930s.

In Germany experimenters had been drawn to the study of liquid propellants and their work was carefully watched by the army, who saw the long-range rocket as a possible substitute for heavy artillery which would evade the provisions of the *Versailles settlement. The Soviets also saw rockets as a cheap substitute for artillery and began work on a simple bombardment weapon.

The British rockets were fully developed and given extensive testing in the West Indies in 1938–9, but the army demanded a closed-breech launcher which proved inaccurate and the programme was shelved in favour of guns. The Royal Navy adopted the 2 in. design and used it with some success as a barrage weapon to protect ships; this system used a simple open-rail launcher which proved satisfactory, with the result that a similar simple launcher to fire the 3 in. rocket was developed for the army in late 1940. It was intended for use against dive-bombers and the rocket was fitted with the first *proximity fuze, an electro-optical sensor which detected the shadow of the aircraft. As this device was useless in darkness, and as the Germans had turned to night attacks (see BLITZ), conventional time-fuzed warheads were adopted. The launchers were re-grouped into batteries of 64 two-rocket launchers and employed for high-altitude barrage fire, principally around seaports so that the expended rocket motors could fall harmlessly into the sea. These 'Z Batteries' remained in service until the end of the war.

When the *Dieppe raid of August 1942 revealed how crucial it was to saturate landing beaches with fire, the RN scaled-up the 3 in. design to 5 in. (12.6 cm.) diameter to produce a weapon for close onshore bombardment. These rockets were fired from fixed frames fitted in special *landing craft and were extensively used during the Normandy landings in June 1944 (see OVERLORD) and elsewhere.

In 1944, in search of a field bombardment weapon, the Canadian Army adopted the 3 in. rocket motor and allied it to the naval 5 in. warhead to produce the LAND MATTRESS (a meaningless codename) which was used with considerable success on Walcheren Island during the *Scheldt Estuary battle and to break through the *West Wall at the start of the battle for *Germany. The launcher was a simple open-frame device holding sixteen rockets and capable of being towed behind a light truck. The same rocket/warhead combination was also used by the RAF as an air-to-ground attack weapon, particularly against tanks and transport during the *Normandy campaign in 1944. With a different warhead, it was also used by RAF Coastal Command against submarines.

German rocket development split into two: the evolution of long-range liquid-fuelled missiles (see V-WEAPONS) and of short-range solid-fuel bombardment rockets for field use. The latter became the Nebelwerfer (smoke thrower), a simple wheeled launcher which fired a volley of six 15 cm. (5.9 in.) rockets; this design was then improved into models firing 21 cm. (8.2 in.) and 32 cm. (12.6 in.) rockets. The name was a hangover from the *First World War, when the larger *mortars were employed to lay down smoke or gas. Various solid-fuel air defence rockets were also developed in Germany. None was ready for service before the war ended, but a rocket-

Rocket weapons, Figure 1: Panzerschreck

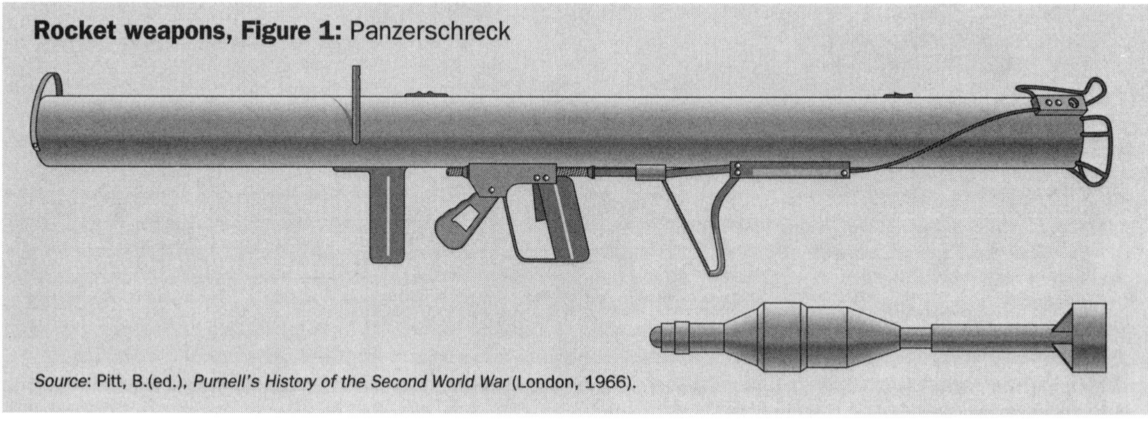

Source: Pitt, B.(ed.), *Purnell's History of the Second World War* (London, 1966).

Rocket weapons, Figure 2: Panzerfaust

Source: General Editor

propelled fighter did become operational (see FIGHTERS, 1).

Soviet development was almost entirely confined to heavy bombardment rockets, familiarly known as Katyusha or 'Stalin's Organ'. They were 21 cm. solid-fuel rockets discharged in volleys from launchers carried on trucks, and became a prime component of Soviet field artillery.

American work began with spin-stabilized field bombardment rockets in 4.5 in. (11.4 cm.) and 7.2 in. (18.2 cm.) calibres, and then extended to air-to-ground rockets for tactical support fighters. However, perhaps the most significant American development was of the 2.36 in. (6 cm.) Bazooka anti-tank rocket, a design based on semi-official pre-war experiments. This small shoulder-carried launcher had been perfected but there appeared to be no tactical use for it until the arrival of the shaped charge (see EXPLOSIVES) as a potential armour-defeating weapon. With a shaped-charge head attached to the rocket, the Bazooka became the progenitor of a host of similar devices extending to the present day. It was first used in the *North African campaign in 1942. Quantities of the earliest ones were supplied to the USSR and a number fell into German hands. The Germans then copied the design and produced the Panzerschreck launcher. This fired a 88 mm. (3.4 in.) rocket grenade whose rocket motor was ignited by an electrical pulse. It was operated by two men, had a range of 150 m., and could penetrate 210 mm. (8.25 in.) of armour (see Figure 1).

The Panzerschreck should not be confused with the Panzerfaust, also a recoilless rocket launcher of German design (see Figure 2). This fired a hollow-charge bomb from a disposable tube launcher, and could be carried and fired by one man. It first appeared in late 1942 and later models had a range of up to 100 m. at which range it could penetrate 200 mm. (7.8 in.) of armour. See also GUIDED WEAPONS.

IAN HOGG

Baker, D., *The Rocket* (London, 1978).
Gusnton, W., *Rockets and Missiles* (London, 1979).

Rokossovsky, Marshal Konstantin (1896–1968), Red Army officer whose earlier career progressed rapidly, but, promoted to corps commander in 1936, he was one still in June 1941. For an indeterminate period before his release in early 1940, he had been imprisoned as a suspect in Stalin's purge of the armed forces. In July 1941, after the first wave of defeats in the *German–Soviet war, he received an army command under *Zhukov, who had once been his subordinate but now outranked him by two grades. His chance came in September 1942 when Zhukov persuaded Stalin to entrust him with Don *front* (army group) in the crucial sector between the Volga and Don rivers north of *Stalingrad.

In January 1943 he conducted the terminal operation against the Stalingrad pocket and received the German surrender. He then shifted his staff and one army by rail to the *Kursk sector, where, reinforced and renamed Central *front*, they arrived at the end of winter and held the north face of the Kursk salient until after the battle in July. In August, Rokossovsky drove towards the River *Dnieper, which he reached and crossed on a broad front in November, having in the meantime combined Central and Briansk *fronts* to form Belorussian *front*.

Since the main effort was in the Ukraine during the winter and spring of 1944, Rokossovsky's mission was to keep pace with the advance there by stretching his line westwards through the Pripet marshes. Consequently the Belorussian, later renamed First Belorussian *front* occupied the entire southern half of the bulge in which German Army Group Centre was destroyed in July and thereafter straddled the most direct route to Berlin. After Rokossovsky reached the River Vistula north and south of Warsaw in September, Stalin advanced him to Marshal of the Soviet Union; but (possibly because, among other reasons, he did not want a marshal with a slightly blemished past as the conqueror of Berlin) turned First Belorussian *front* over to Zhukov and shifted Rokossovsky to Second Belorussian *front*.

In January 1945, advancing across Poland on Zhukov's right, Rokossovsky reached the mouth of the Vistula. For the next two months, on Stalin's orders, he and Zhukov occupied themselves with desultory operations in West Prussia and Pomerania. He redeployed to the lower River Oder in April, helped Zhukov get around Berlin, and made contact with the Americans at Wismar, 200 km. (124 mi.) west of the Oder, on 2 May. EARL ZIEMKE

rolling barrage, see ARTILLERY, 2.

Rol-Tanguy, Colonel Henri (b.1905), French communist resister who fought in the International Brigade in the *Spanish Civil War and took part in the fighting which preceded the fall of *France in 1940. When demobilized, he organized 'popular committees' of saboteurs in Paris motorcar factories working for the Germans. Taking the codename 'Rol', he rose to command the Franc-Tireurs et Partisans in the Paris region (see also FRANCE, 9) was military commander of the *Paris rising in August 1944, and signed the instrument of German surrender.

M. R. D. FOOT

ROMANIA

1. Introduction

Romania entered the war because, as Grigore Gafencu, a former foreign minister, argued in 1944, 'there was no longer order in Europe, nor any feeling of security or collective solidarity.'

Greater Romania was born of the *Versailles settlement in 1919 and its continued existence was linked to the maintenance of, and respect for, the new international order consecrated by the peace treaties. Defence of the European status quo, which implied opposition to revision of the Versailles agreements and to any attempt to readjust Romania's new frontiers, thus became the cornerstone of inter-war foreign policy pursued by all Romanian governments until the *Munich agreement of 1938. There were three bases to this policy: collaboration with France, the strongest western continental military power; alliance with the other post-Versailles states which shared a common interest with Romania; and support for and participation in the *League of Nations which guaranteed the territorial integrity of its members.

2. Domestic life, economy, and war effort

The German–Romanian economic agreement of 23 March 1939 guaranteed the predominance of Germany in the Romanian economy and established an economic plan for the development of agriculture, forestry, mining, and communications with German assistance; in furtherance of these activities joint German–Romanian companies were to be established. This plan was extended under an agreement, concluded on 4 December 1940, which provided long-term credits. Through these arrangements Germany achieved both direct and indirect control, through a monopoly of purchase and supply, of much of the Romanian economy. By 1941, 47% of the country's crude oil output was produced by German-owned companies and Romanian deliveries of petroleum products to Germany rose from 1,177,000 tons in 1940 to 2,963,000 in 1941, 2,192,000 tons in 1942, 2,406,000 in 1943, and to 1,043,000 in 1944 (see also RAW AND SYNTHETIC MATERIALS). Such was the German reliance upon Romanian oil that in August 1944 Hitler declared to General Alfred Gerstenberg, the officer responsible for air defence of the *Ploesti oilfields: 'if we lose the oilfields we can no longer win the war' (quoted in D. Irving, *Hitler's War*, New York, 1977, p. 681).

The major wartime problem for Romanian agriculture was maintaining production in the face of the drain on manpower, and the requisitioning of equipment and livestock for the army. Legislation was introduced to control prices, and exports, to requisition cereals, and to organize labour battalions to work the land. In order to compensate for the shortage of manpower and livestock increased imports of agricultural machinery were made from Germany. The numbers of tractors imported almost trebled in 1942 in comparison with the previous year to 2,800, and there were also significant increases over the same period in imports of harvesters, hoes, and threshing machinery. Despite German optimism that these measures would help to increase Romanian agricultural production by 25% over ten years, and that 40% of the surplus of cereals and vegetables would be available for export to Germany, the total production of cereals dropped from an average of 7.5 billion kg. for the period 1935–9 (without the lost provinces of Bessarabia and Northern Bukovina) to 6.4 billion in 1940–3 for the same land area. What the estimates had overlooked was the sharp decline by one-third in the number of draught animals, caused largely by the presence of both German and Soviet troops on Romanian soil between 1943 and 1945. Since these animals were the most practical form of traction on the small strip farms, the increased numbers of tractors did not have a marked impact upon cereal production. The burden of feeding the German Army on its territory and in southern Russia led to the introduction of bread rationing in Romania in December 1941; rationing continued after the Soviet Army took the place of the Germans in the late summer of 1944.

3. Government

The economic recession of the 1930s fostered a decade of instability in which the xenophobia of the impoverished Romanian peasantry was exploited by right-wing movements, principally by the fascist Iron Guard, and directed against the Jews. The growth in support for the Guard, which stemmed in part from a widespread disillusionment with the experience of parliamentary government, led the king, Carol II (1893–1953), to institute a personal dictatorship in 1938. At the same time, Romania's geographical position, and its economic predicament, forced it into Hitler's arms.

After the Munich agreement of 1938 Romania found itself increasingly drawn into the web of German military and economic policies. With the UK unwilling to buy Romania's wheat in large quantities, and with Germany in control of the Czech Skoda works with which Carol had placed orders for arms, Romania was dependent on Hitler for the means to save its economy and territorial integrity in the face of threats from the USSR and Hungary. The decision to shift towards

Germany was taken by Carol and his ministers on 27 May 1940 after the successful German sweep to the Channel during the fighting which led to the Fall of *France. In June Carol succumbed, on German advice given in accordance with the *Nazi–Soviet Pact of August 1939, to the Soviet demand for Bessarabia and Northern Bukovina; two months later he accepted Hitler's own imposition of the second *Vienna award, by which Romania was forced to cede northern Transylvania to Hungary (see Map 49); and in September, by the treaty of Craiova, South Dobruja, Romanian territory since 1913, was returned to Bulgaria (see Map B). In return Carol obtained Hitler's guarantee of protection for the rump of his country which had been truncated at the German leader's own request; German bombers began to arrive at Brasov in July.

The loss of these provinces cost Romania almost one-third of its territory and population of whom half, some three million, were ethnically Romanian. Unable to resist popular demands for his abdication following these supine concessions, Carol renounced the throne on 6 September 1940 in favour of his son Michael (b.1921) after having appointed General Ion *Antonescu as prime minister. On 12 October the first contingents of the German military mission entered Romania to rebuild the Romanian Army; a German economic mission also arrived to match the Romanian economy to Germany's military needs. But efforts to increase Romania's economic output were threatened by the reign of terror which the Iron Guard, a partner in power with Antonescu, unleashed against its opponents and against Jews. Therefore when Antonescu began to disarm Iron Guardists and strengthen the army, he did so with Hitler's support. On 21 January 1941 the Guard rose against the government and Hitler, anxious to have a stable Romania as a springboard for his invasion of the USSR (see BARBAROSSA) allowed Antonescu to crush the rebellion. On 27 January he appointed a new cabinet formed almost entirely of military officers, and the Iron Guard was dissolved.

A military dictatorship was now established under Antonescu and it received the rubber stamp of a popular plebiscite. Despite alignment with Germany and the presence of German troops on its territory, Romania retained its sovereignty which, because of Hitler's admiration for Antonescu, was respected. Apart from a small number of changes the military government headed by Antonescu remained in power until August 1944.

Throughout this period the opposition parties remained outlawed, having been suppressed when Carol established his own personal dictatorship in February 1938; nevertheless, Antonescu acknowledged the counsels offered to him by Iuliu Maniu and Constantin Brătianu, the respective leaders of the two major democratic parties, the National Peasants and the National Liberals. Thus he received their support when he joined BARBAROSSA on 22 June 1941. According to foreign observers, such as *The Times* correspondent Archibald Gibson, most Romanians were behind Antonescu when he joined Hitler's attack on the USSR, but after Romanian troops crossed the River Dniester into Soviet territory proper, both Maniu and Brătianu protested and demanded Romania's withdrawal from the war.

After German–Romanian forces captured Odessa in October, pressure began to build up from Moscow for the UK to declare war on Romania. The British government had not protested when Romanian forces crossed the River Prut into Bessarabia and Northern Bukovina, but because Romania was at war with the USSR Stalin urged Churchill to act. Churchill was reluctant to do this because he realized that Romania had been overpowered by Hitler but, realizing the need to give the Soviet leader a public gesture of support, finally acquiesced. On 28 November the British government sent an ultimatum via the US legation to the Romanian government pointing out that for several months it had been conducting aggressive military operations on the territory of the USSR, an ally of the UK, in close collaboration with Germany. It warned that unless the Romanians ceased military operations in the USSR by 5 December the British government would have no option but to declare the existence of a state of war between the two countries. The Romanian government did not reply until the day after the expiry of the ultimatum. It offered a justification for Romania's military action against the USSR which, it argued, was one of legitimate self-defence in the face of Soviet aggression which had begun in 1940 with the occupation of Bessarabia and Northern Bukovina. When the UK officially declared war on Romania on 7 December, Antonescu, who had served as military attaché in London in the 1920s and had a great admiration for Britain, expressed regret in a radio broadcast that his people's centuries-old struggle to preserve its existence had not been understood. Romania's present action was, he claimed, a continuation of that struggle. On 12 December Romania, following Germany's lead, declared war on the USA.

Throughout 1942 Maniu and Brătianu kept up the pressure on Antonescu to withdraw Romanian forces from the USSR, but he would not bow. He argued that a withdrawal would be a mistake because the front was 1,500 km. (930 mi.) away, winter was approaching, the stores and railways were in the hands of the Germans, and the Luftwaffe had the power to punish disloyalty. Antonescu asked Brătianu if he realized what would happen to the army, its soldiers, and its equipment, should Romania try to abandon the front without the consent of the Germans. Not only would the army collapse, but the whole country with it, for the Germans would occupy Romania as they had done Serbia and Greece. Antonescu offered to consult the army and the people with a view to handing over the government to Brătianu, and invited him to withdraw the army from the USSR and come to terms with the UK. Brătianu, in his reply of 14 November, ignored this offer. He might not have done so five days later when the major Soviet offensive at *Stalingrad was launched.

As the situation steadily deteriorated after the Soviet victory at Stalingrad in January 1943 Antonescu, no longer certain of an Axis victory, tolerated the extension of peace feelers, both from within his own government and from the opposition leader Maniu. Mihai Antonescu, vice-president of the council of ministers, gave some indication of his own change of heart in January 1943 to the Italian minister in Bucharest. The minister went to Rome to present a report of his conversation with Antonescu to *Ciano, the Italian foreign minister. Ciano saw an about-face in the attitude and words of Mihai Antonescu, but Mussolini was not swayed by the proposal that the Italians and Romanians should make a joint approach to the Allies to withdraw from the war.

This rebuff prompted Mihai Antonescu to attempt direct contact with the diplomatic representatives of the Allies in neutral countries with a view to concluding a separate peace. He himself raised the matter with Andrea Cassulo, the papal nuncio in Bucharest, while the Romanian minister in Berne was instructed to make contact with the nuncio there. In March the Romanian minister in Madrid asked his Portuguese and Argentinian counterparts to let the American ambassador, Carlton Hayes, know of Romania's desire to conclude a peace with the Allies. Similarly, Victor Cădere, the Romanian minister in Lisbon, took soundings in October of *Salazar and of the British ambassador. In December the Romanian chargé in Stockholm, George Duca, contacted the British and American ministers in the name of Maniu and Brătianu. All these efforts foundered on the Anglo-American insistence on *unconditional surrender, which could not be reconciled with Antonescu's desire to guarantee Romania's post-war independence from the USSR. The Romanian side, be it Antonescu, Mihai Antonescu, or Maniu, was unable to secure the joint agreement of the Americans, British, and Soviets to the conditional *armistice proposals which it made between December 1943 and April 1944 in Stockholm (to the Soviets) and in Cairo (to all three Allies). Eventually agreement on armistice terms was reached with the UK and the USA in Cairo in April 1944 and confirmed by the Soviets through the Stockholm channel in June. However, no Romanian representative was empowered by Antonescu to sign the armistice because of his reluctance as a soldier to abandon his German ally. Antonescu's intransigence forced the opposition parties to plot his overthrow and, in the face of a rapid Soviet advance on Romanian territory and the threat of military defeat and occupation, the young King Michael boldly had him arrested on 23 August 1944. The surrender of all Romanian forces opposing the Red Army followed.

Stalin fashioned from the Soviet–Romanian armistice, signed on 12 September, a legal framework for securing a dominant political and economic interest in Romania, one conceded to him by Churchill at their Moscow meeting a month later when the infamous 'percentage agreement' was initialled (see TOLSTOY). The American and British co-signatories, and their representatives on the significantly named *Allied (Soviet) Control Commission in Romania, were reduced to the role of spectators in the armistice's application. Blatant political engineering was employed by the Soviet authorities in order to impose Stalin's will on the Romanian people. On the grounds that they needed stability in a country that was behind their lines in their continuing war effort against Germany, they installed a puppet government under Petru Groza on 6 March 1945. This government oversaw the first steps to communize the country which involved abolition of the freedom of the press and of political assembly, and the arrest and imprisonment of virtually all political opponents. Most of the Romanian Army was demobilized and the policing of the country placed in the hands of the Soviet army of occupation.

4. Armed forces and their part in the German–Soviet war

(a) Army

By 27 July 1941, just over a month after the launch of BARBAROSSA, the combined German–Romanian armies had recovered the two Romanian provinces of Northern Bukovina and Bessarabia—as defined by their boundaries prior to their seizure by the USSR in June 1940—at a cost of 10,486 Romanian dead. Most Romanian political leaders were content with the reconquest and advised Antonescu against crossing the River Dniester into the USSR proper. But Antonescu (who by promoting himself to marshal while commanding the armies had received the nickname 'Auto-Marshal') did not heed this advice. The German–Romanian armies advanced across the Dniester and eventually captured Odessa on 16 October after fierce resistance from Soviet forces. These inflicted heavy Romanian losses which, by then, amounted to 27,061 killed, 89,632 wounded, and 14,624 missing.

Antonescu's participation in the attack on the USSR was not motivated solely by the desire to regain the lost territories of Bessarabia and Northern Bukovina. He saw the German invasion as an ideological crusade against the infidel of *communism and his association with it as an act of Christian righteousness (see also RELIGION). In an order of the day Antonescu told his troops that the hour had arrived for the fight against the yoke of Bolshevism, while his vice-president, Mihai Antonescu, in a broadcast on the same day, began with the words: 'Romanians, today our nation has begun a great holy war'.

In the attack Romanian forces were assigned the task of protecting the right flank of Army Group South. These forces were integrated into a separate Army Group under the nominal command of Antonescu which was made up of the Eleventh German Army and the Third and Fourth Romanian Armies. In effect this Group took its orders from the commander of the Eleventh German

Army, General Eugen von Schobert, in accordance with the guidelines for German–Romanian military co-operation laid down by Hitler in a letter to Antonescu of 18 June. Here Hitler underlined the need for the direction of 'this grandiose attack' to be concentrated 'in a single hand' and requested Antonescu's 'permission to send him from time to time those of his wishes which referred to the Romanian Army and whose execution, in the interests of a unified, co-ordinated direction of operations, must be considered absolutely necessary'.

The escalation of Romania's part in the war prompted further misgivings, not only from political quarters but also from Antonescu's own senior commanders. In a series of memoranda Antonescu's chief of staff, General Iosif Iacobici, fearing a surprise Hungarian attack from the west against southern Transylvania—which was considered at risk because of the withdrawal of forces from there to support the campaign in the USSR—urged the Marshal to limit his involvement east of the Dniester. Iacobici was dismissed for his pains in January 1942 and replaced by General Ilie Şteflea, who endorsed his predecessor's views. When Şteflea took over the Romanian Army had 33 divisions, 15 east of the Dniester in the USSR and 18 in Romania. In February Şteflea learned about the promise given to Hitler by Antonescu to send the divisions in Romania to the front.

A first echelon of 10 divisions was due to be sent in the spring of 1942, followed by a second echelon of 5–6 divisions. That represented almost all the troops in the country. If these plans were implemented there would have remained in Romania only one division in the oilfields, and a division each to protect the Black Sea coast and Bessarabia. Şteflea succeeded in delaying the dispatch of the first echelon by six months and then sent them under strength, keeping much of their artillery in the country. By claiming that these under-strength divisions needed to be augmented by men and equipment from the divisions which were due to be sent in the second echelon, he was able to keep in Romania all the divisions which should have formed the second echelon. By sending the first echelon to the front at only half strength, he was able to keep 120,000 soldiers in reserve, and by keeping the second echelon in Romania he was able to save 100,000.

The major objectives of the German summer offensive of 1942 were the pincers move on Stalingrad, and its capture, and the conquest of the Caucasian oilfields. On 23 July Hitler issued his directive No. 45. The Seventeenth German Army, the Third Romanian Army, and the First and Fourth German Panzer Armies, concentrated under the command of Army Group A, were ordered to advance to the conquest of the Caucasus via Rostov-on-Don, where Hitler proposed to surround and defeat the enemy (see GERMAN–SOVIET WAR, 4). Sixth Army, under the command of General *Paulus, was ordered to capture Stalingrad and throw a cordon between the Don and the Volga. Paulus, because of his family contacts (he was married to a Romanian), was selected for the post of deputy C-in-C of a new Romanian–German Army Group Don, which was to be formed from the Third and Fourth Romanian Armies, the Sixth German Army, and the Fourth Panzer Army, and placed under Antonescu's command after the capture of Stalingrad.

Early in the autumn, the Third and Fourth Romanian Armies were brought up to protect the right and left flanks respectively of the Sixth Army. The Third Romanian Army, under General Petre Dumitrescu, was made up of eleven divisions (1st Armoured, 1st and 7th Cavalry, 5th, 6th, 7th, 9th, 11th, 13th, 14th, and 15th Infantry) and was placed to the north of Stalingrad, while the Fourth Romanian Army, under General Constantin Constantinescu, made up of seven divisions (5th and 8th Cavalry, 1st, 2nd, 4th, 8th, and 20th Infantry) was positioned to the south in the area of the Kalmyk Steppe lakes. Both Romanian formations were very inadequately armed, having neither heavy artillery nor anti-tank weapons.

The German troops suffered heavy losses as they gnawed their way into Stalingrad. Paulus begged for reinforcements, for the strengthening or the protection of his flanks, for better arms for the Romanians. He tried to enlist the co-operation of Dumitrescu in the hope that, via Antonescu, of whom Hitler held quite a high opinion, help might be extended to the Romanians and to his own army. Hitler ignored these requests. In the middle of November he sent Paulus a signal saying that he now expected of the Sixth Army one final, supreme effort to wipe out the Red Army in Stalingrad.

On 19 November the Twenty-First Soviet Army and the Fifth Soviet Tank Army, each with two armoured and two cavalry corps and infantry estimated at 21 divisions, broke through the front of the Third Romanian Army on the Don. The next day, 20 November, the Fifty-First and Fifty-Seventh Soviet Armies, with strong armoured support, broke through the front of the Fourth Panzer Army and Fourth Romanian Army to the south of Stalingrad. Thus the Soviets had succeeded in making deep breaches in the line on both flanks of the Sixth Army; there was a grave danger of encirclement. Paulus realized that his forces, together with elements of the Fourth Panzer Army, stood in danger of being hemmed in between the Volga and the Don. The formations involved were four army corps, one panzer corps, fourteen infantry, three armoured and three motorized Divisions, one Romanian infantry and one Romanian cavalry division, a total of approximately 260,000 men.

Despite stubborn Romanian and German resistance the Soviet Sixty-Fifth Soviet Army cut off any retreat to the west from a bend in the Don, and it was in this area to the south-west of Raspopinskaya that five infantry divisions of the Third Romanian Army (5th, 6th, 13th 14th, and 15th), under General Mihail Lascăr, were forced to surrender after their ammunition ran out on 24 November. The Soviet forces took more than 30,000 Romanian prisoners and all their equipment.

On 24 November Hitler ordered his forces to hold Stalingrad. The new Army Group Don, commanded by

*Manstein, was formed from the encircled Sixth Army of Paulus, the Fourth Panzer Army, part of which was also surrounded, the Fourth Romanian Army and a number of units taken from France and Germany. On 12 December the Fourth Panzer Army and the Fourth Romanian Army tried to battle their way to the encircled forces but were stopped some 40 km. (25 mi.) short of their objective. On 24 December the Soviet armies counter-attacked and virtually destroyed the Fourth Panzer Army and the Fourth Romanian Army. Of the three Romanian divisions only battalions survived. By early January Paulus's supplies were nearly exhausted. German attempts to relieve him by air were thwarted by bad weather and by the Soviet Army Air Force. On 8 January the Soviet command sent Paulus an ultimatum to surrender but it was rejected under Hitler's orders. The Soviet armies went over to the offensive and split the German resistance. On 31 January the southern group, under Paulus, who had just been promoted to Field Marshal by Hitler, surrendered, and two days later the remnants of the northern group also capitulated.

In the course of the Soviet counter-offensive at Stalingrad two German armies, two Romanian armies, and one Italian army were massacred. The Romanian losses in the Third and Fourth Armies in the period from 19 November 1942 to 7 January 1943 were put at 155,010 dead, wounded, and missing, most of the last being taken prisoner. This figure represented over a quarter of all Romanian troops engaged on the Eastern Front. Antonescu now realized that Hitler could no longer win the war and that Şteflea had been wise to advise withholding half Romania's army from the Eastern Front and keeping them in reserve to protect his country's sovereignty. It now seemed that he might have to use them for this purpose.

The volte-face of King Michael's coup in August 1944 exposed the German Army's southern flank and opened the whole of south-eastern Europe to the Red Army which was now able to sweep down into Bulgaria and move on towards Yugoslavia. At a stroke Hitler lost an ally who had 20 divisions on the Eastern Front and 30 divisions in Romania itself. Those at the front were disarmed by the Red Army while those in Romania now turned against the Germans (at the time of the coup there were 612,000 German troops at the front and in Romania, including 26 divisions totalling 390,000 men and 36,000 air force and navy personnel). In this fighting in the week after the coup the Romanians killed about 5,000 Germans and took 53,000 prisoners, including 9 generals and 650 officers. Romanian losses were 5,800 including 116 officers.

Romanian casualties in the German–Soviet war were put in 1946 at 625,000; almost half this figure represented persons missing. More than 100,000 soldiers were lost in the week following King Michael's coup, presumably taken prisoner by the Red Army after having laid down their arms, although the Soviet foreign minister *Molotov had given an undertaking on 2 April, repeated by Moscow radio on 24 August, to leave the Romanian forces their arms if they fought the Germans and Hungarians.

The terms of the Soviet–Romanian armistice, signed in Moscow on 12 September, recognized Romania's entry into the war on 24 August on the Allied side against Germany and Hungary, and stipulated that it should provide no less than twelve infantry divisions to fight alongside Soviet forces. In fact between sixteen and twenty Romanian divisions assisted the Red Army in driving the Germans first from Romanian territory, and later, at the beginning of 1945, from Hungary and Czechoslovakia, thus making the Romanian contribution in the European theatre of war at that time, in terms of troops engaged, the fourth largest after the USSR, the USA, and the UK. Romanian losses during these campaigns totalled 160,000 men, of whom 111,000 were killed or seriously wounded. Romania's military effort on both sides, from 1941 to 1944, and from 1944 to 1945, belied its craven surrenders of territory in 1940.

(b) Navy

Romanian naval forces in the *Black Sea consisted of four Italian-built destroyers, four torpedo boats, three submarines, three minelayers, one submarine depot ship, three gunboats, and one training ship. Operating with this force were five Italian submarines and when Italy capitulated in September 1943 the Romanians forestalled the Germans by seizing them. Although the Soviet Black Sea fleet was much larger, the Romanians, despite participation in convoying and in the evacuation of Odessa on 15 January 1944, lost no warships.

(c) Air Force

At the outbreak of war between Romania and the USSR on 22 June 1941 the Romanian Air Force consisted of 956 aircraft; 586 fighters (49 squadrons), 180 bombers (20 squadrons), 18 naval aircraft (2 squadrons), and 162 reconnaissance aircraft (18 squadrons). More than one-third of these aircraft were engaged in hostilities with the USSR, the remainder being deployed to defend Bucharest and the oilfields at Ploesti north of the capital, and in Transylvania. Between 1941 and 1944 in the war with the USSR 152 Romanian airmen lost their lives. During the Anglo-American raids on the Ploesti oilfields from 1942 to 1944 Romanian fighter aircraft joined locally based Luftwaffe forces in defending them.

After King Michael's coup in 1944 the Romanian Air Force was used in operations to clear Romania of German forces. On Stalin's orders Romanian forces were demobilized in March 1945. Subsequently, officers from all three Romanian services who had fought in the war against the USSR were arrested and tried as 'war criminals' by the communist authorities. A number were executed, while many were sentenced to long periods of imprisonment, including General George Jienescu, chief of the air staff, who spent the years 1945–64 in jail.

5. Merchant marine

This consisted of 28 ships at the outbreak of war. Ten of them were lost to mines in the Black Sea; one was seized by the British in Port Said and a number survived by remaining in Turkish waters during hostilities.

Dennis Deletant

Gafencu, G., *Prelude to the Russian Campaign* (London, 1945).
Hillgruber, A., *Hitler, König Carol und Marschall Antonescu* (2nd edn., Wiesbaden, 1965). An authoritative account of German–Romanian relations from 1938 to 1944.
Pearton, M., *Oil and the Romanian State* (Oxford, 1971).
Porter, I., *Operation Autonomous. With SOE in Wartime Romania* (London, 1989).

Rome–Berlin Axis, see AXIS STRATEGY AND CO-OPERATION.

Rome Committee of National Liberation, see ITALY, 3(b).

Rommel, Field Marshal Erwin (1891–1944), one of Hitler's most charismatic generals, who was best known for his victories during the *Western Desert campaigns. To those who fought against him he became something of a legend, but he is not highly regarded by German historians.

Born in Heidenheim, near Ulm, of middle-class parents with no military connections, Rommel joined the army in July 1910. On the outbreak of the *First World War he immediately displayed the boldness and independence that was to characterize his leadership during the Second, and ended it a captain and the holder of Prussia's highest decoration, the Pour le Mérite.

In 1937 Rommel published a book, *Infanterie greift an*, (English edn., *Infantry Attacks*, 1979) which brought him to Hitler's notice and, as a brigadier, he was put in charge of Hitler's security unit. Always a devotee of mobile warfare, and the exploitation of the surprise it often achieved, he requested command of a panzer division which he led with *élan* during the German offensive in May–June 1940 which culminated in the fall of *France. He ended the campaign as one of its heroes, was promoted maj-general in January 1941, and appointed to command the embryo *Afrika Korps in the Western Desert. Arriving in Tripoli on 12 February 1941, he made his presence felt immediately. Ordered by the Army High Command (OKH) to remain on the defensive he blithely disobeyed and

Rommel at St Valéry en Caux, 12 June 1940, after the surrender of the British 51st Highland Division there. Its divisional commander, Maj-General Victor Fortune, is standing next to him.

launched a blistering attack which drove the British almost out of Cyrenaica. In July 1941 his German–Italian command was enlarged to become Panzer Group Afrika and he was promoted lt-general. Although nominally under Italian command, his prestige was by now so great that he virtually held an independent command. But though he had scored remarkable victories his difficulties were immense—*Tobruk remained untaken and he was acutely short of supplies. He beat off two British offensives (BREVITY and BATTLEAXE) during May and June 1941, but was forced to fall back before a third, CRUSADER, that November.

Undismayed, and bolstered by reinforcements and new supplies, Rommel, now a general commanding an enlarged force, struck back in January 1942. In June he captured Tobruk and was promoted Germany's youngest field marshal, and then pushed the British back into Egypt. But, still starved of essential supplies and far from well, he was held in July at *El Alamein, stopped in September at *Alam Halfa, and finally routed in November at the second battle of El Alamein—though his retreat into Tunisia was as masterly as any of his victories. His advice that North Africa should now be abandoned was ignored. Instead his force, now called the German–Italian Panzerarmee, attacked the Allied line in northern Tunisia and defeated a mixed Allied force at *Kasserine Pass. However, command difficulties, misguided orders from the Italian High Command (see COMANDO SUPREMO) which he was no longer in any position to ignore, and adverse terrain combined to force Rommel to abandon his offensive. On 23 February he was given command of both panzer armies (Army Group Africa) and returned to the south to oversee an attack against *Montgomery's Eighth Army. But the *Medenine battle ended in failure and on 9 March he flew to Germany and was sent on extended sick leave.

In May 1943 Rommel was recalled to plan the occupation of northern Italy if it should prove necessary. It did and by August he had accomplished it. But he lost the argument as to how the Allied *Italian campaign should be opposed and was given instead the job of improving the coastal defences in western Europe (see ATLANTIC WALL). Then, in January 1944, he established Army Group B headquarters with operational control of all forces waiting to repel the expected Allied invasion. When the Normandy landings came (see OVERLORD), Allied successes and Hitler's obstinacy convinced Rommel that the war was lost. On 17 July he was badly wounded by an air attack and, in the aftermath of the July bomb plot to kill Hitler (see SCHWARZE KAPELLE), was unwittingly implicated by a conspirator. He was given two choices: face charges of high treason in the *People's Court, or commit suicide. If he chose the latter, his family would remain unharmed and he would receive a state funeral. He took poison. Those who saw his body noted the look of contempt on his face.

Hart, L. B. (ed.), *The Rommel Papers* (London, 1953).
Schmidt, H., *With Rommel in the Desert* (London, 1951).

Rommel's asparagus, Allied name for poles planted in open spaces in France by the Germans to prevent *gliders landing. This was done in early 1944 when *Rommel began reinforcing the *Atlantic Wall in preparation for the Allied invasion of the continent (see OVERLORD). The British used similar defences in Kent and Sussex during the invasion scare in 1940 (see SEALION).

RONA (Russian National Liberation Army), see SOVIET EXILES AT WAR.

Roosevelt as war leader. As president of the USA from 1933 to 1945, Franklin Delano Roosevelt (1882–1945) played a large part in shaping world events, especially during the Second World War. His effectiveness as an international leader partly rested on a lifelong interest in foreign affairs. As a boy he travelled and studied in France, Germany, and the UK, and he admired the exploits of his distant cousin President Theodore Roosevelt (1859–1919). By defining a new world role for the USA during his presidency in the early years of the century, Theodore helped make Franklin an internationalist. Following in his forebear's footsteps, he served as assistant secretary of the navy under President Woodrow Wilson (1856–1924), and became an advocate of US entry into the *First World War and of Wilson's peace programme. Wilson's failure to win approval from the US Senate for the *Versailles settlement and the *League of Nations in 1919 taught Roosevelt a lesson he consistently applied throughout his own presidency: America's democratic system and long tradition of isolationism required a president to have stable backing at home for any significant commitments abroad.

Up to the outbreak of the Second World War in September 1939 Roosevelt largely followed Congressional and public demands that the country isolate itself from foreign conflicts. In particular, he signed into law a series of *Neutrality Acts that prohibited the USA from supplying arms or financial support to belligerents and forbade American vessels to carry munitions to warring nations and US citizens to sail on belligerent ships. Roosevelt accepted these restrictions as a domestic political necessity, but he viewed them as encouraging aggression by Germany, Italy, and Japan. In the summer of 1939, when the president proposed revising these laws so that victims of aggression could buy munitions with cash and transport them in their own ships, congressional leaders refused. They did not believe a war was about to take place, and if one did, they were determined to keep the USA at peace.

Between the onset of fighting in September 1939 and the attack on *Pearl Harbor in December 1941, Roosevelt consistently sided with the Allies against the Axis. In November 1939, he persuaded Congress to put the neutrality statutes on a cash-and-carry basis, which then allowed the UK and France to buy munitions in the USA. In the winter of 1939–40, when a lull in the fighting followed the *Polish campaign, Roosevelt tried to buy

Roosevelt at the SEXTANT conference in Cairo, November 1943. He is flanked by Chiang Kai-shek and Winston Churchill. On Churchill's left is Madam Chiang Kai-shek. Behind them stand, left to right, Generals Shang Chen, Lin Wei, Somervell, Stilwell, and Arnold, Field Marshal Dill, Admiral Mountbatten, and Maj-General Carton de Wiart.

more time for the Allies to develop their military strength by sending Sumner *Welles on a peace mission to the European capitals. In the spring and summer of 1940, Germany's conquest of western Europe, including France, left the UK and its empire as the only deterrent to Hitler's control of the Atlantic approaches to the USA. The withdrawal of British forces on the Continent by a heroic sealift from *Dunkirk, and Churchill's inspired rhetoric promising ultimate victory, aroused American sympathies. Although the great majority of Americans continued to oppose involvement in the war, their desire to help the UK defeat Germany and Italy increased. In response, Roosevelt agreed to Churchill's request for 50 destroyers in return for 99-year leases on Caribbean bases. Roosevelt, who was a master at reading the national mood, hailed the exchange, which became known as the *destroyers-for-bases agreement, as America's greatest foreign agreement since the Louisiana Purchase. At the same time, he persuaded Congress to pass the first peacetime draft in US history (see SELECTIVE SERVICE SYSTEM) as a prelude to expanding America's defensive capacity. However, isolationist sentiment, as the *America First Committee proved, remained so strong in the country that the president felt compelled to make an unqualified pledge during the 1940 campaign that the country would not go to war. This blanket pledge, devoid of the qualifying phrase, 'except in case of attack' laid him open to later charges that he had lied the country into war.

On 29 December 1940, after winning re-election to an unprecedented third term in November 1940, Roosevelt announced, during one of his 'fireside' radio broadcasts, his intention to make the country the 'great arsenal of democracy'. To fulfil that commitment, he persuaded Congress in March 1941 to enact *Lend-Lease, a programme for continuing to supply the UK, which could no longer afford to buy *matériel* from the USA. In May 1941, after German naval forces had inflicted substantial losses on British shipping during the battle of the *Atlantic and German armies had occupied Yugoslavia and Greece, and threatened the UK's control of the Middle East, Roosevelt publicly declared a state of national emergency. Although he would not say so openly, he now concluded that US air and naval forces would have to take part in the fighting. In June, the Nazi attack on the USSR (see BARBAROSSA) moved him to extend Lend-Lease help to Moscow as well which resulted in the *Three-Power conference that October. In the summer of 1941 he underscored America's identification with Hitler's opponents by holding the *Placentia Bay conference with Churchill and issuing the *Atlantic Charter, a statement of democratic principles separating the UK and the USA from Nazi Germany and fascist Italy.

Although Roosevelt discussed US entry into the war with Churchill at the conference, he saw no means to bring the country into the fighting without a public and Congressional debate that would do more to divide the American people than unite them behind an extended war effort. All the public opinion polls he saw in 1940–1 convinced him that while he could command majority support for US belligerency, he had no means of creating a broad, stable consensus for war. Only a major provocation abroad seemed likely to arouse a strong domestic commitment to fight. For example, in May 1941, the unprovoked sinking by a German U-boat in a non-war zone of an American freighter, **Robin Moor*, had not impressed Roosevelt as a sufficient *casus belli*. Nor did he see the exchange of fire between a German submarine and the American destroyer **Greer* in September 1941 as sufficient to create a public demand for war, despite his misleading description of the attack as unprovoked. As he told the British ambassador, Lord *Halifax, 'his perpetual problem was to steer a course between ... (1) the wish of 70% of Americans to keep out of war; (2) the wish of 70% of Americans to do everything to break Hitler, even if it means war. He [the President] said that if he asked for a declaration of war he wouldn't get it, and opinion would swing against him. He therefore intended to go on doing whatever he best could to help us, and declarations of war were out of fashion.' Not even the sinking of the destroyer, **Reuben James*, moved him from this opinion and it was only the Japanese attack on Pearl Harbor on 7 December 1941 that ended the political debate and brought a strongly united country into the fighting.

Much has been made of the idea that Roosevelt purposely provoked Tokyo into an attack which he knew was coming. According to this explanation of how Japan surprised the USA at Pearl Harbor, Roosevelt allowed it to happen as a 'back door' to the European war. This conspiracy theory rests on very thin evidence. Although Roosevelt had spoken out against Japanese aggression in China (see CHINA INCIDENT) in the Quarantine Address of October 1937, and introduced embargoes in 1940–1 on scrap metal and petroleum in response to Japanese aggression against French Indo-China, the president hoped to avoid a war with Tokyo. He believed that such a conflict would divert American resources from Europe, where he wished to help the UK and the USSR defeat Germany and Italy. He assumed that an Axis defeat in Europe would open the way to effective action against Japan.

While the availability of *MAGIC intelligence—the capacity of American military intelligence to read Japanese diplomatic codes—told Roosevelt that Japan intended to attack somewhere on the weekend of 7 December, he could not be certain where. Japanese military movements suggested that a strike might come against any number of targets. In addition, the president and his military chiefs did not think Japan had the military capacity to attack the fleet in Hawaii. Outdated military intelligence about the distance carrier-based Japanese planes could travel, and the supposed inability of Japanese torpedoes to run the shallow depths of Pearl Harbor, lulled military planners into unwarranted assumptions about Japan's ability to stage an attack. Moreover, in American eyes, the fleet was a deterrent and not a target.

Finally, even if Roosevelt had foreseen the attack and wished to use it as a 'back door' to the European war, it is inconceivable that he would have allowed so much of the American fleet and *air power in Hawaii to have been destroyed. A successful Japanese surprise attack against a small number of ships and planes would have had the same result as their devastatingly successful strike of 7 December. The attack destroyed much of the fleet at Pearl Harbor, though the aircraft carriers, which were at sea, were spared. On 8 December, the US Congress, responding to what the president called 'a day that will live in infamy', declared war on Japan. Three days later, Hitler and Mussolini, believing a conflict with the USA inevitable, declared war. This united the country behind an all-out war against the Axis, and allowed Roosevelt to forge a *Grand Alliance with the UK, China, and the USSR.

The first half of 1942 was the most difficult period of the war for Roosevelt and America. Japan scored a series of battlefield victories in the *Pacific war that brought it control of the Philippines, Burma, Singapore, the Netherlands East Indies, and parts of New Guinea, the Solomons and the Gilbert Islands. At the same time, German armies launched new offensives in the USSR and captured 25,000 British Empire troops at *Tobruk in Libya. These victories threatened the defeat of the USSR and the loss of Australia, India, Egypt, and all of the Middle East.

Roosevelt took a variety of political and military actions to sustain American and Allied morale and avert military defeat. He persuaded the Allies to issue a joint declaration pledging support for 'life, liberty, independence, and religious freedom' and a commitment 'not to make a separate *armistice or peace with the enemies'. He unsuccessfully pressed Churchill to promise post-war independence to India to stiffen Indian resolve to fight and to disarm American suspicions of a war to save the British Empire. He directed the war department to incarcerate 120,000 *Japanese-Americans, most of whom were US citizens, as a safeguard against Japanese sabotage and espionage. Roosevelt also helped develop a plan for sixteen army B25s to bomb Tokyo from the carrier *Hornet*. This successful *Doolittle raid—named after its leader,

Colonel Jimmy Doolittle—took place in April and elated Roosevelt and the nation. More important, American naval forces fought the battle of the *Coral Sea in May, which prevented the capture of Port Moresby, the capital of Papua, and then scored a convincing victory at *Midway in June. However, continuing Japanese expansion in the South and South-West Pacific, provoked a series of battles in the Solomon Islands (see GUADALCANAL, for example) and New Guinea which compelled Roosevelt to send additional resources to the region. Although intent on pursuing a Europe-first strategy (see RAINBOW PLANS), by the close of 1942, Roosevelt had sent 9 of the 17 divisions and 19 of the 66 air groups that had gone overseas to fight in the *Pacific war. At the same time, to keep China going and tie down Japanese forces there, Roosevelt assured *Chiang Kai-shek, the head of the Nationalist government, of China's central place in the Allied coalition and the ultimate return of lost territories. In addition, he committed himself to a dangerous and costly air supply route from India to China over the Himalayas, known as the *Hump.

To advance the Europe-first strategy in 1942, Roosevelt made an unrealizable commitment to an Anglo-American invasion of western Europe before the end of the year. In meetings with the Soviet foreign minister, *Molotov, in May and June, the president, though knowing that insufficient troops, fighter planes, and landing craft would make any cross-Channel attack a sacrificial operation, promised to draw off German forces from the Soviet Front with an assault on Europe in 1942. Later in June, after conferring with Churchill in the USA, Roosevelt agreed instead to an invasion of North Africa in November (see NORTH AFRICAN CAMPAIGN) and a delay in the cross-channel invasion until 1943. Determined to bring American troops into action before the end of 1942 and concerned not to lose the Middle East, where British forces continued on the defensive against the Axis, he wisely allowed realities to dictate US military actions. Churchill, feeling, he said, as if he were 'carrying a large lump of ice to the North Pole', personally brought the news to Stalin in Moscow. Though the Soviet dictator was relieved to know that there would be some kind of additional front in 1942, he complained that the British and Americans were unwilling to make sacrifices in the way the Soviets were and expressed doubts about Anglo-American readiness to sustain a united effort with Moscow against Berlin. It was the beginning of recriminations over the Second Front that would last until 1944.

The start of the North African campaign in November 1942 led to a major Allied victory over the Germans in the Middle East and opened the way to an invasion of Europe. In January 1943 Roosevelt met Churchill at Casablanca (see SYMBOL) to lay plans for a European assault in 1943. Churchill and his military chiefs persuaded him that a cross-Channel attack could not be implemented until the second half of 1943 or the first half of 1944. They convinced him and his chiefs that Allied forces, after clearing the Germans from North Africa, should seize Sicily and then invade Italy. In Churchill's words, they were to strike at the 'soft underbelly' of Europe.

Roosevelt's agreement to the attack in southern Europe, coupled with the suspension of the *Arctic convoys taking Lend-Lease supplies to the USSR, meant renewed difficulties with Stalin. Nothing short of 50 or 60 divisions in France by the spring of 1943 would satisfy him, Churchill said. Roosevelt had tried to persuade Stalin to come to Casablanca, but the Soviet leader said that the major military actions which were imminent in the *German–Soviet war, made it impossible for him to be away from Moscow. Though Stalin had political motives for not wanting a face-to-face meeting early in 1943, there were indeed major military movements afoot that would result in the great Soviet victory at *Stalingrad. As Churchill said at the time, the Allied victories in the winter of 1942–3 did not represent the end or even the beginning of the end, but it was 'perhaps, the end of the beginning'.

Fearful that Stalin would see the delayed invasion of France as a political decision to bleed Germany and the USSR as a prelude to Anglo-American domination of post-war Europe, Roosevelt persuaded Churchill at Casablanca to join him in issuing an *unconditional surrender declaration. Pledging not to accept anything less from the Axis powers, Roosevelt and Churchill assured Stalin that they would not enter into a negotiated settlement with Berlin or any agreement that left Germany in a position to threaten future Soviet security. Some historians have argued that the declaration stiffened German resolve to fight and so extended the war. Since Hitler had no intention of surrendering on any terms, and since opposition to him was all but non-existent in Germany, it is difficult to credit the idea that a demand for Germany's unconditional surrender had a significant impact on the duration of the European fighting.

In addition to military and political planning that would carry the fighting on to the European continent and appease Stalin, Roosevelt faced abrasive tensions with General de *Gaulle at Casablanca. France had been a thorn in Roosevelt's side since its collapse in June 1940. Eager to deter a defeated France from fully co-operating with the Nazis, and particularly to prevent the French fleet from coming under German control, Roosevelt established relations with the collaborationist *Vichy government. This decision brought him under sharp attack in the USA and the UK, where critics complained that it signalled a willingness to negotiate with fascist regimes. No one was more outspoken against this policy than de Gaulle. He declared himself the leader of the Free French everywhere and dismissed American assertions that relations with Vichy had limited French resistance to the invasion of North Africa. Indeed, he complained that American actions undermined Free French morale and readiness to rally to the Allied cause.

After much hectoring by Churchill, de Gaulle agreed

to meet Roosevelt in Casablanca. But Roosevelt was not well disposed towards him. He believed that the defeat of France had deprived it of a central role in future peacemaking or a return to Great Power status. He also wished to prevent the restoration of France's colonial empire and the rebellions he expected would follow if it was restored. De Gaulle was not far from the mark when he later wrote that 'Roosevelt regarded me without benevolence'. He 'meant the peace to be an American peace, convinced that he must be the one to dictate its structure, that the states which had been overrun should be subject to his judgement, and that France in particular should recognize him as its saviour and arbiter.' Although the two men put on a show of unity in Casablanca for the sake of the war effort, the president left the conference confirmed in his judgement that de Gaulle would do more to undermine than advance the war effort, would try to establish himself as France's political chief by undemocratic means, and would resist all efforts to confine France to a secondary role after the war.

The capture of Sicily, the invasion of Italy, and the surrender of its government during 1943 prepared the way for conferences in Cairo (see SEXTANT) and Teheran (see EUREKA) in November–December. Meeting first in Cairo with Churchill and Chiang Kai-shek and then in Teheran with Churchill and Stalin, Roosevelt and the Allies agreed on future war plans. Specifically, they agreed to recapture Burma and cross the Channel into France in the spring of 1944. To Roosevelt's particular satisfaction, Stalin promised to enter the fighting against Japan within three months after the war ended in Europe. Despite the success of the US military against Japan in the Pacific through an *island-hopping campaign, Roosevelt worried that an ultimate invasion of Japan's home islands would cost the USA massive casualties. He hoped to reduce American losses by a Soviet invasion of Manchukuo that would tie down Japanese troops. He also believed that Soviet participation against Japan would shorten the Pacific war.

The meetings in Cairo and Teheran also gave Roosevelt opportunities to begin advancing his post-war plans. He was eager to destroy German and Japanese power and replace it with a coalition of the Big Four—the UK, China, the USA, and USSR—which would police the world through an international organization, or a new version of Wilson's *League of Nations called the United Nations (see SAN FRANCISCO CONFERENCE). Yet Roosevelt believed that post-war peace arrangements were contingent upon persuading the US people and Congress to commit themselves to sustained involvement in international affairs. This meant confirming American hopes that universalist or worldwide solutions could replace regional ones in resolving international conflicts.

Much of what he said and did in public was directed towards this goal. For example, he was not confident that Wilson's proposals for collective security were realistic—a world in which nations relied on collective action rather than self-serving alliances, spheres of influence, and balances of power to protect them. In a meeting with seven US senators from both parties in January 1945, Roosevelt candidly said that spheres of influence were a reality which the USA lacked the power to abolish. The 'idea kept coming up', he explained, 'because the occupying forces had the power in the areas where their arms were present and each knew that the other could not force things to an issue.' He also privately stated that 'the Soviets had the power in Eastern Europe, that it was obviously impossible to have a break with them and, therefore, the only practicable course was to use what influence we have to ameliorate the situation.' Yet Roosevelt never said this to the public. Instead, he emphasized his hope that a new world organization would bring a new era in international relations much like the one Wilson had envisaged in 1918–19.

Roosevelt's private understanding of conditions in China and his public discussions of its wartime and post-war roles further illustrate the point. He knew full well that China was not a Great Power and was unlikely to become one for the foreseeable future. He also understood that Chiang's government was corrupt and unpopular and that there might be a post-war revolution that would replace Nationalist control with a communist regime. Despite this knowledge, the president consistently referred to Chiang's government as democratic and China as a great power that would share in post-war peacekeeping as an equal with its wartime Allies. Aware that China was America's most popular ally and that Americans wanted a major role for a democratic China in the post-war world, Roosevelt encouraged the public's illusions. At the same time, he hoped a Great Power role for China would give the USA an advantage in post-war international affairs. Expecting China to be dependent upon Washington after the war, the president hoped it would side with the USA in the United Nations Security Council and help in the administration of former colonies handed over to trustees assigned to govern them until they were ready for independence.

A similar approach shaped Roosevelt's handling of wartime relations with the USSR. Outwardly, the president consistently encouraged the belief that the USA's wartime alliance with Moscow would continue for as far into the future as anyone could see. After the Teheran conference, when a reporter asked him for his personal impressions of Stalin, Roosevelt replied: 'We had many excellent talks,' which would 'make for excellent relations in the future.' He also described Stalin as 'something like me ... a realist.'

Roosevelt, in fact, had substantial doubts about the extent of post-war Soviet–American co-operation. He hoped that Soviet suspicions of the West could be overcome and that continuing accommodation would be the outcome of the war. But he knew that the end of the fighting might rekindle adversarial relations between them. However, he would not reveal this concern to the public or Congress. He believed that the country would not commit itself to a post-war part in international affairs if it saw Soviet–American relations turning into traditional sphere-of-influence diplomacy or power politics. During 1943, Wendell *Willkie, the Republican Party's 1940 presidential candidate, had caught the public's imagination with a best-selling book, *One World*, which celebrated the similarities between the USSR and the USA and emphasized the necessity of shared international values for a peaceful world. Unwilling to challenge American hopes with the unvarnished truth about possible divisions in the post-war era, Roosevelt encouraged wishful thinking about Soviet–American relations as a way to ensure an end to US isolationism after the fighting stopped.

Post-war issues came to a head at Yalta in February 1945 (see ARGONAUT), Roosevelt's last meeting with Churchill and Stalin. The conference focused on post-war arrangements for Poland, Germany, China, and former colonies, and the need for a new world league. Churchill and Roosevelt were worried that Stalin would set up a Soviet sphere of control in southern and eastern Europe that would threaten western security and cause dissolution among the peoples there. To head off full Soviet control of the Balkans Churchill had gone to Moscow in October 1944 (see TOLSTOY) where he and Stalin had agreed to a sphere-of-influence arrangement. Despite public expressions of opposition to any spheres of influence, Roosevelt privately endorsed Churchill's action. At the same time, he cabled his ambassador in Moscow: 'My active interest at the present time in the Balkan area is that such steps as are practicable should be taken to insure against the Balkans getting us into a future international war.'

At Yalta, where the three leaders hammered out agreements about a *Polish–Soviet frontier, German boundaries, and the post-war Polish government, Roosevelt won Stalin's agreement to a *Declaration on Liberated Europe, which met two of Roosevelt's political concerns. He naïvely believed that it would put a moral burden on the Soviets to act with some restraint in what he knew would be their East European sphere, and would continue to encourage the American illusion that the Soviets would abandon power politics for collective security.

A secret agreement with Churchill in September 1944, covering the development of the *atomic bomb, reflected the depths of Roosevelt's distrust of the Soviets. In an *aide-mémoire*, which recorded a conversation they had at Hyde Park, New York, the president and prime minister agreed that the Soviets were not to share in the control and use of atomic energy. Roosevelt saw the atomic bomb strictly in Anglo-American hands as a way to shore up Britain's post-war power and guard against Soviet domination of all Europe and other parts of the world. His principal scientific adviser recorded after a conversation with Roosevelt at Hyde Park: 'The President was very much in favour of complete interchange with the British on this subject [atomic energy] after the war in all phases, and apparently on a basis where it would be used jointly or not at all ... The President evidently thought he could join with Churchill in bringing about a US–UK post-war agreement on this subject by which it would be held closely and presumably to control the peace of the world.'

In a speech to a joint session of Congress on 1 March 1945, Roosevelt declared Yalta a huge success and asked national support for its results. '... Unless you here in the halls of the American Congress—with the support of the American people—concur in the general conclusions reached at Yalta ... the meeting will not have produced lasting results ... We shall have to take the responsibility for world collaboration, or we shall have to bear the responsibility for another world conflict.' But he advised Americans that this 'collaboration' would no longer be on the basis of 'the system of unilateral action, the exclusive alliances, the spheres of influence, the balances of power, and all the other expedients that have been tried for centuries—and have always failed'. Instead, as a result of the conference, he predicted that there would be a 'new structure of peace ... a universal organization in which all peaceloving nations will finally have a chance to join'. But privately he sounded a different note, telling one sceptical adviser, 'I didn't say the result was good. I said it was the best I could do.' To another adviser, he expressed doubt 'whether, when the chips were down, Stalin would be able to carry out and deliver what he had agreed to'.

In the six weeks before he died on 12 April, as Soviet actions in Eastern Europe generally, and in Poland particularly, began to undermine American confidence in the USSR's willingness to abandon spheres of influence, Roosevelt pressed Stalin to understand that if the American people viewed the Yalta agreement as having failed, it would be a grave blow to 'the successful development of our programme of international collaboration ... All of the difficulties and dangers to Allied unity which we had so much in mind ... at the Crimea [Yalta] will face us in an even more acute form.' When Stalin remained unresponsive, Roosevelt told Churchill that 'we must not permit anybody to entertain a false impression that we are afraid. Our armies will in a very few days be in a position that will permit us to become "tougher" than has heretofore appeared advantageous to the war effort.'

Because he had limited faith in the willingness of nations, including the UK and the USSR, to replace traditional power politics with collective security, Roosevelt tried to ensure that the USA would be in a strong position after the war to defend its national security without the United Nations. In particular, he favoured US control of strategic air and naval bases around the globe. He wanted US forces to establish themselves in Dakar in West Africa, in French Indo-China and in the Pacific islands Japan had controlled under a League of Nations mandate since 1920. But he believed that any open admission of intending to set up these bases would arouse domestic opposition and rekindle isolationist feelings against any Great Power role for the country in world affairs. To solve this political problem, Roosevelt called for trusteeships over former colonies by the Allied powers. The USA, UK, and China, for example, were to be trustees for French Indo-China for 20 or more years, or until it could establish self-rule. In short, Roosevelt tried to use an idealistic idea to mask a concern with power. Evolving world conditions, however, made it impossible for him to fulfil this plan. China proved to be too weak to join the USA in policing parts of Asia and the Pacific, and British and French determination and ability to hold on to their empires forced the president to abandon establishing various trusteeships in the closing months of his life.

In the years since 1945, Roosevelt has come under sharp attack for his handling of foreign affairs. To be sure, historians generally agree that he was an architect of victory in the Second World War, but they find little to compliment beyond that: his endorsement of neutrality laws in the thirties, his pre-Pearl Harbor dealings with Japan, and his wartime approach to China, France, and the USSR have evoked complaints of superficiality and naïvety. Moreover, his readiness to incarcerate Japanese-Americans during the war, his failure to make significant efforts to rescue Europe's Jews from Nazi extermination (see FINAL SOLUTION), his guarded dealings with Congress and the public before the war, and secret agreements with Churchill and Stalin during the fighting, have saddled him with a reputation for timidity in defence of humane values and for deviousness that undermined democracy at home and abroad.

Yet Roosevelt's contribution to the survival of international democracy cannot be in doubt. Moreover, his broad conception of what it would take to assure the post-war peace was fundamentally sound: a greatly expanded American role abroad, a Soviet–American accord or 'peaceful coexistence', a place for a Great Power China, and an end to colonial empires have all become fixtures on the post-war world scene. But these developments emerged neither in the way nor to the extent Roosevelt had wished. His plans for a USA with substantial, but nevertheless limited, commitments abroad, an accommodation with the USSR, a stable, co-operative China, a passive France, and a smooth transition for dependent peoples from colonial to independent rule could not withstand the historical and contemporary forces ranged against them. Roosevelt was mindful of the fact that uncontrollable conditions—Soviet suspicion of the West and internal divisions in China, for example—might play havoc with his post-war plans. But his vision of what the world would need to revive and remain at peace after the war moved him to seek these ends anyway. That he fell short of his aims had less to do with naïvety or idealism than with the fact that even a thoroughgoing commitment to *Realpolitik* or an exclusive reliance on power would not have significantly altered developments in Europe and Asia after the war. Soviet expansion, Chinese strife, and colonial revolutions were beyond Roosevelt's power to prevent.

By contrast with these developments, external events played a central part in helping Roosevelt bring the country through the war in a mood to take a major role in overseas affairs. Much of Roosevelt's public diplomacy during the war was directed towards this goal: the portraits of an effective peacekeeping body, of a friendly USSR, and of a peaceful China had as much to do with creating an internationalist consensus at home as with establishing a fully effective peace system abroad. Principally influenced by Pearl Harbor, which destroyed isolationist contentions about American invulnerability to attack, and by the country's emergence as the world's foremost power, the nation ended the war ready to shoulder substantial responsibilities in foreign affairs.

ROBERT DALLEK

Burns, J. M., *Roosevelt: The Soldier of Freedom* (London, 1971).
Dallek, R., *Franklin D. Roosevelt and American Foreign Policy, 1932–1945* (New York, 1979).
Freidel, F., *Franklin D. Roosevelt: A Rendezvous with Destiny* (Boston, 1990).

Rosenberg, Alfred (1893–1946), Estonian-born member of the Nazi Party whose *anti-Semitism, and anti-Christian theories, made him one of the principal contributors to *Nazi ideology.

Rosenberg obtained an architectural diploma in Moscow in March 1918, and witnessed the revolution there. In November 1918 he went to Germany where he wrote anti-Semitic articles, met Hitler, joined the Nazi Party, became the editor of its newspaper (*Völkischer Beobachter*), then its managing editor, and, as a Russian speaker, was the Nazis' expert on east European matters.

At first his influence over Hitler was all-pervading and he led the party when Hitler was imprisoned after the Munich putsch. But opponents soon forced him to resign and Hitler—who found Rosenberg's principal opus, *Myth of the Twentieth Century*, incomprehensible when it was published in 1930—later froze him out of his inner circle.

However, Rosenberg's early influence on Nazi ideology ensured his survival and a succession of party posts. In 1927 he became head of the new National Socialist Society for Culture and Learning (Combat League for German Culture from 1929); in 1933, after Hitler came to power, he formed the party's foreign policy office; and in 1934 he was made responsible, in his own words, for the party's 'intellectual and ideological education and training'. His foreign policy office was soon eclipsed by *Ribbentrop—though he did ensure Hitler's limited backing for *Quisling (see also NORWAY, 3)—and in striving to achieve a cultural policy he again lost out to more determined rivals such as *Ley. Once Germany was at war he also became the titular head of an organization which bore his name to purloin paintings, books, furniture, and *objets d'art* from occupied territories (see LOOT).

Though Hitler remained distant, in July 1941 he appointed Rosenberg Reich Minister of Eastern Occupied

Territories (Ukraine and *Ostland). Rosenberg abjured genocide and expulsion, preferring to co-opt the territories to fight Stalin, but he proved quite unequal to the machinations of such power-hungry rivals as *Goebbels, *Himmler, and *Göring, and in October 1944 he intimated in a letter to Hitler, which was never answered, that he wanted to resign. He was sentenced to death at the *Nuremberg trials and executed.

Cecil, R., *The Myth of the Master Race: Alfred Rosenberg and Nazi Ideology* (London, 1972).

Rote Drei (Red Three), Soviet *GRU intelligence network established in Switzerland. It was so named by German counter-espionage because of its three radio stations linked to Moscow, one in Lausanne and two in Geneva, though in fact there were sometimes four or five. It was led by a Hungarian-born communist, Sándor Radó (DORA), whose information was gathered from various sources, but primarily from the *LUCY Ring. In October–November 1943 the Swiss, prompted by the Germans, seized the transmitters and broke up the network. Radó escaped to France after ten months living in a cupboard; then in September 1944 went to newly-liberated Paris and made contact with the Soviet military mission there. In January 1945 he boarded an aircraft for Moscow, but at Cairo he sought the protection of the British authorities and the fact that neither they nor the relevant authorities in London knew anything about him belies the story that his network had been used by the British to pass *ULTRA intelligence to the USSR. He did not attempt to defect and his request for protection was denied. He was handed over to the Egyptian authorities who deported him to the USSR in July 1945 where he was imprisoned for ten years on a trumped-up charge. See also ROTE KAPELLE and SPIES.

Radó, S., *Codename Dora* (London, 1977).

Rote Kapelle (Red Orchestra), cryptonym used by the German *Abwehr and Sicherheitsdienst (see RSHA) for a European-wide Soviet espionage network, *Kapelle* being Abwehr jargon for secret wireless transmissions and the counter-espionage operations mounted against them. The term was first used to describe an Abwehr operation against a secret wireless transmitter detected in Brussels in August 1941 and was later extended to cover those operations which were largely directed by *Schellenberg against other transmitters in the Netherlands, Germany, France, Switzerland (see ROTE DREI), and elsewhere.

Headed by a Polish Jew and dedicated communist, Léopold Trepper, the Belgian network was first established during the 1930s by the Soviet espionage organization, Razvedupr (later known as *GRU), when it was led by another dedicated communist, a German radio and forgery expert called Johann Wenzel. This network was later extended to the Netherlands, and then to France—where Trepper settled—and occasional contact was also made with three groups, headed by Harro Schulze-Boysen, Arvid Harnack, and Rudolf von Scheliha, which were active in Germany. Von Scheliha, especially, was highly regarded by the GRU and during the course of the war a number of Soviet agents were parachuted into Germany to help the groups establish radio contact with Berlin. It was later estimated by the head of the Abwehr, Admiral *Canaris, and by others, that the Rote Kapelle in Germany cost the lives of 200,000 men. When Schulze-Boysen, a desk officer at the Reich ministry of aviation, was arrested a message he was about to encode gave detailed information of the whereabouts of 2,500 Luftwaffe aircraft gathered to support the German drive on *Stalingrad.

The network became of primary importance to Moscow after the Germans invaded the USSR in June 1941 (see BARBAROSSA). It was inundated with questions from Moscow, which alerted the Abwehr to a number of transmitters, and the first arrests were made when agents transmitting from Brussels were caught in December 1941. Aware now of the network's existence, the Abwehr's hunt for its other members began.

Trepper himself proved elusive, but his radio was soon found in a Paris suburb. In July 1942 Wenzel was caught in the act of transmitting and revealed his codes. This enabled the Abwehr to decrypt messages they had already intercepted, leading to the arrest of Schulze-Boysen in August 1942, and by October members of all three German groups had been arrested. Of the 118 put on trial, 41 were beheaded, 8 were hanged, and 2 committed suicide.

After his capture, Wenzel began co-operating with the Abwehr by operating a *Funkspiel* (radio game) as did two other captured agents. However, Moscow knew through Trepper that Wenzel had been arrested, and in November 1942 he escaped and was able to get word to Moscow about the *Funkspiel*. Victor Sukolov, who ran the Belgian network after Trepper left, went to Marseilles in January 1942 to start a new network there. But when the Germans occupied *Vichy France in November 1942 Sukolov was arrested and under interrogation he revealed the existence of the Rote Drei in Switzerland.

Trepper was one of the last to remain at liberty but he was cornered at his dentist's surgery in December 1942. He then betrayed other members of the Rote Kapelle and co-operated with the Germans in a *Funkspiel*. But he was probably a *triple agent, still under orders from Moscow, and by betraying some he may have saved others. In September 1943 he escaped and was not recaptured.

Soviet agents connected with the Rote Kapelle were also active elsewhere in Europe, including Scandinavia and the UK, and in the USA. After the war the myth was perpetrated that the organization had played a critical part in the *German–Soviet war. Communist propaganda also asserted that in Germany it had played an important part in the political resistance against Hitler (see SCHWARZE KAPELLE). But although Schulze-Boysen's group is regarded in Germany as part of this resistance the Rote Kapelle's real purpose was espionage by communists for communists.

Those Soviet agents who survived were not well rewarded. Several—Sándor Radó (the head of the Rote Drei), Trepper, Sukolov, and probably Wenzel—were imprisoned in the USSR after the war.

The Rote Kapelle: The CIA's History of Soviet Intelligence and Espionage Networks in Western Europe, 1936–1945 (Annapolis, Md., 1979).
Trepper, L., *The Great Game* (London, 1977).

Rotterdam raid, mounted on 14 May 1940 to force this Dutch city to capitulate quickly after German paratroopers had previously landed to seize its bridges. The raid was cancelled when surrender discussions started, but the abort message did not reach the aircraft and 57 out of 100 dropped their bombs before an emergency flare signal was seen. These were aimed at military targets and used no incendiaries, but 2.8 sq. km. (1.1 sq. mi.) of the city centre was destroyed, between 800 and 980 civilians were killed, and a few hours later the Dutch government surrendered with its army still largely intact.

The raid ended the British *phoney war policy of not bombing Germany for the Allies had threatened Germany with retaliation if it bombed civilian targets; and on 15 May 1940 the first RAF raid on the Ruhr was launched, heralding the start of the *strategic air offensive against Germany.

Rowecki, Maj-General Stefan (1895–1944), Polish Army colonel who used the pseudonym 'Grot' when, from July 1940, he commanded the Polish partisan force, Union for Armed Struggle (Związek Walki Zbrojnej, or ZWZ) which became the Polish Home Army in February 1942 (see POLAND, 4). Promoted maj-general after his capture in July 1943, he was murdered in *Sachsenhausen and was replaced by Lt-General *Komorowski.

***Royal Oak*, sinking of.** On the night of 13/14 October 1939, U-47, commanded by Günther Prien, penetrated the defences of the base of the British Home Fleet at Scapa Flow in Scotland. One of his first salvo of torpedoes found its target, but those aboard the battleship *Royal Oak* attributed the explosion to an internal cause, Prien's second salvo, fired 20 minutes later, capsized the vessel

Rotterdam after the German air raid on it, May 1940.

with the loss of 833 lives. An Admiralty board of enquiry concluded that Prien could not have entered by the channel he had in fact used, and the British remained uncertain how the ship had been sunk until it was announced on German radio. Prien himself was killed the following year when his U-boat was sunk.

Royal Victoria Patriotic Schools, reception centre in Wandsworth, south London, the point through which all foreign arrivals from occupied Europe had to pass, and were vetted by *MI5 to make sure they were not Axis *spies. Normal stays were for two or three nights; doubtful cases might be held for weeks. It was known officially from 1942 as the London Reception Centre.

RSHA. Created by a decree of Heinrich *Himmler on 27 September 1939 (with effect from 1 October), the Reichssicherheitshauptamt, or Reich Security Main Office, brought policing in the Third Reich under a single organizational umbrella and played a key part in the campaigns of mass murder in Nazi-occupied Europe. The establishment of the RSHA brought together within a single framework the state security formations—the Secret State Police (Gestapo) and the Criminal Police (Kripo)—and the Nazi Party security service, the Sicherheitsdienst (SD). It was a central office both of the SS and of the Reich Interior Ministry.

The RSHA was essentially the creation of Reinhard *Heydrich, who assumed the title of Chef der Sicherheitspolizei und des SD (CSSD) and who headed the organization until he died on 4 June 1942 from an attack by the Czech resistance on 27 May. After his death, the day-to-day functions of the CSSD were performed by Bruno Streckenbach, until Himmler appointed Ernst *Kaltenbrunner as Heydrich's successor in January 1943. Kaltenbrunner remained at the head of the RSHA until the end of the war.

The creation of the RSHA did not really signify a major departure. Before it was established Heydrich had already become chief of the security police, heading both the Gestapo and the Kripo, and had already been head of the party's 'Security Main Office' (Sicherheitshauptamt). Essentially the RSHA gave an institutional framework to what in effect was happening already: the centralization of German policing and the placing of parallel state and party security organizations under a single leadership. Furthermore, the security services had, in effect, been freed already from the restraints imposed by an ordered state legal system.

When the RSHA was established in the autumn of 1939, it initially comprised six departments (*Ämter*), but this was soon increased to seven (see Table). With the expansion of Nazi power across Europe, the scope for the activities of the RSHA grew tremendously, and by the beginning of 1944 it employed roughly 50,000 people (more than 31,000 in the Gestapo, more than 12,000 in the Kripo, and more than 6,000 in the SD). It also played a central role in carrying out Nazi policies of genocide, in particular through the Jewish Affairs Section (B4) of Amt IV headed by Adolf *Eichmann, and the *Einsatzgruppen* which, with the co-operation of the German armed forces, murdered hundreds of thousands of people (most of them Jews) following the invasion of the USSR in June 1941 (see BARBAROSSA).

RSHA: Structure and areas of responsibility of the Reichssicherheitshauptamt

Department	*Head*
I Personnel	Bruno Streckenbach
II Organization, Administration, and Law	Werner Best (later Hans Nockemann)
III SD Domestic Intelligence	Otto Ohlendorf
IV Political Police (Gestapo)	Heinrich Müller
V Criminal Police (Kripo)	Arthur Nebe
VI SD Foreign Intelligence	Heinz Jost (later Walter Schellenberg)
VII Ideological Research and Evaluation	Alfred Franz Six

Source: Contributor.

The RSHA had three main areas of activity: intelligence gathering at home and abroad; policing, including the suppression of the Nazis' political opponents, both within the Reich and in the occupied territories; and the extermination of the Nazis' racial victims.

The intelligence-gathering activities of the RSHA were conducted by Amter III and VI of the SD. Within Germany the SD used an extensive network of informers (see V-MAN) systematically to collect material about popular opinion and morale; this information was gathered in the SD's 'Reports from the Reich' (*Meldungen aus dem Reich*) for distribution to leading officials, until they were suspended in 1944 when it was decided that their content was too 'defeatist'. The intelligence-gathering arm of the RSHA competed with the military's counter-intelligence service, the *Abwehr, headed by Admiral Wilhelm *Canaris. In 1944, after it was discovered that a group of resistance conspirators against Hitler had gathered within the Abwehr (see SCHWARZE KAPELLE), it was incorporated into the RSHA.

The policing activities of the RSHA encompassed both the political police and the criminal police (Amter IV and V respectively). The political police—the Gestapo—were able to operate in large measure independently of the legal system. By applying an 'order for protective custody' (*Schutzhaftbefehl*) the Gestapo were able to bypass the court system and imprison people in *concentration camps for indeterminate periods. People thus imprisoned effectively had no legal redress and, during the war and especially after the invasion of the USSR, orders of protective custody were increasingly applied to people simply classified as opponents of the regime without their having been guilty of any specific crime. With the agreement of Himmler and the new, radical Nazi justice minister Dr Otto Thierack in September 1942 (see also PEOPLE'S COURT), the Gestapo was also given an increasingly free hand with so-called 'asocial elements' including alleged habitual criminals as well as members of allegedly 'inferior' racial groups.

Although the numbers employed by the Gestapo may appear large, considering that they came to operate across Europe their numbers were actually rather small. Consequently, they were dependent for success upon the active collaboration of members of the public who were prepared to denounce their neighbours, colleagues, and relatives.

Like the Gestapo, the Kripo also applied racial criteria in its work, viewing criminal behaviour as biologically inherited. Accordingly, justification was provided for the protection of society from alleged potential criminals through the use of protective custody—which usually meant confinement in a concentration camp—and, finally, the destruction of allegedly 'unworthy' lives under the *euthanasia programme.

As the German armed forces conquered much of Europe, the sphere of activity of the RSHA increased accordingly. The RSHA installed a CSSD in each occupied country under whom were a number of regional police commanders. These were responsible for combating all forms of resistance to German rule; they were unfettered by restrictions on the methods they could employ and were able to count on the co-operation of the army in carrying out their tasks. It was in policing the occupied territories that the RSHA made its most terrifying contribution to the Nazi policies of genocide. Its special detachments, the *Einsatzgruppen*, of the Security Police, had already been established for the campaign against Poland, in order to 'combat all elements hostile to the Reich and to Germans behind the fighting forces'. They were charged with, among other things, preventing espionage and arresting 'politically unreliable persons'. However, it was with the campaign against the USSR that the *Einsatzgruppen* really came into their own, when they were charged with eliminating actual and potential opponents of German rule behind the front lines (see COMMISSARS). Four such *Einsatzgruppen* followed the Wehrmacht into the USSR in 1941, and by the spring of 1942, with the co-operation of the army in whose rear operational areas they conducted their grisly business, they had succeeded in murdering half a million people.

RICHARD BESSEL

Buchheim, H., *et al.*, *Anatomy of the SS State* (London, 1968).
Gellately, R., *The Gestapo in German Society: Enforcing Racial Policy, 1933–1945* (Oxford, 1990).

Ruhr air offensive, the first of the three major bombing offensives mounted by RAF Bomber Command during 1943–4 (see also HAMBURG and BERLIN) in pursuance of the Allied POINTBLANK *Combined Bomber Offensive directive. It opened with an attack on Essen by 442 bombers on the night of 5/6 March 1943 and ended with a raid on Gelsenkirchen on the night of 9/10 July, although targets outside the Ruhr continued to be attacked during the battle. The comparatively short distance from the UK, and the use of *electronic navigation systems (OBOE and H2S radar) acted in Bomber Command's favour. Even so, the industrial haze over the region, combined with the German use of decoy targets, meant that bombing accuracy continued to suffer, although much destruction was wrought among the towns and cities and the offensive did force the Germans to move much of their vital war industry to more remote rural areas. During the last phase of the battle the German night fighters, equipped with improved radar and *electronic warfare aids, were steadily reinforced, and these became increasingly effective, accounting for more bombers than the anti-aircraft defences did. Thus the RAF's availability of heavy bombers and crews fell from 726 on 11 June to 623 on 9 July. It was growing aircraft losses which forced *Harris to end the offensive in spite of the continued glowing reports, which post-war bombing surveys revealed to be over-optimistic, on the damage being done to Germany's main industrial centre.

CHARLES MESSENGER

Aders, G., *History of the German Night Fighter Force 1917–1945*, (London, 1979).
Messenger, C., *'Bomber' Harris and the Strategic Bombing Offensive, 1939–1945* (London, 1984).

Rundstedt, Field Marshal (Karl R.) Gerd von (1875–1953), distinguished German Army group and theatre commander who was one of Hitler's most loyal generals.

Rundstedt, who came from the cream of the Prussian aristocracy, was commissioned into the infantry in June 1892 and quickly showed much promise. A graduate of the prestigious Kriegsakademie, he served on the staff on both the Eastern and Western Fronts throughout 1914–18, rising to chief of staff of an army corps and being twice recommended for Prussia's highest decoration, the Pour le Mérite. His marked ability ensured his retention in the much diminished post-war German Army and he quickly rose to lt-general by the time Hitler came to power in January 1933. While he constantly disparaged Hitler in private, in public he displayed unquestioning support for him in accordance with the traditional Prussian military code of honour, duty, and loyalty. It was Rundstedt's rigid adherence to this code, his natural modesty and his belief that officers should not become involved in politics, which made him a figurehead among his brother officers. Hitler was quick to exploit his standing and established a unique relationship with Rundstedt in order to ensure the loyalty of the officer corps. Thus Rundstedt survived the purge of March 1938 and, indeed, was promoted to general. By this time he wanted to retire, but was not allowed to do so until the successful conclusion of the Sudetenland crisis in September 1938 (see MUNICH AGREEMENT), during which he commanded the Second Army.

Rundstedt's retirement was to be shortlived. In May 1939 he was appointed to lead a small planning team for

Field Marshal von **Rundstedt** after Germany's defeat.

the *Polish campaign. This eventually became HQ Army Group South, which Rundstedt commanded with great success in September 1939. After a brief spell as C-in-C East, towards the end of that October he was given command of Army Group A, which was to take the leading role in the fall of *France the following May. Promoted field marshal in July 1940, Rundstedt was given command of the ground forces for the projected invasion of the UK (see SEALION), an operation in which he had little faith. After its postponement he was made C-in-C West, but in March 1941 was ordered to set up HQ Army Group South at Breslau for *BARBAROSSA, the invasion of the USSR. While he viewed this operation with foreboding, Rundstedt made little protest and also passed on Hitler's orders for the extermination of *commissars and others (see also EINSATZGRUPPEN) without question. At the start of the *German–Soviet war Army Group South attacked into the Ukraine and eventually took Rostov-on-Don, gateway to the Caucasus, on 21 November. Ten days later, Hitler peremptorily dismissed Rundstedt, who had recently suffered a mild heart attack, for withdrawing against orders from Rostov-on-Don in the face of determined Red Army counter-attacks. When Hitler was made aware of the facts, he quickly forgave him and sent him into retirement with a large financial reward, a gesture which embarrassed Rundstedt, who, while unable to refuse it, never personally touched the money.

In March 1942 Rundstedt was again recalled to active duty, this time to replace the ailing *Witzleben as C-in-C West. He oversaw the occupation of *Vichy France in November 1942 and later formed a close relationship with Marshal *Pétain. When *Rommel was appointed C-in-C Army Group B, nominally under Rundstedt, at the end of 1943, the two clashed over how best to defeat the expected Allied invasion (see OVERLORD), but made up their differences shortly before it took place. As the situation in Normandy grew more desperate Rundstedt and Rommel increasingly clashed with Hitler over his refusal to countenance any withdrawals. Eventually, on 2 July 1944, Rundstedt was relieved by *Kluge, but again his retirement was to be brief. He was ordered by Hitler to preside over the Court of Honour set up in the aftermath of the July 1944 bomb plot (see SCHWARZE KAPELLE), an action for which many Germans, especially those who had hoped that he would provide a lead in overthrowing Hitler, never forgave him. In early September 1944 he was reappointed C-in-C West and was given credit by both sides for his skill in holding the Allied thrusts towards Germany. The Allies saw him as the mastermind of the December 1944 *Ardennes campaign, but this was mistaken. The plans, to which Rundstedt and *Model, the army group commander concerned, strongly objected, had been drawn up by Hitler's High Command (OKW), and Rundstedt had little say in them or their execution. Eventually, having conducted a skilful withdrawal across the Rhine, Rundstedt was dismissed for a third and final time and replaced by *Kesselring as a direct result of the seizure of the *Remagen bridge by the Americans in March 1945. Captured by the Americans on 1 May 1945, he was later handed over to the British and, after much controversy, was eventually charged with *war crimes in Poland, the USSR, and the west. Only ill health saved him from being tried and he was released from captivity in May 1949.

Both *Eisenhower and *Montgomery regarded Rundstedt as the outstanding German commander of the war, and after it his reputation stood much higher among his former enemies than among his fellow countrymen. While his competence is in no doubt, old age and uncertain health increasingly affected his powers as the war progressed. Never a man to reveal his innermost thoughts, he possessed many fine personal qualities, but his blind observance of the military code in which he had been nurtured proved to be both a strength and also a major weakness, in the end fatal, as it was with so many of his fellow generals.

CHARLES MESSENGER

Messenger, C., *The Last Prussian: a Biography of Field Marshal Gerd von Rundstedt 1875–1953* (London, 1991).

Russia. Strictly speaking the term Russia refers only to the RSFSR, the largest of the sixteen republics which made up the USSR at the time of the Second World War.

By the same token, 'the Russians', whose native language is Russian, were but one of the USSR's 70 recognized nationalities.

During the Second World War, however, it was normal practice among westerners to use 'Russia' as a synonym for the USSR, and to talk of 'the Russians' in reference to all Soviet citizens. This was probably a hangover from The *First World War when the Russian Empire had been an ally of the western powers, and when all subjects of the tsar had commonly been called Russians irrespective of their national or ethnic identity. It also coincided with the demands of Stalinist ideology, which regarded the USSR as a simple continuation of the Russian Empire, and which treated the Russian nation as the 'elder brother' of all other Soviet nationalities. Although Soviet sources usually make the proper distinction between 'Soviet' and 'Russian', western practice inevitably served the official policy of restricting the free expression of the non-Russian nationalities, and of bolstering the fiction of a new Russian-based 'Soviet Man'. In this, it matched entrenched German habits, where old imperial ideas of 'Russland' frequently survived.

The resultant misunderstandings were legion.

In institutional terms, many important nuances were lost. There could be little awareness of the separate structures of the central Soviet government or of the all-Union Communist Party and those of the constituent republics. Although the Red Army changed its official name to Soviet Army in 1944, it was universally referred to in the West as the Russian Army.

In geographical terms, few outside commentators saw the difference between the 'Soviet frontier' and the 'Russian frontier'. When the German Wehrmacht crossed the Soviet frontier in June 1941 (see BARBAROSSA), almost all western comment said that it had invaded 'Russia'. In reality, it had invaded the republics of Lithuania, Belorussia, and Ukraine, that is, from the legal standpoint, the territory of the Soviet-occupied Baltic States and of Soviet-occupied Poland. The zone of German occupation in the USSR never went beyond the outer fringes of Russia proper.

In the realm of statistics, there are endless imprecisions. For example, the phrase '20 million Russian war dead' has become very widespread in western literature. It conceals the fact that, though Russians probably made up the greater part of military casualties, the majority of Soviet civilians who perished during the war were neither Russian by nationality nor victims of military action. See also BALTIC STATES, BELORUSSIA, CAUCASUS, and UKRAINE. NORMAN DAVIES

Russo-Finnish war, see FINNISH–SOVIET WAR.

Ruthenia. In its widest historical sense, Ruthenia relates to the whole of non-Russian Ruś (i.e. Belorussia and Ukraine): but in contemporary usage Ruthenia (Sub-Carpathian Ruthenia or Carpatho-Ukraine) is usually reserved for the easternmost province of inter-war Czechoslovakia. With its administrative capital at Užhorod, the province's Ukrainian peasant population eked out a poor living in a remote corner of the Carpathian mountains. Though Ukrainian in origin, Ruthenia had been an integral part of Hungary for a thousand years.

During the *First World War, émigré Ruthenian political activists in the USA led by Dr Grigory Žatković took Ruthenia out of Hungary and into Czechoslovakia. Czech promises for an elected Diet never materialized, but inclusion in Czechoslovakia undoubtedly bestowed economic and social benefits while fostering Ukrainian nationalism.

The *Munich agreement of September 1938 diminished Czechoslovakia and led to Ruthenian autonomy under the leadership of a Uniate priest, Monsignor Augustine Voloshin. But in November Ruthenia was obliged by the first *Vienna Award to cede its southern districts, including its capital, to Hungary (see Map 49). In March 1939, after Germany annexed Bohemia and Moravia, it declared itself the independent Carpatho-Ukraine, but Hungary reasserted its claim to the province, and although the invading Hungarian Army met organized Ruthenian resistance, annexation brought bloody oppression and a policy of Magyarization to Ruthenia.

The Red Army liberated Ruthenia from Hungarian rule in October 1944. Wartime discussions between the Czechoslovak *government-in-exile and Stalin had pointed towards a return of Ruthenia to Czechoslovakia. Stalin's policy abruptly shifted in the closing stages of the war and Czechoslovakia formally ceded the province to the USSR in June 1945 when it became part of Ukraine. Ruthenia's value to the Soviets was largely strategic, providing as it did a convenient land bridge to Czechoslovakia and Hungary. PAUL LATAWSKI

Rothschild, J., *East Central Europe between the Two World Wars* (Seattle, 1977).

Seton-Watson, H., *The East European Revolution* (3rd edn., New York, 1968).

Seton-Watson, R. W., *A History of the Czechs and Slovaks* (London, 1943).

Ryti, Risto (1889–1956), Finnish politician who was governor of the Bank of Finland from 1923 to 1940. He spoke out for strong resistance when the USSR invaded his country in November 1939 (see FINNISH–SOVIET WAR), and when President Kyösti Kallio (1873–1940) died in December 1940 Ryti was given an overwhelming vote to succeed him. He subsequently allied Finland with Germany, declaring war on the USSR in June 1941. Although he was re-elected in 1943, the defeat of the Finnish Army forced his resignation in August 1944 and he was succeeded by Marshal *Mannerheim. He returned to the Bank of Finland but when Germany surrendered he resigned. In 1946 he was sentenced to ten years' imprisonment as a war criminal but was released in 1949.

Ryūkyū Islands, archipelago situated off the south-west coast of Japan which has a close cultural and racial affinity with its inhabitants. Under the *San Francisco peace treaty they were administered by the USA as trust territories of the United Nations (see also SAN FRANCISCO CONFERENCE). The northernmost Amami group was returned to Japan in 1953, but the largest island, *Okinawa, was not returned until 1972.

SA (Sturmabteilungen, or Storm Detachment), early Nazi paramilitary organization founded by Hitler in 1920, and destroyed by him in June 1934. The stormtroopers, known as Brownshirts from their uniform in imitation of Mussolini's *Blackshirts, were used by Hitler as an effective instrument of street terror in his accession to political power; but from mid-1933 their numerical strength and the increasingly political ambitions of SA leaders, particularly Ernst Röhm (1887–1934), made the SA a liabilty to Hitler. See also CONCENTRATION CAMPS and SS.

sabotage, see SUBVERSIVE WARFARE.

Sachsenhausen was a Nazi *concentration camp situated 50 km. (30 mi.) north of Berlin. It was opened in 1936 and provided *forced labour for local factories. During the war skilled prisoners were employed in Operation BERNHARD making counterfeit documents and bank-notes for the *SS, and so pleased were the Germans with the results that twelve of the prisoners were awarded the War Merit Medal (see DECORATIONS). Though not a death camp (see OPERATION REINHARD), an estimated 100,000 were murdered there including Stalin's son. Kurt von Schuschnigg, the former Austrian chancellor, was one of its inmates. In March 1945 *Bernadotte and the *International Red Cross Committee managed to free Danes and Norwegians in the camp, but on 15 April the remainder were forced to start marching westwards and thousands died before they were found by the Red Army.

St Nazaire raid, mounted on this French port by the British *Combined Operations HQ, in March 1942. Its purpose was to destroy the only dry dock on the Atlantic coast big enough to accommodate the German battleship **Tirpitz*, which, it was feared, Hitler might use to attack Allied *convoys.

On the night of 27/28 March 1942, *Campbeltown*, a US destroyer acquired under the *destroyers-for-bases agreement, bluffed her way past the defences and rammed the dock's outer caisson, while 268 commandos landed to destroy essential machinery. Many of those who had landed had to be abandoned, but the next day five tons of explosives detonated in the destroyer's bows, blowing up the caisson, many Germans who had gone aboard to look around, and two Commando officers who knew the ship was about to blow up, but did not say so.

In all, 83 *decorations were awarded to the participants, who lost 144 killed and more than 200 captured.

St Pierre and Miquelon, France's oldest and smallest colony, situated off the Newfoundland coast, which was occupied by de *Gaulle's Free French forces on 24 December 1941.

In early 1941 the USA concluded an agreement with Admiral *Robert, the *Vichy French high commissioner for the French West Indies whose fief included the islands, for the maintenance of the status quo of all French possessions in the *Western Hemisphere. However, a powerful wireless station on the islands began to cause the UK and Canada concern, and discussions started on how best to control its transmissions. The USA vetoed any Free French interference and suggested Canada take action. But Canada, because of its *French-Canadian population, had no wish to offend Vichy France. While all parties hesitated, de Gaulle, despite agreeing to hold his hand, ordered the islands occupied by Vice-Admiral *Muselier's naval forces, a decision overwhelmingly supported by a local plebiscite. The British were delighted, the Canadians relieved, but the US secretary of state, Cordell *Hull, was furious as he regarded it as a breach of the Havana Act (see HAVANA CONFERENCE). He threatened to use force to oust 'the so-called Free French', and though a compromise was eventually reached, whereby the islands were demilitarized and declared neutral, he barred the Free French from signing the *United Nations Declaration then being drawn up.

Anglin, D., *The St Pierre and Miquelon Affair of 1941* (Toronto, 1966).

Saipan, capture of. One of the most critical battles of the *Pacific war, the seizure of this Pacific island by US forces caused the fall of the Japanese prime minister, General *Tōjō. Its capture brought Japan within range of US B29 bombers (see STRATEGIC AIR OFFENSIVE, 3).

One of the Mariana Islands and a Japanese mandate, Saipan was a vital Japanese administrative base. At 22 km. (14 mi.) long it was large enough to be defended in depth and high ground allowed the defenders to bombard the western landing beaches. These were protected by reefs, a way through which had to be blasted by underwater demolition teams (see FROGMEN) before the 2nd and 4th US Marine Divisions of Lt-General Holland Smith's 77,000-strong 5th Amphibious Corps landed on 15 June 1944. Because of an inadequate pre-landing bombardment, the 32,000 troops of Lt-General Saito Yoshitsugu's Thirty-First Army caused 4,000 marine casualties in the first 48 hours, even though Saito had been expecting the landings elsewhere. He expected, too, to hold the marines in their beachhead, and that they and their transports would be destroyed by the approaching Japanese Mobile Fleet. When neither happened—the Mobile Fleet was defeated in the *Philippine Sea battle—he could only withdraw to the island's centre and fight a delaying action. But his men fought so fiercely that the three days allotted to the island's capture became three weeks.

A crucial objective in the south, Aslito airfield, was overrun on 18 June, but when the marines swung northwards Saito's defensive line, which included the rugged terrain around Mount Tapotchau, proved difficult to penetrate. In the centre the newly committed 27th Infantry Division was forced to attack his most heavily defended area, which included a densely wooded escarpment soon known as Purple Heart Ridge (see DECORATIONS), and when it failed to make any progress the division's commander was relieved.

Helped by accurate naval fire, which was able to find Japanese defensive positions among the valleys, the advance was soon resumed, but the Japanese continued to fight tenaciously and on the night of 6/7 July they launched the war's largest *banzai charge. By some accounts more than 4,300 Japanese bodies were buried afterwards, and though this defeat heralded the end of all organized resistance small groups continued to hold out for a long time. On 9 July, the day the fighting officially ended, many Japanese soldiers, and civilians faithful to the Japanese cause, jumped from Marpi Point.

Sakhalin, island 900 km. (560 mi.) long situated north of Japan, of which the southern half was occupied by Japan and the northern half by the USSR. A secret clause agreed at the Yalta conference in February 1945 (see ARGONAUT) permitted the USSR to occupy the whole island in August 1945 when the Red Army also invaded Manchukuo (see JAPANESE–SOVIET CAMPAIGNS). Under the *San Francisco peace treaty Japan renounced any claim to it.

Salazar, António de Oliveira (1889–1970), Portuguese politician and professor of economics who became prime minister and virtual dictator of his country from 1932 until he suffered a stroke in 1968. He was inclined towards *fascism but detested the Nazis, and impressed one British diplomat as an ascetic who 'lived the plainest of lives, indifferent and indeed hostile to any ostentation, luxury or personal gain'. Though Portugal is the UK's oldest ally, Salazar maintained a policy of strict neutrality until October 1943 when he allowed the Allies an air base on the Azores. See also PORTUGAL.

Salerno landings. The principal opening gambit of the Allied *Italian campaign, and an important move in the battle for the *Mediterranean, this *amphibious warfare operation was mounted on 9 September 1943 with Naples, 48 km. (30 mi.) to the north-west, as its immediate objective (see Map 93).

The landings, in the Gulf of Salerno, were commanded by the Fifth US Army's Lt-General Mark *Clark. They were undertaken by the four divisions of 6th US Corps, commanded by Maj-General Ernest Dawley, and the British Eighth Army's 10th Corps, commanded by Lt-General *McCreery, which comprised two infantry and one armoured division. They started a few hours after *Eisenhower's announcement of an *armistice with Italy and were mounted despite a critical shortage of *landing craft and with the knowledge, gleaned from *ULTRA intelligence, that total surprise would be impossible.

The landing force and its covering warships from *Force H totalled 627 ships. An additional naval force (Force V), of one fleet carrier and four escort carriers, gave extra air cover over the landing beaches which were at the extreme range of Allied air bases in Sicily.

McCreery's Corps landed around Salerno: Rangers (see USA, 5(f)) and commandos on the left, 46th and 56th Divisions to the right, while Dawley landed further south in the Bay to protect McCreery's flank. Initially, the British met light opposition from Lt-General Hans Hube's 14th Panzer Corps which was still in the process of taking over Italian defences, but one US unit became stalled on the beach, and the sole panzer division in the area fought with great skill to prevent the Allies advancing inland. Montecorvino airfield was captured immediately, but when General Heinrich von Vietinghoff (1887–1952), commanding Tenth Army in southern Italy, brought forward 76th Panzer Corps from Calabria and a Panzergrenadier division from Rome, the airfield soon came under heavy fire and could not be used. This hampered Allied air cover and on 11 September two cruisers were damaged by radio-controlled bombs (see GUIDED WEAPONS), as was the battleship *Warspite* later. Airstrips were soon built elsewhere, though they too were under constant attack.

In the week following the landings the Allies were unable to break out of their shallow beachhead. They captured both Salerno and Vietri, but could not push the Germans sufficiently far from either to make use of them as supply ports. The German attacks, piecemeal at first, became more co-ordinated, and their build-up was quicker than Clark's. On 12 September 1943, the day the German garrison on the nearby island of Capri surrendered without firing a shot, Vietinghoff launched a determined counter-offensive and the situation became so desperate that neither the British nor the Americans had any reserves left. Every man who could carry a rifle was fighting, and plans were drawn up for evacuating the beachhead. Reinforcement was extremely difficult without interrupting Allied *logistics, but at the height of the battle two battalions of 82nd US Airborne Division were dropped in to the beachhead; the naval bombardment force was reinforced by two British battleships; and 1,500 troops were transported by three cruisers from Tripoli in Libya to reinforce 10th Corps. These emergency measures, plus massive extra air support supplied by *Tedder's entire Mediterranean strategic air force, which was switched to a tactical role, turned the tide. The offensive petered out and the Germans, partly outfought but partly through a change of tactics, began slowly withdrawing on 16 September to a new position north of Naples. The *Naples rising followed on 27 September 1943. Also on 16 September, American patrols in the southern part of the bridgehead made contact with the balance of *Montgomery's Eighth Army, advancing north from where it had landed at *Reggio di Calabria, and the first Allied unit entered Naples on 1 October.

Salò Republic, Mussolini's Italian Social Republic which he set up in northern Italy on 15 September 1943. See ITALY, 3(b).

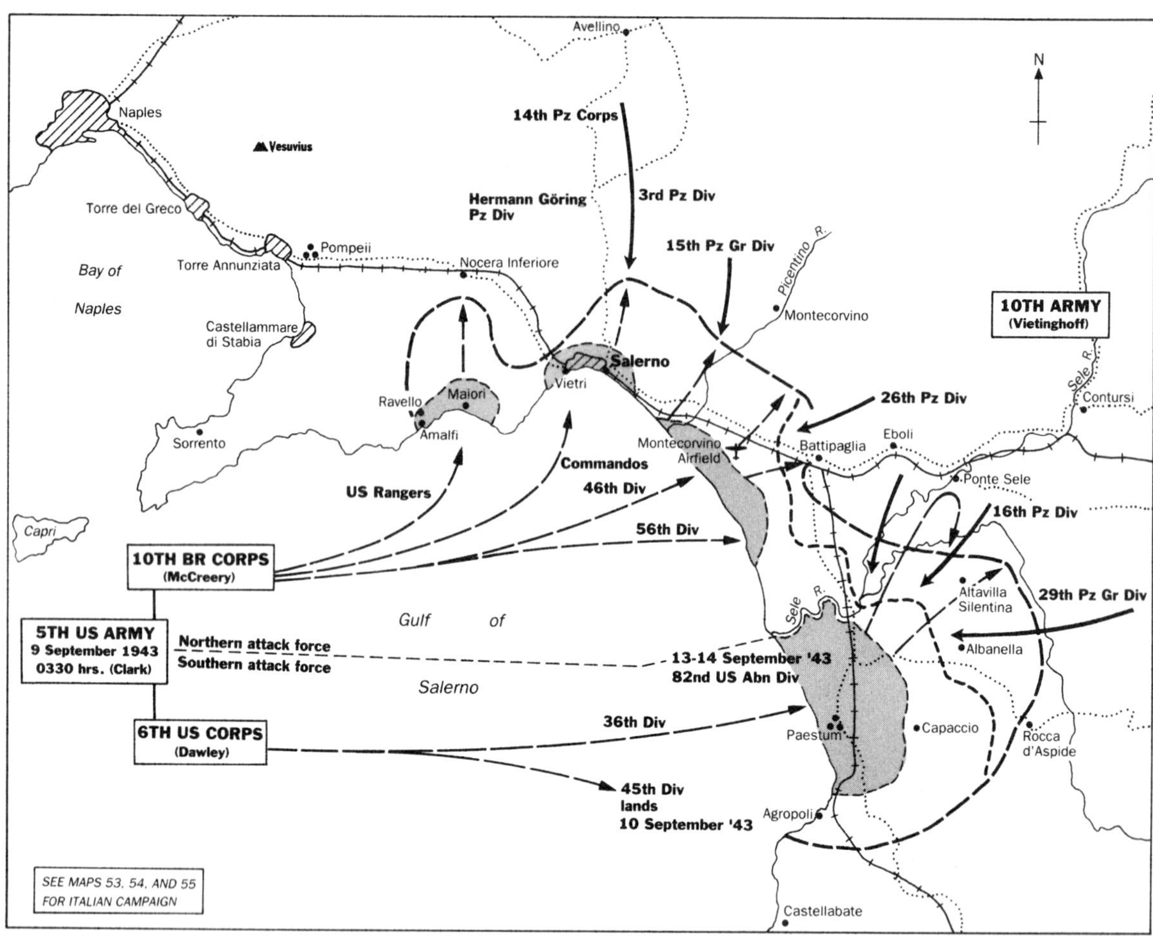

93. **Salerno landings**, 9 September 1943

Samoa, group of Pacific islands divided into eastern, or American, Samoa, which was administered by the US navy department; and western Samoa, a New Zealand mandate. There was a US naval base on the former but neither was involved in the war.

San Francisco conference, the inaugural meeting of the United Nations more formally known as the United Nations Conference on International Organization. It was held in this Californian city from 25 April to 26 June 1945 and was attended by delegates from 50 Allied nations, 45 of which had signed the *United Nations Declaration of January 1942. However, the seat reserved for Poland remained vacant as the USA disagreed with the USSR's claim that the Moscow-backed Polish government (see LUBLIN COMMITTEE) was independent. A United Nations Security Charter based on the draft proposals of the *Dumbarton Oaks conference was drawn up and signed after three main areas of disagreement between the USA and USSR were settled. These were the future of dependent populations (see REFUGEES); regional collective security; and the use of the veto in the Security Council which comprised five permanent members (China, France, UK, USA, and USSR) and six temporary ones. The conference also created a Trusteeship Council for administering the colonies and mandates of the Axis powers, and other non-self-governing territories.

San Francisco peace treaty, signed between Japan and 48 Allied nations at a conference in September 1951, but in the absence of China which was not invited. It gave Japan back its independence, ended its occupation and allowed those imprisoned by the *Far East War Crimes Trials to be released. In return Japan abandoned its claims to Korea, Formosa, the Pescadores, the Kuriles, South Sakhalin and the Spratly and Paracel islands. The Ryūkyū and Bonin chains were to be controlled by the USA under a United Nations trusteeship. Japan also renounced any rights or interests in China and agreed to pay reparations to certain countries. The USSR, Poland, and Czechoslovakia refused to sign and though invited, India, Burma, and Yugoslavia did not attend.

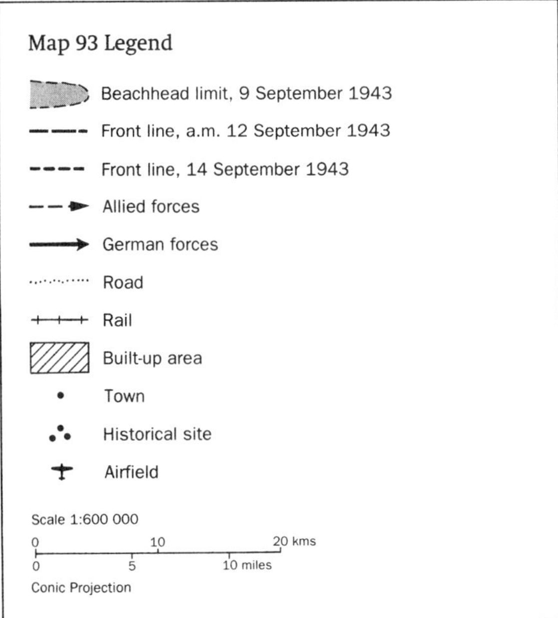

Sansom, Odette (b.1912), French-born member of *FANY who joined *SOE and was arrested in France in April 1943. She pretended to be the wife of Peter Churchill, whose assistant she was, and this prevented her execution as the commandant of *Ravensbrück, where she was eventually sent, thought she was related to the British prime minister. She was awarded the George Cross (see DECORATIONS).

Tickell, J., *Odette* (London, 1949)

Santa Cruz Island, battle of, fought between US and Japanese carrier forces on 26 October 1942 off *Guadalcanal during the *Pacific war. Though the Japanese lost 100 aircraft, against 74 lost by the Americans, it was a tactical victory for them as they sank the US carrier *Hornet*.

sappers, see ENGINEERS.

Sarawak, see BRITISH NORTH BORNEO.

Sardinia, Italian possession, the second largest island in the Mediterranean, which was an important staging-post for convoys supplying Axis forces during the *North African campaign. On 8 September 1943, the day Italy surrendered to the Allies, all German units on the island began moving to nearby Corsica, and on 14 September US paratroopers landed on Sardinia unopposed. It was later used by aircraft of co-belligerent Italy as a base from which to attack German shipping.

SAS, see SPECIAL AIR SERVICE.

Sauckel, Fritz (1894–1946), Nazi Party member from 1923 who was appointed the *Gauleiter of Thuringia in 1927, its minister president in 1932, and then its governor. In March 1942 Hitler appointed him plenipotentiary for the mobilization of labour which made him responsible for Germany's entire workforce including foreigners and prisoners-of-war (see FORCED LABOUR). During the three years in which he worked to build up the workforce Sauckel acquired 5.3 million workers from occupied countries and he estimated in 1944 that only 200,000 of these were volunteers. By the end of 1944, 20% of all workers in Germany were foreigners. His demands on the *Vichy French government to provide sufficient conscripts drove many of those eligible to hide and fight (see MAQUIS). At the *Nuremberg trials he was sentenced to death and hanged.

Smelser, R., and Zitelmann, R. (eds.), *The Nazi Elite* (London, 1993).

Saudi Arabia remained neutral for most of the war under its absolute ruler, Ibn Saud, but revealed pro-Allied leanings by refusing to aid *Rashid Ali's revolt in Iraq, rejecting Axis requests for oil concessions, and allowing a US air base at Dhahran. Commercial oil production, started in 1938, was curtailed during the war with Saudi Arabia receiving *Lend-Lease supplies to protect US oil concessions there. It eventually declared war on Germany and Japan in March 1945.

Savo Island, battle of, encounter during the *Pacific war between an Allied naval force screening US marine landings at the start of the *Guadalcanal campaign, and seven Japanese cruisers commanded by Vice-Admiral Mikawa Gunichi. Immediately the Japanese were alerted to the landings, which started on 7 August 1942, Mikawa was dispatched from *Rabaul, and before dawn on 9 August he surprised the Allied screen off Savo. Without loss to his force, Mikawa sank one Australian and three US cruisers, and badly damaged another US cruiser; the waters in which these ships went down were thereafter known as Iron Bottom Sound. But fearing the air attacks that daylight might bring, Mikawa withdrew without attacking the US landing and supply transports lying helpless in Lunga Bay. In the action 1,270 Allied seamen lost their lives and 709 were wounded.

Saw, U (1900–48), Burma's Myochit (Patriotic Party) leader who was prime minister of Burma from 1940 to 1942. In December 1941 he went to London to negotiate Burma's post-war independence, but failed. While on his way home, *MAGIC intelligence revealed a traitorous conversation he had had with a Japanese diplomat in Lisbon, and he was arrested and interned on the Seychelles. He returned to politics after the war and was executed for the assassination of *Aung San. U is a respectful term of address.

Schacht, Hjalmar (1877–1970), apolitical financial architect of the Third Reich who served as president of the Reichsbank 1923–30 and 1933–9, plenipotentiary for war economy 1935–7, minister of economic affairs from August 1934 to November 1937, and finally minister without portfolio until January 1943. He came to oppose Hitler's policy of increased rearmament, which he considered inflationary. Initially his international reputation gave him immunity domestically but he eventually resigned his ministerial positions in 1937 after making 'it clear to the Four-year Plan commissioner and Hitler himself that he regarded their foreign-currency, manufacturing, and financial policy "as incorrect"' (W. Deist, *et al.*, *Germany and the Second World War*, Vol. 1, Oxford, 1990, p. 314). *Göring, with whom he had frequently clashed over economic matters, took his place. He joined the resistance against Hitler and was arrested after the failure of the July 1944 bomb plot (see SCHWARZE KAPELLE). After spending the rest of the war in *concentration camps, he was acquitted at the *Nuremberg trials. See also WORLD TRADE AND WORLD ECONOMY.

Scharnhorst, 31,000-ton German battle-cruiser with a main armament of nine 28 cm. (11 in.) guns. With another battle-cruiser, *Gneisenau*, she sank the British *armed merchant cruiser *Rawalpindi* in the North Sea in November 1939 and the British carrier *Glorious* and her two escorting destroyers at the end of the *Norwegian campaign in June 1940.

Early in 1941 she broke out into the Atlantic with *Gneisenau* and together they sank 22 merchantmen before entering Brest in March. They were subsequently damaged by bombing raids and remained there until the following February when, in a daring operation, they returned to Germany via the English Channel (see CERBERUS).

Scharnhorst was badly damaged by mines during the operation, but in March 1943 she moved to Norway and on Christmas Day that year sailed to attack the *Arctic convoy JW55B off North Cape. Aided by *ULTRA, intelligence and other signals the C-in-C of the British Home Fleet, Admiral *Fraser, who was aboard the battleship *Duke of York*, ordered 10th Cruiser Squadron to place itself between the battle-cruiser and the convoy. In what was later called the battle of North Cape, *Scharnhorst* twice tried to attack the convoy but each time was driven off by the cruisers. Thwarted, she turned for home but was tracked by *radar and then cut off by Fraser and his heavy squadron. At 1722 on 26 December *Scharnhorst* signalled that she was surrounded. Shells and torpedoes poured into her and at 1745 she sank with the loss of all but 36 of her crew of more than 2,000. See also WARSHIPS and SEA POWER.

Scheldt Estuary, battle for, 85-day campaign, fought from September to November 1944, to open this vital Allied supply route up to the Belgian port of Antwerp.

Having swept across northern France during the last lap of the *Normandy campaign, tanks of *Montgomery's Twenty-First Army Group reached Antwerp on 4 September 1944. The Germans were so totally taken by surprise that they were prevented by local resistance groups from destroying the port's extensive dock installations and lock system. Captured intact these docks, and access to them via the River Scheldt, became the focal point for one of the critical battles of the European war. For without Antwerp to supply them (see LOGISTICS), it would have been all but impossible for *Eisenhower's armies to start, much less finish, the battle for *Germany.

The capture of Antwerp left Lt-General Gustav-Adolph von Zangen's Fifteenth Army isolated on the west bank of the Scheldt. There was therefore little to oppose a thrust by *Dempsey's Second Army into the 112 km. (70 mi.) gap that yawned between von Zangen and the German forces defending the *West Wall. But Montgomery, concentrating on obtaining a bridgehead on the further side of the Rhine (see MARKET-GARDEN), gave insufficient attention, and resources, to the problem of opening the Scheldt. Hitler's intention to stand at its banks was immediately revealed by *ULTRA intelligence. But this intelligence was ignored, its importance perhaps obscured by the euphoric feeling that total victory was not far off. It was 'the first time that plain Ultra evidence on a matter of major importance had been disregarded' (R. Bennett, *Ultra in the West*, London, 1979, p. 143); and so bitter was the first draft of the post-war official US military history about Montgomery's failure to react that Eisenhower felt obliged to suppress it.

The failure of MARKET-GARDEN crushed any hope of opening Rotterdam or Amsterdam as alternative supply ports. If Montgomery's forces had instead been used to cut the South Beveland isthmus, just 32 km. (20 mi.) north of Antwerp, they could have prevented the escape of the Fifteenth Army which was being ferried from Breskens to Flushing. *Crerar's First Canadian Army, which Montgomery thought would stop this exodus, was restricted by the diversion of supplies to those taking part in MARKET-GARDEN and by Montgomery's clear directive to clear the Channel ports first. Two of Crerar's armoured divisions did try to stop it but both failed to reach Breskens in time. On 20 September 1944, a Polish infantry brigade managed to reach Terneuzen, another port being used by the Germans, but an attack by it towards Breskens was soon halted. Bomber Command, too, failed to make much impact on the German evacuation, an operation of brilliant improvisation, for it was primarily committed to supporting Crerar's attacks on the Channel ports. However, from 17 September, it did start attacking the network of gun batteries and other defences sited on Walcheren Island which dominated the mouth of the Scheldt.

On 15 September Crerar's 1st Corps was committed to guarding the flank of the Second British Army during

Allied commandos were employed to take Walcheren Island during the battle for the **Scheldt Estuary** in November 1944. This photograph of a German HQ on fire was taken on the coastal dunes by a Norwegian photographer who landed with Norwegian commandos at Westkapelle.

MARKET-GARDEN, so responsibility for clearing the banks of the Scheldt devolved on his 2nd Corps. His plans included a landing on Walcheren, once its dykes had been breached by Bomber Command and most of the inland German defences flooded or isolated, and the seizure of the area around Roosendaal and Bergen op Zoom before moving into South Beveland. On 26 September he returned to England for medical treatment and his place was taken by the commander of his 2nd Corps, Lt-General *Simonds.

In early October the 2nd Canadian Division started moving north from Antwerp towards the South Beveland isthmus. At the same time an operation (SWITCHBACK) was launched to eliminate the defensive area around Breskens, known to the Germans as Scheldt Fortress South and to the Allies as the *Breskens pocket. By 14 October this had been much reduced, but the supply situation was now so desperate that Montgomery was coming under increasing criticism for his failure to solve it. He finally issued an unequivocal directive on 16 October that enabled Simonds to concentrate the entire First Army on clearing both banks of the Scheldt. The 2nd Canadian Division launched an assault (VITALITY) along the isthmus to clear South Beveland and the eastern bank. Aided by two brigades from 52nd (Lowland) Division—which crossed the Scheldt on 26 October and landed on the coast—South Beveland was overrun by the end of the month. However, to reach Walcheren from the mainland a formidable obstacle, a 1,100 m. (1,200 yd.) causeway, dead straight and without any cover, had to be stormed. The Canadians attacked along it three times but were repulsed each time. They were eventually relieved by the two brigades of 52nd (Lowland) Division, units of which, in a daring operation, found a route across the Sloe channel on to the island. Meanwhile, the 3rd Canadian Division was steadily reducing the Breskens pocket. Breskens itself was taken on 21 October 1944, Knocke was captured on 2 November, and on 3 November patrols were reporting that Zeebrugge was clear. As this operation neared completion two amphibious assaults were launched against Walcheren by a British commando brigade with supporting armour: one at Westkapelle (INFATUATE I) on the westward tip of the island, the other at Flushing (INFATUATE II).

Soon after dawn on 1 November the commandos used American *amphibians and *weasels to disembark through a breach in the dyke at Westkapelle. The defences facing them were formidable, for the heavy naval coastal batteries which dominated the estuary were protected by pillboxes, strong-points, concealed *flame-throwers, and anti-personnel mines. To help neutralize these defences, and in particular the three naval batteries in heavy concrete emplacements that commanded the estuary around Westkapelle, there was a preliminary bombardment by warships. But bad weather aborted the air bombardment and though rocket-firing aircraft were employed the 27 converted landing craft, specially equipped to pour concentrated fire on the beaches, were badly mauled. All but seven were sunk or damaged and there were 300 casualties, but they drew the fire of the

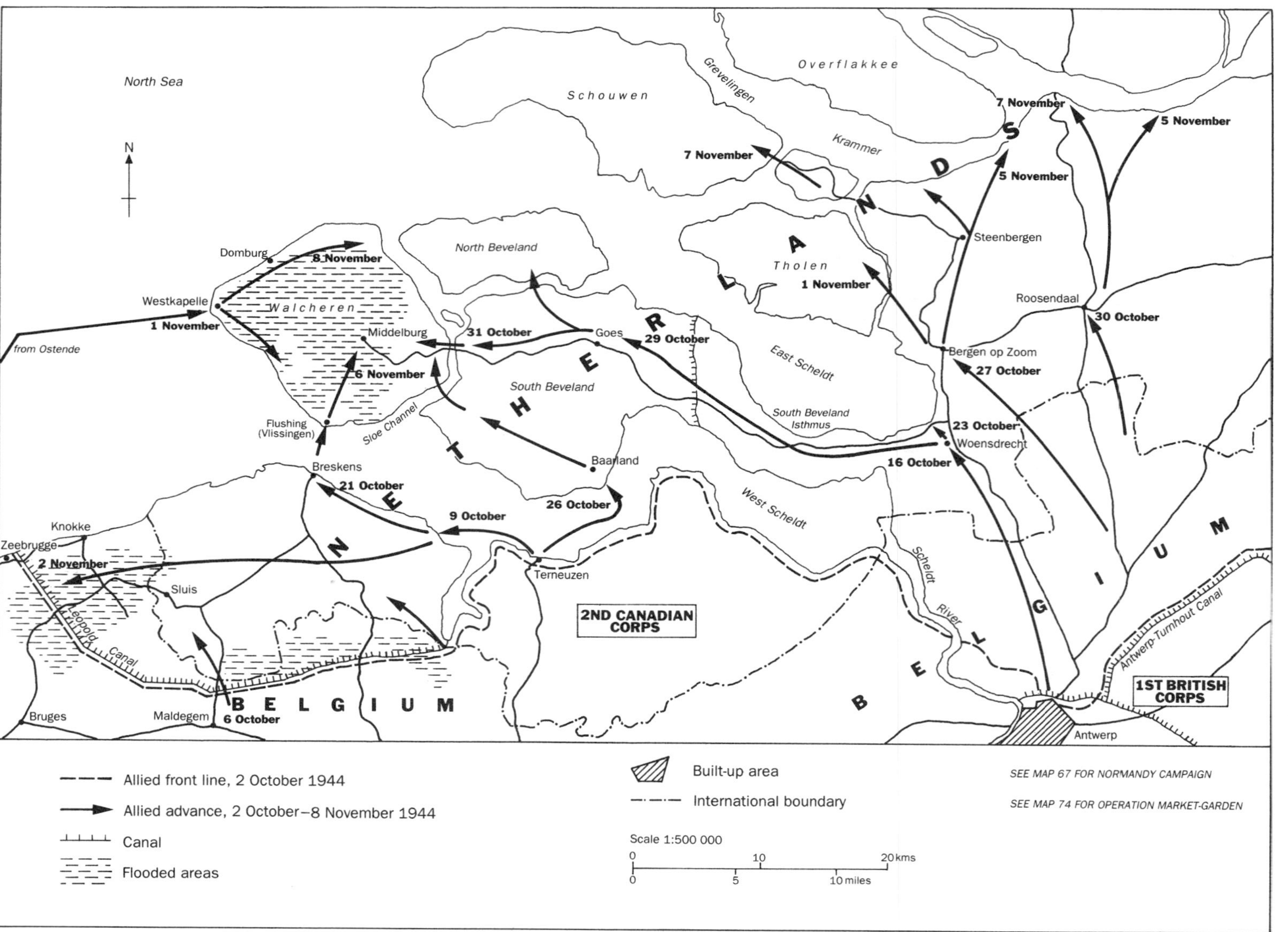

94. **Scheldt Estuary battle**, October–November 1944

batteries and the commandos landed comparatively unscathed.

At Flushing the commandos began landing before dawn after a heavy artillery bombardment on the port. They were closely followed by 155th Brigade of 52nd (Lowland) Division and two days of street fighting followed before the Germans there capitulated. Units of 155th Brigade then crossed the floods in amphibians to reach the island's capital, Middleburg, and the German commander surrendered there on 5 November. By then the commandos at Westkapelle had moved in both directions along the dyke and had captured all the batteries between Domburg and Flushing, enabling minesweeping operations in the River Scheldt to begin. There was residual resistance in the north of the island but by 8 November 1944 the last defenders had surrendered.

The Scheldt was declared free of mines on 26 November and two days later the first supply convoy arrived at the docks. Opening Antwerp brought about a complete revolution in the Allies' supply situation. Hitler realized full well how vital it was to them. Large numbers of the *V-weapons were directed at the city (more than at London); *E-boats and *midget submarines were deployed to interfere with the convoys; and it was the ultimate German objective when they launched their *Ardennes campaign. See also AMPHIBIOUS WARFARE.

Moulton, J., *Battle for Antwerp* (Shepperton, 1978).
Thompson, R., *The 85 Days* (London, 1957).
Whitaker, W. and S., *Battle of the Scheldt* (London, 1985; published in Canada in 1984 as *Tug of War*).

Schellenberg, Walter (1910–52), *SS and police Brigadeführer (brigadier) who ran the Foreign Intelligence Service (Amt VI) of the Reichssicherheitshauptamt or *RSHA.

In November 1939 Schellenberg, who was then head of the RSHA's counter-espionage section (Amt IVe), organized the *Venlo incident which brought him promotion to Standartenführer (colonel). The following July he was dispatched by *Ribbentrop to Spain to organize the kidnapping of the Duke and Duchess of *Windsor who had escaped from France and were about to embark at Lisbon for the Bahamas. But word got back to the UK and Schellenberg's plot failed—*Willi will nicht* ('Willi won't play') he wrote in his diary when the royal couple sailed as planned.

In late 1941 Schellenberg moved to the RSHA's Foreign Intelligence Service (Amt VI) as its *de facto* head, a position in which he was confirmed in February 1943, and was a prime mover in uncovering the European-wide Soviet espionage network, the *Rote Kapelle. When Germany surrendered in May 1945 he was in Sweden trying to negotiate peace terms through Count *Bernadotte. He was extradited and became a witness at the *Nuremberg trials before being sentenced to six years' imprisonment by a US military tribunal in January 1948. He was released in 1951.

Bloch, M., *Operation Willi: The Plot to Kidnap the Duke of Windsor, July 1940* (London, 1984).
Schellenberg, W., *Memoirs* (London, 1956).

Schindler, Oskar (1908–74), German industrialist and Nazi Party member who, under cover of running an enamelware factory in Cracow, Poland, and later a munitions factory in Czechoslovakia, saved the lives of 1,300 Jews from nearby *concentration camps, including *Auschwitz. His story became well known in 1982 when Thomas Keneally's novel *Schindler's Ark* (*Schindler's List* in the USA), based on his exploits, was published. A film version of Keneally's book appeared in 1993.

Schnorchel (German slang for nose), a combined air-intake and diesel gas-outlet that enabled submarines to remain submerged for indefinite periods. The Americans abbreviated it to 'snorkel', the British to 'snork'. It was a pre-war Dutch device which had been offered to, and rejected by, the Admiralty in 1940. Dutch submarines fitted with it were captured by the Germans, but the German Navy was slow to develop it, and it was not operational until early 1944, too late to affect the outcome in the battle of the *Atlantic. It was, nevertheless, a dangerous innovation as it was almost impossible to detect by *radar. See also SUBMARINES.

Schörner, Field Marshal Ferdinand (1892–1973), German Army officer who won Prussia's highest decoration for bravery, the Pour le Mérite, during the *First World War, and was the last German general to be promoted field marshal.

Only *Model and *Keitel among the German generals rivalled Schörner as a devotee of Hitler. From 1940 to 1942 he commanded 6th Mountain Division which fought in the *Balkan campaign and then on *Crete. Promoted maj-general in January 1942, he commanded the German Mountain Corps which stopped the Soviet offensive against Kirkenes in Norway during the *German–Soviet war. He then commanded a panzer corps on the Eastern Front and in March 1944 was promoted general and given command of *Kleist's Army Group A with the title C-in-C Army Group South Ukraine. From July 1944 he was C-in-C Army Group North, but in January 1945 moved back to commanding Army Group A which became Army Group Centre the same month. On 5 April 1945 he was promoted field marshal and in his will Hitler named him his successor as C-in-C of the German Army. But in May Schörner ordered what remained of his Army Group, now in Czechoslovakia, to escape westwards while he flew to take command of the supposed *National Redoubt. After the war he was tried in the USSR for *war crimes and sentenced to 25 years' imprisonment, but was released after nine years.

Schuh-mine, see MINE WARFARE, 1.

Schulte, Eduard (1891–1966), anti-Nazi chief executive of Giesche, which was one of Germany's leading mining firms. As such he had detailed knowledge of his country's position regarding *raw and synthetic materials. On his frequent visits to Switzerland he passed on high-level intelligence to several Allied agents, including Allen *Dulles, and to the Swiss authorities. In July 1942 he was the first person to inform the Allies that Hitler had ordered, as a matter of policy, the extermination of European Jewry (see FINAL SOLUTION). In December 1943, on the advice of Hans Gisevius (1904–74), who worked for the *Abwehr in Switzerland, he took refuge in Switzerland for the remainder of the war to avoid arrest. He wanted his name kept secret, which it was until 1983.

Laqueur, W., and Breitman, R., *Breaking the Silence* (London, 1986).

Schwalbe (swallow), name of the fighter version of the German jet aircraft, the Messerschmitt 262. See FIGHTERS.

Schwarze Kapelle (Black Orchestra), *Gestapo name for the informal group of aristocrats, senior officers, and diplomats in Germany who opposed Hitler and talked about bringing him down, but were unable to do so.

*Himmler and *Heydrich between them had organized a system of terror and espionage so effective that even within this group there were tell-tales. Moreover, none of the group had had any clandestine training; they tended to keep diaries, in which they recorded conversations, wrote down names and addresses they would have done far better to memorize, made appointments by telephone in clear, and committed other elementary indiscretions against personal security.

The figurehead of the group was General *Beck, chief of the general staff (CGS) from 1935 till he resigned in August 1938 in protest against Hitler's plans to overawe Czechoslovakia; no one resigned with him, as he had hoped they would. He was to have been head of state after Hitler's overthrow. A regular Prussian officer with a keen moral sense, he detested Nazi methods of violence and trickery but did not understand how to combat them. Most of his companions were in the same boat.

Their diplomatic adviser, Ulrich von Hassell (1881–1944), married to the daughter of Tirpitz the founder of the imperial German Navy, was German ambassador in Rome 1932–8. He was a diplomat of the old school, and favoured Germany's retention of Austria and of the *Polish corridor when peace terms were discussed, never realizing how wholly unacceptable such terms would be to the Allies.

All of them were devout Christians. Carl Goerdeler (1884–1945), mayor of Leipzig 1930–7, resigned his post when a bust of the composer Felix Mendelssohn was removed by the Nazis from his town hall. He was even more active than von Hassell in travelling round Germany and Europe, trying to organize opposition to Nazism, though he shared von Hassell's views about what post-war frontiers would be acceptable. Goerdeler was the putative new regime's probable chancellor.

Dietrich *Bonhoeffer, the theologian, also took a leading part in conversations and planning, and travelled to Stockholm in 1942 with a set of peace terms, which he tried to submit to the British through Bishop George *Bell: they were turned down. Indeed the British foreign office, like *MI6, having burned their fingers so badly at *Venlo in 1939, were hostile to every approach made from Germany, believing all of them to be Gestapo fronts.

More serious help seemed to be available from *Halder, Beck's successor as CGS, who pronounced himself ready to lead a coup against Hitler in the autumn of 1938, from Admiral *Canaris, the head of the *Abwehr, and from Canaris's deputy Hans *Oster, who was given the task of finding a group of young officers who would storm Hitler's chancellery. Nothing came of these arrangements because of the *Munich agreement; and Halder went on to win Hitler's principal victories for him.

Oster remained available to help what was left of the conspiracy; which could do nothing in 1940–2, the years when the Nazi tide was rising high. As it rose so those plotting Hitler's overthrow became convinced that he would have to be assassinated, not just deposed. One of the most active conspirators in the attempt was Maj-General Henning von Tresckow, chief of operations at the HQ of *Kluge's Army Group Centre. His first attempt, known as the *Smolensk Attentat, took place in March 1943. On another occasion a bomb was placed in the pocket of a new style of officers' greatcoat, which Hitler was to inspect; at the very last moment, the Führer changed his programme, and the would-be hero wearing the coat just had time to retire to a men's room and remove the fuze from his bomb before it went off. Tresckow made several other attempts to kill Hitler and after the abortive July 1944 bomb plot (see below) he committed suicide.

With the *Office of Strategic Services, once it had been formed, Beck and Goerdeler communicated through the German vice-consul in Zurich, Hans Bernd Gisevius (1904–74), who carried messages to *Dulles in Berne. Nothing more than polite talk resulted.

A group centred on Helmut von Moltke (1907–45), great-grand-nephew of the hero of the Franco-Prussian war of 1870, was called the Kreisau circle after his estate in Silesia where it met. Its members sympathized with the conspirators, though most of them—like Moltke himself—did not want actually to get involved in assassinations or *coups d'état*. They combined nobility of thought with practical incapacity; they did not spot the Gestapo informer planted on them. In January 1944 Moltke was arrested and was hanged the following year.

Ernst von Weizsacker (1882–1950), permanent head of the German foreign office from 1938 to 1943, when he moved to be minister in the *Vatican, had (it turned out afterwards) anti-Nazi sympathies, but was not directly involved with the conspirators. However, he did encourage two junior diplomats, the Kordt brothers, Erich and Theo, who had approached the British foreign office in the summer of 1938, trying to get them interested in the plot; they were received with stony indifference.

Another diplomat, Adam von Trott zu Solz (1909–44), a descendant on his mother's side of the first chief justice of the USA, had been a Rhodes scholar at Balliol College, Oxford, in the early 1930s and had many English friends; he also belonged to the Kreisau circle. He was so well placed socially that he was able to meet both *Chamberlain and *Halifax in the summer of 1939, and to try to draw them into negotiations about the future of eastern Europe, attempts that were frustrated by the *Nazi–Soviet Pact. With Weizsacker's backing, he continued to travel in and out of Germany a good deal during the war, but was viewed with suspicion by the British, who suspected him of being an undercover Nazi agent.

In the summer of 1944 the conspirators at last found a competent saboteur to do their work for them: Count Claus Schenk von Stauffenberg (1907–44), a great-grandson of Count Gneisenau, a devout Roman Catholic, an officer in a cavalry regiment in peacetime and a distinguished staff officer in war. He was revolted by what he saw of *SS and Wehrmacht brutality on the Eastern Front. Serving in Tunisia during the *North African campaign, he was severely wounded in April 1943, losing his right hand, part of his left hand, and the sight of his left eye.

While he recovered from his wounds, he devised a plan called 'Valkyrie', which was to set up a military government in Berlin the moment that Hitler was assassinated, neutralize the Gestapo and SS, and sue for peace. Having met Beck and the other principal leaders of the conspiracy, he determined to commit the assassination himself. He was the better placed to do this, because his wounds would make him less likely than usual to be searched on approaching Hitler's presence; and he had a staff post, as chief of staff of the Replacement Army, which gave him frequent access to Hitler's headquarters at Rastenburg in east Prussia.

There, at the fourth attempt, on 20 July 1944 he placed a briefcase containing a kilogram of SOE's plastic explosive, with a ten-minute time pencil working inside it, beneath the table at which Hitler was holding his morning conference. He then slipped out of the room 'to make a telephone call'. By a stroke of bad luck, he had been summoned to his Führer's presence before he had time to put a second kilogram of explosive into the briefcase; and by another, the conference that day was held in a hut out of doors, instead of the usual underground concrete bunker, which was being redecorated.

Stauffenberg saw the hut explode, was confident Hitler was dead, relied on General Erich von Fellgiebel—another conspirator—to cut all communications between the headquarters and the outside world, bluffed his way out of the enclosure, and took an aircraft to Berlin to set the rest of 'Valkyrie' in train.

Several things went wrong. Hitler was severely shaken, debagged, and only lightly wounded, but not killed. Three of his staff died, but most of the bomb's force was dissipated through the hut's thin walls. Fellgiebel was not able to cut off all the telephone, teleprinter, and wireless channels out of the Führer's headquarters at once. By the time Stauffenberg got to Berlin, he found most of the leading conspirators gathered in the war ministry in the Bendlerstrasse, wondering what to do. Teleprinted orders to execute 'Valkyrie' went all over the Wehrmacht; only in Paris were they taken seriously. There, the principal SS leaders were put in prison; they hesitated to come out next day, when the plot was over, because they knew so well the technique of reporting their victims as 'shot while attempting to escape'.

Otto-Ernst Remer, the major commanding the Grossdeutschland guard battalion in Berlin, was sent to arrest *Goebbels. That arch-conspirator outwitted 'Valkyrie': he put Remer in direct telephone touch with Hitler (who promoted him from major to colonel on the spot), and Remer took his battalion back to the Bendlerstrasse where he arrested all the conspirators he could find. One of those on the fringe of the conspiracy was General Friedrich Fromm (1888–1945), the commander of the German Replacement Army, who attempted to cover his tracks by ordering the immediate execution of those involved. (It did him no good. He was arrested the next day, tortured, tried, and executed the following March.) Stauffenberg was shot in the courtyard that night; he was lucky. Most of his co-conspirators, undone by their personal lack of security, came to horrible ends, hanged on hooks by piano wire. Hitler is said to have had their final agonies filmed, and to have enjoyed watching them squirm, as they died. Two officers, Kluge and *Rommel, who still held high commands at the time of the plot, were incriminated, too, and chose suicide to the alternatives that awaited them.

Germans continue to debate whether Stauffenberg did right or wrong. M. R. D. FOOT

Balfour, M., *Withstanding Hitler* (London, 1988).
Hoffmann, P., *The History of the German Resistance 1933–1945* (2nd edn., London, 1977).
Klemperer, K. von, *German Resistance against Hitler* (Oxford, 1992).

Schweinfurt raids. Following the POINTBLANK directive of June 1943 (see COMBINED BOMBER OFFENSIVE), these raids were mounted by the UK-based Eighth US Army Air Force (USAAF) on 17 August and 14 October 1943, and were repeated by it and by RAF Bomber Command during *Big Week in February 1944, and again by the RAF in April 1944.

Schweinfurt contained five ball-bearing factories essential to German fighter production and it was believed that their destruction would cause a bottleneck in the process. Air Chief Marshal *Harris , C-in-C British Bomber Command, called these potential bottlenecks 'panacea targets'. He refused to bomb them, so the task fell to the Americans whose daylight *precision bombing methods on German targets were still unproven.

Out of the 376 bombers sent on the first raid (230 to Schweinfurt, 146 to nearby Regensburg), the largest number yet dispatched by the USAAF, 147 were lost. On the second raid 60 were destroyed out of 291, and 142 were damaged, a loss rate of 19%. This was not sustainable and all raids deep into Germany were suspended until Big Week was launched. The raids prompted the Germans to move some of their ball-bearing production elsewhere. Damaged factories were quickly rebuilt, double shifts were introduced, and production returned to normal.

The attack mounted by Bomber Command in April 1944 was also controversial for Harris was forced, against his better judgement, to abandon the general *area bombing in which he so fervently believed for more selective targeting. His judgement was vindicated, for little long-term damage was done and 9.3% of the force was lost. See also STRATEGIC AIR OFFENSIVE, 1.

Coffey, T., *Decision over Schweinfurt* (New York, 1978).

scientists at war. Science and technology played much greater parts in the Second World War than in any of its predecessors. There was much more scientific knowledge to be applied, and there were more scientists available to follow the trail already blazed in the *First World War, where the onset of *chemical warfare, the military use of the submarine and the aeroplane, and the discovery of radio waves, had all resulted in both sides of the conflict seeking the aid of scientists. The discovery of germs and new drugs enhanced the fighting potential of armies, and the use of X-rays in surgery enabled wounded men to be more effectively treated. Science during the First World War also became important to *economic warfare, in Germany at least, through such inventions as the Bosch-Haber process for fixing atmospheric nitrogen, which enabled Germany to counter the economic blockade that threatened to starve it of *explosives.

However, because the unique contribution that science could make was not at first apparent to governments, many scientists on both sides, from 1914 onwards, enlisted to serve in the front line. In the UK they included at least five future Nobel Prizewinners: E. V. Appleton (physics, Infantry), P. M. S. *Blackett (physics, Royal Navy), W. L. Bragg (physics, Artillery), A. V. Hill (physiology, Infantry) and G. P. Thomson (physics, Infantry). These, fortunately, all survived; but H. G. J. Moseley, a certain Prizewinner in physics had he lived, enlisted in the Royal Engineers and was killed at Gallipoli in 1915. His death helped to ensure that British scientists were more wisely employed in the Second World War.

The rise of Nazi Germany after 1933 led to calls in the UK for the aid of science in countering the bomber, the submarine, and the naval mine. Renewed attention needed to be paid to chemical warfare, on the precedent of its use in the First World War; and *biological warfare, particularly with anthrax and botulism, appeared possible. Prominent among the men of science who concerned themselves were those who had been involved in the First World War, particularly F. A. *Lindemann (later Lord Cherwell) and H. T. *Tizard, who, as former test pilots, were especially concerned with air defence.

In 1935 the British air ministry formed the Committee for the Scientific Survey of Air Defence, and Tizard was made its chairman after Lindemann, in association with Churchill, had provided the main public drive for something to be done. Lindemann and Tizard, previously good friends, now fell out; but the ensuing enmity was fortunately little bar to progress, and the invention of *radar and its development from 1935 onwards under R. A. *Watson-Watt came just in time for a working system to be ready for the battle of *Britain. Fighters would have been far too few for continuous patrols in strength to intercept incoming bombers; the early warning given by radar enabled fighters to be 'scrambled' only when and where necessary. By thus multiplying the effective strength of Fighter Command, it turned the balance in the battle.

The UK was not, of course, the only country to develop radar. But in the USSR development was handicapped because the chief researcher was falsely imprisoned in 1937 as a result of Stalin's purges (see USSR, 6(a)), while Japanese research and development were seriously hindered by inter-service *rivalries, for which the Japanese navy and army were notorious. German radar in 1939 was in some respects technically superior to the British but it was not used so effectively in operation. This was because there was little prospective pressure on the German defences, and serving officers and scientists were not driven together by an imminent threat as were their British counterparts. American thoughts on how best to use radar lagged for the same reason, as Tizard himself noted: 'we were, however, a very long way ahead in its practical application to war. The reason was that scientists and serving officers had combined before the War to study its tactical uses. This is the great lesson of the last war'.

Tizard's Committee on Air Defence was so successful that a further committee, on Air Offence, was formed, with Tizard again as chairman. But the new committee was not nearly as effective, because Bomber Command staff were far less receptive than their Fighter Command counterparts, complacent as they were in the belief that the bomber 'will always get through' and needed no 'adventitious aids' such as science might provide. Later in the war, when bomber losses began to mount, and when it became evident that targets could rarely be found without *electronic navigation systems such as the beams that had guided German bombers in the *Blitz, Bomber Command, too, began to value scientific aid. So besides Tizard's 'great lesson' the British also learned that help can rarely be effective unless the potential recipient realizes that he needs it.

The help that scientists could provide was twofold in nature. First they could conceive new devices, such as the *cavity magnetron, in response to a need to generate shorter radio wavelengths to improve the sharpness of radio beams for radar. Second, they could conduct objective study of operations to improve their effectiveness. What, for example, was the best flight pattern for an aircraft to cover as large an area of ocean as possible in searching for U-boats? Or what telephone line circuitry and capacity were necessary to deal with the flow of plots on incoming bombers from the radar stations back to Fighter Command headquarters? This latter problem was one of the first to be studied by a small detachment from the radar research station at Bawdsey which was sent to Fighter Command in 1937. Its work became known as *operational research, and the Operational Research Section at Fighter Command was later followed by similar sections at the other RAF Commands, and in the Admiralty and in the army. Ultimately, under the title 'Operations Research', the activity also spread throughout the American services.

Operational Research attracted some of the best intellects among British men of science. The nuclear physicist P. M. S. Blackett, for example, became director of Operational Research at the Admiralty, with E. C. Bullard, a geophysicist, as his chief lieutenant. Another nuclear physicist, E. J. Williams, took over at Coastal Command after Blackett had left for the Admiralty. J. D. Bernal became a scientific adviser to Vice-Admiral *Mountbatten, chief of *Combined Operations; and the South African physicist B. F. J. Schonland, became scientific adviser to General *Montgomery and head of the Army Operational Research Group, among whose members was the theoretical physicist, N. F. Mott. J. C. Kendrew, who like Blackett and Mott was later to win a Nobel Prize, was in operational research with the RAF, and the anatomist S. Zuckerman became scientific adviser to Air Chief Marshal *Tedder, the Deputy Supreme Allied Commander.

Another need for scientific aid emerged when the Tizard committee found in 1939 that the British intelligence services knew little about new German applications of science to warfare. R. V. Jones was accordingly transferred to air intelligence from infra-red research on 1 September 1939. This appointment led to the detection in June 1940 of the impending German use of radio beams to guide bombers to their targets. Radio counter-measures were thereupon devised, and although they were not always successful they proved the only effective means of blunting the German attacks in the Blitz until fighters and guns could be equipped with effective radar. The episode demonstrated the value of scientific intelligence, which grew into a major factor in *electronic warfare, both defensive and offensive, in countering Hitler's *V-weapons and in watching for German nuclear and other developments. In November 1940 F. C. Frank joined R. V. Jones who also acted as *MI6's chief scientific adviser, and towards the end of the war F. H. C. Crick (later to share a Nobel Prize for elucidating the structure of DNA) was appointed by the Admiralty. H. P. Robertson, the relativist, who had been sent to London by the US *Joint Chiefs of Staff in 1943, provided powerful support from the American side.

Relations between the Allies in science became so extensive as the war proceeded that scientific attachés were appointed, notably in Washington, starting with A. V. Hill, and in Chungking, where J. Needham's appointment resulted in the monumental scholarship enshrined in his *Science and Civilisation in China*.

Some distinguished scientists served in the resistance movements, including L. Tronstad (Norway), Y. Rocard (France), A. Michels (Netherlands), and J. Groszkowski (Poland): all these contributed to scientific intelligence, as did H. F. Mayer (see OSLO REPORT) and P. Rosbaud (Germany). Tronstad provided intelligence concerning the output of heavy water in Norway, Rocard investigated a new German radio navigational system, Michels ran a technical intelligence service among Dutchmen working in German factories, and Groszkowski analysed the fuels remaining in the V-1s and V-2s which had been fired in trials in Poland. Rosbaud, the anti-Nazi science editor of a German publishing firm, was allowed to travel to neutral countries because of his job, and he was therefore able to feed the Allies occasional information as to the whereabouts of *Heisenberg's group of nuclear physicists.

The technology of intelligence was itself greatly advanced by the efforts of mathematicians and scientists. The German cipher machine, *ENIGMA, was first broken in 1932 by a Polish team of mathematicians led by M. Rejewski; in 1939 they presented their work to their British counterparts at *Bletchley Park, where other mathematicians such as G. Welchman, M. Newman, and A. *Turing made outstanding contributions. Turing's work was instrumental in the development of computers, and the crucial electronic circuitry evolved from the scale-of-two counter devised for nuclear physics by the physicist C. E. Wynn Williams.

Many British scientists were directly concerned with the invention and development of new weapons; and just as the Royal Aircraft Establishment (RAE) at Farnborough had attracted a galaxy of talent in the *First World War, so did the Telecommunications Research Establishment (TRE), first at Swanage and then at Malvern, in the Second. The RAE, of course, continued as the research centre for aeronautics, as did the Chemical Warfare Research Establishment at Porton for chemical and biological warfare.

Most of the research and development for radar was done in the government establishments at Malvern, Portsmouth (Admiralty Signals Establishment), and Christchurch (Air Defence Research Establishment), where the pre-war staffs were powerfully augmented by the scientists who came in from the universities. Among those who went to TRE were the nuclear physicists P. I. Dee and W. B. Lewis, the zoologist J. W. S. Pringle, and two more future Nobel Prizewinners, M. Ryle (physics) and A. L. Hodgkin (physiology). Another future Nobel Prizewinner in physiology, A. F. Huxley, worked on the development of naval radar, and yet another, G. Porter (chemistry), became a naval radar officer.

While many ideas and inventions originated in government establishments and universities (radar in the Radio Research Station, for example, and the cavity magnetron in Birmingham University), a third source was industry which, besides manufacturing the weapons and devices conceived in establishments and universities, sometimes offered inventions of its own. Radar itself owed much to the electronic circuits invented by A. D. Blumlein in the EMI laboratories, while E. C. S. Megaw and his team at the laboratories of the General Electric Company (GEC) took the cavity magnetron into large-scale production; and the development of the jet engine, conceived by A. A. Griffith and F. Whittle, owed much to S. G. Hooker at Rolls-Royce. Another major invention, the *proximity fuze, was due as much to the Salford Electrical Instrument Company as to the Air Defence Research Establishment.

In contrast with its part in the First World War, chemistry was much less militarily prominent in the Second, partly because—against what appeared likely in 1939—neither side resorted to chemical warfare. This was fortunate for the UK, because in Germany G. Schraeder had in 1936 invented the first 'nerve gas', Tabun, and then the even more lethal Sarin. Although these were manufactured in quantity, Hitler withheld their use, partly because he erroneously thought that the British might have them too—an example of effective, if self-inflicted, deterrence.

While the UK was well behind in chemical warfare, it would by 1944 have been armed for biological warfare, thanks to the work of the bacteriologist P. G. Fildes who joined Porton in 1940 and developed bombs for distributing anthrax spores. Anthrax threatened a devastating form of warfare, but despite the precedent set by a German attempt to infect mules, cattle, and sheep with it in Romania and Argentina in the First World War, both sides withheld its use in the Second. Half a million doses fatal to cattle and half a million anthrax bombs had been made in the UK and USA as a deterrent should the Germans threaten to cross the divide into biological warfare. A happier outcome from bacteriology was the discovery and production of penicillin by Alexander Fleming and Howard Florey (see MEDICINE).

Japan and the USSR, too, developed biological warfare agents. Techniques for spreading anthrax, glanders, and paratyphoid were tried by the Japanese, who also dropped plague-infected fleas on civil populations in China; and the notorious Unit 731 under General Ishii Shiro experimented on *prisoners-of-war.

The main fields in which Germans excelled in applying science were aerodynamics (especially supersonics with A. Busemann), *guided weapons with anti-aircraft missiles, using infra-red and radar homing devices, under development, and rocketry (where von *Braun's V-2 rocket set the pattern for intercontinental missiles and space flight). Though leads in all these fields were achieved in Germany, most scientific advances, and the exploitation of them, occurred in the UK and USA as the ideologies of Germany and Italy—and the suspicion and dislike that the Japanese military establishment had for Japanese scientists because many of them were western educated—meant that Axis scientists were not properly mobilized. Many Italian scientists (see FERMI, for example) fled Mussolini's fascist regime well before the war, and the Nazis' hostility towards Jewish scientists is well known—Einstein's Theory of Relativity was declared invalid because he was a Jew—and there was an exodus of them. There was no single German agency or individual to oversee the scientific war effort which was concentrated into three main groups: the 30 research institutes of the Kaiser Wilhelm Gesellschaft, the research departments of the large industrial firms such as I. G. Farben, Siemens, and Krupp, and the research establishments of the Wehrmacht's three services; co-operation between these groups was almost unknown and, indeed, was discouraged. A short war having been anticipated, little effort was made to organize scientists for war until 1942 and it was not until the spring of 1943 that the Kriegsmarine-Arbeitsgemeinschaft (Naval Study Group) was formed to tackle problems of *submarine warfare. Only from 1943 onwards was there a serious effort to co-ordinate the scientific effort in Germany, when *Göring installed Professor W. Osenberg, a mechanical engineer from Hanover, as head of the Reichsforschungsrat Planungsamt (State Research Council's Planning Office), but his appointment came too late to have much effect.

By contrast, the scientific effort in the UK was well co-ordinated from 1939 onwards, and the fact that so many scientists found suitable, even agreeable, niches was partly due to the Central Register of Scientists, headed by C. P. Snow, that had been started before the war to ensure that scientific talent would be employed to best effect, and such tragic losses as that of Moseley in 1915 should be avoided.

At the highest level, Churchill himself had his own scientific adviser, his close friend of 20 years' standing, Lindemann, whose advice sometimes differed from that of Tizard, whose influence—though still important—declined with the ascendancy of Lindemann after June 1940.

In the same month, observing developments in Europe, the Americans set up the National Defense Research Committee, renamed *Office of Scientific and Research Development in 1941, with Vannevar Bush (1890–1974) as its chairman and K. T. Compton, J. B. Conant, J. B. Jewett, and R. C. Tolman as its scientific members. In September 1940 Tizard headed a British mission to the USA with Churchill's authority 'To tell them (the Americans) what they want to know, to give them all the assistance I can on behalf of the British government to enable the Armed Forces of the USA to reach the highest level of technical efficiency.'

An immediate result of the Tizard mission was the realization by Bush and his colleagues of how much could be learned from the British in defence science, and great efforts were made to catch up and to convert new ideas and devices into well-engineered military products. But there were relatively few government laboratories in the USA with the necessary competence, and so the Americans decided to graft new defence laboratories on to the academic scientific institutions in which they excelled such as the Massachusetts Institute of Technology (MIT). Thus, whereas in the UK many scientists had been drawn from universities into government establishments such as TRE, the pattern in the USA was for scientists to join new and specially created laboratories such as the Radiation Laboratory at MIT for radar under the directorship of Lee DuBridge, the Radio Research Laboratory (RRL) for Radio Countermeasures, at Harvard under C. G. Suits, and the Applied Physics Laboratory at Johns Hopkins. The RRL at Harvard also ran the American British Laboratory (ABL 15) under V. H. Fraenkel attached to TRE in Malvern for joint work on radio counter-measures with the British.

The difference between the American and British patterns in defence research had an important legacy after the war. The British continued to build up government establishments at the expense of the universities, and so tended to lock up research staffs in establishments where they had no part in bringing on new generations of students, while in the USA the universities kept research, even of the most applied kind, and teaching together.

Another legacy of the war was the way in which politicians and the public regarded science and technology because of their manifest effects, both good and ill, on human life at all social levels from the international to the personal. The heavy bombing of cities, by both conventional and nuclear weapons, and the prospect of biological warfare in particular, raised questions of conscience for many scientists, and each had to answer them for himself. Some of us were grateful to discover Francis Bacon's classic response: 'Let none be alarmed at the objection of the Arts and Sciences becoming depraved to malevolent or luxurious purpose or the like, for the same can be said of every worldly Good: Talent, Courage, Strength, Beauty, Riches, Light itself, and the rest. Only let mankind regain their rights over Nature assigned to them by the gift of God and obtain that power whose exercise will be governed by right Reason and true Religion.'

In the UK, at least when fighting a Nazi-dominated Germany, the answer was clear for most of us; but the dropping of *atomic bombs on Japanese cities would have been long debated had the decision been left to scientists alone. Also, the effort to build the nuclear bomb raised questions of organizational doctrine. General Leslie Groves, in supreme charge, organized the effort into compartments so tight that any one scientist, except at the highest level, knew only a small part of the whole programme, and might not even know the ultimate purpose of what he was being asked to do. By contrast, in radar in the UK, workers at all levels were encouraged to debate ideas and progress at the 'Sunday Soviets' at Malvern, where air marshals could be questioned by junior scientific officers. While such open informality could risk endangering security, it was more in the spirit of true science than the rigid compartments of the nuclear project: but it has to be admitted that General Groves achieved results. Perhaps only in wartime would scientists for long endure working in closed environments.

R. V. Jones

Baldwin, R. B., *The Deadly Fuze* (London, 1980).
Bower, T., *The Paper Clip Conspiracy* (London, 1987).
Hackmann, W., *Seek and Strike* (London, 1984).
Jones, R. V., *Most Secret War* (London, 1978).
—*Reflections on Intelligence* (London, 1989).
Kevles, D. J., *The Physicists* (New York, 1979).
Macrakis, K., *Surviving the Swastika: Scientific Research in Nazi Germany* (Oxford, 1994).
Ordway, F. I., and Sharpe, M. R., *The Rocket Team* (London, 1979).
Price, A., *Instruments of Darkness* (2nd edn., London, 1978).
Weart, S. R., *Scientists in Power* (Cambridge, Mass., 1979).
A bibliography of some 200 books and papers up to 1974 can be found appended to the record of a meeting held on 28 March 1974 by the Royal Society on *The Effects of the Two World Wars on the Organization and Development of Science in the United Kingdom*, published in *Proc.R.Soc.Lond.A.*, 342 (1975), pp. 439–586.

scorched earth policy, whereby retreating armies destroyed or dismantled everything in the path of their advancing opponents to deprive them of shelter, food, natural resources, working factories, anything that might be of use to them. *Chiang Kai-shek employed it during the *China Incident when he had the dykes of the Yellow River dynamited in June 1938 to slow the Japanese advance on Hankow and to deny them valuable agricultural resources. The resulting floods ravaged three provinces leaving perhaps two million homeless and many thousands dead. Not until 1947 was the Yellow River returned to its pre-1938 channel. The Red Army implemented it with great ruthlessness before the advancing Wehrmacht after the German invasion of the USSR in June 1941 (see BARBAROSSA). They destroyed or removed their factories, blew up the Dnepropetrovsk dam which supplied the Donets industrial region with power, and dismantled the installations belonging to the Maikop oilfields in the Caucasus so that the Germans were unable to extract any oil from them.

The British never exercised the policy with any efficiency. For example, they failed to destroy vessels on the west coast of Malaya during the *Malayan campaign, allowing Japanese troops to use them to outflank British positions on the west coast. During the fighting which preceded the fall of *Singapore, Churchill urged the garrison to implement a scorched earth policy if the island were in danger of falling, but, as the official historian of that British military disaster drily pointed out, it is difficult to carry out on ground you are still defending.

SCU/SLU, see SPECIAL LIAISON UNITS.

SD (Sicherheitsdienst), see RSHA.

Seabees was a name derived from the initials CB (construction battalions). Formed by the US Navy in December 1941, the force eventually grew to 8,000 officers and 250,000 men and its work of constructing naval bases, air strips, and roads, and handling cargos, during the *Pacific war and elsewhere, was an essential foundation to the victories that followed. Its volunteer members were all trained craftsmen or civilian engineers whose pay was the equivalent of at least a petty officer's. The organization's insignia was a flying bee wearing a sailor's cap, and carrying a tommy gun, a wrench, and a hammer. See also ENGINEERS.

SEAC, see SOUTH-EAST ASIA COMMAND.

SEALION (German, *Seelöwe*) was the German codename for the invasion of England. On 13 July 1940 the question of greatest concern to Hitler was why Britain was still unwilling to make peace. *Halder, chief of the Army General Staff, noted in his diary: 'He believes, as we do, that the answer to this question is that Britain is still placing her hopes in Russia. He therefore expects that it will be necessary to force the UK to make peace.'

Three days later, on 16 July, Hitler issued Directive No. 16 'on preparations for a landing operation against England'. As the first prerequisite for it he mentioned that the British Air Force must be eliminated to the point that it would not have the strength necessary to mount a significant attack on a German attempt to cross the Channel. In conferences with the commanders-in-chief of the Wehrmacht services on 21 July, Hitler repeated his doubts about a landing operation: 'If it is not certain that preparations can be concluded by the beginning of September, other plans will have to be considered.' Among these plans was an attack on the USSR.

Above all, the navy voiced serious doubts about the feasibility of a landing. The importance of air supremacy was increasingly emphasized, not only for the crossing but also for the orderly deployment of the transport fleet and the necessary minesweeping operations. On 11 July *Raeder, C-in-C of the navy, explained to Hitler that a landing could only be a 'last resort'. He demanded strong air attacks, for example on Liverpool, 'to make the entire nation feel the effects'. After Raeder had informed him on 31 July that the navy's preparations for a landing could not be concluded before 15 September, Hitler decided that all preparations should take that date as a deadline, but his final decision would depend on victory in the battle of *Britain. Eight or, at most, fourteen days after the start of the 'great air campaign against Britain', which could begin at any time from about 5 August, he intended to decide whether or not SEALION could take place in 1940.

After the fall of *France the Luftwaffe was in a very favourable geographical position for operations against England, but it did not have any overall tactical plan. In spite of Hitler's orders to prepare an invasion, his hesitation about carrying it out greatly complicated the problem of setting consistent priorities and goals in an air war against that country. However, there was general agreement that domination of the air, or at least regional air supremacy, was essential for a landing as well as for an independent strategic air war against the UK.

Preparations for the invasion, which was to be carried out by divisions drawn from Army Group A's Ninth and Sixteenth Armies (see Map 95), included the recording of all available sea and river craft in Germany and the occupied countries, embarkation and disembarkation exercises, and the formation of occupation authorities which planned, among other tasks, the arrest of certain prominent citizens (see BLACK BOOK).

When the battle for air supremacy over England began by 13 August 1940, *Göring's *Adlertag (Eagle Day), seven weeks had passed since the fall of *France, during which time the British had been able further to improve their air defences. Thus the battle of *Britain took the form of a strategically and tactically improvised air offensive against an air defence system which the British had been building up systematically for four years.

On 14 September 1940 Hitler informed the Cs-in-C that the navy had completed preparations for SEALION, but in spite of the 'enormous' successes of the Luftwaffe the preconditions for the operation did not yet exist. Although domination of the air had not been achieved, Hitler did not want to cancel SEALION as yet because that would destroy the effect of the air attacks on British morale. Whereas earlier the purpose of the air war had been to create the preconditions for a landing, Hitler now evidently viewed the landing preparations as a psychological instrument to support the air war, which had been indecisive but might still lead to victory.

Raeder suggested 8 October as the next date for a landing, as the situation in the air would not change before the next favourable invasion dates, 24–27 September. His remark that a Channel crossing would not be necessary if the Luftwaffe, had been completely successful by then and his demand for air attacks 'without regard to SEALION', suggests that by this time he had ruled out a landing in 1940. Hitler, however, ordered preparations to be made for 27 September and named 17 September as the date for confirmation or otherwise. Only after that should 8 October be considered. The main thing was, however, that the air attacks should be continued without interruption.

Göring's remark on 16 September that SEALION must not disturb the operations of the Luftwaffe and his reference to 'subsequent attacks spread all over Britain' show that he, like Raeder, no longer expected the landing operation to be carried out. In view of the first dispersal order of the Wehrmacht High Command of 19 September for the SEALION transport fleet to avoid further losses as a result of British air attacks, and the instructions to halt

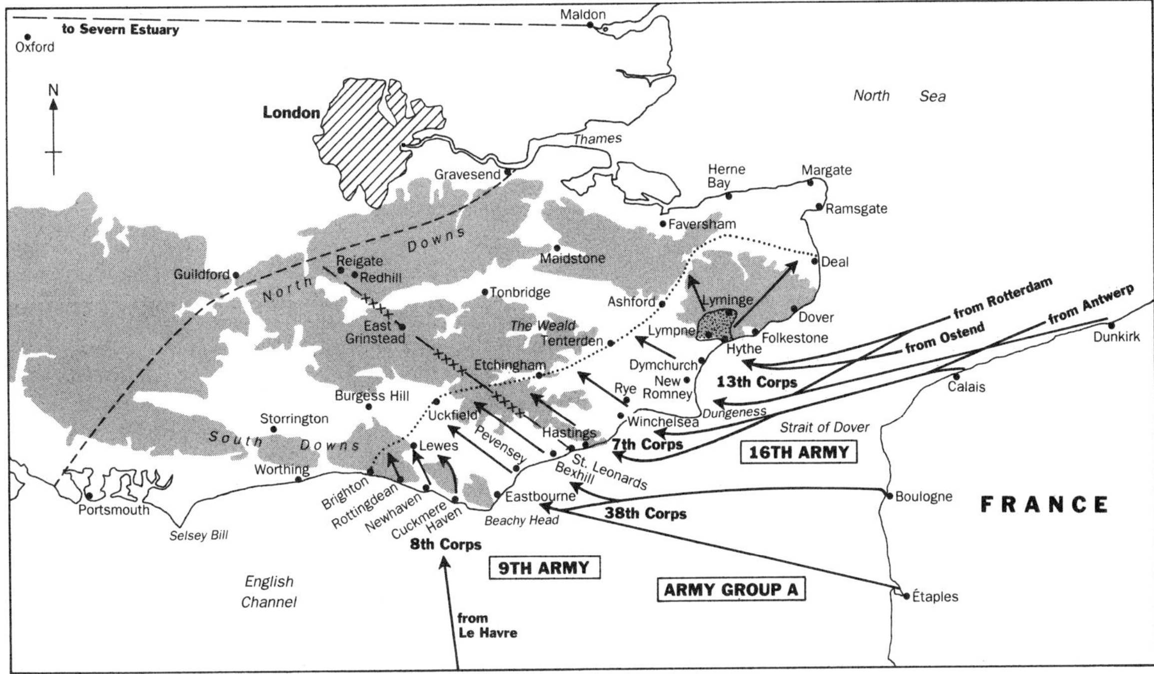

95. Operation **SEALION**

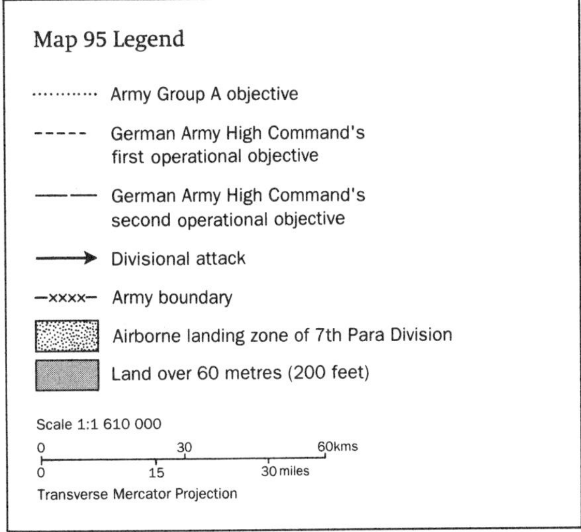

further deployment of the transport ships, any serious preparations by the Luftwaffe for the invasion had become superfluous.

In fact war-economy considerations forced a disbanding of the deployment for SEALION. Because of the losses caused by British air attacks, on 2 October Hitler ordered that all measures taken in conjunction with SEALION were to be 'largely dismantled'. In his Directive No. 18 of 21 November he again stated that changes in the general situation might make it possible, or necessary, to revert to the plan in the spring of 1941; but he evidently expressed himself more plainly on 5 December, when Halder noted: 'SEALION can be left out of account.'

On 18 December 1940 Hitler issued Directive No. 21 in which he ordered the Wehrmacht to be prepared to 'crush Soviet Russia in a rapid campaign', codenamed *BARBAROSSA, even before the UK had been defeated. In this way Hitler attempted to correct the priority of the two fronts, deriving from his basic aim of conquering **Lebensraum* (living-space) in the east. KLAUS A. MAIER

Schenk, P., *Invasion of England 1940* (London, 1990).

seaplanes, see FLOAT PLANES.

sea power. The strategy of sea power in the Second World War remained in essence what it has been since man first took to the water, began trading, and succumbed to a state of war: deny the seas to the other side while retaining control yourself. In the Napoleonic wars, French armies could range across Europe and east as far as Moscow, but the UK's coastline and commerce were usually safe so long as the kingdom could dominate the seas. Admiral Mahan referred succinctly to 'those far distant, storm-beaten ships, upon which the Grand Army never looked', which 'stood between it and the dominion of the world'. With the ultimate defeat of the combined fleets of France and Spain at the battle of Trafalgar, on 21 October 1805, the Royal Navy ensured the security of the nation from invasion and its trade from interference.

One of the crucial roles of Allied **sea power** was escort duty. These British destroyers accompanied the Arctic convoy PQ18 to Murmansk in September 1942. The leading warship is HMS *Fury*; behind her is HMS *Ashanti*.

The control of the seas by the UK remained virtually unrivalled for a hundred years. By 1914, however, the challenge by the German and Austro-Hungarian Central Powers had become highly intimidating. Neither of these empires possessed any naval tradition but the massive German fleet was imbued with professionalism and possessed first-rate material.

The ships and weapons of all navies in 1914 were infinitely more sophisticated than at Trafalgar. The guns mounted on battleships, themselves capable of 24 knots, could fire accurately at an opponent almost beyond the horizon, while submarines could fire their torpedoes unseen to a lethal distance of over 9,000 metres (9,840 yards). Tethered mines, which had paid a crucial part in the most recent naval war, between Russia and Japan in 1904–5, added a new offensive and defensive dimension to weaponry. Aeroplanes and airships ranged the sky on reconnaissance, 'spotted' for the guns and searched the seas for German submarines (U-boats).

Before the *First World War ended in an Allied victory, brought about substantially by the failure of the German Navy to break the blockade which was starving the Central Powers of food and war materials, the submarine had proved to be the most dangerous fighting ship, while the bomber and torpedo-carrying plane posed a threat to the future of old naval weaponry. Yet nothing had altered the strategic principle of sea power.

To replace Germany as a challenger to British naval dominance there emerged from the First World War two new naval powers, already in competition with one another. The naval tonnage figures sum up the situation in 1922. Japan 547,000; the USA 1,100,000; the UK 1,400,000. Nineteen years later, Japan had torn up all the international treaties of limitation in numbers and size of warships designed to prevent a repeat of the 'battleship race' between Germany and the UK in the years between 1900 and 1914. Its naval tonnage had doubled to 1,100,000 while the USA had added only some 250,000 tons to its strength in 1922.

This Imperial Japanese Navy (IJN), scarcely half a century old, had been brought into being by British-built ships, and inherited British traditions and officer training. Before and during the First World War, and between the wars, Japan had built up a large and first-rate shipbuilding industry, and by 1941 Japanese weaponry and the naval air arm were the equal of any other navy. The great weakness was the lack of an industrial base in any way competitive with that of the USA.

The US Navy began to rearm and modernize in the mid-1930s as Japan demonstrated aggressive and truculent attitudes, invading China (see CHINA INCIDENT) and building illegal bases in the Marshall Islands. Simultaneously, the British Royal Navy laid down new tonnage, reacquired control of its neglected air arm from the RAF, and introduced *radar and less inadequate protection against bombing, as Hitler marched into neighbouring nations such as Austria and Czechoslovakia.

At the same time, Germany began the construction of a modern fleet, previously prohibited under the terms of the *Versailles settlement following the First World War. The new navy, designed this time for the *guerre de course* rather than direct confrontational battle, was not due to be ready before 1941–2, but with Hitler's limited faith and interest in sea warfare, that was no deterrent to the opening of his land and air campaigns in September 1939.

German strategy at sea was to attack Allied shipping wherever it could be found with surface raiders (see AUXILIARY CRUISERS and GERMAN SURFACE RAIDERS) and U-boats. During the last weeks of peace, a number of fast, modern, and heavily armed warships, with their supply ships, were dispatched to the North and South Atlantic, and even into the Indian Ocean, to await the order to open hostilities. At the same time, almost the entire U-boat fleet of some 40 vessels put to sea and took up station in the North Sea and the Atlantic approaches to British and French western ports.

For the UK and her allies and Commonwealth, the tasks were closely similar to those in 1914. Again, the U-boats became an instant menace and the surface raiders hard to find and difficult to destroy. By contrast with the days of sail, the raider now had the advantage of speed, *radio communications and even radar, and (in some cases) a spotter seaplane to extend the area of search for prey. But the modern raider also suffered from the need to refuel and avoid damage far from repair facilities; under sail a raider had been largely self-supporting.

There were numerous occasions when the threat of gunfire caused a raider to sheer off at speed. An early British success in damaging the German pocket battleship *Admiral Graf Spee* (see RIVER PLATE), leading to her self-destruction, acted as a salutary lesson and signal for even greater caution among raider commanders. In all, the cost to the Germans of surface raiding was too high for the toll exacted.

There were abundant lessons to be learned on the Allied side, too. It should not have been necessary as the two most important lessons had been acted upon before, and somehow forgotten. In 1917 the maritime war—and therefore the war itself—had been almost lost by the Allies as a result of the failure to introduce *convoys to protect merchant ships, a defensive precaution known and practised in the days of sail.

Fortunately, for the Allies, this mistake was not repeated; the complex machinery for introducing convoys had been set up again in the UK in 1937, and the first convoy sailed within a few days of the beginning of the war at sea. But convoying was of a strictly limited nature, in part because of the shortage of suitable escort craft, a handicap which prevailed for many months.

Churchill, as First Lord of the Admiralty in 1914–15, had called for an offensive strategy towards the U-boats, with hunting groups ranging the oceans. The chances of finding one, conveniently on the surface, proved highly unlikely. When he came back to the Admiralty in 1939, with his same urge to take the offensive, hunting groups, in some cases including precious and vulnerable aircraft *carriers, were again formed, to negligible effect. Only when one large carrier had been torpedoed and sunk and a second brought close to destruction, was Churchill's folly ended, albeit slowly and by stages. 'It is only politicians who imagine that ships are not earning their keep unless they are rushing madly about the ocean,' remarked the British First Sea Lord, Admiral *Pound, sardonically.

Churchill cannot, however, be held to blame for the loss of the treaty bases in Eire, by their voluntary surrender to Dublin in 1938, contrary to treaty obligations. These had proved of inestimable value for the protection of the Western Approaches in the First World War, and now their loss was to cost the lives of many thousands of merchant seamen in the battle of the *Atlantic.

Another renewed threat facing merchantmen and warships alike on both sides was *mine warfare. The sea mine was now a more sophisticated weapon than that one which had restricted the movements of the fleets in the North Sea in 1914–18, and rebuffed the British and French navies in the Dardanelles in 1915. The Germans had perfected a magnetic mine, which could be laid by aircraft or fast small warships in coastal shipping lanes and entrances to harbours. It claimed many victims in the first winter of war before an answer was found to it.

As in 1914, German mercantile trade was reduced to a trickle by the instant Allied naval blockade (see also ECONOMIC WARFARE) which sealed off the northern entrance to the North Sea with cruiser patrols, and RAF Coastal Command air patrols, and effectively prohibited passage of the Dover Straits to U-boats and merchantmen by minefields and light patrol boats. Contraband cargoes destined for Germany in neutral vessels were seized from the first days of war.

At the start of the battle for the *Mediterranean, Italy's navy posed a threat even while at first abstaining from any hostile activity. The British Navy made itself responsible for the eastern basin based on Alexandria, while the French covered the sea west of Malta. The French and Italian navies were comparable in strength, both possessing a few modern heavy ships and numerous fast cruisers and destroyers, backed up by surviving First

World War tonnage. *Air power could be exercised by Italy from land bases.

Substantially, this was the strategic scene in the opening months of hostilities. The similarity with 1914 was almost uncanny. The best survivors of the middle-rank officers of the earlier war were now in senior command, the wiser for their earlier experience. The battleship was still considered effectively the final arbiter of sea power, and more of these behemoths were fitting out or on the stocks of many naval shipyards; while air power was, amazingly, still seen only in terms of reconnaissance, spotting for the big guns, perhaps damaging further a retreating opponent, locating surface raiders, and providing cover for convoys.

The British Home Fleet was again worried about the security of its northern base at Scapa Flow, with reason. The submarine was, once again, surprising both the Germans and the British by its effectiveness. The Royal Navy again efficiently transported the small *British Expeditionary Force to France, without losing a man. *Plus ça change plus c'est la même chose* indeed!

Churchill's 'Gallipoli' of 1940 was the attempt to close off the Swedish iron ore trade (see also RAW AND SYNTHETIC MATERIALS) with Germany down the Norwegian coast by occupying Narvik (see NORWEGIAN CAMPAIGN). But once again political delays and procrastination nipped a brilliant strategic concept in the bud: the Germans got there first. In failing to intercept effectively the German invasion of April–May 1940, the British and French navies suffered a severe setback, which shocked the American president and people.

The Allied navies' successful withdrawal of troops from Narvik and Trondheim, and on a vastly larger scale, the British and French troops blocked in at *Dunkirk, offset the lamentable performance in Norway, even though the German Navy suffered crippling losses there.

With the fall of *France in June 1940, and entry of Italy into the war on Germany's side, the fate of the powerful French Navy became a serious preoccupation. Many of the French warships were neutralized, or turned over to the British Navy. But other heavy units had to be attacked, unsuccessfully as it turned out at Dakar, successfully at Oran in North Africa (see MERS-EL-KÉBIR). Although the loss of lives was regrettable and embittered the French people, the UK's evident determination to pursue the war even without allies greatly impressed the US public.

Alone now in the summer of 1940, the British and Commonwealth navies were fully stretched keeping open the trade routes to North and South America, South Africa, Australasia and the Far East, and through the Mediterranean for the supply of men and materials to the land campaigns and the vital oil of the Middle East. It was an even more complex and critical strategic problem than that posed in the Napoleonic campaigns against the navies of France and Spain at the turn of the 18th–19th centuries.

The Italians suffered major defeats on land in the *Western Desert campaigns and Mussolini's assault on neutral Greece, which began the *Balkan campaign, was blessed with no better fortune. Meanwhile, Hitler, acquisitive eyes for long set on the east, determined to clear up these failing campaigns before invading the USSR (see BARBAROSSA). The effect of this intervention was felt immediately.

The British Navy was deeply and expensively involved in the unsuccessful attempts to hold back the German tide in Greece, and then in *Crete. Much criticism was levelled at what was seen as strategical folly. In fact, it may have delayed BARBAROSSA by 3–4 weeks, and the onset of the Russian winter almost certainly saved Moscow and Leningrad, and the USSR itself. Only sea power could have brought this about. The UK could also claim the moral kudos of meeting its commitment to support Greece, again important to American opinion.

As the war progressed, the USA, while remaining nominally neutral until December 1941, was offering more and more material aid to the UK under *Lend-Lease, especially in aircraft and naval vessels, and co-operating with the Canadian Navy in guarding the western end of the Atlantic convoys.

From the outset of the *German–Soviet war, Churchill pledged the fullest possible support in war materials of all kinds to the Soviet war effort. This put yet more strain on British naval resources. Everything had to be shipped in the *Arctic convoys to northern Soviet ports, or later via the southern route through Persia.

It was at this time that the loss of Norway was most seriously felt. Although the UK had built up bases in Iceland, the Arctic convoys, which carried aircraft, tanks, and all manner of military *matériel* for the hard-pressed Red Army, were vulnerable to shore-based German bomber and torpedo-carrying aircraft, U-boats and surface ships—including the new mighty battleship **Tirpitz*, which lurked among the northern mists in its well-concealed anchorage.

These Arctic convoys, stoutly supported with the aid of the US Navy after Germany declared war on the USA on 11 December 1941, cost many ships and many thousands of lives. To the displeasure of Stalin, they had to be halted from time to time, but the material they delivered proved vital to the survival of the USSR.

Meanwhile, the battle of the Atlantic continued with increased relentlessness, and new tactics and weaponry. Code breaking took an important part in the defeat of the U-boat packs (see ULTRA, 1), but it was the escort carrier with its short-range aircraft, and the advent of very long range heavy bombers and *flying boats, which turned the tide. By May 1943, when convoys were first able to sail the entire Atlantic under land-based air cover (see AIR GAP), German losses reached unacceptable heights, and U-boats were forced away to distant waters for their prey.

A further skill the sailor had to learn and perfect if the war was to be won by the Allies was that of *amphibious warfare. Commando raids on occupied France took place within days of the fall of France. These early amphibious operations, calling for the closest co-operation between the army, the navy, and sometimes the air force, were not notably successful. But knowledge was constantly being built up for the large-scale landings which followed. These required a new strategy on a radical and giant scale, as well as new skills in bombarding defences and bringing men and supplies to land on hostile coasts at minimum cost in lives. The first requisite of successful amphibious warfare was control of the sea, which, in turn, presupposed control of the air.

By the time the men and shipping had been assembled in southern England for the Normandy invasion in June 1944 (see OVERLORD), the techniques and art of amphibious warfare had been thoroughly exercised in the Pacific. The peacetime US Navy of 1941 was a fine service suffering from limited resources but enjoying presidential approval and encouragement. The attempt by an army air force lobby, led by Colonel Billy Mitchell, to prove the superiority of army air power, had a double-edged consequence, resulting as it did in the setting up, in 1921, of a bureau of aeronautics within the navy department which led to the formation of both a navy and a marine corps air arm.

The lack of American bases in the Pacific also led, *faute de mieux*, to fleet self-subsistence and long-range capability. The US Pacific Fleet in the years leading to war with Japan had not only evolved the carrier task force but also the *Fleet Train, including tankers (oilers), transports, repair ships, ammunition and cargo ships. Efficient *landing craft were used in amphibious exercises, and integration between all classes of *warships was refined through the 1930s.

All manoeuvres were conducted on the premise that Japan would be the opponent, and as late as 1938 a surprise 'attack' by carrier-borne aircraft on *Pearl Harbor in the Hawaiian Islands was conducted as an exercise—with complete success, it should be noted. The material strength of the Japanese Navy was understood, but the quality of the personnel and weaponry was under-estimated.

With the real attack on Pearl Harbor in December 1941—'This is no drill! This is no drill!'—and the simultaneous attacks on American, British, French, and Dutch bases and territory in South-East Asia, the Philippines, and the South Pacific, initial Allied strategy was perforce one of confinement and defence. The vulnerability of the battleship—demonstrated earlier by the British who had put out of action the Italian battle fleet at *Taranto with a handful of obsolescent dive-bombers and torpedo-bombers—was evidenced not only at Pearl Harbor. The British attempt to deter the Japanese from attacking Singapore and Malaysia by sending, without air cover, a modern battleship and older battle-cruiser, ended in disaster (see PRINCE OF WALES AND REPULSE).

While the big gun was to prove valuable for bombardment use, and the battleship made an excellent platform for multiple anti-aircraft guns to protect the carrier, it was the carrier itself that at once replaced the battleship as queen of the fleet. For some five months after Pearl Harbor, the Japanese carriers swept the Pacific and Indian oceans almost with impunity, mounting raids from *Darwin, Australia, to Colombo, Ceylon (see INDIAN OCEAN RAID), and on numerous Pacific islands.

The intention of the Japanese High Command was to cripple US naval power, while brushing aside Dutch and British intervention, and so demoralize the American people that a negotiated settlement could be demanded. There was no intention of occupying any part of the US mainland: that would not be necessary in the judgement of Tokyo.

But no greater misjudgement of a nation's character in the face of threat had ever been made. The folly of temporarily wrecking the American battle fleet in a sneak attack only inflamed the determination for revenge. The rate of Japanese successes, which had at first been breathtaking, inevitably slowed. In May 1942, as the industrial might of the American nation geared itself to the production of armaments, and a flood of young men trained for the armed forces, Japanese carrier pilots met serious opposition for the first time when, in the *Coral Sea battle, the IJN lost its first carrier. This engagement, in which the US Navy also lost a carrier, heralded an entirely novel form of naval warfare, as it was conducted, for the first time ever, without the ships of the opposing sides ever sighting one another. And the heavy gun, with its maximum range of around 25,000 m. (27,340 yd.), had been superseded by the bombing/torpedo aircraft with a range limited only by the capacity of the fuel tank, and the wind.

Wind had been a consideration in the days of coal-firing and pre-smokeless shell-propellant; and the laying of an artificial smokescreen was an additional wind-dependent factor. Now, in this new carrier warfare, the wind reverted to almost the same importance as it had had in the days of sail. For carriers, these floating airfields, were required to turn into the wind both to launch and to recover their machines, a time-consuming process. Wind strength and direction was also the paramount factor in judging the safe range of a carrier's aircraft, and this calculation was further complicated by the carrier's present and future speed, and course.

During the *Pacific war, carrier warfare was usually conducted with the opposing ships beyond visual range of each other. This involved accurate reconnaissance and *meteorological intelligence, top-level communications, radio interception and code-breaking, support teams, *air-sea rescue vessels to cover airmen forced to 'splash', and split-second decision-making among the commanders. (The best American carrier fleet commander, Admiral *Spruance, was nicknamed 'Electric Brain'.) Naval *radar, unknown to the Japanese at this time, had been handed over to the Americans by the British. Above all, and as always, successful carrier warfare demanded good luck and individual courage.

American success in early carrier battles such as *Coral

Sea and *Midway contained the Japanese amphibious advance in the central and south-west Pacific, and put heart into the US Navy and Marine Corps just when they were threatened with demoralization. But for many months the situation remained delicately poised. In this new naval warfare the carrier was far more vulnerable than the heavily armoured battleship had been. After Pearl Harbor, the US Pacific Fleet did not lose a single battleship, but at one time it was reduced to a single operational (and damaged) carrier in the South Pacific. Three years later, there were almost 100 carriers operating with the US Navy, the shipyards achieving a launch rate of one per week. How could the Japanese hope to match that?

For the IJN, it was a very different and sorry story. Short of everything but zeal, by a superhuman effort it managed to assemble five fleet carriers and four smaller carriers for the *Philippine Sea battle in June 1944, but this equalled the strength of only a single US task force. Of equally ominous significance for the IJN were its relatively inferior aircrew resources. The Japanese aircrews of Pearl Harbor and Midway had been unequalled in skill and experience. But when, inevitably, most of these were lost, their replacements were of steadily declining skills, while the US Navy's aircraft became as good and then better than Japanese ones.

In the *island-hopping amphibious Pacific campaigns, the greatest integrated combined operations in history until OVERLORD, it is impossible to weigh the relative contributions of any arm. The land-based heavy bombers of the US Army Air Forces took a larger and larger part as the war advanced and bases within flying range of mainland Japan could be constructed. Then there were the marine corps and army infantry who waded ashore or were landed by air on island after island.

It is also impossible to overstate the importance of the contribution of the US Navy's submarine service, which for propaganda reasons was played down at the time, while German U-boat warfare was being condemned for its ruthlessness. But the submarine campaign against Japanese shipping was quite as unrestricted, and even more effective, hastening the end for the Japanese Empire (see JAPAN, 7).

Well before the first *atomic bomb was dropped on Japan its merchant service had ceased to exist, confirming the imminent total collapse of the empire. Two-thirds of its total tonnage, and two-thirds of Japanese warships, had been sent to the bottom by American submarines. But as Admiral S. E. Morison has written in his official history of this magnificent record (see below), 'few stories of the exploits were given out and no correspondent was taken to sea before 1945.'

Casualties among the US submarine crews were severe—though not on the scale of German U-boat losses—but no great naval war in history was won with so few casualties as in the Pacific war. By employing in the later stages an almost excessive superiority in *matériel* and men to attack Japanese-held islands, casualties were kept to a minimum. The principle was sustained that there should be no limit to expenditure of *matériel* if it resulted in saving a single American life.

In these last months, the IJN virtually ceased to exist, and was reduced to mounting *kamikaze suicide attacks. So powerful were the gun and fighter defences of the Allied ships, they generally had a nuisance value only (but see OKINAWA).

The overall strategic concept of the war at sea against the powerful and wholly dedicated Japanese, and the conduct of operations, at first against intimidating odds, are difficult to criticize. While it was almost entirely American in contribution and inspiration, and a remarkable example of the rapid response and resilience of the American people and industry, effective British, Australian, and New Zealand participation was welcomed and recognized, perhaps less by the US Navy's C-in-C, *King, than by his subordinate commanders serving at sea. Relations remained cordial during all active operations.

The scale of the Pacific naval war, which was without precedent in history, would have exhausted the resources of any nation except the USA. But, with the early decision to make the defeat of Germany the first Allied priority, the US Navy was committed to a two-ocean war. From the *North African campaign landings of 8 November 1942, and the subsequent landings in Sicily, Italy, and the south of France (see SICILIAN and ITALIAN CAMPAIGNS, and FRENCH RIVIERA LANDINGS) the US Navy operated in the Mediterranean on a large scale and in the same capacity as in the Pacific. But as in the Atlantic, the British contribution was very much larger.

As far as the grindingly drawn-out battle of the Atlantic, and the Arctic convoys, were concerned, US participation was variable according to priorities elsewhere. But the Canadian contribution (see CANADA, 6(c)) was steady and consistent, and of greater value than has sometimes been credited to that Dominion.

Two late events, long after Taranto, Pearl Harbor, and the sinking of the *Prince of Wales* and *Repulse*, can be seen as marking again the changed nature of warfare at sea in 1939–45. The first was the sinking of the 'unsinkable' modern Japanese giant battleship **Musashi* by carrier-borne torpedo- and dive-bombers, and of the equally formidable German battleship **Tirpitz* in a Norwegian fiord by British heavy bombers. Neither of these monsters, which had demanded such vast resources and manpower in their construction, had taken any useful part in the war except as vague threats.

By contrast, combined operations, when correctly planned and given surprise and control of the air and the sea, invariably succeeded. Churchill, who had unjustly received the blame for the disaster of the failed combined operations at Gallipoli in 1915, had wished to entitle his First World War history, 'The Great Amphibian'. It would have been more suitable for his history of the Second World War.

From the day France fell and mainland Europe was at

the mercy of Hitler; equally, from 'the day of infamy', Pearl Harbor, victory over Germany and Japan could be achieved only by amphibious, or combined, operations, which in turn depended for success on command of the seas. This was as evident in the ferocious struggle for *Guadalcanal in the south-west Pacific as at *Anzio in Italy and the beaches of Normandy. Even Stalin, like Napoleon essentially a soldier, was forced to recognize this truth, and from the early weeks of the German attack in 1941 applied political pressure relentlessly on the Allies to make a seaborne landing in the west—a Second Front.

The strategy of sea power, and of its first cousin amphibious operations, had not fundamentally altered since Medina Sidonia's Great Armada had failed to defeat Queen Elizabeth I's navy, the Dutch sailed up the Medway, and Napoleon's troops were obliged to sit it out on the Boulogne cliffs. As Captain Stephen Roskill (see below), has written, 'When we review amphibious warfare in a modern context, here is a case of a historic principle whose validity, at least over a matter of four hundred years, remains quite unchanged'. RICHARD HOUGH

Hough, R., *The Longest Battle: The War at Sea* (London, 1986).
Kemp, P. K., *Victory at Sea 1939–45* (London, 1957).
Macintyre, D., *The Battle for the Mediterranean* (London, 1964).
—*The Battle for the Pacific* (London, 1966).
—*The Naval War Against Hitler* (London, 1971).
Morison, S. E., *History of United States Naval Operations in World War II*, 15, vols. (Boston, 1948–64).
Roskill, S. W., *The Strategy of Sea Power* (London, 1952).
—*The War at Sea*, 3 vols. (London, 1954–61).
Ruge, F., *Sea Warfare: A German Concept* (London, 1957).

searchlights, used by all armed forces, were primarily employed to help anti-aircraft guns and warships take accurate aim at night, but they had other uses as well. The Germans, for example, shone them on low clouds to give their troops more light by which to advance at the start of the *Ardennes campaign on 16 December 1944 (see also SIMONDS).

The range of early UK searchlights during the *Blitz was only about 3,660 m. (12,000 ft.) and the Germans soon learnt to fly above that height, but once their power was increased, and they became *radar-controlled, searchlights were more effective. Each box of the German defensive *Kammhuber Line had a radar-controlled master searchlight which locked on to an aircraft, and the others then followed it. The British put searchlights on some of their aircraft. The TURBINLITE, used on early night fighters, was soon outdated, but the Leigh Light on anti-submarine Coastal Command aircraft, used in conjunction with radar, helped to destroy several U-boats. British searchlights were also used to help damaged bombers land safely. On the transmission of a codeword every searchlight near a crippled aircraft exposed its beam vertically and then shone it horizontally towards the nearest airfield. It has been estimated that no fewer than 3,000 aircraft were helped in this way.

secrecy is the precondition of surprise, always one of the most effective strokes in warfare. Great care is always taken by commanders to keep their intentions secret; great efforts are expended by security services, in preserving secrecy, and by intelligence services, in trying to pierce through it.

Mid-20th-century armed forces generated huge quantities of paper: the British war office used up more paper in a year, 25,000,000 tons, than the 22,000,000 tons allotted to the whole book publishing industry. Much of this paper bore no security grading, but what did, bore it on an established scale: restricted, confidential, secret, most secret (changed to top secret after *Pearl Harbor, because some Americans thought 'most' meant 'almost' secret). Beyond top secret, a limited group of officers handled *ULTRA top secret material, deriving from *Bletchley Park; an overlapping (but not identical) group handled material, classified as BIGOT, which included details of NEPTUNE, the assault phase of the Normandy landings (see OVERLORD).

There were, moreover, secret services, such as *MI5, *MI6, and *SOE, the mere existence of which was not supposed to be referred to in papers graded lower than secret or in unscrambled telephone conversations. Telephone scramblers, then in their infancy, were available to staff at senior headquarters. They provided no long-term security (see FORSCHUNGSSTELLE, for example) as all an interceptor had to do was to record them, and then play them over at varying speeds, until he hit one that was intelligible, but they were useful for making secret tactical arrangements.

Not only were extra severe precautions taken to keep ULTRA secret material hidden; matters that senior staff regarded as very secret indeed were sometimes (in defiance of a rule of Churchill's) not written down at all—to the confusion of historians, but to the advantage of maintaining secrecy and thus securing victory.

The Americans, coming from a much more open society than the British, were less affected by the passion for secrecy. The Germans were still more affected by it than the British. Hitler put out an order, of which a copy was on the wall in every office in Germany, civil or military, in which he reminded his subjects that nothing declared secret was ever to be discussed by those not entitled to know about it: it was a useful part of the arrangements for persecuting those of whom the Nazis disapproved.

The Germans also graded some documents 'only for officers', just as the British and Americans sometimes used the rubric 'by hand of officer only'. Over-elaborate precautions were taken by the Americans in the limited distribution of *MAGIC decrypts. In 1941 there was a rule that MAGIC messages were carried round Washington, DC, in a locked box by a US Marine officer, who had no key to it and no knowledge of its contents. He visited each of eight key-carriers (president, chiefs of army and navy staffs, and so on), satisfied himself that each was sitting at an empty desk, placed the box on it, retired to the back of room, and picked the box up again after it had been re-locked. Therefore none of the readers of the messages could make any notes about them, at least while he had them in front of him; and analysis of the contents was consequently inhibited. It was an instance of how an obsession with security can defeat its own ends. The rubric THIS DOCUMENT IS NOT TO BE TAKEN INTO FRONT-LINE TRENCHES was discontinued by the British War Office in June 1940; 'not to be taken forward of Divisional headquarters' remained in occasional use until 1942.

Debate continues about whether any secrets are still worth preserving. Few of those who conduct it are aware of all the issues involved. Questions of manners, tact, and discretion are mixed up with questions of national safety; there are various points of method, still perfectly usable, which it would be folly to reveal; while a myriad points of detail are only held back because governments cannot afford the time and money to have the old records securely winnowed.

Secret services, moreover, like to be able to offer to possible recruits the inducement that a person's connection with the service will never, ever, become known to anybody outside it, and indeed only to a restricted number of people within it; such assurances will be valueless if any chance enquirer is ever to be let loose among secret service papers. M. R. D. Foot

secret services, see intelligence services section of major powers.

Security Intelligence Middle East (SIME), British intelligence organization formed in December 1939. It was responsible for security intelligence throughout the Mediterranean and Middle East, including Syria and Persia. Run jointly by *MI5 and *MI6, it described itself as the MI5 of the Middle East and acted through Field Security sections and MI6 Special Counter-Intelligence units. Among its more successful operations were rounding up members of the *Kondor mission and feeding misleading information to the Axis through a *double agent, Renato Levy, codenamed CHEESE.

selective service system, first-ever US peacetime draft of personnel for the armed forces, approved by Congress in September 1940. Under the Selective Service Act every US male citizen aged between 21 and 36 had to register and from November 1942 the ages were 18–45. From those who registered some were selected to serve for a year (later extended) but they had to be employed within the *Western Hemisphere or in US possessions, which included the Philippines. Initially, deferment was granted to students, but this was stopped in July 1941. After *Pearl Harbor the territorial restrictions were removed and during the war years a total of ten million men were inducted, with officers serving at an average of 39 months and enlisted men 33 months. The Act prohibited racial discrimination in drafting recruits and in their training, but as the army banned integrated units few *African Americans were drafted by the time the USA entered the war.

The Selective Service Act also defined *conscientious objectors. About 25,000 of these served in non-combatant roles (after 1943 they were confined to the medical corps), while 11,950, who objected to wearing a uniform, were drafted to civilian public service camps.

self-propelled guns were mobile artillery on tracked carriages which gave fire support, usually indirect, to infantry or tanks. The Americans, who specialized in this type of weapon, called them Tank Destroyers when employed in the anti-tank role. See also ANTI-TANK WEAPONS and ARTILLERY.

Senegal, see FRENCH WEST AFRICA.

Serbia, see YUGOSLAVIA.

Services Reconnaissance Department, see SPECIAL OPERATIONS AUSTRALIA.

Sevastopol, sieges of. The USSR's main *Black Sea naval base was one of the world's strongest fortresses. Its site on a deeply eroded, bare limestone promontory at the south-western tip of the Crimea makes an approach by land exceedly difficult, and cliffs protect the anchorage in Severnaya Bay. The Soviet Navy maintained and modernized forts dating back to the Crimean war of 1854–6 and installed 12 naval gun batteries comprising 42 guns, varying in calibre from 152 mm. to 305 mm. (5.9–11.9 in.), in armoured turrets and concrete emplacements. In the last two weeks of October 1941, early in the *German–Soviet war, Major General I. Y. Petrov and the survivors of his Independent Maritime Army, 32,000 troops, arrived by sea from Odessa. Petrov set about building three defence lines, the outermost on a rough arc about 16 km. (10 mi.) inland.

Between 26 September and 16 November Lt-General von *Manstein's Eleventh Army, with the Third Romanian Army attached, cleared the Crimea except for Sevastopol. The Eleventh Army, seven divisions in all, was the smallest German army on the Eastern Front, and although the Romanians compensated for its numerical deficiency they were lightly armed, poorly trained, and badly led. Torrential downpours and jumbled terrain delayed Manstein's deployment for a month, giving the C-in-C, Black Sea Fleet, Vice-Admiral F. S. Oktyabrsky, who had taken command of the fortress, time to bring in men and *matériel* for Petrov, who was his ground forces commander. Cruisers and destroyers could make the trip from Novorossisk overnight.

Manstein opened the attack on 17 December, sooner than Oktyabrsky, who was preparing to disrupt it by making several simultaneous landings along the coast, had thought he would. In five days, the German infantry at the point breached the first and second defence lines and in another four days they were cutting into the third line, beyond which the outer works of the fortress itself lay. Victory appeared close at hand, but only one German division and the Romanians were protecting 275 km. (170 mi.) of coast from Kerch to Yalta. On 26 December, Soviet troops took a beachhead near Kerch, and two days later a stronger force landed at Feodosiya in position to cut off the entire Kerch peninsula, which it proceeded to do in short order. Manstein then had to stop at Sevastopol and withdraw two divisions to prevent a breakthrough into the interior. In January 1942, the Soviet command activated the Crimea *front* under Maj-General D. T. Kozlov and ordered him to deploy three armies on the Kerch peninsula, which could be done by truck after the Kerch Strait had frozen solid.

When good weather returned in May, Manstein had to deal first with Crimea *front*. He deployed five German and two Romanian infantry divisions plus a panzer division (180 tanks) against Kozlov's 21 infantry divisions and 4 tank brigades (350 tanks). On 8 May, a landing executed under air cover by small craft of the type used for river crossings completely unhinged Kozlov's front, and ten days sufficed to finish the operation. More than 170,000 Red Army men were taken prisoner, largely because Stalin refused to permit a timely evacuation.

With a major offensive on the mainland in the offing, taking Sevastopol hardly seemed worth the effort. Manstein believed three or four divisions could keep the fortress under siege. The success on Kerch and another near *Kharkov, however, persuaded Hitler to conduct additional preliminary operations. Moreover, at Sevastopol he had a chance to show off a spectacular array of superheavy artillery built for use against the *Maginot Line which had not been needed there. The 33 pieces emplaced during April and May ranged in calibre from 280 to 600 mm. (10.9–23 in.). One, known as DORA, could fire an 800 mm. (31 in.) shell 50 km. (31 mi.).

Manstein, the master of the *blitzkrieg, faced a test in positional warfare. The terrain confined the lines of approach to the north, where the first attempt had been made, and to the south-east. Oktyabrsky and Petrov had exploited their five-month respite to the full. Petrov had 106,000 troops, and more than 80,000 naval personnel manned the forts and gun emplacements. Manstein's artillery bombardment, by 600 pieces including the heaviest, began on 2 June. Four divisions attacked from the north on 7 June but failed to find a single weak spot. Three divisions on the south-east had the same experience four days later. The artillery was effective against the forts but not against the hundreds of natural and man-made caves that housed machine guns and light artillery.

After two weeks, the north group was on the shore of Severnaya Bay opposite Sevastopol, and the attack from the south-east was stalled at the Sapun Heights. Hitler had set 23 June as the terminal date for all preliminary operations, but the end was not in sight, and to have stopped then would have seemed to concede defeat. A surprise thrust into Sevastopol by boat from across the bay on 28 June finally unsettled the defence. On the night of 30 June, Oktyabrsky left to organize an evacuation—which did not materialize except for a few hundred in the upper ranks who were taken out by air. Thereafter the resistance crumbled, ending on 4 July with 90,000 prisoners counted.

In the spring of 1944 the positions were reversed. In mid-April the Seventeenth German Army, much weakened and with three Soviet armies on its heels, took refuge at Sevastopol, from which the army commander, Lt-General Erwin Jaenecke, expected it to be evacuated. Hitler, however, demanded that Sevastopol be held to prevent Soviet control of the Black Sea. The Soviet commands, treating the fortress with considerable respect, prepared thoroughly and on 5 May took the Sapun Heights in a mass assault. After Hitler approved an evacuation late on 6 May, ships from Constanta took 38,000 troops off Cape Kherson. The Soviet commands claimed 100,000 killed and captured. Earl Ziemke

Manstein, F. E. von, *Lost Victories* (Chicago, 1958).
Ziemke, E. F., *Moscow to Stalingrad* (Washington, DC, 1988).

SEXTANT, codename for the Allied Cairo conference held from 23 to 26 November and 3 to 7 December 1943 to discuss future strategy (see GRAND ALLIANCE). In between, Churchill and Roosevelt and the *Combined Chiefs of Staff attended *EUREKA, the Teheran conference. EUREKA had been arranged because a Chinese delegation, led by *Chiang Kai-shek, was also attending SEXTANT and Stalin, who unlike China was not at war with Japan, had refused to send a representative or come himself.

In Cairo, both Allied leaders were accompanied by large delegations. As well as the Chinese, there was also a delegation led by *Mountbatten, *South-East Asia Command's supreme commander. Initial discussions centred on South-East Asia and Chiang Kai-shek's desire for *amphibious warfare operations in the Bay of Bengal to coincide with a proposed Chinese intervention in the *Burma campaign. Churchill called these discussions lengthy, complicated, and minor. Despite British reluctance, Roosevelt promised Chiang just such an operation. The consequences of EUREKA later forced him to retract, but the Cairo Declaration that was issued stated that all three powers were agreed upon future operations against Japan. It also stated that Japan would be stripped of all the territories it had acquired since 1914; that those taken from the Chinese would be returned to China, 'such as Manchukuo and Formosa, and the Pescadores', and that 'in due course' Korea would become free and independent.

Discussions during the second part of SEXTANT included those with President *Inönü on the likelihood of Turkey entering the war on the Allies' side, and Roosevelt told Churchill that he had decided to appoint *Eisenhower to command the Normandy landings (see OVERLORD). See also DIPLOMACY.

Seyss-Inquart, Artur (1892–1946), Reich Commissioner of German-occupied Netherlands from 1940 to 1945 who was named as foreign minister in Hitler's political testament.

The son of a teacher, Seyss-Inquart was born near Iglau in Moravia. After serving in the Austro-Hungarian Army during the *First World War, when he was seriously wounded, he studied law at Vienna University, became a barrister, and joined the Austrian Nazi Party in 1931. In May 1937 he became an Austrian state councillor, and, after pressure from Hitler, was appointed Austrian minister of the interior in February 1938. This gave him control of the country's internal security and of its police forces and enabled him to play a leading role in the events which led up to the Anschluss, Austria's union with Germany, in March 1938. His appointment, on 11 March, as the new Austrian chancellor was forced on the Austrian president whose powers Seyss-Inquart acquired when the German Army entered Austria the next day.

Promoted to *SS Obergruppenführer (lt-general) for his services during the Anschluss, Seyss-Inquart remained the Reich Governor of Ostmark—as Austria was now called—until 30 April 1939. Once Poland had fallen (see POLISH CAMPAIGN) he set up the General government (see POLAND; 2(b)) and was then appointed deputy to its governor, Hans *Frank, before being moved by Hitler to the occupied Netherlands where he served as Reich Commissioner until the end of the war. Although at first the Netherlands were not treated as harshly as some Nazi-occupied countries, Seyss-Inquart was not slow in beginning the round-up of Dutch Jews, recruiting *forced labour to work in Germany, confiscating valuable works of art (see LOOT), and making the Dutch economy an adjunct of Germany's. As the war progressed harsher and harsher measures were introduced. The deportation of Dutch Jews to their death was speeded up—117,000 out of a total of 140,000 were killed (see also FINAL SOLUTION)—vicious reprisals were instituted for resistance activities, and so much food and so many goods were extracted from the Dutch economy for German consumption that towards the end of the war its people were living below subsistence level. For this and other reasons, during the winter of 1944–5 some 16,000 died from starvation in those parts of the country which had not yet been liberated.

Compared with other high-ranking Nazi officials Seyss-Inquart appeared outwardly pleasant. He was also more intelligent than most of them, and when those defendants awaiting the *Nuremberg trials were given an IQ test he scored the second highest marks after *Schacht. Nevertheless, he had been directly responsible for mass deportations, summary executions, and the shooting of hostages, and he was found guilty of war crimes and executed.

Sforza, Count Carlo (1873–1952), anti-fascist Italian politician who fled to France in 1927, and then moved to the USA in 1940. He returned to Italy in September 1943 but refused to join *Badoglio's government unless King *Victor Emmanuel, whom he called the '*Pétain of Italy', abdicated. However, in April 1944, he became one of the ministers without portfolio in a restructured cabinet. He was elected president of Italy's preliminary parliamentary assembly in September 1945.

SHAEF, acronym of Supreme Headquarters Allied Expeditionary Force, which controlled Allied forces fighting in north-west Europe.

*Eisenhower was appointed supreme commander in December 1943; SHAEF was formed in February 1944; and the following month it moved to a hutted encampment in Bushy Park on the outskirts of London. It absorbed nearly all the staff of its predecessor, *COSSAC, but Eisenhower decided to retain several senior members of his *Allied Forces Headquarters in North Africa, where he had developed a highly successful, nationally integrated command system. These included his chief of staff, Lt-General Bedell *Smith, and Air Chief Marshal *Tedder who now became his deputy supreme commander.

To Tedder fell the responsibility of co-ordinating all *OVERLORD *air power which included, from 14 April to 14 September 1944, the British and US strategic air forces. Below Smith, who took many administrative problems off Eisenhower's shoulders and acted as a filter for correspondence and interviews, were three deputy chiefs of staff: Lt-General Frederick Morgan, Lt-General Humfrey Gale, and Air Vice-Marshal James Robb (see Chart). Morgan occasionally deputized for Smith; Gale, as the chief administrative officer, had the task of co-ordinating the activities of two of SHAEF's staff divisions, G-1 (Personnel) and G-4 (Supply), and the supply elements of G-5 (Civil Affairs); and Robb co-ordinated all correspondence and planning of the various SHAEF divisions connected with the Allied air forces. Except for the Adjutant General's, all SHAEF divisions had British deputies if commanded by a US officer, and vice versa.

The detailed planning of OVERLORD had already been delegated by COSSAC to the Commanders of the land, air, and sea forces (*Montgomery, *Leigh-Mallory, and *Ramsay). But before the landings Eisenhower retained responsibility for tactical decisions involving any major changes in the OVERLORD plan; and throughout the campaign in north-west Europe he also had wide administrative powers besides the operational ones he wielded after 1 September 1944. These included such diverse matters as health, welfare, *prisoners-of-war, *logistics, and the outlining of administrative plans for future operations.

The political sphere was a particularly vital area for SHAEF. Delicate negotiations had to be undertaken with de *Gaulle and the Free French, and civil affairs administrations had also to be organized for other liberated countries, as had a military government for Germany and Austria (see ALLIED CONTROL COMMISSIONS). SHAEF's G-5 division maintained liaison with the

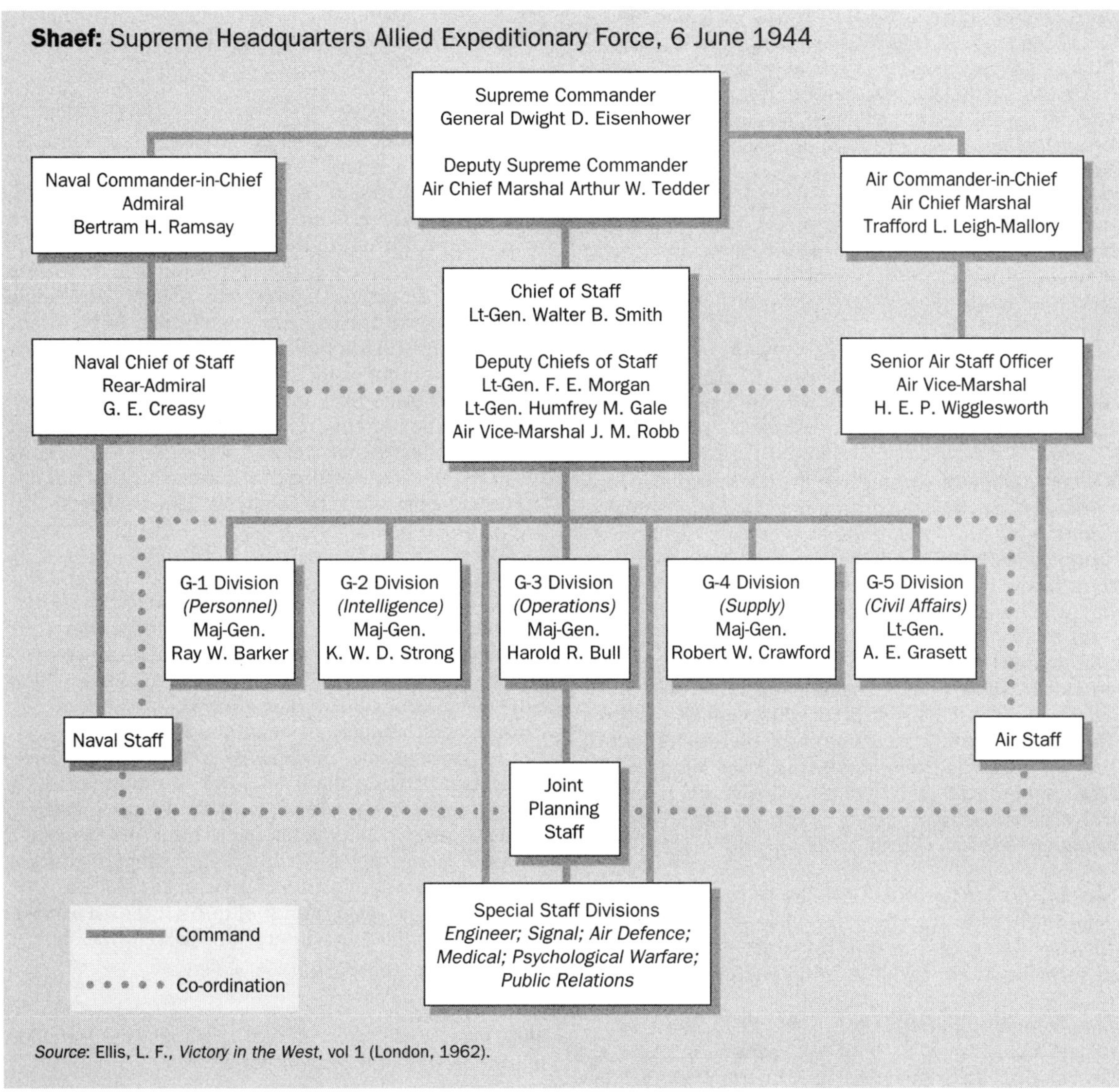

various *governments-in-exile through its European Allied Contact Section and when their countries were liberated sent missions to co-operate with them.

The nerve centre of SHAEF was its operations division, G-3, where planning and operations were combined. It planned operations for every eventuality; directed resistance activities in occupied Europe through its Special Force HQ, into which *SOE and the *Office of Strategic Services were co-opted; co-operated with the Psychological Warfare Division; and maintained the SHAEF War Room. The Intelligence Division, G-2, under Maj-General *Strong, also played a vital role in the success of OVERLORD, as its Ops B was responsible for the supervision of *deception operations within Eisenhower's area of command.

In early May 1944 an advanced command post was opened for Eisenhower near Portsmouth. In early July this was enlarged to become what was known as SHAEF Forward, while those remaining at Bushy Park became known as SHAEF Main. On 7 August Eisenhower established a small advance HQ (SHELLBURST) near Tournières, 19 km. (12 mi.) south-west of Bayeux in Normandy, and at the end of August SHAEF Forward moved to Jullouville just south of Granville. This became Eisenhower's operational HQ when he assumed direct command of Twelfth and Twenty-First Army Groups, and later of *Devers's Sixth Army Group. Jullouville soon proved too far from the front and on 19 September SHAEF Forward moved to Gueux, some 11 km. (7 mi.) north-west of Reims, which was where the Germans signed the document of *unconditional surrender on 7 May 1945. On 20 September SHAEF Main opened at the Trianon Palace Hotel in Versailles and its move was completed on 5 October. The following week what remained of SHAEF Main in the UK, about 1,500 men, was moved to Bryanston Square in central London, and once Germany had surrendered both Main and Forward were transferred to Frankfurt-am-Main to organize the disarmament of the German armed forces, the arrest of leading Nazis, and the formation of a military government. One of its last problems, before being disbanded on 14 July 1945, was handling the crisis of the continued fighting in and around *Prague.

In July 1944 SHAEF numbered 4,914 officers and men. By February 1945 this had jumped to 16,312, but the British contribution, limited by an acute manpower shortage, was only 6,320.

shaker technique, precursor of British *Pathfinder Force methods, first employed during the *thousand-bomber raids in May–June 1942. It was employed on night raids mounted by the RAF's Bomber Command after the *Butt report had revealed how few bombs reached their targets. Aircraft equipped with GEE (see ELECTRONIC NAVIGATION SYSTEMS) flew ahead of the main force and illuminated the area to be attacked with flares. These aircraft would be followed by target markers, also equipped with GEE, which dropped incendiary *bombs. These gave a concentrated area of fire on which the bombers of main force, which were not yet equipped with GEE, could unload their high explosive bombs. It brought about a marked improvement in Bomber Command's accuracy. See also STRATEGIC AIR OFFENSIVES, 1.

Shamir, Yitzhak (b.1915), Polish Jew who immigrated to Palestine in 1935. He joined the *Irgun in 1937 and then the *Stern gang, becoming its leader in 1942. From 1983 he served as Israel's prime minister on several occasions.

Shaposhnikov, Marshal Boris (1882–1945), Red Army officer, highly valued by Stalin, who served as Chief of the General Staff (CGS) from 1928 to 1931, from 1937 to 1940, and during the early part of the *German–Soviet war.

Shaposhnikov was an extremely able and talented staff officer who drew up the plans for the Soviet occupation of eastern Poland during the *Polish campaign and the Red Army's eventual success in the *Finnish–Soviet war. In August 1937 he became deputy to the Defence Commissar, *Voroshilov, as well as CGS, but when Voroshilov was removed in May 1940 so was Shaposhnikov, though the same month he was promoted marshal of the Soviet Union. He left his post as CGS in August 1940 to take charge of the new *Stalin Line which was being constructed on the Soviet Union's new borders. After the German invasion in June 1941 (see BARBAROSSA) he again became CGS and a member of the *Stavka. But his health declined and in May 1942 he was replaced by *Vasilevsky and again became Deputy Defence Commissar. In June 1943 he was appointed to head the Voroshilov Higher Military Academy, a post he held until his death.

Shukman, H. (ed.), *Stalin's Generals* (London, 1993).

Shell House raid, mounted in March 1945 by 18 British Mosquito bombers and 25 American Mustang fighters against Copenhagen's *Gestapo HQ which was situated in the city's Shell Petroleum offices. The raid was requested by resistance workers in Denmark who wanted to free 38 leaders of the resistance who were being held on the top floor and to destroy Gestapo records. Using the technique of *skip-bombing the bombers demolished the building's ground floor which contained the records and destroyed vital evidence that would have led to the arrest and execution of other resistance leaders. One of the bombers crashed, killing 86 children in a nearby school, but 32 of the 38 prisoners escaped. As one of them left the building, he picked up, at random, a card index which turned out to contain a list of all the Gestapo's Danish helpers.

Reilly, R., *The Sixth Floor* (London, 1969).

Shetland Bus, nickname of a British clandestine organization formed by *SOE, the Admiralty's *Naval Intelligence Division, and the Military Intelligence Service of Norway's *government-in-exile. It used Norwegian fishing boats (later three US submarine-chasers) and their crews to maintain contact with Norwegian resistance movements. It ferried agents and equipment between Shetland, Scotland's most northerly islands, and Norway, and often evacuated Norwegian civilians. Several boats were used to transport *human torpedoes across the North Sea in an attempt to attack the German battleship **Tirpitz* in October 1942. The organization operated from 1941 to 1945, the sea passages always taking place in winter when daylight was short.

Howarth, D., *The Shetland Bus* (London, 1951).

shipping, see ARCTIC CONVOYS, CONVOYS, and Merchant marine section of the major powers.

shuttle bombing was a technique whereby aircraft flew between two bases, attacking their target on the way. It was employed by Eighth and Fifteenth US Army Air Forces in Europe, and was first used in August 1943, when aircraft attacking Regensburg (see SCHWEINFURT) from the UK then landed at bases in North Africa. It was also used in mid-1944 when American bombers were allowed by the USSR to use three bases near Kiev (Poltava, Mirgorod, Pinyatin) to bomb Germany, Hungary, and Romania while flying to and from their bases in Italy and the UK. However, on 21 June 1944, when 114 UK-based bombers attacked a synthetic oil plant south of Berlin, a German aircraft shadowed them to Poltava. That night the airfield, along with 58 aircraft, was destroyed by the Luftwaffe, and another 26 aircraft were damaged.

Siam, see THAILAND.

Sicherheitsdienst, the Security service of the *SS. See RSHA.

Sicilian campaign. The decision to invade Sicily as part of the Allies' strategy to win the battle for the *Mediterranean, was made at the Casablanca conference in January 1943 (see SYMBOL). The operation (HUSKY) was given to General *Alexander's newly formed Fifteenth Army Group. It comprised *Montgomery's British and Commonwealth Eighth Army and *Patton's 1st US Armored Corps, which became Seventh US Army on invasion day, a total of eight divisions including airborne, commando, and Ranger units. The supporting sea and air commanders, *Cunningham and *Tedder respectively, worked with Alexander under *Eisenhower and *Allied Forces HQ, a command system which, by allowing the Axis forces to evacuate Sicily almost unscathed, proved to be less than satisfactory.

The planning stage was confused and protracted, the operational one hardly less so. Anglo-American, and inter-service, co-operation was dogged by disagreement and acrimony, which were the foundation of high-level disputes later in the war (see also RIVALRIES). Montgomery's most noteworthy contribution was to improve the invasion plan, for once ashore he acted almost independently of Patton and signally failed to achieve the quick breakthrough he sought. The Americans, on the other hand, highly mobile and aggressive, came of age as a fighting force.

The landings, launched before dawn on 10 July 1943, were the second largest undertaken in Europe during the war after *OVERLORD and involved 180,000 Allied troops and 2,590 ships. The operation succeeded, but with not much margin to spare. Axis airfields had been neutralized, but the air support plan was inadequate and strong winds made the first large Allied airborne operation a disaster, with many of the gliders landing in the sea. However, *ULTRA intelligence had already revealed the success of the *MINCEMEAT deception plan, which had focused German attention elsewhere, and that the morale of the defending forces was low.

The only two German divisions available to oppose the landings, the reconstituted Hermann Göring and the newly formed 15th Panzer Grenadier, proved formidable opponents. Both these were part of General Hans Hube's 14th Panzer Corps which was later reinforced by 1st Parachute Division and most of 29th Panzer Grenadier Division. An Italian, General Alfredo Guzzoni, one of Mussolini's most competent generals, was in overall command though he soon relinquished operational control to Hube.

Despite the adverse weather conditions the landings which followed the airborne drops went fairly smoothly. Montgomery's two corps (10th and 13th) landed between Pozallo and Syracuse on the east coast where there was only isolated opposition, and Syracuse was taken, as planned, by 13th Corps on the day of the landings. The Americans, landing between Cape Scaramia and Licata on the south-west coast, were more exposed to the weather and had some difficulties. Initial opposition was also stronger there but by the end of the day all three divisions were ashore. Fierce fighting on 11 July drove off armoured counter-attacks around Gela, US warships providing much needed support.

Once the Allied forces were firmly ashore Alexander ordered Patton to shield Montgomery's left flank as the Eighth Army advanced on two axes: 13th Corps towards Catania and 30th Corps towards the network of roads around Leonforte and Enna. By doing so he missed the opportunity of allowing *Bradley's 2nd US Corps to cut the island in half quickly and trap 15th Panzer Grenadier escaping from the west.

On 15 July 1943 Patton regrouped his forces to form a Provisional Corps under his deputy, Lt-General Geoffrey Keyes, ready to advance on Palermo. When, the next day, Alexander ordered him to continue protecting Montgomery's flank, Patton flew to see him to protest. New instructions allowed the Provisional Corps to reach Palermo on 22 July after a whirlwind advance in which many Italian *prisoners-of-war were taken, but which was of doubtful value otherwise. By 17 July Hube had established the first of three lines of defence, stretching from south of Catania across to San Stefano on the north coast. The rugged Sicilian landscape confined any armoured advance to the narrow, winding roads, making the terrain ideal for defensive purposes. The defenders made the most of it and Montgomery's forces, now organized into a four-pronged attack, made slow progress. But on 22 July 1943 (three days later than Montgomery had predicted) 1st Canadian Division took Leonforte, while on its left Bradley's 2nd Corps made, too late, the bisection of the island Alexander had originally envisaged Montgomery would achieve. Montgomery's attack towards Catania was even slower and the port did not fall until 5 August.

Hitler was implacably opposed to any withdrawal but when Mussolini fell from power on 25 July he ordered plans for a possible evacuation to be drawn up, and two days later the Germans started withdrawing from the first defensive line. However, they continued to resist stoutly in ideal defensive country, though the Italians had virtually given up. The 1st US Division (see BIG RED ONE) was involved in a fierce five-day battle at Troina while the British launched a powerful attack towards Adrano, both places being key positions in Hube's next line of defence. Their fall prompted Kesselring, the German C-in-C South-West, to start a total evacuation which began on the night of 11/12 August 1943, a brilliantly planned and executed operation. It has been estimated that as many as 40,000 German and 62,000 Italian troops—and most of their equipment and supplies—escaped almost unhindered. The Allies' use of intelligence at the highest level, including ULTRA which gave a clear warning of the Germans' intentions ten days

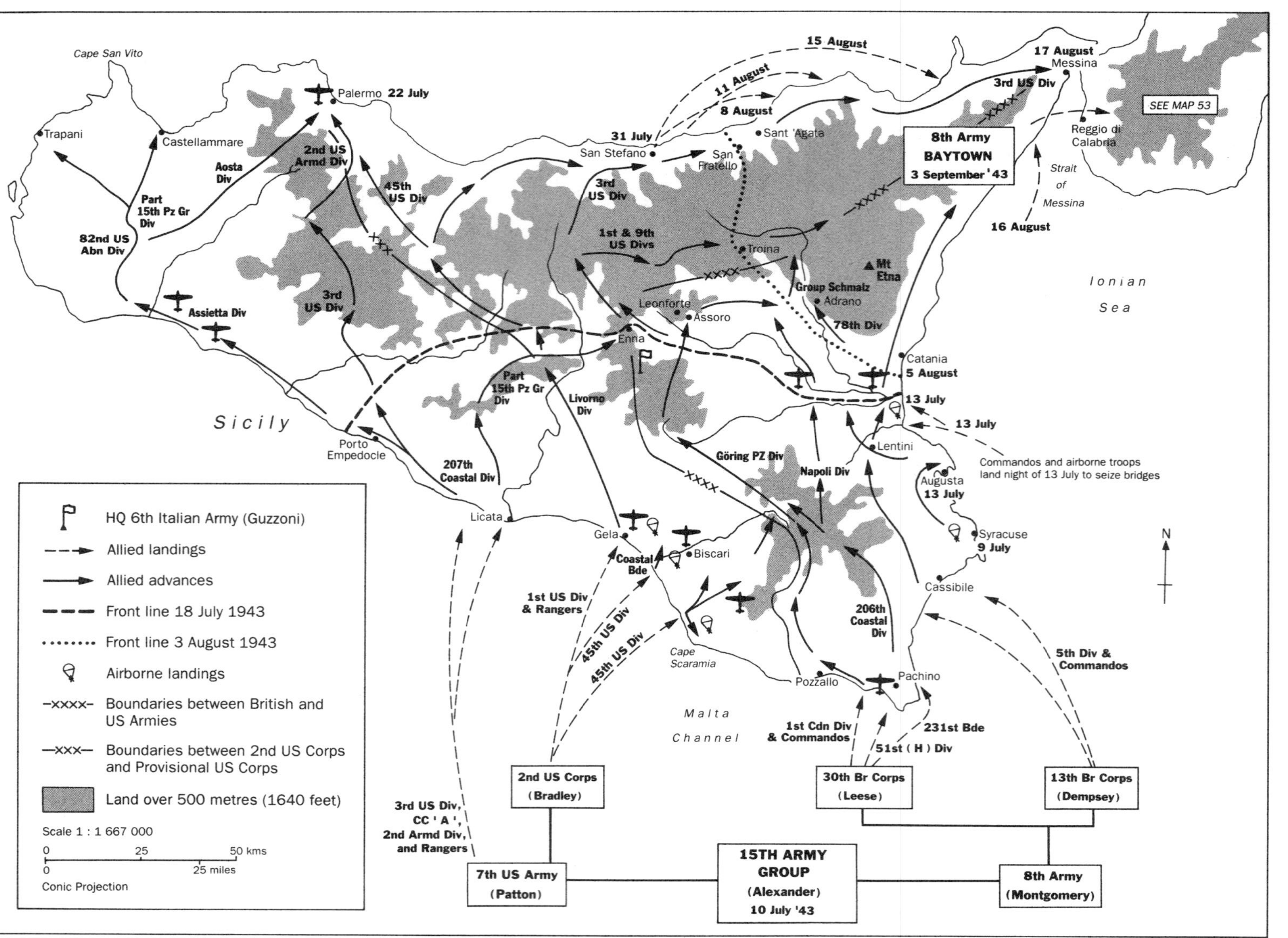

96. **Sicilian campaign**, July–August 1943

in advance, was poor and the Allied commanders, without a co-ordinated plan to stop the exodus, made little concerted effort to intervene.

However, both the Americans on the north coast, who fought their last fierce engagements between San Fratello and Sant' Agata, and the British, who were advancing north-eastwards on either side of Mount Etna, launched fruitless *amphibious warfare operations to cut off their retreating opponents. A final dash by the two allies to reach Messina first was won by the Americans. One of their patrols entered the port on the evening of 16 August; by early next morning the last of Hube's men had been evacuated. Once the island had been liberated the *Allied Military government of Occupied Territories established a civilian administration which was deeply penetrated by the *Mafia.

D'Este, C., *Bitter Victory* (London, 1988).

Sidi Barrani, battle of, British counter-attack (COMPASS), mounted on 9 December 1940, during the *Western Desert campaigns after the Tenth Italian Army, commanded by General Mario Berti, had invaded Egypt in September 1940. It proved to be that rare event, a battle that goes according to plan, the plan being drawn up with the help of *Dorman-Smith. The attack was rehearsed in extreme secrecy and mounted by *O'Connor's Western Desert Force. Although heavily outnumbered, it was equipped with the new Matilda tank against which Berti had no defence. When the battle ended on 11 December 38,300 Italians, including four generals, had been made *prisoners-of-war. British casualties were 624. COMPASS, which started as a raid, became the prelude to the Italians being chased out of Egypt and then out of eastern Libya as well.

Sidi Rezegh battles, fought during the *Western Desert campaigns as part of the British and Commonwealth Eighth Army's offensive in November 1941 (CRUSADER).

The CRUSADER plan envisaged an inland thrust by Eighth Army's armoured corps through *Rommel's forces besieging *Tobruk while the infantry corps advanced along the coast. These thrusts would then link up with a break-out by the Tobruk garrison, and the Allied forces would then sweep westwards across eastern Libya.

Sidi Rezegh, a ridge some 32 km. (20 mi.) south-east of Tobruk, lay between this British thrust and the besieged port. Rommel, who at first thought CRUSADER was only a raid, ordered the *Afrika Korps to the area. As the Tobruk garrison began its break-out towards Sidi Rezegh the ridge was captured, but when 7th Armoured Brigade tried to advance beyond it Afrika Korps units counter-attacked, retook the ridge, and almost destroyed the brigade.

With the British armour reinforced by 1st South African Division the two sides now fought for possession of the ridge. The Afrika Korps and the Italian Ariete Armoured Division scattered and partly destroyed South African supply columns and virtually annihilated a South African infantry brigade. The battle became known as Totensonntag (Sunday of the Dead) as it took place on the last Sunday of the ecclesiastical year, the day when German Protestants pray for the souls of the departed. That same day, 23 November, the British Eighth Army commander, Lt-General *Cunningham, alarmed by his losses, requested the presence of his C-in-C, General *Auchinleck. Convinced by Totensonntag that CRUSADER had failed, Cunningham wanted to withdraw. Auchinleck arrived but ordered the offensive to continue, and on 26 November replaced Cunningham with Maj-General Neil Ritchie.

Having decisively won the battle on Totensonntag, Rommel now decided to relieve his posts at *Bardia and *Halfaya Pass, which had become isolated by the British advance. But while he moved eastwards—his advance is sometimes known as his 'dash for the wire' as the Egyptian frontier was marked by a wire fence—the New Zealand Division retook Sidi Rezegh in one of the hardest, and bloodiest, battles it ever fought. Then, on 26 November, other British units linked up at Ed Duda with those attacking out of Tobruk.

Rommel's lightning thrust failed to achieve its objective and his return put the New Zealanders, already besieged at Sidi Rezegh, under increasing pressure, which 1st South African Brigade and British armour could do nothing to relieve. By 1 December Sidi Rezegh was back in Axis hands, the Tobruk corridor had been cut, and the New Zealand Division badly mauled. This second victory spurred Rommel to try advancing eastwards again, but his casualty figures, increasing Allied pressure, and particularly the paucity of his supplies, soon forced him to withdraw.

Casualty figures for CRUSADER were high on both sides. Out of 118,000 Allied troops taking part, British and Commonwealth losses amounted to 17,700, or 15%. The Axis forces, which had numbered 119,000, lost 24,500, or 20%, and another 13,800 became *prisoners-of-war when Rommel's frontier posts at Bardia and Halfaya Pass surrendered the following January.

Siegfried Line, name used by both sides for the German *West Wall, as was a part of Germany's *First World War Western Front fortifications between Lens and Reims.

Sieg Heil! (hail to victory) was, with the accompanying Nazi salute, the rallying cry of Hitler's faithful followers, particularly at Nazi Party rallies.

Sierra Leone, see BRITISH WEST AFRICA.

SIGABA, US cipher machine produced by the Teletype Corporation in Chicago for the US armed forces (the US Army called it the SIGABA, the US Navy the Electrical Cypher Machine). It was developed from a cipher machine invented by a Swede, Boris Hagelin. The American cryptologist William F. Friedman (1891–1969), who broke the Japanese *PURPLE machine cipher from which *MAGIC intelligence was derived, helped produce it during the 1930s and it was the one most frequently employed by the US Army during the war.

sigint is an abbreviation of signals intelligence, as opposed to humint or human intelligence (for which, see SPIES). In addition to the entry below, see COMBINED BUREAU MIDDLE EAST, FAR EAST COMBINED BUREAU, FORSCHUNGSSTELLE, MAGIC, and ULTRA, as well as the intelligence services section of entries for the major powers.

signals intelligence warfare

1. Introduction

There is a good deal of terminological confusion about the broad field of signals intelligence (sigint) since it was not until 1943 that efforts were made to standardize terms commonly in use in the UK and USA. Sigint was held to consist of four distinct processes: (1) the interception of all signals, known as the *Y-Service in the UK and the Radio Intelligence Service (RI) in the USA; (2) the monitoring of traffic patterns and networks, designated as Traffic Analysis (TA); (3) the decryption or cryptanalysis of encoded or enciphered signals (see CODES AND CIPHERS); (4) the interpretation (including translation) of decrypted signals. These processes were located in the UK in the government Code and Cypher School (GCCS), set up after the *First World War under Foreign Office supervision, but drawing personnel from the armed services (see BLETCHLEY PARK). In the USA, they were organized by separate groups within the Navy's Operations Division and the Army General Staff (see USA, 6).

Even greater organizational diversity prevailed in Germany, where the leading role was taken by the army; former army personnel ran the foreign ministry's small cipher section, while the navy organization was even smaller. In 1928, military Sigint was centralized within the Secret Service, the *Abwehr, but in practice each service kept trained personnel within separate signals services, though in 1938 co-ordination of the three services was established under a Wehrmacht High Command (OKW). Initially, the first two processes were known under the term *Beobachtungs-Dienst* (or *B-Dienst) within the navy—*Horchdienst* in the army and air force—and the third process was called the *Entzifferungs-Dienst* (E-Dienst). In 1933 a new Nazi Party-dominated service, the Forschungsamt, was established and eventually became the largest German sigint agency (see also GERMANY, 7). But no single central agency emerged, such as GCCS in the UK or the 8th Chief Directorate of the *NKVD in the USSR, as each German agency expanded and tended to compete more strongly with the others. Each retained the terminology but, in practice, the *secrecy within which they operated meant that each organization tended to cover all of these processes according to the resources and areas of concentration allocated to them. Italy and Germany began to collaborate from 1933 and Italian sigint organizations developed along parallel lines thereafter. The Japanese Army was influenced by Polish advisers in the early 1920s, while the Japanese Navy had had signals instruction from the UK since the late 19th century; army and navy developed rival sigint establishments, while the foreign and home ministries organized the principal civilian agencies.

Differences emerged in the forms of centralization or co-ordination according to bureaucratic or political demands in each country, but in every country there was a tendency for party political control to prevail and a tendency for each agency to engage in frequent organizational changes to maintain secrecy. Where the internal security of the state or ruling groups might be threatened by the effects of war, the interception of cable, telephone, and voice signals tended to be primarily delegated to the internal security services of the combatant powers, such as *MI5, the FBI (see USA, 6), the NKVD or the Sicherheitsdienst (see RSHA) or divided between civilian (*Tokkō) and military (*Kempei) police in Japan. The onset of war, however, ensured that military agencies would gain resources and influence as a result of operational requirements. All these organizations, together with others concerned with what is nowadays known as electronic warfare intelligence (elint), *photographic reconnaissance, the Radio Security Service (see MI6), the monitoring of the media and mail *censorship, are now seen as integral parts of a country's communications intelligence (comint), the products of which are channelled to higher policy-making and operational bodies.

Sigint in practice related primarily to radio (or wireless) traffic since *radio communications became the most important method of communication for the mobile aerial and land warfare that developed during the Second World War. During the inter-war period, all belligerent states invested heavily in the creation of extensive communications networks and in the monitoring of the preparations of other states, which had a direct impact on the conduct of operations in the early stages of the Second World War (see BLITZKRIEG, for example). Revelations about decryption successes in the First World War and in the early 1920s, directly connected with the revolution in Russia, led to investment in more advanced code and cipher systems aimed at protecting state communications. Soviet cryptographic advances after 1926 in particular stimulated the development of *one-time pad systems for codes (where letter symbols were prevalent) and of electro-mechanical and, later, electronic machine ciphers (where number symbols were prevalent). These advances contributed not only to security in communications, but also to the apprehensions of neighbouring states, such as Poland, Germany, Hungary, Sweden, and Japan, and rapidly spread to the rest of the international system in the 1930s. The crucial balance to be struck was between minimizing losses in one's own communications security and maximizing penetration of the security of one's opponents' communications.

2. Joint and combined sigint

More than ever before, the effectiveness of sigint depended on the joint efforts of all agencies at every national level and the combined efforts of the belligerent coalitions. The success of any side depended to a considerable extent on a superior advance knowledge of an opponent's intentions and movements, particularly when the operational capabilities of each side were relatively evenly matched. Close German sigint collaboration with Italy, Hungary, Finland, and the Baltic States in the 1930s proved more effective in penetrating Anglo-French systems in 1939–40, and in assisting German operational successes during the *Norwegian campaign and the fall of *France in June 1940, than the individual progress made separately by Poland, France, and the UK up to the outbreak of war. British penetration of Italian systems in August 1940 was of direct value in improving communications security and in laying the ground for successful operations in the battles for the *Mediterranean and the *Atlantic in 1940–1. In 1941–2, however, Anglo-American advances with Japanese and German systems were still insufficient, combined with inadequate military preparations in the Pacific, to outweigh their losses of signals security.

Japanese intervention possibly lengthened the Second World War by 12–18 months, as the USA and UK failed to achieve an adequate level of signals intelligence co-operation with the USSR against Japan and were unable to commit Stalin to the war against Japan before the spring of 1945. The serious underestimation of Japanese operational capabilities was matched by an over-estimation of the value of the pre-war penetration of Japanese diplomatic and naval signals security. Direct Anglo-American knowledge of the plans of the Japanese Army was not obtained until April 1943, though knowledge of Japanese naval operations played a crucial part in the decisive battle of *Midway in June 1942 (see ULTRA, 2). Anglo-American ignorance about Japanese preparations for war in 1941 was compounded by an inability to penetrate Soviet signals security sufficiently to recognize the Soviet–Japanese commitment to mutual neutrality, without which Japan almost certainly could not have gone to war. Japanese sigint's most successful contribution (with some Italian and German assistance) lay in the independent confirmation, from a reading of state department radio cables, of the lack of American–Soviet accord on Far Eastern policy.

Severe German underestimation of the capacity of the Soviet system to resist, coupled with an overestimate of Japan's capacity to contain the USA and with an over-readiness to take on the USA at a time when Hitler already had cause to recognize an over-extension of German resources, was compounded by a steadily worsening balance of advantage in sigint warfare. Not only were German sigint organizations unable to make more than tactical inroads into Soviet communications security, and virtually shut out of US operational traffic from 1 January 1942 (and of British from June 1943), but also Anglo-American inroads into German and Axis cipher security became so extensive that the balance swung dramatically in favour of the Allied coalition for the rest of the war.

3. Surprise and deception

Many important cryptosystems in use by all belligerents were never resolved, usually because, even if they were intercepted, there were too few signals for them to be decrypted successfully, as decryption experts needed sufficient quantities of material to break a cipher. In many instances, greater security could be attained by minimizing or eliminating radio communications and resorting to cable, telephone, and landline, or courier services. Strict radio silence increased the surprise impact of offensive operations, and jamming, changes of wavelength, changes of code or cipher table, or changes of system, could have a temporary or more permanent effect on operational sigint agencies. On the other hand, elaborate efforts were made to deceive hostile sigint agencies, usually prior to major strategic moves such as *BARBAROSSA or *OVERLORD by organizing large amounts of dummy radio signals planned to simulate an impending offensive in a different direction from that actually intended, or in the case of the Japanese attack on *Pearl Harbor, to disguise the true location of a striking force. Given the likelihood that success in reading operational signals was bound to be subject to gaps or delays in resolution, the techniques of direction-finding and traffic analysis were often the mainstays available to interpreters of offensive moves. Even when denied any possibility of successful decryption for most of the *Pacific war, Japanese listening-posts were usually alerted to impending US offensives by increases in radio traffic across the Pacific. This ensured that general preparations could be made to make capture of Japanese-held territory a more costly business, especially in the end phase of the war.

4. Physical and covert retrieval

Military operations offered more opportunities for the physical seizure of communications equipment and code materials, but, except in cases where it was difficult to replace compromised systems quickly, or there were delays in confirming compromise, as in the case of the British cabinet papers taken from the liner **Automedon* off Singapore in November 1940, such seizures were of smaller value than covert photography of codes and ciphers. All states engaged in this kind of activity, but it was a favourite method of some states: for example, it was successfully employed by the Italian secret services (see ITALY, 6) against the French, British, and Americans, and extended to their own allies, particularly the Japanese and the Romanians. The use of telephone taps (see also FORSCHUNGSSTELLE and SOURCE K) and listening devices was also a valuable supplementary method of Sigint, as these were not only voice-activated, but could also record sounds of machinery such as typewriters and cipher machines, which could then be transformed into text form.

5. Signal security and alerts

Sigint security at national level was sometimes the responsibility of each agency and sometimes this was delegated to a single body, such as the NKVD's 8th Chief Directorate in the USSR or Bletchley Park in the UK, which were responsible for both diplomatic and military ciphers, or the Amtsgruppe WNV in Germany which supervised armed forces cipher security, but also tested the security of civilian systems unofficially. Generally, the military tended to be unconvinced of the security of their own diplomatic and civilian systems (as in the USA, Germany, and Japan) and tended to instruct military personnel to minimize reliance on such systems for the transmission of operational information. But bureaucratic *rivalries also could lead to silence about insecure communications because that could confer some advantage domestically for one agency over a rival.

Nor were allies in the same coalition as frank as they might be about weaknesses in their systems. The UK, for example, hesitated to draw Soviet attention to some enemy tactical systems known to be penetrated in order not to compromise knowledge of British resolution of the *ENIGMA machine cipher. Equally, the German Navy passed on decrypts of Allied traffic to Japan after 9 December 1941 only in its own cipher because of suspicions about Anglo-American inroads into Japanese systems. A German warning about the insecurity of Japanese diplomatic traffic (see MAGIC) in March 1941, and an Italian warning about the compromise of the traffic of the Japanese military attaché in Lisbon in 1943, led only to checks on the physical security of the relevant diplomatic premises, but not to any serious questioning of compromise through decryption. The Italians had an extensive monitoring network in the Western Atlantic, Indian, and Pacific oceans as well as the Mediterranean area. This considerably assisted German *auxiliary cruiser operations from 1939 to 1941 and gave support to the Japanese Navy from 1941 onwards, but the Italians frequently had their warnings of compromised traffic ignored or rejected by their allies (see also AXIS STRATEGY AND CO-OPERATION).

German suspicions of Italian losses of cipher security to the UK in the autumn of 1940 led to the dispatch of an advisory mission to Rome. But advice that every effort be made to keep German and Italian systems completely separate was ignored and ENIGMA equipment, previously loaned during the *Spanish Civil War but upgraded in 1940, was allowed to be deployed selectively in Italian communications (see CAPE MATAPAN). Fear that this would lead to a compromise of German systems was also ignored; even when leakages in German operational communications occurred in the Mediterranean theatre, it was always attributed to poor Italian security rather than to resolutions of ENIGMA systems. A more concerted effort was made in July 1942 to tighten joint security and this was extended to the Pacific at the same time as a result of the capture of papers from the Combined Operations Intelligence Centre in New Zealand on board the Australian steamer **Nankin* by a German auxiliary cruiser. These seemed to indicate a degree of compromise of Japanese naval systems that was reinforced by the subsequent loss of a Japanese naval codebook on Guadalcanal. The net result was an extensive tightening of security which increased Allied difficulties in reading Axis military systems in the second half of 1942. On the Allied side, by contrast, close Anglo-American co-operation in organizing a standard system for secure distribution of ULTRA intelligence by means of *Special Liaison Units to theatre commands minimized leakages and this was steadily reinforced by a tightening up of British naval systems between the winter of 1941 and the summer of 1943.

6. The strategic value of diplomatic intercepts

The penetration of merchant shipping and diplomatic systems, including those used by military attachés abroad, or of individual members of the opposing coalitions, provided valuable clues about the strategies and operational intentions of the other members of the coalitions. Anglo-Polish collaboration in helping to make the earliest inroads into ENIGMA systems is well-documented. But it is much less well-known that German reading of Polish diplomatic and attaché traffic with Scandinavia provided insights in 1941 into the system most commonly employed by British military attachés for communication with both London and command posts overseas, the Interdepartmental Cypher. Such breaks, combined with information from the Naval Cypher and Naval Code and from Yugoslav and Greek traffic, were of great value for the German *Balkan campaign and on *Crete, as well as in highlighting British activities in the neutral countries of Europe, the Near and Far East and the Americas up to the introduction of one-time pads at the end of 1941. Italian and German successes with the US *Black code up to September 1942 provided a flow of decrypts of detailed reports about British dispositions and plans for the Western Desert campaigns that were of great value for *Rommel's defensive and offensive successes during 1942. German penetration of Merchant Navy Code and Naval Cypher No. 3 compromised Allied convoy movements in the battle of the Atlantic until July 1943 and offset the advantage the Allies had of virtually complete security of US naval systems after the USA entered the war.

Similarly, the US Army's resolution of the main Japanese diplomatic system in 1940 provided access to Hitler's briefings of the Japanese ambassador in Berlin, General *Ōshima, about German offensive plans between 1941 and 1943 and to Ōshima's detailed reports about the state of German defences along the Channel coast. These advantages were enhanced by US resolution of the Japanese military attaché cipher in 1943 and UK resolution of Japanese naval attaché systems in 1944, covering developments in the whole of neutral and occupied Europe to the end of the war. Although it appears that little progress was made in persuading

Soviet sigint agencies to exchange Japanese code materials, it was possible for the UK and USA to utilize the resolutions of Japanese systems, as well as German foreign ministry and Abwehr traffic, to promote frictions between Japan and Germany of the kind that had already been successfully promoted between Italy and Germany. For example, Allied disinformation about Japanese collusion with the USSR to permit a massive transfer of Soviet forces from the Far East to Europe convinced the German foreign minister *Ribbentrop, who confronted and angered senior Japanese Army representatives in Berlin with accusations of disloyalty to the alliance in May and October 1943. Knowledge derived from decrypts was useful in generating frictions, but was much less effective in destroying the credibility of Japan as an ally in Hitler's eyes than had previously been achieved in the case of Italy, mainly by feeding enemy agents and diplomats in neutral countries with misleading, but plausible, information.

Allied penetration of Japanese communications shed much light on the wartime efforts to employ the USSR as a potential mediator in the Pacific war and Japan as a mediator in the *German–Soviet war. But, after the war, even following the seizure of Axis archives and interrogation of participants in wartime decisions, the USSR remained, in Churchill's phrase, an 'enigma wrapped up in a mystery'. Post-war defections and Soviet revelations about wartime intelligence activity in such cases as the RAMSAY ring in Japan (see SORGE) and the *Rote Kapelle in western Europe have lifted only part of the veil from Soviet sigint. The USSR was probably the most successful state in protecting strategic communications from hostile sigint and in cloaking its intentions in 1939 and 1941 in order to avoid being drawn prematurely into the European and Pacific conflicts. But at the same time, its unwillingness to co-operate with the western powers deprived it of access to knowledge that could have significantly reduced the massive manpower and material losses accompanying its entry and involvement in the Second World War. The end of the *Cold War has opened up Soviet archives, which may begin to answer many hitherto unresolved questions about Soviet sigint.

7. The role of the neutral states

The territory of the neutral states provided fertile ground for the sigint activities of the warring coalitions, as well as access to economic resources and technology. States such as Italy, Japan, and Spain early in the war were benevolently neutral towards Germany, which derived useful information-gathering opportunities from a presence on their territory, much as the UK benefited from US and Swedish benevolence. Both sides sought to derive advantage from their ability to read Turkish codes and ciphers as a means of deceiving and misleading their opponents.

Spanish territory was a significant battleground in covert warfare. Permission was given to the Axis states, in spite of constant Allied complaints to the Spanish authorities, to set up radio monitoring facilities on the mainland and the Atlantic islands, along with ship-reporting and supply facilities which directly supported U-boat operations in the Central and South Atlantic. Spanish government agencies provided a good deal of information otherwise inaccessible to each of the principal Axis states which was passed on to their representatives in Madrid throughout the war. On the other hand, the USA and UK derived benefit from their control of Spain's cable and telephone utilities and Allied agencies exploited their presence on Spanish (or Portuguese) soil to obtain Axis code materials and to disseminate misleading information, derived from decrypt evidence and aimed at the creation of frictions between Germany and its allies.

Although Switzerland and Sweden were particularly vulnerable to German threats, they sought to preserve as much independence as possible by an even-handed approach to the belligerent coalitions. Covert links were maintained with both Axis and Allied intelligence services. In the Swiss case, an exchange of intelligence was conducted by Colonel Roger Masson that traded information with both sides. In August 1943, for example, Masson informed the Abwehr that a contact in the US navy department had revealed that the real reason for Allied success in the battle of the Atlantic was the existence of a British Admiralty team responsible for breaking the U-boat cipher (see ULTRA, 1). The German Navy's refusal to accept the validity of this warning helped shorten the war. But it also indicates that, if a positive response had resulted, then the role of the neutrals could have had a more significant impact on both signals intelligence warfare and the length of the war.

The Swedish contribution to sigint was also of some significance. In the 1930s, the Swedish inventor Boris Hagelin (see also SIGABA) had tried unsuccessfully to sell his cipher machines to the German armed forces, but was more successful in parallel dealings with Italy, France, and the USA. In 1942, taps on German teletype lines to Norway passing through Swedish territory facilitated Swedish decryption of part of German military communications at a time when Sweden was particularly worried about a possible German invasion or becoming embroiled in the German–Soviet war. Information was supplied to the British naval attaché in Stockholm about German compromise of the Interdepartmental Cypher in 1941 and other information of value to the UK, such as further early warning of the departure of the battleship **Bismarck*.

On the other hand Swedish counter-intelligence authorities passed on information about Anglo-Polish and Polish–Japanese collaboration on Swedish territory both to the Abwehr and the Sicherheitsdienst, which supplied them with listening devices which were planted in the offices and homes of Allied diplomats. The Swedish foreign ministry allowed Polish military intelligence access to its courier service to send funds to, and exchange information with, the Home Army in occupied Poland until the discovery and arrest of numerous Swedish agents by the *Gestapo in September 1942. These activities were linked to increasing evidence of the growth of a Soviet threat, already manifested in 1942 through Soviet submarine activity in Swedish territorial waters and in the sinking of Swedish shipping. Swedish intelligence agencies extended collaboration in intelligence-gathering against the USSR from 1943 to 1945 with the representatives of all the Axis states, including Finland, Hungary, and Japan, and aided them by putting them in contact with exiles from the former Baltic States, just as they facilitated Allied access to Norwegian exiles and contacts. From 1941 to 1943, the Japanese Army employed Polish contacts in Stockholm to supply information about developments in both the USSR and the UK and employed former Polish officers in Manchukuo to monitor and decrypt Soviet communications in the Far East, even though Poland and Japan were officially at war. After Finland was forced to seek an *armistice in 1944, permission was granted to the Japanese military attaché in Stockholm to move the decrypt section of the Finnish Army General Staff to Sweden to continue its sigint operations against the USSR. In mid-1945, the Japanese were also involved in attempts to infiltrate Estonian agents into the USA, but the Salzburg section of the *Counter Intelligence Corps attached to Seventh US Army had already been forewarned of such a move by interrogation of a former Hungarian attaché in Sweden following the German surrender. Similar Japanese recruitment of Italian and German sigint and intelligence personnel occurred in China following the Italian surrender in September 1943 and the German surrender in May 1945.

8. Theatre and tactical sigint

Even the secure delivery of strategically significant sigint by central agencies to theatre commands was no guarantee that field commanders would invariably be able to exploit it effectively. The Poles and French, for example, were unable even to continue the war despite the successes they enjoyed in the reading of some of the early ENIGMA systems. An important lesson of the campaigns in the *Western Desert, too, was the need for effective inter-service co-operation and for effective corps and divisional sigint organizations which provided intelligence for the higher command, as well as for a regular supply of high-grade ULTRA decrypts which often gave a decisive advantage to those actually fighting the battles. The performance of the *Afrika Korps under Rommel showed what a well-integrated field intelligence system at the disposal of a small, but well-armed and skilfully led force could achieve against superior numbers. The application of systems analysis and *operational research by the Allies to determine intelligence priorities and link them to organizational, logistical, and technical problems was an essential prerequisite for decisive military victory in offence as well as defence.

9. Conclusion

The importance of being able to intercept, decrypt, and analyse signals communications is that it is a highly economical method of building up a more comprehensive picture of a complex, global framework of economic, political, technological, and military interactions than could ever be gathered by huge numbers of spies. The authoritarian states, including the USSR, devoted a larger percentage of sigint manpower to domestic security roles than the Anglo-American states. The latter, therefore, achieved a more effective concentration of resources on the Axis coalition and a more rational division of labour based on a more effective sharing of knowledge and a higher standard of communications security, especially after December 1941. But because of their ignorance of Soviet communications and Japanese military systems, serious misjudgements were made by the western Allies about Japan's relations with the USSR and Germany, and about its operational intentions in 1941. However, the ill-effects of these were offset by a combined pooling of knowledge and allocation of resources in 1942 that stabilized the global balance of power. Drawing on previous experience of successful strategic defence and on vastly superior manpower, material, and technological resources, the western powers expanded sigint capabilities at every level and shaped them to serve offensive needs, while minimizing casualties. The Axis powers contributed to their own defeat by fighting separate wars and by sticking doggedly to the belief that their communications systems were impregnable. But it was also a remarkable tribute to Anglo-American communications security that that belief was not only reinforced at the time but, in the case of ULTRA, was sustained for three decades after 1945. JOHN CHAPMAN

Andrew, C. (ed.), *Codebreaking and Signals Intelligence* (London, 1986).
Drea, E. J., *MacArthur's ULTRA: Codebreaking and the War against Japan* (Lawrence, Kan., 1991).
Hinsley, F. H., *et al.*, *British Intelligence in the Second World War* (London, 1979–90).
Kahn, D., *The Codebreakers* (London, 1973).

Sikorski, General Władysław (1881–1943), Polish Army officer and politician who, having been prime minister and minister of war during the 1920s, took command of the Polish Army which began forming on French soil after the *Polish campaign. On 30 September 1939 he became prime minister of a Polish *government-in-exile in France; and, on 7 November, C-in-C of all Polish forces. He organized Polish forces which fought during the *Norwegian campaign and in the fighting which preceded the fall of *France in June 1940. When France capitulated 24,000 Polish troops were evacuated to the UK, and Sikorski moved his government to London and announced his intention of fighting on. After Germany invaded the USSR in June 1941 (see BARBAROSSA) he signed the Polish–Soviet Treaty (see POLAND, 2(e)); and his meeting with Stalin in Moscow that December resulted in the agreement to form *Anders' Army. He was an untiring and vocal spokesman for the Polish cause and gained an early supporter in Roosevelt whom he visited several times. He was killed when, returning from an inspection of Anders' Army in Iraq, his aircraft crashed on take-off from Gibraltar. He was succeeded as prime minister by Stanisław Mikołajczyk and as C-in-C by General *Sosnkowski.

Simonds, Lt-General Guy (1903–74), English-born but Canadian-educated, Canadian Army officer who rose from being a junior staff officer in September 1939 to command 1st Canadian Infantry Division in the *Sicilian and *Italian campaigns, and then 5th Canadian Armoured Division in the Italian campaign. From January 1944, when he was promoted lt-general, he commanded 2nd Canadian Corps which, as part of *Crerar's First Canadian Army, took part in the Normandy landings in June 1944 (see OVERLORD) and in the fighting in north-west Europe which followed. *Montgomery thought highly of him and during the 85-day battle for the *Scheldt Estuary in the autumn of 1944 he commanded the Second Canadian Army when Crerar was on sick leave.

Simonds proved to be an innovative tactician. He was the first to use artificial moonlight operationally (by playing *searchlights on to clouds), and devised the first armoured personnel carriers, and a variety of direction-finding devices to help armoured columns advance at night. His operations (TOTALIZE and TRACTABLE), which aimed to close the Falaise Gap during the *Normandy campaign, were brilliantly conceived but were less successful than had been hoped as his Canadian troops were slow to implement them and allowed thousands of Germans to escape. J. L. GRANATSTEIN

Simpson, Lt-General Frank (1899–1986), British Army officer who, as a brigadier, served as *Montgomery's chief of staff in the UK and ended the war as assistant *Chief of the Imperial General Staff under *Brooke. Montgomery said he was the best staff officer he had ever met.

Simpson, Lt-General William H. (1888–1980), US Army officer who was a classmate of *Patton and *Eichelberger at West Point Military Academy, where he graduated second from bottom. However, he rose to become commander of Ninth US Army which was activated in north-west Europe in September 1944. He was one of the US Army's most outstanding generals, known for his ability to work with the British, and he served under *Montgomery during the *Ardennes campaign as well as under *Bradley in the battle for *Germany.

Singapore, fall of. This British colony, an island base at the tip of the Malayan peninsula, commanded vital sea routes through the Orient and *Netherlands East Indies, and also guarded India from the east and Australia from the north. The construction of the base between the wars was slow, and in many ways inadequate, and was hindered by Churchill's cutting expenditure on it during his time as chancellor of the exchequer (1924–9). Its capture by the Japanese—after Churchill had urged the garrison to fight to the last and implement a *scorched earth policy if the island should look like falling—was, in Churchill's words, 'the worst disaster and largest capitulation in British history'.

By 31 January 1942, after their defeat in the *Malayan campaign, the British forces had completed their withdrawal across the Johore Straits to Singapore. To defend the base GOC Malaya Command, Lt-General Arthur Percival, divided the island into three sectors. The southern was defended by two Malay and one Straits Settlements volunteer brigades; the western by 8th Australian Division (two brigades) and 44th Indian Infantry Brigade; and the northern by 3rd Corps comprising 11th Indian Division (two brigades), which included the remnants of 9th Indian Division (two brigades). Shortly before the Japanese attacked the newly arrived 18th British Division (three brigades) was also added to the garrison, but took little part in the fighting. Altogether, 13 brigades comprising some 70,000 fighting troops, plus 15,000 administrative and unarmed personnel, were available to Percival. But because he decided—and it was a difficult choice to make—to defend all 112 km. (70 mi.) of the coastline, there were inadequate forces where the Japanese landed and too small a mobile reserve to drive them back into the sea once ashore. It was the first of many errors of judgement.

Although called a fortress, and thought to be one by Churchill and by others who should have known better, Singapore was nothing of the sort. The permanent fixed defences had been primarily designed to guard the naval base from seaward attack; and though the guns could be traversed to fire inland they did not have the ancillary equipment or correct ammunition for land warfare. Defences constructed in Johore in case of attack from across the straits were incomplete but it had, anyway, been generally thought that 320 km. (200 mi.) of Malayan jungle made the island impregnable from that direction. Most of the formations defending the island were under strength, newly arrived, or contained half-trained troops, and sometimes all three. Many had taken part in the defeat on the mainland and were demoralized and short of weapons. Available air cover was far less than the planners had stipulated as necessary and the Japanese were able to make their preparations with little interference.

Opposing the defenders were 35,000 Japanese troops of Lt General *Yamashita's Twenty-Fifth Army, well supported by aircraft and tanks. During the night of 8/9 February 1942 elements of the battle-hardened 5th and

18th Divisions landed on the north-west coast and the next evening the Imperial Guards Division began landing just west of the Causeway. They came ashore in great strength and though there were isolated, and spirited, counter-attacks, and some of the defenders fought tenaciously, it was soon obvious that the island's defence had been poorly planned, was being badly executed, and that its participants were disheartened.

By 12 February 1942 the situation seemed irretrievable and Percival ordered the formation of a perimeter around Singapore town. This did nothing to improve the spirit of those fighting outside it, while in it the numbers of armed *deserters mounted, panic-stricken refugees flooded in, the water supply was damaged by bombing, civil labour had been withdrawn, and morale began to disintegrate. At a conference on 15 February Percival commented that it was pointless to remain on the defensive: he either had to go on to the offensive or capitulate. He favoured the former but his commanders did not; that afternoon he surrendered unconditionally and 14,000 Australian, 16,000 British, and 32,000 Indian troops became *prisoners-of-war; many of the last joined the Japanese-sponsored *Indian National Army. It was an ignominious end, particularly as Yamashita had outrun his supplies and probably would have had to withdraw before a determined counter-attack. But for Yamashita—whose casualties amounted to 1,714 killed and 3,378 wounded—it was the culmination of a brilliant campaign that ranked, alongside the capture of the Malayan peninsula, as the Japanese Army's most outstanding achievement of the war. See also BROOKE-POPHAM.

Allen, L., *Singapore 1941–42* (London, 1977).
MacIntyre, W., *The Rise and Fall of the Singapore Naval Base 1919–1942* (London, 1979).

Sinzweya, battle of, see ADMIN BOX.

Sipo, or Sicherheitspolizei (security police), was the organization formed in 1936 as part of *Himmler's reorganization of the German police. It comprised the state criminal investigation branch, *Kripo and the secret state police, *Gestapo. The remaining branches of the police became integrated into the Ordnungspolizei, or *Orpo. The Sipo, commanded by Reinhard *Heydrich, remained within the German ministry of the interior. It was the forerunner of the *RSHA (Reichssicherheits-hauptamt), a main office of the *SS, which absorbed the Kripo and Gestapo when the RSHA was formed under Heydrich in September 1939.

Sirte, battles of, two naval encounters between British and Italian warships which took place off the Libyan Gulf of Sirte. The first, on 17 December 1941, was a skirmish between a British cruiser and two destroyers of *Force K, and a superior Italian force which included two battleships. The second occurred on 22 March 1942 when the Italian battleship *Littorio*, three cruisers, and eight destroyers attacked a convoy bound for *Malta. The convoy's escort of five cruisers and seventeen destroyers under Rear-Admiral Philip Vian was heavily outgunned, but Vian's aggressive tactics enabled the convoy to escape unharmed under cover of smoke. However, air attacks later sank two of its merchantmen at sea and the other two were hit in harbour, and only 20% of the convoy's cargo was landed. See also MEDITERRANEAN.

SIS, see MI6 and USA, 6.

Sittang river bridge. Outflanked by Lt-General Sakurai Shōzō's 33rd Division early in the *Burma campaign, Maj-General John Smyth, commanding 17th Indian Division, ordered the destruction of this bridge on 23 February 1942. The action delayed the Japanese advance on Rangoon—perhaps by ten days—but it trapped two of Smyth's three brigades on the eastern bank, and 5,000 men, plus nearly all the division's artillery and transport, were lost. Poor *radio communications, the refusal of the C-in-C Burma, Lt-General Thomas Hutton, to allow Smyth to withdraw until it was too late, and Smyth's failure to create a strong enough bridgehead in time, all contributed to the disaster. Hutton was replaced by *Alexander and Smyth was removed from his command and forcibly retired. Smyth's decision, one of the most controversial made by a British general during the war, caused heated debate for years.

SIW stood for self-inflicted wound, a not uncommon occurrence among those who had had enough of the fighting. For example, out of 29,860 battle casualties and injuries suffered by the British Second Army in north-west Europe, 179, or 0.6%, were self-inflicted.

Skelton, Oscar D. (1878–1941), Canadian academic and civil servant who was appointed under-secretary of state for external affairs by the prime minister, Mackenzie *King, in 1925, and held this appointment until he died. He was King's closest adviser on domestic as well as foreign policy, and was the founder of the modern Canadian department of external affairs.

skip bombing, method of bombing ships devised by British Coastal Command early in the war. Light bombers, flying low above the water, released their bombs so that they hit the sea horizontally. This made them bounce and penetrate their target's hull near the waterline. Maj-General *Arnold, chief of what was then the US Army Air Corps, heard of the technique when he visited London in 1941. He had it tested and it was later used, with great effect, against Japanese ships in the *Bismarck Sea battle in March 1943. The term was also used to describe low-level air attacks such as the *Shell House raid where bombs were lobbed by fighter-bombers at buildings to penetrate their walls. See also BOMBERS, 2.

Skorzeny, Otto (1908–75), Austrian-born *SS Obersturmbannführer (lt-colonel) who was appointed to the *RSHA (Reichssicherheitshauptamt) in 1942 to organize special commando units, called Friedenthaler Jadgverbände (Friedenthal Hunting Groups) after their training area in a park not far from Berlin. In September 1943 he and 90 men belonging to *Student's forces landed in gliders to snatch Mussolini from captivity in the mountains at Gran Sasso in the Abruzzi region of Central Italy, and the success of this operation enabled him to expand his force. He was promoted; given command of special weapons such as those operated by *Tenth Light Flotilla; and later supervised the operations of *KG200. Unswerving loyalty to Hitler after the July 1944 bomb plot (see SCHWARZE KAPELLE) brought further promotion and in October 1944 he mounted an operation which dissuaded Hungary's regent, Admiral *Horthy, from withdrawing from the war: he kidnapped Horthy's main negotiator, his son, and then bluffed his way into the Admiral's citadel and forced him to reverse his announcement of an *armistice with the USSR. During the *Ardennes campaign a few of his English-speaking men, dressed in American uniforms, penetrated US Army lines which caused considerable panic and some confusion. He may have organized post-war escape routes for SS officers (see VATICAN) but he was acquitted of war crimes at the *Nuremberg trials.

Slapton Sands, a US Army training area on the English Channel coast in south Devon which was used for exercises prior to the Normandy landings in June 1944 (see OVERLORD). One exercise (TIGER) was started there on 27 April 1944 and an inadequately escorted convoy, bringing a second wave of troops to the beach, was attacked overnight by nine German *E-boats. Amidst scenes of great confusion three *landing craft were hit by German torpedoes. About 749 US servicemen lost their lives, more than were killed on *UTAH beach during OVERLORD, and there were fears that missing officers cognizant of the invasion plans might have been captured by the Germans. The incident was played down at the time and lack of proper documentation led to speculation during the 1980s about the number killed, how they died, where they were buried, and why some of their names were included in the OVERLORD casualty lists.

Lewis, N., *Channel Firing* (London, 1989).

slave labour, see FORCED LABOUR.

Slessor, Air Marshal Sir John (1897–1979), RAF officer who was head of the plans branch of the air staff in September 1939. In April 1941 he was appointed to command No. 5 Group, Bomber Command; a year later he returned to the air staff as Assistant Chief of Air Staff (policy); and in February 1943 succeeded *Joubert as C-in-C Coastal Command at perhaps the most crucial phase in the battle of the *Atlantic. Following the *Washington Convoy conference in March he began to receive more very long-range aircraft and by May the mid-Atlantic *air gap had been closed and the U-boats all but beaten. During his time at Coastal Command his aircraft, which now ranged from Iceland and the Faeroes to Gibraltar and the Azores, destroyed an average of seven U-boats a month. In January 1944 he was appointed C-in-C of all RAF forces in the Mediterranean and Middle East, and was *Eaker's deputy in those theatres. In June 1944 he was responsible for forming the *Balkan Air Force and ended the war as a member of the air council responsible for personnel. He was knighted in 1943.

Slessor, J., *The Central Blue* (London, 1956).

Slim, General Sir William (1891–1970), British Army officer who commanded the Fourteenth Army in the *Burma campaign.

Having fought with the British Army during the *First World War, Slim transferred to the Indian Army in 1919 and by September 1939 held the rank of brigadier. In 1940 he was given command of 10th Indian Infantry Brigade in the *East African campaign and later of 10th Indian Division, which successfully fought *Vichy French forces during the *Syrian campaign in June 1941. In March 1942 Slim was sent to Burma with the rank of lt-general to command *Burcorps retreating from Rangoon. When this was disbanded he led 15th Indian Corps during the fighting in Arakan before being given command, in October 1943, of the newly formed Fourteenth Army. The following year this soundly defeated the Japanese diversionary attack in the Arakan (see ADMIN BOX) and then their *Imphal offensive, and in the retreat that followed the Japanese suffered 50,000 casualties and an overwhelming defeat. The battles earned Slim world-wide renown and a knighthood, but after his reconquest of Burma a disagreement over a new appointment for him ended in his requesting retirement. There was general consternation and *Brooke intervened personally. As a result, *Leese, the Allied Land Forces commander for *South-East Asia Command, was dismissed and Slim was promoted general and took over Leese's post.

Slim's physical presence, with his bulldog jaw, inspired tremendous confidence. 'He has a hell of a face,' Churchill remarked, but he was also extremely experienced, mentally robust, and equable. He gained and held the affection and admiration of his men with whom he could converse in their own language, be it English, Urdu, or Gurkhali: they called him 'Uncle Bill'. He once said 'I must have been the most defeated general in our history', but he also produced some notable victories. After the war he was appointed *Chief of the Imperial General Staff and promoted field marshal. He served as governor-general of Australia from 1953 to 1960 and was created a viscount in 1960.

Lewin, R., *Slim: the Standardbearer* (London, 1976).
Slim, W., *Defeat into Victory* (London, 1956).

slit trench, a defensive position for infantrymen sometimes dug in an L-shape. Unlike the *foxhole, it took a number of soldiers. See also INFANTRY WARFARE.

Slovakia, the eastern part of Czechoslovakia, emerged as a semi-independent client state of Nazi Germany in the wake of the *Munich agreement of September 1938, with Slovak nationalists, led by a Roman Catholic priest, Mgr Josef Tiso (1887–1947), gaining autonomy for Slovakia from the Czechoslovak government. This realignment shifted the future of Slovakia out of the hands of Prague and to those of Berlin. With the first of the *Vienna awards, Germany sanctioned the loss of Slovakia's southern belt of territory (containing a Magyar majority) to Hungary (see Map 49), but for Slovak nationalists German policy also had its benefits. With the German occupation of the rump of the Czech lands in March 1939, Slovakia gained, with German support, nominal independence.

From the very beginning, independent Slovakia was in the firm grip of Nazi Germany. In March 1939, it adhered to a 'Treaty of Protection of the Slovak State by the German Reich'. This instrument subordinated Slovakia's foreign and military policy to Germany and based German troops on Slovak soil. Economically, Germany exploited the territory for the benefit of the German war effort. The German minority in Slovakia obtained a privileged legal position and the right to form paramilitary units known as 'Ordners'.

Tiso, now the Country's president, and his clerical-fascist Slovak People's Party dominated the domestic politics of the new Slovakia. The political system and body of law introduced under the Tiso regime closely emulated Nazi Germany. The Slovak People's Party had its own paramilitary force, the Hlinka Guards, named after the cleric who shaped the political party. It also had its junior Hlinka Youth, modelled on the lines of the *SS and *Hitler Youth. Reflecting Slovak *anti-Semitism, the Tiso government adopted Nazi-style legislation, which placed great disabilities on Slovakian Jewry, and eventually it collaborated openly with the German *Final Solution leading to the elimination of Slovakia's 100,000-strong Jewish community.

Although Tiso's regime satisfied one of the central impulses of Slovak nationalism—a Slovak state—the population's disillusionment with Germany grew as the war progressed, and traditional pan-Slavic sympathies with the USSR asserted themselves. Germany's invasion of the USSR in June 1941 (see BARBAROSSA) saw the commitment of more than 50,000 Slovak troops to the Eastern Front, resulting in enormous Slovak casualties and mass surrenders to the Red Army.

As the war progressed, popular discontent increased and eventually culminated in the Slovak rising in August 1944, the advance of the Red Army into Poland in early 1944 creating the political and military conditions necessary for its outbreak. Senior officers in the Tiso regime's Slovak army established clandestine contact with the Soviet authorities. They sought agreement to coordinate a rising with the Red Army's military operations and planned to secure key mountain passes in the Carpathians for it. Slovak hopes rested on the rapid entry of Soviet forces in order to minimize destruction and loss of life at the hands of the Germans.

However, events in Slovakia pre-empted the army's planning. The Tiso regime's loss of control of many parts of the country, coupled with intense partisan activity which disrupted vital railway communications, prompted direct German military intervention. The rising began prematurely on 29 August 1944 when Slovak units clashed with advancing German forces.

Despite a chaotic start, Slovak regular and partisan forces seized control of a large area of central Slovakia. Banská Bystrica became the centre of the uprising with Lt-Colonel Ján Golian assuming command of the insurgent forces. Later, General Rudolf Viest, dispatched by the Czechoslovak *government-in-exile, took over command, with Golian becoming his deputy, but the rapid German advance quickly overcame the Slovak army's best equipped units in the extreme east and west of the country and deprived him of his potentially most valuable forces.

Throughout September and into October, the insurgent forces maintained a precarious hold on central Slovakia, but German attacks in mid-October led to their final collapse, though some remnants fought on as partisan groups in the Tatra mountains until *liberation by the Red Army in March 1945.

The Czechoslovak government-in-exile under *Beneš sought Allied help for the Slovak insurgents, but American and British aid was constrained for political and operational reasons as Slovakia lay at the limits of the range of Allied air forces without access to Soviet airfields. The USSR, with the Red Army and airfields closest to the rising, was in the best position to help. Soviet aid, however, was grudging and Stalin's attitude toward the Slovak insurgents was not dissimilar to his response to the *Warsaw rising of August 1944. Soviet help eventually came with the insurgents' forces being augmented by elements of *Svoboda's 2nd Czechoslovak Airborne Brigade under the command of Lt-Colonel Vladimír Přikryl. From mid-September it was flown in from Soviet territory, but it took some six weeks for the airlift of this largely Slovak unit to be completed.

Even at the peak of their strength, the Slovak insurgent forces never exceeded 50,000. On the German side, elements of five divisions and numerous independent units were committed to counter the rising and German forces enjoyed an overwhelming superiority in men and *matériel*. Slovak deaths numbered at least 25,000 through military action and German reprisals. Among the victims were the leaders of the uprising, including Viest and Golian.

The Slovak rising showed the bankruptcy of the Tiso regime and marked the beginning of the end of 'independent' Slovakia. The advancing Red Army liberated it and returned it to the Czechoslovak state, and Tiso was tried and executed. A product of Hitler's 'new order' in east-central Europe and Tiso's Slovak People's Party, wartime Slovakia represented a tragic experiment for Slovak nationalism. PAUL LATAWSKI

Letrich, J., *History of Slovakia* (New York, 1955).
Mikus, J. A., *Slovakia A Political History: 1918–1950* (Milwaukee, 1963).

small arms. Those used by the combatant armies in 1939–45 fell into five groups: pistols, sub-machine-guns (the Germans called them machine pistols, the British also called them machine carbines), rifles, machine-guns, and anti-tank rifles (see Table).

The primary weapon of all modern soldiers is, of course, the rifle, and almost without exception the rifles with which all soldiers were armed in 1939 were virtually the same as those which their forebears had carried during the *First World War (in the case of the Japanese, the Russo-Japanese War of 1905); the only changes were minor, intended to make mass-production easier. The British had the Lee-Enfield, the Germans the Mauser, the Soviets the Mosin-Nagant, the Italians the Mannlicher-Carcano and the Japanese the Arisaka, all manually operated, bolt-action magazine weapons. The only exception to this was the US Army, where issue of the semi-automatic Garand M1 rifle had begun, though the majority of troops were still armed with the 1903 Springfield bolt-action rifle.

During the course of the war the US forces were completely equipped with the Garand, and the Red Army developed two or three semi-automatic rifle designs which were not particularly successful. The major advance in this field came from Germany, where a pre-war reassessment of the infantryman's task led to an entirely new type of weapon, the assault rifle. In brief, analysis of wartime experience showed that the infantry rarely fired at ranges in excess of 300–400 m. (330–440 yd.), whereas the contemporary bolt-action rifles were designed to deliver accurate fire up to 1,000 m. (1,100 yd.) or more. By developing a shorter cartridge of less power, a lighter rifle could be made and the soldier could carry more ammunition for a given weight. A suitable 7.92 mm. (0.3 in.) cartridge was designed, using a light bullet in a short cartridge case. Around this an automatic rifle was developed, capable of single shots or full automatic fire. The light bullet and lower charge made it controllable, and thanks to the short cartridge the weapon was compact. It was issued in 1943 as the 'Machine Pistol 43' but was later re-named the 'Sturmgewehr (assault rifle) 44' and proved an excellent weapon. It became the inspiration for an entirely new class of rifle which, by the 1970s, armed the majority of the armies of the world.

The sub-machine-gun had been developed in Germany in 1917–18 as a weapon for storm troops, a short-range automatic weapon firing pistol ammunition. In the 1920s the development of this class of weapon was desultory, some armies seeing no tactical function for such a device. On the outbreak of war in September 1939 only the German Army held them in any quantity, and then largely in armoured formations where a compact weapon was desirable for troops carried in cramped vehicles. Similar weapons—the British Sten gun for example—were adopted by other countries largely because of their cheapness and simplicity, and also because of their attraction as a compact weapon of high firepower for airborne and special forces troops. Their major adoption was by the USSR, which saw them as a cheap and effective method of arming their vast armies; moreover this class of weapon suited Soviet tactics—close-quarters fighting rather than distant sniping.

Machine-guns fell into two groups, light and heavy; the latter were almost entirely the water-cooled tripod-mounted weapons familiar in 1918—the Maxim, Vickers, and Browning designs used for long-range suppressive fire in the attack and for overwhelming defensive fire from fixed positions. The light machine-gun (LMG) was almost entirely a development of the inter-war years, though the principle had been explored in the latter stages of the *First World War. The 1939–45 LMG such as the British Bren, and the American Browning Automatic Rifle (BAR), was a magazine-fed weapon, usually with a barrel which could be quickly removed and replaced with a cool spare barrel when it grew hot from prolonged firing.

However, the German Army felt that the provision of two types of machine-gun for different tactical functions often led to the desired weapon not being readily available, and they set about the development of an entirely new class, the 'general purpose' machine-gun. In this, the basic weapon was the same, a belt-fed gun with a high rate of fire and a quick-change barrel, but the method of mounting varied. Where it was desired to be used in the LMG role it had a bipod and shoulder-butt; for use in the heavy, supporting and defensive, role it was provided with a tripod and long-range sights. The logistical advantage was that only one type of gun had to be manufactured. Experience showed that this system worked well, and in post-war years it was widely adopted by other armies.

Pistols are not as widely employed as is often thought, and very little wartime thought was given to them. The choice between revolver and automatic pistol was still a debating point; the British retained the revolver, adopting automatic pistols only for special forces such as commando and airborne troops; the Soviets retained their 1892 revolver but also gradually introduced an automatic pistol since it was easier to manufacture. The US forces retained the Colt automatic which had been in use since 1911. The Italian and Japanese armies also used automatic pistols, though both also employed quantities of older revolvers since production could not be spared for more automatics. Germany still used the Luger of First World War vintage but had officially replaced it in 1938 by a Walther design which was cheaper and easier to manufacture; even so, such was demand that the Luger remained in manufacture until late in 1943.

Small arms: Principal types of major powers

Title	Calibre	Magazine Capacity	Weight Empty	Rate of Fire (rounds per minute)
Germany				
Pistols				
Parabellum P08 (Luger)	9 mm	8	870 g (31 oz)	n/a
Walther P38	9 mm	8	960 g (34 oz)	n/a
Rifles				
Mauser Kar 98	7.92 mm (.311 in)	5	3.9 kg (8.6 lb)	n/a
Fallschirmgewehr 42	7.92 mm	20	4.5 kg (9.9 lb)	750
Sturmgewehr 44	7.92 mm	30	5.1 kg (11.2 lb)	500
Walther G41	7.92 mm	10	5.0 kg (11 lb)	n/a
Gewehr 43	7.92 mm	10	4.3 kg (9.5 lb)	n/a
Submachine Guns				
MP40 (Schmeisser[a])	9 mm	32	4.0 kg (8.8 lb)	500
Machine Guns				
MG34	7.92 mm	250	12.1 kg (26.6 lb)	850
MG42 (Spandau[a])	7.92 mm	50	11.5 kg (25.3 lb)	1,200
Anti-tank Rifles				
PzB38	7.92 mm	1	15.9 kg (35 lb)	n/a
PzB39	7.92 mm	1	12.4 kg (27.3 lb)	n/a

Penetration 30 mm (1.2 in) of armour at 100m (109 yd) range

[a]Both misnomers: Schmeisser never had anything to do with the design of the MP40 and though the original Maxim guns of the First World War were made at Spandau arsenal, and became known as 'Spandau machine guns', the MG42 was manufactured elsewhere.

Title	Calibre	Magazine Capacity	Weight Empty	Rate of Fire (rounds per minute)
Italy				
Pistols				
Glisenti	9 mm	7	820 g (29 oz)	n/a
Beretta 34	9 mm	7	660 g (23.3 oz)	n/a
Rifles				
Carcano M1891	6.5 mm (.25 in)	6	3.8 kg (8.4 lb)	n/a
Carcano M1938	7.35 mm (.28 in)	6	3.7 kg (8.1 lb)	n/a
Submachine Guns				
Beretta 18/30	9 mm	25	3.3 kg (7.3 lb)	900
Beretta M38A	9 mm	30	4.2 kg (9.2 lb)	600
Machine Guns				
Fiat-Revelli M35	8 mm (.31 in)	50	18.1 kg (40 lb)	500
Breda M30	6.5 mm (.255 in)	20	10.2 kg (22.4 lb)	475
Breda M37	8 mm	20	19.5 kg (43 lb)	450
Anti-tank Rifles				
Solothurn S-18/100	20 mm (.78 in)	10	45.0 kg (99.2 lb)	n/a

Penetration of armour 27 mm (1.05 in) at 300m (328 yd) range

Title	Calibre	Magazine Capacity	Weight Empty	Rate of Fire (rounds per minute)
Japan				
Pistol				
Nambu 14	8 mm	8	900 g (32 oz)	n/a
Type 94	8 mm	6	765 g (27 oz)	n/a

Small arms (*cont.*)

Title	*Calibre*	*Magazine Capacity*	*Weight Empty*	*Rate of Fire (rounds per minute)*
Rifles				
38th Year	6.5 mm	5	4.3 kg (9.5 lb)	n/a
Type 99	7.7 mm (.3 in)	5	4.2 kg (9.2 lb)	n/a
Submachine Gun				
Type 100	8 mm	30	3.8 kg (8.4 lb)	800
Machine Guns				
Type 92	7.7 mm	30	55.3 kg (122 lb)	450
Type 96	6.5 mm	30	9.1 kg (20 lb)	550
Type 97	7.7 mm	30	10.9 kg (24 lb)	500
Type 99	7.7 mm	30	10.4 kg (23 lb)	850
Anti-tank Rifles				
Model 97	20 mm	7	69.0 kg (152 lb)	n/a
Penetration of armour 25 mm (.98 in) at 300 m (328 yd.) range.				
UK				
Pistols				
Enfield No 2	.38 in (9.7 mm)	6	780 g (27.5 oz)	n/a
Browning HP[b]	9 mm (.35 in)	13	992 g (35 oz)	n/a
[b]Commando and Airborne forces only, 1944 onward				
Rifles				
Lee-Enfield No 4	.303 in (7.7 mm)	10	4.1 kg (9 lb)	20
Lee-Enfield No 5	.303 in	10	3.2 kg (7 lb)	20
Submachine Guns				
Lanchester (RN only)	9 mm	50	4.3 kg (9.5 lb)	600
Sten Mk II	9 mm	32	2.9 kg (6.4 lb)	550
Machine Guns				
Lewis	.303 in	47	11.8 kg (26 lb)	550
Bren	.303 in	30	10.2 kg (22.4 lb)	500
Vickers-Berthier[c]	.303 in	30	9.4 kg (21 lb)	500
Vickers Medium	.303 in	250	18.1 kg (40 lb)	450
[c]Indian Army only				
Anti-tank Rifles				
Boys	.55 in (14 mm)	5	16.3 kg (36 lb)	n/a
Penetration 21 mm (.82 in) armour at 300 m (328 yd) range				
USA				
Pistols				
Colt M1911A1	.45 in (11.5 mm)	7	1.1 kg (2.4 lb)	n/a
Colt M1917	.45 in	6	1.1 kg	n/a
Smith & Wesson M1917	.45 in	6	1.0 kg (2.2 lb)	n/a
Rifles[d]				
Springfield M1903	.300 (7.62 mm)	5	3.9 kg (8.6 lb)	n/a
Garand M1	.300	8	4.4 kg (9.7 lb)	n/a
Carbine M1	.30	15	2.5 kg (5.5 lb)	n/a

Small arms (*cont.*)

Title	*Calibre*	*Magazine Capacity*	*Weight Empty*	*Rate of Fire (rounds per minute)*
Submachine Guns				
Thompson M1	.45 (11.43 mm)	20	4.8 kg (10.5 lb)	700
M3 'Grease Gun'	.45	30	3.7 kg (8.1 lb)	450
Machine Guns				
Browning Auto Rifle	.300	20	9.98 kg (22 lb)	550
Browning M1917	.300	250	15.0 kg (33 lb)	500
Browning M1919	.300	250	14.0 kg (31 lb)	500
Browning M2HB	.50 (12.8 mm)	110	38.2 kg (84 lb)	500

[d] All three rifles were the same calibre but the .300 round had a bottle-necked case 63 mm long; the .30 round had a straight-sided case 33 mm long

USSR

Title	*Calibre*	*Magazine Capacity*	*Weight Empty*	*Rate of Fire (rounds per minute)*
Pistols				
Nagant M1895	7.62 mm (.3 in)	7	790 g (28oz)	n/a
Tokarev TT-33	7.62 mm	8	830 g (29oz)	n/a
Rifles				
Mosin-Nagant M1891	7.62 mm	5	4.4 kg (9.7 lb)	n/a
Tokarev SVT40	7.62 mm	15	4.4 kg	n/a
Submachine Guns				
PPD-40	7.62 mm	71	3.7 kg (8.1 lb)	800
PPSH-41	7.62 mm	71	3.6 kg (7.9 lb)	900
PPS-43	7.62 mm	35	3.4 kg (7.5 lb)	650
Machine Guns				
Degtyarev DP	7.62 mm	47	9.1 kg (20 lb)	550
Maxim M1910	7.62 mm	250	23.8 kg (52.5 lb)	560
Goryunov SG43	7.62 mm	250	13.6 kg (30 lb)	650
DShK M1938	12.7 mm (.5 in)	50	35.5 kg (78 lb)	550
Anti-tank Rifles				
Simonov PTRS	14.5 mm (.56 in)	5	20.8 kg (63.4 lb)	n/a
Degtyarev PTRD	14.5 mm	1	17.3 kg (38 lb)	n/a

Penetration 25 mm (.98 in) of armour at 500 m (547 yd) range

Source: Contributor.

Anti-tank rifles were a unique case, since they saw no widespread use before 1939 and were all obsolete by 1945. They stemmed from a Mauser design of 1918, a heavy 13 mm. (0.5 in.) bolt-action weapon capable of penetrating the thin armour of 1918 British tanks. In the inter-war years they were developed and adopted by most armies (the US and Italian being the exceptions), though the execution differed. The British employed the 0.55 in. (14 mm.) bolt-action Boys rifle; the Germans a 7.92 mm. semi-automatic weapon using an enlarged cartridge to generate high velocity; the Poles another 7.92 mm. with over-sized cartridge but with a bolt mechanism; the Soviets two 14.5 mm. (0.56 in.) weapons firing extremely powerful rounds, one a bolt-action, the other a semi-automatic. The Japanese preferred a 20 mm. (0.78 in.) semi-automatic weapon of considerable weight. All these weapons were deployed in 1939 but few stayed the course, since the rapid improvement in the armour strength of tanks and the consequent ineffectiveness of the anti-tank rifle which, at best, could defeat only 15 mm. (0.6 in.) or so of armour plate, made them ineffective. From 1941 onwards the development of hand-held anti-tank *rocket weapons, proved far more effective in defeating armour, and the anti-tank rifle was rapidly abandoned. It survived only in the Red Army, since no effective substitute was devised during the war, but survival did not necessarily mean extensive use. See also ANTI-TANK WEAPONS.

IAN HOGG

Hogg, I. V., and Weeks, J. S., *Military Small Arms of the 20th Century* (6th edn., London, 1991).
Smith, W. H. B. and J. E., *Small Arms of the World* (New York, 1973).

Small Operations Group, British Far East HQ formed in June 1944 to co-ordinate operations by *Combined

Operations Pilotage Parties, the *Special Boat Section, a Sea Reconnaissance Unit, which specialized in long-distance swimming and landing through surf, and Detachment 385, a unit of swimmers and *canoeists trained in raiding in small groups. As part of *Mountbatten's *South-East Asia Command, it mounted 170 operations during the *Burma campaign and was unofficially known as 'Mountbatten's private navy'.

Smaller War Plants Corporation, US agency established in June 1942 as a division of the *War Production Board. Its aim was to finance and aid smaller American businesses, employing fewer than 500 employees, so that they obtained a greater share in service procurement contracts. It was not until Maury Maverick became chairman in January 1944 that it showed any signs of success, but even he could not fundamentally alter the unfavourable statistics: in December 1939 firms with fewer than 100 employees accounted for 26% of total US manufacturing output, but five years later, a period in which production doubled, this figure had declined to 19%. In 1943, the peak year of the US production effort, firms with under 100 employees were awarded 86,000 contracts. This amounted to about 35% of the total number awarded (241,531), but was worth only 3.5% of the total value ($35.3 million) of all the contracts. See also USA, 2.

Small Scale Raiding Force, British commando unit, formed from an *SOE force which mounted the *Fernando Po raid. It used a cover name, No. 62 Commando, and was administered by SOE, but came under the operational control of *Combined Operations. It undertook several cross-Channel raids between August 1942 and April 1943 when it was disbanded. The *Combined Operations Pilotage Parties and No. 2 *Special Boat Section were also part of No. 62 Commando.

SMERSH was the Main Counter-Intelligence Directorate of the USSR's People's Commissariat of Defence (GUKR). Founded on 14 April 1943, it was given the name SMERSH, an acronym for *Smert Shpionam* (Death to Spies) by Stalin himself who rejected the original proposed title, Death to German Spies, on the grounds that the new intelligence service should concern itself with all *spies. It was the successor of the Special Departments (Osobyye Otdeli) which had carried out counter-intelligence duties since 1918, but while these had been part of the *NKVD, SMERSH was subject to the commissariat of defence. However, army commanders had virtually no control over SMERSH units attached to their command. The head of the Special Departments, V. S. Abakumov, became head of SMERSH with the rank of deputy commissar of defence. He probably had direct access to the State Defence Committee whose head was Stalin.

The counter-intelligence duties of SMERSH were so extensive that it became, in effect, a watchdog ensuring the loyalty of the armed forces. Thus a special directorate was charged with surveillance of the armed forces including staff officers attached to the general staff in Moscow. American sources estimate that 3–4% of Soviet military personnel were engaged in intelligence or counter-intelligence while another 12% were agents or informers. Alexander Solzhenitsyn records in the first volume of *The Gulag Archipelago* that he was arrested by SMERSH agents. He shared a prison cell with three other soldiers, whose only crime had been to chase two girls, one of whom was the 'property' of the local SMERSH chief. In fact SMERSH had considerable success in tracking down German spies and in operating behind German lines in co-operation with partisan units. Together with the border troops of the NKVD it re-established Soviet administration in territories liberated by the Red Army, and once beyond the borders of the USSR, it created favourable conditions for the activities of communist and pro-Soviet forces. However, military intelligence was conducted by a separate organization, the *GRU, subordinated to the general staff. SMERSH was disbanded in May 1946 and its duties transferred to the ministry of state security. H. Hanak

Romanov, A. I., *Nights are longest there. Smersh from the Inside* (tr. G. Brooke, London, 1972).

Smith, Lt-General Walter Bedell (1895–1961), US Army officer who served as *Eisenhower's chief of staff from September 1942 until the end of the war.

Smith fought in France during the *First World War after serving as a private in the Indiana National Guard from 1910 to 1916. After the war he gained a regular commission, but promotion was slow, and it was not until April 1941—eighteen months after *Marshall had called him to Washington to help build up the army—that he became a lt-colonel. However, he was soon recognized as a tough and skilful administrator, and advancement followed rapidly. He became a colonel in August 1941, a brigadier-general in February 1942, a maj-general in December 1942, and a lt-general in January 1943.

Though critics saw him as quick-tempered, harsh, abrupt, and arbitrary, practically everyone recognized his genius as a chief of staff. One historian has described Smith's role as follows: 'He decided who could see Eisenhower and who could not, handled much of Eisenhower's civil affairs and diplomatic duties, had almost unlimited responsibility and authority in all matters except promotion of officers and operational directives, was the "no" man in the office, and frequently represented Eisenhower at meetings' (S. Ambrose, *The Supreme Commander*, London, 1971, p. 81). He was promoted four-star general in 1951.

Smolensk, battle of. Having demolished the Soviet West *front* (army group) in the *Białystok–Minsk encirclement, and covered 475 km. (295 mi.) in two weeks at the start of the *German–Soviet war (see also

BARBAROSSA), the German Second and Third Panzer Groups arrived on 6 July 1941 at the historic gateway to Moscow, the gap 80 km. (50 mi.) wide between the *Dnieper and Western Dvina rivers. Their next objective was Smolensk, at the eastern exit from the gap. Opposite them, Marshal *Timoshenko had, on 2 July, taken command of a new West *front*, five armies that had originally been scheduled to sustain a drive towards Germany. The panzer group commanders, Generals *Guderian (Second) and Hermann Hoth (Third), knew when they began receiving counter-attacks on 3 July that they were going to meet more determined resistance than they had encountered thus far.

By 11 July, with support from *Löhr's Fourth Air Fleet, Hoth had a spearhead directed along with Dvina on the north side of the gap and Guderian had thrust across the Dnieper on the south. On 16 July, Guderian's tanks seized Smolensk by a *coup de main*. By 20 July, Hoth's and Guderian's armoured spearheads had both gone 200 km. (124 mi.) deep; but the Soviet troops between them were holding fast and others were attacking their outer flanks, particularly Guderian's, into which two Soviet corps had driven west to the Dnieper. The pocket around Smolensk could not be closed completely until 5 August. Timoshenko kept his troops fighting to the last but lost them in the end. The Smolensk pocket yielded 310,000 prisoners and one around the corps further south another 38,000. EARL ZIEMKE

Smolensk Attentat (*Attentat*, attempted assassination). In March 1943 Lt Fabian von Schlabrendorff, one of those associated with Maj-General Henning von Tresckow's plot to kill Hitler (see SCHWARZE KAPELLE), planted a bomb in Hitler's aircraft before it took off from Smolensk to where the Führer had flown to meet Field Marshal *Kluge. But the bomb—constructed from two captured British Clam mines (see LIMPET MINES) provided by Maj-General *Oster and disguised as a bottle of Cointreau—failed to explode and was later retrieved by other conspirators. See also GERMANY, 9.

Smuts, Field Marshal Jan Christiaan (1870–1950), South African politician of mainly Dutch ancestry who led his country throughout the war.

After fighting against the British during the Boer War of 1899–1902, Smuts fought for them during the *First World War in East Africa, and German South-West Africa, attaining the rank of lt-general in the British Army. He attended the London Imperial conference in 1917 and for the next eighteen months served in the British war cabinet. During this time he was chairman of the committee which organized the air defence of London and created the RAF as an independent service. He attended the Paris peace conference and was in the forefront of those who founded the *League of Nations.

Returning to South Africa in 1919, Smuts became prime minister, a post he retained until 1924. In 1933 he formed a coalition with *Hertzog and was deputy prime minister under him in their United South African National Party (United Party), but when war broke out in Europe he voted against Hertzog and neutrality. Parliament narrowly endorsed his decision and on 6 September 1939 he became prime minister again. He also became minister of defence and, from June 1940, C-in-C of the South African armed forces, an accumulation of power which no other Allied democratic leader acquired and which gave him full control of his country's political and military machinery.

But Smuts initially suffered constant opposition to South Africa's role in the war, both in and out of parliament, and though he felt more at home on the international scene than in domestic politics, he had to give time to retaining his majority and to curbing the activities of Nazi sympathizers (see OSSEWABRANDWAG). However, he steadfastly refused, as many of his supporters urged, to suppress totally his fascist opponents.

Smuts was a strong advocate of holding Egypt at all costs and South African air and ground units, after fighting in the *East African campaign, were by November 1941 fully engaged in the *Western Desert campaigns, and in 1942 were also involved in capturing *Madagascar. In 1941 Smuts was made an honorary field marshal in the British Army, but asked that he still be known by his old rank of general. Churchill who considered him a magnificent man and one of his most cherished friends was in constant telegraphic touch with him and valued his judgement. However, this was not infallible. For example, a month before *Tobruk fell in June 1942, with a resultant heavy loss in South African troops, Smuts had declared himself quite satisfied with the situation there. In 1943 he sat with the British war cabinet, and attended the Cairo conference that December (see SEXTANT). In April 1945 he attended the *San Francisco conference to take part in the opening session of the United Nations whose charter he had helped compose and whose preamble he had written. He remained in office until the 1948 general election when he was defeated by one of his most vociferous wartime opponents, Daniel Malan.

Hancock, W. K., *Smuts* (Cambridge, 1962).
Ingham, K., *Jan Christiaan Smuts* (London, 1986).

Sobibor was a Nazi death camp (see OPERATION REINHARD) situated near Chełm in Poland. It opened in May 1942 and probably at least 250,000–300,000 people were murdered there. A revolt on 14 October 1943 led to several guards being killed and some 600 prisoners escaped. Half that number reached the woods, but few survived long and most were returned by anti-Semitic local inhabitants. It closed in November 1943 and all signs of the camp were then obliterated, and the site planted with saplings. See also CONCENTRATION CAMPS and FINAL SOLUTION.

SOE (Special Operations Executive) was a British secret service intended to promote *subversive warfare in enemy-occupied territory. It was formed in July 1940 by joining together a small sabotage branch of *MI6, section D; a still smaller research branch of the war office, MI(R); and EH, a semi-secret propaganda department of the foreign office.

Politically, it came under the minister of *economic warfare—*Dalton until February 1942, Lord Selborne thereafter—but was quite separate from his ministry in Berkeley Square; its headquarters were in Baker Street, Marylebone, close to the rooms of the fictional Sherlock Holmes. It wrapped itself in a dense veil of *secrecy, and an air of unreality has stuck to it.

Strategically, it came under the *Chiefs of Staff; at first directly, later in the war (Poland excepted) through Cs-in-C in the field. Diplomatically, its chief executive officer, Gladwyn Jebb, kept its policies roughly in step with those of the foreign office, to which he had belonged, till he returned to *diplomacy in mid-1942; thereafter there were sometimes wide divergences. Under the minister and Jebb, its directing heads were in turn Frank Nelson, Charles Hambro, and Colin *Gubbins.

SOE was founded on a misapprehension—the belief that the Germans' successes in overrunning Poland, Denmark, Norway, the Netherlands, Belgium, and France in such short order in 1939–40 had been primarily due to the work of *fifth columnists lodged behind their victims' lines before ever a shot had been fired. There was nothing—or almost nothing—in this, in fact, but the myth, fostered especially by the British minister who had narrowly escaped from The Hague in May 1940, was widely believed in high circles as well as low.

The total strength at its largest, in mid-1944, consisted of some 10,000 men and 3,000 women; nearly half the men, and a few of the women, worked for short or long spells as secret agents in enemy territory or in neutral countries. SOE's scope was indeed world-wide; only in the USSR did it have no influence at all. (It had a mission there, kept on a tight rein by the *NKVD, which told it nothing and made sure it kept out of mischief.) It should be noted that it also absorbed most of the work done by some 40,000 airmen in the special duty squadrons allotted to help clandestine activity by the RAF.

Recruiting for SOE was done mainly—in the early stages, had to be done entirely—on 'the old boy network', those in it from the start invited to join them friends they had known before the war, on whose loyalty and devotion they knew they could rely. It accumulated several characters with personalities like sledgehammers, men and women of enormous energy and originality, who evolved as they went along doctrines of effective clandestine behaviour, and found the agents and invented the tools with which these doctrines could be applied. Not surprisingly, SOE was exceedingly unpopular in Whitehall and in some parts of the older secret services.

With MI6 it often got on particularly badly, partly for an excellent professional reason—SOE's agents sought to create social mayhem, thus attracting police attention, while MI6 's agents desired utmost police somnolence—and partly because of clashes of personality. Relations were more smooth with *MI5, which provided SOE with useful advice and staff.

Jebb and Nelson toured Whitehall together, explaining to permanent secretaries that there was now a new secret service which needed to be handled with diligence and care. They were fortified by a treasury minute which laid down that all SOE's demands were to be met without question; the secret service fund covered running costs.

A fearful political battle in Whitehall, which awaits its historian, resulted in the separation from SOE of its political warfare branch, known as SO1. Dalton had advocated from the start the uniting of all forms of subversive warfare under a single head; the rest of the civil service was not ready for so sweeping a change. In August 1941 SO1 became the *Political Warfare Executive, a separate body under the foreign office's wing again. SO2, the more operational part of SOE, got on with its work.

SOE was organized in two main branches, one to provide facilities, one to act. The former provided money, clothing, forged papers, training, weapons, ciphers and signals, the latter was made up of a number of country sections. Paramilitary training, after a preliminary course at a country house in south-eastern England, was mostly done on a remote part of the west coast of Scotland, arranged by Gubbins (a Highlander by origin) with a pre-war neighbour. Agents who qualified there then went to the New Forest, where Beaulieu House, which belonged to a cousin of Churchill's (it now houses the Montagu Motor Museum) held the staff who trained potential agents in how to behave secretly. One of the most successful tutors here was the Soviet agent, 'Kim' *Philby till he left to join MI6 in September 1941.

Other training arrangements, usually rougher, were made at some of SOE's overseas bases. There was a large camp near Toronto (see CAMP X) popular, after the *Office of Strategic Services (OSS) was formed, with American visitors. Those attending it enjoyed the training in unarmed combat by an expert who had learned it in the Shanghai police. There was also a school on Mount Carmel, in Palestine, from which—with the help of one of the staff, who defected to them—the *Haganah stole their first machine-guns, and one in Singapore which taught future members of the resistance in Malaya the rudiments of sabotage and guerrilla warfare.

Among the most important of the lessons learned at these schools were the techniques of industrial sabotage worked out by G. T. Rheam at Brickendonbury in Hertfordshire. Rheam taught his pupils how to look over a factory, and spot in it the few machines on which the work of the rest depended; and then how to put a vital machine out of action, perhaps by a method as simple as hitting its cast-iron base once, hard, with a hammer. He trained them also in the use of time pencils, developed by SOE from a model brought back from Poland by Gubbins in 1939, to detonate a pre-laid charge of plastic *explosives after a fixed time limit (which varied from

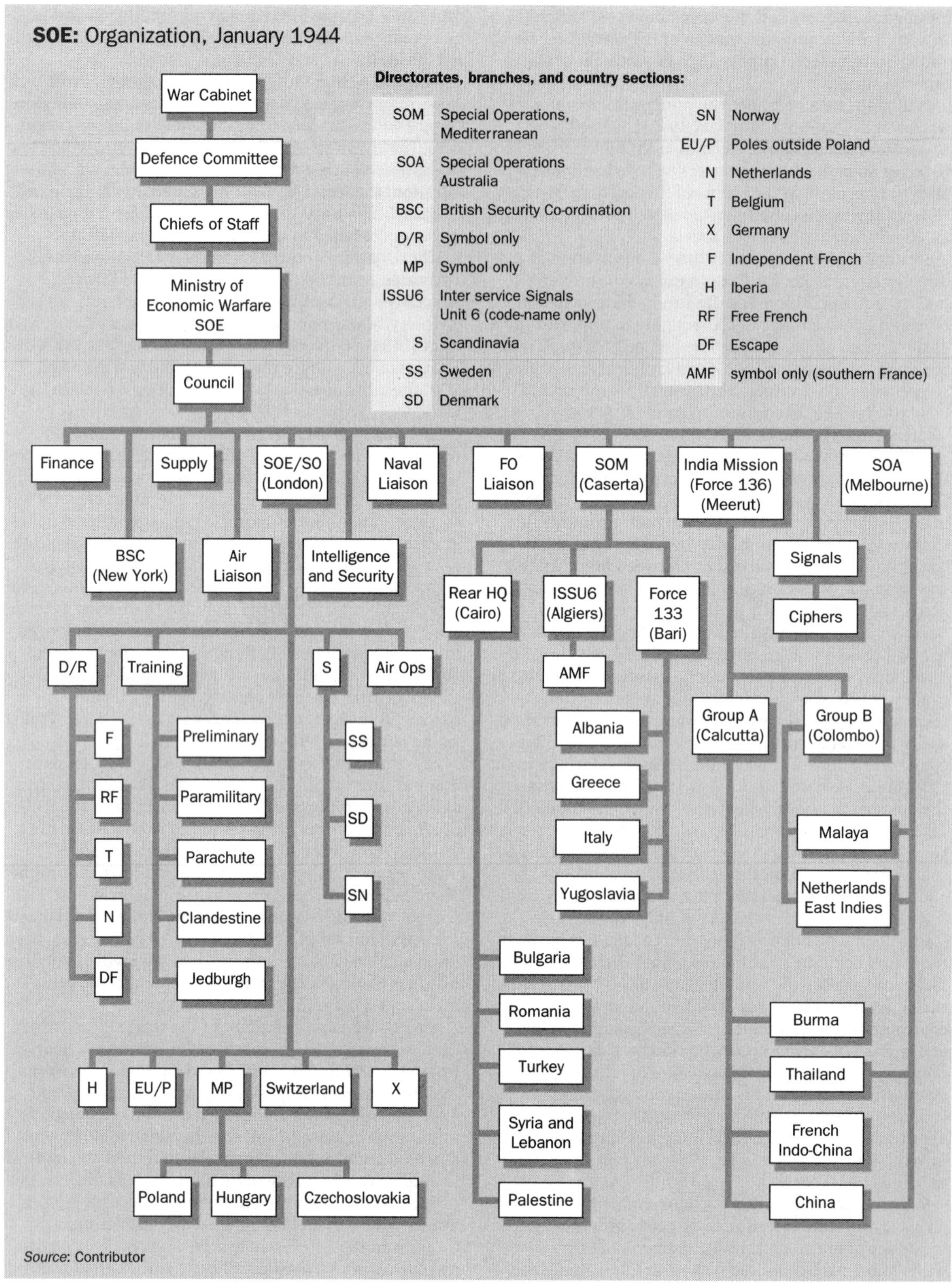
SOE: Organization, January 1944
War Cabinet
Defence Committee
Chiefs of Staff
Ministry of Economic Warfare SOE
Council
Finance
Supply
SOE/SO (London)
Naval Liaison
FO Liaison
SOM (Caserta)
India Mission (Force 136) (Meerut)
SOA (Melbourne)
BSC (New York)
Air Liaison
Intelligence and Security
Signals
Ciphers
Rear HQ (Cairo)
ISSU6 (Algiers)
Force 133 (Bari)
AMF
D/R
Training
S
Air Ops
F
RF
T
N
DF
Preliminary
Paramilitary
Parachute
Clandestine
Jedburgh
SS
SD
SN
Albania
Greece
Italy
Yugoslavia
Group A (Calcutta)
Group B (Colombo)
Malaya
Netherlands East Indies
Bulgaria
Romania
Turkey
Syria and Lebanon
Palestine
Burma
Thailand
French Indo-China
China
H
EU/P
MP
Switzerland
X
Poland
Hungary
Czechoslovakia
Directorates, branches, and country sections:
SOM Special Operations, Mediterranean
SOA Special Operations Australia
BSC British Security Co-ordination
D/R Symbol only
MP Symbol only
ISSU6 Inter service Signals Unit 6 (code-name only)
S Scandinavia
SS Sweden
SD Denmark
SN Norway
EU/P Poles outside Poland
N Netherlands
T Belgium
X Germany
F Independent French
H Iberia
RF Free French
DF Escape
AMF symbol only (southern France)
Source: Contributor

ten minutes to 30 hours, according to the colour marked on the pencil). Plastic explosive had been invented in England just before the war began and SOE was its first large-scale user. It had all sorts of clandestine advantages: it did not smell, it was readily mouldable into any required shape, and it was stable—it did not go off when jolted by anything less than a detonator (one or two agents, who ate it by mistake, survived).

Even more critical to SOE's successes than methods of sabotage were methods of signalling, which Gubbins described in a post-war lecture as absolutely critical. At first SOE had to depend entirely on MI6, for cumbrous equipment and infantile codes; but from June 1942 it manufactured its own more compact and more efficient short-wave transceivers (see also RADIO COMMUNICATIONS) and shortly thereafter introduced *one-time-pad ciphers, then at least unbreakable. Almost all its effective groups of secret agents at work included at least one wireless operator; and it was through their wireless-operators, readily enough detected by direction-finding, that most of such groups as came to grief were caught. The best wireless operators, like the best agents, kept on the move as much as they could and evaded arrest altogether.

Next to signals, transport into the field was the critical problem for SOE. Transport by sea was seldom possible, though submarines could occasionally be spared to put a very few agents ashore, or collect them; and a few sailors in the free Polish navy ran a successful small boat line between Gibraltar and the south coast of France in 1941–2. There was also a frequent small boat service, known as the *Shetland Bus, between the Shetlands and Norway, and there were other interesting small-boat operations in the Mediterranean. But the way most agents had to take into occupied territory was by parachute, and there were seldom enough dropping aircraft available. The Chief of the British Air Staff, *Portal, used to say that his bombers were a gilt-edged investment, while SOE only represented a gamble on which he resolutely refused to stake too much of his effort. Competition with MI6 and *MI9, who also occasionally required secret drops, made further complications.

The first agents always had to drop 'blind', with no one to meet them, hoping that their pilots had taken them close to the exact spot they had chosen beforehand. Once some organization had been started up on the ground, drops—sometimes aided by the *Eureka homing device—could be made to reception committees, gatherings of resisters who would break curfew, meet arriving agents, and collect and hide arriving stores of arms. This was doubly risky work, not only because breaking curfew might be regarded by the occupying forces as a serious offence, but because every effort was made by the Axis police to get *double agents on to reception committees, so that they could find out what was going on.

Both in North and in South America SOE had agents standing by, in case Axis fifth column activities broke out. The agents' existence in South America had to be kept from J. Edgar *Hoover, head of the FBI (see USA, 6); the need for them to be active fortunately never arose.

In northern Europe, SOE managed in co-operation with the navy to extract some special steels and ball-bearings by sea from Sweden (see BLOCKADE RUNNERS)—a small but vital contribution to the British armaments industry—and played a leading part in helping the Norwegians to organize and arm their resistance movement. One nine-man SOE party succeeded in dislocating entirely the Nazis' plans to make an *atomic bomb with heavy water from a Norwegian plant (see VEMORK): this coup alone provides justification enough for SOE's existence. In Denmark, resistance developed comparatively late; SOE helped to stimulate it, and armed it extensively. SOE was also made responsible by MI6 for securing military intelligence from Denmark; this task was usually outside its remit.

Poland was close to Gubbins's heart; he had visited it both shortly before and at the start of the war in 1939, and had excellent relations with the Polish intelligence staff in exile in Paris and later in London. It was to Poland that SOE made its first successful clandestine parachute drop, in February 1941; but distance made it extra hard for SOE to help the Poles, because the USSR forbade RAF aircraft on secret duties to land in its territory. With SOE's help, the Poles carried out extensive sabotage of German rail traffic towards the Eastern Front, putting some 6,000 locomotives out of action. Into what had been Czechoslovakia SOE only mounted one operation of importance, but that disposed of *Heydrich—at a ghastly cost in reprisals at *Lidiče and elsewhere.

SOE got some of its earliest field experience in the *East African campaign, in the winter of 1940–1, when it provided an irregular expedition, *Gideon Force, to escort *Haile Selassie, the exiled emperor of Abyssinia, back to his throne in Addis Ababa.

In Cairo SOE had a large branch headquarters, constantly revised, often inefficient; so bent on secrecy that its cipher clerks once fell three weeks behind in clearing even most immediate messages. It nevertheless supervised some useful activity in the Balkans (see FORCE 266). In Greece SOE's *Force 133 armed several thousand guerrillas, only to discover that those of them under communist domination were using the arms, not against the Germans, but against fellow guerrillas who were anti-communist, a few of whom SOE was able to rescue. Some useful railway sabotage was also accomplished.

In Yugoslavia, SOE was at first ordered to back *Mihailović's Četniks. Later, it was switched to support the communist-led partisans under *Tito, who, with substantial SOE backing, secured control of the country as the Red Army swept past it. In Albania, too, SOE tended to support the communist-dominated partisan movement rather than more right-wing forces.

SOE could get nothing useful done in Italy before 1943, but then by a stroke of luck provided the channel through which *Eisenhower could arrange with Marshal *Badoglio, the Italian prime minister, the conditions for

Italy's *unconditional surrender; and thereafter it took part in organizing and arming partisan activity against the occupying Germans. Here the communists were persuaded to join in a common anti-fascist front with all the rest, with valuable results.

In France, on the other hand, the communists tried to keep aloof from other resisters, though they made approaches to de *Gaulle, who brought communists on to his *French Committee for National Liberation. In France SOE did not have its usual single country section, but no fewer than six separate sections, four large and two small: F, the independent French section run by *Buckmaster, which worked directly for the Chiefs of Staff; RF, which supported General de Gaulle; AMF (the largest), which worked out of Algiers into southern France after the *North African campaign landings in November 1942; and the *'Jedburgh' teams, who provided a steel core for several groups of *Maquis after the Normandy landings on 6 June 1944 (see OVERLORD); as well as DF, a secret escape service, and EU/P which worked among the Polish minority in the French coal-mining areas. With the RAF's help, SOE provided arms for nearly half a million Frenchmen, whose effort Eisenhower said was worth half-a-dozen divisions to him.

SOE's work into Belgium, hampered by incessant quarrels with the *government-in-exile in London, turned out almost without effect, because the campaign swept across the country so fast in September 1944. There had been some useful sabotage meanwhile, and resisters captured Antwerp docks all but intact: a splendid gift to the invading Allied forces, which they were slow to exploit.

In the Netherlands there was a catastrophe in 1942–3: the *Abwehr and the Sicherheitsdienst (see RSHA), co-operating, succeeded in capturing almost all of the first 55 agents SOE sent in, unknown to the staff in London (see ENGLANDSPIEL). Two escaped, and turned up in Switzerland in November 1943 to report their companions' fate. By this time it was almost too late to get the arming of Dutch resistance, which might have been formidable, properly organized; a little, but only a little, could be done in the eastern Netherlands in the spring of 1945.

In Australia SOE formed *Special Operations Australia and in the Far East it was active also during the last two years of the war; sometimes in co-operation, sometimes in acute rivalry, with OSS. It operated under the codename Force 136. Its head was Colin Mackenzie (1898–1986), a Scottish textile manufacturer who had a secret commission as a maj-general—useful for securing places on aircraft during his constant voyages round his command—and a strong grasp of security and of politics.

Force 136 operated extensively in Burma, rather less so in Thailand and French Indo-China, and with difficulty in Malaya. SOE's best agent in Malaya, F. Spencer Chapman (1907–71), had done his extraordinary work before the codename was adopted. In Burma the force was somewhat, in French Indo-China it was extensively, and in Thailand it was extravagantly, at odds with the OSS: the two services' work was nothing like as well co-ordinated in Asia as in Europe. Each was unnecessarily suspicious of the other's aims. With the help of the regent of Thailand, SOE was able to do something towards getting the Japanese to relax their hold on the country; in French Indo-China its attempts to assist Free French subversion came to nothing, while the OSS was then working with the *Viet Minh.

In Burma it undertook, against the European rules and indeed its own charter, a good deal of intelligence-collecting work, for which the British Secret Intelligence Service, MI6, could provide no facilities on the spot; it also organized some formidable bodies of guerrillas, particularly in the Karen Hills. These guerrillas killed nearly 17,000 Japanese troops in the closing months of the war, and *Slim bore witness to them in his final report as 'a most valuable asset'. Force 136 moreover persuaded the Burma National Army (see BURMA INDEPENDENCE ARMY), organized by the Japanese as an armed gendarmerie, to change sides in April 1945 and work against their Japanese occupiers instead of for them.

Force 136 also sent two missions into China, where SOE was specifically forbidden to operate. One, under Walter Fletcher (1892–1956), was a purely personal venture—not, Fletcher assured everybody, an operation—which cleaned up £77,000,000 profit, partly from dealings in foreign exchange and partly from smuggling. The other, extra secret (for knowledge of it had to be kept from *Chiang Kai-shek as well as from the Americans) offered *Mao Tse-tung's Eighth Route Army advice on sabotage methods acquired by SOE in western Europe.

SOE was disbanded in January 1946, its work done. It had done a great deal to sustain morale in occupied Europe, and to justify a remark made by one of its agents in Abyssinia: 'Perhaps God fights on the side of the great hearts and not of the big battalions.' Moreover, thanks to Fletcher's achievement, it ended with its accounts in the black, and paid over a profit of several million pounds to the treasury with its expiring breath. M. R. D. FOOT

Chapman, F. S., *The Jungle is Neutral* (London, 1949).
Cruickshank, C. F., *SOE in the Far East* (Oxford, 1983).
Foot, M. R. D., *SOE in France* (Frederick, Md., 1984).
Gilchrist, A., *Bangkok Top Secret* (London, 1970).
Gubbins, C., 'Resistance Movements in the War', *JRUSI*, xciii.210 (May 1948).
Stafford, D., *Britain and European Resistance 1940–1945* (London, 1980).

Solomon Islands, double-chained Pacific archipelago 965 km. (600 mi.) long which was the scene of some of the severest fighting in the *Pacific war. It includes *Bougainville and Buka, which were part of the Australian mandated territory of the north-eastern part of the island of New Guinea, while those islands situated to the south-east—including Choiseul, New Georgia, and Guadalcanal—were British protectorates (see Map 83).

Somerville, Admiral of the Fleet Sir James (1882–1949), retired British vice-admiral who was recalled in September 1939. In May 1940 he helped *Ramsay organize the *Dunkirk evacuation and he then commanded *Force H. In February 1942 he was appointed C-in-C of the Eastern Fleet which was defeated by a Japanese task force in April 1942 when it made a raid into the *Indian Ocean. In August 1944 he was replaced by Admiral *Fraser and he then headed the Admiralty delegation to Washington. Promoted to admiral on the retired list in May 1942, he was later reinstated on to the active list and was promoted admiral of the fleet in May 1945. On his death Admiral *Cunningham wrote that 'he was a great sailor and a great leader: shrewd, imaginative, determined, and farseeing'. He was knighted in 1941.

MacIntyre, D., *Fighting Admiral* (London, 1961).

SONAR, acronym derived from Sound-Navigation, Ranging. It was a US device which, like *ASDIC, was developed between the wars to detect submerged submarines. In 1943 the Royal Navy adopted SONAR as the name for its ASDIC equipment.

Sonderführer (special leader), rank given to civilians who were attached to the German Wehrmacht.

Sonderkommandos (special detachments) was the name of **Einsatzgruppen* sub-units. But it was also used to describe squads of inmates in the death camps (see OPERATION REINHARD) who were used by their guards as work parties to clear the gas chambers and bury or burn the victims. They were given extra food and privileges, but were eventually shot to cover all traces of what they had been forced to do. See also FINAL SOLUTION.

Soong Tsu-wen ('T. V.') (1891–1971), brother-in-law of *Chiang Kai-shek and one of the ablest financial brains in the Chinese Nationalist government. He read economics at Harvard University and was minister of finance in Chiang Kai-shek's government from 1928 to 1931 before becoming chairman of the Bank of China. When the Japanese invaded in 1937 (see CHINA INCIDENT) Soong was put in charge of *economic warfare and was later sent to the USA as a special envoy where he negotiated a $100 million loan for his country. He remained in Washington throughout the war, serving first as China's minister of foreign affairs and, from December 1944, as its prime minister as well. See also CHINA, 3(a).

Sorge, Richard (1895–1944), Soviet agent of German-Russian parentage who was one of the war's most effective *spies.

Sorge went to Japan as the *Frankfurter Zeitung*'s correspondent during the 1930s where, as a close friend and confidant of the German military attaché (later ambassador) in Tokyo, he became the German embassy's press attaché. A member of the Nazi Party who was, in fact, a dedicated communist, he established a network of agents, codenamed RAMSAY, which included Ozaki Hotsumi, a close adviser to the Japanese prime minister, Prince *Konoe. Ozaki and other high-level contacts enabled him to obtain accurate intelligence which included indications, and eventually the date, of the German invasion of the USSR in June 1941 (see BARBAROSSA). But Stalin was as sceptical of Sorge's warnings as he was of the other sources from which he received the same unwelcome news, and the head of Soviet military intelligence (see GRU), General *Golikov, to whom Sorge reported, wanted him recalled and punished. But when, in September 1941, Sorge relayed that the Japanese had decided against attacking the USSR through Manchukuo and had decided to move southwards against the colonies of the western powers instead, his intelligence must have been received with interest. For it was then that Stalin decided to move his armies from Siberia, which were there to counter a Japanese offensive, so that they could help stem the German onslaught against *Moscow.

In October 1941 Sorge and 35 members of his network were arrested by the *Tokkō, and after being held in prison for three years he was executed. Twenty years later he was posthumously awarded the title Hero of the Soviet Union (see DECORATIONS).

Johnson, C., *An Instance of Treason: Ozaki Hotsumi and the Sorge Spy Ring* (rev. edn., Stanford, Calif. 1990).

Sosnkowski, General Kazimierz (1885–1969), Polish Army officer who was deputy commander of the army during the *Polish campaign in September 1939. After the death of General *Sikorski in July 1943, he commanded the armed forces controlled by the Polish *government-in-exile and became the successor of the new Polish president, Stanisław Mikołajczyk. His strongly patriotic views offended the Soviet Union, which urged the British government to press for his resignation, and in 1944–5 he was, *de facto*, interned in Canada.

Source K. In January 1942 Robert Keller, a French telephone engineer, succeeded in tapping the long-distance telephone between Paris and Hitler's headquarters in east Prussia; for some months he drew valuable intelligence from it, which he passed to *Vichy by safe hand, whence in turn it reached London. (Some of Vichy's intelligence staff were ready to work with *MI6.) The information of naval interest was often important. Keller made the original tap himself, with a German sentry at his elbow; all his workmen also had to operate under similar close watch, but succeeded in bluffing the sentries with technical jargon. Keller decided to extend his work to cover a second major trunk telephone line from Paris into Germany; this attempt led to disaster in December, because the Germans spotted it at once. He and several of his accomplices were arrested and deported to *forced labour camps, and the source ceased to work. See also FORSCHUNGSSTELLE.

South Africa, Union of. In 1939 South Africa was a British dominion, comprising the provinces of the Cape of Good Hope, Natal, the Orange Free State, and the Transvaal, with the additional mandated territory of South West Africa. Rich in gold and diamonds, as well as coal and iron ore, and other strategic *raw materials, South Africa possessed an industrial base capable of ready expansion. Yet compared to Australia, Canada, and New Zealand, its contribution was limited. 'Viewed from outside', concluded W. K. Hancock (*Smuts, The Fields of Force*, Cambridge, 1968, p. 330), 'the South African war effort was not massive'.

The reasons for this are not hard to find. South Africa entered the war against Germany deeply divided. As far as the overwhelming majority of black South Africans (Africans, Coloureds, and Indians in the tortured local lexicon) were concerned, the war was a matter of little concern. Unenfranchised Africans in particular saw no point in getting involved in a white man's war. 'There is one thing certain', noted one newspaper early in 1940, 'there is no enthusiasm among them [Africans] for the war. The reason ... is that they are not convinced of the truth of the causes and aims of this war and that they as an oppressed people do not figure anywhere in its aims'. Others were blunter. 'Why should we fight for you? We fought for you in the Boer War and you betrayed us to the Dutch. We fought for you in last war. We died in France, in East Africa ... and when it was over, did anyone care about us? What have we to fight for?'. Not surprisingly some Africans even 'privately cheered the military advance of the Third Reich ... because of an emotional alliance with the enemy of South Africa'. At the same time, a large section of the ruling white minority were strongly opposed to the war. Embittered by the British victory in the South African War (the 'Anglo-Boer' War of 1899–1902) and alienated by the subsequent policy of anglicization, most Afrikaners wanted nothing to do with what they saw as the UK's latest war. Only English-speaking whites, actually a minority of a minority; were unequivocally prepared to die for King and a far-away country.

As a result, when General *Smuts, a junior partner in the coalition United South African National Party government, narrowly defeated the prime minister on General *Hertzog's motion that South Africa should remain neutral, his mandate was considerably less than popular. On the 6 September 1939 the South African 'herrenvolk democracy' declared war on Nazi Germany. The irony was not lost on black political organizations. In December 1939 a resolution passed at the annual conference of the African National Congress (ANC) declared that 'unless the government grants the Africans full democratic and citizenship rights, the ANC is not prepared to advise the Africans to participate in the present war, in any capacity'.

Although the ANC leadership later modified its position, in such circumstances the Smuts government had to move with great caution. Afrikaner hostility to the war found expression in two main channels. One of these was broadly constitutional; the other explicitly non-parliamentary. In parliament itself the combined Nationalists, including a faction of Hertzog's old National Party, the Purified National Party led by D. F. Malan, made up the Opposition. However, Malan, who later, as prime minister from 1948, was to secure Afrikaner domination of South African political life and to introduce apartheid, was pro-Nazi and the long-standing animosity between him and Hertzog made unity short-lived. Malan also fell out with a yet more extreme element of his own supporters, the *Ossewabrandwag who became committed to the violent overthrow of the government. Both movements found much to admire in Nazi racism and openly sought German victory. Nazi propaganda in Afrikaans beamed from the radio station at Zeesen near Berlin further inflamed this extremely vocal anti-war constituency.

The Smuts government made no attempt to introduce conscription and it shied away from banning extremist organizations. *Internment for enemy aliens and those suspected of subversion (*c.*2,000 and numbering amongst them another future prime minister, John Vorster) was eventually introduced, and to prevent the possibility of rebellion all private rifles were confiscated. But even so, dissent against the country's involvement in the war persisted. Early in 1941 the Ossewabrandwag provoked clashes between civilians and soldiers in Johannesburg; the following January saboteurs attacked power and telephone lines; and in June 1942 preliminary legal hearings revealed the presence of 8,000 extremists in the Transvaal, including members of the police, who were plotting to overthrow the government. From 1943, though, with hopes of German victory fading, the influence of the extra-parliamentary extremists fell sharply.

British reverses during the fighting which preceded the fall of *France in June 1940, and the entry of Italy into the war the same month, speeded South Africa's war preparations and threw it onto its own resources. These included vast amounts of iron ore, huge reserves of coal and electricity, and two of the world's largest explosives factories. In particular, railway and harbour workshops, and the gold mining industry provided important productive capacity and valuable engineering skills for the South African Engineer Corps which served with great distinction throughout the *Western Desert and *Italian campaigns, and elsewhere.

By 1945 South Africa's industrial output had nearly doubled, most growth occurring in mining, steel, and textiles. Factories turned out 12 million pairs of boots and shoes, 2 million steel helmets, and a mass of other war material which included armoured cars, tyres,

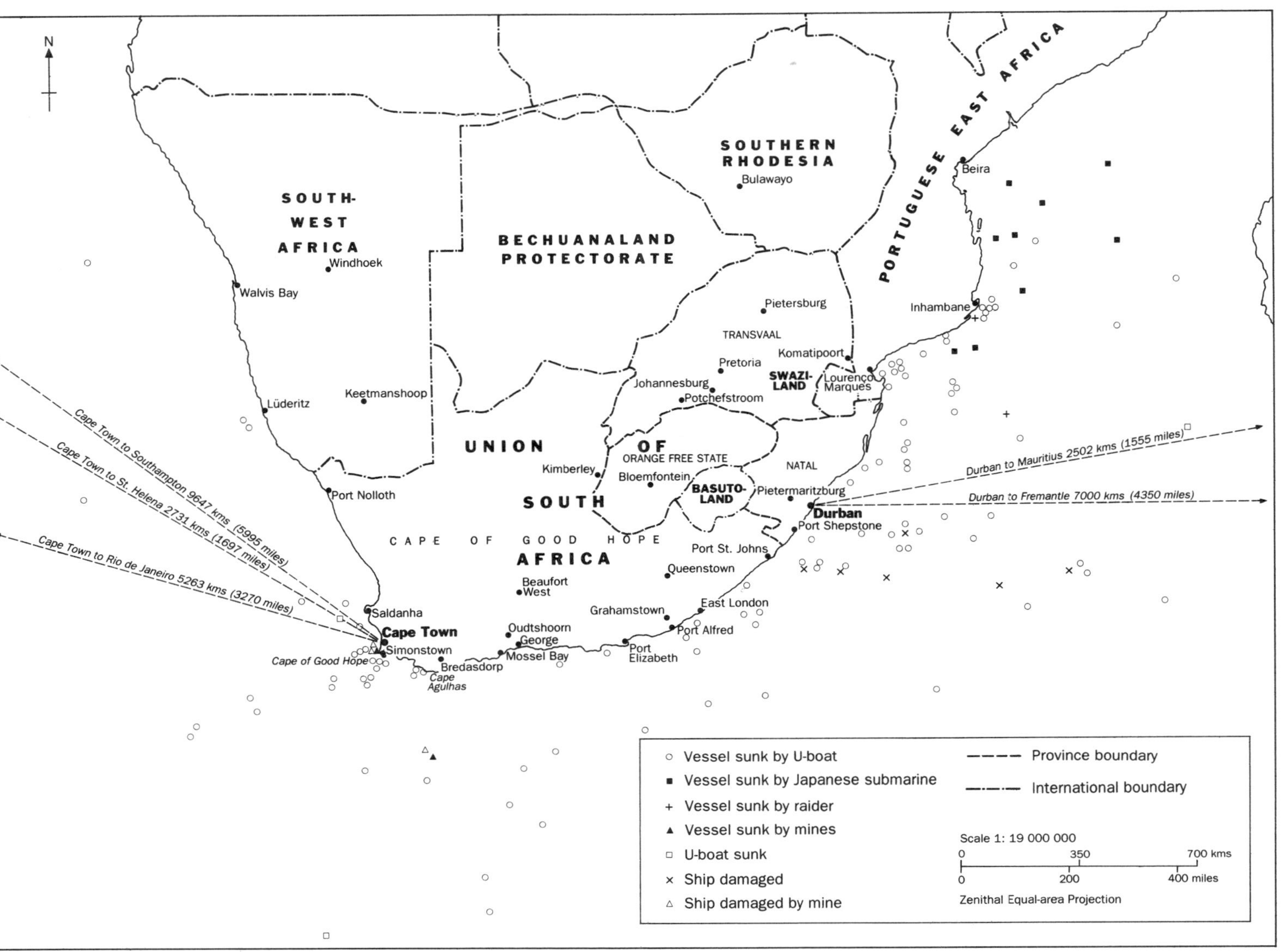

97. War at sea in **South African** waters, 1939–45

howitzers, mortars, and ammunition. These were manufactured not only for South Africa's own armed forces, the Union Defence Force (UDF) but also for the UK and India. Food was exported in large quantities too. With the virtual closure of the Mediterranean and then the entry of Japan into the war, South Africa's ports and ship repair industry became a vital aspect of the Allied war effort, and both were expanded and improved. Four hundred *convoys carrying six million men used South African ports during the war, and 13,000 ships were repaired.

For many white South Africans, however, the war remained remote for the first two years, and though in May 1941 the government restricted the use of white flour and attempted to make voters live more frugally—whites were enjoined 'not to keep more servants than you really need', thereby freeing black labour for 'more useful purposes'—it was not until the end of 1941, when Japan entered the war, that its effects began to be noticed. By then there were shortages as stocks ran low, shipping space contracted, and import sources dried up. Petrol rationing, and price and import controls were introduced, and a Food Controller was appointed.

The main impact of the war in fact was felt elsewhere. It opened up a range of previously closed opportunities to white women and semi-skilled black factory operatives. *Women worked in munitions factories and ultimately *c.*65,000 served in the South African Women Auxiliary Services (SAWAS). As increased industrial output could only be sustained by employing more black workers, their numbers grew by three-quarters during the war. Grim living conditions exacerbated by overcrowding and inflation set off a wave of strikes in 1941–2, while in the countryside rumours of an imminent Japanese invasion in 1942 made it clear that many people would welcome Japanese soldiers as liberators. Desperate to bind black and white together in the face of danger, the Smuts government suspended influx control measures (so-called 'pass laws' which denied most black South Africans the right to dwell permanently in urban areas). But this relaxation of segregatory laws was short-lived. Once the Japanese threat receded, the old laws were reintroduced. This provoked an anti-pass campaign the following year, and accelerated the radicalization of black political movements. In 1943 the militant Congress Youth League was founded.

The Union Defence Force, which comprised the country's land, air, and sea forces, was commanded by Maj-General Pierre van Ryneveld, who acted as his own Chief of Staff. In September 1939 its regular component, the Permanent Force, totalled only 5,385 men. Coastal defences were antiquated, the land forces had no modern tanks or artillery, the South African Naval Service (SANS) had no warships, and the South African Air Force (SAAF) had only six modern aircraft. Part-time forces like the Active Citizen Force, the Defence Rifle Associations (Burger Commandos), and the South African section of the British Royal Navy Volunteer Reserve (RNVR)—which anyway came under the Royal Navy's C-in-C Africa Station at the British naval base at Simonstown—were equally unready and, with few exceptions, were neither properly trained nor armed for war.

During the *First World War, black South Africans saw active service in the Cape Corps, but in the Second, with very few exceptions, they only served as non-combatants, in the Non-European Army services (NEAS). This predominantly comprised the Cape Coloured Corps, which enrolled 45,000 men after it was reformed in May 1940, and the Native Military Corps (NMC) which enrolled 76,000 men. Recruitment for the Cape Corps was undertaken by the Director of Recruitment, but recruitment for the NMC was controlled by the Native Affairs Department. By far the majority of them came from rural areas devastated by drought. Destitute peasants joined up even though their basic pay was less than half that of white servicemen. The Cape Corps provided gunners for the Coast Garrison Force. Motor transport, and engineering works companies, and performed guard and security duties, while the Native Military Corps provided mess servants, hygiene personnel, and specially trained men for SAAF and Engineer units.

From March 1940 White volunteers joining the UDF had to take an oath, which obliged them to serve anywhere in Africa, but this remained optional for those already serving. Those taking the oath wore an orange strip, known as the 'Red Tab', on their shoulder straps. In January 1943 a new oath was introduced for those willing to serve anywhere. Some servicemen had refused to take the original oath and others refused to renew it when it changed; and throughout the war the government, while continuing to refuse black South Africans combatant roles, remained desperately short of white recruits for the ground forces.

The nucleus of these ground forces were three infantry divisions. The 7th Motorized Brigade Group of the 3rd SA Division took part in the capture of *Madagascar, but the balance of the division never saw action as it acted as a reserve for the other two divisions. The 1st SA Division, and armoured cars of the 2nd SA Tank Corps, fought in the *East African campaign before moving, with the SA Division, to the Middle East in 1941. By September 1941 there were nearly 60,000 South African troops in Egypt, including 15,000 blacks. This proved to be the peak of South Africa's war effort on the ground because the 1st SA Division lost one-third of its strength during the *Sidi Rezegh battles of November 1941 and the 2nd SA Division had 353 casualties while capturing *Bardia in January 1942, and a further 10,722 became prisoners of war when *Tobruk fell in June 1942. The 1st SA Division was withdrawn after taking part in both *El Alamein battles and its survivors then formed the nucleus of a new formation, the 6th Armoured Division, which fought in the Italian campaign from April 1944 until the end of the war.

The SAAF, however, remained in combat without a

break and by the end of the war it totalled four SAAF wings and 28 squadrons, as well as supporting other units. It served under RAF command in East Africa and Madagascar, in the Western Desert—making almost one third of the striking power of the *Western Desert Air Force—and in the Central Mediterranean, where it was part of the *Balkan Air Force. Besides contributing significantly to victory in the battle for the Mediterranean, the SAAF played a vital role in training Allied air crew.

At sea the SANS, aided by the SAAF's Coastal Air Force, patrolled South Africa's coast line, and its minesweepers dealt with mines laid by German *auxiliary cruisers (see Map 97). In January 1940 it was absorbed into the newly-formed Seaward Defence Force (SDF) which also absorbed those members of the RNVR's South African section not already manning ships of the Royal Navy. By November 1940 the SDF had expanded enough to provide a flotilla of four modern Antarctic whalers, converted for minesweeping, for service in the Mediterranean. In August 1942 the SDF and RNVR (SA) officially amalgamated to become the South African Naval Force (SANF). By 1945 this totalled 78 vessels, including three new frigates, one of which sank a U-boat.

Altogether 334,224 South Africans volunteered for full-time service. Of this total, 132,194 whites, and most of the 123,131 Blacks who had volunteered, served in the ground forces, while 44,569 whites served in the SAAF and 9,455 in the SANF. A total of 21,265 white women served in various branches of the women's Auxiliary Defence Corps and 3,710 in the Military Nursing Service. Casualties amounted to nearly 9,000 dead, over 8,000 wounded and over 14,000 taken prisoner. IAN PHIMISTER

Davenport, T., *South Africa: A Modern History* (4th edn., London, 1991).
South Africa at War Series, 8 vols. (Cape Town, 1968–79).

South-East Asia Command (SEAC), established in October 1943 after Anglo-American agreement at the first Quebec conference in August 1943 (see QUADRANT). Its operational area contained Burma, Malaya, Sumatra, and, for clandestine missions only, Thailand and French Indo-China. Its supreme commander, Admiral *Mountbatten, a compromise choice, had his HQ at New Delhi, India, which he moved in June 1944 to Kandy, Ceylon. His deputy was an American, first *Stilwell and then *Wedemeyer (see Chart for command structure). His instructions, issued by the *Combined Chiefs of Staff, were to increase pressure on the Japanese in the *Burma campaign and elsewhere, in the hope of drawing off their strength from the *Pacific war; to maintain the *Hump air supply route to China; and to open a land route for supplies through northern Burma as quickly as possible (see LEDO ROAD).

From the first, SEAC was bedevilled by staff problems (see AXIOM MISSION, for example); by Mountbatten's conception of his role which clashed with that of his Cs-in-C; by differences between British and US strategy (an American wit said that SEAC's initials stood for 'Save England's Asiatic Colonies'); by shortages of *matériel*; and by the intransigence of *Chiang Kai-shek. As a result, operations to invade Sumatra, to land on the Andaman Islands, and to take the offensive in the Burma campaign, were all frustrated. An operation (PIGSTICK) to land on Burma's Arakan coast met the same fate. 'PIGSTICK,' Churchill informed Roosevelt, 'has become PIGSTUCK.' Eventually, it was the Japanese who rescued SEAC from its inactivity by launching the *Imphal offensive in March 1944 which ended in their defeat by *Slim's Fourteenth Army the following year.

In November 1944 General George Gifford, C-in-C of Eleventh Army Group which administered all British land forces in SEAC, was replaced by General *Leese who headed a new land forces organization, Allied Land Forces South-East Asia (ALFSEA). This incorporated US troops who had formerly come under Stilwell's Northern Combat Area Command (see CHINA–BURMA–INDIA THEATRE). In May 1945 Leese was replaced by Slim, whose Fourteenth Army HQ moved to India to plan the invasion of Malaya (ZIPPER), and a new Twelfth Army was formed under Lt-General *Stopford to control British and Indian formations in Burma. On 15 August 1945 SEAC's boundaries were altered to include the *Netherlands East Indies and French Indo-China. ZIPPER went ahead on 9 September 1945, after the formal Japanese surrender, but there was no fighting and Mountbatten held a surrender ceremony in Singapore on 12 September. In June 1946 he handed over to Stopford, and on 30 November 1946 SEAC became defunct.

South Pacific Area, from 1 August 1942 that part of Admiral *Nimitz's Pacific Ocean Areas which lay south of the equator between longitude 159° East and 110° West. It included New Zealand, New Caledonia, New Hebrides, Fiji, and some of the Solomon Islands, and was commanded first by Vice-Admiral Ghormley and, from October 1942, by Vice-Admiral *Halsey (see Map F). Though Nimitz was his superior, Halsey, after March 1943, was also responsible to the commander of the *South-West Pacific Area (SWPA), General *MacArthur, for the strategic direction of the war in the Solomons. His naval forces, designated Third US Fleet (Fifth Fleet when commanded by Admiral *Spruance) from March 1943, were mostly drawn from the US and New Zealand navies, but no warships, apart from the New Zealand ones, were permanently assigned to him, Nimitz allotting them to him as the need arose. Halsey's principal permanent forces comprised: the South Pacific Amphibious Force, commanded by Rear-Admiral Kelly *Turner, to which landing forces were attached for *amphibious warfare operations; land-based Allied air units commanded by Vice-Admiral Aubrey Fitch; and two ground forces. One of the ground forces was commanded by an airman, Lt-General Millard Harmon, who had overall command of four infantry divisions as well as Thirteenth USAAF (later transferred to SWPA), and these normally fought under the tactical command of 14th US Corps. The other was

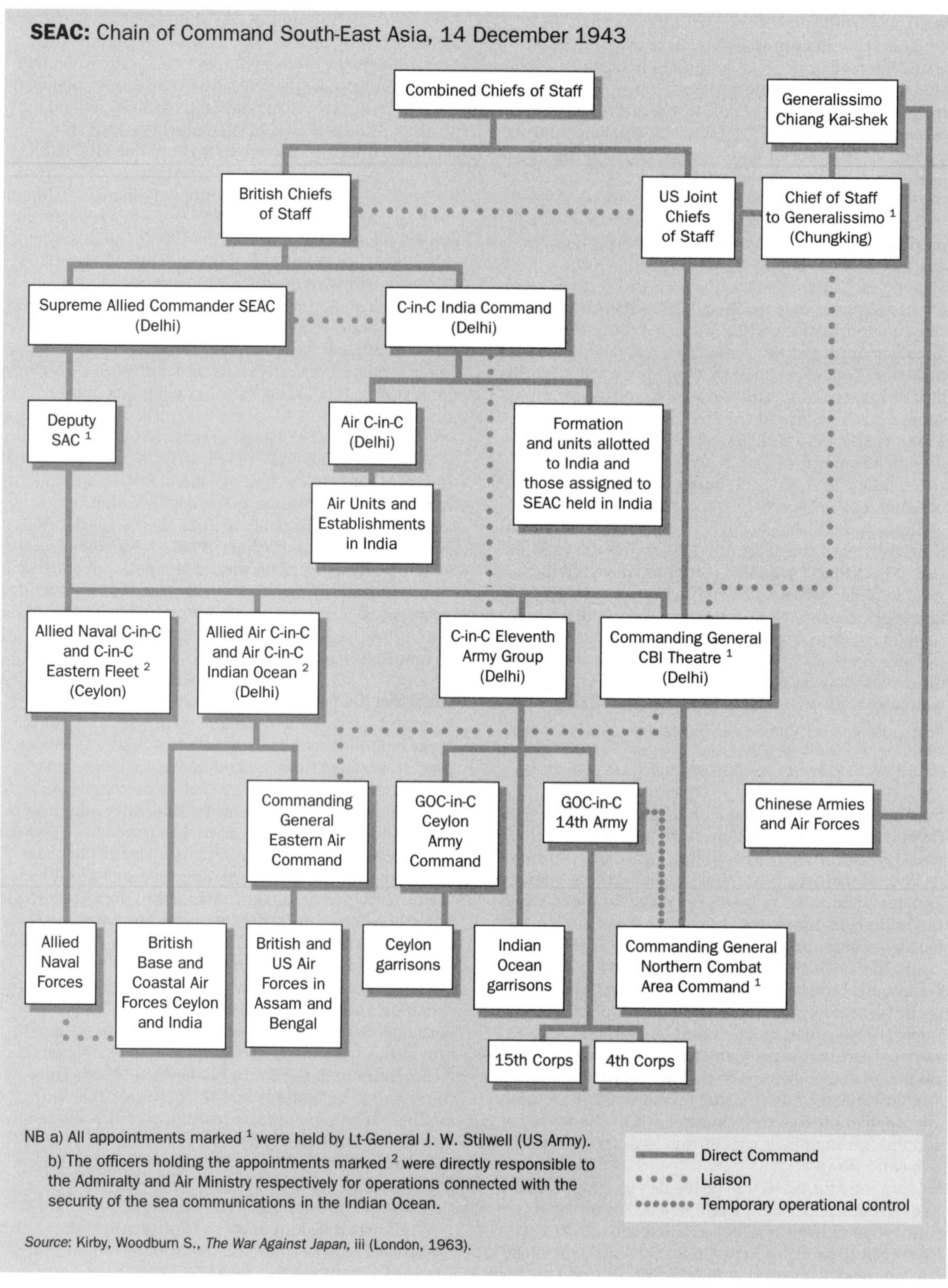

NB a) All appointments marked [1] were held by Lt-General J. W. Stilwell (US Army).
b) The officers holding the appointments marked [2] were directly responsible to the Admiralty and Air Ministry respectively for operations connected with the security of the sea communications in the Indian Ocean.

Source: Kirby, Woodburn S., *The War Against Japan*, iii (London, 1963).

Maj-General Clayton Vogel's 1st Marine Amphibious Corps which comprised two marine divisions and ancilliary units.

South-West Pacific Area (SWPA), US theatre of operations commanded by General *MacArthur during the *Pacific war (see Map F). Its GHQ, established in Brisbane in April 1942, commanded an area which took in Australia, the Philippines, New Guinea, Bismarck archipelago, Solomon Islands, and the Netherlands East Indies (except Sumatra). In August 1942 the boundary was changed to exclude Guadalcanal and certain other Solomon islands, which the US *Joint Chiefs of Staff had ordered the commander of the *South Pacific Area to seize.

All Allied combat echelons in the area were assigned to MacArthur. An Australian, General *Blamey, was appointed his Allied Land Forces commander, while two US officers, Lt-General George Brett and Vice-Admiral Herbert Leary, were appointed his Allied Air Forces and Allied Naval Forces commanders. In July 1942 Lt-General George C. Kenney, who also commanded SWPA's Fifth USAAF (and later Thirteenth USAAF as well), replaced Brett; in September 1942 Vice-Admiral Arthur Carpender, who also commanded SWPA's Seventh Fleet, replaced Leary; and in November 1943 Vice-Admiral Thomas Kinkaid replaced Carpender. In August 1942 Lt-General *Eichelberger was appointed corps commander of two US infantry divisions (32nd and 41st) which had been sent to reinforce Australia. These initially came under Blamey's command, but in June 1943 MacArthur formed *Alamo Force which effectively removed all US ground forces from Blamey's operational command. These forces became part of Sixth US Army, formed in February 1943 under Lt-General Walter Krueger, and Eichelberger's Eighth US Army, formed in October 1944.

The two organizations formed to provide MacArthur with intelligence were the *Allied Intelligence Bureau, which controlled all intelligence operations in SWPA, and Central Bureau, MacArthur's decoding establishment. Central Bureau played a major role in providing *ULTRA intelligence and by August 1945 numbered more than 4,000 men and women from several Allied countries.

Soviet exiles at war. The German armed forces made use of Soviet citizens because of manpower shortages. Very rapidly this became a political matter and heralded attempts to alter Nazi policy towards the population of the USSR.

The unprovoked attack by the Third Reich on the USSR on 22 June 1941 (see BARBAROSSA) produced a very confused situation. Stalin had refused to believe reports of an imminent attack. Troops were unprepared. While some units fought valiantly against the invader, others surrendered or deserted to the German side, their attitude to the invasion reflecting the unpopularity of Stalin's regime. The civilian population, which often greeted the German troops as liberators, was convinced that the Germans understood what had been happening within the Soviet Union and were coming to free them from Stalinist tyranny. Between June and November 1941 the Germans took more than 3,800,000 *prisoners-of-war (POW).

Throughout the *German–Soviet war the position of Soviet citizens under the jurisdiction of the Third Reich was influenced by the assumptions underlying German policy towards the USSR and the occupied territories (*Ostpolitik*). The origins of this policy can be found in **Mein Kampf*, in which Hitler maintained that the German nation needed living-space (**Lebensraum*) which could only be found in the east. In Soviet Bolshevism he saw the embodiment of the aspirations of world Jewry to achieve global domination, and he viewed the Slavs as an inferior race. All achievements of the Soviet state, he argued, were a result of the influence of the German minority (see VOLKSDEUTSCHE). Slavs were to be used to serve Germany's interests and the USSR was to be exploited to the same end. These views received further elaboration after the outbreak of the German–Soviet war and resulted in the implementation of a very harsh policy in the occupied territories, particularly by party fanatics such as Erich Koch, the **Gauleiter* of the Ukraine.

Because Hitler regarded the Slavs as inferior to the Aryans, he considered that they should not be afforded the privilege of serving in the German armed forces. Furthermore, he did not believe that it was worth considering any of the political aspirations of the population of the USSR as these people were not capable of appreciating and did not need the benefits of a freer or more just society.

Increasingly, this view came to be challenged by German officers on the Eastern Front who saw that the unmerciful treatment of the population was not in the German interest. The population, too, had realized, by the winter of 1941, that Nazi policy saw the whole situation in racist terms. This stiffened resistance. Some German officers such as *Kleist tried to find a way to alter Nazi policy so that the population would meet with less harsh treatment and anti-Stalinist feelings might be utilized for German benefit. To this end, Fremde Heere Ost, the section of the German Army High Command dealing with intelligence in the USSR, looked for a potential leader for a Russian Liberation movement and on 12 July 1942 a suitable candidate, General *Vlasov, was captured. He was sent to a camp for high-ranking POW in Vinnitsa where he met other Soviet officers, opposed to the Stalinist regime and was visited by German officers, one of whom, Captain Wilfred Strik-Strikfeldt, became Vlasov's friend and protector. These German officers persuaded Vlasov to write a letter to the Nazi authorities pointing out that anti-Stalinist feeling should be utilized in such a way that Soviet citizens did not feel themselves to be *traitors and that an anti-Stalinist movement would still have to be patriotic. His argument was not understood by the authorities, who moved Vlasov to the German High Command's

These **Soviet exiles** were Cossacks serving with a Waffen-SS cavalry division.

propaganda centre at Viktoriastrasse in Berlin, where attempts were made to make him write appeals to Soviet soldiers to defect.

In December 1942 Vlasov signed the so-called Smolensk Declaration which was dropped on the German side of the Eastern Front. This document spoke of the need to form a Russian Liberation Army to fight Stalin. It reached Soviet citizens serving in the Wehrmacht and they took it as a sign that German policy towards the USSR was changing. This propaganda move was followed by further attempts to show that there was considerable support for a political, not a racial, approach towards the population of the occupied territories. In the spring of 1943 Vlasov was allowed to visit towns such as Pskov and Riga, and he issued an 'Open Letter' explaining why he had decided to oppose Stalin. He was greeted with great enthusiasm by the local population, but Hitler disapproved of this display of Russian *nationalism and on 18 April 1943 *Keitel issued an order forbidding further trips. Then, at the Berghof conference in June 1943, Hitler forbade all further attempts to form a Russian army; Vlasov was kept under virtual house arrest and all activity was confined to the training camp at Dabendorf, set up by Colonel Claus von Stauffenberg in 1942.

The question of using Russians was brought up again in 1944, when Standartenführer (Colonel) Günther d'Alquen, an *SS officer who had been dealing with propaganda on the Eastern Front, raised the matter with *Himmler. A meeting was arranged for 21 July but the meeting was postponed to 16 September because of the attempt to assassinate Hitler (see SCHWARZE KAPELLE). At this meeting Himmler agreed to the formation of Russian divisions and a Committee for the Liberation of the Peoples of Russia (Komitet Osvobozhdeniya Narodov Rossii, or KONR) which produced the Prague Manifesto, the main programme of the movement published in Prague on 14 November 1944. But it came too late, as the Germans no longer occupied any areas of the USSR, and the population of these areas was therefore not available to support the movement. The manifesto presented a fourteen-point programme and tried to explain why its adherents had considered it their duty to fight Stalin in the best interests of Russia. Despite Nazi pressure to do so, the authors of the manifesto avoided any derogatory reference to the Jews.

The period following the publication of the manifesto saw the KONR and the Germans seeking different aims. The KONR argued that Himmler had originally promised that ten divisions could be formed, not the two divisions finally agreed upon. Also, the Russian commanders had no wish to be used as cannon fodder and tried to discuss ways in which all anti-communist forces might unite against Stalin. The Germans, on the other hand, saw the KONR divisions as last-ditch reinforcements and had no time for the committee's political aspirations. In January 1945 two Russian KONR divisions were formed under Vlasov. The 2nd KONR Division never saw active service, but 1st KONR Division fought with the Czech nationalists in *Prague in May 1945 against Wehrmacht and SS troops stationed there. When it became clear that the Americans were not going to advance on the Czech capital, the division left Prague and tried to enter the American zone of Germany, but was refused permission to do so. Vlasov then gave the order to disband and approximately half his force fled westward while others turned eastward towards the advancing Red Army and were captured by it.

Other units were also formed from Soviet citizens who fought on the German side. The principal ones were:

Osttruppen

The earliest form of co-operation between Soviet citizens and the Wehrmacht took the form of auxiliary troops (*Hilfswillige*, or 'Hiwis'), who worked in non-combatant positions: drivers, ammunition carriers, grooms, translators. They were recruited as a result of decisions made at the level of divisional commanders or below who incorporated Soviet civilians or military personnel into their formations; they, in their turn, were glad to escape some of the privations of prison life. Gradually, these auxiliaries were utilized in military capacities as local militia, against Soviet partisans and even as regular units with German officers. These troops had been acquired through unofficial channels, and the statistics were not accurate, so that the Nazi authorities did not realize the extent to which these subhumans (*Untermenschen*) were playing a role in the Wehrmacht. However, their role was officially recognized on 15 December 1942 when General Heinz Hellmich was appointed General der Osttruppen under the aegis of the organization section of the German Army High Command (OKH). In 1943 he was replaced by General Ernst Köstring and on 1 January 1944 this post was renamed General der Freiwilligeverbände (volunteer units). It is estimated that there were more than 800,000 Soviet nationals in the Wehrmacht by the end of the war. They manned anti-aircraft guns and filled non-combatant roles. By the end of 1943 it was not uncommon for a German battalion to contain a company of *Osttruppen*.

Ostlegionen

The use of non-Slav troops was authorized by the Nazi authorities in 1941. The formation of these legions represented a major victory for the ministry of the Eastern Occupied Territories (Ostministerium). Alfred *Rosenberg, in charge of this ministry, argued that in the future a truncated Russian state, Muscovy, should be surrounded by a ring of buffer states of the non-Russian nationalities of the USSR. He fostered collaborationist movements within these areas and promoted the use of military formations. He opposed the use of Russians in these units or in any united anti-Soviet movement. Six national legions were formed: the Armenian, Azerbaijani, Georgian, North Caucasian, Turkestan, and Volga Tatar legions. There was also a cavalry corps of Kalmyks (who came from an area south of the Volga bordering the Caspian Sea) and a Crimean Tatar military formation. The Armenian and Azerbaijani legions were fairly homogeneous, the others contained a great many nationalities. It is not possible to give the precise strengths and locations of these formations, but they were stationed with other Wehrmacht units largely, though not exclusively, on the Eastern Front. One historian considers that the main point of forming them was for propaganda purposes.

Cossacks

These originated from communities which had existed on the frontiers of the Russian Empire, forming a social and cultural entity without being a specific national group. The main groups were the Don, Kuban, Terek, and Zaporozhian Cossacks, but there were other smaller groups from a wide range of different areas. In Nazi Germany they were in an anomalous position because they were not regarded as Slavs. Émigré Cossacks had supported Hitler in the 1920s for his anti-Bolshevism. It was argued, therefore, that Cossacks were descended from the Goths and were Aryans.

Nazi policy on the Cossacks was never consistent. Rosenberg envisaged creating 'Cossackia' in the Don and Volga regions, but this plan was abandoned. Attempts to establish self-governing areas in the Kuban were opposed by the Ostministerium and the SS.

On 15 April 1942, Hitler sanctioned the formation of Cossack units. A division under the command of Lt-General Helmuth von Pannwitz consisting of regiments from the Don, Kuban, Terek, and Siberia was formed. Subsequently this became the 15th Cossack cavalry corps.

Émigré Cossacks such as General P. N. Krasnov, General A. G. Shkuro, and General V. G. Naumenko sided with the Germans because Germany was the only Great Power fighting the Bolsheviks. Younger Cossacks, such as Major I. N. Kononov, who had deserted with his regiment from the Red Army and joined von Pannwitz, did not agree with the more reactionary attitudes of this older generation and tended to look to General Vlasov for leadership.

In March 1944 a directorate of Cossack forces, headed by Krasnov, was created. His forces, several thousand strong, moved through Poland and Southern Germany to the foothills of the Italian Alps. He would not agree to unite with Vlasov's forces. Von Pannwitz was sent to Yugoslavia to fight *Tito and the partisans and on 19 May 1945 he surrendered to the 2nd British Armoured Division.

The term Cossack—and Ukrainian—was often used loosely to denote Soviet citizens serving in the Wehrmacht.

Other Units

Various other units, including the Roland and Nachtigall *formations from Ukraine, were created in attempts to utilize anti-Soviet feeling. The German High Command's propaganda centre at Viktoriastrasse in Berlin was used to train those who might be willing to be involved in *collaboration. Local commanders formed small units with names like Dnieper or Volga which were used in anti-partisan warfare. Larger ones included the Russian National Army of Liberation (Russkaya Osvoboditelnaya Armiya, or RONA) led by Bronislav Kaminsky. Better known as the Kaminsky Brigade, it numbered, very approximately, some 5,000 men in 1942 and double that in 1943.

Kaminsky held sway in the Briansk–Lokot region, as a quasi-warlord, was equipped by the Germans and espoused, at least theoretically, a National Socialist platform. Mostly engaged in anti-partisan activity, he was shot in 1944 by the SS and his brigade was used in the suppression of the *Warsaw rising that August, and then disbanded. The Gil-Rodionov Brigade, also known as SS Druzhina 1, was led by a Soviet lt-colonel, Vladimir Rodionov, who deserted back to the Soviet side in 1943. The Russian National People's Army, (Russkaya Narodnaya Natsionalaya Armiya, or RNNA), first known as the Osintorf Brigade (Osintorf being where it was formed), was initially led by old émigrés, including Colonel K. G. Kromiadi, also known as Colonel Sanin, later to head Vlasov's secretariat. In 1942 Kromiadi was replaced by G. N. Zhilenkov and Colonel V. I. Boyarsky, both of whom were later closely associated with Vlasov. Field Marshal von *Brauchitsch considered that the RNNA had an important role to play on the Eastern Front. Field Marshal von *Kluge gave the go-ahead for its formation, but its German and Russian leaders found it almost impossible to co-operate in the field and the RNNA was dissolved in 1943.

At the end of the war captured Soviet nationals in German uniform—the KONR divisions, members of the *Freiwilligeverbände* who considered themselves part of RONA, the Cossack Cavalry Corps, and other formations—presented a difficult problem for the western Allies. The Soviet authorities were unwilling to explain how so many of their nationals had come to fight on the side of the Germans. The western Allies, who had grown used to seeing the conflict in terms of fascist and democratic forces, did not understand the views of those who said that they had fought for Russia against the Soviet government on the German side, but were not fascists and who did not wish to be handed over to the Soviet authorities to be returned home. Under the terms of the Yalta agreement (see ARGONAUT), those who had Soviet nationality before the *Nazi–Soviet Pact of August 1939 were to be repatriated: the British sent back approximately 2,250,000 and the Americans about 2 million. Other ranks were mostly sent to the *GUlag on arrival in the USSR, officers were shot. Vlasov, thirteen of his subordinates, and Krasnov, were tried *in camera* in 1946 and hanged. As a German citizen, Pannwitz could have remained a British prisoner, but he chose to stay with his troops and in January 1947 he and five senior Cossack leaders were hanged in Moscow.

Nicholas Bethell and Nikolai Tolstoy in their books published in 1974 and 1977 (see below) raised the question of how far the British government had been aware that they were sending back men to Soviet labour camps and almost certain death. The argument advanced by the British authorities was that they had to send back captured Soviet citizens not only to comply with the agreement made at the Yalta conference in February 1945, but to guarantee the release of British POW. Tolstoy has argued that this latter reason could not have been a determining factor since it was not in Stalin's interest to reveal the extent to which the Soviet regime had been opposed by its own citizens, which would have become public knowledge if he had refused to release British POW freed by the Red Army. Tolstoy also tried to show the extent to which officials within the Northern Department of the British foreign office, as well as certain politicians and army officers, were acting in the Soviet interest, or in response to Soviet pressure. All these allegations have been denied, but the reasons behind the decision to repatriate millions of Soviet citizens have not been fully clarified. C. ANDREYEV

Andreyev, C., *Vlasov and the Russian Liberation Movement* (Cambridge, 1987).
Bethell, N., *The Last Secret* (New York, 1974).
Dallin, A., *German Rule in Russia* (2nd edn. London, 1981).
—'The Kaminsky Brigade', in A. and J. Rabinowitch (eds.), *Revolution and Politics in Russia. Essays in Honour of B. I. Nicolaevsky* (Bloomington, Ind., 1972).
Elliot, M. R., *Pawns of Yalta* (Urbana, Ill., 1982).
Fischer, G., *Soviet Opposition to Stalin* (Cambridge, Mass., 1952).
Hoffmann, J., *Die Ostlegionen* (Freiburg, 1976).
Longworth, P., *The Cossacks* (London, 1969).
Tolstoy, N., *Victims of Yalta* (2nd edn., London, 1979).

Soviet–Finnish war, see FINNISH–SOVIET WAR.

Soviet–German Pact, see NAZI–SOVIET PACT.

Soviet–German war, see GERMAN–SOVIET WAR.

Soviet–Japanese campaigns, see JAPANESE–SOVIET CAMPAIGNS.

Soviet Union, see USSR.

Spaatz, General Carl A. ('Tooey') (1891–1974), US airman of German immigrant stock who, from January 1944, commanded the USA's strategic air forces in Europe and then its strategic air forces bombing Japan.

Spaatz was one of the earliest US military aviators. He first saw action on the Mexican border in 1916 and in France during the *First World War. With the rank of colonel, he was sent to the UK in 1940 as an official observer where he was quick to realize that the Luftwaffe was misdirecting its efforts by bombing London (see BLITZ), and to appreciate the quality of the RAF pilots who opposed it. His report to this effect helped convince Roosevelt that the UK could survive and should be given every possible help.

In 1941 Spaatz was promoted and appointed chief of air staff to the US Army Air Forces (USAAF) Headquarters. In January 1942 he was promoted major-general and that July he took command of Eighth USAAF in England and its Bomber Command, under *Eaker, began operating in August. In November 1942 he handed over to Eaker when he was appointed Allied Air Forces commander under *Eisenhower in the *North African campaign and was promoted lt-general in March 1943. As well as always being a firm believer in precision daylight bombing, he became an advocate of the analysis of bombing raids of the kind carried out by the British scientist Solly Zuckerman. Their collaboration brought about the bombing of the Mediterranean island of *Pantelleria along lines suggested by scientific analysis. When a unified air command for the battle of the *Mediterranean was established under *Tedder in February 1943, Spaatz became his deputy, and in December 1943 he was appointed C-in-C of the newly formed US Strategic Air Forces (Eighth and Fifteenth USAAF) in Europe, reporting directly to the *Combined Chiefs of Staff. With them he masterminded the *Combined Bomber Offensive for which he was forced to introduce new tactics, because of high losses in earlier raids such as *Ploesti and *Schweinfurt. Primarily, this meant the use of long-range fighters which he employed with consummate skill during early 1944. 'He insisted that the fighters not be tied to the bombers as escorts, that they surge ahead of the bomber formations, seek out the German fighters in the air and on the ground, and destroy them' (M. Carver (ed.), *The War Lords*, London, 1976, p. 571). Within months of the introduction of long-range fighters Spaatz had turned round the war in the air over Germany, had brought the Luftwaffe to battle, and had soundly defeated it.

To facilitate the Normandy landings of June 1944 (see OVERLORD), and the *Normandy campaign which followed them, the American and British strategic air forces were placed directly under *Eisenhower from April to October 1944. Spaatz, ever mindful of his basic tenet that the ground battle could only be won if air supremacy was achieved, wanted to destroy the Luftwaffe by continuing to attack vital German targets, primarily oil installations. Eisenhower used the bombers to isolate the landing beaches from reinforcements, but was persuaded by Spaatz that they should continue to be used against Germany whenever possible. In fact, by *D-Day the Luftwaffe had already been decimated by Spaatz's long-range fighters. But the tactic of continuing to bomb German oil targets did ensure that the surviving fighters were forced to continue defending them so that they could not be moved to France to oppose the landings. It also caused an acute lack of fuel in Germany which became a major factor in its collapse. After Germany surrendered Spaatz, who had been promoted general in March 1945, was sent to form US Strategic Air Forces in the Pacific and to oversee the *strategic air offensive against Japan which ended in *atomic bombs being dropped on *Hiroshima and *Nagasaki in August 1945.

Spaatz was an unassuming man who actively rejected personal publicity. This made him less well known than most of his contemporaries but only heightened the esteem in which he was held by them. This genuine modesty was no drawback when it came to high command, for he knew his own mind, was decisive in utilizing this knowledge, was in awe of no one, and had the capability of thinking big.

He succeeded General *Arnold as commander of the USAAF in 1946 and became the first chief of staff of the independent US Air Force in September 1947. He retired in April 1948.

Mets, D. R., *A Master of Air Power* (Calif., 1988).

Spahis, a term which originated from the Persian word *Sipahi* (Turkish irregular cavalry), were irregular mounted levies, conscripted from the local populations of Algeria, Tunisia, and French Morocco into the French Armée d'Afrique (see FRANCE, 6(b)). But each of these French possessions also had its own Spahi regiments which were regular cavalry of the highest quality. During the fighting which preceded the fall of *France in June 1940 six of the thirteen Spahi regiments fought as three brigades; the others formed reconnaissance groups. None was mechanized. All but three then returned to North Africa. One squadron of the three sent to Syria deserted to de *Gaulle and the Free French, expanded, and fought at the second *El Alamein battle. After the *North African campaign landings, the Americans mechanized six regiments for reconnaissance, nearly all the indigenous troops being replaced by Europeans. Three regiments, equipped with Sherman tanks, later fought with the *French Expeditionary Corps in the *Italian campaign and one was part of *Leclerc's 2nd Armoured Division in north-west Europe. Other Spahi regiments, some still mounted, fought in de *Lattre de Tassigny's First French Army which took part in the *French Riviera landings (as Armée B) and then in the battle for *Germany.

Clayton, A., *France, Soldiers and Africa* (London, 1988).

Spain was ruled during the war by the fascist dictator General *Franco (el Caudillo), who maintained its neutrality throughout it. Its geographical position, dominating Gibraltar and the Western Approaches (see UK, 7(c)), made Spain's neutrality an essential factor in enabling the Allies to win the battles for the *Mediterranean and *Atlantic. Though pro-Axis, the country was exhausted by the *Spanish Civil War (in which Franco had received Axis help) and in no position to become a belligerent even if it had wished to. Also, the Allies' sea blockade (see ECONOMIC WARFARE) made Spain reliant on them for food, fuel, and *raw materials, a reliance that was counter-balanced by Allied eagerness to keep Spain out of the war.

In March 1939, before the official conclusion of the civil war on 1 April, Spain joined the *Anti-Comintern Pact and then signed a Treaty of Friendship with Germany. When the war began in September 1939 it declared its neutrality, but changed this to a state of non-belligerency after Italy entered the war on 10 June 1940. Four days later Franco exploited the chaos in Europe by occupying the international zone of Tangier and the same month he informed Hitler that he was prepared to enter the war on the side of the Axis after a brief interval in which to convince public opinion. In return he demanded Gibraltar, French Morocco, and parts of French West Africa, as well as food and arms, a price Hitler thought too high. However, the following month Franco declared he was ready to forge an empire (Spain's few remaining colonies—the Canaries, Spanish Guinea, Spanish Morocco, and Spanish Sahara—were of little consequence), and in August he wrote to Mussolini that since the start of the war he had been making the necessary preparations to allow Spain to enter the war at the most propitious moment. But in October 1940, when he met Hitler at Hendaye in south-western France, he refused to commit himself and merely spent the day expressing his sympathies for the Axis cause.

At this meeting Hitler revealed a plan (ISABELLA-FELIX) for German forces to attack Gibraltar via Spain, which would close the western Mediterranean to the British. But Franco demurred and, to Hitler's irritation, renewed his territorial demands. Further negotiations to implement ISABELLA-FELIX proved equally inconclusive and on 11 December the plan was shelved. But Hitler, now knowing that Franco would not co-operate, was still considering the invasion of Spain, or the toppling of Franco, as late as 1943 in order to achieve his aims.

Throughout the war Spain harboured many Axis *spies and saboteurs. They targeted British ships and established observation posts on Spanish territory, while the Italian *Tenth Light Flotilla launched attacks on Gibraltar from southern Spain. Italian aircraft overflew Spanish territory to bomb Gibraltar and Axis warships were given shelter in Spanish ports. Axis air crews who had been forced to land in Spanish territory were repatriated. Allied ones were interned as were escaping *prisoners-of-war (see also MI9); and they were often kept in terrible conditions. However, pro-Axis as it was, Spain was never prevented by the British naval blockade of occupied Europe from receiving the essentials it needed. This ultimately allowed it to become reasonably prosperous, but initially the devastation of the civil war, which had begun in 1936, brought the country close to famine. In early 1941 a typhus epidemic, brought about by malnutrition and the large increase of beggars in the streets, swept Madrid, and in November 1941 the death penalty was introduced for certain food offences.

In the early days of the war the pro-German faction of the Spanish population, with the press and radio behind it, was the most vocal. British propaganda, and even newspapers, were forbidden. In June 1941 the British embassy was attacked by Falangists (the Spanish fascists) and the same month the Spanish foreign minister and Falangist leader, Ramon Serrano Suñer, made a number of virulent anti-Allied speeches. The recruitment for the *Blue Division to fight in the *German–Soviet war was also started and was followed in August 1941 with an agreement that allowed Spanish workers to be recruited for work in Germany. In February 1942 Franco made his celebrated remark that 'If the road to Berlin were ever open to the enemy, Spain would raise a million men to defend the capital of the Reich.' In September 1942 he replaced Suñer, who was his brother-in-law, with a less outspoken foreign minister, but Franco himself continued to make pro-Axis speeches and much of the Spanish press remained hostile to the Allies until the end of the war.

During the build-up of ships and aircraft at Gibraltar which preceded the *North African campaign landings in November 1942, Franco ordered partial mobilization. Though he did not take any other action—a quiescence Churchill noted with appreciation during a speech in 1944—it was not until Mussolini fell in July 1943 that Spain's stance against the Allies began to soften. As evidence of this change of heart, the Blue Division was steadily reduced in strength throughout the latter half of 1943; and by the end of it, when Franco dissolved the Falangist militia, it had been almost totally withdrawn—though a rump, the *Spanish Legion, remained.

With the war now running strongly against the Axis powers, in early 1944 Allied *diplomacy put increasing pressure on Franco to stop the export of tungsten to Germany as part of the Allies' economic warfare plans, to prevent the recruitment of men for the Spanish Legion, and to stamp on the widespread activities of Axis agents and saboteurs based in Spain. Negotiations on these points continued to drag on until the USA decided to withhold Spain's oil supplies for February 1944. A premature leak of this decision resulted in a US press agency announcing it as an ultimatum. Except for the withdrawal of the Spanish Legion, which Franco ordered in February 1944, this caused a further delay in the solution of the disputed points until May 1944. Then Spain at last agreed to reduce drastically its tungsten exports, to hand over all interned Italian ships, to close the German consulate in Tangier, and to expel all German agents on Spanish territory—though in fact Madrid continued to give Germany intelligence aid right up until the end of the war, and after it gave refuge to large numbers of Nazi and *Vichy French refugees.

In October 1944 Spain recognized the government of de *Gaulle and the Free French, and in April 1945 it severed diplomatic relations with Germany and Japan. But no invitation was extended to it to attend the founding conference of the United Nations that May (see SAN FRANCISCO CONFERENCE), and it was not admitted to the United Nations Organization until 1955.

Spanish Civil War. In 1931 King Alfonso XIII of Spain (1886–1941) was deposed. The resulting republic seemed to right-wingers to be drifting further and further to the left; particularly after the Popular Front's victory in the elections of February 1936. In July that year the regular army revolted against the Republican government; brisk fighting at once began, and did not officially end until 1 April 1939. Tens of thousands of soldiers from the defeated Republican army had by then fled across the Pyrenees and were interned in France, and many later escaped to join various *Maquis. Others fled to North Africa (see ZOUAVES).

In November 1936 the Nationalist regime of the head of the army, General *Franco, was recognized as the government of Spain by Germany and Italy which provided armed support for the Nationalists. The Republicans received fighter aircraft (but no spares), and a great deal of advice, from the USSR; but as the war coincided with the depths of Stalin's great purge, he was ill-placed to provide substantial help. France also provided fighters, and a number of communist-inspired International Brigades fighting on the Republican side included volunteers from France, the UK, and the USA among others.

Communist civilian leaders in Spain learnt a great deal which was put to good use when it came to waging partisan warfare in their occupied countries. But militarily the USSR was adversely influenced by the war. Stalin was told that the fighting showed that tank formations were unsuited to playing an independent operational role, and in 1939 the Red Army's armoured formations were broken up and used for supporting infantry. After the *Polish campaign and the fall of *France Stalin reversed this decision, but it came too late for the German invasion of the USSR in June 1941 (see BARBAROSSA). The apparent ineffectualness of strategic bombing also induced the Soviets to stop production of a new heavy bomber (the TB7), dismantle the strategic arm of their air force, and concentrate on producing aircraft that were subordinated to supporting the infantry.

The French, too, drew wrong conclusions, preferring to see the fighting in Spain as evidence that the defensive battle was still the stronger form of warfare and that the fear of a swift, highly mechanized form of warfare (see BLITZKRIEG) was exaggerated. 'They even believed a German émigré writer, Helmuth Klotz, who, after a few weeks in Spain, wrote in his *Leçons militaires de la guerre d'Espagne* that the tank had been mastered by the anti-tank gun' (see H. Thomas, *The Spanish Civil War*, new edn., London, 1986, p. 770). The Italians learned valuable lessons, particularly in the air, but then failed to implement them.

The Germans benefited most from their experience in Spain, and put it to the best use at the start of the Second World War. General von Thoma, who commanded the German troops there, regarded the war as 'the European Aldershot' (quoted in A. Millett and W. Murray, *Military Effectiveness*, Vol. 2, New York, p. 261). The Luftwaffe's Kondor Legion perfected the fighter tactics Luftwaffe pilots employed during the battle of *Britain. *Dogfights, thought to be a thing of the past once fighters reached speeds in excess of 320 kph (200 mph), were found to be still practicable. The RAF was slow to realize this. The Germans also drew from the Kondor Legion's operation the conclusion that the Luftwaffe should be used for close tactical air support not strategic bombing.

Apart from being a testing-ground for several of the major combatants of the Second World War, the Spanish Civil War produced some important advances in surgical techniques and blood transfusion (see also MEDICINE).

I. C. B. DEAR/M. R. D. FOOT

Spanish Legion, the Legion Españolo de Voluntarios, or LEV, volunteer force commanded by Colonel Antonio Navarro, who were recruited mostly from the *Blue Division when it was withdrawn from the *Soviet–German war in 1943 and returned to Spain.

At 1,500 strong, the maximum size allowed by the Spanish government, LEV was divided into three *banderas* (small battalions). After operating against partisans on the borders of Latvia it was attached to a German division in December 1943. It fought near Kostovo and took part in the retreat that followed the liberation of *Leningrad before it was ordered home in February 1944. Despite losing their citizenship for serving in a foreign army, some subsequently formed a Spanish battalion in 28th *SS Wallonian Division and were among the last troops fighting to prevent the fall of *Berlin.

SPARS, acronym derived from *Semper Paratus* (Always Ready), the US Coast Guard's motto. It was the name of its women's branch which was formed in November 1942 and had a peak strength of 11,000.

Special Air Service (SAS), British special forces unit formed in October 1941 by Lt David Stirling (1912–90) from members of *Layforce. It came directly under the C-in-C Middle East, General *Auchinleck, who was persuaded by Stirling that small groups of specially trained parachutists could wreak havoc among the Axis desert airfields before being exfiltrated by the *Long Range Desert Group (LRDG). Brigadier Dudley Clarke, who was in charge of *deception in the Middle East, had just created a fictitious unit, 1st Special Air Service Brigade, to deceive the Germans into believing that a powerful airborne force existed in Egypt. To make the deception more convincing Stirling's unit, as 'L Detachment', was, notionally, made part of it. In fact, it was, initially, No. 2 Troop of *Middle East Commando.

The LRDG and Stirling's men proved a successful combination. One of Stirling's officers, Paddy Mayne, destroyed 47 aircraft in a single night, possibly more than the RAF's highest-scoring fighter ace ('Pat' Pattle who shot down 40–50 aircraft), and Stirling's force was soon expanded to include Free French paratroopers. In November 1942, after it had become 1st SAS Regiment, the SAS also absorbed the *Special Boat Section which, with a troop of the *Greek Sacred Regiment, became 1st SAS's D Squadron in January 1943. A second regiment, 2nd SAS, raised by Stirling's eldest brother Bill, became operational in early 1943. Both regiments undertook sabotage and reconnaissance operations behind the Axis lines in the *North African campaign, but after David Stirling was captured in February 1943 1st SAS was dissolved. D Squadron became the Special Boat Squadron, the other squadrons the *Special Raiding Squadron (SRS), though both retained the SAS insignia and beret.

Both 2nd SAS and SRS fought in the *Sicilian and *Italian campaigns, mounting long-range penetration patrols and seaborne raids against German lines of communication. In early 1944 both returned to the UK to form a real SAS Brigade which comprised SRS (now called 1st SAS again), 2nd SAS, two French regiments, one Belgian squadron, and a squadron of the *Phantom Regiment. On the night of the Normandy landings (see OVERLORD) ten SAS men executed TITANIC, part of a *deception operation (FORTITUDE) that simulated major airborne landings. This distracted a German regiment away from *OMAHA beach for the whole morning of 6 June. Thereafter members of the brigade established bases well behind German lines in France from which they attacked German lines of communication and relayed intelligence. Later, SAS units were also dropped into Belgium and the Netherlands, and some saw action with British and Canadian forces during the battle for *Germany. In December 1944 a newly formed SAS squadron worked with Italian partisans and at the end of the war the brigade disarmed 300,000 German troops who were garrisoning Norway.

Hoe, A., *David Stirling* (London, 1992).
Strawson, J., *A History of the SAS Regiment* (London, 1984).

Special Boat Section (SBS), British sabotage and reconnaissance unit founded in July 1940 by a commando officer, Roger Courtney, which later became two distinct organizations. Initially known as the Folboat Troop, after the type of folding canoe employed in raiding operations (see also CANOEISTS), and then the Special Boat Section, it worked with *Layforce from April 1941 carrying out several successful operations during the battle for the *Mediterranean before becoming, briefly, part of the *Middle East Commando. In December 1941 Courtney returned to the UK where he formed 2nd SBS, and 1st SBS became attached to the *Special Air Service (SAS). In September 1942 1st SBS lost irreplaceable men during a raid on Rhodes, was absorbed into the SAS in November, and together with a troop of the *Greek Sacred Regiment became its D Squadron in January 1943. In April 1943, after SAS was dissolved, D Squadron was re-formed as the Special Boat Squadron, became part of *Raiding Forces, and operated among the Dodecanese and Cyclades groups of islands in the Aegean, raiding a total of 70 islands 381 times. In August 1944 it joined Land Forces, Adriatic (see BALKAN AIR FORCE) and worked with the *Long Range Desert Group in operations in the Adriatic, on the Peloponnese (see BRITISH EXPEDITION TO GREECE), in Albania, and, finally, Istria. It was disbanded in 1945.

The 2nd SBS, which retained its name, Special Boat Section, throughout the war, took Maj-General Mark *Clark ashore before the *North African campaign landings in November 1942 (TORCH) and later one group, Z SBS, based in Algiers from March 1943, undertook eighteen Mediterranean operations, including the beach reconnaissance for the *Salerno landings and a raid on Crete, before moving to Ceylon to work with *SOE's Force 136 and later with *Special Operations Australia. The rest of 2nd SBS became part of *South-East Asia Command's *Small Operations Group, operating on the Chindwin and Irrawaddy rivers, and in the Arakan, during the *Burma campaign. See also UK, 7(e).

Courtney, G., *SBS in World War Two* (London, 1983).
Pitt, B., *Special Boat Squadron* (London, 1983).

Special Forces, see under armed forces sections of major powers.

Special Intelligence Service, see USA, 6.

Special Liaison Units (SLU) were part of the British Secret Intelligence Service (see MI6), formed in 1940 to convey *ULTRA intelligence to British, and later US, Cs-in-C in the field. SLUs, which worked in the utmost secrecy, were attached to the HQ of those commanders cleared to receive ULTRA. They comprised two sections: the Special Communications Unit (SCU), manned by army personnel, and the Special Liaison Unit, mostly manned by RAF personnel. The former received the ULTRA intelligence—transmitted from the British Code and Cypher School at *Bletchley Park by the *one-time pad method of encodement or later by the *TYPEX machine—and the latter deciphered and disseminated it. After it had been digested by the army commander, or by one or his staff officers who had been cleared to receive it, the SLU officer ensured it was destroyed.

Prior to the Normandy landings in June 1944 (see OVERLORD) the Americans began using an 'ULTRA representative' who received the deciphered signals from the SLU, digested the information in them, and then presented it at regular briefings to the commander in the field or his senior staff officers. The ULTRA representative was also empowered to combine it with intelligence from other sources and to give operational advice on its use in such a way as to protect its origin. They were trained at Bletchley Park and numbered only 28 in all.

Lewin, R., *ULTRA Goes To War* (London, 1978).

Special Operations Australia was part of the British clandestine organization *SOE, some of whose members became its local nucleus after they had escaped from

*Singapore. It was proposed in March 1942 by the C-in-C Australian Forces, General *Blamey, and approved by the Allied commander of the *South-West Pacific Area (SWPA), General *MacArthur. It was initially given the local cover name of Inter-Allied Services Department, or ISD, but when relations with its parent organization, SWPA's *Allied Intelligence Bureau, became strained it was reorganized the following year and given a new cover name, the Services Reconnaissance Department (SRD). 'Z special Unit' administered its Australian personnel and is the name by which SOA is most commonly known in Australia. Until May 1943, it also had a Dutch section, the head of which later ran Section III (Secret Intelligence and Special Operations) of the Netherlands Forces Intelligence Service (NEFIS) based in Melbourne. It operated principally within SWPA, but also had the remit to operate in Thailand and China.

During 1942 SOA infiltrated parties to support guerrilla actions by Australian army units in Portuguese Timor and landed eight intelligence parties in Japanese-occupied Netherlands East Indies territory, six of which were betrayed and captured. (Other parties were dispatched there by NEFIS-III during the following years, with no success.) In September 1943 SOA *canoeists mounted a successful operation (JAYWICK) against Japanese shipping in Singapore but a repeat operation (RIMAU) mounted the following year ended in disaster. Equally disastrous was the capture of a SOA signaller in Portuguese Timor in September 1943. He was forced to reveal his cipher and to contact SOA's HQ with messages written by his captors. This enabled the Japanese to ambush other SOE parties sent to Timor and though the Australian signallers deliberately broke their security procedures SOA HQ ignored their warnings and assumed they were still free. (For other examples of what the Germans called a *Funkspiel*, 'radio game', see ENGLANDSPIEL and ROTE KAPELLE.)

From February 1945 SOA supported Australian forces operating against the Japanese in British and Dutch colonies in the SWPA by raising local resistance groups and undertaking various reconnaissance missions which preceded Australian landings at *Balikpapan, *Tarakan, and elsewhere. In Sarawak, for example, SOA-led guerrillas killed 1,500 Japanese and captured another 240. Altogether SOA sent 81 parties, totalling 380 men, into Japanese-occupied territory from 1942 to 1945. Its casualties were 69 dead and 7 captured. At 15 August 1945 its total strength was 1,700, 1,250 of whom were Australian.

Courtney, G. B., *Silent Feet* (Melbourne, 1993).

Special Operations Executive, see SOE.

Special Raiding Squadron, British special forces unit formed from part of 1st *Special Air Service after this had been disbanded in March 1943. It operated during the *Italian campaign, taking part in the *Reggio di Calabria and *Termoli landings, and in several smaller operations. It returned to the UK in early 1944 and, as 1st SAS Regiment, became part of a newly formed SAS Brigade.

Speer, Albert (1905–81), German architect who became a close confidant of Hitler and served as minister for armaments and munitions from 1942 to 1945.

Speer was an early admirer of Hitler but did not join the Nazi Party until 1932. He then also became a member of the *SS and arranged the spectacle of the 1934 Nuremberg Rally. His first war appointment was to oversee the construction of armament factories and military installations. When the head of the *Todt Organization died in a plane crash in February 1942 Speer succeeded him as minister for armaments and munitions, and as head of the organization; and the following year he was given overall responsibility for the direction of Germany's war economy (see SPEER PLAN, below). He proved himself an outstanding and ruthless administrator who, despite the Allied *strategic air offensive, which unleashed almost constant bombing raids on Germany's industrial centres, managed to triple armaments production between 1942 and 1944. His foresight in planning the production of synthetic oil (see also RAW AND SYNTHETIC MATERIALS) enabled the German war machine to keep running almost until the end.

After Hitler's death in April 1945, which Speer, so he said, had earlier contemplated trying to achieve by poison gas, he served as economy minister in *Dönitz's seven-day government. At the *Nuremberg trials he disassociated himself from Hitler's regime but dramatically accepted 'collective responsibility' for its crimes. This did not save him from a 20-year sentence for his complicity in using *forced labour, which he served in full. But it gave birth to the spurious belief—which Speer perpetuated in his two memoirs, *Inside the Third Reich* (London, 1970) and *Spandau: the Secret Diaries* (New York, 1976)—that he had been an apolitical technocrat who had known nothing of the *Final Solution, a master builder too involved in his work to understand the criminality of the regime he served.

Schmidt, M., *Albert Speer: The End Of A Myth* (New York, 1984).

Speer Plan. In February 1942 Hitler appointed Albert *Speer, his chief architect, to the post of minister for armaments and munitions. Hitler wanted a great increase in the output of finished weapons. Under Speer's administration the German war economy expanded military production threefold in two years.

Speer's appointment did not initiate the programme of increased production as Hitler had set the economy very large goals from the start of the war. By the summer of 1941 two-thirds of the German industrial workforce were working on war orders, and civilian consumption had been cut further than in the UK. But with the invasion of the USSR in June 1941 (see BARBAROSSA) it became clear to Hitler that the war economy was not producing what it was capable of with the large quantity of resources at its disposal. The failure was a result of the poor central direction of the economy, particularly by *Göring's Four Year Plan organization, coupled with high levels of unhelpful military intervention in industrial affairs. War output was riddled with inefficiency, waste, and confusion. From early 1941 efforts were being made to rationalize the production of army weapons under Fritz Todt (see TODT ORGANIZATION); and from May 1941 the rationalization of the aircraft industry was set in motion by Field Marshal *Milch, Göring's energetic deputy in the air ministry. But in the end it took the intervention of Hitler himself, who in December 1941 issued a decree which set the framework for the rationalization of production and the simplification of design and production methods. When in February 1942 Todt (1892–1942) was killed in an air crash, Speer was appointed as armaments overlord to put the new decree into effect.

Speer had no master plan: he continued the policies initiated by his predecessor and endorsed by Hitler. However, he had one big advantage over any possible rivals in securing the personal backing of Hitler; he was able to bypass the military leaders and the Four Year Plan and agree policy directly with Hitler in regular 'Führer Conferences' held between the two men until 1944. Speer was responsible for important administrative changes to improve war output. In April 1942 he set up Central Planning, an executive board under his direction which decided on the allocation and distribution of *raw materials and capital equipment on a national scale. He also set up an interlocking system of production committees for all major weapons, each committee being responsible for all the firms involved in the production of a particular weapon group. The main committees became the forum for planning and supervising all military output, and the system led to great improvements in efficiency, co-operation, and centralized control.

Speer was also successful politically, pushing the armed forces out of their role in the war economy and reducing the level of military interference in industrial matters. At the same time he insisted on bringing industrialists and engineers into the war economic apparatus, so that production could be run by people who knew about it. The principle of 'industrial self-responsibility', as Speer called it, brought rich dividends. In two years, and despite the effects of the Allied *strategic air offensive, armaments production trebled, and output of aircraft increased almost fourfold, from 11,000 to 39,000. Only intensive bombing from the summer of 1944 brought a gradual decline, and then in the first few months of 1945 a sharp collapse.

There were limitations to Speer's achievement. By 1944 he no longer enjoyed the complete backing of Hitler, and the *SS was able to gain a greater say in running war production. Speer did not control aircraft production until 1944, though he co-operated closely with Milch, who shared his aims and methods. Nor did he control labour supply, one of the critical limiting factors for the war economy. Hitler placed this under the Nazi *Gauleiter* Fritz *Sauckel, who refused to co-ordinate his plans with Speer's strategy for raw materials and industrial rationalization. Finally, the bombing of Germany hit the rationalization plans by compelling de-centralization of production, and interrupting the delicate web of distribution and sub-contracting set up by the committee system. When Hitler wanted to shift all production underground, Speer was unenthusiastic. The SS promised to complete this programme instead, and this caused the rapid erosion of Speer's standing and the rise of new SS economic leaders, Xavier Dorsch and Hans Kammler. By the end of the war Speer was disillusioned with Hitler. He refused to implement his orders for a *scorched earth policy as German forces retreated into the Reich, leaving much of Germany's new military industries to help with the post-war economic revival. See also GERMANY, 2.

RICHARD OVERY

Mierzejewski, A. C., *The Collapse of the German War Economy 1944–1945* (Chapel Hill, NC, 1988).
Overy, R. J., *Goering: the 'Iron Man'* (London, 1984).
Schmidt, M., *Albert Speer: the End of a Myth* (New York, 1982).
Speer, A., *Inside the Third Reich* (London, 1970).

Sperrle, Field Marshal Hugo (1885–1953), German Luftwaffe officer who, in 1936–7, commanded the German Kondor Legion during the *Spanish Civil War. This record earned him promotion to maj-general, then lt-general, and he was then appointed to command the formation that became Luftflotte 3 in September 1939. It did not participate in the *Polish campaign of September–October 1939 but supported *Rundstedt's Army Group A during the fighting which led to the fall of *France in June 1940; and its success in this campaign earned Sperrle his field marshal's baton in July 1940. By then Luftflotte 3, based in northern France, was embroiled in the battle of *Britain during which Sperrle vainly urged that Luftwaffe attacks should continue to be concentrated on British fighter airfields. Luckily for the British he was overruled.

By May 1941, with nearly all German air strength needed for the invasion of the USSR (see BARBAROSSA), Luftflotte 3 had been reduced from 44 bomber groups to 4 and Sperrle, with his HQ in Paris, became disillusioned and lax. *Goebbels accused him of living the life of a sybarite and said that Hitler wanted to replace him, but Sperrle continued to command Luftflotte 3 in its role of defending Belgium, France, and the Netherlands from air attack, and mounting occasional operations against the UK. However, by June 1944 the demand for aircraft on other fronts had reduced his striking power to such impotence that his fighters could only mount a handful of sorties against the Normandy landings on D-Day (see OVERLORD) and his command's poor performance led to his dismissal in August. He was never re-employed.

S-Phone: Vertical and horizontal sections of beam transmitted by S-phone. Range of communications was directly proportional to the altitude of the aircraft. The phone's range at ground level was, at most, 1.6 km. (1 mi.) and this made it very secure.

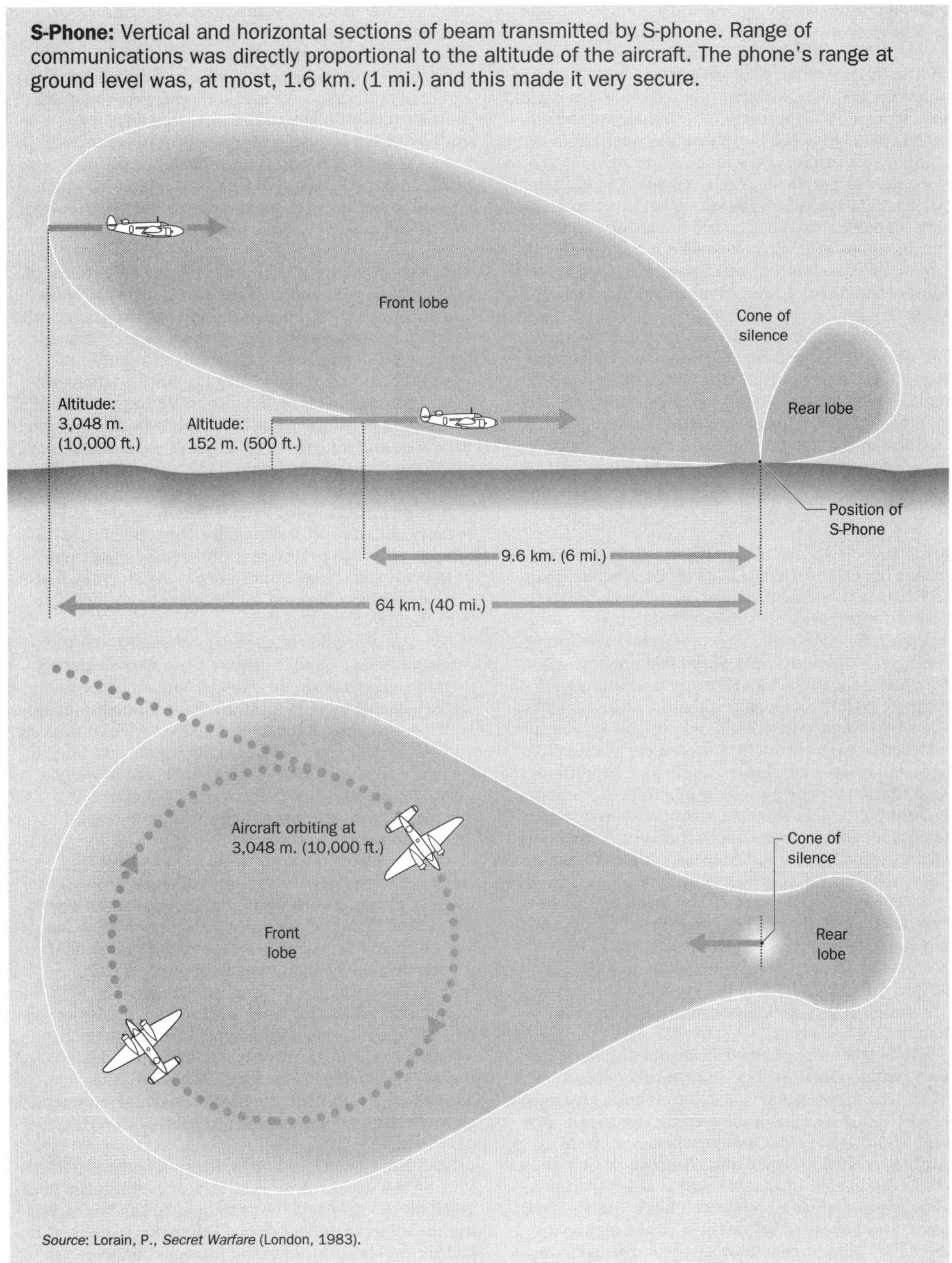

Source: Lorain, P., *Secret Warfare* (London, 1983).

S-phone, British device developed by *SOE, which was used by resistance groups in occupied Europe to communicate with friendly aircraft, or by commandos raiding the French coast. It was also employed to guide supply aircraft to resistance dropping zones. The aircraft (or ship, or submarine) carried the master set, the other, which could be packed into a suitcase, was carried by the agent or commando. The S-phone's theoretical range when used as a radio-telephone was about 65 km. (40 mi.) by air and 24 km. (15 mi.) by sea, these distances being almost doubled when it was used as a navigational device. Transmissions to an aircraft could not be picked up by ground detectors more than 1,500 m. (5,000 ft.) from the point of transmission, and it was therefore relatively safe to use (see Figure).

The Americans developed a similar, more advanced, much smaller device called 'Joan-Eleanor' which was used by agents belonging to the *Office of Strategic Services who penetrated into Germany during the last months of the war. 'Joan' was carried by the agent, 'Eleanor' by the aircraft. Any conversation could be recorded aboard the aircraft on a spool of wire, an early form of tape recorder. See also RADIO COMMUNICATIONS.

spies. In 1939–45 *signals intelligence warfare was of far greater importance than it had ever been before and overshadowed human intelligence, the work of spies. Nevertheless, there were subjects that signals intelligence (sigint) could not cover, and that human intelligence (humint) could. Sigint seldom provided evidence of the character of enemy commanders, which might be vital to those making plans to defeat them. Moreover, the yield from sigint was patchy; so was that of the other primary intelligence source, *photographic reconnaissance, which hinged on weather conditions; the yield from a properly placed spy might be continuous and full. Sigint did not often cover intentions, except that it could sometimes reveal impending moves; spies might, with a great deal of luck, be in a position to know them. There was still, in fact, much of value that could be done by a well-placed, well-informed spy, provided that he or she could deliver the intelligence gained, in time for it to be acted on (see POPOV for a botched example). *Menzies, the head of the British Secret Intelligence Service, *MI6, said of one of the war's best spies, Paul *Thümmel, 'A-54 is an agent at whose word armies march.'

Several types of spy need to be distinguished. There were casual sources, as the intelligence services called them, who sometimes provided information on a once-only basis and were not available again (see OSLO REPORT, for example); *Coast Watchers, who were carefully trained to recognize and report passing ships, and were valuable and active in areas as far apart as Norway and the Solomon Islands; and the professional agent, most of whom, before the war, had diplomatic cover and ran their own network of sub-agents in the field. Service attachés in embassies and legations were not, technically, spies at all; but were well known to be on the look-out for any military information that came their way. On the other hand, press and commercial attachés, and passport control officers, were sometimes only nominally diplomats, because they were really engaged either in spying themselves or in organizing networks of spies to observe for them. The spy ring centred on the Japanese consulate at Honolulu, which worked to facilitate the Japanese attack on *Pearl Harbor (see below), is one example of spies using diplomatic cover.

But *diplomacy was far from being the only source of, or cover for, spies—and was, anyway, of little use once war had actually begun. About a third of the effort of the wartime US intelligence agency, the *Office of Strategic Services (OSS), was devoted to intelligence-gathering, some of it through spies. *SOE was a British sabotage organization, not an intelligence-collecting one, but of course its agents needed to have their own information networks, and sometimes collected valuable nuggets of intelligence; all of which they had to pass over to MI6, and were not allowed to circulate themselves. Counter-espionage organizations such as *MI5 were also intimately connected with spying, for they often relied on *double agents to penetrate the other side's networks or to plant false information (see XX-COMMITTEE); first-class spies might look out for double agents, and try to turn them into *triple agents.

The dual aspect of the spy's role—the need to transmit intelligence, as well as to acquire it—is often neglected by those who write on the subject, but was of cardinal importance: of such importance that counter-espionage bodies sometimes contented themselves with controlling and observing a spy's communications, not troubling to interrupt the traffic that (if they could read it) would provide valuable information for their own side. It is always a gain to one side to know what questions the other side wants answered.

Another aspect of a spy's work, quite outside his or her control, was the need to analyse reports he or she sent in, to tie them up with whatever else was known about the subject, and to make sure that appropriate action was taken. Military history is littered with tales of vital reports delayed by dunderheads, or overlooked by harassed staff officers: or simply not believed by high commanders. Richard *Sorge's warning to his Soviet masters of the German invasion of the USSR (see BARBAROSSA) is a classic case of the last. (Incidentally, the world's intelligence services all believed that BARBAROSSA would fell the USSR in six or seven weeks: an interesting example of the weakness of expert opinion.)

Spies had to have good cover. Sorge, a German born on Russian soil who became a convert to *communism, had excellent cover: he was the correspondent in Tokyo for a number of serious German and Dutch newspapers, and had secured personal letters of introduction to members of the German embassy staff in Tokyo. Cover, to be any good, must have some bearing on reality; indeed the more real it is, the better it will work. Ideal cover was available for 'Rygor' Slowikowski who ran *Agency Africa while based in Algiers: that of a Polish refugee business man, who had a little capital, and invested it in a porridge factory. He was the only porridge manufacturer in north-west Africa; as such, he could travel widely, and recruit large numbers of business agents—most of whom he also employed as spies, through intermediaries, never revealing to them that they were working to their own managing director until the *North African campaign landings (TORCH) in November 1942 had taken the area over for the Allies. The success of TORCH depended largely on Slowikowski's information; though he got no personal benefit from it, as he had passed most of it (for convenience) through OSS channels, and OSS took all the credit.

The spymaster's difficulty was always to find the spy, and then to put him (or her) unobtrusively where he (or she) could make notes, or even take photographs, and afterwards transmit the results to where the spymaster could make use of them. In order to communicate fast, most spies needed access to a radio transceiver (see also RADIO COMMUNICATIONS). This might well expose them to being traced, quickly, by direction-finders; and if they were not trained to transmit themselves, gave them the additional peril of needing an extra member of their spy group in the person of the radio operator. Even before the war, *Dansey reckoned that the Germans had penetrated most of MI6's spy networks in Europe, through their radio traffic; it was a cast-iron rule of his 'Z' networks that they were never to use radio at all.

Alternative methods of communication were usually available. Much time and attention at spy schools went on teaching how to prepare and develop secret ink (at a pinch, semen could be used). As a counter to these inks, censors often criss-crossed suspect pieces of paper with developing chemicals, which would show hidden inks up at once, as would careful use of a magnifying glass. Much ingenuity was also expended on methods of carrying written messages—whether in cipher or in clear—which would not be easy to detect or intercept. The Germans developed a miniature photograph, called a microdot, which reduced a foolscap page to the size of a full stop; this might easily pass a censor unnoticed. It could be enlarged, or read through a microscope. Casual sources in France were encouraged to report *radar sites or V-1 sites (see V-WEAPONS) in their area by using *carrier pigeons which the RAF dropped in canisters.

The aura of *secrecy and subterfuge created by spies also created a feeling, throughout the old officer class (a body which transcended national boundaries) that spying was off-colour, ungentlemanly, unfair; most high commanders, whatever side they were on, mistrusted any information that came to them from spies, because they thought them necessarily an unreliable lot.

It was for this reason that early efforts by the British to hide the source of *ULTRA intelligence by telling commanders in the field that it had originated from a well-placed agent (codenamed BONIFACE) resulted in the intelligence being sceptically received. Army commanders in the field were therefore soon let in on its source, which did not stop ULTRA remaining a closely guarded secret in the UK until 1974. Doubtless the secrecy which deliberately surrounded it for so long accounts for the mythical stories of some spies which still flourish in the public's memory. These spies were allowed, by higher authority, to go public because their tales provided satisfactory cover for how such intelligence was really obtained. For example, this is probably the reason for the reputation of Betty Pack (who died under the name of Elizabeth Brousse), whose alleged spy coups in neutral legations in Washington were published in the 1960s (see H. M. Hyde, *CYNTHIA: The Spy who changed the Course of the War*, London, 1966). The Germans only once came near to discovering that their machine ciphers were being broken (see SIGNALS INTELLIGENCE WARFARE, 7).

The Soviet Union's greatest wartime intelligence successes were not achieved against its opponents but against its allies. In the opinion of the *NKVD, its ablest group of agents were five Cambridge graduates recruited in the mid-1930s; Anthony Blunt, Guy Burgess, John Cairncross, Donald *Maclean, and 'Kim' *Philby. They were dubbed collectively the 'Five' or the 'London Five' (since they were controlled from the London NKVD residency). The first to penetrate Whitehall was Maclean, who began a sixteen-year career in the foreign office in 1935. Cairncross also entered the foreign office in 1936, moved to the treasury in 1938, became private secretary to Maurice Hankey in 1940, entered *Bletchley Park in 1942, and joined MI6 in 1943. Burgess joined the *BBC in 1936, entered the newly created covert action branch of MI6 (section D) in 1938, returned to the BBC in 1940, and entered the foreign office in 1944. Anthony Blunt joined MI5 in 1940. Kim Philby was turned down by Bletchley Park, but succeeded in entering SOE in 1940 before moving a year later to MI6, where he established himself as a high-flyer.

In Washington the NKVD ran two agent networks of government officials headed respectively by Nathan Gregory Silvermaster and Victor Perlo. A number of other agents, the state department official Alger Hiss and the treasury official Harry Dexter White among them, were run individually. OSS contained perhaps a dozen Soviet agents. The NKVD and the *GRU (Soviet military intelligence) also both penetrated the *atomic bomb research establishments at Los Alamos and at Montreal. In August 1945 the British atomic scientist Alan Nunn May gave the GRU details of the bomb dropped on *Hiroshima and two samples of uranium.

There was thus an enormous disparity between what the West knew about the USSR and what Moscow knew about its allies. Neither MI6 nor OSS had a single agent worth the name in Moscow. But there was a vast gulf also between the amount of intelligence which Moscow received from London and Washington, and its understanding of the West. The USSR remained constantly suspicious that its allies were considering stabbing it in the back. Philby later admitted that what most interested his wartime controllers was intelligence on the UK's non-existent plans for a separate peace with Nazi Germany and schemes, equally non-existent, to enter the war against the USSR.

The Soviet Union also had the *Max Organization, designed to penetrate its own dissident groups (see SOVIET EXILES). It formed, too—initially using *Comintern cover—some useful spy rings that worked against the Nazis. These rings, called the *Rote Kapelle (Red Orchestra) by German counter-espionage, were started in several European countries before the war began and were quite widespread—a survivor of the Rote Kapelle's Berlin branch claimed that the branch had as many as 283 members. Some were quite junior clerks in the German armed forces or government offices; that did not prevent them from seeing and copying useful material. The best branch, for the *LUCY Ring was working for it, was the *Rote Drei in Switzerland.

It is worth emphasis that real spies, quite unlike the spies of melodrama or public myth, are as a rule inoffensive-looking, clerkly types, whose cover is so dense that they never attract a second glance from passers-by or serious attention from security officers. One of the Allies' most valuable spies was a clerk at a large Belgian railway junction, who simply took home with him every night a copy of every document he had typed during the day: these precious lists of war materials in transit were smuggled away to London.

Few spy networks resisted the temptation to recruit many sub-agents, to widen the base from which they could supply data to their distant masters; few sub-agents were given proper training in how to remain obscure, or what not to say when captured; hence many networks' undoing. Both Sorge and Leopold Trepper, who ran the Rote Kapelle in France, fell into enemy hands because sub-agents of theirs were captured and said more than they should have done. Sorge was executed; Trepper survived the war, to undergo a long spell in Siberia as a reward for his services to the USSR. Ideally, a spy's sub-agents can only reach him through cut-outs, so that their arrests do not imperil him; few spies operate in an ideal world.

All sorts of military data were easy for sub-agents to obtain, particularly for those brought up to be observant, as most countrymen and countrywomen were. Any housewife, pushing a pram along a path beside an airfield, could count the aircraft in sight on it, and the number of engines on each; and could spot which were real, and which were dummies (see DECEPTION). Any bright lad could count how many guns there were in a horse-drawn battery passing through his village (most German artillery was horse-drawn). Any drinker in a bar could notice the colours on the shoulder-strap edges of the German soldiers who drank there too (white for infantry, red for artillery, and so on). It did not take much training to equip the housewife and the lad with the extra, telling details which would enable them to distinguish one type of aircraft or tank or armoured car from another, or to guess at the calibres of guns. Observant drinkers could learn to look out for formation signs on sleeves as well as arm-of-service colours on shoulder-straps. It was this kind of information that the 'Noah's Ark' circuit (see below) passed on with such good effect.

This sort of spying was available, in theory, to both sides. Even in battledress, soldiers in the British Army usually wore arm-of-service colour patches on their sleeves (red for infantry, scarlet and blue for artillery, and so on). Many regiments insisted on bearing some ancient badge, or even the regimental name, visibly on their uniforms. Every division, and many other formations, had a separate badge, worn near the shoulder of every man and on the front and back of every vehicle. A spy at a busy railway station or crossroads, watching which signs moved in which directions, could get some notions of an order of battle together. For this reason alone, it was as well for the Allied cause that *all* the German spies in the UK were captured and that a number became useful double-agents.

The *Abwehr office in Hamburg ran spies (it believed) in the British Isles, in South Africa (see also OSSEWABRANDWAG), and in North and South America, and it also attempted, with the *Kondor mission, to establish a network in Egypt. Its spies were also landed in Eire to contact the *Irish Republican Army, but were nearly of as little use as those landed in England—and nearly all were equally quickly captured. A few were lodged on the coast of Greenland (see METEOROLOGICAL INTELLIGENCE) to provide the Luftwaffe with weather reports (as did the German legislation in Dublin); it was not in the Allied interest to clean them out entirely, because their messages were so useful for decipher staffs.

Several German spies were sent to the USA (see USA, 6) and a few to Canada; all of them were rounded up, sooner or later, by the security forces, and between them hardly produced any useful intelligence at all—except that a pre-war agent provided the drawings for the Norden bomb-sight, then the US Army Air Forces' principal secret.

In South America the Abwehr was a little more successful, because it had established agents in Brazil, Argentina, and Chile before the war, who could report (by radio—posts were very slow) on economic affairs. Industrial espionage, now a business commonplace, was attempted by the Nazis, with some degree of success. SOE—unknown to the Federal Bureau of Investigation (see USA, 6) or to the *Office of the Co-ordinator of Inter-American Affairs—had an elaborate network of agents in South America, who marked down these and other German agents, and stood by to attack them (it never did), a classic case, common with intelligence services, of not allowing the left hand to know what the right is doing. Extra care was taken to make sure that the FBI knew nothing of this potential infringement of the Monroe Doctrine of 1823. The Nazi Sicherheitsdienst or SD (see RSHA) also ran spies (see V-MAN), some of whom, like *Déricourt, were double-agents. The SD's most famous coup was in Turkey, where the British ambassador's valet, Elyeza *Bazna, provided the German embassy for several months in the winter of 1943–4 with the contents of his master's safe. Exactly what use his information was to the Germans remains doubtful—*Ribbentrop and *Kaltenbrunner never settled a quarrel about which of them was to lay it before Hitler, who never saw it—and it is possible that the British early detected his treachery, and made use of him (also ineffectively) for purposes of deception.

Bazna, like many wartime spies, was an amateur: professionals were seldom available to either side. Enormous anti-Nazi enthusiasm, almost all of it amateur, undirected, and dangerous to those who felt it, was available in occupied Europe; some of it turned into useful spying. Dansey's links with *governments-in-exile in London were often here turned to useful effect; even without such a link, he ran some remarkably useful spies.

One of the largest and best of these amateur spy circuits working to MI6 was nicknamed 'Noah's Ark' by the *Gestapo, because its agents all had animals or birds for their cover names. Its founder, Georges Loustaunau-Lacau, an eccentric right-wing French officer, was soon arrested; his secretary, Marie-Madeleine Fourcade, took over, and established more than 3,000 informants, more than 500 of whom died in German hands. They provided, from all over France, minutely detailed information about German defences and order of battle; some of it already known, to a very limited circle, from ULTRA intelligence, much of it new and of great tactical value. Much of the 'Noah's Ark' material, as of other spy networks, was carried out of France by light aircraft of the RAF, which could carry whole suitcases-full of reports too cumbrous to be condensed and sent by wireless: a facility seldom available elsewhere. The reports of amateur spies were of particular value to British intelligence staffs working on German radar and on *V-weapon sites. One spy in Belgium, Walther Dewé, had the distinction of running a large and efficient spy network both in the *First World War and in the Second; he was killed in a street fight with the SD in 1944.

The Japanese had widespread spy circuits in South-East Asia. There was a spies' training school, run by the army, in the Tokyo suburb of Nakano, which trained men (only men) in techniques of espionage as well as sabotage and subversion. Some of this school's pupils were trained to act as stay-behind parties in areas the Allies reconquered from Japan; one of them, more devoted than intelligent, did not surrender until 1974. Before even the war began, captains and majors in the Japanese Army were happy to take on jobs as mess waiters in the lavish service establishments of the British armed services in the Malay States, and picked up a great deal of gossip from officers' indiscretions, and they were equally active in Burma, the Netherlands East Indies, Hong Kong, and the Philippines. Personnel of the Japanese Army's No. 82 Research Unit, run by Colonel Tsuji Masanobu, surveyed many of the landing beaches Japanese forces were to use in these areas. Only days before the Japanese launched their *Malayan campaign, Tsuji himself flew over southern Thailand, northern Malaya, and Singapore, and was able to build up, without any interference, an accurate picture of the defences laid out below him. The Japanese also had an espionage network on the US west coast which had links to New York and Mexico. Until he was forced to return to Japan in May 1941, it was organized by a Japanese naval commander, Yamamoto Hirashi, whose cover was running a chain of 'comfort houses' (see also COMFORT WOMEN) in Los Angeles.

Japanese intelligence-gathering before *Pearl Harbor is probably the best-known example of the Japanese use of spies. When Roosevelt based the US Pacific Fleet at Hawaii in May 1940 the Japanese consulate at Honolulu began sending regular reports on its movements, nearly all of which were conveniently chronicled in the local newspapers. The following March an ex-naval officer, Yoshikawa Takeo, who was a trained intelligence agent, joined the staff of the consul-general, Kita Nagao. Yoshikawa and a team of helpers compiled detailed notes on the fleet's routines and composition and how it was protected, as well as gathering information on military installations such as airfields, the direction of air patrols, and the whereabouts of storage facilities. They discovered the fleet, contrary to the most elementary security precautions, had a regular routine, one of which was that its capital ships (but not its carriers) were nearly always in harbour on a Sunday. All this they managed to ascertain without actually infringing any local security regulations and the information fed back to Tokyo built up as detailed a picture of the target as any attacking force could hope for, Yoshikawa even thoughtfully provided an aerial panoramic picture postcard of the harbour, copies of which accompanied the Japanese pilots to help them to orientate themselves before attacking.

Small wonder that the Japanese, throughout the remainder of the war, were exceptionally spy-conscious. As it happened, this proved to be of great advantage to the Allies because, instead of suspecting their codes had been broken (see ULTRA, 2), the Japanese blamed enemy agents when any particularly disastrous leakage of information occurred. In fact, humint played a minimal role in Allied intelligence-gathering in South-East Asia. However, the Americans did have one spy at work in the Philippines. This was a Nisei (see JAPANESE-AMERICANS) sergeant called Richard Sakakida who, over time, managed to persuade the Japanese *Kempei in Manila that he was a seaman who had jumped ship before the war. While working as a handyman in the Japanese judge advocate general's office in Manila, he used Filipino runners to take his information to the guerrilla bands in Luzon's mountains who then transmitted it to Brisbane.

A concluding example of the value of spies may be

given from France. When the *Todt Organization set out to build the *Atlantic Wall of coastal defences against seaborne attack, it ran the scheme from a headquarters in Caen which was decorated by local French labour, just after work on the wall had begun. A painter, René Duchez, tucked into his blouse a copy of the detailed instructions for building blockhouses—exactly what dimensions of concrete and of reinforcing rods were to be used—and took it away. The Germans noticed a copy was missing. It could not have been the painter, they thought, as the commandant had always been in the room with him. They forgot how busy the commandant had been on the telephone; they shot the electrician instead. Duchez had friends in an intelligence network; the document was in London a few weeks later, and was a godsend to artillery and engineer officers planning how to break through the wall, as they did during the Normandy landings in June 1944 (see OVERLORD).

CHRISTOPHER ANDREW/M. R. D. FOOT

Andrew, C., *Secret Service* (London, 1985), *ad fin.*
Fourcade, M.-M., *Noah's Ark* (London, 1973).
Jones, R. V., *Most Secret War* (London, 1978).
—*Reflections on Intelligence* (London, 1989)
Kahn, D., *Hitler's Spies* (London, 1978).

Spitzbergen, group of Norwegian islands lying some 645 km. (400 mi.) north of Norway in the Arctic Sea. They include Bear Island, about 210 km. (130 mi.) south of the group, either side of which, depending on the state of the ice, the *Arctic convoys sailed to and from the USSR. The islands had gypsum and asbestos mines which a Canadian force destroyed in August 1941 to prevent them from falling into German hands. They became a battleground in the 'Weather War' (see METEOROLOGICAL INTELLIGENCE), with both sides establishing meteorological stations on them. In September 1943, a German squadron, which included **Tirpitz* and **Scharnhorst*, bombarded shore installations there, but by then Allied dominance of the island group was assured.

Spruance, Admiral Raymond A. (1886–1969), US naval officer who commanded the Fifth US Fleet in some of the most crucial campaigns of the *Pacific war.

As a rear admiral Spruance commanded the cruiser division which acted as the surface screen for *Halsey's carrier task force during the first months of the war. When Halsey fell ill Spruance took his place commanding one of the carrier groups which ambushed the Japanese force advancing on *Midway which, after the fall of *Wake Island, was the Americans' most westerly Pacific outpost. Spruance emerged from this turning-point of the Pacific war with the reputation of being one of the foremost fighting and thinking admirals the US Navy had ever produced.

He then served for fourteen months as chief of staff to the C-in-C of the Pacific Fleet, *Nimitz, being for part of that time deputy C-in-C. He was promoted vice-admiral and in August 1943 was named Commander Central Pacific Force (later designated Fifth Fleet, called Third Fleet when commanded by Halsey). He put together a talented team which included Rear-Admirals Marc Mitscher (see TASK FORCE 58) and Kelly *Turner, and Maj-General Holland Smith (1882–1967) of the US Marine Corps; and later the British Pacific Fleet, *Task Force 57, served under him.

After planning the capture of *Tarawa atoll, accomplished in November 1943, he planned the seizure of the *Marshall Islands, and his success there gained him promotion to admiral. Then came the capture of the *Mariana Islands and finally *Iwo Jima and *Okinawa. After the *Philippine Sea battle in June 1944 he was criticized for failing to follow up his success during it, but posterity has largely exonerated him as his primary task was to protect the *Saipan landings, which he did.

'Power of decision and coolness in action were perhaps Spruance's leading characteristics,' wrote the US Navy's official historian. 'He envied no one, rivaled no man, won the respect of almost everyone with whom he came in contact and went ahead in his quiet way, winning victories for his country' (S. E. Morison, *History of US Naval Operations in World War Two*, Vol. 8, Boston, 1953, pp. 235–6).

Buell, T., *The Quiet Warrior* (Boston, 1974).
Larrabee, E., *Commander in Chief: Franklin D. Roosevelt, His Lieutenants, and Their War* (New York, 1987).

SS. The SS (Schutzstaffeln, or protection squads) became, from 20 July 1934, an independent organization within the German National Socialist, or Nazi, Party (NSDAP). Like no other institution of the Third Reich, the SS represents the arrogance of *Nazi ideology and the criminal nature of Hitler's regime.

Origins and general character

The early history of the SS dates back to 1923, when Hitler founded a so-called *Stabswache* (Headquarters Guard), which was banned, after his abortive Munich Beer Hall putsch of 9 November 1923. With the re-launching of the Nazi Party in 1925 a small *Stabswache* reappeared, named Schutzstaffel soon after. From then on, it expanded more or less continuously, albeit in decentralized form, with the establishment of new tiny echelons (*Staffeln*) in various cities of the Reich. Placed from their very beginning directly under Hitler's command, these SS squads functioned primarily as bodyguards, orderlies for mass meetings, and party propagandists. Thus, in contrast with the stormtroopers (Sturmabteilungen, or *SA) under Ernst Röhm, they were originally party cadres, not offshoots of the tradition of the Weimar Republic's paramilitary *Wehrverbände*.

The growth of the SS accelerated with the appointment of 29-year-old *Himmler as its head (Reichsführer-SS) on 6 January 1929. Membership sharply increased from a few hundred in early 1929 to about 52,000 in December 1932 and reached 209,000 by the end of 1933. At the same time, the areas of SS activity expanded rapidly. By crushing a

SS, Table 1: Ranks in the SS and Waffen-SS

Rank	*Comparable Wehrmacht rank*	*British Army*	*US Army*
SS-Oberstgruppenführer und Generaloberst der Waffen-SS	Generaloberst	General	General
SS-Obergruppenführer und Generaloberst Waffen-SS	General	Lt-General	Lt-General
SS-Gruppenführer und Generalleutnant der Waffen-SS	Generalleutnant	Maj-General	Maj-General
SS-Brigadeführer und Generalmajor der Waffen-SS	Generalmajor	Brigadier	Brigadier-General
SS-Oberführer } SS-Standartenführer }	Oberst	Colonel	Colonel
SS-Obersturmbannführer	Oberstleutnant	Lt-Colonel	Lt-Colonel
SS-Sturmbannführer	Major	Major	Major
SS-Hauptsturmführer	Hauptmann	Captain	Captain
SS-Obersturmführer	Oberleutnant	Lieutenant	1st Lieutenant
SS-Untersturmführer	Leutnant	2nd Lieutenant	2nd Lieutenant

Source: Wegner, B., *The Waffen SS* (Oxford, 1990).

revolt of Berlin SA formations (the so-called Stennes-Revolte) in 1930 and creating the following year an intelligence bureau of its own, Ic-Dienst, the SS developed beyond its original functions into a kind of party police within the growing Nazi movement. In addition, the establishment of an SS Race and Settlement Office (SS-Rasse- und Siedlungsamt) in 1931 indicated Himmler's ambition to create out of the SS a new, biologically-defined, aristocracy, a modern knighthood, destined to become the ideological avant garde of National Socialism.

The core of the SS was the General SS (Allgemeine SS), a term introduced to distinguish the bulk of the organization from its various special branches such as the SD and the armed SS formations. Its structure was modelled partly on military organizations, partly on monastic orders, and its members were given special ranks (see Table 1). While its unarmed formations were organized on lines somewhat resembling a regimental system, the SS as a whole regarded itself as an exclusive order: candidates for admission had, as a rule, to meet special demands as to their racial origin, physical appearance, political loyalty, and character. They had to undergo pseudo-religious initiation rites and were, as members of the order, subject to a quasi-monastic rule which governed questions of honour, obedience, and social behaviour. All this, as well as a great number of obscure Germanic rituals and military symbols, served to create among SS members the self-image of a chosen few and to justify their pretensions to domination.

Fields of activity

During the first months of the Third Reich, the SS, despite the expansion of its membership and its loyalty to the Führer, did not play a particularly decisive role. In the shadow of Röhm's powerful SA until the so-called 'Night of the Long Knives' on 30 June 1934, the SS did not look like one of the real winners from Hitler's accession to power. Starting from the apparently modest position of temporary chief constable of Munich, Himmler nevertheless managed quietly to build up the most impressive power base for the further development of the SS. Within fifteen months he had gained control over the political police in all the German states. (The political police were special departments each state had during the Weimar Republic to defend the constitution against politically motivated attacks. In Prussia this department developed in 1933 into the *Gestapo.) After another two years he controlled the police apparatus as a whole and on 17 June 1936 was given the title 'Reichsführer-SS and Head of the German Police'. In the following years, step by step, the police forces were integrated into the administrative structure of the SS. This process, the aim of which was the complete amalgamation of both organizations into a gigantic state Protection Corps (Staatsschutzkorps), which never actually materialized, led to a fundamental change in the function of the police service. It now gradually lost its character as an institution of public service and became—as the SS always had been—an instrument of the Führer's personal will. The SS, on the other hand, now acquired the position of a quasi-state agency and, as a result, benefited from many of the privileges usually reserved for the country's civil service.

All this helped to increase the efficiency of SS operations, most obviously so in the case of the Ic-Dienst, the SS intelligence bureau, which became known as the Sicherheitsdienst or SD. Having managed, since 1934, to monopolize all intelligence activities within the Nazi movement the SD, from late 1938, also officially operated on behalf of the Reich minister of the interior. One year later, the administration of the SD and the Security Police (Sicherheitspolizei, or Sipo) was combined in the newly established Reich Security Main Office (Reichssicherheitshauptamt, or *RSHA).

Alongside the police and the SD, the *concentration camps, taken over from the SA in the summer of 1934, formed the third pillar of SS power. Theodor Eicke, a notorious former commander of the *Dachau camp, was appointed inspector of concentration camps and reorganized them within a few years into a centralized and strictly regulated repressive machine. To guard the camps he also formed special armed units, the Death's Head Units (SS-Totenkopfverbände), which had rudimentary military training. By early 1939 they reached an overall strength of about 9,000 men; later in that year they were incorporated into the military formations of the new Waffen-SS (Armed SS) as the nucleus of the SS Death's Head division while their original duties were taken over by members of the General SS who were too old for military service.

Through its control of the police, the SD, and the concentration camps the SS had already achieved before the war a monopoly of domestic security and kept it until the collapse of the regime. Perhaps the most important aspect of this monopoly was that it gave the SS almost unlimited freedom of action, independent of the existing law and administration of justice. It was this parallel existence of traditional public service organs and SS-agencies which led Ernst Fraenkel to describe it as the 'Dual State' (E. Fraenkel, *The Dual State*, New York, 1941).

The range of SS activities went far beyond mere terror. Claiming to be not only the pioneers of the Nazi movement but also a model for, and the educator of, the German people, the SS did much to promote ideological indoctrination and propaganda. Convinced that Germany had been led astray for the last thousand years by Christianity, Himmler saw the restoration of the old pre-Christian, Germanic culture and lifestyle as a main task of the SS. To this end, the SS sponsored many different cultural and scientific activities. Countless articles, books, and films were produced for ideological indoctrination. Through a special office, headed by SS-Obergruppenführer August Heissmeyer, it also exerted a considerable influence on the Nationalpolitische Erziehungsanstalten, a system of élitist National Socialist schools, and established a network of student hostels at the German universities. Moreover, it encouraged research on Germanic history and archaeology and founded a research society of its own, the *Ahnenerbe* (literally, ancestral heritage), exclusively for this purpose. Another institution formed by the SS was the **Lebensborn*, which encouraged the birth of 'racially sound' babies.

Quite another sector in which the SS contrived, unobtrusively, to gain some measure of influence was the economy. The economic plans of the SS sprang from its desire to use the concentration camps and their large manpower reservoirs more systematically and efficiently. In this endeavour it founded a few enterprises of its own and after 1938 began systematic expansion in certain key fields of production. By the end of the war, the SS owned more than 40 different businesses embracing about 150 plants and factories. It was involved in quarrying, in the production of food and drink, in agriculture and forestry, in timber and iron processing, in leather and textiles, and in publishing. All these activities were co-ordinated by the Main office for Economy and Administration (SS-Wirtschafts und Verwaltungshauptamt) into which in March 1942 the concentration camp system was also integrated.

This official entrepreneurial activity was supplemented by semi-official contacts with influential circles in the German economy. These contacts were supported mainly by the Freundeskreis Reichsführer-SS (Circle of Friends of the Reichsführer-SS), a group of a few dozen industrialists, bankers, and high-ranking civil servants who were interested in having some degree of connection with the SS without actually joining it. For the SS, these contacts paid off—literally—as members of the Freundeskreis supported its work with substantial sums of money and were also prepared to help in other ways, for example in granting cheap loans.

The Waffen-SS

Of all activities of the SS, the 'black order' as it was called, its penetration into the prerogative of the Wehrmacht, while unspectacular at first, eventually had the greatest impact on the German war effort, as by May 1945 more than 800,000 men, formed into 38 divisions (see Table 2), had served in the ranks of the armed SS, the Waffen-SS, some 20 or 25% of whom had been killed in battle. SS formations fought on all battle fronts with the exception of the *Western Desert campaigns, and frequently played a critical role in the *German–Soviet war and in the fighting in north-west Europe. Names such as Rostov, *Kharkov, Demyansk, *Kursk and Cherkassy, Caen and Falaise (see NORMANDY CAMPAIGN) are closely associated with important offensive, and even more defensive, successes of Waffen-SS divisions. More than 400 officers of the Waffen-SS were awarded the *Ritterkreuz* (see DECORATIONS); several of them even commanded armies and army groups.

Though it undoubtedly achieved an impressive military record, the Waffen-SS (a name adopted only in late 1939) was neither an ordinary army nor, as has been often suggested, merely a fourth service of the Wehrmacht. Rather, the first armed SS units had been established as so-called Political Readiness Squads (Politische Bereitschaften) independently of the government by the regional SS commands (SS-Oberabschnitte). Only Hitler's personal guard (Leibstandarte), under the command of Sepp *Dietrich, was formed on Hitler's direct order in March 1933, and that, too, was done unconstitutionally. Before the war, all these squads seemed to serve primarily internal political purposes; this was clearly demonstrated in June 1934, when some of them were used in the liquidation of the SA leadership. Moreover, Hitler confirmed in various decrees that the Political Readiness Squads, known as the SS-Verfügungstruppe from autumn 1934, were intended to be the Führer's

SS, Table 2: List of armies, corps commands, and division of the Waffen-SS, 1944–5

Key to Symbols

[a] Units that were divisions in name only, often no larger than regiments
F+ Units composed largely of foreign personnel
F– Units including a sizeable number of foreign personnel
V+ Units composed largely of Volksdeutsche
V– Units including a sizeable number of Volksdeutsche

Army and Corps Commands

Armee-Oberkommando 6th SS-Panzerarmee
Generalkommando Ist SS-Panzerkorps 'Leibstandarte Adolf Hitler'
Generalkommando IInd SS-Panzerkorps
Generalkommando IIIrd (German) SS-Panzerkorps
Generalkommando IVth SS-Panzerkorps
Generalkommando Vth SS-Gebirgskorps
Generalkommando VIth SS-Freiwilligenkorps (Latvian)
Generalkommando IXth Waffen-Gebirgskorps der SS (Croatian)
Generalkommandos XIth–XVth SS-Armeekorps (mixed Army–SS staffs)
Generalkommando XVIIIth SS-Armeekorps (Rhine front)

Divisions

1st	SS-Panzerdivision 'Leibstandarte Adolf Hitler'	
2nd	SS-Panzerdivision 'Das Reich'	
3rd	SS-Panzerdivision 'Totenkopf'	
4th	SS-Polizei-Panzergrenadierdivision	
5th	SS-Panzerdivision 'Wiking'	F– (Norwegians)
6th	SS-Gebirgsdivision 'Nord'	
7th	SS-Freiwilligen-Gebirgsdivision 'Prinz Eugen'	V+ (Croatia)
8th	SS-Kavalleriedivision 'Florian Geyer'	V–
9th	SS-Panzerdivision 'Hohenstauffen'	
10th	SS-Panzerdivision 'Frundsberg'	
11th	SS-Freiwilligen-Panzergrenadierdivision 'Nordland'	F– (Norwegians and Danes)
12th	SS-Panzerdivision 'Hitler Jugend'	F+ (Latvians)
13th	Waffen-Gebirgsdivision der SS 'Handschar'	F+ (Croatians)
14th	Waffen-Grenadierdivision der SS	F+ (Ukrainians)
15th	Waffen-Grenadierdivision der SS	F+ (Latvians)
16th	SS-Panzergrenadierdivision 'Reichsführer SS'	V–
17th	SS-Panzergrenadierdivision 'Götz von Berlichingen'	V–
18th	SS-Freiwilligen-Panzergrenadierdivision 'Horst Wessel'	V+ (Hungary)
19th	Waffen-Grenadierdivision der SS	F+ (Latvians)
20th	Waffen-Grenadierdivision der SS	F+ (Estonians)
21st	Waffen-Gebirgsdivision der SS 'Skanderbeg'.	F+ (Albanians)
22nd	Freiwilligen-Kavalleriedivision der SS 'Maria Theresia'	F+/V–(Hungarians/Hungary)
23rd	Waffen-Gebirgsdivision der SS 'Kama'; dissolved late in 1944, and numerical designation given to SS-Freiwilligen-Panzergrenadierdivision 'Nederland'	F+ (Croatians then Dutch)
24th	Waffen- Gebirgskarstjägerdivision der SS	F+ (Italians, Slovenes, Croats, Serbs, Ukrainians)
25th	Waffen-Grenadierdivision der SS 'Hunyadi'	F+ (Hungarians)
26th	Waffen-Grenadierdivision der SS	F+ (Hungarians)
27th	SS-Freiwilligen-Grenadierdivision 'Langemarck'	F+ (Belgians)
28th	SS-Freiwilligen-Grenadierdivision 'Wallonien'	F+ (Belgians and Walloons)
29th	Waffen-Grenadierdivision der SS; transferred to the Vlasov Army, and numerical designation given to Waffen-Grenadierdivision der SS as of April 1945	F+ (Belorussians)
30th	Waffen-Grenadierdivision der SS	F+ (Russians and Ukrainians)
31st	SS-Freiwilligen-Panzergrenadierdivision 'Böhmen-Mähren' (established in 1945, around a nucleus of personnel from the various Waffen-SS schools and training establishments in Bohemia-Moravia)	F–/V– (Hungarians/Hungary)

SS, Table 2 (*cont.*)

32nd	SS-Panzergrenadierdivision '30. Januar' (created by mobilizing the students and instructors at the various panzer and panzergrenadier schools)	
33rd	Waffen-Kavalleriedivision der SS; annihilated early in 1945 during the battle for Budapest, and numerical designation given to Waffen-Grenadierdivision der SS 'Charlemagne'	F+ (Hungarian then French)
34th	SS-Freiwilligen-Grenadierdivision 'Landstorm Nederland'	F+ (Dutch)
35th	SS-Polizei-Grenadierdivision (created in 1945 by mobilizing members of the Ordnungspolizei)	
36th	Waffen-Grenadierdivision der SS (a titular upgrading of the notorious Dirlewanger penal brigade)	
37th	SS-Freiwilligen-Kavalleriedivision 'Lützow'	F+
38th	SS-Panzergrenadierdivision 'Nibelungen' (composed in part of the staff and students of the SS-Junkerschule 'Bad Tölz')	

Source: Stein, G. H., *The Waffen SS* (Oxford, 1966).

personal instrument 'for special internal political tasks'. Himmler's ambition, however, went far beyond that. While pretending to create a kind of police force, he militarized his formations and transformed them into a professional military body. Recruited exclusively from volunteers, the Verfügungstruppe was supposed to outshine the army by achieving higher standards of training and better equipment as well as through political loyalty and attempts to abolish the more antiquated customs which characterized the German Army at that time (see also RIVALRIES). However, efforts to realize these goals met with considerable difficulties, for their success depended heavily on the professional support of the Army High Command (OKH). After its experience with SA Stormtroopers in 1933–4, the OKH rejected, for obvious reasons, the idea of a competing SS army outside its control. Thus, the pre-war years were dominated by a perpetual struggle between the army and the SS on the strength, organization, and function of the Verfügungstruppe. The result was that numerically the OKH's policy of limiting SS growth was fairly successful; until the eve of the war, the overall strength of all armed SS units, including the Death's Head formations, did not exceed about 23,000 men. On the other hand, the military establishment had had to recognize service in the Verfügungstruppe as the equivalent of military service. In a decree of 17 August 1938 Hitler finally confirmed the military character of armed SS forces as well as their formal independence. He thus abandoned the principle that the Wehrmacht was to be the nation's only bearer of arms (*einziger Waffenträger*), which he himself had repeatedly stressed on earlier occasions.

With the approach of war the scales shifted further in favour of the SS. It was now no longer a question of whether the SS formations would be allowed to share in military conquests; the disputes now concerned only their assignments, size, and organization. As the first months of the war demonstrated, the SS was well prepared for a rapid expansion of its armed formations. All of them—including the Death's Head units and two *Junker* cadet schools at Braunschweig and Bad Tölz—were united in November 1939 under the collective term Waffen-SS. At about the same time, in October 1939, the first three SS divisions were formed, one each from the Verfügungstruppe (later called SS-Division Das Reich), the Death's Head units (SS-Divisions Totenkopf), and the police (Polizeidivision, which became formally part of the Waffen-SS only in 1942). As a reinforced motorized regiment, Hitler's Leibstandarte formed the nucleus of a fourth division (Leibstandarte-SS-Adolf-Hitler, or LSSAH), raised in 1941.

As the Waffen-SS had no general staff training programme, the commander and senior officers for the new formations were largely recruited from former Wehrmacht and police officers, who for personal, career, or political reasons had transferred to the SS. Former Army NCOs (non-commissioned officers) made up part of the junior officer corps, the majority of which was provided by the SS *Junker* cadet schools.

The SS front line divisions were deployed by the army in various operational theatres and fully integrated into its command structure. At the same time they remained subordinate to the SS High Command in all other respects (personnel, replacement training, indoctrination, court-martial matters, and so on). This division of responsibility led not only to further friction with the Wehrmacht, but also to a permanent power struggle within SS Headquarters. The main reason for this was the failure of its organization to keep pace with the growth of the 'black empire' as a whole. In 1939–40 Himmler had created several new *Hauptämter*, or Main Offices, which functioned as an SS equivalent to ministries, without defining clearly their respective jurisdictions. This policy of 'divide and rule' helped to strengthen Himmler's personal position, but it caused serious frictions between the various Main Offices. The competition was particularly acute between the old SS Central Bureau (SS-Hauptamt) under the command of SS-Obergruppenführer Gottlob Berger and the new Leadership Main Office (SS-Führungshauptamt), a kind of SS general staff, headed by SS-Obergruppenführer Hans Jüttner.

One of the major disputes between Berger's and Jüttner's agencies concerned the question of how rapidly the Waffen-SS should grow. The Leadership Main Office, responsible for the SS formations' military training and organization, argued for moderate growth in order to preserve the image of the Waffen-SS as a professional élite force. But Berger's institution, with Himmler's support, tried to recruit as many volunteers as possible. Since its arrangements with the Wehrmacht allotted the SS only a small share of German conscripts, Berger, from 1940 onwards, enlisted more and more volunteers from outside the German borders. Two manpower pools proved to be particularly responsive: the so-called **Volksdeutsche*, ethnic Germans living abroad (especially in Hungary, Romania, and the Balkans), and foreign volunteers from 'Germanic' countries such as the Netherlands and Flanders, Norway and Denmark. Though up to 1945 several hundred thousand *Volksdeutsche* and 'Germanic' men were recruited for the Waffen-SS, these figures still proved insufficient to compensate for the dramatic casualties suffered in the German–Soviet war and, at the same time, expand the Waffen-SS into a pan-Germanic mass army. So, from 1943, 'non-Germanic' volunteers from France and Italy, and in much greater numbers from eastern Europe (Ukraine, Belorussia, Latvia, Estonia) and the Balkans, were accepted to fill the ranks of the Waffen-SS, though without becoming members of the 'SS order' in the strict sense. Towards the end of the war, more than half of all Waffen-SS soldiers were either foreigners or ethnic Germans recruited from abroad. Some of the foreign formations such as the Muslim divisions (Handschar, Skanderbeg, and Kama), the *Indian Legion, or the tiny *British Free Corps, served from the outset almost exclusively for propaganda purposes and the combat effectiveness of most other SS formations raised after 1941 did not usually correspond to the élitist claim of the Waffen-SS. The reasons for this were not only shortcomings in training and equipment, but often also lack of motivation. A growing number of Germans, and particularly *Volksdeutsche*, were more or less pressed into 'volunteering' by bribery and intimidation. Foreigners, too, were often seduced to join the SS forces by false promises. For them, political frustration often caused a further decline in motivation, for Hitler and the other Nazi leaders refused to make any binding statement about the political future of the volunteers' native countries after Germany's final victory. For all these reasons, the number of first-class fighting formations barely exceeded half a dozen, among them being the LSSAH, Das Reich, Totenkopf, and Wiking. Receiving preference in equipment, these were transformed into panzer divisions in 1942–3 and henceforth deployed mainly as a kind of 'fire brigade' at any trouble-spots on the front. Their endurance in battle soon became as legendary as their involvement in a number of *war crimes and *atrocities.

The SS and German occupation policy

The war brought massive expansion not only for the Waffen-SS but also other branches of Himmler's empire. With the extension of German rule over large parts of Europe, the concentration camp organization changed most dramatically both in scope and in structure. The increase in the number of camp inmates, from about 25,000 in 1939 to more than 700,000 in January 1945, indicates the magnitude of this change. Seen in the total context of SS policy of repression and extermination, these figures represent, however, only the tip of the iceberg: they do not include those hundreds of thousands who died in the camps from inhuman living and working conditions, let alone those millions of Jews and gypsies, murdered by the mobile **Einsatzgruppen* of the SD and the security police, or gassed in the specially designed extermination camps of *operation REINHARD.

The expansion of the concentration camp system was accompanied by a fundamental change in its role. Before the war, the camp's main purpose was to neutralize the regime's internal enemies. After 1942 this function was increasingly superseded by two other tasks: mass extermination and economic exploitation. These were mutually contradictory: while the latter required the preservation of the prisoners' capacity for work, the former meant its destruction. The SS never managed to solve this problem.

With the rapid expansion of its military and repressive instruments, the SS tried to carve for itself a key position in German *occupation policy. As a political *tabula rasa*, the occupied countries offered the SS a unique opportunity for realizing most of its administrative, economic, military, racial, and settlement ambitions. By seizing this chance, Himmler hoped to ensure a decisive share for the SS in the future reconstruction of post-war Europe according to the tenets of Nazi ideology. The main executive organ created to achieve these goals was a network of territorial Higher SS and Police Leaders (*Höhere SS- und Polizeiführer*, or HSSPF). These tried to extend and consolidate the power of the SS High Command, often in fierce competition with the civil and military administration in the occupied areas, and their efforts, particularly in eastern Europe, met with considerable success. Following special agreements with the Wehrmacht High Command (OKW), the SS became largely responsible for 'pacifying' the rear areas. This euphemism meant in reality not only the containment of partisan and resistance movements but also a rule of terror, characterized by ruthless economic exploitation and enslavement of the Slavic population and the annihilation of real or apparent opponents on an unprecedented scale. Initially justified as 'war necessity', these mass killings soon became part of the *Final Solution programme as envisaged at the *Wannsee conference. At the same time the Reichsführer-SS, who in 1939 had also been appointed Reichskomissar für die Festigung deutschen Volkstums (Reich Commissioner for the Strengthening of Germandom), worked out far-reaching plans for the colonization of the conquered Polish and Soviet territories. According to the *Generalplan Ost* (1941–2), many millions of Slavs were to be deported to western Siberia, while a small minority of the native population was to be selected for 'Germanization'. As the pillar of German rule in the east, the SS correspondingly intended to create a network of settlements, for which it hoped to attract not only German farmers and veterans, but also *Volksdeutsche* and 'Germanic' volunteers from the Reich's neighbouring countries. The selection and *Eindeutschung* (Germanization) of the settlers as well as their transfer into the annexed eastern territories was largely the task of the Liaison Office for Ethnic Germans (Volksdeutsche Mittelstelle), headed by SS-Obergruppenführer Werner Lorenz. Due to the unfavourable course of the war, the SS was forced first to postpone, then give up most of these plans.

Given the megalomaniac character of its ambitions in the east, it is hardly surprising that the SS developed a special interest in northern and western Europe as well. Occupied Norway and Denmark, the Netherlands and Flanders were seen as integral parts of a future Greater Germanic Reich and as an additional manpower pool for populating the **Lebensraum* (living-space) in the east. Consequently the SS did not confine its role in these countries to merely supporting the German occupation authorities. By close co-operation with, and control of, the various collaborationist movements, and even the creation of a Germanic SS—the equivalent to the General SS in the 'Germanic' countries—Berger's Central Bureau tried, with only partial success, to establish a political power base for a lasting influence of the 'black order'.

Undoubtedly the Second World War offered the SS a historically unique chance to extend dramatically its power on a European scale. Paradoxically, Himmler's empire owed this increase in power not only to the victories of German weapons but also to their defeats. The more the bad news from the battlefields accumulated to become a threat to existence of the Nazi rule the faster the SS increased its power. It was to this tendency that Himmler and the SS owed their last triumphs. In the summer of 1944—after the attempted putsch against Hitler, the breakdown of the central sector of the Eastern Front, and the Allied invasion in Normandy (see OVERLORD) had led the Nazi regime to the brink of ruin—the power of the SS reached its zenith. The consequence of this was another intensification of National Socialist terror, which was now directed primarily against supposed 'defeatists', without being able, however, to prevent Hitler's thousand-year empire from collapsing earlier than almost any other in German history.

BERND WEGNER

Birn, R. B., *Die Höheren SS- und Polizeiführer. Himmlers Vertreter im Reich und in den besetzten Gebieten* (Düsseldorf, 1986).
Buchheim, H., *et al.*, *Anatomy of the SS State* (London, 1968).
Koehl, R. L., *The Black Corps. The Structure and Power Struggles of the Nazi SS* (Madison, Wis. 1983).
Stein, G. H., *The Waffen SS. Hitler's Elite Guard at War, 1939–1945* (London, 1966).
Wegner, B., *The Waffen-SS. Organization, Ideology and Function* (tr. R. Webster, Oxford, 1990).

Stalag, abbreviation of *Stammlager* (main camp), German camps holding Allied other ranks, see also PRISONERS-OF-WAR.

Stalin as war leader.

Iosif Vissarionovich Djugashvili-Stalin (1879–1953), was the only leader on the Allied side who dominated the war machine of a major power throughout the Second World War. His military experience was limited. He was exempted in the *First World War on grounds of physical unfitness. In the Russian Civil War, after the Bolsheviks had seized power, he was appointed as a political *commissar on the southern front; he also worked in the Red Army in the Soviet invasion of Poland in 1920. While he had never been a soldier, he had always fancied himself as a commander. He had interpreted his political duties in 1918–20 very broadly and had intervened on strategical and tactical questions. The death of Vladimir Lenin (1870–1924) opened the doors to a struggle for political power which, by the end of the decade, Stalin had convincingly won; and military matters continued to engage him as master of the Kremlin. The First Five Year-Plan, with its forced-rate dash for industrialization, contained an emphasis on military production. Stalin also stressed the need to produce a young generation of Soviet commanders: his suspicion of the existing officer corps was such that he exterminated most of them in the bloody purges of 1937–8.

Throughout the 1930s he and his government confronted threats to the USSR's security from Japan in the east and Germany in the west; and he could draw no comfort from the reluctance of the democratic western states to combat the advance of *fascism energetically. His worries were, however, underpinned by a judgement that the next world war would probably be between coalitions of capitalist powers. He declared a belief, in line with Lenin's predictions, that the world's only socialist state ought to be able to stay out of such a conflict.

It was with this mental framework that Soviet diplomatic manoeuvres were undertaken in 1939, the year when a short but intensive war was fought in Manchukuo against the Japanese (see JAPANESE–SOVIET CAMPAIGNS). Therefore, the search for security in the west seemed a logical priority and there have been suggestions that Stalin had always favoured a pro-German orientation in international relations. The merely tentative overtures of the UK and France in the summer of 1939 put the matter beyond doubt. Stalin had never had moral scruples in foreign policy. Relations with Italy, for example, had not been adversely affected by Mussolini's fascism. Nevertheless, Nazism had been castigated as a transcendent evil in the Soviet press and the sudden signing of the *Nazi–Soviet Pact in August 1939 therefore took Soviet citizens, as well as the rest of the world, by surprise.

Stalin's military and political dispositions once the war started have incurred odium. He completed the seizure of eastern Poland before Hitler had captured Warsaw, and a Nazi–Soviet friendship treaty on 28 September (see NAZI–SOVIET PACT) consolidated his gains as falling within the new formal boundaries of the USSR. Lithuania, Latvia, and Estonia were swiftly forced into the USSR in June of 1940. Finland, too, was invaded by the Red Army, and the bitter *Finnish–Soviet war of 1939–40 ensued to the north of Leningrad.

The resistance in eastern Poland, Lithuania, Latvia, and Estonia was short-lived and brutally repressed. The Great Terror in the USSR had abated by 1939, but now it was repeated in the newly incorporated territories. Poles, Lithuanians, Latvians, and Estonians suffered as others had before them. Particularly vulnerable to arrest and execution were persons from professional, commercial, and cultural strata. Officers in the old armies of the republics were also searched out, captured, and either sent to the *GUlag or killed. Stalin had determined on the decapitation of the nations he had conquered. This was war in every sense except that most of the victims were not soldiers and the killing was in the main done not by the Red Army but by the *NKVD.

Finland, however, resisted strongly. Stalin sought a redrawing of the boundaries as the minimum aim and the establishment of a Finnish Soviet republic if all went well. But incompetence and complacency pervaded the Soviet military effort. The commanders co-ordinated the attack badly; they also evinced little understanding of the superiority of mechanized units over infantry. Finland capitulated in March 1940, but on terms which involved chiefly a shifting of the Soviet–Finnish border at Finland's expense.

The difficulties that his force had in subduing a small state annoyed Stalin (and cheered Hitler). His personal and political hostility to his first deputy commissar for defence, Marshal Mikhail Tukhachevsky (1893–1937), whom he had had executed in 1937, had induced him to overlook the marshal's merits as a military thinker—Tukhachevsky, had been a long-term advocate of tanks and other mechanized formations. But finally Stalin learned the necessary lesson. Cavalry and infantry, so much touted by cronies of Stalin like *Voroshilov and *Budenny, could no longer be accepted as more useful than tanks and other modern weaponry. This in turn pushed Stalin into redoubling his programme of aircraft and tank production. Factory output quotas were raised still further. Labour disciplinary codes were tightened even more. Stalin wanted to be ready for the contingency of war, be it against Japan in the east or Germany in the west.

The rapidity of the fall of *France took him unawares, and his medium-term planning was thrown into disarray. In particular, his insistence on rebuilding Soviet defences at the extremity of the territory newly incorporated in the USSR left the country with the worst military scenario: the old defence system was half-dismantled (see STALIN LINE), but the new one had not been built. Stalin, of course, was not the only political or military figure to have overestimated French power. German generals had doubted Hitler's optimism. Japan's absorbtion in the extension of its Pacific empire diminished its threat to the USSR; but, through the first half of 1941, Stalin talked privately about the strong possibility of an eventual war with Germany. Even so, he believed that his diplomatic deal with Hitler would hold for longer than it did. Indeed he was unrivalled in his obtuseness about the precise and accurate intelligence he received regarding the nature of German aggressive plans. Not only his spy Richard *Sorge in Tokyo but also a series of informants, from German soldier-defectors through to Churchill, warned him about them. He even contrived to overlook the significance of German reconnaissance flights over Soviet soil.

The burden of his effort was to appear conciliatory to Hitler. In 1940 he had prevailed upon the Germans to accept that the USSR's interests in the Balkans and Turkey should be respected; but in the following year he softened his tone in messages to Berlin. Shipments of grain and oil to Germany continued to be arranged in strict accordance with the official trade agreements, even though the Germans stopped supplying their set quotas of machinery in return.

In addition, Stalin turned down the request of *Timoshenko and *Zhukov to order mobilization in mid-June 1941. Subsequently Stalin was to remark that, if Germany and the USSR had stuck together, they would have been invincible. His prognosis, then, was based upon the hope that Hitler would—at least for a time—share his own perspective on political and military realism in Europe. In the meantime he sent frenzied messages out to his subordinates to raise output levels for tanks and aircraft, to maintain morale in the armed forces, to indicate to an anxious (but, because of the heavy state censorship, ill-informed) populace that nothing could trouble the friendly relations between Germany and the Soviet Union.

The *blitzkrieg across the River Bug on 22 June 1941 (see BARBAROSSA) astounded him. For hours he refused to sanction retaliation: he still hoped against hope that what was happening was a mere 'provocation'. Eventually he came to his senses; but, although he participated in the emergency decision-making, several days passed before he recovered from the shock. He left it to *Molotov to broadcast the appalling news to the public. Stalin's private thoughts were despairing: 'Everything which Lenin created we have lost for ever!'

Stalin pulled himself back from what was nearly a complete mental collapse. In the first month of the war he operated cautiously and without his previous confidence. The débâcle of Soviet arms was awesome to contemplate, let alone to reverse in practice. The German advances were so rapid that towns and villages in Soviet-held territory were overrun before the inhabitants knew that a war was in progress. By the end of 1941 the German Army had lodged itself only a few dozen kilometres from *Moscow and in the suburbs of *Leningrad; and the south of Russia, including the entire Transcaucasus, lay in imminent danger. Half the industrial and agricultural resources of the USSR had been seized; half the population had been caught in the wake of the rapid German invasion. Stalin, self-styled military and political genius, had led his country to a greater defeat even than had been suffered by Alexander I at the hands of Napoleon in 1812.

Yet Stalin recovered his confidence to some extent within a fortnight of the invasion. On 3 July 1941 he agreed to address the public by radio. Careful listeners could discern a vocal tremulousness as well as the sound of clinking glass as he refreshed his throat. Yet his iron determination was also on display. Hitler was to be resisted with all the resources, human and material, at his command.

The speech began with the invocation: 'Comrades! Friends! Brothers! and Sisters!' These words were notable for including the whole population and not merely the supporters of the Communist Party. Class struggle, Bolshevism, Marxist terminology: these were largely missing. To the fore was the call to arms, to the unity of all patriots, to the defeat of the hated invaders. Stalin, man of steel (as his name implies in Russian), had come through his personal trauma. He had little choice but to make this endeavour: neither he nor his regime would survive defeat by Hitler. The facts about the genocide and mass starvation practised by the *Gestapo and the German Army were not yet widely known, but enough information was available to inspire Stalin and his confederates to stiff resistance.

Not that public statements were the whole story. In July 1941 a meeting took place between Stalin and the Bulgarian envoy Stamenov. *Beria and Molotov were in attendance. Stalin proposed that an overture should be made to Hitler offering a separate peace with Germany involving the cession by the USSR of vast areas then under German occupation. It would be an arrangement similar to the treaty of Brest-Litovsk accepted by Lenin in 1918. The Bulgarian refused to make the overture, and the idea was dropped. Thereafter an unequivocal policy of resistance was pursued.

A state committee of defence, uniting the organs of army, party, government, and police, was formed on 30 June 1941. All other public institutions were subordinated to it. Stalin was its chairman and remained in the post throughout its existence. He refused at first to assume the title of Supreme Commander. Probably the knowledge that further grievous disasters would befall the Red Army discouraged him from identifying himself too closely with military leadership. Possibly he also bore in mind that Tsar Nicholas II had attracted nothing but grief from a similar decision in 1915. But other counsels prevailed in the state committee of defence. If he wanted popular support, he had to take a fuller obvious responsibility. On 10 July he appointed himself Supreme Commander.

Stalin's formal qualifications were much greater than Roosevelt's and Hirohito's, but weaker than Hitler's and Churchill's. He had plenty to learn. At the beginning of his political career he had been a party functionary. In 1912 he had risen, by co-option, to membership of the Bolshevik faction's Central Committee and after the October Revolution he had entered the Bolshevik-led government as People's Commissar of Nationalities Affairs. Subsequently he became the chairman of the Workers' and Peasants' Inspectorate. His activities as a political commissar had not increased his reputation for military competence among those who worked with him; indeed he was blamed by Lenin and Leon Trotsky (1879–1940) as a major reason why the Red Army's advance on Warsaw was botched in mid-1920. Thereafter, he concentrated his career inside the central party apparatus. Giving up his governmental jobs, he became the party's general secretary in 1922. Since the party controlled and directed the government, his power was immense as soon as Lenin, the chairman of the government (or Sovnarkom), died. And yet it was only on 6 May 1941, a few weeks before Hitler's invasion of the USSR, that Stalin took up the governmental chairmanship for himself.

Stalin's limitations as military expert did not inhibit him. He had anyway thoroughly intimidated his command staff by means of the recent bloody purges; and the Red Army's forced retreat towards Moscow was blamed by the Supreme Commander not on himself but on his commanders. General D. G. Pavlov became his scapegoat and was summarily shot. Stalin took control. By November 1941, he was already demanding that the Red Army should launch a counter-attack on the German forces as they dug in for the winter short of Moscow. This request was regarded as a military nonsense by the Soviet High Command. Their battered forces needed to be regrouped, re-equipped, and re-trained for the battles in prospect along the front that sprawled from Leningrad in the north down towards the Black Sea. But Stalin had his way, and some kilometres of ground were won back in severe wintry conditions. He was unworried by the human cost. He considered that, in demographic and industrial capacity, the USSR could afford to be much more wasteful than Germany and intended to show that the Germans were not invincible. Hitler's forces, moreover, were going to be denied a winter of leisurely reinforcement, and he also rightly foresaw that an improvement in civilian as well as military morale would occur if even a small victory could be extracted.

By early 1942 he was telling his commanders that Hitler was doomed. Always driving the Red Army ever forward, he had insisted in September 1941 that *Kiev, the capital of the Ukraine, should not be surrendered. This was the utmost folly. As was anticipated by his generals and political commissars, the result was that hundreds of thousands of Soviet troops were trapped in a German pincer movement.

But the defensive mode remained uncongenial to him. In the spring of 1942 he ordered preparations to be made for a Soviet offensive to the south of Moscow in the direction of *Kharkov in the eastern Ukraine. Again he trampled on informed advice. Again the amassment of troops, machines, and *matériel* was insufficient. Despite *Shaposhnikov's last-minute remonstrations, the offensive took place. Defeat followed, with large Soviet losses, and the German Army could move still more freely in the region of the River Volga. The experience sobered Stalin somewhat. His Commanders noted that his military knowledge increased substantially by the end of the first twelve months of the *German–Soviet war. He had bought this knowledge at huge cost, but it was to be put to good use in the ensuing period.

Stalin felt that the key to victory was as much political and economic strategy as military. The integrity of his system of power was crucial to him. But he changed style considerably. His appeal to his listening public as brothers and sisters was an attempt to appear homely, patriotic, and even rather non-political. Despite his Georgian accent, he wished to appear a fitting leader for Russians.

For Churchill or Hitler, such a *démarche* was unnecessary. For years they had used the forms of national pride without equivocation. Stalin, however, led the *Comintern which directed the activities of communist parties around the world and which was committed to 'proletarian internationalism'. Russian nationalism had grown in the 1930s, but had been handled with some finesse. Yet the wartime emergency threatened the regime's collapse and Stalin wrapped himself unashamedly in the flag of Russian nationalism. Tsarist commanders from previous centuries like Suvorov and Kutuzov were elevated in esteem (see DECORATIONS, USSR). Traditional Russian values were stressed. Stalin did not quite strut the stage as a tsar—for instance, he appealed in his broadcast to his 'brothers and sisters' rather than to mere lowly subjects—yet the patriarchal style was otherwise prominent.

On the whole, Stalin conducted his propaganda at long range. Unlike Churchill or even Hitler, he rarely appeared in public. The great exception was the annual parade on the anniversary of the October revolution, when he saluted troops and tanks heading directly out to the front. But he visited the front itself only once, and then only fleetingly (although he made much of it in his letters to the Allies).

Among his other devices to rally popular opinion was a relief of pressure on the Orthodox Church (see RELIGION). Inviting the patriarch to the Kremlin, he had the gall to enquire why so few priests were available. The patriarch refrained from replying that Stalin had killed thousands of them in the GUlag. Tanks were now paid for and blessed by priests as they rolled off the factory assembly lines. Cultural self-expression also became somewhat freer. Poets like Anna Akhmatova were allowed to broadcast, so long as they did not stray into commentary prejudicial to the regime. Composers such as Dmitri Shostakovich produced symphonies which inspired everyone, regardless of faith or political opinion, behind the war effort (see also USSR, 10).

The official cult of Stalin as an omniscient leader was not dismantled. His ludicrous autobiography, which he had secretly edited, was printed in millions of copies; and the history of the Communist Party, written in his image (and again under his attributed supervision) continued to be published. Only in outlying villages was the apparatus of official propaganda weakly established.

Things also changed in the daily press. *Censorship in the Soviet-held areas was never removed, and lies, big and small, were told daily by the regime's spokesmen; but the contents of newspapers and radio broadcasts became more believable than for many years. The truth of Nazi *atrocities was seen by Stalin to be a highly effective means of summoning up national support, and *Pravda* was allowed to reduce its previous quotient of ideology. *War correspondents such as Vasili Grossman toured the frontal areas and recounted how the German invaders were exterminating Jews and communists wherever they caught them and reducing the rest of the population to levels below those of human subsistence.

Other relaxations, too, were allowed. There were food shortages in the towns of central and northern Russia, even though the quotas of procurements were maintained at a high level. Consequently a blind eye was frequently turned to the urban black market: getting the population fed by any means to hand was considered the priority. Stalin could bide his time until, with the defeat of Hitler, he could reimpose the old forms of control.

And, if there were wartime relaxations, there were also measures to increase the demands on society. Stalin was aware of historical precedents. He knew from the textbooks that few tsars had been unwilling to sacrifice vast material resources (as had Alexander I in the retreat before Napoleon in 1812) or vast numbers of people (as had Peter the Great in his several wars or Nicholas II in 1914–17). The ruthlessness of Ivan the Terrible was greatly to Stalin's taste. At a banquet in 1937 he had declared—off the record—that, if anyone thought of betraying the country's cause, he would 'physically destroy him together with his clan'. Like Ivan, he considered that people worked best when they walked in 'holy terror' of what would happen to them if they failed to fulfil their duties to the state.

Stalin arriving at Churchill's residence for dinner during the TERMINAL conference in Potsdam, July 1945. He is saluting a guard of honour provided by the Scots Guards.

Accordingly two infamous instructions were given to Red Army generals by Stalin. The first was Order No. 227, issued on 28 July 1942. It bluntly demanded that no further territory whatsoever, once the initial German invasion had been halted, should be surrendered. To give up territory even for sound strategical reasons was considered treason.

The other had been issued earlier, on 16 August 1941: Order No. 270. It stated that any Soviet soldier taken prisoner should be deemed a traitor. Men were required to die fighting rather than fall into enemy hands. Not even Hitler was so ruthless. Stalin could not trust his men to face up to the horrors of Hitler unless they knew they would surely otherwise encounter the horrors of Stalin. The risk he ran became obvious in the summer of 1942 when General *Vlasov's forces, about to be cut off and captured by the Germans in northern Russia, asked Stalin's permission to effect withdrawal. Vlasov's bravery and competence were beyond question, but Stalin would not yield; the forces were duly overwhelmed and taken prisoner.

Vlasov's fury was such that he offered to form units from Soviet *prisoners-of-war to fight on the Eastern Front against the Red Army (see SOVIET EXILES), his immediate aim being the overthrow of Stalin. But he also intended, as a patriot, to turn on Hitler whenever he had the chance. Thousands of Russians, starved and demoralized in German *concentration camps, joined him. They sensed there was little to lose since Stalin already regarded them as *traitors for allowing themselves to be captured. In fact both Vlasov and his men were cruelly deceived by Hitler, for few of them were allowed to fight on the Eastern Front as they had wanted.

But the episode indicated that Stalin, while cognisant that a war must be fought politically as well as militarily, made some egregious mistakes. His own son Vasili was captured in the middle of the war. Strictly speaking, compliance with Order No. 270 would have entailed that members of Vasili's family in Russia, including the supreme commander, should have had their rations withdrawn. But nobody pointed this out to Stalin; and, in any case, he got round the problem with glacial aplomb by simply disowning his son. When Hitler arranged for approaches to be made for a bartering of Vasili Stalin in return for some German generals, Stalin felt no need to respond. Thus he stressed that his will to defend every inch of Soviet-held territory to the last drop of blood of the last Red Army infantryman was infrangible.

The situation in mid-1942 still seemed far from promising from the Soviet viewpoint. Various meetings between representatives of the Allies had evinced no firm promise by the UK and the USA to launch a rapid invasion of France. The brunt of the war against Hitler would therefore be borne by the USSR for the foreseeable future. Supplies were in the meantime sent to Moscow. Crucial to the Soviet war effort were the *Lend-Lease jeeps, the canned beef, and the sugar shipped, often by the *Arctic convoys in danger from German aircraft, submarines, and surface warships.

The Eastern Front was fought over intensively. The siege of Leningrad grew tighter; and, on the Volga, *Stalingrad became a cockpit of the struggle between the Soviet and German armies. The fact that the city bore Stalin's name added to its singularity as a prize of war. Stalin favoured Stalingrad as the springboard for a strategic counter-attack in mid-summer 1942. *Zhukov firmly faced him down on operational grounds. But in September 1942 Stalin got his way. Stalingrad was fought for to the last square metre. The city became a huge, baking graveyard. As German forces steadily lost the battle under weight of Soviet superiority in numbers and equipment, so Hitler—like Stalin before him—refused to sanction retreat. By the end of January 1943 Stalingrad was again a Soviet city.

By then the USSR's output of tanks and aircraft was vastly greater than Germany's. In the summer of 1943 the Germans tensed themselves for one last massive offensive. They chose a bulge in the Soviet line of defence near *Kursk and hurled their tanks at it. Stalin and his commanders threw men and machines into the gaps made by Hitler's forces. As usual, Stalin advocated counter-attack as the best means of defence. But now he hearkened to advice. A defensive posture, aimed to defeat the Germans by remorseless attrition, was adopted and was effective. And defeat at Kursk was the death-knell of Nazism on the Eastern Front.

Still Stalin drove his men on. Not sparing his own health, his working day lasted twelve to fourteen hours, and he continued to toil into the small hours of the night. This had become natural for his body clock, but he imposed his habits on everyone else: his colleagues had to be ready to receive a call from him at any time of night. His memory was as impressive as his resilience. Commanders and politicians were frequently surprised by his detailed recollection of the names of middle-ranking officers and their geographical locations. His growing technical comprehension had not altered a reliance on his tried and tested methods of rule. He harangued his colleagues in person and, in case they should fail to remember who was boss, he usually kept one of their close relatives in a *GUlag. It was as if Churchill had taken the precaution of holding Mrs Eden in the Tower of London on below-subsistence rations while his foreign secretary, Anthony *Eden, conducted state affairs.

This was an unusual pattern of governance. No other Allied, or indeed Axis, leader so humiliated his colleagues. He would not tolerate high-ranking functionaries meeting in groups away from his presence. Nobody was to have the chance to plot against him. Stalin also had the habit of inviting the members of the state committee of defence to country dinner parties where he would get them drunk (and perhaps make them do a dance) so as to loosen their tongues.

He frequently reinforced any decisions with telephone calls to impress urgency on his subordinates. But systematic and intimidatory informality was part of the pattern of his rule. And yet even he needed a regular administrative centre, and successive chiefs of staff (particularly *Vasilevsky) were empowered to keep tight control over communications and files. His commanders grew to respect as well as fear him. Not only Vasilevsky but a large number of other youngish commanders earned promotion at his hands: *Timoshenko, Zhukov, *Rokossovsky, *Konev. Zhukov made a name for himself by daring to say the unsayable to the supreme commander. As his trust in their expertise increased, their scope for initiative was expanded. Success was be rewarded with fame, medals, and privileges. Epaulettes, titles, modes of address: all reverted to the tsarist customs. In October 1942, Stalin demonstratively abolished the system of political commissars in the Red Army in order to exhibit his confidence in the High Command.

Not that Stalin's hyper-centralized oversight was dispensed with. The Soviet bureaucracy, civilian and military, had always been very chaotic; and resistance to Moscow's instructions had typically taken the form of time-wasting and the formation of local cliques. The terror inflicted on the administrative strata of state and society in the late 1930s had increased this tendency. Only fools were unaware of the possibilities of being purged. Prudence induced people into making 'arrangements' with dependable friends and associates.

Stalin persisted in trying to eradicate these trends. He did not succeed: they were inherent to the nature of his regime. And yet, whatever his difficulties may have been, he virtually always got his way in matters of domestic or foreign policy which were thought by him to be crucial. In other matters, too, he frequently interfered. For example, he offered authoritative judgements on both biology and linguistics in the 1940s. Yet he recognized that he needed active assistants to break through the lines of bureaucratic retrenchment, and he often used plenipotentiaries to investigate, control, and bully on his behalf. The state committee of defence was in some ways like an 18th century royal court. Stalin had *Beria to run the security policy, Georgy Malenkov (1902–79) to co-ordinate the party, N. I. Voznesensky to handle the economy. These vigorous, ambitious, and merciless men were employed to shake up their respective bureaucracies and to act as a counter to the authority of the military High Command. And among themselves they engaged in competition for Stalin's favour, for he cunningly arranged for their various areas of competence to overlap. They consumed themselves in mutual exhaustion and had little time or energy to plot against him. Stalin, by his own lights, was loyal to them in wartime, but they all had vivid memories of the recent purges. Ruthless in the performance of their tasks, they could never forget that they served a ruthless terrorist as their master.

In fact Stalin had slackened the pace of arrests since early 1939, but he did not empty the GUlags of their surviving victims. The generals who were released at his whim in order to fight the Germans were the exceptions, and the millions of other convicts toiled on with nothing but death to look forward to. And while repression on the scale of the Great Terror did not return to the Soviet population as a whole, it was applied intensively to certain large groups. The Poles and Balts in Stalin's prisons continued to be treated vengefully; and all nationalities suspected by Stalin and Beria of a probable pro-German orientation were uprooted *en masse* and transported by cattle trucks into the inhospitable depths of the country. Such was the fate of the Chechens and other peoples of the north Caucasus; of the Crimean Tatars; of the Volga Germans (see DEPORTATIONS).

Not that the rest of the population had an enviable life. Consumer needs were subordinated to the demands of the armaments industries under Voznesensky's direction. Tanks and aircraft were being speedily produced from the Urals and western Siberia after the feats of evacuation achieved in 1941. Soviet prospects had improved to such an extent by the winter of 1942–3 that the contingency plans for the transfer of the capital from Moscow to Kuibyshev on the Volga were never carried out, though the staffs of foreign embassies were moved there.

After the battle of Kursk in the summer of 1943, the Germans were constantly on the retreat. The Ukraine, Belorussia, the Baltic republics: all were steadily hauled back into the zone of Soviet administration under Stalin. His reprisals against those who had collaborated with the Germans were as terrible as they were predictable. On and on he drove his commanders through the last months of 1943 and the spring of 1944. Repeatedly he indicated to the Allies that it was the blood of the population of the USSR that was winning the war and conserving the blood of others. Only in June 1944 did he obtain what he had been demanding since 1941: the opening of a so-called 'Second Front' (see OVERLORD), though the western Allies had been engaged against German troops on mainland Europe since September 1943 (see ITALIAN CAMPAIGN). The British were especially galled by his use of this term since they had fought Nazi Germany for nearly two years before the USSR's entry into the war. Even so, the crucial and predominant contribution made by the USSR to Allied victory over Germany was beyond dispute.

As Hitler's imminent demise was scented, Stalin rose to new heights of prestige at home and abroad. He made himself Marshal in 1943. His fame among western Allied troops as 'Uncle Joe' the indefatigable anti-Nazi was understandable but exaggerated: it had been he, after all, who had sanctioned the Nazi–Soviet non-aggression and friendship treaty in 1939, and had contemplated suing for peace with Hitler in July 1941.

There were others fighting against Hitler who had a realistic viewpoint of him, chief among them the Poles. Stalin's fears about a resurgent Poland had led him to order the massacre of thousands of defenceless Polish army officers in *Katyń forest and elsewhere in the year following the Nazi–Soviet Pact; and his will to stamp Poland under his heel was undiminished as Soviet troops again advanced on Polish territory in 1944. Poland's future had already been discussed, much to Stalin's chagrin, at the first meeting of the main leaders of the Allies—Churchill, Stalin, and Roosevelt in Teheran in November 1943 (see EUREKA). Stalin wanted no further interference in his dirty business. His intentions were revealed implicitly when, on the first major occasion since Soviet entry into the war, he stopped his forces from advancing. This occurred in summer 1944 as they reached the River Vistula. Instead of crossing the banks to help the *Warsaw rising, the Red Army was ordered to wait while Hitler carried out Stalin's butchery for him.

International issues were now at the top of Stalin's political agenda. Despite what he said to his fellow Allied leaders, he wanted his forces to be the first to enter Berlin. At the Teheran conference he had proposed the extermination of 50–100,000 German officers. Roosevelt diplomatically assumed that he was joking, but Churchill felt physically sick: he saw all too clearly that Stalin was proposing the geographical extension of methods of dominion which had served him effectively for more than a decade in his own country.

Nevertheless, the frightful chaos and carnage that awaited their forces in the final campaigns against the Germans, put enormous pressure on his allies to come to terms with Stalin. At their Yalta conference in February 1945 (see ARGONAUT) an agreement was made about spheres of military and political influence. Stalin was left in potential control of all eastern and east-central Europe. The period of operation of the agreement was left unclear, but Stalin discerned no reason why it should not be made permanent. He even managed to extract concessions for the USSR in the Far East, including the promise of a military base in China. Reparations, too, were to be secured from Germany. Characteristically Stalin attributed his own deviousness to his rivals: 'I think that Roosevelt won't break the Yalta agreements; but, as for Churchill, that one might do anything!'

As the Yalta conference broke up, Soviet armies stood on the Oder and the Danube and the armies of the western Allies on the Rhine. The race was on, as Stalin saw things, for the fall of *Berlin. If he had been deliberately dilatory before Warsaw, he was recklessly demanding of his commanders now. Drawing a line on the German map between the forces of Zhukov and of Konev, he left them to compete for the honour of entering the German capital first. The various forces converged in April 1945, and the Berlin garrison commander capitulated on 2 May. The official national surrender to all Allied forces followed, and was ratified on 8 May.

Stalin, his regime, and his country had been pulled back from the brink of disaster in four years. Defeat would have brought swift death, slow starvation, or a lifetime's gruelling servitude to the entire Soviet population under Nazi domination. Stalin's personal contribution to victory was double-edged. The contemporary official praise in the USSR was extreme and would be merely comic if it had not been inflicted on millions of people while Stalin lived. His determination to win the war, to drive his colleagues and subordinates to the utmost, and to inspire his society is well-attested. His capacity to intervene decisively at the points of military or economic bottleneck was abundantly in evidence. He also learned fast how to run the war machine more or less competently and even to hearken to advice.

And yet the price was high for his leadership. The miscalculations before and during BARBAROSSA were stupendous. The subsequent human and material losses caused by his rigid insistence that no unit should retreat and no soldier surrender were awesome. The liquidation of generals who sustained defeat and of 'suspect' ethnic groups was gruesome. The peoples of the USSR would have fought hard against Hitler because they knew what Hitler would do to them without the necessity for Stalin to outmatch Ivan the Terrible in brutality.

The manner of Stalin's victory, furthermore, left a murderous regime intact at home and able to replicate itself in eastern and east-central Europe. At the very end of the war, as the Americans moved in to defeat Japan, Stalin declared war on the Japanese and seized some of their islands (see JAPANESE–SOVIET CAMPAIGNS). He would undoubtedly have imposed Stalinism as widely in the Far East as in Europe if only he had had the opportunity. As it was, his desires were unopposable only in the West. With his backing, mini-Stalins seized power in most countries to the east of the line drawn down the middle of Europe at the Yalta conference and set the scene for the *Cold War.

The Allies met again in Potsdam in July (see TERMINAL). By then Roosevelt had died and his successor, Harry *Truman, took a stronger line against Stalin. Churchill, too, was replaced, by the Labour leader Clement *Attlee who hated *communism as much as Churchill did. Yet Stalin's power was untouched by them. His image as a war hero was assiduously cultivated. He agreed, with sham modesty, to accept the title of Generalissimo as a token of reward for his services. Not all the acclaim for him, however, was forced. Despite the repression he had organized and maintained against his own citizens, he also enjoyed widespread respect and admiration. The demonic figure in the Kremlin was secure in power until his death in March 1953. ROBERT SERVICE

Deutscher, I., *Stalin* (Oxford, 1949).
McNeal, R. H., *Stalin: Man and Ruler* (London, 1988).
Medvedev, R., *On Stalin and Stalinism* (Oxford, 1979).
Volkogonov, D., *Stalin: Triumph and Tragedy* (London, 1991).

Stalingrad, battle of. This was the turning-point of the *German–Soviet war. Hitler had expected the German *blitzkrieg, after having swept across the Ukraine and into the Caucasus, to complete the Soviet Union's reduction to military impotence there, on the River Volga, at the edge of Asia. But before the battle had ended, the USSR had made its debut as a military superpower, blitzkrieg was no more, Hitler was the beleaguered one, and he would henceforth have to fight on Stalin's terms.

General *Paulus's Sixth Army had the mission of taking Stalingrad and, together with General Hermann Hoth's Fourth Panzer Army, extending downstream on the Volga to Astrakhan, which would give Army Group B, under General Maximilian von Weichs, a solid line on the Don and Volga rivers covering the eastern Ukraine and the Caucasus. Paulus and Hoth faced a problem generals prefer never to contemplate: having to take a large city street by street. An even more unpleasant possibility confronted Stalin: having an already disastrous summer end with the loss of the city that bore his name. On 12 September 1942, the day German troops entered it, Stalin decided some part of the city would have to be held regardless of the cost; and Maj-General *Chuikov, whose Sixty-Second Army was in Stalingrad, began receiving heavy reinforcement.

In a radio speech on 30 September, Hitler assured the German people and the world that Stalingrad would be taken. Paulus and Hoth then had two-thirds of the city, but counter-attacks by Don *front* (army group) on the north and Stalingrad *front* on the south, and the constant stream of fresh troops to Chuikov were bringing them to a stop.

The next seven weeks were crucial for both sides—in the battle and the war. To increase the concentration in Stalingrad, Weichs turned over half of Paulus's front on the Don and half of Hoth's south of Stalingrad to the Romanian Third and Fourth Armies, both of which had poor performance records (see ROMANIA, 4). For *Zhukov and *Vasilevsky, the Romanian armies were a godsend from which they derived the basis for a counter-operation (URANUS, see Map 98). Opposite the Third Romanian Army and its neighbour on the left, Eighth Italian Army, they built a new South-West *front* (four field armies and a tank army), and they attached the equivalent of a tank army (two armoured corps) to Stalingrad *front*'s Fifty-First Army opposite the Fourth Romanian Army. URANUS, however, was vulnerable: because it had to wait until the autumn rains ended, it could become a wasted effort if Stalingrad fell or the Germans detected the build-up in the interim. The last two weeks, when ice floes blocked the Volga, were the most hazardous.

On 19 November, Lt-General N. F. Vatutin, the South-West *front* commander, threw two field armies and his tank army against the Third Romanian Army. At Stalingrad *front*, Lt-General *Eremenko joined in against Fourth Romanian Army with his armour and Fifty-First Army a day later. The Romanian armies collapsed under the first assaults, and the Soviet armour completed

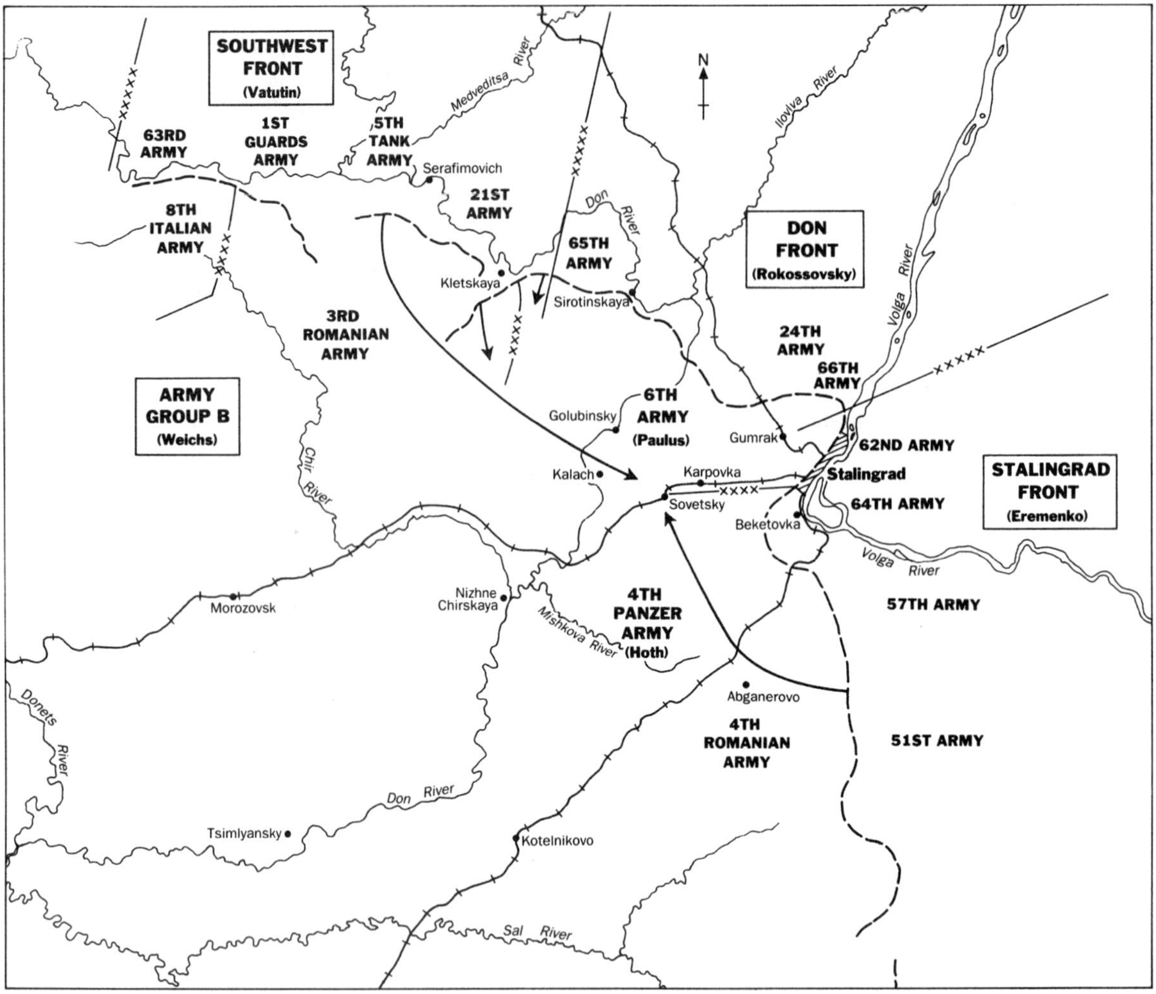

98. **Battle of Stalingrad:** Operation URANUS, 19–23 November 1942

Map 98 Legend

- – – – Approximate front line, 19 November 1942
- ——→ Direction of Soviet attack
- -xxxxx- Army group boundary
- –xxxx– Army boundary
- —+—+— Railway
- Built-up area

Scale 1:2 500 000

0 25 50 75 100 kms

0 25 50 miles

Conic Projection

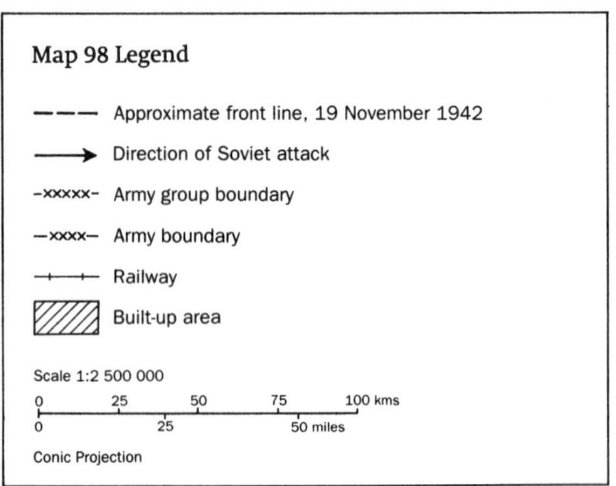

an almost perfect encirclement near Kalach on 23 November.

Paulus—who had twenty divisions, six of them panzer or motorized, nearly a quarter of a million troops in all—asked permission to break out. Hitler, insisting that Stalingrad was the 'most substantial achievement of the 1942 campaign', demanded that the pocket be held until contact was restored from the outside, and he promised massive air supply. To make the contact, he created Army Group Don (initially, two panzer divisions, one infantry division, Hoth's Fourth Panzer Army headquarters, and the remains of the Romanian armies) and gave the command to Field Marshal von *Manstein. *Göring pledged his air force to deliver 300 tons of supplies a day to the pocket.

Zhukov and Vasilevsky had apparently not anticipated the German response; and while they and Stalin deliberated on what to do next, Manstein had time to assemble a relief force of three panzer and two infantry divisions under Hoth. The operation (WINTER STORM) began 100 km. (62 mi.) south of the pocket on 12 December. Four days later, Zhukov opened an operation (LITTLE SATURN) to force Army Group Don away from Stalingrad. South-West *front* overran the Eighth Italian Army and struck south deep behind Manstein's north flank. Stalingrad *front*, with WINTER STORM going on literally in its midst, turned south-westward, towards the River Donets and the lower Don.

On 23 December, after Hoth's armour had been stopped for four days on the River Mishkova, 57 km. (35 mi.) south of the pocket, Manstein told Hitler that he was going to have to take at least a panzer division away from the river and Paulus would have to attempt a breakout even though he was perilously short of motor fuel and rations. (The airlift had averaged barely 90 tons per day.) Hitler talked about taking 'some elements' from Hoth's forces on the Mishkova, and also holding there until the advance could be resumed, but by 28 December Hoth's entire force had been engulfed, and Manstein had to allow him to withdraw.

LITTLE SATURN left the final reckoning with Sixth Army to Lt-General *Rokossovsky's Don *front* as a separate operation (RING). In early January, the pocket had about the same dimensions as in November, roughly 60 km. (37 mi.) east–west and 45 km. (28 mi.) north–south. For three weeks, Hitler managed to force the airlift up to 120 tons a day. Rokossovsky began RING on 10 January. Driving across the pocket from west to east, he covered about half the distance by 17 January; but then, having underestimated the German resistance, he had to pause for four days to regroup. On 22 January, after having lost his last airfield, Paulus suggested—and Hitler rejected—a surrender, and by 29 January, Sixth Army was confined to two small pockets in Stalingrad. On 31 January, a day after Hitler advanced him to field marshal, Paulus surrendered the pocket in which his headquarters was located, but refused to order the other to do the same. Hitler, who had expected more of Paulus after his promotion, ordered the six divisions in the second pocket to fight to the last man. Contact with them ceased on 2 February. According to German Red Cross estimates the Germans lost 200,000 troops at Stalingrad, a figure which did not include any of the 30,000 wounded evacuated by air.

EARL ZIEMKE

Chuikov, V. I., *The Battle For Stalingrad* (New York, 1964).
Goerlitz, W., *Paulus and Stalingrad* (London, 1963).
Schröter, H., *Stalingrad* (New York, 1958).

Stalin Line, a system of deep defences and deep deployment of troops built during the 1930s deep inside the USSR's Western frontier. Consisting of a series of thirteen fortified regions it was constructed as a springboard for an offensive as well as for defensive purposes. Unlike the *Maginot Line it could not be outflanked on land as it stretched from the Baltic to the Black seas. After the Soviet occupation of eastern Poland in October 1939 it was largely dismantled as it was too far away from the new Soviet border for offensive purposes, and Stalin was no longer thinking in defensive terms.

Stark, Admiral Harold R. (1880–1972), US naval officer who, as Chief of Naval Operations (CNO), held the highest post in the US Navy at the time the Japanese attacked *Pearl Harbor in December 1941. Soon afterwards he was suceeded by Admiral *King when Roosevelt resurrected the post of C-in-C of the US Fleet and appointed King to it. Stark remained as CNO until March 1942 when he was appointed to command US naval forces in Europe, a liaison post which he retained until August 1945.

The apportioning of blame for the attack on Pearl Harbor clouded much of Stark's later career. The findings of the navy's court of enquiry, released in August 1945, led to King ordering that Stark should not again hold a post requiring the exercise of superior judgement, a decision King later admitted had been too harsh. In 1946, when a Congressional inquiry was established on Pearl Harbor, two Republicans on it wanted Stark accused of being part of a conspiracy to force the US into the war, but this was voted down by other members of the committee.

Larrabee, E., *Commander in Chief: Franklin D. Roosevelt, His Lieutenants, and Their War* (New York, 1987).

statistics. Accurate historical statistics are notoriously difficult to procure even under the most propitious of circumstances. The Second World War is no exception. It is true that under wartime regulations, and the mountain of additional paperwork that they generated, greater efforts were made to provide accurate statistics in areas vital to the war effort. But wartime dislocation and destruction created additional difficulties. The figures in the tables that follow are as complete as the published sources will allow; where a figure is simply not available, or is an estimate, this is indicated in the text.

A second problem is the comparability of statistics. The figures for aircraft or naval production, for example, say little about the weight or technical quality of the end product. In the last years of war German and Japanese aircraft production shifted to large numbers of fighter aircraft to combat bombing, while British and American

Statistics, Table 1: The costs of the War

State	*Bills. of national currency*
UK (1939–45)	£20.5
USA (1941–5)	$306.0
Germany (1939–45)	RM414.0
Japan (1941–5)	yen174.7
Italy (1940–3)	lire278.5
USSR (1941–5)	rbl582.0

Source: Contributor.

Statistics, Table 2: Military production

State	Weapons Category	1939	1940	1941	1942	1943	1944	1945[a]
UK	Aircraft	7,940	15,049	20,094	23,672	26,263	26,461	12,070
	Tanks	969	1,399	4,841	8,611	7,476	5,000	—
	Artillery[b]	—	1,900	5,300	6,600	12,200	12,400	—
	Major naval vessels[c]	57	148	236	239	224	188	64
USA	Aircraft	5,856	12,804	26,277	47,836	85,898	96,318	49,761
	Tanks	—	*c.*400	4,052	24,997	29,497	17,565	11,968
	Artillery	—	*c.*1,800	29,614	72,658	67,544	33,558	19,699
	Major naval vessels	—	—	544	1,854	2,654	2,247	1,513
Germany	Aircraft	8,295	10,247	11,776	15,409	24,807	39,807	7,540
	Tanks	c.1,300	2,200	5,200	9,200	17,300	22,100	—
	Artillery[b]	—	5,000	7,000	12,000	27,000	41,000	—
	Submarines	15	40	196	244	270	288 (+99 midget submarines)	103 (midget submarines only)
Japan	Aircraft	4,467	4,768	5,088	8,861	16,693	28,180	11,066
	Tanks	—	1,023	1,024	1,191	790	401	142
	Major naval vessels	21	30	49	68	122	248	51
USSR	Aircraft	10,382	10,565	15,735	25,436	34,900	40,300	20,900
	Tanks	2,950	2,794	6,590	24,446	24,089	28,963	15,400
	Artillery	17,348	15,300	42,300	127,000	130,000	122,400	93,000 (Jan–Mar)
	Major naval vessels	—	33	62	19	13	23	11

[a] figures for UK Jan–Aug, for US Jan–Aug, for Japan Jan–Aug, for Germany Jan–April, for USSR whole year
[b] over 37mm
[c] excludes landing-craft, torpedo boats, and smaller auxiliary vessels

Source: Contributor.

aircraft industries built large numbers of heavier and more technically complex machines. In 1944 Axis output was 40% of the number of Allied 'planes; but it was only 20% of Allied structure weight. Again German and Japanese naval production by the middle of the war was concentrated on submarine output or, in the case of the Japanese, the building of small suicide boats. American shipyards built a whole range of vessels, including more than 100 aircraft carriers, and hundreds of cruisers and destroyers. There are clear dangers in comparing raw figures on numbers produced, and this should be borne in mind when using the figures cited below.

There were also marked differences in the structures of the different war economies (see WORLD TRADE) which are not immediately apparent from the raw data. Take the figures on female employment (Table 4). Both

Statistics, Table 3: Strength of the Armed Forces (millions)

	UK	USA	USSR	Germany	Japan
1939	0.5	0.6	1.6	1.3	1.6
1940	2.3	0.7	4.2	5.6	1.7
1941	3.4	1.9	4.2	7.2	2.4
1942	4.1	4.8	10.9	8.6	2.8
1943	4.8	11.1	11.0	9.5	3.8
1944	5.0	14.8	11.2	9.1	5.3

Source: Contributor.

Statistics, Table 4: Women workers as a percentage of the civilian workforce

	Germany[a]	UK	USA	Japan	USSR Ind.	USSR Agric.
1939	37.3	26.4	—	—	—	52.0
1940	41.4	29.8	25.8	39.4	41.0	
1941	42.6	33.2	26.6	—	—	—
1942	46.0	36.1[b]	28.8	—	53.0	—
1943	48.8	37.7[b]	34.2	—	57.0	73.0
1944	51.6	37.9[b]	35.7	41.9	—	—

[a] figure for May each year. UK figure for June each year. Japanese figure for Oct 1940 and Feb 1944.
[b] includes part-time workers (2 part-time = 1 full-time)

Source: Contributor.

Statistics, Table 6: Sources of oil supply for major combatant powers

Germany (000 tonnes)

	Total Imported	Home Production Natural	Home Production Synthetic	from the USSR	from Romania	War booty
1939	5,165	1,465	2,200	5	848	745
1940	2,075	1,465	3,348	617	1,177	112
1941	2,807	1,562	4,116	248	2,963	n.a.
1942	2,359	1,686	4,920	0	2,192	140
1943	2,766	1,883	5,748	0	2,406	0
1944	961	1,681	3,822	0	1,043[a]	0

N.B. The United States is not included as it was self-sufficient in oil supplies
[a] includes oil delivered direct to the German armed forces

Japan (000 barrels)[a]

	Crude oil imports	Refined oil imports	Home production (natrual & synthetic)	Total domestic stocks	Imported from Netherland East Indies	Produced in Netherlands East Indies[c]
1939	18,843	11,818	2,332	51,398	*c.*3,000	—
1940	22,050	15,110	2,063	49,581	*c.*3,500	59,109
1941	3,130	5,242	1,941	48,893	0[b]	60,100
1942	8,146	2,378	1,690	38,229	10,524	25,939
1943	9,848	4,652	1,814	25,327	14,500	49,626
1944	1,641	3,334	1,585	13,816	4,975	36,928
1945	0	0	809	4,946	0	6,546

[a] It is not possible to equate barrels with tonnage acurrately as it depends on the type of oil being transported. Very roughly, one metric tonne of crude oil (average density) equals 7.5 barrels; One metric tonne of aviation fuel (Kerosene) equals .128 of a barrel.
[b] During 1941 the Dutch embargoed oil supplies to Japan. Imports came mainly from Mexico and the Middle East.
[c] The bulk of production in the period 1942–5 was consumed by Japanese army and navy forces in the South Pacific or was sunk in transit to the home islands.

United Kingdom

	Total imports (000 tons)	Home production (shale oil)	from USA	from Caribbean[a] (per cent)	from Iran (per cent)	from East Med.[b]	Other[b]
1939	11,618	517	19.2	46.2	23.8	7.0	3.8
1940	11,271	660	16.9	47.7	16.8	11.0	7.6
1941	13,128	784	54.5	41.7	0.8	0.0	3.0
1942	10,258	950	60.0	40.0	—	—	—
1943	14,795	1,046	75.7	24.3	—	—	—
1944	20,344	1,057	79.0	21.0	—	—	—
1945	15,617	997	not known	not known	—	—	—

[a] Mainly from Mexico, Trinidad, and Venezuela.
[b] In 1939–40 these supplies came principally from Romania and the Persian Gulf. In 1941 imports from Romania ceased, and Middle East output was sent direct to forces in North Africa, Iraq, and India rather than to the British Isles. In 1939 Romania supplied 5.5% of British imports, and 4.2% in 1940.

Soviet Union (million tonnes)

	Home production	Lend-Lease supplies	
1941	33.0	1941–5 total 2.84 Incl.	
1942	22.0	aviation fuel	1.163
1943	18.0	oils for blending	0.834
1944	18.2	fuel oil	0.287
1945	19.4	motor oil	0.267

Source: Contributor.

Statistics, Table 5: A Comparison of the German and British war effort

	Index of consumer spending (per capita, 1938 = 100)		*War expenditure as a % National Income*	
	Germany	*UK*	*Germany*	*UK*
1939	95.0	97.2	32.2	15.0
1940	88.4	89.7	48.8	43.0
1941	81.9	87.1	56.0	52.0
1942	75.3	86.6	65.6	52.0
1943	75.3	85.5	71.3	55.0
1944	70.0	88.2	—	54.0

Source: Contributor.

Germany and the Soviet Union had very large agricultural sectors characterized in the one case by small peasant farms, in the latter by the collective farm. Both were compelled to use large quantities of female labour power to keep the farms going since the armed forces took a large proportion of the able-bodied male workforce. The result was an unusually high proportion of *women in the overall workforce. Female workers in the UK and the USA, on the other hand, were largely drawn from a pre-war pool of unemployed women, who were recruited to work in the new war industries. In the UK male farmers were regarded as a necessary skilled workforce and were kept for the most part at home to secure much-needed food supplies.

Under these circumstances it might well be asked why statistics are used at all. They are supplied here as a rough guide to the quantitative picture of wartime economy and society. If they sometimes tell only part of the story, they do provide a starting point. For all their limitations they make clear the extraordinary scale of the domestic war effort in mobilizing men for the front, in diverting the civilian economy to the many purposes of war and in trespassing on the lives and livelihoods of non-combatants. All the major warring states, save the US, devoted well over half their national product to fighting the war, and mobilized in the forces or in industry almost two-thirds of their active population. This was an exceptional feat of organization and mobilization; it is difficult to imagine that states today could afford its cost and level of sacrifice without intolerable strain. Behind the printed figures lies another story of populations subjected for years to extraordinary strains and losses. On issues such as these statistics remain dumbly eloquent. See also DEMOGRAPHY.

RICHARD OVERY

Statistics, Table 7: Civilian production (coal, steel, aluminium, oil)

State	*Material*	*1939*	*1940*	*1941*	*1942*	*1943*	*1944*	*1945*
UK	coal	231.3	224.2	206.3	204.9	198.9	192.7	182.7
	steel	13.2	12.9	12.3	12.7	13.0	12.1	11.8
	aluminium	24.9	18.9	22.6	46.7	55.6	35.4	31.9
	oil (shale oil)	517	660	784	950	1,046	1,057	997
USA	coal	394.8	460.8	514.1	582.7	590.2	619.6	577.6
	steel	47.1	59.8	73.9	76.8	79.3	80.0	71.1
	aluminium	163.5	206.3	309.1	521.1	920.2	776.4	496.5
	oil	1,265.0	1,353.2	1,402.2	1,386.6	1,505.6	1,677.9	1,713.7
Germany	coal	240.3	267.7	315.5	317.9	340.4	347.6	—
	steel	23.7	21.4	28.2	28.7	30.6	25.8	—
	aluminium	199.4	211.2	233.6	264.0	250.0	245.3	—
	oil[a]	3.6	4.8	5.7	6.6	7.6	5.5	1.3
Japan	coal	52.4	57.3	55.6	54.1	55.5	49.3	—
	steel	5.5	5.3	5.1	5.1	5.6	4.3	—
	aluminium	29.5	40.8	71.7	103.0	141.0	110.3	—
	oil[a]	2.3	2.0	1.8	1.7	1.8	1.6	0.8
USSR	coal	146.2	165.9	151.4	75.5	93.1	121.5	149.3
	steel	17.6	18.3	17.9	8.1	8.5	10.9	12.3
	aluminium	—	—	—	51.7	62.3	82.7	86.3
	oil	30.3	31.1	33.0	22.0	18.0	18.2	19.4

[a] German and Japanese production of synthetic oil and domestic supplies of natural crude oil

figures for UK: coal and steel in million long tons, aluminium and shale oil in thousands of tons
figures for USA: coal and steel in millions of US tons (2,000 lbs), aluminium in thousands of US tons, oil in millions of barrels
figures for Germany: coal, steel, and oil in million metric tons, aluminium in thousands of metric tons
figures for Japan: coal, steel, oil in millions of metric tons, aluminium in thousands of metric tons
figures for USSR: coal, steel, oil in millions of metric tons, aluminium in thousands of metric tons

Source: Contributor.

Statistics, Table 8: Sources and use of strategic raw materials (excl. iron ore, oil, and coal)

Material	*Chief sources, 1938*	*Chief wartime use*
Bauxite ore	France, 16.5%; British Guiana, 13.8%; Hungary, 13.1%; USA, 7.7%	ore for aluminium, chiefly used for aircraft production
Antimony ore	China, 22.2%; Mexico, 22.2%; Bolivia, 25.8%	lead hardener, used for shells and bullets
Chrome ore	Turkey, 20.6%; S. Rhodesia, 17.5%; USSR, 17.3%; S. Africa, 15.3%	steel alloy, used in armour plate and for warships
Cobalt	Belgian Congo, 32%; N. Rhodesia, 28%; French Morocco, 16%	steel alloy, used for machine tools
Copper	USA, 24.9%; Chile, 17.3%; Canada, 12.7%; N. Rhodesia, 12.6%	cartridge cases, radio sets, aircraft
Cotton	USA, 41%; India, 14%; USSR, 10%; China, 10	clothing
Lead	USA, 18.7%; Mexico, 15.7%; Australia, 15.6%; Canada 11%	bullets, shells, batteries
Magnesite	USSR, 37%; Austria, 21%; USA, 16%; Manchuria, 14.5%	incendiary bombs
Manganese	USSR, 41.3%; India, 17.6%	steel production
Mercury	Italy, 44.4%; Spain 27.9%; USA, 11.9%	detonating agent, electrical equipment
Molybdenum	USA, 92.4%	steel alloy for machine tools, aircraft parts
Nickel ore	Canada, 87% equipment	steel alloy used for aero-engines, marine
Phosphates	USA, 26.8%; USSR, 15.8%; Tunisia, 14%; French Morocco, 11.9%	fertilizers
Potash	Germany, 62.2%; France, 19.4%; USA, 9.6%	fertilizers
Pyrites	Spain, 22.2%; Japan, 16.7%; Norway, 11%; Italy, 10%	steel production
Rubber	Malaya, 41.5%; Netherlands East Indies, 33.3%	tyres
Sulphur	USA, 78%; Italy, 12.8%	explosives
Tin ore	Malaya, 26.7%; Netherlands East Indies, 16.9%; Bolivia, 15.8%	alloy for bronze, gun-metal etc.
Titanium	India, 68%; Norway, 25%	smoke-screens, steel alloy for cutting tools
Tungsten	China, 37.7%; Burma, 16.5%	steel alloy for machine tools, armour plate, armour-piercing shells
Vanadium ore	Peru, 31.2%; USA, 27.3%; S.W. Africa, 17%; N. Rhodesia, 13%	steel alloy for high-speed tools, engine parts, locomotives
Wool	Australia, 26%; Argentina, 10%; USA, 12%	clothing
Zinc ore	USA, 25.1%; Australia, 11.9%; Germany, 11.9%; Canada, 10%	electrical components, electroplating, wire, propellers

Source: Contributor.

Stavka. From June 1941, the Soviet armed forces did not have an explicitly designated commander-in chief. The function was assumed to be vested in the People's Commissar (minister) of Defence, Marshal *Timoshenko, who, upon the outbreak of a general war, would organize a *stavka* (general headquarters) under himself. However, Stalin alone possessed the authority to make the kind of decisions necessitated by the German invasion (see BARBAROSSA), and he was not disposed to delegate it. On 19 July 1941, after an attempt to run a *stavka* in which Timoshenko was chairman and he a member, Stalin, having also recovered somewhat from the first shock of the war, took over as chairman and defence commissar.

In early August, when the situation appeared to be stabilizing, Stalin named himself Supreme Commander-in-Chief, formed the Stavka of the Supreme Commander and charged it with directing military operations in accordance with strategic requirements determined by the State Defence Committee, which he also headed. He and Marshal *Shaposhnikov, chief of the general staff, which was the Stavka's planning and executive agency, were the only members with regularized functions in a body that was otherwise consultative. *Molotov and Admiral N. G. Kuznetsov represented their commissariats, foreign and naval affairs respectively. Marshals Timoshenko, *Voroshilov and *Budenny, and General *Zhukov served as Stalin thought they could be best used at a given time. Zhukov, particularly, and Timoshenko, quickly proved effective at high-level field command. Voroshilov and Budenny failed about as quickly, but Stalin kept them on for personal and political reasons. The Stavka only met on Stalin's call, which as time passed came more and more infrequently, and the greater part of the decisions attributed to it were Stalin's alone.

During the winter offensive of 1941–2, when he believed victory was in sight, Stalin regarded the Stavka as no more than the means of ensuring total compliance

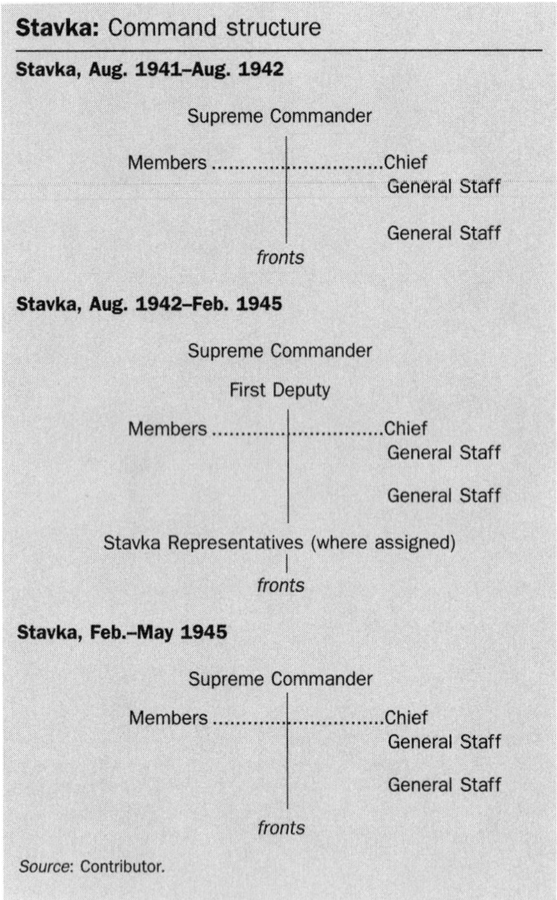

with his orders. The following summer's defeats forced him to revise his command style; and in August 1942, he made Zhukov first deputy C-in-C and first deputy defence commissar, which placed him a clear second in the command channel and gave him access to the general staff apparatus. Together with its chief (since June 1942), General *Vasilevsky, Zhukov organized the *Stalingrad counter-offensive and solved a major Soviet command problem which was an inability to perform sophisticated large-scale manoeuvres, such as encirclements. Soviet *fronts* (army groups) possessed only about a third the span of control of German army groups, and their performance was uneven. At Stalingrad, as Stavka representatives, Zhukov and Vasilevsky personally co-ordinated three fronts in the preparation and the battle, and they brought in—also as Stavka representatives—the army branch chiefs for air, armour, and artillery to supervise their contingents. The result was a masterly encirclement that, with Hitler's help, culminated in a shattering German defeat.

In early 1943, the Red Army was as close to having a professional C-in-C as it ever would be. Zhukov appears to have had the deciding voice in military operations. But Stalin's self-confidence was reviving as well. Very likely because they were the most proficient but also, no doubt, to protect his own position, Stalin kept Zhukov and Vasilevsky in the field co-ordinating fronts from June 1943 to April 1944 and from June to October 1944. As successes multiplied, he increasingly asserted his prerogatives.

In October 1944, when preparations for the final offensives began, he gave Zhukov command of First Belorussian *front* and recalled Vasilevsky to Moscow to plan a campaign against the Japanese *Kwantung Army (see JAPANESE–SOVIET CAMPAIGNS). He told Zhukov that although two *fronts* besides his would be involved in the drive to *Berlin, his services as co-ordinator would not be needed because everything could be handled from Moscow.

On 17 and 18 February 1945, Stalin sent Vasilevsky to take command of Third Belorussian *front* in east Prussia and reorganized the Stavka. General A. I. Antonov, who had substituted for Vasilevsky during his absences, became chief of the general staff and a member. N. A. Bulganin (1895–1975), a political *commissar with the assimilated rank of general, became a member. Kuznetsov represented the navy. Zhukov and Vasilevsky were retained in the anomalous position of members functioning at a subordinate command level. Vasilevsky's memoirs indicate that he had not previously known he was a member, which may disclose much about the Stavka's collegial status. The Stavka terminated before the war against Japan, in which Vasilevsky, as C-in-C, Far East, served directly under Generalissimo of the Soviet Union Stalin. See also USSR 6(a). EARL ZIEMKE

steel helmets were reinvented on the Western Front in 1915 and worn by most troops engaged in close-quarter fighting. They gave no protection against *small arms, but they gave some confidence under fire to the wearer and gave him a measure of protection against shell or grenade fragments, falling masonry, and so on. The British pattern had a horizontal brim, above the ears; German helmets came lower down over the back of the neck; American, French, Japanese, and Soviet designs were nearer to the German than to the British shape. Commandos and parachutists, out of panache, preferred not to wear them, and suffered accordingly; Waffen-*SS were more professional. They were also worn by civil defence workers. M. R. D. FOOT

Stephenson, Sir William (1896–1989), Canadian-born *First World War fighter ace and pugilist who in August 1940 formed *British Security Co-ordination. His influence was wide and varied, and his role, especially during the early years of the war, of establishing a close Anglo-American relationship in security and intelligence matters, was important enough to earn him a knighthood in 1944 and for him to be the first non-American to receive the highest US civilian decoration, the Medal of Merit (see DECORATIONS). But he never acted as a secret liaison between Churchill and Roosevelt, was not codenamed INTREPID by Churchill, whom he probably never even met, nor did he contribute to unravelling the mysteries of the *ENIGMA cipher machine, or play any part in secret activities outside the *Western Hemisphere.

Stern gang. Also called Lehi, an acronym derived from Lohamei Herut Yisrael (Fighters for the Freedom of Israel). It was a splinter group of the *Irgun formed in Palestine in 1940 whose leader, Abraham Stern, opposed Irgun's truce with the British. He sought a *modus vivendi* with the Nazis, which lost him much support, and he lacked the resources for a terror campaign that went beyond assassinating policemen. He was killed by British security forces in February 1942, but the gang survived under its new leader, Yitzhak *Shamir. In November 1944 it killed Lord Moyne, the British minister in the Middle East.

Stetsko, Yaroslav (1912–86), born in Tarnopol (Ternopil) in Austrian Galicia and a member of the pre-war Organization of Ukrainian Nationalists (OUN). He was prime minister of the independent Ukrainian state proclaimed in *Lwów (Lviv) on 30 June 1941. Having refused to collaborate with the Nazis, he was arrested on 12 July and interned in *Sachsenhausen along with another Ukrainian nationalist, Stepan *Bandera. After the war Stetsko served as chairman of the OUN and was active in the Anti-Bolshevik Bloc of Nations and the World Anti-Communist League. See also UKRAINE. L. Y. Luciuk

Stettinius, Edward R. Jr. (1900–49), wealthy US industrialist who became chairman of the War Resources Board in 1939 and in May 1940 a member of the Advisory Commission to the Council of National Defense. In January 1941 he became director of the Office of Production Management and that August he was appointed administrator of the *Lend-Lease programme, a task he performed with great distinction. He succeeded Sumner *Welles as under-secretary of state in September 1943 and played a leading role at the *Dumbarton Oaks conference the following year. In November 1944 he succeeded Cordell *Hull as secretary of state, a position he held until June 1945 when he attended the *San Francisco conference as the first US ambassador to the United Nations. See also USA, 3.

Campbell, T., and Herring, G. (eds.), *The Diaries of Edward Stettinius Jr, 1943–46* (New York, 1975).

sticky bomb, British hand grenade (no. 74), developed by *MD1, which stuck to armoured targets such as tanks to maximize the explosion. It was a glass (or plastic) sphere with a handle attached for throwing. The sphere broke on contact allowing an adhesive 'sock' of plastic *explosive inside it to spread like a poultice on to the armour. As the Boys rifle (see SMALL ARMS) proved useless, it was the only effective weapon the British infantryman had against armour until the *PIAT was introduced.

Stilwell, General Joseph W. (1883–1946), US Army officer who, as *Chiang Kai-shek's Allied chief of staff in Chiang's capacity as a Supreme Allied Commander, commanded US and Chinese forces in the *China–Burma–India theatre.

After serving in France during the *First World War, where he rose to the rank of colonel, Stilwell had four tours of duty in China which made him fluent in the language and familiar with its people. The US Army chief of staff, General *Marshall, thought him one of the most brilliant and cultured men in the US Army and in February 1942 he was appointed to head the US military mission to China, to supervise *Lend-Lease to the country, and to be Chiang Kai-shek's Allied chief of staff with the rank of lt-general. In March he took nominal control of two Chinese armies (equal to two reinforced US divisions) in the *Burma campaign and, when the Japanese were driving all before them, led a small group of refugees 225 km. (140 mi.) across the mountains to India. When asked about the 'glorious retreat' and 'heroic voluntary withdrawal' described by the British generals, Stilwell replied with typical forthrightness that 'no military commander in history ever made a voluntary withdrawal. And there's no such thing as a glorious retreat. All retreats are as ignominious as hell. I claim we got a hell of a licking.' This did not increase his popularity with the British whom he anyway disliked.

Operating primarily from Chiang's capital Chungking, he tried to improve the fighting efficiency of the Chinese forces and increase the effectiveness of US aid, tasks which proved political minefields. A meeting with Roosevelt at the Cairo conference in December 1943 (see SEXTANT) did nothing to clarify his mission which had become no simpler when, two months previously, he had been made deputy Supreme Allied commander under *Mountbatten in the newly formed *South-East Asia Command.

In October 1943 Chinese troops belonging to Stilwell's Northern Combat Area Command, who were led by his deputy, Brig-General Hayden Boatner, began the battle to recapture northern Burma. When Boatner fell ill Stilwell took command and, with the help of Merrill's Marauders (see GALAHAD) and the *Chindits, eventually retook *Myitkyina, the strategic key to the area, in August 1944. This campaign, which opened a shorter air route for supplies to China than the *Hump, proved Stilwell's point that Chinese troops, if properly treated, could fight, and gained him promotion to four-star general.

Meanwhile, the Japanese had begun an offensive (ICHI-GŌ) which swept across central and southern China, but when Roosevelt suggested Stilwell command all Chinese forces to resist it, Chiang, no ally of Stilwell's, demurred, and in October 1944 had Stilwell recalled. From June to October 1945 Stilwell commanded Tenth US Army on *Okinawa. He died of cancer five months before he was due to retire.

Stilwell possessed a fierce integrity, and a hatred of incompetence and pretentiousness, but as Mountbatten found out, he could also be devious and secretive (see

AXIOM MISSION). He was probably unsuited to the intricate problems he faced, as temperamentally—and despite being purblind—he was a fighting general not a diplomat. His cantankerous personality earned him the nickname 'Vinegar Joe', but, as has been pointed out, if Saint Francis of Assisi had been sent to China in Stilwell's place, he would now probably be known as Vinegar Frank.

Carver, M. (ed.), *The War Lords* (London, 1976).
Tuchman, B., *Sand Against the Wind: Stilwell and the American Experience in China, 1911–45* (New York, 1970).
White, T. H. (ed.), *The Stilwell Papers* (New York, 1948).

Stimson, Henry L. (1867–1950), US Republican lawyer and statesman who from 1940 to 1945 served as Roosevelt's, and then *Truman's, secretary of war, a position he had first held from 1911 to 1913.

Stimson fought as a lt-colonel in the field artillery in France in 1917 and between the wars served as governor-general of the Philippines and then secretary of state in President Herbert Hoover's cabinet. Though his name was attached to the doctrine of non-interference when Japan occupied Manchuria in 1931, throughout the 1930s he was an ardent opponent of *fascism and was against neutrality as a policy to avoid war. In June 1940 Roosevelt appointed him secretary of war and Stimson immediately began to give order and direction to a department which needed both. He quickly surrounded himself with a group of able aides, established a good working relationship with the army's chief of staff, General *Marshall, and gave increasing independence to the Army Air Forces. He was also an early backer of *radar-equipped aircraft to hunt U-boats—though he could not get the navy to collaborate in the methods he espoused—and some avow that his greatest contribution was to persuade the military to acquaint itself with the flow of new scientific ideas and their application.

One of Stimson's first decisions after the USA entered the war, and one of his hardest, was to evacuate all *Japanese-Americans from the Californian coastline. He was a strong advocate for the earliest possible landing on continental Europe and argued his case in this and other matters with frankness and persistence. In his diaries he frequently condemned Roosevelt's 'topsy-turvy' system of administration—it was he who said that conferring with the president was 'very much like chasing a vagrant beam of sunshine around a vacant room'—but Roosevelt said he could trust him with anything, which he often did.

As the war progressed, Stimson, to his annoyance, was increasingly bypassed by Roosevelt on questions of strategy, tactics, and operations, as the president chose to confer with Marshall direct on these matters. From its earliest days Stimson bore the responsibility for the development of the *atomic bomb: in 1943 he negotiated with Churchill in London on total exchange of information and ideas about nuclear energy, and in 1945 chaired the interim committee which advised Truman on the use of the atomic bomb.

To many Stimson was stern, reserved, and forbidding. But he was a man of high principle—it was he who between the wars, opposed the breaking of codes, saying that gentlemen did not read other people's mail—and of rocklike determination. He also possessed a strong humanity: the removal of Japanese-Americans from the west coast disturbed him greatly and he called the *Morgenthau Plan 'a crime against civilization itself'.

Hodgson, G., *The Colonel* (New York, 1990).
Stimson, H. L., and Bundy, M., *On Active Service in Peace and War* (New York, 1948).

stonk, see ARTILLERY, 2.

Stopford, Lt-General Montagu (1892–1971), British Army officer who, from the end of 1943, commanded 33rd Indian Corps, part of *Slim's Fourteenth Army fighting the *Burma campaign. He played a critical role in stemming the Japanese *Imphal offensive of March 1944 by raising the siege of *Kohima. In March 1945 he captured *Mandalay and after Rangoon fell that May he took command of the newly formed Twelfth Army. He commanded *South-East Asia Command from June 1946 until it was disbanded later that year.

Stormvogel (stormbird), name of the bomber version of the German jet, the Messerschmitt 262. See BOMBERS.

strategic air offensives.

1. Against Germany

The immediate origins of the campaign are to be found in the long-range bombing of the *First World War. The Germans, who could not invade or effectively blockade the UK due to their relative lack of sea power, tried a direct attack by bombing. This was done by Zeppelins and increasingly, from May 1917, by aeroplanes, of which the Gotha was the most effective. These raids, and especially those of the Gothas on London in June and July 1917, caused alarm bordering on panic in Lloyd George's cabinet. *Smuts was appointed to produce a solution to this new threat. His conclusion was that direct defence against long-range and high-level bombers, even in daylight, was not feasible and that the only answer was a counter-offensive of greater power. He thought this offensive would be so important that he recommended the creation of a new and separate fighting service with its own independent staff to bring the campaign into action. The result was the creation on 1 April 1918 of the Royal Air Force with the central task of waging a direct bombing offensive aimed at the sources of Germany's war effort, such as its war industries and transport system.

Little progress had been made towards a test by experience of what long-range bombers could achieve when the war was determined by conventional means in November 1918. This meant that those who were

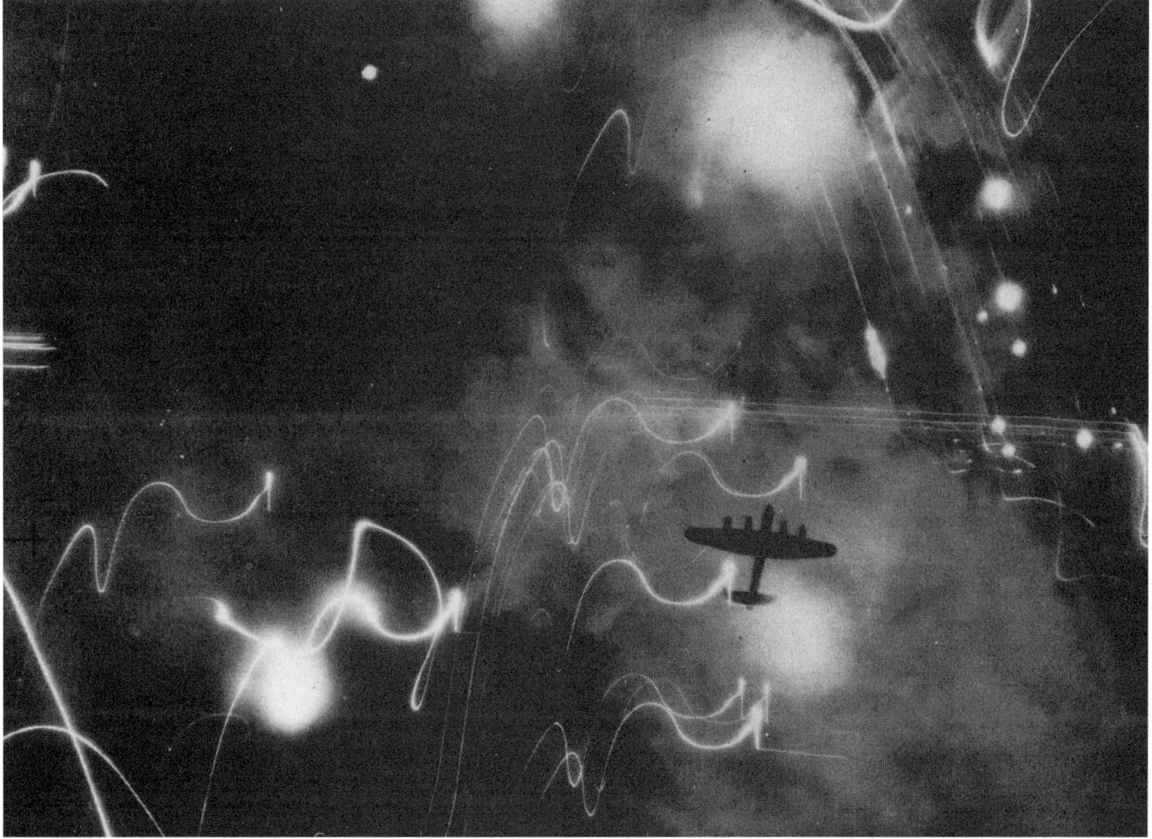

A British Lancaster bomber over Hamburg as seen from another Lancaster during the **strategic air offensive** against Germany.

advocates of the decisive prospect of what soon became known as strategic bombing could not be proved by the sceptics to be wrong; it meant in effect that the British air staff, under the dynamic leadership of Marshal of the Royal Air Force Hugh Trenchard (1873–1956), was able to develop a theory of war which said that victory would come to the power which mounted the heaviest and most sustained bombing offensive. To a large extent, however, the idea remained a theory as opposed to the basis of an experiment; the Conservative Party in the UK was reluctant to devote financial and industrial resources to the arming of the country and the Labour Party was inclined to fall in with the view that bombing should be declared illegal by international agreement. So while the air staff produced memoranda setting out in increasing detail how an enemy, and, in particular, the German, war economy could be destroyed by bombing, they had little scope for testing the plans by realistic air exercises. Such exercises as were held did reveal a substantial gap between what was aimed at and what was possible, but shortcomings were largely disregarded on the grounds that the force was inadequately trained and equipped and that the aircraft were of obsolete vintage.

Hitler's arrival in power in 1933 produced a re-armament policy in the UK and the air staff proposed to give an overriding priority to the expansion of Bomber Command, which was created in 1936. Though a heavy bomber specification was issued, which eventually produced the Stirling, the Halifax, and, via the Manchester, the Lancaster, this did not produce effective operational results until March 1942. Indeed, the government over-ruled the air staff's priority and substituted one in favour of fighters, which were much cheaper per unit and therefore produced better figures to announce in the Commons when the subject was air parity with the Luftwaffe.

When war broke out in September 1939 the British had much the most advanced doctrine of strategic bombing, but the Germans had the larger air force and the Americans, as events were soon to prove, had far the greatest long-term potential. As the USA was neutral, the Germans had no theory of strategic bombing, and the British were unwilling to provoke an air attack by what they saw as a more effective opponent, the strategic air offensive was deferred, but in this breathing-space, first the British and then the Germans thought they had

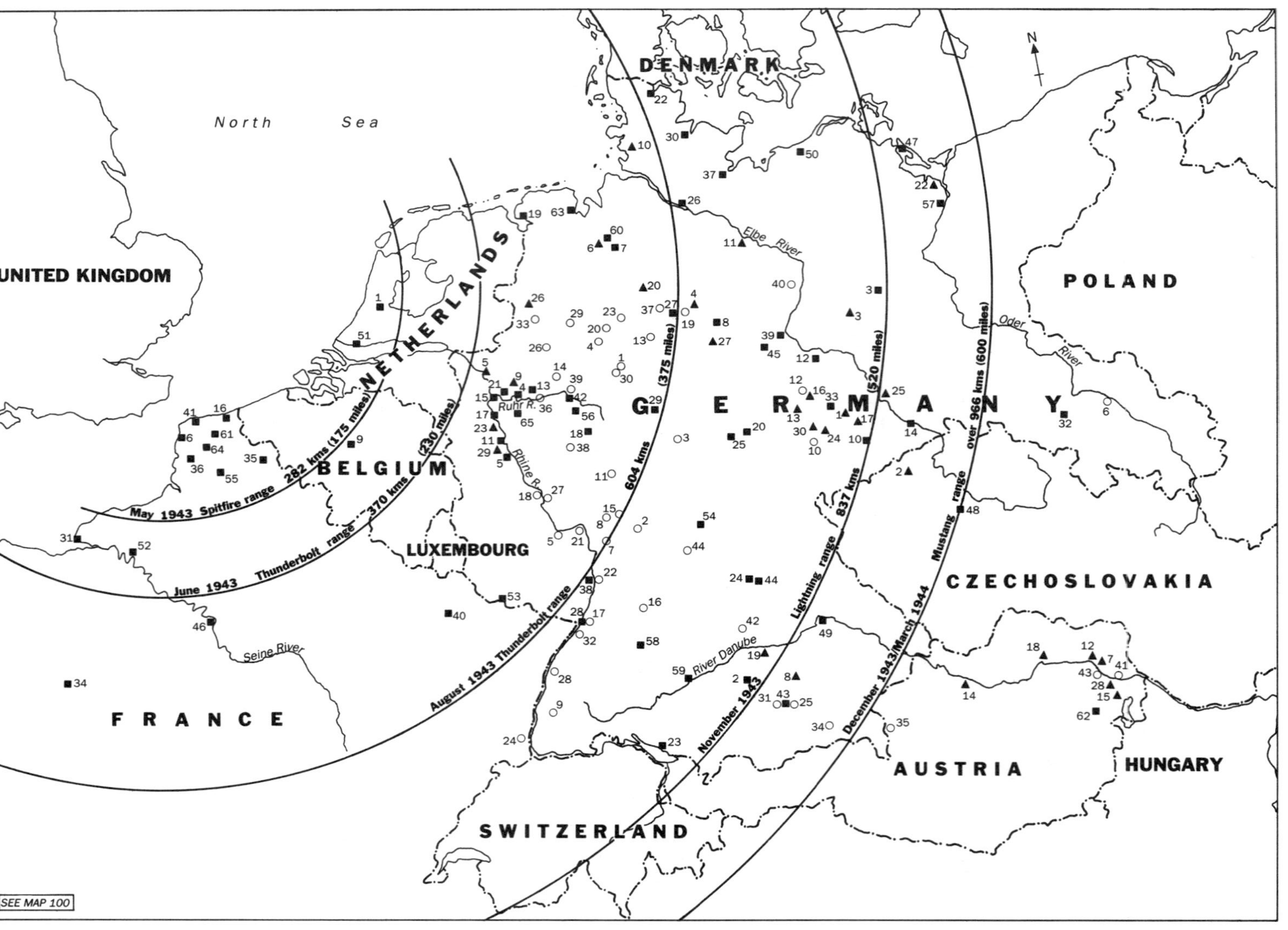

99. **Strategic air offensive** against Germany: principal targets of UK-based bombers, and limits of fighter cover, 1940–5

Map 99 Legend

—·—·— International boundary, January 1938

Scale 1:7 500 000

0 — 150 — 300 kms

0 — 75 — 150 miles

Conic Projection

Key Bombing Targets
(numbers refer to list below)

▲ Oil

1 Böhlen
2 Brüx (Most)
3 Derben
4 Dollbergen
5 Dülmen
6 Farge
7 Floridsdorf
8 Freiham
9 Gelsenkirchen
10 Heide
11 Hitzacker
12 Korneuburg
13 Leuna
14 Linz
15 Lobau
16 Lützkendorf
17 Mölbis
18 Moosbierbaum
19 Neuburg
20 Nienburg
21 Ploesti
22 Pölitz
23 Reisholz
24 Rositz
25 Ruhland
26 Salzbergen
27 Salzgitter
28 Schwechat
29 Wesseling
30 Zeitz

○ Railways

1 Altenbecken Neuenbecken
2 Aschaffenburg
3 Bebra
4 Bielefeld
5 Bingen
6 Breslau
7 Darmstadt
8 Frankfurt
9 Freiburg
10 Gera
11 Giessen
12 Halle
13 Hameln
14 Hamm
15 Hanau
16 Heilbronn
17 Karlsruhe
18 Koblenz
19 Lehrte
20 Löhne
21 Mainz
22 Mannheim
23 Minden
24 Mulhouse
25 Munich
26 Münster
27 Oberlahnstein
28 Offenburg
29 Osnabrück
30 Paderborn
31 Pasing
32 Rastatt
33 Rheine
34 Rosenheim
35 Salzburg
36 Schwerte
37 Seelze
38 Siegen
39 Soest
40 Stendal
41 Strasshof
42 Treuchtlingen
43 Vienna
44 Würzburg

■ Industrial

1 Amsterdam
2 Augsburg
3 Berlin
4 Bochum
5 Bonn
6 Boulogne
7 Bremen
8 Brunswick
9 Brussels
10 Chemnitz
11 Cologne
12 Dessau
13 Dortmund
14 Dresden
15 Duisburg
16 Dunkirk
17 Düsseldorf
18 Eder Dam
19 Emden
20 Erfurt
21 Essen
22 Flensburg
23 Friedrichshafen
24 Fürth
25 Gotha
26 Hamburg
27 Hanover
28 Karlsruhe
29 Kassel
30 Kiel
31 le Havre
32 Leignitz
33 Leipzig
34 le Mans
35 Lille
36 Lottinghem
37 Lübeck
38 Ludwigshafen
39 Magdeburg
40 Metz
41 Mimovecques
42 Möhne Dam
43 Munich
44 Nuremberg
45 Oschersleben
46 Paris
47 Peenemünde
48 Prague
49 Regensburg
50 Rostock
51 Rotterdam
52 Rouen
53 Saarbrücken
54 Schweinfurt
55 Siracourt
56 Sorpe Dam
57 Stettin
58 Stuttgart
59 Ulm
60 Vegesack
61 Watten
62 Wiener Neustadt
63 Wilhelmshaven
64 Wizernes
65 Wuppertal

Strategic Air Offensive (Germany): RAF Bomber Command and Eighth USAAF: sorties flown, approximate tonnage of bombs dropped, and operational losses, September 1939–May 1945

The figures shown in brackets after RAF Bomber Command's monthly losses were those lost in crashes and are included in the monthly total. The figures for total losses before March 1942 are unreliable as it is not known if all the aircraft which crashed had to be written off. Sorties flown for sea and flying bomb patrols, and for minelaying and Special Duties, are not included.
The figures shown in brackets after Eighth USAAF monthly losses were those aircraft lost operationally for reasons other than being shot down by hostile A-A fire or aircraft, and they are included in the monthly total of losses.

[a] only night raids mounted during these months

A = number of sorties, B = approximate tonnage of bombs dropped in long tons,
C = operational losses.

	RAF Bomber Command			*Eighth USAAF*		
Dates	*A*	*B*	*C*	*A*	*B*	*C*
1939						
Sep	123	6	17(3)	–	–	–
Oct	32[a]	–	4(2)	–	–	–
Nov	19	–	1(1)	–	–	–
Dec	159	25	19(2)	–	–	–
1940						
Jan	44	1	0	–	–	–
Feb	58	1	3(2)	–	–	–
Mar	292	31	12(6)	–	–	–
Apr	656	112	41(8)	–	–	–
May	2,419	1,668	76(6)	–	–	–
Jun	3,296	2,300	65(8)	–	–	–
Jul	2,338	1,257	79(7)	–	–	–
Aug	2,605	1,365	81(11)	–	–	–
Sep	3,239	2,339	87(21)	–	–	–
Oct	2,414	1,651	60(32)	–	–	–
Nov	2,007	1,316	86(34)	–	–	–
Dec	1,441	992	62(23)	–	–	–
1941						
Jan	1,126	777	27(13)	–	–	–
Feb	1,741	1,431	52(34)	–	–	–
Mar	1,890	1,744	75(36)	–	–	–
Apr	2,925	2,396	98(19)	–	–	–
May	2,689	2,846	76(17)	–	–	–
Jun	3,759	4,310	116(18)	–	–	–
Jul	3,825	4,384	188(31)	–	–	–
Aug	3,812	4,242	206(50)	–	–	–
Sep	2,884	2,889	153(63)	–	–	–
Oct	2,639	2,984	126(41)	–	–	–
Nov	1,756	1,907	104(21)	–	–	–
Dec	1,562	1,794	51(16)	–	–	–
1942						
Jan	2,240	2,292	88(32)	–	–	–
Feb	1,414	1,011	48(15)	–	–	–
Mar	2,355	2,675	101(21)	–	–	–
Apr	3,998	4,433	174(31)	–	–	–
May	2,807	3,234	136(21)	–	–	–
Jun	4,997	6,845	241(40)	–	–	–
Jul	4,227	6,368	212(22)	–	–	–
Aug	2,640	4,162	173(21)	114	151	–
Sep	3,616	5,595	214(39)	183	188	2(0)
Oct	2,604	3,809	130(27)	284	278	10(2)

Strategic Air Offensive (Germany) *(cont.)*

	RAF Bomber Command			*Eighth USAAF*		
Dates	*A*	*B*	*C*	*A*	*B*	*C*
Nov	2,194	2,423	87(23)	519	604	13(3)
Dec	1,958	2,714	112(24)	353	340	17(0)
1943						
Jan	2,962	4,345	122(21)	338	594	18(0)
Feb	5,456	10,959	132(25)	526	568	23(2)
Mar	5,458	10,591	194(26)	956	1,483	21(3)
Apr	5,887	11,467	290(25)	449	858	29
May	5,490[a]	12,920	284(31)	1,672	2,555	69(8)
Jun	5,816[a]	15,271	290(15)	2,107	2,330	90(0)
Jul	6,170[a]	16,830	219(31)	2,829	3,475	118(10)
Aug	7,807[a]	20,149	308(33)	2,265	3,999	117(10)
Sep	5,513[a]	14,855	225(34)	3,259	7,369	98(27)
Oct	4,638[a]	13,773	180(21)	2,831	4,548	186(9)
Nov	5,208[a]	14,495	210(48)	4,157	5,751	95(17)
Dec	4,123[a]	11,802	217(47)	5,973	10,655	172(22)
1944						
Jan	6,278[a]	18,428	352(38)	6,367	10,532	203(37)
Feb	4,308	12,054	223(24)	9,884	16,480	271(20)
Mar	9,049	27,698	322(39)	11,590	19,892	345(55)
Apr	9,883	33,496	239(25)	14,464	22,447	420(1)
May	11,369	37,252	303(29)	19,825	32,450	376(43)
Jun	15,963	57,267	335(30)	28,925	54,204	320(46)
Jul	17,798	57,615	274(33)	23,917	40,784	352(71)
Aug	20,284	65,855	244(23)	22,967	44,120	331(32)
Sep	16,071	52,587	152(15)	18,268	36,332	374(30)
Oct	16,906	61,204	153(26)	19,082	38,961	177(29)
Nov	14,644	53,022	173(34)	17,003	36,091	209(13)
Dec	14,895	49,040	162(43)	18,252	36,826	119(17)
1945						
Jan	10,907	32,923	190(57)	17,702	34,891	314(43)
Feb	17,400	45,889	233(60)	22,884	46,088	196(25)
Mar	21,191	67,637	301(86)	31,169	65,962	266(39)
Apr	13,823	34,954	108(35)	20,154	41,632	190(41)
May	1,417	337	6(1)	2,276	—	7(2)
TOTALS	373,514	955,044	10,123(1,796)	332,904	621,877	5,548(657)

Sources: Webster, C. and Frankland, N., *The Strategic Offensive against Germany, 1939–45*, Vol. 4, (London, 1961), and Freeman, R., *The US Strategic Bomber* (London, 1975).

learned the same lesson. This was that the vulnerability of heavy bombers to defending fighters meant that long-range bombing by day beyond the range of high-performance escorting fighters such as Me109s or Spitfires was not a feasible operation of war. When therefore, in May 1940, the desperate situation of the war on land drove the British to embark upon the long-planned strategic air attack on Germany, the Wellingtons, Whitleys, and Hampdens went into action at night. Similarly, when the Germans were frustrated in their attempt to destroy RAF Fighter Command in the battle of *Britain, they too turned to night attack (see BLITZ). The cover of darkness, which afforded the bombers a substantial degree of protection, also prevented the crews from seeing their targets, or indeed, for the greater part, getting anywhere near them. Thus, the original targets, which had been individual installations, such as oil plants or factories, or complexes, such as marshalling yards or dock areas, were abandoned in favour of larger ones. In the course of 1941, it became clear from photographic evidence (see BUTT REPORT) that the smallest targets which were operationally feasible at night with the aircraft and equipment in service were whole towns. Thus, the British had the choice between abandoning the bomber offensive, which at the time was the only available means of striking direct blows at Germany, or of adopting the policy of attacking the centres of large towns. In the situation of the war at the end of 1941, it is scarcely surprising that the latter course was selected and a tactical policy known as *area bombing was adopted.

The British attack upon German towns was thus

dictated by operational and tactical reasons, but there also seemed to be strong strategic arguments in favour of it. These were cogently urged in the government and in the *Chiefs of Staff Committee by Churchill's scientific adviser, Lord Cherwell (see LINDEMANN), and they were readily accepted, and, indeed, also advocated by the chief of the air staff, *Portal, and by *Harris, who took over as AOC-in-C of Bomber Command in February 1942. Harris seized this new initiative by mounting dramatic fire raids on Lübeck and Rostock in the spring of 1942. At the end of May 1942 he called up the whole of his second line of operational training units and launched a thousand bombers in a single attack upon a single target, Cologne (see also THOUSAND-BOMBER RAIDS). Thereafter, with massive reinforcements of men and machines, the introduction of aids to navigation and bomb aiming (see ELECTRONIC NAVIGATION SYSTEMS), and the development of increasingly ingenious tactics, he embarked upon a systematic attempt to tear the heart out of the major German industrial and transport towns from the Ruhr to Berlin. In March 1942, serious damage was done in the Ruhr; in July 1943 *Hamburg was set alight and upwards of 40,000 people killed; and in November 1943 the prime aim was shifted to the middle of Berlin. Harris declared that the battle would cost Bomber Command 400–500 aircraft but that, if the Americans would come in on the attack, it would cost Germany the war.

During the air offensive against *Berlin, between 18 November 1943 and 31 March 1944, Harris dispatched some 9,111 bomber sorties in 16 major attacks. He also sent another 11,113 against other major towns elsewhere for he could never concentrate exclusively on one target since that would have enabled the defences to concentrate too. From all these operations 1,047 bombers failed to return and a further 1,682 were damaged, many of them beyond repair. In the attacks on Berlin itself, 492 bombers were lost. These losses had to be viewed in the context of the front-line strength of Bomber Command, which, throughout the battle, averaged, some 892 bombers. If Bomber Command was to survive as an effective fighting force, this was a casualty rate which could not be sustained. The battle had to be broken off; moreover, though Berlin and many other German towns suffered catastrophic damage, it did not cost Germany the war. On the contrary, a self-destructive element in the British night area offensive began to appear. In the race between, on the one hand, the admittedly vast destructive power which Bomber Command had now developed and, on the other, the resilience, ingenuity, and rate of repair on the German part, it was the latter which was beginning to win. Yet through one of the great ironies of military history, Bomber Command was on the verge of its greatest triumph.

The Americans hardly came in on the air offensive against Berlin, for the simple reason that they were unable in this period to mount sustained attacks on German targets. The problem which this created for them is the key to the outcome of the strategic air attack on Germany. *Arnold, the commanding general of the United States Army Air Forces (USAAF), had been greatly impressed by the British theory of strategic bombing, but neither he nor his subordinates thought much of the tactics or the results of night area bombing. Moreover the principal American bomber, the B17, was unsuited to night flying. The Americans determined to mount their attack in daylight, which they thought would enable them to employ *precision bombing methods to hit 'pinpoint' targets, such as oil installations, aircraft factories, and, above all ball bearing plants. Thus they would achieve with the surgeon's knife what the British had been driven to attempt by the sledgehammer. Despite British attempts to convince them that heavy bombers could not stand up to high performance short-range fighters, the Americans built up in England within the Eighth USAAF a formidable bomber force under *Eaker's command and in October 1943 the Fifteenth USAAF was activated in Italy, for use mainly against targets in northern Italy and the Balkans. From August 1942 onwards Eaker's B17s and B24s rehearsed the part, usually within range of fighter cover, over targets in France. In January 1943, soon after the *Combined Bomber Offensive was discussed and approved at the Casablanca conference (see SYMBOL), they flew beyond the range of friendly fighters and opened their attack on German targets. A series of disasters culminated in a raid on the ball bearing plants at *Schweinfurt on 14th October 1943 from which, out of a force of 291 bombers, 60 failed to return and more than 100 others were damaged. This showed that the British warning had been right; the Americans had to break off the attack and the German war economy continued to function with remarkable efficiency.

Instead of turning to night attack, as in like circumstances the British had done, the Americans adopted a second and radical alternative. This was the provision of fighter cover for the day bombers all the way from base to target and back even at the longest ranges, including Berlin. Though the British had pronounced such an idea a technical impossibility (they believed that a fighter given the range of bomber would cease to be a fighter), the Americans found a solution in an aircraft which had originally been built in the USA, rejected by the American authorities and bought by the British—the P51 Mustang. Re-engined with a Packard Merlin and progressively equipped with longer and longer range droppable petrol tanks, strong forces of Mustangs were able to fly from British bases by the end of March 1944 and match, and usually outmatch, anything German, even at the extreme range of Berlin. By the end of the war, some 14,000 of these aircraft had been produced in the USA. This changed the prospects of long-range daylight bombing and indirectly it released the potential of night bombing as well.

The Eighth USAAF bombers, now, with Fifteenth USAAF, under *Spaatz's overall command, were used to draw up the German defending fighters which were then engaged by his Mustangs at long range or by other types at shorter range. In the great air battles from January 1944 onwards, the Americans gradually wore down the Luftwaffe and began to establish an increasing degree of air superiority (see BIG WEEK), enabling the American bombers to begin systematic bombing operations without prohibitive casualties. The decline of the Luftwaffe then began to engulf the night fighter force and from September 1944 onwards there was diminishing resistance to Bomber Command's night attacks. Thus, the way was opened for an effective bombing offensive against Germany by day and night.

In this final phase British Bomber Command, which could now regularly dispatch a thousand front-line bombers, most of them Lancasters, developed a destructive power and an accuracy of aim at night which far exceeded what the American B17s and B24s could do in daylight. Techniques of bombing, notably those developed by Group Captain Leonard Cheshire on principles which had first been indicated by Group Captain Guy Gibson in the *Dam Busters raid of May 1943, enabled Bomber Command to devastate relatively small targets and especially oil refineries, or, alternatively, to achieve fearful concentrations of destruction in area attacks on towns, which culminated in the ruin of *Dresden in February 1945. The effort was, however, unduly dispersed between the top objects and within the former group between the alternatives of attacks on oil and on other industrial and communications targets. This was due to severe and unresolved differences of opinion between Portal, who was now convinced that oil was the best target, *Tedder, who favoured transport, and Harris who adhered to the policy of general area bombing against the main towns. With bitter experience on his side, Harris was sceptical of intelligence, which got nearly everything except the German oil position wrong, and of 'panacea' solutions to the problem of cracking the German war economy.

Despite these differences, and the enormous diversion of effort into supporting the land forces launching the Normandy landings (see OVERLORD), British Bomber Command and the Eighth USAAF did produce an oil famine in Germany, the collapse of its transport system, and a fearful levelling of most of its great cities. These results were too late to win the war on their own, but they did make a decisive contribution to the defeat of Germany which could not have been achieved without the campaign in which Spaatz brought the Luftwaffe to action and defeated it.

The strategic air offensive against Germany cost the lives of about 50,000 British aircrew and a like number of Americans. It resulted in the death of between 750,000 and a million Germans. The destruction of the German war economy, which was eventually achieved, proved to be a far more formidable task than even cautious advocates had estimated. Spaatz stands out as the most brilliant commander, since it was he who grasped the principle that the way to victory lay in the achievement of command of the air and that the only effective method was the pursuit of the air battle. On Harris's side it must be recognized that intelligence estimates of German dependence on this or that commodity were usually wrong and, on Tedder's, that his policies related the air effort more directly to the operations of the armies, thus, as he put it, exploiting the common denominator factor. Portal, too, often the victim of bad intelligence, was certainly right in the end when he accepted their view of the German oil position. Arnold created and sustained an independent air effort on the part of what was still, theoretically, a subordinate service. A. N. FRANKLAND

2. Against Europe outside Germany

The Allied strategic air offensive in Europe, though directed mainly at Germany, also involved attacks on targets in occupied countries used for the German war effort, and on Germany's allies and satellites. Italian cities were subject to intermittent attack from 1940 onwards; a great deal of bombing in the autumn and winter of 1942–3 was directed at the submarine bases and facilities in France; and from late 1943 the Fifteenth US Army Air Force based in Italy attacked targets from the southern French coast to the Black Sea.

The attacks on occupied areas and on Germany's allies fulfilled the same purposes as the attacks on Germany itself: they were designed to destroy military and economic targets deemed vital to the Axis war effort. The bulk of the attacks outside German soil were against heavy industrial targets, the oil industry, and the European transport network. Many of the attacks on transport were tactical rather than strategic in character, preparing the way for the Allied assault on Sicily and then the Italian mainland, and in 1944 preparing the way for the Normandy landings. Towards the end of the war transport attacks became more strategic in purpose, disrupting rail links between industrial centres or destroying the supply routes for essential *raw materials out of the Balkans or Italy.

The bombing of Italy followed very much the same pattern as the offensive against Germany. In 1940 RAF Bomber Command launched small and largely ineffective attacks against Italy's northern industrial cities. In the light of all the difficulties encountered in attacking such distant targets with any accuracy, the RAF adopted morale as the key target, and area bombing of key industrial suburbs as the instrument. When bases were secured in 1942 and early 1943 for attacks from the Mediterranean, both British and American bombers attacked Italian industry by day and night, bringing high casualties and a calculated reduction of Italian industrial output of 60% by the time Italy capitulated in September 1943. Much of this loss was due to widespread panic among the urban populations which had been left virtually defenceless against air attack. After Italy's surrender the Allies kept up the bombing of the northern part occupied by the Germans and more than 50,000 Italians were killed in these raids. Much of the later

Strategic Air Offensive (Europe): Fifteenth USAAF: sorties flown, tonnage of bombs dropped, and operational losses, November 1943–May 1945

H = high explosive, I = incendiary

Dates	*Sorties*	*Bombs dropped*		*Operational losses*
1943		*H*	*I*	
Nov	1,785	5,392	–	28
Dec	2,039	7,752	–	36
1944				
Jan	4,720	11,051	–	54
Feb	3,981	6,611	136	128
Mar	5,996	9,842	534	85
Apr	10,182	20,657	599	194
May	14,432	29,606	749	175
Jun	11,761	23,637	829	196
Jul	12,642	30,621	1,562	317
Aug	12,194	27,660	179	254
Sep	10,056	20,645	211	94
Oct	9,567	15,712	545	140
Nov	9,259	16,153	1,144	132
Dec	10,050	18,308	449	205
1945				
Jan	4,002	6,784	–	88
Feb	13,444	24,417	91	147
Mar	14,939	30,265	–	149
Apr	15,846	29,181	77	83
May	42	84		14
TOTALS	166,937	334,378	7,105	2,519

Source: Freeman, R., *The US Strategic Bomber* (London, 1975).

bombing was undertaken by the Fifteenth USAAF which attacked steel and ball-bearing production in Milan, Genoa, and Turin.

The bombing of occupied Europe raised more delicate issues. The Allies were aware that bombing would bring civilian casualties and so might alienate the very populations they were trying to liberate. Attacks on France began in earnest in 1942, but were governed by a directive agreed between the British and Americans that they would be confined only to clearly identified military targets and that every effort was to be made to avoid hitting civilian targets in the vicinity. This proved impossible in practice. From October 1942 to the spring of 1943 top priority was given to bombing the German submarine bases in St Nazaire, Lorient, Brest, and La Pallice. The attacks by day and night utterly destroyed the towns surrounding the submarine pens but did virtually no damage to the targets themselves. Harris, RAF Bomber Command's C-in-C, regarded the attacks as 'completely wasteful', and after the spring the bombers were increasingly used against industrial targets in France, disrupting much of the work being done for the Germans in the French aircraft and motor industries. It was in France that the Eighth USAAF, based in the UK, began its bombing career, testing the American tactics of daylight bombing of precision targets against light resistance. The lessons learned in France convinced its commander, Eaker, that daylight attacks were 'feasible and practicable'.

The same tactics were adopted by the Fifteenth USAAF when it was activated in southern Italy in October 1943. Its purpose was primarily to contribute to the aims of the *Combined Bomber Offensive in attacking German oil supplies, the aircraft industry, and transport. The most important attacks were against the Romanian oilfields at *Ploesti. First attacked in August 1943, the oilfields were repeatedly bombed until August the following year when production ceased. The Fifteenth USAAF dropped 13,469 tons of bombs on Ploesti, but lost 350 heavy bombers in the effort. The loss rates for the Fifteenth were higher than those of the Eighth, partly because the oil targets were so well-defended, partly because of the dangers of long flights over mountainous terrain. The Fifteenth also attacked a wide range of other oil targets, damaging, by June 1944, 29 out of the 60 oil refineries within its range. The bombers, sometimes by *shuttle bombing, also attacked industrial and transport targets in Hungary, Czechoslovakia, Yugoslavia, and Greece. Only at this later stage of the war did Austria come within range of Allied bombers, and much less damage was inflicted on Austrian cities and industries than was the case elsewhere in Greater Germany. The exception was

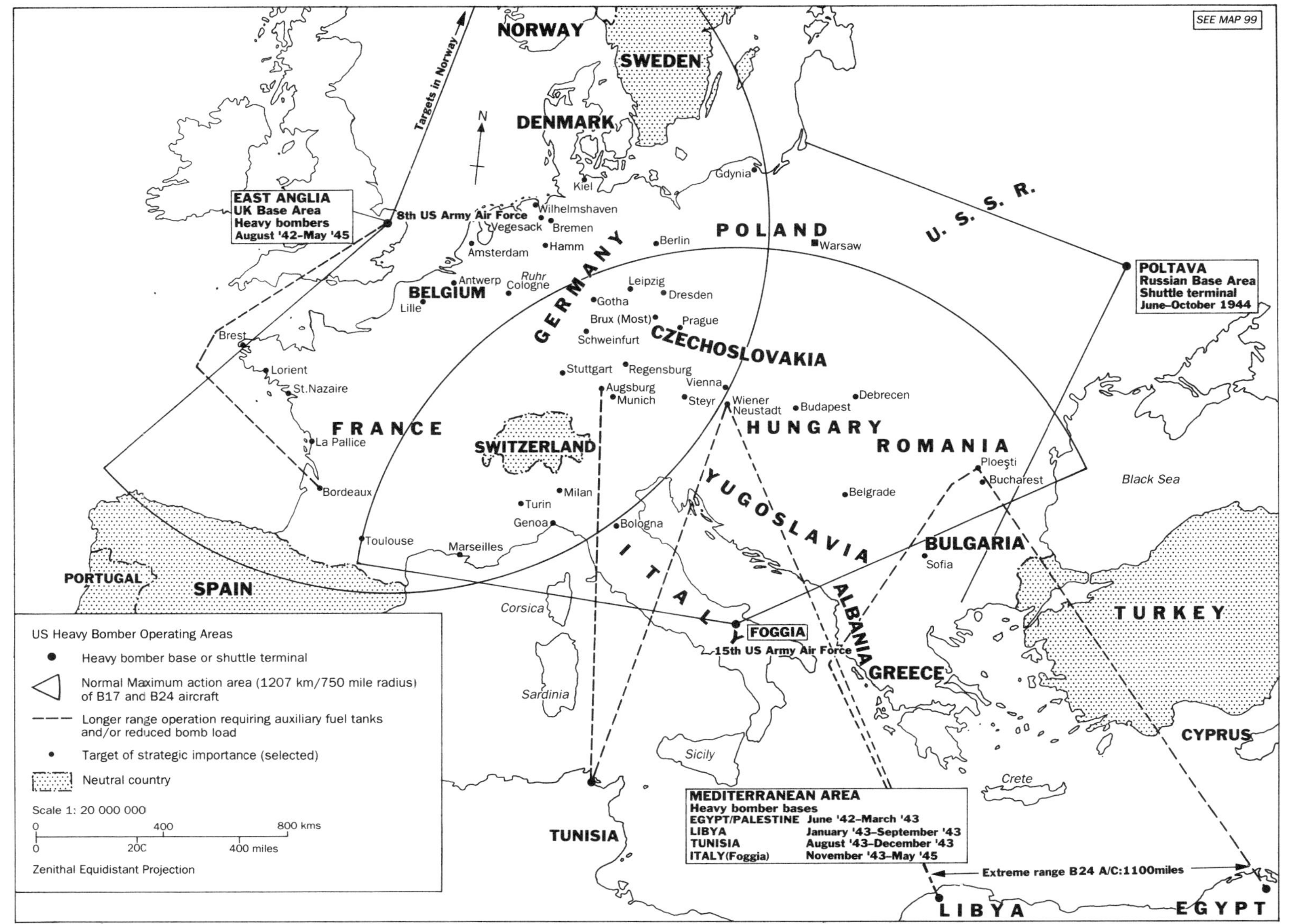

100. Operational range of US Army Air Forces employed in **strategic air offensive** against Europe, 1942–5

the industrial area of Wiener Neustadt where the large Messerschmitt aircraft factories became a key target in 1944. After *Vichy France was occupied in November 1942 attacks were started against oil and industrial targets in southern France. American experience in the southern theatre showed that despite efforts to bomb precisely, they only achieved the *area bombing of selected targets instead, and, in Germany, it proved impossible to separate the material from the moral target, to destroy factories without killing workers. More French and Italian citizens were killed by bombing than Britons. RICHARD OVERY

3. Against Japan

The strategic air offensive against Japan began on 15 June 1944 when 50 B29 Superfortresses of the Twentieth US Army Air Force bombed steel mills at Yawata, Kyūshū. Over the course of the next fifteen months, B29s would bring the war home to all of Japan with cruel and shocking effectiveness, destroying its cities, laying waste its industrial capacity, killing hundreds of thousands of its citizens, and finally delivering the *atomic bombs that forced the *unconditional surrender of its armed forces.

This great aerial assault rested on the wings of the new B29. Ready for action by early 1944, the huge plane could carry a greater bomb-load over longer distances than any other aircraft. But the Superfortresses required bases within 2,575 km. (1,600 mi.) of the Japanese home islands in order to strike the heart of their target. These became available that summer with the seizure of the *Mariana Islands which were within B29 range of Tokyo and all other important Japanese cities.

The general strategy of the bombing campaign had been approved by Roosevelt and Churchill at the Cairo conference in December 1943 (see SEXTANT), and final plans were completed by the US *Joint Chiefs of Staff the following April. The implementing agent was the newly created Twentieth USAAF, an independent organization operating directly under the control of General Arnold, commander of the US Army Air Forces.

Until the Marianas could be captured and developed as a base, the air offensive would be launched from India. The B29s would stage through central China to strike iron and steel targets in Manchukuo and south-western Japan. But these attacks were subject to severe logistical limitations and in any event could reach only as far as Kyūshū. They were thus simply a temporary measure until occupation of the Marianas allowed a full-scale assault on all of Japan.

On 15 June 1944, even as the invasion of the Marianas began, B29s of Twentieth USAAF's 20th Bomber Command struck Kyūshū from China. The China-based raids, however, proved of limited value. Of nearly 50 B29 attacks flown from China in 1944 and early 1945, only nine actually hit Japan, and these and others against targets in Manchukuo, Korea, China, Formosa, and South-East Asia did little strategic damage. They provided valuable experience for the bomber crews, but otherwise hardly justified their cost and effort.

The first B29 attack from the Marianas came on 24 November 1944. Approximately 80 unescorted Superfortresses of Twentieth USAAF's 21st Bomber Command, commanded by Brig-General Haywood S. Hansell, struck Tokyo's Nakajima aircraft factory in the first of a series of raids designed to cripple the Japanese aircraft industry. For the next two months Hansell, an outspoken advocate of precision bombing, carried out high-level daylight precision attacks on aircraft plants in Tokyo and Nagoya. These attacks were severely hampered by bad weather, extremely strong winds, mechanical difficulties with the new B29s, and losses to Japanese fighters. While they none the less inflicted considerable damage and lowered Japanese aircraft production, this was not immediately evident since poor weather and heavy cloud cover limited *photographic reconnaissance.

The apparent inability of 21st Bomber Command to inflict greater damage brought increasing criticism from General Arnold in Washington. Arnold questioned the value of continued precision bombing efforts and urged the initiation of massive fire-bombing raids against Japan's inflammable cities. Flying at night at low altitudes, the incendiary attacks could carry a heavier bomb-load, avoid opposing fighters in the dark, and spread destruction over huge areas. The indiscriminate nature of these raids was exactly the effect that Hansell was determined to avoid. In mid-December, however, Arnold ordered him to make a full-scale incendiary attack on the city of Nagoya.

Hansell protested vigorously, but carried out the raid on 3 January 1945. The results were inconclusive. By comparison, a heavy precision bombing attack on a town near Kobe two weeks later was extremely effective, knocking out a major aircraft production facility.

By now, however, Arnold had decided to relieve Hansell. On 20 January, he replaced him with Maj-General Curtis E. *LeMay, who had headed 20th Bomber Command in India and China. In his new command, LeMay continued to fly the high-level precision attacks but began to mix in a few incendiary raids. Although the latter were flown in daylight at high altitudes, they showed impressive results and Arnold directed that they be increased.

On 25 February, some 150 B29s carried out a huge incendiary attack on Tokyo, burning out over two and a half square kilometres (nearly a square mile) of the city. LeMay thereupon decided to make a major tactical change designed to further increase effectiveness. In place of the high-level daylight raids, he would have his bombers attack at night at low altitudes. They would thus escape the clouds and strong winds encountered on high as well as the Japanese fighter planes that had plagued daylight missions. Flying at low altitudes also reduced engine strain and fuel consumption, allowing the Superfortresses to carry more bombs. And without enemy fighter opposition, most of the B29 gunners, along with their weapons and ammunition, could be left behind, further increasing the feasible bomb-load. This drastic change in tactics would prove to be one of the

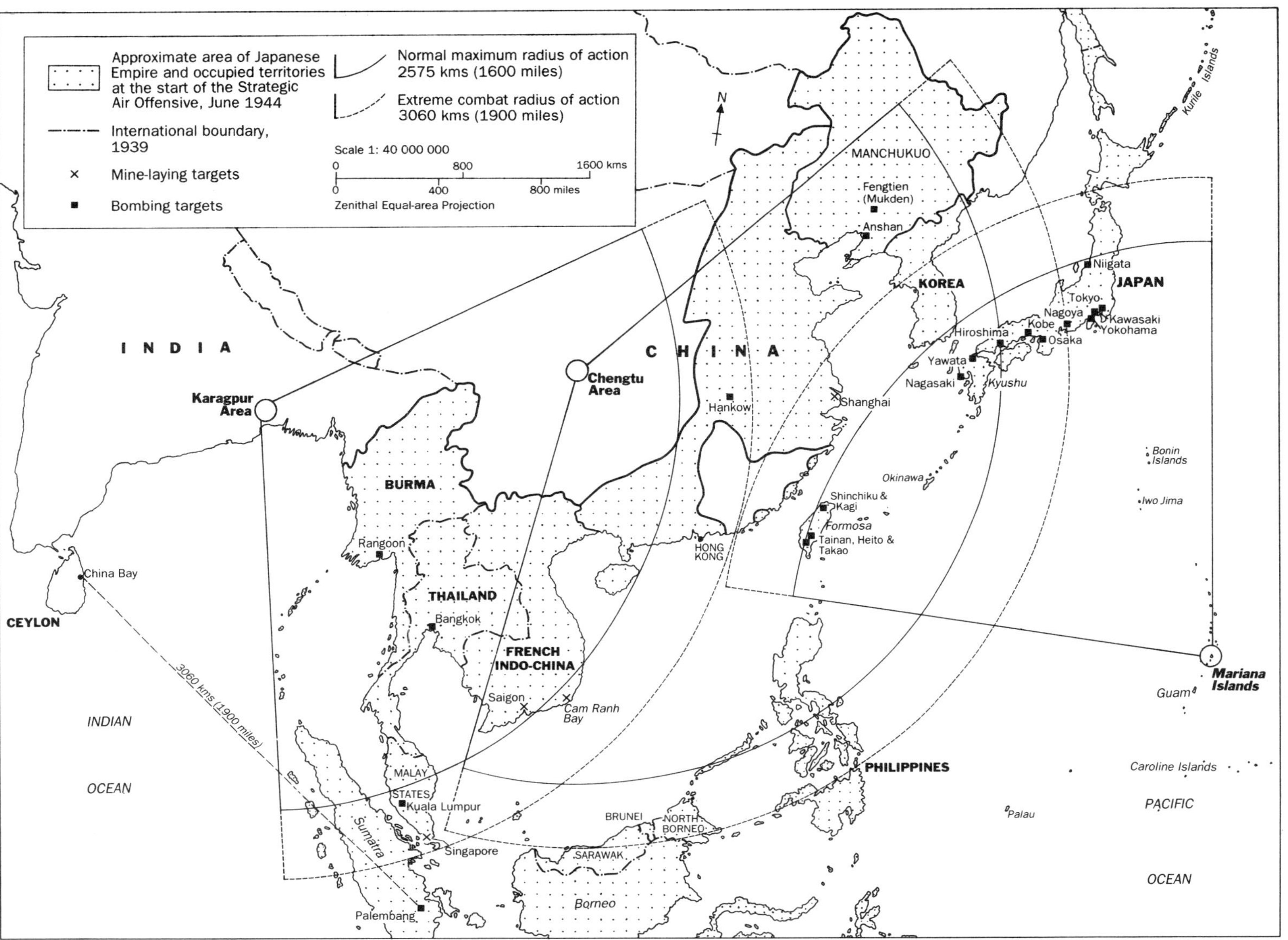

101. US Army Air Forces' **strategic air offensive** against Japan and Japanese-held territory, 1944–5

Strategic Air Offensive (Japan): Twentieth USAAF B29 losses and estimated tonnage of bombs dropped, April 1944–August 1945

A = combat losses, B = non-combat losses, C = estimated tonnage of bombs dropped

	20th Bomber Command			*21st Bomber Command*		
Dates	*A*	*B*	*C*	*A*	*B*	*C*
1944						
Apr	–	7[a]	–	–	–	–
May	–	5	–	–	–	–
Jun	10	8	547	–	–	–
Jul	3	5	209	–	–	–
Aug	14	5	252	–	–	–
Sep	3	7	521	–	–	–
Oct	5	16	1,669	–	–	–
Nov	19	2	1,631	4	5	575
Dec	16	6	1,556	21	6	2,105
1945						
Jan	4	3	2,006	27	–	1,404
Feb	4	2	1,865	26	3	2,155
Mar	2	1	1,436	34	–	13,847
Apr	–	–	–	57	1	117,492
May	–	–	–	88	3	24,285
Jun	–	–	–	44	7	32,542
Jul	–	–	–	22	5	42,551
Aug	–	–	–	11	7	21,029
TOTALS	80	67	11,691	334	37	157,985

[a] unconfirmed

Source: Freeman, R., *The US Strategic Bomber* (London, 1975).

most important innovations of the war (see BOMBERS, 2).

On the night of 9/10 March 1945 nearly 300 B29's dropped about 2,000 tons of incendiaries on Tokyo. Attacking at altitudes of from 1,500–2,750 m. (5,000–9,000 ft.) for almost two hours they spread fires over a densely populated area. The flames, fanned by winds, became a vast *firestorm that destroyed a quarter of the city, including more than 20 important industrial targets, killing nearly 85,000 Japanese civilians and injuring tens of thousands more.

Over the next ten days, similar incendiary attacks burnt out large sections of Nagoya, Kobe, and Osaka. Two more fire raids struck the Tokyo–Kawasaki area before the B29s were diverted to support the April invasion of *Okinawa. By mid-May, however, 21st Bomber Command had been reinforced and resupplied and long-range P51 fighter escorts were flying from newly captured *Iwo Jima, midway on the attack route.

For a month beginning on 14 May, B29s ravaged Japan's six most important industrial cities. Tokyo, Nagoya, Kobe, Osaka, Yokohama, and Kawasaki were reduced to smouldering ruins in nine devastating 500-bomber incendiary assaults. More than 100,000 civilians were killed and millions of others rendered homeless or forced to flee. Some of these attacks were daylight raids, which lured defending Japanese fighter planes into uneven combat with the escorting American P51s. By early June, so many of the defenders had been shot down that the Japanese grounded their remaining fighters to preserve them for use against the expected invasion of their homeland. LeMay now began a furious assault on 60 smaller Japanese cities and towns. These attacks were primarily incendiary strikes, but high-level precision raids on selected oil refineries and other targets destroyed the Japanese oil industry and inflicted further damage elsewhere. The tempo of these assaults was not at all slowed by an organizational change on 16 July 1945 when, in preparation for a planned invasion of Japan, Twentieth USAAF became the nucleus of the newly created US Army Strategic Air Forces (USASTAF), commanded by General Spaatz.

By the end of July, the B29s had just about run out of targets. Almost every Japanese city and large town had been devastated and all normal processes completely disrupted. The nation's economy was shattered, its industry crippled, transport and communication fragmented, and war production cut by more than half. Civilian casualties exceeded 800,000, including 300,000 dead; an estimated 8.5 million or more were rendered homeless. But the most important impact of the strategic air offensive was its effect on Japan's willingness to continue the war.

The punishing bombing campaign had raised serious concerns within the Japanese civilian leadership about the wisdom of continuing to fight. Although military domination of the government prevented any real steps towards peace, by April 1945 Emperor *Hirohito had become determined to end the struggle somehow. Military leaders, however, remained adamant in their belief that if Japan could survive the B29 attacks, high American casualties in the expected invasion would bring a negotiated peace on relatively favourable terms. The official Japanese response to the Allied ultimatum contained in the 26 July Potsdam Declaration (see TERMINAL) was therefore simply to ignore it.

The atomic bombing of *Hiroshima and *Nagasaki on 6 and 9 August, along with the Soviet entry into the war on 8–9 August (see JAPANESE–SOVIET CAMPAIGNS), brought matters rapidly to a head. Despite the continued opposition of his military chiefs, the emperor took the unprecedented step of announcing his decision to yield to Allied demands. On 14 August he directed that Japan should accept the Potsdam Declaration and surrender. The crushing fury of the B29 attacks, the mounting horror and devastation of the great fire raids, and the shocking atomic destruction of Hiroshima and Nagasaki had finally ended the war. STANLEY L. FALK

Cooke, R. C., and Nesbit, R. C., *Target: Hitler's Oil: Allied Attacks on German Oil Supplies 1939–1945* (London, 1985).
Craven, W. F., and Cate, J. L. (eds.), *The Army Air Forces in World War II*, 9 vols., (Chicago, 1948–58).
Frankland, N., *The Bombing Offensive against Germany, Outlines and Perspectives* (London, 1965).
Hansell, H. S., Jr., *The Strategic Air War Against Germany and Japan* (Washington, DC, 1986).
Harvey S., 'The Italian War Effort and the Strategic Bombing of Italy', *History*, 70 (Feb. 1985).
LeMay, C. E., with MacKinley Kantor, *Mission with LeMay* (Garden City, NY, 1965).
Webster, C., and Frankland, N., *The Strategic Air Offensive against Germany*, 4 vols., (London, 1961).
Wolff, L., *Low Level Mission: the Story of the Ploesti Raids* (London, 1958).

Streicher, Julius (1885–1946), founder of the anti-Semitic German Socialist Party which amalgamated with the Nazi Party in 1921. In 1923 he founded the newspaper *Der Stürmer*, whose obscene outpourings encouraged and exacerbated German hatred for the Jews. He was an early supporter of Hitler and in 1935 he staged that year's Nuremberg rally at which Hitler announced his anti-Semitic laws. In 1940 he was dismissed as Franconia's **Gauleiter* for dishonesty, though he continued editing his paper. Crude, sadistic, and corrupt, Streicher called himself 'Jew-baiter number one'. He was universally loathed and but for Hitler's protection would probably not have survived so long. At the *Nuremberg trials he was sentenced to death and executed. See also ANTI-SEMITISM.

Strong, Maj-General Kenneth (1900–82), British Army officer who was appointed *Eisenhower's chief of intelligence in March 1943 and subsequently served in the same capacity with *SHAEF. He was a confidant of Eisenhower and one of his strongest supporters. This did not endear him to some of his British superiors who criticized him for not predicting the German *Ardennes campaign in December 1944. See also ULTRA, 1.

Strong, K., *Intelligence at the Top* (London, 1968).

Stroop, Jürgen (1895–1951), *SS Oberführer (brigadier) who became an expert in the subjugation of the civilian populations of the Nazi-occupied areas of the USSR, Poland, and Greece. His most notorious act was the savage repression of the *Warsaw ghetto rising of April–May 1943. After being sentenced to death by an American military tribunal for shooting pilots and hostages in Greece, he was deported to Poland and executed.

Struma. In December 1941 this 100-year-old, 180-ton cattleboat sailed for Palestine from Constanta, on Romania's Black Sea Coast, with 769 Jewish refugees aboard including 269 *women and 70 *children. She soon proved unseaworthy and was forced into Istanbul. As with those abroad the **Patria*, the British authorities refused all appeals to allow the refugees into Palestine. After two months the ship was forced to leave Istanbul by the Turkish authorities, and the loss of all but one aboard when she foundered led to an international outcry. See also FINAL SOLUTION.

Student, General Kurt (1890–1978), Luftwaffe officer whose innovative ideas helped form the German airborne forces which played a crucial role (see EBEN EMAEL) in Hitler's western offensive in May 1940 (see FALL GELB) and which captured *Crete a year later.

During the *First World War Student commanded a fighter squadron and, as Germany was banned from having an air force by the *Versailles settlement, later helped foster the art of gliding. In early 1938 he was appointed to command Germany's first paratroop division, Fliegerdivision 7, and when he became inspector of German airborne forces later that year he began developing *gliders which would land his newly formed 22nd Division. On 14 May 1940 he was severely wounded in Rotterdam, but returned to duty in September and was promoted maj-general.

Student's largest operation was the capture of Crete by his Fliegerkorps 11 in May 1941. Losses were so heavy that Hitler forbade any more large-scale offensive airborne operations, and Student's forces were thereafter mostly employed as ground troops; but it was his forces, and his planning, that helped *Skorzeny rescue Mussolini in September 1943. He was promoted general in September 1944 when his First Parachute Army helped defend Arnhem (see MARKET-GARDEN), and from October 1944 until February 1945 he commanded Army Group H in the Netherlands. A prison sentence by a British military court in May 1946 was not confirmed.

Stumpff, General Hans-Jürgen (1889–1968), Luftwaffe officer who was appointed the Luftwaffe's chief of personnel in 1935 and then its chief of staff in June 1937.

In February 1939 he was succeeded as chief of staff by *Jeschonnek and the following year commanded Luftwaffe air operations in the *Norwegian campaign. He then became Air C-in-C Norway as well as commander of Luftflotte 5 which was based there. This took only a minor part in the battle of *Britain as its strength was only 123 bombers and 34 twin-engined fighters and these, of course, had much further to fly than those based in France. From mid-1941 to the end of 1943 Stumpff supervised attacks on the *Arctic convoys and support for German and Finnish troops fighting in the *German–Soviet war on the Northern Front. In January 1944 he took command of the home air fleet (Luftflotte Reich) which was responsible for the air defence of Germany. From September 1944 this included *Sperrle's Luftflotte 3 but lack of fuel, and of trained pilots, resulted in his forces being overwhelmed.

Stumpff was one of the three principal signatories to Germany's *unconditional surrender in Berlin on 8 May 1945 and ended the war as one of the few high-ranking Luftwaffe officers without a blemish on his reputation.

submarines. (See also ANTI-SUBMARINE WEAPONS, MIDGET SUBMARINES, SEA POWER, and TORPEDOES.)

1. Design and development

Submarines during the Second World War only dived when necessary: most were designed primarily for good *surface* speed and endurance on diesels (see Table 1 for principal types). Submerged, typical storage batteries (recharged by diesels), powered electric motors for one hour at 8–9 knots or four days at 2 knots; but air became foul after about a day despite oxygen supplies and carbon dioxide absorption methods (French and German equipment was the best, followed by American, and later, British, equipment).

The surface range of big submarines was many times that of a destroyer: and the bigger a boat the further and faster it could go—hence large American and Japanese submarines, for Pacific distances, and German 'U-cruisers'. The Germans employed large Type 14 'Milch Cow' submarines for refuelling and re-supplying smaller U-boats in the South Atlantic and Indian oceans.

By mid-1942 German U-boats could not safely surface at all, even at night, in areas covered by centimetric Allied airborne *radar. A means of running diesels submerged therefore became essential and a Dutch invention, a **Schnorchel* pipe, which reached to the surface from periscope depth, was widely fitted in U-boats from early 1944.

Germany, then seeking optimum submerged performance in the face of new Allied anti-submarine measures, developed the streamlined Type 21 'Electro' boat with a greatly increased battery capacity. Its top speed submerged was 17.2 knots and at 5 knots range was 365 nautical miles (667 km.) without using its *Schnorchel* except, briefly, to refresh the air. The six bow torpedo tubes could all be reloaded mechanically in five minutes against about 20 minutes per tube manually. Fortunately for the Allies, although the tiny sister 'Electro' Type 23 saw some coastal fighting, the powerful Type 21 came too late for active operations. Nor, in a radically different design tested in 1944, did the wholly air-independent 'Walter' turbine-propulsion system, supplied with oxygen and steam from the breakdown of hydrogen peroxide, become operational.

Meanwhile, the German workhorse was the Type 7c of 865 tons dived—a thoroughly good boat which underwent successive improvements to increase extreme diving depth to 300 m. (985 ft.) and range to 12,600 nautical miles (23,000 km.). Four bow tubes and one stern were sufficient for merchant ship targets.

Second after Germany in wartime evolution, but without a single-minded aim, Japan produced a number of remarkable submarines. Some carried bomber or reconnaissance aircraft—the huge 6,560-ton I-400 class could carry three aircraft—while others, normal attack types, could carry midget submarines or *human torpedoes. Other boats were designed specifically to take supplies and reinforcements to besieged island garrisons.

There were some 30 Italian submarine classes; but, although impressive in peace—after the USSR, Italy had the world's largest submarine fleet—too many were ill-prepared for the rigours of war.

Among the Allies there were few noteworthy wartime developments. However, from 1942 British yards employed welding more widely (it was standard for German and American boats) instead of weaker riveting. Allied ancillary equipment—radar, *ASDIC, fire control, communications—was steadily improved, with the US Navy making the speediest advances.

The Royal Navy was justifiably satisfied with its three principal classes—ocean-going T-boats; middling-sized versatile S-boats; and the handy little U-class (with the similar V-class) so suitable for Mediterranean work. None was innovative and none was fast; but all were dependable and well armed. The 3 in. (76 mm.) or, better, 4 in. (102 mm.) guns fitted on all classes were devastating against small vessels.

The American force consisted predominantly of excellent fast, long-range Fleet boats with four or six bow tubes, four stern tubes and quite good habitability for long periods at sea. Up to 32 mines could be embarked in reload torpedo stowages instead of 20–24 torpedoes. (Most submarines in all navies could substitute mines for torpedoes and carry a mix; but there were also purpose-built minelayers.)

Soviet designs ranged from the 'baby' 256-ton coastal M-class to formidable long-range 2,095-ton K-boats. Substantial numbers were available but they were not put to good use.

2. Warfare

Submarine strategy and tactics differed among the underwater belligerents; and objectives sometimes changed. The Samurai spirit of the Japanese demanded

Submarines, Table 1: Some principal types

Country	*Class*	*Dived Displacement (in tons)*	*Speed (Surf/Sub)*	*Usual Armament*	*Remarks*
France	*Rubis*	925	12/9	2 TT(B) 2 TT(S) 1 TT in revolving tower amidships. 32 mine-chutes 76 mm A-A gun	Minelayer
Germany	Type VIIc	865	17/7.6	4 TT(B) 1 TT(S) 88 mm (3.4 in) gun 20 mm (.78 in) A-A gun	Atlantic. Guns from 1944 replaced by 1 37mm (1.44 in) and 2 x twin 20 mm A-A guns
	Type IXD/42	1,804	19.2/6.9	4 TT(B) 2 TT(S) 105 mm(4.1 in) gun 37 mm and 20 mm A-A guns	U-cruiser: range 32,300 nautical miles 21 torpedoes, 200 x 105mm rounds carried Minelayer: range 21,000 nautical miles
	Type XB	2,177	17/16.4	2 TT(S) Mine chutes: 66 mines 105 mm gun 37 mm and 20 mm A-A guns	
	Type XXIII	256	9.7/12.5	2 TT(B)	Coastal 'Electro'
Italy	'Calvi'	2,060	17.1/7.9	6 TT(B) 2 TT(S) 2 x 119 mm (4.6 in) guns, 4 x 13.2 mm (.51 in) A-A guns	Atlantic
	'Perla'	852	14.2/8.1	6 TT(B) 99mm (3.8 in) gun, 4 x 13.2 mm A-A guns	Med/Aegean
Japan	RO-series K6	1,447	19.7/8	4 TT(B) Light A-A guns	General purpose attack, range 11,000 nautical miles
	B1 Typ *I-15* series	2,584	23.5/8 A-A guns	6 TT(B) 140 mm (5.4 in) and miles	Scouting. Carried 1 float plane. Range 14,000 nautical
	STo Type *1–400* series	6,560	18.7/6.5	8 TT(B)	3 float planes (bombs or torpedoes). Range 37,500 nautical miles
UK	'S'	960–99	14.7/9	6 TT(B) 1 TT(S) in some 3 in or 4 in (76 mm, or 102 mm)	General purpose
	'T'	1,571	15.2/8.7	8 TT B 3 TT (5:2 amidships + 1 aft) 4 in (102 mm) gun, light A-A weapons.	Ocean-going. Amidship tubes initially pointed forward. Welding increased range from 8,000 to 11,000 nautical miles by enabling certain ballast tanks to carry fuel.

Submarines Table 1 *(cont.)*

Country	*Class*	*Dived Displacement (in tons)*	*Speed (Surf/Sub)*	*Usual Armament*	*Remarks*
	'U'	730–5	11.7/9	4 TT(B) (early boats 6) 12 pdr or 3 in (76 mm) gun, light A-A weapons.	Originally intended for training but proved ideal for Mediterranean patrols.
USA	Fleet Gato-class	2,410–24	20.2/8.7	6 TT(B) 4 TT(S) 3 in (76 mm) gun	Habitability good for patrol endurance 75 days, range 11,000 nautical miles
USSR	K-class	2,095	18/9	6 TT(B) 4 TT(S)	Long-range but not deployed far

Source: Contributor.

that their submarine arm operate against their opponents' warships; the clear aim of the Germans, on the other hand, was to destroy Allied merchant shipping, particularly those *convoys around which the battle of the *Atlantic raged; but submarines were also used, by both sides, as *blockade runners and for delivering agents on to the opposing side's shores (see SPIES).

Just as in the First World War, U-boats nearly brought the UK to its knees. In 68 months about 2,000 Allied merchant ships, amounting to some 14.5 million tons, were sent to the bottom (see also UK, 9). Against that, 781 U-boats were lost—66% of the 1,170 commissioned, nearly 80% of the (approximate) 1,000 that actually operated. (Figures in this entry do not take account of midget submarines.)

At the outset, Hitler insisted on prize regulations being observed, though this did not prevent the sinking of the **Athenia*. Ordinary merchantmen were to be stopped and searched before being sunk; and the safety of crews had to be ensured. But the danger to U-boats from merchant ships which were armed, which attempted to ram, or which reported their position by radio, to say nothing of naval escorts, was plain, and the restrictions were lifted step by step. By August 1940 virtually no holds were barred. Then, after the **Laconia* affair in 1942, Dönitz directed that all efforts to rescue survivors were to cease: 'Be severe.'

During their heyday (from 1940 to the end of 1942) U-boats were directed from shore HQ, in surface Wolf-packs, against convoys whenever possible. The exchange rate of ships destroyed to U-boats lost was then profitable at 14:1; but, when Allied anti-submarine measures began to take full effect, and when it became difficult for submarines to surface, it became unacceptably low—about 2:1 for the full year of 1943. Thereafter, U-boats continued to achieve isolated sinkings in all theatres but there was no longer any hope, despite new devices like the *Schnorchel*, of breaking the supply chain from the USA.

In 1939 British submarines had Axis warships, including U-boats, as priority targets. They were generally disposed along lines of individual patrol areas where, instead of chasing their prey, they waited, submerged, for it to come within range. However later, in the Aegean, the eastern part of the Mediterranean, and in South-East Asia, they were often given roaming commissions, to attack anything found, together with covert tasks such as landing agents. The 'U'-class 10th Flotilla, operating under extreme difficulty from *Malta during the siege of the island, demonstrated the effect of submarine warfare on a land battle. The havoc wreaked on *Afrika Korps supply lines during the *Western Desert campaigns caused Lt-General Fritz Bayerlein, *Rommel's chief of staff, to admit: 'We should have taken Alexandria and reached the Suez canal if it had not been for the work of your submarines.'

In all theatres, British submarines sank 169 warships (35 U-boats among them) and 493 merchant vessels, but 74 were themselves sunk—33% of those available.

The US Navy's submarine force in the *Pacific war was hampered until mid-1943 by defective torpedoes; but subsequently its performance was magnificent. Like the UK, Japan was dependent on its merchant fleet as imports were essential, both for the economy and the war industry, while a very substantial outward flow of troops, arms, ammunition, aircraft, and food was needed to capture and hold Pacific island territories. Thus, in December 1941, the USA resolved, despite earlier protestations, on unrestricted submarine warfare against Japan's merchant marine. This strategy demanded different tactics; and peacetime caution was abandoned by fresh, spirited commanding officers who discounted the dangers of attacking on the surface or at periscope

Unrestricted **submarine warfare** was waged by both sides against each other's shipping. Here a sinking Japanese destroyer is photographed through the periscope of the US submarine which has just torpedoed it.

depth. Radar and sophisticated fire-control methods came to be employed with great success while *ULTRA intelligence enabled USN submarines, using their high surface speed, to intercept their targets. Submarine warfare, amounting from mid-1944 to blockade, arguably spelled the end of Japan's fighting ability. Nearly 1,300 Japanese merchant ships, as well as one battleship, eight aircraft carriers, and eleven cruisers were sunk for the loss of 52 US submarines—18% of 288 in the force.

The Japanese Navy started the war with 60 submarines and continually added widely assorted types including boats which carried aircraft. Despite superb oxygen-fuelled torpedoes their score was relatively small because the attack boats were frequently sent, as part of the battle fleet, against heavily defended naval units instead of the more vulnerable American lines of communication. However, although fewer than a score of US naval warships were sunk by Japanese submarines, more than 170 merchant 'supply' and transport ships were lost to them. Japanese submarine losses amounted to 128 or 64% of the 200 available, but many of these were not engaged in combat operations.

When Italy entered the war in June 1940 it had 113 submarines which, after the USSR, was the world's largest submarine fleet. At the time its submarine equipment was thought to be modern and only 32 boats had been built before 1932. They were Mussolini's great pride, but the clarity of the waters they operated in—an aircraft could spot a submarine down to a depth of 40 m. (110 ft.)—the efficiency of British anti-submarine defences, and the immediate grip the Royal Navy imposed led, despite much activity, to poor results at the start of the battle for the *Mediterranean (see Table 2). Total sinkings by Italian submarines during the war amounted to six warships and half a million tons of merchant shipping for the loss of 86 of their number, or 57% of the 150 which became operational.

The Soviet submarine fleet was strong numerically, but weak tactically. Exact numbers are not known (nor losses) but 75 may have operated in the *Baltic—where one sunk the **Wilhelm Gustloff*—50 in the Arctic, and 50 in the *Black Sea. Grossly inhibited by political over-control, robbed of good officers by Stalin's 1937 purge, often used purely for defence, and lacking proper fire-control procedures or reliable torpedoes, they made little impact on the *German–Soviet war. According to one source (S. Breyer, *Guide to the Soviet Navy*, 2nd edn., Cambridge, 1977) their losses were as high as the losses they inflicted, and sometimes higher. In the Baltic one submarine was lost for each ship sunk (51 each); in the Arctic they sank 45 ships but lost 25 of their number; while in the Black Sea 34 submarines were destroyed for the loss of 32 ships.

Among other Allied submarine services, the Dutch were exceptionally efficient, making a notable contribution in the Mediterranean and Far East; the Polish submariners, especially the crews of *Sokol* and *Dzik*, were experts; but of the seven French boats that escaped the German occupation to work on behalf of Free French forces, only the *Rubis* gained distinction—for a record-breaking 38 minelaying operations (683 mines) which claimed 21 victims. RICHARD COMPTON-HALL

Alden, J., *The Fleet Submarine in the US Navy* (Annapolis, Md., 1979).
Blair, C., *Silent Victory—The US Submarine War against Japan* (New York, 1975).
Compton-Hall, R., *The Underwater War 1939–1945* (Poole, Dorset, 1982).

Submarines Table 2: Italian submarine activity, June–October 1940

Month	Submarines employed	No. of actions	Naval tonnage sunk (t.)	Merchant tonnage sunk (GRT)	Submarines lost	Submarines damaged
June	97	105	4,180	9,920	6	12
July	59	65	1,350	5,141	none	4
Aug	36	42	uncertain	uncertain	1	none
Sept	27	32	none	none	1	1
Oct	27	37	1,475	none	5	none

Source: *La marina italiana*, xiii. 60, 73, 82, 92–3, 102. Maier, K.A., *et al*, *Germany and the Second World War*, Vol. 2 (Oxford, 1991).

Friedman, N., *Submarine Design and Development* (London, 1984), chs. 1–4.
Polmar, N., and Carpenter, D., *Submarines of the Imperial Japanese Navy 1904–1945* (London, 1986).
Terraine, J., *Business in Great Waters—The U-Boat Wars 1916–1945*, Part III (London, 1989).

subversive warfare. In parallel with war at sea, on land, and in the air, another aspect of warfare flourished from 1939 to 1945: war by propaganda and sabotage, aiming at the subversion of the opposing side so that soldiers folded up without fighting. This was in accord with a very ancient principle of war, laid down by the Chinese sage Sun Tzu in the fourth century BC: that the supreme art of generalship is to subdue the enemy without any battles.

All the principal war leaders (being politicians) paid close attention to propaganda, and to what would now be called the polishing of their own images as almost superhuman—a fact kept secret by all of them at the time, as a matter at once of political decency and of expediency. One could not be seen admiring oneself in a looking-glass; but one could make sure the glass was kept polished bright. All affected to despise their opponents, as criminal warmongers; all encouraged cartoonists to do their worst in illustrating this. Many savage results of this policy are on file; a few are still familiar.

At the start of the war, *Chamberlain's government in London believed that Germans would listen to reason. For months, RAF Bomber Command scattered over western Germany leaflets compiled by the foreign office and the ministry of information, setting out the reasonableness of the Allied case against Nazi expansion. They had no perceptible impact on German opinion, though the leaflet raids gave aircrew some essential training in night navigation.

Leaflet-dropping went on all through the war, even after the dropping of bombs became much more common; it was practised by the Luftwaffe as well as by the British and US air forces. New methods for delivering leaflets by artillery shell were developed, as had been done (with considerable success, in rotting German Army morale) in the last year of the *First World War. The Americans invented a leaflet bomb, to improve distribution from the air. Leaflets had several objects: to attempt to sap the morale of enemy troops and civilians, to the point of provoking desertion or riot; to provide cover for drops nearby of agents or stores for secret resisters (see SOE); and to supply occupied countries where wireless sets had been confiscated with news of the progress of the war. No one has ever established how much, or how little, impact these leaflets had.

Forged pamphlets were also frequently used by both sides (see POLITICAL WARFARE EXECUTIVE for a British example). They were called black propaganda, because inadmissible by the government that produced them. White propaganda was based on facts, albeit distorted to favour those disseminating it; black depended largely on lies and deceit. Disseminating leaflets sometimes called for less haphazard means than scattering them from aircraft, but seems not to have been beyond several secret services' capacities. Though the results are unquantifiable, the effort was presumed, by all the countries that used it, to have had some weakening influence on their opponents' war effort.

Occupying forces, the Germans in particular, made lavish use of posters, to instruct civilians in what to do, or to announce uses made by the occupiers of their power to punish. It was neither very difficult nor very dangerous to deface posters, by simply tearing them down or painting them out, or by adding slogans to them such as the variants on H7, by which Norwegians signified loyalty to their exiled King Haakon VII (1872–1957), or the ubiquitous V for Victory sign.

Broadcasting was more important and more effective. This was on the whole a pre-televisual age, though in Paris television continued to broadcast for two hours daily, to a small audience of the well-to-do. Sound broadcasting became the essential wartime news medium; called, behind the scenes, white propaganda. It provided news much faster, if less permanently, than any newspaper, as well as providing a steady source of entertainment in blacked-out cities and in countrysides deprived of the means of transport. In all the warring nations, government exercised control over what—particularly what news—was broadcast. In the Soviet Union, wireless sets were confiscated or were untuneable: they could only receive official programmes. In many parts of Nazi-occupied Europe, wireless sets were confiscated, sooner or later, by the occupiers. While the *BBC retained its independence of the British government (only during the general strike of 1926 has it ever come directly under crown control) it never made difficulties about withholding anything that government did not want publicly known, and provided a regular channel through which ministers could address the country. Churchill in particular made use of radio; some of his broadcast speeches, such as the one on the night the Germans attacked the USSR on 22 June 1941 (see BARBAROSSA), are still vividly remembered. Roosevelt also was master of the 'fireside chat', through the much more diffuse radio networks of the USA. Mussolini, Hitler, and *Goebbels, on the other side, broadcast occasionally to sustain their nations' morale; as, rather rarely, did Stalin.

In the USA, *Stephenson, who ran all British secret activities west of the Atlantic, brought off an important coup in 1940–1: he succeeded in persuading a great many newspaper owners and broadcasters that anti-Nazism was a more constitutional attitude to adopt than the hitherto prevalent isolationism. It was not he alone who did this; but the fundamental change-round in American press and hence public opinion was of great importance.

Once the habit of listening to broadcasts had been formed, an opening was made for subversives: users of black rather than white propaganda. Leon Trotsky (1879–1940) had seen this first, back in the 1920s. Goebbels took the idea over. German broadcasts helped to undermine French morale in the winter of 1939–40, before the fall of *France in June 1940. French morale was in fact under attack from two sides: from the Germans and from the French Communist Party, acting under the *Comintern's orders and seeking to persuade the French that capitalism was in its death-throes, not worth the slightest struggle. This two-sided attack helped to drain from one of the world's most prestigious armies its will to fight, and played a large part in securing the Germans' overwhelming triumph in May–June 1940.

Goebbels then turned his broadcasts against the UK; never realizing that 'Lord Haw-Haw', as his Berlin announcer was scornfully nicknamed from his Mayfair accent, promptly became to the English a figure of fun (see JOYCE).

Was it possible that what did not work against the UK would work against its originator, Germany? SO1, the propaganda branch of SOE—removed in August 1941 to become the Political Warfare Executive (PWE)—attempted through two short-wave stations to weaken the morale of the Wehrmacht by black propaganda broadcasts. Sefton Delmer's *Soldatensender Calais*, aimed at the German Army, and Donald McLachlan's *Kurzwellensender Atlantik*, aimed at U-boat crews, pretended to come from Wehrmacht sources that were both anti-British and anti-Hitler. They used a frankly scabrous tone, mixing news items with descriptions of the private lives of German high commanders and of the wives and girlfriends at home of German soldiers and sailors on duty at the front, for this, they thought, would attract a bored audience. (Stafford *Cripps once picked up one of these broadcasts by accident and was so shocked, when he discovered where the broadcasts came from, that he tried to get the whole enterprise suppressed.) Again, how much actual impact these programmes exerted has never been established.

More than 170 broadcasting stations worked, at one time or another, in Europe during the war; most of them black, like the Italian Radio Himalaya which pretended to work from northern India, or the Voix Chrétienne through which Moscow sought to influence the occupied French. More publicly, Moscow Radio provided, throughout the war, a platform from which the central committee of the Communist Party of the Soviet Union could proclaim to the world what communist policy was; it gave essential guidance to foreign comrades, who might have trouble in keeping up with the twists and turns of the party line and, again, exercised a no doubt appreciable if unquantifiable impact.

Vatican radio was less outspoken, as the Pope's concordat with Mussolini had mildly muzzled it; but another voice could be heard in central Europe, which provided fresh, unvarnished news of the course of the war. This was Radio Suisse, broadcasting from Lausanne, valuable to those who could pick up its broadcasts as a check on all the combatants, for it gave a clear, neutral account of events. The BBC, early in the war, took the decision also to publish the news unvarnished, even if markedly unfavourable to the British; when the BBC and Radio Suisse both said the same thing, as they usually did, the listener could believe it to be true.

The Japanese also made effective use of radio during the war; but until they precipitated the *China Incident in July 1937, they despised propaganda. They even refused to use the word, preferring the appropriate phrase 'thought war'. However, they then realized that they needed to adopt western techniques; and once they had overrun American, British, and Dutch colonies in South-East Asia in early 1942, they wasted no time in establishing several short-wave transmitters there. (It is interesting to note that short-wave receivers had been banned in Japan since 1932.) They broadcast the benefits of the *Greater East Asia Co-prosperity Sphere to those who lived in the lands the Japanese now occupied, and emphasized the downfall of their former colonial masters; they also carried on an intensive radio war against Australia as well as one against Allied forces fighting the *Pacific war (see TOKYO ROSE for an example).

These broadcasts struck the right chord among their Asian listeners when, during the early—and, for the Japanese, successful—months of the war they questioned Australia's 'White Australia' policy. Other successful programmes, which certainly had their eager listeners in Australia and in the USA, were those in which *prisoners-of-war sent messages home. These broadcasts were sent out unscheduled between other propaganda items, so that anyone wanting to hear the prisoners had to listen to the complete programme. But on the whole Japanese broadcasts aimed at Australia showed that, in order to have any impact, propaganda must be relevant and is better based on truth than on falsehood. As the Japanese were losing their war within a year of entering it, it was difficult for them to fulfil either of these preconditions. So, for example, when Japanese broadcasters described Japan's material shortages as being 'only psychological' and the fall of *Okinawa as 'the quintessence of Japanese strategy' (quoted in L. Meo, *Japan's Radio War on Australia 1941–1945*, Melbourne, 1968, pp. 152–3) it is not surprising that they were not taken very seriously. (For the subjects of Japanese broadcasts about the course of the war, see Chart.)

Another useful medium for influencing opinion was film (see also CULTURE sections of the major powers). All warring governments kept close control over the brief newsreels that then prefaced almost every cinema show, just as they controlled newspaper communiqués of *war correspondents and made sure that their own leaders and armed forces were well depicted in them, by contrast with the other side's. In the dark of a cinema, fairly brave citizens might dare to boo a leader they greatly distrusted; this was sometimes an early sign that the other side's propaganda was beginning to bite.

Films could also be used directly as propaganda vehicles. The British film industry had begun to show great skill in documentary film-making in the 1930s, and many films useful to the war effort followed; while, on the German side, *Victory in the West* (*Sieg im Westen*) at least has become a classic—a brilliant evocation of the Wehrmacht's triumphs in the Netherlands, Belgium and France in 1940.

The other principal formative influence on opinion was the *press. One of the first steps Axis occupying forces always took, to secure their hold on a newly-conquered country, was to take over the principal newspaper offices as well as the broadcasting stations. Newspapers thereafter printed the Wehrmacht or other official communiqués, with leading articles carefully slanted to secure obedience to the conquerors' will.

Almost at once, a clandestine press began to appear in most occupied countries. Bernard Ijzerdraat, who published the very first Dutch clandestine broadsheet as early as 15 May 1940, the day after the Dutch Army surrendered, was unusually quick off the mark; he had thousands of followers, all over occupied Europe. The Dutch in the end produced more than a thousand clandestine titles, the French even more; some of these were, like Ijzerdraat's, merely cyclostyled sheets, sometimes only a single sheet; others were well printed, up to a dozen pages long, and distributed in tens of thousands.

Distributing a clandestine newspaper was quite as dangerous as any other form of *resistance; quite as liable to lead to prison, *concentration camp, gallows. Receiving one was not quite so dangerous—one could always say it had simply been pushed through the letterbox by an unknown hand; but to be found in possession of several different sheets, or several copies of a single one, was certainly counted as a crime and might involve heavy penalties.

Much attention has been devoted by historians to the clandestine press, because historians like to handle archival evidence, and this is the obvious archival side of resistance. Yet as sources for what life in occupied territory was like, clandestine newspapers have several faults: their coverage could not help being incomplete, they were produced under severe and dangerous conditions, and many of them were intended to promote the aims of a particular political party, with consequent bias in their outlook. They must not be conflated with the morning newspaper produced in a free country, which the biggest of them did their best to resemble, for their sources and origins were entirely different. Naturally, they were most prevalent in the most highly developed and literate societies, where there were plenty of small presses available on which they could be printed. In general, it can safely be said that they had a sizeable (though, again, unquantifiable) impact on public opinion, turning it away from the idea that people ought to do what they were told to the idea that an Allied victory was not only desirable but attainable.

Their news-carrying function mattered; when men and women could read for themselves how the war was going on distant fronts, they could form a sounder opinion of how well-based Axis control in their immediate neighbourhood might be; hence the awesome importance of the battle of *Stalingrad, because it was a manifest, colossal setback for the German Army that had hitherto been presented by Goebbels as invincible. The fall of Tunisia three months later, at the close of the *North African campaign, with an even larger toll of Axis prisoners-of-war, had a reinforcing if a less dramatic effect.

The fate of the intelligentsia, which considered it had a duty to keep public opinion up-to-date, varied from one occupied area to another. In Poland and in south-east Europe and Asia anyone with any sort of academic qualification was at once interned (the Soviet authorities took as much trouble over this in Poland and the Baltic States as the Germans did), and kept from any sort of public pronouncement at all. In Norway all the history teachers were at one time arrested, and interned in nasty conditions on moored ships; they succeeded in maintaining their peaceful protest against teaching history on the lines to be laid down for them by the *Gestapo. In the rest of occupied Europe some teachers took the side of the occupier, and were allowed to remain at work, while others tried to take up a more resistant stance—usually after some months or years had passed. Axis *censorship of all publications was automatic. It was possible for the ingenious to introduce *doubles entendres* into their work, which their compatriots would see but the censors would miss: hence, for example, a spurt of publications in Dutch discussing resistance to the Spaniards during the Eighty Years War of 1568–1648, using methods that could be used against the Nazis.

One other subversive influence over public opinion was

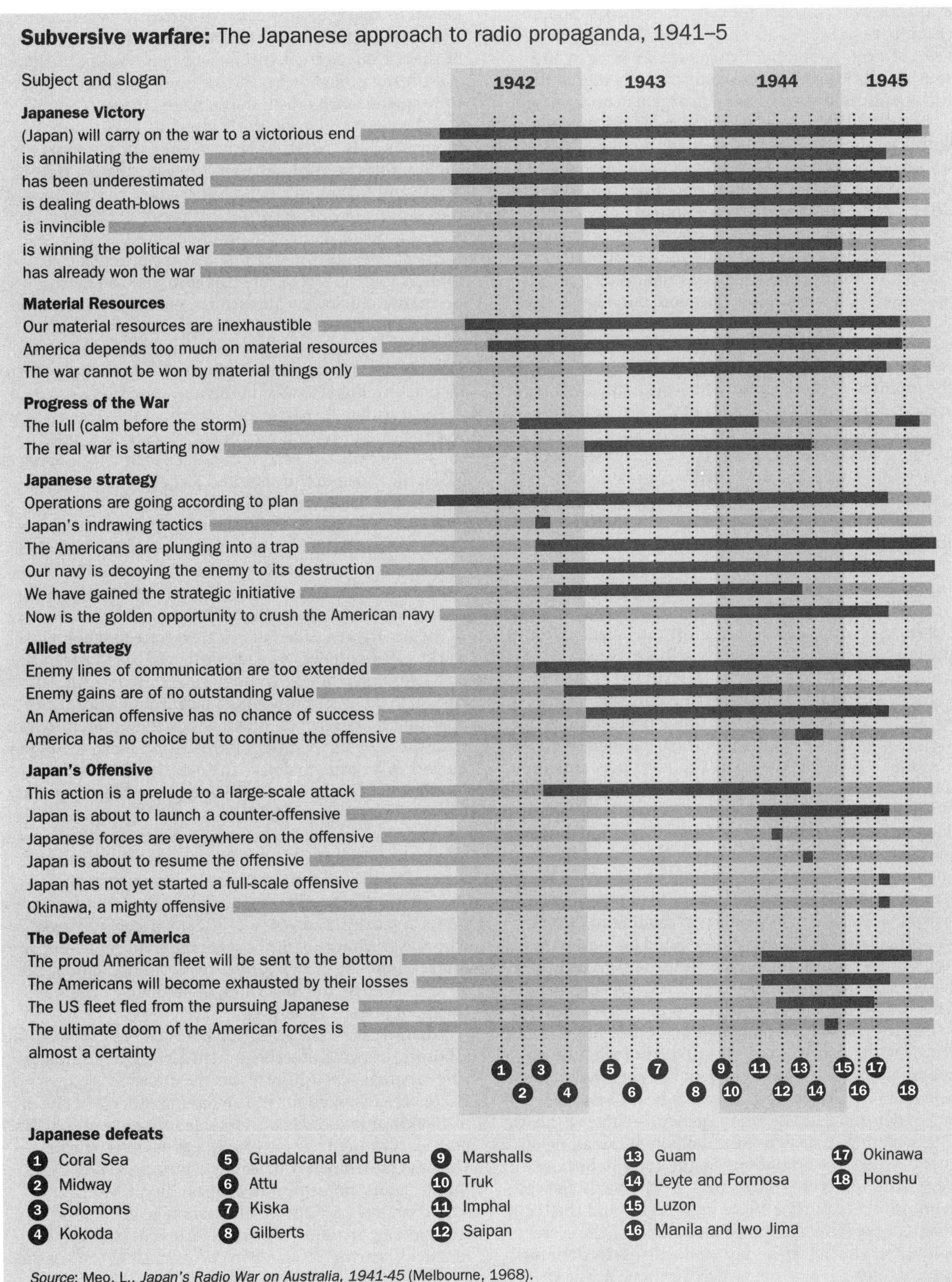

Source: Meo, L., *Japan's Radio War on Australia, 1941-45* (Melbourne, 1968).

available, as it had been for centuries: the sermon, in church or chapel (see also RELIGION). Though priests had few openings left to them in Poland, in western and southern Europe they were comparatively undisturbed. It was noticed by those trying to organize escapes (see MI9) that, outside Iberia, a stranger could throw himself with confidence on the mercy of any country priest, who would be unlikely as a Christian to hand him over to the Gestapo or to the local police, even if he could provide no actual help. The more senior Roman Catholic Church hierarchy was much less reliably anti-Axis, with a few notable exceptions such as Canon Kir of Dijon.

What public opinion then was remains a largely unanswered, unanswerable question; but a few solid points do emerge from attempts to study it. One of these is that, as the war progressed, public opinion in the Axis-occupied countries went through a 180-degree turn. At the moment of catastrophe, when the occupiers first arrived, survivors thought only of the simplest things: where to sleep, how to eat, how to keep the children warm. It was manifestly necessary to do whatever the occupying powers laid down: to be courteous and obedient to them, in all their manifestations. Years later, as the moment of liberation visibly and audibly approached, the turn-around was complete; hardly anybody took any more notice of the occupation rules, almost everybody was looking out for opportunities to work with the incoming Allied forces. A very few, very obstinate resisters had been against the invaders from the start; a very few, very obtuse adherents to *collaboration tried to stick to them at the end.

There was an interesting intermediate stage, when the occupied had got over the first shock of defeat, had got used to the sight of enemy uniforms, and had not necessarily decided that occupation was permanent. At this moment, as a later famous French clandestine leaflet pointed out, it was no longer necessary to be quite so deferential to the conqueror. If a passing soldier asked the time, one's watch had stopped; if he asked the way, one had never heard of the place he wanted to go to; it was not, indeed, necessary to speak to him at all. The age-old schoolchild's technique of 'sending to Coventry'—what the Irish called boycotting—could be used with some effect against the morale of third-line Axis forces in garrison towns. Such a line might be followed generally when public opinion had turned round far enough.

This turn-around was largely the product of press and broadcasting; partly it was the product of what neighbours said to each other, but what the neighbours said depended in turn on what they had heard and read; which depended, again, on the general course of the war.

Whispering campaigns—the deliberate spreading of gossip, which the originators might know to be false—were used, sometimes with effect, by the Nazis and the communists in the late 1930s in Germany and the USSR, both as a means of enforcing the control of the secret police over the public, and to weaken trust in their own governments in countries which Germany or the USSR meant to take over. It became generally known in both countries that a horrible fate in a concentration camp or the *GUlag awaited anyone who came out publicly against the government: this sufficed. Similar rumours were spread, with effect, in occupied lands.

SO1 made some some early attempts at rumour-mongering also, starting by launching the rumours in London pubs and studying how they circulated. How to devise and to launch a rumour became a routine part of the training of British subversive agents thereafter; results abroad, again, remain unobserved.

Direct appeals by megaphone to the other side's soldiers to desert were sometimes made—the British, Germans, and Soviets all used the technique, sometimes with effect. These appeals had extra strength if they could be addressed to a particular unit, or at least to a particular nationality, which depended on how good the tactical intelligence was on the megaphonic side.

The training, dispatch, and control of subversive agents was the task of several wartime secret services, notably the British SOE, the American *Office of Strategic Services (OSS), the German *Abwehr and Sicherheitsdienst (see RSHA), and the Soviet *NKVD. Their tasks were to be distinguished sharply from those of *spies—intelligence agents—who in the UK and sometimes in the USSR had different controlling bodies, *MI6 and the *GRU, but in the American and the German secret services came ultimately under the same head.

The Americans called political warfare psychological warfare. *Eisenhower's headquarters in North Africa had an Anglo-American psychological warfare branch, 60 strong, to conduct propaganda locally and against the opposing Italo-German forces, which moved on into Italy with the Allied Expeditionary Force and reckoned to play its part in helping to defeat the Axis. It was recruited jointly from OSS and from PWE. An even larger, similar branch formed part of *SHAEF.

Subversive agents might have specific tasks of sabotage, of purely military or industrial importance, or more general tasks, political in their aim. Large advances in sabotage technique were made during the war, principally under the inspiration of G. T. Rheam, a steel engineer who was in charge of SOE's sabotage training school at Brickendonbury in Hertfordshire, north of London; they were assisted by the invention, in England as the war began, of plastic *explosives.

A distinction was early made between readily traceable sabotage, blowing objects up with a bang, and undetectable sabotage—*insaississable* was the almost untranslatable French word for it. The foreign office, which in 1940–1 at least had considerable influence over SOE's policies, favoured the latter and less obvious course. This was far from easy to arrange, but, by an odd irony, the Germans' notorious orderliness did provide opportunities for undetectable sabotage. All trains transporting material for the Wehrmacht had to carry it in trucks bearing, low on one corner, a label stating the content, origin, and destination of the truck. Railway procedures ensured that, every two or three hundred kilometres, goods trains would pause in marshalling yards, where they had to be re-labelled. The staff officers who had laid down the rule, far from the noise and dirt of the yards, did not take in that all the railwayman who held the pile of labels had to do to cause confusion was to put the top label at the bottom of the pile. Many railwaymen thought of this for themselves; many more were encouraged to do it by SOE and OSS agents; it caused a great deal of minor nuisance, for which no individual could be blamed.

Equally effective was the technique of Hasek's Good Soldier Schweik: pretending to be willing, while working maddeningly slowly and not quite right. The BBC encouraged those who were sent on *forced labour into Germany to imitate Schweik, and not work too industriously for their Axis masters. In *DORA for instance, French intellectuals making V-2s (see V-WEAPONS) under murderous conditions, including close SS supervision, managed to sabotage more than they completed by taking care not to do anything exactly as they ought, unless they were under an SS man's immediate eye. This helps to account for the large proportion of V-2s that failed to reach their intended targets.

Clerks and telephone operators compelled to work for the Germans could also use imperceptible sabotage with ease; misrouteing calls was as easy as mislaying files, as exasperating to the enemy and as difficult to blame on an individual.

These tactics were often not much more than pinpricks; more serious troubles could be brought on by traceable sabotage. Telephone lines, then almost essential for the running of a large army or air force's supply services, were vulnerable both to interception, which might provide invaluable intelligence (see SOURCE K), and to direct attack, which might spread untold confusion. Blowing up a telephone pole was so simple an exercise that hundreds were demolished by resisters under training, not all of whom remembered that more trouble was caused by felling a pole at a corner than by felling one in a straight line, and that it was indispensable to gather up plenty of the fallen wire and carry it away—not only for the price it would fetch on the black market, but because the occupying force would have to replace it. And might it not be possible to ambush the replacing party?

More sophisticated attacks could be mounted on buried long-distance telephone cables, or even—given luck and the right friends—on telephone exchanges. Here it was necessary to be careful: if an Allied invasion was anywhere near imminent, the Allies would themselves need to use the telephone exchanges, and would not want them permanently damaged. An invaluable side-effect of telephone sabotage in Europe was that it compelled the Germans to make more use of wireless; thus providing more material from which the decipher staff could conjure up intelligence (see ULTRA, 1).

Similarly, guerrillas in touch with an Allied High Command which intended attacks on road or railway bridges were instructed, in such cases, not to cause damage that would be likely to take more than a week to repair. It was not something that an amateur could judge with any ease. For instance, an enthusiastic but ignorant party of OSS saboteurs in south-west France lay low in the hills, and—meaning only to make a temporary break in a main railway line—issued forth to destroy, by miscalculating the amount of explosive they used, three arches of a railway viaduct: just when the local railway authorities wanted to send trains over it to feed the population. Unknown to the OSS, the Germans had just left.

Industry had by this time become so intricate that extra attractive sabotage targets could be found in mines producing valuable *raw materials, notably chrome and wolfram, needed by the German armaments industry to make some kinds of armour. Factories were another fruitful target for sabotage. Many worked with mass production methods; any intelligent saboteur could be taught how to spot the one or two machines on which a production line depended, and how to put them out of action, thus bringing the whole line to a standstill. When a factory depended on electric power, it was likely to contain a transformer station: burn up the transformer, and the factory must stop.

Aircraft were fragile; by breaking a small part, a whole machine might be rendered unserviceable. Railway engines were more robust, but were often laid up for the night in round-houses; bold saboteurs could raid a round-house, and damage (say) the right-hand piston on every steam locomotive, putting them all out of action. Railway track was vulnerable; the best railway saboteurs made sure that they had excellent intelligence from friends on the railway staff, so that they attacked troop or ammunition trains, rather than trains full of civilians.

Ammunition's vulnerability to sabotage goes without saying. Dumps were therefore carefully guarded; so were airfields (the RAF Regiment was formed specifically for this purpose). It would be interesting to know what proportion of the enlisted force of each combatant power was spent in guarding such vulnerable points; this was certainly something about which strategists bothered. A single saboteur, R. B. Mayne, a member of the *Special Air Service, once destroyed 47 Axis aircraft in a single night by putting a small incendiary bomb in each—more than any pilot in Fighter Command shot down in the whole war. But there were not many men as brave as Mayne; and high commanders mostly preferred to stick to the methods of war they had learned in staff college, instead of trusting to devices they thought underhand.

By spreading disinformation, diplomats could occasionally be persuaded to play a part in subversive warfare, though many of them, like high commanders, liked to feel they were fighting with their hands clean. SOE in its early stages had trouble finding diplomatic cover in British legations; as the war went on, British ministers became more bellicose. The ambassador in Madrid was persuaded to let his staff do what they could to foment German–Italian antagonism, by suggesting to the Italians that the Germans were too suspicious of them; and the minister in Stockholm was able to make judicious use of a homosexual on his staff to mislead the Germans about British diplomatic inclinations. A former Polish officer who happened to have links with Japan was able to sow some Japanese–German dissension by calculated indiscretions in Lisbon. All this was in addition to the more direct methods of *deception in use through *double agents working to the Abwehr.

Sometimes subversive agents had to get in touch with smugglers; the British armaments industry, short of ball-bearings and special steels, was to some extent dependent on quantities of both that SOE managed to smuggle out of Sweden in *blockade runners. There is an unwritten chapter of SOE's history that would cover its dealings in the international diamond market.

However, sabotage apart, the main task of subversive agents was not economic, but politico-military. This was particularly the case on the Eastern Front, where a highly developed partisan movement came under rigid control by the Soviet secret police, the NKVD, acting for the Communist Party of the Soviet Union. Partisan units usually began spontaneously, where a few Red Army soldiers, separated from their units but still combatant-minded, fell in with villagers past whom the German Army had swept who were also prepared to resist occupation. Where villagers did not want to join in, committed partisans were quite ready to apply some judicious terror to make sure that they did. By the end of 1941, *Beria, who had charge of the NKVD, had succeeded in establishing radio contact with a few partisan units, and eventually the partisans received orders by radio, and supply and reinforcements by air, in much the same way as SOE or OSS agents at work among the local populations in occupied countries in western or southern or northern Europe, though on a less sophisticated scale. In all these cases, the objects were the same: to put the other side into a state of lasting unease about the security of their communications with the fighting fronts, to unsettle the morale of rear-area troops, to sabotage dumps, trains, road transport, and airfields, and to keep the local population up to the task of detesting the invaders and all their works.

When the Allied advance came closer, agents' and partisans' tasks became more specifically tactical: sometimes to hold open, sometimes to demolish or obstruct particular bridges or defiles, to report precise locations and identities of enemy headquarters and forces, and as soon as the area was overrun to provide guides and guards. Considerable successes were reported, both on the Eastern and on the Western and Southern Fronts, and there were innumerable examples of gallantry; just as there were innumerable examples of penetration by double agents, betrayal by locals who changed their minds about which side they wanted to support, and fearsome *atrocities of reprisal.

Occasionally, whole areas would come out in support of the Allied advance; the Guards Armoured Division for example was mobbed when eventually it reached Brussels, as *Leclerc's 2nd Armoured Division (Deuxième Division Blindée) had been mobbed when it entered Paris a fortnight earlier. Many towns in southern France and northern Italy cherish the myth that they liberated themselves; a myth that usually, on close inspection, means that the local resistance forces took over an hour or two after the last serious German forces had left. Just as the French Army had surrendered in many areas, in 1940, in 1944–5 in a few areas outside Germany there were widespread German surrenders; and inside Germany in the closing stages there were many more.

In the Far East conditions were by no means the same, partly for a simple racial reason: it was impossible for agents of European origin to disguise themselves as Asiatics and blend in with the local population, as British, American, and Soviet personnel could easily enough manage to do in Europe. Moreover, morale in the Japanese Army was high enough for most of the war to ensure that very few Japanese ever surrendered—it had come to be regarded as the ultimate disgrace for a soldier.

There was also a political difference. The Japanese presented themselves at first as the heralds of the Greater East Asia Co-prosperity Sphere, an Asiatic replacement for the European- or American-dominated colonial regimes that had preceded them; though before long it became clear to occupied Malays, Javanese, Sumatrans, Filipinos that they had simply changed one imperial master for another. Rules imposed by Japanese rear-area troops (for example that civilians passing a Japanese sentry had to bow, even if the sentry was sitting down, smoking a cigarette) soon made it clear who the new bosses were.

In these circumstances, the sort of clandestine work that had been attempted in Europe was all but impossible. SOE in the Far East did nevertheless manage in one case at least to organize local resistance thoroughly enough to kill 10,000 Japanese soldiers as they retreated from the Karen hills during the *Burma campaign in 1945.

M. R. D. Foot

Balfour, M., *Propaganda in war 1939–1945* (London, 1979).
Rhodes, A., *Propaganda: the Art of Persuasion: World War II* (London, 1976).

Sudan, theoretically under joint Anglo-Egyptian sovereignty since the Condominium Agreement of 1899, but in fact ruled by a succession of British governor-generals until independence in 1955. In 1939 the Sudanese formed the Graduates' General Council, whose formation the British encouraged although they refused to recognize it as a political body. None the less, in April 1942 it demanded post-war self-determination. When Italy declared war in June 1940 Italian troops occupied the Sudanese frontier town of Kassala. At the start of the *East African campaign these were soon driven back by British forces, which included the Sudan Defence Force, a generic name for 4,500 regular Sudanese soldiers of the Camel Corps, Eastern Arab Corps, Western Arab Corps, and Equatorial Corps. See also ANTI-IMPERIALISM.

Sudetenland, originally the mountainous rim of Czechoslovakia's north-eastern Bohemia and northern Moravia that contained an overwhelmingly German population. Its broader definition encompasses all the German-inhabited regions of the Czechoslovakia contiguous to Austria and Germany.

The *Versailles settlement put the Sudetenland in Czechoslovakia (see Map A). The ethnic composition of Bohemia and Moravia made the Sudetenland a highly contentious issue as, in these provinces, roughly 3 million Germans lived in the mountainous perimeter while the Czechs dominated the heartland. Czechoslovakia won control of the Sudetenland for historic and economic reasons, but at the cost of self-determination for its people. Although Czech policy towards its German population was relatively benign, the Sudeten Germans, led by Konrad *Henlein, turned in the mid-1930s to Nazi Germany for support and by 1938 the future of Sudetenland had precipitated a major crisis between Czechoslovakia and Germany. Wishing to avoid a major European war, Britain, France, Italy, and Germany forced Czechoslovakia to cede the Sudetenland to Germany in the *Munich agreement. At the end of the Second World War, Czechoslovakia regained the Sudetenland and expelled its German population on the basis of Allied agreements reached at the Potsdam conference of July–August 1945 (see TERMINAL).

PAUL LATAWSKI

Bruegal, J. W., *Czechoslovakia before Munich: The German Minority Problem and British Appeasement Policy* (Cambridge, 1973).
Rothschild, J., *East Central Europe between the Two World Wars* (Seattle, 1974).
Wiskemann, E., *Czechs and Germans: A Study of the Struggle in the Historic Provinces of Bohemia and Moravia* (London, 1967).

Sugiyama Hajime, Field Marshal (1880–1945), Japanese war minister during 1937–8 and a strong supporter of war with the western powers and for the policy of striking southwards into South-East Asia. He supervised Japanese operations at the start of the *China Incident before succeeding *Terauchi as C-in-C of the North China Area Army in December 1939. He was appointed army chief of staff in 1940, was promoted to the honorary rank of field marshal in 1943, and remained chief of staff until 1944 when he again became war minister after the fall of *Tōjō's government that July. In April 1945 he took command of the First General Army designated to defend Japan against the expected US invasion. He committed suicide after Japan's surrender.

Sukarno, Achmad (1901–70), Indonesian engineering graduate from Bandung Technical College who, during the 1930s, led the nationalist movement against the Dutch authorities ruling the Netherlands East Indies (NEI). He was imprisoned and exiled but returned to chair a committee of four (Empat Serangkai, or Four-Leaf Clover) which, under Japanese occupation, ran an association of most of the island's nationalist parties. He worked with the occupiers (see COLLABORATION) to gain his country's independence, which was eventually promised in September 1944. On 7 August 1945 he became chairman of the Japanese-approved Committee for the Preparation of Indonesian Independence whose members came from all over the NEI. However, an extremist group of young Indonesians—who believed independence had to be taken from, not granted by, the Japanese if the Allies were to support it—kidnapped Sukarno and his deputy at gun-point, and threatened to rise against the occupiers. But violence was averted and, with Japanese consent, Sukarno announced Indonesia's independence on 17 August 1945. He was then proclaimed first president of the Republic of Indonesia which was finally recognized by the Netherlands in 1949. See also ANTI-IMPERIALISM and JAVA.

Legge, J., *Sukarno. A Political Biography* (London, 1972).

Sultan, Lt-General Daniel I. (1885–1947), US Army officer who was *Stilwell's deputy in the *China–Burma–India theatre. When Stilwell was recalled in October 1944, his functions were divided into two. *Wedemeyer became *Mountbatten's deputy at *South-East Asia Command (and *Chiang Kai-shek's Allied chief of staff), while Sultan took command of the India–Burma theatre, and it was Sultan's US–Chinese forces which opened the *Burma Road during the latter part of the *Burma campaign. In June 1945 he became inspector-general of the US Army.

Sumatra, see NETHERLANDS EAST INDIES.

Supreme Headquarters Allied Expeditionary Force, see SHAEF.

Supreme War Council, the Anglo-French co-ordinating committee which oversaw Anglo-French strategy before and during the fall of *France in June 1940, but which had no operational powers. It first met at Abbeville on 12 September 1939. The last meeting took place near Tours on 13 June 1940 when British representatives included Churchill, *Dill, and *Beaverbrook, and French representatives included *Reynaud, *Pétain, and de *Gaulle who had just been made under-secretary for National Defence.

Sussex teams, 50 two-man Allied intelligence teams jointly run by the *Bureau Central de Renseignements et d'Action, the *Office of Strategic Services, and *MI6. Recruited from the French forces in North Africa, they were trained by MI6 before being dropped into France to transmit information about German movements at the time of the Normandy landings in June 1944 (see OVERLORD). Five pathfinder agents were dropped in

February 1944 and by the end of May thirteen teams were operating. As the Allied armies swept across France (see NORMANDY CAMPAIGN), some volunteered to be dropped behind the German lines, but they were all withdrawn in October 1944. Unlike the *Cooney, or *Jedburgh, teams, they did not wear uniform. See also SPIES.

Suzuki Kantarō (1867–1948), retired Japanese admiral who spent the war as a member of the privy council until, in April 1945, following the resignation of the prime minister, *Koiso Kuniaki, he formed Japan's last wartime government. A universally popular figure in Japan, who was backed by those fervently seeking peace, this venerable and moderate gentleman was then aged 78, and it was beyond his means to give the country the lead it needed to bring the war to its conclusion. He unsuccessfully sought terms through various intermediaries, but his response to the Allies' Potsdam conference declaration in July 1945 (see TERMINAL), given at a press conference, was ambiguous, and on 6 August the first *atomic bomb was dropped on *Hiroshima. He resigned when Japan surrendered on 15 August 1945. See also JAPAN, 3.

Svoboda, General Ludvik (1895–1979), Slovak Army officer who, after the German invasion of Czechoslovakia in March 1939, escaped to Poland and raised a Czech Legion which fought the Germans during the *Polish campaign that autumn. The Legion then escaped to the USSR and in February 1942 Svoboda formed the 1st Czech Independent Infantry Battalion which fought on the Eastern Front during the *German–Soviet war. In December 1943 he was promoted general and made C-in-C of the Czech Army by the Czech president, Edvard *Beneš. By 1944 Svoboda's command had become a corps which took part in the fighting in Slovakia. He was president of Czechoslovakia and C-in-C from 1968 to 1975.

swastika (*Hakenkreuz*), the hooked black cross which became part of the German national flag in 1935. Its origins go back to the ancient world, in which it was a fertility symbol. In early Christian and Byzantine art it was known as the Gammadion Cross. In 1910 the German poet and ideologist Guido von List suggested it as the symbol for all anti-Semitic organizations and for this reason—and because it was thought, incorrectly, to be Teutonic in origin—it was adopted by Hitler's National Socialist Party in 1919. The word swastika comes from Sanskrit, meaning 'well-being'. See also ANTI-SEMITISM.

Sweden. In September 1939 Sweden was a peaceful democracy on the northern periphery of Europe with a population of just under 6.5 million. Although full parliamentary democracy had only been introduced less than 20 years earlier, the country had a centuries-old tradition of constitutional government and the rule of law. Neither the far right nor the far left had been able to achieve any real strength in Swedish politics, which were dominated by four parties committed to the existing political system: the Conservatives, the Liberals, the Agrarian Union, and the Social Democrats. The government was a stable, majority coalition of the Social Democrats and the Agrarians, headed by Per Albin Hansson, the Social Democratic leader. In December 1939 a national government was formed under Hansson's leadership by extending the existing coalition to include the Conservatives and the Liberals.

Sweden had not been at war since 1814 and by 1939 was one of Europe's long-standing, traditional neutrals. This, of course, was no guarantee of future safety and in a number of important respects Sweden was in a weak position in 1939. Although a rearmament programme had been initiated in 1936, the Swedish armed forces still lacked modern military equipment in significant quantities and military weakness remained a factor underlying Swedish policy until the last years of the war. In 1937 the total personnel of the Swedish Army was 403,000 men and it possessed 79 anti-aircraft guns and no tanks. In 1945 the corresponding figures were 600,000 men, 2,750 anti-aircraft guns, and 766 tanks. The strength of the Swedish Air Force grew from 257 aircraft of all types in 1936 to 596 in 1940 and 1,018 in 1945, while the Swedish Navy had 47 vessels of all types in service in September 1939 and 126 in May 1945.

Economically, Sweden was dependent on foreign trade. It needed to import a number of vital commodities, above all oil and coal and, in trying to sustain this trade, lost no fewer than 241 ships, 26 of which were seized by the Germans. A factor which compensated for military and economic vulnerability was Sweden's geographic remoteness from the centre of Europe. It also had the advantage of being surrounded by neighbours that served as buffer states: Norway in the west, Denmark in the south, and Finland in the east. Moreover, Swedish territory in itself was unlikely to be of overriding importance to any belligerent, except in one respect: Germany obtained well over half its vital iron ore imports from the far north of the country (see Table).

Within Sweden, the neutralist tradition was long-established and widely supported. This did not mean that Swedes had no views or sympathies in relation to the fate of Europe. Conservative and military circles were anxious that the USSR might try to reconquer Finland and that communist revolution might sweep through Europe in the wake of a German collapse. The pre-war balance in Europe between Moscow, Berlin/Rome, and Paris/London was not disadvantageous to Sweden, and the prospect that the war would end (as in fact it did) with Germany's removal as a Great Power and Soviet domination of much of Europe was unwelcome to mainstream Swedish opinion. On the other hand, there was widespread distaste for German Nazism, and not only on the left of the political spectrum. Many Swedes regarded the prospect that Hitler would ultimately triumph as a catastrophe for Europe.

However, such views and sympathies did not, broadly

Sweden: German imports of Swedish iron ore (all figures are in millions of tons)

	German domestic production of iron	*Total German iron ore imports*	*German iron ore imports from Sweden*
1939	14.7	19.6	10.0
1940	19.2	9.9	8.4
1941	18.1	17.4	9.2
1942	15.3	17.8	7.9
1943	15.2	19.6	9.6
1944	–	8.2	3.4

Source: Contributor.

speaking, lead to the conclusion that Sweden should abandon its neutral stance. The greatest difficulty about neutrality for Swedish opinion related not to the war as a whole but to Sweden's Nordic neighbours: Denmark, Finland, and Norway. Feelings of Nordic solidarity, combined with Sweden's interest in the continuing independence of its three neighbours, were a factor in Swedish policy throughout the war, though never one which could override the demands of power politics.

The first year of the war was marked by two serious crises for Sweden. The first was unleashed by the Soviet invasion of Finland on 30 November 1939, which shattered the relative tranquillity of the region and drew the attention of the belligerents northwards. It was after the outbreak of the *Finnish–Soviet war (the Winter War) that Germany began serious planning for WESERÜBUNG (the occupation of Denmark and Norway) and that France and the UK developed a scheme to occupy the Swedish orefields under the guise of assisting Finland. In Sweden, the new national government chose to steer a middle course between neutrality and intervention in the Finnish war. Armaments and other supplies were sent to Finland on a large scale, and by the end of the Winter War about 8,000 Swedish volunteers were serving in Finland, but the government repeatedly ruled out intervention by the Swedish Army and resisted Anglo-French pressure to allow Allied troops to enter Sweden *en route* for Finland. This refusal to intervene fully to help Finland created a moral crisis in the minds of many Swedes, but the government succeeded in retaining the support of majority opinion. During the last six weeks of the war, after Stalin's decision to seek a settlement with Finland, Sweden acted as an intermediary between the two parties in the negotiations which led to the conclusion of the Winter War in mid-March 1940.

The restoration of peace in the region proved short-lived. Less than a month after the Peace of Moscow, on 9 April 1940, Germany invaded Denmark and Norway. Once again, Nordic sentiment in Sweden was outraged, but—in contrast to its policy towards Finland—Stockholm followed a policy of strict neutrality during the two months of the *Norwegian campaign and no assistance was given to Norway. On the other hand, Sweden did mobilize its army and resisted German pressure to allow the transit of munitions. What weakened Swedish resolution was the failure of Allied arms in Norway and, even more, the fall of *France. In these circumstances, the government yielded on 18 June 1940 to German demands that parts of the Swedish railway network be made available for the passage of armaments to Norway and of German soldiers on leave travelling between Norway and Germany.

The presence of large German forces in Denmark and Norway made Sweden far more vulnerable to German attack and cut it off from any possibility of assistance from the west. The country remained a non-belligerent, but was enclosed within the area of German control. The transit agreement with Germany in the summer of 1940 was one manifestation of this state of affairs. So were the government's efforts to curtail the most vociferous anti-Nazi comment in the Swedish press. However, the best known of Sweden's concessions during the period when German power was at its height was the decision to allow the so-called Engelbrecht Division through Sweden. On 22 June 1941, the day of the German invasion of the USSR (see BARBAROSSA), the Germans demanded that a division stationed in Norway should be allowed to cross Sweden to Finland. After several days of intense discussion in Swedish political circles, the government acceded to the German demand.

As such concessions demonstrate, what Germany demanded was that Sweden should be responsive to the needs of the German war effort but not that it depart from actual non-belligerency. Sweden emerged from the years of German domination of the European continent as an unoccupied, independent state able, during the last years of the war, to adopt a much firmer attitude towards Germany. Large German forces remained in the Nordic region around its frontiers, but a German attack became less and less practical: the Swedish armed forces were considerably stronger than they had been in the earlier part of the war and Germany was under growing military pressure on all sides. The first and most striking indication of how the position had changed was the Swedish decision, taken under strong British and American pressure, to cancel the 1940 transit agreement with Germany from August 1943, and during the remainder of the war Sweden continued to pursue a policy which was generally accommodating to the Allies and unhelpful towards Germany.

Sweden survived the war as a non-belligerent state by following a flexible policy which responded to the political realities of the moment while retaining some freedom of manoeuvre for the future. It was a policy that was sometimes offensive to significant sections of political and public opinion, but an essential measure of national unity was always maintained. In the last resort, however, it was also a policy which only succeeded because none of the belligerents ever concluded that its interests required that Sweden be forced into the war at all costs. See also BLOCKADE RUNNERS.

THOMAS MUNCH-PETERSEN

Carlgren, W. M., *Swedish Foreign Policy during the Second World War* (London, 1977).
Munch-Petersen, T., *The Strategy of Phoney War. Britain, Sweden and the Iron Ore Question 1939–1940* (Stockholm, 1981).

Switzerland, a democratic state with strong traditions of neutrality, though its German- and Italian-speaking cantons made its political position a sensitive one. Its geographical position was equally delicate: sandwiched between the two Axis powers of Germany and Italy, the Swiss government (the Federal Council) knew invasion was a real possibility and on 2 September 1939 it mobilized the Swiss Army, some 435,000-strong. The army's commander, General Henri Guisan, initially deployed most of it in the north-west of the country in case the Germans attempted to outflank the *Maginot Line by entering Switzerland north of Basle.

Though numerically strong, the Swiss Army was not mechanized, its artillery was still being modernized, and the air force comprised only 150 Swiss-built fighters of poor performance, and 50 modern Messerschmitt 109 fighters. A mobile battle was therefore out of the question and Guisan decided he had only sufficient strength to defend one position properly. The one he chose, opposite the most likely invasion route, stretched from the still-incomplete fortress of Sargans, through Zurich, up to the Gempen Heights overlooking Basle. If the Germans attacked, secret plans (which later fell into German hands) allowed the French, at the request of the Swiss, to occupy the heights south of Basle and the Gempen plateau, where they would link up with units of the Swiss Army. However, once Italy had declared war on the Allies, and the fall of *France had taken place in June 1940, Guisan announced that the only effective means of defence, if Switzerland were invaded, was for the army to abandon most of the country and form a National Redoubt in the southern Alps. This strategy meant that most of the Swiss population of 4.2 million would be left behind; nevertheless, the plan was positively received, for though the Federal Council had to temporize, most Swiss, and especially the *press, were anti-Nazi.

During May 1940 a German attack was expected daily. When both French and German aircraft violated Swiss air space, there were clashes in the air, and in June several German aircraft were shot down. These losses infuriated *Göring who sent a sabotage team to attack Swiss air bases, but it was immediately captured. Later, when British bombers nightly violated Swiss space to raid Germany and Italy, the Swiss were accused by the Germans of doing little to hinder them. In fact, the Swiss did try, but neither their air force nor their anti-aircraft guns were equipped for night fighting. The Germans then demanded that the Swiss use *blackout in their brightly-lit cities which, they said, were useful navigational aids for the British aircraft. At first this was resisted, but it was eventually implemented in November 1940 and remained in force until September 1944. As the Swiss had feared, it resulted in the accidental bombing of Swiss cities. The worst incident was when Schaffhausen was bombed by US aircraft in April 1944, but later the towns of Rafz and Stein were also hit, and in 1949 the US government paid $62 million compensation for the damage.

After the fall of France three-quarters of the Swiss Army was demobilized and the president of the Federal Council, Marcel Pilet-Golaz, gave the impression that Switzerland, like France, was a defeated nation. However, in November 1940, public confidence was restored when both the Fascist National Movement of Switzerland—strong in the German-speaking cantons where assimilation into a greater Germany was by no means ruled out—and the Communist Party were banned. The announcement of the creation of a National Redoubt also improved morale, with Guisan giving the Swiss the strong leadership they were seeking.

Switzerland was tied by treaty to allow the transportation of non-war materials between Italy and Germany, and the Swiss railways carried coal, steel, and agricultural products between the two Axis powers, via the Simplon and St Gotthard tunnels, both of which lay within the National Redoubt. This traffic was essential to the Germans, as it left the Brenner Pass clear for military traffic, but the Swiss prepared both tunnels for demolition, and left the Germans in no doubt that both would be destroyed if they attacked. This proved a powerful negotiating weapon for the Swiss, who needed essential materials and trading concessions from Germany, for much of their food and all their fuel had to be imported.

To ensure that the inward flow of essential goods for the Swiss economy was maintained, fifteen Greek steamers were chartered and others were purchased, and in 1941 Basle was designated a Swiss port. This permitted ships carrying goods to Italian ports for transportation to Switzerland to be registered there so that they could fly the Swiss flag at sea. Rationing of certain essential foods was imposed in October 1939, and by October 1942 even bread had been rationed. In November 1940 the 'Wahlen Plan' was introduced which in four years doubled the country's cultivated surface.

Situated as it was in the centre of Nazi-dominated Europe, Switzerland was a valuable refuge for escaped *prisoners-of-war, members of the French Resistance, and Italian partisans. *Refugees posed a constant moral dilemma. When, at the beginning of 1942, *Vichy France declared 170,000 Jews undesirable residents (see also FINAL SOLUTION), the Swiss borders were closed to them. Some were given asylum, but others were turned back—a number committed suicide in front of the Swiss frontier guards. By May 1945 there were 115,000 refugees, interned military personnel, and escaped prisoners-of-war in Swiss camps. Altogether 400,000 refugees and emigrants reached or passed through the country, many of whom were helped by the *International Red Cross Committee whose headquarters was in Geneva.

Besides being a refuge, Switzerland was a convenient conduit for information about Nazi-occupied Europe (for example, see SCHULTE). This made it an ideal centre for espionage: the *LUCY Ring and the *Rote Drei both operated from there, while *Dulles, the head of the *Office of Strategic Services in Europe, worked from Berne. The Swiss also had their own very efficient intelligence service, headed by Colonel Roger Masson, which had its own high-level intelligence network (WIKING LINE) in Germany. Swiss counter-intelligence was very effective, too, and 387 *spies, mostly Swiss but including 100 Germans, were captured and brought to trial of whom 17 were executed.

In waging *economic warfare against the Axis the Allies were often in conflict with Swiss interests. But though irritated by Swiss compliance with German economic demands the British understood the reasons for it, and when Stalin called the Swiss 'swine', Churchill wrote to his foreign secretary, Anthony *Eden, that the UK should stand by them: 'Of all the neutrals Switzerland has the greatest right to distinction. She has been the sole international force linking the hideously sundered nations and ourselves. What does it matter whether she has been able to give us the commercial advantages we desire or has given too many to the Germans, to keep herself alive? She has been a democratic state, standing for freedom in self-defence among her mountains, and in thought, in spite of race, largely on our side' (see Churchill, *The Second World War: Triumph and Tragedy*, vol. 6, London, 1954, p. 616).

Garlinski, J., *Swiss Corridor* (London, 1981).
Schwarz, U., *The Eye of the Hurricane* (Boulder, Colo., 1980).

SWORD, codename for assault beach in British sector on which 3rd British Infantry Division disembarked at the start of the Normandy landings on 6 June 1944 (see OVERLORD). It lay between St Aubin sur Mer and the mouth of the River Orne in the Baie de la Seine. By the end of the day 28,845 troops had been landed there.

Sydney, 6,830-ton Australian cruiser which sank, and was apparently sunk by, the German *auxiliary cruiser *Kormoran*, off the west coast of Australia on 19 November 1941. Although 318 of the *Kormoran*'s crew of 398 survived, none of the cruiser's complement of 645 did. The theory that a still-neutral Japanese submarine helped in the cruiser's destruction, and then ensured there were no survivors, remains a speculative one as files that might help clarify what happened are still closed.

Montgomery, M., *Who Sank the Sydney?* (Melbourne, 1981).

Sydney harbour, attack on, night raid by three Japanese *midget submarines which, on 31 May 1942, tried to torpedo Allied warships in this large natural harbour in south-east Australia. The alarm was raised after one of the midget submarines became tangled in anti-torpedo netting and scuttled itself. The US cruiser *Chicago* fired at another, but her shells only caused damage ashore. After firing its torpedoes—one was a dud, the other hit an accommodation ship, killing nineteen seamen—this submarine disappeared, and the two-man crew of the third committed suicide after being hunted for some hours. The Japanese submarines which had transported the midgets shelled Sydney and Newcastle, and sank three merchantmen, before departing. One midget submarine was exhibited around Australia in 1942 as a boost to public morale when Australian troops were fighting on the *Kokoda trail during the *New Guinea campaign.

SYMBOL, codename for the Allied conference held from 14 to 24 January 1943 at a hotel complex in Anfa, a suburb of Casablanca in French Morocco. Churchill and Roosevelt, and the *Combined Chiefs of Staff, were present, and Generals *Alexander and *Eisenhower also took part in some of the discussions which centred primarily on future strategy (see GRAND ALLIANCE). Stalin was invited, but he declined because of the critical situation at *Stalingrad. The Allied policy of *unconditional surrender was first announced there, and the decision to launch a *Combined Bomber Offensive from the UK against Germany, was made. De *Gaulle and *Giraud, who then represented different factions of the French armed forces opposing the *Vichy French regime, were, with difficulty, brought together to attempt a political settlement between them, and this eventually led to the formation of the *French National Committee for Liberation.

Syria. Formerly part of the Ottoman Empire, this French mandate in the Levant sided with the *Vichy regime after the fall of *France in June 1940. In December 1940 General *Dentz became the country's high commissioner and in May 1941, on instructions from the Vichy government, which had just negotiated the *Paris protocols, he allowed German aircraft to land in Syria while on their way to support *Rashid Ali's revolt against the British in Iraq. An invasion by Australian, British, and Free French forces followed on 8 June 1941 (see SYRIAN CAMPAIGN). An *armistice was signed five weeks later and the Free French commander, General *Catroux, then became Syria's 'Delegate-General and Plenipotentiary'. An independent Syrian republic was proclaimed by the

One of the midget submarines which attacked shipping in **Sydney harbour** in May 1942 being raised from the seabed.

French in September 1941 and elections in 1943 returned a large nationalist majority. Independence was finally granted on 1 January 1944, but the country remained under Anglo-French occupation. Rioting broke out on *V-E Day and later there was fighting between the French and the Syrians which ended in Damascus being bombarded by the French. British forces then intervened, but it was not until April 1946 that British and French forces withdrew. See also ANTI-IMPERIALISM and NATIONALISM.

Syrian campaign, fought in June–July 1941 when Australian, British, and General Paul Legentilhomme's Free French forces, all commanded by Lt-General Maitland *Wilson, invaded the French mandates of Syria and Lebanon to prevent supposed German plans to establish a base there from which to attack Egypt.

When *Rashid Ali rose against the presence of British troops in Iraq in April 1941 the Germans decided to help him. Under the *Paris protocols they arranged with the *Vichy French government to use Syrian airfields as staging posts for German aircraft supporting Rashid Ali, and for the high commissioner, General *Dentz, to provide the Iraqis with arms. Some of these moves were known to the British through *ULTRA intelligence, but the extent of German designs on Syria remained uncertain until after the Allied invasion was launched. It then became clear that German interest was limited; in fact all its forces were withdrawn before the fighting began, though German aircraft, based in Greece and the Dodecanese, flew sorties in support of the French, and Hitler permitted Dentz's troops to be reinforced.

Hopes of an unopposed occupation, after both British and French had openly guaranteed the independence of Syria and Lebanon, were soon dashed; for Dentz, well aware that the Paris protocols were being negotiated, and that France's future could depend on them, was determined to show solidarity with Germany. Opposing Wilson's forces, which included elements of the French Foreign Legion, was a mixed force of 45,000 local and French colonial troops, and four battalions of a French Foreign Legion regiment. There was fierce fighting at the River Litani, and at Kissoué where French fought against French, and on 19 June 1941 two Indian battalions and one British battalion were surrounded and forced to surrender at Mezze. But two days later Free French and Australian units entered Damascus where the two factions of the French Foreign Legion fought one another in the streets. It fell the next day and a mixed force of British troops (HABFORCE), including the Arab Legion, entered Syria from Iraq and advanced on Palmyra. This was attacked on 25 June—the Legionnaires there held on

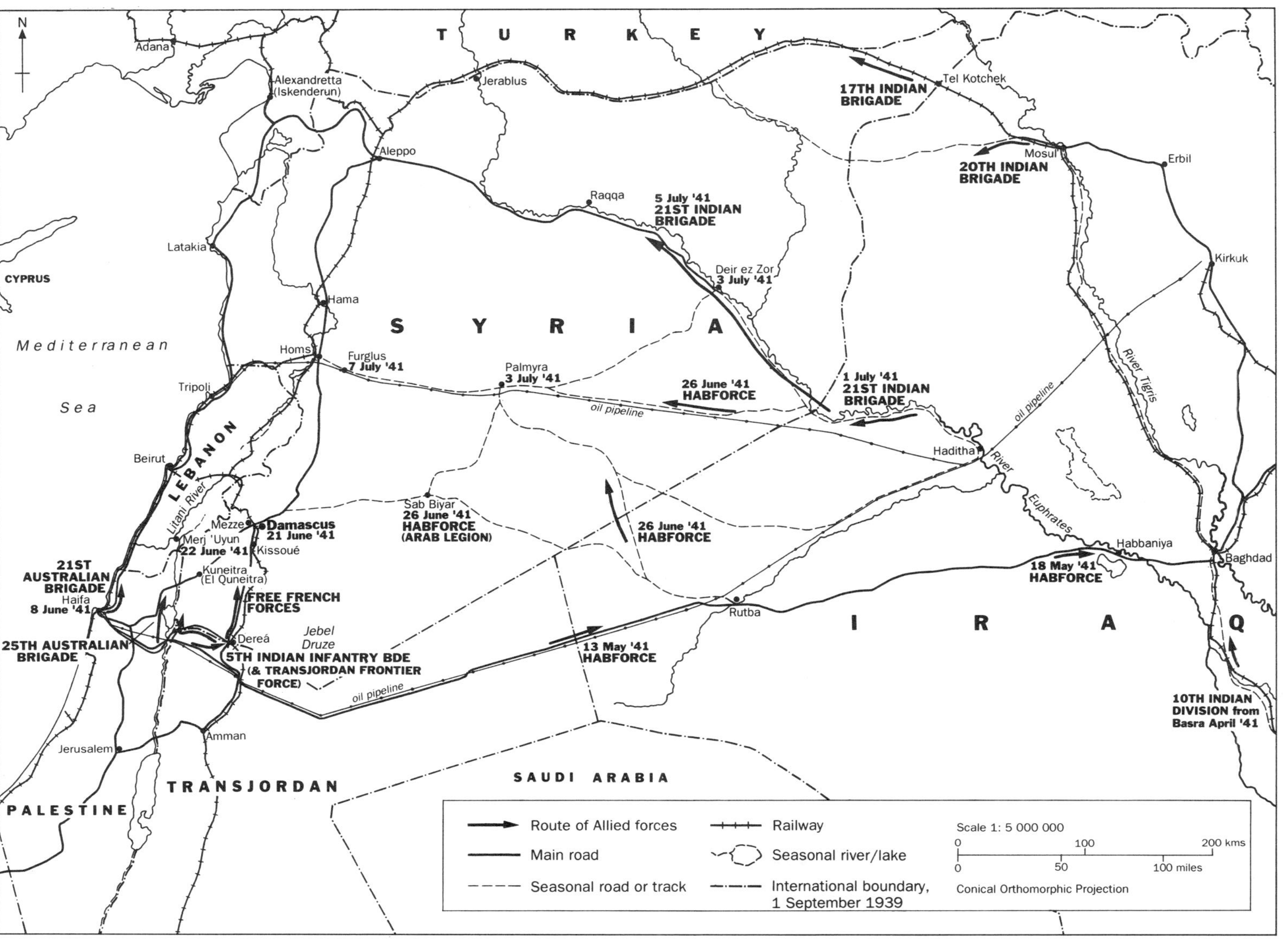

102. Iraqi and **Syrian campaigns**, May–July 1941

for nine days—and at sea a Vichy French naval flotilla was defeated. Then *Slim's 10th Indian Division also entered Syria from Iraq, and Dentz's forces became isolated. On 10 July, when the Australians were within 8 km. (5 mi.) of Beirut, Lebanon's capital, Dentz requested an *armistice. Known as the Acre Convention, and signed on 14 July, its terms were generous to the Vichy French who had fought so hard, and they were accorded all the honours of war. The fact that the Free French were not a party to the Acre Convention infuriated de *Gaulle, but a compromise was eventually reached whereby, among other concessions, he was allowed to seek recruits from among the Vichy French troops. Some 6,000 joined him but many more chose to return to France.

Szabo, Violette (1921–45), Anglo-French shop assistant who, after her husband was killed during the second *El Alamein battle in November 1942, joined the *ATS and then *FANY and the *SOE, and in June 1944 was parachuted into the Limoges area to strengthen local resistance groups. She was captured, and executed at *Ravensbrück; and was posthumously awarded the George Cross (see DECORATIONS).

Minney, R. J., *Carve Her Name With Pride* (London, 1956).

Szilard, Leo (1898–1964), Hungarian-born nuclear physicist who, after serving in the *First World War, studied physics in Berlin. He was the first to propound what then seemed the highly implausible idea of a nuclear chain reaction, crucial to the development of an *atomic bomb. When Hitler came to power in January 1933, Szilard went to the UK and then to the USA where he worked with Enrico *Fermi who supervised the first nuclear chain reaction in Chicago in December 1942.

More politically aware than most of his fellow nuclear physicists, Szilard encouraged the US government to continue research into the development of a nuclear weapon. In September 1939 he drafted the letter signed by Albert Einstein to Roosevelt which voiced his anxieties, and those of Fermi, that Germany might also be building one (see also HEISENBERG and SCIENTISTS AT WAR).

Takoradi air route, used to fly Allied aircraft reinforcements between the Gold Coast and Egypt, and to ferry *Lend-Lease aircraft to the USSR. The route was pioneered between the wars and in 1936 Imperial Airways began running a weekly service over part of it, between Lagos in Nigeria and Khartoum in the Sudan. When Italy entered the war, in June 1940, it was decided to use the route with its series of landing strips to fly reinforcements to the *Western Desert Air Force fighting in the *Western Desert campaigns. Aircraft were either shipped to Takoradi, assembled there, then flown the 6,450 km. (4,000 mi.) across Africa to Khartoum, and then up to Abu Sueir on the Suez canal near Cairo; or they were flown to Takoradi from the USA using Brazil and Ascension Island as staging posts. The Free French *Fezzan campaigns kept the Italians from encroaching on the route's airfields.

Tallboy bomb, British 12,000 lb. (5,430 kg.) bomb, a scaled-down version of the *Grand Slam bomb. It was developed by Barnes *Wallis and was first used operationally in June 1944. Altogether, 854 were dropped by the *Dam Buster squadron on targets which included the German battleship **Tirpitz*. They were used in combination with Grand Slam bombs when those became operational in March 1945. See also BOMBS.

Tanaka Raizō, Rear-Admiral (1892–1969), Japanese destroyer commander who played an important part in the *Java Sea battle and was involved in many major naval actions during the *Pacific war. These included *Midway and those around *Guadalcanal, where he was responsible for the *Tokyo Express and where he defeated superior US naval forces off *Tassafaronga. But in July 1943 he had his flagship sunk under him while trying to reinforce troops on Kolombangara during the *New Georgia campaign. When Tanaka protested about the waste of resources in carrying out such operations he was dismissed and never received another sea command. He was a hard-headed, first-class destroyer leader, probably the best the Japanese had. Allied naval commanders had a great respect for him, but he was not so highly thought of by some of his colleagues. He ended the war as overall commander of all naval units in Burma.

Tanganyika, see BRITISH EAST AFRICA.

Tangier was an international zone, and port, within Spanish Morocco. In June 1940, when it appeared that Italy might take the zone over, Spain occupied it and dismantled the international administration. The port of Tangier soon became a centre of German espionage (see also SPIES) until Allied diplomatic pressure forced the closure of the German consulate in May 1944. After the war it reverted to international control.

tanks

1. Design and development

Tracked Armoured Fighting Vehicles (AFVs, called tanks by the British) were first used in battle in 1916 as a weapon system incorporating firepower (two 57 mm./2.2 in. guns plus machine-guns), protection (10 mm./.39 in. armour plate) and mobility (a 105 hp engine driving endless tracks to give a maximum speed of 6.4 kph/4 mph across country and obstacles). But after the *First World War the original British 28-ton, rhomboid tanks were replaced by lighter types armed with anti-tank guns up to 50 mm. (1.95 in.) calibre mounted in revolving turrets, with 14 to 20 mm. (.54 to .78 in.) homogenous steel armour, speeds up to 29 kph (18 mph), and marginally improved mechanical reliability. Most were modelled on the Vickers Medium of 1922 and were similar in layout to Second World War tanks (see table for principal types).

Experiments in tank warfare during the 1920s and 1930s centred on infantry support tactics, long-range so-called independent operations, and tank versus tank action, all controlled by *radio communications. The first role called for 'infantry tanks', proof against existing *anti-tank weapons but slower than those for the second role which demanded tanks with lighter armour and a wide radius of action. The size of anti-tank weapon dictated a tank's size—the bigger the gun, the larger the turret; therefore the heavier the vehicle and the more powerful the engine. But increased complexity in search of a universal machine, capable of fulfilling all roles, only placed extreme demands on technical feasibility and manufacturing capacity—as well as cost when governments were insisting upon cheapness. Compromise ruled.

British and French tanks in 1939 were either very light (up to 10 tons), fast, and machine-gun armed; slower 20-ton mediums with light armour and an anti-tank gun; and very slow 30-ton machines armoured against 37 mm. (1.44 in.) high velocity (HV) guns. The Germans also built light tanks but no heavies yet; instead their mediums, the Mark III with a 37 mm. gun and Mark IV with a short 75 mm. (2.9 in.) piece firing only shells and smoke, had only 30 mm. (1.17 in.) armour, or less, compared with opponents up to 60 mm. (2.34 in.). The Soviets, on the other hand, built light and heavy tanks (mostly based on British Vickers designs) and 48 kph (30 mph) mediums based on the designs of the American J. Walter Christie (whom the British also copied for one of their medium types, the so-called cruiser tanks). Both the Japanese and Italians were influenced by pre-war Vickers designs and concentrated on infantry support vehicles which, in due course, fell well below the standards of other major combatants in all respects.

After gaining experience in the battles of 1940, the Germans and British accelerated the classic gun versus armour contest. The first German reaction was to equip

Tanks: Armoured fighting vehicles, 1939–45

Type	*Year entered service*	*Length*	*Width*	*Armour max.*	*Weight tons*	*Power plant hp*	*Max. speed*	*Main armament*	*Crew*
France									
D 1A	1931	4.9 m (16 ft)	2.2. m (7 ft 3 in)	30 mm (1.2 in)	12	150	19.3 kph (12 mph)	1 x 37 mm (1.44 in)	3
Somua S 35	1936	5.4 m (17 ft 8 in)	2.1 m (7 ft 1 in)	55 mm (2.1 in)	20	190	40 kph (25 mph)	1 x 47 mm (1.83 in)	3
Renault R 35	1935	4.1 m (13. ft 4 in)	1.9 m (6 ft 2 in)	45 mm (1.8 in)	9.8	82	20 kph (12.5 mph)	1 x 37 mm	2
B 1 *bis*	1939	16.6 m (21 ft 9 in)	2.5 m (8 ft 3 in)	60 mm (2.3 in)	32	300	28.2 kph (17.5 mph)	1 x 75 mm (2.9 in)	4
Hotchkiss H 35	1935	4.3 m (14 ft 1 in)	1.8 m (6 ft)	34 mm (1.3 in)	11.4	75	28.2 kph	1 x 37 mm	2
Germany									
PzKpfw IA	1934	4 m (13 ft 2 in)	2 m (6 ft 7 in)	13 mm (0.5 in)	5.4	60	40 kph	2 mg	2
PzKpfw IIC	1937	4.8 m (15 ft 10 in)	2.1 m (7 ft 1 in)	30 mm	8.8	140	25.7 kph (16 mph)	1 x 20 mm (0.8 in)	3
PzKpfw IIID	1938	5.5 m (18 ft)	2.9 m (9 ft 8 in)	30 mm	19.3	320	40 kph	1 x 37 mm	5
PzKpfw IVA	1936	5.7 m (18 ft 8 in)	2.8 m (9 ft 4 in)	20 mm (0.8 in)	17.3	250	30 kph (18.5 mph)	1 x 75 mm	5
PzKpfw IIIJ	1941	5.4 m (17 ft 9 in)	2.9 m (9 ft 7 in)	50 mm (2 in)	22	320	45 kph (28 mph)	1 x 50 mm (1.9 in)	5
PzKpfw IVG	1942	5.9 m (19 ft 4 in)	2.9 m (9 ft 7 in)	50 mm	23.6	300	40 kph	1 x 75 mm	5
PzKpfw Panther D	1943	7 m (22 ft 11 in)	3.5 m (11 ft 5 in)	80 mm (3.1 in)	43	650	45 kph	1 x 75 mm	5
PzKpfw Tiger I	1942	6.9 m (22 ft 8 in)	3.8 m (12 ft 5 in)	100 mm (3.9 in)	55	700	37 kph (23 mph)	1 x 88 mm (3.4 in)	5
PzKpfw Tiger II	1944	7.4 m (24 ft 2 in)	3.8 m (12 ft 5 in)	150 mm (5.9 in)	68	700	37 kph	1 x 88 mm	5
Italy									
CV 3/33	1933	3 m (9 ft 11 in)	1.4 m (4 ft 6 in)	14 mm (0.5 in)	3.35	43	42 kph	2 mg	2
M 11/39	1939	4.7 m (15 ft 6 in)	2.2 m (7 ft 3 in)	30 mm	11	105	32.2 kph (20 mph)	1 x 37 mm	3
M 13/40	1940	4.9 m (16 ft 2 in)	2.2 m	40 mm (1.6 in)	14	105	30.6 kph (19 mph)	1 x 47 mm	4
Japan									
Type 89A	1929	5.1 m (16 ft 8 in)	2.2 m (7 ft 3 in)	17 mm (0.7 in)	13	118	24.1 kph (15 mph)	1 x 57 mm (2.22 in)	4
T95 Kyu-go	1935	3 m (10 ft 1 in)	2 m (6 ft 7 in)	14 mm	7.4	110	45 kph	1 x 37 mm	3
T97 Chi Ha	1937	5 m (16 ft 7 in)	2 m (6 ft 7 in)	25 mm	14	170	38.6 kph (24 mph)	1 x 57 mm	4
T97 Chi-nu	1937	5.1 m (16 ft 8 in)	2 m (6 ft 7 in)	50 mm	18.8	240	38.6 kph	1 x 75 mm	5
UK									
Vickers Medium I	1923	5.3 m (17 ft 6 in)	2.8 m (9 ft 1 in)	6.25 mm (0.24 in)	11.7	90	24 kph	1 x 47 mm	5
Cruiser Mark I	1938	5.8 m (19 ft 3 in)	2.5 m (8 ft 4 in)	14 mm	12	150	40 kph	1 x 40 mm (1.5 in)	6
Infantry Mark I	1938	4.9 m (15 ft 11 in)	2.3 m (7 ft 6 in)	60 mm	11	70	12.9 kph (8 mph)	1 mg	2
Light Mark VIB	1936	3.9 m (13 ft)	2 m (6 ft 7 in)	14 mm	5.5	89	56.3 kph (35 mph)	2 mg	3
Cruiser Mark IV	1939	6 m (19 ft 9 in)	2.5 m (8 ft 3 in)	30 mm	15	340	48.3 kph (30 mph)	1 x 40 mm	4
Infantry Mark II (Matilda)	1940	5.6 m (18 ft 5 in)	2.5 m (8 ft 3 in)	78 mm (3 in)	26.5	2 x 87	24 kph	1 x 40 mm	4
Infantry Mark III (Valentine I)	1940	5.5 m (17 ft 11 in)	2.7 m (8 ft 9 in)	65 mm (2.5 in)	17	135	24 kph	1 x 40 mm	3

Tanks (*cont.*)

	Year					*Power*			
entered			*Armour*	*Weight*	*plant*		*Main*		
Type	*service*	*Length*	*Width*	*max.*	*tons*	*hp*	*Max. speed*	*armament*	*Crew*
Infantry Mark IV (Churchill I)	1941	7.4 m) (24 ft 5 in)	3.3 m (10 ft 8 in)	102 mm (4 in)	38.5	350	27.4 kph (17 mph)	1 x 76 mm (2.9 in)	5
Light Mark VII (Tetrarch)	1941	4.3 m (14 ft 1 in)	2.3 m (7 ft 6 in)	10 mm (0.4 in)	7.5	165	64.3 kph (40 mph)	1 x 40 mm	3
Cruiser Mark VI (Crusader I)	1941	6 m (19 ft 8 in)	2.6 m (8 ft 8 in)	40 mm	19	340	42 kph	1 x 40 mm	5
Cruiser Mark VII (Cromwell IV)	1943	6.3 m (20 ft 10 in)	2.9 m (9 ft 7 in)	76 mm (2.9 in)	27.5	600	61.1 kph (38 mph)	1 x 75 mm	5
Churchill VII	1944	7.4 m (24 ft 5 in)	3.5 m (11 ft 4 in)	152 mm (5.9 in)	40	350	19.3 kph	1 x 75 mm	5
Comet	1944	6.5 m (21 ft 6 in)	3 m (9 ft 10 in)	101 mm (4 in)	32.5	600	46.6 kph (29 mph)	1 x 77 mm (3 in)	5
USA									
M 3 Light (Stuart I)	1940	4.5 m (14 ft 9 in)	2.3 m (7 ft 6 in)	43 mm (1.7 in)	12.3	250	56 kph	1 x 37 mm	4
M 3 Medium (Grant)	1942	5.6 m (18 ft 6 in)	2.7 m (8 ft 9 in)	50 mm	27	340	42 kph	1 x 75 mm 1 x 37 mm	6
M 4 Medium (Sherman I)	1942	6 m (19 ft 7 in)	2.7 m (8 ft 9 in)	76 mm	30	353	40 kph	1 x 75 mm	5
M 24 Light (Chaffee)	1944	5.9 m (19 ft 4 in)	3 m (9 ft 10 in)	38 mm (1.5 in)	18	2 x 110	56 kph	1 x 75 mm	4
M 4 A3 E8 Medium	1944	6.2 m (20 ft 7 in)	2.7 m (8 ft 9 in)	100 mm	33	450	40 kph	1 x 76 mm	5
M 26 (Pershing)	1945	6.5 m (21 ft 4 in)	3.6 m (11 ft 8 in)	102 mm	41	500	48 kph	1 x 90 mm (3.5 in)	5
USSR									
T 26B	1931	5 m (16 ft 3 in)	2.4 m (8 ft)	15 mm (0.6 in)	9.4	91	28.2 kph	1 x 45 mm (1.7 in)	3
BT 2	1931	5.8 m (19 ft 2 in)	2.2 m (7 ft 3 in)	13 mm	10.2	343	61 kph	1 x 37 mm	3
T 35	1935	9.8 m (32 ft 4 in)	3.3 m (10 ft 8 in)	30 mm	45	500	29 kph (18 mph)	1 x 76.2 mm (3 in) 2 x 45 mm	10
BT 7	1935	5.7 m (18 ft 10 in)	2.3 m (7 ft 6 in)	22 mm (0.9 in)	13.8	450	53 kph (33 mph)	1 x 45 mm	3
Heavy KV1A	1940	6.8 m (22 ft 6 in)	3.4 m (11 ft)	90 mm (3.5 in)	43.5	600	33.7 kph (21 mph)	1 x 76.2 mm	5
Medium T 34/76A	1941	6 m (19 ft 9 in)	3 m (9 ft 10 in)	45 mm	26.3	500	53 kph	1 x 76.2 mm	4
Light T 70	1942	4.4 m (14 ft 4 in)	2.4 m (8 ft)	45 mm	9.2	2 x 70	43.4 kph (27 mph)	1 x 45 mm	2
T 34/85	1943	6.2 m (20 ft 3 in)	3 m (9 ft 10 in)	75 mm (2.9 in)	32	500	499 kph (31 mph)	1 x 85 mm (3.3 in)	4
JS II	1944	6.8 m (22 ft 6 in)	3.1 m (10 ft 2 in)	160 mm (6.2 in)	46	600	35.4 kph (22 mph)	1 x 122 mm (4.7 in)	4
T 44	1945	6.2 m (20 ft 3 in)	3.2 m (10 ft 6 in)	90 mm	32	520	515 kph (32 mph)	1 x 85 mm	4
JS III	1945	6.7 m (22 ft 2 in)	3.3 m (10 ft 8 in)	230 mm (9 in)	46	600	40 kph	1 x 122 mm	4

Source: Contributor.

their infantry, instead of tanks, with the improved 50 mm. anti-tank gun. The British aimed to mount 57 mm. guns and also fit 80 mm. (3.1 in.) armour to their newest medium tanks. The Soviets meanwhile, in great secrecy, produced in quantity in 1941 two revolutionary models—the 43-ton KV 1B, with 110 mm. (4.3 in.) armour, and the 26-ton Christie medium T34/76A with 45 mm. (1.75 in.) sloped armour. The former was proof against the German 88 mm. (3.4 in.) dual-purpose gun and both were armed with the dual-purpose 76 mm. (2.9 in.) gun. These tanks shook the Germans into emergency up-armouring and arming of their Mark III and IV mediums, and hastening the design and production of the 56-ton Tiger I Tank, with 88 mm. gun, and the 45-ton Panther with an extra-long 75 mm. gun.

Concurrently with developments in Europe there were advances in the USA, where the need for a medium tank with a 75 mm. gun led first to the stop-gap Lee/Grant design, with 75 mm. gun in a side sponson and 37 mm. in a turret, first used by the British during the *Gazala battle in June 1942. Then came the reliable Sherman, with 75 mm. gun in turret, which would be the principal universal battle tank of the Allies for the rest of the war, ousting the British concept of specialized slow Infantry and fast Medium tanks.

After 1942 rapidly expanding Allied production left the Germans far behind in numbers. Only quality and superior tactics could redress the balance. This their Panthers and Tigers—supplemented by an increasing number of tracked assault guns and Jagdpanzers (more easily produced tank hulls mounting guns with limited traverse)—managed to achieve against the British and Americans; but they found it more difficult against the Soviet 46-ton JS tanks, with 100 or 122 mm. (3.9 or 4.7 in.) guns, and the latest mark of T34, with an 85 mm. gun, which provided very tough technical opposition. Indeed, British tanks were outclassed in every respect from 1942 onwards, while the American decision in 1943 to postpone development of the Sherman's successor, and depend upon vast numbers of improved Shermans, was nearly disastrous, a situation which was only partially redeemed when the British fitted the Sherman with their own good 17-pdr. (76.2 mm.) gun in 1944.

In one department the British excelled: the development of specialized AFVs, such as *flame-throwers (called Crocodiles) and infantry carriers (Kangaroos), adapted from obsolescent tanks (see also AMPHIBIANS and ENGINEERS, 1(d)).

From their debut in action in 1916 the tanks' demise at the hands of the latest anti-tank weapons had been foretold. Yet in 1945, out of need for mobility and due to improved technology and techniques, they dominated battlefields by the tens of thousands.

2. Tank warfare

Tracked Armoured Fighting Vehicles (AFVs) made their battle debut in September 1916 during the First World War. At first they were used as auxiliaries to infantry, operating within the limits of their slow speed, short range, and poor mechanical reliability. But as improvements were made Colonel J. F. C. Fuller of the British Tank Corps advanced ideas for penetration in depth of the enemy lines by armoured forces, supported by aircraft: a concept he expanded in his celebrated Plans 1918 and 1919 which were blueprints for *blitzkrieg (see also LAND POWER).

In the 1920s, while most armies regarded AFVs as infantry adjuncts alone, the British experimented with the so-called 'independent' role of all-arms mechanized forces, in which the tank was the dominant weapon and from which horses were excluded. In the 1930s, while the French and the Soviets were forming mixed divisions either for infantry support or in the traditional cavalry roles of reconnaissance and exploitation of success, the Germans (inspired by *Guderian) copied the British by creating armoured (*Panzer*) divisions. Armoured divisions were organized for all phases of land warfare—reconnaissance, advance to contact, attack, exploitation, defence, and withdrawal by day and night. Ideally, their combat vehicles were to be fully armoured, although this, for economic and industrial reasons, was never achieved. Essentially, however, their flexibility and ability to concentrate rapidly against decisive points, was dependent upon efficient radio communications enabling fluent command and control with maximum economy.

Tank tactics at their most sophisticated, under Guderian's tutelage, revolved around close co-operation by tanks, armoured cars, infantry, artillery, and engineers within ad hoc battle groups, supported by aircraft. After careful reconnaissance they would seek out and attack the opposing side's weak spots to occupy vital ground. This ground they would then hold with infantry and anti-tank weapons as a pivot for further offensive action. Although most tanks were armed for tank versus tank combat, it was hoped to provoke the opposing side into expending tanks against the pivot's anti-tank guns. This conserved the more valuable tanks to spearhead thrusts into their opponents' rear with mobile columns, logistically self-contained for three or four days, which were aimed at strategic and politically sensitive objectives.

In the *Polish campaign of September 1939 these methods proved themselves, although the Germans found (as the British and French had realized when providing special infantry support tanks) that the ordinary infantry divisions needed AFVs to stiffen their offensive spirit. Prior to the German invasion of western Europe in May 1940 (see FALL GELB), therefore, a number of armoured assault guns (self-propelled guns) were produced for infantry support—with a significant outcome. For thereafter assault guns, with tanks, played a dominant role in tank warfare, particularly in tank versus tank combat as far larger, high velocity guns were needed to defeat improved armour in the classic gun versus armour race.

Tank warfare dominated campaigns in open terrain—in western Europe, the Eastern Front, the Western Desert, and North Africa—where freedom of movement was least impeded and static defences were easily outflanked and logistical support relatively easy to sustain. It was also effective in the mountains during the *Balkan campaign in 1941 when the Yugoslavs, Greeks, and British were hopelessly outclassed. The tank thrived against smaller opponents, even in defensively favourable surroundings, but this superiority tended to diminish once forces of rough equality were pitted against each other in built-up areas, such as *Stalingrad, or in adverse terrain.

As the Axis forces lost the initiative after 1942, and their initial offensive superiority was eroded, they developed highly effective anti-tank defences. These were founded upon the maximum utilization of employing counter-strokes within a framework of strategically located static defences keyed to natural or man-made obstacles. The laying of mines, to delay tanks and channel them into killing zones dominated by artillery and anti-tank guns, meant expensive and time-consuming Allied set-piece attacks by all arms; and attacks also frequently needed specialized AFVs to create gaps in minefields, cross water obstacles, and demolish obstructions and strong points (see ENGINEERS, 1(d)).

Having at last refined the blitzkrieg technique, the Allies were frequently compelled to indulge in attritional warfare to wear down their opponents' tank and logistical strength before achieving the breakthrough and thrusting enormous armoured forces deep into their opponents' rear. The second battle of *El Alamein, successive Soviet offensives from Stalingrad onwards, and the latter phase of the *Normandy campaign are outstanding examples of tank warfare in the modern style—offensives which as often as not were halted more by logistical factors (notably fuel shortage) than by force of arms.

Notwithstanding the magnetic drama of massed armoured forces in motion, the effects of small groups or even individual tanks in special situations must not be overlooked. On narrow frontages, such as the jungle trails of Burma, the effect of a single tank pushed forward by immense engineer effort, could be as decisive as a regiment of 60 tanks in a European setting. Regardless of improved anti-tank measures, the mobility, firepower, and protection of tanks, regardless of numbers, was as potent in 1945 as in 1939. KENNETH MACKSEY

Macksey, K., *Tank versus Tank* (London, 1991).
—*Guderian* (London, 1992).
Orgorkiewicz, R., *Armour* (London, 1960).

Tarakan, an island 24 km. (15 mi.) long, situated off the eastern coast of Dutch Borneo in the *Netherlands East Indies, which had valuable oilfields producing about 500,000 tons of oil annually. It was occupied by the Japanese in February 1942. On 1 May 1945 the 13,000-strong Australian 26th Brigade Group, commanded by Brigadier D. Whitehead, with 5,000 men of the Royal Australian Air Force under command, were landed there by a US Amphibious Group with the objective of establishing an air base to support later operations in Borneo. The island was defended by about 2,000 Japanese soldiers and sailors who resisted strongly. Fighting continued until the end of July 1945 and cost the Australians 894 dead or wounded. It was then found that the airfield was beyond immediate repair.

Taranto raid, mounted on 11 November 1940 by units of Admiral *Cunningham's Mediterranean Fleet against this southern Italian naval base. It strongly influenced Japanese plans for their attack on *Pearl Harbor in December 1941 and together with that operation proved an important landmark in naval history, for it brought to a close the battleship era (see also SEA POWER).

The raid was undertaken by 21 Swordfish biplanes which were flown from the British carrier **Illustrious*, positioned 290 km. (180 mi.) from Taranto. They attacked in two waves an hour apart. Each wave included two aircraft which illuminated the targets with flares before flying on to attack ships in the inner harbour to divert the attention of the anti-aircraft guns. Last-minute *photographic reconnaissance averted probable disaster by showing that the anchorage had recently been protected by barrage balloons, and the battleships by nets, which enabled the pilots to avoid these obstacles.

Surprise was total. One new and two old battleships were torpedoed, a cruiser was hit, and the dockyard damaged. Two British aircraft were lost, but at one bold stroke the balance of naval power in the battle for the *Mediterranean was tilted in favour of the Allies. The next day every seaworthy Italian ship left Taranto for safer harbours on Italy's west coast, thus reducing the threat to British *convoys.

Tarawa, capture of, one of the epic battles of the *Pacific war, which opened the way to the *Marshall Islands for US forces and started their drive across the central Pacific.

Part of the Gilbert Islands, the atoll's main island, Betio, 4 km. (2.5 mi.) long and no larger than New York's Central Park, had more than 4,500 top-grade Japanese troops concealed in intricate defences. Makin and Apamama islands, also part of the atoll, were less heavily defended but Betio's defences were so strong that the Japanese commander, Rear-Admiral Shibasaki Keiji, boasted that it could not be taken by a million men in a hundred years. It seemed impervious to the pre-landing air and sea bombardment, though communications were disrupted which prevented a concerted Japanese counter-attack the first night.

Employing LVTs (see AMPHIBIANS) as armoured personnel carriers for the first time in battle, 2nd Marine Division, commanded by Major-General Julian Smith, and a company of tanks, landed on 20 November 1943 after a delay in the assault which gave Shibasaki time to transfer troops to the landing beaches. Insufficient LVTs meant that back-up troops had to be ferried ashore in landing craft. But the tides, which were not constant, had been predicted incorrectly. Many craft became stuck on the reefs and there were heavy casualties among those who had to wade ashore.

The situation remained critical throughout the first day, but by the following afternoon marines had managed to divide the defences by occupying positions on the south shore, and others established a defensive line at the island's western end which allowed reinforcements to land there on the third day. These moved eastwards meeting violent, but isolated, resistance until the remaining Japanese were pinned down at the eastern end. They counter-attacked with **banzai* charges but were held, and by 23 November the island had been overrun.

The US casualty list—1,009 killed, 2,101 wounded—shocked the American public. But it was not the worst, merely the first in a long series of bitterly contested Pacific island battles. See also AMPHIBIOUS WARFARE.

Task Force 38, see TASK FORCE 58.

Task Force 57 was the designation of the combined British Pacific Fleet (Task Force 112) and its *Fleet Train (Task Force 113), which operated in the *Pacific war from March to August 1945 as part of Admiral *Spruance's US Fifth Fleet. The use of it had been offered by Churchill, and accepted by Roosevelt against Admiral *King's advice at the *OCTAGON conference in Quebec the previous September. Under the overall command of Admiral *Fraser, who was appointed in November 1944, it was commanded tactically by Vice-Admiral Bernard Rawlings and comprised two battleships, four carriers, five cruisers, and fourteen destroyers, making it by far the largest and most powerful British fleet of the war. It helped cover the invasion of *Okinawa—where 4 ships were damaged and 98 aircraft lost—and mounted attacks on Formosa and mainland Japan.

Marder, A., *Old Friends, New Enemies*, 2 vols. (Oxford, 1981–92).
Smith, P., *Task Force 57* (London, 1977).

Task Force 58. In March 1943 Admiral *King, C-in-C US Navy, numbered all the units of the US fleets, and the Fast Carrier Force of Vice-Admiral *Spruance's Fifth US Fleet was designated Task Force 58. Under the command of Rear-Admiral Marc Mitschner, TF58—or TF38 when Fifth US Fleet became Third US Fleet under Vice-Admiral *Halsey—was the US Navy's primary strike force in the *Pacific war. By January 1944, when it established air supremacy over the *Marshall Islands prior to the landings there, it comprised four task groups. Together these totalled 12 carriers with 650 aircraft—later increased to 15 carriers—8 new fast battleships, and a powerful escort of cruisers and destroyers. Thereafter, it was involved in nearly all the major sea actions and amphibious landing operations in the Pacific, including the *Philippine Sea and *East China Sea battles, and the landings on *Iwo Jima and *Okinawa. In December 1944, while under Halsey's command, the Task Force was caught in a typhoon as it was refuelling near the Philippines, and lost 3 destroyers, 146 aircraft, and 790 men.

Tassafaronga, battle of, the last of several fierce naval night encounters between Japanese and US warships off *Guadalcanal during the *Pacific war. It took place off the island's Tassafaronga Point and was a prime example of the Japanese Navy's skill at night actions and the supremacy of their Long Lance *torpedoes.

On 30 November 1942, as a Japanese force of two destroyers and six transport-destroyers approached the Point to drop drums of supplies for Japanese troops ashore, it was attacked by five US cruisers and six destroyers of Task Force 67 under Rear-Admiral Carleton Wright. But the Americans were spotted early and Wright was slow to open fire. He sank only one destroyer before the Japanese commander, Rear-Admiral *Tanaka, ordered a torpedo attack which severely damaged three of Wright's cruisers and sank a fourth.

Tedder, Air Chief Marshal Sir Arthur (1890–1967), British airman who served as *Eisenhower's deputy from December 1943 to May 1945.

After serving in the British Army during the *First World War, Tedder transferred to the Royal Flying Corps, rose to command a fighter squadron, and in 1919 was given the rank of squadron leader in the newly formed RAF. In 1937, while AOC, Far East, he was promoted air vice-marshal and in 1938 was appointed to the newly created post of director-general of research and development at the air ministry.

When the ministry of aircraft production was created in 1940 he worked with it, becoming deputy member of the air staff for development and production. However, he had conflicts of opinion with *Beaverbrook, the minister concerned, and this did not enhance his reputation with Churchill. In December 1940, early in the battle for the *Mediterranean, he became *Longmore's deputy in the Middle East and succeeded him in May 1941 with the rank of air marshal. But when Churchill thought his estimate of RAF strength needed for the relief of *Tobruk was too conservative he tried to have him sacked. *Portal, the chief of air staff, threatened to resign and Tedder stayed.

During his time in the Middle East Tedder did much to improve army—air co-operation, one notable contribution being the bombing technique of clearing a path for ground troops through the Axis defences which came to be known as 'Tedder's carpet' (see also BOMBERS, 2). He was promoted air chief marshal in 1942 and served as vice-chief of the air staff before becoming Allied Air Commander in the Mediterranean in February 1943, the start of a long and successful partnership with Eisenhower and also a turning-point in his relationship with the prime minister.

In December 1943 Tedder returned to England as Eisenhower's deputy for the Normandy landings which took place the following June (see OVERLORD). He orchestrated the vast array of Allied aircraft with such effectiveness that the Germans had little chance of intervening during the landings and were severely hampered in bringing up supplies and land reinforcements after them. But in his role as Deputy Supreme Commander at *SHAEF Tedder was also an outstanding mediator: like Eisenhower he truly understood the meaning of unified command and of co-operation.

Tedder was a quiet man with a quizzical sense of humour, but he could be tough, too. *Harris, with whom Tedder clashed more than once, thought Tedder had one of the most brilliant minds of any serviceman. He was knighted in 1942, promoted Marshal of the Royal Air Force in September 1945, created a baron in January 1946, and became Chief of Air Staff the same month. See also AIR POWER.

Tedder, A., *With Prejudice* (London, 1966).

Teheran conference, see EUREKA; see also GRAND ALLIANCE.

Tellermine, see MINE WARFARE, 1.

TEMPEST, codename of the Polish Home Army's uprising against the Germans which started in January 1944. Its objective was to maintain Polish autonomy from the USSR, whose troops were entering Poland, and to counter propaganda that it was the Red Army alone that was freeing Poland from *occupation.

On orders from General *Sosnkowski, the Polish C-in-C in London, the Home Army (see POLAND, 4) offered military co-operation with the advancing Red Army against the retreating Germans, while resisting any efforts to infringe Polish independence.

Militarily, TEMPEST could be counted a success, even though the *Warsaw rising of August 1944, which was part of it, failed. The Home Army inflicted heavy losses on the retreating Germans, captured valuable equipment, and liberated several cities such as Lublin and *Lwów. But politically it was not a success. It failed either to pressure Stalin to recognize the Polish government-in-exile in London (see POLAND, 2(e)), or to strengthen the hand of those negotiating with Moscow. In the Polish province of *Volhynia Home Army units did at first work successfully with the Red Army, but at *Wilno they were arrested. Whatever the initial reaction the end result was the same: any agreements were always abrogated by the commanders of *NKVD units which replaced Red Army ones and Home Army commanders were shot or imprisoned. Their men were disarmed and ordered to join *Berling's Army. If they refused they were deported, and eventually 50,000 were sent to the *GUlag.

tenkō Japanese word for recantation, or thought reform, usually by coercion, as practised by the *Tokkō, particularly on communists during the 1930s. During the period 1937–45 it evolved into a method of showing loyalty to the regime and political organizations and liberal thinkers issued *tenkō* statements even when their loyalty had not been in doubt. *Tenko*, with no accent, is the Japanese word for roll-call.

Tenth Light Flotilla, unit of the Italian Navy equipped with 'special attack weapons'.

The Italians pioneered the *human torpedo, *frogmen, and the *explosive motor boat (EMB), and were early developers of the *midget submarine. These were weapons which the Tenth Light Flotilla, which was commanded by Commander Vittorio Moccagatta and from mid-1942 by Commander Prince Junio Borghese, used to good effect during the early years of the war. Most notably, three of the unit's human torpedoes penetrated Alexandria harbour in December 1941 and severely damaged two British battleships, *Valiant* and *Queen Elizabeth*, along with a tanker and a destroyer, thereby altering the balance of *sea power in the battle for the *Mediterranean. The unit also launched an EMB and human torpedo attack on Valetta harbour, Malta, in July 1942, in which Moccagatta was killed; raided Gibraltar harbour several times from Spain and sank eleven merchantmen; and mounted other attacks on Allied shipping in the Mediterranean, one of which sank the British cruiser *York* in Suda Bay, Crete, with an EMB. When Italy surrendered Borghese himself remained loyal to the Germans—who began to exploit his expertise by forming 'small battle groups' armed with similar weapons (see GERMANY, 6(e))—but some of his men fought on the Allied side and took part in Anglo-Italian human torpedo and frogman operations.

Borghese, J., *Sea Devils* (London, 1952).

Terauchi Hisaichi, Field Marshal Count (1879–1946), Imperial Japanese Army (IJA) officer, the eldest son of Field Marshal Terauchi Masatake, a one-time war minister and prime minister from whom he inherited the title of count in 1919. He was about to retire into obscurity when the purges which followed the *coup d'état* of February 1936 (in which he was not involved) left him the IJA's senior general. The following month, despite his political inexperience, he was appointed war minister in the cabinet led by Hirota Koki. When that fell, he was appointed, in February 1937, inspector-general of military training, one of the top three offices in the IJA hierarchy, and the following August, just after the start of the *China Incident, he became commander of the North China Area Army.

In accordance with the decision of the Imperial Conference on 5 November 1941 (see JAPAN, 3) to enter the war on the Axis side, Terauchi was appointed to command the Southern Expeditionary Army, comprising Fourteenth, Fifteenth, Sixteenth, and Twenty-Fifth Armies and 3rd and 5th Air Divisions, and on 4 December he set up an advance HQ at Saigon. *Singapore fell in February 1942 and that June Terauchi moved his HQ there and made the former governor-general's residence his own.

Terauchi was less a strategist than a skilful co-ordinator of his commanders and staff officers, in whom he had complete trust, permitting them unusual freedom of action. On one of the rare occasions he asserted himself he dismissed General Kuroda Shigenori, Fourteenth Army's commander in the Philippines, over a strategic disagreement, and replaced him with General *Yamashita. Terauchi also made no secret of his displeasure when the prime minister, General *Tōjō (whom Terauchi disliked), announced the transfer of the four northern Malay states to Thailand in July 1943 without consulting him. Terauchi was also strongly opposed to the transfer of his HQ to Manila, which Tōjō ordered in May 1944. He obeyed but then moved his command post to Dalat 225 km. (140 mi.) north-east of Saigon. He suffered a cerebral haemorrhage the following year and was unable to attend the surrender ceremony in Singapore on 12 September 1945. Instead, he surrendered personally to *Mountbatten in Saigon on 30 November 1945. In March 1946 Mountbatten arranged for him to be transferred to a bungalow in Rengam, near Johore Bahru, Malaya, where he died that June.

Terauchi's high reputation for good relations with his subordinate commanders and staff officers, his magnanimous personality, and his seniority (he was given the honorary rank of field marshal in June 1943), resulted in his being the only senior general in the IJA to hold the same post throughout the war. So high was his reputation that, after Tōjō's resignation in July 1944, Terauchi was seriously considered as his possible successor, but the idea was dropped as he was considered too important as the Southern Expeditionary Army's supreme commander. AKASHI YOGI/IAN NISH

Terboven, Josef (1898–1945), German politician who was a member of the Reichstag from 1930 and an early supporter of the Nazis. In April 1940 he was appointed Reich Commissioner of occupied Norway. During the war years he ensured that Norway's economy was geared to Germany's needs, encouraged the collaborators around *Quisling, and suppressed the Norwegian *resistance with great severity. He committed suicide before he could be captured. See also NORWAY, 3.

TERMINAL, codename for the Allied conference held in Potsdam, Germany, from 17 July to 2 August 1945. It was the third, last, and longest conference in which all the principal leaders of the *Grand Alliance took part. But *Truman had replaced Roosevelt, after the latter's death in April, and Churchill, defeated in the general election results announced on 26 July, was replaced midway through the conference by his deputy, *Attlee, who returned to Potsdam as prime minister on 28 July with *Bevin, his foreign secretary.

The principal topics were the surrender terms for Japan, the boundaries and peace terms for Europe, which the Council of Foreign Ministers was formed to draw up, and Poland's future frontiers (see ODER–NEISSE LINE) and government. The last occupied many of the discussions, with representatives of the provisional government (see LUBLIN COMMITTEE) taking part in some of them; but the conference will, perhaps, be best remembered for the Potsdam Declaration which stated the surrender terms for Japan.

Via the Japanese ambassador in Moscow, Emperor *Hirohito had already expressed his wish to end the war, but Stalin intimated to his western partners that Japan would not accept *unconditional surrender, a fact the Americans already knew through *MAGIC intelligence. On 26 July the Potsdam Declaration was issued after it had been approved by China, which was a signatory. It called on the Japanese government to proclaim the unconditional surrender of its armed forces and stipulated that 'The authority and influence of those who have deceived and misled the people of Japan into embarking on world conquest' had to be eliminated; that Japan would be occupied until this had been achieved; that the Cairo Declaration, issued at the Cairo Conference in November 1943 (see SEXTANT), would be adhered to; and that Japanese sovereignty would be confined to its four main islands. All Japanese forces would be disarmed and permitted to return to their homes. It was not intended to enslave Japan, but justice would be meted out to war criminals (see FAR EAST WAR CRIMES TRIALS), 'the Japanese government shall remove all obstacles to the revival and strengthening of democratic tendencies', and freedom of speech, religion, and thought, and respect for fundamental human rights, would be established. See also DIPLOMACY.

Termoli landings, executed on 3 October 1943 during the *Italian campaign by two British commando units and the *Special Raiding Squadron. They were mounted to outflank any German attempt to form a defensive line on the River Biferno as the British 13th Corps advanced up the eastern coast of Italy. The three units landed north of Termoli and, with the help of two British brigades landed from the sea, secured the town three days later after heavy fighting.

Teschen, up to 1918, the German name for a rich and heavily industrialized east European Duchy within the Austro-Hungarian empire whose population was 55% Polish. Following the *First World War both Poland and Czechoslovakia claimed one of its regions, also called Teschen, and after a bitter dispute it was divided in July 1920 along the River Olse. The larger part, including the eastern half of the city of Teschen, became Polish (Cieszyn); the western part remained Czech (Český Těšín). However, the dispute remained and after Czechoslovakia was weakened by the *Munich agreement Poland occupied the whole of the region in October 1938. In 1945 Poland attempted to retain it but the USSR reimposed the borders agreed in 1920.

Thailand was nominally ruled by a council of regency, as the king, Ananta Mahidol, remained in Switzerland throughout the war. The real power lay with the country's C-in-C and prime minister, Field Marshal Pibul Songgram, a pro-Japanese military dictator. In June 1939 he changed the country's name from Siam. As *thai* means 'free' this did not please the British, who saw it as symbolic of Pibul's intentions of aligning his country against western colonial influence and co-operating with Japan.

The peacetime strength of the Thai army was 26,500 men organized into two corps; by November 1940 this number had risen to 50,000. The air force had 150 of varying types and age, plus 120 training aircraft. The navy had a British-built destroyer of *First World War vintage, nine large, modern Italian-built torpedo boats, and a miscellany of smaller vessels. Two light cruisers were being built in Italy but these were commandeered by the Italians in December 1941.

In 1940, the two major colonial powers in South-East Asia, France and the UK, signed pacts of non-aggression with Thailand, which declared its neutrality. Despite this, in early 1941 Pibul attacked the French protectorates of Laos and Cambodia in French Indo-China to regain disputed border territories. Though victorious on land, Pibul lost at sea (battle of Koh-Chang, January 1941) and both sides accepted Japanese mediation. As a result the *Vichy French administration in French Indo-China was forced to sign a treaty in May 1941 which gave Thailand the territories it claimed; and the Japanese southward advance against British and Dutch colonial territories then used French Indo-China and Thailand as staging-posts for its campaigns.

The first of these campaigns started in the early hours of 8 December 1941 when the Japanese landed on the Thai coast at Singora and Patani in order to facilitate their *Malayan campaign. Initially, the Thais resisted, as they did a British advance from Malaya the same day, but on 9 December Pibul ordered all resistance to cease. On 25 January 1942 he declared war on the UK and USA, but not on China with whom Japan was also at war. The UK reciprocated, but the USA, believing the country was being coerced, did not, an early sign of policy differences which reflected American suspicions of British post-war intentions towards Thailand. 'For the British, Siam had become, quite simply, an enemy country. For the Americans, who had not reciprocated Siam's declaration of war, she was an enemy-occupied country' (L. Allen, *The End of the War in Asia*, London, 1976, p. 32).

*Collaboration with the Japanese brought Thailand liberal awards of neighbouring territories. Following its declaration of war the Thai government was allowed to occupy the four northerly Unfederated States of Malaya, and when Burma was granted independence in August 1943 Thailand received the Shan states of Kengtun and Mongpan. But though outwardly compliant with the Japanese, many Thais were sympathetic to the Allies. Pibul's political rival, Nai Pridi Bhanomyong, had been made regent by Pibul to keep him quiet. But Pridi started a Free Thai Movement which later linked up with another resistance movement to become the 'XO group'. This worked with *SOE and with the *Office of Strategic Services to foster resistance within Thailand, though the two Allied organizations reflected their countries' differing political attitudes towards Thailand by acting independently of one another. In July 1944 Allied successes and pressure from the Free Thai Movement resulted in the fall of Pibul's government. Khuang Aphaiwong now became prime minister of a government which followed Pridi and by August 1945, when Japan surrendered, local guerrillas had already been in control of northern Thailand for some months.

The terms on which the British were prepared to make peace with Thailand were regarded as too harsh by the Americans, who thought the UK was attempting commercial domination of the country. The USA backed the Thais who achieved the terms they sought. See also ANTI-IMPERIALISM and NATIONALISM.

Thakin (master), the common name for the Dobama Asi-ayone (We Burmans) Society, an amalgamation of two nationalist, communist-minded student groups, mostly from Rangoon University, who sought *collaboration with the Japanese to gain Burma's independence from the UK. 'Thakin' was the usual manner of addressing Europeans and its members wanted to show their equality with them. Their leader, *Aung San, fled Burma and helped create the *Burma Independence Army with 30 other Thakins. This eventually gave them political dominance in Burma under the Japanese occupation and the Thakin Party flag became the national flag, and the party song the national anthem. See also NATIONALISM.

Theresienstadt was the German name for the walled town of Terezin in the Protectorate of Bohemia and Moravia. Situated 56 km. (35 mi.) from Prague it was opened as a camp for Jews in November 1941 on the orders of Reinhard *Heydrich, after its Czech inhabitants had been expelled. Called a *ghetto by the Nazis, it contained elderly Jews unfit for hard work and certain categories of privileged Jews (war veterans, distinguished individuals, senior civil servants). As such it acted as a suitable cover for those implementing the *Final Solution and representatives of the *International Red Cross Committee were even allowed to visit it. But it was really a transit camp and out of the 141,162 Jews who were sent there 88,162 were subsequently deported to death camps (see OPERATION REINHARD), 1,623 were released to Sweden or Switzerland in 1945, but 33,456 died there. At the end of the war 16,832 remained alive as did a few thousand non-Jews who were also incarcerated there.

Third Reich (empire), the term adopted by Hitler during the 1920s to describe the thousand-year regime he intended to create. He regarded it as the successor of the First Reich, the Holy Roman Empire which ended in 1806, and the Second, founded by Prince Otto von Bismarck (1815–98) in 1871, which lasted until 1918.

thousand-bomber raids, mounted in May–June 1942 against German cities by RAF Bomber Command using the bomber-stream technique for the first time (see BOMBERS, 2). They were ordered by *Harris, C-in-C Bomber Command, to publicize—at a time when Roosevelt wanted to cut back on the delivery of US-built aircraft (see ATLANTIC FERRY ORGANIZATION)—the importance of the *strategic air offensive against Germany. The raids, employing the *area bombing technique, used four or five times more aircraft than normal and Harris had to use training units to increase his serviceable bombers, then numbering 400, to the required figure. The first raid, on 30 May 1942, used 1,050 bombers which caused massive damage to Cologne. A second used 956 bombers and the new *shaker technique to bomb Essen two nights later. This, from the British point of view, was less successful, and a third, on 25 June, using 1,006 aircraft (including some from Coastal Command) to bomb Bremen, was also disappointing to Harris, with 49 aircraft being lost. The strain on resources, and the poor results of the last two operations, led to the size of raids being scaled down.

Barker, R., *The Thousand Plan* (London, 1965).

Three-Power conference, held in Moscow in September 1941. Churchill and Roosevelt, while they were together at the *Placentia Bay conference in August 1941, cabled Stalin to propose that it should be held to discuss the distribution of *Lend-Lease supplies. *Beaverbrook representing the UK, and Averell *Harriman the USA, met Soviet representatives to find out what *matériel* the USSR required immediately. The conference was held in a grim and unfriendly atmosphere for Stalin failed to acquire the level of help he requested, but on 1 October a protocol was signed which listed the supplies the UK and USA would provide to the USSR from October 1941 to June 1942. It stated that these would be 'made available at British and American centres of production', but the British undertook to help in its transportation. In fact 90% of the ships used in the *Arctic convoys, and on other supply routes to the USSR, were either British or American owned or controlled, as were the escort ships that protected them. See also GRAND ALLIANCE.

Thümmel, Paul (?–1945), Dresden-based high ranking member of the *Abwehr who, from March 1937, supplied Czechoslovakia with reliable information about Germany's intentions and order of battle. He continued to do so via the Czech underground when the Czech government-in-exile was established in the UK. Code-named A-54, Thümmel's intelligence was passed to both *MI6 and the USSR and helped maintain the credibility of Edvard *Beneš, the exiled Czech leader.

Thümmel was a highly decorated Nazi Party veteran and so many protests followed his arrest in October 1941 that the *Gestapo released him. Rearrested the following March, he was imprisoned without trial and murdered by his *SS guards a few days before the war ended.

The motives for his treachery remain a mystery. He received payments, but not enough to compensate for the dangers to which he exposed himself, and the information he passed was too valuable for him to have been a *double agent. See also SPIES.

Tibet, a country which was, *de facto*, independent and neutral under its Dalai Lama. But it was constantly under pressure from China, which claimed suzerainty over it, and from the UK, to allow transit of war supplies for China. After a Chinese show of force, which the Tibetans defied, and which the Allies told China to desist from, permission for non-military supplies to pass through was granted in 1943. For other supply routes to China see BURMA ROAD, FRENCH INDO-CHINA, HUMP, and LEDO ROAD.

Timor. In 1941 this island 450 km. (280 mi.) long, which lies only 800 km. (500 mi.) from northern Australia, was half-Portuguese and half-Dutch. The Japanese had planned, after occupying the whole island, to station troops in the Portuguese eastern half while allowing the Portuguese to continue ruling. It was a method they had already followed in Thailand and French Indo-China, but in December 1941, 1,320 Australian troops reinforced local Dutch troops at Koepang in Dutch Timor which was part of the *Netherlands East Indies. Some of this joint garrison then occupied Portuguese Timor until Portuguese reinforcements were able to arrive from Portuguese East Africa. However, the Japanese successfully isolated this garrison, firstly by forcing a reinforcement to return to Australia and then mounting a devastating raid on *Darwin.

The day after the Japanese air attack on Darwin, 20 February 1942, Maj-General Ito Takeo, commanding 38th Infantry Group, mounted the 'First classic combined amphibious assault and vertical envelopment (a parachute drop) in history' (M. Bartlett (ed.), *Assault from the Sea*, Annapolis, Md., 1983, p. 202) against the Allied forces holding Koepang, and within three days the defenders had been forced to surrender. Some escaped into the island's rugged interior and, along with those in Portuguese Timor, began a successful guerrilla campaign. Their activities tied down an increasing number of Japanese who were convinced that continued resistance indicated that an attack from Australia was imminent. In September 1942 the guerrillas' numbers rose to about 300 when an Australian Independent Company (see AUSTRALIA, 5(e)) was landed. But overwhelming Japanese superiority, sickness, and the diminishing loyalty of the local people, forced the Australians' withdrawal by January 1943.

Timoshenko, Marshal Semyon (1895–1970), Red Army officer who had been a non-commissioned officer in the Tsarist cavalry and commanded a division in Stalin's creation, the First Cavalry Army, during the Civil War. Subsequently he commanded cavalry divisions and corps until the late 1930s, when the military purge brought him rapid advancement to the highest ranks. In September 1939, he commanded the provisional Ukrainian *front* (army group) in the occupation of eastern Poland during the *Polish campaign. After a similar attempt at an unopposed march into Finland failed bloodily in December (see FINNISH–SOVIET WAR), he assumed command and mounted a ten-week battle of attrition. In March 1940 this enabled the USSR to secure sufficiently stringent terms to claim a victory and gained Timoshenko a Hero of the Soviet Union award (see DECORATIONS), his only one in the war. In May 1940,

Stalin appointed him People's Commissar for Defence and advanced him to Marshal of the Soviet Union.

The Finnish–Soviet war, which exposed pervasive weaknesses in the Soviet command system, and the fall of *France in June 1940, which left the USSR alone on the continent with a rampant Germany, imposed massive pressure and problems on Timoshenko as defence commissar. He worked manfully to reorganize, retrain, and expand the armed forces, but some intangible requisites, such as initiative and flexibility, were exceedingly difficult to instil under a political system that demanded passive subservience. Moreover, making the same error as the British and French with regard to Poland, he and his staff concluded that *blitzkrieg was only possible against a weak and irresolute opponent. Therefore, they believed a *German–Soviet war would be prolonged and difficult but devoid of major surprises. In early 1941, they were as well prepared as they needed to be for the kind of war they expected to fight.

When Germany invaded the USSR in June 1941 (see BARBAROSSA), Timoshenko automatically became chairman of the *Stavka and therefore titular C-in-C of the armed forces, although Stalin held all the authority. On 10 July Stalin sent him into the field to take command of West Front and five reserve armies in the River *Dnieper sector due west of Moscow. There, at the cost of almost all his men and equipment, he managed to keep the battle around *Smolensk going into early August. By then, Stalin had become the supreme C-in-C, but Timoshenko stayed on in the Stavka throughout the war as a member without portfolio.

In September, after the disaster at *Kiev, he took over the remnants of South-West and South *fronts* then retreating across the eastern Ukraine. Co-ordinating the two, he regained enough equilibrium by late November to stage a counter-attack that drove two SS panzer divisions back 65 km. (40 mi.) from Rostov-on-Don. As the first Soviet advance of the war, and the first German retreat since September 1939 (see KUTNO), this success had a great psychological impact.

In April 1942, while trying to meet Stalin's requirement for 'pre-emptive blows' against the German deployment for a summer offensive, Timoshenko lost a quarter of a million men along with their tanks and artillery in an ill-timed thrust towards *Kharkov. The losses could not be made good before the German offensive began in June. In the ensuing retreat, which rapidly became a near-rout, he lost control of his armies. On 23 July, Stalin recalled him to Moscow, probably to preserve his reputation, since he was then regarded at home and abroad as the most competent Soviet general.

He returned to the field in October to command North-West *front*, which had been trying all summer to reduce a German salient at Demyansk. After that succeeded in March 1943, he turned to co-ordinating operations on secondary fronts as a representative of the Stavka, first (March–June) at *Leningrad, then (June–November) against a German bridgehead on the eastern coast of the *Black Sea, and later (February–June 1944) in the *Baltic littoral.

From August 1944 to May 1945, Timoshenko co-ordinated the First, Second, and Third Ukrainian *fronts* in the drive through the Danube basin towards Vienna. The advance went splendidly for two months but then stalled for three at and around *Budapest. Thereafter, Timoshenko's forces took Vienna on 13 April 1945 and made contact with the Americans at Linz on 6 May.

EARL ZIEMKE

Tinian. One of the Pacific Mariana Islands chain, this island 16 km. (10 mi.) long, which lies just 5 km. (3 mi.) from *Saipan, was garrisoned by 8,350 Japanese troops during the *Pacific war. Following a 43-day air and sea bombardment, 2nd and 4th US Marine Divisions of Maj-General Harry Schmidt's 5th Amphibious Corps (see also AMPHIBIOUS WARFARE) landed there on 24 July 1944. They overcame all organized opposition in twelve days, though it took three months to eliminate pockets of resistance. So well did the marines fight and co-ordinate with the supporting forces that the commanding general of the Marianas Expeditionary Troops, Lt-General Holland Smith (1882–1967), considered it the best amphibious operation in the Pacific war. It was from Tinian that B29 bombers delivered the *atomic bombs on *Hiroshima and *Nagasaki.

TINSEL, British codename for a small transmitter fitted on some British bombers adjacent to one of their engines. When operating, it jammed the *radio communications of German controllers with their night fighters by transmitting the noise of the engine on the same frequency. First used in the autumn of 1943, it was soon neutralized when the Germans began employing more powerful transmitters on several frequencies. See also KAMMHUBER LINE and STRATEGIC AIR OFFENSIVES.

Tirailleurs (sharpshooters), the name given to the infantry regiments of the Armée d'Afrique and the Troupes Coloniales (see FRANCE, 6(b)). Originally, the term was applied to indigenous troops used for skirmishing or as scouts, not as infantry of the line. The Armée d'Afrique conscripted them from the local populations of Algeria, Tunisia, and French Morocco; the Troupes Coloniales conscripted them from other French colonies with French subject status. Twenty-one regiments of Tirailleurs Algériens and Tirailleurs Tunisiens took part in the fighting which preceded the fall of *France in June 1940, eight fought in the *North African campaign, four in the *French Expeditionary Corps in the *Italian campaign, and five in the *French Riviera landings. The Tirailleurs Sénégalais, the generic description for infantry units raised from the populations of French sub-Saharan colonies, also fought in France in 1940 and suffered heavy casualties. They were then used by the *Vichy French government and by the Free French, so that they sometimes fought each other (see GABON and SYRIAN CAMPAIGNS, for example). Tirailleurs opposed the Allies at the start of the North African campaign, but then fought with them, and, with de *Lattre de Tassigny's First French Army, some took part in the French Riviera landings and the battle for *Germany.

Clayton, A., *France, Soldiers and Africa* (London, 1988).

Tirpitz was the sister ship of the 42,000-ton German battleship **Bismarck*. She was armed with eight 38 cm. (15 in.) guns, but the only time she employed them was against shore installations on Spitzbergen, for the stringent conditions Hitler put on the vessel's use rarely allowed her to put to sea.

In March 1942 she left Trondheim in Norway to attack an *Arctic convoy. The British Admiralty, alerted by *ULTRA intelligence, had already ordered the Home Fleet to sea. But errors aboard the flagship and by the Operational Intelligence Centre of the Admiralty's Intelligence Division, then inexperienced in handling ULTRA in such a complex situation, allowed her to escape. The threat of her attacking another Arctic convoy, PQ17, led to *Pound's orders for it to scatter, with disastrous results, though *Tirpitz* was at sea for only a few hours before being ordered to return. So great a threat was she that desperate measures were taken by the British to try and sink her. An abortive operation with *human torpedoes was mounted in October 1942, and in September 1943 *midget submarines crippled her for six months. A series of daring air attacks then damaged her again, making her non-operational. She moved south to Tromsö to act as a floating battery in case of invasion, but constant air attacks—there were 22 altogether including one by Soviet aircraft—eventually reduced her to a hulk. Rubble was dumped under her to prevent her capsizing, but on 12 November 1944 she received two direct hits from *Tallboy bombs delivered by *Dam Buster bombers, and capsized with the loss of 1,204 lives. Her crew were heard singing '*Deutschland über alles*' as she sank.

Kennedy, L., *Life and Death of the Tirpitz* (London, 1979).

Tito and the Partisans. Josip Broz (1892–1980) was born near Klanjec in Croatia. He was, from the 1920s, a clandestine communist revolutionary using many pseudonyms, one of which, Tito, he eventually adopted permanently. From 1935 he spent more time in Moscow than elsewhere, working for the *Comintern, before being chosen to take over the Communist Party of Yugoslavia (KPJ). After almost three years on probation and under investigation, he was fully confirmed in October 1940 as its political secretary, entrusted with the task of reorganizing a party that had come close to being dissolved by the Comintern.

By the time Yugoslavia was attacked in April 1941, Tito had successfully carried out his task, he had selected a team of lieutenants, including Milovan Djilas, and the KPJ had a membership of some 8,000. Uneasy coexistence with the German occupation allowed the party to establish the basic network of its military organization in anticipation of action, so that when Hitler invaded the USSR in June 1941 (see BARBAROSSA), and Tito issued his call to arms, he was both responding to an appeal by the Comintern to assist the USSR and seizing the opportunity provided by the war to launch a revolution.

The armed struggle initiated by the KPJ would soon be officially designated the 'People's Liberation Struggle', described as a patriotic enterprise against foreign occupation troops and their native auxiliaries, and as a revolutionary undertaking against the forces of domestic and international reaction. In the summer of 1941, as it gradually advanced from sabotage to guerrilla warfare in competition with General *Mihailović's Četnik guerrillas who were loyal to the Yugoslav *government-in-exile in London, the KPJ called for the liquidation of domestic enemies, in the belief that the Red Army would soon arrive, and that preparations had to be made for a take-over. With several risings, but especially with an upsurge of pro-Allied optimism in Serbia, Russophilia and a reaction against the establishment that had just been defeated helped the KPJ increase its membership to 12,000. The communists' revolutionary sanguine disposition would hold out throughout the year and beyond, in spite of the Comintern telling them that it actually needed the co-operation of all anti-fascist patriots rather than a premature revolution. As military repression turned the popular mood against the communists, both in German-held Serbia and in Italian-held Montenegro, only their ideological projection into the future could keep them in the field.

Nevertheless, the partisans (named after Soviet irregulars), with Tito and the KPJ cadres, had to slip out of Serbia to a remote area of south-eastern Bosnia in the 'Independent State of Croatia' (Nezavisna Drzava Hrvatska, or NDH) where, in January 1942, they set up their headquarters at Foča, restructuring the bands that had been driven out of Serbia and Montenegro. It was there that Tito and his partisans went through their first serious crisis as they shed the illusions that had accompanied the first phase of their struggle.

Serbia and Montenegro had been largely pacified by the end of 1941, but occupation commands realized this would not be so easy in the NDH where Ustaša anti-Serbian terror fanned guerrilla warfare. Worried by the concentration around Foča, which could threaten mines that were important to their war economy and could even spread back to Serbia, through which went important communications, the Germans mounted operations to suppress it. The partisans had to move again, in search of a safer haven in the more variegated countryside of western Bosnia, where the Serbian peasantry had suffered most, and where local partisans had held out against *Pavelić's pro-Axis Ustaša forces.

This was when Tito understood that victory and power would not come soon. After more critical warnings from the Comintern, in view of the approaching *Anglo-Soviet Treaty of May 1942, the KPJ leadership decided to give up its revolutionary extremism. Meanwhile they had reorganized their militant combatants into 'proletarian brigades', as disciplined mobile shock units (which actually contained few proletarians). By June they had disengaged themselves, and set out on their 'long march' to the rugged mountainous regions of the NDH where, generally speaking, occupation forces and Ustašas had not been able to eliminate the Serbian insurgents. Thereafter, the revolutionary conflict waged by the communists would gain its own momentum in the civil strife that ravaged partitioned Yugoslavia for the rest of the war. They would benefit from intra-Axis rivalry, and would always surge in the direction of least resistance.

During the summer of 1942, Tito's force of 4,000–5,000 fighters moved westwards along a route that followed the German–Italian demarcation line. In the Serbian pale astride western Bosnia and inner Croatia, not only had partisans held out, but they had gained in prestige among Muslims and Catholic Croats as well as Orthodox Serbs, for they were always on the side of those fighting for their lives. By going there, Tito's proletarian nucleus would overcome the crisis of the KPJ-led movement in the eastern provinces, for the partisans brought hope with them. They were Serbian fighters, but they were also making themselves acceptable to other communities.

That summer, the climate was right for Soviet propaganda to come out in support of the Yugoslav partisans, who now enjoyed several advantages apart from their increased combativeness. Their leadership as well as their intentions were clearly pan-Yugoslav, and going from the Serbian lands in the east to the 'Independent State of Croatia' helped to foster the belief that they were not, as the Četniks were, exclusively Serbs, which enabled them to make a start in attracting Croats to the resistance. Axis propaganda also helped the partisans by branding all insurgents 'communists'. Tito's communications with the Comintern were secret, and it was not known to the outside world that the partisan force had had to flee the consequences of the KPJ's mistakes in some areas, to other areas where options had been reduced to dying or fighting for one's life. The propaganda about the partisans originated to a large extent with the KPJ itself, before it was taken up and adapted in Moscow, to be fed through Comintern channels for Allied and neutral consumption. It gave an enormous boost to their cause, coming as it did when the Allies, anxious to see Yugoslavia both restored and reorganized after the war, were beginning to grant priority to anyone ready to fight.

By taking them out of their Orthodox, Muslim, and Catholic milieux, the KPJ turned the adolescents of the territory it had come to control into members of supranational units, the only ones in the mixed areas whose recruitment was not on an ethnic basis, although political commissars were busy indoctrinating these uprooted peasant youths into another sectarian mould. By the end of the year, they were not territorial units defending their own villages against other militias, but the People's Liberation Army. Tito was its supreme commander, and the original partisans who had come with him from the east formed the cadres of a force that had increased tenfold since June. The meeting of an Anti-Fascist Council for the National Liberation of Yugoslavia at Bihac in Western Bosnia, in November, was meant to convey the impression that what was now called the People's Liberation Movement was a broadly-based patriotic grouping rather than an instrument of communist revolution.

The fear of an Allied landing in the Balkans in the spring of 1943 led Hitler to demand another cycle of combined anti-insurgent operations in the NDH. Carried out in January–March, they were a military defeat for Tito, but they did not achieve lasting success, and the partisans' retreat back to the south-east, accompanied by sporadic resistance and much suffering, was presented by their propaganda as a great victory. March 1943 was, nevertheless, the second and the most critical period Tito's movement went through.

The main operative group of some 20,000 combatants under his command, with many more refugees and wounded, was hard-pressed by the increasing tightness of the ring closing in on them. Anxious to free himself in order to destroy Mihailović and the Četniks before the expected British landing, Tito used existing contacts to initiate talks with the German command, and sent high-level delegates to Zagreb. Having stated that their main enemies were the Četniks, whom they denounced as being tolerated by the Italians and linked to the British, they offered to stop harassing Axis forces if the partisans were allowed to return to their homes, or go east to fight the Četniks. The possibility was also envisaged of joint partisan–German action against Anglo-American forces should these land. The consistent line of Tito's high command in early 1943 was to go for a truce with the Axis, followed by a showdown with Mihailović.

The common ground that the Germans in the NDH had with the partisans was their opposition to Mihailović, seen as dangerous in the event of an Allied landing. During the talks, the Germans called a halt to their anti-partisan operations, while Tito issued orders that the struggle against Axis forces be stopped along with sabotage on the Zagreb–Belgrade railway. The truce probably made it easier for the partisans to win a difficult victory over the Četniks who had massed to block their advance across the Neretva valley in Herzegovina, but it also caught Tito off his guard when the talks failed and the Germans resumed their operations, causing heavy losses before the partisans managed to slip back to the relative safety of the uplands of eastern Bosnia.

Hitler had killed the attempt stone dead, but the Comintern was also not pleased when Tito reported, with some economy of truth, that talks had been held for the exchange of prisoners. At the time the USSR was busy demolishing Mihailović's reputation in the west on the grounds of his alleged *collaboration, so any leak of what Tito was up to would have been highly embarrassing; and it would not have suited Moscow to give Hitler too much respite in the Balkans while he was trying to recover after *Stalingrad.

The partisans still came out on top eventually. Almost destroyed in eastern Yugoslavia in 1941, they were able to surface again in the west by penetrating the desperate struggle of the Serbs to survive the Ustašas' reign of terror. The People's Liberation Movement then developed out of the anarchy of the NDH, as Croats themselves turned away from it. Tito's main mobile force of combatants could be defeated; it always managed to dissolve into the landscape and to regroup, with the help of communist-controlled guerrilla groups throughout the country, of propaganda and, later on, of Allied support.

The situation in Yugoslavia changed dramatically to the partisans' advantage with the collapse of Italy in September 1943. By then the Allies were anxious to engage the Germans on the Yugoslav side of the Adriatic, and had become convinced of the effective superiority of the partisans. Most of those who, in the Italian zone, had been attracted to or neutralized by the Axis, and now wanted to find themselves on the winning side after Italy's surrender in September 1943, threw in their lot with the partisans, who were thus able to recruit and equip (with captured Italian *matériel*) four divisions of 4,000 men each, and take over much of the coast. A number of Italian troops also joined the partisans and formed the *Garibaldi Division.

The Germans soon recovered control of the coast, but at the cost of allowing large areas of Bosnia and of inland Croatia, which had previously been cleared of insurgents, to fall to the partisans again. Having thus recovered, and with Allied help now forthcoming from Italy, the KPJ leadership felt sufficiently strengthened at home and abroad to set up a counter-government. At Jajce in Bosnia, in November 1943, a second session of the Anti-Fascist Council virtually set up a new regime: the exiled monarch and his government were denied any rights, Tito was made marshal and president of a National Committee for the Liberation of Yugoslavia.

He now posed as a statesman, but kept putting off the political settlement the British wanted to make with him, while taking care not to risk losing their military help which he badly needed. 'England' remained a bogey, as the partisans were convinced the class enemy there was conspiring to destroy them under the mask of liberation by Allied troops.

By the time the Allies had definitely turned to Tito in the wake of the Teheran conference in November 1943 (see EUREKA), German anti-insurgent operations had once again drastically reduced all resistance in Yugoslavia. Tito, whose headquarters had been on the move, was back in western Bosnia, at Drvar, at the beginning of 1944. His movement had grown in the NDH over the winter. The more obvious the coming defeat of the Reich, and the nearer the break-up of the Ustaša state, the greater was the number of Croats who wanted to leave that sinking boat. The People's Liberation Movement offered a way out. Allied support, and the fact that in Croatia the partisans welcomed almost any one who would co-operate with them, caused many people to believe Tito's movement would moderate its communism.

Making one last effort to clear those territories which they considered to be important of insurgent concentrations, the Germans made a surprise airborne attack on partisan headquarters at Drvar in May 1944. Tito, with his staff, the Allied military missions, and their escort, barely escaped capture, and he lost touch with his forces. Fearing for the co-ordinated control of his movement, the Soviets advised Tito to get out of Yugoslavia to Allied-occupied Bari, in Italy, the HQ of the inter-service *Balkan Air Force which was then being formed to support him. He was air-lifted there, then taken by British destroyer to Vis, the only Yugoslav island not to have been retaken by the Germans. It had been turned into a British-protected base through which Allied supplies reached the partisans on the mainland. Large-scale intervention by the western Allies from Italy saved the movement in its third major crisis, but for the first time since he had taken the field two years earlier, Tito was separated from the bulk of his forces.

In order to obtain political, as well as military, recognition from the Allied powers, Tito concluded an agreement that summer with the prime minister of the government-in-exile in which he made a few token temporary concessions. He also went to Italy again, reluctantly, on Soviet advice, to meet Churchill. He could afford some transient concessions, for he already held almost all the cards. Practically, the only serious hurdle left on the KPJ's path to power was Mihailović in Serbia, and Tito turned his energies to conquering that region which was vital to the establishment of a new regime.

In July he began to ask Stalin to help him in the task, complaining that the British were not to be trusted, and eventually requested a meeting to avert the danger of a Serbian-based, western-assisted counter-revolution. Over the summer, operations against Serbia were planned with the Soviet military mission, at the same time as 'Ratweek', the British-conceived action to harass the German evacuation from the Balkans through Serbia. This was used by the partisans to push their way against Mihailović's guerrillas, as the Germans proceeded with their orderly retreat. When the Red Army came up to Yugoslavia's eastern border, Tito 'levanted' from Vis for his pre-arranged visit to Moscow.

The meeting there resulted in the Soviet decision to provide support with armour and heavy artillery, to arm fourteen partisan divisions, and to help the Bulgars change sides. A joint communiqué gave the impression that the Soviet government had asked Tito's National Committee to allow the Red Army a short cut through Yugoslav territory to Hungary, in exchange for acknowledging the partisans' administration in newly-liberated territories. Tito needed the military help of Soviet troops, and he also needed a Soviet presence so as to be accepted in Serbia. Soviet support duly enabled the partisans to install themselves in the capital earlier than they could have done alone. On 1 November 1944, the impending formation of a united provisional government and of a regency was announced in liberated Belgrade.

After that, and with an army of several hundred thousand well-armed combatants, the KPJ-led People's Liberation Movement really was the only possible solution for the future of Yugoslavia. It could turn westward again to finish off its task of liberating Yugoslavia, and also to increase its territory at the expense of Austria and Italy (including *Trieste). On 19 March 1945 the Fourth Yugoslav Army launched its offensive northwards along the coast. Two other Yugoslav Corps (4th and 7th) supported it inland by playing a guerrilla role north of Bihac and Novo Mesto, and the Balkan Air Force gave it logistical and air support, as well as some backing with units of its Land Forces, Adriatic. The partisans were opposed by Croat and German divisions but on 30 April Tito announced that his forces had reached Trieste. However military operations against the Germans would not end until 15 May 1945. Meanwhile, in March, Tito finally formed his provisional government, with 23 communists, two fellow-travellers, and three non-communist politicians who had returned from London, and was granted formal recognition by the Allies. Thereafter these concessions became worthless in the run-up to the general elections for a constituent assembly which would set up a communist regime. Marshal Tito was subsequently prime minister, minister of defence, and supreme commander until 1953, when he was elected to the new office of president of the republic, eventually to become life president.

The occupation provided an ideal situation for the propagation of a radical movement. The partisans fought a revolutionary war in a constantly shifting pattern, and their leadership did so with a political aim. Only as leader of a patriotic resistance could Tito hope to retain the support of his non-communist combatants and followers, but his primary long-term aim was the conquest of power. The concept of 'national liberation' was used as an instrument of social revolution and political conquest, in the course of the civil war that raged under a multiple foreign *occupation. A physically terrorized, economically deprived, and politically naïve peasantry supplied most of the manpower for that operation.

The communists quickly established an overall unity of strategy, which enabled them to exploit the situation, and practise a variety of tactics, while showing a bold, single, face to the world outside. There was no such unity of purpose among the anti-communists. Tito placed a patriotic movement in the service of world *communism, with the object of destroying all forces that opposed the transformation of the war of liberation into a war for the establishment of communist rule. The partisans initially obtained the support of those who had been radicalized by the upheavals of war; thereafter, their successes at home and abroad attracted further support, and they snowballed to victory. The war of the partisans would remain the legitimizing source and inspiration of Tito's regime to his death. STEVAN PAVLOWITCH

Djilas, M., *Wartime* (New York, 1977).
Pavlowitch, S., *Yugoslavia's Great Dictator, Tito—A Reassessment* (London, 1992).
Roberts, W., *Tito, Mihailović and the Allies 1941–45* (2nd edn., Durham, NC, 1987).

Tizard, Sir Henry (1885–1959), British chemist and scientific administrator who, after serving as a pilot during the *First World War, was chosen to head the air ministry's committee for the Scientific Survey of Air Defence (later of Air Warfare) in November 1934. The Tizard committee, as it came to be called, first met in January 1935 and subsequently oversaw the development of *Watson-Watt's radio echo system. This became the *radar air defence system which helped win the battle of *Britain and Tizard was also responsible for encouraging the development of airborne radar (see ELECTRONIC NAVIGATION SYSTEMS), a possibility he had first suggested in 1936. In June 1940, after expressing his scepticism about the existence of the German *Knickebein beam, he resigned as chief scientific adviser to the air staff. Antipathy between him and Churchill's scientific adviser *Lindemann, led to his talents being underused for the rest of the war, but in September 1940 he led what became known as the Tizard mission to the USA to explain British scientific advances in radar (most notably the *cavity magnetron) and *ASDIC, as well as new developments such as the RDX *explosives and the *proximity fuze. This information enabled much valuable war *matériel* to be produced in the USA and established Anglo-American scientific co-operation during the war years which culminated in the development of the *atomic bomb. He was knighted in 1937. See also SCIENTISTS AT WAR.

Clark, R., *Tizard* (London, 1965).

Tobruk, sieges of. *Rommel's victories in the spring of 1941 during the *Western Desert campaigns failed to include this Libyan port which contained two Australian brigades under Maj-General *Morshead. Rommel realized he must eliminate Tobruk before advancing into Egypt, but his forces twice failed to take it, and then a raid by the garrison netted two Italian infantry battalions. After he had received reinforcements, Rommel tried again, but was again repulsed.

By now Tobruk had become a *cause célèbre*. Churchill signalled Morshead, 'The whole Empire is watching your steadfast and spirited defence of this important outpost of Egypt with gratitude and admiration.' But after two British offensives (BREVITY and BATTLEAXE) failed to relieve the siege the Australian government insisted its men be withdrawn, and between August and October 1941 they were partially replaced by British troops and those of the Polish *Carpathian Brigade.

Rommel was now obsessed with taking this stubborn enclave behind his lines, but he was pre-empted from another all-out attack when the CRUSADER offensive was launched on 18 November 1941 by *Auchinleck. As part of Auchinleck's plan, the garrison broke out of Tobruk and on the night of 26/27 November linked up with the 2nd New Zealand Division. This connection was temporarily severed by Rommel but within days his inadequate *logistics forced his withdrawal and the siege was lifted. However, in June 1942, after his successes in the *Gazala battle, Rommel attacked the port from the least expected point, the south-east. By then Auchinleck regarded it as indefensible; on 20 June it fell, and nearly all the 35,000-strong garrison, which included one-third of South Africa's ground forces in Libya, became *prisoners-of-war. The port remained in Rommel's hands until his retreat after the second *El Alamein battle that November.

Todt Organization. In scarcely five years, according to a 1945 British Intelligence report, the Organization Todt (OT) carried out the most impressive construction programme since the days of the Roman Empire. More than 1,400,000 men built bunkers and bridges for the Wehrmacht, but though they wore uniforms with swastika armbands they were neither soldiers nor members of a party organization. A Nazi body, though independent of party control, the OT was the only organization in the Third Reich besides the *Hitler Youth to bear the name of a member of the party élite. The reactions it provoked varied from amazement to fear.

In 1938 Fritz Todt (1892–1942), Hitler's young engineer and chief architect, had been commissioned to complete the building of the giant *West Wall on the German–French frontier as quickly as possible. To do this he brought in gangs from his newly-built autobahns, mobilized the Reich Labour Service, and used the Wehrmacht's construction battalions. Todt placed his trust in the principles of private enterprise, the art of improvization, and the triumph of technical rationality over red tape. Under his leadership, almost half a million workers built 5,000 concrete bunkers in record time, freeing Hitler to invade Poland without the need to worry about his western borders.

Following the outbreak of war, Todt as a close confidant of the Führer, was given an ever increasing number of construction tasks vital to the war effort (see Table). The OT followed the conquering Wehrmacht across Europe, repairing bridges, dams, road systems, and bombed factories, and in the process playing a large role in exploiting the occupied countries. In the Balkans it took care of the mining of ores essential to the war effort and their shipment to the Reich; and the roads on which Hitler's Wehrmacht marched to Yugoslavia and Greece were brought up to scratch by it. In the west its building gangs were put to work from Norway to the Bay of Biscay to construct the *Atlantic Wall intended to protect Hitler's conquests against the British and American forces. The great U-boat pens in France and the airfields used in the bombardment of Allied *Arctic convoys en route for Murmansk were also its work as, later, were the V-1 launching ramps (see V-WEAPONS).

After February 1940, when Fritz Todt became minister for weapons and munitions, he was given ever more responsibility for the war economy. The OT expanded in consequence, recruiting large numbers of foreign workers. But it attracted few Germans and those it employed had an average age of 53. Some 80% of the OT's members were young non-Germans, many of them volunteers taken in by clever propaganda. But most were *forced labour and *prisoners-of-war (POW), uniformed and drilled and in a position which was little better than those working in the *concentration camps.

The OT's greatest task came in June 1941 as Hitler's Wehrmacht invaded the USSR (see BARBAROSSA). The military construction battalions alone were incapable of building the necessary railway links, bridges, and repair facilities in the vast expanses of the USSR. Even at this stage the OT was no more than an improvised construction organization rather than an official institution of the Third Reich, and thus avoided being taken over by either the party or the armed forces.

In February 1942 Todt was killed in a mysterious air accident; thereafter his successor, Albert *Speer, maintained the OT as his predecessor had run it. Under Speer it reached its maximum size. From 1943–4, in addition to its many tasks abroad, it became heavily engaged in clearing up air raid damage in Germany and building more facilities for the war effort. In this latter regard it became more and more obvious that the OT were not just 'soldier-workers', but part of the Nazi system of terror and annihilation. Its members were committed in anti-partisan campaigns and supervised teams of Jewish slave-workers and Soviet POW. They were technicians, slave-drivers, and in some cases murderers. Their technical ability was doubtless greater than their discipline. Complaints about corruption in the OT and other signs of organizational degeneration dramatically increased in 1944 as the Germans retreated on all fronts.

At no time did the authorities succeed in welding the military and civilian construction units together. The OT remained independent—even when, in the autumn of 1944, it was renamed the 'Front-OT', armed, and committed to the defence of the Reich. Most of the buildings it created were now destroyed and after the German defeat the OT itself was broken up and banned. Speer, its last head, was convicted at the *Nuremberg trials of forced recruitment and employing slave labour. While the ruins left by the Romans can still be seen and marvelled at today, most of the buildings erected by the OT for Adolf Hitler's 'Thousand Year Reich' have long since disappeared in the dust of history. See also SPEER PLAN and RAW AND SYNTHETIC MATERIALS.

ROLF-DIETER MÜLLER

Todt Organization: Concrete used by OT-Operation Group West, 1940–4 in 1,000 cubic metres

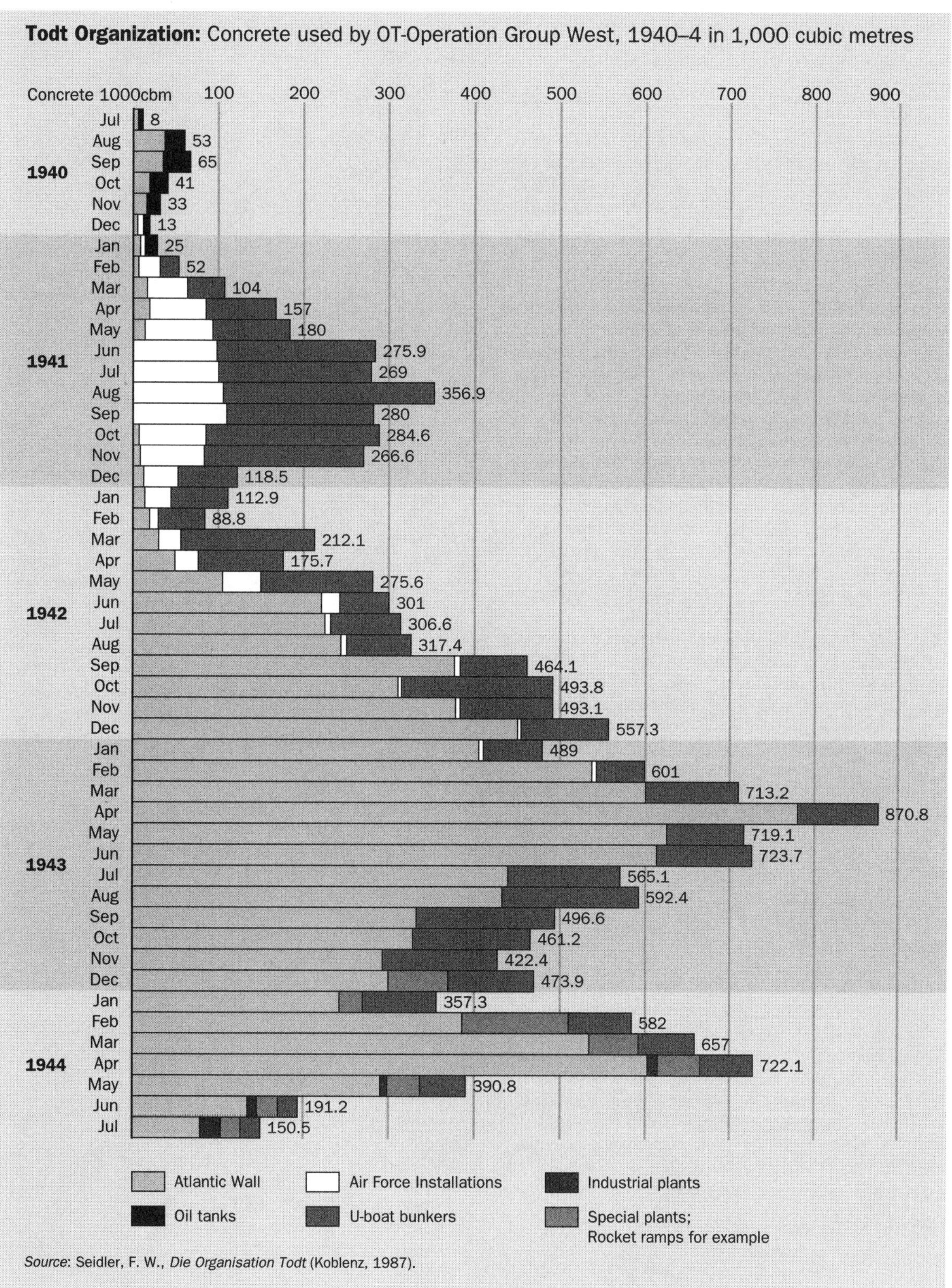

Source: Seidler, F. W., *Die Organisation Todt* (Koblenz, 1987).

Guse, J. C., *The Spirit of the Plassenburg. Technology and Ideology in the Third Reich* (Ann Arbor, Mich., 1983).
Seidler, F. W., *Die Organisation Todt* (Koblenz, 1987).
—*Fritz Todt* (Munich, 1986).

Togliatti, Palmiro (1893–1964), Italian Communist Party leader who, until Italy surrendered in September 1943, broadcast propaganda to his country from Moscow under the name of Mario Correnti. He then returned to Italy and served in Marshal *Badoglio's government, and the others that followed. See also ITALY, 3(b).

Tōgō Shigenori (1882–1950), prominent Japanese diplomat who became foreign minister before the outbreak of the *Pacific war in December 1941, and at its end. Born in Kagoshima, he studied at Tokyo University. After a brief career as a university teacher he became a diplomat in 1912. He capped a long diplomatic career overseas by becoming in 1937 ambassador to Germany, though he was thought to be opposed to the *Anti-Comintern Pact reached between Germany and Japan during the previous year. In 1938 he was transferred as ambassador to the USSR and conducted important negotiations over fisheries in Soviet far eastern waters and the Japanese military defeat at the battle of Nomonhan in September 1939 (see JAPANESE–SOVIET CAMPAIGNS). In July 1940 Tōgō presented Moscow with the draft of a neutrality pact with the USSR, but he was almost immediately recalled to Tokyo. He was out of favour for a year but in October 1941 returned to service as foreign minister in the cabinet of General Tōjō and was involved in the last-minute negotiations with Washington, which eventually failed with the outbreak of war. Tōgō was in favour of an early peace with the USA during the Pacific war and fell out with Tōjō over the founding of the Greater East Asia Ministry. He resigned in September 1943 and became a member of the House of Peers.

When a new cabinet was formed in April 1945 Tōgō agreed to become foreign minister on the understanding that he would work towards peace. He tried to exploit his contacts in Moscow to persuade the USSR to mediate just before the Potsdam conference (see TERMINAL). Although the terms of the Potsdam Declaration were much more severe Tōgō, following the dropping of the *atomic bomb on *Hiroshima on 6 August, favoured the acceptance of it. Emperor *Hirohito accepted the views of the peace party and Japan capitulated on 14 August. Almost immediately the whole cabinet resigned. In 1946 Tōgō was arrested and prosecuted (see FAR EAST WAR CRIMES TRIALS) and two years later was sentenced to 20 years' hard labour, but died in an American military hospital after writing his autobiography, *Jidai no ichimen*, which covers his career as a diplomat.

IAN NISH

Butow, R. J. D., *Japan's Decision to Surrender* (Stanford, Calif., 1954).

General **Tōjō**.

Tōjō Hideki, General (1884–1948), Japan's political and military leader during the greater part of the Second World War in the east, as prime minister from 1941 to 1944 and as army minister from 1940 to 1944. Born in Tokyo, the son of an army general, he graduated from the military academy (1905) and the army staff college (1915). Hard-working but not particularly bright, he distinguished himself as an administrator rather than as a field commander. After serving as a military attaché in Switzerland and Germany (1919–22), he taught at the army staff college (1922–6), was attached to the army ministry (1926–9), commanded the First Infantry Regiment (1929–31), served with the army General Staff (1931–4), and commanded the 24th Infantry Brigade (1934–5). It was at this period that he gained the nickname 'Razor' (Kamisori) Tōjō for his strictness and adherence to details.

In the factional struggles within the army in the 1930s Tojo was one of the leaders of the control faction (*tōseiha*), which favoured stronger discipline in the ranks, an enhanced role for the army in the state, and expansion in China. In 1935 he was appointed commander of the *Kempei (military police) of the *Kwantung Army in Manchukuo, where he suppressed the more radical elements of the imperial way faction (*kōdōha*). In March 1937 he became chief of staff of the Kwantung Army and in that position played a major role in the Japanese attack on China in July of that year (see CHINA INCIDENT). The war with China provided Tōjō with his only combat experience when, in late 1937, he led two brigades to conquer Chahar (Inner Mongolia). Tōjō's position on China was that only a show of force, in the form of an occupation of Chinese territory, would persuade the Chinese to collaborate with Japan. In this stand he clashed with General Ishiwara Kanji, who cautioned against a full-scale war with China. Ishiwara's removal from the General Staff in September 1937 marked the victory of the hardliners, of whom Tōjō was one of the leading figures.

In May 1938 Tōjō was appointed army vice-minister under General *Itagaki, in the first cabinet of Prince *Konoe. In that cabinet Itagaki and Tōjō represented the position of the army, which opposed any compromise or accommodation with the Chinese Nationalist government of *Chiang Kai-shek. After the fall of the Konoe cabinet in January 1939, Tōjō became inspector-general of army aviation. When Konoe formed his second cabinet in July 1940, Tōjō was appointed army minister and he remained in that post in Konoe's third cabinet, which was formed in July 1941. As army minister he wielded a strong influence over the cabinet, pressing for a hardline policy towards the western powers and China and for a controlled economy at home.

In 1940, with the blessing of Tōjō and the army, the political parties dissolved and set up the Imperial Rule Assistance Association (see JAPAN, 3). Following Hitler's military victories in Europe, Tōjō pushed for the *Tripartite Pact with Germany and Italy which was formed in September of that year. In July 1941 he induced the cabinet to dispatch troops to southern Indo-China, a move which made the Americans impose a total trade embargo on Japan. As relations with the western powers deteriorated, the Imperial Conference, upon Tōjō's recommendation, decided on 6 September 1941 that Japan would go to war with the UK and USA if a solution was not found by early October.

Prince Konoe, having failed to accommodate the Americans as well as his own military leaders, resigned on 16 October and Emperor *Hirohito, upon the recommendation of Lord Keeper of the Privy Seal, Kido Kōichi, asked Tōjō to form a cabinet. Kido hoped that Tōjō's appointment would serve a warning to the USA and restrain the army at home, but the results were the reverse. On 26 November 1941, Washington notified Japan that it must withdraw from China as a precondition for the resumption of trade (the 'Hull Note'), and the Tōjō cabinet, viewing this as a hostile move, decided to go to war. Tōjō justified this decision by saying that in the life of every nation, as in the life of every individual, there is a moment when a momentous risk has to be taken, and one must be ready 'to jump with closed eyes from the veranda of the Kiyomizu Temple'. Under his direction, Japan launched the attack on *Pearl Harbor, in December 1941, conquered most of East and South-East Asia, and set up the *Greater East Asia Co-prosperity Sphere.

Tōjō was the first prime minister of Japan to hold concurrently the posts of army minister and general on the active list. During the first four months of his cabinet, which coincided with the outbreak of the Second World War in the east, he was also home minister and in that capacity directed the arrests of leftists and liberals. These powers made him the strongest prime minister in modern Japanese history, and he used them to harass his opponents and establish the supremacy of the military. The Tōjō cabinet imposed strict controls on the economy, the press, and all political and public organizations. In April 1942 Tōjō called a general election, in which the government helped 'recommended' candidates to be elected to the Diet. He also tried to enhance his public image by addressing rallies, reviewing troops, and riding in open cars.

But unlike his allies Hitler and Mussolini, Tōjō was not a dictator. He assumed office in the traditional way through being recommended to the Emperor, and his rise to power was not accompanied by constitutional changes. There was no mass movement behind him and no ideology attributed to him. Despite all his posts, he had to contend with other centres of power such as the civil bureaucracy, the navy, the industrial conglomerates (*zaibatsu*), senior statesmen, and the imperial court, all of which protected their autonomy. His ability to dictate to other ministers, or to the Imperial Headquarters conducting the military and naval operations, was also limited. One of his major problems was how to increase war production in view of the great losses which had to be made up and the competition between the army and the navy over *raw materials. To solve this problem, in November 1943 he established the ministry of munitions with himself as minister, but it was only a partial solution.

The weakness of Tōjō's position became evident when Japan began to suffer serious military setbacks in 1944. In February of that year he also assumed the office of army chief of staff, in order to direct the campaigns personally, but this infuriated his critics. After the fall of the strategic island of *Saipan in June, a coalition of his opponents, made up of senior statesmen, naval officers, and court officials, pressed for his resignation. Tōjō tried to placate and intimidate them, but failed. In July 1944, bowing to pressure to assume responsibility for operational losses, he resigned all his positions. This was done without any *putsch* and he stepped down in the same constitutional way in which he rose to power. After his resignation he was neither arrested nor denounced, but withdrew to the obscurity of a former prime minister, leaving the stage to his successors, Lt-General *Koiso Kuniaki (until April 1945) and Admiral *Suzuki Kantarō. Japan was thus the only major belligerent which changed its leaders peacefully twice during the Second World War.

When Japan surrendered, Tōjō did not commit suicide as some other military officers did. Only when American military policemen arrived to arrest him did he shoot himself in the chest, but he missed vital organs and recovered from the wound. He was put on trial as a war criminal (see FAR EAST WAR CRIMES TRIALS) and the court found him guilty of conspiracy, waging an aggressive war, and ordering, authorizing, and permitting *atrocities. In December 1948 he was hanged, together with six other convicted wartime leaders, at the Sugamo Prison in Tokyo.

There was little public sympathy for Tōjō in Japan in the post-war period. His responsibility for the war, his oppressive regime, and his failure to commit suicide turned him into a notorious figure. Later revelations about his personal integrity, impeccable family life, devotion to duty, and loyalty to the emperor somewhat improved his image. In 1978 Tōjō's name, together with those of thirteen other 'class A' war criminals, was commemorated in the Yasukuni shrine, Japan's foremost memorial for its fallen soldiers. There was a wave of protests, mainly from Christian and pacifist groups, but as the shrine was then a private institution the government could not interfere. In 1980, when the site of Sugamo prison was converted into a residential and shopping complex, a monument was erected at the place where Tōjō and the other war criminals had been executed. This act too elicited many protests. See also JAPAN, 3.

BEN-AMI SHILLONY

Butow, R. J. C., *Tojo and the Coming of the War* (Princeton, 1961).
Peattie, M., *Ishiwara Kanji and Japan's Confrontation with the West* (Princeton, 1975).
Shillony, B.-A., *Politics and Culture in Wartime Japan* (Oxford, 1981).

Tokkō. 'If you say "Tokkō", even a crying child falls silent,' (Takagi Takeo, 1954). Even today the name of the Tokkō (Special Higher Police) carries a fearful resonance to the Japanese as the words *Gestapo does to westerners. In fact, critics of the repressive pre-1945 Japanese political system have frequently made analogies between the Tokkō and its German—and Soviet—counterparts.

The Tokkō played the role of front-line agency in the government's efforts to suppress radical leftist ideologies and organizations, particularly communist ones, during the 1930s and 1940s; it was Tokkō officers who arrested the Soviet agent Richard *Sorge, in October 1941. During the war the Tokkō, which worked almost exclusively in the home islands, spread its net to include certain new Buddhist religions, liberals, and any others who did not support the government's policies. Its main legal weapon was the Peace Preservation Law of 1925, which after a 1928 revision made it a capital crime to attempt to form an organization aimed at destroying the *kokutai*, Japan's unique national polity centred on the emperor. Persecution of new Buddhist religions was sufficiently significant for the 1941 revision of the Peace Preservation Law to include two new clauses aimed at regulating religious groups and individuals seen to be threats to the *kokutai* or to the sanctity of shrines and the imperial house (see also RELIGION).

In their zeal, Tokkō officers, who numbered about 2,000, frequently violated the procedural rights of suspects and became notorious for brutality and torture. Despite it being illegal since 1879, regular police officers as well as Tokkō officers not uncommonly used torture, which resulted in the deaths of a number of leftist activists during the 1930s and some well-known liberal journalists during the war. Prolonged detentions (even up to two years) also represented abuses of authority which even defenders of the Tokkō admit were widespread.

A number of factors help to explain the brutality and abuses of authority and in addition, throw light on the relationship between the Tokkō and other groups or institutions in wartime Japanese society and politics. The Japanese police in modern times, despite a number of attempts by leaders to professionalize them and improve police–public relations, had had poor relations with the public. Such efforts were hampered by an underlying assumption of the superiority of Japanese bureaucracy over the people. The Tokkō was part of the bureaucracy, being a section of the civil police under the home ministry with designated responsibility for control of so-called social or ideological movements. Under the Meiji constitution (1889), government officials remained outside the jurisdiction of the regular courts, which dealt with civil and criminal cases, and only the banning of organizations by the Tokkō could be questioned in the administrative court. Consequently, individual victims of Tokkō abuse had very limited means of redress for their grievances.

Furthermore, because the Tokkō's responsibilities were regarded as the most important among police functions, and this was emphasized by the French-derived name of Special Higher Police, it became the 'aristocracy' of the police. Its officers were recruited for their nationalistic fervour and were inculcated with a high sense of mission which was reinforced by wartime conditions. Secrecy and a separate chain of command and appointment of officers also contributed to Tokkō arrogance and insulation from criticism.

Although the Tokkō's application of the Peace Preservation Law widened after the nation began war preparations in the early 1930s, the goal shifted from prosecution and imprisonment of violators to conversion of those harbouring 'dangerous thoughts' and the remoulding of converts—by torture or, more often by the appropriate social and/or psychological pressure—into loyal Japanese subjects. In 1936 a system of 'protection and supervision' centres was established to keep converts from backsliding. As a result, relatively few prosecutions and no executions occurred for Peace Preservation Law violations, and the Tokkō never established *concentration camps. Increased emphasis on 'guidance of thought into proper channels' raised the importance of preventing the propagation of illegal ideologies and extended the Tokkō's involvement in the daily lives of Japanese people. However, although wartime pressures to mobilize support for the government's policies elevated the Tokkō's institutional status and expanded its sphere of operations, it neither acted wholly independently nor created a 'state within a state', as did the German *SS. ELISE K. TIPTON

Mitchell, R., *Janus-Faced Justice: Political Criminals in Imperial Japan* (Honolulu, 1992).
Tipton, E. K., *The Japanese Police State: The Tokkō in Interwar Japan* (Sydney, 1990).

Tokyo Express, Allied nickname for regular convoys of Japanese destroyer-transports which carried reinforcements and supplies for Japanese troops fighting during the *Pacific war on *Guadalcanal and, later, on other islands in the Solomons. They were dispatched from *Rabaul, down the channel between the islands which the Allies called 'The Slot', and were first given this name by *Coast Watchers who reported their movements. The mainstay of the Tokyo Express was Rear-Admiral *Tanaka's Transport Group. See also CONVOYS.

'Tokyo Rose', name given by US troops in the *Pacific war to various female propagandists employed by the Japanese on their 'Zero Hour' radio programme broadcast from Tokyo. Several women were employed—*Japanese-Americans, an Australian, and several Filipinos—and one of them, Iva Toguri Ikoku (b.1916), an American citizen of Japanese parents, was put on trial for treason in 1948, sentenced to ten years' imprisonment, and given a $10,000 fine. She was released after six years and in January 1977 received a presidential pardon. For propaganda, see SUBVERSIVE WARFARE.

Tolbukhin, Marshal Fedor (1894–1949), Red Army officer who served as a captain in the tsarist army. He did not join the Communist Party until 1938, and was rumoured to have a strong religious bent. In short, he was not the preferred type for Soviet high-level command, and his career most significantly exemplifies the dearth of fully competent leadership in the Soviet wartime forces.

In July 1942 he was deputy commandant of a rear area command, the Stalingrad military district, when the fighting suddenly arrived on its doorstep. He then commanded an army at *Stalingrad and in the Soviet counter-offensive that followed, and in March 1943 he took over South *front* (army group), which became Fourth Ukrainian *front* later in the year. In May 1944, he moved to Third Ukrainian *front*, which he commanded in the August 1944–May 1945 march through the Danube Basin.

In September 1944, after Stalin refused to accept Bulgaria's surrender without an occupation, Tolbukhin took his armies into the country, and Stalin advanced him to Marshal of the Soviet Union to enhance his status *vis-à-vis* the British and American representatives on the *Allied Control Commission for Bulgaria.

In March 1945, after participating in the nearly four-month battle for *Budapest, his armies beat off a German counter-offensive in the Lake Balaton area and advanced on Vienna, which they occupied on 13 April. In July, Tolbukhin became the commander of Soviet forces in Romania and Bulgaria, staying on thereafter until January 1947, when peace treaties were signed and the *Allied Control Commission was dissolved.

EARL ZIEMKE

TOLSTOY, codename for the Allied conference held in Moscow from 9 to 19 October 1944. Present were Churchill and Stalin, and their military and diplomatic advisers. Averell *Harriman, the US ambassador, was present at most meetings as an observer, and the head of the US military mission in Moscow, General John Deane, was present whenever military topics were discussed.

Churchill primarily wanted to establish the timing for the USSR to enter the war against Japan, which Stalin had promised to do at the Teheran conference the previous November (see EUREKA), but he first came to an agreement with Stalin over the degree of influence the two countries should have in the Balkans. He wrote on a piece of paper the following percentages:

Romania—USSR 90%, others 10%
Greece—UK (in accord with USA) 90%, USSR 10%
Yugoslavia—50–50%
Hungary—50–50%
Bulgaria—USSR 75%, others 25%

Stalin agreed by ticking the piece of paper and this enabled Churchill to dispatch the *British expedition to Greece later that month. However, in subsequent haggling between *Eden and *Molotov the percentages for Bulgaria and Hungary were changed to 80%–20% in favour of the USSR. Poland's future was also discussed after Churchill requested that Stanisław Mikołajczyk, the prime minister of the Polish government in London, should meet the Soviet government to discuss the *Polish–Soviet frontier, but nothing was achieved. See also DIPLOMACY and GRAND ALLIANCE.

TORCH, see NORTH AFRICAN LANDINGS.

Torgau, German village on the River Elbe where, on 25 April 1945, Soviet and US troops made contact during the last phase of the battle for *Germany which meant that the country had been cut in two. The first contact had been made a few hours earlier near the village of Stehla, 16 km. (10 mi.) south-east of Torgau.

torpedo bombers, see CARRIERS, 2; see also PEARL HARBOR and TARANTO.

torpedoes were widely employed during the Second World War. *MTBs and their equivalents, destroyers, cruisers, and even some battleships, were equipped with torpedo tubes for use in fleet actions; and they were also launched from aircraft, notably at *Taranto by the British, at *Pearl Harbor by the Japanese, and in the carrier *v.* carrier naval actions during the *Pacific war (see CARRIERS, 2). But a 'fish' ('eel' in the German Navy) was most deadly when fired, without warning, by a submarine (see Figure for typical torpedo).

Torpedoes: American Mark XIV Torpedo

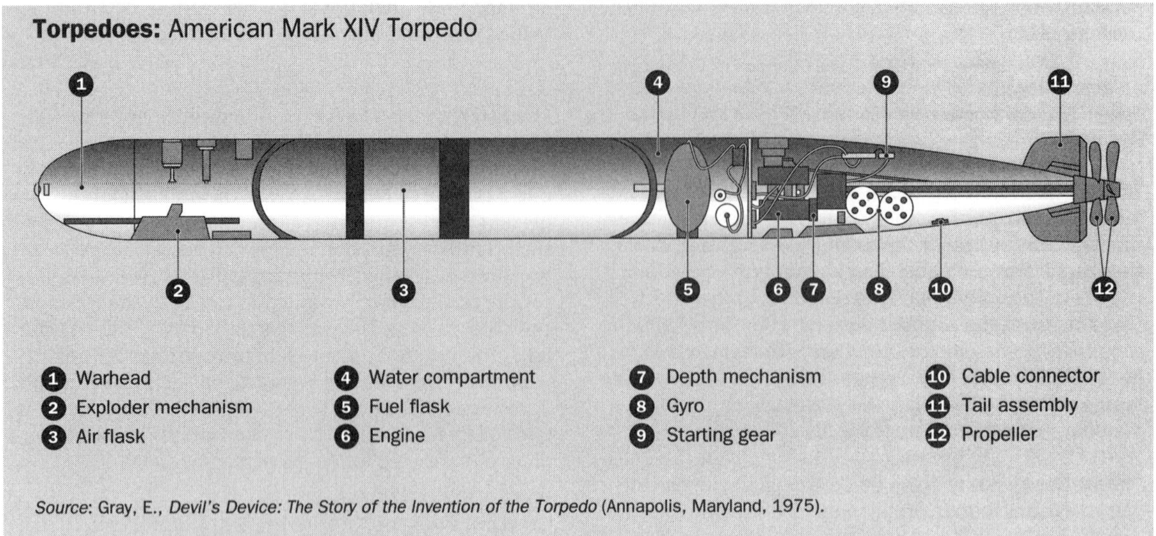

1 Warhead
2 Exploder mechanism
3 Air flask
4 Water compartment
5 Fuel flask
6 Engine
7 Depth mechanism
8 Gyro
9 Starting gear
10 Cable connector
11 Tail assembly
12 Propeller

Source: Gray, E., *Devil's Device: The Story of the Invention of the Torpedo* (Annapolis, Maryland, 1975).

A torpedo was, in fact, a miniature submarine in itself; but the depth-keeping and steering mechanisms were fully automatic. Until mid-1940 the depth-keeping of German torpedoes was erratic and there were numerous failures. American submariners, for some 20 months, also suffered from faulty weapons which did not explode and one German naval historian also comments on the lack of reliability of 'the depth keeping and firing mechanisms' of Soviet torpedoes used by the *Black Sea Fleet (F. Ruge, *The Soviets as Naval Opponents*, Cambridge, 1977, p. 101).

Typically, a semi-internal-combustion or turbine-propulsion torpedo was 533 mm. (21 in.) in diameter and 6.1 m. (20 ft.) long. An air bottle, to supply the engine,

Torpedoes: Principal types

Origin	*Propulsion*	*Speed/Range (n. miles) nautical miles = 2,000 yards = 1,829 metres*	*Explosive Weight*	*Use*
France				
549 mm (21.6 in)	Thermal	35/3.8	308 kg (678 lb)	S/M
Germany				
533 mm G7e	Electric	30/2.7	297 kg (653 lb)	S/M
533 mm G7a	Thermal	44/3.3	299 kg (658 lb)	General
Italy				
533 mm Veloce	Thermal	49/2.2	113 kg (249 lb)	General
450 mm (17.7 in)	Thermal	44/1	110 kg (242 lb)	MAS (Torpedo) boats
Japan				
610 mm (24 in) 93	Oxygen	49/12	499 kg (1,098 lb)	Surface ships
533 mm 94	Oxygen	45/2.5	393 kg (865 lb)	S/M
UK				
533 mm (21 in) MkVIII	Thermal	45/2.5	350 kg (550 lb)	S/M
457 mm (18 in) MkXII	Thermal	40/0.75	176 kg (387 lb)	Aircraft
533 mm MkIX	Thermal	40/5	340 kg (748 lb)	Destroyers/Cruisers
USA				
533 mm 14	Turbine	46/2.25	272 kg (598 lb)	S/M

Source: Contributor.

occupied about one-third of the length. It could take a heavy warhead of 270–393 kg. (595–866 lb.) 3–5 km. (2–3 mi.) at 45 knots or nearly 13 km. (8 mi.) at 30 knots, but the ideal range was about 1,100 m. (1,200 yd.). The longer ranges were academic unless a large number of fish were fired in a spread salvo like the opened fingers of a hand or successively in a 'hosepipe' which had the same effect by virtue of target travel. The chances of hitting an evasive target with only one or two torpedoes at more than a mile (1.6 km.) were low, though the Germans improved the odds at long range by using the Federapparat (spring apparatus) torpedo, or FAT, and Lagenunabhängiger (independent of target's inclination) torpedo, or LUT, which crossed and recrossed a convoy's path. Against 'easy' merchantmen, however, U-boats usually employed single-shot 30-knot, cheap and simple battery-powered electric 'eels' which, unlike 'thermal' oil-fuelled (or alcohol for USN turbine-drive) torpedoes, left no revealing wake on the surface. American submarines were similarly equipped from late 1943 and by 1945 were using them in 65% of attacks. The Royal Navy clung to oil-air thermal weapons scarcely changed from a 1928 design except that a magnetic-influence pistol—which was unreliable but could be more damaging because it exploded the 350 kg. (770 lb.) warhead beneath a target's pull—was sometimes used.

The Japanese secretly developed exceptionally fast, reliable, long-range, and virtually trackless oxygen-fuelled torpedoes in the 1930s. The type 93 'Long Lance' for surface ships was huge—610 mm. (24 in.) in diameter, 9 m. (30 ft.) long—delivering half a ton of explosive (508 kg.) out to 19 km. (12 mi.) at 49 knots. Fired in sufficient numbers to create a broad swathe of 'torpedo water', it was extremely effective against Allied warships in several naval engagements during the Pacific war (see TASSAFARONGA, for example). The smaller oxygen-fuelled submarine version had a shorter range (4 km./2.5 mi.) than the conventional German air-oil 'eel' (5.3 km./3.3 mi.), but a larger warhead (393 kg./866 lb. against 299 kg./659 lb.). Italy had some fast (48–50-knot) torpedoes but range was only 3.2 km. (2 mi.) and warheads were comparatively small at 250–270 kg. (551–95 lb.). For homing torpedoes see GUIDED WEAPONS; see also HUMAN TORPEDOES.

RICHARD COMPTON-HALL

Totensonntag, see SIDI REZEGH.

Tovey, Admiral Sir John (1885–1971), British naval officer who, as second-in-command of *Cunningham's Mediterranean Fleet, fought in early skirmishes with the Italian Navy. In October 1940 he was appointed C-in-C Home Fleet whose warships sank the German battleship **Bismarck* in May 1941 and guarded the *Arctic convoys. He was promoted admiral in 1942, became C-in-C the Nore, one of the navy's five home commands, and in May 1943 was promoted admiral of the fleet. He was knighted in 1941.

Admiral **Toyoda**.

Toyoda Soemu, Admiral (1885–1957), C-in-C of the Japanese Combined Fleet from March 1944 in succession to Vice-Admiral *Koga. He ordered Operation *A-GŌ which resulted in a resounding defeat for his fleet by the US Navy in the *Philippine Sea battle of June 1944. In May 1945 he was appointed Chief of the Naval General Staff and was on the side of those who wanted to continue the war. He was tried by an Allied military tribunal, but acquitted.

Tragino raid. This, the first British attempt at *airborne warfare, was undertaken by 35 men of No. 2 Commando (later 11th Special Air Service Battalion, then 1st Parachute Battalion) on 10 February 1941. They destroyed their target, an aqueduct across the River Tragino 58 km. (36 mi.) south of Foggia, which supplied the toe of Italy with fresh water. All were subsequently captured, and one, Italian-born but of British nationality, was executed. The aqueduct was quickly repaired and the operation failed to cause, as had been hoped, any disruption at the ports of Taranto, Brindisi, and Bari which supplied Italian forces fighting in the *Western Desert campaigns.

Foxall, R., *The Guinea-Pigs* (London, 1983).

traitors and treachery, like *liberation and *occupation these words tended to be used subjectively. For example, members of the German *Rote Kapelle, quickly executed as traitors by the Nazis, were considered heroes in the Soviet Union. See also BRITISH UNION, JOYCE, PHILBY, SCHWARZE KAPELLE, and VLASOV for further examples of traitors and treachery.

Transjordan, an integral part of the British mandate of Palestine until 1921 when Emir Abdullah ascended the throne. Transjordan's independence was recognized in 1928, but the British Resident retained important powers, and it remained a British mandate until 1946. The Arab Legion, a police force lead by British officers, had been raised in Transjordan during the 1920s. This helped as part of HABFORCE to quell the revolt in Iraq in May 1941. With the country's regular army, the Transjordan Frontier Force which was also led by British officers, it also helped to overrun *Vichy French forces in the *Syrian campaign. Otherwise, apart from a Vichy air raid on the capital, Amman, the country, with its population of some 300,000 Arabs, was untouched by the war. From 1946, when full independence was achieved, it was known as the Kingdom of Jordan and became the Hashemite Kingdom of Jordan in 1949.

Transnistria was the name given to the area of the Ukraine between the Dniester and Bug rivers, over which Marshal *Antonescu, the Romanian leader, proclaimed sovereignty in August 1941, and which he was forced to abandon in April 1944 (see Map 80). This region contained only a small number of Romanian settlements and had never before been claimed by Romania. Its civilian governor, Gheorghe Alexianu, first based his administration in Tiraspol and, until the capture of Odessa, controlled only largely rural areas of the province. The Fourth Romanian Army advanced to Odessa in early August 1941 but encountered fierce Soviet resistance. Fighting lasted until 16 October when the city fell, at a cost of some 70,000 Romanian dead and wounded. The Transnistrian government was publicly proclaimed on the following day but the governor's headquarters were not moved from Tiraspol to Odessa until December 1942.

One of the first, and most notorious, acts of the Romanian authorities was their response to the blowing-up by Soviet partisans on 22 October 1941 of the Romanian headquarters in the city which caused the deaths of 16 officers, 9 non-commissioned officers (NCOs), and 35 other ranks. Antonescu ordered that 200 citizens of Odessa should die for every officer killed, and 100 for every NCO and other ranks. The number of people actually executed in retaliation is not known, but *Pravda* in the summer of 1944 accused the Romanians of having massacred 200,000 on this occasion. The figure of 20,000 was mentioned in May 1945 when a 'People's Tribunal' in Bucharest tried Generals Macici and Trestioreanu and other Romanian officers who had carried out Antonescu's orders.

Transnistria was designated by Antonescu a resettlement area for Jews and gypsies deported from Bucovina and Bessarabia (see also DEPORTATIONS). In December 1941 it was reported to Antonescu that these deportations had been completed and that 108,000 Jews had been resettled there. In 1942 the Romanian authorities announced that the number of Jews in the province was 80,087 and by December 1943 this figure, according to a neutral source, had fallen to 54,300. Antonescu put a stop to wholesale deportations of Jews early in 1942 and in March 1943 he gave the Central Jewish Office in Romania permission to repatriate all Jews deported to Transnistria. This body managed to bring back only some 10,000. Many of those deported had perished on the way to Transnistria since the railway wagons into which they were loaded were not provided with sufficient food or water for the week-long journey. It is estimated that between 70,000 and 90,000 Jews and Gypsies from Romania, together with an unknown number of Soviet Jews, were shot or starved to death by German and Romanian units in Transnistria. In May 1946 Alexianu was tried with Antonescu for war crimes and executed on 1 June.

For non-Jews Romanian rule in Transnistria was less draconian and considerably more benevolent than German rule in other parts of Soviet territory. Money was invested in the economy and Romanian laxity encouraged bribery and speculation which allowed the inhabitants to display a measure of private enterprise and personal initiative. Some 7,000 Soviet citizens accompanied the Romanian Army when it withdrew from Transnistria in April 1944 in the face of the Red Army.

DENNIS DELETANT

Dallin, A., *Odessa 1941–1944: A Case Study of Soviet Territory Under Foreign Rule* (Santa Monica, Calif., 1957).
Fisher, J. S., *Transnistria: The Forgotten Cemetery* (London, 1969).

Treblinka was a Nazi death camp located on the River Bug 72 km. (45 mi.) from Warsaw. As part of *Operation REINHARD, it opened in July 1942 and was used to exterminate the inhabitants of the Warsaw ghetto (see also WARSAW RISINGS). Its efficiency in implementing the *Final Solution was horrific: at least 900,000 Jews are said to have died there, making it second only to *Auschwitz in this respect. In August 1943 a camp revolt by 700 prisoners resulted in the death of 15 guards. But only 12 prisoners managed to escape, the rest being killed, and in November 1943 the camp was razed to the ground. See also CONCENTRATION CAMPS.

TRIDENT, codename for the second Allied Washington conference held from 11 to 25 May 1943 at which Churchill and Roosevelt, and their diplomatic and military advisers, were present. Their discussions centred upon future strategy, which included a decision to delay the invasion of France until May 1944. It was also agreed that Portugal should be approached to allow air bases on the Azores; and that the policy of *unconditional surrender, first enunciated at the Casablanca conference the previous January (see SYMBOL), should be pursued with Italy, despite requests by *Eisenhower and Maitland *Wilson for a more lenient approach. The deficit in available shipping and the satisfactory progress of the battle of the *Atlantic were also discussed. See also DIPLOMACY.

Trieste is situated in the north-eastern corner of the Adriatic sea (see Map B). Until 1918, when its population was nearly two-thirds Italian, it was the Austro-Hungarian empire's principal port. At the end of the *First World War it was ceded to Italy; at the end of the Second it was the scene of the first clash of the *Cold War, for the region of Venezia Giulia, of which Trieste is a part, was claimed by both Italy and Yugoslavia, and in March 1945 *Tito and the Partisans launched an offensive into the area. After occupying most of it Tito then abrogated an agreement he had made that the western Allies could establish a military government there, and on 2 May demanded that all Allied forces withdraw behind the River Isonzo. On 12 May Churchill, concerned about Soviet intentions, cabled *Truman that an 'Iron Curtain is drawn down upon their front. We do not know what was going on behind. There seems little doubt that the whole of the regions east of the line Lübeck–Trieste–Corfu will soon be completely in their hands...'

During the negotiations which followed Tito's forces entered Austria, but on 9 June an agreement was signed in Belgrade and the Partisans withdrew from Austria, and from Trieste and its environs. The peace treaty with Italy signed in Paris in 1947 created the Free Territory of Trieste, but this failed to work and eventually the area was partitioned between the two countries with the port remaining in Italian hands.

Tripartite Pact, negotiated in Tokyo and signed in Berlin on 27 September 1940 by Germany, Italy, and Japan. It was primarily intended to forestall US intervention in the war, for the terms included promise of mutual aid if any one of the signatories was attacked by a power not already involved in the European war or in the *China Incident. However, secret clauses added at Japan's request more or less nullified these terms as Japan wanted to obtain concessions from the USA, using its withdrawal from the pact as a bargaining point. But Washington was not intimidated by the pact; on the contrary, the USA intensified its help to China, which made any negotiations impossible for the Japanese.

One of the pact's articles specifically guaranteed the existing German–Soviet relationship (see NAZI–SOVIET PACT), and in November 1940 the USSR was asked to join. However, the conditions Stalin proposed for doing so did not suit Hitler and negotiations ceased, but Romania, Hungary, and Slovakia signed the same month, Bulgaria and Yugoslavia (which repudiated it almost immediately) signed in March 1941, and the Nazi puppet state of Croatia signed on 15 June 1941. Unlike the *Grand Alliance, the Axis coalition formed by the pact had no agreed strategy for fighting the war. See also AXIS STRATEGY AND CO-OPERATION.

triphibious warfare was Churchill's name for *amphibious warfare because it involved all three services. He called *Mountbatten, the chief of *Combined Operations and the British expert in this form of warfare, 'young, enthusiastic, and triphibious...'

triple agents. A very few brave and cunning *double agents managed to change sides back again, thus enabling their original secret employers to turn the tables again. Such cases were always viewed with extra suspicion by the side that benefited from them. See GARBY-CZERNIAWSKI, for example. M. R. D. FOOT

Tripolitania, western province of the Italian colony of Libya.

Trobriand Islands, situated north-east of the Papua peninsula. The Japanese did not occupy them during the *Pacific war, but a US airstrip was built on the principal one, Kiriwina, after troops of *MacArthur's *Alamo Force landed there and on another, Woodlark Island, on 30 June 1943. The landings, the first Allied ones of any size in the *South-West Pacific Area, heralded the start of MacArthur's offensive (CARTWHEEL) to capture *Rabaul, the main Japanese base in the area, as the Kiriwina airfield brought it within fighter range. However, at the Quebec conference in August 1943 (see QUADRANT) it was decided to bypass Rabaul instead and the airfields were used to help neutralize it.

Truk Atoll is one of the Pacific Caroline Islands chain. Its lagoon harboured the Japanese Combined Fleet and it was also an important Japanese air base. During the *Pacific war it was attacked frequently by US aircraft of *Task Force 58 and as *Eniwetok was being assaulted in February 1944 they mounted the first-ever *radar-guided night bomber attack on shipping there. The Combined Fleet had left, but 265 Japanese aircraft were destroyed, 140,000 tons of shipping was sunk, and the naval base was badly damaged. A final strike on 29/30 April destroyed what remained, by which time the US *Joint Chiefs of Staff had decided to bypass Truk, which released the troops earmarked to invade it for *amphibious warfare landings on the Mariana and Palau Islands.

Truman, Harry S (1884–1972) was president of the USA, 1945–52. On 12 April 1945, Roosevelt's death catapulted Truman, as incumbent vice-president, into the American presidency. Millions in the country worried that 'the little man from Missouri', as he was initially described, would not be an effective replacement for Roosevelt, one of the greatest presidents in US history. Truman, however, had attributes that would allow him to rise to the challenge. A captain of artillery in the *First World War, a Missouri county judge, and, from 1935, a senator, he had almost ten years of experience in the Senate when Roosevelt selected him as his vice-presidential running mate in 1944. Despite ties to the corrupt Democratic machine in Kansas City, Missouri, Truman had a reputation as an honest, hard-working, loyal Democrat. He gained national prominence during the Second World War as chairman of the Senate Special Committee to Investigate the National Defense Program. Credited with saving the government billions of dollars and protecting the Roosevelt administration from criticism over war production, the Truman Committee, as it was called, gave him standing with Roosevelt. More important, a split in the Democratic Party, between southern conservatives opposed to the incumbent liberal vice-president, Henry Wallace, and liberal labour leaders opposed to the leading conservative candidate, James *Byrnes of South Carolina, made Truman, a border state Democrat and moderate, the compromise choice for the job.

During his 83 days as vice-president, the 60-year-old Truman had little contact with Roosevelt and no clear idea of what his chief intended in foreign affairs. The president, for example, had never informed him of the programme to build an *atomic bomb nor taken him into his confidence on any of the great post-war issues the country would shortly confront. On assuming the presidency, Truman relied on Roosevelt's advisers and his own instincts to fashion a response to events in Europe, where the war ended on 8 May. To reassure Americans and the country's allies that there would be no break with Roosevelt's policies, Truman announced in his first speech on 16 April that he would insist on *unconditional surrender by Germany and Japan.

By the time Truman had become president, Germany's defeat was assured and the emerging problem in Europe was Soviet expansionism. Aggressively asserting their self-interest in eastern Europe generally and in Poland in particular, the Soviets angered Truman, who accused them of breaking the Yalta agreements made with Roosevelt in February 1945 (see ARGONAUT). Truman believed that Soviet treatment of Poland signalled whether the world would enter a new era of collective security in international relations or a return to traditional Great Power politics. In meetings with the Soviet foreign minister, *Molotov, on 22–23 April, the president, believing it would save American lives, echoed Roosevelt's hopes for Soviet participation in the war against Japan while emphasizing that good relations with the USA depended on Moscow's fulfilment of the Yalta accords.

Truman took some hope for continued co-operation with the Soviets from the successful *San Francisco conference in April and May, which established the United Nations. He took particular satisfaction from Stalin's acceptance of American insistence on limiting vetoes in the Security Council to matters of substance. No nation would have a veto over agenda items for debate, assuring freedom of discussion on all international questions. He also took comfort from the thought that the likely development of an atomic bomb would give the USA the power to shape the course of post-war affairs. His decision to go ahead with the production of the bomb, however, rested principally on the expectation that it would serve to end the war more quickly against Japan (but see ATOMIC BOMB, 2).

Soviet reaffirmation in June of a readiness to fight Japan and acceptance of Truman's suggestion that there be a Big Three meeting (see also GRAND ALLIANCE) in July further encouraged the president's hopes for post-war co-operation with Moscow. As a consequence, Truman rejected suggestions from Churchill that US troops, who ended the war deep inside the previously determined Soviet zone of occupation, be left there as a way to put pressure on Moscow regarding eastern Europe. Truman believed that this would do more to undermine than advance Soviet–American relations and might delay the movement of US forces from Europe to the Far East.

Truman's conference with Churchill and Stalin at Potsdam from 17 July to 3 August (see TERMINAL) jolted the president's hopes for sustained Allied co-operation. Towards the end of July, elections in the UK replaced Churchill with *Attlee, leader of the Labour Party, and raised questions in Truman's mind about continuities in British foreign policy. More important, the conference produced sharp quarrels with Stalin over a number of issues, including western recognition of Moscow's East European satellites, Poland's western boundary with Germany (see ODER–NEISSE LINE), and German reparation payments. Although agreements were hammered out on some of these issues, and Truman put the best possible face on the discussions in a report to the American people, he had few illusions about the results of the meetings. Agreements with Moscow were more the exception than the rule, and the Big Three papered over their differences by referring them to a council of foreign ministers for further discussion.

Truman's face-to-face encounter with Stalin and the Soviets convinced him that the essential ingredient of relations with them must be toughness. News of the successful test of an atomic bomb in the New Mexico desert on 16 July stiffened his resolve to follow a hard line. When he received a cable about the test, Secretary of War Henry *Stimson remembered that 'the president was tremendously pepped up by it.' Churchill saw Truman as 'emphatic and decisive ... telling [the Soviets] as to certain demands that they absolutely could not have.' Partly out of a desire to avoid future recriminations with the Soviets over hiding the development of the bomb, Truman now decided to inform them of its existence. At the close of the day's proceedings on 24 July, he casually told Stalin that the USA had a weapon of unusually destructive force that it planned to use against the Japanese to end the war. Stalin, who already had knowledge of America's atomic project from *spies,

President **Truman** announces Japan's surrender during a press conference at the White House, 14 August 1945.

coolly expressed pleasure at the news and the hope that the Americans would make good use of the weapon against Japan. Three days before the end of the conference Truman wrote to his mother, 'You never saw such pig-headed people as are the Russians. I hope I never have to hold another conference with them—but, of course, I will.' In fact, he never did.

A constant concern Truman faced during and after Potsdam was how to end the war against Japan quickly but without sacrificing American determination for an unconditional surrender. Suggestions to Truman and his secretary of state James Byrnes that they issue a call for Japan's surrender while promising not to abolish the monarchy were rejected. The president believed that Japan might take such a statement as a sign of weakness and might lead to terrible repercussions in the USA. Although the Japanese asked the Soviets to explore the possibility of mediation, and Stalin passed the request to Truman at Potsdam, the president was unresponsive. He believed it was a ploy to divide the Allies and weaken their will to fight. Moreover, deciphered cables (see MAGIC) from Tokyo to the Japanese ambassador in Moscow, saying that Japan would not accept unconditional surrender, persuaded the president that Japan intended to hold on to some conquered territory. On 27 July, the UK, USA, and China issued an ultimatum to Japan to proclaim unconditional surrender or face 'prompt and utter destruction'. Nothing was said about the future of the monarchy. Tokyo dismissed the ultimatum as a rehash of past declarations.

The Japanese response triggered final preparations for using atomic bombs against Japan at *Hiroshima on 6 August and *Nagasaki on 9 August. Much has been written about Truman's fateful decision to drop the bomb. In a sense there never was a decision. As General Leslie R. Groves, the army officer in charge of the bomb's development, said, Truman's 'decision was one of noninterference—basically a decision not to upset the existing plan.' All the momentum was in the direction of using the bomb. Having invested $2 billion in its development, fearful that the alternative was a longer war with hundreds of thousands of additional Allied casualties, and hardened by repeated Axis and Allied air raids, which had already taken hundreds of thousands of civilian lives, Truman and his military chiefs saw no compelling reason against the earliest possible use of the bomb. Considerations of power politics—the extent to which use of the 'winning weapon', as some called it, would increase the USA's ability to compel Soviet compliance with post-war peace arrangements—were distinctly secondary; but they were not entirely absent from Truman's mind.

Soviet entry into the war against Japan on 8 August and Japanese acceptance of US surrender terms, which Tokyo interpreted as not eliminating the emperor's rule, brought an end to the war on 14 August. Although Truman understood that the future peace might hold difficulties as great as any he had faced in ending the war, he took satisfaction from having presided over a rapid conclusion to the most terrible war in human history. ROBERT DALLEK

Donovan, R. J., *Conflict and Crisis: The Presidency of Harry S. Truman, 1945–1948* (New York, 1977).
Gaddis, J. L., *The United States and the Origins of the Cold War, 1941–1947* (New York, 1972).
Sherwin, M. J., *A World Destroyed: The Atomic Bomb in the Grand Alliance, 1941–1945* (New York, 1975).

Truscott, Lt-General Lucian K. (1895–1965), US Army officer who commanded 3rd US Division during the *Sicilian campaign, at *Salerno, and at *Anzio where, from 23 February 1944, he took command of Allied forces (6th US Corps) and broke out of the precarious bridgehead.

In May 1942, Truscott, as a colonel, was seconded to *Combined Operations headquarters in London. Promoted brigadier-general the same month, he formed the first Ranger battalion (see USA, 5(f)), a part of which participated in the *Dieppe raid at which he was present. His command of a small task force which captured Port Lyautey during the *North African campaign landings in November 1942 established him as a battle-proven commander and during the subsequent fighting in Tunisia he commanded *Eisenhower's Advanced Command Post. In September 1944, after 6th Corps had taken part in the *French Riviera landings, he was promoted lt-general; and in November he was given command of Fifth US Army fighting in the *Italian campaign which he led successfully until the end of the war.

Truscott, L., *Command Missions* (New York, 1954).

Tulagi Island. This small Pacific island, 3,600 m. (4,000 yd.) long, in the Solomons was occupied during the *Pacific war by the Japanese prior to the battle of the *Coral Sea in May 1942 to establish a seaplane base there. It was retaken by US marines on 7 August 1942, at the start of the *Guadalcanal campaign.

Tunisia, French protectorate with a population of 2.6 million, including 204,500 Europeans, and nominally ruled by the Bey of Tunis who pledged support for France in September 1939. When Italy declared war in June 1940 French troops from Tunisia entered Libya, but these withdrew when the Franco-Italian *armistice was signed.

In 1942 a new Bey, Prince Mohammed el-Moncef, supported the nationalist leader, *Bourguiba, by appointing his own cabinet without reference to the *Vichy resident-general, Admiral *Estéva. They were still in dispute when the *North African campaign started in November 1942 and the Germans occupied Tunisia. This involved Estéva in *collaboration and the Tunisians in a war where some sided with the Germans and others with the Allies. When the Axis forces occupying Tunisia surrendered in May 1943 the Bey was overthrown by General *Giraud and Estéva was replaced by Maj-General Charles-Emmanuel Mast.

Six Tunisian regiments of *Tirailleurs took part in the fighting which preceded the fall of *France in June 1940 and one was raised to fight with Giraud's forces in the North African campaign.

Turing, Alan (1912–54), British mathematician whose theories, and work at the British government Code and Cypher School at *Bletchley Park, resulted in the modern computer. With another mathematician, Gordon Welchman, he developed a British 'bombe', the name the Poles gave to their machines for deciphering early *ENIGMA signals that produced *ULTRA intelligence. He led the deciphering of German naval ENIGMA signals, so vital during the battle of the *Atlantic, and was involved in breaking the *Geheimschreiber transmissions. But he was a solitary, eccentric genius, not an administrator, and in 1943 he left Bletchley Park to develop a speech encipherment system. His post-war career was marred by personal tragedy that ended in his suicide.

Hodges, A., *Alan Turing: the Enigma* (London, 1983).

Turkey was the only major participant in the *First World War which managed to avoid fighting in the Second. It was the experience of 1914–18 which helped to determine its policy. Virtually all the political and military leaders of Turkey during 1939–45 had direct personal experiences of the disasters of the earlier struggle, which had finally destroyed the Ottoman Empire, and they were determined not to repeat them. They were also aware that, by 1939, their armed forces were woefully out of date: in any serious encounter with either the Allied or the Axis forces, they would be faced with the severe risk of defeat. Domestically, Ismet Inönü, who had succeeded Kemal Ataturk, as president on the latter's death (1881–1938), maintained an authoritarian single-party regime. Since Inönü and his advisers all seem to have been in favour of *de facto* neutrality, there was no serious internal challenge to this policy.

Neutrality was certainly the most sensible policy for

Turkey, but it was not easy to maintain. Historically, its main enemy had been Russia, but, in 1925 the two countries had signed a Treaty of Friendship, renewed in 1935, which appeared to neutralize the potential threat from the north. During the 1930s, Turkey's main concern was the threat to Balkan security posed by the ambitions of Italy. By 1939, France and the UK were also becoming worried by the threat to their own interests in the eastern Mediterranean, and began to look for an alliance with Turkey. The Turks were happy to reach arrangements which would provide themselves with assistance if they were attacked by Italy or Germany, but did not want to be dragged into the war for the sake of the Allies.

In May 1939, Turkey and the UK issued a joint declaration stating that they would aid one another in the event of an act of aggression leading to war in the Mediterranean. Following an agreement with France which resulted in the transfer of the disputed province of Alexandretta from Syria to Turkey, the Turkish and French governments issued a similar declaration in June 1939. Soon afterwards, however, Turkey received a rude shock from the signature of the *Nazi–Soviet Pact of August 1939, which created the serious danger that Hitler and Stalin might combine against it. Accordingly, the Turkish foreign minister, Şükrü Saraçoğlu, visited Moscow in September 1939 for what turned out to be a fruitless attempt to negotiate mutual security arrangements. Faced with this failure, Turkey returned to negotiations with France and the UK. In October 1939, the three governments signed a tripartite treaty providing that the two countries would aid Turkey if it were attacked by another European power. If there were an act of aggression leading to war in the Mediterranean area involving France and the UK, then Turkey would assist them, but would be exempted from any action in the case of a war between its two allies and the USSR.

Once the war had begun in Europe, Turkey entered a period of grave danger which lasted until June 1941. Italy's entry into the war in June 1940 began the battle for the *Mediterranean. The collapse of France meant that the UK was unable to aid Turkey; however, it also meant that the British recognized that there was no point in obliging the Turks to fulfil their commitments under the tripartite treaty. Subsequently, the German occupation of the Balkans in April 1941 brought the war to the frontiers of Turkey. Faced with the danger of a Nazi attack on Istanbul and the straits, and with British concurrence, Turkey signed a Treaty of Territorial Integrity and Friendship with Germany on 18 June 1941.

Four days after the signature of the German–Turkish Pact, Hitler invaded the USSR (see BARBAROSSA). This opened a second phase in the war for Turkey, since it virtually removed the danger that either Germany or the USSR would attack her, at least in the near future. However, Inönü strongly resisted efforts by Franz von *Papen, the German ambassador in Ankara, to bring Turkey into the war on Germany's side.

The second phase ended in the autumn of 1942, as the battle of *El Alamein and Soviet resistance at *Stalingrad indicated that the Allies were likely to win the war eventually. Until 1943 the UK, the USSR, and later the USA were prepared to accept Turkey's *de facto* neutrality, since the USSR was naturally preoccupied by the German invasion, and the other Allies were as yet in no position to launch a counter-offensive in Europe. Once the turning-point was passed, these concerns ceased to apply. Churchill, in particular, was keen to bring Turkey into the war, so as to attack Germany from the Balkans. However, his 'soft underbelly' strategy was not fully supported by the USA, which was anxious not to divert resources away from the west. Turkey came under very strong pressure to join the Allies in the war in February 1943, when Churchill visited Inönü at Adana, and again at the Cairo conference in the following December (see SEXTANT). The Turks insisted on, and received, increased quantities of Allied war *matériel*, but dragged their feet over implementing their undertakings of 1939. By 1944, relations between Ankara and the Allies (the UK and the USSR in particular) had reached a low point. Turkey officially declared war on Germany on 23 February 1945, but only to establish its status as a founder member of the United Nations (see SAN FRANCISCO CONFERENCE).

In the meantime, Stalin reacted to Turkey's non-belligerence by demanding political and territorial concessions. In June 1945, Moscow insisted that the Turkish–Soviet Friendship Treaty could not be renewed unless Soviet bases were established in the straits, and the provinces of Kars and Ardahan, on Turkey's eastern frontier, were ceded to the USSR. Hence, as the Second World War turned into the *Cold War, a new threat opened up for Turkey, and the main lines of her post-war foreign policy were determined. WILLIAM HALE

Ataöv, T., *Turkish Foreign Policy, 1939–1945* (Ankara, 1965).
Deringil, S., *Turkish Foreign Policy during the Second World War* (Cambridge, 1989).
Weisband, E., *Turkish Foreign Policy, 1943–1945: Small State Diplomacy and Great Power Politics* (Princeton, 1973).

Turner, Admiral Richmond Kelly (1885–1961), US naval officer who proved to be the most gifted amphibious commander the *Pacific war produced.

Though he was one of the US Navy's most outstanding pre-war planners—he wrote the early drafts of the *Rainbow 5 war plan—the army chief of staff, *Marshall, had him removed from the joint planning staff for being too abrasive. This assessment is supported by Turner's behaviour as director of war plans before the Japanese attack on *Pearl Harbor in December 1941 when his political infighting was at least partly responsible for the failure of vital intelligence to reach the Hawaii command. However, the navy's C-in-C, Admiral *King, called Marshall's decision the Army's greatest single contribution to the war in the Pacific, for Turner, whose capacity for hard work was legendary, went on to command the successful amphibious landings at *Guadalcanal, *New Georgia, *Tarawa, *Eniwetok, the

*Mariana Islands, *Iwo Jima, and *Okinawa. See also AMPHIBIOUS WARFARE.

Dyer, G., *The Amphibians came to Conquer: the Story of Admiral Richmond Kelly Turner*, 2 vols. (Washington, DC, 1969).

Twining, Lt-General Nathan F. (1897–1982), US airman who served as a corporal in the US National Guard during the *First World War. By 1943 he had risen to command Thirteenth USAAF based in New Caledonia and in July that year he took tactical command of all Allied and US air units for operations in the Solomons (Airsols), the first joint air command in US history. From January 1944, as commander of Fifteenth USAAF in Italy, and of the Allied Strategic Air Forces fighting in the battle for the *Mediterranean, he planned the raids on the *Ploesti oilfields and directed his command's role in the *strategic air offensive in Europe. In August 1945 he succeeded *LeMay as commander of Twentieth USAAF on the Marianas, which had been created to bomb Japan with the new B29 Superfortress (see STRATEGIC AIR OFFENSIVE, 3), and it was Twining's aircraft that dropped the *atomic bombs on *Hiroshima and *Nagasaki.

Typex, British cipher machine, the result of the deliberations of a committee formed in 1926 to investigate whether the three services, the foreign office, and the colonial and India offices, should employ machine ciphers instead of book codes. The investigation, which included the purchase of two German *ENIGMA cipher machines, concluded in 1935 that '3 sets of cypher machines of an improved "Enigma" type through the agency of so-called "Type X" attachments' should be constructed (quoted in F. H. Hinsley *et al.*, *British Intelligence in the Second World War*, vol. 2, London, 1981, p. 631). The army and the RAF adopted the Typex which proved secure (though lower grade book codes used by both services were broken by the Germans). However, the Admiralty refused to use it, almost certainly because signals enciphered by machine took longer to transmit than those based on a code book, a practical consideration in ship-to-shore communications. As a result, the German Navy's *B-Dienst broke a number of Admiralty high grade *codes and ciphers, which had disastrous consequences for the British during the early years of the battle of the *Atlantic, and aided the German Navy during the *Norwegian campaign and in the operations of its *auxiliary cruisers.

By January 1943 all British naval shore commands were equipped with Typex but it was never used aboard British warships. Instead, by November 1943 they were using the Combined Cypher Machine which was in operation aboard all warships for British–Canadian–US communications in the Atlantic. The Combined Cypher Machine was based on the Typex and on the US Navy's Electrical Cypher Machine (see SIGABA), both of which were adapted so that they could communicate with it. So far as is known, no Allied machine cipher was ever broken by any of the Axis powers.

U-boat or *Unterseeboot* (undersea boat), the name commonly given to German *submarines.

Udet, General Ernst (1896–1941), German *First World War fighter ace when he served in *Göring's Richthofen Squadron. In 1936 Göring put him in charge of the Luftwaffe's technical office where he became largely responsible for the construction of fighters and medium bombers at the expense of heavy bombers, and for the design and manufacture of several famous German aircraft such as the Stuka dive-bomber and the twin-engined Ju88. In 1939 he became the director of air armament, but his inability, among other failures, to improve aircraft production, lowered his prestige in the eyes of Hitler and Göring. His depressions, exacerbated by alcohol and narcotics, increased to such an extent that he eventually committed suicide. The facts were covered up and he was given a state funeral.

Uganda, see BRITISH EAST AFRICA.

UK

1. Introduction

At 1100 on Sunday 3 September 1939, the UK's ultimatum to Germany expired and, for the second time in 21 years, the two countries were at war. The mood of sombre determination with which the UK entered the Second World War—in marked contrast to the rapturous enthusiasm people had displayed in August 1914—reflected not only apprehension about the future but also a recognition of the failure of British policies and British politicians over the previous decade.

Between 1931 and 1935 the UK's global security was shattered by the appearance of three potential enemies. Japan's invasion of Manchuria in September 1931 (see MANCHUKUO), Hitler's accession to power in Germany in January 1933, and Italy's attack on Abyssinia in October 1935 produced a situation in which appeasement of one or more of these ambitious powers was unavoidable. The contemporaneous collapse of the European security system, marked by Germany's withdrawal from the Geneva disarmament conference in October 1933, the remilitarization of the Rhineland on 7 March 1936 and the discrediting of the *League of Nations in the wake of Japanese aggression in Manchuria and the Italian conquest of Abyssinia, caused British politicians to focus their efforts on Germany as the greatest threat. To meet it, the UK developed a dual policy of arms limitation and appeasement. Both Stanley Baldwin (1867–1947) and Neville *Chamberlain sought to allay Germany's ruffled feelings, return it to the international fold, and at the same time prevent an arms race.

Between 1934 and 1936, when the occupation of the Rhineland signalled the start of a more aggressive phase in German policy, the UK put much of its faith in the parity deterrent: a policy of limited bomber construction at a rate Germany could not outpace which was calculated to deter Hitler from unilateral repudiation of the 1919 *Versailles settlement. Hitler's announcement of German rearmament in March 1935, and his claim that the Luftwaffe was already the equal of the RAF, vitiated this policy, though the conclusion of an Anglo-German naval agreement in June 1935 and the temptation of a western air pact (which was never secured) encouraged British statesmen to put continued faith in the prospects for arms limitation.

Events in the Rhineland and Abyssinia, combined with the evident bankruptcy of the parity deterrent, forced a reconsideration of British defence policy; in December 1937 the government allocated £1,500,000,000 for defence over the next five years and switched priority from bombers to an integrated air defence system. At the same time, Chamberlain made it plain that the UK was prepared to see possibly extensive changes in Austria and Czechoslovakia in Germany's favour, provided they were achieved by peaceful means. This policy was influenced by the hostility of the Dominions to any war in Europe and by Chamberlain's desire to avoid unrestrained rearmament, which would distort the British economy and mean the loss of exports. It was also the preference of a man with a profound horror of war who misread the temper of his opponent.

After Germany's absorption of Austria on 12 March 1938 it became plain that Czechoslovakia was next on Hitler's shopping list. Military unreadiness and the UK's detachment from European affairs in general and eastern Europe in particular led to the *Munich agreement of 30 September 1938—the high point of appeasement and the low-water mark of British foreign policy. After the Anschluss rearmament was at last allowed to go ahead unfettered; but in March the British *Chiefs of Staff decided that nothing could be done to help Czechoslovakia (not least because they were unwilling to enter into military conversations with the French) and thereafter they urged the government to appease the UK's opponents. British policy at Munich was in part the inescapable consequence of military vulnerability: in September 1938, the cabinet knew that the Luftwaffe could not launch the much-feared 'knock-out blow' from the air, but it was also aware that British air defences were still in disarray (only four *radar stations were operational and all the guns on Spitfires needed modification before they could fire at heights at which German bombers would probably be encountered). A second strand in British policy was the view that Germany had a moral right to the Sudetenland. Whether the Munich agreement was also a conscious policy of buying time remains debatable.

Chamberlain's return from Munich with 'peace in our time' was greeted with popular relief; but he remarked privately to Lord *Halifax, the foreign secretary, that in three months the wild celebrations would be over. His pessimism was fully justified. Germany's occupation of the rump of Czechoslovakia on 15 March 1939 demonstrated that British policies could neither deter Hitler nor assuage his mounting territorial appetite. Guarantees to Poland and Romania in March, the imposition of conscription in April and the rapid development of joint military plans with France signalled a late turn in the UK's attitude. By July the final details of the concentration areas of the *British Expeditionary Force in France had been agreed. Already, in February 1939, the Chiefs of Staff had evolved a long-term strategy for war against Germany which involved exerting economic pressure (see ECONOMIC WARFARE), building up British strength, and using command of the sea to strike at vulnerable points.

In 1938, Chamberlain had regarded war against Germany to preserve the European balance of power as 'preventive war' and had opposed it; in September 1939, faced with the German invasion of Poland (see POLISH CAMPAIGN) and a tide of national anger, he was forced to commit a country which was by no means fully prepared to a war in defence of France, of the concept of a European balance of power, and ultimately, of democracy.

JOHN GOOCH

2. Domestic life, war effort, and economy

(a) Attitudes on the home front

As people in the UK perceived it, the war presented several distinct phases:

1. September 1939–April 1940: the *phoney war when mobilization seemed sluggish, unemployment remained high, and, in the absence of major war news, the pacifist minority was still quite numerous and vocal. However, the mass evacuation of *children and the imposition of a *blackout at nights meant sharp departures from peace-time normality.

2. April 1940–May 1941: military disaster in the *Norwegian campaign precipitated a political crisis in which the Conservative prime minister, Neville Chamberlain, despite his party's huge parliamentary majority, was forced into resignation on 10 May 1940. On that very day, the German Army moved into the Low Countries (see FALL GELB). Its rapid successes produced an atmosphere of extreme urgency, in which the new ruling coalition led by Churchill had to be seen to act decisively. An extension of the Emergency Powers Act introduced the previous year gave the government, from 22 May 1940, 'complete control over persons and property, not just some persons of some particular class of the community, but of all persons, rich and poor, employer and workman, man or woman, and all property,' as *Attlee, now deputy prime minister, explained to the Commons. The leading trade unionist, Ernest *Bevin, who was appointed Minister of Labour by Churchill, could now direct any person to do any job, and set wages, hours, and conditions. Excess Profits Tax, designed to prevent profiteering, was raised to 100%. The basis was laid for what some called 'War Socialism'. After the fall of *France in June 1940 the UK and its empire fought on virtually without allies, and the battle of *Britain in the air that summer and early autumn inspired those working overtime in war factories. Fear of invasion, at this time not unjustified, gave everyday life a febrile quality. Many parts of the country experienced bombing, and on 7 September the *Blitz began when the Luftwaffe attacked London's East End in force. Thereafter London was bombed for all but one of 76 consecutive nights. A heavy raid on *Coventry on 14 November marked a shift in the Luftwaffe's attentions away from the capital, though London continued to receive intermittent heavy attacks. Certain western ports, vital to the country's links with overseas, were especially hard hit—Plymouth, Merseyside, Southampton, and Portsmouth. But Clydeside experienced only one major raid and production of munitions and other war essentials was not greatly affected. The conviction that the UK was 'taking it' as London had 'taken it' helped to alleviate depression in the grim early months of 1941. In May, after a particularly heavy raid on London, the Luftwaffe let up, as Hitler moved his forces to the Eastern Front. The heroic phase of the civilian war—the country's 'finest hour', as Churchill had called it—was over.

3. May 1941–November 1942: though Hitler's invasion of the Soviet Union on 22 June 1941 (see BARBAROSSA) gave the UK a popular new ally, and Japan's strike at *Pearl Harbor on 7 December brought the economic might of

UK: Londoners learned to survive during the Blitz by sleeping in the underground. This photograph by Bill Brandt was taken at the Elephant and Castle station on 11 November 1940.

WAY OUT
PHILIPS

the USA fully into the war on the UK's side, this was a phase of discontent. War news, mostly bad in 1941, was still worse in 1942 when Japan overran the Far Eastern portions of the British Empire, and *Rommel's forces were rampant in the *Western Desert campaigns. According to opinion polls, approval of Churchill as prime minister never dropped below 78%, but between February and October 1942 his political position was believed insecure: for much of this period Sir Stafford *Cripps seemed to some, in and out of high political circles, to be a likely successor. Cripps was applauded for his calls for further austerity. Rationing of food, clothing, and petrol was now intense, yet there is ample evidence that such controls, to help win the war, were not resented. However, there was much well-publicized discussion of inefficiency in industry, the coalition government lost four by-elections to independent candidates, there was clamour for a Second Front in Europe to help the USSR, and public opinion was generally truculent. *Montgomery's victory over Rommel at *El Alamein early in November came as a vast relief, and reconsolidated Churchill's position as war leader. From now on, over-optimism about early victory replaced anguish over frequent reverses as a 'morale problem'.

4. November 1942–August 1945: with the fear of invasion entirely dissipated, talk of a better world after the war serged to the headlines. On 1 December 1942 the Beveridge Report was published (see GOVERNMENT, below). William Beveridge (1879–1963) gathered to a head the widespread conviction that Planning (now so often given a capital P), such as had governed the country's now successful-seeming war effort, could guarantee a secure post-war life for all citizens. Since 1941, many official and non-official committees had been devising post-war schemes for various areas of economic and social concern (including blueprints for the rebuilding of blitzed cities). While Conservative businessmen protested that ambitious undertakings such as the Beveridge plan would have to be paid for by improved export performance, public opinion swept past them. Churchill's lack of enthusiasm for post-war planning confirmed the widespread belief that he was a great war leader, not suitable for peacetime. In May 1944 parliament passed an Education Act (rationalizing and broadening school provision on lines prefigured by pre-war planning) which was the most that Churchill would concede in the way of immediate major reform, though family allowances were introduced before he left office in July 1945.

In less than two and half years, from January 1942 to *D-Day in June 1944, more than a million and a half US servicemen arrived in the UK. The lifestyle and values of their homeland were well-known already through *Hollywood films, and American dance music was very popular. Nevertheless, 'oversexed, overpaid and over here', the *GIs provoked friction. Many *women, from teenagers to grandmothers, seem to have been eager to trade their virtue for luxuries from the PX stores and nights out dancing to the excellent bands which served the US bases. But this increased resentments felt by men, in and out of the UK services, who saw that GIs were better paid and better dressed than they were. Despite the tragic courage of the USAAF's 'mighty Eighth', which flew daylight bomber sorties out of East Anglia during the *strategic air offensive against Germany, and sustained more than 45,000 casualties, the slur that the 'Yanks' were cowards was commonplace. As in the *First World War, it was said the USA had entered late, after others had born the brunt of the battle. While the US 'occupation' increased mutual understanding in some quarters it also generated anti-American feeling. A symptom of the complex factors at work was the general sympathy for black GIs (see AFRICAN AMERICANS)—subjected to colour bars in their own army—expressed by British civilians who contrasted their kindly courtesy with the arrogance attributed to white GIs.

The Normandy landings of 6 June 1944 (see OVERLORD) produced high hopes of swift victory, dampened by the arrival from 13 June of V-1 'flying bombs' over south-eastern England, followed by V-2 rockets from 8 September (see V-WEAPONS). These preyed on the nerves of war-weary civilians, caused considerable casualties, and aggravated the housing problem which was a legacy of the 1940–1 raids. However, high spirits were everywhere seen on *V-E Day. On 23 May the coalition ended, after the Labour Party's National Conference had refused to continue in it and Churchill's 'caretaker' Conservative government was decisively defeated in the ensuing general election, in which Labour swept to power with 393 Commons seats out of 640. The public had opted for a 'planned' peace.

(b) *Manpower and war production* (see Table 1)

The UK mobilized civilians more fully than any other combatant nation. In June 1944, when 22% of the country's labour force was in the armed services, 33% was in civilian war work. Even this impressive figure omits the efforts of part-time volunteers in Civil Defence (see below) and the *WVS and the work done by pensioners, while women occupied in household work (nearly 10 million out of a population of 47,700,000) were in a truly essential occupation when there were 9 million children under 14 and some 6 million old people to be looked after, not to speak of husbands and lodgers who worked in mines and factories.

Since May 1940 control over manpower—including 'womanpower'—had been exercised at the top, by Ernest Bevin. In December 1940, his ministry of labour was still under fire for not making sufficient use of its powers of compulsion. In that month, Sir William Beveridge unveiled in secret a report on manpower requirements which was as much a turning-point in the economic history of the war as its author's report on social security was to be in its political history. It pointed out that one and a half million women would have to be drafted into

UK, Table 1: The British war effort 1940–4

The following statistical table is subject to familiar caveats. It is based on figures prepared by the Central Statistical Office and published in 1951 in a *Statistical Digest of the War* to accompany the 'United Kingdom Civil Series' of official histories. As victors, the British could afford to be honest, and the official histories are thorough and candid. Indeed, we can learn from them to recognize (for instance) that many of the aircraft built at the peak of production were of obsolescent types unfit for battle, and that statistics about strikes need very careful interpretation. The picture is most clearly seen if 1944, the year of D-Day, is taken as the terminus of 'total' war effort. Unless otherwise stated all figures refer to mid-year (June) and are given in thousands. Some have been rounded.

	1940	*1942*	*1944*
Total Population of Great Britain, excluding N. Ireland	47,000	47,000	47,750
Total Working Population			
male	15,104	15,141	14,901
female	5,572	6,915	7,107
Total in Armed Forces and Auxiliary Services			
male	2,218	3,784	4,500
female	55	307	467
Total in Civil Employment			
male	12,452	11,296	10,347
female	5,306	6,582	6,620
agriculture and fishing	925	1,002	1,048
mining and quarrying	886	823	813
metals, engineering, vehicles, and shipbuilding	3,198	4,372	4,496
chemicals, explosives, paints, oils, etc.	361	618	515
textiles	1,074	723	635
clothing, boots, and shoes	748	550	455
food, drink, and tobacco	621	567	508
building and civil engineering	1,064	893	623
national and local government	1,448	1,728	1,809
Civil Defence, Fire Service, and Police	345	384	282
Strength of Home Guard	1,456	1,565	1,758
Annual coal production (000 tons)	224,229	204,944	192,746
Annual imports of petroleum (000 tons)	11,381	10,232	20,176
Annual production of aluminium (000 tons)	57	126	140
Annual aircraft production	15	24	26.5
Annual aircraft production: (structure weight in millions of lb)	59	133	208.5
Index of Ministry of Supply Munitions Production (Sept–Dec 1939 = 100), figures for third quarter.			
guns, small arms, instruments	212	701	385
filled shells and bombs	214	1,009	529
small arms ammunition	358	2,679	4,188
propellants and high explosives	161	513	480
armoured fighting vehicles	324	1,727	–
wheeled vehicles	343	341	280
radar and searchlight	124	198	670
Naval vessels built annually (no.)			
major combat	52	114	76
smaller craft	375	1,049	1,651
merchant vessels completed annually (gross tons)	810	1,301	1,014
Area of arable land by acres (GB)	13,203	16,175	17,936
wheat	1,797	2,504	3,215
potatoes	695	1,116	1,219
vegetables	301	418	499

UK, Table 1 *(cont.)*

	1940	*1942*	*1944*
Numbers of livestock (GB)			
cattle	8,361	8,248	8,616
sheep and lambs	25,465	20,764	19,435
pigs	3,631	1,872	1,631
poultry	62,121	43,212	38,481
Monthly milk sales through marketing schemes (by million gallons)	128	137	143
Working days lost in strikes (annual)	940	1,527	3,714
Absenteeism in coal mines (%)	7.26	10.06	12.89

Source: Contributor.

war industry from housework and from less essential work. From March 1941, the registration of women began, eventually extending to all between 18 and 60, along with that of men over 41. In the same month, the Essential Work Order tied workers to jobs in establishments deemed vital. By the end of 1941, under the provisions of this order, nearly six million workers had been guaranteed job security with decent minimum pay and conditions.

The war abolished unemployment, to the point where many people—such as factory workers who were in the Home Guard, bank clerks who were ARP volunteers—were, in effect, doing more than one job. This gave new strength to the trade union movement: between 1938 and 1943 the number of unionized workers increased by over a third, to 8,174,000, and Bevin's own Transport and General workers became the first union to top a million members.

By 1943, it was almost impossible for a woman under 40 to avoid war work unless she had heavy family responsibilities or was looking after a war worker billeted on her. Scotland, Wales, and the north of England exported 'surplus unskilled mobile woman labour' to the munitions factories of the Midlands. Women replaced 100,000 railway workers drafted into the forces. Controversially, they worked as bus conductors, wearing trousers. 'Numbers of passengers believe that the last act of conductress and her driver or motorman each night before going home is the exercise of sexual intercourse', noted one of these outrageous females—but women wearing trousers were becoming a common sight. Women even worked as welders in shipyards, traditionally almost as macho in ethos as coalmines: in lighter engineering 'dilution' by women might reach 80% or higher. The *Women's Land Army (WLA) repeated a First World War experiment. In June 1939 there had been 546,000 regular male workers in agriculture and 55,000 regular female workers. By June 1944 there were 150,000 more land workers, though regular men had dropped to 522,000. The WLA stood at 80,000. A former hairdresser won a horse-ploughing competition in Yorkshire against a field of men.

But the filthy and dangerous work of coalmines remained a male preserve. The industry at this time combined, as one critic put it, 'the worst features of decaying and restrictive monopoly with the most brutal evils arising from cut-throat competition'. Relations between colliers and their employers were uneasy, often bitter; after decades of struggle, strikes were commonplace, absenteeism widespread. During the war the miners were an ageing workforce, depleted by enlistment in the army and not over-willing to co-operate with government's attempts to rationalize the industry. Production of deep-mined coal fell from 204 million tons in 1942 to 175 millions in 1945, though manpower, 766,000 in 1939, had been stabilized at 710,000. Miners' sons were forced down the pits, and from December 1943 *Bevin boys were employed.

Statistically, however, war industry was a success story. Aircraft production, for instance, rose from 3,000 warplanes in 1938 to 15,000 in 1940. It trebled between January 1940 and January 1942, and doubled again by March 1944. At this time, 1,700,000 were employed by firms under contract to the ministry of aircraft production. But the biggest British factories had only 3,000 to 15,000 employees, compared to up to 40,000 in their US counterparts, and efficiency was accordingly much lower, so the industry was subjected to constant criticism. High wages were one focus for disapproval from outsiders: in the Midlands, where labour was scarce, firms paid huge bonuses, to which overtime was added, and some workers took more in a day than a railwayman could earn in a week, while the wives of servicemen struggled on tiny allowances.

Strikes had all but disappeared in the hectic year of 1940 when the country stood alone, and Bevin's Order 1305 of July that year had made them illegal. Yet 1944 set a new record for aggregate number of stoppages: 2,194, involving the loss of 3,700,000 working days. Two-thirds of those lost were in coal mining, but engineering—that is, war industry—came second. However, most strikes were short: the typical stoppage was a swift outburst over piece rates, in which communist shop stewards—committed, after Hitler's invasion of the Soviet Union, to the maximization of production—would attempt to restrain their aggrieved brothers and sisters. Though a relative handful of workers were fined for striking, Order 1305 was in general ineffectual.

(c) Rationing and domestic life

Total war progressively diverted resources and labour away from the production of consumer goods, and reduced food supplies from overseas. Like many other policies developed during the *First World War, rationing was reintroduced early in the Second. Petrol was rationed from September 1939, with evidence of strong popular support for the move. Chamberlain's government introduced rationing of meat, butter, and sugar early in 1940. Clothes rationing, after prices had soared, came in June 1941. War meant that many commonplace items were in short supply, and generated incessant 'salvage drives'. When rationing reached a peak in August 1942, each citizen was entitled to 1*s.* 2*d.* worth of meat per week (nearly 1 lb./450 gm. per person), to four ounces (113 gm.) of bacon and ham, eight (225 gm.) of sugar, eight of fats, and eight of cheese, though the cheese allowance dropped to a mere two ounces (57 gm.) in April 1944. Over a four-week period a consumer might purchase 16 oz. of hard soap, 16 oz. of jam, marmalade, or mincemeat, and 8 oz. of sweets. Over eight weeks, an adult could get one packet of dried eggs equal to 12 eggs: children under six were allowed two packets and, like invalids and expectant mothers, were guaranteed a pint of milk per day. For each month, a ration-book holder had twenty 'points' which could be used on scarce goods ranging from tinned salmon at (say) 32 points for a pound, to dried peas for as little as one point per pound; such items as breakfast cereals, syrup, and biscuits came under the 'points' scheme. Tea was also rationed, but important foods such as bread, potatoes, vegetables, fruit, and fish were not.

Rationing tied customers to particular retailers, and bore hard on working-class men who had traditionally been heavy consumers of meat, but it was generally approved of. It seemed to guarantee 'fair shares'. Cooks became expert in making puddings without eggs, preserving fruit without sugar, and creating dishes out of strange canned meats from the USA such as the famous Spam. While the black market might satisfy a craving for such rare items as oranges, many citizens heeded the 'Dig for Victory' campaign and grew food for themselves in gardens and allotments (the number of the latter rose from 815,000 in 1939 to 1,400,000 in 1943). Poultry-keeping and pig-keeping increased. Meanwhile, farmers prospered as they put every possible acre to use for food production, assisted in summer by volunteer workers such as schoolchildren and weekending adults.

Overall there is no doubt that in terms of essential vitamins and calories the UK's population was better fed in wartime than before, when malnutrition had accompanied unemployment and low wages. Meals eaten in canteens, often provided for the first time at workplaces, and in the new, cheap British restaurants, were 'off the ration', and the government used these to make extra meat and cheese available to workers in heavy industry. However, for most people the diet was restricted and monotonous.

Even after the major disruptions caused by bombing in 1940–1 had ceased, travel on crowded public transport was subject to delays. Housing accommodation was in short supply, particularly in areas where new or expanded war factories brought in many newcomers. Population in the blitzed centres of several cities, including London, fell markedly, but new workers continued to arrive in the engineering industries of Coventry and Manchester. Building workers were largely employed on camp and factory construction. By the end of 1942, some 300,000 families were living in houses unfit for habitation by pre-war standards, and two and a half million occupied bombed houses which had received only temporary repairs.

From the outbreak of war to the end of 1945, some 60 million changes of address took place among a civilian population of about 48 million, an indication of the disruption and inconvenience which war brought to non-combatants. It is hardly surprising that, while some women moving into war work revelled in new experiences, work place friendships, and the freedom given by rates of pay which, though lower than men's, might seem very considerable, many others could not wait to return to civilian life. The end of the war produced a rush back to domesticity, though married couples separated for years by war service, and children meeting fathers they had never known, often found readjustment very difficult.

The UK birthrate had been falling before the war: it rose sharply, from 13.9 per thousand of population, the lowest point in the history of registration, in 1941 to 17.5 in 1944 (see DEMOGRAPHY). Long-term demographic factors rather than wartime circumstances were responsible for the boom (in 1947, the rate would be 20.6), but the war accounted for a rising proportion of illegitimate births, despite the increased spread of knowledge of contraceptive methods which was promoted. Divorce petitions rose from just under 10,000 in 1938 to 25,000 in 1945. The paradoxical effect of war overall seems to have been that it loosened family ties and eroded moral constraints, while simultaneously creating a yearning for settled home life.

(d) Morale, national unity and wartime spirit

In 1940 and 1941 approximately 43,000 civilians in the UK were directly killed by *bombs, and about 17,000 more over the remaining years of war. About half of these 60,000 deaths were in London. At least 86,000 people were seriously injured (see Table 2). This compares with deaths in the armed forces of 260,000. Both figures are small compared to losses from war causes suffered by European, Japanese, and Chinese forces and civilians. Nevertheless, the sustained nightly bombing of London

UK, Table 2: Civil Defence and civilian Casualties. Casualties to United Kingdom civilians due to enemy action as reported to 31 July 1945

	Total Civilian					*Civil Defence workers* [a] *on duty*		
	Total	*Men*	*Women*	*Children under 16*	*Unidentified*	*Total*	*Men*	*Women*
Killed and missing believed killed	60,595	26,923	25,399	7,736	537	2,379	2,148	231
Injured and detained in hospital	86,182	40,738	37,822	7,622	–	4,459	4,072	387
TOTAL	146,777	67,661	63,221	15,358	537	6,838	6,220	618

[a] Civil Defence General Services, National Fire Service, Regular and Auxiliary Police, also included in total civilian casualties.
Source: Mellor, W. Franklin (ed.), *Casualties and Medical Statistics,* (UK Official History Series), (London, 1972).

in the autumn of 1940 was unprecedented in history and represented the fiercest exposure of any section of the UK population to armed conflict in centuries.

Morale was never tested as severely as it was in Germany, where war production soared in spite of raids which killed half as many people again in *Hamburg in one night as died from bombing in London throughout the war. Even in Japan, it took a new weapon of devastating power, the *atomic bomb, to induce the surrender of a people whose cities had been devastated by the strategic air offensive mounted against it. That British morale survived the Blitz of 1940–1 is not, therefore, at all surprising. Nevertheless, the endurance shown by civilians in that period was a cause for local and national pride at the time, and has been since. Post-raid emergency services were often sadly inadequate. In the absence of deep shelters, and justifiably suspicious of the brick communal shelters erected in city streets, hundreds and thousands of Londoners, in the autumn of 1940, slept in underground stations. Many others evacuated themselves to safer parts. But London was seen to be 'taking it' and inhabitants of other cities were generally determined to show that they, too, could 'take it'. 'Trekking' by inhabitants of heavily bombed cities to sleep under cover or without cover in suburban and rural areas was commonplace, but bombs caused surprisingly little voluntary absenteeism from work. In public shelters, communal entertainments were often organized. The shared experience of the raids generated spontaneous fellow-feeling, strangers spoke to each other, neighbours were lavish with cups of tea, publicans gave out free drinks, class divisions (it seemed to many) broke down.

Other factors made for greater national cohesion. Among other effects, the greater mobility of the population brought Scots, Welsh, and Irish people in large numbers to dynamic centres of industry in England, as well as scrambling them together in the armed forces. The *BBC before the war had already provided a common standard of information and entertainment for the nation: during the war it became less stiffly genteel, and began to use personalities with regional accents.

The war had the effect of cutting down (though not eradicating) conspicuous consumption by the well-to-do—it was hard to hold on to domestic servants, for instance—and of improving levels of feeding and income among the poorest, now guaranteed work if they could do it. Even the proliferation of 'red tape'—controls, regulations, and bureaucracy—at least had the effect of uniting the public against their tormentors, the civil servants.

Nevertheless, the war revealed, and confirmed, social problems and fissures between groups and classes. Crime rates rose sharply—there were just over 300,000 indictable offences in England and Wales in 1939, 478,000 in 1945—though increased theft, rather than violence, accounted for this increase. Juvenile delinquency was fostered by the disruption of schooling caused by evacuation and bombing, and by the preoccupation of adults with war work. Evacuation of poor slum dwellers, like the arrival later of refugees from blitzed areas, produced paroxysms of class hatred among well-to-do householders in safe areas, who often did all they could to avoid billeting such riff-raff, and as figures for strikes showed, class feeling remained strong in industry. That Labour in 1951 secured a higher vote than any recorded before or since in a general election by any party, and nevertheless lost to Churchill's resurgent Conservatives, suggests, as analysis confirms, working-class self-assertion confronting middle-class resistance.

But the UK won the war, after 'standing alone' in 1940, suggesting to the British public that British ways of doing things were better than those of other people. While the country's actual bankruptcy, a result of the all-out war effort, reduced the empire to the status of a satellite of the globally triumphant USA, British industry maintained its old-fashioned methods and attitudes prevalent during the war. While European nations earnestly created new constitutions, the Mother of Parliaments was now more than ever sacrosanct, and

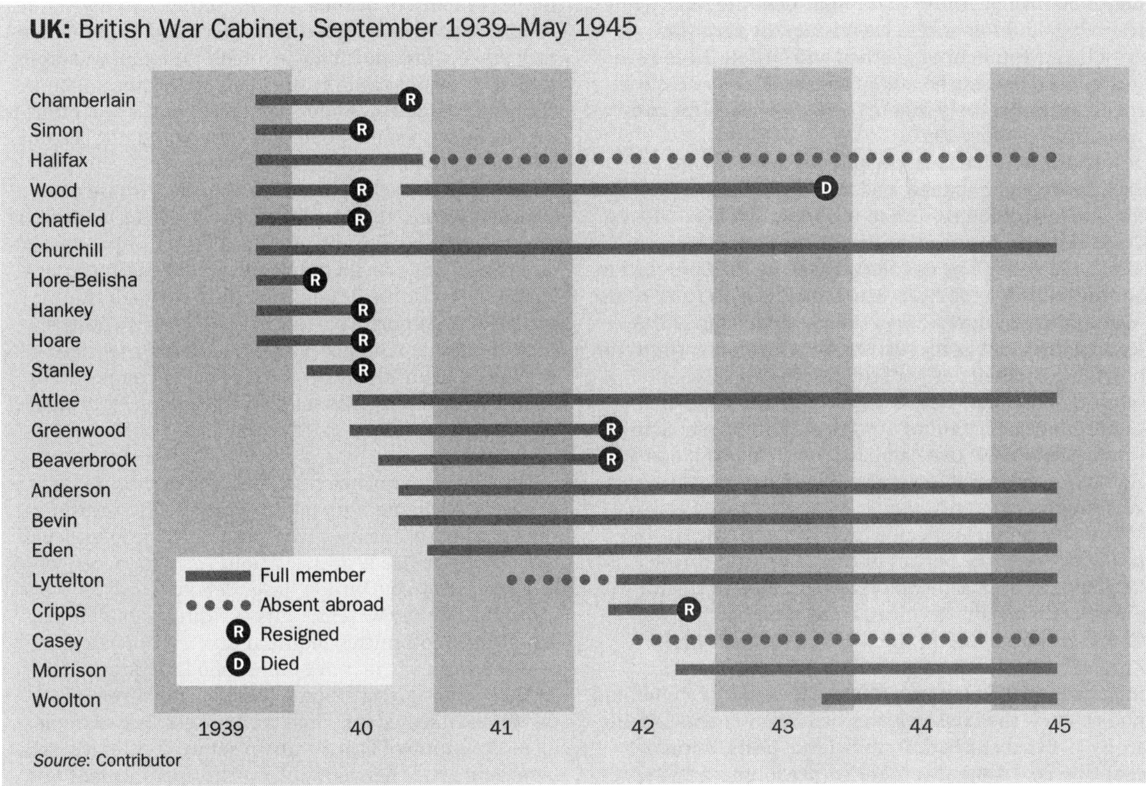

other salient British institutions basked in complacency. Talk, in the 1940s, of wartime social revolution, in hindsight seems ludicrously inappropriate. See also WORLD TRADE AND WORLD ECONOMY. ANGUS CALDER

3. Government

When the war began on 1 September 1939 the prime minister, Neville Chamberlain, offered the Labour and Liberal parties a coalition with his Conservative government, which had a comfortable majority of some 250 in a House of Commons of 615 members; they refused. However, they did not oppose any of the wartime legislation the cabinet proposed; and the addition of Churchill and *Eden to the cabinet's ranks visibly strengthened it.

Chamberlain had excellent reasons, dating back to the previous world war, for distrusting any scheme put up by Lloyd George (1863–1945, prime minister 1916–22), but nevertheless appointed a war cabinet, eight strong (see Chart); in spite of urgings from Churchill, who sat in it (Eden did not), it took no warlike action for months (see PHONEY WAR). In consultation with the French, at the Allied *Supreme War Council, the war cabinet did decide to offer covert support to Finland in midwinter (see FINNISH–SOVIET WAR); and again acting jointly, nerved itself in the spring of 1940 to sanction an attack on Norway, pre-empted by the Germans.

The *Norwegian campaign went so badly that the Commons insisted on debating it, on 7 and 8 May 1940. Several of Chamberlain's old supporters turned against him; one of them, Leo Amery used to his government Cromwell's words to the Long parliament: 'You have sat here too long for any good you have been doing. Depart, I say, and let us have done with you. In the name of God, go'. When the house divided, 200 members voted against Chamberlain, including 41 of his own supporters, and 281 for him, showing how unpopular he had become, even in the Commons. On 10 May, having failed to persuade his foreign secretary Lord Halifax to succeed him, he resigned and recommended King *George VI to send for Churchill, who became prime minister that evening.

Churchill enjoyed a unique standing. To many Americans, he *was* the government of the UK. The Emergency Powers (Defence) Act, passed through all its stages from first reading to royal assent on the single day of 22 May 1940, gave the crown power to command any subject to perform any action; the power to be exercised through defence regulations, which would be laid before parliament. Regulations allowed government to control civil unrest and to impose *censorship on the media; these reduced public discussion of appeasement policies and muted political discontent. Almost all journalists, moreover, accepted the justice of the war and were happy not to publish anything that might help the Axis, while reserving, and sometimes exercising, the right to criticize government on method and on detail (see PRESS). If they overstepped the mark they were banned, as was the Communist Party organ, the *Daily Worker*, for two years from January 1941.

Technically, Chamberlain had not lost a vote of confidence; he remained leader of the Conservative Party until ill-health forced him to resign in October 1940 (he died the following month). But his hold on it was weakened enough by the Norway debate for Churchill to be able to form a coalition which included all three of the major parties, Conservative, Labour, and Liberal. The leading dissident Conservatives he rewarded with useful posts; he disposed deftly of the leading appeasers, sending John Simon (1873–1954) to become Lord Chancellor, the height of any lawyer's ambition; Samuel Hoare (1880–1959) to be ambassador in Madrid; and Halifax, after a brief interval, to be ambassador in Washington.

The new cabinet reflected the formal balance of power between the parties in the Commons: fifteen Conservative ministers, four Labour, and one Liberal (Archibald Sinclair, the air minister who had been Churchill's adjutant on the Western Front in 1916). Among all the government ministers together (not including parliamentary private secretaries), cabinet and non-cabinet, the Conservatives had 52 posts and Labour 16. By 1945 Labour had 27 ministerial posts, but the coalition government was always predominantly Conservative; though it often adopted socialist methods. As the Labour leader and Churchill's deputy, Clement Attlee once put it, 'When one came to work out solutions they were often socialist ones, because one had to have organization and planning, and disregard vested interests.' Labour ministers thought that they were unlikely to win the next general election, and decided they should take what advantage they could of the opportunities they got to further working-class interests.

After 1939 many conventions of parliamentary democracy were suspended while the war lasted. Even before the coalition was built, the party leaders had agreed on an electoral truce. The general election, due to be held in 1940, was regularly postponed by amendments to the Septennial Act of 1716—a reminder to the political public of parliament's ancient roots. The Commons whips—those officers of the three major parties who discipline members of the House—agreed not to contest by-elections caused by death or resignation, and to recommend to the electorate the candidate who was put forward by the party which already held the seat. Such uncontested vacancies provided government with a means of admitting potential ministers to parliament. For example, Churchill brought Ernest Bevin into the cabinet (and, later, into the war cabinet) as minister of labour; months later, a seat in parliament was found for him through a vacancy at Wandsworth in south London. The whips also agreed conventions which allowed a number of MPs to be on active military service without resigning their seats. The verbatim record of parliamentary proceedings normally printed in *Hansard* was from time to time not made public. This gave Churchill a chance to explain confidential details of the war effort to members, with some hope that they would not become known too soon to the Axis.

Churchill held the post of leader of the House of Commons himself, although he devolved the work of it to Attlee. The coalition had a joint whips' office. Formal opposition was provided through an opposition front bench in the House of Commons and through the activities of minority parties in the country. Those Labour MPs who did not hold office in the coalition elected an 'administrative committee' to compose this front bench, and the Parliamentary Labour Party elected an acting chairman to perform as leader of the opposition.

The select committee on national expenditure was the principal parliamentary body empowered to scrutinize the workings of the executive. Its chairman interviewed, tête-à-tête, the heads of the various secret services, whose budgets are by convention never debated, to satisfy himself that they were not misspending public funds grossly; the committee inquired much more extensively into the work of the other main spending departments. As the war progressed, some backbenchers from all parties established informal committees. For example, in 1942 a group of Conservatives set up the 'Active Back-Benchers', who then agitated for the appointment of a 'Scrutinizing Committee' which would examine the statutory rules and orders laid on the table of the house. A combination of Conservatives from both the Commons and the Lords, called the 'Watching Committee', became less important after 1941. Opposition in the country, such as it was, was seen largely at by-elections contested by minority parties. The Independent Labour Party and the Communist Party were free to challenge the candidates nominated by the coalition parties.

The communists' position was peculiar. On 2 September 1939 the party secretary, Harry Pollitt, had put out an impassioned pamphlet in which he argued that 'To stand aside from this conflict, to contribute only revolutionary-sounding phrases while the Fascist beasts ride roughshod over Europe, would be a betrayal of everything our forebears have fought to achieve in the course of long years of struggle against capitalism.' For this robust stance he was rebuked from Moscow, and demoted. The disappearance of the *Daily Worker* from the newspaper stalls concealed from the public the extent to which the Communist Party adhered to Moscow's line of support for Berlin, until 22 June 1941 when Hitler attacked the USSR; thereafter the communists, changing sides overnight, flung themselves ardently into support for the war effort and for an immediate Second Front.

The Common Wealth party, formed by Sir Richard Acland in the late summer of 1942 on the news, shocking to the general public, of the fall of *Tobruk, enjoyed three by-election successes. Another eleven independents of various political shades were also elected during the course of the war.

Churchill survived every attack on his position as leader of the coalition because he retained ample, indeed overwhelming, support in the House of Commons, backed by enormous popularity in the country. The formal vote of confidence in his direction of the war, at a black moment—2 July 1942—was carried by 476 to 25: it was the largest number of MPs to vote against him in any substantial division in his first three years in office. His frequent BBC radio broadcasts helped him to retain the respect, even the affection, of the nation at large. Within the coalition itself, his personal supremacy led to difficulties, particularly when he obstructed the consideration of major post-war issues.

Between October 1943 and June 1944 the government machine was geared to two major tasks: the Allied invasion of Europe and the plans for post-war reconstruction. Churchill was prevailed upon to appoint a minister of reconstruction in November 1943. By then the prolongation of parliament's life without a general election could not be disconnected from the plans being made for a transition from war to peace, sometimes called the 'two-stage ending', because it was assumed that the war against Japan would continue well after the defeat of Germany. The question arose, whether the coalition could be prolonged under Churchill's leadership into the peace. By October 1944 he was committed to dissolving parliament as soon as the victory over Germany had been achieved. Some Labour ministers would have preferred to continue the coalition, but they were overruled by their party's executive, which called for a withdrawal at the time of Germany's surrender.

There was no equivalent of coalition at the local level. The conventions of local authorities were suspended by statute, which authorized them to fill any vacancy among the body of elected councillors by co-option. There were no local government elections between 1939 and 1946. The local authority associations (national organizations, representing different kinds of council) remained in existence, but became apprehensive about the consequences for local government of wartime emergency regulations and of the formation of national organizations, such as the Auxiliary Fire Service, for civil defence. Part of their anxiety also stemmed from the appointment of regional commissioners, who were empowered to supervise the local authorities under their charge and to create 'seats of government' if the country were invaded.

These contingency plans emphasized the importance of co-ordinating the activities in each region of the representatives of the major departments of state. The management of the war effort was undertaken through regional boards of production and their committees, which allocated scarce supplies. County war agricultural executive committees, for instance, so re-ordered English agriculture that the balance of grassland to plough was exactly reversed—more than 17 million acres to 12 million before the war, 11 million to 18 million by 1943. This saved a lot of shipping space.

Critical observers noticed during the first Luftwaffe air attacks on London that there were far too many overlapping local authorities and boards, likely only to get in each others' way rather than to help those made homeless by German air raids. These attacks caused some confusion at first among this plethora of bodies; and the laying of sea mines from the air in the Thames estuary brought on a restructuring of the import distribution system, London being replaced for a time by Liverpool and Glasgow among the UK's busiest ports. The central government machine was mildly, but only mildly, disrupted by bombing: ministers and civil servants alike, in civil as well as in military branches of government, rapidly got used to walking to work across piles of rubble and broken glass; to the shortage of sleep; to the occasional house move, because one had been bombed out of one's home. Getting on with the war was clearly more important than any domestic imbroglio, even at a time when one Londoner in six was bombed out.

Parliament continued to sit at the usual times, bombs or no bombs. The great fires of the night of 10/11 May 1941 burnt out, among many other buildings, the chamber of the House of Commons; MPs simply moved to the Lords' chamber, and their lordships to Church House across the way. Neither house missed a sitting; and Westminster Hall, for centuries the seat of justice, was saved from fire by a passing MP (Walter Elliot) who saw the danger from some incendiary bombs lodged in its roof, seized a fireman's axe, and hacked open the great north door (of which the key had been mislaid) so that the firemen could tackle the blaze.

When reconstruction was placed on the political agenda in 1943 there were doubts about the future allocation of administrative functions to local authorities. Official descriptions of the wartime structure of British government concentrated on the centre and on its centralizing tendencies, not on the future of the balance between centre and locality. Such accounts divided the structure into military affairs, the Home Front, supply, and, later, reconstruction. In all four areas, government seemed to consist chiefly of administrative controls. Battles were deemed to be won or lost according to the efficiency of the authorities in regulating supply.

The three critical resources were labour, materials, and food. Their flow had to be planned, and they sometimes competed for space. For example, imports of rationed foodstuffs might limit the volume of military *matériel* that could be carried by ship. Major administrative achievements lay in the design of shipping budgets which allocated cargo space in the most economical manner, and skills in 'manpower budgeting' were also developed. Manpower—and womanpower—were indeed more thoroughly organized in the UK than in any other warring nation.

The greatest impact of government on the population as a whole lay in this direction of labour and in the rationing of food and of *raw materials. The regulations needed for all this involved an expansion of the civil service, and of the scale and scope of public expenditure. The number of non-industrial civil servants rose from 399,600 in 1939 to 722,200 in 1944, when it was calculated that 5 million people were in the armed services and a further 3.5 million in other public services of various kinds—excluding war industry in private ownership.

Government expenditure in 1944 was 60% of the national total, of which 55% was borne out of revenue. Only New Zealand reached a comparable concentration of financial effort. The basic rate of income tax rose to 50%, and it reached 95% for large unearned incomes. National Savings filled the gap, aided and supplemented by special local appeals, the wartime variant of peacetime pageantry. The RAF received ardent public support, not only during the battle of Britain but thereafter, when a substantial slice of the nation's effort went into servicing Bomber Command. On one day during the battle of Britain, Fighter Command reported the loss of seven aircraft; next morning a blank cheque arrived at the air ministry from a manufacturer, with a request that it be used to pay for their replacements. Similarly, a Scotswoman called MacRobert, who lost a son in the RAF, sent the ministry a cheque for £5,000 to purchase a Stirling bomber, to be called 'MacRobert's Reply.' After BARBAROSSA began, support for the USSR also attracted enormous public enthusiasm, accompanied by cash gifts at rallies.

When Japan also entered the war, the Treasury warned—as the Admiralty had long predicted—that the UK could not afford to fight in Asia as well as in Europe. The defence committee of the war cabinet decided that even if national bankruptcy threatened, national honour demanded a full-scale British share in the Asian war: strategy was adapted accordingly.

The major departments of state, like the secret services, recruited extensively in the universities, whose staff and teaching were greatly reduced. Regulations also extended the scope of government activity abroad. British officials in Washington, DC, who collaborated with the Americans on supply and on the administration of *Lend-Lease became an essential element in the planned flow of raw materials and food.

The organization of military affairs was dominated by the war cabinet and its defence committee, which was serviced by the Chiefs of Staff. Churchill acted as his own minister of defence, assisted by Major-General *Ismay who ran the defence side of the cabinet office. The war cabinet as a rule had six to eight members—ten was the maximum, with two usually overseas—who concentrated on strategy and on major questions of politics. They were deliberately excluded from routine Home Front business. Their officials spent much of their time in an underground bunker, where they also slept, which had been built by the south-east corner of St James's Park, beneath the public offices in Storey's Gate (now a museum). They also handled communications with the prime minister when he was abroad. The Chiefs of Staff had their own committee system, and were closely connected with their American counterparts through a series of joint planning meetings.

In the UK the two key institutions over which Ismay presided were the Joint Intelligence Committee (see also INTELLIGENCE, below) and the Joint Planning Staff; they were responsible for effecting analysis of military intelligence drawn from all sources, and for strategic planning for all three armed forces. The decoding of intercepted signals was the work of the Government Code and Cypher School at *Bletchley Park, which came under remote foreign office control, via *MI6. The circulation of decrypts from the German *ENIGMA and *Geheimschreiber machines, which were known by the codename *ULTRA, was carefully controlled under the direct authority of the prime minister, who ensured that the list of those in the know was kept to a minimum. Even some members of the war cabinet were left off his list.

The Home Front was managed by the Lord President's Committee of the full cabinet. This committee brought together those ministers principally concerned with the administrative controls which regulated the supply of labour, materials, and food. It was also the authority which sanctioned the submission to Parliament of the legislation deemed necessary for the war effort, and of the statutory rules and orders by which so many emergency arrangements were implemented. It was designed to overlap with the civil defence committee, which would have been obliged to instruct the regional commissioners and other provincial authorities if the Germans had landed.

The lord president of the council chosen by Churchill was for a significant proportion of the war (October 1940 to September 1943) John Anderson (1882–1958), who had been a distinguished civil servant before he accepted ministerial office. He had worked both in Ireland and in India, in turbulent conditions. A significant group of official inquiries and agencies was committed to his charge, including the research unit developing an atomic bomb. Anderson was moved to the Treasury when Sir Kingsley Wood (1881–1943) the chancellor of the exchequer, died suddenly. The line between the responsibilities of the lord president and those of the production executive was difficult to draw. The lord president's committee was directly concerned with all the questions which affected civilian morale. The ministry of information was created in order to regulate the flow of information to the public at large. It devised ways of judging civilian morale, and became the home of a government social survey which conducted regular interviews as a means of testing public opinion.

The expansion of government on the Home Front necessitated the creation of new departments of state, some of which existed as 'shadow ministries' before the war began. A ministry of home security was attached to the home office, and one of national service to the ministry of labour (both in 1939). The arrangements for rationing civilian access to food and raw materials were made the responsibilities of new ministries of food (1939) and of fuel and power (1942). A critically important step in planning the production of war *matériel* was the setting up the ministry of aircraft production (1940). The ministry of production (1942) itself was never a major organization; it had to work by persuading other departments to co-operate because they had the statutory authority to create controls. The ministry of war transport (1941), created from the mercantile marine department of the board of trade, played an important role in the management of shipping space, particularly that in transatlantic *convoys. The ministry of economic warfare (1939) was not concerned with rationing civilians, but rather with the best means of depriving the Axis of supplies; it also provided cover for *SOE, which came to take up four-fifths of its minister's time.

From the start of the war, even before the coalition was formed, many politicians had been concerned with the definition of war aims and with the opportunities for social reform which mobilization seemed to present. Their discussions precipitated the notion that there was a 'progressive centre' in British politics which would encourage all the major parties to consider programmes of social reform. For example, in response to this mood, officials of the board of education, then evacuated to Bournemouth, began in 1941 to draft papers which led eventually to the Education Act of 1944, bringing 'secondary education for all'.

The most dramatic political event was the reception given to the Beveridge report on its publication in December 1942. Sir William Beveridge, a don at Oxford, had been asked to consider the existing schemes of social insurance—health, unemployment, pensions. He recommended that a single new ministry of social security should be formed to replace the sections of seven different departments which paid cash benefits of various kinds. A ministry of national insurance was created in 1944. Beveridge also assumed that a post-war government would be committed to the maintenance of full employment, the payment of family allowances, and the creation of a national health service. Putting these ideas into practice spanned the general election of 1945. Reconstruction plans from the coalition were taken up by the Labour government at the end of the war.

A major consideration in post-war reconstruction planning was the future of British influence in world affairs. Two official cabinet committees considered, in parallel, 'internal economic problems' and 'external economic problems'. Britain's war effort was dependent on American *Lend-Lease; its peacetime reconstruction seemed likely to depend heavily on help from overseas. The foreign office, taking stock of the position at the time of the defeat of Germany, noted that there was a feeling in the USA and the USSR that 'Great Britain is now a secondary power and can be treated as such'.

When the war in Europe ended, Churchill proposed to Attlee that the coalition should continue until the war in Asia was over, too. The Labour Party insisted on a general election instead, which was held on 5 July. Men serving overseas voted by post; this put off the counting of votes, and the announcement of the result, to 26 July. By that date the Potsdam conference (see TERMINAL) had already begun; Churchill and Eden represented the UK, accompanied by Attlee as an observer.

To the world's astonishment—indeed, to Attlee's as well—the Labour Party won a large majority, with 393 seats in an enlarged house of 640 members. The forces' vote was understood to have been powerfully anti-Conservative. It was not a vote against Churchill as a war leader; it was a vote against the perceived ineptitude of Conservative policy during the great recession of 1929–33 and in the run-up to the war, as well as a vote against Authority, against what Cobbett used to call The Thing, what later radicals called the Establishment. Attlee returned to Potsdam with the new foreign secretary, Bevin, and continued to put the British case.

J. M. Lee/M. R. D. Foot

4. Northern Ireland

The six north-eastern Irish counties remained part of the UK after 1922 when the Irish Free State—or Eire as it was called after 1937—achieved independence. The most significant wartime role of the province was in providing facilities during the battle of the *Atlantic. Londonderry became a major base for convoy protection vessels with by 1943 a shore-based complement of 2,000 servicing some 20,000 British and Canadian personnel in more than 130 warships. An extensive American naval operating base at the port, for which construction began in June 1941, was never fully used by the US Navy, but the repair yard remained open until 1945. Naval units were also based at Belfast and Larne, while RAF Coastal Command squadrons (eventually ten in all) flew from four airfields and a flying boat base. Catalina aircraft from this base played a major role in the operation against the German battleship **Bismarck* in May 1943. A sustained airfield construction programme provided a further fifteen for the use of British and American forces. From January 1942 the province acted as a bridgehead for American troops and aircraft being sent to Europe. The Eighth US Army Air Force established a very large repair and maintenance depot at Langford Lodge near Lough Neagh and in 1944 the province served as a training area for over 100,000 US troops preparing for Normandy landings.

Socially, Northern Ireland was less harshly affected than some other parts of the UK. Belfast suffered only two major air raids, although the first of these, on 15/16 April 1941 when 745 people were killed, was one of the UK's most costly single bombing attacks of the war outside London. In the second raid three weeks later 150 died. In all 56,000 houses were damaged and 100,000 people left homeless, 15,000 of them permanently. Bomb damage also temporarily held up production at Belfast's substantial shipbuilding, aircraft, and engineering works. During the war years the Harland and Wolff shipyard completed more than 90 warships (including three aircraft carriers) and 50 cargo vessels, as well as building tanks and aircraft. The relative security of Northern Ireland, which for some time was believed to be beyond the range of German bombers, made the province an attractive location for dispersed strategic industries. In 1936 the aircraft company Short Brothers had established a presence in Belfast. During the war their factory chiefly produced Stirling heavy bombers (more than 1,500 in all) and Sunderland flying boats.

In employment terms the war was good for Northern Ireland. The very high structural levels of unemployment before 1939 were greatly reduced, although never entirely eliminated. In June 1943 an estimated 5% remained jobless. Some of the surplus was absorbed by other parts of the UK, with up to 60,000 workers crossing the Irish Sea. Although considered on a number of occasions, conscription was never applied in the province. It would certainly have provoked bitter opposition among the Roman Catholic minority community, and in the end it was reckoned that the manpower gains would have been outweighed by the social and political costs of the measure. During the war, however, some 37,000 men and women from Northern Ireland served in the British forces.

In Northern Ireland the shared experience of the war undoubtedly brought the two local communities closer together and the fact of Eire's neutrality also entrenched the partition of Ireland. But the Northern Unionist government were unwilling—or unable—to exploit the opportunity to draw the minority community more fully into the whole life of the province. For them Eire's neutrality merely confirmed the perceived disloyalty of all Irish nationalists, north and south of the border. At the end of the war Churchill contrasted the vital contribution of loyal Ulster with the position of neutral Ireland. 'A strong, loyal Ulster', he asserted, 'will always be vital to the security and well-being of our whole empire and commonwealth.' Keith Jeffery

5. Empire

The British Commonwealth of Nations, then still informally called the British Empire (see Map D) centred on the person of the king-emperor, George VI. It covered a quarter of the world's land surface, the largest area ever to submit to a single political control. George VI was king of England by direct descent from William the Conqueror, and of Scotland by direct descent from James I and VI. Wales came under the crown by Edward I's conquest, the Channel Islands (once part of the duchy of Normandy) by inheritance from the Conqueror, the Isle of Man by purchase from the duke of Atholl in 1765, and Northern Ireland by an act of parliament passed as recently as 1922. These territories combined to form the United Kingdom, the empire's core.

Ireland's case was special. Under the 1922 act, six of the nine counties of Ulster formed Northern Ireland (see above), part of the UK. The remaining 26 Irish counties formed the Irish Free State (Eire from 1937), a quasi-independent republic, with its own president, but which did not then issue its own passports. Those of its citizens who needed a passport for travel outside the British Isles had to use a British one (see JOYCE); to this extent, it formed part of the empire.

Outside this geographical core were many different types of attached or dependent territories, where links with the UK originated in migrations of peoples of British stock, or in variations of conquest or cession. Closest to the UK in ethos were the four 'old dominions': Canada, Australia, New Zealand, and South Africa. These, along with what was then the Irish Free State and Newfoundland, comprised the original Commonwealth of Nations created by the Statute of Westminster (1931) which recognized they were all fully independent states in international law while sharing the same monarch as the UK. The old dominions each had a high commissioner in London, as the Irish Free State did; British relations with them were conducted through the secretary of state for the Dominions, usually a cabinet minister. He also dealt with Southern Rhodesia, though it was still officially a self-governing colony. For decades, their politicians had conferred with British leaders on matters of common concern, particularly trade and defence, and this pattern was of great value during the war.

India had its own special status within the empire. The king's representative in the recently opened capital, New Delhi, was the viceroy, formally responsible to the king and working closely in practice with the secretary of state for India, also normally a cabinet minster, who answered on Indian affairs to parliament. The viceroy controlled India's armed forces, police, and civil service and with them governed directly two-thirds of the whole subcontinent that was later divided between India, Pakistan, and Bangladesh. The remaining one-third remained under various Indian princes, who were politically dependent on the crown and the viceroy. Until 1937, when it was given a measure of self-government, Burma was also governed by the viceroy. Ceylon did not come under India, but was a colony.

The colonies, under their own secretary of state, formed an outer circle: remote alike from the crown and from independent status. Some of the more ancient, such as Bermuda and Jamaica, had their own legislatures, and some say in how they were run; others, such as Gibraltar or Aden, were little more than garrison towns under direct military rule.

Another category of dependent imperial territory was formed by League of Nations mandates. Mandates, predecessors of today's United Nations trusteeships, were created by the Versailles settlement for former parts of the German and Turkish empires. Australia and New Zealand had mandates in the Pacific and South Africa had a mandate over South-West Africa, formerly a German colony. One British mandate, Palestine, was a

UK, Table 3: Volunteer defence forces, 1940–5 (000s)

	Home Guard		*Royal Observer Corps*	
	Men	*Women*	*Men*	*Women*
June 1940	1,456	–	27.9	–
June 1941	1,603	–	33.2	–
June 1942	1,565	–	33.1	1.0
June 1943	1,784	4	30.7	2.2
June 1944	1,727	31	28.5	4.1
June 1945	(stood down Dec 1944)		6.6	2.1

Source: Contributor.

cause of constant concern. The foreign office did its best to keep it under its own control; as it did Egypt, which was neither a mandate nor a colony, but, until 1922, a protectorate. Protectorates were independent, but client, states. They came under the protection of powers that had the right of garrison in them, and were understood by other powers to be specially interested in their territories; but the protecting power was not responsible for local detail inside the protectorate. Egypt and the UK shared the government of the Sudan. India, too, had a protectorate, Sikkim.

The king's signature to the declaration of war against Germany on 3 September 1939 committed both the UK and the Indian and colonial parts of the empire to war. The mandates' participation seems to have been taken for granted also. By mid-September the four 'old dominions' had all resolved to join. Eire remained neutral; the Germans retained a legation in Dublin all through the war.

The automatic assumption that India would go to war, without consultation with Indian politicians, precipitated a major imperial crisis, which was not finally resolved till India—with Pakistan split off from it—became independent in 1947. However, the empire as a whole constituted a far more formidable fighting machine than the UK could ever have been alone. The effort it expended in the war exhausted it: it was fatally affected. Soon after 1945 came a period of de-colonization, a loosening of ties, and a reassessment of its role, but the voluntary association of most of the countries involved continued, and is known as the British Commonwealth. See also ANTI-IMPERIALISM and NATIONALISM. M. R. D. FOOT

6. Defence forces and civil defence

The formation of a defence force, announced on 14 May 1940, was a direct response to the German invasion of the Low Countries. At this stage the new force was called the Local Defence Volunteers, and within 24 hours more than a quarter of a million men had come forward (see Table 3 for total annual figures). Men over the age for military conscription could 'do their bit' in 'Dad's Army'. Organization at first was spontaneous and haphazard, equipment extremely scarce. After the British Expeditionary Force was evacuated from *Dunkirk, weapons were even scarcer.

Eventually, khaki overalls became standard issue to the force, soon renamed the Home Guard, but in the beginning dress was variable, weapons mostly improvised. Training began on a freelance basis, organized by veteran commanders or provided by training establishments set up on private initiative, such as the one created at Osterley Park near London, by wealthy backers. Run by Tom Wintringham, an ex-communist who had commanded the British contingent in the International Brigade during the *Spanish Civil War, this, between July and August, trained 5,000 men before being taken over as 'War Office No. 1 School' for the Home Guard.

In the summer of 1940, when fears of invasion were well justified, the Home Guard performed a useful if humble function, keeping vigil over coastline, airfields, and factories, and manning roadblocks, so giving the army breathing space in which to train its raw soldiers. The fervent desire of some Home Guard to fight, as Churchill had suggested in a famous speech, on the beaches and in the hills against German invaders, was, of course, frustrated, though rounding up Luftwaffe personnel who parachuted from their planes provided excitement during the battle of Britain.

From August 1940, Home Guard units were affiliated to county regiments of the army: in February 1941 ranks, as in the regular army, were introduced. Recruiting was temporarily suspended in October 1942: when this ban was lifted, the government used the Home Guard as a training-ground for boys of seventeen and eighteen prior to call-up. Compulsory service was introduced early in 1940; by the summer of 1943 there were 1,750,000 Home Guards in 1,100 battalions, whose average age was now under 30. Equipment and training in specialist duties (including Civil Defence) progressively improved the Home Guard which continued to show a variety of local colorations: a bus depot platoon would naturally be commanded by a bus driver, former regular soldiers who were commissionaires drilled the higher officials of the BBC. Military exercises were, in effect, a substitute for peacetime sporting activities. Though some of the 140,000 Home Guard serving in anti-aircraft batteries in September 1944 resented the compulsion which had sent them there, the 'standing down' of the force in December 1944 marked, for many, the end of a hobby.

Another organization which played an important part in defending the UK was the Observer Corps (later Royal Observer Corps). This had been formed between the wars by civilian volunteers whose main task once the war had begun was to supplement the radar network by reporting the direction, numbers, height, and type of any aircraft which might be hostile. They were especially useful in alerting the fighter defences to raiders which flew under the radar screen. Mostly unpaid, Corps members worked in pairs and by 1944 there were 1,500 observation posts, on duty day and night (for wartime personnel totals see Table 3). These were linked to a number of Group Centres which controlled up to 36 posts, each Centre being linked to the fighter defences in that particular area (see diagram in battle of Britain entry). When Hitler's V-weapons began to fall on the UK, observer posts were concentrated at half-mile intervals where the V-1s crossed the coast. These were equipped with signal rockets to indicate to intercepting fighters the position of the V-1 as it flew over.

In 1937, experts had estimated that in a new war, bombing would feature on a scale vastly greater than the German raids on the UK in the First World War which had killed 1,413 people. They believed that Germany would bomb the UK at once and continue the attack for 60 days, and that each ton of high explosive would cause 50 casualties, killed and wounded, a total of nearly two million casualties. Such fatalism had already inspired a government circular to local authorities in September 1935 which had encouraged them to organize Air Raid Precautions (ARP). In April 1937, an Air Raid Wardens' Service was created and by the middle of 1938 this had some 200,000 recruits. Over half a million more people enrolled in the ARP services during the 'Munich crisis' of 1938 (see MUNICH AGREEMENT) when trench shelters were dug in public parks. By the outbreak of war, enough covered trenches were available to shelter half a million people and nearly one and a half million *Anderson shelters had been issued free to householders with gardens. Citizens, provided with masks against gas attack, were told how to gas-proof a room in each home, and ordered to *blackout their windows.

Since no great raids occurred immediately, air raid wardens' chief duty in the early months was to enforce blackout regulations: not a popular role. However, during the Blitz of 1940–1 wardens and other Civil Defence personnel often performed heroically, and suffered a considerable number of casualties (see Table 2). Their work overlapped with that of people maintaining peace time roles—doctors, nurses, ambulance drivers, and policemen—and that of the WVS. At the height of the Blitz in December 1940 most of the 200,000 or 250,000 people serving in various post-raid services and in shelter organizations were volunteers, and volunteer part-timers were preponderant in the designated Civil Defence services. The Civil Defence (General) services included wardens, rescue and stretcher parties, staffs of control centres, and messenger boys. Casualty services embraced emergency ambulance workers and first-aid post staff. The Fire Service included full-time and part-time regular firemen and part-time auxiliaries. Together, all these numbered more than 1,500,000 people. There were also more than 250,000 full-time and part-time policemen, and hundreds of thousands of active WVS volunteers. The duties of the Home Guard often involved its members in raids and rescue work, so that out of the UK's total civilian population at this time up to a tenth were active, or prepared to be active, in Civil Defence.

Air raid wardens operated from local posts—about ten to the square mile (2.6 sq. km.) in London. They mounted regular patrols and reported bombs as they fell, supervised public shelters, and acted as the eyes and ears of Civil Defence. Rescue teams summoned to 'incidents' (the euphemistic term for bomb damage) comprised stretcher bearers and 'heavy rescue men', mainly peacetime building workers knowledgeable about house construction. Firemen were commonly needed too. From 31 December 1940, after the so-called 'Second Fire of London' had exposed the disastrous consequences of leaving small commercial and industrial premises unattended at night, compulsory 'fire watching' was introduced. But regulations were hard to enforce, and incendiary bombs kept the Fire Service busy. Its paid full-timers served 48 hours on, 24 hours off: they were joined at night by part-time auxiliaries. During the Blitz, the difficulties of their work were compounded by the division of responsibility between many hundreds of local authorities, resulting in chaos when the fire service of one locality had to call for help from others. In May 1941, when the worst was almost over, all forces were combined in one National Fire Service.

The Civil Defence services were maintained at the ready long after heavy bombing ceased: there were still hundreds of thousands of volunteers in June 1944, though the number of full-time Civil Defence personnel, 127,000 at the height of the Blitz, had fallen to 70,000 by the end of 1943. Women increasingly joined: a fifth of the quarter-million part-time fire-fighters were eventually female. An attempt was made to excite enthusiasm among the millions of citizens now compelled to undertake 48 hours' firewatching per month by naming them the 'Fire Guard'. But it was said that, 'anyone not a congenital idiot could easily evade fire guard duty, and in any case a congenital idiot was entitled to exemption.'

ANGUS CALDER

7. Armed forces and special forces

(a) High Command

The UK waged the Second World War with three major independent branches of the armed forces: the Royal Navy, the Army, and the Royal Air Force. Up to the eve of war in 1939 their strategic and operational direction was vested, at the highest level, in the Committee of Imperial Defence (CID) which formulated strategy and defence requirements through a number of sub-committees, and reported to the cabinet through the minister for co-ordination of defence. On 1 September 1939 the prime minister, Neville Chamberlain, set up a war cabinet (see GOVERNMENT, above), as Lloyd George had done in 1916, and dissolved the CID. The minister for co-ordination of defence was given a seat in the war cabinet which also included the three armed services ministers, the first lord of the Admiralty, secretary of state for war, and secretary of state for air. When Churchill succeeded Chamberlain in May 1940 he immediately created an inner war cabinet, making himself minister of defence, as well as prime minister, and excluding the armed services ministers. He preferred to deal directly with the uniformed heads of the armed forces who formed the Chiefs of Staff Committee. The armed forces ministers thus had little influence on operations and largely concerned themselves with organizational matters, operating through their ministries—the Admiralty, War Office, and Air Ministry.

(b) Army

The titular head of the army was the *Chief of the Imperial General Staff (CIGS) and its affairs were, and still are, conducted through the Army Council. Presided over by the secretary of state for war it had six military members, including the CIGS. The others were the adjutant-general, responsible for personnel matters, quartermaster general (*logistics), vice-chief of the Imperial General Staff (operations, plans, intelligence, and training), deputy chief of the Imperial General Staff (organization for war), and the master general of ordinance. They exercised their staff functions through the war office.

At the outbreak of war the army was made up of the Regular and Territorial Armies (TA), but limited conscription was already in place, having been introduced in April 1939. Part of the reason for this was the decision, in view of the bomber threat, to create an Anti-Aircraft Command of five TA divisions. At home the army was organized in a number of geographic commands and districts—Aldershot (later renamed South-Eastern Command), Southern, Western, Northern, Scottish, and Eastern Commands, London and N. Ireland Districts (see Map 103). Within these were five regular infantry divisions, and a number of TA divisions, the bulk of which were to make up the British Expeditionary Force (BEF), which began to cross to France in September 1939. There was also a mobile (later armoured) division in the process of being formed, but this would not be ready for action until the end of May 1940, and then only in truncated form. There was a second mobile division (later 7th Armoured Division, the Desert Rats) in Egypt and 8th Infantry Division in Palestine, which had been coping with the Arab rebellion there. Beyond that the British Army overseas was largely deployed in its traditional manner in scattered small garrisons. A large part of the army overseas was in India at the outbreak of war, as each Indian brigade had one British battalion in it, a policy instituted after the 1857 mutiny (see also INDIA, 4(a)).

The main cornerstone of the British Army, in the cavalry and infantry, was the regimental system. Many regiments had been in existence since the 17th century and had long and illustrious histories. Each had its own cap-badge and particular distinguishing features in uniform. The object was that once a man joined a particular regiment he stayed with it throughout his service. It generated in the individual soldier a special sense of belonging, especially since most regiments recruited from a particular part of the country so that he served with men of the same background. In turn this attachment developed both pride and loyalty, which enhanced the regiment's fighting spirit. Nevertheless, as had happened during 1914–18, it became increasingly difficult to maintain regimental 'purity', especially when casualties were high. Reinforcements often had to be posted to regiments wearing a different cap-badge.

The army was made up of three main elements. The teeth arms, those that actually closed with the enemy, the supporting arms, and the service arms. The teeth arms were the Royal Armoured Corps (RAC), which had been formed in 1938 from the cavalry, now largely mechanized (although the 1st Cavalry Division, comprising horsed cavalry and yeomanry regiments, was sent to Palestine in 1939 before being later converted to 10th Armoured Division), the Royal Tank Corps, which became the Royal Tank Regiment (RTR), and the infantry. After the fall of France in June 1940 the RAC was rapidly expanded in order to create additional armoured divisions. This was done by converting a number of infantry battalions into RAC regiments, and guards battalions into the Guards Armoured Division. Six additional cavalry and three RTR regiments were also raised. In 1940 the Reconnaissance Corps was formed to provide reconnaissance regiments for the infantry divisions, a role which cavalry had fulfilled, but had surrendered when its regiments were required for the new armoured divisions being raised. The Reconnaissance, Corps did not become part of the RAC until January 1944, and it was disbanded after the war.

The infantry expanded as it had done in the First World War, with each regiment raising additional battalions. Apart from the normal infantry battalion, other types were introduced to fulfil special roles. Each infantry division had a machine gun battalion, instead of the Machine-Gun Corps during the First World War. Motor battalions were created to serve in armoured formations and later in the war a few infantry battalions were also converted to the glider-borne role and became part of the airborne forces. Early in the war when there were plans to aid the Finns in their fight against the USSR (see FINNISH–SOVIET WAR), one or two battalions were even trained as ski troops. There were also those battalions which were incorporated in the *Chindits in Burma. By mid-1944, however, there was a serious shortage of infantry and a number of battalions had to be disbanded and even surplus RAF personnel transferred to make good the shortfall. Part of the reason was casualties, but also

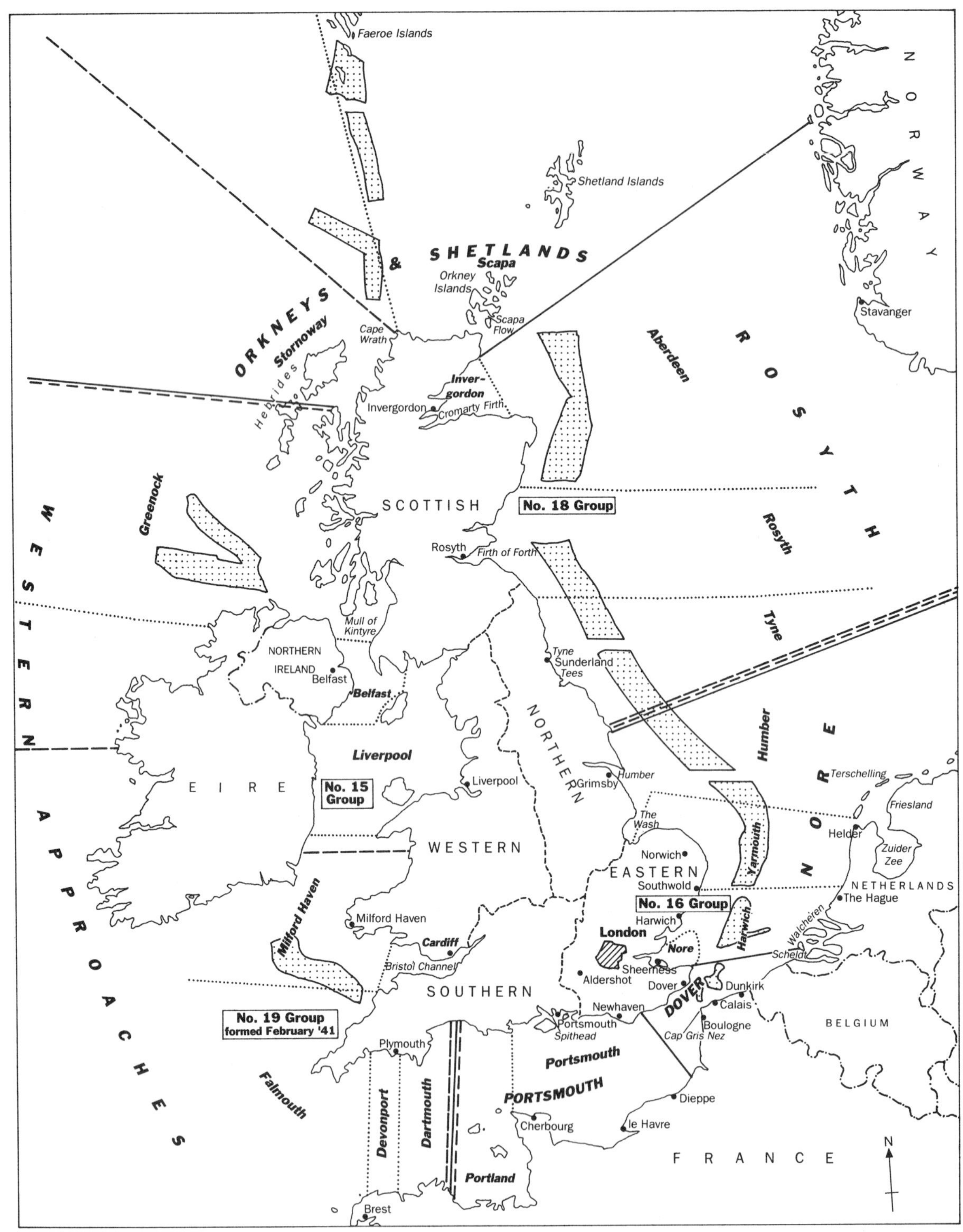

103. **UK**: Home Defence Organization, Summer 1940, and RAF Coastal Group boundaries, 1939–45

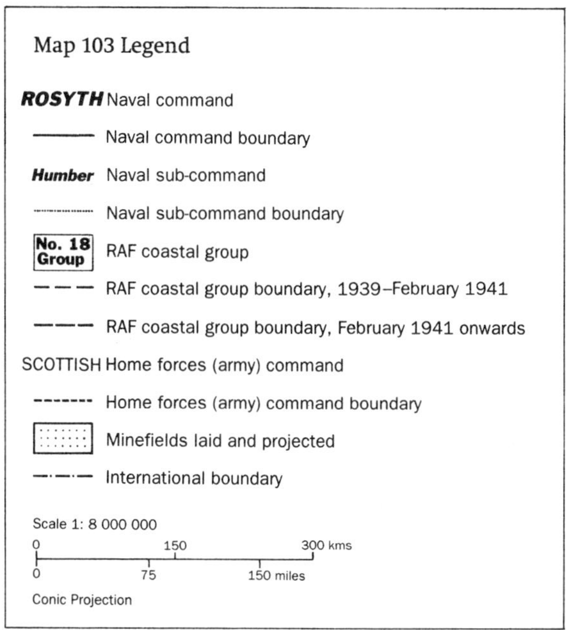

because the increasing sophistication of weapons systems meant ever rising demands for manpower by other arms and services both to operate and to support them.

Of the three supporting arms, the Royal Artillery had the largest proportion of manpower among all the arms and services. Indeed, it lived up to its motto *Ubique* (Everywhere). Besides manning the *artillery (field, medium, heavy) directly involved in the ground battle, it was also responsible for anti-aircraft (known as 'Ack Ack') defence and coastal artillery, and manned as well some of the heavier *anti-tank weapons. It even, through the Royal Maritime Artillery, provided gun crews for merchant vessels and operated light aircraft as air observation posts to spot targets and direct artillery fire on to them.

The Royal Engineers—the sappers—also undertook a wide range of tasks. Apart from mine laying and clearance, bridge-building, and demolitions, they were also responsible for the construction of defences, camps, airfields, roads, and railways. They became heavily involved in the operation of ports and in the latter half of the war Armoured Engineers became a vital element of armoured warfare (see ENGINEERS, 1). Another very important role, especially in overseas theatres, was water purification, and engineers also ran the military postal system.

Finally, the Royal Corps of Signals was responsible for the army's communications—telephone, *radio, and teleprinter. The increasing reliance on good communications was reflected in the fact that the Royal Signals increased its strength six-fold during the war.

The main services within the British Army in 1939 were the Royal Army Service Corps (RASC), the Royal Army Ordnance Corps (RAOC), and Royal Army Medical Corps (RAMC). The RASC was primarily responsible for maintaining supplies to the troops in the field. This involved both transportation and handling of fuel, ammunition, and food (including bread baked in the RASC's own bakeries). The RAOC, on the other hand, was essentially responsible for all types of stores. These included clothing, general stores—ranging from tools to barracks furniture—and warlike stores (weapons, vehicles, ammunition, radios). The RAOC was also responsible for the repair and maintenance of warlike stores, but in 1942 this was taken over by the newly formed Royal Electrical and Mechanical Engineers (REME).

There were also a number of smaller corps. These included the Royal Army Chaplains Department, the Corps of Military Police, Royal Army Pay Corps, Army Educational Corps, Army Dental Corps, and the Auxiliary Military Pioneer Corps (title changed to Pioneer Corps in 1940), the last performing the same mission as its First World War predecessor, the Labour Corps. Besides the REME, two new corps were formed during the war: the Intelligence Corps, whose function had previously been carried out by the Staff, and the Army Catering Corps, a reflection of the fact that good food is important in maintaining high morale. For every infantryman and tank soldier in the front line there were nine in the supporting arms and services.

Women in khaki supported the army through the Auxiliary Territorial Service (ATS), formed in 1939 and initially composed of volunteers. They fulfilled much the same tasks as the WRNS did in the Royal Navy, but they additionally made a significant contribution to the work of Anti-Aircraft Command, doing everything except actually fire the guns. Army nurses were drawn from two sources, Queen Alexandra's Imperial Nursing Service and the Territorial Army Nursing Service, amalgamated in 1949 as Queen Alexandra's Royal Army Nursing Corps (see also FANY).

After *Dunkirk, command of the British land forces in the UK was vested in GHQ Home Forces, which operated through the geographical commands. Based in Cairo, GHQ *Middle East Command initially controlled British and empire forces which fought in the Western Desert, *East African, and *Syrian campaigns, but in August 1941 East Africa Command was formed to administer troops in that theatre. During early 1942 Middle East Command was also required to take responsibility for Iran and Iraq. These countries had previously come under C-in-C India (as did Burma) but in August 1942 Persia and Iraq Command was formed to administer the few troops in them (see PAIFORCE).

In the UK, when Montgomery took over South-Eastern Command in 1941, he renamed it South-Eastern Army. Otherwise, army commands existed only overseas and were placed, according to the theatre in which they operated, under a British or Allied GHQ. First Army, under *Eisenhower's *Allied Forces HQ, was formed for the

UK, Table 4: Strength of Armed Forces (000s)

	Navy (inc. Royal Marines)	*Army (exc. Home Guard)*	*RAF*
Sept 1939	180	897	193
Sept 1940	307	1,888	420
Sept 1941	424	2,292	767
Sept 1942	529	2,494	895
Sept 1943	710	2,697	982
Sept 1944	776	2,741	992
Jun 1945	783	2,920	950

At the outbreak of war the strength of the Royal Marines was 12,390 men. This grew to 74,000 men by 1945.

	Women			
	Nurses	*WRNS*	*ATS*	*WAAF*
Sept 1939	2.4	–	–	–
Sept 1940	7.9	7.9	36.1	17.4
Sept 1941	10.4	15.1	42.8	37.4
Sept 1942	13.9	33.3	162.2	141.5
Sept 1943	17.5	60.4	212.5	180.3
Sept 1944	20.3	74.0	198.2	171.2
Jun 1945	21.4	72.0	190.8	153.0

Source: Contributor.

*North African campaign landings; Second Army, ultimately controlled by *SHAEF, took part in *OVERLORD and the fighting in north-west Europe; Eighth, Ninth, and Tenth Armies were all formed within Middle East Command, but the last two never numbered more than a few divisions, never saw combat as formations, and were used to reinforce the Eighth Army when necessary and as cover for the *deception operation which created an imaginary Twelfth Army. A real Twelfth Army was also created as part of Allied Land Forces South-East Asia (ALFSEA) in May 1945 to control British troops fighting in the *Burma campaign. Finally, there was Fourteenth Army, formed in October 1943 under GHQ Delhi, which fought the Burma campaign until it was withdrawn to India to prepare for the invasion of Malaya, and was replaced by Twelfth Army.

Where two armies operated together, they formed army groups under army group commanders. British armies formed Eighteenth Army Group (First and Eighth), which fought in the North African campaign; British and US armies formed Fifteenth Army Group, which fought the *Sicilian (US Seventh and British Eighth) and the *Italian campaigns (US Fifth and British Eighth); and a Canadian (First) and British (Second) army formed Montgomery's Twenty-First Army Group which fought in north-west Europe. The exception to this was Eleventh Army Group, based in India. This had Ceylon Army Command and the garrisons of the Indian Ocean bases under it and was also the administrative structure for Fourteenth Army, before ALFSEA, part of *South-East Asia Command, replaced it in November 1944.

In all, at the peak of its strength, the British Army had 11 armoured divisions, 9 of which saw action, 34 infantry divisions, of which 9 saw no combat, and 2 airborne divisions. In all, just over 3.5 million men and women enlisted in it between 1939 and 1945, and 144,000 lost their lives (see Tables 4, 5, and 6). For the Home Guard see DEFENCE FORCES AND CIVIL DEFENCE above.

(c) Navy

The Admiralty is the oldest of the British war ministries, founded during the reign of Henry VIII, and the Royal Navy is the UK's senior service. Its work was directed by the Admiralty Board, which consisted of the First Lord, First Sea Lord, who was also the Chief of Naval Staff, Second Sea Lord (responsible for manning and recruiting), Third Sea Lord, also known as the Controller of the Navy (ship building and repair, naval dockyards), Fourth Sea Lord (victualling, supplies, naval hospitals), and Fifth Sea Lord (Fleet Air Arm matters).

Operations were under the direct control of the First Sea Lord, in his capacity as Chief of the Naval Staff. He exercised this control through the Vice-Chief of the Naval Staff, whose responsibilities also covered intelligence, plans, signals communications, hydrography, and navigation, and three Assistant Chiefs of the Naval Staff (ACNS), Home, Foreign, and Trade. Within these three broad divisions the ACNS looked after local defence, operations, training, gunnery, and minesweeping.

Uniquely, the Admiralty exercised world-wide command and control of naval operations through various commands and stations: these were North Atlantic and South Atlantic Commands, and the China (Singapore), America and West Indies, and East Indies

Stations. Each had a varying number of *warships, including those of Commonwealth navies (and, during the war, those belonging to the various *governments-in-exile) under its operational control. There were also six home commands—Orkney and Shetlands, Rosyth, Nore, Dover (from October 1939), Portsmouth, Western Approaches—which were, with one exception, responsible for the defence of territorial waters around the British Isles (see Map 103). To this end they had light forces of destroyers, minesweepers, and motor gun/torpedo boats under command.

The exception was Western Approaches, whose headquarters was initially at Plymouth, but was then moved to the more central position of Liverpool. This command had direct responsibility for the day-to-day conduct of the battle of the *Atlantic, under the overall direction of the ACNS (Trade) at the Admiralty. While the Admiralty Trade Division worked out the routes of the *convoys, in conjunction with the Submarine Tracking Room, which was part of the *Naval Intelligence Division, the composition of merchant ships within them was the responsibility of the Naval Control Service, which had a representative at each port. Western Approaches controlled and allocated escort vessels, which were organized into groups.

The RN's main offensive power was built round its fleets. Each contained all the warships operating within a fleet's designated area of command. 'Battlefleet' was the term used to describe a fleet's battle squadron and all those warships manoeuvring with it. Unlike the First World War, when the Grand Fleet had a number of battle squadrons, there was normally only one battle squadron within each fleet.

At the outbreak of war there were two main fleets, the Home Fleet, which immediately deployed to Scapa Flow in the Orkney Islands, and the Mediterranean Fleet based at Alexandria, Egypt. A third was formed at Singapore on 2 December 1941 when the post of C-in-C China Station as an operational command was discontinued. Instead, Admiral Tom Phillips was appointed C-in-C Eastern Fleet. This comprised warships which formerly came under the China Station, and Force 'Z' (see PRINCE OF WALES AND REPULSE). In April 1942, when commanded by Admiral *Somerville, the Eastern Fleet tried to oppose the Japanese raid into the *Indian Ocean. It was subsequently based at Kilindini (Mombasa) in British East Africa, and eventually became the basis of the British Pacific Fleet (see TASK FORCE 57), the largest British fleet of the war.

Ships of all these fleets were organized into numbered squadrons for cruisers and above, and into numbered flotillas for destroyers and below. Squadrons had a minimum of two ships, flotillas a maximum of eight. If there were enough ships, squadrons and flotillas could be divided into numbered divisions and subdivisions. Unlike squadron divisions, the numbers allotted to destroyer divisions had no connection with how many there were in any particular flotilla. There were also, at various times, formations based on major surface vessels which were smaller than a fleet. These were termed 'Forces'. Two of the best-known were *Force H and *Force K.

As submarines operated independently, any number could belong to a submarine flotilla which was a purely administrative unit. The most famous was 10th Flotilla, which was based at *Malta for much of the war. It suffered heavy casualties in boats lost, but also achieved spectacular successes. Besides attacking enemy shipping, British submarines were also one of the main means of landing agents and Special Forces on hostile shores. Motor Torpedo Boats (*MTBs) and Motor Gunboats (*MGBs) were termed Coastal Forces and had their own dedicated bases in home waters. However, they also operated overseas, notably in the Adriatic during, 1944–5, and in support of the final ground offensive in the Burma campaign.

The RN also devoted a significant part of its resources to *Combined Operations, the organization set up to develop techniques for, and to mount, *amphibious warfare operations which involved all three services. All landing ships and *landing craft came under the Combined Operations umbrella.

In terms of manpower, the RN was made up of three elements: the standing regular navy, the Royal Navy itself; the Royal Naval Reserve (RNR), comprising officers and men who had previous RN service or were professional Merchant Navy officers; and the Royal Naval Volunteer Reserve (RNVR). This last consisted only of officers, distinguished by the waved rings of rank worn on their cuffs, hence its nickname the Wavy Navy (the ranks of RNR officers were two interlinked wavy rings). RNVR officers were drawn from those who had volunteered for naval service in time of war, and those conscripted and given naval commissions during the war. Conscripted ratings, on the other hand, were merely classified as 'Hostilities Only' and wore no distinguishing insignia. The reason for the difference was the traditional Royal Navy view that all officers were volunteers, but that, recalling the press gang, ratings were generally not so in wartime. RNR officers were often Merchant Navy officers of liners, trawlers, and other ships which were taken into Royal Navy service as troopships, *armed merchant cruisers, and vessels employed in laying or sweeping mines (see MINE WARFARE, 2). Another category was retired senior Royal Navy officers brought back to active service as commodores of convoys. But RNVR officers accounted for over three-quarters of the total officer strength of the wartime navy. The battle of the Atlantic especially fell on their shoulders, since it was they who almost entirely manned the corvettes, frigates, and destroyers which made up the escorts.

The Royal Navy was made up of a number of branches, reflecting specialities. The largest of these was the seaman's or executive branch, but both ships and shore establishments had others. These included the Engineering, Medical, Supply, Instructional, Paymasters, and Chaplains branches. In terms of insignia, they were identified by different colours between an officer's rings of rank, and by the various qualification badges worn by ratings on the upper arm. Each branch had its own promotion ladder. Both officers and ratings tended to specialize in one type of ship, but could, and did, serve in others.

A unique branch of the service was the Fleet Air Arm. Up until 1937 it had been the RAF's responsibility to provide naval aircraft and pilots on the grounds that the Fleet Air Arm's predecessor, the Royal Naval Air Service, had been absorbed into the RAF when it was created in 1918 and it would be illogical for the navy, or the army for that matter, to recreate its own air wing. It was, however, an unsatisfactory situation, especially since the RAF accorded low priority to the navy's aviation needs. When, to the air ministry's dismay, the Fleet Air Arm was handed back to the navy and responsibility for it vested in the newly created Fifth Sea Lord, aircrew were drawn from the General List, as the seaman's promotion ladder was called. This policy was maintained throughout the war, even though those who joined the Fleet Air Arm stayed in it. It was, like the RAF, organized in squadrons, numbered from 800 upwards to distinguish them from RAF squadrons.

In September 1939 the Fleet Air Arm possessed 232 obsolete aircraft operating in the main from five aircraft *carriers. By June 1945 the number of carriers of all types had grown to more than 50 and the front-line aircraft strength was 1,336 organized in 73 squadrons. However, 55% of the aircraft were US types.

Mention must be made of the Women's Royal Naval Service (WRNS), known affectionately as the Wrens. Founded in 1918, but stood down at the end of the First World War, in 1939 it was reactivated, initially relying on volunteers. As the wartime navy expanded, so did the WRNS, taking over many shore-based tasks from their male counterparts and thus making more men available for service at sea. Their contribution to the Royal Navy can best be summed up in the decision in 1949 to make the WRNS part of the standing Royal Navy and it remained in being until 1993. During the war Wrens did, on rare occasions, serve aboard MTBs, but it was not until 1990 that they were allowed to go to sea as part of a warship's complement on a regular basis. The other major contribution made by women was Queen Alexandra's Royal Naval Nursing Service, which had been founded in 1902 and provided the nursing staff at all naval hospitals.

The Royal Marines were also an integral part of the Royal Navy. Their role in time of war had been redelineated in 1923 by the Admiralty's Madden Committee, which recommended that, apart from their traditional role afloat of helping man the guns of the larger warships, the marines should also raise a striking force for amphibious warfare and a mobile force for defending naval bases overseas. These recommendations were not implemented and in September 1939 the marines, then 12,390 strong, had the manpower only to fulfil their role afloat. But steps were immediately taken to raise an RM brigade—expanded to a division of three brigades (101–103) in 1941—which took part in the abortive *Dakar expedition in September 1940. Anti-aircraft batteries and an RM Fortress Unit were also raised, as was the first of two *Mobile Naval Base Defence Organizations (MNBDO) which fought on *Crete. Later, large parts of this MNBDO were sent to defend Indian Ocean bases while the second, formed from the Fortress Unit, took part in the Sicilian campaign in July 1943. In the meantime, the RM Division, whose HQ had controlled the *Madagascar landings, began to be broken up, its battalions gradually being converted into RM commandos (see SPECIAL FORCES, below). The MNBDOs were also disbanded to form commandos or to provide crews for landing craft which participated in the landings in Normandy and on Walcheren Island during the *Scheldt Estuary battle. During the course of the war marines also flew with the Fleet Air Arm, formed an RM Armoured Support Regiment and an anti-aircraft brigade for OVERLORD, and raised special units such as *Force Viper and the Royal Marine Boom Patrol Detachment (see CANOEISTS).

For numbers of personnel and casualties see Tables 4, 5, and 6.

(d) Air Force

The Royal Air Force was only 21 years old when the Second World War began, and was thus very much the junior service. This, however, did not mean that it was any less important than its older counterparts. In terms of High Command, it was structured similarly to the other two services, with policy being evolved through the Air Council, presided over by the Secretary of State for Air. The head uniformed member was the Chief of the Air Staff (CAS), who had operations, plans, and intelligence as his remit, besides being the overall commander-in-chief of the RAF. He was assisted in this by the Deputy CAS (DCAS), the focus for planning, and the Assistant CAS (ACAS), who was the day-to-day link between the Air Ministry and the operational commands. The other members were the Air Member for Personnel (AMP), Air Member for Supply and Organization (AMSO), Air Member for Training (AMT), Vice Chief of the Air Staff (VCAS), as CAS's deputy, and the Air Member for Development and Production (AMP). The last-named, lost his seat when the Ministry of Aircraft Production (MAP) was set up under *Beaverbrook in May 1940, but was brought back on to the Air Council in 1941 as the Controller of Research and Development, and MAP's representative on it.

Until 1936 the RAF at home had one operational command, the *Air Defence of Great Britain (ADGB), but in that year there was a major reorganization and a number of separate commands by role were created: Bomber, Fighter, Coastal, Reserve, and Training Commands. Reserve Command was absorbed by Training Command, which was split into Flying Training and Technical Training Commands, shortly after the

UK, Table 5: Casualties to all ranks of the Armed Forces of the United Kingdom during the war as reported to 28 February 1946

	Total	*Royal Navy*	*Army*	*Royal Air Force*
Killed	264,443	50,758	144,079	69,606
Missing[a]	41,327	820	33,771	6,736
Wounded	277,077	14,663	239,575	22,839
Prisoners-of-war	172,592	7,401	152,076	13,115
TOTAL	755,439	73,642	569,501	112,296

[a]Including the following who were still missing on 28 February 1946; Royal Navy 340, Army 2,267, Royal Air Force 3,089; Total 5,696

Source: Mellor, *Casualties and Medical Statistics*.

outbreak of war, and later additional commands were added. These were Army Co-Operation, Balloon, Maintenance, and Ferry Commands. The last-named, with the *Air Transport Auxiliary, was responsible for delivering aircraft from factory to operational units. It was taken over by Transport Command when that was set up in 1943. Army Co-Operation Command was formed in December 1940 to develop air operations in direct support of the ground forces. The main overseas commands were RAF Middle East (later Mediterranean and Middle East), whose main operational element was the *Western Desert Air Force, and Air Command South-East Asia. Unlike the commands at home those overseas carried out all operational air roles. Often, too, their forces were merged into Allied air commands. Thus, in the Mediterranean theatre from 1943 onwards British and US air forces operated together under the overall umbrella of Mediterranean Air Command. For most of the war Coastal Command was placed under the operational control of the Admiralty in order to have unified command for the battle of the Atlantic. By the same token, RAF Fighter Command had operational control over the army's Anti-Aircraft Command for the air defence of Britain. In August 1941 Coastal Command (see Map 103 for RAF Coastal Command Group boundaries) assumed responsibility for *air-sea rescue operations in the open ocean from the Air Ministry's Directorate of Air-Sea Rescue, but Fighter Command remained in charge of operations around the coast.

Each command comprised a number of groups, each made up of a number of squadrons, except in the case of fighter groups, which, from the autumn of 1940 had an intermediary level of command, the fighter wing. Within the Metropolitan Air Force, as the RAF in Britain was sometimes termed, Bomber Command initially consisted of Nos. 2–5 Groups, which were operational, and No. 6 Group for training. Of these, No. 2 Group was to be largely dedicated to daylight bombing and was passed to the command of 2nd Tactical Air Force, formed in 1943 for support of OVERLORD and replacing Army Co-Operation Command. No. 6 Group was later joined by No. 7. These were then redesignated Nos. 91 and 92 Groups in May 1942. Their purpose was to control the Operational Training Units (OTU), which every command had. These represented the final stage of training for aircrew before they joined operational squadrons. No. 6 Group did, however, reappear in Bomber Command as an all-Canadian Group at the beginning of 1943 (see CANADA, 6(d)). No. 1 Group, which had been sent to France as part of the Advanced Air Striking Force (AASF) at the beginning of the war, came back into the Bomber Command fold after Dunkirk. Also formed in January 1943 were No. 8 (*Pathfinder Force) Group and, towards the end of that year, Nos. 80 and 100 (Special Duties) Groups, responsible for handling the ever more sophisticated *electronic warfare that was fought in the skies above Germany and occupied Europe. Fighter Command had Nos. 10–13 Groups, Coastal Command Nos. 15–19 Groups, Balloon Command Nos. 30–33 Groups, and Army Co-Operation Command Nos. 70 and 71 Groups.

During the war the RAF drew its strength from a number of different sources. First, there was the RAF, the standing air force. There was also the Royal Auxiliary Air Force (R Aux AF), formed in 1924 to provide a reserve of manpower and air squadrons; and it also found the manpower for Balloon Command. In 1937, in the midst of the RAF's expansion, it was realized that the existing organization would be unable to keep pace with the additional aircrew required. Consequently, the Royal Air Force Volunteer Reserve (RAFVR) was formed to create a pool of aircrewmen who could be brought on to the active list as soon as war seemed imminent. The 'weekend fliers' as its members were called, and who numbered over 10,000 at the outbreak of war, were a vital part of the RAF, especially during the battle of Britain.

The Dominion air forces—Australian, Canadian, New Zealand, and South African—were also incorporated in the RAF, as were those of continental nations overrun by Hitler. These included the Czech, Belgian, Dutch, French, Norwegian, and Polish air forces, many of whom had their own national squadrons within the RAF order of battle. Lending their support to all these disparate elements were the Women's Auxiliary Air Force (WAAF) and Princess Mary's RAF Nursing Service. Besides providing much administrative support, WAAF personnel performed invaluable service as plotters in the operational control rooms, especially during the battle of Britain, as *radar operators, and in the RAF's *Y-service, which eavesdropped on airborne radio communications.

Finally, there was the RAF Regiment. The RAF had assumed a ground role in 1922 when, through air control, it had taken over the policing of the British mandates and other territories in the Middle East. It formed armoured car companies, which took part, under army command, in the Western Desert and North African campaigns and ran the Iraqi and Aden Protectorate Levies. During 1939–41 the RAF provided some lighter anti-aircraft weapons for defence of its airfields, but after the fall of Crete in May 1941, a study on the threat of airborne troops was set up. The result was the formation, in February 1942, of the RAF Regiment to protect airfields from this threat. More than 220 RAF Regiment squadrons were raised before 1945, but the armoured car squadrons did not come under the RAF Regiment umbrella until 1946.

While conscription applied to the RAF in the same way as the other two services, throughout the war all aircrew were volunteers. Given their high losses—Bomber Command alone lost almost 56,000 killed—it became clear very early on that resources were simply not sufficient to train the required numbers for an ever-expanding force. The solution was the *British Empire Air Training Scheme, established in December 1939. The aircrew training process was, however, a long one. The volunteer initially had to pass medical and intelligence tests and was then sent to the Air Crew Reception Centre at Regent's Park in London. Twelve weeks' ground training at an Initial Training Wing (ITW) followed. Those who had opted for crew positions other than that of pilot were then sent to specialist schools—navigation, wireless, gunnery—while the pilots attended Elementary Flying Training School (EFTS). Here those without the required flying aptitude were identified and remustered in other air trades and the remainder underwent advanced flying training, often abroad, under the Training Scheme. On return they were assigned to the type of aircraft for which they were best suited and then sent to an OTU. There multi-seater aircrewmen formed their operational crews and were posted as such to squadrons. Often it would be eighteen months or more from the time that a pilot originally reported to Regent's Park to his first operational sortie in a squadron. It was this, rather than the rate of aircraft production, that acted as the limiting factor on the rate of increase of the RAF's front-line aircraft strength. See DEFENCE FORCES AND CIVIL DEFENCE above, for Royal Observer Corps. See Tables 4, 5, and 6 for personnel numbers and casualties.

(e) Special forces

For much of the inter-war period little thought was given to what were called 'irregular operations', although T. E. Lawrence had demonstrated in the Near East during 1917–18 how effective they could be. However, the War Office did eventually establish a small branch to study the subject and at the outbreak of war it put forward a number of proposals, including destroying the Romanian oilfields by sabotage, but none came to anything. The first Special Forces units actually raised were the ten Independent Companies, formed in 1940 for the Norwegian campaign with the mission of preventing the Germans from setting up U-boat bases on the coastline between Narvik and Namsos. Five companies were sent; they achieved little. But from them evolved the commandos when, in the summer of 1940, Churchill ordered that hit-and-run raids be mounted against the occupied coastline of Europe—his 'butcher and bolt' policy, as he called it. The commandos were initially formed into battalion-sized units called Commandos which were trained to fight as self-contained groups. They were then renamed Special Service battalions but reverted to being called Commandos in March 1941. Numbered 1–9, 11, and 12, each totalled about 500 men. During the early part of the war they mounted numerous raids against the occupied coastline (see DIEPPE, LOFOTEN, and ST NAZAIRE, for example). Later, they were joined by No. 10, an inter-Allied unit made up of anti-Nazi German personnel and others drawn from the forces belonging to the various *governments-in-exile No. 14, raised for raids on occupied Norway; No. 30, an inter-service intelligence-gathering unit; and by a number of Royal Marine (RM) Commandos. The first RM Commando, raised in 1942, was simply called the Royal Marine Commando, but this later became No. 40 and Nos. 41–48 were also raised. All Army and Marine Commandos were contained in four Special Service (Commando from December 1944) Brigades, which were in turn controlled by a Special Service (Commando) Group.

However, Special Forces initially thrived in the Middle East. First on the scene was the *Long Range Desert Group, quickly followed by the raising of three Middle East Commandos (nos. 50–52) independent of those formed in the UK. But apart from the LRDG, and, to a lesser extent the *Special Boat Section, early attempts to employ Special Forces in the Middle East were not overly successful, basically because the higher command had little understanding of them. Out of this frustration was born the *Special Air Service (SAS), but other organizations were formed as well, including *Popski's Private Army. Indeed, such was the plethora that controlling and co-ordinating their activities proved very difficult (see LAYFORCE and MIDDLE EAST COMMANDO). Burma, too, generated its own Special Forces. Among them were *V-Force and, of course, the *Chindits; and after South-East Asia Command was formed in October 1943 it, too, had its own group of Special Forces (see SMALL OPERATIONS GROUP).

By mid-1943 Special Forces could be categorized in a number of types. First, there were those primarily dedicated to supporting the major Allied landing operations; they came under the umbrella of Combined Operations HQ. These included not just the commandos, but the *Combined Operations Pilotage Parties which carried out beach reconnaissance; Royal Naval commandos for organizing the beaches during the

UK, Table 6: Casualties to the Women's Auxiliary Services during the war as reported to 28 February 1946

	Total	*Women's Royal Naval Service*	*Auxiliary Territorial Service and Army Nursing Services*	*Women's Auxiliary Air Force*
Killed	624	102	335	187
Missing	98	–	94[a]	4
Wounded	744	22	302	420
Prisoners-of-war	20	–	20	–
TOTAL	1,486	124	751	611

[a]Including 18 women who were still missing at 28 February 1946

Source: Mellor, *Casualties and Medical Statistics.*

landings themselves; and the RAF Servicing Commandos, who made captured airfields operational. Then there were the *Raiding Forces, who by this stage in the war had primarily an intelligence-gathering function and included the commandos in part. Finally, there were those who operated behind the enemy lines, with the resistance or partisans (also the function of SOE), or independently, as in the case of the SAS in Italy and France (see COONEY TEAMS) and the Chindits in Burma.

Special Forces provided an escape for many who were frustrated by the strict confines of conventional soldiering, but often they were those that their units could ill afford to lose. The consequent resentment, and the significant number of abortive operations during the first half of the war, gave Special Forces a bad name in many quarters. However, once it was realized that they could be a valuable weapon if their activities were closely tied to overall theatre plans—and that they often required the close support of all three armed forces—they became very much more effective and undoubtedly justified the effort put in to creating and nurturing them.

CHARLES MESSENGER

8. Intelligence

Each of the armed services included a few secret or very secret branches—planning staffs, designers of future equipment, cipher staffs, wireless interception or Y-Service staffs. Moreover, there were several secret services, so classified—officially undiscussable in parliament, in the press, in open correspondence, or on unscrambled telephones. Unlike the German *Abwehr, these were separate organizations and therefore prone to rivalry and intrigue.

The oldest and weightiest of these, generally known as *MI5, the security service, and *MI6, the secret (or special) intelligence service (SIS), dated back formally to a cabinet decision in 1909, though both had earlier and deeper roots. They were numbered as being part of the Directorate of Military Intelligence (see Table 7), but were independent of it. In principle, MI5 was a defensive body, whose writ ran within the crown's territories and 4.8 km. (3 mi.) out to sea beyond them, while the more offensive MI6 operated into foreign countries. They were powerful, although if any arrests were necessary they had to be made by the ordinary civil police force. In practice, MI5 needed some outstations outside the empire; there were joint MI5–MI6 missions in New York, called *British Security Co-ordination and in Cairo, called *Security Intelligence Middle East, as well as in New Delhi and elsewhere.

Under MI5, though transferred to MI6 in May 1941, came the Radio Security Service (RSS), which listened to every broadcast made on British soil and investigated any that were unauthorized. Also under MI5 came the *Royal Victoria Patriotic Schools at Wandsworth in south London.

Technically under the head of MI6—though, as it developed, both larger and more important than its nominal master—came the Government Code and Cypher School, the cover name for the decipher service which was located at *Bletchley Park. This interservice body was of cardinal importance for strategy and quite beyond price (see ULTRA); its diplomatic role, no doubt also important, remains unexplored as most of the files are still closed.

MI6's supposed monopoly on overseas operations outside crown territories was broken by the formation in December 1939 of *MI9 the escape service. MI9's head also controlled MI19, which dealt with intelligence from *prisoners-of-war and from refugees from occupied territory; MI19 ran the Combined Services' Detailed Interrogation Centre (CSDIC).

A more formidable rival overseas to MI6 was SOE (Special Operations Executive) set up in July 1940 to organize sabotage and subversion in enemy-occupied territory, which grew to be an almost world-wide body, with a perceptible impact on the course of the war. SOE originally included a propaganda branch, which was wrested from it in August 1941 to become the *Political Warfare Executive, also of worldwide reach and closely controlled by the foreign office.

The smallest and most secret service was the London Controlling Section (LCS) which ran deception. It depended largely on Bletchley Park for information about how far the Germans took the baits that it laid, and on a small branch of MI5, B1a (see XX-COMMITTEE), which handled *double agents through whom the LCS could influence German intelligence opinion and even reach Hitler himself.

All these secret services in fact needed to co-operate, though they often purported to be rivals; and inter-service *rivalries did sometimes do actual harm—for instance, when MI6 withheld for some months from MI5 decipher material vital for MI5's progress in the business of double-crossing the Germans. A self-appointed body, the W Board, met occasionally to co-ordinate them all. It consisted of the heads of the regular service intelligence departments and of MI5 and of MI6. The XX-Committee was, formally, a sub-committee of the W Board. Later in the war the task of co-ordination was taken over by Victor Cavendish-Bentinck who forged in the Joint Intelligence Committee a body of central significance. A sub-committee of the British Chiefs of Staff committee, it comprised the three service heads of intelligence, and the heads of MI5 and MI6. Between them they analysed such intelligence as was available, advised the Chiefs of Staff about probable Axis moves, and supervised the dissemination of intelligence through the armed forces.

All in all, the secret services deserved reasonably well of their country. Traditionally, work in them was supposed to be its own reward, but they were not wholly overlooked when it came to handing out *decorations.

M. R. D. FOOT

UK, Table 7: British directorate of military intelligence *c.*1942

MI1	administration
MI2	E. Europe and Asia
MI3	W. Europe and Americas
MI4	maps
MI5	security[a]
MI6	espionage[a]
MI7	press[b]
MI8	signals
MI9	Allied prisoners; escapes and evasions
MI10	technical
MI11	field security police
MI12	postal security[b]
MI14	Germany
MI15	photographic reconnaissance
MI16	science
MI17	co-ordination
MI19	enemy prisoners; refugees from Continent
MIL	liaison with Allies
CMIR	research[c]
MIX	intelligence corps

[a] secret service, independent of DMI
[b] later handed over to Ministry of Information
[c] absorbed into SOE 1940

Source: Contributor.

9. Merchant marine

Britain's dependence on merchant shipping was an economic fact which total war heavily underlined. In addition to the need to import huge quantities of food and *raw materials, soldiers and airmen had to be shipped overseas, equipped, and then sustained. The shipping industry—which became the Merchant Navy in wartime—was so stretched that maintenance of supplies to the UK and the armed forces overseas was regularly in crisis for the first four years of the war. It was not until 1944, when regular deliveries of US mass-produced *Liberty ships to the British merchant fleet had been established, that shortages were overcome.

The shipping crisis had little to do with the operation and management of merchant ships. Shipowners, though generally conservative, were effective managers and seafarers were competent. In 1939 the British merchant fleet was still the world's largest, accounting for some 33% of total tonnage. The country's share had shrunk by some 12% since 1914, but this was only to be expected as economic development unfolded in other world regions. British shipowners, however, had been slow to build tankers and in the tramp traders had lagged behind in adopting diesel propulsion. Technological backwardness was common also among the cargo liner companies. While they owned the fastest and most up-to-date ships in the UK, they were still outstripped by best practice in Scandinavia, Germany, and the Netherlands. The problem lay largely with the shipbuilding industry. Even in the inter-war period British yards were notoriously inefficient and in the war years they proved incapable of raising productivity sufficiently to make a significant contribution to repairing the losses due to enemy action.

If the first cause of the permanent wartime shipping crisis lay in the deficiencies of the shipbuilding industry, the second lay in the inability of the Admiralty to provide adequate protection for merchant ships in convoy. UK coastal and outward North Atlantic convoying began within a matter of days of the outbreak of war and within a month inward convoys were organized from Freetown, Gibraltar, and Halifax, Nova Scotia. Routine convoy organization of mustering and then controlling merchant ships in formation quickly became efficient. The problem lay in the Royal Navy's lack of suitable escort ships and anti-submarine tactics, resulting in high losses of merchant ships during the battle of the Atlantic. Air cover and statistical analysis of U-boat operations were also critical and it was not until mid-1943 that all the elements were in place (see AIR GAP).

The first phase of managing the shipping crisis saw the gradual integration into the British fleet of shipping from other European countries which had evaded German occupation (see Table 8). Politically unwilling to attempt requisition even where feasible, the British government sought to negotiate with governments-in-exile and foreign shipowners. On average, 26% of the Norwegian, Danish, Dutch, and Belgian fleets were in their

UK, Table 8: Dry-cargo merchant shipping under British control, 1,600 gross tons and over, 3 September 1939 to 30 September 1945 (In thousand deadweight tons)

		British flag			*Foreign vessles*		*Foreign[a] flag vessels time-chartered to United Kingdom*
	Total	*Total*	*United Kingdom and Colonies*	*Dominions*	*Bareboat charter*	*Requisitioned*	
1939							
Sept 3	18,710	18,710	17,691	1,019	–	–	–
Dec 31	18,579	18,418	17,314	1,096	8	–	161
1940							
Mar 31	18,764	18,403	17,258	1,102	43	–	361
June 30	21,096	18,911	17,264	1,276	68	303	2,185
Sept 30	23,459	19,831	17,718	1,343	45	725	3,628
Dec 31	21,963	18,453	16,362	1,330	46	715	3,510
1941							
Mar 31	21,622	18,050	15,858	1,305	81	806	3,572
June 30	20,858	17,037	14,828	1,282	131	796	3,821
Sept 30	21,115	17,085	14,807	1,302	153	823	4,030
Dec 31	21,324	17,221	14,851	1,316	206	848	4,103
1942							
Mar 31	20,994	16,809	14,452	1,272	245	840	4,185
June 30	20,505	16,336	13,921	1,250	346	819	4,169
Sept 30	19,722	15,826	13,333	1,219	488	786	3,896
Dec 31	18,758	15,135	12,411	1,225	826	673	3,623
1943							
Mar 31	18,449	14,937	12,059	1,168	1,066	644	3,512
June 30	18,528	15,067	11,514	1,480	1,456	617	3,461
Sept 30	19,163	15,725	11,810	1,746	1,548	621	3,438
Dec 31	20,082	16,738	11,801	2,232	2,093	612	3,344
1944							
Mar 31	20,765	17,426	11,892	2,364	2,546	624	3,339
June 30	21,967	18,245	11,996	2,650	2,997	602	3,722
Sept 30	21,962	18,282	11,841	2,901	2,971	569	3,680
Dec 31	22,225	18,597	12,000	3,104	2,945	548	3,628
1945							
Mar 31	22,228	18,638	11,996	3,202	2,910	530	3,590
June 30	22,143	18,844	12,234	3,246	2,918	446	3,299
Sept 30	21,210	19,043	12,426	3,345	2,977	295	2,167

[a] for the earlier months of the war the information about foreign flag vessels on time-charter is incomplete

Source: *Statistical Digest of the War*, Table 153; Behrens, C. B. A., *Merchant Shipping and the Demands of War* (London, 1955).

home ports and captured during German *occupation. While none of those ships away on voyages returned home, they did not all rally to the British cause with equal enthusiasm. Most Danish shipowners were pro-German and ordered their masters to put into neutral ports. About half did so. The remaining ships, although still manned by Danes, were seized and sailed thereafter under the British flag. The whole of the much smaller Belgian fleet was made available to the UK. The most significant fleets were the Norwegian and the Dutch and half of each were sailing under British direction by November 1939. Greek ships were a later and important addition. Approximately half a million tons of French shipping came into British hands after the fall of France in June 1940—but this was almost exactly matched by the tonnage of British ships caught in French ports at the same time.

By the spring of 1941 the crisis reached another peak when estimates of importing capacity were steadily reduced from 42 million tons to 28.5 million tons—less than had been imported in 1917. Relief came from the USA as elderly, laid-up ships were released on bareboat charter (that is, without crews) and French, Italian, and Yugoslav ships being held in US ports were requisitioned and handed over to the British. The shipping crisis was not resolved by American entry into the war: indeed, early in 1943, as a result of the shipping needed to mount and supply the Anglo-American North African campaign landings, the situation was worse than in 1941. Again, resolution depended upon American help—this time by the USA agreeing to divert shipping from the Pacific to the Atlantic.

Formal ownership of merchant shipping was left unchanged although the government, via the Ministry of Shipping, incorporated into the Ministry of War Transport (MOWT) in May 1941, had requisitioned all vessels by the summer of 1940 and agreed terms with the owners. The ministry now decided where ships would go and what cargoes should be carried. Senior managers and directors were recruited from shipping companies to ministry posts for the duration of the war while other shore staffs continued to organize crewing, provisioning, and maintenance of ships. Shareholders, for their part, had their dividends regulated. In short, the general direction, management, and operation of shipping remained in the hands of those who had run the industry in the pre-war years.

It was a combination of MOWT direction and Admiralty control of merchant shipping at sea which justified the use of the term 'Merchant Navy'. This honorific title was conferred on the industry in 1928 when the Prince of Wales adopted the title 'Master of the Merchant Navy and Fishing Fleets' in recognition of merchant seafarers' role in the First World War. From 1936 successive monarchs adopted the title. In peacetime the industry had no more coherence than any other and the title had only the substance of rhetoric. In wartime, however, the industry did indeed become a quasi-service and the fourth arm of the state.

In the first nine months of war, 150 ships were sunk. These early losses were made good through new building and captured Axis ships. The need for additional ships did not become a matter of pressing urgency until after the fall of France and Italy's entry into the war. The former entailed the closure of the English Channel to deep-sea ships while the latter closed the Suez route to the east. The route to UK east coast ports was now via the north of Scotland, adding eleven days to merchant ships' average voyage length. Ships supplying the armed forces in the Middle East had now to go via the Cape of Good Hope and travel 21,000 km. (13,000 mi.) instead of 4,800 km. (3,000 mi.) as before; Bombay was now nearly 18,000 km. (11,000 mi.) distant instead of 9,600 km. (6,000 mi.). These and other re-routings, together with delays such as those involved in assembling convoys, led to an increase in average round voyage time from about 90 to 122 days and effectively reduced importing capacity by 25%.

Ships' patterns of trading were, of course, transformed. A handful of the smaller passenger ships continued their normal services to India and Australia but 50 of this type of ship, together with most of their officers and crew, were transferred to the Royal Navy to become *armed merchant cruisers. The remainder of the deep-sea passenger ships were used for trooping. The larger and faster of these had originally been designed for the North Atlantic routes but now travelled world-wide. Cargo liners, also built for particular trades, were retained as far as possible for their normal routes and cargoes. Refrigerated ships designed for the Argentinian and Australasian meat trades, for example, continued to sail to those regions. Tramps, on the other hand, no longer scoured the globe in seasonal search of bulk cargoes and were overwhelmingly employed in the main North Atlantic supply line. Ships in the coastal trade mostly stayed in UK waters although a number were sent to the Mediterranean in 1942 to supply troops in that theatre. Some 24 North Sea and home trade passenger ships were allocated more heroic tasks. They sailed with the Atlantic and Arctic convoys as rescue ships.

Some merchant ships were cast in unaccustomed roles. A number were adapted to launch aircraft to help protect the convoys in which they sailed (see CAM and MAC SHIPS); and, beginning in 1943, five high-speed MGBs, crewed by merchant seamen, operated from Hull, on the English eastern coast, as *blockade runners.

In 1938 there were 192,375 persons employed on British merchant ships, 50,700 of whom were Indian and Chinese. Constant official anxiety about the adequacy of shipping capacity, and heightened public awareness of dependence upon imports, focused an unusual degree of attention on merchant seamen. On the one hand they were uniformly portrayed in films, books, newspapers, magazines and radio programmes as archetypal stoical Britons who without fuss brought home food and the *matériel* of war. On the other hand, and quietly, Defence Regulations and the disciplinary provisions of the Merchant Shipping Acts were used by shipmasters, magistrates, and consuls to fine and gaol seafarers for shipboard offences in the UK and abroad on a scale without precedent. Another and wholly new disciplinary problem was provided by the Indian and Chinese seamen: hitherto considered docile, they engaged respectively in strikes and mass desertions as they successfully attempted to close the gap between their own and British seamen's wages. For their part, industrial action by British crews was rare. Although seafarers' average working week (before overtime) was ten hours longer than the all-industry average, and shipboard conditions were greatly inferior to those of Norwegians, monthly rates of pay had become relatively good and paid leave and continuity of employment were introduced for the first time. At no time during the war was there a scarcity of men to match the scarcity of ships. At those rare moments when seafarers were in short supply numbers were made up by recruitment in Aden and the West

Indies as they had been in the First World War. When the war ended 29,180 merchant seamen had died and some 4,700 British-flagged ships had been sunk. TONY LANE

10. Culture

The outpouring of cultural activities and achievements in the UK during the years of the Second World War, notable at the time, seems in retrospect a truly remarkable, even unparalleled phenomenon. The achievements at their most impressive, and, as it has turned out, at their most enduring, have transcended national boundaries and historical circumstances to become a permanent part of western culture in the 20th century. Even the most selective list would include Virginia Woolf's *Between the Acts*, George Orwell's *Animal Farm*, T. S. Eliot's *Four Quartets*, the poems of Dylan Thomas gathered in *Deaths and Entrances*, the wartime films by Humphrey Jennings, especially *Fires Were Started*, the 'Shelter Drawings' by Henry Moore, and Benjamin Britten's first true opera, *Peter Grimes*. These are the examples that immediately come to mind but they were not isolated achievements. Rather, they can be seen as the most outstanding in their respective genres, surrounded by an impressive array of work approaching them in quality.

Indeed, to have so distinguished a creative outpouring in a period of six years would be remarkable at any time. That it should have occurred in wartime, in a country engaged in a struggle that threatened its very existence, seems almost incredible.

There seems to have been, from the first, a determination on the part of such responsible and farseeing public figures as the economist John Maynard Keynes and the art critic Kenneth Clark, editors such as John Lehmann of *Penguin New Writing* and Cyril Connolly of *Horizon*, and senior authors such as E. M. Forster and Osbert Sitwell that 'culture' was not to be put aside 'for the duration'; in the act of fighting to save the UK, the nation's culture must not be sacrificed. The commitment of the government to art in all its manifestations was established as a principle early on. The creation of the War Artists's Advisory Committee, under Clark, and of the Committee for the Encouragement of Music and the Arts, under Keynes, would play a significant role in bringing art to the people even as the Blitz brought the war itself into their lives. The 'Home Front', a cosy-sounding phrase, was anything but comfortable as the bombs fell night after night on London, Manchester, Coventry, and elsewhere. Life in the wartime years went on at something like battle pitch. The emotional level was high, and it was a level at which it was possible for artists, composers, and writers to create works of art—not as a way of escape, but to express the tension under which they lived. But their mood at the start of the war was subdued and was well captured by C. Day Lewis. In answer to the call for heroic war verse, he wrote: 'It is the logic of our times, / No subject for immortal verse— / That we who lived by honest dreams / Defend the bad against the worse.'

Perhaps the most emblematic events of the role of culture in the UK during the Second World War were the concerts given at the National Gallery in London (cleared of its pictures in anticipation of the bombing raids). From 10 October 1939, when they started with Myra Hess playing Beethoven's 'Appassionata' sonata and her own arrangement of Bach's 'Jesu, Joy of Man's Desiring', until 1945, there were 1,698 concerts by 700 performers attended by a total audience of 825,000.

Severe paper rationing was soon instituted and created a shortage of reading material, just at a time when long periods of boring wartime duty gave people more time to read. Penguin Books, eminent in the cheap paperback market since the mid-1930s with books priced at sixpence (under 3p) each, provided a mass of crime and adventure stories, suitable for reading in air-raid shelters, as well as more serious books, both literary and political. Largely through Penguin's influence, books began to form part of the English domestic furniture in a much wider range of houses than had been the case before the war—another foretaste of a new age.

John Lehmann had started to edit a book magazine, *New Writing*, before the war broke out, but it transformed itself quite rapidly into *Penguin New Writing*, a highly popular paperback that reprinted old material as well as new pieces, frequently by Europeans and by servicemen. Even more an exponent of high art was *Horizon*, edited by Cyril Connolly, committed to the best of European culture, with a slightly disdainful attitude towards the war. Distractions at all levels were prized, and the long novels of Trollope enjoyed a revival that has lasted to the present day.

In literature it was not necessarily those who were directly involved in the war who wrote the most memorable works, among them T. S. Eliot, Virginia Woolf, and George Orwell, who published powerful essays dwelling on what was the essence of the good parts of English life, and on the necessity of keeping language honest against the claims of propaganda.

More directly depicting the effect of war on the Home Front were the novels and stories of Elizabeth Bowen, and the stories of the fire service by William Sansom. Otherwise, there seemed to be two main streams in the writings of the war. There was a high Bohemian and romantic strand found in what came to be known as Fitzrovia, centring on the personal style, and the poetry, of Dylan Thomas, the short stories of J. Maclaren-Ross, and James Tambimuttu and his *Poetry (London)*. The emphasis was upon the personal, as in the developments to be found in one of the more public of the 1930s poets: Stephen Spender. Yet they wrote about the war, as in some of the best known of Thomas's poems, 'Deaths and Entrances' and 'A Refusal to Mourn the Death, by Fire, of a Child in London'. There were also extremely fine soldier poets such as Alun Lewis (killed in Burma), Roy Fuller, Keith Douglas (killed in

Normandy in 1944), and Henry Reed whose well-known poem 'The Naming of Parts' is characteristic of the rueful irony that was the dominant note in the poetry of the time. There are two voices in it—the sergeant's, explaining the different parts of the rifle; and the civilian soldier's which gives the military phrases a private meaning.

> Today we have naming of parts. Yesterday,
> We had daily cleaning. And to-morrow morning,
> We shall have what to do after firing. But to-day,
> To-day we have naming of parts. Japonica
> Glistens like coral in all of the neighbouring gardens,
> And to-day we have naming of parts.

At a more popular level, Patience Strong, the pen-name of Winifred Cushing, wrote a set of verses for every issue of the *Daily Mirror* and *Sunday Pictorial* for 40 years, including all those of the war. Through a mixture of sentiment, piety, and common sense she helped to sustain the morale of several million readers, and ran an unofficial forces' welfare bureau. The monthly magazine *Lilliput* also had its attractions, for in every number, supported by short stories, nature photographs, and snippets of news, was an artistic photograph of a naked girl; and in spite of the paper shortage, there was a steady demand for sporting and popular newspapers (see PRESS).

Other than controlling paper, and hence restricting how many books could be printed, there was little official influence on what was published in the ordinary way. But in other aspects, the government was deeply involved, most notably in the world of art and the newest medium of all, the cinema. This was conducted through the new Ministry of Information, which in the course of the war helped produce 1,887 films as well as vetting 3,200 newsreels and 380 features. By 1942, these films, or others approved by the ministry, were being shown to 20–30 million filmgoers weekly. The ministry was not in charge of making commercial films but its approval (and also financing) was extremely important in terms of supplies and exemption from armed service of those involved. Perhaps the most famous made during the war were *Henry V* (1945), starring and produced by Laurence Olivier, and *In Which We Serve* (1942), starring and produced by Noël Coward. In vastly different ways, they both emphasized quiet heroism by all classes. The line between documentaries and commercial films was blurred, with documentaries, moving on from the tradition of John Grierson, likely to have somewhat more plot than they had had before, and commercial films having some sense of the actuality of war. Perhaps the most distinguished documentary, or rather docu-drama, of the war was Humphrey Jennings's *Fires Were Started* (1942). It told of 24 hours in the life of a fire service unit in London during the Blitz which had ended the previous year. The Germans were not mentioned by name, and the emphasis, with very little sentimentality, was on carrying on with the job, even at the cost of a life.

What were the contribution of those in the visual arts? Artists were to provide a record of the war; and in some instances, though it was very much a lesser consideration, they might even create something of greater artistic merit. That had certainly been true of such painters as Paul Nash, Stanley Spencer, and Wyndham Lewis in the First World War, so there was little resistance to the idea that something similar should be encouraged during this war as well. In August 1939, Kenneth Clark proposed a War Artists' Advisory Committee to the Ministry of Information and it came into being the following January.

A few artists' organizations outside the government had been already formed by that time, such as Paul Nash's Oxford Art Bureau. Nash was concerned that artists might too hastily be called up as servicemen, and he established a panel of authorities—John Betjeman, Lord David Cecil, Lord Berners, and John Piper—to compile lists of possible *war artists, and the lists were sent to ministries. But Nash's efforts were superseded by Clark's committee, which would appoint certain artists as official war artists and have the right of first refusal for all of their work.

Thanks to the war artists' scheme important work was done outside the UK by such painters as Anthony Gross, Eric Ravilious, Edward Bawden, Leonard Rosoman, and Edward Ardizzone. Yet it is striking that the greatest art work of the war was produced on the Home Front. Not only were there Moore and Sutherland in London, but Stanley Spencer paintings in the shipyards on the Clyde and Paul Nash with extraordinary paintings of fighter planes in the air war over Britain, culminating in the greatest single oil masterpiece of the war, *Totes Meer* (*Dead Sea*) of wrecked German planes. It was perhaps the most extensive patronage scheme for British artists that has ever existed, and it resulted in nearly 6,000 works of art, eventually most of them distributed to museums, with the Tate Gallery and the Imperial War Museum having the first pick. It also resulted in a higher evaluation placed by the public, and those who were seriously concerned with art, upon British art not only of the present but of the past.

Light music was for everyone and wartime Britain was deluged with it. It came primarily from the *BBC and from innumerable private or public-house gramophones, playing fragile 78 r.p.m. records. 'Music while you work', an American slogan imported in the 1930s, helped to relieve monotony in war factories, where the machinery was not too noisy to drown out the music. Jack Payne and Henry Hall, dance band leaders, were better known than most generals.

So were Gracie Fields the comedienne and Vera Lynn the singer, who sang mixtures of old favourites and new, sentimental songs. Gracie Fields with her Lancashire accent and working-class airs was a symbol of the growing power of democracy, and Vera Lynn's good looks enchanted thousands of serving men at forces' concerts. Theatres and music-halls suffered severely from blackout and call-up—acting was not a reserved occupation; but, by arrangement with the service ministries, many actors and actresses were spared call-up if they consented to take part in travelling shows to entertain the armed forces.

Air attack damaged many theatres and put many more out of business. One that was proud to boast, after the war, that 'We never closed' was the Windmill Theatre off Piccadilly Circus, in central London.

The BBC competed, often with success, against theatres and cinemas as a vehicle of popular entertainment. One show in particular, Ted Kavanagh's ITMA ('It's That Man Again'), starring Tommy Handley, was reckoned to have 16 million listeners every Thursday evening, among whom George VI was one of the most devoted. ITMA gently satirized wartime bureaucracy, in a dazzling interchange of epigrams and catch-phrases, many of which passed into the common currency of speech.

M. R. D. FOOT/PETER STANSKY

Domestic Life, economy and war effort
Addison, P., *The Road to 1945: British Politics and The Second World War* (London, 1975).
Barnett, C., *The Audit of War* (London, 1986).
Calder, A., *The People's War: Britain 1939–1945* (London, 1969).
Jefferys, K., *The Churchill Coalition and Wartime Politics 1940–1945* (Manchester, 1991).
Marwick, A., *The Home Front* (London, 1976).
Smith, H. (ed.), *War and Social Change: British Society in the Second World War* (Manchester, 1986).

Government
Addison, P., op. cit.
Jefferys, K., op. cit.
Lee, J. M., *The Churchill Coalition* (London, 1980).
Schoenfeld, M. P., *The War Ministry of Winston Churchill* (Iowa, 1972).

Northern Ireland
Blake, J. W., *Northern Ireland in the Second World War* (Belfast, 1956).

Armed forces and Special Forces
Barnett, C., *Engage the Enemy More Closely: The Royal Navy in the Second World War* (London, 1991).
Fraser, D., *And We Shall Shock Them: The British Army in the Second World War* (London, 1983).
Messenger, C., *The Commandos 1940–1946* (London, 1991).
Richards, D., and Saunders, H., *The Royal Air Force 1939–45*, 3 vols. (London, 1974).
Seymour, W., *British Special Forces* (London, 1985).
Terraine, J., *The Right of the Line: The Royal Air Force in the European War 1939–1945* (London, 1985).

Intelligence
Hinsley, F. H., *et al., British Intelligence in the Second World War*, 4 vols. (London, 1978–90).

Merchant marine
Behrens, C. B. A., *Merchant Shipping and the Demands of War* (London, 1955).
Lane, T., *The Merchant Seamen's War* (Manchester, 1990).

Culture
Aldgate A., and Richards, J., *Britain Can Take It: The British Cinema in the Second World War* (Oxford, 1986).
Blythe, R. (ed.), *Writing in a War: Stories, Poems and Essays of 1939–1945* (Harmondsworth, 1982).
Coultass, C., *Images for Battle: British Film and the Second World War, 1939–1945* (London, 1989).
Davin D., *Short Stories from the Second World War* (Oxford, 1982).
Foot, M. R. D., *Art and War* (London, 1990).
Harries, M. and S., *The War Artists* (London, 1983).
Haskell, A., Powell, D., Myers, R., Ironside, R., *Ballet, Films, Music, Painting Since 1939* (London, 1948).
Hewison, R., *Under Siege: Literary Life in London, 1939–45* (London, 1977).
Ross, A., *Colours of War* (London, 1983).

Ukraine (see Maps 104 and 105). Arguably, no other European country suffered as much as Ukraine during the Second World War. The calamities that befell it then added to the agonies of a people whose eastern lands had only a few years earlier been subjected to Stalinist terror, including the politically engineered famine of 1932–3 which caused an estimated 7 million deaths.

Historically, Ukraine's western territories had been partitioned between the Polish, Romanian, Hungarian, and Czechoslovak states and on 1 September 1939, at the start of the *Polish campaign, its eastern part was one of the constituent republics of the USSR. It was therefore a nation, not a sovereign state. But its Slavic people had for long struggled for the unification of their country and their independence from the Russian and Soviet empires—a struggle which partly came to fruition for certain periods between 1917 and 1921 when Ukraine became an independent republic.

Surprisingly, Ukraine's wartime experiences are little understood. Many students of the war overlook Ukraine altogether. They often classify Ukrainians as Russians or over-emphasize the image of Ukrainians welcoming the Germans as liberators. Ukraine is not Russia, as Ukrainians have asserted throughout modern times; and, rather than being overjoyed by the German invasion, most Ukrainians were cautious, welcoming the overthrow of an increasingly oppressive Soviet regime but remaining suspicious of the new overlords. It is ironic then that most non-Ukrainian historians have accepted views similar either to those of Soviet propaganda or to that of the Nazi officials who declared that: 'Ukraine does not exist ... it is merely a geographical concept.' They have forgotten what the American journalist Edgar Snow wrote on 27 January 1945 in the *Saturday Evening Post*: 'This whole titanic struggle, which some are apt to dismiss as "the Russian Glory" has been, in all truth and in many costly ways, first of all a Ukrainian war ... No single European country has suffered deeper wounds to its cities, its industry, its farmlands and its humanity.'

Ukrainian lands were first embroiled in conflict on 15 March 1939, when Hungarian troops, with the approval of Nazi Germany and fascist Italy, invaded Ruthenia (Carpatho-Ukraine). They quickly overwhelmed this small country, which had emerged in the wake of Czechoslovakia's dissolution after the *Munich agreement of September 1938, although indigenous self-defence units and Ukrainian nationalists from western Ukraine attempted resistance. A policy of Magyarization was imposed on the region for the next five and half years, after which it was absorbed into Soviet Ukraine.

The next Ukrainian territories to be occupied were

Ukraine

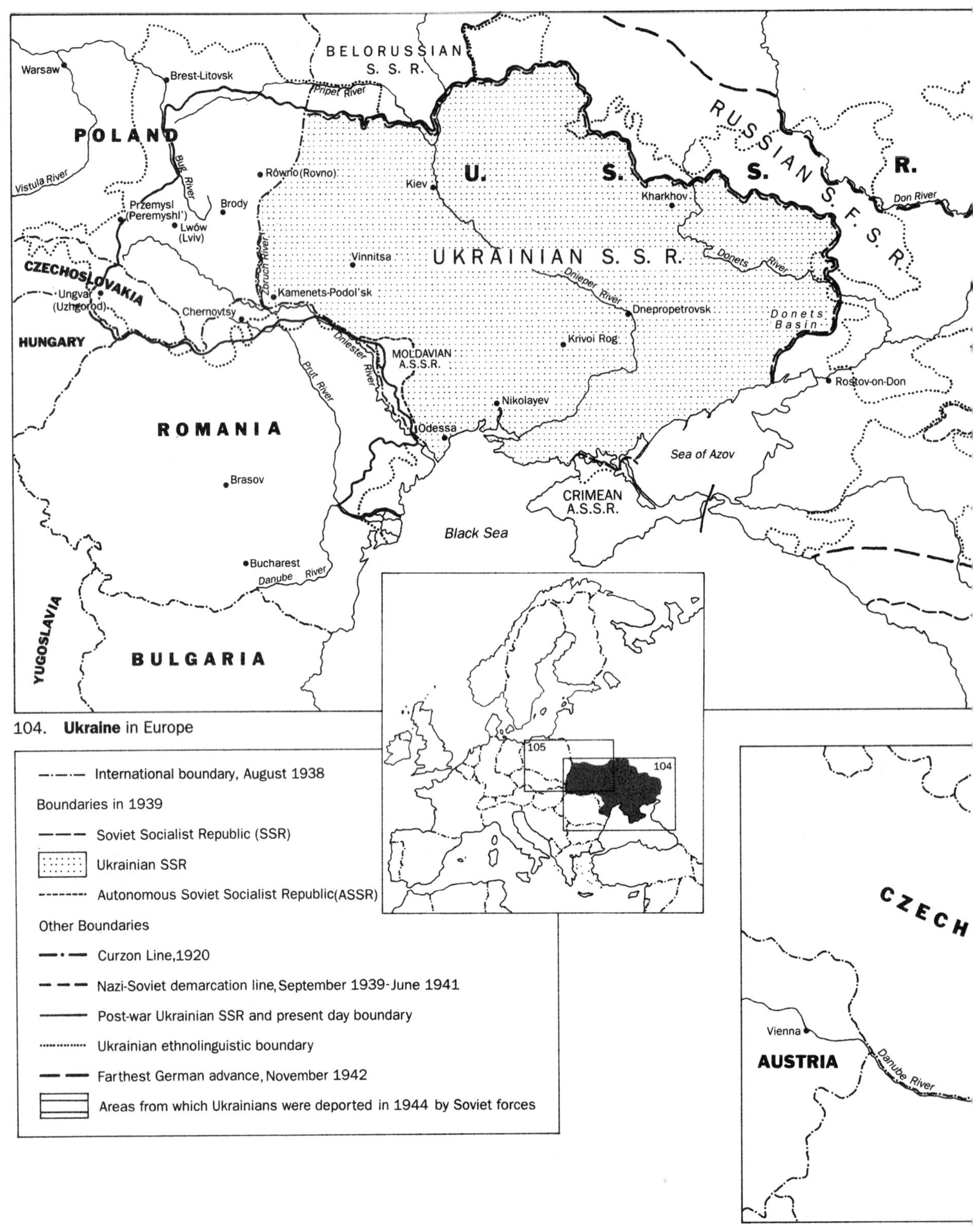

104. **Ukraine** in Europe

105. Western **Ukraine**

Galicia and *Volhynia, controlled by Poland in the inter-war period and assigned to the Soviets by the *Nazi–Soviet Pact. In concert with the Germans, the Red Army moved in on 17 September 1939, ostensibly to protect the Ukrainian and Belorussian populations in Poland. The lands east of the San and Bug rivers were annexed by 1 November 1939 to the Ukrainian SSR, a process continued with the incorporation of the formerly Romanian-dominated areas of northern Bukovina and parts of Bessarabia in June 1940, again with the acquiescence of Germany. The first mass movement of Ukrainian refugees began at this time when some 20,000–30,000 fled from the Soviet-held zone into the General Government which had been set up by the Germans to control what remained of Poland. These refugees joined nearly half a million Ukrainians in the Lemko, southern Podlachia, and Chełm regions, which had passed under German control after the dismemberment of Poland. It was from this population, particularly from the refugees clustered around Cracow, that the Ukrainian Central Committee, headed by Professor Volodymyr Kubijovyć, was formed. The committee, while avoiding *collaboration with the Nazis, nevertheless attempted to protect Ukrainian interests by instituting educational, social welfare, co-operative, and cultural programmes, efforts that were modestly successful in easing the burden of occupation.

After western Ukraine's incorporation into the USSR, and a brief period of Ukrainianization, the *NKVD, the Soviet secret police, began consolidating control through arrests, *deportations, and executions. More than a million Polish citizens, including Poles, Ukrainians, and Jews, were affected. According to a letter from Metropolitan Andrei Sheptytsky, the influential primate of the Greek Catholic Church in western Ukraine, which was sent to the Vatican on 7 November 1941, some 400,000 Ukrainians fell victim as members of the intelligentsia, clergymen, political figures, and nationalists were killed or dispatched to the *GUlag in Siberia and Kazakhstan. During their hurried retreat from these same territories in the summer of 1941, NKVD forces again committed war crimes, massacring more than 19,000 political prisoners in *Lwów (L'viv), Sambor (Sambir), Stanisłowów (Stanyslaviv), Równo (Rivne), Łuck (Lutsk), and elsewhere. For example, recent excavations at two Ukrainian cities, now called Drohobych and Ternopil, have uncovered victims' remains and there is no doubt as to who was responsible.

Mass death and destruction were unleashed on Soviet Ukraine when the German invasion began on 22 June 1941 (see BARBAROSSA). By 19 September 1941 the capital, Kiev, was taken and Ukraine's second city, Kharkov, fell on 24 October. In the south, Germany's ally Romania occupied Ukrainian lands between the Bug and Dniester rivers and renamed them Transnistria. By the time the furthest eastward advance of the German armies was attained, in the summer of 1942, when the front stretched along the River Don to Stalingrad on the Volga, and Kuban region, the whole of Soviet Ukraine had been encompassed. By way of comparison, only a small fraction of Russian territory was occupied.

In what has been described as one of the largest evacuations in history, the retreating Soviets moved about 1,500 factories and more than 10 million people to the Urals and Central Asia, more than a third of these from Ukraine. Ufa, the capital of the Bashkir republic, became the wartime seat of the Soviet Ukrainian government. A *scorched earth policy destroyed what could not be moved. In this period Kiev suffered more damage from the retreating Soviets than from the advancing Germans. In the Donets basin most mines were flooded, the huge Dnieper hydroelectric power works were blown up and all of Ukraine's 54 blast furnaces were destroyed. When the tide turned against Germany in the winter of 1943 the retreating German troops obeyed a similar order from Hitler and created a 'zone of destruction' east of the River *Dnieper.

German-occupied Ukraine was divided into three sectors. The land closest to the front came under direct military rule. Galicia and Volhynia in contrast were added to other occupied Polish territory as the fifth district of the General Government, ruled from Cracow by Hans *Frank (August 1941). His attitude towards the peoples in his domain was reflected in a speech delivered on 14 January 1944: 'Once we have won the war, then for all I care, mincemeat can be made of the Poles and the Ukrainians and all the others who run around here.' Most Ukrainian lands, however, were included in the Reichskomissariat Ukraine, presided over by *Gauleiter Erich Koch, whose administrative centre became the Volhynian city of Równo (Rivne). The treatment of civilians differed in each of these territories, with probably the worst befalling those in Koch's jurisdiction. A fanatical Nazi who described himself as 'a brutal dog' mandated 'to suck from Ukraine all the goods we can get hold of, without consideration for the feelings or the property of the Ukrainians', Koch declared that 'if I find a Ukrainian who is worthy of sitting at the same table with me, I must have him shot.'

Germany's brutal and irrational policies in Ukraine were one of the great wartime blunders. The Nazi leadership held a racist conception of eastern Europe in which Ukraine was nothing more than a colonial **Lebensraum* (living-space) fated to be ruled over by an Aryan *Herrenvolk* (master race) whose duties included the eradication or enslavement of the native population, referred to as *Untermenschen* (subhumans). Instead of exploiting the national aspirations of Ukrainians and other peoples subjugated by the Soviet empire, the Nazis attempted to set up an empire of their own.

Through overseers such as Koch, the Nazis hoped to terrorize the population of Ukraine into submission. A mass destruction of the intelligentsia was orchestrated; thousands of hostages, including *women and *children, were executed, and millions were sent to the Third Reich as *forced labour. Others were incarcerated in *concentration camps or simply massacred, including

600,000 Jews (see FINAL SOLUTION). But instead of cowing the Ukrainians the Nazis' behaviour provoked large-scale resistance and a new Ukrainian patriotism. Although a communist partisan movement emerged, enjoying Soviet military and political support, the core of the national Ukrainian resistance was formed by the Organization of Ukrainian Nationalists (OUN), a revolutionary movement in existence from 1929. A significant political force in Polish-controlled Ukraine in the inter-war period, the OUN was weakened after February 1940 when it fractured into two competing movements. Members of the younger generation, more militant and uncompromising than their elders, broke with Colonel Andrii Melnyk (OUN-M) to form a new revolutionary leadership headed by Stepan *Bandera (OUN-B). Attempting to take advantage of the Soviet retreat and resulting chaos, the OUN-B proclaimed an independent Ukrainian state in Lwów on 30 June 1941.

The Germans had no intention of recognizing an independent Ukraine. Within days of its formation the government was disbanded and most of its leaders were imprisoned, both Bandera and Yaroslav *Stetsko, the prime minister, being sent to *Sachsenhausen concentration camp, where they remained until the autumn of 1944. Many members of OUN-B expeditionary groups, who had moved into eastern Ukraine in the wake of the advancing Germans to press for Ukrainian independence, fell prey to the mobile killing units of the **Einsatzgruppen* or were imprisoned. The OUN-M, which founded a Ukrainian National Council in Kiev on 5 October 1941, was also suppressed. Melnyk was placed under house arrest in 1941 and, in January 1944, imprisoned in Sachsenhausen for several months. In Ukraine itself thousands of members and supporters of the nationalist movement perished while others were executed for hiding Jews. The first determined campaign against the Ukrainian national movement, begun on 31 August 1941, had by the end of September spread throughout occupied Ukraine. By January 1942 most advocates of Ukrainian independence had been caught in the Nazi net. Under these conditions, not surprisingly, many Ukrainians concerned themselves less with resistance and more with simple survival.

Armed resistance to Nazi rule emerged first in the backwoods of Volhynia, where the Ukrainian Insurgent Army (Ukrainska povstanska armiia, or UPA) was established in 1942, based on self-defence units that had formed the year before under Taras Bulba-Borovets. After the UPA came under the control of the OUN-B, in the autumn of 1942, operations were extended throughout Polissia and into Galicia. By 1944 the UPA consisted of some 40,000 insurgents, aided by an even larger covert network of OUN members and supporters that may have reached a peak strength of 100,000, geographically concentrated in western Ukraine. Under the command of General Roman Shukhevych (*nom de guerre*, Taras Chuprynka), the UPA carried on a two-front war, first against the Nazis and then, after their defeat, against the Soviet reoccupation of Ukraine. As a result of their contact with eastern Ukrainians and wartime experience, both the OUN-B and UPA issued manifestos condemning Nazi and Soviet imperialism and affirming their commitment to political pluralism and democratic freedoms of the sort commonly associated with western liberalism. This commitment was confirmed in July 1944 after a meeting of OUN-B delegates and representatives from eastern Ukraine near Sambor, in Galicia, when the formation of the Ukrainian Supreme Liberation Council (Ukrainska Holovna Vyzvolna Rada, or UHVR) was proclaimed.

In areas of mixed ethnic settlement, such as Volhynia, Polissia, and Chełm, where Polish and Ukrainian partisans both fought to assert control over areas that they claimed, tens of thousands of civilians were slaughtered.

After the surrender of German forces at *Stalingrad the Ukrainian Central Committee supported the formation of the 14th Volunteer Grenadier Division of the Waffen-*SS, 1st Galician Division (renamed towards the end of the war as the 1st Ukrainian Division of the Ukrainian National Army). The hope that this division would constitute a nucleus around which an army could be formed for the purpose of reasserting Ukrainian independence proved false. Most of its soldiers perished in battle against the Red Army near the Galician town of Brody in mid-June 1944.

The return of Soviet forces to western Ukraine in 1944 did not quell Ukrainian resistance. The independence movement was suppressed only through the mass deportation of Ukrainians from the Lemko and Chełm regions, the forced collectivization of agriculture in 1948–51, a massive influx of Russians and the incarceration of the hierarchy of the Greek Catholic Church in the GUlag, including Sheptytsky's successor, Metropolitan Iosyf Slipy. The formal liquidation of the Greek Catholic Church, an ally of the independence movement, was accomplished through its forcible union with the Russian Orthodox Church in March 1946 (see also RELIGION).

Militarily, it took the combined action of Polish, Czechoslovak, and Soviet forces to liquidate the Ukrainian partisans, largely in the spring of 1948, in a search-and-destroy plan known as Operation VISTULA. By that time the nationalists were acting in concert with the anti-Communist Polish Home Army (Armija Krajowa, or AK) and had despatched small units to western Europe to solicit aid from the Anglo-American powers for what they described as their anti-imperialist war of *liberation against the Soviets. Their faith in the West, which never wanted a free Ukraine, proved unfounded, and the nationalist leaders concluded that independence, if it were ever to come, would have to be won by Ukrainians for themselves. Still, even without foreign aid, dispersed OUN and UPA forces continued to fight for liberation for several years, General Shukhevych himself not being killed until March 1950 when his entourage was surrounded by Soviet security troops near Lwów.

Thousands of those not killed in battle or executed after capture were banished to the GUlag, where they formed self-defence groups that, as Alexander Solzhenitsyn has attested, protected political prisoners from criminal elements in the camps and their gaolers.

The groundwork for a nationalist movement in eastern Ukraine was laid down by those OUN expeditionary groups that had eluded the Nazis and were able to promote the goals of Ukrainian unity and independence. Their anti-Nazi and anti-Soviet resistance consisted mostly of propaganda and agitation. Their political impact should not be underrated. The nationalists became important in industrial cities such as Dnepropetrovsk and Krivoi Rog, and in the Donets basin, eastern Ukraine's industrial heartland—a region that had been under Soviet rule for over two decades. Marked for destruction by the Nazis, confronted by an antagonistic Communist underground and, later, by a Soviet administration equally determined to eradicate them, the nationalists nevertheless managed to spread their views.

Ukrainians fought in a variety of military formations during the war. Thousands, for example, could be found in the ranks of various Polish armies, with the Czech formations of General *Svoboda and even in two Ukrainian battalions fighting alongside the French resistance. Other Ukrainians soldiered in the armies of Romania and Hungary, with the Serbian monarchist *Mihailović or against him in the ranks of *Tito's Yugoslav partisans. Uncounted numbers were organized by the Germans into guard (see OPERATION REINHARD), construction, auxiliary police, and fire brigade units. Some were attached to General *Vlasov's Russian Liberation Army (see SOVIET EXILES). Nearly 60% of the 250,000 Soviet partisans in Ukraine were Ukrainians, but the largest number, some 4.5 million, served in the ranks of the Red Army. According to Soviet statistics, these Ukrainians made a major contribution to Soviet victory in the *German–Soviet war. Nearly half a million were awarded medals for bravery, and 961 became Heroes of the Soviet Union (see DECORATIONS). Many thousands of others took part in armed resistance against both the Nazis and the Soviets.

Over 7 million inhabitants of Ukraine, more than one-sixth of the pre-war population, were killed during the Second World War. Of a total population in January 1941 of 41.9 million, of whom 14 million lived in the cities, only 27.4 million remained in 1945, 7.6 million of them in the cities, a loss of 14.5 million people through deaths, deportations, and evacuations. Among these losses must be counted the 1.4 million Ukrainian *prisoners-of-war who were among the 5.8 million Red Army soldiers who were captured by the Wehrmacht and of whose number 3.3 million died of ill-treatment, disease, and starvation. In sheer numbers, no nation lost so many civilians as Ukraine. Further, more than 700 Ukrainian towns and cities and 28,000 villages were destroyed, 42% of the urban centres devastated by the war in the USSR, leaving 19 million people homeless. The capital of Kiev suffered a 60% reduction in population. Kharkov's pre-war population of 700,000 was reduced to under 500,000 as 120,000 citizens were transported to Germany, another 80,000 starved, and 30,000 were executed. For every village that was obliterated in occupied France or Czechoslovakia, such as *Oradour and *Lidiče, some 250 villages and their inhabitants were destroyed in Ukraine. The destruction of more than 16,000 industrial enterprises and 28,000 collective farms meant the loss of much of the industrial and agricultural infrastructure that the country had gained at such great sacrifice in the 1930s. Direct material damage amounted to 285 milliard roubles (at 1941 prices) or over 40% of the USSR's wartime losses. Soviet authors have estimated the costs of the war to Ukraine at an astronomical one trillion two hundred milliard roubles, approximately 30% of its national wealth.

In addition, nearly 3 million Ukrainians were press-ganged into the service of the Third Reich as *Ostarbeiter* (east workers). In the wake of this cataclysm, several million Ukrainian displaced persons (DPs) were marooned in western Europe (see also REFUGEES). Most were repatriated against their wishes to the Soviets by British, American, and French troops acting according to a now questioned interpretation of the Yalta agreement (see ARGONAUT). Large numbers of those handed over were summarily executed or interned in concentration camps. A minority of the Ukrainian refugees escaped repatriation by hiding, declaring that they were citizens of Poland, or claiming to be stateless. Most of these ended up in DP camps run by *UNRRA or, after 1947, by the International Refugee Organization. Most remained in that limbo for several years before resettling in the USA, Canada, UK, South America, Australia, and elsewhere.

Although the war devastated Ukraine, it also resulted in the unification of almost all ethnic Ukrainian territories into one state which achieved some international prominence by becoming a founding member of the United Nations (see SAN FRANCISCO CONFERENCE). The new *Polish–Soviet frontier, agreed at Yalta in February 1945, gave most of eastern Galicia as far as the River San, Volhynia, and Polissia as far west as the River Bug and northern Bukovina, Transnistria, Bessarabia, and Ruthenia to the Ukrainian Soviet Socialist Republic. This acquisition added 11 million people and some 163,200 sq. km. (63,000 sq. mi.) that is, over one quarter the size of the whole country, to Ukraine. Ethnic problems that had plagued Ukrainian lands earlier were much reduced with the elimination, through deaths and deportations, of the country's Polish and Jewish communities, and through a series of population exchanges between Poland, Czechoslovakia, and the USSR between 1945 and 1948.

The democratic popular front Rukh ('Movement') and related organizations, such as the Memorial Society, have begun the laborious process of collecting evidence about Soviet and Nazi crimes against humanity in Ukraine. An independent Ukrainian Catholic Church has emerged from the catacombs, as has an autocephalic Ukrainian Orthodox Church. Through public subscription, a monument to Bandera, the OUN leader assassinated by a KGB agent in Munich in 1959, was erected in his birthplace, Staryi Uhryniv, in 1990, but it was blown up soon afterwards. Similar monuments to the founder of the OUN, Colonel Yevhen Konovalets, and to the soldiers of the Galician Division, were also bombed in the summer of 1991. Nevertheless, an all-Ukrainian brotherhood of OUN and UPA veterans has formally been established in Ukraine.

Controversy still continues to surround what happened in Ukraine before, during, and immediately after the war, and this cannot be resolved without full access to archival material in émigré Ukrainian repositories and inside the former USSR. Given Ukraine's proclamation of independence of 24 August 1991 it is to be hoped that an unfettered history of the country during the Second World War will finally be written. L. Y. Luciuk

Armstrong, J. A., *Ukrainian Nationalism* (3rd edn. Englewood, Colo., 1990).
Boshyk, Y. (ed.), *Ukraine during World War II: History and Its Aftermath: A Symposium* (Edmonton, 1986).
Kamenetsky, I., *Hitler's Occupation of Ukraine, 1941–1944: A Study of Totalitarian Imperialism* (Milwaukee, 1956).

Ulster, see UK, 4.

ULTRA. Section 1 deals with the intelligence derived from decrypts of signals enciphered on the German *ENIGMA and *Geheimschreiber cipher machines; section 2 covers the intelligence gleaned from the codes of the Japanese armed forces. The former therefore describes the influence of ULTRA intelligence on the war in the northern hemisphere while the latter is almost wholly concerned with the war in the Far East. The two articles have been labelled UK and USA to indicate the main—but far from the only—nationality of those involved in decrypting these signals, and in translating and assessing their value.

Both the Germans and Japanese used many codes and ciphers, some of which were never broken. The Japanese possibly had more than 50; the Germans had nearly 200 ENIGMA variants alone as well as several Geheimschreiber and hand cipher systems.

See MAGIC for intelligence derived from diplomatic signals enciphered on the Japanese cipher machine, codenamed *PURPLE. See also SIGNALS INTELLIGENCE WARFARE, SIGABA, and TYPEX.

1. UK

ULTRA was the British security classification chosen in 1940 to denote the new and highly secret intelligence produced by the decryption of intercepted German (and some Italian) radio messages enciphered in the ENIGMA machine cipher or transmitted on the Geheimschreiber, or, in the case of Italian signals, enciphered in the C38m's machine cipher. The C38m was very similar to the ENIGMA. The ENIGMA was used by all three German armed services, the *SS, the *Abwehr, and the German state railways.

Translations of naval ENIGMA messages teleprinted from the British Code and Cypher School at *Bletchley Park to the Admiralty's *Naval Intelligence Division, and copies of the signals sent to commands abroad based on army and Luftwaffe messages (but not translations of the actual decrypts), can be seen in the Public Record office in London and in the National Archives in Washington. It is upon them that this article is mainly based.

ENIGMA was supposed to be unbreakable, and this, together with the portability of the enciphering machine, encouraged its widespread use by the Wehrmacht. There was a consequent dilution in the quality of the signals personnel, of the Luftwaffe in particular (see FLIVOS), who operated the machine, and in their observation of the proper security procedures. This greatly assisted decryption. The degree of dilution and other variables, such as the occasional capture of a month's ENIGMA key-lists, varied from service to service and from time to time. The number of decrypts from a particular service or theatre of war therefore varied from nil upwards, and so did the usefulness of the derived intelligence, though on the whole both gradually rose throughout the war. Thus, for example, fewer than 200 army/air signals were sent to commands abroad in the six months ending in November 1941, and only about 8,000 by June 1942, but 15,000 by October 1942. By the end of the war almost 100,000 had been sent, together with more than half a million of the usually far shorter naval teleprints to the Admiralty for operational action.

The seeds of what was to become ULTRA were sown by an anti-Nazi German, a far-sighted French intelligence officer, and a trio of brilliant young Polish mathematicians. In the late 1920s the German armed forces bought up the rights to the ENIGMA machine, which had failed in the commercial market for which it was designed, and were developing it for military purposes even before the Nazis rose to power; machine ciphering was then a novelty. In 1931 Hans-Thilo Schmidt (cover name Asche), a member of the German defence ministry staff, gave some sheets of the ENIGMA instruction manual to Captain *Bertrand of the French military cryptographic bureau; it was the first of several such contacts. Bertrand offered to share his new and potentially valuable knowledge with the British and the Poles. The British, believing the cipher to be as insoluble as was claimed, showed little interest, as did Bertrand's own superiors; the Poles, on the other hand, accepted Bertrand's proposal with alacrity, though with little hope of being able to exploit it.

However, using Asche's guidelines and a commercial ENIGMA, Marian Rejewski—he was one of the three bright young Poles—worked out the theory of the machine, and by the late 1930s the Poles were reading a great deal of the traffic passed in the new cipher. Seeing the threat to their independence, in July 1939 they presented both the British and the French with one of the machines they had reconstructed, together with details of the knowledge they had accumulated.

By this time British cryptographers were alert to the possibility of breaking ENIGMA and to the military advantages of doing so. A group of university mathematicians was established at Bletchley Park, and before long they had advanced beyond the point the Poles had reached, in spite of new procedures introduced by the Germans on the outbreak of war. These procedures were often ignored and the resultant breaches of security played into the hands of the cryptographers; hence the repeated remark by Gordon Welchman, one-time head of the army/air cryptographic section at Bletchley Park, 'We were lucky.' A system which should have been invulnerable, as the British *Typex was, proved not to be so. Army and navy ENIGMA were more difficult to break, but entry into the Luftwaffe version eased the way into them.

The Germans' belief that ENIGMA guaranteed the security of their communications had two consequences for the British and their Allies.

First, the cryptographers' awareness that the complexities of the cipher could easily be increased and that it might thus be put beyond their reach, or that a new and unbreakable cipher might be substituted if serious doubt were cast on ENIGMA, demanded extreme care to preserve the secret that it had been broken. Careless talk could cost more than lives, and so might military action which could only have resulted from Allied knowledge of information transmitted in ENIGMA. By 1945 many thousand British and American men and women were engaged in the successive stages between interception and use in battle, and not the least remarkable feature of ULTRA's history is that none of them ever leaked the secret, but kept it inviolate for the next 30 years. Similarly, the loyalty and security-mindedness of the French and Polish personnel who remained silent under the stress of enemy *occupation of their countries are quite beyond praise. In the field, commanders accustomed themselves to shaping their actions so as not to rouse suspicions that they were using ULTRA, after a few sharp rebukes in the early days reminded them of the overriding claims of security (but see MEDENINE).

Secondly, because ULTRA was the result of unsuspected eavesdropping on German official correspondence, information derived from it was absolutely reliable factually. Information from other sources always required subjective evaluation before it could be acted on: had an agent been duped or misinformed, did a prisoner-of-war really know as much as he suggested under interrogation, and so on. ULTRA was free from this confusing element. But because it was necessarily only a random selection of German correspondence—the Germans naturally preferred to use landlines where they existed—it always needed to be interpreted and set in its probable context. This need was particularly acute in the early days, when intelligence staffs were inexperienced and few keys were being broken, but it always remained paramount for the full utilization of decrypted intelligence even when experience had been gained and new keys had widened and deepened the foundations of ULTRA intelligence.

So necessary was it to protect the guarantee of ULTRA's reliability—that it was the product of supposedly impossible decryption—that in the early days it was passed off as the work of an omnipresent spy called 'Boniface' who had access to German military secrets at all levels from the lowest to the highest. As an agent, 'Boniface' had to be represented as subordinate to 'C', the head of *MI6, and the information he provided cast in the form of an agent's report. The illogicality of this arrangement not only led to friction between MI6 and the service ministries but also had the unfortunate side-effect that, because so few were allowed to know the truth, it discredited ULTRA in the eyes of military commanders, who could not of course believe any agent to be entirely trustworthy. The chosen disguise, in fact, was so successful that for a time it reduced the effectiveness of the intelligence it was designed to protect. As more officers were indoctrinated, after suitably severe warnings, the pretence was silently dropped.

ULTRA is a collective, not a singular, noun. It was not the product of a single cipher, but of several, all closely related. Almost 200 ENIGMA keys were known by 1945, not all of which were broken; some (the Luftwaffe general key, for instance) were in use throughout the war, others (the variant employed in the *Norwegian campaign, for example) disappeared when the reason which had called them into existence no longer applied. In one form or another, ENIGMA was an integral component of the Wehrmacht command system at all levels, from an airfield reporting the number of serviceable fighters it housed at the end of each day, to Berlin's directions for the conduct of the war to the U-boat fleet, or to individual theatre commanders.

Over the years, the cryptographers progressively widened their hold, and (as will be seen) this was reflected in the improving quality and value of the derived intelligence. Thus there was no question of one gigantic effort uncovering the whole ENIGMA mystery. On the contrary, the cryptographers' work was never complete; they waged a continuous, fluctuating, and ultimately victorious struggle to enlarge and maintain their mastery over keys which underwent regular monthly, daily, or sometimes even thrice-daily modifications.

Decryption of the Luftwaffe general key on a regular and current basis began on 21 May 1940, which has been called the birthday of ULTRA. This was too late for it to have any influence on the fighting which led to the fall of *France, then approaching its climax. In any case the British armed services were as unprepared to use high-grade intelligence as they were in other respects, and no arrangements secure enough for the distribution of such intelligence had been made in advance. The same situation had prevailed in Norway, where the special key being used by the Germans was successfully broken. However, the reading of Luftwaffe traffic currently from May 1940 had one immediately important consequence: the revision downwards of previously inflated estimates of German air strength, which had hitherto been very inaccurate, because no sound information on which to base them had been available. During the coming battle of *Britain it was of the greatest assistance to know how long the Germans could maintain their offensive at the current rate of aircraft loss, and future estimates of aircraft numbers could usually reflect truth rather than guesswork.

From July 1940 onwards ULTRA's chief service was to give general warnings of the state of preparations for the invasion of England (see SEALION) and in September to furnish strong indications that invasion had been postponed; but no precise details of German invasion intentions were ever revealed. This was doubtless because of the extensive use of landlines for the most important orders. Except in the desert, where they did not exist, landlines were always to restrict the completeness of ULTRA intelligence.

A special ENIGMA key came into use for the autumn and winter *Blitz of British cities. The inner meaning of the cryptic messages which were enciphered in it defied interpretation until a young MI6 scientist attached to the air ministry, Dr. R. V. Jones, realized the way in which bombers were being directed to their targets by radio beams (see ELECTRONIC NAVIGATION SYSTEMS), and was able to counteract the beams sufficiently to reduce substantially the damage the bombers using them were causing. Four years later the same key gave clues to the development of the V-1 and V-2 (see V-WEAPONS), and in combination with evidence from *photographic reconnaissance and reports from the *resistance in France and Poland made it possible to foresee and, to some extent, counter the V-weapon attacks of the summer and autumn of 1944.

With the postponement of SEALION in 1940, and the move of German bombers away from France to take part in the invasion of the USSR (see BARBAROSSA) the volume of ENIGMA traffic declined for several months. The lull gave the opportunity for an enlargement of staff which was already plainly desirable. At its fullest extent, this staff combined men and women, civilians and members of the uniformed services, into a single whole, subdivided into a number of mutually supportive sections on the sole basis of individuals' qualifications and abilities in different aspects of the work. From December 1943 onwards, American officers were also drafted into it, 'some to remain at Bletchley, some to be trained in ULTRA before heading the US equivalent of the British *Special Liaison Units.

Soon after regular daily decryption of the Luftwaffe key came on stream in the summer of 1940, it became clear that the best results would be obtained if the functions of decryption, translation, and intelligence servicing were formally separated, while of course remaining closely interconnected. This represented a radical departure from previous practice and undoubtedly raised the quality of the end product, intelligence for operational use.

The new arrangements were just settling into place when the *Western Desert campaigns erupted into violent action with the arrival of *Rommel in February 1941. A new Luftwaffe ENIGMA key for the Mediterranean had just been broken, and it was soon obvious that for the first time enough information was likely to be available to provide field commanders with urgent intelligence of great if sometimes ephemeral value (Rommel's tactical plans, or orders for aircraft movements, for instance). A special radio channel, exclusive to ULTRA, was opened between London and Cairo. The intelligence staff at Bletchley Park was authorized to draft and transmit signals over it on their own initiative and these were then disseminated by Special Liaison Units to those cleared to receive them. By 1944 there were two or three dozen such stations operating at the same time.

Both these innovations, of fundamental significance for the future of ULTRA, are associated with the name of Group Captain F. W. Winterbotham, but the precise extent of his contribution has never been disclosed.

Decryption and translation of naval ENIGMA material were the responsibility of a separate section at Bletchley, but the drafting of signals to fleets at sea was the province of the Admiralty. This was because the Admiralty was an operational headquarters as well as an organizational and administrative centre, and consequently had functions which the other service ministries were compelled to delegate to commanders in the field.

Hitler invaded Greece and Yugoslavia in April 1941 (see BALKAN CAMPAIGN), only a few weeks after the break into the new Mediterranean key had sharpened interest in the Western Desert war. Regular intercepts, decrypted with unprecedented speed, justified the new radio link, which was extended briefly to Yugoslavia and GHQ Greece, but only a very few signals could be delivered quickly enough to protect the British force as it retreated southwards. Determined to press home his advantage, in April Hitler sanctioned a project to capture *Crete—where the tiny British garrison was reinforced only by men exhausted by their hasty retreat through Greece—with parachutists and glider-borne detachments. So completely were the arrangements revealed by the Luftwaffe key that the whole plan was in British hands a fortnight before the invasion on 20 May. This was the first convincing demonstration of what ULTRA could do. It would also have been ULTRA's first operational test had not the material weakness of the defenders loaded the dice too heavily against them. In spite of the forewarning, Crete fell on 31 May.

Although it was only dimly recognized at the time, Greece and Crete had shown that tactical intelligence could not be ULTRA's strongest suit. This was because in most cases it was impossibly difficult to carry out the whole process—from interception to the delivery of a signal to the officer who could use it—before the land battle had moved on. Very occasionally the process could be completed in about three hours, but six hours may have been nearer the average. When, at Churchill's insistence, *Wavell launched attacks in the desert which quickly collapsed, this conclusion should have been drawn. *Auchinleck, Wavell's successor as C-in-C *Middle East Command, resisted similar demands more stubbornly, but ULTRA was still too novel and too mysterious to command the attention it was beginning to deserve. Half the ground gained by Auchinleck's CRUSADER offensive of November 1941 was lost in the new year, partly through misinterpretation of ULTRA and partly through military error, although some German army traffic was now being read for the first time. A truer, but not yet fully appreciated, pointer to the future had been given six months earlier: analysis of successive supply returns showed that the navy and the RAF, assisted by a combination of Italian naval decrypts with German reports of Luftwaffe cover of trans-Mediterranean shipping, had almost strangled Rommel's air component by reducing its petrol stocks by 90% between May and October. Military strategy, often based on logistical analysis like this, was gradually recognized as potentially ULTRA's greatest contribution to victory.

Government cryptographers, some with over 20 years' experience, formed the nucleus of the cryptographic party at Bletchley, and the university mathematicians who joined them found little difficulty in adapting their skills to new requirements. The translators possessed first-class degrees in German. But since in 1939 hardly anyone in England had experience of intelligence at the level of ULTRA, the new intelligence officers received no guidance and had to discover the rules of their craft for themselves as they went along; small wonder that their first steps sometimes faltered. The same applied in the field. The necessary skills had been learned at both ends by mid-1942. The defensive battle of *Alam Halfa at the beginning of September first showed how much progress had been made; less happily, it also contributed to the foundation of the 'Montgomery legend'. *Montgomery had taken command of the Eighth Army only a fortnight earlier; but he never openly admitted that his victory was due to ULTRA as well as to his own genius.

Rommel could have broken through to Cairo and the Nile in July had his men not been exhausted by their efforts, and it was obvious that he would make another attempt as soon as he could. On 15 August he explained to Hitler, via ENIGMA, what he would do, announcing that his tanks would advance at the end of the month. A translation was in Montgomery's hands 48 hours later. It showed that Rommel would swing south round the end of the British line and then strike north to isolate the Eighth Army from its base, but that the Alam Halfa ridge would then bar his way. This was exactly what Montgomery had prophesied after his first reconnaissance of the front line two days earlier; the confirmation not only gave him time to strengthen the defences of the ridge still further, but also invited the navy and the RAF to redouble their assault on Rommel's Mediterranean supply line. They sank so many tankers that on 1 September petrol shortage immobilized the *Afrika Korps in front of Alam Halfa, where it was bombed mercilessly. Rommel withdrew to his starting-point three days later, having gained nothing.

The forewarning given by ULTRA resembled that over Crete, but with the immense difference that this time there were resources enough to take full advantage of it. This first victory of a British army over the Germans after three years of retreat and failure silenced those who had doubted the value of intelligence in general and ULTRA in particular, and the frosts of former scepticism soon melted away. The second battle of *El Alamein in October was by comparison a lesser intelligence triumph, and when the move south of 21st Panzer Division (which opened the way for the decisive breakthrough) was reported by the *Y service several hours before ULTRA, the latter's relative tactical incapacity was underlined.

Decrypts of the Italian naval ENIGMA cipher had laid the foundations of the Mediterranean fleet's victory over the Italians at *Cape Matapan in March 1941, and continued to assist air and sea attacks on the Axis supply route to Libya until it was withdrawn in that summer. The Admiralty had always recognized the enormous advantage the breaking of German naval ULTRA would bring, if it could be achieved. Unfortunately the inherent complexities of the naval key and the naval operators' superior security long stood in the way. The first breaks, in the spring of 1941, into the key then used by surface vessels and U-boats in common (once mastered, it was read regularly from August until the end of the war, though only used by surface vessels from February 1942 onwards) made it possible to plot the U-boats' present and likely future positions and to re-route Atlantic *convoys accordingly, thus restricting the successes of the newly-introduced wolf-packs in the battle of the *Atlantic. However, decryption was still too intermittent and often too late to give much help in the hunt for the **Bismarck* when she broke out into the north Atlantic in May 1941; most of the intelligence which led to her destruction came from air reconnaissance.

Reliance on ULTRA to maintain a continuous U-boat plot became so routine and so vital a feature of the Admiralty's control of the battle of the Atlantic that the sudden separation of surface and U-boat communications, and the introduction of a new and still more complicated key for the latter at the beginning of February 1942, was a shattering blow. So greatly were the cryptographers' difficulties increased that the new U-boat key could not be broken until December, with the result that the convoys suffered badly during the intervening months: when 700,000 tons of shipping were sunk in November, it began to look as if the UK might starve and American armies be unable to cross the Atlantic for the liberation of Europe. An added handicap to the defence against the U-boats was that at this time the Germans were reading the British convoy code (see B-DIENST). This was changed in mid-December, just as the new U-boat key was broken; the Admiralty's sight improved as the Germans grew blind. (By curious coincidence, the same pattern had just occurred in the desert. Rommel's advance in the summer of 1942 was assisted by reading low-grade British codes as well as the American military attaché's telegrams to Washington: see ITALY, 6. Both leaks were stopped before the summer was over.)

The improved situation for the British brought relief to the hard-pressed Atlantic supply route, though the extent of the relief was not fully felt until May 1943, when so many U-boats were being sunk that *Dönitz withdrew the remainder; they never returned in such numbers.

A major part in this ocean victory was played by new methods of finding and destroying U-boats which had recently been developed: high-frequency direction-finding techniques (see HUFF-DUFF) and centrimetric *radar, very-long-range reconnaissance aircraft, reinforced escort groups with escort carriers, and so on. The respective shares of responsibility cannot profitably be assessed, but the reading of the U-boat key may well have been the chief.

Having thus played so significant a role in winning the war at sea, from which final victory flowed, naval ULTRA's essential work was done. It never exercised so decisive an influence on events again, though later on it gave welcome assurance that the production of U-boats of a new type, able to move much faster under water and to breathe through a pipe (see SCHNORCHEL)—boats which might have renewed the Atlantic danger in still more alarming terms—was being retarded by bombing more even than had been hoped.

Critical turning-points, then, in the exploitation of both naval and army/air ULTRA were reached in the course of 1942, and great dangers were overcome by the end of the year. In the former case, cryptographic skill, assisted by the capture of several of the monthly lists of settings which Berlin issued to naval vessels, had found a way out of an apparent impasse, prevented the loss of a valuable source and gained what was, perhaps, a war-winning victory. In the latter, respect for ULTRA and the acceptance of intelligence as a leading instrument of command had been secured at last.

On land, however, the winter of 1942–3 saw much that seemed to contradict this. Montgomery flatly disregarded ULTRA's indications that if he moved smartly he could probably trap Rommel's army and annihilate it as it retreated across Libya; notably, he hesitated too long at Mersa el Brega in December instead of pushing on. In Tunisia, during the *North African campaign, their lack of experience of fighting Germans afflicted some of both the British and the American forces engaged. Intelligence was not accorded the place it had now won with the Eighth Army, and this delayed the Allied advance as much as military mistakes, although it must be admitted that the serious set-back which the Allies suffered at *Kasserine Pass in February 1943 was partly the result of unusual problems of interpretation posed by current ULTRA, so that accurate forecasting was abnormally difficult.

The *Sicilian campaign, which opened in July 1943, saw a new and profitable aspect of ULTRA. Because the island was so obvious a target after Tunisia, efforts were made to persuade the Axis that the landings would be elsewhere. ULTRA soon showed beyond doubt that Sicily was not being reinforced but that a panzer division, newly re-equipped after bruising battles in the *German–Soviet war, was being hastily transferred from France to southern Greece. No other source could have proved the efficacy of the *deception planners' rumour-mongering so conclusively, thus relieving the operational commanders' minds as they prepared an amphibious undertaking on an unprecedented scale.

The Italian surrender and the Allied landing in Italy in September 1943 (see REGGIO DI CALABRIA and SALERNO) gave prominence to another new aspect of ULTRA's capabilities. What would Hitler's reaction be? Would he protect Rome and contest every inch of ground, as he had told Rommel to do at El Alamein, or would he prudently retire to the Alps to economize on men and *matériel*? He hesitated for several weeks, and ULTRA showed him doing so. Finally he decided to stand on successive defence lines across the peninsula (see WINTER LINE, for example), and ULTRA reported the decision as soon as he made it in early October. This was a strategic prize of the greatest moment; it enabled the Allies to design the *Italian campaign to draw maximum advantage from the willingness Hitler thus displayed to allow Italy to drain away his resources. Nothing subsequently during the war in Italy could bear comparison with it, though the steady flow of decrypts was maintained surprisingly well, given the availability of landlines. Among the most important were those which showed *Kesselring had decided to make no further attempt to wipe out the *Anzio bridgehead after the failure of his big attack in February 1944.

In spite of the Germans' natural preference for landlines, which restricted the amount of ENIGMA traffic in France before the Normandy landings of June 1944 (see OVERLORD), enough intercepts were collected to identify all the divisions manning the coastal defences and to locate all but two of them with sufficient precision. Directly the Allies landed the volume of traffic grew enormously. The most pressing question now was whether the three panzer divisions in the Pas de Calais would move to Normandy at once and counter-attack the beachhead before it was properly consolidated. Would the FORTITUDE deception plan which had held them away until now, still carry conviction? ULTRA was able to keep watch on all three divisions closely enough to show that they were all remaining in place for the first crucial ten days (the first to move was not ordered to Caen until 19 June, D+13), a service of prime importance in complementing the deception plan, and again one which no other source could have rendered as reliably.

After usefully demonstrating that the German troops east of Avranches, where the First US Army was to attack at the end of July, were weak and exhausted, ULTRA could claim the initiative in what was to become the German disaster of the Falaise pocket (see NORMANDY CAMPAIGN). *Bradley had already directed the Third US Army up the Loire valley towards Paris when on 6 August ULTRA gave notice that armour was being assembled for an attack near Mortain; in consequence, the attack was stopped in its tracks. Then in the early hours of 10 August came the *coup de grâce*. On the previous evening Hitler ordered a renewal of this attack, with the object of driving through to the sea at Avranches and cutting the American supply line. News of the move reached Allied headquarters less than twelve hours later. The certainty that the Germans were facing west, when they should have been extricating themselves from the risk of encirclement by looking to their rear in the east, lent extra force to the Allied onslaught.

Elements retreating from the pocket in August and September filled the air with reports of their movements and strength, and among much else these showed that 1st SS Panzer Corps was to refit in the general area of Arnhem where Montgomery was planning to make a bridgehead across the lower Rhine. So firmly entrenched, however, was the conviction that German resistance was nearing its end that this knowledge was not enough to cast doubt on the wisdom of launching operation *MARKET-GARDEN.

The myth, mistakenly put about in the late 1970s, that German radio silence prevented ULTRA from giving warning of the *Ardennes campaign in mid-December is still current in some quarters. It must be flatly contradicted. For the previous three months ULTRA evidence had been accumulating that a large armoured force was being assembled in north Germany for an undisclosed purpose. From early November the movement of its component divisions westwards across the Rhine by rail was steadily reported, and at the end of the month there began a stream of urgent requests for air reconnaissance of just those parts of the Ardennes into which the German spearheads thrust on 16 December. None of this evidence was wholly unambiguous, and no intention to attack was ever expressed. Nevertheless, it is regrettably plain that neither SHAEF nor Twenty-First Army Group ever analysed it impartially enough to allow the deduction that it might as easily represent preparations for an attack, as for a counter-attack when the Allies next moved forward.

While it would be foolish to attempt to apportion responsibility for the eventual Allied victory between the various strands (including other sources of intelligence) which made up that victory, there can hardly be any doubt that the regular provision of absolutely reliable—if sometimes incomplete—intelligence about German actions, resources, and intentions was certainly among the foremost.

Two further aspects of Allied co-operation call for mention. The US armed forces came into the ULTRA picture remarkably late. Hitler's declaration of war on the USA on 11 December 1941 was quickly followed by the first Washington conference (see ARCADIA), which confirmed the policy that the new allies should concentrate their main effort on Germany first. Yet it was not until more than a year later, on 25 April 1943, that an American cryptological and intelligence reconnaissance party arrived at Bletchley Park. A formal agreement to share ULTRA followed in May. But, no doubt because of the natural reluctance of the British to risk their priceless secret without fully satisfactory safeguards, for many months to come the authorities of the two countries seemed to be, in the words of the official US historian, 'walking round each and eyeing each other like two mongrels who have just met'.

The first American recruits reached Hut 3 only in January 1944, and the same historian (who was one of them) reckoned that the party did not come of age until *D-Day. The American contingent never numbered more than 68, as against several hundred British; a dozen were absorbed into the British staff on a completely equal footing, and the remainder were attached, after training, to US field commands as the channels though which ULTRA was delivered in accordance with regulations laid down by General *Marshall, the US Army's Chief of Staff, on 15 March 1944. The experiences of these officers, recorded directly after the end of the war, shed interesting light on the degree to which they managed to 'educate the generals to the value of intelligence' and provide illuminating examples of the way in which ULTRA assisted operations.

Secondly, how much did Stalin and the USSR learn, directly or indirectly, about the intelligence content of ENIGMA? The short answer is: directly, nil, indirectly a good deal in 1941–2, but not thereafter.

Churchill's declaration of common cause with the Soviet Union immediately upon the German invasion in June 1941 had been preceded the previous month by an ENIGMA-based warning (which he ascribed to 'a trusted agent') of troop movements towards the Soviet frontier. Stalin did not reply. Churchill's motive was clearly not so much altruism or an appeal to left-wing sentiment at home (Clementine Churchill's 'Aid to Russia Appeal' took care of this) as national self-interest—the more the Germans faced east and spent their strength in the USSR, the less possible a new SEALION and the more probable eventual victory.

Only a month after BARBAROSSA he persuaded 'C' the head of MI6, and the *Chiefs of Staff to agree to send suitably camouflaged information on a regular basis 'provided no risks are run'. The service continued at a steady rate while air and army ULTRA provided advance information about German tactics and intentions during the crisis in front of *Moscow in the late autumn, but fell off about midsummer 1942; nevertheless information about German plans probably gave some slight assistance towards preventing a breakthrough in the Caucasus and in the defence of *Stalingrad. The USSR showed scant gratitude and no reciprocity, and by the winter of 1942–3 was cold-shouldering the Allies in intelligence matters. The Red Army rejected any idea of cryptographic partnership in December 1942, for instance, while the painfully slow progress towards a similar partnership with the USA reflected the fears of many on the British side that by sending so much Churchill was wearing the disguise thin and endangering the precious ULTRA secret. Reluctance on both sides reduced the service to a trickle in 1943 and brought it to an end in 1944.

There is no evidence that the Soviets ever broke ENIGMA themselves, though they could read German army and airforce hand ciphers. Gordievsky, the high-level KGB defector, considers that 'the odds are that Soviet cryptanalysts were unable to read ENIGMA on any regular basis, though they sometimes captured key-tables.

RALPH BENNETT

2. USA

In the *Pacific war the Allies used the same designator as they did in Europe for the special intelligence derived from the interception and decryption of enciphered Axis army and navy *radio communications. Although the Americans also often used *MAGIC to cover all Japanese communications broken into by cryptanalysis, the two sources were distinct: ULTRA was military, MAGIC diplomatic.

ULTRA was a secret weapon of enormous importance. Without it, the war against Japan would have been far more perilous and difficult than it was. Logically the Americans and British would make the best use of their interception and breaking of Japanese codes (as well as German) by pooling their interception, cryptanalysis, and finished intelligence, and they approached that point by the end of the war. Nevertheless, the sharing was very slowly and painfully achieved and integration was never complete.

The sharing of precious national assets such as the techniques and successes of cryptanalysis was shocking to the military services. Furthermore, American intelligence was rigidly compartmentalized, army separate from navy and cryptanalysis from evaluation, so that the more centralized British had to deal individually with a set of American rivals. At one point, the US Navy refused to provide the US Army with ULTRA material it was already passing to the British. The same pattern of parochialism, *rivalries, and compartmentalization obstructed the flow of intelligence among and within the South-East Asia, South-West Pacific, and Central Pacific combat theatres.

As Allied power mounted and wider engagement with the enemy proved the value of ULTRA, the demand for it grew and the need for pooling resources, integrating management, and widening access became apparent. Facing the enlarging role of the USA in the war and its dominant position against Japan, the British were the more inclined to tie their efforts to those of the Americans. Enhancing the US advantage was the advanced state of American communications technology, especially in high-speed calculators, permitting grand scale attacks on the most difficult codes and ciphers.

Most important in the forming of a British–American partnership in special intelligence (ULTRA and MAGIC) was the BRUSA (Britain and the United States of America) agreement of 17 May 1943. According to Bradley F. Smith (see below), this provided for the sharing of ULTRA between the British cryptanalytic centre at Bletchley Park and its US Army counterparts in Washington. The US Army took responsibility for Japanese military and air codes and ciphers, the British for those of Germany and Italy. The US Navy made its own arrangements with the British, so that for the war against Japan two special intelligence networks evolved, navy and army, each connected to Bletchley Park. More limited sharing occurred between networks. ULTRA was never shared with the Chinese and Free French, and only on rare occasions, and then in disguised form, with the Soviets (see above). The rising demand for ULTRA, the multiplicity of Japanese codes and changes therein, and the growing complexity of cryptanalytic methods and devices, created a voracious demand for personnel whose numbers at Arlington Hall, the US Army's cryptanalytic centre in Washington, reached 7,000 during the course of the war.

In the months of Allied weakness, and Japanese ascendancy and triumph following *Pearl Harbor, it was vital to learn where the next blow would fall. The Japanese admirals' code had proved impervious to attack, but the Japanese Navy's operational code, JN-25, had yielded some ground. This was an enciphered code. To encrypt, the sender would substitute five-digit numbers from a code 'dictionary' for the words and phrases of a message, then add to each (without carrying) another five-digit number from a second book of 100,000 randomly selected groups, using an enciphered key which indicated where to start. Place names had their own two or three-letter designators.

The breaking of JN-25 was never as final and complete as that of MAGIC. The code was first introduced in 1939, and the eve of war with Japan, the British *Far East Combined Bureau at Singapore had penetrated JN-25 to the point of monitoring Japan's main fleet movements, according to F. H. Hinsley, the authority on British intelligence. The smaller Dutch unit at Bandung, Java, it is claimed, was also reading some fleet communications, as was the cryptanalytic unit of the Office of Naval Intelligence in Washington (Op-20-G). However, JN-25 became unreadable again when the Japanese Navy replaced its book of random additives on the eve of Pearl Harbor. No evidence has yet been found that the American–British–Dutch–Australian coalition had foreknowledge of the Japanese attacks of 7/8 December 1941.

After Pearl Harbor the US Navy made an all-out effort to break the new version of the JN-25 code. Working on the task were the codebreaking units at Washington,

Pearl Harbor, and Corregidor. With the fall of the *Philippines the unit in Malinta Tunnel on Corregidor was evacuated to Melbourne where it joined forces with Australian navy cryptographers and continued to work on JN-25. In addition the British unit evacuated from Singapore continued its work at Colombo. Leading the way was the navy radio intelligence unit at Pearl Harbor under Commander Joseph Rochefort, who possessed a powerful intuitive faculty, command of Japanese, extensive experience in cryptanalysis, and an extraordinarily retentive memory.

Rochefort and his team worked relentlessly for months in their cluttered, windowless 'dungeon' in the basement of Fourteenth Naval District Headquarters. At the height of activity in 1942 the Rochefort unit was using three million IBM punch cards a month for storage and retrieval of every five-digit code group received. Gradually a small but usable portion of the messages became clear.

One advantage was that American carrier raids on Japanese-controlled islands in the central Pacific and on Tokyo (see DOOLITTLE RAID) stirred up intensive signalling in the Japanese fleet, allowing more intercepts and fodder for cryptanalysis. A second advantage was that while additives had changed the code itself had not, so equivalents discovered before Pearl Harbor were still usable once the cipher was stripped away. A third advantage was that the Japanese Navy was so widely deployed, with so many ships and air groups to command by radio, that it proved impossible to distribute new code books in time for a scheduled revision on 1 April 1942. Because of this, Rochefort's team gained nearly two more months' use of the old code, a crucial benefit as it turned out.

In March 1942 evidence from several sources began to accumulate of a forthcoming Japanese drive towards Australia with JN-25 decrypts showing that ships and air groups were being staged southwards. A British JN-25 decrypt revealed dispatch of two carriers from the Indian Ocean to the great Japanese anchorage and base at *Truk in the Caroline Islands. Estimating Japanese intentions required inspired guesswork, for at this time Pearl Harbor was decrypting on average only about 12–15% of a message. Nevertheless, Rochefort correctly concluded that the Japanese build-up was aimed at Port Moresby, on the south-eastern coast of New Guinea, and at the Solomon Islands. That estimate was repeatedly confirmed by decrypts in April to the point where Admiral *Nimitz, C-in-C of the Pacific Fleet, was prepared to take the risk of sending a second precious carrier, the *Lexington*, to join the *Yorktown* in the south-west Pacific.

The result was the battle of the *Coral Sea of May 1942. The Americans suffered heavily, with the sinking of the *Lexington* and damage to the *Yorktown* as compared with the Japanese loss of a light carrier and damage to the attack carrier *Shōkaku*. However, both Japanese warships suffered plane losses that kept them out of the forthcoming battle of *Midway, while the *Yorktown* was repaired in time for it.

Above all, the Japanese purpose was foiled; the invasion forces withdrew. Japan had sought New Guinea, from which air attacks could be launched against northern Australia, as a barrier for defence of the southern rim of its new empire. New Guinea and the Solomons would also open its way across the Coral Sea to the New Hebrides, New Caledonia, and Fiji Islands, severing the American supply route to Australia. ULTRA therefore played a key role in securing this vital flank for the Allies.

Even as they were predicting a southward thrust, the Rochefort group detected signs that Japan was preparing a larger naval offensive against some other unknown objective. They were correct: the objectives were Midway, some 1,816 km. (1,135 mi.) west of Pearl Harbor, and, to create a diversion, Kiska and Attu in the western Aleutians (see ALEUTIAN ISLANDS CAMPAIGNS). In the view of Admiral *Yamamoto, commander of the Combined Fleet, seizure of Midway would so threaten Hawaii that it would force the Pacific fleet to sail out and counter-attack, whereupon a far-flung net of Japanese carrier and battleship groups would close in and destroy it. Next would come invasion of Hawaii and then the Americans would sue for peace.

American intelligence was groping to learn what sort of operation to expect, and where and when it would occur. By now a substantial portion of JN-25 intercepts were being read and scraps of information from these were suggestive: frequent mention of a 'forthcoming campaign', requests for the type of hose used in mid-ocean refuelling and for maps of the Aleutians and Hawaiian waters, summonses to staff conferences aboard flagships, and plans for reconnaissance of a place intelligence identified as Hawaii. Decrypts and traffic analysis indicated that warships were gravitating towards Saipan, the logical assembly base for a central Pacific campaign. A 'hot' decrypt linked the proven equivalent for 'invasion force' with 'AF', a geographic designator. Rochefort guessed AF was Midway, while another designator linked the invasion force with Saipan.

By mid-May Nimitz was convinced that Midway was the target. Nevertheless Washington remained sceptical, fearing a Japanese deception plan. To lock Midway firmly in place as the object of all these Japanese preparations, Rochefort hit upon a trick, which Nimitz approved. By undersea cable—and therefore secure from Japanese interception—Midway was ordered to radio that its fresh-water supply equipment had broken down. This information was of course important to the Japanese, intent on occupation of the islet, and it was soon rebroadcast by them which confirmed that the AF indicator meant Midway.

There remained the question of when. Instructions for a Combined Fleet departure from Saipan on 27 May suggested 2 or 3 June, but so much hinged on timing that an unquestionable source was needed. The date was in a separately enciphered code group of a Combined Fleet operational order and on this Rochefort's group concentrated their most intense efforts for three days and nights, finally unlocking the secret that the occupation force transports were to arrive at Midway on 6 June. Since a decrypt revealed that the air strike on the island was to commence two days earlier than the landings, the date for the beginning of the Midway operation could be set at 4 June. The fleet intelligence officer was then able to predict almost exactly the spot and time where the carriers would launch their attack. Only days later the JN-25 code was changed and again became undecipherable.

As a result of these intelligence estimates, Nimitz had time to withdraw his carriers from the south-west Pacific, hastily repair the *Yorktown*, and position his forces to surprise the Japanese. At the battle of Midway four Japanese aircraft carriers, the heart of the Imperial Japanese Navy's striking power, were sunk. The invasion force retreated and the tide of Japanese conquest turned.

Revisions of JN-25 after Midway and again in August 1942 made the code unreadable until the end of that year. Traffic analysis and the Australian *Coast Watcher system supplied vital information during the ferocious and costly naval battles of *Guadalcanal, but the fleet code was sorely missed. By 1943, with more and more codebreakers and translators at work, combined with the capture of Japanese code books, JN-25 again became readable and, with temporary lapses, remained so until the end of the war. ULTRA struck a deadly blow in April 1943 when the itinerary of Yamamoto's inspection trip to the Solomons was decrypted, giving precise times and places. P38 Lightning fighters intercepted the admiral's plane and shot it down, killing him.

Most difficult to penetrate were the Japanese Army codes, on which no progress was made until the spring of 1943. The British Wireless Experimental Centre (WEC), in New Delhi, an outstation of Bletchley Park, led the way, but opinion is not unanimous as to how much *Slim was helped by ULTRA intelligence during the *Burma campaign. Also working on the army codes were *MacArthur's Australian–American cryptology unit at Brisbane, called Central Bureau, and the US Army's establishment at Arlington Hall in Washington. Successively, the water transport, or shipping, code, the code disguising addressees of messages (which WEC probably penetrated first), the army's general administrative code, and the Army Air Force code, were broken. But this took time and it was the US Navy's success in breaking the Japanese naval code which greatly aided MacArthur's early air and land operations (see the defence of Milne Bay in NEW GUINEA CAMPAIGN, for example, and the BISMARCK SEA battle).

On the mistaken assumption that lower-level codes would be easier to decrypt, MacArthur's Central Bureau first tried to break the low-level three-digit, regimental one used by the Japanese Army. But because each regiment had its own code and communicated in it only to its divisional HQ and not laterally, to other regiments—and because the close proximity of a regiment to its divisional HQ meant only low power was used to transmit signals—the Bureau was never able to intercept sufficient messages to work on. However, this was not the case with the army's mainline four-digit code which was used between the higher commands (divisions, armies, area armies). Successes with this were achieved from 1943 onwards because, as the Japanese spread into MacArthur's vast *South-West Pacific Area, the numbers of signals in the four-digit code proliferated; also, because of the distances involved, these took more power to transmit and were, therefore, easier to intercept.

In mid-1942 the stresses and strains of holding such a huge perimeter forced the Japanese Army to reorganize its shipping administration and in December of that year an Army Water Transport Code was introduced to enable the large number of independent commands to communicate with each other and with their superior HQ. So pressed were the Japanese that they made the Water Transport Code a simplified version of their mainline one but failed to make it as secure. This was discovered by an astute cryptanalyst at Central Bureau and in April 1943 that code was broken.

The Japanese Navy's Water Transport Code had already been partly penetrated when code books had been salvaged from a Japanese submarine sunk off Darwin in January 1942. Now, between them, the two Water Transport codes yielded invaluable intelligence on the army's shipping movements and provided US submariners with copious information about convoys, including the number and names of ships, their cargoes, destinations, routes, and often the noon positions. Submarines were now in a position to intercept effectively and sinkings rose dramatically: by the end of 1944 the majority of Japan's merchant ships had been sunk and its supply of oil was cut off. Indeed, it was discovered after the war that US Navy information on *V-J Day about the number and location of Japanese merchant ships was more complete than the Japanese government's.

The next significant advance for codebreakers came when the Japanese military attachés' code was broken. Inroads into it had first been achieved in the summer of 1942 at Bletchley Park. By the following September the daily signals between the attachés and Tokyo were being read on a regular basis, and these provided high-level intelligence which included Tokyo's assessments of its operations in the Pacific war and in the *China Incident. Between July 1943 and mid-August 1944 Arlington Hall decrypted over 5,000 of these signals, 2,100 of which the war department considered were of strategic significance. They included details of new U-boats, German jet aircraft, and the fortifications of certain French ports which were of invaluable help in planning the Normandy landings (see OVERLORD). As Edward Drea remarks on p. 76 of his book (see below) it is little wonder that Arlington Hall described the Japanese military attachés as the most efficient *spies the USA had in Europe.

By mid-1943, therefore, some Japanese army codes had begun to yield up their secrets, but often the process was too slow to be of operational use. The big breakthrough in the Japanese Army's mainline four-digit code did not come until January 1944 when the code books of the retreating 20th Division on New Guinea were found. They had been buried in a steel trunk which was discovered when the area was swept by a mine detector. This piece of carelessness enabled the US Army for a time to decrypt army signals with all the speed and precision its naval counterparts had achieved with the Japanese Navy's signals. In January 1944 Arlington Hall decrypted under 2,000 army messages; in March it decrypted over 36,000. It was this breakthrough that allowed MacArthur to pinpoint Japanese forces on New Guinea and to bypass them by landing at *Hollandia. In the same manner, intelligence from the Japanese fleet code provided Nimitz with precise troop strengths in the *Marshall Islands, leading him to invade Kwajalein in January 1944 rather than more heavily defended islands.

Even when the Japanese Army changed the key to its mainline code after the Hollandia landings, MacArthur's luck held: material relating to the new key was found. When this, too, was discontinued by the Japanese for a new key the old one was used by Central Bureau to decode a backlog of signals which it had previously not been able to break. One of these revealed that a barge carrying the new code books had been sunk off Aitape and it was supposed they had been destroyed by the fire that had sunk the vessel. But though books turn to ash they do not disintegrate unless burnt page by page, and it is still possible to read their contents. A diver was sent to Aitape, the steel trunk containing the codebooks was recovered, and 85% of the key was eventually reconstructed.

But ULTRA intelligence could not, and did not, reveal every move the Japanese made in the Pacific. For example, soon after MacArthur invaded Luzon in January 1945 (see PHILIPPINES CAMPAIGNS) the Japanese Army again changed the key of its mainline code and it took some time for Central Bureau to accumulate sufficient signals for the new key to be broken. The invaluable Water Transport Code also failed to produce the necessary intelligence as the Japanese High Command had abandoned Luzon and so was not sending either reinforcements or supplies there. The Japanese Army Air Force had been destroyed, so this produced nothing either, and as the batteries of Japanese radios failed, and could not be replaced, internal and external radio links gradually petered out. Because of this dearth of signals intelligence, US intelligence for the Luzon campaign was particularly flawed and the numbers of Japanese on the island were constantly underestimated. However, more code books were captured on Luzon, and then on *Okinawa, and from 1 July 1945 all Japanese signals relating to the build-up of Japanese forces on their home islands were monitored. These revealed the determination with which the Japanese were preparing for the US invasion and the surprisingly (to the Americans) large forces at their disposal. To some extent this ULTRA intelligence also ran counter to MAGIC decrypts which seemed to indicate that a faction of the Japanese government wanted to surrender. Drea has suggested (p. 201) that ULTRA's revelations on Japan's military build-up, and the military's determination to resist, was a factor in influencing the Americans to employ the *atomic bomb.

WALDO HEINRICHS

Bennett, R. F., *Ultra and Mediterranean Strategy* (London, 1989).
—*Ultra in the West* (London, 1979).
—*Behind the Battle* (London, 1994).
Drea, E., *MacArthur's Ultra: Codebreaking and the War against Japan, 1942–1945* (Lawrence, Kan., 1992).
Hinsley, F. H., *et al.*, *British Intelligence in the Second World War*, Vols. 1–3 (London, 1979–88).
Layton, E. T., *'And I Was There': Pearl Harbor and Midway—Breaking the Secrets* (New York, 1985).
Lewin, R., *The American Magic: Codes, Ciphers, and the Defeat of Japan* (New York, 1985; published in London as *The Other Ultra*).
—*Ultra Goes to War* (London, 1978).
Parrish, T., *The Ultra Americans* (New York, 1986).
Smith, B. F., *The Ultra-Magic Deals and the Most Secret Special Relationship* (Novato, Calif., 1993).

Umberto II (1904–83), son of King *Victor Emmanuel III of Italy who, as crown prince, commanded the Italian Army of the Alps which attacked France in June 1940. He changed sides when his father signed the armistice with the Allies in September 1943 and when Victor Emmanuel was obliged to step down in June 1944, Umberto, as lt-general of the realm, acted as regent. In May 1946 his father abdicated in his favour but Umberto, who became known as the May King, was narrowly ousted by a referendum in favour of abolishing the monarchy after he had reigned for only 35 days. See also ITALY, 3(b).

unconditional surrender, Allied policy first enunciated by Roosevelt at the press conference after the Anglo-American summit meeting at Casablanca in January 1943 (see SYMBOL). The phrase did not appear in the communiqué of the conference, and both Roosevelt and Churchill later tried to claim that its use was unpremeditated. It is now known that Roosevelt had discussed the matter with his staff before leaving Washington, and that Churchill had had the opportunity to consult the war cabinet in London. The absence of the phrase from the communiqué, and its subsequent use by Roosevelt, suggest disagreement between the two leaders, and at that stage in the war the likely cause of the difference was the treatment of Italy. Although the invasion of Sicily was agreed at Casablanca, the invasion of the mainland was still under discussion. Churchill hoped for some way of easing Italy out of the war; Roosevelt thought it more important to restate Allied war aims firmly and unambiguously. He did so not, as has sometimes been suggested, in order to reassure Stalin, restive over continuing delay in mounting the Second Front, but in order to reassure American public opinion, unhappy with *Eisenhower's deal with the *Vichy French authorities in Algiers which had eased the American landings at the start of the *North African campaign.

Although the phrase 'unconditional surrender' was

indeed used for the first time at Casablanca, other phrases implying no less had been common enough. What other meaning can be attached to 'complete victory', for example? After the entry into the war of the USA it was clear that there was no possibility of Allied defeat and no doubt that the war could be fought to the unconditional surrender of the Axis, if that was what the Allies chose to do. The demand was even extended to the Allies' lesser opponents during the *Moscow conference later in 1943. On the other side, the *Atlantic Charter and the *United Nations Declaration had already attempted to sketch at least the western view of the post-war order, making it clear that the world would have a place for vanquished as for victors. In longer perspective the important question is not why the policy was announced at Casablanca, but rather whether it was a wise one. Did it either lengthen the war or contribute to preventing a satisfactory settlement—satisfactory, by implication, to the western Allies? In answering such questions it is important to remember how different the circumstances and interests of the three major Axis powers were, and how little co-operation there was among them.

The lesser states of eastern Europe can be ignored. They were necessarily overrun as the Soviets fought their way towards Germany, and Soviet policy determined their later fate. The first of the Allies' major opponents to come under consideration was also the least, Italy. Some historians have tried to argue that Italy might have been removed from the war earlier and at less cost had an offer of terms been made. That is hard to sustain because by September 1943 Italy was in effect an occupied country. The Italians' surrender to the Allies was in form only, for in practice they had already surrendered to the Germans. If the Italian *armistice could have led to the quick and painless occupation of Italy, it would have been worth paying a price to get it. It was not, however, an Italian army that the Allies faced in Italy but a German one. Italy became a battleground rather than either an opponent or a conquered territory. It remains a moot point whether the time and effort expended on driving the German forces out of Italy were well spent by the Allies, but the debate need take no account of Italian considerations. It may be that the last stages of the war did some damage to future Italian politics that might have been avoided in other circumstances, but it was the Germans and not the Allies who controlled those circumstances. The Allies gave no great thought to the political future of Italy, and indeed they differed over such matters as whether the monarchy should be retained or not (see VICTOR EMMANUEL).

The case of Germany was the central case, recognized by all to be so. Of the Axis powers, only Germany had been an opponent of the UK and the USA in the *First World War, and the defects of the *Versailles settlement were widely regarded as an important contributory factor to the coming of the Second World War. It was important that mistakes then made, whatever they were, should not be repeated. It was common ground that the Nazi regime must be overthrown. There could be no bargaining with Hitler or his followers. If he were overthrown by the Germans themselves, the successor regime must surrender. But what should follow? It was easy to argue that Hitler could never have succeeded without support from the barons of German heavy industry and from many ordinary Germans, so that the establishment of German democracy was no matter of form but one requiring a prolonged period of re-education. Beyond that, however, there were those who argued that the essence of the problem was one of German power, so that its solution required the limitation of that power, either by constraints on Germany or by permanent partition.

The partition of Germany as a permanent solution was abandoned, even if reluctantly before the end of the war (see MORGENTHAU PLAN). However convenient in other respects, it was thought likely to be a cause of permanent German resentment, unless perhaps particularism were to revive in the historic provinces such as Bavaria. The post-war division of Germany was along artificial lines and was never intended to be lasting, as the arrangements for four-power control made clear (see ALLIED CONTROL COMMISSIONS). Yet in spite of much thought and hard work, it proved impossible either to decide in advance what the Allies should do in Germany, or to devise any formula which might be broadcast before or shortly after the Normandy landings (see OVERLORD) to encourage the Germans to give in. That difficulty did not derive from a foolish commitment to the doctrine of unconditional surrender. The more the effort was made to find some other formulation, the more clear it became that any statement was open to misinterpretation both by Germany and by the USSR and that, if it came to competition among the Allies, it was the Soviets and not the western Allies who had real concessions to offer—for example, over the eastern frontiers of post-war Germany (see ODER–NEISSE LINE).

Once Germany had surrendered, it was clear that the surrender of Japan was no more than a matter of time, but time and the cost in Allied lives, chiefly American, were none the less matters of great concern. In historical discussion of the Japanese case, a great deal of attention has naturally been given to the decision to drop the *atomic bomb. The Soviets had undertaken to enter the war against Japan, in which they had not hitherto been engaged, once Germany was defeated. Some historians have therefore argued that the use of the bomb was no longer justifiable on grounds of military necessity and so must have had some concealed purpose, such as denying the USSR a voice in the peace settlement with Japan, or even modifying Soviet policy elsewhere. The argument can hardly be settled, but may be over-ingenious. Recent Pacific island battles such as *Iwo Jima had shown just how costly it would be for the Allies to fight their way into Japan, and there is some evidence that the atomic bomb gave the Japanese peace party their most compelling argument in their struggle against the diehards, and may at least have saved the lives of *prisoners-of-war in Japanese hands. Nevertheless, it was the Japanese who succeeded in laying down one condition of surrender, the continued rule of Emperor *Hirohito, in spite of the fact that many in the west regarded him as a war criminal. Military considerations overrode political ones in that instance at least.

The experience of the Second World War suggests several general conclusions. First, in a war presented from the start as a necessary war of good against evil, not as a conflict of national interests, and a war in which, after the entry of the USA, the Allies had the capacity for complete victory, any war aim other than unconditional surrender would have been inappropriate. Second, that same nature of the war determined what could be done by the victorious Allies after it. Moral constraints proved as compelling as national interests might have been. The demand for unconditional surrender neither lengthened the war needlessly nor did anything much to determine the shape of the post-war world. The rivalries of the major Allies after the war served to maintain an international balance quite as well as any agreement among them that balance was desirable could have done. It also allowed, over time, for the return of the defeated states into the international system. Ideological rivalries are not easily accommodated in systemic analysis, yet an international system of considerable stability proved possible.

A. E. CAMPBELL

Campbell, A. E., 'Franklin Roosevelt and Unconditional Surrender', in R. T. B. Langhorne (ed.), *Diplomacy and Intelligence during the Second World War. Essays in Honour of F. H. Hinsley* (Cambridge, 1985).
O'Connor, R. G., *Diplomacy for Victory. FDR and Unconditional Surrender* (New York, 1971).
Villa, B. L., 'The US Army, Unconditional Surrender and the Potsdam Proclamation', *Journal of American History*, 63:1 (June 1976).

underground movements, see resistance sections of relevant major powers and under names of relevant countries; see also SUBVERSIVE WARFARE.

Union of Soviet Socialist Republics, see USSR.

United Kingdom, see UK.

United Nations Declaration. Following the *Atlantic Charter a statement of Allied war aims was agreed during the first Washington conference in December 1941 (see ARCADIA). This became the basis for a war alliance, the first the USA had made since 1778. It was signed on 1 January 1942 by China, the UK, USA, and USSR, and was later signed by 22 other nations which were named as joint declarers. All signatories agreed to employ their full resources against the Axis powers; to continue such employment until those powers were defeated: to co-operate with the others; and not to make a separate peace with any Axis power. It concluded that this declaration could be adhered to by other nations which were already rendering, or might in the future render, 'mutual assistance and contributions' towards the defeat of the Axis, and in due course 19 others signed. The Declaration was the first official use of the term 'United Nations'. See also GRAND ALLIANCE and SAN FRANCISCO CONFERENCE.

United States of America, see USA.

UNRRA (United Nations Relief and Rehabilitation Administration), established in November 1943 by delegates from 44 countries meeting in Atlantic City in the USA. It was initially set up to provide help for the peoples of liberated countries and it first began its work in North Africa. In the immediate post-war period it looked after displaced persons (see REFUGEES), and altogether it dispensed over $4 billion to 17 countries before it ceased operating in June 1947. See also CONSEQUENCES OF THE WAR.

Untermenschen (subhumans), Nazi term for 'inferior' races, meaning the Slavs and the Jews.

Uruguay was the most consistently pro-Allied, and anti-Axis, of all the South American states before the USA entered the war in December 1941, and its government maintained a strictly neutral stance when the German pocket battleship *Admiral Graf Spee* sought refuge in Montevideo after the *River Plate battle in December 1939. Uruguay severed relations with the main Axis powers in January 1942. On 22 February 1945 it declared war on Germany and Japan, and signed the *United Nations Declaration two days later. See also LATIN AMERICA AT WAR.

USA

1. Introduction

The road by which the USA entered the Second World War was long and tortuous, and reluctantly taken. The nation had historically adhered to an isolationist foreign policy, departing briefly from that line in 1917–18, when it became a belligerent against Germany in the *First World War. The experience was not a happy one. It cost some 50,000 American lives and failed to produce the equitable, durable peace that President Woodrow Wilson (1856–1924) had promised as the fruit of American participation. American diplomacy reverted thereafter with quickened dedication to its customary isolationism which did not release its grip on American foreign policy until the Japanese attacked *Pearl Harbor on 7 December 1941.

Disillusionment with the results of US intervention in the First World War was vividly manifested in the rejection by the Senate of the *Versailles settlement, including its provisions for American membership in the *League of Nations. The Senate further evidenced the renewed isolationist tenor of American diplomacy when it ratified the several treaties issuing from the Washington Naval Armament Conference of 1922. Their most important provisions called for the USA to scrap nearly a million tons of warships, and to limit further naval construction, in order to comply with a mandated ratio of 5:5:3 in capital-ship tonnage among the UK, the USA, and Japan, respectively. In addition, Washington agreed not to fortify its Pacific possessions west of Pearl Harbor, including Guam and the Philippines.

In practice, the USA did not maintain even a 'treaty strength' fleet in the 1920s. Throughout that decade and much of the next, the US Navy had a complement of fewer than 100,000 men; the army in that same period averaged about 135,000 men. The Roosevelt administration authorized some new naval construction beginning in 1933, but the continuing constraints of isolationism and the economic crisis of the Great Depression kept the size of the American military to a minimum. As late as 1940, the army numbered 269,023 personnel; the navy 160,997; the marines 28,345.

Those numbers, and the political philosophy that underlay them, made for a weak diplomatic hand. Just how weak was revealed in 1931, when Japan seized control of Manchuria from China and established the puppet state of Manchukuo. The USA condemned the Japanese action, but was unprepared to give force to its disapproval by either economic or military means. Washington contented itself with enunciating the *Stimson doctrine which withheld recognition from the Manchukuo regime while invoking the hoary principles of the 'Open Door', the policy of respecting Chinese Sovereignty and claiming equal commercial access to China by all nations, first enunciated by Secretary of State John Hay in 1899.

Such toothless moral posturing foreshadowed the agonizing attenuation of the American response to the outbreak of full-scale war between Japan and China in July 1937 (see CHINA INCIDENT). Even when Japanese aircraft sank the US gunboat *Panay* in the river Yangtze on 12 December 1937, no warcry swept the USA. Indeed, the following month the House of Representatives narrowly defeated the Ludlow resolution, calling for a Constitutional amendment that would require a national referendum on a declaration of war. As the British prime minister, *Chamberlain, accurately observed at the time: 'It is always best and safest to count on nothing from the Americans but words.'

From 1934, isolationist sentiment was especially aroused by the hearings of the Senate Munitions Investigating Committee (the Nye Committee), where many witnesses alleged that American financiers and arms manufacturers had manipulated American entry into the First World War. Public outrage over these inflammatory accusations produced a disposition in Congress to erect statutory barriers against the possibility that the USA might again be lured into a mistaken internationalist adventure. Accordingly, the first of three *Neutrality Acts was passed in 1935, which prohibited, among other restrictions, arms sales to belligerents.

Throughout this period in the mid-1930s, Roosevelt appeared personally inclined toward a more active international role for the USA, but his assessment of congressional and public opinion, his competing domestic priorities, and the absence of vigorous diplomatic initiatives by the other democratic states, all inhibited him from strenuously moving in an internationalist direction.

When war broke out in Europe in September 1939, Roosevelt induced Congress to repeal the arms embargo, but the Neutrality Act of 1939 still placed limitations on arms sales by including a 'cash-and-carry' provision. American opinion was strongly anti-German and anti-Japanese, but the expectation prevailed that France and the UK could contain Hitler in Europe, and that some *modus vivendi* might yet be worked out in Asia.

The fall of *France in June 1940, leaving the UK and its

empire the only Great Power facing Hitler, shattered those comfortable assumptions. A memorandum drafted that month by the army's War Plans Division predicted the UK's early defeat, called for the husbanding of all American military resources for hemispheric defence, and advocated a purely defensive posture in the Pacific.

Roosevelt, however, made the crucial decision to bet on the UK's survival. Throughout 1940, he undertook simultaneously to strengthen American military capacity, and to aid the UK by all means short of war itself. More than $10 billion was appropriated for a military build-up, including, on 20 July, an act authorizing the creation of a two-ocean navy. In September the nation's first peacetime conscription law was passed (see SELECTIVE SERVICE SYSTEM). The president created a National Defense Research Committee (later the *Office of Scientific Research and Development) to bring scientific expertise to bear on the military effort. Remembering the damage that political partisanship had inflicted on Woodrow Wilson's diplomacy, Roosevelt in June named two internationalist-minded Republicans to his cabinet—Henry Stimson as secretary of war, and Frank *Knox as secretary of navy. In November Roosevelt conveniently won re-election to an unprecedented third presidential term, while pledging that the USA would not go to war.

The 'short of war' strategy appeared to be Roosevelt's sincere hope. He intended to leave the actual fighting to the UK, while making the USA, as he said in a radio address of 29 December, 'the great arsenal of democracy' but not a belligerent. Already, on 3 September 1940, he had concluded with the UK the *destroyers-for-bases agreement and on 11 March 1941 he signed the *Lend-Lease Act. From 9 to 12 August 1941 Roosevelt and Churchill met at *Placentia Bay, Newfoundland, and drew up the *Atlantic Charter. In November 1941 Congress revised the neutrality laws to allow the arming of merchant ships, and to permit sending them into war zones. American naval vessels had by that time begun escorting British convoys carrying Lend-lease goods across the Atlantic, which led to an undeclared naval war between Germany and the USA as part of the battle of the *Atlantic. German submarines torpedoed the escort destroyer **Kearny* on 17 October 1941, and sank the **Reuben James* on 1 November 1941. Yet neither Hitler nor Roosevelt used these incidents to create a *casus belli*. The former was preoccupied with his invasion of the Soviet Union, launched on 22 June 1941 (see BARBAROSSA), the latter was restrained by his 'short of war' electoral promises and by continuing signs of isolationist strength in Congress. The House of Representatives, for example, still powerfully influenced by isolationist lobbies such as *America First, passed an extension of the Selective Service Act on 18 August 1941 by the margin of just a single vote. Additionally, Roosevelt appreciated the woeful unpreparedness of American military forces, and he had scant need of engagement in the war in Europe while events in Asia remained so volatile.

In the *ABC-1 Plan talks of January–March 1941, American and British military planners had agreed that in the event of American belligerency with both Germany and Japan, the defeat of Germany would be the first priority. But it was at Pearl Harbor in the Pacific that war eventually came to the USA, and it was on the *Pacific war that much popular American feeling would focus. Among American strategists the precise interpretation of the 'Germany first' doctrine would remain controversial throughout the conflict.

The story of the road to Pearl Harbor is a story in which both protagonists, Japan and the USA, writhed for years on the horns of their respective dilemmas. To continue its war against China, Japan depended upon purchasing critical materials in the USA, particularly scrap metals and petroleum products. Yet the Americans made no secret of their disapproval of the Japanese role in China. The Japanese government was chronically worried about the dependability of its American supplies of metal and oil, and constantly sought alternative sources. Under the circumstances, the Japanese looked naturally to the special opportunity presented by the German subjugation of France and the Netherlands in the spring of 1940. The collapse of the French and Dutch governments left their colonies in French Indo-China and the Netherlands East Indies, rich in oil and strategic metals, tantalizingly vulnerable to Japanese penetration.

Debate divided both the Japanese and American governments over the question of Japanese pressure on French Indo-China and the East Indies, and the proper response to that pressure. In some ways the controversies within the two governments were mirror images of one another. For the Japanese, the issue was what degree of aggression could be pursued in the South Pacific without precipitating conflict with the USA. For the Americans, the question was what degree of resistance could be posed to Japanese aggression without driving Tokyo to a declaration of war.

On both sides of the Pacific, statesmen delicately adjusted these fateful balances throughout 1940 and 1941. In Tokyo, army leaders pressed for more aggressive moves towards the south. Some civilian members of the government, and some navy leaders, urged restraint. In Washington, Stimson and secretary of the treasury, Henry Morgenthau, advocated embargoing the shipment of strategic materials to Japan. But secretary of state *Hull, usually backed by the navy, rather consistently opposed a strict embargo as too provocative. His influence remained paramount at least until the summer of 1941, dampening the tempo of American *diplomacy directed against Japan, and delaying the moment of the final showdown.

In the summer of 1940, Washington announced its intention to limit shipments of scrap metals and oil to Japan; it imposed a formal embargo on iron and steel scrap on 26 September 1940. The following day Tokyo announced its adherence to the *Tripartite Pact with Germany and Italy. In November 1940 Japan wrung a limited oil-supply agreement from the government of the Netherlands East Indies. Japanese troops occupied French Indo-China on 24 July 1941. On 26 July 1941 Roosevelt froze all Japanese assets in the USA, in effect embargoing all shipments to Japan including, most crucially, oil. Though Roosevelt apparently intended to release some oil shipments in return for promises of Japanese good behaviour—thus pursuing even at this late hour the hope of reaching some kind of *modus vivendi*—the public announcement of the American action gave the impression of an iron-clad embargo, and Roosevelt concluded that it would be a sign of weakness to amend it.

The die was now all but cast. On 6 September 1941 a Japanese Imperial Conference stipulated that if an agreement with the USA was not in prospect by early October, Japan should move towards war. Prime Minister *Konoe sought a secret meeting with Roosevelt to hammer out an accord. From Tokyo, Ambassador Joseph Grew advocated the meeting as the last chance to avoid war. But the US government, privy to Japanese intentions thanks to *MAGIC intercepts, saw no hope for significant Japanese concessions—especially over China—and spurned the offer. Konoe's government fell on 16 October 1941, and the following day General *Tōjō became prime minister. An Imperial Conference of 5 November 1941 directed that war plans go forward, to be confirmed on 25 November if a last effort to secure American agreement to Japanese terms for a settlement failed.

But China, especially, remained the sticking-point. Washington simply would not give any official approval to the Japanese invasion of China. Hull made this point repeatedly to Ambassador Nomura Kichisaburo during their final, fruitless round of talks in Washington from 20 November to 7 December 1941.

Yet ironically, on the same date of 5 November that Tōjō's government slipped its war machine into gear, American army and navy planners advised that, 'considering world strategy', further Japanese aggression in China 'would not justify intervention by the United States against Japan' (H. Feis [below], p. 302). No matter. The Americans had stood on principle—the principles of the Open Door and the Stimson doctrine of non-interference in the affairs of other nations. The Japanese acted from what they regarded as economic and political necessity, but most of the world regarded it as naked aggression. Aiming to secure their access to the *raw materials of French Indo-China and the Netherlands East Indies, they had first to eliminate the threat to their eastern flank posed by the US Pacific Fleet. On 7 December 1941, Japan attacked the US base at Pearl Harbor, Hawaii, and the following day, with a sole dissenting vote, Congress declared war on Japan. DAVID M. KENNEDY

2. Domestic life, war effort, and economy

The fall of France had finally galvanized Washington into action. The political stalemate was broken; there was near unanimity that the USA must rearm immediately. By the end of the summer Congress had approved $78 billion for future war spending (the total GNP was only $101 billion). In late summer the National Guard (state-based reserves totalling 300,000 men) was called up and, with the introduction of the Selective Service Act, the first peacetime draft began, with a target of two million men in one year. These early moves were a harbinger of a national commitment that would expand even more dramatically in the next five years. Mobilization was managed by the war and navy departments, and by new emergency agencies that were abolished when peace returned. They were headed by conservative Republican lawyers, financiers, and businessmen, as were the war and navy departments. In the latter, however, the generals and admirals minimized the influence of civilians.

Roosevelt, despite his experience in running naval affairs in the First World War, had considerable difficulty in managing the war effort. Congress was not the problem—generally, it gave all the authority and money requested—the problem was in the New Deal's style of divided responsibility. The army and the navy feuded incessantly, over grand strategy, manpower allocations, and munitions priorities (see also RIVALRIES); inside the army, the air force carved out a large and semi-autonomous domain with its own priorities. Roosevelt's management style encouraged such divided responsibility, with feuding agencies having to return to him again and again to settle disputes. His goal of maximizing his personal control proved inefficient and confusing during the war, and more and more he had to yield authority on economic affairs. Compounding his problem was a mysterious failure of his skills in mobilizing public opinion: with few radio talks, public appearances, or dramatic statements, the president kept a low profile.

The economy in 1940 had been weakened by a decade of depression. Unemployment at nearly 15% was the highest among major nations, profits were low, and the factories were rusting because little investment had been made. Furthermore, businessmen were hostile towards Roosevelt's administration, and were doubly suspicious of the powerful new labour unions, which were themselves divided into two feuding camps: the larger, older, more conservative American Federation of Labor (AFL) and the leftist Congress of Industrial Organizations (CIO). Guaranteed large increases in membership, the unions suppressed wildcat strikes that threatened to interrupt war production, but also tried to keep overtime pay and other perks. On a positive note, the people were sick of internal dissension and depression and, when the call to arms sounded, proved ready to work harmoniously for the goal of a better life after the war. The economic challenge was to provide 12 million thoroughly trained soldiers and sailors, plus a huge supply of aircraft, warships, transports, electronic gear, and other *matériel* for American and Allied armies, plus oil and food for everybody, plus money to pay for it all (see Table 1 for US economic indictors 1939–46).

USA, 2, Table 1: Basic economic indicators, 1939–46

Year	*1939*	*1940*	*1941*	*1942*	*1943*	*1944*	*1945*	*1946*
real GNP-1940 ($)	92	100	116	131	149	159	156	138
inflation	98	100	108	121	129	133	136	152
% of GNP to war	1.0	2.2	10.9	30.7	41.4	41.5	35.3	
consumer prices	99	100	105	118	126	130	133	143
real weekly $ mfg	95	100	112	124	136	141	132	122
real hourly wage mfg	97	100	105	110	115	119	116	115
TOTAL EMPLOYMENT	95	100	113	124	131	129	125	129
non-war employment	96	100	108	111	109	108	109	121
war employment	87	100	135	184	237	234	199	165
% of women in labour force	28.0	27.9	28.5	31.0	35.8	36.5	35.9	31.1
civilian women at work		100	109	127	152	157	155	136
civilian men at work		100	105	109	102	99	96	110
% unemployed	17.2	14.6	9.9	4.7	1.9	1.2	1.9	3.9
working week, av. hours		43.8	44.2	45.2	47.3	46.2	44.3	42.4
structure of civilian labour force								
% youth under 20		7.5	9.1	11.1	12.0	11.4	10.5	8.4
% adult men		70.0	68.9	64.5	59.7	58.8	59.2	66.2
% adult women		22.5	22.0	24.4	28.4	29.8	30.3	25.4
earnings, full-time men	95	100	109	121	139	146	141	125
earnings, full-time women	98	100	105	110	126	136	133	134
women's pay as % men	57.4	55.6	53.5	50.8	50.4	51.8	52.7	59.5
durable mfg output	78	100	145	201	259	254	197	138
non-durable mfg output	95	100	123	137	153	149	144	143
railway freight ton-miles	89	100	127	171	195	198	182	159
railway passenger miles	95	100	123	226	369	402	386	272
war construction	27	100	528	1,540	805	377	263	55
non-war construction	99	100	111	69	48	39	54	153
corporate taxes	48	100	280	481	624	585	424	345
corporate after-tax profit	87	100	137	160	175	168	151	235
exports to the UK	50	100	162	250	446	519	217	85
income share of top 5%	26.8	25.4	23.0	19.0	16.7	15.8	16.7	17.7
personal spending	95	100	108	106	110	117	126	141
personal taxes	93	100	121	196	542	560	603	504
personal savings	69	100	276	618	696	757	585	280
births	96	100	106	117	121	115	112	133
marriages	88	100	106	111	99	91	101	144

Source: Contributors.

Under the Lend-Lease programme, the USA provided a quarter of the munitions for the UK, and perhaps a tenth of what the USSR used. Two-thirds of all supplies shipped abroad consisted of oil. The USA pumped nearly two-thirds of the world's oil from its rich Texas and California fields, and at only $1.15 a barrel it was cheap. At first, moving it safely was another matter, because of the German submarines off the coast (see CONVOYS). The nation's tanker capacity reached 11.4 million tons by 1945, compared to 2.5 million tons in 1941, much of which was sunk. Civilian demand for petrol was cut 28% by rationing, and all the increased production (up 29% in 1945 over 1941) went into the war effort. In 1942 Japan captured 90% of the world's rubber supplies, but, despite early confusion, by late 1943 a highly successful synthetic rubber industry had met the increased war demands.

On US farms the recent memories of surpluses, low prices, and hardship vanished, though many young people, blacks, and marginal farmers left, shrinking the rural farm share of the population from 23% to 20%. However, Congress made sure that prices stayed high, and exempted most young farm workers from the draft. As a result, crop production increased by 15%, beef production by 37%, and pork production by 63%. A tenth of the food was exported through Lend-Lease, chiefly to the UK (43%) and the USSR (28%). Though this abundance strained the transportation and storage system, Americans ate more and better food during the war than ever before, and tightly enforced rationing ensured they were more equal in their diets. In 1938 protein, calorie, calcium, and iron consumption among the poorest one-third of the population was 74% of that consumed by the richest third. By 1942 this had increased to 89%, and to 93% by 1948. Even so, people who until the war had not been able to afford mince, now complained that even their high wages could not buy them steak.

The USA never adopted a comprehensive manpower programme. The draft reached most young men by 1944, and physical standards remained high. Draft boards were reluctant to take fathers or men under 19; if drafted they were rarely sent to combat formations. The government decided, after much debate, not to draft *women or force them to enter the labour force (see Graph 1 for labour force structure 1938–47). No coercion was used to move men into war jobs, either, but the lure of very high pay proved quite sufficient. Employment in durable goods manufacturing leaped from 4.7 million in May 1940, to a peak of 10.7 million in December 1943—an astonishing gain of 6 million jobs in 3½ years. At the end of the war there were still 10.1 million workers, but overnight the munitions factories dismissed 85 to 95% of their employees and durable goods employment dropped to 6.5 million in December 1945.

With the enormous demand for construction workers to erect camps, hospitals, shipyards, and munitions plants, unemployment vanished in 1940–2. The previously dirt poor rural South became the favourite site for most military camps, and for many shipyards and munitions works. Millions of families moved from rural areas and small towns to work in overcrowded production centres like Los Angeles, San Francisco, Chicago, Detroit, Pittsburgh, Mobile, and Baltimore, but the shortage of skilled workers threatened to delay full production. During the Depression the government, on ideological grounds, had refused to fight unemployment through job training programmes or wage subsidies. It now reversed its policy and paid for massive training programmes through its 'cost-plus' contracts with private industry. (The contracts paid all legitimate costs, plus a small percentage profit.) Semi-skilled workers and high school drop-outs suddenly found themselves well-paid skilled specialists, or even foremen. More had to be done, so industry systematically 'diluted' or redesigned jobs so that less skilled workers could handle them. In peacetime dilution had been fiercely opposed by the unions; now they co-operated, for they obtained new rules that made most of the new workers join unions. Dilution allowed the hiring of millions of women, blacks, youth, and older people who had previously been in low-paid jobs, or unemployed.

To increase productivity further, factories stayed open for a second or even a third shift, and workers added long hours of overtime (with a 50% wage premium paid beyond the basic 40 hours). The average working week in manufacturing durable goods jumped from 38 hours in 1939 to 47 hours in 1943, and efficiency experts looked for ways to increase production. A favourite solution was to use assembly-line techniques and prefabrication, so as to minimize the amount of skilled labour needed and allow many people to work on a project simultaneously. The productivity gains were striking: it took only a third as many worker-hours to build a ship in 1945 as in 1942. Despite the disruptions caused by the draft, and by the confusion of producing new products under pressure, the overall productivity of the economy, per worker-hour, rose by 21% between 1940 and 1945. Railway workers were 63% more productive in 1943 than in 1940.

In 1940 the nation's steel mills operated at 82% capacity, producing 67 million tons; by 1944 they were working at full stretch pouring 89 million tons of steel, about half the world total. The numbers employed did not change—all the gains came from enhanced productivity. As tens of thousands of factories tooled up for their production runs, the machine tool industry was overwhelmed. Orders in 1942 were five times higher than in 1940, but very long working weeks helped the industry manufacture $4.7 billion of tools between 1940 and 1945, or 20 times more than in the previous decade. Engineers redesigned the tools to be more durable, more versatile, and simpler to operate; the skills the operators lacked had to be designed into the machines and jigs themselves. The total stock of machine tools in all American factories soared from one million in 1940 to 1.7 million in 1945. With many in operation for three shifts a day, the sinews of economic mobilization were ready, and in five years the USA produced $181 billions worth of munitions, of which aircraft made up 24%; ships, 22%; food, clothing, and medicine, 20%; tanks and trucks, 12%; ammunition, 10%; guns and fire control equipment, 6%; and radio and radar, 6% (see Table 2 for munitions output 1940–5). Employment in war industry as a whole peaked at 8.8 million in late 1944, 29% of them women and 8% black.

Roosevelt's promise in 1940 to build 50,000 aircraft was received with amazement. In the end, 300,000 were built, at a cost of $45 billion. The Army Air Forces took 185,000; the navy, 60,000; the UK, Canada, Australia, and New Zealand, 33,000; the USSR, 18,000; and China, 4,000. Measured by weight, the production totalled 2.9 billion pounds, of which 61% represented bombers and 22% fighters. Overnight, executives at Douglas, Consolidated Vultee, Boeing, North American, Lockheed, and smaller aircraft companies, transformed their small workshops into the world's largest and most complex factories. Riveters with just three or four weeks' training were employed extensively. Virtually all the warplanes had been designed before Pearl Harbor, though they were continually modified and upgraded. With car production suspended for the duration, the great automobile companies retooled radically. They converted their old assembly lines to make aircraft and tank gear, and the government built new plants for them, such as Ford's gigantic *Willow Run bomber plant or the even larger Dodge engine plant in Chicago. The rifles, cannon, shells, and ammunition for the forces were made primarily in government arsenals. Located typically in small towns known to have a surplus of labour, they employed 486,000 workers in 1943, as against 22,000 in 1940. Shipyards

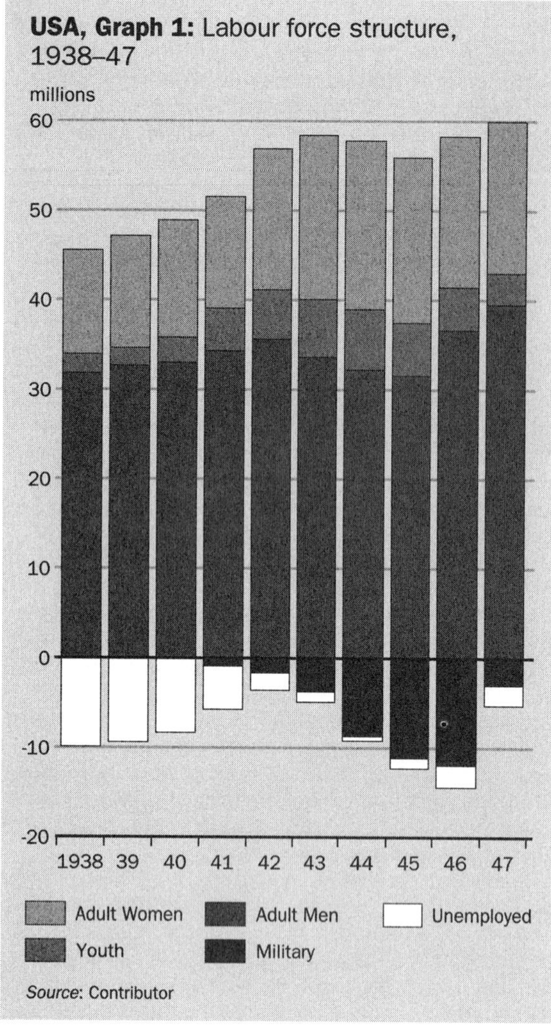

USA, Graph 1: Labour force structure, 1938–47

Source: Contributor

launched 88,000 landing craft, 215 submarines, 147 aircraft carriers, and 952 other warships, aggregating 14 million tons. They also welded together 5,200 merchant ships totalling 39 million gross tons (see LIBERTY SHIPS). The war geared up not only armies and industries but also science and technology. Chemists made possible the daily production of 80 million litres of 100-octane aviation fuel, which gave aircraft a distinct edge in speed, climb rate, and manoeuvrability. Physicists and electrical engineers perfected the *proximity fuze—which made Japanese Zeros 50 times easier to hit—but the most astonishing scientific and engineering achievement of the war was the invention of the *atomic bomb. In the long run, however, arguably the most important technical achievement of the war was America's first programmable electronic computer. Developed at the University of Pennsylvania in 1945 (some two years after *Bletchley Park's COLOSSUS II), the ENIAC (Electronic Numerical Integrator and Computer) was designed to calculate artillery tables.

The change in gross national product from $101 billion in 1940 to $214 billion in 1944 can be hypothetically broken down into different factors. The departure of the soldiers (−17%) was offset by increases due to inflation (26%), new workers (11%), elimination of unemployment (12%), population growth (4%), extended hours (4%), and increases in capital and worker productivity (60%). These factors did not just happen: they required the deliberate efforts of government, the services, executives, engineers, unions, workers, and the community as a whole to make them happen. The establishment of open-ended contracts on a cost-plus basis guaranteed that corporations would aggressively search out new workers and train them. The government would pay. The patriotic willingness—even eagerness—of people to switch from stable jobs to the better paying but dead-end munitions jobs was essential. Above all, the nation's engineers and managers were inspired to design, plan, and organize vast economic potential without regard to profit.

Since nearly half the GNP had to be devoted to the war, the workers could not be allowed to spend more than half their wages. Price controls and rationing were imposed so that essential items would remain cheap. Consumer durables like automobiles, domestic appliances, and houses were no longer produced. The government spent $350 billion ($318 for direct war purposes), but only took in $147 billion in taxes. The deficit had to be borrowed. Six million volunteers whipped up patriotism and drained surplus money by selling $157 billions worth of war bonds. (Those assets would play a decisive role in maintaining prosperity after 1945.) The consequence was that the national debt of $259 billion in 1945 exceeded the GNP of $212 billion; since interest rates were kept artificially low, at about 1%, the burden was bearable. Taxes soared during the war. Previously only the wealthiest tenth paid income taxes; now 90% of all families paid, and at stiff rates. A typical worker with a wife and child earned $2,600 in 1944. Of that $253 went to federal income tax (23% after exemptions of 3 × $500), and $26 went to Social Security. Of the $2,600, 11% went to taxes, 33% to food, 33% to clothing and housing, 5% to transportation, 10% to medical costs (private medical insurance was just becoming popular), and 8% was saved or used to pay off old depression debts. Corporate taxes were raised to guarantee that profits would remain at about 1936–7 depression levels of 10% of net worth.

Americans were patriotic during the war, and more united than ever before. They therefore sacrificed some of their famed individualism in exchange for community purposes. The refrain 'Don't You Know There's a War On!' silenced grumblers and emboldened the community minded. While most families felt that material conditions had worsened, cold statistics showed they were distinctly better fed and better clothed than in the depression years. No matter, for Americans had recalibrated their sensibilities towards a new post-war standard of prosperity. Against that gauge the war years were uncomfortable yet optimistic. The deliberate national policy of keeping casualties to a minimum (and especially not subjecting fathers to combat) meant there were few orphans and widows to plunge a community into mourning. Indeed, for an average group of 1,000 soldiers, more fathers died a natural death on the Home Front than sons in combat. Americans were confident the soldiers would march home safe.

The demand for housing was exceptionally high in the major industrial centres, and shopping, transportation, and community services were almost overwhelmed. Fat pay checks assuaged much of the discomfort. The federal government, under the Lanham Act, provided modest support facilities for towns inundated by war industry. The act also provided for day-care centres for pre-school children. Surprisingly, they were highly controversial, as any number of social forces (mothers, factories, sundry local and federal agencies, social workers, educators, unions, clergymen) made the centres into political footballs that reflected distinctive socio-political ideologies. An apparent upsurge in juvenile delinquency heightened concerns about teenagers. There was no epidemic of delinquency; rather the youth who had been so repressed because of hard times were suddenly allowed to move about. Much of the mischief involved youth staying out beyond curfew; their older brothers were off to war, and excitement was in the air. The upsurge in high school enrolments from 1920 gave teenagers more intellectual skills and social resources. A new quasi-autonomous youth culture was beginning to flourish. Its taste in fashion, music, food, and egalitarian, consumer-oriented, informal lifestyle would soon become the norm.

Marriage, setting up a new household, and starting a family all required ingenuity and help, given the shortage of housing, furniture, and appliances. Servicemen's wives usually returned to their parents' home, a doubling up that would not be relieved until the post-war housing boom finally caught up with demand around 1948. Worse than the inconvenience and the waiting was the loneliness. Young couples discarded much of the tradition that had separated husbands and wives into different spheres. They sought egalitarian, companionable marriages. Divorce rates changed little: 27% of the wartime marriages eventually ended in divorce, compared to 26% for the late 1930s and 26% for the late 1940s. Couples were child-oriented and in 1940 they began a 'baby boom' that lasted until 1960. Between 1940 and 1942, the rate of first births jumped from 293 per 10,000 women to 375 (the rate of subsequent births went from 506 to 540). The increase in childbearing took place among all groups of young women, but was greatest among the best educated, who had the most resources and the most opportunities to understand and control their lives.

The nation puzzled over new roles for women, Most long-standing prohibitions against married women working were dropped. For the first time, large numbers

USA, 2, Table 2: US munitions output, 1940–5

	May 1940– Dec 1941	*1942*	*1943*	*1944*	*Jan–July 1945*	*Total*
Munition budget	$10,384	$30,168	$51,745	$57,594	$30,767	$180,658
aircraft	$2,152	$5,817	$12,514	$16,047	$7,716	$44,246
ships	$2,221	$6,957	$12,498	$13,429	$5,534	$40,639
guns	$429	$1,794	$3,180	$2,926	$1,373	$9,702
ammunition	$509	$2,743	$4,908	$5,768	$3,930	$17,858
vehicles	$1,508	$4,778	$5,926	$4,951	$2,942	$20,105
radar/radio	$250	$1,512	$3,043	$3,739	$2,119	$10,663
Munitions purchases						
Aircraft, 000s	23	48	86	96	43	296
Aircraft weight, m kg	43	125	297	437	221	1,123
Aircraft bombs[a]	41	57	135	198	100	531
Warships[b]	270	847	2,562	3,223	1,341	8,243
Naval ammunition[a]	32	558	658	1,191	1,039	3,478
Landing vessels, 000s	1	7	16	27	13	64
Depth charges, 000s	17	141	147	170	54	529
Torpedoes, 000s	2	5	16	24	7	54
Rifles/carbines, 000s	357	1,541	5,683	3,489	1,503	12,573
Ground artillery ammunition[a]	52	615	726	1,313	1,145	3,851
Tanks	4,203	23,884	29,497	17,565	11,184	86,333

[a] million metric tons [b] thousand displacement tons

Source: Contributor.

Women became part of the war effort in the **USA** just as much as they did in other combatant countries. This poster of 'Rosie the Riveter', is typical of the propaganda disseminated to encourage them.

of mothers entered the workforce. Nevertheless, social values still strongly preferred that husbands be the primary breadwinners and wives focus their attention on home duties, especially child-rearing. Women saw two kinds of jobs open up. In some munitions plants women replaced young men called up into the services, but much more often the women did not replace anyone, for over 90% of the munitions jobs were new. The image of 'Rosie the Riveter' doing traditionally male work was a propaganda device; the real 'Rosies' either did traditional woman's work, like assembling radios, or else they did a new sort of job that no one had done before, such as riveting an airplane or welding a ship. When women did replace men it was only after compromises with the unions. Fearing the old bogies of cheap/unskilled/female workers replacing their permanent male members, the unions insisted that women were temporary employees and should be paid the same as men, so that, when the men returned from war, the employers would dismiss the less efficient highly-paid women. In fact most of the new women workers did not enter munitions plants, but took office and factory jobs where they often did replace men. These jobs were non-union, and after the war the women held on to them. The workforce became distinctly more feminized, especially in the white collar sector. After the war 4.1 million women left the labour force: 50% told census takers they did so because of the demands of family; another 18% said their husbands insisted on being the sole breadwinner; 13% cited age or disability; 11% cited their return to education or to a rural home as the reason. A few left because of lack of suitable jobs (6%), or poor working conditions or lack of child care (2%). Wives were especially clear in their determination to leave their paid jobs. They had been doing double duty, and their home chores had increased because of poor services, overcrowded public transport, shortages, and increased childcare responsibilities.

Eleanor Roosevelt (1884–1962), Oveta Culp Hobby of the Woman's Army Corps (WAC), Congresswoman/playwright/society leader Claire Boothe Luce, and Jackie Cochran (director of the *WASP, the organization which ferried Air Force planes), along with numerous *Hollywood celebrities, were the most prominent women of the day. In contrast to the depression years, which put a premium on nurturing female roles, the war years extolled masculinity. The 'Rosie' and *WAC propaganda always featured women excelling in male roles, but it was really the change in the role of females that counted. Women invested in the future—in return for high morale, hard work, and general support for the nation's war goals, they demanded control over post-war society. They gained in power and importance inside the family, especially among better educated younger couples. The soaring birth rates and the idealization of the child-centred, egalitarian suburban home was their ultimate achievement. Government policy quickly ratified the new ideals. The EMIC (Emergency Maternal and Infant Care) programme provided free prenatal and obstetric care for servicemen's wives. The *GI Bill provided very cheap home ownership, loans to start up businesses, and free college tuition for ex-servicemen. Unlike the New Deal, which targeted its aid to the poor, these programmes fitted the conservative ideal of reward for actual service to the nation.

Egalitarianism was the rule in the war years, reinforced by rationing, shortages, price controls, and the universalism of the draft. Income differentials narrowed, and relief was once more concentrated on people outside the labour force. The share of total income received by the richest 5% fell from 27% in 1939 to 16% in 1944. The communal spirit dramatically softened the lines that divided ethnic and religious groups. *Anti-Semitism and anti-Catholicism declined sharply (see also RELIGION). Desperately poor Slavic and Italian ethnic groups rapidly improved their economic status, earning about 94% of average by 1950.

The question of the loyalty of enemy aliens, and those of Axis origins, was troublesome. When in 1942 the army proposed that citizens of Germany and Italy be relocated away from the West Coast, public opinion would not accept wholesale removal; only 10,000 were moved. Of the 20 million Americans of German descent, only a few thousand sympathized with the Nazis (see GERMAN–

AMERICAN BUND). Mussolini was a good deal more popular among Italians, but obviously posed a negligible military threat. Public and élite opinion was loud and nearly unanimous that *Japanese-Americans were dangerous and, at the minimum, had to be removed from strategic localities. Until 1950 federal law prevented people born in Japan (Issei) from becoming citizens; their children (Nisei) born on US soil automatically acquired citizenship, but they were mostly minors and would share the fate of their parents. Both groups were considered Japanese citizens by Tokyo. Although most proclaimed their loyalty to the USA, the level of distrust was high. Those living along the West Coast were sent to inland relocation centres, but there was no way to relocate or incarcerate the Issei in Hawaii, so the entire island was put under martial law for the duration. By 1988 public opinion had totally changed round, and the government offered an apology and cash payment to those who had been relocated. Mexicans, considered during the depression low-wage competitors for jobs and welfare benefits that ought to go to natives, had been given one-way tickets back to their home villages. During the war the buses and trains ran in the other direction, as thousands of Mexicans and Caribbeans replaced native farm workers (see BRACERO PROGRAMME). Since a main reason for the war in the Pacific was the USA's protective attitude towards China and the Philippines, the country's 100,000 Chinese and Filipino residents were given new recognition and their legal rights expanded (though not to fully equal status).

The economic status of blacks improved sharply during the war, as millions moved from unemployment in the city or under-employment in the cotton South, to manual labour jobs vacated by whites. In 1939, blacks comprised 10% of the non-farm labour force, but only 8.3% of the men and 4.3% of the women held jobs outside farming and domestic service. The median annual wages were 33% of the white rate for men, 46% for women. By 1944 black men and women were up to 10.1% and 9.1% of male and female employees, and their wages were 46% of the white rate for men and 42% for women. Except for government-run munitions plants, blacks were the last hired and the first fired. Segregation was still ironclad in the South, and prevailed in practice in the North. Rioting in Detroit in 1943 killed 34 as the acute housing shortage pitted newly arrived black families against newly arrived whites from the Appalachians. Observers were convinced that far more inter-racial bloodletting was inevitable, but apart from a few limited incidents in Mobile, Alabama, and Beaumont, Texas, trouble was averted for the time being (see also AFRICAN AMERICANS AT WAR).

The national mood during the war displayed little of the crusading fervour that characterized the First World War. There was a job to be done, then everyone could go home. Hatred of the Japanese was strong, but propaganda efforts to personalize the war against Hitler and Tōjō were not persuasive. The egalitarianism which gained a strong boost during the war had some negative effects in the military: US soldiers resented the artificial privileges that set officers apart from the enlisted men. Unions vastly increased their presence in the labour force and their power inside the Democratic Party. Bargaining with management became a matter of dollars and cents, not life and death. The antics of the labour leader John L. Lewis (1880–1967), however, created powerful resentment against labour 'barons' who supposedly ruled their domains in non-democratic fashion without regard to the national interest. Patriotism surged during the 1940s, as business and labour, farms and factories, men and women, white and black worked together for communal goals with a degree of harmony that presaged an era of consensus. Foreign policy battles faded as a recognition developed of the value of allies and the glowing promise of collective security through the United Nations (see SAN FRANCISCO CONFERENCE). The community spirit forged in countless scrap drives, air raid drills, Red Cross meetings, draft board hearings, and volunteer activities helped dissolve the class lines that had come into sharp relief a decade before. The practical value of education, the necessity of expertise, the limitless promise of technology, and the economic power of systematic organization all burned themselves deeply into the national mind, providing a fount of conventional wisdom that would last for two more decades. The enormous pride in having won a world war in decisive fashion, with their enemies prostrate and the Allies desperate for American help, led to an uncritical self-confidence. It would inspire politics, diplomacy, military policy, and even the media, academe, and the corporations until the crises of the 1960s. See also WORLD TRADE AND WORLD ECONOMY.

D'ANN CAMPBELL/RICHARD JENSEN

3. Government

For the USA, as for other major participants, the Second World War imposed one overriding task on the national government—marshalling the resources of the nation for the maximum feasible production of military might. Accomplishing that task accentuated one of the dominant trends of the 20th century, centralization of authority in the executive. However, centralization proceeded less far in the USA than in other countries, including the UK. Until the attack on Pearl Harbor, the USA moved only slowly away from reliance on markets and prices to allocate resources. The administrative machinery of war eventually emerged, but in 'a crazy-quilt pattern of new emergency agencies and old departments', according to one expert on wartime mobilization. Roosevelt initially resisted the creation of centralized control over the US economy, in part because he did not wish to inflame isolationist sentiment with overt preparations for mobilization, but also because he disliked the idea of placing one individual or agency in charge of the war effort. Additionally, the constitutionally induced conflicts between the executive and legislative branches hampered centralization and co-ordination, as did the wartime backlash against the New Deal, disagreements about the government's post-war programme, and clashes among powerful private interest groups representing agriculture, business, and organized labour.

By the end of the 1930s, Roosevelt's New Deal had produced a partial recovery from the Great Depression but had also generated intense controversy. In the summer of 1939, opposition to the administration's legislative programme had become so strong in Congress that any significant extension of New Deal reforms had become unlikely. In any case, the outbreak of war in Europe in September 1939 caused Roosevelt to reorder his priorities. Convinced that he could lead on only one front at a time, and blocked by Congressional opposition from continuing his domestic reforms, he moved national defence and foreign policy to the top of his agenda. As he would later explain, 'Dr New Deal' was giving way to 'Dr Win-the-War.' To bolster public and Congressional support, the president needed to broaden his political base. Facing vigorous isolationist opposition, he could not govern with support only from the New Deal wing of the Democratic Party. Accordingly, he considered forming a coalition cabinet, an idea he modified in June 1940 when he appointed Frank Knox and Henry Stimson, two leading Republican warhawks, to be secretaries of navy and war. He later named Jesse Jones (1874–1956), a conservative southern Democrat and the administration's chief spokesman for big business, to be secretary of commerce.

As the appointments of Knox, Stimson, and Jones signified, the president hoped to improve relations with groups that opposed the New Deal but supported his foreign and defence policies. He pursued rapprochement with the business community, which during the 1930s had become estranged from the administration. An expanded national defence programme would require the involvement and co-operation of business interests, and so in 1940 he appointed a National Defence Advisory Commission that included Edward R. *Stettinius Jr. of US Steel and William S. Knudsen (1879–1948), a former General Motors executive. But this new group had no authority and no single individual in charge, for Roosevelt remained reluctant to create an agency to control economic mobilization and defence production.

As military appropriations and the federal deficit soared in the spring and summer of 1940, the Roosevelt administration prodded Congress to raise taxes. At first the president and the secretary of the treasury, Henry Morgenthau Jr., favoured a progressive tax programme that would confiscate excessive profits arising from defence expenditures. In the end, the president proved willing to accept revenue legislation that deviated from principles of progressive taxation. The First and Second Revenue Acts of 1940 granted substantial concessions to business. Roosevelt accepted those concessions because he was convinced that unless corporate management got what it wanted on taxes, businessmen would not sign defence contracts. Therefore he surrendered to pressure for higher profits in order to induce corporations to produce arms.

Appeasement of the business community disenchanted New Dealers, who feared that the president had completely abandoned reform. It was partly to allay such fears that Roosevelt in 1940 chose as his vice-presidential nominee the secretary of agriculture, Henry A. Wallace (1888–1965). In 1940 the Roosevelt–Wallace ticket faced a stiff challenge from the Republican Wendell L. *Willkie, an attractive and articulate businessman who asserted that the New Deal had disabled the American economy and interfered with national defence. During the final weeks of the campaign, Willkie attacked Roosevelt's foreign policy as likely to lead the nation into war, but in November 1940 the president won re-election, although by a smaller margin than on the two previous occasions.

Even as the election campaign proceeded, the president and Congress moved to remedy American military weakness by introducing conscription (see SELECTIVE SERVICE SYSTEM) and by extending aid to the UK. Then, to speed up the defence production needed to implement these decisions, Roosevelt created, in January 1941, a new agency called the Office of Production Management (see Table 3 for principal government war agencies). This had somewhat broader scope and authority than its predecessor, the National Defense Advisory Commission, and, because it was jointly administered by William S. Knudsen and by union leader Sidney Hillman, it ensured that both management and labour were represented in the defence programme. But it was not a comprehensive mobilization organization. Jealous of his own prerogatives, Roosevelt still refused to establish a ministry of supply under a mobilization tsar.

By the summer of 1941, when American rearmament had still not shifted into high gear, it was becoming obvious that civilian production would have to be curtailed to increase military production, and that the president would have to relinquish his role as the day-to-day boss of the defence programme. Nevertheless, it was not until after Pearl Harbor, in January 1942, that he established the *War Production Board (WPB) with significantly greater power over defence production than the Office of Production Management. To direct the WPB, Roosevelt selected Donald M. Nelson (1888–1959), a former executive with the giant retailer Sears, Roebuck. Nelson was not, however, a mobilization tsar, for he shared authority over war production with a bewildering array of officials and agencies, which caused overlapping responsibilities and much friction.

The president also had to deal with friction between the executive and legislative branches of government and among powerful and competing private interest groups. Control of agricultural prices—part of the larger problem of economic stabilization in wartime—proved especially disruptive and a major source of controversy during 1942. Following an angry debate that pitted farm lobbies and

USA, 3, Table 3: Principal US Government war agencies, 1940–5

Board of Economic Warfare (later Office of Economic Warfare)
National Defense Advisory Commission
National Housing Agency
National War Labor Board
Office of Civilian Defense
Office of Defense Transportation
Office of Emergency Management
Office of Economic Stabilization
Office of Lend-Lease Administration
*Office of Price Administration
Office of Production Management
*Office of Scientific Research and Development
*Office of Strategic Services
*Office of War Information
Office of War Mobilization (later Office of War Mobilization and Reconversion)
Petroleum Administrator for War
Rubber Administration
*Smaller War Plants Corporation
War Food Administration
War Manpower Commission
War Labor Board
*War Production Board
War Relocation Authority
War Shipping Administration

* see separate entries

Source: Contributor.

farm bloc legislators against administration loyalists, Congress passed the Stabilization Act of 1942, which finally granted the *Office of Price Administration the authority to regulate farm prices.

The dispute over agricultural price control took place shortly before the congressional elections of November 1942 and proved costly to the Democratic Party. Farming belt voters elected Republicans, who were considered more inclined to support higher farm prices and incomes. These results reflected a national trend towards the Republicans, who gained 44 seats in the House of Representatives and 9 in the Senate. Low turnout contributed to Republican success, for many low-income workers and young people, who tended to vote Democratic, had not gone to the polls, while young men and women serving in the armed forces had found voting difficult. Although the Democratic Party retained nominal control of both houses of Congress, a conservative coalition of Republicans and anti-administration Democrats now exercised *de facto* control of the House of Representatives and exerted substantial influence in the Senate. Roosevelt faced a hostile Congress filled with anti-administration legislators who believed they had a mandate to repeal the New Deal and prevent a post-war revival of reform.

This situation confirmed Roosevelt's perception that ancillary issues would have to be subordinated to the lowest common denominator of national unity—a military victory speedily won. Vice-President Wallace and other reformers portrayed the war as a 'people's revolution' that compelled attention, at home and abroad, to a wide range of social and economic concerns. Roosevelt had become convinced that emphasizing these concerns would enrage his domestic opposition, divide the country, and imperil his leadership. Therefore he was ready to sacrifice social and economic reform, and concentrate almost exclusively on those things necessary to military victory. He even acquiesced as his Congressional adversaries carried out a retroactive revenge against the New Deal. They argued that enormous government expenditures for war required deep cuts in non-war spending and proceeded to eliminate several depression-era agencies and programmes.

The Congressional backlash against the New Deal also affected several war agencies. Critics complained that the Office of Civilian Defense, the *Office of War Information, and the Office of Price Administration had become sanctuaries for New Dealers who were more interested in perpetuating or initiating social and economic reforms, than in effective performance of proper wartime functions. All these agencies became targets of Congressional investigations and efforts to reduce their appropriations. Such legislative reprisals reflected the irritation of anti-administration congressmen who were compelled by the war to delegate authority to an executive branch that they distrusted and despised. Having granted power with one hand, Congress frequently tried to revoke or constrain that power with the other. Ambivalence towards delegation of power accounted for much of the friction between legislative and executive branches during the war years.

In early 1943, a serious clash took place between the president and Congress over agricultural and labour policy. Farm bloc congressmen won approval for legislation intended to raise price ceilings on agricultural commodities. On 2 April 1943 Roosevelt issued a stinging veto that warned Congress against igniting a fire storm of 'wartime inflation and post-war chaos'. With little chance of mustering a two-thirds majority in both House and Senate, anti-administration leaders made no attempt to override the veto. Nevertheless, the episode widened the breach between farm bloc legislators and the Roosevelt administration, as did a subsequent confrontation over agricultural prices in July 1943 that produced a second presidential veto.

The farm bloc reacted bitterly to agricultural price ceilings and blamed the Roosevelt administration for 'coddling' urban workers and consumers. In this context, legislation aimed at punishing unions for strikes in wartime began to attract support. A series of stoppages in the bituminous coal industry intensified anti-labour sentiment in Congress. In May and June 1943, John L. Lewis, the boisterous head of the United Mine Workers, ordered shutdowns intended to extract higher wages from the coal industry and the National War Labor Board.

Those strikes infuriated a large proportion of the American people who thought strikes in wartime delayed victory and threatened the lives of American soldiers. A Congressional majority agreed and adopted the Smith-Connally Act (War Labor Disputes Act) of 1943, which was designed to curb the activities of labour unions. On 25 June 1943, Roosevelt vetoed the measure because it contained features more likely to foment strikes than prevent them and because the bill contained a section prohibiting political contributions by unions. The House and Senate quickly overrode the president's veto, and the Smith-Connally Act became law. It foreshadowed a post-war labour policy less favourable to unions.

With Congress in a defiant mood, Roosevelt responded by creating buffers between irritable legislators and the executive branch. On 27 May 1943 he established the Office of War Mobilization (OWM) to oversee all the federal agencies engaged in the war effort. As director of OWM, the president chose James F. *Byrnes, a former Democratic senator from South Carolina. Fred Vinson, another former congressman, replaced Byrnes as head of the Office of Economic Stabilization, the principal agency for resolving domestic economic problems. Late in June 1943, the president appointed Marvin Jones, former chairman of the House Agriculture Committee, as War Food Administrator. Byrnes, Vinson, and Jones were moderate Democrats who maintained friendly relations with Capitol Hill. If those men could not get along with Congress, no one could. With these appointments, Roosevelt in effect divested himself of detailed involvement in domestic political and economic affairs, and allowed his subordinates to run the Home Front. Under Byrnes, an unofficial 'assistant president,' the office of War Mobilization became the central administrative mechanism for directing the war economy.

Meanwhile, Congress began to concentrate on post-war policy, as the furore over the National Resources Planning Board (NRPB) revealed. Since 1 July 1939, the NRPB had functioned as the planning arm of the executive office of the president. With the outbreak of war, the Board had started developing plans and programmes for the post-war period. A 'new economic bill of rights' for the American people, drafted by the NRPB in 1939, guided its work. Two reports, released in March 1943, outlined plans and programmes designed to assure the American people of the right to education, health care, housing, employment, and economic security. What the Board proposed was nothing less than the completion of the welfare state begun during the New Deal. On Capitol Hill Republicans and anti-administration Democrats exploded with indignation. In June 1943, Congress voted to eliminate the Board and specified that none of its functions could be transferred to any other government department. Having destroyed the NRPB, anti-administration congressmen proceeded to create their own instruments for post-war planning, the special Senate and House Committees on Post-War Economic Policy and Planning, whose recommendations were limited and conservative in character.

Only in the area of veterans' benefits was Congress prepared to adopt welfare state measures. On 27 October 1943, Roosevelt transmitted a message calling for generous unemployment, social security, and educational benefits for returning servicemen. In January 1944, Congress started work on a comprehensive veterans' readjustment plan that became popularly known as the 'GI Bill of Rights'. After prompt passage by the Senate, the House scaled down the benefits, but then passed the measure substantially intact in June 1944. The Servicemen's Readjustment Act provided educational assistance, readjustment allowances, and low interest loans for housing. It won approval because it applied exclusively to veterans: Republicans and anti-administration Democrats did not intend the Act to become a model for broader welfare programmes, though the president had that possibility in mind.

Trying to minimize conflict with Congress, Roosevelt had offered little more than token resistance to the elimination of New Deal agencies and the destruction of the NRPB. Even when he did fight back against Congressional opponents, he had little success. In February 1944, the House and Senate passed a tax bill that fell far short of treasury department recommendations. Roosevelt's advisers urged him to veto the bill, and on 22 February 1944 he did so. This measure was not a tax bill at all, he declared, 'but a tax relief bill providing relief not for the needy but for the greedy'. Infuriated by his harsh language, Congress speedily overrode the president's veto.

Having defeated Roosevelt on taxes, anti-administration congressmen turned to the issue of absentee voting by men and women in the armed forces. Public opinion polls suggested that a majority of servicemen would support the Democrats, and the president and his political advisers wanted as many soldiers as possible to cast their vote. Republicans, on the other hand, feared that a large soldier vote would jeopardize their chance of defeating Roosevelt and his fourth term programme. They formed an alliance with southern Democrats who opposed any plan that might enfranchise black soldiers (see also AFRICAN AMERICANS AT WAR). After a protracted struggle lasting from December 1943 until March 1944, the coalition of Republicans and southern Democrats killed the administration's absentee voting bill, which provided a federal ballot, and substituted a state-controlled voting plan that would keep most southern black soldiers from participating in the election. Republicans eagerly backed that bill because it was more cumbersome than a federal ballot and would discourage voting by servicemen. The president considered the 'states rights' bill unacceptable, but in March 1944 let it become law without his signature.

In mid-1944, Roosevelt interrupted his concentration on war and diplomacy to consider election-year politics.

When the Democratic Party held its national convention in July, his renomination was assured, but there were still decisions to be made. Because of the belief that the ill and weary president might not survive another term, the various factions of the Democratic Party fought over the vice-presidential nomination. Reformers and union leaders favoured the incumbent vice-president, Henry A. Wallace. The president, though he liked and respected Wallace, refused to insist on his renomination because he thought he had moved too far ahead of public opinion. To replace Wallace he chose Senator Harry S *Truman of Missouri, who had directed a highly respected Senate investigation of war production and who was on reasonably good terms with all factions of the Democratic Party.

During the campaign of 1944, Roosevelt called for fulfilment of the new economic bill of rights to ensure housing, education, medical care, and economic security. He endorsed the goal of post-war full employment, defined as 60 million jobs, and urged the creation of a permanent Fair Employment Practices Committee to prevent job discrimination against ethnic minorities. With heavy support from organized labour and from urban voters, the president received 53.4% of the popular vote and 432 electoral votes. His victory over the Republican candidate Thomas E. Dewey (1902–71) was the narrowest of his four presidential contests and the closest election since Woodrow Wilson edged out Charles Evans Hughes in 1916.

With the election over and the war moving towards a climax, New Dealers expected Roosevelt to lead a revival of reform. Those expectations were doomed to disappointment. The elections of 1944 had strengthened Democratic control of Congress but had not shattered the anti-administration coalition of Republicans and conservative Democrats that now dominated Capitol Hill. The fate of two presidential appointments in early 1945 revealed the continuing strength of the anti-administration coalition. On 1 March 1945 the Senate confirmed former vice-president Henry A. Wallace as secretary of commerce, but only after Congress had drained most of the power from that office. On 23 March 1945, the Senate decisively rejected Aubrey W. Williams, Roosevelt's choice to head the Rural Electrification Administration. The president faced the same kind of opposition in the new Congress that had characterized the earlier war years.

Roosevelt died on 12 April 1945 with his plans for the post-war era only half formed. His successor, Truman, had not been taken into Roosevelt's confidence and was uncertain about key national policies and decisions. During his first months as president, Truman was preoccupied with military and diplomatic concerns, including the decision to use the atomic bomb against Japan, and provided little leadership on the Home Front. He tended to defer to congressional committee chairmen and was willing to let Congress set priorities, draft bills, and pass legislation.

Squabbles over reconversion policy also clogged the channels of the executive and legislative branches. Some officials in the Roosevelt administration had urged partial reconversion before the war ended so that small business firms could start civilian production. This arrangement would compensate for the fact that most war contracts had gone to big business and that the government had never made effective use of small enterprise in the war production effort (see also SMALLER WAR PLANTS CORPORATION). However, the military services objected to piecemeal reconversion on the grounds that it might interfere with the war effort and delay victory. Large firms opposed partial reconversion because it would give smaller competitors a head start on producing for post-war markets. In the struggle over reconversion, the alliance of the military and big business prevailed.

For the American government, the Second World War proved an ambiguous experience. Executive power was enhanced, but Congress became more assertive, especially in the area of domestic policy. A conservative coalition of Republicans and anti-administration Democrats matured during the war years, rolled back part of the New Deal, and blocked passage of new domestic programmes, but the basic framework of the welfare state survived intact. The war boom ended unemployment and created a 'politics of inflation' that lessened support for new federal welfare measures and intensified pressures exerted on government by business, labour, and agricultural interests. In national politics and federal policy, the patterns of the post-war years had emerged before the war itself was won.

RICHARD CHAPMAN

4. Defence forces and civil defence

Civilian defence served to calm fears of sabotage and attack; to turn aside demands for protection by organizing civilians to protect themselves; to generate enthusiasm for the war effort; and to provide useful services. The FBI (see INTELLIGENCE, below) wanted to handle all anti-subversion activity by itself, with no public involvement. It did a good, quiet job, but only the relocation of the West Coast Japanese-Americans, satisfied public thirst for visible action. Loud demands for anti-aircraft defences threatened to divert scarce military resources; better to have worried civilians get out and do the job themselves. By 1941, 42 states had created their own defence programmes, modelled after the successful state defence councils of 1917, New York State drew up elaborate plans to evacuate the metropolis, and in May 1941 Roosevelt created the Office of Civilian Defense, with the colourful Fiorello LaGuardia (1882–1947) as head and Eleanor Roosevelt (1884–1962), the president's wife, as assistant director for volunteers.

LaGuardia, who continued as full-time mayor of New York City, proved incompetent; he rarely showed up at OCD headquarters. The day after Pearl Harbor he alarmed millions by warning of imminent attacks on the East Coast. The president soon gave OCD to James Landis, an efficient lawyer. With a federal staff of only 1,000, Landis stressed co-ordination with the much larger and more important state and local agencies. Manuals sent to 12,000 local offices covered the basics of organization, air raid sirens and shelters, camouflage, and defence against poison gas. Some federal money was usefully spent on fire engines; much was wasted on millions of gas masks, which cities desperately wanted. Mrs Roosevelt, interested mostly in involving blacks in the programme, was forced out. By early 1943, 12 million Americans (mostly men, nearly all white) had volunteer roles, half in protective services like air-raid warden. There were 600,000 serving as aircraft spotters; unfortunately, they turned in many false alarms. The *blackout exercises saved a little electricity, but disrupted the round-the-clock movement of workers to munitions factories. Washington, of course, knew there were no enemy bombers to fear, but was distressed at the failure of one-third the population to take the war seriously, and it wanted to give the all-out enthusiasts something harmless to keep them busy. Blackouts were late coming to the Atlantic coast, where the bright lights of resort hotels silhouetted ships that were often sunk by German U-boats (see CONVOYS). One OCD operation, the *Civil Air Patrol, had civilian pilots flying their own planes. Some were armed and sent searching for German submarines; they made 57 attacks. In some large cities block organizations helped people understand the rationing scheme and hunt for war jobs; often they brought local problems to the attention of city hall.

OCD was a minor wartime agency. More effective use of volunteers was made by private agencies such as the Red Cross (which recruited nurses and collected blood), and the United Service Organization (which supported soldiers' families). With the National Guard called into service, state and local civilian defence organizations provided significant help in disasters, such as major floods in the Midwest. Disaster planning became a permanent function of government, and was the chief legacy of wartime civilian defence.

D'ANN CAMPBELL/RICHARD JENSEN

5. Armed forces

(a) High Command

All the armed forces of the USA operate under the supreme control of the president. Roosevelt, like Churchill, insisted on retaining overall direction of the American war effort, though generally speaking the US military were given a much freer hand than their British counterparts. But the demands of global coalition warfare soon exposed the inadequacy of the civilian–military command structure and the lack of army–navy co-operation, and the first meeting of the *Combined Chiefs of Staff committee on 23 January 1942 underlined the necessity for an American equivalent of the British *Chiefs of Staff. Such an equivalent was formed in February 1942 when the highest US military authority, the Joint Board, was replaced by the *Joint Chiefs of Staff (JCS). Later that year the command structure was further strengthened when Admiral *Leahy became JCS chairman and the president's chief of staff. The strong professional bond between Leahy and Roosevelt enabled the JCS to dominate planning and co-ordination, and exercise total control over the country's armed forces. It also achieved primacy in advising the president on national strategy, production requirements, manpower allocation, and shipping.

(b) Army

Civilian control of the army, including its air arm (see below), rested with the secretary of war. He acted through the war department which contained the offices of the chiefs of the arms (infantry, field artillery, coastal artillery, and so on) and services (the suppliers and administrators) and the general staff (the planners and organizers). The secretary of war from July 1940 was Henry Stimson. His under-secretary, Robert Patterson (1891–1952), was mainly concerned with procurement so an assistant secretary, John McCloy (1895–1989), acted as Stimson's general deputy. The other assistant secretary, Robert Lovett (1895–1986), was, in effect, Stimson's air force equivalent, though nominally subordinate to him. As Roosevelt exercised his function as commander-in-chief principally through his military commanders, Stimson's responsibilities were mostly confined to the war department's civilian functions, but included development of the atomic bomb.

In September 1939 the US Army comprised, besides its air arm, the Regular Army, the National Guard, and the Organized Reserves. The Regular Army, 190,000 strong, including the territorial indigenous Philippine Scouts, was the nation's standing army. It was well trained but was under-strength and under-equipped and relied on short-term enlistments and a minuscule corps of professional officers. The National Guard comprised 200,000 civilian volunteers who were raised and trained by the individual states. They drilled for 48 evenings a year and had two weeks of federally directed training. Once the Selective Service Act had been passed in August 1940 the units of the Organized Reserves, which already had on hand a cadre of reserve officers, began to expand.

From March 1941 the USA, otherwise known as the Zone of Interior, was divided into four Defense Commands (see Map 106) which corresponded with the areas allotted to the existing four armies (numbered 1–4), while outside the continental USA were the old established Hawaii and Philippines departments and the newly formed Alaska and Caribbean Defense Commands. In March 1942 GHQ, the central training command and operational centre, was abolished and three new, co-equal, autonomous organizations were formed instead: Army Ground Forces, commanded by Lt-General Lesley McNair (1883–1944), assumed GHQ's training functions and controlled all ground combat troops within the USA; the air arm, which was given its own command structure; and Services of Supply (later Army Service Forces),

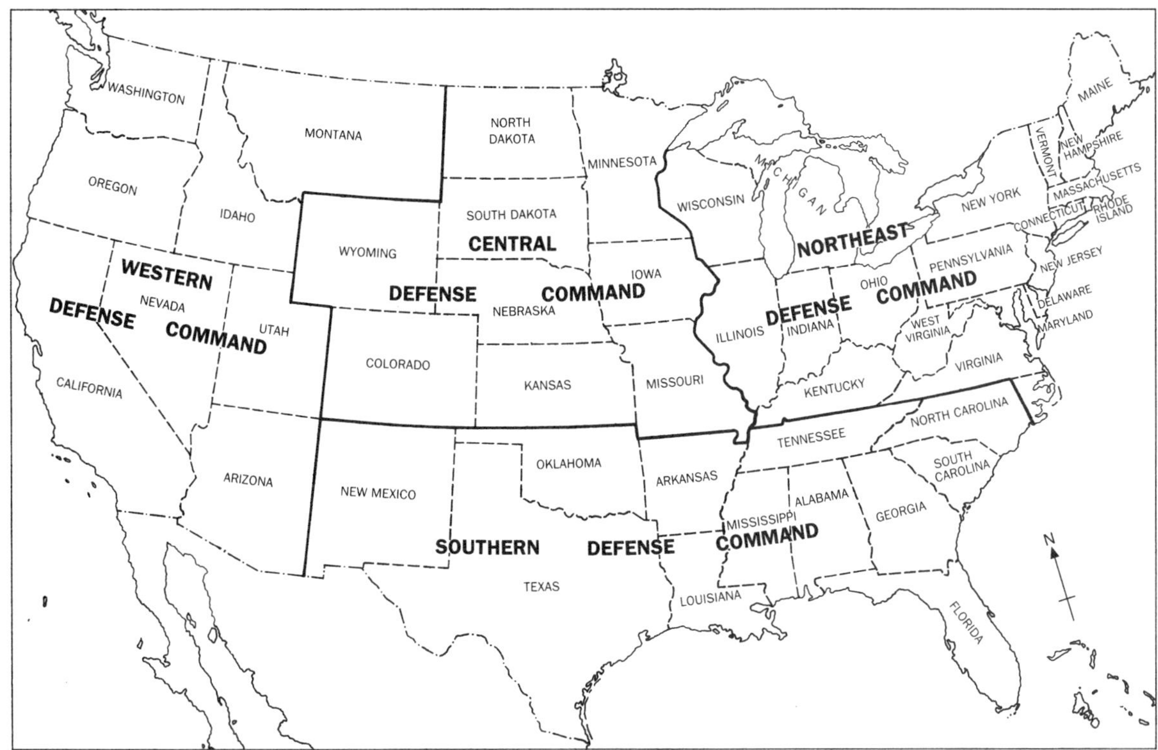

106. **USA**: Defense Commands established 17 March 1941

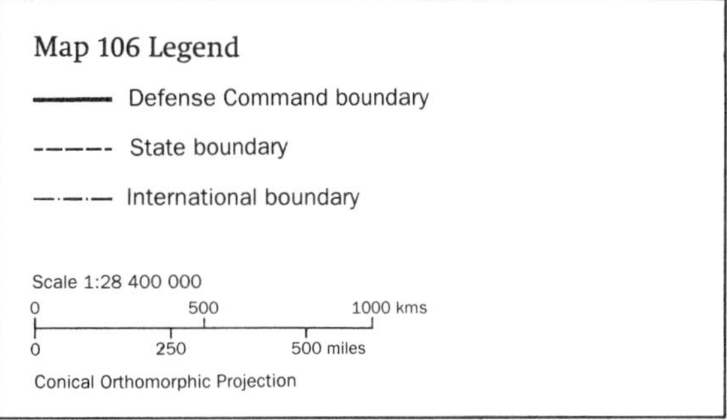

commanded by Lt-General Brehon Somervell (1892–1955), which assumed responsibility for the war department's *logistics and procurement.

McNair had the formidable task of building an army suitable for global conflict and finalizing its training before overseas deployment. To do this he created a number of new HQ for training and development: Armored Force, Anti-Aircraft Command, Tank Destroyer Center, Airborne Command (first organized as the Provisional Parachute Group), Amphibious Training Command/Center, Desert Training Center, and Replacement and School Command. Once trained, combat-ready troops were delivered to embarkation ports as required by theatre commanders. The Victory Program (see WEDEMEYER), drawn up in early 1942, specified an army of 213 divisions, but this was later reduced to 90 (excluding 2nd Cavalry division which was disbanded).

Large though McNair's organization became it was dwarfed by Somervell's powerful and influential Army Service Forces which, as the war progressed, absorbed an increasing percentage of the army's manpower (see Table 4). Within its jurisdiction were such diverse units as the military police, chemical warfare service, corps of engineers, and quartermaster, ordnance, signal, medical, and transportation corps, but it did not administer air units as the air force insisted upon, and received, its own parallel supply organization. The Chemical Warfare Service activated about 375 air and ground chemical units, including those for gas warfare and 30 chemical mortar battalions (see MORTARS), which supported the infantry with high explosive, white phosphorus, and smoke shells. Its *engineers performed herculean efforts in combat in virtually every major engagement, and they were sometimes also employed as infantry.

The creation of these three administrative commands allowed *Marshall, the army's chief of staff, and his general staff to control operations and plans. To fight a war of unrivalled complexity in several theatres simultaneously Marshall reorganized the War Plans Division into an expanded Operations Division (OPD). This was the linchpin for the central direction of all

USA, 5, Table 4: Growth of the Army by branch, 1941–5 (reported actual strength and per cent of total Army)

	31 December 1941		*31 December 1942*		*31 December 1943*		*31 March 1945*	
Branch	*Strength*	*Per cent*	*Strength*	*Per cent*	*Strength*	*Per cent*	*Strength*	*Per cent*
Infantry, Cavalry, Field Artillery (includes Armoured and Tank Destroyer)[a]	690,083	41.7	1,512,730	28.0	1,960,068	25.8	2,423,075[b]	29.7
Coast Artillery Corps (includes Anti-aircraft)[a]	177,379	10.7	425,187	7.9	590,939	7.8	330,442	4.1
TOTAL GROUND ARMS	867,462	52.4	1,937,917	35.9	2,551,007	33.6	2,753,517	33.8
Adjutant General	966	0.1	4,418	0.1	15,688	0.2	56,116	0.7
Engineers	91,476	5.5	333,209	6.2	561,066	7.4	688,764	8.4
Signal	50,596	3.0	241,227	4.5	309,641	4.1	331,105	4.1
Medical[c]	129,512	7.8	469,981	8.8	622,227	8.2	670,151	8.2
Ordnance	34,278	2.1	235,350	4.3	316,174	4.2	332,042	4.1
Quartermaster	122,672	7.4	327,794	6.1	453,419	6.0	491,301	6.0
Chemical	6,269	0.4	46,182	0.8	66,610	0.9	61,458	0.7
Military Police			147,840	2.7	222,639	2.9	203,823	2.5
Transportation			51,041	0.9	167,612	2.2	260,260	3.2
TOTAL SERVICES	435,769	26.3	1,857,042	34.4	2,735,076	36.1	3,095,020	37.9
Air Corps	270,535	16.3	1,270,677	23.5	1,810,900	23.9	1,831,091	22.4
All Other (includes Women's Army Corps, Warrant and Flight Officers, and No Branch Assigned)	83,391	5.0	333,252	6.2	485,451	6.4	477,758	5.9
GRAND TOTAL	1,657,157	100.0	5,398,888	100.0	7,582,434	100.0	8,157,386	100.0

[a] Armoured, Tank Destroyer, and Anti-aircraft were not reported as separate arms. Because of inclusion of these specialities in the basic ground arms, exact breakdown of the ground arms cannot be made.
[b] This figure, at this date, includes perhaps 300,000 carried in the Troop Basis as 'Hospital Population,' most casualties occurring in the ground arms and to a less extent in the Air Corps.
[c] Includes Army Nurse Corps, Dietitians, and Physiotherapists.

Source: Greenfield, K., Palmer, R., and Wiley, B.,*US Army in World War II: The Organization of Ground Combat Troops* (Washington, DC, 1947).

operations, and through it Marshall controlled and monitored the various theatre commands, and co-ordinated their supply requirements. These included Iceland; North-West Service Command in the Yukon Territory of Canada; US Army Forces, South Atlantic (which co-operated with the Brazilian armed forces); the North African Service Command which ensured supplies to US forces serving in the Allied North African Theatre of Operations (redesignated Mediterranean Theatre of operations in November 1943); the Iran–Iraq Service Command (redesignated Persian Gulf Command in December 1943), which expedited the flow of Lend-Lease to the USSR; the European Theatre of Operations (see ETOUSA); and US Army Forces, Pacific Ocean Areas, which, with the Hawaiian Department, was responsible for administering, training, and supplying all army and air force personnel involved in the Pacific war.

In May 1942 the first of the American women's wartime services, the Women's Army Auxiliary Corps, was established under Colonel Oveta Culp Hobby. In 1943 it ceased to be an auxiliary force and became part of the US Army as the Women's Army Corps. Its peak strength was 99,000 women who worked in almost every military occupation except combat and from January 1943 served in every overseas theatre of war.

The US Army's highest operational field structure, the Army Group, reflected the nature of coalition warfare as its commander supervised two or more armies which often contained several nationalities. *Bradley's Twelfth Army Group, which fought in north-west Europe, was almost wholly American in content, but *Devers's Sixth Army Group, which fought its way into southern Germany after the *French Riviera landings, was half French; and Fifteenth Army Group, formed for the *Sicilian campaign and commanded by Mark *Clark in the *Italian campaign from December 1944, had originally been led by a British general and though predominently Anglo-American had units from many nations, including the co-belligerent Italian forces.

During the war the USA deployed eleven field armies. First, Second, Third, and Fourth were already in existence at the commencement of hostilities; Fifth, Sixth, and

Seventh were raised during 1943; the Eighth, Ninth, Tenth, and Fifteenth in 1944. Second and Fourth Armies remained in the Zone of Interior on training and administrative duties; the First, Third, Ninth, and Fifteenth Armies fought in north-west Europe; the Fifth Army took part in the Italian campaign; the Seventh Army fought as part of Devers's Sixth Army Group; and Sixth (see also ALAMO FORCE), Eighth, and Tenth Armies were formed for service in the Pacific, the first two under *MacArthur in his *South-West Pacific Area, the last for the invasion of *Okinawa under General Simon Buckner.

Each army comprised two or more corps of which the US Army formed 26 during the war, all but one being deployed overseas. It was the corps commander who fought the battles and he usually had at his disposal one armoured and two infantry divisions, plus supporting arms and services. The division was the basic military formation, 68 being deployed in Europe and 22 in the Pacific. The four-regiment 'square' infantry division was replaced in May 1940 by the slimmer, more flexible three-regiment 'triangular' division, 14,250 strong, which eliminated brigade HQs. A regiment comprised three battalions (each of which had three rifle companies and one heavy weapons company), a headquarters company with six 105 mm. howitzers, a service company, and an anti-tank company. When tanks and engineers, and extra support if necessary, were attached, it was known as a Regimental Combat Team (RCT). As well as the *Americal and Philippine infantry divisions, the following numbered divisions were raised; 1–9, 24–38, 40–45, 63, 65, 66, 69–71, 75–100, 102–104, and 106.

German *blitzkrieg tactics encouraged the belief that the US armoured division could act as a self-sufficient task force that could, by virtue of its protective armour, fire-power, and mobility, strike deep into enemy-held territory. Altogether 16 were raised as were 60 non-divisional tank battalions. The 1st, 2nd, and 3rd Armored Divisions were raised under 'heavy' tables of organizations with 390 tanks, while 4–14, 16, and 20 were organized as 'light' *formations having 263 tanks each (1st Armoured Division also became a 'light' formation later). All armoured divisions were eventually deployed in Europe, but unfavourable terrain and the superiority of German tanks and anti-tank weaponry prevented them from operating as originally envisaged until German resistance collapsed in the spring of 1945. Initially, an armoured division of 14,620 men was divided into two tank regiments and one armoured infantry regiment, each of three battalions, plus three artillery battalions, but for greater flexibility this organization was abolished in 1943 and replaced by three battalions each of infantry, tank, and artillery. These were allotted, as appropriate, by the division's HQ, to two smaller HQ, known as combat commands (CC), which could be reinforced as necessary by non-divisional tank battalions.

Important as armour was in offensive, mobile warfare, it was the combination of infantry and artillery that proved the key to success.'I do not have to tell you who won the war,' General *Patton said. 'You know our artillery did.' High quality *radio communications and spotting, combined with great flexibility, accuracy, and sheer weight of fire-power, ensured the advancing infantry maximum support. Apart from its three artillery battalions a division could also request support from non-divisional artillery under corps or army command. Altogether, the US Army raised 326 artillery battalions, around 400 anti-aircraft battalions, and 86 tank destroyer battalions. In December 1942 non-divisional regiments of anti-aircraft artillery and field artillery were converted into separate battalions. When several battalions were employed together they were controlled by a group HQ; several groups had a Brigade HQ.

Specialized divisions were also raised for a variety of purposes. In the winter of 1942–3 three light divisions—89th (Truck), 71st (Pack, Jungle), and 10th (Pack, Alpine)—were created for jungle warfare in the Pacific. Each had 9,000 men equipped with lightweight gear that could be either animal- or man-packed. However, the concept was soon discarded as combat conditions were not as expected and the US Navy and Army amphibious engineer brigades furnished the required mobility. More importantly, the higher strengths and endurance of the regular infantry divisions were found to be necessary to combat the Japanese in tropical terrain and only the 10th (Pack, Alpine) was retained. This was brought up to the strength of a normal infantry division and as 10th Mountain Division fought in the Italian campaign. The army also experimented briefly with five motorized divisions, but their equipment would have filled so much shipping space that theatre commanders rejected them in favour of receiving additional ordinary formations, and they were therefore converted to standard infantry divisions.

More successful were the five airborne divisions that were raised. Like the light divisions they were formed as smaller counterparts to the standard infantry division, but this was not found to be successful. The 13th, 17th, 82nd, and 101st Divisions, which were deployed in Europe—where they were organized into two parachute regiments and one glider regiment, plus a battalion of 105 mm. howitzers—were increased from 8,500 to 12,799 men, but the fifth formation, 11th Airborne Division, which fought in the south-west Pacific, retained its own unique structure and size.

Two cavalry divisions were also raised: 2nd Cavalry Division, which had a high proportion of African Americans and, was disbanded (twice), and 1st Cavalry Division, which fought in the south-west Pacific. The 1st Cavalry retained the old 'square' divisional formation of four regiments as well as the names and traditions of some of the US Army's most famous regiments, including Custer's 7th Cavalry, and was theoretically still organized as horse cavalry which fought dismounted.

Unlike in the First World War, when some divisions had had to be stripped for replacements, all 90 divisions

USA, 5, Table 5: Deployment of the Army, 30 April 1945 (reported actual strengths)

Type of Troops	*European Theatre*	*Mediterranean Theatres*	*European and Mediterranean Theatre Combined*	*South-West Pacific Theatre*	*Pacific Ocean Theatre*	*China and India-Burma Theatres*	*Principal Theatres Combined*
Divisional combat troops	819,342	102,485	921,827	183,798	80834		1,186,459
Non-divisional combat troops[a]	595,418	37,797	633,215	113,318	102,076	15,766	864,375
TOTAL GROUND COMBAT TROOPS	1,414,760	140,282	1,555,042	297,116	182,910	15,766	2,050,834
Non-divisional service troops	828,726	128,307	957,033	214,835	142,579	69,898	1,384,345[b]
Army Air Forces	439,425	153,005	592,430	173,343	75,438	90,949	932,160
Replacements	171,933	34,551	206,484	34,203	20,371	4,365	265,423
Patients	128,305	15,679	143,984	41,135	6,423	1,439	192,981
Overhead	54,758	17,080	71,838	29,500	19,851	10,447	131,636
Miscellaneous	27,598	4,972	32,570	12,372	3,380	5,966	54,288
ARMY IN PRINCIPAL THEATRES	3,065,505	493,876	3,559,381	802,504	450,952	198,830	5,011,667
Percentage of Army in principal theatres to total Army (8,290,993)	37.0	6.0	43.0	9.7	5.4	2.4	60.4
Percentage of ground combat units in principal theatres to all ground combat units in Army (2,233,854)	63.4	6.3	69.7	13.3	8.2	0.7	91.9

[a] Including as combat troops all men in engineer, signal, and chemical units of AGF type.
[b] In addition, air forces totalling approximately 200,000, under direct command of the commanding general of Army Air Forces, were engaged in overseas operations, chiefly in the Pacific, without being assigned to a theatre.

Source: Greenfield, Palmer, and Wiley.

were kept in being and were deployed all round the world (see Table 5). as by the start of the final year of the war 47 infantry regiments had sustained a casualty rate which varied from 100% to 200% this was no mean achievement (see also GROUND FORCE REPLACEMENT SYSTEM). But 90 proved to be barely sufficient (the Red Army raised 400, Germany 300, Japan 170) and all saw combat. When the German *Ardennes offensive began in December 1944 the few remaining in the USA were moved to Europe and no more were then being formed.

Excluding Army Air Force personnel, by the end of the war US Army strength had risen to over 6,000,000. Casualties, including those *en route* to combat theatres, amounted to 820,877 including 182,701 dead.

(c) Army Air Forces

In September 1939 the army's air arm was administratively organized into the US Army Air Corps, commanded by Maj-General *Arnold, and GHQ Air Force. A series of changes in this administrative structure, influenced by the air force's desire for greater autonomy, by the growing realization that its mission implied more than support for the ground forces, by the war in Europe, and by the unsatisfactory nature of the chain of command, culminated in the US Army Air Forces (USAAF), as it was called from June 1941, becoming, in March 1942, one of the army's three co-equal commands. In reality, however, it achieved equal status with the army and navy, for its commanding general, Arnold, sat with the other two service chiefs on the Joint Chiefs of Staff and Combined Chiefs of Staff committees, and directed air operations without formal reference to the army's chief of staff. After March 1942 the Air Corps remained the USAAF's main component, but GHQ Air Force (called Air Force Combat Command from June 1941 to March 1942) was dissolved and its responsibilities taken over by the newly formed USAAF HQ.

The expansion of the USAAF during the war years was phenomenal. In 1939 there were 17 air bases in the USA; by 1943 there 345 main bases, 116 sub-bases, and 322 auxiliary fields. It grew in strength from 20,196 men in June 1938 to nearly 1,900,000 men and women in March 1945, rising from 11% of the army's strength to over 22%. In September 1939 it had 2,470 aircraft; in July 1944, when the maximum number was reached, it had 79,908. In September 1939 it possessed only 23 B17 bombers, its one modern aircraft type; by 1945 it had at least one aircraft type in each conventional class (but not in jets), which was equal to the best of its opponents and in some cases, such as transport aircraft and heavy bombers, its superiority was unchallenged.

Administratively the USAAF relied on a number of Commands or similar organizations, for such support functions as supply, transport, and *meteorological intelligence, and the larger ones had sub-commands under them. The world-wide network of radio communications was organized by the Army Airways Communications System. Training was the responsibility of Troop Carrier Command—initially called *Air Transport Command until this name was transferred to the Air Ferrying Command in June 1942—and of the four home-based air forces (see below) which in May 1945 were grouped together as the Continental Air Forces (see Chart).

The USAAF employed 422,000 civilians, including *WASP pilots and those who manned the Civil Air Patrol,

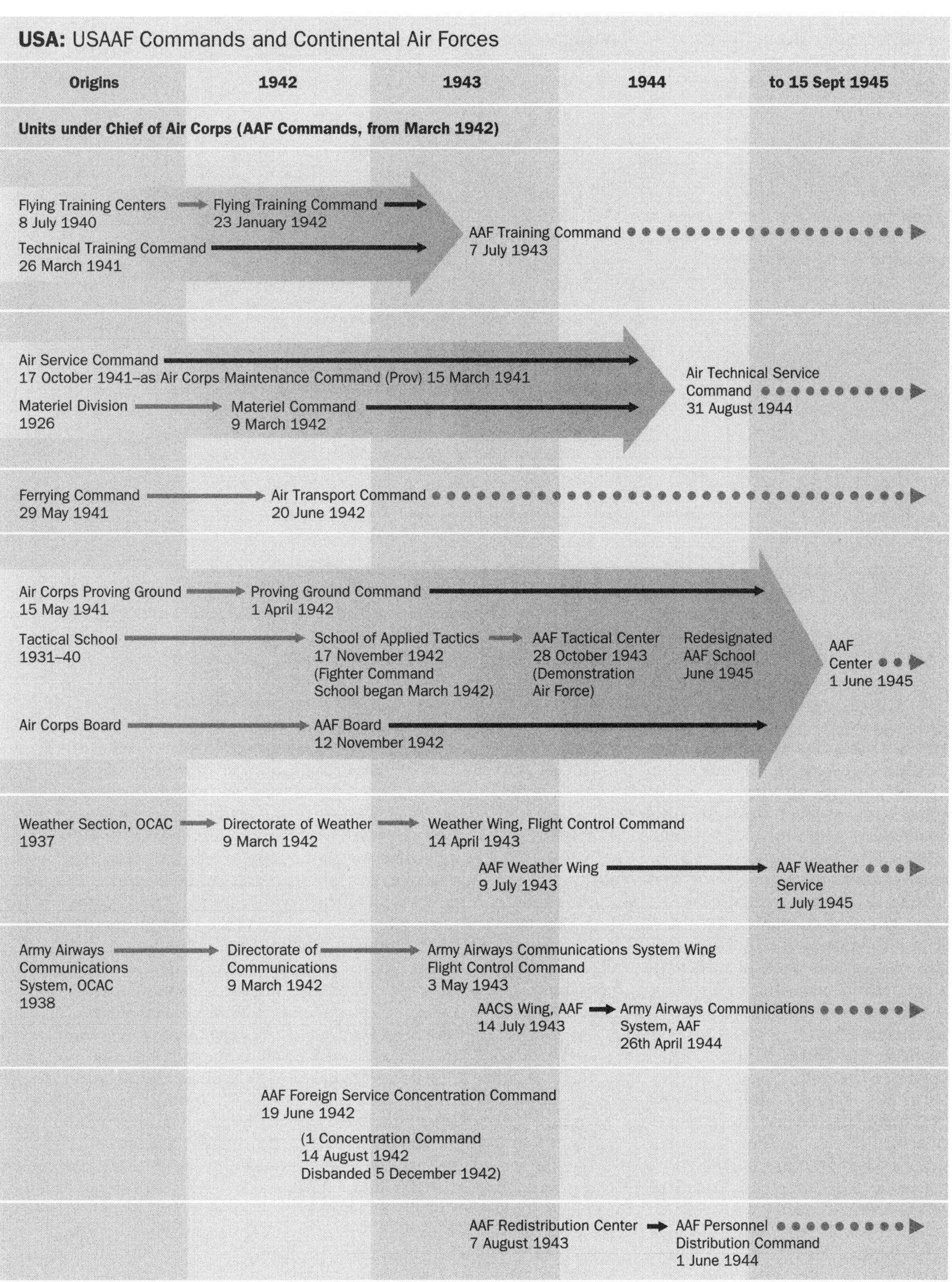
USA: USAAF Commands and Continental Air Forces
Origins
1942
1943
1944
to 15 Sept 1945
Units under Chief of Air Corps (AAF Commands, from March 1942)
Flying Training Centers 8 July 1940
Flying Training Command 23 January 1942
Technical Training Command 26 March 1941
AAF Training Command 7 July 1943
Air Service Command 17 October 1941–as Air Corps Maintenance Command (Prov) 15 March 1941
Materiel Division 1926
Materiel Command 9 March 1942
Air Technical Service Command 31 August 1944
Ferrying Command 29 May 1941
Air Transport Command 20 June 1942
Air Corps Proving Ground 15 May 1941
Proving Ground Command 1 April 1942
Tactical School 1931–40
School of Applied Tactics 17 November 1942 (Fighter Command School began March 1942)
AAF Tactical Center 28 October 1943 (Demonstration Air Force)
Redesignated AAF School June 1945
AAF Center 1 June 1945
Air Corps Board
AAF Board 12 November 1942
Weather Section, OCAC 1937
Directorate of Weather 9 March 1942
Weather Wing, Flight Control Command 14 April 1943
AAF Weather Wing 9 July 1943
AAF Weather Service 1 July 1945
Army Airways Communications System, OCAC 1938
Directorate of Communications 9 March 1942
Army Airways Communications System Wing Flight Control Command 3 May 1943
AACS Wing, AAF 14 July 1943
Army Airways Communications System, AAF 26th April 1944
AAF Foreign Service Concentration Command 19 June 1942
(1 Concentration Command 14 August 1942 Disbanded 5 December 1942)
AAF Redistribution Center 7 August 1943
AAF Personnel Distribution Command 1 June 1944

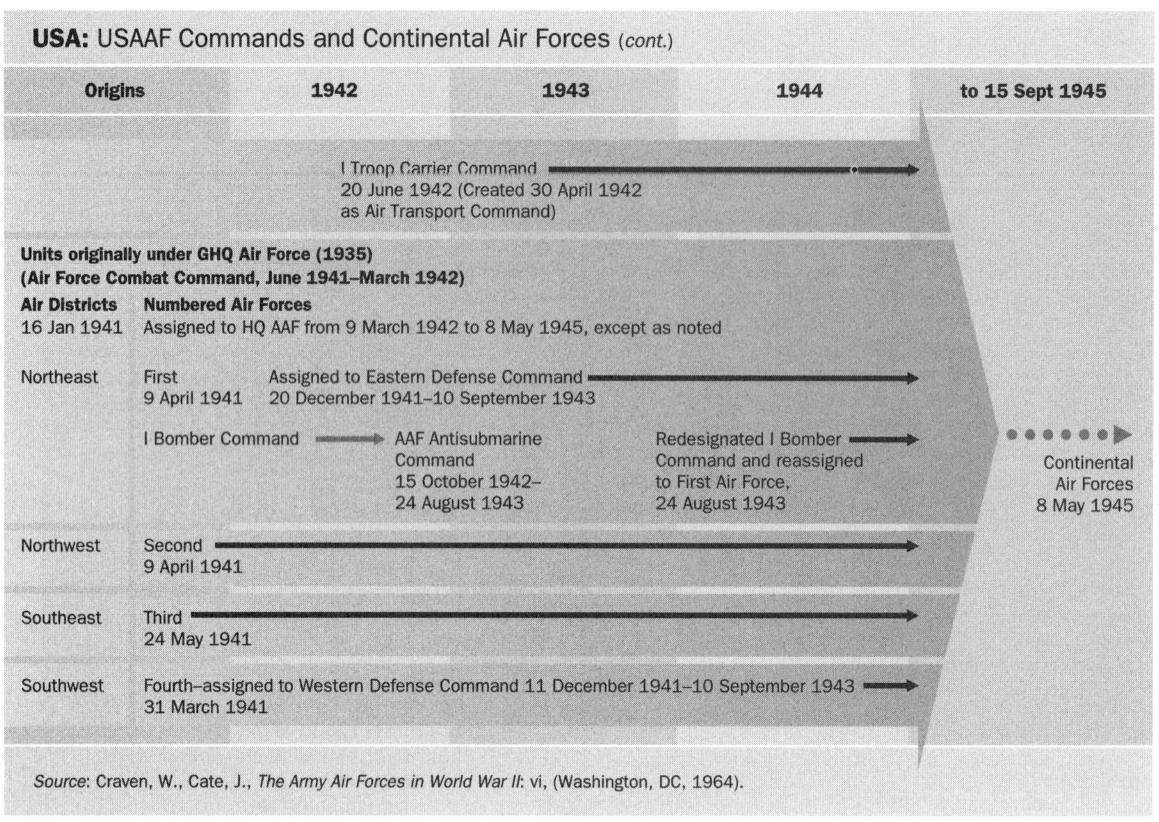

and more than 39,000 members of the Women's Army Corps. It also controlled a wide variety of ancilliary units drawn from the army (for example, medical, police, and signal services) which were officially designated Arms and Services with AAF (ASWAAF), and an estimated 1,500,000 volunteers joined its Ground Observer Corps (see DEFENCE FORCES AND CIVIL DEFENCE, above).

To carry out combat missions sixteen separate air forces were formed, numbered in the order in which they were raised. These were usually divided into a number of subordinate commands, some of which were Allied ones. A Fighter, a Bomber, and an Air Service Command was the normal minimum, but air force organizations varied widely and a system of directorates and divisions, abandoned by USAAF HQ in 1943, continued to be employed by some.

The First, Second, Third, and Fourth Air Forces, which supported First, Second, Third, and Fourth Armies, remained within the Zone of Interior for defence purposes and for training. Fifth Air Force, originally created as the Philippine Department Air Force, was part of MacArthur's South-West Pacific Area command; Sixth protected the Panama Canal and adjacent shipping lanes; Seventh protected Hawaii and then participated in the Central Pacific offensive; Eighth was based in the UK and took part in the *strategic air offensives against Germany and German-occupied Europe; Ninth was employed during the *North African campaign before moving to the UK to provide tactical air support for Allied ground troops in north-west Europe; Tenth, based in India, organized the *Hump supply route and supported ground troops in Burma and China; Eleventh was based in Alaska; Twelfth served in North Africa and then in the Italian campaign, becoming the Mediterranean Theatre of Operations tactical air force in November 1943; Thirteenth, based in New Caledonia, provided tactical air support to Allied forces in the Solomon Islands, *New Guinea campaign, and the Philippines; Fourteenth, formed as a consequence of the *American Volunteer Group, augmented Tenth in operations in South-East Asia; Fifteenth, based in Italy, aided Eighth in the strategic air offensives against European targets; and Twentieth, based first in China and later in the Marianas, mounted the strategic air offensive against Japan and dropped the atomic bombs that devastated *Hiroshima and *Nagasaki. Eighth and Fifteenth Air Forces formed *Spaatz's US Strategic Air Forces in Europe in January 1944; Fifth, Seventh, and Thirteenth Air Forces made up Lt-General George C. Kenney's Far East Air Forces when this was formed in August 1944; and Twentieth,

USA, 5, Table 6: Norms for AAF Combat groups, February 1945 (includes allowance for reserve)

Type of Unit[a]	Major type of Plane	Number of Plans	Number of Crews	Men per Crew	Personnel Total	Officers	Enlisted	No. of Groups formed
Very Heavy Bombardment Group	B-29	45	80	11	2,078	462	1,616	26
Heavy Bombardment Group	B-17 B-24	72	96	9–11	2,261	465	1,796	72.5
Medium Bombardment Group	B-25 B-26	96	96	5–6	1,759	393	1,366	28.5
Light Bombardment Group	A-20 A-26	96	96	3–4	1,304	211	1,093	
Single-engine Fighter Group	P-40 P-47 P-51	111–26	108–26	1	994	183	811	71
Twin-engine Fighter Group	P-36	111–26	108–26	1	1,081	183	898	
Troop Carrier Group	C-47	80–110	128	4–5	1,837	514	1,323	32
Combat Cargo Group	C-46 C-47	125	150	4	883	350	533	
Because of employment of variations in Group Composition, the following are best defined in terms of squadron strength (normally three or four squadrons would make up a group)								included in I Fighter Groups
Night Fighter Squadron	P-61 P-70	18	16	2–3	288	50	238	13
Tactical Reconnaissance Squadron	F-6 (P-51) P-39 P-40 L-4 L-5	27	23	1	233	39	194	
Photo-reconnaissance Squadron	F-5 (P-38)	24	21	1	347	50	297	
Combat Mapping Squadron	F-7 (B-24) F-9 (B-17)	18	16	9	474	77	397	

[a] Air Commando Groups were composite units. Usually they had 2 Reduced strength Fighter Squadrons, Troop Carrier Squadron, and Liaison Squadrons.

Source: Craven, W., and Cate, J. (eds.), *The Army Air Forces in World War II*, Vol. 6 (Washington, DC, 1964).

controlled directly by Arnold from the *Pentagon, was redesignated US Strategic Air Forces, Pacific, in July 1945.

The combat units in an Air Force, and their size and content, also varied considerably. Before the war the wing had been the key tactical and administrative organization with which GHQ Air Force had controlled its combat units. It continued in limited use during the war, but it was the group, roughly parallel to an army regiment, which was administratively and operationally the most important unit. Altogether, 243 fully equipped groups were raised, each of which usually contained three or four squadrons. Squadrons were the USAAF's basic permanent combat unit as well as the basic organization for supporting services. They, and the group or wing to which they belonged, were always described by function (see Table 6) as well as being numbered, and they normally did their advanced training together and fought as a unit—though squadrons could, and often did, operate separately. In 1944 a squadron, which comprised flights of three or more aircraft, contained from 7 B29 Superfortresses to 25 fighters and numbered from 200 to 500 men. A composite group or wing, as the term implies, had a mixture of squadrons.

By the end of the war the USAAF had taken delivery of 158,800 aircraft, including 51,221 bombers and 47,050 fighters, of which 22,948 were lost in action. During the 2,363,800 combat sorties which had been mounted 2,057,000 tons of bombs had been dropped—75% of them on Germany—and 459,750,000 rounds of ammunition fired. Casualties of 115,382 included 40,061 dead, 17,021 of whom were officers.

(d) Navy

Civilian control rested with the secretary of the navy. He acted through the navy department and its various bureaus, and was advised by a navy board. In July 1940 the then secretary, Charles Edison, was replaced by Knox, and in August *Forrestal assumed the new post of under secretary. When Knox died in May 1944, Forrestal replaced him.

In September 1939 the US Navy was still oriented towards capital ships, of which it had fifteen, though one dated back to 1912 and two others to 1923. It also had 5 carriers, 18 heavy cruisers, 19 light cruisers, 61 submarines, and a miscellany of destroyers, patrol craft, gun boats, and wooden submarine chasers. It controlled

USA 7, Table 7: US Navy, US Marine Corps, US Coast Guards. Officers, men, and women on active duty, 1 July 1940–31 August 1945

	1 July 1940	*31 Dec 1941*	*30 June 1942*	*31 Dec 1942*	*30 June 1943*	*31 Dec 1943*	*30 June 1944*	*31 Dec 1944*	*31 Aug 1945*
Navy									
Officers, Men	13,162	38,601	67,786	117,268	170,418	212,820	260,143	291,357	316,675
Officers, Women	0	0	0	770	3,827	6,459	7,611	8,744	8,399
TOTAL OFFICERS	13,162	38,601	67,786	118,038	174,245	219,279	267,754	300,101	325,074
Nurses	442	823	1,778	2,907	5,431	7,022	8,399	8,893	10,968
Enlisted, Men	144,824	332,274	556,477	1,099,109	1,486,696	1,995,893	2,542,653	2,735,270	2,935,695
Enlisted, Women	0	0	0	3,109	21,083	38,450	57,500	72,864	73,685
TOTAL NAVY	160,997	383,150	640,570	1,259,167	1,741,750	2,381,116	2,981,365	3,201,755	3,408,347
Marine Corps									
Officers, Men	1,819	4,067	7,138	13,151	21,140	27,588	31,991	34,598	36,851
Officers, Women	0	0	0	0	244	605	797	824	813
Enlisted, Men	26,545	70,908	135,688	223,243	284,481	356,533	415,559	414,561	427,017
Enlisted, Women	0	0	0	0	3,313	9,720	16,669	17,012	17,350
TOTAL MARINE CORPS	28,364	75,346	143,528	238,423	310,994	405,169	472,582	472,380	485,833
Coast Guard									
Officers, Men	1,360	1,854	3,507	5,462	8,104	10,038	11,275	11,697	11,766
Officers, Women	0	0	0	15	235	514	704	918	855
Enlisted, Men	12,261	25,575	55,142	135,231	142,631	154,251	149,589	147,865	148,629
Enlisted, Women	0	0	0	69	2,956	5,570	7,392	8,911	8,646
TOTAL COAST GUARD	13,766	27,730	58,998	141,769	154,976	171,939	169,258	169,871	170,275
GRAND TOTAL	203,127	486,226	843,096	1,639,359	2,207,720	2,958,224	3,623,205	3,844,006	4,064,455

Annual totals and grand totals also include numbers of officer candidates.

Source: *Annual Report of the Secretary of the Navy*, 10 Jan. 1946 pp. A 14–15.

its own aviation which operated land-based sea patrols and the specialized aircraft employed on its carriers (see CARRIERS, 2). Between July 1940 and August 1945 more than 75,000 aircraft were delivered and naval air personnel rose from 10,923 (2,965 pilots) in mid-1940 to 437,524 (60,747 pilots) by August 1945, while the navy as a whole expanded at a similar rate (see Table 7). It also manned the guns of armed American merchantmen with personnel of the Naval Armed Guard; and inducted a large number of women (see WAVES).

Between the wars the navy's highest commander was designated Chief of Naval Operations (Opnav), a position held in September 1939 by Admiral *Stark. The preponderence of the navy's strength lay in the Pacific Fleet, commanded by Admiral James O. Richardson as C-in-C US Fleet (CINCUS), which was based in the Hawaiian Islands. But there was also a small Asiatic Fleet, based on Manila, and the Atlantic Squadron. On 5 September 1939 the Atlantic Squadron started the *Neutrality Patrol with its four old battleships, one carrier, four cruisers, and one destroyer squadron, and on 1 November 1940 it was redesignated Patrol Force United States Fleet before becoming the Atlantic Fleet in February 1941.

The same month the position of C-in-C, US Fleet, was abolished, and a true 'two-ocean navy' came into being when an Atlantic and a Pacific Command were created. Vice-Admiral *King, who had commanded the Patrol Force since the previous December, was appointed C-in-C Atlantic Fleet, while Rear-Admiral *Kimmel took command of the Pacific Fleet; but after the USA entered the war in December 1941 the position of C-in-C US Fleet was resurrected and King was appointed to it. At King's insistence his abbreviated title was known not as CINCUS, because it was pronounced 'sinkus', but COMINCH, and he was granted unprecedented powers. They excluded control of the bureaus, traditionally accountable to the navy secretary, but he was made directly responsible to the president and for current plans. Stark continued to have responsibility for long-term plans but in March 1942 he moved to London as C-in-C US naval forces in Europe and the office of Opnav was merged with COMINCH.

In July 1940 Congress authorized a large increase in construction (see Table 8) and the same month Roosevelt declared his intention of giving the UK all possible help 'short of war' a policy which, by the following year, committed King's forces to actions hardly distinguishable from those of the belligerents (see GREER, KEARNY, and REUBEN JAMES).

The US continental coastline, and some adjacent sea areas such as the Hawaiian Islands, were divided into numbered Naval Districts, but these were administrative areas not geared to directing modern anti-submarine warfare. So in July 1941 Stark formed four Sea Frontiers. Designated Eastern, Gulf, Caribbean, and Panama (which covered both ends of the canal), their areas of responsibility extended not only along a length of the coastline but about 350 km. (200 mi.) out to sea. Their task was to protect local convoys within their areas with Coast Guard cutters, *blimps, and whatever other units were allotted them. (Air cover for transatlantic convoys was initially the responsibility of the USAAF's No. 1 Bomber Command—Anti-Submarine Command from October 1942—but in September 1943 the command was disbanded. The Navy then took over its aircraft and assumed its responsibilities, though the air crews remained members of the USAAF.) The Eastern Sea Frontier, which operated the few *Q-ships the US Navy used during the war, was the parent organization. Working closely with Anti-Submarine Command at his New York HQ, the frontier's commander had complete operational control over all forces allocated to him, and he continued to be responsible for any coastal convoys that originated from his frontier when they left it.

In December 1941, when the Japanese launched their surprise attack on Pearl Harbor, the Pacific Fleet comprised 9 battleships, 3 carriers, 21 heavy and light cruisers, 67 destroyers, and 27 submarines. The attack caused heavy losses, especially to the battleships, but the carriers were at sea, and many of the ships were later salvaged and put back into commission. The Asiatic Fleet, which in December 1941 comprised 3 cruisers, 13 destroyers, 29 submarines, 2 seaplane tenders, and 6 gunboats, became part of *ABDA Command and its commander, Admiral *Hart, was appointed its naval commander (ABDAFLOAT). But he lost his principal base when the Japanese overran Luzon (see PHILIPPINES CAMPAIGNS) and nearly all his ships in a number of naval actions when the Japanese moved into the Netherlands East Indies (see JAVA SEA BATTLE).

In March 1942 Admiral *Nimitz, who had succeeded Kimmel as C-in-C Pacific Fleet (CINCPAC), was also appointed to command all US forces in the Pacific Ocean Areas (CINCPOA) which was divided into three geographical zones: North Pacific, Central Pacific, and South Pacific (see Map F). But the two separate offensives which were launched in the Pacific war—Nimitz's Central Pacific one and MacArthur's towards the Philippines—were co-ordinated by the Joint Chiefs of Staff.

In February 1943 the naval forces in MacArthur's *South-West Pacific Area (SWPA) were redesignated Seventh Fleet and in March *Halsey's South Pacific command became Third Fleet (established 15 March 1943) and Central Pacific command became Fifth Fleet (established 26 April 1944). In June 1944 these two fleets merged to become the Pacific Fleet's main strike force with their commanders taking it in turns to command it (called Third Fleet when commanded by Halsey; Fifth Fleet when commanded by *Spruance). In the Atlantic and Mediterranean South Atlantic command became Fourth Fleet in March 1943; Naval Forces, North-West African Waters, became Eighth Fleet; and Naval Forces, Europe, became Twelfth Fleet.

USA 7, Table 8: Strength of the US Navy, 1940–5

Date	*Number of Vessels of all Types*
30 June 1940	1,099
30 June 1941	1,899
30 June 1942	5,612
30 June 1943	18,493
30 June 1944	46,032
30 June 1945	67,952
Warships completed or acquired between 1 July 1940 and 31 August 1945	
Battleships	10
Aircraft carriers (CV, CVL)	27
Escort carriers (CVE)	111
Cruisers (CB, CA, CL)	47
Destroyers	370
Destroyer escorts	504
Submarines	217
Minecraft	975
Patrol ships and craft	1,915
Auxiliary ships	1,612
Landing ships and craft	66,055
District craft (yard craft)	3,053
TOTAL	74,896

Source: *The United States Naval Chronology, World War II* (Washington DC, 1955).

Tenth Fleet, the shore-based anti-submarine command, was formed by King in May 1943. Though designated a fleet this command had no ships, but brought together a number of organizations, such as those which dealt with convoy routing and with intelligence, which were already in existence when it was formed. By combining them under one roof King achieved greater co-ordination as well as greater security, and from it was monitored the movement of every merchant ship, warship, and aircraft in the US-controlled western Atlantic (US Strategic Zone).

The strength of each of the sea-going fleets varied, but their offensive units were always formed into task groups and task forces. By far the most powerful of these was Third Fleet's Task Force 38 (*Task Force 58 when Third Fleet was operating as Fifth Fleet), which was built around the Pacific Fleet's fast carriers and was supplied across the vast stretches of the Pacific by the *Fleet Train, one of the war's most outstanding feats of logistics. So powerful did this force become that by 1944 Nimitz was able to muster 14 battleships, 15 fleet carriers, 10 escort carriers, 24 cruisers, and a host of smaller vessels to support the invasion of the Marianas. The navy's submarine forces, by applying a stranglehold on Japan's shipping routes, also played a crucial role in winning the Pacific war, as did the amphibious forces of the US Marine Corps (see below), which did much of the fighting on land.

During the war years the US Navy also administered and controlled the US Coast Guard. This organized the auxiliary *Coastal Picket Patrol and performed a variety of tasks on land, in the air, and at sea under the command of the four Sea Frontier commanders. Its primary function was the protection of coastal convoys, but its personnel also regulated merchant shipping in port and at wharves; patrolled beaches; manned look-out stations, and some troop transports and landing craft; and undertook *air-sea rescue operations. Its personnel strength grew from 13,766 in 1940 to 170,275 in 1945, including 9,501 women (see SPARS). It was then operating more than 800 vessels over 20 m. (65 ft.) in length, and was also manning 351 naval vessels and 288 USAAF aircraft.

(e) Marine Corps

A separate service within the navy department, the USMC had the traditional marine role of being the navy's soldiers, but unlike any other marine force in the world it controlled its own aviation. The highest serving marine officer, the Corps Commandant (General Thomas Holcomb, 1936–43; General Alexander Vandegrift, 1944–7), had his own HQ and staff, but aboard ship marines were always subordinated to naval command and, until 1947, the USMC was not represented on the JCS Committee.

In 1933 the Fleet Marine Force (FMF) was established to undertake amphibious landings and by mid-1939 a quarter of the corps' total strength of nearly 20,000 men were part of it. The FMF was organized into two brigades (1st and 2nd) which were each supported by a Marine Aviation Group (AVG). One brigade was based at Quantico, Virginia, the other at San Diego, and there were also marine units scattered all over the world on guard and garrison duties. In February 1941 the two FMF brigades were redesignated 1st and 2nd Marine Division, each made up of three infantry regiments, an artillery regiment, and various support units, and their supporting aviation became 1st and 2nd Marine Aircraft Wings. It was these formations under an administrative and co-ordinating corps HQ (First Marine Amphibious Corps, or IMAC) which undertook the marines' first operation of the war when they landed on *Guadalcanal in August 1942, and IMAC (redesignated Third Amphibious Corps in April 1944) became the amphibious operations planning HQ for the South Pacific area.

The USMC expanded as quickly as the other services (see Table 8) and altogether six marine divisions were activated: 3rd, 4th, and 5th in the USA between August and November 1943 and 6th, on Guadalcanal, in September 1944. The marines also raised Raider battalions (see SPECIAL FORCES, below), parachute battalions (paramarines), a glider group, *barrage balloon squadrons, and seven defence battalions for guarding island bases such as *Wake and *Guam.

Marine Corps aviation kept up with this growth. In December 1941 there were 641 pilots and 13 squadrons; by September 1945 there 10,049 pilots and 128 squadrons formed into 5 aircraft wings (1st–4th, and 9th, a training wing), plus 106,475 ground officers and enlisted men and women. Squadrons were designated by numbers and by the letters VM to which was added another letter for identification (e.g. VMF for fighter squadrons, VMB for bomber squadrons).

Before the start of Nimitz's Central Pacific offensive V Amphibious Corps (VAC) was formed in September 1943 and this subsequently oversaw the invasions of the Gilbert Islands (see TARAWA) and the *Marshall Islands. Both Amphibious Corps came under the Fleet Marine Force which was redesignated Fleet Marine Force, Pacific (FMFPac) in 1944. Initially, both FMFPac and VAC were commanded by Maj-General Holland M. Smith (1882–1967) during the Central Pacific offensive, but he relinquished the latter post to Maj-General Harry Schmidt in October 1944. Marine Corps casualties during the war amounted to 91,718; 24,511 of whom were killed or died.

(f) Special Forces

The Marine Corps raised the first special forces when 1st and 2nd Raider Battalions were formed in February 1942 to spearhead amphibious landings on normally inaccessible beaches, mount surprise raiding expeditions, and conduct guerrilla-style missions. At the start of the Guadalcanal campaign 1st Raider Battalion landed on Tulagi and Savo islands, but the troops were then used in an infantry role, for which their training had not fitted them, on Guadalcanal. The 1st Raider Battalion took part in the battle for Edson's Ridge (so called after the battalion's commander) and 2nd Raider Battalion, known as *Carlson's Raiders, pursued and destroyed a Japanese regiment during the course of a 240 km. (150 mi.) patrol through the jungle.

Two more Raider Battalions (3rd and 4th) were raised in the Pacific theatre in September–October 1942 and all four became part of 1st Raider Regiment formed in the New Hebrides in March 1943, but they did not always operate together. In September 1943 2nd Raider Regiment (Provisional) was formed from 2nd and 3rd Battalions which fought on *Bougainville, but the increasing need for Marine Corps reinforcements, and the lack of opportunity to employ the raiders in their specialist role, led to their disbandment in January 1944, and all four battalions became 4th Marine Regiment to replace the one which had been lost in the Philippines in 1942.

The army's special forces were called the Rangers. The first battalion, the idea of Brig-General *Truscott who modelled it on the British commandos, was raised from US troops stationed in Northern Ireland in mid-1942, and 50 rangers participated in the *Dieppe raid that August. The 29th Ranger Battalion (Provisional), formed in the UK in December 1942, participated in raids on Norway while attached to the British commandos, and two more (3rd and 4th) were raised in Morocco during May 1943. The 1st, 3rd, and 4th took part in the Sicilian campaign and then landed at *Salerno (September 1943) and *Anzio (January 1944). They took their objective, the town of Anzio, with relative ease; but though specifically trained for raiding, and therefore lightly equipped, they were then used as conventional infantry. On 29 January two battalions (1st and 3rd) were used to spearhead the attack on Cisterna but were ambushed and almost totally annihilated. When the remaining battalion tried to reach them it suffered heavy casualties and out of the original 1,500 men only 449 remained. Two more Ranger Battalions (2nd and 5th) were activated in the USA and took part in the Normandy landings in June 1944 (see OVERLORD), 2nd landing on *OMAHA beach while 5th stormed Pointe du Hoc. The 6th Ranger Battalion was formed in New Guinea in September 1944 and was employed in raids on the Japanese-occupied Philippines.

A joint US–Canadian brigade-sized unit called the First Special Service Force was also raised. It was trained in amphibious, mountain, and arctic warfare techniques with the idea of making a large-scale raid on Norwegian industry in tracked vehicles which were being developed in the UK for arctic warfare. The Norwegian *government-in-exile vetoed the raid but the force, which was commanded by a US Army officer, Brigadier R. Frederick, remained in being. It landed on Kiska unopposed during the Aleutian Islands campaigns and then took part in the Italian campaign and landed at Anzio. It was also employed during the French Riviera landings in August 1944 when it took two of the Hyères islands to protect the invasion's left flank. It then operated as part of Devers's Sixth Army Group in southern France, but by then its specialist techniques were no longer required—it also proved to be highly complicated to administer—and it was disbanded in December 1944. See also GALAHAD, MARS TASK FORCE, and OFFICE OF STRATEGIC SERVICES.

I. C. B. Dear
Shelby Stanton

6. Intelligence

In the Second World War, the gathering and processing of military intelligence depended less on the traditional methods of espionage agents and clandestine reconnaissance, and more on the sophisticated technologies of electronic eavesdropping and communications intelligence.

The American military intelligence units, designated G-2 in the army and N-2 in the navy, were transformed almost beyond recognition by the incorporation of scientific techniques into the age-old quest to 'see to the other side of the hill'. The army also had the *Counter Intelligence Corps (Corps of Intelligence Police until January 1942), but most important was the Signal Intelligence Service—later called the Special Branch, Military Intelligence Service—established in 1929 under the cryptologist Colonel William F. Friedman (1891–1969). The analogous navy organization was the Communication Security Unit, also known as OP-20-G, formed in 1924 under Commander Laurence F. Safford. Rivalling these units in size and importance was the *Office of Strategic Services (OSS), created on 13 June 1942 under William J. *Donovan.

Communications intelligence was broken into two broad categories: cryptanalysis and traffic analysis. Cryptanalysts engaged in the traditional practice of code-breaking, or deciphering the other side's encoded messages (and, reciprocally, devising and constantly revising codes for the secure transmission of their own nation's messages). But modern codes had become so complex—for example, the Japanese naval code, JN-25, comprised some 45,000 five-digit groups, each signifying a word or phrase, and each further embedded in additive five-digit groups taken from a continually changing list of 50,000 random numbers—that rudimentary computers and advanced mathematical theory were required to crack them.

American cryptanalysts led by Friedman had broken the Japanese diplomatic code, known as PURPLE, even before the outbreak of war. In the doomed negotiations between Tokyo and Washington (see INTRODUCTION, above) just before Pearl Harbor, deciphered Japanese diplomatic messages, called *MAGIC by the Americans, were often in the hands of Roosevelt and *Hull before the messages were formally presented to the Japanese diplomats who were their intended recipients. Probably the greatest triumph of American cryptanalysis in the war was the accurate prediction by the Pearl Harbor branch of OP-20-G, under Commander Joseph J. Rochefort Jr. of the Japanese attack on *Midway, 3–6 June 1942 (see ULTRA, 2).

Traffic analysis (see SIGNALS INTELLIGENCE WARFARE), depended not on actually reading encrypted enemy communications, but on identifying patterns in the volume, sources, destinations, and other characteristics of radio transmissions. In the battle of the *Atlantic, traffic analysis of data provided by high-frequency direction finders (see HUFF-DUFF) enabled the British and American navies to plot the approximate locations of German U-boats, by monitoring the frequent radio communications between submarines at sea and their bases in Germany. This kind of intelligence ultimately proved crucial in breaking the back of the German submarine warfare campaign.

On the Home Front, primary responsibility for intelligence gathering and analysis rested with the Federal Bureau of Investigation (FBI) under J. Edgar *Hoover. The Bureau existed principally to investigate violations of federal law, and to collect evidence to support criminal prosecutions, its enabling statute also authorized it to investigate any matters referred to it by the state department. Accordingly, President Roosevelt on 25 August 1936 directed Secretary of State Hull officially to request the FBI to collect information on 'subversive activities'.

That request provided the FBI with the authority it needed to create a General Intelligence Section, without formally notifying Congress or the public. The creation of that section vastly amplified the scope of the FBI's activity, and helped to fuel the growth of the FBI from 391 agents in 1933 to some 3,000 in 1942, and 4,886 in 1944.

Even before the USA entered the war, the FBI conducted

an investigation into the legality of the camps run by the *German-American Bund, and also made an extensive investigation of Nazi espionage activities in America, resulting in the indictment of eighteen persons in 1938. In that same year Hoover began attaching security specialists to each of the Bureau's 45 field offices. On 21 May 1940 Roosevelt authorized wiretapping of 'persons suspected of subversive activities'. The FBI also established a Custodial Detention Programme in 1940, identifying 'dangerous' individuals for arrest in case of emergency. Included on this list by December 1941 were 770 Japanese aliens whose arrest Hoover ordered after the attack on Pearl Harbor. (Hoover remained convinced that the FBI could contain any threat of Japanese subversion with individually targeted arrests of this kind, and he was critical of the later decision to intern the entire West Coast population of some 110,000 Japanese-Americans.)

A presidential directive on 26 June 1939, allocating intelligence duties among the army, navy, and FBI, assigned responsibility for both domestic and Latin American intelligence to the FBI. The Bureau investigated some 19,649 reports of sabotage in the USA during the war (none of which was definitively established to be sabotage), and foiled several German efforts to land saboteurs by submarine. In early 1941 it rounded up and imprisoned 33 Nazi suspects which accounted for all the German agents in the USA. In June 1942 eight saboteurs were landed by submarine, four on Long Island and four near Jacksonville, Florida. The FBI rounded up these as well before they could do any damage. Six were subsequently executed and two imprisoned as were some of those who helped shelter them. Another two agents were landed by submarine in Frenchman's Bay in Maine in November 1944. Their mission was to discover for *Goebbels how effective his propaganda broadcasts were, but they, too, were quickly captured by the FBI and sentenced to death, though this was later commuted to life imprisonment. In Latin America, the approximately 360 agents of the FBI's Special Intelligence Service (SIS) co-operated with the *Office of the Co-ordinator of Inter-American Affairs in denying strategic raw materials to enemy powers, and monitoring enemy intelligence and propaganda activity.

A major purpose of the FBI's wartime role was to forestall the kind of hysteria and vigilante disruption that had swept the USA during the First World War. Accordingly, the Bureau undertook extensive training and liaison activities with local police forces, established a network of informants in defence plants, and pre-empted a scheme by the American Legion to organize its own counter-espionage force by recruiting some 60,000 legionnaires into its American Legion Contact Program.

David M. Kennedy

7. Merchant marine

One way to understand the Second World War is to appreciate the critical role of merchant shipping in its prosecution. Throughout the entire conflict, the availability or non-availability of merchant shipping determined what the Allies could or could not do militarily. This was most evident in the early stages of the war when sinkings of Allied merchant vessels exceeded production, when slow turnarounds, convoy delays, roundabout routeing, and long voyages taxed transport severely, or when the cross-Channel invasion planned for 1942 had to be postponed for many months for reasons which included insufficient shipping. But in time, the bottoms required to help turn the tide became a reality. These were provided overwhelmingly by the USA, primarily through construction. From 1939 to 1945, the US Maritime Commission built 5,777 ships, mostly large cargo carriers and tankers, for a total of 56.3 million deadweight tons, or almost five times the size of the nation's entire 1939 fleet (see Graph 2); it was the most prodigious construction of ships ever undertaken. Had these ships not been produced, the war would have been in all likelihood prolonged many months, if not years—some argue the Allies would have lost—as there would not have existed the means to carry the personnel, supplies, and equipment needed by the combined Allies to defeat the Axis powers. The US wartime merchant fleet, built by a labour force which, at its peak, numbered more than 600,000 men and women at 70 principal private and government shipyards at a cost of $13 billion, constituted one of the most significant contributions made by any nation to the eventual winning of the Second World War.

Few could have predicted such an extraordinary American maritime growth before the outbreak of war. In 1937 the US merchant fleet was on the verge of obsolescence. In late 1938, however, the newly constituted US Maritime Commission (USMC) under Admiral Emory S. Land inaugurated a long-range construction programme geared to provide 50 ships a year for 10 years. This timely undertaking provided the nation with just enough ships, shipyards, and expertise to enable it and the Allies to weather the storm in the early stages of the war.

One of the more conspicuous manifestations of its gradual move away from neutrality was the shipping assistance the USA provided the Allies. The USMC sold large numbers of its First World War reserve fleet to the British, which, while helping the USA dispose of obsolete ships at reasonable prices, provided the UK with much needed tonnage. The USMC also constructed vessels for the Allies, in particular the UK. To facilitate mass, rapid, and efficient construction of these, a British design for an emergency 11 knot, 10,800 dwt dry cargo ship with reciprocating steam engines, the famous *Liberty ship, was adopted, and orders for 260 of these, including 60 for the UK, were placed in early 1941. These and other ship type orders more than doubled with the establishment of Lend-Lease. Following Hitler's invasion of the USSR in June 1941, and reflecting continued enormous losses of Allied shipping to German attacks,

USA, Graph 2: Vessels delivered in US Maritime Commission Programme, 1939–45

	Number	Tonnage (000s tons) Deadweight (Gross)
Grand Total	**5,777**	**56,292 (39,920)**
By Type of Contract		
Maritime Commission	5,601	54,102 (38,490)
Private	111	1,581 (997)
Foreign	65	608 (433)
By Type of Ship		
Standard Cargo	541	5,349 (3,834)
Emergency Cargo (Liberty)	2,708	29,182 (19,447)
Victory Cargo	414	4,492 (3,151)
Tankers	705	11,365 (7,061)
Minor Types	727	2,601 (1,980)
Military Types	682	3,303 (4,452)

Deadweight Tonnage
Long Tons (1,000,000s)

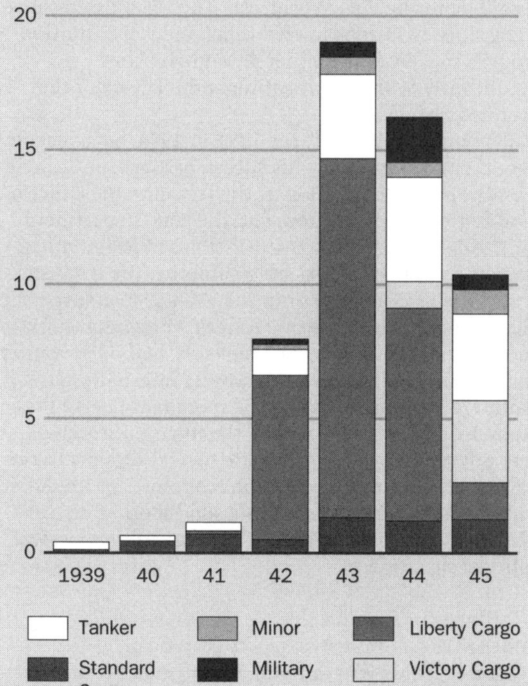

Note: The deadweight tonnage of a ship is the weight of cargo it carries (based on the long ton of 2,240 lb./1,017 kg.). Gross registered tonnage is a volume measurement (in cubic feet where 100 cubic feet equals one long ton) of a ship's hull but includes engine-spaces, crew quarters, and other spaces below the upper deck not assigned to storing cargo. Net registered tonnage is when these non-cargo spaces have been deducted from the gross registered tonnage.

Source: Lane, F. C., *Ships for Victory: A History of Shipbuilding under the United States Maritime Commission during World War II* (Baltimore Md., 1951).

the building programme was supplemented yet again. Once the USA entered the war, the main task facing the USMC was to produce merchant vessels faster than the Axis could sink them. In 1941 and 1942 the Allies were not only losing the war on land, they were losing it at sea, and a successful Axis severing of their line of supply seemed possible. Not until 1943 was the disparity between sinkings and construction overcome.

But the neutralization of the submarine menace did not diminish the need for ships, as supply lines to American and Allied forces fighting abroad on ever widening and remote fronts had to be assured. It took seven to eight tons of supplies to sustain a soldier in Europe in 1942, and double that in the Pacific. The shipyards under the USMC met the challenge admirably. In 1943 alone they launched 18 million tons. Although the USMC built some warships, including LSTs, escort carriers ('baby flattops'), and attack cargo ships (see LANDING CRAFT), most of its types, or about 77% production, were of commercial design. These included progressively more advanced vessels. The Liberty ship design, for example, was replaced by that of the Victory ship, a minimally larger, but much faster and rangier, and more commercially desirable, turbine-driven cargo carrier.

The allocation and control of the government's ships was just as significant as their construction. Once launched, the ships had to be supervised. The most efficient employment and turnaround of all ships, new or old, government or private, had be accomplished. Some balance had to be achieved between the USA's incoming strategic materials needs, and its outgoing military shipping requirements. Lend-Lease had to be serviced. The UK's minimal domestic requirements alone exceeded 25,000,000 annual tons of imported food and supplies for its civilian population. The USSR had to be supplied via long and extremely hazardous sea lanes (see ARCTIC CONVOYS). In 1943, US merchant ships in Lend-Lease made 2,267 voyages to the UK, 328 to the USSR, and 281 to other Allied nations.

In order to effect efficient control and operation of the vast flotilla of merchant ships, in February 1942 Roosevelt created the War Shipping Administration (WSA), under the direction of Lewis W. Douglas. Admiral Land, as head of the USMC, continued, with his deputy, the indispensable Admiral Howard L. Vickery, to oversee shipbuilding. Douglas ultimately succeeded in creating a co-ordinated, scientifically managed, and balanced pool of ships for both war and civilian cargoes, including in the latter the critical United Kingdom Import Program. Among Douglas's and the WSA's major obstacles were the US service branches, as the US Army and Navy naturally favoured military over civil programmes, resented civilian handling of military cargoes, and actually sought to use the distribution or denial of US tonnage to the Allies as a means of influencing Allied strategic thinking, particularly during 1942 and early 1943 when British military planning was dominant. Douglas's long-range

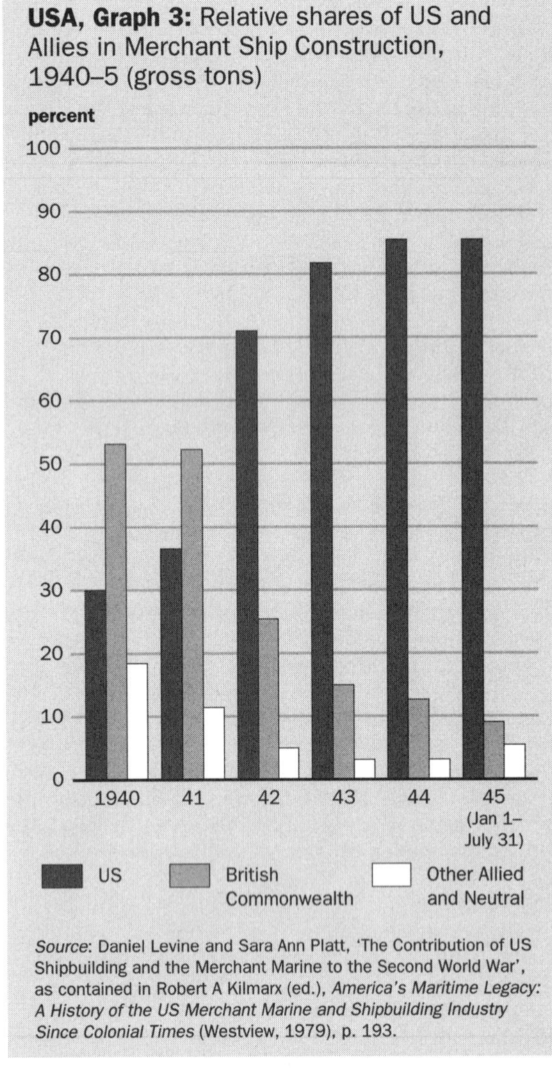

USA, Graph 3: Relative shares of US and Allies in Merchant Ship Construction, 1940–5 (gross tons)

Source: Daniel Levine and Sara Ann Platt, 'The Contribution of US Shipbuilding and the Merchant Marine to the Second World War', as contained in Robert A Kilmarx (ed.), *America's Maritime Legacy: A History of the US Merchant Marine and Shipbuilding Industry Since Colonial Times* (Westview, 1979), p. 193.

view was also in conflict with Admiral Land's and the USMC's goal of rebuilding the USA into a great post-war merchant shipping power. As Douglas saw it, the USA, with its general economic superiority, could not justify wresting control of the seas from Allied nations whose prosperity depended upon maritime revenues. For Douglas and the WSA the *Atlantic Charter of 1941—the Roosevelt–Churchill agreement of fair play and global interdependence between nations allied in war—and not the Merchant Marine Act of 1936, with its strong nationalistic commitment to the economic welfare of the US shipping industry, provided the preferable guideline. In this interpretation Douglas enjoyed the invaluable support of Harry *Hopkins, Roosevelt's closest aide. Together, Douglas and Hopkins, with periodic support from the president, formed the staunchest pro-British team in the US war administration.

Even so, the WSA frequently had to devote as much time to soothing British anxiety about the potential post-war commercial uses of America's huge new fleet—a 'floating avalanche' was one British name for it—as it did to the US service branches' attempts to commandeer it. British concerns were understandable; in 1943 the US merchant fleet equalled that of the UK's in tonnage, and in 1945 had doubled it (see Graph 3). Ultimately, the British reconciled themselves to the inevitability and necessity of US shipping growth, and throughout the war were increasingly beneficiaries of it, as the WSA laboured to make up the UK's shipping losses and guarantee its post-war maritime recovery. The benefits included the continued allocation of US ships to the UK Import Program, the loan of two million tons of US vessels to London on bareboat charters, and the formalization of an Anglo-American authority, the United Maritime Authority, over all Allied shipping to prevent the chaotic and ruinous competition that followed precipitous decontrol in the First World War. The WSA also assigned many ships to European civil relief and rehabilitation programmes in 1944–5, thereby contributing significantly to the stabilization and recovery of the liberated nations.

Although Douglas left the WSA in 1944, his concepts were carried through by his successor, Captain Granville Conway, by the White House, the treasury, the Office of Lend-Lease Administration, and the state department. For the degree to which the principles of the Atlantic Charter prevailed in respect to shipping, the Potsdam accords of 1945 and the Ship Sales Act 1946 assured both the maintenance of a strong American merchant marine for foreign trade and national defence, and the beneficent policy which helped restore post-war international commerce by rehabilitating the merchant fleets of the Allies. In the final assessment, the huge US merchant fleet not only provided critical logistical support to the war effort, but helped place the economies of the Allied and liberated nations on a more solid footing, thereby adding a substantial degree of stability to the post-war political situation. JEFFREY J. SAFFORD

8. Culture

(For the US film industry, see HOLLYWOOD.)

The war, filled with human drama vivid action, and exotic locales, suffused US culture during most of the 1940s. Americans, flushed with prosperity and eager for relief and relaxation, created a boom in popular entertainment. Although both popular and serious culture were characterized more by quantity than quality, a hungry public turned to a wider variety of outlets for reassurance, enlightenment, and sheer escape.

The theatre—which still chiefly meant Broadway—offered relatively little of a serious nature about the war. Lillian Hellman's *Watch on the Rhine* (later made into a movie) delivered a ringing call to anti-fascist arms in 1941 before Pearl Harbor, but its topical material left it time-bound. John Steinbeck's 1942 play *The Moon Is Down* (based on his novel of the same title) probed the human dilemmas of the German occupation and the Norwegian resistance, but was hotly controversial for its treatment of a German officer as a likeable boy-next-door caught up by irresistible forces. The few plays that entered the repertory during the war had little to do with the global conflict. The most memorable was *The Glass Menagerie*, which in 1945 heralded the arrival of one of America's major playwrights, Tennessee Williams.

The war, curiously, played better as a musical. Irving Berlin, the leading US song-writer, recast *Yip Yip Yaphank*, his light-hearted look at First World War military life, as *This Is the Army* (1942) featuring big chorus numbers performed by 300 servicemen. It was an all-male, white-dominated show, casting blacks all too aptly as second-class citizens, and with the women's roles played by men in drag. (*This Is the Army* was made into a popular movie, starring future politicians George Murphy and Ronald Reagan as father and son.) If *This Is The Army* looked backward in time, *On The Town* (1944) forecast the future. A happy collaboration of Leonard Bernstein, a major figure in American music for the next half-century, and choreographer Jerome Robbins, it celebrated high-spirited sailors who romped through New York on shore leave. It was brassy, sexual, and urban, but nostalgia for a simpler, halcyon America also continued to be big box office, notably in the enduring Richard Rodgers–Oscar Hammerstein collaboration *Oklahoma!* (1943).

Popular music took on a patriotic, martial air. The industry boomed as huge audiences were glued to their radios for war news and a mobile population with money to spend flocked to big-city clubs and country music venues. Irving Berlin's 'God Bless America', written in 1938 and rocketed to instantaneous recognition by Kate Smith, became the unofficial national anthem. Tin Pan Alley tried to equal such memorable hits from the First World War as 'Over There' and 'K-K-K Katy', but the innocence that had buoyed such tunes was missing in this greater, more terrible war: efforts such as 'Goodbye Mama, I'm Off to Yokohama' and 'You're a Sap, Mr Jap' fell flat. The reality of the war was captured more by such songs as Frank Loesser's 'Praise the Lord and Pass the Ammunition'. Domestic dislocations received bittersweet recognition in a woman's lament, 'They're Either Too Young or Too Old'. Nostalgia for a vanished world fuelled hits like 'The Last Time I Saw Paris' by Jerome Kern and Oscar Hammerstein.

New musical forms and entertainers came into the spotlight. Country music was less narrowly defined by region and class as military and industrial demands brought people of diverse backgrounds side-by-side. 'There's a Star-Spangled Banner Waving Somewhere', which claimed to be the most popular song of the period, suggested the fusion of patriotism and nostalgia as country music went mainstream. GIs in Europe ranked Roy Acuf their favourite performer, and 25 country music groups played at army camps in the European theatre alone.

Big band jazz enjoyed great popularity, even though conscription and travel restrictions made staffing a nightmare. War audiences wanted loud, full music with a lively beat. From the big band scene emerged one of the biggest stars of the post-war era: Frank Sinatra. His 'nice guy' image combined with jazz-inspired phrasing and supple microphone work propelled him to stardom in 1943. Simultaneously the 'bebop' or 'bop' movement, an antidote to the bland commercialism of jazz and popular music, began to grow under the influence of the legendary Charlie 'Bird' Parker. Though initially ridiculed by many critics, bop's voice from the inner city was destined to have a major effect on post-war jazz and rock. Carried abroad by GIs and their bands, the dazzling variety of American music attained new international influence.

The classical music scene languished during the war as symphony orchestras and opera companies lost musicians to military bands. American composers sometimes turned to war subjects, although few had the lasting appeal of Aaron Copland's *A Lincoln Portrait*, written as a declaration of faith in 1942 during the dark night of Allied losses. The most lasting compositions came from the pen of Béla Bartók, in particular his *Concerto for Orchestra*. Like many members of Europe's intelligentsia, Bartók, a Hungarian émigré, took refuge in the USA in the 1930s and enormously enriched American cultural life.

For serious discussions of the war the public found a flood of books, mostly by *war correspondents and politicians. Non-fiction overtook novels in popularity, a trend evident with the two best-sellers of 1941. William L. Shirer's *Berlin Diary* chillingly portrayed Hitler's Germany, and then surrendered its lead to Joseph E. Davies's *Mission to Moscow*, which offered a reassuring, if over-credulous, view of the Soviet ally. In 1943 Wendell Willkie, the Republican presidential candidate of 1940, distilled his passionate internationalism into the suggestively titled *One World*, which sold two million copies in two years, a record to that point in American publishing. Sober readers worked through Walter Lippmann's *US Foreign Policy* and Sumner *Welles's *The Time for Decision*.

The murkiness of geopolitics was leavened by human-interest stories about average GIs. Private Marion Hargrove's cosy sketches of boot camp in *See Here, Private Hargrove* (1942) became a phenomenal best-seller. As GIs moved from camp to battlefield, an obscure newspaper-man named Ernie Pyle rocketed to fame with his loving portraits of ordinary soldiers. Late in the war in *Up Front*, Sergeant Bill Mauldin's writings and drawings conveyed a first-hand authenticity that could only have come from one who was there.

For American fiction the war would be a catalyst. During the conflict religious novels, like movies offering the reassurance of faith, proved popular. A harbinger of war-inspired subject matter and a new generation was the youthful John Hersey's *A Bell for Adano*, a tale of the Italian campaign, which won the Pulitzer Prize in 1945. Major works of the war-inspired generation led by men such as Norman Mailer, James Jones, Herman Wouk, and Gore Vidal lay over the horizon.

The war spurred economic developments that shook up the genteel book trade and helped democratize American reading. It abetted the paperback revolution, begun in 1939 with Pocket Books' cautious release of ten paperbacks selling for 25 cents each. Wartime paper rationing, which squeezed books into smaller formats, helped make paperbacks respectable, and a mobile public liked the slim, light volumes. The Armed Services Editions became the biggest mass publishing venture in American history. Sixty million books, ranging from Charles Dickens and Joseph Conrad to mysteries and westerns, poured into the hands of soldiers and sailors—free. Charges of censorship flared as zealous officers tried to circumscribe what GIs, whose experiences outran many writers' imaginations, might read.

In the end the war transformed American culture. Freed from previous constraints, 12 million soldiers and sailors experienced worlds vastly different from the conventional pieties in which they had been raised. If the depression had coloured the outlook of an era, the war shaped the attitudes of a new generation prematurely powerful, sceptical, and worldly. When the veterans returned home they began reshaping the American cultural imagination to account for their experience.

Clayton R. Koppes

Introduction/domestic life/government

Blum, J. M., *V Was for Victory: Politics and American Culture During World War II* (New York, 1976).

Burns, J. M., *Roosevelt: the Soldier of Freedom, 1940–1945* (New York, 1970).

Campbell, D'A., *Women at War with America: Private Lives in a Patriotic Era* (Cambridge, Mass., 1984).

Chapman, R., *Contours of Public Policy, 1939–1945* (New York, 1981).

Dallek, R., *Franklin D. Roosevelt and American Foreign Policy, 1932–1945* (New York, 1979).

Feis, H., *The Road to Pearl Harbor* (Princeton, 1950).

Freidel, F., *Franklin D. Roosevelt: A Rendezvous with Destiny* (Boston, 1990).

Hartzel, K., *The Empire State at War: World War II* (New York, 1949).

Kennett, L., *For the Duration: The United States Goes to War, Pearl Harbor–1942* (New York, 1985).

Lingeman, R., *Don't You Know There's a War On?* (New York, 1970).

Polenberg, R., *War and Society: The United States, 1941–1945* (Philadelphia, 1972).

US Civilian Production Administration, *Industrial Mobilization for War: History of the War Production Board and Predecessor Agencies 1940–1945* (Washington, DC, 1947).

Armed forces

Maurer, M. (ed.), *Air Force Combat Units of World War II*, Air University (1961; repr. Washington, DC, 1980).

Stanton, S., *Order of Battle: US Army, World War II* (Novato, Calif., 1984).

Updegraph, C., *US Marine Corps Special Units of World War II* (Washington, DC, 1972).

Intelligence

Powers, R. G., *Secrecy and Power: The Life of J. Edgar Hoover* (New York, 1987).

Merchant marine

Land, E., *Winning the War with Ships: Land, Sea, and Air—Mostly Land* (New York, 1958).

Lane, F. C., *Ships for Victory: A History of Shipbuilding under the United States Maritime Commission During World War II* (Baltimore, Md., 1951).

Safford, J. J., 'Anglo-American Maritime Relations During the Two World Wars: A Comparative Analysis', *The American Neptune*, 41:4 (October 1981), pp. 262–79.

Culture

Schuller, G., *The Swing Era: The Development of Jazz, 1930–1945* (New York, 1989).

USAAF (United States Army Air Forces), see USA, 5(c).

USSR

For the fighting in the USSR, see BARBAROSSA and GERMAN–SOVIET WAR; see also entries for BALTIC STATES, BELORUSSIA, BESSARABIA, BUKOVINA, CAUCASUS, RUSSIA, and UKRAINE.

1. Introduction

The USSR was an active participant in the Second World War from start to finish, from September 1939 until August 1945. Official Soviet propaganda, which came to be widely accepted in the West in relation to events in eastern Europe, made great efforts to conceal this fact. Soviet histories always preferred the label of 'The Great Patriotic War, 1941–5' and propaganda consistently maintained, for example, that the Soviet Union was neutral in the period before 22 June 1941, the date when Germany invaded the USSR (see BARBAROSSA), and that Soviet operations were defensive in nature throughout.

In reality, the Soviet Union supported Nazi Germany in a substantial way between the conclusion of the *Nazi–Soviet Pact of August 1939 and the German invasion. Also, the Red Army was heavily engaged against the Japanese in August 1939 (see JAPANESE–SOVIET CAMPAIGNS); against the Poles in September 1939 (see POLISH CAMPAIGN); against the Finns during 1939–40 (see FINNISH–SOVIET WAR); and was used in the forcible annexation of the Baltic States and the former Bessarabia in the summer of 1940. In fact, Soviet military operations represent an important component of the changing European scene during the currency of the Nazi–Soviet Pact; and the incorporation into the USSR of a broad belt of occupied territory formed an important political and military prelude to the *German–Soviet war (see Map 107).

In September 1939, before it acquired any of that territory, the USSR's population was 170.5 million inhabiting an area of 21.4 million sq. km. (8.25 million sq. mi.). The country then consisted of several theoretically sovereign republics which were constituted on 29 December 1922 by the Union's founding members, the Russian, Ukrainian, Belorussian (White Russian), and Transcaucasian republics. When a new constitution was adopted in 1936 the USSR consisted of eleven member republics, some of which contained within themselves other autonomous republics and regions. The largest republic was the Russian Federation (RSFSR) with 63.8% of the total Soviet population. The RSFSR itself consisted of fourteen autonomous republics, including one for German colonists whom Catherine the Great had summoned to the country, and seven autonomous regions. Only 73.4% of the RSFSR's population were Great Russians who, within the USSR as a whole, amounted to 58.4% of the population, a percentage which dropped to 52.7% with the annexation of Polish territory (largely inhabited by White Russians and Ukrainians), of Moldavia, and of the Baltic States. The second largest Soviet people were the Ukrainians with 16.6%, followed by the White Russians (Belorussia) with 3.1%, and then there were the Uzbeks, Tatars, Kazakhs, Azeris, Armenians, Georgians, Lithuanians, Jews, and so on. There were at least fourteen nationalities with around one million and more members. Depending on definitions there existed more than 80, 120, or even 170 different languages within the USSR.

Thanks to its victory in the German–Soviet war, the USSR emerged in 1945 as the political and military master of eastern Europe. Soviet *communism reached its zenith, for the western powers possessed neither the means nor the will to oppose Stalin's designs. In their eagerness to enlist Soviet support for the final phase of the *Pacific war, they proved ready at the Yalta conference (see ARGONAUT) to sanction Soviet territorial annexations contrary to the *Atlantic Charter and were in no position to extract more tangible guarantees from the Soviet Union to protect Polish independence. In fact, no effective steps were taken to challenge Soviet political machinations in countries recently liberated by the Red Army. Most of the new frontiers (see ODER–NEISSE LINE, for example) and new political regimes of eastern Europe, including the Soviet frontier itself (see POLISH–SOVIET FRONTIER), were organized in the last year of the war according to Stalin's wishes. However, in the absence of a formal peace treaty, the settlement of 1945 contained the seeds of future conflict, fuelling the *Cold War which did not cease until the terminal collapse of the USSR in 1991.

The Communist Party benefited greatly from the war. Military membership had been only 15% in June 1941 in the wake of the Red Army purges; just over half of party members were service personnel by the end of the war. The party began to grow in influence in 1943 and something like a revival occurred in 1944. Many members favoured a flowering of party debate and the updating of the ideology. Stalin appears to have considered this a threat to his authority and debate was stifled. He also viewed the increasing prominence of victorious Soviet generals as alarming and these heroes were dispatched to minor posts after 1945.

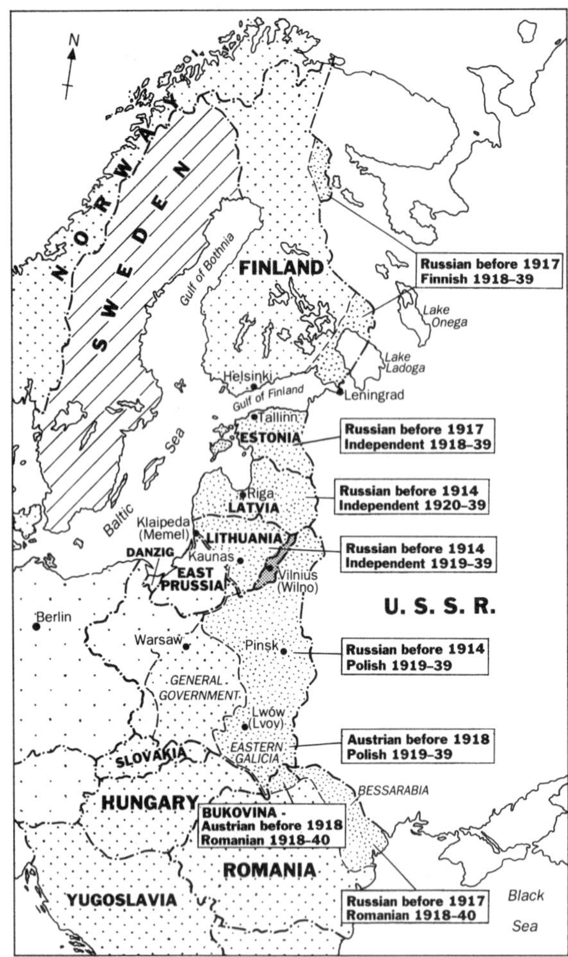

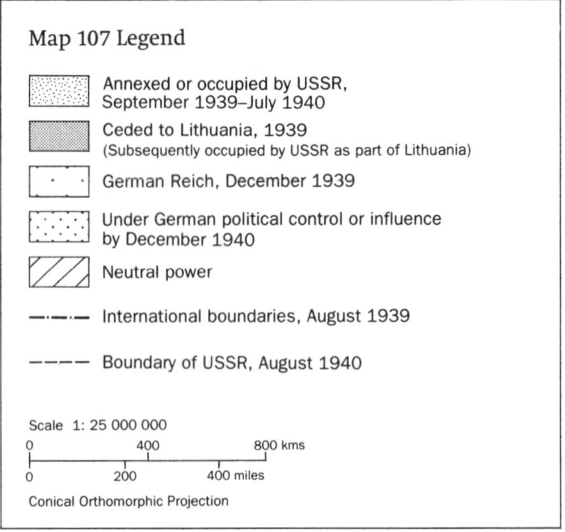

107. Status of territories prior to occupation by **USSR** between September 1939 and July 1940

The war transformed the Soviet Union. It welded party and people together for the first time. The USSR was now a great power. However, the political and economic system which had been fashioned so successfully during the war was only permitted to evolve within narrow limits. This major flaw was later to become a fatal weakness.

Norman Davies
Heinz-Dietrich Löwe
Martin McCauley

2. Domestic life, economy, and war effort

From about 1929 the USSR went through major social and economic transformation even more traumatic than the 1917 revolution. A determined policy of collectivizing the peasantry and industrializing the country was pursued. This massive, accelerated development forced through from above may have been motivated by military considerations, but the system was also forced to balance the interests of the agricultural areas and those of the workers and the cities. Although the New Economic Policy (1921) had ended forced quotas and brought other concessions, which resulted in economic and political normalization, peasants were still disadvantaged through pricing and planning decisions. Serious crises in feeding the cities resulted, in 1922–3, 1925–6, and 1928–9, as the peasants seemed to withdraw from the market. The crises were not only economic, they reflected a deep crisis of legitimacy caused by the alienation and distrust between the rural classes and the urban-based communist system, threatening the very existence of the proletarian state. It seemed obvious that a policy which destroyed the peasantry as a social force and turned the agricultural USSR into an industrial state would solve this conflict for good and secure the 'socialism in one country' the system was bent on building.

Collectivization was meant to facilitate massive transfers of resources from agriculture to industry. Even Soviet historians of pre-*perestroika* times admit that this transfer did not take place. Rather, the state had to invest massively in agriculture. Only manpower transfers took place as millions of uprooted peasants moved to industrial centres. And this was of doubtful benefit because it reinforced the emphasis on quantity and the neglect of quality so characteristic of Stalinist industrialization and of Soviet industry later.

Still, in crude, quantitive terms, this 'third revolution'—after the (by the Russian old-style calendar) February and October revolutions of 1917—starting with the first Five Year Plan in 1929, was fairly successful. Growth rates were considerably higher than those of capitalist countries at the time and they stand comparison with any major industrialization. During the first and second Five Year Plans the country developed an industrial base that enabled it to withstand the onslaught of the Wehrmacht in June 1941. None the less, industrialization was chaotic, belying the very idea of a planned economy.

USSR: A Urals tank assembly factory in 1943.

The industrial workforce became rather volatile, quickly moving from one factory or from one region to another, exacerbating the problem of low per capita productivity. Plans served mainly as tools to motivate. The regime reacted to difficulties with witch-hunts, show-trials, and death sentences for 'saboteurs'. The balance between urban and rural sectors changed palpably; from 18% in 1929 the share of the urban population had risen to 33% by 1939.

Collectivization proved disastrous. Agricultural production sank dramatically between 1929 and 1933, only just regaining the 1928 level in 1939. Particularly drastic was the loss of livestock slaughtered by peasants in protest against collectivization. Official figures say that by 1933 livestock was reduced by half, to regain the level of 1926–7 only by 1953–4. Collectivization was pushed through brutally and peasants were forced to deliver more produce than they could afford. There were massive famines in the Ukraine and on the lower Volga, and millions of deaths followed. The famine in the Ukraine was possibly intentional and used to break the back even of passive resistance. Millions of peasants fled to the cities and further millions were deported to Siberia. Altogether, 15 million peasants perished or were killed in this most horrifying attempt at social engineering.

Under these circumstances the total subservience of the population could be taken for granted. But it also has to be stressed that industrialization was supported with great enthusiasm. Fast economic growth and schooling programmes created opportunities for hundreds of thousands to move into better jobs—a movement accelerated by the fact that the Great Terror emptied so many positions. Even for the dirty work of collectivization thousands of determined and hardened party and civil war veterans could be mobilized to apply themselves with their usual zest.

By 1939 the leadership had promised and granted an end to massive terror, though it continued on a reduced, less visible, level. Emphasis on 'class warfare' and the 'class enemy' was toned down and the 'Stalin Constitution' of 5 December 1936 no longer disenfranchised anybody on the basis of class origin. The Stalin cult helped to stabilize the system, however improbable that may seem. It gave an ideological coherence which appealed, if only in a superficial way, to the men of humble background and rudimentary education who by now had moved upwards into the higher regions of party and state bureaucracy. With them the belief in the scientific value of the maxims of Marxism-Leninism seems to have been strong.

Contributing to stability and cohesiveness was the fact that the cultural experiments of earlier Soviet years were abandoned. Now the new élites shared readily and willingly the values, attitudes, and tastes of ordinary people. This communality of largely conservative views was a very important element in holding the system together. Similarly, by the mid-1930s family values were re-emphasized. 'Free love' was condemned as a 'bourgeois institution', divorce was made more difficult, and abortion became illegal. Schools put emphasis on discipline and proper learning, and reintroduced examinations. History teaching had to avoid 'abstract sociological schemes' and to employ a 'chronological . . . sequence . . . firmly fixing in the minds of the pupils important events, personages and dates'. School uniforms returned, with compulsory plaits for girls. In arts and literature a semi-religious cult of heroes and morality developed which catered to many tastes. The proclamation of Socialist Realism as the only acceptable, rather conventional, form of art also facilitated the return of Russian and foreign classics. A form of nationalism foreshadowed the unashamed rejection of internationalism and a return to Russian traditions, institutions, and values which took place during the war.

Society became characterized by an élite of technical graduates—represented by figures such as Nikita Khrushchev (1894–1971), Alexei Kosygin (1904–80), and Leonid Brezhnev (1902–82)—who rose quickly in the 1930s and were to remain prominent until the 1980s. This new élite was no longer composed of old revolutionaries of middle-class origin, but was drawn from the trained and educated offspring of peasants and proletarians who stood nearer to the masses. For the ordinary man the 'Stalin Revolution' brought the first, still patchy, elements of a welfare state, and he could also be impressed by the architecture of the time, clearly built to inspire awe. *Edinonachal'e* (one-man rule) enabled factory managers or officers to decide matters on their 'technical', rather than their ideological, merits and reduced the influence of party officials or political *commissars. The system of bringing workers from the factory floor into higher education was discontinued, as was positive discrimination on entrance. Fees for higher education emphasized the increasingly hierarchical character of Soviet society.

If ordinary people were drawn nearer to the élite in terms of values, taste, and attitudes, this was not necessarily so in politics. True, most members of society became part of an institutional framework that mobilized them for carefully selected and carefully supervised political activities. But a full picture of events and the possibility of discussing them were not available to the masses or even to party members relatively high up. It was extremely difficult for ordinary people to follow the politics that led to war between Germany and the western powers, and to the German attack on the USSR; and the motives and actions, and the surprising about-turns, of their leadership also remained unclear to them. In 1938 the Soviet Union offered to fight against Nazi Germany in defence of Czechoslovakia. During the first half of 1939 Stalin criticized Germany for being the main aggressor and the western powers for not acting decisively. But the Nazi–Soviet Pact of August 1939 changed everything. Nazi Germany was now an ally and anti-German propaganda stopped. German–Soviet friendship was celebrated to suggest it was neither tactical nor short-term. At times the Soviet press seemed to appeal to the Germans to invade England (see SEALION), and newspapers stressed the support the USSR was giving to the Nazis. This did not change, though with the fall of *France in June 1940 it was emphasized that Soviet neutrality was armed, and that the Red Army stood ready to repel any aggressor. While the battle of *Britain was raging, reporting, always subordinate to the aims of official policy, became more objective and sympathetic towards the people of the UK. But no hint of the impending danger of a German attack could be found in contemporary Soviet newspapers. The Soviet people were completely surprised and deeply shocked when the Wehrmacht invaded in the early hours of 22 June 1941.

Soviet industrialization was always planned with one eye on the demands of any wartime mobilization of the economy. A special mobilization administration was formed, first under VSNKH (Verkhovnyi Soviet Narodnogo Khoziaistva, or Supreme Council for the National Economy) and then under the Commissariat for Heavy Industry. With the increase of tensions internationally economic mobilization became the centre of attention. On 30 April 1938 a military-industrial commission was set up under the Defence Committee of the USSR Council of People's Commissars, or Sovnarkom (see Chart 1 for the USSR's party, armed forces command, and administrative structure). A Sovnarkom decree followed on 15 July 1939 appointing representatives of the People's Commissariat for Defence to major plants to check on the fulfilment of defence contracts and to develop plant mobilization plans. In September 1939 an experimental partial mobilization of industry was conducted, and after the Politburo's discussion of the Finnish–Soviet war, conversion planning was again reviewed in detail. None the less, mobilization plans for different industries and especially at plant level were not complete when the German–Soviet war broke out. In the crucial field of ammunition a mobilization plan was only approved on 6 June 1941.

Yet in many fields the conversion of civilian factories to military production had begun much earlier. A policy of subcontracting military production to civilian firms was used to spread expertise and to stimulate partial conversion. In some branches of industry reserve capacities had been created. In the first half of 1941, for example, 1,500 modern tanks (KV and T-34) were produced, with the two largest factories having the capacity to produce twice that number.

On 31 July 1940 the Praesidium of the Supreme Soviet, the state administration's highest legislature, intro-

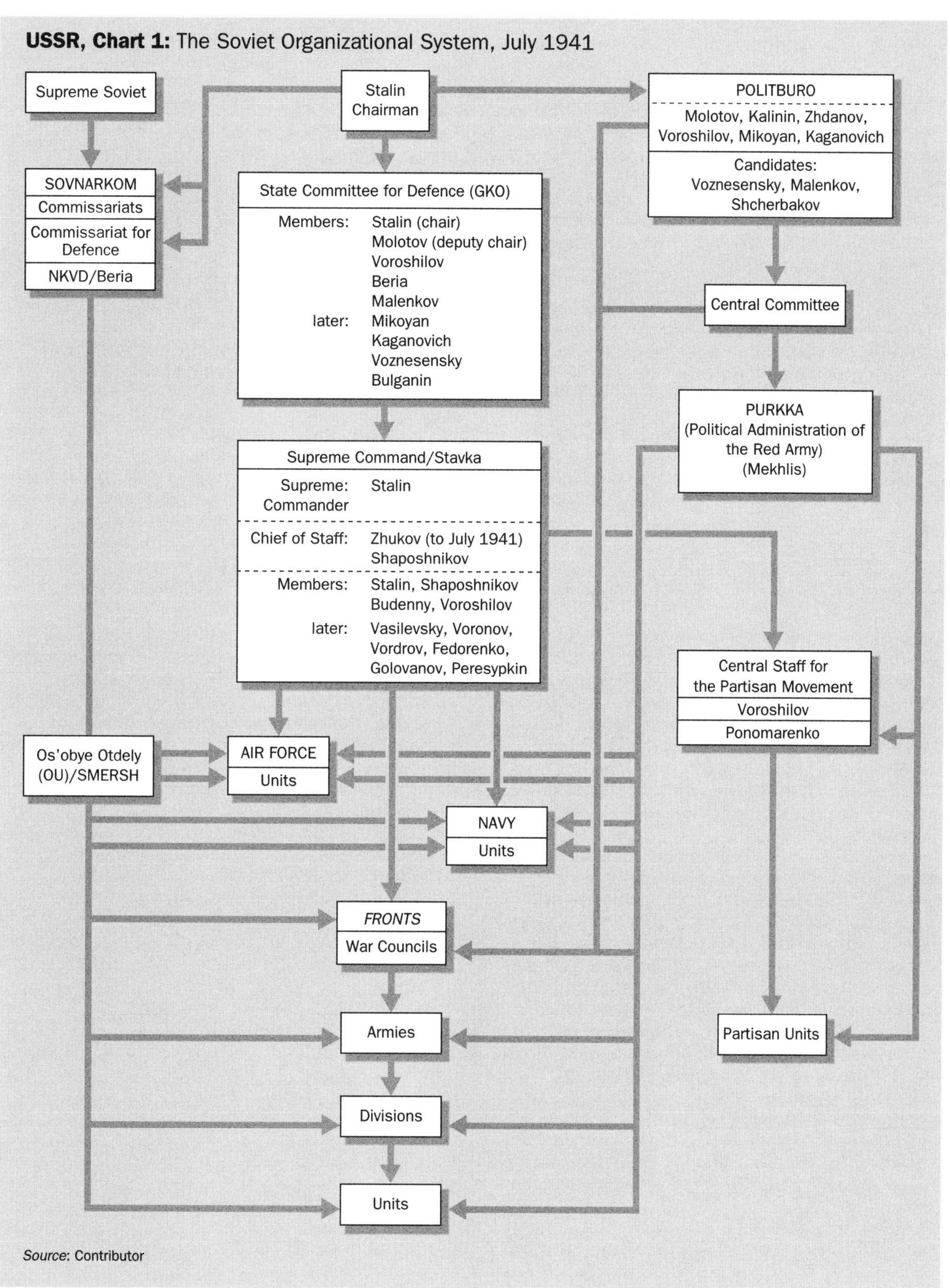

Source: Contributor

duced the seven-day working week and the eight-hour day. At the same time unauthorized changing or leaving of workplaces was made illegal. However, a nationwide plan for wartime economic mobilization was only botched together after the German attack. This was because the political climate before the war did not allow for the consideration of worst-case scenarios which were condemned as defeatist. Instead, economic planning for a war was largely based on the assumption of a Soviet offensive which would, as Field Regulations stressed and as Stalin had so often repeated, immediately be carried into enemy territory.

Because they had not developed a realistic framework of strategic expectations, Soviet authorities underestimated the economic burden of a war and its economy-wide dimensions. Plans for dispersing or relocating industries, for the accumulation of reserves, and for finding alternative resource and energy bases, were not persistently pursued.

From 1938 special emphasis was put on increasing the production and the reserves of strategic commodities. Stockpiling of strategic *raw materials began seriously in January 1940. In 1939 and 1940 reserves of the main metals doubled. Between January 1940 and the outbreak of hostilities the rouble value of all strategic reserves also nearly doubled. But this was still inadequate for a long war. There were barely enough foodstuffs and fodder to last six months at wartime consumption levels. Under peacetime conditions the stockpiles of petro-chemicals would have lasted eighteen days, those of pig-iron four days, and those of rolled steel six days. Reserves of strategic materials were located too near to the western frontiers. The general staff wanted them safely stored behind the River Volga, but Commissar First Grade Lev Mekhlis, the chief of the Red Army's political administration (PURKKA), regarded the suggestion as defeatist and Stalin, in 1940, sided with his trusted henchman.

Despite these errors, rapid industrialization had greatly increased the abilities of the USSR to conduct a war. But the regional distribution of industries still resembled pre-*First World War patterns, which exposed most Soviet production to German attacks. In 1940, less than 30% of steel and iron production came from the eastern territories and only 7% of aircraft, 26% of tank, and 34% of munitions factories were situated there; many specialized production processes were exclusively in the war zone (see Map 108). So when German forces invaded on 22 June 1941 they conquered an area containing 40% of the USSR's population, 60% of its armaments industries, 38% of its cattle, 60% of its pigs, 74% of its coke, 63% of its coal, 71% of its iron ore, 68% of its pig iron, 60% of its aluminium, 58% of its crude steel, 57% of its rolled steel output, and 42% of its electricity generation.

Evacuation was essential for survival. For this the State Committee of Defence (Gosudarstvennv Komitet Oborony, or GKO) set up a special Council for Evacuation on 3 July 1941, with L. M. Kaganovich as chairman and N. M. Shvernik (who soon took over as chairman) and Kosygin as deputies. The council had three sub-departments, for the evacuation of industries and their workforce, for *refugees, and for transport. On 14 October, Kosygin was appointed to conduct the evacuation of Moscow. Another, general, Committee for Evacuation was also created, under Anastas Mikoyan (1895–1970), which worked alongside the old council until the middle of December to save stocks of producer and consumer goods. Theoretically all decisions should have been made by the council, but local initiative was considerable though it was frequently denounced from above as defeatism, as evacuations tended to increase panic.

Evacuation of the population from Minsk, largely *women and *children, began on the second day of the war, ordered locally by the Central Committee of the Belorussian Republic. But not many were evacuated in an organized way—only a few tens of thousands from the Baltic, a million from Belorussia—and tens of thousands simply fled spontaneously, clogging up transport and interfering with troop movements. On 6 and 7 July the evacuation council ordered children and women to be sent away from Moscow and Leningrad and then, in September, from Tula, Orel, Kursk, Voroshilovgrad, the Donbass region, Rostov-on-Don, and Murmansk. The council managed to evacuate 400,000 people from Leningrad and 1.4 million from Moscow during the autumn. But orders frequently came too late. Transport was violently disrupted, people (and *matériel*), were abandoned in the middle of nowhere or ended up back where they had come from. Passengers went for days without food and drink. Although cities in the east made great efforts to accommodate new arrivals, they often found the demand beyond their means.

Evacuation and flight have been put as low as 7.5 million and as high as 25 million. One estimate (see Harrison [below], p. 71 f.) arrived at 16.5 million, with 6.5–10 million having fled outside official channels. This was below one-fifth of the population of the territories overrun by the Germans. Large quantities of goods were lost and undamaged installations fell into German hands when Stalin refused Khrushchev permission to begin the necessary preparations in the Ukraine. From the Donets Basin only 17 out of 64 steelworks were successfully evacuated. At one Ukrainian depot alone more than 200,000 tons of rolled metals, ingots, castings, pipes, and so on were left behind, a loss comparable to the country's whole strategic reserves of 177,000 tons of pig-iron or 204,000 tons of rolled steel at the beginning of 1941. By the end of July 1941 only 20.3%, or 261,832 tons, of the grain earmarked for the interior was saved. Evacuation of livestock proved more successful in the initial phase, but then the problem of feeding it arose. However, the evacuation council was spared major catastrophes as the Germans did not take Leningrad or Moscow, where orders for evacuation had gone out too late.

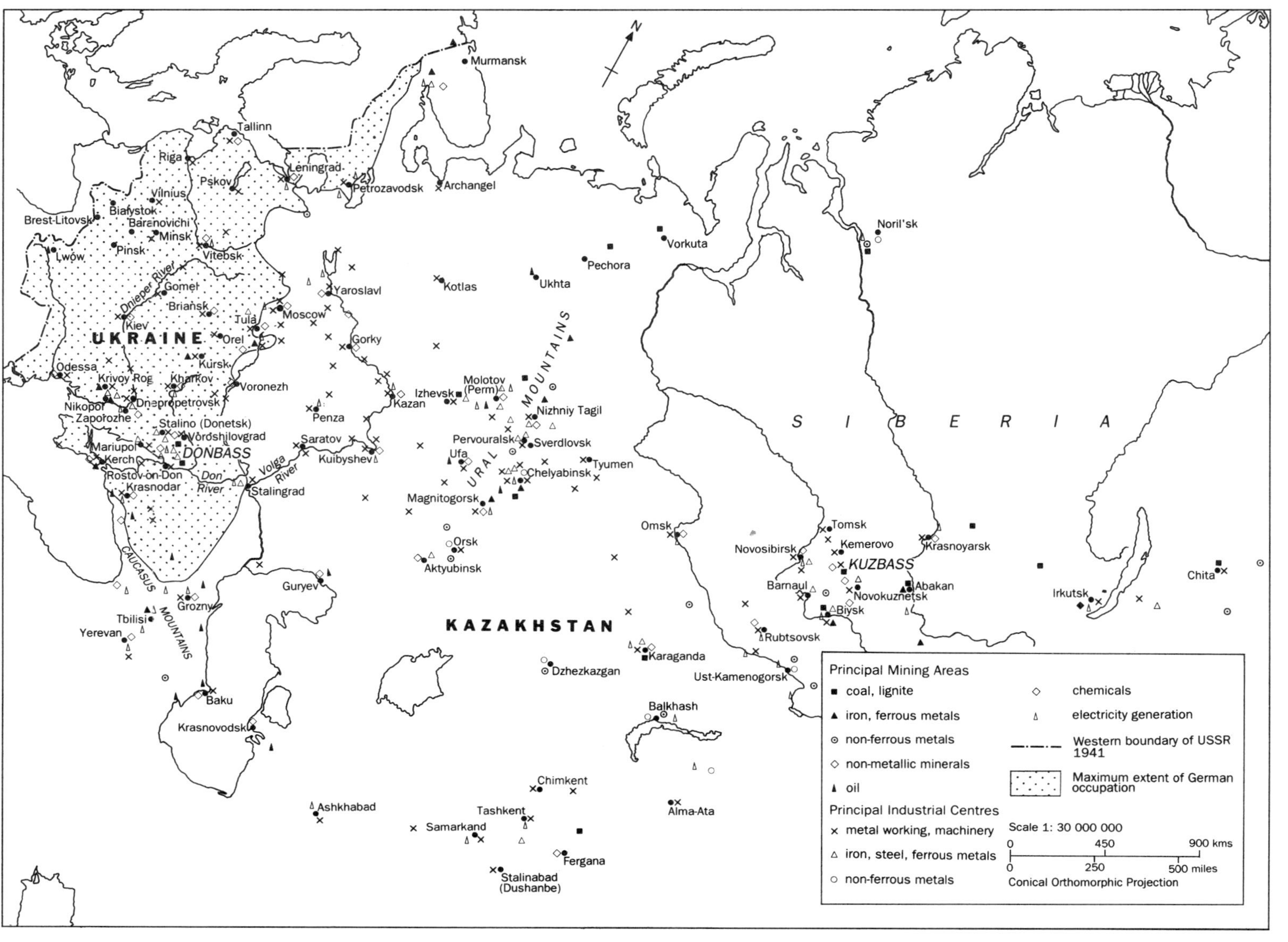

108. Industrial and mining areas of **USSR**, 1941–5

On 25 December 1941 the first Council for Evacuation was supplanted by a Committee for Freight Dispersal under Mikoyan which had to deal with the chaos on the overburdened railways. Almost half the rolling stock was used for evacuation. The daily travelling distance halved from 160 km. (100 mi.) to 84 km. (52 mi.). By November 58,000 loaded trucks had piled up on the main lines to the eastern and south-eastern regions. Materials and machinery were often simply dumped and left to rot but at least the statisticians quickly conducted a census of vacant factory accommodation, and building space, to which plants could be moved. But not until November 1941 was a central schedule established for re-erecting the evacuated factories.

Altogether 2,593 plants were evacuated, 1,523 of them major ones. Of the latter, 226 were moved into the Volga region, 667 to the Urals, 244 to western and 78 to eastern Siberia, and 308 to Kazakhstan and Central Asia. Of the 1,523 evacuated during the second half of 1941, 1,200 were in operation again by the middle of 1942. About 30–40% of the workers and technical personnel were also evacuated, together with their factories. Some factories were very quickly dismantled and reassembled: the first train with equipment from the Dnepropetrovsk tube-rolling mill left the original site on 9 August for Pervouralsk; production re-opened on 24 December of the same year. An evacuated tractor factory from Kharkov sent its first 25 tanks from the Urals to the front on 8 December 1941. Parts of the Leningrad Kirov factory that had been removed early in August began producing tank steel in Novo-Tagilsk in the Kuzbass Basin by 1 September.

Evacuation, because of the sheer volume and the organizational demands, was a tremendous task. For example, early in August 1941, 450 transports from Kiev evacuated parts of the equipment of 197 large factories, together with 350,000 people. In the middle of August the evacuation of the Zaporozhe and Dnepropetrovsk industrial complexes began (notably the hydro-electric power station), which had to take place under enemy fire. In Zaporozhe alone 5,500 workers and some 8,000 railway carriages were needed to evacuate the local population. Literally, workers had to evacuate their factories on one day and fight the Germans the next.

The first official decisions at the top to evacuate factories and reserves from front-line zones were made by the Politburo on 29 June 1941: eleven aircraft factories were to be moved. On 2 July the CC of the CPSU and the Council of People's Commissars ordered, for example, the Mariupol (Ukraine) 'Ilich Tankplate Factory' and ten munitions factories from Leningrad to Magnitogorsk. The Council for Evacuation ordered the relocation of 26 factories of the Commissariat for War from the centre to regions around the Volga, to the Urals, Siberia, and Central Asia, and on 7 August ordered the evacuation of the 'Serp i Molot' and 'Elektrostal' factories from the Moscow region. The part of the Kirov factory that produced steel for tanks was also evacuated and ordered to move to Novo-Tagilsk in the Kuzbass Basin. However, the swift advance of the Wehrmacht prevented any evacuations from the areas around Brest-Litovsk, Białystok, Baranovichi, and Pinsk. Only in the eastern parts of Belorussia were evacuations more successful, started on local initiative. The Homel party organization ordered and successfully executed the evacuation of 38 factories, among them the biggest factory of the area ('Gomselmash'), the equipment of which was moved to the Urals.

A new wave of evacuations was made necessary by the German advance in 1942. On 22 June a Commission for Evacuation, again under Shvernik, was created to organize the relocations from the Don, Volga, and Caucasus regions. Another 150 enterprises were to be moved, but again, many trains could not leave the front areas in time. The evacuation of Stalingrad was not seriously undertaken, because Stalin opposed it: only one plant was saved. In spite of intense efforts and extreme hardships endured by those involved—more than 30,000 youth groups helped with the evacuation, the party and the Komsomol mobilized their members—32,000 enterprises of all sizes fell into German hands. Yet the one-eighth of productive capacity of the western provinces that was saved proved sufficient. For, low as this may seem, the most crucial industries had been successfully moved.

Transport problems, however, were not solved by these measures. The basic situation was that the radial system from Moscow—with the denser network to the west—was not suited to the task it had to perform. Also, the railways were hopelessly overloaded in trying to supply the armies, the cities, and industries while, at the same time, evacuating factories, materials, civilians, and soldiers from the front-line areas. In January 1942 the average daily haulage on the railways was down 50% compared to peacetime. Nearly 3,000 trucks were standing idle without locomotives, two-thirds of them loaded with evacuated equipment. Chaos reigned during the initial phases of the war, and threatened to bring the railways to a complete halt. At the most critical points during the war a few lines into the hinterland of Moscow had to carry most of the burden. New lines had to be built, especially when the German Army stood at the banks of the Volga and because new industrial centres in the east had to be connected. In the third quarter of 1941 the railways had received 90% of the 64,000 tons of rails they had asked for. But then supplies virtually broke down. In December 1941 they only received 8 km. of the 846 km. (530 mi.) of rails they had requested just to repair damaged track. For 1942 as a whole they were supplied with 300,000 tons of iron and steel (2.9 million tons in 1940), eight locomotives, and no new railway trucks.

The transport crisis was tackled by the usual dose of centralization. On 4 February 1942 the GKO formed a special transport committee under Stalin and from 25 March the head of army *logistics controlled it. Military and civilian transport were thus put under one head. The situation then improved, only to worsen again by the end of 1942. The central authorities stepped in again and sent Central Committee secretary, A. A. Andreev, to the worst hit area, the Urals, to sort things out. A decree of 15 April 1943 put the railways under martial law, and a military code of discipline was introduced for railway workers, to tackle serious problems of indiscipline and morale. Perhaps in order to strengthen managerial powers, the political departments of the railway institutions were closed on 31 May 1943. At the same time martial law was also extended to river and sea transport—in other branches of industry it had been rescinded in the spring of 1942. A period of sustained improvement followed and lasted until the end of 1944. The reconquest of occupied territory also allowed the network to expand under Soviet control. In January 1943 it was possible to put back into operation 725 km. (450 mi.) of railway lines, in February 2,139 km. (1,328 mi.) in March 3,175 km. (1,970 mi.); in all, 18,800 km. (11,675 mi.) were restored in 1943—four and a half times what had been achieved in 1942. Double tracks and often treble tracks became widespread in the Urals during early 1942, and in general the situation there eased early enough not to hamper the war effort seriously. Still, the freight transport volume of the railways was down to 52% of the pre-war level, reaching only 58% in 1943, 68% in 1944, and 76% in 1945—and railways accounted for 83% of all freight transfers and 70% of military freight transfers.

Fuel, transport, and the production of pig-iron and steel became the major bottlenecks in the USSR's war production effort. The balance between the three sectors was particularly critical during the last months of 1941 and again in the second half of 1942. The decrease in the production of fuel was especially critical by the end of 1941, largely because of the German advance and the capture of the Donbass coal mines.

During the second half of 1942, the most serious crisis in production (except machine tools) was of basic investment goods and raw materials, especially fuels. In September 1942 the GKO ordered a crash programme for exploration and drilling in the oil regions of the interior. The party organizations of the Kuzbass and Karaganda coalfields received stinging rebukes, tens of thousands of workers were drafted into the mines, new machinery was earmarked for these regions, and new pits were opened. From October 1942 an upswing was noticeable in the Karaganda area, although mines in the Kuzbass basin showed hardly any improvement. For the north of European Russia the Pechora mines (Vorkuta and Itinsk) became the main source of coal (see GULAG), after many new mines had been built and a new North Pechora railway line had linked this area to the areas of consumption. The reopening of the Moscow coal basin contributed most to the re-establishment of industry there and to providing the population of the region with a meagre ration of coal. During the fourth quarter of 1941 and in 1942 large investments in the oil industry were planned and carried through. By 1943 the output of coal was increasing nationwide, and oil soon followed suit. Although the fuel crisis seems to have been solved by that time, energy production—particularly crucial as the evacuation of industries had created new demands—fell further below capacity. The main reason was an imbalance between construction of new power-plants and the availability of equipment. Other reasons were the inexperience of a greatly altered or newly recruited workforce and the resulting inefficiency, particularly in the management of equipment and fuel stocks.

A great number of special metals had to be mined from new sites. Manganese now no longer came from Nikopol, but from the Northern Urals, to where the miners from Nikopol had been evacuated. Similarly, manganese from Eastern Siberia and Kazakhstan helped to fill the gap. In Kazakhstan and Uzbekistan the mining of wolfram, vanadium, and molybdenum had to be increased to compensate for the loss of sites in German-occupied territory. Production of aluminium was begun in the area of Sverdlovsk and the Kuzbass Basin. But by the second half of 1942 the situation in the Soviet war economy was still critical, particularly because the production of several sorts of steel and iron and of copper declined or stagnated. Only after 1943 did a general improvement set in and the newly constructed sites and plants were able fulfil most of the targets.

Military production kept up well and, in the third quarter of 1941 and overall in 1941, even increased more steeply than envisaged by the wartime economic plan. But it remained far behind requirements. Although aircraft factories produced 16% of the air force's front-line strength each month, monthly losses amounted to no less than 45%. While 18% of the front-line strength in armoured vehicles was replaced monthly, losses reached a staggering 57%. During the initial phases high losses had to be anticipated, but problems remained extremely severe. By the winter artillery ammunition had been rationed to one or two shells per gun per day. During the last quarter of 1941 military production actually lagged behind the plan as strategic reserves were eaten up and production of basic industries declined. Transport proved to be the second major constraint. Army *logistics had become so strained that in December horse battalions were reintroduced.

These economic and logistical imbalances had to be rectified during 1942, but they did not prevent Stalin impetuously ordering—against the advice of both N. I. Voznesensky, the head of the war economy, and General *Zhukov, the *Stavka's chief of staff—a general offensive which petered out because of shortages. Emergency measures, increasingly administered through Gosplan, the state planning institution, tried to deal with this situation. Tasks were increasingly dictated from the centre to individual plants. The number of planned production indicators, by which production processes, speed of production, measurements, quality standards, and so on were determined, rose steeply. Fulfilment checks on quotas and standards were conducted on a daily basis, and the number of centrally planned products doubled, but basic statistical reporting remained chaotic until the end of 1942.

At the same time centralization was complemented by a decentralization of rather less important areas of economic life. In particular, local authorities and people in general were encouraged to make use of local resources not subject to central planning.

Figures for overall production are unreliable, but it is clear that during 1941 Soviet military production (see Table 1) was already surpassing Germany's. Even during the second half of 1941 production of aircraft and tanks nearly equalled Germany's for the whole year. By comparison German industry produced only 4,800 tanks and 17,400 aircraft in 1942, 25,200 aircraft in 1943, and 34,300 aircraft in 1944, 10% of which were trainers; tank production reached 11,800 in 1943, and 17,800 in 1944; and the output of infantry rifles and carbines was 1.4 million in 1942.

Soviet war production was also supplemented by the Allied *Lend-Lease programme. Altogether, during the years 1941 to 1945, 21,621 combat aircraft and 12,439 tanks and self-propelled guns arrived in the USSR, 12,869 and 7,747 respectively coming from the USA, the rest Anglo-Canadian deliveries. Compared to an overall Soviet production during the same period, of 136,364 aircraft and 99,507 tanks or self-propelled guns, Allied supplies seem insignificant. But during the critical year 1942 they provided the margin which allowed the USSR to have adequate aircraft and tank forces. Of acknowledged importance was the delivery of trucks and jeeps. Only these provided the mobility which gave the Red Army the opportunity to turn tactical and operational gains into strategic victories.

Despite some Soviet manipulation of the figures—especially with respect to the initial strength—Table 2 shows the relative importance of Allied deliveries and home production during certain phases of the war.

Western support to the USSR was not restricted to military *matériel*, which represented only 47% of all American help (including motor vehicles, trucks, and tractors, deliveries of which significantly surpassed Soviet production). Foodstuffs accounted for 17%, amounting to 4.4 million tons, topped up by another 200,000 tons from the UK and Canada. There were also 15.4 million pairs of army boots, nearly 2,000 locomotives, 11,155 freight trucks, more than 3.7 million tyres, 90 cargo vessels, 98 million metres (107 million yards) of cotton cloth, and 57 million metres (62.5 million yards) of wool cloth. Aid filled some critical equipment gaps such as telephone wire and aviation fuel, and supplies of alloy steel, for example, helped ease some particular bottlenecks. At its peak in 1944 western help amounted to 10–12% of Soviet GNP.

While Soviet military production surpassed Germany's, production of coal, oil, and steel declined (see Table 3). This led to a deep cut back in civilian consumption in the USSR as compared to Germany, where life remained comparatively comfortable until late in the war. Other figures give a similar impression. The share of the armaments industries in the Soviet budget rose from 32.8% in 1940 to 59% in 1942. (These figures cannot be compared internationally because of the nature of the Soviet economic system.) Budget spending on the economy—excluding direct military outlays—fell from 33.5% in 1940 to 21.5% during the war. Of the budget for industry, 90% went into heavy industry and machine building, only 10% at best into consumer industries. General indices of industrial development, agricultural production, and turnover in the retail business point in the same direction (see Table 4).

Production for civilian needs was obviously cut to a bare minimum, with these figures probably understating the full decline in the standard of living. Investment in housing decreased drastically during wartime and the consequences of the destruction and evacuation had to be suffered by the population for long after the war. Goods available to civilians became extremely scarce (see Table 5).

Agriculture was left mainly to its own devices. A minimum of agricultural machinery had been saved and brought into the interior to ease the burden of labour, although the army took most of the tractors and lorries. By the end of 1945 agriculture had only 75% of the tractors, 81% of combine harvesters, and 25% of the lorries available in 1940, and by the middle of the war the situation was probably much worse. In 1943 only 58% of the pre-war stock of draught animals remained. Farms had lost 13.5 million workers, 12.4 million of them men who either entered the army or migrated into industry. From 1940 to 1945 the Soviet agricultural workforce (both sexes) dropped by roughly a third, from 36.6 to 24.7 million, while the industrial workforce dropped by only 12.5%, from 31.2 to 27.3 million. By 1943 the male workforce as a whole had declined to under one-third of

USSR, Table 1: Soviet arms production

	1940	*1941*	*1942*	*1943*	*1944*	*1945*
Aircraft	10,565	15,735	25,436	34,845	40,246	20,102
Tanks and self-propelled guns	2,794	6,590	24,446	24,089	28,963	15,419
Artillery and mortars (000s)	53.8	67.8	356.9	199.5	129.5	64,6
Rifles and carbines (000s)	1,461	2,660	4,049	3,437	2,450	574

Source: Harrison, M., *Soviet Planning in Peace and War 1938–45*, (Cambridge, 1985), p. 118.

USSR, Table 2: Lend-Lease v. home production of selected weapons. Arms balance for selected categories 1941–5

	Period beginning on first day of June 1941	Dec 1941	May 1942	Nov 1942	July 1943	Jan 1944	June 1944	Jan 1945
	duration, months 5.3	5	6	8	6	5	7	6
Combat aircraft								
Initial force	8,105[a]	2,495	3,160	3,088	8,290	8,500	11,800	14,500
Domestic supply	7,042	6,323	11,928	18,537	16,100	13,583	19,627	16,418
External supply	0	1,441	2,601	4,355	4,851	3,103	3,356	1,914
Estimated losses	12,652	7,099	14,601	17,690	20,741	13,386	20,283	?
Tanks and self-propelled guns								
Initial force	7,000	1,730	4,065	6,014	9,580	4,900	8,000	11,000
Domestic supply	4,090	7,767	12,960	15,708	12,900	11,500	17,463	15,419
External supply	0	1,678	2,904	2,413	1,385	1,310	1,913	836
Estimated losses	9,360	7,110	13,915	12,142	18,965	9,710	16,376	?
Artillery and mortars								
Initial force	34,965	22,000	43,640	72,500	98,700	88,900	83,200	91,400
Domestic supply	61,532	129,683	182,433	175,067	81,600	54,417	75,083	64,600
Estimated losses	74,497	108,043	153,753	148,777	91,490	60,117	66,883	?

[a] as of 22 June 1941

Source: Harrison, *Soviet Planning*, p. 264.

its pre-war strength. To alleviate the scarcity of labour those working on the collective farms were forced to increase their working days by up to 50% compared to pre-war norms. It was rural women, supported by minors and old people, who bore the brunt of farm work–including literally working as draught animals. As manpower was the ultimate bottleneck, more and more depended on women; they not only penetrated into the least likely areas of industrial and agricultural work, but 800,000 were also enlisted into the Red Army.

As industry remained more attractive than rural work, migration to the factories had to be prohibited in certain areas. of the high quotas demanded, rural consumption of even basic foodstuffs declined markedly. Life on the collective farms, never easy, became extremely harsh. Production of grains contracted from 95.6 million tons in 1940 to a mere 26.7 million in 1942, potato production fell from 76.1 to 23.8 million tons, and meat and fat from 4.7 to 1.8 million tons. However, to balance this drop in production the number of people who had to be fed shrank from 194.1 million to only 130 million. So while the population decreased to 67% of its size in 1940, the available amount of potatoes dropped to 31.3% of its 1940 crop, grain dropped to 27.9%, and meat and fats to 38.3%. To use private plots more intensively *kolkhozniki* (those who worked on collective farms) were allowed to sell

USSR, Table 3: Soviet and German production of selected raw materials (million tons)

	1940	1941	1942	1943	1944	1945
Coal						
USSR	165.9	151.4	75.5	93.1	121.5	149.3
Germany		246.0	258.0	269.0	281.0	
Steel						
USSR	18.3	17.9	8.1	8.5	10.9	12.4
Germany		31.8	32.1	34.6	35.2	
Oil						
USSR	31.1	33.0	22.0	18.0	18.3	19.4
Germany	4.8	5.6	6.6	—		

Sources: Istoriia Vtoroi Mirovoi Voiny, Vol. XII, *History of the Second World War*, 12 Vols (Moscow, 1973–82), p. 161; *Die Deutsche Industrie im Kriege, 1939–1945* (Berlin, 1954), p. 52.

USSR, Table 4: Index figures of economic development (1940 = 100)

	1941	1942	1943	1944	1945
Net material product	92	66	74	88	83
Gross industrial production	98	77	90	104	92
Arms production	140	186	224	251	173
Light industry	88	48	54	64	62
Gross agricultural output	62	38	37	54	60
Turnover of state-owned Retail net (constant prices)	84	34	32	37	42

Sources: Istoriia Velikoi Otechestvennoi Voiny, Sovetskogo Sojuza 1941–45, Vol. 6, p. 45; *The History of the Great Patriotic War of the Soviet Union 1941–45*, 6 Vols (Moscow, 1960 ff); *Kravchenko: Ekonomika*, pp. 125, 228, 351; Malafeev, A., *Istoriia tsenoobrazovaniia v SSSR, 1917–1963 gg.* (Moscow, 1964), p. 407.

products from them on the *kolkhoz* markets and these became an important factor in feeding the population. The people in general were also called upon to use their gardens, and even flower pots, to grow foodstuffs. Rationing applied to the urban population, peasants had to look after themselves. By the end of 1942 central distribution of bread reached 62 million people, by the end of 1945, 81 million.

The normal calorie allowances for dependents (780 calories) and employees (1,074–1,176 calories) were dangerously low. Workers in heavy industry and particularly in mining received a much higher allocation (3,181–4,418 calories), but, with the exception of bread, supplies hardly ever reached the required level. This system of rationing was a deliberate policy to direct workers into production, into heavy industry, and into mining in particular. Low rations for dependents were meant to force them to look for employment.

Working conditions in industry, in spite of preferential treatment, were very hard. A partly juvenile, partly overage industrial workforce toiled to exhaustion on meagre rations. Living quarters were cramped. In the east, where new or evacuated industries were erected, workers initially had to live and sleep in the open, and later to brave the climate in hovels barely fit to house human beings.

The suffering inflicted on the people of the USSR by war and occupation defies description. Figures of overall Soviet losses took decades to emerge as post-war authorities were most reluctant to reveal their real extent. As many as 27 million people may have died, the vast majority of them civilians from the western republics of the Baltic, Belorussia, and the Ukraine. The 900-day siege of *Leningrad was especially horrific. Here alone at least 635,000 people died, with many sources putting the figure as high as one million. But the Soviet population also suffered at the hand of their own regime. Even during the war hundreds of thousands, maybe millions, died in the GUlag.

USSR, Table 5: Index of goods available to civilians (1940 = 100)

	1941	1942	1943	1944	1945
clothing	61	10	10	11	18
cloth	73	14	14	19	29
shoes	65	8	7	10	15

Source: *Istoriia Velikoi Otechestvennoi Voiny*, Vol. 6, p. 63f.

Total demographic losses in the USSR, including so-called 'indirect losses' due to premature deaths, to children unborn, and to desertion and emigration, must have been in the region of 48 million, and another 2.4 million Soviet citizens were deported to Germany as *forced labour. Material losses are even more difficult to establish, but 1,710 cities and 70,000 villages were partly or completely erased, and 30% of the national wealth was destroyed. These losses represent a value of 679 billion pre-war roubles. HEINZ-DIETRICH LÖWE

3. Government and legal system

See also COMMUNISM.

Between the two world wars the USSR experienced more violent changes and hardships than any other country in the world. The revolution of 1917 and a long civil war with foreign intervention had put a new class into power. The old élites emigrated, perished, or were submerged. The new, highly ideological, regime established a class-dictatorship of the proletariat through the party of the proletariat, the Communist Party. It abolished private ownership of land and industrial enterprises.

But in spite of its collectivist ideology the system rested on a charismatic leader and a personality cult around him. From the beginning terror was an integral part of it. The man who through skilful manipulation rose to absolute power after Lenin's death in 1924, Iosif Vissarionovich Stalin (born Djugashvili), both perfected the cult around his person and advanced the regime's indiscriminate terror to dimensions until then unknown by stamping out every form of open debate, public criticism, and opposition. He first defeated Leon Trotsky (1879–1940) and the Trotskyites, then the 'Left Opposition' and the 'Right Opposition'. After the 1934 17th Party Congress, which probably tried to moderate party policies—and after the murder of Sergei Kirov, the Leningrad party boss who had been regarded as the champion of moderation—the Great Terror unfolded indiscriminately. Hundreds of thousands of the political class, in particular old Bolsheviks, were killed or perished in the GUlag and prominent leaders such as N. A. Bukharin and G. E. Zinoviev, and others were condemned to death in show trials and then executed. Even before this, purges had already begun to affect the old intelligentsia and others, and in particular the technical intelligentsia. Peasants also fell victim to the GUlag in their millions when collectivization unfolded.

Stalin reigned supreme. Through his private secretariat (*Poskrebyshev*), and his cronies in important branches of the state machinery, he determined all major and many minor aspects of policy. This system of personal rule bred lack of initiative, a tendency to shirk responsibility, to refer matters upwards for decision, which led to often highly capricious and catastrophic decisions by the *Velikii Vozhd* (Great Leader).

In theory the Communist Party governed the country. Through its collective wisdom it was to arrive at scientifically correct decisions and to implement them in a rational way. Stalin, indeed, always took great trouble to posture as the representative and embodiment of party opinion, and as its defender against 'Right' and 'Left' deviations. Though internal democracy disappeared—on the basis of the anti-faction decision at the Tenth Congress (1921) which forbade the formation of groups inside the party—the now thoroughly hierarchical party always was, and remained, an important instrument of power, in particular an instrument of social transformation and mobilization. To some degree it had become 'militarized' during the Civil War when at least half of all party members were fighting in the Red Army. Even later the army remained the most important recruiting ground for the party. This reinforced its authoritarian streak and encouraged a certain predilection for pragmatic and radical solutions to political, social, and economic problems.

At the head of the party stood a general secretary who was also the head of the Secretariat of the Central Committee with its different departments which doubled up the different branches of the state administration (see Chart 1 for wartime organization). The office of general secretary had been created, and Stalin appointed to it, in April 1924. The party's leading body, the Politburo, in theory determined policy, though in fact Stalin controlled it from as early as 1930. From 1937, with the Great Purge, it had become totally subservient to him. It was 'elected' by the Central Committee which in turn was determined by the Party Congress. By June 1941 the Politburo only met irregularly and infrequently, and no minutes were kept. There was considerable overlap in terms of personnel between it and other high government offices. From time to time certain members took on the responsibility of overseeing certain branches of government or whole sets of ministries, or, in certain cases, of overseeing especially important tasks, such as the railways. During the war the Politburo was largely supplanted by the State Committee for Defence (Gosudarstvenny Komitet Oborony, or GKO, see below), but this did not meet in any regular and formal fashion either.

The party controlled every aspect of civilian and military life, actively governing, administering, and directing the country at all levels down to the grass roots. As the USSR boasted a planned economy, the role of the party became paramount in this field also. Every important organization, each factory, and each institution had a party cell which kept watch. The party had, as it claimed, become the 'leading and directing' force of Soviet society. It was extremely difficult for anybody to make a career without belonging to it or its youth organization (Komsomol). Tight censorship of broadcasting and publishing carefully filtered the information the public was allowed to receive.

The USSR did have a constitution, drawn up in 1936, but it cannot be compared to its western counterparts. It was not meant to limit the power of the state, or the party, or other organs. Its promises were not enforceable. It was not intended to secure the independence of the judiciary. Its stipulations about the procedures of government or the delineation of authority between different agencies were never really observed.

The 'sovereignty' of the Union Republics, of which the USSR consisted, had no real substance. For example, the constitution's Article 17, which theoretically gave the Union Republics the right of secession, was, it was explicitly stated, never to be used. Individual rights also lacked meaning, even in the realm of the so-called 'social' rights on which the regime often prided itself. Describing the all-important feature of constitutional reality, Article 126 declared 'the most active and politically conscious citizens in the ranks of the working class, working peasants, and working intelligentsia voluntarily unite in the Communist Party of the Soviet Union, which is the vanguard of the toilers in their struggle to build a communist society and is the guiding nucleus of all organizations of the toilers, both social and state.' This made it clear that the party was not open to everybody and—as a monopoly party—was the one which called the tune.

The state administration, which ran parallel to the party, mushroomed into large numbers of very specialized and less powerful ministries called People's Commissariats. Its highest legislatures were the two houses of the Supreme Soviet: the Soviet of the Union, with one deputy for each 300,000 inhabitants; and the Soviet of Nationalities, with 25 deputies for each Union Republic, 11 for each Autonomous Republic, 5 for each Autonomous Region, and 1 for each National Area. In 1937 the two houses had 569 and 574 members respectively and they ran for four years concurrently. The constitutions of the Union Republics and Autonomous Republics were copies of the central constitution, with the exception that they were unicameral even where the Republics contained Autonomous Republics.

The governments and ministries of the Union Republics were subordinate to their counterparts at the centre, and their importance was further limited because no clear delineation of responsibilities, or power, existed. Also, the USSR Council of People's Commissars, or Sovnarkom, had the right to suspend all decisions and orders of a Republic's Council of Commissars, and the Praesidium of the Supreme Soviet could annul them. Probably such action was never taken.

The only area clearly reserved for one side was foreign policy, which remained the prerogative of the Union. The centre could and did absorb the ministries of Union Republics into its own administration or set them up itself. Ministries at the Autonomous Republic level were directly responsible both to their Union Republic's Council of People's Commissariat and to the central Supreme Soviet. Legislative powers belonged to the Supreme Soviet and its counterparts in the Union Republics. But it was by no means clear what a law was. The Praesidium of the Supreme Soviet could issue edicts (*ukaz*) and, according to Article 66, 'the Council of People's Commissars of the USSR issues decrees (*postanovlenie*) and dispositions (*rasporiazhenie*) on the basis, and in pursuance, of the laws in operation.'

Defying all rules of incompatibility, the Praesidium of the Supreme Soviet interpreted the laws, and it also exercised the right, between sessions of the Supreme Soviet, to pardon those found guilty under them, to ratify and rescind international treaties, to proclaim martial law, to issue mobilization orders and to declare war. It convened and dissolved the Supreme Soviet and fulfilled the role of head of state. The Supreme Soviet convened rarely—the constitutional minimum was twice a year—and for rather short periods. During the war it did not function in any serious sense. Even the Praesidium itself decided in 1938 to meet only four times a year and Stalin's appointment as Chairman of Sovnarkom did not lead to a meeting of the Supreme Soviet or its Praesidium. This clearly showed that all executive and administrative authority was vested in the Sovnarkom which, in theory, was responsible to the Supreme Soviet and its Praesidium.

Sovnarkom was not a western-style cabinet. Probably it never met regularly. In 1938 it met nine times. It had a Praesidium, also not a cabinet, rather a co-optive body providing a platform for individuals who were powerful because of their standing outside the government proper. Some Commissariats were clearly more powerful than others. Only the People's Commissariat for Internal Affairs, the *NKVD, headed by *Beria, had any real power, but this was tightly controlled by the Politburo and by Stalin himself. It had unrestricted powers to arrest, to send to the GUlag, and even to execute without trial. However, to a very large degree, death penalties were sanctioned at the very top by Stalin and other members of his Politburo, irrespective of court cases still pending and even if legal proceedings had not even been started.

The NKVD combined the normal functions of administering the country's internal affairs with the responsibility for the secret police and the ordinary police, or *militsia*. It commanded all penal institutions, the fire departments, the frontier guards, internal security troops, the highway administration and civil registry offices, and the ones responsible for statistics, surveying, and cartography. It also had a vast economic empire, based largely on the GUlag. The Commissariats apart, a host of commissions further reduced the power of Sovnarkom. Gosplan, nominally its organ, became a very powerful institution slowly assuming the functions of long-term economic planning. Below the commissariats a huge bureaucratic *apparat* had developed which in 1941 employed eight times more officials than in 1913.

pBelow the level of the Union Republics were both Autonomous Republics and *oblast* (provinces), *okrug* (districts), settlements and villages, towns, and districts within towns, which all had their own soviets which were 'elected' for two years. There were also *Krai*, large economic and administrative units in the RSFSR. Voting (in theory secret, in reality open) was, in contrast to earlier custom, direct. The local soviets 'selected' their executive committees (*ispolkom*) which were in theory dependent on them. Standing commissions of local soviets, to which non-elected personnel could be co-opted, played a considerable role in overseeing the work ordered by the soviets. There was never more than one candidate in any election and an unmarked ballot paper counted as a vote. Nomination of a candidate belonged to the so-called 'social' organizations of the working people, the factories and collective farms, and the Communist Party with its branch organizations. Pre-election constituency conferences were called to consider possible candidates, but final nominations would always be decided somewhere else beforehand. Very rarely were those nominated not elected—and this only locally. In 1939, out of 1,400,000 places to be filled, only 125 candidates did not gain the necessary absolute majority.

Local soviets met rarely and at irregular intervals, betraying their subordinate position to their Executive Committees. They were not instruments of representation, deliberation, and decision-making, but rather of control of subordinate agencies, of mobilization, and of measuring organizational efficiency. The Executive Committees met in private and did not publish minutes. They commanded large staffs and organizations, and according to Soviet sources they had the same tasks as central government with its emphasis on economic administration, especially in the countryside. However, in many instances, organs of local government were not responsible for what happened within their districts because large areas, industrial enterprises, and many other matters were under the jurisdiction of the NKVD, and factories and collective farms largely ran their own affairs. But there was still scope for local government agencies in public works and in food supply, and social aspects (like housing) and cultural affairs were an important part of their activities. They had to organize the military call-up and to keep records of defence obligations (for example, to provide horses or other forms of transport, especially in case of mobilization). But ultimately local government was to a considerable degree dependent on directives from above, and these had to be fulfilled without proper consideration for, and without regard to, local needs.

The court system paralleled the different levels of the Soviets which elected judges for a fixed time—usually five years. A 1938 law also gave them the right to supervise judges and to dismiss them. At the lowest level judges of People's Courts were popularly elected, but even they could be dismissed. In factories, more concerned with production than justice, special comradely courts functioned. After 1938 only one method of appeal was left and bias against those doing so was obvious, the statutes calling an appeal by an individual a 'complaint', one by the public prosecutor a 'protest'.

The public prosecutor became completely independent from the Commissariat of Justice and the courts. His offices also had to check on all government departments, including the NKVD. During the great purges the jurisdiction of ordinary courts was restricted and special 'colleges' at all levels took over political trials. A 'Lex Kirov', issued after Kirov's assassination, rode roughshod over remaining procedural niceties: investigation and trial had to be finished within ten days, a summary of the accusation was handed over to the accused only 24 hours before the trial, and the proceedings would take place without public prosecutor or defence counsel. Appeals or petitions were inadmissible, death sentences had to be carried out by firing squad immediately after pronouncement. Political crimes were to be investigated by the NKVD and its 'special councils' could also pass judgement without any court proceedings. Torture was a common feature of political investigations.

No systematic reorganization of the country's government was undertaken during the war. The initial shock of the invasion and the lack of contingency planning led to ad hoc solutions which were altered in the light of experience. It was not institutions but individuals that were of paramount importance. The hallmark was personalized power. Perhaps this was not surprising in the light of Stalin's approach to decision-making. The specially created State Committee for Defence, GKO, with Stalin in the chair, played the key role. Its members were Molotov (deputy chairman). Budenny, Timoshenko, *Voroshilov, Malenkov, and Beria, who were later joined by Mikoyan, Kaganovich, Voznesensky, and N. A. Bulganin (1895–1975). For pressing needs special ad hoc commissions were organized. The GKO was given unlimited powers and its decisions carried the force of law. It did not develop a local network, but relied on a host of specially appointed plenipotentiaries of party and industrial leaders who were superimposed on local governments but were formally independent of them. The GKO did not work as a normal bureaucratic organization. It had no formal agenda, no secretaries; no minutes were kept. It rarely assembled formally, attended by all its members. In this it was a true mirror of Stalin's leadership style, a style which was faithfully copied down the ladder. A sharp increase of personalized, dictatorial administration at all levels was the consequence.

Being a decision-making body without an executive arm, implementation of GKO's orders became the responsibility of the party, soviet, and government bodies. Here the Central Committee of the Communist Party, the Sovnarkom, and the People's Commissariats were of key importance. GKO and the *Stavka worked closely together. Members of the GKO delivered reports on the sector of the economy or problem area they headed and had direct access to the chairman of the GKO. Military leaders, people's commissars, and other responsible officials came and went and there was no formal agenda. It was like a permanently functioning think-tank. Each GKO official was responsible for finding a technical solution to his problem. This was often done by calling together a group of specialists and mulling over the problem until a solution suggested itself. Once a solution had been found, Gosplan, the people's commissariats, and other bodies were instructed to implement it. The GKO official played Stalin *vis-à-vis* other institutions. Stalin himself was a good chairman, thanks to his phenomenal memory and his ability to put rapier-like questions which penetrated to the core of the matter. Offsetting these qualities was his capriciousness. Nevertheless, he normally used experts to check on the officials and often sought out differing views. He appears to have favoured a discussion of conflicting opinions as a way of reaching a solution.

A new task confronted the regime when territory was liberated, that of reincorporating it into Soviet life. By mid-October 1944 Ukraine was wholly free of the Wehrmacht.chose nikita khrushchev as his plenipotentiary and ordered him to restore Soviet rule and its economy as quickly as possible. The NKVD swept through the republic but met stiff opposition from the nationalist Ukrainian insurgents. These were strongest in west Ukraine which had passed to the Soviet Union in 1940. In April 1944, 3,000 officials from the Russian east were transferred to Ukraine and given leading positions. Ukrainian nationalists continued their resistance from Polish territory. By the end of 1946 half of the leading party and government officials in Ukraine were new.

The Baltic States resisted incorporation in the Soviet Union even more vigorously than western Ukraine. Many Balts had served in the German forces and there were two Latvian and one Estonian *SS divisions. Lithuania put up the strongest struggle, with partisans holding out until 1953. The NKVD systematically deported certain categories of persons from the Baltic States. In early 1945 those who had served in the Wehrmacht were dispatched east. They were followed by the intelligentsia and cultural élites. They were replaced predominantly by Russians, followed by Ukrainians and Belorussians.

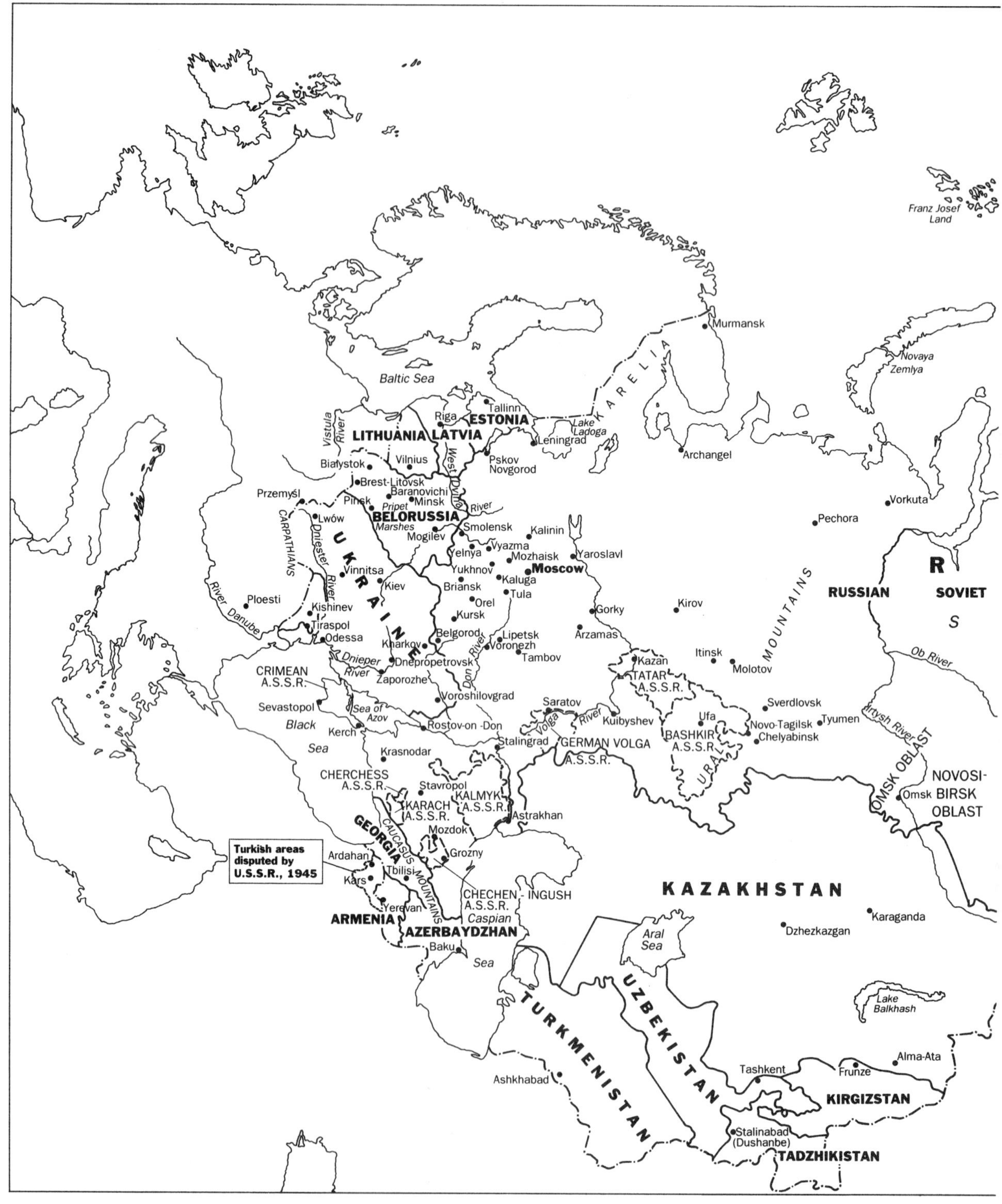

109. **USSR**: republics and selected administrative areas, 1941

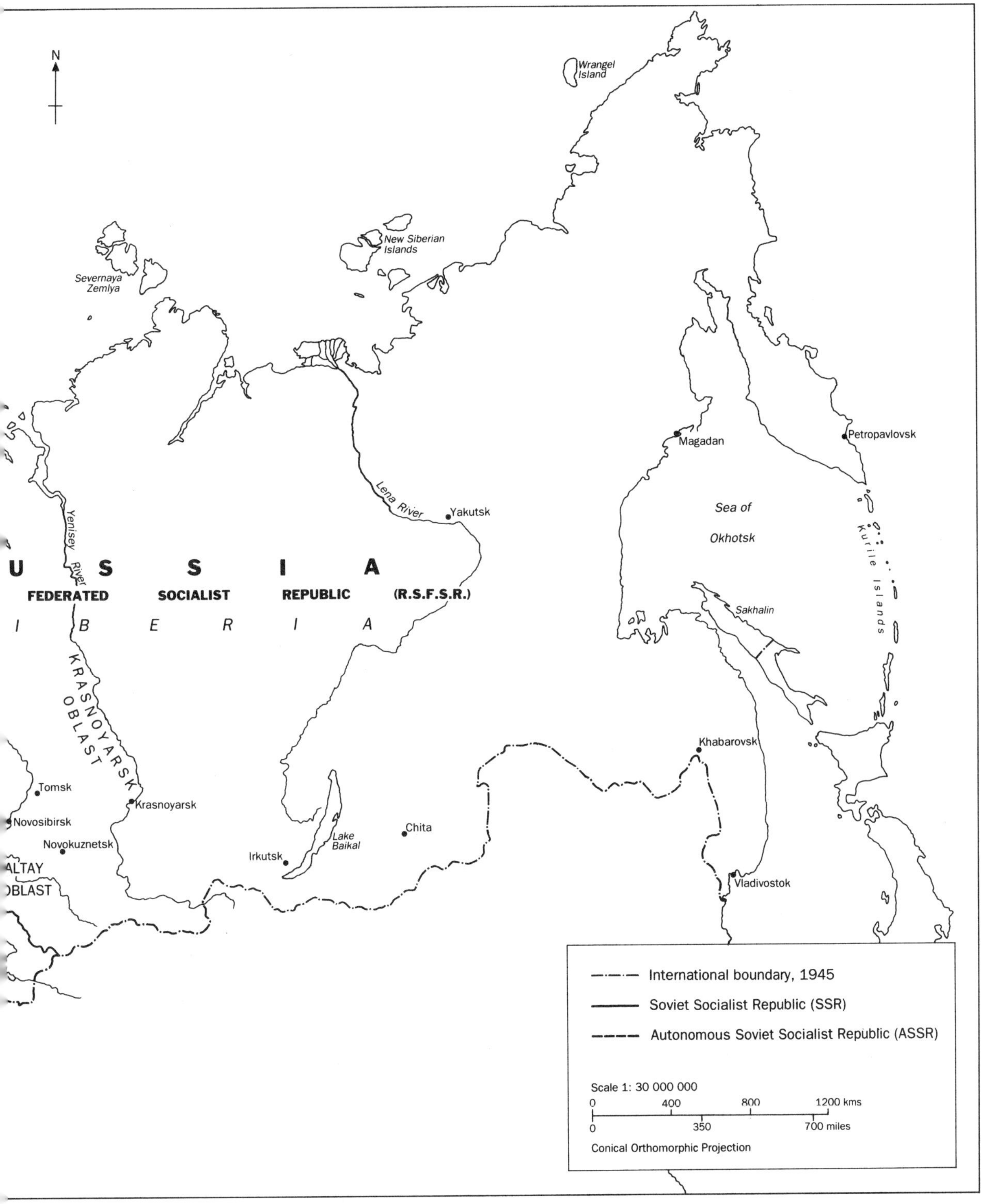
N
Wrangel Island
New Siberian Islands
Severnaya Zemlya
Magadan
Petropavlovsk
Lena River
Yakutsk
Sea of
Okhotsk
Kurile Islands
Yenisey River
U S S I A
FEDERATED SOCIALIST REPUBLIC (R.S.F.S.R.)
I B E R I A
Sakhalin
KRASNOYARSK OBLAST
Khabarovsk
Tomsk
Krasnoyarsk
Novosibirsk
Novokuznetsk
Lake Baikal
Chita
Irkutsk
ALTAY
OBLAST
Vladivostok
International boundary, 1945
Soviet Socialist Republic (SSR)
Autonomous Soviet Socialist Republic (ASSR)
Scale 1: 30 000 000
0 400 800 1200 kms
0 350 700 miles
Conical Orthomorphic Projection

However, in Moldavia, which the Red Army recaptured in late 1944 after driving the Wehrmacht out of Ukraine, there was almost no partisan resistance when the Moldavian Soviet Socialist Republic was reimposed (see inset, Map 80). But as the indigenous Communist Party was minuscule large numbers of Ukrainian and Russian officials were posted to the republic and, unlike many other places within the USSR, there were no organized *deportations after *liberation. HEINZ-DIETRICH LÖWE
MARTIN MCCAULEY

4. Preparations for war and reaction to BARBAROSSA

It cannot be said that the Red Army command had failed to take preparatory measures for a war against Germany: formidable troop movements and a considerable military build-up were under way well before the German attack. On 15 May 1941 Zhukov suggested to Stalin that he forestall the Wehrmacht by attacking before it was properly deployed. Stalin's reaction is not known, but on 21 February 1941, the Soviet general staff had already passed the necessary documents for major troop transfers to the People's Commissariat for Railways. Many *formations had already been moved into their locations by that date and others were in transit. By the end of 1940 Sixteenth Army of the Trans-Baikal Military district—where a war involving hundreds of aircraft and tanks and tens of thousands of troops had recently taken place (see JAPANESE–SOVIET CAMPAIGNS)—began secretly to move west. The Nineteenth Army, which had been formed in Trans-Caucasia, had also moved westwards, as did 57th Tank Division, 18th and 31st Rifle Corps, and 211th and 212th Airborne Assault Brigades. During May 1941 Twenty-Second and Twenty-Fourth Armies were also preparing to head westwards; by the end of May 1941 the 31st Rifle Corps had arrived in the Kiev Military District; and on 13 June the 62nd Rifle Corps of the Urals Military District received orders to move.

Altogether five armies moved westwards from the heart of the country, while three more were prepared for redeployment. In May and June 800,000 reservists were called up and brought to their units; on 13 May, Stalin ordered a further 28 divisions to the western borders; and in June he ordered an additional 25 divisions to the South-West *front* (army group). However, deployment by no means went smoothly. Troops and headquarters sometimes ended up in locations far from each other, artillery and anti-aircraft battalions found themselves at the front line without ammunition.

The policy of freeing high-ranking officers from the tentacles of the GUlag had also begun well before the outbreak of hostilities. Altogether about 4,000 were brought back. Prominent examples were General Aleksandr Gorbatov and the future Marshal of the Soviet Union *Rokossovsky, who were sent to resorts to recover their health and given new command posts before war began. The most senior and able commanding officers of the east were secretly transferred to new positions in the west.

As early as February 1941 war councils of the frontier Military Districts had been ordered to set up *front* HQ and to move the *fronts* westwards. The last moved on 20 June 1941 from the Odessa Military District to Tiraspol with Ninth Army, whose HQ was also to serve as HQ for the South *front*. By the middle of June the structures of frontier districts had been divided into their military and administrative branches. A secret directive from the Politburo of 21 June ordered Marshal *Budenny, who was to be their commander, and Marshal *Timoshenko, then the commissar for defence, to set up HQ for the reserve armies at Briansk. This was the second strategic echelon for which, on 13 May, Stalin had ordered 28 divisions and four army HQ to move to the Mogilev region on the Dnieper Line from the Urals, the Caucasus, and the Far East. Also during May instructions went out to the Ural, North Caucasus, Volga, and Kharkov Military Districts to have elements of their forces ready for deployment to the line of the Dnieper and Dvina rivers.

Zhukov, while retaining his position as chief of staff, was instructed by the same Politburo directive of 21 June to oversee the South and South-West *fronts*, and during the first days of the war he took command in this region, in particular the forces around *Lwów. General *Meretskov had received a similar order for the North *front*. But when the Germans attacked the Red Army's deployment was by no means finished and many of its commanding staffs were, literally, trapped on the railways. As one Soviet historian has commented: 'The Nazi command simply succeeded in forestalling our troops in the two weeks preceding the outbreak of war' (S. P. Ivanov, *Nachal'nyi period voiny* ['The Starting Phase of the War'], Moscow, 1974, p. 212).

Soviet *historiography has maintained that two plans had been worked out for the eventuality of war: a 'special plan for the defence of the State frontier' (in early 1941) and an 'operational plan' (in late 1940). The former included 'active air operations' to achieve air superiority, the liquidation of break-ins and, should general headquarters so direct, directives for carrying the war into enemy territory. Deployment was in any case offensive. The 'operational plan' dealt with counter-offensives and 'possibly' carrying the war into enemy territory before the main (Soviet) forces were assembled. In that event a 'second strategic echelon' would be formed behind the first to develop any retaliatory offensive 'in accordance with the general strategic concept' (ibid., pp. 204–6).

These plans meant that the deployment of troops and *matériel* did not meet the requirements of a defensive war. As the *Stalin Line had been largely dismantled, there was no defence in depth. Also, far too many formations and supply dumps were positioned too close to the frontier. Men and *matériel* were not dispersed and stationed in depth, but were concentrated mainly in advance positions, making them easy targets for any surprise attack. Troops had not dug in and were concentrated where an attack was unlikely. For example,

Twelfth and Eighteenth Mountain Armies were at the foot of the eastern Carpathians (useless, because of their light equipment, in defending the Ukrainian steppes) and massively at the Danube estuary. Ninth Army, probably the strongest formation of all, was concentrated in the south with a strong force of bombers to threaten the Ploesti oilfields in Romania. A German attack was not expected here because of the long lines of supply, and the difficulties presented by the Carpathians for any kind of transport. So when the Wehrmacht advanced Ninth Army had to beat a hasty retreat to avoid encirclement by German armies moving south from the centre of the front.

Deployment—and other indications which pointed towards the offensive character of Soviet intentions, such as Stalin's assumption of the chairmanship of Sovnarkom from *Molotov on 6 May 1941—have been interpreted as a Soviet plan to conduct a massive first strike against Germany. But for almost all of its history the Red Army had singularly neglected defensive strategic thinking and defensive military training.

When it was attacked, on 22 June 1941, the Red Army had not only not completed its deployment and reorganization but, for reasons difficult to explain, Stalin had refused until a couple of hours before the attack to put the armed forces on full alert. The shortage of commanders was still acute, they lacked experience, and most of them had been in their positions only a short time. Tank corps and air force units had not been fully deployed or concentrated properly. No plans for *strategic* defence were available; all plans envisaged forward movement by the Red Army very soon; positional warfare had never been tested in exercises. Commanders thus found themselves at a loss, a situation which was compounded by totally unrealistic orders from Stalin to attack.

Top political and military echelons in the USSR were, of course, aware of the heightened danger of getting involved in the war, as is shown by the increased military production from 1937 and particularly from 1939 onward. Still, when the Germans attacked they were able to achieve a major strategic surprise.

This lack of preparedness could not have stemmed from a lack of information. The Soviet leadership had ample knowledge of the German preparations and had been warned of the impending attack through diplomatic and other channels (see SORGE, for example). It is difficult to believe that Stalin trusted Hitler. If for some time he thought a German invasion unlikely, it was because he could not imagine that Hitler, already stalemated in one war he could not win, would voluntarily embark on another. This could also go some way to explain the robustness, even aggressiveness with which Moscow pursued its interests in the Balkans—the annexation of Bessarabia and northern Bukovina; the military occupation of some Romanian islands in the Danube; the treaty concluded in 1941 with the new regime in Belgrade that triggered off the German attack on Yugoslavia—and the, by diplomatic standards, extraordinarily rude behaviour of Molotov during his visit to Berlin in December 1940. With the German invasion of the Balkans in April 1941 (see BALKAN CAMPAIGN) Stalin's attitude softened, because this extension of the war seemed to him irrational on Hitler's part and may have sown doubts in his mind about the improbability of Hitler attacking the USSR. If before he had slowed down delivery of goods to Nazi Germany, he now became extremely punctual. According to Soviet historians, in an attempt to stave off the German attack into the next year, he also avoided doing anything which Hitler could construe as provocation—and that was why he declined the request of the military to put the army on full alert.

One of Stalin's Soviet biographers (D. Volkogonov, *Stalin: Triumph and Tragedy*, London, 1991) says that Stalin believed a war between Germany and the USSR was inevitable, but would take place two or three years later because he could not imagine that Hitler would risk a war on two fronts. This presupposes, if the option of the USSR starting a war is excluded, that Stalin assumed a German victory over the UK, or at least a peace treaty between the two countries, was a certainty, a not very satisfactory interpretation.

According to some historians (see, for example, J. McSherry, *Stalin, Hitler and Europe*, vol. 2, Cleveland, Ohio, 1970), Stalin concluded the Nazi–Soviet Pact not in order to keep the USSR out of the war as long as possible, or to make the territorial gains which it brought, but rather to see France and the UK get entangled in a war with Germany. Even the Soviet argument, that Stalin wanted a breathing-space before a German–Soviet war broke out, presupposes war in the west, because his only safeguard would be the fact that the Wehrmacht was engaged in fighting the British and the French: a treaty alone would not bind Hitler. In a clear, logical calculation it must have been obvious to Stalin that after the British and French guarantees of Poland (see POLAND, GUARANTEE OF) and its borders a German attack on Poland meant war between Hitler and the western Allies. Through the Nazi–Soviet Pact Hitler received the freedom to attack Poland, as he had made clear he intended to. If he had wanted to prevent war, Stalin should have refrained from a non-aggression treaty with Nazi Germany because at that time Hitler still feared war on two fronts. But as early as 1925 Stalin had declared that a war between the capitalist countries was inevitable. What he did not say was that the USSR would keep out of it as long as possible and enter at its own choosing to maximize possible political gains. But evidence that he intended to follow this course is circumstantial and may never become available.

In 1939 and 1940 Stalin's major miscalculation lay in the underestimation of German military capabilities: Poland and France were overrun much faster than he had expected. The capitalist countries did not get bogged down in a war of attrition, as many had expected. This made his country vulnerable to an untimely German attack. According to some historians (see, for example, Werth, below) Stalin, in a speech given on 5 May 1941, even predicted that the USSR would take the initiative militarily to enter the war. In his biography, Volkogonov merely reports that Stalin hinted at the possibility of a German–Soviet war, implying that Germany would attack first. Yet in October 1938, Stalin had made clear that a socialist country was not a pacifist one and that circumstances might arise in which the Bolsheviks could attack first. But to see the Nazi–Soviet Pact, as one historian does (see E. Topitsch, *Stalin's War*, London, 1987), as a master plan to drive the Anglo-Saxon powers from the Continent in order to extend Soviet power all over Europe—and to portray Hitler as being tricked into attacking the USSR—is rather far-fetched.

First reactions of the political leadership after the German attack bordered on panic. Only on the evening of 22 June was the Soviet public informed officially of what had happened. Not Stalin, head of government, but Molotov, deputy chairman of Sovnarkom and people's commissar for foreign affairs, addressed the nation over the radio. Stalin did not speak until 3 July. One of the first measures of the government was to demand the handing in of private radios to the authorities. Information should only come through public loudspeakers and the official press. The NKVD deported and even killed 'undesirable' elements and civilians were threatened with the death penalty for spreading rumours or other minor misdemeanours. Considerable distrust of the Red Army was also shown. Dual command was reintroduced, that is commissars once again became the equals of professional officers, and thousands of reliable communist cadres were drafted into particularly sensitive units to intensify party work and boost morale. The arrest in June 1941 and subsequent execution of General D. G. Pavlov, the commander of the West *front*, and several of his generals was meant to stiffen resistance, but it also stemmed from a paranoid fear of espionage and sabotage which was characteristic of Stalin and his entourage.

On 22 June 1941 half of European Russia, from Archangel to Moscow and Krasnodar, was put under military law. Party control over public life was drastically reinforced. Thousands of party and Komsomol members were mobilized for the army. Party agitators swept the country. Heavy and war industries were put under direct party supervision. The political sections of the machinery and tractor stations in collectivized agriculture were reintroduced, and though many such measures were rescinded in May 1943, as was the dual command system in the army, Stalin's response to a harsh situation was, at the time, to make it even harsher. On 21 September 1941 he dictated: 'They are saying the German swine who are advancing on Leningrad are driving old folk and women and children in front of them. They are saying there are Bolsheviks in Leningrad who find it impossible to use their weapons against such deputies (people). I think that if there are such people among the Bolsheviks, then they should be destroyed first, because they're more dangerous than the German Fascists' (quoted in Volkogonov, op. cit., p. 420).

Stalin was equally harsh with his armed forces. On 16 August 1941 he dictated order no. 270: 'I order that: (1) anyone who removes his insignia during battle and surrenders should be regarded as a malicious deserter, whose family is to be arrested as the family of a breaker of the oath and betrayer of the Motherland. Such *deserters are to be shot on the spot. (2) those falling into encirclement are to fight to the last and try to reach their own lines. And those who prefer to surrender are to be destroyed by any available means, while their families are to be deprived of all state allowances and assistance . . . This order is to be read to all companies, squadrons, batteries' (ibid., p. 427).

He was confirmed in this rigorous attitude by reports that soldiers took fright too easily and magnified German successes and strength in their imagination. At critical moments the old tension between the military and the political leadership resurfaced. The commissar of the war council of the North-West *front* accused commanders of 'defensive-mindedness' and on 8 July advocated a counter-attack, asking the Stavka, the Red Army's GHQ, to order it. Things were different when the *Kiev tragedy unfolded. The war council wanted to retreat in time, but Stalin threatened Khrushchev and Kirponos, to prevent them giving up the left bank of the *Dnieper. He must therefore be given full responsibility for the ensuing catastrophe. But at least in military matters he soon learned to concentrate on general directives. Although petty meddling never stopped, he learned to accept the judgement of the military and to leave details to generals whom he trusted. There were not many of them, for Stalin distrusted even those who (following his orders) had fought their way out of encirclements. The same applied to soldiers who had fallen into German hands, but escaped or were liberated. These were either transferred to *penal battalions or sent to special camps where the NKVD could 'check' on them.

Harsh measures originated from others, too. The war council of the South *front* demanded the expulsion of German settlers, reporting from the Dniester that they had shot at retreating Soviet soldiers and greeted the Wehrmacht with bread and salt. On 29 August 1941, the committee for the defence of Leningrad ordered the immediate expulsion of 96,000 Soviet citizens of German or Finnish descent to be resettled in Kazakhstan, Krasnoyarsk, Novosibirsk, Altay, and Omsk *oblasty* (provinces) and only the swiftness of the German advance prevented this. On 31 August the Politburo ordered 'Germans living in the Ukrainian SSR' (i.e. Soviet citizens) to be arrested. The commissariat for defence was to mobilize all able-bodied German men between 16 and 60 into construction battalions and hand them over to the NKVD 'to be used in the eastern regions of the USSR'. During the same month Moscow ordered the deportation of Germans in the Volga region to Central Asia and other eastern areas. In a small, but typical, incident Stalin ordered all 170 inmates of a prison near Orel to be shot without any trial after the NKVD's head, Beria, had reported on 6 September 1941 that prisoners had spread defeatist propaganda before preparing to flee. Among the high-calibre victims were two old communists and one old foe of the Bolshevik regime: Christian Rakovsky, Olga Kameneva (sister of Trotsky), and Maria Spiridonova.

Nonetheless, the regime felt forced to loosen, at least partially, the fetters with which Soviet society was held down so that the war effort could gain the widest possible support. Poets such as Boris Pasternak (1890–1960) and Anna Akhmatova (1889–1966) were allowed to appear in public again. Official propaganda discarded Marxist elements, appealed to nationalist sentiments and made the war the Great Patriotic War on the model of 1812. Figures from Russian history, such as the princes Alexander Nevsky and Dmitri Donskoi who had beaten foreign invaders in previous centuries, became celebrated heroes and the subject of films. The state sought and found an arrangement with the Russian Orthodox Church (see RELIGION). Atheist propaganda was discontinued and by the end of the war the church again had 46 bishops, 16,000 churches, and 30,000 priests.

Panic and confusion reached a high point as the Germans advanced rapidly towards Moscow. The evacuation of industries (see DOMESTIC LIFE, ECONOMY, AND WAR EFFORT above) had already begun, and as early as 5 July the NKVD received orders to evacuate the state archives from the capital. First steps to defend *Moscow were taken on 9 July, accompanied by special orders to foil German 'diversionist' activities. Many new units were created, always with an eye to political reliability. Air defence forces in particular had to be packed with party and Komsomol members. Beyond this, every battalion had to have fifteen NKVD men among their personnel. On 16 July Stalin ordered General Artemev, head of the Directorate of Operational Troops of the NKVD and also of the Moscow Military District, to organize ten divisions of the 'Home Guards' (Narodnoe Opolchenie; see DEFENCE FORCES AND CIVIL DEFENCE, below) and intermingle them with a further five NKVD divisions for deployment on the Mozhaisk front. But it still remained unclear that Moscow would and could be defended. On 8 October 1941 Stalin created a special commission under the Deputy People's Commissar for the Interior, General Ivan Serov, to plan the destruction of industrial enterprises. Local troikas comprising the party secretary, the chief of the local NKVD intelligence units, and a Red Army engineer, were to make the necessary preparations. The next day Serov presented to Stalin a list of 1,119 plants, 412 of them military, to be destroyed. Shortly afterwards the city soviet ordered all women with children under 14 to prepare for immediate evacuation; and on 15 August Stalin ordered the evacuation of foreign embassies, the Supreme Soviet, and the government to Kuibyshev, and the general staff to Arzamas. This announcement created panic. The directive also ordered the NKVD to blow up all factories and power plants that could not be evacuated, should the Wehrmacht appear at the gates of the capital.

On 19 October Moscow was put under martial law. General Artemev, who wielded all military and civil authority, was under orders to suppress any outbreak of 'panic' by the severest measures. From 20 October to 13 December 1941 in the city of Moscow alone more than 47,000 *deserters, or people who had somehow avoided military service, were detained. Sixteen people were shot on the spot for desertion, 'fascist' agitation, or 'espionage'. A further 357 were executed after courts-martial. Deserters were shot in front of the troops, 'to support the educational work'. Altogether during this time nearly 122,000 people were arrested in the city, for spreading rumours, for anti-Soviet pronouncements, and for other transgressions, and only 24,000 of them were released after their cases had been investigated. According to incomplete data 779 senior personnel—directors, chief accountants, and others—fled from 438 factories, many of them attempting to enrich themselves in the process. Still, discontent seems only to have really surfaced with grumbling and sullen faces. But the authorities did not take any chances and all public places were closely controlled. In particular the bomb shelters and the metro were supervised by the Komsomol, and the leadership, Stalin included, were informed that as a consequence of insufficient political education people had started to play cards for money in the shelters. Stalin's decisions to stay in Moscow, to hold the traditional military parade on the anniversary of the October Revolution, and to receive the British foreign minister, Anthony *Eden, did much to restore confidence.

At the top of government and party, centralization reached extremes. Stalin had already become chairman of Sovnarkom. On 30 June 1941, he assumed the chair in the specially created State Committee for Defence (GKO), and on 10 July he took over from Timoshenko the chairmanship of the Stavka, formed on 23 June, and on 19 July the People's Commissariat for Defence. On 8 August he became Supreme Commander of the Red Army and 14 February 1942, when a Transport Commission was attached to GKO, he became its chairman, too.

Particularly during the first phases of the war Stalin busied himself with minutiae mostly referred to him by others. On his desks landed reports on which trains had gone to the wrong places and where they had ended up. Ordinary soldiers wrote to him and he read their letters. Especially in the early stages he received reports minimizing Soviet losses and giving fanciful accounts of success. Local commanders pleaded with him for reinforcements and he would release them in small quantities. The chairman of the Moscow Soviet, Pronin, related a typical story. On 5 October 1941 the Germans had broken through between Vyazma and Kaluga and a tank column had appeared near Yukhnov. A member of the political administration of the West *front*, who nearly fell into their hands, got on the phone to contact Alexander Shcherbakov, Moscow's party boss.

Shcherbakov immediately rang Stalin, who personally ordered the commander of Moscow's air defences to send two aircraft to reconnoitre, and then another two. The facts established, Stalin himself ordered all Moscow air defence aircraft to attack the German tank column and to deploy artillery against it.

Seen from below, this incident showed it would not do to go through the normal military channels. Everything had to be decided by the man at the top. The same Pronin brought Stalin's anger upon himself by distributing flour to the population of Moscow on Mikoyan's directive, to save it from German bombs. For this he was brought before Stalin, who saw the action as aggravating the general panic. Pronin's life hung on a thread, but Mikoyan owned up. During the ensuing altercations between Stalin's entourage (among them Beria) and Mikoyan, the latter, obviously frightened, repeatedly pleaded with Stalin: 'Comrade Stalin, you know how I acted during the year 1937!' (the worst year of the purges and of the decapitation of the army).

HEINZ-DIETRICH LÖWE

5. Defence forces and civil defence

The Local Air Defence (Mestnoe PVO) was responsible for air raid shelters, special preparations in case of enemy attacks and fire-fighting as a result of these, providing individual means of defence against air raids and fires, and for the anti-chemical defence of the population. Originally administered at the centre through the administration of the PVO of the People's Commissariat of Defence, in 1940 a Main Administration of the MPVO was created and integrated into the NKVD. Regionally, the MPVO was under the command of the Military Districts. Locally, the city and regional soviets had to organize all citizens between 16 and 60 for the purpose of civil defence. The work of the MPVO was very extensive and rather varied. According to Soviet sources it prepared shelters for more than 20 million people, fought more than 90,000 fires, defused hundreds of thousands of bombs and millions of mines, helped after innumerable accidents in industry, repaired thousands of buildings, and provided first aid.

The Narodnoe Opolchenie (NO, or Home Guards) were makeshift units recruited locally from men who had not been subject to the first call-up and women who not infrequently volunteered. Such units were as a rule formed in emergency situations, and they first appeared during the defence of Brest-Litovsk and Przemysl. They were often part of a spontaneous patriotic movement, but sometimes they were simply the state organizing something like the draft system locally through the party. In extreme cases NO units were sent into battle after only a few hours of training and sometimes not even that.

The Home Guards varied tremendously in shape, training, and the tasks they were given. For example, on 24 June 1941 a government order called for the creation of volunteer guards to fight Wehrmacht diversionary activities. By the end of July there were already more than 300,000 men and women in such units. The initiative for the direct recruitment of new troops through local channels was taken in Leningrad, with the approval of the Stavka, and Stalin, in a radio broadcast on 3 July, demanded the formation of Home Guards in every city where an enemy attack threatened. On 4 July GKO published an order 'On the voluntary mobilization of the workers of Moscow and Moscow district into divisions of Home Guards'. Similar orders were given for the Ukraine, Karelia, and Belorussia. Local party units took on local recruitment and organization of the units and officers of the regular army took over their command. Factories formed regiments and brigades, cities or districts formed divisions. Workers and Komsomol members played a particular role and a troika of officer and party workers commanded the larger units. NO units were incorporated into the regular army and then complemented and filled up with regular units. But often there was no time for such preparation. Home Guards played a considerable role in the defence of Moscow and Leningrad. Altogether, 60 divisions totalling two million people were organized as NO during the war.

HEINZ-DIETRICH LÖWE

6. Armed forces

(a) Background and High Command

From its formation in 1918 the Red Army was under the contradictory influences of ideological thinking and military exigencies. Initially, the revolutionaries who had just taken power aimed at the creation of a workers' militia, but the Bolsheviks were immediately confronted by the realities. The Red Guards that had successfully won and defended the revolution proved small fry for the German Imperial Army after a breakdown in the negotiations for what was to be the peace of Brest-Litovsk. The civil war finally made it imperative to build a more traditional army that would be able to defeat the Whites. It was Leon Trotsky who, with an iron fist, guided the Red Army on its path towards professionalism. A major step in this direction was the decision to accept officers of the old imperial army, and 48,409 officers and 214,717 non-commissioned officers joined between June 1918 and August 1920. Although always treated with distrust by functionaries and ordinary soldiers alike, some of the former tsarist officers were to have distinguished careers under the new regime, among them I. Vatsetis, A. Svechin, and Marshals M. Tukhachevsky (1893–1937) and *Shaposhnikov. The distrust of these 'military specialists' (*voenspetsy*) found expression in a dual command structure unique to the Red Army: to every commander (the word 'officer' was banned until 1935) a political commissar was assigned who had to confirm orders before they became valid. This form of institutionalized non-confidence was scaled down during the years after the civil war until commanders became solely responsible for military matters, with the political commissar being responsible only for party work and political instruction. But at times of crisis (during the years of collectivization and terror, for example, and immediately after the German attack in 1941) the regime reintroduced dual control. Tensions between the two rather different groups of command personnel never quite disappeared.

The Red Army was always the army of a class and of the party. The Political Administration of the Red Army (Politicheskoe Upravlenie Respubliki, or PUR, then PURKKA) which directed and organized the work of the commissars, and which from 1925 was controlled by the Party's Central Committee, made sure it remained so. From 1937 on PURKKA was in the hands of one of Stalin's creatures, Commissar First Grade Lev Mekhlis, who presided over the purges in the army. The social composition of the Red Army, especially of the corps of commanders, was carefully watched and the party made sure that the proletarian element remained strong enough to secure its loyalty. Troops for use internally, especially the early motorized units, showed a particularly high percentage of workers and once the war had begun demoralized or unreliable Red Army formations would be swamped by mass drafts of reliable party workers.

Political instruction in the army put particular emphasis on winning supporters for the new regime and many of the former peasant-soldiers developed into the only important rural element the party could win. With the beginning of collectivization the party ordered the army to train peasant soldiers for political, administrative, and specialist work in the countryside. The army proved reliable against peasant unrest during collectivization as it been earlier, in 1920–1, during the risings in Tambov and other provinces.

Strategic and tactical thinking in the Red Army had been largely determined by the lessons drawn from the civil war. In particular the so-called 'Red Commanders'—Bolsheviks who had mostly risen from the ranks of non-commissioned officers of the old army (among them Budenny, Voroshilov, Timoshenko, and Zhukov), or political commissars, such as *Konev, who joined the commanding staff—fervently defended a military doctrine that saw in a war of movement and in an offensive spirit the essence of everything they thought was new in their 'proletarian military doctrine'. They were supported in this by more senior officers such as Tukhachevsky. The representative of the Red Commanders, M. Frunze, who became Trotsky's deputy in 1924 and supplanted him in 1925 as People's commissar for war, fully shared the predilection for an offensive 'proletarian' strategy combined with a disdain for defensive thinking, and an unrealistic optimism that deemed the armies of the capitalist countries incapable of an offensive war of movement. The commanders and Frunze believed that once a war had been carried into enemy territory the oppressed workers would rise and ensure victory and revolution. Trotsky—the theorist of permanent revolution—warned against such facile optimism and denied a relationship between the class-character of the Red Army and its ability to conduct a war of manoeuvre. Frunze aggravated faulty strategic thinking by denouncing the *blitzkrieg theory as a bourgeois deviation. The Red Army did not expect to have to face it.

Frunze and the Red Commanders insisted on keeping a professional army after the civil war, though Trotsky wished to create a militia army based on the centres of production, in keeping with the idea of dictatorship of the proletariat. The peacetime army that developed out of demobilization during 1924–5 was a professional army of the 'cadres', with a territorial militia element where recruits would be trained. The professional elements of the army provided two-fifths of the infantry, four-fifths of the cavalry, and all the technical units (air force, tank units, and engineers). Between one-sixth and one-tenth of the territorial militia units were regular cadre troops; the balance was composed of recruits who came for three-month courses but who had to be available to the army for five years. Every male, with the exception of members of the 'exploiting classes', had to do military service.

From 1939 on all male Soviet citizens were liable to the draft. At the same time commanders who had received only the barest military education during the civil war were dismissed—as were large numbers of 'military specialists'—and a new corps of commanders developed. However, improvement proved slow in coming as educational qualifications for entry to military schools were lowered and deserving rank-and-file soldiers were moved up in order to strengthen the proletarian element among the commanders.

Something like a general staff had been nominally extant since 1921, but only when Frunze became commissar for war did it assume a leading role and begin to work on improving the army's training, tactical and strategic planning, and organizational structure. Under him the first, provisional, Field Service Regulations for the Red Army were issued. But the army had problems handling modern technology and strong elements of the general staff underestimated its importance. A soldier's day had three hours' less military training in it than in the old tsarist army, although this included four and a half hours of political and general education. Because of the low level of military spending more defensively-minded military men moved into the general staff, and the Stalin Line was built. However, this emphasis on the defensive was reflected neither in military teaching and practical training, nor in the new Field Service Regulations of 1929.

From the mid-1930s onwards the Red Army became a fully professional modern army. In 1935 officer ranks were reintroduced, though the title of general had to wait until May 1940. Pay for officers and pay differentials increased markedly between 1934 and 1939 and special shops and restaurants for officers were introduced. By January 1936 only 23% of the army were still of the territorial-militia type; by 1939, when its numbers had increased to three million, they had been phased out. Because of the vast size of the USSR and its underdeveloped transport system, two independent armies were created, one in the west and the other in the east, each of which could take on an opponent on its own.

During the 1930s technology and mechanization became major characteristics of the Red Army. Particular emphasis was laid on air and tank forces, but not yet on artillery. The brain behind this modernization was Tukhachevsky. He assembled a group of competent commanders who organized new branches such as a strategic bomber fleet which became the strongest in Europe, and a special tank corps to enable the army to conduct a modern war of movement. In developing modern tactics for these new branches the Red Army benefited considerably from its co-operation with the Reichswehr at the Soviet–German air base at Lipetsk and the Soviet–German Tank School at Kazan. Technical assistance was also given by the French and the Americans.

Although it has always been maintained that the military motive was a particularly strong factor in the USSR's rapid industrialization, it was a long time before the Red Army received an important share of the national budget (see Table 6) and new weapons in any sizeable number. A war scare like that of 1927, made much of mainly for internal reasons, did not make any difference. The reason may be that the industrial capacity had to be created first, before the army could even order more sophisticated weapons. The production of new weapons for the army developed as in Table 7.

The military power of the USSR grew rapidly in the late 1930s. Figures for the introduction of new models of military aircraft and tanks might even understate the dramatic increase in production, because they do not allow for qualitative improvements. Certainly the Red Army was well equipped when hostilities broke out.

But although equipped with modern weapons, and with a training that emphasized technology—and in spite of Tukhachevsky's experiments with modern warfare—the Red Army remained ideologically wedded to the idea that wars were decided not by technology and new military weapons, but by the masses and their motivation. 'Bourgeois' military theorists such as J. F. C. Fuller and Basil Liddell Hart (see LAND POWER) were taken note of and their works translated into Russian; but their strong emphasis on modern systems, or on one system—the tank or the air force—was dismissed as a symptom of the class-bound nature of bourgeois armies. Soviet thinking strongly insisted on the co-operation of all arms, but centred on a strong infantry. In terms of tactics and strategy this posed the difficulty of persuading 'the masses' to accept a concept that stressed, as Tukhachevsky did with great emphasis, the necessity of high mobility and technical efficiency. The Field Service Regulations issued in 1936 did not solve this problem, as Tukhachevsky's influence was not strong enough to marry the two concepts successfully, and the omission was not corrected later on. The chief instrument of war remained the infantry. Defensive elements were neglected, although in the early 1930s they had received some attention under the guidance of Shaposhnikov and others.

From this overestimation of the importance of infantry followed the directive that was to have catastrophic results in the first phase of the German–Soviet war: soldiers had to let themselves be overrun by the first wave of enemy tanks in order to separate these from their infantry.

Further deeply flawed changes followed as a consequence of the purges in the military and because of erroneous conclusions drawn from the experiences of the *Spanish Civil War. Stalin's creatures, G. Kulik, D. Pavlov (who had served in Spain), and Mekhlis, could, after Tukhachevsky and the officers supporting him had been liquidated, push through their view without resistance. They believed that neither tanks nor the air force could play an independent strategic role. Therefore, all tank corps were dissolved and their tanks shared out among infantry divisions where they assumed more or less the role of a self-propelled artillery. The air force was treated similarly. When, following the fall of France in June 1940, the Red Army Command realized that these earlier decisions were catastrophically wrong, a hasty regrouping began which had not been fully completed when the Wehrmacht attacked.

The reasons for the purges and mass killings of officers that decapitated the Red Army in 1937 and 1938 are difficult to gauge. No open or organized opposition against Stalin existed in the military and PURKKA controlled tightly any political activities within it. The only element virtually immune to repression, and the only ones Stalin trusted, was the group around the First Cavalry Army led by Marshal Voroshilov, the commissar for war, and Marshal Budenny, with whom Stalin had worked during the civil war and who had raised men such as Timoshenko and Zhukov. But many military men owed nothing to Stalin. Tukhachevsky, and a number of other generals, were heroes in their own right and they commanded the loyalty of many others. Maybe the purges occurred because under them the army had voiced its concern about the consequences of the massive collectivization and had tried to protect Nikolai Bukharin, Stalin's last great rival. Whatever the reason, almost everybody connected with Tukhachevsky disappeared or was shot, and they were those most intimately connected with the modernization of the army. Some 35,000 officers out of an officer corps of roughly 80,000 fell victim to the purges; among them three of the five Marshals of the Soviet Union, all eleven deputies of the commissar for war, 75 of the 85 corps commanders, and 110 out of the 195 divisional commanders were killed. Of the naval commanders only one survived.

Not only was the Red Army under the strict control of the regime's political institutions, but Stalin had also developed a direct personal grip on it, and on 3 March 1938 a Main Military Council for the Peasants' and Workers' Red Army, and a parallel Main Military Council for the Navy, were created to supervise the commissariats for defence and the navy (the latter having been established on 30 December 1937). Stalin became a member of the first and made his trusted henchman, Andrei Zhdanov, chairman of the other. The independence of the commissariat of defence and of its head, Voroshilov, was therefore drastically reduced.

Since 1934 a 'Staff of the Peasants' and Workers' Red Army' had existed under the commissariat for defence. In 1935 this was renamed the 'General Staff'. The first chief of staff was Marshal A. Egorov, who was followed in 1937 by Shaposhnikov. In 1940 Meretskov took over, then Zhukov (February to July 1941), who was followed in August 1941 by Shaposhnikov again, then by Vasilevsky (June 1942) and, finally, in February 1945 by A. Antonov. The general staff had departments for operations, organization, mobilization, and intelligence and it also retained some control over the inspectorates, although the inspectorate apparatus as such was under the control of an inspector-general of armaments. The general staff, was not as powerful as its German counterpart the OKH (see GERMANY, 6(b)), for it had to compete with the Main (Central) Administration which was also under the commissariat for defence and commanded departments for the command staff, military schools, recruiting, replacements, and military topography. Other Main Administrations were to follow, most of whose heads became deputy commissars of defence. These powerful agencies restricted the powers of the general staff. In the second half of 1941 the general staff was in fact, under the Stavka, explicitly restricted to its tasks of planning and directing operations in the theatre of war. The Main Administrations were, like most other military institutions, not very stable in their existence and it would be impossible to follow the fluctuations in their numbers.

Under the commissariat of defence fourteen military districts covered the entire USSR. At the head of this commissariat stood a military, or war, council on which sat two political commissars. These faced the military commander, whose staff was subordinate to the council not to him. Military districts possessed roughly the same administrative structure as the commissariat for defence itself. They were responsible in their areas for the formation of military units; the training and political education of officers and soldiers; mobilization and, together with the local soviets, conscription; the requisitioning of transport; communications; the scrutiny and selection of commanding personnel for the troops and the administrative offices; supply, sanitary, and veterinary arrangements; anti-aircraft defences including the supervision of civil defence or paramilitary organizations; pre-army military training; and the supervision of defence construction work and of civilian participation in it.

In 1990 the Chief of the Soviet General Staff made public the results of two official commissions set up to calculate human losses in the Soviet armed forces during

USSR, Table 6: Percentage of the annual budget spent on the army

1922–3	*1924–5*	*1927–8*	*1933*	*1934*	*1935*	*1936*	*1937*	*1938*	*1939*	*1940*	*1941*
15.6	14.5	12.3	3.4	9.1	11.1	16.1	16.5	18.7	25.6	32.6	43.4

Source: Contributor.

USSR, Table 7: Production of new weapons (yearly average production of)

	1930–1	*1932–4*	*1935–7*	*1938*	*1939*	*1940*	*1941*
aircraft, total	860	2,595	3,578	5,467	10,382	10,565	15,735[b]
including fighters	120	326	1,278		6,995	4,574	7,086[c]
bombers	100	252	568			3,571	3,748[d]
tanks	740	3,371	3,139	2,271	2,950	2,794	6,590
including KV and T34	—	—	—	—	—	358[a]	4,322[e]
artillery, total	1,911	3,778(?)	5,020	12,340	17,348	15,300	42,300
including small calibre	1,040	2,196	3,606				
large calibre	870	1,602	1,381	5,214	8,863		
rifles (000s)	174	256	397	1,175	1,503	1,461	

[a] planned 600 T34 alone [b] planned 20,150 [c] planned 8,150 [d] planned 6,070
[e] planned 4,000

Source: Contributor.

the German–Soviet War and the campaign against Japan in August 1945. The commissions' figures, which included those killed in action, missing in action, prisoners-of-war who did not return, and those who died of other causes, were 8,509,300 (Army and Navy), 97,700 (Internal troops), and 61,400 (Frontier troops), a total of 8,668,400 (see J. Erickson & D. Dilks (eds.), *Barbarossa*, London, 1994, p. 259).

(b) Army

The war councils of the five military districts on the western frontiers had to assume, with their staffs, the role of *fronts* (that is, army groups) in case of war. Each *front* controlled a number of armies and each had a highly placed political functionary from the orbit of the Politburo added to it just before the Germans attacked. This policy somewhat obscured the chain of command. However, potential conflicts were mediated by Stalin who assumed all important political and military positions either before the war or during its first weeks. Thus the *fronts* were firmly under his control.

Below the military districts, or the *fronts*, armies were the largest military formations. Normally they existed only during wartime, but by 22 June 1941 there were almost 30 armies, and this number quickly grew. They were normally created on the basis of a military district, but there was no real continuity, as most armies were reconstituted during the war (or even before) by a different military district from the one which first established them. The word 'Army' could mean very different things. An ordinary army in 1940–1 might have two rifle—that is, infantry—corps, one cavalry corps, and one mechanized corps (see Chart 2), but it could be smaller or much larger depending on the theatre of war or the special role that it was assigned. Soviet military doctrine also recognized the so-called shock army (*udarnaia armiia*) which was trained and equipped to make large-scale attacks to punch through the opposing side's lines. It was much larger than a normal army and had between four and five rifle corps, one or two mechanized corps, a much higher share of artillery brigades, and more independent divisional tank and artillery units.

A rifle corps consisted of three rifle divisions, two corps artillery brigades, an independent anti-aircraft battalion, a pioneer battalion, a signals battalion, and service troops. A rifle division had three rifle regiments and two artillery regiments in addition to corps artillery, one anti-tank, one anti-aircraft, one engineer, and one signals battalion—all in addition to the corresponding units of the corps. Many rifle divisions still had their own tank battalion and rifle regiments also had their own artillery of fourteen guns of various calibres.

A mechanized corps consisted of two tank divisions and one motorized rifle division, a tank division of two tank regiments, one motorized rifle regiment, one artillery regiment, and one anti-aircraft battalion. A motorized rifle division had two rifle regiments, one tank regiment, one anti-aircraft battalion, and one anti-tank battalion.

Before BARBAROSSA, the shortcomings of the Red Army had already been exposed during the Finnish–Soviet war which started on 30 November 1939, even though this was fought only by the forces of the Leningrad Military District. The political and military leaderships attempted to address the apparent problems. Scrutiny of the German success against France initiated a major reorganization of the Red Army. The mechanized corps was reinstated so that armoured forces could be heavily concentrated to increase the army's mobility and offensive capabilities. Even then this return to Tukhachevsky's thinking ran into considerable resistance and the reorganization had not been completed when the Germans launched BARBAROSSA.

On paper the Red Army looked very impressive. More than 5.37 million men stood under arms; during the ten days following the invasion another five million were mobilized. It had more than 20,000 tanks, albeit mostly outdated models, but at least 1,861 (according to Volkogonov, op. cit., p. 375, about 2,000) of the newest make that were superior to anything the Wehrmacht could muster. The air force possessed about 10,000 aircraft of which 2,640—or even as many as 2,739—conformed to modern standards. According to Soviet historians there were at least 2.9 million men immediately facing the Wehrmacht, reinforced by 100,000 NKVD border troops and additional smaller units. It is quite possible that this number only included forces equipped by the local military districts and not the strategic reserve in the rear. As many as 8,000 aircraft, 1,450 of them modern designs, could have been deployed in the west, as were up to 10,000 *tanks, of which 1,475 were of the KV or T-34 type, most of which were in forward positions. German and other forces amounted to some three million men equipped with somewhere between 2,800 and 3,580 (according to some Soviet sources 3,712) tanks and 2,740 aircraft.

It is not particularly meaningful when Soviet sources say that Red Army formations in the west were not fully equipped when BARBAROSSA was launched, because the planned strength of Soviet formations was considerably higher than in other armies. For example, a Red Army tank division (61 had been formed) was meant to have 375 tanks, a Wehrmacht tank division (21 were deployed in the east) had only between 135 and 209; a Red Army motorized division (31 had been formed) should have had 275 tanks, the Wehrmacht equivalent (14 at the Eastern Front) did not have any. Similarly, a fully equipped Soviet rifle division had 1,204 machine-guns, whereas a German infantry division had only 486.

Therefore, Red Army formations should have been sufficiently well equipped to repel any aggressor even if they were not up to planned strength. But the army did suffer from a shortage of traction power for its artillery and had only half the number of trucks envisaged for its motorized units. Another drawback was that *radio

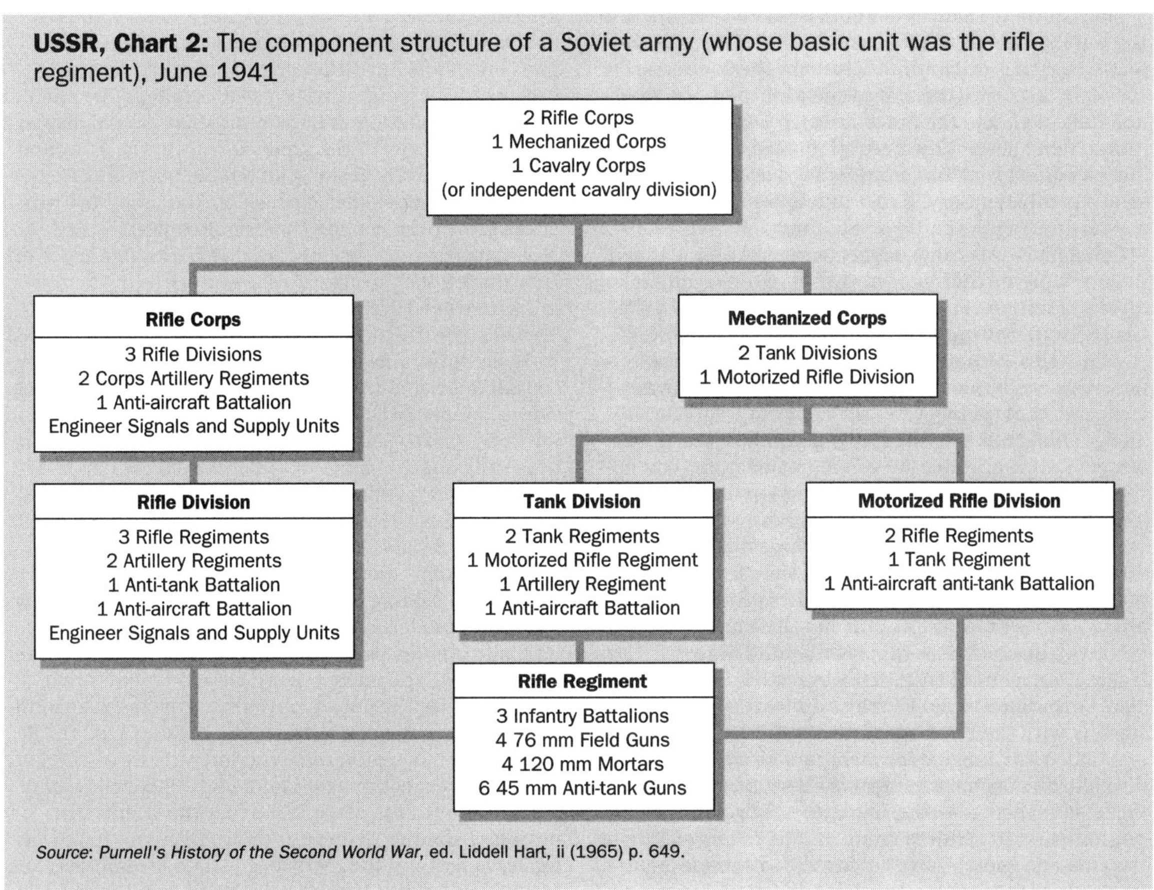

communications had been sadly neglected; after the Germans launched their attack communications between Soviet commanders and their troops, and especially to headquarters, broke down because land-lines had been severed, a situation which could not be remedied for some while. Mistakes in training and in tactics produced catastrophic results.

The regime quickly drew a number of lessons from the initial disasters of BARBAROSSA. Co-ordination between *fronts* and large formations proved an immediate problem. Officers lacked initiative and a willingness to shoulder responsibility—a typical consequence of the conditions of the Stalinist command system—the staffs at corps level were found to be overburdened, while those at divisional level were also deemed unsatisfactory. The corps, as a level of command, were therefore abolished and the *fronts* received overseers in the form of three Main Commands for Strategic Direction; the Northern Direction co-ordinating the Northern and North-west *fronts*, the Northern (Atlantic) and the Baltic Fleets; the Western Direction in charge of the West *front* and the Pinsk River Flotilla; and the South-Western Direction overseeing the South and South-West *fronts*, the troops of the Briansk area, and the Black Sea Fleet. Lines of communication could have been shortened in this way and some decentralization achieved, but the Stavka, which meant Stalin, still insisted on directing *fronts* and even armies. Divisions were considerably reduced in size and for a while, particularly in the tank forces, were completely supplanted by brigades. To tackle the glaring inadequacies of the officer corps half a million men, often directly from the front, were given special courses for commanders.

Other changes were also implemented to improve the command system. The air force became independent of the army again and received its own commander, as did parachute and air defence forces, and formations and units from these forces were combed out of divisions and *fronts*—as were many artillery and tank units—and put directly under the Stavka. This put the Stavka in a position to intervene constantly in operational decisions of the *fronts* and individual armies which, of course, suited Stalin's habits. At the same time the Stavka created new guards formations as élite troops—something that had been ideological anathema until then (for airborne, cavalry, and guards units, see SPECIAL FORCES, below).

Many of these changes did not last long. Over much of the war experimentation was one of the distinguishing features of the Soviet military system. The commands of the Main Strategic Directions were abolished during May and June 1942, and the ten to fifteen *fronts* (depending on military and geographical requirements) reverted to the Stavka's direct control. Occasionally the Stavka would send a plenipotentiary to co-ordinate two *fronts*, as was the case during the battle of *Stalingrad. In August 1942 Marshal Zhukov became deputy commissar for war and deputy supreme commander, therefore the second man after Stalin in the Stavka and senior to the chief of the general staff. During 1942 the corps was reintroduced step by step as a command level as army staffs were obviously overburdened when attacks had to be organized, and 28 corps HQ were created during the year. The gradual and then fast-growing supply of technical weapons also suggested certain reorganizations had taken place. In March 1942 the formation of tank corps began first comprising two tank brigades, and one motorized rifle brigade, then with three tank brigades. From September, mechanized corps were formed with one tank brigade, three mechanized brigades, one anti-aircraft artillery regiment, and one anti-tank artillery regiment. But sufficient supporting units were still lacking, a structural fault that was rectified later. In May 1942 tank armies began to be formed for offensive actions, starting with the Third and Fifth Armies. Each comprised two tank corps, one independent tank brigade, one rifle division, one regiment of light artillery, one regiment of rocket launchers or *katyusha* (see ROCKET WEAPONS), and one anti-aircraft artillery group. In July the formation of the First and Fourth Tank Armies with a similar organization began. But this structure still proved somewhat deficient and was modified later. Tank armies had their own HQ and war councils. By September the creation of 1st and 2nd Heavy Guards Rocket Launcher Regiments had started and at the beginning of 1943 tank guard armies also began to be formed, these initially belonging almost exclusively to the Stavka reserve.

From the first the Stavka had combed out artillery units from the *fronts* and had concentrated them in its own hands. Although artillery units were later built up within smaller formations the Stavka also started to create huge concentrations of artillery fire-power. By the autumn of 1942 it had begun to form whole artillery divisions as part of its reserve, which would only be incorporated into a *front* for special offensive or defensive operations and then withdrawn. There were two types: one for attacks, consisting mainly of mine-throwers, howitzers, and rocket launchers with only a few field guns; and one for defensive purposes consisting mainly of field guns and howitzers for counter-bombardment. In 1943 artillery corps were formed which had about 700 artillery pieces. At the end of the war there were ten of these.

During 1943 the *fronts* and armies in particular received special communications units and independent artillery units that were to increase efficiency considerably. Divisions received additional artillery on several levels and had their numbers of machine- and sub-machine-guns increased. But although the army's equipment became much better the Stavka still clung to the habit of building up all kinds of large reserves at its own disposal. However, as a sign of the growing trust in the army and its officer corps the number of political deputies of commanders was reduced considerably, a measure which at the same time provided additional officers.

Despite even the serious initial setbacks, at almost any time during the German–Soviet war Red Army forces must have been vastly superior in numbers to the Wehrmacht. The most comprehensive figures published by Soviet historians overestimate German strength considerably and understate the numbers for the Soviet side (see Table 8). A Soviet publication put Soviet tank forces at 20,500. German reports claimed that 13,405 had been captured and more than 9,372 destroyed up to 1 January 1942. Stalin told Roosevelt's envoy, Harry *Hopkins, that the Red Army possessed 24,000 tanks at the time of BARBAROSSA. A figure well above 20,000 therefore seems more than likely. This picture is not changed by the fact that the majority of Soviet tanks were outmoded models, as a large number of German tanks were also obsolescent. The Soviet T-34 and KV tanks proved so superior to the most modern German models that German experts seriously considered copying them. But even as late in the war as the battle of Stalingrad the Red Army could not exploit this superiority to the full because of poor optical equipment and tactical ineptitude, and it was not until the end of 1943 that the Wehrmacht possessed sizeable quantities of the Tiger and King Tiger tanks, superior to the KV type, and also the improved Mark IV and Mark V, which were comparable to the T-34.

The Wehrmacht's initial successes cannot therefore be attributed to a lack of Soviet troops, or to the quality or quantity of their tanks. However, the Luftwaffe's technical superiority was a definite factor in the Germans' favour as was the fact that German troops were better trained and that their technical equipment, such as optical aiming devices and radio communications, was superior to the Red Army's. Another decisive factor was the Germans' ability to co-ordinate large fighting forces and the resourcefulness of their middle-ranking officers. Two overriding reasons turned German operational successes into strategic catastrophes for the USSR. Firstly, the Red Army had deployed for offensive, not defensive, operations. This had created a concentration of Soviet forces which enabled the Germans to wipe out large numbers of tanks and aircraft in a first devastating blow. Secondly, Stalin refused to use strategic withdrawal as a means of avoiding large-scale encirclements.

Soviet losses remained extremely high throughout the war, particularly in lives and numbers of wounded. The costly practice of attacking without tanks, holding them back until a breakthrough was achieved, was never discontinued. Because of this tactic the battle which led to the fall of *Berlin alone cost more Soviet lives than the

USSR, Table 8: Balance of personnel and selected categories of arms 1941–5

	June 1941	*Dec 1941*	*May 1942*	*Nov 1942*	*July 1943*	*Jan 1944*	*June 1944*	*Jan 1945*
Combat aircraft								
Soviet forces	8,105	2,495	3,160	3,088	8,290	8,500	11,800	14,500
German estimates								*16,600*
German forces	4,950	2,500	3,400	3,500	2,980	3,000	2,800	1,960
Tanks and self-propelled guns								
Soviet forces	7,000	1,730	4,065	6,014	9,580	4,900	8,000	11,000
German estimates.	*15–20,000*		*5,200*				*9,300*	*13,400*
German forces	2,800	1,500	3,230	6,600	8,550	5,400	5,200	3,950
German sources	*3,300*		*1,870*	*495*[c]	*2,800*	*2,300*[a]	*3,500*	
Artillery and mortars								
Soviet forces	34,965	22,000	43,640	72,500	98,700	88,900	83,200	91,400
German forces	47,260	26,800	43,000	70,980	54,300	54,000	49,000	28,500
Service personnel *thousand*								
Soviet forces	2,900[b]	4,200	5,500	6,154	6,442	6,165	6,500	6,000
German estimates	*4,700*				*13,200*			*12,400*
German forces	5,500	5,000	6,200	6,270	5,325	4,906	4,000	3,100
German sources	*3,200*	*(5,000)*	*2,850*		*3,100*	*2,800*	*2,160*	*1,800*

[a] October 1943
[b] Only those facing the Wehrmacht directly, German estimates counted 4,700 'at the European *front*'
[c] Briefly in January 1943

Source: Harrison, *Soviet Planning*, p. 111 (German), 264 (Soviet forces).

whole war had cost the Americans. Stalin repeatedly ordered his commanders not to spare lives. From December 1942 to the end of 1943, 2.5 million were killed or went missing, with equal losses incurred during 1944 and 1945. Soviet figures estimate losses of tanks at 15,100 in 1942, 23,500 in 1943 (8,000 at *Kursk alone), 23,700 in 1944, 13,700 in 1945 (the Germans reported much lower Soviet losses from 1943 onwards). About ten million Soviet servicemen (including partisans) were killed in action during the German–Soviet war, went missing, or did not return from German prisoner-of-war camps, and 18 million were wounded of whom one million died.

On 8 August 1945 the USSR declared war on Japan, this act being justified by the supposed Japanese refusal to accept the Potsdam ultimatum (see TERMINAL). Contrary to the long-standing official interpretation that Japan in 1940–5 had stopped the imperialist expansion of tsarist Russia, the war was now justified as the revenge for that defeat. After a few days the strong Soviet forces (seven armies, two air force armies, and a mechanized corps, all supported by the Pacific Fleet) had already advanced deep into Manchukuo and fighting continued even after the Japanese capitulation of 14 August, the *Kwantung Army not surrendering until 20 August. For this campaign Soviet troops used parachute formations on a large scale to occupy the ports of Dairen and Port Arthur to pre-empt an anticipated American landing. In a number of *amphibious warfare operations, which ended with the occupation of the Kurile Islands, southern Sakhalin Island, and North Korea, the Soviet Pacific Fleet played a major role. This theatre of war alone devoured 30,000 Soviet lives (see JAPANESE–SOVIET CAMPAIGNS).

Many Soviet soldiers fought hard and German commanders often commented on their stubbornness, even in hopeless situations. However, this has to be balanced by the extremely high numbers taken prisoner—at least 5.25 million—and commanders and commissars often complained about the unwillingness of their troops to fight on, and they applied draconian measures against such 'defeatism'. For example, in a report to Stalin a high-ranking official complained that in Orel *okrug* (district) only 45,000 out of 110,000 men could be mobilized and that on the way to the front large numbers of the men were often 'lost'. He called for increased political education and commented that there were too few executions. Commanders issued threats frequently, often to whole groups, but, he continued, an example should be made of individuals rather than merely threatening large numbers.

The very high numbers of deserters who went over to the German side (see SOVIET EXILES AT WAR) also raises doubts about the loyalty of many Red Army personnel. Even at the end of 1944, when a Soviet victory was not in doubt, one in every sixteen Soviet *prisoners-of-war was a deserter. The disregard for human life on the part of commanders, the refusal to allow tactical withdrawals that so shattered morale, and the fact that totally untrained troops, the Home Guards (Narodnoe Opolchenie), were frequently dispatched to the front, may explain such a high desertion rate. But it might also be indicative of a widespread disaffection with the political system that developed during the years of collectivization and the purges. The political and military leadership certainly behaved in a way that suggests they were aware of a lack of legitimacy from which their regime might have suffered.

(c) *Navy*

From October 1939 Admiral N. Kuznetsov was both the navy's C-in-C and the people's commissar of the navy. Below him was a Supreme Naval Staff, headed from 1938 by Admiral L. Galler. The Soviet Navy was grouped into four principal fleets: the Pacific Fleet (Admiral I. Iumashev), the Polar Fleet (Rear-Admiral A. Golovko), the Red Banner Baltic Fleet (Vice-Admiral V. Tributs), and the Black Sea Fleet (Vice-Admiral F. Oktiabrsky). There were also a number of river flotillas, the two main ones being the Pinsk River Flotilla, and the Danube River Flotilla. The Caspian Sea Flotilla participated in the Anglo-Soviet invasion of Persia in August 1941 before moving, via the USSR's large river system, to help in the defence of Moscow. There was also the Volga Flotilla, which operated around Stalingrad; the Ladoga Flotilla, which helped defend Leningrad; the sea of Azov Flotilla; and the Dnieper Flotilla, which took part in the fall of Berlin.

The ocean-going fleets had their own war councils and staffs, which commanded warships, coastal artillery, marines and a naval air force. The navy had long been neglected and was seen as purely defensive. In 1938 this changed and a massive construction programme was decided upon. But only very few big units had been completed by the time of BARBAROSSA and the programme became irrelevant. During the course of the war 2 light cruisers, 19 destroyers, 54 submarines, and 900 torpedo-boats, minesweepers, and other small craft, were built, but many of the bigger warships were outdated, they were difficult to operate, and their crews were badly trained. Figures on the Soviet Navy vary: western estimates are somewhat higher than Soviet ones (in brackets) or they have a different definition of warship type. There were 4 (3) battleships, 1 (0) heavy cruiser, 7 medium cruisers, 5 (0) light cruisers, 78 (54) destroyers, more than 200 (212) submarines, 55 (80) minesweepers, 269 (287) torpedo-boats, some minor units, 2,800 aircraft, and 260 coastal batteries. The Baltic Fleet was the strongest. Only the submarine force played any substantial role in the war and major surface units were rarely engaged. The damage inflicted on Axis shipping was small (negligible with respect to warships), and even when the Allied *Arctic convoys were being run the Soviet Navy played hardly any part in protecting them. According to German sources Soviet military forces sank 831,357 tons of shipping, with 272,203 tons being sunk by submarines and only 7,527 tons by surface units.

By the beginning of the war there was a brigade of marines (*Morskaia Pekhota*)—the largest unit employed—within the complement of the Baltic Fleet. After this a number of units totalling some 100,000 men were formed and trained. As a part of the fleets and flotillas they operated with land forces to defend ports and installations. When necessary these soldiers, and very often the sailors, fought as ordinary infantry. Mainly during a later phase of the war the fleets and river flotillas conducted more than 100 amphibious operations in which many thousands of marines took part. Not only the big ocean-going fleets had marines aboad their ships, but also the fleets of much smaller river boats. See also BALTIC SEA and BLACK SEA. Heinz-Dietrich Löwe

(d) *Air Force*

The Red Army Air Force and Long-Range Bomber Aviation were administered by Main Directorates of the people's commissariat for defence, while the Naval Air Forces were administered through a directorate within the people's commissariat for the navy. Operationally, the Red Air Force was subordinated at the outbreak of war to either army or *front* commands, and Naval Air Forces to their respective fleet commands. Long Range Bomber Aviation (DBA, subsequently retitled ADD) was directly subordinate to the Stavka. The largest tactical formation was the air division. Air divisions attached to the *front* commands each consisted of fighter, ground-attack, or bomber aircraft, with a single composite air division of mixed types provided at army level. Each division consisted of from four to six regiments, with fighter regiments made of four squadrons, each of twelve aircraft, and bomber regiments of four squadrons of fifteen aircraft.

The enormous Soviet air losses over the first six months of the war, the defects of the dual army–*front* command system, the unwieldy size of existing air regiments and divisions, and the need for more vigorous leadership, saw changes introduced into the Red Army Air Force in April 1942. General P. Zhigarev was replaced by General A. Novikov (air marshal from 1943 and air chief marshal from 1944) and a new tactical air command, the air army (*vozdushnaya armiya*) introduced. The new air army was a unified command supporting an army group on a designated front. In all, thirteen air armies were created during 1942 and committed to support Soviet *fronts* in the west, with three subsequently formed in the Soviet Far East and a further two in the interior.

As the supply of new aircraft improved after the industrial evacuations of late 1941 (see DOMESTIC LIFE, ECONOMY, AND WAR EFFORT, above) obsolescent I16 and I153 fighters were increasingly replaced by new Yak1, Yak7, LaGG3, and MiG3 machines; the practical and rugged I12 Shturmovik ground attack aircraft was available in greater numbers as was the fast and manoeuvrable Pe2 dive-bomber. With the arrival of these more modern types of aircraft, though still in inadequate numbers, the air regiment was reduced to include, on average, three squadrons of ten aircraft in fighter and ground attack regiments, or three squadrons of nine aircraft in daylight bomber regiments. The remodelled air division now usually comprised two or three air regiments.

An air army consisted, on average, of a command staff, two or three fighter divisions, a Shturmovik division, and one or two night-bomber divisions, equipped with obsolete light bombers or adapted training aircraft, together with reconnaissance and liaison units amounting to some 400 to 500 aircraft. It could, however, be rapidly augmented to meet a strategic contingency with the addition of formations 'loaned' from the Supreme Command Air Reserve. This Air Reserve was developed from special Reserve Air Groups of the State Committee for Defence (GKO) which was formed in the autumn of 1941 to reinforce critical sectors. The Sixteenth Air Army formed to defend Stalingrad in August 1942 began its existence with no more than 300 aircraft, but had been expanded to field 2,183 machines by the opening of the battle which led to the fall of Berlin and was thus numerically superior to what remained of the Luftwaffe. The Air Reserve consisted of air corps, usually of two divisions, and contained most of the day light bomber formations available. It enabled massive concentrations of aircraft to be deployed for major offensives; 2,650 aircraft in three air armies at Kursk in July 1943; 5,700 in four air armies for the Belorussian offensive in June 1944; and 7,200 in three air armies for the fall of Berlin in April 1945. In these huge build-ups of air strength, the Supreme Command Air Reserve contributed, on average, half the aircraft required. By May 1945 twelve fighter corps, eleven Shturmovik corps, seven tactical day light bomber corps, and thirty independent divisions had been formed. Of the 17,000 Soviet Air Force combat aircraft then deployed in eastern Europe, 43% belonged to the Supreme Command Air Reserve.

Novikov, unlike his predecessor, took an active part in operational planning when major offensives were being co-ordinated. Together with his first deputy, General G. Vorozheikin, and his chiefs of air staff, Generals S. Khudyakov and F. Falaleyev, he served as a Stavka representative, closely consulted by front-line commanders and with his professional experience respected and utilized.

Long-Range Bomber Aviation suffered particularly in desperate and often unescorted raids against the advancing Wehrmacht during the first weeks of the war, with such heavy losses of its obsolete TB3 and DB3 bombers that it was soon compelled to fly by night only. In March 1942 the force was reconstituted as Long-Range Bomber Aviation under General (air chief marshal from 1944) A. Golovanov. The main bombardment function of ADD lay in the preliminary night bombing of Axis positions, railheads, and depots as a prelude to major ground offensives or counter-attacks. No less important was the part ADD aircraft played in flying supplies, ammunition, and reinforcements to isolated Soviet ground units or partisans when aircraft previously operated by the Soviet Civil Air Fleet (GVF) were pressed into service. The purely tactical role of Long-Range Bomber Aviation led to its redesignation as Eighteenth Air Army in December 1944. Equipped primarily with twin-engined Il4 bombers and armed Li2 (Soviet-built DC3) transports and with a handful of surviving four-engined TB3 and more modern TB7 bombers, Eighteenth Air Army possessed nine corps with some 1,600 aircraft by January 1945.

While aircraft of the Naval Air Forces were subordinated to the commands of the four Soviet fleets, overall administrative command was in the hands of C-in-C of naval aviation, General S. Zhavoronkov. Equipped primarily with land-based aircraft, Soviet naval air units were used mainly to support the flanks of the land war. Of all operational sorties flown by Soviet naval aircraft during the war, 31% were in air defence, 23% in support of ground forces and 14% for reconnaissance. Less than 10% were flown against Axis vessels or naval bases.

From November 1940 Soviet Air Defence (Protivo-Vozdushnaya Oborona or PVO) was an independent branch of the armed forces and its commander, General N. N. Voronov, was made a deputy people's commissar for defence. A new chief administration for air defence was created within the people's commissariat defence and made responsible for the administration of PVO's anti-aircraft artillery and fighter aviation units, whose role was to defend rear areas from attack. Operational control of the PVO was vested in military district commands, or *fronts*, and in the naval fleets. The PVO, which flew the same types of fighters as the Army Air Force also included the Soviet Union's observer corps. PVO zones of defence were formed with the military district structure and these were divided into regions and specific areas. Particularly important areas such as Moscow and Leningrad were defended by fighter corps. The corps was normally the largest formation except that in 1943 the First Air Defence Fighter Army was formed to defend Moscow.

Luftwaffe bomber raids on Moscow from July 1941 were opposed by 796 76 mm. (3 in.) and 85 mm. (3.3 in.) anti-aircraft guns, and by almost 600 mainly new fighters of 6th PVO Fighter Corps based on airfields guarding the approaches to the capital. Raids on Leningrad were similarly contested, although 7th PVO Fighter Corps defending the city was smaller, had fewer modern fighters, and was restricted by the smaller number of usable airfields available to it. Overall experience indicated, however, that the separation of operational direction into army-controlled A-A artillery and air force controlled fighters was unsatisfactory, and in November 1941 the Chief Administration for Air Defence was replaced by a National Air Defence Command, the Red Army Artillery Command assuming responsibility for front-line air defence.

The new National PVO Command was placed under General M. S. Gromadin as C-in-C with full operational control. Gromadin's deputies, General A. F. Gorokhov and

General I. D. Klimov, headed directorates for anti-aircraft artillery and fighter aviation and were responsible respectively for some 3,300 anti-aircraft guns, 1,500 fighters in 40 air regiments, and some 182,000 men.

In the spring of 1942, the Moscow PVO zone was redesignated the Moscow PVO *front* and air defence armies were formed for Leningrad and Baku. Moscow, however, continued to receive the most—and the best—equipment available. The 102nd PVO Fighter Division confronting the Luftwaffe at Stalingrad in the late summer of 1942 could only field five fighter regiments flown by inexperienced pilots and equipped mainly with obsolescent machines.

Although the Luftwaffe had been slow to mount a campaign of strategic air attacks on Soviet armament factories relocated to the east, a number of bombing raids on key factories at Gorky, Saratov, and Yaroslavl were made in the early summer of 1943. These raids soon petered out as Luftwaffe bombers were switched to tactical targets in preparation for the battle of *Kursk. None the less the threat was taken seriously and Soviet air defence resources were divided between two new *fronts*—a western covering Moscow and the industrial centre, and an eastern covering the Urals, the Volga, and the Caucasus. The Transcaucasus was, in itself, a special air defence zone. However, at this time, the post of C-in-C National Air Defence was abolished and merged with that of C-in-C Red Army Artillery, but the posts of PVO Chief of Air Defence Staff, Commander of PVO Fighter Aviation, Head of PVO Inspectorate, Head of PVO Operational Training and Head of the VNOS were retained.

At the conclusion of the European war in May 1945, the Soviet Air Defence Command covered four *fronts* with a force of some 3,200 fighters and 9,800 medium-calibre anti-aircraft guns. At the close of hostilities in the west it claimed 3,930 aircraft brought down by its fighters and 2,654 by its anti-aircraft guns. ALEXANDER BOYD

(e) Special Forces

Guards

The Red Army did not have guards or élite units before the Second World War. This policy may have been ideologically motivated, as Soviet military theorists stressed the superiority of mass armies over technical armies. When guards units came into being they did so in two different ways, perhaps wedding the concept of the superiority of an army of the masses with that of an élite. Units that had distinguished themselves in battle were honoured with the title 'guard'. This happened first after the battle of *Smolensk on 18 September 1941 when 100th, 127th, 153rd, and 161st Rifle Divisions were renamed 1st, 2nd, 3rd, 4th Guards Rifle Divisions respectively. Technology and professionalism were also reasons for allowing a unit to have the prefix 'guards' and a number of special ones, such as the rocket launcher (*katyusha*) regiments, were given the title as were certain tank units. The title was also awarded to units of the air force and navy. However, guards units did not develop traditions and were not regarded as permanent.

Airborne troops (Vozdusno-Desantnye Vojska, VDV)

The Red Army was the first to experiment with dropping paratroops from aircraft and in April 1941 it began to form five corps which during the first weeks of the war had to be used mainly as infantry. This also happened later, during the battle for Stalingrad and the attacks on Prague and Vienna, but during the battles for *Kiev and Odessa, and on the Kerch peninsula in the Crimea, smaller tactical airborne operations were undertaken. By August 1941 airborne units were taken out of the *fronts* and united under their own independent command. During September 1941 the formation of ten air transport squadrons began, which were later transformed into two glider and two air transport regiments. Corps formations of three brigades, one tank battalion, an artillery division, and air transport capacity came into being around the turn of the year 1941–2.

At the end of 1942 airborne corps were regrouped into divisions, but in the summer of 1943 these were supplanted by 20 guards airborne brigades. Parachutists and airborne troops were rarely used behind enemy lines in major operations. However, for crossing the Dnieper on the Voronezh front airborne operations were of great importance in 1943; here three brigades were again united into a corps. In October 1944 most VDV units were brought together into a Guards Airborne Army and in January 1945 this became part of Ninth Guards Army. Units of the VDV also played an important role in the rout of the Japanese *Kwantung Army in August 1945.

Cavalry

The Red Army before the war still believed in the operational and strategic capabilities of the cavalry, although between the Finnish–Soviet war and BARBAROSSA this emphasis had been criticized. At the beginning of the war there were thirteen divisions organized into four cavalry corps. A division was equipped with 64 light tanks, 18 armoured cars, and a variety of small artillery units. By the end of 1941 the number of divisions had grown to 82, with a division on paper being more than 9,000 men strong (in reality about 6,000). Because of their high vulnerability these forces were reduced to 26 divisions or 8 corps in 1943, after which they were mainly used for diversionary tactics behind German lines, for attacking any retreating forces, and for mopping up dispersed German units in sudden advances. A short-lived attempt to form a force combining cavalry and a mechanized corps was not successful, but cavalry played a role in defeating the Kwantung Army in August 1945. HEINZ-DIETRICH LÖWE

7. Intelligence

The operation of intelligence is always two-fold: the gathering of information and its interpretation. Also, a distinction has to be made between military intelligence and political and economic intelligence. Of course, Soviet intelligence was not only collected on Germany, but also on Allied countries (see SPIES).

Economic intelligence was collected from many sources and Soviet organizations were extremely successful where political intelligence was concerned. For example, the *GRU, the Red Army's espionage organization headed by General Golikov, collected highly reliable information on Hitler's intentions before the Nazi–Soviet pact was signed in August 1939. It was divulged by the German General *Kleist during a visit to Warsaw and amounted to firsthand accounts of Hitler's conversations with *Ribbentrop and an eastern specialist, Peter Kleist. In them Hitler disclosed his intention of conquering Poland and then defeating France and the UK in the unavoidable war that was to follow; only then would he attack the Soviet Union.

The GRU had an extensive espionage network in Europe. Called the *Rote Kapelle (Red Orchestra) by the Germans, its cell in Switzerland, known as the *Rote Drei, was particularly effective as it obtained high-level intelligence from the *LUCY Ring. In 1943 one of the Ring's sources disclosed the strategic direction of the German offensive (CITADEL) at the Kursk salient; and until the autumn of 1943, the same source passed other top secret information—including the daily *Lageorientierung* (situation reports)—which was transmitted to the USSR. However, other networks, which had been established in Belgium, France, Germany, and the Netherlands, were quite quickly tracked down by the *Abwehr and Sicherheitsdienst (see RSHA), and eliminated.

The GRU also received abundant reports about German troop concentrations on the Eastern Front. On 15 June 1941 a GRU agent in Tokyo Richard Sorge, reported the precise date that BARBAROSSA would be launched. But Stalin distrusted agents' reports, and it was even dangerous to disclose such information to him. This innate suspicion of any intelligence which stemmed from the opposing side was characteristic of the Soviets during the war—it was one their Allies largely shared (but not the Germans: see XX-COMMITTEE), except where *ULTRA was concerned—and even the LUCY Ring's 'Werther', whose information had proved consistently accurate, was ignored over CITADEL. Even after a German aircraft with detailed plans of CITADEL abroad fell into Soviet hands, the Red Army preferred to rely on its own reconnaissance.

Soviet battlefield intelligence was very poor in the beginning, as air force losses and German air superiority rendered *photographic reconnaissance flights practically impossible. The Soviet side could not even gain a clear picture of the strategic thrust of the German attack. This proved disastrous when, after the first phase of war, Hitler redirected *Guderian's Panzer Army towards the Ukraine. Stalin refused to trust the patchy findings of army intelligence or to heed Zhukov's advice to take the necessary precautions against such a move. When the first major Soviet offensive around Kalinin succeeded in January 1942, the Soviet High Command did not see how well they had done and were not therefore able to exploit their operational advance fully. Similarly, in 1942, offensives were conducted on almost the whole front because German weak spots could not be detected in advance. The defeat at *Kharkov in May 1942 must partly be explained by lack of intelligence because the Stavka had expected another attack on Moscow.

By the middle of 1942 the situation had begun to improve and Stavka correctly predicted the impending attack on Stalingrad. Both 'Werther' and British intelligence, based on ULTRA, had also predicted this offensive, but Soviet operational decisions were based only on information from the battlefield. It was then that photographic reconnaissance came into its own and 10% of all flights were now devoted to it (later this proportion rose to 40%). Another important factor in assessment of intelligence before Stalingrad was that Soviet traffic analysis (see SIGNALS INTELLIGENCE WARFARE) had now reached a stage where the Soviet side could, for the first time, study the disposition of the German forces and pin-point the Romanian troops, who were regarded as inferior and therefore vulnerable. This was of critical value for the Soviet counter-offensive which destroyed not only the Romanian forces but the Sixth German Army as well.

During 1943 the Soviets fully developed their system of battlefield intelligence through reconnaissance in force (small units sent behind German lines) in co-operation with the partisan movement, radio interception, and the pin-pointing of German field headquarters and units through traffic analysis and photo reconnaissance. In addition to the normal military intelligence units—which were formed down to the regimental level and whose information was collated by the intelligence staff of the various *fronts*—special artillery intelligence and engineer intelligence units were formed, the former to target German positions accurately, the latter to predetermine the most promising axes of attack. Special counter-espionage units (see SMERSH) were also organized from the old Osobye Otdely (OO, or Special Departments) of the NKVD, and put under the commissariat for defence.

The first time that Soviet battlefield intelligence worked satisfactorily was during CITADEL, though the Soviet High Command still covered all possible advance routes, and from then on intelligence played an important and increasing role. In the battles on the River Vistula the Soviet command was able to pinpoint the location of German reserves and it also became highly accomplished at hiding its own intentions and deployment (see DECEPTION). HEINZ-DIETRICH LÖWE

8. Resistance

Partisan warfare was not prepared in any significant way. The first steps to organize diversionary actions directed against German installations and the advancing Wehrmacht were taken by the Central Committee of the Belorussian Communist Party, and for most of the war its

USSR: Young Soviet partisans being hanged at Minsk, 1941.

head, P. K. Ponomarenko, commanded the movement. Initially, partisans—often Soviet regulars encircled or left behind the front—were soon cut off because of the moving front line and were faced with unsuitable terrain and the hostility of local populations. As 50% of all partisans were party or Komsomol members (that is, party officials and NKVD personnel ordered to stay behind) they had the additional disadvantage of being part of the regime and were regarded as aliens by the rural populations among whom they had to operate. In certain areas, such as the western Ukraine, they were completely wiped out because of the hostility of the inhabitants. Elsewhere, as in the steppes and particularly in the Crimea, they found it extremely difficult to operate for the whole period of German occupation. The harsh climate did not favour them, either. The terrain, the hostility of the population, and their reliance on air support, also forced partisans to operate in large groups.

What made partisan warfare particularly brutal was that neither of the opposing sides paid much attention to the needs of local people. Nor were they constrained by considerations of humanity or morality. However, the movement was strengthened in the early months by the way Soviet prisoners-of-war (POW) were treated and this motivated many encircled Red Army soldiers to hide or fight on. For a while many settled down and formed relationships with local women. An example of relatively successful partisan activity during this first phase was the area around the cities of Yelnia and Dorogobuzh, east of Smolensk, where it was mostly undertaken by Red Army stragglers. But because these partisans were not trained in irregular warfare, the Wehrmacht found it relatively easy to wipe them out to prevent a resurgence of activity.

In the second phase, which lasted until the end of 1942, surviving elements of the Political Administration of the Red Army (PURKKA) managed to bring the roaming forces under their control. PURKKA personnel were also reinforced by trained party, Komsomol, and NKVD personnel brought in by air or through the German lines. This, and the continued existence of a dual command structure of commanders and commissars in the partisan forces, points to Stalin's overriding intention to demonstrate that Soviet power could not be permanently excluded from occupied areas. During this time the partisan movement developed a rather varied command structure which, however, bound the majority to higher echelons and to the underground party organizations.

In a third phase partisans undertook military activities to disrupt German communications. Considering the relatively large numbers of partisans involved, and the resources made available to them, the effect remained small. After the victory at Stalingrad partisans began to penetrate from the Briansk region, where they were strong around the fringes of the Pripet marshes, and they hampered German communications considerably during the battle of Kursk. They also infiltrated into the woods and swamps towards the River Dnieper, and into the forests of the northern Ukraine, which, up to then, had been free of them. However, they were loath to move south. Those who did faced extinction, for the Ukrainians did not welcome their presence. But the fact that the Germans had preserved the collective farms had angered the peasantry, and the growing likelihood of a German victory—and brutal German repression—induced many to turn to the partisans.

Before and during the Red Army's Belorussian campaign in 1944 partisans were used successfully to disrupt German communications. None the less, their impact was limited. Altogether 400–500,000 (German estimates) to 700,000 fighters were involved (one million according to Soviet sources), but they never exceeded 250,000 at any one time and only tied down a similar number of Axis forces. The losses they inflicted probably did not exceed 35,000. An important element of partisan activities was the gathering of intelligence. Although local populations, under the impact of the German regime, became more favourably inclined over time, partisans never received their full support. They had to force compliance and right up until the end of the war deserters turned bandits roamed the woods, refusing to come out in support of either side. The commissar system reflected the distrust the regime felt towards its partisans. Overall direction of the partisan forces rested with a special branch of the NKVD and from July 1941 onwards with PURKKA. HEINZ-DIETRICH LÖWE

9. Merchant marine

The Soviet merchant fleet did not have the same vital role to play as merchant ships elsewhere. In 1939, according to one source (J. Meister, *The Navy*, October 1957, pp. 32–4), 716 merchant ships totalling 1,300,000 tons were registered in the USSR, and another 200,000 tons fell into Soviet hands when the Baltic states were absorbed in 1940. About 36% of the carrying capacity of this shipping was employed in the Caspian Sea, 25% in the Baltic, 24% in the Black Sea, 8% in the Far East, and 6% in the Arctic. Losses during the war amounted to 500,000 tons but the Soviet merchant fleet received more than this tonnage in Lend-Lease, including a number of *Liberty ships, and after the war it acquired ships from Germany, Finland, Romania, and Bulgaria.

More important during the German–Soviet war was the USSR's inland fleet of small vessels and barges which worked on the country's large lakes and numerous navigable rivers. In 1936 this fleet comprised nearly 10,000 small self-propelled vessels and barges, 80% of which were lost during the war. When the railway network was interrupted, or stretched to its limits, the merchant flotilla on the Caspian Sea and on the River Volga had a vital role in transporting oil from the Caucasus to the north, or to the army. The volume of this traffic is difficult to gauge, but it can safely be said that without it the Red Army might have been immobilized at times.

HEINZ-DIETRICH LÖWE

10. Culture

Soviet writers and poets were active from the onset of the German–Soviet war, the 'holy war' as they called it. Almost all of them—more than a thousand—became *war correspondents and went to the front and reported back in a concerted effort to strengthen the will to resist, and 417 of them lost their lives in doing so. They also took part in organizing and writing (not only in Russian) newspapers produced at the front for the soldiers, and, to boost morale, they held innumerable meetings with soldiers where they read from their work.

These wartime activities were organized by Alexander Fadeev who, with Maxim Gorky (1868–1936), had founded and run the Soviet Union of Writers. Alexei Surkov's poem 'We swear Victory' appeared the day after the Germans attacked, and on the day after that the poem 'Holy War' by Lebedev-Kumach (the pen name of V. I. Lebedev) was published. Set to music, it became the battle hymn of the Soviet people.

Many songs and poems were written that expressed the patriotic mood and showed its virulent loathing of the invader. 'The Song of the Avengers', whose first public performance was given in Moscow's Hall of Columns, became one of the most popular partisan songs. Mikhail Sholokhov wrote 'A School of Hatred' (published in 1942, and in English the same year), Aleksei Surkov the poem 'I Hate', and Konstantin Simonov—whose play *The Russian People* was published in *Pravda* and performed countrywide and at the front—wrote the poem 'Kill Him'.

Well-known writers also participated in propaganda and what they wrote was widely read. A. N. Tolstoy, for example, produced such articles and sketches as 'what we defend', 'The motherland', and 'Shame is worse than death'; while with others—'The Russian Character', 'Russian warriors', 'To all Slavs'—he described the main sources of Soviet heroism as being the Russian heritage. The cruelties and crimes of the enemy were also, of course, a major topic.

In spite of the coarsening of tastes some great pieces of art were created. Alexander Tvardovsky's poem, 'Vasilii Terkin' was one example. The first serious attempt at depicting the war realistically in high literary form was V. S. Grossman's collection of short stories called *The Immortal People* (1942, translated into English in 1946 as *The Years of the War*). Ilya Ehrenburg's novel *The Fall of Paris* received the Stalin prize in 1942, and Simonov's *No Quarter* and *Days and Nights*, both published in 1943, were received with acclaim. But the efforts of these writers to portray the war realistically were often thwarted and brought heavy criticism upon them after the war.

Officially prescribed glorification of the war posed a tricky problem for the authorities, because millions had experienced the unbearable hardships and the follies of the military and civil authorities. The post-war debate on how it should be presented seems to have been undecided for some time. In 1946, F. Panferov, editor of the journal *October*, who had himself written a trilogy on the 'heroes of the home front', wrote a ringing condemnation of the literary bureaucracy and its attempts to suppress the realities of war. Panferov wrote that Soviet writers had been told to forget the negative aspects of the war. 'Forget how? It is possible to forget that the Germans were at Stalingrad, at Mozdok, at Moscow? How is it possible to forget the burdens our people shouldered during the war? Indeed, sometimes our shoulders cracked under these burdens.' He went on to mock the way officials wanted to see the war pictured: 'the workers arrived in the Urals and immediately settled into the best cottages; pork chops were immediately placed on their tables; they went at once into warm shops, immediately found what they wanted, and began at once to "fulfil and overfulfil". But, Panferov continued, the Soviet reader was not stupid. He was not a non-participant 'like you crocks and potsherds. He was at the *front*, he retreated, attacked, and he lived through terrors and joy' (quoted in M. Gallagher *The Soviet History of World War II, Myths, Memories and Realities*, New York, 1963, p. 109 f).

Fadeev's novel *The Young Guard* (1945), which depicted the true experience of a partisan group, was attacked in November 1947 for not giving a prominent enough role to the party. This was understood, and meant, to be a directive to writers. Immediately afterwards Alexander Tvardovsky's *Motherland and Foreignland: Pages from a Notebook* was severely criticized for 'pacifism'. At a public discussion many writers courageously defended the work, and honest accounts of the wartime experience found support from highly placed military leaders, partisan heroes, and writers of letters to the press. Panferov and Tvardovsky did not—yet—lose their positions. None the less, for a while it became very difficult for writers to present their views artistically. During the thaw of 1955–6 new accounts appeared, and writers or poets such as Simonov and Surkin recorded their ordeal of being prevented from writing the truth.

In spite of the restrictions placed upon it, literature provided for a long time the only outlet for an honest rendering of the war. Tvardovsky's poems, published in 1946, expressed eloquently and poetically the human sufferings and the feelings of those who had lost a loved one, and in 1956 Sholokhov published *The Destiny of Man*. But Simonov's literary account of the battle of Stalingrad, *Days and Nights*, which was published in 1943 (in English in 1945) probably became, because of its realism, one of the most widely read books of the Second World War.

Film directors were also fully integrated into the war effort. Their most common form of work was propaganda films, clearly intended to boost morale, and a kind of documentary which had of course, the same aim. But the documentaries did give some information and tried to convey the heroism of the front to the home audiences. The first films of this type, with titles like *All Efforts for the Smashing of the Enemy* and *In the Defence of our Moscow*, were released at the end of 1941, and others, such as *The Smashing of the German Forces at Moscow*, *Leningrad at War*, and *Stalingrad* followed.

Many feature films used the heroic exploits of the Red Army during the civil war as a subject to mirror their current bravery. *The Defence of Tsaritsyn* (the previous name of Stalingrad) was one example of this genre, and the great historic military figure, Kutuzov, also became the subject of a film of that name. Films appealing to the feelings of certain national minorities, such as the Ukrainians, the Armenians, and Georgians, also played some role; while others, which could claim some artistic merit, were based on wartime productions of Russian and Soviet writers. For instance, *Raduga*, about the Soviet resistance against fascist occupation, was based on V. L. Vasilevskaya's novel of the same name, and *Wait for Me* was based on Simonov's writings. Even satirical films were produced in considerable numbers—one described the further exploits of the Good Soldier Schweik—but the greatest artistic achievement of the war years in film-making was, without doubt, the first part of Eisenstein's *Ivan the Terrible* which was produced in 1945.

The war also saw the creation of important music. Shostakovich's Seventh (Leningrad) Symphony, written in the besieged city of Leningrad, was first performed in Kuibyshev on 5 March 1942 and in Leningrad, under K. I. Eliasberg, on 9 August. It became a symbol of the will of the Soviet people to hold out under the most severe circumstances and it was immediately performed, with great success, in the West (in London first, on 22 June 1942, and in the USA, under Arturo Toscanini, on 19 August, as a sign of Allied solidarity. His Eighth and Ninth symphonies were also dedicated to wartime themes and proved very successful.

During the first months of the war Serge Prokofiev wrote his symphonic suite 'The year 1941', and later his Fifth Symphony, as did Aram Khatchaturian his Second. Also very topical was Prokofiev's monumental opera *War and Peace*, based on Tolstoy's famous novel. Dimitri Kabalevsky produced his cantata *The Great Motherland*, and a suite for choir and orchestra, *The People's Avengers*, in 1942, and his opera *Under Fire*, in 1943, a setting of the words of the poet E. A. Dolmatovsky and others. A number of lesser works were also composed, many of which imitated the cantata or oratorio style, which can seem somewhat embarrassing today in their vulgar plagiarization of religious styles.

Musical life continued not only in the big cities, even in Leningrad, but also for the soldiers at the front and in the rear. Tens of thousands of artists gave hundreds of thousands of concerts, which, must, of course, have included a large majority of concerts of more 'popular' music. These popular songs—still largely compositions by professional musicians who often put to music the words of their writing colleagues—played a major propaganda role and were regarded as a spiritual weapon in the fight against *fascism.

Soviet war art was necessarily tied to official propaganda. Before the war reached Soviet territory, years of discipline had accustomed Soviet artists to painting in a style called Socialist Realism (remarkably similar to the realist paintings then fashionable in Nazi Germany and fascist Italy). It was not hard to apply the same sorts of principles to pictures of soldiers, sailors, and weapons as had earlier been applied to proletarians, tractors and factories.

The horrors and tensions of war heightened the effects artists might obtain; several remarkable pictures resulted, such as Anatoley Smirnov's 'The Last Stop' of machine-gunners who have taken a Leningrad tram to the edge of their battlefield, or Mikhail Savitsky's 'The Partisan Madonna' of a young peasant woman feeding her baby while older women reap corn under militia guard in the background.

Artists were not exempt from call-up; lucky ones had notebooks with them at the front, and could make pencil sketches at least, which they could work up on to larger canvases at the end of the war, if they survived it—or much later. Yuri Neprintsev's popular 'Resting after Battle' was not painted until 1955; Savitsky's 'Partisan Madonna' not until 1967; and Tatiana Nazarenko, not born till 1944, did not paint her 'The Partisans have come', a deposition scene deliberately reminiscent of much religious art, till 1973. This was not the sort of war art as reportage that was being produced in western Europe in 1940–5. The war, in short, provided subject-matter for post-war Soviet painting rather more than it provided subject-matter for paintings done and reproduced at the time.

Similarly, sculptors were no more exempt from call-up than were graphic artists; but when their war service was done, there was plenty of work waiting for them in the design and carving of war memorials. Vast chunks of stone and marble were distributed, under communist party guidance, all over Soviet-occupied eastern Europe as well as within the USSR, as permanent reminders of the sacrifices made by the Red Army in order to free these territories from Nazi occupation. Such sculptors as Daniel Mitylanski (born 1924), with several years' fighting experience of their own and many dead friends, were well placed to design and carve these memorials; of which the artistic merits hardly came into question, compared with the importance the party attached to their lasting value as propaganda.

HEINZ-DIETRICH LÖWE
M. R. D. FOOT

Armstrong, J. A. (ed.), *Soviet Partisans in World War II* (Madison, Wis., 1964).
Boyd, A., *The Soviet Air Force* (London, 1977).
Conner, A. Z., and Poirier, R. G., *The Red Army Order of Battle in the Great Patriotic War* (Presidio, Calif., 1985).
Conquest, R., *Nations Killed. The Soviet Deportation of Nationalities*, (London, 1970).
Dallin, A., *German Rule in Russia, 1941–1945. A Study of Occupation Policies* (2nd edn., London, 1981).
Glantz, D. M., *Soviet Military Intelligence in War* (London, 1990).
Harrison, M., *Soviet Planning in Peace and War* (Cambridge, 1985).
Herring, G. C., *Aid to Russia: Strategy, Diplomacy, the Origins of the Cold War* (New York, 1973).
Linz, S. J. (ed.), *The Impact of World War II on the Soviet Union* (Princeton, 1985).
Moscoff, W., *The Bread of Affliction: Food Supply in the USSR during World War II* (Cambridge, 1990).
Voznesensky, N. A., *The War Economy of the USSR in the Period of the Great Patriotic War* (Moscow, 1948).
Werth, A., *Russia at War 1941–1945* 2 vols (London, 1964).

UTAH, code name for assault beach in American sector on which the 4th US Division landed at the start of the Normandy landings on 6 June 1944 (see OVERLORD). It lay along the eastern coast of the Cherbourg peninsula northwards from the mouth of the River Vire in the Baie de la Seine and the division landed south of Les Dunes de Varreville. By the end of the day 23,250 troops had disembarked there.

UXB stood for unexploded bomb.

V

Vaagso raid, mounted by British and Norwegian commandos on 27 December 1941 against these German-occupied islands at the entrance to Nordfjord, central Norway. It was a pinprick operation designed to prevent German troops being moved to the Eastern Front to take part in the *German–Soviet war, and was an early British effort in *Combined Operations and *amphibious warfare. German military installations were wrecked while the Royal Navy neutralized nearby batteries. A diversionary raid was carried out at the same time against the *Lofoten Islands.

VAD (Voluntary Aid Detachment), British nursing organization which functioned in both world wars.

Vasilevsky, Marshal Aleksandr (1895–1977), Red Army officer who, although he was among the foremost in ability, was one of the least celebrated Soviet marshals. This was probably because his education for the priesthood, service as an officer in the tsarist army, and belated entry into the Communist Party (in 1938) did not fit the preferred image. He may himself have considered a certain obscurity advisable.

The *German–Soviet war accelerated his career. A colonel with twenty years' service transferred into the general staff in 1938, he became its chief and a member of the *Stavka, in May 1942. Four months later Stalin, his faith in his own military genius badly shaken, gave *Zhukov and Vasilevsky a free hand in planning and managing a Soviet winter offensive. The results were the victory at *Stalingrad, recovery of the Caucasus, and a German retreat to the line from which they had started their summer campaign. Vasilevsky, who was at the front throughout the winter, received a two-step promotion to Marshal of the Soviet Union in February 1943. Thereafter, although he retained the title until early 1945, he did not resume the duties of chief of the general staff. Zhukov, distinctly abrasive, and Vasilevsky, somewhat benign, both highly competent, had given Stalin what he sorely needed: a team capable of handling operations equalling in scale those the German field marshals had conducted.

The collaboration continued in the battle of *Kursk and the 1943 summer offensive, which evolved into winter and spring offensives in 1944 during which Vasilevsky co-ordinated Third and Fourth Ukrainian *fronts* (army groups) in the advance from the lower *Dnieper to the Dniester and Prut rivers. In June and July 1944, after organizing it, he and Zhukov co-ordinated *fronts* in the operation that destroyed Army Group Centre, the strongest German Army Group.

The subsequent course of his *fronts*—Third Belorussian and First and Second Baltic—took him off the direct line of approach to Germany and towards east Prussia, Lithuania, and Latvia, which no longer figured significantly in the military outcome of the war but were extremely important to Stalin. Until February 1945, Vasilevsky co-ordinated the *fronts* on the north flank, and thereafter, until May, he commanded Third Baltic *front*. From 9 August to 2 September, as C-in-C of Soviet Far Eastern Forces he conducted operations against the *Kwantung Army in Manchukuo.

EARL ZIEMKE

Vatican City, the independent neutral Catholic state in Rome, whose sovereign ruler is the pope. It was established under the terms of the Lateran treaty concluded in February 1929 between Mussolini and Pope Pius XI. His wartime successor *Pius XII adopted a policy of keeping open diplomatic channels with all the belligerents, maintaining a strictly non-partisan stance that infuriated the envoys of both sides. Inevitably, the Vatican was the centre of much diplomatic lobbying and intrigue: it was used by members of the German resistance against Hitler to channel some of their messages to the Allies (see X-REPORT). After the fall of Mussolini, the independence of the Vatican itself was at risk: in July 1943 Hitler seriously considered occupying it and was only dissuaded by *Ribbentrop and *Goebbels. Vatican property provided refuge for numbers of Jews, *refugees, and Allied *prisoners-of-war after Italy's surrender in September 1943. In 1944 right-wing priests in the Vatican began, unofficially, to establish escape lines, or ratlines as they were called, for Nazis and their collaborators. This organization, obsessively anti-communist, was itself deeply penetrated by Soviet intelligence. See also DIPLOMACY.

Aarons, M., and Loftus, J., *Ratlines* (London, 1991).
Chadwick, O., *Britain and the Vatican during the Second World War* (Cambridge, 1986).

V-E Day, 8 May 1945, the day victory in Europe was celebrated in Allied countries.

Vella Lavella, battle of. US troops landed on this Pacific island on 15 August 1943 during the *New Georgia campaign to try to bypass and isolate a strong Japanese garrison on nearby *Kolombangara Island. On 18 September the 3rd New Zealand Division replaced the Americans and began attacking 600 Japanese who had recently landed on the island. But control of the island was mostly disputed in the air—the Japanese mounted 108 raids in the first month—and at sea where the campaign's last action, known as the battle of Vella Lavella, took place on the night of 6/7 October. Both sides lost a destroyer when the Americans, who also had two destroyers damaged, failed to prevent the Japanese on the island being evacuated.

Vemork raid, British operation (FRESHMAN) mounted in November 1942 to try to sabotage a Norwegian hydro-electric plant at Rjukan that was producing the only heavy water available for Germany's *atomic bomb programme. It was undertaken by 34 British engineers who were to be flown into the area in two gliders where they were to be met by local *SOE agents. It was the first time the British had used gliders operationally; one of the towing aircraft and both gliders crashed, and the 20 survivors were, under Hitler's *Commando Order, executed by the local *Gestapo. In February 1943 six Norwegian SOE agents under Lt Joachim Rönneberg parachuted into Norway and, in what the C-in-C of German forces there thought the best coup he had ever seen, sabotaged the plant. This, plus an air raid, prompted the Germans to try to transfer the heavy water and equipment to Germany in February 1944, but a ferry transporting it across Lake Tinnsjoe was sabotaged by SOE and sunk. By this time the Germans had abandoned the search for an atomic bomb.

Haukelid, K., *Skis against the Atom* (London, 1954).
Wiggan, R., *Operation Freshman* (London, 1986).

Venezuela remained strictly neutral until the USA entered the war in December 1941 when it took a pro-Allied stance by severing relations with the main Axis powers. Operations by U-boats in the Caribbean swung public opinion against Germany, and badly inhibited the country's trade. But once a proper system of *convoys had overcome this problem Venezuela flourished, and its oil—of which it was then the world's greatest exporter and which was mostly refined on the nearby Dutch West Indies island of Aruba—was of crucial importance to the Allied war effort (see also RAW AND SYNTHETIC MATERIALS). In February 1945, Venezuela declared war on Germany and Japan, and signed the *United Nations Declaration. See also CARIBBEAN AT WAR.

Venlo incident, German counter-intelligence operation in the Netherlands which resulted in the kidnapping of two British *MI6 officers on the Dutch–German border in November 1939.

By the beginning of the war the MI6 network in the Netherlands had been penetrated by a *V-man of the Nazi security service, the Sicherheitsdienst or SD (see RSHA). This enabled the SD to dupe one of the network's officers, Captain Sigismund Payne Best, into believing that a group of conspirators against Hitler wished to negotiate peace. Best reported his meeting to London and *Chamberlain, the prime minister, was among those who believed the contacts were genuine. At a subsequent meeting the head of the SD's counter-espionage section, Walter *Schellenberg, posing as a conspirator called 'Major Schaemmel', requested British peace terms. When, on 31 October 1939, the British cabinet learned about these negotiations, some—especially Churchill—objected strongly, which delayed an agreed reply until 6 November. Schellenberg then chose a café between the Dutch and German customs barriers near Venlo to receive the reply, and during a third meeting there, on 9 November, Best and another MI6 officer, Major Richard Stevens, were kidnapped and a Dutch intelligence officer was killed.

Until *Himmler chose to reveal what had happened, on 22 November, the British remained mystified as the 'conspirators' continued to communicate with MI6 in The Hague. The Germans then scored a propaganda success by accusing Best and Stevens of plotting Hitler's demise; and one of the reasons they gave for invading the Netherlands in May 1940 was the collusion of Dutch military intelligence with the British.

Payne and Best were sent to *concentration camps. They survived the war but the information one of them revealed under interrogation severely compromised other European MI6 networks. The only grain of comfort the British subsequently gained from the incident was that Schellenberg missed a valuable opportunity to establish the kind of double-cross system later employed in **Englandspiel* and by the *XX-committee.

Kessler, L., *Betrayal at Venlo* (London, 1991).

Vercors. This 900 m. (3,000 ft.) plateau, 48 km. (30 mi.) long by 19 km. (12 mi.) wide, is situated south-west of Grenoble in France. It is screened by a formidable rock barrier and the Free French wanted to make it a *National Redoubt, an impenetrable fortress for the *Maquis gathering there, to give them a safe base from which to harass German supply routes after the *French Riviera landings of August 1944. The local maquis leaders, expecting a plan of flying in reinforcements and heavy weapons to be implemented immediately after the Normandy landings (see OVERLORD), closed the passes into the Vercors on 10 June 1944, flew a tricolour from the heights in full view of the Germans at Grenoble, and created a Free Republic of the Vercors. But large-scale reinforcements for the 3,500 lightly-armed maquis never arrived, though supplies were dropped and both *SOE and the *Office of Strategic Services sent missions. Fighting escalated with German patrols and the local *Milice until, on 19 July, the Germans launched a full-scale attack on the plateau with 10,000 men. Three days later 200 *SS troops landed there in gliders, forcing the surviving maquis to disperse and hide. In overrunning the area the Germans committed many *atrocities.

Pearson, M., *Tears of Glory* (London, 1978).

VERITABLE, codename for an operation carried out by *Crerar's First Canadian Army, with the British 30th Corps under command, to clear the Germans from east of Nijmegen in the Netherlands south-east to the Lower Rhine in preparation for the *Rhine crossings. After a preliminary operation (BLACKCOCK) in mid-January 1945 to clear the Roermond triangle, VERITABLE opened on 8 February 1945 with the largest artillery barrage (from 1,050 guns) so far laid down during the campaign in north-west Europe. This helped the four assaulting divisions to break through the first line of German defences on the first day, with the second, which represented part of the *Siegfried Line, being breached the following day. The attacking troops reached the

Rhine at Emmerich, east of Nijmegen, on 13 February, but, in the face of poor weather and tenacious resistance by the German First Parachute Army, clearance of the area to the south (codenamed BLOCKBUSTER) was slow, with fierce fighting, especially in the *Reichswald. Not until the Ninth US Army's *GRENADE operation, a thrust from the south designed to join hands with VERITABLE, began to make progress did the Germans begin to withdraw across the Rhine. The completion of this on 9 March marked the conclusion of VERITABLE. It cost *Montgomery's Twenty-First Army Group 15,000 casualties; the Germans lost 70,000.

CHARLES MESSENGER

Verona trials, special tribunal set up, at Hitler's insistence, in Mussolini's Italian Social Republic (see ITALY, 3(b)) to try those who had forced the Duce's resignation by voting against him in the Fascist Grand Council in July 1943. The tribunal was established by a decree which Mussolini issued on 24 November 1943 and the trial of the nineteen accused was held from 8 to 10 January 1944. Only six appeared in court: Marshal Emilio De Bono, Count *Ciano, Tullio Cianetti, Giovanni Marinelli, Luciano Gottardi, and Carlo Pareschi. The others were tried *in absentia* and all were sentenced to death. Of the six who appeared in court only Cianetti, the minister of corporations, was reprieved because the day after Mussolini had been defeated in the Grand Council, Cianetti had withdrawn his vote against him. Instead, he was given a sentence of 30 years' imprisonment.

Versailles settlement. The armistice of 11 November 1918 that ended the *First World War led to a peace congress in Paris at which the French, British, and American delegations, assisted by a myriad of diplomats from other allied powers, worked out a new map of Europe and, under pressure from the American President Woodrow Wilson (1856–1924), the structure of a new international organization, the *League of Nations, designed to prevent future world wars. Revolutionary Russia was not invited; nor did its leaders wish to be present. German delegates were summoned in May 1919 to receive the final text of a treaty that was signed at Versailles on 28 June 1919. Germany meanwhile remained under strict blockade, and its people suffered from hunger.

The treaty's opening clauses constituted the covenant of the League. Germany's boundaries were revised, to the benefit of most of its neighbours: France retook *Alsace and Lorraine, Belgium and Denmark took some frontier districts, and newly independent Poland secured the free and secure access to the sea guaranteed to her by one of Wilson's Fourteen Points (of January 1918), to which Germany had agreed at the armistice (see DANZIG). This access, through the *Polish corridor, separated east Prussia from the rest of Germany and was particularly resented. So were the clauses which severely restricted German armaments, and the one which affirmed German guilt for the outbreak of war in 1914.

Under the treaty, Germany accepted the principle of paying reparation for war damage inflicted on Belgium and France; the details, left to be worked out later, were never satisfactorily settled, and remained a focus for international resentment.

Separate treaties handled the affairs of Austria (Saint-Germain, 10 December 1919) and Hungary (Trianon, 4 June 1920) as well as Bulgaria (Neuilly, 24 November 1919). Austria and Hungary were separated, and the new states of Czechoslovakia and Yugoslavia were created from the defunct Austro-Hungarian Empire; Romania also secured large gains of territory at Hungary's and some at Bulgaria's expense. A treaty signed with Turkey at Spa in August 1920 was repudiated by the regime of Kemal Atatürk (1881–1938); a fresh settlement was eventually reached at Lausanne in 1923, after a Greco-Turkish war.

Hitler repudiated the settlement in March 1935. However, that June he did come to an arrangement with the UK under the Anglo-German Naval Treaty which allowed Germany to construct up to 35% of the Royal Navy's tonnage and which, under certain circumstances, allowed the German Navy a submarine fleet of equal size. In April 1939 Hitler repudiated this treaty, too. See also DIPLOMACY and ORIGINS OF THE WAR.

M. R. D. FOOT

V-Force, British guerrilla organization formed by the C-in-C India, General *Wavell, in April 1942, to attack Japanese lines of communication should the Japanese invade Assam during the *Burma campaign. It was built around units loaned from the Assam Rifles, which were supplemented by 1,000 Burmese hill tribesmen, and each of its six groups was responsible for an area that bordered India and Burma. When the Japanese attack did not materialize it operated intelligence-gathering patrols which were especially useful in collecting information of short-term tactical value. Z-force patrols were much smaller and were used to gather intelligence much deeper inside Japanese-held territory.

v-girls were very young American girls—some only twelve—who hung around US base camps and recreational areas in the USA to proposition, or be picked up by, US servicemen. The 'v' stood for victory.

Vichy was the name given to Marshal *Pétain's French collaborationist regime whose government was based in the city of that name. See FRANCE 3(c).

Victor Emmanuel III (1869–1947), king of Italy from 1900 to 1946 (also emperor of Abyssinia from 1936 and king of Albania from 1939) who acquiesced in Mussolini's takeover of the state in 1922. With the war obviously lost he had already arranged for Mussolini's arrest when the Grand Fascist Council voted, on 25 July 1943, to restrict the Duce's powers, and he then appointed *Badoglio prime minister. 'With the disappearance of Mussolini the king was truly in command for the first time in his reign' (D. Mack Smith, *Italy and its Monarchy*, London, 1989, p. 306), but in the weeks of hesitation that followed he emerged with little credit; and when the *armistice with the Allies was announced on 8 September 1943 he was forced to flee Rome before the Germans occupied it. With Allied support, he and his government were established in Brindisi (he later moved to Ravello and the government to Salerno), where it soon became obvious he was more concerned with saving his throne than with helping his country's plight. At first he resisted pressures to abdicate, but when the Allies captured Rome in June 1944, Count *Sforza and other liberal politicians forced him to step aside and his son, *Umberto II, became Lt-General of the Realm, or regent. He abdicated in May 1946 and died in Egypt. See also ITALY, 3(b).

victory program, See WEDEMEYER.

Vienna awards, agreements made in November 1938 and August 1940. They were part of the Axis powers' rearrangement of south-eastern Europe after the *Munich agreement of September 1938 gave Hitler the green light to dismember Czechoslovakia. In November 1938 the first award forced the transfer of the southern areas of Slovakia from Czechoslovakia to Hungary and Ruthenia was forced to cede its southern districts, including its capital Užhorod, to Hungary. In August 1940 northern Transylvania, whose population exceeded 2 million, was transferred from Romania to Hungary. This second award and the loss of other territories, led to the abdication of Romania's King Carol (see ROMANIA, 3). See also AXIS STRATEGY AND CO-OPERATION and DIPLOMACY.

Viet Minh, an abbreviation of Vietnam Doc Lap Dong Minh Hoi (League for the independence of Vietnam), a communist guerrilla organization formed in southern China in 1941 to fight both the Japanese in French Indo-China and the French administration which the Japanese had retained (see COLLABORATION). Its forces were led by Vo Nguyen Giap, under *Ho Chi Minh as its general secretary, and by the end of 1944 with the help of US supplies, and of the *Office of Strategic Services in the field, it had captured large areas in the northern part of the country (Tongkin). Five days after the Japanese capitulated on 15 August 1945, Viet Minh detachments entered Hanoi, and on 2 September 1945 Ho Chi Minh proclaimed the Democratic Republic of Vietnam.

Vis is one of the Dalmatian Islands off the Yugoslav coast. It became an Allied stronghold, and a base for *Tito and the partisans after the Germans, at the end of 1943, had overrun the Italian garrisons on most of the other islands and occupied the Yugoslav coastline. By May 1944, when German pressure forced Tito to make his HQ on the island for five months, the forces there included a British commando brigade, artillery units, elements of the *Long Range Desert Group, the *Raiding Support Regiment, and an *Office of Strategic Services detachment. Aided by *MTBs, these raided nearby German garrisons and ran supplies to the partisans on the mainland. See also BALKAN AIR FORCE.

V-J Day was 15 August 1945, the day victory over Japan was celebrated in Allied countries, and the day after Japan accepted Allied terms for *unconditional surrender. The date the Japanese signed the document for their unconditional surrender, 2 September 1945, is also known as V-J day.

Vlasov, Lt-General Andrey (1900–46), Red Army Officer who was prominent in the defence of *Moscow before becoming deputy commander of the Volkhov *front* (army group), in March 1942, and the commander of Second Shock Army. Captured by the Germans in July 1942, he agreed to try to form an anti-Stalinist Russian Liberation Movement recruited from *prisoners-of-war (see SOVIET EXILES AT WAR).

The youngest son of a peasant, Vlasov broke off his seminary and agricultural studies at the time of the revolution. In the spring of 1919 he was called up. He served in the Red Army during the civil war, was promoted rapidly, and became a professional soldier during the reorganization of the Red Army. Steady promotion in the 1920s and 1930s was accompanied by party membership from 1930 and in 1938 he was appointed to Marshal *Timoshenko's staff. His subsequent appointment as chief of staff to General A. I. Cherepanov, the Soviet military adviser to *Chiang Kai-shek, shows that he was seen as politically trustworthy. However, the decoration given to him by the Chinese leader and a watch from Madam *Chiang Kai-shek were removed from Vlasov on the border when he returned in 1939; but he was reappointed to the Kiev military district. He was then appointed commander of the 99th Infantry Division. It had been notorious for its indiscipline, but in 1940 it was awarded the Order of the Red Banner for the best division in the Kiev military district, and Vlasov received the Order of Lenin (see DECORATIONS).

Vlasov's early war service was exemplary. In command of Thirty-Seventh Army defending *Kiev he fought his way out even after losing contact with HQ. Appointed commander of the Twentieth Army in November 1941, he took part, together with *Rokossovsky's Sixteenth Army, in the December counter-attack outside Moscow and in January 1942 his army spearheaded the main Soviet counter-offensive in the Mozhaisk–Gzhatsk–Vyazma area. On 24 January he was awarded the Order of the Red Banner and was promoted Lt-General.

In March 1942, he was made deputy commander of the Volkhov *front* created to relieve the pressure on *Leningrad; it was a significant appointment in a precarious

Celebrations in Times Square, New York, on **V-J Day**, 15 August 1945.

situation where inadequately trained troops were under severe pressure. But for reasons which are still unclear GHQ failed to provide Vlasov's Second Shock Army with the necessary support, nor was Vlasov allowed to withdraw, and the army was subsequently surrounded. Vlasov gave his men the order to disband and spent the next three weeks in the forests and swamps.

Subsequently, he explained that he had been horrified by the treatment afforded his men and asked himself why this had occurred. He could not rejoin the Soviet forces as he faced severe punishment for the loss of the army, regardless of where the blame lay. Eventually, he was located by German troops and was well treated in captivity, which predisposed him to agree to try to form a Russian Liberation Movement with the intention of persuading the Nazi authorities to alter political policy towards the USSR. This decision led him to become embroiled in a complex political situation for which he lacked the experience or temperament. He was recaptured by the Red Army in May 1945 and was hanged on 1 August 1946. C. ANDREYEV

Andreyev, C., *Vlasov and the Russian Liberation Movement* (Cambridge, 1987).
Dallin, A., *German Rule in Russia* (2nd edn., London, 1981).
Fischer, G., *Soviet Opposition to Stalin* (Cambridge, Mass., 1952).
Steenberg, S., *Vlasov* (New York, 1970).
Strik-Strikfeldt, W., *Against Stalin and Hitler* (London, 1970).

V-man (*V-Mann* or *Vertrauensmann*, trusted man), or *V-Leute* (trusted people) in the plural, were agents recruited by the *Abwehr and the Nazi security service, the Sicherheitsdienst or SD (see RSHA). The recruits, who were primarily used to maintain surveillance of the civilian populations in Germany and in occupied countries, then organized their own network of sub-agents and informers who often had no idea whom they were working for. According to an SD instruction issued in 1937, V-men were to be recruited among those having as little culture, common sense, objectivity, and logic as possible. But as they included individuals such as Henri *Déricourt, and one V-man was able to penetrate the *MI6 network in the Netherlands (see VENLO INCIDENT), this instruction was obviously often ignored. The word was also used to describe a confidential agent on a much higher plane, such as the individuals employed in the attempted *SS abduction of the Duke and Duchess of

*Windsor in July 1940 (see SCHELLENBERG). See also SPIES.

Volcano Islands, group of three Japanese islands—*Iwo Jima, Kita Iwo, and Minami Iwo—situated south of the Bonin Islands some 1,065 km. (660 mi.) south of Tokyo. They were administered by the US from 1945 to 1968.

Volhynia, a province of eastern Poland, where the Polish Home Army first implemented operation *TEMPEST in an abortive attempt to maintain Poland's autonomy from the USSR.

Partisan units of the Home Army, formed into 27th Infantry Division, attacked German lines of communication, and established contact with the Red Army when it entered Poland in February 1944. In March the first joint operation against the Germans was mounted and an agreement was made with the Soviet commander, General Sergeyev, that the Home Army division was a unit of the Polish armed forces subject to the orders of its own government; that it would be properly equipped by the USSR; and that operationally it was under Soviet command. From then on the division and the Red Army fought side by side, but in April 1944 the *NKVD refused to honour the agreement Sergeyev had made, and most of 27th Division was disarmed or merged with *Berling's Army.

Volksdeutsche were communities of German-speaking minorities living outside Germany. In European countries which had been awarded German territory after the *First World War (see Map A) *Volksdeutsche* were often accused of being *fifth columnists (see Chart). But though they played a substantial role in the Sudetenland, and some in Poland and Yugoslavia, their importance in helping the invading German armies was exaggerated at the time.

Volksgrenadier (people's grenadier), German divisions formed within *Himmler's Replacement Army (see GERMANY, 6(b)) from September 1944 onwards and mostly used to defend the *West Wall. They were raised to replace divisions lost in the *German–Soviet war and in the *Normandy campaign, and recruits came from rear echelon units, or from remnants of other units destroyed in battle. There were about 50, each almost half the strength of a normal division. They had few supporting arms and little mobility, but were well armed with automatic weapons (see SMALL ARMS) and Panzerfaust (see ROCKET WEAPONS).

Volkssturm, the German home guard. See GERMANY, 5.

Voroshilov, Marshal Kliment (1881–1969), Stalin's earliest and most intimate military associate, who became the Soviet defence minister in 1925 and a marshal in 1935. His incompetence, and Stalin's obstinacy, resulted in profound embarrassment in the 1939–40 *Finnish–Soviet war and his removal from the defence ministry.

In July 1941 he was appointed to command North-West *front* (army group) to stem the German onslaught on *Leningrad. However, by September he had conclusively demonstrated his unsuitability for field command and was replaced. For two months in 1942, he was the nominal C-in-C of the partisan movement; and in January and December 1943, he lent his presence—briefly, in the planning stage—to offensives at Leningrad and in the Crimea. Nevertheless, Stalin retained him in the *Stavka throughout the war. He was also a member of the Soviet delegation at several Allied conferences (see GRAND ALLIANCE) and was prominent in post-war Soviet politics.

EARL ZIEMKE

VT fuze, see PROXIMITY FUZE.

V-weapons was the British name for the so-called Vergeltunsgwaffen (retaliation weapons) developed by the Germans as a means of exacting retribution for the destructive Allied bombing raids on Germany cities.

The V-1 flying bomb was a small pilotless (but see KG 200) aircraft powered by a pulse-jet engine (see Figure 1). Due to shortages of aluminium alloys, wherever possible parts of the weapon were manufactured from steel pressings. The missile could be catapulted to flying speed from an inclined ramp on the ground, or air-launched. It made its first flight launched from a ground ramp at the test establishment at *Peenemünde on the Baltic, where Wernher von *Braun was the technical director, in December 1942. In 1943 the weapon was ordered into mass production and responsibility for its operational deployment was assigned to the anti-aircraft arm of the Luftwaffe.

The first flying bombs were launched against London before dawn on 13 June 1944. Between then and the end of June, 2,452 were launched against England. About one-third of these crashed or were shot down, by fighters or anti-aircraft fire, before they reached the coast and one-third crashed or were shot down over southern England outside the target area. The remaining third, about 800 missiles, crashed on Greater London. The most serious single incident was on 18 June, when one landed on the Guard's Chapel at Wellington Barracks while a service was in progress and killed 121 people including 63 soldiers.

The majority of the flying bombs fired at England came from ground launchers, but a small proportion were launched from Heinkel 111s of 3rd Group of Kampfgeschwader 3 against London, Southampton, and Gloucester. Between a third and half of the air-launched bombs failed to function correctly and crashed soon after release, and the accuracy of the rest was far lower than those fired from ground launchers. Throughout these operations the German aircraft suffered continual harassment from RAF night fighters. In the autumn of 1944 the V-1 air-launching force was expanded to a full

***Volksdeutsche*:** Survey of factors that could have furthered the rise of a political fifth column among *Volksdeutsche* groups (1933)

	1	2	3	4	5	6	7	8	9
Saar (99%)	●	●	●	●	●	●	○	○	○
Eupen-Malmedy (0.5%)	○	●	●	●	○	●	○	○	○
Danzig (98%)	●	●	●	●	●	●	○	●	●
Memel (4%)	◐	●	●	●	◐	●	●	●	◐
Alsace (2%)	○	●	●	●	◐	○	◐	○	○
Northern Schleswig (1%)	○	●	◐	◐	◐	●	◐	○	○
Corridor, Posen, Eastern Upper Silesia (3%)	◐	●	◐	◐	●	●	●	●	○
South West Africa (35%)	●	○	○	◐	○	●	●	○	◐
Austria (98%)	●	●	●	●	●	●	○	○	●
Sudeten area (22%)	●	●	●	●	●	●	●	●	●
Southern Tyrol (0.5%)	○	◐	●	◐	○	●	●	◐	○
Estonia (1.5%)	○	◐	○	●	○	◐	●	●	○
Latvia (3%)	◐	◐	○	●	○	◐	●	●	○
Hungary (2%)	○	◐	◐	◐	○	○	●	◐	○
Romania (2%)	○	◐	◐	◐	○	○	●	●	◐
Yugoslavia (3%)	◐	◐	◐	◐	○	○	●	●	○
Soviet Union (0.5 %)	○	○	◐	○	●	○	●	●	○
USA (1%)	○	○	○	●	◐	○	○	○	◐
Brazil (1.5%)	○	○	◐	◐	◐	○	◐	◐	◐
Argentina (1.5%)	○	○	◐	◐	◐	○	◐	◐	◐
Chile (0.875%)	○	○	◐	●	○	○	○	●	◐

The German group

1. Is proportionately of considerable size
2. Lives near Germany
3. Lives in strong geographical concentration
4. Is highly developed economically
5. Is in a position of social distress
6. Has been separated from Germany against its will
7. Feels oppressed as a minority
8. Has a historical feeling of superiority
9. Possesses a National Socialist cadre

The factor is applicable

● To a large degree

◐ To a small degree

○ Not or hardly at all

The figure given between brackets indicates the percentage the *Volksdeutsche* group formed of the total population of the political unit in which they lived.

Source: de Jong, L., *The German Fifth Column in the Second World War* (London, 1956).

V-weapons, Figure 1: V-1

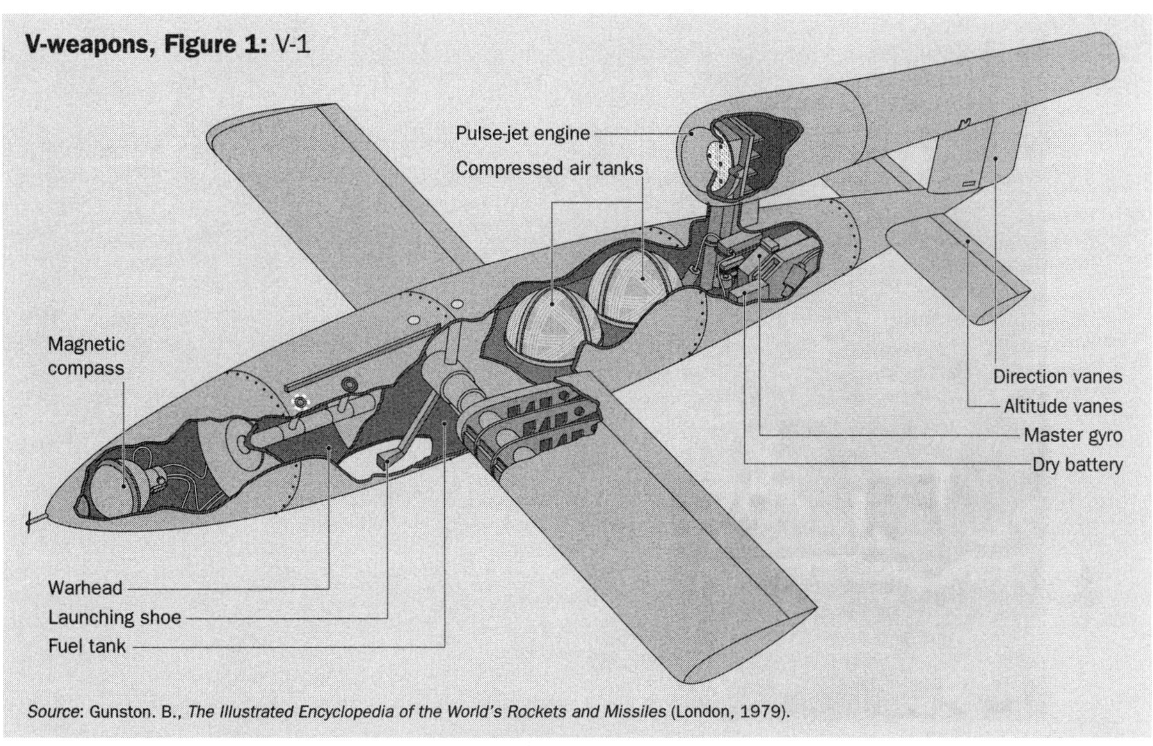

Source: Gunston. B., *The Illustrated Encyclopedia of the World's Rockets and Missiles* (London, 1979).

V-weapons, Table 1: The V-1 (Fieseler Fi 103) Flying Bomb

Role:	Pilotless bombardment weapon.
Guidance:	Preset, compass, and automatic pilot.
Power:	One Argus pulse jet engine, developing 335 kg, (740 lb.) thrust at take-off.
Warhead:	850 kg, (1,875 lb.) high explosive warhead, impact fused.
Performance:	V-1s were not manufactured to aircraft tolerances, and speed varied between missiles. Maximum speed recorded was 670 kph (420 mph) at 1,200 m. (4,000 ft.); maximum range (normal version) 200 km. (125 mi.).
Weight at Launch:	2,180 kg. (4,800 lb.).
Dimensions:	Span 5.3 m. (17 ft. 4.5 in.), length 8.32 m. (27 ft. 3.5 in.).

Source: Contributor

Geschwader, Kampfgeschwader 53, with about a hundred aircraft. But fuel shortages imposed severe restrictions on the pace of these operations and brought them to a halt in mid-January 1945. From October 1944, Belgian cities came under attack from V-1s. The main target was Antwerp, the chief supply port for Allied forces in Europe, which suffered considerable damage. In March 1945 the bombardment of London was resumed, using an extended-range version of the V-1 fired from launchers in the Netherlands. The new attack opened on 3 March 1945 and closed at the end of the month, after 275 missiles had been fired.

Altogether, just over 10,000 flying bombs were launched against England. Of those 7,488 crossed the

V-weapons, Figure 2: V-2

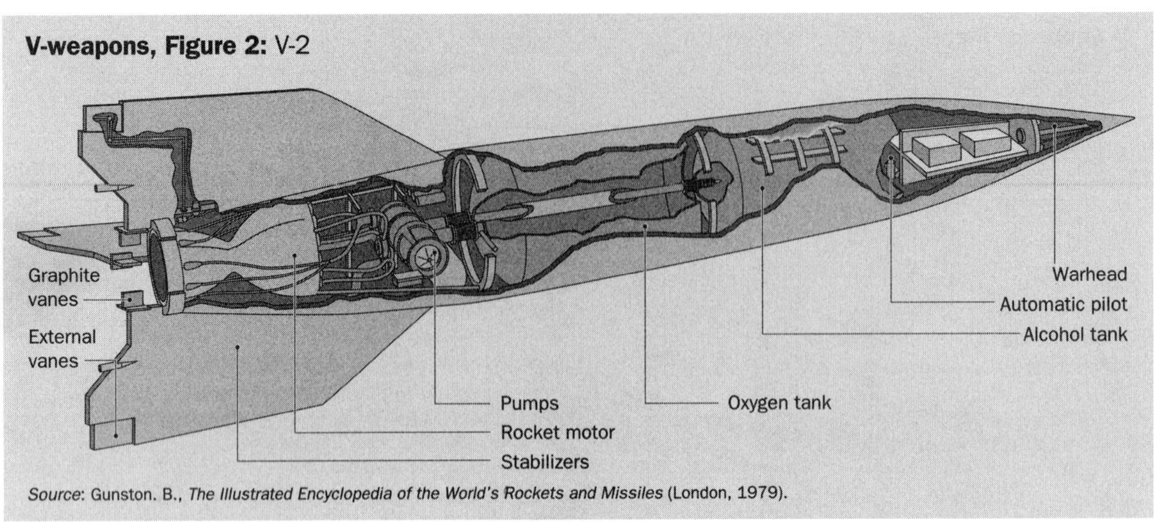

Source: Gunston. B., *The Illustrated Encyclopedia of the World's Rockets and Missiles* (London, 1979).

V-weapons, Table 2: The V-2 (A4) Bombardment Rocket

Role:	Ummanned long-range bombardment rocket.
Guidance:	Preset, employed integrating accelerometers to measure the velocity at which the motor was shut down.
Power:	Liquid fuelled rocket motor, running on liquid oxygen and 3:1 alcohol-water mixture. Maximum thrust, 25 tons. Maximum burning time, 65 seconds.
Warhead:	975 kg. (2,150 lb.) high explosive warhead, impact fused.
Performance:	Maximum velocity reached, 5,750 kph (3,600 mph); velocity at impact, about 4,000 kph (about 2,500 mph); maximum altitude reached in ballistic trajectory (long-distance shot), 96 km. (60 mi.); maximum range 320 km. (200 mi.).
Weight at launch:	13,000 kg. (28,665 lb.).
Dimensions:	Length 14.04 m. (46 ft. 1.25 in.), fin span 3.56 m. (11 ft. 8.25 in.).

Source: Contributor

British coast and 3,957 were shot down before reaching their targets. Of the 3,531 which eluded the defences, 2,419 reached London, about 30 reached Southampton and Portsmouth, and one hit Manchester. These bombs caused 6,184 deaths and 17,981 cases of injury.

The V-2 bombardment rocket (see Figure 2) was developed in parallel with the V-1, for the German Army. The rocket motor ran on alcohol and liquid oxygen, with a secondary power system using hydrogen peroxide and calcium permanganate to drive the fuel pumps. Guidance was preset, with an integrating accelerometer to measure when the missile had reached the requisite speed to reach the target. At that point the fuel to the rocket was cut off and the missile coasted along its ballistic trajectory to the target.

The V-2 made its first successful firing in October 1942, but it was a complicated and expensive weapon to develop and produce, and large-scale production did not begin until May 1944 at the huge underground factory at Nordhausen in the Harz mountains, with *forced labour being employed in its construction (see DORA).

The first V-2 to reach England was launched from a site near The Hague in the Netherlands, some 310 km. (194 mi.) from its target. It crashed on Chiswick, in south-west London, on the afternoon of 8 September 1944, killing three people and injuring seventeen. It was launched from a small square of flat concrete that was easy to conceal, and all equipment for firing the weapon was easily transportable, so there was little for attacking aircraft to hit even if the sites could be found.

The port of Antwerp also came under attack from these missiles, more than 900 being fired at it during the final three months of 1944. Between 8 September 1944 and 27 March 1945, a total of 1,054 rockets fell on England (an average of about 5 per day); of that total 517 rockets (an average of fewer than 3 per day) hit London. Just over 2,700 Londoners were killed in the attack.

The V-3 long-range gun, code-named by the Germans *Hochdruckpumpe* (high-pressure pump) or *Fleisigges Leichen* (begonia), was a long-range smooth-bore gun, designed to fire fin-stabilized shells. Several designs of shell were considered for use with the gun, of which the largest was 3 m. (9 ft. 10 in.) long with a diameter of 11 cm. (4.3 in.), weighing 127 kg. (280 lb.) of which 10 kg. (22 lb.) was the high explosive warhead. The shells were held in the centre of the barrel by sabots arranged around their circumference, which fell away after the missile left the barrel. The gun was of unusual design, with a series of explosive charges placed in side chambers extending obliquely from the barrel along its length, rather like the ribs on a fish-bone. These charges were fired electrically in sequence as the missile came past each, to accelerate the shell by a series of propulsive 'kicks' until it reached the muzzle with a speed of about 1,500 m. (4,900 ft.) per second.

In the autumn of 1943, even before the weapon had demonstrated the required capability, work began to excavate two firing sites for it at Mimoyecques near Calais in northern France, 152 km. (95 mi.) from London. Together, the two sites would be capable of raining shells on London at a rate of about ten a minute. Each firing site was to have 25 barrels, each barrel 150 m. (492 ft.) long and with a bore of 15 cm. (5.9 in.). Inclined at an angle of 45 degree to the horizontal, each barrel was housed underground inside an oblique concrete-lined shaft.

Following an air attack on the workings in November 1943 one of the firing sites was abandoned. Development work on the weapon continued throughout the first half of 1944, but by July the longest range achieved was only 93 km. (58 mi.) and even at that inadequate distance the gun barrels demonstrated a disconcerting propensity to split open during firing. Also during that month RAF bombers attacked the surviving site at Mimoyecques using *Tallboy bombs, causing serious damage to the underground installations. Little had been done to repair the damage when, in the following months, Allied troops overran the area.

Work on the novel gun continued, however. In December 1944 two simplified installations went into action, each with a single 60 m. (197 ft.) barrel and using reduced charges to give a range of about 65 km. (40 mi.). The guns bombarded the port of Antwerp and American troop positions in Luxemburg, but appear to have had little military effect. After a short time they were blown up by retreating German forces to prevent them from falling into Allied hands.

ALFRED PRICE

Gunston, B., *Rockets and Missiles* (London, 1979).
Irving, D., *The Mare's Nest* (London, 1964).
Young, R. A., *The Flying Bomb* (Shepperton, 1978).

WAAC, Women's Army Auxiliary Corps, a US formation which, at its peak, totalled 100,000 women. In mid-1943 it became part of the US Army and became the Women's Army Corps, or WACs. Some 39,000 served with the US Army Air Forces. See also USA, 5(b).

WAAF, Women's Auxiliary Air Force; see UK, 7(d).

Waffen-SS, see SS.

WAFS, Women's Auxiliary Ferrying Squadron, see WASP.

Wainwright, Lt-General Jonathan M. (1883–1953), US commander of the Philippine Division when the Japanese landed on Luzon in December 1941 (see PHILIPPINES CAMPAIGNS). He then commanded 1st Philippine Corps on *Bataan before *MacArthur, ordered to Australia in March 1942, made him commander of all ground forces on Luzon. However, this proved an unsatisfactory command system and Wainwright was soon promoted lt-general and given command of all forces in the Philippines. He surrendered on 6 May 1942 after making a last-ditch stand on *Corregidor which secured his reputation as a first-class fighting general. He chose not to escape capture and after spending the rest of the war as a prisoner-of-war in Manchukuo, went home to a hero's welcome, and was awarded the Congressional Medal of Honor (see DECORATIONS).

Wake, Nancy (b.1916), Australian-born wife of a French businessman who lived in Marseilles. She helped run an escape line (see MI9) until forced to flee across the Pyrenees, eventually reaching the UK in the summer of 1943. She joined the *FANY and then *SOE and was parachuted into the Auvergne in April 1944 to work with the *Maquis.

Braddon, R., *Nancy Wake* (London, 1956).

Wake Island, capture of. Within hours of attacking *Pearl Harbor at the start of the *Pacific war, the Japanese started to bomb Wake, the most westerly US Pacific base, from air bases in the Marshall Islands. It was defended by marine-manned shore batteries and a Marine Fighter Squadron which between them, on 12 December 1941, drove off Rear-Admiral Kajioka Sadamichi's invasion force and escort, sinking two destroyers and damaging a transport.

Rear-Admiral *Kimmel, C-in-C of the US Pacific Fleet, wanted to reinforce the island and trap any renewed attempt with his naval forces, but he was superseded on 17 December and his plan was not implemented with any resolution by his temporary replacement, Vice-Admiral William Pye, or by Rear-Admiral *Fletcher commanding the task force sent to relieve the island. So when Kajioka attacked again on 23 December, this time reinforced by two carriers returning from the Pearl Harbor raid, he overwhelmed the defence and occupied the island. But he did so only after the garrison had accounted for four more Japanese warships, twenty-one aircraft, and nearly a thousand Japanese troops. Wake remained in Japanese hands for the rest of the war, having been bypassed when the Americans began their Central Pacific advance.

Heinl, R., *The Defense of Wake* (Washington, DC, 1945).

Walcheren Island, see SCHELDT ESTUARY.

Wallenberg, Raoul (1912–47), Swedish diplomat who saved tens of thousands of Jewish lives after the Germans occupied Hungary in March 1944 and *Eichmann began deporting the Jewish population to *Auschwitz.

Prompted by the US *War Refugee Board, Sweden's neutral government sent Wallenberg to Budapest to organize, under diplomatic cover, the rescue of as many Jews as possible. He arrived on 9 July 1944, by which time 437,402 provincial Jews had already been deported leaving 230,000 in Budapest. Soon after his arrival, the deportations were suspended by Hungary's regent, Admiral *Horthy, and Wallenberg then co-ordinated the work of the neutral nations, the Papal nunciature, and the *International Red Cross Committee in giving succour to those who remained. In October 1944, after Horthy's removal from power, the remaining Jews were herded into two Budapest *ghettos and the deportations resumed. Wallenberg, it has been estimated, saved between 30,000 and 100,000 from certain death by issuing special passports, bribing guards and officials, interceding wherever possible, and often simply by bluffing.

On 17 January 1945, after the Soviet Army had entered Budapest, Wallenberg went to Debrecen in eastern Hungary to meet the Soviet commander, Marshal *Malinovsky. He was not heard from again. At first the Soviet government denied any knowledge of him but in 1957, after several ex-inmates of the *GUlag prison system had claimed meeting him or his driver, it announced that he had died of natural causes in July 1947. Rumours persisted that he was still alive but in 1991 a Soviet historian, leading an investigation into Wallenberg's disappearance, announced that, although the final documentary evidence was missing, Wallenberg had been shot in Moscow's Lubianka prison on 17 July 1947. See also FINAL SOLUTION.

Bierman, J., *Righteous Gentile* (New York, 1981).

Wallis, Barnes (1887–1979), British engineer whose early work on airships led him into aircraft design during the 1930s. He was responsible for the Wellesley bomber, and for the later Wellington of which nearly 12,000 were built. He is best remembered for his invention of the cylindrical, rotating bomb which the *Dam Busters used to destroy the Möhne and Eder dams in May 1943. This success enabled him, against the current thinking, to develop the *Tallboy and *Grand Slam bombs which were so effective against heavily fortified targets.

Wang Ching-wei (1883–1944), Canton-born politician who, from November 1940, led a Nanking-based puppet government of Japanese-occupied central China.

Wang was an early political opponent of *Chiang Kai-shek before forming a coalition with him in 1931. The Japanese, believing him a useful go-between with Chiang to end the *China Incident, persuaded him to defect in December 1938. Wang's original intention was to form an independent government in the unoccupied provinces of South China which would gradually take control of the ones occupied by the Japanese, but his position quickly deteriorated into almost pure *collaboration. He went first to *French Indo-China and then Shanghai and, after protracted negotiations with the increasingly obdurate Japanese, in March 1940 became president of the Reformed government, sponsored by the Japanese Central China Expeditionary Army and a carbon copy of the one he had left in Chungking. Eventually, in November 1940, he signed a treaty with Japan, which formalized his regime. But his government, dominated by its Japanese advisers, had no real power, while the treaty merely confirmed Japan's violations of China's sovereignty.

As the war progressed, Wang was pressed to declare war on the Allies. He eventually did so on 9 January 1943 and that June he was allowed to assume the administration of the International Settlement in Shanghai, perhaps the most significant move towards autonomy that the Wang regime achieved. In October the 1940 treaty was replaced with a 'Pact of Alliance', but though Wang's government now began to have an aura of independence, and its 900,000-strong army took over the role of rural pacification from Japanese garrisons, he could do nothing to lessen the Japanese grip on China. In November 1943 he attended the Greater East Asia conference in Tokyo (see GREATER EAST ASIA CO-PROSPERITY SPHERE), but by then his health was failing. In March 1944 Ch'en Kung-po became acting president of the Reformed government when Wang was flown to Japan for treatment; but that November he died from complications caused by an assassin's bullet which had wounded him nine years previously. See also CHINA, 3(b).

Bunker, G., *The Peace Conspiracy: Wang Ching-wei and the China War, 1937–1941* (Cambridge, Mass., 1972).

Wannsee conference, held in the offices of Interpol, of which Reinhard *Heydrich was the current chairman, in the Berlin suburb of Grossen-Wannsee on 20 January 1942. It was conducted in great secrecy to settle the concluding programme for the *Final Solution which was already under way, Heydrich, the conference's chairman, having been ordered by *Göring the previous July to find 'a final solution of the Jewish question'. Besides discussing how best to implement the last stages of the Holocaust, through *operation REINHARD and other means, the fourteen other Nazi bureaucrats present—who included Heinrich Müller, head of the *Gestapo, and Adolf *Eichmann—considered Heydrich's question of what to do with those who were half-Jewish or of mixed race, but no decision was taken as to how they were to be treated.

war artists. During the *First World War scores of artists, some already famous, were put into uniform and encouraged to paint scenes of war, with interesting results, both as art and as propaganda. Many striking pictures resulted, and a few great ones.

The propaganda possibilities of war art were perceived early, both in fascist Italy and in Nazi Germany. Both these regimes, and painters working in *Franco's Spain during the *Spanish Civil War, had developed by 1939 a style which might be called Fascist Realism—strikingly similar to the Socialist Realism then insisted upon in the USSR, but with warplanes and tanks instead of dynamos and tractors.

The British mobilized artists again in 1939. Some stalwarts from the previous war, notably Sir Muirhead Bone, Eric Kennington, Paul Nash, and Norman Wilkinson, were still available: Wilkinson, who had been present at the Dardanelles on 25 April 1915, painted the *Dunkirk evacuation; Nash, who had painted the unforgettable *Menin Road* outside Ypres in 1917, painted both the battle of *Britain and the pitched air battles which took place during the *strategic air offensive against Germany.

There was hardly ever room for an artist on the spot during tactically critical actions, whether on land or sea or in the air; though Ronald Searle, then a private in the Royal Engineers, was able to sketch from a corner of the room the act of British surrender at *Singapore in February 1942. *Pace* Edvard Munch, it is not easy to depict fear on canvas; but Edward Ardizzone proved that you can capture both boredom and apprehension, in his sketches of shelterers during air raids, and Henry Moore made some exceptionally moving and memorable drawings of Londoners sheltering in underground railway stations, which provided motifs for much of his later sculpture.

Soviet, American, German, Italian, and Japanese as well as British artists were awake to the new visual possibilities presented by the war in the air, as well as on the ground; numerous striking pictures resulted. Such artists as Aleksandr Deineka, in his *The Defence of Sevastopol 1942*, were able to combine the strictest rules of Socialist Realism with a passion for displaying defenders of the USSR in hand-to-hand combat. Japanese war art looks somewhat stilted to western eyes, in conformity with western judgements of the restraint with which no Japanese artist could then help painting; the artists felt as strongly about their subjects as any westerner could.

War art was both of artistic and of historical value. Quite apart from their merit as works of art, which was often high, these pictures could provide striking evidence of what life in wartime looked like to a trained, intelligent observer; observers in later ages can benefit directly, by using their own eyes. Obviously, the pictures dealt much more with life in wartime than with acts of war; but life in wartime remains a matter of historical interest, for which these pictures provide useful evidence.

Another important wartime role for artists lay in the design of posters, often a useful arm of propaganda. The German slogan *Feind hört mit!* was echoed by the English 'The enemy is listening'. Cartoonists on both sides busied themselves in warnings of the dangers of careless talk; war finance depended largely on loans, which in turn depended largely on the efforts of poster designers. See also CULTURE sections of the major powers.

M. R. D. FOOT

Foot, M. R. D., *Art and War* (London, 1990).
McCormick, K., and Perry, H. D., *Images of War* (London, 1991).

war correspondents have existed for as long as newspapers have been printed, but the first to be given the designation was William Howard Russell who, in 1854, began reporting the Crimean war for the London *Times*. During the Second World War the US alone fielded 1,646 accredited correspondents, including 127 *women, and the numbers world-wide during the war has been estimated at 10,000.

On both sides the truth was suppressed and correspondents, knowingly or not, fuelled their countries' propaganda machines. One of them, the American novelist John Steinbeck, later wrote that 'we were all part of the war effort. We went along with it, and not only that, we abetted it . . . we wrote only a part of the war but at that time we believed, fervently believed, that it was the best thing to do' (*Once There Was A War*, New York, 1958, p. xviii).

Nearly every national newspaper had accredited war correspondents at the front—as did agencies such as Reuters and Associated Press—though in the UK the *Daily Worker* was refused facilities in case the interests of the Communist Party were put before the security of the state. Allied correspondents had to agree to submit their copy for military *censorship before they could become accredited to formations taking part in the fighting. They were the élite. Some, such as the Australian Alan Moorehead, who reported the *Western Desert campaigns, and Ernie Pyle, the American journalist who lauded the ordinary *GI, became household names. It was a risky business: 37 US correspondents, including Pyle, died, and 112 were wounded; by July 1941, 29 German reporters and 4 radio journalists had been killed; and 33 Japanese reporters perished in the Philippines in 1944.

Allied war correspondents were civilians in uniform; they wore no badges of rank, but the *Geneva Convention entitled those captured to be treated as captains. The Convention's rules forbidding war correspondents to bear arms were often ignored: one British journalist, during the *Italian campaign, took temporary command of a platoon and there are numerous examples of similar incidents. Soviet war correspondents, not restricted by the Convention as the USSR had not signed it, automatically served as combatants and over 400 were killed in action (see also USSR, 10).

The tone of American and British reporting was more realistic than in the *First World War. Censorship was more relaxed in the USA than in the UK—though the truth about the losses at *Pearl Harbor, accurately reported in Japanese newspapers, was rigorously suppressed. Roosevelt's *caveat*, that news issued under the American War Powers Act 'must be true and must not give aid and comfort to the enemy', was an accepted guideline on both sides of the Atlantic where newspaper censorship was self-imposed. But it did not prevent confusion, serious breaches of security, and double standards, and only occasionally did the truth emerge before the censors could get at it. So total was censorship for Allied newspapermen during the fighting that led to the fall of *France that neutral correspondents turned to German communiqués, and to the output of *Goebbels's *Propaganda-Kompagnien*, for accurate news which Allied statements failed to provide. These propaganda companies did not employ civilian correspondents. Instead, Goebbels recruited into them all available journalists, *war photographers, and radio announcers. They were 12,000 strong at the height of the *German–Soviet war, and produced graphic copy in their 'Front Reports' as they rode with the victorious Wehrmacht in tanks, flew in their aircraft, and dropped with their parachutists, a form of co-operation which the Allies soon adopted. However, once the war turned against Germany, Goebbels's dictum that 'news policy is a weapon of war: its purpose is to wage war and not give out information' was rigorously applied.

Only the Japanese public were less informed than their German counterparts when victory turned to defeat, for the Japanese government controlled the press totally and organized it for war. Its Cabinet Information Bureau dealt with civilian matters such as controlling the press and disseminating information on the war was left to the press department of the Japanese Imperial HQ (see JAPAN, 5(a)). This 'deployed its own war correspondents and occasionally drafted civilian reporters for on-the-spot coverage of military operations' (B. A. Shillony, *Politics and Culture in Wartime Japan*, Oxford, 1991, p. 94), and its vice-president, along with the official spokesmen for the army and navy, briefed the press, broadcast, and wrote leading articles for the newspapers. Many intellectuals (*bunkajin*) were drafted as war correspondents who served in a propaganda corps similar to the Goebbels's *Propaganda-Kompagnien*. This had groups attached to Japanese armies during the *China Incident and the *Pacific war which propagated cultural policy, such as introducing the Japanese language in place of English, and assumed responsibility for cultural and academic

War correspondents accompanied the armed forces on many operations. Here a British one, Alan Wood, types his dispatch during the battle for Arnhem, September 1944.

institutions such as the Raffles Museum in Singapore.

During the *Finnish–Soviet war the USSR would not let any foreign correspondent near the fighting, and alone among the belligerents was, during the German–Soviet war, as secretive in victory as it had been in defeat. The best-known Soviet war correspondent was the virulently anti-Nazi writer Ilya Ehrenburg, but there were also a number of novelists and poets—Konstantin Simonov and Mikhail Sholokhov among them—who had their articles published in the official organs of the Communist Party. Their style was literary and as censorship was total they became expert at writing atmospheric pieces that were long on sentiment and short on facts. There was no tolerance for anyone who deviated from a total commitment to the communist cause. Ehrenburg told a British correspondent that in wartime all objective reporters ought to be shot. Foreign correspondents, who were accredited to the Soviet foreign office not to the Red Army, were only rarely allowed anywhere near the front. After much haggling, one party was allowed to watch the arrival of US bombers at Poltava after a *shuttle bombing operation, but mostly correspondents were forced to glean their news from official communiqués. The British correspondent Alexander Werth, being Russian-born, could at least detect their nuances, and was able to differentiate between 'fierce', 'stubborn', and 'heavy' fighting when a particular battle was described.

The finest war reporting of the German–Soviet war, 'perceptive, analytical, and accurate' (P. Knightley, *The First Casualty*, London, 1975, p. 255), probably emanated from Curzio Malaparte, who worked on the Eastern Front for the Italian newspaper *Corriere della Sera*. He alone was able, though not without trouble, to recount truthfully what he saw and have it published at the time.

On one occasion at least correspondents did have a profound and genuine effect on the course of the war that transcended their propaganda functions. This was when 120 US correspondents reported the progress of the battle of *Britain, and then of the *Blitz. These reports, which included Ed Murrow's famous radio broadcasts, confirmed that the UK was standing firm. They helped swing American public opinion away from the neutralist lobby (see AMERICA FIRST COMMITTEE) and enabled Roosevelt to enact the *destroyers-for-bases' agreement and then *Lend-Lease. See also PRESS.

Collier, R., *The Warcos* (London, 1989).
Mathews, J., *Reporting the Wars* (Minneapolis, 1957).
Wagner, L., *Women War Correspondents of World War II* (New York, 1989).

war crimes belong to a separate legal category that has to be distinguished from all other crimes that happen to be committed in wartime. The Interallied War Crimes Tribunal, established in 1945 by the victorious Allied powers, distinguished war crimes, crimes against humanity, and crimes against international peace. The first was mainly concerned with breaches of the *Geneva and *Hague Conventions committed during the conduct of warfare, and hence offences against *prisoners-of-war (POW), offences against non-combatants caught up in the fighting, offences of wanton violence under cover of war. The second concerned campaigns of mass terror, repressions, deportations, and genocide. The third concerned the planning and execution of wars of aggression.

Examples of all these categories of crime can be found in all theatres of the Second World War, although conditions were particularly atrocious on the Eastern Front in Europe and in the mainland campaigns in Asia.

There were important differences in the official attitudes and practices of the various combatant powers. The armies of the western powers—France, Poland, the UK, and later the USA—were ordered to observe the Geneva Conventions. They did not indulge in mass terror or genocide in occupied countries; and they saw themselves as prosecuting a just, defensive war. The most serious accusations of (untried) crimes allegedly committed by the western powers centre on the indiscriminate bombing of civilian targets during the *strategic air offensive against Germany and on the transfer of POW to the Soviet Union in 1945 to almost certain death (see SOVIET EXILES AT WAR).

The armies of the USSR and of imperial Japan did not operate under the same restraints. They did not observe the Conventions; they openly defied international law; they committed crimes against humanity in all countries they occupied; and they repeatedly initiated campaigns of aggression. The list of Soviet crimes includes the mass murder of 26,000 Polish officer POW in the *Katyń forest and elsewhere; the *deportations and repressions carried out in countries forcibly incorporated into the USSR in 1939–41 and throughout eastern Europe in 1944–5; and the unprovoked invasions of Poland (1939), Finland (1939), and the Baltic States (1940). The Soviet Union was unique in rejecting the POW status of its own soldiers captured by enemy forces. About 1 million ex-Soviet POW, who survived captivity in Germany, were treated as traitors by the *NKVD on their return to the USSR in 1945 and sent to the *GUlag.

The list of Japanese crimes includes the murder and maltreatment of Allied POW and civilian internees; the genocidal campaigns against civilians during the *China Incident; the unprovoked attack on the USA at *Pearl Harbor (1941); and the series of aggressive invasions throughout South-East Asia.

The armies of the Axis, Italy and Germany, generally observed the niceties of international law when fighting against western powers. Elsewhere, they ignored them. There was a marked contrast in Italian conduct between their restraint when facing the British in North Africa, and their depredations in Albania, Greece, Yugoslavia, and especially Abyssinia. Despite notorious lapses, there was a world of difference between the Germans' comportment on the Western Fronts and their heinous behaviour in the east. Many observers noted a difference between the attitudes of the *SS and other special Nazi formations, and those of the regular Wehrmacht.

None the less, the catalogue of German crimes is very extensive, covering all known categories. (It filled 23 volumes of the record of the Nuremberg tribunal; documentary evidence took up another 19.) On the Western Front, there were several grave incidents such as the shooting of US prisoners at *Malmédy during the *Ardennes campaign, or the reprisals taken against villages such as *Oradour in France. There were numerous acts of limited repression and deportation against members of the Resistance and especially Jews (see FINAL SOLUTION); and clear acts of aggression against Belgium, the Netherlands, Denmark, Norway, and France. (The UK declared war on Germany, not vice versa.)

In the east, however, no holds were barred. On 31 August 1939 Hitler specifically ordered his forces to show no mercy in Poland. The strafing of *refugees, bombing of civilian targets, the shooting of hostages, and the murder of Jews were commonplace. In the *German–Soviet war German soldiers were expressly absolved from crimes which would have been an offence under regular German law; prisoners were not usually taken in combat; political *commissars and Jews were shot on sight; and 3–4 million Soviet and Italian captives were systematically starved to death. In Yugoslavia and Greece, partisan warfare inspired atrocities on all sides. Occupied Poland was the main location of *operation REINHARD and of other genocidal campaigns. The suppression of the *Warsaw rising in 1943 was attended by the slaughter of about 40,000 non-combatants; in the main Warsaw rising of 1944 about 250,000 were killed. The fate of *Lidiče and Lezaky was meted out to literally hundreds of villages in Poland, Belorussia, and Ukraine.

The International War Crimes Tribunals were the product of a consistent Allied policy originating in 1942 when the decision was taken to prosecute all enemy war criminals at the end of hostilities. Two main trials were held—one in *Nuremberg 1945–7 and the other in Tokyo (see FAR EAST WAR CRIMES TRIALS). The Allied organizers were strongly criticized at the time both for failing to entrust proceedings to a neutral court and for the retrospective definition of offences, thereby infringing a basic legal tenet, *Nulla poena sine lege* (no punishment without law). The main failing, however, lay in the fact that Allied prosecutors were only empowered to consider crimes committed by the defeated enemy. The colossal criminal record of the Soviet Union did not come into the reckoning. When defence lawyers at Nuremberg attempted to draw comparisons with Allied conduct, they were ruled out of order.

Trials for war crimes, collaboration, and genocide continued in several countries for many years after the war. In the Federal Republic of Germany they were staged at regular intervals in the 1950s and 1960s. The State of Israel, which was not in existence during the war, none the less took on the prosecution of crimes connected with the Final Solution (see EICHMANN). In France, the trial and sentencing of Klaus *Barbie, the 'Butcher of Lyons', took place as late as 1987, and the head of the Lyons *Milice, Paul Touvier, was in 1994, the first

Frenchman to be sentenced for crimes against humanity.

A new wave of war crime investigations began in 1970s with the creation of the Office of Special Investigation (OSI) in Washington. The main instigators were Jewish organizations in the USA, notably the Wiesenthal Center in Los Angeles, which demanded the pursuit of alleged war criminals who had obtained US citizenship through false declarations of their wartime activities. Since most of the offences had occurred in eastern Europe, the Soviet KGB inevitably became a prime source of evidence. Lengthy enquiries led to a number of false accusations, such as those against a resident of Chicago, Frank Waluś, who was later cleared. In 1986 a resident of Cleveland (Ohio), John Demaniuk was administratively extradited for trial in Israel on charges of being the camp guard 'Ivan the Terrible' at *Treblinka. Demaniuk was convicted in Jerusalem in 1988 in a highly publicized trial, but subsequent evidence threw doubt on the verdict. His appeal was upheld and he was released in September 1993.

Under pressure from the USA, similar war crimes legislation was instituted in Canada, Australia, and the UK. The British War Crimes Act (1991) exceptionally limits its competence to crimes 'committed in Germany or in German-occupied territory', thereby eliminating the possibility of prosecuting alleged Soviet or other Allied criminals. NORMAN DAVIES

Warden, Colonel, a cover name Churchill sometimes used when travelling abroad.

war effort, see in domestic life section of major powers or in entries on countries; see also RAW MATERIALS and WORLD TRADE AND WORLD ECONOMY.

war photographers and ciné cameramen of both sides, like *war correspondents with whom they often worked closely, recorded just about every aspect of the war.

Roger Fenton, Queen Victoria's court photographer, was the first war photographer when he covered the Crimean War (1854–6). 'No dead bodies,' were his instructions from Prince Albert, a principle official censorship followed about American casualties during the Second World War until a photograph of three dead US soldiers on a beach at *Buna was released by *Life* magazine in September 1943. But Axis *censorship was more rigorous than that of the Allies. As an extreme example, when a Japanese newsreel cameraman recorded the Japanese Navy's defeat at *Midway, his film was confiscated and he was kept in virtual isolation for the rest of the war.

Both military and civilian photographers were employed by both sides. German photographers and cameramen were recruited into the Propaganda Ministry's PK units (*Propaganda-Kompagnien*) which also contained war correspondents. The British used civilian photographers, who wore uniform and were attached to all three services, and in October 1941 the Army Film and Photographic Unit was formed for Army Film Unit personnel and civilian official photographers. US service photographers and cameramen were mostly part of the US Signals Corps; the US Navy had its own group of photographers, organized by the fashion photographer Edward Steichen.

Most US civilian photographers came from Associated Press, Acme Newspictures, International News Photos, and *Life* magazine. There were no exclusives: they pooled all photographs. *Life* had 21 war photographers, including Margaret Bourke-White, whose photographs of *Moscow under attack in 1941 went round the world, and Robert Capa, famous for his *Spanish Civil War photograph of a Republican infantryman being struck by a bullet. Capa was one of the first ashore during the Normandy landings (see OVERLORD). 'If your pictures aren't good enough,' he would say, 'you aren't close enough.' To be close enough, war photographers took enormous risks. By July 1941 fifteen stills photographers from German PK companies had been killed, and during the course of the war 37 US photographers lost their lives and 112 were wounded.

Some photographers, such as Capa, became famous with just one shot. The picture of the Stars and Stripes being raised over *Iwo Jima's Mount Suribachi made photographer Joe Rosenthal a household name after the war (see p. 602). The fact that, like *MacArthur wading ashore (see p. 704), it was a posed shot and that a much smaller flag had been raised—and photographed by Sgt Louis Lowery—three hours earlier while fighting was still continuing on the mountain, did not detract from its universal appeal. Others became well known for their photographic record on the Home Front. Heinrich Hoffman, Hitler's personal photographer, helped to create the cult that surrounded the Führer by producing images of a leader at one with his people, while Bill Brandt's name will always be associated with his photographs of sleeping Londoners who had taken night-time refuge from the *Blitz in the underground and elsewhere (see p. 139).

Some wartime photographs were taken in unusual, or terrible, circumstances, or for unusual reasons. Johannese Lange, a German photographer who lived near *Colditz, was ordered to record life there and the means and methods used by *prisoners-of-war to escape; an Australian soldier, George Aspinall, not only managed to take photographs in *Changi prison and of scenes on the *Burma–Thailand railway, but was able to process them with chemicals smuggled in to him; and Matsushige Yoshito, a civilian press photographer, was in a suburb of *Hiroshima when the first *atomic bomb was detonated above the town. His pictures of the devastation—just five negatives survived radioactive contamination—were taken only hours after the city's destruction, a unique record. He never accepted any money for their use. 'It is enough,' he said, 'that their publication helps to make a second Hiroshima out of the question.'

Fabian, R., and Adam, H., *Images of War* (New York, 1985).
Moeller, S., *Shooting War* (New York, 1989).
Roeder, G., *The Censored War* (New Haven, 1993).

War Production Board, US civilian agency, headed by Donald M. Nelson (1888–1959), which was formed in January 1942 to organize economic mobilization for the war, encourage industrial expansion, and develop policies controlling every aspect of production. One of its main tasks was to divide scarce materials between the military and civilian production sectors which it was authorized to do under the Second War Powers Act passed in March 1942. It also had the power to stop or ration the production of civilian goods and in agreement with the military, which retained responsibility for procurement contracts, to set production quotas and schedules to eliminate bottlenecks and cut down on waste. To speed the conversion of industry to war production, its first decision was to outlaw the production of all cars and light trucks after 31 January 1942; and by June, when the *Smaller War Plants Corporation was formed as part of it, the production of consumer durable goods had been cut by 29%. It was, Nelson later commented, not so much industrial conversion as industrial revolution.

Though effective at first, the Board's authority was undermined by other, autonomous, agencies and Nelson had difficulty in dealing with the services and keeping the Board unified. In February 1943 Roosevelt agreed to replace him with Bernard Baruch. He then changed his mind, but power soon shifted to Nelson's deputy, and in May 1943 Roosevelt created the Office of War Mobilization which assumed much of Nelson's role as a policy-maker. The following June, Nelson's premature plans for reconversion to a civilian economy were so strongly opposed by the services that he was forced to resign and was replaced by Julius A. Krug in September 1944. Krug, too, wanted reconversion to start, but the military won the argument and it was not until April 1945 that wartime economic controls began to be dismantled. See also USA, 2.

War Refugee Board, established in January 1944 by the US secretary of the treasury Henry Morgenthau Jr. (see also MORGENTHAU PLAN), to assist the immediate rescue and relief of European Jews, and of any other victims of Nazi persecution. It worked with other US agencies, and with international ones, to this end and $1 million was set aside for initial administrative expenses. Its members were Morgenthau, the secretary of state, Cordell *Hull, and the secretary of war, Henry *Stimson, but they left the initiation and the execution of policy to the Board's director, John Pehle (later William O'Dwyer). The removal of Jewish refugees from France, including 5–6,000 *children, was arranged, as was the transportation of Jewish children from Bulgaria to Palestine via Turkey, and safe havens were established for others in the USA and Libya. See also FINAL SOLUTION and REFUGEES.

Warsaw risings. There were two risings against the Nazis in the former Polish capital, one in the city's ghetto, the other as part of operation *TEMPEST. The uprising in the Warsaw ghetto which broke out on 19 April 1943 was a symbolic fight; victory, other than moral, was never anticipated. Knowing that death and extermination were inevitable (see FINAL SOLUTION) the Jews of Warsaw decided to die with dignity and honour by staging armed resistance. They saw their fight as part of the general Polish struggle for freedom and a revenge for the crimes of the *concentration camps and death camps (see OPERATION REINHARD).

In July 1942 the transportations of the Jews from the Warsaw ghetto to *Treblinka death camp began. By the end of September 300,000 had been deported; only 60,000 remained. As a result the organization of Jewish underground resistance in the ghetto was speeded up, and in December the Jewish Fighting Organization (ZOB), commanded by Mordechaj Anielewicz, was created. Its object was to stage armed resistance when the ghetto's final liquidation started. It began to collect and produce arms, and build underground bunkers.

On 19 April 1943 German forces launched their onslaught on the ghetto using about 3,000 men, including some 2,600 *SS and also the Wehrmacht and police. They attacked with a tank, armoured vehicles, heavy machine-guns, and artillery, and set fire to and blew up buildings where Jews were sheltering and hiding. SS Brigadeführer (Brigadier) *Stroop commanded these German units and the attack. A force of 600 men from ZOB and 400 from the Jewish Military Union (ZZW) units, stubbornly defended themselves from their bunkers, using one machine-gun, pistols, hand grenades, and *Molotov cocktail bombs. This resistance took the Germans completely by surprise and it was not until 16 May that Stroop was able to claim that the operation was concluded, although armed resistance by individual Jewish units continued into the middle of July.

Several times during the fighting Polish Home Army and *People's Guard units (see POLAND, 4) tried unsuccessfully to breach the ghetto's walls to provide an escape route for the Jews. On 8 May Anielewicz and the ZOB command committed joint suicide in their bunker. About 50 ZOB fighters escaped through the sewers, some later to fight in the Second Warsaw rising. The battle and fires claimed the lives of 14,000 Jews, 7,000 were transported to Treblinka to be exterminated, and most of the remainder were sent to *Majdanek. German losses are not known but at the time they were estimated to be about 400 dead and 1,000 wounded.

This unprecedented fight by the Jews quickly became legendary and provided inspiration for similar revolts in the Białystok ghetto and Treblinka and *Sobibor death camps.

The second Warsaw rising, part of operation TEMPEST, broke out on 1 August 1944. It was planned to last, at the longest, ten days, but fighting went on for 63 days. The city was originally excluded from TEMPEST, but in July

A German photograph of Jews being rounded up during the first **Warsaw rising**, April 1943, in the Warsaw ghetto.

1944 General *Komorowski, the C-in-C of the Polish Home Army, decided to stage a rising in the capital, believing control of the city was essential if the political aims of TEMPEST were to be realized. Thus it was aimed militarily against the Germans and politically against the Soviet Union.

Commanded by General Antoni Chrusciel, about 37,600 Polish insurgents fought in this second rising of whom 36,500 were Polish Home Army members. At first, less than 14% of the men were armed, having only 20 heavy machine-guns, 98 light machine-guns, 844 sub-machine-guns, 1,386 rifles, and 2,665 handguns between them, but during the rising further arms and ammunition were received from western Allied and Soviet drops, or captured from the Germans. Much of the fighting was done with hand grenades and Molotov cocktails.

The rising broke out at 1700, as it was thought this hour would most surprise the Germans. In fact the Germans knew a rising was being planned, and seem to have known the time it would commence, but had insufficient troops available to crush it immediately. In the initial battles the greater part of the city was taken by the insurgents, and was split up into several disconnected districts by the fighting, but they did not manage to capture any strategic points or control the main communication arteries or railway stations. The rising was greeted with virtually unanimous support and enthusiasm by the city's inhabitants, and Komorowski decided to continue the fight by going on the defensive, and await help from the Allies or the Soviets, or the collapse of Germany. However, *Himmler quickly organized a German counter-attack and by 20 August 21,300 German troops, including Oberführer Oskar Dirlewanger's Police Brigade, made up of criminals, the Kaminsky Brigade (see SOVIET EXILES AT WAR), and an Azerbaijan infantry brigade, had been brought in, although they were never all engaged simultaneously. SS Obergruppenführer (Lt-General) Erich von dem Bach-Zelewski commanded the operation. *Himmler ordered that all Poles, insurgents or not, should be shot and during the first five days more than 40,000 Poles were massacred. These orders were quickly modified by Bach-Zelewski and the mass executions of unarmed civilians ceased. On 25 August the Germans started their counter-attack.

The unequal battle, between the well-equipped German

forces backed by aircraft and the home-made arms of the Polish insurgents, was bitter and unrelenting. Every street and house was fought over. But Warsaw fought alone as the Soviet advance was stopped on the outskirts of eastern Warsaw by a German counter-attack and Stalin did not renew the offensive. Between 16 and 21 September Polish troops of *Berling's Army did land on the western bank of the Vistula and tried to establish a bridgehead, but heavy casualties forced them back. Stalin's attitude to the rising is still not clear; at the time he dismissed it as an 'adventurist affair' and refused landing facilities on Soviet airfields to Allied planes bringing help. In spite of their closeness to Warsaw the Soviets did not start their drops of humanitarian and military aid until 13 September, and night sorties from British bases in Italy (see BALKAN AIR FORCE) with arms and other aid were soon stopped because of the excessively high level of losses. On 9 September Stalin agreed, just once, to let US aircraft land on Soviet airfields, but when these dropped supplies on 18 September the part of Warsaw still in Polish hands had shrunk so much that most of the containers fell into German-occupied areas.

During the rising fire-fighting and anti-air attack squads were organized by the insurgents, soup kitchens were set up, wells sunk, accommodation for refugees and bomb victims arranged. Communication was often only by underground passages, through cellars, tunnels, and the sewers, but newspapers were published, radio broadcasts transmitted, and an insurgent postal service was organized. Hospitals and medical units worked efficiently in appalling conditions, and in spite of the desperate living conditions, terrible food shortages, and continual threat of death, the civilian population stayed loyal and uncomplaining. At the beginning of September, when it seemed the rising would collapse, an evacuation was arranged by the Red Cross, but less than 10% of the population opted to leave. This unity was an important factor in enabling the rising to continue. But district by district the Germans regained control of the city and by 30 September only part of the central district was still being defended insurgents. On 1 October, Komorowski, seeing no hope of external help, decided to surrender. The capitulation agreement recognized the insurgents as combatants and stipulated the capital was to be totally evacuated, an event unprecedented in modern history.

During the rising more than 15,000 insurgents were killed and between 200,000 and 250,000 civilians (of a population of 1,000,000). Bach-Zalewski claimed German losses were exceedingly high: 17,000 dead and missing. Before Warsaw fell to the Soviets, the Germans systematically destroyed 83% of the city.

The rising was the subject of intense debate, political manipulation, and falsification during the years of post-war communist rule in Poland. Certain myths were created around it, and it has come to play an indelible and important role in the political and historical awareness of all Poles. Without access to Soviet archives no complete assessment of the Soviet reaction can be attempted, but it would seem that Stalin saw it as advantageous to his future plans to stand back and let the city and the Polish underground élite be destroyed. The Soviet reaction, however, was not without impact on western Allied attitudes to their eastern ally. The Polish Home Army was broken up; the confidence of the Poles in their government in London (see POLAND, 2(e)) which had been unable to organize help for the beleaguered city, was severely shaken; and many Poles came to accept that accommodation with their eastern neighbour was unavoidable. See also GHETTOS. JOANNA HANSON

Ciechanowski, J., *The Warsaw Rising of 1944* (Cambridge, 1974).
Gutman, Y., *The Jews of Warsaw 1930–1943: Ghetto, Underground, Revolt* (London, 1982).
Hanson, J. K. M., *The Civilian Population and the Warsaw Uprising of 1944* (Cambridge, 1982).
Zawodny, J. K., *Nothing but Honour. The Story of the Warsaw Uprising, 1944* (London, 1978).

warships. In 1939 the battleship, the capital ship, still laid credible claim to being the primary naval striking unit. Although the German **Bismarck* was crippled by torpedo bombers in May 1941, not until December 1941 were capital ships sunk at sea by aircraft (see PRINCE OF WALES AND REPULSE), and not until October 1944 did American carrier-based aircraft sink the Japanese super-battleship **Musashi*. The *First World War had demonstrated that the idea of skimping on protection in some ships—fast battle-cruisers—was unwise, and that if speed was required it could only be acquired on a sufficiently well-protected hull by building a very large ship. The British *Hood* was the first such vessel, officially a battle cruiser but in reality a fast battleship of over 40,000 tons. She was armoured to contemporary battleship standards but the distribution of this protection reflected only a partial absorption of wartime lessons and she was easily sunk in May 1941 by the *Bismarck*, a more modern ship.

During the inter-war period the size of warships was controlled by international treaties. The British were forced to sacrifice speed in the two 35,000-ton 16 in. (41 cm.) gun battleships, *Nelson* and *Rodney*, allowed to them under the Washington Treaty of 1922. The Germans built unique 28-knot diesel-powered armoured ships that looked as if they might not exceed the *Versailles settlement limit of 10,000 tons, which mounted six 11 in. (28 cm.) guns. These pocket battleships proved not entirely successful in service but they caused a stir at the time, and encouraged the French to build two 30,000-ton 29.5-knot capital ships armed with 13 in. (33 cm.) guns. These relatively lightly protected ships are sometimes referred to as battle-cruisers as are the larger and more heavily armoured ships the Germans built immediately after abrogating Versailles, the 35,000-ton **Scharnhorst* and *Gneisenau* armed with nine 11 in. guns. The British hoped that naval rearmament in the late 1930s could still be controlled by treaty, at least qualitatively, and produced a balanced and economical 14-inch gun battleship design, the King George V class. All the other naval powers, however, went for 15, 16, and even 18 in. guns (38, 41, and 46 cm.) and greater displacement (see Table). As well as new construction, much work was done rebuilding older capital ships with longer-range main armament, anti-aircraft guns, and improved protection against long-range fire, bombs, and torpedoes. The war proved the need for still further increases in anti-aircraft armament in both new and old vessels. After *Pearl Harbor the Americans gave their badly damaged old battleships further reconstruction, producing ships that proved especially valuable supporting *amphibious warfare landings.

Second World War cruisers were smaller, faster, and more lightly protected than battleships and were divided into two categories, heavy—armed with 8 in. (20.3 cm.) guns—and light—armed with 5 in., 5.25 in., or 6 in. (12.7 cm., 13.3 cm., 15.2 cm.). The inter-war treaty system had the effect of enlarging cruisers into latter-day battle-cruisers, despite the best efforts of the British to limit size and armament to allow the maximum number to defend her maritime trade from enemy commerce raiders. The Royal Navy only built heavy cruisers in the 1920s; in the 1930s it constructed large general-purpose cruisers, armed with eight or twelve 6 in. guns, together with smaller fleet cruisers armed either with six 6 in. guns or, later, 5.25 in. dual-purpose weapons. The need to increase anti-aircraft armament during the war led to the larger British cruisers losing a quarter of their anti-surface armament to mount extra light A-A guns.

The Japanese concentrated on large, powerful heavy cruisers which also carried *float planes for reconnaissance duties, a role other navies abandoned as war experience revealed the vulnerability of these aircraft. Older ships of the small First World War light cruiser type largely sufficed the Japanese as destroyer leaders and their striking power along with that of the larger cruisers was greatly increased by the addition of 24 in. (61 cm.) Long Lance *torpedoes that, uniquely, could be used at long gun ranges. The Japanese had, however, to sacrifice surface gun armament to increase A-A potential as the lessons of war were learned.

The Americans built large numbers of heavy cruisers, enlarging their 10,000-ton Washington treaty designs for wartime construction. The pre-war 10,000-ton London Treaty 6 in. light cruiser was also retained with the main armament slightly reduced from fifteen to twelve guns to improve A-A potential. In addition special small anti-aircraft cruisers entirely armed with 5 in. dual-purpose guns were constructed.

Italy had impressive and good-looking cruiser designs in both the heavy and light categories, with the accent on speed. Many could keep up with destroyers, but the price paid in lack of protection was significant. The Germans, who were limited to 6,000-ton light cruisers in the 1920s and early 1930s, built heavy cruisers once they had the chance after 1935. Only three were completed, the two Hipper class of 14,000 tons and the huge *Prinz Eugen* of 17,000 tons. These ships suffered from very unreliable high pressure engines which vitiated their primary role as *German surface raiders.

Pre-war destroyers had been designed primarily for high-speed anti-surface warfare with maximum speeds of 36 knots or more. The Japanese set the shape of Second World War destroyers in the late 1920s with the Fubuki class of 1,750 tons armed with six 5.1 in. (13 cm.) guns and nine 24 in. torpedo tubes. This design had grown to 2,000 tons by 1940. The British, who were standardizing on 1,400-ton designs armed with four 4.7 in. (12 cm.) guns and eight 21 in. (53 cm.) torpedoes, were forced to build 1,900-ton answers to the Fubukis, the Tribals, with double the normal British gun armament and half the torpedoes. Before the war the Americans had standardized on a mix of 1,600-ton destroyers armed with four or five single 5 in. guns supplemented by destroyer leaders of 1,850–2,000 tons armed with eight 5 in. guns in twin mountings. The 38 calibre 5 in. gun was an excellent dual-purpose weapon with good A-A capability. From 1939 onwards the USA built three successive destroyer types. The first, of just over 1,850 tons, had to sacrifice both 5 in. guns and torpedoes to acquire sufficient light A-A armament. Much superior was the Fletcher class launched from 1942 onwards, much larger and able to mount a good all-round armament. These were supplemented before the end of the war with the related Allen M. Sumners class which replaced single 5 in. gun mounts with three twin mountings.

Although the Japanese Navy built a class of large destroyers armed with eight quick-firing, dual-purpose 3.9 in. (10 cm.) guns and only four torpedo tubes for use as carrier escorts, both the Americans and the Japanese tended to retain heavy torpedo armaments for fleet destroyers as night surface actions remained the norm during the *Pacific war. The British on the other hand, being involved in escorting *convoys which were subject to air attack, found it necessary to sacrifice torpedoes for A-A guns. One reason for their having to do this was their lack of an effective dual-purpose destroyer gun until high-angle 4.7 in. and later 4.5 in. (11.4 cm.) weapons became available during the war. Even then, lack of production facilities meant that many fleet destroyers had to go to sea with 4 in. (10.2 cm.) A-A guns as main armament. By the late war years the standard British fleet destroyer had become a ship of just over 1,700 tons armed with four dual-purpose guns, six light A-A guns, and eight torpedo tubes.

Prior to 1939, France had built in addition to more conventional destroyers, high-speed *contre-torpilleurs* of well over 2,000 tons, and the Germans built similar oversized ships from 1939 onwards. They were designed for six 5.9 in. (14.9 cm.) guns but proved top-heavy and suffered from ammunition handling problems. Their machinery was also unreliable. Germany and France also built smaller torpedo boats in the 600–1,200-ton category for general destroyer-type duties in coastal waters. Italy did the same, while its fleet destroyers like its cruisers

Warships: Comparative Second World War warships

Germany

Battleship: Bismarck Class

Standard displacement: 42,000 tons. Armament: 8 x 15 in (381 mm) guns, 12 x 5.9 in (150 mm) guns, 16 x 4.1 in (105 mm) A-A. Maximum armour: 12.5 in (31.8 cm) belt and 14.25 m (36.2 mm) turrets. Speed: 29 knots. *Bismarck* and her sistership *Tirpitz* were commissioned in 1940–1. They proved very hard to sink but their low armoured deck made them relatively easy to put out of action.

Heavy Cruiser: *Prinz Eugen*

Standard displacement: 14,600 tons. Armament: 8 x 8 in (203 mm) guns, 12 x 4.1 in (104 mm) A-A, 12 x 21 in (533 mm) torpedo tubes. Maximum armour: 3.25 in (8.3 cm) belt and 6.25 in (15.9 cm) turrets. Speed: 32.5 knots. One of the largest cruisers ever built; neither of her two sisters was completed.

Light Cruiser: 'K' Class

Standard displacement: 6,700 tons. Armament: 6 x 5.9 in (150 mm) guns, 2–4 x 3.4 in (86 mm) A-A guns, 12 x 21 in (533 mm) torpedo tubes. Maximum armour; belt 2.75 in (7 cm), turrets 1.25 in (3.2 cm). Speed: 32 knots. Built in the 1920s under the Treaty of Versailles restrictions, they had combined steam and diesel propulsion. *Königsberg* of this class was the first major warship sunk by aircraft, at Bergen in April 1940.

Destroyer: 1936A Type

Standard displacement: 2,600 tons. Armament: 6 x 5.9 in (150 mm) guns, 8 x 21 in (533 mm) torpedo tubes. Speed: 38.5 knots. These ships, numbered in the Z series, were plagued with problems. Some had a single gun forward instead of the designed twin turret. They carried A-A armaments of 37 mm (1.44 in) and 20 mm guns that were increased as the war went on.

Japan

Battleship: Yamato Class

Standard displacement: 64,170 tons. Armament: 9 x 18 in (457 mm) guns, 12 x 6.1 in (156 mm), 12 x 5 in (127 mm) dual-purpose; 6 x 6 in (152 mm) guns later removed to allow augmentation of A-A armament, that eventually totalled up to 130 x 25 mm (0.97 in) guns. Maximum armour: 16.1 in (41 cm) belt, 25.6 in (65 cm) turrets. Speed: 27 knots. There were only two, the largest and most powerful battleships ever built; a qualitative reply to American quantitative superiority. Their armour protection had flaws and both were sunk by American carrier-based torpedo bombers, *Musashi* in late 1944 and *Yamato* in 1945.

Heavy cruiser: Takao Class

Standard displacement: 13,400 tons. Armament: 10 x 8 in (203 mm) guns, 8 x 5 in (127 mm) dual-purpose guns, 16 x 24 in (61 mm) torpedo tubes. Maximum armour: 4.9 in (12.4 cm) belt, 1 in (2.5 cm) turrets. Speed: 34.2 knots. Originally completed in 1932, the four ships in this class were rebuilt in 1939–40, two to the above specifications. One of the other, less modified pair, *Maya*, was rebuilt again after battle damage when two of her 8 in guns were replaced with extra anti-aircraft armament.

Light cruiser: Nagara Class

Standard displacement: 5,600 tons. Armament: 7 x 5.5 in (140 mm) guns, 8 x 24 in (610 mm) torpedo tubes; 2 dual-purpose 5.5 in were substituted for a pair of the original guns in 1943 and the torpedo armament was increased to 24 tubes. Maximum armour: 2.5 in (6.4 cm). Speed: 36 knots. A classical First World War light cruiser type built in the early 1920s, but still used extensively during the war.

Destroyer: Yugumo Class

Standard displacement: 2,100 tons. Armament: 6 x 5 in (127 mm) guns, 8 x 24 in (610 mm) torpedo tubes; 2 guns were removed from 1943 to enhance light A-A armament from 4 to 15 25 mm guns; the remaining after turret was sometimes replaced with a more effective dual purpose 5 in (127 mm) mounting. Speed: 35 knots. The final development of the Fubuki Special Type, launched in the early war years; all were sunk.

UK

Battleship: King George V class

Standard displacement: 36,700 tons. Armament; 10 x 14 in (356 mm) guns, 16 x 5.25 in (133 mm) dual-purpose guns. Maximum armour: 15 in (38 cm) belt and 13 in (33 cm) turrets. Speed: 28 knots. These ships were exceptionally well protected for their size and sacrificed gun power to achieve this.

Heavy cruiser: Kent Class

Standard displacement: 10,700 tons. Armament: 8 x 8 in (203 mm) guns, 8 x 4 in (102 mm) A-A guns. Maximum armour: 4.5 in (11.4 cm) belt. Speed: 31.5 knots. These 1920s ships were reconstructed between 1935 and 1939.

Warships (*cont.*)

Light cruiser: Fiji Class

Standard displacement: 8,500 tons. Armament: 12 x 6 in (152 mm) guns, 8 x 4 in (102 mm) A-A, 6 x 21 in (533 mm) torpedo tubes; later altered to 9 x 6 in guns with addition of more light A-A guns. Maximum armour: 3.5 in (8.9 cm) belt, 2 in (5.1 cm) turrets. Speed: 31.5 knots. These ships were the latest British large light cruisers on the outbreak of war.

Destroyer: 'K' Class

Standard displacement: 1,690 tons. Armament: 6 x 4.7 in (119 mm) guns, 10 x 21 in (533 mm) torpedo tubes; 1 4 in (102 mm) A-A gun could be substituted for five tubes. Speed: 36 knots. This was the standard fleet destroyer on the outbreak of war. The light A-A armament increased during the war from 1 quadruple 2-pdr to 10 20 mm (0.78 in) or 4 40 mm (1.5 in) guns.

USA

Battleship: Iowa Class

Standard displacement: 48,100 tons. Armament: 9 x 16 in (406 mm) guns, 20 x 5 in (127 mm) dual-purpose guns. Maximum armour: 12.1 in (30.7 cm) belt and 19.7 in (50 cm) turrets. Speed: 32.5 knots. These fine ships were built to operate with fast carrier groups. They were retained after the war and saw action off Korea, Lebanon, and Kuwait.

Heavy cruiser: Baltimore Class

Standard displacement: 14,500 tons. Armament: 9 x 8 in (203 mm), 12 x 5 in (127 mm) dual-purpose. Maximum armour: 6 in (15 cm) belt, 8 in (20 cm) turrets. Speed: 33 knots. These large and powerful vessels were commissioned from 1943 onwards.

Light Cruiser: Cleveland Class

Standard displacement: 11,700 tons. Armament: 12 x 6 in (152 mm), 12 x 5 in (127 mm) dual-purpose. Maximum armour: 5 in (12.7 cm) belt, 6.5 in (15.9 cm) turrets. Speed: 32.5 knots. From 1942 onwards 29 of these ships were completed.

Destroyer: Fletcher Class

Standard displacement: 2,325 tons. Armament: 5 x 5 in (127 mm) dual purpose, 10 x 21 in (533 mm) torpedo tubes. Speed: 38 knots. Perhaps the best all-round destroyer of the war. They were able to mount 5 twin 40 mm and 7 single 20 mm A-A guns with no diminution of other armament. No fewer than 175 were built.

Wartime modifications

Most warships were progressively modified as the war progressed. Here are two typical examples drawn from the Royal Navy

Battleship *King George V*

1941: A-A rocket launchers removed; quadruple 2-pdr A-A mounting fitted on after turret, octuple 2-pdr mounting added on twin forward turret; 18 20 mm A-A guns added; no: 271 (surface-warning) radar added but soon replaced by longer-range no: 273; no: 282 (fire control) radars added to five 2-pdr directors.

1942–3: 20 more 20 mm A-A guns added; no: 285 (five control) radars added to 5.25 in (133 mm) directors, FM2 medium frequency direction finder added.

1944–5: Octuple 2-pdr A-A replaces quad on after turret; 2 quadruple 2-pdrs added to after superstructure; 2 quadruple 40 mm Bofors gun mountings also put on after superstructure; 6 twin 20mm mountings replace 12 singles; two more later replaced by single 40 mm Bofors. No: 279B (air search) radar replaces original no: 279; no: 274 (main battery fire control) radar replaces original no: 284 and no: 285 (fire control) radar added to after main armament director; no: 273 radar replaced by no: 277 (surface search) radar; no: 293 (surface/air target indicator) radar added. No: 282 sets provided for new 2-pdr installations; FC2 high-frequency direction finder replaced by RH2 direction finding installation. All the ships's original 1940 electronic sensors had now been replaced.

Cruiser *Sheffield*

1941: Nos: 284 and 285 (fire control) radars added for main armament; 2 quadruple .5 in (12.8 mm) machine guns removed and replaced by 6 20 mm A-A guns

1942: No: 279 (air search) radar removed and replaced by no: 281; nos: 282 and 283 radars added for short- and long-range A-A fire control respectively, no: 273 (surface search) radar added; 3 more 20 mm A-A guns added.

1943: 5 more 20 mm A-A guns added.

1944: 8 more 20 mm A-A guns added.

1945: 1 triple 6 in (152 mm) turret removed and 4 quadruple 40 mm A-A guns added; 15 single 20 mm replaced by 10 twin 20 mm; no: 273 radar replaced by 277.

Source: Contributor.

emphasized high speed. There was a large 1,900-ton design to counter the French ships, but the normal Italian destroyer was around 1,700 tons with four or five 4.7 in. guns and six torpedo tubes; it could make 38 knots. As usual, light A-A armament was progressively increased.

Destroyers of all sizes found themselves pressed into service as mercantile convoy escorts, duties for which they were not necessarily best suited because of their anti-surface armaments and limited range. Just before the war the British had begun converting old fleet destroyers into specialized escort vessels with A-A and enhanced anti-submarine armament, and this process continued with older destroyers into the war years. To produce ocean-going escorts one set of boilers and machinery was sometimes removed. Before the war, the Admiralty had developed a sloop design for convoy escort work, but these 1,250-ton ships with eight (later six) 4 in. A-A guns were impossible to produce in quantity. The Admiralty had made coastal convoys its priority and in 1939 began construction of short-range Hunt class escort destroyers of 1,050 tons and 1,000-ton vessels based on a whale-catcher design, known as corvettes. The latter type, armed with single 4 in. gun, a light A-A armament and depth charges, proved a useful if uncomfortable ocean escort. It was developed into a larger 1,400-ton twin screw truly ocean-going frigate that proved the definitive answer to the mercantile escort problem. The original River class frigates were armed with two 4 in. guns, depth charges, and the new Hedgehog ahead-throwing weapons (see ANTI-SUBMARINE WEAPONS). Later, frigates were larger and were armed either with more guns for A-A purposes (the Bay class) or the new Squid anti-submarine mortars (the Loch class). The Americans produced in large numbers an excellent ocean-going destroyer escort (DE) design of 1,200–1,400 tons which was rated a frigate by the British. These escort vessels were only capable of about 20 knots, but this was sufficient to deal with the contemporary submarine and to escort slow merchantmen over long distances.

The ever-increasing dependence on *radar and *ASDIC meant that if the information was to be properly utilized spaces had to be set aside for its collation and display; in British ships this was the 'action information organization', in American vessels the 'combat information centre'. With this extra demand on the internal volume of ships, already overloaded by the sensors themselves, their operators, the enhanced armaments, and their ammunition supplies, wartime ships could become very overcrowded and uncomfortable.

See also LANDING CRAFT, SEA POWER, and SUBMARINES; see under name for smaller warships such as MTB; see also ARMED FORCES, NAVY, under major powers.

ERIC GROVE

Chesneau, R. (ed.), *Conways All the World's Fighting Ships, 1922–1946* (London, 1980).
Brown, D. K., *The Eclipse of the Big Gun, the Warship 1906–1945* (London, 1992).
Grove, E., *Fleet to Fleet Encounters* (London, 1991).

Wartheland, part of western Poland annexed to Germany. See POLAND, 2(b).

Washington conferences, see ARCADIA and TRIDENT; see also GRAND ALLIANCE and WASHINGTON CONVOY CONFERENCE (see below). For Pacific Military conference held in Washington see PACIFIC WAR.

Washington Convoy conference, planned at the Casablanca conference in January 1943 (see SYMBOL) and held from 1 to 12 March 1943. Present were representatives of the British, Canadian, and US navies, and the RAF and USAAF Anti-Submarine Command, who made various recommendations to the *Combined Chiefs of Staff. To the surprise of the British and Canadians it soon became apparent that the Americans wanted to withdraw their escort vessels from the battle of the *Atlantic. A compromise was reached by which the British and Canadian navies took complete control of northern transatlantic *convoys, except for the short leg between Halifax and Boston or New York. As part of this reorganization, Rear-Admiral *Murray headed a newly formed North-West Atlantic Command during the final phase of the battle of the Atlantic. The conference also decided that 20 very-long-range aircraft be supplied to the Royal Canadian Air Force to start covering the principal mid-Atlantic *air gap south of Greenland. It was also agreed that new convoy cycles be set up; the *huff-duff network be increased; escort carrier groups be introduced to protect Atlantic convoys.

Wasilewska, Wanda (1905–64), Polish Communist politician who fled to the USSR when Germany invaded in September 1939 (see POLISH CAMPAIGN). She was subsequently elected to the Supreme Council of the USSR, became one of Stalin's trusted advisers and was 'the most servile exponent of Soviet ideology' (J. Garlinski, *Poland in the Second World War*, London, 1985, p. 156). She suggested forming *Berling's Army to Stalin and became chairman of the executive council of the Union of Polish Patriots when it was formed in March 1943 (see POLAND, 2(e)).

WASP, Women Airforce Service Pilots, a US civilian organization formed in August 1943 from the Women's Auxiliary Ferrying Squadron and the Women's Flying Training detachment. Its pilots were used by *Air Transport Command for ferrying tasks but principally for operational duties with Training Command. It was run by the well-known aviator Jacqueline Cochran, and more than 1,000 *women completed the training.

Watson-Watt, Sir Robert (1892–1973), British inventor of *radar. He developed his discovery at the radio department of the National Physical Laboratory at Teddington where he was superintendent, and then, after receiving the backing of the *Tizard committee in 1935, at the air ministry's Bawdsey research station which he set up in 1936. In 1938 he became director of communications development at the air ministry. He was knighted in 1942. See also SCIENTISTS AT WAR.

Watson-Watt, R., *Three Steps to Victory* (London, 1957).

Wavell, Field Marshal Sir Archibald (1883–1950), British Army officer who served as C-in-C Middle East during part of the *Western Desert campaigns and as C-in-C and later Viceroy of India.

After serving in the Boer War and *First World War (during which he lost an eye) Wavell became C-in-C *Middle East Command in July 1939. During 1940 and 1941 he defeated the Italians, first beating them at *Sidi Barrani and then driving them out of Cyrenaica. But his command was far-flung and sparsely garrisoned and when, in August 1940, British troops fighting the invading Italians in British Somaliland were given permission to evacuate, Wavell supported the decision. Churchill, however, abhorred it and demanded the general concerned be dismissed. Wavell refused and cabled Churchill that a big butcher's bill was not necessarily evidence of good tactics. This riposte infuriated the prime minister and exacerbated a mutual antipathy which remained throughout Wavell's life.

Success in the *East African campaign soon followed the setback in British Somaliland and Wavell's victories there and in the early Western Desert campaigns brought him well-deserved fame; his formation of A-Force created a system of *deception which was to serve the Allied cause well in the Middle East. However, bled of his best troops for the *Balkan campaign, which he oversaw, Wavell was forced into retreat by *Rommel in the Western Desert, and when trouble flared in Iraq and then Syria (see SYRIAN CAMPAIGN) he was obliged to fight there, too. He protested, was overruled, and though he managed to contain some of his problems his offensives (BREVITY and BATTLEAXE) in the Western Desert failed, and in July 1941 Churchill replaced him with *Auchinleck whose post as C-in-C India Wavell now filled. In January 1942 Wavell was appointed to head *ABDA Command, with his HQ in Java in the *Netherlands East Indies. But the Japanese advance proved irresistible, as it did in the *Malayan campaign, and no sooner had Wavell set up his HQ than he had to dissolve it and pull out. He then reverted to being C-in-C India. His command now included Burma where he also tried, without success, to stem the Japanese tide (see BURMA CAMPAIGN). But even as the remains of the British forces escaped into India he was planning to return. Apart from forming *V-Force, his positive steps in 1942 and 1943 amounted to no more than a disastrous thrust into the Arakan and the use of *Wingate's *Chindits, operations launched with inadequate resources and for which Wavell received no help but much criticism.

He was meant by Whitehall to be only a stop-gap viceroy—a post to which he was appointed in October 1943—to hold the fort till the war's end. But he showed unexpected political skills. The Bengal famine, horribly expensive in lives (see INDIA, 2) was technically his responsibility, if hardly his fault; he pressed relief measures forward with vigour. He maintained an uneasy truce with *Gandhi, of whose astuteness he thought highly; and he almost resolved the conflict, that turned out irresolvable, between Hindus and Muslims about the control of all India after the British had left. His successor, *Mountbatten, solved it in 1947 by partition.

Wavell rated physical and mental toughness as the first qualities of a general. They were qualities he had himself in full measure. But he was not a man of social graces and his silences and inability to hide his boredom were proverbial. He was knighted in 1939, promoted field marshal in January 1943, created a viscount that July, remaining as viceroy until 1947 when he was created an earl.

Lewin, R., *The Chief* (London, 1980).
Moon, P. (ed.), *The Viceroy's Journal* (London, 1973).
Wavell, A. P., *Generals and Generalship* (London, 1941).

WAVES, Women Accepted for Volunteer Emergency Service, the US naval women's service, established in June 1942. More than 900 shore stations were staffed by 86,000 of them.

wavy navy, the Royal Naval Volunteer Reserve: see UK, 7(c).

weasel, multi-purpose tracked vehicle designed for carrying cargo or personnel across surfaces, such as snow, sand, or marshland, impassable to heavier transport. An American invention, it was 5.45 m. (16 ft.) long and could carry about 453 kg. (1,000 lb.). A development of a tracked *jeep, it was used by US forces during the *Pacific war from 1944 onwards and by the British during the *Scheldt Estuary battle.

weather intelligence, see METEOROLOGICAL INTELLIGENCE.

Wedemeyer, Lt-General Albert C. (b.1897), US Army officer who succeeded *Stilwell as *Chiang Kai-shek's Allied Chief of Staff.

The grandson of a German emigrant, Wedemeyer served in China during the early 1930s and learned the language. In the spring of 1941 he started work in the War Plans Division (later Operations Division) under *Eisenhower and became the principal author of the Victory Program, a comprehensive study of what manpower and *matériel* resources would be needed to defeat the Axis powers. Wedemeyer calculated that, after the needs of industry, civilian life, and the other services had been satisfied, a maximum of 8,795,658 men could be mobilized for the army. This proved close to the numbers actually mobilized (8,291,236 men as at 31 May 1945, including US Army Air Forces personnel). But it did not prove practicable to raise the 213 divisions he calculated were necessary, and the 90 that were raised proved barely sufficient.

Rapid promotion followed—from major to brigadier-general in just over a year—and as a war plans expert he accompanied the army chief of staff, General *Marshall, to most of the Allied conferences (see also GRAND ALLIANCE). After being promoted maj-general in September 1943 he became *Mountbatten's deputy chief of staff at *South-East Asia Command, heading the unsuccessful *Axiom Mission and wrestling with the problems this theatre continually generated. In October 1944 he became Chiang Kai-shek's Allied Chief of Staff, commander of US Army forces in China (mostly military advisers) and the administrator of US aid to China, difficult tasks to which Wedemeyer, with his tact and firmness, was better suited than Stilwell. He was promoted lt-general in January 1945 and continued in his post until April 1946, dealing primarily with the repatriation of Japanese troops and civilians. He retired in 1951 and was promoted four-star general three years later.

Wedemeyer, A., *Wedemeyer Reports!* (New York, 1958).

Wehrmacht, the German armed forces. See GERMANY, 6.

Welles, (Benjamin) Sumner (1892–1961), US under-secretary of state from 1937 until his resignation in September 1943. He was highly thought of by Roosevelt who liked to deal with him direct. He represented the US at the *Panama conference in September 1939 and in early 1940 was dispatched by Roosevelt on a peace mission to Europe, possibly to attempt to woo Mussolini away from Hitler. He was present at the *Placentia Bay conference in August 1941, assisting in drafting the *Atlantic Charter which was issued there, and took part in the negotiations with Japan which preceded that country's attack on *Pearl Harbor (see USA, 1). He then represented the USA at the *Rio conference and worded the diluted statement which merely recommended all South American states to break with Germany (see also LATIN AMERICA). This compromise infuriated Cordell *Hull, the secretary of state, but Roosevelt approved it. His career was ended when an ambitious rival, William Bullitt, whom Roosevelt never forgave, presented the president with an affidavit about Welles's homosexuality.

Wenck, Lt-General Walther (1901–82), German Army officer who was operations officer of the German Army High Command (OKH) from July 1944 and then commander of German Twelfth Army. In April 1945 during the battle which preceded the fall of *Berlin Hitler ordered Wenck to break the ring of Soviet troops around the German capital, but by then Wenck's army, which included teenage members of the *Hitler Youth, was not much more than a figment of the Führer's imagination. Wenck was supposed to command the *Werewolves which were to hold out in the *National Redoubt in southern Germany, but the Redoubt never materialized.

Werewolves, putative Nazi guerrilla organization which was to man the *National Redoubt and carry out sabotage and resistance in occupied Germany. It was given a commander, Lt-General *Wenck, but the Redoubt was never formed and the Werewolves amounted to nothing more than a handful of fanatical young Nazis whose best-known action was to murder the mayor of *Aachen in March 1945 for *collaboration with the Allies. Soviet disinformation exaggerated their importance, to distract the western Allies.

Western Approaches, British naval shore command. See UK, 7(c).

Western Desert Air Force (WDAF), formed from the RAF's Middle East 204 Group (Air HQ, Western Desert) in October 1941 after the unsuccessful BATTLEAXE offensive, launched during the *Western Desert campaigns, had made it clear that greater ground-air co-operation was needed.

It was initially commanded by Air Marshal *Coningham who set up his HQ with the commander of Eighth Army (to which WDAF gave close support for much of the war), and as a tactical formation it quickly became known for its mobility and ability to work closely with ground troops. It comprised personnel of several nations, but predominantly South African, and initially had sixteen squadrons of aircraft (nine fighter, six medium bomber, one for tactical reconnaissance). At first losses were high, for no Allied fighter was then the equal of the German Messerschmitt 109F; and in a six-month period during 1941 one squadron commander lost 120% of his pilot strength. But during the summer of 1942 the WDAF began to be supplied with the Spitfire Mk5, and in August 1942 three USAAF squadrons, flying Warhawks, joined it, and the Allies began to gain the upper hand. By the second *El Alamein battle in October 1942 the WDAF had grown to 29 squadrons (including nine South African) which were equipped with Boston, Mitchell, and Baltimore bombers and Hurricane, Kittyhawk, Tomahawk, Warhawk, and Spitfire fighters, or fighter-bombers.

During the *North African campaign, in which Air Vice-Marshal Harry Broadhurst commanded it from 1 February 1943, the WDAF became, from 23 February 1943, part of the North West Africa Tactical Air Force; and then, for the *Sicilian campaign which started in July 1943, part of the Mediterranean Allied Tactical Air Force. On 21 July 1943 it was renamed the Desert Air Force. It took part in the *Salerno and *Anzio landings; and in the rest of the *Italian campaign, where it developed new methods of close support bombing, it helped the *Balkan Air Force supply Italian and Yugoslav partisans, operating over the Adriatic Sea west of a line drawn between Fiume and Ancona. Air Vice-Marshal W. Dickson commanded it from April 1944 and Air Vice-Marshal R. Foster from December 1944.

Western Desert campaigns, fought in Libya and Egypt from June 1940 to January 1943, principally by British and Commonwealth forces, to prevent Axis forces severing the Suez Canal, a vital Allied supply and communications artery. The first campaign was a débâcle for the Italians. The second, with *Rommel leading a combined German–Italian force, was a 2,145 km. (1,500 mi.) seesaw affair (see Map 110) dominated by the struggle for air and sea superiority in the battle for the *Mediterranean and by the *logistics of supplying both armies through inadequate ports and over hundreds of kilometres of desert, mostly via a single coastal road.

In most of the confrontations between the two sides Rommel's force was numerically inferior, but his troops were more professional, better led, and thoroughly steeped in the co-operation of all arms. By contrast, British reinforcements for the original Western Desert Force were slow to adapt to desert warfare; the infantry and armour floundered in mutual mistrust and rarely co-ordinated their efforts; and the professional *élan* of Lt-General *O'Connor's early Western Desert Force soon became an indifferently commanded army whose worst faults were not corrected until the arrival of *Montgomery in August 1942.

Fighting in the vast expanse of the Libyan desert was unlike any other theatre of war. The distances involved were great, the problem of supply constant, yet the numbers of men involved—compared, say, with those committed to the *German–Soviet war—were tiny. The conditions in which both sides fought were harsh and the sickness rate was high (see MEDICINE). But helped by the absence of *SS units and large numbers of civilians it was a chivalrous war; and, with the exception of *El Alamein—and, of course, the siege of *Tobruk—a very mobile one. Rommel, writing to his wife in March 1941, said that speed was the one thing that mattered, and he later wrote that territory was less important than to keep moving until a tactically favourable position for battle was found, and then to fight.

The fighting, in which British special forces such as the *Long Range Desert Group and *Popski's Private Army played a notable part, was often confused and confusing: the terrain was mostly flat and featureless; dust and sand, churned up by artillery fire and tanks, obscured the battlefield; each side used the other's vehicles and armour, often making identification impossible until too late; *radio communications were unreliable; and desert navigation was an art few could master. Close air support was another crucial factor (see WESTERN DESERT AIR FORCE) and *signals intelligence warfare also played its part. For the British, *ULTRA intelligence gave unique insight into German plans, though sometimes the intentions Rommel signalled his superiors were not what he actually did. For the Germans, Rommel's radio monitoring unit, and what he called the 'Good Source'—decrypted messages despatched by the US military attaché in Cairo in the *Black code (see also ITALY, 6)—gave him equally vital insights into British plans until the one was destroyed and the other ceased in mid-1942.

Italy declared war on 10 June 1940, but it was not until 13 September that the C-in-C of Italian forces in Libya, Marshal *Graziani, was ordered by Mussolini to launch his Tenth Army, commanded by General Mario Berti, on an invasion of Egypt. The Western Desert Force, comprising only two partially equipped, but mobile, divisions, withdrew before Berti's five (later nine) ill-equipped divisions. But when Berti arrived at *Sidi Barrani on 16 September he stopped to await supplies, and on 9 December, after receiving additional tanks from the UK, the C-in-C *Middle East Command, *Wavell, launched a successful surprise attack (COMPASS). The Italians suffered heavy losses and these increased further when *Bardia fell the following January. They then withdrew to Tripolitania, which Hitler helped them defend by sending a 'special blocking detachment' (5th Light Division), the first of two German formations that were to comprise the legendary *Afrika Korps. He also ordered Fliegerkorps 10, then assembling in Sicily, to extend its operations to the Western Desert. But these moves did not immediately affect O'Connor's triumphant advance westwards: Tobruk fell to him on 22 January and then, with a daring inland cross-desert thrust, he cut off the retreating Tenth Army at *Beda Fomm before the threatened German invasion of Greece (see BALKAN CAMPAIGN) siphoned off his best troops. All that remained was a weak screening force, commanded by Lt-General Philip Neame, but Wavell calculated that Rommel would not attack before May, a judgement ULTRA appeared to support by revealing the determination of the German Army High Command, to keep Rommel in a defensive mode. But neither Wavell nor the German High Command had reckoned with Rommel. Within a week of landing he had pushed a reconnaissance screen up to Nofilia; he then captured El Agheila on 24 March 1941 and Mersa Brega on 1 April.

Initially, Rommel had regarded his attack as just a raid, but once he saw his chance he ignored the orders of both Hitler and his immediate superiors—he was always, at least nominally, under the Italian High Command (see COMANDO SUPREMO)—and, with the Italian Ariete Division under Afrika Korps command, launched himself further into Cyrenaica. Order, counterorder, and disorder followed for the British. Neame and O'Connor were captured, Tobruk was invested, and Rommel was not halted until he reached Sollum. This dramatic advance, which reversed nearly all O'Connor's successes and gave the Germans vital airfields from which the siege of *Malta could be imposed by air raids on the island, was an unwanted success for the German Army High Command, whose attention was focused on Greece and the forthcoming invasion of USSR (see BARBAROSSA). Its chief of staff, General *Halder, commented that Rommel had gone 'stark mad'. His deputy, Lt-General *Paulus, sent to

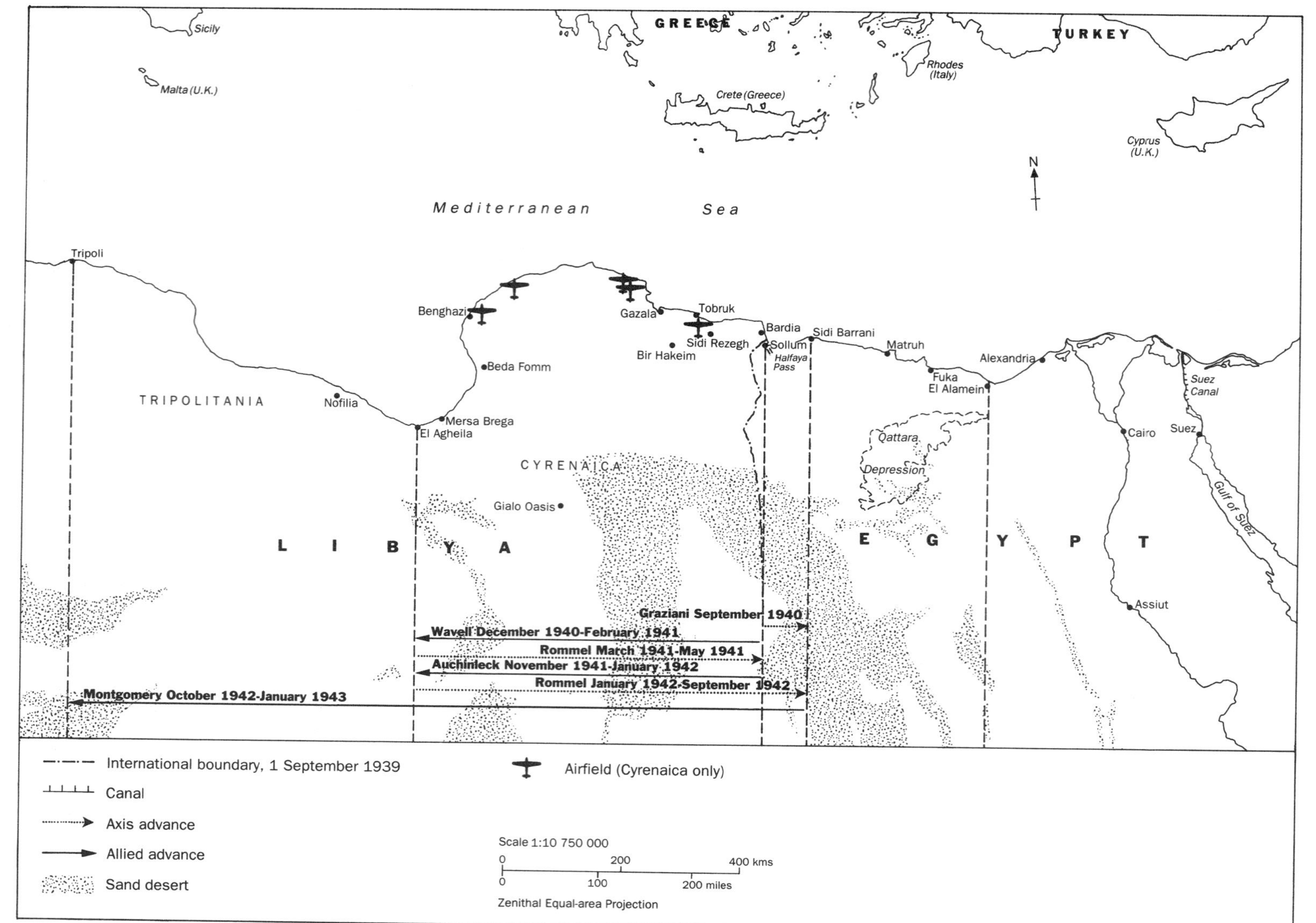

Map 110. **Western Desert campaigns**, 1940–3

investigate, recommended to Rommel that he stay on the defensive, even after he had been reinforced by 15th Panzer Division, then in the process of arriving in Libya.

By contrast, Churchill wanted success, and quickly. He had a fast convoy (TIGER) containing tanks and fighters dispatched to bolster Wavell; and when Paulus's signal recommending caution was decrypted at *Bletchley Park, he made the first operational use of ULTRA intelligence in North Africa by urging Wavell to attack. But both BREVITY (15 May), and the more powerful BATTLEAXE (15 June), were hastily planned and executed. Bad radio security, and Rommel's first use of his 88 mm. anti-aircraft guns as *anti-tank weapons against the British tanks during BATTLEAXE, played a crucial part in their failure. They also led to Wavell being replaced by *Auchinleck on 1 July.

Auchinleck knew that Wavell had been forced to act prematurely and he refused to budge until he was ready. He also cabled Churchill demanding a 50% reserve of tanks, inspiring the prime minister's remark that, 'Generals only enjoy such comforts in Heaven. And those who demand them do not always get there.'

The date for another offensive (CRUSADER) was eventually agreed and Lt-General *Cunningham was appointed to command a newly formed Eighth Army made up of 13th Corps (the Western Desert Force) and a new formation, 30th Corps. Auchinleck, having accumulated a marked superiority in tanks and aircraft, launched CRUSADER on 18 November against Rommel's force (renamed Panzer Group Afrika, July 1941) which now comprised the Afrika Korps and 21st Italian Corps. The attack pre-empted yet another assault by Rommel on Tobruk, the thorn in his side which precluded any advance into Egypt until it had been removed. At first, Rommel thought Cunningham's armoured thrust a raid. But once the size of the threat had been established his forces reacted with their usual vigour. In a series of hard-fought actions around *Sidi Rezegh ridge they inflicted such severe casualties on the Eighth Army that Cunningham requested Auchinleck's presence to decide whether to withdraw. This pessimism caused Auchinleck to replace Cunningham with his own deputy chief of staff, Maj-General Neil Ritchie. But these battles, and an impulsive advance, had inflicted heavy losses on Rommel's forces, and had strained his logistics to the limit and beyond, and on 8 December he began withdrawing towards Cyrenaica.

In some respects the Eighth Army had repeated O'Connor's success of the previous year, but this time there was no Beda Fomm. Also, Rommel's supply lines now became more secure as additional Axis U-boats and aircraft began to exert their influence in the central Mediterranean. On 5 January 1942 he received extra tanks and fuel, and on 21 January pre-empted Auchinleck's plan to invade Tripolitania (ACROBAT) by striking at Mersa Brega. The next day his Panzergruppe Afrika, which now included the Ariete and Trieste divisions (20th Corps), was renamed Panzer Army Afrika, and its probing raid again precipitated a hasty British retreat. Ignoring all orders to halt, Rommel surged forward to take Benghazi before his advance ran out of steam.

A somewhat acrimonious debate followed between London and Cairo as to when the Cyrenaica airfields, lost once again and once more helping to neutralize Malta, were going to be recaptured. Auchinleck finally agreed to move in June 1942, but then ULTRA revealed that Rommel intended launching an attack (VENEZIA) in May and the Eighth Army turned its attention to defensive preparations. But though it was known when Rommel was going to strike it was not known where, and, after outflanking the British and French positions at *Bir Hakeim, he defeated Ritchie in the *Gazala battle, and on 21 June finally took Tobruk.

The crisis was now such that Auchinleck dismissed Ritchie and took personal command. The Eighth Army, efficiently protected by the Western Desert Air Force, retreated to *Mersa Matruh where at the end of June it suffered another defeat. The nadir of British fortunes in the Middle East had been reached. The Eighth Army now fell back to the partially-built *El Alamein line, and reserves from Syria and Egypt were brought forward. On 30 June Auchinleck told his men to show Rommel 'where he got off'. But the mood of some of the British commanders was gloomy, if not openly defeatist. The Mediterranean fleet left Alexandria and in Cairo there was an air of panic.

Auchinleck's generalship had created an atmosphere where, as a New Zealand officer memorably described it, 'the whole attitude of Eighth Army was that of having one foot in the stirrup'. But Rommel's attack when it was launched on 1 July was too hastily mounted and Auchinleck's plans, ably drawn up by *Dorman-Smith, were sound. In what is now known as the first El Alamein battle, the Axis forces were held. Both sides introduced reinforcements, but in a series of further confrontations neither gained a decisive advantage.

In early August Churchill and General *Brooke arrived in Cairo. They replaced Auchinleck with *Alexander and Montgomery was given the Eighth Army after Churchill's first choice, Lt-General William Gott, was killed. Montgomery, supplying badly needed, incisive leadership, made changes to Auchinleck's defensive plans; ULTRA, by revealing Rommel's exact intentions, confirmed that Montgomery's reading of the situation was correct; and at the end of August Rommel, now a sick man, was beaten back at *Alam Halfa.

Montgomery then concentrated on training his army for a new offensive (LIGHTFOOT). This was launched on 23 October and in the twelve-day second El Alamein battle that followed Montgomery's tactics of attrition finally broke open Rommel's defences. However, heavy rain, the exhaustion of his pursuers, his own defensive skills, and Montgomery's caution, combined to allow Rommel to extricate his most valuable troops, though he left behind 30,000 *prisoners-of-war. Montgomery's inability to destroy Rommel's forces subsequently earned much criticism, but his advance across Libya was a logistical triumph. Rommel stood at several places, but each time he was prised from his positions. On 23 January 1943 Montgomery took the surrender of Tripoli and three days later Rommel withdrew into Tunisia where he then participated in the *North African campaign.

Behrendt, H., *Rommel's Intelligence in the Desert Campaign* (London, 1985).
Carver, M., *Dilemmas of the Desert War* (London, 1986).
Pitt, B., *The Crucible of War*, 2 vols. (London, 1980–2).

western hemisphere. In July 1940 Roosevelt declared at the *Havana conference that the USA would be responsible for the defence of the western hemisphere. This area was then defined by Admiral *King by drawing a line between the two hemispheres so that the western one extended from about 26° West, which is the meridian that passes some 80 km. (50 mi.) west of Reykjavik in Iceland, to the International Date Line. In the Atlantic this included Greenland, the Azores, the Gulf of the St Lawrence, the Bahamas in the British West Indies, the Caribbean Sea, and the Gulf of Mexico. Entry into the western hemisphere by warships or aircraft of belligerent nations, other than those powers who had sovereignty over territory there, would be viewed as possibly having hostile intent. On 15 July 1941, a week after US troops took over from British forces in Iceland, King redefined the western hemisphere to include that country.

Westerplatte, a mile-long strip of land by the port of *Danzig where Poland was entitled to maintain a naval depot and a small garrison. At 0445 on 1 September 1939, just minutes after Luftwaffe attacks on Polish airfields heralded the start of the war, the old German training cruiser *Schleswig Holstein*, on a goodwill visit to the port, opened fire on Westerplatte at close range. An attempted German landing on it failed, and several hundred Germans were killed before the Polish survivors eventually surrendered on 7 September 1939.

Westmark, Nazi *gau* created after the fall of *France in June 1940 from Lorraine, the Saar, and the Palatinate. Josef Burckel was appointed its **Gauleiter*. See also GERMANY, 4.

West Wall, German fortifications which ran for 480 km. (300 mi.) opposite the French *Maginot Line from Basle to Cleves. Construction started in 1936 and accelerated in 1938 when the *Todt Organization employed 500,000 workers and consumed one-third of Germany's annual output of cement to complete it. It consisted mainly of mutually supporting pillboxes, in two bands in some places, and, where geographical features provided no natural barrier, concrete anti-tank defences. It was not designed to thwart a full-scale offensive, but merely to delay it while reserves could be brought forward. It deterred the French during the *phoney war that lasted over the winter of 1939–40 and was first broken by the US Army at the start of the battle for *Germany in the autumn of 1944 when it was partly manned by **Volksgrenadier* divisions. From 1940 to 1944 the line was neglected and much of its armament removed. Both sides also called it the Siegfried Line.

Weygand, General Maxime (1867–1965), French Army officer, born in Brussels of unrevealed parentage. He was Foch's chief of staff during the *First World War and commanded the Polish forces which successfully defended Warsaw against the Red Army in 1920. On 20 May 1940 he succeeded *Gamelin as supreme Allied commander during the fighting which preceded the fall of *France, having been brought out of retirement the previous year to command French forces in the Levant (Syria and Lebanon). His Weygand Plan, to attack from two directions the German corridor which stretched to the coast, came to nothing; the *Dunkirk evacuation followed; soon after, his Weygand Line, which stretched along the Seine and Aisne rivers to the *Maginot Line at Montmédy, was breached; and on 5 June he called on the politicians to arrange an *armistice. He then served as defence minister in Marshal *Pétain's *Vichy government before becoming its delegate general in North Africa in September 1940.

According to the Nazis' ambassador in Paris, Otto Abetz, Weygand was an irreconcilable enemy of Germany and a major factor in ensuring that the *Paris protocols remained unratified. Hitler forced his resignation in November 1941 but he continued to influence Pétain and was at least partly responsible for the marshal's strongly worded protest when the Germans invaded unoccupied France in November 1942. Soon afterwards he was arrested and imprisoned in Germany. After the war he was charged with treason but was acquitted.

white propaganda, see SUBVERSIVE WARFARE.

Wilde Sau (wild boar), German night-fighter tactics used from the summer of 1943 to attack British bombers in the *strategic air offensive against Germany. Instead of being tied to, and controlled by, the *Kammhuber Line, single-engined fighters roamed at will over a German city under attack. *Flak was restricted to a certain height above which the fighters were free to attack the bombers, which were silhouetted by the fires they had created. The first such unit was formed by Major Hajo Herrmann shortly before the British first used WINDOW as a form of *electronic warfare during a raid on *Hamburg on the night of 23/24 July 1943. This was highly effective and forced the Germans to use the Wilde Sau tactics, which they did with increasing success. Eventually Herrmann's command increased to divisional strength and the technique was used by nearly all Kammhuber Line twin-engined fighters as well. See also FIGHTERS, 2; and ZAHME SAU.

Wilhelm Gustloff, 25,484-ton German liner, named after a Swiss Nazi leader assassinated in 1936, which was torpedoed in the *Baltic Sea by a Soviet submarine on 30 January 1945. She was carrying 8,000 service personnel and refugees from Gdynia which was about to fall to Soviet troops during the last phase of the *German–Soviet war. More than 7,000 died, the largest single loss of life in maritime history.

Willkie, Wendell (1892–1944), US lawyer, American born but of German origin. He was a delegate at the 1924 Democrat Convention, but opposed two of Roosevelt's New Deal projects and in 1940 he changed sides. He was nominated as the Republican presidential candidate that year but lost heavily. In the following year he did much to unify the USA behind Roosevelt's policies by turning the Republican Party away from its long-standing isolationism (see also AMERICA FIRST COMMITTEE) and by backing the president's *Lend-Lease programme. In August 1942 he became a goodwill ambassador to the Middle East (and later to the USSR and China) a task he performed extremely well; his book describing that journey; *One World* (1943), became a best-seller. But his backing of so many Democratic measures had incurred the wrath of his more conservative Republican colleagues and he failed to become the party's presidential choice in 1944. He refused to back the chosen candidate, Thomas Dewey, but would not support Roosevelt either. He died in October, the month before the president was re-elected.

Willow Run Plant, the largest aircraft assembly factory in the world, was conceived by the Ford Motor Company's production chief, Charles Sorensen. It was built by Ford 48 km. (30 mi.) west of Detroit, its isolation being deliberate to minimize union influence. Construction began in March 1941 and the first B24 bomber was completed that December. The bombers were built, like Ford cars, on an assembly line in a building 1.6 km. (1 mi.) long and 400 m. (440 yd.) wide. At one time the factory employed 42,000 workers. But though it was a symbol of American industrial capacity, it also revealed the flaws and waste that much of American industry suffered from early in the war. The temporary living accommodation was inadequate and insanitary, so that half the workers preferred to commute from Detroit. The absentee and turnover rates were high, and teething problems gave it the nickname 'willit run?' The production and morale problems were eventually resolved when half its operations were farmed out to Ford subsidiaries, the workforce was scaled down, and it became a final assembly line. By August 1944 production had increased to 500 bombers a month, and in its 43 months of operation it produced 8,685 aircraft, or one every 103 minutes.

Wilno was annexed by Poland in 1922. It was occupied by the Red Army in September 1939 (Rus.: Vilna) and ceded to Lithuania (Lith.: Vilnius) before being occupied by the Germans (Ger.: Wilna) in June 1941. It was near Wilno, in July 1944, that the Polish Home Army (see POLAND, 4) made contact for the second time—*Volhynia had been the first—with the advancing Red Army as part of the Home Army's operation *TEMPEST. By then local Home Army units had already fought about 30 encounters with the Germans, and had captured several towns. On 6 July 1944 they attacked Wilno itself and the next day the Red Army joined in. After it fell on 13 July the Soviet commander ordered the Home Army from the city but subsequently agreed to equip and arm them properly. However, the Home Army commander, General 'Wilk', never returned from a second meeting, his officers were imprisoned by the *NKVD, and Wilno's civilian administration was deported. Most of the Home Army personnel who had taken part in the city's capture, about 5,700 in all, were rounded up and, when they refused to join *Berling's Army, were sent to the *GUlag. Some who escaped later preferred to fight than flee, and in the battle of Surkonty they killed 132 Soviet soldiers while losing 36 themselves.

Wilson, Field Marshal Sir (Henry) Maitland (1881–1964), British Army officer who commanded British and Empire troops during the *Balkan campaign in April 1941. He was appointed C-in-C *Middle East Command in January 1943, and succeeded *Eisenhower as Supreme Allied Commander in the Mediterranean in January 1944.

In September 1939 Wilson was a lt-general in command of British troops in Egypt. Early successes against the Italians were followed by a brief spell as military governor of Cyrenaica. He was then given command of Allied troops in the Balkan campaign and handled the hasty retreat from Greece with skill. On his return to the Middle East *Wavell appointed him to command British troops in Palestine and Transjordan which Wilson used to quell *Rashid Ali's revolt in Iraq in May 1941 and then in the *Syrian campaign the following month.

Although he was a very competent commander in the field, circumstances now conspired to keep Wilson at posts which required his considerable political and diplomatic skills. Churchill lobbied strongly for him to command the Eighth Army, but the new C-in-C, *Auchinleck, preferred *Cunningham. In December 1941, by which time he had been promoted general, his command became Ninth Army which covered the Levant (Syria and Lebanon) as well as Palestine and Transjordan; in August 1942 he took command of the new Persia–Iraq command (see PAIFORCE); and he then succeeded *Alexander as C-in-C Middle East where his only operational involvement was against the *Dodecanese Islands. He was strongly criticized for the British failure there, but he later made it clear that it had been mounted against his better judgement on direct orders from London. During his time as Supreme Commander in the

Mediterranean he oversaw the *Italian campaign as well as the last two large amphibious operations there, *Anzio and the landings on the *French Riviera. In December 1944 he handed over to Alexander, was promoted field marshal the next month, and became British representative to the *Combined Chiefs of Staff committee in Washington, a post he held until it was abolished in 1947. He was knighted in 1940.

Keegan, J. (ed.), *Churchill's Generals* (London, 1991).

WINDOW, see ELECTRONIC WARFARE.

Windsor, Edward, Duke of (1894–1972), former British monarch, Edward VIII, whose abdication on 10 December 1936 soured his relationships with his family and the British government. He married the divorcée Mrs Wallis Simpson, the cause of his abdication, in 1937 and the same year made an ill-advised visit to Hitler, who announced himself 'entranced'. When war broke out he returned to the UK and was appointed to a military mission in Paris, dropping in rank from field marshal to major-general. He undertook a series of goodwill tours of the French front with orders to report back on the *Maginot Line and other French defences about which the French were being very secretive. After the fall of *France in June 1940 he went with his wife to Madrid and then Lisbon. His request for suitable employment in the UK was refused, but he was offered, and accepted, the governorship of the Bahamas. While he was in the Iberian peninsula the Nazi foreign minister, *Ribbentrop, attempted to detain him there (see SCHELLENBERG), but the royal couple, who were unaware of the plot, sailed from Lisbon on 1 August 1940 and remained in the Bahamas for the rest of the war.

Some assert that though the duke may have made some indiscreet remarks during his stay in Portugal, and may have entertained the possibility of being a useful intermediary in any peace negotiations, there is no evidence that he either sympathized with the Nazis or was in contact with them. On the other hand, the historian Martin Gilbert records the contents of a telegram which was drafted by the colonial secretary, Lord Lloyd, for Churchill to send over his own name to the dominion prime ministers. Part of it read: 'The activities of the Duke of Windsor on the Continent in recent months have been causing HM [*George VI] and myself grave uneasiness as his inclinations are well known to be pro-Nazi' (*Winston S. Churchill*, Vol. 6, London, 1983, p. 700). However Churchill, a longstanding friend of the duke's, rejected the draft and wrote of the duke's 'unimpeachable' loyalties.

Bloch, M., *The Duke of Windsor's War* (London, 1982).

Wingate, Maj-General Orde (1903–44), British Army officer whose methods of irregular warfare led to the formation of the *Chindits during the *Burma campaign.

Wingate was born in India of parents who were Plymouth Brethren. Between the wars he gained experience of guerrilla warfare in Palestine and became a fervent Zionist. In January 1941, as a lt-colonel and a member of *SOE, he accompanied the exiled Emperor *Haile Selassie back into Italian-occupied Abyssinia. At the head of a mixed band of troops, which he called *Gideon Force, Wingate fought a series of brilliant guerrilla actions, marked by sheer bluff and guile, which ended with Haile Selassie being returned to his capital. But by achieving this feat of arms Wingate had stepped beyond his military brief and, after writing a report that was less than flattering about higher authority, he was virtually dismissed from his command. Exhausted by his efforts, he attempted suicide and spent some months in hospital.

In March 1942 *Wavell, under whom Wingate had served in Palestine and East Africa, summoned him to India to organize guerrilla warfare behind Japanese lines in Burma. Wingate proposed self-contained 'long range penetration' groups, or Chindits, which would operate while being totally supplied by air. His plans were accepted and in June 1942 he was promoted brigadier and given a force to train with which he operated behind Japanese lines in Burma between February and June 1943. A third of the force was lost but he was hailed as a hero and Churchill asked to meet him. 'We had not talked for half an hour before I felt myself in the presence of a man of the highest quality', the prime minister later wrote (*The Second World War*, Vol. 5, p. 62), and at the time he thought Wingate should command the army in Burma. He took him to the *QUADRANT conference (see also GRAND ALLIANCE) in Quebec in August 1943 where Wingate created such a favourable impression that he was given more resources than he could ever have expected. He returned to India a maj-general, trained his new, much larger, force during the winter of 1943–4, and, after many political vicissitudes and a severe bout of typhoid, took it behind the lines of the Japanese then moving forward for their *Imphal offensive. But on 24 March 1944 he was killed in an air crash and in the months that followed his Chindits, through no fault of their own, failed to achieve the grand designs Wingate had planned for them.

Wingate's personality and the originality of his thinking—some would say genius—have made him one of the most controversial military figures of his time, and one who continues to cause conflicts among historians. Churchill, always drawn to the more unorthodox methods of warfare, was intrigued by his fervour and vision, and his men were devoted to him. By supplying his troops totally by air, and substituting air support for artillery, he showed himself to be a brilliant innovator. But the multitude of books on the Burma campaign nearly all have comments to make on his insubordination, ruthless ambition, calculated rudeness, and emotional instability.

Sykes, C., *Orde Wingate* (London, 1959).
Tulloch, D., *Wingate in Peace and War* (London, 1972).

Winter Line, Allied name for the series of defensive lines the Germans built during the *Italian campaign to defend Rome: see BERNHARDT, GUSTAV, and HITLER LINES.

Winter war, see FINNISH–SOVIET WAR.

wireless bombs, see GUIDED WEAPONS.

Witherington, Pearl (b.1914), eldest daughter of the last male heir of an ancient Northumbrian fighting family; she lived in Paris with her mother and three younger sisters, and worked as an extra cipher clerk in the British embassy. In June 1940, when the embassy fled south-westward, she took her family down to a boat for England and then turned back herself to help France. After a year's work in an escape line at Marseilles (see MI9), she returned to England, where she joined *SOE's F section and was parachuted back into France early in 1943 as courier to a particularly widespread network of secret agents, whom she helped to arm for work on sabotage in preparation for the Normandy landings (see OVERLORD). When on 1 May 1944 her organizer was arrested, she took over a network of her own, concentrating on the northern half of the Indre *département*; by July 1944, with a price of a million francs on her head, she was running a private army some 3,000 strong, specializing in cutting railway lines. Neither the German nor the French police ever caught her. M. R. D. FOOT

Witzleben, Field Marshal Erwin von (1881–1944), German Army officer who spent much of the *First World War on the Western Front and was decorated for valour. Between the wars he rose steadily but unspectacularly in rank and by 1936 was a lt-general. The dismissal in 1938 of the army's C-in-C, *Fritsch, on trumped-up charges turned his disapproval of the Nazis into open hostility and he was deeply involved in the 1938 conspiracy to remove Hitler (see SCHWARZE KAPELLE). His First German Army manned the *Siegfried Line during the *Polish campaign of September–October 1939 and made a diversionary attack against the *Maginot Line during the fighting which led to the fall of *France in June 1940. Having been promoted general in November 1939, he received his field marshal's baton in July 1940, and in April 1941 became C-in-C of the newly formed Army Group D which guarded the Atlantic and Channel coast, and garrisoned France. In March 1942 he went on sick leave. Hitler saw this as an opportunity to retire him and replace him with *Rundstedt, and he was never re-employed. In the July 1944 bomb plot to assassinate Hitler, Witzleben was to assume the position of C-in-C of the Wehrmacht. When the plot failed he was tried by the *People's Court and hanged.

Mitcham, S., *Hitler's Field Marshals and Their Battles* (London, 1988).

Wolff, Lt-General Karl (1906–84), early *SS member who was a pre-war chief of staff to *Himmler. After Italy's surrender in September 1943 he became military governor of northern Italy and head of the SS there. In March 1945, realizing Germany had lost the war, he met Allen *Dulles in Switzerland to arrange the capitulation of all German forces in Italy which took place on 2 May 1945. This saved him from prosecution at the *Nuremberg trials but, having served one week of a four-year sentence in 1949, he was sentenced in 1964 to 15 years' imprisonment for murdering 100 Jews and sending 300,000 more to the death camps (see OPERATION REINHARD). He was released in 1969 because of ill health.

wolf-pack, see ATLANTIC, BATTLE OF THE.

WOLFSCHANZE (Wolf's Lair), codename for Hitler's HQ situated near Rastenburg in East Prussia. It was used by Hitler and his High Command from June 1941 to November 1944 and was the scene of the attempted assassination of 20 July 1944 (see SCHWARZE KAPELLE).

women at war. 'The last was a soldier's war. This one is Everybody's', commented the editor of the British magazine *Mother and Home* in November 1939. The American ambassador in London, John G. Winant, went further: 'This war, more than any other war in history, is a woman's war.' Yet the age-old tradition that warfare was the business of men, not women, which was challenged in the Second World War, was a misleading one. Women had always been involved in wars. They had serviced armies as camp-followers and, since the mid-19th century, served as army nurses. In zones of combat and enemy occupation they had never been immune from injury. In national and revolutionary conflicts, such as the Greek war of independence and the Russian revolutionary war, they had fought with partisan armies. They had supplied armies with uniforms and boots and where, as in the Napoleonic wars, diversion of manpower into the armed forces created labour shortages, they had substituted for men in the civilian workforce. Twentieth-century warfare, engaging the resources of entire societies, employing new and powerful weapons of destruction, waged in an age of mass politics and mass media, merely increased women's involvement and made it more visible. The *First World War, remembered as a soldier's war chiefly because of the overwhelming predominance of military over civilian casualties, had drawn women into 'men's work' in munitions factories and on the land. They had served in the field as nurses and ambulance drivers and performed military support roles as cooks and orderlies, clerical workers, telephonists, and signallers. In the UK, for example, The first Zeppelin raid on London in April 1915 and the introduction of food rationing in 1918 also foreshadowed developments that would, between 1939 and 1945, bring war and its demands into the home and co-opt housewives into the war effort.

women at war

For women, as for men, the Second World War differed from its predecessors chiefly in its scale and impact on civilian populations, which were targeted systematically by strategic bombing designed to break morale. Women experienced the war differently from men chiefly because more than any previous war it tended to disrupt domestic life and to cast them in unfamiliar gender roles, most conspicuously as uniformed servicewomen. However, patterns both of women's participation in the military and of civilian losses varied in different nations. The UK became in 1941 the first country to conscript women, the Soviet Union in 1942 the first to use them in combat with regular armed forces. Other nations did not follow suit, although all major combatant powers except Japan used uniformed women volunteers as auxiliaries to the military. More British civilians than military personnel died under enemy attack in the first two years of the war, most in the London *Blitz of 1940–1: by December 1942 the numbers of UK civilians killed included 20,629 women and 24,203 men. *Area bombing of German cities by the RAF from 1942 and American raids on Japan's industrial cities in 1943–5 (see STRATEGIC AIR OFFENSIVES, 1 and 3) equally placed women alongside *children and the elderly in the front line, and where conscription had depleted the male population, as in *Hamburg in 1943, the dead included more women than men. By contrast, the USA, apart from a few *balloon bombs, escaped aerial bombardment, and suffered hardly any civilian war deaths. Elsewhere, civilians became casualties of war in much the same ways as in the past: in war-induced famines in India, Greece, and the Netherlands, in the sieges of *Leningrad and *Sevastopol, or as victims of terror and reprisal at the hands of occupying forces in Europe and South-East Asia. Yet the audit of deaths in Europe at the end of the war showed that only countries under German occupation had suffered more civilian than military losses. These victims were predominantly men. In the Soviet Union in 1959 women outnumbered men in the age-range 37–48 by five to three. Where the slaughter of civilians was not indiscriminate, from the air, it was still men who were chiefly identified and killed as potential fighters. In that sense, this remained a soldier's war, a men's war, and soldiers were often confused about the place of women in it. American troops who liberated *Auschwitz were surprised, according to a survivor, Vera Laska, to find women in *concentration camps, even though their own government had interned as enemy aliens *Japanese-Americans of both sexes.

No woman exercised significant influence over the conduct of the war—except, perhaps, the indirect influence wielded by such wives as Clementine Churchill, Eleanor Roosevelt, and Madam *Chiang Kai-shek—but in most combatant countries women were more actively identified, as citizens, with public policy and national defence than ever before. In the UK and its Dominions, in the USA and in Germany women had the vote. In the Soviet Union in 1941 one in seven party members in the CPSU was a woman and the Komsomol youth organization provided rudimentary military training for members of both sexes. Axis regimes, though more conservative in their emphasis on women's traditional roles in home and family, nevertheless sponsored women's and youth organizations that brought them into public life and engaged in propaganda and voluntary work. The 400,000 women of Italy's Fasci Femminili joined in the campaign against *League of Nations' sanctions during the Abyssinian war of 1935–6. Japanese women's 'patriotic' organizations, merged in 1942 in a single Dai Nihon Fujinkai (Greater Japan Women's Association), worked under government direction to promote the 'National Spiritual Awakening' and when the *China Incident started in July 1937 they campaigned against extravagance and cared for the wounded and bereaved. Nazi Women's organizations—the Frauenschaft and Frauenwerk—and the Bund Deutscher Mädel (see HITLER YOUTH) worked to identify women, as transmitters of culture and mothers of the Aryan race, with the values of the regime. In 1938 it became compulsory for single German girls of 17 to 25 to do six months' labour service (increased in 1941 to a year) as farm workers or domestic servants, or a longer period in nursing, welfare, or kindergarten work. In Allied countries, too, before war broke out, women' organizations prepared for the work of national defence and women volunteers did military training. In the UK they served with *FANY, the Women's Legion, and the Voluntary Emergency Service, and these organizations provided officers for the British women's auxiliary services, reconstituted in the last year of peace: the ATS in September 1938, the WRNS in February 1939, the WAAF in June 1939. The Women's Voluntary Services for Civil Defence (*WVS), organized by Lady Reading in 1938, attracted 300,000 members within a year. Women of all nations also belonged to organizations that performed first-aid and social work on an international basis such as the Red Cross and YWCA.

Feminists had been prominent in the inter-war peace movement, yet many—among them Virginia Woolf, Maude Royden, Helen Keller, and Simone Weil—became converts to the view that war was a lesser evil than Nazism. Feminists are divided in their attitude to women's war service and the significance of women's identification with the war effort is controversial: did it fulfil women's claim to equal citizenship or subject them to the military? Historians are also divided on the consequences of war for women: does it promote or undermine equality between the sexes?

The Second World War did little to clarify these issues. Women's right to serve their country was pressed by such equal-rights feminists as the British MPs Irene Ward, Lady Astor, and Edith Summerskill, who criticized delays in mobilizing womanpower in 1940–1. But war service could also be seen as patriotic duty, a response to emergency, without implications for women's conventional peacetime roles. Poland, Catholic and conservative but fearing invasion from both east and west, made military

Some **women** bore arms during the war. Here, women of the Rani of Jhansi Regiment, a part of the Indian National Army, form a guard of honour in Singapore.

training, including the use of firearms, compulsory for young women in 1937. The enfranchisement of women had been justified in Britain in 1918 by their contribution to the war. In France and Italy, where anti-clerical parties had denied them the vote after the First World War, women's role in the resistance was cited as a reason for enfranchising them in 1944 and 1946 respectively. In the USA, however, women had gained the vote in 1919 partly because of President Woodrow Wilson's conviction that they would use it in the cause of peace. Evidence that American women were indeed less hawkish than their men is provided by an *Office of War Information survey conducted two months after *Pearl Harbor: 57% of men but only 35% of women favoured all-out war against Japan. The masculine basis of militarism was recognized by General *MacArthur, who regarded the enfranchisement of Japanese women, decreed by the occupying authorities in 1945, as 'the most effective single barrier [against] future jingoism' and hoped it would 'bring to Japan a new concept of government directly subservient to the well-being of the home'. Yet the previous decade had shown, if nothing else, that women, though not initiators of war, could be conditioned as citizens and patriots to play their part in it.

Mobilization of women during the war was nowhere more effective than in the UK (despite a slow start) and the Soviet Union. In the UK by September 1943 an estimated 7.75 million women were in paid employment, by comparison with 5.09 million in 1939, and over a million more were in the WVS. More than 470,000 were in the women's services or forces nursing services, 80,000 were in the *Women's Land Army, and over 400,000 were employed as full-or part-time civil defence workers or in the Home Guard and Royal Observer Corps (see UK, 6). Munitions industries—engineering and metals, explosives, chemicals, and shipbuilding—employed about two million women, more than four times as many as in 1939. The number of women in civil service or local government white-collar jobs had grown by 500,000. Many women transferred to war work from traditional 'women's jobs', in domestic service or industries like textiles and clothing, and the great majority in the forces were volunteers. But from March 1941 women became liable to direction into war work and under the National Service (No. 2) Act of December 1941 single women aged 20–30 became liable to conscription. Between 1942 and 1945 nearly 125,000 recruits were 'called up' into the women's auxiliary services—though women, unlike men, were given the choice of serving instead in civil defence, industry, or the Land Army. In 1943 the age for conscription was lowered to 19 and direction of labour, originally restricted to women of 18–40, was extended to 'grandmothers' of 40–50. Mothers with a child of under 14 living with them remained exempt, but other exemptions for married women, generous at first, were whittled down from 1943 as the government began to direct them into part-time work and industrial out-work. The acute shortage of manpower that prompted these measures also hit the Soviet Union after the German invasion (see BARBAROSSA). Between June and December 1941 nearly a million Soviet housewives and schoolgirls joined the paid workforce. A decree of February 1942 made all women aged 16–45 liable for war service. By the end of the war women accounted for 55% of the civilian workforce, compared with 30% in 1940, and on the collective farms there were four women workers for every man. About 800,000 women served with the Soviet military and a further 200,000 as partisans in occupied regions.

The USA, with its superior resources and pool of unemployed male workers, faced less severe manpower problems. Yet even there the mobilization of women has been compared favourably with that of Germany and Japan. A sustained propaganda campaign aimed chiefly at housewives increased America's female workforce by six million, or 32% between 1941 and 1945. The great majority worked in industry but women's branches of the services created in 1942–3 included at peak strength nearly 272,000 recruits. In Japan, where the prime minister, General *Tōjō, made a virtue of his refusal to conscript women in deference to the family system, a combination of propaganda and inducements increased the female workforce between 1940 and 1944 by only 1.5 million, under 10%. As for Germany, although women accounted for about 1.5 million of the 7 million foreign volunteer or *forced labour workers employed in the Reich during the war, the number of German women in employment hardly increased at all. But comparison between Germany and Allied countries is not straightforward. In 1939 women had formed 37.4% of the German workforce, a higher proportion than in the UK in 1943 (36.4%). There was a much smaller pool of unemployed housewives to draw on. As in Japan, many married women worked in agriculture and their labour became more vital—and harder—as male farm workers were conscripted. Within the manufacturing sector, working-class women did move into heavy industry, which in Germany by May 1943 employed 1.5 million women, nearly twice as many as in May 1939. Moreover, in Germany, unlike Japan, the armed forces had, since the First World War, employed women civilians in clerical and manual jobs and from 1940 uniformed women auxiliaries, the Helferinnen, were attached for the first time to all branches of the armed forces.

A widespread tradition has it that the German war effort was greatly handicapped by failure to exploit womanpower, caused by Nazi eugenic policies and belief in restricting women's sphere to *Kinder, Küche, Kirche* (children, kitchen, and church), and also by the inability of a dictatorship to impose sacrifices on a population that had been led to expect easy victories. There is something in this view, but it has been exaggerated (see GERMANY, Table 2 and STATISTICS, Table 4). Nazi pronatalism did lead to measures likely to keep women out of the workforce: exceptionally generous allowances for servicemen's wives, exhortations to young Aryan women to have babies, even (to the disgust of respectable Frauenschaft leaders) outside marriage (see also LEBENSBORN). But Nazi notions of 'womanly work' did not exclude productive employment in the cause of the nation. Women were exhorted to make 'Munitions for their Sons' and those who did take factory work, though they often worked in grim conditions and under military discipline, were well provided with day nurseries, which cared in 1944 for 1.2 million *children—ten times as many as found places in the federally-funded child care centres set up to help working mothers in the USA. But propaganda to recruit women was less sustained than in the USA and advocates of their compulsory mobilization, like Hermann *Göring and Albert *Speer, were overruled by Hitler. The government acquired the authority to conscript women as early as 1935, but never used it. In 1943 a law was passed requiring women aged 17–45 to register for directed war work, but it was not systematically enforced. As in Japan, middle-class women found it easy to avoid war work and to keep their domestic servants. Nor were they attracted into the civil and armed services by the kind of responsible and interesting jobs that were open to British and American women. But the suggestion, sometimes made, that failure to mobilize women led to Germany's defeat is certainly a myth.

In the regular armed forces of all the combatant powers women remained a small minority. The UK women's services included at peak strength just under one woman to ten servicemen, while Soviet women made up about 8% of total armed forces manpower. In the USA, where the army's chief of staff, General *Marshall, had trouble overcoming army resistance to women in the military and the Senate passed the 'WAAC Bill' on 14 May 1942 by a mere eleven vote majority, the number of servicewomen never exceeded 2% of fighting strength. The civilian status of Helferinnen was emphasized by uniforms adapted from that of the Red Cross. British and American servicewomen also began the war as civilians, though the British ATS and WAAF (but not the WRNS) were given military status in 1941, as were the American WAAC, renamed WAC, in 1943, largely in order to check the growing number of *deserters. The range of tasks performed by servicewomen was subject to restrictions, varying in different countries, but it was everywhere wider than ever before, reflecting the growth of service bureaucracy and changes in weapons and communications technology. By 1943 the British ATS worked in more than 80 different army trades. Over a quarter served in anti-aircraft batteries where they came under fire and operated searchlights and targeting instruments. They did not, in theory at least, fire guns since a Royal Warrant limited women to non-combatant roles, but Churchill conceded that they should be known as 'gunners'. In Germany, too, women served as Anti-Aircraft Auxiliaries (Flakwaffenhelferinnen), and, like the UK's WAAFs, they manned *radar stations, performed the heavy work of handling air defence *barrage balloons, and trained as aircraft mechanics. American servicewomen served in the field in the Pacific, Africa, and Europe, but the general staff abandoned the experiment of using them in anti-aircraft batteries in 1942 for fear of public criticism. Women also performed more traditional roles in the nursing services and as cooks, orderlies, and drivers. 'Forces Sweethearts' like Vera Lynn, Marlene Dietrich, Anne Shelton, and Carol Landis toured with *ENSA and America's USO, supplying the troops with entertainment. By 1943 women outnumbered men by over four to one on the staff of *NAAFI, vastly expanded to provide catering and recreation facilities for British forces at home and overseas.

Only in the Soviet Union, and there only in desperate response to losses inflicted in the *German–Soviet war, were servicewomen used in combat roles with regular troops—as snipers, tank drivers, and air force pilots—some serving alongside men and some in separate women's units. Among the latter were three regiments organized by Marina Raskova, the celebrated Russian woman aviator. The 586th Women's Fighter Regiment included the ace pilot Lily Litvak, the 'White Rose of Stalingrad', while the 588th Women's Night Bomber Regiment, known to the Germans as the 'Night Witches', harassed the enemy so effectively in their ancient biplanes that they were given the title of a Guards Regiment in recognition of outstanding service (see also USSR, 6(e)). Even the Soviet Navy which shared the widespread sailors' belief that women were bad luck on ships, was induced to let a few women serve at sea.

The policy of using women to release men for combat may in part explain the hostility encountered by servicewomen in the English-speaking world. In the UK, the Dominions, and the USA the recruitment of women was hampered by persistent rumours of immorality among servicewomen. In fact, where statistics were available, they showed that rates of illegitimate pregnancy and infection with venereal disease (VD) were lower than for civilian women of the same age group. Official investigations showed that these rumours originated not with enemy *fifth columnists but with Allied servicemen, though they were spread by the *press and civilians of both sexes. ATS women were known as 'officers' groundsheets' and WAAFs as 'pilots' cockpits'; in the UK only the WRNS, the smallest and most exclusive of the services, were exempt from such calumnies. Soviet women veterans were similarly abused as 'campaign wives' (not, however, as they recall by men who served with them at the front). Deep-rooted anxieties about the place of women in a war machine were present in all societies and gave rise to policies that sometimes seemed perverse. German women auxiliaries were forbidden to use firearms even to defend themselves against capture and, as civilians, they were not entitled to be treated as *prisoners-of-war. Those captured by the Soviets sometimes disguised themselves as men for fear of being used as army prostitutes. Outside the Soviet Union no air force accepted women as pilots, yet women aviators did vital and dangerous work in the war. Most renowned among women test pilots of experimental planes was Hanna Reitsch, who flew Germany's V-I before it was adopted as an unmanned bomb (see V-WEAPONS). In the British *Air Transport Auxiliary one in eight pilots was a woman and fifteen, Amy Johnson among them, were killed on missions (see also CIVIL AIR PATROL and WASP).

The urge to protect women was less strong than the cultural stereotype that made them bearers, not destroyers, of life. As Sybil Irving, controller of the Australian Women's Army Service, put it, 'These girls will be the mothers of the children who rebuild Australia. They must not have the death of another mother's son on their hands.' But the belief that it was not a woman's role to kill did not extend to clandestine and partisan warfare—in which women played an important part—though Pearl *Witherington, an *SOE agent and one of the few women who led *Maquis groups in France, did share it.

SOE is known for its departure from the tradition that banned women from combat: it sent 50 women agents to occupied France and trained women in the use of weapons and explosives, evading armed service regulations by enrolling them in the civilian Women's Transport Service or FANY. Partisan armies in eastern and southern Europe—the Home Army in Poland (see POLAND, 4), as well as *Tito's followers in Yugoslavia and the resistance forces of *ELAS in Greece—included a higher proportion of women soldiers than the French *Maquis, the core of which consisted of men determined to avoid conscription by the Germans. An estimated third of Italian partisans were women; but although even the communists, according to the Italian resistance veteran 'Elena' (Carla Capponi), were happy for women to carry bombs, because they were less liable to be challenged by the Germans, they were reluctant to accept them as equal combatants. As in regular armies, women played vital support roles: they acted as nurses, radio operators, and couriers, and smuggled weapons and supplies. Yet in many aspects of resistance work women had special advantages to offer. In escape lines used by Allied servicemen and Jewish or political refugees, safe houses—private homes, hotels, brothels, and convents—were crucial. Women guides were indispensable, since couples were less conspicuous than men travelling alone. Major escape lines in France averaged 40% of women among their members and four were headed by women: the Belgian nurse 'Dédée' de Jongh; 60-year-old Marie Louise Dissard of Toulouse; Mary Lindell, comtesse de Milleville, a veteran nurse from the First World War who used the French Red Cross as cover; and Pauline, comtesse de St Venant. Intelligence *réseaux* (networks) included an estimated 18% of women and individuals played important roles. An American agent, Virginia Hall, posing as a journalist in *Vichy France, helped SOE to establish early secret resistance connections in 1941, while British-born Pearl Witherington ran a sabotage network. Women who headed *réseaux* linked with Britain's *MI6 or the American *Office of Strategic Services included a publisher's secretary, Marie Madeleine Fourcade (see SPIES); a nurse, Jeannine Picabia, daughter of the well-known surrealist painter; and an industrialist's wife who worked for the Vichy *censorship, Suzanne Bertillon. Women also organized and largely staffed the illicit social service network for prisoners and their families that was initiated by Bertie Albrecht, women's unemployment officer at Lyons. A Dutch housewife, Mrs Kuipers-Rietberg, was co-founder of an organization that gave assistance to the *onderduikers* (divers), most of them Jews like Anne *Frank and her family, who lived in hiding during the German occupation of the Netherlands. The production and distribution of the clandestine press (see SUBVERSIVE WARFARE) in occupied Europe also relied heavily on women.

Unlike regular armies, which recruited mostly young women—and some of the 'Night Witches' were mere teenagers, too small to see out of the windscreens of their planes unless they perched on cushions—resistance groups drew in women of all ages. Post-war books and films told the stories of individual women agents—Odette *Sansom, Violette *Szabo, Nancy *Wake, and Mathilde *Carré in France, Christine Granville and Hannah Senesh in central Europe—but clandestine warfare relied on many part-time women workers whose contribution was never recorded. The social conventions that gave them some protection from suspicion and allowed them to operate 'above ground' equally discouraged women from claiming credit for resistance work after the war. Yet those who were captured were tortured, imprisoned, and often killed. Of 10,000 French women who were sent to *Ravensbrück, 85% of them resistance workers, only 500 survived. Reprisals for resistance activities were sometimes visited on entire communities. The men might be killed outright and women and children sent to concentration camps, as in the Czech village of *Lidiče, or hostages be slaughtered regardless of gender or age, as in the case of the massacre at the *Ardeatine catacombs in March 1944.

The wartime *internment of women, like their military involvement, was not a new phenomenon but in the Second World War it came about in unfamiliar circumstances. In the UK about 500 of the 6,500 *conscientious objectors imprisoned between 1940 and 1945 were women who had refused conscription or compulsory fire-watching duties. In the Far East about 20,000 British civilians, men and women, were left stranded after the unexpected fall of *Singapore in 1942, together with civilians of other nationalities, mostly Dutch and Australian. In the fifteen main internment camps set up by the Japanese for women, the survivors—teachers, nurses, missionaries, business and service wives—were held for the remainder of the war. Nazi racial policies had led to the internment of women before the war, although political prisoners as well as Jews, gypsies, and prostitutes were consigned to the concentration camp established for women at Moringen in 1933 and the larger, wartime women's camp at Ravensbrück, through which passed about 123,000 victims. The war and the *Final Solution brought women also to camps originally set up for men. At one stage there were nearly 100,000 at *Auschwitz. Other predominantly male camps, such as *Buchenwald, included female labour details employed on munitions work. In contrast to the regime in the Soviet *GUlag, where men and women often mixed freely and contracted 'sub-marriages', both Germans and Japanese rigidly segregated male and female prisoners. The Germans, unlike the Japanese, made use of women as guards. These *SS Helferinnen were often recalled as crueller to women prisoners than the men. Irma Grese of Auschwitz and *Bergen-Belsen, the 'Blonde Angel of Hell' who whipped women to death, was among those hanged in 1945. Hermine Braunsteiner Ryan, the 'Mare' of *Majdanek, trampled prisoners to death with steel-studded boots: she was among those sentenced to life imprisonment in Dusseldorf in 1981.

Hunger, disease, brutality, extremes of cold in Europe and heat in Asia, sometimes long hours of forced labour—these were the lot of all inmates of Axis camps. As Alexander Solzhenitsyn remarked of women in the GUlag, 'it seems that things were no harder for them and maybe even easier.' A third of the women imprisoned in Japanese camps died, but over half the men. German records suggest that women survived starvation for longer periods than male inmates, perhaps because they had better housekeeping skills and strategies for sharing. Children of both sexes were imprisoned with the women and in Japan helped women maintain the rituals of home life more effectively than men. Survivors of Ravensbrück recall that networks of mutual aid, surrogate 'families', helped women in the struggle to hold on to life. Women ceased to menstruate not, as was believed in the German camps, because of chemicals in the prison soup, but through malnutrition and stress. European women accustomed to subservience from colonial peoples found particular humiliation in aspects of Japanese camp discipline that reflected their captors' contempt for them, both as women and as prisoners—the deep bow required from prisoners to guards, the blow to the face as punishment for insubordination. In German camps women had their heads and bodies shaved on arrival and often experienced sexual humiliation and abuse: naked parades before guards, forced abortion or sterilization. In both instances they were less liable to be raped by their captors than were the Soviet Union's women *zeks* (GUlag prisoners).

For the great majority of women, however, the Second World War was spent on the Home Front. Films popular in the UK and USA—*Hollywood's *Mrs Miniver* and the British Ministry of Information-backed *In Which We Serve* for example—portrayed women as wives and mothers bravely supporting the military and sustaining morale. Propaganda slogans aimed at attracting women into war industry often used similar imagery: '"The Girl He Left Behind" is Still Behind Him'. In wartime women's domestic roles became more, not less, important. As *Good Housekeeping* pointed out, 'If those who keep house went on strike, the war would be lost in a week.' Women played a key role in adapting economies to war, promoting war loans and salvage drives, and coping with reduced levels of consumption. Recurring themes in women's memories of the war are the disruption of everyday living and the traditional 'woman's sphere'. In areas subject to bombardment there was *blackout, nights were spent in air-raid shelters, and children were evacuated with or without their mothers. In country areas other women received evacuees and *refugees, not always hospitably, into their homes. Bereavement and separation, hunger and homelessness, struck unevenly but with similar effect. Women from the cities scoured the countryside on bicycles for food and fuel, families were fed on black bread or turnips, soap was scarce, Italians learned to cook without oil, Japanese without rice, Parisians kept rabbits on their balconies, British and Canadian women grew vegetables in 'Victory Gardens'. In Germany by 1945 over half the houses in big cities were in ruins and rations at starvation level. Even in the USA there were shortages of food, clothing, and domestic equipment, and the number of households with domestic servants fell by 50%—it was not just conservatism that led seven out of eight Americans surveyed in 1946 to see home-making as a full-time activity. British austerity regulations included a ban on the manufacture of shoes with heels over two inches high. Japan banned perms and required even geisha girls to wear the unbecoming peasant *mompe* (baggy trousers). Women in trousers, though denounced by the Vatican, became for the first time a common sight in the west. On the other hand make-up, a compensating symbol of femininity, became more socially acceptable and Tampax was promoted with the slogan 'Women are winning the War—of Freedom'.

Some increase in sexual freedom for women resulted from a war that saw unprecedented movement of armies around the world and relaxation of the disciplines of family life. British and American divorce rates rose and it has been estimated that in the decade after 1942 nearly a million American servicemen married foreign 'war brides', three-quarters of whom eventually joined them in the USA. But in both countries moral panics caused by rising illegitimacy and VD rates (see MEDICINE) reinforced the 'double standard', as purity movements blamed *v-girls or 'good-time girls'. Black propaganda used by both sides in subversive warfare played on servicemen's fears of infidelity by wives and sweethearts at home. For many women these years were far from liberating. The estimated 42,000 part- or full-time prostitutes found by the Americans in Naples in 1944 were often providing for starving families. At the end of the war Soviet women who had served as 'German bedstraw' were sent to the GUlag. The 'horizontal collaborators' of Vichy France had their heads shaved in public (see p. 247). The conflicting pressures of war on sexual norms were reflected in the inconsistent policy of the western Allies towards official brothels for serving troops—sanctioned in the earlier stages of the war in the hope of containing VD but later banned—and 'fraternization' with conquered populations, encouraged by MacArthur in Japan but (somewhat ineffectively) banned in Germany. Germany criminalized its own prostitutes and within Japan almost all brothels were closed down, yet both powers used official or supervised brothels for troops in the field (see COMFORT WOMEN).

In the UK and the USA women who wanted employment did find that the war eased their path. The Paramount comedy *Rosie the Riveter* (1944), inspired by Norman Rockwell's cartoon of a muscular, overalled housewife working in the shipyards, was more popular with female than male filmgoers. But under government pressure industrialists became less reluctant to employ older women and women from ethnic minorities. Roosevelt insisted in 1944 that the American services should recruit black women (see also AFRICAN AMERICANS AT WAR). Some trade unions which had excluded women, such as the British Amalgamated Engineering Union, now accepted them as members. The proportion of married women in the workforce rose, partly reflecting a wartime increase in the marriage rate, partly the increased availability of part-time work. The marriage bar in teaching was lifted on both sides of the Atlantic. More middle-class women found clerical or responsible administrative or management jobs, more working-class women undertook 'men's work' in industry. Land girls also did 'men's work' such as ploughing. Equal pay was conceded in industry where a woman took over a 'man's job' without modification, but trade unions ensured, as in the First World War, that this rarely happened: changes in the production process were used to create new categories of 'women's work', paid at a lower rate. In the UK, though not in the USA, equal pay was denied to government employees, civilian and military, and it became an issue. An all-party caucus of women MPs secured in 1943 equal compensation for women for war injuries; in 1944 they carried an amendment to Butler's Education Act to give equal pay to teachers, although that vote was reversed when Churchill made it an issue of confidence. Public nurseries were provided in the UK for only a quarter of the under-fives whose mothers were in employment. The spread of part-time working, and the concession by employers of 'shopping-time' to women who worked the standard wartime 57–60-hour week, though welcomed at the time, underlined the assumption that housekeeping was a woman's job. The end of the war brought efforts to persuade women that they really wanted to withdraw from employment: there is conflicting evidence about how far this was true.

Feminist historians now tend to see the mid-20th-century cult of domesticity and femininity as a reaction against deprivations endured in a war that had confused rather than undermined traditional gender roles. In the distribution of *decorations for bravery women were everywhere less likely to gain recognition than men. The UK's highest honour, the Victoria Cross, was reserved for military combatants and even SOE heroines were ineligible for it. Some Italian resistance groups excluded women from their post-war parades. America's Veterans of Foreign Wars organization banned women from membership. In the Memorial National Cemetery of the Pacific in Honolulu it is the timeless suffering of bereaved mothers that is commemorated in an inscription quoting Lincoln's tribute to a mother who lost five sons in the American Civil War: 'The solemn pride that must be yours to have laid so costly a sacrifice upon the altar of freedom'. Women who had served with the military sometimes found it wisest to conceal the fact (even in the Soviet Union the reputation of veterans for roughness and immorality did not improve their chances of marriage) and the urge to protect children from knowledge of the horrors of wartime caused memories to be repressed. Only in recent years have women veterans, prisoners, war wives, and widows, and those who suffered internment been encouraged to recall the more positive side of their experiences—the unfamiliar sense of independence and personal autonomy, the unexpected discovery of women's strengths and capacity for collective action. Four decades passed before the publication of words written by a Soviet anti-aircraft gunner, Nonna Alexandrovna Smirnova: You must tell your children, Putting modesty aside, That without us, without women, There would've been no spring In 1945.

JANET HOWARTH

Campbell, D'A., *Women at War with America* (Cambridge, Mass., 1984).
Goldman, N. L. (ed.), *Female Soldiers—Combatants or Non-combatants? Historical and Contemporary Perspectives* (London, 1982).
Higonnet, M. R., Jenson, J., Michel, S., and Weitz, M. C. (eds.), *Behind the Lines. Gender and the Two World Wars* (New Haven, 1987).
Laska, V. (ed.), *Women in the Resistance and in the Holocaust. The Voices of Eyewitnesses* (Westport, Conn., 1983).
Summerfield, P., 'Women, War and Social Change: Women in Britain in World War II', in A. Marwick (ed.), *Total War and Social Change* (London, 1988).
Warner, L., and Sandilands, J., *Women Beyond the Wire* (London, 1982).

Women's Land Army, British organization re-formed in 1939 whose members worked in agriculture. See also UK, 2.

world trade and world economy. The Second World War was an economic as well as a military conflict. The war effort made enormous demands on the economic resources of all the combatant powers, and the Axis states were finally worn down by the sheer material strength of the *Grand Alliance they faced. The war also altered the international economy, bringing to an end the period of stagnation and protectionism of the 1930s; creating the circumstances for greater economic co-operation under the guidance of the USA; and, after 1945, launching the world economy on a great economic boom.

The world economy in the decade before war was dominated by the Great Depression, the slump of 1929–32 which brought a collapse of world trade, prices, and employment from which most economies failed to recover before the coming of war. The slump destroyed international economic co-operation as states struggled to look after their own economic interests. The pre-war years were the high-water mark of economic nationalism, of tariffs and trade discrimination, of managed currencies and barter trade. The old imperial states, France, the Netherlands, and the UK, fell back more and more on their empires as a source of cheap food and materials, and safe markets for their exports. Other states, most significantly Japan, Italy, and Germany, saw the solution to their relatively weak position in the world economy in pursuing 'autarky', or self-sufficiency, cutting off dependence on the world economy. They also sought a solution to their shortages of *raw materials and other economic resources in imperialism. Japan saw China and the western Pacific as a natural area of political and economic expansion; Italy sought new resources in Africa; Germany looked to eastern Europe and the Soviet Union as an area for potential economic exploitation. By the late 1930s all three states had begun to create closed economic areas or blocs which would provide economic security and an economic base for military strength. War was seen as a natural part of this process of economic empire-building.

The rise of protectionism and imperialism in the 1930s was partly a response to the obvious weaknesses of the world economy. The gold standard broke down after the slump and it proved impossible to stabilize the currency system in the 1930s; international investment declined to negligible levels in the 1930s, making it difficult to increase trade and reducing the transfer of skills and technology; the migration of labour also came to a halt. For the poorer primary-producing states, low prices for food and materials meant greater poverty and a sharp slow-down in efforts to modernize. The greatest problem of all, however, was the withdrawal of the two major international economies, the UK and the USA, from any active leadership of the world economy. America was the largest and potentially most powerful of the developed industrial economies; it was also one of the major protectionist states, withholding loans from other countries and using high tariffs to block their exports. Without American or British willingness to play the role their economic strength justified, the world economy continued to stagnate and the pursuit of political or military solutions could not be restrained.

Economic insecurity and imperial conflict led to a rapid increase in rearmament from the mid-1930s onwards. This had the paradoxical effect of boosting the world economy by increasing industrial output and the demand for raw materials. By 1938 the scale of rearmament had begun to distort patterns of trade and output. The increases in military spending were substantial for all the great powers except the USA. In the 1930s most states expected a future war to make very great demands on economic resources and capability. Rearmament was seen not just in terms of finished weapons but in terms of industrial capacity, trained labour, and access to raw material and energy resources, nowhere more so than in Germany where the idea of 'total war' was developed most fully. From 1936 the German economy was transformed to meet the strategic demands of future warfare. By 1939 almost one-quarter of the national product was devoted to military spending, and two-thirds of industrial investment went to war-related industries, particularly iron and steel, aluminium, chemicals, and synthetic fuel. Germany was not alone in this. By 1939 France was spending three and a half times as much on the military as in 1913, and British rearmament rose from £185 million in 1936 to £719 million in 1939. The UK, like Germany, was preparing for a war of attrition, stockpiling scarce resources, retraining labour, expanding industrial capacity in key engineering sectors. By 1939 the major European states were all heavily committed to military effort. The Soviet Union had the world's largest armed forces, thanks to the military priorities of the Five Year Plans. In 1930 the USSR produced 890 aircraft; in 1939, 10,000.

Rearmament brought a great number of economic headaches. By the late 1930s military demands made it necessary to increase state intervention in the economy to balance civilian and military needs. In Germany this meant complete control over trade, investment, prices, and wages. In the UK it brought the state into a more active role in trade and industrial production. For the western states there were limits to intervention, and it proved difficult to interfere in international transactions. As a result the balance of payments deteriorated rapidly by the late 1930s and the UK suffered heavy losses of gold and foreign exchange. Heavy military spending also encouraged inflationary pressures. Preparation for war reversed the long price decline in the world economy. This made it more expensive to get the quantities of scarce resources needed for war. Oil was a particular difficulty, on which the military industries and forces of all states depended (see STATISTICS Tables 6 and 7). Germany tried to solve the problem of high dependence on overseas sources by producing synthetic 'oil-from-coal'; the UK sought to find overseas supplies, that it could dominate commercially, in the Middle East and Far East, in Iran, Burma, and Iraq. Fierce competition for raw material resources set in before the outbreak of war, and encouraged Hitler to move eastwards so that he could engross there the food, labour, and raw material supplies needed for the German military build-up. The war against Poland was part of this process. Against his expectations, the western states obstructed the move and Hitler found himself faced with 'total war' sooner than he had expected, before his grand economic and military plans were complete.

The war had an immediate and far-reaching effect both on the domestic economy of the combatant powers and on the world economy as a whole. Military demands distorted the patterns of consumption and trade; military spending increased government debt and raised taxes. All the major states faced severe financial pressure, but were anxious to avoid the mistakes of the *First World War when prices rocketed and state debt escalated. While there were very great increases in military spending (see Table 1), much more of it was covered by tax revenue. Tax receipts more than doubled in Germany; they more than trebled in the UK. In the USA, where tax was low before the war, federal expenditure rose from $12 billion in 1941 to $100 billion in 1945, of which 43% was financed by taxation. To prevent these high levels of spending from producing inflation, all governments controlled prices and reduced consumption. Rationing of food and household goods not only reduced domestic consumer spending, but also ensured a fairer distribution of what goods were available. By the end of the war Germans consumed almost a third less than at the start; in the UK consumption fell by about one-fifth by 1943 but then began to revive again. Only in the USA was the war effort accompanied by an increase in consumption, thanks to the vast resources at its disposal and the large-scale re-employment of previously idle capacity and labour.

The great increases in military spending and cuts in consumption made possible very large increases in the output of weapons and equipment (see STATISTICS Table 2). This was achieved by converting much civilian production to military contracts and by expanding investment in new plant and machinery. In the UK and Germany much of the new capacity for armaments was found in idle car factories, furniture workshops, locomotive plants, and a host of other civilian firms. By 1941 almost 50% of the output of German consumer industries went to the armed forces. In the USA, where there existed only a very small military industry before 1941, huge investment programmes were set up to provide new factory capacity. By 1945 there was 50% more productive plant in the USA than there had been in 1940.

The demands of war industry made it necessary to control the distribution of raw materials and of labour. This was not done in Germany until 1942 when a new Central Planning agency to rationalize the whole raw materials situation was set up (see SPEER PLAN). In the UK this was done from the outset of the war, and with American entry the two western states co-ordinated their raw material needs and distribution. Labour supply was a problem because of the demands of the armed forces for manpower. In Germany 12 million men were taken out of the German workforce and were replaced with *women or *forced labour taken from occupied Europe. By 1945 over 50% of the native German workforce was female. Though this level of female employment was never reached in the UK or USA, women did take up many of the jobs previously done by men (see STATISTICS Table 4). The only other way of coping with high demands for labour was the rationalization of factory methods and labour use. In most industrial states great gains were made in efficiency over the war period by increasing automation in factories, reorganizing the work processes, and making better use of existing equipment. Labour productivity in Germany increased by 60% in war industries between 1939 and 1944. In the USA the most spectacular example of this change was the output of

World trade, Table 1: Military expenditure of the major powers, 1938–44 (in billions of national currency)

	1938	*1939*	*1940*	*1941*	*1942*	*1943*	*1944*
Germany (RM)	17.2	38.0	55.9	72.3	86.2	99.4	n.a.
UK (£)	0.4	0.7	2.6	3.6	3.9	4.5	4.5
USSR (rbls)	27.0	40.8	56.8	82.0	108.0	124.0	138.0
USA ($)	0.1	0.1	1.9	14.2	52.4	85.2	90.9
Japan (yen)	6.0	6.4	7.2	8.8	12.4	17.9	27.3
Italy (lire)	15.0	27.7	58.8	64.2	83.8	—	—

Source: Contributor.

cargo ships—nicknamed *Liberty ships—by mass production. The time taken to make one ship was cut from 260 days to 40 over the course of the war.

Every war economy had its own strategic priorities and its own peculiar problems. The British war economy was faced with the difficulty of importing much of its raw materials and food; hence great efforts were made from early on to use resources as rationally as possible. The Japanese economy was always short of sufficient raw materials and factory capacity, and had to restrict consumption as much as possible. The Soviet Union, following the German attack on its prime industrial region, had to reorganize war production in new areas in eastern and central Russia (see USSR, 2). The Soviet priority was output at all costs, with low living standards and poor working conditions. In Germany the problem was not so much resources as poor administration and organization of the war effort. Not until the middle of the war was the economy thoroughly reorganized to achieve what it was capable of producing. By then the *strategic air offensives against both Germany and Italy, and later Japan, began to place a real ceiling on the further development of productive resources. For the USA the only real difficulty lay in the very low level of military preparedness in 1941 and the sheer speed with which the war economy had to be developed. Though this brought its share of friction and crisis, the vast material resources of the USA and its position as the leading industrial power gave it the human and material capacity necessary to produce an extraordinary transformation in two years.

The effect of the war on the international economy was just as far-reaching. By the time the USA entered the war in December 1941 a 'world market' no longer existed. Germany and Japan dominated large enclosed blocs in Europe and Asia which fuelled their war efforts. The British Empire world-wide was organized economically for the war effort. Normal flows of trade and investment were interrupted or distorted. *Economic warfare was carried on all over the world. The usual methods of buying and selling goods no longer applied, for most of the major combatants could not pay for their imports by exporting goods. The export industries in the UK, Germany, and Japan were busy producing weapons. International lending also came to halt. Memories of the unpaid war debts of the First World War made neutral investors rightly shy of making loans to the warring states. The only 'normal' trade that survived was British and American trade with the suppliers of raw materials, oil, and food in the Third World.

The economic blocs dominated by Germany and Japan were essentially siege economies. Under the title of *Greater East Asia Co-prosperity Sphere, Japan sought to integrate the economies of the areas captured by its forces in Manchukuo, eastern China, French Indo-China, Malaya, and the Netherlands East Indies (NEI) with the Japanese economy, primarily to feed the war effort but ultimately with the object of creating a large autarkic economic bloc which would be self-sufficient in food and materials. Other Asian states would be invited or pressured to join the Co-prosperity Sphere, but Japanese interests would remain paramount. There is no doubt that without the additional resources, particularly oil, seized in South-East Asia the Japanese could not have sustained their war effort for as long as they did. A flow of materials and food came from the conquered areas: by 1943 the NEI supplied 80% of Japan's crude oil and almost all its coal came from Manchukuo and northern China.

The German 'New Order' in Europe (see GERMANY, 4) was run on very similar lines. The process of controlling the resources of eastern Europe began before September 1939 with the incorporation of Austria, the Sudetenland, and the rump of Czechoslovakia, and trade treaties with Romania and Yugoslavia. When war came Germany was immediately subjected to blockade and had to rely on what it could get from continental Europe, but the victories of 1939–41 gave access to the resources of almost the entire continent, and largely freed it from the effects of sanctions. Europe under the New Order economy was divided into areas directly incorporated into Greater Germany (including the coal and iron ore regions of Silesia and Alsace-Lorraine); states that were occupied and run by military governors or puppet regimes (Norway, Belgium, Netherlands, Yugoslavia, Bohemia, and others) which had to supply Germany with goods and labour on very unequal terms; and finally neutrals which were compelled by circumstances to trade with Germany.

Like Japan, Germany used the new economic bloc to supply the resources for war, but also planned to exploit the area after the war in the German interest. The New

Order was to have a rich industrial Germany at its core with the European economy, linked to the Reichsmark, centred on Berlin, Vienna, and new industrial capitals to be built up in central Europe and the captured areas of the western USSR. German planners sought a single, unitary European market, though nothing like the modern European Union. The new Europe was to be run on imperial lines, primarily to meet German needs. But while the war continued the top priority was using Europe to win the war. By 1944 seven million workers had been brought into the Reich to solve its labour problems, mostly Soviet citizens or Poles. European states funded one-quarter of the German war effort through forced levies, occupation costs, and blocked trading accounts. Vital raw materials—oil from Romania, bauxite from Yugoslavia, coal from Poland, and so on—were supplied at low cost and the money earned by other states was held in Berlin for the duration. Germany continued to trade with states such as Spain, Sweden, or Switzerland because they refused to supply Germany without getting German exports or foreign exchange in return. Almost all Germany's trade outside Europe was cut off by the blockade except for limited supplies from the Far East which, until 22 June 1941, entered Germany via the USSR or arrived in *blockade runners.

Although Germany had a continental economy under its military control by 1942, the level of exploitation was less than it had hoped for. The Soviet Union provided only a fraction of the output expected from the captured areas because of widespread destruction (see SCORCHED EARTH POLICY). Food from the Soviet Union was largely consumed by German forces fighting there, rather than being sent back to Germany. Food supplies remained low throughout the war, and although rationing provided a steady and monotonous diet of black bread and potatoes, the German diet remained well below the calorie level of the western states, and even lower than in some of the German-occupied areas. Moreover, Germany found it necessary to send food and materials to some of the captured areas, so that the flow was by no means all one-way. The problems of exploiting European resources stemmed partly from the difficulties of working with a hostile population, but also from the shortages of equipment, skilled labour, and raw materials in the occupation zones. As the war effort failed, the borders of the economic bloc contracted and Germany faced growing resource difficulties. When strategic bombing was added to blockade as a means of economic warfare, the siege economy gradually collapsed.

The situation facing the Allies was very different. The UK could not hope to provide the resources for a prolonged war from within the British Isles and depended on acquiring resources overseas. This posed a very serious difficulty because the demands of war production made it impossible to export to acquire these resources, or to invest heavily overseas to build up British assets. Instead, the UK was compelled to run very large balance-of-payments deficits and to sell off most of its overseas assets. In 1939 the balance was £400 million in the red; by 1944 the figure was £2,500 million. Over the whole war British exports were only one-quarter of the value of its imports. Access to the world market was only an advantage if it could acquire the needed resources without facing bankruptcy. The problem was solved in a number of ways. First, the UK had to liquidate most of its foreign assets, including over $4 billions-worth in North America. Second, the other empire states and friendly neutrals were induced to accept postponement of payment until the end of hostilities. Third, and most significant, the UK came to rely on direct economic aid from the USA and Canada.

Economic assistance from the USA became essential after the fall of *France in June 1940. By December 1940 the UK was no longer able to buy supplies in the dollar areas and had to throw itself on the mercy of the USA. Roosevelt faced strong resistance to making commitments to the UK from isolationist opinion, but was able to persuade Congress to approve aid on the basis that it was the best form of defence for the USA. He promised to make America the 'arsenal of democracy'. In March 1941 an aid package was approved under the name of *Lend-Lease. Under this scheme America undertook to supply military equipment, food, and materials to the British Empire without a corresponding commitment to repay, and the scheme was eventually extended to a further eight countries. Over the whole course of the war the USA gave aid totalling $50 billion ($27 billion for the UK, $10 billion for the Soviet Union), and received $7.5 billion in reciprocal aid, mainly from the UK. About half the aid to the UK was in the form of weapons and military equipment. For the Soviet Union most of the goods were food or industrial capital equipment. Over $4 billion of aid was supplied by Canada to the UK on the same basis (see CANADIAN MUTUAL AID).

The American contribution was essential to the Allied war effort. Lend-Lease supplied one-quarter of all the weapons of the British Empire. The 427,000 trucks and 13,000 combat vehicles sent to the Soviet Union provided Soviet forces with essential mobility during the *German–Soviet war. The USA also made a vital contribution to the Allied war effort in producing the ships to deliver the supplies and in fighting to keep world sea lanes open. Trade everywhere was threatened by submarine attack. At the height of the battle of the *Atlantic in 1942–3 the UK was losing more ships than it could replace. Instead of the planned import of 42 million tons of supplies a year, only 22 million got through. The crisis was averted by American shipbuilding. In 1942 American shipyards produced 3 million tons of shipping; in 1943, 9 million. By the end of the war the USA had replaced the UK as the foremost shipping power. Much of the new shipping was to carry oil, the supply of which was vital for the western war effort. Despite the loss of over 5 million tons of oil tankers, the western states had 75% more tanker capacity in 1945 than in 1942. During this period the UK became very largely dependent on American supplies of

World trade, Table 2: American trade during the Second World War (1939–45) (million $)

	1939	*1940*	*1941*	*1942*	*1943*	*1944*	*1945*
Imports	2,361	2,599	3,269	2,821	3,418	3,911	4,125
Exports	3,138	3,938	5,026	8,005	12,872	14,288	9,676
Lend-Lease[a]	—	—	999	4,525	8,659	9,967	3,781

[a]British Empire only
Source: Contributor.

oil. Even the oil-rich USSR needed imports of American high-grade oil for aviation fuel.

Not only was the US economy capable of large quantities of weapons and shipping output, but it proved able to expand the level of its exports where most of the other combatant powers had to reduce them (see Table 2). The pace of US trade expansion had slackened in the 1930s; but during the war the USA took the opportunities created by the crisis to replace Europe or Japan as supplier to the rest of the world and the value of its exports rose from nearly $4 billion in 1940 to $14.2 billion in 1944. Imports rose over the same period from $2.6 to 3.9 billion, and by the end of the war the USA was conducting most of the world's trade in manufactured goods. Its economy supplied half the world's manufactures, and half of its shipping. All the other warring states were debtors by 1945; the USA was a net creditor. The success of the American economy owed a great deal to simple geographical good fortune. The USA was not directly attacked in the war, and the continental economy possessed ample raw materials, agricultural resources, and modern industrial capacity. American businessmen and engineers were given a great deal of the responsibility for running the war economy, and the American administration took a very 'economic' view of the war. Gross corporate profits rose almost threefold between 1940 and 1944, and record levels of investment and labour input were reached. When the American production record was added to that of the UK and the USSR, the gulf between the productive performance of the Allies and the Axis became unbridgeable. In 1943 the Allies produced 147,000 aircraft, the Axis only 44,000; in the same year the figures for tank production were 61,000 and 18,000 respectively. Though the mere possession of material resources is not a full explanation of Allied victory, it goes a long way towards explaining Axis defeat.

Mobilization for war affected a wide circle of states outside the combat zones. The poorer primary producers suddenly found their products in high demand. In Latin America economies weakened by the slump found themselves with large export surpluses. Price deflation was replaced with a sustained inflation of commodity prices. In a great many states industrial output expanded to meet war needs or to replace goods which could no longer be imported from Europe. The supply of equipment and expertize from the UK or USA speeded up the diffusion of technology. This process of renewed economic expansion ended ten years of decline and stagnation, and paved the way for the sustained post-war boom. But there were costs to be borne. Inflation was higher in the poorer and less-developed states and eroded incomes there. Many workers in Third World countries ended the war poorer. In many countries the presence of Allied troops led to very large increases in money supply, with a much slower expansion of output. The developed world, even at war, produced higher increases in output, lower rates of inflation, and gains in real income.

In any balance sheet of the impact of war on the world economy some account must be taken of the sheer level of destruction wrought by the conflict. Industrial expansion during the war was not felt in terms of improved living standards and consumer goods in the shops. Ordinary consumers had much less available to buy, and put their surplus income into savings, much of which was then taken by the government as loans to pay for the war. A very great deal of the industrial output of the world between 1939 and 1945 was blown up, shot down, or sunk. In Europe physical destruction extended much further than this, for much of the Continent was a combat zone. In the USSR 17,000 towns and 70,000 villages were destroyed by the fighting. In Germany almost every major city was bombed, and 90% of the housing stock was destroyed or damaged. In the occupied zones industrial and transport facilities were looted or destroyed. The French government calculated that France lost 45% of its national wealth during the war; in Italy the figure was estimated at one-third. In Japan the situation was the same: the destruction of the major cities through fire-bombing and the *atomic bombs, the loss of its merchant marine, the destruction of much of its industrial fabric. Prospects for economic revival in 1945 looked bleak.

Nor were the problems confined only to physical damage. All the major warring states, save the USA, lost export markets during the war and built up substantial internal and external debts. The UK, a major foreign creditor in the 1930s, lost over £4 billion of assets and overseas investment and ended the war with debts of £16 billion. In weaker, war-damaged economies high government debt and shortages of goods and food led to growing inflation. In Italy and Greece serious food shortages almost produced famine in 1943–4. In Bengal in 1944 harvest failures and the disruption of transport to meet British war needs led to a famine that killed three million Indians. When the war ended, dislocation of international shipping and the abrupt ending of Lend-Lease aid in August 1945 produced further food shortages. Most of the food surplus was produced in the dollar areas; at the end of the war it was difficult for states outside that area to produce sufficient exports to buy what they needed. In Europe industrial production was 33% of the 1938 level; agricultural production was 50%. The so-called 'dollar gap' facing the post-war world could in the end only be made good by further help from the USA in terms of food and industrial aid and generous loans.

Yet despite the extensive destruction and economic dislocation, the war did contribute in many ways to shaping the post-war economy and the great boom after 1945. Historians have now demonstrated that a great deal of industrial capacity and capital equipment survived the destruction, even in the bombed areas. In Germany there was more industrial capacity available in 1945 than there had been in 1938. In the Soviet Union and the USA a great deal of additional capacity was built during the war years. In occupied Europe the German administration had set up new industrial plant, and transport facilities to meet their needs. In Czechoslovakia and Austria, relatively undamaged by bombing, new chemical, machinery, and iron and steel capacity existed. In Norway improvements had been made to the hydroelectric system. Japanese economic imperialism in China left extensive industrial facilities for the post-war regime.

The war also witnessed the extensive exchange and diffusion of scientific discoveries and technology (see also SCIENTISTS AT WAR). The most obvious example was the flow of advanced machine-tools and equipment sent from the USA to Canada, the Soviet Union, and the UK. In the Soviet case this transfer included whole factories and hydroelectric plants. The machinery sent to the UK helped to speed up the modernization of British factory methods and increase industrial efficiency. The stream of scientific discoveries during the conflict provided a range of important developments, particularly in chemical and electronic goods, which could be exploited after the war as was German rocket development (see V-WEAPONS) on which the USA founded its space age programme. Improvements in aviation—large multi-engined aircraft, pressurized cabins, jet engines—transformed post-war air travel. Finally, the war witnessed a great increase in the power and variety of weapons themselves, whether through the development of rocket technology and atomic bombs or steady improvements in bombing accuracy, artillery range, and *radar-controlled firing; and so on. The Second World War produced the weapons which characterized all post-war conflicts, and diffused this technology world-wide. The ships, aircraft, and guns of the war were sold to smaller states after 1945 and saw service long after the major states had shifted to more sophisticated technology.

Above all, the war created circumstances which led to the USA to assume a dominant role in the world economy. The German and Japanese view of 'New Orders', self-contained protectionist blocs sustaining a military empire, was replaced by a new liberal trading order, regulated by institutions backed by American economic power. It was the bankruptcy of the UK in 1941 that finally brought home to a suspicious business establishment in the USA that the British were no longer able to play the role in the international economy that they had played since the 19th century. American leaders sought an international economy with as much free trade as possible, backed up with credit and assistance from the USA where necessary. Maintaining stability in the world economy was seen as the surest way to guarantee American economic interests; by 1945 it was clear that no other state posed a serious short-term economic threat. It was also evident that without American assistance the revival and reconstruction of the world economy would not be possible. From Lend-Lease to post-war Marshall Aid, American actions were governed by a mixture of political responsibility and economic self-interest.

The Lend-Lease programme symbolized America's new role. Although Roosevelt did not expect very much to be repaid, the Lend-Lease Master Agreement made it clear that in return for the economic assistance, the USA expected the western states which received it to co-operate in reducing tariffs and other trade restrictions after the war. This commitment was honoured after 1945 with the signing in 1947 of the General Agreement on Tariffs and Trade (GATT). Trade in the western world expanded rapidly after 1945 on the basis of greater openness and a genuine political willingness to avoid the beggar-my-neighbour strategies of the 1930s, which had led to economic stagnation and war. Americans also recognized that they would have to assume the responsibility for oiling the wheels of world commerce, since the American economy was the only one with sufficient funds to do so. Lend-Lease began the process. In 1944 the American administration insisted on planning the reconstruction of the world economy before the war was over. At *Bretton Woods agreement was reached for the establishment of an International Monetary Fund to provide credit for states facing payments difficulties. At the same meeting plans were drawn up for an International Bank for Reconstruction and Development to provide a channel for investment in the post-war economy. Under the aegis of the proposed United Nations Organization (see SAN FRANCISCO CONFERENCE) the USA and its allies agreed to set up other reconstruction agencies, the most important of which, *UNRRA, provided generous assistance for European recovery.

The net effect of all these initiatives was to pave the way for greater international economic co-operation and to place at the centre of the economic stage a state whose economic strength was sufficient to make the system work. But the reconstruction did not include the USSR. The advance of the Red Army into eastern Europe produced a different outcome there. The states brought under Soviet political domination became part of a single economic bloc, dominated at first by the interests of the USSR which extracted extensive reparations from the region and set up centralized, state-run economies in each of the satellite states. The world economy, like world politics, was divided on the lines of the *Cold War. One factor the two sides shared: a commitment to greater planning in economic affairs. The war saw very great increases in state planning for the economy and governments everywhere assumed responsibility for a greater share of the national product. In the west the Allies co-operated through Combined Boards for food, raw materials, and shipping which planned output and allocation. State planning in Germany and the UK turned both countries into temporary command economies. Though much of the wartime planning was scaled down after the war, the experience of demand management and state regulation provided important lessons for post-war economic development. The free market was in practice replaced by what came to be called 'mixed economies', with a good degree of state regulation, advice, and control to maximize economic growth. The post-war growth record, achieved by limited planning and the managed liberalization of trade, demonstrated that there were much more successful means of solving the world's economic problems than war.

See also DOMESTIC LIFE, ECONOMY AND WAR EFFORT sections of the major powers. RICHARD OVERY

Dobson, A. P., *US Wartime Aid to Britain 1940–1946* (London, 1986).
Hancock, W., and Gowing, M., *The British War Economy* (London, 1949).
Harrison, M., *Soviet Planning in Peace and War 1938–1945* (Cambridge, 1985).
Maddison, A., *Economic Growth in the West* (London, 1964).
Milward, A. S., *War, Economy and Society 1939–1945* (London, 1977).
Prest, A. R., *War Economics of Primary-Producing Countries* (Cambridge, 1948).
Vatter, H. G., *The US Economy in World War II* (New York, 1985).

Wormhoudt massacre. In May 1940, during the fighting which preceded the fall of *France, about 100 British *prisoners-of-war were herded into a barn near the French town of Wormhoudt by a company of Waffen-*SS troops commanded by SS-Hauptsturmführer (Captain) Wilhelm Möhnke. The Germans then proceeded to throw hand grenades into the barn and to shoot its occupants. There were about sixteen survivors. Möhnke, who later rose to command an SS division, was also linked to other *atrocities during the *Normandy campaign and at *Malmédy. He was a prisoner-of-war in the USSR for ten years after the war but escaped prosecution.

WRNS, Women's Royal Naval Service; see UK, 7(c).

WVS, Women's Voluntary Services, a British organization formed in 1938 to assist in Air Raid Precautions. See UK, 6, and WOMEN AT WAR.

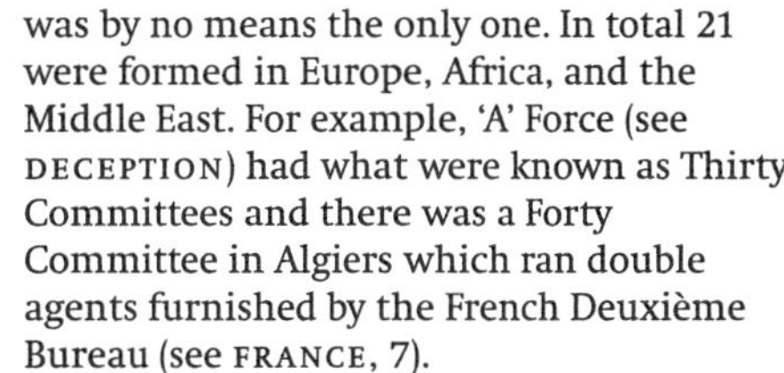

X-craft, see MIDGET SUBMARINES.

X-report, written specifically to encourage two German generals, *Halder and *Brauchitsch, to overthrow Hitler, which it failed to do. It purported to summarize British terms for peace which Dr Josef *Müller, a Vatican emissary of German opponents of the Nazi regime, had obtained in February 1940 by using the Pope, *Pius XII, whom he never actually met, as an intermediary.

Müller conveyed his notes of the terms to one of the conspirators, Hans von *Dohnanyi, who wrote a twelve-page memorandum based on them and called it the X-report as Müller's codename was Mr X. Dohnanyi subsequently deposited the report in a safe which was burgled by the *Gestapo in September 1944 and no copy of it has survived. But the relevant British foreign office papers show that the negotiations were taken very seriously by both sides in an effort to bring about a negotiated peace during the *phoney war before Hitler could unleash his offensive in the west (see FALL GELB). There was no definite agreement, but there probably was 'a general understanding or even a "gentleman's agreement" which emerged in the course of the intricate mutual sounding. Thus, with all the caution necessary in view of the delicate documentation, it can be assumed that there was agreement that the territorial integrity of the German Reich as of 1937 was to be respected . . . and that the Munich Agreement would after all be respected' (K. von Klemperer, *German Resistance against Hitler*, Oxford, 1992, p. 175). Halder saw the report on 4 April 1940; he and another general, Georg Thomas, later recalled that it 'called for the restitution to Germany in the west of Alsace-Lorraine and in the east of the borders of 1914' (ibid.). This would never have been acceptable to the UK—France was just kept minimally informed and was not involved—and was probably added by other conspirators who were trying to extract a higher price. Both Halder and Brauchitsch considered it futile to pursue the matter.

XX-committee, a sub-committee of the W Board established by the British director of military intelligence in September 1940 to co-ordinate the dissemination of false information. It was set up in January 1941 to operate what was known as the double-cross system.

The aims of the XX, or Twenty, committee, were: to control, as far as possible, the German espionage system in the UK; to catch new *spies immediately they arrived; to acquire knowledge of the personalities, methods, codes, and ciphers of the *Abwehr which operated the spies, and to obtain information about German plans and intentions from the questions asked by it; to influence German plans by the answers sent to these questions; and, finally, to deceive the Germans about British plans and intentions. Though the first of such committees it was by no means the only one. In total 21 were formed in Europe, Africa, and the Middle East. For example, 'A' Force (see DECEPTION) had what were known as Thirty Committees and there was a Forty Committee in Algiers which ran double agents furnished by the French Deuxième Bureau (see FRANCE, 7).

The XX-committee was headed by an *MI5 officer, J. C. Masterman and one of its members was Lt-Cdr Ewen Montagu of the Admiralty's *Naval Intelligence Division. It assessed on a weekly basis what information could be passed to the Germans via their agents working under British control, and weighed the likely gains of doing so against the losses which could be caused by releasing it, a process likened by the chairman to handling dynamite.

MI5 had employed *double agents before the war. Every aspect of an agent's life, and what he transmitted either by wireless or by secret writing, was controlled by a sub-section of MI5's B Division, known as B.1A, headed by T. A. Robinson. This allotted a case officer, backed by technical and administrative staff, to each double agent. The case officer knew the agent's background and circumstances intimately, and made a careful assessment of his psychology.

One of MI5's earliest double agents, Arthur George Evans, codenamed SNOW, had been recruited by the Abwehr in the 1930s. Though he had to be imprisoned in March 1941 he did much useful work for MI5 before then. In April 1940 he tipped it off to the presence of an Abwehr control station aboard a ship in Norwegian waters. Signals from this ship in an Abwehr hand cipher were decrypted at *Bletchley Park, and it was on these, and later on *ULTRA intelligence, that the double-cross system relied to discover if the messages it was planting were still being accepted as genuine.

From 1940 onwards the Abwehr attempted to establish a number of agents in Britain but with the help of SNOW and other double agents they were all, with one exception, rounded up. The exception was Jan Ter Braak whose body was found in a Cambridge air-raid shelter in April 1941 after he had committed suicide, probably because he had run out of money.

MI5 had files on about 120 double agents, some of whom operated outside the UK. Those who did not come up to scratch for one reason or another—and they were the majority—were imprisoned and some were hanged. Altogether sixteen spies were executed in the UK during the war, two of whom were British.

Among the early recruits two of the most successful were a Dane called Wulf Schmidt (TATE) and a well-connected Yugoslav named Dusko *Popov (TRICYCLE). TATE, who was captured after landing by parachute in September 1940, became one of the XX-committee's most faithful wireless agents despite being a committed Nazi Party member. It was his messages about false minefields that, by the spring of 1945, kept 9,300 sq. km. (3,600 sq.

mi.) of the Western Approaches (see UK, 7(c)) clear of U-boats. The Germans also thought sufficiently highly of him to naturalize him by wireless so that he could receive the Iron Cross, First and Second Class (see DECORATIONS), and he was also sent large sums of money (the whole double-cross system was almost entirely funded by the Abwehr). TRICYCLE had been recruited by the Abwehr in Belgrade and then sent to London to collect intelligence. He, and the network of notional agents he created, eventually became an important part of the XX-committee's *deception plans, as did two other important double agents: a Spaniard called Juan *Pujol (GARBO), who entered Britain in April 1942, and a Polish air force officer called Roman *Garby-Czerniawski (BRUTUS), who had been recruited by the Abwehr while heading the *Interallié network in France. The latter arrived in the UK in October 1942.

By the time the XX-committee was established it appeared virtually certain that the complete German espionage network was under British control, but the double-cross system was always run on the assumption that there might be undetected spies at large who could check the truth of the controlled agents' messages. If there were any, they have never revealed themselves.

During 1941 the XX-committee implemented a number of deception plans and one of double-cross sabotage. These operations were small-scale affairs, early tests of the double-cross system, and most, for one reason or another, failed to work. However, some did, including 'Plan Midas' in which TRICYCLE successfully extracted £20,000-worth of US dollars from his German masters.

Another useful double agent whom the XX-committee ran was a London safe-breaker called Edward Chapman who had been recruited by the Abwehr while awaiting trial for burglary in the Channel Islands. He was parachuted into Cambridgeshire in December 1942 and promptly gave himself up. After a rigorous interrogation he was allowed to make contact with his Abwehr controller and was given the codename ZIGZAG. Chapman had been told to sabotage an aircraft factory at Hatfield. This was duly rigged and ZIGZAG returned in triumph to the Germans via Lisbon. In June 1944 he was again parachuted into the UK, this time to report, among other things, on the damage caused by the *V-weapons. Though he had retained the confidence of the Germans the British found him indiscreet, and his case was terminated in November 1944.

In the middle of 1942 the double-cross system began to be employed as part of larger scale deception plans associated with deceiving the Germans about the timing and place of the Normandy landings (see OVERLORD), plans that came under the control of *SHAEF's Ops B when SHAEF was formed in early 1944. It was said that the XX-committee's main achievement during 1942 and 1943 was that, despite some narrow escapes, the double-cross system was preserved intact so that it could be employed in this fashion and GARBO, supported by BRUTUS and TATE, succeeded brilliantly in planting the necessary information. It was thought that the system was bound to be 'blown' by this grand deception, but in two instances at least the Germans chose, after the Normandy landings, to act on information received from the XX-committee: the final phase of the German U-boat campaign (the role of TATE in this has already been mentioned) and the targeting of V-weapons, where the Germans were persuaded to shorten the range so that many fell outside London.

The XX-committee has been criticized for being less professional than its counterpart in the Middle East, A-Force, and it was certainly helped in its task, wittingly or otherwise, by Abwehr officers who were either venal in the extreme or hostile to the Nazi regime. But its contribution to the success of the Normandy landings was undeniably an intelligence coup of the greatest strategic value.

Howard, M., *Strategic Deception* (London, 1990).
Masterman, J. C., *The Double-Cross System in the War of 1939 to 1945* (New Haven, 1972).

Yalta conference, see ARGONAUT; see also GRAND ALLIANCE.

Yamamoto Isoroku, Admiral (1884–1943), Japanese naval officer who planned and directed the pre-emptive strike against the US Pacific Fleet in *Pearl Harbor on 7 December 1941.

Born in Nagaoka, Yamamoto was the son of a schoolmaster. He joined the naval academy at Etajima and passed out in 1904, just in time to participate in the Russo-Japanese war which had begun that February. He served in a cruiser and participated in the battle of Tsushima Strait where he lost two fingers from his left hand and was wounded in the leg. In 1919 he was sent to the USA to study English. He lived in Boston where he learnt to play poker, its mixture of bluff, luck, and anticipation appealing to his temperament. But besides studying the language he was learning about oil, which he knew to be fundamental to the existence of a modern navy.

He returned to Japan in 1921 and in 1924 was given his first major assignment, as executive officer of a naval air station, becoming one of Japan's foremost experts in military aviation. In 1926 he was made naval attaché in Washington and returned two years later with a low opinion of the US Navy which he described as a club for golfers and bridge players, though he never had illusions about American power as a whole. By the time of the 1930 London naval conference, which he attended, he was a rear-admiral and in September 1930 was assigned to Naval Air Corps headquarters. There he did much to improve the quality of naval aircraft as well as demanding the development of a fast carrier-borne fighter which eventually produced the Zero. In October 1933 he took command of 1st Carrier Division and by 1935 was a vice-admiral and vice-minister of the navy. He was a fervent supporter of *air power and had, unlike some of his colleagues, little faith in battleships. 'They are like elaborate religious scrolls which old people hang in their homes,' he said, ' a matter of faith, not reality ... In modern warfare battleships will be as useful to Japan as a samurai sword.' When his fellow admirals pointed out that only a battleship could sink a battleship he quoted an oriental saying: 'The fiercest serpent may be overcome by a swarm of ants' (see M. Carver, ed., *The War Lords*, London, 1976, p. 396).

But though he understood the basis of future naval power, and how to exploit it, Yamamoto opposed those who wanted war, and therefore the *Tripartite Pact. He was so outspoken against war that during the late 1930s he was in danger of being assassinated by extremists and in July 1939 a plot to kill him was uncovered. To save his life the navy minister promoted him to admiral and sent him to sea as C-in-C of the Combined Fleet. When asked by the prime minister, Prince *Konoe, what chance Japan had against the USA and the UK if there was a war, Yamamoto replied prophetically: 'we can run wild for six months or a year, but after that I have utterly no confidence. I hope you will try to avoid war with America' (ibid).

Staff studies also soon convinced him that the only hope Japan had in such a war was to destroy the US Pacific Fleet by a pre-emptive strike at its base, Pearl Harbor. His colleagues demurred. It was too risky. Two or three carriers would be lost and that was too high a price to pay. But Yamamoto continued to argue, cajole, and threaten, and eventually his plan was adopted. Its success, and Japanese victories in the *Pacific war which followed, brought Yamamoto enormous prestige and though the navy general staff at first rejected his plan to bring the US Pacific Fleet to battle at *Midway the *Doolittle raid on Tokyo soon resulted in its acceptance. But *ULTRA intelligence had forewarned the Americans of the plans and a crushing defeat was inflicted on his forces. During the next six months he had some success against the US Navy around *Guadalcanal, directing operations from the super-battleships *Yamato* and **Musashi*, but his forces were unable to prevent the Americans from gaining the upper hand at sea and eventually winning the island.

On 3 April 1943 Yamamoto moved his headquarters

Admiral **Yamamoto**.

from *Truk to *Rabaul and fifteen days later he flew out to inspect Japanese bases in the northern Solomons. ULTRA intelligence revealed his itinerary in advance and *Nimitz, C-in-C Pacific, asked Washington if it was in America's best interests that he be eliminated. The answer was 'yes' and on 18 April 1943 a flight of fighters intercepted Yamamoto's aircraft as it approached *Bougainville and shot it down.

Agawa, H., *The Reluctant Admiral: Yamamoto and the Imperial Navy* (New York, 1979).
Potter, J., *Yamamoto, the Man Who Menaced America* (New York, 1965).

Yamashita Tomoyuki, General (1885–1946), Japanese Army officer who was the conqueror of Malaya and Singapore, and who in 1944–5 defended the Philippines against *MacArthur's forces (see PHILIPPINES CAMPAIGNS).

The son of a village doctor, Yamashita was born on Shikoku, the smallest of Japan's main islands. He passed out fifth from the Central Military Academy in Tokyo in 1908 and by 1926 he was a colonel. He seemed destined for high command and was promoted maj-general, but his role in an attempted military coup in 1936 incurred Emperor *Hirohito's displeasure. He was removed from the promotions lists and sent to command a brigade in Korea and was later transferred to Manchukuo. However, his reputation continued to grow and the promotion ban was eventually lifted. He was promoted lt-general in November 1937, and in July 1940 was recalled to Tokyo to replace *Tōjō as inspector-general of air aviation when Tōjō became war minister. But Tōjō was an old political enemy—the two men belonged to rival military factions—and Yamashita soon found himself heading a military mission to Germany. On his return in March 1941 he was again dispatched to Manchukuo, this time to command the *Kwantung Army, a banishment that lasted until November 1941 when he was appointed to command the Twenty-fifth Army for the invasion of Malaya.

Yamashita's *Malayan campaign, culminating in the fall of *Singapore in February 1942, made him a national hero. But he did not revel in his success as many would have done. He treated his *prisoners-of-war humanely and when asked the date of his victory march into Singapore replied tersely that there would be no parade but that 'a funeral ceremony is fixed for 20 February'. As a victorious general he was now entitled to expect a further major role in the war, an interview with the emperor, and the acclaim of his people. Instead, Tōjō saw to it that he was appointed to what was virtually a non-operational (although strategically vital) command of First Army Group in Manchukuo, was refused an audience with the emperor, and was ordered to travel direct to Manchukuo so that he would not receive a public welcome in Japan.

Though promoted general in 1943 Yamashita remained in Manchukuo until Tōjō fell from power and he was then given command of Fourteenth Area Army in the Philippines. He flew to Tokyo, obtained his long-desired interview with the emperor, and then flew on to Manila, arriving there on 5 October 1944. But his appointment had come too late to prepare properly for the American onslaught and by July 1945 he and his headquarters staff had been reduced to hiding in the mountains from the advancing Americans. On 2 September he left his staff and walked to the American lines to sign the document of surrender and to go into captivity.

General **Yamashita**, the 'tiger of Malaya'.

In October 1945 he was tried by the US Military Commission for permitting the barbarous acts committed against the civilian population during the defence of Manila. Despite having no idea that they had occurred—they were, anyway, committed by naval troops probably not under his direct command—Yamashita was found guilty and sentenced to death. MacArthur refused to consider his appeal, and the civilian courts felt unable to uphold it; after his proposed execution had been described by the two dissenting Supreme Court judges as 'legalized lynching', he was hanged.

Yamashita was described by one of his contemporaries as halfway between clever and cunning. He was a gifted general, probably the best Japan had. Ruthlessly ambitious and physically gross, he was nevertheless very fastidious and highly emotional.

Barker, A., *Yamashita* (New York, 1973).
Potter, J., *A Soldier must hang: the Biography of an Oriental General* (London, 1963).

Yemen, independent Arab republic which remained neutral under its Imam, though disputes with the British over Aden continued.

Yeo-Thomas, Wing Commander (Forest F.) Edward (1902–64), English-born, but French-educated, member of *SOE one of whose codenames was WHITE RABBIT. He joined the RAF in 1939 before moving to SOE in February 1942 where his sledgehammer personality had scope. He parachuted three times into occupied France to help co-ordinate *resistance movements there (see also FRANCE, 9), and on the last occasion was captured. He was tortured, and then imprisoned, but escaped execution at *Buchenwald by exchanging his identity with a fellow prisoner dying of typhus. He later twice evaded his captors to reach Allied lines and was subsequently awarded the George Cross (see DECORATIONS).

Marshall, B., *The White Rabbit* (London, 1952).

'Y' service was the British codename for the interception of enemy radio and telephone traffic. 'Y' service detachments formed part of the signals branch of each of the three armed services and were treated, like cipher staff, with special *secrecy. All the principal warring powers, and the Poles, had similar detachments, listening to what their enemies were saying among themselves. Their results were divided into traffic analysis, location (see HUFF-DUFF), normal intelligence analysis, and decipher. See also SIGNALS INTELLIGENCE WARFARE.

M. R. D. FOOT

YUGOSLAVIA

1. Introduction

Founded on 1 December 1918 as the Kingdom of the Serbs, Croats, and Slovenes, Yugoslavia united for the first time the bulk of the South Slav lands of the disintegrating Habsburg Empire with the previously independent kingdoms of Serbia and Montenegro (see Map B). Those who inspired the foundation of the new state, which in 1941 covered an area of 247,542 sq. km. (95,550 sq. mi.) with an estimated population of 15.97 million, believed it must have a common national identity as well as a common government; but their doctrine of Yugoslav 'national oneness' served in practice to abet the assertion by the country's largest people, the Orthodox Serbs, and their dynasty, the Karadjordjevićes, of dominion over the rest. Far from fostering 'national oneness', Serbian centralism stimulated feelings of national separateness. Whether under ineffectual parliamentary rule between 1918 and 1929 or royal dictatorship thereafter, the country was riven by national and constitutional dissension. The Catholic Croats, the second most numerous nation, were least reconciled to their subordinate status in a unitary state, but the other Yugoslav peoples, including the Serbs, and the many national minorities also had fundamental grievances.

Yugoslavia declared itself neutral in September 1939, but that did not spare it from Axis and Allied pressure or from an intensification of its domestic quarrels. The two were interrelated. The Serbs, recalling their comradeship in arms with France and the UK on the Salonika Front in 1915–18, were both overwhelmingly pro-Allied in sentiment and inclined to feel that no war could be fought successfully without them. Serb domination of the Yugoslav officer corps, and the anglophilia of the Regent Prince Paul (1893–1976), reinforced the government's portrayal of its neutrality to the Allies as a temporary expedient, necessitated by the country's strategic vulnerability and economic subordination to the Axis, as well as by the faint heartedness of the non-Serbs.

The leaders of the other Yugoslav peoples were both more impressed by Axis power than were the Serbs and less keen to fight for a state and regime which they did not really regard as theirs. The Slovenes, for whom no alternative was on offer, were expected to remain loyal. But radical Croat nationalists had not been satisfied with the belated granting of home rule in August 1939; and even the mainstream Croatian Peasant Party, despite entering government, remained susceptible to Italian blandishments concerning statehood. The Macedonian Slavs (classed as Serbs in the inter-war years) tended to look to Bulgaria as a possible liberator. The Slav Muslims of Bosnia and Herzegovina (claimed by both Serbs and Croats as co-nationals) were another doubtful element, while some Montenegrins (also defined as Serbs) hankered after a restored independence under Italian patronage. Finally, the large Albanian, German, and Hungarian national minorities constituted potential *fifth columnists if and when their putative motherlands should beckon.

2. Domestic life and economy

By 1940 the German Reich possessed both a stranglehold on Yugoslavia's foreign trade and an enhanced share of the ownership of its important mines of non-ferrous metals. The dependency of an underdeveloped economy on the export of its peasant proprietors' agricultural surpluses gave Germany political influence as well as economic control. Prince Paul's government felt obliged not only to meet Germany's ever-increasing demands for foodstuffs and *raw materials, but also to make the occasional anti-Semitic gesture. Meanwhile, the progressive absorption of Hungary, Romania, and Bulgaria into the Axis camp (Albania was already there) meant that Yugoslavia was virtually surrounded by hostile states with claims on its territory. The UK was in no position either to contest Germany's economic domination or to outbid the Axis in making offers to Yugoslavia's neighbours. Nor could London make good the country's deficiencies in armaments and aircraft. Prince Paul sought to find a counterweight in the Soviet Union, but Stalin was unwilling to push his rivalry with Hitler in the Balkans to the point of jeopardizing the *Nazi–Soviet Pact.

Before the Axis occupation of Yugoslavia in April 1941 the Germans had developed elaborate schemes for the economic exploitation of Yugoslavia, as for south-eastern Europe generally. In the event, however, they sought merely to maintain their hold over those mines (of copper, chrome, lead, zinc, and bauxite), rich lowland agricultural areas, and lines of rail, road, and river communication which were deemed essential to their war effort. Even where a facility fell within the zone of occupation of one of their allies, as in the case of the bauxite mines near Mostar, the Germans demanded and got control over the installation and its output.

The 'Independent State of Croatia' (Nezavisna Država Hrvatska, or NDH) which was set up by the Germans after their occupation of the country, was also compelled to supply Germany with such of its products as the Germans required, and to pay the costs of the German and Italian occupation forces. In the rump of Serbia, the value of the minerals and foodstuffs taken by the Germans was simply offset against the huge occupation costs imposed on the Belgrade government. This was not necessarily disadvantageous to peasant farmers in areas of food surplus. They tended to prosper as forcible requisitioning was abandoned in favour of bulk purchases. The residents of cities and towns might also prosper financially, but they were also vulnerable to being rounded up for execution in reprisals or deportation to Germany. Several hundred thousand Yugoslavs were sent to work in the Reich: some as *prisoners-of-war (all Serbs), some as volunteers, and some as forcible deportees. The Germans also employed *forced labour in some of the mines under their control.

The Italians, in contrast, discovered that their share of the Yugoslav spoils was an economic liability, and even had to be fed from Italy. The Bulgarians and Hungarians concentrated on integrating their portions by expelling post-1918 Serb colonists and imposing their own teachers and administrators. In Macedonia this provoked native resentment, both on account of the high costs to be paid and the absence of the expected opportunities for advancement by the local intelligentsia.

3. Government

(a) Pre-occupation

After King Alexander (1888–1934) was assassinated, Prince Paul ruled on behalf of the young King Peter II (1923–70). Paul moderated but did not dismantle his late cousin's dictatorship. The prospect of war had moved the Prince Regent to grant home rule to Croatia. Yet his failure, simultaneously, either to restore democracy or to devolve powers to the other national-historical units ensured that Yugoslavia entered the wartime period as disunited as ever.

The Italians' failure to subdue the Greeks following Mussolini's invasion in October 1940 (see BALKAN CAMPAIGN) compelled Hitler to come to the Duce's rescue. This meant, in turn, that Yugoslavia had to be enrolled in the Axis. The Germans did not need Yugoslav help or the use of Yugoslav territory to attack Greece, but they did require a guarantee of access via Bulgaria and the isolation of the British. From November Hitler began bludgeoning Prince Paul to sign the *Tripartite Pact.

The prince, hoping for deliverance by the outbreak of Nazi–Soviet hostilities, played for time, failing to appreciate that it was running out. He wavered until early March 1941 when, after submitting to a harangue from Hitler at *Berchtesgaden, he concluded that the only alternative to signing the pact was state suicide.

Yugoslav ministers journeyed to Vienna to sign the Tripartite Pact on 25 March 1941. It committed Yugoslavia to little more than acquiescence in Germany's conquest of Greece; the various let-out clauses and the bribe of a post-war acquisition of Salonika remained secret. Demonstrations against the Axis erupted in Serbia and Slovenia. Conspirators drawn from the army, air force, and Serbian nationalist groups seized power in Belgrade in the early hours of 27 March, abolishing the regency, and proclaiming King Peter to have come of age. Serbs took to the streets to celebrate the recovery of their honour and the prospect of a just war alongside the UK and Greece. Communists among them shouted instead for an alliance with Moscow. From London Churchill hailed the Yugoslavs' recovery of their 'soul'. Croats sulked at home over such folly and expected the worst.

An all-party government was established under the presidency of the conspirators' nominal leader, General Dušan Simović. It seemed an impressive embodiment of Yugoslav unity, but its cohesion was illusory. The makers of the coup had acted to expunge the dishonour which partnership with the Axis would do to Serbian traditions: the politicians whom they summoned to share power had other concerns. The representatives of those Serb parties which had been in opposition since 1929 were as hostile to the iniquities of Prince Paul's domestic policy as they were to his appeasement of the Axis. They resented, in particular, the manner in which Croatia had won autonomy. On the other hand, Vladko Maček, leader of the Croatian Peasant Party and vice-premier of Paul's ousted government, made his participation in the new cabinet conditional upon its reaffirmation of both Croatian home rule and Yugoslavia's adherence to the Tripartite Pact. This was agreed as the enormity of the country's peril sank in.

Hitler was enraged by the insult dealt to him by the coup. Within a few hours he had issued Directive No. 25, decreeing Yugoslavia's obliteration and assigning secondary roles in its conquest to Italy and Hungary. The invasion, on 6 April 1941, took place simultaneously with the German attack on Greece (see BALKAN CAMPAIGN).

The Luftwaffe inaugurated the Axis offensive with punishing raids on Belgrade (killing some 5,000 people in the supposedly 'open city') and the main military airfields. These set the king, government, and High Command in flight, disrupted communications, and destroyed from the outset any possibility of a concerted defence. German forces in Bulgaria struck deep into Macedonia, cutting off by 8 April the Yugoslavs' line of retreat towards Greece and nullifying the premise of their strategic plan. The Wehrmacht then turned its attention to Belgrade (which fell on 13 April) and the north and west of the country. As German troops entered Zagreb on 10 April the Ustaša—Croat Fascists led by Ante *Pavelić—were permitted to declare the independence of Croatia, Maček having spurned German offers that he do so. Italy and Hungary invaded on 11 April to claim their shares of the spoils. (Bulgaria was not obliged to fight for its share.) In total, the Axis invaders employed 52 divisions, 24 of which were German, and their casualties were negligible. The Germans, for example, lost only 151 dead.

Although the Yugoslavs offered occasional local resistance, and some effort was made to attack the Italians across the Albanian frontier, their rout was complete. It took the Germans longer to locate men competent to sign an instrument of surrender than it did to create the conditions of chaos that made Yugoslav capitulation inevitable. The king and most of his ministers fled by air to Greece on 14 and 15 April. Simović left behind instructions to seek an armistice (blaming the Croats' defection for the need), but it was, in effect, an unconditional surrender which was signed in Belgrade on 17 April.

(b) Government under occupation

Hitler had sketched out the lineaments of the country's occupation and partition on 12 April. This was now put into effect (see Map 111). The aim of the new regime was to secure for Germany what it required in the area (principally, control over the main lines of communication and certain economic assets) while rewarding (and making use of) the Reich's allies and those Yugoslav peoples thought by Hitler to be amenable to his purposes. It was also designed to give expression to Nazi racial doctrines (e.g. Germanization for northern Slovenia, now incorporated into the Reich; 'Aryan' status for the Croats and Slav Muslims of an independent Croatia which included Bosnia and Herzegovina; self-government for the German minority in Banat) and to eradicate the very idea of a South Slav state. This meant that the Serbs, as the Yugoslav *Staatsvolk* and authors of the insult of 27 March, were singled out for condign punishment. Hitler did not originally intend that the rump of Serbia should have even a spurious statehood. The establishment during the summer of a *Quisling regime under General Milan Nedić came in response to a predictable outbreak of Serbian rebellion.

The rebellion happened, above all, because of the Ustašas' initiation in May 1941 of a campaign of terror and genocide against greater Croatia's nearly two million Serbs. (The far smaller numbers of Jews, gypsies, and communists were, of course, also targeted for destruction.) The Ustašas' aim was to produce an ethnically and ideologically 'pure' Croatia by expelling to Serbia, converting to Roman Catholicism, and murdering its 'oriental' minorities in roughly equal proportions.

Less predictable was the dissatisfaction and rivalry which soon came to prevail among both Hitler's allies (who wanted more than they had got) and the Yugoslav beneficiaries of his largesse (who gradually found reasons to repent of their initial enthusiasm for the 'new order'). The super-nationalistic pretensions of the NDH had in any case been crippled at the outset by its enforced cession of much of Dalmatia to Italy and by the designation of an Italian prince as Croatia's future king. The subsequent revelations of Ustaša barbarism against Croatia's Serbs and of the nullity of NDH 'independence' completed its delegitimation. The oppressive Bulgarian regime in Macedonia eventually disabused people there also of their inclination to regard Sofia as a deliverer. Hitler's 'new order' (see GERMANY, 4) was, in fact, to prove a principal cause of both the resistance struggle and the accompanying civil wars, as well as of the Axis powers' inability to extirpate the former while making use of the latter.

(c) Government-in-exile

King Peter and his ministers arrived in London in June 1941 to find themselves regarded as heroes. Their army's performance in April may have been lamentable, but that did not appear to have diminished Allied admiration for their March defiance of Hitler. The fragmentary reports of ongoing resistance which filtered out of their homeland in July and August and, by September, of the self-proclaimed leadership of it by Colonel Draža (Dragoljub) *Mihailović, the foremost of the Serb royalist officers who called themselves Četniks, enhanced their sense of being no mere collection of impotent exiles. They set about promoting Mihailović's cause (and their own) among the Allies and made him a general. They also nourished hopes of using the thousand or so of their servicemen who had joined the British evacuation from Greece to Egypt as the nucleus of an army to be raised among Yugoslav emigrants in the Americas. With forces fighting both at home and in the Near East, they were

Map 111. Division of **Yugoslavia**, April 1941

confident of translating Allied pledges to restore Yugoslavia into reality.

It was not long, however, before divisions appeared in their ranks. These reflected both the unresolved national and constitutional questions which they had brought with them into exile and the weaknesses inherent in their detached and dependent existence. King Peter, the fount of their legitimacy, was immature, impressionable, and wilful. His premier, General Simović, was inept and inconsistent, and soon alienated both cabinet colleagues and the king. News of the Ustašas' massacres of Serbs in the NDH destroyed all trust between Serb and Croat ministers, and of both in their premier, who bungled his handling of this explosive issue. King Peter, meanwhile, had fallen under the influence of junior officers who resented Simović's effort to monopolize credit for the 27 March coup, criticized his conduct of the April war, and accused him of failing to mobilize adequate aid for Mihailović. Despite British reservations, the king dismissed Simović in December and entrusted his government to a distinguished but elderly Serb academic, Slobodan Jovanović. In an effort to undo any consequent damage, the king and Jovanović promoted Mihailović again and made him their war minister. By this action the Yugoslav exiles entrusted their fate to a movement about which they knew little and over which they could exercise even less control.

The dangers of such a policy would not become apparent until August 1942, when the Soviets began to attack Mihailović for collaborating with the Italians and, even worse, at the end of the year, when the British began to reassess their exclusive commitment to him. In the first half of 1942, however, it was *mutinies among the Yugoslav forces in Egypt which did most to undermine the government's prestige. The displaced war minister, the senior officers, and the majority of their men refused to accept the new government's replacement commander. British GHQ, regarding the mutineers as the true authors of the March putsch and the first officer sent out from London as incompetent, refused, in turn, to help the government impose its will. Only the nomination of another commander and *Rommel's June eruption into Egypt put an end to this farce.

The inability of the Yugoslav exiles either to manage their own affairs or to assert their relevance to their compatriots at home by any means other than cleaving to Mihailović led their British hosts to treat them with ever-diminishing respect. Their own efforts to lessen their dependency on the British by strengthening ties with the Americans, Soviets, and de *Gaulle's Free French were unsuccessful. Personal, party, and national dissension among them and the large Yugoslav-American community led to cabinet crises and, in the summer of 1943, to two changes of government. These, however, had more to do with King Peter's determination to defy his ministers' opposition to a wartime marriage than with increasing British reservations about Mihailović. When, by August, the king contrived to provide himself with a non-party government under Bozidar Purić which was prepared to sanction his marriage, the British had come to see him not only as the sole element among the émigrés worthy of their support, but also as the only one likely to repay it.

As the British moved towards abandoning the inactive Mihailović in favour of the more warlike communist partisan leader, *Tito, it was the king's legitimacy, pliability, and assumed popularity with the Serbs that appeared to offer the only chance of reconciling the UK's short-term military requirements with long-term political interests. Having decided in December 1943 to break with Mihailović, Churchill laboured to persuade Tito to work with the king. By doing so, he argued, Tito might acquire international recognition, the material assets of the exile government, and the support of royalist Serbs. He worked simultaneously to compel Peter to dismiss the Purić government (and, with it, Mihailović) and to name a premier willing to deal with Tito. By May 1944 he had succeeded. Ivan Subasić, the former *ban* (governor) of Croatia, formed a one-man government charged with effecting a merger between the monarchy and the revolution, and in June he signed an agreement with Tito's Anti-Fascist Council of National Liberation (AVNOJ) which envisaged the eventual formation of a united Royal-AVNOJ government.

(d) Post-occupation government

Although Tito could by 1944 expect to take control in most of the country when the Germans withdrew, the Četniks still dominated Serbia. It was with this in mind that he appealed to Stalin in July 1944 to divert the Red Army from its course into Central Europe and to help hasten the conquest of Serbia. Stalin graciously complied; and the Četnik movement, its morale sapped by three years of equivocation over its role, disintegrated under the triple blows of a Partisan–Soviet attack, western Allied abandonment, and King Peter's endorsement of the Partisans. Belgrade was liberated on 20 October. The Red Army then decamped for Hungary, leaving the Partisans (now fighting as a regular army) to finish the job as the Germans and their Yugoslav auxiliaries slowly fell back to the north and west. An internationally recognized coalition government, with Tito as premier and Subasić as foreign minister, had been formed under communist domination in March 1945, but complete liberation did not come until the German surrender in May 1945.

Over the next few months the communists consolidated their power, took revenge on those of their enemies who had failed to escape to Italy or Austria, and began to remake their country in the image of the only other authentically revolutionary Marxist-Leninist state—the USSR.

4. Armed forces

(a) Army

The Yugoslav Army's war establishment was 1.2 million, with a further half-million in the reserves. At the end of

March 1941, when both a 'general activation' (not mobilization) and a new war plan were promulgated, the army's strength stood at 700,000. At least half of its 110 light tanks were obsolescent. Despite relatively lavish expenditure on defence in recent years, this was an army which still moved at the pace of a bullock cart and was led by men whose conceptions had advanced little since 1918. The army's only possible advantage over the Wehrmacht lay in the use it might make of its rugged native terrain, but that was vitiated by demoralization, disaffection, and paralysis in the face of German might. At less than half-strength and with its dispositions in flux on account of the new war plan, the Yugoslav Army was no match for its enemies in April 1941. A Yugoslav infantry battalion composed largely of ex-Italian prisoners-of-war of Slovene nationality was later formed in Egypt.

(b) Navy
The Yugoslav Navy had an old German training cruiser, four modern destroyers—a fifth was under construction—four submarines, sixteen old torpedo boats, and a number of miscellaneous craft including a seaplane tender. None was lost to enemy action but the cruiser seaplane tender, and three of the destroyers were captured. The fourth destroyer was scuttled by its crew. A submarine, two torpedo boats, and eleven seaplanes of the Yugoslav Fleet Air Arm escaped to Alexandria where they were used for local patrol duties. Later, a number of small British warships were manned with Yugoslav crews based on Malta. Their return, along with vessels seized by the Italians in 1941, was sought by Tito in 1944.

(c) Air Force
With a total of 419 aircraft the airforce comprised one fighter and one bomber air brigade, each with two wings; two mixed air brigades, each with one wing of fighters and one of bombers; and a bomber air brigade of two wings. There were also seven squadrons of obsolete army aviation aircraft. The aircraft were of mixed British, French, and German types, some modern, some not. The fighter air brigade which protected Belgrade was equipped mostly with Hurricanes and Me109s, and these inflicted some losses on the Germans when the Luftwaffe raided the capital on 6 April 1941. Altogether, 49 Yugoslav aircraft were lost in the air and 85 on the ground before the *armistice. About 50 escaped to Greece, some of which eventually reached Egypt. The bulk of the several hundred air force personnel who reached Egypt mutinied against the Jovanović *government-in-exile early in 1942. The mutineers were eventually enrolled in the RAF Volunteer Reserve. Most returned to the Yugoslav colours in 1944 when the UK began to train fighter squadrons for Tito.

5. Resistance and civil war
Resistance to the Axis was to be expected in lands where the traditions of fighting alien rule were still living parts of most people's national identities. Fragments of the army and gendarmerie, who adopted the traditional Serbian name of Četniks (from *četa*, regiment), had taken to the hills as the magnitude of their defeat became obvious in April 1941. There they regrouped, awaited developments, and rallied gradually to the command of Mihailović. The communists, or Partisans as they came to call themselves, were also organizing themselves under their party secretary since 1937, Josip Brož Tito, though they too were few in number. Unlike the Serb loyalists, they were awaiting the revolutionary situation they trusted Soviet entry into the war would unleash. Both movements sought to take control and advantage of the spontaneous and inchoate Serb risings which the Ustaša pogroms were provoking in the Independent Croatian State, or NDH. Not wanting to be left out, and encouraged by the Soviet Union's entry into the war and the communists' consequent call to arms—as well as by the Germans' earlier transfer of front-line troops to the east—the Serbs of Montenegro and the rump of Serbia rose in rebellion in July and August. Such unity as these various local uprisings possessed was not destined to endure, as their would-be leaders, the communists and the Serb officers, were fighting for different ends. These, in turn, implied different strategies.

Mihailović's movement sought Yugoslavia's restoration as a Serb-dominated monarchy. Its appeal to non-Serbs was thus small. But in the summer of 1941, the popular demand was for resistance; and Mihailović and his commanders went along with it so as to maintain their claim to both wartime and post-war leadership. By the autumn, however, the mass reprisals against Serb civilians (on a ratio of 100 executions for every German soldier killed) which had become Hitler's answer to revolt confirmed Mihailović in his original belief that the uprisings were premature and that the communists were no better than criminals for seeking to provoke and prosecute them. In this assessment lay the seeds of the Četniks' *collaboration with the Axis and a long civil war; although in November the Germans rejected Mihailović's offer to fight the communists in return for arms.

The communists, on the other hand, were fighting for a revolutionary transfer of power. Although this, their ultimate objective, was more or less effectively camouflaged after the spring of 1942, from the start they sought to appeal both individually and collectively to all the Yugoslav peoples. Militarily, they differed from the Četniks by emphasizing unremitting war on the Axis and its Yugoslav helpmates: at first in order to lend assistance to the embattled 'first country of socialism', but later because to do otherwise was to serve the enemy and to betray one's own people. They denounced Mihailović, the various Croat and Slovene leaders, and parties who refused to concede their right to command the resistance as collaborators. Most of these anti-communist potential resisters fell into the trap, becoming what the communists alleged they were.

So the lands of the dismembered Yugoslav state became not only the scene of Europe's greatest resistance struggle, but also one of its bloodiest civil wars. Partisans and Četniks fought the occupiers, their servants, and each other in order to win anti-Axis leadership and the right to organize the post-war state. The several regimes and movements involved in collaboration fought the resisters and occasionally each other under the benevolent or worried gaze of their rival Axis patrons. For example, the Serb anti-communist militias organized by the Italians in their zones of occupation (and which also proclaimed their allegiance to Mihailović) not only participated in Axis offensives against the Partisans, but also fought Croatian forces (Ustaša and regulars) armed and directed by the Germans. General Nedić, the Serb Quisling, pressed the Germans to detach eastern Bosnia from the Ustaša state and to re-assign it to Serbia. Meanwhile, in German-occupied eastern Bosnia itself, the local Četniks forged anti-communist alliances with the very elements they had come into existence to oppose—the Ustaša. Catholics, Orthodox, and Muslims massacred each other in the name of *religion. Brother fought brother in the name of politics. Most of the 1.2 million Yugoslavs who died in the Second World War perished at the hands of other Yugoslavs.

Mihailović's movement was in the ascendant during 1942. By partially 'legalizing' itself with the Nedić regime, it had managed to escape destruction in the German offensive which chased the Partisans out of Serbia at the end of 1941. Its natural appeal to Serbs as a reincarnation of 19th-century insurgencies against the Turks was buttressed by the legitimacy accorded to it by King Peter's government and by the propaganda backing it received from the Allies. Outside narrow Serbia, in Montenegro, Herzegovina, and inland Dalmatia, Mihailović's sub-commanders joined with the Italians in waging war on the communists and/or in keeping the Ustašas at bay. By such means they expected both to preserve themselves and to eliminate their rivals against the day when the Italians, quitting the war, should bequeath their arms, equipment, and control of the coast. The British, unable themselves at this stage to supply the Četniks, did not oppose these arrangements.

The Partisans, however, were recovering from their set backs of late 1941 and early 1942. Their 'long march' from south-east to north-west Bosnia in the summer of 1942 translated them from an area in which they had worn out their welcome to one sympathetic to their now less revolutionary demeanour. When they convoked the first meeting of their all-national front, the Anti-Fascist Council of National Liberation (AVNOJ), in Bihać in November they gave it a moderate and patriotic guise. In the first half of 1943 they survived—just—two great Axis offensives, while inflicting crippling defeats on the Četniks outside Serbia in the process. They also extricated themselves from negotiations with the Germans for an anti-Četnik *modus vivendi* without being found out by the British, who had chosen this moment (April) to send their first missions to them. By the end of 1943 they claimed to have more than 200,000 men and women under arms. More importantly, from the Allied point of view, they were credited with holding down some 35 Axis divisions which might otherwise have been available for service on the Italian or Eastern Fronts.

MARK WHEELER

Clissold, S., *Whirlwind: An Account of Marshal Tito's Rise to Power* (London, 1949).
Deakin, F. W. D., *The Embattled Mountain* (London, 1971).
Djilas, M., *Wartime* (London, 1977).
Roberts, R., *Tito, Mihailović and the Allies, 1941–1945* (2nd edn., Durham, 1987).
Tomasevich, J., *War and Revolution in Yugoslavia, 1941–1945: The Chetniks* (Stanford, Calif., 1975).
—'Yugoslavia During the Second World War', in W. S. Vucinich (ed.), *Contemporary Yugoslavia: Twenty Years of Socialist Experiment* (Berkeley, Calif., 1969).
Mark Wheeler, 'Pariahs to Partisans to Power: The Communist Party of Yugoslavia', in T. Judt (ed.), *Resistance and Revolution in Mediterranean Europe, 1939–1948* (London, 1989).

Zahme Sau (tame boar), German night-fighter tactics used against RAF bombers employed in the *strategic air offensive against Germany from late 1943 onwards. It was a development of the *Wilde Sau (wild boar) tactics but the larger twin-engined fighters of the almost defunct *Kammhuber Line were used, not over the cities being attacked, but on the bombers' route to and from their target. As a result bombing raids often became air battles fought over hundreds of miles, the *Nuremberg raid of 30/31 March 1944 being an example of this. The fighters were kept constantly informed as to their whereabouts by a 'running commentary' from the ground, but they picked their targets by *radar or even visually. See also FIGHTERS, 2.

Zamość, region (and town) in the General Government area of Poland (see POLAND, 2(b)) where the Nazis' largest single so-called pacification programme was started in November 1942 after they had decided that it should become a German region. Some 150,000 Poles from nearly 300 villages were either deported as *forced labour, sent to *concentration camps, or distributed elsewhere in Poland. They included 30,000 *children, most of whom disappeared, though it is known that 4,454 of the more Aryan-looking ones became part of the **Lebensborn* programme. The Polish inhabitants were replaced by settlers from Germany and the Ukraine, but the *SS lacked the manpower to deport everyone—400 villages were untouched—and when those who remained began attacking the new settlers the operation was abandoned.

Żegota, secret name of the Polish Council for Aid to Jews (Rada Pomocy Zydom) formed in December 1942. It helped Jews, and in particular *children, find suitable hiding-places to escape the *Final Solution, and it also gave financial assistance and false documents to those living underground. Its work was concentrated in Warsaw, but it also functioned elsewhere in occupied Poland. In all, it possibly saved over 100,000 people.

Zeitzler, General Kurt (1895–1963), appointed chief of the German Army's High Command (OKH) in September 1942 after serving as *Kleist's chief of staff during the fighting which led to the fall of *France in June 1940, in the *Balkan campaign, and in the German invasion of the USSR in June 1941 (see BARBAROSSA). Hitler rarely took his advice and refused Zeitzler's pleas for him to allow *Paulus to break out at *Stalingrad. When the rations of those trapped there were reduced Zeitzler visibly lost weight by eating the same rations himself, but Hitler was unmoved. Successive defeats in the *German–Soviet war, particularly the failure of the *Kursk offensive in July 1943, gradually undermined his position and his health. He resigned before the July 1944 bomb plot against Hitler (see SCHWARZE KAPELLE) and the following January he retired from the army.

Zhukov, Marshal Georgi (1896–1974), Red Army officer, a one-time NCO (non-commissioned officer) in the Imperial Russian cavalry who, when war broke out in Europe in September 1939, was dealing the Japanese *Kwantung Army a sharp defeat on the Halha River or Khalkin-Gol (*Gol* means river in Mongolian) in Outer Mongolia (see JAPANESE–SOVIET CAMPAIGNS). In January 1941 Stalin selected him to be chief of the general staff, a posting which he regarded with misgivings since he had neither training nor interest in staff work. In late July 1941, apparently because he was too outspoken, Stalin dismissed him from the general staff but retained him in the *Stavka, the general headquarters committee responsible for strategic planning.

In early September, Zhukov was deploying reserve armies west of Moscow when Stalin ordered him to take over Leningrad *front* (army group), which appeared about to lose the city. Zhukov arrived at the same time as the German commander received an order to isolate but not enter *Leningrad; consequently, in a few days he appeared to have worked a miracle. Needing another miracle in October, as the Germans approached *Moscow, Stalin gave Zhukov West *front* to halt them. Two weeks after he arrived, rain and mud stopped German Army Group Centre for three weeks 65 km. (40 mi.) west of Moscow. Resuming the advance in mid-November, German spearheads closed in on the Soviet capital, one getting within 20 km. (12.5 mi.) of the suburbs before a drastic freeze stopped them on the night of 4 December. Two days later, using reserve armies Stalin had mustered during the pause, Zhukov counter-attacked. Thereafter, he stayed on the offensive until the thaw in March 1942, driving deep bulges in the German lines but not achieving his assigned objective, the destruction of Army Group Centre.

Expecting another attack towards Moscow, Stalin kept him at West *front* during the summer, while two German army groups moved swiftly towards the Caucasus (see GERMAN–SOVIET WAR, 4). Finally, on 27 August, Stalin summoned him to Moscow, named him deputy supreme commander and gave him and the chief of the general staff, A. M. *Vasilevsky, a free hand to deal with the situation in the south. The result was Operation URANUS, which destroyed the German Sixth Army at *Stalingrad and together with its successor, SATURN, forced a German retreat to the River Donets. In January 1943, Zhukov received his marshal's star, the first awarded in the war.

In the spring of 1943 Zhukov and Vasilevsky planned and organized Operations KUTUZOV and RUMYANTSEV in the Kursk sector, and in July, they co-ordinated the six *fronts* deployed there. When the battle at *Kursk merged into the first Soviet summer offensive, he co-ordinated First and Second Ukrainian *fronts* in the drive to and across the River *Dnieper between Kiev and Dnepropetrovsk. After the First Ukrainian *front* commander was wounded in late February 1944, Zhukov took command of the *front* and in the next month and a half drove into the gap 400 km. (250 mi.) wide between the Carpathians and the western edge of the Pripet marshes.

In June and July, after supervising the deployment for the operation, Zhukov and Vasilevsky each co-ordinated fronts in BAGRATION (see GERMAN–SOVIET WAR, 9), which, owing in good part to Hitler's refusal to permit a timely retreat, destroyed Army Group Centre. Zhukov then marched his *fronts*, First and Second Belorussian, through the ensuing gap and closed to the River Vistula north and south of Warsaw in August. In November, Stalin gave him command of First Belorussian *front*, on the most direct line to Berlin and told him he would no longer be needed for higher level planning and co-ordination.

Out of bridgeheads on the Vistula, Zhukov, with *Konev's First Ukrainian *front* on his left and *Rokossovsky's Second Belorussian on his right, began the drive towards Berlin on 12 January 1945. He reached the River Oder, 57 km. (35 mi.) east of Berlin, in fourteen days, but Stalin ordered him to stop there and divert forces north towards the Baltic coast. Stalin, seeming almost to have forgotten Berlin, prolonged the halt more than two months.

The fall of *Berlin, although it made him a world figure, was not Zhukov's most brilliant victory. Begun on 16 April as a triumphal march, it bogged down first in the swamps along the Oder, then on the heights behind the river, and did not end until 2 May, after Konev and Rokossovsky had joined it from the south and the north.

On 1 August 1945, as military governor of the Soviet zone, Zhukov became the Soviet member of the Allied Control Council for Germany (see ALLIED CONTROL COMMISSIONS). EARL ZIEMKE

Chaney, O. P., *Zhukov* (Norman, Okla., 1971).
Zhukov, G. K., *Memoirs* (London, 1971).

Zog I (Ahmed Zogu 1895–1961), prime minister of Albania from 1922 to 1924 before being voted president in January 1925 which meant he was virtually a dictator. In 1928 he was proclaimed king but was forced to flee when Italy invaded Albania in April 1938, and spent the war in the UK. Elections in 1945 voted in a communist government and he never returned to his throne.

zoot-suit riots, sparked off in Los Angeles, California, in June 1943 when a rumour spread that a gang of young Mexican-Americans or *pachucos* (unemployed slum-dwellers who were often petty criminals) had attacked a sailor. For several nights US servicemen beat up any young Mexican they found, stripping him naked so that he was then arrested for indecency, and the riots spread to other Californian cities. Zoot suits were the *pachucos*' uniform: long, loosely-cut coats with wide, padded shoulders, baggy trousers cut tight around the ankles, thick-soled shoes, and a wide-brimmed hat.

Zouaves, élite infantry units of the Armée d'Afrique (see FRANCE, 6(b)) which originally drew their manpower from the Zwawa who lived in the Djurdjura mountain range in northern Algeria. However, by September 1939 the fifteen Zouave regiments were composed of metropolitan Frenchmen, European settlers in North Africa, and Spanish republicans (at least 100,000 of whom had sought refuge in Algeria after the *Spanish Civil War), although there were also a few Algerian Muslims. Ten regiments took part in the fighting which preceded the fall of *France in June 1940, three took part in the *North African campaign, and two in the *French Riviera landings.

Clayton, A., *France, Soldiers and Africa* (London, 1988).

Z Special Unit, see SPECIAL OPERATIONS AUSTRALIA.

zyklon-B was the trade name in Germany for prussic acid when used as a commercial pesticide. After successful experiments were carried out on Soviet *prisoners-of-war in *Auschwitz in August 1941 it was employed in the gas chambers of the Nazi *death camps, though not in those of *operation REINHARD.

Colour Maps

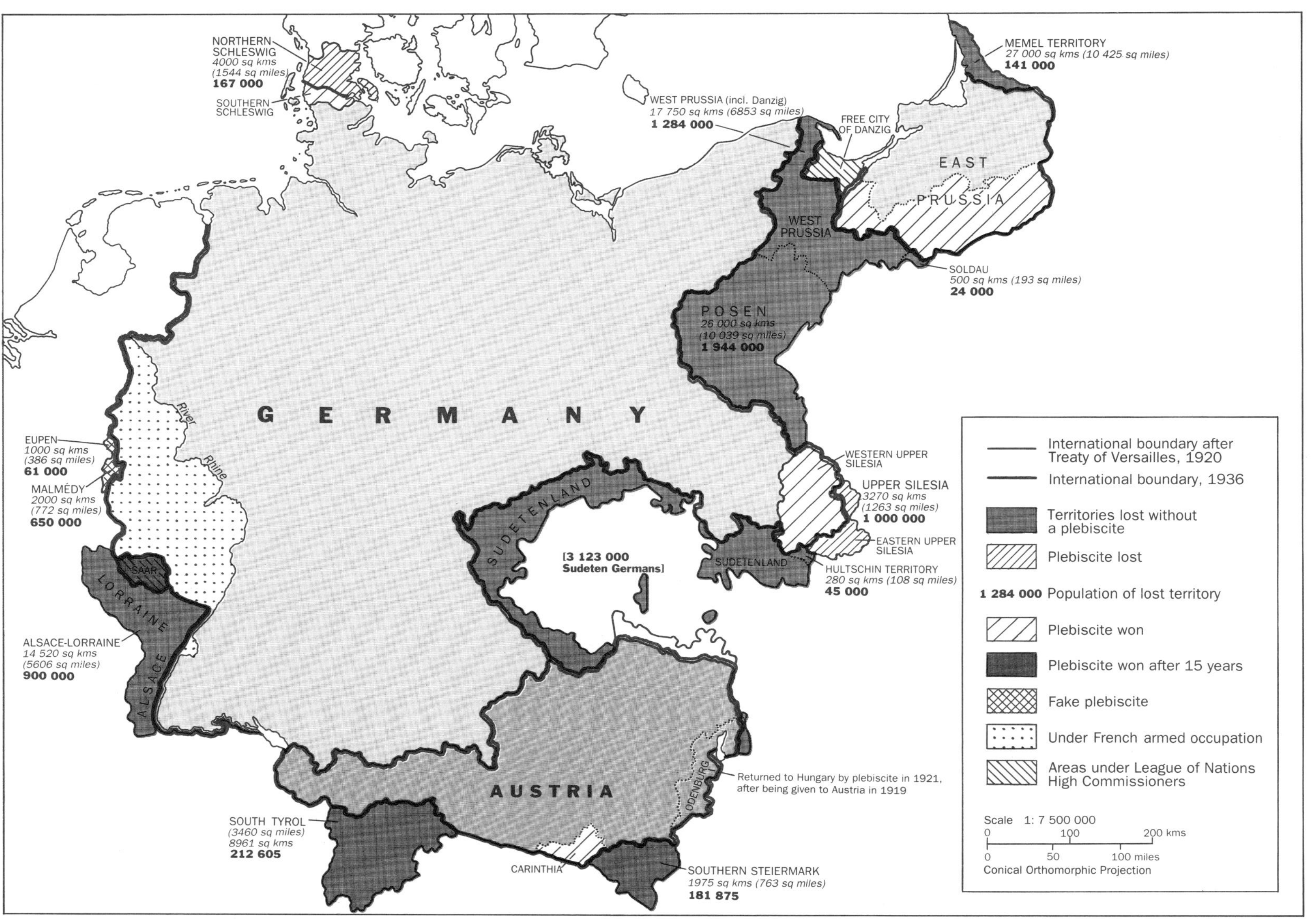

A. German and Austrian territorial losses after the First World War

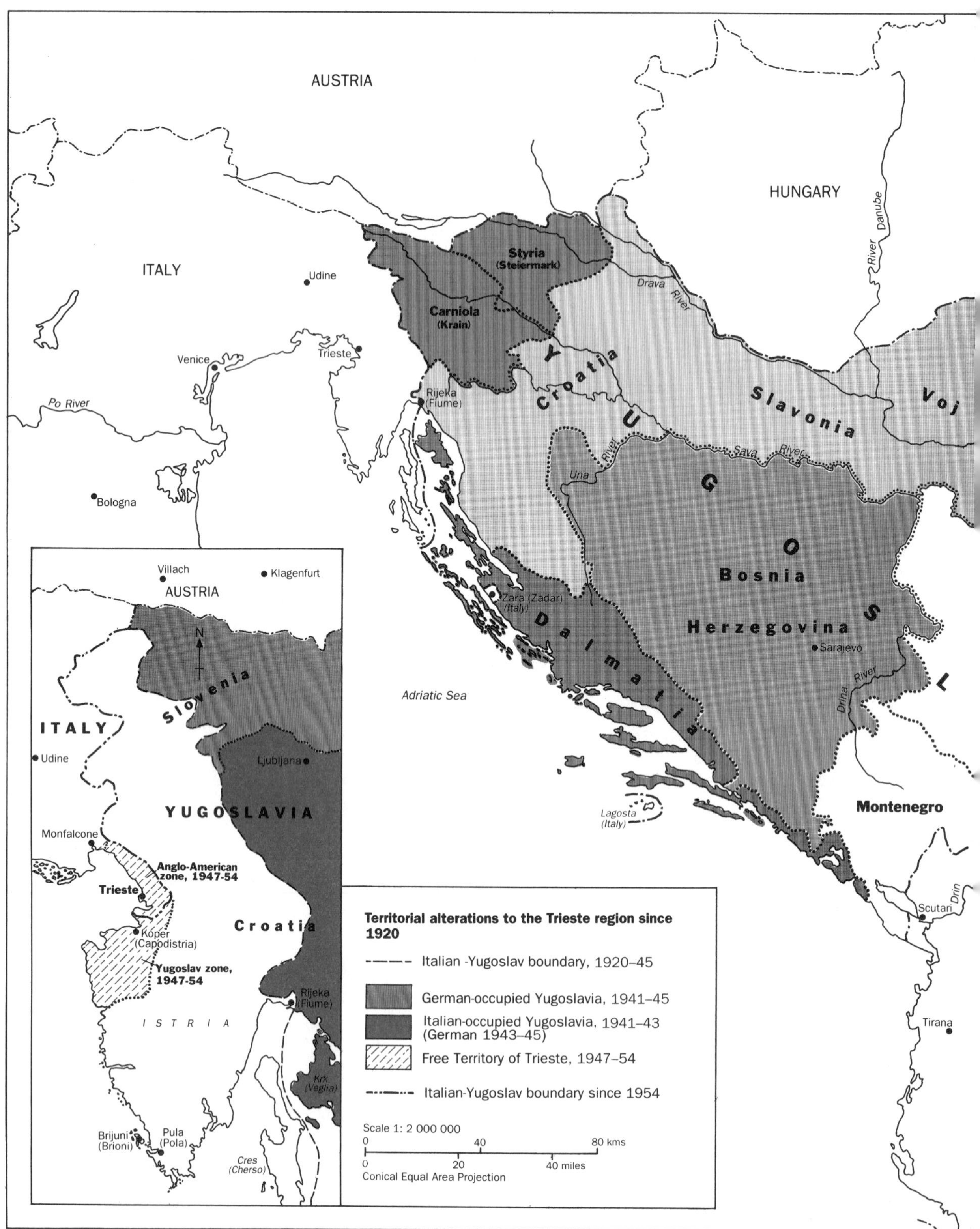

B. Territorial changes to Yugoslavia and Bulgaria, 1918–March 1941

Yugoslavian gains
1918 former Austrian territory
1918 former Hungarian territory
1918 former Austro-Hungarian province of Bosnia-Herzegovina
1918 former Albanian territory
1919 former Bulgarian territory
Bulgarian losses
1919 to Greece
1919 to Romania (returned to Bulgaria in September 1940)
International boundary, 1919
Scale 1: 4 500 000
0 50 100 150 kms
0 50 100 miles
Conical Orthomorphic Projection
ROMANIA
Tisza River
vodina
River
Belgrade
Danube
N
Bucharest
DOBRUJA
River Danube
Varna
Serbia
BULGARIA
Sofia
Black Sea
Maritsa River
Skoplje
Adrianople (Edirne)
THRACE
Mesta River
MACEDONIA
TURKEY
ALBANIA
GREECE
Salonika
Thasos
Aegean Sea

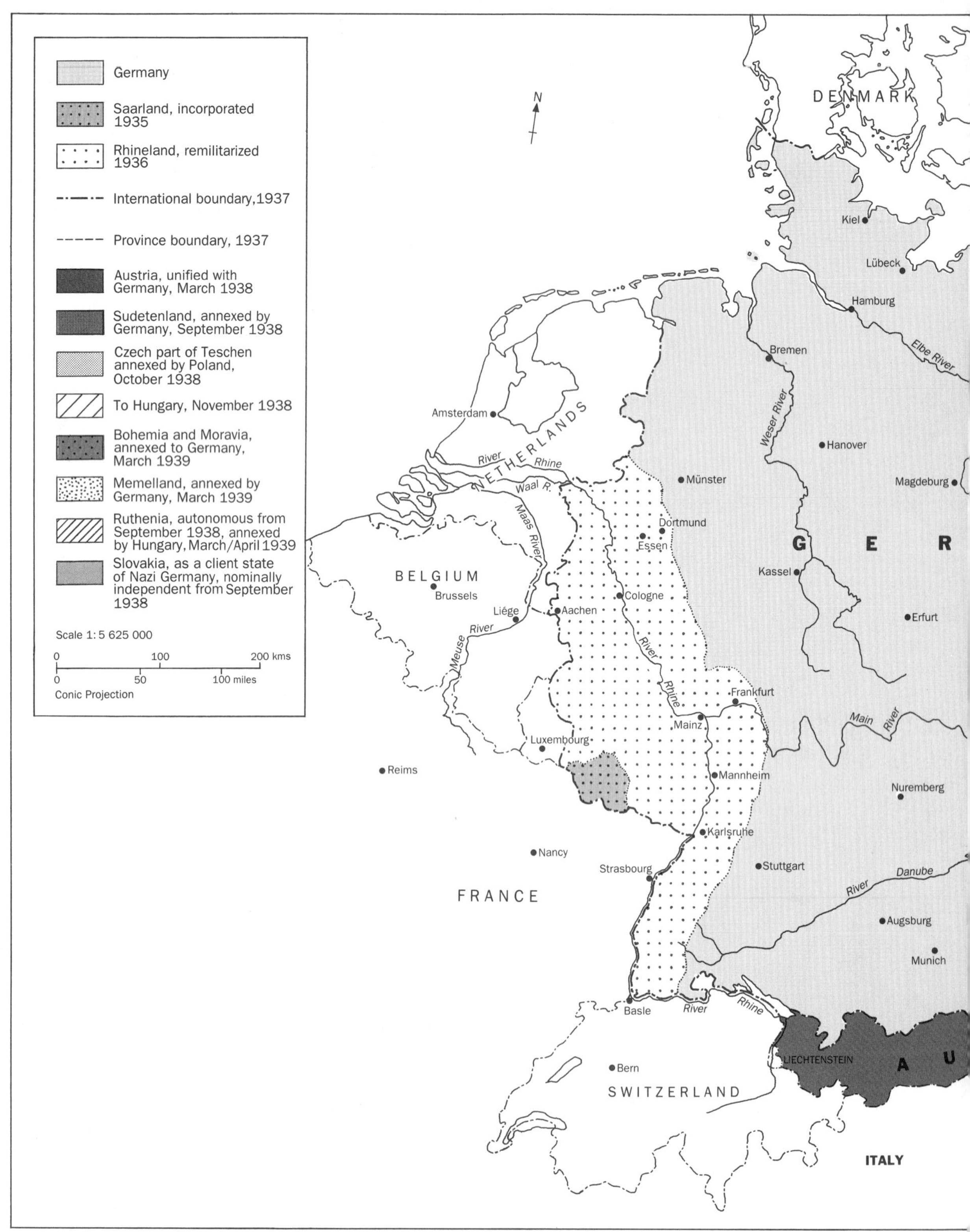

C. Territorial changes to Czechoslovakia and Germany, 1935–April 1939.

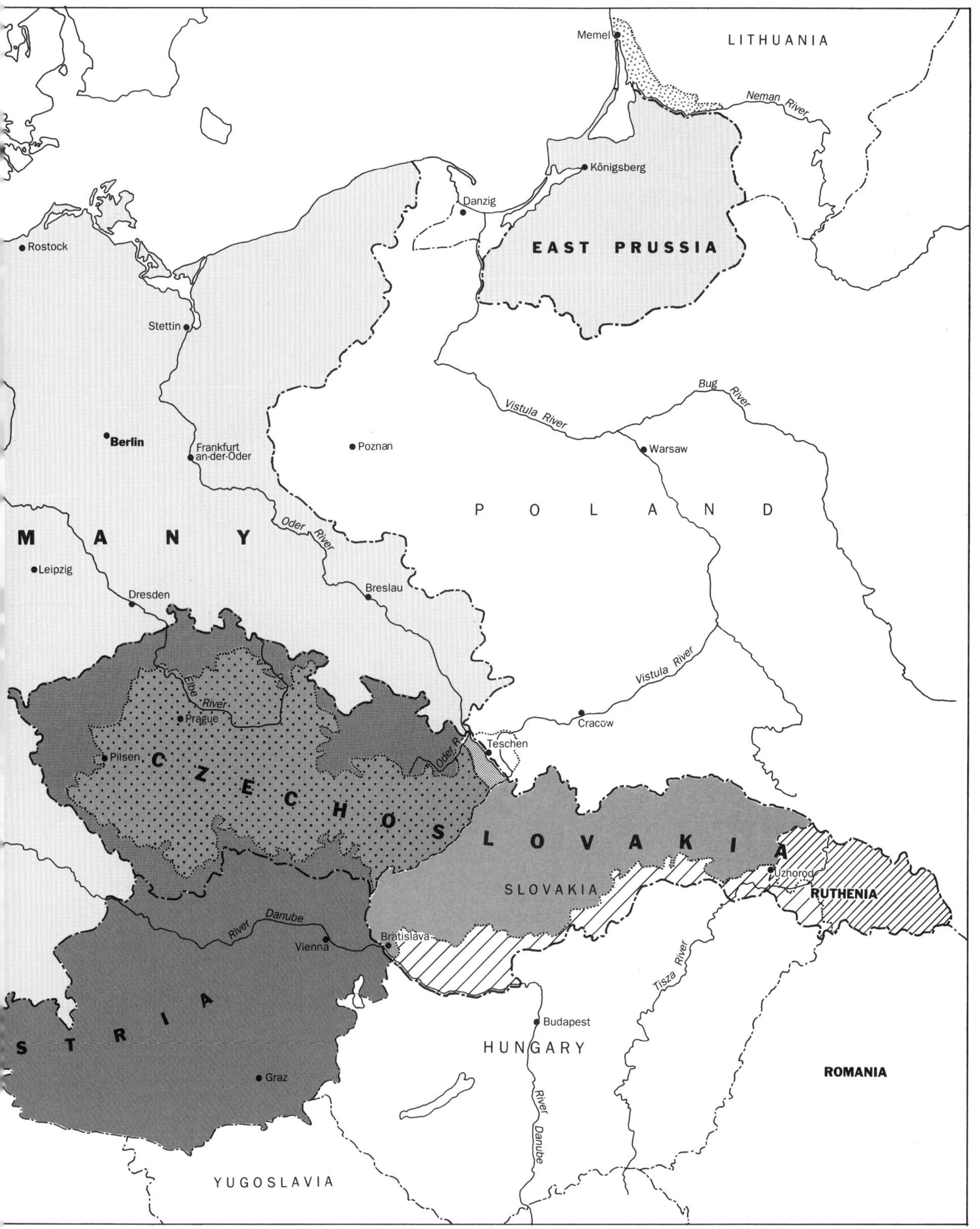
Memel
LITHUANIA
Neman River
Königsberg
Danzig
EAST PRUSSIA
Rostock
Stettin
Bug River
Vistula River
Warsaw
Berlin
Frankfurt an-der-Oder
Poznan
POLAND
Oder River
MANY
Leipzig
Dresden
Breslau
Vistula River
Elbe River
Prague
Cracow
Teschen
Pilsen
Oder R.
CZECHOSLOVAKIA
SLOVAKIA
Uzhorod
RUTHENIA
Danube River
Vienna
Bratislava
Tisza River
STRIA
Budapest
HUNGARY
ROMANIA
Graz
River Danube
YUGOSLAVIA

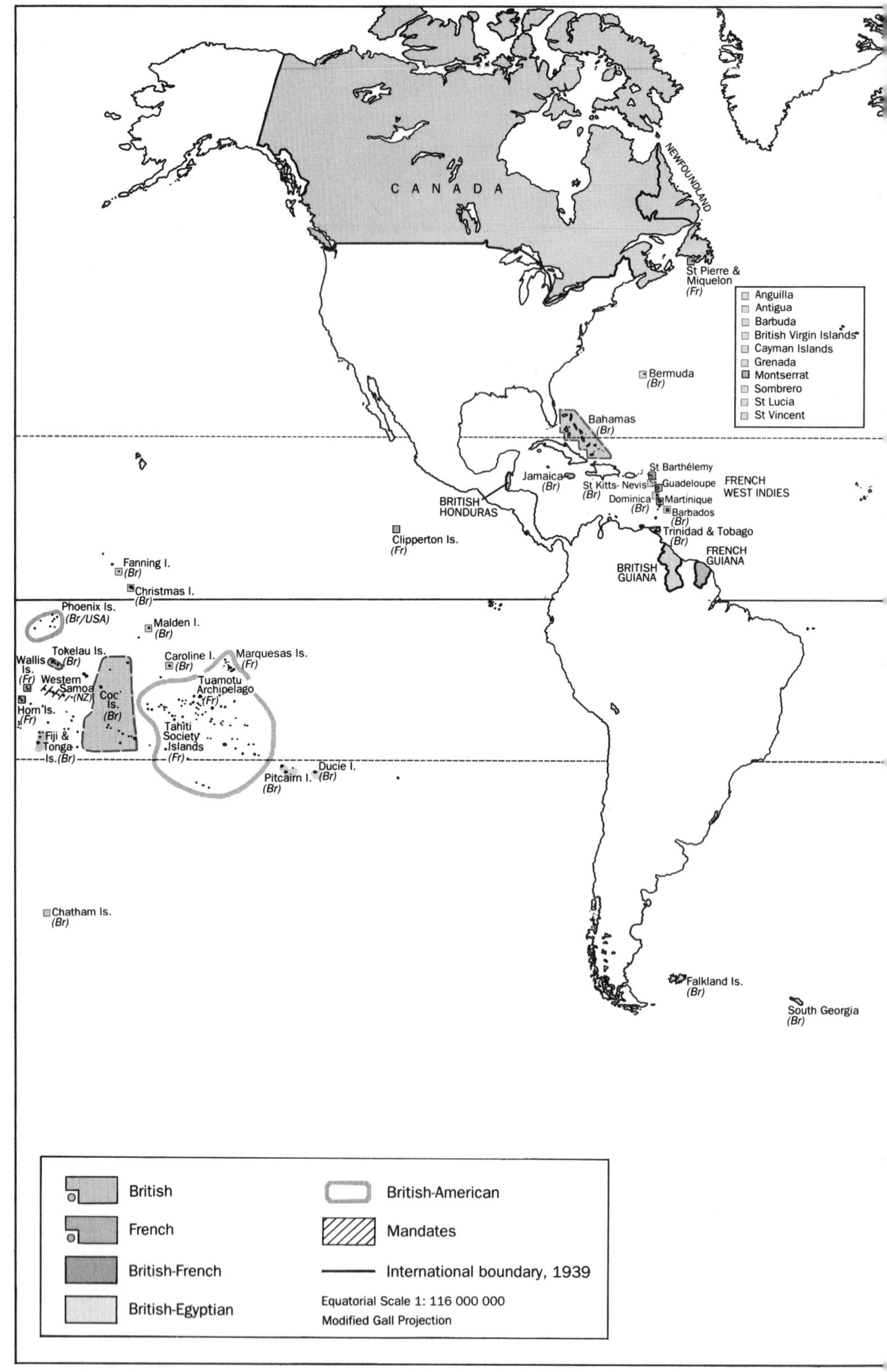

D. British and French Empires, 1 September 1939

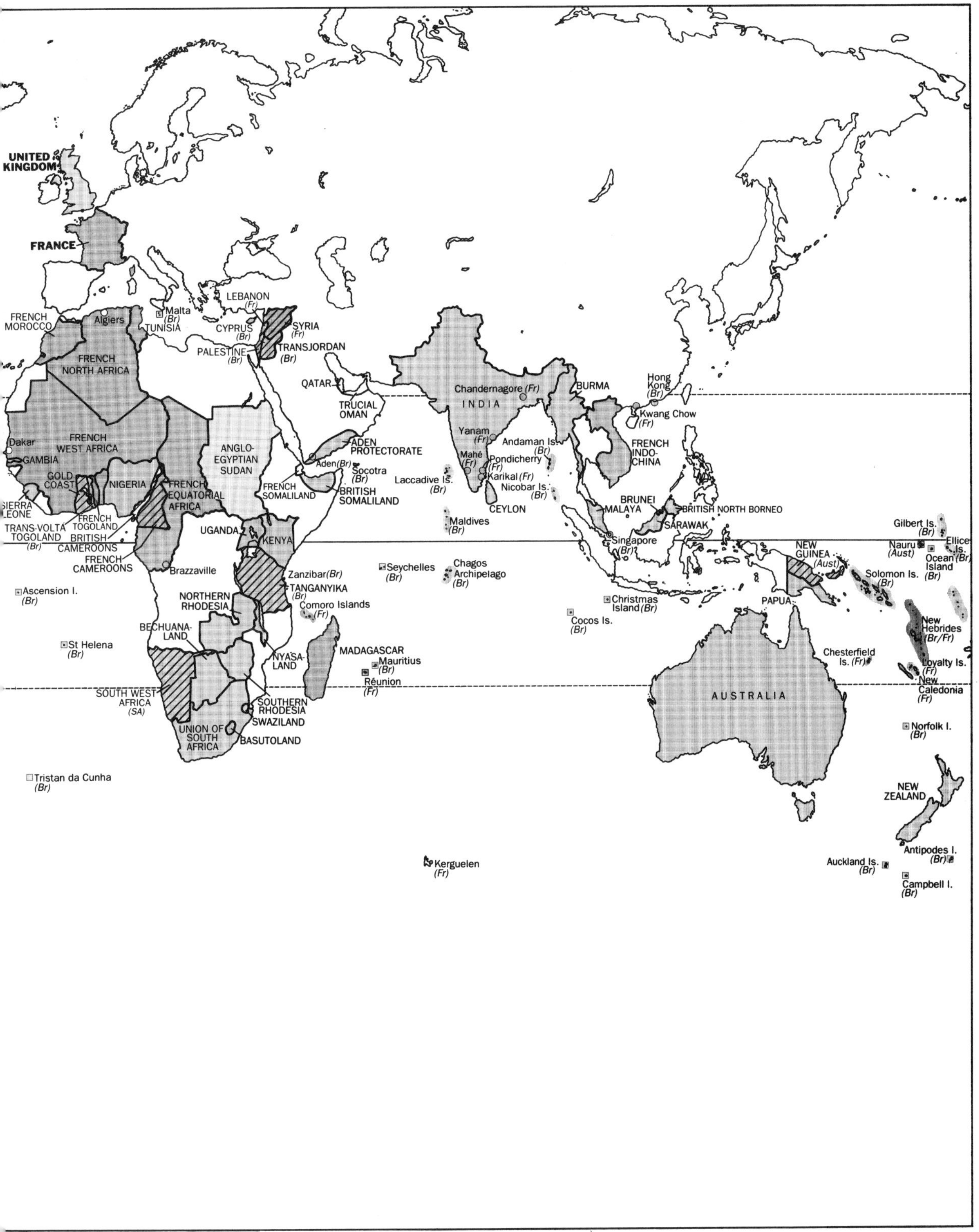

UNITED KINGDOM
FRANCE
FRENCH MOROCCO
Algiers
Malta (Br)
TUNISIA
LEBANON (Fr)
CYPRUS (Br)
SYRIA (Fr)
PALESTINE (Br)
TRANSJORDAN (Br)
FRENCH NORTH AFRICA
QATAR
TRUCIAL OMAN
Chandernagore (Fr)
INDIA
BURMA
Hong Kong (Br)
Kwang Chow (Fr)
Dakar
FRENCH WEST AFRICA
GAMBIA
ANGLO-EGYPTIAN SUDAN
ADEN PROTECTORATE
Aden (Br)
Socotra (Br)
Yanam (Fr)
Mahé (Fr)
Andaman Is. (Br)
Pondicherry (Fr)
Karikal (Fr)
Nicobar Is. (Br)
Laccadive Is. (Br)
FRENCH INDO-CHINA
GOLD COAST
NIGERIA
FRENCH EQUATORIAL AFRICA
FRENCH SOMALILAND
BRITISH SOMALILAND
CEYLON
SIERRA LEONE
FRENCH TOGOLAND
TRANS-VOLTA TOGOLAND (Br)
BRITISH CAMEROONS
FRENCH CAMEROONS
UGANDA
KENYA
Maldives (Br)
BRUNEI
MALAYA
BRITISH NORTH BORNEO
SARAWAK
Singapore (Br)
Gilbert Is. (Br)
Nauru (Aust)
Ellice Is.
Ocean Island (Br)
NEW GUINEA (Aust)
Brazzaville
Zanzibar (Br)
Seychelles (Br)
Chagos Archipelago (Br)
Solomon Is. (Br)
Ascension I. (Br)
TANGANYIKA (Br)
NORTHERN RHODESIA
Comoro Islands (Fr)
Christmas Island (Br)
PAPUA
Cocos Is. (Br)
New Hebrides (Br/Fr)
BECHUANA-LAND
St Helena (Br)
MADAGASCAR
Mauritius (Br)
NYASA-LAND
Chesterfield Is. (Fr)
Loyalty Is. (Fr)
Réunion (Fr)
SOUTH WEST AFRICA (SA)
SOUTHERN RHODESIA
AUSTRALIA
New Caledonia (Fr)
SWAZILAND
UNION OF SOUTH AFRICA
BASUTOLAND
Norfolk I. (Br)
Tristan da Cunha (Br)
NEW ZEALAND
Antipodes I. (Br)
Kerguelen (Fr)
Auckland Is. (Br)
Campbell I. (Br)

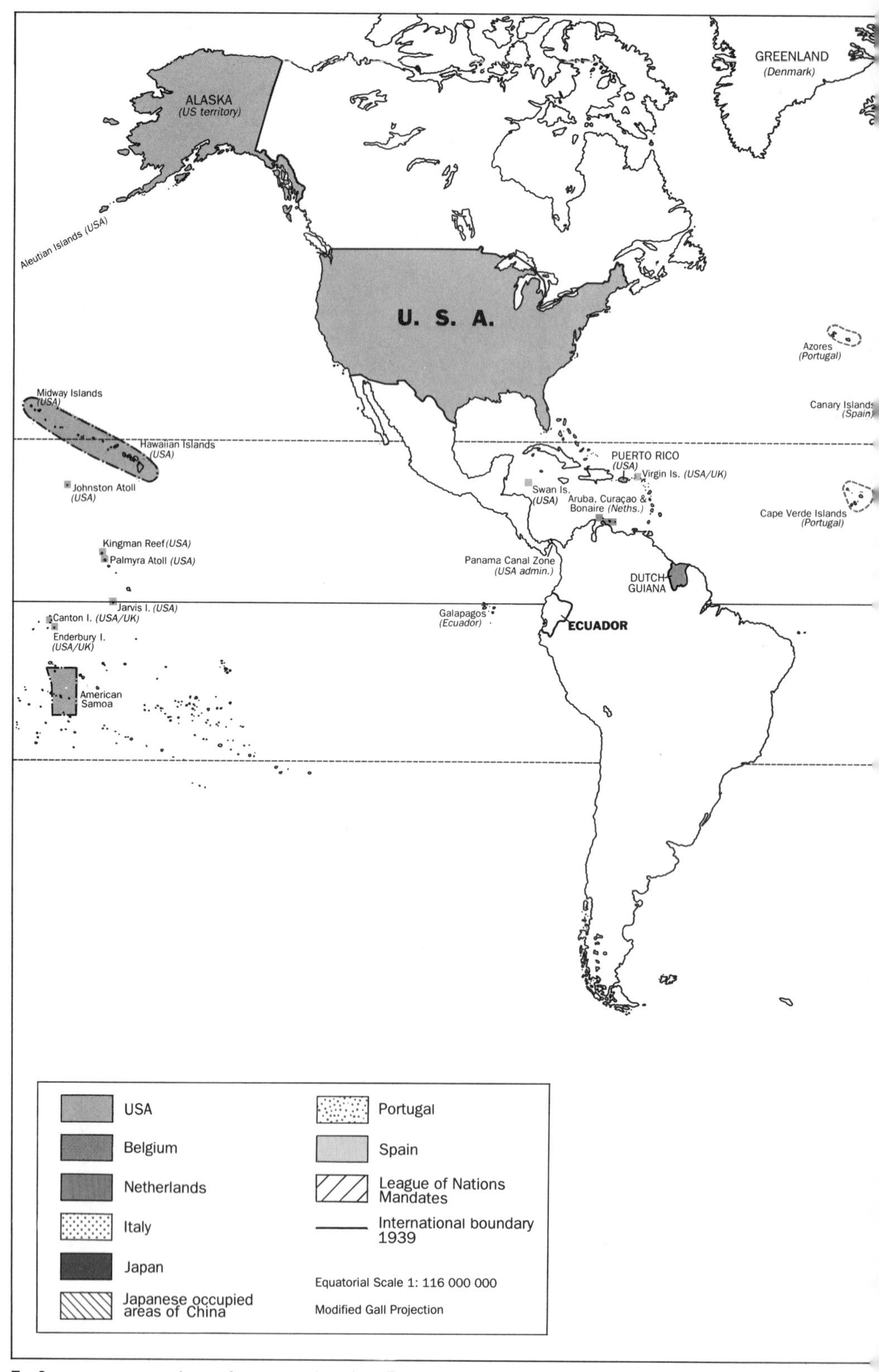

E. Overseas possessions of powers other than France and UK, 1 September 1939.

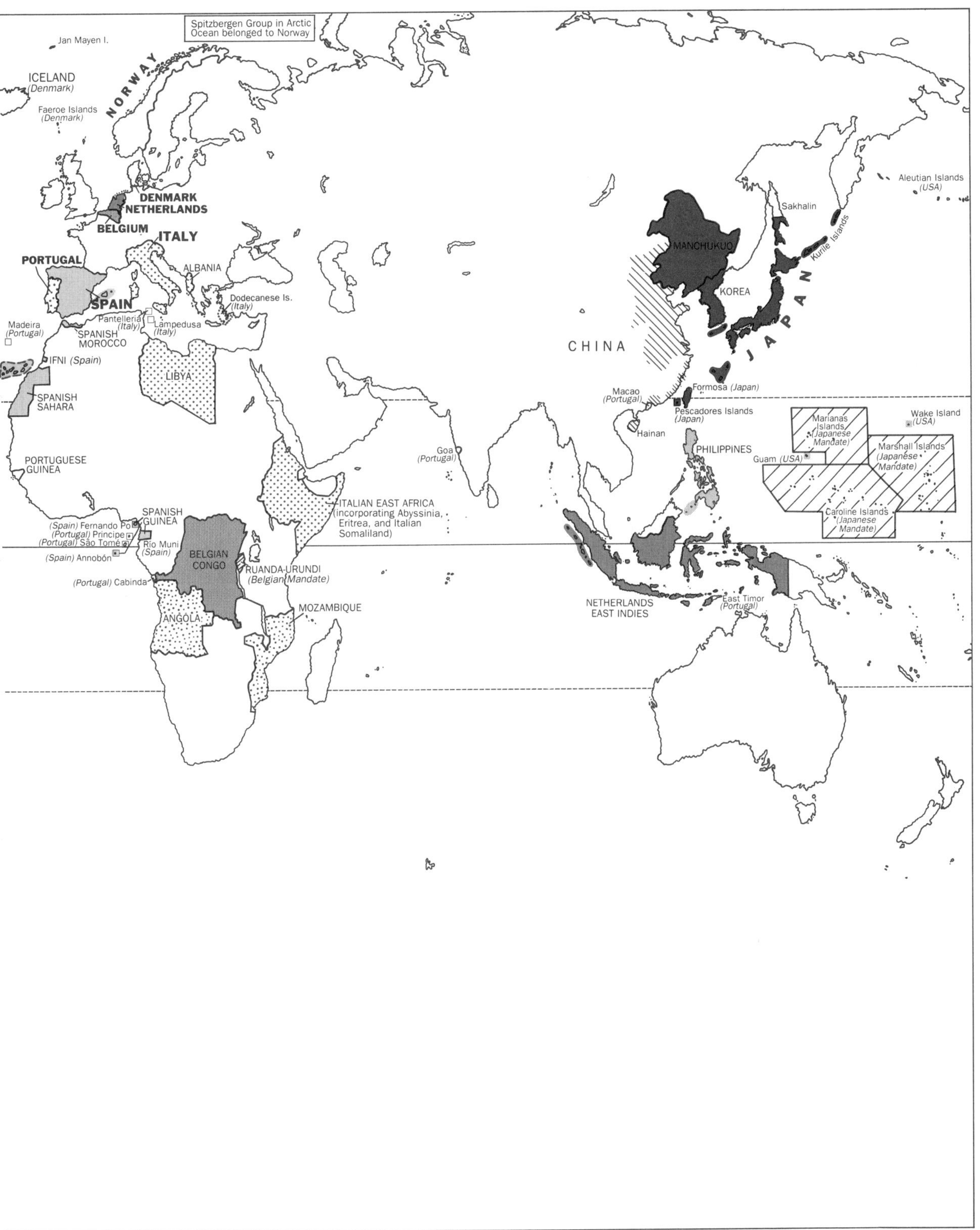
Spitzbergen Group in Arctic Ocean belonged to Norway
Jan Mayen I.
ICELAND
(Denmark)
Faeroe Islands
(Denmark)
NORWAY
DENMARK
NETHERLANDS
BELGIUM
ITALY
PORTUGAL
ALBANIA
SPAIN
Dodecanese Is.
(Italy)
Pantelleria
(Italy)
Lampedusa
(Italy)
Madeira
(Portugal)
SPANISH
MOROCCO
IFNI (Spain)
LIBYA
SPANISH
SAHARA
PORTUGUESE
GUINEA
SPANISH
GUINEA
(Spain) Fernando Po
(Portugal) Principe
(Portugal) São Tomé
Rio Muni
(Spain)
(Spain) Annobón
(Portugal) Cabinda
BELGIAN
CONGO
RUANDA-URUNDI
(Belgian Mandate)
ANGOLA
MOZAMBIQUE
ITALIAN EAST AFRICA
(incorporating Abyssinia, Eritrea, and Italian Somaliland)
Goa
(Portugal)
CHINA
MANCHUKUO
KOREA
JAPAN
Sakhalin
Kurile Islands
Aleutian Islands
(USA)
Macao
(Portugal)
Formosa (Japan)
Pescadores Islands
(Japan)
Hainan
PHILIPPINES
Marianas Islands
(Japanese Mandate)
Wake Island
(USA)
Guam (USA)
Marshall Islands
(Japanese Mandate)
Caroline Islands
(Japanese Mandate)
NETHERLANDS
EAST INDIES
East Timor
(Portugal)

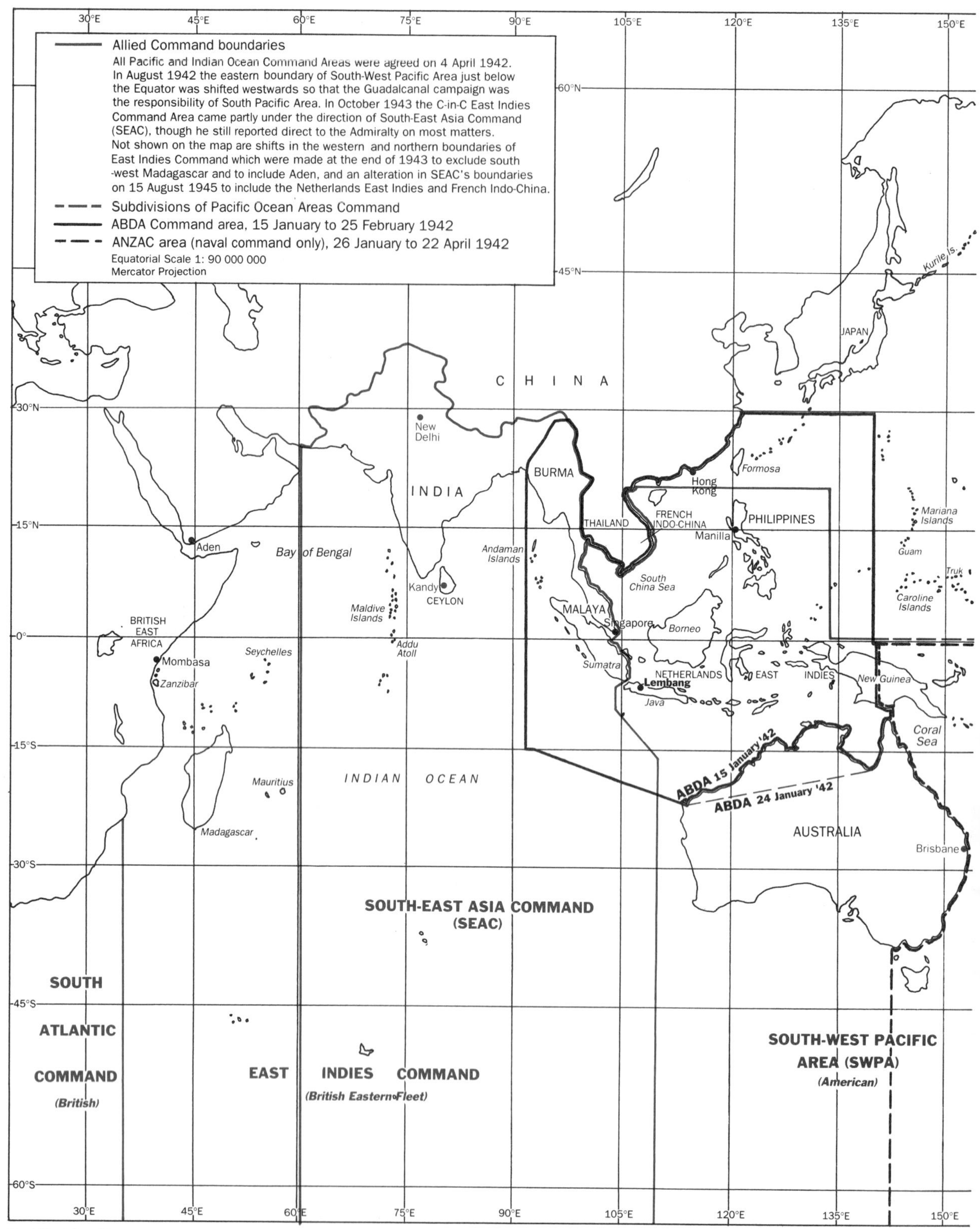

F. Allied Pacific and Indian Ocean Commands, 1942–5

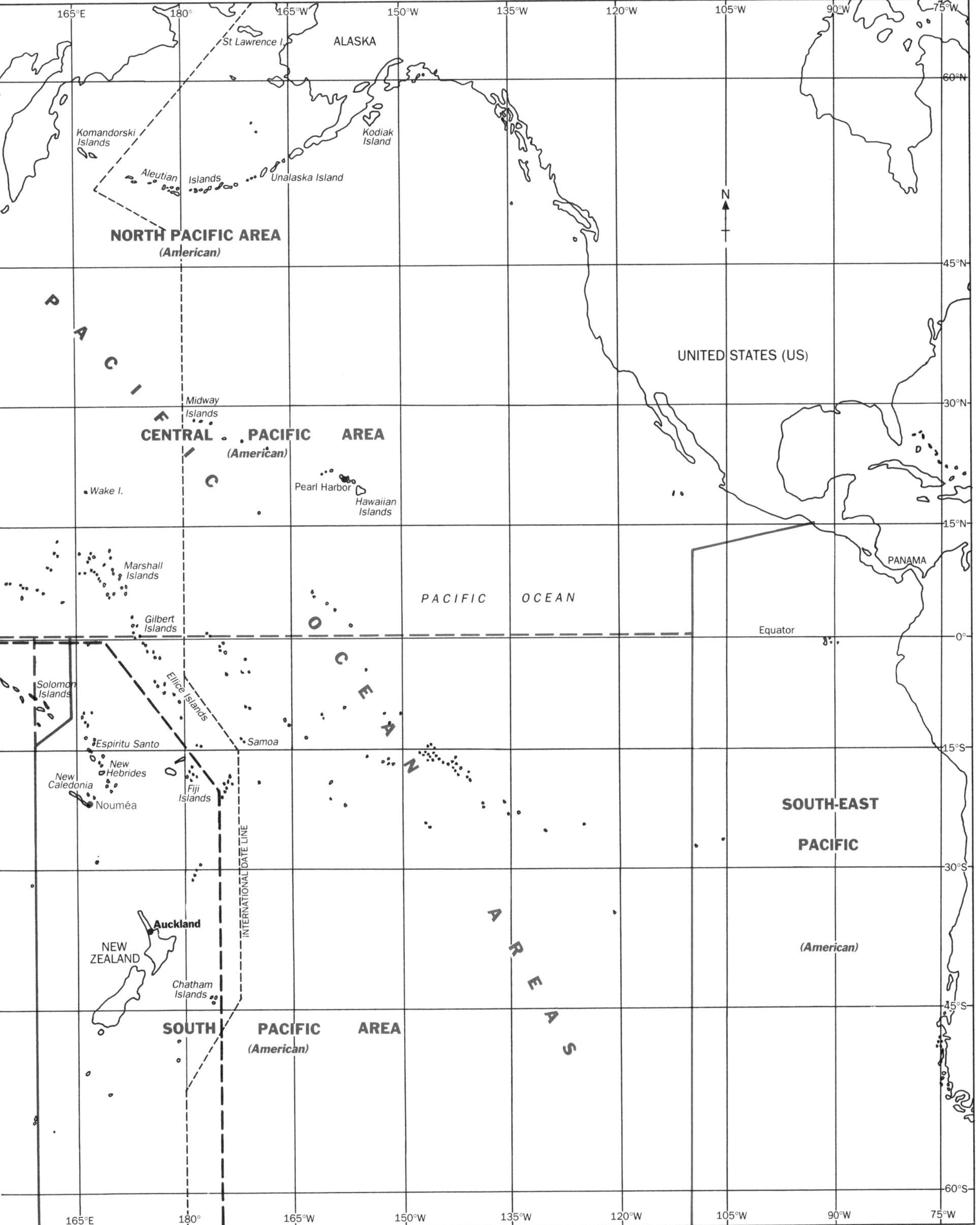
165°E
180°
165°W
150°W
135°W
120°W
105°W
90°W
75°W
60°N
45°N
30°N
15°N
0°
15°S
30°S
45°S
60°S
St Lawrence I.
ALASKA
Komandorski Islands
Kodiak Island
Aleutian Islands
Unalaska Island
N
NORTH PACIFIC AREA
(American)
UNITED STATES (US)
PACIFIC OCEAN AREAS
Midway Islands
CENTRAL PACIFIC AREA
(American)
Wake I.
Pearl Harbor
Hawaiian Islands
Marshall Islands
PANAMA
PACIFIC OCEAN
Gilbert Islands
Equator
Solomon Islands
Ellice Islands
Espiritu Santo
Samoa
New Hebrides
New Caledonia
Nouméa
Fiji Islands
SOUTH-EAST PACIFIC
INTERNATIONAL DATE LINE
Auckland
NEW ZEALAND
(American)
Chatham Islands
SOUTH PACIFIC AREA
(American)

G. Pacific theatre: Japanese defensive perimeters and Allied Offensive against Japan, 1942–5

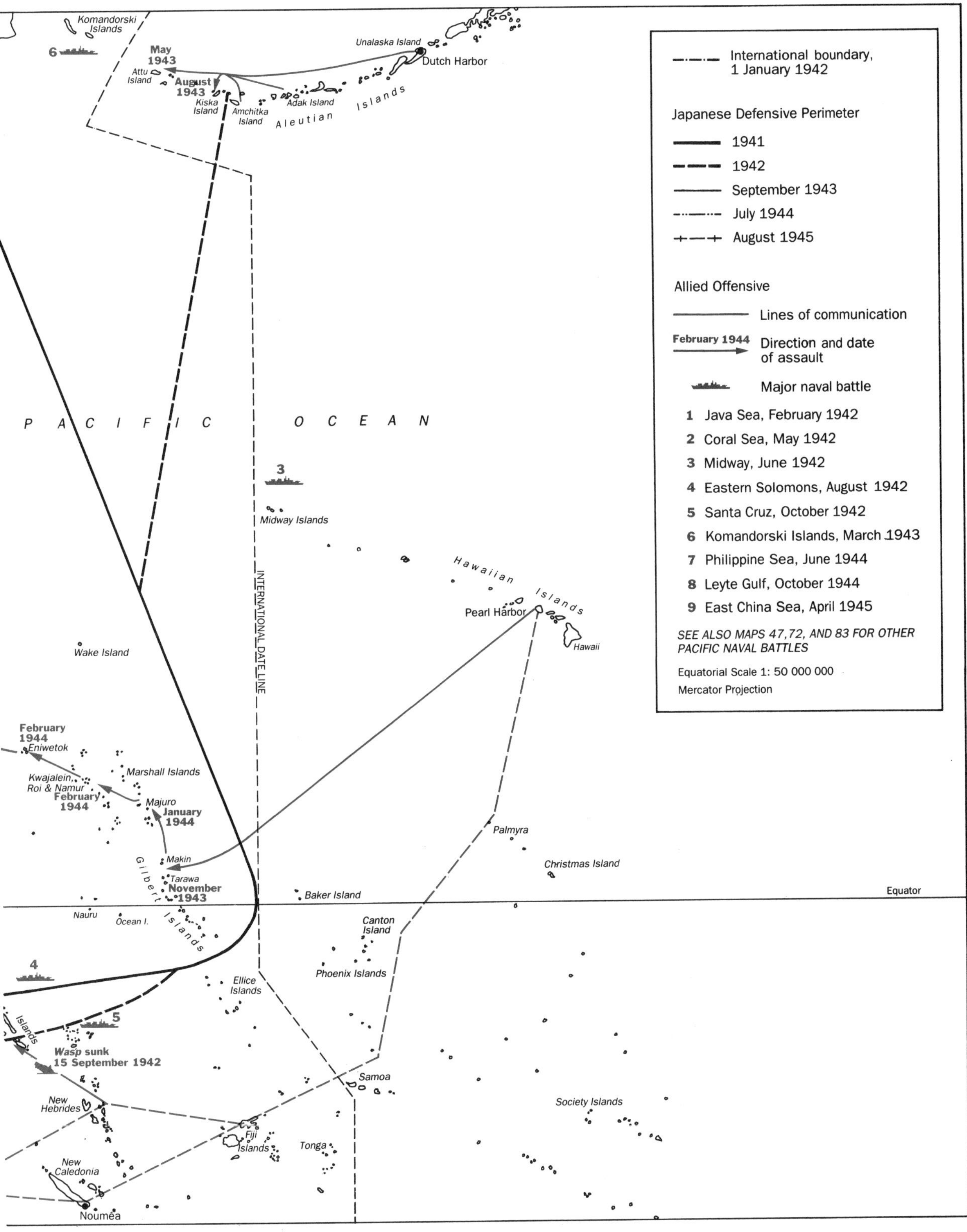

International boundary, 1 January 1942
Japanese Defensive Perimeter
1941
1942
September 1943
July 1944
August 1945
Allied Offensive
Lines of communication
February 1944
Direction and date of assault
Major naval battle
1 Java Sea, February 1942
2 Coral Sea, May 1942
3 Midway, June 1942
4 Eastern Solomons, August 1942
5 Santa Cruz, October 1942
6 Komandorski Islands, March 1943
7 Philippine Sea, June 1944
8 Leyte Gulf, October 1944
9 East China Sea, April 1945
SEE ALSO MAPS 47,72, AND 83 FOR OTHER PACIFIC NAVAL BATTLES
Equatorial Scale 1: 50 000 000
Mercator Projection
Komandorski Islands
Unalaska Island
Dutch Harbor
May 1943
Attu Island
August 1943
Kiska Island
Amchitka Island
Adak Island
Aleutian Islands
PACIFIC OCEAN
Midway Islands
Hawaiian Islands
Pearl Harbor
Hawaii
Wake Island
INTERNATIONAL DATE LINE
February 1944
Eniwetok
Marshall Islands
Kwajalein, Roi & Namur
February 1944
Majuro
January 1944
Makin
Tarawa
November 1943
Gilbert Islands
Palmyra
Christmas Island
Baker Island
Equator
Nauru
Ocean I.
Canton Island
Phoenix Islands
Ellice Islands
Wasp sunk 15 September 1942
Samoa
New Hebrides
Fiji Islands
Tonga
Society Islands
New Caledonia
Nouméa

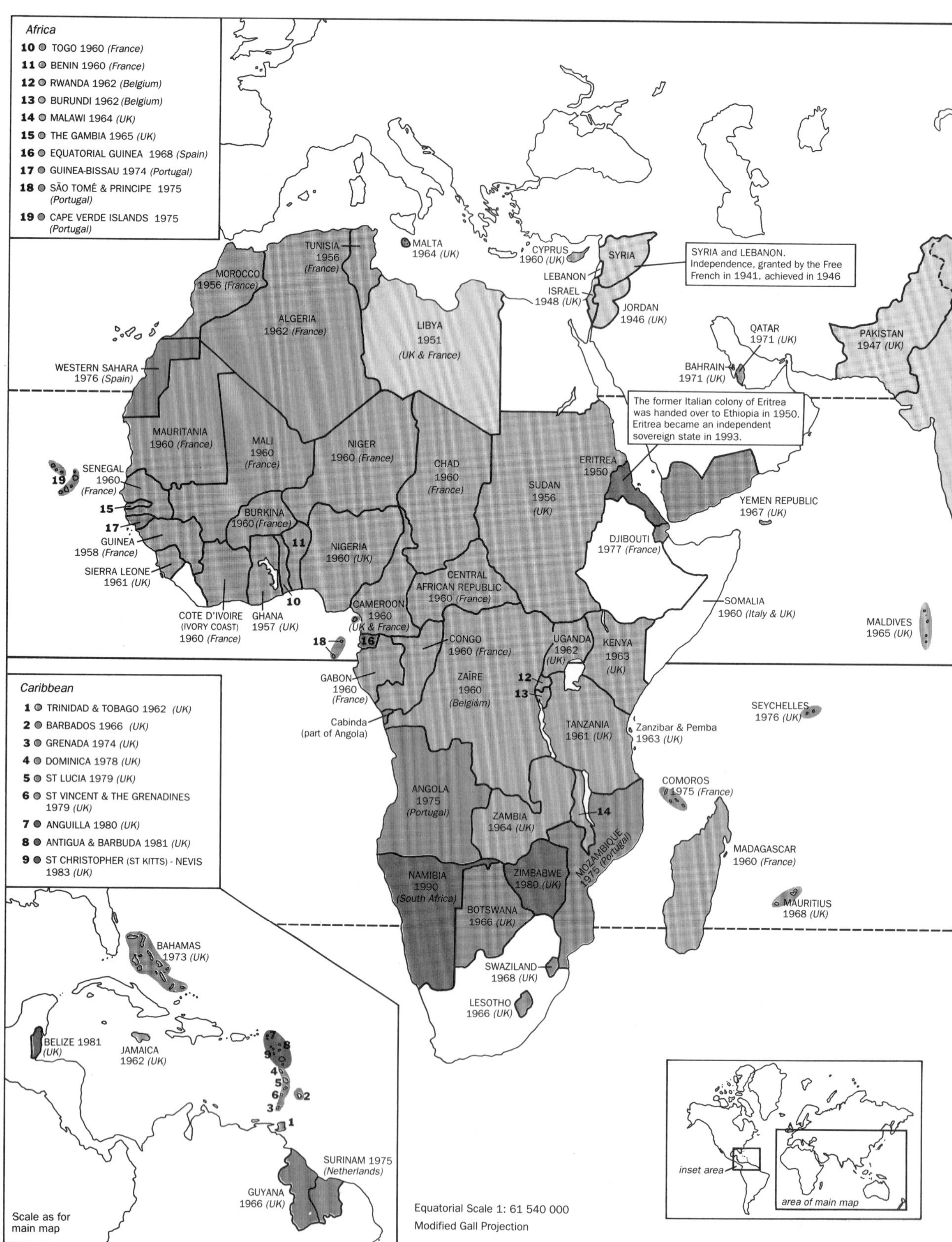

H. Post-war independence from Colonial Powers

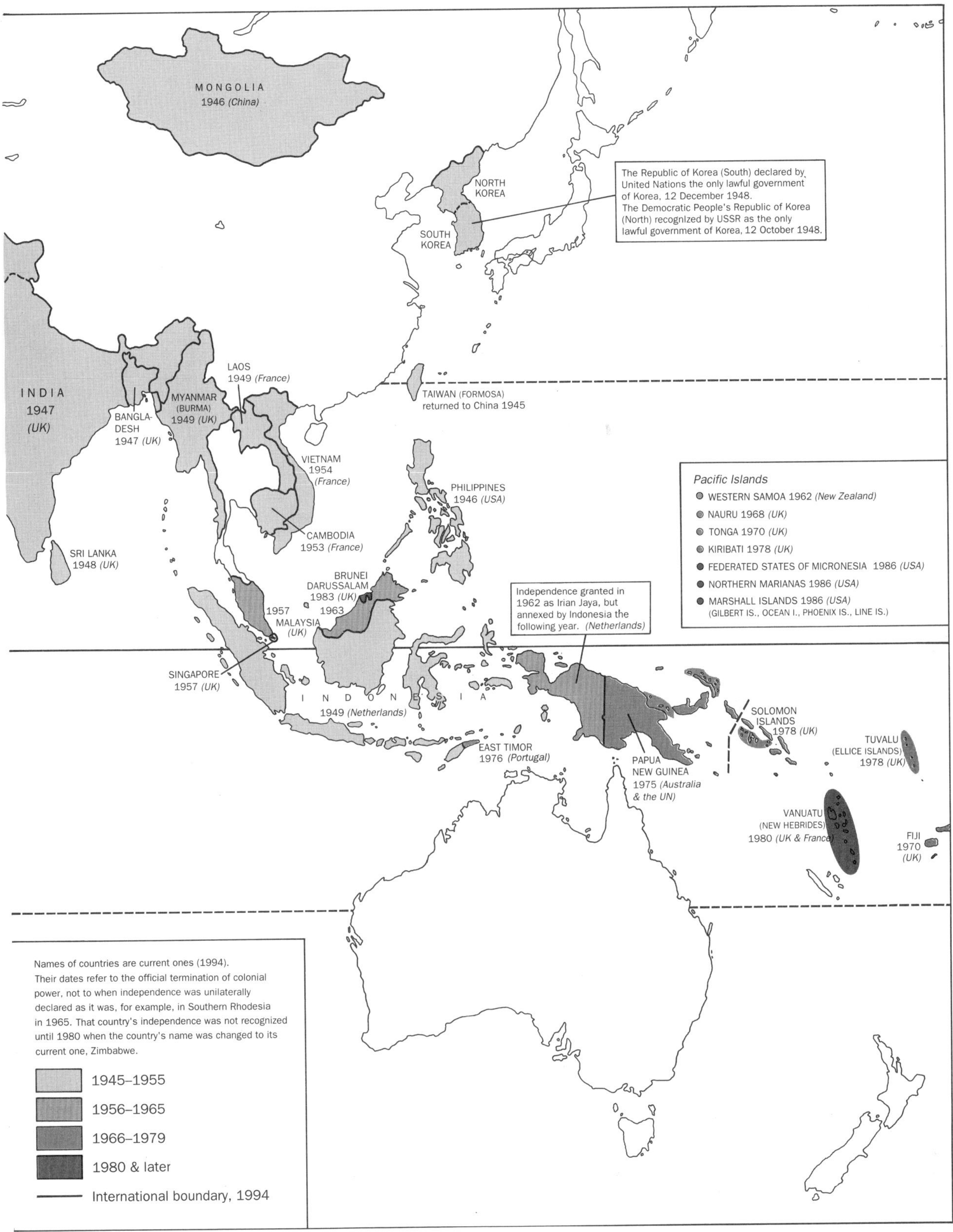
MONGOLIA
1946 (China)
NORTH KOREA
SOUTH KOREA
The Republic of Korea (South) declared by United Nations the only lawful government of Korea, 12 December 1948.
The Democratic People's Republic of Korea (North) recognized by USSR as the only lawful government of Korea, 12 October 1948.
INDIA
1947
(UK)
BANGLA-DESH
1947 (UK)
MYANMAR (BURMA)
1949 (UK)
LAOS
1949 (France)
TAIWAN (FORMOSA)
returned to China 1945
VIETNAM
1954
(France)
PHILIPPINES
1946 (USA)
CAMBODIA
1953 (France)
SRI LANKA
1948 (UK)
BRUNEI DARUSSALAM
1983 (UK)
1963
1957
MALAYSIA
(UK)
SINGAPORE
1957 (UK)
INDONESIA
1949 (Netherlands)
Independence granted in 1962 as Irian Jaya, but annexed by Indonesia the following year. (Netherlands)
EAST TIMOR
1976 (Portugal)
PAPUA NEW GUINEA
1975 (Australia & the UN)
SOLOMON ISLANDS
1978 (UK)
TUVALU
(ELLICE ISLANDS)
1978 (UK)
VANUATU
(NEW HEBRIDES)
1980 (UK & France)
FIJI
1970
(UK)
Pacific Islands
WESTERN SAMOA 1962 (New Zealand)
NAURU 1968 (UK)
TONGA 1970 (UK)
KIRIBATI 1978 (UK)
FEDERATED STATES OF MICRONESIA 1986 (USA)
NORTHERN MARIANAS 1986 (USA)
MARSHALL ISLANDS 1986 (USA)
(GILBERT IS., OCEAN I., PHOENIX IS., LINE IS.)
Names of countries are current ones (1994).
Their dates refer to the official termination of colonial power, not to when independence was unilaterally declared as it was, for example, in Southern Rhodesia in 1965. That country's independence was not recognized until 1980 when the country's name was changed to its current one, Zimbabwe.
1945–1955
1956–1965
1966–1979
1980 & later
International boundary, 1994

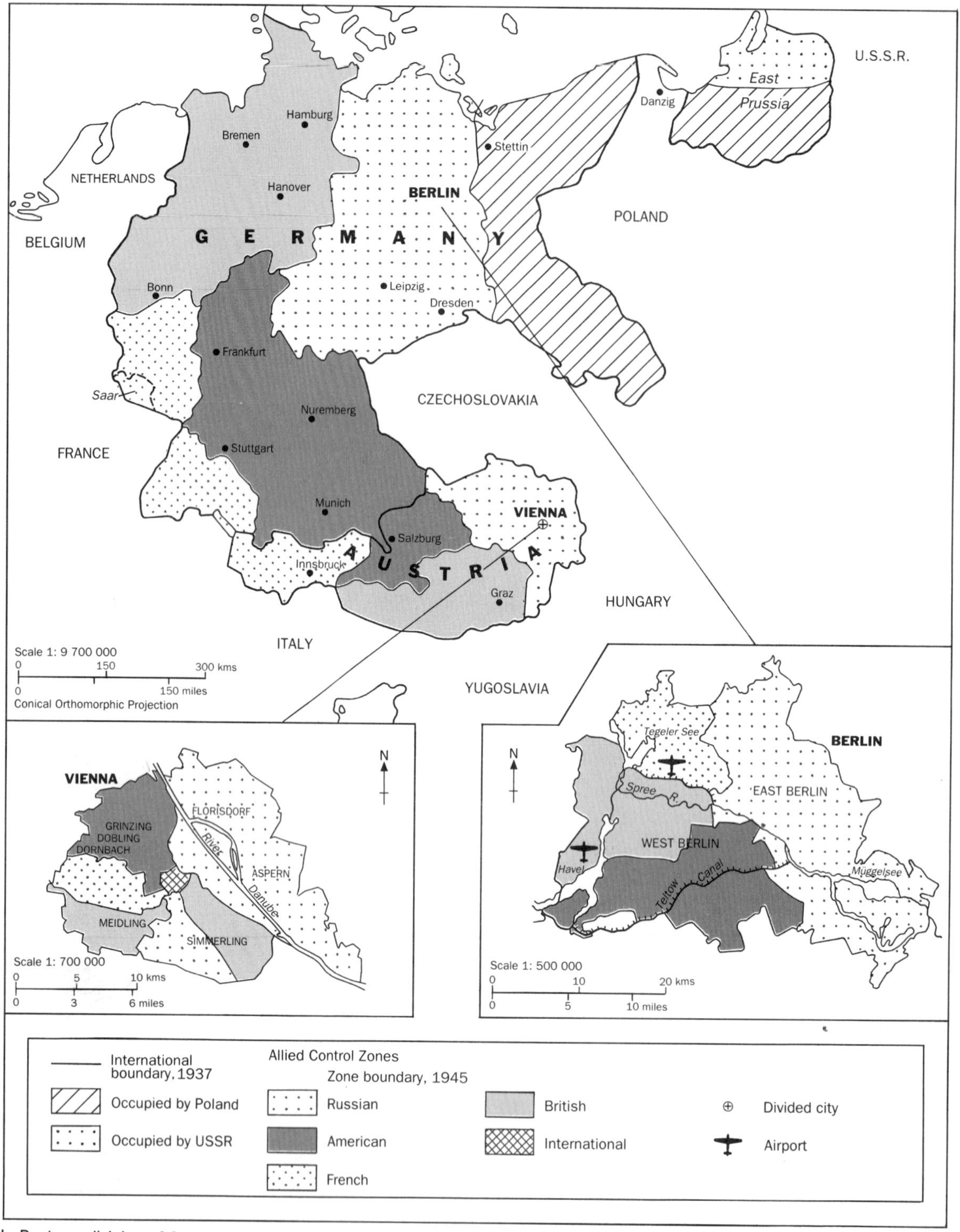

1. Post-war division of Germany and Austria

Chronology

Atlantic/Northern and Western Europe (except Italy)	Central and Eastern Europe	Balkans/Mediterranean/ Italy/Near and Middle East/Africa	North and South America	Pacific/Far East/ Australasia
		1931		
				18 Sep Japanese troops begin occupying Manchuria
		1932		
			8 Nov Franklin D. Roosevelt elected President of USA	**9 Mar** Pu-Yi installed as emperor of Japanese puppet state of Manchuria (now Manchukuo)
		1933		
30 Jan Hitler becomes chancellor **28 Feb** Reichstag fire **14 Oct** Germany withdraws from League of Nations				**25 Mar** Japan leaves League of Nations
		1934		
30 Jun Röhm purge in Germany **25 Jul** Assassination of Austrian Chancellor, Engelbert Dollfuss. Kurt von Schuschnigg replaces him **19 Aug** Hitler becomes head of state on death of Hindenburg		**16 Dec** Border incidents between Abyssinia and Italian Somaliland		**21 Oct** Mao Tse-tung's communist forces in China begin Long March to Shensi province
		1935		
1 Mar The Saar is returned to Germany **11 Mar** Existence of Luftwaffe made public **16 Mar** Hitler introduces conscription **18 Jun** Anglo-German Naval Treaty signed **10 Oct** League of Nations agrees to impose sanctions on Italy		**3 Oct** Italy invades Abyssinia from Eritrea		**20 Oct** Long March ends

Atlantic/Northern and Western Europe (except Italy)	Central and Eastern Europe	Balkans/Mediterranean/ Italy/Near and Middle East/Africa	North and South America	Pacific/Far East/ Australasia
		1936		
7 Mar Germany occupies Rhineland				
		2 May Emperor Haile Selassie flees Abyssinia **5 May** Italian troops enter Addis Ababa **9 May** Italy annexes Abyssinia		
17 Jul Spanish Civil War starts				
		26 Aug Anglo-Egyptian treaty signed		
3 Nov Roosevelt re-elected President of USA **25 Nov** Germany signs Anti-Comintern Pact with Japan				**25 Nov** Japan signs Anti-Comintern Pact with Germany
		1937		
28 May Neville Chamberlain becomes British prime minister				
	12 Jun Stalin's purge of Soviet armed forces results in execution of Marshal Tukhachevsky and eight other high ranking officers			
				7 Jul Start of China Incident
1 Aug Buchenwald concentration camp opened				
		11 Dec Italy leaves League of Nations		
				13 Dec Nanking falls to Japanese, inhabitants massacred
		1938		
11 Mar Germany annexes Austria **29 Sep** Munich agreement signed				
	5 Oct Germany occupies Czech Sudetenland; Poles seize Teschen **2 Nov** First Vienna Award			
9 Nov *Kristallnacht*—attacks on Jews and their property throughout Germany				
		1939		
	14 Mar Czechoslovakia is dismembered as Slovakia declares its independence; Hungary occupies those parts of Ruthenia not already given it by the First Vienna Award; Germany occupies Bohemia and Moravia			
31 Mar Chamberlain announces France and UK to guarantee Poland **1 Apr** Spanish Civil War ends				
		7 Apr Italy invades Albania		
				24 Apr Robert Menzies succeeds Joseph Lyons as Australia's prime minister

Atlantic/Northern and Western Europe (except Italy)	Central and Eastern Europe	Balkans/Mediterranean/ Italy/Near and Middle East/Africa	North and South America	Pacific/Far East/ Australasia
26 Apr Conscription introduced in UK				
22 May Germany signs Pact of Steel		**22 May** Italy signs Pact of Steel		
28 Jun Hitler repudiates Anglo-German Naval Treaty				
	23 Aug Nazi–Soviet Pact signed			
	1 Sep Germany invades Poland			
3 Sep France and UK declare war on Germany. SS *Athenia* torpedoed				**3 Sep** Australia, India, and New Zealand declare war on Germany
		6 Sep South Africa declares war on Germany		
			10 Sep Canada at war with Germany	
	17 Sep USSR invades Poland			
		23 Sep Panama Conference starts		
			26 Sep Agreement signed to establish British Empire Air Training Scheme in Canada	
	27 Sep Warsaw falls			
	28 Sep German–Soviet Treaty of Friendship, Co-operation, and Demarcation signed			
14 Oct *Royal Oak* torpedoed				
			4 Nov US Neutrality (Cash and Carry) Act passed	
	30 Nov Finnish–Soviet war starts			
	14 Dec USSR expelled from League of Nations			
			17 Dec *Admiral Graf Spee* scuttled in River Plate	
		1940		
8 Jan Ration books introduced in UK				
	12 Mar Finnish–Soviet war ends			
				27 Mar Peter Fraser becomes New Zealand's prime minister on the death of Michael Savage
9 Apr Germany invades Norway and Denmark				
14 Apr Allies land in Norway				
10 May Germany launches offensive in the west (FALL GELB). Churchill succeeds Chamberlain as prime minister				
15 May British Strategic Air Offensive against Germany starts. Dutch army surrenders				
26 May Dunkirk evacuation starts				
28 May Belgian army surrenders				
2 Jun Allies withdraw from Norway				
4 Jun Dunkirk evacuation completes				

chronology

Atlantic/Northern and Western Europe (except Italy)	Central and Eastern Europe	Balkans/Mediterranean/ Italy/Near and Middle East/Africa	North and South America	Pacific/Far East/ Australasia
		10 Jun Italy declares war on France and UK **11 Jun** South Africa declares war on Italy		
14 Jun Germans enter Paris				
			18 Jun Canadian government introduces conscription, but service overseas remains voluntary	
		21 Jun Italy attacks France		
22 Jun France signs armistice with Germany **24 Jun** France signs armistice with Italy **28 Jun** De Gaulle recognized by UK as leader of Free French **30 Jun** Germans begin occupying Channel Islands	**28 Jun** USSR occupies Bessarabia and northern Bukovina			
		3 Jul Royal Navy bombards French fleet at Mers-el-Kébir **4 Jul** Italian troops from Abyssinia occupy frontier posts in Sudan		
10 Jul Battle of Britain begins				
	14 Jul Baltic States incorporated into USSR			
			22 Jul Havana conference begins	
		4 Aug Italian troops invade British Somaliland		
	30 Aug Second Vienna Award			
			2 Sep Destroyers-for-bases agreement finalized	
		6 Sep King Carol of Romania abdicates		
7 Sep Blitz on UK begins				
		12 Sep Italians invade Egypt from Libya		
			16 Sep US Selective Service Act becomes law	
17 Sep Hitler postpones the invasion of England (SEALION) until further notice				
21 Sept Tripartite Pact signed by Germany		**20 Sep** Opening of Takoradi Air Route **21 Sept** Italy signs Tripartite Pact **25 Sep** Anglo-French Dakar expedition abandoned		
			26 Sep USA imposes embargo on sale of iron and steel scrap to Japan	
				27 Sep Japan signs Tripartite Pact
		12 Oct Gabon campaign begins **28 Oct** Italy invades Greece from Albania		
			5 Nov Roosevelt wins third presidential term	
		11 Nov British raid on Taranto		
14 Nov Air raid on Coventry				
	20 Nov Hungary joins Tripartite pact			

Atlantic/Northern and Western Europe (except Italy)	Central and Eastern Europe	Balkans/Mediterranean/ Ital/ Near and Middle East/Africa	North and South America	Pacific/Far East/ Australasia
21 Nov Belgian government-in-exile declares war on Italy				
		22 Nov Romania joins Tripartite Pact		
	23 Nov Slovakia joins Tripartite pact			
		9 Dec British defeat Italians at Sidi Barrani		
	18 Dec Hitler issues Directive no. 21 for the invasion of the USSR (BARBAROSSA)			
			29 Dec Roosevelt in radio broadcast says USA should be the 'arsenal of democracy'	
		1941		
			6 Jan Roosevelt delivers 'Four Freedoms' speech to US Congress	
				10 Jan Thailand invades French Indo-China
		19 Jan British launch offensive in East African campaign **22 Jan** Australian trops enter Tobruk		
			24 Jan Anglo-US staff talks which were to produce ABC plan begin in Washington	
				31 Jan Thailand and French Indo-China accept Japanese mediation
		6 Feb British forces capture Benghazi **11 Feb** Rommel arrives in Libya **1 Mar** Free French forces enter Kufra in Fezzan campaigns. Bulgaria joins Tripartite pact		
			11 Mar Lend-Lease Bill becomes law	
		24 Mar Rommel captures El Agheila **25 Mar** Yugoslavia joins Tripartite Pact **27 Mar** *Coup d'état* in Belgrade. Yugoslavia leaves Tripartite pact **28 Mar** Naval action off Cape Matapan **3 Apr** *Coup d'état* brings Rashid 'Ali to power in Iraq **6–8 Apr** Bulgarian, German, and Italian forces invade Yugoslavia and Greece. British enter Addis Ababa		
11 Apr USA extends neutrality patrols in Atlantic to 25 degrees west				
	13 Apr Japanese–Soviet neutrality pact signed in Moscow			
		17 Apr Yugoslavia surrenders **19 Apr** Iraqi rebels surround British air base at Habbaniya		
			20 Apr Hyde Park Declaration	

chronology

Atlantic/Northern and Western Europe (except Italy)	Central and Eastern Europe	Balkans/Mediterranean/ Italy/Near and Middle East/Africa	North and South America	Pacific/Far East/ Australasia
		24 Apr British forces begin evacuating Greece **7 May** Habbaniya relieved		
10 May Rudolf Hess, Hitler's deputy, flies to Scotland				
		16 May East African campaign virtually ends when Italians surrender at Amba Alagi **20 May** German airborne forces land on Crete		
24 May *Bismarck* sinks *Hood* **27 May** *Bismarck* sunk by Home Fleet			**27 May** Roosevelt declares 'unlimited national emergency'	
28 May Paris Protocols signed				
		30 May Iraqi revolt collapses **1 Jun** British forces withdraw from Crete **8 Jun** Syrian campaign begins		
			14 Jun German and Italian assets frozen in USA	
		15 Jun Croatia joins Tripartite pact		
22 Jun Italy declares war on USSR	**22 Jun** Germany invades USSR (BARBAROSSA) **27 Jun** Hungary declares war on USSR	**22 Jun** Romania declares war on USSR		
			5 Jul Peru invades Ecuador	
7 Jul US troops relieve British garrison in Iceland				
	11 Jul Romania leaves League of Nations			
		14 Jul Acre armistice ends Syrian campaign		
	16 Jul Germans take Smolensk **21 Jul** First German air raid on Moscow			
			26 Jul Japanese assets in USA frozen which prevents all shipments to Japan including oil	
				27 Jul Japanese troops start occupying French Indo-China
	30 Jul Soviet–Polish agreement signed **6 Aug** General Anders appointed C-in-C Polish forces in USSR			
			9 Aug Placentia Bay conference begins at which Atlantic Charter is issued	
		25 Aug UK and USSR invade Iran		
	19 Sep Germans capture Kiev			
23 Sep De Gaulle forms French National Committee				
	28 Sep Start of Three Power conference in Moscow **2 Oct** Germans start their offensive to capture Moscow (TYPHOON)	**28 Sep** Free French proclaim independence of Syria and Lebanon		
				7 Oct John Curtin becomes Australia's prime minister

Atlantic/Northern and Western Europe (except Italy)	Central and Eastern Europe	Balkans/Mediterranean/ Italy/Near and Middle East/Africa	North and South America	Pacific/Far East/ Australasia
10 Oct German plebiscite in Luxembourg ignored by 97% of the country's inhabitants				
	12 Oct Red Army evacuates Briansk **13 Oct** Red Army evacuates Vyazma **14 Oct** Red Army evacuates Mariupol **16 Oct** Red Army evacuates Odessa			
				18 Oct General Tōjō replaces Prince Konoe as Japanese prime minister
	19 Oct State of siege announced in Moscow and evacuation of government to Kuibyshev begins **24 Oct** Germans capture Kharkov			
31 Oct US destroyer, *Reuben James*, sunk by U-boat in Atlantic				
	3 Nov Germans capture Kursk			
			13 Nov US Neutrality Act revised	
	16 Nov Germans capture Kerch			
		18 Nov British CRUSADER offensive begins in Western Desert		
				19 Nov HMAS *Sydney* sunk
6 Dec UK declares war on Finland, Hungary, and Romania	**28 Nov** Fourth Panzer Group 20 km. (12.5 mi.) from Moscow **6 Dec** Red Army counter-offensive in front of Moscow starts			
			7 Dec Canada declares war on Finland, Hungary, and Romania	**7 Dec** Japanese attack Pearl Harbor. New Zealand declares war on Finland, Hungary, and Romania
8 Dec UK declares war on Japan as do the Free French and the following governments-in-exile: Czechoslovakia, Luxembourg, Netherlands, and Yugoslavia		**8 Dec** South Africa declares war on Japan, Finland, Romania, and Hungary	**8 Dec** USA declares war on Japan as do Canada, Costa Rica, Dominican Republic, Haiti, Honduras, Nicaragua, and El Salvador	**8 Dec** Japanese invade Malaya and Thailand (0115, 7 December east of the International Date Line). Free French proclaim state of war between Japan and all Free French territories. China declares war on Germany, Italy, and Japan. Australia declares war on Finland, Hungary, and Romania
			9 Dec Cuba, Guatemala, and Panama declare war on Japan	**9 Dec** Australia and New Zealand declare war on Japan, effective from 8 December **10 Dec** *Prince of Wales* and *Repulse* sunk off Malaya. Japanese troops land on northern Luzon in the Philippines
11 Dec Germany declares war on USA. The Dutch government-in-exile declares		**11 Dec** Italy declares war on USA	**11 Dec** Costa Rica, Cuba, Dominican Republic, Guatemala, and Nicaragua	

Atlantic/Northern and Western Europe (except Italy)	Central and Eastern Europe	Balkans/Mediterranean/ Italy/Near and Middle East/Africa	North and South America	Pacific/Far East/ Australasia
war on Italy, the Polish government-in-exile declares war on Japan			declare war on Germany and Italy	
		12 Dec Romania declares war on USA	**12 Dec** Haiti, Honduras, Panama, and El Salvador declare war on Germany and Italy	
		13 Dec Bulgaria declares war on UK and USA. South Africa declares war on Bulgaria		**13 Dec** New Zealand declares war on Bulgaria
		14 Dec Croatia declares war on UK and USA		**14 Dec** Japanese start invasion of Burma by occupying Victoria Point
16 Dec Czech government-in-exile declares itself at war with all countries at war with the UK, USA, and USSR				
				17 Dec Japanese land in British Borneo
	18 Dec Hitler appoints himself C-in-C German army when Brauchitsch resigns			
			19 Dec Nicaragua declares war on Bulgaria, Hungary, and Romania	
20 Dec Belgian government-in-exile declares war on Japan				**20 Dec** Japanese attack Netherlands East Indies
			22 Dec–14 Jan 1942 ARCADIA conference held in Washington	
			24 Dec Haiti declares war on Bulgaria, Hungary, and Romania. St Pierre and Miquelon occupied by Free French forces	**24 Dec** Wake Island captured by Japanese
				25 Dec Hong Kong falls to Japanese **27 Dec** Curtin announces that 'Australia looks to America' for protection
		1942		
			1 Jan United Nations Declaration signed by China, UK, USA, and USSR **3 Jan** Washington conference decides to form ABDA Command	
		13 Jan Italy declares war on Costa Rica, Dominican Republic, Haiti, Honduras, Nicaragua, Panama, San Salvador		
				14 Jan Australia declares war on Bulgaria, effective from 6 January
			15 Jan Rio de Janeiro conference begins	
25 Jan Luxembourg's government-in-exile declares war on Germany, Italy, and Japan **26 Jan** US troops arrive in Northern Ireland **5 Feb** UK declares war on Thailand **10 Feb** Pacific War Council meets in London				

Atlantic/Northern and Western Europe (except Italy)	Central and Eastern Europe	Balkans/Mediterranean/ Italy/Near and Middle East/Africa	North and South America	Pacific/Far East/ Australasia
11 Feb Operation CERBERUS: German battle-cruisers escape from Brest		**11 Feb** South Africa declares war on Thailand as from 25 January		
			13 Feb Roosevelt signs executive order which results in evacuation of 110,000 Japanese-Americans from west coast	
				15 Feb Singapore falls to Japanese **19 Feb** Japanese bomb Darwin **25 Feb** ABDA Command dissolved
27 Feb Bruneval raid				**27 Feb** Java Sea battle **28 Feb** Japanese invade Java **8 Mar** Japanese land in New Guinea **17 Mar** General MacArthur appointed to command South-West Pacific Area **22 Mar** Cripps mission arrives in India
27 Mar St Nazaire raid				
			1 Apr First meeting of Pacific War Council in Washington	
				5 Apr Japanese navy's raid into Indian Ocean **9 Apr** US troops surrender in Bataan peninsula
			10 Apr Roosevelt announces US forces to be sent to Greenland	
14 Apr Laval returns to power in Vichy France				
		16 Apr Malta awarded George Cross		
				18 Apr Doolittle raid on Tokyo
24 Apr Start of German Baedeker raids on the UK				
	26 Apr Anglo-Soviet treaty signed			
			27 Apr Plebiscite in Canada on overseas conscription. Quebec votes 'non'	
		5 May Allied forces land on Madagascar		
				6 May Corregidor Island falls to Japanese **7 May** Coral Sea battle starts **20 May** British troops complete withdrawal from Burma
			22 May Mexico declares war on Germany and Japan	
		26 May Rommel attacks at Gazala		
30 May First RAF Thousand-bomber raid				
				31 May Attack on Sydney Harbour
			3 Jun Japanese bomb Aleutian Islands. **5 Jun** USA declares war on Bulgaria, Hungary, and Romania. Japanese land on Aleutian Islands	**4 Jun** Battle of Midway starts

chronology

Atlantic/Northern and Western Europe (except Italy)	Central and Eastern Europe	Balkans/Mediterranean/ Italy/Near and Middle East/Africa	North and South America	Pacific/Far East/ Australasia
	9 Jun Germans avenge assassination of Heydrich in Prague with Lidiče massacre			
		21 Jun Tobruk falls to Rommel		
	28 Jun Germans launch their summer offensive (BLUE) towards the Caucasus **1 Jul** Sevastopol falls to Germans	**1 Jul** First El Alamein battle begins		
2 Jul Churchill's government survives censure motion in House of Commons **4 Jul** Arctic convoy PQ17 ordered to scatter and suffers heavy losses				
				7 Aug US troops land on Guadalcanal
	8 Aug Red Army evacuates Maikop			
		11 Aug Arrival of PEDESTAL convoy alleviates siege of Malta		
	12 Aug Churchill attends Moscow conference			
19 Aug Dieppe raid				
			22 Aug Brazil declares war on Germany and Italy	
		31 Aug Alam Halfa battle begins **12 Sep** *Laconia* sunk		
22 Oct Male call-up age in UK lowered to 18				
		24 Oct Start of second El Alamein battle **8 Nov** Allied landings in Algeria and French Morocco (TORCH) start North African campaign		
11 Nov Germans and Italians occupy Vichy France **27 Nov** French fleet scuttled at Toulon				
		1 Dec Abyssinia declares war on Germany, Italy, and Japan		
	12 Dec Slovakia declares war on UK and USA **13 Dec** Hungary declares war on USA			
		1943		
		14–24 Jan SYMBOL conference held at Casablanca **16 Jan** Iraq declares war on Germany, Italy, and Japan **23 Jan** British troops enter Tripoli **26 Jan** Fezzan campaigns end when Free French forces reach Tripoli		
27 Jan Eighth USAAF mounts its first raid on Germany (Wilhelmshaven)				
	2 Feb German forces capitulate at Stalingrad **8 Feb** Red Army captures Kursk			
				13 Feb First Chindit operation launched into Burma

Atlantic/Northern and Western Europe (except Italy)	Central and Eastern Europe	Balkans/Mediterranean/ Italy/Near and Middle East/Africa	North and South America	Pacific/Far East/ Australasia
		19 Feb Battle for Kasserine pass begins		
			1 Mar Start of Washington Convoy conference	
				2 Mar Bismarck Sea battle
		6 Mar Medenine battle starts		
			7 Apr Bolivia declares war on Axis nations	
	16 Apr First report of Katyń Forest massacre received in London **19 Apr** First Warsaw rising starts		**19 Apr** Bermuda conference begins	
		3 May Tunis captured		
			11 May Canadian and US forces land on Aleutian Islands **11–25 May** TRIDENT conference held in Washington	
		13 May Axis forces capitulate in North Africa		
15 May French National Council for Resistance formed **16 May** RAF 'Dam Buster' squadron breaches Möhne and Eder dams				
			18 May Conference starts at Hot Springs, Virginia, which sets up Food and Agriculture Organization	
24 May U-boats withdrawn from north Atlantic				
		3 Jun French Committee for National Liberation formed in Algiers		
	8 Jun Formal dissolution of Comintern			
		11 Jun Italian held island of Pantelleria capitulates		
				20 Jun US campaign in New Georgia begins
		4 Jul General Sikorski killed in Gibraltar air crash		
	5 Jul Kursk battle begins when Germans launch CITADEL			
		10 Jul Allied forces land in Sicily		
24 Jul RAF raids on Hamburg begin				
		25 Jul Mussolini resigns and is arrested. Marshal Badoglio becomes Italian prime minister		
				1 Aug Japanese declare Burma independent
	5 Aug Red Army captures Orel			
17 Aug RAF Peenemünde and Eighth USAAF Schweinfurt raids		**17 Aug** Axis resistance ends in Sicily		
			17–24 Aug QUADRANT conference held in Quebec	
	23 Aug Red Army captures Kharkov			
		26 Aug UK and USA recognize French Committee for National Liberation		

chronology

Atlantic/Northern and Western Europe (except Italy)	Central and Eastern Europe	Balkans/Mediterranean/ Italy/Near and Middle East/Africa	North and South America	Pacific/Far East/ Australasia
28 Aug Danish government resigns				
		3 Sep Allies land on Italian mainland **8 Sep** Announcement that Italy surrenders **9 Sep** Allies land at Salerno **10 Sep** Germans occupy Rome and much of northern Italy. Dodecanese campaign begins **19 Sep** Germans evacuate Sardinia		
	23 Sep Red Army captures Smolensk			
		4 Oct Corsica liberated		
				7 Oct Admiral Mountbatten arrives in India to take up his position as supreme commander of South-East Asia Command
12 Oct Azores becomes an Allied base **13 Oct** Italy declares war on Germany				
				14 Oct Japanese declare independence of the Philippines
	19 Oct Foreign Ministers' Moscow conference **6 Nov** Red Army captures Kiev			
			9 Nov UNRRA established	
				20 Nov US forces land on Tarawa as first US move in Central Pacific offensive
		23–26 Nov first part of SEXTANT conference held in Cairo		
			27 Nov Colombia declares war on Germany	
		28 Nov–1 Dec EUREKA conference held in Teheran		
			2 Dec Development of atomic bomb: first chain reaction achieved at Chicago university	
		3–7 Dec second part of SEXTANT conference continued in Cairo		
24 Dec Eisenhower named as supreme commander for Normandy landings (OVERLORD) **26 Dec** *Scharnhorst* sunk				
		1944		
	4 Jan Red Army crosses prewar Polish border			
		22 Jan Allied landings at Anzio		
	27 Jan Leningrad siege ends	**27 Jan** Liberia declares war on Germany and Japan **30 Jan** Brazzaville conference begins		
				31 Jan US forces land on Marshall Islands
1 Feb Creation of FFI unifies most resistance movements in France		**1 Feb** First battle of Monte Cassino begins		

Atlantic/Northern and Western Europe (except Italy)	Central and Eastern Europe	Balkans/Mediterranean/ Italy/Near and Middle East/Africa	North and South America	Pacific/Far East/ Australasia
		14 Feb Second battle of Monte Cassino begins		
18 Feb Amiens prison raid **20 Feb** 'Big Week', Anglo-US air offensive against Germany, starts				
				2 Mar Second Chindit operation launched into Burma
		15 Mar Third battle of Monte Cassino begins		**15 Mar** Japanese Imphal offensive from Burma begins
	18 Mar German troops start occupying Hungary **10 Apr** Red Army captures Odessa			
				22 Apr MacArthur's forces land at Hollandia, New Guinea
	9 May Red Army captures Sevastopol			
		11 May Alexander's Italian offensive (DIADEM) and fourth battle of Monte Cassino begins **4 Jun** US troops enter Rome		
6 June Operation OVERLORD starts: Allies land in Normandy **13 Jun** Start of V-1 bombardment against England				
		15 Jun Formation of Balkan Air Force		**15 Jun** strategic air offensive against Japan begins. US forces land on Saipan
		16 Jun Free French troops land on Elba		
				19 Jun Philippine Sea battle starts
			1 Jul Bretton Woods conference starts	
	3 Jul Red Army captures Minsk **13 Jul** Red Army captures Wilno			
				18 Jul Tōjō falls from power
20 Jul Attempt by members of *Schwarze Kapelle* to assassinate Hitler fails				
	27 Jul Red Army captures Lwów **28 Jul** Red Army captures Brest-Litovsk **1 Aug** Second Warsaw rising starts			
		4 Aug Allies enter Florence **15 Aug** Allied French Riviera landings (DRAGOON)		
19 Aug Paris rising begins				
		20 Aug Red Army launches attack on Romania **23 Aug** Romania accepts Soviet armistice terms		
25 Aug Germans surrender in Paris		**25 Aug** Romania declares war on Germany **28 Aug** First French Army takes Toulon		

chronology

Atlantic/Northern and Western Europe (except Italy)	Central and Eastern Europe	Balkans/Mediterranean/ Italy/Near and Middle East/Africa	North and South America	Pacific/Far East/ Australasia
	29 Aug Slovak rising begins			
4 Sep Allies capture Antwerp				
		5 Sep USSR declares war on Bulgaria		
8 Sep First V-2 rocket lands on England		**8 Sep** Red Army enters Bulgaria. Bulgaria surrenders and declares war on Germany		
10 Sep Finland surrenders				
			12–16 Sep OCTAGON conference held at Quebec	
				15 Sep US forces land on Peleliu
17 Sep Operation MARKET GARDEN launched to establish bridgehead at Arnhem				
			21 Sep Dumbarton Oaks conference starts	
			22 Sep Tokyo news service reports declaration of war by Philippines on the USA	
			26 Sep President of Philippines announces his country at war with the USA	
1 Oct Allied operations begin to clear Scheldt Estuary				
	3 Oct Warsaw rising ends			
	5 Oct Red Army enters Hungary			
		7 Oct Germans decide to evacuate Greece		
	9 Oct TOLSTOY conference in Moscow starts			
	13 Oct Red Army takes Riga			
		14 Oct British Expedition to Greece enters Athens		
	16 Oct Germans depose Admiral Horthy, Regent of Hungary, after he announces armistice			
		18 Oct Greek government returns to Athens		
		20 Oct Red Army and Yugoslav partisans enter Belgrade		**20 Oct** US troops land on Leyte in the Philippines
21 Oct First German city captured when Aachen falls to US troops				
23 Oct UK and USA recognize de Gaulle as head of French provisional government				
				24 Oct Battle of Leyte Gulf begins
			1 Nov Conference which forms International Civil Aviation Organization starts in Philadelphia	
			6 Nov Roosevelt wins fourth presidential term	
12 Nov *Tirpitz* sunk				
			22 Nov Canadian government sends 16,000 conscripts overseas	
28 Nov First Allied supply convoy reaches Antwerp up the Scheldt estuary				
16 Dec Germans launch Ardennes campaign				

Atlantic/Northern and Western Europe (except Italy)	Central and Eastern Europe	Balkans/Mediterranean/ Italy/Near and Middle East/Africa	North and South America	Pacific/Far East/ Australasia
	22 Dec Soviet sponsored Hungarian government formed at Debrecen **31 Dec** Moscow makes Lublin Committee Provisional government of Polish Republic			
		1945		
				9 Jan US forces land on Luzon
	14 Jan Red Army attacks into East Prussia **17 Jan** Red Army takes Warsaw **20 Jan** Hungarian government signs armistice			
		30 Jan–3 Feb first part of ARGONAUT conference held at Malta		
			2 Feb Ecuador declares war on Germany and Japan	
		4–11 Feb second part of ARGONAUT conference held at Yalta		
6 Feb Colmar pocket cleared			**8 Feb** Paraguay declares war on Axis nations	
13 Feb Air raid on Dresden	**13 Feb** Germans surrender Budapest		**13 Feb** Peru declares war on Germany and Japan **14 Feb** Chile declares war on Japan **16 Feb** Venezuela declares war on Germany and Japan, Chile declares war on Germany	
				19 Feb US forces land on Iwo Jima
			21 Feb Inter-American conference in Mexico City begins at which Chapultepec Act is signed	
		23 Feb Turkey declares war on Germany and Japan with effect from 1 March **24 Feb** Egypt declares war on Germany and Japan	**23 Feb** Uruguay declares war on Axis nations	
26 Feb US Ninth Army reaches Rhine south of Dusseldorf				
		27 Feb Syria and Lebanon declare war on Germany and Japan **1 Mar** Iran declares war on Japan. Saudi Arabia declares war on Germany and Japan		
4 Mar Finland declares war on Germany backdated to 15 September 1944 **7 Mar** US Third Army crosses Rhine at Remagen				
				9 Mar Japanese seize control in French Indo-China
		19 Mar Yugoslav partisans launch offensive towards Trieste		
				20 Mar British capture Mandalay
			27 Mar Argentina declares war on Germany and Japan	

Atlantic/Northern and Western Europe (except Italy)	Central and Eastern Europe	Balkans/Mediterranean/ Italy/Near and Middle East/Africa	North and South America	Pacific/Far East/ Australasia
	30 Mar Red Army enters Austria and Red Army takes Danzig			
				1 Apr US forces land on Okinawa
			12 Apr Roosevelt dies. Truman becomes President	
	13 Apr Red Army takes Vienna			
		21 Apr US Fifth Army takes Bologna		
25 Apr Soviet and US troops meet at Torgau			**25 Apr** San Francisco Conference starts	
		28 Apr Mussolini shot by partisans **29 Apr** Germans sign surrender terms for their troops in Italy, to take effect from 2 May		
30 Apr Hitler commits suicide				
	2 May Red Army takes Berlin			
				3 May British enter Rangoon
4 May Germans in the Netherlands, northern Germany, and Denmark surrender to Montgomery at Lüneburg Heath **5 May** Germans surrender in Norway **7 May** At 0241 Jodl signs unconditional surrender of Germany at Reims to take effect at 0001, 9 May **8 May** V-E Day. Before midnight, Keitel ratifies the Reims surrender in Berlin				
	10 May Red Army takes Prague			
			6 Jun Brazil declares war on Japan	
		9 Jun Agreement in Belgrade to withdraw Yugoslav partisans from Austria and Trieste		
	5 Jul Polish provisional government recognized by the UK and USA			
		14 Jul Italy declares war on Japan		
			16 Jul Atomic bomb tested at Alamogordo	
	17 Jul–2 Aug TERMINAL conference held in Potsdam			
26 Jul Churchill resigns after being defeated in general election. Attlee becomes prime minister. Broadcast of Potsdam Declaration				
				6 Aug Atomic bomb dropped on Hiroshima
	8 Aug USSR declares war on Japan, with effect from 9 August, and invades Manchukuo			
				9 Aug Atomic bomb dropped on Nagasaki

Atlantic/Northern and Western Europe (except Italy)	Central and Eastern Europe	Balkans/Mediterranean/ Italy/Near and Middle East/Africa	North and South America	Pacific/Far East/ Australasia
				14 Aug Emperor Hirohito announces Japanese forces' unconditional surrender **17 Aug** Sukarno announces Indonesia independent **2 Sep** Japanese surrender signed aboard USS *Missouri* in Tokyo Bay

Place-Name Changes

Wartime Name	*Current Name*
Abyssinia	Ethiopia
Acre	'Akko
Addis Ababa	Adis Abeba
Addis Derra	Adis Dera
Aden Protectorate	People's Democratic Republic of Yemen
Akyab	Sittwe
Aleppo	Halab
Alexandretta	Iskenderun
Amba Alagi	Amba Alage
Amboina	Ambon
Amoy	Xiamen
Anhwei	Anhui
Annam	part of Vietnam
Asmara	Asmera
Assab	Aseb
Assiut	Asyut
Bardia	Al Bardi
Basra	Al Basrah
Batavia	Jakarta
Bechuanaland	Botswana
Beda Fomm	Bayda' Fumm, Bi'r
Belgian Congo	Zaire
Bielgorod	Belgorod
Benghazi	Banghazi
Bir Hakeim	Abyar al Hakim
Bône	Annaba
Bonin Is	Ogasawara Guntō
Bougie	Bejaïa
Breslau	Wrocław
Brest-Litovsk	Brest
Briansk	Bryansk
British Cameroon	northern area part of Nigeria, southern area part of United Republic of Cameroon
British Guiana	Guyana
British Honduras	Belize
British North Borneo	Sabah
British Somaliland	part of Somalia
Burma	Myanmar
Canea	Khaniá
Canton	Guangzhou

Wartime Name	*Current Name*
Carinthia	Kärnten
Castelrosso	Megisti
Celebes	Sulawesi
Ceram	Seram
Cetatea-Albă	Belgorod-Dnestrovski
Ceylon	Sri Lanka
Chahar	divided amongst other Chinese Provinces
Chandernagore	Chandannagar
Changteh	Changde
Chekiang	Zhejiang
Chengchow	Zhengzhou
Chengtu	Chengdu
Chining	Jining
Chungking	Chongqing
Cocanada	Kakinada
Cochin-China	part of Vietnam
Czechoslovakia	divided into Czech and Slovak Republics
Dahomey	Benin
Dairen	Dalian
Danzig	Gdańsk
Debra Markos	Dabra Markos
Deutsch-Brod	Havličkuv Brod
Diégo Suarez	Antseranana
Dnepropetrovsk	Dnipropetrovsk
Dobruja	Dobrogea
Dutch Borneo	Kalimantan, which is divided into four Indonesian provinces
Dutch Guiana	Suriname
Dutch New Guinea	Irian Jaya, a province of Indonesia
Dutch Timor	East Nusa Tenggara, a province of Indonesia
Eire	Republic of Ireland
El Agheila	Al-'Uqaylah
Ellice Is	Tuvalu
Etorofu I.	Ostrov Iturup
Fanning I.	Tabuaeran

place-name changes

Wartime Name	*Current Name*
Fengtien (Mukden until 1932)	Shenyang
Fernando Po I.	Bioko
Fiume	Rijeka
Formosa	Taiwan
Fort Lamy	N'Djamena
French Cameroon	part of United Republic of Cameroon
French Guinea	Guinea
Fench Indo-China	Vietnam, Cambodia, Laos
French Morocco	part of Morocco
French Somaliland	Republic of Djibouti
French Sudan	Mali
French Togoland	Togo
Fushih	Yanan
Gavutu I.	Ghavutu I.
Gazala	Ghazalah, 'Ayn al
Genzan	Wŏnsan
Gilbert Is	Kiribati
Gleiwitz	Gliwice
Gojjam	Gojam
Gold Coast	Ghana
Gona	Garara
Gondar	Gonder
Gorky	Nizhniy Novgorod
Gzhatsk	Gagarin
Halha river	Ha-lo-hsin river
Hangchow	Hangzhou
Hankø	Hangö
Hankow	Hankou
Harar	Harer
Heraklion	Iráklion
Hollandia	Jayapura
Honan	Henan
Hopeh	Hebei
Hsinking	Changchun
Hsüchow	Xuchang
Hupeh	Hubei
Ichang	Yichang
India	divided into Bangladesh, India, and Pakistan
Inner Mongolia	Nei Mongol Zizhiqu
Irrawaddy river	Ayeyarwady river
Ismail	Izmail
Italian Somaliland	part of Somalia
Ivory Coast	Côte d'Ivoire
Java	Jawa
Jehol (province)	divided between Chinese provinces of Nei Mongol Zizhiqu (formerly Inner Mongolia), Hebei, and Liaoning
Johore Bahru	Johor Baharu
Juba river	Jubba river
Kalinin	Tver
Karen state	Kayin state
Kassa	Košice
Katanga	Shaba
Kiangsu	Jiangsu
Kirgizia	Kyrgystan
Kissoué	Kiswe
Knocke	Knokke-Heist
Konigsberg	Kaliningrad
Koritsa	Korcë
Kota Bharu	Kota Baharu
Kovno	Kaunas
Kronstadt	Kronshtadt
Kuibyshev	Samara
Kulm	Chełmno
Kunashiri I.	Ostrov Kunashir
Kurile Is	Kurilskiye Ostrova
Küstrin	Kostrzyn
Kwangtung	Guangdong
Leningrad	St. Petersburg
Lourenço Marques	Maputo
Lunga Pt	Lungga Pt
Lwów	L'viv
Majunga	Mahajanga
Makin I.	Butaritari I.
Malacca	Melaka
Malaya	part of Malaysia
Maldive Is	Maldives
Massawa	Mits'iwa
Mengkian	Jingyu
Mersa Brega	Al Burayqah
Mersa Matruh	Marsa Matruh
Middle Congo	People's Republic of Congo
Moulmein	Mawlamyine
Moluccas	Maluku
Mosul	Al Mawsil
Mozhaisk	Mozhaysk
Mukden	see Fengtien
Murzouk	Murzuq
Naga Hills	Nagaland
Nanking	Nanjing

Wartime Name	*Current Name*
Netherlands East Indies	Indonesia
New Guinea (Australian mandate)	now part of Papua New Guinea
New Hebrides	Vanuatu
Ninghsien	Ningbo
Ningsia	Ningxia
Noemfoor	Numfor
Northern Rhodesia	Zambia
Nyasaland	Malawi
Ocean I.	Banaba
Okhotsk Sea	Okhotskoye More
Onega Lake	Onezhskoye Ozero
Oranienbaum	Lomonosov
Pahlevi	Bandar-e Anzali
Palestine	Israel
Palmyra	Tadmur
Papua	part of Papua New Guinea
Patani	Pattani
Pegu	Bago
Peking	Beijing
Petsamo	Pechenga
Ploeşti	Ploïesti
Pomerania	Polish provinces of Szczecin and Koszalin, and part of Gdańsk province
Pomerelia	Polish provinces of Gdańsk and Bydgoszcz
Pomorze	Polish province of Bydgoszcz
Port Arthur	Lüshun
Port Lyautey	Kenitra
Port Swettenham	Pelabohan Kelang
Portuguese East Africa	Mozambique
Portuguese Guinea	Guinea-Bissau
Portuguese Timor	East Timor
Portuguese West Africa	Angola
Prussia	divided between Germany, Poland, and Russia
Rangoon	Yangon
Rastenburg	Kętrzyn
Retimo	Réthimnon
Ruanda-Urundi	two independent states: Rwandi and Burundi

Wartime Name	*Current Name*
Salonika	Thessaloniki
Salween river	Thanlwin river
Scarpanto	Karpathos
Schneidemühl	Pila
Seishin	Chŏngjin
Sian	Xian
Sidi Rezegh	Sidi Rizq
Sidon	Saïda
Singora	Songkhla
Sinkiang	Xinjiang
Skoplje	Skopje
Smyrna	Izmir
Sollum	Salum
Southern Rhodesia	Zimbabwe
South-West Africa	Namibia
Spanish Guinea	Equatorial Guinea
Spanish Morocco	part of Morocco
Spanish Sahara	part of Morocco
Sphakia	Sfakíon
Spitzbergen	Spitsbergen
Stalingrad	Volgograd
Stalino	Donetsk
Stanyslaviv	Ivano-Frankivsk
Stettin	Szczecin
Stutthof	Sztutowo
Sumatra	Sumatera
Swatow	Shantou
Szechwan	Sichuan
Taierhchwang	Teierzhuang
Takao	Keo-hsiung
Tanganyika	Tanzania
Tangier	Tanger
Tarnopol	Ternopil
Tassafaronga	Tasivarongo
Teheran	Tehran
Terijoki	Zelenogorsk
Teschen	Český Těšín
Thereseienstadt	Terezín
Tientsin	Tianjin
Tilsit	Sovetsk
Tobruk	Tubruq
Tolvajarvi	Tolvayarvi
Tongkin	part of Vietnam
Transjordan	Jordan
Trans-Volta Togoland	part of Ghana
Trengganu	Terengganu
Truk Is	Chuuk Is
Tsinan	Jinan
Tulagi I.	Tulaghi I.
Tungan	Mishan

place-name changes

Wartime Name	*Current Name*
Ubangi-Shari	Central African Republic
Ungvár	Uzhgorod
Upper Volta	Burkina
USSR	dissolved December 1991
Vaagso	Vágsøy
Valetta	Valletta
Viipuri	Vyborg
Vileika	Molodechno
Voroshilovgrad	Lugansk
Wilno	Vilnius
Yangtse River	Jinsha Jiang
Zhdanov	Mariupol

Places in the former Soviet Union are given their most up-to-date current name, but these are liable to change.

Illustration Sources

The editors and publishers wish to thank the following who have kindly given permission to reproduce the illustrations on the following pages:

(IWM—The Trustees of the Imperial War Museum, London; NA—National Archives, Washington)

10 IWM BU1163; **17** NA 59056AC; **31** NA W&C1150; **37** NA W&C870; **53** NA 111-SL-199507; **63** IWM C5816; **70** UPI/Bettmann; **100** NA 208-N-16757; **101** NA 111-SC-329440; **115** NA W&C 1144; **126** Novosti; **133** IWM HU381; **139** NA 306-NT-3173V; **151** Mainichi Shimbun; **159** IWM HU49253; **175** IWM SE3281; **181** IWM A9422; **193** NA W&C1132; **201** Australian War Memorial negative no 139316; **209** Mainichi Shimbun 11943-57; **228** Mainichi Shimbun; **236** NA 111-SC-178042; **243** NA 111-SC-191850; **247** NA 111-SC-193785; **261** *top* NA 208-AA-206K-31; *bottom* NA 111-SC-204811; **268** NA 80-G-42023; **311** IWM D1417; **312** IWM HU44924; **332** IWM C5635; **336** *The Funnies: History of 79th Armoured Division*, Geoffrey W. Futter, 1974; **337** *top Vehicles at War*, David Bishop & C. Ellis, HarperCollins Publishers Limited; *bottom The Funnies: History of 79th Armoured Division*, Geoffrey W. Futter, 1974; **338** Royal Engineers Museum; **340** IWM MH27176; **377** NA 110599; **409** IWM PL68706; **419** IWM C3293; **427** IWM OWIL36141; **435** IWM HU3418; **491** IWM MH13143; **512** NA A702372; **528** IWM NAP284316; **531** NA W&C1244; **535** IWM NYP68066; **543** NA 111-SC-354696; **567** NA 111-SC-196947; **573** NA 111-SC-239682; **602** NA W&C1221; **616** Mainichi Shimbun; **633** NA W&C780; **640** NA 111-SC-191850; **642** Mainichi Shimbun; **646** NA W&C1353; **649** NA 111-SC-205656; **654** Australian War Memorial negative no 26837; **663** NA 109598; **665** IWM HU5165; **676** NA 111-SC-354693; **684** Novosti; **690** NA W&C1158; **699** IWM EA63016; **704** NA W&C1207; **714** NA 111-SC-226838; **729** IWM E16493; **752** NA 111-SC-184220; **754** NA 80-G-700777; **758** NA 111-SC-439454; **765** NA 111-SC-195879; **767** NA W&C746; **775** NA W&C1242; **781** NA W&C990; **792** Australian War Memorial negative no 60587; **802** NA 80-G-250000; 813 NA 111-SC-174707; **825** NA W&C1296; **853** NA 80-J0-63425; **856** NA 64013; **866** NA 111-SC-193339; **871** NA 80-G-32691; **876** The Hulton Deutsch Collection; **885** NA 80-G-238024; **914** NA 111-SC-203905-S; **921** Royal Air Force Museum U114; **930** NA W&C795; **936** NA 111-SC-340859; **939** NA W&C1033; **951** NA 111100; **959** IWM RML5; **961** NA 111-SC-182216; **968** NA W&C1334; **971** NA 111-SC-207164; **979** Norwegian Commando Association; **990** IWM A10296; **1030** IWM MH6804; **1054** IWM BU9192; **1067** IWM C3371; **1083** NA W&C1315; **1096** Australian War Memorial Postcard Collection; **1116** NA 306-MT-353-E-1; **1121** NA 80-J0-63365; **1125** NA 79-AR-508Q; **1131** IWM D1568; **1184** NA W&C798; **1209** Novosti; **1240** Robert Hunt Library; **1248** NA 80-G-377094; **1257** IWM BU1146; **1261** NA 238-NT-282; **1277** Mainichi Shimbun DB87360; **1291** NA 80-J0-63430; **1292** NA 111-SC-211907

Picture research by Sandra Assersohn.
Diagrams prepared by Russell Birkett.